NEW HANOVER COUNTY
PUBLIC LIBRARY
201 CHESTNUT STREET
WILMINGTON, N. C. 28401

Compendium of the Confederacy

An Annotated Bibliography

Books • Pamphlets • Serials

Compiled by
JOHN H. WRIGHT

Volume I
A-L

BROADFOOT PUBLISHING COMPANY
Wilmington, North Carolina
1989

BROADFOOT PUBLISHING COMPANY
CIVIL WAR BOOKS
Route 4, Box 508-C
Wilmington, North Carolina 28405

Catalog Upon Request

THIS VOLUME IS PRINTED ON ACID-FREE PAPER

Copyright © 1989
FRIENDS OF FONDREN LIBRARY
Rice University
ISBN 0-916107-74-4

BROADFOOT PUBLISHING COMPANY
Route 4, Box 508-C
Wilmington, North Carolina 28405

01307894

To
Ruby

INTRODUCTION

This is a simple, short-title compilation of books, pamphlets, and serials relating to the Confederacy, made over several decades. It derives, basically, from booksellers' catalogues, periodicals, and journals, some dating back a hundred years.

Early in the 50's, while inventorying my Confederate collection, I started clipping dealer-catalogues to save typing. At the same time, I compiled a "want-list" of desirable books and in time I had thousands of titles. Dealers, collectors, and friends, noting the size of the three-ring binder, suggested that I should consider publishing a volume, a Howes CSAiana. Around this time, O'Hare (Schenectady, NY) offered me his entire priced card catalogue of CSAiana if I would make a concerted effort to expand it as far as possible... I accepted. Larry Foster (Tuscaloosa, AL), (?) Hawkins (Birmingham, AL), J.E.D. Shipp (Americus, GA), and Bill Morrison (Waco, TX) also encouraged me along.

Meanwhile, catalogues were piling up faster than I could peruse them. I was fortunate to have people like the order-clerk at Texas University and Dr. Hoole at Alabama University, who had a house cleaning and gave me his cache of catalogues, some back as far as 1880's-90's. Boxes appeared on my doorstep, gifts from Winston Broadfoot, curator of the "Flower's Collection" at Duke University. Current catalogues, with more up-to-date pricing, have also been incorporated into this work; Broadfoot, Carolina Books, Goodspeed, Jenkins, MacManus, and Younger. Without booksellers, this compendium would have been impossible. No finer bunch of personalities exist and I thank them all.

Since so much Confederacy has been written and published in serials and can only be found therein, it was decided to include them also. The entire run of the *Southern Historical Society Papers* has been incorporated in this work, as well as *Confederate Veteran*, Miller's *Photographic History, Battles & Leaders, Annals of the War, Century Magazine, Southern Bivouac, Land We Love, Our Living & Our Dead,* and many, many others too numerous to mention.

"Writings in American History" (AHA), as well as the *Journal of Southern History* have been indispensable, as were the Library of Congress cards, to "flesh-out".

Since this work relies largely on secondary sources, it will be noted that no provenance is shown as will be found in Dornbusch's scholarly bibliography. An effort has been made to find every title possible on the Confederacy in hopes that some future researcher will complete a definitive bibiography of the Confederacy.

Even as this is typed, a revised, corrected edition is being planned, with additions of hundreds of titles too late to be included herewith.

John H. Wright
St. Petersburg, 1989

COMPENDIUM OF THE CONFEDERACY
— WHAT IT IS AND HOW TO USE IT —

When John Wright sent me the preliminary copy for this compilation I studied it for several days from different angles. Finally, I called him and asked, "What is it?" And you, my friend, may be the finest Confederate bibliographer that ever turned a page, but a few words of explanation will help greatly in understanding and using this work.

In short, John has tried to gather, under one cover, a listing of every book, pamphlet, and article ever published which relates to the Confederacy. As Charles Dornbush noted in his bibliography of the Civil War, "The very magnitude of this undertaking precludes even the hopes of a definitive checklist." The same sentiment holds well here, but a bibliography can be successful without being definitive. The good bibliographies are someone's best shot at the impossible.

There is no other compilation of this scope. Dornbush's *Military Bibliography of the Civil War* does not include naval or civilian related topics, politics, or fiction. This volume has no limitations as to subject area and thus is much broader and more extensive. However, the two titles do not compete, but compliment— this volume presents a mass of raw data useful for futher research— Dornbusch gathers and organizes titles in one area: military.

This volume is not all-comprehensive. Books and pamphlets that didn't appear in dealers catalogs are not listed; thus, there are in this volume perhaps a third of the 7,984 Confederate imprints in Parrish and Willingham.

This compendium is especially valuable for the listing from serials, many of which have never been indexed. John plowed through them page by page and extracted the articles of Confederate import. This was done — not only with serials of predominately Confederate content, but for the minor serials as well. A look at the index of serials will affirm the scope of the undertaking.

Also of import for Confederate researchers is the extensive listing of material from dealers' catalogs. Much of what is listed here came from catalogs dating from the 40's and is not preserved elsewhere. When I met John I had been selling Confederate material for 20 years and I had never seen a copy of the greatest Confederate rarity, *1491 Days In The Confederate Army*. John knew the locations of over fifteen copies, had a copy himself, and had records of six copies offered in dealers catalogs, along with the catalogs.

— HOW TO USE THIS COMPENDIUM —

Material is listed alphabetically, by author: last name, first name, middle name or initials. All material written by a particular author is grouped under his name. Items for which the author was unknown are listed by title. Since the author and title listings are alphabetical in this work, they are not incorporated into the index— to do so would have been repetitive and cumbersome.

Thus, if "Stonewall" Jackson (i.e. Thomas Jonathan Jackson) is your interest, look first under his name within the text. There will be listed any material which he wrote. Next, look in the index under his name for a listing of all titles about or related to him. Having determined what is available (and there are 190 Jackson items listed) define what you need and hope the library will have it. If they don't, ask them about inter-library loan.

Though establishing values is not a primary purpose of this volume, with some common sense and a little interpolation, it becomes an important side benefit. If a listed book or pamphlet does not have a price, or only one or two prices, and the title in question is not a recent publication, then it's scarce— not having been listed frequently in the thousands of dealers catalogs that were perused in compiling this volume. Scarce doesn't necessarily mean valuable, but further evaluation is called for. Also the prices given establish a value range for the titles (an "old" price of $100 can say a lot).

This volume unlocks a wealth of Confederate material. Scholars, students, and those interested in the Confederacy are indebted to Mr. Wright. Thanks, John, from all of us.

Tom Broadfoot
April, 1989

INDEX TO SERIALS

The following serials were searched for material of Confederate interest; the resulting extracts constitute the majority of entries in this volume. Serials preceeded by an asterisk were either checked in their entirety, as in the case of defunct serials, or through the third quarter of 1988 for ongoing serials.

Agricultural History
*AlaHQ .... Alabama Historical Quarterly
*Ala.Rev. .... Alabama Review
American Economic Review
Amer.Hist.Mag. .... American Historical Magazine
Amer.Hist.Rev. .... American Historical Review
Amer.Jew.Hist.Soc.Pub. .... American Jewish Historical Society Publications
American Journal of Legal History
American Law Review
American Military History Foundation Journal
American Military Institute Journal
*Amer.Neptune .... American Neptune
Amer.Quart. .... American Quarterly
Amer.Rifleman .... American Rifleman
Ann.Med.Hist. .... Annals of Medical History
Annals Army Tenn. .... Annals of Army of Tennessee
*AW .... Annals of War
*Arizona Historical Review
*ArkHQ .... Arkansas Historical Quarterly
*AHQ .... Arkansas Historical Quarterly
Armor
Army Ordnance Journal
Army Quart. .... Army Quarterly
Army Quarterly & Defense Journal
*Atl.Hist.Soc. .... Atlanta Historical Society
Atl.Monthly .... Atlantic Monthly
Baton Rouge Historical Society Proceedings
*B & L .... Battles & Leaders
*Benton County (Ark) Historical Society
*Black.Edn.Mag. .... Blackwood's Edinburgh Magazine
B & G .... Blue & Gray
British Columbia Historical Quarterly
Bulletin: History of Medicine
Cand.Hist.Rev. .... Canadian Historical Review
Cavalry Journal
*ChO .... Chronicles of Oklahoma
*Chr.Okl. .... Chronicles of Oklahoma
Charleston, SC, City Yearbook
Christopher Gist HSP .... Christopher Gist Historical Society Papers
*CWH .... Civil War History
*CWTI .... Civil War Times Illustrated
Clark County (Ark) Historical Quarterly
Coast Artillery Journal
*CV .... Confederate Veteran
*Confed.Vet. .... Confederate Veteran
Conservative Review
'The Dial', Fortnightly Journal of Literature & Criticism
East Tenn HS .... East Tennessee Historical Society Publications
ETHSP .... East Tennessee Historical Society Publications

Emory University (Ga) Quarterly
Field Artillery Journal
Forney's "Progress"
*FCHQ .... Filson Club Historical Quarterly
*FHQ .... Florida Historical Quarterly
*FlaHQ .... Florida Historical Quarterly
Frank Leslie's Pop. Monthly .... Frank Leslie Popular Monthly
*Frontier Times (Texas)
Genealogical Magazine
Ga.Genealog.Soc.Quart. .... Georgia Genealogical Society Quarterly
*Ga.H.Q. .... Georgia Historical Quarterly
*Ga.Hist.Quart. .... Georgia Historical Quarterly
*GHQ .... Georgia Historical Quarterly
Great Plains Journal
*Gulf Mag. .... Gulf States Historical Magazine (2 vol.)
Hispanic American Historical Review
Hist.Mag.Prost.Episc.Ch. .... Historical Magazine of Protestant Episcopal Church
P.E.,Ch.Hist.Mag. .... Historical Magazine of Protestant Episcopal Church
Ind.Mag.Hist. .... Indiana Magazine of History
*Independence County (Ark) Historical Society
Inf.Journ. .... Infantry Journal
Irish Sword
Jour.Amer.Hist. .... Journal of American History
Jour.Amer.Studies .... Journal of American Studies
*Jour.Confed.Hist.Soc. .... Journal of Confederate Historical Society (London)
Journal of Military History (Texas)
Jour.Mil.Ser.Inst. .... Journal of Military Service Institute
JMSI .... Journal of MIlitary Service Institute
*Jour.Miss.Hist. .... Journal of Mississippi History
*JMH .... Journal of Mississippi History
Jour.Soc.Studies .... Journal of Social Studies
*JSH .... Journal of Southern History
*Journ. Southern Hist. .... Journal of Southern History
Journal of US Artillery
JUSCA .... Journal of US Cavalry Association (also: Cavalry Journal)
Kansas Historical Society
"LaRoyale" (pts. 7 & 8) vol. 1-6
Lancashire & Cheshire Antiquarian Society Transactions
Lincoln Herald
*LaHQ .... Louisiana Historical Quarterly
*LHQ .... Louisiana Historical Quarterly
*Louisiana History
*LWL .... Land We Love
Magazine of Albemarle County History (Va)
The Magnolia
Magnolia-Literary Magazine for the Confederacy
Marine Corps Gaz. .... Marine Corps Gazette
*Md.H.M. .... Maryland Historical Magazine
*MHM .... Maryland Historical Magazine
Medical Journal
Methodist History
Mil.Affairs .... Military Affairs
Mil.Collector & Hist. .... Military Collector & Historian
MC & H. .... Military Collector & Historian
Mil.Engineer .... Military Engineer
Military Historian & Economist

*MHT-Sw	Military History of Texas & Southwest
*Mil.Hist.Tex. & SW	Military History of Texas & Southwest
Military Medicine	
Military Surgeon	
MVHR	Mississippi Valley Historical Review
*Mo.Hist.Rev.	Missouri Historical Review
Neale's Monthly Magazine & Youth's Companion	
*New Eclectic Magazine	
*NMHR	New Mexico Historical Review
*New Mex.Hist.Rev.	New Mexico Historical Review
Nineteenth Century (XIXth Century)	
N.Ala.Hist.Association Bul.	North Alabama Historical Assoc. Bul.
*NAR	North American Review
*No.Amer.Rev.	North American Review
*NCHR	North Carolina Historical Review
*N.Caro.Hist.Rev.	North Carolina Historical Review
North Carolina Literature & Historical Association Proceedings	
North West Georgia Society Bulletin	
North Dakota University Quarterly	
Northern Neck of Va. Historical Magazine	Northern Neck of Virginia
OHS	Ohio Historical Society Magazine
Old Guard	
*OLOD	Our Living & Our Dead
Palimyssest	
Pan American Medical Congress Transactions	
Panhandle-Plains Hist.Rev.	Panhandle Plains Historical Review (Tex)
Pasquatank Historical Society Yearbook	
Password	'Password' El Paso (Tex) Historical Society
Pensacola Hist.Soc.Quart.	Pensacola (Fla) Historical Society Quarterly
Phillips CHQ	Phillips County (Ark) Historical Quarterly
Political Science Quarterly	
PMHS	Publication Mississippi Historical Society
Pub.Miss.Hist.Soc.	Publications Mississippi Historical Society
*Pulaski County (Ark) Historical Review	
Railway & Locomotive Historical Society	
Records of American Catholic Historical Society	
*Reg.Ky.HS	Register, Kentucky State Historical Society
*RKHS	Register, Kentucky State Historical Society
Quarterly Journal of Speech	
Quartermaster Rev.	Quartermaster Review
RHS	Rockbridge Historical Society Proceedings (Va)
Rockbridge Hist.Soc.Proc.	Rockbridge Historical Society Proceedings
Rocky Mountain Social Science Journal	
Sabin	
Scott's Monthly Magazine	
Sewanee Rev.	Sewanee Review
Sigma Chi Quarterly	
So.Atl.Quart.	South Atlantic Quarterly
So.Caro.Hist.Mag.	South Carolina Historical & Genealogical Magazine
SCHM	South Carolina Historical & Genealogical Magazine
*So.Biv.	Southern Bivouac
*SB	Southern Bivouac
Shetler (WVa) Civil War	
So.Hist. Monthly	Southern Historical Monthly
SHAP	Southern History Association Publications

*SHSP	Southern Historical Society Papers
SHSTrans.	Southern Historical Society Transactions
SHST	Southern Historical Society Transactions
Southern Illustrated News	
South.Mag.	Southern Magazine (Baltimore)
SoMag.	Southern Magazine (Baltimore)
Southern Quarterly Review	
Southern Speech Communication Journal	
*SwHQ	Southwestern Historical Quarterly
Studies in Social History & Politics	
Taylor-Trotwood Magazine	
*Tennessee Historical Magazine	
*THQ	Tennessee Historical Quarterly
*TennHQ	Tennessee Historical Quarterly
*Tx.Mil.Hist.	Texas Military History
*TMH	Texas Military History
Unit.Serv.Mag.	United Service Magazine
United States Armed Forces	
United States Cavalry Association	
US Naval Inst.Proceed.	United States Navy Institute Proceedings
USN Inst.Proc.	United States Navy Institute Proceedings
VaMag.Hist.Biog.	Virginia Magazine of History & Biography
VMHB	Virginia Magazine of History & Biography
Watson's Jeffersonial Magazine	
Watson's Magazine (Atlanta)	
Vermont Hist.	Vermont History
*Wash.Co.Hist.Soc.	Washington County (Ark) Historical Society Papers
W.Tenn. HSP	West Tennessee Historical Society Papers
WTHA	West Texas Historical Association
W.Tex.HAssn.	West Texas Historical Association
*Wm. & Mry. Quart.	William & Mary College Quarterly Magazine
Winchester-Frederick County (Va) Historical Society	
*WTHSP	West Tennessee Historical Society Papers
*W.Tenn.Hist.Soc. Papers	West Tennessee Historical Society Papers
*W.Va.Hist.	West Virginia History
*'Writings in American History', AHA	

A

1 **ABBOT, Haviland Harris**
"General John D. Imboden." In: W. Va. Hist., 1959, v.XXI, p. 88-122, port.

2 **ABBOTT, Lawrence F. "**
Jefferson Davis." In: Outlook, Oct. 17, 1923, v.CXXXV, p. 259-261.

3 **ABBOTT, Martin**
"President Lincoln in Confederate Caricature (1860-1865)." In: Ill. Hist. Soc. Jour., Autumn, 1958, v.51, p. 306-319, cartoons, $7.

4 ...."Southern reaction to Lincoln's assassination." In: Abr. Lincoln Quar., Sept., 1952, v.7, p. 111-127, notes.

5 ...."The First Shot at Fort Sumter." In: CWH, Mar., 1957, v.III, #1, p. 41-45.

6 **ABEL, Annie Heloise**
"The American Indian as Slaveholder and Secessionist; an omitted chapter in diplomatic history of the Southern Confederacy." Cleveland: Arthur H. Clark Co., 1915, 8vo, cl, 394pp, front, ports, maps, plans.

7 ...v.II, "Participants in the Civil War." 8vo, cl, 403pp., 3vo: $17.50, $40, $65.

8 ...v.III, "The American Indian Under Reconstruction." 419pp. Mrs. George Cockburn Henderson, Ex-Lib. $300. Bright set $400-bmk
...N.Y., Johnson Reprints(1970). Series in American Studies, v.31. Reprint in three parts. v.III, $14.75 16-y

9 ..."The Indians in the civil war." In: Amer. Hist. Rev., Jan. 1910, v.XV, p. 281-296.

10 **ABERCROMBIE, Irene**
"The Battle of Prairie Grove." In: Ark. Hist. Quart., 1943, v.II, p. 309-315.

11 **ABERCROMBIE, John J.**
"Battle of Honey Hill, S.C." Chicago: Samuel Harris, 1911, 8vo, wraps, 15pp. See: "Battle of Honey Hill."

12 **ABNEY, James A. (Md., Confed. Vet.)**
"An Abridged Autobiography, Some of Many Incidents & Experiences of..." Brownwood, Texas, 1928, 12mo, wraps, (18)pp.

13 **ABOLITION Traitor, An**
"There are traitors in the North as well as in the South, etc." Signed at end(printed) A Democratic Workingman. New York, Aug. 29, 1863. Broadside, sm. folio, 1p. (old) $11.50. "Free Society a monstrous abortion & slavery, the beautiful, healthy & natural state of being, etc."

14 **ABRAHAMS, Robert D.**
"The uncommon soldier: Maj. Alfred Mordecai." N.P., 1959, 12mo, cl, dj, 179pp. Juvenile biography of a North Carolina soldier. $10.

15 **ABRAM ,**
A Military Poem. By a Young Rebelle, Esq. of the Army. Richmond, Va., Macfarlane & Ferguson, 1863. 16mo, wraps, 66pp.

16 **ABRAM LAND Letters**
"The Abram Land Letters, Edt: Mrs. John B. Kittrell." In: "Rivers, roads & points between." Summer. 1980, v.8, p. 2-16, Civil War letters.

17 **ABRAMS, Alexander St. Clair**
"A full & detailed history of the seige of Vicksburg." By A.S. Abrams of New Orleans. Atlanta: Intelligencer Press, 1863. 8vo, cl, 80pp. Crandall-2612 Bmk-94-$300 $85.

18 ..."President Davis & his administration. Being a review of the "Rival Administration", lately published in Richmond, and written by E.A. Pollard", by A.S. Abrams. Atlanta, Ga., for the author, 1864. 8vo, wraps, 20pp. (Crandall-2613).

19 …"The trials of the Soldier's Wife: a tale of the second American revolution." Atlanta, Ga. Intelligencer Press, 1864. 12mo, cl, 188pp. (Wright II-5) $1000-gdsp.

20 **ABRAMS, Ray H.**
"Copperhead newspapers & the negro." In: Jour. Negro Hist., 1935, v.XX, p. 131-152. Attitude of country towards negro & abolitionists as found in "Age", a Phila., Copperhead Jour., in the '63's-'64's.

21 **ABSHIRE, David M.**
"The South Rejects a Prophet; the Life of Senator D.M. Key, 1824-1900. Foreword by Ralph McGill." N.Y., F.A. Praeger (1967). 8vo, cl, illus., ports, xii, 250pp. $15. US Senator(Tenn.) CSA regiment during war.

22 **ABZUG, Robert H.**
"The Copperheads: Historical Approaches to Civil War Dissent in the Midwest." In: Ind. Mag. Hist. 1970, v.LXVI, p. 40-55.

23 **ACCEPTANCE,**
Of statues of George Washington & R.E. Lee. Presented by the State of Virginia Proceedings in the Congress & in the rotunda, United States Capitol. Washington: Gov. Print Off., 1934. 8vo, cl, 2-pls., 62pp. U.S. Congr., 73rd, 2nd sess. HR Doc-410. See: Robert E. Lee, Statue of…

24 **ACCOUNT, of the Battle of New Bern, N.C.**
In: OLOD, 1875, ii, 281-290pp.

25 **ACCOUNT, of the Celebration**
Of the 34th Anniversary of the Washington Artillery, with the oration of Gen. Samuel McGowan, & the transfer & reception of the war guidon of Hart's Battery, at Charleston, S.C., Washington's Day, Feb. 22, 1878. Charleston, S.C., News & Courier, 1878. 8vo, wraps, 48pp. See: Saml. McGowan, Henry Hart, Lee C. Harby, James F. Hart.

26 **ACHISON, David R., et al**
"The Voice of Kansas, let the South Respond. Appeal by the law & order party of Kansas Territory to their friends in the South, & to the law abiding people of the Union." n.p., 1856. 8vo, wraps, 8pp. (Westn. Hemisp.) $75. DeBow's Review for August.

27 **ACT,**
For the Needy Confederate soldiers & sailors, resident citizens of Alabama & their widows. Montgomery, Ala. (1899?) 8vo, wraps, cover title, 8pp. Montgomery, Ala., 14pp. 1901. Bmk-$10.

28 **ACT,**
To provide an armed military force; & an act to establish a Board of Ordnance Bureau, & for other purposes, passed Dec. 17, 1860. Columbia, S.C., Chas. P. Pelham, 1860. 8vo, wraps, 10pp. $25.

29 **ACTS,**
…Passed at the Called Session of the general assembly of the State of Arkansas, which was begun & held in the courthouse, in the town of Washington, Hempstead County, on Thursday, Sept. 22, 1864 & ended on Sunday, Oct. 2, 1864. Heretofore printed in a newspaper only. Washington, D.C., Statute law book co., 1896. sm.8vo, wraps, iv, 27pp. Not printed until 1896 from scarcity of paper.

30 **ACTS,**
Passed at the 14th Session of the general assembly of the State of Arkansas, which was begun & held in the capitol, in the city of Little Rock, on Monday the third day of November, 1862 & ended on Monday Dec. 1, 1862. Now first printed--. Washington, D.C., 1896. 8vo, wraps, iii, 98pp. Not printed until 1896 from scarcity of paper.

31 **ADAM, Graeme Mercer**
"The Life of Gen. Robert E. Lee…the life career & military achievements of the great Southern general, with a record of the campaigns of the Army of Northern

Virginia." N.Y., A.L. Burt Co. (c.1905) 12mo, cl, front(port) illus., 321pp. $5.

32 **ADAM, William Robert**
"Confederate History of Alexandria, Va." This essay won first prize in a contest sponsored by the Virginia Division, United Daughters of the Confederacy. n.p., n.d. 8vo, cover title, (8)pp. $2.50

33 **ADAMS, Charles Francis**
"Wolseley & the Confederate Army." Mass. Hist. Soc. Proc., XLVII, p. 9-24. Reprints from Blackwood's Magazine of January 1863: "A month's visit to the Confederate Headquarters."

34 ..."McHenry on the Cotton Crisis, 1865." Mass. Hist. Soc. Proc., XLVII, p. 279-287. Resume'of pamphlet by Geo. McHenry, who sympathized with the CSA, relates to the Lancashire "cotton famine" of 1861-1864."

35 ..."The Golgotha year." Mass. Hist. Soc. Proc., XLVII, p. 333-340. A study of the Lancashire, England, cotton industry for 1862 & its relation to the CSA. England's trade conditions responsible for the cotton crisis.

36 ..."A Crisis in Downing Street." Mass. Hist. Soc. Proc., XLVII, p. 372-424. Britain's policy in American civil war in 1862, recently available to Adams.

37 ..."The Confederacy & The Transvaal", "Peoples Obligation to Robert E. Lee." Speech at American Antiquarian Society, Oct. 30, 1901. Boston: Houghton, Mifflin Co., 1901. 8vo, wraps, 25pp. $10, $3.

38 ...Concerning the right of secession." In: CV, Jan. 1902, v.XI, p. 12-13.

38a ..."Lee at Appomattox" in his 'Lee at Appomattox & other papers.' Enlarged & 2nd edt. 1902. p.1-30.

39 ..."Lee's Centennial. An Address by...delivered at Washington & Lee Univ. Lexington, Va., Sat. Jan. 10, 1907..." n.p., n.d., 750 copies printed, some copies with author's atg. slip tipped-in. (Boston: Houghton, Mifflin?) 1st Edt. $15. 8vo, orig. wraps, 76pp. ($5, $8.50, $10) Chicago: Americana House, 1948. $7.50, $15.
...Richmond, Va., n.d. 8vo, wraps, 24pp., frontis. ($3., $6.)

40 ..."Toast to R.E. Lee." In: SHSP, v.30, p. 121-123.

41 ..."Lee at Appomattox, & other papers." Bost.-N.Y., Houghton, Mifflin Co., 1902, 12mo, cl, 387pp. ($4, $6, $7.50) $15.
...2nd enlarged edt., 12mo, cl, 442 pp. (1903?) (Edt: 1923)
...Freeport, N.Y., Books for Libraries Press(1970) reprint. 22-y $16.

42 ..."Trans-Atlantic Historical Solidarity: Lecture before the University of Oxford." Oxford: University Press, 1913. 8vo, cl, 184pp. B-$25, $15-R, $5 CSA Cotton campaign, Lancashire, 1861-1862. Gen. Lee's Character, etc.

43 ..."The Constitutional Ethics of Secession & "War is Hell." Two speeches delivered at Charleston, S.C., Dec. 22, 1902 and N.Y. Jan. 26, 1903. Boston: Houghton, Mifflin Co., 1903. 12mo, wraps, 41pp. $10-jk, $5.

44 ..."Shall Cromwell have a statue? An oration by...before the Phi Beta Kappa Society of the University of Chicago, Tuesday June 17, 1902." Boston: Charles E. Lauriat Co., 1902. 8vo, wraps, p. 44. Essentially a study of R.E. Lee having a statue. See: SHSP, v.30, p. 1-33.

45 ..."Sectional feeling in 1861." In: MHSP, 1913, v.XLVI, p. 306-315. Wm. H. Russell's letter in London Times, May 28, 1861, giving his description of the feelings of S. Carolinians re the Northern sts.

46 ..."Lee at Appomattox." Suffolk, Va., Robt. Hardy Pub., 1986, 8vo, wraps, 36pp. illus.

47 **ADAMS, Ephraim Douglas**
"Great Britain & the American Civil

War." 2 Vols. London: N.Y., Longman's, 1925. 8vo, cl, ports, illus., 307, 340pp. $15.
...N.Y., Russell & Russell (1960?) 2 vols. in 1. $25-McM $3.50 $10-15-Y
...Gloucester, Mass., Peter Smith, 1957. Full Mor. $30.

48 **ADAMS, Francis F., Jr.**
"Robert E. Lee & the Concept of Democracy (1832-1868)." In: Amer. Quart. Fall, 1960, v.12, p. 367-374, notes.

49 **ADAMS, George W.**
"Confederate Medicine." In: Jour. South. Hist., VI(1940) p. 151-166. Bmk-$8.

50 **ADAMS, Henry**
"Henry Adams silenced by the cotton famine. Edt.: Joseph A. Borome." In: NEQ, June 1960, v.33, p. 237-240. notes.
"Private & confidential" letter to NY Times Edt. Henry J. Raymond, 24 Jan. 1862, on danger of British intervention in favor of the CSA.

51 **ADAMS, James Truslow**
"America's Tragedy." N.Y., Chas. Scribner's, 1934. 8vo, cl, vii, 415pp. "The Northerner's resentment & the Southerner's fear. The Northerner may have hated slavery but he hated quite as much the aristocratic slave owner..."

52 **ADAMS, Julia Davis**
"Stonewall." "The Shenandoah." See: Julia Davis.

53 **ADAMS, Michael C.C.**
"Our Masters the Rebels: a Speculation on Union Military Failure in the East, 1861-1865." Cambridge: Harvard University Pr., 1978. 8vo, cl, dj, x, 256pp. $12.50

54 **ADAMS, Wirt, Brig-Gen.**
"Report of General Adams. Hdq. Cavalry Brigade, Mar. 12, 1864." In: SHSP, 1881, v.IX, p. 340-344.

55 **ADAMSON, Augustus Pitt, Rex, Ga.**
"Brief History of the Thirtieth Georgia Regiment." Griffin, Ga., Mills Print, 1912. $600., $25. 8vo, wraps, ports (inc. front), 157pp., $35. 1/2 lt. slip case $750-bmk-105.
..."Brief History of the 30th Georgia Regiment." Jonesboro, Ga., Freedom Hill Press, 1987. 8vo, wraps, 161p. ills. Rosters. $15. Reprint of 1912 edition, 400 copies.

56 **ADAMSON, Nellie**
"The Secession Movement in Georgia." In: Ga. Hist. Assoc. Proceed., 2nd Annual sess., Apr. 6, 1918, p. 10 $10.

57 **ADDEY, Markinfield**
"Stonewall Jackson. The Life & Military Career of Thomas Jonathan Jackson, Lt. Gen. in the Confederate Army." 12mo, cl, front(port), 240pp. N.Y., C.T. Evans; Chicago: J.R. Walker(etc., 1863. $30-Ch. Hill, $7.50, $10, $12.50, $15, $65-jk-135.

58 ..."The Life & imprisonment of Jefferson Davis, together with the life & military career of Stonewall Jackson, from authentic sources." New York: M. Doolady, 1866. 12mo, cl, ports: Davis, Jackson & Lee, p. 140, 300. 1st Edt. (old)$5. (Reissue of "Old Jack", N.Y., 1864, in 2nd part)

59 **ADDRESS of Congress**
To the people of the Confederate States-(adopted Dec., 1863) joint Resolution in relation to the war." In: SHSP, 1876, v.1, p. 23-38.

60 ..."Address of Congress to the People of the Confederate States, by T.J. Semmes, et. al." Richmond, Va., 1864, caption title. 8vo, sewn, 8pp. South in a struggle for preservation of liberty & civilization. $100-jk-127.

61 **ADDRESS,**
To Christians throughout the World by the Clergy of the Confederate States of America. 8vo, stitched, 16pp.(London), 1863, Sabin-408, shows date (1862). (old) $2.50

62 **ADDRESS of Southern Delegates**
In Congress to their Constituents. (Washington: Towers Print, 1848?) 15pp., 8vo,

captin title. $35, $75. Signed: R.M.T. Hunter & 47 other members of both branches of 30th Congress. Fugitive slave law & extension of slavery in the states & territories.

63 ...Address of the Southern Delegates in Congress to their Constituents." (Washington, 1860?), 8vo, sewn, 15pp. Movement to Secession, list of delegates at end, by states. $25-bmk, $50-bmk, $75, Jk $45- (122)

64 **ADDRESS to the State-Rights Opposition** voters of Alabama. (caption title) Montgomery, Ala., (1860) 8vo, sewn, 16pp. (old) $12.50. Speech endorsing Breckenridge-Lane.

65 **ADEN, R.F., Mrs.**
"In Memoriam, Seventh Tennessee Cavalry, C.S.A." In: WTHSP, 1963, v.17, p. 108-117.

66 **ADKINS, William M.**
"Obadiah Jennings Wise, '50', Sketch of His Life." Indiana Univ., Alumni Quarterly, in 4 installments., Sec't of Publications Office, n.p. (Reviewed in Va. Mag. Hist. Biog. Oct., 1938, v.XLVI, #4, p. 371.

67 **ADLER, Herbert F.**
"Jefferson Davis at Fort Monroe." In: Mil. Rev., 1967, v.XLVII, p. 71-76.

68 **ADOLPHSON, Steven J.**
"An Incident of Valor in the Battle of Peach Tree Creek, 1864." In: Ga. H.Q., Fall, 1973, v.LVII, #3, p. 406-420.

69 **ADTS, Nicholas Joseph**
"Le Monitor et le Merrimac; systeme de projectile se forcant dans l'ame au moyen d'un sabot." Paris: Tanera, 1862. 8vo, wraps, 29pp.

70 **ADVENTURES of Lena Rouden,**
a "Southern Letter Carrier", or Rebel Spy: a story of the late war. Chicago: Horton & Leonard Print, 1872, 12mo, wraps, 69pp. (Wright II-1830) Signed at end "Oliver Outwest". Laid in Tenn.

71 **ADVENTURES of the Marion Hornets** Co. H., 7th Regt., Fla. Vols." Verse. Knoxville, Tenn., Pub. for the Author, 1863, 16mo, wraps, 32pp.

72 **AFFLECK, C.J. & B.M. Douglas**
"Confederate Bonds & Certificates. A listing with a description of the Confederate States of America Bonds & Certificates, showing degree of rarity & price." (Boyce, Va., Carr Pub. Co., 1960) 8vo, stiff wraps(color flag) facsms, 38pp. $3, $30pbmk-104.

73 **AFFLECK, Issac Dunbar**
"A Cadet at Bastrop Military Institute. The Letters of Isaac Dunbar Affleck. Edited by Robert W. Williams, Jr. & Ralph A. Wooster." In: TMH, Spring, 1967, v.6, #1, p. 89-106.

74 ..."With Wharton's Cavalry in Arkansas. The Civil War Letters of Private Isaac Dunbar Affleck. Edited by Robert W. Williams, Jr. & Ralph A. Wooster." In: AHQ, 1962, v.XXI, p. 247-268.

75 ..."With Terry's Texas Rangers: Letters of Dunbar Affleck." Edts: Robert W. Williams, Jr. & Ralph A. Wooster." In: CWH, v.IX, #3, p. 299-319.

76 ..."Camp Life in Civil War Louisiana: The Letters of Private Isaac Dunbar Affleck." In: La. Hist., v.V, p. 187-201. Edt: Robert W. Williams & Ralph A. Wooster.

77 ..."With the Confederate Cavalry in East Texas: The Civil War Letters of Private Isaac Dunbar Affleck." In: ETHJ, v.1, p. 17-28.

78 ..."A Texas War Clerk: Civil War Letters of Isaac Dunbar Affleck. Edt. Robert W. Williams, Jr. & Ralph A. Wooster." In: Tx. Mil. Hist., Nov. 1962, v.2, #4, p. 279-294, illus., maps.

79 **AFFLECK, Thomas, Mr. & Mrs.**
"Life in Civil War Central Texas, Letters from Mr. & Mrs. Thomas Affleck to Private Isaac Dunbar Affleck. Edt: Robert

W. Williams & Ralph A. Wooster." In: Texana, Summer, 1969, v.VII, #2, p. 146-162. See: Robert W. Williams, Ralph Wooster.

80 **AGEE, Rucker**
"Forrest-Streight campaign of 1863; preliminary report. Prepared for the 100th meeting of the Civil War Round Table." Milwaukee, 1958. CWRT. 4to, wraps, illus., maps, 34pp. $25-bmk-atg.

81 ..."Lets keep the record straight. (A vaudeville of historical incidents.)" Birmingham, Ala., 1963. 4to, wraps, illus., ports, 42 lfs. $10bmk. Supplementary remarks to members of Ala. Hist. Assn. meeting, Apr. 27, 1963. See: Dabney H. Maury, Jno. A. Wyeth, Nathan Bedford Forrest.

82 **AIKEN, Leona Taylor**
"Letters of Offield Bros., Confederate soldiers from upper East Tennessee." In: East TennHS, 1979, #46, p. 116-125. Subject: John & Joseph Offield.

83 **AILENROC, M.R. (pseud.)**
See: Murrell, Cornelia Randolph.

84 **AIMONE, Alan Conrad**
"Reinvestigation of the Battle of Hartsville, Tennessee." (London) Jour. Confed. Hist. Soc., Summer, 1967, v.5, #2, p. 41-48, map.

84a **AITKEN, Roy E.**
"The Birth of a Nation." Middleburg, Va., 1965, Wm. W. Denlinger. 8vo, wraps, 96p. Roy Aitken as told to Al P. Nelson. $15.

85 **AKEHURST, Jennie**
"To raise myself a little: the diaries & letters of Jennie, a Georgia teacher, 1851-1886." Edt: Thomas Dyer. Athens: University of Georgia Press, 1982, 8vo, cl, dj, illus., notes, index, xiv, 284pp. "The South did more for Jennie than she did for it." $10.

86 **AKIN, Warren & Mary Frances**
"Letters of Warren Akin, Confederate Congressman. Edt: Bell Irvin Wiley." Athens: Univ. of Georgia Pr., (1959), 8vo, cl, dj, ports, notes, 151pp. Reprinted (with 3 added letters) from Ga. H.Q., Mar., 1958-Sept., 1959, letters while a member CSA congress to wife in Elberton, Ga. $15

87 **ALABAMA ,**
"Report of the majority & minority of the committee of thirteen made in the Alabama State Convention, Jan. 10, 1861. Convention, 1,000 copies. Montgomery, Ala., Shorter & Reid Print, 1861. 8vo, sewn, 8pp. Owen(p. 878) Maj.-by Wm. L. Yancey. Minor-Jere Clemens.

88 ..."Proposed amendment to the State Constitution on changing the mode of electing circuit judges." Montgomery, Ala., 1861. 8vo, sewn, 7pp. no title page. Owen(p. 878) Report of Comm. to Secession convention made by John T. Morgan of Dallas Co.

89 ..."Ordinances adopted by the people of the State of Alabama, at Montgomery, commencing on the seventh day of Jan., 1861. Andrew B. Moore, Gov. Wm. M. Brooks, Pres. of Convention." Montgomery, Ala., Shorter & Reid, Print, 1861. 8vo, wraps, 30pp. Owen(p. 878)

90 ..."History & Debates of Convention." See: Wm. Russell Smith.

91 ..."The Alabama Soldier. Devoted to the Alabama Soldier. Devoted to the Alabama State Troops." v.1(-10) Birmingham, Ala., July 30, 1891(-July 11, 1892) 4to, each issue c. 8pp., numbered separately. T.J. & E.B. Jones, Edt. & Pub. Only 40 numbers issued. Pub. weekly, but irregular toward end. Current events of State Troops, but a column by veterans of "late war", reminiscences, poems & short articles.

92 **ALABAMA Civil War Centennial Commission.**

"A manual for Alabamians." University, Ala., n.d., (c.1960) 8vo, wraps, 27pp. $4.50

93 **ALABAMA Claims**
"The Case of the United States, to be laid before the Tribunal of Arbitration, to be convened at Geneva, under the provisions of the treaty between the U.S. & Her Majesty the Queen of Great Britain, concluded at Washington, May 8, 1871." Washington, D.C., Gov. Print. Off., 1871. 4to, cl, (or 1/2 Mor.) 501pp. $22.50, $65 jk-135.

94 **ALABAMA Claims North America.**
No. 1, 1872. "Case presented on the part of the Government of Her Britannic Majesty to the Tribunal of arbitration constituted under Article 1 of the Treaty concluded at Washington on the 8th May, 1871, between Her Britannic Majesty & the United States of America. Presented to the House of Commons..." London, 1872. 4to, blue printed wraps, 168pp. $75. Blockade, steamers "Florida", "Alabama", "Georgia" & "Shenandoah". British side of the court case of "Alabama Claims."

95 **ALABAMA Confederate Civil War**
Centennial Commission. Whole issue of the AHQ, 1961, v.23, #1 & 2 (listed individually by author) #3 &4 as follows: Editorial (207): "Col. Jas. F. Armstrong of Montgomery Co., rendered unusual service to Confederacy" by Floelle Tongblood Bonner (231); "Alabama Conscripts Act, 1863"; "A Memorial Sermon by the Right Rev. Nicholas H. Cobbs, by Rev. Geo F. Cushman" (249);

96 "A contemporary account of the Inauguration of Jefferson Davis, Edt. Virginia K. Jones." (273); "A University Cadet's Letter." (289); "Turkeytown, CSA, Letters." (300);

97 "Shelby Springs, CSA Hospital." (305); "Confederate Memorial Day." (308); "Recent Centennial" additions of Dep't. of Archives & History." (310); "Alabama's Representatives in the Confederate States Congress, by William Letford." (312);

98 "Montgomery Military Academy, 1862." (317); Index v.23, 1961.

99 **ALABAMA Historical Society, new series.**
"Transactions of the Alabama Historical Society, v.2-5; 1897/1898-1904." Tuscaloosa, Ala., T.M. Owen, Editor. 4 vols (v.1, not published), all published. 4 vols. front(port) $100-bmk. Number of CSA articles.

100 **ALABAMA Secession:**
Entire issue of v.3, #3 & 4, 1942. Introduction, p. 269-276; Events preceding Secession, p. 277; The Alabama Secession Convention, p. 287; History of the Document, p. 357; The Alabama Secession flag, p. 364; Delegates to the Secession Convention, p. 368; Withdrawal of the Alabama Delegation from the Congress of the U.S., p. 427; Withdrawal Speech of Jefferson Davis, p. 447. Index of V.3, 453.

101 **ALABAMA, C.S.S.**
"Sinking of the "Alabama"." Colored photogravure after painting by J.O. Davidson, 1881. Print, 23x31" India proof before letters, mounted. N.Y., C. Klackner, 1892. $17.50

102 ..."What the Alabama Did." In: SHSP, 1896, v.XXIV, p. 249-250.
..."C.S.S.-ALABAMA." A mssc. by G. J. Fullam, acting Master's Mate, log covers entire period of the cruise. Sotheby's sale, 12, 16-1963 to Mrs. Clara Fields, Mobile Ala. $3,640.00.

103 ..."Life on the Alabama." (London) Jour. Confed. Hist. Soc., June, 1964, v.II, #2, p. 58-93, ports(3), plates(5), map, includes reprint of Philip Drayton Haywood Century Mag. article & note by the editor of Century.

104 **ALABAMA, Claims**
"The case of Great Britain as laid before

the tribunal of arbitration, convened at Geneva under the provisions of the treaty between the United States of America & Her Majesty the Queen of Great Britain." Washington, D.C., Govt. Print Off., 1871. 8vo, cl, maps, charts, some folding, some color, 3vols+ counter case. 1105pp. (4vols.) bm-$150. Treats of neutral rights, blockade running, CSA raiders & privateers.

105 **ALABAMA, Imprints**
See: Jessie E. Cobb, Rhoda Ellison. Crandall-Harwell.

106 **ALABAMA, Memorial & Biographical Record**
See: Brant & Fuller.

107 ..."Farewell address to the People of Louisiana." In: LWL, Aug., 1866, v.1, #4, p. 275-277. Governor of the state.

108 **ALABAMA, Office Commandant Conscripts for State of Alabama**
Montgomery, Ala., Oct. 12, 1864. Broadside: folio, 1pp. Circular. $16.75. Instructions for number slaves to be provided army, if not hired, to be impressed.

109 **ALABAMA, Office of Secretary of State**
"An Ordinance to Make Provisional Postal Arrangements in Alabama." President of Alabama Convention: William M. Brooks. Montgomery, Ala., Jan. 18, 1861. Not in Crandall/Harwell/Sabin.

110 **ALABAMA, The**
"A statement of fact from official documents, with the sections of the Foreign Enlistment Act violated by her equipment..." London: J.Snow, etc., 1863. 8vo, wraps, 16pp.

111 ..."Proceedings of the Chamber of Commerce of the State of New York, on the burning of the Ship "Brilliant", by the Rebel Alabama." N.Y., 1862, wraps, 22pp. $15
See: "The Career of the "Alabama"."

112 **ALABAMA, The C.S.S.**
"The U.S. Sloop of war "Kearsarge", 7 Guns, sinking the Pirate "Alabama." 8 guns. Off Cherbourg, Francs, June 19, 1864. N.Y., Currier & Ives, small folio litho hand colored. $35

113 ..."Alabama in the War, 1861-1865." Williamsbridge, N.Y., Ambrose Lee Pub. (1908). Revised by Marcus Wright, now in the press. (Not here, Ghost? Adv. in back of Wright's "Tenn. in the War."

114 **ALABAMA: Adjutant General's Reports**
see: "List of maimed soldiers...", "Payments to needy soldiers...", "Compilation of records, corresp...muster roll."

115 **ALABAMA: Adjutant General's Reports:**
"Biennial report..." Montgomery, Ala., Brown Print, 1894. 8vo, wraps, 224pp. "Statement of records relating to the Confederacy." p. 200-224.

116 **ALABAMA: Vicksburg Monument Memorials.**
See: Wallace Malone, Kathleen Carson, Annie F. Daugett, Dr. Joseph Dill Alison, Arthur M. Schaw, Stanley Arthur, Carolyn T. Foreman, Walter B. Jones.

117 **ALAMANCE County, N.C.**
"Confederate Memoirs, Alamance County Troops in the War Between the States, 1861-1865." See: Jm. G. Albright. n.p., n.d. (c. 1965) Centennial Edt., 8vo, wraps, 43pp. $15-bmk-84 $35-bmk

118 ..."The North Carolina Union Men of 1861." In: North Carolina Booklet, July 1911. 12mo, wraps, 16pp. $10-bmk-84.
"Confederate Memoirs: Alamance County Troops, CSA. See: "Confederate Memoirs of...

119 **ALBAUGH, William A.**
"Cadet gray to butternut: the evolution of Johnny Reb's uniform." In: Amer. Arms Col., Jan. 1957, v.1, p. 4-10.

120 ..."Confederate Arms". In: "Encyclopedia of Firearms", Edt: Harold Peterson, London: 1962.

121 ..."Confederate Firearms".In: "The Collection of Guns". Edt.: Jas. E. Serven, Harisburg, Pa., Stackpole Co., 1964.

122 ..."C.S. or U.S.". In: "Amer. Arms Col., Jan., 1958, v.2, #1.

123 ..."The Confederate Naval Official Regulation Sword." In: Amer. Arms Col., July 1958, v.2, #3.

124 ..."The Spiller & Burr Confederate Revolver." In: John Amber's Gun Digest." Chicago: 1956.

125 ...All following titles: Texas Gun Collector. "Relationship of price & value", March. 1952. "The Revolvers of George Todd of Alabama & Texas." May, 1954. "Schneider & Glassich of Memphis" Tenn., June, 1954. "Thomas W. Cofer-Portsmouth, Va." Sept., 1954. "Columbia, S.C. & the Palmetto Armory." Jan. & Feb., 1955. "Gun News of the 1860's." March 1955. "An Ordnance Officer's Nightmare." June, 1955. "Fact & Fiction." Dec., 1955. "The Richmond Sharps Carbine." three part story in Sept./Oct./Nov., 1955.

126 **ALBAUGH, William A., III**
"Tyler, Texas, C.S.A." Harrisburg, Pa., Stackpole Co. (1958) Wilson, 8vo, cl, d/w, illus., maps, 235pp. $5.95, $25-jk, $10, $15-nc

127 ..."Confederate Edged Weapons." New York: Harper & Bros., (1960). 4to, cl, d/w, illus. from orig. sketches, 198pp., xxiv. N.Y. Bonanza Rep $10-, $3, $5, pub: $7.50 $25, $30, $17.50-b.

128 ..."Confederate Handguns-Collector's Detailed Study of Southern Pistols." Reprint: Ordnance Journal of the American Ordnance Association, 1951, Nov-Dec. 4to, caption title, 11pp., illus.

129 ..."The Confederate Brass-Framed Colt & Whitney." n.p., Pub. privately by William A. Albaugh, 3rd., Falls Church, Va., & Edward N. Simmons.

130 ..."Confederate Handguns Concerning the Guns the men who made them & the times of their use." Philadelphia: Riling & Lentz, 1963. 4to, cl, d/w, color endsheets, xix, 250pp., index, illus., facms. $9.95, $20 ...Bonanza Reprint $15, $20, $25-bmk.

131 ..."Confederate Faces: A Pictorial Review of the individuals in the Confederate Armed Forces." Solana Beach, Cal., Verde Pub., (c. 1970) 4to, cl, illus., ports (part color), xx, 229pp. $20.

132 ..."More Confederate Faces: a Pictorial Review." Washington, D.C., ABS Printers, 1972. sm. 4to, ports, illus., 233pp.
..."Confederate Handguns." N.Y., Bonanza Books (197?) reprint of 1963. $15, $20, $25-bmk.

133 ..."Col. R. Milton Cary." In: North South Trade, 1977, v.V, p. 25-30.

134 **ALBAUGH, William A., III, & Edward N. Simmons**
"Confederate Arms." Harrisburg, Pa. (1957)...$1969, $6, 4to, cl, d/w, sviii, 278pp., diagrams, views, bibliography, $9, $12.50, $15, $65-jern., $15

135 ...DeLuxe Edt., padded blue Mor. Lim. Edt. signed by both authors. Includes 83pp. directory of makers, gunsmiths, dealers, places & men connected with Confederate Ordnance. $25. Bonanza Reprint $12.

136 **ALBAUGH, William A., III, & Richard D. Steuart**
"Handbook of Confederate Swords." Harriman, Tenn., Pioneer Press, 1951. 8vo, cl, (also stiff wraps), 127pp. (1)p. Index, illus. from orig. sketches. $3, $5, $6, $12.50

137 ..."A Photographic Supplement of Confederate Swords." (Washington, D.C.?, c.1963) Private printing, for the author & Wm. A. Bond. 8vo, xv, 205pp. illus., ports.

$25, $12.50
...Orange, Va., 1979 rep., 54pp, $20.

138 ..."The Original Confederate Colt. The Story of Leech & Rigdon & Rigdon-Ansley Revolvers. New York: Greenberg: Publisher(1953). Tall 8vo, decr. d/w, boards, illus., facsm. 62pp. $3.50, $35-bmk-105.

139 **ALBEMARLE, County, Va.**
See: "Magazine of Albemarle County History, Civil War Issue", v.22, v.25 & 30; See: Caroline M. Brown, James O. Breeden, Herbert A. Thomas, Jr., M.M. Clarke.

140 **ALBERT, Alphaeus Homer**
"Buttons of the Confederacy; descriptive & Illustrated Catalogue of buttons work by the troops of the Confederate States of America, 1861-1865." Hightstown, N.J., 1963. 8v, wraps, facsms., illus, xvii, 93pp. op

141 **ALBERTHAL, Vernell**
"Bushwhackers in them thar hills." In: Jr. Historian (Tex.), Sept. 1952, v.13, #1, p. 21-22. On loyalists ("rebels against rebellion." In the hill country of Texas. (German settlement)

142 **ALBERTS, Don E.**
"Brandy Station to Manila Bay: biography of General Wesley Merritt." Austin, Texas, Presidial Press, 1981, 8vo, cl, 352pp.+xp. maps, photos. Objective treatment of Union/CSA cavalry at Brandy Station, later Indian wars.

143 ..."Rebels on the Rio Grande: the civil war journal of A.B. Peticolas." Albuquerque: University of New Mexico Press, 1984, (8vo, cl, 187+ix, maps, illus.
..."Rebels on the Rio Grande . . ." Edt. See: A. B. Peticolas Journal.
..."The Battle of Peralta." In: NMHR, Oct. 1983, v.58, #4, p.369-79. Port, notes.

144 **ALBRIGHT, James W.**
"Books made in Dixie." In: SHSP, Sept. 1916, v.XLI, p. 57-60.

145 **ALBUM, For Reproductions of Confederate Currency.**
A collection of copies of Confederate Currency issued by the C.S. of A." Folder: 17x25", folded to 17x8 1/4", with 9 examples of CSA currency: $1, $2, $5, $10, $20, $50, $100, $500, & $1000, or 1861. Color scene of Mississippi steamboat, description of money.

146 **ALCORN, James Lusk**
"Letters of..., Edt. P.L. Rainwater." In: Jour. Miss. Hist., 1937, v.III, p. 196-209. CSA contraband trade & morale of people during the war. See: Mary Fisher Robinson.

147 **ALDEN, John Richard**
"The First South." Baton Rouge: Louisiana State University Press(1961) 12mo, cl, d/w, vii, 144pp. $3.50
...Gloucester: Peter Smith, 1968. $2.50

148 **ALDERMAN, Edwin Anderson & Armistead Churchill Gordon**
"J.L.M. Curry (1825-1903) a biography." N.Y., Lond: Macmillan, 1911. 8vo, cl, xx, (2), 468pp., port. $7.50, $10, $12, $12.50, $25-bmk. Comdr. 5th Ala. Reg., member congr. before in CSA, minst. to Spain, prf. Law, coll. pres.

149 **ALDERMAN, J.T., Prof.**
"Memories of 1865-1871." In: N.C. Booklet, April, 1914, v.XIII, #4, p. 199-213. Civil War & Reconstruction. $15 Bmk-106.

150 **ALDERSON, J. Coleman**
"Virginia in the war tragedies." In: CV, Oct, 1911, v.XIX, p. 465-466.

151 **ALDREDGE, George N.**
"Robert E. Lee, eulogy on unveiling of statue by Daughters of the Confederacy, April 19, 1897." Dallas, Texas, 1897. 8vo, 3, (1)pp. folder.

152 **ALECKSON, Sam**
"Before the War & After the Union, an Autobiography." (Priv. Print?) Boston

(1929), Gold Mind Pub. Co., 8vo, cl, 171pp. $8.50. Born Charleston, S.C., a slave, discusses plantation life, War Between States, in the Confed. army as officer's boy, thence to Springlake, Conn., Windsor, Vt. (1852-1914)

153 **ALEXANDER, Adam Leopold**
"The Alexander Letters, 1787-1900. Edt: Marion Alexander Boggs, foreword by Richard Barksdale Harwell." Athens: University of Georgia Pr, 1979. 8vo, cl, dj, illus., ports, 394pp.(wraps. $6) cloth-$16.95.

154 ...(1st Edt.) Savannah, Ga., Privately printed for George J. Baldwin, 1910. 8vo, ,s, genealogical table 387pp. 131 copies, for the family.

155 **ALEXANDER, E. Porter, Brig-Gen.**
"The great charge & artillery fighting at Gettysburg." In: B & L, v.3, p. 357-368, illus., port.

156 ..."Longstreet at Knoxville." In: B & L, v.3, p. 744-752, illus., ports.

157 **ALEXANDER, E.P.**
"E.P. Alexander & Pickett's Charge." In: CWTI, April 1978, v.17, #1, p. 22-25, illus., ports. Letters of Longstreet, Pickett & Alexander.

158 **ALEXANDER, Edward P.**
"Pickett's charge & artillery fighting at Gettysburg." In: Cent., Jan. 1887, v.33, #3, p. 464-471, illus.
..."Pickett's Charge". In: Cent. Mag., Jan. 1887.

159 **ALEXANDER, Edward Porter**
"Confederate Artillery Service." In: So. Hist. Soc. Tran., 1875, v.II, p. 27-41.
...(same) In: SHSP, 1883, v.XI, p. 97-113.

160 ..."Battle of Fredericksburg-crossing the river & occupying the town." In: SHSP, 1882, v.X, p. 382-392, 445-464.

161 ..."Causes of Lee's Defeat at Gettysburg." In: SHSP, Sept., 1877, v.IV, #3, p. 97-111.

162 ..."Battle of Bull Run." In: Scribners Mag., 1907, v.XLI, p. 80-94, plan.

163 ..."Great Charge & artillery fighting at Gettysburg." In: B & L, port, illus., v.III, p. 357-368.

164 ..."Letter from Gen. E.P. Alexander." In: SHSP, 1878, v.V, p. 201-203.

165 ..."Letter from General Early." In: SHSTransact., 1875, v.II, p. 71-74.

166 ..."Longstreet's Brigade." In: SHSTransact., 1875, v.II, p. 53-62.

167 ..."Longstreet at Knoxville." B & L, v.III, illus., plan, p. 745-751. In: JMSI, Mar., 1911, v.XLVIII, p. 264-267.

168 ..."Records of Longstreet's Corps., ANV. The Seven Days Battle." (cont'd. from Southern Mag., June, 1875) In: SHSP, 1876, v.I, p. 61-76, chart.

169 ..."Movement against Petersburg." In: Scribner's Mag., 1907, v.XLI, p. 180-194, plans.

170 ..."Seven Days' Battles." In: SHSTrans., 1875, v.II, p. 99-116.

171 ..."Sketch of Longstreet's Division-Winter of 1861-1862." In: SHSP, 1881, v.IX, p. 512-518, 1882, v.X. 'Yorktown & Williamsburg', p. 32-45.

172 ...(Printed circular letter, pertaining to the history of his command which he was preparing at the request of Gen. Longstreet. 8vo, one page, Columbia, S.C., Sept. 12, 1866.

173 ..."The Confederate Veteran." Reprint of the New York Times, June 15, 1902. Cleveland, Ohio, Burrows Bros. (1902). 12mo, 15pp. Head of title-"Address of...delivered alumni day, West Point Military Academy Centennial, June 9, 1902." 10,000 copies for distribution $5. Also, N.Y., G.P. Putnam's, 1902(?).

174 ..."The Wilderness Campaign." (1) Grant's conduct of Wilderness by E.P. Alexander. (2) Lee's Conduct at Wilderness, by Col. Wm. R. Livermore. (3) Wilderness Cam-

paign from our present point of view, by Maj. Eben Swift. Washington: American Historical Association Annual Report, 1908, vol. 1, p. 223-247, 1909, 8vo, wraps. $3.50, $5.

175 ..."Lee at Appomattox. Personal recollections of the break-up of the Confederacy." In: Century, 1901-1902, v.63, p. 921-931, port.

176 ..."Military memoirs of a Confederate, a critical narrative by...Brig.-Gen. in the Confederate Army, Chief of Artillery, Longstreet's Corps. New York: Charles Scribner's Sons, 1907, 8vo, cl, xviii, 634pp., 2 ports (incl. front), maps (1-fldg.). $150 jk-137, $100-bmk, $75, $40-y, $16.50, $20, $30, $35, $37.50.
...1908. $40, $17.50, $32.50.
...1910. $36, $50-bmk-75, $13.50, $20, $25
...1912. $45-bmk, $12.50, $15
...1914. $20, $12.50
...1918. $12.50, $25
...1962. Civil War Centennial Series. Bloomington, Ind., University Press. 8vo, cl, d/w, xii, 652pp. with a new introduction & notes. T. Harry Williams. $7.95, $22.50, $27.50.
...Dayton, Ohio, Morningside Press, 1977. New introduction by Dr. Maury Klein. $23, $30-y, $35-y

177 ..."The American Civil War, a critical narrative by..., with sketch maps by the author." London: Siegle, Hill & Co., 1908, 8vo, cl, xviii, 634pp., pl., 1 ports (incl. front maps (1-fldg.) First published: "Military Memoirs of a Confederate." NY-Scribner's, 1907. $5, $15, $50-brf.
Portrait, signature in facsimile, half-length to waist. Oval: 3 1/2x2 3/4" (Plate: 7x5") n.d. (c.1885).

178 **ALEXANDER, Edward Porter, Col.**
"Report of the Battle of Gettysburg." In: SHSP, 1877, v.IV, p. 235-239.

178a **ALEXANDER, Gen. E. P. and Col. Charles Marshall**
"Articles on Appomattox," in: Cent., April 1902. $30 Bm.

179 **ALEXANDER, Frederich Warren**
"Stratford Hall & the Lees connected with its history. Biographical, Genealogical, & historical." Coat-of-Arms. Park Grove, Va., The author, 1912. 8vo, cl, illus., pl, port, facsm., 332pp. $10, $15.

180 **ALEXANDER, Herbert L. Rice**
"The Armstrong Raid including the battles of Bolivar, Medon Station & Britton Lane." In: Tenn. HQ, 1962, v.XXI, p. 32-46.

181 **ALEXANDER, Holmes Moss**
"Washington & Lee; a study in the will to win." Boston: Western Islands (1966). 12mo, cl, xii, 114pp. $10.

182 ..."The hidden years." Richwood, W.Va., Press Club, (1981) 8vo, cl, dj, xiii, 187pp., illus. $18.50. Human interest biography of Stonewall.

183 **ALEXANDER, John Brevard**
"History of Mecklenburg County (N.C.) 1740-1900." Charlotte, N.C., Observer print, 1902. 8vo, cl, front, pl., port, map, iv, (3)431pp. Roster of 21 companies from county in the civil war. $10, $20, $40.

184 ..."Reminiscences of the past sixty years, by Dr. John Brevard Alexander." Charlotte, N.C., Ray print, 1908. 8vo, cl, port, 513pp. Gettysburg, Manassas & Richmond experiences in war. Dornbusch, 814.

185 ..."Roster of the twenty-one companies furnished by Mecklenburg county, N.C. in the War of 1861-1865." In: author's "Mecklenburg Co. History." Charlotte, N.C., Observer, 1902. p. 333-359. $20, $40.

186 **ALEXANDER, John Henry**
"Mosby's Men, by..., of Mosby's Rangers (Co. A)". N.Y., Wash., 1907, Neale Pub.

Co., sm. 8vo, buck., d/w, 14-ports, 180pp. $15, $18, $25, $30, $40, $50, $75-nc-384, Va. Cavalry-43rd Bat., $150-bmk-105.

..."Mosby's Men." Gaithersburg, Md., (1983), Butternut Press., sm8vo, cl, 180pp., reprint. $22.50.

187 **ALEXANDER, Thomas B.**
"Whiggery in Alabama & the lower south, 1860-1867." In: ARev., Jan. 1959, v.12, #1, p. 35-52.

188 ..."Neither peace nor war; conditions in Tennessee, 1865." In: East TennHS, 1949, #21, p. 33-51.

189 **ALEXANDER, Thomas B. & Rich. E. Beringer**
"The Anatomy of the Confederate Congress." Nashville, Tenn: Vanderbilt Univ. Press, 1972, 8vo, cl, xi, 435pp., append., tables, maps, bibliog., index. $16-bmk, $10

190 **ALL Quiet along the Potomac Tonight...**
Written by.... See: Thaddeus Oliver.

191 **ALLAN & HOTCHKISS, Wm. & Jed**
"Battlefields of Virginia, Chancellorsville..." Baltimore, Md., Butternut & Blue, 1984, 8vo, cl, 152pp., (5)fldg. maps, Lim. Edt. 600 numbered copies. Reprint of 1867 edt. $41.50.

192 **ALLAN, Francis D.**
"Allan's Lone Star Ballads. A Collection of Southern Patriotic Songs, Made During Confederate Times. Let me write the Ballads of a nation & I care not who makes the Laws. Montesquieu. Compiled & Revised by Francis D. Allan." Galveston, Texas: J.D. Sawyer, Pub., 1874. $150. 16mo, cl, (or, roan), iv, (5)-200, ads, 201-222, (2) $30, $85, $100, $135, $50, $125. Orig. pub. during war in pamphlet form, titled "Allan's Lone Star Ballads, #1." Also printed in broadside form as individual poems/songs.

193 ..."Allan's Lone Star Ballads. Galveston-Houston." Southrons, Hear Your Country Call You! by Albert G. Pike, or Arkansas. Tune of Dixie." (Houston, Texas Printing House, n.d., this printer dates from 1862-1864). Broadside 6x9.

...N.Y., Burt Franklin (1970). "Research & Source Works series-578." American Classics in History & Social Science, #153. $17, $21-y.

194 ..."Allen's Lone Star Ballads, No. 1: A Collection of Southern Patriotic Songs." Galveston-Houston: Francis D. Allen, 1863. 16mo, cover title, 64pp. Brick-Row, $1500. Only known copy.

195 ..."No. Eight, Allan's Lone Star Ballads. Galveston-Houston. There's Life in the Old Land Yet!", by James R. Randal, n.p., n.d. Broadside, 7 1/4x9 1/2" (c. 1862-1864, Houston) This must be James Ryder Randall. See: Crandall-3886-91, author "Maryland, My Maryland." Winkler Imprints, II, pg. 81 notes. "Lone Star Ballads, #1 (Patriotic) & #2 (Sentimental) from an ad in "Tri-Weekly Telegraph," Jan. 13, 1863. A collection of 94 of the most popular sentimental songs of the day. Send $1 by mail to Allen's Bookstore, Houston, Texas.

ALLAN, William
"The Army of Northern Virginia in 1862." Dayton, Oh., Morningside Press, 1983, 8vo, cl, 548pp., 5 colored fldg. maps, $60. New introduction by Robert Krick.

..."Hist. of campaigns T.J. Jackson..." Dayton, Oh., Morningside Press, 1987(sic) e.g., 1986, facsm, #19.

196 **ALLAN, William, Lt. Col.**
"Causes of Lee's Defeat at Gettysburg, Letter from Col. Wm. Allan, of Ewell's staff." In: SHSP, 1877, v.IV, p. 76-80.

197 ..."Confederate Artillery at Second Manassas & Sharpsburg." In: SHSP, July, 1883, v.XI, #7, p. 289-91.

198 ..."Contributions to the History of the Confederate Ordnance Department." In: SHSP, 1884, v.12, p. 66-94.

199 ..."Is the "Eclectic History of the US a proper book to use in our schools?" In: SHSP, 1884, v.XII, p. 235-237.

200 ..."First Maryland Campaign. Review of Gen. Longstreet by Col. Allan." In: SHSP, 1886, v.XIV, p. 102-118.

201 ..."Fredericksburg." In: Pap. Mil. Hist. Soc. Mass., 1899, v.III, p. 122-149.

202 ..."Invasion of Maryland." In: So. Biv., 1886, ns, v.II, p. 300-306, map.

203 ..."Jackson's Valley Campaign. Address delivered before Va. Div., ANV., Oct. 31, 1878, by..., late chief of ordnance, 2nd. (Stonewall) Corps, ANV." In: SHSP, Jan., 1879, v.VII, #1, p. 1-30.

204 ..."Lee's Campaign against Pope in 1862." Mag. Amr. Hist., 1886, v.XVI, p. 483-489.

205 ..."Lee's Strength & Losses at Gettysburg." In: SHSP, 1877, v.IV, p. 34-41.

206 ..."Military Operations of Gen. Beauregard by Alfred Romans. A review by Col. Allan, formerly chief ordance, 2nd Corp., ANV." In: SHSP, 1884, v.XII, p. 258-266.

207 ..."Pope's campaign again, a noteworthy review of facts & figures." In: Mag. Amer. Hist., 1886, v.XVI, p. 483-489.

208 ..."Relative numbers & losses at Slaughter's Mountain("Cedar Run")" In: SHSP, 1880, v.VIII, p. 178-183.

209 ..."Relative strength at Second Manassas." In: SHSP, 1880, v.VIII, p. 217-221.

210 ..."Reminiscences of Field Ordnance Service with the Army of Northern Virginia, 1863-1865." In: SHSP, 1886, v.XIV, p. 137-146.
...(same). "Arms Collector," Apr., 1957, v1, p. 37-41, views.

211 ..."A reply to Gen. Longstreets: Lee's invasion of Penna. & Lee's right wing at Gettysburg." In: B & L, v.III, p. 355-356.

212 ..."Review of Bat's Battle of Gettysburg." In: SHSP, 1876, v.I, p. 365-370.

213 ..."Review of Gen. Doubleday's Campaign of the Civil War-Chancellorsville-Gettysburg." In: SHSP, 1882, v.X, p. 170-174.

214 ..."Review of Alex S. Webb's Peninsula McClellan's Campaign of 1862." In: SHSP, May, 1882, v.X, #5, p. 193-206.

215 ..."A Review of Geo. E. Pond's Shenandoah Valley in 1864." In: SHSP, 1883, v.XI, p. 270-282.

216 ..."Stonewall Jackson's Valley Campaign." In: Annl. of War, Phila: 1879, p. 724-49.

217 ..."Strategy of the Gettysburg Campaign objects, progress, results." In: Pap. Mil. Hist. Soc. Mass., 1887, v.III, p. 415-448.

218 ..."History of the Campaign of Gen. T.J. (Stonewall) Jackson in the Shenandoah Valley of Virginia from November 4, 1861, to June 17, 1862, by William Allan, formerly Lieutenant-Colonel & Chief Ordnance Officer, Second Corps, ANV. With full maps of the region & the battlefields by Jed Hotchkiss, formerly Captain & Topographical engineer, second Corp., ANV." In: SHSP, Sept. 1920, v.XLIII, pt. II, p. (3). (113)-294, (1) note. 9-maps, color, some folded. Dayton, Ohio: Morningside Press, 1974. Reprint, 175pp. color maps. $15

219 ..."The Invasion of Maryland." In: SB, ns, v.II, 1886-1887, p. 300-306, map.

220 ..."Strategy of the campaign of Sharpsburg or Antietam, Sept., 1862." In: Pap. Mil. Soc. Mass., 1888, v.III, p. 73-103.

221 ..."Strategy of the Sharpsburg campaign." In: Md. Hist. Mag., 1906, v.I, p. 247-271.

222 ..."Strength of the forces under Pope & Lee, contributed by..., late Lieut-Col. chief of Ordnance, 2nd corp. ANV. CSA to which is append: a note by John C. Ropes. In: Pap. Mil. Hist. Soc. Mass., 1886, v.II, p. 195-219.

223 ..."The Virginia Campaign of 1864-1865." by Gen. Humphreys, a review by..." In: SHSP, 1883, v.XI, p. 454-460.

224 ..."Jackson's Valley Campaign. An address by...Col. Wm. Allan, formerly Chief of Ordnance of Jackson's 2nd Corp., of McDonough institute, Md., before the Virginia division Army of Northern Virginia, at annual meeting, held in the capitol in Richmond, Va., Oct. 30, 1878." Richmond: G.W. Gary & Co., 1878. 8vo, wraps, 30pp. $7.50, $15, $100-bmk-105.

225 ...S.H.S.P., 1979, v.VII, p. 1030.

226 ..."The Army of Northern Virginia in 1862. With an introduction by John C. Ropes." New York & Boston: Houghton, Mifflin Co., 1892. 8vo, cl, x, 537pp. front(port) fldg. maps, (6). $40, $7, $15, $32.50, $22.50, $50, $70-nc, $100-brd, $150-bmk-105.

227 ..."History of the Campaign of Gen. T.J. (Stonewall) Jackson in the Shenandoah Valley of Virginia." London: Rees Print, 1912. 8vo, cl, 8-maps, xvi, 284pp. Pall Mall Military Series.

228 **ALLBRITTON, Orval E.**
"The 3rd Arkansas Regiment from formation to Fredericksburg." (Fayetteville, Ark., Ark. Hist. Quar., 1957, v.XVI, p. 150-162.

229 **ALLEAU, M.Th.**
"La Auerre et la Paix. Discours Prononce le 17 Juin, 1864, a la Nouvelle Orleans par, Au Profit des Prisonniers et des Victimes de la Guere." Nouvelle Orleans ("Plume De Bronze") 1864. 8vo, wraps, 20pp. A New Orleans Catholic priest. Tinker locates only his copy. $10

230 **ALLEN, A. Hall**
"Major General Frederick Steele & Staff." In: AHQ, 1964, v.XXIII, p. (191), plate. Steel & staff, Dept. of Arkansas, Hdq. Little Rock.

231 **ALLEN, C.T.**
"Rich Mountain in 1861." The second battle of the late war. In: SHSP, 1889, v.XXVII, p. 44-48.

232 **ALLEN, Cuthbert Edward, O.S.B., A.B.**
"The Slavery Question in Catholic Newspapers, 1850-1865." N.Y., United States Catholic Historical Society, 1936, in v.XXVI, Historical Records & Studies, p. 99-169.

233 **ALLEN, George W.**
"Civil War Letters of George W. Allen. Edt: Charleen Plumly Pollard." In: SWHQ, July, 1979, v.LXXXIII, #1, p. 47-52, (1)-drawing.

234 **ALLEN, Glenn C. & Wayne C. Piper**
"The Battle Flags of the Confederacy." Rushville, Ind., 1975. 8vo, pict. wraps, 55pp. $15, $10, Reissue of the Cotton Belt Route title. "The Returned Battleflags." sepia-tone.

235 **ALLEN, H.D.**
"The paper money of the Confederate States, with historical data." In: Numismatist, Jan/Feb., 1919, v.XXXII, p. 2-10, 50-56.

236 ..."The treasurer of the Confederate States of America." In: Numismatist, April, 1919, v.XXXII, p. 145-147. Edward C. Elmore.

237 **ALLEN, Hall**
"Center of Conflict. A Factual Story of the War Between the States in Western Kentucky & Tenn." Pub: Paducah(Ky.) Sun-Democrat in Observance of the Civil War Centennial, 1861-1961. (1961). 8vo, soft-wraps, decr., illus., ports, ix, 179pp. $3

238 **ALLEN, Hervey**
"Action at Aquila." N.Y., Farrar & Rinehart (1938). 12mo, cl, illus.(maps) 7, 3-369pp. $17.50
...London: V. Gollanca, Ltd., 1938. 12mo, cl, 448pp. $35, $25-jk-122, $15

239 **ALLEN, Hugh (pseud.)**
"The James City Cavalry. Its Organization

& First Service." In: SHSP, 1896, v.XXIV, p. 353-358.

240 **ALLEN, James Lane**
"The Sword of Youth." N.Y., Century, 1915, 12mo, cl, 261pp. Lee saves soldier on AWOL, fiction.

241 **ALLEN, James S.**
"Reconstruction; the Battle for Democracy, 1865-1876." N.Y., International Pubs., (1937). 8vo, cl, illus., 256pp. $10

242 ..."The Struggle for Land during the Reconstruction period." In: Sci. & Society, 1937, v.I, p. 378-401.

243 **ALLEN, John James, Hon.**
"Preamble & Resolution, offered in a large mass meeting of the people of Botetourt Co., Dec. 10, 1860, by...& adopted with but two dissenting voices." In: SHSP, 1876, v.1, p. 13-19.

244 **ALLEN, L.W., Capt.**
"A Plan to Escape, in 1863, from the Federal Prison on Johnson's Island." In: SHSP, 1891, v.XIX, p. 283-289.

245 **ALLEN, Lee N.**
"John Allen Wyeth: historian." In: ARev., July 1971, v.24, #3, p. 182-191.

246 **ALLEN, Lyman Whitney**
"The Gray Cavalier; The Story of Robert E. Lee." N.Y., Thornton W. Allen Co., 1929, 12mo, cl, illus., front, ports, 228pp. $5. 500 copies, atg. edt., "An Epic Trilogy, v.III" (Washington, Lincoln, Lee)

247 **ALLEN, Merritt Parmlee**
"White Feather." N.Y., Longmans, Green, 1944. 12mo, cl, 196pp. Lad with Morgan & Duke. Fiction.

248 **ALLEN, R.N.**
"Guy's Battery. Another Roll of the Company made from memory." In: SHSP, 1901, v.XXIX, p. 311-314.

249 **ALLEN, Randall**
"Census enumeration of Confederate soldiers residing in Randolph County, Ala. in 1907." In: W. Cent. Genea. (Ga.) So. News letter, 1984, v.6, (102), 9-20.

250 **ALLEN, Theodore F.**
"The Flag Still There. Dedicated to the Vanishing Army of "Morgan's Men"." Cincinnati, (1906). 12mo, port, cl, 26pp. Remarks about Renfrew & his island, with CSA flag still there after 25 years. $7.50

251 ..."Breech-loading cannon in the Confederate army." In: Jour. Mil. Ser. Inst., May, 1909, v.XLIV, p. 440-444.

252 **ALLEN, V.C.**
"Rhea & Meigs Counties (Tennessee) in the Confederate War." n.p., n.d. (1908) 12mo, cl, front(color flag) 6-ports. (A previous sale $75, until a small cache was found) Many rosters of the various companies listed.) $50-bmk, $75-bmk-84, $35-mcm, $25

253 **ALLEN, W.G.**
"Reminiscences of Chickamauga." In: CV, Nov., 1911, v.XIX, p.511.

254 **ALLEN, Walter**
"Governor Chamberlain's administration in South Carolina; a chapter of Reconstruction in the Southern States." N.Y., Lond: E.P. Putnam's sons, 1888. 8vo, front, port, xv, 544pp. $75-jk-137.

255 **ALLEN, Ward**
"A note on the origin of the Ku Klux Klan." In: Tenn. HQ, 1964, v.XXIII, p. 182-202.

256 **ALLEN, William, Hon.**
"The Southland Columbiad & other Poems." Nashville, Tenn., M.E. Church, south, 1897. 12mo, cl, 316pp. Author not only soldier but chaplain thru entire war.

257 **ALLENTUCK, Andrew**
"James G. Blaine & Reconstruction." (London) Jour. Confed. Hist. Soc., Summer, 1968, v.6, #2, p. 72-86.

258 **ALLISON, Joseph Dill, Dr.**
"I have been through my first battle & have had enough to last me..." In: CWTI,

Feb. 1967, v.5, #10, p. 40-, illus., map. Stationed near Pensacola, the Alabama doctor camp life boring and shocking.

259 ..."War Diary of J.D.A." In: AHQ, 1947, v.9, p. 385-398. J.D. Allison of Carlowville Ala.

260 **ALLISON, Young Ewing**
"Sue Mundy: an account of the terrible Kentucky guerrilla of Civil War Times." In: KyHSR, Oct., 1959, v.57, p. 295-316. notes. From the "Courier Journal." See: Sue Mundy, pseud.
..."Select works of Young E. Allison-Literature-biography-history-insurance, with a biography of the author & a list of his writings." Louisville, Ky., 1935. 12mo, cl, 2pp, (iii)-vii, 469pp., front, illus., pls, ports, facsms (incl. music). Edt: Young E. Allison, Jr., J. Christina Bay, commemoration of the Filson Club. Included herein is a reprint of "Sue Mundy", itself reprinted from the 1887 Feb. 6, "Courier-Journal". Note: Allison wrote this 22 years after Mundy's hanging.

261 **ALLSOPP, Frederick William**
"The Life Story of Albert Pike (1809-1891)." Little Rock, Ark., Parke-Harper News, 1920. 8vo, cl, illus., plates, ports, 130pp.

262 ...(same), 1928. Revised & extended edt. of above, xix, 369, (7)pp. $10. Gen. Pike organized Indians for CSA. $35-y.

263 **ALMAND, Bond**
"Judicially it was a civil war." In: Ga. Bar Jour., Feb., 1956, v.18, p. 245-252. Legal nature of relations between CSA & US as determined by court decision, 1868ff.

264 **ALSPAUGH, Granville L.**
"Letters of a Confederate soldier, 1862-1863. Edt: Mary Elizabeth Sanders." In: LHQ, 1946, v.29, p. 1229-1240.

265 **ALSTON, Joseph Blyth**
"Sumter". Large 8vo, wraps, (3), 4-11pp. (verso title-"These verses are published for the Benefit of the South Carolina Monument Association to aid their design of erecting a monument at Columbia, S.C., in memory of those who fell in defence of their country." A.S. Salley gives Allston as author, c. 1870.

266 **ALSTON, Robert C. (Cotten)**
"Lucius Q. Cincinnatus Lamar. Speech before the Symposium, Feb. 15, 1937 in Atlanta, Georgia." n.p. (Atlanta, Ga.?) 8vo, wraps, cover title, 33, (1)p. speech taken from Cate's Life of Lamar.

267 **ALTSHELER, Joseph Alexander**
"Before the Dawn; a story of the Fall of Richmond." N.Y., Doubleday, Page co., 1903. 12mo, viii, 372. Prolific Kentuckian writer.

268 ..."The Guns of Bull Run; story of the Civil War's Eve." N.Y., D. Appleton, 1914. 12mo, 347pp. front, col. pls.

269 ..."The Guns of Shiloh; story of the Great Western Campaign." N.Y., D. Appleton, 1914.

270 ..."The Last Rebel." Phil: J.B. Lippincott, 1900. 12mo, cl, illus., front, 219pp.

271 ..."The Scouts of Stonewall; Story of the Great Valley Campaign." N.Y., D. Appleton, 1914. 12mo, cl, 351pp., col. front & pls. "Civil War Series". Other edts. 1917 & 1928, $3.50, $5

272 ..."The Shades of the Wilderness, a Story of Lee's Great Stand." N.Y., D. Appleton, 1916. 12mo, cl, 311pp., col. front & pls.

273 ..."The Star of Gettysburg; a story of the Southern High Tide." N.Y., D. Appleton, 1915. 12mo, cl, 370pp., col. front, & pls. $3.50, Also 1919 edition.

274 **ALVAREZ, Robert L.**
"The Death of the "Old War Horse" Longstreet." In: Ga. H.Q.,March, 1968, v.LII, #1, p. 70-77.

275 **ALVES, Jo Ann**
"A Muster Roll of 1862." In: AHQ, 1954, v.XIII, p. 127-131. Of Co. A., Sixth Regi-

ment, Arkansas Volunteers, CSA.
..."A Muster Roll of 1862." In: ArkHQ, v.13, p. 127-131.

276 **AMANN, William Frayne**
"Personnel of the Civil War," reprint in part of Marcus Wright's Local Designation of CSA Troops & Memorandum Armies & General Officers. N.Y., Thos. Yoseloff, 1961, 2vols. Boxed, vii, 376, 373pp. $10, $20-y, full calf. $40
...2nd Edt: (Mar., 1964) $18, $30-bmk-108
...3rd Edt: (1968) 2vol. in 1 $5.95, $10

277 **AMBLER, Charles Henry**
"The Cleavage between Eastern & Western Virginia." In: Amer. Hist. Rev., July, 1910, v.15, #4, P. 762-780.

278 ..."General R.E. Lee's Northwest Virginia Campaign." In: W. Va. Hist., 1943, v.V, p. 101-115.

279 ..."Romney in the Civil War." In: W. Va. Hist., 1943, v.V, p. 151-200.

280 ..."The Life & Diary of John Floyd: Governor of Virginia, an apostle of secession, father of the Oregon country." (Richmond, Va., Richmond Press, 1918) 8vo, cl, port, 248pp.

281 ..."Sectionalism in Virginia." Chicago, 1910, Univ. of Chicago Press, 8vo, cl, ix, 366pp., 12-maps.

282 ..."Thomas Ritchie (1778-1854) a Study in Virginia Politics." Richmond: Bell Book & Stationery, 1913, 8vo, cl, xvi, 303pp. plates, ports. $10
..."Gen. R.E. Lee's Northwest Virginia campaign." In: WVaH, 1943-1944, v.V, p. 101-115.

283 **AMBROSE, Stephen E.**
"By enlisting negroes, could the South still win the war?" In: CWTI, Jan. 1964, v.III, #9, p. 16-21. illus., port. Pat Cleburne's proposal, to give up slavery in exchange for independence. Hushed up & Prs. Davis's request to keep it quiet.

284 **AMERICAN Battle Art, Album of, 1755-1918.**
Washington: Government Printing Office, 1947. 4to, cl, 318 pp., Civil War prints: #72-126; descp. of plates, p. 165-210. Both original drawings & lithographs. $5

285 **"AMERICAN State Papers."**
In: Black Edn. Mag., May 1863, v.XCIII, p. 626-644. Takes Seward to task, the strange weakness of the North & it's futility of diplomacy.

286 **AMES, Susan M.**
"Federal policy toward the eastern shore of Virginia in 1861." In: VMHB, Oct. 1961, v.69, #4, p. 432-459, facsm.

287 **"ANATOMY of the Confederate Congress, The,**
a study of the influence of member characteristics on legislative voting behavior, 1861-1865." Nashville, Tenn., Vanderbilt University Press, 1972. 8vo, cl, xi, 43pp. (wraps.) $10. See: W. Buck, A.B. Moore, Frank Owsley.

288 **ANDERS, Curt**
"Fighting Confederates." New York: G.P. Putnam's (1969), 8vo, cl, d/w, maps, 315pp. $3.50, $6.50, $20-bmk, $1.98, $15

289 **ANDERS, Leslie**
"Fighting the ghosts at Lone Jack." In: MHR, April, 1985, v.79, #3, p. 332-356, ports, illus., maps.

290 **ANDERSON, Archer**
"Sorrel's 'Recollection of a Confederate Staff Officer', a correction & a vindication of Gen. D.H. Hill." In: SHSP, 1905, v.33, p. 25

291 ..."Robert Edward Lee, an address delivered at the dedication of the monument to General Robert Lee at Richmond, Virginia, May 29, 1890, by Archer Anderson. Published by the Lee Monument Association." Richmond, Va., W. Ellis Jones, 1890, 8vo, wraps, 45pp. $20-bmk, $4.50, (atg.) $7.50, $15

292 ...Also in: SHSP, 1889, v.XVII, p. 303, p. 312-335.

..."Address on the opening of Lee Camp soldier's home, May 20, 1885." Richmond, Va., R.E. Lee Camp #1. 8vo, wraps, 12pp.

..."An Appreciation. . . ." See: Egbert G. Leigh, Jr.

293 **ANDERSON, C.C.**
"Who was responsible for Andersonville?" In: CV, May, 1921, v.XXIX, p. 168.

294 **ANDERSON, Charles**
"Speech on the State of the Country, at a meeting of the people of Bexar County, at San Antonia(!), Texas, November 24, 1860." Washington: L. Towers, 1860." 8vo, wraps, 16pp. Appeals staying in the Union. $125-jk-127.

295 **ANDERSON, Charles C.**
"Fighting by Southern Federalism which the author places the numerical strength of the armies that fought for the Confederacy at approximately 1,000,000 men & shows that 296,579 white soldiers living in the South, and 137,676 colored soldiers, and approximately 200,000 living in the North that were born in the South, making 634,255 southern soldiers, fought for the preservation of the Union." N.Y., Neale pub., 1912. 8vo, cl, front(map), 408pp., general index, and index of battles. Men mainly living in Maryland, Kentucky & Missouri. $100-bmk-43, $125, $45-y, $75, $15, $120-bmk-48, $150-bmk-48.

296 **ANDERSON, Charles T.**
"Campaigning in Southern Arkansas, a memoir by C.T. Anderson. Edited by Roman J. Zorn." In: Ark. HQ, 1949, v.VIII, p. 240-244. Newton's Regiment.

297 **ANDERSON, Charles W., Maj, Adj. & Inspt. Gen.**
"The true story of Fort Pillow." In: CV, Nov. 1895, v.III, #11, p. 322-326, map.

298 **ANDERSON, David Daniel**
"Robbery or Warfare: Port Clinton's Unresolved dilemma-the case of Confederate Agent Bennett G. Burley, 1861-1865." Northwest Ohio Quart., Spring 1960, (not in '60 AHA)

299 **ANDERSON, David W., Maj.**
"The Bloody Angle. Maj. D.W. Anderson's Relation." In: SHSP., 1885, v.XIII, p. 251-254. Anderson was Major 44th Va. Reg. Jone's Division.

300 **ANDERSON, Dice R. (Robins)**
"R.M.T. Hunter." In: Branch Hist. Pap. II, June, 1906, p. 4-77.

301 **ANDERSON, Edward C., Maj.**
"Confederate Foreign Agent: The European Diary of Major Edward C. Anderson." Edt. W. Stanley Hoole. University, Alabama: Confederate Pub. Co., 1976, 8vo, cl, dj, 161pp. $12.50

302 **ANDERSON, Edward Maffitt**
"Letters from a Georgia Midshipman on the C.S. Alabama. Edited by W. Stanley Hoole." In: Ga. Hist. Quart., 1975, v.LIX, p. 416-432. $8-bmk

303 **ANDERSON, Edward Willoughby, et al**
"Letters of a West Pointer, 1860-1861." (Lancaster, Pa., Lancaster print, 1928) 8vo, wraps, cover title, p. 599-617. Reprint: Amer. Hist. Review, XXXIII, #3, April, 1928.

304 **ANDERSON, Ellen Graham**
"The Wounding & Hospital Care of William A. Anderson." (Richmond) Va. Mag. Hist. Biog. Apr., 1954, v.62, #2, p. 205-207.

305 **ANDERSON, Ephraim McD(owell)**
"Memoirs, historical & personal, including the campaigns of the First Missouri Confederate Brigade." St. Louis, Times Print, 1868, 8vo, cl, 2, vi, (9)-436, (2)pp. front(port) plates(4). $50-y, $250-bmk-94

...Dayton, Ohio: Morningside Bookshop (1972) Second Edition-Notes & Foreword by Edwin C. Bearss, Index by Margie Riddle Bearss." 8vo, cl, added pages:

foreword, port., ix-xv, Appendix: (2), 439-590pp., incl. index, map lines. $30-y, $20.

..."Memoirs: Historical & Personal--Campaigns of Missouri Confed. Brig." Dayton, Oh., Morningside, 1988. 8vo, cl, 590p, ills, map, ports. $35.

306 **ANDERSON, Frank**
"Missouri's Confederate State Capitol at Marshall, Texas." (Columbia, Mo., Mo. Hist. Review, Apr., 1933, v.XXVII, #3, p. 240-243.

307 **ANDERSON, Fulton, et al**
"Address delivered before the Virginia State Convention by...(of Mississippi), Henry L. Benning (Georgia) & John S. Preston (South Carolina), Feb., 1861." Richmond: Wyatt M. Elliott, 1861. 8vo, wraps, 64pp. Presenting strong reasons why Virginia should seceed. Crandall-2257 $$25., $32.50, $35., $150-Ginsberg, $27.50, $60-bmk, $100-bmk.

308 **ANDERSON, George Burgwyn, Gen.**
See: Maj. Seaton Gales.

309 **ANDERSON, Henry W.**
"Virginia First & Lee an Address by.-..delivered at Richmond, Va., Virginia Day, Jan. 22, 1917." (Richmond, Va., Jan. 31, 1917), 8vo, wraps, cover title, (1), 88pp. $2, $4, $5

310 **ANDERSON, James LaVerne**
"Robert Mercer Taliaferro Hunter." (Richmond), Va. Cavl., Autumn, 1968, v.XVIII, #2, p. 8-13, illus., ports. "Conservative in both manner & politics, he served the old Union & the Confederacy equally well."

311 **ANDERSON, James Patton, Maj-Gen.**
"Civil War Letters of Major General James Patton Anderson. Edited by Margaret Anderson Uhler." In: FHW, Oct., 1977, v.LVI, #2, p. 150-175.

312 ..."Autobiography." In: SHSP, 1896, v.24, p. 57-72. (JPAPapers (autobiog.) at P.K. Yonge Lib., Univ. of Florida.

313 **ANDERSON, James W.**
"A Confederate Prisoner at Camp Chase, letters & diary of Private..., by George C. Osborn." (Columbus, Ohio State Archaelogical & Historical Quarterly, 1950. LIX, p. 38-67. Also: Tenn. H.Q., March-June, 1951, v.X, p. 74-90, R161-84.

314 **ANDERSON, James, Capt.**
"A captured Confederate officer; nine letters from James Anderson to his family (1862-1864)." In: Md.HM, Spring, 1981, p. 63-39. George M. Anderson, Edt.

315 **ANDERSON, John H.**
"The American Civil War, the operations in the eastern theatre from the commencement of hostilities to May 5, 1863. And in the Shenandoah Valley from Apr., 1861-Je., 1862." London: H. Rees, 1910. 8vo, cl, 120pp, 14-fldg. maps in pocket at end.

316 ..."Notes on the Battles of Antietam & Fredericksburg." London: H. Rees, 1912. 8vo, wraps, 34pp. 2-fldg. maps.

317 ..."Notes on the Life of Stonewall Jackson & on His Campaigning in Virginia, 1861-1863." London: H. Rees, 1904. 8vo, cl, 64pp., 12-fldg. maps, rear pocket. $65-jk, $14.50, $27.50.

...London: Hugh Rees, 1905. Second revised & enlarged edt." Including papers set at the promotion examinations, Nov. 1904, with answers." 8vo, cl, 80pp., 13-fldg. maps at end. $16.50, $20, $100-bmk-105.

318 **ANDERSON, John Huske, Mrs., (Lucy London)**
"North Carolina Women of the Confederacy." Reprint History N.C., U.D.C., 1926. (Raleigh, N.C., Confederate Centennial Comm. (1964?) 8vo, wraps, port on covers, 141pp., illus. (op)

..."North Carolina Women of the Confederacy, written & published by..., historian North Carolina Div., U.D.C." 1926. (Fayetteville, N.C., Cumberland Pr. Co.) 8vo, port on stiff wraps, illus., 141pp. $25, $7.50, $12.50, $18.50.

...Reprint, n.p., n.d., (1964?) $2.50, $20-bmk-105.

319 ..."Confederate arsenal at Fayetteville, N.C. In: CV, June, 1928, v.XXXVI, p. 222-223, 238.

320 ..."The Life of Samuel A'Court Ashe, Dean of North Carolina Historians." n.p., n.d. (UDC, North Carolina Div. Prize Essays, offprint, 1936) 8vo, wraps, 12pp. $5.

321 ..."Value of the Jefferson Davis Historical Foundation(a foundation founded by the United Daughters of the Confederacy, for the purpose of preserving the history of the state(South Carolina)." In: South. Mag., 1936, v.II, #10.

322 ..."What Sherman did to Fayetteville, N.C." In: CV, April, 1924, v.XXXII, p. 138-140.

323 ..."The old arsenal at Fayetteville, N.C." In: CV, April, 1926, v.XXXIV, p. 134-135.

324 ..."Foreign relations of the Confederacy." In: CV, 1932, v.40, p. 13-16, 56-59.

325 ..."The University of North Carolina, in the war between the states." III-parts. In: CV, 1930, v.38, p.12-15, 51-53, 91-94. Prize essay, N.C. Div., UDC.

326 ..."War days in Fayetteville, N.C." Fayetteville, N.C., 1910, 8vo, wraps, 60p. $75-r

...See: Mrs. John Huske (Lucy London), N.C. Women of the CSA.

327 ANDERSON, John Q.
"A Texas Surgeon in the C.S.A." Tuscaloosa, Ala: Confed. Pub. Co.,, 1957, Confederate Centennial Studies, #6. 12mo, stiff wraps, 123pp. Lim. Edt. 450 copies. $25-bmk, $5, $7.50

328 ANDERSON, John Q., Edt.
"Campaigning with Parson's Texas Cavalry Brigade, CSA The War Journals & Letters of the Four Orr Brothers, 12th Texas Cavalry Regiment." (Hillsboro, Texas) Hill Junior College Press (1967) Waco, Texas: Texian Press. 8vo, cl, d/w, xiii, (2), 173pp. ports. $6$12-chill, $8

329 ANDERSON, John T.
"General Hunter in the Valley." In: Tyler QHM, 1931, v.XII, p. 197-198. Letters of Anderson to J.D. Imboden, April 2, 1877, re depredations by Hunter's troops, June, 1864.

330 ANDERSON, Joseph R., Gen.
"Hero of an incident of the Battle Gaines' Mill." In: SHSP, 1891, v.19, p. 416-417.

331 ANDERSON, Joseph Reid
"Anderson's Brigade in battles around Richmond." In: Confed. Vet., Dec., 1923, v.XXXI, p. 448-451.

332 ..."Genr. Joseph R. Anderson. Hero of an incident of the Battle of Gaines' Mill." (From: Rich "Times", Jan. 24, 1892.) In: SHSP, 1891, v.XIX, p. 416-417.

333 ..."The V.M.I., Her Past." Lexington, Va., VMI, 1910. See: Chas. B. Dew's "Ironmaker of the Confederacy: Joseph R. Anderson & the Tredegar Iron Works."

334 ANDERSON, L.B., Dr.
"The Execution of Dr. David Minton Wright by the Federal Authorities, at Norfolk, Va., October 23, 1862." In: SHSP, 1893, v.XXI, p. 326-337. See: Alex W. Weddell.

335 ANDERSON, Lee Stratton
"Valley of the Shaw; the Battles of Chickamauga & Chattanooga, 1863." Chattanooga, Tenn., Hudson Pr., 1959. 8vo, wraps, maps, ports, views, 64pp.

336 ANDERSON, Lucy Work London
"Handbook of historical facts about North Carolina in the War Between the States, 1861-1865." Compiled for chapters of N.C. Div. of U.D.C. (Fayetteville, N.C., Cumberland Print. 12mo, wraps, (10)pp.

..."War days in Fayetteville, N.C." Fayetteville, N.C., 1910. 8vo, wraps, 60pp. $75.

337 ANDERSON, Mabel Washbourne
"Life of General Stand Watie, the only In-

dian Brigadier General of the Confederate Army & the Last General to Surrender." Pryor, Okla., Mayes Co. Republican, 1915. Decr. wraps, 8vo, 58pp. Born near Rome, Ga., a full blood-brother of Elias Boudinot & most prominent men of Cherokee Nation. $200-jk-142, $95, $150.
...Pryor, Okla., 1931, Rev. ed. 2nd. 8vo, wraps, illus., port., 85pp. cover title "Life of Gen. Stand Watie & contemporary Cherokee History." $10, $15, $17.50, $20, $25, $47.50, $30, $70-bmk

338 ..."Chronicles of Okla., X, p. 540-548. 46pp., 1936, (See: Frank Cunningham)

339 ..."Excerpts from the Life of General Stand Watie." In: So. Mag., Winter, 1936-1937, v.III, p. 7-8, 46.

340 **ANDERSON, Patton, Maj-Gen.**
"Report: Operations from July 30th to Aug. 31st, 1864, including the Battle of Jonesboro, Ga." In: SHSP, 1877, v.IV, p. 193-202. (See: H.D. Clayton), v.V, p. 127-128,; R.L. Gibson's Letter, v.V, p. 132-133; Letter S. D. Lee, V.V, p. 130-131.

341 ..."Autobiography of Gen. Patton Anderson, transcribed by Mrs. Anderson." In: SHSP, 1896, v.24, p. 57-72.

342 **ANDERSON, Richard B.**
"Civil War Experiences of..." (Lometa, Texas, 1928) 16mo, wraps, cover title, port, (7)pp. Text in double columns.

343 **ANDERSON, Richard Henry, Lieut-Gen.**
"Official Diary of First Corps., ANV, while commanded by Lt.-Gen. R.H. Anderson, from May 7 to 31st, 1864." In: SHSP, 1879, v.VII, p. 491-494; 503-512.

344 ..."Report of the Battle of Gettysburg." In: SHSP, 1877, v.III, p. 49-54.

345 **ANDERSON, S.T.**
"Diary of S.T. Anderson, Confederate Prisoner of War, 1864-1865." (Chester, S.C., no. Pub., 1908) 8vo, wraps, 16pp.

346 **ANDERSON, Samuel James Pierce**
"The Dangers & Duties of the Present Crisis! Discourse delivered in Union Church, St. Louis, Jan. 4, 1861." St. Louis, Mo., Schenk & Co., 1861. 8vo, wraps, 18pp. Anti-Union (old)$4

347 **ANDERSON, Sterling P., Jr.**
"Edmund Ruffin, Editor & Publisher." (Richmond), Va. Cavl., Summer, 1967. v.XVII, #1, p. 32-38, illus., ports (2-color) Re: his agricultural achievements, not his secessionist bend.

348 **ANDERSON, William A.**
"Stonewall Jackson." In: SHSP, ns, II, 1915, p. 149-161. Address at laying cornerstone of the equestrian statue of Jackson, Richmond, June 3, 1915.

349 **ANDERSON, William Alexander**
"Address of..., upon the laying of the corner-stone of the equestrian statue of Stonewall Jackson in Richmond, Va., June 3, 1905, at the request of the Stonewall Jackson monument corp." Richmond, Va., 1915. 8vo, wraps, 12pp, reprint. In: SHSP, 1915, v.XL, p. 149-161. $2.50

349a **ANDERSONVILLE, Georgia**
See: Edward W. Boaten, Walter L. Fleming, Michigan Post & Tribune, New Orleans, La. Picayune, Joshua Peterkin, Rufus Bryan Richardson, Isaiah H. White.

350 **ANDERSONVILLE, Stockade, Georgia**
Colored lithograph, 17x23", showing inmates in various activities. n.p., n.d. (1903) $7.50, $25

351 ..."Andersonville Prison from the Southeast." color litho., 17x23", n.p., n.d. (1860's) $25

352 ..."Andersonville Prison, sketched by John Burns Walker, P.V.I., 17 1/2x22", black & white, North View. Phila: T. Sinclairs, 1865. $20

353 ...Same, "South View" $20

354 ..."Bird's-Eye View of Andersonville Prison from the South-East." 19x14", Color litho, J.W. Morton, Jr. (c.1890) $30

355 **ANDERSONVILLE: The Other Side.**
In: CV, 1907, v.15, p.57-60. Capt. J.M. Bryant, M.J. Haley, et.al., their opinions dissected.

356 **ANDREANO, Ralph Louis**
"A Theory of Confederate Finance." In: CWH, December, 1956, v.II, #4, p. 21-28.

357 **ANDREWS, Andrew J.**
"A sketch of the boyhood days of...of Gloucester County, Va., & his experience as a soldier in the late War between the States. Written by self. Richmond, Va., Hermitage Press, 1905, 12mo, cl, front(port), 163pp. "To which are added selected poems by the author." $20, $25, $45, $150-bmk-105

358 **ANDREWS, E. Benjamin, Dr.**
"Dr. Andrews on General Lee." In: SHSP, September, 1915, v.XL, p. 320-321.

359 **ANDREWS, Eliza Frances**
"The War-Time Journal of a Georgia Girl, 1864-1865." N.Y., D. Appleton & Co., 1908. 8vo, decr. cl, illus., ports (incl. front) (4), 387, (4)pp-ads. teg. $12.50, $14, $17.50, $20, $25, $30-nc $40-bmk
...Louisville: Lost Cause Pr., microcard, 1957. $6
...Macon(Georgia). The Ardivan Press, 1960. Edt: Spencer Bidwell King, Jr., 8vo, cl, map-endsheets, xvii, (1), 396pp., index, front(port). $5.50, $20-bmk
...Atlanta, Ga.: Cherokee Pub., 1976, Edt: Spencer Bidwell King, Jr., 8vo, cl, port, index, p. 387 $10, $20

360 ..."Seven great battles of the Army of Northern Virginia. A program of study & entertainment, arranged for J.E.B. Stuart chapter of Children of the Confederacy.-..Sophie Bibb Chap. U.D.C." Montgomery, Ala., Brown print. (c.1906) 12mo, wraps, 16pp. Swem-129

361 **ANDREWS, George Leonard**
"The Battle of Cedar Mountain, Aug. 9, 1862." In: Pub. Miss. Hist. Soc., 1895, v.II, p. 387-442.

362 **ANDREWS, J. Cutler**
"The Confederate Press & Public Morale." (Houston, Tex.) JSH, Nov., 1966, v.XXXII, #4, p. 445-465. $8

363 ..."The South Reports the Civil War." Princeton, N.J., University Press, 1970. Large 8vo, cl, d/w, xiii, 611pp. dble-pg., map, ports, facsms, illus., maps, bibliog: p. 548-586; index: 587-611. $15
...1971, $34, $20-bmk
..."The South reports the civil war." Pittsburg, Pa., University of Pittsburg, 1985. 8vo, paper, 627pp. $20.

364 ..."The Southern Telegraph Company, 1861-1865: a Chapter in the History of Wartime Communications." (Houston, Tex.) JSH, Aug., 1964, v.XXX, #3, p. 319-344. $8

365 **ANDREWS, Marietta Minnigerode**
"Scraps of Paper." N.Y., E.P. Dutton & Co., (1929), 8vo, cl, illus., ports, front, xv, 381pp. All CSA, except p. 247-381. $10, $30-bmk,

366 **ANDREWS, Matthew Page**
"The Dixie Book of Days." Phila., Lippincott, 1912. 12mo, cl, col. front, 294pp. Quotations illus. of history & literature of South.$3, $6, $15-bmk

367 ..."The Dixie Calendar.", N.Y., Dodge Pub. Co. (1913) 8vo, (54)pp. loose pages tied with ribbon, illus. on cover, boxed. Quotes from southern authors prose & poetry, day by day. $7.50
...1st appeared in 1912 under auspices: Page Pub. Ass'n.

368 ..."Women of the South in War Times." Baltimore: Norman, Remington, 1920. 2nd Edt. $10, $3, $4, $6, $8.50, $16-bmk, $20-bmk. 12mo, cl, d/w, pl, ports, xvii, 466pp.
...New, revised edt. 1923. $5, $15.
...New, revised edt. 1924. $40-bmk, $4, $14

...New, revised edt. 1925. $20-bmk
...New, revised edt. 1927. $20, $3.50-bmk

369 ..."The treatment of prisoners in the Confederacy." In: Confed. Vet., April, 1918.
..."Also in: "The Gray Book", pub. by Sons of Confed. Vets., (15)pp.

370 **ANDREWS, Richard Snowden, Lieut-Col.**
"Richard Snowden Andrews, Lt.-Col. commanding 1st Maryland Artillery (Andrew's Battalion) C.S.A. A Memoir Edt: Tunstall Smith, Baltimore." (Baltimore) Sun job print, 1910. tall, 8vo, cl, illus., ports (inc. front color), $10, $14, $17.50, $25-Wentz, $45-Ginsis, $30, (atg.) $20.

371 ..."Andrews' mounted artillery drill; compl. according to latest regulations from standard military authority." Charleston: Evans & Cogswell, 1863. 12mo, cl, 164pp., 61-plates $425(Gdsp-590)

372 ..."The Gettysburg Campaign, Report of Colonel R. Snowden Andrews, Aug. 5, 1863. In: SHSP, 1882, v.X,p. 67-69.

373 **ANDREWS, Robert W.**
"The Life & Adventures of Capt....of Sumter, S.C., extending over a period of 97 years, replete with startling situations & interesting incidents. Together with Reminiscences of the War of 1812, & the recent "unpleasantness" between the North & South. Printed for the Author." Boston: E.P. Whitcomb, 1887. 8vo, wraps, front(port)87, (1)pp. Veterinary surgeon in Gardners Battery. $7.50, $12.75, $10, $15, $50-bmk-105, $35-jk-122.

374 **ANDREWS, Roland Franklin**
"How "unprepardness" undid St. Albans." In: Outlook, Nov. 22, 1916, v.CXIV, p. 673-684. Acct. CSA raid on St. Albans, Vt., in 1864. See: Under St. Alban's Raid.

375 **ANDREWS, W.H.**
"Diary of W.H. Andrews, 1st Sgt. Co. M., 1st Georgia Regulars, from FEb., 1861, to May 2, 1865." (East Atlanta, Ga.? 1891?) 8vo, wraps, 16, (8)pp(addenda)

376 ..."Hardships of Georgia Regulars." In: CV, May, 1909, v.XVII, p. 230-232.

377 **ANDREWS, W.J.**
"Sketch of Co. K., 23rd S.C. Volunteers in the Civil War, from 1862-1865." Richmond, n.d., Whittet & Shepperson. 8vo, wraps, 33pp. (c.1910?) Complete Muster Roll of Co. K (Reprint: Sumter, S.C., Wilder & Ward, Offset Printing Co.
..."Sketch of Company K, 23rd S.C. Volunteers in the civil war, from 1862-1865." Suffolk, Va., Robt. Hardy Pub., 1986, 8vo, wraps, 36pp.

378 **ANGLE, Paul M.**
"The End of the Civil War." In: Chicago Hist., 1965, v.VII, p. 193-197. Surrender of the CSS Shenandoah, Oct. 23, 1865, at Mersey, Scotland.

379 ..."The Last Years of the "Shenandoah." In Chicago Hist., 1965, v.VII, p. 242-245.

380 **ANGLE, Paul M. & Earl Schench Miers**
"A Ballad of the North & South." Kingsport, Tenn. Privately printed at Kingsport Press, February, 1959. Tall 8vo, blue/gray buckram, boxed. Edt. of 1,240 copies, Keepsake #4. Vignettes, 48pp. $18, $25-Bmk.

381 **"ANNALS of the War, The**
Written by leading participants North & South. Recently published in the Philadelphia Weekly Times." Philadelphia: Weekly Times, 1879. Tk. 8vo, cl, illus., 800pp. $10, $22.50, $50-mcm, $30-jk

382 **"ANNIE CLEVELAND:**
a Romance from Real Life connected with the Second Great American Revolution." New Orleans (Crescent Job Print), 1867. 8vo, wraps, 72pp. $17.50

383 **"ANNUAL Report**
of the State Historian of Confederate Records: John P(eyre) Thomas, for the year 1897." Columbia, S.C., 1899. 8vo, wraps, 16pp.
...1898, Columbia, 1899, pp. 74

384 ...1899, Columbia, 1900, pp. 89. Raising troops in S.C., for the State & Confed. Service, beginning of war in S.C., incl. rosters.

385 ..."Report of the Historian of the Confederate Records to the Gen. Assembly of South Carolina." Columbia, S.C., The Bryan Print., 1898-1900, Tables, 5 Vols. Turnbull, IV, p. 387, "there are 5 vols & (State Co., imprint) this is evidently a preliminary report." See: W.J. Rivers' Acc't., same series.

386 **"ANNUAL Reunion**
of the Virginia Division A.N.V. (Speeches: A.M. Keiley & Marcus J. Wright." In: SHSP, 1878, v.VI, p. 283-289. "Annual Reunion of the Association of the Army of Northern Virginia." With an address of Gen. E.M. Law-" The Confederate Revolution." In: SHSP, 1889, v. 85-112.

387 **ANSON, Charles H., Bvt. Maj.**
"Gen. Robert E. Lee, read Mar. 6, 1890. MOLLUS, Wisconsin Commandery, War Papers, v.1. Milwaukee: Burdick, Amitage & Allen, 1891. , #16, p. 241-150. (Anson, U.S. Bols., Adj., 1st Vermont Artillery.

388 **ANTHONY, Allen**
"Kentucky Bend-the lock that had to be released." In: RKHS, Spring 1979, v.77, #2, p. 108-111, maps.

389 **ANTI-ABOLITION Tracts, #1-**
"Abolition & Secession; or, Cause & Effect. Together with the Remedy for our sectional troubles." See: Unionists, 1st Edt., 1862. New York: Van Evrie, Horton & Co., 1864. 8vo, sewn, 30, (2)pp. Sabin-81715.

390 ...Tract, #2: "Free Negroism; or, Results of Emancipation in the North, & the West India Islands. With Statistics of the Decay of Commerce-idleness of the Negro-His Return to Savageism, & the Effect of Emancipation upon the Farming, Mechanical & Laboring Classes." 2nd Edt. Rev. & enlarged. Sabin-81982. New York: Van Evrie, Horton & Co., 1863.

391 ...1st Edt: 32pp.

392 ...Tract #3: "The Abolition Conspiracy to destroy the Union; or, a Ten Years' Record of the "Republican" Party. The Opinions of William Lloyd Garrison (& others)..." New York: Van Evrie, Horton & Co., 1866. 8vo, sewn, 31pp. Sabin-81717.

393 ...Tract, #1: "Abolition is National Death or, the Attempt to Equalize Races the Destruction of Society." New York: Van Evrie, Horton & Co., 1866. 8vo, sewn, 30pp. Sabin-81722.

394 ..."Abolitionism Unveiled! Hypocrisy Unmasked! & Knavery Scourged! Luminously portraying the whining Philanthropists-...practical atheists & the hollow-hearted swindlers of labor, the "Northern Abolitionists." N.Y., T.V. Paterson Print, 1850. 8vo, wraps, 32pp. Sabin-81730. See: H.F. James.

395 ..."Abolitionism exposed, corrected. By a physician, formerly a resident of the South, etc., etc." See: "A Tennesseean."

396 ..."Abolition a Sedition. By a Northern man." Phila: Geo. W. Donohue, 1839. 16mo, cl, vii, 187pp. Pro-slavery. Sabin-81713 $15

396a **"ANTICIPATIONS of the Future...**
Extracts of Letters from an English Resident..."
See: Edmund Ruffin.

396b **ANTIETAM Nat'l. Park**
See: Frederick Tilberg.

397 **D'ANTIGNAC, Munroe**
"Georgia's Navy 1861." Griffin, Ga. Private print, 1945. 8vo, wraps, port, 16pp. Letters from John M. Kell during period when Georgia had its own Navy, prior to joining the CSNavy. $50-bmk-120, $15.

See: Norman Delaney's work on Kell(1972).

398 **ANTRIM, Earl**
"Civil War Prisons & their Covers." (N.Y., Collector's Club, 1961) Collector's Club Hornbook #12. 12mo, cl, dj, illus., 215pp. $10.

399 ..."Confederate packet markings." In: Amer. Philatelist, July, 1949, v.62, p. 791-792. Facsms. On packet-boat postal markings, 1863.

400 **APPEAL for Pecuniary Aid**
to care for & monument the remains of the Confederate dead buried on Johnson's Island & at Columbus, Ohio." Cincinnati, Cohen & Co., 1892. 12mo, wraps, 71, (1)p. fldg. table. List arranged by state & regiment. Dorn: II-71, UCV, Northwest Division.

401 **"APPEAL for contributions**
for the erection of a Memorial tablet in honor of the Confederate dead of St. Michael's Parish-to be erected in the vestibule of the church." Charleston, S.C., Lucas & Richardson, 1900. "Remembrance of our soldier dead erected by congregation, 1901." 8vo, wraps, (10)pp., (1) at end.

402 **APPEAL to Democrats & Union Men**
against Northern Fusion & Sectionalism. From the Democracy of Boston & Suffolk. Adopted by the Ward & County Committees, in Convention, October 1855." (Boston) Printed by office of Boston Post. 8vo, wraps, 7pp. Practical appeal to warring factions of the North to not let 25 million whites lock in combat over 3 million blacks; quit meddling in affairs of other states.

403 **"APPEAL to thinking men.**
From the Natches (Miss.) Dailey Courier, 1860." (Natches, Daily Courier(?), c.1960) 8vo, wraps, 15pp. Right of secession, states rights. $15.

404 **APPERSON, John S.**
"Smyth Blues." Muster Roll Co. D., Fourth Virginia Infantry." In: SHSP, 1906, v.XXXIV, p. 359-362.

405 **APPLER, August C.**
"The Guerrillas of the West; or, the Life & character & daring exploits of the Younger brothers; with a sketch of the life of Henry W. Younger, father of the Younger brothers...The war record of Quantrill...also a sketch of the Life of the James boys." St. Louis, Eureka Pub. Co., 1876. 12mo, cl, illus., incl. front, iv, 5-208pp.
..."The Younger brothers, their life & character, with foreword by Burton Rasco." N.Y., F. Fell(1955). 12mo, cl, illus., 245pp. $15-dab, $5.

406 **APPLER, Augustus C.**
"The life, character & daring exploits of the Younger brothers, with a sketch of the life of Henry W. Younger." Chicago: Belford, Clarke & Co., (c.1875) 12mo, cl, viii, (9)-287pp., illus.

407 **APPLETON, J.M.W.**
"That Night at Fort Wagner. By One Who Was There." In: Putnam's Magazine, IV, 1869, p. 9-16. CSA loss was 12; Union was 339 in their assault.

APPOMATTOX Nat'l. Park
See: Ralph Happel.

408 **APPOMATTOX Roster.**
Intro: Philip Van Doren Stern. N.Y., Antiquarian Press, 1967. 8vo, cl, illus., ports, 508pp. $15, $22.50
...Do: 1962. Reprint of "Paroles of the Army of Northern Virginia." See also under this title. Original edition.

409 **ARCENEAUX, William**
"Acadian General: Alfred Mouton & the Civil War." Lafayette: Center for Louisiana Studies, University of Southwestern Louisiana, 1981, 8vo, cl, xvi, 188pp., photos, maps. $11.

410 ARCHAMBEAU, Ernest A., Jr.
"The defense of Petersburg on the 9th June, 1864." In: Geo. Bernard's "War Talks". Petersburg, Va., 1892. p. 107-148.

411 ARCHER, G.W.
"A few papers of the Army of the Tennessee." (Balt: South. Mag., 1873, v.XIII, p. 194-199, 313-320. Hardee's Corp.

412 ARCHER, James Jay
"The James J. Archer Letters: a Marylander in the Civil War." Edt: C.A. Porter Hopkins. (Baltimore, Maryland Historical Magazine, 1961, v.LVI, p. 72-93; 125-149.
...Issued, 440 wraps. $8-bmk.

413 ARCHER, Mary Brown
"A Letter from Occupied Tallahassee." In: FHQ, July, 1969, v.XLVIII, #1, p. 70-75, port, plate.

414 ARCHER, Stevenson
"Capt. Evans & his Texas Scouts." In: Wash. Co. Hist. Soc. Papers, 1910-1915, p. 223-227. Reminisc. (1912) of activities on Yazoo river 1864, & of their (unnamed) capt.

415 ARCHER, W.P.
"History of the Battle of Atlanta, also Confederate Songs & Poems." Knoxville, Ga., C.B.H. Moncrief (1940) 12mo, wraps, illus., ports, 35pp.

416 ARCHER, William S.
"Letter of Lieutenant W.S. Archer, re: "The Bloody Angle." In: SHSP, 1893, v.XXI, p. 242-244.

417 ARCHIVES Bureau at Washington
(War Department) Criticism of...) In: SHSP, 1878, v.V/VI, p. 255-256; p. 239-240(v.6). The latter-J. Wm. Jone's "History of our relations with the "Record Office" at Washington. Its settlement, with the appointment of Gen. Marcus J. Wright.

418 AREHART, W.H.
"Diary of W.H. Arehart." In: Rockingham(Va.) recorder, Dec., 1948, v.1, p. 271-282. Service in the 12th Va. reg. in central Va., Aug-Oct., 1863.

419 ARENA, Frank C.
"Southern Sympathizers in Iowa During the Civil War Period." In: Annals of Iowa, 1951, p. 486-528.

420 ARENT(S)CHILDT, Friedrich von
"Instructions for Officers & Non-commissioned Officers of Cavalry, on Outpost Duty...with an abridgment of them by...F. Ponsonby...(with illustrations in text)." Richmond, 1861 Crandall-2393. 12mo, (72)p., limp cloth. $750-goodspeed, Gdsp. note: Pub. for CS cavalry by Gen. Phil St. George Cocke. One other edt. Streeter's unique Edt. Fort McCulloch in Indian Territory sold 1967-$3750.

421 ARKANSAS C.S.A. Soldiers.
(Census of Confederate Veterans) Transcribed & edited by Bobby J. McLane & Capitola H. Glazner." Hot Springs, Ark., Arkansas Ancestors, 1980. Vol. I, Surnames A thru D, p. 160, $14; Vol. II, Surnames E thru Mc., p. 171, $14; Vol. III, Surnames M-Z, p. 200, 1982, $16. The 1911 act provided for a census by each tax assessor of counties. The above represents all counties enumerated, since no records can be found for remaining 31 counties. The 1,751 questionnaires list full names, address, date & place of birth, date state & county of enlistment full name & place of birth for subject's parents, grandparents, maiden name of wife, date & place of marriage, names of her parents, full list of children, with spouses.

422 "ARKANSAS Confederate records:
in Arkansas History Comm., of Clara Barton Eno Collection. Edt: Ted R. Worley, Exec. Sect. Little Rock, 1956. pp.(2), 23 leaves.

423 ARKANSAS Democrat, Confederate Reunion Edition,
Little Rock, Ark., Capital City, Confeder-

ate Veterans Reunion, May 16-18, 1911." Little Rock, Ark., Arkansas Democrat, 1911-cover title. 4to wraps, illus., ports, 95, (1)pp.

424 **ARKANSAS History Commission:**
Bulletin of information #5, March, 1913. Dallas T. Herndon, Sect., p. (2), 107-173. Calendar of Documents re political & military affairs of Arkansas, 1861-1865.

425 ...Bul. of information #6, June, 1913., Little Rock, Ark., 1914. p. 177-284. Dallas T. Herndon, Sect. Re: Roster of Arkansas Volunteers, Civil War, p. 185-264.

426 ..."Seven Battles Fought in Arkansas, 1861-1865." Little Rock: Arkansas History Comm.(1960) cover title, 4to, (7)pp. plans. Pea Ridge, Prairie Grove, Ark. Post, Helena Poison Spring, Marks Hill & Jenkins Ferry.

427 **ARKANSAS Peace Society...**
"Documents relating to the Arkansas Peace Society of 1861. Edt: Ted Worley." In: AHQ, 1958, v.XVII, p. 82-111. In mountainous north Arkansas, group to resist CSA or participation in war.

428 **ARKANSAS in the Second Year**
of the Civil War. In: PCHR, June 1969, v.7, p. 23-33.

429 **ARKANSAS' Battle Flags Used in Action:**
"Flag gallery located in Former Supreme Court Library Old State House..." 8 1/2x14" (3)p. sheets, mimeographed, sketches of the 21 flags.

430 **ARKANSAS, The**
the stirring saga of the Confederate Gunboat "Arkansas." In: Pulaski Hist. Rev., Winter, 1979. XXVII, #4, p. 97-104, 113-118, map. 1st article, Summer, 1979, #2, p. 42-50, dble-pg. plate.

431 **ARKANSAS:**
"Journal of the Senate of Arkansas, sessions of 1864,"1864-1865 & 1865. And-Journal of the Convention of Delegates of the People of Arkansas. Assembled at the Capitol, Jan. 4, 1864; also, journal House of Representatives of sessions of 1864, 1864-1865, & 1865." (old)$35 Little Rock, 1870. Price & Barton Print. (The Senate: P. 345, 162, 8vo, 1/2 sheep.) (Del. & Hse., p. 58, 309, 67pp. 2Vols. Details events war years, troublesome conditions during turbulent period.
...1864 Sess-Nov. -60-Jan. -61, LR, 1861, p. 900, $50-bk

432 ...(Northwest Arkansas Special Order #50, May 8, 1863...the men formerly belonging to Clarkson's Regiment Cavalry & Adams Reg. of Infantry, who are now absent from their regiments...are hereby notified that unless they enroll themselves in some of said companies, within ten days from publication of this order, they will be arrested..." W.L. Cabell, Brig-Gen. Broadside, 17.5x24.5, 5cm. (not in Crandall-Harwell)

433 **ARKANSAS: District of..**
Office Commandant Conscripts. Special instructions to enrolling officers. Endorsed(margins) Maj. Jas. S. Sparks. Broadside: 19 1/2x24cm (double columns) $75.

434 **ARKANSAS: Headquarter,**
Trans-Mississippi Department, Little, Rock, Dec. 8, 1862. Gen. Ord. #45: for the purpose of carrying into effect the conscript act...following regulations are adopted for the trans-Mississippi Department..." 3pp. 8vo. $75. Not in Crandall-Harwell.

435 **ARLINGTON, Va., Confederate Monument...**
Account of the dedication to Confederate dead June 4, 1914. In: CV, July, 1914, v.XXII, p. 292-199, illus. Also: speech by Mrs. Daisy McLaurin Stevens, p. 346-347.

436 **ARMES, Ethel**
"The Story of Coal & Iron in Alabama." Birmingham, Ala: Chamber of Commerce, 1910. Cl, 8vo, ports, illus., maps,

xxxiv, 581pp. fine index. Many copies destroyed in fire. Confederate conditions at war's start, Arsenal & Naval foundry, coal & ironmaking, p. 121-195. $10, $15, $85-orko.

...Birmingham, Ala., Book-Keepers Press, 1972. p. 20a, xxxvi, 581. $15.

437 ..."Stratford on the Potomac, an address by Ethel Armes; on Robert E. Lee by Sidney Lanier." Greenwich, Conn., William Alexander jr., Chapter, United Daughters of Confederacy. 1928. 4to, stiff wraps, illus., 44pp. $5, $35-y, $40-appler.

438 ..."Stratford Hall, the great house of the Lees, with an introduction by Franklin D. Roosevelt." Richmond, Va., Garrett & Massie Pr., 1936. Imp. 8vo, cl, front, illus., ports, maps, plans, facsms. coats of arms, xxiv, 575pp. illus. liners. Lim. Edt., 1200 copies atg. by author. $100-bmk-105, $125-b, 124, $100.

439 **ARMISTEAD, Drury L.**
"The Battle in which General Johnston was wounded. Described by his courier Drury L. Armistead, March 28, 1891." In: SHSP, 1890, v.XVIII, p. 185-188.

440 **ARMISTEAD, Lewis Addison, Gen.**
"Did Gen. Armistead fight on the Federal side at First Manassas?" In: SHSP, 1882-1883, v.X & XI, p. 284; p. 335; 423-429; v.XI, p. 283-286. See: James E. Poindexter.

441 **ARMSTRONG, A.F.H.**
"The Case of Major Isaac Lynde." (Albuquerque, New Mexico-Historical Review, Jan. 1961, v.XXXVI, #1, pl-35. Surrender of US forces at Ft. Fillmore. See also: Jas. Cooper McKee; "Memoirs of Hank Smith"; Ralph Emerson Twitchell, Chas. S. Walker; W.H. Watford; Martin H. Hall.

442 **ARMSTRONG, I.R.**
"The Kearsarge & the alabama." In: Nation Mag., Oct., 1917, v.XLVII, p. 112-115.

443 **ARMSTRONG, J.L.**
"Biographical Sketch of John Esten Cooke with selections from his writings." In: Alderman, E.A. Library Southern Literature, 1909, v.3, p. 1021-1062.

444 **ARMSTRONG, James, Col.**
"Carolina Light Infantry's Record in the great war, the story of a gallant company, most of the members of which were boys in years though inspired with the spirit of heroes, by Col. James Armstrong." Charleston, S.C., Walker, Evans & Cogswell Co., 1912 $25. 8vo, orig. pict. wraps, 12pp (dble-column)

445 ..."McGowan's Brigade at Spotsylvania." In: CV, Oct., 1915, v.XXXIII, p. 376-379. In the fighting at Bloody Angle.

446 **ARMSTRONG, Zella**
"The last of the Confederate generals." In: Munsey's Mag., 1904, v.XXXI, p. 387-393, ports.

447 ..."A National Memorial Park, Battlefields of Chickamauga & Chattanooga." In: Munsey's Mag., 1903, v.XXX, p. 65-72, illus.

448 **ARMY Songster, The.**
dedicated to the Army of Northern Virginia. Richmond, Va., Geo. L. Bidgood, 1864, 16mo, wraps, 72pp., Crand:3252.

...Richmond, Va., J.W. Fergusson & Son, 1901. CM $15-bmk

449 **ARMY of North Virginia:**
In: SHSP. See: "Annual Reunions," "Articles of surrender,", J.L. Chamberlayne, Gen. R.H. Anderson, F.M. Colston, Robert A. Hardaway, D.H. Hill, Bradley Tyler Johnson, John Wm. Jones, Thomas G. Jones, Fitzhugh Lee, "List of Virginia Chaplains," Edward McCrady, "Organizatio of the A.N.V.," "Paroles of the ANV," W.N. Pendleton, "Field Letters from Hdqs., 2nd Corp." Charles S. Stringfellow.

450 **ARMY of Northern Virginia, Association:**
See: Archer Anderson, Jno. W. Daniel,

Jas. N. Dunlop, Dan. H. Hill, In Memoriam: Otey Battery, Rich. Irby, Thos. G. Jones, Brad T. Johnson, Chas. T. Loehr, Wm. G. McCabe, Ed. McCrady, H.B. McClellan, Chas. Marshall, Leigh Robinson, Alfred M. Scales, Chas. S. Vanable, A.M. Waddell. Gens-Wm. H. Fitzhugh & Lee & A.L. Long.

451 **ARMY of Tennessee:**
In: SHSP. See: Wm. Preston Johnston, Joseph Jones, Thos. R. Markham, "Org. Army of Tenn." P.D. Stephenson. Jefferson Davis

452 **ARMY of the Confederate States: Army Regulations.**
Richmond, Va., West & Johnston, 1861, Greenville, SC, A Press, 1984. 12mo, paper, tables, append., index. $18. III, 198pp.

453 **ARMY-Department of Western Louisiana.**
(Correspondence between E. Warren Moise & Simon Boliver Buckner) (Nachitoches, La., 1864) 8vo, 8pp. $37.50. Not in Crandall-Harwell, Duke suppl. See: J.L. Brent.

454 **ARNETT, Ethel Stephens**
"Confederate guns were stacked at Greensboro, North Carolina." Greensboro, N.C., Piedmont Press, 1965. 4to, cl, 178pp. illus., maps, ports, bibliog. $20.

455 **ARNOLD, Benjamin William**
"Virginia Women & the Civil War." (Washington, D.C., Southern History Assn. Publications, v.2, 1898, p. 256-271.

456 **ARNOLD, Edwin**
"Address made before the assembled members & guest of the Harris Co., Hist. Society at its annual dinner, June 14, 1960, at the Milford House, 1110 Milford Ave., Houston, Texas by...lawyer, who has practiced law at the Houston Bar for some four decades last past." n.p. (Houston, Texas, 1960). 8vo, wraps, cover title, 37pp. $1.50. Material taken from author's Land of Fadeless Start." On Secession & causes of the War Between States.

457 ..."Land of Fadeless Stars." Boston: Chistopher Pub(1948), tk, 8vo, d/w, x, (13)-587pp. bibliography 585-587, $15, $20.
..."Fadeless Stars." Houston, Texas, Alpha Law Brief Co., (1942) 8vo, cl, 2p, 1, iv, 627, 3p, bibliog. (3)p. 1st.
..."Land of Fadeless Stars." Houston, Texas, Alpha Law Brief Co., (1942) CSA, in fictional form but factual. 8vo, 2p, iv, 627, (3)p-index. 2nd.

458 **ARNOLD, Eugenia Hill**
"The Christian character of our great leaders." In: CV, Feb., 1920, v.XXVIII, p. 53-55. CSA.
..."Recollections of Mrs. Stonewall Jackson." In: CV, Nov., 1922, v.XXX, p. 412-414. Anna Morrison Jackson, wife of Stonewall.

459 **ARNOLD, R.A. (Arthur)**
"History of the Cotton Famine, from the fall of Fort Sumter to passing of the Public Works Act." London: Saunders & Otley, 1864. 8vo, cl, xiv, 570pp., Sabin-2078.
...1865, with postscript, new edt. Post 8vo, viii, 350pp.

460 **ARNOLD, Richard Dennis, Dr.**
"Letters of Richard D. Arnold, M.D., 1808-1876, mayor of Savannah, Georgia, first secretary of the American Medical Ass'n. Edited by Richard H. Shryock." Durham, N.C., Duke University Pr., 1929. Hist. Papers, pub. by Trinity College Historical Society, double ser., xviii-xix. 8vo, cl, port, 178pp.

461 **ARNOLD, Samuel Bland**
"Defence & Prison Experiences of a Lincoln Conspirator Statements & Autobiographical Notes by..." Hattiesburg, Miss., The Book Farm, 1943 (Heartman's Hist. Series #66) 8vo, cl, 133pp., 199 copies printed. CSA soldier, from Maryland, for 2 years before returning;

schoolmate of Booth, in plan to abduct Lincoln. See: Albert C. Manucy. $15, $10.

462 **ARNOLD, Thomas Jackson**
"Early Life & Letters of Gen. Thomas J. Jackson "Stonewall" Jackson, by his nephew." N.Y., etc., Fleming H. Revell Co (1916) 8vo, cl, illus., facsms, ports (incl. front) 379, (4)pp. adds. $10, $15, $17.50, $20, $40-bmk, $60, $75
...(Richmond, Va., Dietz Pr., 1957) $7, (1916) 1st Edt.-atg. $90-bmk-105, $20.

463 ..."The Battle of Rich Mountain." In: CV, Sept., 1921, v.XXIX, p. 342-343.

464 ..."Hunter as Lincoln's agent." In: CV, Nov., 1925, v.XXXIII, p. 410-411. Gen. David Hunter's conduct in campaign of 1864, in Valley of Va.

465 **ARNOLD, William E.**
"An Analysis of Some Speeches of Jefferson Davis." (Jackson, Miss.) Jour. Miss. Hist. Nov., 1971, v.XXXIII, #4, p. 351-355.

466 **ARP, Bill (pseud.), Charles Henry Smith**
"Bill Arp, so called. A Side Show of the Southern Side of the War..." N.Y., Metropolitan Record office, 1866. 12mo, cl, 204pp. (Y)-$100
...Same, 1867 (old) $3. See: Charles Henry Smith---Jas. C. Austin.

467 ..."Bill Arp's Peace Papers." N.Y., G.W. Carleton; London: S. Low, 1873. 12mo, cl, illus., 271pp., front. (old) $6. Civil War & Reconstruction, humorous.

468 ..."Bill Arp. From the Uncivil War to Date. (1861-1903) Memorial Edt. Atlanta, Ga., Hudgins Pub. co., 1903. 8vo, cl, illus., port, 378pp. $12.

469 **ARTHUR, Stanley Clisby**
"Pioneer", the First Submarine boat." In: AHQ, 1949, #3, p. 405-411.

470 **ARTICLES of Surrender**
of the Army of Northern Virginia at Appomattox Court House, Va., April 10th, 1865. (Longstreet J.B. Gordon & W.N. Pendleton-Sigs. for the CSA.) In: SHSP, 1888, v.XVI, p. 107-108.

471 **ARTILLERY Officers, C.S.A.**
(Washington, D.C., 188-) 12mo, cl, 186, 37pp. Contents: Organizations; Artillery battles. Memorandum of artillery officers, CSA. List of officers corps of artillery, CSA on register (US) of 1861; Index. (Binder's title) Dorn-II, 820.

472 **ARTILLERY Organizations**
of the Confederate States, 1861-1865, compiled in Rebel Archives, etc.
See: "A List of the Artillery Organizations in the Confed. States Service."

473 **ARTILLERY of the Confederate States Army**
See: E.P. Alexander, J.L. Brent, H.C. Cabell, W.N. Pendleton.

474 **ASBURY, A. Edgar, Col.**
"My experience in the war of 1861-1865." (Higginsville, Mo., 1892) 8vo, wraps, 48pp. (with Kirby Smith) Also wrote of his prison experiences in the St. Louis "Republican", in 1886.
...In: CV, 1912, v.XX, p. 242-243, illus. (2)

475 **ASBURY, Richard Thomas**
"A Lecture-lesson on the Confederate War." n.p., n.d. (c. 1900) (Macon, Ga., 511 Forsyth St.) 8vo, wraps, 15pp. Very pro-Confederate. (Folk-#37) $5.

476 **ASBURY, William Henry**
"A Confederate soldier's view of Johnson's Island Prison (May-Aug., 1862)." In: Ohio Hist., Spring 1970, p. 101-111.

477 **ASH, Stephen V.**
"A community at war: Montgomery County, 1861-1865." In: THQ, Spring 1977, v.36, #1, p. 30-43.

478 **ASHBROOK, Stanley B.**
"Some Notes on the Harold C. Brooks Collection of Confederate States of America." N.Y., The Stamp Specialist (1945) Facsms., p. 32-45.

479 ..."Confederate States of America. Some Notes on the Postal Legislation, Postal Rates, Postal Uses & Earliest Known dates of use of the Stamps of General Issues." N.Y., The Stamp Specialist (1946). Facsms., p. 3-54.

480 ..."Some notes on the Postal Legislation of the Confederate States of America, 1861-1865. Postal rates earliest known dates of use of the stamps of the General Issues." reprint from "The Stamp Specialist. n.p., March, 1946. sm. 4to, wraps, facsms., 54pp. $3.50, $7.50.

481 **ASHBROOKE, W.B.**
"Roster of the Alstadt Grays." In: SHSP, 1908, v.XXXVI, p. 26-27. From Chesterfield Co., Va., Mahone's Brig. Anderson's Div., of A.P. Hill Corp., Army of Northern Virginia.

482 **ASHBURN, Karl E.**
"Slavery & cotton production in Texas." In: SWSoc. Sci. Quart., 1933, v.XIV, p. 257-271. Cotton/slavery from time of Stephen Austin. estb. his colony.

483 **ASHBY, General Turner**
"Sketch of General Ashby." In: LWL, August, 1968, v.V, #4, p. 287-290, plate(port)

484 ..."Life of General Turner Ashby." In: The Old Guard, Apr., 1867, V, #7, p. 305-308., dbl. column.
...See: Thomas Almond Ashby, Jas. Battle Avirett, Frank Cunningham, Wm. Naylor McDonald, Wm. Goldsborough, Clarence Thomas.

485 **ASHBY, John William**
"Met His Death in Last Fight. John William Ashby is man who fell at Appomattox in Gordon's Last Assault." Letters from John W. Daniel, Bushrod Rust & Gen. R.D. Funkhouser." In: SHSP, 1906, v.XXXIV, p. 218-221.

486 **ASHBY, Thomas Almond**
"Life of Turner Ashby (1828-1862)." N.Y., Neale Pub. Co., 1914. 8vo, cl, front(port) 275pp. $12.50, $17.50, $20, $27.50, $35, $40, $275-bmk-105, $275-bmk, $225-bmk.

487 ..."The Valley Campaigns, being the Reminiscences of a Non-combatant while between the lines in the Shenandoah Valley during the War of the States." N.Y., Neale Pub. Co., 1914. 8vo, cl, 327pp. $15, $17.50, $20. $70/with pj, $60-nc, $100-nc, $100-nc, $45-y, $125-bmk-105.
...Dayton, Oh., Morningside, 1979. (op) $17.50

488 **ASHCRAFT, Allan C.**
"Confederate Indian Department Conditions in August, 1864." Oklahoma City: Chron. Okla., Autumn, 1963, v.XLI, #3, p. 270-285.

489 ..."Confederate Indian Territory Conditions in 1865." Oklahoma City: Chron. Okla. Winter, 1964-1965. v.XLII, #4, p. 421-428.

490 ..."Civil War Naval Weapons That Might Have Been." Amer. Neptune, Oct., 1962, Vol. XXII, #4, p. 280-289. diagrams.

491 ..."Confederate Beef Packing at Jefferson, Texas." In: SwHQ, October, 1964, v.LXVIII, #2, p. 259-270.

492 ..."The Confederate "Inspector of Railroads" for Texas." In: Tx. Mil. Hist., 1963, v.III, p. 33-35.

493 ..."The Defense of Houston." In: Tx. Mil. Hist., 1964, v.IV, p. 189-191.

494 ..."San Antonio Defenses, 1863." In: Tx. Mil. Hist., 1964, v.IV, p. 25-26.

495 ..."Staff Functions in the Confederate District of Texas." In: Tx. Mil. Hist., 1963, v.III, p. 114-119.

496 ..."Confederate Indian Troop Conditions in 1864." Oklahoma City: Chron. Okla., Winter

497 ..."Texas in the Civil War: A Resume' History." Austin, Texas, January, 1962. Texas Civil War Centennial Commission. 8vo, stiff decr. wraps, 53pp., notes, bibliog., p. 31-41. Chronology. $1.50

498 ..."East Texas in the Election of 1860, & the Secession Crisis." In: "East Texas History, Edt: By Archie P. McDonald, p. 95-110, v.1, #1, July 1963, p. 7-15.

499 ..."The Union Occupation of the lower Rio Grande Valley in the Civil War." In: TMH, 1969, v.8, #1, p. 13-26.

500 ..."Texas in Defeat: The early phase of A.J. Hamilton's Provisional Governorship of Texas, June 17, 1865 to February 7, 1866." In: TMH, 1970, v.8, #4, p. 199-219.

501 **ASHE, S.A., Capt.**
"Steps leading to war." In: CV, 1921, v.39, p. 453-457.

502 **ASHE, Samuel A'Court**
"The Charge at Gettysburg." n.p., n.d., Ashe's name does not appear, but atg. inscription. (Raleigh) Reprinted from News & Observer (1890?) Weeks' Bibliog., 8vo, dbl-column, 15pp. map.

503 ..."Life at Fort Wagner." In: Conf. Vet., 1927, v.XXXV, p. 254-256.

504 ..."History of North Carolina." Raleigh: Edwards & Broughton, 1925. v.II, from 1783-1925. 8vo, cl, xiv, 1449pp. $50- CSA, about 400pp. Vol. I, published in 1908 in Greensboro: C.L. Van Noppen., V.II, $27.50, Spartanburg, S.C., Reprint Co. (1971), $30.

505 ..."Slavery in the South." In: TylerQHGM, 1933, v.XIV, p. 138-141.

506 ..."Secession, Insurrection of the Negroes, and Northern Incendiarism." (Richmond, Va.) Revised & reprinted from Tyler's Quarterly Historical & Genealogical Magazine, v.XV, July, 1933. 8vo, wraps, 21, (1)pp. $8, $15, $9.50, $6.50

507 ..."The War Between the States." In: Tyler's Quart., July, 1928, v.X, p. 3-11. $8.

508 ..."How President Davis became free." In: Conf. Vet., Nov., 1928, v.XXXVI, p. 411-412.

509 ..."North Carolina History." "Slavery agitation", p. 318-546. "Southern Confederacy", p. 547-1012. "Reconstruction." p. 1013-1091.

510 **ASHE, Stephen V.**
"Sharks in an angry sea: civilian resistance & guerrilla warfare in occupied middle Tennessee, 1862-1865." In: THQ, Fall, 1986, v.xlv, #3, p. 217-229.

511 **ASHLEY, Robert Paul**
"The St. Alban's Raid." In: CWTI, Nov. 1967, v.VI, #7, p. 18-27, illus., group port, plan.

512 **ASSOCIATION Confederate Soldiers,**
Tennessee Division: Minutes of the 9th Annual Meeting. Nashville, Tenn., 1896. 8vo, pict., wraps, 56pp. $15-bmk. Constitution, charter, list inmates at CSA Home, pensioners.

513 **ASSOCIATION of Confederate Soldiers,**
Tennessee Division. Minutes of the Fifth Annual Meeting, held in the city of Franklin, Sept. 14, 1892. 8vo, full leather, 98pp. $30.

514 **ASSOCIATION of Maryland Line in CSA.**
See: Brig. Bradley T. Johnson, Wm. W. Goldsborough.

515 **ASSOCIATION of medical officers**
of the army & navy of the Confederacy. Samuel Preston Moore, M.D., Surgeon-General of the Confederate States of America. (Washington, D.C., Judd & Detweiler Pr., 1910) 8vo, wraps, (9)pp. Swem-184.

516 ..."Association of Medical Officers of the Confederate Army & Navy." In: OLOD, Nov., 1874, v.1, #3, p. 219.

517 **"ASSOCIATION of the Army of Tennessee: Louisiana Division.**
Charter, Articles of Organization & Rules & Regulations...of." New Orleans, La., L.R. Simmons, 1904. 8vo, wraps, 53pp. $25-jk Group of United Confederate Veterans.

518 ...New Orleans, La., McCrane & Lesslie, 1892. 8vo, wraps, 43pp.

519 ...New Orleans, 1915, revised, 8vo, wraps, 23pp.

520 **ASTON, B.W.**
"Federal Military Reoccupation of the Texas Southwestern Frontier, 1865-1871." In: TMH, 1970, v.8, #3, p. 123-134.

521 **ATCHISON, Ray M.**
"Land We Love: a Southern Post-Bellum Magazine of Agriculture & Military History." In: NCHR, Oct., 1960, v.XXXVII, p. 506-515. $8-bmk.

522 ..."Our Living & Our Dead." In: NCHR, Autumn, 1963, v.XL, p. 423-433.

523 **ATHENS (Georgia), 1861-1865.**
As Seen through letters in the University of Georgia Libraries. Edt: Kenneth Coleman. Athens: University of Georgia Libraries Misc. Pub. #8, paper-$4.50, $3. 8vo, wraps, viii, 123pp. See also: John F. Stegman. Chs. J. Brockman.

524 **ATHERTON, Lewis E.**
"Life, Labor & Society in Boone County, Missouri, 1834-1852, as revealed in the correspondence of an immigrant family from North Carolina." in 1-parts. (Columbia, Mo., Mo. Hist. Review, April & July, 1944, v.XXXVIII-#3 & 4; p. 277-304; 408-429. The Lenoir Family letters.

525 ..."Mercantile Education in the Ante-Bellum South." (Cedar Rapids, Ia.) MVHR, March, 1953, v.XXXIX, #4, p. 623-640.

526 ..."The Southern Country Store, 1800-1860." (Baton Rouge, La.) JSH, FEb., 1950. v.XVI, #1.

527 ..."The Southern Country Store, 1800-1860." Baton Rouge: Louisiana State Univ., 1949. 8vo, cl, dj, bibliog., xii, 227pp.

528 **ATKINS, John Black**
"The Life of Sir William Howard Russell, the first special correspondent." London: J. Murray, 1911. 8vo, cl, plates, ports (incl. front), facsm. 1vols. $16. London Times reporter's war reports in 1861-1862 influenced Anglo-American public opinion.

529 **ATKINSON, Edward**
"The Battle of Marks mill, Edt: By J.H. Atkinson." In: AHQ, 1955, v.XIV, p. 381-384.

530 **ATKINSON, James Harris**
"The action at Prairie De Ann(near Prescott, Ark., 10-13 Apr., 1864)" In: Ark. Hist. Quart., Spring, 1960, v.XIX, p. 40-50, plans.

531 ..."The Brooks-Baxter Contest." In: AHQ, 1945, v.IV, p. 124-149. Reconstruction in Arkansas. See: John M. Harrell's "Brooks & Baxter War...St. Louis, 1893, 276pp.

532 ..."The Action at Prairie De Ann." In: AHQ, 1960, v.XIX, p. 40-50, p. maps(2). Near Prescott, Ark., Apr. 10-13, 1864.

533 ..."Forty Days of Disaster. The Story of Gen. Frederick Steel's Expedition into Southern Arkansas, Mar. 23-May 3, 1864." Little Rock, Ark., Pulaski County Hist. Society, Bulletin Series, #1, Nov., 1955. 4to, soft back, (3), 42pp. map. $4.50, $15

534 **ATKINSON, John Wilder**
"Col. Ulric Dahlgren, the Defeated Raider." In: SHSP, 1909, v.XXXVII, p. 351-353. Atkinson: Comm. 10th & 19th Bat. Artillery, CSA.

535 **ATLANTA (Ga.) in the Civil War:**
The Personal Perspective; a Multimedia Exhibition at the Atlanta Historical Society, March-November, 1979. In: Atl. Hist. Journ., (1979), v.23, included 24pp (between p. 64-65) pictures in exhibit.

536 **ATLANTA Campaign, The**
Special issue of: Atlanta, Ga., Atlanta Historical Journal, 1984, 8vo, paper, 112pp. $10. Richard M. McMurray & Stephen Davis-"A reader's guide to the Atlanta Campaign."

537 ...The Atlanta Campaign & Kennesaw Mountain National Battlefield Park, Georgia. (Wash: US Dept. of Interior, Na-

538 **ATLANTA Century, The**
(March, 1860-May, 1865.) (Atlanta, Ga., I.D. Publishers, Tucker-Castelberry Print, Dec., 1965.) Folio, fabricoid, ports, illus., maps, unpaginated (276)pp. 2nd edt. Feb., 1966. Intro: Norman Shavin.

539 **ATLANTA in the Civil War,**
The Atlanta Historical Bulletin, Summer 1979. n.p., n.d., 1879, wraps, 149pp. Articles: "Life at the crossroads of the Confederacy, Atlanta 1861-1865 by Robert Gibbons"; "Foraging, scouting, & skirmishing: the Federal occupation of Atlanta as seen in the letter of Maj. William C. Stevens, 9th Michigan Cavalry by Albert Castel"; "A Georgian's view of the war in Virginia: The Civil War letters of A.B. Simms." Edt: Jane Peacock.

540 **ATLANTA, Georgia, Confederate Map.**
"Map of Atlanta as of 1938, showing the field & fortified lines of the Confederate Forces, together with those of the Federal Armies. Also fields of the three major engagements, during the summer, 1864." (Atlanta, Ga., Ivan Allen-Marshall Co.) Atlanta Chamber of Commerce, 19x24" map Wilbur G. Kurtz historical data, Aug., 1938.

541 **ATTEMPT of the North, The**
to subdue the Southerners, & the attempt of Spain to subdue the Netherlanders. Is there any analogy between them? An offhand inquiry. By the author of "Uncle John's Cabin, next door to Uncle Tom's Cabin. London: Simpkins, Marshall co, 1865. 12mo, wraps, 16pp., Sabin-2322.

542 **ATWOOD, Evans**
"Prisoner of War Diary of..." Edt: W.J. Lemke. (Fayetteville, Ark. Hist. Quart., 1953, v.XII, p. 340-369. Johnson's Island & Point Lookout, Md., 1863-1865. Roster of 66 prisoners.

tional Park Service, 1942) 4to, pict. wraps, illus., ports, map, 15, (1)p.

543 **AUCHAMPAUGH, Philip Gerald**
"Black, Thompson & Stanton, in 1864." April (1929) Tyler's Quar. Hist. & Geneal. Mag., X, p. 237-250. Letters in LC, re: peace negotiations of 1864 between Judge J.S. Black & Jacob Thompson, CSA comm. in Canada.

544 ..."Robert Tyler, Southern Rights Champion, 1847-1866." Duluth, Minn., H. Stein Print, 1934. 8vo, cl, port, ix, 387pp. Documentary study chiefly of antebellum politics: Robt. Tyler, son of Pres. J. Tyler, Henry A. Wise, Va. Gov., Jas. Buchanan. $35-bmk.

545 ..."James Buchanan & his cabinet on the eve of secession." (Lancaster, Pa.) Priv. print, 1926. 8vo, cl, ix, 224pp. port. $8.50 Reprinted, Boston: 1966. See: James Buchanan. Review: Tyler's Qrt. Hist. Mag., ix, #1, (1927).

546 ..."James Buchanan, the court & the Dred Scott case." In: TennHM, Jan. 1926, issued Oct., 1928, v.IX, #4, p. 231-240.

547 ..."Everett Abolitionized." In: Tyler's Quart. Hist. & Genea. Mag., July, 1925, v.VII, #1, p. 141-144. Supports Edward Everett, who is denigrated by the North.

548 ..."Charles O'Connor's views of the prosecution of Jefferson Davis, 1867." In: TylerQHGM., Jan., 1948, v.29, p. 181-183. Notes. Includes letter of O'Connor, N.Y., Oct. 19, 1867.

549 **AUER, J. Jeffery, Edt.**
"Antislavery & Disunion, 1858-1861. Studies in the Rhetoric of Compromise & Conflict." N.Y., Harper & Row(1963). $3.75. 8vo, cl, xii, 427pp. Auspices of the Speech Association of America.

550 **AUER, John Jeffery**
"The little fight." Duke's raid on Augusta(Ky) Sept. 27, 1862." In: KyHSR, Jan., 1951, p. 28-34. Notes. A raid under Col. Basil Duke, CSArmy.

551 **AUGUSTIN, John Alcee**
"War Flowers, reminiscences of four years campaigning. Respectfully dedicated to the ladies of New Orleans, by F.B." (New Orleans, Hinton Print, July 5, 1865) 16mo, boards, 103pp., errata slip. $7.50, $10, $17.50, $175-jk-142.

552 **AUMAN, William T.**
"Neighbor against neighbor." The inner civil war in the Randolph County area & Confederate North Carolina." In: NCHR, Jan. 1984, p. 59-92.

553 **AUMAN, Wm. T. & David D. Scarboro**
"The Heroes of America in Civil War North Carolina." In: NCHR, v.LVIII, Autumn, 1981, 37pp. $8-bmk.

554 **AUSTERMAN, Wayne R.**
"Those Damn Yankee Rifles." In: Va. Cavalcade, Winter 1985, v.34, #3, p. 100-107pp., illus., incl. double-pg. color, ports.

555 ..."Rebel Rimfires, the Henry Rifle in the Confederacy." In: "Men at Arms", Oct. 1985, v.7, #5, p. 36-42, facsm., illus., ports.

556 **AUSTILL, Hurieosco**
"Fort Morgan in the Confederacy." In: AHQ, 1945, v.VII, p. 254-268. A member of the 1st Battl.

557 ..."Letters by..." In: AHQ, 1945, v.VII, p. 547-573. Prison experiences.

558 **AUSTIN, Aurelia**
"Georgia Boys with "Stonewall" Jackson, James Thomas Thompson & the Walton Infantry." Athens, Ga., University of Georgia pr, 1967. 12mo, cl, dj, ports, xii, 99pp. $4.75, $7.

559 **AUSTIN, Charles W.**
"The First Ironclad." In: South. Hist. Assn. Pub., 1902, v.30, p. 196-204. Texas Confederate officer.

560 **AUSTIN, J.P.**
"The Blue & the Gray, sketches of a portion of the unwritten history of the great American Civil War, a truthful narrative of adventure with thrilling reminiscences of the great struggle on land & sea. By J.P. Austin of 9th Ky. Cavalry." Atlanta, Ga., Franklin Print, 1899. 12mo, gray cl, front, xi, (1), 246pp. color illus. $10, $12.50, $15, $20, $25, $30, $60-bmk, $40, $100-jk-117.

561 **AUSTIN, James C.**
"Bill Arp." N.Y., Twayne Pub., (1969) 12mo, cl, d/w, 120pp. $2.50. Twayne's U.S. Authors Series, #162. A study of Chas. Henry Smith, creator of Bill Arp & a cross-section of Southern Life from antebellum times.

562 **AUSTIN, Robert A.**
"Battle of Wilson's Creek." In: Mo. Hist. Rev., 1932, v.XXVII, p. 46-49.

563 **AUTAUGA Rifles, 1861-1865.**
(Montgomery, Alabama Print, 1891) sm 4to, 13pp. Unit roster & individual records of their participation in battle

564 **"AUTOGRAPHS of Prominent Men**
of the Southern Confederacy Historical Documents, E.M. Bruce Collection." (Houston, Texas, Cumming Print, 1903) Comps-Passenger Dept., Southern Pacific RRy., n.d. $20-bmk, $3.50. Oblong, 8vo, stiff wraps, 32pp., facsms.

565 **AVARY, Myrta Lockett, Edt.**
"A Virginia Girl in the Civil War 1861-1865. Being a record of the actual experiences of the wife of a Confederate officer." N.Y., D. Appleton & Co., 1903 (1st, Feb. 1903) 12mo, cl, x, 384, (6)pp-ads. $9, $12.50, $15, $20. Edts: N.Y., Lond: 1910, $3.50; NY, 1917, $7.50. ..." An account taken from..." A Virginia girl & the Romance of War." In: Harold Straubig's Civil war eyewitness reports., Hamden, Conn., Archon books, 1985. p. 235-236.

566 ..."Dixie After the War. An exposition of social conditions existing in the South, during the twelve years succeeding fall of Richmond with Intro: Gen. Clement A. Evans. Illus. from old paintings, daguerreotypes, rare photos." N.Y., Doubleday,

Page & Co., 1906. Imp. 8vo, decr. cl, teg, x, 435pp. illus., ports-incl. front. $10, $12.50, $15, $30-bmk

...Boston: Houghton, Mifflin Co., 1937. Reissue omission of chap. 1, slight changes in text. $9.

...N.Y., Da Capo, 1970 (The American Scene Da Capo reprint series. $22.50, $15, $25-y. See: Alex H. Stephens, she edited.

567 ..."A Lincoln souvenir in the South. A letter from Abraham Lincoln to Alexander H. Stephens which hangs on the wall of a Southern Home." In: Cent. Mag., FEb., 1907, v.LXXIII, p. 506-508.

568 **AVERA, William Franklin**
"Extracts from the Memoirs of William Franklin Avera. Edited By Henry Cathey." In: AHQ, 1963, v.XXII, p. 99-116, port. Largely CSA, in 5th Ark. Artillery Co.

569 **AVERASBORO, Battle of,**
North Carolina Southern Historical Society Papers. Gen. Wm. B. Taliaferro's Report, v.7, p. 31-34; also his letter of explanation, p. 195. Capt. Graham Dave's correction, v.7, p. 125-126. See: Alex. C. McClurg. See: Harnett Co., N.C. in civil war.

570 **AVERILL, J.H., Col.**
"Richmond, Virginia. The Evacuation of the City & the days preceding it." In: SHSP, 1897, v.XXXV, p. 267-273.

571 **AVERILL, J.P., Compl.**
"Andersonville prison park. Report of its purchase & improvement. Accompanied by a plat of ground made from actual survey." Atlanta, Ga. (c. 1898) 8vo, wraps, illus., map, 21, (3)pp. $15-bmk-89.

572 **AVERY, Alfonso Calhoun**
"Memorial address on life & character of Lt. Gen. D.H. Hill, May 10, 1893." Raleigh, N.C., Edwards & Broughton, 1893. 8vo, wraps, 41pp. $3.50, $10, $12, $25-y, $15.

573 ...So. Hist. Soc. Papers, XXI, p. 110-150.

574 **AVERY, Hester S., Jr., Mrs.**
"The Story of Co. I, 16th Ark. Inf. Regt. Army of Confederate States." In: Wash. Co. Hist. Soc., "Flashback". Aug. 1970, v.XX, #2, p. 27-31.

575 **AVERY, Isaac Wheeler**
"The History of the State of Georgia, from 1850 to 1881, embracing the three important epocs: The decade before the war of 1861-1865; The War; the period of Reconstruction, with portraits of the leading public men of this era." N.Y., Brown & Derby, Pubs., (1881) Tk. 8vo, cl, front(port), ports(steel & engr.) facsm some copies with fldg. colored map, (12), 714, (1)p. Ga. Officers in CSA, p. (657)-694; Append-B, Jeff Davis & Gov. Joe E. Brown, p. (695)-714. The CSA period, p. 161-335. $15, $38.50-y, $20. Other copies have Index, (715)-754pp., errata slip.

576 ..."In Memory. The Last Sickness, Death, & Funeral Obsequies of Alexander H. Stephens, Gov. of Georgia." Atlanta, Ga., 1883, V.P. Sisson, pub., 8vo, wraps, 84pp. $5, $10, $12, See: Kemp P. Battle.

577 ..."Recollections of the "Lost" Cause." By a Southern Cavalry Officer. In: LWL, Nov. 1867, v.IV, #1, p. 38-49.

578 **AVERY, Roy C., Mrs., Edt.**
"The Second Presbyterian Church of Nashville during the Civil War." In: Tenn. HQ, Dec. 1952, v.XI, p. 356-375. Letters of Adam G. Adams & Rev. J.S. Hays, 1861-1862.

579 **AVILLO, Philip, Jr.**
"John H. Reagan: Unionist or Secessionist?" In: ETHJ, Spring 1975, v.XIII, #1, p. 23-33, notes.

580 **AVIRETT, James B., Rev.**
"Memoirs of Gen. Turner Ashby..." Gaithersburg, Md., Butternut Press, 1985. $28.50.

580a **AVIRETT, James Battle**
See: Frank Cunningham, Adolphus Edward Richards, Clarence Thomas.

581 **AVIRETT, James Battle, Rev.**
"The Memoirs of Gen. Turner Ashby & his compeers."...and other officer of Army of Northern Virginia, C.S.A." Baltimore: Selby & Dunlaney, 1867. 12mo, cl, xi, (13)-408pp. port. $12.50, $20, $35, $50, $45-nc, Mint-$250-bmk-105, $85-ginsb-9, Ex-Lib-$150. Avirett was chaplain in Ashby's Cavalry.

582 ..."The Old Plantation. How we lived in great house & cabin before the War." N.Y., F. Tennyson Neely Co., 1901. 8vo, cl, ports, x, 220pp. Plantation in Onslow County, N.C. Preface by Hunter McGuire, Late Surgeon-General, Stonewall Jackson. $25.

583 ..."Who Was the Rebel-the traitor-the Trans-Susquehannan man or the Cis-Susquehannan man?" An oration by...on occasion of laying the foundation stone to the central shaft in the North Carolina plot in Stonewall Cemetery, Winchester, Va. Sept. 17, 1897. The 35th Anniversary Battle of Sharpsburg." (Winchester, 1897) 8vo, wraps, 30pp. (Louisburg, N.C., Kittrell's, Oct. 5, 1897) Pub. thru the generosity of Mr. Charles B. Rouss.

584 **AVIS, John**
"Exact copy of affidavit made by Captain John Avis, the jailer & Executioner of Captain John Brown." In: SHSP, 1885, v.XIII, p. 339-342.

585 **AWTREY, Hugh**
"War paper news of the sixties." In: Regional Rev., (1939), v.III, #6, p. 15-20. Being printed on wall-paper because the scarcity of paper.

586 **AYER, Isaiah Winslow**
"The Great Northwestern Conspiracy in all its Startling Details, Plot to Burn New York, piracy on the lake-ports for the Sons of Liberty-trial of the Chicago conspirators, inside views of the temples of Sons of Liberty, names of prominent members." 3rd Edt. Chicago: Rounds & James, 1865. 8vo, cl, iv, (5)-112pp., illus., ports. $27.50.
...Do: Chicago: John R. Walsh, 1865.
...Do: Howes shows an 1864 edition.

587 ...Do: "The Great Treason Plot in the North during the War." Chicago: U.S. Publishing Co., (1895). xix, (20)-453pp., illus., ports, 8vo. $20.

588 **AYER, Lewis Malone, Jr.**
"An address, on the question of Separate State Secession, to the People of Barnwell District." Charleston, S.C., Walker & James, 1851. 8vo, wraps, p.(3), 4-22.

589 ..."Southern Rights & the Labour Question. An address delivered at Whippy Swamp, on 4th of July, 1855, by Gen. Lewis M. Ayer, published by the People to whom it was delivered." Charleston,S.C., A.J. Burke, 1855. 8vo, wraps, p.(3)-4-23.

590 ..."Patriotism & State Sovereignty; an oration delivered before the Two Societies of the South Carolina College, on 4th of December, 1868." Published by the Euphradian Society." Charleston, S.C., A.J. Burke, 1859. 8vo, wraps, 26pp.

591 ..."Biographical Sketch of Gen. Lewis M. Ayer from Annals of Barnwell Col., by Hartzog & Bonham. Caption title, no imprint. 1896. 8vo, wraps, (1)-4-31. Errata slip. All above from Turnbull, III, IV.

592 **AYERS, George R.**
"Cotton & sugar through the Federal Blockade. By Ella J. Deasy & Edmund J. Deasy, Edts." In: Tyler QHGM, 1940, v.XXII, p.-. Letter from New Orleans, Mar. 10, 1863.

593 **AYLETT, William Roane, Col.**
"Women of the South. Address before Pickett Camp in behalf of a Monument to

the women of the Southern Confederacy." In: SHSP, 1894, v.XXII, p. 54-63.

594 **AYLOTT, F.G.**
"A Confederate Dilemma." (London) Jour. Confed. Hist. Soc., Nov., 1962, v.I, #2, p. 41-48, plate guns. Refers to guns & ammunitions.

B

1   **BABCOCK, Bernie**
"Lighthorse Harry's Boy: The Boyhood of Robert E. Lee." Phila: Lippincott Pr., 1931. 12mo, cl, color front, illus. by Walter Pyle, 255pp. juvenile. $4.50

2   **BACHMAN, J.**
"Panorama of the Seat of War. A collection of four lithographs in color, depicting the physical aspects of the south. Drawn, lithographed & published by J. Bachman. N.Y. (1861) J. Bachman. folio, cloth $12.50. Va., Md., Del., & D.C.; N. & S. Carolina, part Ga.; Fla. pt. of Ga. & Ala.: La., Miss., Ala., Fla.

3   **BACHMAN, Robert, Mrs., Compl.**
"Tennessee Confederate Soldiers in the Battle of Shiloh, Apr. 6-7, 1862." U.D.C.-Tennessee Division, n.p. (c.1941) 4to, typescript copy.

4   **BACHMANN, John, Map**
"Panorama of the seat of War. Birds eye view of Louisiana, Missipi, Alabama & part of Florida. Drawn from nature & lithographed by..." New York: John Bachmann, 1861. 28x18 3/8". $250-y. More geographical than cartography, many ships in water foreground, La. delta.

5   **BACON, Augustus Octavius**
"Participation of the Southern States in the War of the American Revolution. Speech of Hon. Augustus O. Bacon, of Georgia, in the Senate of the United States, Wednesday, Jan. 29, 1902. n.p., 1902. 8vo, wraps, 8pp. caption title.

6   ..."The Civil War was not a "Rebellion". A Rebel has no claim of right except the right of force; the South claimed the right of law." Speech of Hon. A.O. Bacon, of Georgia in the Senate of the US, Friday, Jan. 11, 1907. Washington, 1907. 8vo, wraps, 7pp.

7   **BADEAU, Adam**
"The relative strength of the two armies in Virginia, 1864-1865." In: Hist. Mag., s.2, (Morrisania, 1871) p. 102-111, v.IX. Letters of Gen. Badeau to London Std. occasioned by an editorial on Gen. Lee together with Gen. Early's reply to Badeau. Dorn-II, 1103.

7   **BAENZIGER, Ann Patton**
"The Texas State Police during Reconstruction: a Reexamination." In: SwHQ, April, 1969, v.LXXII, #4, p. 470-491.

8   **BAGBY, Alfred, Rev.**
"King & Queen County, Virginia." N.Y., Wash., Neale Pub., 1908. 8vo, cl, front, pls., ports, maps, (7)-402pp.
...Baltimore: Regional Pub. Co., 1974. 8vo, cl, illus., 402pp. $13.50, $21-y

10 **BAGBY, George William, Dr.**
"The Old Virginia Gentleman & Other Sketches." Edt: Thomas Nelson Page. N.Y., Charles Scribner's sons, 1910. 12mo, cl, front(port), xxix, 312pp. $5.
...Richmond, Va., Dietz Press, 1938. Edt: By his daughter, Ellen M. Bagby. Intro: Douglas Southall Freeman, $30-bmk. 8vo, cl, illus., bibliog., xxvii, 296pp. $3.50, Deluxe Edt., $7.50.

11 ..."John M. Daniels Latch-Key. Being a Sketch of his life." Lynchburg, Va., J.P. Bell, 1868. 12mo, wraps, 40pp. First published in the "Native Virginian." A memoir of the late editor of Richmond Examinor.

12 ..."John Brown & Wm. Mahone. An historical parallel foreshadowing civil trouble." Richmond, Va., C.F. Johnson, 1880. 16mo, wraps, 23pp. Swem-217. Signed: Edmund Riffin's Shade. After receiving his degree, really didn't practice but Edt. Lynchburg Express, later:

Southern Literary Messenger & correspondent other papers. A delineator of not only the Southern character but humor.

13 ..."John M. Daniel's latch-key. Being a sketch of his life." n.p., 1868. 12mo, wraps, 40pp. (See also under title)

14 ..."Original Letters of Mozis Addums to Billy Ivvins." Richmond, Va., Clemmitt & Jones, 1878, sq. 12mo, wraps, 118pp. Orig. pub. by West & Johnson in a small edt., 87pp. 1862. Author states in preface mainly distributed among soldiers in the field & lost or destroyed. Originally published in the Southern Literary Messenger.

15 ..."Selections from the miscellaneous writings of Dr. Geo W. Bagby." Richmond, Va., Whittet & Shepperson, 1884-1885. 12mo, cl, 2vols. port.

16 **BAGGETT, James Alex**
"Origins of Upper South Scalawags leadership." In: CWH, March 1983, v.29, #1, p. 53-73, notes charts. See: Otto H. Olsen.

17 **BAGLEY, William Chandler**
"Soil Exhaustion & the Civil War." Washington, DC: American Council on Public Affairs, 1942. 8vo, cl, ix, 101pp. Claims was cause of the war. See: Ramsdell(Chs.) "Limits of Slavery."

18 **BAGWELL, Alexander**
"Confederate generals killed in the war." In: CV, Oct. 1919, v.XXVII, p. 386-387.

19 **BAHNSON, Henry T.**
"The Last Days of the War." Hamlet, N.C., Capital Print, 1903. 16mo, wraps, 22, (1)pp. $3. $20-bmk-105. North Carolina Booklet, v.II, #12. Great Events in North Carolina Hist. Author: Co. B., 1st N.C., Batt'n. S.S., A.N.V. As seen by a confed. private.

20 ..."Days of the War, 1863-1865. By Henry Theodore Bahnson." (Clemmons (?) Mrs. T. Holt Haywood, N.D. 16mo, wraps, port, 31pp. Note: In Winston Salem, N.C., the Moravians published a small pamphlet on Dr. Bahnson & reprinted it once.?

21 **BAHOS, Charles**
"On Opothleyahola's trail Locating the Battle of Round Mountain." In: ChO, Spring, 1985, v.1xiii, #1, p. 58-89, map, port, extensive notes.

22 **BAILEY, Anne J.**
"Henry McCulloch's Texans & the defense of Arkansas in 1862." In: AHQ, Spring, 1987, v.46, #1, p. 46-59, maps, port.

23 **BAILEY, David C.**
"Farewell to valor; a salute to the brothers Coleman...of Asheville days remembered." Ashville, N.C., 1977. 8vo, wraps, 68pp., illus. David, Thad & Robert, N.C. mountain regs. $10.

24 **BAILEY, Fred A.**
"Class & Tennessee's Confederate generation." In: JSH, Feb. 1985, v.51, #1, p. 31-60.

25 **BAILEY, Fred Arthur**
"Class & Tennessee's Confederate generation." Chapel Hill: University Press, 1986. 8vo, cl, dj, 180pp. $21.

26 **BAILEY, Hugh C.**
"Disaffection in the Alabama Hill Country, 1861." In: CWH, June, 1958, v.IV, #2, p. 183-193.

27 ..."Alabama political leaders & the Missouri Compromise." In: Ala. Rev., April, 1956, v.9, p. 120-134, notes.

28 ..."Hinton Rowan Helper, Abolitionist Racist." Montgomery, Ala., University of Alabama Press (1965) Southern Hist. Pub. #7. $6.75. 8vo, cl, port, xi, 256pp. Bibliog. p. 221-229. Helper was catipulted into national fame with his violent anti-slavery writings.

29 ..."Hinton Rowan Helper & "The Impending Crisis(1857)." In: LaHQ, April, 1957, v.40, p. 132-145. Notes. Sentiments of the

Southern yeoman, contributes to mutual fear & hatred, culminating in the war.

30 **BAILEY, Hugh Coleman**
"Disloyalty in Early Confederate Alabama." In: JSH, Nov., 1957, v.23, p. 524-528. $10.

31 **BAILEY, James H.**
"Henrico Home Front 1861-1865. A picture of life in Henrico Co., Va., from May, 1861, through April, 1865. Based upon selections from the Minute books of the Henrico county court." (Richmond, Va., Whittet & Shepperson) 1963. A project sponsored by the Henrico Co. Civil War Centennial Commission. 8vo, wraps, illus. (incl. front) ports, xxiv, 275pp., list of CSA soldiers of Henrico co., p. 243-257; index. $25-bmk-105, $3

32 ..."Anthony M. Keiley & the Keiley incident." In: VaMHB, 1959, v.67, p. 65-81.

33 **BAILEY, John W., Jr.**
"The McNeill Rangers & the Capture of Generals Crook & Kelley." In: Md. Hist. Mag., 1967, v.LXII, p. 47-63.

34 **BAILEY, W.**
"The star company of Ector's Texas (cavalry) brigade." In: CV, Sept., 1914, v.XXII, p. 404-405. Service of Co. D, 14th Texas dismounted cavalry.

35 **BAILEY, William H.**
"Sketch of Col. Benjamin Harvey Hill." In: NC Univ. Mag., 1890, #3, ix, p. 41-52, 143.

36 ..."The Battle of Great Bethel Church." In: B & G, v, 1895, p. 153-156.

36a **BAIRD, Nancy Disher**
"David Wendel Young, physician of old Louisville, by Nancy Disher Baird." Lexington: University of Kentucky Press 1978. 8vo, cl, dj, x, (1), 115p. (1)p. ills, plan, ports.

37 **BAIRD, Samuel John, Rev.**
"Southern Rights & Northern Duties in the present crisis. A Letter to Hon. William Pennington." Phila., Lindsay & Blakiston, 1861. 8vo, wraps, 32pp. $5.

38 **BAIRD, W. David**
"Fort Smith & the Red Man." In: AHQ, 1871, v.XXX, p. 337-348, illus.

39 **BAIRD, William**
"Dismemberment of Virginia." In: So. Hist. Ass'n., Jan, 1898, v.II, #1, p. 34-50. Formation of West Va.

40 ...Same. In: SHSP, 1898, v.XXVI, p. 39-62.

41 ..."A foreign view of the Civil War in America", a review by Baird of the Comte de Paris book, same title. SHSP, 1876, v.II, p. 209-222.

42 **BAKELESS, John**
"Catching Harry Gilmor." In: CWTI, April 1971, v.10, p. 34-40, illus., ports. Late in the war this "thorn in the side" was caught.

43 ..."James Harrison: Rebel Enigma." In: CWTI, April 1970, v.IX, #1, p. 12-20, illus., facsms., ports.

44 ..."The Mystery of Appomattox." In: CWTI, June, 1970, v.IX, #3, p. 18-34, illus., map, ports. Sidelight on march of ANV & Lee seriously crippled by Federal spies.

45 **BAKELESS, John Edwin**
"Spies of the Confederacy." Phila: Lippincott & Co. (1970) tk. 8vo, cl, dj, viii, 456pp. $7.50, $15-bmk
...2nd printing. 3rd., $7.50, $8.50-y

46 ..."Confederate Spy Stories." Phila: Lippincott Pub. Co., (1973) 12mo, cl, map, 159pp. $6., $9-y.

47 **BAKER, Alpheus**
"Island No. 10." In: SB, 1882-1883, v.1, p. 54-62.

48 **BAKER, Andrew J.**
"Speech of...delivered to the Camp of Ex-Confederates at Walnut Springs, Aug. 11, 1897." Austin, Texas, 1897. 8vo, wraps, 29pp. $12.50.

48a **BAKER, Charles Estell**
"The Palmyra Massacre Oct. 18, 1862, Palmyra, Missouri, Marion County." In: CV, ns, Jan-Feb. 1988, v. 26, #1, p.24-34, ills, maps, ports.

49 **BAKER, Cullen**
"Life of the Notorious Desperado Cullen Baker, from his childhood to his death, with a full account of all the murders he committed. Thos. Orr, Editor." n.p., n.d. (1870) 16mo, wraps, (46)pp.(LC, only known copy). Said to have fought with pro-slave group in Kansas War; in CSA service, reconstrn. in NE Texas area. See: Bartholomew(Ed). See: Mrs. Viola Cobb, J.K. Bivins "Memoirs." 1 chapter on Cullen Baker.

50 **BAKER, Henry H.**
"A Reminiscent Story of the Great Civil War. First (-second) paper. A Personal experience by Henry H. Baker." New Orleans, La., Ruskin Press, 1911. 12mo, wraps, cover title, , plates (3-ports) 1-illus. in 2 Vols. 65pp. (V.2) 18pp. $15.

51 ..."Battle of Fredericksburg by Col. Henry H. Baker, New Orleans, 1911. 12mo, 18pp. bound in same vol. $100-bmk-105.

52 **BAKER, Jean H.**
"The Loyal Opposition: Northern Democrats in the Thirty-seventh Congress." In: CWH, June, 1979, v.25, #2, p. 139-155, notes, chart.

53 ..."The Politics of Continuity: Maryland Political Parties from 1858 to 1870." Baltimore: Johns Hopkins Press, 1973. 8vo, cl, notes, bibliog., index, xv, 239pp. $11. See also: Wm. J. Evitts

54 **BAKER, Jeffrey J.W.**
"Strike the Ten." Color photos: Lawrence O. Holmberg, Jr. Garden City, N.Y., Doubleday & Co. (1970) Sm. oblong 4to, (64)pp. unnumbered. $5.95. Descp. text to photos. d/w subtitle: "The steps of Robert E. Lee's Army of N. Va."

55 **BAKER, L.S., Colonel**
"Report of Colonel L.S. Baker, 1st N.C. Cavlary." In: OLOD, Mar., 1875, v.2, #1, p. 29-30.

56 **BAKER, Marion A.**
"Farragut's demands for the surrender of New Orleans. By the Mayor's private secretary." In: Cent., July, 1886, n.s. X, p. 459-464. port of Soule. See: Beverly Kennon.

57 **BAKER, Thomas H.**
"Refugee Newspaper: The Memphis "Daily Appeal" 1862-1865."(Houston, Tex.) JSH, August, 1963. v.XXIX, #3, p. 326-344.

58 ..."The Memphis Commercial Appeal. The History of a Southern Newspaper." Baton Rouge: Louisiana State University Press, (1971). 8vo, cl, dj, (5), 336pp. $12.50

59 **BALACE, Francis**
"La Guerre de Secession, et la Belgique: documents d'Archives Americaines, 1861-1865." Leuven: Editions Nauwelaverts: Paris Beatrice-Nauwelaerts, 1969. 8vo, cl, xxviii, 320pp. $500-bfr.

60 **BALCH, Thomas Bloomer**
"My manse during the war: a decade of letters to the Rev. J. Thomas Murray, editory of the "Methodist Protestant." Balt: Sherwood & Co., 1866. 12mo, wraps, 42pp.

61 **BALDINGER, Nancy Shepard**
"Genealogy, the Wright-Hawkins-Edwards family & the Civil War." In: RKHS, Jan. 1962, v.60, #1, p. 50-67.

62 **BALES, Richard**
"The Confederacy." A cantata based on music of the South during the years 1861-1865." Wed. Jan. 20, 1954, Columbia, Columbia Museum of Art. 4to, stiff decr. wraps, official program ports, (12)p., pl. $15. A recording by the National Gallery, Wash., DC. "The Confederacy by Bales.

63 **BALFOUR, Daniel T.**
"13th Virginia Cavalry." Lynchburg, Va.,

H.E. Howard, 1986, 8vo, cl, dj, (6) 115pp., ports, pl. 1000 copies numbered, signed.

64 **BALIR, Asa Jordan**
"Asa Jordan Blair's part in the Civil War." In: AHQ, Fall 1958, v.20, #3, p. 476-478.

65 **BALLAIGUE de BUGHAS, Louise Dubois**
"Nos Americains de la Guerre de secession Paris: Societe generale de librairie Catholique, 1882. 12mo, cl, or wraps, 384pp. $12, $10. Another edt., 1881, with 385pp. $50-ginz. Refugee life in and around Charleston in war.

66 **BALLARD, Effie**
"Ridgeley Greathouse. Copied form the "Shelby record" dated Friday, Aug. 8, 1902, & contributed by Wm. E. Railey." In: KyHSR, 1935, v.XXXIII, p. 273-275. Activities on behalf the CSArmy, imprisonment, escape during war.

67 **BALLARD, Michael B.**
"Yankee Editors on Jefferson Davis." In: JMH, November, 1981, v.XLIII, #4, p. 316-332, notes.

68 ..."A long shadow: Jefferson Davis & the final days of the Confederacy." Jackson, Miss., University Press, (1986) 12mo, cl, dj, xi, 200pp., illus., port.

69 **BALME, Joshua R., Rev.**
"American States, Churches & Slavery." Edinburgh: Nimmo Church Pub., 1862. Tk, 8vo, lxviii, 546pp. Sabin-2977.
...London: Hamilton Pub., 1863 (2nd Edt.)

70 ..."Amer. States, Churches, Slavery & a Snyopsis of the American War." London: Hamilton Pub., 1865. Tk. 12mo, cl, lxviii, 776pp.

71 ..."Letters on the American Republic, or, Common Fallacies & Monstrous Errors refuted & exposed." London: Hamilton, Adams Co., 1863. 12mo, cl, p. 547-776. $12.50. Pro-Southern, condems Northern hardheartedness, hypocrisy & negro-hating emancipationists.

72 **BALTIMORE & ANNISTON.**
(Tune-Maryland, My Maryland) (Baltimore: 1861) Broadside: 8 1/2x3 1/2, 1p. See: James R. Randall. $35.

73 **BALTIMORE, Lester B.**
"Benjamin F. Stringfellow. The Fight for Slavery on the Missouri Border." (Columbia, Mo., Mo. Hist. Review, Oct., 1967, v.LXII, #1, p. 14-29, illus., ports.

74 **BALTZ, Louis J., III**
"Let us say no more about it." In: CV (new) Nov. 1985, v.33, #6, p. 24-29, tint map, ports, plate(color. Bristoe Station disaster.

75 **BALTZELL, George F.**
"The Battle of Olustee (Ocean Pond) Florida." (Gainsville, Fla.) Fla. Hist. Soc. Quart. (1931) v.IX, p. 199-223. Fldg. map. See also: Ruth Cole.

76 **BANCROFT, A.C., Edt.**
"The Life & Death of Jefferson Davis, ex-president of the Southern Confederacy. Together with comments of the press, funeral sermons, etc." Edt. by... N.Y., J.S. Ogilvie (1889) Fireside series, #102. 12mo, wraps (or, cloth) port of Davis on cover, front, illus., port, 256pp. (cheap paper) 3/4 Mor. $50-bk, $25-bmk, $3.50, $6., $10. $12.50, $15, $20,
...Louisville, Ky., Lost Cause Press, microcd. $3.95

77 **BANCROFT, Frederic**
"Calhoun & the South Carolina Nullification Movement." Baltimore: Johns Hopkins Press, 1928. 8vo, wraps, vi, 199pp. $7.50

78 **BANE, John P., Major**
"Report of Major J.P. Bane, Fourth Texas Regiment, Hdq., July 9, 1863." In: SHSP, 1885, v.XIII, p. 190-191.

79 **BANJAMIN, L.N.**
"The St. Albans Raid; or, Investigation into the Charges against Lieut. Bennett H. Young & Command, for their acts at St.

Albans, Vt. On the 19th Oct., 1864. Being a Complete & Authentic Report of all the Proceedings on the Demand of the U.S. for their Extradition, under the Ashburton Treaty. Before Judge Coursol, j.s.p., & the Hon. Mr. Justice Smith, j.s.c." Montreal, 1865. 8vo, wraps, 480pp.
...Boston: A. Williams & Co., 1865. $17.50, $20, $32.50, $40, $225-ginz-9.

80 **BANKHEAD, John Hollis, Capt.**
"Capt. John Hollis Bankhead, C.S.A., 1842-1920." In: CV, June, 1920, v.XXVIII, p. 207-208.

81 **BANKHEAD, Smith P., Col.**
"Letter on Battle of Shiloh." In: SHSP, 1879, v.7, p. 41-42.

82 **BANKS, Dean**
"Autobiography of John Banks, Columbus, Georgia, 1797-1870." n.p. (c.1938) 2nd printing. 1936. $35-bmk. 8vo, cl, 38pp., less than 250 copies of both edts., printed exactly from a contemp. mssc., on Seminole War, Civil War to Nov. 23, 1865. (old) $10

83 **BANKS, John**
"A Short Biographical Sketch of the Undersigned by Himself." (Austell, Ga., c. 1936/1938) 8vo, wraps, 38pp.

84 **BANKS, Robert W.**
"Civil War Letters of Robert W. Banks Atlanta Campaign. Edt: George C. Osborn." In: Ga. H.Q., June, 1943, v.XXVII, #2, p. 208-216. $10
..."The Civil War Letters of Robert W. Banks." Edt: Geo. C. Osborn. (Jackson, Miss., Jour. of Miss. Hist. July, 1842, v.V, #3, p. 141-154.

85 **BANKS, Robert Webb**
"The Battle of Franklin, Nov. 30, 1864, the bloodiest engagement of the War between the States, by R. W. Banks, Capt. Co. 3, 37th Miss. consolidated infantry." N.Y., Neale pub., 1908. 12mo, cl, 88pp. $10, $12.50, $15, $22.50, $100-bmk-105, $90-bmk, $40-nc.

86 ..."Civil War Letters: the Atlanta Campaign", in Ga. Hist. Quar. XXVII, 1943, p. 208-216.
..."Battle of Franklin..." Dayton, Oh., Morningside Bks., 1982, Reprint of 1908 edition, 500 copies op. $40.

87 **BANKSTON, Marie Louis Benton**
"Camp-fire stories of the Mississippi valley campaign." Louisiana Series. New Orleans, La., L. Graham Co, 1911, 16mo, cl, front, port, illus., 171pp. $15.
...2nd edt., 1914.

88 **BANNISTER, Don**
"Long Day at Shilah." London & Henly: Routledge & Kegan Paul, 1981. 12mo, cl, 277pp. Fictional account of bloodiest day of civil war. $12.

89 **BAPTIST CHURCH, Georgia.**
Hephzibah Baptist Association, August. "Minutes of the sixty-ninth anniversary Hephzibah Baptist Association, held at Hephzibah Chapel, Richmond County, Ga., on the 12th & 14th of September, 1863." Augusta, Ga., Chronical & Sentinel, 1863. 8vo, cover title, 15pp. Not in Crandall/Harwell(69th Anniv. only)

90 **BAPTIST CHURCH, North Carolina**
"Minutes of the Little River Baptist Ass'n., held at Juniper Meeting House, Johnson County, N.C., 26th Sept., 1862." 8vo, sewn, 8pp. (Hook-cat-#30, fall, 1940)

91 **BARBEE, David Rankin**
"Dr. (John Joseph) Craven's "Prison Life of Jefferson Davis" (1867)...an expose." Tyler's Quarterly History & Genealogical Magazine, April, 1951. v.32, p. 282-295. Attributes this work to Charles Graham Halpine. $10-bmk-84.

92 ..."An excursion in Southern history briefly set forth in correspondence between Sen. A.J. Veberidge & D.R. Barbee." (Asheville (N.C.) Service print), 1928. 8vo, wraps, 64pp. $5., $15-bmk. Originally published in the Asheville Sunday Citizen, May

93 ..."How Lincoln rejected peace overtures in 1861." In: Tyler's Quar. Hist. & Geanal. Mag., 1924, v.XV, p. 137-144. $10-bmk-84.

94 ..."The North in Arms! Lincoln's Responsibility!" In: Tyler's Quar. Hist. & Genal. Mag, 1934, v.XV, p. 129-130.

95 ..."The Line of Blood; the coming of the Civil War, 1860-1861." In: Tenn. HQ, March, 1957, v.XVI, p. 3-54, notes.

96 ..."Historic Letters." Tyler's Quar. Hist. & Geneal. Mag., 1934, v.XV, p. 232-236. Letters: Jacob Thompson & Mrs. Archibald Dixon.

97 ..."Hinton Rowan Helper, 1829-1909." In: Tyler's QHG Mag., 1934, v.XV, p. 145-172, 228-231. $10-bmk

98 ..."Letters on the Issues of 1850-1865." In: Tyler's QHGMag., 1932, v.XIV, p. 90-103.

99 ..."Hinton Rowan Helper's mendacity." In: Tyler's QHGMag., April, 1934, v.XV, p. 5 $5.

100 ..."Lincoln & Andersonville." In: Tyler's QHGMag., April, 1934, v.XV, p. 12. $5

101 ..."A lost incident in Lincoln's life." In: Tyler's QHGMag., July, 1945, v.XXVI, p.8 $8-bmk

102 ..."The plain truth about the Bixby Letter." In: Tyler's QHGMag., Jan. 1945, v.XXVI, p. 23 $8-bmk.

103 ..."Secession & Coercion." In: Tyler's QHGMag., Oct. 1933, v.XIV, p. 8 $8-

104 ..."The Capture of Jefferson Davis. Reprint: Tyler's Quart. History & Genealog. Mag., July, 1947. 8vo, sewn, illus., 37pp. Reprint: n.p., n.d., #9, $6-bmk, $15-bmk.

105 ..."Lincoln, Chase & the Rev. Dr. Richard Fuller." In: Md. HM., June, 1951, v.46, p. 108-123. Notes. Dr. Fuller & Baltimoreans persuade Lincoln to recognize independence of South. April, 1861.

106 ..."Who wrote Dixie??? Origin of America's most stirring song challenged by historians." In: Musical Digest, 1948, v.XXX, p. 6-9, April-May. Facsms, ports, views. See: Alfred Human's editorial-"Cloud Over Dixie", p. 4, for references, 1858-1861. See: Chas. B. Galbreath.

107 **BARBET, Paul**
"Naval encounter between the 'Kearsarge' & 'The Alabama.' fought in the sight of Cherbourg, on June 19, 1864." In: USN Inst. Proc., Aug., 1926, v.LII, p. 1681-1686. Reprint: Marine Jour., June 19, 1926.

108 **BARBIERE, Joseph**
"Scraps from the prison table, at Camp Chase & Johnson's Island. By Joseph Barbiere, Lieut-Col. late CSA." Doylestown, Pa., W.W.H. Davis Print, 1868. 8vo, cl, front (plan) 7-pls., 397, (2)pp. Roster of prisoners on Johnson's Island, p. 335-391. $13.50, $25, $28.50, $35, $40-b, $47.50wh, $200-bmk-105.

109 **BARBOUR COUNTY, Alabama**
in the War. See: Mattie Thompson.

110 **BARCLAY, Alexander Tedford**
"The Liberty Hall Volunteers from Lexington to Manassas." Address at Washington & Lee University, Feb. 21, 1900. Lynchburg, Va., J.P. Bell, 1904. p. 123-136. In Historical Papers, #6, Washington & Lee University, Lexington, Va., See: Dr. Givens Brown Strickler, W.G. Bean $20-bmk

111 **BARDOLPH, Richard**
"Inconstant Rebels: Desertion of North Carolina Troops in the Civil War." In: NCHR, 1964, v.41, p. 163-189.

112 ..."Malice toward one: Lincoln in the North Carolina press (1861-1865)." In: Lincoln Herald, Winter, 1951, v.53, #4, p. 34-45. facsms.

113 **BARDSLEY, Virginia O., Edt.**
"Frederick Diary: Sept. 5-14, 1862." In:

Md.Hist.Mag., 1965, v.LX, p. 132-128. A Southern sympathizer.

114 **BARGER, W.D.**
"The field of Sharpsburg." In: CV, Oct. 1911, v.XIX, p. 484-485.

115 **BARKER, Daisy King**
"Echoes of the Old South." (Leaksville,N.C., Leaksville Pub., (1930's) 8vo, boards, 168pp. atg. $35. Collection of 19 stories about the war, 12 of which relate to N.C.

116 **BARKER, Eugene C.**
"The influence of slavery in the colonization of Texas." In: Miss. Val. Hist. Rev., June, 1924, XI, p. 3-36; So-west Hist. Quart., July, 1924, XXVIII, p. 1-33.

117 ..."The African Slave Trade in Texas." In: QTSYA, Oct., 1902, v.VI, #2, p. 145-158.

118 **BARKER, Jacob**
"Mr. Jacob Barker's advocacy of peace." New Orleans, La., March 21, 1864." New Orleans, La., 1864. 8vo, wraps, 20pp. $100-g. N.O. Banker who opposed Butler's rule.

119 **BARKER, Theodore Gaillard**
"Address of..., before the Washington Artillery Club on their Anniversary, 22nd February, 1876, at Hibernian Hall, Charleston, S.C." Charleston, S.C., Lucas & Richardson pr, 1876. cover title, 8vo, wraps, (3)-4-15pp.

120 **BARKER, Walter B.**
"Two Anecdotes of General Lee." In: SHSP, 1884, v.XII, p. 328-329.

121 **BARLOW, M.R., Mrs. (Manassas, Va.)**
"History of the Prince William Cavalry." In: CV, 1907, v.15, p. 353-355.

122 **BARNARD, Daniel Dewey**
"Truths for the Times. Hon. D.D. Barnard on the Presidential Question. The whole field surveyed. Why no friend of the Union can be a Republican. Reasons why no lover of the Union can vote for Lincoln. Doctrine of the Fathers restated. Relative position of whites & negroes in this Republic. Republicanism against Constitution. Republicanism against the Declaration of Independence. Republicanism against the Union." St. Louis, Mo., George Knapp & Co (1860). 8vo, wraps, cover title, dble-column, 15pp. Prophecy of disunion in event Lincoln's election. Monaghan-v.I, #19.

123 **BARNARD, Frederick Augustus Porter, Dr.**
"Autobiographical Sketch of Dr. F.A. P. Barnard." (Oxford, Miss., Publ. Miss. Hist. Soc., 1912, v.XII, p. 107-121, port. A letter largely about his war career.

124 ..."Report on the Organization of Military Schools made to the Trustees of the University of Mississippi, Nov., 1861." Jackson, 1861, Mor. 8vo, p. 36. Not in Crandall.

125 **BARNARD, Harry Vollie**
"Tattered Volunteers. The Twenty-Seventh Alabama Infantry Regiment, CSA." Northport, Ala., Hermitage Press(1965). 12mo, cl, dj, maps(incl. front), illus., vii, (2), 182pp. Roster, p. 88-158. $5, $14.50

126 **BARNER, Absalom B.**
"Selected letters (civil war) June 1862-Nov., 1863, by Absalom B. Barner. Edt. by Wm. F. Hawn." In: Reg. Ky. HS, July 1973, p. 296-306.

127 **BARNES, Eric Wollencott**
"The War Between the States." N.Y., Whittlesey House (1959). 8vo, cl, illus., 148pp. juvenile $6. Reprinted: 1961.

128 **BARNES, F.C., Col. and Capt. R.E. Frayser**
"Imprisoned Under Fire. Six hundred gallant Confederate Officers on Morris Island, S.C., in reach of Confederate Guns." In: SHSP, 1897, v.XXV, p. 365-369. $77.

129 **BARNES, Frank**
"Fort Sumter National Monument South Carolina, by Frank Barnes." Wash: Nat'l.

Park Ser. Hist. Handbook, #12, 1952, (revised 1962). 8vo, pict. color stiff wraps, facsm. maps, 1-dbl. pg., illus., ports, (4), 47pp.

130 **BARNES, John B.**
"Boonville (MO); the first land battle of the civil war." (Washington, D.C.) Infantry Journal, Dec., 1929, v.XXXV, p. 601-607.

131 **BARNES, Ruffin**
"The Confederate Letters of..., Wilson County (N.C.) Edt: Hugh Buckner Johnston, Jr." N.C. Hist. Rev., (1954), v.XXXI, p. 75-99. $10-bmk-86.

132 **BARNETT, James**
"Munfordville in the civil war." In: RKHS, Oct. 1971, v.69, #4, p. 339-361. Map of 1st battle Dec. 17, 1861 at Rowletts Sta., 2nd Sept. 14-17, 1862. One a Federal victory, the other by CSA.

133 **BARNETT, W.R., Jr., Mrs.**
"The Flags of the Confederacy." In: CV, Apr., 1928, v.XXXVI, p. 139-140.

134 **BARNETT, William W., Jr.**
"Shelby's expedition to Mexico." In: Field Art/Jour., May/June, 1949, v.39, p. 121-122.

135 **BARNEY, William L.**
"The Secession Impulse: Alabama & Mississippi in 1860." Princeton: University Press, 1974. 8vo, cl, dj, maps, tables, append., index bibliog., xv, 371pp. $17.50-y, $16, $14.50

136 ..."The Road to Revolution; the Social Basis of Secession in Alabama & Mississippi." N.Y., 1971. (c.1973) Columbia University thesis. Sm. 4to, 2Vols. (iii, 580 lfs.) Bibliography leaves 540-580.

137 ..."The Road to Secession, a new perspective on the Old South." With a foreword by James P. Shenton. N.Y., Praeger Print(1972). 12mo, cl, xv, 235pp. $8.

138 ..."Flawed Victory: a new perspective on the civil war." Lanham, Md., 1980. 8vo, cl, 225pp. $10-paper, $25.

139 **BARNWELL, John**
"Letters of Robert Woodward Barnwell to Robert Barnwell Rhett." In: SCHM, 1976, v.77, #4, p. 236-256.

140 ..."Love of Order: South Carolina's First Secession Crisis." Chapel Hill: North Carolina University Press, 1982. 8vo, cl, dj, x, 258pp. $25.

141 **BARNWELL, Robert W. to James H. Hammond.**
"In the Hands of the Compromisers", letters of Robert W. Barnwell to James H. Hammond." In: CWH, June, 1983, v.29, #2, p. 154-168, notes.

142 **BARNWELL, Robert Woodward, Sr.**
"The Lines & Nature of Lincoln's Greatness." Columbia, S.C., The State Co., 1931. 8vo, wraps, 137pp. anti-Lincoln worship. $5.

143 ..."Southern Rights & Co-operation, Doc. #2. Remarks of the Hon. R.W. Barnwell before the Convention of Southern Rights Association in Charleston, May, 185." Charleston, Walker & James, 1851. 8vo, wraps, (1)-9pp.

144 ..."Fort Sumter, 1860-1861." In: CV, Nov., 1927, v.XXXV, p. 414-418.

145 ..."General Lee's strategy from the Wilderness to Cold Harbor." In: CV, July, 1927, v.XXXV, p. 260-262.

146 ..."A view on the Crater battle." In: CV, May, 1925, v.XXXIV, p. 453-355. Conferred on precise share between Lee & Jackson at Chancellorsville, May 2, 1863, when Jax struck Federals right & rear.

147 ..."The Teamwork of Lee & Jackson." n.p., n.d. (Florence, S.C.?) 12mo, wraps, (8)pp. atg. copy $15.

148 ..."Bentonville, the last Battle of Johnston & Sherman." In: Proceedings of S.C. Hist. Ass'n., 1943, p. 42-54.

149 ..."Armistead's brigade at Seven Pines." In: CV, Sept., 1928, v.XXXVI, p. 337-338.

150 ..."The battle of Seven Pines." In: CV, Feb., 1928, v.XXXVI, p. 58-61.

151 **BARR, Alwyn**
"The Battle of Bayou Bourbeau, Nov. 3, 1863: Colonel Oran M. Roberts Reports." In: La. Hist., v.VI, p. 83-91.

152 ..."Confederate Artillery in Arkansas." (Little Rock) Ark. Hist. Qurt., XXII (1963) p. 238-272. plate.

153 ..."Texas Confederate Field Artillery." In: Texas Military History (Aug. 1961) p. 1-8.

154 ..."Confederate Artillery in Western Louisiana, 1862-1863." In: CWH, March, 1963, v.IX, #1, p. 74-85.

155 ..."Texan Losses in the Red River Campaign, 1864." In: TMH, Summer, 1963, v.3, #2, p. 103-110, tables.

156 ..."Confederate Artillery in the Trans-Mississippi." In: Mil. Affairs, 1963, v.XXVII, p. 77-83. $10.

157 ..."The Battle of Calcasieu Pass." In: SwHQ, July, 1962, v.LXVI, #1, p. 59-67.

158 ..."The Battle of Blair's Landing." In: LS, v.II, p. 204-212.

159 ..."Polignac's Texas Brigade." (Houston, Texas) Texas Gulf Coast Hist. Ass'n. Nov. 1964. Publication Series, v.VIII, #1. 8vo, wraps, ports, maps, (6), 72pp. See: Roy O. Hatton, #3, $8-bmk

160 ..."Sabine Pass, September, 1863." In: Tx. Mil. Hist., February, 1962, v.2, #1, p. 17-22, map.

161 ..."A Bibliography of Articles on the Military History of Texas." Civil War period: Tx. Mil. Hist., Spring, 1963, v.3, #1, p. 26-30, part IX; Winter, 1964, v.4, #4, p. 286-287,

162 ..."Texas Civil War Historiography." In: Tex. Libraries, 1964, v.XXVI, p. 160-169.

163 ..."Texas Coastal Defense, 1861-1865." In: SwHQ, July, 1961, v.XLV, #1, p. 1-31, illus., map.

164 ..."Records of the Confederate Military Commission in San Antonio (Texas)." In: SWHQ, July, 1969, p. 83-104, 243-274.

165 ..."The making of a secessionist: the antebellum career of Roger O. Mills." In: SWHQ, Oct., 1975, v.LXXXIX, #2, p. 129-144.

166 **BARR, Amelia Edith**
"All the days of my life: an autobiography the red leaves of a human heart." N.Y., Appleton's, 1913. 8vo, cl, pls., ports, vii, (5), 527pp. $10. Largely in Austin, Texas & thru war CSA.

167 ..."Texas Memoirs of Amelia E. Barr, Edt: Philip Graham." In: SwHQ, April, 1966, v.LXIX, #4, p. 473-498.

168 **BARRETT, Charles G., Mrs.**
"Official programs for March & April, 1913: Dept. of History-Texas Division: United Daughters Confederacy. Mrs. C. G. Barrett, historian, Texas Div. U.D.C. Huntsville, Texas." Narrow, 8vo, (5)pp. folder, tied ribbon, with port: "Prince John" (Bankhead) Magruder on cover.

169 ..."The battle field of Shiloh." In: CV, July, 1912, v.XX, p. 321-333.

170 **BARRETT, John G.**
"Edmund Dewitt Patterson Yankee Rebel." In: ARev., Jan. 1975, v.28, #1, p. 32-47.

171 **BARRETT, John Gilchrist**
"The Civil War in North Carolina." Chapel Hill: Univ. of N.C. Press (1963) 8vo, cl, dj, viii, (2), 484pp. Notes & Index, p. 395-484. map endsheets, maps illus. (old prints) $12.50-y, $10.

172 ..."North Carolina as a Civil War Battleground, 1861-1865." Raleigh, N.C., State Dept. of Archives & Hist., 1960. 8vo, wraps, viii, 99, (2)pp. fold, map, ports, illus., bibliog. p. 101.

173 ..."Sherman's March Through the Carolinas (Jan-Apr., 1865)." Chapel Hill: North Carolina University Press, 1956.

Cloth, 8vo, viii, (2), 325pp. maps, with bibliog. (p. 282-309) notes. $3.50, Reprinted: 1979:, $12-bmk, $7, $8.50.

174 ..."Sherman & Total War in the Carolinas." In: NCHR, July, 1960, v.XXXVII, p. 367-381.

175 ..."North Carolina as a Civil War Battlefield, 1861-1865." Raleigh, N.C. State Dept. of Archives & History, 1960. 8vo, decr. wraps, ports, illus., facsms, (8), 99, (1)pp. fldg. map at end. $7.50
...2nd edt., 1964, $10, $12.

176 **BARRETT, Thomas**
"The Great Hanging at Gainesville, Cooke County, Texas, October 1862." Suffolk, Va., Robt. Hardy , Pub., 1986. 8vo, wraps, 36pp. map, port.

177 **BARRETT, W.H.**
"Robert Edward Lee." Athens, Ga., 1925, 8vo, wraps, 14pp.

178 **BARRINGER, John W.**
"Railroads of the Civil War." (London) Jour. Confed. Hist. Soc. Summer, 1967, v.5, #2, p. 48-66, pls(2)

179 **BARRON, Samuel B.**
"Lone Star Defenders." Washington, DC, Zenger Pub. Co., 1983, 8vo, cl, illus., 393 pp., end-paper map, index, + new illus. & maps. $20.

179a **Bartholomew, Ed. Ellsworth**
"Cullen (Montgomery) Baker (1835-69) Premier Texas Gunfighter." Houston, TX: Frontier Press, 1954. 12mo, cl, (7)-139pp. ports, views. Note: PP.85-132 photolith of T. Orr's Life of C. Baker. Only known copy at LC. Baker was an E. Tx Bushwhacker in US.

180 **BARTLETT, Catherine Thom., Edt.**
"My Dear Brother" A Confederate Chronicle, compiled & edited by..." Richmond, Va., Dietz Press, 1952. 8vo, cl, dj, ports (incl. front) illus., facsms. xiii, 224pp. index, notes, bibliog. $7.50. $12, $14-bmk, $9, $25. Largely letters from Joseph Pembroke Thom from Wm. Alex. Thom, CSA officer in Richmond & other Maryland family.

181 **BARTLETT, John Russell**
"The Literature of the Rebellion. A Catalogue of books & pamphlets relating to the civil war in the U.S., & on subjects growing out of that event, together with works on American slavery & essays from reviews & magazines on the same subject." Boston: Draper & Halliday, 1866. 8vo, cl, iv, (5)-477pp. Reprint: $16.50. Westport, Conn., Negro Univ. Press (1970).

182 **BARTLETT, Napier**
"Military Record of Louisiana, including biographical & historical papers relating to the military organizations of the State. A soldier's story of the late war, muster rolls, lists of casualties in the various regiments (so far as now known), cemeteries where buried, company journals, personal narratives of prominent actors, etc." New Orleans, La., L. Graham & co., 1875, 8vo, cl, (1-mounted port) 68, (3-mounted ports)54, (1-mounted port)62, iii, x, (2)pp. $22.50, $65, $75, $125, $175. $225-y, 259pp.
...Baton Rouge: Louisiana State University Press(1964). 8vo, cl, dj, xv, 68, (2), 54, 62, iii-s, (5)-259--. OP $7.50.
..."Confed. Dead, CSA, Buried in Va.(93)-7p; "Battles in Va." (8)-19; "Biog. & Hist. papers relating to La. During & since the war. Organizations of La. Brigades in Va." 20-23pp; "La Brigades in Va. & their last commander. Journal of 10th La." (24)-56pp. "The 6th La. Reg." (57)-63; "Muster Roll Co. G., 1st La. Reg. from Aug.-Oct., 1861: (63)-64; "Roll of Capt. E.D. Willett, Co. G, 1st Reg. La. Vols., Month of Feb., 1864. (64)-"Muster Roll Donaldsonville Artly. (65)-66; "Crescent Rifles-Co. A. (Co. B., Dreux's La. Bat." (66)-68pp.; "Complete roll Fenner's La. Bat. from

time of org. May 16, 1862 under surrender of Gen. Taylor, at Meridian, Miss., May 10, 1865." (2)p; "La. Troops in the West. Brig. of the Army of Tenn." 10pp; "Orleans Guard & Bat. Org. & Muster Roll." (10)-16pp; "Journal of the Orleans Guard." (17)-20; "13th La. Reg., Muster Roll of Officers & Men." (21)-26; "Orleans Guard Battery." (27)-30; "Movement of Orleans Lt. Horse & 1st Commander." (31)-34; "11th La." (35)-36; "Memorable Deaths-Capts. Fortin & Vienne," (36)-47; "Muster Roll Capt. A. Picolet, Co. D, 30th La. Reg." (47)-50; "3rd La. Brig." (50)-51; "Le Gardeur's Bat." (52); "Bridge's Battery" (53)-54; "Trans-Miss., 1st Paper." 14pp.; "Muster Roll co. A Confed. Guards Response." 16; "Trans-Miss., 2nd paper," (17)-28; 3rd Paper, (28)-32; 4th Paper, (33)-34; "Sub-division of N. La." (34)-6; "Record of 18th La. Reg." (37)-44; "Capture of Federal Ironclad Gunboat Indianola." (45)-53; "La. Batteries in Army of Western La. (54)-60; "28th La." (61)-62; "Washington Arty. record of newly elected field, staff & Co. officers." (iii)-x, (2)p; "Last Chap. placed 1st Reorganization Washington Arty, since War." (2)p.

183 ..."A Soldier's Story of the War; including the marches & battles of the Washington Artillery, & of other Louisiana Troops." New Orleans: Clark & Hofeline, print, 1874. Tall 8vo, cl, 252, (1)Append: Camp Stories & Tales of the Crescent City, before & since the war.", 13, (35), (6)-ads. $125. Note: many editions have the "Soldier's Story", published anon., bound in with the second edition, titled "Military Record." Various editions show a wide variation of pagination: Howes: p. 60, 30, 40, (12), 259 & 9-plates; others as 262pp. 311pp. & 235pp.

184 ..."Clarimonde: a tale of New Orleans life & of the present war. By a Member of the N.O. Washington Artillery." Richmond: M.A. Malsby, 1863. 12mo, cl, (or, wraps), 79pp. $75. Crandall-3070 & Wright-229.

185 ..."Stories of the Crescent City." New Orleans: Steel & Co, 1869. 8vo, wraps, cover title, 100pp. dble. colm.

186 ..."Extracts from a Soldier's Story of the War, 1861-1865." New Orleans: Jackson Barracks, 1937. 8vo, wraps, 63pp.

187 ..."The Defence of Fort Gregg." In: SHSP, 1877, v.III, p. 82-86.

188 **BARTLETT, Ruhl J.**
"New Light on Confederate prisons." In: Am. Mil. Inst. Jour., 1940, v.IV, p. 256-258.

189 **BARTMAN, Roger J., The Rev., OFM**
"Joseph Holt & Kentucky in the Civil War." In: FCHQ, April, 1966, v.40, #2, p. 105-122.

190 **BARTON, J.M., Brig.-Gen.**
"Letter of General Barton, on operations against Newbern in 1864." In: SHSP, 1881, v.IX, p. 7-11.

191 **BARTON, Lon Carter**
"Reign of terror in Graves County, Ky." In: RKHS, Apr. 1948 (#155), v.46, p. 434-495. Largely Confederate sympathizers & Breckinridge Democrats.

192 **BARTON, Michael**
"Goodmen: the character of Civil War soldiers." University Park: Pennsylvania State Univ. Press, 1981. 8vo, cl, dj, tables, notes, append., sources, index, viii, 135pp. $13. Diff. in character between Northern & Southern soldiers. Diaries & letters of 400 men. "Southerners expressed values more than Northern counterparts.

193 **BARTON, Michael, Edt.**
"The End of Oden's War: a Confederate Captain's Diary, Edt: Michael Barton." In: AHQ, 1981, v.43, #2, p. 73-98.

194 **BARTON, O.S.**
"Three Years with Quantrill." See: John McCorkle.

195 **BARTON, Randolph**
"Recollections 1861-1865." (Baltimore, Md., Thomas & Evans) 1913. Preface notes: (Revised 1913) Dated April 24, 1897. 8vo, cl, ports(incl. front84, (1), lf, 9pp-"Memorial services held in honor of Major Randolph Barton." with two columns: Baltimore Sun & American editorials, dated Mar. 16, 1921. Priv. print, family, friend $75.

196 ..."Stonewall Jackson, by Capt. Randolph Barton, Adj.-Gen. of Stonewall Brigade." In: SHSP, 1910, v.XXXVII, p. 268-287. Reviews G.T.R. Henderson's "Stonewall"

197 ..."Wounding of Stonewall Jackson." In: SHSP, 1902, v.XXX, p. 116-117.
..."Stonewall Brigade at Louisville. An address to the survivors at the reunion, June, 1900." In: CV, 1900, v.8, p. 481-484. ports, Barton was Asst. Adj-Gen. of the brigade.

198 **BARTOW COUNTY**
formerly Cass Georgia, in the Civil War. See: Lucy Josephine Cunyus.

199 **BARTOW, Francis S., Col.**
"Proceedings of the Congress on the Announcement of the death of Col. Bartow of the Army of the Confederate States & late a delegate from Georgia." Richmond: Enquirer, 1861. Crand-77. $350-gdsp.

200 **BARUCH, Simon, Dr.**
"Confederate Surgeon." In: Jacob Marcus Rader's "Memoirs of Amer. Jews." Phila: Jewish Pub. Soc. of Amer., 3vols, 1955. v.3, p. 269-281. From "Reminiscences" by the author, 1915. His services as surgeon in S.C. July/Sept., 1863 & death of Marcus Baum.

201 ..."Reminiscences of a Confederate Surgeon." (New York, 1915) Priv. Print. 4to, stiff wraps, (12)pp.-3columns. pl & port. from "Long Branch Record Sept. 24, 1915. "Hist. Soc., Dr. Baruch Guests-200 hear host's address, etc."

202 ..."Robert Edward Lee-the man & the soldier address at the university of the birthday of the Southern Commander, before the Confederate veteran camp of N.Y. & its guests, at Hotel Astor, Jan. 19, 1918." N.Y., 1918. portrait on cover. 8vo, wraps, caption title, illus., port, 14pp.

203 ..."Bernard Baruch's father recounts his experiences as a Confederate surgeon." In: CWTI, Oct., 1965, v.IV, #6, p. 40-47, illus., port.

204 **BARWELL, Stephen B.**
"The Confederate Episcopacy, Slavery & Stephen Elliott." In: Michigan Academician, 1969, v.I, iii & iv, 57-67.

205 **BARZIZA, Decimus et Ultimus**
"The adventures of a prisoner of war, & life & scenes in Federal prisons: Johnson Island, Fort Delaware & Point Lookout, by an escaped prisoner of Hood's Texas Brigade." Houston, Texas: Richardson & Owen, 1865. 16mo, wraps, 112pp.(2-known copies)

206 ...Austin: University of Texas Press(1964) "Decimus et Ultimus Barziza The adventures of a prisoner of war 1863-1864." Edt: R. Henderson Shuffler. (see also under Shuffler) 8vo, cl, dj, port(front) illus., xiv, 140pp. $4.50, $7.50

207 **BASHINSKY, L.M., Mrs.**
"The proposed memorial to General Robert Edward Lee in the Washington Cathedral." In: VMHB, July 1949, v.57, p. 301-306.

208 **BASINGER, William S., Major**
"Crutchfield's Artillery Brigade. Report of its operations, April 3-6, 1865, when it was captured with Lee's Division at Sayler's Creek." In: SHSP, 1897, v.XXV, p. 38-44. With list of casualties in the 18th Ga. Batt., G.W.C. Lee's Div., Ewell's Corps, in Battle of Hillman's Farm, or Sayler's Creek, Va., April 6, 1865. See also: "Sayler's Creek, Battle of."

209 **BASKERVILLE, William Malone**
"Southern Writers: biographical & critical studies." Nashville, Tenn: Pub. M.E. Church South, 1902-1903. Vol. 1-1897. 12mo, 2vols. (1)-vii, 404pp. $4. Suppl. vol. by author's pupils, pub. 1903, vol. II, Dallas, Texas: M.E. Church South, 1903. sm. 8vo, cl, ports, v.392pp. First issued in monthly parts, 1896, '97, no more published.

210 **BASOCO, Richard M.**
"The Cruise of 'Savez' Read." In: CWTI, Dec., 1963, v.II, #8, p. 10-15, illus., map, port. One ship & 20 men, burned 16 ships "bonded" 6 others."

211 ..."A sequel: "Savez" Read's adventures after his capture at Portland Harbor." In: CWTI, FEb. 1964, v.II, #10, p. 32-33.

212 **BASS, James Horace**
"The Attack upon the Confederate Administration in Georgia in the Spring of 1864." In: Ga. Hist. Quart., 1934, v.XVIII, p. 228-247. Against CSA's policies: impressment, conscription, suspension writ habeas corpus. $10-bmk-

213 ..."Civil War Finance in Georgia." In: Ga. H.Q., Sept.-Dec., 1942, v.XXVI, #3 & 4, p. 213-224. $10-

214 ..."The Georgia Gubernatorial Elections of 1861 & 1863." In: Ga. H.Q., Sept., 1933, v.XVII, #3, p. 167-189.

215 **BASSETT, George W.**
"A northern plea for the right of secession." Ottawa, (ill) Office of the Free Trader, 1861, 22x13cm, cover title, 24pp.

216 **BASSETT, John Spencer**
"Running the Blockade from Confederate Ports." Historical Papers Trinity College Historical Society, SeriesII, p. 62-68. Durham, N.C., 1898, 8vo. $20.
...Reprint, wraps, 6pp. $12-bmk,

217 ...Do: "Slavery & Servitude in the Colony of North Carolina." Johns Hopkins Studies in History & Political Science, 14th Series, IV-V, 8vo, p. 86. Baltimore-Johns Hopkins Press, 1896.
...Do: Reprint, 1899, Ser. XVII-#7-8, p. 111. $22-y, $12.50

218 ..."The Southern Plantation Overseer as revealed in his letters." Taken from the corresp. of John Knox Polk. Smith College 50th Anniversary publication.(vol. V) Northampton, Mass: Print for Smith College, 1925. p. vii, 280. facsms. $30-bmk, $17.50.

219 ..."Slavery in the State of North Carolina." Baltimore: Johns Hopkins pr., 1899. J.H. Univ. Studies in Hist. & Pol. Science, Ser. XVII, #7-8. Herb. B. Adams, Edt. 8vo, wraps, 111, (11p. ads)pp. $30, $15.

220 ..."How the Southerners supported the War for Seccession." In: Hist. Outlook, Oct. 1918, v.IX, p. 373-375. Both financial & moral support.
..."Secret Service in the Confederate States of America." In: NCBooklet, 1903, v.II, #11.

221 **BASSHAM, Ben L.**
"Conrad Chapman's Charleston & its defenses." In: CWTI, April 1977, v.16, #1, p. 34-41, facsms, illus., ports.

222 **BASSO, Hamilton**
"Beauregard The Great Creole." N.Y., Charles Scribner's Sons, 1933. 8vo, cl, xiv, 333pp. ports, facsms, illus. political cartoons $7.50, $10, $15, $20, $30-bmk.

223 **"BATCHELOR-TURNER LETTERS 1861-1864",**
written by Two of Terry's Texas Rangers Annotated by H(elen) J.H. Rugeley." (Austin, Texas. The Steck Co, 1961). 8vo, stiff wraps, (6)pp. ports, facsms, xi, 99pp., Index. $10.

224 **BATE, R. Alexander**
"Robert E. Lee. A Play." Boston: The Stratford Co., 1927. 12mo, cl-bds., illus., 83pp. $3.50, $4.50

225 **BATE, William Brimage**
"The dedication of the Chickamauga &

Chattanooga National Park. Address by Gen. Wm. B. Bate, one of the speakers appointed by the Secretary of War for the above occasion. Delivered on Sept. 20, 1895." Nashville, Brandon Print, 1895. 8vo, wraps, 38pp.

226 **BATE, William Brimage, Maj-Gen.**
"Address delivered by..., on the occasion of dedicating the "Battle-ground academy", on the field of Franklin. Franklin, Tenn., Saturday, Oct. 5, 1889." (Franklin?1889) 8vo, wraps, 15pp.

227 ..."Oration of..., U.S. Senator, on occasion the unveiling of the Confederate monument at Knoxville, Tenn., May 19, 1892. With history Ladies Memorial Association & other orations & ceremonies incident to erection of the monument." Knoxville, Tenn., S.B. Newman, 1892. 8vo, wraps.

228 ..."Memorial address by..., of Tenn., upon the life & character of Hon. Edward C. Walthall (late senator from the state of Miss.) delivered in the senate of the US, May 26, 2898." Washington, DC, GPO, 1898. 8vo, wraps, caption title, 8pp. See: under Walthall (Edward Cary) Brig.-Gen. CSA, & senator from Mississippi.

229 ..."Oration delivered by... on occasion of the Confederate commenoration services, at Elmwood cemetery, Memphis, Tenn., on Sat. May 7, 1870." Nashville: Union & American off., 1870. 8vo, wraps, 28pp. $5, $7.50.
...Nashville, Tenn., Brandon Pr., 1904 8vo, wraps, 28pp. Dornbusch-2594.

230 **BATEMAN, John M.**
"A Sketch of the History of the Governor's Guards of Columbia, S.C., 1843-1898." Columbia, S.C., 1910, Turnbull, V-67.

BATES, Allan
231 "The Letters of Quntus Curtius Snodgrass." In: "American Literature, Mar., 1964, v.XXXVI, p. 31-37.

232 **BATES, E.W., Mrs.**
"Heroes of the Southland." Toledo, Oh., Wooson Spice Co., n.d., 12mo, wraps, 22pp., ports.

233 **BATES, Finis Langdon**
"The Escape & Suicide of John Wilkes Booth or the First True Account of Lincoln's Assassination containing a complete confession by Booth many years after the crime Giving in Full Detail the Plans, Plot & Intrigue of the Conspirators, & the Treachery of Andrew Johnson, then Vice-President of the U.S. written for the Correction of History." Memphis, Tenn., Pilcher Print, 1907. 12mo, decr. cl, port. illus., 309pp. $17.50, $100-bmk-116, $12.50, $100-ginz, $17.50. Also may be found in wrappers. Monaghan-1519 lists following: Memphis: Historical Publishing Co., with tab on top-Bates Pub. Co. Boston: Geo. M.Smith Co. (c.1907) Napierville, Ill.: J.L. Nichols & Co. One of the best selling Lincoln books & hawked along with alleged corpse of Booth. 75,000 copies were sold."
...Detroit, Mich., (c.1900) $5, $12.50
...n.p., n.d., wraps. $7.50. Naperville, Atlanta, Memphis: J.J. Nichols, n.d., (c.1903) $80-bmk-116. 12mo, cl, 309pp. illus., cheap paper. $15.

234 **BATES, Robert L.**
"Battle of Smithfield (Va.) 1864." In: Jefferson Co.(Va.)HSM., 1952, v.18, p. 8-14. map.

235 **BATES, William M.**
"The last stand for the Union in Georgia (debate in Jan., 1861). In: Ga. Rev., winter 1953, v.6, p. 455-467.

236 ..."McGuffeys of the Confederacy." In: Ga. Rev., Fall 1954, v.VIII, #3, p. 290-300.

237 **BATHE, Greville**
"Ship of destiny; a record of the US Steam Frigate Merrimac, 1855-1862: with an appendix on the development of the United

238 **BATTAILE, J.E.**
"Unveiling of Monument to Defenders of Vicksburg & Poem to the occasion, by J.E. Battaile." In: SHSP, 1893, v.XXI, p. 201-202.

239 **BATTERY Wagner, Life in:**
In: LWL, Mar. 1867, v.II, #5, p. 351-355.

240 **BATTEY, George Magruder**
"A history of Rome & Floyd County, state of Georgia, United States of America, including numerous incidents of more than local interest, 1540-1922." Atlanta, Ga., Webb & Vary Co., 1922. Imp. 8vo, cl, front, illus. (incl. maps, ports, facsms, col. plates. Lim. Edt. $75. Around one third re civil war.

241 **BATTEY, George Magruder, Jr.**
"A history of Rome & Floyd county, state of Georgia, United States of America, including numerous incidents of more than local interest, 1540-1922. 8vo, cl, illus., ports, maps, facsms, color plates, v.1 (all pub.) 640pp. $15, $45, CSA-eight chps., 150pp.

242 **BATTINE, Cecil William**
"The Crisis of the Confederacy; a History of Gettysburg & the Wilderness." N.Y.-Lond: Longmans, Green Co., 1905. 8vo, cl, col. front., 6-fldg. maps, xv, (1), 424pp. $10, $15, $17.50, $20, $32.50, $35, $45,-mcm, $100-bmk-105.

243 **BATTLE ABBEY**
"The Location of the Battle Abbey Decided" (from "News Leader", Jan. 1, 1909). In: SHSP, 1908, v.XXXVI, p. 156-160.

244 **BATTLE FIELDS OF THE SOUTH.**
From Bull Run to Fredericksburg: with sketches of Confederate commanders, & gossip of the Camps. By an English Combatant, Lieutenant of Artillery on the field staff. London: Smith, Elder & co., 1863. $75, $250-jk-135, $100, $40, $125. 12mo, cl, xliii, 339, 399pp. 2 maps, $15, $27.50(also, 2vols. in one) $20. $180-nc-133, $200-nc-133, $75.
...N.Y., John Bradburn, 1864. $32.50, $75, $12.50, $20, $150-bmk, $325-mem, $17-'73avc't. Title on backstrip. "Southern History of the War. Battle Fields of the South." written by T.E.C.

245 **BATTLE OF BATON ROUGE,**
August 5th, 1862.Sketched by Pt. James J. Kelly. Co. F., 6th Mich. Regiment. (n.p., 1862?) Lithograph, black & white, 14x18" incl. margins. Birdsview: gunboats in foreground, town in middle area, battle beyond. Gdsp. ('61) See: Edward Cunningham. $100.

246 **BATTLE OF BIG BETHEL.**
(Camp Benning, Ga., Infantry school press, 1921. 8vo, wraps, 38pp., fldg. plan. Official reports of participants of battle. Dept. of Research, Infantry school, Camp Benning, Ga., Course in historical research 1920-1921, Military history pamphlet, #3.

247 **BATTLE OF BULL'S RUN, The.**
A Political Caricature. Lithograph from a pen sketch 22x14". Illustrating Beauregard's Hdq., Generals McDowell & Tyler, Fire Zouzves Blenker's Brigade, Ladies as Sputatiers & ten other scenes. n.p., n.d. Weitenkampf describes it as Confederate or Copperhead cartoon. $35.

248 **BATTLE OF CEDAR CREEK.**
In: SHSP. See: Samuel D. Buck, G.B. Gerald, Clarence R. Hatton, C.S.M. (Surgeon CSA.) J.S. McNeily, Marcellus N. Moorman.

249 **BATTLE OF CEDAR RUN,**
described by an Old "F" Company Man, who took part therein. In: SHSP, 1899, v.XXVII, p. 144-151.

250 **BATTLE OF CHANCELLORSVILLE**
In: SHSP. See: William Allan, George W. Beale, Theodore A. Dodge, R.T. Hubard, Thomas J. Jackson, Fitzhugh Lee, R.E. Lee, Albert Reynolds, Robert E. Rodes, C.C. Sanders. J.E.B. Stuart, Thomas Talcott, William Terry.

251 **BATTLE OF CHANCELLORSVILLE,**
Special edition by the editors of: CWTI. August 1971, v.10, #5, 50pp.

252 **BATTLE OF CHICKAHOMINY:**
"What I saw of the battle of Chickahominy." In: South. M., Jan. 1972, v.X, p. 1-15. $15. See also under Battles of Gaines' Mill, Cold Harbor & 'Seven Days battle before Rich.'" See: Ed. P. Alexander, Clifford Dowdey, Daniel H. Hill, Gan. Evander McI. Law, James Longstreet, Jno. B. Magruder, Ed. Al Pollard, Harold B. Simpson.

253 **BATTLE OF CHICKAMAUGA**
SHSP. See: Archer Anderson, Henry Lewis Benning, Henry Van Ness Boynton, et al, Braxton Bragg, John Cabell Breckinridge, Simon Bolivar Buckner, W.W. Carnes, T.T. Clay, James Dinkins, James N. Goggin, Thomas Carmichael Hindman, Benjamin Grubb Humphreys, James T. Hunter, Bushrod Rust Johnson, Joseph Brevard Kershaw, James Longstreet, William T. Martin, James D. Nance, Joseph Palmer, Wm. M. Polk, William Preston, Jerome B. Robertson, Alex P. Stewart.

254 **BATTLE OF CHICKAMAUGA, The**
An eye-witness' thrilling story of the great conflict, as seen from the Federal side. From: New Orleans "Picayune", Nov. 9, 1902. In: SHSP, v.XXX, p. 178-188.

255 **BATTLE OF CRATER**
"The Crater Legion. In loving remembrance of comrades of Mahone's brigade, Anderson division, A.P. Hill's Corps, A.N.V. who lost their lives in the Battle of Crater, July 30, 1864." Broadside. Swem-1207.

256 ..."Battle of Crater, July 30, 1864. Roster of Members of the 12th Virginia Infantry, Mahone's Brigade, who were engaged." In: SHSP, 1903, v.XXXI, p. 271-274.
...See: Geo. Smith Bernard "Battle of Crater" & "War Talks C. Vets.", James C. Coit, Wm. H. Etheredge, John C. Featherstone, Henry G. Flanner, Fitz William McMaster, "Battle of Crater & Roster of 12th Va.", Mahone's Old Brigade at Crater, Wm. H. Stewart.

257 **BATTLE OF DEAD ANGLE**
on the Kennesaw Line, near Marietta, Georgia (June 17, 1864). In: SB, v.III, (1884-1885, p. 71-74. signed: M.

258 **BATTLE OF DREWRY'S BLUFF.**
In: SHSPs. See: Wm. Izard Clopton, Pierre G.T. Beauregard, Augustus H. Drewry, "Drewry's Bluff, 1864." Johnson Hagood, Robert F. Hoke, Charles Theo Loehr, John W. Sumter.

259 **BATTLE OF FORT GREGG, Louisiana, The**
Survivors tell the story of the fight. In: SHSP, 1900, v.XXVIII, p. 265-267.

260 **BATTLE OF FORT SUMTER**
& first victory of the Southern troops, April 13, 1861. Full accounts of the bombardment, with sketches of the scenes, incidents, etc. Compiled chiefly from the detailed reports of the Charleston press. Published by request. Charleston: Evans & Cogswell, 1861. 8vo, wraps, 32pp. $450-jk-135, $275-gosp, $150-ebert. ($15, $20, $25, $37.50, $65)
...Do: with 35pp. & map Streeter sale. $75.
...Charleston, S.C., Shaftsburg Press, 1961. 8vo, wraps, dble. map, 35pp. $6.50.

261 **BATTLE OF FORT SUMTER:**
its mystery & miracle--God's Mastery &

mercy. So. Presbyterian Review, Oct., 1861, v.XIV, #3, p. 365-400.

262 **BATTLE OF FORT SUMTER & First Victory, The**
of the Southern troops, April 13, 1861. Full accounts of the bombardment, with sketches of the scenes, incidents, etc. Compiled chiefly from the detailed reports of the Charleston press. Suffolk, Va., Roct. Hardy Pub., 1986, 8vo, wraps, 36pp. facsm.

263 **BATTLE OF FRANKLIN (TENN.)**
"Williamson County, Franklin, Tennessee. Civil War Centennial 1864-1964. November 28-29-30, 1964. Official guide book & program, price, $.50." (cover title) 4to, decr. color wraps, illus., maps, incl. fldg. map, 16pp.

264 **BATTLE OF FRANKLIN.**
(Sims Crownover) Franklin, Tenn., n.d. 8vo, wraps, fldg. maps & plates. $10. From: TennHQ, Dec. 1955, v.XIV, p. 291-322.

265 **BATTLE OF FREDERICKSBURG, The**
a Special Edition of Civil War Times Illustrated. Edts: Edward J. Stackpole & Wilbur S. Nye. In: CWTI, Dec. 1965, v.4, #8, p. 1-50. illus., maps, ports.

266 **BATTLE OF GALVESTON**
recounted in an Extra to "The Era." Folio Broadside, 4-columns. New Orleans, 4 p.m., 25 February, 1863. The fight at Galveston, statement of crew, on "Harriet Lane", course of battle & capture of ship. Hundreds of prisoners sent to Houston to be enrolled by the "fat, tall & savage" CS officer, Lt. Todd (brother-in-law Lincoln) $150.

267 **BATTLE OF GETTYSBURG & Campaign**
in Pa., extracts from the diary of an English officer present with Confederate army. In: Blackwoods, Sept., 1863, v.94, p. 365-394.

268 **BATTLE OF HONEY HILL, S.C.**
Charles C. Jones-7th Annual Survivors... William A. Courtenay, John J. Abercrombie, Chas. C. Jones. SHSP, v.13, p. 355-367.

269 **BATTLE OF LEXINGTON**
Fought in & about the city of Lexington, Missouri, Sept. 18-20, 1861. Under command of Col. James A. Mulligan, USA- Gen. Sterling Price, M.S.G. The Official Records of both parties to the conflict, to which is added memoirs of participants with maps, & cuts. (Lexington, Mo.) Missouri Historical Society, May, 1903. Intelligencer Print. $.25. 12mo, stiff wraps, illus., ports, fldg. map, 68pp.

270 **BATTLE OF MANSFIELD,**
Mansfield, Louisiana. Fought April 8, 1864. Gen. Richard Taylor, Commander Confederate Forces & Gen. N. P. Banks, Commander Federal forces. 8vo, wraps, illus., map, 20pp. 1949. (Picture on covers.) $20-bmk.

271 **BATTLE OF NEW MARKET**
& the Cadets of V.M.I., May 15, 1864. See: D.H. Bruce, Holmes Conrad, Howard Morton, Richmond Times-Dispatch.

272 **BATTLE OF OLUSTEE**
Centennial Observance, Feb. 1864-1964. (Jacksonville, Fla., H & W.B. Drew) 4to, decr. colored wraps, 20pp. ads in text. See: Jas. A. Harley & J.G. Rice.

273 **BATTLE OF PEA RIDGE 1862.**
Published in commemoration of the 100th anniversary of the Battle of Pea Ridge & dedication of the Pea Ridge National Military Park to be held May 31, 1963. Rogers, Ark., Pea Ridge Nat'l. Mil. Centennial Committee, n.d.(1963). 4to, pict. wraps, ports, illus., facsms. ads through text, 72pp. See: Benton County "Pioneer". $2.50

274 ...Do: n.p., n.d. (c.1967) same format, not all illus. as above, no ads, sold at park,

44pp. $.50.

...Rogers, Ark., Shofner's Print, n.d. 8vo, wraps, illus, 44pp. Article by Nat'l Park Historian John W. Bond & earlier articles from Okla. Hist. Society Quarterly + a 7pp. history of the Butterfield Overland Mail.

275 **BATTLE OF PRAIRIE GROVE, ARKANSAS,**
Dec. 7, 1862. Published by the Washington County Historical Society, Fayetteville, Ark., as a Souvenier of the visit to battlefields by the Civil War Round Table of Chicago on April 21, 1967. Edt: W.J. Lemke. 4to, wraps, facsms, illus., ports, maps, (3), 16pp.(18)p. unnumbered plates $5.

276 ..."Special issue in Commenration of the 100th Anniversary of the Battle of Prairie Grove, Dec. 7, 1862. W.J. Lemke, Edt.." In: Wash. Co. Hist. Soc., "Flashback", Dec., 1962. v.XII, #4, facsms, illus., ports, incl. group, 48pp.

277 ..."The Battle of Prairie Grove, Dec. 7, 1862." In: Wash. Co. Hist. Soc., "Flashback", Dec. 7, 1952. Published on the 90th Anniversary of the Battle. W.J. Lemke, Edt., Fayetteville, Arkansas." v.II, #6, 2-maps, 45pp.

278 **BATTLE OF SAILOR'S (SAYLER'S CREEK),**
part taken in it by the Savannah guard." In: SHSP, 1896, v.XXIV, p. 250-254.

279 **BATTLE OF WILSON'S CREEK: CSA & UNION ACCTS.**
Adamson, Hans C. - "Rebellion in Missouri." Chilton Co., Phila., 1961.
...Castel, Albert - "Gen. Sterling Price & C.W." Baton Rouge, La., Univ. Press, 1968.
...Crawford, Saml. J. - "Kansas in the Sixties." Chi: A.C. McClurg, 1911.
...Edwards, Jno. N. - "Shelby & His Men." Kansas City, Mo., 1897.
...Holcombe, R.I. & Adams - "Acct. of Battle." Springfield, Mo., Pub. Library reprint.
...McElroy, Jno. - "Struggle for Missouri." Wash., D.C., National Tribune, 1909/1913.
...Monaghan, Jay Jas. - "Civil War Western Border, Boston, Mass., 1955.
...Schofield, Jno. M. - "Forty-six Years in Army." NY, Century Co., 1897.
...Snead, Thos. L. - "Fight for Missouri." NY, Scribners, 1886.
...Ware, Eugene F. - "Lyon Campaign in Mo." Topeka, Kan., Crane Print, 1907.
...Woodruff, W.E. - "With Light Guns in '61." Little Rock, Ark., 1903.

280 ...War of Rebellion Records, Official Records: Ser.I, v.III, p. 53-130; Ser.I, v.LIII, 1898. Battle & Leaders of the Civil War. NY, Barnes/Yoseloff, 1956. v.I, p. 263-306, accts: Snead, Fremont, Wherry, Pearch & Sigel.

281 **BATTLE, Cullen A., Gen.**
"Extract from a speech, at Tuscumbia." In: OLOD, Feb., 1875, v.1, #6, p. 559-561.
..."Cullen Andrews Battle, Patriot, Orator, Soldier & Christian." n.p., n.d., (1905?). 8vo, wraps, 16pp. $75-bmk.

282 ..."Report of Colonel C. A. Battle, of 3rd Alabama, Hdq. July 9, 1863." In: SHSP, 1885, v.XIII, p. 177-178.

283 ..."Edwin La Fayette Hobson, glowing tribute from an Old Commander." In: SHSP, 1901, v.XXIX, p. 281-284.

284 **BATTLE, J.H., W.H. Perrin & G.C. Kniffin**
"Kentucky, a History of the State, origin & development of the Virginia Colony, etc." Louisville, Ky., F.A. Battey Pub., 1885. 4to, 3/4Mor., ports, pls., maps, 1058pp. Chaps: XV-XIX, p. 349-487. "First phase of war, " Mil. Opr. in Ky., Tenn., "Ky. troops in Tenn., Ga. campn." "Morgan's Cavalry & Ky. Confederate Brigade." 450-473.

285 **BATTLE, Jesse Sumner, CSA**
"Civil War Letters of Jesse Sumner Battle, CSA & James Norman Adams, CSA. Edited : John D. Battle, Jr., Cleveland Heights, Ohio. The Clinic Center, 1979. 8vo, wraps, illus., map, 86pp. $4.50

286 **BATTLE, Kemp Plummer**
"The Legislation of the (North Carolina) Convention of 1861." In: Jas. Sprunt Hist. Monograph, #1, p. 98-144. Chapel Hill, NC, 1900. University of N.C. Publications.

287 ..."Col. Isaac Erwin Avery." In: NC Univ. Mag., 1890, #2, wraps, 4pp. $10-bmk-124.

288 ..."Commodore Maury & Gen. Pettigrew." In: NC Univ. Mag., May, 1893, wrap, 8pp. $10.

289 ..."Memoirs of an old-time Tar-hell, Edt: by his son William James Battle." Chapel Hill: Univ. of NC Press, 1945. 8vo, cl, dj, ports, illus., xii, 296pp. $17.50. 4 chaps. relates to his non-combatant experiences in war. $25-bmk
...2nd print. $20.

290 ..."Legislation of the Convention of 1861." Part of the "Personnel of the Convention of 1861", see: John Gilchrist McCormick's title.

291 ..."The Secession Convention of 1861." Raleigh, N.C., N.C. Daughters of the Revolution, Apr., 1916. v.XV, #4. The North Carolina Booklet. 8vo, wraps, p. 177-202. $20-bmk, $12-bmk-84, $2.50

292 ..."Sketch of Col. Isaac Erwin Avery." In: N.C. Univ. Mag., 1890/1891, X, p. 89-93.

293 ..."Sketch of Senator Z.B. Vance." In: N.C. Univ. Mag., 1886/1887, VI, p. 257-262. Port. $10-bmk

294 ..."A Secret Session Debate of the North Carolina Secession Convention of 1862. (Delegate to the convention). In: SHSP, 1895, v.XXIII, p. 314-318.

295 **BATTLE, Laura Elizabeth Lee, Mrs.**
"Forget-Me-Nots of the Civil War; a Romance, containing reminiscences & original letters of two Confederate soldiers." St. Louis: A.R. Fleming Print(1909) 12mo, cl, front(port), 10pls, 355pp. Personal narrative of the CSA. $100-bmk.

296 **BATTLE, Richard H.**
"Z(ebulon) B. Vance (1830-1894)." In: N.C. Hist. Com. Pub., I, 1907, p. 375-415.

297 **BATTLE, Richard Henry**
"Chapel Hill at the close of the Civil War." In: N.C. Univ. Mag., 1900-1901, ns, v.XVIII, p. 272-275.

298 **"BATTLEFIELD Markers Association,**
Western Division." Charlottesville, Va., 1929. 8vo, wraps, 31pp. ($10-bmk) Text of markers.

299 **BATTLEFIELD OF PEA RIDGE**
Arkansas. The Glamorous Struggle Behind the Battle of Pea Ridge. 12mo, wraps, cover title, map, 16pp. (Garfield, Ark., Battlefield Museum)

300 **BATTLEFIELD OF PEA RIDGE, ARK.,**
Battlefield Folklore, Battlegrams & Generals. Garfield, Ark., n.d. 8vo, wraps, cover title, 65pp.

301 ...Fayetteville, Ark., Washington County Historical Society, 1958. 12mo, wraps, (2), 18pp. First published by Castle Battlefield Museum, Rt. 1, Garfield, Ark.

302 **BATTLEFIELD OF SHILOH, The**
n.p., n.d., 16mo, wraps, 6pp. Letter dated Field of Shiloh, Tenn., April 14, 1862. Text sig: "W".
...Same: 8vo, wraps, 8pp, Signed: W.W.W. See: Dornbusch-2932-3, Sabin-3962.

303 **BATTLEFIELDS IN DIXIE**
& Chickamauga Military Park. Nashville, n.d. (1917) 8vo, wraps, illus., maps, 63pp. $10-bmk-104.

304 **BATTLEFIELDS OF THE SOUTH,**
from Bull Run to Fredericksburg... By an English Combatant. (New York, 1984 Time-Life Books-"Collectors Library of

the Civil War." Leather bound, edges gilt. $25.

305 **BATTLEFIELDS in Dixie Land**
& Chicakamauga National Military Park. With description of the important battles fought along these lines & the story of the engine "General". National Chattanooga & St. Louis Ry-Western & Atlantic R.R. (Chicago: Poole bros., Jan. 1928) 12mo, decr-color wraps, illus., ports, maps (l-dbl-pg) 64pp. $5.

306 **BATTLES & LEADERS of the Civil War.**
Being for the most part contributions by Union & Confederate officers. Based upon the "Century War series". Edited by Robert Underwood Johnson & Clarence Clough Buel, of the editorial staff of "The Century Magazine." N.Y., The Century Co. (1884-1887). $60, $400-jk, $100-y. Grant-Lee Edition. sm. 4to, t.e.g., cl, 4vols in 32 parts, printed & bound in 8vols: xxiii, 750; xix, 760, xix, 752; xix, 835(Index: p. 769-835) illus., maps. $50.

307 ...N.Y. (1894) "People's Pictorial Edt., in 20 parts, oblong folio, wraps, $40-mm, $25, $150-bmk. Also: In cloth, leather label, ports, illus., maps. type-set in four columns, 324pp., index. $22.50.
...Same: 1/2Mor., condensed & arranged for popular reading. $17.50.
...N.Y., 1956, reprint of complete edition in 4 vols. YOSELOFF, Box $50-y, $30.
...Same: Lim. Edt. 100 copies, leather $55. NY, 1884-1887, "Grant-Lee Edt", t.e.g., $150-jk.

308 **BATTLES LOST & WON,**
Essays from Civil War History. Edt: John T. Hubbell. Westport, Conn., Greenwood Press, 1975. 8vo, cl, dj, xv, 290pp. $14. A book for arm-chair Generals, largely modern-day historians critical essays on each others' books.

309 **BATTLES OF ATLANTA.**
Short Sketch of the Battles around, siege, evacuation & destruction of Atlanta, Georgia, in 1864. With map, historic places, directory to battle lines, prominent characters who participated, etc. Prepared under the direction of the Committee of the Atlanta Camp, United Confederate Veterans, for the information of visitors, & sold for the benefit of the Camp. Atlanta, Ga., (Bergstrom Print) Sept., 1895. 8vo, wraps, 2pp. (7)-31pp. Color fldg. map. $10.

310 **BATTLES OF CHATTANOOGA,**
fought Nov. 23-25, 1863, by the Armies of the Cumberland & Tennessee, under Generals Grant, Thomas, Sherman, & Hooker. General Bragg commanding Confederate forces. Chattanooga, Lookout Mountain, Missionary Ridge & localities made famous by the battles of Chicamauga, Wauhatchie, Graysville, Ringgold, etc. A resume' of the situations shown in the panorama of Missionary Ridge, & very full extracts of official reports & papers from the library of Willain Wehner's panorama studio, Milwaukee, Wisconsin. Chicago, Ill., W.J. Jefferson, 1886. 8vo, wraps, 2fldg. maps, 71, (2)pp.

311 **BATTLES OF THE CIVIL WAR,**
1861-1865. A Pictorial Presentation. (Little Rock, Ark., Pioneer Press (1960) 48x64cm, consists of 36 color plates from original Kurtz & Allison prints. Each plate has a (2)p. text(2,3, & 5 columns length) by various authors, e.g., (4)p., (72)p., (36)p. pls. Spiral bound, color cover cardboard, each plate on 2-ply cardboard, boxed. $100.
...Remaindered & reissued at $250. by: Oxmoor House, Birmingham, Ala. 1976. folio, blue/gray buck., dj, $125. text in separate 4to, cl, vol.

312 **BATTLES OF THE CIVIL WAR:**
The complete Kurtz & Allison Prints.

N.Y., Fairfax Press, 1976. 4to, cl, 36 full page prints in color. $10.

313 **"BATTLES OF WHITE HOUSE, Oct. 3d, & Corinth, Oct. 4th"**
(n.p., 1863?) Broadside, 20x15cm. Dorn-II, 1901. Sig: "One of the 2d division." Strait lists as 1862.

314 **BATTLES of Fredericksburg, Chancellorsville, Wilderness & Spotsylvania...National Park.**
See: Joseph P. Cullen.

315 **BATTS, William**
"A Foot Soldier's Account: Letters of William Batts, 1861-1865. Edt: Jan Bonner Peacock." In: Ga. H.Q., March, 1966, v.L, #1, p. 87-100. $10.

316 **BAUER, Charles J.**
"The odd couple who hanged Mary Surratt." Silver Springs, Md., Silver Springs Press, 1980. 8vo, cl, dj, ix, 107, (30)pp., 118pp. illus., facsm, ports. Much on Surratts & anti-Union cartoons by Adalbert Volck.

317 **BAUMGARTEN, Julius B.**
"Seals, Stamps & Currency for the Confederate States made by Julius B. Baumgarten." In: SHSP, 1905, v.XXXIII, p. 188-190.

318 **BAXLEY, Houghton**
"Dr. Edward Warren of North Carolina." In: CV, May, 1926, v.XXXIV, p. 172-173. Surgeons of the CSA.

319 **BAXTER, Alice**
"Battle Flag of the Third Georgia." In: SHSP, 1910, v.XXXVIII, p. 210-216.

320 **BAXTER, Charles N. & Jas. M. Dearborn**
"Confederate literature: a list of books & newspapers, maps, music & miscellaneous matter printed in the South during the Confederacy, now in the Boston Athenaeum with introduction by James Ford Rhodes. Printed from the income of the Robert Charles Billings Fund." Number 5. $10. Boston: The Boston Athenaeum, 1917. Tall 8vo, cl, x, 213, (1)pp. (Thomas Todd co.) $22.50-wh, $100-bmk-114.

321 **BAXTER, Ed Dellahunty**
"Address of Capt..., before Tennessee Association of Confederate Soldiers at Nashville, Oct. 3, 1889." The True Status of the Confederate Soldier." Nashville: Oster & Webb(c.1899). 8vo, wraps, cover title, 23pp.

322 **BAXTER, George D., Mrs.**
"Contributions of the South to the civilization of Missouri." In: CV, March, 1924, v.XXXII, p. 135-137.

323 **BAXTER, James Phinney, III**
"The introduction of the Ironclad Warship." Cambridge: Harvard University Pr., 1938. 8vo, cl, plates, x, 398pp. Last 4-chaps: XI-XIV, deals with ironclads in Civil War. Based on research in British Admiralty papers, French archives U.S., as well as personal papers.
...Hamden, Ct., Archon Bks., Shoestring Press, 1968. $19.50-y.

324 **BAXTER, Lucy W.**
"Through the Union Lines into the Confederacy." (Charleston, So. Caro. Hist. & Genea. Mag., July, 1953, v.LIV, #3, p. 135-140.

325 **BAXTER, William**
"Pea Ridge & Prairie Grove; or, scenes & incidents of the war in Arkansas." Cincinnati: Poe & Hitchcock, 1864. 16mo, cl, 262pp. $18.50, $22.50, $30, $40-y. English clergyman but lived most of his life in Arkansas. $50-bmk, $150-jk, $75-bmk-105.
...Van Buren, Ark., 1957 $10

326 **BAYLOR, George**
"Bull Run to Bull Run; or, Four Years in the Army of Northern Virginia. Containing a detailed account of the career & adventures of the Baylor Light Horse, Company B, 12th Virginia Cavalry, CSA, with leaves from my scrap-book.(poem)" Rich-

mond: B.F. Johnson Pub. co., 1900. Tall 8vo, cl, ports(incl. front), 412pp. $75-bmk-105, $80-bmk-106, $40-nc(worn), $17.50, $20, $25, $30, $32.50.
"Bull Run to Bull Run; or, four years in the Army of Northern Virginia." Washington, DC, Zenger Pub. Co., 1983, 8vo, cl, dj, illus., endpaper map, new index. 427pp. $22.

327 **BAYLOR, George Wythe**
"John Robert Baylor Confederate Governor of Arizona." Edt: Intro: Odie B. Faulk. Tucson, Ariz., Pioneers' Historical Society, 1966. 8vo, fabricoid, map, facsm., front(port) 500 copies, index, 38pp. $5.

328 **BAYLOR, George Wythe, Col.**
"With Gen. A.S. Johnston at Shiloh." In: CV, Dec. 1897, v.V, #12, p. 609-613, illus., map, ports.

329 **BAYNE, Thomas L.**
"A Sketch of the Life of General Josiah Gorgas, Chief of Ordnance of the Confederate States." Richmond, 1885. Tall 8vo, wraps, port, 15pp. $10.
...South. Hist. Soc. Papers, v.13, p. 216-228, for 1885 under same title with port. of Gorgas as front. A. Lt.-Col. Thomas L. Bayne, Chief of Bur. Foreign Supplies is noted in book.

330 ..."Our Fallen Comrads", speech of Col. Bayne, of the Washington Artillery." In: SHSP, 1883, v.XI, p. 328-330.

331 ..."Report of Bureau of Foreign Supplies." In: SHSP, 1876, v.II, p. 103-105.

332 **BEACH, Elizabeth Jane**
"The Yankees in New Albany: Letter of Elizabeth Jane Beach, July 29, 1864." (Jackson, Miss., Jour. of Miss. Hist., Jan. 1940, v.II, #1, p. 42-48.

333 **BEALE, George W.**
"Maryland campaign, the cavalry fight at Boonsboro, graphically described, ninth Virginia & 8th Illinois regiments cross swords." In: SHSP, 1897, v.XXV, p. 276-280.

334 **BEALE, George William**
"A Lieutenant of Cavalry in Lee's Army." Boston: Gorham Press, 1918. 12mo, cl, 231pp. $750-bmk-105, $30, $38.50
...Louisville: Lost Cause, micro-cd, $4.28

335 ..."Address of Rev. G.W. Beale at the Northern Neck Soldier's Reunion, Nov. 11, 1884." In: SHSP, 1888, v.XVI, p. 109-116.

336 ..."The Battle of Greatest luster, incident in Chancellorsville Campaign." In: SHSP, 1906, v.XXXIV, p. 206-210.

337 ..."Company C, Ninth Virginia Cavalry, CSA. Its Roster & gallant record." In: SHSP, 1895, V.XXIII, p. 330-332.

338 ..."A soldiers account of the Gettysburg Campaign, letter from Geo. W. Beale." In: SHSP, 1883, v.XI, p. 320-327. See: R.L.T. Beale (father of Geo.)

339 **BEALE, Richard Lee Tuberville**
"History of the Ninth Virginia Cavalry." Amissville, Va., American Fundamentalist, Gaithersburg, MD., Butternut Press, 1984. 8vo, cl, 192pp. front (port) 350 copies $28.50. See: Robert Krick's "9th Va. Cav."
..."History of the 9th Virginia cavalry in the War between the States." by the late Brig.-Gen. R.L.T. Beale." Richmond, Va., B.F. Johnson Pub., 1899. 8vo, cl, front(port), 192pp. $15, $18, $40, $87.50. Written in 1865, found among author's papers at his death & published. $1000-bmk-105.

340 ..."List of Officers & Men of the Cavalry brigade of Brig.-Gen. R.L.T. Beale; CSArmy surrendered at Appomattox, Apr. 9, 1865." In: Va. Hist. Soc., collections, NS, v.6, p. (347)-355. Signed S.H. Burt, Capt. Richmond, Va., Va. Hist. Soc. Colle., 1887.

341 ..."Part taken by the Ninth Virginia Cavalry in repelling the Dahlgren Raid." In:

SHSP, 1877, v.III, p. 219-221. See: Geo. W., his son.

342 **BEALL, John Bramblett, Lt. Col.**
"In Barrack & Field. Poems & Sketches of Army Life." In three parts. Nashville: Smith & Lamar, 1906. 12mo, decr. cl, 420pp.(largely sketches, only 75pp. poems) front(port) $32.50. Author with 19th Georgia Vols. scarce. $35op.

343 **BEALL, John Yates**
"Trial of..., as a Spy & Guerrillero by Military Commission." New York: D. Appleton & Co., 1865. 8vo, wraps, 94pp. $7.50, $10, $35, $50-y. Beall, a Virginian, spied in Ohio & N.Y., captured steamship "Philo Parsons" in Ohio, in 1864.

344 ..."Memoir of..., His Life, Trial, Correspondance, Diary & Private Miscellany Found Among His Papers, including His Own Account of the Raid on Lake Erie." Montreal: J. Lovell, 1865. 8vo, cl, port pasted-in as front, vi, 297pp. $22.50, See: Wm. W. Baker, J.H. Crawford, Wm. R. Riddell.

345 **BEALS, Carleton**
"Brass-Knuckle Crusade. The Great Know-Nothing Conspiracy, 1920-1860." N.Y., Hastings House (1960) American Procession Series. 8vo, cl, d/w, viii, 312pp. ports, illus. $6.

346 **BEAN, R.T.**
"The Battle of Hartsville, Tenn." In: CV, Mar. 1915, v.XXIII, p. 125-126.
..."Seventeen months in Camp Douglas." In: CV, June/July, 1915, v.XXII, p. 268-270, 310-312. Camp Douglas near Chicago, Ill.

347 **BEAN, W.G.**
"A House Divided: The Civil War Letters of a Virginia Family." John P. & James L. Welsh. (Richmond) Va. Mag. Hist. Biog., October, 1951, v.59, #4, p. 397-422.
...Reprint, wraps, 25bp, atg. sign letter. $10

348 ..."Captain James Keith Boswell." (Richmond) Va. Cavl., Winter, 1970. v.XIX, #3, p. 30-35, illus., ports.

349 ..."John Letcher & the Slavery Issue in Virginia's Gubernatorial Contest of 1858-1859." (Lexington, Ky.) JSH, Feb., 1954. v.XX, #1, p. 22-49.
..."The unusual war experience of Lt. Geo. G. Junkin, CSA." In: VMHB, Apr. 1968, v.76, #2, p. 181-190.

350 **BEAN, W.G., Dr.**
"Lee blamed Ewell & Longstreet for his failure in the Wilderness." In: CWTI, Apr. 1966, v.5, #1, p. 4-7, ports. Recent undiscovered letters revealing above.

351 **BEAN, William Gleason**
"The Ruffner Pamphlet of 1847: An Antislavery aspect of Virginia Sectionionalism." (Richmond) Va. Mag. Hist. Biog. July, 1953, v.61, #3, p. 260-282. See: "Address to the people of West Virginia, etc..." Ruffner pamphlet.

352 ..."The Liberty Hall Volunteers Stonewall's college boys." Charlottesville, University Press of Virginia, (1964). 12mo, cl, x, (1), 227pp. op $4, $7, $15-bmk-84, $20-bmk-84.

353 ..."Stonewall's Man Sandie Pendleton." Chapel Hill, University of North Carolina Press, (1959). op $17-k, $20, $8-y. 8vo, cl, dj, port(front)viii, (1), 252pp. $5.

354 ..."An aspect of Know Nothingism-The immigrant & slavery." p. 319-334, South Atl. Quart., XXIII, Oct., 1924.

355 **BEARD, Dan W.**
"With Forrest in West Tennessee, winter campaign of 1862." In: SHSP, 1909, v.XXXVII, p. 304-308.

356 ..."Forrest men rank with bravest of brave." In: SHSP, 1909, v.XXXVII, p. 364-368.

357 **BEARD, William Ewing**
"Battle of Nashville including an outline of stirring events occurring in one of the

	most notable movements of the civil war- Hood's invasion of Tennessee." written for the Nashville Industrial Bureau. (Nashville: Marshall & Bruce Co) 1913. 12mo, wraps, front(fldg. plan) illus., ports, 44pp.
358	..."The Log of the "C.S. Submarine." In: USN Inst. Proc., Sept. 1916, v.XLII, p. 1545-1557. CS submarine "H.L. Hunley."
359	..."The Battle of Nashville. The limit of the last aggressive movement of the armies of the Confederacy. Hood's grand maneuver designed to prevent Sherman's March to the Sea, fought in the southern suburbs of Nashville, Dec. 15-16, 1864." Nashville: Benson print (1913) for the Nashville Industrial Bureau. $37.50, $15, $25. 8vo, wraps, 16pp.
360	..."The Confederate Government, 1861-1865." In: T.H.M., June, 1915, 9p.
361	**BEARD, William M.** "Stonewall" Jackson." In: UDCMag. June 1949, v.12, #6, p.18-20. A tribute to Gen. Jackson.
362	**BEARDEN, Robert E.L., Jr.** "The Episcopal Church in the Confederate States." In: AHQ, 1945, v.IV, p. 269-275. In: Americana, 1940, v.XXXIV, p. 471-475.
363	**BEARSS, Edwin C.** "Morgan's Second Kentucky raid, Dec., 1862, Parts: I, II," In: Reg. KyHS, July 1972, p. 200-218. Gen. John Hunt Morgan's Second Ky. Raid, Dec. 1862, part 2, Morgan attacks Elizabethtown; part 3, Morgan begins his return to Middle Tennessee." In: Keg. Ky. HS, April, 1973, p. 177-188. Oct., 426-438.
363a	..."Rebel Victory at Vicksburg." Wilmington, N.C., Broadfoot Pub., 1988, 8vo, cl, 299pp. Reprint. $25.
364	..."Rousseau's raid on the Montgomery & West Point Railroad." In: AHQ, 1963, v.XXV, p. 7-48, maps, 1 fold. See: Mark E. Fretwell.
365	..."Vicksburg is the key: the campaign for Vicksburg." Vol. I, Dayton, Oh., Morningside House, 1985, 8vo, cl, dj, 769, illus., maps. $37.50. ..."Unvexed to the sea." Vol. II.
	BEARSS, Edwin C. & Chris Calkins
366	"The Battle of Five Forks." Lynchburg, Va., H.E. Howard, 1986, 8vo, cl, lim. edt., 131pp., illus, maps, ntoes.
367	..."The Battle of Hartsville & Morgan's second Kentucky raid, part 1." In: RKHS, Jan. 1967, v.65, #1, p. 1-19; pt. II, Apr. 1967, #2, p. 120-133; pt. III, July 1967, p. 239-252; pt. IV, Oct. 1967, p. 304-323.
368	..."Construction of Fort Henry & Donelson." In: WTenn. HSP, 1967, #21, p. 24-47.
369	..."Morgan attacks Elizabethtown." pt. II, In: RKHS, April 1973, v.71, #2, p. 177-188. pt. II. Morgan begins his return to Middle Tenn., Oct. 1973, v.71, #4, p. 426-438. Pt. IV, Morgan, in a hard night march, evades trap." Jan. 1974, v.72, #1, p. 20-37.
370	**BEARSS, Edwin C. & Warren Grabau** "The Destruction of the Cairo." (Jackson) Jour. Miss. Hist., July 1961, v.XXIII, #3, p. 141-163.
371	**BEARSS, Edwin Cole** "The Armed Conflict, 1861-1865." In: A History of Mississippi by Rich. A. McLemore, Edt. Vol. 1, p. 447-492.
372	..."The Army of the Frontier's First Campaign: Confederate's Win at Newtonia." (Columbis, Mo., Mo. Hist. Review, April, 1966, v.LX, #3, p. 283-319, maps, illus.
373	..."The Army of the Frontier invades Washington County(Arkansas)." In: Wash. Co. Hist. Soc., "Flashback", Feb., 1970, v.XX, #1, plate, p. 1-20.
374	..."The Battle of Jackson, May 14, 1863 & the Siege of Jackson, July 10-17, 1863." Jackson, Miss., Civil War Round Table, 1981, 8vo, cl, 158pp. illus., 5 maps. $12.

375 ..."The Battle of Jenkins' Ferry Grant County, Arkansas." (Sheridan, Ark., Grant County Chamber of Commerce) Aug. 1961, $50, only 50 copies printed. 4to, mimeograph(one side) (7), 246pp.

..."The Battle of Wilson's Creek, with battle maps by David Whitman." Boseman, Montanna-Artcraft print, 1975. 8vo, cl, xii, 170p, ills, maps, ports.

..."Brice's Cross Roads." Dayton, Oh., Morningside, 1987. 8vo, cl, 379p. $30.

376 ..."Cavalry Fight at Cane Hill." In: AHQ, 1961, v.XX, p. 65-73.

377 ..."Calendar of events in Mississippi, 1861-1865." In: Jour. Miss. Hist., 1959, v.XXI, p. 85-112. Chronology.

378 ..."The Battle of the Post of Arkansas." In: AHQ, 1959, v.XVIII, p. 237-279, 3pp. maps.

379 ..."Battle of Huntsville & Morgan's 2nd Kentucky Raid." In: Ky. Hist. Reg., 1967, v.LXV, p. 1-19.

380 ..."The Battle of Pea Ridge.. Chap. 1-"Curtis" Army retires behind Little Sugar Creek.", Chap. II-"Van Dorn's advance-the engagement at Bentonville." In: AHQ, 1961, v.XX, p. 74-94, map.

381 ..."The Battle of Helena, July 4, 1863." In: AHQ, 1961, v.XX, p. 256-197, maps, 2.

382 ..."The Battle of Pea Ridge." (Des Moines: Annals of Iowa) pt-1, 3rd Ser., v.XXXVI-#8, Spring 1963. p. 569-589; pt-2, v.XXXVII-#1, summer 1963, p. 9-41; pts-III & IV, v.XXXVII-#3, Winter, 1964, p. 207-239.

383 ..."The First Day at Pea Ridge, March 7, 1862." In: Ar.HQ, 1958, v.XVII, p. 132-154.

384 ..."The Battle of Baton Rouge." In: JLHA, Spring, 1962, v.III, #2, p.77-128, maps(3).

385 ..."The Battle of Wilson's Creek. Greene & Christian Counties, Missouri." Wilson's Creek National Battlefield Park, U.S. Dept. Interior, National Park Service. July 1960. $7.50, $10, 4to, soft back, (2), (1)fldg. map, 213pp. (10pp. illus.(not numbered) append: xxxix, xipp.

386 ..."The Battle of Wilson's Creek." In: Annals of Iowa, 1961-1962, v.XXXVI, p. 81-109, 161-186. map, ports. $7.

387 ..."General Breckinridge leads the Confederate advance into middle Tennessee." In: RKHS, July, 1962, v.60, #3, p. 183-208.

388 ..."General Bragg abandons Kentucky." In: RKHS, July 1961, pp.

389 ..."General William Steele fights to hold onto Northwest Arkansas." In: AHQ, 1966, v.XXV, p. 36-99, 3-maps.

390 ..."General Cooper's CSA Indians threaten Fort Smith." In: AHQ, 1966, v.XXVI, p. 257-284, 2-maps.

391 ..."Cavalry operations in the Battle of Stone's River." In: Ten. Hist. Quart., XIX (1960)p. 23-53; 110-144.

392 ..."The Civil War Comes to Indian Territory, 1861: The Flight of Opothleyoholo." "Journal West", Jan. 1972, p. 9-42.

..."The Civil War Comes to Indian Territory, 1861." In: Journal of the West, v.XI, p. 9-42. The flight of Opothleyhola.

393 ..."Civil War Operations in & Around Pensacola." In 3 parts. (Jacksonville, Fla.) Florida Historical Quarterly, 1957-1958. V.36, p. 125-165; pt.II, p. 231-255; pt.III, p. 330-353. Final part in 1961 April issue. Parts were also issued as separates.

394 ..."The Confederate Attempt to regain Fort Smith." In: AHQ, 1969, v.XXVIII, p. 342-380, map, ports.

395 ..."Confederate Action against Fort Smith Post: Early, 1864." In: AHQ, 1970, v.XXIX, p. 226-251, maps, ports.

396 ..."Decision in Mississippi. Mississippi's Important Role in the War Between the States." Jackson: Miss. Comm. on War Between the States(1962) (Little Rock, Ark: Pioneer Press). Tk. 8vo, fabricoid, maps (3-fldg.) xvi, 636pp. bibliog., Index.

(609-635) $45-dabney, $20-bmk, $30, $6. ...Dayton, Oh., Morningside, 1980 $30.

397 ..."McArthur's May Expedition Against the Mississippi Central Railroad." (Jackson, Miss.) Jour. Miss. Hist., v.XXVIII, #1, p. 1-14.

398 ..."Marmaduke attacks Pine Bluff." In: AHQ, 1964, v.XXIII, p. 291-313, maps, illus. ports.

399 ..."The Fall of Fort Henry Tennessee." Dover, Tenn., Eastern National Park & Monument Ass'n., Fort Donelson National Military Park (c.1963) reprint from West Tennessee Historical Society, v.XVII, 1963. Large 8vo, decr. wraps, 30pp, illus., ports, p.85-107.

400 ..."The Federals raid Van Buren & threaten Fort Smith." In: AHQ, 1967, v.XXVI, p. 122-142, maps.

401 ..."The Federals capture Fort Smith, 1863." In: AHQ, 1969,, v.XXVIII, p. 156-190, pl, maps-2.

402 ..."Federal Generals squabble over Fort Smith, 1863-1864." In: AHQ, 1969, v.XXIX, p. 119-151, maps, ports.

403 ..."Federal Expedition against Saint Marks ends at Natural Bridge." In: FHQ, April, 1967, v.XLV, #4, p. 369-390, map.

404 ..."From Rolla to Fayetteville with Gen. Curtis." In: AHQ, 1960, v.XIX, p. 225-259, maps.

405 ..."The Federal Struggle to hold on to Fort Smith." In: AHQ, 1965, v.XXIV, p. 149-179, maps.

406 ..."Fort Smith serves General McCulloch as a supply depot." In: AHQ, 1965, v.XXIV, p. 315-247, illus., map, port.

407 ..."Forrest at Brice's Cross Roads." Dayton, Ohio, Morningside Books, 1979, 8vo, cl, ix, 382. illus., maps, index $10. Bearss finishes the book, begun by Glenn Tucker.

408 ..."Forrest at Brice's Cross Roads & in North Mississippi in 1864." Dayton, Oh., Morningside, 1979. 8vo, cl, illus., maps, ix, 382, (21)pp. pls. bibliog. 357-362. $20.

409 ..."Grand Gulf's Role in the Civil War." In: CWH, March, 1959, v.V, #1, p. 5-29, map.

410 ..."Protecting Sherman's Lifeline. The Battles of Brices Cross Roads & Tupelo, 1864." Wash: Nat'l. Park Serv., 1971, sq. 8vo, wraps, sketches, color maps, (40)pp. $.70.

411 ..."Military Operations on the St. Johns, Bluff(Florida), Sept.-Oct., 1862." In: Fla. Hist. Quart., XLII (1963-1964) p. 232-247 (pt.I); p. 331-351 (pt. 2), 2-maps.

412 ..."Calendar of events in Mississippi, 1861-1865." In: Jour. Miss. Hist., XXI(1959) p. 85-112.

413 ..."The Vicksburg River defenses & enigma of "Whistling Dick." In: Jour. Miss. Hist., XIX(1957), p. 21-30.

414 ..."Mississippi in the War Between the states 1861-1865." n.p., n.d.(c.1961) Tall, narrow 8vo, (12)pp. brief chron. history distributed by the Miss. Civil War Centennial Commission.

415 ..."Morgan's Second Kentucky Raid, December, 1862." Part I. Kentucky Historical Society Register, v.LXX, p. 200-218.

416 ..."Rebel Victory at Vicksburg." Vicksburg Centennial Commemorative Comm.(Little Rock, Ark: Pioneer Print, July 4, 1963. 8vo, cl, d/w, xi, 299pp. maps op $25, $5, $15-y, $10-y.

417 ..."Sherman's Demonstration Against Snyder's Bluff." (Jackson, Miss.) Jour. Miss. Hist., May, 1965, v.XXVII, #2, p. 168-186.

418 ..."The Trans-Mississippi Confederates Attempt to relieve Vicksburg." Part I. In: McNeese Review, 1964, v.XV, p. 46-70. Pt. II, 1965, v.XVI, p. 46-47.

419 ..."Texas At Vicksburg." Dedication of Monument of Texas at Vicksburg, Nov. 4, 1961. A Texas Civil War Centennial Ob-

servance. 8vo, wraps, 31pp., maps. $2.50, $1.

420 ..."The Vicksburg Centennial Commemorative Association, June 30-July 4, 1963." (Vicksburg, Miss.) 4to, decr. wraps, cover title, ads thru-out. $3.50

421 ..."Unconditional Surrender: The Fall of Fort Donelson." (Nashville:Tennessee Historical Quarterly reprint, Mar./June, 1962, vol.XXI-#1 & 2, p.47-66, 140-162, $.50. 8vo, decr. stiff wraps, 47pp., ports, illus.

422 ..."Steele's Retreat from Camden & the Battle of Jenkin's Ferry." (Little Rock) Arkansas Civil War Centennial Comm. Pioneer Press(c.1966) 8vo, cl, d/w, xiv, (1)190pp., maps, ports. op $10, $14.

423 ..."The Vicksburg River Defenses & the Enigma of "Whistling Dick"." In: Jour. of Miss. Hist., Jan, 1957, p. 10, v.xix, #1, Legend of CSA gun used against Union gunboats.

424 ..."The White River Expedition, June 10-July 15, 1862." The Federals prepare to strike. In: AHQ, 1962, v.XXI, p. 305-362. map, illus., port.

425 **BEARSS, Edwin L.**
"Asboth's Expedition up the Alabama & Florida Railroad." In: FHQ, October, 1960, v.XXXIX, #2, p. 159-166.

426 **BEASLEY, W.F.**
"The 48th N.C. Troops at Sharpsburg." In: OLOD, Dec., 1874, v.1, #4, p.330.

427 **BEATTY, Richmond Croom & Floyd C. Watkins & Thomas Daniel Young, Edts.**
"The Literature of the South." Chicago: Scott, Foresman(1952) tk. 8vo, cl, xxiii, 1106pp. Selections from Southern writers arranged in four periods: "The rise of the Confederate South, 1815-1865." with extensive introductions.

428 **BEATY, John O.**
"John Esten Cooke, Virginian (1830-1886)" N.Y., Columbia Univ. press, 1922. Columbia Univ. studies in English & comparative literature. Also as a thesis. 8vo, cl, viii, 173pp. (Reprinted, 1965) $7.50. Port Washington: Kennikat Pr. $35. op

429 **BEAUMONT, Betty Bentley, Mrs.**
Twelve Years of My Life. An Autobiography."...of Woodville, Miss. Phila: T.B. Peterson & Bros., 1887. 12mo, cl, 366pp. (27pp. ads) 17 lines fine print on t/p, a blurb much on CSA, born in England, settled in Miss. $45-jk-122.

430 **BEAUMONT, Henry Francis**
"Behind Prison Bars." In: CV, 1901/1902, v.10, p. 413-415, port. Re: William Stewart Hawkins, CSA officer, poet.

431 **BEAUREGARD, G.T., Gen.**
"The Campaign of Shiloh." In: B & L, v.1, p. 569-593, illus., ports.

432 ..."The Battle of Drewry's Bluff." In: South Mag., Mar., 1872, v.III, #3, 10pp. $10

433 ..."The defense of Charleston." In: B & L, v.4, p. 1-23, illus., maps, ports, diagrams.

434 ..."Four days of battle at Petersburg." In: B & L, v.4, p. 540-544, illus.

435 ..."General Beauregard." In: Atl. Monthly, June 1884, v.53, p. 551-560.

436 **BEAUREGARD, Pierre G.T.**
"Some mistakes of Rear-Admiral Taylor (William Rogers Taylor)." In: NAR, v.143, p. 413-418.

437 ..."A rejoinder to Gen. Beauregard by Admiral Taylor." In: NAR, 1887, v.144, p. 308-312.

438 ...Reply: NAR, v.145, p. 572-573.

439 **BEAUREGARD, Pierre Gustave Toutant, General**
Autograph: holograph conclusion of letter New Orleans, May 5, 1866. framed, port. $50.

440 ...Autographed Letter, signed-to Marcus Wright, Sept., 1882. Blue Ridge Springs, Va., 4pp. Critical of Jeff Davis. $85. (Goodspeeds, '73)

441 ..."The Defense of Drury's Bluff." In: B & L, IV, p. 195-205.

442 ..."Drewry's Bluff & Petersburg, May & June, 1864." N.Y. (March) North American Review, 1887. Tall 8vo, wraps, 17pp. From: North Amer. Rev., 1887, v.CXLIV, p. 244-260.

443 ..."First Battle of Bull Run." In: B & L, v.I, p. 196-227.

444 ..."Gen. Beauregard on the situation at Richmond, May, 1864." In: LWL, 1866/1877, v.II, p. 389-190. See also: Wm. Allan, Hamilton Basso, Alfred Romans, T. Harry Williams, Charles Gayarre, Hagood Johnson, Thomas Jordan, Theo. F. Dwight.

445 ..."General Pierre Gustave Toutant Beauregard." In: Illinois Central Mag., Mar. 1914, 11-27; II 10(April 1914) 9-24, illus., ports. (Dornbusch II-2602).

446 ..."General Order, No. 4, Corinth, Miss., May 19, 1862. Hdq. Western Dept." Broadside, 6 11/16x4 7/16". Beauregard's answer to "Beast Butler's" Gen. Order, #28. New Orleans, La., May 15, when he ordered arrest of any woman insulting Union men & "treated as women plying their trade." His answer "drive back from the soil, these infamous invaders." (Gdsp. '50) $35.

447 ..."General Order No. 14." facsimilie of his order to fire on Fort Sumter, April 11, 1861. contained in the Fifth Yearbook." Boston, Mass., Bibliophile Society, 1906. Limited 500 copies, uncut. $12.50.

448 ..."Orders for Battle of Manassas (Bull Run.)" In: Confed. War Jour., 1893, v.1, p. 66-69, 71-76, pl. 90.

449 ..."Battle of Shiloh or Pittsburg Landing." In: Confed. War Jour., 1893, v.1, p. 149, 151, 154-157.

450 ..."Principals & maxims of the art of war outpost service; general instructions for battle; review." Third edition. New Orleans, La., Brandao print, 1890, 8vo, wraps, 28pp.
...1st Edt: Charleston, 1863, wraps, 32pp.

451 ..."The Unification Question. Address of...to the people of Louisiana." (New Orleans, La., 1873) 16mo, caption title, 4pp.

452 ..."Beauregard monument association, organized in New Orleans, La., Feb. 21, 1893, to raise funds for the erection of a monument commemorative of Gen. G.T. Beauregard. New Orleans, La., 1917. 8vo, wraps, 16pp. $3.50.

453 ..."A Commentary of the Campaign & Battle of Manassas, of July, 1861. Together with a summary of the art of war." N.Y., G.P. Putnam's Sons, 1891. 8vo, cl, maps(fldg), xiv, 187pp. $7.50, $12.50, $10.75, $13.75, $80-bmk. Written in answer to a magazine article by Joseph E. Johnston. "Century" Mag., May, 1885.

454 ..."Gen. Pierre Gustave Toutant Beauregard." in Illinois Central Magazine, March & April, 1914, vol.II, p. 11-27; p. 9-24, illus., ports.

455 ..."Proceedings in New Orleans, La., & Charleston, S.C., relative to the presentation of the sword of Gen. Beauregard by his grandson, its reception by delegates from Charleston, with the official action of the City council of Charleston, 27th March, 1893, upon their formal acceptance of this trust." Charleston, Walker, Evans & Cogswell, 1893. 8vo, wraps, bds., port(front), illus., 23pp. $7.50.

456 ...Also, in Yearbook for the city of Charleston, for 1893. p. 273-292. $12.50.

457 ..."The Battle of Petersburg." In: North Amer. Rev., 1887, v.CXLV, p. 367-377; 506-515.

458 ..."Defence of Petersburg in June, 1864, Letter of Gen. Beauregard." In: So. Hist. Soc. Tr., 1874, v.1, 1, 134-137.

459 ..."Letter of Beauregard to Gen. C.M. Wilcox." In: Pub. Miss. Hist. Soc., 1906, v.V, p. 119-123.

460 ..."Sketch of Operations for the Spring Campaign of 1865." In: LWL, 1866, v.1, p. 188-189.

461 ..."Defense of Charleston." In: B & L, v.IV, p. 1-23.

462 ..."Defense of Charleston, S.C., in 1862-1863-1864." In: N. Amer. Rev., 1886, v.CXLII, p. 419-436; 564-571.

463 ..."Gen. Beauregard's official report on Morris Island, during month of July, August & Sept., 1863." In: So. Mag., 1871, v.VIII, p. 581-589; 679-688; v.IX, p. 45-57.

464 ..."Report of Gen. Beauregard of the Defense of Charleston, pub. by Order of Congress." Richmond: R.M. Smith, Print, 1864. 8vo, cl, p. 91, (2). Crandall-1417.

465 ..."Torpedo Service in Charleston Harbor." In: Annals of War, p. 513-526.

466 ..."The Shiloh Campaign." In: N. Amer., 1886, v.CXLII, p. 1-24; 159-194.

467 ..."Review of Beauregard's "Military Operations" by Alfred Romans, by Wm. Allan." In: SHSP, v.XII, p. 258-266.

468 ..."Battle of Drewry's Bluff." In: SHSP, v.XI, p. 1-10; v.XXV, p. 206-207.

469 ..."Battle of Ocean Pond, Florida. (Battle of Olustee, Fla.)" In: SHSP, v.IX, p. 11-15.

470 ..."Review of A. Roman's Military Operations", by Charles Gayarre." In: SHSP, v.XII, p. 402-416; 432-447.

471 ...Johnson Hagood's "Gen. P.G.T. Beauregard". In: SHSP, v.XXVIII, p. 318-336.

472 ...Thomas Jordan's "Recollections of Genl. Beauregard's Service in the Spring of 1862." In: SHSP, v.VIII, p. 404-417.

473 ..."Torpedo Service in the Harbor & Water Defenses of Charleston." In: SHSP, v.V, p. 145-161. $7.

474 ..."Letter of General Beauregard to Gen. C.M. Wilcox." In: Mil. Hist. Soc., Mass Papers, Bost: 1906, v.5, #5, p. 117-123.

475 ..."The Beauregard Manassas Quickstep", by A. Noir(Armand Edward Blackmar) New Orleans, La., A.E. Blackmar, 1861, 5pp., last pg. "Southern Military Music! For Piano." Differs from Crandall-3320-1, no port of Beauregard on cover. $60.

476 ..."Notes relative to obstructions designed by Col. G.T. Beauregard for the Mississippi River at Fort Jackson & Fort St. Philip, La. in Feb'y. 1861." In: LaHQ, Oct. 1919, v.II, p. 451-453.

477 ..."Official Report Battle Manassas." Rich: 1861, see Crandall-1380-1 ($75)

478 ..."Defense of Charleston." Rich: 1864. See: Crandall-1417; Sabin-4199 note. "These two reports very scarce, having been mostly destroyed by fire."

479 ...(Charles J. Villere) Presidents remarks when requested to restore Beauregard to Command of Dept. #2. Crandall-2873.

480 ...See: Gamaliel Bradford's "Confed. Ports." for a biography; also, his Biog. in Neale's I, March, 1913, p. 259-268.

481 ...See: Beatrice Van Court Meegan's Biog.

482 ...See Y.R. Le Monnier, GTB at Shiloh.

483 ..."Gen. Beauregard's report of the Battle of Drewry's Bluff." In: LWL, May, 1867, v.III, #1, p. 1-8. South. Mag. Mar., 1972, wrap. 10pp. $10.

484 ...Beauregard to J.E. Johnston-"Plan of the Campaign for 1865(May 15)." In: SHSP, 1914, v.39, p. 59-60.

485 ..."A Short History of Gen. G.T. Beauregard." Park Place, N.Y., Knapp & Co, 1888. 2 3/4x1 1/2" colored booklet, 16pp. facsm. signature(packed in Duke's cigarettes.) See: "Heroes of the C.W." & W. Duke Co.

486 ..."Treatment of Prisoners-Letter of Genl. Beauregard." In: SHSP, 1916, v.41, p. 184-187.

487 ..."A South-side History of the War shown in the Letters of & to General P.G.T. Beauregard...to be sold. April 4, 1916." Phila: Stan V. Henkels Auction Commission Merchant, 1916. Cat. #1148, pt.II, Pts I-II $50.

488 ..."The First Manassas, Corresp. between Ewell & Beauregard, etc." See: under R.S. Ewell.

489 ..."Suppressed part of Gen. Beauregard's report of the Battle Manassas." LWL, 1867, v.II, #4, p. 259-260.

490 **BEAUREGARD, R.T.**
"A sketch of General G.T. Beauregard." In: LaHQ, July, 1919, v.II, p. 276-281. Written by his son.

491 **BECK, Nemias Bramlette**
"Alexander H. Stephens (1812-1883) Orator." In: "Wisconsin", University. Summaries of doctoral dissertations, v.3, Madison: Univ. of Wisc. pr., 1938, p. 275-277.

492 **BECK, R. McC.**
"General J.E.B. Stuart at Brandy Station, June 9, 1863." In: Cavalry Jour., 1935, v.XLIV, #189, p. 5-10.

493 **BECKER, Stephen**
"When the war is over." N.Y., Random House, 1969, 8vo, cl, 240pp. $10. Based on incident in which a CSA soldier was executed May 11, 1865, near Cincinnati, 32 days after war was over.

494 **BECKETT, Richard Capel**
"Some effects of military Reconstruction in Monroe County, Mississippi." In: Pub. Miss. Hist. Soc., Oxford, Miss., 1904, v.VIII, p. (177)-186.

495 ..."A sketch of the career of Company B, Armistead's Cavalry Regiment." In: Pub. Miss. Hist. Soc., Oxford, Miss, 1904, v.VIII, p. 33-50.

496 **BECKHAM, Elihu C., Sgt., Co.K, 21st Arkansas**
"Where I was, What I saw During the War." An account of the civil war as seen by a soldier. Written by Elihu C. Beckham shortly after the War from memory & handed down from generation to generation." recently published in serial form by Stone County Leader, Mountain View, Arkansas, n.d. (1962) 12mo, soft wraps, 39pp. Melbourne, Ark., (c.1898?) 1st edt. $1.

497 **BEDFORD, A.M., Capt.**
"Diary kept by..., 3rd Missouri Cavalry, while on Morris Island, S.C. prisoner of war, Hilton Head & Fort Pulaski." In: John Ogden Murray's "The Immortal Six-hundred." p. 250-319.

498 **BEDFORD, H.L.**
"Fight between the Batteries & Gunboats at Fort Donelson." In: SHSP, 1885, v.XIII, p. 165-173.

499 **BEDFORD, Henry F.**
"The Union Divides/Politics & Slavery, 1850-1861." N.Y., The Macmillan Co(1963). "New Perspectives in American History." 12mo, decr. stiff wraps, bigs., map, chart, (6), 89pp, index. $1.50

500 **BEDINGER, Singleton Berry**
"Defenders in Gray." Dallas: Royal Pub. Co., 1962, 8vo, wraps, 32pp., ports.

501 ..."Kentuckians, C.S.A." Intro: W. Clyde Odeneal, Taylor, Texas: Merchants Press, 1965, 8vo, wraps, illus., ports, 32pp.

502 ..."Missouri's Confederates, 1861-1865." Intro: J. Winston Coleman, Jr. Taylor, Texas: Merchants Press, 1967, 8vo, wraps, ports, 44pp. $3.50.
...All: OP-Xerox, Ann Arbor, $6.ea.

503 ..."Texas & the Southern Confederacy, with an introduction: Dale Oliver Turner. Dedicated to the memory of all Texans who served the Confederacy during the War Between the States. The Bonnie Blue Flag." Taylor, Texas: Merchant's Press, 1970. 8vo, stiff wraps, illus., ports, 58pp. $3.50

504 **BEE, Hamilton P.**
"Battle of Pleasant Hill-an Error Corrected." In: SHSP, 1880, v.VIII, p. 184-186.

505 **BEEBE, Gilbert J.**
"A Review & Refutation of Helper's 'Impending Crisis'." Middletown, N.Y., 1860. 8vo, printed wraps, 64pp. (old) $7.50. Like Saml. Wolfe, attacks Helper's statistics.

506 **BEER, William**
"The 'Dixie bill'." In: Mag. of Hist., Jan., 1915, v.XX, p. 1-3. A bill issued by Citizens bank of New Orleans, for a number of years before the war. Many believe the term "Dixie" originated by its popular use.

507 **BEERS, Fannie A., Mrs.**
"Memories. A record of personal experience & adventure during four years of war." Phila: J.B. Lippincott Co., 1888. 12mo, cl, port(front) 336pp. (16)pp. ads. $35, $12.50, $25.
...1889 edt. ($17.50); 1891 edt. ($10); 1891 edt. ($35-jk; $90-bmk-105, $40.

508 **BEERS, Henry Putney**
"Guide to the Archives of the Government of the Confederate States of America." Washington: National Archives, 1968. 8vo, cl, ix, 536pp., index(427)-536. $3.75, $7-bmk.

509 **BEGERON, Paul H.**
"Tennessee's Response to the Nullification Crisis." (Houston, Tex.) JSH, Feb. 1972, v.XXXIX, #1, p. 23-44.

510 **BEITZELL, Edwin Warfield**
"Point Lookout prison camp for Confederates." (Abell, Md., The Author, 1972), 4to, cl, dj, illus., x, 217pp. $8, $15, $20.

511 **BEITZINGER, A.J.**
"The Father of Copperheadism in Wisconsin." In: Wis. Mag. Hist., Autumn, 1955, v.XXXIX, p. 17-29. On Edward G. Ryan, Democratic party leader in Wisc. 1860-1863.

512 **BEJACH, Wilema Roberts**
"Civil War letters of a mother & son." In: W.TennHSP, 1950, #iv, p. 50-71.

513 **BEJACK, L.D.**
"The Battle of Moscow, Tenn., Dec. 4, 1863." In: W. Tenn. HSP, 1973, p. 108-112.

514 **BELCHER, James R., Jr. & Ronald L. Heinemann**
"Heros von Borcke Knight-errant of the Confederacy." In: Va. CAvl. Autumn, 1985, #2, v.35, p. 86-95, illus. (3-color), ports.

515 **BELDEN, Bauman Lowe**
"War Medals of the Confederacy." N.Y., American Numismatic Society, 1915: reprint, Amer. Jour. Numis., vXLVIII. 100 copies. 4to, wraps, 12pp. 1-illus. Read before the society, Dec. 7, 1914.
...Glendale, N.Y., Benchmark Pub. Corp., 1970. $2.h

516 **BELIN, H.E.**
"The Civil War as seen through Southern glasses." In: Amer. Jour. Sociol., Sept., 1903, v.IX, p. 259-267.

517 ..."A Southern view of Slavery." In: Amer. Jour. Sociol., Jan., 1908, v.XIII, p. 513-522.

518 **BELKNAP, William Worth**
"Information relative to an alleged unlawful traffic with rebels in the State of Texas during the late war." Washington, DC, Senate Doc. 10, 8vo, wraps, 97pp. $45-jk-127. Blockade running in Texas. Senator Thurman also reports such traffic in a Mar. 3, 1871, Senate #377, 41st. Cong. 3rd sess. traffic not implicating Senator Sprague. 18pp.

519 **BELL, Alfreda Eva**
"The Rebel Cousin; or, Life & Love in Secessia. The autobiography of the beautiful Bertha Stephens, the accomplished

niece of the Hon. Alexander Hamilton Stephens, Vice President of the Southern Confederacy. Written by herself, & prepared for Publication by her friend, Alfreda Eva Bell." Phila: Barclay & Co., 1864. 12mo, cl, 48pp., illus. WrightII-254) "New Era in American History". "Not based on fact".

520 **BELL, Clarence**
"The Confederate Soldier." In: "The Bivoacan Independent Mil. Jour., Bost: E.F. Rollins, Jan., 1883-Dec., 1885, v.III, p. 201-205.

521 **BELL, Earl L. & Kenneth C. Crabbe**
"The Augusta Chronicle: Indomitable Voice of Dixie, 1785-1960." Athens: Univ. of Georgia Press, 1960. 8vo, cl, illus., append., index, xii, 273pp.

522 **BELL, George**
"Diary of George Bell, a Record of Captivity in a Federal Military Prison, 1862. Edited by Whitfield J. Bell, Jr." In: Ga. H.Q., June, 1938, v.XXII, #2, p. 169-184. $8.

523 **BELL, Hiram P.**
"Men & Things. Being Reminiscent, Biographical & Historical." Atlanta, Ga., 1907, Foote & Davis Print. 12mo, cl, port, viii, 449pp. $7.50, $10. Formed & in com'd. 43rd. reg. Ga. Vols.

524 **BELL, J.F.**
"Price's 1861 Missouri campaign." In: CV, Sept., 1914, v.XXII, p. 416.

525 **BELL, John P.**
"Price's Missouri campaign, 1861." In: CV, June/July, 1914, v.XXII, p. 271-272, 318-319.

526 **BELL, John Thomas**
"Civil War stories; compiled from Official Records-Union & Confederate." San Francisco, Cal., Whitaker & Bay Co., 1903. 12mo, cl, front(port), 189pp. Anecdotal.

527 **BELL, John W.**
"Memoirs of Gov. William Smith, of Va. His political, military, & personal history. By John W. Bell, priv. in the Culpeper minute-men, & 13th Va. Reg., etc." N.Y. Moss Engr. co, 1891. 8vo, cl, xvi, 461pp., front(port), pls, facsm. $125-bmk-105, $15. See: Ed. F. Heite.

528 **BELL, Landon C.**
"The Old Free State. A contribution to the History of Lunenburg Co., & Southside Virginia." Richmond, 1927. 2vols. About 225pp. on slavery, secession, Civil War & post bellum. $80-bmk-105.

529 **BELL, Landon Covington**
"An address at Johnson's Island in memory of the Confederate Soldiers who while prisoners died & are buried on the island." (Columbus, Ohio 1929) Deliv., May 26, 1929. 8vo, wraps, 22pp. $10.

530 ..."Robert E. Lee; an address before the Dixie chapter, U.D.C., Columbus, Ohio., in celebration of Gen. Lee's birthday, Jan. 19, 1929. Append: Letter of Gen. Lee to Lord Acton. Dec. 15, 1866." (Columbus, Ohio, 1929) 8vo, wraps, 27pp. $25-atg-bmk.

531 ..."The Lincoln Myths are passing-But Slowly Bowers Tragic Era." Reprinted from Tyler's Quarterly Hist. & Genealogical Magazine, Jan. 1930. Cover title, 8vo, wraps, 16pp. debunks Lincoln myths & Bower. $5.

532 **BELL, Ovid**
"Political conditions in Callaway before the civil war began." (Calloway County, Mo., 1860-1861) Fulton, Mo., 1952. 8vo, wraps, 25pp.

533 ..."The kingdom of Calloway." Fulton, Mo., 1952. 8vo, wraps, 31pp. Reprint: Mo. HSB, Apr., 1952, v.8, p. 226-243. Calloway Co., "in sentiment was truly a detached fragment of Southern Confederacy.

534 **BELL, Patricia**
"Gideon Pillow." In: CWTI, Oct. 1967, v.VI, #6, p. 12-19, illus., ports.

535 **BELL, Robert T.**
"11th Virginia infantry." Lynchburg, Va. H.E. Howard, 1985, (J.P. Bell Print), 1st, Lim. atg. edt., 415, 8vo, cl, dj, (3), 103pp., maps, ports. $17.50.

536 **BELL, Stephen Hugh**
"Phillip Phillips Neely & Secession." In: AHQ, 1976, v.38, #1, p. 45-50.

537 **BELL, T.F., Adj. Gen., Louisiana**
"Report of the Adjutant General, Jan. 2, 1892. A record of civil & military officers C.S.A., their time of service. Louisiana Colonels killed, roster of Louisiana troops mustered in the provisional army, CSA." New Orleans, La., 1892. 8vo, wraps, plates, 2-fldg., 79pp.

538 **BELL, William**
"Camp Jackson prisoners." In: CV, July 1923, v.XXXI, p. 260-261.

539 **BELLAH, James Warner**
"The Valiant Virginians." With a foreword: Fletcher Pratt & maps by Rafael Palacios. N.Y., Ballantine Books(1953). 12mo, cl, illus., 146pp. $1. (Shorter version of "Tales of Valarous Virginians, serially in Sat. Eve. Post.

540 ..."Soldiers' battle: Gettysburg." N.Y., preface: Henry Graff. N.Y., D. McKay. (1962) 8vo, cl, 204pp. illus., bibliog. dj. $40.

541 **BELLAMY, Ellen Douglas**
"Back with the tide; Memoirs." (Wilmington, N.C., 1940?) Private Print. 8vo, wraps, 35pp., front. CSA personal narrative.

542 **BELLAMY, James W.**
"The political career of Landon Carter Haynes, 1816-1875." In: ETenn.HSP, 1956, v.28, p. 102-126, notes. His legal practice, activities in Tenn. & CSA politica.

543 **BELLIGERENT RIGHTS AT SEA**
and changes proposed in them." In: Black. Edn. Mag., Jan, 1863, v.XCIII, p. 116-1132. "The Alabama", "Privateering", "Trent Affair".

544 ..."Our neutrality", In: Black. Edn. Mag., Apr. 1864, v.XCV, p. 447-461.

545 **BELLOW, Saul**
"Mosby's Memoirs & other stories." N.Y., Viking, 1968, 8vo, cl, dj, 1st edt. $15.

546 **BELLOWS, Donald**
"A study of British conservative reaction to the American civil war." In: JSH, Nov. 1985, v.51, #4, p. 505-526.

547 **BELMONT, MO., Battle of**
"The Battle of Belmont." Camp Benning, Ga., 1921. 8vo, wraps, fldg. maps, 108pp. $25-bmk. Probably a training exercise. See: Geo. B. Wilds article in CV, XXXII, 1924, p. 485.

548 **BELO, A.H., Col.**
"The Battle of Gettysburg." In: CV, 1900, v.8, p. 165-168, port. Belo, 59th N.C. Inf., reminiscences before Sterling Price Camp, Dallas, Tex., Jan. 20, 1900.

549 **BELO, Alfred Horatio**
"Memoirs of..., dictated by him to & with a short introduction, by Charles Peabody, May, 1902." Bost: Alfred Mudge & Son, 1904. 12mo, wraps, 75pp. Cap't. of his company from N.C., after Gettysburg, made colonel. To Texas & estb. Galveston & Dallas News.

550 **BELPERRON, Pierre**
"La Guerre de Secession, 1861-1865, Ses Cause s et ses Suites." Paris: Plon print(1947) 8vo, cl, maps(part fldg.)ports, illus., iv, 760pp. Bibliog. 737-740. $30, $450-frs.

551 **BELZ, Herman**
"The Etheridge Conspiracy of 1863: A Projected Conservative Coup." (Houston, Tex.) JSH, Nov., 1970, v.XXXVI, #4, p. 549-567. Radicals maintain control, finally

keep any dissident elements out of control of congress.

552 **BELZUNG, L.D. & G. Hayden Green**
"Slavery was only an excuse-resource shortages caused, decided America's civil war." In: Arkansas Business & economic Review, Fayetteville, Ark., Spring, 1973, v.6, #1, p. 21-27.

553 **BENECKE, Louis**
"Some light upon a Charlton County episode of '64." n.d., c.1891, 8vo, wraps, 13pp. $50-ginx-41. His defense of a charge of murder when he led Missouri buschwhackers.

554 **BENEDICT, James Bell, Jr.**
"General John Hunt Morgan, the Great Indiana-Ohio Raid." In: FCHQ, April, 1957, v.31, #2, p. 147-171.

555 **BENJAMEN, J.P., Hon.**
"The right of secession." Wash: Lemuel Towers, 1861, 8vo, 16pp. (G. Hendershott) $75.

556 **BENJAMIN, Judah P.**
"Confederate period vieux Paris painted & gilded porcelain portrait & scenic plate of Benjamin, signed on reverse-painted & guilded by Rudolph L. Lux, New Orleans, La., April 1861." Reverse eight red stars, represent "T" for Tex/or Tenn, "A"/Ala., etc.

557 **BENJAMIN, Judah Philip**
"Intercepted Instructions to L.Q.C. Lamar, Styled Commissioner. The African Slave Trade. The Secret Purpose of the Insurgents to Revive it." Philadelphia: C. Sherman & Co. 1863. 8vo, wraps, 24pp. $25-bmk-90, (old) $., $50-ginz (Sabin's copy-4703, shows 34pp.)

558 ..."Relation of States. Speech of...delivered in the Senate of the U.S., May 8, 1860, on the Resolutions submitted by Hon. Jefferson Davis, Mar. 1, 1860." Baltimore: Murphy & Co., 1860. 8vo, sewn, 8pp, Sabin-4704.

559 ..."Kansas Bill. Speech of..., of La., delivered in the Senate...Mar. 11, 1858. Slavery Protected by the Common Law of the New World. Guaranteed by Constitution. Vindicated by the Supreme Court of the U.S." Washington: G.S. Gideon, 1858. 8vo, sewn, 29pp. Sabin-4705.

560 ..."Speech of...On the Kansas Question. Delivered in the Senate, May 2, 1856." Washington, 1856. 8vo, sewn, 28pp. Sabin-4706.

561 ..."Extracts from the Speech...on the Kansas Question: showing the True Meaning of the Kansas Law, & his Reasons for joining the Democratic Party. Delivered in the Senate May 2, 1856." Washington, 1856. 8vo, sewn, 8pp, Sabin-4707. See: Jno. W. Delehant.

562 ..."Judah P. Benjamin", from Charleston "News & Courier, Jan. 1898." In: SHSP, 1897, v.XXV, p. 378-379.

563 ..."Official Correspondence of Confederate State Department, Letter from Hon. J.P. Benjamin, (concerning Confederate mission to Canada.) In: SHSP, 1879, v.VII, p. 99-101.

564 ..."Two witnesses on the "Treatment of prisoners"-Hon. J.P. Benjamin & General B.F. Butler." In: SHSP, 1878, v.VI, p. 183-187.

565 ...Lithograph Portrait by Albert Rosenthal, after a daguerreotype of 1859, n.p., 1924. Signed proof Imp., 24x19" $25.

566 ..."Speech of Hon. J.P. Benjamin on the Right of Secession. Delivered in the senate of the United States, Dec. 31, 1860." n.p., n.d., 8vo, sewn, 16pp. $5, $25-bmk-108, $7.50

567 ..."Address upon the General Changes of the Practical Operation of our Constitution Compared with its Theory, etc." San Francisco, 1860. 8vo, wraps, 25pp. Sabin-4700.

568 ..."Defence of the National Democracy against the attacks of Judge Douglas Constitutional Rights of the States. Speech of Hon. J.P. Benjamin, of Louisiana. Delivered in the senate, May 22, 1860." Washington, 1860. 8vo, wraps, 24pp. $8.50, $12.50

569 ...(n.p., n.d.)8vo, 16pp. Sabin-4701.

570 ..."Official Correspondence of Confederate State Department. Letter from Mr. Benjamin, Richmond: April 20, 1864." In: SHSP, 1879, v.VII, p. 132-139.

571 ..."The Life of...(1811-1884) Publication of the Louisiana State Museum. Mar., 27, 1937." (New Orleans, La.: T.J. Moran, 1937) 8vo, wraps, illus.(incl. ports) 26pp. See: E.M. Gates, Burton Hanson., Owen Maurice Peterson.

572 ..."Pius IX & the Confederacy." U.S. Catholic Hist. Soc. Rec.XXXI, (1940), p. 149-151. Text of instruction sent by JPB to Bishop P.M. Lynch, CSA Commissioner to the Pope. See: Father Jerome.

573 ..."The letters of Judah Philip Benjamin to Ambrose Dudley Mann, minister of the Confederacy to Belgium & special commissioner to the Vatican, together with the correspondence with the Pope. Edt: James A. Padgett." Louisiana Hist. Quar., XX(1937, p. 738-793) Papers of Pickett in LC, papers of CSA.

574 **BENJAMIN, Mary A.**
"A little known tragedy of the Civil War." In: Collector, Nov. 1954, v.67, p. 97-100. Letters, news clippings, relates to trial of Col. Lawrence Orton Williams & Lt. Walter G. Peters, CSA, as spies, Franklin, Tenn., 9 June, 1863, with text of some letters.

575 ..."The Vicksburg Daily Citizen", July 4, 1863." In: Collector, June, 1954, v.67, p. 49-51. facsm. Issue set in type by CSA, then "struck-off" by Union soldiers, who added their capture of the city.

576 **BENNER, Judith Ann**
"Fraudulent Finance: Counterfeiting & the Confederate States: 1861-1865." (Hillsboro, Texas) A. Hill Junior College Monograph, No. 3, 1970. 8vo, stiff wraps, facsms, ports, vii, 70pp. Bibliog. 59-66, index. $5-y

577 ..."Sul Ross, Soldier, Statesman, Educator." College Station: Texas A & M Univ. pr., 1982, Centennial Series of Association of Former Students, #13. 8vo, cl, illus., bibliog., index, 286pp. $10. Lawrence Sullivan Ross, CSA soldier & Tex. Ranger, Senator & Pres. of A & M College.

578 ..."Lone Star Rebel." Woodcuts: R.B. Dance. Winston-Salem, N.C., John F. Blair (1971) $5. 12mo, cl, dj, decr. endsheets, (6), 232pp. CSA, Col. Lawrence Sullivan Ross & later a governor of Texas. Fiction based on fact.
..."The Lone Star Rebel, by J.A. Benner, woodcuts: R.B. Dance." Winston-Salem, N.C., J.F. Blair (1971) 8vo, cl, 232pp., illus., Fiction (Jr.Hi) Joins 6th Tex. Cav. courier for Col. Ross.

579 **BENNETT, Alice B.**
"Pinckney Barfield(born 1831)" In: UDC mag. April, 1949, v.12, #4, p. 13-14. On service of her grandfather in CSArmy, 1861-1863.

580 **BENNETT, John B.**
"Albert Taylor Bledsoe: Transitional Philosopher of the Old South." In: Methodist Hist., 1972, v.XI, p.i, 3-14.

581 **BENNETT, L.**
"The case of the mysterious Confederates." In: S.P.A. Jour., May, 1953, v.15, p. 437-438. Facsm., on ultramarine, gray, & carmine stamps surreptitiously printed in Ohio from a captured plate of the CS $.10 stamp, some time after 1865.

582 **BENNETT, Martha Haines Butt**
"Antifanaticism: A Tale of the South." Phi-

la: Lippincott, Granbo co, 1853. 12mo, cl, 268pp. Wright-288. In defense of slavery.

583 **BENNETT, P.T., Hon.**
"General Junius Daniel. An address before Ladies' Memorial Association, in Raleigh, N.C., May 10, 1888." In: SHSP, 1890, v.XVIII, p.340-349.

584 **BENNETT, Risden Tyler**
"Address of..., Late Colonel 13th N.C. Inf., CSA at laying corner-stone of the Confederate Monument at Raleigh, N.C., May 22, 1894." "Morale of Confederates." In: SHSP, 1905, v.XXXIII, p. 65-70.

585 ..."Address before the Ladies' Memorial Association." In: SHSP, 1906, v.XXXIV, p. 52-56.

586 ..."The Confederate Soldier." In: SHSP, 1890, v.XVIII, p. 272-275.

587 ..."The Private soldier of the C.S.Army, & as exemplified by the representation from North Carolina. An address before Ladies' Memorial Association at Raleigh, N.C., May 10, 1897." In: SHSP, 1897, v.XXV, p. 302-308.

588 **BENNETT, William Wallace**
"A Narrative of the great revival which prevailed in the Southern armies during the late Civil War between the States of the Federal Union." Philadelphia: Claxton, Remson & Heffelfinger, 1877. 8vo, cl, illus., 427pp. (micro-cd, $6.19) $25.
..."A narrative of the Great Revival..." Harrisonburg, Va., Sprinkle Press, 1976. wraps, 427pp.

589 **BENNING, Henry Lewis, Gen.**
"Report of General Benning, Battle of Chickamauga." In: SHSP, 1885, v.XIII, p. 373-376.

590 ..."Notes by General H.L. Benning on Battle of Sharpsburg." In: SHSP, 1888, v.XVI, p. 393-395.

591 ..."Notes on the Final Campaign of April, 1865." In: SHSP, 1879, v.VII, p. 193-195.

592 ..."Report of...Battle of Gettysburg." In: SHSP, 1877, v.IV, p. 167-178.

593 **BENNINGTON, Bill**
"Revolvers of the Confederacy." In: Gun Jour., May, 1981, v.1, #3, p. 12-18, illus., port.

594 **BENNISON, Richard T.**
"Gen. Braxton Bragg." In: Field Artillery Journal (1931), XXI, illus., port, p. 600-611. Dornbusch-2623.

595 **BENNY, John, Mrs. (qualified guide)**
"Brief History of Battle of Shiloh & Corinth including Pickwick Dam." Michie, Tenn: Shiloh Park, n.d. (c.1938) 16mo, wraps, illus., 23pp. $1.

596 **BENSON, B.K.**
"Old Squire; the romance of a black Virginian." N.Y., Macmillan Co.; London, 1903. 12mo, cl, x, 1, 432pp., incl. maps. $20. Black servant who accompanies master throughout war. Author a South Carolinian serving in S.C. Vols. (Gregg's) (Carolina Book)

597 **BENSON, Berry**
"Berry Benson's Civil War Book. Memoirs of a Confederate Scout & Sharpshooter. Edt: Susan Williams Benson." Athens: University of Georgia press(1962) 8vo, cl, dj, ports, illus., xi, 203pp. $20, $4.50, $25-bmk-104, $7.

598 ..."My escape from a Yankee Prison. Edt. by Susan William Benson." In: Ga. Rev., Winter, 1961, (13)pp. $8.

599 **BENSON, Blackwood Ketcham**
"Who Goes There? The story of a spy in the Civil War." N.Y., Macmillan co, 1900. 12mo, cl, illus.(maps), xviii, 485pp. (Author was brother, Berry Benson, see under this name.

600 ..."Bayard's Courier: a story of love & adventure in the cavalry campaigns." N.Y., Macmillan co, 1902, Re: Stuart & Jackson, $25-bmk-105. 12mo, cl, maps, front., pl., vii, 402pp.

601 ..."A Friend with a Countersign." N.Y., Macmillan co, 1901. 12mo, cl, front, 7-pls., 4-maps, front, vii, 455pp. civil war, virginia hist.

602 **BENTLEY, H. Blair**
"Morale as a Factor in the Confederate Failure at Island Number Ten." In: West Tenn. Hist. Soc. Papr., Fall, 1978.

603 **BENTON COUNTY PIONEER (Arkansas)**
"100th Anniversary Battle of Pea Ridge." (Rogers,Ark.) Benton Co. Historical Society. vol.7, #3, March, 1962. 4to, mimeo., cover title, illus., facsms, 75pp. Muster Rolls, short biogs. soldiers of Benton County. $5.

604 ...Mar., 1957, v.II, #3, Commemoration, 12pp. illus.

605 **BENTON, Lee David**
"On the border of Indian Territory/the Oklahoma adventures of William Quesenbury." In: Chron. Okla., Summer 1984, v.62, #2, p. 134-155, pl, port, facsm., dble-pg. map. Newspaper editor, Brig. Qtr. master under Pike.

606 **BENTONVILLE, N.C.**
"Battle of Bentonville." In: NCHR, 1956, v.33, p. 332-358. (Gen. Joseph E. Johnston)

607 ..."Battle of Bentonville, March 19-20, 1865." Raleigh, N.C., Confederate Centennial Commission, 1965. (Fayetteville, N.C.) Worth Print (1965). 8vo, pict. colored stiff wraps, (36)pp. See: Jay Luvaas' "Johnston's last stand, Bentonville. Report reprinted from NCHR.

608 **BERESFORD-HOPE, A.J.B.**
"The American Disruption. 1. A Popular View of the American Civil War. 2. England, The North, & the South. 3. The Results of the American Disruption. In three lectures, delivered by request...before the Maidstone Literary & Mechanics Institute." London: James Ridgway, 1862. 8vo, cl, 116pp.
...6th Edition, as above. Sabin-32895. Strongly pro-South, against Lincoln.

609 ..."England, the North, & the South." London: James Ridgway, 1862. 8vo, cl, 40pp. $4, $6.
...Above, 4th Edition.

610 ..."A Popular View of the American Civil War." London: James Ridgway, 1861. 8vo, cl, 39, 28pp. $4.
...Same, 3rd Edition.

611 ..."The Results of the American Disruption: A Lecture...in Continuation of a Popular View of the American Civil War, & England, The North & South." London: James Ridgway, 1862, third edt. 8vo, cl, 40pp. $4.

612 ..."The Social & Political Bearings of the American Disruption." London: William Ridgway, 1863. 8vo, cl, 42pp.
...Same, Second & Third Editions.

613 ..."The American Church in Disruption." London: James Ridgway, 1863. (Reported by Robt. McElroy Bibliography of Davis. Also an "enlarged edt." 78pp. of "Eng., the North & South."

614 **BERGERON, Arthur W.**
"They Bore Themselves with Distinguished Gallantry: The Twenty-Second Louisiana Infantry." In: Louisiana History, v.XIII, p. 253-282.

615 ..."Robert C. Kennedy: Louisiana Confederate Secret Agent." In: Louisiana Review, Winter, 1977. (See: O. Edward Cunningham)

616 **BERGERON, Arthur W., Jr.**
"Free men of color in Grey." In: CWH, Sept. 1986, v.32, #3, p. 247-255.

617 ..."General Richard Taylor as a military commander." In:aH., 1982, v.23, p. 25-47.

618 ..."Prison life at Camp Pratt." In: LaH, 1973, v.14, p. 386-391.

619 ..."The twenty-second Louisiana Consolidated Infantry in defense of Mobile,

1864-1865." In: AHQ, 1976, v.38, p. 204-213.

620 **BERGERON, Arthur W. and Lawrence L. Hewitt**
"Boone's Louisiana Battery: A History & Roster." Baton Rouge: Louisiana University Press, 1986. 8vo, dj, 76p, wraps, ills, maps. $12. 500 copies.
..."Mile's Legion: A History & Roster." Baton Rouge: Louisiana University Press, 1983. 8vo, wraps, 104p, ills, maps. $12. 500 copies, sig. both authors, numbered

621 **BERGUIN, H.K.**
"Considerations relative to a Southern Confederacy, with Letters to the North, on the preservation of the Union, & a note from the secret history of the Emancipation in the English West Indies. By a Citizen of North Carolina." Raleigh, 1860. 8vo, wraps, 40pp. $15. Strong worded warning to North for meddling in Southern affairs & threatens secession.

622 **BERINGER, Richard E.**
"There is too much talking: the Congress of the Confederate States of America, 1861-1865." In: N. Dakota Quart., 1975, v.XLIII, p.II, 5-22.

623 ..."A Profile of the Members of the Confederate Congress." (Houston, Tex.) JSH, Nov. 1967, v.XXXIII, #4, p. 518-541. tables. $8.

624 ..."The Unconscious "Spirit of Party" in the Confederate Congress." In: CWH, Dec., 1972, v.18, #4, p.312-33; tables.

625 **BERINGER, Richard E., Herman Hattaway, Archer Jones & William N. Still, Jr.**
"Why the South lost the Civil War." Athens, Ga., University of Georgia Press, 1985. 8vo, cl, dj, xi, 582pp. illus., bibliog. index. $30.

626 **BERKELEY BORDER GUARDS**
"Constitutional Articles of the Berkeley Border Guards. A Volunteer Company, Organized in Martinsburg October 31, 1859." Martinsburg, Va., American & Gazett print, n.d. 8vo, wraps, 8pp. Org. by J.Q.A. Nadenbousch in Berkeley Co., became Co.D, 2nd Va. Inf., CSA. (Shetler-140)

627 **BERKELEY, C. Edmund, Col.**
"The Berkeley Brothers of the Eighth Virginia Regiment, CSA." In: SHSP, 1906, v.XXXIV, p. 371-372.

628 **BERKELEY, F.M., Capt.**
"Imboden's Dash into Charlestown." In: SHSP, 1903, v.XXXI, p. 11-19. From Balt. Sun., Aug. 30-1903.

629 **BERKELEY, Henry Robinson, Private**
"Four Years in the Confederate Artillery.-.The Diary of..." For Virginia Historical Society by Chapel Hill: Univ. of N.C. Press, 1961. Tall 8vo, cl, ports(incl. front) maps, facsm., xxv, 156pp. Edt: William H. Runge. $4, $40, $25-bmk-111, $12-bmk-111.

630 **BERKELEY, Norbonne**
"Eighth Virginia's part in Second Manassas Co., N.B. tells how his Regiment shared in the memorable victory over John Pope." In: SHSP, 1909, v.37, p. 313-316.

631 **BERNARD, George S.**
"Great Battle of the Crater. The work of Mahone & Weisiger at the fight." In: SHSP, 1890, v.XXVIII, p. 204-221.

632 ..."Malvern Hill. Recollections of the fight by one who was there.(Extracts from Official Federal & Confederate Records.)" In: SHSP, 1890, v.XVIII, p. 56-71.

633 ..."War Talks of Confederate Veterans, compiled & edited by..., Petersburg, Va. An address delivered before A.P. Hill Camp of Confederate Veterans, of Petersburg, Va., with addenda giving statements of participants, eye-witnesses & others, in respect to compaigns, battles, prison-life & other war experiences."

Petersburg, Va., Fenn & Owen, Pub. 1892. Tall 8vo, cl, printed dble-column, ports, incl. front, maps(2-fldg) illus., diagrams, xxiii, 335, (2)pp.errata at end. $15, $20, $35, $40-bmk.

..."War Talks of Confederate Veterans." Dayton, Oh., Morningside Press, 1981. $35.

634 ..."The Battle of Crater, in front of Petersburg, July 30, 1864...an address delivered before A.P. Hill Camp Confederate Veterans, Petersburg, Va., June 24, 1890. Published by A.P. Hill Camp C.V., proceeds to be applied towards erection of a monument to Gen. A.P. Hill." Petersburg: Index-Appeal press(1890) 8vo, wraps, 18pp. $10, $7.50, $25-bmk-94.

635 ...See also, S.H.S.P., v.XVIII, p. 3-38. Excerpt originally published in his "War Talks", above, p. 149-230. $50-bmk-121, $6, $20-bmk.

...Reprinted, April, 1937, wraps, 90pp. same imprint on cover, dated 1892. $2.50.

636 **BERNARD, George Smith**
"The Battle of Crater...(being) advance sheets...War Talks of Confederate Veterans..." Petersburg, Va., Feen & Owen, 1892. 8vo, wraps, dbl. column, view of battlefield rear cover, p. 149-230; including a chapter (in the press) advance sheets, p. 1-76. Two pamphlets. $50.

..."War talks CSA Vets." Dayton, Oh., Morningside, 1981. $20-y.

636a **BERNARD, Mountague**
M.A. Chichele Professor of Law & Diplomacy in the University of Oxford. "A Historical Account of the Neutrality of Great Britain during the American Civil War." London: Longmans, Green, Reader & Dyer, 1870. 8vo, cl, xv, (1), 511p, uncut. $250.

637 **BERNATH, Stuart L.**
"Squall Across the Atlantic: The "Peterhoff" Episode." (Houston, Tex.) JSH, Aug. 1968. v.XXXIV, #3, p. 382-401. Running the Union blockade by a British ship, resulting legal difficulties with the US.

638 ..."Squall Across the Atlantic: American Civil War Prize Cases & Diplomacy." Berkeley: University of California Press, 1970. 8vo, cl, x, 229pp. (11pp. bibliog) $15-y, $12-nc, $7

639 **BERNATH, Stuart W.**
"British Neutrality & the Civil War Prize Cases." In: CWH, December 1969, v.XV, #4, p. 320-331. Notes.

640 **BERNEY, Saffold**
"Major Henry Churchill Semple (1822)." In: AlaHQ, 1952, v.14, p. 163-169. port. On his service in CSArmy in Ala. & Tenn., 1862-1865. Winter. 1956, v.18, p. 522-528. (achievements in CSArmy.

641 **BERRIGAN, Joseph Richard**
"B.L. Gildersleeve: Confederate Classicist." In: Classical Bul. 1965, v.XLI, ii, p. 52-55. (Taught during school year & served in army in the summer.)

642 **BERRY, J.M.**
"Prison Life in Camp Douglas." In: CV, Jan. 1903, v.XI, p. 37-38.

643 **BERRY, James H.**
"Report of the committee marking Confederate Graves. Letter of secretary of war. Final report on continuing work on locating & marking graves of C.S.A. dead. House doc. #1105, 62nd Congress, 3rd Session, 1913." Washington: GPO, 1913. 8vo, sewn, 28pp. $3.50, See: "Marking of Graves."

644 **BERRY, Mary F.**
"Negro troops in Blue & Gray: the Louisiana Native Guards, 1861-1863." In: LaH., 1967, v.8, p. 165-190.

645 **BERRY, Thomas F., Col.**
"Four Years with Morgan & Forrest." Oklahoma City: Harlow-Ratliff co., 1914. 12mo, cl, ports(incl. front) illus., xv, 476pp.

$25, $32.50, $40, $75. (fine)$100-y, $175-border, $2.50-bmk-105, $125-bmk-94.

646 ..."Prison experiences on Rock Island." In: CV, Feb. 1912, v.XX, p. 65-69.

647 **BERRYER, Pierre Antoine**
"Replique de M. Berryer pour les Etats-Unis d'Amerique contre M. M. Arman et consorts-audience du 1, Juillet, 1868." Paris: Impr. S. Rocon et cie, 1868. 8vo, wraps, 2p, lf, 55pp. US Gov. suit against French builders of boats for the C.S.N.

648 **BERRYHILL, William Harvey, Lt.**
"The Gentle Rebel: The Civil War letters of 1st Lt. William Harvey Berryhill, Co.D, 43rd Regiment, Mississippi Volunteers." Edt: Mary Miles Jones & Leslie Jones Martin." Yazoo City, Miss., Sassafras Press, 1982, 8vo, cl, 159pp. index. $13.

649 **BERTHRONG, Donald J. & Odessa Davenport**
"A Confederate in the Colorado Gold Fields." Norman: Oklahoma Univ. press, 1970. 8vo, cl, dj, illus., 186pp. $10.

650 **BESSE, Sumner Bradford**
"C.S. Ironclad Virginia, with data & references for a scale model." Newport News, Va., Mariners' Museum Museum Publication #4. 1937. 12mo, stiff wraps (color illus.) Illus., incl. front, facsms, fldg. pl., 47pp. $7.

651 ..."C.S. Ironclad Monitor, with date & references for a scale mode." Museum pub. 2, Newport News, Va., Mariner Museum, 1936. 12mo, stiff wraps, illus., 2fld. pls. front $10.

652 **BESSELEU, T.E.**
"Address of...delivered before the Confed. Vets Ass'n., of Savannah, Ga. "With Stuart & Hampton from Upperville to Gettysburg." p. 11-23. (Savannah: Braid & Hutton, 1893, pp.

653 **BESTON, Daniel Perrin**
"Letters from a Southern Opponent of Sectionalism, Sept. 1860 to June 1861." Edt: Arthur E. Bestor, Jr. (Baton Rouge, La.) JSH, Feb., 1946, v.XII, #1, p. 106-133.

654 **BETHEL, Battle of**
"Topographical sketch of the Battle of Bethel, June 10, 1861." n.p., n.d., 1861? $400-bmk.

655 **BETHEL, Battle of...North Carolina**
"Letter from the Secretary of War...Mar. 31, 1862. Communicating copies of official reports, on file in this department, of the Battle of Bethel on 10th June, 1861." Richmond, Va., 1862. $100-ginzb.30. 8vo, sewn, 31pp. $150-jk-137. Reports of Magruder, D.H. Hill, Wm. D. Stuart, Geo. Randolph, E.B. Montague, W.H. Werth. See: "First North Carolina regiment..." W.H. Bailey, Danial H. Hill, Walter, Clark. 1, p. 69-133 by Maj. Ed. J. Hale.

656 **BETHEL, Elizabeth, Compl.**
"Preliminary Inventory of the War Department Collection of Confederate Records (Record Group 109)." Washington: National Archives & Records Service, General Service Administration, 1957. 4to, wraps, ix, 310pp. $12-bmk, $10-bmk.

657 **BETHEL.,**
n.p., n.d., (186?) 12mo, wraps, 4pp. Harwell-1631 $150.

658 **BETTERSWORTH, John Knox**
"Confederate Mississippi, the People & Politics of a cotton state in wartime." University Station, Baton Rouge, La., Louisiana State University Press, 1943. $12.50, $35-bmk, $20-y. 8vo, cl, dj, front, pls., ports, map, mapliners, facsm., xi, 386pp. bibliog. 351-374.
...Reprint: Peter Smith, 1970, $36-y.

659 ..."The Home Front, 1861-1865." In: A Hist. of Miss., Edt: Rich. A. McLemore, Vol. 1, p. 492-541.

660 ..."Mississippi in the Confederacy, as they saw it." Jackson, Miss., Dept. of Archives & History. Louisiana State Univ. Press.

(1961). 8vo, cl, dj, xxxii, 362pp. illus., maps, facsms., 2vols, $50-bmk-105, $5.95, $18-nc. See: James W. Silver, vol.II.

...1970, N.Y., Kraus reprint, 2vol. in 1; xxxii, 362; xx, 319pp. $36-y, $30.

661 **BETTS, Alexander Davis**
"Experience of a Confederate Chaplain, 1861-1864(i.e., '65), by..., chaplain 30th N.C. troops". Edt: W.A. Betts, n.p., n.d.(Greenville, S.C., 1907) 12mo, wraps, illus., ports, 103, (1)pp. $28.50. Confed. Museum, Coulter-29; reprint: 1963, n.p., 12mo, 109pp. $15.

...N.Y., Scholarly Reprints, 1976. $10, $30-bmk-105.

662 **BETTS, Edward Chambers**
"Early History of Huntsville, Alabama 1804 to 1807." Montgomery, Ala., Brown print, 1916, 8vo, stiff wraps, 122pp. $12.50, CSA & Reconstruction, p. 88-122.

663 **BETTS, Edward E., Compiler**
"Atlas of Chickamauga, Chattanooga & Vicinity." n.p., 1901, folio(40x27"), 13 multicolored plates similar to "Official Records Atlas". Under supervision of the Battlefield Park Comm. $200-bmk.

664 **BETTS, Vicki**
Private & amateur hangings: the lynching (by Confederate troops near Brownsville, Texas) of W.W. Montgomery, Mar. 15, 1863." In: SWHQ, Oct., 1984, p. 145-166.

665 ..."Smith County, Texas in the civil war." Tyler, Texas: Jack T. Greer Memorial Fund of Smith Co., Historical Society, 1979. 8vo, cl, xi, 106pp., illus., bibliog., index. $10.

666 **BEVANS, W.E.**
"Reminiscences of a private." Newport, Ark., Jackson County Historical Society, 1985. 8vo, cl, 40, illus.

667 **BEVENS, W.E.**
"Reminiscences of a Private. Company "G", First Arkansas Regiment Infantry, by...May, 1861, to April, 1865." (Newport, Ark., 1913?) 8vo, cl, ports, 89pp. $85.

...Louisville: Lost Cause Pr., micro-cd. $2.72. Both Dornbusch/Coulter show as 58pp. Newport, Ark., 1977 reprint 96pp. $10.

668 **BEVIER, Robert S.**
"History of the First & Second Missouri Confederate brigades, 1861-1865, (1/2 title, part 1)"personal remiscences, From Waukarusa to Appomattox. An anagraph from my diary of the war." Appended: a list of survivors of the 1st & 2nd Missouri brigades." $250-mcm, $30, $20, $42.50, $50, $95-jk, $200-bmk. St. Louis: Bryan, Brand & Co., 1879. 8vo, cl, front(ports)xii, 480, 27pp. (Ark. Hist. Comm., State Participation in civil war.)

...N.Y., Scholarly Press, (c.1976) Regency Press...$30.

669 **BEVIER, Robt. S.**
"The Confederate First & 2nd Missouri..." Florissant, Mo., Inland Print., 1985, Lim. Edt., 750 copies. $25.

670 **BEYMER, William Gilmore**
"On Hazardous Service. Scouts & Spies of the North & South. Illus-Howard Pyle." N.Y., Lond: Harper & bros., 1912, $7.50. 8vo, cl, color illus., ports, xiii, 287pp. $10. $25-nc. From chaps. in Harper's. Confederates: Williams, Bowie, Grenhow & Beall.

671 ..."Williams, C.S.A." In: Harper's, Sept. 1909, v.CXIX, p. 498-510. Incident of June 8, 1863, Franklin, Tenn., "First rebel officers hung during war, as spies."

672 **BIBLIOGRAPHIES ,**
Broadfoot's Guide to CW Books; Coulter, E. Morton; Dornbusch, Charles E.; Harwell, Richard B., In Tall Cotton, "Cornerstones", "Confed. 100." Nevins, Alan; Robertson, Jas. I.; Kennerly, Sarah Law; "Bibliog. of State Participation..."; Baxter, Charles N.; Breckenridge, James M.; Crandall, Marjorie L.; "Civil War Lib-

rary."; "Finding list of Military Biographies."; Freeman, Douglas S., "South to Posterity"; Grimes, Maxine M.; Hargrett, Lester; Hodgkins, Wm. Henry; Krick, Robt. K., Neale books; McCabe, Jas. D.; Mebane, John; Morrison, Hugh A.; Nevins, Alan; Nicholson, Jno. Page; Pumphrey, Wm. F.; "Rare CSA Books"; Randolph, J.W. & Co.; Robinson, Raymond V.; Ryder CSArchives (Tufts College); Snowden, Yates; Swem, Earl, Va.; "The South: History & Literature.: Watters, Willard O.; Wynne, Thos. H.; Bartlett, John R.

673 **BICKEL, Karl A.**
"Robert E. Lee in Florida." In: FHQ, July, 1948, v.XXVII, #1, p. 59-66.

674 **BIDDLE, George C.**
"Florida Prepares for War, 1869-1861." In: FHQ, October, 1972, v.LI, #2, p. 143-152.

675 **BIDGOOD, Joseph Virginius**
"Further recollections of Second Cold Harbor. By Joseph B. Bidgood, Late Adj. 32nd Va. Inf." In: SHSP, 1909, v.XXXVII, p. 319-320.

676 ..."List of General Officers & their staffs in the Confederate Army, furnished by Virginia, as far as I have been able to get them." In: SHSP, 1910, v.XXXVIII, p. 156-183, p. 290-291.

677 **BIECIUK, Hank & H.G. "Bill" Corbin**
"Texas Confederate County Notes & Private Scrip. A comprehensive listing of currency printed, issued & used by Texas counties, cities & private individuals during the period of the Civil War." (Tyler, Texas, 1961) Private printed. 8vo, wraps, facsms, 110pp.(2)p. blak. $5, $20-jk-129.

678 **BIER, Justus**
"A forgotten work by Ferdinand von Miller, the younger, a contribution to the history of Confederate monuments." In: KyHSR, Apr. 1956, v.54, p. 125-133. The bronze figure of CSA memorial at Louisville, Ky., cast by Miller in Munich. Sketch.

679 ...Bibliography of State Participation in the Civil War Dept. Library, Subject Cat. #6-" 3rd Edt. Washington: GPO, 1913. Tk. 8vo, wraps, x, 1140pp. $15, $25, $35, $45
...Reprint, 1961, Burt Franklin, N.Y., $29.50, $45. First Edt., 1897; 2nd Edt., 1899; Suppl. to 2nd Edt., 1902.
...2nd Edt., 1899-"Military Literature in the War Department Library relating chiefly to the participation of the individual states in the War for the Union. Dir: Hon. Russell A. Alger, Sect. War. Subject Cat. #6.

679a **BIERCE, Ambrose**
"Tales of Soldiers & Civilians." San Francisco: E.I.G. Steele, 1891. 16mo, cl, 300p. $150 Bm. Entered here only as a literary figure & experiences in the war. Some travels in the South.
..."Battle Sketches." London: Printed at the Shakespeare Head Press Saint Aldates Oxford for the First Edition Club Bedford Square. Imp. 8vo, slip case, (6), 88, (1)p. 1930. $100 Bm.

680 **BIGELOW, John**
"France & the Confederate Navy 1862-1868, an International Episode." N.Y., Harper & Bros., 1888. $27.50mcm, $10, $20, $40-bmk. 12mo, cl, x, 247pp. index, 4p-ads. From Northern point of view. Was US consul-general in France during the war.
...Louisville: Lost Cause pr., micro-card, $4.21.
...N.Y., Bergman print, 1968, $7.50.

681 ..."Lest we Forget. Gladstone, Morley & the Confederate loan of 1863; a rectification by John Bigelow." N.Y., De Vinne Press, 1905. 8vo, wraps, 65pp.

682 ..."The Southern Confederacy & the Pope." In: NAR, 1893, v.157, p. 462-275. See: Father Jerome's CSA & the Vatican.

683 BIGELOW, Martha M., Edt.
"Plantation Lessee Problems in 1864." (Houston, Tex.) JSH., August, 1961. v.XXVII, #3, p. 354-367.

684 ..."Vicksburg: Experiment in Freedom." (Jackson, Miss.) Jour. Miss. Hist., Feb. 1964, v.XXVI, #1, p. 28-44. Working slaves during war.

685 BIGHAM, Robert Williams (Ga.)
"Joe: A Boy in the War-times." Nashville, Tenn., Sunday School Dept. Methodist Pub. House., (1889) 16mo, decr. cl, plate, 226pp. Scenes & exp. home life during war. $8, $15.

686 BIGLOW, John
"The Confederate Diplomatists & their shirt of Nessus, a chapter of secret history." In: Cent., May 1891, v.20, p. 113-126.

687 ...Edwin DeLeon denial, p. 638. $20.

688 BILBO, William
"The Past, Present, & Future of the Southern Confederacy: an oration delivered by..., in the city of Nashville, Oct. 12, 1861." Nashville, Tenn., J.D.W. Green & Co., 1861. 8vo, wraps, 47pp. $10, $85.

689 BILL ,
to provide more effectually for the reduction & redemption of the currency, A. Senate, Dec. 26, 1864." (Richmond, Va., 1864.) 8vo, sewn, 8, (3)pp. Not in Crand/Harw.

690 BILL, Alfred Hoyt
"The Beleagured City Richmond, 1861-1865." " Richmond must not be given up; it shall not be given up!" Robert E. Lee." N.Y., Alfred A. Knopf, 1946. 8vo, cl, dj, illus.(incl. front) 2fldg. maps, xiv, (1), 313, xviii, (i)pp. $5, $7.50, Atg. copy-$10, 2nd Edt. $4.

691 BILLMYER, M.J.
"The Last Charge at Appomattox." From "Baltimore Sun", Feb. 7, 1906. In: SHSP, 1905, v.XXXIII, p. 191-192.

691a BINGHAM, R. W.
"Justice for the South." In: CV, Sept./Oct. 1987, ns, v.35, #5, p.10-17. Reprinted: Mobile Daily Item, Apr. 26, 1910. Address before Sons CV plate.

692 BINGHAM, Robert
"Annual address of President State Library & Historical Association of N.C., at 9th Annual Session. Raleigh, N.C., Oct. 13, 1908. "Secession in Theory, as the Framers of the Constitution Viewed it; Secession as Sustained by the U.S.A.; Secession as Attempted by the C.S.A." Ashville, N.C., Col. R. Bingham, Supt. of the Bingham School. wraps, 8vo, 32pp.

693 ..."An ex-slaveholder's view of the negro question in the south." By Col. R. Bingham. (Ashville, N.C., Printing Co., 1900) 8vo, wraps, 16pp.

694 ..."Sectional Misunderstandings." (Ashville, N.C., Hackney & Moale Co., 1904?) cover title, 8vo, wraps, 20pp. Reprinted: from North American Review of Sept. 1904, cover title-"The misunderstandings between the sections of our common country." (secession)
...Do: Ashville, 1911 & 22pp. wraps(?) $1.50. If dissolved, reverts back to orig. states. $12-bmk.

695 ..."Response to a toast: "The Status of the South in the past; the decadence of the status; Its restoration". at Annual banquet New York Southern Society of Walforf, Dec. 14, 1904. Repeated Mar. 9, 1905: Pen & Plate Club, Ashville, N.C., 8vo, wraps, (16)pp.

696 ..."A reminiscence of 1863." (Ashville, N.C., 1916) 8vo, wraps, 8pp, Dornbusch-822. From Bingham H.S. yearbook for 1916.

697 ..."We saved Gen. Lee's communications with Richmond. Two companies of North Carolina defends bridge across the South Anna, June 26, 1863." In: CWTI, DEc., 1966, v.5, #8, p. 22-27, illus., ports.

697 **BINKLEY, William C.**
"The contribution of Walter Lynwood Fleming to Southern Scholorship." Offprint: JSH, 1939, v.V, #2, 12pp., 8vo, wraps, $10.

699 **BIOGRAPHICAL Catalogue of Portraits**
in the Confederate Memorial Institute, "The Battle Abbey"." Richmond, Va., R.E. Lee Camp. #1, n.d., 8vo, cover title, 2-pls (1-color) 45pp. $10-nc.

700 **BIOGRAPHICAL MEMORANDA**
of the Confederate Veterans of Jackson County, Arkansas. In: "Stream of History", July 1974, v.12, p. 3-32.

701 **BIOGRAPHICAL Sketches & Pictures**
of Co. B., Confederate Veterans of Nashville, Tennessee. Nashville: Foster & Webb, 1902. 12mo, wraps, 78-ports, 88pp. $12.50. Oct. 12, 1895 some Veterans met at Cheatham Bivouac, forming a military co., & on Nov. 14, 1895, sworn in, 111-members. Margin notes many deaths.
...Brentwood, Tenn., July 2, 1974(B.P. Barney) 12mo, stiff wraps, ports, 88, (8)pp. Addenda: M.M. Barnes-"Memarabilia of a Confederate Soldier." reprint, $5, $12-bmk-84.

702 **BIRCH, A.C.**
"The Confederate Constitution." In: Ala. State Bar. Assn., Annual meet, July 1/2, 1926. p. 108-122.

703 **BIRCH, Edmund Pendleton**
"The Devil's Visit to "Old Abe." By Rev. E.P. Birch, of La Grange, Ga. Written on the occasion of Lincoln's Proclamation for prayer & fasting after the battle of Manassas. Revised & improved expressly for the La Grange Reporter, by the author." (La Grange, Ga., 1862?) 16mo, caption title, 8pp. Crandall-3134. Satirical verse.
..."The Refined Poetry of the South (from the "Southern Confederacy") The Devil's Visit to "Old Abe". By Rev. E.P. Birch, of La Grange, Ga." 8vo, caption title, 4p-folder. Monaghan-#119, A variant of above.

704 **BIRD'S Eye View**
of Confederate Prison Pen at Salisbury, N.C., taken in 1864. Cotton Factory, Old Blacksmith Shop, used Guard House & afterword as Dead House, Old Well, 4,5,6,7,8, & 9 brick houses used as officers prison, Confederate Hdqrs., Soup House, hold from which prisoners tunneled and escaped. Boston, N.Y. & Chicago: J.H. Buford Sons, Lith., 1886-C.A. Craus(copywr.) Lithograph: 28x38" tinted. 23x34. $25, $450-bmk-98.

705 **BIRD, W.H.**
"Stories of the Civil War, by W.H. Bird of Co.C, 13th Regiment, Alabama Vols." Columbus, Ga. (1910?) 12mo, wraps, 39pp. Dornbusch has TxU: Columbiana, Advocate Print(n.d.), with 60, (1)pp.

706 **BIRDSONG, James C.(ook)**
"Brief sketches of the North Carolina State Troops in the War between the States. Sketches include: 1st, 2nd, 3rd, 4th, 6th, 7yh, 11th, 12th, 13th, 37th Regs., together with 1st. Bat. hvy. artly., 2nd bat. lt. infty. return of flag to Co. I, 6th reg. N.C. troops, Gen. Lane's Brig., sketch of Henry L. Wyatt, 1st Confed. Martyr, Lane's brig. Corps. Sharpshooters. Compil. Edt. by..., Ex-State Librarian. printed under resolution ratified Mar. 6, 1893." Raleigh, N.C., Jos. Daniels, state print., Edwards & Broughton, 1894. 8vo, wraps, color-flags, 213pp. Full lt. $275-bmk-105, $45, $18, $20, $25, $28.50, $32.50, $35.

707 ..."The Petersburg Grays." (List: officers & privates in Petersburg "A Grays", 4th Va. Batt., After: Co.B, 12th Va. Reg.

Mahone's Brig. A.P. Hill's Corps." In: SHSP, 1908, v.XXXVI, p. 360-362.

708 BIRKHIMER, William Edward, Maj.
"Service of Graduates in the Civil War." In: "A Century of U.S. Military Academy at West Point, 1802-1902, addresses & histories." Wash: GPO, 1904. 2vols. 4to, p. (632)-749. map, ports: Jeff Davis, Bragg, Lee, J.E. Johnston & A.S. Johnston.

709 BIRNEY, Alison
"Civil war sketches." In: Boston Pub. Lib. Qrt. Jan. 1951, v.4, p. 27-33, view. On Adalbert John Volck's sketches of the civil war, 1861-1863.

710 BISHOP, Carter R., Capt.
"The Cockade City of the Union." Petersburg, Virginia. Written for the Council of the City of Petersburg, by-..."n.p., 1907. 8vo, wraps, fldg. map. 16pp. Largely devoted to the War. $20.

711 BISHOP, Harry G.
"Beau Sabreur." In: Mil. Engineer, 1934, v.XXVI, p. 98-100. Jeb Stuart reconnoiters McClellan's army on the Chickahominy in '62.

712 BISHOP, Merrill & Joseph Roemer
"The Gentleman Commander. Character Portrayal of Robert E. Lee." Oklahoma City, et.al., Economy Co(1937) Copy. 1936. Texas School adoption, stamped. 12mo, decr. cl, port(front) illus., 224pp. $3.50, $5.50

713 BISSET, Johnson
"The Mysteries of Chancellorsville Who Killed Stonewall Jackson." N.Y., Hobson Book press, (1945) 16mo, wraps, xi, (1), 37pp. $3.75, $15-nc, $20, $7.50-y. Various authors: Early, Wilbourn, Moorman & Official Records.

713a "BITS of Camp Life."
N.Y., n.d. (1870?). 5 x 6 1/2", wraps, ills with 5p color lithos, pict. covers, foraging, letter writing, sentry duty, etc. $75-bmk.

714 BITTLE, George C.
"Fighting Men View the Western War, 1862-1864." In: FHQ, v.XLVII, #1, July, 1968, p. 25-33.

715 BIVINS, Viola Cobb (Mrs. J.K.)
"Echoes of the Confederacy." Longview, Texas: Mrs. J.K. Bivins(1950) (Dallas: Banks Upshaw Co.) $12.50, $20. 8vo, cl, dj, illus., (incl. front) (16), 197pp.

716 ..."Memoirs & biographical sketches of East Texas Pioneers." n.p., n.d. (1930). 8vo, cl, front, plates, ports, 138pp. $27.50, $40. Has one chapter on Cullen Baker. Author was wife of a CSA veteran, Longview, Texas.

717 BLACK HORSE TROOP.
Some reminiscences of this famous command. In: SHSP, 1902, v.XXX, p. 142-146.

718 ..."The Members of the House of Delegates, who served in the famous body. Pilcher, Lewis & Talliaferro. A brief sketch of the Black Horse & its commanders." In: SHSP, 1896, v.XXIV, p. 218-225. From Richmond "Times", Feb. 23, 1896.

719 BLACK, Edna M., Mrs.
"Daughter of Old Kentucky." N.Y., Fortuny's Print, 1940. 12mo, cl, 87pp. In Louisville during war, emigrates west.

720 BLACK, James Conquest Cross
"Address of..., on Confederate Memorial Day, Apr. 26, 1890." Augusta, Ga., 1890, 8vo, wraps, 20pp.

721 ..."Confederate memorial record. Anniversary address Confederate memorial day, April 26, 1890, by...Published for distribution as a presentation of historical truth & fact..., by an ex-Confederate." Augusta, Ga., Confederate pub. co., 1890, 8vo, wraps, 20pp. Dornbusch-2611.

722 ..."Address of J.C.C. Black, at the Unveiling of the Hill statue, Atlanta, Ga. May 1, 1886." In: SHSP, 1886, v.XIV, p. 163-179.

723 BLACK, John Logan, Col. CSA
"Crumbling defenses; or, memoirs & re-

miniscences of...Edt. & Pub. by Eleanor D. McSwain." Macon, Ga. (J.W. Burke Co) 1960. 8vo, cl, facsms(some fldg.) port, map, 133pp. $7.50, $15.

724 **BLACK, May Gardner**
"Confederate surgeons & hospitals." In: CV, May, 1928, v.XXXVI, p. 183-185.

725 **BLACK, Patti Carr, Compl.**
"Guide to Civil War source material in Department of Archives & History State of Mississippi, compiled by...Edt: by Charlotte Capers, Maxyne Madden Grimes." Jackson, Miss., Dept. Archives & Hist., 1962. 8vo, wraps, 71pp.

726 ..."Civil War Manuscripts in the Mississippi Department of Archives & History." In: JMH, July 1961, v.XXIII, #3, p. 164-195.

727 **BLACK, Robert C., III**
"The Railroads of the Confederacy." Chapel Hill, Univ. North Carolina pr. (1952, N.Y., Van Rees Press.) 8vo, ck, dj, illus., facsms, maps, xiv, 360pp. large fldg. map of RRy. at end. notes & bibliog. p. 301-360, index. $6, $10, $16, $15-atg.

728 ..."Railroads in the Confederacy." In: CWH, September 1961, v.VII, #3, p. 231-238.

729 ..."Thoughts on the Confederacy." In: Donald Sheehan & Harold C. Syrett, Edts: "Essays in Amer. Historiography: Papers presented in honor of Allan Nevins." N.Y., Columbia Univer. Pr., 1960, p. 20-36, notes. Causes for the failure of the Confederacy but survival of its "essential substance."

730 ..."The Railroads of Georgia in the Confederate War Effort." (Baton Rouge, La.) Nov. 1947, v.XIII, #4, p. 511-534. $10.

731 **BLACK, Sallie M.A.**
"Kindness to Enemies (Poem)." (Columbia, S.C., 1901. 8vo, wraps, illus., 16pp. Rich. Kirkland heroically brings water to a wounded enemy.

732 **BLACKBURN, Benjamin M.**
"Life & Character of Jefferson Davis." Atlanta, 1905, Atlanta Chap., UDC. 8vo, wraps, 22pp. Address in Georgia House of Representatives, June 3, 1905. On life & character of Jeff. Davis.

733 **BLACKBURN, George Andrew, Edt.**
"The Life Work of John L. Girardeau." Columbia, S.C., State Print, 1916. 12mo, cl, 432pp. $9. CSA Chaplain, 23rd S.C.V.

734 **BLACKBURN, James Knox Polk**
"Reminiscences of Terry Rangers." (Austin, Texas) Pub. by Littlefield Fund for Southern History, Univ. of Texas., 1919 (Orig. pub.: Southwestern Hist. Quar., XXII, p. 38-77; 143-179. $10, $15, Tall 8vo, wraps, vii, 79pp. index. $17.50, 1918, $75.
...Louisville: Micro-cd. $2.61, $10, $22.50, $25, $37.40, $60-ginz.
...Austin, Texas, Ranger Press civil war series #2, 8vo, wraps (1979) vii, 79pp. $8. Fac. reprint of 1919 edt., with foreword by Steve L. Perkins. The 8th Texas cavalry.

735 **BLACKBURN, John S. & W.N. McDonald**
"A Grammar-school history of the United States; from the discovery of America to the present time." Baltimore: W.J.C. Dulany & co., 1871. 12mo, cl, maps, 241pp. $12. "A history free from false statements & misrepresentations that fill Northern hist.
...Do: 1888, xii, 248pp.

736 **BLACKBURN, John W.**
"Gray jackets with blue collars." Beaver Dam, Ky., Embry Newspapers (1963) 12mo, pls., ports, xi, (1), 104, 8, (1)pp. op. Index, 8pp-Dornbusch-406A.

737 **BLACKBURN, Joseph Cial Styles**
"Address of..., at unveiling of statue of Gen. John C. Breckinridge, at Lexington, Ky., Nov. 16, 1887." Frankfurt, Ky., Western Argus, 1887. 8vo, wraps, 8pp. cover title, printed in double column. Dornbusch-2628.

738 **BLACKFORD, William Willis, Lieut-Col.**
"War Years with Jeb Stuart." N.Y., Charles Scribner's Sons, 1945. 8vo, cl, dj, illus., ports (incl. front) append: Rosters & index, xiii, 322pp. $10, $15, $25-bmk-89, $23-nc.

...same, for 1946 $35-op, $7.50

...(1945) same as above, but for front. port of Blackford, taken from earlier photo. & opposite copy. pg., dedicated to Capt. Jas. C. Motley (1920-1944). Paper is thicker than "wartime" of 1945 edt. (1945, 1946, $3-dj) $4.50, $12-y

739 ..."An Incident of Lee's Surrender." In: SHSP, 1885, v.XIII, p. 454-455.

740 **BLACKFORD, Charles Minor**
"The trials & trial of Jefferson Davis. A paper read before the 12th Annual meeting of the Virginia State Bar Ass'n., held at Old Point Comfort, Va., July 17-19, 1900." Richmond, Va., J.T. West, 1900. 8vo, wraps, 46pp. $7.50, $12.50, $15.

...Also in Va. State Bar Ass'n. 12th annual report, 1900, p. 232-274.

...In: SHSP, 1901, v.XXIX, p. 45-81.

...Lynchburg, Va., J.P. Bell Co., 1901. 8vo, wraps, 70pp. cloth, $12.50. $75-b, Atg. Pres. Inscrip. $750-bmk-105.

741 ..."Annals of the Lynchburg Home Guards, prepared by request, by Charles M. Blackford chairman of comm., & pub. by the Company." Lynchburg, Va., John W. Rohr, print., 1891. 12mo, cl, illus., ports, 185pp. Dornbusch-. $2.50-bmk, $16.50, $300-bmk-106, $28.50.

742 ..."Campaign & Battle of Lynchburg, Va. delivered by request of Garland-Rodes Camp of Confederate Veterans, Lynchburg, Va. June 18, 1901." (Lynchburg, Va., J.P. Bell co, 1901) 12mo, wraps, front(port) 72pp. Roster. $150-bmk- 105, $25-bmk, $5.

...Reprint, SHSP, v.XXX(1902), p. 276-332.

743 **BLACKFORD, Eugene, Maj., 5th Ala.**
"Report of Major Blackford, of Sharpshooters of Rone's Brigade. July 17, 1863. In: SHSP, 1885, v.XIII, p. 178-179.

744 **BLACKFORD, Launcelot Minor**
"The great John B. Minor & his cousin Mary face the war: correspondence between the professor of law & Lynchburg Blackfords, 1860-1964." Virginia Mag. Hist. & Biog., Oct. 1953, v.LXI, p. 439-449.

...Reprint, 11pp, wraps. $8. See also his "Mine Eyes Have Seen, etc."

745 ..."The Spirit of '76 & the Spirit of '61." In: SHSP, 1895, v.XXIII, p. 336.

746 ..."Mine Eyes Have Seen the Glory. The story of a Virginia Lady, Mary Berkeley Minor Blackford, 1802-1896, who taught her sons to hate slavery & to love the Union." Cambridge, Mass., Harvard Univ. Press, 1954. 8vo, cl, dj, ports (incl. front) facsm., chart, xix, 292pp., notes & index, p. 261-292. $12, $6., $7., $20-atg. Though against slavery (she owned one to her death) & pro-Union, she furnished five sons to the CSArmy.

747 **BLACKFORD, Susan Leigh Colston, Mrs.**
"Memoirs of life in & out of the army of Virginia during the War between the States. Compiled by Susan Leigh Blackford from original & contemporaneous correspondence & diaries. Annotated & edited exclusively for the private use of their family by her husband, Charles Minor Blackford." Lynchburg, Va., J.P. Bell, 1894-1896. 8vo, cl, vi, 292; 279, viiipp. Edition of 35 copies printed, not published.

748 ..."Memoir. Chapter one of life in and out of the army in Virginia during the War Between the States. Reproduced by photo-lithography, for the Lynchburg Historical Society from the original, printed in 1894." Lynchburg, Va., J.P. Bell Print,

1959. 8vo, wraps, plate, 28pp. $30-bmk-116.

749 ..."Letters from Lee's Army; or, memoirs of life in & out of the army in Virginia during the War betwen the States. Compl. by Susan Leigh Blackford, from original & contemporaneous memoirs, correspondence & diaries. Annotated by her husband Charles Minor Blackford. Edited & abridged for publication by Charles Minor Blackford, III." N.Y., Scribner's Sons, 1947. sm. 8vo, cl, dj, vii, 312pp. $7.50, $10, Pres $35-bmk-116, Atg $13-C.Hill, $25, $20-bmk. Some copies in full red calf. $20.
...Reprint, 1962 in cloth ($6) paper, $1.25, "Encore Library of the Civil War." $2.25

750 BLACKFORD, William M., Hon.
"Blackford Letters, 1860-1865." Jacksonville, Fla., Historical Records Survey, WPA, 1939. 4to, stiff wraps, typescript:v.1(1860) 101pp.; v.2(1862-1863) (103)-265pp.; v.3-(1864-1865) (266)-435pp. Blackford was editor of the "Virginian", of Lynchburg, Va., a banker.

750a "BLACKHORSE TROOP of Fauquier County, (Va.), The
Compiled by the Black Horse Chap., U.D.C. (Va.)" Warrenton, Va., 1972. 8vo, wraps, 32p. ills, ports. $20. See: W. W. Blackford. Roster CSA soldiers buried in the Warrenton Cemetery. Sketch of Clack Horse Troops, 4th Va. Cav.

751 BLACKMAN, Ed Lewis
"Our relations with America." Manchester, Eng., Committee of Manchester (Eng.) Southern Club., 1863. Wanted immediate recognition of South, a reply to Richard Cobden's speech in House of Commons.

752 BLACKMAN, Edward Lewis
"Shall we recognize the Confederate States? The question considered in three letters with reference to our national interest & duty, & to slavery as illustrated in the history of our West Indian possessions" reprinted "Ipswich Journal, with remarks suggested by the present state of affairs." Ipswich, Henry Knights, 1863. 8vo, wraps, 24pp. (Western Reserve Hist. Soc.)

753 BLACKMAN, R.H., Mrs.
"History of the Shreveport (La.) chapter, United Daughters of the Confederacy, 1898-1948." In: UDCMag., Sept. 1948, v.11, #9, p. 16-18.

754 BLACKMAN, W.H.H.
"Johnson's Island. A visit to the Confederate Cemetery of the Prison, with a list of those buried there." In: SHSP, 1899, v.XXVII, p. 102-108.

755 BLACKMORE, Bettie Ridley & Rebecca Crosthwaite Ridley
"Behind the Lines in Central Tennessee, 1863-1865. The Journal of Bettie Ridley Blackmore. Edt: Sarah Ridley Trimble." In: Tenn. HQ, 1953, v.XII, p. 48-80.

756 BLACKNALL, O(scar) W(illiams)
pseud: David Dodge. "Domestic economy in the Confederacy." In: Atl. Month., 1886, v.LVIII, p. 241.

757 BLACKNALL, O.W.
"Lincoln as the South should know him. Can the man who suffered his lieutenant, Sherman, to ruthlessly devastate twice as much Southern territory as all Belgium combined be the Southern ideal? Can the man whose life work was to tear from the Declaration of Independence its immortal part, its very soul, "That governments derive their just powers from the consent of the governed," be the American ideal, if the truth is looked full in the face? Second edition." Reprinted by Manly's Battery Chapter Children of the Confederacy, Raleigh, N.C. (Edwards & Broughton Co., Raleigh, N.C., 1915) Signed: O.W. Blacknall, Kittrell, N.C., 8vo, wraps, 21pp. $4.
...Raleigh, N.C., Commercial Print, 1915,

8vo, wraps, 23pp. $3. Dislike of Lincoln, "let South idealize its own kitch & kind."

758 **BLACKSHEAR, Perry Lynnfield**
"Blacksheariana: genealogy, history, anecdotes, a compilation." Atlanta (Ga.), 1954. 8vo, cl, xxx, 476pp., coat-of-arms, facsms., ports, views, etc. "Diaries of Capt. James Appleton Blackshear CSA in the civil war & while teaching school in Sumter co., Ga., 1862-1865. (p. 190-204) "Civil War letters of James Everard Blackshear, Savannah, 16 Dec., 1864, (p. 213-214).

759 **BLACKWELL, Robert**
"Original Acrostics on some of the Southern States, Confederate Generals & various other persons & things." St. Louis, 1869, Southwestern book co., 12mo, illus., 100pp., iv, $7.50, $12.50, $15-y, $35-bmk.
..."Original acrostics on all the states & presidents of the United States, & various other subjects, religious, political, personal." Nashville, Tenn., for the author, 1861. 12mo, cl, x, (11)-224pp. illus., incl. front, ports.
...Loudoun Co., Va. 1863, Z.F. Milbourn. 24pp., Crand-3135, cover title, wraps.
...Macon, Ga., John L. Jenkins, 1862. 32pp., wraps. Harwell-3135.
...Cincinnati: The author, 1868. 12mo, co, x, (13)-224pp. illus., ports.
...Nashville, Tenn., The author, 1870, 12mo, wraps, 75pp., illus.
...Baltimore: J. Young, 1873, 12mo, wraps, 169, 9, (1)p. front(port) illus.

759a **BLACKWOOD'S Edinburgh Magazine, Dec. 1863**
"Reviews of Books on the Civil War." 12mo, wraps, 19p. $30. Includes Fremantle & 'Battlefields of the South.' (Rowe).

760 **BLADA, V. (pseud.)**
"Sketches from the Civil War in North America, 1861, '62, '63." London: 1863. 4to, "series of 45 sketches, chiefly scenes in CSArmy, really pub. in Baltimore. Only 12-copies struck off for friends, plates destroyed for fear of exposing artist, a dentist in Baltimore. Sabin-5709.
...See: Dr. A.J. Volck.

761 ...Tarrytown, N.Y., Magazine of History, Extra #60. 1917. $7.50. 8vo, wraps, reprint of above '63. cl, front, 24pp.(i.e., 30 etchings) 12x9"
...(Volck, Adalbert J.)

762 ..."Confederate War Etchings." n.p., (Baltimore, 1863?) 29 plates & "Index" leaf, printed on india paper mounted on cardboard, & loose in cardboard folder. 8x10 1/2". $40, $65, $82.50, $150, Auct-'63 @ $230. Issued under anagram - "V. Blada", but uncertain if there was ever a London edt., although it's said only a dozen copies made; however LC notes 200 copies of 30 etchings. Plates were said to have been sent to London for that edt. but do not know if genuine. Goodspeed notes plates destroyed but before this Murray Halstead pulled some impressions.
...Reissued "Confederate War Etchings", (cover title) n.p., n.d.-Phila., c.1880-1894) 100 sets printed, numbered 1-29, india pap. mounted on white paper, 15x11 1/2". Index leaf printed red ink, in portfolio, boards, cloth back & ties. $100, $50, $150. Goodspeed's notes a recently found pub.; notice shows it a Porter & Coates, who bought the plates & printed this edition. Says 1st edt. no more than 4/5 sets known.
...Same edt., 29 plates on India paper, mounted, with index. Cloth back portfolio, probably issued after the Porter & Coates. Goodspeed's (cat-466) $30. See also: McLaughlin, James F.

763 **BLAIN, William T.**
"William Felix Brantley, 1830-1870." In: Jour. Miss. Hist., Nov. 1975, v.XXXVII, #4, p. 359-380. Became Gen. in CSArmy, org. "Wigfall's Rifles, in Army of Tenn., 15th Miss. & in Walthall's Brig.

764 **BLAINE, James Gillespie (Augusta, Me.)**
"Jefferson Davis Amnesty." Wash: G.P.O., 1876. 8vo, sewn, caption title, 32pp. H.R., Jan. 10, 1876. $5, $8.50, $10-y.

764a **LAIR, Asa Jordan**
"Asa Jordan Blair's part in the Civil War." In: AHQ, Fall 1958, v.20, #3, p.476-8.

765 **BLAIR, Carvell Hull (C.H.M.)**
"Submarines of the Confederate Navy." 1862-1865. Annapolis, Md., 1952. 8vo, wraps, views, 7pp. $7. From: U.S. Navy Inst. Pro., Oct., 1952, v.78, p. 1114-1121.

766 ..."An historical sketch of the Confederate Navy." In: Unit. Ser., May 1903, v.XLI, p. 1155-1183.

767 **BLAIR, Gist**
"Lincoln, Jefferson Davis & Francis Preston Blair." In: Ky. H.S.R., May, 1917, v.XV, p. 35-40. Blairs trip to Richmond, confers with Davis in 1864.

768 ..."Annals of Silver Spring." In: Columbia Hist. Soc. Rec., 1918, v.XXI, p. 155-185. Mrs. Jeff. Davis's letter to Blair on capture of Davis by Federals. (June 6, 1865 letter)

769 **BLAIR, John L.**
"Morgan's Ohio Raid." In: FCHQ, July, 1962, v.36, #3, p. 242-271.

770 **BLAIR, Maria, Miss**
"Matthew Fontaine Maury." By... Honorary president of Matthew Fontaine Maury Ass'n. Richmond, Va. A paper read at annual meeting May 13, 1918. Publication ordered by the Association." Richmond, Va., Whittet & Shepperson, 1918. 8vo, cover title, port, 13pp. (1)p. $6.50, $20, $15, $12.50-y

771 **BLAIR, Ruth, Miss**
"Confederate Military Records. Georgia Military Districts. 1st & 2nd: Chatham, Bryan & Effingham; 2nd: Liberty, Tattnail & McIntosh." In: Ga. H.Q., Dec. 1927, v.XI, #4, p. 344-347; Mar. 1928, v.XII, #1, p. 105-108; v.XII, #2, p. 199-202.

772 **BLAIR, W.C.**
"Realism & romanticism of a fourteen-year-old Tennessee soldier boy." (Austin, Texas) Austin Print Co.(1915?) 12mo, wraps, 112pp. Dornbusch-2612. Intro: J.M. Dunn, Princ. State School for the Blind.

773 **BLAKE, Harold R.**
"The compromises in the Federal Constitution." In: CV, July 1917, v.25, #7, p. 309-314. As it relates to the CSA, secession, etc.

774 **BLAKE, Minnie E.**
"The Quantrill raid, with introductory poems." (Lawrence, Kan. 1929) 8vo, cl, 4, 11-42pp., incl. illus(port) $15.

775 **BLAKE, Nelson Morehouse**
"William Mahone of Virginia (1826-1895). Soldier & Political Insurgent." Richmond, Va., Garrett & Massie, 1935. 8vo, cl, port, illus., maps, xv, (1), 323pp. $7.50, $10, $12.50, $15, $30-y, $35-nc. CW-p. 38-70, Reconst-70-111, $50-dj, $40-bmk

776 **BLAKE, Thomas Ballard**
"Retreat from Richmond, Colonel Crutchfield & the "Artillery Brigade" Interesting Reminiscences." In: SHSP, 1897, v.XXV, p. 285-287.

777 **BLAKE, W.H.**
"Coal barging in war times, 1861-1865." In: Gulf States Hist. Mag., May, 1903, v.1, #6. p. 409-412.

777a **BLAKE, William (pseud)**
See: William James Blech.

778 **BLAKELY, John R.**
"Early civil war days in Covington & northern Kentucky (1861-1862)." In: Christopher Gist HSP, 1950-1951, 106-17 leaves.

779 **BLAKELY, Stephen L.**
"Belle Boyd (1844-1900), a phantasy based on logic." In: Christopher Gist Hist. Soc. Paper, 1952-1953, leaves, 80-91. Political history of the US since 1865 had the war been won by the CSA.

780 **BLANCHARD, Julian**
"An essay for a North Carolina Confederate note (1863)." In: Essay-proof jour., July 1954, v.12, p. 139-142. facsms.

781 **BLAND, Schuyler Otis**
"Robert E. Lee Memorial Foundation. An address delivered at acquition of title to Stratford." Washington, DC, 1930.

782 **BLANDFORD CEMETERY, Petersburg, Va.**
"Unveiling of Soldier's Monument, June 7, 1890." In: SHSP, 1889, v.XVII, p. 388-403. Twenty thousand Confederaet Dead."

783 **BLANKENSHIP, Lela McDowell**
"Fiddles in the Cumberlands." See: Armanda McD. Burns.
..."When yesterday was today." Nashville: Tennessee Book Co., 1966. 8vo, cl, dj, 194pp. $15. Novel of guerrilla warfare in the Tenn. highlands during the civil war.

784 **BLANTON, L.H.**
"Well Done thou good & faithful servant." funeral sermon on the death of Rev. John W. Griffin, chaplain of 19th Va. Regt., Aug. 1st, 1864. By Rev. L.H. Blanton, Salem, Roanoke Co., Va." Lynchburg, Va., Virginia Power Pr., 1865. 8vo, wraps, (10)pp. Swem-432; Crandall.

785 **BLANTON, Margaret Gray**
"Moments of truth-a CSA spy Geo. Hughes." In: CWTI, Oct. 1967,v.VI, #6, p. 20-23, illus., port.

786 **BLANTON, Wyndham B.**
"Medicine in Virginia in the Nineteenth Century." Richmond: Garrett & Massie, 1933. 8vo, cl, illus., xii, 466pp. "Va. Surgeons in Civil War." p. 393-420.

787 **BLASER, Kent**
"North Carolina & John Brown's Raid." In: CWH, September 1978, v.24, #3. p. 197-212.

788 **BLEASE, Coleman Livingston, Hon.**
"Destruction of Property in Columbia, S.C. by Sherman's Army, Speech by...in the Senate May 15, 1930." Wash: G.P.O., 1930. Senate Doc. 149, 8vo, wraps, 112pp. $5, $15-bmk, $20

789 **BLECH, William James**
"The Copperheads, by William James Blake, (pseud). N.Y., The Dial Press, 1941. 8vo, cl, vii, 9-741pp. fiction.

790 **BLEDSOE, Albert Taylor**
..."The artillery brigade at Sailor's Creek." In: CV, June 1920, v.XXVIII, p. 213-216. Apr. 6, 1865.

791 ..."An essay on liberty & slavery, by..., Prof. math. in Univ. of Va." Phila. Lippincott & Co., 1856, 12mo, cl, 4, 9-383pp. $10, $15, $30. Also an Edt., 1857. Author a Col. in CS Army, an ass't sect. war, with Davis who later sent him to Eng. to gather hist. issues between North & South.

792 ..."Is Davis a Traitor, or, was Secession a constitutional right previous to the war of 1861?" (this book caused US Gov. drop Davis prosecution) Baltimore: Innes & Co., for author, 1866. 8vo, cl, vi, 263, (1)pp. $10, $15, $25-strand, $40-jk-122.
...St. Louis, 1879, edt. of 262pp.
...Richmond, Va., Hermitage press, 1907. (republished by Mary Barksdale Newton in memory of her husband, Virginius Newton of Richmond, Va.)$7.50, $20-bmk-84. 12mo, cl, viii, 263pp. Lynchburg, Va., 292pp., $12-y. See also: "Southern Review", 1873. Essay on Lincoln with suppressed chapters of Lamon's & Herndon's Life of Lincoln.

793 ..."Liberty & Slavery; or, Slavery in the light of moral & political philosophy." In: E.N. Elliott's "Cotton is King & pro-slavery arguments." p. 271-458.

794 ..."The War Between the States or was Secession a Constitutional Right previous to the War of 1861-1865? Arranged without verbal changes from "Is Davis a Traitor" Lynchburg, Va., J.P. Bell Co., 1915. 12mo, cl, illus., ports(incl. front),

242pp. $10, $20-bmk, $14. See also Harry E. Pratt.

795 ..."Chancellorsville." Baltimore, 1867. credited to Dr. Bledsoe by D.S. Freeman. Bledsoe had office 8 years next Lincoln in Ill.

796 ..."Jefferson Davis & Robert E. Lee." In: Southern Review, vol. 2, n.s., p. 232-242. See: Sophia Bledsoe Herrick.

797 **BLESSINGTON, Joseph Palmer**
"The Campaigns of Walker's Texas Division. By a Private Soldier. Containing a complete record of the compaigns in Texas, Louisiana & Arkansas, the skirmish at Perkins' Landing & battle of Milliken's Ben, Bayou Bourbeaux, Mansfield, Pleasant Hill, Jenkins' Ferry, etc. Including the Federal's Report of the Battles, names of the officers of the division, diary of marches, camp scenery, anecdotes, description of the country through which the division marched., etc." N.Y., Published for Author by Lange, Little & Co., 1875 $50, $60, $75, $85, $100.
...Pine Bluff, Ark., 1983. $45.
...Append: signed-J.P. Blessington. After organization of the Div., officially known as M'Culloch's. Div., later assumed the name Walker's Div., & known by that name to end of the war.
...Austin, Texas, Pemberton Press, 1968. Brasada Reprint Series, with an introduction by Alwyn Barr. $9.50, $10. 8vo, cl, port, (4), 314pp. index (14pp. ads-(8). See: Harry M. Henderson, Walker's Div.

798 **BLIED, Benjamin J.**
"The Bishops of the South & the Civil War." In: Salesianum, 1938, v.33, p. 57-66. See: Willard Eugene Wight.

799 **BLISS, George Newman**
"Cavalry affairs at Waynesboro." In: SHSP, 1885, v.13, p. 427-430.

800 **BLOCH, Charles J.**
"States' Rights: the law of the land." Atlanta, Ga., Harrison co., (1958) 8vo, cl, xi, 381pp. "Table of cases", p. 339-353. Ten chapters in chronological order, 1607-1957.

801 **BLOCK, W.T.**
"A History of Jefferson County, Texas, from Wilderness to Reconstruction." Nederland (Texas), Pub. Co., 1976. 8vo, cl, bibliog., index, 129pp. $12. Covers area as seaport, blockade runs tribulations of Reconstruction.

802 ..."Sabine Pass in the Civil War." In: ETHJ, Oct., 1971, v.IX, #2, p. 129-152. Notes.

803 **BLOCKADE RUNNERS**
See: Henry Blun; Wm. W. Belknap; Leslie S. Bright; Francis B.C. Fradlee; Dundas, Wm.O. Cobden; Hamilton Cochran; Robert W. Glover; Katherine A. Hanna; Frank E. Hamilton; Dr. Warren W. Hassler; H.J. Heagney; W. Edwin Hemphill; Paul Henderson; Henry Hollyday; Leonard V. Huber; Clarence Jeffries,; John Johns; Klaxon; Ethes S. Nepveux; T.L. Outerbridge; Wendell Pierce; Marcus W. Price; "Report Sect. Navy: Messages, Docs. 1865; A. Sellew Roberts; Wm. M. Robonson; James Sprunt; Reston Stevenson; Alice Strickland; Albert Wagner; Harry Wandrus; Arthur C. Wardle; Stanley Waterloo; J. Wilkinson.

804 **BLOCKADE RUNNING**
"Experience of a Northern Man in the Confederate Army-Blockade Running." In: SHSP, 1881, v.9, p. 369-378.

805 ..."Blockade Runners: The American Neptune Pictorial Supplement." In: Amer. Neptune, vol. XXI: Between p. 48-49(15-ships, 8pls); Between p. 92-93(2-pls); Between p. 124-125(16-ships), 8-pls); Between p. 216-217(14-ships, 8-pls.); Between p. 268-269(3-pls). $10-bmk, $5.

806 **BLOODY ANGLE, The,**
the Confederate disaster at Spotsylvania

Court-house, May 12, 1864, by which the "Stonewall Brigade" was annihilated...accounts by Gen. James A. Walker, Col. Thomas H. Carter, Lt. Wm. S. Archer, M.S. Stringfellow & Maj. D.W. Anderson." In: SHSP, 1893, v.XXI, p. 228-254. See: Gen. Jas. Walker.

807 **BLOOM, Lansing B., Edt.**
"Confederate Reminiscences." (Albuquerque, N.M., New Mexico Historical Review.) July, 1930, v.V, p. 315-324.

808 **BLOUNT, Lois Foster**
"Captain Thomas William Blount & his Memoirs." In: SwHQ, July, 1935, v.XXXIX, #1, p. 1-14. Under Gen. Bragg. (Texas)

809 **BLOW, William N., Capt.**
"Company H, Thirteenth Virginia Cavalry. Its Roster from Apr. 22, 1862 to April 9, 1865. With the killed, wounded, captured & promoted-a summary." In: SHSP, 1899, v.XXVII, p. 380-383.

810 ..."Sussex Light Dragoons. A Roll of this gallant organization. Something of its history." In: SHSP, 1897, v.XXV, p. 273-275.

811 **BLUE & GRAY;**
the patriotic American magazine, v.1, Jan. 1893. J.W. Morton, Jr., Edt. Phila: Patriotic Pub. Co., 1893. 4to, illus., plates, monthly. Pub. Washington, D.C., Feb. 1895. v.IV, #4, Oct. 1894, article on Stonewall Jax. $20. v.V, #1, Jan. 1895, $15.

812 ...or, Two Oaths & Three Warnings. By Louisiana. New Orleans (La.) (L. Graham & Son) 1885. 12mo, decr. wraps, & t/p, 169pp. Civil War & Reconstruction.

813 **BLUE, B.B.**
"Gen. Marmaduke's expedition into Missouri April/May, 1863." In: SoMag., 1871, v.IX, p. 333-339. Marmaduke's report, Jacksonport, Ark., May 19, 1863. Dorn-II3274.

814 **BLUE, John, Lt.**
"Lieutenant Blue's Escape." (London) Jour. Confed. Hist. Soc., Autumn, 1969, v.7, #1, p. 13-27.

815 **BLUM, Virgil C.**
"The Political & Military Activities of the German Element in St. Louis, 1859-1861." (Columbia, Mo., Mo. Hist. Review, Jan., 1948. v.XLII-#2, p. 103-129. Largely responsible in swinging to Union, otherwise Mo. would have joined South.

816 **BLUMENTHAL, Henry**
"Confederate Diplomacy: Popular Notions & International Realities." (Houston, Tex.) JSH, May, 1966. v.XXXII, #2, p. 151-171. $8.

817 **BLUMENTHAL, Walter Hart**
"An incendiary book: were three men hanged for having it?" In: Amer. Book Collector, Oct., 1956, v.7, #2, p. 14-17. On Hinton Rowan Helper's "Impending Crisis".

818 **BLUN, Henry**
"Reminiscences of My Blockade Running." (Savannah, Ga., Baird & Hutton, 1910) cover-title, 8vo, wraps, 10pp.

819 **BLUNDELL, (B)ezer**
"The Contributions of John Lewis Peyton to the History of Virginia & the Civil War in America, 1861-1865., reviewed by B. Blundell." London: John Wilson, 1868. 8vo, wraps, 46pp. See also: John Lewis Peyton. $7.50.

820 **BLUNT, Joseph**
"A historical sketch of the formation of the Confederacy, particularly with reference to the Provisional Limit of the General Government over Indian Tribes & the public territory, 1825. $20.

821 **BLUNT, Maria**
"In the Wake of Battle. A woman's Recollections of Shepherdstown during Antietam week." In: Cent., July, 1886, NS, v.X, p. 435-443, illus.

822 **BLYTHE, Vernon**
"A History of the Civil War in the United

States." N.Y., Neale Pub., 1914. 8vo, cl, front, maps, 411pp. Objective but still strongly Southern. $60-bmk.

823 **BOATE, Edward Wellington**
"The True Story of Andersonville told by a Federal Prisoner." In: SHSP, 1882, v.X, p. 25-32.

824 **BOATNER, Mark Mayo, III**
"The Civil War Dictionary. Maps & Diagrams by Major Allen C. Northrop & Lowell I. Miller." N.Y., David McKay & Co., (1959). Tk. 8vl, cl, dj, maps, incl. map liners, xvi, (1), 974pp. Reprinted: 1961. $15, $25, $20-y, $20. 8th print-1976.

825 **BOBBITT, B. Boisseu**
"Our Last Capital. Danville's part in the closing hours of the Confederacy. What Davis did while there." In: SHSP, 1903, v.XXXI, p. 334-339.

826 ..."Last Capital of the Confederacy at Danville, Va." In: SHSP, 1903, v.XXXI, p. 80.

827 **BOCAGE, J.W.**
"Four years service during the Civil War." In: Jefferson Co. HQ, Ark., 1975, #2, v.6, p. 34-43.

828 **BODDIE, William Willis**
"History of Williamsburg. Something about the people of Williamsburg County, South Carolina, from the first settlement by Europeans about 1705 until 1923." Columbia, S.C., The State Co., 1923. 8vo, cl fldg. maps, viii, (1) 611pp. $75-bmk. 90pp. of Williamsburg in the CSA, includes co. muster rolls, soldier photos, extracts diary of Wm. Clarkson, 10th SC, Mar/Dec. 1862.

829 **BODER, Bartlett**
"Jeff Thompson (1828?)-1876 & the ordinance that dethroned a city." In: Mus. graphic, Fall, 1952, v.4, #4, p. 6-7. 11. On life of Merriweather Thompson, St. Joseph Mo., & his services in Mo/Ark., as an officer in the CSArmy.

830 **BOEHM, Robert B., Dr.**
"Mountains & mud were chief obstacles of Jones-Imboden raid in West Virginia." In: CWTI, May 1964, v.III, #2, p. 14-21, illus., map ports.

831 **BOETHEL, Paul C.**
"The Big Guns of Fayette." Austin, Texas: Von Boeckmann-Jones Co., 1965. 8vo, pict. stiff wraps, maps, facsm., (7), 98pp. index, notes. $7.50

832 **BOGGAN, G.S., Mrs.**
"War record of Pvt. John Steward (1840-1930)" In: Crawford Co. Hist. Soc. Heritage. July, 1957, v.1, p. 25-26. On his service, 1861-1865, as pvt. in CSArmy.

833 **BOGGS, Marion Alexander, Compl.**
"The Alexander Letters, 1787-1900." Savannah, Ga., 1910, Priv. Prt. by George J. Baldwin, Lim. Edt. 131-copies. 8vo, cl, front, 13-pls., fldg. genealogical table, illus., 387pp. $37.50. Southern Plantation life before the War, few CSA letters reprint from other source.

834 **BOGGS, William Ellison**
"The South vindicated from the charge of treason & rebellion, being the substance of an address before the Survivor's association of the 6th Reg. S.C.V. at their reunion in Chester, S.C., Aug. 4, 1881, by.- ..late chaplain of the same." Columbia, S.C., Presbyterian Pub. Hse., 1881. wraps, 8vo, 56pp. errata slip. $56-gin.

835 ..."Secession of South Carolina & her ten sister states vindicated from the charge of treason & rebellion. Being the substance of an address before his comrads of the South Carolina Div., U.C.V. reunion, Columbia, S.C., Apr. 22, 1915. 8vo, wraps, 52pp.

836 **BOGGS, William Robertson, Gen. CSA**
"Military Reminiscences of..., with Intro., notes by William K. Boyd." Durham, N.C., Seeman Printery, 1913. The John Lawson Monographs of the Trinity College His-

torical Society, Ill." 12mo, cl, port(front)xxiii, 115pp. $20, $10, $12, $15, $75-nc, $35-nc, $30-jk, $160-jk, $22.50-y, $50-bmk.

...Louisville: Lost Cause pr., micro-cd. $3.01

837 **BOGLE, James G.**
"The Locomotive Texas". In: "The Landmarker", 1979/1980, v.4, p. 3-14. On locomotive in the Civil War chase with the "General".

839 **BOGLE, Joseph**
"Some Recollections of the Civil War, by a private in the 40th Ga. Regiment, CSA." Dalton(Ga.) Daily Argus, 1911. 8vo, wraps, 26pp. Dornbusch-291.

839 **BOGLE, Joseph, Private**
"Historical sketches of Barton's (later Stovall's) Georgia Brigade, Army of Tennessee, CSA. By Private Joseph Bogle Co. I, 40th regiment & Captain William L. Calhoun Co.K, 42nd regiment with complete roster of the 40th, 41st, 42nd, 43rd, & 52nd regiments. Edited with an introduction by William Stanley Hoole & Martha DuBose Hoole." University, Ala., Confederate Pub. Co., 1984. Confederate Regimental series #5. 8vo, stiff wraps, 108pp.

...University, Ala., Confederate Pub. Co., 1977. Reprint of Bogle's "Reminiscences". See: Wm. L. Calhoun's reprint in this vol., page 33.

840 **BOGLE, Robert V.**
"Defeat through default: Confederate Naval strategy for the upper Mississippi River & its tributaries, 1861-1862." In: THQ, 1967, v.26, p. 62-71.

841 **BOHANNAN, Willis W.**
"Surry County at War 1861-1865." Sketches by Kathleen P. Horne. n.p., (1963) $3.50, $15-bmk-105, $20. 8vo, soft wraps, drawings, 64, (1)p. Roster: Scurry Co. Confed. soldiers.

842 **"BOHEMIAN", "War Songs of the South."** See: Dr. William G. Shepperson.

843 **BOISSEAU, Sterling**
"The Virginia convention of 1861." In: CV, Jan. 1924, v.XXXII, p. 8-10.

844 ..."Why did Virginia secede?" n.p., n.d., (Adv. circular)

845 **BOISSONNAS, B. de La Touche, Mme.**
"Un Vaincu. Souvenirs du General Robert Lee." 3rd Edt. (old) $5. 12mo, wraps, front(port), fld. map, vii, 291pp. Paris, Bibliotheque d'education et de recreation, J. Hetzel et cia, edt., 1875. $55-jk-129.

846 **BOKER, George Henry**
"The Second Louisiana, May 27, 1863." n.p., n.d.(c.1863). 8vo, broadside verse.

847 **BOLAND, Marvin Dement**
"Re-interpreting History or, the Fight for Democracy." Tacoma, Wash., Marland Bookcraft (1947), 12mo, cl, 188pp. pro-South.

848 **BOLANDER, Louis H.**
"The C.S.S. Stonewall; Ship of Many Names & Many Flags." (Salem, Mass.) Amer. Neptune, July, 1941. p. 242-254. plate.

849 **BOLDRICK, Charles C.**
"Father Abram J. Ryan, "The Poet Priest of the Confederacy." In: Filson Club Hist. Quart., 1972, v.XLVI, p. 201-218.

850 **BOLEY, Henry**
"Lexington in Old Virginia." Richmond, Va., Garrett & Massie (1936). 8vo, decr. cl(color flags on cover)pict. endsheets, illus. (incl. front) ports, xii, 235pp. Much on Jackson & Lee. $20-bmk, $30-bmk, $12.50.

851 **BOLGER, Margaret C., Mrs.**
"The Fiat of Fate or Ambition's Dream." Minneapolis: Harmon & Moen, 1887. 12mo, cl, front(port), 298pp. $10. Patriotic poems re CSA people, events.

852 **BOLLES, John A.**
"Escape from Fort Warren. CSN sea

raider "Savez" Read in Boston Harbor." In: CWTI, July, 1966, v.5, #4, p. 44-48, plan, group ports.

853 **BOLLING, Eugene S.**
"The bill of fare of the Hotel de Vicksburg-1863. Edt: Mattie Russell." In: JMH, Oct., 1955, v.17, p. 282-285. notes. Fictitious menu of a fictitious hotel by a CSA major, memorializing a narrow escape from slaughter of Morgan, a saddle mule.

854 **BOLLS, James**
"A Complete Roster of the Soldiers & Sailors of Warren County During the Civil War." n.p., n.d., (c. 1928) sm. 4to, wraps, (28)pp. Copy distr.(?) J.G. Sherard, Clerk of Chancery Court, of Vicksburg, Miss.

855 **BOLTON, Channing M.**
"With General Lee's engineers." In: CV, Aug., 1922. v.XXX, p. 298-302.

856 **BOMAR, Thomas, Captain**
"Muster Roll of the Company known as the Chestatee Artillery, Commanded by Captain Thomas Bomar, stationed at Camp Lee, Skidaway Road, 3 1/2 miles from Savannah, December 31, 1862." In: Ga. H.Q., Sept., 1917, v.1, #3, p. 266-267.

857 **BOND, Christiana**
"Memories of General Robert E. Lee." Baltimore: Norman Remington, 1926. 12mo, boards, dj, illus., 52pp. $4, $7.50, $25
...Second printing. $3, $4, $10-bmk. First in S. Atlantic Quart.

858 ..."Recollections of General Robert E. Lee." In: So. Atl. Quart., Oct., 1925, v.XXIV, p. 333-348. (Her book first appeared here.)

859 **BOND, Daniel**
"Songs of the Confederacy." In: CV, Jan. 1896, v.IV, #1, p. 2-5, ports.

860 **BOND, E. Holmes**
"The Conrad Boys in the Confederate Service." In: SHSP, 1908, v.XXXVI, p. 224-225.

861 **BOND, Frank A.**
"Company A. First Maryland Cavalry." In: CV, 1898, v.6, p. 78-80.

862 **BOND, John W.**
"The History of Elkhorn Tavern." In: Ar. HQ, 1962, v.XXI, illus., p. 3-15.

863 **BOND, Lewis H.**
"The Capture & trial of a Confederate Spy sent to Ohio by Jefferson Davis, a paper read before the Ohio commandery of the military order of the loyal legion of the U.S., Feb. 2, 1887." Cincinnati: H.C. Sherick & co., 1887. 8vo, wraps, 10pp. (old) $2.50. From: MOLLUS-Ohio, II, p. 153-160.

864 **BOND, Oliver James**
"The Story of the Citadel." Richmond: Garrett & Massie (1936). 8vo, cl, dj, illus., ix, 242pp. $5. Hist. S.C. Military academy, 1822 to 1936.

865 **BOND, William R.**
"Pickett or Pettigrew? An Historical Essay." Weldon, N.C., Hall & Sledge (c.1888). $75-bmk-105, $50-bmk-99, $125-r. 8vo, wraps, 49pp. $10, $12.50, $22.50. (in preface mentions edt., 2000 copies exhausted, 2nd print, c. 1901) Claims honor of assault, 3rd day Gettysburg for Pettigrew's N. Carolinians over Pickett's Virginians.
..."Pickett or Pettigrew? An Historical Essay, (Revised & Enlarged by..., sometime officer Brig. Staff Army Northern Virginia." "Tell the truth & the world will come to see it at last." Emerson. 2nd edition, single $.25, 5-copies $1." Scotland Neck, N.C., W.L.L. Hall, pub., (c.1901) 8vo, wraps, 91pp. (4)pp. folder, loosely inserted-"Appreciative Opinions of the Second Edition." $20-sh-111, $40-bmk, $12.50, $25.
..."Pickett or Pettigrew? North Carolina at

Gettysburg. A historical monograph, Third edition." Scotland Neck, N.C., W.L.L. Hall, 1901. 8vo, wraps, 94pp. Swem-461.

..."Pickett or Pettigrew, an historical essay." Gaithersburg, Md., Butternut Press, 8vo, wraps, 91pp. $20, (p.4.50) 1984)

866 BONDURANT, Alexander L.
"Did Jones County Secede?" In: Pub. MHS, 1898, v.1, p. 103-106. See: Goode Montgomery.

867 BONE, John Wesley
"A personal memorial of the Civil War services of John Wesley Bone, Confederate soldier from Nash County, N.C. Intro: Hugh Buckner Johnston." Wilson, N.C., H.B. Johnston, 1978. 8vo, wraps, 7, 38, 9 leaves.

868 BONEY, F. Nash
"Southerners All." Macon, Ga., Mercer University, 1984. 8vo, paper, x, 217pp. $13. A crucial period 1830-1860, recalls W.J. Cash's "Mind of the South" & Daniel R. Hundley's "Social Relations of Our Southern States". "Plain people of the South". A good course on the South.

869 BONEY, F.N.
"Governor Letcher's Candid Correspondence." In: CWH, June, 1964, v.X, #2, p. 167-180.

870 ..."Virginian, Southerner, American." (Richmond) Va. Cavl., Summer, 1967, v.XVII, #1, p. 11-19, ports (1-color), illus. (1-color). John Letcher, Virginia's Civil War Governor.

871 ..."Governor John Letcher, Virginian. A reluctant Rebel, this old Democrat proved to be one of the most loyal of the South's war governors." In: CWTI, Dec. 1972, v.XI, #8, p. 10-19, illus., ports.

872 ..."John Letcher of Virginia: The Story of Virginia's Civil War Governor." Southern Historical Publications, #11, (Tuscaloosa) Univ. of Alabama pr, (1966) $20-b, $15-y, $7, $12.50-jk, $15-y. 8vo, cl, dj, 319pp. front(port)

873 ..."The Politics of Expansion & Secession 1820-1861." In: Kenneth Coleman's History of Georgia(Athens), 1977).

..."The conqueror. Sgt. Mathew Woodruff in war & peace 1861-1866." In: Ala. Rev., July 1970, p. 193-211.

875 ..."John Letcher's secret criticism of the Confederate Cabinet." In: VMHB, July, 1964, v.72, #3, p. 348-355.

876 BONHAM, Milledge L., Jr.
"The British Consuls in the Confederacy." N.Y., Columbia University. Longmans, Green & Co, agents, 1911. Columbia studies in Economics & Hist., v.XLIII, #3. 8vo, wraps, 267pp. bibliog. $75-bmk, $22.50, $18.50. 8vo, wraps, 267pp. bibliog.
...NY, AMS Press (1969) cloth, $8.50, $12.50-y

877 ..."The Expulsion of the British Consuls by the Confederate Govmt." In: Americana, Apr. 1918, v.XII, p. 224-226.

878 ..."Louisiana's seisure of the Federal arsenal at Baton Rouge, Jan., 1861." In: East & West Baton Rouge Hist. Soc. Proc., 1918, v.II, p. 47-55.

879 ..."Man & Nature at Port Hudson, 1863." In: Mil. Hist. & Economist, Oct., 1917, v.II, p. 372-384, #4, v.III, #1, Jan., 1918, p. 20-38. Reprinted: n.p., 1917, map, 33pp.

880 ..."An undergraduate's views on the crisis of 1860." In: Hist. Outlook, May 1928, v.XIX, p. 209-211. A letter written by Henry Martyn Dodd, a student at Hamilton College, Dec. 11, 1860. See: Abner M. Perrin.

881 ...A convention that made history." In: S.C. Hist. Assoc. Proc., 1940, v.X, p. 3-9, 1859 convention in Syracuse, NY, its effects on 1860 Democratic convention Charleston, S.C.

882 ..."The Rebel Reefer furls his last sail." In: La. Hist. Quart., Oct., 1928, v.XI, p. 582-

606. Sketch of Jas. Morgan, born N.O., Mar. 10, 1845, died Apr. 21, 1928. Author of "Recoll. of a Rebel Reefer." CSNavy.

883 ..."Financial & economic disturbance in New Orleans on the eve of secession." In: LHQ, Jan. 1930, v.13, #1, p. 32-36.

884 **BONNER, James C.**
"Georgia's last frontier: Development of Carroll County." Athens: University of Georgia Press, 1971, 8vo, cl, dj, illus., maps, 236pp., index $20. Good material on civil war & Reconstruction.

885 ..."Milledgeville: Georgia's Antebellum capital." Macon, Ga., Mercer University Press, 1985. 8vo, cl, illus., 257pp., bibliog., index. $20.

886 **BONNER, James Calvin**
"Charles Colcock Jones: The Macaulay of the South." In: Ga. H.Q., Dec., 1943. v.XXVII, #4, p. 324-338.
..."Journal of a Milledgeville Girl..." See: Cook, Anna Maria Green.

887 ..."David R(udolphus) Snelling (1836/1901). A study of desertion & defection in the civil war." In: Ga. rev., fall, 1956, v.10, p. 275-282. Brief service in CSArmy, desertion to Union in 1st Ala. Reg., Union Cavalry.

888 ..."Milledgeville: Georgia's Antebellum Capital." Athens: University of Georgia Press, 1978. 8vo, cl, dj, xii, 307pp. $14.50. Good section relates to the War & Reconstruction.

889 ..."Plantation Architecture of the Lower South on Eve of the Civil War." (Baton Rouge, la.) JSH, Aug., 1945. v.XI, #3, p. 370-388.

890 ..."War Crimes Trials, 1865-1867." Reprint: Social Science, v.22, #2, April, 1947. Large 8vo, cover title, p. (127)-134. On Wirz, Davis & Surratt.

891 ..."Sherman at Milledgeville in 1864." (Lexington, Ky) JSH, v.XXII, #4, Nov. 1956, p. 273-291.

892 **BONNER, Thomas Reuben, 18th Tex. Inf.**
"Sketches of the Campaign of 1864. Walker's Division-Retreat up Red River-Battle of Mansfield." In: LWL, Oct. 1868, v.V, #6, p. 459-466; Nov. 1868, v.VI, #1, p. 7-12. See: Mansfield, Battle of.

893 **BOOKER, H. Marshall**
"Thomas Roderick Dew, Forgotten Virginian." (Richmond) Va. Cavl., Autumn 1969. v.XIX, #2, p. 20-29, illus., ports (2-color) dbl-pg. color. Prof. hist., political economy, Germans influenced his thinking on superior white race pro-slavery, expressing the local views.

894 **BOOKER, John A.**
"Record of Confederate Generals, giving states of each, rank, full list of battles, dates from 1861-1865." Richmond: Everett Waddey Co., 1897, 8vo, wraps, 12pp.
...Dorn, III, cites 42pp.

895 **BOONE, Benjamin**
"A letter of Lieutenant Boone, C.S.A. Edited by his granddaughter Mrs. Nora Boone Carlisle." In: AHQ, 1944, v.III, p. 63-65.

896 **BOOTH, Alan R.**
"Alabama at the Cape, 1863." In: Amer. Neptune, April, 1966, Vol. XXVI, #2, p. 96-108.

897 **BOOTH, Andrew B.**
"List of Organized Camps of the United Confederate Veterans, corrected to Aug. 31, 1921." New Orleans, 1921. 8vo, wraps, 19pp. $4.50

898 ..."Records of Louisiana Confederate Soldiers & Louisiana Confederate Soldiers & Louisiana Confederate Commands." In 3 vols (i.e., 4) Lists of CSA Commands, etc., in v.1. Compiled by Andrew B. Booth, Comm. La. Mil. Records. New Orleans, La. (Ramires-Jones, Print. 1928) to.p., date 1920. $37.50, $50, $75, $400-bmk, $1000-bmk. 4to, cl, 200, 1000, 1312, 1195pp. v.1-"Alphabetically: list of local

designations of La. organizations in CSArmy, comprising Inf., artly., Cav. & militia. 982 mil. companies org. in La. (400 militia, mostly home guards, some served to end of war); Index of battles, campaigns, engagements, etc. fought within limits of state of La., 1861-1865, alphabetically arranged. Alphabetical roll of such official records of individual Confed. soldiers, as are to be found in U.S. records & state off. records.

899 ..."Louisiana Confederate Military Records." In: La. Hist. Quart., IV(1921). p. 369-418. "Alphabetical list & local designations of La. organizations in the CSA army; Index to battles, campaigns, engagements, etc., fought within the limits of the State of Louisiana, 1861-1865." See: Louisiana: Comm. of Mil. Records.

..."Records of Louisiana Confederate Soldiers & Louisiana Confederate Commands." Easley, S.C., Southern Historical Press, 3 vol. set. $187.50. 1984. Vol1 & 2 (200, 1000pp), Vol. 3, Book 1, (1312pp), Vol. 4, Book 2, (1195 pp.)

900 ..."Louisiana Confederate Military Records." In: LHQ, 1921, v.4, p. 369-418. Large list of companies.

901 **BOOTH, Edwin Gilliam**
"In War Times. Two years in the Confederacy & two years north. With many reminiscences of the days long before the war." Phila: J.D. Avil & co., 1885. 8vo, cl, illus., pls, ports, (3)-141, xii, 142-221pp. $15, $25, $50, $150-jk-135, $100, bmk. Originally in Forney's "Progress".

902 **BOOTH, G.W.**
"Personal reminiscences of a Maryland soldier in the war between the states, 1861-." Baltimore, Md., Butternut & Blue, 1986, 8vo, cl, 177pp. 1898 reprint. $22.50.

903 **BOOTH, George Wilson, Capt., Compl.**
"Maryland Line Confederate Soldier's Home, Pikesville, Maryland, compiled by. Pub. in interest of & under the supervison of the board of Governors & managers of the home, 1894; heading-"Illustrated Souvenir." n.p., (Baltimore, Md. Commercial Print.) Tall 8vo, decr. cl, illus., ports, (8), 133pp. ads thru text. $30-nc, $10, $15, $20, $350-ob, $50-bmk. The 1894 Edt: contains Muster Rolls of Md. Line P.A. of the Confederate States. Co.A, p.59; 2nd Md. Inf., p.67; 1st Md. Cavalry, p.75; 1st Md. Arty., p.84; 2nd Md. Arty., p.86; 3rd Md. Arty., p.87; 4th Md. Arty., p.90; "Roster of Officers & Members of the Society of the Army & Navy of the C.S., in state of Maryland, inc. recorded in liber G.R., #19, folio 294, one of the charter records of Baltimore City, with Constitution, Balt., 1894, p. 91-133.

904 ..."Personal Reminiscences of a Maryland Soldier in the War Between the States, 1861-1865. For private circulation only." Baltimore (Fleet, McGinley & co.) 1898. 8vo, cl, 177pp. $85, $22.50, $250-bmk, Atg-$325, $150.

905 ..."We've played Cards & Lost", the last days of Confederate New Orleans..." In: CWTI, Jan., 1973, v.XI, #9, p. 16-24, facsm., illus., map, ports.

906 ..."Running the Inland Blockade." In: CWTI, June 1972, v.11, #3, p. 12-19

907 **BOOTH, Helen Sutton**
"Old Christ Church & the Civil War." (Richmond) Va. Cavl., Summer, 1961, v.XI, #1, p. 12-17, illus. (1-color).

908 **BOOTH, John Wilkes**
"Patriotic Cover-Booth." "Hunt the villian down. Scatter his likeness in every of the Country; scan every face..." Sent out to assist in hunt for Booth. Cover: 3 1/16x5 3/8", port of Booth 2 x 2 1/4 head & shoulder. (Borderland) $125. One of two known copies. G.C. Jenks, Wash., D.C.

909 ..."Unexplored Lincoln material: the pursuit & capture of John Wilkes Booth."

In: MoHSB, Jan. 1951, v.7, p. 167-181. Texts of official telegrams & messages, Apr. 15-30, 1865.

910 ..."Booth's Diary (1864)." Wm. Hatchett, Edt. In: Jour. Ill. State HS, Feb. 1979, p. 39-56.

911 **BOOTHE, J.B.**
"The Siege of Knoxville & its results." In: CV, June, 1914, v.XXII, p. 266-267.

912 ..."The Tallahatchie rifles-" "Cap" Houston." In: CV, Dec. 1924, v.XXXII, p. 458-460.

913 **BOOTS, E.N.**
"Civil War letters of E.N. Boots from New Bern & Plymouth. Edt: Wilfred W." In: NCHR, April 1959, v.36, p. 205-223.

914 ..."The Civil War letters of E.N. Boots. Edt: Wilfred W. Black." In: VMHB, April 1961, v.69, #2, p. 194-219.

915 **BOOZER, Marie**
See under title, "Checkered Life of Countess Pourtales

916 **BORCKE, Heros von**
"Memoirs of the Confederate War for Independence." Gaithersburg, Md., ButterNut Press, 1985. 12mo, cl, 438pp., fldg. map $35.
..."Memoirs of the Confederate war for independence..." In: Blackwoods: Sept. 1865, v.98, p. 269-288 (part I; Pt. II, p. 389-437, Pt. III, p.557-580, Pt. IV, p. 635-655; Pt. V, p. 83-102, Pt. VI, p. 173-196, Pt. VII, p. 307-321, Pt. VIII, p. 448-468, Pt. IX, p. 543-564, Conclusion: p. 749-770.
..."Memoirs of the Confederate war." Dayton, Oh., Morningside Press, 1985, 8vo, 1vols in one, color fldg. map. $25.

917 ..."The Prussian remembers. Edt: Stuart Wright." In: CWTI, Feb. 1981, v.19, #10, p. 40-43, (pt. I); Apr. 1981, v.20, #1, p. 44-49, illus., ports.

918 **BORCKE, Johann August Heinrich Heros von**
"Swi Jahre im Sattel und am Feinde, Erinnerungen aus dem Unabhangigkeitskriege der Konfoderirten, von Heros v.Borke. Aus dem Englischen ubersetz von Kaehler." Berlin: Ernst Siegfried Mittler, Sohn, 1877. 2 vols in 1. 12mo, cl, fldg. map, 256, 244pp. front (port) $20.
...Other edts: 1886 & 1898. $275-bmk-105. 1886 edt. 2 vols in 1: 1898 edt. 2 vols. 8vo, cloth, 1886; 1898 edt. in wraps, vii, 281pp, v, 304pp., 8vo, $75-jk, $200-b

919 ..."Die grosse reiterschlact bei Brandy Station, 9 juni, 1863. Bearb. von Heros von Borcke...(und) Justus Scheibert...mit 6 portrats, 5 karten und 7 vollbildern nacheinem Kreigsskizzenbuch gezeichnet vom schlactenmaler C. Sellmer." pict. battle scene/cover, wrap, $50, $60, $350, $500-r, $85-ginzb.9. 8vo, cl, 179pp., incl. 7pl., 6ports, 5 maps. The great cavalry battle at Brandy Station; book never trans. into English.

920 ..."Ein Reis von altem Stamm, Roman aus dem Leben von Heros von Borcke, herausgegeben von Hermann Muller-Bohn." Berlin: verlag von Paul Kittle, 1895-1896. 8vo, cl, 3 vols., illus., ports. Vol 1-"Junges Blut; II-"Auf dem Kriegsfade; III-An des Grabes Rande., II-"On the war path."; III, "On the brink of the grave.". This edition has variants as follows: "An des Grabes Rande." Berlin: P. Kittel, 1896, 8vo, wraps, illus., port, 294pp. $125-bmk-128.

921 ..."Auf dem Kriegsfade." Berlin: P. Kittel, 1895, 8vo, wraps, illus., 365pp. $125-bmk.

922 ..."Dritte Auflage, mit einem Nachtrage "Zwangig Jahre spater". Berlin: Ernst Siegfried Mittler, Sohn, 1898. 8vo, cl, front(ports) fldg. map, 2 vols. See: Maj. Edgar Erskine Hume(biog) & Jas. R. Belcher.
..."Memoirs of the Confederate War for Independence." Blackwoods Edinburgh Magazine-xcvii, July 1865-June 1866. In

ten installments. 1st printing of book. 8vo, 3/4 calf, 2 vols. $25, $50, $75. Borcke was Jeb Stuart's chief of staff & privy to much inside information as well as in line of action.

...Edinburgh & London: 1866, W. Blackwood & son. 2 vols. $325-b, $150-bmk, nc in ap. 8vo, cl, fldg. map, x, 323; vii, 318pp. $30, $37.50, $42.50, $50, $55, $75.

...Philadelphia: J.B. Lippincott, 1867. 12mo, cl, fldg. map, 4p, lf, (vii)-x, 438pp. $27.50, $45, $55, $125-bmk

....N.Y., Peter Smith, 1938. 8vo, cl, map, 323, 318pp. $7.50, $10, $15, $17.50, $32.50-mcm, $20, $40-bmk, $60-bmk.

...N.Y. Kraus Reprint co., 1969, $25.

923 ..."Colonel Heros von Borcke's Journal, 26 Apr.-8 Oct., 1862. Trans: Stuart Wright." n.p., 1981, 224pp. 180pp. Lim. Edt., sig. translator. Pg. of origi. narrative, pict. slipcase, extra bound. $125-bmk

924 ..."The Great Cavalry Battle of Brandy Sta. Trans: Stuart Wright & F.D. Bridgewater, Winston-Salem, NC, 1976, Palaemon Pr., 8vo, cl, 143pp. lim. 1M copies. $10, $45-op, See: Wm. V. Kennedy. Fore: Bell Wiley.

925 **BORGLUM, John Gutzon de la Mothe**
"Gutzon Borglum & Stone Mountain." In: Emory Univ. quart., June 1952, v.8, p. 111-115. Excerpts of letters, 1915, re gigantic sculpture for a CSA memorial near Atlanta.

926 **BORGWALD, Lucille**
"Desertions from the Confederate Army (1861-1865). In: Davis & Elkins Hist. Mag., Mar. 1950, v.3, p. 15-17.

927 **BORLAND, William P., Hon.**
"Gen. Jo. O. Shelby." An address by... Rep. in Congress, at unveiling of the monument to the Confederate dead, erected by the Fed. Gov., in Union Cemetery, Kansas City, Oct. 22, 1911. (Columbia, Mo.), Oct. 1912, v.VII, #1, p. 10-19. Reprint, in wraps, of above...

928 **BOSAND, James N.**
"Memoirs of a Pulaski Veteran of the Stonewall Brigade, 1861-1865. Cap't. of Co.C, 4th Virginia infty, Stonewall Brigade, Pulaski, Va." (Pulaski, Va., B.D. Smith & Bros., 1930) 12mo, pict., wraps, cover title, 25pp. $10, $25, $50-bmk-105.

929 **BOSHER, Kate Langley (Mrs. Charles)**
"Bobbie", by Kate Cairns. Richmond, Va., B.F. Johnson Pub, 1899, 12mo, cl, front, pls., 134pp. $3.50.

..."Bobbie" A story of the Confederacy. Phila: Henry Altemus co. (1905). sq. 8vo, decr. cl-color, illus., 128pp. $3.

930 **BOSWELL, E.M.**
"Rebel Religion." In: CWTI, Oct., 1972, v.XI, #6, p. 26-33, illus., ports. In camp Johnny Reb thought "God was on his side".

931 **BOSWELL, James Keith, Capt.**
"Diary of a Confederate officer-Jackson's staff Boswell." In: CWTI, April, 1976, v.15, #1, p. 30-38, facsms, illus., ports.

932 **BOTELER, Alexander R., Col.**
"Stonewall Jackson & Campaign of 1862." In: SHSP, Sept., 1915, v.XL, p. 162-182. pt. 2, Oct., 1917, v.XLII, p. 174-180.

933 ..."Why "Stonewall" Jackson did not drink." In: SHSP, 1882, v.X, p. 287.

934 ..."Recollections by a Virginian who witnessed the fight. The John Brown Raid." In: Century, May/Oct. 1883, p. 399-411.

..."My Ride to the Barbecue; or, Revolutionary Reminiscences of the Old Dominion." In: Mag. Jefferson Co. HS, v. 39, p.13-61, 1973.

935 **BOTKIN, Benjamin Albert, Edt.**
"A Treasury of Southern Folklore: stories, ballads, traditions, & folkways of the people of the South." N.Y., Crown Pub., (1949). music, notes, xxiv, 776pp. $12.50, $20-Ch-Hill.

936 **BOTSFORD, T.F.**
"A Sketch of the 47th Alabama Regiment, volunteers, C.S.A." Co. D. 47th. Montgomery, Ala., Paragon press (1909) 12mo, wraps, cover title, (1), 19pp.
...2nd Edt., 1910, wraps, 22pp.

937 ..."Memories of the War of Secession." Montgomery, Ala., Paragon press, 1911. 16mo, 22pp. $7, $22.50, $200-al. "Reprint of another by me in 1909 & '10, however its more than a mere revision."

938 **BOTSFORD, Theophilus F., Pvt.**
"Sketch of the 47th Alabama Regiment Vols. CSA." Montgomery, Ala., Paragon Press, 1909. 8vo, wraps, 36pp.
...1914 Edt. 3, titled "A boy in the Civil War." differs only of a photo of the author & at least 7 reprints within the year. See: Capt. Joseph Q. Burton.

939 **BOTT, Elizabeth Catherine**
"Admiral Semmes, C.S.N." Baton Rouge, La., Ortlieb's print, 1911. sq.8vo, wraps, port, 8pp. cover title. La. State Univ., Bul. #2, vol.II, NS, Feb., 1911. Reprinted from Americana, Dec.,1910. The Joanna Waddill prize offered by the Joanna Waddill Chap. UDC, was awarded to the writer of this paper, at commencement, 1910, La. State Univ.

940 **BOTTOM, Raymond B.**
"John Mitchel, Irish Patriot & Defender of the Southern Cause in the War Between the States, an address delivered at the dedication of the Mitchel Plaque, Fort Monroe, Virginia, Oct. 6, 1951." (Richmond)Va. Mag. Hist. Biog., April, 1952, v.60, #2, p. 326-328, port.

941 **BOUCHER, Chauncey Samuel**
"The Nullification Controversy in South Carolina." Chicago: University Press (1916). 12mo, cl, maps (incl. fldg. front), xi, 300pp. 350 copies printed. (Univ. of Mich. thesis) ...N.Y., Russell & Russell, 1968. 8vo, cl, dj, xiv, 399pp. $10.

942 ..."The Ante-Bellum Attitude of South Carolina towards manufacturing & Agriculture." caption title. St. Louis, Mo., Washington Univ., 1916. Wash. Univ. Studies series IV, v.1, pt. 2, 8vo, p. 243-270.

943 ..."Sectionalism, Representation & the Electoral Question in Ante-Bellum South Carolina." Caption title. St. Louis, Mo., Washington Univ., 1916. Wash. Univ. Studies series, Oct., 1916. vol.IV, pt. 2, #1. 8vo, wraps, 62pp.

944 ..."In re. that aggressive slavocracy." In: Miss. Val. Hist. Rev., June, 1921, v.VIII, p. 13-79. Examines charge the South controlled events as a powerful, aggressive slavocracy. Mex. War & Texas Annex.

945 ..."The Secession & Co-Operation Movement in South Carolina, 1848-1852." St. Louis, Mo., Washington Univ., Apr., 1918. In: Humanistic Series, vol.V, #2; Series IV, whole #-XX. Large 8vo, wraps, (4), 67-138pp. maps, $7.50.

946 ..."South Carolina & the South on the Eve of Secession, 1852-1860." As above, April, 1919, Vol. VI, #2; Series IV, Whole #XXIV, (4), 81-144pp., maps, $7.50.

947 ..."Sectionalism, representation, & the electoral question in ante-bellum South Carolina." In: Wash. Univ. Stud., Oct., 1917, v.IV, p. 3-62.

948 **BOUGHTON, Joseph S.**
"The Lawrence massacre by a band of Missouri ruffians under Quantrill, August 21, 1863. 150 men killed, eighty women made widows & 250 children made orphans..." Lawrence, Kan., J.S. Boughton, (1885-?) 12mo, wraps, cover-title, 36pp.
...Do: another copy with (4)p. ads. $175-jk-142.

949 ..."The Quantrill Raid! An account of the burning & sacking of the city of Lawrence,

Kansas and the murdering of one hundred fifty of her citizens by a band of ruffians under Quantrill, Aug. 21, 1863, as given by Rev. R. Cordley, Hon. Joseph Savage, J.G. Sands, F.W. Read & others, who were eye witnesses of the barbarous scene-unparallel(!) in the history of civilized warfare." Lawrence, Kansas, J.S. Broughton, 1884. 12mo, wraps, 36pp.

950 **BOULDIN, Edwin E.**
"Charlotte Cavalry. A brief history of the gallant command." In: SHSP, 1900, v.XXVIII, p. 71-81. With revised Roll. Bouldin was formerly Captain, Co. B., 14th Va. CSA.

951 ..."Historical Memorial of the Charlotte Cavalry, with chronological list of engagements." In: SHSP, 1906, v.XXXIV, p. 75-81.

952 ..."The Last Charge at Appomattox." SHSP, 1900, v.XXVIII, p. 250-254.

953 **BOULGER, Margaret C. (sic) Bolger**
"The Fiat of Fate or Ambition's Dream." Minneapolis: Harmon & Moe, print, 1887. 12mo, cl, port(front)1887. Largely verse on battles, secession, etc.

954 **BOULIGNEY, John Edmund**
"Remarks of..., on the secession of Louisiana. Delivered in the House of Representatives, FEb. 5, 1861." (Washington, DC? 1961) 8vo, 1-lf, caption title.

955 ..."Speeches of Mr. Boligney of La., & Mr. Sickles of N.Y., delivered in House of Representatives, Feb. 5, 1861. Secession of Louisiana." caption title. (Washington, DC?) 8vo, 8pp.

956 **BOUNDS, Charles L.**
"Ben H. Bounds, 1840-1911, Methodist minister & prominent Mason, biography & highlights from his early life & Civil War Memoirs. Prepared & edited by his son, Rev. Charles L. Bounds, Dallas, Tex. (Columbus, Ohio, n.d., 1911?) 8vo, wraps, cover title, 25pp. Dornbusch-574. Arranged in book form by his grandson, James Orris Moore, Columbus, Ohio.

957 **BOURLAND, Hal**
"Plantation life in Texas." In: CV, June 1923, v.XXXI, p. 222-223. On Stephen F. Austin's plantation during Republic & pre-war days of '60s.

958 **BOVEY, Wilfred**
"Confederate agents in Canada during the American civil war." In: Cand. Hist. Rev., Mar., 1921, v.II, p. 46-57.

959 **BOWDEN, J.J.**
"Exodus of Federal forces from Texas in 1861." Austin, Texas: Eakin Press (1986). 8vo, cl, dj, xi, 149pp., illus., ports, map.

960 **BOWDOIN, Maggie**
"A Virginia Girl in the Civil War, 1861-1865." Edt: Mrs. Myrta L. Avary. See: Myrta L. Avary. Mrs. Anne M.D. Wingfield of Petersburg, Va. identifies author as Maggie Bowdoin, "the youngest daughter is the wife of one of my cousins in Richmond." She having dictated this experience to Myrta Lockett." Note in Jenkins cat. #154. $85.

961 **BOWEN, Clarissa Adger**
"The Diary of Clarissa Adger Bowen, Ashtabula Plantation, 1865, with excerpts from other Family Diaries & comments by her grandaughter, Clarissa Walton Taylor; & many other accounts of the Pendleton Clemson Area, South Carolina, 1887-1889." Comp: Mary Stevenson, Pendleton, S.C., Research & Publication Committee, Foundation for Historic Restoration in Pendleton Area, 1973. 8vo, wraps, 126pp., illus., maps, pls. $8. 1000 copies printed.

962 **BOWEN, Don R.**
"Quantrill, James, Younger, et al: Leadership in a Guerilla Movement, Missouri, 1861-1865." In: Mil. Affairs, February, 1977, v.XLI.

963 ..."Guerilla War in Western Missouri, 1862-1865: Historical Extensions of the

Relative Deprivation Hypothesis." In: Comp. Studies in Sociology & History, February, 1978.

964 **BOWEN, John Joseph**
"The Strategy of Robert E. Lee." By J.J. Bowen, formerly member of the 1st Co. of Richmond Howitzers. N.Y., Thomas Y. Crowell (1914) (c. by Neale Pub. Co.) $50, $75-bmk, $40-bmk, $24-r. 8vo, cl, ports, illus., 256pp. $7.50, $10, Orig. in Neale's, I(Jan-June) p. 3-16; 179-193; 285-301; 399-415; 541-562; 671-685; II(july) p. 55-66.

965 **BOWEN, Nancy Head**
"A Political Labyrinth: Texas in the Civil War." In: ETHJ, Fall, 1973, v.XI, #2, p. 3-11, notes.

966 **BOWEN, William A.**
"Uncle Zeke's Speculation. A Story of War & Reconstruction Days in Texas." Arlington, Texas: Arlington press (1910) 16mo, illus. on stiff wraps, 125pp. $37.50.

967 **BOWEN, William R.**
"The history & archaeology of a civil war soldier." In: Atlanta Hist. Jour., v.25, #3, p. 67-77. 1981. On Jacob Wheeler of Liberty County.

968 **BOWERING, Andrew Benjamin**
"Andrew Benjamin Bowering (died 1923) He didn't like "Dixie!"...Edt: Chester Goolrick. In: Va. Caval., spring 1960, v.9, #4, p. 4-10, facsms, ports (1-color), views. Undated reminiscences by the bugler & band leader of the 10th Va. Inf. CSArmy, 1863-1865.

969 **BOWERS, Claude G.**
"The Tragic Era; the Revolution after Lincoln." Cambridge: Houghton Mifflin Co., 1929, 8vo, cl, plates (inc. facsms) ports, xxii, 567pp. $5. "A person finds himself a partisan or an apologist for crime", sources as diaries, letters, newspapers, leave no doubt of the crimes committed on the South by carpetbaggers.

970 **BOWES, Frederick P.**
"The Culture of Early Charleston." Chapel Hill, N.C., Univ. N.C. Press, 1942. 8vo, cl, vii-xi, 156pp.

971 **BOWES, John**
"The Fall of Abraham Lincoln. Slavery Vanquished in Arms, Resorts to the Pistol & the Dagger: Thus the South is Avenged. A Lecture delivered in the Corn Exchange Hall, Dundee, May 5, 1865." (Metuchen, N.J., Wayside Press by R.H. Pickersgill, 1941) Heartman Hist. Ser. #59, 8vo, wraps, 16pp. (old) $8.50. Reprinted: "The Truth Promoter, etc." as described below.

972 ..."The Truth Promotor: or, the Truth, the only way to the Freedom, Elevation, & Happiness of Man." Dundee, 1863-1866. 8vo, (4), 300pp., #1, March 1863-#38, April, 1866. Cloth. Underscribed, not in Monaghan. Contains a lecture, "Fall of Abe Lincoln", as described above reprint. (old) $42.50.

973 **BOWIE, Marshall**
"A time of adversity & courage." Montgomery, Ala., 1961. 8vo, wraps, 16pp. $7.50. "Montgomery & West Point RRy during the war.

974 **BOWIE, Sidney J., Hon.**
"Address of..., to United Daughters of the Confederacy of Camp W.H. Forney, & the U.C.V., of Camp Pelham on Memorial Day, June 3, 1903, Anniston, Alabama." Anniston, Ala., n.d. (1903) 8vo, wraps, 16pp. Atg. present. $10.

975 **BOWLBY, Elizabeth**
"The role of Atlanta during the war between the states." In: Atl. Hist. Bul, V., 1940, p. 177-196. Stresses economic role during the war.

976 **BOWLES, R.C.**
"The Ship Tennessee. A description of the Conflict in Mobile Bay. One of the men aboard tells of surrender & why." In: SHSP, 1893, v.XXI, p. 290-294.

977 **BOWLES, Richard C.**
"Company D, Forty-Fourth Virginia. A Brief History & Roster of the Command." In: SHSP, 1900, v.XXVIII, p. 259-260.

978 **BOWMAN, Forest J.**
"Capture of Generals Crook & Kelley, "The most brilliant exploit of the war." In: CWTI, Feb. 1969, v.VII, #10, p. 28-37, illus., map, ports McNeil's Rangers captures generals before 8000 Union troops.

979 ..."Confederate Constitution-copy of the U.S., or an improvement?" In: CWTI, Nov. 1967, v.VI, #7, p. 12-18, illus., ports.

980 **BOWMAN, Robert**
"Reconstruction in Yazoo County." In: (Oxford), 1903, Pub. Miss. Hist. Soc., v.VII, p. 115-130.

981 ..."Yazoo County in the Civil War." In: (Oxford), 1903, Pub. Miss. Hist. Soc., v.VII, p. 57-73.

982 **BOWMAN, Thornton Hardie**
"Reminiscences of an ex-Confederate soldier; or, forty years on crutches." Austin, Texas: Gammel-Statesman (1904). 12mo, wraps, 2-ports (incl. front) 126pp. (old)$12.50, $30, $350-r, $75.

983 **BOWSER, O.P.**
"Notes on Granbury's Brigade." In: Dudley Wooten's "Comprehensive History of Texas", v.II, p. 741-754.

984 **BOWYER, N.B.**
"Reminiscences of Appomattox." In: CV, 1902, v.10, p. 77-78, port.

985 **BOX, Eugene, Mrs.**
"Ante-Bellum Travelers in Mississippi." (Jackson, Miss., Jour. Miss. Hist., April, 1955, v.XVII, #2, p. 110-126.

986 **BOX, Sam**
"End of the War-Exiles in Mexico." In: CV, March 1903, v.XI, p. 121-123.

987 **BOY'S EXPERIENCE IN THE CIVIL WAR, A,**
See: Thomas Hughes.

988 **BOYCE, Joseph**
"The evacuation of Nashville (Tenn.) In: CV, FEb. 1920, v.XXVIII, p. 213-216.

989 ...Missourians in battle of Franklin." In: CV, Mar. 1916, v.XXIV, p. 101-103, 138.

990 **BOYCE, William W. & Hammond, Jas. H.**
"Boyce-Hammond Correspondence." Edt: Rosser H. Taylor. (Baton Rouge, La.) JSH, Aug. 1937, v.III, #3, p. 348-54. Critics of Davis & promoted peace.

991 **BOYD, Belle Hardinge**
"Belle Boyd, in Camp & Prison. With an Introduction by a Friend to the South." London: Saunders & Otley, 1865, 2vols, 8vo, cl, xi, 291, xv, 280pp. port. $15, $25, Fine: $275, $100-bmk. 3/4Mor.
..."Belle Boyd in Camp & Prison. Written by Herself. With Introduction by George Augustus Sala." New York: Blelock & Co., 1865. 12mo, cl, p. 464. $75-jenk-151, $30, $17.50, $20, $50.
...Do: N.Y., 1866. $30, (old)$3.
...Do: N.Y., 1867, (old)$4.50, $40-bmk, $50-bmk.
..."A new edition prepared from new materials, by Curtis Carroll Davis." South Brunswick, N.J., Thomas Yoseloff, c. 1968. $10. 12mo, cl, dj, front(port), facsm., illus., ports. Seventeen year old girl from Martinsburg, Va. Spy for Jackson. Claimed she seduced Hardinge, Lt. in U.S.N., who fell in love with her & later married.

992 ..."Belle Boyd, Southern Spy of the Shenandoah." (Front Royal, Va.) Warren County Rifles Chap., U.D.C., n.d. (1936). 8vo, wraps, 8pp, caption title $1. See: H.E. Cole.

993 **BOYD, Casper**
"Casper W. Boyd, Campany I, 15th Alabama infantry, CSA. A casualty of the battle of Cross Keys, Va. His last letters written home." In: AHQ, 1961, v.XXIII, p. 291-299.

994 **BOYD, Charles H.**
"An incident on the coast of Maine in 1861." In: Mag. of Hist., Jan 1912, v.XV, p. 38-41. Capture of CSNavy ships "Express" & "Alice Ball" by US schooner "Arago".

995 **BOYD, David French**
"Address of Col. D.F. Boyd on the anniversary of the Delta Rifles, 4th Louisiana regiment, Confederate States Army, at Port Allen, West Baton Rouge, La., May 20th, 1887." Baton Rouge: Capitolian-Advocate print, 1887. 8vo, wraps, 20pp. Dornbusch-449.

996 ..."Life & services of David French Boyd." Baton Rouge, LSU Bulletin series 2, #2, June 1904. Complete issue devoted to Boyd. His CSA services. $9.50

997 ..."Gen. Richard Taylor, CSA." In: Confed. Vet., Nov. 1928, v.XXXVI, p. 412-413.

998 **BOYD, J.L.R.**
"John Angus Campbell, pfc. CSA, 1840, 1933." (Photo:c.1912). 8vo, wraps, 6pp at end: Distr., compl. Standard Federal Savings & Loan Assn. 48 Broad St., NW, Atlanta, Ga. (Emory) $16.

999 **BOYD, J.N.**
"The Battle of Oak Hills or Wilson's Creek." In: CV, Jan. 1911, v.XIX, p. 9-10.

1000 **BOYD, James**
"Marching On." N.Y., C. Scribner's Sons, 1927. 12mo, cl, 3-426pp. $12. Novel of a N.C. CSA private.
...5th print. $20, $20-bmk, $30-bmk.

1001 **BOYD, LeRoy**
"Thunder on the Rio grande, the Great Adventure of Sibley's Confederates for the Conquest of New Mexico & Colorado." In: Colorado Mag., v.XXIV, p. 131-140.

1002 **BOYD, Mark F.**
"The Joint Operations of the Federal Army & Navy Near St. Marks, Fla. March, 1865. - "Battle of Natural Bridge"." Tallahassee, Fla., 1950. Reprint: Florida Historical Quarterly, Oct. 1950, wraps, 30pp. $10, $5, $3. Largely the CSA account of battle.

1003 ..."The Federal Campaign of 1864 in East Florida (Olustee Battlefield)". Tallahassee, Fla: Historical Quarterly, July, 1950, v.XXIX-#1, Reprint. $10, $3, $8. 8vo, wraps, fldg. maps, 37pp.

1004 ..."The Battle of Marianna." Tallahassee, Fla: Historical Quarterly, April, 1951, v.XXIX-#4, Reprint. $5-bmk, $3, $10. 8vo, wraps, 17pp. See: Fannie B. Chapman

1005 **BOYD, Thomas M.**
"General Stonewall Jackson". In: SB, ns, v.II, 1886/1887, p. 355-360. $10.

1006 **BOYD, William Kenneth & Robt. P. Brooks**
"A selected bibliography & syllabus of the history of the South, 1584-1876." Athens, Ga., McGregor co, 1918. Univ. Ga. Bul., v.XVIII, #6, 8vo, cl, 133pp. $25-ginz.

1007 ..."North Carolina on the Eve of Secession." Wash: 1912, in Amer. Hist. Ass'n. Yearbook for 1910, p. 165-177.
...Reprint, 8vo, wraps, above, also in cloth.

1008 ...See: his Intro. & notes, Gen. Wm. R. Boggs.

1009 ..."Fiscal & Economic Conditions in North Carolina during the war." In: N.C. Booklet, April 1915, v.XIV, #4, p. 195-219, 8vo, wraps, 25pp. $10-bmk-84

1010 ..."Military Criticisms, by Gen. W.R. Boggs." In: So. Atl. Quart., April 1912, p. 154-166. A review of Bogg's "Reminiscences." Made introduction/notes to Bogg's book.

1011 ..."Three Letters relating to conditions in Eastern Carolina in 1864." Durham: Duke University, 1906. Historical Papers Trinity College Historical Society, Ser.VI, p. 99-102. $14-bmk

1012 ..."Robert E. Lee." In: So. Atl. Quart., 1935, v.XXXIV, p. 211-219. Review of

Douglas Freeman & Robert W. Winston's biographies of Lee.

1013 **BOYER, Margrette**
"Morgan's Raid in Indiana." In: Ind. Mag. of Hist., Dec. 1912, p. 149-165.

1014 **BOYERS, Thomas**
"General Sam Houston. Explanation of causes why the Soldier-Governor forsake the three-month bride to live with Cherokee Indian Tribe." In: SHSP, 1907, v.XXXV, p. 146-150.

1015 **BOYKIN, Burwell**
"Address delivered before the Southern Rights Association of Alabama, of Mobile. Mobile, 1850. 8vo, wraps, 11pp. $75-gdsp.

1016 **BOYKIN, Edward**
"Beefsteak Raid." N.Y., Funk & Wagnalls co(1960), 8vo, cl, dj, illus., ports, map, (4), 305pp. $25-bmk-84, $4.95, $10, $40.

1017 ..."Congress & the Civil War." N.Y., McBride Co(1955). 8vo, cl, dj, illus., ports, 352pp. $5, $8, $8.50.
...Special Vista House Edition, n.d., $5, (cheaper binding & paper).

1018 ..."Ghost Ship of the Confederacy. The Story of the Alabama & her captain, Raphael Semmes." N.Y., Funk & Wagnalls Co(1957). 8vo, cl, dj, illus., ports, map, viii, (2)-404pp. Pub: $4.95, $8.50, atg-edt.-$7.50, $10, $27.50, $20-bmk-95, $12.50-y, $14-bmk.

1019 ..."Sea Devil of the Confederacy. The Story of the Florida & her captain, John Newland Maffitt." N.Y., Funk & Wagnalls Co.(1959), 8vo, cl, dj, illus., ports, map, xii, 306pp. Pub: $4.95, $6.50, $30-b, $11, $16-bmk, $25-bmk.

1020 **BOYKIN, Edward M.**
"The Falling Flag. Evacuation of Richmond, Retreat & Surrender at Appomattox. By an officer of the rear guard." N.Y., E.T. Hale & Son, 1874. 12mo, wraps, 67pp. $10, $30, $35, $350-os, $200-bmk-105, $125-bmk-85, '73 auction-$32, $65-bmk.
...3rd Edt., same, illus., by Edward M. Boykin, Lt.-Col. 7th regt., S.C. cavalry. decr.cf. $200-ob, $35.

1021 ..."Boys' & Girls' Stories of the War. Contents: Gen. Jackson, Com. Foot, Col. Small, etc." Richmond, Va., West & Johnston (c.1864) 32mo, wraps, cover title, illus., 32pp.

1022 **BOYKIN, James H.**
"Negro in North Carolina Prior to 1861; an Historical Monograph." N.Y., Pageant Press, (1958), 12mo, wraps, 84pp. bibliog.

1023 ..."North Carolina in 1861." N.Y., Bookman Associates (1961), sm.8vo, cl, 237pp. Social, secession, politics & gov.

1024 **BOYKIN, Laura Nisbet**
"Shinplaster & homespun: the diary of Laura Nisbet Boykin." Edt: Mary Wright Stock." (Rockville, Md., Printex, 1985. 8vo, stiff wraps, xvi, 76pp. illus. Personal narrative of Civil War.

1025 **BOYKIN, Richard Manning**
"Captain Alexander Hamilton Boykin, one of the South Carolina's Distinguished Citizens. by...a Grandson." Privately printed for Family & Friends (#481) New York, 1942. (Pandick Press) 8vo, cl, ports, pl, sketches, facsms, map & map endpapers, ii, (2), 263pp. $22.50, $5, $7.50, $10, Lim. sig. edt.-$52.50, $45-y, $36-bmk-86, $45-bmk-84.

1026 **BOYKIN, Samuel, Edt.**
See: Cobb, Howell, "Memorial Record of..."

1027 **BOYLE, Francis Atherton**
"The Prison Diary of Adjutant Francis Atherton Boyle, C.S.A." Edt: Mary Lindsay Thornton. (Raleigh) NCHRev., Winter 1962, v.XXXIX, #1, p. 58-84. $10-bmk.

1028 **BOYLE, Rockwell S.**
"Virginia's mineral contribution to the Confederacy." In: Va. Geological Surv.,

contributions to Virginia geology. University, Va., 1936, in Bul. 46, p. 117-123.

1029 **BOYLE, Virginia Frazer**
"Brokenburne, A Southern Auntie's War Tale." N.Y., E.R. Herrick, 1897. 8vo, cl, illus. (incl. front) 75pp. $25, $3.50.
...N.Y., Arno Press, 1977. "Black Heritage Library Collection." $12.75.

1030 **BOYLES, J.R.**
"Reminiscences of the Civil War. By Lt. J.R. Boyle of Company "C", 12th S.C.V., Gregg's Brigade (afterwards McGowan's)." Columbia, S.C., Bryan Printing co, 1890, 8vo, 66pp. cover title. Turnbull, v.IV.

1031 **BOYLSTON, Raymond P., Jr.**
"The battle of Aiken...Sketches by Samuelton L. Boylston." (Belvedere, S.C., 1960. 8vo, wraps, illus., dbl. map, 22pp.

1032 **BOYNTON, Henry Van Ness, Gen.** "The Blue & the Gray United. The Chickamauga Memorial Association." In: SHSP, v.XVI, p. 339-349.

1033 ..."Chickamauga & Chattanooga National Military Park, Sept. 18-20, 1895." Washington, DC, 1896. 8vo, cl, illus., maps, 374pp. Dedication of the Park. $12.

1034 ..."Chickamauga & Chattanooga National Military Park Commission Organization of the Union Forces & of the Confederate Forces." Washington, DC, 1893. 8vo, wraps, map, 34pp. $20-bmk.

1035 ..."The National Military Park, Chickamauga-Chattanooga. An Historical Guide." Cincinnati: Robert Clarke Co., 1895." 8vo, wraps, front, illus., map, xviii, 307pp. "Roster of the Union & Confederate Armies at Chickamauga." p. 60-87. "Rosters of the Union & Confederate Forces at Chattanooga." p. 140-166. Compil.: J.W. Kirkley. $20-bmk.

1036 **BOYNTON, James W.**
"The South Atlantic Blockading Squadron: The Diary of James W. Boynton, Edited by Abbott A. Brayton." In: So. Car. Hist. Mag., 1975, v.LXXVI, p. 112-117.

1037 **BOYNTON, Thomas**
"Oration delivered at Key West (Fla.), July 4, 1861." Key West, (Florida), 1861. 8vo, wraps, 23pp. (Eberstadt-Cat. 115, #398) $5.

1038 **BOYS & GIRLS Stories of the War.**
See: Edward M. Boykin.

1039 **BOZEMAN, Nathan**
Portrait, steel-engraved, by H.B. Hall Sons, New York (c.1880) 4to. Confederate surgeon. $3.50

1040 **BRACKENBURY, Henry**
"Stonewall Jackson." In: Blackwood's Edinburg Mag., Dec. 1898, 18pp.

1041 **BRACKETT, Albert G., Gen.**
"Sketch, Colonel Theodore O'Hara." In: SHSP, 1891, v.XIX, p. 275-281. See: George Washington Ranck, Theodore O'Hara, Edgar E. Hume.

1042 **BRACKETT, Jeffrey Richardson**
"The Negro in Maryland; a study of the institution of Slavery." Baltimore, N. Murray, pub. agt., Johns Hopkins University, 1889. Half-title: Johns Hopkins University Studies in Historical & Political Science. Extra Vol. vi. 8vo, wraps, 268pp. $35.

1043 **BRADBEER, William West**
"Confederate & Southern state currency; historical & financial data, biographical sketches, descriptions with illustrations." Mt. Vernon, N.Y., 1915 private print. 8vo, cl, illus., 162pp. $25, $10, Auct-$65, $75.
...Chicago, Ill., 1945 Reprint, 1000 copies. 8vo, cl, illus., port, facsm, (9)-277 (i.e., 291pp.) Ex-pages inserted (156A-156N, incl. 163-277) most of H.D. Allen's, which appeared in Numismatist 1917, 18, & 19. Also Wismers' Tex. Treas. Notes of civil war, Sept. 1927 Numismatist. (1956) $10, $15, Auct-$10.

1044 ..."North Carolina State Currency (From Confederate & Southern State Currency.)

1045 In: N.C. Booklet, July-Oct. 1919, v.XIX, #1-2, p. 36-46. $20-bmk.
..."Southern state currency." In: Numismatist, Feb. 1913, v.XXVI, p. 72-74. (civil war period.)
...(Racine, Wisc., Whitman pub., 1960, p. 199-201, facsms, reprint of 1913 edt.

1046 **BRADEN, George**
"The Ku-Klux Klan: An Apology." In: SB, ns, v.1, 1885/1886, p. 103-109. $10.

1047 ..."An apology explained." In: SB, ns, v.1, #8, p. 507-508. (1885/1886). Answers D.L. Wilson's "Beginnings of Ku-Klux Klan & George Braden's KKK: an apology. See: above author's articles.

1048 **BRADEN, W.H.**
"Reconstruction in Lee County." Oxford, Miss., PMHS, v.X, 1909, p. 135-146.

1049 **BRADEN, Waldo W.**
"Oratory in the Old South, 1828-1860." Baton Rouge: La. State Univ. Pr., 1970. 8vo, cl, d/w, viii, 311pp. $10.

1050 ..."C. Alphonso Smith on Southern Oratory before the War." In: South. Speech Jour., 1970, v.XXXVI, p. 127-138.

1051 **BRADFORD, Gamaliel**
"Lee & his Army." In: Atlantic, July, 1911, v.108, p. 83-93.

1052 ..."J.E.B. Stuart." In: Atlantic, Jan. 1913, v.CXI, p. 98-109.

1053 ..."Robert Toombs; a Confederate Portrait." In: Atlantic, Aug. 1913, v.CXII, p. 208-219.

1054 ..."Joseph E. Johnston (Confederate Portraits I)." In: Atlantic, Nov. 1912, v.CX, p. 637-648.

1055 ..."A Hero's conscience; a study of Robert E. Lee." In: Atlantic, Dec. 1910, v.CVI, p. 730-739.

1056 ..."Lee & the Confederate Government." In: Atlantic, Feb. 1911, v.CVII, p. 192-202.

1057 ..."Portrait of Edwin Booth." In: Scribner's Feb. 1925, v.LXXVII, p. 143-155. Same, trans: In: Inter-America, July 1925, v.IX, p. 114-128.

1058 ..."First lady of the Confederacy; port of Mrs. Jefferson Davis." In: Harper's, Aug. 1925, v.CLI, p. 355-366.

1059 ..."Alexander H. Stephens, A Confederate Portrait." Excerpt: The Atlantic Monthly, Boston, 1913, July, v.CXII, #1, p. 62-73.

1060 ..."James Longstreet." In: Atlantic, Dec. 1912, v.CX, p. 834-845.

1061 ..."Confederate Portraits." Bost., N.Y., Houghton Mifflin Co., 1914, 8vo, cl, ports (incl. front), xviii, (1), 291pp. Johnston, Longstreet, Stuart, Beauregard, Benjamin, Stephens, Toombs, Semmes. All reprinted from Atlantic Monthly, Neale's Monthly Mag., & Youth's Companion. $25, $7.50, $10, $15-y, 1/2 Mor. edt. atg. $12.50, 1922-$25, $35-b.
...Same (1942), dj, $35-bmk, $6., $7.

1062 ..."Lee, The American." Bost., N.Y., Houghton Mifflin Co., 1912. 8vo, cl, front, ports, facsm, xvi, 324pp. $10, Mor. edt.-$15. $16-bmk.
...London, 1912. $5.
...Revised Edt., 1927-"Riverside Library" Reprint. Same., n.d. $2.50, $7.50-y, $5. Same: 1929; and Edt: (1940)1949. $2.50.

1063 ..."Lee after the War." So. Atl. Quart., 1911, X(July), p. 232-247.

1064 ..."Lee in Battle." Atlantic, CVIII(Aug.), p. 220-227.

1065 ..."The Social & Domestic Life of Robert E. Lee." So. Atl. Quart., X(Apr), p. 103-118.

1066 ..."The Spiritual Life of Robert E. Lee." Atlantic, CVIII(Oct.), p.501-512.

1067 ..."Lee Before the War." Sewanee Rev., XX, (Jan), p. 12-25.

1068 ..."Lee & psychography." So. Atl. Quart., XI(Jan), p. 63-74.

1069 ..."General Robert E. Lee as a college president." Rev. of Rev., XLV(Jan), p. 102-103.

1070 ..."Lee & Davis." Atlantic, CVII(Jan)1911, p. 62-72.

1071 ..."Lee & Jackson." Atlantic, CVII(June), p. 778-788.
..."Raphael Semmes; a last Confederate Portrait." In: Atlantic, Oct. 1913, CXII, p. 62-73.

1072 **BRADFORD, S. Sydney**
"The Negro Ironworker in Ante-Bellum Virginia." (Lexington, Ky.) JSH, May, 1959, v.XXV, #2, p. 194-206.

1073 **BRADLEE, Francis B.C.**
"A forgotten chapter in our naval history. A sketch of the career of Duncan Nathaniel Ingraham, commander U.S.N. & Commodore C.S.N." $10, $15. Salem, Mass: Essex Institute, 1923. 8vo, wraps, front(port) illus., 25pp. $25.

1074 ..."Blockade Running during the Civil War & the effect of water & land transportation on the Confederacy." Salem, Mass: Essex Institute, 1925. 8vo, cl, front, maps, facsm., ports, 340pp. Reprint: Hist. Colls. Essex Inst., v.LX, LXI, 1924-1925. $15, $20, $8, $25, $100-bmk, $150-bmk-105.
...Phila: Porcupine Press, 1974, rep: $20. $25-y. LX(Jan/Oct), p. 1-16, 153-177, 233-256, 349-372. LXII(Jan/Oct), p. 33-64, 129-160, 321-352. LXIII(Jan. 1927), p. 42-44.

1075 ..."An Essex county vessel the first to hoist the Southern colors at the breaking out of the civil war in 1860." In: Essex Inst. Hist., Apr. 1927, v.LXIII, p. 133-134. Charleston, S.C., Nov. 1860 the "James Gray" of Newburyport, Mass., 1st vessel to publicly display & salute the Palmetto(Secession) flag of South Carolina.

1076 ..."The Kearsarge-Alabama Battle, the story as told to the writer by James Magee of Marblehead, seaman on the Kearsarge." Salem, Mass: Essex Institute, 1921, 8vo, wraps, plates, ports(groups), 25pp. Reprint: Hist. Coll. Essex Inst., July, 1921, v.LVII, p. 217-241. $20, $12.

1077 **BRADLEY, Bert E. & Jerry L. Tarver**
"John C. Calhoun's Argumentation in Defense of Slavery." In: South. Speech Journ., 1969, v.XXXV, p. 163-175.

1078 **BRADLEY, Chester D.**
"Dr. Craven & the Prison Life of Jefferson Davis." (Richmond)Va. Mag. Hist. Biog. Jan. 1954, v.62, #1, p. 50-94, pl, port, facsm. Craven's book was based on his diary & help from his friend, Charles G. Halpine, a well-known journalist's.

1079 ..."Dr. John J. Craven, physician to Jefferson Davis." reprint from Virginia Medical Monthly, v.78, Aug. 1951. 4to, p. 433-437; also in UDC Mag. Feb/Mar. 1952, p. 23-24, 5.

1080 ..."Craven & O'Meara: Medical Boswells, Jefferson Davis & Napoleon Bonaparte." Reprint: Bul. Hist. of Med., vol. xxvi-#2, Mar-Apr. 1952. 8vo, wraps, p. 141-152, illus. & ports. $3.50

1081 ..."Dr. Craven & the Prison Life of Jefferson Davis." From: Va. Mag. of Hist. & Biog., vol.62, Jan. 1954, 8vo, wraps, p. 50-94.

1082 ..."Jefferson Davis in Prison." In: Manuscripts, 1958, v.10(2), p. 35-39, 52(spring) on shackling Davis' legs by Capt. Titlow. $5.

1083 ..."Was Jefferson Davis disguised as a woman when captured?" (Jackson)Jour. Miss. Hist., Aug.1974, v.XXXVI, #3, p. 243-268, illus.

1084 ..."Dr. Craven & the Prison Life of Jefferson Davis." (Richmond)Va. Mag. Hist. Biog., Jan. 1954, v.LXIII, p. 50-94.

1085 **BRADLEY, James**
"The Confederate Mail Carrier or from Missouri to Arkansas, through Mississippi, Alabama, Georgia & Tennessee. An Unwritten Leaf of the "Civil War". Being an account of the battles, marches & hard-

ships of the 1st & 2nd brigades, Mo., CSA. Together with the thrilling adventures & narrow escapes of Capt. Grimes & his fair accomplice, who carried the mail by the "underground route" from the Brigade to Missouri." Auct-$78.50. Mexico, Mo., The Author, 1894. $17.50, $35. 12mo, cl, ports(incl. front), 275pp. $27.50, $50, $200-bmk. p. 231-"Part Second Introduction The Confederate Home its origin & its objects by Mrs. Elizabeth Ustick McKinney. Biography & an explanatory index to engravings. See: Absalom Grimes.

1086 **BRADLEY, Jesse N.**
"A Rebel Officer's revenge, in spades, against the Navy." In: Smithsonian, Nov. 1976, v.7, #8, p. 122-131. Color illus., port.

1087 **BRADLOW, Edna & Frank**
"Here Comes the Alabama. The Career of a Confederate Raider." Capetown-Amsterdam: A.A. Balkema (1958). Tall 12mo, cl, dj, illus.(1-color) facsms, port (front), index. 128pp. $3.25, $5, $7.50, $25-bmk-104.
...Same book, with inprint on title page: "Distributed in USA, Southern University Press, Birmingham, Alabama." (1975) $6.95.

1088 **BRADMORE, Michael**
"Some aspects of the Confederate Medical Service." (London)Jour. Confed. Hist. Soc., Summer, 1972, v.10, #2, p. 48-62, port.

1089 **BRADSHAW, George S.**
"The History of the 1st N.C. Reunion at Greensboro, N.C., Oct. 11-13, 1903. compl. & edt. by Geo. S. Bradshaw." Greensboro, N.C., J.J. Stone, 1905. sm.4to, 176pp. incl. map, 3-pls.(incl. front), 66-ports on 54 plates. $10.

1090 **BRADWELL, I.G.**
"After the Surrender at Appomattox." In: Conf. Vet., Sept. 1909, XVI, p. 467.

1091 ..."Battle of Cedar Creek, Va." In: CV, July 1914, XXII, p. 315-316.
...Same: CV, Nov. 1919, v.XXVII, p. 411-412.

1092 ..."Battle of Fisher's Hill." In: CV, Sept. 1920, v.XXVIII, p. 338-240.

1093 ..."In the Battle of Monocacy, Md." In: CV, Feb. 1928, v.XXXVI, p. 55-57.

1094 ..."Battle of the Wilderness." In: CV, Dec. 1919, v.XXVII, p. 458-459.
...Same: CV, Sept. 1908, v.XVI, p. 447-448.

1095 ..."Burning of Wrightsville, Pa. (1863). In: CV, Aug. 1919, v.XXVII, p. 300-301.

1096 ..."Capture of Winchester, Va., Milroy's Army in June, 1863." In: CV, Sept. 1922, v.XXX, p. 330-332.

1097 ..."Chancellorsville." In: CV, July 1922, v.XXX, p. 257-260. (Below: "Cold Harbour.")

1098 ..."Early's demonstration against Washington in 1864." In: CV, Oct. 1914, v.XXII, p. 438-439.
..."Early's march to Washington, 1864." In: CV, May, 1920, p. 176-177.

1099 ..."With Early in the Valley." In: CV, Nov. 1914, v.XXII, p. 504-506.

1100 ..."Early's Valley Campaign, 1864." In: CV, June 1920, v.XXVIII, p. 218-221.

1101 ..."The Flight at Winchester, Va.-Jim Graham." In: CV, Sept. 1907, p. 411.

1102 ..."First of Valley Campaign by Gen. Early." In: CV, May 1911, XIX, p. 230-231.

1103 ..."From Cedar Mountain to Sharpsburg." In: CV, Aug. 1921, v.XXIX, p. 296-298.

1104 ..."From Cold Harbor to Cedar Mountain." In: CV, June 1921, XXIX, p. 222-225.

1105 ..."General Lee at Sharpsburg, 1862." In: CV, Oct. 1921, v.XXIX, p. 378-380.

1106 ..."The Georgia Brigade at Fredericksburg." In: CV, Jan. 1922, XXX, p. 18-20.

1107 ..."Gordon's Brigade after the Valley Campaign." In: CV, Nov. 1920, v.XXVIII, p. 418-420.

1108 ..."Gordon's Georgia Brigade in the Wilderness." In: CV, Dec. 1908, XVI, p. 641-642. (Below: "Grant Rev.)

1109 ..."Last Days of the Confederacy." In: CV, FEb. 1921, v.XXIX, p. 56-58.

1110 ..."Making Our way home from Appomattox." In: CV, Mar. 1921, V.XXIX, 102-103.

1111 ..."Morton's Ford, Jan. 4, 1864." In: CV, Nov., 1925, v.XXXIII, p. 412-414.

1112 ..."On Picket duty in front of Fort Steadman." In: CV, 1930, v.38, p. 302-307.

1113 ..."Picturesque Soldiery." In: CV, June 1923, v.XXXI, p. 212-214. An acct. of Buck Tails, Zouaves, Garibaldi.

1114 ..."Second day's battle of the Wilderness, May 6, 1864." In: CV, Jan. 1920, v.XXVIII, p. 20-22.

1115 ..."Soldier life in the Confederate Army." In: CV, Jan. 1916, v.XXIV, p. 20-25.

1116 ..."Spotsylvania, May 12-13, 1864." In: CV, Mar. 1920, v.XXVIII, p. 102-103.
..."Same: May 8-9, 1864." In: CV, Feb. 1920, v.XXVIII, p. 56-57.

1117 ..."The Valley Campaign after the Battle of Cedar Creek." In: CV, Oct. 1920, v.XXVIII, p. 374-376.

1118 ..."Cold Harbor, Lynchburg, Valley Campaign, etc., 1864." In: CV, Apr. 1920, v.XXVIII, p. 138-139.

1119 ..."The Grand Review." In: CV, Jan. 1923, v.XXXI, p. 16-18. Gen. Lee reviews CSArmy, south Rapidan in 1864.

1120 ..."In front of Fort Steadman, 1865." In: CV, Sept. 1917, v.XXV, p. 408-409.

1121 ..."Fort Steadman & subsequent events." In: CV, Jan. 1915, v.23, p. 20-23.

1122 **BRADY, Cyrus Townsend**
"The Patriots; story of Lee & the last hope." N.Y., Dodd, Mead & Co., 1906. $3, $6.50. 12mo, cl, col. front., plates, 12, (3)-348pp.

1123 ..."The Southerners. A Story of the Civil War." N.Y., Charles Scribner's sons, 1903. 12mo. decr. cl., illus. tinted pls. (incl. front), xii, (1)407, (1), (4)pp. $15-bmk-109, $4.50

1124 ..."Three Daughters of the Confederacy, a story of their hatreds, their joys & their sorrows, during many surprising adventures on land & sea." N.Y., G.W. Dillingham co(1905). $10, $12.50. 12mo, cl, 6-color pls. (incl.front) 440pp. All Brady's books fiction.

1125 **BRADY, Lewis**
"Notice of Chew's Battery." In: SHSP, 1888, v.XVI, p. 214-215. Brady was late private Chew's Battery, Breathed's Battalion, Stuart's Horse Artillery.

1126 **BRAGG, Braxton, Gen.**
"A Short History of Braxton Bragg." Park Place, N.Y., Knapp & Co., 1888. 2 3/4x1 1/2" colored booklet, 16pp. facsm. signature. (packed in Duke's cigareetes) See: "Heroes of the C.W. & W. Duke co.

1127 ..."Confederate love-taps, General Braxton Bragg & the Generals of his command." In: Morrisania, 1873-Historical Magazine, v.1, p.257-274, 334-351; v.2, p.32-36.

1128 ..."Kentucky Headquarters, Dept. #2, Glasgow, Ky., Sept. 14, 1862." Quarton, 1p. Broadside. $25. "Kentuckians-I have entered your state with the CSArmy of the West & offer you an opportunity to free yourself from the tyranny of a despotic ruler."

1129 ..."Report made by Gen. Bragg of the Kentucky Campaign." In: OLOD, 1874/1875, v.1, p. 15.

1130 ..."Gen. Braxton Bragg's report of the Battle of Chickamauga." In: OLOD, 1874, '75, v.1, p. 122-134.

1131 ..."Official report of the Battle of Chickamauga." Pub. by Order of Congress, Richmond: R.M. Smith, Print, 1864. 8vo, cl, 234pp. Crandall-1372. $250-r.

1132 ..."We Sowed & We Have Reaped"; a Post-war letter from Braxton Bragg." (Houston, Tex.) JSH, Feb. 1965, v.XXXI, #1, p. 75-79. $8-bmk

1133 ..."Battle Shiloh & Pittsburg Landing." In: Confed. War Jour., v.I, p. 178-181. See: "Memoranda of facts, re: Ky. camp."

1134 ..."The Battle of Chickamauga. Report of General Braxton Bragg, Dec. 28, 1863." In: SHSP, 1883, v.XI, p. 49-65.

1135 ..."Lookout Mountain & Missionary Ridge. Report of General Braxton Bragg, Nov. 30, 1863.

1136 ..."Defence & Fall of Fort Fisher. Letter from General Braxton Bragg, Jan. 20, 1865." In: SHSP, 1882, v.X, p. 346-349.

1137 ..."General Bragg's Proclamation on entering Kentucky. Sept. 18, 1862." In: SHSP, 1879, v.VII, p. 172. See also: John Cabell Breckinridge, W.T. Martin, E.T. Sykes.

1138 ..."Bragg & His Generals." In: SB, v.1, #5, ns, 1885/1886, p. 278-283. From Liddell's Record. $6. See: C.C. Gilbert, L.H. Stout.

1139 ...Bragg's Campaign of 1862. See: Bragg, Braxton; Duke, Gasil; Fisher, Horace N.; Gilbert, C.C.; Hammond, Paul F.; McWhiney, Grady; Messmer, Charles K.; Quisenberry, Anderson C.; Rankin, Walter H.; Seitz, Don C.; Urquhart, David; Wheeler, Joseph.

1140 **BRAGG, Jefferson Davis**
"Louisiana in the Confederacy." Baton Rouge: Louisiana Univ. Pr. (1941) 8vo, map-endsheets, ix, 341. $8.50, $10.
...Gloucester, Mass. Peter Smith, $12.50, $16-bmk, $20-y.

1141 **BRAGG, Junius Newport**
"Letters of a Confederate Surgeon, 1861-1865." Edt: Mrs. T.A. Gaughan. (Camden, Ark., The Hurley co, 1960) 8vo, cl, illus., 4, 276pp. $10, $15, 500 copies printed.

1142 **BRAGG, William C. & Frank B. Screven**
"Robert E. Lee in Georgia." In: Ga. Rev., Winter, 1962, (5)pp. $8.

1142a **BRAGG, William Harris**
"Joe Brown's Army: the Georgia State Line, 1862-1865." Macon, Ga., 1987. 8vo, cl, dj, 175p, ills, roster. $30.

1143 **BRALY, Mary Gramling**
"If I had a thousand lives." In: Tenn. Hist. Mag., July, 1931. (9)pp. (p. 261-269). Story: Sam Davis. $8.

1144 **BRAMANTIP, Bocardo**
"The Abraham Lincoln Myth." See: Buel, Oliver Prince

1145 **BRANCH, John**
"St. Albans Raid, St. Albans, Vermont, Oct. 19, 1864." St. Albans, Vt. (1935?) 8vo, wraps, ports, 67pp. Raid on St. Albans from Canada by the Confederates. Articles from files of St. Albans Daily Messenger.

1146 **BRANCH, L. O'B., Gen.**
"From the Correspondence of...Extract from a private letter, from Fairfax C.H." In: OLOD, Sept. 1874, v.1, #1, p. 41-42.

1147 **BRANCH, Mary Emerson**
"The story behind the story of the "Arkansas" & the "Carondelet"." In: MHR, April 1985, v.79, #3, p. 313-331, illus., port.

1148 **BRANCH, Mary Polk**
"Memoirs of a Southern Woman "within the lines", and a genealogical record." Chicago: Joseph G. Branch Pub. Co, (1912). 12mo, 1/2 cl-bds., illus., ports, 107pp. $15.

1149 **BRANCH, Paul, Jr.**
"The Siege of Fort Macon." Morehead City, N.C., The Author, 1982. 8vo, wraps, 106pp., illus., bibliog. $6.

1150 **BRAND, W.H., Col.**
"The 2nd Missouri Cavalry." In: LWL, Aug. 1867, v.III, #4, p. 273-282.

1151 **BRANDENBURG, Kurt**
"The great military antique swindle." In: CWTI, Feb. 1976, v.14, #10, p. 22-28, illus.

1152 **BRANDER, Thomas Alexander**
"Reception address, before the Pegram Battalion Association." In: SHSP, 1886, v.XIV, p. 21-22.

1152a **BRANDT, Nat**
"The South in the North." In: CV, new, Nov./Dec. 1987, v. 33, #6, p.24-31, ills., ports. Based on author's book 'Man who Tried to Burn N. Y.
..."The Man Who Tried to Burn New York." Syracuse, N.Y., University Press. 8vo, cl, dj. $20.

1153 **BRANHAM, Alfred Iverson, Capt.**
"The Story of the Alabama: Interview with Captain John McIntosh Kell, Executive officer of the Alabama, given forty-six years ago, June, 1883." (Atlanta, Ga.? 1930. 8vo, wraps, 13pp.

1154 ..."The sinking of the Alabama." In: AHW, 1939, v.1, #1, p. 91-98.

1155 **BRANNON, C.H.**
"A true story of the Old South, notes from a Confederate diary." In: RKHS, Jan. 1939, v.37, (#118) p. 40-53.

1156 **BRANNON, Peter Alexander**
"Medical sources of the Confederacy." In: Ala. Hist. Quart., Spring-Summer, 1955, v.17, p. 28-32. On medical practice in CSA 1861-1865.

1157 ..."General Stand Watie, Cherokee Indian, CSA." In: AHQ, 1943, v.5, p. 66-67.

1158 ..."The Organization of the Confederate Postoffice Department at Montgomery & a Story of the Thos. Welsh Provisional Stamped Envelope, together with the activities of Montgomery Postoffice in the Confederate Period." Montgomery, Ala., Peter A. Brannon, 1960 (Paragon Press). sm.4to, illus., facsms, 164, (2)pp. xi, $6, $45.

1159 ..."The Origin of the Confederate Post Office Department & comments on some stamps." In: Ala. HQ, Spring 1958, v.XX, p. 65-69, view.

1160 ..."The Cahawba Military Prison, 1863-1865." In: Ala. Rev., July 1950, v.3, p. 163-173. diagr., notes.

1161 ..."Russell County, Ala., 1775-1865." Montgomery, Ala., State Dept., Archives & History, 1959 (c.1960). 8vo, wraps, (6), 127pp., facsm., maps, fold-pl. ports, tables, views. (The Ala. Hist. Quart.) v. 21, #1-4. In part: an account of the 15th Alabama Infty. CSA.

1162 ..."The Stars & Bars." In: AlaHQ, winter 1956, v.18, p. 427-442. One CSA flag, probably designed by Nicola Marschall of Marion, Ala.

1163 **BRANSCOM, Alexander C.**
"Mystic romances of the Blue & Grey, mask of war, commerce & society." N.Y., Mutual Pub. Co., (1883). 12mo, cl, illus., 324pp. print dbl. columns. Wright, III, 657. $75, $100-bmk.

1164 **BRANSON, Thomas A.**
See under: "Jack Morgan Songster."

1165 **BRANT & FULLER, Compilers**
"Memorial record of Alabama. A concise account of the State's political, military, professional & industrial progress, together with the personal memories of many of its people." Madison, Wisc., Brant & Fuller, 1893. Tk. 4to, cl, v.1, p. viii, 17-1144; II, p. 17-1100. portraits. Chap. II, Gen. Joseph Wheeler's "Military History, p. 95-153. v.1 only... About half of biographical sketches relate to civil war vets & their service records. $100-bmk-111.

1166 **BRANTLEY, Raburn Lee**
"Georgia Journalism of the Civil War Period." Nashville, Tenn., George Peabody College for Teachers, 1929. Contributions to education of Geo. Peabody College for Teachers, #58. 8vo, wraps, map, fldg.

facsms, xvi, (1) 134pp., bibliog. $10, $12.50, $20, $25-r, atg. $14-bmk.

1167 **BRANTLEY, William H(enderson)**
"Alabama Secedes." In: Ala. Rev., July, 1954, v.VII, p. 165-185, notes.

1167a **BRANTLEY, William Henderson, Jr.**
"Unparalleled Audacity of Mobile Bay, Capt. Maffitt Runs the 'Florida' through Farragut's Blockade in Broad Daylight." Birmingham, Ala., 1954. 8vo, wraps, 12p, ills. $50.

1168 **BRATCHER, James T.**
"An 1866 letter on War & Reconstruction." Edt: Bratcher. In: Tenn. HQ, 1963, v.XXII, p. 83-86.

1169 **BRATTON, J.R.**
"Letter of a Confederate surgeon on Sherman occupation of Milledgeville (Ga.)." In: GaHQ, Sept. 1948, v.32, p. 231-232. Milledgeville, Ga., Nov. 25, 1864.

1170 **BRATTON, John, Col.**
"Colonel Bratton's Report (Lookout Valley) Hdq., Nov. 1, 1863." In: SHSP, 1880, v.VIII, p. 509-511.

1171 ..."Report of operations of Bratton's Brigade from May 7th, 1864 to January, 1865." In: SHSP, 1880, v.VIII, p. 547-559.

1172 ..."The Battle of Williamsburg. Narrative of Colonel Bratton, Sixth South Carolina Regiment." In: SHSP, 1879, v.VII, p. 299-302.

1173 ..."The Sixth South Carolina at Seven Pines." (Address at Seven Pines, Aug. 6th, 1885 to survivors of the regiment." In: SHSP, 1885, v.XIII, p. 199-133.

1174 ..."Tribute to General "Dick" Anderson." In: SHSP, 1885, v.XIII, p. 419-420.

1175 ..."Bratton's Brigade...Resolutions adopted by Bratton's Brigade, South Carolina Volunteers, Jan. 30, 1865 (pledging loyalty to the cause of the Confederacy)." (Richmond, Va., 1865) 8vo, 3p. folder. Heading: "House" House of Representatives, FEb. 6, 1865-ordered to be laid on the table & printed. (Presented by Mr. Simpson) John B. Erwin, Chm., J.C.G. Wardlaw, Sectry.

1176 **BRAUER, Kinley J.**
"British Mediation & the American Civil War: A Reconsideration." IN: JSH, Feb. 1972, 16pp. $8.

1177 ..."Cotton Versus Conscience: Massachusetts Whig Politics & Southwestern Expansion, 1843-1848." Lexington: University of Kentucky Press, 1967. 8vo, cl, d/w, p. vi, 272pp. index, bibliog. $7.50

1178 **BRAUN, Herman A.**
"Andersonville, an object lesson on protection. A critical sketch." Milwaukee, Wis., C.D. Fahsel, 1892. 12mo, cl, plans, (iii)-xi, (13)-164, (2)pp. Defends Wirz, legal & otherwise.

1179 **BRAWLEY, William H.**
"Address...May 10, 1905, at the laying of the cornerstone of a monument to the Confederate dead at Chester, S.C." Charleston, S.C., Walker, Evans & Congswell Co., 1905. 8vo, wraps, 15pp. McKissick-252.

1180 **BRAXTON, A. Caperton**
"The Fifteenth Amendment: an Account of its Enacment." Fore: Wyndham R. Meredith. Lynchburg, Va., J.P. Bell, (1934). 8vo, cl, d/w, port, x, 78pp. $12.50, jk-122, $6, $7.50. Reprint of address before Va. Bar Assn., 1903. Lawyer questioning wisdom of negro voting.

1181 **BRAXTON, Carter M.**
"Map of the battlefield of Fredericksburg, explained by extracts from official reports; also, Gen. R.E. Lee's report of the battle." Lynchburg, Virginian press, 1866. 12mo, wraps, fldg. map, 44pp. Swem-548.

1182 **BRAYER, Herbert O.**
"The fall of Fort Filmore, 1861." In: Westerners Denver Posse Brandbook, 1951. p. 411-156. fold. facsms., pls, illus., ports. See: M.L. Crimmins

1183 **BREAKING of the Light, The**
In: Wm. & Mary Quart., April, 1913, v.XXI, p. 211-220. Growth of a more liberal interpretation of the civil war, as shown by Jno. D. Long, Chs. F. Adams & other eminent historians of age.

1184 **BREAZEALE, B.B.**
"Co. J, 4th South Carolina Infantry at the first battle of Manassas." Manassas, Va., Manassas Journal, 1912. 8vo, wraps, 28pp., illus., plates, map. Writings in Amer. History-#973.

1185 **BRECKENRIDGE, James Malcolm**
"William Clark Breckenridge (1862-1927), historical research writer & bibliographer of Missouriana; his life, lineage, writings." St. Louis: The Author, 1932. 8vo, cl, illus., 380pp. Doniphan Expedition. Missouri in the Kan. struggle, Slavery & Civil War in Missouri, p. 249-349.

1186 **BRECKINRIDGE, John Cabell**
"Escape of Confederate Secretary of War." See: A.J. Hanna

1187 **BRECKINRIDGE, John Cabell - Lane**
"Breckenridge & Lane Campaign Documents." Wash: National Democratic Campaign Committee, 1860. $40. 8vo, wraps, Nos. 1-13, (Approx. 170pp.) The Southern delegates left Democratic Convention (1860), in Charleston, held their own convention in Baltimore & nominated Breckenridge for president on a pro-slavery platform. Sabin-7672 lists 12-pamphlets.

1188 ..."Battle of Chickamauga-Report of Gen. J.C. Breckinridge, Hdq. October 1863." In: SHSP, 1879, v.VII, p. 161-168.

1189 ..."Last Letters & Telegrams of the Confederacy-Correspondence of General John C. Breckinridge." In: SHSP, 1884, v.XII, p. 97-105.

1190 ..."Battle of Murfreesboro, Report of General J.C. Breckinridge, Hdq. Jan. 1863. In: SHSP, 1878, v.V, p. 209-217.

1191 ..."General Breckinridge's Reply to General Bragg's Report of the Battle of Murfreesboro, March 31, 1863." In: SHSP, 1886, v.XIV, p. 475-477. See: Josiah Stoddard Johnston sketches. Lucille S. Williams.

1192 ..."A rebel leader's flight." In: CWTI, June 1967, v.VI, #3, p. 4-10. See: Wm. C. Davis.

1193 ..."A Short History of John C. Breckinridge." Park Place, N.Y., Knapp & Co, 1888. 2 3/4x1 1/2" colored booklet, 16pp. facsm. signature. (packed in Duke's cigarettes) See: "Heroes of the C.W." & W. Duke co.

1194 **BRECKINRIDGE, John Cabell, Maj.-Gen.**
"Portrait, Lithograph, 18x23. Chicago, Ill., n.d., Kurz & Allison. $25.

1195 ...N.Y., Currier & Ives, n.d., Lithograph 12x14" $35.

1196 ..."Speech of the Hon...., delivered at Ashland, Ky. Sept. 5, 1860, repelling the charge of didunion & vindicating the National Democracy." Washington: Nat'l. Democratic Exec. Comm. 8vo, sewn, 16pp. Extension slavery in Tenn. (Breckinridge & Lane Campaign Doc. #18)

1197 ..."Speech of..., of Ky., on executive usurpation, delivered in Senate of U.S., July 16, 1861." Washington: Congressional Globe, 1861, 8vo, sewn, 16pp.

1198 ..."Substance of a speech by..., delivered in the Hall of House of Representatives at Frankfurt, Ky., Dec. 21, 1859." Washington: Natl. Democratic Comm., 1860. 8vo, sewn 8pp. caption title. (Breckinridge & Lane Campaign Doc. #10.

1199 ..."Breckinridge & Lane Campaign Document, No. 19." see: "Great Issue, No. 19."

1200 ..."The Great Document of the Campaign. Speech delivered at Ashland, delivered at Ashland, near Lexington, Kentucky, Sept.

5, 1860. Revised & corrected." Frankfurt, Ky., 1860. 8vo, wraps, 16pp. (old)$5.

1201 **BRECKINRIDGE, Lucy**
"Lucy Breckinridge of Grove Hill, the Journal of a Virginia girl, 1862-1864. Edited by Mary D. Robertson. Kent, Ohio, University Press, 1979, 8vo, cl, dj, 233pp. $15.

1202 **BRECKINRIDGE, Lucy G.**
"The Dusky Wings of War: The Journal of Lucy G. Breckinridge, 1862-1864." In: CWH, March 1977, v.23, #1, p. 26-51. Edt: Mary D. Robertson.

1203 **BRECKINRIDGE, Robert J.**
"The Secession Conspiracy in Kentucky & Its Overthrow." In: Danville Quarterly Review, II, June, 1862. p. 226-238.

1204 **BRECKINRIDGE, W.C.P., Col.**
"The opening of the Atlanta Campaign." In: B & L, v.4, p. 277-281, Pl.

1205 **BRECKINRIDGE, William Campbell Preston**
"A Plea for a history of the Confederate War, an address at the decoration of the Confederate graves in Cave Hill cemetery, Louisville, Ky., May 26, 1879." Louisville, Ky., J.P. Morton Co., 1887. 8vo, wraps, illus., ports, 45pp. Cover title.

1206 ..."The Confederate dead: two addresses, "Who were the Confederate dead? Address at the unveiling ceremonies of the Confederate monument, Hopkinsville, Ky., May 19, 1887." P. (15)-45.

1207 ..."The ex-Confederate & what he has done in peace." An address delivered before the Association of the Army of Northern Virginia, at the meeting held in Richmond, Va., Oct. 26, 1892. by..." Richmond, Va., J.L. Hill Print, 1892. tall 8vo, wraps, 22pp. $35-jk, (old)$3.50, $22.50. See: "Confed. Monument Ass'n."

1208 ..."What the Ex-Confederate has done in Peace." In: B & L, v.IV, p. 277-281.

1209 **BREEDEN, Pompey O.**
"Letters from a Civil War Soldier." In: Faulkner Facts & Fiddlings, Spring, 1975, v.XVII, #1, p. 1-10. Arkansas.

1210 **BREEDLOVE, J.W.**
"Company I, 56th Virginia. Roster of the Command-Some of its Movements." In: SHSP, 1896, v.XXIV, p. 210-212. Organized in Charlotte Co., Va., June 1861, known as "Charlotte Grays."

1211 **BREEDON, James O.**
"Andersonville-A Southern Surgeon's (Joseph Jones) Story." In: Bul. of Hist. of Med., 1973, v.XLVII, p. 317-342.

1212 ..."Joseph Jones, M.D.:Scientist of the Old South." Lexington: University Press, 1975. 8vo, cl, dj, illus., maps, tables, 308pp. $15.50. See: Dr. Joseph Jones. $15.50-y. Activities as inspector of Confederate Camps.

1213 ..."Joseph Jones & Confederate Medical History." In: Ga. H.Q., Fall 1970, v.LIV, #3, p. 357-380.

1214 ..."A medical history of the later stages of the Atlanta Campaign." In: JSH, Feb. 1969, 29pp., v.35, #1, p. 31-59. $8.

1215 ..."Insights into the Medical Statistics of the Charlottesville General Hospital 1861-1865." In: "Magazine of Albemarle County History", v.30, 1972, p. (42)-59. Facsm.

1216 **BREEN, Walter**
"Coinage of the New Orleans Mint in 1861." In: Numismatist, Apr. 1951, v.64, p. 387-394. Coins minted for U.S., Louisiana & CSA. Includes documents.

1217 **BREEZE, Lawrence E.**
"The Battle of Olustee: Its meaning for the British." In: FHQ, January, 1965, v.XLIII, #3, p. 207-216.

1218 **BREIHAN, Carl William**
"Cullen Baker-First of the Gunfighters." In: "The West-true stories of the old West." July 1967, v.7, #2, p. 16-19, 42-47. ports, illus., facsm. Conscript in CSA, Lit-

1219 ..."Gen. James Longstreet." In: Frontier Times, Jan/Mar. 1954, v.31, p. 36-44. On his activities in US/CSArmy, later on during Reconstruction. 1848 ff.

1220 ..."Battle of Fair Oaks or Seven Pines (Virginia) 1862." In: Gun Rep., June 1957, v.3, #1, p. 14-17.

1221 ..."Younger Brothers." San Antonio, Texas, Naylor Co., (c.1961) 12mo, cl, xiii, 260pp., illus., ports. War era, 1-57.

1222 ..."Quantrill & His Civil War Guerrillas." Denver: (A Swallow) 1959 (Sage Books) 8vo, cl, dj, illus., 174pp. $15-pres. cpy, $10-nc, $3.50
...N.Y., Promontory Press (1959). 12mo, cl, dj, 174pp., NY, 1973. $10-bmk, $5-op. CSA guerrillas in Mo. & Kan., 1861-1865, with roster of 296 men.

1223 ..."Battle of Sabine Pass (Texas & La. in 1863) Gun Rep., 4(6), Nov. 1958, p. 19-21.

1224 ..."The killer legions of Quantrill." Seattle, Wash., Hangman Press, Superior Press (1971). sm4to, cl, illus., ports, 144pp. $5.

1224a ..."Sam Hildebrand: Guerrilla." Wauwatosa, 1984. 8vo, pict. wraps, 184p. $7.50. See also under Hildebrand.

1225 **BRENT Joseph Lancaster**
"Capture of the Ironclad, "Indianola"." New Orleans, La., Searcy & Pfaff, 1926, 12mo, wraps, 84pp.

1226 ...In: SHSP, 1876, v.I, p. 91-99. $20.

1227 ..."The Lugo Case; a personal experience, written by..." New Orleans, La. Searcy & Pfaff, 1926, 12mo, wraps, 69pp. $47.90. Both pamphlets privately printed, scarce.

1228 ..."Operations of the Artillery of the Army of Western Louisiana, after the Battle of Pleasant Hill. Report of Col. J.L. Brent, Hdq., May 20, 1864." In: SHSP, 1881, v.IX, p. 257-264.

1229 ..."Memoirs of the War Between the States." (New Orleans, La., Fontana Print, 1940) Private print-100 copies. 8vo, wraps, 238pp. front(port) cover title: "Memoirs of Joseph Lancaster Brent, Brig-Gen., CSA. $37.50, $75, $100, $650-r, $250-nc'76.

1230 ...Mobilizable fortifications & their controlling influence in war." Bost., N.Y., Houghton, Mifflin pr., 1885. 12mo, cl, vi, 142pp. $100-bmk-105.
...Baltimore: Williams & Wilkins co., 1916, 2nd edt., viii, 143pp.

1231 **BREWER, George E.**
"The defenders of Vicksburg." In: CV, Oct. 1914, v.XXII, p. 457-459.

1232 ..."How Lee's corps crossed Duck river." In: CV, July 1910, v.XVIII, p. 326-329.

1233 ..."Incidents of the retreat from Nashville." In: CV, July 1010, v.XVIII, p. 327-329.

1234 ..."Why Missionary Ridge was lost by the Confederates." In: CV, May, 1914, v.XXII, p. 232.

1235 **BREWER, George Evans, Captain**
"History of the Forty-sixth Alabama Regiment Volunteer Infantry, 1862-2865. Introduction & Edited by William Stanley Hoole with a Roster of the Regiment." University, Ala., Confederate Pub. Co., 1985. Confederate Regimental Series #8. 8vo, stiff wraps, 51pp., port. First published in the "Montgomery Advertiser", Feb. 9, 1902. This being the 1st edition in book form.

1236 ..."Brief historical sketch of military organizations raised in Alabama." See: Willis Brewer.

1237 **BREWER, James H.**
"The Confederate Negro: Virginia's Craftsmen & Military Laborers, 1861-1865." Durham: Duke Univ. Press, 1969, 8vo, cl, dj, illus., maps, xvii, 212pp. $9.75-y, $7.50, $10-b.

1238 **BREWER, John M.**
"Prison Life, by...Late Reading Clerk of

the Maryland Senate of 1860-1861, and still later of Fort Delaware & Warren." Baltimore: S.S. Mills, n.d., 8vo, wraps, 31pp. At outbreak of war, prisons used for some legislators accused of disloyalty & likely to forestall passage of act of secession. Ft. Delaware (on Del. river); Ft. Lafayette & Warren (in N.Y., & Boston Harbor, resp.)

1239 ..."Prison Life in Forts Lafayette & Warren (Clerk of Maryland Senate)." (Harper's '04), n.p., n.d., 8vo, wraps, 31pp.

1240 **BREWER, William M.**
"Some effects of the Plantation System upon the Ante-Bellum South." In: Ga. H.Q. September, 1927, v.XI, #3, p. 250-273.

1241 **BREWER, Willis**
"Alabama: Her History, Resources, War Record, & Public Men. 1540-1872." Montgomery, Ala., Barrett & Brown, 1872. 8vo, cl, 712pp. CSA, p. 61-74; 586-705 sketch each Co. & officers $20, $65-y, $125, $175.
...Tuscaloosa, Ala., 1964 reprint. $12.50.
...Spartanburg, S.C., 1975, Reprint Co., 712pp., indexed. $27.

1242 ..."Brief Historical Sketches of Military Organizations Raised in Alabama during the Civil War." From his-"Alabama: Her History, Resources, War Record & Public Men, from 1540-1872." Montgomery: Alabama Civil War Centennial Commission, 1962. 8vo, wraps, p. 589-705.

1243 **BREWTON, William W.**
"The Son of Thunder; an epic of the South." Richmond, Va., Garrett & Massie, 1936. 8vo, cl, dj, ix, (2), 468pp. $7.50, $9, $10. "Sone of Thunder", acct. of politics & gov., of South (1775-1865) is Robert A. Toombs, historically accurate but fiction.

1244 **BRICE, Marshall Moore**
"Conquest of a Valley." Charlottesville, Va. University Press (c.1965) 8vo, cl, front, vii, 184pp. maps-1-foldg., primarily a study of Piedmont, Va., battle June 5, 1864. $12.50, $6-b, $30-b, $7-y.
...Verona, Va., 1974, $10-bmk.

1245 ..."The Stonewall Brigade Band." Verona, Va., McClure Print (1967) 8vo, cl, viii, (2), 213pp., illus. $7, $8.50, $15-bmk-84.
...1982. 2nd printing, pict. cl, index. $12.50.

1245a ..."Augusta County during the Civil War." In: Augusta Hist. Bul. 1, #1, Spring 1969, 5-19p.

1246 **"BRICE'S Crossroads National Battlefield Site.**
Confederate Gen. Nathan Bedford Forrest won here a memorable tactical victory against larger Union forces on June 10, 1864." (Wash., DC) U.S. Dept. Interior, Natl. Park Service. (Reprint, 1961). 8vo, (6)pp folder, caption title, port, sketches, maps.

1247 **BRIDGES, C.A.**
"The Knights of the Golden Circle: A Filibustering Fantasy." In: SwHQ, Jan. 1941, v.XLIV, #3, p. 287-302.

1248 **BRIDGES, Hal**
"Civil War & Reconstruction." Washington: Amer. Hist. Assn., (1962) 8vo, wraps, 25pp. $7.50. Essay on civil war Books published between 1950-1960.

1249 ..."A Confederate hero: Gen. William Y(arnell) Slack (1818-1862)." In: Ark. HQ, Autumn 1951, v.10, p. 233-237. notes. Legal & political activities in Missouri, service as an officer of CSArmy.

1250 ..."D.H. Hill's Anti-Yankee Algebra." (Lexington, Ky.) May, 1956, v.XXII, #2, p. 220-222.

1251 ..."Lee's Maverick General Daniel Harvey Hill." N.Y., McGraw-Hill Book co(1961), 8vo, cl, dj, maps, facsm, viii, (2) 323pp., notes, bibliog., index, p. 281-323. $7.50(pub), $10, $12.50, $45, $30-b, $25-16c.hill.

1252 **BRIDGES, Herb**
"The filming of Gone With the Wind." Macon, Ga., Mercer University Pr. 1984. 8vo, cl, dj, viii, 284pp. photos. $28.

1253 **BRIDGES, Lamar W.**
"The Memphis Daily Appeal's "Dixie": Civil War capital correspondent." In: THQ, 1967, v.26, p. 377-387.

1254 **BRIDGES, Richard C.**
"Letters from Private Richard C. Bridges, CSA, 1861-1864." (Jackson, Miss.) Jour. Miss. Hist. Nov. 1971, v.XXXIII, #4, p. 357-372.

1255 **BRIDGES, Toby**
"Dixie Buckles." Harriman, Tenn., Pioneer Press.

1256 **BRIDGFORTH, Lucie Robertson**
"Mississippi's response to Nullification, 1983." In: JMH, Feb. 1983, v.XLV, #1, p. 1-21. "was not a prelude to civil war."

1257 **BRIGHAM, Clarence Saunders**
"Wall-paper newspapers of the civil war." (Cambridge, Mass: Harvard Univ. Press) 1924, reprinted from Bibliographical essays a tribute to Wilberforce Eames. a checklist of issues: p. 205-209) 8vo, wraps, p. 203-209.

1258 **BRIGHT, John M(organ)**
"The States in the Confederate War; inside information about the Army of Tennessee." In: CV, Aug. 1909, v.XVII, p. 393-399.

1259 **BRIGHT, Leslie S.**
& Wm. H. Rowland, James C. Bardon, Division of Archives & History, North Carolina Dept. Cultural Resources. "C.S.S. Neuse, a Question of Iron & Times." Raleigh, N.C., 1981. 4to, illus., 165pp., stiff wraps. Ill-fated ironclad, never saw action, destroyed by crew Mar. 10, 1865. Story of its career & largely salvage of artifacts.

1260 ..."The Blockade Runner 'Modern Greece' & her cargo." Raleigh, N.C., 1975, 8vo, wraps, 210pp. $15-bmk. Salvage of the cargo, ship sunk June 1962 off Ft. Fisher.

1261 **BRIGHT, Leslie S. & William H. Rowland & James C. Bardon**
"C.S.S. Neuse-a question of iron & time." Raleigh: North Carolina Dep't of Cultural Resources. Division of Archives & History. 8vo, wraps, 165pp., illus. $10, 1981.

1262 **BRIGHT, Robert A.**
"Pickett's Charge. The story of it as told by a member of his staff." In: SHSP, 1903, v.XXXI, p. 228-236.

1263 **BRIGHT, Simeon Miller**
"The McNeill Rangers: a study in Confederate Guerrilla Warfare." In: West Va. His., July 1951, v.12, p. (338)-394. Also as a thesis: W. Va. Univ., 1950, See: "Roster of McNeill's Rangers."

1264 **BRIGHTWELL, Juanita S.**
"Roster of the Confederate Soldiers of Georgia, 1861-1865, an INDEX." Spartanburg, S.C., The Reprint co., 1982, 8vo, cl, 513pp. $30.

1265 **BRINEGAR, Claude S.**
"Mark Twain & the...Snodgrass Letters." In: "Journal of American Statistical Association", Mar. 1963, v.LVIII, p. 85-06.

1266 **BRISTOW, E.H.**
"Vindication of the South, her statesmen soldiers & citizens, delivered by...at Aberdeen, Miss., on obsequies of Pres. Jefferson Davis." Aberdeen, Miss., Examiner print, 1901. 8vo, wraps, 13pp.

1267 **BRITISH OFFICIAL PAPERS**
relating to the Rebellion, 1862-2867. Apparently a Complete set in 4 Vols., folio, 1/2 clf. London: 1862-1867. (old, Harper's '04) 1862 (12 numbers); 1863 (14 numbers); 1864 (19 numbers); 1865 (9 numbers); 1866 (corresp. on "Shenandoah", 181pp.); 1867 (British-American Claims from the Civil War, p. 45, 4). 1862-; "Papers relating to Blockade of Ports of the C.S., p. 126." (#1)"Corresp. Relating to

C.W., 141pp."; "Corresp. on Internatl. Maritime Law", p. 37. (#4)"Withdrawal of Mr. Bunch's Exequatur as H.M. Consul, Charleston, 27pp." (#5)"Corresp. seizure of Mason & Slidell from "Trent", p. 37." (#6)"Corresp. rel. Steamers Nashville & Tuscarora at Southampton." p. 30.; "Corresp Obstruction of Southern Harbors", p. 4. (#12)Further Corresp. on C.W.", p.6. 1863: (Dispatch resp. C.W. p.2; (#1) Corresp. resp. C.W., p. 53; (#2)"Corresp. with Mr. Mason resp. Rocognition of the CS." p.17; (#3)"Corresp. resp. the "Alabama". p.48; (#6)"Corresp. with Mr. Adams resp. Neutral Rights", p. 6; (#8)"Corresp. with Mr. Adams resp. Confed. Aganets in England." p. 18;1864: (#1)"Corresp. resp. "Alabama", p. 57; (#3)"Corresp. resp. "Alabama", p. 18; (#4)"Corresp. resp. Shipment Guns." p. 4; (#6)"Corresp. resp. the "Tuscaloosa", p. 32; (#7)"On Enlistment of British Seamen on "Kearsarge", p. 10; (#12)Further Corresp. resp. "Kearsarge", p. 7; (#13)"Resp. removal of British Consuls from so-styled C.S." p. 39. 1865: (#3)"Corresp. arising out of Conflict between "Kearsarge" & "Alabama", p. 4; Cont'd: British Parliamentary Papers, presented to Parliament, 1864. Largely Cruisers & final results settlement "Alabama Claims" PP: 57, 43, 18, 3, 32, 10, 14, 96, (1), 20, 7, 39, 37, 17, 5, 59, 6, 5, plus a lp. circular on the "Belligerent Cruisers" & their prizes if captured in British waters. (See: Bartlett's Lit. of the Rebellion, p. 59-60.) $850-jk-135.

1268 **BRITISH PARLIAMENTARY PAPERS,**
North America, presented to Parliament, 1864. London(1864). folio, blue cloth, 57, 43, 18, 3, 33, 32, 10, 14, 96, (1), 20, 7, 39, 37, 17, 5, 59, 6, 5pp. Plus a 1p. circular on Belligerant Cruisers", & prizes if captured in British waters. Bartlett's "Lit. of the Rebellion", p. 59-60. Largely activities of CSNaval vessels, other diplomatic controversies with USA, with settlement of "Alabama Claims." $6.50-jk-144.

1269 **BRITISH SESSIONAL PAPERS-**
British House Commons, Parliament. See: Robert Huhn Jones.

1270 **BRITON IN THE (AMERICAN) CIVIL WAR.**
(London) Jour. Confed. Hist. Soc., v.d., v.I, #4, p. 117-118; II, #3, p. 119-120; IV, #1, p.2-11, port (Col. Robt. A. Smith, 10th Miss. Inf., from Edinburgh, cont'd--v.V, #2, p. 66-69, pl., p. 52-53; IV, #3, p. 97-98, port. (Thos. Lander, CSA, lived Augusta, Ga., pub. "Chronicle". V., #3, p. 101-106, pl. (Wm. Isham Kendrick of 16th S.C. Reg.); V, #4, Col. Harry M. Campbell; pt. VIII, p. 122-124, pl. Britons in the Amer. Civil War, British born Generals of the CSA (Cleburn, Finegan, Lane, Leventhorpe & Moore); pt. X-Old St. Leger by Milton Overley, 9th Ky. Cavl., v.8, #4, p. 79-83, port.

1271 **BROADFOOT, Thomas & Marianne Pair, Edts.**
"Civil War Books: a priced checklist, 2nd. Edition, revised." Wendell, N.C., 1983. 4to, cl, 350pp. Some 7000 titles. Largely CSA. Roger Hunt updates the Union titles. $30.
BROADFOOT, Tom, Edt.
"Civil War Books a Priced Checklist. Compiled by Ann Sterling & Marianna Pair, General Books & Regimentals, Stuart Wright, CSA Imprints." Wendell, N.C., Avera Press, 1978. sm.4to, cl, ix, 503pp. $25.

1272 **BROADWATER, John D.**
"Ironclad at Hampton Roads/CSS Virginia the Confederacy's formidable warship." In: Va. Cavalcade, Winter 1984, v.33, #3, p. 100-113, diagrams, illus., incl. dbl. page color+cover, ports, map.

1273 **BROCK Robert Alonzo**
"The Appomattox Roster: a List of the

Paroles of the Army of Northern Virginia Issued at Appomattox Court House, April 9, 1865." Reprint of Vol. XV-Southern Historical Society Papers. p.xxxiii, 508. N.Y., Antiquarian Press. $12.50, $22.50, N.Y., Antiquarian Press, 1962, Rep. $20-bmk-40, $30

1274 ..."Gen. Robert Edward Lee; soldier, citizen & Christian patriot by Mrs. Roger A. Pryor, Dr. Edmund Jennings Lee, Col. John J. Garnett, Mrs. Sally Nelson Robins, Gen. T.L. Rosser, et.al. Also an interesting early history of the Lee Family in England & America..." $75-bmk-110, $45-jk-97, $25. Richmond, Va., B.F. Johnson Pub. Co. (1897) 8vo, cl, illus., ports, map, facsms., 586pp. Beauregard's "Battle Manassas", Jackson "Seven days battle before Richmond", also by Gen. Lee, as well as his "Maryland", etc.
...Richmond, Va., Royal Pub. co, (1897) Sq. 8vo, otherwise same collation. $10.
...Atlanta, Ga., Hudgins co. (1897) Sq. 8vo, same. $10.

1275 ..."A Memorial. Moses Drury Hoge, D.D." In: SHSP, 1898, v.XXVI, p. 255-291.

1276 ..."General John Rogers Cooke." In: SHSP, 1890, v.XVIII, p. 322-327. In memory of Gen. Cooke, member of SHSoc.

1277 ..."Escape of prisoners from Johnson's Island." In: SHSP, 1890, v.XVIII, p. 428-431.

1278 ..."General Birkett Davenport Fry." In: SHSP, 1890, v.XVIII, p. 286-288.

1279 ..."Joseph Jones, M.D., LL.D." In: SHSP, 1895, v.XXIII, p. 382-383.

1280 ..."The Southern Historical Society: Its Origin & History." In: SHSP, 1890, v.XVIII, p. 349-365.

1281 ..."Miscellaneous papers, 1672-1865, now first printed from the manuscript in the collections of the Virginia historical society, etc., etc." Richmond, Va., The Society, 1887. 8vo, cl, 4, 374pp. Va. Hist. Soc. Coll. new series, v.6, i.e., "Career of the Ironclad Virginia, 1862"; "Memorial of Johnson's Island, 1862-1864."; "Beale's Cavalry brigade parole, 1865." CSA covered in p 195-335. $35.

1282 **BROCK, Irving A., Capt.**
"Cleburne & his Division at Missionary Ridge & Ringgold Gap." In: SHSP, 1880, v.8, p. 464-475.

1283 **BROCK, Sallie A., Miss, Edt.**
"The Southern Amaranth; a carefully selected collection of poems growing out of & in reference to the late war." New York: Geo. S. Wilcox, 1869. Tall 8vo, gilt edges, xii, (13)-651pp. front. Tinted decr. t/p & half-title. (old) $7.50.
...see also: Putnam, Sallie A. Brock.

1284 **BROCKENBROUGH, Eleanor, Miss**
"The Confederate Signal Bureau & the Secret Service." (London) Jour. Confed. Hist. Soc., Summer, 1966, v.4, #2, p. 75-84, pl.

1285 **BROCKMAN, Charles L., Jr.**
"Life in Confederate Athens, Georgia." In: Ga. Rev., 1967, v.XXI, p. 107-125. $8.

1286 ..."The Confederate armory of Cook & Bro.," In: Gun Digest, 1959, v.14, p. 74-79, views, note Arms mfg. by Ferdinand W.C. Cook (died in 1864) & Francis L. Cook at New Orleans, late at Selma, Ala., & Athens, Ga., 1861-1870.

1287 ..."A rebel secret weapon." In: Amr. rifleman, Aug. 1956, v.104, #8, p. 28, view. Dbl-barreled cannon, designed by John Gilleland & produced by Athens (Ga.) Foundry & Machine Works, 1862, never used by CSArmy.

1288 **BROCKSTOCE, John**
"War at the top of the world." In: CWTI, Oct. 1986, v.25, #6, p. 12-18, 36-42, illus., map, ports.

1289 **BROGAN, D.W.**
"The origins of the American civil war."

In: History, Apr. 1930, v.XV, n.s., p. 47-51. Some of difficulties & perplexities of the political & social situation leading to war.

1290 **BROGLIE, Prince Albert duc de**
"Les tranchees dns la guerre de secession; lettres au duc Albert de Broglie." In: Corresp., ns, CCXXVI, Jan. 10, 1916, p. 72-83. Letters in 1867 recounts visit to battlefield of Richmond & Petersburg, describes the system of trenches used there.

1291 **BROMBERG, Alan B.**
"An Unconventional Confederate. Extra Billy Smith & the Civil War." In: Va. Cavl. Spring 1981, v.XXX, #4, p. 148-155. ports, on in color, plan, facsm., illus.

1292 ..."The Virginia Congressional Elections of 1865: a test of Southern loyalty." In: VMHB, Jan. 1965, (23)pp. $8.

1293 **BROMBERG, Frederick George**
"The Reconstruction period in Alabama. (Mobile, Ala.?)." Papers of the Iberville Historical Society, no.iii. For the Bienville monument fund. 8vo, wraps, 18pp.

1294 **BRONAUGH, Warren Carter**
"The Younger's Fight for Freedom. A Southern soldier's twenty years campaign to open Northern prison doors-with antecdotes of war days. By W.C. Bronaugh of Co.K, 16th Missouri Inft., CSA. Who spent the period from 1882 to 1902 to secure the release of Jim Cole and Bob Younger from the Minnesota State Penitentiary. Last relics of the War Between the States." Columbia, Mo., E.W. Stephens Pub. Co for the Author, 1906. 8vo, cl, ports (incl. front) illus., 398pp. $18.50, $20, $25, $35, $40, $75-bmk, $65-jk-138.

1295 **BROOK CHURCH FIGHT, The**
& something about the Fifth North Carolina Cavalry. Death of James B. Gordon. From the Charlotte "Observer", Jan. 8, 1902." In: SHSP, 1901, v.XXIX, p. 139-144.

1296 **BROOK, Michael**
"Confederate Sympathies in Northeast Lancashire, 1862-1864." In: Lancashire & Cheshire Antiq. Soc. Trans., 1965-1966, v.LXXV & LXXVI, p. 211-217.

1297 **BROOKE, Bissell**
"A young Confederate describes "the beloved General". In: Hobbies, May 1958, v.63(3), p. 108-109, 121. Recollects Sidney Lanier's 1870 address, Confederate Memorial.

1298 **BROOKE, George**
"John Mercer Brooke (1826-1906)." In: Rockbridge Hist. Soc., Proc., 1954, v.4, p. 32-34. As officer in USNavy & chief of ordnance CSNavy. 1841-1865.

1299 **BROOKE, George Mercer, Jr.**
"John Mercer Brooke (1826-1906) Naval scientist." In: NCUniv., Research in progress, 1956, v.34, p. 125-126. His career as officer in US/CSNavy, 1841-1865. Chief: Bureau of Ordnance & Hydrography. See: Jno. Mercer Brooke.

1300 ..."The Virginia or Merrimac; her real Projector. A statement of the facts connected with her conversion into an Iron-Clad, by John M. Brooke, late Commander C.S. Navy." Richmond: 1891, W.E. Jones Pr. tall 8vo, wraps, 34pp. diagrams, rep: SHSP, XIX, p. 3-34. See: Geo. Mercer Brooke.

1301 **BROOKE, St. George Tucker**
"The Merrimac-Monitor Battle." In: Transalleghenny Hist. Mag., Oct. 1902, v.II, p. 30-42. Remins, CSA naval soldier.

1302 **BROOKMAN, L.G.**
"Southern Censorship of the South Mail." N.Y., The Stamp Specialist (1944). Ills., p. 38-42.

1303 **BROOKS COUNTY, Georgia**
Folks Huxford's "History of Brooks Co., Ga." Quitman, Ga., 1948, maps, index, xiv, 608pp.
...Spartanburg, S.C., Reprint Co.,

1978($25). Extensive treatment of the Civil War, muster rolls of all companies in county of CSA ser., & deaths of individual soldiers.

1304 **BROOKS, Aubrey Lee**
"Walter Clark, Fighting Judge." Chapel Hill: Univ. N.C. Press (1944). 8vo, cl, dj, 278pp. $8.50, $13, $15-y. Clark served as Lt. 22nd, N.C. Reg. Later Lt.-Col. 70th N.C. Reg. See: W. Clark (Edt.) Press. $15.

1305 **BROOKS, Carlton P.**
"The Magnolia, A Literary Magazine for the Confederacy." In: Va. Caval., Spring 1983, #4, v.XXXII, p. 150-157, ports, illus., facsms.

1306 **BROOKS, Charles Walker**
"Rhymes of a Southerner." Richmond, Va., Dietz Pr., 1936. 12mo, cl, ix, 143pp. dj. $10-jk

1307 **BROOKS, Edward**
"American letter express company, Louisville & Nashville, 1861. By Edward Brooks; Sam Adkins, associate." Louisville, Ky., Standard Print, 1946. Large 8vo, cl, illus. (incl. ports, facsms.) 60, (1)pp. $10. Not only U.S., but the Confederacy.

1308 **BROOKS, Fred Emerson**
"Pickett's Charge & Other Poems." Boston-Chi., Forbes & Co., 1903. 12mo, cl, front (port) xi, 211pp. $6.
...1902 Edt., same. $7.50.
...1915 Edt., same. $10-b.

1309 **BROOKS, James, Hon., N.Y.**
"Not Reconstruction, but Destruction. Speech of Hon. James Brooks, of N.Y." Washington, 1867. 8vo, sewn, 8pp. $6.

1310 **BROOKS, Preston Smith**
"Speech of Hon. S.P. (sic) Brooks, on resigning his seat in Congress, in the House of Representatives, July 14, 1856." (Washington, 1856) 8vo, 4pp folder. Sabin-8367. Assaulted Sumner & resigns his seat. In following work exhorts his constituents in S.C. to tear up constitution & form a Southern Confederation.

1311 ..."Disunion Document, #1. Speech of Hon. Preston S. Brooks. Delivered at Columbia, S.C., Aug. 29, 1856." Boston: John P. Jewett & Co., 1856. 12mo, sewn, port, 12pp. Sabin-8366.

1312 **BROOKS, Robert Preston**
"Conscription in the Confederacy." (Athens, Ga., 1917) University of Ga. Bul., March 1917, v.XVII, #4, p. 417-442. Read before the Miss. Val. Hist. Ass'n. Nashville, Tenn., 1916. Reprint from Military Historian & Economist, v.1, #4. $15, $30.
...(Cambridge, Mass., n.d., 1916?) 8vo, wraps, 24pp. $5. See: Albert B. Moore.

1313 ..."Howell Cobb & the Crisis of 1850." In: Miss. Val. Hist. Rev., Dec. 1917, v.IV, #3, p. 279-298.
...Athens, Ga., University Bul. v.XVIII, #1, p. (279)-298.

1314 **BROOKS, Ulysses Robert**
"Butler & His Cavalry in the War of Secession, 1861-1865." Columbia, S.C., The State co., 1909. Tall 8vo, cl, ports, illus., ports, 591pp. Index & index of titles, $10, $25, $30, $40, $35, $50, $65-y, $100-g, $75-bmk-105. Colonel in 2nd S.C. cavalry, brigade consisted: 1st, 2nd, 4th, 5th, 6th regs. Sketches: Hampton's Cav., Hart's & Bachman's Battery.

1315 ..."Stories of the Confederacy, Edt. by U.R. Brooks." Columbia, S.C., The State co., 1912. Tall 8vo, cl, plates & ports, 410pp. $125, $22.50-y, $40-ng, $100-bmk-105, $65-bmk. Includes a reprint of an Anon. 1864 pamphlet, "Sketches of Hampton's Cavalry 1861-1862-1863. Being a reprint of a pamphlet published in Columbia latter part of 1864, author unknown printing press & pamphlets destroyed by Sherman's Army-copy from which this is reprinted loaned by J.H. White of Graham, N.C." p. (67)-218. Note:

D.B. Rea's "Sketches from Hampton's cavalry, embracing the principal exploits of the cavalry in the campaigns of 1862 & 1863." Columbia, S.C., 1864 has 158pp. & this may be the pamphlet above.

1316 ..."Battle of Reams Station." In: CV, Dec. 1914, v.XXII, p. 554-555.

1317 ..."Hampton & Butler. Some pages of hertofore unwritten history. A paper read by Capt. U.R. Brooks before the meeting of Camp Hampton Confederate Veterans, at Columbia, S.C., Sept. 6, 1895." In: SHSP, 1895, v.XXIII, p. 25-37.

1318 **BROOKS, W.R., Capt.**
"Hot Night Fight at Stony Creek. Movement which broke Wilson's Great Raid." In: SHSP, 1908, v.XXXVI, p. 152-155.

1319 **BROOKS, William E.**
"Lee of Virginia a Biography by..." Indianapolis, Ind., Bobbs-Merrill (1932) 8vo, cl, ports (incl. front.) plates, xix, -(23)-361pp. $6, $20-bmk, $15-nc, $8.50.
...N.Y., Garden City (1932) reprint, $5.

1320 **BROOKSHER, William R. & David K. Snider**
"Around McClellan again." In: CWTI, 1974, v.13, #5, p. 4-8, 39-48, illus., dble-pg., maps, ports, color port Stuart (cover). "Three day raid from Va. to Pa., Stuart outrode & outwits McClellan.

1321 ..."A visit to Holly Springs." In: CWTI, June 1975, v.14, #3, p. 4-9, 40-44. illus., ports, map.

1322 ..."Devil on the river." Forrest at Johnsonville." In: CWTI, Aug. 1976, v.17, #5, p. 12-19, illus., map, sketch, ports-incl. color port of Forrest on cover.

1323 ..."Stampede in Kentucky: John Hunt Morgan Summer raid." In: CWTI, June 1978, v.17, #3, p. 4-10, 43-46, illus., map, ports.

1324 ..."Stuart's ride-the great circuit around McClellan." In: CWTI, April, 1973, v.12, #1, p. 4-10, 40-47, illus., map, ports.

1325 ..."The War Child" rides-Joe Wheeler at Stones River." In: CWTI, Jan. 1976, v.14, #9, p. 4-10, 44-46, illus., map, ports. color portrait of Wheeler on cover.

1326 **BROPHY, Patrick**
"Bushwhackers of the Border: the Civil War period in Western Missouri." Nevade, Missouri: Vernon County Historical Society, 1981. 8vo, paper, 62pp. illus., map, index, cloth, $3.50, $10.

1327 **BROUN, Catherine Barbara Hopkins**
"Family events, 1854-1889...Compiled by Philip H(opkins) Broun." n.p., Brandt & Lawson, 1959. 8vo, cl, (1), iii leaves, 130, (15)p. Chron. record of domestic occupations, Civil War (p. 6-79) marriages, births, deaths at Sunny Bank, Midddleburg," Va., with 9 letters from Maj. Thomas Lee Broun, CSA to sister Ann Eliza Broun, 1861.

1328 **BROUN, Thomas L., Compl.**
"Dr. William LeRoy Broun, compl. by... assisted by Bessie Lee Broun & Sally F. Ordway." N.Y., Neale pub., 1912. 8vo, cl, ports, (8), 247pp. $5, $40-b, $25-bmk, $85-r, $16.

1329 ..."Recollections of Cloyd's Mountain Battle." In: SHSP, 1909, v.XXXVII, p. 349-350.

1330 ..."General R.E. Lee's War-Horses, Traveller & Lucy Long." In: SHSP, 1890, v.XVIII, p. 388-390; 1891, v.XIX, p. 333-335; 1907, v.XXXV, p. 99-101. (Latter, sketch by a man who owned him, T.L. Broun)

1331 **BROUN, William LeRoy, Lieut-Col.**
"The Red Artillery. Confederate Ordnance During the War. The difficulty of obtaining it." In: SHSP, 1898, v.XXVI, p. 365-376. Contributed to: "Jour. of the US Artillery." April, 1898. Also in Jan. & Feb., 1898.

1332 ..."Letter to Senator M.C. Butler." In: SHSP, 1888, v.XVI, p. 286-289.

1333 ..."Confederate Ordnance during the war." In: CV, 1904, v.12, p. 20-23. Formerly Lieut-Col. Ordnance, CSArmy. From Jour. US Artillery.

1334 **BROWIN, Frances Baker Williams**
"The mails went through (sometimes)." In: Tex. quar., summer 1959, v.2, #2, p. 145-154. On postal service inthe CSA.

1335 **BROWN(E), S.H.**
"Diary of S.H. Brown(e) Aboard the Blockade Runner S.S. Dee." In: Amer. Neptune, July, 1963, Vol. XXIII, #3, p. 225-227.

1336 **BROWN, A. Theodore**
"Business 'Neutralism' on the Missouri Kansas Border: Kansas City, 1854-1857." (Houston, Tex.) JSH, May, 1963. v.XXIX, #2, p. 229-140.

1337 **BROWN, A.F., Colonel**
"Van Dorn's Operations in Northern Mississippi-Recollections of a Cavalryman." In: SHSP, 1878, v.VI, p. 151-161.

1338 **BROWN, A.J.**
"History of Newton County, Miss. from 1834 to 1894." Jackson, Miss., Clarion-Ledger Co., 1894. 8vo, cl, illus., xv, 472pp. (old) $10, $100-jk-122. Largely devoted to period, five years during the war.

1339 **BROWN, Aaron V.**
"Speech of Gov. A.V. Brown, on the Issues of the Presidential Canvass, delivered at Columbia, Aug. 6, 1852." Nashville, Tenn., American Office, 1852. 8vo, sewn, 15pp. pro-slavery (old)$5.

1340 ..."Address on the Parties & Issues of the Presidential Election, delivered at Philadelphia, Aug. 15, 1856." Nashville, Tenn., 1856. 8vo, sewn, 29pp. (old)$5. Dissented at Nashville Convention 1850, drew up the Tenn.-Platform.

1341 ..."Address before the Democratic Association of Nashville, June 24, 1856." Nashville, Tenn., 1856. 8vo, sewn, 22pp. (old)$5.

1342 **BROWN, Albert Gallatin**
"Speech of..., in house, Mar. 14, 1852, on the Southern Movement & Mississippi Politics." (Wash: Congress. Globe Office, 1852) 8vo, 7pp. fldg. $5.

1343 **BROWN, Andrew**
"The First Mississippi Partisan Rangers, CSA." In: CWH, Dec. 1955, v.1, #4, p. 371-399, plates (2).

1344 ..."Sol Street, Confederate Partisan Leander." (Jackson, Miss., Jour. Miss. Hist., July, 1959, v.XXI, #3, p. 155-173.

1345 **BROWN, Bedford**
"Remarks of Hon..., of Caswell, made in the Senate of North Carolina, Dec. 19, 1860, on the Resolution of Mr. Hall, of New Hanover of Federal Relations." (Carolin printing, 1861). 8vo, sewn, caption title, 16pp. (old) $8.50. Favored secession. See-Houston G. Jones. See also: N.C. Hist. Rev., 1955 (july-Oct.) v.XXXII, "The Senator", p. 321-345; The Conciliator", p. 483-511.

1346 ..."Selections from the Correpondence of Bedford Brown." In: Trinity Col. Hist. Soc. Papr., 1907, v.VII, p. 16-31. Second installment of Brown's Correspondence.

1347 ..."Personal experience in observing result of good & bad sanitation in the Confederate Army." In: Pan Amer. Medical Congr. Trans. Pt. 1, p. 705-730.

1348 **BROWN, Benjamin F.**
"McGowan's South Carolina brigade in the Battle of Gettysburg." In: CV, Feb. 1923, v.XXXI, p. 51-53. See: Jas. F. Caldwell.

1349 **BROWN, Campbell H., Col., of Ewell's staff.**
"Forrest's Johnsonville Raid." In: CWTI, June 1965, v.IV, #3, p. 48-57, illus., maps, ports. In which 3700 troops sank a fleet of river boats, devasted a $2.2 million Federal supply depot.

1350 ..."Carter's East Tennessee raid, the sailor on horseback who raided his own backyard." In: THQ, 1963, v.22, p. 66-82.

1351 ..."The First Manassas, Correspondence between Generals R.S. Ewell & G.T. Beauregard, to which is added extracts from a letter to Gen. Fitz Lee." Nashville: Wheeler, Osborn & Duckworth, 1885. 8vo, wraps, 8pp. Caption title. Memoranda on the civil war of Gen. Ewell at Bull Run, with pub. letters of Generals Fitzhugh Lee, Ewell, and Beauregard. (reprint: Century for March 1885) $15-k, See: S.H.S.P., Jan. 1885, xiii, p. 41-47.
...Louisville, Jy., 1970. 8vo, wraps, 8pp. reprint of 1885 edt. 100 copies, 70 for sale. $10.

1352 ..."Notes on Ewell's Division in the Campaign of 1862." In: SHSP, June 1882, v.X, #6, p. 255-261.

1353 ..."General Ewell at First Manassas. Col. Campbell Brown's reply to Gen. Beauregard." In: SHSP, 1885, v.XIII, p. 41-47. These letters appeared in "Century Mag." March, 1885.

1354 ..."The Myth of the 5 dead Rebel Generals." In: CWTI, Aug. 1969, v.VIII, #5, p. 14-15, illus.

1355 ..."How Ewell lost his leg." In: CWTI, June, 1965, v.IV, #3, p. 16-20, illus., map, ports. From an unpublished journal of Ewell's step-son.

1356 **BROWN, Carolina Morrill, Mrs.**
"War-Time Memories by an Old Lady who was then young." In: "Magazine of Albemarle County History." v.30, 1972, p. 29-41. port., pl. Originally presented by Ms. Brown before a literary club at the Univ. of Virginia around 1910.

1357 **BROWN, David**
"The Planter; or, Thirteen Years in the South, by a Northern Man." Phila: H. Hooker, 1853, 12mo, cl, 275pp. Wright-377. Arguments condoning slavery interspersed with tales.

1358 **BROWN, Dee Alexander**
"The Battle of Brice's Cross Roads-June 10, 1864, Nathan Bedford Forrest inflicted most decisive defeat of the civil war." In: CWTI, April 1968, v.VII, #1, p. 4-9, 44-48, illus., maps, ports.

1359 ..."The Battle of Westport-Sterling Price's bold raid across Missouri, ends biggest battle of the war west of the Mississippi." In: CWTI, July 1966, v.V, #4, p. 4-11, 40-43. Illus., maps, ports.

1360 ..."The million dollar wagon train raid, in Indian Territory." In: CWTI, Oct. 1968, v.VII, #6, p. 12-20, illus., map, ports.

1361 ..."The Bold Cavaliers. Morgan's 2nd. Kentucky Cavalry Raiders." Phil: J.B. Lippincott Co. (1959). 8vo, cl-bds., dj, map endsheets, illus. ports, 353pp. $6, $15, $17.50. $50-bmk, $25.

1362 ..."The Battle of Pea Ridge-"Gettysburg of the West." In: Civil War Times 1967, 1vol. (unpaged), illus.

1363 ..."The Northwest Conspiracy." In: CWTI, May 1971, v.X, #2, p. 10-19. See: Frank L. Klement, Jno. B. Castleman, Oscar Kinchen. "Copperheads."

1364 ..."The Galvanized Yankees." Urbana, University of Illinois press, 1963. 8vo, cl, dj, 243pp., illus., prots, map-lines, $10.

1365 ..."Galvanized Yankees." In: CWTI, FEb. 1966, v.4, #10, p. 12-21, illus., maps, ports. CSA prisoners who fought Indians in the west for the Union.

1366 **BROWN, Fred E.**
"The Battle of Allatoona." In: CWH, Sept. 1960, v.VI, #3, p. 277-297, maps, port, pl.

1367 **BROWN, Gayle Ann**
"Confederate Surrenders in Indian Territory." In: Jour. of West, 1973, v.XII, p. 455-461.

1368 **BROWN, George W.**
"Trends toward the formation of a

Southern confederacy." In: Jour. Negro Hist., 1933, v.XVIII, p. 256-281. Events leading to Southern states secession.

1369 **BROWN, George William**
"Baltimore & the Nineteenth of April, 1861. A Study of the War." Baltimore: Johns Hopkins Unvi., 1887. Studies in Historical & PoliticalScience Extra vol. III. Herbert B. Adams, Edt. Tall 8vo, cl, map-frontis. 176pp.(10p. ads. Mayor of Baltimore, unusually sympathetic presentation of a Southern point of view re Marylands' near joining the CSA. See: "Baltimore in 1861." $10, $20, $15, $17.50-y.

1370 **BROWN, Isaac N., Capt., CSN**
"The Confederate gunboat "Arkansas"." In: B & L, v.3, p. 572-580. illus., ports. Also CSA Torpedos in the Yazoo.

1370a **BROWN, James Earl**
"Life of Brig.-Gen. John McCausland." In: W. Va. Hist., vol. 4, 1943.

1371 **BROWN, John**
"Old John Brown, a Song for Every Southern Man." (Richmond, Va.? 1860) small Broadside 20x15cm, seven four-line stanzas & a chorus, very anti-Brown & warns of Northern Agents in South to incite slaves to leave. Probably printed at Richmond Religious Herald, with notes of sermon by Dr. Shaver, its editor. $100-jk-122.

1372 **BROWN, John & William Mahone**
"An historical parallel, foreshadowing civil trouble, 1860-1880." Richmond, Va., Johnston pub., 1880. 8vo, wraps, 23pp. (Canner-485) $5.

1373 **BROWN, John Calvin, Brig.-Gen.**
"Lookout Mountain! Report of Brigadier General J.C. Brown. Hdq., Nov. 30, 1863." In: SHSP, 1884, v.XII, p. 182-183.

1374 **BROWN, John Henry**
"The Paths of Glory"-a Wartime diary of Maj. John Henry Brown,CSA. Edt: W.J. Lemke." In: AHW, 1956, v.XV, p. 344-359. Concerns Gen. Ben McCulloch vs Gen. Sterling Price.

1375 **BROWN, John Henry, Chairman Comm.**
"A Report & treatise on slavery & the slavery agitation. Printed by order: House of Representatives of Texas. December, 1857." Austin, Texas: John Marshall & Co., 1857." 8vo, wraps, 81. vi, pp(append., a list of works on slavery by a Southern Editor). $125-jk, $275-jk, $75. Urges congress to abolish all laws hindering slave trade, Winkler-#958, reports Streeter copy had a Broadside "addressed to Editors & pres. of colleges in Texas; signed: "Men from all parts of Texas." following...
...Galveston, Texas: Die Union Office, an edition in German of 1500 copies.

1376 ..."War-time diary in northwest Arkansas." In: "Flashback", Nov. 1956, v.6, #6, p. 3-11. Record kept by a CSA (Texas) major, his travel from East Texas (Marshall) to Fayetteville & his service with Gen. Ben McCulloch & his publishing an army newspaper "The War Bulletin." 11 Sept.-31 Dec. 1861.
..."War-time editorials from the "War Jour." a CSA army newspaper published in Fayetteville, Ark., by Brown." In: "Flashback", May 1957, Jan., Mar., Oct. 1958, v.7, #3; v.8, #1, 2 & 6. Reprinted from issues of 9 & 22 Jan. & 4 Feb. 1862. A letter to J.S. Tucker of Missouri defending Gen. Ben McCulloch & Arkansas record in the war.

1377 **BROWN, John Thompson, Col.**
"The Gettysburg Campaign-Operations of the Artillery. Report of Col. J. Thompson Brown, Hdq., Aug. 13, 1863." In: SHSP, 1882, v.X, p. 59-62.

1378 **BROWN, John Wilcox**
"Why Jefferson Davis was never tried." In: SHSP, 1910, v.XXXVIII, p. 347-349.

1379 **BROWN, John, Harper's Ferry**
"Trial of John Brown, its Impartiality & Decorum Vindicated." In: SHSP, 1888, v.XVI, p. 357-365. See: John Avis (Jailor), Rev. Abner C. Hopkins.

1380 **BROWN, Joseph Emerson**
"An Act, to further provide for the Suppression of unlawful distillation of grain, & other commodities in this State(Ga.)." Milledgeville, Ga., 1863. Broadside: 13x6.5" dble. column $450. Unrecorded, Jenkins-#197(cat.)

1381 **BROWN, Joseph Emerson, Gov. of Ga.**
"Correspondence between Gov. Brown & President Davis on the Constitutionality of the Conscription Act." Atlanta, Ga., Atlanta Intelligencer print, 1862. 8vo, wraps, 52pp. $10. Brown for States' Rights & Davis: power is vested in the government itself (same as the Lincoln position). See also, Crandall #606, Richmond, 1862 imprint of 20pp.

1382 ..."Executive Dept., Letter to Gen. Joseph E. Johnston on the campaign, 1864. (Feb. 10)." In: SHSP, 1914, v.39, p. 60-61.

1383 ..."Official Correspondence of Governor Joseph E. Brown 1860-1865, Inclusive." In: Allen D. Candler's "Confederate Record, v.III, 746pp., incl. Index.

1384 ..."State Papers of Governor Joseph E. Brown relating to the Public Defense, the Organization & Equipment of Troops, Provision for the Families of Soldiers, etc. 1860 to 1865, inclusive." In: Allen D. Candler's "Confederate Records." v.II, 905pp., incl. index.

1385 ..."A Proclamation, November 21, 1860." Milledgeville, Ga. Executive Dept't. To hold an election Jan. 16, 1861, for delegates to the Convention." In: Allen D. Candler's "Confederate Records", v.1, p. 209-211.

1386 ..."The Governor of Georgia urges the Secession of Arkansas. Edt: Willard E. Wight." In: AHQ, 1957, v.XVI, p. 192-202.

1387 ..."Proclamations & Orders calling into active Military Service & sending to the Front the Civil & Military Officers & the Reserved Militia of the State of Georgia to the Army of Tennessee." sewed, 8vo. (July 9, 1864). Milledgeville: 1864. $50. Not in De Renne, Crandall-Harwell.

1388 ..."Read & hand to your neighbor. Correspondence between the Secretary of War & Gov. Brown, growing out of a requisition made upon the Governor for the Reserve Militia of Georgia to be turned over to Confederate Control." Milledgeville, Ga., Boughton, Nisbet, Barnes & Moore, State Printers, 1865. 8vo, 43pp. DeRenne, II, p. 673.
...Do, 37pp. Crandall-1331-2.

1389 ..."St. Valentine Feb. XIV, MDCCCLXXXVIII." (N.Y., Press of Fleming, Brewster & Alley 1888). 8vo, wraps, illus., ports, (7)pp. Union & CSA recovering bodies at the battle of Kennesaw Mt., June 27, 1864.

1390 ..."The story of a song. Saint Valentine's day, 1889." (N.Y., Press of Fleming, Brewster & Alley 1889. 12mo, wraps, cover title, illus., (8)pp.

1391 ..."Special Message to the Legislature of Georgia, on Our Federal Relations, Retailitory State Legislation, the Rights of Secession, etc., Nov. 7, 1860." Milledgeville, Ga., Broughton, Nisbet & Barnes, 1860, (copy: 28pp.) $35-jk-122, (old)$7.50. 8vo, wraps, 22pp.
...Reprint: in Allen D. Candler's "Confederate Records", v.1, p. 19-57.

1392 ..."Annual Message to the Georgia Legislature, Nov. 7, 1860." Milledgeville, Ga. (above) 1860. 8vo, sewn, 28pp. $35-jk, $10-j. Refers to Ga. Mil. Acad., preparedness, on defense of our rights purchase of arms from the North, trade with Europe, etc.

...Biographies or references to: Fielder, Herbert; Hill, Louise B.; Avery, Isaac W., Hist. of Ga.; Clark, Richard H., Memories relate to; Brown, Alex Stephens & Cobb; Hay, Thomas R.; Bass, James Horace.

1393 BROWN, Joseph Mackey
"The Battle of Allatoona, Oct. 5, 1864. One of the gamest & bloodiest fights of the war. Some facts never before published." Atlanta, Ga., Record pub. co., 1890. 4to, wraps, illus., maps, 24pp.

1394 ..."Kennesaw's Bombardment. How the Sharpshooters woke up the batteries." Atlanta, Ga., Record pub. co., 1890. 12mo, wraps, illus., errata slip, 172pp. $7.50, $10, $12.50, $100-bmk-104, $60, Factual material in guise of fiction.

1395 ..."The Great Retreat. Could Johnston have defended Atlanta successfully. The policy of the great Southern general defended & the field looked over the light of events. A review of his plan of campaign." Atlanta, Ga., (188-?) Railroad record print. 8vo, wraps, illus., 16pp.

1396 ..."The Mountain Campaigns in Georgia; or, War scenes on the W. & A." (Buffalo, 1886. Art printing co. of Matthews & Northrup.) 4to, wraps, illus., (11)-51pp, (1)p. maps. $17.50. Another copy: same, but with front, errata slip at end. atg-$10-bmk.
...Louisville: Lost Cause Pr., micro-cd.
...Same, 1887.
...(Buffalo, 1888) 3rd Edt., ports, 60pp. $60-ob
...(Buffalo, 1895) 6th Edt., 2, 1, (11)-72pp.
...(Buffalo, 1890) 5th Edt. 72pp.

1397 BROWN, Joseph Newton
"An address delivered by...at the Nov. (1900) meeting of the R.E. Lee Chapter of the Daughters of the Confederacy, who requested him to address them on the battle of "Boody Angle", May 12th, 1864." Anderson(S.C.) Advocate Pub. Co., 1900. 8vo, 11pp. Dornbusch-930.

1398 ...Supplement to Col. J.N. Brown's account of the battle of Gettysburg. (Anderson, S.C., 1901) 8vo, 4pp. caption title.

1399 BROWN, Joshua
"The story of Sam Davis." In: Amer. Irish Hist. Soc. Jour., 1914, Dec., XXII, p. 554-555. Also in: "Historic Pulaski, birthplace of the Ku Klux Klan, etc." See title. Author: Wm. Thomas Richardson.

1400 BROWN, Kent Masterson & Edgar G. Archer
"Order A.P. Hill to prepare for action." The career of Lieut. Gen. Ambrose Powell Hill. (part I)" In: Lincoln Herald, Summer, 1979, p. 79-87.

1401 ..."Mechanichsville to Sharpsburg; the ascendance of the "Light Division"; the military career of Lieut. Gen. Ambrose Powell Hill. (part II)." In: Lincoln Herald, Fall 1979, p. 149-158.

1402 BROWN, Louis A.
"The Salisbury Prison. A Case Study of Confederate Military Prisons, 1861-1865." Wendell, N.C., Avera Press; Broadfoot's Bookmark, 1980. sm. 4to, fabricord, facsms., map, illus., ports, xvii, 204pp, index, bibliog. op-$25, $15.

1403 BROWN, Maud Morrow
"The University Greys Company A., Eleventh Mississippi Regiment Army of Northern Virginia 1861-1865." Richmond, Va., Garrett & Massie (1940). 8vo, cl, front(port) xii, (1)80pp. $8.50, $45, $35-bmk, $25-bmk, $17.50-y. See: Maud Morrow.

1404 ..."The War Comes to College Hill." (Jackson, Miss., Jour. Miss. Hist., Jan. 1954, v.XVI, #1, p. 22-30.

1405 BROWN, Norman D.
"Edward Stanly: Whiggery's Tarheel" Conquerer." University, Alabama University

pr., (1974). Southern Historical Publication #18. 8vo, cl, xiii, 365pp. (bibliog. 333-350). Brown was first military Governor of N.C. $20-b, $10.

1406 ..."One of Cleburne's command." Austin: 1980, 8vo, cl, 192pp. See: Saml. T. Foster, $15.

1407 **BROWN, Philip Francis**
"A Guide to Fortifications & Battlefields around Petersburg with a splendid map." Prepared & published as a handbook by Proprietor of Jarratt's Hotel." Petersburg, Va., Jno. B. Ege's Print, 1869. 8vo, wraps, fldg-map, 26pp. front-CSA flag. $30.
...1st Edt., 1866, same, (2), 27pp. (ads, 10pp). $10, $15.

1408 ..."Reminiscences of the war of 1861-1865." (Roanoke, Va., Union Print, 1912) (altho last page shows Blue Ridge Springs, Va.) 8vo, wraps (cover title), illus., ports (incl. front), 54pp. $15, $26.50, $75, $110, $150-bmk, $200-bmk-105.
...Richmond, Va., Whittet & Shepperson, 1917. Only port(front), no illus., color flag on cover. Author in Co. "C", 12th Va. Inf., Mahone's Brigade. $7.50, $12.50, $15, $20.
...Louisville, Ky., Lost Cause Press, microcard, $2.33

1409 **BROWN, R. Shepard**
"Stringfellow of the Fourth." N.Y., Crown Pub. (1960) 8vo, cl, dj, ports, illus., map, (1), 307pp. $3.95(pub.) $6, $12, $30-dj, $20-bmk-105, $45-b, $19.50.

1410 **BROWN, Ralph Minthorne**
"Bibliography of Com. Matthew Fontaine Maury, including a biographical sketch." (Blacksburg, Va.) Virginia Polytechnic Institute, Bul, vol. XXIV, #2, 8vo, wraps, 61pp., port.

1411 **BROWN, Robert B.**
"Texans in Leopard skin pants." N.Y., Bibliog. Soc. Amer. Papers (1950) 44: p. 373-378. (4th quart.) Reviews W.W. Heartsill's 1491 Days in CSArmy. $4.50

1412 **BROWN, T.L.**
"General Lee's horse "Traveller." In: SHSP, 1890, v.18, p. 388-390; 1891, v.19, p. 333-335, 1907, v.35, p. 99-101.

1413 **BROWN, Tom Watson**
"The military career of Thomas R.R. Cobb." In: Ga. H.Q. Dec. 1961, v.XLV, #4, p. 345-362. $8.

1414 **BROWN, Varina Davis**
"A Colonel at Gettysburg & Spotsylvania." Columbia, S.C., State Co., 1931. Tall 8co, cl, ports, maps, xvi, 333pp., dj. $15, $9.50, $12, $17.50, $20, $150, $75-r, $35-bmk, $40-bmk, $60-n
..."A colonel at Gettysburg & Spotsylvania. Part 1, the life & character of Col. Joseph Newton Brown correspondence of 1861-1862, papers of Colonel Newton Brown, South Carolinians at Gettysburg, the Bloody Angle at Spotsylvania. Part II, the Battle of Gettysburg, July 1, 1863; the Battle of Spotsylvania, May 12, 1864." Columbia, S.C., State Co., 1931. 8vo, cl, xvi, 333pp. pls (3 maps, 1-fold) ports. $75.
..."A Colonel at Gettysburg & Spotsylvania." Baltimore: Butternut & Blue, 1988. 8vo, cl, ills, maps, ports, 333p. $25.

1415 **BROWN, W. LeRoy**
"The Richmond Arsenal." In: LWL, New Eclectic Magazine, April 1869, v. , p. 455-458.

1416 **BROWN, Walter L.**
"Albert Pike & the Pea Ridge Atrocities." In: Ark. HQ, Winter 1979, v.XXXVIII, #4, p. 345-359.

1417 ..."Rowing against the stream: the course of Albert Pike from National Whig to Secessionist." In: ArkHQ, Autumn, 1980, v.XXXIX, #3, p. 230-246.

1418 ..."Pea Ridge, Gettysburg of the West." In: Ar. HQ, 1958, v.XV, fldg. map, p. 3-16.

1419 **BROWN, William Garrott**
"A Gentleman of the South, a Memory of the Black Belt from the manuscript

memoirs of the late Col. Stanton Elmore, edt. without change by..." N.Y. Macmillan Co., 1903. $7.50. 12mo, cl, decr. t/p, front, illus., pl, 232pp.

1420 ..."The lower South in American history." N.Y., Lond: Macmillan co., 1902. 12mo, cl, xi, 271pp. (1903 edt., $25) 2nd print.
...N.Y., P. Smith reprint. Secession, resources, KKK.

1421 ..."The Orator of Secession: A Study of an Agitator." (William L. Yancey) Atlantic Monthly, 1899, v.LXXXIII, p. 605-617.

1422 ..."The Ku Klux Movement." In: Atlantic Monthly, 1901, v.LXXXVII, p. 634-644.

1423 ..."The Resources of the Confederacy." In: Atlantic Monthly, 1901, v.LXXXVIII, p. 827-838.

1424 ..."Foe of Compromise." (1902) (The Compromise of 1850, with Rufus Choate as the orator of compromise & William L. Garrison as its foe) considered his finest work. Reprinted in 1903, in N.Y., p. 11-64, titled "Foe of Compromise & Other Essays."

1425 **BROWNE, A.K.**
"The Story of the Kearsarge & Alabama." San Francisco, H. Payot & Co., 1868. 8vo, wraps, (27)leafs.

1426 ...See: Century, April 1886, v.31, p.911-922. Re: John M. Kell.

1427 **BROWNE, Douglas G.**
"The Boy's Battle." In: Blackwood's, Dec. 1915, v.CXCVIII, p. 807-816. VMI's cadets at Newmarket in 1864.

1428 **BROWNE, Francis Fisher**
"Bugle-echoes; a collection of poems of the Civil War, northern & southern." N.Y., White, Stokes & Allen, 1886. 12mo, cl, x, (11)-336pp. t.p., in red; title vignette.
...Do., new & revised edt., with illus., front, plates & ports. $15.
...Do., F.A. Stokes & Bro., 1890. Illustrated edt.
...Do., Chicago: A.C. McClurg, 1916.

12mo, 11, (13)-329pp. From his editorial desk in Augusta, Ga., a history of Randall's "Maryland".

1429 **BROWNE, G. Waldo**
"A daughter of Maryland, a narrative of Pickett's last charge at Gettysburg, a novel." N.Y., Novelist Pub. Co., (1895) 12mo, wraps, viii, 179pp., illus. (cheap paper)

1430 **BROWNE, M.S., Dr., Winchester, Ky.**
"Confederate Coinage." In: CV, 1, p. 118-119, facsm.

1431 **BROWNE, P.D.**
"Captain T.D. Nettles & the Valverde Battery." In: Texana, Spring 1964, v.II, #1, p. 1023, ports, illus., Muster Roll.

1432 **BROWNE, W.B.**
"Stranger than Fiction. Capture of U.S. Steamer "Maple Leaf", near Cape Henry, half century ago." In: SHSP, Apr. 1914, v.XXXIX, p. 181-185.

1433 **BROWNING, O.H., Hon., of Ill.**
"Speech of...On the Confiscation Bill." To confiscate property & free slaves of the Rebels. Against, as unconstitutional." (Washington: L. Towers & Co., 1862) 8vo, sewn, 16pp. $1.50

1434 **BROWNLEE, Richard S.**
"The Battle of Pilot Knob, Iron County Mo. Sept. 27, 1864." (Columbia, Mo., Mo. Hist. Review. Oct. 1964, v.LVIV, #1, p. 1-20, illus., ports.

1435 ..."Gray Ghosts of the Confederacy. Guerrilla Warfare in the West, 1861-1865." Baton Rouge: Louisiana State Univ. Press (1958). 8vo, cl, dj, map endsheets, illus., ports, maps, xi, 274pp. Roster of guerrillas. $5, $6.50, $25, $12-nc.
...1963 (2nd Edt); 1968(3rd Edt); 1973 & 1975 Edt. $23, $20, $17.50.
..."Gray Ghosts of the Confederacy." Baton Rouge: La. State Univ. Pr., 1984. 8vo, cl, dj, viii, 246pp., illus. $20.

1436 **BROYLES, Nash R.**
"A historic bail-bond." In: Ga. Bar Ass'n. 47th annual report, May 19-21, 1930. Macon, Ga., p. 257-260. Copy of Jeff Davis' bond, May 13, 1867, from prison.

1437 **BRUBAKER, John H., III**
"The Last Capital, Danville, Va., & the final days of the Confederacy." Danville, Va., Danville Museum of Fine Arts & History (1979). 8vo, wraps, iii, 74pp. illus. See: Burke Davis. $12-b, $7.80

1438 **BRUCE, D.H.**
"The Battle of New Market, Va., by the Captain who witnessed it." In: SHSP, 1907, v.XXXV, p. 155-158.

1439 **BRUCE, Edward C.**
"In & around Richmond." In: Harper's Dec/May, 1865/1866, v.XXXII, p. 409-430.

1440 **BRUCE, George Alexander**
"President Davis." In: Military Historical Society of Mass. Papers, v.13, 1913, Boston, Mass., Athenaeum, 1913. p. 347-389, compact & able sketch.

1441 **BRUCE, Horatio W.**
"Some Reminiscences of the Second of April, 1865." In: SHSP, 1881, v.IX, p. 206-211.

1442 **BRUCE, Kathleen**
"Economic factors in manufacture of Confederate Ordnance." Washington: Army Ordnance Ass'n. (1926) 8vo, wraps, illus., incl. port, (13)pp. Reprint: Army Ordnance Journal, Army Ordnance Ass'n., v.VI, p. 33-34, Nov-Feb., 1926, p. 166-173; 259-264.

1443 ..."Slave Labor in Virginia iron industry." William & Mary Quarterly, 2nd Ser., VI (October 289-302pp. 1926; VII (Jan. 1927, p. 21-31. "Virginia Iron Manufacture in the Slave Era." Head title: Amer. Hist. Ass'n. N.Y., Century co, 1930, 8vo, cl, illus., xiii, 482pp.

1444 **BRUCE, Philip Alexander**
"Brave Deeds of Confederate Soldiers." Phila: George W. Jacobs co. (Oct. 1916). 8vo, decr. cl, illus., (old prints), 351pp. $20, $6, $9. $25-bmk.

1445 ..."The Plantation negro as a freeman; observations on his character, condition, & prospects in Virginia." N.Y., G.P. Putnam's sons, 1889. 12mo, cl, ix, 262pp. Swem-631.

1446 ..."Robert E. Lee." Phila: G.W. Jacons Co. (1907). Half-title: American Crisis Biographies, Edt: E.P. Oberholtzer. 12mo, cl, front(port), 380pp. $5, $6, $12, $35-b.

1447 ..."Hist. of University of Virginia-(The War Years, 1861-1865, Reconstruction. In: v.III, IV, NY, Macmillan, 1921.

1448 ..."The National Spirit of General Lee." In: So. Atl. Quart., Jan. 1911, v.X, p. 23-30.

1449 ..."Plantation Memories of the Civil War." In: So. Atl. Quart., Jan. 1915, v.XIV, p. 28-46.

1450 ..."Recollections of my Plantation Teachers." In: So. Atl. Quart., Jan. 1917, v.XVI, p. 1013.

1451 **BRUCE, William Cabell**
"Address on General Robert E. Lee." Baltimore, 1930. 8vo, wraps, 11pp.

1452 **BRUCE, William G.**
"The battle of the crater." In: Marine Corps. Gaz., June 1954, v.38, #6, p. 36-41. ports, views. Disastrous failure of Lt. Col. Henry Pleasants' upon Petersburg.

1453 **BRUCHEY, Stuart**
"Cotton & the Growth of the American Economy: 1790-1860." New York: Harcourt, Brace, World, 1967. 8vo, cl, xi, 275pp. $3.95.

1454 **BRUGGER, Robert J.**
"Beverly Tucker: Heart over head in the Old South." Baltimore: Johns Hopkins pr, 1978, 8vo, cl, dj, xvii, 294pp. $15.

1455 **BRUMGARDT, John R.**
"Alexander H. Stephens & the State Con-

vention Movement in Georgia: A Reappraisal." In: Ga. H.Q., v.LIX, Spring, 1975, #1, p. 38-49.

1456 ..."The Confederate career of Alexander H. Stephens: the case reopened." In: CWH, Mar. 1981, v.27, #1, p. 64-81.

1457 **BRUMMER, Sidney David**
"The Judicial Interpretation of the Confederate Constitution." In: Studies in Southern History & Politics, N.Y., Columbia University Press, 1914. p. 107-133., v.VIII, p. 387-409. Also: "Lawyer & Banker." Dec. 1915.

1458 **BRUNKER, Howard Molyneux Edward, Lt. Col.**
"Story of the Campaign in Eastern Virginia, April, 1861 to May, 1863. Including "Stonewall Jackson's" Operations in the Valley." London: Forster Groom & Co., 1910. 8vo, cl, xxvii, 109pp., table, 13-fldg. maps in pocket (i.e., 14-two maps of #12) $10, $15, $30, 2nd $25.

...1st Edt., 1904 prepared for competitive examinations Nov. 1904 & May 1905 in conjunction with Henderson's "Stonewall Jackson." $16.50.

1459 ..."Grant & Lee in Virginia, May & June, 1864. Summary of the Campaign, with sketch maps to illustrate the operations, & comments on the campaign." London: F. Groom & Co., 1908. 16mo, cl, 63pp., 6-fldg. maps in pocket, at end.

1460 **BRUNSON, Joseph W.**
"Historical sketch of the Pee Dee light artillery, ANV, by orderly Sergeant J.W. Brunson, together with a roll of McIntosh's battery artillery." Columbia, S.C., R.L. Bryan Co., 1904. 8vo, wraps, 20pp. (O'Brien 450.) $750.

1461 **BRUNSON, Joseph W., Sgt.**
"Historical Sketch of the Pee Dee light artillery, Army Northern Virginia, by..., together with a roll of McIntosh's battery artillery." Winston-Salem, N.C., Stewart Pr., 1927. tall 8vo, wraps, 25, (1)p. $15, $30, $38.50, $250-lb. Hoole notes: three known copies: Columbia Univ., University of S.C. & Francis Marion College Library.

1462 **BRUNSON, Joseph Woods, Sgt.**
"Pee Dee Light Artillery of McGregg's-later Samuel McGowan's Brigade First South Carolina Volunteers (Infantry) CSA. A Historical Sketch & Roster by Sgt. Joseph Woods Brunson (1839-1923). To which has been added the rosters of the three Pee Dee Infantry companies (from Darlington, Horry, & Marion counties) which were supported by the Pee Dee Artillery. Introduction & edited by William Stanley Hoole." University, Ala, Confederate Pub. Co., 1983. Confederate Regimental Series #4. 8vo, stiff wraps, 60pp.

1463 **BRUNSWICK BLUES, The**
"In: SHSP, 1900, v.XXVIII, p. 261-262.

1464 **BRUNSWICK GUARD, The**
"A detailed account of its fine record. Its marches, fights, & Roll of Members." In: SHSP, 1900, v.XXVIII, p. 8-14. See also: George E. Mitchell.

1465 **BRUTUS (pseud.)**
"The Crisis: Or, Essays on the Usurpations of the Federal Government." Charleston, S.C., A.E. Miller, 1827. 8vo, wraps, 166pp. (Henkels-#1118) Sabin-8776. States rights (Robt. Jas. Turnbull - 97465.

1466 **BRYAN, Anna Semmes**
"The "Virginia" & the "Monitor"." In: CV, Sept. 1924, v.XXXII, p. 346-347. Battle of Hampton Roades, Mar. 9, 1862.

1467 **BRYAN, Charles F., Jr.**
"I mean to have them all": Forrest's Murfreesboro raid." In: CWTI, Jan. 1974, v.12, #9, p. 26-34, illus., map, ports.

1468 ..."The Marooned Brigade." (London) Jour. Confed. Hist. Soc., Winter, 1971, v.9, #4, p. 112-130. Port of Gen. Early.

1469 ..."Nashville under Federal occupation." In: CWTI, Jan. 1975, v.13, #9, p. 4-11, 40-47, illus., ports.

1470 ..."Stalemate at Seven Pines." In: CWTI, Aug. 1973, v.12, #5, p. 4-11, 39-47, illus., maps, port.

1471 ..."A gathering of Tories: the East Tennessee Convention of 1861." In: THQ, Spring 1980, #1, p. 27-48.

1472 **BRYAN, Emma Lyon, Mrs.**
"1860-1865. A Romance of the Valley of Virginia." Harrisonburg, Va., J. Taliaffero, 1892. 12mo, cl, 228pp. $7.50, $10, $12.50, $25-bmk-84.

1473 **BRYAN, George S.**
"The Great American Myth." N.Y., Carrick & Evans (1940). 8vo, cl, xii, 436pp., index, bibliog., 396-407..., illus., facsms (incl. front) ports, illus., $10. Study of Booth, events leading to Lincoln assassination, what happend to Booth.

1474 **BRYAN, Goode, General**
"Report of General Goode Bryan, the Battle of Wilderness. August 14th." In: SHSP, 1878, v.VI, p. 83-84

1475 **BRYAN, Guy M.**
"Address to the people of the State of Texas (Head: Galveston County, Texas. Committee of Safety & Correspondence.)" In: SWHQ, Jan. 1954, v.57, p. 389-391. Sign: Guy M. Bryan, 29 Dec., 1860, Corresp. Sect. Urges formation of convention to resist Northern action on the South. (Sam Houston, Gov. Tex. refused to convene such a convent)

1476 ...Folder, one page of print (three columns) 21.5x26.5 cm (17x18.5cm) Winkler, 1-1334. Issued as a broadside. (See: Earl Fornell)

1477 **BRYAN, John Stewart**
"Joseph Bryan (1845-1908): His Times, His Family, His Friends, a Memoir." Richmond, Va. (1935) Private print. 4to, cl, illus., 408pp. Lim. Edt. 400 copies $17.50, $35, $75, $150-ob, $51-cw-108. Bryan was with Mosby's Rangers. See: Joseph Bryan. 2nd Print, 1938.

1478 **BRYAN, Joseph**
"Oil-cloth coat in which Jackson received his mortal wound. Story of its loss & recovery." In: SHSP, 1891, v.XIX, p. 324-326. See: John S. Mosby's "participant..." Re: Joseph Bryan's character. See: John Stewart Bryan.

1479 **BRYAN, Joseph, III**
"The Sword Over the Mantel, the Civil War & I." N.Y.: McGraw-Hill Book Co (1960) 12mo, cl, dj, sketches, (2), 123, (1)pp. $4, $750-b

1480 **BRYAN, King, Lieut.-Col.**
"Report of Lieutenant-Colonel K. Bryan Fifth Texas Regiment. Hdq. July 8, 1863." In: SHSP, 1885, v.XIII, p. 192-193.

1481 **BRYAN, Thomas A., Capt.**
"Bryan's Battery, 13th Battalion, Virginia Artillery, C.S.A., 1862-1865." Richmond, Va., n.d. 12mo, wraps, ill. colored flag, wraps, 24pp., (old) $15, $28.50.

1482 **BRYAN, Thomas Conn**
"The Churches in Georgia during the Civil War." In: Ga. H.Q., Dec., 1949, v.XXXIII, #4, p. 283-302. $10-bmk.

1483 ..."Confederate Georgia." Athens: Univ. of Ga. Press (1953) 8vo, cl, dj, x, 299pp. $25, $4.50, $16-bmk, $10, $12.50-y.

1484 ..."General William J. Hardee & Confederate Publication rights." In: JSH, May 1946, 8pp. $8.

1485 ..."The Secession of Georgia." In: Ga. H.Q., June 1947, v.XXXI, #2, p. 89-111. $10.

1486 **BRYANT, John Randolph**
"Balloon used for scout duty in C.S.A." In: SHSP, 1905, V.XXXIII, p. 32-42. See: Capt. Langdon Cheeves, Jr., Jenkins Cornish. Also: CV, Apr. 1914, v.22, #4, p. 161-165.

1487 **BRYANT, Victor S.**
"Let the South & West Unite." In: N.C. Unvi. Mag., 1890, ns-v.X, p. 93-98. "Unite South & West against haughty oppression of the North."

1488 **BRYCE, Campbell, Mrs.**
"Reminiscences of the Hospitals of Columbia, S.C., during the four years of the Civil War." Phila: J.B. Lippincott, 1897. sq. 12mo, wraps, 31pp.

1489 ..."The personal experiences of Mrs. Campbell Bryce during the Burning of Columbia, S.C. by Gen. W.T. Sherman's Army Feb. 17, 1865." Phila: (Lippincott press) 1899. 12mo, wraps, 53pp. Turnbull-IV. $35.

1490 **BRYCE, Clarence Archibald**
"Kitt Dixon, belle of the South Anna; a wee bit of love & war, by C.A. Bryce, M.D." (Richmond, Va., "Southern Clinic Press, 1907) 12mo, cl, front, pl, (vi), (7)-102pp. Southern War Songs, p. 87-102. Swem-651.

1491 **BRYDON, G. MacLaren**
"The "Confederate Prayer Book"." (Garrison, N.Y.) "Hist. Mag. of Protestant Episcopal Church", Vol. XVII-#4, Dec. 1948, p. 339-344.

1492 ..."The Diocese of Virginia in the Southern Confederacy." In: same magazine above, p. 384-410.

1493 **BRYSON, Thomas A.**
"A Lawsuit conserning the publication of Jefferson Davis's "Rise & Fall of the Confederate Government." In: Ga. H.Q., Winter 1970, v.LIV, #4, p. 540-552. $8.

1494 ..."A Note on Jefferson Davis' Lawsuit against Appleton Pub. Co." (Jackson, Miss.) Jour. Miss. Hist. May, 1971, v.XXXIII, #2, p. 149-165. $8.

1495 **BUBECK, A. Eric**
"Colonel Lee & the marines at Harper's Ferry." In: Marine Corps gaz., Dec. 1949, v.33, (#12), p. 50-54. Ports, views. Lt.-Col. Robert E. Lee commands marines Oct. 18, 1859.

1496 **BUCHANAN, Elliott M.**
"The part Indians played in the Confederacy." In: AlaHQ, 1943, v.V, p. 59-65.

1497 **BUCHANAN, Franklin**
"Battle of Hampton Roads-Confederate Official Reports, April 10, 1862." In: SHSP, 1879, v.VII, p. 305-324.

1498 ..."Fight between the "Virginia" (Merrimac) & "Monitor." In: Confed. War Jour., 1893, v.1, p. 82-85, 87-90, illus.

1499 ..."The Naval Fight in Mobile Bay, Aug. 5, 1864-Official Report of Admiral Buchanan." In: SHSP, 1878, v.VI, p. 220-224.

1500 ...Also: New Eclectic Mag., Aug. 1969, v.V, #2, p. 201-206.

1501 ..."Official Report of the Battle between the C.S.S. Virginia (formerly U.S.S. Merrimack) & the U.S.S. Monitor, on March 9, 1862, by Flag Officer Franklin Buchanan." Washington: Naval Historical Foundation (1962?) 12mo, wraps, caption title, 8pp. $1.

1502 **BUCHANAN, James**
"Mr. Buchanan's administration on the eve of the rebellion." N.Y., D. Appleton, 1865 (also for 1866) 8vo, cl, xx, 11-296pp., 6-ads. $12.50. See: Philip G. Auchampaugh. Democratic pres. in 1856; both northern & southern men in cabinet; believed in "sacred balance" between slave & free states, tho disliked slavery, believed the constitution protected slavery where it exists; North accuses his southern expansion as increasing slave power; he hated Abolitonists; if South secedes the Fed. Gov. should only protect Fed. property & desperately tried to keep union.

1503 **BUCHANAN, Lamont**
"A Pictorial History of the Confederacy." N.Y., Crown Pub. (1951). 4to, cl, dj, illus., facsms, cartoons, ports, 288pp. $25-b, $15,
...1959, $20

...1961, 9th printing, $7.50
...(1963) Bonanza reprint '59 $15, '69 $15.
...(1975)

1504 **BUCHANAN, W. Jefferson**
"Maryland's Crisis: a political outline." Richmond: J.W. Randolph, 1863. 12mo, wraps, 16pp. Crandall-2700, $26.50.

1505 ..."Maryland's hope; her trials & interests in connection with the war." Richmond: West & Johnson, 1864. 8vo, wraps, 62pp. Crand-2701. $50. Reasons for Md. joining C.S.A.

1506 **BUCK, Charles W.**
"Colonel Bob & a Double Love A Story from the civil side behind the Southern Lines, by...authors of "Under the Sun, or, the Passing of the Incas." Louisville, Ky., Standard Press (1922), tk. 12mo, decr. cl, sketches, x, 433pp. $5, $20, $15-bmk.

1507 **BUCK, Irving Ashby**
"Cleburne & His Command, by... Former Capt. & A.A.G. Cleburne's Division." N.Y., Wash: Neale Pub., 1908. 8vo, cl, maps, front(port), 1-illus. $175, $275-bmk-105, $20, $22.50, $30, $37.50, $50, $57.50, $62.50. p.xii, (13)-382.
...Jackson, Tenn., McCowat-Mercer Press, 1959. Fore: Bell Irvin Wiley. 378pp. (2000 copies) $6, $8.50, $12.50, $20-y, $35, $30-bmk, $22.50-y, $16.
...Dayton, Oh., Morningside bks, 1982. 8vo, pict. covers, reprint of 1908 edt. $27.50.

1508 ..."Cleburne & his Division at Missionary Ridge & Ringgold Gap." In: SHSP, 1880, v.VIII, p. 464-475. Buck was A.A. Gen., Cleburne's Division.

1509 ..."Negroes in Our Army. General Pat Cleburne to the first to advocate their use. His plan was turned down." In: SHSP, 1903, v.XXXI, p. 215-218.
..."Cleburne & his command...Edt. Thomas R. Hay. Foreword by Bell Wiley. Dedicated to Wiley by Maury Klein (6pp. with a bibliog. of Wiley." Dayton, Oh., Morningside Press, 1985. 8vo, cl & leatherette spine. Facsm. #63.

1510 **BUCK, Lucy Rebecca**
"Sand Earth, Sweet Heaven. The Diary of ..., during the War Between the States, Front Royal, Virginia, Dec. 25, 1861-April 15, 1865." Birmingham, Ala., Cornerstone pub. (1973) $20. 8vo, cl, dj, ports, illus., maps, 304, (16)pp. $11.

1511 ..."Diary of Lucy Rebecca Buck, 1861-1865." n.p., 1940. Edited: L. Neville Buck." 4to, mimeo. pict. covers (wraps), ports, plates, map, (orig. photos tipped-in) 240 numbered lfs. $150-bmk.

1512 **BUCK, Martina E.**
"A Louisiana prisoner of war on Johnson's Island, 1863-1865." In: LaH., 1963, v.4, p. 233-242.

1513 **BUCK, Nina Kirby-Smith**
"All's Fair in Love & War, or-The Story of how a Virginia Belle Won a Confederate Colonel, written by...about 1901. "For my two little grandaughters" Juliana & Rowena." n.p., Pub. by author, 1945, 8vo, wraps, color flag, 37pp. $7.50.

1514 **BUCK, Samuel D.**
"With the Old Confeds. Actual Experiences of a Captain in the Line, by.-..Co. H, 13th Va. Inf." Baltimore: H.E. Houck co, 1925. 8vo, cl, illus., ports, xii, (13)-141pp. $15, $600-b.

1515 ..."Battle of Cedar Creek, Va., Oct. 19, 1864." In: South. Hist. Soc. Papers, XXX, (1902), p. 104-110.

1516 ..."General Joseph (James) A. Walker." In: CV, 1902, v.10, p. 34-36, port. Virginia CSA General.

1517 **BUCK, Samuel D., Capt.**
"With the Old Confederates..." Gaithersburg, Md., Butternut Press, 1983. 8vo, cl, dj, ix, 141, (3)lfs, (10)p. Intro: Jim D. Moody.

1518 **BUCKHOLTZ, Louis von**
"On Infantry Camp Duty. Promulgated at Fort M'Culloch, May 1862." (Fort McCulloch, 1862) 8vo, marbled paper wraps, 12pp. bound with: "Instructions on Outpost Duty, for Officers & Non-Commissioned Officers of Cavalry. By Lt.-Col. Von Arentschildt...with an Abridgement of them by Lt. Col. the Hon. F. Ponsonby. Fort McCulloch, June 1861." t.p. (35)-37, lf. contents. Streeter-$3750.

1519 ..."On Infantry Camp Duty, prepared & arranged by L.v.B." Washington: Selmar Siebert, 1860. 16mo, limp cloth, paper label, 39pp.

1520 ...(bound with)-"On Field Fortifications, Fortresses, Attack & Defence of Houses & Villages: Compiled for Use of Infantry. By L. V. Buchholtz." Wash: Selmar & Siebert, 1860, pp. 24, green wraps bound in.

1521 ...(bound with)-"Coast Defence: A Supplement to Field Fortifications." blue wraps, 8p., errate (1). fldg. pl.

1522 **BUCKHOLZ, Louis von**
"Tactics for officers of infantry, cavalry & artillery." Richmond, Va., 1861. 8vo, boards, 121p+advs., Crand-2400, $175-b

1522a **BUCKLEY, William**
"Buckley's History of the Great Reunion of the North & South & of the Blue & Gray." Staunton, Va., 1923. 12mo, cl, 244p, ills, ports. Survivors at reunion, Niagra Falls, hosts 5th Va. reg., who returned a Northern reg. Flay (Cedar Mountain) May 1883.

1523 **BUCKNER, Simon Bolivar, Maj.-Gen.**
"Report of Major-General S.B. Buckner of the Battle of Chickamauga, Hdq. Nov. 11, 1863." In: SHSP, 1883, v.XI, p. 313-317. See: Leslie J. Perry.

1524 ..."A.L.S., 1p 4to, Kentuck, 1903. gdsp. $75.

1525 ..."Gen. Simon Bolivar Buckner." In: CV, March 1914, v.XXII, p. 100-103. See: Arndt M. Stickles, Leslie J. Perry, John B. Floyd.

1526 **BUEL, Oliver Prince**
"The Abraham Lincoln Myth An Essay in "Higher Criticism" by Bocardo Bramantip, Huxleyan professor of dialectics in the University of Congo from the 37th Century Magazine of Apr. A.D. 3663." N.Y., Mascot Pub. co., 1894. $45-jk-122, $12.50. 12mo, wraps (or 3/4 Mor.), 88pp. $5.

1527 **BUEMYER, Walter L.**
"Texas & the riddle of Secession." In: SWHQ, Oct. 1983, p. 151-182.

1528 **BUENGER, Walter L.**
"Secession & the Texas German community: Editor Lindheimer vs. Editor Flake." In: SWHQ, Apr. 1979, v.LXXXII, #4, p. 379-402.

1529 ..."Secession revisited: the Texas experience." In: CWH, Dec. 1984, v.30, #4, p. 293-305, notes.

1530 ..."Secession & the Union in Texas." Austin: University of Texas Press, 1984. 8vo, cl, 267pp. $17.50.

1531 **BUFFALO GUARDS, Virginia**
"Roll of Buffalo Guards. Mustered as Virginia State Troops, May 13, 1861, Buffalo, Va., afterwards Co. A, 36 Va. Reg. n.p., n.d. Broadside, Shetler-683.

1532 **BUFORD, J.H.**
"War map of the middle states. Balloon view of Virginia, Maryland, Kentucky, Tennessee...Arkansas, Missouri, Illinois, Indiana, Ohio." Boston: Bufford, 1861.

1533 ...Large folding litho panoramic map 40.5x28.5", mounted in sections on canvas, three colors. $1500-jk-169.

1534 **BUFFORD, Jefferson**
"Address delivered before the Southern Rights Association, in Eufaula, by Maj. Jefferson Buford. Published by order of

the Association, Jan. 21, 1851." Eufaula, Ala., Office of "Spirit of the South", 1851, 8vo, wraps, 23pp. Owen.

1535 **BUFORD, M.N.**
"Surrender of Johnston's army." In: CV, May 1920, v.XXVIII, p. 170-172.

1536 **BUGBEE, Lester G.**
"Slavery in Early Texas." Boston, Mass: Atheneum Press, 1898. 8vo, wraps, 24pp. $35. First appeared in Sept./Dec. "Political Science Quarterly." 1898. Largely material unpublished, p. 389-412; 648-665.

1537 **BUGEAUD DE LA PICONNERIE, Thomas Robert, duc d'Isly**
"The practice of war: being a translation of French military work entitled "Maxims, counsels & instructions on the art of war, or a handbook for the practice of war. For the use of military men of all arms & countries. From a manuscript written, in 1815, by a general of that time, & revised, in 1855, to be put in harmony with the knowledge & organization of the present day. 4th edt., pocket size, 15plates, 1857: Paris." To which the translator has added Marshal Bugeaud's letters of instruction to the Fifty-Sixth Regiment of French Infantry also, the second appendix of Baron Jomimi to "Precis de l'art de la guerre." By C.F. Pardigon, Richmond, Va., West & Johnston, 1863. 12mo, cl, xiii, (1), (13)- 216pp. plates. Crandall-2401. $200, $450- jk- 144.

1538 **BUISSON, B., Captaine**
"Instruction pour le Service et les Manoeuvres de L'Artillerie Legere, redigee pour la Batterie des Gardes D'Orleans." Nouvell-Orleans, 1861. 16mo, orig. vellum covers. 44pp. $30, From Eberstadt- #113 (112) (1938).

1539 **BULL, Emily L.**
"Lucy Pickens: first lady of the South Carolina Confederacy." In: PSCHA, 1982, p. 5-18.

1540 **BULL, Gustavus Adolphus, Lt. Col.**
"Lieutentant-Colonel Gustavus Adolphus Bull." In: Scotts Monthly Magazine, July 1869, p. 561-568.

1541 **BULL, Henry DeSassure**
"Ashley Hall Plantation." (Charleston: So. Carol. Hist. & Genea. Mag., April, 1952, v.LIII, #2, p. 61-66, illus., plan. First destroyed in Revolution, the last owner Col. Bull set it afire himself on approach of Sherman's firemen.

1542 **BULLARD, F. Lauriston**
"Lincoln pardons conspirator on pleas of an English statesman." In: Am. Bar. Assn. Jour., 1939, v.XXV, p. 215-220. An Alfred Bubery, who was aiding the CSA cause & granted request of John Bright.

1543 **BULLARD, K.C., Compl.**
"Over the dead-line; or, Who Killed "Poll Parrot", by..." N.Y., Neale Pub., 1909, 12mo, wraps, 33pp. $150-ob, $10. An Irishman's defense (Wilkinson Co., Ga.) by Jas. T. Kolpatrick, tried 1873, appeal to jury, re: Andersonville Prison.

1544 **BULLARD, Lucille Blackburn**
"Marion County, Texas 1860-1870." Jefferson, Texas: Published & mimeogr. by Lucille Blackburn Bullard, 1965. 4to, stiff wraps, (1), (2), v,(1), 115pp., illus., printed on-side. Muster roll Capt. W.H. Duke's Co. Inf. "Jefferson Guards", Co. G. 3rd. Texas Cavalry; Roll of Capt. W.L. Crawford's Co., John K. Cocke's Co. D, 18th Reg. Texas Inf.; Roll Capt. T.D. Sedberry, Co. F., 19th Reg. Index.

1545 **BULLITT, Thomas Walker, Col.**
"Lee & Scott. paper read at the Reunion of Morgan's Men at Lexington, Ky." In: SHSP, 1883, v.XI, p. 443-454.

1546 ..."More of General Morgan's Escape." In: SB, 1885/1886, v.I, ns. p. 116-119.

1547 **BULLOCK COUNTY, Alabama**
"Reconstruction in Bullock County." In: AHQ, 1953, v.15, #1, p. 75-125.

1548 **BULLOCK, James D.**
"The Secret Service of the Confederate States in Europe or, How the Confederate Cruisers were Equipped. By..., Naval Representative of the Confederate States in Europe during the Civil War." 2 vols. London: Bentley print, 1883. v.1, 8vo, cl, errata slip, x, 460, v, 438pp. $75, $300 bmk- 105, $40.
...N.Y., G.P. Putnam's sons, 1884 (this edt. printed Billing & Sons, Guildford & London, $35, $37.50, $50(Parke-Ber., $75, $125-bmk.
...N.Y., Lond: Yoseloff, (1959). 2vols, Intro: Philip Van Doren Sterne. cartoons, illus., ports, maps, xl, 460, x, (1), 459pp. facsms, boxed. $15, $17.50, $20-bmk-84, $30-nc, $50, $43.50, $23.
...N.Y., Burt Franklin, 1972. "Research & source works series, American Classics in history & social science."

1549 ..."Building Confederate Vessels in France (from his "Secret Service in CS in Europe)." In: SHSP, 1886, v.XIV, p. 454-465.

1550 **BULLOCK, Rufus B.**
"Reconstruction in Georgia, 1865-1870." In: Indep., Mar. 19, 1903, v.LV, p. 670-674.

1551 **BUMMERS in Sherman's Army."**
(New York: Excerpt: "Beadle's Monthly". v.1, May 1866. 8vo, illus, p. (389)-398. DeRenne, II, p. 680.

1552 **BUNCH, Robert**
"Dispatch from the British Consul at Charleston to Lord John Russell, 1860." In: Amer. Hist. Rev., July 1913, v.XVIII, p. 783-787. Reports conversation with R.B. Rhett, forecasts policy of CSA, after secession & attitude of GB.

1553 **BUNDLE OF LETTERS, A**
In: Univ. N.C., mag. 1916/1917, v.XLVII, p. 205-211, 265-270, 316-320.

1554 **BUNN, Henry G., Judge**
"Early Days of the War in the West." In: CV, 1902, v.X, p. 449-453, port.

1555 **BUOHL, George W.**
"Buohl's Illustrated Map & Guide to Tour the Gettysburg Battlefields." Gettysburg, Pa., 1936. Narrow 8vo, decr. color front, (18)pp. folder, illus., ports, verso-panoramic air-view locates 77 points. $3.50.

1556 **BURCH, John P.**
"Charles W. Quantrill A True History of his Guerrilla Warfare on the Missouri & Kansas Border during the Civil War of 1861 to 1865. As told by Captain Harrison Trow one who followed Quantrill through his whole course." (Vaga, Texas, J.P. Burch, 1923) $20-jk-127, $30-bmk-104, $15-mor, $5, $10. 12mo, decr. cl, port, illus., sketches, 266pp.

1557 **BURCKMYER, Cornelius L. & Charlotte R.**
"The Burckmyer Letters, March, 1863-June, 1865." (c)Charlotte R. Holmes. Columbia, S.C., The State Co., 1926. 8vo, cl, 476pp. $10, $12.50, $20, $25, $35-bmk. Interest in economic data, life of CSA colony in europe & in Charleston.

1558 **BURDETT, Samuel Swinfin**
"The Lee Statue, remarks of S.S. Burdett comrad(sic) of the Grand army of the Republic before the Middlesex Club, Boston, Mass., March 24, 1910 (vererans' night)" n.p., 8vo, 12pp. caption title, Dornbusch.

1559 **BUREAU OF CONSCRIPTION,**
Richmond, March 18, 1864. Circular #(?)8. Caption title. (Richmond: 1864) 8vo, sewed, 20pp. $8. Contains all laws, rules & regulations pertaining to enrollment into Confed. Army. Not in any references.

1560 **BURFORD, Thomas P., Chm. Historical Comm.**
"Lamar Rifles, a history of Company G,

Eleventh Mississippi regiment, CSA, with the official roll giving each man's record from time of enlistment to twenty-ninth March, eighteen hundred & sixty-five; individual & company sketches; incidents of the camp, the march, & the battlefield; & is intended to be of special interest to the relatives & friends of members of this company , which was popularly known as the "Lamar Rifles", & which served in the Army of Northern Virginia, from May 1861 to April 1865. This work was done under the auspices & by the authority of "the Survivors association of Lamar Rifles. Historical committee: Thos. P. Burford, Chairman, Thos. H. Chilton & BemPrice, Jr. Secretary." (Roanoke: Stone print, 1903). 8vo, wraps, front(port), ports, 93pp.

1561 **BURGE, Dolly Sumner Lunt, Mrs.**
"A Woman's Wartime Journal; an account of the passage over a Georgia Plantation of Sherman's Army on the march to the sea, as recorded in the diary of Dolly Sumner Lunt(Mrs. Thomas Burge); with an introduction & notes by Julian Street." N.Y., The Century Co., 1918. 16mo, cl, front, xi, 54pp. $17.50, $30, $45.
...Macon (Ga.), J.W. Burke Co., 1927. 16mo, cl, xii, 1, 15-65pp. $12, $24, $40-bmk-106.

1562 ..."The Diary of Dolly Lunt Burge. Edt: James I. Robertson, Jr." Athens: Unvi. of Ga. Press (1962). 8vo, cl, dj, xv, 141pp. index. $4, $20-bmk.

1563 ..."The Diary of Dolly Lunt Burge. Edt: James I. Robertson, Jr." In: Ga. H.Q. in 8-parts: June 1960-march 1962. 202-219; 321-337; 434-455; 57-72; 155-170; 257-274; 367-384; 59-78.

1564 **BURGE, Louisiana**
"Louisiana Burge: the diary of a Confederate college girl." (Wesleyan Female College, 1861-1862) Edt: Richard Barksdale Harwell (Athens: Georgia Historical Quarterly, reprint, vol. XXXVI, June 1952) 25pp. 8vo, wraps, p. (144)-163. with a biographical sketch of Burge. $5, $8-bmk, $15, $12-bk.

1565 ..."The Diary of a Confederate College Girl." Edt: Richard Barksdale Harwell, Reprinted Georgia Hist. Quart., Vol. XXXVII, June 1852, 8vo, wraps, port, 25pp. $5.

1566 **BURGER, Nash K.**
"Confederate Spy: Rose O'Neale Greenhow." Hidden Heroes Series, A Giniger Book pub: New York: Franklin Watts, (1967). 12mo, cl, d/w, 230pp. port on d/w. $3, $4.95, $25-b. "A Giniger book", 3rd print., 1967. $4.95.

1567 ..."The Diocese of Mississippi & the Confederacy." In: P.E. Church Hist. Mag., 1940, v.IX, p. 52-77, March. $10.

1568 ..."South of Appomattox." N.Y., Harcourt, Brace (1959). 8vo, cl, d/w, illus, 376pp. viii. Ten CSA leaders, what happened to each after the war. $25-b, $5.75, $12.50, $15, $20-bmk-84.

1569 **BURGES, Samuel Edward**
"The Diary of...1860-1862. Edited by Thomas W. Chadwick." (Charleston) So. Car. Hist. Geneol. Mag. (1947), XLVIII, p. 63-75; 141-163; 206-218.

1570 **BURGESS, George W.**
"The Ram "Arkansas", & the Battle of Baton Rouge." In: East & West Baton Rouge Hist. Soc. Proc., 1918, v.II, p. 34-37.

1571 **BURGESS, John W.**
"Reconstruction & the Constitution 1866-1876." N.Y., Charles Scribner's Sons, 1902. sm.8vo, cl, xii, 342pp.

1572 ...1905. A stinging rebuke to congress for the insults, ignorant & venal judges & acts of humiliating to South; hardly a line of the bill would stand test of Constitution, "The most brutal one ever sent to congress." Scandalous corruption.

1573 **BURGESS, Mary Abigail, Mrs.**
"History of the battlefields around the city of Richmond, & how to reach them. Distance from the city & full information concerning them." Richmond, Va., M.A. Burgess Pub., 1905. 16mo, wraps, map, 24pp. Swem-666.

1574 ..."Richmond guide book; sketches & views of Richmond, Va., suppl. by sketches of Williamsburg, Jamestown, Yorktown. Description & map, historic battlefields. Location given of all pictures in the book." Richmond, Va., M.A. Burgess, 1909. 16mo, wraps, front (fldg. map) illus., 87pp. Revised & largely rewritten from her "Sketches & views, points of interest." Published, 1903.

1575 **BURGESS, W.W.**
"Soldier's story of J.E.B. Stuart's death. Account of Yellow Tavern from a man in the ranks." In: SHSP, 1908, v.XXXVI, p. 121-124.

1576 **BURGET, Russell L.**
"Rebs Sink the Cairo." (Houston, Texas: Historical Communications, v.1, #1, 1970." In: "VIA", Rodeway Inns of America. 4to, color wraps, (4)pp. illus. See: Edwin C. Bearss-"Hardluck ironclad; the sinking & salvage of the Cairo, etc." (Baton Rouge, La., LSU press, 1966))

1577 **BURGWYN, William Hyslop Sumner**
"An address on the military & civil services of Gen. Matt W. Ransom (Matthew Whitaker), delivered in the Senate chamber at Raleigh, N.C., before the Ladie's Memorial ass'n., & citizens, May 10, 1906." n.p., n.d., 8vo, wraps, 2-ports, 52pp. $20. Against secession but joined forces after Lincoln elected.

1578 ..."Unparalleled loss of Company F. 26th. North Carolina Regiment, Pettigrew's Brigade, at Gettysburg." In: SHSP, 1900, v.XXVIII, p. 199-204.

1579 **BURIAL OF CONFEDERATE DEAD, etc.**
See: Appeal for pecuniary aid; Berry, Jas. H.; Brawley, Wm. H.; Ceremonies attending..., of...etc.; Confederate Buried; Confederate Dead; Confederate Graves; Confederate Memorials; Confederate Soldier, Sailors & civiln.; Descriptive list of burials; Goote, Frank H.; Garnett, Alex. Y.P.; Griffith, L.D.; Girardeau, Jno. Lafayette; Hollywood Memorial Ass'n; Index to compiled Ser. Records; Jones, Richard W.; Jones, Walter B.; Kurtz, Lucy F.; Keiley, A.M.; Ky. CSA buried at Douglas; Ladies Memorial Ass'n; Letter relating to CSA cemetery; Marking CSA graves; Memorial of...; Poffinberger, Moses; Pompey, Sherman Lee; Register of CSA dead. Camp Douglas; Register of CSA dead. Hollywood; Report of the Comm...marking; Roster of Departed comrads; Report on reburial...; Titus, W. Allen; Underwood, Jno. C.; "Our Confederate dead..."; Otey Battery; Camp Morton, Walthall, E.C.; Young, Gen. Bennett H.; Montgomery, Walter A.; Confederate gravestone records: NC; Krick, Robert K.

1580 **BURKE COUNTY, Georgia**
"The Burke Sharpshooters." In: CV, Dec. 1924, v.XXXII, p. 464-466. First volunteers from Burke Co.

1581 **BURKE, Joseph C.**
"The Proslavery Argument & the First Congress." In: Duquesne Rev., 1969, v.XIV, p. 3-15.

1582 **BURKER, Walter E., Jr.**
"Quartermaster, a brief account of the Life of Col. Abraham Charles Myers, Quartermaster Gen'l. C.S.A., by the author, n.p., 1976, February, 14. $5. 8vo, wraps, 43pp. illus., facsms, maps, ports.

1583 **BURKHIMER, Eloise Bernheim**
"Rise & Fall of the Confederate History Pageant." Wilmington, N.C., 1922. Cape

1584 **BURKHOLDER, N.M.**
"The Barn-Burners. A chapter of Sheridan's Raid up the Valley." In: SHSP, 1900, v.XXVIII, p. 98-106.

Fear Chapter UDC Southern Playwrights & Producers for history & Dramatic Presentation. 8vo, wraps, 26pp.

1585 **BURNE, Alfred H.**
"Early's valley campaign." In: Fighting Forces 1940, v.XVI, p. 236-246. Early's campaign in the valley, in 1864.

1586 ..."Lee, Grant & Sherman; a study in leadership in the 1864-1865 campaign." Aldershot (England): Gale & Polden, 1938. 8vo, cl, xv, 216pp. ports, maps, $7.50. "to strike a balance between the rival protagonists." by an Englishman. N.Y., Scribners, 1939, XXIII, 216, illus. fldg. maps, $10, $15, $7.50, $75-r.

1587 **BURNET, T.L.**
"The Battle of Saltville." In: SB, 1883/1884, v.II, p. 20-22.

1588 **BURNING OF BRENHAM, Texas**
"Washington, DC, March 3, 1871; 41st Congress, 3rd Session, Ex-Doc., #145. 8vo, sewn, 27pp.

1589 ...Washington, DC, House Ex-Doc. 237, 43rd Congress, 1st session, Apr. 30, 1874. 8vo, boards, 28pp. $35. Brenham was a military post in 1865. The Federals & citizens in a controversy resulting in a partial burning of the city in late 1867. Military rule lasted to '69.

1590 **BURNING OF CHAMBERSBURG**
In: CV, Oct. 1903, v.XI, p. 444-445.

1591 **BURNING OF COLUMBIA, The**
Letter of Gen. Wade Hampton, June 24, 1873, with Appendix. II-Report of committee of citizens, Ex-Chancellor J.P. Carroll, Chairman, May, 1866. (From the News & Courier, Charleston, S.C., Jan 15 & Feb. 5, 1888) Charleston, S.C., Walker, Evans & Cogswell Co., 1888. 8vo, wraps, 24pp. $75-ob, $12.50. See also: Anna T. Swindell; William A. Nicholson; Mrs. Campbell Bryce, Coleman L. Blease, Jas. P. Carroll, Alex R. Chisolm, Aug. Conrad, Jas. W. Davidson, Wade Hampton, Jas. G. Gibbes, Jas. D. Hill, Agnes Law, Thos. J. Myers, Jas. F. Rhodes, Ed. Sill, Wm. G. Simms, D.H. Trezevant, Ed. Wells, "Who Burnt Co.?", "Mixed Comm. Amer. & British...Marion B. Lucas.

1592 **BURNING OF COLUMBIA. See:**
Bryce, Mrs. Campbell; Conrad, August; Goodlett, Emily Geiger; Hampton, Wade; Nicholson, Wm. A.; Swindell, Anna Tillman; Trezevant, Daniel Henry.

1593 **BURNS, Amanda McDowell**
"Fiddles in the Cumberlands, by ... A Diary of Amanda McDowell Burns with narrative chapters by Lela McDowell Blankenship." N.Y., Richard R. Smith, 1943. Tall 8vo, cl, ix, 310pp. $17.50-y, $6.50, $39.50, Bordered-$15-nc. Woman's view of war, living in the middle grounds, pillaged by both sides. Her two brothers on opposite sides.

1594 **BURNS, Zed H.**
"Abel D. Streight Encounters Nathan Bedford Forrest." (Jackson, Miss.) Jour. Miss. Hist., Nove. 1968, v.XXX, #4, p. 345-359.

1595 ..."Ship Island & the Confederacy." Hattiesburg, 1971, University & College Press of Mississippi. 8vo, stiff wraps, in color, illus., maps, xi, 52pp. $2.50, $20-bmk.

1596 ..."Confederate Forts, Foreword by Porter L. Fortune." Natchez, Miss., Southern Historical Publications, 1977. 4to, 107pp. color photos, maps, biblio. index, $20-bmk, atg.-$10.

1597 **BURPO, Robert S., Jr.**
"Notes on the First Fleet Engagement in the Civil War." (Fort Pillow) In: Amer. Neptune, Oct. 1959, Vol. XIX, #4, p. 265-273, plates (8).

1598 **BURR, C. Chauncey**
"See: "The Old Guard." Joseph George, Jr., Wm. W. Rogers, Copperheads.

1599 **BURR, Frank A.**
"Jefferson Davis, the ex-Confederate President, at home. (Beauvoir, Miss.)" Tyler's Quart. Hist. & Geneal. Mag., Jan. 1951, v.32: p. 163-180 (reprint: Phila. Press, July 10, 1881. Interview on civil war, future of South, etc.

1600 ..."The great battle of Chickamauga." Memphis, Tracy Print, 1883. 12mo, wraps, 32pp. Burr's narrative, 3-17; Longstreet's, 17-23; Cap't. W.W. Carnes of Macon, 26-32, "Chickamauga, a battle of which half has not been told."

1601 **BURR, Samuel Engle, Jr.**
"Mrs. Varina Howell Davis, wife of the Confederate States of America." In: UDCMag., Jan. 1951, v.14, #1, p. 6-7, 8-19, 21. On her married life, 1845 ff.

1602 **BURRELL, Charles Edward**
"A History of Prince Edward County, Va., from its formation in 1753, to the present. Compiled mainly from original records & personally contributed articles. With a brief sketch of the beginnings of Virginia, summary of the history of the county seat & a special chapter on the churches of the county." Richmond, Va., Williams Print, 1922. 8vo, cl, ports Iincl. front) map, illus., 408pp. $15. CSA: p. 87-188; Reconstr: to 193. with Muster Roll of the county.

1603 **BURROWES, John F.**
"Burrowes' Piano-Forte Primer, containing the rudiments of music, calculated either for private tuition, or, teaching in classes. Revised & enlarged, with additions & alterations." Crandall-3257. Richmond: J.W. Randolph, 1864. 8vo, wraps, 48pp. Goodspeeds-$750.

1604 **BURROWS, John Lansing**
"The Christian Scholar & Soldier. Memoirs of Lewis Minor Coleman, Lt. Col. of First Regiment Virginia artillery." Richmond: Smith Bailey & co., 1864. 12mo, wraps, 44pp. Head of title: Virginia Baptist Sunday School & pub. board, Richmond, No. 109.
...(Raleigh?) 1864, p. 32. Type reset in small type. See Crandall-4600/4601.

1605 ..."Palliative & prejudiced judgements condemned. A discourse delivered in the First Baptist Church, Richmond, Va., June 1, 1865, the day appointed by the president of the U.S. for humiliation & mourning on account of the assassination of President Lincoln, together with an extract from a sermon, preached on Sunday, Apr. 23, 1865, upon the assassination of President Lincoln." Richmond, Va., Commercial Bull., 1865, 8vo, wraps, 12pp. (an answer to accusations of South's guilt pub. in northern presses.)

1606 ..."Recollections of Libby Prison. (read before the Louisville Southern Historical Ass'n." In: SHSP, 1883, v.XI, p. 83-92.

1607 **BURT, Jesse C.**
"Fighting with "Little Joe" Wheeler, cavalry genius in west knew just one command: "Charge"." In: CWT, May 1960, v.II (OS) #2, p. 18-19, plate, port.

1608 **BURT, Samuel H.**
"List of officers & men of the cavalry brigade, Gen. R.L.T. Beale, CSArmy, surrendered at Appomattox Court Hse., Virginia, Apr. 9, 1865." Richmond, Va., Va. Hist. Soc. Collect., New series, v.6, p. 347-355. 1887.

1609 **BURTON, David L.**
"Pawnee" Sunday." In: Va. Cavalcade, Summer, 1982, v.XXXII, p. 4-9, port, illus.. Union gunboat shells Richmond, Apr. 21, 1861.

1610 **BURTON, E. Milby**
"Siege of Charleston." Columbia, SC Press, 1971 (2nd) $45.
..."The Siege of Charleston 1861-1865."

(Columbia: Univ. of S.C. Press, 1970. 8vo, cl, d/w, xvii, 373pp., illus., $14.95, $10, paper-$5, color front, $19.50-y, $16.

1611 BURTON, H.W.
"The History of Norfolk, Virginia, Review of Important Events & Incidents 1736-1877. Record of personal reminiscences & political, commercial, & curious facts, by H.W. Burton, "Harry Scratch", (pseud), Norfolk, Va." Norfolk, Va., Norfolk Virginian Print., 1877. $15., 8vo, cl, illus, vi, 264, (2)pp., (20pp. ads in text).

1612 BURTON, J.Q., Capt.
"Forty-seventh regiment Alabama Volunteers, CSA, by..., commanding company H. A historical sketch covering the time from muster in to muster out." (n.p., 18-?) 8vo, (4)pp. triple columns.
...1902 reprint of 100 copies. See: T.F. Botsford memories of 47th.

1613 BURTON, Joseph Q., Captain
"Historical sketches of the Forty-seventh Alabama Infantry Regiment, CSA. By Capt. Joseph Q. Burton, Co. H & Private Theophilus F. Botsford, Co. D. With Introduction by William Stanley Hoole." University, Ala., Confederate Pub. Co., 1982. Confederate Regimental Series, #2. 8vo, stiff wraps, 36pp. See: T.F. Botsford + reprints.

1614 BURWELL, Letitia M.
"A Girl's Life in Virginia Before War." New York: F.A. Stokes (1895). 12mo, decr. cl, front, illus., 209pp. (old)$1.50, $7.50.
...2nd Edt. $6., $45-jk.

1615 BUSHNELL, Belle Johnston, Mrs.
"John Arrowsmith-Planter." Cedar Rapids, Iowa, Torch Pr., 1910. 8vo, cl, 466pp. Plantation on Atchafalaya (La.) CSA, interest & sympathies; siege Vicksburg making 1st CSA flag.

1616 BUSHONG, Millard K., Dr.
"Old Jube." $10. Shippensburg, Pa., Biedel Print, 1984.

1617 BUSHONG, Millard Kessler
"A History of Jefferson Co., West Va." Charles Town: Jefferson Pub. Co., 1941. A 1941 Ph.D. dissertation from West Va. Univ., 1941, p. 438. "Civil War", p. 142-189; Roster: p. 362-386. $50-bmk-84. Many Confederates from this county.
...Boyce, Va., 1972. 8vo, cl, 604pp. illus., $20-bmk-106.

1618 ..."General Turner Ashby & Stonewall's Valley Campaign." Verona, Va., 1980. (McClure Print), 8vo, cl, dj, 261pp., pres. copy. $15.

1619 ..."Fightin' Tom Rosser, C.S.A." Shippensburg, Pa.: Beidel Print., 1983. 8vo, cl, illus., maps, bibliog., index, p. 281, $17.50. 5th Va. Cav., commands Laurel Brigade with roster.

1620 ..."Old Jube, a biography of Gen. Jubal A. Early." Boyce, Va., Carr Pub. Co., (1955). illus. & maps by Timothy T. Pohmer. 8vo, cl, d/w, illus., 343pp. $50.
...1961 Edit. $20-bmk, $4, $6.50, $50, $7.
...1969 edition, $10-carrier, $40-bmk, $17.50-y

1621 BUSYN, Helen
"Peter Kiolbassa-maker of Polish America." In: Polish Am. sutdies, July/Dec., 1951, v.8, p. 65-84. notes. Life in Texas, service in CSA & Union armies Catholic layman in Chicago.

1622 BUTLER, Edward
"Civil War Letter from Paris, Texas, 1861." Oklahoma City: Chron. Okla., Autumn, 1966, v.XLIV, #3, p. 322-324.

1623 BUTLER, John C.
"Origin of the banner "Lone Star" & coat of arms of Texas." In: SHSP, 1881, v.9, p. 219-224.

1624 BUTLER, Lorine Letcher
"John Morgan & His Men." Philadelphia:

Dorrance Co. (1960). 8vo, cl, d/w, front(port), 357pp., $15-bmk.

1625 BUTLER, M.C., Maj-Gen.
"The Cavalry fight at Trevilian Station." In: B & L, v.4, p. 237-239, illus., port.

1626 BUTLER, Matthew Calbraith
"Address of Gen. M.C. Butler on the Life Character & Services of Gen. Wade Hampton of South Carolina, on 23rd Jan., 1893." Wash: Gibosn Bros., 1893. 8vo, wraps, 23pp. $7.50, $15, $75-bmk.
..."Address: Life, Character & Services of Gen. Wade Hampton. . . Washington: Gibson Bros., 1903. Removed from bound vol., wraps, 23p.

1627 ..."Address at the laying of corner stone of the Confederate monument at Orangeburg, S.C., Times & Democrat, 1892. 8vo, wraps, 14pp.

1628 ..."Southern Genius. How war developed it in an Industrial & Military Way." In: SHSP, 1888, v.XVI, p. 281-295. See: U.R. Brooks "Hampton & Brooks; W.L. Browns's Letter to Butler, & "Proceeding at unveiling of Monument to Charleston."

1629 BUTLER, P.R.
"The cruise of the "Sumter"." In: Blackwood's May 1948, v.245, p. 351-362. Capt. Semmes cruises to Gibraltar, 1864.

1630 BUTLER, Pierce
"Judah P. Benjamin." Phila., Jacobs Print (1906), American Crisis Biographies. 12mo, cl, port, 459pp., index. $10, $12.50. Same: (1907) Edt. $7.50, $15. See: Gamaliel Bradford's Confed. Portraits.; also, J.P.B., Confederate Portrait, in Atlantic, CSI (June) 1913, p. 795-806.

1631 ..."The Unhurried Years: Memoirs of the Old Natchez Region." Baton Rouge, LSUniversity (1948). 8vo, cl, dj, illus., 198pp.

1632 BUTT, Marshall W.
"Portsmouth (Va.) Under Four Flags, 1752-1961. Published by the Portsmouth Historical Association." Portsmouth, Va., Messenger Print, 1961. 12mo, stiff wraps, ports, facsms, maps, illus. (3), 170pp. (largely pictorial, text 35pp.) $5.

1633 BUTTONS: CSA Uniform
(Alphaeus K. Albert, Dan Jenkins. See: Stanley Kerksis, Sydney K. Richard Dennis Stuart.

1634 BUTTS, Donald C.
"The irrepressible conflict: slave taxation & North Carolina's gubernatorial election of 1860." In: NCHR, 1981, v.58, p. 44-66, facsms. map, ports. Fight over taxes, the slaveholders for taxation. Non-slaveholders wanted a tax on value of slaves as "property".

1635 BUXTON, Virginia
"Clayton's Militia in Sevier & Howard Counties." In: AHQ, 1961, v.XX, p. 344-350. Martial Law in county with militia & the KKK.

1636 ..."By This We Conquer: For President: Salmon P. Chase, of Ohio. For Vice-President: Jefferson Davis, of Miss. United We Stand(clasped hands) Divided We Fall." Election Broadside. (n.p., 1860) 12mo (Eberstadt) $15. A Compromise ticket of Abolition & Slavery! $100-jk-122.

1637 BUZHARDT, Beaufort Simpson
"Beaufort Simpson Buzhardt, 1838-1862, Newberry, S.C., prepared by Carrie Buzhardt Traywick." (Newberry, S.C., 1916?) printed for private distribution. $10. 12mo, cl, ports (incl. front), 73pp. "Diary" imprinted on cover, after Buzhardt.
...Louisville: Lost Cause Pr., micro-card, $2.54.

1638 BYNUM, Hartwell T.
"Sherman's Expulsion of the Roswell Women, in 1864." In: Ga. H.Q., Summer, 1970, v.LIV, #1, p. 169-182. $8.

1639 BYRD, Ethel Maddox, Edt. & Zelda Haas Cassey

"Memoirs of the War Between the States, commemorating its Centennial, 1861-1961." Richmond, Va., Whittet & Shepperson, 1961. 8vo, stiff wraps, 64pp. verse & prose. Pres. copy, Mrs. Byrd, $25-bmk.

1640 **BYRD, Ruth Carolyn**
"Lucy Holcombe Pickens, "Queen of the Confederacy"." In: Jr. Historian (Texas). Sept. 1949, v.10, #1, p. 1-3, 31. Subject: wife of wartime Gov. S.C., of Texas. Appears on the CSA $100 bill.

1641 **BYRD, William**
"The Capture of Fort De Russy, La." In: LWL, Jan. 1869, v.VI, #3, p. 185-187. Close to Mansfield Battle & Texans.

1642 **BYRNE, Barbara Ann**
"Charles C. Jones & the Intellectual Crisis of the Antebellum South." In: Southern Studies, Fall, 1980, v.XIX, p. 274-285.

1643 **BYRNE, Clifford**
"Jesse James: folk-hero." In: Tenn. Folklore Soc. Bul., Sept. 1954, v. 20, p. 47-52. notes. On ballads, 1882 ff. Represents James as "gallant, chivalrous & defender of poor & oppressed", & here attributed to CSA sympathizer. See: Anderson Conner.

1644 **BYRNE, Frank L.**
"Libby Prison: A study in emotions." (Lexington, Ky.) JSH, Nov. 1958, v.XXIV, #4, p. 430-444. $8.

1645 ..."A Terrible Machine": General Neal Dow's Military Government on the Gulf Coast." In: CWH, March 1966, v.XII, #1, p. 5-22. Plundered booty from homes under a military officer.

C

1 **"C.S.A. HALF DOLLAR, The"**
N.p., n.d., (c.1960) 32mo, (4)p. folder, with picture of coin on cover, $25 in silver. Only four originals made; "500 restrikes were made a generation ago & bring $175 to $350 according to condition." Only two known copies of original known. In 1879 the mint director, Dr. B.F. Taylor of New Orleans, own copy was sold, $3000. See: Telamon Euyler.

2 **C.S.H.,**
"Oh, slander not the South! or, two Virginians (Lee & Thomas)" Bost: Stillings Press, n.d., 8vo, wraps, p. 23.

2a **CABANIS, Jim**
"Civil War Journal & Letters of Washington Ives 4th Florida CSA." Tallahassee, Fla., 1988. 8vo, cl, 109pp. $15.

3 **CABEEN, Richard McP.**
"Camp Douglas & its prisoner of war letters." In: Amer. Philatelic Congr., (1951), "Original Papers", 17th., fldg. plan, facsms., views, notes, p. 76-99. $16.

4 **CABELL, David Shepherd Garland**
"Lee as an Educator. His zeal for Washington College's Welfare." In: SHSP, 1889, v.XVII, p. 357-362.

5 **CABELL, George Craighead, Lieut-Col.**
"Account of the Skirmish at Swift Creek." In: SHSP, 1888, v.XVI, p. 223-223. Cabell was with the 18th Va. Inf.

6 ..."Col. H.A. Carrington, C.S.Army. A sketch of his life & service." In: SHSP, 1904, v.XXXII. p. 216-220.

7 **CABELL, Henry Coalter, Col.**
"Report of Colonel H.C. Cabell, on the Artillery of the Gettysburg Campaign." In: SHSP, 1882, v.X, p. 164-169.

8 **CABELL, Sears Wilson**
"The 'Bulldog' Longstreet at Gettysburg & Chickamauga in the light of the official records, by..., Treas., Longstreet Memorial Ass'n. The Gettysburg story was first published in the Richmond, Va. Times Dispatch, August 7, 1938." $3, $4, $5, $8-bmk, $10. Atlanta, Georgia: Ruralist Press, 1938. 8vo, color flags on wraps, port, pl, 16pp.

9 **CABELL, William Lewis, Brig. Gen.**
"The Confederate States' Flag. How the Flag was made." In: SHSP, 1903, v.XXXI, p. 68-70.

10 ..."Gen. W.L. Cabell tells how Confederate flag was devised." In: SHSP, 1909, v.XXXVII, p. 255-256. Note: See: v.XXVIII, 1900, p. 89-90.

11 ..."Living Generals of the C.S.A." In: SHSP, 1892, v.XX, p. 34-39.

12 ..."True history of our battle flag." In: CV, Aug., 1903, v.XI, p. 339.

13 ..."Special Order No.50. Hdq.", May 8, 1863. Broadside, 17.5x24.5 cm. (Little Rock, 1863) $17.50. Not in Crandall - Harwell -Allen. Men formerly in Clarkson's & Adams regiments, if not enrolled in 10 days in some company, will be arrested.

14 ..."Report of the part Cabell's Brigade took in what is called Price's Raid in Missouri & Kansas, in the Fall of 1864." n.p. (Dallas, Texas-Jan. 1, 1900) 8vo, wraps, 16pp.

15 **CABELL, William Preston**
"Woman saved Richmond City. Story of Dahlgren's Raid & Mrs. Seddons' Old Blackberry Wine." In: SHSP, 1906, v.XXXIV, p. 353-358. See: C.V., May 1923, v.XXX, p. 177-178.

16 **CABLE, George Washington**
"George W. Cable's Recollections of General Forrest." Edt: Arlin Turner. (Lexi-

ngton, Ky.) JSH, May 1955., v.XXI, No.2, p. 224-228.

17 ..."The Cavalier," Ills.: Howard Chandler Christy. N.Y., Charles Scribner's Sons, 1901. 12mo, decr. cl, 311pp., illus.(front). $15-bmk.

18 ..."Kincaid's Battery." Illus.: Alonza Kimball. N.Y., Charles Scribner's Sons, 1908. 12mo, cl, decr., illus., color front, x, (1), 396, (4) pp.-ads. $12, $16.50.
...Same, 1911 reprint, $20 -wilson, $35 -atg. Cable, at 18, joined the 4th Miss. Cav.

19 ..."George W. Cable's recollections of General (Nathan Bedford) Forrest. Edited by Arlin Turner." In: JSH, May 1955, v.XXI, p. 224-228, notes. Reprinted from Current Lit., 1897, Memories of 1864-1865. See: A. Turner. $5.

20 **CADDALL, J.B.**
"Some Confederate letters of I.B. Cadenhead Co.H., 34th Ala. Inf. Reg." In: AlaHQ, Winter, 1956, v.18, p. 564-571. To his wife, dated Miss., Ala., Ga. 1862-2864. Three letters to her from others on his death.

21 **CADMAN, S. Parkes**
"English clergyman on Stonewall Jackson." In: CV, May 1912, v.XX, p. 217-220. Rep: Meth. Rev. (qrtly) Apr. 1911, v.LX, p. 302-315.

22 ..."Stonewall Jackson." In: Meth. Quart. Rev.,

23 **CAFFEY, Thomas**
"Letters from the front." In: Confed. Vet. Feb - Aug., 1918, v.XXVI, p. 64-65, 107-108, 157-158, 198-199, 246-247, 307, 353-355.

23a ..."Battlefields of the South, from Bull Run to Fredericksburg, by an English Combatant." N.Y., John Bradburn, 1864. 8vo, cl, 517pp. $275.

24 **CAGE, William L.**
"The civil war letters of Wm. L. Cage, Edt: T. Harry Williams." In: LaHQ, Jan. 1956, v.39, p. 113-130, notes. From a Lt. in Co.D, 21st reg. Miss. vols. to his wife Josephine (Posey) & his son John. Va., 14, July 1861-19 Apr. 1863.

25 **CAIN, J. Isaiah**
"The Battle of Atlanta as described by a Confederate Soldier. Edt: Andrew Forest Muir." In: Ga.H.Q., March 1958, v.XL, No.1, p. 109-111.

26 **CAIRNES, John Elliott**
"The Southern Confederacy & the African Slave Trade. The Correspondence between Professor Cairnes, A.M., & Geo. McHenry with an introduction & notes by Rev. Geo. B. Wheeler, A.M." Dublin: McGlashan & Gill, 1863. 8vo, wraps, xxviii, 61pp. $50 -ob. Reprinted from Daily News, Nov.-Dec., 1862. See also: George McHenry. (pro-slavery)

27 **CAISON, Albert Stacey**
"Southern Soldiers in Northern Prisons. Experience at Johnson's Island & Point Lookout." In: SHSP, 1895, v.XXIII, p. 158-165.

28 **CALATRELLO, Robt. L.**
"Jeff Davis' relations with his Military Commanders in the field." In: Social Studies, Oct., 1962.

29 **CALBERT, Jack**
"The Jackson Purchase & the End of the Neutrality Policy in Kentucky." In: FCHQ, July, 1964, v.38, #3, p. 206-223.

30 **CALDWELL, James E., Mrs. (May Winston)**
"A Chapter from the Life of a Little Girl of the Confederacy." Nashville: Parthenon Press, for the Author. (c.1937). sm.4to, cl, ports, illus., 25pp. Pres. $50-bmk.

31 **CALDWELL, James Fitz James**
"The History of a Brigade of South Carolinians known first as "Greggs" & subsequently as "McGowans Brigade." Philadelphia: King & Baird, Print., 1866. 12mo, cl, 247pp.(addenda sheet is often

missing). $50, $75, $85, $115, $750, $600-op, $500-g, $400-bmk, $150-y.
..."The history of a Brigade of South Carolina known first as 'Greggs'...Intro. & notes by Lee A. Wallace." Dayton, Oh., Morningside Books, 1984. 8vo, cl, 326pp., illus., notes $25. Many changes made in text, with append. by Gregg years later.
...Marietta, Ga., Continental Book co., 1951. 12mo, cl, dj, 247, (1)pp. addenda (casualties among officers) 2nd Manassas. $6, $15, $17.50, $35,
...Dayton, Oh., Morningside Press (1974). Facsimilie #16, paper $7.50, cl.-$12.50. See: Benj. F. Brown.

32 **CALDWELL, Ron S.**
"Civil War action in Arkansas." In: The Record, 1968, v.9, p. 68-73. A chronological listing.

33 **CALFEE, Berkeley G., Mrs.**
"Confederate History of Culpeper Co.(Va.) Culpeper County in the War Between the States. Together with a Complete Roster of the Confederate Soldiers From this County." (Culpeper, Va., Star-Exponent/c.1960's) 1958. 8vo, stiff wraps, 22pp. (roster 10pp.) $1, $10-bmk, $3, $8, $6.
...Berryville, Va., Chesapeake Book Co., (1962). Reprint, 2nd Edt., 22pp. $10-bmk-84, $10, $15.

34 **CALHOUN, Alfred Rochefort**
"A Story of the civil war." N.Y. Robert Bonner Print,1890. 12mo, cl, 350pp. Two Jessamine brothers CSA & Union in Ky. & Tenn. campaigns, irregular guerilas. Fiction.

35 **CALHOUN, C.M.**
"History of Greenwood. Some causes of Secession, Early battles of the war. Sketches of Butler's Brigade." Greenwood, S.C., Index Job Print, n.d., 8vo, cl, 118pp. (McKissick-341)

36 ..."Liberty Dethroned. A concise history of some of the most startling events before, during, & since the Civil War." (Greenwood, S.C., 1903). 12mo, cl, ports, plates, 385, (2)pp. erratta at end. Not in Turnbull. $50, $100, $150, $500-ob, $225, $250-bmk. Author of Co. K. 7th SCV & Co.C, 6th SCC. Hist. Greenwood Co., Cause of secession. Sketch of Butler's Brig. Story of Sam Puckett, Sam Davis, Bedford Forrest, Conf. at Hamilton Roads, Burning of Columbia, Lee Strategy & Reconstruction. Author's note(atg.) front flylf., disavows the book, failed to place on sale because of many typographical errors, being printer's first book, altho overall substance matter may pass judgement!

37 **CALHOUN, William Lowndes**
"History of the 42nd Regiment, Georgia Volunteers, Confederate States Army, infantry, by Capt. W.L. Calhoun, Historian." Atlanta, Ga., (Sisson Print) 1900. 8vo, wraps, col. illus.(incl. front) 45pp. $10, $17.50, $22.50, $25, $50, $125-bmk-105, $275-jk-138, $75-bmk, $15-bmk, Reprint-$7.50.
..."History of the 42nd regiment, Georgia Volunteers, Confederate States Army, Infantry, by Captain W.L. Calhoun, Historian." Atlanta, Ga., Sisson Print, 1900. 16mo, wraps, color illus. (incl. front), port, 45pp. Unit roster, 5-28. $50, $65.
...Reprint, n.p., n.d., (1977) $20.

38 **CALISCH, Rabbi**
"Hon. Judah P. Benjamin." In: SHSP, 1915, v.40, p. 240-243. See: Geo. L. Christian, p. 244-252.

39 **CALKINS, Christopher M.**
"36 hours before Appomattox." Lynchburg, Va., Civil War Roundtable, 1980. Farmville, Va., Farmville Herald, 8vo, 80pp. $5. Battles: Sayler's Creek,

High Bridge, Farmville & Cumberland Church, Apr. 6-7, 1865. $15.

40 ..."From Petersburg to Appomattox." Petersburg, Va., The Farmville Herald." 8vo, wraps, 48pp. $2.25. illus, maps, 1983. Eastern National Park & Monument Ass'n.

41 **CALL TO ARMS, The.**
Secession from a feminine point of view. Edited by Samuel Proctor. In: FHQ, January 1957, v.XXXV, #3, p. 266-270. "The ladies of Broward's Neck, Duval County, East Florida, Nov. 6, 1860.

42 **CALL, Richard Keith**
"Union-Slavery-Secession. Letter from R.K. Call, of Florida, to John S. Littell, of Germantown, Pa." Phila: C. Sherman & Son, 1861. 8vo, pamph., 30, (1)pp. $25. Altho a slaveholder, he's against slavery. $45-Lighthouse.

43 **CALLAHAN, James Morton**
"The Diplomatic History of the Southern Confederacy." Baltimore: Johns Hopkins Press, 1901. Albert Shaw lectures on Diplomatic history, 1900. $22.50, $25, Pres-$60-bmk, $40-bmk, $65-bmk. 12mo, cl, 2, (7), 304pp. $12.50, $15, $17.50.
...Springfield, Mass., Walden Press, 1957. Foreword: Benj. Keen.
...N.Y., Frederick Ungar Pub. Co. (1964). "American Classics". $14.25-y, $25, $5.

44 ..."Diplomatic Relations of the Confederate States with England (1861-1865)." Washington, DC, Amer. Hist. Ass'n., 1899. 8vo, wraps, 18pp. $4. Offprint: AHA Annual Report, 1898, p. 265-283.

45 ..."The Confederate Diplomatic Archives-the Pickett Papers." In: So. Atl. Quart., Jan. 1903, v.2, p. 1-9.

46 **CALLAWAY, Felix Richard**
"Bloody Links, The Four Years from 1860-1864. Description of Events before & after the War." (Shreveport, La., 1907. 8vo, boards, ports (2)facsm., plates(3), 75, (1)pp. cover title, a slip, "Tribute to Bog's Mother", tipped-in, chap. vi. (old) $6, $15. Pendleton's Reserve Arty., A.P. Hill Corps. Author was priv. in Cutts' Arty. Battl, Ga. Vols.

47 **CALROW, Charles James**
"Cold Harbor: A Study of the operations A.N.V. & Army of Potomac, May 26 - June 13, 1864." (Norfolk, Va., 1933) typescript, maps in pocket, at end, 319pp.

48 **CALVIN, Martin V.**
"The Bloody Angle, thrilling events of the 12th of May, 1864." In: CV, Dec. 1924, v.XXXII, p. 460-461.

49 **CAMBELL, Josiah H. Patterson, Hon.**
"Address upon the life & character of Jefferson Davis, delivered before the Legislature of State of Mississippi, in Joint Memorial session, Jan. 22, 1890." Jackson, Miss., R.H. Henry Pr., 1890. 8vo, wraps, 19pp. (R. McElroy bibliog). $50-jk-122.

50 ..."Oration of...at the third annual reunion grand camp Confederate Veterans." Jackson, Miss., July 12, 1892. caption title, double columns. 8vo, wraps, 17pp, Dornbusch-2636. Author, last surviving member CS Congr.

51 ..."The Lost Cause. A masterly vindication of it by Judge J.A.P. Cambell. Address at Canton(Miss.), May 1, 1874, on occasion of the decoration of Graves of Confederate soldiers." In: SHSP, 1888, v.XVI, p. 232-245.

52 **CAMERON, Alexander**
"A Soldiers Fare is Rough. Letters from A. Cameron in the Indian Territory, Arkansas Campaign, 1862-1864." In: TMH-MHT-Sw., 1974, v.XII, #1, p. 39-61. See: J.S. Duncan

53 **CAMERON, C.B.**
"The last days of "Stonewall" Jackson." In: Mil. surgeon, 1936, v.LXXVIII, p. 135-140. A more medico-historical review of treatment & death of Jackson. Taken from

Sarah Randolph & Mary Ann Jackson's life. of Jax.

54 **CAMERON, C.W.E.**
"The life & character of Robert E. Lee, an address to A.P. Hill Camp, UCV, Dept. of Va. 14th Annual Meeting at Petersburg, Va., 1901." 8vo, wraps, 72pp.

55 **CAMERON, Corinne**
"Haenger Bande." In: Junior Hist. (Tex.) Mar. 1955, v.15, #5, p. 28-29, 32. Gang of pro-Confederate outlaws, murderers in Gillespie Co., Texas, 1863-1873.

56 **CAMERON, John D.**
"Sketch of Thomas L. Clingman, U.S. Senator & Brig.-Gen., C.S.A." In: Univ. N.C. Mag., 1888-1889, viii, p. 249-257.

57 **CAMERON, Simon**
"Did Gen. George H. Thomas hesitate to draw his sword against his native state Virginia?" In: SHSP, 1884, v.XII, p. 468-470.

58 **CAMERON, W.J.**
"Robert E. Lee. A talk given on the Ford Sunday Evening Hour, Jan. 19, 1941." Dearborn, Mich., Ford Motor Cp. (1941) 16mo, (3)p. folder.

59 **CAMERON, William Evelyn**
"Historic Waters of Virginia. The Battle in Hampton Roads as viewed by an eye witness. The Improvised Confederate Naval Fleet." In: SHSP, 1904, v.XXXII, p. 347-354.

60 ..."The Life & Character of Robert Edward Lee. Address delivered before A.P. Hill Camp Confederate Veterans. By Ex-Governor Wm. Evelyn Cameron at Petersburg, Va., Jan. 19, 1901." In: SHSP, 1901, v.XXIX, p. 82-99.
..."The Life & Character of Robert E. Lee, an address to A.P. Hill Camp, CV by William E. Cameron, Petersburg, Virginia, January 19th, 1901." n.p. (Petersburg, Va.? 1901?). 8vo, wraps, title on cover, 23pp.

61 ..."The Southern Cause." Address to R.E. Lee Camp, Confederate Veterans, Richmond, Va., FEb. 20, 1903. Presentment of a portrait of Gov. James Lawson Kemper, Maj-Gen. CSArmy." In: SHSP, 1902, v.XXX, p. 360-368.

62 ..."Chancellorsville, a sketch of the Battle of the part taken by Mahone's Brigade with incidents & personal recollections of the campaign." In: Bernard's "War Talks". p. 45-76.

63 ..."The Career of General A.P. Hill." In: Annl. of War, 1879, p. 693-704.

64 **CAMERON, William Lochiel**
"The Battles opposite Mobile." In: CV, July, 1915, v.XXIII, p. 305-308.

65 **CAMMACK, John Henry**
"Personal recollections of..., a soldier of the Confederacy, 1861-1865, written at the urgent request of his family & friends, during the last years of his life, & published that the story may be read by those who knew & honored him. To which is added press notices & other papers containing a final tribute to his memory." Huntington: (W.Va.) Paragon Print (1920) 12mo, cl, front(port), 164, (1)pp. 50 copies for family and friends. $1400 -bmk, $50. Borderland -$175. Presention slip signed by author's son.

66 **"CAMP CHASE CEMETERY-Columbus, Ohio."**
(London) Jour. Confed. Hist. Soc., Sept. 1965, v.III, #3, p. 101-103.

67 **CAMP CHASE, Ohio-Memorial Service."**
"In: CV, 1903, v.11, p. 313-317, illus., ports.

68 **CAMP FORD, Texas**
A portfolio of contemporary illustrations of Tyler, Texas, Civil War prison from the collection of F. Lee Lawrence. In: Smith Co. (Texas) Hist. Soc. Fall, 1967, v.6, #2, 50pp. illus. See: Randal B. Gilbert, F. Lee Lawrence.

69 **CAMP JESTER, The**
Or, Amusement for the Mess. Augusta, Ga., Blackmar & Bro., 1864. 16mo, wraps, 71pp. Jokes & stories.

70 **CAMP MORTON, Indianapolis, Indiana.**
"Confederate dead buried in Indiana." In: CV, Jan. 1914, v.22, #1, p. 24-29, 76-82.

71 **CAMP, Cordelia**
"Governor Vance; a life for young people." Asheville, N.C., Stephens Press, (1961). 8vo, wraps, 58pp., illus., ports, map. $10.

72 **"CAMPAIGN FOR ATLANTA, The, from the editors of Civil War Times.**
By leading experts." In: CWTI, July 1964, v.III, #4, p. 3-50, illus., maps, ports.

73 **"CAMPAIGN IN FREDERICKSBURG,**
Nov.-Dec., 1862. A Study for Officers of Volunteers by a Line Officer." London: 1888. See under: Col. Chas. C. Chesney, also G.F.R. Henderson, same title.

74 **CAMPAIGN OF GETTYSBURG, The**
By "Miles." London: Groom & Co., (1912?) 8vo, cl, 201, (1)pp. 3-fldg. maps (pocket). Author: Walter E. Day.

74a **CAMPAIGNS,**
Wirt Adams; Wm. Allan; Henry L. Benning; A.F. Brown; James R. Chalmers, CSA, Adj. Gen.; "Memorandum of Info." Edward Dillon; W.O.Dodd; Jubal A. Early; Richard S. Ewell; Saml. W. Ferguson; Chas. W. Field; "Field Telegrams around Richmond; Nathan Bedford Forrest; Moses Gobson; Jas. R. Hagood; Paul F. Hammond; M.W. Humphreys; Bradley T. Johnson; Bushrod R. Johnson; Edward Johnson; Wm. E. Jones; B.P. Lee; Robert Edward Lee; Stephen D. Lee; Wm. Henry F. Lee; Armistead L. Long; Jas. Longstreet; Saml. McGowan; Jno. S. Marmaduke; Dabney H. Maury; Thomas T. Munford; New Orleans Picayune;

75 ..."Off. Reports Officers of Field Artillery."; "Opr. in Trans. Miss. Dept.; "Wm. F. Perry; Stirling Price; Stephen D. Ramseur; Thomas J. Riddle; Lawrence Sullivan Ross; Thomas L. Rosser; William R.Scurry;Jas. P. Simms; Edmund Kirby Smith; P.D. Stephenson; Carter L. Stevenson; "Strategic Points of War."; J.E.B. Stuart; E. T. Sykes; Richard Taylor; Isaac R. Trimble; Earl Van Dorn; Chs. S. Vanable; A.D. Warwick. Al so: Under names of battles.

76 **CAMPBELL, A.A., Mrs.**
"The First Fight of ironclads." In: CV, Aug. 1921, v.XXIX, p. 290-291.

77 ..."Secession." In: CV, Jan. 1922, v.XXX, p. 16-17.

78 **CAMPBELL, Albert H., Major**
"Lost War Maps of the Confederates." In: Cent. Mag., Jan. 1888, v.XXXV, p. 479-481.

79 **CAMPBELL, Andrew Jackson**
"The Civil War Diary of Andrew Jackson Campbell. Edited by Jill Knight Garrett." (Columbia, Tenn., 1965) 8vo, stiff wraps, 132pp. $15. See: Jill Knight Garrett. Was in Tenn. Inf. (CSA) 48th Reg.

80 **CAMPBELL, Bernard T.**
"Shiloh National Military Park." In: Tenn. HQ, 1962, v.XXI, p. 3-18, also in "Landmarks of Tenn." p. 301-316.

81 **CAMPBELL, Harry M., Col.**
"Which General...?" (London)Jour. Confed. Hist. Soc., Winter, 1971, v.9, #4, p. 120-124. Name confusion in CSA & Union.

82 ..."Robert E. Lee, a victim of circumstances (London) Jour. Confed. Hist. Soc., Spring, 1970, v.8, #1, p. 6-11, port Lee.

83 ..."Rebellion an outgrowth of many issues." (London) Jour. Confed. Hist. Soc., Autumn, 1969, v.7, #1, p. 27-32, map.

84 **CAMPBELL, Helen Jones**
"The Case for Mrs. Surratt." N.Y., G.P. Putnam's Sons (1943). 12mo, cl, front(port), dj, 272pp. $10-y, $25, $17.50.

85 ..."Confederate Courier." N.Y., St. Martin's Press (1965, c.1964) 8vo, cl, dj, xvi, 301, illus., ports, $8, $10, $15. The historic trial of Johnny Surratt for the murder of Lincoln.

86 **CAMPBELL, J.A.**
"Resources of Confederate Government at the opening of 1865." In: South. Mag., Dec. 1874, v.8, #6, (also in SHSP)

87 **CAMPBELL, James B.**
"East Tennessee during the Federal occupation, 1863-1865." In: East TennHS, 1947, #19, p. 64-80.

88 **CAMPBELL, James M., Maj.**
"Report of Maj. Campbell, Forty-seventh Alabama Regiment. Hdq. Aug. 7, 1863." In: SHSP, 1885, v.XIII, p. 181-182.

89 **CAMPBELL, John**
"Letter of John Campbell, Unionist, Edt: James J. Johnston." In: AHQ, 1970, v.XXIX, p. 176-182, port. Was 1st Lt. Co. K, Fourteenth Arkansas Infantry, CSA.

90 **CAMPBELL, John Archibald**
"An address upon the life & public services of John C. Calhoun delivered at Mobile, on 13th December, 1850." Mobile (Ala.) Dade, Thompson & Co., 1851. 8vo, wraps, 45pp.

91 ..."In the matter of liability of Officers who were compelled to surrender moneys of the United States to the Officers of the seceeding states, after the passage of the Acts of Secession in 1861." (n.p., n.d.) 12mo, wraps, 21pp. Regarding the New Orleans Mint.

92 ..."Papers of Hon. John A. Campbell, 1861-1865." (To Daniel Chandler, Esq.) In: SHSP, Oct., 1917, v.XLII, p. 3-81.

93 ..."Efforts for Reconstruction in April 1865." In: SHSP, 1908, v.XXXVI, p. 250-260.

94 ..."Evacuation Echoes. Asst. Sect. of War Campbell's interview with Lincoln." In: SHSP, 1896, v.XXIV, p. 351-353.

95 ..."An alleged Proclamation of President Lincoln." In: SHSP, 1879, v.VII, p. 95-98.
..."Reminiscences & Documents relating to the Civil War during the year 1865." Baltimore: J. Murphy & Co., 1887. 8vo, wraps, 69pp. $12.50, $35, $75-ob.
...Louisville: Lost Cause Press, micro-card, gives date: 1886. $3.24.

96 ..."The Administration & the Confederate States." n.p., n.d., 1861. 8vo, sewn, 127pp. caption title. (old) $7.50. Probably printed in Montgomery of Charleston. Corresp. relates to his efforts to get assurances from Seward that military forces not be sent to Fort Sumter. Crandall-2702 gives a copy with just 7pp.

97 ..."Recollections of the Evacuation of Richmond, April 2, 1865." Baltimore, Md., 1880. 8vo, cl, 27pp.

98 ..."Letter to Gen. Fitzhugh Lee." Answering an invitation to attend placing corner stone to Lee Monument in Richmond. Baltimore, 1877. 4to, 3pp. folder. (old)$2.

99 ..."The Institutions, duties & relations of Alabama. An oration before the Erosophic & Philomathic societies of the University of Alabama. July 12, 1859." Tuscaloosa, J.F. Warren Print, 1859. 12mo, wraps, 34pp. Relates to U.S. constitution, secession.

100 ..."Rights of the Slave States, by a Citizen of Alabama. From the Southern Quarterly Review, for Jan., 1851. Published by the Southern Rights Association. (1850). n.p., 8vo, wraps, 47pp.

101 ..."The Prospects before us." n.p., (1850) no t.p., 8vo, wraps, 50pp. Owen. Discusses slavery, anti-slavery agitation, sectional differences, etc.

102 ..."Letters from John A. Campbell, addressed to Daniel Chandler, Mobile, Ala., Nov. 24-26, 1860, on the present crisis in Southern affairs. Wash., DC, G.S. Gideon Print, (1860). 8vo, sewn, no t.p., , 12pp.

Owen. Campbell was a Justice of US Supreme Ct., later on CSA Ass't. Sect. War.

103 ..."The administration & the Confederate States...Corresp. between Hon. John A. Campbell & Hon. Wm. H. Seward, all of which was laid before the provisional congress on Saturday by President Davis, n.p., 1861." 8vo, caption title, 7pp.

104 ..."Recollections of the evacuation of Richmond, April 2nd, 1865." Balt: J. Murphy & co., 1880. 8vo, wraps, 27pp.

105 ..."Reminiscences & Documents relating to the Civil War during the year 1865." Balt: J. Murphy & Co., 1887. 8vo, wraps, 68pp. Gdsp.-$75. Campbell's CSA Comm. meets Lincoln.

106 **CAMPBELL, John Archibald, Judge, Asst. Sect. War**
"A view from the inside of the Confederacy." In: Cent., Oct. 1889, v.16, p. 950-954.

107 **CAMPBELL, John F.**
"The Campbells of Drumaboden, on the River Lyennon, near Rathmelton, county Donegal, north of Ireland." (Nashville: Foster & Parkes) 1925. 8vo, cl, plates, ports, 147pp. $10. 44pp. devoted to War in Tennessee.

108 **CAMPBELL, Mary**
"Lucy Long." In: Wm. & Mary Quart., 2nd ser., 1939, v.XIX, p. 471-473. Notes & letters re Gen. Lee's sorrel mare "Lucy Long", which he rode when "Traveller" was resting.

109 **CAMPBELL, Mary Emily Robertson**
"Attitude of Tennessee Toward the Union, 1847-1861." New York: Vantage Press (1961). 12mo, cl, 308pp., illus. $25, $15-bmk-84, $4.50.

110 ..."Tennessee & the Union, 1847-1861." (Nashville, Tenn: Mary R. Campbell, 1938) Printed, edited & distributed by Joint-Libraries of Nashville, 1938. Reprinted from the East Tennessee Historical Society, publication #10, bibliog., footnotes, 8vo, wraps, (22)pp. A summary of a thesis (PHd) at Vanderbilt University, 1938.

111 ..."Tennessee's Congressional delegation in the sectional crisis of 1859-1860." In: TennHQ, Dec. 1960, v.19, p. 348-371. notes. On the 2 Senators & 10 Representatives from Tenn., in the 36th Congr., 1st session.

112 **CAMPBELL, Mary R.**
"Unionist victory in the election of Feb. 9, 1861." In: East Tenn HS, 1942, #14, p. 11-30.

113 **CAMPBELL, Robert M.**
"History in Relation to some principals & practices of Confederate Surgeons." In: Va. Medical Monthly, 1967, v.XCIV, p. 600-608.

114 **CAMPBELL, W.P.**
"Travelers Series Number Seven." The Escape & Wanderings of J. Wilkes Booth until ending of the trail by suicide in Oklahoma. The way of the transgressor is hard." Copyright 1922. Oklahoma City, Okla., all rights reserved, price $1." 8vo, wraps, cover title, illus., 142pp. $50. A variant has separate lf., p. 143-144, tipin.

115 **CAMPBELL, William A.**
"The Child's First Book. By Campbell & Dunn. Approved by the Educational Association of Virginia through their committee." Richmond, Va., Ayers & Wade, 1864. 12mo, 48pp. Crandall-4036 (Bohl.) $250-copy, $150-bmk.

116 **CAMPBELL, William, Hon.**
"Stuart's Ride & death of Latane." In: SHSP, April 14, 1914, v.XXXIX, p. 86-90. Campbell was in Co. F., 9th Va. Cavalry.

116a **CANALE, Allen**
"A diplomatic wrangle." In: CWTI, Oct. 1987, v.26, #6, p.38-48, ills.

117 **CANAN, Howard V.**
"Maps of the civil war." In: Armor, Sept./Oct. 1956, v.65, p. 34-42. maps,

notes. On maps available for military use at the beginning of war & development of military cartography by Union & CSA forces.

118 ..."The Missouri Paw Paw Militia of 1863-1864." (Columbia, Mo., Mo. Hist. Review, July, 1968. p. 431-448. illus., ports.

119 ..."Confederate Military Intelligence." In: Md. H.M., March 1964. p. 34-51

120 **CANAVELLA, Charles A.**
"The Confederate Diary of Charles A. Canavella, Co. E., 3rd Alabama Infantry 1861-1864." Jacksonville, Fla., Historical Records Survey, 1938. 4to, stiff wraps, typed copy of 8pp. Largely names & lists. $15.

121 **CANDLER, Allen D.**
"The Confederate Records of the State of Georgia, compiled & published under authority for the Legislature. Message of Gov. Joseph E. Brown on Federal Relations, Nov. 7, 1860. Resolutions of Various Counties. Address of Thos. R.R. Cobb, Alex H. Stephens, Act Calling Convention, Relating public defense." Atlanta, Ga., Chs. P. Byrd, State Printer, 1909. Tk, sm. 4to, cl, 773pp. 905, 746. $40. Vol.II-"State papers Gov. Joseph E. Brown, relating to the public defense, Organization & equipment of troops, provisions for the families of soldiers, etc., 1860-1865, inclusive." Vol. III-"Official Correspondence of Gov. Joseph E. Brown, 1860-1865, inclusive." $150-ea. b., $500, $400-bmk-105. 8-vols.Vols. IV & VI (v.5 never printed) relates to Reconstruction in Georgia. $50, $275
...Reprint: 1970 at $348. See: Lillian Henderson & Allan D. Candler's Report...and Ga. Soldiers.

122 ..."Watch on the Chattahoochee, a Civil War Letter. Edt: Elizabeth Hulsey Marshall." In: Ga. H.Q., December 1959, v.XLIII, #4, p. 427-428.

123 **CANDLER, John S., Judge**
"Address: upon the occasion of the memorial service at Atlanta Camp #159, United Confederate Veterans, for members of the camp who died during the year. First Presbyterian Church, Oct. 15, 1905." Atlanta, Ga., Franklin Press, 1905. 8vo, wraps (also cover title), 8pp.

124 **CANDLER, Mark Allen**
"The beginnings of slavery in Georgia." In: Mag. of Hist., July 1911, v.XIII, p. 342-351.

125 **CANFIELD, Cass**
"The Iron Will of Jefferson Davis." N.Y., Lond: Harcourt Brace Jovanovich, (1978). 12mo, cl, dj, illus., maps, ports, incl. front, facsm. liners, xiv, 146pp. $10, $8.

125a **CANNON, Devereaux D.**
"The Flags of the Confederacy: an illustrated history." Wilmington, N.C., Broadfoot Pub., 1988 with St. Luke's Press. 4to, cl, 128pp, ills (56 in color), index. $30. Paper, $10.

126 **CANNON, Jabez P.**
"Inside of Rebeldom, the daily life of a Private in the Confederate army, by H.P. Cannon, late 27th Alabama." Washington, National Tribune, 1900. 12mo, cl, xx, 21-288p. front, ports, illus., "Old Glory Library, #32."

127 **CANNON, Joseph P.**
"Inside of Rebeldom: the daily life of a private in the Confederate Army." Washington, D.C., National Tribune, 1899. 8vo, wraps, front(port) illus.(drawings), xx, (21)-288pp. $15, $25, $37.50, $40, $50.
...Reprint: 1900. "Old Glory Library", as above. Cheap paper. Front. notes, "M.D." $25-bmk, $75.

128 ..."Confederate Diary of Joseph P. Cannon." In: Cooper's Coffee Cooler, Sturgis, Mich., 1893-1896. v.VI, #6; v.IX, #2, & 3, June, 1893-Feb.-Mar., 1896. Note in Bibli-

og. State Participation, C.W. Alabama, 27th Inf. Dornbusch #61. Notes: As Jabez.

129 **CANNON, Newton, Sergeant**
"Reminiscences of Sergeant Newton Cannon." Franklin, Tenn., Carter House Association. (Jackson, Tenn., McCowat-Mercer Press, 1963) 8vo, stiff wraps (battle scene front to back) port front., ports, facsms. illus., 84pp. $15-bmk-105, $25, $6, $2.50

130 **CANNON, Ralph**
"Lee on the Levee." N.Y., Saravan House (1940). 8vo, cl, front(map), 183pp. $4. Period: 1837-1840 when Lee a hydraulic engineer on Mississippi. A historical novel based on letters to Dr. Wm. Beaumont of St. Louis.

131 **CANONGE, Alphonse**
"Exercises et Manoeuvres de l'Infanterie." Nouvell Orleans, La., 1861. See: Under title.

132 **CANTRELL, Mark Lea(Beau) & Mac Harris**
"Kepis & Turkey Calls. An anthology of the War Between the States in Indian Territory. Edt: Mark Lea(Beau) Cantrell & Mac Harris. Foreword by Kenny A. Franks." Oklahoma City: Western Heritage Books, 1982. 8vo, paper, x, 222pp., illus., maps, index. $10. 12 articles appeared in Chronicles of Okla., between 1921-1980.

133 **CANTRELL, Oscar Alexander**
"Sketches of the First Regiment Georgia. Vols. together with the history of the 56th Regiment Georgia Vols. to Jan. 1, 1864." Atlanta, Ga., Intelligencer Steam Press, 1864. 8vo, wraps, 73pp. Crandall-2617.

134 **CANTWELL, Edward**
"Oration before the Wilmington Light Infantry, on their 24th anniversary, May 20, 1877." Wilmington, N.C., S.G. Hall Print, 1877. 8vo, wraps, cover title, 26pp.

135 **CAPE FEAR, (N.C.) Div.: U.D.C., Chap. No.3**
"Catalogue of relics in history & relics room of the Cape Fear Chap., U.D.C." (Wilmington, N.C., n.d.) 12mo, wraps, 20pp.

135a **CAPERS, Charlotte, Edt.**
"Guide to Civil War Source Materials in the Mississippi Department of Archives & Hist." Jackson, Miss., Archives & History, 1962. 8vo, wraps, 71pp.

136 **CAPERS, Ellison, Brig-Gen.**
"South Carolina." v. 6, 8vo, cl, 931pp. Wilmington, N.C., Broadfoot, 1987.

137 ..."Agreement between the US Government & South Carolina as to 'preserving the status' of the forts at Charleston." In: SHSP, 1884, v.12, p. 60-63.

138 ..."An address on Memorial Day, May 20, 1890. Greenville, S.C." Greenville, S.C., Ladies Memorial Association of Greenville, 1890. 8vo, wraps, 19pp. McKissick-375 $10.

139 ..."The last commander of Fort Sumter, Thomas A. Huguenin, (Class of 1859). Tribute read before the Association of Graduates of the South Carolina Military Academy." Charleston, S.C., Walker, Evans & Cogswell Co., 1898. 8vo, wraps, 8pp (McKissick-378) See: Maj. John Johnson's CSA defense of FS.

140 ..."South Carolina" , v.V of Clement Evans Confederate Military History. Atlanta: Confederate Pub. Co., 1899. 8vo, cl.(or, 3/4 Calf) (or, 3/4 Black Mor.), ports, 3-maps (2-dble), 424pp. $10.
...Same, with Biographical Suppl., p. 931. From $50 to $75, when available. See: Walter Branham Capers (Biography)

141 ..."Captain Francis Huger Harleston." In: SHSP, 1884, v.XII, p. 361-366. Address delivered at the "Citidel", unveiling the monument to Capt. Harleston.

142 ..."The Twenty-Fourth South Carolina at the Battle of Jonesboro, official report of Colonel Ellison Capers." In: SHSP, 1883, v.XI, p. 481-484. See: Jno. W. DuBose.

143 **CAPERS, Francis W.**
"Report of the military service of the Georgia military cadets." Milledgeville, Ga., 1864. 8vo, wraps, (2)p. "Hdq. Battl. of cadets & Georgia mil. inst., Milledgeville, Oct. 27, 1864." Crandall-1597. See: Robert L. Rogers & Robt. L. Rodgers.

144 **CAPERS, Gerald A.**
"Occupied City: New Orleans Under the Federals, 1862-1865." Lexington: University of Kentucky Press, 1965. Cloth, 8vo, d/w, p.ix, 248. $25-bmk, $6.75. From viewpoint of the conquered inhab.

145 ..."A Reconsideration of John C. Calhoun's Transition from Nationalism to Nullification. (Baton Rouge, La.) JSH, Feb. 1948. v.XIV, #1, p. 38-48.

146 **CAPERS, Gerald M., Jr.**
"Confederates & Yankees in Occupied New Orleans, 1862-1865." (Houston, Tex.) JSH, Nov. 1964, v.XXX, #4, p. 405-426. $8.

147 ..."John C. Calhoun-Opportunist, a Reappraisal." Gainesville, (Fla) Univ. of Florida Press, 1960. 8vo, cl, dj, port(front), viii, 275pp.

148 ..."Stephen A. Douglas: Defender of the Union." Boston: Little, Brown Co., 1959. 8vo, cl, dj, bibliog. essay, x, 239pp. Tries to right misconception of Douglas, not understood by other writers. A struggle between two secions for control of Gov.

149 **CAPERS, Henry D.**
"The Life & Times of C.G. Memminger." Richmond, Va., 1893. Everett Waddey Co. 8vo, cl, illus., port(front)ports, illus., 604pp. $6, $8, $10, $15, $17.50, $20, $25. Memminger was Sect. Treasury. Important source of growth of the CSA to secession & history. $32.50-y, $75 jk-137, $50 bmk-84.

150 ..."Recollections of the Civil Service of the Confederate Government." pt. 1(all pub.) Atlanta, Ga.: Constitution Pub., 1887. 8vo, wraps, 48pp. Capers was chief clerk under Meminger.

151 ...Capers, H.D., Major, C.S.A. "To the People of Jacksboro & Campbell Co., Tenn. For 12 months you have been distracted in all relationships of life. Fields barren, Academies in ruins, roving bands of thieves & murderers have found shelter. I invite shelter of the Confederate flag, return to the allegiance which you owe Tenn. & C.S." Broadside: 5x10", note in his own hand-"this proclamation printed on Confed. paper with type & press of Knoxville Whig, "Parson Brownlow's " outfit, requested by me at Jacksboro, Tenn., Aug., 1862. $100.

152 ..."The Defense of Fort Wagner." In: SB, ns, v.II, p. 195-196, (1886/1887).

153 ..."Maj. H.D.D. Twiggs at Battery Wagner." In: CV, 1902, v.10, p. 23-24.

154 ..."Treasurer of the Confederate Government." In: CV, Apr., 1916, v.XXIV, p. 150-151. Treas: Edward C. Elmore.

155 **CAPERS, John G., of S.C.**
"An address-Winchester, Va.-Memorial Day, 1899-published by special request. (a son of an ex-Confederate soldier.)" (Washington, D.C., Law Reporter Press) n.d. (c.1900) 8vo, wraps, 23pp.

156 **CAPERS, Walter Branham**
"The Soldier Bishop, Ellison Capers." New York: Neale Pub. Co., 1912. 8vo, cl, 367pp. $10, $18.50, $25, atg & ds-$80-nc, $32.50-y, $100-bmk-75.

157 **CAPITOL OF THE C.S., The, Richmond, Va."**
Colored lithograph, by E. Sachse & Co., 1865.

158 **CAPPLEMAN, Josie Frazee, Mrs.**
"Confederate Memorial Coin, by..." n.p., n.d., Broadside, 12mo. Poem. Head of title: "These poems dedicated to Stone Mt. Confederate Memorial & to valor of the soldiers of the South. Distr. by J.R. Riley, Jr., Ark. cmp. dir."

159 ..."Importance of the local history of the Civil War." In: V.III, 1900, Publications Mississippi State Hist. Society.
..."Importance of Local History of the Civil War." (Oxford, Miss., Pub. Miss. Hist. Soc., 1900, v.III, p. 107-112.

160 ..."Local Incidents of the War Between the States." In: PMHS, v.IV, p. 79-87.

161 **CAPPON, Lester Jesse**
"Government & Private Industry in the Southern Confederacy." In: Humanistic studies in honor of John Calvin Metcalf. Charlottesville, Va. (NY-Columbia Univ. Press, 1941) 8vo, cl, x, 338pp., 1-illus., pl. (University of Va. Studies, v.1, bibliographical foot-notes.

162 ..."A Note on Confederate Ordnance Records." Amer. Military Inst. Jour., IV (1940), p. 94-102. CSA Ordnance records Natl. Archiv.

163 ..."Trend of the Southern Iron Industry under the Plantation System." Jour. of Economic & Business Hist., (Feb., 1930), p. 353-381.

164 ..."Government & Private Industry in the Southern Confederacy." Reprint: "Humanistic Studies in Honor of John Calvin Metcalf."

165 ..."The Yankee press in Virginia, 1861-1865." In: Wm. & Mary Quart., 1935, v.XV, 2nd Ser., p. 81-88. Papers pub. in a dozen Va. towns by northern troops, on life of soldiers & civilians behind the lines.

166 **CAPPS, Claudius Meede**
"The Blue & the Gray; the best poems of the Civil War." Compiled & edited by..." Boston: B. Humphried (1943). 12mo, cl, 281pp. $5, $7.50, $20-bmk.
...N.Y., Arno's Granger Index Reprint series. 1970. $14.25.

167 **CAPRON, John D.**
"Virginia Iron Furnaces of the Confederacy." (Richmond) Va. Cavl., Autumn, 1967. v.XVII, #2, p. 10-18, port, chart, map, illus., 2-colored, one on back cover.

168 **"CAPTURE OF FORT HENRY."**
Camp Benning, Ga., Dept. of Research the Infantry School. Course in Historical Research 1920-1921, Mil. Hist. Pamphlet #5. Printed at the Infantry School Press, 1921. 8vo, wraps, fldg. map, 23pp. $3.

169 **CAPTURE of a Confederate Blockade Runner, The**
Extracts from the journal of a Confederate Naval Officer. Edt.: Frank E. Vandiver. In: NCHR, April 1944, p. 136-138.

170 **CARAWAY, L.V.**
"The battle of Arkansas Post." In: CV, May, 1928, v.XXXVI, p. 171-173. Union captures port, Jan. 11, 1863.

171 **CARDOSO, Jack J.**
"Southern Reaction to the 'Impending Crisis'." In: CWH, March 1970, v.XVI, #1, p. 5-17.

172 **CARDOZO, Jacob Newton**
"Reminiscences of Charleston." Charleston: Joseph Walker, 1866. 12mo, wraps, 144pp. (War period, 81-142) (ginz)atg-$150, $10, $17.50, $30-bmk.
...Louisville: Lost Cause Pr., micro-card, $3.25.

173 **CARDWELL, D., Col.**
"A brilliant coup. How Wade Hampton captured Grant's entire beef supply. Col. Cardwell's thrilling story. The greatest cattle raid of the war-2,486 beeves driven from Coggin's Point into the Confederate lines." In: SHSP, 1894, v.XXII, p. 147-156.

174 ..."The Battle of Five Forks." In: CV, March, 1914, v.XXII, p. 117-120.

175 ..."The career of the "Alabama" (no. 290) from July 29, 1862, to June 19, 2864." London: Dorrell & Son, 1864. reprinted: N.Y., W. Abbatt, 1908. The Magazine of history with notes & queries. Extra numbers, #2(pt.2. sm. 4to, wraps, 35, (3)pp. Published anonymously. Appended (3)pp: "Aboard a Semmes prize", by Capt. Strout.

176 **"CAREER of the Confederate Ironclad Neuse, The"**
In: NCHR, 1966, v.43, p. 1-13. (William M. Still)

177 **CARLETON, Fred**
"Roll of Co.G., 16th Texas Infantry, compiled from memory & from a partial copy of the roster of the company, officers as they were at the original organization of tthe company." (Austin, Texas, Bryant P.Dickens, 1899?) 12mo, wraps, 8pp. TU

178 **CARLETON, G.W., Late of C.S. Navy**
"David & Goliath on the Deep. An incident of the Siege of Charleston." In: Confederate Annals, Aug. 1883, v.1, #2, p. 41-47.

179 **CARLISLE, James Mandeville**
"A tribute to the memory of General Lee, by J.M. Carlisle, being one of several addresses at the memorial meeting held in Washington, Mr. Corcoran prisiding, Friday Oct. 14, 1870." Washington, DC, M'Gill & Witherow, 1870. 8vo, wraps, 10pp.

180 **CARLTON, Mabel Mason**
"Robert E. Lee." Boston, Mass., 1926, 8vo, cl, 16pp.

181 **CARMACK, E.W.**
"Record of a Confederate & a Senator." Tributes paid by colleagues to William Brimage Bate, Maj-Gen., CSA. Address delivered in the US Senate, Jan. 17, 1907, on his life, character & public service.

182 **CARMICHAEL, Emmett B.**
"La Fayette Guild (1825-1870)." Ann. Med. Hist., n.s., VIII, p. 147-155, (1935). Services in war as surgeon and Med. Dir. in A.N.V.

183 **CARMICHAEL, Maude**
"Federal Experiments with Negro Labor on abandoned plantations in Arkansas, 1862-1865." In: ARQ, March 1942, v.1, #1, p. 101-116.

184 **CARNAHAN, J. Worth**
"4000 Civil War Battles, from Official Record." Ft. Davis, Texas: Frontier Book Co., 1975. 12mo, cl, illus., 128pp. $4.

185 **CARNES, Eva Margaret**
"The Battle of Philippi." In: NS, v.3, #4, p. 56-59; 76(summermap, ports., views(1 color)

186 ..."Centennial History of Philippi Covered Bridge, 1852-1952." Philippi: Barbour Co. Hist. Soc. (1952) 8vo, cl, 101pp. diagrs., ports, views. by several contributors. Battle Philippi by Mary R. Hoge, p. 77-86.

187 ..."(Bishop) George W. Peterkin at Valley Mountain." August 1861. Randolph Co. Hist. Soc., W.Va., Mag. of Hist. & Biog., Apr. 1961, p. 97-99. A sketch of Peterkin's service with the 21st Va. Inf.

188 ..."The Tygarts Valley Line, June-July, 1861." Philippi: First Land Battle of the Civil War Cent. Commemoration. (1961). 8vo, illus., maps, ports, 105pp.

189 **CARNES, W.W., Major**
"Chickamauga." In: SHSP, 1886, v.XIV, p. 398-407.

190 **CARNZTHAN, W.J.**
"The proposal to reopen the African slave trade in the South." In: So. Atl. Quart., Oct. 1926, v.XXV, p. 410-429.

191 **"CAROLINA & THE SOUTHERN CROSS"**
Kinston, N.C., (1913-1914). v.1-2; Mar. 1913-Aug. 1914. Monthly. Edt: L.V. Archbell, no more pub.? "Official organ of the North Carolina United Daughters of

the Confederacy. Sm.4to, wraps, illus., much on the C.S. $5. ea.

192 **CAROLINA BOOKSHOP (Charlotte, N.C.)**
Cat. #9-"The War Between the States." 120pp. (Summer 1984) Civil war fiction, 1266-1442. Good descriptive on ephymeral items.

193 **CAROLINA RIFLE CLUB, The,**
June 12, 1875. Presentation of the Battle Flag of the Tenth Regiment, S.C.V., Confederate States Army, July 12, 1875. Tall 8vo, wraps, 23pp. $15. Charleston, Walker, Evans & Cogswell Printers, 1875. Address of Col. C. Irvine Walker on presenting the flag.

194 **CARPENTER, Bonnie**
"Old Mountain City an Early Settlement in Hays County." San Antonio, Texas: Naylor Print (1970). $8. 12mo, cl, dj, x, 105pp. (p. 39-95 CSA) Mountain City rallies to support CSA.

195 **CARPENTER, Horace**
"Plain living at Johnson's Island, described by a Confederate Officer." In: Cent. Mag., 1891, v.XLI, p. 705-718, facsms, illus.

196 ..."Poor Johnnies", plain living at Johnson's Island, described by a Confederate Officer." (n.p., c.1890's) 12mo, wraps, caption title, dbl. column, (12)pp.
..."Plain living at Johnson's Island, described by a Confederate Officer." In: Cent., April 1891, v.19, p. 705-718, facsms, illus.

197 **CARPENTER, Kinchen Jahu**
"War Diary of Kinchen Jahu Carpenter Company I, Fiftieth North Carolina Regiment War Between the States, 1861-1865." Prepared for publication by Mrs. Julie Carpenter Williams, Rutherfordton, N.C., 1955. (Rutherfordton, N.C., April 5, 1955) 8vo, stiff wraps, color-flags, front-port, 17pp. $25-bmk-105, (pub)$1.25, $30-b, $10-nc, $15-nr.

198 **CARPENTER, Stephen D.**
"Logic of History. Five hundred political Texts: being concentrated extracts of Abolitionism; also, results of Slavery agitation & emancipation; together with sundry chapters on Despotism, Usurpations & their Frauds, 2nd Edt.(?)" $57.50. Madison, Wisc., S.D. Carpenter, Pub., 1864. 8vo, cl, (4), 351pp. Howes: "1st & only edt. voices unregenerate Copperhead belief of Abolition Republicans strove to effect sectional rupture & didn't want union restored."

199 **CARR, B.B. & others**
"History of Co.E., 20th N.C. Reg. 1861-1865; The Confederate Greys." Goldsboro, N.C., 1905. 8vo, wraps, 23pp. $15, $22.50.
...Do: Goldsboro: Joe F. Morris Press, 1932. 8vo, stiff wraps, 27pp. illus., ports. (from Walter Clark's History "Several Regs")

200 **CARR, Julian Shakespeare**
"Address of...' The Confederate Soldier', at the reunion, Richmond, Va., June 2, 1915." (Durham, N.C. ? 1915) 8vo, cover title, 29pp.

201 ..."Address to Veterans of Southern Confederacy, delivered at Wilmington, N.C., May 10, 1894." n.p., (c.1894) 8vo, wraps, 23pp.

202 ..."In Loving Remembrance of our Brother in Gray; address of..., at Windsor, Bertie County, N.C., before the Bertie County Veterans Association, Thursday, August 1, 1895." n.p. (c.1895). 8vo, wraps, 20pp. cover title.

203 ..."These remarks affectionately dedicated to Confederate Soldiers of the 'Rank & File', & to Henry L. Wyatt, first hero who fell in defence of the South, at Wilmington, N.C., May 10, 1894." (Wilmington, 1894?) 8vo, wraps, cover title, 23pp.

204 ..."The Hampton Roads Conference. A refutation of the statement that Mr. Lincoln said if Union was written at the top the Southern Commissioners might fill in the balance." Durham, N.C., n.d. (Jan. 15, 1917) 12mo, wraps, cover title, port, 36pp. $5. See: "Hampton Roads Conference."

205 ..."The Hampton Roads Conference." In: CV, Feb. 1917, v.25, #2, p. 57-66, illus., port.

206 ..."President's Report of Confederate Memorial Institute or 'Battle Abbey' to U.C.V., assembled at New Orleans, Richmond, 1923, wraps, 11pp. $1.

207 **CARRIE, David C.**
"Dundee & the American Civil War. 1861-1865." In: Abertay Hist. Soc. Pub., 1953, #1, p. 24. University Library, Dundee Scot.

208 **CARRIER, John P.**
"Bullets, Ballots & Bayonets: Reconstruction Politics & elections in Smith County, Texas, 1866-1873." In: Chron. Smith Co., Tex., Summer, 1974.

209 **CARRIGAN, Alfred Hold & Jess N. Cypert**
"Reminiscences of the Secession Convention." In: Pub. Ark. Hist. Assn., v.I, 1906, p. 305-323.

210 **CARRIGAN, C.H. or Joseph G. Carrigan**
Godspeed's cat-599 cites: "Authorship written on t.p., as C.H. Carrigan but Union Cat. notes Joseph G. Carrigan. Both C.H. & Joe G., are here in roster of 8th Tenn., where 'writer' in penciled in after C.H."
See: Under title- "Cheat Mountain"

211 **CARRIGAN, Jo Ann**
"Yankees versus Yellow Jack in New Orleans, 1862-1866." In: CWH, September 1963, v.IX, #3, p. 248-260.

212 **CARRINGTON, James McDowell, Maj.**
"First Day on Left at Gettysburg. General Early's advice-an oft-repeated incident corroborated by a witness who was there." In: SHSP, 1909, v.XXXVII, p. 326-337.

213 **CARROLL, Daniel B.**
"Henri Mercier & the American Civil War." Princeton: University Press, 1971. 8vo, cl, d/w, xxi, 396pp. $12.50. Mercier pro-southern, wanted a common-market for the South.

214 **CARROLL, James Parsons**
"Report of the Committee appointed to collect Testimony in relation to the Destruction of Columbia, S.C., on the 17th February, 1865." Columbia, S.C., Bryan Print, 1893. 8vo, wraps, 20pp. $15.

215 ..."The Burning of Columbia, South Carolina-Report of the Committee of citizens appointed to collect testimony." In: SHSP, v.VIII, 1880, p. 202-214.

216 **CARROLL, John William**
"Autobiography & reminiscences of John W. Carroll." Henderson, Tenn., (1898). 12mo, wraps, port, 66pp. CSA, p. 20-42. Experience in army, 27th Inf.

217 **CARROLL, Karen C.**
"Sterling, Campbell & Albright; textbook Publishers, 1861-1865." In: NCHR, April, 1986, v.63, #2, p. 169-98, facsms, illus, ports.

218 **CARROLL, Thomas F.**
"Freedom of speech & of the press during the civil war." In: Va. Law Rev., May 1923, v.IX, p. 516-551.

219 **CARSE, Robert**
"Blockade: the Civil War at Sea." N.Y., Rinehart & co., (1958). 8vo, cl, dj, ports, views, (8)-279, (1)p. bibliog., notes. $5, $7, $10, $14-bmk, $20-bmk, $30-b.

220 ..."Department of the South, Hilton Head Island in the Civil War." Columbia, S.C., State Print, 1961. 4to, cl, dj, map endsheets, illus.(some color), plan, x, 156pp. $75, $25, $15.

221 **CARSEL, Wilfred**
"The slaveholders indictment of Northern

wage Slavery." In: JSH, 1940, v.VI, p. 504-520. The South's counter attack on abolitionists by an expose' of factory conditions, 1830-1860.

222 **CARSON, J.R., Mrs.**
"Wade Hampton, 1818-1902." In: S.C. Mag., v.XI, #7, p. 19-22. Port, 1948. On political career of Hampton(Military), 1861-1897.

223 ..."The great triumvirate of Reconstruction period in S.C." In: UDCm, Sept. 1948, v.11, #9, p. 6-8. (Wade Hampton, M.C. Butler, M.W. Gary, & the Red Shirts.

224 **CARSON, James Petigru**
"Life, letters & speeches of James Louis Petigru, the Union man of South Carolina. With Intro: Gaillard Hunt." Washington: W.H. Lowdermilk, 1920. 8vo, cl, pls., ports, facsm. xxiii, 497pp. Against secession but during war was loyal to South. $30, $25-bmk.

225 **CARSON, John M.**
"Missing link or unwritten reminiscences, 1896." In: UDCMag., Nov. 1951, v.14, #11, p. 10, 31, 34-35, 37-38. On 21st Tenn. Reg. CSArmy, 1862-2863.

226 **CARSON, Kathleen Daugette**
"Alabama Memorials at Vicksburg." In: AHQ, 1949, v.9, p. 352-360.

227 **CARSON, Robert T. & L.D.**
"Letter from Robert T. Carson, St. Matthews Rifle Eutaw Regt., James Island to his mother, March 6, 1863. Mrs. Eva Baker (owner) Bristol, Fla." Copies by Historical Records Survey State Archives Survey. April, 1937." (Bound-in)..."Letter from L.D. Carson Walker Hospital, Columbus, Ga. to his mother Nov. 27, 1864. Mrs. Eva Baker (owner) Bristol, Florida." 4to, stiff boards, (2), (3)pp. $15.

228 **CARSON, William Waller**
"Joseph Carson (1843-1902), Louisiana Confederate soldier. Edt: John Q. Anderson." In: La. Hist., Winter 1960, v.1, p. 44-69, notes. Reminiscences (1917) of service of author & brother Joseph, the latter in 28th Miss. Cavalry, both in 4th La. Cavalry, 1862-1865.

229 **CARTA PASTORAL que El Illmo. Sr.**
Obispo de Linares Dirije a Los Fieles Catolicos de la Parroquia de Santa Barbara. Brownsville, Texas. Imprenta Del. "Centinela Del Rio Grande." 1861. 8vo, sewn, 8pp. (C. Dorman David) $125.

230 **CARTER HOUSE, Franklin Tennessee.**
See: Will Spencer McGann, Sergeant Newton Cannon, John W. Copley, S.A. Cunningham, Daniel M. Robison.

231 **CARTER, Dan T.**
"When the war was over: the failure of self-Reconstruction in the South, 1865-1867." Baton Rouge: Louisiana State University Press, 1985. 8vo, cl, dj, xiv, 285pp. (paper-$13), $27.50

232 **CARTER, George E.**
"A Note on Jefferson Davis in Canada-His Stay in Lennoxville, Quebec. (Jackson, Miss.) Jour. Miss. Hist. May, 1971, v.XXXIII, #2, p. 133-139.

233 **CARTER, Hodding**
"Robert E. Lee & the Road of Honor." N.Y., Random House (1955). 12mo, cl, d/w, Landmark Books, tint, illus., 186pp. 8th printing. $1.95.

234 ..."Their words were bullets, the Southern Press in War, Reconstruction, & Peace." Athens, Ga., University Press, 1969. 8vo, wraps, 78pp. $8.

235 **CARTER, Howell**
"A Cavalryman's Reminiscences of the Civil War." New Orleans (La.) American Print. (c.1900) (Frontispiece, "The Author 1900.") 12mo, pict. cl, 30-ports, 212pp. $35, $12.50, $18.50, $75 nc-'76, $125 bmk, $110, $175 bmk. 1st. La. Cavalry muster roll & the Army of Tenn.

236 ..."The Pelican Boys in Gray & their Inspiration. Thoughts Suggested at a Con-

federate Re-union at the Louisiana State University Grounds, Baton Rouge, La." (Baton Rouge) "The Felicianas" (1905?) narrow 12mo, title cover, 10pp. Poem.
..."Cavalryman's Reminiscences of the Civil War." Baton Rouge, La., FPHC, Inc. Reprint $11.50.

237 **CARTER, J.H., Capt.**
"Sixty-nine Federals in sight of their Army captured by seven Confederates." In: SHSP, 1880, v.VIII, p. 122-123.

238 **CARTER, Rosalie**
"Captain Tod Carter-Confederate States Army." Franklin, Tenn., Carter Crafts, 4to, stiff wraps, 60pp. $6.50.

239 **CARTER, Samuel, III**
"The Final Fortress, the Campaign for Vicksburg, 1862-1863." N.Y., St. Martins Press, 1980. 8vo, cl, dj, illus., 384pp. $20-y.
...Wilmington, N.C., Broadfoot Pub., reprint. 8vo, cl, 384pp. $25.

240 ..."The Siege of Atlanta, 1864." N.Y., St. Martin's Press (1973). 8vo, cl, dj, map-endsheets, maps,
...N.Y., Bonanza, (1973), $8.50, $15.

241 ..."The Riddle of Dr. Mudd." N.Y., G.P. Putnam's Sons, (1974). 8vo, cl, dj, facsm., illus., ports, map liners, 380pp. op. $8.95.

242 ..."The Last Cavaliers-Confederate & Union Cavalry in the Civil War." N.Y., St. Martin's Press (1979). 8vo, cl, & boards, dj, facsms, illus., maps, ports, (5), xiii, 338pp., bibliog. index. $16.
...1969 First Edt. $10.

242a **CARTER, Sidney**
"Dear Bet, the Carter Letters, 1861-3, the letters of Sidney Carter, Co. A, 14th Reg. S.C. Vols., Gregg-McGowan's Brig., CSA, to Ellen Timmons Carter. Edt. Bessie Mell Lane." Greenville, S.C., Keys Print, 1978. 8vo, cl, xxv, 165pp, facsms, ills, map, port on cover. Muster roll.

243 **CARTER, Sidney, Lt., & Ellen**
See: Edt-Bessie Mell Lane.

244 **CARTER, Thomas Henry, Col.**
"The Bloody Angle, letter of Colonel Thomas H. Carter." In: SHSP, 1893, v.XXI, p. 239-242.

245 ..."Captured guns at Spotsylvania Court-House, a letter from Colonel T.H. Carter." In: SHSP, 1879, v.VII, p. 540.

246 ..."The Gettysburg Campaign. Report of Colonel T.H. Carter, Aug. 5, 1863." In: SHSP, 1882, v.X, p. 65-67.

247 ..."Letter of Colonel Thomas H. Carter, Apr. 14, 1899, re: General R.S. Ewell." In: SHSP, 1914, v.XXXIX, p. 5-7.

248 **CARTER, William Harding, Maj. Gen.**
"General Robert E. Lee (A Lee Miscellany)" In: Va. MH, Oct. 1925, v.XXXIII, p. 371-382.

249 **CARTER, William Page**
"Rodes' Brigade at Seven Pines (Poem)." In: SHSP, 1905, v.XXXIII, p. 288-289.

250 **CARTER, William, of Defiance, Ohio.**
"Joint Resolutions concerning the usurpation of Congress & their encroachments upon other depts. of the Federal Gov." 58th Gen. Assembly, Reg. Sess., S.J.R. 46. (Columbus, Ohio, 1860) Broadsheet 14x8 1/2" $10. Pro-southern resolution, on eve of War. "attempt to make negro an element of political power in U.S., a servile imitation of British example in West Indies & brings contempt on Republican institutions.

251 **CARTWRIGHT, Samuel A., Dr.**
"Essays, being Inductions drawn from the Baconian Philosophy proving the Truth of the Bible & the justice & benevolence of the decree dooming Canaan to the Servant of Servants." 1843. Natchez, Miss., Vidalia, opposite Natchez, 8vo, wraps, 68pp. Also an essay "Prognathous Species of Mankind", in Eric McKitrick's "Slavery Defended."

252 ..."The pro-slavery arguments of Dr. Samuel A. Cartwright." In: La., 1968, v.9, p. 209-227.

253 **CARY, Clarence Fairfax**
"The War Journal of Midshipman Cary, Edts: Brooks Thompson & Frank Lawrence Owsley, Jr." In: CWH, June 1963, v.IX, #2, p.187-202, map.

254 **CARY, Harriette**
"Diary of Miss. Harriette Cary, kept by her from May 6, 1862, to July 24, 1862." In: TQHGM, Oct. 1927, v.IX, p. 104-115. $15-br.
..."Diary of Miss Harriet Cary." In: TylerQHGM, 1931, v.XII, p. 160-173. Cont'd. from v.IX, 1928. Civil war diary in & around Williamsburg, Va.

255 **CARY, R. Milton**
"Skirmisher's Drill & Bayonet Exercise (as now used in the French Army)." Richmond, Va., West & Johnston, 1861. 16mo, limp boards, 56pp. cover-cut shows soldier in action with bayonet. $300-bmk. This edition varies from Crandall-2401 in pagination & identifies Cary as "Capt. F. Company, 1st Regiment, Va. Vols."

256 **CARY, Wilson Miles**
"From the diary of WMC." In: Tyler's Qr. 1942/1943, v.24, p. 106-109. Diary: April 2-3, 1865.

257 **CASADA, James A.**
"A history of the 48th Virginia Infantry Virginia Volunteer Army of the Confederate." In: Hist. Soc. Washington Co., Va. Ser.II, #7, Winter-Spring, 1968-1969. p. 5-38. Abingdon, Va., offprint, 42pp. 1969. $5, $10.

258 **CASDORPH, Paul Douglas**
"The Bogus Texas Delegation to the 1860 Republican National Convention." In: SwHQ, April, 1962, v.LXV, #4, p. 480-486.

259 **CASE OF THE SEIZURE**
Of the Southern Envoys. Reprinted, with additions, from the "Saturday Review." London: James Ridgway, 1861. 8vo, wraps, 26pp.

260 **"CASE OF THE TRENT EXAMINED..."**
London: James Ridgway, 1862. 8vo, wraps, 24pp. Sabin-11317-11318.

261 **CASE, Leverette N.**
"Personal recollections of the siege of Petersburg by a Confederate officer--(P.C. Hay)", read Apr. 1, 1897, War papers Commandery State of Michigan, MOLLUS (Detroit, 1897?) v.2, p. 153-166.

262 **CASEY, Powell A.**
"Early history of the Washington artillery of New Orleans." In: La. H.Q., 1940, v.XXIII, p. 471-484. Seen service in every war of US, last 100 years.
..."The story of Camp Moore." Baton Rouge, La., FPHC, Inc, 1985. 8vo, wraps, x, 158pp., illus., maps. Named for Gov. Thos. O. Moore of La.

264 **CASEY, Silas**
"Infantry tactics, for the instruction, exercise, & maneuveres of the soldier, a company, line of skirmishes, battalion, brigade or corps D'Armee. By Brig-Gen. Silas Casey, USArmy. Vol. III. Evolutions of a brigade & corps D'Armee." Charleston, S.C., Evans & Cogswell, 1864. 16mo, cl, 160pp., 29 litho plates. (Edts: NY-1863, $150; Phila. 1862, $150, Crandall-2403. Yates Snowden notes he saw only v.III. (reprint) possibly only one republished. Gen. Thos. Jordan of Gen. Beauregard's staff requested that it be republished. To supplement Hardee.

265 **CASH, W.T.**
"Taylor County history & Civil War deserters." In: FlaHQ, July 1948, v.27, p. 28-58. Reviews history of Taylor Co., Fla. 1839-1865.

266 **CASH, Wilbur Joseph**
"The Mind of the South." N.Y., Alfred Knopf, Feb. 10, 1941. 8vo, cl, d/w, XI, 429,

index-xvpp. $100.

...Reprinted, five times.

...1954, N.Y., Doubleday Anchor Books A-27. 444pp.

...June 1965-seventh printing. $6.

267 **CASKEY, Thomas W.**
"The Oxford(Miss.) Hospital, 1862. Edt. by Willie D. Halsell." In: JNH, 1946, v.VIII, p. 36-44.

268 **CASKEY, Willie Malvin**
"Secession & restoration by Louisiana." Foreword: Frank Lawrence Owsley. University, La., La. State Univ. Pr., 1938. 8vo, cl, xi, (1), 318pp., 9-maps, half-title: La. State Univ. Studies, #36, bibliog: 301-309. N.Y., DaCapo Press, 1970. $12.50, $25-bmk, $10.

269 **CASKIE, Jaquelin Ambler**
"Life & Letters of Matthew Fontaine Maury." Richmond, Va., Richmond Press, 1928. 12mo, cl, port(front), pl, 191pp. $8, $16.50, $40-bmk-105, $20-bmk-105, $75.

270 **CASLER, John Overton**
"Four Years in the Stonewall Brigade, by..., Private, Company A, 33rd Regiment Virginia Infantry, Stonewall Brigade, 1st Division, 2nd Corps., Army of Northern Virginia, Gen. Robt. E. Lee, commanding..." Guthrie, Oklahoma, State Capital Print, 1893. 12mo, cl, illus., ports, facsms (& foldg.) 495pp. $100-bmk, $350-bmk-105, $450-jk, $50, $65, $75, $100, $140-y.

..."Four Years in Stonewall Brigade, by... Ex-commander Oklahoma Division, U.C.V." Private Company A, 33rd Reg. Va. Inf. Stonewall Brigade, 1st Div., 2nd Corps, A.N.V., Gen. Robert E. Lee, commanding. With illustrations. Containing the daily experiences of four year's service in the ranks from a diary kept at the time. A truthful record of the battles & skirmishes, advances, retreats & maneuvers of the army. Of incidents as they occurred on the march, in the field, in bivouac & in battle, on the scout, in hospital, prison. Replete with thrilling adventures & hair-breadth escapes." Second Edition, revised, corrected & improved by Maj. Jed Hotchkiss, topographical engineer, 2nd Corps, Army of Northern Virginia." Girard, Kansas, Appeal Pub. Co., 1906. 12mo, cl, (or, stiff wraps), illus., ports, facsms, (7), 365pp. $47.50, $55, $75, $90, $100. $350 b-124, $300-bmk, $300-jk

...Marietta, Georgia., Continental Book Co., 1951, Reprint 2nd Edt. $9.50, $15, $25-bmk-84.

...Morningside Bookshop-Dayton, Ohio, 1971. 12mo, cl, dj, map endsheets, xvi, 362, (8)pp. Foreword: James I. Robertson, Jr. $10, $15, $20.

271 **CASON, Charles**
"The Confederate soldier & the South's call to youth; address delivered at the Annual Confederate Reunion, Rome, Tenn., Sept. 1911." Nashville, McQuiddr Print, 1911. 8vo, wraps, 15pp. port.

272 **CASS, Michael M.**
"Charles C. Jones, Jr. & the "Lost Cause." In: Ga. H.Q., Summer, 1971, v.LV, #2, p. 222-233.

273 **CASSEDAY, Morton M.**
"The Surrender of Fort Donelson." In: SB, ns, v.II, 1886/1887, p. 694-697.

274 **CASSELMAN, A.B.**
"The numerical strength of the Confederate Army." In: Cent. Mag., 1892, v.XLIII, p. 792-796; 1892, v.XLIV, p. 957-959; his rejoiner to Joseph T. Derry's "Sou. view of the question, same, p. 956-957. See: Randolph H. McKim.

..."The numerical strength of the Confederate Army." In: Cent., April 1892, v.21, p. 792-796.

275 ..."Casselman's rejoinder to Joseph T. Derry's "Southern view" in Cent., Oct. 1892, v.22, p. 956-959.

276 **CASSIDY, Vincent H. & Amos E. Simpson**
"Henry Watkins Allen of Louisiana." Baton Rouge, La., State Univ. Pr. (1964) 8vo, cl, d/w, vii, 201pp. port. $8-y, $5, $30, $6.

277 ..."The Travelling Man; the life story of Henry Watkins Allen." Baton Rouge: Claitor's Book Store, 1967, 8vo, cl, 79pp., illus., port. $2.

278 **CASTEL, Albert**
"Earl Van Dorn-the loser at Corinth." In: CWTI, April 1967, v.VI, #1, p. 38-42, illus., port.

279 ..."Fiasco at Helena, everything went wrong for the CSA in ill-fated campaign to sieze this Arkansas river port." In: CWTI, Aug. 1968, v.VII, #5, p. 12-17, illus., map, ports.

280 ..."Fort Sumter-1861" In: CWTI-Entire Issue..Oct. 1976, #6, v.17, p. 50. illus., facsm., ports.

281 ..."Theophilus Holmes-pallbearer of the Confederacy." In: CWTI, July 1977, v.16, #4, p. 10-17, illus., map, ports.

282 ..."Victory at Corinth." In: CWTI, Oct. 1978, v.17, #6, p. 12-22, illus., map, ports.

283 ..."The Historian & the General: Thomas L. Connelly versus Robert E. Lee." In: CWH, March 1970, v.XVI, #1, p. 50-63. (See: Connelly's CWH, v.XV, p. 132.)

284 ..."The Jayhawkers & Copperheads of Kansas." In: CWH, June 1959, v.V< #3, p. 283-293.

285 ..."Quantrill's Bushwhackers: a Case Study in Partisan Warfare." In: CWH, March 1967, v.XIII, #1, p. 40-50.

286 ..."Kansas Jayhawking Raids into Western Missouri in 1861." (Columbia, Ma., Mo. Hist. Review, Oct., 1959, v.LIV, #1, p. 1-11, illus., ports.

287 ..."A New View of the Battle of Pea Ridge." (Columbia, Mo., Mo. Hist. Review, Jan. 1968, v.LXII, #2, p. 136-151. ports, illus., map.

288 ..."Quantrill's Missouri Bushwhackers in Kentucky. The End of the Trail." In: FCHQ, April 1964, v.38, #2, p. 125-132.

289 ..."William Clarke Quantrill: His Life & Times." N.Y., Frederick Fell, Inc., 1962. 8vo, cl, d/w, 250pp. index. $6, $15-bow, $30-jk, $10.

290 ..."Quantrill in Texas." In: CWTI, June 1972, v.11, #3, p. 20-27, illus., ports.

291 ..."General Sterling Price & the Civil War in the West." Baton Rouge: Louisiana Univ. Press, 1968. 8vo, cl, d/w, illus., maps, xvi, 300pp. $8.95, $65-r, $25-bmk-11.

292 ..."The Fort Pillow Massacre: A Fresh Examination of the Evidence." In: CWH, March 1958, v.IV, #1, p. 37-50.

293 ..."The Siege of Lexington (Mo.)" In: CWTI, Aug. 1969, v.VIII, #5, p. 4-13, illus., map, port. Sterling Price captures 3500 Federals but strategically was useless.

294 ..."War & politics: the Price raid of 1864." In: KanHQ, 1958, v.XXIV, p. 129-143, illus.

294a ..."Mars & the Reverend Longstreet: or Attack & dying in the Civil War." In: CWT, June 1987, v.33, #2, p.103-14. Longstreet's pamphlet uncovered.
See: Under Rev. Augustus Baldwin

295 **CASTELMAN, T.W.**
"Report of...Commissioner of Louisiana Military Records to the Governor of the State of Louisiana, May 11, 1910." New Orleans: Schumert & Warfield, 1910. 8vo, wraps, 10pp. Relates to Booth's compilation of CSA Record of La. Soldiers.

296 **CASTLEMAN, John B.**
"Active Service, by Jno. B. Castleman, CSA-USA." Louisville, Ky., Courier-Journal Job Printing Co., 1917. sm.4to, cl, ports, illus., facsms, 369pp.(not counting 42 plates). $150 nc-'76, $45-y, $178 bmk-100, $10, $18, $20, $22.50, $25, $27.50, $35. With Morgan's Cavalry, detailed to

Canada in release CSA prisoners. $130-mil.hist.

297 **CASTLEN, Harriet Gift**
"Hope bids me onward...Biography of George Gift arranged by his daughter, from letters George Gift wrote to her mother before they were married." Savannah, Ga., Chatham Print, 1945. 8vo, cl, 198pp. Lt. Gift, CSN letters now in Ellen Shackleford Gift Papers, Univ. of N.C. Blockade, CSS "Arkansas", "Chattahoochee."

298 **CASTLES, Calvin C.**
"Reminiscences of an Old Confederate, anecdotes of Civil War, by C.C. Castles, Palestine, Texas. Only living spy of the Confederacy." (Palestine, Texas: Record Journal Print, 1912. 8vo, wraps, cover title, front(port) 24pp. TxU. $375-b

299 **CATALOGUE of Portraits**
& library of R.E. Lee Camp, No. 1, Confederate Veterans, Richmond, Va. Richmond, Va., 1911. 8vo, wraps, 11pp. $25-bmk.

300 **CATALOGUE of Rebel Flags**
Captured by Union Troops since April 19, 1861., deposited in the Ordnance Museum. (Washington, DC, n.d.) War Department. 8vo, wraps, 31pp. $22.50. Lists 540 flags & those who captured them.

301 **CATALOGUE of Relics**
In the history & relics room of Cape Fear chapter of the United Daughter of the Confederacy." n.p., n.d., 12mo, dec. wraps, 20pp.

302 **CATALOGUE of the Confederate**
Relic Room, Columbia, South Carolina. n.p., n.d. (c.1900) 8vo, wraps(pict.) 32pp. $4.

303 **CATALOGUE of the Confederate Museum**
Maintained by the United Daughters of the Confederacy. Texas Division. First floor of Museum building corner of Eleventh & Brazos. Austin, Texas. (c.1945) 8vo, wraps, color-flag seal, front, (8), 51pp. $5.

304 **CATALOGUE of the Confederate Museum,**
Maintained by the United Daughters of the Confederacy-Texas Division. Austin, Texas: 1st Floor Museum Bldg., 1935. 8vo, wraps, front, port, xiv, 64pp., supplement. 14pp, pasted in back. $10, $15.

305 **CATE, Margaret Davis**
"Mistakes in Fanny Kemble's Georgia Journal." In: Ga. H.Q., March 1960, v.XLIV, #1, p. 1-17, illus., port., map.

306 **CATE, Wirt Armistead**
"Lucius Q.C. Lamar, secession & reunion." Chapel Hill: Univ. of North Carolina Press, (1935). Tall 8vo, cl, illus., ports. (incl. front), xiii, 594pp. (An autographed Edt., 425 copies $15.) $5.(pub.), $6.50, $10, $12.50, $15-y. Lamar an officer in 19th Miss. Reg. CSA. US Senator, Sect. Interior, Assc. Justice, Supreme Ct. Book emphasizes his effort toward healing wounds between North & South after war.

307 ..."Lamar & the Frontier Hypothesis." Journ. Southern Hist., 1, p. 497-501. Is an amplification of the above book.

308 ..."Two Soldiers The Campaign Diaries of Thomas J. Key, CSA. Dec. 7, 1863-May 17, 1865, & Robert J. Campbell, USA. Jan. 1, 1864-July 21, 1864. Edited with an introduction, Notes & Maps by Wirt Armistead Cate." Chapel Hill: University of North Carolina Press, 1938. 8vo, cl, dj, maps, ports, facsms (incl. front) xiii, 277pp. $4.50, $8.50, $12.50, $30-y, $50-b, $35-bmk-105.
...Louisville: Lost Cause micro-cd. $4.79.

309 **CATECHISME IMPRIME Par Ordre**
de Monsig. Antoine Blanc, Archeveque de la Nouvelle-Orleans, Lib. Michon et Desportes, 166, Rue Royale, Ancien 200,

1861. Orig. bds., Verso t.p., Paris, Impr. de Edouard Blot, Rue St. Louis, 46) $25.

310 "CATECHISMO DE LA DOCTRINA CHRISTIANA."
Nueva-Orleans, La., 1864. 16mo, 1/2 Lt., 136pp. $17.50.

311 **CATER, Douglas John**
"As it Was", by D.J. Cater, Confederate Soldier. Edt: William D. Cater." San Antonio, Texas, 1981. 4to, typescript, paperbound, 270pp. 3rd Texas Cavalry & 19th Louisiana Infantry Regiment, at Wilson's Creek & Pea Ridge.

312 **CATHERWOOD, T.B.**
"The Confederate private soldier in camp & conflict. In addresses delivered before the Confederate Association of Savannah, Georgia, 1893." Savannah, Ga., Braid & Hutton, 1893. 8vo, wraps, 57-66. See: Confed. Vets. Ass'n., Savannah, Ga.

313 **CATHEY, Clyde**
"Battle of Pea Ridge." In: South. Mag., II, 1935, No.4, p. 29-30, 44.

314 ..."Slavery in Arkansas." In: AHQ, 1944, v.III, p. 66-90, 150-163. tables.

315 **CATHEY, Cornelius Oliver**
"The impact of the Civil War on agriculture in North Carolina (1861-1865). Edt: Joseph Carlyle Sitterson." In: Studies in Southern history (Chapel Hill, N.C., University of NC Press. 1957), p. 97-110. notes.

316 **CATHEY, James Harrison**
"Truth is Stranger than Fiction; or the True Genesis of a wonderful man." (Bryson City, N.C., Feb. 18, 1899) $10., 16mo, cl, illus., ports, incl. front, 185pp.
...Atlanta, Ga., Franklin Print, 1904, 3rd Edition. $20., 12mo, cl, (or wraps), ports, incl. front. 307pp. (first 185pp. same as 1899 edt.)
...Canton, N.C., 1939, new material 206pp. $40 -bmk, $25., N.C. tradition of Nancy Hanks' marriage to Abraham Enloe whose physical characteristics resembled that of Lincoln.

317 **CATLETT'S STATION**
See: J.C. Cooke, Richmond Dispatch (Stuart raid).

318 **CATO, A.Q., Dr.**
"A study in Artillery -Fort Pulaski." (Houston, Texas: Civil War Round Table, Address March 1956. 8 1/2 x 11, heavy paper covers, folded to 8vo. 11pp. $10-b.

319 **CATTON, Bruce**
"A Bibliography of the American Civil War." N.Y., New York & Pennsylvania Co., 1962. Oblong 4to, decr. stiff wraps, illus., 18pp, cover title. $7.50

320 ..."Black pawn on a field of peril. Dred Scott vs Sandford." In: Amer. Hert. Dec. 1963, v.XV, #1, p. 66-71, 90-91, ports.

321 ..."The famous Cyclorama of the great Battle of Atlanta." In: Amer. Hert., FEb. 1956, VII, #2, p. 32-45, ports, illus., incl. 5-dbl. pg. color, map.

322 ..."A Southern Artist (Volck) on the Civil War." In: Amer. Hert., Oct., 1958, IX, p. 117-120, sketches.

323 ..."Prison Camps of the Civil War-Andersonville was merely the worst of a bad lot, North & South alike-more lethal than shot & shell." In: Amer. Hert. Aug. 1959, X, #5, p. 4-13, 96-97. John T. Omenhausser color sketches, life at Point Lookout, Md. prison.

324 **CATTS, Samuel W.**
"Two Confederate surgeons." In: AHQ, 1947, v.7, #3, p. 352-354.

325 **CAUBLE, Frank P.**
"The proceedings connected with the surrender of the Army of Northern Virginia, April 1865." Appomattox Court House National Historical Park, 1962. Springfield, Va., Nat'l. Tech. Info. 4to, stiff wraps, 256, viii, p. $20. With all the conflicting reports presented.

326 **CAUSBY, Thomas Espy**
"Stoming the stone fence at Gettysburg." In: SHSP, 1901, v.XXIX, p. 339-341.

327 **"CAUSES of the Confederate War."**
See: John Archibald Campbell, Robert Lewis Dabney, Graham Daves, Robert M.T. Hunter, Julian I. Wells, Joseph Wheeler, Richard Grant White, Edwin Charles Rozwenc.

328 **CAUSES of the Defeat**
Of Gen. Lee's Army at the Battle of Gettysburg-Opinions of leading CSA soldiers. SHSP, v.4, p. 48-87. See: J.A. Early, A.L. Long, Fitz Lee, Wm. Allan, Walter H. Taylor, E.P. Alexander, John B. Hood, C.M. Wilcox, Henry Heth, Jas. H. Lane, Jas. Longstreet, Jno. S. Mosby, Count of Paris, Robt. M. Stribling, Jas. B. Waltor.

329 **"CAUSES of the War in the South."**
In: Confed. Annals, June 1883, v.1, #1, p. 5-20.

330 **CAUSEY, Jerry**
"Please Send Buttons": Correspondence from Confederate Mississippi." In: Manuscript Fall 1980, v.XXXII, p. 260-270.

331 ..."Selected correspondence of the Adjutant-General of Mississippi." In: JMH, Feb. 1981, v.XLIII, #1, p. 31-58.

332 **CAUTHEN, Charles Edward, Edt.**
"Family Letters of the Three Wade Hamptons 1782-1901." Columbia: University of South Carolina Press, 1953. 8vo, cl, dj, illus., facsms, ports, xix, 181pp. (CSA, p. 73-114) $5, $12.50, $15, $30pbmk. (South Caroliniana Sesquicentennial Series, #4.)

333 ..."South Carolina's decision to lead the Secession movement." In: N.C. Hist. Rev., 1941, v.XVIII, p. 360-372.

334 ..."South Carolina Goes to War 1860-1865." Chapel Hill: University of N.C. Press, 1950. (The James Sprunt Studies in Hist. & Political Science, vol. 32) 8vo, cl, vii, (1), 256pp. bibliog. 231-245, index, $4.50, $7.50, $8.50, $10, $15, $30-bmk-op, $17.50-y.

335 **CAUWET, Alfred**
"Les Confederes A Mon Ami, M.B.W.S....Du Mississippi(poem)" Paris: Imp. Dubuisson, 1864. 8vo, wraps, 4pp.

336 **CAVALIER SONGSTER, The**
Containing a splendid collection of original & selected songs. Compiled & arranged expressly for the Southern public. Crandall-3258. Staunton, Va., 1865. 6 1/2" tall, 48pp. Godspeed-$450. Shenandoah Valley songster with heroes as Ashby & Jackson.

337 **CAVALRY RAID, The**
By Custer, Kilpatrick & Dahlgren. In: SHSP, 1874, v.1, 155-175.

338 **CAVALRY TACTICS**
Single Rank Formations & Skirmish Drill for Mounted Rifles. For instruction of forces of the Confederate States, in the Department of Indian Territory. Boggy Depot, C.N., May, 1863. 16mo, wraps, 37pp., Crandall-753.
...Tulsa, Okla., Gilcrease Institute of American History & Art, 1965. reprint. $4.

339 **"CAVALRY of the Confederate War."**
In: SHSP, See: J.N. Dunlop, R.F. Gross, John Lamb, Fitzhugh Lee, Stephen D. Lee.

340 **CAVANAUGH, John**
"Historical Sketch of the Obion Avalanche Co. H., 9th Tennessee Infty., C.S.A." Union City, Tenn., Commercial Print, 1922. Titleheading: "Confederate Record." 8vo, wraps, 1p, 52pp. (Xerox print) Tenn State Library. See: Rebel C. Forrester's "Glory & Tears", reprint, p. 168-222.

341 **CAVE, Robert Catlett**
"Address at Unveiling of Soldiers & Sailors Monument." In: SHSP, 1894, v.XXII, p. 336-380.

342 ..."Ungenerous Criticism of Rev. Dr. R.C. Cave's Oration." (Above) In: SHSP, 1894, v.XXII, p. 381-186.

343 ..."Charles S. Stringfellow's reply to ungenerous criticism..." In: SHSP, 1894, v.XXII, p. 383-386.

344 ..."The Men in Gray." Nashville Tenn., Confederate Veteran, 1911. 12mo, cl, front(port)pl, 1-p. color flags. $10, $17.50, $30, $50-bmk-105.

345 **CAVELYN, Edward (pseud.)**
"Memories of some courageous Southerners, before & after the Civil War." Boston: Christopher Pub., (1940) 12mo, cl, 3pp., ix-xi, 13-66pp. Memories of author's father, mother, grandmother. His father going against prevailing sentiment of the South.

346 **CAVERLY, Robert B.**
"The Merrimac & its Incidents. An Epic Poem." Boston: Innes & Niles, 1866. 12mo, wraps, 80 lfs, 1-steel engr., 14-woodcuts. $15.

347 **CAVETT, E.D.**
"A Ring Tournament in 1864. A Letter from a Mississippian in the Army of Northern Virginia." Edt: Joseph C. Robert. (Jackson, Miss., Jour. of Miss. Hist., Oct., 1941, v.III, #4, p. 289-296.
...Reprint-8vo, wraps, 8pp, atg. $10-bmk.

348 **CAWTHON, John Ardis**
"The Inevitable Guest/Life & Letters of Jemima Darby." San Antonio, Texas: Naylor Co., (1965) 8vo, cl, dj, ports, illus., front, bibliog. index (369-412) xix, (8), 412pp. $10. Letters from South Carolina, between 1853-1883. copious notes.

349 **CEDAR CREEK, Battle of**
See: Saml. D. Buck, G.B. Gerald, Clarence R. Hatton, "C.S.M." surgeon CSA, J.S. McNeily, Marcellus N. Moorman.

350 **CEDAR MOUNTAIN, Battle of**
See: Wm. Allan, Richmond Times-"Battle of Cedar Run."

351 **CELEBRATION,**
Of the Seventy-fifth Anniversary of the Chatham Artillery of Savannah, May 1, 1861. Savannah (Ga.) John M. Cooper Co., 1861, 8vo, wraps, 65pp. Charles C. Jones oration, p. 9-62.

352 **CEMETERIES, Confederate Dead**
See: Burial of CSA dead.

353 **CENSER, Jane Turner**
"North Carolina Planters & their children, 1800-1860." Baton Rouge: Louisiana University, 1984. 8vo, cl, dj, xxv, 191pp., notes, maps, tables, append., bibliog., index. $20.

354 **CENTRAL CONFEDERACY, A**
"Effort made to establish a Central Confederacy in 1861. Efforts taken by Maryland's executive & others to form the proposed new government." In: SHSP, 1900, v.XXVIII, p. 144-148. States: Md., Pa., NY, NJ, Del., Va., Mo., & Oh.

355 **CENTRAL RAILROAD & BANKING CO., Georgia**
28th Annual Report of the Pres. & Supt., of, to the Stockholders. Macon, Georgia, 1862. 8vo, wraps, fldg. tables, 43pp. $15. Not in Crand/Harw/deRenne.

356 **CENTZ, P.C. (pseud.)**
See: Bernard J. Sage.

357 **CEREMONIES,**
At the unveiling of the South Carolina Monument in the Chickamauga Battlefield, May 27, 1901. Together with the Record of the Commission who suggested & were instrumental in erecting the Monument, etc... n.p., 1901. 12mo, wraps, 50pp. $7.50, $15. Addresses: Gov. McSweeney, Bishop Ellison Capers, Gen. Henry V. Boynton.

358 ..."Attending the dedication of the Virginia Memorial on the battlefield of Gettysburg, Friday, June eight, nineteen hundred & seventeen." (Richmond, Va., E. Waddey Co., 1917) 8vo, wraps, plates, ports, 48pp.

359 ..."Attending the Presentation & Unveiling of the North Carolina Memorial on the Battlefield of Gettysburg, Wednesday, July 3, 1929." (n.p., 1929?) 8vo, wraps, plates, 44pp. $20 bmk-95. Program of exercises presenting marker by N.C. Div., U.D.C., p. 25-44.

360 ..."Attending the unveiling, of the monument to the Confederate Dead of Florida at Jacksonville, June 16, 1898. Presented by Charles C. Hemming of Gainesville, Texas, formerly of Jacksonville, Fla., & a member of 3rd Fla. Infantry, CSA." Jacksonville, Fla., n.d. 8vo, wraps, 25pp. $7.50

361 ...In: SHSP, 1899, v.27, p. 109-131.

362 ...In Augusta, Georgia, Laying the Cornerstone of the Confederate Monument: with Oration by Gen. Clement A. Evans & Col. Charles C. Jones, Jr., Augusta, Ga., 1878." 8vo, wraps, 33pp. $10. See also: Chs. C. Jones. Similar titles.

363 ...Of Marking Confederate Graves, in Colquitt County, Georgia. In Commemoration of the War Between the States, Sunday, October 15, 1961." n.p., n.d. (1961). 12mo, oblong stiff blue wraps, ribbon-tied, seal, cover title, (12)pp. $1.50. Roster of all CSA buried in county, by towns. Sponsors: Colquitt Co. Civil War Centennial Committee.

364 ...Of unveiling the Confederate Monument, Augusta, Ga., Oct. 31, 1878." Broadside, 7x14" (old) $2. Address: Charles Colcock Jones, Jr., see also under C.C. Jones, 9pp. pamphlet.

365 ...Attending the unveiling of the monument erected by Colonel Thomas W. Smith at Suffolk, Va., to the memory of the Confederate dead on Thursday, Nov. 14, 1889. Including incidents addresses, description of the monument, etc. (Suffolk, Va., 1890?) 8vo, wraps, 28pp.
...Reprint: Suffolk, Va., Robt. Hardy Pub., 1986. 8vo, wraps, 28pp., facsm. t/p.

366 **CHADICK, W.D., Mrs.**
"Civil war days in Huntsville." In: AHQ, 1947, v.9, #2, p. 199-333.

367 **CHADSEY, Charles Ernest**
"The Struggle between President Johnson & Congress over Reconstruction." N.Y., 1896. Columbia University Studies in History, Economics & Public Law. v.VIII, #1. 8vo, wraps, pp. vi-142. $11.50-y, $7.50.

368 **CHADWICK, French E.**
"The organization of the Confederate Navy." In: Photo. Hist. CW, v.6, p. 71-90, illus., ports.

369 ..."The Confederate Cruisers & the "Alabama"." In: Photo. Hist. CW, v.6, p. 287-306.

370 **CHADWICK, W.D., Mrs.**
"Civil War Days in Huntsville (Ala.) as taken from the Diary of..., which appeared in irregular editions of the "Huntsville Times", 3rd edition. $.10." Heading: "The Huntsville Times-North Alabama's Leading Newspaper." (Huntsville, Ala. (193?), n.d. Folio, cover title, 14, (2)pp. $5, $10, $20-b.

371 **CHAFFIN, William W.**
"John Warwick Daniel's speech honoring Robert E. Lee, Lexington, Va., 1883." In: South. Speech Jour., Summer 1960, v.25, p. 305-313.

372 **CHAILLE, Stanford Emerson, Dr.**
"Intimidation & the number of white & colored voters in Louisiana in 1876, as shown by statistical data derived from Republican official reports." New Orleans, La., Picayune Print, 1877. 8vo, wraps, 36pp. $125-jk-129.

373 **CHALARON, J.A., Capt.**
"Battle Echoes from Shiloh." In: SHSP, 1893, v.XXI, p. 215-224.

374 ..."Hood's Campaign at Murfreesboro." In: Confed. Vet., Oct. 1903, v.XI, p. 438-440.

375 ..."The Washington Artillery in the Army of Tennessee." An address by..." In: SHSP, 1883, v.XI, p. 217-222.

376 **CHALMERS, Anna Mead**
"Brown & Arthur: an episode from "Tom Brown's school days." Arranged for the press by A Mother. Richmond: West & Johnston, 1861. 16mo, cl, xvi, (17)-184pp. (old)$7.75. Not in Crandall/Harwell. Swem-842a.

377 **CHALMERS, James Ronald, Gen.**
"Forrest & His Campaigns." In: SHSP, 1879, v.VII, p. 451-486. $10, $15 bmk-109.

378 ..."General Chalmers' report of operations of Cavalry Division on Line of Memphis & Charleston RR from 5th to 13th October, 1863. Oct. 20, 1863. Hdq. North Mississippi." In: SHSP, 1880, v.VIII, p. 222-229.

379 ..."Capture of Fort Pillow-Vindication of General Chalmers by a Federal Officer." In: SHSP, 1879, v.VII, p. 439-441.
..."Forrest & his campaigns." Robert Hardy Pubs., 1986. 8vo, wraps, 40pp.

380 **CHAMBERLAIN, Hope Summerell**
"Old days in Chapel Hill, being the life & letters of Cornelia Phillips Spencer." Chapel Hill: University of N.C. Press, 1926. 8vo, cl, x, 3-lfs., 325pp., illus., incl. front, ports. Good study of Chapel Hill during the war & reconstruction. Thornton-1967. $20.

381 **CHAMBERLAIN, Joshua Lawrence, Gen.**
"The Last Salute of the Army of Northern Virginia. Details of the Surrender of General Lee at Appomattox Courthouse, April 9, 1865. Lenient terms of Gen. Grant. In: SHSP, 1904, v.XXXII, p. 355-363.

382 **CHAMBERLAINE, William W., 6th Reg. Va. Infty.**
"Memoirs of the civil war between the northern & southern sections of the United States of America." Washington, D.C., B.S. Adams, 1912. 8vo, cl, front(port) 138pp. $20, $45, $200-fine, $650-b-139, $500 bmk-105.
...Do: Louisville, Ky.: Lost Cause Pr., micro-cd. $3.26.

383 **CHAMBERLAYNE, Edwin H.**
"War History & Roll of the Richmond Fayette Artillery, 38th Va. Battalion Artillery, C.S.A., 1861-1865." Richmond: Everett Waddey, 1883. 8vo, wraps, 23pp. $15, $28.50, $100, $250-ob.

384 ..."Record of the Richmond City & Henrico County, Va., Confederate States Army (series #(1)-10. Compiled by... Sergt. "D" Co., 1st Va. Regt. Inf. C.S.A." Richmond: Wm. Ellis Jones, Printer, 1879. (1-2: Henry Schott, p. 16, 8); #3: J.W. Ferguson & Son; #4: Baughman Bros.; #5: Jas. E. Goode. $50 bmk-84; #6-7: Geo. W. Gary (p. 13, 9); #8(8pp.) thru #10: 1883. Folding table. I-Vol. All 10 Series & Fayette Art. $750 bmk-105.
..."Record of the Richmond City & Henrico County Virginia troops, Confederate States Army, Series #6, self wraps. 8vo. $75-r

385 **CHAMBERLAYNE, John Hampden**
"Ham Chamberlayne-Virginian; letters & papers of an artillery officer in the war for southern independence, 1861-1865; with introduction, notes & index, by his son C.G. Chamberlayne." Richmond, Va., Press of Dietz Printing, 1932. 8vo, cl, front, plates, ports, maps (2-fldg.), facsms., xxx, 440pp., 1000 copies, signed, but some copies unsigned. $6, $7.50, $10, $12.50, $15, $135-r, $100, $75-bmk, $65-mcm, $40-bmk, $50-bmk, $35, $20, $27.50, $30.
...Louisville, Ky: Lost Cause Press, microfilm reproduction. $6.59.

386 **CHAMBERLAYNE, John Hampden, Capt.**
"Address on the character of General R.E. Lee, Delivered in Richmond, Jan. 19,

1876, on Anniversary of Lee's Birth." In: SHSP, 1877, v.III, p. 28-37.

387 **CHAMBERS, Henry A., Capt.**
"Civil War diary. Edt.: T.H. Pearce, with a biographical sketch by Selby A. Daniels." Wendell, N.C., Broadfoot Pub., 1983, 8vo, cl, 348pp., illus. $25.

388 **CHAMBERS, Lenoir**
"Notes on life in occupied Norfolk, 1862-1865." In: VMHB, Apr. 1965, v.73, #2, pl, pl. 131-144, ports.

388a ..."Stonewall Jackson." Reprint. Wilmington, N.C., Broadfoot Pub., 1988. 8vo, 2 vol. $60.

388b **CHANCE, CHANCE & TOPPER**
"Tangled machinery & charred relics: the historical & archaeological investigation of the C.S.S. Nashville." Orangeburg, 1985. 4to, color wraps, 267pp, ills, 1,000 copies. History of boat, archaeological work, dives & artifacts, legal difficulties. $35.

389 **CHANCE, Joseph E.**
"The Second Texas Infantry; from Shiloh to Vicksburg." Austin, Tex., Eakin Press, (1984). 8vo, cl, xiv, 216pp., illus., bibliog. (195)-211pp.

390 ..."The Texas Second Infantry: from Shiloh to Vicksburg." Austin, Texas: Eakin Press, 1984, 8vo, cl, dj, xiv, 216pp. $14.

391 **CHANCELLOR, Sue M., Mrs.**
"Personal recollections of the battle of Chancellorsville." In: RKHS, April 1968, v.66, #2, p. 137-146. Chancellorsville, not a village but a country home (Fannie Underwood was a great-granddaughter of Wm. Underwood, a member of House of Burgesses 1652 & husband of a great granddaughter of Pocahontas.

392 **CHANDLER, Greene Callier**
"Journal & speeches of Greene Callier Chandler, 1829-1905." Foreword: Walter Chandler. (Memphis, Tenn?) 1954(c.1953) 8vo, cl, coat of arms, ports, (8), 244, (1)p. Early life in Miss., officer in CSArmy, Miss. Assembly.

393 **CHANDLER, Hatchett**
"Little gems from Fort Morgan." (Foley, Ala., Howell Pub. Co., 1953. 8vo, wraps, 105pp. $35. Fort Morgan in Mobile Bay, Ala.

394 ...Fort Morgan, Ala., The Author, 1960. 8vo, wraps, 84pp. $25.

395 **CHANDLER, Porter R.**
"How my grandfather (Ralph Chandler) nearly lost the Civil War. (USS "San Jacinto" vs CSS "Alabama", Nov. 1862)." In: Amer. Neptune, Jan. 1973, p. 5-15.

396 **CHANDLER, Robert J.**
"The Release of the "Chapman" Pirates: A California sidelight on Lincoln's Amnesty Policy." In: CWH, June 1977, v.23, #2, p. 129-143.

397 **CHANDLER, Walter**
"Diplomatic history of the Southern Confederacy." In: CV, Dec. 1922, v.XXX, p. 453-458.

398 **CHANNING, Edward**
"The War for Southern Independence." N.Y., Macmillan & sons, 1925. 8vo, cl, illus., maps (part fldg.) vii, 645pp. v.VI of "A Hist. of the U.S."

399 **CHANNING, Steven A.**
"Crisis of Fear. Secession in South Carolina." N.Y., Simon & Schuster (1970) 8vo, cl, d/w, 315pp., map, ports, bibliog. (295)-308pp. paper-$5, $15, $8, $20-b, $12-nc-84, $3.

400 ..."Confederate ordeal: the Southern homefront." N.Y., Time-Life Books, 1984. Civil war series. $20. 8vo, Kivar bnd., gilt edges, marbled endsheets.

401 **CHAPALA, John D.**
"42nd Virginia Infantry." Lynchburg, Va. H.E. Howard, 1983. (J.P. Bell Print) Lim. Atg. Edt. $17.50. 8vo, cl, (5), 149pp. maps, ports.

402 **CHAPIN, E.Y.**
"Stonewall Jackson & Trust, Chattanooga, Tenn." In: CV, 1931, v.39, p. 254-261.

403 **CHAPIN, Sallie F. Moore, Mrs.**
"Fitz-Hugh St. Clair, the South Carolina Rebel Boy; or, It Is No Crime to Be Born a Gentleman." Philadelphia: Claxton, Remsen & Haffelfinger, Charleston, S.C., John M. Greer & Son, 1872. 12mo, cl, 252pp., illus., $8.50.
...Do: Philadelphia, 1873. Novel, against North. (old)$3., $10.

404 **CHAPLA, John D.**
"Quartermaster operations in the Forty-second Virginia Infantry Regiment." In: CWH, Mar. 1984, v.30, #1, p. 5-30.

405 **CHAPLAIN, C.T. & J.M. Keeling**
"Operations on the Blackwater River." In: CV, August, 1919, v.XXVII, p. 304-305. Fed. expd., Sept., 1862, against Franklin, Va., on Blackwater River.

406 **CHAPLAINS in the CSA**
See: Robert E. Bearden; Judah P. Benjamin; Benjamin J. Blied; G. McLaren Brydon; Alex Davis Betts; T. Conn Bryan; Army N. Va. Chaplains; Joseph B. Cheshire; Church in the CSA; Walter B. Capers; W. Harrison Daniel; Rev. Nicholas A. Davis; Wm. E. Dunston; Bishop Stephen Elliott; Mike Gannon; Wilson Gregg; Slex. Gregg; Edna H. Fowler; Jospeh Cross; Wm. Thos. Hall; Jno. Wm. Jones; John Lipscomb Johnson; Bertram W. Korn; Lawrence F. London; Bishop Henry A. Lay; Wm. A. Love; Mrs. Sue F. Mooney; Herman Norton; Edgar L. & Lawrence Pennington; Joseph J. Pitts; Beulah M. Price; Bishop John & Charles Todd Quintard; John Quinlan; Sidney Romero; Archibald Thomas Robertson; Roy H. Schmandt; James Sheeran; John Shepard; James W. Silver; Anthony Toomer; Geo. G. Smith; Richard H. Smith; Bishop August Verot; Art. L. Walker; Robert L. Dabney.

407 **CHAPLIN, Jane Dunbar, Mrs.**
"Out of the Wilderness." Bost: Henry A. Young & Co., 1870. 12mo, cl, 330pp. (WrightII-490) Plantation problems during civil war & lives of a slave family after war.

408 **CHAPMAN, Fanny B.**
"Battle of Marianna, Fla." In: CV, Oct. 1911, v.XIX, p. 483-484. See: Mark Boyd.

409 **CHAPMAN, John Abney**
"History of Edgefield County from the Earliest Settlements to 1897, biographical & Anecdotal; with sketches of the Seminole War; Nullification; secession; reconstruction; churches & literature; with roll of all the companies from Edgefield in the War of Secession. War with Mexico & with the Seminole Indians." Newberry, S.C., E.H. Aull Print, 1897. 8vo, cl, fldg. map, 521, vi. $18-y, $65-bmk. Spartanburg, S.C., Reprint Co., 1980, new index. $30.

410 **CHAPMAN, Katherine Hopkins**
"Sketch of Dr. LaFayette Guild, Medical Director & Chief Surgeon of the Army of Northern Virginia." $6.50, $9.50. (Charleston, S.C., Mar. 24, 1909) 8vo, wraps, n.d., 21pp. (1)p. addenda. See also: James M. Phalen, Emmett B. Carmichael.

411 **CHAPMAN, Robert Duncan**
"A Georgia Soldier in the Civil War, 1861-1865." Houston, Texas, (1923). 12mo, stiff wraps, 108, (1)pp., 2-ports. Co. "E", 55th Ga. Regt. $12.50, $18.50, $32.50, $35, $65-jk-117, $175-jk-138, $200-b.
...Louisville: Lost Cause Micro-cd.
...(Little Rock, Ark., Gen. T.J. Churchill, Chap. U.D.C., 1932. Reprint(Coulter-76)
...(Houston, Texas, Harry G. Wood, c.1929) 8 1/2x14", reprint from typed copy, printed one side, 36pp. Blue paper covers, with port, dated: 1839-1929. (Emory)

..."A Georgia Soldier, CSA." In: CV, 1930, v.38, p. 230-232, 270-272, 308-311, 347-350, 390-393, 431-433, 470-473.

412 ..."Confederate Treasury Notes: the chemicograbachs." In: Numismatist, April 1960, v.73, p. 403-411. Agreement between S. Straker(London) & Jos. Walker, CSAgent, to produce plates for printing backs of $5, $10-50, & $100 & $500 notes. 1 Sept., 1863. Describes designs, why never used & reproduces a print for each back & accounts for word-"chemicographed."

413 ..."The mysterious chemicograph backs of Confederate Currency (1863-1864)." In: Numismatist, Mar. 1950, v.63, p. 123-129. Views. Offprint. Auct-$15.

414 ..."C.S.A. Issues of 1861 in Panorama." Reprint from "Numismatist 1962. 8vo, wraps, illus., 23pp. $1.50.

415 ..."A mystery of Confederate Treasury notes unraveled: varities of the $10 note 'Hope with anchor' type #124/5." In: Numismatist, Feb. 1952, v.65, p. 130-138. facsms.

416 ..."Paper Money of the Confederacy: new findings of counterfeit & bogus Confederate Treasury Notes." In: Numismatist, October, 1951, v.64:1080-1092, facsms.

417 **CHAPPELL, Jimmie**
"General Albert Sidney Johnston." In: AHC, 1952, v.14, #1, & 2, p. 109-114.

418 **CHASE of the Rebel Steamer of war "Oreto", The**
Commander J.N. Maffitt, CSN, into the Bay at Mobile, by the US Steam sloop "Oneida", Comm. Geo. Henry Preble USN, Sept. 4, 1862." Cambridge: Private circulation, 1862. 8vo, wraps, 60pp.
...Cambridge: Allen Farnham Pr. 1862. 8vo, wraps, 48pp. Sabin-12217.

419 **CHASE, William C.**
"Story of Stonewall Jackson. A Narrative of the Career of Thomas Jonathan (Stonewall) Jackson, From Written & Verbal Accounts of His Life. Approved by his Widow Mary Anna Jackson." etc. Atlanta, Ga., D.E. Luther Pub. Co., 1901. 4to, full red Mor., pix of Jackson on cover, illus., ports, facsm. 569pp. gilt edges. $10, $225-bmk-121.

420 **CHASE, William Henry**
"The Secession of the Cotton States; its status; its advantages & its power." (Pensacola, 1860?) 12mo, wraps, 8pp. UWF. Two letters addressed to N.Y. Express & (Pensacola?) Observer, Oct. 22, 1860. Reprint: DeBow's Review, v.30, (Jan.1861) p. 93-101.

421 **CHATHAM ARTILLERY COMPANY:**
"Celebration of the 75th Anniv. "Historical Sketch Savannah vol. Chs. C. Jones' Chatham Artly." John E. Ward, John F. Wheaton.

422 **CHATHAM ARTILLERY, The**
One-hundred & seventy-fifth Anniversary Celebration, May 5 $ 6, 1961. Savannah, Ga., (1961?) 8vo, wraps, cover title, illus., (unpaged) See: Charles Colcock Jones.
..."The Chatham Artillery." In: CV, Jan., 1922, v.XXX, p. 22-24. Chatham Artillery of Savannah, Ga.

423 **CHATTAHOOCHEE VALLEY Historical Society.**
"War Was the Place; a Centennial Collection of Confederate soldier letters. Old Oak Bowery, Chambers Co., Alabama. (Alexander City, Ala., Outlook Pub. Co.) (n.p.) 1961. bulletin #5. 8vo, stiff wraps, illus., map, 198pp.

424 ..."Pioneer Members & History of Temple Beth-El 1859-1959." n.p. 8vo, stiff wraps, 47pp. Muster Roll of West Point Guards (p. 46-47)$12, $10-bmk

425 **CHAUDRON, Adelaide De Vendel**
"Chaudron's Spelling Book, carefully prepared for family & school use." Mobile, Ala., S.H. Goetzel, 1865. 12mo, wall-paper

covers, illus., 48pp. $200. cover title: 5th Edt., fortieth thousand.

426 **CHEAT MOUNTAIN;**
Or Unwritten Chapter of the Late War. By a Member of the Bar, Fayetteville, Tenn. Nashville: Albert B. Tavel, 1885. 8vo, cl, 128pp. (Shetler-121) Cheat Mt., Big Springs & Sketch-Col. Alf. S. Fulton. $12.50-ob, $150, $750-G, $100-G. 3-known copies (?J.H. Carrigan) Avc '30).

427 **CHEATHAM, Benjamin Franklin**
"The Lost Opportunity at Spring Hill, Texas. General Cheatham's Reply to General Hood." In: SHSP, 1881, v.IX, p. 524-541.

428 ..."Maj.-Gen. B.F. Cheatham's tribute to the Memory of Bishop C.T. Quintard." In: SHSP, 1888, v.XVI, p.349-354.

429 ..."The Battle of Perryville." In: SB, ns, v.1, #11, 1886/1886. p. 704-705.

430 **CHEAVENS, Henry Martyn**
"Journal of the Civil War in Missouri, 1861, by..." Edt: Virginia Easley. (Columbia, Mo., Mo. Hist. Review, Oct., 1961, v.LVI-#1, p. 12-25, illus., port., map.

431 **CHECKERED LIFE, A**
Being a brief history of the Countess Pourtales, formerly Miss Marie Boozer of Columbia, S.C. Her Birth, Early Life, Marriage, Adventures in New York & Europe, Separation from her husband, Marriage to a French Count, off to China, etc., etc. Compiled by "One Who Knows." Heading: Read this-you'll like it. Columbia, S.C., Daily Phoenix Office, 1878. 12mo, 64pp. stiff paper covers. $25.
...(Columbia, S.C., S & H Pub. Co., 1915. $7.50, $15, $50-bmk, $35. This scandalous account of a native South Carolinian turned "Yankee courtesan" when Sherman invaded Columbia, is attributed to a well known South Carolinian editor. See: Julian Selby, Elizabeth B. Coker.

432 **CHEEK, Charles D.**
"Honey Springs, Indian Territory Search for a Confederate Powder House. An Ethnohistoric & Archeological Report." Oklahoma City, Oklahoma Hist. Soc. Series in Anthropology, #2, 1976. 4to, stiff cover, plastic bnd., illus., drawings, tables, bibliog., vii, 151pp. $5.50. See: Chas. R. Freeman.

433 **CHEMICALS ,**
"How the South got chemicals during war." See: J.W. Mallett.

434 **CHENAULT, John Cabell**
"Old Cane Springs; a story of the War Between the States in Madison Co., Ky.' Revised & Supplemented by Jonathan Truman Dorris, Ph.D., from the original by...John Cabell Chenault, Atty., an Intro. by Ivan E. McDougle, Ph.D., published in recognition of the Sesquicentennial of the Organization of Madison County, Ky., 1786." Louisville, Ky., Standard Printing Co., 1936. 8vo, cl, illus.(incl.front) ports, map endsheets, map, xvi, 257pp. $10, $27.50, $25, $60 bmk-105.

435 ...Same, 1927, (2)pp. added at end, 259pp. $10, $35-y.

436 **CHEPESIUK, Ron**
"Eye witness to Fort Sumter: Letter 1860-1861 of Priv. John Thompson." In: SCHM, Oct. 1984, p. 271-179.

437 **CHEROKEE COUNTY, Ga., in the War.**
See: Lloyd Garrison Marlin.

438 **CHEROKEE TREATY-CSA**
"A Treaty of Friendship & Alliance, made & concluded at Tahlequah, in the Cherokee Nation, on October 7, 1861, between the Confederate States of America. By Albert Pike, Commissioner, & the Cherokee Nation of Indians, by John Ross, the principal chief, Joseph Verner, James Brown, John Drew, & Wm. P. Ross, executive councellors,...authorized to enter into this treaty by General Conven-

tion of the Cherokee People, etc." (Richmond, 1862?) 8vo, sewn, 26pp. (Harvard & LC (old)$100, $150.

439 **CHESHIRE, Joseph Blount**
"Bishop Thomas Atkinson & the Church in the Confederacy." Raleigh, N.C., Edwards & Co., 1909. 8vo, wraps, 21pp.

440 ..."The Church in the Confederate States. A History of the Protestant Episcopal Church in Confederate States." N.Y., London: Longmans, Green Co., 1912. 12mo, cl, ix, 291pp. $10, $12.50, $15, $30, $35-nc, $50-b.
...N.Y., 1914, New edt., corrections. $50, $8, $15, $17, $30. See: Edgar L. Pennington, L.F. London.

441 **CHESNEY, Charles Cornwallis**
"Essays in Military Biography." N.Y., Henry Holt, 1874. 12mo, cl, vi, 398pp. $3.50. Memoir of Lee, p. 81-135. Author a Sandhurst professor of history.

442 ..."A military view of recent campaigns in Virginia & Maryland." London: Smith, Elder & Co., 1863-1865. 12mo, cl, xii, 230, (2-fldg. maps), viii, erratum, 234, (2)p.-ads, 4-fldg. maps. $15, $25, (vol. 1, only $10) Emory.$100-Dabney, $40-bmk.
...2nd Edt., revised & enlarged, 1864.
...3rd Edt., 1865.

443 ..."The Campaign of Fredericksburg, Nov.-Dec., 1862; a study for officers of volunteers, by a Line Officer." London: K. Paul, Trench & Co., 1886. 12mo, cl, maps (part fldg.) plans, xviii, 1p., 145, (1)p.
...London: 1888, maps in color, $90. "An amplification of the chapter on Fredericksburg in Colonel Chesney's "Campaign in Virginia"." p.xi. See also: G.F.R. Henderson's title.

444 ..."Lee's Second Year Campaigns in Defense of Richmond." In: British Army & Navy Review, v.1, #1, July, 1864; other articles on the Navy of the CSA by Commander Bedford, the Volunteers." (London), 1864, p. 115. $10.

445 ..."Memoir of General Robert E. Lee." In: Edinburgh Review, 1873, v. 137, p. 363.

446 **CHESNUT, James, Jr., Hon., South Carolina**
"Relations of States" A Speech of...In Senate U.S., April 9, 1960 on the Resolution submitted by Hon. Jeff. Davis of Miss., on 1st March, 1860. Baltimore: Jno. Murphy & Co., 1860. sewed, 8vo, 24pp. $15-jk-122, $3.50

447 **CHESNUT, Mary Boykin**
"Mary Chestnut's Civil War, Edited: C. Vann Woodward." New Haven: Yale Univ. Pr., 1981?, facsm. 8vo, cl, dj, 1viii, 886pp., front(port) illus. $30. See: Elizabeth Muhlenfeld.
...Tarrytown, N.Y., Reprinted, W. Abbatt. The Magazine of history, with notes & queries, Extra number 58(pt.1) 1917. 8vo, wraps, 35pp.

448 ..."A Diary From Dixie, as written by Mary Boykin Chesnut, wife of James Chesnut, Jr., U.S. Senator from South Carolina, 1859-1861, & afterward an Aide to Jefferson Davis & a Brigadier-Gen. in the Confederate Army; Edited by Isabella D. Lockett Avary." N.Y., D. Appleton & Co.(March)1905. 8vo, cl, t.e.g., ports (incl.front), illus., facsms, xxii, (1), 424, (2)pp. index. $25, $75-b, $10, $12.50, $15, $20, $33-nc, $125-jk.
...London: 1905($10.15); N.Y.: 1906($25, $6.50, $10); N.Y.: 1914($10); N.Y.: 1926($6); N.Y.: P. Smith, 1929($35, $15); Boston: Houghton Mifflin Co., 1949, xii, 572pp. ($12.50, $6, $7.50, $8.50); Boston: 1950($7.50), 1945 ($10); same in flex. cl, $3.85; Gloucester, Mass., Peter Smith, 1961 ($9-y, $3.50); Boston: Houghton Mifflin, 1961. Both the 1949 editions & 1961 has Ben Ames Williams, Edt., "Sentry Edition", pict. cl, soft back, $2.45, $6.95, $20-y.

...1979: Cambridge, Mass., Harvard Univ. Pr., 8vo, cl, 608pp.(paper, $6.95) $20. See: Elizabeth Muhlenfeld biog.

449 **CHESSER, Mysie Abernethy & Mrs. Wm. R.**
"Our Southern Flags both Secession & Confederate." (Pensacola, Fla., Engraving Co., 1948) 8vo, color flags on cover, 37pp. $17.50

450 **CHESTER COUNTY, S.C.**
See under: "Honor Roll of CVs Chester Co., S.C."

451 **CHESTER, Samuel H.**
"African slavery as I knew it in southern Arkansas." In: Tenn. HM, Oct., 1925, issued May, 1928, v.IX, #3, p. 178-184. Chap. from his "Pioneer days in Ark."

452 **CHESTERMAN, William D.**
"Guide to Richmond & the Battlefields." Richmond, Va., James E. Goode, 1881. 16mo, wraps, 72pp., pl. map. $32.
...Do: 1884 and 1894, as above; 1890, p. 77. $15.

453 **CHESTNEY, M. Jemison, Mrs.**
"The Service of the Confederate flags, with history & description & designs of five flags. With Instructions for the service. n.p., (Macon, Ga., c.1926) 8vo, wraps, cover title with colored flags on covers, 14pp. $3.50.

454 ..."The History of the Confederate Flags." n.p. (c.1925) By author. 8vo, narrow, illus-flags, (12)pp. cover title.

455 **CHEVALIER, M. Michel**
"France, Mexico & the Confederate States." trans: Wm. Henry Hurlbut. New York: C.B. Richardson, 1863. 8vo, wraps, 16pp. $12.50. Author, a French economist. Designs of Napoleon, III, in Mexico.

456 **CHEVES, Langdon**
"Letter on Southern Wrongs, Sept. 1844, in Southern Rights, Free Trade & Anti-Abolition Tract #1." 8vo, wraps, 40pp. Charleston, Walker & Burker, 1844.

..."Capt. Langdon Cheves, Jr., & the Confederate silk dress balloon." In: So. Caro. Hist. Mag., 1944, v.XLV, p. 1-11, 99-110. Edt: J.H. Easterby. See: Jno. Randolph Bryan.

457 ..."Speech of..., in the Southern Convention at Nashville, Tenn., Nov. 14, 1850. Pub. by: Southern Rights Association." (Nashville, Tenn.?) 1850?) 8vo, sewn, 30pp. $45.
...Same, "Revised edition." Exhorts South to unite & protect states rights, slavery, make Calif. a slave state, restore dismembered terr. of Tex.

458 ..."Letter of the Hon. Langdon Cheves, to the Charleston Mercury, September 15, 1850." Columbia, S.C., A.S. Johnson Print, 1850. 8vo, wraps, 32pp.

459 **CHEW, Roger Preston**
"Stonewall Jackson: address of Col. R.P. Chew, chief horse artillery, Army of Northern Virginia, delivered at the Virginia Military Institute, Lexington, Va. on the unveiling of Ezekiel's statue of Gen. T.J. Jackson, June 19, 1912." Lexington, Va., Rockbridge County News, 1912. Wraps, 8vo, front(port) map, 64pp. $12.50

460 ..."Letters & papers relating to services of Lt. Colonel R.P. Chew, CSA." n.p., n.d. 8vo, wraps, 12pp. (o'Brien) $100. Signed on wrap: Chew 1-29-07.
See: "Military operations in Jefferson County, Va."

461 **CHEWING-GUM: ,**
Confederate notes. Harold Hill: A & B.C. Chewing Gum of Romford, England. Issued Confederate Notes, half-size, color cards in second wrappers, with gum in 1970(?) (not seen). Note in "Confed. Hist. Soc. Jour." (England)

462 **CHEWNING, Charles R.**
"Journal of Charles R. Chewning, Co.E, 9th Virginia Cavalry, CSA." n.p., n.d. 8vo, wraps, 20pp.

463 **CHICAGO COPPERHEAD CONVENTION, The.**
"The Treasonable & Revolutionary Utterances of the men who composed it. Extracts from all the notable speeches delivered in & out of the National "Democratic Convention." Wash., D.C., 1864. 8vo, wraps, 16pp. $15.

464 **CHICKAMAUGA, Battle of**
See: Archer Anderson, Henry L. Benning, Henry van Ness Boynton, Braxton Bragg, John C. Breckinridge, Simon B. Buckner, W.W. Carnes, T.T. Clay, Jas. Dinkins, Jas. N. Goggins, Thos. C. Hindman, Benj. G. Humphreys, Jas. T. Hunter, Bushrod R. Johnson, Joseph B. Kershaw, Jas. Longstreet, Wm. T. Martin, Jas. D. Nance, New Orleans Picayune, Joseph Palmer, William M. Polk, Wm. Preston, Jerome B. Robertson, Alex P. Stewart, Edward E. Betts Atlas.

465 **CHICKASAW BAYOU, Battle of**
See: Stephen Dill Lee.

466 ..."Chickasaw Souvenir. Indian Territory." Ardmore, I.T., The Ardmoreite, (c.1899) Oblong, 4to, wraps, cover title, illus., port, (front), (40), (1)p. $125. Contains 14pp. Confederate Vets., in I.T.

467 **CHIDSEY, Donald Barr**
"The American Privateers." N.Y., Dodd, Mead Co., 1962. 8vo, cl, dj, illus., bibliog., x, 182pp. $4. From Capt. Kidd to the CSN-"Savannah" & "Jefferson Davis."

468 **CHILDE, Edward Lee**
"Le General Lee; sa vie et ses campagnes, par Edward Lee Childe." Paris: Hachette et cie, 1874. 12mo, full mor.(wraps bound-in) front(photo) fldg. map, iii, 382pp. $40-b, (old)$10, $17.50. (Issued in wraps, in France, & owner can choose his own binding)$7.50. This is the 1st Edt., preceeding by one year the Eng. translation edition.

469 ..."The Life & Campaigns of General Lee. By his nephew, Edward Lee Childe. Translated from the French, with the consent & approval of the author, by George Littig." London: Chatto & Windus, 1875. sm.8vo, cl, front(port), xi, 336pp. $25, $8.50, $18.50, $20.

470 **CHILDS, H.T.**
"The Battle of Seven Pines." In: CV, Jan. 1917, v.XXV, p. 19-20.

471 ..."The Second Battle of Manassas." In: CV, Mar. 1920, v.XXVIII, p. 100-101.

472 ..."Turney's First Tennessee regiment." In: CV, Apr., 1917, v.XXV, p. 164-166.

473 **CHILTON, Frank B., Comp.**
"Unveiling & Dedication of Monument to Hood's Texas Brigade on the Capitol Grounds at Austin, Texas, Thursday, Oct. 17, 1910. Minutes of the 39th Annual Reunion of Hood's Texas Brigade Association held in Senate chamber at Austin, Texas, Oct. 26, 27th, 1910. Together with a short monument & brigade association history & Confederate Scrap Book, etc." Houston, TExas: Compl. & published by F.B. Chilton, 1911. (Press of Rein & Sons) 4to, 3/4 calf, ports(incl. front) plates, 372, (1)pp. $25, $57.50, $70, $85, $125. First org. 1861 by Hood orig. of 1st, 4th, 5th Tex. Inf., 18th Ga. Inf. & Hampton, S.C., Legion. In '63, the 3rd Ark. Inf. was substituted for last two named.

474 **CHILTON, T.H.**
"A History of Co. "G", 11th Mississippi Regt., CSA. (Lamar Rifles)...May 1861, April 1865." (Roanoke, Va., 1901?) n.p., n.d., 8vo, decr. cl., 93pp. $35-oh.

475 **CHIMBORAZO Hospital**
See: J.R. Gildersleeve

476 **CHIPMAN, N.P., General**
"The tragedy of Andersonville Trial of Captain Henry Wirz." San Francisco, Cal., Blair-Murdock, 1911. 8vo, cl, 511pp., illus., index. $75-r.

477 **CHISOLM, Alexander Robert**
"The Battle of Antietam, comments by Alexander Robert Chisholm(sic)." In: SHSP, 1903, v.XXXI, p. 43-45. Chisolm was former aid to Gen. Beauregard.

478 ..."Beauregard's & Hampton's Orders on evacuating Columbia-Letter from Colonel A.R. Hisolm." In: SHSP, 1879, v.VII, p.249-250.

479 ..."How the War began & I became a soldier." In: B & G, 1893, v.1, p. 226-228.

480 ..."Some corrections of Sherman's Memoirs." In: SHSP, 1879, v.VII, p. 295-298.

481 ..."The Confederate battle flag." In: CV, May 1903, v.XI, p. 223.

482 **CHISOLM, Alexander Robert, Colonel**
"Beauregard's & Hampton's Orders on Evacuating Columbia-Letter from A.R. Chisolm." In: SHSP, v.VII, 1889, p. 249-250.

483 **CHISOLM, John Julian, M.D.**
"A Manual of Military Surgery, for the use of Surgeons in the Confederate Army with an appendix for the rules & regulations of the Medical Department of the Confederate Army." Charleston, S.C., Evans & Cogswell, 1861. 12mo, cl, tables, xi, 447pp. $750-bmk-114, $200.
...Richmond, Va., West & Johnston, 1861.(author's title added-"Professor of Surgery in the Medical College of the State of South Carolina." $125.
...Same, Second Edition-revised & improved, 1862. xii, 514pp. $137.50.
...Columbia, S.C., Evans & Cogswell, 1864. Third edition-carefully revised & improved. (title addition-"with explanatory plates of all useful operations.") $150.

484 **CHISOLM, Robert**
"Correspondence of R. Chisolm, CSA, with J.P. Devereaux, Gen. Johnson Haygood, et.al., regarding charges of alleged cowardice of Capt. Chisolm." n.p., (Charleston, S.C., Aug. 10, 1886) 8vo, wraps, 10pp.

484a **CHITTUM, Charles H.**
"The Story of finding the coffin which Gen. Robert E. Lee was afterward buried." Lexington, Va., n.p., n.d. (1932 ?) 16cm, 1 leaf, folded, 4-illus. $30 Bm.

484b **CHITTUM, Charles R.**
"Company E, 5th Regiment, Stonewall Brigade." Part I, Augusta Hist. Bul. 15, #1, Spring 1979: 23-7pp.
...Part II, Fall 1979, #2, p.23-6.
..."Company D, Fifth Virginia regiment, Stonewall Brigade." Bul. 23, #2, Fall 1987, p.14-27.
..."Recovered Civil War Records." In: Augusta Hist. Bul. 12, #2, Fall 1987, p.28-41.

485 **CHITTY, Arthur Benjamin, Jr.**
"Reconstruction at Sewanee. The Founding of the University of the South & its First Administration 1857-1872." Pub. in anticipation of the Centennial of the University in 1957." Sewanee, Tenn., University Press, 1954. 8vo, stiff wraps, ports, illus., map endsheets, 206, (1)p. (Many notables of CSA connected with Sewanee: Gorgas, Leonidas Polk, Robt. Dabney, Kirby-Smith, Dr. Quintard, Brig.-Gen. Shoup, Stephen Elliott, Gen. Fairbanks.

486 ..."Leonidas Polk, a mediocre General but a Gerat Bishop." In: CWTI, Oct., 1963, v.II, #6, p. 16-20, illus., ports.

487 **CHITWOOD, W.R.**
"Doctor Spotswood & the Confederate Navy." n.p., 1976. 8vo, wraps, illus., 5pp. $7-bmk. From: Virginia Medicine, Oct. 1976, (8)pp.

487a **"CHIVALROUS C.S.A."**
...Broadside 4 1/4 x 8 1/2", decr. borders. Baltimore, Sept. 21, 1861. $50-Bmk.

488 **"CHOICEST SONGS of the Civil War:** the sweet sixteen. Edt.: by student body, "Oklahoma History, 162." Oklahoma State

University. Foreword: Charles Evans." n.p., Oklahoma Historical Society, 1960. 4to, wraps, 56pp., music, text & tunes of 16 Union & Confederate songs, with a brief account of each, 1856-1864.

489 **"CHRISTIAN ASSOCIATION of Stonewall Brigade.**
Constitution, by-laws & catalogue of members of the Christian Association of the Stonewall Brigade, Johnsons Division, ANV. Organized May 19, 1863." Richmond, Va., Wm. H. Clemmitt Pr., 1864. 12mo, cl, 11, (1)p. Crandall-4956.

490 **CHRISTIAN, Charles B.**
"The Battle of Bethseda Church. Graphic description of it by Lieutenant Colonel C.B. Christian." In: SHSP, 1905, v.XXXIII, p. 57-64.

491 ..."Battle at Bethesda Church. One among the boodiest contests of the great war of the Sixties-The color bearer killed." In: SHSP, 1909, v.XXXVII, p. 236-242.

492 **CHRISTIAN, George L., Hon.**
"Abraham Lincoln, an address delivered at Richmond, Va., Oct. 29, 1909. 8vo, wraps, 36pp., Lee Camp, #1, UCV. Suffolk, Va., Robt. Hardy Pub., 1986.

493 **CHRISTIAN, George Llewellyn**
"Abraham Lincoln. An address delivered before the R.E. Lee Camp, #1, Confederate Veterans, at Richmond, Va., Oct. 29, 1909." Richmond: W.E. Jones, 1909.
...Richmond, Va., L.H. Jenkins, 1909. 2nd Edt., 31pp. $15.
...Richmond, Va., Richmond Press, 1927. 8vo, wraps, 32pp. $5-(3rd edt), $25-bmk.

494 ..."Hon. Judah P. Benjamin." In: SHSP, 1915, v.40, p.244-252. See: Rabbi Calisch.

495 ..."A comparatively unknown incident in the life of Daniel Webster." In: SHSO, June, 1923, v.XLIV, p. 209-214. Webster inconsistently supported New England threatened withdrawal from Union on the Embargo Act.

496 ..."The capitol disaster. A chapter of reconstruction in Virginia. Sold for benefit of Ass'n. Charities of Richmond, Va." (Richmond: Richmond Press, 1915) Feb. 12, 8vo, wraps, cover title, illus., 46pp. $18.50.

497 ..."Confederate memories & experiences by...An address at annual commencement of the training school for nurses, connected with St. Luke's Hospital, Richmond, Va., 11-"Reminiscences & a contrast", giving some experiences of the writer as a student at the University of Virginia during the war;111-"Recollections of the Evacuation of Richmond, April 1865." Richmond: Clayton Print, (1915) 8vo, wraps, cover title, 37pp.

498 ..."The Confederate Cause & its defenders." Address at the Grand Camp of Confederate Veterans of Virginia Annual meet at Culpepper Courthouse, Oct. 4, 1898. reprint. Southern Historical Society Papers, XXVI. Richmond: Wm. Ellis Jones, 1898. p.323-347, 8vo, wraps, 27pp. $3, $5, $10-nc.

499 ..."General Lee's Dispatches." In: SHSP, 1916, v.41, p. 192-194.

500 ..."General Lee's Headquarters Records & Papers-the present location of some of these." In: SHSP, June 1923, XLIV, p. 229-240.

501 ..."Memorial of Gen. Jubal Early, remarks by Judge Christian." In: SHSP, 1894, v.XXII, p. 283-285.

502 ..."North Carolina & Virginia, report of History Comm. GCCvets of Va." In: SHSP, v.XXXI, 1903, p. 340-364.

503 ..."Official report of the history committee of the Grand Camp, C.V., department of Virginia, Oct. 11, 1900. (1)The right of secession established by northern testimony. (2)The North the aggressor in bringing on the war, established by their

504 ..."Official report of the history committee of Grand Camp, C.V., department of Virginia...read at Petersburg, Va., Oct. 25, 1901, published by order of Grand camp of Virginia. A contrast between the way the war was conducted by the Federals & the way it was conducted by the Confederates, drawn almost entirely from Federal sources." Richmond: O.E. Flanhart(1901) cover title. 8vo, wraps, 32pp. $40, $15-bmk, $3.50
...In: SHSP, 1901, v.XXIX, p. 99-131.
..."Report of the U.C.V. history commission regarding the causes & conduct of the war." n.p., n.d., 8vo, wraps, cover title, 16pp.

[Entry continues from previous page:] own testimony." n.p., 8vo, wraps, 19pp. $3.
...In: SHSP, 1900, v.XXVIII, p. 169-198.

505 ..."Official report of the history committee of Grand Camp, C.V., department of Virginia. Read at Wytheville, Va., Oct. 23, 1902, published by order of the Grand Camp of Virginia. On the treatment & exchange of prisoners." (Pulaski, Va., B.D. Smith, 1902) 8vo, wraps, cover title, 29pp. $3.50, $42, $4.50, $20-bmk.
...In: SHSP, 1902, v.XXX, p. 77-104.

506 ..."Official report of the history committee of Grand Camp, C.V., department of Virginia. Read at Newport News, Va., Oct. 28, 1903 & published by order of the Grand Camp of Virginia. North Carolina & Virginia in the Civil War." n.p., 8vo, wraps, cov er title, 26pp. $20, $30, $5.
...CV, 1907, v.15, p. 314-418, ports. First published in the Confederate Veteran, April, 1904, v.12, p. 161-169.

507 ..."Sketch of the origin & erection of a Confederate Memorial Institute at Richmond." (Richmond, Va., n.p., n.d. ?1920. 2nd edt. 8vo, wraps, cover title, 32pp. $30-bmk-104, $1.25. 2nd edt. (Rich. Whittet & Shepperson, 1931?) front(port). See also: Hunter H. McGuire.

508 **CHRISTIAN, Rebecca**
"Georgia & the Confederate Policy of Impressing Supplies." In: Ga. H.Q., Mar. 1944, v.XXVIII, #1, p. 1-33. $10.

509 **CHRISTIAN, William Asbury**
"Richmond, Her Past & Present." Richmond, Va., L.H. Jenkins, 1912. 8vo, cl, vi, 2, 618pp. color front(port) plates (1-fldg.) map. $10. $20-nc, $40-ob. McElroy bibliog., "wealth of material on affairs there while seat of Davis Gov."
...Spartanburg, S.C.-Reprint Co., 1973, $24.

510 **CHRISTIE, Anne M.**
"Bill Arp." In: CWH, September 1956, v.II, #3, p. 103-119.

511 **CHRISTIE, D.H., Col.**
"Sketch of Col. D.H. Christie, 23rd. N.C. Troops." In: OLOD, Dec. 1874, v.1, #4, p. 325-329.

512 **CHRISTIE, Fay, & Hortense Woodson.**
"Come out brave men of Edgefield." (Edgefield, N.C.) Edgefield Advertiser, 1960. 8vo, stiff wraps, 94pp. $35. Companies from Edgefield in CSA service.

513 **CHURCH in the Confederate States, The."**
Entire issue "Historical Magazine of the Protestant Episcopal Church. Dec. 1948, v.XVII, #4. See: Edgar L. Pennington, Willard Eugene Wight. $20-bmk-114.

514 **CHURCH, William Conant**
"The arbitration of the "Alabama Claims"; with a series of cartoons from London-"Punch"." In: Cent. Mag., Mar. 1913, v.LXXXV, p. 703-720.

515 **CHURCHILL, Winston S.**
"If Lee had not won Gettysburg." In: Scribner's Mag., v.88, #6, Dec. 1930, p. 587-597. 8vo, wraps. $15.

516 ..."If Lee had won the Battle of Gettysburg." In: John Collins Squire's "If; or, History rewritten." NY, Viking Press, 1931, p. 259-286.

517 **CHURCHVILLE CAVALRY**
"Roster of Churchville Cavalry." In: SHSP, 1908, v.XXXVI, p. 218-219. Augusta Co., Va., Apr. 19-June 30th, 1861. Capt. Franklin F. Sterrett, Com.

518 **CIMPRINCH, John**
"Military Governor Johnson & Tennessee Blacks, 1862-1865." In: THQ, Fall, 1980, v.39, #4, p. 459-470.

519 **CIMPRINCH, John & Robert C. Mainfort**
Editors: "Dr. Charles Fitch's report on the Fort Pillow Massacre (Apr. 2, 1864)." In: THQ, Spring 1985, v.44, p. 27-39.

520 **"CINCINNATUS" (pseud.)**
"Address of the Atlanta Register, to the people of the Confederate States." (Atlanta, Ga., 1864) January 1st, 1864. 8vo, 16pp.

521 **"CIRCULAR.,**
To the committees heretofore appointed by the Military Board, to purchase clothing for Arkansas Volunteers." (Little Rock, Ark., 1861) Broadside: 24cm. (Hargrett)

522 **CITIZEN SOLDIER, The,**
devoted to the interests of the Alabama State Troops. Motto...v.1, #1(-8) Tuskaloosa, Ala., Sept. 1, 1893 (April, 1894). 4to, 116pp. Some biographical sketches with occasional items of CSA history. Owens (p.859)

523 **"CITY BATTALION, Richmond Va.,**
Roster of officers in the Twenth-fifth battalion of infantry." In: SHSP, 1903, v.XXXI, p. 323-325. From Richmond Times-Dispatch, Feb. 14, 1904.

524 **"CITY INTELLIGENCER, The;**
or, Stranger's Guide by V. & C." Richmond (Va.): Macfarlane & Fergusson, 1862. 12mo, wraps, 24pp.(incl. ads)

525 ...Richmond, Va., Confederate Museum Valentine Museum (1960) reprinted & bound-in with "Illustrated Guide to Richmond, The Confederate Capital, etc."

526 **"CITY furnished many officers**
in the War Between the States-Logan & Bunn among Colonals." In: Ouchita Co. (Ark) HQ, June, 1980, v.11, p. 20-25.

526a **"CIVIL WAR, The.**
...A Pictorial Guide to the Virginia Peninsula." Hampton Roads, compiled & published by the Junior League, 1961. 8vo, wraps, 32pp. $10.

527 **"CIVIL WAR & the Battles**
of Corinth & Shiloh, The Daily Corinthian Special Civil War Centennial Souvenir Edition, 1961-1965." (cover title) (Corinth, Miss.) Daily Corinthian, 1964. Folio, ports, illus., ads with text, 5-sects. 16pp. each, i.e., 90pp. $7.50.

528 **"CIVIL WAR ACTION**
in Rockingham County, Virginia 1861-1865. Including the engagements of Harrisonburg, Cross Keys, Port Republic, Bridgewater, Mt. Crawford, Lacey Springs, Brock's Gap." Harrisonburg, Va., Rockingham-Harrisonburg Civil War Centennial Comm. (McClung Print, Waynesboro, Va.) (1961) 8vo, wraps, maps, (12)pp. cover title. $3, $10.

528a **"CIVIL WAR at Charleston, The."**
Charleston, S.C., Evening Post, (1960s) 11 x 14 3/4", color wraps, 66pp, ills. $25. Supp'l. by The Post commemorates the Centennial of the war.

529 **"CIVIL WAR BATTLE**
of Lexington, Missouri's Civil War Centennial Feature. Re-enactment by the Cadet Battle Group of Wentworth Military Academy Assisted by Regular Army, National Guard & ROTC Units. May 18, 1961." cover title. 12mo, decr. color stiff wraps, illus., ports, maps, 16pp. $1.50.

530 **"CIVIL WAR BATTLES**
in Winchester & Frederick Co., Va. 1861-1865." Winchester-Frederick Co. Civil War Cent. Commission, (24)pp., maps,

8vo, wraps. Boyce, Va., Carr Pub. Co.) 1960. $4, $15.

531 ...in the West. Essays by Leroy H. Fisher, Kel N. Pickens, Maynard J. Hanson, David Perrine, Henry F. Hartsell & Ival L. Gregory.

532 **"CIVIL WAR BLOCKADE RUNNERS"** Pictorial Supplements to the American Neptune. #III. Salem, Mass: Peabody Museum, 1966. wraps, 32pp. $1.

533 **"CIVIL WAR CENTENNIAL, City of Atlanta.** Showing the area of the three major engagements & deployment of Union & Confederate Forces during the summer of 1864." Folding map, 22x34". (Atlanta) State Highway Dept. of Georgia.

534 **"CIVIL WAR CENTENNIAL, The** an opportunity for all Virginians..." (Richmond, Va., 1960) Virginia Civil War Centennial Commission. 12mo, wraps, cover title, form, 44pp. Manual for observance in the counties & cities of the Commonwealth of Va.

535 ...to commemorate the War Between the States. To Honor Our Confederate Heroes to tell the true story of Georgia's role in the conflict, to dramatize the great ideals that are the basis of our freedom & tradition." (Atlanta: Georgia Civil War Comm., 1961) 12mo, decr. color flag stiff wraps, ports, 35, (1)pp.

536 **"CIVIL WAR CENTENNIAL COMMISSION:** Guide to Observance of the Centennial of the Civil War." (Dedicated to the memory of the Union & Confederate Soldiers & Sailors of the Civil War.) Washington, Feb. 1959. (Press of Byron & Adams); Civil War Centennial Comm., 8vo, wraps, plate, 16pp.

536a ...May 1958 - June 1965, v.1, #1, v.8, #6, complete run of 86 numbers. Washington, D.C., Bell Wiley's set in ring binder. $150.

537 **CIVIL WAR Centennial Series-** Indiana University. See under individual author: Jno. Esten Cooke, "Wearing the gray."; E.H. Alexander, "Military memoirs of Confed."; Sarah Dawson Dawson, "Confederate girl's diary."; Basil, "History of Morgan's cavalry."; Ge. Eggelston, "Rebel's Recollection."; Jubal Early, "War Memoirs."; J.F.C. Fuller, "Grant & Lee."; A.J. Hanna, "Fight into oblivion."; Jno. B. Hood, "Advance & Retreat."; J.E. Johnston, "Narrative of Military Oper."; T.L. Livermore, "Numbers & Losses in CW."; Jas. Longstreet, "From Manassas to Appomattox."; H.B. McClellan, "Life & Campaigns Jeb. Stuart."; Jno. S. Mosby, "Memoirs."; Carlton McCarthy, "Detailed Minutiae soldier life." In: Sterne's "Soldier life in Union/CSA..."; Raphael, Semmes, "Memoirs afloat."; Phil Van Doren Stern, "Prologue to Sumter."; Walter Taylor, "Four years with Lee."

538 **"CIVIL WAR DIARIES** of Edwin F. Stanton, USA & William Quensell, CSA: Yank & Reb under one cover. Edt.: Edgar E. Lackner." In: East Tex. Hist. Jour., Fall, 1980.

539 **"CIVIL WAR EXTRA, The:** from the pages of the Charleston Mercury & the New York Times. Intro: Eugene P. Moehring & Arleen Keylin." N.Y., 1975 (Arno Press)Pub. $50, $16. sm. folio, facsms, illus., 309pp. cloth.

540 **"CIVIL WAR Eyewitness Reports,** Edt: Harold E. Straubing." Hamden, Ct., Archon Books, Shoe String Pr., 1985, 8vo, cl, 236pp. $25. Articles reprinted from c.1865-1962 from various sources, e.g., Myrta L. Avery, Mary A. Gay, James Dinkins & "Diary of a pro-Union woman..."

541 **"CIVIL WAR HISTORY."** Iowa City, March 1955, volume 1. Quarterly. 8vo, stiff wraps, facsms, illus., ports, maps. Pub: State University of Iowa.,

Clyde C. Walton, Edt. Vols. 1-18, $300. Vols. 1-6 (1955-1960) $144-y, v.1960, 1961, $4-each issue., V.9-12(#2)18-issues $90. 1955-1984, (30 vols.) $400-b.

542 **"CIVIL WAR IN VIRGINIA, THE."**
(Richmond, Va., The Commonwealth, Magazine of Virginia, 1962. 4to, wraps, (36)pp., illus., ports, map. $6, $10, bound, $25-bmk.

543 **"CIVIL WAR LIBRARY, A**
offered as a collection by International Bookfinders." Beverly Hills, Calif., 1963. 8vo, wraps, 56pp. illus., $20-bmk-114. Over 2M items, many CSA imprints.

544 **"CIVIL WAR MAPS in the National Archives."**
Washington: 1964. The National Archives National Archives & Records Service General Service Administration. sm.4to, decr. cover map, facsm. maps, plate, xi, (2), 127pp. index. Made up of largely Union maps. See: Rich. W. Stephenson. $7.

545 **"CIVIL WAR Naval Chronology,**
1861-1865. (Part 1-1861) Edited by E.M. Eiler, Rear Admiral, USN(Ret.) Dir. of Naval History, Washington, D.C." Washington, D.C., Naval History Division of the Chief of Naval Operations, Navy Department, Washington, D.C.) Washington: U.S. Government Print (1961) 4to, pict. wraps, contemp. photos., illus., facsms., maps, ports, line drawings. iv, 41pp.; Part II-1862, iv, 117pp.; Part III, iv, 169pp.; Part IV, iv, 151pp.; Part V, iv, 134pp.; Part VI-"Sammary of Significant Events & Calendar for 1861-1865." 447pp. (Index-409-477);. Part VI has special articles, private Journals, life on shipboard, naval sheet music; list of CSA forces, table of illustrations, Blockade Runners, etc. Published 1971, reprint in one volume. xxvii, 41, 117, 169, 151, 477pp. Same pagination but for the ivpp. introduction to each part, in the first edition. 6 parts-wraps. $15.50, $40, $37.50-wh.

546 **"CIVIL WAR PRISONS.**
Edited by William B. Hesseltine." (Kent, Ohio) Kent State University Press (1962). From "Civil War History", v.8, #2, 1962. Various authors. 8vo, stiff wraps, illus., 123pp. $2. See: Hesseltime's book, same title.

547 **"CIVIL WAR ROUND TABLE of Wilmington, Deleware,**
"To those who wore the Gray." (n.p., n.d., 1960) 8vo, wraps, cover title, maps, 47pp.

548 **"CIVIL WAR SOLDIERS:**
Muster Roll of Company D, 53rd Regiment Georgia Volunteer Infantry Army of Northern Virginia, CSA. Coweta & Heard Counties." In: Heard Heritage, 1981, v.6, #1, p. 9-13.

549 **"CIVIL WAR TIMES**
in St. Augustine (Florida)." St. Augustine, Fal., The St. Augustine Journal of History, v.23, 1986, "El Escribano." 8vo, stiff wraps, 135pp., Entire issue, illus., ports, 6-chapters, various authors. $20.

550 **"CIVIL WAR TIMES."**
Gettysburg, Pa., Historical Times, 1952, v.1-3; April 1959-Feb., 1962. 3 vols., 30-43cm., monthly (except Sep't., May) Superseded "Civil War Times, Illus. Supplements accompany some issues, e.g., "Hood's Nashville Campaign", "Struggle for Vicksburg", "Gettysburg", etc.

551 ..."Civil War Times Illustrated." vol. 1-April, 1962. 30cm., illus(part colored), maps, ports. Monthly, except March & September. R.H. Fowler, Editor. 20 yr. run, v.1, #1-41-XXI, #8(1982) $600-Vol.1-19(lax #7), $450-bmk.

552 **"CIVIL WAR Through the Camera, The**
Hundreds of vivid photographs actually taken in Civil War times. Together with Elson's New History in sixteen parts. Comprising a complete history of the Civil

War. Containing Records of the War Between the States by General Marcus J. Wright, CSA." (Springfield, Mass., Patriot Pub. Co., 1912) 4to, decr. stiff wraps, illus., ports, 16-parts, each with a front. in full color. Issued of auspices Civil War Semi-Centennial Society. Partly illus. by Brady. $35. $150-175-bmk-105. Also issued as bound copies, without the wraps. (N.Y., Trow Directory & Printing 1912). $25.

553 **"CIVIL WAR in Florida, The"**
Miami Herald, Oct. 9, 1960. Folio, 8pp. color repro: Kurtz & Allison "Battle of Olustee" Most articles by John L. Boyle. Sunday Magazine section.

554 **"CIVIL WAR in Kentucky, The**
Centennial 1861-1981." (Louisville, Ky) Courier Journal, November 20, 1960. 32cm, ads thru copy, 112pp., illus., some color, facsms, ports, $3.50, $7.50.

555 **"CIVIL WAR in Middle Tennessee,**
(Part 1, 1861-1862) (Part II, 1863) (Part III, 1864) Part IV, Nov. 30, 1864. April 9, 1865 (conclusion)." Nashville, Tenn: Nashville Banner, Dec. 16, 1961-Nov. 14, 1964. Commemorating the Centennial. Folio, 36, 36, 36, 48pp. illus., some in color facsms, ports, maps (1-color coded)

556 **"CIVIL WAR, The**
a Catalogue of books in the Army Library pertinent to the American Civil War." Washington, D.C., GPO, 1965, 2nd Centennial Edition. sm.4to, pict. wraps, 111pp. $10.

557 **"CIVIL WAR, The:**
a Centennial Exhibition of Eyewitness Drawings." Wash: National Gallery of Art, 1961. Imp. 8vo, cl, illus., bibliog., 153pp. See: Vizetelly drawings.

558 **CLACK, Louise, Mrs.**
"General Lee & Santa Claus. Mrs. Clack's Christmas Gift to her little Southern Friends. Illustrated." N.Y., Blelock & Co., 1866. sm.4to, 6-plates, 36pp.
...New Orleans, La., J.C. Eyrick, 1867.

559 ..."Our Refugee Household. By Mrs. Louise Clack, of Louisiana. N.Y., Blelock & Co., 1866. 12mo, cl, 226pp. $7.50, $50, $40-b, $20. Civil War in Louisiana.
..."Our Refugee Household." N.Y., Blelock & Co., 1866. 12mo, cl, 226pp. $5, $7.50. La. during Civil War. $20-bmk.

560 **CLACK, Tommie H.**
"A soldier of Co.A, First Tenn. Cavalry." In: West Tex. Genealogical Soc: Bul. #3, July 1961, p. 28-30.

561 **CLAGHORN, Joseph S.**
"Abstract of heavy artillery drill by Captain Commanding, Chatham Artillery." Savannah, January 26th, 1861. 8vo, sewn, 8pp. (unrecorded) Goodspeed-$850.

562 **CLAIBORNE GUARDS (Alabama)**
"Flag of the "Claiborne Guards." In: AHQ, 1957, v.19, #2, p. 352+

563 ..."Death of Lieutenant Wilcox." AHQ, 1957, v.19, #2, p. 228-231.

564 **CLAIBORNE, John Francis Hamtramck**
"A Sketch of Harvey's Scouts, formerly of Jackson's Cavalry division, Army of Tenn. Being a part of the second volume, Claiborne's History of Mississippi." Printed for private distribution. Starkville, Miss: Southern Livestock Journal Pr., 1885. Wraps, 8vo, 1, 1f, 24pp. $38.50. First published in the "Clarion" at Jackson, Miss., & partly in the "East Mississippi Times", of Starkeville, Miss.

565 **CLAIBORNE, John Herbert**
"Personal Reminiscences of the "Last Days of Lee & his Paladins, "read before the A.P. Hill Camp, C.V., by request, on the 6th of March, 1890, by John Herbert Clairborne, lately Major & Surgeon, PACS & repeated by request, at the Academy of Music, City of Petersburg, Va., on the 15th May, 1890." Petersburg, Va., G.M. Bozel Print (1890). 8vo, wraps,

1p., 42pp. $350-g. In: SHSP, 1900, v.XXVIII, p. 18-58. See also: Geo. Bernard's "War Talks of Confederate Veterans", for a reprint of "Last Days of Lee & His Paladins.", p. 237.

566 ..."Seventy-five Years in Old Virginia; with some account of the life of the author & some history of the people amongst whom his lot was cast, their character, their condition, & their conduct before the war, during the war & after the war." N.Y. & Wash., The Neale Pub., 1904. 8vo, cl, xvi, (17)-360pp., ports, (front) $100-bmk, $75-nc, $125-jk-135, $10, $15, $17.50
...1905 Edt. $25, (1906 Edt.-$15.)

567 ..."Address to his constituents of Petersburg & Prince George." Richmond, 1861. 8vo, sewn, 14pp. $35. "We have not the sort of stuff here in Va., to make white slaves..."

568 **CLAIBORNE, John M.**
"Muster Roll of Terry's Texas Rangers with Historical Remarks compiled by Jno. M. Claiborne. Reunion in Galveston, Feb. 20, 1882." Limp full calf, 13 3/4"x8 1/2", lettered: "Terry's Texas Rangers L.B. Giles, Company D." 108pp. One-half each facing page blank, for "additional remarks." $400.
...First printed in The New Birmingham Times, New Birmingham, Texas (ghost town near Lufkin, Texas), 1881. Complete roster in two editions of the newspaper.

569 **CLAIBORNE, Marie Evans, Mrs.**
"A woman's memories of the sixties, some interesting letters not heretofore published." In: CV, 1905, v.13, p. 61-64. ports.

570 **"CLAIM of certain Confederate Officers.** Statement of Maj. J. Ogden Murray before the committee on war claims, House of Representatives. Sixty-third Congress, 2nd Session, in support of H.R. 14170, a bill for the relief of certain officers of the CSA in the War Between the States. Mar. 28, 1914." Wash: GPO, 1914. 8vo, wraps, 43pp.

571 **CLAPP, Theodore**
"Parson Clapp of the Stranger's Church of New Orleans, Edited by John Duffy." Baton Rouge, Louisiana Univ. Pr. (1957). 8vo, cl, dj, illus., facsm., port, ix, 191pp. Clapp's life, from 1792-1866.

572 **CLARE, Virginia**
"Thunder & Stars. Life of Mildred Rutherford." (Milledgeville, Ga.) Oglethorpe University (1941) 8vo, cl, 245pp., port. $16, $20-bmk, $5. One of the original unreconstructed Rebels, prolific writer on the CSA.

573 **CLARK, Carrol Henderson**
"My Grandfather's Diary of the War. Carrol H. Clark, Co. I, Sixteenth Regiment Tennessee Volunteers, C.S.A." n.p., August, 1963. Tall 4to, decr. color flag-stiff cover, port front, facsm. diary, (62)pp. $16.

573a **CLARK, Champ**
"Gettysburg: the Confederate High Tide." Alexandria, Va., Time-Life Books, 1985. 8vo, lt. binding, gilt, Civil War Series. 176pp, ills, maps (some color). $10.

574 **CLARK, Charles Branch**
"Suppression & control of Maryland, 1861-1865. A study of Federal-State relations during the civil conflict." In: MdHM, Sept. 1959, v.54, p. 241-271. notes.

575 **CLARK, Covington**
"Mosby's Night Hawk." Chicago: Reilly & Lee Co.(1931). 12mo, cl, 290pp. topo-map end-sheets. Fiction. $4, $6.

575a **CLARK, Daniel**
"Speech of Hon. Daniel Clarke, of Prince Georges County, Md., in Constitutional Convention, of Maryland, in opposition to abolishing slavery in Maryland." Baltimore, Md., 1864, 8vo, wraps, 23pp. See: Samuel Johnson. "Resolution of the Comm. on Federal relations...

576 **CLARK, Douglas**
"Rhythmic Ramblings in Battle-Scarred Manassas." Phila., 1905. 8vo, wraps, illus., 26pp. $15-bmk-106. Port of Stonewall.

577 **CLARK, Edward, Gov. of Texas**
"Proclamation to people of Texas. Aug. 26. (Austin, Texas), 1861" Broadside: 20 1/2x32cm. Crandall-2209. Reprint: Waco, Texas: Morrison's (c.1964) Calls for 2000 troops service in Valley & along Gulf Coast. Original only 2 copies?

578 ..."Governor's Message to the Senators & Representatives of the ninth Legislature of the State of Texas." Austin: John Marshall Print, 1861. 12mo, sewn, 17pp. Speech Nov. 1, 1861, near end of his term of office as successor to Sam Houston, who refused to give oath of office to the CSA.
...Reprint: in Tex. State Hist. Ass'n., 66th Annual Meeting, April 27-28, 1962. Austin, Texas, 17pp. $5.

579 **CLARK, George**
"A Glance Backward; or Some events in the past history of my life." Houston, Texas: Press of Rein & Sons (1914?) 12mo, cl, 93pp. $17.50, $40, $35, $60-jenk.
...Louisville: Lost Cause Press (micro-cd) $2.76.

580 ..."From Rapidan to Petersburg; Wilcox's Alabama Brigade in that memorable campaign." In: CV, Aug. 1909, v.XVII, p. 228-230.

581 ..."Chancellorsville & Salem Church; special features of battle of the latter." In: CV, March 1910, v.XVIII, p. 125-126.

582 **CLARK, Gibson**
"Reminiscences of Civil War Days." In: Annals of Wyoming, 1943, v.XV, p. 377-386. Dorn-II, 1158.

583 **CLARK, James C.**
"Last train South. The flight of the Confederate Government from Richmond." Jefferson, N.C., McFarland & Co., 1984. 8vo, cl, 192pp., illus., maps, bibliog., $18.

584 **CLARK, James Lemuel**
"Civil War recollections of James Lemuel Clark. Edited with an introduction by L.D. Clark." College Station, Texas: Texas A & M Press, 1984. 8vo, cl, 124pp. $12.50. Served both the CSA & Union army as sympathetic to the Union & secession.

585 **CLARK, Mary B., Mrs.**
"Great Seal of the Confederate States." In: CV, Aug. 1912, v.XX, #8, p. 376-379(307). Mrs. Clark was Hist. Musadora C. M'Corry Chap. UDC, Jackson, Tenn. See: Annie Payne Pillow, John T. Pickett.

586 **CLARK, Micajah H.**
"Retreat of the Cabinet. Described by President Davis' Confederate Secretary." In: SHSP, 1898, v.XXVI, p. 96-101.

587 ..."The Last Days of the Confederate Treasury & what became of its specie." In: SHSP, 1881, v.9, p. 542-556.

588 ..."Twilight of a Treasury. The last acting treasurer of the Confederacy tells his own story of the fleeing government & its money in the days after Appomattox." In: CWTI, Dec. 1972, v.XI, #8, p. 38-45, facsms., illus., ports.

589 **CLARK, Myron Holley, Captain**
"The Last Days of the Confederate Treasury & what became of the specie." In: SHSP, 1881, v.IX, p. 542-556.

590 **CLARK, Robert T., Jr.**
"The New Orleans German Colony in the Civil War." New Orleans: LHQ, October, 1937, v.20, #4, p. 990-1015.

591 **CLARK, Sam L., Edt.**
"A Confederate officer visits Richmond." In: THQ, 1952, v.11, p. 86-91.

592 ...& H.D. Riley, Jr., Edt.: "Outline & the organization of the Medical Department of the CSArmy & Dept. of Tenn." By S.H. Stout. " In: THQ, 1957, v.16, p. 55-82. See also: Dr. S.H. Stout, W.J. Holman, Jr.

593 **CLARK, Thomas D.**
"Pleasant Hill in the Civil War." Shakertown, Ky., Pleasant Hill Press, 1972. 8vo, wraps, illus., x., 76pp. $4.50. Largely the same as found in Nancy Greene's "Ye Old Skaker Bells."

594 **CLARK, W.M. (William Martin)**
"A Confederate Officer visits Richmond. Edt: Sam L. Clark." In: Tenn. HQ, Mar. 1952, v.XI, p. 86-91. Letters to wife, on journey from Knoxville to Richmond, with yankee prisoner, his observations on Richmond.

595 **CLARK, Walter Augustus, Sgt.**
"Under the Stars & Bars; or, Memories of Four Years Service with the Oglethorps of Augusta, Georgia." $750-ob, $500. Augusta, Ga., Chronicle Print, 1900. Decr. cl, 8vo, 239, (3)pp. $15, $75, $80.
...Louisville, Ky., Lost Cause Press, 1956, Travels in CSA, #82.
...Jonesboro, 1987. 2 vols. $30. 8vo, cl, 248pp, rosters, index. $15.

596 **CLARK, Walter, Chief Justice**
"Address by..., of N.C. Supreme Court at Cooper Union, New York City, 27 Jan., 1914. "Government by Judges", 2nd Edt." n.p. (1914) cover title, 8vo, wraps, 24pp. $4.

597 ..."The Battle of Sharpsburg, personal incidents." Wake Forest Student, xviii. (Winston-Salem, 1897) p. 83-97, 2-maps, Dornbusch-813.

598 ..."Caldwell County, N.C. in the Great War 1861-1865: address unveiling the Monument to Confederate States Soldiers for Caldwell Co., at Lenoir, June 3, 1910-The 58th Reg. Inf. N.C. Troops." Hickory, N.C., Clay Print, 1910. 8vo, wraps, ports, illus., 53pp.

599 ..."Histories of the several regiments & battalions from North Carolina in the Great War 1861-1865, written by members of the respective commands, edited by Walter Clark, published by the State." Raleigh: E.M. Uzzell, 1901. Goldsboro: Nash Bros., 1901, 5vols. Tk. 8vo, cl, ports, illus., maps $60, $85. (I, III, IV, V-$70) (v.III-$17.50, $35.) IV, V-$12.50, $25, each. Index in V.
..."Histories of the Several Regiments & Battalions from North Carolina in the Great War 1861-1865." Wendell, N.C., Avera Press, Reprinted by Broadfoot's Bookmark, 1982. tk. 8vo, cl, decr. covers with flags in color. $150.

600 ..."Memorial Address upon the life of Gen. James Green Martin, delivered at Raleigh, N.C., by Walter Clark (1916). 8vo, wraps, 21pp. Dornbusch-3004.

601 ..."North Carolina at Gettysburg & Pickett's Charge A Misnomer. Also Sixty Years After & the Rearguard of the Confederacy...address delivered Durham, N.C., 24 Aug. 1921 cover title, illus., maps, pict. wraps, 8vo, 31pp. $12.50, $60, $100-ob, $25-bmk

602 ..."North Carolina in the Navy." See Vol. V, p. 296-451, in his "Hist. of Several Regs. & Batts. from North Carolina".

603 ..."North Carolina in South America. North Carolina in War-Her Troops & Generals." Raleigh, N.C., 1904, N.C. Booklet, v.4, #6. 8vo, wraps, 24pp. $10, $8.

604 ..."North Carolina's Record in War-Her Troops & Generals." In: N.C. Booklet, Oct. 1904, wraps, 7pp. article. $10., $15

605 ..."North Carolina Troops at Gettysburg. Address before N.C. Confederate Veterans Ass'n., Durham, N.C., 24 Aug., 1921. p. 91-208.

606 ..."North Carolina in the Civil War." In: South. Hist. Assn., July 1902, v.VI, #4, p. 328-334.

607 ..."North Carolina Troops in the Great War, 1861-1865." Vol. 1, pub. by the State. Raleigh, E.M. Uzzell, 1901. 8vo, wraps, color-flags, maps, ports, 39pp. cover title.

608 ..."Raising, Organization & Equipment North Carolina Troops during Civil War." Raleigh: 1919, North Carolina Booklet, v.19. #1/2, p. 55-65; a reprint of proceedings of N.C. Historical Ass'n., 1917. $35-bmk-105, $10-bmk-84.

...Also in: N.C. Lit. & Hist. Assoc. Proc., 1918, v.XVIII, p. 104-111.

609 ..."The Papers of Walter Clark. Edited by Aubrey Lee Brooks & Hugh Talmage Lefler, Vol. 1, 1857-1901:. Chapel Hill: Univ. of N.C. Press (1948). 8vo, cl, xv, 607pp. facsms., ports, views. $45-b. Letters rec'd. & sent by Clark, relates to his exp. as an officer in CSArmy, 1861-1065, a lwyr., jurist in N.C., etc. $8.50.

...Vol. 1, p. vii, 608, (1950) covering years 1902-1924.

...1st Edition $13.

610 ..."William Alexander Graham (1804-1875)" In: N.C. Booklet, July, 1916, v.XVI, p. 3-16. See: Wm. A. Graham.

611 ..."Maj. Gen. Stephen Dodson Ramseur, an address delivered at the presentation of the portrait of...7 June, 1916." North Carolina Booklet, XVI, plate, p. 69-75. 8vo, wraps, Dornbusch-3066. $10.

612 ..."Gen. James Johnston Pettigrew, C.S.A., address at Bunker Hill, West Va., Sept 17, 1920, n.p., n.d. (1920) 12mo, pict. wraps, 11pp. 1-illus. $60, $15. Also: N.C. Booklet, XX, p. 171-180. $125-ob.

613 ..."The term "Pickett's Charge" is a misnomer." In: N.C. Booklet, 1922, v.XXI, p. 21-27.

614 **CLARK, William Henry Harrison**
"History in Catoosa County." (Ringgold, Ga., Privately Pr., 1972) 8vo, cl, vi, 302pp. $9.50. 180pp. devoted to the War, 6pp.illus., map, 6pp soldiers in the CSA

615 **CLARKE COUNTY, Alabama**
"A glance into the great southeast, or,

Do: Reprint(c.1962) Franklinville(N.C.) Store.

Clarke County, Alabama from 1540-1877, by T.H. Ball." Grove Hill, Alabama, 1882, p. 782. Civil War & list of soldiers, p. (258)-290.

616 **CLARKE, Asia Booth**
"The Unlocked Book; a memoir of John Wilkes Booth (1828-1865) by his sister Asia Booth Clarke; with a foreword by Eleanor Farjeon." N.Y., Putnams Sons, 1938. 8vo, cl, illus., 205pp. $35-bmk, $7.50

617 **CLARKE, George Herbert**
"Some Reminiscences & Early Letters of Sidney Lanier." $20-bmk. (Macon, Ga., J.W. Burke Co., 1907) $50-bmk. Tall 8vo, cl, front(port), 27, (1)pp. $5.

618 **CLARKE, H.C., of Vicksburg, Miss.**
"Diary of the War for separation, a daily chronicle of the principal events & history of the present revolution, to which is added notes & descriptions of all the great battles, including Walker's narrative of the battle of Shiloh." (Augusta, Steam Press of Chronicle & Sentinel, 1862) (Georgia) 8vo, wraps, 191pp. Sabin-13404, Crandall-#2618. $100, (old)$65, $68.50.

..."Diary of the war for separation, being a daily chronicle of the leading events & history of the present revolution, from the inauguration of Abraham Lincoln to the battle of Shiloh; containing full & minute statements of all the battles, skirmishes & engagements, lists of killed & wounded, number of forces engaged, etc. Also, notes of the war, with biographical sketches of Confederate generals, remarkable events, etc. Edited by H.C. Clarke." Vicksburg: Clarke's Southern Pub. House, 1862. 8vo, wraps, 56pp. Cover title-"First Year of War." (Was originally prepared for the "Confederate States Almanac for 1862." Pref.) Sabin-13405, Crandall-2619 (old) $50.

...See also: Crandall-4981-4 Almanacs, $35.

619 ...Confederate Souvenir: "The Confederate State Almanac & Repository of useful knowledge, for 1862." Compl: H.C. Clarke. (Atlanta, Ga., H. Krouse & D.C. Black, 1895) 12mo, wraps, illus., pls, ports, 96pp. $250. Cover title: "Confederate Souvenir 1862 reissue, with additions of the C.S. Almanac for 1862, 1st published in Vicksburg, Miss., by H.C. Clarke. (12mo, wraps, 176pp. $85.) (Mobile: 1865, p. 23-$15; Vicksburg: 1863-23pp-$35.; Lynchburg, Va., 1861-31pp.-$20) Mobile: 1863, p. 119-$25.

..."Clarke's Confederate Almanac for 1863." Massapequa, N.Y., Political Heritage, Inc. 1961. 12pp. woodcuts of uniforms & other illus.

620 **CLARKE, Henry S., Hon.**
"Incidents of Quantrill's Raid on Lawrence, August 21, 1863. The remarkable & heretofore unpublished experience of Hon. Henry S. Clarke." Lawrence, Kan., 1898. 8vo, sewn, illus., 17pp. $30.

621 **CLARKE, Jennie Thornley, Edt.**
"Songs of the South. Choice Selections from Southern Poets from colonial Times to the Present." Intro: Joel Chandler Harris. Phila., 1896, J.B. Lippincott. 12mo, cl, xix, 333pp., illus., cl. $8.

..."Songs of the South. Choice Selections from Southern Poets from Colonial Times to the Present. With an appendage of brief biographical notes, intro: Joel C. Harris.

...Another edt., same date, with "Photogravure illus. (ports)

...Same edt., with title in red & black, with front. ports.

...Garden City, N.Y., Doubleday, Page & Co., 1913. 12mo, cl, 3pp., 1, v-xix, 333pp. $20-bmk.

622 **CLARKE, M.M.**
"Midway Hospital: 1861-1863; the Diary of Miss. Clarke of South Carolina. Edt: by Chalmers L. Gemmill." (Charlottesville, Va., Albemarle County Historical Society, 1964) v.24, p. 162-189.

623 **CLARKE, Robert L.**
"The Florida Railroad Company in the Civil War." (Lexington, Ky.) JSH, May, 1953. v.XIX, #2, p. 180-192. $10.

624 ..."Northern Plans for the Economic Invasion of Florida, 1862-1865." In: FHQ, April, 1950, v.XXVIII, #4, p. 262-270.

625 **CLARKSON, Charles Ervine, Rev.**
"A Rose of Old Virginia, A Romance of the Old South & the War Between the States." (Ft. Smith, Ark., Calvert-McBride, 1927) 12mo, cl, 59pp. privately printed) $5, $15-bmk, $20-b.

626 **CLARKSON, Henry Maxyck**
"Story of the Star of the West." In: CV, May 1913, v.XXI, p. 234-236. Account of firing on US "Star of the West" in Charleston Harbor, Jan. 9, 1861.

627 ..."Evelyn: a romance of the "War Between the States"." With an Appendix of minor poems. Charleston: Walker, Evans & Cogswell, 1871. 12mo, wraps, 69pp. (McKissick-465)

628 ..."Songs of Love and War." Manassas, Va., Journal & Print, 1898, 12mo, cl, front(port) 158pp. Do: 2nd Edt. enlarged, 1910. 8vo, cl, port, vii-(9)-198. $10-bmk.

..."Songs of Love & War...2nd Edt. enlarged." Manassas, Va., Manassas Journal Pub., 1910. 8vo, cl, vii, (9)-198pp. front(port) $5. Scarce Southern poet.

629 **CLAUSEN, C.A. & Derwood Johnson**
"Norwegian-American Soldiers in the Confederate Forces." In: v.25 "Norwegian-American Studies (Hist. Society, Northfield, Minn.) 1972, 36pp. Contains a list of 50 Norge-Texans, serving in CSA, with trans. 17 letters. Members of McCord's Frontier Reg., Tex. Cav., 31st Cav. & 15th Tex. Inf.

630 **CLAUSS, Errol MacGregor**
"Sherman's Failure at Atlanta." In: Ga. H.Q., Sept. 1969, v.LIII, #3, p. 321-329.

631 **CLAUSSEN, Martin P.**
"Peace factors in Anglo-American relations, 1861-1865." In: MVHR, 1940, v.XXVI, p. 511-522.

632 **"CLAY COUNTY, Missouri,**
Confederate soldiers who were killed or who died while in service, 1861-1865; transcribed from "Liberty Tribune", Liberty, Mo., June 21, 1901 by Nadine Hodge." (Kansas City, Mo., n.d.) 4to, wraps, 5-leaves.

633 **CLAY, A.B.**
"On the right at Chickamauga." In: CV, July 1911, v.XIX, p. 329-330. (The CSA right).

634 **CLAY, Brutus J.**
"Selections from the Brutus J. Clay Papers 1861-1865. Edt: Cassius M. Clay." In: FCHQ, Jan. 1958, v.32, #1, p. 3-37. Brother's War, the divided Clay's.
...Part II, April 1958, v.32, #2, p. 136-150.

635 **CLAY, Clement Claiborne**
"Another leaf from history." (Report to Judah P. Benjamin) Folio Broadside in two wide columns, 12 Sept., 1864. St. Catherine's, C.W. $150-jk, $65. Neither in Crandall/Harwell, possible print in Richmond. Davis sends Clay on secret mission to Canada, re St. Albans Raid, observe North. Attempt negotiate peach thru Greeley.

636 **CLAY, Green**
"Old Cane Springs: a border-land tale of the civil war." In: KyHSR, 1931, v.XXIX, p. 184-189, 246-277.

637 **CLAY, H.B.**
"On the right at Murfreesboro." In: CV, Dec. 1913, v.XXI, p. 588-589.

638 **CLAY, James Brown**
See: Sarah Agnes Wallace, Edt.

639 **CLAY, Tacitus T., Capt.**
"The War Letters of..." Edt: Judy & Nath Winfield. (Chappell Hill, Texas. Dec. 1, 1968) $7.50. 8vo, stiff wraps, port(front) 29pp. $1.

640 ..."Report of Captain T.T. Clay, commanding Fifth Texas Regiment in the Battle of Chickamauga, Sept. 21, 1863." In: SHSP, 1888, v.XVI, p. 381-384.

641 **CLAY - CLOPTON (Virginia)**
"Confederate Cruiser, Sumter." In: AHQ, 1948, #1, p. 8-12, Front: Adm. Raphael Semmes. +Review of "Rebel Raider by editor", p. 13-14.

642 **CLAY - CLOPTON, Virginia, (Clement Claiborne)**
"A Belle of the fifties; Memoirs of Mrs. Clay of Alabama, covering social & political life in Washington & the South, 1853-1866, gathered & edited by Ada Sterling." New York: Doubleday, Page & Co., 1904. $45-jk-122. 8vo, cl, t.e.g., xxii, 386pp. 24ports (2,light colors, incl. front) $5, $8.50, $10, $15-b, $12, $25-bmk. Do: 1905, $30-bmk-84, $40, $7.50. Lond: Wm. Heinemann (N.Y. World's Press) '05. Instead of blue, London copies dk. green cover. N.Y., Da Capo, 1969. $15, $32.50-y, $25-y, $7.50, $9.

643 ..."Official Correspondence of Confederate State Department. Letters from Honorable C.C. Clay, Jr., August 11, 1864." In: SHSP, 1879, v.VII, p. 333-343.

644 **"CLAYTON & CATTERSON Rob Columbia County.**
Edt: J.H. Atkinson." In: AHQ, 1962, v.XXI, p. 153-157. Embittered county against Catterson & Powell, who falsely accused people of murdering Freedmen & Union men.

645 **CLAYTON, Alexander M.**
"Letter of Judge Alexander M. Clayton, relative to Confederate courts in Mississippi. Edt: Nannie M. Tilley." In: JSH,

1940, v.VI, p. 392-401. Letter, Sept. 5, 1864, details of functions of CSA courts in Mississippi.

646 **CLAYTON, Henry De Lamar**
"A correction of General Patton Anderson's report of the Battle of Jonesboro", Ga. Dec. 31, 1877." In: SHSP, 1878, v.V, p. 127-129; p. 134-135.

647 ..."Report of the operations of Clayton's division north of the Tennessee River in the Campaign of the Winter of 1864." In: SHSP, 1878, v.VI, p. 86-90.

648 **CLAYTON, Powell**
"Aftermath of the Civil War in Arkansas." N.Y., Neale Pub. Co., 1915. $50-jk-135, $37.50, $30, $25. 12mo, cl, front(port), 378pp.
...N.Y. (1969) Rep. Negro Univ. Press., $18, $12.

649 **CLAYTON, Victoria V.**
"White & Black Under the Old Regime." Milwaukee-London(1899) Young Churchman. 16mo, cl, port, illus., 195pp. $7.50, $25, $30-bmk. By widow of Maj-Gen. Henry D. Clayton, CSA becomes slaveholder again, his Kansas War experiences, in Alabama & Georgia.

650 **CLAYTON, W.F.**
"A Narrative of the Confederate States Navy, by W.F. Clayton, Ex-Passed Midshipman C.S. Navy & Secretary of the Survivor's Association, C.S. Navy. Bulletin Pee Dee Historical Association, 1910." Weldon, N.C., Harrell's Print., 1910. 8vo, cl, port(front), 116pp. $10, $15, $20, $22.50, $400-nc-124, $500-bmk-105.

651 **CLEARY, W.W., Judge**
"The attempt to fasten the assassination of President Lincoln on President Davis & other innocent parties." In: SHSP, 1881, v.IX, p. 313-325.

652 **CLEBSCH, William A., Edt.**
"Journals of the Protestant Episcopal Church in the Confederate States of America." Austin, Texas: The Church Historical Society, 1962. 8vo, cl, dj, xvi, 451pp. $7.50.

653 **CLEBURNE, Patrick Ronayne**
"General Cleburne's Report of the Battle of Chickamauga." In: LWL, 1866, v.1, p. 249-254, map.

654 ..."Cleburne's report of the Battle of Ringgold Gap, Dec. 9, 1863." In: SHSP, 1881, v.IX, p. 65-70.

655 ..."Negroes in Our Army. General Pat Cleburne the first to advocate their use. His plan was turned down." In: SHSP, 1903, v.XXXI, p. 215-228. SHSP, 1901, v.XXIX, p. 173-174. See: Irving A Buck, Geo. W. Gordon, Wm. J. Hardee, Briscoe Hindman, Chs. E. Nash, Thomas O. Moore, Sam T. Foster.

656 ..."A Sketch of Maj. Gen. P.B. Cleburne." In: LWL, Apr. 1867, v.II, #6, p. 460-463.

657 **CLEGG, Henry Clay**
"War Record from 1862 to 1865. As published in the Chatham Record, Pittsboro, N.C. by H.C. Clegg (82 years old)." n.p., n.d. Cover title. (16)pp. 8vo, $9.50. Was in 48th N.C., Co. "G".

658 **CLEGGETT, D.A.H.**
"An instance of plagiarism by Pres. Jeff Davis." In: VMHB, Oct. 1964, v.72, #4, p. 490-495.

659 **CLELAND, Robert Glass**
"Jefferson Davis & the Confederate Congress." In: QTSHA, Jan. 1916, v.XIX, #3, p. 213-231.

660 **CLEMENS, Samuel L. (Mark Twain)**
"The Twainian." March 1940. (Elkhorn, Wisc., Etc., 1939-. 4to, monthly, new series. (6)p. from typed copy. George Hiram Brownell, Edt. Article re. Mark Twain's service in CSArmy, refutes assertion that Twain was a coward, deserter from the CSArmy & unworthy of having a US Postage stamp commemorative. Published by the Mark Twain Society of

Chicago: Mark Twain Association of America.

661 ..."Mark Twain's war experiences; his graphic recital of them at dinner to the Boston Ancient & Honorable Artillery Company." In: Twainian, Mar/Apr. 1954, v.13, #2, p. 1-2. Speech at Hartford, facetious recollections of military service in Missouri, c.1861. Reprint from NYTimes 7 Oct. 1877.

662 ..."Mark Twain-The Letters of Quintus Curtius Snodgrass." Edt: Ernest E. Leisy. Dallas, Tex: Southern Methodist Univ. Pr., 1946. (re: Twain's short stint in CSArmy) thin 8vo, cl, front(portxii, (1), 76pp. $10. Letters appearing in New Orleans Daily Crescent, never acknowledged by Twain. $17.50-jk.

663 ..."Mark Twain's "Private campaign", Edt: John Gerber." In: CWH, Mar. 1954, v.1, p. 37-60. notes. First pub. in 1885, with editorial review of the known participation in the war, proportion of fact & fiction.

664 ..."The private history of a campaign that failed." Sketches by E.W. Kemble. In: Cent. Nov. 1895, v.31, p. 192-204. See: Fred Lorch, J. Stanley Mattson.

665 **CLEMENS, Sherrard**
"State of the Union. Speech of the Hon. Sherrard Clemens of Virginia, in the House of Representatives, Jan. 22, 1861." (Wash., Congressional Globe, 1861) 8vo, sewn, 8pp.

666 **CLEMENT, Abram Wilson**
"Diary of Abram W. Clement, 1865. Edt: Slann L.C. Clemmons." In: SCHMag., Apr. 1958, v.59, p. 78-83. Note. Record of brief service in 11th Reg. S.C. Vols. & imprisonment at Fort Monroe. See: Joseph Julius Wescoat.

667 **CLEMENT, Maude Carter, Mrs.**
"War Recollections of the Confederate Veterans of Pittsylvania County Virginia 1861-1865." Chatham, Virginia: U.D.C. (C. 1961) (Danville, Va., J.T. Townes) 8vo, wraps, illus., ports, 84pp. (500 copies, author) $3.

668 **CLEMSON, Floride**
"A Rebel Came Home. Wartime Adventures, 1863-1864." Edt: Charles M. McGee & E.M. Lander. Columbia, S.C., University Press, 1961. 8vo, cl, d/w, pp.xxiv, 153, maps, illus., ports. $4.50, $20-b.

669 **CLENDENEN, Clarence C.**
"A Confederate Spy (Captain H. Kennedy, C.S.) in California." In: Southern California Quart., 1963, v.XLV, p. 219-234.

670 ..."Mexican Unionists: A Forgotten Incident of the War Between States." (Albuquerque) New Mex. Hist. Rev., Jan. 1964, v.XXXIX, #1, p. 32-39.

671 ..."Soldier or Bandits-the Westernmost Fights of the Civil War." (London) Jour. Confed. Hist. Soc., Summer, 1969, v.7, #2, p. 43-47.

672 ..."Was Sylvester Mowry a Secessionist?" In: Ariz. Quart., Autumn 1953, v.9, p. 260-266. Notes. Activities in southern Ariz. & his mine there 1858-1862.

673 **CLEUGH, Eugenie Clark**
"Stonewall" Jackson, Southern Teacher, Statesman, Soldier. An Appreciation by..." Paducah, Ky.,n.d. 16mo, wraps, port, 25pp. $10.

674 **CLEVELAND, Annie**
"A Romance from real life connected with the second great revolution." New Orleans, 1867. wraps, 72pp.

675 **CLEVELAND, Charles Boarman**
"With the Third Missouri Regiment; reminiscences of Charles Boarman Cleveland." In: CV, Jan. 1923, v.XXXI, p. 18-21.

676 **CLEVELAND, Charlotte & Robert Daniels, Edts.**

"Diary of a Confederate Quartermaster." In: THQ, 1952, v.11, p. 78-85.

677 **CLEVELAND, Henry**
"Alexander H. Stephens, in Public & Private. With Letters & Speeches, before, during, & since the war." Phila., et.al. National Pub. Co., (1966). 8vo, full calf, (1/2 Mor., or cloth), ports (2-incl. front) 2-illus., 833pp. errata sheet at end. $10, $12.50, $17.50, $25, $30-bmk, atg-$130-bmk.

...2nd copy (DeRenne II, p. 680) adds New Orleans to Natl. Pub. Co., & lacks illus. at p. 23, 102, 232. front. port by Sartain is changed for original printing.

678 ..."Alexander Hamilton Stephens", excerpt: Harper's Mag., Feb. 1876, v.LII, #309, illus., p. 387-393. See: Paul H. Hayne on Lee.

678a **CLEVELAND, Henry Whitney**
"Robert Toombs." In: SB, ns, 1885/1886. v.1, #8, p. 449-459. port. $10.

..."Old Scipio." In: SB, ns, 1886/1887. v.II, p. 670-678. Siege Vicksburg, North trades South.

679 **CLEWS, Henry**
"Great Britain & the Confederacy." In: NAR, v.149, p. 215-222.

680 **CLIFFORD, B.G., Mrs.**
"Why John Wilkes Booth Shot Lincoln." In: SHSP, 1904, v.XXXII, p. 99-101.

681 **CLIFORD, Roy A.**
"The Indian Regiments in the Battle of Pea Ridge." (Okla. City) Chron. Okla., Winter, 1947, v.XXV, #4, p. 314-322, map.

682 **CLIFT, G. Glenn**
"Civil War Engagements, Skirmishes, etc. in Kentucky, 1861-1865." A finding list designed for use by Researchers, Speakers & Students during the Civil War Centennial 1961-1965." Head: Kentucky Historical Society Research Contribution #2, Lexington, Ky., Ky. Civil War Cent. Com., n.d., 4to, (2), 29pp. stiff wraps, cover title.

683 **CLIFTON, James M., Edt.**
"Life & Labor on Argyle Island: Letters & Documents of a Savannah River Rice Plantation, 1833-1867." Savannah, Ga., Beehive Press, 1978, 8vo, cl, dj, xlvi, 365pp. illus., maps. $30.

684 **CLINE, Inez. E.**
"A synopsis of the activities of Co. F, 3rd Arkansas Cavalry." In: The Record, 1964, v.5, p. 76-88.

685 **CLINE, William R.**
"The ironclad Ram "Virginia"-Confederate States Navy. Memorable Engagement of March 8-9, 1862. One of her Crew." In: SHSP, 1904, v.XXXII, p. 243-249.

686 **CLINGMAN, Thomas L.**
"Selections from the Speeches & Writings of Hon...., of North Carolina, with additions & explanatory notes." Raleigh: John Nichols, 1877. 8vo, boards, roan back, v, 623pp. Clingman's Brigade composed of: 8th, 31st, 51st, 61st Reg. Infty. Cold Harbor. $7.50. 2nd Edt., 1878, p. 623, append. 52pp.

687 ..."Clingman's Brigade at Cold Harbor." In: OLOD, May 1875, v.2, #3, p. 291-292.

688 ..."Official Report of Gen. Clingman." In: OLOD, June 1875, v.2, #4, p. 409-412, v.3, p. 448-454.

689 **CLINTON, Thomas P. & James A. Anderson & Samuel W. John**
"The Federal Invasion of Tuscaloosa, 1865." Northport, Ala., American Southern (Apr. 1965) sq.8vo, CSA-flag, wraps, 63pp. $1.

690 ..."The Military Operations of Gen. John T. Croxton in West Alabama, 1865." Montgomery, Ala., Transactions of Ala. Hist. Society, Reprint #22, 1904. $3.50, From: Ala. Hist. Soc., Trans.IV, 1899/1903. p. 449-463.

691 **CLOPTON, John Jones, Rev.**
"The True Stonewall Jackson." Baltimore:

Ruth's Sons, Print, 1913. 8vo, wraps, 28pp. $5.

692 **CLOPTON, William Izard, Judge**
"New Light on the great Drewry's Bluff Fight." In: SHSP, 1906, v.XXXIV, p. 82-98.

693 **CLOWER, George Wesley, Edt.**
"Confederate life at home & in camp: seven letters." In: GaHQ, Sept., 1956, v.40, p. 298-309, notes. Oak Hill, Ga., near Decatur-Camp near Fairfax, Va., & Camp Sam Jones, Oct. 1861-Feb. 1862. The Davis family: Moses, Ezekiel, Frances, Fredonia, etc.

694 **CLUBBS, Occie**
"Stephen Russell Mallory, United States Senator from Florida & Confederate Secretary of the Navy." In: FHQ, January 1947, v.XXV, #3, p. 221-245; pt. 2: Apr. 1947, #4, p. 295-318; pt. 3: July 1947, v.XXVI, #1, p. 56-76.

695 **COBB COUNTY, Georgia:**
See: Sarah B. Temple's "First 100 Years..."

696 **COBB, Andrew J., Judge**
"The Constitution of the Confederate States; its influence on the Union it sought to dissolve." In: Ga. H.Q., June 1921, v.V, #2, p. 7-15.

697 **COBB, Howell**
"Howell Cobb Papers. Edt: R.P. Brooks." In: Ga. H.Q., Mar-June-Sept-Dec. 1921. v.V, p. 50-61; 29-52; 35-55; 43-64; 1922, Mar-June-Sept-Dec., v.VI, p. 35-84; 147-173; 233-264; 355-394. Private & public papers, state, national political affairs.

698 ..."In Memory of Georgia's Gifted Statesman, Noble Patriot, Generous Friend, eloquent orator, sage, counsellor, & brave defender. Gen. Howell Cobb, born Sept. 7, 1815, died Oct. 9, 1868, etc., etc., dedicated to the people of Georgia by B.B. Euston, prof. of penmanship." Philadelphia: Moss & Co.(c.1868) Stell engraving, 19"x15", embellished portrait from Brady. $10.

699 ..."A Memorial Volume of the Hon. Howell Cobb, Edited by Samuel Boykin." Phila: J.B. Lippincott & Co., 1870. 12mo, cl, port, 280pp. $15, $17.50, $20, $75-b.

700 ..."Letter of Hon. Howell Cobb to the People of Georgia on the present condition of the country." $15. Washington: McGill & Witherow, 1860. 8vo, wraps, 15(i.e., 16)pp., DeRenne, III. See: U.B. Phillips-"Toombs, Stephens & Cobb Letters." Robt. Preston Brooks. See: Joseph Lamar Rucker's "Howell Cobb", in Men of Mark in Ga., 1911. v.III, p. 566-581.

701 ..."Howell Cobb's account, a dialogue with Charles C. Jones." In: CWTI, Aug., 1981, v.20, #5, p. 28-33, illus., ports.

702 **COBB, Howell, Gen.**
Portrait: Litho 19x15" (oval inset 7x5 1/4"). "In Memory of Georgia's gifted statesman, noble patriot, generous friend, eloquent orator, sage, counsellor, & brave defender Gen'l Howell Cobb, Born Sept. 7, 1815-Died Oct. 9, 1868." "O gracious God! not gainless in our loss: a glorious sunbeam gilds thy sternest frown; & while his country staggers with the cross, he rises with the crown." Dedicated to the people of Georgia. By B.B. Euston Prof. of penmanship." (seal) "State Agricultural College. Athens, Ga." "The above if a facsimile of the original executed entirely with a steel pen portrait from a photograph by Brady in possission of the family." Engr. by Moss & Co., Phila. (1868?) Elaborate wreath around a small oval portrait of Cobb, Old English lettering.

703 **COBB, J.**
"Augusta's(Ga.) Big Bang: the story of the Confederate Powder Works." In: Augusta Mag., 1981, v.7, #2, p. 17-19+.

704 **COBB, James C.**
"The Making of a Secessionist: Henry L.

Benning & the Coming of the Civil War." In: Ga. H.Q., Winter, 1976, v.LX, #4, p. 313-323.

705 **COBB, Jessie E., Librarian, Ala. Archives.**
"Publications in Alabama during the Confederacy located in the State Department of Archives & History." In: Alabama Historical Quarterly, Spring Issue, 1961, vol. 23, #1 & 2. p. 73-137. Largely in Crandall-Harwell. $15-bmk.

706 **COBB, John A.**
"Civil War incidents in Macon, Georgia." In: Ga. HQ, Sept., 1923, v.VII, p. 282-284.

707 **COBB, Thomas Read Rootes**
"The Correspondence of...1861-1862." In: Southern Historical Society Papers, 1900. v.XXVII, p. 280-301. Extracts, to his wife.

708 ..."The Correspondence of... 1860-1862." In: Southern Historical Association Publications. Washington, D.C., 1907. cl, 8vo, v.11: p. (147)-185, (233)-260, (312)-328. Incomplete, three installments above end May 1861. Sketch of Cobb by A.L. Hull, p. 148-156. LC.

709 ..."Substance of Remarks made by..., in the Hall of the House of Representatives, Monday evening, Nov. 12, 1860." Atlanta, Ga., John H. Seals, 1860. 8vo, sewn, 17pp.
...Reprint: in Allen D. Candler's "Confederate Records." v.1, p. 157-182.

710 ..."Code of the State of Georgia prepared by R.H. Clark, T.R.R. Cobb & D. Irwin." Atlanta, Ga. John H. Seals, Crusader Book & Job Office, 1861. 8vo, xxiii, 1057, (1)pp. The convention of the people of Ga., in sesseion at Savannah, resolved the new c ode be adapted to conform to the gov. of CSA instead of the U.S.A.

711 **COBB, William H.**
"Story of Moses & Margaret Phillips." Randolph Co. Hist. Soc. Mag. of Hist. & Biog., v.7, 1933, p. 30-33. Help for the CSA, Margaret as spy in that area.

712 **COBDEN, M.P. (Britain)**
"Speech of Mr. Cobden, on the "Foreign Inlistment Act", in the House of Commons, Friday, April 24, 1863." London: Wm. Ridgway, 1863. 8vo, sewn, 25pp(2pp. ads) $35. Blockade Running & Case of the Alabama.

713 **COBLENTZ, David Herr**
"Military dispatches from Yellow Tavern." In: Manuscripts, Fall 1956, v.8, p. 282-286, facsm. On 2 military dispatches of Maj. Gen. J.E.B. Stuart, 11 May 1864. See: Samuel H. Miller.

714 **COCHRAN, Hamilton**
"Blockade Runners of the Confederacy." Indianapolis: Bobbs-Merrill Co. (1958) 8vo, cl, dj, illus., (incl. front) ports, 350p. $12.50, $5(pub.), $7.50, $10. $15-$20-bmk, $35. $20-bmk-84, $16.50-y.
...Westport, Ct., Greenwood Pr., 1973, $18.

715 **COCHRAN, John Salisbury, Judge**
"Bonnie Belmont a Historical Romance of the Days of Slave & Civil War." (Wheeling, W.Va.), c.1907) Wheeling News Litho. Co. $7.50. 8vo, cl, ports, 2-pls, 1-fldg. 291, (1)pp. $15.

716 **COCHRAN, William C.**
"The dream of a Northwestern Confederacy." In: Wis. HSP, 1917, v.LXIV, p. 213-253. "Force states with watershed of Mississippi to join the CSA or break with New England, Atlantic states & join the CSA by treaty.

717 **COCHRANE, Harden Perkins**
"The letters of Harden Perkins Cochrane, 1862-1864. Arranged by Harriet Fitts Ryan." In: Ala. Rev., Oct. 1954-Dec. 1955, v.7, p. 277-294; v.8, p. 55-70, 143-152, 219-228, 277-290. Letters from a member of Co.D., 2nd Ala. cavalry, dated in Ala., Miss., Fla., & Ga.
..."The letters of Harden Perkins Cochrane, 1862-1864." In: ARev., Jan. 1955, v.8,

#1, p. 55-70; 1954, v.7, p. 277-294; Apr. 1955, p. 143-152; July, p. 219-228; Oct., p. 277-290.

718 **COCKE, Preston**
"The Battle of New Market & the cadets of the Virginia Military Institute, May 15, 1864; salient features of the battle in connection with the part taken by the cadets, with map of battlefield & key. By a V.M.I. New Market Cadet." (Richmond, Va.?) 1914. $50-b, $10, $5. 8vo, wraps, 11pp. double map. Prefatory note signed: Preston Cocke. Reprint-7-new.

719 **COCKRELL, Monroe Fulkerson**
"After Sundown-Dropped Stitches in the War Between the States, a few unknown & long forgotten bignettes, graphic, pathetic, tragic & even ludicrous." (Chicago, Ill., 1959) Vol.X, 12mo, wraps, (28)pp., illus., facsms. 1142 Hinman Ave., Evanston, Ill.

720 ..."First Manassas-Wilmer McLean Appomattox." Evanston, Ill., 1965. 4to, 1-vol. (various pagings) illus., maps. Includes bibliography.

721 ..."The Lost Account of the Battle of Corinth & Court-Martial of Gen. Van Dorn by an Unknown Author. Intro. & Informal Essay on the Battle by..." 8vo, stiff decr. color wraps, plates, port, 78pp. $3.50, $5, $7.50, $37.50, $20-bmk, $9, $12.50-y, $15-nc. Jackson, Tenn., McCowat-Mercer, 1955. See: G.W. Dudley.

722 ..."The Military Campaigns of Nathan Bedford Forrest, Forrest's Cavalry CSA, 1861-1865. Historical map prepared by... & reprinted from "As They Saw Forrest", Edt. by Robert Selph Henry, Jackson, Tenn., McCowat-Mercer Press (1956) $1. 8vo, stiff folder, map-17" sq., (1)p. facsm. of "Address Maj-Gen. N.B. Forrest to His Troops", Jan. 12, 1865. (Map omits Sturgis' March to Cross Roads by Andrew Brown, in the Robert S. Henry volume, & remainder of Forrest's address to troops.)

723 ..."Notes & Articles by..., for his maps of the War Between the States." (Evanston, Ill., 1950) 4to, wraps, front(port), illus., ports, fldg. maps in pocket, mimeogr. (various paging) Priv. print, 22 copies. Cover title: "Civil War studies, with maps." N.B. Forest, Federal Occupation of Corinth, May 30, 1862, "Fight of nearby Iuka, Sept. 19, 1862, Battle of Corinth, Oct. 5, 1862, Siege of Vicksburg, May 18, 1862-July 4, 1863, Fight at the Hatchie, Oct. 5, 1862.

724 ..."The Siege of Vicksburg, May 18, 1862, to July 4, 1863." (Evanston, Ill.?) 1949. Map 78x55cm. showing Mississippi Valley from Memphis to the Louisiana line, with chronological & milage table & notes.

725 ..."Stonewall Jackson." Evanston, Ill., 1955. 4to, wraps, 12pp. Limited Edt. 25 copies. Biographical notations. $20.

726 ..."General Nathan Bedford Forrest, CSA." (Houston, Texas. Civil War Round Table, Address Feb. 21, 1955. 8 1/2x11, heavy paper covers, folded to 8vo, 10pp.

727 ..."Where did Confederate General Nathan Bedford Forrest cross the Sipsey River in Alabama on March 29, 1865? Where are the bridge & the two ferries named in his order & where are the graves of the two alleged deserters who had been shot at the bridge?" n.p. (Evanston, Ill.?) 1956. 4to, (12) 1, maps.

728 ..."The Bivouac of the Dead" & "The Old Pioneer" by Theodore O'Hara; a venture into the shadows of yesterday." (Evanston, Ill? 1951?) 4to, (11)pp.

729 **COCKE, St. Geo., Brig. Gen.**
"Headquarters, Potomac Department, Culpeper, C.H., May 5, 1861." (Richmond, Va., 1861) Narrow quarto, 1p Broadside. $35. Appeals to citizens of Va. to enlist in the Confederate Army.

730 **COCKRELL, Francis Marion**
"A.L. Sig." 8vo, 4pp. Missouri, 1875. $95-gdsp. Brig. Gen. CSA, re: reunion in Caldwell, Ohil.

731 ..."The Senator from Missouri, The Life & Times of Francis Marion Cockrell." N.Y., Exposition Press, 1962. 8vo, cl, d/w, 114pp. $3. In Battles Wilson Creek, Pea Ridge, Iuka, Corinth, Vicksburg & became Brig.-Gen. in CSA.
..."Francis Marion Cockrell of Missouri; a sketch of his life & military record, with documentary evidence." n.p. (Evanston, Ill?) 1954.

731a **COCKRELL, Monroe Fulkerson**
"Nathan Bedford Forrest, General CSA. An outline of an address by Monroe Cockrell before the Houston Civil War round table, Feb. 21, 1955." Houston, Texas, Civil War Roundtable. 4to, folder, 10 leaves, mimeograph.

732 **CODDINGTON, Edwin B.**
"Prelude to Gettysburg: The Confederates Plunder Pennsylvania." In: Penna. Hist., 1963, v.XXX, p. 123-157.

733 ..."The activities & attitudes of a Confederate business man: Gazaway L. Lamar." In: JSH, Feb. 1943, p. 34, v.9, #1, p. 3-36, $8-bmk.

734 ..."Soldiers' Relief in the Seaboard States of the Southern Confederacy." (Cedar Rapids, Ia.) MVHR, June 1950, v.XXXVII, #1, p. 17-38.

735 **CODY, Annie E.**
"History of the Tennessee Division, United Daughters of the Confederacy." (Nashville, Tenn., c.1947) 8vo, cl, 374pp. $6, $10.

736 **CODY, Barnett Hardeman**
"Letters of Barnett Hardeman Cody & others, 1861-1864. Contributed, with notes, by Edmund Cody Burnett." In: Ga.H.Q., Sept. 1939, v.XXIII, #3, p. 265-299, Dec. 1939, #4, p. 362-380.
...(Savannah?) 1939, cover title, (265)-315pp., $15.

737 **COFFIN, C.H.**
"Reminiscences of the Confederacy, J.U. Payne, of New Orleans, La.-devotion to & sacrifice to the Cause." In: SHSP, 1907, v.XXXV, p. 127-131.

738 **COFFIN, James P.**
"Confederate Cemeteries in Arkansas." In: Pub. Ark. Hist. Assn., v.II, 1908, p. 296-306.

739 **COFFMAN, Edward M.**
"Captain Thomas Henry Hines & his Feb., 1863 raid." In: RKHS, 1957, v.LV, p. 105-108.
..."Capt. Hines adventures in the Northwest Conspiracy." In: RKHS, Jan. 1965, v.63, #1, p. 30-38. See: SB, II, Jan. 1887, p. 502; DEc. 1886, Feb./Apr. 1887.

740 **COFFMAN, Richard M.**
"A vital unit-true history of 10,000 volunteers, Phillips Legion." In: CWTI. Jan. 1982, v.20, #9, p. 40-45, illus., ports.

741 **COGGIN, James M.**
"Chickamauga, a reply to Major Sykes." In: SHSP, 1884, v.XIII, 219-224pp.

742 **COGGINS, Jack**
"Arms & Equipment of the Civil War." 4to, cl, d/w, profusely ill. by author, 160pp. N.Y., Doubleday & Co., 1962, $2, $10, $5.95, $35-bmk-84.

743 **COHEN, Barry M.**
"The Texas-Mexican Border, 1858-1867. Along the Lower Rio Grande Valley during the decade of the American Civil War & the French Intervention in Mexico." In: Texana, Summer, 1968, v.VI, #2, p. 153-165.

744 **COHEN, Fanny**
"Fanny Cohen's Journal of Sherman Occupation of Savannah. Edt: Spencer B. King, Jr." In: Ga. H.Q., December 1957, v.XLI, #4, p. 407-415.

745 **COHEN, Henning**
"Florena Budwin-woman of mystery." In: SC Mag. Feb. 1949, v.12(#2), p. 21, 46, facsms. On death of Capt. Budwin & his alleged wife, Florena, enlisted in disguise as his orderly in the military prison at Florence, SC, 1864.

746 **COHEN, Henry**
"A modern Macabean, by Rev. Henry Cohen, Galveston, Texas." Baltimore: Friedenwald Press, 1897. 8vo, wraps, (31)-37, cover title. From the Publication of the American Jewish Historical Society, #6, 1897.

747 **COHN, Douglas A., Capt.**
"Jackson's Valley Campaign, with maps from the West Point Atlas of the Civil War." Wash., American Pub. Co., 1986. Sq. 8vo, stiff wraps (pict) 120pp., illus., ports, maps.

748 **"COINS, connected with**
the Confederate states." In: Numismatist, Mar. 1919, v.XXXII, p. 101-104. See: Sr. S.N. Browne.

749 **COIT, James C.**
"The Battle of the Crater, a Letter from Major J.C. Coit, Aug. 2, 1879." In: SHSP, 1882, v.X, p. 123-130.

750 **COIT, Joseph H.**
"The Civil War Diary of Joseph H. Coit." In: MdHM, Sept. 1965, v.60, #3, p. 245-260.

751 **COKE, John A., et al**
"Memorials of three great Virginians, Matthew Fontaine Maury, Robert Edward Lee, Thomas Jonathan ("Stonewall") Jackson." Richmond: United Daughters of the Confederacy, 1924. 8vo, wraps, 16pp. $4.

752 **"COKER HOUSE**
prominent landmark on Champion Hill Battlefield." (Jackson, Miss., 1985) 12mo, stiff pict. wraps, (14)pp. illus., map tint cover.

753 **COKER, Charles Frederick**
"North Carolina Civil War records: an introduction to printed & mssc. sources." Raleigh, N.C. Archives Information circular #4, Revised, 1972. 8vo, wraps, 10pp.

754 **COKER, Elizabeth Boatwright**
"La Belle; a novel based on the life of the notorious Southern Belle, Marie Boozer." N.Y., Dutton Pub., 1959, 8vo, cl, 320pp. bibliog. See: "A Checkered Life..." $15.

755 **COKER, Hannah Lide, Mrs.**
"A Story of the Late War, written at the request of her children, grandchildren & many friends." Charleston, S.C., Walker, Evans, Cogswell. 1887. Privately printed for the family. 12mo, cl, 47pp.

756 **COKER, James Lide**
"History of Co.G, 9th SC Reg., S.C. Army, & Co. E, 6th S.C. Reg., S.C. Army. Prepared & published by request of the survivors of these companies, by..., formerly Maj. 6th S.C. vs Inf." Charleston: Walker, Evans & Cogswell, 1899, 12mo, cl, 210pp. 150 copies printed. $17, $37.50, $50, $75, $1250-ob, $600.
...N.Y. Attic Books, 1979. See: E.L. Wilkins, $12.50-y, $20.

757 **COKER, W.B.C.**
"Letters to the head writer's brother, F.M. Coker. Edt: Sylvia Head." In: Ga. Rev., Winter, 1960, v.14, p.355-360. From Camp Cutts (a mile from Manassas) 28 July 1861, & Camp, Mercer's Brig. Army of Tenn., 15 Sept. 1864. His military experiences in Va. & Ga.

758 **COKER, W.C.**
"Sketch of the organization of the Darlington companies in the 8th Reg. S.C. Volunteers of the Confed. Army." "Treasured Reminiscences" collected by John K. McIver Camp, UDC-Columbia, SC, State Press, 1911.

759 **COLBERT, Laura A., Mrs.**
"Broken Links & Southern Soldiers, with

Sketches & Poems." Nashville, Tenn., 1873, 12mo, cl, 269pp. $5.50

760 **COLBURN, Warren**
"Colburn's First Lessons-Intellectual Arithmetic, upon the inductive method of instruction." Houston, Texas: E.H. Cushing, 1865. 12mo, printed boards, 124pp. Crandall-4046 lists only Nashville imprint.

761 **COLBY, C.B.**
"Civil War Weapons Small Arms & Artillery of the Blue & Gray." N.Y., Coward-McCann, Inc., (1962) Sm.4to, cl, illus., 48pp. $4.50-y

762 **COLBY, Elbridge**
"A battle of civilians." In: Mil. Engineers, 1939, v.XXI, p. 49-57, Battle "Big Bethel", Va. in 1861.

763 ..."Introducing a new Lee." In: Mil.Engineer, 1935, v.XXVII, p. 123-124. Review of Douglas Freeman's Lee.

764 **COLBY, Leonard Wright**
"Return of a Confederate Flag to its original owner." In: SHSP, 1891, v.XIX, p. 263-266.

765 **COLD HARBOR, Battle of, 1862-1864**
See: Edward McCrady; Joseph Virgininius Bidgood; A. DuBois; William Worthington Goldsborough; B.M. Parham; Thos. Lanier Clingman; Evander McIvor Law; Martin Thomas McMahon.

766 **COLE, Arthur Charles**
"The South & the right of Secession in the early fifties." In: Miss. Valley Hist. Rev., Dec. 1914, v.1, p. 376-399. $3.75.

767 ..."The Era of the Civil War, 1848-1870." Springfield, Ill: Illinois Centennial Commission, 1919. 8vo, cl, front, ports, maps, 7p, 499pp. Good bibliography.
...N.Y., Arno Press, (1972) "Select bibliographies Reprint series. Facsimilie Edition. $26-y, $12.50.

768 ..."President Lincoln & his war-time critics." In: Hist. Teach. Mag., May 1918, v.IX, p. 245-249.

769 ..."The Irrepressible Conflict, 1850-1865." New York: Macmillan Co., 1934. 8vo, cl, xv, 468pp., pls, ports, map, facsms. "A history of American life.", v.VII, $4, $7.50-y. A conflict between two different civilizations contesting, one for supremacy, the other for independence. $12.50-can
...N.Y., Scholarly Press Reprints, 1971. $29.50. Also: Paperback-"History of American Life Series" $4.45.

770 **COLE, Birdie Haile**
"The Battle of Pilot Knob." In: CV, Sept. 1914, v.XXII, p. 417.

771 **COLE, C.M., Memphis Tenn.**
"Vivid war experiences at Ripley, Miss." In: CV, 1905, v.13, p. 262-265. Letter written by Cole's mother to "Cousin Blance" of Franklin, Tenn., but never received.

772 **COLE, Ellen Bryant**
"Recollections (ca.1907) of the battle of Appomattox Court House (1865)." In: Tyler QHGM, Apr. 1952, v.33, p. 233-241. notes. Info. about site from N.R. Featherston.

773 **COLE, Fred C. & C.W. Darden**
"Robert Augustus Toombs." Schenectady, N.Y. (1961) Union College Pub., (Union Worthies, #16) cover title. 8vo, wraps, port, 26pp. $2.50. Books by & about Toombs, p. 25-26.

774 **COLE, H.E.**
"Belle Boyd, Rebel Spy." In: Wis. Mag., May 1924, v.II, p. 32, 42-43.

775 **COLE, J.R.**
"Sketches of the 22nd Reg. North Carolina State Troops First Two Years of the War." In: OLOD, Dec. 1874, v.1, #4, p. 305-313.

776 **COLE, James Reid**
"Miscellany by James Reid Cole. President of Cole's Classical & Military School, Dallas, Texas." Dallas, Texas: Ewing B. Bedford Press, 1897. 12mo, cl, 303pp. $12.50. CSA, chaps: 1, XVI, XXVI-

XXVII. Life: C.V., August 1918, v.XXVI, p. 334-346.

777 COLE, Robert G.
"Feeding Paroled Confederates." In: SHSP, 1891, v.XIX, p. 266.

778 COLE, Ruth H.
"The Battle of Olustee, a description of Florida's major battle in the War Between the States, which took place near Lake City, Feb. 20, 1864 by Ruth H. Cole, a senior in Rollins College.(Winter Park, Fla.) Florida Division United Daughters of the Confederacy." Winter Park, Fla., Rollins College, 1929. 12mo, wraps, 15pp. See also: Geo. F. Baltzell, Milton M. Woodford. $7.50, $35-ob.

779 COLEMAN, Aruthr C.
"Roster: 38th Regiment, Ga. Volunteer Infantry." In: Armchair Researcher, 1981, v.2, #2, p. 66-80+. Soldiers from DeKalb, Milton, Emmanuel, Hart Bulloch, Oglethorpe, Elbert, Jefferson, Dawson & Fulton counties.

780 COLEMAN, Carolina S.
"Origin of the "Red Shirts", & adoption of uniform." In: UDCM, July 1948, v.11, #7, p. 12-13. Followers of Wade Hampton.

781 COLEMAN, Charles H.
"The Election of 1868: the Democratic Effort to Regain Control." N.Y., Columbia Univ. Press, 1933. Columbia Univ. Studies, #392. 8vo, cl, 407pp. (iisued also as a thesis)

782 ..."The Charleston Riot, Mar. 28, 1864." In: Ill. State HSJ, 1940, v.XXIII, p. 7-56. Charleston, Ill. riots between union soldiers & "Copperheads", illustrating factionalism of the time. (by Coleman & Paul H. Spence)

783 ..."The use of the term "Copperhead" during the Civil War." In: MVHR, Sept., 1940.

784 COLEMAN, Chew
"War's Bravest Deeds." See sketch by Charles P. Young, late of Crenshaw's Battery, CSA.

785 COLEMAN, Edith Stetson
"Alexander Smith Atkinson, 1815-1894." In: Ga. H.Q., June 1939, v.XXIII, #2, p. 154-169. Camden Co., Ga. planter, Legislature of Ga., & Capt. Co.B, 26th Ga. Reg.

786 COLEMAN, Elizabeth Dabney
"The captain was a lady." In: Cavalcade (Va.) Summer 1956, v.6, #1, p. 35-41. facsms, port views(1 col.). On Sally Louise Thompkins (1829-1916) Capt. in CSArmy, managed a military hospital in Richmond Aug. 1861-June 1865.

787 ..."Laurel twined with cypress." In: Va. Cav., Spring 1956, v.5, #4, p. 32-38. facsms, ports, views (1 dbl-column) On funeral of Stonewall Jackson, 11/15 May 1863.

788 COLEMAN, Hannah Hemphill, Edt.
"Stories of Of't told tales of Confedcy." n.p., n.d., S.C.(?) (not all CSA) spiral bnd., 63pp. $14-bmk.

789 COLEMAN, Hubert A.
"Notes on the Civil War Correspondence of Private Henry Tucker." (Baton Rouge, La.) JSH, Aug. 1944, v.X, #3, p. 343-355.

790 COLEMAN, J. Winston, Jr.
"Lexington During the Civil War." Lexington, Ky., Commercial Print, 1938. 8vo, stiff wraps, illus., 51pp. $15. Limited Edt., 150 copies.
...Lexington: Henry Clay Press, 1968, 8vo, wraps, illus., notes, 48pp. $7.50.

791 ...Lexington Slave Dealers & their Southern Trade." In: FCHQ, January 1938, v.12, #1, p. 1-23.

792 COLEMAN, Johnnie
"Centennial in Commemoration of the Civil War Marietta-Cobb & North Georgia 1861-1865/1961-1965. Battle of Kennesaw Mountain." Marietta, Ga.,

Johnnie W. Coleman. (1961) 4to, color pict. wraps, ports, illus., maps (96)pp.

793 **COLEMAN, Kenneth**
"Confederate Athens." Athens: University Press of Georgia, (1967) 12mo, cl, dj, illus., maps (partly fold.) ix, 214pp. $10.

794 **COLEMAN, R.B.**
"Indian tribes in the Confederacy." In: CV, Nov. 1916, v.XXIV, p. 509.

795 ..."More of scouting in Missouri & Arkansas." In: CV, Nov. 1911, v.XIX, p. 525-526.

796 ..."Secession of Indians from the U.S., full text/negotiations." In: CV, 1903, v.11, p. 444-460.

797 **COLEMAN, S. James, Mrs.**
"Maj-Gen. James Lawson Kemper (1822-1895)." In: UDCMag. June 1948, v.11, #6, p. 20-22. Career in CSArmy & Va. politics.

798 **COLEMAN, Wiliam M.**
(copywrighted) Price $.25. "The Evidence that Abraham Lincoln was not born in Lawful Wedlock, or the Sad Story of Nancy Hanks." Caption title(1899?) signed: Wm. M.C., Dallas, Texas. 8vo, cl, 18pp. $3.

799 **COLEMAN, William, Ky.**
"Appeal to the People of the North." (Louisville, Ky., Hanna & Co., 1861) 8vo, sewn, 16pp. Sabin-14315.
...2nd Edition. (4 editions in all) signed: "A Voice from Kentucky."

800 **COLEY, C.J.**
"The Battle Horseshoe Bend." In: AHQ, 1952, #1 & 2, p. 129-134. (See: Paul Ghioto)

801 **"COLLECTION of Louisiana Confederate Letters, A.**
Edt: Frank E. Vandiver." In: LaHQ, 1943, v.XXVI, p. 937-974. Henry E., E. Jefferson, George M. & William C. Lee.

802 **"COLLECTION of War Songs of the South, A.**
By the Ladies of the Marietta Memorial Association for the benefit of the Confederate Cemetery at Marietta, Ga.(eight lines of verst)." Atlanta, Ga., Franklin Print, 1895. 8vo, wraps, 16pp. (unnumbered). Cover title: Southern War Songss. DeRenne III, 929.

803 **"COLLEGE HOSPITAL in Gettysburg."**
"In: LWL, Feb. 1867, v.II, #4, p. 290-295.

804 **COLLIER, Bryan Wells, Mrs. (Margaret Wooten)**
"Biographies of representative women of the South 1861-1920." Volume I. n.p., n.d., (1920?) 8vo, cl, 324pp. $10-bmk. Emphasis on service to the CSA.

805 **COLLIER, Calvin L., Capt.**
"They'll do to Tie To" The Story of the third Regiment Arkansas Infantry, C.S.A." (Little Rock, Ark., Pioneer Press, 1959) Published by Maj. James D. Warren, USAF, 8vo, cl, dj, maps, vi, 233pp. $5, $7.50, $15-y, $35-b, $25-bmk-105. Muster rolls: p. 15-32, 221-231.

806 ..."First in-Last Out/The Capitol Guards, Ark. Brigade." Little Rock, Ark., Pioneer Press (1961). 8vo,cl, dj, maps, illus., ports, (4)vi, 161, (1)p. Muster Roll-11-15pp. $7.50, $12, $15.

807 ..."The War Child's Children. The Story of the Third Regiment, Arkansas Cavalry, Confederate States Army." 1965 (Little Rock, Ark., Pioneer Press) o.p., 8vo, cl, dj, ports, illus., maps, ix, 129pp. $12.50-7, $10, $37, $16-bmk, $20, $22.50. Muster Rolls: p. 9-20, 135-138.

808 **COLLIER, Charles F.**
"War Recollections, story of the Evacuation of Petersburg, by an eye-witness." In: SHSP, 1894, v.XXII, p. 69-73.

809 **COLLIER, William Armistead, Jr., Chairman**
"Report of the History Commission of United Sons of Confederate Veterans at

8th Annual Reunion." n.p., n.d., 8vo, wraps, cover title, 20pp.

810 **COLLINS, Clarence B.**
"Tom & Joe. Two farmer boys in war & peace & love. A Louisiana memory." Richmond, Va., E. Waddey, 1890. 12mo, cl, front(port), 259pp. $7.50. A story based on fact.

811 **COLLINS, Andy**
"To the victor belongs the spoils." In: MHR, Jan. 1986, v.70, #2, p. 176-195, illus., maps, ports.

811a **COLLINS, Bruce W.**
"Governor Joseph E. Brown, economic issues & Georgia's road to secession, 1857-1859." In: GHQ, Summer 1987, v.71, #2, p.189-25, ills, ports.

812 **COLLINS, Elizabeth**
"Memoirs of the Southern States (1859-1865) By Elizabeth Collins...(An English Servant Maid)." Taunton, England: Barnicutt Print, 1865. 12mo, cl, (6), 116pp. Sabin-14435. Sympathtic to C.S.A.- Southern way of Life.

813 **COLLINS, R.M., Lt.**
"Chapters from the unwritten history of the War Between the States; or, the incidents in the life of a Confederate soldier, in camp, on the march, in the great battles, & in prison, by Lieut. R.M.Collins, Co. B., 15th Texas Granbury's Brigade, Cleburne's Division, Army of Tennessee." St. Louis: Nixon-Jones Print, 1893. 12mo, cl, illus., facsm., ports(incl. front), 335pp. $300-jk-145, $300-bmk-105, $12.50, $27.50, $35, $50, $65, $95-jk, $90-mor., $75, $200-jk-97.
...Dayton, Ohio, Morningside Pr., 1982, Intro: Norman D. Brown. Index. Edition of 300 copies. $31.50

814 **COLLINS, Richard H.**
"Civil War Annals of Kentucky, 1861-1865." by Richard H. Collins. Edt: Hambleton Tapp." In: FCHQ, July 1961, v.35, #3, "Civil War Centennial Number." p. 205-322. Extract from Collins' larger 2vol. work, Louisville, 1924; a reprint of the Louisville 1877 edition of 909pp. Collins played a part in the war period, a definite Southern tone. $15-bmk.

815 **COLLINS, Thomas Benton**
"A Texan's Account of the Battle of Val Verde." In: Panhandle-Plains Hist. Rev., 1964, v.XXXVII, p. 33-35. 5th Texas Cavalry.

816 **COLLINS, William B.**
"Herschel V. Johnson in the Georgia Secession Convention." In: Ga. H.Q., Dec., 1927, v.XI, #4, p. 330-333.

817 **COLONNA, B.A.**
"The Battle of New Market, Va. By B.A. Colonna, cadet Capt. "D" Co., V.M.I., May 15, 1864." In: JMSIUS. New York, 1912, v.51, #180, Nov/Dec. 8vo, wraps, map, p. (341)-351.

818 **"COLORS of the First South Carolina volunteers (Gregg's Regiment).**
Presented by the ladies of Charleston, on departure of the regiment for Virginia, Apr. 22, 1861." n.p., 186-. Broadside, 56x55 1/2cm. Dorn-II, 885. List of officers, record of deaths, wounds.

819 **COLQUITT, Alfred Holt**
"Battle of Ocean Pond, Florida (Olustee, Fla.)" In: SHSP, 1881, v.9, p. 20-23.

820 **COLSTON, Frederick M., Capt.**
"Recollections of the last months in the Army of Northern Virginia." In: SHSP, 1910, V.XXXVIII, p. 1-15.

821 ..."Efficiency of General Lee's ordnance: recollections of the last month in the Army of Northern Virginia." In: CV, Jan. 1911, v.XIX, p. 22-26.

822 **COLSTON, Raleigh Edward, Gen.**
"Address before the Ladies' Memorial Ass'n., Wilmington, N.C., May 10, 1870." In: SHSP, 1893, v.XXI, p. 38-49.

823 ..."General Raleigh E. Colston, C.S.A.-Army, a tribute to the memory of the Gallant & Accomplished Soldier." In: SHSP, 1897, v.XXV, p. 346-351.

824 ...(Washington, D.C., Confederate Veterans Association, 1897.) 8vo, wraps, 8pp, (reprint of above article)

825 ..."General Colston's Ode to the Confederate Soldier's Monument in Oakdale Cemetery, Wilmington, N.C." In: SHSP, 1897, v.XXV, p. 352-353.

826 ..."Lee's knowledge of Hooker's movements." In: B & L, v.III, p. 233.

827 ..."Official report of the operations of General Colston's division during the battle of Chancellorsville, May 2 & #, 1863." In: So.Mag., 1863, v.XI, p. 57-63. Dorn-II, 1669.
...Same, July 1872, v.4, #1, 128pp., wraps, $15.

828 ..."Watching the Merrimac." In: Cent. Mag., Mar., 1885, v.XXIX, p. 763-766. Also in B & L.

829 **COLSTON, William E.**
"An old letter & a epitaph. Edt: J.A. Campbell Colston." In: Md.HM, June 1956, v.51, p. 158-160., notes. Letter to Fred M. Colston, Suffolk, Va., June 4, 1861, from an officer in CSArmy; with an acct. of his death in action, reprinted from Baltimore Sun.

830 **COLTON, Ray Charles**
"The Civil War in the Western Territories: Arizona, Colorado, New Mexico & Utah." Norman, University Oklahoma Press(1959). 8vo, cl, dj, illus., ports, maps, ix, 230pp. $9.50, $30-b.

831 **COLTRANE, Daniel Branson**
"The Memories of...Co. 1, 63rd Reg. North Carolina Cavalry, C.S.A." Raleigh: Edwards & Broughton, 1956, 8vo, wraps, 64pp., xiiipp. ports, op, $100-b. Preface: Stuart Chevalier, foreword: Mrs. Inglis Fletcher.

832 **COLUMBIA COUNTY, Florida**
Keuchel, Edward P. - "A history of Columbia County, Florida." Tallahassee, Fla., Sentry Press, 1981. 8vo, cl, xii, 267pp., illus., append., bibliog. $12.40. Covers secession & CSA in war, Battle of Olustee. Append: Columbia Co. Men in War.

833 **"COLUMBIA RECORDS proudly presents**
"The Confederacy", based on the music of the South during the years 1861-1865. by Richard Bales. The National Gallery Orchestra & Cantata Choir of Lutheran Church of the Reformation, Washington. Issued as a record, also in a cloth bound book describing origin & presentation of the music. Illustrated & with essays by Bruce Catton & Clifford Dowdey." N.Y., Columbia Records, n.d. (1960's) 4to decr. color cloth, ports, group ports facsms, music, illus., Pocket for record.

834 **COLUMBIA, S.C., Burning of**
"See: J.P. Carroll, Alex R. Chisolm, James W. Davidson, Wade Hampton, Mrs. Agnes Law, Thos. J. Myers, Edward L. Wells.

835 **COLVER, J. Newton**
"Lee the American. An Address by... Jan. 19, 1924." n.p., n.d., 8vo, wraps, 16pp. $2.

836 **COLVIN, R.M.**
"A visit to Point Lookout Prison." In: CV, Dec., 1914, v.XXII, p. 548. Reminiscences of imprisonment at Point Lookout, Md.

837 **COLWELL, Stephen**
"The Five Cotton States & New York; or remarks upon the social & economical aspects of the Southern political crisis." (Phila.?) 1861. 8vo, wraps, 64pp. Swem-1067.

838 **COMMAGER, Henry S. & Lynd K. Ward**
"America's Robert E. Lee." Boston: Houghton Mifflin Co., 1951, 8vo, cl, illus., 111pp. Young Peoples Biography. $3.

839 **COMMAGER, Henry Steele**
"The Blue & the Gray. The Story of the Civil War as told by participants." Indianapolis: Bobbs-Merrill Co.(1950). tk. v8o, cl, pict. end-sheets (illus., incl. front, maps, index, bibliog. 1155-1186pp., xxxv, 588, xv, (589)-1201. $7.50, $14, $12.50, $50, 1979 rep. #40-y, $22.50-jk, $4-30-bond.

840 **"COMMISSIONER'S REPORT,**
commission appointed to cooperate with the National Park Commission in locating positions of Texas Troops during the siege & defense of Vicksburg." Greenville, Texas: Herland Print (1901?) 8vo, wraps, cover title, 12pp. Dorn-II, 2896.

841 **"COMMITTEE of the 7% Cotton Bond-holders Report**
Report of the Committee of the 7% Cotton Bond-Holders of the Confederate States of America." London: W. Clowes & Sons, 1865. 8vo, wraps, 28pp.

842 **"COMPANY B, Twenty-first Virginia."**
In Worthington's 'Maryland Line." p.160-162.

843 **"COMPANY C, Thirty-seventh Virginia Infantry."**
A list of the officers & privates & brief history." In: SHSP, 1903, v.XXXI, p. 185-189. From Richmond, Va., Dispatch, May 16, 1902.

844 **"COMPANY D, Eighteenth Virginia Infantry.**
Reunion of survivors-War Roster of the Company." In: SHSP, v.19, p. 120-122.

845 **"COMPANY E, 37th Tennessee Infantry Regiment."**
n.p., n.d., 8vo, sewn, 4pp. Raised in Madison Co., but remained with 37th Tenn., through the War.

846 **"COMPANY E, Third Regiment Georgia Cavalry."**
In: Helen Terrill's "Hist. Stewart Co., Ga. 1958."

847 **"COMPANY G of the 18th Virginia Cavalry."**
In: SHSP, 1907, v.35, p. 161-165. From: Times Dispatch (Richmond).

848 **"COMPANY G, Twenty-sixth Virginia Regiment, muster Roll."**
In: Goldsborough's "Maryland Line", p. 249-256.

849 **"COMPANY G, 19th Regiment, Henry County, Ga., C.S.A."**
In: NW Ga. Geneal. & Hist. Soc. Qurt., 1980, v.12, No.2, p. 46-48.

850 **"COMPANY of Military Collectors**
& Historians (Providence, R.I.)" Uniforms, in Quart., Mar. 1953-June 1955: 5th Company, Washington Artillery of New Orleans, CSA, 1862 (Plate 81). "5th Company, Washington Artillery of New Orleans, CSA, 1862 (Plate 81)." "Terry's Texas Rangers (8th Texas Cavalry CSA, 1864 (Plate 84)." "Sussex Light Dragoons, Virginia State Cavalry, 1861 (Plate 100)."

851 ..."Company of Military Collectors & Historians (Providence, R.I.)" Spring - Winter, 1958, v.10, p. 20-22, 46-50, 111-114, partial contents: Frederick P. Todd's "Confederate Shoes", Lee A. Wallace, Jr. 1st Sgt. Charles Stevens Powell, North Carolina Volunteers, 1861, Stanley J. Olsen- "US & Confederate Artillery Driver's saddles."
...Do: p. 71-82, 105-110. Fall - Winter, views. No.146 - "Battalion of Washington Artillery of New Orleans, 1861."

852 **"COMPANY ROLL**
& a Brief Historical Sketch."
See: J.H. Savage.

853 **"COMPARATIVE GENERALSHIP."**
e/g., Lee & Grant. In: LWL, August 1868, v.V, No.4, p. 292-299.

854 **"COMPILATION of laws**
relating to accounts due deceased officers & enlisted men of the army; claims of Confederate soldiers for horses, side-

arms, & baggage alleged to have been taken from them by Federal troops at & after the surrender at Appomattox, in violation of the terms of the surrender, etc." Wash., GPO, 1909. 8vo, sewn, 11pp.

855 **"COMPILATION of narrative histories, The,**
or historical sketches of Alabama commands, 1861-1865." (Montgomery, Ala., Dept. of Archives & History, circular no. 6. 8vo, caption title, 7pp, paper $5.

856 **"COMPILATION of records,**
correspondence, muster rolls, etc. on file in the Adjutant General's office." by W.S. Ford. Adjutant General's Biennial Report, 1894, p. 193-224. Owens (P.860) Alabma.

857 **"COMPLETE ROLL, famous Co. A, 7th Va. Cavalry, ANV."**
See: Joshua C. Fletcher.

858 **"COMPLETE Set of Forms, A**
intended to aid the officers of the Army & Navy in the performance of the painful duty of drawing up charges & specifications for trial of courts martial & military courts." By an experienced Judge Advocate of the CSArmy." Richmond, 1864. 1.vol. Notes: v.XX, #4, p. 428, 1912, Va. Mag. Hist. & Biog.

859 **"COMPREHENSIVE HISTORY**
of the Great Civil War, from Bull Run to Appomattox, containing correct accounts of the leading statesmen & Generals, both in the Union & Confederate councils & battlefields. Together with full & vivid accounts of all the important sieges, battles, & naval engagements." N.Y., World Manufacturing Co., (1885). 12mo, cl, front, illus., 552pp.

860 **COMPREHENSIVE SKETCH**
of the Merrimac & Monitor Naval Battle, giving an accurate account of the most important Naval Battle in the annals of war." Theophile Poilpot, N.Y., New York panorama Corp., 1886, 8vo, wraps, 15pp. Their exhibit of a pix of engagement, engravings.

861 **"COMPREHENSIVE Sketch, A,**
of the battle of Manassas; or, second battle of Bull Run, giving a brief account of one of the most important engagements of the late civil war." ts. Washington, DC, Manassas Panorama Co., 1886. Large 8vo, wraps, 24pp., illus., maps $40.

862 **COMPTON, James**
"Memoirs of...Lieut. Co. A, Jackson railroad rifles." In: Illinois Central Mag., Sept. 1913 & Oct., v.II, #3 & $. p. 13-18, 13-18, port.

863 **COMSTOCK, Anthony**
"A Jefferson Davis Document." In: Jour. Amer. Hist., 1911, v.V, #4, p. 599-600. Inventory personal effects of Davis when captured at Waldo,Fla., 6-15-65.

864 **"CONDITIONS of Peace**
required to the So-Called Seceded States. Article 1. Unconditional submission to the Gov. of the United States. Article 2. To deliver up One Hundred of the Arch Traitors, to be hung (8 articles in all, followed by a short paragraph): The above is the least that indignant people will accept, outraged a they have been, by the foulest most heinous, & gignatic instance of crime recorded in history." New York, April 24, 1861. Broadside, 48x30cm. frayed edges. (Streeter believes the item may be Confederate propagnada & consequently a Confederate imprint) no place, 1861. Streeter-$40.

865 **CONE, Mary**
"Morgan's Raid." In: Mag. of Western Hist., 1886, v.IV, p. 748-766.

866 **CONERLY, Luke Ward**
"Pike County, Mississippi, 1798-1876. Pioneer families & Confederate Soldiers, Reconstruction & Redemption." $100. Nashville, Tenn., Brandon Print, 1909. 8vo, cl, illus., ports, front, col. pl. 368pp.

...Spartanburg, S.C., The Reprint Co., 1978. Reprint in E. Russ Williams/Conerly's-"Resource Records of Pike/Walthall Co., Miss., 1798-1910. (reprint 1909 edt. $30)

867 **"CONFEDERACY-the Starting Point**
of the Great War Between the states Inauguration of Jefferson Davis, at Montgomery Alabama, Feb. 18, 1861." Lithograph 26 1/2x20 1/2" (plus margins) hand-colored. $250. Balt: A. Hoen & Co., 1887.

868 **"CONFEDERATE AIRSHIP, A.**
The "Artis Avis" which was to destroy Grant's Army." In: SHSP, 1900, v.XXVIII, p. 303-305.

869 **CONFEDERATE ARMY Signal Corps**
See: Edmund H. Cummins.

870 **"CONFEDERATE ARMY, The**
Its Numbers-Troops Furnished by States-Its losses by States, & contrasted with Grant's Forces in 1865." In: SHSP, v.XIX, p. 253-256.

871 **CONFEDERATE ARMY-Engineers**
"Engineer Bureau of C.S. Army, Report, Feb. 16, 1865." In: SHSP, 1876, v.2, p. 123-125.

872 **CONFEDERATE ASS'N. of New Orleans, La.**
"Suggestions for the celebration of the one-hundredth anniversary of the birth of Gen. Robert E. Lee, Jan. 19, 1907." N.O., Confederate Ass'n. of N.O., La. nd, 8vo, illus., unpaged.

873 **"CONFEDERATE ASSOCIATION",**
Marshall, Texas Aug. 20, 1863-Head: CIRCULAR. Broadside: 21x27cm, unlisted. Printed on blue paper. G. Hendershott $500. Announces organization of the "Confederate Association by the governors of the Trans-Mississippi Department to "harmonize & infuse vigor into the patriotic efforts of the people.-..discourage disloyalty, spies & secret agents, etc." Signed: Thos. C. Reynolds, Chm. Trans-Mississippi Comm. of Public Safety.

874 **"CONFEDERATE Annals"**
St. Louis, Mo: J.W. Cunningham, Edt. Pub. (Nixon-Jones Printing Co.) Vol. 1-#1, June, 1883; #2, August 1883. All published. 8vo, wraps, #1(40pp.); #2 (p. 41-84) published under auspices of Southern Historical & Benevolent Association of St. Louis. $50.

875 ..."Union & Confederaet Annals." St. Louis: Jan. 1884, Jan., v.1, #1, Cited by Mo. Hist. Rev., v.II, #3, p. 245.

876 **"CONFEDERATE Armies & Generals. The"**
In: Photo. Hist. C.W., v.10, p. 239-286, illus.

877 **CONFEDERATE Artillery**
See: Edward P. Alexander, Joseph L. Brent, Wm. N. Pendleton.

878 **CONFEDERATE BILL-Verses:**
Verses found on the back of a Confederaet Bill, representing nothing on God's earth now. Broadside, 10"sq. Shows replica of a CSA $20 bill, with four stanzas verse around it. Chattanooga, (Tenn.) n.d., $25. At end: "These verses were found written on the back of a CSA $20 bill in pocket of a dead soldier. Name of composer lost."

879 **CONFEDERATE BOOKS - reviews...**
"Books on the American War." In: Black. Edn. Mag., Dec. 1863, v.XCIV, p. 750-768. Reviews: Capt. Chesney's Campgn. in Va. Md. Pollard's First year of war, Estvan's War Pictures of So., Official Rep. of Battles, "Battlefields of South", "Three months in Southern States".

880 **"CONFEDERATE BULLETIN."**
Philatelist, Edt: Aug. Dietz Richmond, Va., See notes under "Southern Philatelist."

881 **"CONFEDERATE BURIALS**
in Rose Hill Cemetery, Macon, Georgia."

In: Ga. Geneal. Mag., 1983, #88, p. 129-139.

882 **"CONFEDERATE Battle Flags**
in the Museum of the Wisonsin Historical Society; II-Photographs of Confederate officers & monuments in the Library of the Society. With thirteen illustrations of flags. (From Report of Executive Comm., in Proceedings of the State Historical Society of Wisconsin, 1905)." Madison: State Hist. Soc. of Wisc., 1906. 8vo, wraps, illus., (2), 2lf, (1)pp. 39, (2pls) 42, (1pl), p. 103-107 (heading: "Miscellaneous Accessions") A total of 15pp. printed, incl. front & plates.

883 **"CONFEDERATE CAMP During the Late American War."**
London: M & N Hanhart, 1871. Chromolithograph after painting by Conrad Wise Chapman, 59th Va. Regiment Wise's Brigade.

884 **"CONFEDERATE CAPITAL & Monuments, The**
in Bronze & Stone. Dedicated to veterans attending the reunion of 1896." Richmond, Va., Taylor & Taylor (1896). 12mo, wraps, illus., ports (incl. front) plate, (facsm.) 120pp. $65-jk-122, $40-bmk.

885 **"CONFEDERATE CATECHISM of Session**
in Abbeville County, 1860-1865." (Abbeville, S.C., 1930?) Abbeville Chap. UDC, 12mo, wraps, (8)pp. S.C. Division.

886 **"CONFEDERATE CAVALRY at**
the First Manassas." In: SB, II, 1883-1884. p. 529-534, map. Sig: J.S.B.

887 **"CONFEDERATE CAVALRY attacking**
a Federal Supply Train near Jasper, Tenn." (Civil War in the U.S.) Hand colored print, 11x16: n.p., n.d. (c.1870). $25.

888 **CONFEDERATE CONGRESS - Laws & Resolutions, etc.**
"Laws & Joint Resolutions of the Last Session of the Confederate Congress..." See under Charles W. Ramsdell, Edt.

889 **CONFEDERATE CONSTITUTION, The**
CSA Congress." (Athens, Ga., pub. for the University of Ga. Libraries by the Wormsloe Foundation, 1979. 8vo, xii, 22pp. Intro: R.B. Harwell, a reprint of 1861 edition by Broughton, Nisbet *Barnes of Milledgeville, Georgia, bibliographical references.

890 **"CONFEDERATE CRUISER SHENANDOAH, The"**
Insurance against capture, & Geneva Award." New York: Powers, Macgowan & Slipper, 1873. 8vo, sewn, 13, (1)pp. $9.50.

891 **CONFEDERATE CURRENCY**
"Valuable information concerning the Notes issued. The Best Collection. (State of North Carolina). Includes all rare specimens, where & how printing was done." In: SHSP, 1903, v.XXXI, p. 145-151.

892 ..."Examples of Confederate Currency, issued by the Confederate States of America." Cover title: "Album for Reproductions of Confederate Currency. A Collection of copies of Confederate Currency issued by the Confederate States of America." A tri-fold 17x24 1/2" (folds to: 17x8 1/4") Colored drawing "The 'Robert E. Lee' on the Mississippi", & short history of bills:: $1, $2, $5, $10, $20, $50, $100, $500, $1000. facsimiles individually (loosely) mounted. See: Numismatics.

893 **CONFEDERATE Centennial Studies**
William Stanley Hoole, Edt. Tuscaloosa, Ala., Edition limited to 450 copies each title. All in orig. stiff ptd. wraps, 16 vols: $150, $900-Haslam, $400-bmk, $200-nc, $20ea.-bmk. See: each listed by author, following: E.M. Coulter, "Lost Generation." $10, $20; Jay Monaghan, "Swamp Fox of Confed." $25; J.W. Silver, "Conf. Morale & Church." $5; W.S. Hoole,

"Vizetelly Covers Conf." $10; J.L. Nichols, "Confed. Engineers." $6; J.Q. Anderson, "Texas Surgeon, CSA." $8, $25; W.T. Jordan, "Rebels in Making." $6; R.E. Yates, "Confed. & Zeb. Vance." $9, $15; J. Scheibert, "7 Months in Rebel States." $7, $20; H. Montgomery, "Howell Cobb, CSA Career." $7.20; J.L. Hunnicutt, "Reconstr. W. Alabama." $6, $20; M.S. Jones, "Yankee A'Coming." $7, $15; W.H. Hesseltine, "Lincoln Plan Reconst." $10; J.P. Moore, "Ever Dearest Friend." $5; A.J. Hanna, "Conf. Exiles Venezuela." $6; W.S. Hoole, "Alabama Tories." $6; Charles S. Davis; "Colin J. McRae, Fin. Agt." $15; Jesse L. Keene, "Peace Convention of 1861." $15; Wilbur D. Jones, "Confederate Rams at Birk." $15; Wm. C. Harris, "Leroy Pope Walker." $15; Chas. Cirard, "Visit to CSA in 1863." $20; Wm. W. White, "Confederate Veteran." $5; Paul duBellet Pecquet, "Diplomacy of Cab." $5; Henry Graves, "Confederate Marine." $15; Geo. Cholson Walker, "Private Journal." $7.50; Wm. S. Hoole, "Lawley Covers the CSA." $7.50; Chs. G. Summersell, "Cruise of CSS Sumter." $20.

894 **"CONFEDERATE DAUGHTER, The"**
(Austin, Texas) Mrs. E.G. Myers, Edt. Published monthly in the interest of the Daughters of the Confederacy. Vol. 1, #1, Jan. 1900, Feb. #2. Large 8vo, wraps, color flags (covers) ports, 18pp (#2) ads.

895 **"CONFEDERATE DEAD-**
Memorial Day at Elmwood Cemetery-Norfolk, Va." Norfolk, Va., Landmark Steam Press, 1884. 8vo, wraps, 19pp.

896 **CONFEDERATE DEAD:**
"Confederate dead buried in the Cemetery at Arlington. Inscriptions on the headboards." In: SHSP, 1901, v.XXIX, p. 354-357.

897 ..."Confederate dead buried in Mt. Olivet Cemetery Frederick, Md., compiled by Fitzhugh Lee Camp. #279-United Daughters of the Confederacy, Maryland Division." n.p., 19--, 12mo, wraps, (8)pp. cover title.

898 ..."Confederate Dead at Hopkinsville, Ky. List of the "List of the "Unknown" found rubbish." In: CV, 1899, v.7, p. 106-107. Soldiers of the 1st & 3rd Miss., 7th Texas, 8th Ky. & Forrest's Cavalry, found in a small book of Geo. K. Anderson.

899 ..."Confederate Dead in Stonewall Cemetery, Winchester, Va., Memorial Service, June 6, 1894. Eulogy: Capt. Wm. N. McDonald on Maj. Jas. W. Thomson. Career of Chew's Battery." In: SHSP, 1894, v.22, p. 41-48.

900 **"CONFEDERATE DIARY of the Retreat, A,**
from Petersburg Apr. 3-20, 1865. Edt: Richard Barksdale Harwell." Atlanta, Ga., Library Emory University, 1953. 8vo, wraps, 23pp. $5. Emory Pub., Sources & Reprints, Ser. 8, #1. By a participant in the Appomattox Campaign, incorrectly identified as Samuel Howard Gray.

901 **"CONFEDERATE ECHOES."**
Mobile, Ala., v.1, #1, 1964. Edts: Wm. Ray Armistead & Dorothy I. Moffett. $5.50yr (1970)-$7.50yr. 4to, decr. stiff wraps, mimeog. 20/35pp. each issue; v.1-June 1964, #12, May, 65, v.2, #1-12(1966) all issued. Renewed in Theodore, Ala., Jan. 1970(Jan-Nov) as Bi-Monthly, "Historical-Genealogical." 40/45pp. each issue. Jan-Dec. 1971 (1-6); 1972, Jan-Apr. (1-2) end publication.

902 **CONFEDERATE ENGINEERS & Troops**
See: Confederate Army Engineers, Thomas M.R. Talcott.

903 **CONFEDERATE ENGINEERS:**
See: James L. Nichols, CSA Centennial Studies.

904 **CONFEDERATE EXILES IN LONDON.**
See: Sarah Agnes Wallace.

905 **CONFEDERATE FINANCE (in SHSP)**
See: "Charlotte, N.C., 'Observer'. Columbia, S.C., 'State'. John W. Harris, Wm. H. Parker, Raleigh, N.C. 'News & Observer'. Jno. F. Wheless, Myron Holley Clark, Judah P. Benjamin.

906 **CONFEDERATE FLAG**
"The Confederate Flag." (Richmond, Va.) Southern Historical Society Papers, v.VIII, #4, 1880, p. 155-162. Various articles regarding Flag. 8vo, wraps, 8pp, separate. $5.

..."Confederate Flags." Richmond, Va: Confederate Museum. (Whittet & Shepperson, n.d.) 12mo, (16)pp., illus.-color flags $1.

907 ..."Confederate Flags Adopted by the Confederate Congress." Broadside, 12x16", within border, 18 lines of type. Nashville: Foster & Webb Print, n.d. John P. Hickman, Secty. Appears to be same flags on cover of Confederate Veteran, Oct. 1894, X, vol. 2.

908 ...Colored flags on heavy paper, 12"x30", on gray background, blank scroll around edges. Four flags: Stars & Bars, Battle Flag Campaign Flag & last flag of the CSA.

909 ..."Confederate Flags. Creation & Adoption...of the Flags of the Confederate States Army & Navy." Text: L. Brockenbrough. Richmond, n.d., 12mo, wraps, illus. in full color, (14)pp. $1, $1.50.

910 ..."The Confederate Flags & the Flag of the Independent Republic of Alabama. Data compiled from Official Records in the Ala. Dept. Archives & History." Montgomery, Alabama, 1961. Civil War Centennial Bul. #1 Peter A. Brannon, Dir., Ala. Dept. Arch. & Hist., 8vo, wraps (color flags), 1pl., 7pp. $2.

911 ..."Confederate States Flags. List of 544 of those of Virginia Troops, & when captured. In the U.S. War Dept." In: SHSP, 1904, v.XXXII, p. 195-200. See also: Wm. L. Cabell, Bradley T. Johnson, Carlton McCarthy, Geo. H. Preble, Arthur L. Rogers, Alfred Roman, "Flags of the CSA."

912 ..."Much about returning Confederate Flags." In: CV, 1898, v.6, p. 252-255, illus.

913 ..."Confederate flags at Washington." In: CV, Aug.-Sept., 1893, v.1, #8 & 9, p. 247-248, 278-279.

914 ..."Confederate seven-star flag flying, print in red & blue on cloth, with "Southern rights" on banner above, & "Let us alone" emblazoned below. Souvenir hankerchief 8 1/4x10 1/4" n.p., (1861) Goodspeed-601-$500. Note: sent from Washington by Geo. Warren in 1861 while in the 8th Reg. Mass. Vols.

915 **"CONFEDERATE FORTS**
their role in history." Montevallo, Ala., Univ. Montevallo Foundation Sta. #301. 35115 $10.

916 **"CONFEDERATE Field Manual."**
Arendtsville, Pa., Thomas Pub., 1974, 12mo, cl, dj, 176pp. $15. Includes a 32pp. photo suppl. A reprint of "The Field Manual for the use of Officers on Ordnance Duty, prepared by the Confederate Ordnance Bur. in 1862.

917 **"CONFEDERATE GENERALS**
killed or died of wounds or disease during the progress of the war." In: CV, 1907, v.15, p. 236.

918 **CONFEDERATE GENERALS**
"Confederate Generals. Lithographs by Charles Magnus." 24-portraits of Generals, Statesmen. Incl: Lee, Johnston, Jackson, Stephens, Beauregard, Jeff Davis & Naval men. 4to light cardboard(folded) 11 1/4x19, each port 2 1/4x3 1/2", red decr. border around each port. Made to be cut into individual cartde visites. N.Y., Chas. Magnus, n.d.(c.1861). $35, $50, $65, $150-bmk-95.

919 ..."Confederate Generals. Most of them passed their closing years in poverty. Twenty-five unpensioned heroes who suffered the stings & arrows of outrageous fortune." From the "Brooklyn Eagle". In: SHSP, 1894, v.XXII, p. 65-66.

920 "CONFEDERATE GOVERNMENT, The"
In: CV, Mar. 1919, v.XXVII, p. 99-102. List executive officers & congressmen of CS.

921 "CONFEDERATE GRAVES
in the city (Oak Hill) Cemetery, Newman, Coweta County." In: Armchair Researcher, 1981, v.2, #1, p. 41-45.

922 "CONFEDERATE GRAVESTONE RECORDS:
collected by Cape Fear Chapter, United Daughters of the Confederacy, of Wilmington, N.C. (n.d.) 4to, 15 stapeled mimeographed sheets. $5.

923 CONFEDERATE GRAY BOOK
"Confederate Gray Book: John B. Hood, Camp #103. United Confederate Veterans, Austin, Texas." Austin, Texas, 1914. 8vo, wraps, illus., ports.
..."Confederate Gray Book, 1912. Raphael Semmes Camp, #11, United Confederate Veterans, Mobile, Alabama." (Mobile, 1912) 8vo, wraps, cover title, illus., incl. ports, (52)pp. Contains list of camp members, with CSA monuments in various cities as illus.
..."Confederate Gray Book, 1909. Tennessee Division. Confederate Historical Association, Camp #28, Memphis, Tenn." 8vo, wraps, cover title, (8)p, pl, 27ports on 14 lf. Advertising matter interspersed.
...Confederate Gray Book: Monuments to Hood's Texas Brigade." (Austin, Texas, Von Boeckman-Jones, 1914?) 8vo, wraps, (56)pp. illus., ads scattered through text.
..."Confederate Gray Book, 1909. Lafayette McLaws Camp, #596. United Confederate Veterans." Savannah, Ga., M.S. & D.A. Byck Co., (1909) 8vo, cover title, 22pp. (unnumbered) illus.

924 "CONFEDERATE HISTORIC HANDKERCHIEF:
c.1863." Faded green cloth, 34" square. Portraits & ornaments in sepia. n.p., $175. Jeff Davis, in center; Lee, Jackson, Morgan & Beauregard in four corners; Mason, Slidell, Semmes & Joe Johnson, smaller four. In Old Print Shop, Feb. 1959, v.XVIII, #6.

924a CONFEDERATE HISTORICAL Institute Journal,
Summer 1981." Little Rock, Ark., 1981. 8vo, wraps, 47pp. $10. Article on CSA Gen. W.H.T. Walker of 13pp. (Rowe).

925 "CONFEDERATE HISTORY SYMPOSIUM,
1986-Proceedings of...Hillsboro, Texas: Junior College. Battles of the Army of Tennessee, April 19, 1986." 4to, hardback, 129pp. $40. Four essays on Shiloh, Stones River, Chickamauga, Franklin by leading historians.

926 "CONFEDERATE HOME & school,
Charleston, S.C. Founded 1867." Charleston, S.C., News & Courier Pr., 1886. 8vo, wraps, 12pp. Reprinted from the city Yearbook, 1885.

927 "CONFEDERATE HOME ASSOCIATION
of Missouri to to-day; progress & prospects of the great commercial state & center of population; its chief cities & towns, including reminiscences of "Missouri in 1861." St. Louis? Higginsville, Mo., 1893. 4to, wraps, 191, (1)pp. illus. (incl. ports) Note: Mohr-II, apr. 1908, #3, p. 235.

928 "CONFEDERATE HOME MESSENGER."
v.1-4, Oct., 1907-Dec., 1911. (v.1, #1, title: "The Confederate Messenger.") Pewee Valley, Ky., 1907; Louisville, Ky., 1909-

1911. 4 vols in 1. Monthly. 4to, cl, illus. No more published.

929 **CONFEDERATE HOME:**
State of Texas. Austin. "Annual reports of the Confederate Home of the State of Texas. 1897, 1898, 1900, 1904, 1906; Biennial reports for: 1908, 1910, 1914, 1916, 1918. Austin, Texas. 8vo, wraps, v.pp. Complete lists of "inmates", outfits, hometown. $125-jk.

930 "**CONFEDERATE INDIAN Sinking of the 'J.R. Williams'.**"
In: Jour. West., Jan. 1972, p. 43-50.

931 "**CONFEDERATE INFLATION CHART.**"
Richmond: Civil War Cent. Comm., (Jan. 1963) 8vo, (2)p. leaf, illus. $20 CSA bill. #13.

932 "**CONFEDERATE INVASION of New Mexico-1861-1862. The,**"
In: Old Santa Fe, Jan. 1916, v.III, p. 5-43. pt. I-Military operations in the Mesilla Val. & battle of Valverde, Feb. 20, 1862.

933 "**CONFEDERATE IRONCLAD "Missouri"**"
In: La. Studies, 1965, v.4, p. 101-110.

934 "**CONFEDERATE KNAPSACK,**
published monthly by A(rthur) Meynier, Jr., Private Co. "C", 8th La. Vals." New Orleans, 1883-1884. 2 nos. illus., 32cm. v.1, no. 1 & 2, Dec. 1883-Jan. 1884. Dorn. II, 340. See" Col. Charles D. Dreux.

935 **CONFEDERATE LEADERS**
"Confederate Leaders in the Forty-Fourth Congress. Who they are...their aims & opinions. A Democratic Counter Rebellion. Conquering the Union they failed to destroy." N.P. (1876?) caption title. 8vo, 8pp. $35-jk-122. Republican campaign document identifies CSA vets, their wartime wartime deeds of "dishonor."

936 ..."Confederate leaders & other citizens request House of Delegates (Va.) to repeal resolution of respect to Abe Lincoln, the Barbarian." See: Lyon G. Tyler

937 "**CONFEDERATE LETTERS, Some:**
Alabama, Georgia & Tennessee, Edt: Edmund Cody Burnett." In: Ga. Hist. Quart., 1937, v.XXI, p. 188-203.

938 "**CONFEDERATE LETTERS.**"
In: TylarQHGM, Jan. 1929, v.X, p. 185-190.

939 "**CONFEDERATE LOAN OF 1863.**" (from England)
See: Jno. Bigelow's, "Lest We Forget."

940 "**CONFEDERATE MARYLAND'S**"
Foreign Agent, the Bastile in America; or Democratic Absolutism, by an Eye-Witness." London, 1861. 8vo, wraps, 19pp. (old) $7.50. Edw. Johnson, Mayor Brown of Balt., Henry May & 13 other Baltimoreans incarcerated in Fts. McHenry & LaFayette with a British subject.

941 "**CONFEDERATE MEDICINE 1861-1865.**"
Richmond Academy of Medicine, Medical Society of Va., Virginia Civil War Comm., 1961. 4to, wraps, ports, illus., 56pp. $15.

942 "**CONFEDERATE MEDICINE & SANITARY AFFAIRS**"
In: SHSP. See: Joseph Jacobs, Joseph Jones, Samuel E. Lewis, Hunter H. McGuire, Claudius H. Mastin, George Moorman, Francis Porcher, Samuel P. Moore.

943 "**CONFEDERATE MEMOIRS;**
Veteran souvenir, May, 1899." Atlanta, Ga., Byrd Print, 1899. cover title. 8vo, wraps, 1-vol. (unpaged), illus., ports.

944 "**CONFEDERATE MEMOIRS:**
Alamance County troops of the War Between the States, 1861-1865. Centennial Edition, Mabel S. Lassiter, et.al. editors." n.p., n.d. (c.1965?) 4to, stiff wraps, 43pp. mimeo., port of Col. Chs. F. Fisher. Roster of men from Hillsboro & vicinity who surrendered at Appomattox.

945 **CONFEDERATE MEMORIAL**
Literary Society, Richmond, Virginia

"Catalogue of the Confederate Museum, of the Confederate Memorial Literary Society, corner Twelfth & Clay Streets, Richmond, Va." Richmond, Va., Ware & Duke Print, 1905. 8vo, wraps, front, 300pp. $7.50, $6, $37.50. (1898 edition, wraps, 218pp.

946 ..."In Memoriam Sempiternam. Confederate Museum, Richmond, Va., 1896." (Richmond, Va., E. Waddey Co., 1896) 12mo, wraps, front, illus., 98pp. The action of each state seceeding. $4.50, $10, $7.50, $30-bmk.

947 ..."Year Book of the Confederate Memorial Literary Society containing Annual Reports & Membership Lists, Organized 1890." Richmond, Va., Swem(#1078) lists years: 1907, 1909, 1910, 1911, 1912, 1913; The 1926 Yearbook lists it as being the 14th Issue--Richmond, Va., Central Pub., 1927, 8vo, wraps, 90pp. v.9, $15-y, $4.50.

948 ..."List of Relics: Alabama Room Confederate Museum, Richmond, Va., Regiment. Mrs. J.A. Rountree, Birmingham, Ala., V-Regent: Mrs. James H. Drake, Richmond. June, 1922, n.p., 8vo, (8)pp. leaflet. $3.

949 ..."Catalogue of the Confederate Museum, Richmond, Va., 1898." cover title. Georgia. (Richmond, Va., I.N. Jones Print) 1898. 8vo, wraps, color flags, (2) (83)-105pp. $5.

950 ..."Catalogue of the Confederate Museum, of the Confederate Memorial Literary Society, Corner Twelfth & Clay Streets, Richmond, Va., GEORGIA DEPT." Richmond, Va., Ware & Duke Print, 1905. 8vo, wraps, color flags, 40pp. $5.

951 ..."Catalogue of the North Carolina Room of the Confederate Museum, Corner 12th & Clay Streets, Richmond, Va." Richmond, Va., Dietz Press, 1933. $5. 8vo, wraps, color flags, front, plate, 53pp.

952 "CONFEDERATE MEMORIAL ADDRESSES
at New Bern, N.C., 11 May, 1885." Richmond, Va., 1886. 8vo, wraps, 32pp. pl. L.C. Vass' "Hist. Sketch, Ladies Memorial Association of New Bern, N.C., H.C. Graham's Sketch of J.J. Pettigrew. $25-bmk-106.

953 CONFEDERATE MEMORIAL ASSOCIATION
"Text of suit against trustees of the Confederate Memorial Association." In: CV, 1902, v.10, p. 460-463.

954 ...of Frederick County, Frederick, Md. "Memoria exercises on the occasion of the decoration of the graves of Confederate dead at Mt. Olivet cemetery, Frederick, Md., June 18, 1869, with the articles of incorporation of the Confederate Memorial Association of Frederick County, respectfully submitted to the Legislature of Maryland." Frederick, Md., Citizen Print, 1870. 12mo, wraps, 27pp.

955 CONFEDERATE MEMORIAL ASSOCIATION of the South
"History of the Confederate Memorial Association of the South." New Orleans, La., Graham Press, 1903. 8vo, cl, illus., 229pp. ports. $20. Comm: M. Louise Benton Graham, Chm. Daisy M.L. Hodgson, Virginia Frazer Boyle.
...(1904) Revised & Authorized Edition, 8vo, cl, illus., ports, errata slip, 318pp. $15.

956 ..."Minutes of the Tenth Annual Convention, held at Memphis, Tenn., June 7-10, 1909. 8vo, wraps, 62pp. $12. Officers from each state, their reports.

957 "CONFEDERATE MEMORIAL DAY
at Charleston, South Carolina. Re-Interment of the Carolina Dead from Gettysburg. Address of Dr. Girardeau, Odes, etc." Charleston, S.C., Wm. G. Mazyck Pr. 1871. 8vo, wraps, 42pp. (old) $1.75

958 ..."The First Confederate Memorial Day." (from Richmond Times-Dispatch, July 15,

1906) In: SHSP, 1907, v.35, p. 369-370. Origin of Memorial Day-v.37, p. 368.

959 ..."Confederate Memorial Day at Charleston, S.C. Reinterment of the Carolina dead from Gettysburg. Address of Rev. Dr. Girdeau, odes, etc." Charleston, S.C. William C. Mazyck, 1871. 8vo, wraps, 36pp. Dorn:II-66.

960 "CONFEDERATE MEMORIAL."
n.p., n.d., 1p. print of the famous 8-verse poem, originally written on the back of a $10 Confederate Note & found on a dead Confederate soldier." See also: "Confederate Souvenir." $1.

961 "CONFEDERATE MEMORIAL SCROLL to the Indian Officers in the War Between the States." Oklahoma City: Chron. Okla. Summer, 1950, v.XXVIII, #2, p. 206. A double page scroll (facsm.) pf 640 names, officers officers who commanded approx. 11,875 troops in CSArmy. Confederate Memorial Hall, Okla. Hist. Soc., Confederate Room.

962 "CONFEDERATE MILITARY RECORDS."
In: Georgia Genealogical Survey, 1981, v.1, #4, p. 14-22. Records of various CS soldiers of Georgia.
...Do: Abstracted from Microfilm at the Ga. Dept. of Archives & History. v.1, #1, p. 29-44; v.1, #2, p. 28-44.

963 "CONFEDERATE MONUMENT at Pensacola, Florida. Order of Exercises in its dedication, Wednesday 17, June (1891)." (Pensacola, 1891?) Broadside, 44x23cm. TTW Museum.

964 "CONFEDERATE MONUMENT ASSOCIATION
Confederate Memorial. Dedication Address by Col. Wm. C.P. Breckinridge of Ky." (Nashville: Foster & Webb Print, c.1889) 8vo, wraps, front, cover title, 48pp.

965 ..."A History of the Confederate Monument Association & Roster of 'Forbes Bivouac'." Clarksville, Tenn., 1893. 8vo, wraps, (59)pp. incl. ads, front, illus., ports.

966 "CONFEDERATE MONUMENT Unveiled at
New Market, Va., July 21, 1898-Herbert Barbee, sculptor." (New Market, Va., 1898) 8vo, wraps, 20pp. $2.

967 CONFEDERATE MUSEUM
"The South's Museum. The Davis Mansion formally thrown open for the reception of relics/The Battle Abbey of the Confederate States. Oration of General Bradley T. Johnson, etc." In: SHSP, 1895, v.XXIII, p. 354-381. ports (2), sketches (2).

968 ..."Jeff. Davis House. Reminiscences connected with its Ante-Bellum history-the Brockenbroughs, Morsons, Seddons, & Crenshaws, etc." In: SHSP, 1891, XIX, p. 326-329. "Virginius."

969 "CONFEDERATE NAVY in Europe."
See: Chs. P. Cullop's CSA propaganda in Europe; Jas. D. Bulloch; Norman C. Delaney's "Kell"; kalzell's "Flight from Flag"; Doug. French Forrest's "Diary"; Jim Dan Hill's "Sea Dogs"; Tom H. Wells' "CSA Navy".

970 "CONFEDERATE NAVY;
the first submarine boats; sinking of "Housatonic" by one; sad fate of the former's crew; reminiscences of a Confederate Naval Officer." n.p., n.d., 4to, (2)p.

971 CONFEDERATE NECROLOGY.
"Confederate Necrology." In: GaHQ, 1934, v.XVIII, p. 194-196, 283-286, 376-279. Reprinted from "Southern Watchman", 1863. 1935, v.XIX, p. 85-86, 163-167, 264-267, 334-341. 1936, v.XX, p. 85-90, 173-178, 262-268, 366-370. "Southern Watchman", Je. 29, 1864-Jan. 11, 1865.
..."Confederate Necrology." In: Ga. Hist. Quart., 1937, 38; v.XXI, 83-85, 204-205, 298-301, 393-395. XXII, 107-108, 199-201,

294-296, 398-400. Obits. of CSA soldiers, notices in "Southern Watchman", Je. 21, 1865 to Oct. 18; Augusta Weekly Chronicle, Jly. 22, 1862-to Nov. 11, 1862. 1939, v.XXIII, p. 93-95, 205-207, 305-306, 396-398, 1940, v.XXIV, p. 87-90, 163-165, 277-180, 385-388. 1948, v.32, p. 68-70, 143-144, 230-231, 323-324. (from: "Central Georgian", Sandersville) Mar/Dec. 1949, v.33, p. 81-83, 181, 271-273, 355-356. (1950)v.34, p. 63-65, 156-157, 257-258, 343-354.

...March 1948-Dec. 1953, v.32, #1-v.37(4) Texts of obituaries CSA officers & enlistees reprinted from Columbus & Sandersville newspapers, 1861-1865.

971a "CONFEDERATE NORFOLK:
the letters of Virginia lady of the Mobile Register, 1861-2. By William Stanley & Addie Shirley Hoole." University, Ala., Confederate Pub. Co., 1984. 8vo, wraps, 48pp.

972 "CONFEDERATE NOTE, A"
(A CSA note, i.e., $10 or $20, with poem on the back, the authorship is still in doubt. In the Smithsonian Institute, Wash., DC, is one with Miss. M.J. Turner of N.C., insig. but no proof of genuineness. Authorship has been ascribed to Mrs. R.E. Lytle (Louisville, Ky.) & Maj. S.A. Jonas (Aberdeen, Miss.) the latter is more favored. See also under Confederate: "Bill", "Memorial", "Souvenir".

973 CONFEDERATE NOTES & BONDS:
John W. Hazelton, Wm. West Bradbeer, Hank Bieciuk (Texas)-Corbin, C.J. Affleck-Douglas, Robert Werlich, Grover C. Criswell.

974 "CONFEDERATE OFFICER, A..."
See: W.J. Holman, Jr., "War Experience". Sam L. Clark, Edt., "Visits Richmond...

975 CONFEDERATE OFFICERS of Randolph Co. (W. Va.), 1861-1865."
Randolph County Hist. Soc., Mag. of Hist. & Biog., v.8, 1936, p. 10-16.

976 CONFEDERATE OFFICERS, CSA-in SHSP.
See: J.V. Bidgood, W.L. Cabell, J.W. DuBose, C.C. Jones, C.E. Jones, "Nashville Banner", "Richmond Dispatch". "T.M.R. Talcott, Virginia Generals in CSArmy". "Rank in the US & CSArmies".

977 CONFEDERATE ORDNANCE:
"See: Wm. Allan, Wm. LeRoy Broun, Josiah Gorgas, Horace E. Hayden, Jno. W. Mallet, Fred A. Olds, Levi S. White, Louis Zimmer.

978 "CONFEDERATE PATRIOT INDEX, The"
Vol. 1 1894-1924. Originally pub., 1974, vo. 2, 1924-1978. Easley, S.C., Southern Pub., 1978. 4to, mimeographen, paper, 734pp. United Daughters of the Confederacy-Tennessee Division. Reprint: 1985.

979 "CONFEDERATE PENSIONERS"
In: AHQ, 1940, v.2, #2, p. 208-217.

980 CONFEDERATE PERSONAL NARRATIVES" SHSP
See: Saml. Z. Ammen, Launcelot M. Blackford, Thos. B. Blake, U.R. Brooks, J.H. Carter, Thos. R.R. Cobb, Fred. M. Colston, J. Churchill Cooke, S.A. Cunningham, Henry G. Damon, Henry K. Douglas, Frank H. Foote, Robert D. Funkhouser, Jas. M. Garnett, John B. Gordon, John U. Green, John A. Hamilton, George N. Hollins, Geo. J. Hundley, Iredell Jones, James H. Lane, John G. Law, M.T. Ledbetter, J.W. McClung, John McGrath, Clara D. Maclean, Dabney H. Maury, Robt. W. North, Robert Nixon Northen, Chs. H. Olmstead, Jno. N. Opie, Richard C.M. Page, Benj. M. Parham, Robt. E. Park, Wm. W. Parker, Alex S. Paxton, Geo. A. Porterfield, S.F. Power, Jno. G. Pressley, Mrs. Robert C. Randolph, Warren D. Reid, "Richmond Dis-

patch", "Running the Blockade", David M. Sadler, W.F. Shippey, Mrs. Kate C. Starritt, Harry C. Townsend, "Two specimen cases of desertion", E.L. Welles, Henry M. White, W.S. White, Mrs. G. Griffing White.

981 **CONFEDERATE PHILATELIST**
pub: Bi-monthly. Patricia A. Kaufmann, Edt., 8vo, wraps, 32pp., Wash., D.C. Landmark Bldg. See: "Southern Philatelist."

982 **"CONFEDERATE PHILATELIST, The"**
See notes "Southern Philatelist".

983 **"CONFEDERATE PLAN for arming slaves. The,"**
In: Southern Workman, 1901, v.30, p. 475-476.

984 **CONFEDERATE POINT, N.C.**
See: Mrs. Wm. Lamb.

985 **"CONFEDERATE PORTRAIT ALBUM**
of the Civil War, 1861-1865." Louisville, Ky., American Chicle Co., n.d. (c.1900) $17.50-y, $10, $5, $6. Tall 8vo, decr. cl, 12pp. 141 ports (1 1/2") pasted in place. Jeff Davis, Cabinet members, General, Admirals & the CSA flag. This album was sent for $.15 plus 10-"Kis-Me" gum wraps.
...(First noticed by compiler in Confederate Veteran Jan. 1915, v.23, #1, p.2) "140 portraits will be sent on receipt of $.25 & 25 Kis-Me Gum wraps."

986 **"CONFEDERATE PORTRAIT ALBUM.**
Orphan Brigade Souvenir of Civil War, 1861-1865." (n.p., 1917) 7 leaves, plate, ports.

987 **"CONFEDERATE POSTAL HISTORY:**
An Anthology from the "Stamp Specialist. Edited by Francis J. Crown, Jr." Lawrence, Mass., Quarterman Pub., 1976. 8vo, cl, dj, illus., xvi, 313pp. $30-y.

988 **"CONFEDERATE PRISONERS**
in Northern prisons during the war...(189?)." n.p., n.d., 8vo, wraps, 19pp.

989 **CONFEDERATE PRISONERS OF WAR**
"How a Dutch General was circumvented by an actress." In: OLOD, Feb. 1875, v.1, #6, p. 568-572. signed "Rebel."

990 **"CONFEDERATE PRISONERS OF WAR who died in Federal Prisons."**
See: Frances Terry Ingmire, reprint.

991 **CONFEDERATE PRIVATE at Fort Donelson, 1862. A,"**
In: AmHist. Rev. 1925/1926, v.31, p. 477-484.

992 **CONFEDERATE PUBLISHING COMPANY**
University, Alabama. 35486. 1. M.B. Hurst-"14th Alabama Vols." 2. Jos. Q. Burton & Theo F. Botsford-"47th Alabama Inf." 3. Morgan S. Gilmer-"Shockley's Ala. Escort Company." 4. Joseph W. Brunson-"Pee Dee Light Inf." 5. Joseph Bogle-"Barton's Georgia Brigade, Tenn." 6. James M. Thompson-"Autauga Rifles, 6th Alabama." 7. John D. Taylor-"48th Alabama Inf." 8. George Evans Brewer-"46th Alabama Rd." 9. Adam H. Whetstone-"53rd Alabama Vols." 10. "History of 8th Reg. Alabama Inf., ANV." 11. William Stanley Hoole-"5th Alabama Inf." 12. Col. Charles Forsyth-"3rd Alabama Inf. Reg.

993 **"CONFEDERATE RECEIPT BOOK.**
A compilation of Over One Hundred Receipts, Adapted to the times." Intro: E. Merton Coulter. Athens, Ga. University of Georgia (1960). 12mo, boards, facsm. 38pp. d/w, $2.50.
...Reprint-1981, $20-bmk.
..."Confederate Receipt Book", cover "Reprint of rare 1863 Confederate Cook Book." Rich., Va. West & Johnston, 1863. Harriman, Tenn., Pioneer Press (1961). 12mo, wraps, 28, (1)p.

994 **CONFEDERATE RECORDS-South Carolina**
"Report of the Historian of the Confeder-

ate Records of the General Assembly of S.C." Columbia, S.C., Bryan Print, 1898-1900. 8vo, cl, 5 vols. Tables. Turnbull, IV, p. 387.

...Same title above, 1898. Evidently a preliminary Report to the 5 vol. set. p. 280-294.

995 **CONFEDERATE REGISTERS**
See: Joseph B. Bidgood, Robert W. Hunter, Charles C. Jones, John Wm. Jones, Thomas M.R. Talcott.

996 **CONFEDERATE RELIEF BAZAAR ASS'N. of Maryland**
"Confederate Relief Bazaar of Maryland, to be held in Fifth Regiment Armory, Baltimore, April 7 to 11, inclusive, 1885." (Baltimore, Md., 1885) 8vo, wraps, 19, (1)pp.

997 ..."Confederate Relief Bazaar Journal." Edt: Mrs. Russell Wetmore, issued daily, except Sunday, v.I, #1-9; Apr. 11-20, 1898. Baltimore, Md., 1898. 4to, cl, (154)pp. (no more pub.?) To raise money for families of CSA not included in regular channels.

998 **"CONFEDERATE REPORTER, 1861-1864."**
CSA Newspapers, editorial columns, letters from the front, first-hand accounts from Southern newspapers. Edna, Texas: Beulah G. Green (P.O. Box 358) Stiff wraps, 4to, 143pp. Index $12.50, No index, $8.50.

999 **"CONFEDERATE RESEARCH REVIEW."**
Portsmouth, Hampshire, England: Grosvenor Press, Blackfriars Rd., The Confederate Research Club. 4to, #1(Nov.) 1953; #2(Aug.)1954. See also under: R.C. Jarvis, Thos. W. Green, "The New Index".

1000 **"CONFEDERATE REVEILLE MEMORIAL EDITION. The"**
Published by Pamlico Chap. Daughters of the Confederacy, Washington, N.C., Edwards & Broughton, 1898. 8vo, stiff wraps, ports, 164pp. (14pp. advs.) $75, $125-bmk-85.

...Raleigh, N.C., North Carolina Cent. Comm., (Raleigh, N.C. Prison Enterprise Central Duplicating Service., 1964) Same title, with added "Centennial Edt." Foreword (2)pp., 2pp. list members, end. 800 copies printed. $1.25, $30-bmk, $20-bmk-84.

1001 **"CONFEDERATE SCRAPBOOK**
copies from a scrapbook kept during the War..." See: Lizzie Cary Daniel.

1002 **CONFEDERATE SEAL**
See: Great Seal of the Confederacy.

1003 **"CONFEDERATE SHIP 'NASHVILLE'**
sinking the Federal Ship 'Harvey Birch'." Berlin: Lithographed in color by Isidor Roccam. 10 1/2"x15.

1004 **"CONFEDERATE SOLDIER"**
or, Confed. Scout." (An Ex-Confederate). See: John Cussons.

1005 **CONFEDERATE SOLDIER'S & SAILOR'S MONUMENT ASS'N.**
Souvenir, unveiling soldier's & sailor's monument, Richmond, Va., May 30, 1894." Richmond, Va., J.L. Hill Print, 1894. cover title, 8vo, wraps, illus. (partly color, ports, 25, (41)pp.

1006 **"CONFEDERATE SOLDIERS & PATRIOTS"**
of Maury, Co., Tenn., 1970 edition. See: Maury Co., Tenn.

1007 **CONFEDERATE SOLDIERS & SAILOR'S MONUMENT**
See: "Unveiling of..."

1007a **"CONFEDERATE SOLDIERS GRAVES,**
Vol. 1. United Daughters of the Confederacy, Chap. #2243, Baytown, Texas." Houston, Tex., D. Armstrong Co., 1988. 4to, cl, 540p. + index. $50. Over 7000 listings.

1008 **"CONFEDERATE SOLDIERS Who Enlisted**
from Randolph Co. (W.Va.) 1861-1865." U.D.C., Randolph Chap. #267, Hist: Sal-

lie Wellford Scott Hoover, from a list compiled by Maj. Joseph French Harding. (Elkins, W.Va. ?1920) 8vo, cover title, 10pp. Shetler-#875. $30-r.

1009 **"CONFEDERATE SOLDIERS who died** in the service of their country & are buried in Columbia, S.C., 1861-1865." Columbia, S.C., 1924. $5. 12mo, stiff wraps, cover title, 32pp.

1010 **"CONFEDERATE SOLDIERS"** burried in the Confederate section of Westview Cemetery, Fulton County." In: Ga. Arnchair Researcher. 1984, v.5(2):24-31.

1011 **CONFEDERATE SOLDIERS' HOME of Georgia** Acts of the General Assembly Board of Trustees, Officers & Committee Reports, Rules & Regulations governing the Home." Atlanta, Oct. 8, 1902. 8vo, wraps, 70pp. $3.50 See: "In Memory of Soldiers in Gray.

1012 **"CONFEDERATE SOLDIERS,** Sailors & Civilians Who Died as Prisoners of War at Camp Douglas, Chicago, Ill. 1862-1865." Kalamazoo, Michigan. Edgar Gray Pub., n.d., (1968) 4to stiff wraps, (112)pp. illus., frontis, intro., remainder alphabetically lists 4,454 CSA prisoners of war, rank, co. Reg., date of death & burial. $6. Comp-Alex A. Praus, Dir. Kalamazoo Pub. Museu.

1013 **"CONFEDERATE SONG BOOK, The."** by a Confederate Veteran, member Camp 756, U.C.V. Containing the Old War Songs familiar to soldiers of our Southland; also an appendix of principal battles & other important events." Savannah, Ga., 1899. 12mo, wraps. $8-f. See: "Chosen Songs of Civil War."

1014 **"CONFEDERATE SONGS & BALLADS."** 53-Broadside songs, ballands, patriotic, satirical, comic & sentimental, issued in, or for circulation in, the South during the war. Mounted in album, 4to buckram. Includes: "Battle Song of Black Horseman", "Stars & Bars", "Georgia Volunteers","Southron War Song", "The Southrons are Coming", "Battle Song of the Maryland Line", "Lone Star Camp Song", "Kentuckians to Arms", "Downtrodden Maryland", "Chivalrous C.S.A.", etc. Single sheet leaflets, sold in camps & street for a penny & of ephemeral nature. (Henkel cat. #1090, May 1913)

1015 **CONFEDERATE SOUTHERN MEMORIAL ASS'N.** "History of the Confederate Memorial Ass'n. of the South...Pub. by the Confederate Memorial Ass'n. Revised & authorized edt." (New Orleans, La., Graham Pr., 1904) 8vo, cl, pls., ports, 318pp. $15, $7.50, $8-nc. Foreword sig. by M. Louise Benton Graham, Daisy M.L. Hodgson, Virginia Frazer Boyle, comm.
...1st Edt., 1903, p. 229- $12.50.

1016 ..."The Confederate Southern Memorial Association, the Minutes & Meeting held for the Organization of..., Louisville, Ky., May 30, 31, & June 1, 1900." New Orleans, La., 1900. 12mo, wraps, 10pp. $3.50.

1017 **CONFEDERATE SOUVENIR, The** "The Confederate Souvenir. Portraits of leading Confederate Generals, leading spirits of Secession, & Illustrations." Atlanta, Ga., (c.1884/1886) Walter A. Taylor. 8vo, wraps, 16pp. covers printed both sides, Jeff. Davis & his cabinet on front as he appeared when inaugurated, Feb. 18, 1861. Davis on back cover at the laying of a monument, 25 years after inauguration.
..."The Confederate Souvenir." Atlanta, (1886) Walter A. Taylor. vo, wraps, (12)p., illus., covers printed both sides, front: Jeff Davis, the first & last President of the CS as he appeared when inauguration, Feb. 18, 1861. back cover as he appeared on his visit at the laying of the monument.

..."Confederate Souvenir-1861-1865. C.S. Veterans' Reunion May 7, 8, 9, 1912. Macon, Georgia." Marian Wells, designer. Verse: "The Confederate Note". narrow 8vo, cover with an original $20 CSA note. Note: Viola Cobb Bivins'-"Echoes of the Confederacy", pg. 184, "Walter Raleigh Vaughan wrote "Ode to a Confederate Dollar Bill", when a youth in Va. It was immediately printed on the back of CSA money & sold for a burial fund. Enough copies were sold to bury 20 CSA & 10 Union soldiers. See: "Confederate Memorial."

1018 ..."The Confederate Souvenir." H.C. Clark's Confederate Almanac for 1862. Pub., Vicksburg, Miss. 96pp. Republished 1900 with supplemental 16pp. containing Jeff Davis Thanksgiving proclamation, Gen. Lee's order on death of Stonewall Jackson & his correspondence with Grant, Gen. J.E. Johnston's address to Army of Tenn., with Hood's address to same, strength of ANV at surrender. This souvenir was given for renewal of the Confed. Vet.

1019 **"CONFEDERATE STAMP ALBUM."** Philatelist, See notes under "Southern Bulletin, etc." Philatelist. J.B. Baumgarten.

1020 **CONFEDERATE STATE DEPARTMENT. In: SHSP** See: "Corresp. on campaign '64." C.C. Clay, Jr., James P. Holcombe, Judah P. Benjamin, Jacob Thompson, Wm. J. Almon, L. Quinton Washington.

1021 **"CONFEDERATE STATES** Almanac & Repository of Useful Knowledge for 1862." Vicksburg, Miss., Comp-Pub. H.C. Clark. (Atlanta, Ga., Mutual Print, 1895) 12mo, wraps, CS flag, ports, illus., 96pp. Reprint of Crandall-4988. For 1864, p. 20, $375-jk-117.

1022 ...Court Records, 1862, Filed in the U.S. Land Office, Baton Rouge." (New Orleans: Survey of Federal Archives in Louisiana, 1940) 4to, 3, lf, 74, 8pp.

1023 ...Army Casualties: lists & narrative reports, 1861-1865." Wash: National Archives & Records, General Services Administration, 1970. 7 reels-microfilm Pub., #M-836, RG 109.

1024 ...Army Memorial Hall Gray Book. A Chronological Record of Texas, as a state in the Confederacy & a Genealogy of the Daughters of the Confederacy comprising the Texas Division UDC." Dallas: CSA Memorial Hall Ass'n., n.d. (1911) 4to, wraps, illus., 52pp. $15. A Roster of "Texas Troops in Confederate Service (officers) by E.W. Winkler, p. 33-47.

1025 **"CONFEDERATE STATES Medical/Surgical Journal"** 4to, facsimile, xiii, v.I, #1, (80)pp. v.I, #6, (80)-200pp; #12, (201)-224; v.II, #1, 48pp. $45.

1026 ...Medical & Surgical Journal, with an introduction by William D. Sharpe, M.D." N.Y., New York Academy of Medicine, History of Medicine Series, No. 47, 1976. 4to, cl, illus., 290pp. $22.50. Reprint of Journal, begun Jan. 1864 & ends with Feb., 1865. Fourteen issues. (Pub., by Scarecrow Press, Metuchen, N.J., 1976) $40-b.

1027 **"CONFEDERATE STATES, The.** A Government de Facto, & the effects of the war on Existing Contracts: Argument before the court of Appeals of Maryland in Johnson et ux vs. Robertson." (Baltimore, October Term, 1868) 8vo, printed wraps, 22pp. $20.

1028 **CONFEDERATE STATES.** (House Bill #17) House of Representatives, Jan. 15th, 1863. (By Mr. Russell). A Bill to be entitles An Act to prevent the employment of negroes in war against the Confederate States of America." (Richmond, 1863) 8vo, caption title, 2pp. not in Crand/Har.

1029 **CONFEDERATE State Steamer,** 'William A. Webb'." In: South. Mag. June 1874, v.VII, #6, p. 679-691. Also: "Trans. South. Hist. So." Balt: Turnbull Bros., 1874-1875, p. 81-90.

1030 "**CONFEDERATE States Marine Corps.**" (London) Jour. Confed. Hist. Soc. March 1963, v.I, #3, p. 79-82, plate. Lt. Francis Hawkes Cameron, CSMC, 1862.

1031 **CONFEDERATE States Navy, in SHSP** See: Jefferson Davis-"Privateersmen, Dabney H. Maury, Robert D. Minor, Virginius Newton, John W. Porter, Charles W. Read, "Operations CSNavy", & "Confederate States Navy." Jas. D. Bulloch.

1032 "**CONFEDERATE States Navy.** Partial List of Survivors." (from Richmond Times-Dispatch, June 30, 1907) In: SHSP, 1907, v.35, p. 290-297.

..."Confederate States Navy. It was not strong but it made a very good record, partial list of survivors, etc." In: SHSP, 1907, v.XXXV, p. 290-297.

1033 ...C.S.N. - "David." "Our Torpedo Boat. The Original "David", constructed for the Confederate Navy. Sold for junk." In: SHSP, 1901, v.XXIX, p. 292-295.

1034 **CONFEDERATE States of America** "Confederate States of America. 2nd Congress, 1st Session. "Proceedings of the Second Confederate Congress, 1st Session, 2nd Session in part, 2 May-14 June, 1864; 7 November-14 December, 1864. Edt: Frank E. Vandiver." Richmond, Va., Historical Society, 1958. 8vo, cl, xi, 475pp. Southern Historical Society. Papers, new ser. no. 13, whole no. 51. "Copies mainly from the Richmond Examiner." Concludes with v.52, the series of publications of the Southern Historical Society, founded in 1869 & dissolved by its last surviving member, Douglas Southall Freeman, in 1953. Includes a tribute to Freeman by the editor.

..."C.S.A., 2nd Congr., 2nd Sess. "Proceedings of the Second Confederate Congress, second session in part, December 15, 1864-March 18, 1865." Edt: Frank E. Vandiver, Richmond: Virginia Historical Society, 1959. 8vo, cl, xx, 500pp. Southern Historical Society. Papers, new ser. no. 14; whole no. 52.

1035 ...Stampless Cover Catalogue. Edt: Benjamin Wishnietsky, Edt. Asst.: Gordon L. Hudson. 1st Edt. North Miami, Fla., D.G. Phillips Pub. Co., 198, 8vo, illus. 93pp. 1980.

1036 **CONFEDERATE States of America-Constitution**
..."Confederate States of America-Constitution. In Congress-March 9, 1861-Amended Constitution-100 copies ordered to be printed. Constitution of the Confederate States of America. (Caption title) 35cm. (Montgomery, 1861) 29 leaves, printed one side, loose as issued. Printed draft, with lines of sections numbered, and with mssc. endorsement & verso last leaf: "Constituion as reported by the Committee." Unrecorded copy of the final draft of the Constitution. (Streeter) $4250.

..."Confederate States of America-Constitution: A facsimilie of the Constitution of the Provisional Government of the C.S.A." N.Y., Photolithography by J. Laing 1883. From original parchment, an oblong (37 1/2x46cm) folio, cloth-back (2)p., from original in possession of F.G. de Fontaine. (Facsimilie (9)pp. print one side.) $50.

1037 "**CONFEDERATE States of America.** Provisional Congress. Committees of the Congress." Broadside, folio. Montgomery, Ala., May 1861. Argosy Cat. #171, pt. 1- "Hitherto unknown, not in Bost. Athen., issued only for 50 odd members of congress. Earliness of issue indicated by very names of committees. "To arrange for Gov. buildings; flag & seal of CSA; to organize the executive dep't. Includes the Texas members." $75.

1038 **CONFEDERATE States of America;**
Dept. of Justice. "The Opinions of the Confederate Attorneys general, 1861-1865. Edited by Rembert W. Patrick, with a foreword by Harold L. Sebring." Buffalo (NY) Dennis & Co. (1950) 8vo, cl, xxiv, 608pp. $30, $50.

1039 **CONFEDERATE Statistics, In the SHSP**
See: Dr. Joseph Jones, Gen. Samuel Cooper, J.A. Early, Chas. Marshall, Joseph E. Johnston, Wm. F. Fox, J.F. Gilmer, Charles C. Jones, Robert G. Hill, A.R. Lawton, Casenove G. Lee, John S. Ward, "The Confederate Army, Its numbers, etc."

1040 **"CONFEDERATE Steamer, 'Florida':**
Pursuit & Capture of the ship 'Jacob Bell'." Tinted lithograph by J.H. Bufford, Boston (c.1863) 11x15(plate size) $35. See: Thomas K. Porter.

1041 **CONFEDERATE Survivors Association**
"Confederate Memorial Association: Memorial Resolution introduced by Col. Jos. B. Cumming at the 16th Annual Reunion of the C.S.A., of Augusta, Ga. on Memorial Day, April 26, 1894, in honor of its late president, Col. Charles C. Jones, Jr., together with the speeches of Mssrs. F.M. Stovall & Salem Dutcher seconding resolution. The remarks of Capt. Chas. E. Coffin; and the Historian's Report, submitted by Charles Edgeworth Jones." Augusta, Ga., Chronicle Job Print, 1894. 8vo, wraps, cover title, 20pp.

1042 ..."In Memoriam, 1801-1883. To Their Late Comrade, Lewis De Sassure Ford, Surgeon in the Army of the Confederate States." Augusta, Ga., 1884. 8vo, wraps, 8pp. (old) $2.

1043 **CONFEDERATE Survivors Association;**
See: Col. C.C. Jones, F. Edgeworth Eve.

1044 **CONFEDERATE Survivors' Association,**
Augusta, Ga. "Memorial Resolution introduced by Col. Jos. B. Cumming at the Sixteenth Annual Reunion of the Confederate Survivors' Ass'n., of Augusta, Ga. on Memorial Day, Apr. 26, 1894, in honor of the late President Col. Charles C. Jones, Jr., LL.D. Together with the speeches of Messrs. F.M. Stovall & Salem Dutcher seconding the Resolution; the Remarks of Capt. Chas. E. Coffin; & the Historian's Report, submitted by Charles Edgeworth Jones. Printed by order of the Association." Augusta, Ga., Chronicle Job Print., 1894. 8vo, wraps, 20pp. $10.

1045 ..."Address delivered before the Confederate Survivors' Association of Augusta, Ga. upon the occasion of its Seventeenth Annual Reunion, on Memorial Day, April 26, 1895, by Capt. F. Edgeworth Eve, President of the Ass'n. And the Historian's Report, submitted by Charles Edgeworth Jones. Together with Col. Joseph B. Cumming's Speech introducing Gen. M.C. Butler, Gen. Butler's Narrative, & John R. Thompson's Poem, "Lee to the Rear." Printed by Order of the Association." Augusta, Ga., Chronicle Job. Print, 1895. 8vo, wraps, 33, (1)pp. $15.

1046 **CONFEDERATE Treasury Dept., In: SHSP**
See: M.H. Clark, J.W. Harris, W.H. Parker, J.F. Wheless

1047 **"CONFEDERATE Trenches at Petersburg."**
In: CV, Nov. 1925, v.XXXIII, p. 418-420.

1047a **CONFEDERATE VETERAN ALUMNI REUNION,**
July 1912. In Alumni Bulletin University of Virginia, Third Ser. Vol. V, #3. Char-

lottesville, Va., University of Va. Press, 1912. 8vo, wraps, front, folding group portrait, p.225-360. $60.

1048 **"CONFEDERATE VETERAN Magazine, The**
1893. (Nashville, Tenn., Blue & Gray Press, 1974. sm.4to, xix, 384pp., illus., index. $20. A facsm. reprint of the first year of CV.

..."Confederate Veteran Magazine." Atlanta, Georgia, 1890. 8vo, wraps, vol. 1-#1, Jan. 1890 (96pp.) Feb. (-192); Mar. (-288); Apr. (-384); May (-476); June (-576). Vol. II-July (94p.); Aug.(-192); Sept. (-272) paged continuously (all?) $17.50.

...The Confederate Veteran. Edited by Ronald Clemmons. Murfreesboro, Tenn., Sons of Confederate Veterans, 1985. 4to, wraps, $10-year.

..."The Confederate Veteran. Published Monthly in the interest of confederate Veterans & kindred topics." Edt.: S.A. Cunningham, founder. Nashville, Tenn., 1893-1932. 4to, wraps, Jan. 1893-Dec. 1932. (Sales: v.I & 2, $400, Wathen; Full set, bound, $3500, Morrison; unbound $1600, West. Hemsp.; v.II, $100; v.III, IV, V, @ $75 ea.; VI, VII, VIII, @ $60 ea.; IX-XIV, @ $50 ea.; XV-XXXII @ $35 ea.; v.I @ $10 ea., II, @ $8.50. (v.I, #1 reprint $3.50 ea.) (Index, reprint, $25.) Reprint: v.I-IV, @ $15 ea. $35 ea. $2500-b-124, Reb: $3300-4000.

...Bookmark (12-01-82) #124 (item #354) 1893-$25 per issue; 1894-1896 $15 per issue; 1897-1900 $12 per issue; 1901-1913 $10 per issue; 1914-1920 $7.50 per issue; 1921-1932 $5 per issue.

1049 ..."The Confederate Veteran, INDEX. Published Monthly in the Interest of Confederate Veterans & Kindred Topics Vol. I-XL. S.A. Cunningham, Founder." Nashville, Tenn., 1893-1932. (Dayton, Ohio, Morningside Bookshop, n.d. (1972) 4to, cl, facsimilie #6, (281pp.) paged as originally printed, in 4 to 10pp. folders. $25, $35-y.

..."The Confederate Veteran." Wendell, N.C., Broadfoot Pub. Co., 1984. Reprint, gray cloth, acid free paper, 8 1/2x11" 40 vols.-$1000, 3 vol. Index-$300, Odd vols. $30-ea.

1050 **"CONFEDERATE VETERAN Magazine-Index**
Cumulative Index, 1893-1932. Dr. Louis H. Manarin, Edt., Robert S. Bridgers, Ass't. Editor." Wilmington, N.C., Broadfoot Pub., 1986. 4to, cl, 3vols, cxxxii, 2387pp. (1). $300. Continuously paged.

1051 **CONFEDERATE VETERANS**
"Relief of Confederates by National Appropriation. Hon. P.J. Otey's Bill. R.E. Lee Camp, C.V., protests against the consideration of the bill by Cong." In: SHSP, 1895, v.XXIII, p. 337-341.

1052 ..."Pensioning of the Confederate Soldier by the United States. Strong protest by Pickett-Buchanan Camp, C.V., Norfolk, Va." In: SHSP, 1898, v.XXVI, p. 312-315.

1053 ...Program: "Reunion of Confederate Veterans Association, Reunion grounds, Hillsboro, Texas. July 23-26, 1912." Tall 8vo, wraps, (20)pp. largely ads.

1054 **CONFEDERATE VETERANS ASS'N.**
Savannah. "Address delivered before CVA of Savannah, Bradd & Hutton, 1893, 8vo, wraps, 92pp.

1055 **CONFEDERATE VETERANS- Austin, Texas**
"Charter, Constitution, By-Laws of the John B. Hood Camp, Confederate Veterans of Austin, Texas." Austin, Texas, 1886. 32mo, wraps, 30pp. $20.

1056 **CONFEDERATE VETERANS- Charleston, W.Va.**
"Charter & By-Laws of Stonewall Jackson Camp, Confederate Veterans, Adopted March 12, 1894." Charleston: Moses W.

Donnally, 1894. 8vo, wraps, 25pp. (Orgn. Sept. 25, 1893.)

1057 **CONFEDERATE VETERANS- Danville, Va.**
"The Cabell-Graves Camp at Danville Virginia, 1888-1896." sm.4to, stiff wraps, unpaginated, illus. Facsm. minute book Danville UCV. $15-carolina.

1058 **CONFEDERATE VETERANS-Florida**
"Constitution & By-Laws of Camp Ward, Confederate Veterans. Pensacola, Florida." Pensacola: H.S. White, 1902. 12mo, wraps, 12pp. List: members, p. (11)-12.

1059 **CONFEDERATE VETERANS-Georgia to Texas**
"Confederate Veterans from Georgia to Texas." In: Georgia Genealogical Survey, 1981, v.1, #4, p. 4-5.

1060 **CONFEDERATE VETERANS - Grand Camp**
"History Committee, Report of..." In: SHSP, 1900, v.28, p. 169-198; 1901, v.29, p. 99-131.

1061 **CONFEDERATE VETERANS-Kentucky**
"Confederate Veterans Ass'n. of Kentucky. Constitution, By-Laws, Membership with Name, Rank, Command, & Residence." n.p., n.d., (Lexington, Ky., 1890?) 8vo, cl, 16pp. $3, $12.50.
..."Confederate Veteran Association-Ky. Constitution, by-laws & membership, Confederate Association of Kentucky, with name, rank, command & residence." (Lexington, Ky.) 1891. 12mo, wraps, pict, 31pp. $35-bmk-116.
..."Confederate Veteran Association of Kentucky (Port: Brig-Gen. Roger W. Hanson on t.p.) 4th edition." (Lexington, Ky., Transylvania Print, 1893) oblong, 8vo, decr. cl (flag), ports, CSA-flags (8, dup.2) 87pp. $25. Contains: articles of incorp., cons't., membership CSA vets of Ky., and by counties. All Morgan's Men.
..."Confederate Veteran Association of Ky. Constitution, by-laws & list of membership, arranged by Counties & Camps. With name, rank & residence & command of every member in his own county camp, if one has been organized, or in the John C. Breckinridge Camp. 5th Edition. All members of the Confederate Veteran Ass'n of Ky. are also members of the Ky-Div., United Confederate Veterans." Lexington, Ky., Transylvania Print, 1895. Oblong 8vo, decr. cl(flag), ports, color flags, 217, (1)pp. $22.50, $15.

1062 **CONFEDERATE VETERANS-Macon, Ga.**
"Confederate Veterans, Re-union Souvenir Badge, Macon, Ga., Oct., 1887. Souvenir lapel ribbon with contemp. photo Jeff Davis, blue letters on white, CSA flag at bottom." $35-jk-132.

1063 **CONFEDERATE VETERANS-Memphis, Tenn.**
"Meeting of the Confederate Veterans at Memphis, Tenn., address: Col. Bennett H. Young. Achievement of CSA Cavalry." In: SHSP, 1910, v.38, p. 216-220.

1063a **CONFEDERATE VETERANS-Richmond, Virginia**
"R. E. Lee Camp, Charter, by-laws, rules of order & list of officers & members." Richmond, Va., Baughman Stationary Co., 1900. 12mo, wraps, 48pp.
..."Memorial Services, Lee camp hall," Jan. 8, 1909. "The deceased of 1908." n.p., (4)p.
..."Roster of officers & members." Richmond, Va., Jan. 1, 1919. 12mo, wraps, 8p. cover title.

1064 **CONFEDERATE VETERANS-Savannah, Georgia.**
"Confederate Veterans Association of Savannah, Georgia. "Addresses delivered before the Confederate Veterans Association of Savannah, Ga. To which is added the President's Annual Report pub. by the Association." Savannah, Ga., Braid & Hut-

ton, 1893-1902, 8vo, wraps, 5 vols., various paging. Comprises separate vols: 1893, 1895, 1896, 1898 & combined issues 1898-1902. DeRenne(908)III

..."Constitution, By-Laws, Roll of Members of CVA of Savannah, Ga." Morning News, 1892, 12mo, 15, (1)pp.-7 lf.

1065 ...Addresses(1893) wraps, 98pp. "With Stuart & Hampton", "Battle of Mobile Bay", "Battle of Cedar Creek", etc. $35.

1066 ...Addresses(1895) Tall 8vo, wraps, 114pp. "Memory of Confed. Dead", "The Defense Charleston Harbor", "Blockade Running", "A Daring Deed", "Our Last Retreat", Recollections of Petersburg, Va.", "Battle of Fredericksburg." & "Reception of Wade Hampton".

...Addresses(1898), wraps, 92pp. Walter Charlton, et al. $100-ob.

1067 **"CONFEDERATE VICTORIES In the Southwest."**
Prelude to Defeat, from the official record." Edt. by Publishers. Albuquerque, N.M., 1961. (Stagecoach Press). 8vo, cl, d/w, 201pp. 1000 copies. $7.50. Maps, incl. front, $27.50(border), $14-bmk.

1068 **"CONFEDERATE WAR JOURNAL."**
N.Y., Lexington, Ky: "The Printery". Val. 1, April, 1893, to March, 1894. Vol. II, April, 1894, to March, 1895. Vol. I, II, 1 & 2 $125-bmk-105. 4to(cl. or 1/2 lt.) v.1, p. 192, ports., illus.(many dbl. pg.) maps, $75-bmk-V.I, v.1, $18, $20, $25, $65, $7.50ea., Edts: Gen. Marcus J. Wright, associate, Ben La Bree, v.I & II, #2-$125-bmk, V.I, #1,2,7,8, wraps, $150-jk-135, (lax #1 &7)

1069 **"CONFEDERATE WOMEN OF ARKANSAS**
in the Civil War 1861-1865. Memorial Reminiscences. Pub: United Confederate Veterans of Arkansas. November, 1907." Little Rock: Order of J. Kellog (H.G. Pugh Co.) 8vo, cl, ports, 2-pls, 221pp. $15, $20, $25, $75. (Bibliog. of State Participation in C.W., gives book as (90)pp., in addition to above). $27.50.

...Little Rock, Ark., H.G. Pugh Print, 1907. 8vo, cl, pls, ports, 7p. (17)-221pp.

...Do: (90)pp., illus., incl. ports, 32x26 1/2cm. In: The Women of the Southern Confederacy, suppl. to leading newspapers in Tenn. & Miss. together with Arkansas memorial; clipped from original publications. Charleston, S.C. (1908) The leaves of the original publications clipped & mounted; pagination not preserved.

1070 **"CONFEDERATE, The, by a South Carolinian..."**
See: South Carolinian.

1071 **"CONFEDERATE, The."**
Edts: Miss. Rowland & Mrs. E.D. Taylor. Published daily during the Confederate Bazaar, held in Richmond, April-1903: Vol. 1-#1-14, April 15-30, 1903. Richmond, Va., 1903. United Daughters of the Confederacy, benefit of Jeff Davis Monument, 38cm, complete 14 issues.

1072 **"CONFEDERATES BURIED at Camp Douglas,**
Illinois, nearly all under Gen. Jno. Hunt Morgan." In: RKHS, Jan. 1948, (#154)v. 46, p. 404-409.

1073 **"CONFEDERATES UNTANGLED,**
By Seeing Eye." In: SPA, (Soc. Philatelics Amer.) Mar. 1951, v.13, p. 351-353; June 1951, v.13, p. 519-521; rejoiner, Sept. 1951, v.14, p. 32-33.

1074 **CONKLIN, Forrest**
"Footnotes on the death of John Hunt Morgan." In: THQ, Fall 1976, v.35, #3, p. 376-388.

1075 **CONLEY, Philip Mallory**
"The First Land Battle of the Civil War(Philippi)." In: West Virginia History, Jan. 1959, v.20, p. 120-123. port, view.

1076 **CONN, Charles Augustus**
"Conn-Brantley Letters, 1862." In: Ga. H.Q., Fall, 1971, v.LV, #3, p. 437-441.

1077 **CONN, Jack T.**
"Civil War Centennial 1861-1865, 1961-1965." Ada, Oklahoma: Oklahoma State Bank(1961). 8vo, stiff decr. wraps (cover title) ports, vigs. 38pp. presented by bank as a Civil War Centennial feature. $2.50.

1078 **CONN, W.A.**
"Desperate picket fight against superior force, at Fisher's Hill." In: SHSP, 1908, v.XXXVI, p. 220-223. Conn was in Co.C, 7th Va. Cav., 2nd Brig., 2nd Div. ANV.

1079 **CONN, William Thomas & Charles A.**
"Letters of two Confederate Officers: William Thomas Conn & Charles Augustus Conn. Edt: T. Conn Bryan." In: Ga. H.Q., June 1962, v.XLVI, #2, p.169-195. $10.

1080 **CONNELLEY, William Elsey**
"Quantrill & the Border Wars." Cedar Rapids: Torch Press, 1910. Large 8vo, cl, ports (incl. front) facsms, maps (part dbl.) ix, 542pp. $50, $74, $125.
..."Quantrill & the Border Wars." Intro: Homer Croy. N.Y., Pageant Books, 1956. 8vo, cl, ports, views, notes, maps (part dbl.) is, 5-542pp. $12.50. Civil War Book Club edt., atg. Croy, who wrote introduction. $50, $30-bmk, $18.

1081 **CONNELLY, Henry C.**
"Recollection of the War Between the States." Morgan's Raid." In: Ill. Hist. Soc. Jour., Jan, 1913, v.V, p. 458-474; Apr., p. 72-111.

1082 **CONNELLY, Henry, Governor**
"Proclamation by the Governor, Santa Fe, 9 September, 1861." sm.4to, broadside $600-jk. The Gov. exhorts citizens to arm at once & repel the Confederate forces.
..."Proclamacion del Governador." The same as the English version. See Imprints Inventory #149. $650.

1083 **CONNELLY, T.L.**
"The cycle of Military & Economic interests: a theory of Confederate defeat." In: AHQ, 1968, v.30, #3 & 4, p. 111-126.

1084 **CONNELLY, Thomas Lawrence**
"Autumn of Glory. The Army of Tennessee, 1862-1865." Baton Rouge: Louisiana State University Press(1971). tk.8vo, cl, d/w, ix, 558pp. illus., ports, sketch maps. $15.
..."Army of the Heartland: The Army of Tennessee, 1861-1862." Baton Rouge: Louisiana State Univ.(1967) 20, 8vo, cl, d/w, xvi, 306pp. bibliog., maps, illus. $8.50. 1972 Edt. $15, $20, 1982 Edt. $22.50.
..."Autumn of Glory: The Army of Tennessee, 1862-1865." Vol. II, 8vo, cl, d/w, 558pp. 1971 1st., $15. 1974 $27.50, 1982 $27.50.

1085 ..."Civil War Tennessee, Battles & Leaders." Knoxville, University of Tennessee Press, 1983. 8vo, cl, dj, illus., 110pp. $8.50, paper-$3.50. 1st Edt., 1979.

1086 ..."The Image of the General: Robert E. Lee in American Historiography." (Kent, Ohio) Civil War History, v.19, #1, March, 1973, p. 50-64, notes.

1087 ..."Robert E. Lee & the Western Confederacy: a Criticism of Lee's Strategic Ability." In: CWH, June 1969, v.XV, #2, p. 116-132.

1088 ..."The Johnston mystique-why did he rate so high among civil war generals?" In: CWTI, Feb., 1967, v.5, #10, p. 14-23, illus., map, ports.

1089 ..."The Marble Man, Robert E. Lee & His Image in American Society." N.Y., Alfred A. Knopf, 1977. 8vo, cl. spine, boards, dj, xv, 249pp., (2)p. illus., ports, facsm. paper-$6, $12.50, $10.
...Baton Rouge: Louisiana State University Press, 1979, 8vo, paper, 270pp. $6.

1090 **CONNELLY, Thomas Lawrence & Archer Jones**
"The Politics of Command: Factions & Ideas in Confederate Strategy." Baton Rouge: Louisiana State Univ. Pr., 1973. 8vo, cl, dj, xvi, 235pp. $10., $12-y, $17.50-y.

1091 CONNELLY, Thomas Lawrence & Barbara L. Bellows
"God & General Longstreet: The Lost Cause & the Southern Mind." Baton Rouge: Louisiana State University, 1982, 8vo, cl, dj, ix, 158pp., notes. $13.

1092 CONNER, Anderson
"The Return of Jesse James... or did he?" In: Westerners Brand Book, Mar. 1954, v.11, p. 1-3. J. Frank Dalton claimed he was Jesse James, with an account of the CSA underground, 1865 ff. See: Clifford Byrne.

1093 CONNER, Daniel Ellis
"A Confederate in the Colorado Gold Fields." Edt-Intro: Donald J. Berthrong & Odessa Davenport. Norman: University Oklahoma Pr. (1970) 8vo, cl, d/w, xiii, 186pp. port, illus. $4, $13-y, $6.95, $15, $14-bmk. Kentuckian, hiding in Colorado, conspires to wrest control for CSA.

1094 CONNER, Henry G.
"John Archibald Campbell, Associate Justice US Supreme Court, 1853-1861." Bost: Houghton Mifflin Co., 1920. 8vo, cl, viii, 310pp. $35, $50. Much on South, secession, Dred Scott, Hampton Roads Conference, Lincoln conferences, etc. Ass't. Sect. War.

1095 ..."The character & motive of Gen. Robert E. Lee." In: CV, May 1917, v.XV, p. 203-208.

1096 CONNER, James, General
"Letters of General James Conner, CSA." (Columbia, S.C., The State Co., 1933) 8vo, cl, 226pp. Edt: Mrs. Mary C. Moffatt. 20 copies printed for priv. distribution. Coulter #88. Turnbull. $200.
...Columbia, S.C., The R.L. Bryan Co., 1950. 8vo, cl, port, 246pp. $67.50, $500-b, $125-y

1097 ..."James Conner. Born 1st September, 1829, Died 26th June, 1883. In Memoriam. (Charleston, S.C.) Walker, Evans & Cogswell Print, (1883). 8vo, cl, 113pp. $175-r.

1098 CONNOR, Daniel A.
"Civil War Operations in West Texas & New Mexico: 1861-1862." In: Password, Aug., 1956. v.1, p. 90-98. Map ports. Part of thesis (AM) Texas Western College.

1099 CONNOR, Henry G.
"George Davis", Speech delivered at unveiling of his statue at Wilmington, N.C., Apr. 20, 1911. Cape Fear Chap. #3, U.D.C. 8vo, stiff wraps, 54pp. ports. Davis was Senator & Atty-Gen. for CSA.

1100 CONNOR, Orange Cicero & Mary America
"Dear America: Some Letters of Orange Cicero & Mary America (Aikin) Connor." Edt: Seymour V. Connor. Austin, Texas: Jenkins Pub., 1971. 8vo, cl, dj, xv, 132pp., illus., notes, index. $6.95.

1101 CONNOR, Robert Diggs Wimberly, comp.
"Addresses at the unveiling of the memorial to the North Carolina women of the Confederacy presented to the state by the late Ashley Horne." Raleigh: Edwards & Broughton Print, 1914. (Publication of the N.C. Hist. Comm. Bul-16) 8vo, wraps, 26pp., plates, port. $20-bmk-116.

1102 ..."Ceremonies attending the presentation & unveiling of the North Carolina Memorial on the Battlefield at Gettysburg, Wed. July 3, 1929." North Carolina Gettysburg Memorial Comm., n.p., 44pp. plates.

1103 ..."Memorial Day: an interpretation (to the soldier of the Confederacy from Wilson County, N.C.) An address before the John W. Dunham Chap. U.D.C., Wilson, N.C., May 11, 1909." Raleigh: Edwards & Broughton, 1909. 8vo, wraps, 22pp. $1, $3, $15.

1104 ..."Address on Alfred Moore Scales (1927)1892." Raleigh, N.C., Uzzell Print, 1908. 8vo, wraps, 33pp.

1105 ..."The University of North Carolina & the Civil War." In: Univ. N.C. Record, June 1911, #93, (7pp.) See: Henry A. London.

1106 **CONRAD, August**
"The Destruction of Columbia, S.C. A translation from the German by Wm. H. Pleasants of 19th, 20th, 21st, & 22nd Chapters of "Lights & Shadows in America Life During the War of Secession", by... Published at Honover (Germany), 1879." Roanoke, Va., Stone Printing, 1902. 8vo, gray stiff wraps, 31pp.
...Columbia, S.C., 1926. Reprinted & distributed by the Wade Hampton Chap. United Daughters of the Confederacy. (Roanoke, Va., Stone Print) 8vo, 32pp.

1107 ..."Schatten und Lichblicke aus dem Amerikansischen Leben Waehrend des Secessions-Kriege." (Trans: "Shades & Bright Spots in American Life During the War of Secession.") Hanover: 1879, T. Schulze Pub. 8vo, orig. limp leather, (2), 205pp. $200-b, $25, $37.50, $50, $90. Consul from Hanover to Charleston, later in Wilmington, N.C., & Columbia, S.C., the above trans. of Columbia's Destruction is only English trans. of above book. See: Wm. Gilmore Simms title. Also: "Lady of Georgia" (pseud), Dr. D.H. Trezevant, J.G. Gibbes.

1108 **CONRAD, Bryan**
"The Seven Days Campaign, 1862." In: Wm. & Mary Quart., 2nd Ser., 1934, v.XIV, p. 216-221. The campaign around Richmond, June 25-July 1, 1862.

1109 **CONRAD, Daniel B.**
"Capture of the C.S. Ram Tennessee in Mobile Bay, August 1864. By Dr. Daniel B. Conrad, Fleet Surgeon, C.S. Navy." In: SHSP, 1891, v.XIX, p. 72-82.

1110 ..."Capture & Burning of the Federal Gunboat "Underwriter", in the Neuse, off Newbern, N.C., in February, 1864." In: SHSP, 1891, v.XIX, p. 93-100.

1111 ..."History of the First Battle of Manassas & the organization of the Stonewall Brigade, how it was so named." In: SHSP, 1891, v.XIX, p. 82-92.
..."History of the First fight & organization of Stonewall Brigade & how it was so named." In: Phila: United Serv., 1892, v.VII, p. 466-475.

1112 ..."The Stonewall Brigade at Bull Run." In: B & G, 1894, v.IV, p. 359-395, port., illus.
..."With Stonewall Jackson before Bull Run." In: Mag. Hist., 1909, v.IX, p. 148-152.

1113 **CONRAD, Georgia Bryan, Mrs.**
"Reminiscences of a Southern Woman." Hampton, Va., Hampton Institute Pr., (1901) Reprinted from the "Southern Workman", Hampton, Va., 1901. V.XXX, Feb., Mar., May, June, July, 1901. 8vo, wraps, 26pp. Before, during & after the War. Plantation Days or woman rice-planter, mostly on the Altamaha River, in southern Georgia. A privately printed booklet for children, family.

1114 **CONRAD, Holmes**
"The Confederate Cavalry in the East." In: "Photographic Hist. of Civil War.", v.4, N.Y., 1911, p. 71-114, illus., ports. Reprint: Glendale, Cal., 1970.

1115 ..."Ceremonies & address attending the presentation of Hunter McGuire Memorial Association-Statue-its acceptance by the State, Jan. 7, 1904." Richmond, Va. (c.1904). 8vo, wraps, 30pp. $5.
...Also in: SHSP, 1903, v.XXXI, p. 253-266.

1116 ..."Virginia Mourning her dead. Address at Lexington, Va., on occasion of the Unveiling of the statue by Sir Moses Ezekiel. In: SHSP, 1910, v.38, p. 221-241. (See also: E. Holmes Bond.) $38.

1117 **CONRAD, Holmes**
"The Confederate Cavalry in the East." In: Photo. Hist. CW, v.4, p. 71-114, illus., port.

1118 **CONRAD, James L.**
"Forrest's great gamble-the Battle of Ebenezer Church." In: CWTI, Apr. 1981, v.20, #1, p. 30-39, illus., map ports.

1119 **CONRAD, Mary Lynn**
"Confederate Banners, a paper read before the Turner Ashby Chapter & before the Virginia Division State Convention of the U.D.C., Harrisonburg, Va." (Roanoke, Va., 1908?) Stone Print. 16mo, pict. wraps, color flags, 20pp., tied. $5, $25-bmk.

1120 **CONRAD, Thomas Nelson, Capt.**
"A Confederate Spy." Eureka Detective Stories, #8. New York: J.S. Ogilvie, 1892. $125-bmk-105, $40-nc, $50-y. 12mo, wraps, 142pp., facsms. $75.
...Same, But "Peerless series, #63." Dornbusch-2658.
...Same, But n.d., $6.50, $15.
...Lynchburg, Va., Artcraft Pr., 1961, front(port) Dornbusch, 1659. $6.
...N.Y., Ogilvie & Co., 1894, Sunset Series #93. 12mo, wraps, 142, (18)pp. $12.50.

1121 ..."The Rebel Scout. A Thrilling History of Scouting Life in the Southern Army." by.-..of the Army of Northern Virginia, C.S.A., $150-jk-117, $175-bmk-105. Washington City: National Pub., 1904. 12mo,cl, 220pp. $20, $25, $35, #38.50, $45, $150-jk-117, $150-gins.9, $80-nc.

1122 **"CONSTITUTION & BY-LAWS**
of the New York Division United Daughters of the Confederacy. Organized Jan. 13, 1916." (New York, ? 1916) 12mo, wraps, cover title, 3-14pp.

1123 **CONSTITUTION of the Confederate States of America**
"Constitution of the Confederate States of America...(&) United States of America." (Montgomery, Ala., 1861) 8vo, sewn, 21pp. (Together with) Howell Cobb. (Printed letter of transmittal to D.F. Jamison, President of the South Carolina Secession Convention). Montgomery, Alabama, March 12, 1861. Comprising one page of text & a conjugate blank leaf, thus forming a loose cover for the constitution itself. This is the first issue of the permanent Confederate Constitution, the only other known copy being at the University of Ga. Only a small number being printed for submission to the seven secession conventions of the lower South for ratification. The Howell Cobb letter being the only known copy. Cobb had both the CSA & US constitutions printed in parallel columns. List: Jenkins-cat/142. $8500.
..."Constitution of the Confederate States of America." (Charleston? 161) Atg: Robt. B. Rhett (4500) 12mo, sewn, caption title, 21pp. Felix Hargrett. Harwell: 1-5-1.
..."Constitution of the Confederate States of America. Adopted Unanimously by the Congress of the Confederate States of America, March 11, 1861." New Orleans, La., J.O. Nixon, Printer to the Convention, 1861. 8vo, printed self-wraps, 22pp. $400. Ebe rstadt-#166(1964). Apparently only known copy. Earliest one, in which only seven states represented: Ala., Fla., Ga., La., Miss. S.C., & Texas. See: Russell H. Quynn.
...Milledgeville: Boughton, Nisbet & Barnes, State printers, 1861. 12mo, self-wraps, 2299. (old) $30-jk-128, bound with #1, 7 & 15 (Crandall-6) $150. bound in yellow printed wraps.
...Athens, Ga., 1979. 8vo, wrps, 22pp. 12pp. intro., by Richard B. Harwell. $10-bmk.
..."The Constitution of the Confederate States of America, adopted March 11, 1861." Printed, self-wraps, 15, (1)p. $250-jk. Apparently unrecorded.
...(caption title)". In: Congress-March 9, 1861-Amended Constitution-100 copies ordered to be printed (above title in

smaller type) 29 galley proofs or leaves, 12x8 1/2", printed one side only, tied at top, folded. Montgomery, 1861. Goodspeed-601 $15,000. Note: Final printed draft (only two copies known, other: Streeter). For use of committee, spaced for corrections or changes, each line being numbered. Precedes over a dozen printings for public after Constitution was adopted Mar. 11. Ranks with preliminary printed draft (27 leaves). One complete copy known of 13 printed) changed by Congress before printed in final form here. "Cornerstones" lists later pamphlet edition for public. Crand-#7.

...& United States of America." (Charleston, S.C., 1861, (Evans & Cogswell) 16mo, caption title, 21pp. Harwell-1 $4500. Jenkins: "One of only 3 known copies, bears initials of Robert Barnwell Rhett. This particular edition was meant for distribution to the secession convention."

1124 **CONSTITUTION of the Provisional Govermnent**
of the Confederate States of America. "Constitution of the Provisional Government of the Confederate States of America. At a Congress of the Sovereign & Independent States of S.C., Ga., Fla., Ala., Miss. & La. begun & holden at the Capitol, Montgomery (Feb. 4, 1861, & cont. to Feb. 8). Lithographic facsimilie of the manuscript, mounted on linen: 1' 5 1/2"x9'x8", with wood rollers. New York, Joseph Laing, 1883. $50. $150-jk-127. See: "facsimile..."

..."Constitution of the Provisional Government of the Confederate States of America, Feb. 8, 1861." Letter presenting the original document to SHSociety." In: SHSP, 1884, v.XII, p. 140-141. Presentation by William Wilson Corcoran of Washington, D.C., Feb. 6, 1884.

1125 ..."Manuscript of Confederate Constitution on exhibit for Historians." In: SHSP, 1908, v.XXXVI, p. 371-372. From: "NewsLeader", Dec. 30, 1908. In the Confederate Museum but not on display after the exhibit.

1126 **"CONSTITUTION of the Society**
of the Army & Navy of the Confederate States in the State of Maryland." (Baltimore) King Bros., 1871. 12mo, 8pp. folded. $15-jk-122. One of the earliest CSA Vets. formed to preserve materials & memorials.

1126a **"CONSTITUTION of the United Sons of Confederate Veterans...**
third Annual Reunion...1898." Atlanta, Ga., Franklin Print, 1900. 8vo, wraps, 23pp. $15.

1127 **CONSTITUTION of the United States of America**
"The Constitutuion of the United States of America, with a summary of the actions of the States in ratification of the provisions thereof. To which is appended, for its historical interest, the Constitution of the Confederate States of America. Prepared & distributed by the Virginia Commission on Constitutional Government." (Richmond, Va. 1961) 8vo, cl, or wraps, (13), 94pp. $7.50.

..."The Constitution of the United States; also a Document entitled "The Constitution of the Confederate States." Arranged in parallel columns, with the differences indicated, for convenient reference & comparison." Cincinnati: E. Watkin, 1862. 8vo, wraps, 24pp., Sabin-16123.

1128 **"CONSTITUTION, OBJECTS, ROSTERS**
of officers, members, etc., United Daughters of the Confederacy, Mississippi." Louisville, Ky., Courier Press, 1897. 12mo, wraps, illus. (incl. ports), 24pp. cover title.

1129 **"CONSTITUTIONALIST EXTRA.**
Sunday evening, April 30, 1865. Terms of

agreement between Gens. Johnston & Sherman (Caption-title)." Broadside 7x7". (Augusta, Ga., 1865) Hummel-557. Goodspeed-601 $750. One known copy.

1130 "CONSTITUTION of the State of Texas, as amended in 1861. The Constitution of the Confederate States of America. The ordinances of the Texas Convention: & an address to the people of Texas. Printed by order of the Convention & the Senate." Austin: John Marshall, State Printer, 1861. 12mo, sewn, 40, 40pp. $650-jk-152.

1130a "CONSTITUTIONS & BY-LAWS For the Government of the United Confederate Veterans of North Caromer, 1894. 8vo, wraps, color ills of U.C.V. badges, 48pp. Chicago, Ill., Rand, McNally, 1894. $25.

1131 "CONTEMPORARY REPORTS of Confederate Privateers in the 'Charleston Mercury' 1861. The War on the Seas (The Brig 'Jefferson Davis'.)" In: American Neptune, April, 1951, Vol. XI, #2, p. 150-155.

1132 "CONTRIBUTIONS TO A HISTORY of the Richmond Howitzer Battalion." Pamphlets, #1-4. Carlton McCarthy, Editor. Richmond, Va., Carlton McCarthy & Co. 1883-1886. J.W. Randolph & English. 8vo, wraps, 84, (85)-304; 64, 64pp. $150, $50, $12.50, $400-ob.
...Capt. Henry Hudnall - "Organization of First Company & John Brown Raid."; Capt. W. Gordon McCabe - "Our Dead."; Rev. E.C. Gordon - "The Battle of Big Bethel." & "All Official Reports (C.S. & U.S.) Battle of Big Bethel."; William S. White - "A Diary of the War, or, What I Saw of It."; "Rolls of Third Co. Richmond Howitzers as Mustered in & as Surrendered." ; T. Roberts Baker - "Diary, of Second Co."; John Waldrop & William Y. Mordecai - "Diaries" of Second Co., combined.; Reuben B. Pleasants - "First Detachment at Fredericksburg." Col. W.E. Cutshaw - "William S. White's Diary Corrected."; "Roll of Second Co., as mustered in & as surrendered, April 9, 1865."; Creed T. Davis - "Prison Diary, of, Second Co."; J.V.L. McCreery - "That Hog Hole, of First Co."; "Extracts from an old "Order Book", of First Co., Richmond Howitzers." See: Fred S. Daniel; "Richmond Howitzers"; Leigh Robinson, Carleton McCarth, T.J. Macon, Fred S. Daniel, Wm. M. Dame, Andrew J. Andrews, George L. Christian, Henry C. Tinsley, Harry C. Townsend, Robt. Stiles.

1133 "CONTRIBUTIONS of the Confederacy to Naval Architecture & Naval Warfare." In: CV, Sept. 1923, v.XXXI, p. 334-338.

1134 "CONVENTION ACT passed both houses of the General Assembly on Jan. 14, 1861." (Little Rock, Ark., 1861) Broadside, 32.5cm. text 2-column. (Hargrett) Found also in Gov. Rector's Message. #420.

1135 CONVENTION DOCUMENTS-South Carolina
"Report of the Special Committee of Twenty-one, on the Communication of His Excellency Governor Pickens, together with the reports of Heads of Departments & other papers." Columbia, S.C., R. W. Gibbes Print, 1862, Printer for the Convention. 8vo, sewn, 181pp. $25.

1136 CONVENTION of Border Slave States "Journal of Proceedings of Convention of Border Slave States, begun & held in the city of Frankfort, & state of Kentucky on the 27th day of May, 1861." Frankfort, Ky., Yeoman Office, J.B. Major State Printer, 1861. 8vo, sewn, 24pp. Delegates from Kentucky, Missouri & one representative from McMinn & Sevier counties, Tenn.

1137 "CONVENTION of South Carolina. Report & resolutions from the committee on relations with the slaveholding states providing for commissioners to such states." Charleston: Evans & Cogswell, 1861.

1138 **"CONVULSIONS OF AMERICA, The"**
In: Black. Edn. Mag., Jan. 1862, v.XCI, p. 118-130. "Every day tends to justify judgement & policy of the South withdrawing from Union."

1139 **CONWAY, Catlett**
"Richardson Guard. Muster Roll of this Madison County Company (Va.)" In: SHSP, 1896, v.XXIV, p. 361-363. Which became Co. A, 7th Va. Reg.

1140 **CONWAY, Elias Nelson, Gov. Arkansas.**
"Message of the Governor to both houses of the General Assembly; November 6, 1860." Little Rock, Ark., Johnson & Yerkes, 1860. 8vo, wraps, 29, 8pp.
..."Special Message from the Governor relative to commissioner from Mississippi." caption title, title head (House Doc.) sm.8vo, sewn, 8pp.
..."See: Henry M. Rector, Gov. Ark.

1141 **CONWAY, Moncure D. & James M. Mason.**
"Abolitionism & Southern Independence." In: Wm. & Mary Quart., Apr. 1913, v.XXI, p. 221-223. Corresp. between them as pub. in "London Times", 1863.

1142 **CONWAY, William B.**
"The Surrender of Gen. R.E. Lee. He did not offer his sword to Gen. Grant." In: SHSP, 1907, v.XXXV, p. 159-160.

1143 ... "Talks with J.A. Early. Valley Campaign & movement on Washington." In: SHSP, 1902, v.XXX, p. 250-255. Dr. Conway was in Co. C, 4th Reg. Va. Cav.

1144 **CONYER, Luther**
"Last Battle of the War. It was fought on the Rio Grande in Texas." In: SHSP, 1896, v.XXIV, p. 309-315.

1145 **COOK OF THE CONFEDERATE ARMY, The**
In: Scribner Mag., Aug., 1879, illus. by Allen C. Redwood, 10pp. $15-bmk.

1146 **COOK, Anna Maria Green**
"The Glory of the Old South & the Greatness of the New. Reform & the divided mind of Charles Hillman Brough." In: AHQ, 1975, v.XXXIV, p. 226-241.

1147 **COOK, Edward Tyas, Sir**
"Delane of the Times." N.Y., H. Holt & Co., 1916. 8vo, cl, front(port), x, 319pp. "Makers of the Nineteenth Century." Edt: London "Times", during war & supported the South."

1148 **COOK, Giles B.**
"Confederate Leaders & other citizens requests the House of Delegates to Repeal the Resolution of Respect to Abraham Lincoln, the Barbarian." n.p., (c.1928). 8vo, caption title, 16pp. $3.50. Maj. G.W.B. Hale, Lyon G. Tyler.

1149 ..."Final Reply to Westerner. (From the (Richmond, Va.) "Times-Dispatch", Sunday, Jan 8, 1928. n.p., (1928), 8vo, caption title, 19, (1)pp. Reprints of letters to newspapers by the critics of Lincoln.

1150 **COOK, Harvey Toliver**
"Sherman's March through South Carolina in 1865, by Harvey T. Cook, an ex-Confederate." Greenville, S.C., 1938. 8vo, wraps, 25pp. $3.75, $12-bmk, $8, $10.

1151 **COOK, Henry Howe, Judge**
"The story of the Six Hundred." In: CV, March, 1897, v.V, #3, p. 116-118; #4, p. 148-150; #5, p. 219-220.

1152 **COOK, James F.**
"The 1863 raid of Abel D. Streight: why it failed." In: ARev., v.22, #4, p. 254-269.

1153 **COOK, James M.**
"Reminiscences of the civil war, by James M. Cook, Company H. Forty-ninth regiment." Glover, S.C., 1929. 18x9cm, 15pp. Dorn-II, 955.

1154 **COOK, Mary Louise Redd, Mrs.**
"Ante-Bellum. Southern Life as it was. By

Mary Lennox (pseud)." Phila: J.B. Lippincott Co., 1868. 12mo, cl, vii, (9)-322pp.

1155 **COOK, Philip C.**
"Lake Bistineau Salt Works & Civil War Operations." (Ruston, La., Polytechnic Institute, 1963. 4to, 17pp., illus., bibliog. Term paper in history.

1156 **COOK, Robert Cecil, Dr.**
"A Memoir: Two Uncles of a long time ago." In: JNH, May 1978, v.XL, #2, p. 167-181. Memory of two CSA soldiers of Forrest Cavalry Brigade.

1157 **COOK, Roland J.**
"Letters of Roland J. Cook." In: Phillips CHQ, March 1965, v.3, p. 29-37. Civil War letters.

1158 **COOK, Roy Bird**
"Albert Gallatin Jenkins. A Confederate Portrait." In: West Va. Review, May 1934, v.11, p. 225-227. In 8th Va. Cavalry.

1159 ..."Battle of Droop Mountain." In: Confed. Vet., Sept. 1928, v.XXXVI, p. 338-340. "Last stand of the CSA. West of main Alleghanies, Nov. 6, 1863."

1160 ..."Stonewall Jackson in Lewis County (W.Va.)." In: Confed. Vet., July 1924, XXXII, p. 269-269.
..."Battle of Droop Mountain." In: W.Va. Review, Oct. 1928, v.6, p. 14-15. Map, CSA's Jno. Echols, W.L. Jackson.

1161 ..."Capt. Edwin Duncan Camden." In: Confed. Vet., Feb. 1923, XXXI, p. 57-58. In Co.E, 25th Va. Inf.

1162 ..."First Battle of Great Kanawha Valley." In: Confed. Vet., Apr/May, 1931, XXXIX, p. 143-145; 183-186. Reprint West Va. Rev., Dec., 1926, p. 69-71; p. 85-88.

1163 ..."West Virginia at First & Second Manassas." In: Confed. Vet., June 1929, XXXVII, p. 217-218. Lists both CSA & Union units & command.

1164 ..."The Family & Early Life of Stonewall Jackson." Richmond, Va., Old Dominion Press, 1924, 8vo, wraps, plates, ports, 96pp. facs., $5.50, $12.50, or cloth, $40-bmk, 1925-$22.50, $70.
...Charleston, W.Va., Educational Foundation, Inc., 1967. 8vo, cl, 206pp., illus., index. $5, $12.50-y, $30-b, $20-nc. Same: paperbound $3. 2nd Edt: 1925-Rich: Old Dominion Press. atg-$40, $35-mcm, $8.50, $10,$50-b. 3rd Edt: Charleston, W.Va., 1948, p. 198. $15-y, 4th Edt: 1963 & revised before author's death., 5th Edt: 1967, same as above. $20, $10-nc, $30.

1165 ..."Thomas J. Jackson, a God-Fearing Soldier of the C.S.A." n.p., n.d. (1961) (Cincinnati, Ohio.) Christmas gift of Krehbiel Co., 1961. 12mo, fabricoid, 48pp. illus., ports. $10.

1166 ..."Lewis County in Civil War, 1861-1865." $40-bmk, $10, $12.50. Charleston, W.Va., Jarrett Pr., 1924, 8vo, cl, 155pp., pl., ports, map. $3.75, $30.

1167 ..."Joseph Andrew Jackson Lightburn (1824-1901)." In: W.Va. Hist., Oct., 1953, v.15, p. 5-57, notes. On his career as an officer in CSA in W.Va. & Georgia, 1861-1865. With copies of letters to various persons.

1168 ..."The battle of Carnifex Ferry...an address at Carnifex battlefield, Kesler Cross Lanes, W. Va., before 5000 people assembled at commemorate the 70th anniversary of battle, Sept. 10, 1931." n.p., 1931. 8vo, wraps, (8)pp. Dorn-2337 $35.

1168a **COOK, Virgil Young**
"List of General & Field Officers in the Confederate Army from Arkansas." In: Pub. Ark. Hist. Assn., v.I, 1906, p. 411-422. See: UCV Reunion-Ark Report, 21st Annual
..."Forrest's effort to save Selma." In: C.V., Apr. 1918, v.XXVI, p. 151-152.

1169 **COOKE, John Esten**
"Autobiography of John Esten Cooke. Edited by: Hennig Cohen." In: Amer. Lit. v.30, May 1958, p. 234-237, notes. From a

mssc. addressed to Wm. G. Simms, about 1866, on author as "Cavalier" & "Virginian."

1170 ..."John Esten Cooke on Publishing, 1865. Edited: I.B. Cauthen, Jr." In: "Studies in Bibliog., v.8, p. 239-241. 1956. Letters to "Overton", June 23, 1865. Author's plans to publish works in North rather than Va.

1171 ..."Confessions of John E. Cooke, one of the participants in the Harper's Ferry invasion." n.p., Published for Sam'l C. Young (1859) 8vo, wraps, 16pp. Swem-1122.

1172 ..."The Battles of Virginia (including Sharpsburg & Gettysburg)." (In the "Old Guard, a Monthly Magazine." N.Y., Van Evrie & Horton, 1867, v.V) I-"Manassas", p. 21-32; II-"Port Republic", p. 105-119; III-"Seven Pines & the Seven Days", p.177-189; IV-"Second Manassas", p. 340-352; v-"Sharpsburg", p. 422-436; VI-"Fredericksburg", p. 501-513; VII-"Chancellorsville." p.577-591; VIII-"Gettysburg", p. 651-667; IX-"Wilderness, May 1864." p.745-753; X-"By Left Flank from 'Horseshoe' to 'Crater', p. 811-821; XI-"Early's Battles", p.887-896.

1173 ...Bibliography: Oscar Wegelin. Biography: John O. Beaty, Richard Harwell.

1174 ..."General Stuart in camp & field." In: AW, 1879, p. 665-676.

1175 ..."Hammer & Rapier." N.Y., Carleton, London: S. Low, 1870. 12mo, cl, x, (12)-307pp. $20, $25, $50-bmk-116, $40, $12.50; 1871 Edt., $5; 1889, $4; 1890, $20; Charleston, S.C.; 1892, $20; 1893, $20; 1893, $3.50; 1896, $6; 1898, $5.50 (1888 edt. of 397pp., Swem.) Virginia in the Civil War.

1176 ..."Hilt to Hilt; or, Days & Nights on the Banks of the Shenandoah in the Autumn of 1864. From the Mss. of Colonel Surry of Eagle's Nest." N.Y., G.W. Carleton. London: S. Low & Son, 1869. 12mo, cl, vi, (8)-270pp. $35-bmk, $20. 1890, $12.50; 1896, $6; 1893, $20.

1177 ..."A Life of Gen. Robert E. Lee." N.Y., D. Appleton & Co., 1871, 8vo, cl, ports(incl. front) plates, maps (10), 1-fldg., vi, 577pp. $30. (covers: Morocco, sheep & 1/2clf). Editions: 1871($45, $60, $100); 1873 ($75); 1875 ($40); 1876 ($60); 1877 ($60, $100); 1883 ($25); 1887 ($60); 1899 ($12)

1178 ..."The Song of the Rebel." Foreword, Richard Harwell. Richmond, Va., n.d., 1957, (Confederate Museum) reprint of broadside. 8vo, wraps, 19pp (one quote 24pp), $20, $25. See Harwell-#1255, broadside, 1863, only recorded copy?, ViRC

1179 ..."The War Diary of John Esten Cooke, edt: Jay B. Hubbell." In: Jour. South. Hist., 1941, v.VII, p. 526-540. $8, $1.50.

1180 ..."The Life of Stonewall Jackson, from official papers, contemporary narratives & personal acquaintance, by a Virginian. Richmond: Ayres & Wade, 1863. 12mo, cl, xi, (13)-305. (printed paper covers, with Jackson port.) ports(front) litho by Ernest Crehan. $300-ob, $40-bmk, $85. New York Edition has new portrait of Jackson, by O'Neil.

1181 ...N.Y., Charles B. Richardson, 1863, reprinted from the advance sheets of the Richmond edition. $17.50, $25, $60, 1864-$25, $90-b, $100. Since John M. Daniel's name appears on spine, some have attributed it to Daniels. See: Sabin-100578.
...London: S. Low & Son, 1863.
...N.Y., Charles B. Richardson, 1866. (Daniel's name is dropped from spine & printer-R. Craighead, version t.p. also removed, otherwise the same.) Some copies of this edt. has also the name of the London: S.Low & Co. $75-b, $15, $40-bmk
...N.Y., D. Appleton & Co., 1866. "Stonewall Jackson, a Military Biography with a portrait & maps. By John Esten

Cooke, formerly of General Stuart's staff." Crown 8vo, cl, port & 6-maps, part fold., 470pp. Enlarged with new material. $15, $200-r, $37.50, $150, $40-bmk.

..."Stonewall Jackson: A Military Biography. By John Esten Cooke. With an appendix containing personal reminiscences, & a full account of the ceremonies attending the unveiling of Foley's statue, including the oration of Moses D. Hoge, D.D., by Rev. J. Wm. Jones." N.Y., D. Appleton & Co., 1876. $150-bmk-105, $100-bmk, 8vo, cl, front, plates, ports, maps, 7, (9)-587pp. $17.50, $20, $35-bmk, $75, $65-4mor. Other Edts: 1867, $10; 1875, $15.

...N.Y. Dillingham & Co., 1894, 1897, with 464pp. 12mo, ports, pl, maps. $10.

...Freeport, N.Y., Books for Libraries (1971) 8vo, cl, ports, 305pp. Reprint of 1863 edition, new $19-y, $25-b, $13.25.

1182 ..."Stonewall Jackson & the Old Stonewall Brigade." Edt: Richard Barksdale Harwell. Charlottesville, Va., Univ. of Va. Press. from the Tracy W. McGregor Library (1954). 8vo, cl, d/w, front(port) 76pp. $3.50, $8.50, $10, $50-r, $30-bmk, $25-bmk, $35-bmk. Articles Cooke wrote for the Southern Illustrated News, v.I, #22-24, Feb. 7, 14, 21, 1863 make the present volume.

1183 ..."Mohun, or the Last Days of Lee & His Paladins. Final memoirs of a staff officer serving in Virginia. From the Mss. of Colonel Surry, of Eagle's Nest." N.Y., F.J. Huntington & Co., 1869. 12mo, cl, illus., port Lee by O'Neill, facsm., 6lf, 509pp. $40, $20, $50, $25. Sequel to "Surry of Eagle's Nest."

...N.Y., G.W. Dillingham, 1889. 12mo, decr. cl, facsm., but no illus., $7.50, Edt: (1896) $5, (1893) $20., 1936, 8vo, cl, dj, facsms (incl. front) 376pp. $5, $8, $50-b, $25-bmk, $12.50, $30, $50.

...Ridgewood, N.J., Gregg Print (1968) $9.

1184 ..."Our Leader & Defender, Gen. Robert E. Lee." n.p., Collins & Campbell, 1889. 8vo, 3/4 Mor., illus., ports, fldg. map, vi, 577pp. $7.50.

...N.Y., G.W. Dillingham, 1893. 8vo, cl, vi, 501pp. $5. 1899 edtl, in wraps, $5, NY, n.d., 509pp. $4.

1185 ..."Outlines from the Outpost." Heading: The Lakeside Classics. Edt: Richard Harwell." Chicago: R.R. Donnelley & Sons, The Lakeside Press, Christmas, 1961. 12mo, cl, xxiv, 413pp. front(port) $10, $30, $25. All "Outlines" appeared in "Southern Illustrated News" & others, i.e., from "Wearing of the Gray." Revisions.

1186 ..."Personal portraits, scenes & adventures, comprising sketches of the late war, with thrilling narratives of the daring deeds, dashing charges, toilsome marches, willing sacrifices & patient sufferings incident to "wearing of the Gray". N.Y., E.B. Treat, 1871. 8vo, cl, xvi, (17)-601pp. plates, ports, $35.

...same, 1872, $17.50. Reprint: "Wearing of the Gray."

...Bloomington, Indiana Unvi. Press (1959) sm. 8vo, cl, dj, xxii, 572pp., illus. ports. $17.50

1187 ..."Surrey of Eagle's Nest; or, The Memoirs of a Staff-Officer serving in Virginia." Edt. from Mss. of Colonel Surrey by Esten Cooke. $50. N.Y., Bunce & Huntington, 1866. $25-b, $22.50. 12mo, p. 484, woodcuts(4) ('45-50: $8, $10, $16.) 1879, Hartford: W.W. Huntington; N.Y., 1866, p. 490, $60-bmk, ('56) $11, $50-bm; N.Y., 1866, 4th Edt., $37.50, ('60) $35; 5th Edt., $25; N.Y., 1867, 6th Edt.; N.Y., 1869, illus. Winslow Homer, 12mo, cl.; N.Y., (1899) G.W. Dillingham, $7, fine-$10-bmk.' N.Y., (1894), decr. cl, 484pp. illus., $20, $8, $25.; Chi., (1894) Donohue & Co., $30-bmk, $2.50; N.Y., (1898)-G.W. Dillingham. See: Helen Chappell White. N.Y., 1897-G.W.

Dillingham, Ridgewood, N.J., Gregg Print (1968) $14-y, 8vo, cl, port, 484pp.

1188 ..."The Broken Mug." In: SHSP, 1886, v.XIV, p. 222-226. Carried by Cooke thru war.

1189 ..."Wearing of the Gray, being personal portraits, scenes & adventures of the war, by John Esten Cooke, formerly of General Stuart's staff(quote)." N.Y., E.B. Treat & Co., et.al. 1867. Large 8vo, cl, ports(incl. front) plates, xvi, (17)-601pp. $20, $30, $125-bmk, $37.50, $70, $85, $50-ch.hill, $100-nc-76.

...Same, being a sample used for canvassing subscriptions in & around Alexandria, Va., with list headed by Fitzhugh Lee. $10.

...Augusta, Ga., 1870, decr. cl, thick 8vo, $18.50; Other Edts: 1871, $35; 1887, $15 & n.d., $10.

...Bloomington: Indiana Univ. Pr. (1959), N.Y.-Kraus, 1969, $15, $40, $30-y, $35. tk. 8vo, cl, dj, illus., ports, xxii, 572pp. Civil War Cent. Series, Intro-notes by Philip Van Doren Stern. op $15-y.

..."Mohun." Charleston, S.C., Martin & Hoyt Co., 1893, 12mo, wraps, 509pp.

1190 ..."Personal character of General Lee." In: Appelton's Jour., July 9, 1875. (4p)

1191 **COOKE, Giles Buckner, Maj.**
"Just Before & after Lee Surrendered to Grant." n.p., n.d. (Houston, Texas, Chronicle, 1922) cover title. $25, $32.50. 4x9 1/4", printed wraps, tied silk cord. 8pp. (errors corrected in ink) $35. Taken from the Houston Chronicle of Oct. 8, 1922. $150-ob.

1192 ..."Rev. Maj. Giles Buckner Cooke." In: Tyler. QHGM, 1937, v.XIX, p. 1-10, 87-94. Excerpts from diary 1864-1865.

1193 **COOKE, J. Churchill**
"Catlett's Station Raid Again." In: SHSP, 1908, v.XXXVI, p. 213-214. Cooke was in Co. G, 4th Va. Cavalry.

1194 **COOKE, James D.**
"A History of the Thirty-first Virginia Regiment Volunteers, CSA." Morgantown: W. Va. University, 1955. Thesis (M.A.) 4to, 158 lfs. Shenandoah Valley, Jones-Imboden raid. Shetler-162.

1195 **COOKE, Samuel Alonza**
"The Civil War Memoirs of Samuel Alonza Cooke. Edited by Bill O'Neal." In: SwHQ, April, 1971, v.LXXIV, #4, p. 535-548.

1196 **COOL SPRING (Clarke County, Va.)**
Civil War Engagement, July 18, 1864. See: Peter J. Meaney, OSB.

1197 **COOLIDGE, Calvin, President**
"Address of President Coolidge at the Confederate Memorial Arlington National Cemetery, Virginia, May 25, 1924." Washington: 1924, GPO. 8vo, wraps, pp.1, lf, 2pp.

1198 **COOLING, Benjamin Franklin**
"Alabamians in the Forts Henry & Donelson Campaign." In: AHQ, 1964, v.XXVI, p. 217-234, map. Ala. 26/27th Inf. Regs.

1199 ..."The Battle of Dover, Feb. 3, 1863." In: Tenn. HQ, 1963, v.XXII, p. 143-151. Also as Donelson, or Dover.

1200 ..."The Attack on Dover, Tenn." In: CWTI, Aug. 1963, v.II, #5, p. 10-13, illus., map, ports. Forrest & Wheeler failed to overcome a stubborn Federal garrison.

...Edt., see, John Henry Guy.

1201 ..."Fort Sumter & the "Lesson" of History." (London) Jour. Confed. Hist. Soc. Sprg. Summer, 1971, v.9, #1 & @, p. 31-34, pl.

1202 ..."Gee's Fifteenth Arkansas Infantry in the Forts Henry & Donelson Campaign." In: AHQ, 1964, v.XXIII, p. 329-342, map.

1203 ..."Virginians at Fort Donelson, FEb. 1862." (London) Jour. Hist. Confed. Soc., Winter 1966, v.4, #4, p. 142-163, pl, maps (2).

1204 ..."When were Southerners first admitted to the United States Army after the C.W.?" (London) Jour. Confed. Hist. Soc., Summer, 1972, v.10, #2, p. 76-79.

1204a ..."Forts Henry & Donelson, the key to the Confederate Heartland." Knoxville, University of Tennessee Press, 1988. 8vo, cl, dj, 368pp, ills.

1205 **COOMBS, Thomas Monroe**
"Confederate letters." In: RKHS, Jan. 1948, v.46 (#154), p. 397-403. Prisoner of war in Ohio & Columbus, Oh.

1206 **COOMBS, Thomas Monroe**
"Letters written by...to his wife while a prisoner of war in the Ohio State Penitentiary." Columbus, Ohio. In: RKHS, 1948, v.XLVI, p. 397-403.

1207 **COONS, Margaret**
"A Portrait of his Times. John Elder paintings reflect people & events during a critical period in Virginia History." (Richmond) Va. Cavl., Spring 1967., v.XVI, #4, p. 15-31, illus(2-color) ports. 2-color, 1-dbl. page. Largely CSA.

1208 **COOPER, Charles R.**
"Chronological & Alphabetical Record of the engagements of the great Civil War, with the casualties on both sides, & full & exhaustive statistics & tables of the Army & Navy, military prisons, national cemeteries, etc., compiled from the official records of the War Department & Confederate Archives, Washington, DC." Milwaukee, Wisc., Caxton Press, 1904. 8vo, cl, front (port), 211pp. Also: a 2nd Edition, 1904.

1209 **COOPER, Everett K.**
"Confederate Treasure Hunt." (London) Jour. Confed. Hist. Soc., Autumn, 1971, v.9, p. 59-65, pl.

1210 ..."Printing presses financed Southern war effort." In: CWTI, Aug., 1963, v.II, #5, p. 14-18, facsms, plate. CSA started war with $718,000 in the Treas.

1211 **COOPER, Jacob, Rev.**
"William Preston Johnston a Character Sketch. Prepared for the Class of 1852 in Yale University by..." n.p., n.d. (L.C., 1899?) 8vo, wraps, port, 32pp.

1212 **COOPER, James Litton**
"The Civil War Diary of James (Captain) Litton Cooper, Sept. 30, 1861 to Jan. 1865. Edt: Wm. T. Alderson." In: Tenn. HQ, June, 1956, v.XV, p. 141-173, notes. Service in the 20th Tenn. Inf. Reg., CSA.

1213 ..."Reminiscences of two gallant regiments." In: CV, 1909, v.XVII, p. 113. See: Gen. Thomas Burton Smith, W.J. McMurray.

1214 ..."Service with the twentieth Tennessee regiment." In: CV, Jan./June, 1925, v.XXXIII, p. 14-16, 57-58, 100-101, 138-140, 180-183, 222-224. Diary of Capt. Cooper, Edt: Deering J. Roberts.

1215 **COOPER, Norman Lee**
"A Confederate soldier & his descendants, with battle narratives by Stewart Sifakis." Bowie, Mo., N. Cooper Assoc's. 1982, 8vo, cl, 256pp. illus., bibliog., index.

1216 **COOPER, Norman V.**
"How they went to war: an Alabama brigade in 1861-1862." In: AR, Jan. 1971, v.24, #1, p. 17-50.

1217 **COOPER, Samuel, General**
"Confederate Losses during the War. Correspondence between Dr. Joseph Jones & General Samuel Cooper." In: SHSP, 1879, v.VII, p. 287-290.

1218 ..."Letter from Ex-President Davis on the character & services of Gen. Cooper." In: SHSP, 1887, v.III, p. 274-276.

1219 ..."Sketch of the Late General S. Cooper by Gen. Fitz. Lee." In: SHSP, 1887, v.III, p. 269-274.

1220 ..."L. Sig., 4to, 1p. Washington, 1835. $75-gdsp.

1221 ...Adj. & Insp-Gen. office: "General Orders no.3...to provide for the appointment of a General in chief of the Armies of the Confederate States." Broadside, 8vo, 1p. Richmond, Va., Feb. 6, 1865 (Crandall-1351) Appoints Gen. Lee commander-in-chief CSA. $125-jk.

1222 **COOPER, W. Raymond**
"Four Fateful Years, 1858-1861." In: W. Tenn. Hist. Soc. Papers, 1957, v.XI, #1, p. 36-75, notes.

1223 **COOPER, Walter G.**
"The Atlanta campaign." In: Americana, 1938, v.XXXII, p. 702-739. This is part of a four vol. work "Story of Ga." by the same author.

1224 ..."Official History Fulton Co., Ga." Confederate soldiers from: See: Fulton County.

1225 **COOPER, William J., Jr.**
"The South & the Politics of Slavery, 1828-1856." Baton Rouge: La. State Univ. Pr., 1978. 8vo, cl, dj, notes, appends. bibliog., index, xv, 401pp. $22.50. The demise of Whiggery.

1226 ..."A reassessment of Jefferson Davis as war leader: the case from Atlanta to Nashville." In: JSH, 1970, v.36, p. 189-204.

1227 ..."Liberty & Slavery: Southern politics to 1860." N.Y., Alfred A. Knopf, 1983. 8vo, cl, dj, vii, 309pp. Illus., maps, notes, index. $17.50 cloth, $7-paper.

1228 **COPELAND, Catherine**
"Bravest surrender; a Petersburg Patchwork." Richmond, Whittet & Shepperson, 1961. Imp. 8vo, cl, 132pp., illus., bibliog. much on war & origin: Memorial Day.

1229 **COPELAND, J.E.**
"The fighting at Brandy Station." In: CV, Dec. 1922, v.XXX, p. 451-452. Cavalry battle there on Juen 9, 1863.

1230 **COPELAND, James E.**
"Where were the Kentucky Unionist & Secessionists?" In: RKHS, Oct. 1973, v.71, #4, p. 344-363. Tables, maps.

1231 **COPLAND, Mary Ruffin**
"Confederate History of Charles City County Virginia." (West Point, Va., Tidewater Press, Oct. 1957) 8vo, wraps as title-page, color flag, 33pp. $20, $25.

1232 **COPLEY, John M.**
"A sketch of the Battle of Franklin, Tenn., with reminiscences of Camp Douglas." Austin, Texas: Eugene Von Boeckmann, 1893. 12mo, decr. cl, plates, 202pp. $30, $60, $65.

1233 **COPPERHEADS,**
(Copperheads) "The Chicago Copperhead Convention. The treasonable & revolutionary utterances of the men who composed it..." Washington, 1864. sewed, 8vo, p. 16. $15, $10. "Extracts from all the notable speeches delivered in & out of the National "Democratic Convention". title.
..."The Chicago Copperhead Convention, Aug. 19, 1864." (other articles on Lincoln in same pamphlet) "Magazine of History with Notes & Queries, Extra No. 58; reprinted by William Abbatt, Tarrytown, N.Y., 1917. From the Phila. 1864 edition, 16pp.

1234 ...Copperheads-(Mr. Funk) pseud. "Copperheads under the heel of an Illinois farmer." (N.Y., c.1864)? sewn, 8vo, 3pp. $5, $8. See: Analytical view..."

1235 ..."Copperhead Catechism for the instruction of such Politicians as are of tender years. Carefully Compiled by Divers Learned & Designing Men. Authorized & with Admonitions by (F. Wood) Fernando the Gothamite, High Priest of the Order of Copperheads." 12mo, Title, pp. ix-30. London: Sinclair Tousey, 1864. (old) $6., $25. "What is the chief aim of a Copperhead in this life?" "The Chief aim is to abuse the President, vilify the Administration & glorify himself before the people." Copyrighted by & probably written by Montgomery Wilson. (Sabin)

1236 ..."Copperhead Minstrel. A Choice Collection of Democratic Poems & Songs, for the use of Political Clubs & the Social Circles." New York: Feeck & Bancker, 1863. 12mo, wraps, 60pp. Ray H. Abrams, Chs. Ray Wilson, H.H. Wubben.

1237 ...Copperhead Broadside: "Copperheads in Council. Declaration of the leaders. Read & ponder what they say...Men of New Hampshire. Vote the ticket made up by such men?" (Concord, c.1863) 12"x18 3/4" $47.50.

1238 ..."Copperhead Conspiracy in the North West. An Expose' of the Treasonable Order of the "Sons of Liberty," Vallandigham, Supreme Commander." (New York: J.A. Gray & Green, 1864) 8vo, p. 8. border-$55, $20-bmk-84.

...Do: Another edition printed for the Cong. Comm. $200-bordered.

1239 ..."Accuses Knights of Golden Circle aiding in Forrest's attack on Paducah, Ky., on Morgan's Pond's Gap, & Mt. Sterling, Ky..."

1240 ..."Copperheads vigorously prosecuting Peace. Is it the Peace you want?" Broadside. New York: A.D.F. Randolph, 1863.

1241 ..."Notes of Copperheads in Congress of the United States." (Washington, D.C., 1864) 8vo, sewd, 8pp. (old) $. See: Robert H. Abzug, Isaiah W. Ayer.

1242 ..."Official Proceedings of the Democratic National Convention, held in 1864 at Chicago." Chicago, 1864. 8vo, sewn, 64pp. (old) $50. Imp. Inv. #807, where only copy located in Chicago Hist. Society.

1243 ..."Copperhead Platform" (caption), n.p., (c.1864) 8vo, 4pp. sewn (old) $4.50

1244 ..."The Venom & the Antidote, Copperhead declarations." Head: Loyal Reprints #2. Also: "Loyal Publications Society, Loyal Reprints-No.9." (New York, 1863) see Sabin-98891. 8vo, 4pp. folded sheet. $20.

1245 ...(Charles Godfrey Leland) "Ye book of Copperheads." 24 cartoons with satirical captions, followed by verse about Copperheads. Philadelphia, 1863. Leypoldt Pr., 30pp, wraps, $20, $35-bmk, $20, fine-$425-jk.

1246 ..."Ye Sneak Ycleped Copperhead". A Satirical Poem, Woodcuts. 16mo, wraps, Philadelphia, 1863. (old) $15. Mentions Lincoln by name & as president. Atgs: Jno. A. McAllister & Benson J. Lossing.

1247 ..."Copperheads & Unionist: An Ex-Vermonter tells his father why he opposes the Civil War." In: Vermont Hist., 1973, v.XLI, p. 1-6. See: A.J. Beitzinger.

1248 **COPPLESTONE, Bennett**
"Old Beeswax." In: Blackwood's, March 1926, v.CCXIX, p. 330-344. Story of CSNavy ship "Alabama", whose Capt. was called "Old Beeswax" by his men.

1249 **CORBIN, Diana Fontaine Maury**
"Life of Matthew Fontaine Maury, USN, CSN. Compiled by his daughter Diana Fontaine Maury Corbin." London: Sampson Low, Marston, Searle & Rivington, 1888. 8vo, cl, front, (port), (viii), 326pp. $22.50, $12, $75-g, Pres-$125-b.

1250 ..."Son of South. Life & services of Commodore Maury & proposed monument to his memory." In: SHSP, 1890, v.XVIII, p. 365-371.

1251 **CORBIN, Richard W.**
"Letters of a Confederate Officer to his family in Europe during the Last Year of the War of Secession." Paris(?) Neal's English Library. $250, $2000-or, $1000-g, $4500-ob. (only two known copies of the original)

...N.Y., W.Abbatt, 1913, contained in the Magazine of History, Extra #24, one of only 75 copies, 4to, wraps, 96pp. $27.50, $32.50.

...Ann Arbor, Mich. 1967, wrap, 94pp. $15-bmk.

1252 **CORBITT, David Leroy**
"Pictures of the Civil War Period in North Carolina." Raleigh, N.C., State Department of Archives & History, 1958. 8vo, wraps (color flags) ports, illus., facsms, fldg. map, 8, (37)pp-printed one sided. 1st Edt. $4.
...Reissued, 1961.
...Revised & enlarged, 2nd print, 1964, plate on cover, 87, (2)pp. $3.

1253 **CORCORAN, Patricia**
"Stars, Bars & Shamrocks: Battle of Sabine Pass." In: "Friar", 1963, v.XIX-iii, 10-11p. (1st Tex. Hvy. Artly.)

1254 **CORCORAN, W.W.**
"Manuscript of Confederate Constitution on Exhibition for Historians." (from Richmond News-Leader, Dec. 30, 1908). In: SHSP, 1908, v.36, p. 371-372. (Mrs. Mary DeRenne gave it to Confederate Memorial Literary Society.)

1255 **CORDER, Eric**
"Prelude to Civil War; Kansas-Missouri 1854-1861." N.Y., Crowell-Collier Press (1970) 12mo, cl, illus., map, ports, x, 168pp. (paper) $5.

1256 **CORINTH, Mississippi**
"Daily Corinthian. Special Civil War Centennial Issue." Corinth, Miss, Folio, 60pp. illus. $5.

1257 **CORLEW, Robert E.**
"Some aspects of Slavery in Dickson County(Tenn.)" In: Tenn.HQ, Sept. 1951, v.X, p. 224-248, 344-365.

1258 **CORLEY, Daniel B.**
"A visit to Uncle Tom's Cabin." Chicago: Laird & Lee, 1892. 12mo, cl, 78pp., front(port), illus. A cabin on the former estate of Robert McAlpin (supposed original of Simon Lagree) in Natchitoches parish.

1259 **CORLEY, Florence Fleming**
"Confederate City, Augusta, Ga., 1860-1865." Columbia: University of South Carolina Press, 1960. 4to, cl, dj, map, ports, illus., facsms., color flag front., pict. view endhseets, xiv, 130pp. $16-bmk, $35-bmk, $20-bmk, $12.50-y, $6, $10-nc.
...2nd printing.

1260 **CORN, James Franklin**
"Jim Witherspoon: A Soldier of the South, 1862-1865." cover title. (Cleveland, Tenn., 1962. 8vo, wraps, 5p, 36pp., illus., facsms., ports. In Morgan's Cavalry. $30, $12-bmk, $5.

1261 **CORNELL, Nancy J.**
"Campbell County, Ga., Confederate pension roll, 1890-1928." Riverdale: Private printed, (1980) (Not in LC-'81)

1262 **CORNISH, Joseph Jenkins, III**
"The Air Arm of the Confederacy. A History of Origins & Usages of War Balloons by the Southern Armies During the American Civil War." Richmond, Va., Richmond Civil War Centennial Comm., 1963 #11, 8vo, decr. stiff wraps, illus., ports, maps, facsms., 48pp. $35, $7-bmk, $5.

1263 **CORPORATE & FOREIGN BONDHOLDERS:**
"Defaulted debts of Southern States of USA. Extracts from annual report of C of F.B." (London: Williams, 1927) 8vo, wraps, 36pp.

1264 **"CORRESPONDENCE & Orders**
relating to military departments & commands, with Supplement, 1861-1865." Washington, DC: GPO, 1877. 8vo, cl, Note: See-"Letters Sent by CSA War Dept."

1265 **"CORRESPONDENCE BETWEEN the Mayor & Federal Authorities**
relative to the Occupation of New Orleans, together with the proceedings of the Common Council." New Orleans: Bulletin & Job Office, 1862. 8vo, wraps, cover title, 29pp. $5. $275-jk-122

1266 "CORRESPONDENCE Between Her Majesty's Government and Messrs. Laird Brothers respecting the Birkenhead Ironclads." London: (1864) 8vo, wraps, 60pp. Sabin-16853. Laird was an intimate of the CSA secret agent Bulloch.

1267 "CORRESPONDENCE Between the Commissioners of the State of South Carolina, to the Government at Washington & the President of the US together with the Statement of Messrs. Mills & Keitt. Print by order of the Convention." Charleston: Evans & Cogswell, 1861. 8vo, wraps, 26pp. $300-ob, $35.

1268 ..."Corresp. between the Comms. of South Carolina & the Pres. of the U.S. "Buchanan." Washington, 1861, hse. doc-#26, 36th Congr., 2nd, 8vo, sewn, 12pp. $15, $7.50. contains ordinance of S. Carolina secession.

1269 "CORRESPONDENCE Between the President & Gen. Joseph E. Johnston, together with that of the Secretary of War & the Adjutant & Inspector general, during the months of May, June & July, 1863. Pub. by order of Congress. Richmond: R.M. Smith Print, 1864. 8vo, wraps, 64pp. Crandall-605. $40.

1270 "CORRESPONDENCE Concerning Claims against Great Britain, transmitted to the Senate of the United States in answer to the resolutions of December 4 & 10, 1867 & of May 27, 1868..." Washington, Govt. Print, 1869-1871. 8vo, cl, fldg. table, 7 vols. (5 vols. in 1/2 Mor., $75) Much on Alabama Claims.

1271 "CORRESPONDENCE Relating to Fortification of Morris Island & operations of engineers." (Charleston, SC ? 1864) $500-r. 8vo, cover title, 44pp. Crandall-1334.

1272 "CORRESPONDENCE between the Secretary of War & Gov. Brown, growing out of a requisition made upon the governor for the reserve militia of Georgia to be turned over to Confederate control." Milledgeville, Boughton, Nisbet, Barnes & Moore, 1865. 8vo, wraps, 43pp. Crandall-1332.
...Do: 37pp. Crandall-1331.

1273 "CORRESPONDENCE with Mr. Adams respecting Confederate agents in England." London: Parliamentary Papers of North America, #8, 1863. Folio, 18pp. Ginz.-$50.

1274 CORRINGTON, John William
"And wait for the night." N.Y., Putnam's, 1964. 8vo, cl, 508pp. $10-carolina bk. Novel laid in Miss/La., in final days of war much around Shreveport.

1275 CORSAN, W.C.
"Two months in the Confederate States; including a visit to New Orleans under the domination of General Butler, by an English Merchant." London: Richard Bentley, 1863. 12mo, cl, 299pp. $97.50, $140-bmk, $175-jk-135, $200-g, $165-nc-76, $125-jenk, $18. Sympathetic to South. Came primarily to see about debt of South to England.

1276 CORSE, Montgomery Dent
"Second Manassas. Report of Colonel M.D. Corse, commanding Kemper's Brigade." In: SHSP, 1880, v.VIII, p. 538-541.

1277 CORTADO, James W.
"Florida's relations with Cuba during the Civil War." In: FHQ, July 1980, LIX, #1, p. 42-52. See: Clifford L. Egan.

1278 CORY, Chappell, Mrs. (Marielou Armstrong)
"Alabama legislature declares Nicola Marschall designer first Confederate flag, Stars & bars, supported by affidavits of

Marschall's contemporaries & others, including "The true story of the first Confederate flag", by Mrs. Chappell Cory." Publications Historical, patriotic series, #12. Alabama State Department of Archives & History. 8vo, wraps, illus., 71pp. Montgomery, Alabama, (1931) $4.50, $7.50.

1279 **COTTER, W.J.**
"My Autobiography by W.J. Cotter, who has lived nealy a quarter century beyond the alloted three score years & ten & has been a Methodist preacher in Georgia for 73 years. Edt: Charles C. Jones." Nashville, Tenn., Methodist Episcopal Church South, 1917. 8vo, cl, 190pp., front(port) Ministry in Georgia, among Cherokees, much on the Civil War.

1280 **COTTERILL, Robert S.**
"The Louisville & Nashville Railroad, 1861-1865." In: AmHist. Rev., 1923/1924, v.29, p. 700-715.

1281 **"COTTON Field Melodies."**
Augusta, Ga., Blackmar & Bro., 1863. 12mo, wraps, cover title, 36pp.

1282 **COTTON SOLD TO CONFEDERATE STATES**
"Letter from the Secretary of the Treasury transmitting, in accordance with a resolution of the Senate of April 22, 1912, report of sales of cotton to the Confederate States." Washington, Gov. Print. Off., 62nd Congr., 3rd Sess., Senate Doc. 987. 8vo, cl, 314pp. $16-bmk, $25, $6.75. Shows all persons who sold their cotton, price, weight, number of bales, etc.

1283 **"COTTON Sold to the Confederate States..."**
See: "Letter from the Secretary of the Treasury...

1284 **COTTON, J.A.**
"The Cotton Letters." In: Va. Mag. Hist., Jan. 1929, v.XXXVII, p. 12-22. Cotton family of Georgia, 1861-1865, served in Va. in 1861.

1285 **COTTON, John W.**
"The Civil War letters of John W. Cotton. Edt.: Lucille Griffith." In: AR, v.3, p. 207-231, 286-299.

1286 **COTTON, John Weaver**
"Yours Till Death: Civil War Letters of John W. Cotton. Edt: Lucille Griffith." (Tuscaloosa) Univ. of Alabama Pr., 1951. 8vo, cl, dj, port, ix, (3), 128pp. $7, $25-bmk, $35-bmk, $47.50. Private in CSA cavalry, Apr. 24, 1862, Feb. 1, 1865. Ala., Tenn., Ky., Ga., S.C.
...(Tuscaloosa) Ala. Rev., 1950, v.III, p. 207-230; 286-299. $16.

1287 **COTTRELL, Sue**
"Hoof Beats North & South: Heroes & Horsemen in the Civil War." Hicksville, N.Y., Exposition Pr., 1975. 8vo, wraps, illus., 87pp, (6)lfs. plates. $10.

1287a **COULLING, M. P.**
"The Lee Girls." Winston-Salem, N.C., 1987. 8vo, cl, dj, 242pp, ills, ports. $20. Letters & diaries of Gen. Lee's four daughters, 'life with father.'

1288 **COULTER, E. Merton**
"What the South has done about its history." In: JSH, 1936, v.2, #1, p. 3-28.

1289 **COULTER, Ellis Merton**
"Amnesty for all except Jefferson Davis: the Hill-Blaine debate on 1876." In: Ga. H.Q., Winter 1972, v.LVI, #4, p. 453-494, facsm.

1290 ..."Alexander H. Stephens Challenges Benjamin H. Hill to a Duel." In: Ga. H.Q., Summer, 1972, v.LVI, #2, p. 175-192.

1291 ..."William Montague Browne: Versatile Anglo-Irish American, 1833-1883." Athens: University of Georgia Press, 1967. 8vo, cl, d/w, viii, 328pp. atg-$20, $7.50, $10. Helped organize CSA, aide-de-camp to Jeff Davis, Asst. Secty-State, unreconstructed Rebel, never but a southern point of view.

1292 ..."The Civil War & Readjustment in Kentucky." Chapel Hill: Univ. of N.C. Press, 1926, 8vo, cl, dj, illus., maps, viii, 468pp. $37.50, $15, $20, $25, $27.50, $40-nc, $45-bmk-105, $65-bmk-105, Pres-$75-bmk-112, $55-jk-129, $20-b.
...Gloucester, Mass, 1966.

1293 ..."The Confederate Monument in Athens Georgia." Savannah, Ga., 1956. 8vo, wraps, 20pp. Reprint: Ga. Hist. Quart., v.40, p. 230-247. (Sept.) notes; Also printed without notes, Georgia Review (Spring), v.10, p. 56-68.

1294 ..."Commercial Intercourse with the Confederacy in the Mississippi Valley." (Cedar Rapids, Ia.) MVHR, March 1919, v.V, p. 377-395.

1295 ..."The Confederate States of America. 1861-1865." v.VII-The History of the South. (Baton Rouge) Louisiana State University Press/Littlefield Fund for Southern Hist., of the University of Texas, 1950. Tk.8vo, cl, dj, map(fld) illus., facsms, x, (4), 644pp. bibliog., index-p. 569-644. $25, $20, $15. 2nd print(1962); 4th print(1968) $10, $20-y, $17-nc.; 1976-$22.50, $27.50.

1296 ..."Coulter Bibliography." In: GaHQ, Fall, 1977, v.LXI, #3, p. 268-278.

1297 ..."The Effects of Secession upon the Commerce of the Mississippi Valley." (Cedar Rapids, Ia.) MVHR, Dec. 1916, v.III, p. 275-300.
...Issued, wraps, 23pp reprint, $7., $10-atg.

1298 ..."Father Sherman's March to the Sea." In: GaRev., Winter, 1956, v.X, p. 375-392. Also: Offprint, wraps, n.p., 1956, p.17, Atg. copy $8.

1299 ..."The Flags of the Confederacy." In: GaHQ, 1937, v.XXXVII, p. 188-199 color pl.
..."The Flags of the Confederacy." Savannah, Ga., 1953. 8vo, wraps, 12pp(1p.color), $8, $3, Reprint: Ga. Review, v.6, p. 39-49. color views.
...Also in: United Daughters of the Confederacy Magazine, May 1952, v.15, p.20-22, 35; June 1952, p. 15-22.

1300 ..."Lost Generation: The Life & Death of James Barrow(1841-64), C.S.A." Tuscaloosa, Ala., Confederate Pub., 1956, 12mo, stiff wraps, Confed. Cent. Studies-1, 118pp., notes, bibliog. p. 107-110. 45o copies. $20-bmk, $10-b, $5, $9.
...Editor: "Confed. Receipt Book." See under this title.

1301 ..."Memoranda of a Raid Through the Southern States in 1865." In: GaHQ, Sept-Dec., 1942, v.XXVI, p. 291-307.

1302 ..."The Movement for Agricultural Reorganization in the Cotton South during the Civil War." (Raleigh) NCHRev., January 1927, v.IV, #1, p. 22-36. $8.
...Reprint: "Agric. Hist." Jan., 1927, v.1, p. 3-17.

1303 ..."The Myth of Dade County's Seceding from Georgia in 1860." In: Ga.H.Q., December 1957, v.XLI, #4, p. 349-364. $8.

1304 ..."The Nullification Movement in Georgia." In: GaHQ, March 1921, v.V, p. 3-39.

1305 ..."A Name for the American War 1861-1865." Savannah, Ga., 1952. 8vo, wraps, 23pp. (See: Ed. S. Meany) $17.50, $8-bmk, $3. Reprint: Ga. Hist. Quart. (June) 36:109-131pp.; Ga. Rev. 5: 305-335, 1951; Reprinted from Georgia Review, notes added.

1306 ..."Planter's wants in the Days of the Confederacy." In: Ga. H.Q., March 1928, v.XII, #1, p. 38-52.
...Reprint, wraps, 15pp., atg-$10.

1307 ..."Robert Gould Shaw & the Burning of Darien, Georgia." In: CWH, Dec. 1959, v.V, #4, p. 363-373.

1308 ..."Sherman & the South." In: GaHQ, 1931, v.XV, p. 28-45. pres-$10-atg.; also in: NCHR, Jan. 1931, v.8, p. 42-54. $10.

1309 ..."The Speech of Henry R. Jackson at the Macon Fair, 1887: What the South Fought For, 1861-1865." In: Ga.H.Q., Dec. 1966, v.L, #4, p. 366-381.

1310 ..."Travels in the Confederate States, a Bibliography." Norman: Univ. of Oklahoma Press, 1948. 8vo, cl, dj, xiv, 289pp. index. $7.50, $15, $25, pres: $75; Reprint: 1961, p. 303. $50pbmk, $17.50, $25, Wendell, N.C., Broadfoots Bookmark, 1980, $25.

1311 ..."William D. Wash, CSA, Bravest of the Brave." In: Ga. H.Q., March, 1965, v.XLIX, #1, p. 44-56.

1312 **COUNTESS POURTALES**
See under title: "Checkered Life."

1313 **COUPER, William, Col.**
"Address delivered by Col. Wm. M. Couper." In: Rockbridge Hist. Soc., Proc., 1954, v.4, p. 34-36. On the burial of Latane, a painting by Wm. D. Washington, on Latane, a CSA cavalry Capt.

1314 ..."Battle of New Market, May 15, 1939- The 75th Anniversary of...", Virginia Military Institute Centennial year, 1839-1939." n.p. (Lexington, Va.) (1939). 8vo, wraps, illus., facsms, port, 28pp. $2.50.

1315 ..."Claudius Crozet, soldier-scholar-educator-engineer (1789-1864)." Charlottesville, Va., Historical Pub., 1936. (Southern Sketches, #8, 1st Ser.) 8vo, cl, d/w, 221pp. $8, $4, $10, $25-jk-22, $14-bmk, #35-bmk. Material on Stonewall Jackson. De: West Virginia History, Vol. 1(1940), p. 255-269. "Colonel Claudius Croz".

1316 ..."One Hundred Years at V.M.I." Foreword: Gen. George C. Marshall. Richmond: Garrett & Massie (1939). 8vo, cl, 1600pp., illus., 154 maps, photos drawings. I-360pp. Being the establishment of VMI (vo. 1) Civil War (vol.2) (complete-4 vols) $45-y, $80-bmk-94, $12, $100.

1317 ..."The V.M.I. New Market Cadets. Biographical Sketches of all Members of Virginia Military Institute Corps. of Cadets who fought in the Battle of New Market, May 15, 1864." $6, $8.50, $12, $50-b, $33, $24, $30, $40-bmk, $50-bmk-105. Charlottesville, Va: The Michie Co., 1933, 8vo, cl, front, fld. map, illus., port, 272pp.

1318 ..."Virginia Military Institute & the Battle of New Market May 15, 1864." n.p., n.d. (c.1939) 12mo, stiff wraps, illus. 24, (1)pp. $2.50, $10-bmk.
..."The Virginia Military Institute & the Battle of New Market." In: CV, n.s., v.37, #2, p.24-33, ills. ports, map.

1319 ..."War & Work with some account of the coming to Lexington of Generals Lee & Jackson." Address delivered before the Rockbridge County (Va.) Historical Society, Apr. 22, 1940. n.p., n.d., 8vo, wraps, 12pp.

1320 ..."War & work. An address before the Rockbridge County Historical Society, April 22, 1940. In: Proceedings of the RHS. v.1, p. 26-42. Re: R.E. Lee.

1321 **"COURIER, The**
EXTRA. Charleston, S.C., February 18, 1861 - 5 P.M. by Telegraph Southern Congress. Inaugural Speech of President Davis (caption-title) Broadsides: single column, (1) 15X5 1/2" (2)29 1/2x5 1/2". Charleston, S.C., 1861. Goodspeed-601 $1500. Unrecorded but for Gdsp. cat. 1942. Earliest known separate printing of his inaugural address delivered only four hours before.

1322 **"COURIER-EXTRA, The**
Charleston, S.C., Feb. 18, 1861-5 P.M., by Telegraph, Southern Congress, Inaugural Speech of President Davis." Broadsides: 15"x5" & 29 1/2"x5". (Goodspeeds, Feb. 1942, $15.)

1323 "COURIER of the Teche, The." St. Martinsville, (Parish of St. Martin), La. Dec. 17, 1864. Folio, 1-pg. printed on wall paper. $35. Not in Brigham.

1324 COURNOS, John
"Robert E. Lee, strong in defeat." In: His "A modern Plutarch", Indianapolis, 1928, p. 325-346.

1325 COURTENAY, William Ashmead
"Charles Colcock Jones. A typical citizen & soldier of the Old Regime." In: SHSP, 1898, v.XXVI, p. 32-39.

1326 ..."Fragments of War History, relating to Coast Defence of South Carolina, 1861-1865 & the hasty preparations from the Battle of Honey Hill, Nov. 30, 1864." In: SHSP, 1898, v.XXVI, p. 232-241.

1327 ..."Tribute to the Memory of Charles Colcock Jones, commander of the 3rd South Carolina Cavalry." n.p., n.d., (c.1900) 12mo, wraps, 13pp. $10.

1328 ..."A Permanent Confederate Benefaction for Capt. William A. Courtenay." Walhalla, S.C., Keowee Courier Press, 1903. Priv. print, 300 copies, circulation among the Washington Light Infantry & their friends. sq. 8vo, wraps, 16pp. $7.50.

1329 ..."Washington Light Infantry. Proceedings Upon the Resignation of Capt. Wm. A. Courtenay, June 22, 1874." Charleston, S.C., News & Courier, 1874. 8vo, wraps, 22. One ornamented leaf. In: SHSP, 1903, v.XXXI, p. 1-11.

1330 COURTNEY, Patrick C.
"The Seven Days Battles around Richmond: an address given before members of the Confederate Research Club, Jan. 30, 1960." (London, 1960?) Title head: "Civil War Round Table of London, England." 4to, wraps, 15pp. $15-bmk, $9.

1331 COURTNEY, W.J.
"Guerrilla warfare in Missouri." In: CV, Mar. 1921, v.XXIX, p. 104.

1332 COURTWRIGHT, David T.
"Opiate addiction as a consequence of the Civil War." In: CWH, June 1978, v.24, #2, p. 101-111.

1333 COUSINS, Paul M.
"Joel Chandler Harris, a Biography." Baton Rouge: Louisiana State University Press, (1968) 2nd Printing (1969) 8vo, cl, dj, illus., ports, xiv, (2), 237pp. $7.50.

1334 COVELL, Edward M.
"War sentiment in the Sixties. Letters to Dr. Andrew G. Grinnan." In: Tyler Q. H.M., April 1926, v.VII, #4, p. 248-250.

1335 COVINGTON, James W.
"The Camp Jackson Affair, 1861." In: MHR, April 1961, v.LV, #3, p. 197-212.

1336 COWAN, Thomas A., Lieut.
"Memorial sketch of Lieut. Thomas A. Cowan, 33rd Reg., N.C.T." In: OLOD, July 1875, v.3, #1, p. 36-38.

1337 COWARD, Asbury, Col.
"The South Carolinians, Col. Asbury Coward Memoirs. Edited & arranged by Natalie Jenkins Bond & Osman Latrobe Coward." N.Y., Vantage Press (1968) Sm. 8vo, cl, dj, facsms, ports, 188pp. $25-bmk, $15, $5.

1338 COWELL, John Welsford
"A Letter addressed to Capt. M.T. Maury, Confederate Navy, on his Letter to Admiral Fitzroy." London: Robert Hardwicke, 1862. 8vo, cl, 99pp. $10. "Setting forth the justice of her cause hitherto so entirely misapprehended in Eng."

..."Southern Secession. A Letter addressed to Capt. M.T. Maury, Confederate Navy, on his letter to Admiral Fitzroy." London: Robert Hardwicke, 1862. 8vo, wraps, 99pp. Sabin-17240. $75-ginz.

1339 ..."La France et les Etats Confederes. Par John Welsford Cowell agent et representatif de la Banque d'Angleterre aux Etats-Unis dans les annees 1837, 1838, et 1839."

Paris: Dentu, 1865. 8vo, wraps, 30pp. Sabin-17239.

1340 ..."France & the Confederate States." London & Paris: R. Hardwicke, 1865. 12mo, wraps,37pp.

1341 **COWEN, E.G.**
"The Battle of Johnsonville." In: CV, Apr. 1914, v.XXII, p. 174-175.

1342 **COWEN, Ruth Carolina**
"Reorganization of Federal Arkansas, 1862-1865." In: AHQ, 1959, v.XVIII, p. 32-57, notes.

1343 **"COWETA COUNTY, Georgia."**
Mary G. Jones, Lily Reynolds, Edts. "Coweta County Chronicles for One Hundred Years, etc." Atlanta, Ga., Stein Print, 1928. tk8vo, cl, 869pp. CSA p. 143-193, plate, ports (2).

1344 **COWLES, William Henry Harrison**
"Memorial Day. Subject: the life & services of Gen. James B. Gordon. An address by Wm. H.H. Cowles, delivered in Metropolitan Hall, Raleigh, N.C., May 10, 1887." Raleigh: Edwards, Broughton & Co., 1887. 8vo, wraps, 20pp. $50-b, $10, $40-bmk-106. Gordon Comm. N.C. Cav. Brig., composed of 1st, 2nd, 3rd, & 5th N.C. Regs. Cavalry.

1345 **COX, Abner R.**
"South from Appomattox, Diary of..., Edt: Royce Gordon Shingleton." In: SCHM, 1974, v.75, #4, p. 238-244.

1346 **COX, Albert L.**
"Brief...stating North Carolina's claim that the Stars & Bars was designed by Orren Randolph Smith." n.p., 1925. 4to wraps, 27 folios, mimeographed. Detailed argument by Mrs. J. Dolph Long, Pres. N.C. Div., UDC, at the General Convention, Hot Springs, Ark. 1925. $20-jk-122. See: Fannie R. Williams.

1347 **COX, Benjamin B.**
"Mobile in the war between the states." In: CV, May 1916, v.XXIV, p. 209-213.

1348 **COX, Cornelius C.**
"Reminiscences of C.C. Cox." In: QTSHA, Jan. 1903, v.VI, #3, p. 213-230, the Civil War period.

1349 **COX, Edwin P.**
"Alabma's Heroes-Pelham & Wheeler." Address on the occasion of the presentation of a portrait: "The Gallant Pelham", to R.E. Lee Camp, C.V." In: SHSP, 1898, v.XXVI, p. 292-295.

1350 **COX, F.H.**
"Lee, Virginia & the Union." In: Sewanee Rev., July 1901, v.9, p. 302-311.

1351 **COX, James M.**
"Shelby Foote's Civil War." In: South. Rev., April 1985, v.21, p. 329-350.

1352 **COX, James Melville**
"Whitman, Twain & the Civil War." In: Sewanee Review, Spring, 1961. p.(20) $80bmk. See: Alan M. Hollingsworth as co-author "Pickett".

1353 **COX, Millard F.**
"The Legionaries, by Henry Scott Clark (pseud), a story of the great raid." 4th Edt. Indianapolis, Ind., Bowen-Merrill Co., (1899) 12mo, cl, 2, 1, ix-xiii, 385p. front, pl, map.

1354 ..."The Legionaries; a story of Morgan's Raid, by Henry Scott Clark (pseud)." N.Y., Grossett & Dunlap, 1899, 5th Edt. 12mo, decr. cl, 385pp. $15.

1355 **COX, Stella**
"Jeanie the Civil War Bride." Jackson: Purser Bros, 1961. 8vo, wraps, 31pp. atg. $17.50.

1356 **COX, Virginia Lee**
"In prison & ye visited me." In: CV, June 1924, v.XXXII, p. 212-214. Dr. Chs. Minnegerode visits Davis when a prisoner at Fortress Monroe, Nov. 1866.

1357 **COX, William Freeman, Lieut-Col.**
"The Confederate Armies-commands from several Southern & border states." In: SHSO, 1896, v.24, p. 200-202.

1358 **COX, William Ruffin**
"Address on the life & services of Gen. James H. Lane...before the R.E. Lee Camp Confederate Veterans, #1, Dec. 4, 1908." (Richmond, 1908) 8vo, wraps, 23pp. $50-bmk-104, $75-bmk-104, $7.50.

1359 ..."Address on the life & character of Maj-Gen. Stephen D. Ramseur." May 10. Raleigh, N.C., 1891, E.M. Uzzell. 8vo, wraps, front(port) 54pp. $7.50, $10. Before the Ladies Memorial Association of Raleigh, N.C., May 10, 1891.
...(Abridged) In: W.J. Peele's "Lives of Distinguished North Carolinians...Raleigh, 1898, cl, 8vo, p. (456)-494.
...In: SHSP, 1890, v.18, p. 217-260.

1360 ..."Address by Gen. William Ruffin Cox." Richmond, Va., 1911, 8vo, pict. wraps, 16pp. $50-bmk, $20. Southern cause, noble & just.

1361 ..."A sketch of the life & service of Gen. William Ruffin Cox. Including address of Hon. Frank S. Spruill." Richmond, 1921, 8vo, wraps, 41pp. $7.50, $10, $35-bmk-104, $60.

1362 ..."Address on the life & service of Gen. Marcus J. Wright, Feb. 26, 1915." (Richmond, Va., 1915) 8vo, wraps, port, 15, 2pp. $3.25, $17.50, $75-bmk-105.

1363 ...Gen. William Ruffin Cox, 1832-1919." In: CV, Feb. 1920, v.XXVIII, p. 45-46. See: Gary W. Gallagher Biography: WRC.

1364 **COXE, Elizabeth Allen**
"Memoirs of a South Carolina Plantation During the war. By..., daughter of Charles Sinkler of Belvedere." Philadelphia, 1912. Priv. print for my Family & Friends. sq.8vo, front, 96pp. Turnbull, V,p. 97, 3/4lt. $80-bmk-44, $50-bmk.

1365 **COXE, John**
"Battle of First Manassas." In: CV, Jan. 1915, v.XXIII, p. 24-28.

1366 ..."The Battle of Gettysburg." In: CV, Sept., 1913, v.XXI, p. 433-436.
..."In the Battle of Chancellorsville." In: CV, April 1922, v.XXX, p. 138-140.

1367 ..."Last struggles & successes of Lee." In: CV, Aug. 1914, v.XXII, p. 356-359.
..."Recollections of Gen. S(tephen) D. Lee." In: CV, March 1924, v.XXXII, p. 95-96.

1368 ..."Seven days battle around Richmond." In: CV, March 1922, v.XXX, p. 91-92, 117.

1369 ..."The Siege of Knoxville," In: CV, Sept. 1922, v.XXX, p. 340-343.

1370 ..."Chickamauga." In: CV, August, 1922, v.XXX, p. 291-294.

1371 ..."With Hampton Legion in the Peninsula Campaign." In: CV, Nov. 1921, v.XXIX, p. 414-416.

1372 **COZART, A.W.**
"Memorial address delivered Apr. 26, 1927, of the Columbus, Ga. Bar at Opelika, Ala." n.p., cover title, colored flags on cover, 8vo, 11pp., limp cl., cover title (Confederate Generals." the 2nd edt. cloth, 1st edt. wraps.

1373 **CRABB, Alfred Leland**
"Home to Tennessee, a Tale of Soldiers Returning." Indianapolis: Bobbs-Merrill, 1952. 8vo, cl, dj, 299pp. $20-bmk. Fictional acct. Jno. B. Hood's invasion of 1864. Battle of Franklin & Nashville & Tod Carter.

1374 **CRABTREE, Beth G., Compiler**
"Guide to Civil War Records in the North Carolina State Archives." Raleigh: State Dept. Archives & History, 1966, 8vo, wraps, x, 128pp. $2.

1375 **"CRAIG'S SHARE**
in the War Between the States, 1861-1865. Craig Chapter #121, United Daughters of the Confederacy." Roanoke, Va., n.d. 8vo, wraps (pict.) illus., 26pp. $25. With rosters.

1376 **CRAIG, Berry F.**
"Northern conquerors & Southern deliverers: the civil war comes to the Jack-

son Purchase." In: RKHS, Jan. 1975, v.73, #1, p. 17-30.

1377 ..."Kentucky's Rebel Press: the Jackson Purchase Newspapers in 1861." In: RKHS, Jan. 1977, v.75, #1, p. 20-27.

1378 ..."Henry Cornelius Burnett; champion of Southern rights." In: RKHS, Autumn, 1979, v.77, #4, p. 266-274.

1379 **CRAIG, J.M.**
"The diary of Surgeon Craig, fourth Louisiana Regiment, CSA, 1864-1865." In: LaHQ, Jan. 1925, v.VIII, p. 53-70. Edt: John S. Kendall." Experiences during closing months of war. with roster of Delta rifles.

1380 **CRAIG, James**
"James Craig's Tennessee Volunteers at Claiborne (Alabama)." In: AHQ, 1957, v.19, #2, p. 220-219.

1381 **CRAIG, Locke**
"Legacy of the Confederacy; a speech accepting the monument to women of the Confederacy, on occasion of it's unveiling at Raleigh, June 10, 1914." Raleigh, N.C., Edwards Print, 1914. 8vo, wraps, cover title, 8pp.

1382 **CRAIG, William J.**
"The War Journal of Private William J. Craig, Company A., Waller's Texas Cavalry Battalion." In: Chas. Spurlin "West of the Mississippi, with Waller's 13th Texas Cavalry Batt., CSA."

1383 **CRAIGHILL, Edley**
"Lynchburg, Va. in the War Between the States." In: Iron Worker, 1960, v.24, p.5-13.

1384 **CRAIK, Elmer LeRoy**
"Southern Interest in Territorial Kansas 1854-1858." Thesis, Unvi. of Kan., 1923. (Topeka, Kan., 1923) $4. 8vo, wraps, cover title, illus(ports) 334)-450pp. Reprint: Kan. Hist. Soc. Coll., XV, p. 334-450.

1385 **CRANDALL, Marjorie Lyle**
"Confederate Imprints; a check list based principally on the collection of the Boston Athenaeum. With an Introduction by Walter Muir Whitehill." Boston, Mass., Boston Athenaeum, 1955. 8vo, cl, facsms, xxxv, 408, (409)-910pp. $15, $20, $35, $75-y, 4-vol. $175-bmk, $200, $85-jk. See: addenda, Richard B. Harwell.
...Richmond, Va., Va. State Library, 1957. 8vo, 4vols. $400, $250.
...Woodbridge, Conn., Research Publications, 1879. Microfilm collection, complete $4275.

1386 **CRANE, William Carey**
"Memorial of Robert E. Lee, an address delivered at the fair grounds, Brenham, Texas, Oct. 30, 1870. Published by the Washington Co. Committee." Baltimore: John F. Weishampelm, Jr. (1870). 12mo, wraps, 14pp.

1387 **CRANWELL, John Philips**
"Spoilers of the Sea: Wartime Raiders in the Age of Steam." N.Y., W.W. Norton & Co., 1941. 8vo, cl, dj, illus., fldg. charts, 308pp. $3. Confederate raiders "Sumter", "Florida", "Alabama", "Tallahassee", and "Shenandoah", each is devoted one chapter.

1388 **CRARY, John Williamson, Sr.**
"Reminiscences of the Old South: From 1834-1866. With biographical sketch of John Williamson Crary, Sr., by May Crary Weller." Pensacola, Fla., Perdido Press, 1985. 8vo, cl, xi, 163pp.

1389 **"CRATER LEGION, The**
In loving remembrance of comrads of Mahone's Brigade Anderson's Division, A.P. Hill's Corps, ANV. who lost their lives in the battle of the Crater, July 30, 1864." Broadside.

1390 ..."The Crater". Who was its hero. The truth of history vindicated by competent authorities." (Richmond, 1880) Large folio broadside. Statement by members of Mahone's Old Brigade to settle forever the question by eye-witnesses' accounts. (entry from old Heartman's Cat. 297. See: H.A. Chambers.

1391 **CRATER, Battle of the**
See: Geo. S. Bernard, Jas. C. Coit, Wm. H. Etheredge, Jno. C. Featherstone, Henry G. Flanner, Fitz. Wm. McMaster, Richmond News-Leader & Dispatch, Wm. H. Stewart.

1392 **CRAVEN, Avery**
"Lee's dilemma." In: VMHB, April 1961, v.69, #2, p. 131-148.

1393 **CRAVEN, Avery O. & Frank E. Vandiver**
"The American Tragedy: The Civil War in Retrospect." Craven's "Background Forces in Civil War" & Vandiver's "Jefferson Davis & Confederate Strategy!" Hampden-Sidney College: April 1959(Va.) 8vo, wraps, 32pp. $10, $4.

1394 ..."Civil War in the Making, 1815-1860." Baton Rouge: Louisiana State University Press, (1959) 2nd Edt: 1961. 12mo, cl, dj, xiv, (1), 115pp. (The Walter Lynwood Fleming Lectures in Southern History.) 1st $6-nc, $12-atg., $3, 1968-$10, $20.

1395 ..."The Coming of the Civil War." N.Y., C. Scribner's Sons, 1942. 8vo, ix, 2491pp. notes (443)-480. $15, $20.
...N.Y., Scribner's, 1950, $5.
...University of Chicago Pr. (1957), 2nd revised Edt. (only a slight change) 8vo, cl, xi, (1), 491pp. $7.50. Also: a "Civil War Book Club Edt."
...University of Chicago Press, 1960. atg-$16, $20, 3rd Edt., 8vo, cl, x, 491pp. $7.50.
..."Chicago: Univ. of Chicago Pr. (1966) (Phoenix Books) 5th edt. revised $1.

1396 ..."The coming of the war between the states: an interpretation." In: JSH, 1936, v.II, p. 303-32. Study of sectional differences in the US during period from 1829 to 1860.
..."The Coming of the War Between the States: an Interpretation." In: JSH, Aug. 1936. 20pp. $8.

1397 ..."An Historian & The Civil War." Chicago: University Press, 1964, 8vo, cl, d/w, 233pp. $5.95, $6.95.

1398 ..."The Repressible Conflict, 1830-1861." Baton Rouge: La. State Univ. Press, 1939. 8vo, cl, xi, 97pp. $12-bmk. The Walter Lynwood Fleming lectures in Southern History. Deals with causes particularly slave background of C.W.

1399 ..."Edmund Ruffin Southerner. A Study in Secession." N.Y., D. Appleton & Co., 1932. 8vo, cl, ports (incl. front), illus., facsm. (2), 284pp. $10, $20, $35-b.
...Hamden, Conn., Archon Books, 1964. reprint of 1932. $9.
...Baton Rouge: Louisiana Univ., (1966) paperback edition.

1400 ..."Southern Attitudes toward Abraham Lincoln." In: Papers in Ill. Hist., 1942, Springfield, 1944, p. (1)-18.

1401 ..."Slavery & the civil war." In: South. Rev. 1938, v.IV, p. 243-255. (struggle between So. & North, industrial/agric. hidden under emotional appeal against slavery.

1402 ..."The "Turner Theories" & the South." (Baton Rouge, La.) JSH, Aug. 1939, v.V, #3, p. 291-314.

1403 **CRAVEN, John J., Bvt. Lieut-Col.**
"Prison Life of Jefferson Davis. Embracing Details & Incidents in his Captivity, Particulars concerning his Health & Habits, together with many conversations on topics of great public interest, by...Late Surgeon of U.S. Vols. and physician of the prisoner during his confinement in Fortress Monroe, May 25, 1865, up to Dec. 25, 1865." See: David Rankin Barbee, "Espose'". N.Y., Carleton, 1866, '73ave-$13, $22-nc, $40, $50-g, $30-chic. 12mo, cl, frontis, p. 377, 8pp. ads, $5, $7.50. De: Few copies printed on large paper(Sabin); Do: Edition of 1867; Do: London, 1866, cl,

310pp. rare, $35, $27.50; Do: N.Y., G.W. Dillingham (1905) 319pp. $10, $5, $12.50-y, $20, $30-bmk.

1404 ..."La Vie de Prison de Jefferson Davis Ex-President des Etats Confederes au Ft. Monroe. Scenes tirees du journal redige par le de Craven chirurgien de la garnison. Trans. de Anglais--Wallace S. Jones par l'Ecole Militaire de Saint Cyr." Paris, 1866, wraps. $7.50.
...Biloxi, Miss., Souvenir Shop, Jefferson Davis Shrine, 1960. 12mo, cl, facsm., 377pp. $4.50, $12.50.

1405 CRAVEN, William H.
"History of the Rebel muster roll captured at Pine Bluff, Arkansas." In: Ann. Iowa, 3rd. ser. Jan, 1929, v.XVI, p. 542-544. Roll captured by Mo. Vol. Cav., Aug. 17, 1864.

1406 CRAVENS, John Nathan
"James Harper Starr(1809-1890), financier of the Republic of Texas." Austin, Tex: Daughters of Republic of Texas, 8vo, cl, facsms, map, ports, views, 1950, notes, (Bibliog 187-194) xiv, 194pp. $35-jk. Sect. Treas. Rep. of Texas & officer of the CSArmy in Texas.

1407 CRAWFORD, Charles W.
"A Note on Forrest's Race for Rome." In: Ga.H.Q., Sept. 1965, v.L, #3, p. 288-290.

1408 CRAWFORD, J. Marshall
"Mosby & his men..." Gaithersburg, Md., Butternut Press, 1987. 8vo, cl, dj, 375pp., reprint of 1867 edt. $30.

1409 CRAWFORD, J. Marshall, Company B
"Mosby & his men: a record of the adventures of the renowned partisan ranger, John S. Mosby (Colonel CSA) including the exploits of Smith, Chapmen, Richards, Montjoy, Turner, Russell, Glasscck, & the men under them." Dedicated to: Soldiers of 43rd. Batt. Va. Cavl., 12mo, cl, ports (incl. front) 375pp. (8p. ads), $35, $20, $25, $45-e:nsb, $150-bmk-105, 1867, $100-jk-135. N.Y., G.W. Carleton & Co., London: S. Low & Co.

1410 CRAWFORD, J.H.
"John Yates Beall, Gallant Soldier." In: SHSP, 1905, v.XXXIII, p. 71-78.

1411 CRAWFORD, Martin
"William Howard Russell, & the Confederacy." In: Jour. Amer. Studies, Aug. 1981, v.XV, p. 191-210.

1412 CRAWFORD, W.T.
"The Mystery of Spring Hill." In: CWH, June 1955, v.1, #2, p. 101-126, maps., "Jno. B. Hood's Campaign in Ala. & Tenn."

1413 CRAWFORD, William Ayers, Col., CSA
"A Saline Guard: The Civil War Letters of Col. William Ayers Crawford, CSA, 1861-1865." Edited: Charles G. Williams. (Fayetteville, Ark.) Ark. Hist. Quart., v.XXXI, 1972-1973, #4, v.XXXII-#1, p. 328-355; 70-93, port.

1414 CREAGER, J.A.
"Ross's Brigade of Cavalry." In: CV, Aug. 1920, v.XXVIII, p. 290-292. See: Victor Rose.

1415 CREASON, Joe
"Incredible is the word for John Hunt Morgan's Raid." In: Courier-Journal Mag. June 30, 1963. p. 10-20. Account of the raid June 1863, in Ohio & Indiana.

1416 CREEL, Virginia
"Missouri, Dixie's affinity." In: CV, Feb. 1923, v.XXXI, p. 53-54. Hist. acct. Missouri's Southern affiliations.

1417 CREIGH, Thomas
"A brief sketch of the Life & Character of the late David S. Creigh, Esq., with an authentic account of the circumstances of his cruel & lamented death." Lewisburg: Weekly Times Print, 1865. 8vo, wraps, cover title, 20pp. Execution for Creigh's murder of a Union soldier at Creigh's home, 11-8-63.

1418 **CREIGHTON, Wilbur F., Jr.**
"Wilbur Fisk Foster, soldier & engineer." In: THQ, 1972, #3, v.31, p. 261-275.

1419 **CREIGHTON, Wilbur Foster**
"The Life of Wilbur Fisk Foster(Major), a civil engineer, Confederate Soldier, builder, churchman & Free Mason; with personal recollections." (Nashville, Tenn., Ambrose Print, 1961) 12mo, wraps, ports, maps, 58pp. atg-$50-bmk. With Rock City Guards, served under Johnston & Bragg, A.P. Stewart. Did fine battlefield maps.

1420 **CRENSHAW'S Battery**
See: John C. Goolsby, Charles P. Young, "Roster of..."

1421 **CRENSHAW, Edward**
"Diary of Capt. Edward Crenshaw, of the Confederate States Army." In: AHQ, Fall, 1939, v.1, p. 261-270, 438-462, 1940, v.II, p. 52-71, 221-238, 365-385, 465-382. With 17th Ala.

1422 **CRENSHAW, Ollinger**
"General Lee's College: The Rise & Growth of Washington & Lee University." New York: Random House, (1969). 8vo, cl, d/w, p.xvi, 366pp., illus., ports, $10.

1423 ..."Knights of the Golden Circle; Career of George Bickley." In: Amer. Hist. Rev., Oct. 1941, v.XLVII, p. 23-50.

1424 ..."Christopher G. Memminger's Mission to Virginia, 1860." (Baton Rouge, La.) JSH, August 1942. v.VIII, #3, p. 334-349. $8.

1425 ..."The Psychological Background of the Election of 1860 in the South." (Raleigh) NCHRev., July 1942, v.XIX, #3, p. 260-279.

1426 ..."Governor Conway's Analysis & proposed solution of the Sectional controversy 1860." In: AHQ, 1943, v.II, p. 12-19.

1427 ..."The Slave states in the presidential election of 1860." Baltimore: Johns Hopkins Press, 1945, Tall 8vo, cl, 332pp. $15-bmk, $25-bmk, $8-y, $6.50. Reprint from Johns Hopkins studies in history & political science, ser. LXIII, a thesis PHd in 1945. #3. Glouchester, Mass., P. Smith, 1969

1428 **CREOLE of Louisiana, A.**
See: Eugene Musson.

1429 **CRESAP, Bernard**
"The career of General Edward O(tho) C(resap) Ord (1839-1864)." Nashville (Tenn.) Joint Libraries) 1951, 4to, 29pp. notes, Vanderbilt University.

1430 ..."The Confederate Veteran." In: Ala. R., 1959, v.XII, p. 243-257.
..."Frank L. Owsley & King Cotton Diplomacy." In: AR, Oct. 1973, v.26, #4, p. 235-251.

1431 **CREWDSON, Robert L.**
"Burning Columbia." In: CWTI, Oct. 1981. v.20, #6, p. 9-19, illus., map, ports.
..."Bishop (Leonides) Polk & the crisis in the church: Separation or unity?" In: Hist. Mag. Prost. Episc. Ch., March 1983, p. 43-51.

1432 **CRIGLER, T.W., Jr.**
"Autographs, 1861-1862." (Jackson, Miss.) Jour. Miss. Hist., Feb. 1971, v.XXXIII, #1, p. 51-57. CSA officers (90) confined at Fort Warren, Boston Harbor, & several civilians from Maryland. Autographs & comments.

1433 **CRIM, Matt**
"Adventures of a Fair Rebel." N.Y., Chas. L. Webster Co., 1891. 12mo, 3/4 Mor., 323pp., gilt. $10. Authoress from La., lived in Ga. contributed to magazines, etc.

1434 **CRIMMINS, M.L., Colonel**
"Fort Fillmore." (Albuquerque) NMHR, Oct., 1931, v.VI, #4, p. 327-333.

1435 ..."Colonel Charles Anderson Opposed Secession in San Antonio (Tex.)" In: WTHAYB, v.XXIX, p. 67-78, Oct., '53.

1436 ..."The Battle of Val Verde." In: MNHR, 1932, v.VII, p. 348-352.

1437   **"CRISIS of the American Civil War. The"**
In: Blackwoods, Nov. 1862, v.XCII, p. 636-646.

1438   **"CRISIS of the American War. The,"**
In: Black, Edn. Mag., Nov. 1862, v.XCII, p. 636-646. "A war of extermination, letting loose savage 4000 negroes, to make the South a desert."

1439   **"CRISIS, The"**
Editor: Samuel Medary Columbus, Ohio, 1861-1863, Vol. 1, #1, Jan. 31, 1861 to Vol. II, #52, Jan. 21, 1863. Issued weekly, 8pp. an issue. 2 vols. $85. Six states of South had seeceded, Lincoln was elected without any southern elect. vote. Medary espoused case of South, later to become voice of the Copperheads. v.1 & v.3, 1861-1863, $500-bmk-89, (52 issues each)

1440   **CRISLER, E.T.**
"Battle of Helena. (Arkansas)" Helena, Ark., Centennial Association, 1963. 8vo, wraps, illus., 23pp.

1441   **CRISLER, Robert M.**
"Missouri's 'Little Dixie'." (Columbia, Mo., Mo. Hist. Review, Jan. 1948, v.XLII-#2, p. 130-139. Audrain, Boone, Callaway, Chariton, Howard, Ralls, Randolph, Monroe & Shelby counties.

1442   **CRISP, W.H., Mr./Mrs.**
"Last night of the season, by desire of many patrons (the Crisps) will take their farewell of their Mobile patrons & friends. Burlesque, Fun & Frolic." Broadside: 17 1/2x40cm, Unlisted. G. Hendershott $1000.

1443   **CRIST, Lynda Lasswell**
"A bibliographical note: Jefferson Davis personal library: all lost, some found." In: JMH, August 1983, v.XLV, #3, p. 186-193.

1444   **CRIST, Robert Grant**
"Confederate invasion of the West Shore, of the Susquehanna, in 1863. A paper presented before the Cumberland County Historical Society & Hamilton Library Ass'n., on Mar. 23, 1962." Lemoyne, Pa., Lemoyne Trust Co., 1963. 8vo, wraps, illus., plans, 44pp. $3.

1445   ..."Highwater 1863: The Confederate Approach to Harrisburg." In: Penn. Hist., 1963, v.XXX, p. 158-183.

1446   **CRISWELL, Grover C. & Clarence L.**
"Criswell's Currency Series, Vol. 1, Confederate & Southern State Currency. A Descriptive Listing, Including Rarity. The Confederate States of America & All of the Southern States including the Territory of Florida & Republic & Government of Texas." Pass-A-Grille Beach, Florida, 1957. Sm 4to, fabricoid, d/w, (10), 277pp. facsms., $15, $25, $35.

1447   ..."Price List & Supp'l. to Vol. 1 of Criswell's Currency Series, 1957, Current Market Values on Notes Listed by Criswell Numbers." Pass-A-Grill, Fla., Jan. 1957. Wraps, 16pp. 1958-1959 (facsms) 24pp; 1960 (facsms), 23pp. $30-bmk-84, $60, $25.
..."Criswell's Currency Series Vol. 1. First Revised edition. Confederate & Southern States Currency a descriptive listing, including rarity & prices. "The Confederate States of America" & all other Southern States, including "The Territory of Florida", "Republic & Government of Texas". St. Petersburg Beach, Fla., Grover C. Criswell, Jr., 1964. $12.50, $8.95, $30. Tall 8vo, cl in color, (8), 291pp. facsms.
...1976, iv, 294, $15-y, $20-m.

1448   ..."Criswell's Currency Series, Vol. II. Confederate & Southern States Bonds, a descriptive listing, including rarity, "The Confederate States of America" & all the Southern States of America" & all the Southern States including "The Territory of Florida" & "The Republic & Government of Texas". St. Petersburg Beach, Fla., The authors, 1961, N.Y., 1964-$10. Tall

8vo, pict., fabricoid, illus., facsms, some color, (12), 310pp. (1979, p. 374) $25, $16, $10. 1979, Ft. McCoy, Fla., 2nd edt. 374pp. $25.

1449 ..."Price List & Supplement to Vol. II, Criswell's Currency Series-Current market values of bonds listed by Criswell numbers." St. Petersburg Beach, Fla. Grover C. Criswell. Large 8vo, wraps, (7)pp-facsms.

1450 ..."Official Guide to Confederate Money & Civil War Tokens (Tradesmen & Patriotic)" N.Y., Official Publication of HC Publishers (1971). 16mo, colored stiff covers, facsms, illus., (4), 144, (6-advs)pp. $10-bmk, $1. On cover: First edition. Listing & pricing Confederate Money & Civil War Tokens. Fully illustrated.

1451 **CRISWELL, Robert**
"Uncle Tom's Cabin" contrasted with Buckingham Hall, the Planter's Home, or, A Fair View of both sides of the Slavery Question. By Robert Criswell, Esq..." N.Y., D. Fanshaw, 1852. 12mo, illus., cl, 152pp. (old) $6.50.

1452 **CRITCHER, John, Lieut-Col.**
"Dahlgren's Ride into Fredericksburg." In: SHSP, 1877, v.III, p. 87-89.

1453 **CRITTENDEN, Henry Huston**
"The Battle of Westport & National Memorial Park." Kansas City, Mo., Lowell Press, 1938. 8vo, cl, pls, ports, xiii, 202pp. $12.50.

1454 ..."The Crittenden Memoirs." N.Y., G.P. Putnam's Sons, 1936. 8vo, cl, ports (incl. front), pls, facsm., fldg. genealog. tble, crest, xv, 542pp. Bushwhackers, war in Mo. Kan. $35. See: Paul B. Jenkins' Battle of Westport.

1455 **CROCKER, Helen Bartter**
"The war divides Green River County." In: RKHS, Oct. 1972, v.70, #4, p. 295-311.

1456 **CROCKER, James Francis**
"Gettysburg-Pickett's Charge. An address before Stonewall Camp, C.V. Portsmouth, Virginia, Nov. 7, 1894." Suffolk, Va., Robt. Hardy Pub., 1986. 8vo, wraps, 32pp. port.

1457 ..."My personal experiences in taking up arms & in the Battle of Malvern Hill. An address before Stonewall Camp Confederate Veterans, Portsmouth, Va., Feb. 6, 1889." Suffolk, Va., Robt. Hardy Pub., 1986, 8vo, wraps, 16pp., illus., port.

1458 ..."My capture at Gettysburg & prison reminiscences. An address before Stonewall Camp, Confederate Veterans, Portsmouth, Va., Feb. 2, 1904. Suffolk, Va., Robt. Hardy Pub., 1986, 8vo, wraps, 40pp., illus., port.

1459 ..."Colonel James Gregory Hodges, Confederate hero of the 14th Virginia Infantry. An address before Stonewall Camp, Confederate Veterans, Portsmouth, Virginia Infantry, June 18, 1909." Suffolk, Va., Robt. Hardy Pub. 1986. 8vo, wraps, 24pp., illus., port.

1460 **CROCKER, James Francis, Judge**
"Prison Reminiscences. Read before Stonewall Camp, Confederate Veterans, Portsmouth, Va., Feb. 2, 1904." Portsmouth, Va., W.A. Fiske, 1906. 8vo, wraps, 33pp. With Pickett at Gettysburg. $75.
...SHSP, v.34, p. 28-51. "Prison reminiscences." In: CV, 1906, v.14, p. 503-508, port.

1461 ..."My personal experiences in taking up arms & in the Battle of Malvern Hill. Address before Stonewall Camp, Confederate Veterans, Portsmouth, Va., Feb. 6, 1889." Portsmouth, Va., W.A. Fiske, 1905, 8vo, wraps, 12pp. $7.50, $12.50, pres: $50-bmk-106.
...SHSP, v.33, p. 111-118, v.37, p. 257-263.

1462 ..."War Addresses. Gettysburg-Pickett's Charge. Address before Stonewall Camp, Confederate Veterans, Portsmouth, Va., Nov. 7, 1894." Portsmouth, Va., W.A. Fiske, 1905. 8vo, wraps, 33pp.
...2nd Edt., 1905, wraps, 25pp. $75, $7.50.

...SHSP, v.33, p. 118-134.

...3rd Edt., 1915, wraps, 132pp., port(front), illus., $125-bmk-111, $150-atg., $30, $175-r.

1463 ..."Colonel James Gregory Hodges, his life & character. Address before Stonewall Camp, Confederate Veterans, Portsmouth, Va., June 18, 1909. Portsmouth, Va., W.A. Fiske, 1909, 8vo, wraps, 22pp. front (port) $15. Col. Hodges, 14th Va. Reg., was killed in Pickett's Charge. Also: SHSP, v.XXXVII, p. 184-197.

1464 ..."Gettysburg-Pickett's Charge & other War Addresses." Portsmouth, Va., W.A. Fiske Print, 1915. 8vo, cl, illus., port, 132pp. "Taking up arms", Malvern Hill, Gettysburg: Pickett's Charge, Prison reminiscences, Our CSA dead, Jas. Gregory Hodges (also in SHSP). $175-0b.

1465 **CROCKETT, Cary Ingram**
"The Battery that saved the day." In: Field Artillery, 1940, v.XXX, p. 26-33, plan, 2-ports. Imboden's stepson recounts part played by the marine brigade under Imboden. See: other accounts under "Imboden, Jno. D."

1466 **CROFTS, Daniel W.**
"A Reluctant Unionist: John A. Gilmer & Lincoln's Cabinet." In: CWH, Sept., 1978, v.23, #3, p. 225-249.

1467 **CROMWELL, Giles**
"The Virginia manufactory of arms." Va., 1975, 8vo, cl, dj, 208pp., index. $25.

1468 **CROOK, Carland Elaine**
"Benjamin Theron & French Designs in Texas during the Civil War." In: SwHQ, April, 1965, v.LXVIII, #4, p. 432-454.

1469 **CROOK, D.P.**
"The North, the South, & the Powers, 1861-1865." N.Y., Lond: John Wiley & Sons (1974). 8vo, cl, dj, x, 405pp. $6.50. Index, readings, p. 381-405.

1470 ..."Portents of War: English Opinion on Secession." In: Jour. Amer. Studies, 1971, v.IV, p. 163-179.

1471 **CROOK, George**
"Capture of Generals Crook & Kelley of the Federal Army, one of the coolest deeds on record." In: SHSP, 1891, v.XIX, p. 186-188.

1472 **CROOK, Wiley M.**
"Autobiography & Reminiscences." Star City, Ark., (1917) 8vo, wraps, 70pp. (life, manners CSA soldier, Tenn.

1473 **CROOM, Wendell D.**
"The War History of Co. "C" (Beauregard Volunteers) 6th Georgia Reg. (infantry) with a graphic account of each member. Written by Wendell D. Croom & pub. by survivors of the company." Fort Valley, Ga., Advitiser Off., 1879. 8vo, wraps, errata sheet, 37pp. $15.

1474 **CROSBY, Ernest**
"If the South had been allowed to go." In: No. Amer. Rev., Dec., 1903, v.CLXXVII, p. 867-871.

1475 **CROSLAND, Charles**
"Reminiscences of the Sixties." Columbia, S.C., 1910? 8vo, wraps, 70pp., ports. Civil War, chaps-III-X. Member Co. I, 13th, Tenn. Infty.

1476 **CROSS, Fred W., Edt.**
"William & Mary College as a hospital in 1862." In: Wm. & Mary Quart., 2nd ser. 1939, v.XIX, p. 181-186. Letters: Dr. Alfred Hitchcock to Surg-Gen. of USArmy, May 20, 1862; and Dr. S. Cabot to J.A. Andrew, Gov. Mass., May 22, 1862, reporting on medical care of the wounded at W & M.

1477 **CROSS, Henry Martyn**
"A Yankee Soldier Looks at the Negro." In: CWH, June 1961, v.VII, #2, p. 133-148. 2-plates.

1478 **CROSS, Joseph, Rev.**
"Camp & Field. Papers from the Portfolio

of an army chaplain." Macon, Ga., Burke, Boykin & Co., 1863. 12mo, book 1 & 2, 141-160pp. Book 3 & 4, have: Columbia, S.C., Evans & Cogswell, 1864. Wraps, 36pls, 3 & 4, 390pp. $27.50, $50, $85. Admirable invective & denunciation of the North. 1, 3 & 4 $450.

..."Camp & Field. Papers from the Portfolio of an Army Chaplain. By the Rev. Joseph Cross, D.D." Macon, Ga., Burke, Boykin & Co., 1864. 12mo, cl, iv, 9-141pp. Sabin-17657.

1479 **CROSS, R.R.**
"Attack on Fort Gilmer." In: Annals Army Tenn. Early Western Hist., 1878, v.1, p. 127-130.

1480 **CROSSLEY, Martha Jane (Mrs. James David Rumph)**
"A patriotic Confederate woman's war diary, 1862-1863. Edt., with introduction by H.E. Sterks." In: Ala. HQ, Winter 1958, v.20, p. 611-617. Excerpts, 10 Aug-1 Dec. 1862, from a diary kept at Perote, Ala.

1481 **CROUCH, F. Nicholls**
"C.S.A. to G.A.R. A waif on the past, written for the Advance-Gazette, Pensacola, Florida, by a volunteer soldier of the Southern cause." (Pensacola, 1885?) Duke, UWF (copy) Broadside, 38x11cm.

1482 **CROUCH, R.G., Dr.**
"A Confederate Woman's kind act finely told, letter from soldier boy to mother." In: SHSP, 1910, v.38, p. 309-312.

1483 ..."The Dahlgren Raid. Paper read at R.E. Lee Camp, C.V., March 9, 1906." In: SHSP, 1906, v.XXXIV, p. 179-190.

1484 **CROW, L.P., Mrs.**
"The furled banners of the South, a grand carnival of the Southern States, contesting for the keeping of the old battle flag of the Confederacy." Gatesville, Tex: Don C. Curtis Pr. (1903) 12mo, wraps, 1p., 16pp., illus. A Play.

1485 **CROW, Vernon**
"Storm in the mountains: Thomas' Confederate Legion of Cherokee Indians & Mountaineers." Press of the Museum of the Cherokee Indian, North Carolina, 1982. 8vo, cl, 275pp., illus. $15.

1486 **CROW, Vernon H.**
"The Thomas Legion." In: CWTI, June 1971, v.X, #3, p. 40-48, illus., ports. Wm. H. Thomas & his Cherokees war in the Southern Appalachians, N. Carolina.

1487 ..."Storm in the Mountains: Thomas' Confederate Legion of Cherokee Indians & Mountaineers." Cherokee(N.C.): Press of the Museum of the Cherokee Indian, 1982. $15. 8vo, wraps, xv, 275pp., 34 photos, 12-maps, notes bibliog., appendices & Co. Muster ro lls. Mssc., of Col. Wm. H. Thomas & Lieut. Col. W.W. Stringfield. Col. Jas. R. Love.

1488 **CROW, Z.H.**
"A Smith County Confederate writes home: Letters of Z.H. Crow. Edited by F.Lee Lawrence & Robert W. Glover." In: Chron. Smith Co. (Texas), v.IV, p.11-14.

1489 **CROWE, Charles Robert, Edt.**
"The Age of Civil War & Reconstruction, 1830-1900; a book of interpretative essays, edited by Charles Crowe." Homewood, Ill., Dorsey Press, 1966. The Dorsey Series in American History. 8vo, cl, x, 479pp. bibliographies.

1490 **CROWLEY, R.O.**
"The Confederate Torpedo Service." In: Cent. Mag., 1898, v.LVI, p. 290-300. Formerly electrician of torpedo division CSNavy.

1491 ..."Making the "Infernal Machines". A memoir of the Confederate Torpedo Service." In: CWTI, June 1973, v.XII, #3, p. 24-35, illus., diagrams.

1492 **CROWLEY, William J.**
"The Ordeal of Emily Weaver a True-spy story of the Civil War & the Life of Edwin

Tucker Burr." In: Independence Co. Chronicle, Batesville, Ark., Oct. 1975, v.XVII, #1, p.(2) 1-70, (1). Entire number, facsms, ports, illus.

1493 ..."Tennessee Cavalier in the Missouri Cavalry: Major Henry Ewing, CSA, of the St. Louis Times." Columbia, Mo., Kelly Press, 1978. 8vo, cl, dj, illus., index, xii, 229pp., $16-y, $13.50.

1494 ...See also: Oct. 1979, v.XXI, #1, Independence County Chronicle, p. 4-10, ports. Review of Crowley book & Maj. Henry Ewing.

1495 **CROWN, Francis J., Jr.**
"Confederate Postal History." Boston: Quarterman Pub., 1976, 8vo, cl, illus., 313pp. $30-y.

1496 **CROWN, Francis J., Jr., Edt.**
"Surveys of the Confederate postmasters provisionals." Lawrence, Mass., Quarterman Pub., 1982, 8vo, cl, xx, 726pp. $100.

1497 **CROWNOVER, Sims**
"Battle of Franklin." (Nashville: Tenn. Hist. Quart., 1955) v.XIV, #4, Dec. 1955, p. 291-322. Reprint: Sales donated to Carter House Ass'n., of Franklin, Tenn. $1, $8, $15-r, $10-bmk, $4. 8vo, wraps, cover title, 32, (3)pp. port(front) of Gen. Hood. maps.

1498 **CROWSON, E. Thomas**
"Aftermath of Battle. Manassas was not the end...it was just the beginning." (Richmond) Va. Cavl., Spring 1969. v.XVIII, #4, p. 31-40, ports, illus., map.

1499 ..."The High Tide of Confederate Fighting." In: W. Va. Hist., 1975, v.XXXVI, p. 140-145. Battle of Chancellorsville.

1500 **CROWSON, T.W.**
"Run Yank or die." n.p., ca. 1861. small octavo, printed letter-sheet, folded, print in two colums, pict. vigs. surrounds port, of Jeff Davis. $325-jk-142. Penned by T.W. Crowson of "Alabama Hickories." unrecorded.

1501 **CROY, Homer**
"Last of the great outlaws: the story of Cole Younger." N.Y., Duell, Sloan, & Pearce (1956). 8vo, facsm., ports, views, bibliog: 214-235, x, 242pp. Life in Missouri, membership in Quantrill's guerrillas & as an officer in CSArmy.

1502 **CROZIER, Robert Haskins**
"The Confederate Spy: A Story of the War of 1861." novel. Gallatin, Tenn: R.B. Harmon, 1866. 12mo, cl, 406pp. stiff colored wraps, 1st, Panola Col., Miss., 5-27-65? $7.50

..."The Confederate Spy; or, Startling Incidents of the War Between the States." Louisville, Ky: J.P. Morton, 1885, 5th Edt., a novel., 1871.

1503 ..."The Bloody Junto; or, The Escape of John Wilkes Booth. A story containing many interesting particulars in regard to the trial & execution of Mrs. Surratt & other so-called conspirators." Little Rock, Ark., Woodruff & Blocher, 1869. cloth, 146pp. double-column print. Louisville, Ky., Lost Cause Press, micro-card. $3.10.

1504 **CRUDEN, Robert**
"The War that never ended: The American Civil War." Englewood Cliffs, N.J., Printice-Hall, 1973, 8vo, cl, dj, illus., maps, bibliog., index, x, 208pp. $6.

1505 **"CRUISE of the Alabama, The."**
See: G.T. Fullam, George, P.D. Haywood, Norm Delaney.

1506 **CRUISE of the Clarence-Tacony-Archer, The**
by an officer of the United States navy, with addenda by an officer of the three vessels." In: Md. Hist. Mag., March, 1915, v.X, p. 42-55. Three vessels used by Confederates in a commerce destroying curise, June 6-27, 1863.

1507 **CRUMP, Nannie Mayes**
"The attitude of the Southern leaders on the Crittenden compromise." In: CV, Jan. 1919, v.XXVII, p. 12-17.

1508 **CRUMP, S.A., Hon.**
"Speech delivered at the reunion of North Carolina Confederate Veterans, Aug. 20, 1902, Greensboro, N.C." (Macon, Ga., Evening News) 8vo, wraps, cover title, 14pp.

1509 **CRUMPTON, H.J. & Washington Bryan**
"Adventures of two Alabama Boys efforts to reach the Gold Fields in 1849, return from California & through Confederate Lines." Montgomery, Ala., 1912. 12mo, cl, 238pp. ports. $200-ob, $15.

1510 ..."A Book of Memoirs 1842-1892." By Washington Bryan Crumpton. Montgomery, Ala., Baptist Mission Board, 1921. $20-bmk-84. 8vo, cl, front(port), xii, 339, (6)pp. CSA & Alabama material.

1511 **CRUPI, Dominick, Jr.**
"A brief survey of disaffection, disunity, & disloyalty in the Confederacy." In: Jour. Soc. Studies, Spring 1951, v.7, #2, p. 52-61, notes.

1512 **CRUSE, Mary Anne**
"Cameron Hall: a story of the Civil War by M.A.C." laid in Alabama, Huntsville. Philadelphia: J.B. Lippincott & Co., 1867, 12mo, cl, 543pp. (old) $3.50, $20, $15, $25-bmk.

1513 **CRUSH, Charles W.**
"The Montgomery County (Va.) Story, 1776-1957." n.p., 1957. 8vo, cl, 167pp., illus. Rosters. $35.

1514 **CRUTCHFIELD, S., Colonel**
"Report of Col. Crutchfield of the Second Battle of Manassas." In: OLOD, April 1875, v.2, #2, p. 152-156.

1515 **CRUTE, Joseph H., Jr.**
"Confederate Staff Officers 1861-1865." Wendell, N.C., Broadfoot's Bookmark, 1982, 8vo, cl, 267pp. $25.

..."Confederate Staff Officers, 1861-1865." Powhatan, Va., Derwent Books, (c.1982) 8vo, cl, vi, 267pp. $15. Michael Mullins: "One of the most useful of Wright's products was a listing of CSA staff officers in a tiny edition in 1891, listing almost 5000 names. Another version of the same list was not published. The above list was a direct transcription of the second list." See: Marcus Wright, Claud Estes, John M. Carroll.

..."Units of the Confederate States Army." Caithersburg, Md., Olde Soldiers Books, 1987. 8vo, cl, dj, 475pp. $45. 1,300 CSA units, artillery, cavalry, infantry numerically, alphabetically by state, place & time of organization, campaigns & battles.

1516 **"CSA-TRANS-MISSISSIPPI,**
Dept. H.Q., Gen. Order #45. For purpose of carrying into effect the Conscript Act, passed, last sess. Confederate Congress." Little Rock, Ark. Dec. 8, 1862. 8vo, 3pp. sewed. Not in Crand/Harwell. $75.

1517 **CUBAGE, Annie Rosser**
"Engagement at Cabin Creek, Indian Territory, July 1 & 2, 1863." Oklahoma City: Chron. of Okla., March, 1932, v.X, #1, p. 44-51.

1518 **CULBERSON, Charles Allen**
"Sam Houston & Secession." In: Scribner's Mag., 1906, v.39, p. 584-591.

1519 **CULBERSON, Jr.**
"The greatest Confederate commander." Washington, D.C., 1907, 8vo, wraps, 38pp.

1520 **CULBRETH, David Marvel Reynolds**
"The University of Virginia; Memoirs of her Student-life & Professors, by David M.R. Culbreth, M.D." NY & Wash., Neale Publ., 1908. 8vo, cl, plates, ports, incl. front, 501pp. $75-bmk. Articles on Lee's Family, Chs. S. Venable (Lee's staff), Francis H. Smith & John W. Mallet, the ordnance expert.

1531 **CULLEN, Joseph P.**
"Battle of the Wilderness-Lee & Grant first met May 5-7, 1864." In: CWTI, April, 1971, v.10, p. 4-11, 42-47, illus., maps, ports.

1532 ..."The Civil War in Virginia." The Commonwealth Magazine of Va. (Richmond: Virginia State Chamber of Commerce, n.d., 1961) 4to, wraps, (40)pp. ports, illus., dble-page map, facsms $1.

1533 ..."Drugs in the Confederacy." In: CWTI, June, 1965, v.IV, #3, p. 58-62, illus., ports. The South was not short of medicines as it was in distribution.

1534 ..."Gaines's Mill." In: CWTI, Apr. 1964, v.III, #1, p. 10-17, 24-illus., maps, ports. CSA lost 8000 & Federals 7000 June 27, 1862. A draw, neither side really won.

1535 ..."At Malvern Hill, it was not war, it was murder. Poor CS coordination & superior Federal artillery spoiled Lee's last chance to destroy McClellan." In: CWTI, v.5, #2, p. 4-14, illus., maps, ports.

1536 ..."Richmond National Battlefield Park, Virginia. By Joseph P. Cullen." Wash: National Park Ser. Hist. Handbook, #33, 1961. 8vo, pict. color stiff wraps, illus., maps, ports, (4), 46pp.

1537 ..."The Siege of Petersburg." In: CWTI, August, 1970, v.IX, #5, p. 3-50. "A Souvenir Album of the Final Campaign of the War." facsms, illus., color-coded maps, diagrams, ports.

1538 ...."Where a Hundred Thousand Fell." The Battles of Fredericksburg, Chancellorsville, the Wilderness & Spotsylvania Court House... Wash: Nat'l Park Serv. Hist. Handbook series, #39, 1966. 8vo, pict. wraps, ports, maps, facsms, 2-color illus., 56pp. $.70

1539 ..."Chimborazo Hospital, charnel house of living suffering." In: CWTI, Jan. 1981, v.19, #9, p. 36-42, illus. ports.

1540 **CULLEN, William B. & Richard Beard**
"Incidents of Gen. M'Pherson's death." In: CV, March 1903, v.XI, p. 118-119.

1541 **CULLOP, Charles P.**
"Confederate Propaganda in Europe, 1861-1865." Coral Gables, Fla., University of Miami Press, 1969. 8vo, cl, 160pp. $12- bmk, $6.95.

1542 ..."Edwin De Leon, Jefferson Davis' Propagandist." In: CWH, December, 1962, v.VIII, #4, p. 386-400.

1543 **CULMER, Frederic A.**
"A Snapshot of Alexander W. Doniphan, 1808-1887." (Columbia, Mo., Mo. Hist. Review, Oct., 1943, v.XXXVIII-#1, p. 25-32. Worked for peace in Washington Peace Conference, then took no part in war. Interest herein, pungent remarks on current politicians & Lincoln.

1544 **CULP, Frederick M.**
"Captain George King's Home Guard Company CSA." In: WTHSP, 1961, v.23, p. 55-78.

1545 **CUMBEE, David E.**
"Confederate Memorial & Memorial Chapel Riverside Cemetery, Hopkinsville, KY." In: FCHQ, October 1969, v.43, #4, p. 353-354.

1546 **"CUMBERLAND CHURCH**
or the Heights of Farmville: The Last Stricken Field of the Army of Northern Virginia, April 7, 1865; with, "The Last Twenty-four Hours of the Army of Northern Virginia." New York, 1872-1874, in "La Royale", parts VII & VIII. 8vo, wraps, maps, illus. (listed in Jas. A. Williams, cat. #10; quotes Gen. de Peyster that first six numbers of "La Royale" are unobtainable)

1547 **"CUMBERLAND GRAYS, The**
Company D Twenty-first Virginia Infantry, Its Roster, with brief record of its service." In: SHSP, 1897, v.XXV, p. 264-266.

1548 **CUMBERLAND, Charles C.**
"The Confederate Loss & Recapture of Galveston, 1862-2863." In: SwHQ, October, 1947, v.LI, #2, p. 109-130.

1549 **CUMMING, J.D.**
"The Last Sad Days. From Petersburg to Appomattox Courthouse. Last hours of the ANV by one of its Artillery Officers." In: SHSP, 1908, v.XXXVI, p. 261-266.

1550 **CUMMING, Joseph Bryan**
"A Sketch of the Descendants of David Cumming & Memoirs of the War Between the States." Edt: Mary Gairdner Cumming (Mrs. Bryan Cumming)." n.p., privately published for members of the Cumming family, 1925. 8vo, mounted ports (2), 93, 4pp. $15, $25.

1551 ..."Address of..., at the unveiling of the monument to Maj. Gen. William Henry Talbot Walker, on the Battlefield of Atlanta, July 22, 1902." (Augusta, Ga., Chronicle office, 1902) 8vo, wraps, 11pp. See also: Honor to Gen. W.H.T. Walker in Confed. Vet., v.10(1902), illus., port, p. 402-407. Speeches of J.B. Cumming in 15th & 16th Annual reviews "Confed. Survivors Ass'n."

1552 ..."Memorial Resolution introduced by Colonel Jos. B. Cumming at the Sixteenth Annual Reunion of the Confederate Survivors' Association of Augusta, Ga., on Memorial Day, April 26, 1894, in honor or its late president, Colonel Charles C. Jones. Together with speeches of Messrs. F.M. Stovall & Salem Dutcher seconing the Resolution; the remarks of Capt. Chas. E. Coffin; & the Historian's Report, submitted by Charles Edgeworth Jones. Printed by order of the Association." Augusta, Ga., Chronicle Job Print, 1894. 8vo, wraps, 20pp. $15-bmk.

1552a ..."Address delivered before the Confederate survivors association, April 26, 1893 on Chickamauga." Augusta, Ga., Chronicle office, 1893. 8vo, wraps, 32pp.

1553 **CUMMING, Kate**
"A journal of hospital life in the Confederate Army of Tennessee, from the battle of Shiloh to the end of the war; with sketches of life & character, & brief notices of current events during that period." Louisville: J.P. Morton; New Orleans: W. Evelyn (1866) 8vo, cl, printed double column, 199pp. $55, $325-jk-142. (Streeter, atg: $120, $12.50, $20, $30, $35, $40) $150-bmk-106.

1554 ..."Kate: The Journal of a Confederate Nurse." Edt: Richard Barksdale Harwell. Baton Rouge, Louisiana State University (1959) 8vo, cl, d/w, port(front) illus., facsm., xx, 321pp. $6, $25-bmk, $16-atg., $15-y, $40-b.
...Savannah, Ga., Beehive Press, 1975, vii, 288pp. $28, $40.

1555 ..."Gleanings from the Southland. Sketches of life & manners of the people of the South before, during & after the war of secession, with extracts from the author's journal & an epitome of the new wouth." 12mo, cl, 2, ports(front, 277pp. ($12.50, $17.50, $60.) Birmingham (Ala.), Roberts & Sons, 1895.

1556 **CUMMING, Katherine Hubbell**
"A Northern Daughter & a Southern Wife, the Civil War Reminiscences & Letters of Katherine Hubbell Cumming, 1860-1865. Edited by W. Kirkwood." Augusta, Ga., (Augusta College) Richmond County Historical Society, 1976. 8vo, cl, illus., xvii, 126pp. (wraps, $6) $12.

1557 **CUMMINGS, Arthur C.**
"Thirty-third Virginia at First Manassas & Col. J.W. Allen's Report." In: SHSP, 1906, v.XXXIV, p. 363-371.

1558 **CUMMINGS, C.C.**
"Capture of Harper's Ferry." In: Confed. Vet., Apr. 1897, v.V, p. 173-174. Both

Miss. & S.C. Troops at capture, Sept. 13, 1862, by a participant.

..."Leesburg at Balls Bluff." In: CV, 1902, v.10, p. 69.

1559 **CUMMINGS, Charles Martin**
"Fruit of the Restless Spirit: Ohio's Confederate Generals." In: Ohio History, 1964, v.LXXIII, p. 144-156.

1560 ..."Forgotten man at Fort Donelson: Bushrod Rust Johnson." In: THQ, 1968, v.27, p. 380-397.

1561 ..."Otho French Strahl: "Choicest spirit to embrace the South." In: THQ, 1965, v.24, p. 341-355.

1562 ..."Robert Hopkins Hatton: Reluctant Rebel." In: Tenn.HQ, 1964, v.XXIII, p. 169-181.

1563 ..."Seven Ohio Confederate Generals: Case Histories of Defection (Vol. I & II)Ph.D. dss., Ohio State University, 1963. Univ. Micro. 63-6233; MHRC Micro. D. C42.

1564 ..."Yankee Quaker Confederate General. The Curious Career of Bushrod Rust Johnson." Rutherford, N.J., Fairleigh Dickinson University Press, 1871. 8vo, cl, dj, 417pp., illus., ports, facsms, $35, $15, $25, $20.

1565 **CUMMINGS, Edward**
"Marmaduke of Tennessee." Chicago: A.C. McClurg & Co., 1914. Illus: Frank E. Schoonover. 8vo, cl, front-illus(color)(5), 372pp. CSA, divided loyalties in Tenn. $10-nc, $20.

1566 **CUMMINS, A.B.**
"The Wilson-Kautz Raid, More Commonly referred, The Battle of the Grove, June 21, July 1, 1864." (Blackstone, Va., Nottoway Pub. Co., July 1961) 8vo, wraps, map, 39pp. $8, $4-bmk, $.50,

1567 **CUMMINS, Edmund H.**
"List of names of officers of the Signal Corps, Confederate States Army." In: SHSP, 1888, v.XVI, p. 91-107. See: Chs. E. Taylor.

1568 **CUMMINS, Jim**
"Jim Cummins' Book...The Life Story of the James & Younger Gang & their Comrades, including the operations of Quantrill's Guerrillas by One Who Rode With Them." Denver, Colo: Reed Print, 1903, 12mo, pict., cl, illus., 191pp. (13 pls) $100.

1569 **CUNNINGHAM, Edward**
"Battle of Baton Rouge, 1862." (Baton Rouge, La., Kennedy Print Shop (1962) (cover title) Folio, plastic spiral-bound, heavy paper as all sheets. Pages unnumbered, 43cm. (15)p, type-set (12)p. (6)dbl-pg 43x54 1/2 cm. Reproduced from Frank Leslie & Harper's Weekly. Published by the committee for the preservation of Port Hudson Battlefield in an edition of 2000 copies. $50, $20.

1570 ..."The Port Hudson Campaign, 1862-1863." (Baton Rouge) Louisiana State University Press (1963). $45-b, $5, $10-nc. 8vo, cl, dj, illus., xiii, notes/bibliog. 131-168pp.

..."Battle of Baton Rouge." In: LaH., 1962, v.3, p. 77-128.

1571 **CUNNINGHAM, Frank**
"General Stand Watie's Confederate Indians." San Antonio, Texas: Naylor Co. (1959) 8vo, cl, pict. endsheets, ports (incl. front) illus., sketches, xiv, 242pp. atgd-#618, $12.50, $60-#123, $50-bmk-104, $25-jk-97, $15, $30.

1572 ..."Knight of the Confederacy/Gen. Turner Ashby." San Antonio, Texas: Naylor Co. (1960) 8vo, cl, dj, color flag endsheets, ports, illus., facsms, sketches xvi, (20), 225pp. bibliog. index, p. 195-222. atg.-$25, $15-y,

1573 **CUNNINGHAM, Frank Harrison**
"Sidney Smith Lee, forgotten brother of a great General." In: "Traditions" (Detroit)

Nov. 1961, v.4,(11), p. 36-46. Smith served in USN, 1818-1861, CSN 1861-1865.

1574 **CUNNINGHAM, Horace Herndon**
"The Confederate Medical Officer in the field." In: US Armed Forces Med. Jour., Nov. 1958, v.9, p.1580-1604, notes. offprint, 15pp. Based on thesis: Univ. N. Carolina. $35-r.

1575 ..."Confederate General Hospitals: Establishment & Organization." (Lexington, Ky.) JSH, August 1954, v.XX, #3, p. 376-394. $8.

1576 ..."The medical service & hospitals of the Southern Confederacy." In: University of N.C. Research in progress, 1953, v.31, p. 137-138. Abstract of thesis.

1577 ..."Edmund Burke Haywood & Raleigh's Confederate Hospitals." (Raleigh) NCHRev., April 1958., v.XXXV, #2, p. 153-166, port, pls.

1578 ..."Organization & Administration of the Confed. Medical Dept.: In: NCHR, July, 1954, v.XXXI, p. 385-409. $8, $8-bk

1579 ..."Doctors in Gray. The Confederate Medical Service." Baton Rouge: Louisiana State University Press (1958) 8vo, cl, dj, ports, facsms., plate, xi, 339pp. bibliog. 291-321pp., index. $6, $35-bmk-84, $25, $8, $60. 2nd Edition, 1960, Gloucester, Mass., 1970, p. 339, $30-bmk, (wiley copy) $70, $8, $16.

1580 ..."Field Medical Services at the Battle of Manassas (Bull Run)." Athens: Univ. of Georgia Pr., 1968. University Monographs #16, 8vo, wraps, xii, 116pp. More CSA than Union. op, $25-b, $2.50, $6-nc, $10.

1581 **CUNNINGHAM, J.W.**
"Memories of Morgan's Christmas Raid (1862)." In: CV, Feb. 1909, v.XVII, p. 79-80.

1582 **CUNNINGHAM, O. Edward**
"In Violation of the Laws of War: the Execution of Robert Cobb Kennedy." In: La. Hist., Spring, 1978. (see: Arthur W. Bergeron) v.18, p.189-201.

1583 ..."Captain Frank B. Gurly, Fourth Alabama Cavalry, CSA, murderer or victim?" In: AR, Apr. 1975, v.28, #2, p. 83-103.

1584 **CUNNINGHAM, Sumner Archibald**
"Memorials-Col. Richard Owen the good Samaritan of Camp Morton-Sam Davis the Boy Hero of Tennessee." Nashville: Confederate Veteran, (c.1912) 12mo, wraps, cover-title, ports, illus., 47, (1)pp. (The author, deceased, Cunningham material was used here)

1585 ..."Reminiscences of the 41st Tennessee Regiment." Of Company B. 1st published in the "Shelbyville (Va.) Commercial", n.p., n.d. (c.1870) 8vo, wraps, 57pp. double column. See: W.J.Davidson, $100, $75.

1586 ..."Story of a Terrible Battle. The Carnage at Franklin, Tennessee, next to that of Crater." In: SHSP, 1896, v.XXIV, p. 189-192.

1587 ..."Events leading to the Battle of Franklin, Tenn." In: CV, Jan. 1910, v.XVIII, p. 17-20.

..."Sam Davis." In: Amer. Hist. Mag., July 1899, 14pp. wraps. $10-bmk. In: CV, 1899, v.7, p. 538-542, ports, pl.

1588 ..."Samuel Davis, an unexcelled illustration of highest honor in man." In: CV, Oct. 1908, v.16, p. 523-528, port. Paper read before the Tenn. Hist. So.

1589 **CUNNINGHAM, W.H.**
"A History of the Battle of Chickamauga, Sept. 19th & 20th, 1863." (Evergreen, Ala., Orphans' Call Press, 1900. 9cm, wraps, cover title, 11pp. Dated: Camp near Tyner's Sta. on E. Tenn & Knoxville Rrd., Hamilton County, Tenn. Sept. 27, 1863. Dorn-II, 2615.

1590 **CUNYUS, Lucy Josephine**
"The History of Bartow County, formerly Cass." (Cartersville, Ga., Tribune Pub.

Co., 1933) 8vo, cl, front, illus., maps, plates, ports, ix-xv, 343, (1)pp. $50-bmk. 47pp. relates to the Confederacy.

1591 **CUPPLES, George, Dr.**
"Two Battle of Galveston letters, edt: Dorman H. Winfrey." In: SwHQ, October 1961, v.LXV, #2, p. 251-257.

1592 **CURLEE, Abigail**
"The History of a Texas Slave Plantation." In: SwHQ, Oct. 1922, v.XXVI, #2, p. 79-127. charts. Period: 1831-1863.

1593 **CURRAN, Charles**
"The Three Lives of Judah P. Benjamin." In: Hist. Today, 1967, v.SVII, p. 583-592.

1594 **CURRAN, John W.**
"Lincoln conspiracy trial-mysterious phases." In: "Notre Dame Lawyer, 1935, v.X, p. 259-276. Discussion between un-identified professor & a student about trial of eight conspirators leagued with Booth.

1595 **CURRENT, Richard N.**
"The Confederates & the First Shot." In: CWH, Decembe 1961, v.VII, #4, p. 357-369.

1596 ..."God & the strongest battalions. Donald (David) Edt: "Why the north won the civil war." Baton Rouge: Louisiana University Pr., 1960. p. 3-22. On the "chief errors" of CSA "economic policy" 1861-1865.

1597 **CURRIE, John**
"Some letters from John Currie to his family...1862-1865." In: Northern Neck of Va. Historical Magazine. 1969, v.19, p. 1847-1854.

1598 **CURRIN, Jean McCulley**
"Why Indian Territory Joined the Confederacy." In: Lincoln Herald, 1967, v.LXIX, p. 83-91.

1599 **CURRY, William**
"Raid of the Confederate Cavalry through Central Tennessee in October, 1863, comm. by Gen. Joseph Wheeler. A paper read before the Ohio commandery of the loyal legion, April 1, 1908." (Columbus? 1908?) 8vo, wraps, map, 21pp. US cavalry Assoc. Jour. Apr. 1909, v.XIX, p. 815-835.

1600 **CURTIS, Finley P., Jr.**
"The Black Shadow of the Sixties." In: CV, Aug. 1916, v.24, #8, p. 353-357, 401-405, port.

1601 ..."Typical guerrillas of the war period-representing the character of the Home Guard enemy." In: CV, April 1919, v.27, #4, p. 132-136. See: "Home Guard" article in March issue, p. 86-88, port.

1602 **CURTIS, Newton Martin, General**
"Mrs. Jefferson Davis. Visit by Ex-Congressman Curtis to Confederate President's widow." In: SHSP, 1900, v.XXVIII, p. 314-416.

1603 **CURTIS, Richard**
"History of the famous battle between the iron-clad Merrimac, CSN, and the iron-clad Monitor & the Cumberland & Congress of the U.S. Navy. Mar 8-9, 1862, as seen by a man at the gun." (Norfolk, Press of S.B. Turner & Son, 1907) 16mo, wraps, 17pp. Swem-1256.

1604 **CURTIS, William A.**
"Annual address delivered at the Charles L. Robinson Camp #947, U.C.V., Franklin, North Carolina, March 31, 1899." (n.p., n.d., 1899?) 8vo, wraps, port, 16pp.

1605 ..."A Journal of Reminiscences of the war. (1-Sketches of Company "A", 2nd regiment of North Carolina cavalry, from May 1st, 1861, to January 1st, 1862; 2, Battle of Newbern, March 14, 1862." In: OLOD, 1875, v.II, p. 36-44, 281-290. Unit roster Cherokee Rangers.

1606 ..."The battle of New Bern & the retreat to Kinston (March 1862)." In: West. Carolina College Faculty studies, 1958, v.34, p. 3-13, notes. (CSA reminiscences, 1874)

1607 **CURTO, James J., Compl.**
"Sutler issues of the Civil War: a supplemental listing, with other related is-

sues." In: Numismatist, June, July, Sept/Oct. 1959, v.72, p. 643-648, 789-796, 1095-1098, 1211-1117. facsms, suppl. to a list in "Numismatist", 1946. Metal & cardboard tokens, script issued in lieu of currency, in denominations usually from $.02 to $.50, by persons assigned to US & CSArmy posts or units to operate stores or concessions of the soldiers.

1608 **CUSHING, E.B.**
"Edward Hopkins Cushing, an appreciation by his son." In: SwHQ, April 1922, v.XXV, #4, p. 261-273. Cushing was an important publisher during the war, in Houston, Texas.

1609 **CUSHMAN, C.V.B.**
"Jeb Stuart, the Virginia Cavalier." n.p., 1957, 4to, wraps, 48lfs. As an officer in the CSArmy.

1610 **CUSHMAN, Joseph D., Jr.**
"The Blockade & Fall of Apalachicola, 1861-1862." In: FHQ, July 1962, v.XLI, #1, p. 38-46.

1611 ..."The Episcopal Church in Florida during the Civil War." In: FHQ, April, 1960, v.XXXVIII, #4, p. 294-301.

1612 **CUSSONS, John**
"A Glance at Current American History." By An Ex-Confederate. 8vo, wraps, bound. Glen Allen, Va., 1897, Scarce 1st Edt. 32pp. Cussons, May & Co., $20, $8.50, $12.50.
...Do: 1899, cl, port, 12mo, 172pp. $3.75, $10. Cussons Past Grand-Master Va. Confed. Vet.

1613 ..."The Passage of Thoroughfare Gap & the Assembly of Lee's Army for the Second Battle of Manassas, by a Confederate Scout. With an introduction by Senator Daniel, chairman of the History Comm. of Grand Camp of Confederate Veterans." York, Pa., Gazette Print, 1906. 12mo, wraps, 31pp. $7.50, $10, $125-ob, $75, $20-jenk.

1614 ..."Jack Sterry, the Jessie Scout, an incident of the second battle of Manassas, on which turned the course of the campaign & the fate of the Southern army. From the notebook of a Confederate Soldier." n.p., Gazette Print, 1906, 8vo, wraps, 24pp., Swem-1261, $22.50-jk, $75-ob.
...(as above, with addition) by John Cussons, Glen Allen, Va., Confederate Scout, past grand comm. of Confederate Veterans of Virginia, ex-chairman of history committee of the grand camp." Harrisburg, The Star-Independent Pr., 1907, 8vo, wraps, cover title, 20pp, Swem-1262. $8.50, $17.50, $40-r.
...Richmond, Va., Whittet & Shepperson, 1908. 8vo, wraps, 23pp. $16-bmk, $40-bmk, $12.50, $75-b.

1615 ..."United States History as the Yankee makes & takes it, by a Confederate soldier. Glen Allen, Va., Cussons & May, 1900. 12mo, wraps, 99pp, Swem-1263 states its same as "Glance of Current History" but for additions of "Criticisms", p. 11-17. $20-jk, $15, $50-b, $35.

1616 **CUTCHINS, John Abram, Colonel**
"A Famous Command, the Richmond Light Infantry Blues." Richmond, Va., Garrett & Massie (1934) $75-dj, $60, $50-bmk-84. sm.4to, cl, dj, ports, illus. (incl. front), xx, 399pp. append-index, p. 291-399. CSA, C.pp. 38-195, $12.50, $17.50, $20, $25, $25.

1617 **CUTHBERTSON, Gilbert**
"Coller of the Sixth Texas. Correspondence of a Texas Infantry Man, 1861-1864." In: TMH, 1971, v.IX, #2, p. 129-136.

1618 **CUTSHAW, Wilfred E., Colonel**
"The Battle Near Spotsylvania Courthouse on May 18, 1864. An address delivered before R.E. Lee Camp #1, C.V., on the night of Jan. 20, 1905." Confederate Veterans. (Richmond, Va., Wm. Ellis

Jones) (1905) 8vo, wraps, 17pp.
...Reprint: (Rich., So. Hist. Soc. Papers) 1914, v.XXXIX, p. 195-212. $75-ob.
...Do: SHSP, 1905, v.XXXIII, p. 320-334.

1619 **CUTTING, Elizabeth B.**
"Jefferson Davis, Political Soldier." N.Y., Dodd, Mead & Co., 1930. 8vo, cl, front, pls., ports, facsms, x, 361pp. $12.50, $15, $17.50, $30, atg-$20-bmk.

1620 **CUTTS, Allen S.**
"Letter concerning number of guns in Cutt's Battalion at Sharpsburg." In: SHSP, 1882, v.X, p. 430-431.

1621 **CUYLER, Telamon Smith**
"A roster of the surviving general officers of the Confederate States Army, 1861-1865." Mamaroneck, N.Y., Private Print, 1905. 4to, (5-folios), limited: 50 copies. "Of the Beverwyck Quartos this is the first." Note: 2nd & last leaf blank. half-title: "Roster of the Surviving General Officers of the Confederate States Army. Telamon S. Guyler, 1905. Covers.

1622 ..."The Confederate Half Dollar." In: CV, 1907, v.15, p. 507, plate.

1623 **CYPERT, Jesse N.**
"Secession Convention (in Arkansas)." In: ArkHQP, I, 1906, p. 314-323.

D

1 **DABNEY, Robert L.**
"Chaplains in the Army of Northern Virginia. A list compiled in 1864-1865 by Robert L. Dabney. Edt: W. Harrison Daniel." In: VMHB, July 1963, v.71, #3, p. 327-340.

2 ..."Life and Campaigns, Jackson..." Harrisonburg, Va., Sprinkle Pub., 1983.

3 **DABNEY, Robert Lewis**
"Life and campaigns of Stonewall Jackson." Tulsa, Okla., Columbia Press, 1985. 8vo, cl, 742pp. $20.

4 ..."A defense of Va. and the South." Tulsa, Okla., Columbia Press, 1985, 8vo, cl, 356pp., hardback. $10.

5 ..."Secession." Tulsa, Okla., Columbia Press, 1985. 8vo, paper, 64pp. $4.

6 **DABNEY, T.G.**
"When Hood superseded Johnston." In: Confed. Vet., Sept. 1914, v.XXII, p. 406-407. In the command of the army at Atlanta, July 17, 1864.

7 ..."On Hood's Campaign into Tennessee." In: Confed. Vet., Nov. 1922, v.XXX, p. 408-409.

8 **DABNEY, Virginius**
"The Last Parade: the Confederate Reunion, Richmond, 1932." Chapel Hill, NC, Algonquin Books, 1984. 8vo, cl, 184pp., illus., facm. of official program of the 42nd and last reunion of the UCV and GAR. $17.50. Included Douglas Southall Freeman's "Last Parade" from the Richmond News Leader of June 24, 1932. See: Douglas Freemen's "Last Parade".

9 ..."Liberalism in the South." Chapel Hill, N.C. University Press, 1932. 8vo, cl, xix, 456pp. Study of liberalism in the South since the revolution, including states of the CSA and Kentucky.

10 ..."The original of Lee's last order." In: Jour. Am. Hist., Apr. 1926, v.XX, p. 160-174.

11 ..."The Last Review. The Confederate Reunion, Richmond, 1933." In: CV(new), Nov. 1985, v.33, #6, p. 36-46, group pictures, color t.p.

12 **DACUS, Robert H.**
"Reminiscences of Co. 'H', First Arkansas mounted rifles, by Dr. Robert H. Dacus." (Darnanelle , Ark, Post-Dispatch Print, 1897, 8vo, wraps, cover title, (47)pp. $75, $85.
...Dayton, Oh., Morningside Bookshop, 1972, Stiff wraps, exact reprint above. $20, $5, cloth-$15, $7.50-y

DACUS, Robert H., Dr.
"Reminiscences of Company "H", First Arkansas Mounted Rifles." Suffolk, Va., Robt. Hardy Pub., 1986, 8vo, wraps, 52pp.

13 **DADDYSMAN, James W.**
"Matamoros trade, Confederate commerce, diplomacy and intrigue." Newark, Md., University of Delaware Press, 1984. 8vo, cl, 215pp., illus., index. $27.50.

14 **DADE, Virginia E.**
"The Fall of Richmond." (Charleston, S.C., 1885) in "Our Women of the War." p. 99-108.

15 **DAFFAN, Katie**
"My Father as I Remember Him." Houston: Private Print, 1907. 4to, cl, 110pp. $25, $75. Lawrence Aylett Daffan in Co. "G", 4th Texas Reg. Hood's Brig., Battle of Sharpsburg, Manassas, etc. CSA Vets Tributes, etc. See: "Tribute in the "Confed. Vet.", 1907, v.XV, #4, p. 184-186.

16 **DAHLGREN, Ulric**
"Dahlgren's ride into Fredericksburg." John Critcher's letter re: the Dahlgren Memoirs.

17 ...Also re. "Manufactured History" and a sensational press. In: SHSP, 1877, v.III, p. 87-89. See: John Wilder Atkinson, Rich. L.T. Beale, Wm. P. Cabell, Richard G. Crouch, John Wm. Jones, "War time Story of..."

17a **DAILEY, Daphne Lowell**
"Bethel Baptist Church, Caroline County, Virginia, Memorial Service, May 10, 1970 documenting a Funeral Service held in this church on May 11, 1863, for Gen. Thomas Jonathan "Stonewall" Jackson." Published on May 1, 1971, by friends of Bethel church. Edited by Daphne L. Dailey. 4to, wraps, 35p, ills, ports. $6.

18 **"DAILY CITIZEN, The"**
Vicksburg, Miss., July 2, 1863. 1p. folio, 4-columns. Printed on decorative wallpaper. $3500-jk-144. Type-set by CSA printer, but Union captured city and added postscript under last column that "banner of the Union floats over the city." etc. Most copies largely reprints but originals very rare.
...Vicksburg, 1863. Dated June 18, 1863. 14x20", news printed verso wallpaper in purple and brown pattern. $150-bmk.

19 **"DAILY DISPATCH."**
Osyka, Mississippi. Nov. 3, 1864. Pub.: M. Heuman. Quarto, 1pg. Broadside.

20 **DAILY EVENING TRAVELLER,**
Tuesday, Dec. 20, 1870. "A relic of the past." This is the eleventh anniversary of the passage of the "Ordinance of Secession by the Convention of the State of South Carolina (Boston, 1870) Small Broadside. A reprint of the Charleston Mercury broadside of Dec. 20, 1860. "Charleston Mercury Extra". (see also under that title)

21 **"DAILY REPUBLIC EXTRA."**
Columbus, Miss., August 15, 1861. Broadside: 9cm x 27 3/4cm $25. Spec. Bul. relating to war. Not in Crandall.

22 **DAINGERFIELD, Foxhall, Jr.**
The Southern Cross: a play in four acts." Lexington, Ky., 1909. 8vo, pict. wraps, 62pp. $6-bmk-24. Pro-South.

23 **DAINGERFIELD, Henriette Gray**
"That Dear Old Sword." Richmond: Presbyterian Comm. of Publications. (1903) 12mo, cl, front, 99pp. juvenile. Married Foxhall Daingerfield, a Major in CSArmy.

24 **DALBIAC, Philip Hugh, Colonel**
"The American War of Secession, 1863." London: Sonnenschein, 1911. Special Campaign series, #13. 8vo, cl, vii, 187, (1)pp., maps. L2/15s

25 **DALE, Edward Everett**
"The Cherokee in the Confederacy." (Baton Rouge, La.) JSH, May, 1947, v.XIII, #2, p. 159-185, $8.

26 **DALE, Edward Everett, and Gaston Litton, Edts.**
"Cherokee Cavaliers: forty years of Cherokee history as told in the correspondence of the Ridge-Watie-Boudinot family." Norman: Univ. of Okla. Press, 1939. 8vo, cl, illus., xxii, 319, (1)pp. $10, $30. (Civilization of the American Indian) Reprint: 1969, $16-y, $8. Edt: 1940, $7.95, $40. Three chapters, Watie-CSA.

27 ..."Some Letters of General Stand Watie." (Okla. City) Chronicles of Okla., 1921, Jan., v.1, p. 30-59. Civil War corresp. of noted Cherokee-CSA leader in Oklahoma.

28 ..."Arkansas and the Cherokees." In: AHQ, Spring, 1949, v.VIII, p. 104-114. Relates CSA and Union military activities in Arkansas.

29 **DALRYMPLE, Lucinda Lee**
"Journal of a young lady of Virginia." Edt: Emily V. Mason. Baltimore, Lee Memorial Association of Richmond, 1871, (J. Murphy Print) 12mo, wraps, 56pp.

30 **DALTON, Kit**
"Under the Black Flag, by...", Capt. Kit

Dalton, a Confederate soldier, a guerrilla Cap't. under the fearless leader Quantrill and a border outlaw for seventeen years, following the surrender of the Confederates. Associated with the most noted band of free-booters the world has ever known." (Memphis, Tenn., Lockard Publishing, 1914) 12mo, stiff pict. wraps, 252pp., front, illus(ports), pl. $125-jk-138, $15, $22.50, $55-nc, $35-y, $20, $65, $25.

31 **DALTON-ATLANTA Campaign**
See: C.L. Stevenson.

32 **DALY, Louise Porter Haskell**
"Alexander Cheves Haskell, the Portrait of a man." Norwood, Mass., Plimpton Press, 1934. 8vo, cl, front(port), vii, 224pp. $25, $35, $40, $350-b, $3, $125-bmk, $75, $60-nc, $250-bmk-105, 300 copies.

33 **DALY, Robert Welter**
"How the Merrimac won: the strategic story of the C.S.S. Virginia." N.Y., The Crowell Co., (1957) 8vo, cl, d/w, xi, 211pp., notes: p. 189-198, maps, bibliog. (p. 199-204) $. Battle of Hampton Roads, engagement of Monitor and Merrimac, 1862. $20-dabney.

34 ..."Raphael Semmes, Confederate Admiral." N.Y., P.J. Kennedy and Sons, 1965. 12mo, cl, illus., 191pp. (juvenile) $15.

35 **DALZELL, George Walton**
"The Flight from the Flag; the continuing effect of the Civil War upon the American carrying trade." Chapel Hill: Univ. of N. Carolina Pr., 1940, $35. 8vo, cl, dj, front, pls., ports, facsms, xviii, (2), 292pp. $7.50, $10, $17.50.

36 **DALZELL, W.T., Rev.**
"Our Country's Appeal. An address delivered before the Freemasons on "Free Masons who died in the Confederate Army." Shreveport, La., 1867, 8vo, wraps, cover title, 14pp. $20.

37 **DAME, William Meade**
"From Rapidan to Richmond and the Spotsylvania Campaign, a sketch in Personal Narrative of scenes a soldier saw, By William Meade Dame, Private, First Company, Richmond Howitzers." Baltimore: Green Lucas Co., 1920. 8vo, cl, ports(incl. front), xvi, 213pp. $12.50, $15, $16, $18.50, $27.50, $85, $125, $35-y, $40-bmk,$100-b, $50-bmk-105.
..."From Rapidan to Richmond, Spotsylvania . . . Intro: Richard Bowles." Richmond, Va., Owens Civil War Books, 1988. 8vo, cl, dj, 213p, ills, ports, map. $25. Lim. Edt., 500 copies.
...Louisville: Lost Cause micro-cd. $4.08.

38 **DAMON, Henry G.**
"A Florida Boy's Experience in Prison and in escaping." In: SHSP, 1884, v.XII, p. 395-402.

39 ..."Perils of escape from prison." In: CV, 1907, v.15, p. 223-226.

40 **DANA, Charles Anderson, Edt. N.Y. "Sun"**
"Testimony of the Assistant Secretary of War of the United States, Mr. Charles A. Dana." In: SHSP, 1876, v.1, p. 151-153.

41 **DANA, Richard Henry**
"The reasons for not prosecuting Jefferson Davis." In: Mass. Hist. Soc. Pro., 1932, v.LXIV, p. 201-209. Considered needless and embarrassing.

42 **DANCY, James M.**
"Reminiscences of the Civil War." In: FHQ, July 1958, v.XXXVII, #1, p. 66-89.

43 **DANDRIDGE, Danske Bedinger, Mrs.**
"Historic Shepherdstown." Charlottesville, Va., Michie Co., 1910. 12mo, cl, front(map), vi, 362pp. $30. Largely Civil War content.

44 **DANIEL, Charles T.**
"William and Annie, or a tale of love and war and other poems." Guelph, Ontario, Canada, 1864. 16mo, boards. By a soldier of the command of Gen. John H. Morgan, CSA, who was captured and escaped to

Canada where this volume was issued, contains "Song of Morgan's Legion."

45 **DANIEL, Earl S.**
"Lauderdale County (Ala.) soldiers in the Confederate States Army." In: N. Ala. Hist. Assn. Bul., 1960, v.5, p. 13-18. On their units and their officers, 1861-1865.

46 **DANIEL, Edward M.**
"Speeches and Orations of...Compiled by Son." Lynchburg, Va., J.P. Bell, 1911. 8vo, cl, (& full morocco) port (front) 9-787pp. $6, $10, $12.50, $15, $17.50, $20-wan, $40-bmk, $50-109, atg-$60-123. See also: Davis (Jefferson) "Reminiscences Life of Jeff Davis by Distinguished Men of his Time." Intro: John W. Daniel.

47 **DANIEL, Ferdinand Eugene**
"Recollections of a Rebel Surgeon and other sketches; or, In the Doctor's sappy days." Austin, Texas: Von Boeckmann, Schutze, 1899. 12mo, cl, port(front), 264pp., errata slip. $30, $50, $60-bmk, $100-g.
...Chicago: Clinic Pub. Co., 1901, 12mo, cl, illus., 315pp. $15, $17.50, $22.50.

48 **DANIEL, Frederick S.**
"Richmond Howitzers in the War. Four Years Campaigning with the Army of Northern Virginia. By a member of the company." Richmond, 1891. Published anon. 12mo, wraps, 155pp., $10, $13.50, $25, $65, $45, $450-ob.
...See: John M. Daniel "Richmond Examiner". $225-bmk-123 (bound) $150-bmk- 84, $105- bordered.
..."Richmond Howitzers in the war." Gaithersburg, Md., Butternut Press, 1984. $22.50.

49 **DANIEL, James Randolph Vivian**
"Jack Jouette and Paul Revere in petticoats: the heroine of the Battle of Wytheville." (Richmond) Va. Cav., Summer, 1951, v.I, #1, p. 33-35, map, port, view. All night ride of Mary Tynes warning of impending Federal attack, 1862.

50 **DANIEL, John Moncure**
"The Richmond Examiner during the war; or, The writings of John M. Daniel. With a memoir of his life, by his brother, Frederick S. Daniel." New York: American News Co., 1868. $7, $13.75. 8vo, cl, port, 232pp., printed for author. $20, $75-g.
...Do: Same as above, reprint in 1969. $17.50-y.
...N.Y., Arno (1970) "Amer. Journalist Ser." $15.

51 **DANIEL, John W.**
"Robert Edward Lee." Savannah, Ga., 1933. 8vo, wraps, 55pp.

52 **DANIEL, John Warwick**
"The campaign and battles of Gettysburg. An address of...of Lynchburg, Va., before the Va. division: Army of Northern Virginia, at their annual meeting, held in-...Richmond, Va. Oct. 28, 1875." Lynchburg: Bell, Browne Co., 1875, 8vo, wraps, 45pp. $8.50, $25, $100-r, $50-n

53 ..."Character of Stonewall Jackson...by..." Lynchburg: Schaffter and Bryant, 1868. 8vo, wraps, 63pp., errata slip, copy: 3/4Mor. $18. Swem, Dornbusch, $6, $10, $15, $40-bmk, $125-ob.
...See: Edward M. Daniel and Geo. L. Christian.

54 ..."Ceremonies connected with the inauguration of the mausoleum and the unveiling of the recumbent figure of Gen. Edward Lee, at Washington and Lee University, Lexington, Va., June 28, 1883. An oration by...Historical sketch of the Lee Memorial Association, by Wm. Allan. Lynchburg, Va., J.P. Bell, 1883, 8vo, cl, (some wraps) 83pp. $3, $7.50, $25-bmk, $12-nc.
...Richmond, Va., West and Johnston, 1883, $45.

55 ..."Robert Edward Lee an Oration pronounced at the unveiling of the recumbent figure at Lexington, Va., June 28, 1883. By..." Philadelphia: Pawson and Nicholson, n.d. (c.1903). Private Print of 100 copies for Mrs. George Wymberley Jones De Renne. 75 copies, 8vo, iv, 58pp, blue cl, gilt top, plates, gravure of Lee(front). 25 copies, 4to, as above $7.50, $20, $75-bound. In pocket, back cover, 1) clipping from Savannah Morning News, June 10, 1903-"Emory Speer speaks on life of Lee; 2) Letter from Mary Curtis Lee, Aug. 20, 1870; 3) small port of Lee; 4) copy of Lee's coat-of-arms.

..."Appreciations of Robert Edward Lee. An oration pronounced at the unveiling of the recumbent figure at Lexington, Va., June 28, 1883." Strasburg, Va., Shenandoah Pub. House, (1931) 8vo, port, 84pp., wraps ($1.), cloth-$2., $15-bmk.

...Also in: SHSP, 1883, v.XI, p. 340-388. $45.

56 ...John Warwick Daniel (late Senator from Virginia) Memorial Addresses delivered in the Senate and the House of Representatives of the United States. Proceedings in the Senate Feb. 20, 1911, Proceedings in the House June 24, 1911. Compiled under the direction of the Joint Committee on Printing." Washington: 1911 (Gov. Print. Office) sm.4to, gilt cl., engraved port(front), 158pp. $20-bmk. (61st Congress, 3rd Sess., Sen. Doc. 876.

57 ..."Jefferson Davis". In: his "Speeches and Orations...compl. by his son Edward M. Daniel. Lynchburg, Va., J.P. Bell, p. 295-344.

58 ..."Character of Stonewall Jackson." In: "Speeches and Orations", Compl. by son, Edward M. Daniel, Lynchburg, Va., J.P. Bell, p. 41-64.

59 ..."Lee." In: his "Speeches and Orations compl. by his son, Edward M. Daniel, J.P. Bell Col., Lynchburg, Va., p. 187-238.

60 ..."Lee's Birthday." In: SHSP, 1889, v.XVII, p. 350-351.

61 ..."Lee." In: SB, 1883/1884, v.II, p. 1-10.

62 ..."General Jubal A. Early, memorial address by..., before the Association of the Army of Northern Virginia, at the annual meeting in Richmond, Va., Dec. 13, 1894." (Richmond, Va., Southern Historical Society Papers, 1894.) p. 281-335.

63 ..."Gettysburg." In: his "Speeches and Orations...compl. by son, Edward M. Daniel, Lynchburg, Va., J.P. Bell. p. 65-103.

64 ..."One of the Gamest of Modern Fights "Sharpsburg or Antietam"." 15th Va., Semmes Brig., McLaw's Div., at the crisis." In: SHSP, 1905, v.XXXIII, p. 97-99. (cont'd., by Col. E.M. Morrison)

65 ..."The Pulaski Guards, Co. C, 4th Va. Inf. at 1st Battle of Manassas, July 18, 1861. The Original Rebel Yell." In: SHSP, 1904, v.XXXII, p. 174-175. (Cont'd. by J.B. Caddall)

66 ..."Thirty-third Virginia at First Manassas." In: SHSP, 1906, v.XXXIV, p. 363-870. Col. J.W. Allen's report and Col. Arthur C. Cumming's account.

67 ..."Oration at King's Mountain." In: CV, May 1910, v.18, p. 217-124.

68 ..."Oration by... on the life, services and character of Jefferson Davis, delivered under the auspices of the General Assembly of Virginia, at Mozart Academy of Music, Jan. 25, 1890." Richmond: J.W. Randolph and English, 1890. J.L. Hill, Print. 8vo, wraps, 51pp. $15, $6.

...Do: Rich: O'Bannon Print, 46pp. $10-nc, $4.50, $40-jk-122.

...In: SHSP, 1889, v.17, p. 113-159.

69 **DANIEL, Joseph A.**
"The Escape of Captain Joe and Lieuten-

ant Dock Daniel, by Glenn G. Martel." In: "Ark. Hist. Quart., 1947, v.VI, p. 302-343.

70 **DANIEL, Junius, General**
"Battle of Gettysburg, Report of General Junius Daniel, Hdq. Aug. 20, 1863." In: SHSP, 1880, v.VIII, p. 83-92.
...See: P.T. Bennett

71 ..."A sketch of General Junius Daniel." In: LWL, June, 1868, v.V, #2, p. 97-106. See: P.T. Bennett.

72 **DANIEL, Larry J.**
"Manufacturing cannon in the Confederacy." In: CWTI, Nov. 1973, v.12, #7, p. 4-10, 40-46. illus., facsm. ports.

73 ..."Cannoneers in Gray: the field artillery of the Army of Tennessee, 1861-1865." University: University of Alabama, 1984. 8vo, cl, dj, xii, 234pp., illus., index. $20.

74 **DANIEL, Larry J. and Riley W. Gunter**
"Confederate cannon foundries." (Union City, Tenn., Pioneer Press, 1977) 4to, cl, dj, xii, 112pp., illus., facsms, ports, $35, $18.

75 **DANIEL, Lizzie Cary, Mrs., Compl.**
"Confederate Scrapbook. Copied from a scrap-book kept by a young girl during and immediately after the war, with additions from war copies of the "Southern Literary Messenger" and Illustrated News", loaned by friends, and other selections as accredited. Pub. for the benefit of the Memorial Bazaar, held in Richmond, April 11, 1893." Richmond, Va., J.H. Hill Print, 1893. 8vo, cl, color pls.(incl. front) iv, 254pp. $15, $27.50, $37.50, $42.50.

76 **DANIEL, Raleigh Travers**
"The unveiling of the monument to Confederate dead of Alexandria, Va. Speeches of Capt. Raleigh T. Daniel and Gov. Fitzhugh Lee, May 24, 1889." (Alexandria Va., 1889?) 8vo, wraps, cover title, 35pp. Roster: R.E. Lee Camp Confed. Vets.

77 **DANIEL, W. Harrison**
"An Aspect of Church and State Relations in the Confederacy: Southern Protestantism and the Office of Army Chaplain." (Raleigh) NCHRev. January 1959, v.XXXVI, #1, p. 47-71. $8.

78 ..."The Christian Association, a religious society in the Army of Northern Virginia." In: Va. Mag. Hist. and Biog., 1961, p. 93-100.

79 ..."Protestantism and Patriotism in the Confederacy." In: Miss. Quart., 1971, v.XXIV, p. 117-134.

80 ..."Protestant Clergy and Union Sentiment in the Confederacy." In: Tenn. HQ, 1965, p. 284-290, v.XXIII.

81 ..."An aspect of Church and State relations in the Confederacy: Southern Protestantism and the Office of Army Chaplain." In: NCHR, Jan. 1959, v.XXXVI, p. 47-71.

82 ..."The effects of the Civil War on Southern Protestantism." In: Md.H.M., Spring, 1974, v.69, p. 44-63. Hardships during the civil war. $8.

83 ..."Bible Publication and Procurement in the Confederacy." (Lexington, KY.) JSH, May, 1958, v.XXIV, #2, p. 191-201.

84 ..."A Brief Account of the Methodist Episcopal Church South in the Confederacy." In: Methodist Hist., 1968, v.VI, ii, 27-41p.

85 ..."The Southern Baptists in the Confederacy." In: CWH, December 1960, v.VI, #4, p. 389-401.

86 ..."Southern Presbyterians in the Confederacy." In: NCHR, July 1967, 25pp. $8.
..."Southern Protestantism-1861 and After." In: CWH, June 1959, v.V, #3, p. 276-282.

87 ..."Southern Protestantism and Secession." In: Historian, 1967, v.XXIX, p. 391-408.
..."Virginia Baptist, 1861-1865." In: VMHB, Jan., 1964, v.72, #1, p. 94-114.

88 **DANIELL, Elizabeth Otto**
"The Ashburn Murder Case in Georgia Reconstruction, 1868." In: Ga.H.Q., Fall, 1975, v.LIX, #3, p. 298-312. Ashburn was

a white Southern, who turned radical politician.

89 **DANIELS, G.W.**
"American cotton trade with Liverpool under the Embargo and Non-intercourse acts." In: Am. Hist. Rev., Jan. 1916, v.XXI, p. 276-287. Trade between Charleston and Liverpool, 1807-1812, based on Charleston Comm. agt.

90 **DANIELS, Jonathan Worth**
"Mosby: Gray Ghost of the Confederacy." Illustrator: Albert Orbaan. Phila: Lippincott Co., (1959). sm.8vo, cl, illus., 122pp. juvenile litr.

91 ..."Robert E. Lee." Illust: Robt. Frankenburg. Bost: Houghton Mifflin, 1960. North Star Books, #21, juvenile Lit., 8vo, cl, illus., 184pp.

92 ..."Stonewall Jackson." Illustr: William Moyers. N.Y., Random House (1959) Landmark Books, #86, 8vo, cl, illus., 183pp. 3rd printing $1.95.

93 **DANIELS, Josephus**
"John Newland Maffitt." In: CV, June 1922, v.XXX, p. 218-221. See: Mrs. Emma (Martin) Maffitt.

94 **DANNELLY, Elizabeth (A Lady of Georgia, pseud.)**
See: "Destruction of the City of Columbia."

95 **DANNETT, Sylvia G.L.**
"Confederate Surgeon; Aristide Monteiro, by Sylvia G.L. Dannett and Rosamond H. Burkart." N.Y., Dodd, Mead. (1969) 8vo, cl, illus., map, plan, ports, xxii, 226pp. $10. See: Monteiro Memoirs. $20-bmk.

96 ..."And the show went on...in the Confederacy." 1966, Md. Hist. Mag., v.LXI, p. 105-119.

97 **DANNETT, Sylvia G.L. and Katharine M. Jones**
"Our Women of the Sixties." Wash., U.S. Civil War Cent. Comm., 1963, 8vo, pict. wraps, ports, illus., 44pp. $3.50

98 **DANVILLE, Va.-Last Capital of the CSA.**
See: B. Boisseau Bobbitt, New York Herald.

99 **DARDEN, David L.**
"Alabama Secession Convention." (Wetumpka, Ala., Wetumpka Print, (1942). In: Alabama Historical Quarterly, vo. 3, #3 and 4, Fall-Winter 1941. 8vo, wraps (color flags) ports, facsm. (5), (268)-468pp., index. $5. Many biographies, ports of members.

100 **DARGAN, Edwin Charles**
"Harmony Hall; recollections of an old Southern home, 1852-1882." Columbia, S.C., The State Co. (1914) 8vo, cl, 118pp.

101 **"DARING DEED, A**
A True Story of the Confederacy, by an Eye Witness." See: A.J. Rogers.

102 **"DARK Days in Arkansas in 1862."**
In: PCHR, Pulaski CHR, Sept. 1962, v.10, p. 41-51.

103 **DARLING, Jasper Tucker**
"Purify Lee in the Hall of Fame: Put Blood on the Hands of Lincoln." an address in Chicago (1910), wraps, 17pp. $1.50, $2, $5. Jan.1-port, Chi: Libby and Sherwood Print.

104 ..."Praise or Passion, the Capt. Henry Wirz Monument." address delivered May 13, 1909 in Cook County (Ill)." Memorial Hall. Staff Ass'n. With United Daughters of the Confederacy resolution on a slip sheet. n.p. Erection of monument at Andersonville, Ga. cover title. 8vo, wraps, port, (8)pp. See also, Capt. Henry Wirz.

105 ..."Cold Facts. The pen of Col. Lee writes the indictment against the sword of General Lee...an address delivered by Jasper T. Darling of Freeport, Ill., May 30, 1910." 1st edt., 50,000 copies. Chicago, Ill., Libby & Sherwood, 1910. 12mo, cover title, wraps, illus. (port) 15, (1)p.

106 **DARR, John C.**
"Price's Raid into Missouri." In: C. Vet., August 1903, v.II, p. 359-362.

107 **DARROW, Carolyn Baldwin, Mrs.**
"Recollections of the Twiggs Surrender." In: B and L, 1887, v.1, p. 33-39.

108 **DARSEY, B.W.**
"A War Story, or My Experience in a Yankee Prison." Statesboro, Ga., News Print, n.d. (c.1901) Introduction states: "Its been over 36 years since the close of our Civil War..." 8vo, wraps, (24)pp. copy from Georgia Dept. History and Archives. Author was in Co. D, 5th Georgia Cavalry.

109 **DARST, Maury**
"Six Weeks to Texas." In: Texana, Summer, 1968, v.VI, #2, p. 141-152. A new German immigrant family experiences thru South to Texas at outbreak of War.

110 ..."Robert Hodges, Jr.: Confederate Soldier." In: ETHJ, March 1971, IX, #1, p. 20-49, port, notes.

111 ..."Artillery Defenses of Galveston, 1863." In: MHT and Sw., 1974, v.XII, #1, p. 63-67, plates, map.

112 **DASHEW, Drois W.**
"The Story of an Illusion: The Plan to Trade the "Alabama" Claims for Canada." In: CWH, December, 1969, v.XV, #4, p. 332-348.

113 **DAUGETTE, Annie Forney, Mrs.**
"The Life of Major General John H. Forney written by his daughter." In: Ala. Hist. Qu., 1947, v.IX, p. 361-383. See: Gen. John H. Forney.
..."General John H. Forney." In: AHQ, 1949, v.9, #3, p. 362-384.

114 **DAVES, Frank**
"All Quiet Along the Potomac Tonight." Proof that it was written by Thaddeus Oliver, of Twiggs Co., Georgia." In: SHSP, 1880, v.VIII, p. 255-256.

115 **DAVES, Graham**
"Twenty-second North Carolina infantry, its history." In: SHSP, 1896, v.XXIV, p. 256-267.

116 ..."Artillery at the Southern Arsenals. Battery at Fayetteville, N.C." In: SHSP, 1884, v.XII, p. 360.

117 ..."The Battle of Averasboro." In: SHSP, 1879, v.VII, p. 125-126. Add'l. to Gen. W.B. Taliaferro's Report.

118 ..."The Causes of the War, 1861-1865 and events of its first year. Address at Raleigh, N.C., May 10, 1901." In: SHSP, 1904, v.XXXII, p. 275-298.

119 **DAVIDSON, Albert, Lieut.**
"Letters Oct. 1860-Nov. 27, 1864, of a Virginia soldier." In: W.Va.H., Fall, 1979, p. 49-71.

120 **DAVIDSON, Charles A., Major**
"Major Charles A. Davidson: Letters of a Virginia Soldier." In: CWH, March 1976, v.22, #1, p. 16-40.

121 **DAVIDSON, Donald**
"Still Rebels, Still Yankees and other Essays, with wood engravings by Theresa Sherrer Davidson. Introduction: Lewis P. Simpson." (Baton Rouge) Louisiana State University Press (1957) Reprinted (1972). 8vo, cl, dj, front, incl. other woodcuts, xx, 284pp. $7.50

122 ..."Lee in the Mountains and other poems, including the "Tall Men". By Donald Grady Davidson." Boston: Houghton Mifflin Co., 1938. 8vo, cl, dj, x, 137pp. $75-bmk-99.

123 **DAVIDSON, Greenlee, Capt.**
"Captain Greenlee Davidson, CSA, Diary and letters, 1851-1863." Verona, Va., McClure Press, (1975) Charles W. Turner. 4to, wraps, 90pp., (4)lfs, plates, illus.
..."Captain Greenlee Davidson: Letters of a Virginia Soldier. Edt: Charles W. Turner." In: CWH, September 1971, v.XVII, #3, p. 197-221.1ts

124 **DAVIDSON, Hunter**
"Electrical Torpedoes as a System of Defence." In: SHSP, 1876, v.II, p. 1-6.

125 ..."Davis and Davidson. A chapter of War History concerning Torpedoes. Corresp. between Jefferson Davis and Capt. Davidson in relation to the Services of the latter officer." In: SHSP, 1896, v.XXIV, p. 284-291.

126 ..."Mines and Torpedoes during the Rebellion." In: Mag. Hist., Nov. 1908, v.VIII, p. 459-460.

127 **DAVIDSON, James D.**
"Life Behind Confederate Lines in Virginia. The Correspondence of James D. Davidson. Edt: Bruce S. Greenawalt." In: CWH, September, 1970, v.XVI, #3, p. 205-226.

128 ..."Stonewall Jackson in Lexington, Va." In: SHSP, 1881, v.IX, p. 45-46.

129 **DAVIDSON, James Dorman**
"Unionist in Rockbridge County, Va. The correspondence of James Dorman Davidson, concerning the secession Convention, 1861." Edt: Bruce S. Greenawalt." In: VMHB, Jan. 1965, v.73, #1, p. 78-102.

130 **DAVIDSON, James Wood, Colonel**
"Who Burned Columbia? A Review of General Sherman's version of the affair." In: SHSP, v.VII, 1879, p. 185-192. $7-bmk.

131 **DAVIDSON, John M.**
"A wartime story, the Davidson letters, 1862-1865. Edt: Jane Bonner Peacock." Atlanta, 1975, Atlanta Hist. Bul., 109pp., Co. C., the 39th one of three N.C. Regs. with Army of Tenn. Thru Ky., Ga., Tenn. and Miss., illust. $10.

132 **DAVIDSON, Laura Lee**
"The Services of Women of Maryland to the Confederate States." Baltimore, 1920, Prize essay in Balt. Chap., U.D.C. competition. 8vo, wraps, 16pp., tied.
...In: CV, Sept., 1920, v.XXVIII, p. 332-336. $25-bmk.

133 **DAVIDSON, Nora Fontaine M.**
"Cullings from the Confederacy. A collection of Southern poems, original and others, popular during the War Between the States, and incidents and facts worth recalling, 1862-1866. Including the doggerel of the camp, as well as a tender tribute to the dead, compiled by Nora Fontaine M. Davidson." Washington: Rufus H. Darby Print, 1903, 8vo, cl, illus., ports, 163pp. $7.50, $12.50, $15, $35-bmk-109, $20-bmk, $25-bmk.

134 **DAVIDSON, Robert H.M., Col.**
"Oration and Tender of the Monument. Oration on Confederate Dead of Florida." In: SHSP, 1899, v.XXVII, p. 116-124.

135 **DAVIDSON, Victor**
"History of Wilkinson County." Pub: by John Ball Chap. Daughters of the American Revolution. Macon, Ga., J.W. Burke Co.(1930). 8vo, cl, illus., maps, front, ports, fldg. genealogical tables, 645pp. Roster of Wilkinson Co. companies in Civil War, p. (395)-423.
...Spartanburg, S.C. Reprint Co. (1978) $25.

136 **DAVIDSON, W.J.**
"Diary of Private W.J. Davidson, Company C, Forty-first Tennessee Regiment." In: "Annals Army of Tenn." 1878, p. 16-23, 65-70, 122-127, 165-170, 214-219, 279-282, 325-329, 366-369. See: Sumner A. Cunningham.

137 **DAVIE, W.R., Jr.**
"Fort Sumter. Report of the Bombardment, as given in the Charleston "Courier" April 13, 1861. With some account of the beginning of the News Association in the U.S." In: SHSP, 1898, v.XXVI, 1101-1109.

138 **DAVIES, A.M.**
"Petersburg, the battle of the Crater." In: B and G, 1894, v.III, p. 249-252.

139 **DAVIES, Wallace E.**
"The Problem of Race Segregation in the Grand Army of the Republic." (Baton Rouge, La.) JSH, May, 1947, v.XIII, #3, p. 354-372. The Northerner, down South, out-segregated the Southerner!

140 ..."Was Lucius Fairchild a demagogue?" In: Wis. MH, June 1948, v.32, p. 418-428, port. notes. Denounces Grover Cleveland for ordering return of CSA battle flags (1887) to Southern states.

141 **DAVIESS, M.T.**
"Col. Joseph H. Daviess." In: LWL, 1868/1869, v.6, p. 293-301.

142 **DAVIS, Archie K.**
"Col. Harry Burgwyn of the 26th N.C. Regiment." Jackson, N.C., 1961, 8vo, wraps, front, 12pp.

143 ..."She disdains to pluck one laurel from a sister's brow: disloyalty to the Confed. in N.C." In: VMHB, April 1980, v.88, #2, p. 131-147.

144 **DAVIS, Burke**
"The Long Surrender." N.Y., Random House, 1985. 8vo, cl, 319pp., illus., bibliog., index. See: Jno. Brubacker. $20.

145 ..."Appomattox Closing Struggle of the Civil War." N.Y., Haper and Row (1963). 12mo, cl, d/w, 167, (4)pp., illus. $3. ports, maps. "Breakthrough Books."

146 ..."To Appomattox, nine April days, 1865." N.Y., Rinehart and Co. (1959). $6, $12.50-y, $20, $7.50. 8vo, cl, illus., ports, maps, facsm., 433pp. Other editions: 2nd Edt. (1959); the Book Club Edt., slightly smaller, boards/cl. spine. (Jan. 1971) 5th Edt., large 8vo, cl, $8.95, also in paper, $.75, 1967-$6, $15-bmk.

147 ..."Gray Fox: Robert E. Lee and the Civil War." N.Y., Rinehart and Co. (1956) and (1967) $12.50-y, $20, $18. 8vo, cl, maps, ports, illus., xi, 466pp. $7.50. Same: Book Club Edt., signed by author. $25.

148 ..."Jeb Stuart, the last cavalier." N.Y., Rinehart and Co. (1957). 8vo, cl, dj, illus., ports, maps, 462pp. $7.50, $15-y, $12, $12.50. Edition: 6th print. (1967) (c.1975) N.Y., Bonanza Print, $25-atg. $32.50.

149 ..."Lee takes command (Army of N. Va., 1862) In: CWH, Dec. 1957, v.3, p. 377-383.

150 ..."Our incredible Civil War." N.Y., Holt, Rinehart and Winston, 1960. 8vo, cl, dj, 249pp., illus. $15. Anecdotes, coincidences, oddities. (Feb. 1961) 2nd Print, $5, (1966) $20-bmk, $5.

151 ..."They Called Him Stonewall, a life of Lt. Gen. T.J. Jackson, CSA." N.Y., Rinehart and Co. (1954). sm.8vo, cl, illus., ports, maps and liner-map, 470pp. $12.50, $18, $25. Other editions: Dec. 1957-6th printing, $6. (1967)-7th print. $10; 11th print-$15; (1968)-$8.50; (May 1972), 12th print, $15, $20.

152 ..."Boy colonel of the Confederacy. The life and times of Henry King Burgwyn, Jr." Chapel Hill: University of N.C. Press, 1983. 8vo, cl, 420pp., illus., $30.

153 **DAVIS, Charles Hall**
"What became of the Confederate Treasury gold?" In: TylerQHGM, Oct. 1950, v.32, p. 121-126. Account of Wm. T. Davis' daughter's letter to Joseph Claiborne Davis (Apr. 17, 1914) of Dunn, NC. Re: a carpetbag (2) contents unknown in temporary custody of Wm. T. Davis, shortly after Lee's surrender.

154 **DAVIS, Charles S.**
"Colin J. McRae: Confederate Financial Agent." Tuscaloosa, AL.: Confed. Pub. Co., 1961, Confed. Centennial Studies, #17, 12mo, stiff wraps, 101pp. port. Lim. Edt. 450 copies $15-bmk, $5.

155 **DAVIS, Charles Shepard**
"Stephen R(ussell) Mallory: leader of Confed. sea power (1861-1865)." In: Fla.

State Univ. Studies, 1953, v.10, p. 49-61. notes.

156 **DAVIS, Creed T., Second Co.**
"Diary..." In: "Contributions to a History of Richmond Howitzers." Richmond, Va., Carlton McCarthy, 1884, p. 9-35, v.3.

157 ..."Prison Diary of..." In: "Contributions to a History of Richmond Howitzers." Richmond, Va., J.W. Randolph and English, 1886, v.4, p. 3-28.

158 **DAVIS, Curtis Carroll**
"Belle Boyd in Camp and Prison. A new edition prepared from new materials, by Curtis Carroll Davis." South Brunswick, N.J., Thos. Yoseloff (c.1968) 448pp. $35. 12mo, cl, dj, facsm., ports, illus., $9.50. "A catalogue of Civil War spy memoirs separately." 401-414.

159 ..."A Catalogue of Civil War Spy memories separately published." See: his edt: Belle Boyd for 1968.

160 ..."Effie Goldsborough-Confederate courier." In: CWTI, April 1968, v.VII, #1, p. 29-31, illus.

161 "...The Pet of the Confederacy." Still?, Fresh findings about Belle Boyd (Confederate spy)." In: Md. Hist. Mag., Spring 1983, p. 35-53.

162 **DAVIS, Curtis Carroll and Innes Randolph**
"Elegant Old Rebel." (Richmond) Va. Cavl. Summer 1958, v.VIII, #1, p. 42-47. ports, facsms, map, illus., "author of the classic hate poem in the English tongue." See: Innes Randolph.

163 **DAVIS, Edwin Adams**
"Fallen Guidon. The Forgotten Saga of General Jo Shelby's Confederate Command. The Brigade that never surrendered, and its expedition to Mexico." Santa Fe, New Mexico: Stagecoach Pr., 1962. 8vo, cl, dj, illus., ports, incl. front, maps, xiii, 173, (2)pp. 1000 copies. $7.50.

164 ..."Heroic Years. Louisiana in the War for Southern Independence.-WBRZ-TV 1964. Lecture in Louisiana History." Baton Rouge: Louisiana State Univ. (1964) 8vo, cl, dj, illus., xv, 130pp. $25-b, $3.

165 **DAVIS, Edwin Arnold**
"Heritage of Valor. The Picture Story of Louisiana in the Confederacy." Baton Rouge: Louisiana State Archives and Records Comm., 1964. 4to, stiff wraps, illus., maps, 212pp. $3.

166 **DAVIS, Emma-Jo L.**
"Mulberry Island, Va., and the Civil War, Apr. 1861-May 1862." In: Archaelogical Society of Virginia. Quarterly Bul. June 1971. 27pp(of 52) 4 maps, cover port. of Gen. John B. Magruder. $7.50.

167 **DAVIS, Evangeline and Burke**
"Rebel Raider: a Biography of Admiral Semmes." Phila: Lippincott (1966) 8vo, cl, illus., map, ports, 149pp. $6. juvenile.

168 **DAVIS, Ezekiel Andrew**
"Confederate life at home and in Camp, seven letters by...Edt: George W. Clower, Jr." In: Ga. Hist. Quart., 1956, v.XL, p. 298-309.

169 **DAVIS, Garrett Morrow**
"Hugh Darnaby a story of Kentucky." Wash: Gibson Bros., 1900, 12mo, cl, 253pp. Fiction. Adventures in central Ky. with CSA.

170 **DAVIS, George, Hon.**
"Letter from the Hon. George Davis, late Attorney-General of the Confederate States. Sept. 4, 1877." In: SHSP, 1878, v.V, p. 124-126.

171 ..."Memorial of the Hon. George Davis." (Wilmington, N.C., 1896) Chamber of Commerce. 8vo, wraps, 33pp. Senator from N.C., last Atty-Gen. of the CSA. Life of and extracts from his speeches.

172 **DAVIS, Granville D.**
"Arkansas and the Blood of Kansas."

173 ..."An uncertain Confederate Trumpet; a study of erosion in morale." In: W.Tenn.HSP, Dec. 1984, v.38, p. 19-50.

174 **DAVIS, Hugh C.**
"Hilary A. Herbert: Bourbon Apologist." In: AR, July, 1967, v.20, #3, p. 216-225.

175 **DAVIS, J.L.**
"Grant's failure at Lake Providence." In: CV, Oct. 1914, v.XXII, p. 459-460. Grant's failure to enter Vicksburg via Lake Providence in 1863.

176 **DAVIS, Jackson Beauregard, Edt.**
"The Life of (Col.) Richard Taylor." New Orleans, La., 1941. 8vo, wraps, 80pp. Also in: LHQ, 1941, v.XXIV, p. 49-127.

177 ..."Slavery in the Cherokee Nation." In: Ch.Okl., Dec. 1933, v.XI, p. 1056-1072.

178 **DAVIS, James A.**
"51st Virginia Infantry." Lynchburg, Va. H.E. Howard, 1984, (J.P. Bell Print) Lim. Atg. Edt., 8vo, cl, dj, (3)102pp. maps. $17.50

179 **DAVIS, James Lucius**
"The trooper's manual: or, Tactics for light dragoons and mounted riflemen. Comp. abridged and arranged by Col. J. Lucius Davis, graduate of US Mil. Acad., West Point, formerly an officer in the US Army many years commander and instructor of volunteer cavalry." Richmond, Va., A Morris, 1861. 12mo, cl, 284, 19pp. $375-jk, $175-bmk.

180 **DAVIS, Jane R.**
"Please assassinate my brother.: N.Y., Vantage Press, 1973. 8vo, cl, dj, 325pp. $10. Author claims Lincoln as illegitimate half-brother of Jefferson Davis, who hired Booth to kill Lincoln. Also, that she's a descendant of Davis and the story handed down in family.

181 **DAVIS, Jefferson**
"Acceptance and Unveiling of Statues of Jefferson Davis and James Z. George." Presented by the State of Mississippi, proceedings in Congress and in Statuary Hall United States Capital." Washington, D.C., Gov. Pr. Off. 1932. 8vo, cl, ports(front), 60pp. $7.50-y, $5, $25.

182 ..."An Address to the People of the Free States by the President of the Southern Confederacy." Richmond, Jan. 5, 1863. Broadside: 11 1/2x8 1/2. Richmond Enquirer Print (1863). $100. (Spurious response of Davis to Lincoln's Emancipation Proclamation, obviously a Yankee propaganda trick to discredit CSA cause in European eyes. $400-streeter, $450-eberstat.

183 ..."Amnesty: in the House of Representatives, Monday, Jan. 10, 1876." (Washington, 1876). 8vo, sewed, 32pp. $10-bmk, $5. Speeches: Mr. Blaine and Benj. H. Hill.

184 ..."Andersonville and other War Prisons." In: Belford's Mag., Jan/Feb., 1890, v.IV, #20/21, p. 161-178, 337-353. Slip: "passing notes", inserted, p. 161. Jan. issue has "Autobiography of Jeff. Davis." p. 255-266; Edt. Dep: "Andersonville and other War-Prisons", p.273-275.
...N.Y., Belford Co., (Pub. Belford Mag.) 1890. 8vo, wraps, 19 unnumbered leaves. Also: CV, Mar/Apr., 1907, v.XV, p. 107-113, 161-166.
...Dorn-II, 628 copy has (27)pp. $75-ob.

185 ..."Autobiography of Jefferson Davis." In: Belford's Magazine, Jan., 1890." 8vo, 12pp. $10-bmk.

186 ..."Autobiography written in Nov. 1889." In: CV, May, 1907, v.XV, p. 217-222, ports.

187 ..."Beauvoir-Jefferson Davis Shrine. Last Home of Jefferson Davis." (Gulfport, Miss: Gulfport Print, 1939) 8vo, color wraps, 32pp., port, illus.
...1945, note by compiler, $12-bmk.

188 ..."Bibliography-see Robert McElroy's Life of Davis." fine, critical bibliog., p. 699-759.

189 ..."Broadside printed on silk, 9"x12", contains two ports, one in 1861, the other in 1866. Below are a few lines of biography. Issued as a Veteran Soldiers' Souvenir. Atlanta, Ga., (1886). $25.
...See: "By this we conquer..."

190 ..."Calendar of the Jefferson Davis postwar miscellany in the Louisiana Historical Association collection." New Orleans, La., Confederate Memorial Hall, 1943. Biblio.and Ref. Ser. 314, 8vo, cl, 325pp.
...1970 reprint, $29.50-y, NY, Burt Franklin "Research and source works series, American classics in history and social science." $15.

191 ..."Capture of Jefferson Davis." Selma, Alabama, May 17, 1865. Folio, 1pp., $25. Federal Union, capture of Davis and Staff; Davis sent to Washington. Proclamation of the Governor.

192 ...Carte de visit: Mr. Davis by Brady, Pub. by Anthony, showing head and shoulders; Mrs. Davis in full length by Anthony. $20.

193 ..."The Celebrated Bail Bond. Jefferson Davis, Pres. Late Confederate States, accepted by the U.S. Courts at Richmond, Va., Nov. 1867." Broadside: Quarto, facsimilie of original bond and signatures of Bondsmen, i.e., Horace Greely, Aug. Schell, Cornelius Vanderbilt and seventeen other prominent citizens of the U.S. Richmond: Lito. of Ch. I Ludwid, 1895. $5.

194 ..."A citizen of Mississippi." By Oscar L. Davis. In: South. Mag., 1936, v.II, #11, p. 16-17, 45.

195 ..."A floral ship of state; last honors of Texas men to their chieftain." In: South. Mag., 1936, v.II, #12, p. 12, 28-29, 48.

196 ..."Jefferson Davis by Lyon Gardiner Tyler." In: Tyler QHGM, 1936, v.XVII, p. 203-207.

197 ..."Communication from the President of the Confederate States, transmitting the credentials of Hon. Alexander H. Stephens." (Montgomery, c.1861) 8vo, sewn, 5pp. $47.50.

198 ..."Correspondence between the President and General Joseph E. Johnston, together with that of the Secretary of War and the Adjutant and Inspector General, during months of May, June and July, 1863. Pub. by order of Congress." Richmond, Va., R.M. Smith, Pub. Print., 1864. 8vo, sewed, 64pp. $15, $30(auc-68) $40.

199 ..."Correction of errors in statement of Gov. Anderson and letter of Gen. Echols." In: SHSP, 1883, v.11, p. 559-564.

200 ..."Correspondence of Jefferson Davis and J. Thomas Scharf." Edt: Frank F. White, Jr. (Jackson, Miss., Jour. Miss. Hist., April 1948) v.X, #2, p. 118-131.

201 ..."Debate on the pensioning of Jefferson Davis...condensed from Proceedings of the U.S. Senate, March 3, 1879." Washington, 1879. 8vo, sewn, caption title, 8pp. $2.50, $5.

202 ...Davis, Jefferson and Judah P. Benjamin

203 ..."Document, signed, 12 1/2x16". Richmond, Va., April 3, 1863. $1500-gdsp-1982. Printed document, sig: both Davis and Benjamin appointing Philip A. Clayton Marshal of the Distr. of Georgia. (framed 17 1/4x19 1/3".

204 ..."Election, Wednesday, November 6th, 1861. For President, Jefferson Davis, of Mississippi. For Vie-President, Alexander H. Stephens, of Georgia..." Broadside, 12mo. $45-jk.

205 ..."Election ticket for Jefferson Davis for President and Alexander H. Stephens as Vice-President. Lists Roger Pryor for Congress and 18 other names. 4x6", printed on blue paper. $48-resnick.

206 ..."Escape of a Confederate officer from prison. What he saw at Andersonville.

How he was sentenced to death and saved by the interposition of President Abraham Lincoln." Norfolk, a., Landmark Pub. Co., 1892. 12mo, wraps, 72pp. $20, $40, $50. Served under Wirz at Andersonville.

207 ..."Ex-President Davis' last paper of a public nature, written from a sick bed 5 weeks before his death. Occasion, the Centennial Celebration of the Ratification of N.C. of the Constitution of the U.S., at Fayetteville, Nov. 21, 1889. Dated Beauvoir, Miss., Oct. 30, 1889." Richmond, Va. (1896). Litho. A Hoen and Co. Colored Broadside folio, 16 1/2x21", port of Davis and 3 CSA flags. $15.

208 ..."Jeff Davis in the White House. Air - "Ye Parliments of Old England." Broadside verse, 4 1/2 x 11", ornamental borders. $25-bmk. Rudolph-136.

..."Jefferson Davis on Conscription; recently discovered letter of Confederate President to war-time Governor of Georgia is strong defense of the war draft act." In: CV, July 1922, v.XXX, p. 253-255.

209 ..."Jefferson Davis. An Illustrated description of the Home Life and Surroundings of the Sage of Beauvoir." New Orleans, la., n.d.(c.1880) 12mo, wraps. $5.

210 ..."Jefferson Davis recalls the past: notes of a wartime aide, William Preston Johnston." (Jackson, Miss.) Jour. Miss. Hist., May, 1971, v.XXXIII, #2, p. 167-178.

211 ..."A letter by Jefferson Davis relating to events preceding his capture." Ga. Hist. Quart., 1947, XXXI, p. 30-33.

212 ..."Letter from President Davis-Reply to Mr. Hunter." In: SHSP, 1878, v.V, p. 222-227.

213 ..."Letter from Jefferson Davis to General Beauregard." In: Ala. HQ, 1940, v.II, p. 460-462. Richmond, Oct. 16, 1861, CSA military affairs.

214 ..."Jefferson Davis: leader of a lost cause, refuted." In: TylerQHGM, 1938, v.XX, p. 4-12. Review of article-"Jeff Davis leader of, etc."

215 ..."Life of..., From Authentic Sources. By a South Carolinian." London: G.W. Bacon and Co., (1865). 12mo, cl, iv, 96pp. (Sabin-88115, 18839) "Yale copy attributes to G.W. Bacon, who presented it to them in 1871."
...London, 1871.

216 ..."Life and Reminiscences of Jefferson Davis by Distinguished Men of his time." with an introduction by John Warwick Daniel, U.S. Senator from Virginia. 8vo, cl, illus., front(port), xviii, 490pp. $50, $40. Baltimore: R.H. Woodward Co., 1890. $5, $7.50, $12.50, $17.50.

217 ...Lithograph folded sheet, 4 1/2x2 3/4". Front a portrait of Davis-"Jeff Davis after the surrender of Fort Sumter, Apr. 13, 1861 and Jeff Davis after the Surrender of Vicksburg, July 4, 1863." A small window, with a pull-tab, changes the expression from smile (Sumter) to a frown (Vicksburg). $50. Boston (c.1863) Designed and pub. by D.C. Johnston. (The "American Cruikshank") Devices such as this are very scarce.

218 ..."A Memorial of the 6th Annual reunion of United Confederate Veterans Ass'n., and the laying the cornerstone of the Jefferson Davis monument. Richmond, Va., June 30, July 1 and 2, 1896." (Richmond, Va., 1896) (Swem-3649) 8vo, wraps, pls., map, unpaginated.

219 ..."The Jefferson Davis Memorial in the Vicksburg National Military Park." Vicksburg, Miss., Printing Co., 1927, 8vo, wraps, 28pp. (McElroy bibliog.)

220 ..."In Memoriam. Jefferson Davis. State of Texas: House of Representatives, 22nd Legislature." (Austin): Henry Hutchings,

March 7, 1891. 8vo, black wraps, 59pp., borders in black. $15, $25.

221 ...Long address by F.R. Lubbock, long friend of Davis and with him when captured. See also under F.R. Lubbock.

222 ..."Inaugural address of President Davis, delivered at the Capitol, Monday, Feb. 18, 1861, at 1 o'clock, P.M., Montgomery, Ala." Montgomery, Ala., Shorter and Reid, 1861. 8vo, wraps, 8pp. $35, #37.50, $125, $50. Also in: SHSP, 1874, v.1, p. 19-23.

223 ..."Jefferson Davis, Constitutionalist; His Letters, papers and Speeches. Collected and edited by Dunbar Rowland. Jackson, Miss., Mississippi Department of Archives and History, 1923, (J.J. Little and Ives Co., N.Y.) 10 volumes. Tall 8vo, cl, port(front) ea. vol., 2-pls. capitol, 1-composit photo, xxxviii, 603; viii, 608; v.598; v.581; xv, 598; svi, 591; ix, 592; ix, 607; x, 605; v, 458. Bibliog-Index, p. 283-458. $125, $175, $200, $275, $295-y, $30-ea.
...N.Y., AMS Press, 1971. 10vol., $425 or $42.50 per vol.
..."Oh, Jeff! Why don't you come?" Broadside 5 1/8 x 9", $150-bmk. Satiric poetical appeal for Davis to liberate Baltimore.

224 ..."Reviews of Jefferson Davis, Constitutionalist, his letters, papers and speeches." Jackson, Miss., Miss. Dept. Archives and Hist., 1924, 8vo, wraps, ports, plates, 88pp. $12.50, Lim. edt., 1000 copies. $30-n, $14-nc. Same: 8vo, wraps, 11pp., silk cord tied. $3.50

225 ..."Jefferson Davis and "Stonewall Jackson". (Thomas Jonathan Jackson). The Life and Public Services of Each, with the military career and the death of the latter." Phila: John E. Potter and Co. (1866) (copy: M. Doolady) Tk. 12mo, decr. cl, 149,3000pp. ports of Jefferson and Jackson. $18-reb, $10. Append. of 52pp. shows evidence against Davis was bribery by Judge Adv.-Gen. Holt. See also: M. Addey's similar title.

226 ..."Life of Jefferson Davis, with an authentic account of his private and public career, and his death and burial; together with the Life of Stonewall Jackson...including his glorious military career and his tragic death on the battlefield." Phila: Keystone Pub. Co., 1890. 12mo, cl, illus., ports, 197, 300pp. $15. Largely a reprint, chaps. II thru XVII exact as Addey's 1863 edition.

227 ..."Message du President...au Senat et a la Chambre des Etats Confederes..." Richmond 12 Jan. 1863." Paris: Impr. de Dubuisson. sm.4to, wraps, 12pp., double column.
...Do: "le 7 Decembre 1863..." Paris, 1864, 8vo, wraps, 46pp. (old) $10.

228 ..."In Memoriam Jefferson Davis. A Tribute of Respect offered by the Citizens of Charleston, S.C." Charleston, S.C., Walker, Evans and Cogswell, 1890. 8vo, wraps, 79pp. $20, $12.50, $10. 8vo, wraps, 79pp.
...Louisville, Ky., Lost Cause Press, microcard, $2.45.

229 ...New Orleans, La., 1889, Broadsheet card, port. above 4 lines of verse $30-jk-122.

230 ..."In Memoriam." Broadsheet Card. New Orleans, La., 1889. Portrait above 4-lines of verse. $30-jk-127.

231 ..."In Memoriam." State of Texas, Joint Session of the 22nd Legislature, House of Representatives (1891). 3000 copies for joint session, for Senate. Folder, 16pp. $10.

232 ..."Concurrent Resolution adopted by the Senate and House of Representatives, State of South Carolina on the occasion of the Death of Jefferson Davis." n.p., n.d., Folder 4pp. hard-back sheep, tied with black ribbons.

233 ..."In Memoriam." Wilmington's Tribute of respect to Ex-President Jefferson Davis. Containing the exercises of memorial services, Mr. Davis' letter to the Fayetteville Committee and Mr. Davis' reply to Gen. Wolseley." Wilmington, N.C., Messenger Steam Pr., 1890. (cover, all pages with black border) 8vo, wraps, cover title, 36pp.

234 ..."Message of...to the House, Mar. 10, 1863." (Richmond, 1863) Claim of D.J. Turner against Com. T.T. Hunter sinking dredge in Dismal Swamp, "in public interest"." folder, 8vo, 4pp. (not in Cran-Har) $10.

235 ..."Message of...Jan. 6, 1865." (Richmond, 1865) "Relative to impressment of brandy by CSA officers for Medical Dept." (not in Cran-Har.) 8vo, folder, 8pp., sewed. $20.

236 ..."Relations of States. Speech of...of Miss., delivered in the Senate of the U.S., May 7, 1860, on the resolutions submitted by him, Mar. 1, 1860." Baltimore: John Murphy and Co., 1860. 8vo, wraps, 15pp. $3, $6, $10.

237 ..."Message of the President. To the Senate and House of Representatives of CSA." n.p., (1862) 3pp. $12. Confirming report of Gen. Albert Sidney Johnston's death, at Shiloh, Apr. 6, 1862.

238 ..."Message (Jan. 7, 1864) relating to Cherokee Indians." n.p., 2pp. sheet. (Henkel Cat. 1090)

239 ..."Message of the President. To the Senate and House of Representatives of Confederate States." Richmond: Jan. 12, 1863. Sewed, 8vo, 16pp. $80-streeter, $60-gdsp. $50.

240 ..."Message of the President. To the Senate and House of Representatives of the Confederate States of America, April 7, 1862." (Richmond, Va., 1862) 12mo., 3p-fold. Victory at Shiloh and death of Gen. Johnston.

241 ..."Message to the Senate and House of Representatives." Richmond, Va., Dec. 7, 1863." 8vo, sewn, 29pp. $100-jk-127. Reports fall of Vicksburg, Port Hudson, the Union invasion of Arkansa, CSA defeat in Tenn. "grave reverses", Crandall 627.

242 ..."The Obsequies of Jefferson Davis, the Only President of the Confederate States of America; in the city of New Orleans, Wednesday, Dec. 11, 1889." New Orleans, La., Brandao and Gill, 1890. 8vo, wraps, 73pp. (McElroy bibliog.)

243 ..."The Papers of Jefferson Davis, Vol. 1, 1808-1840. Haskell M. Monroe, Jr. and James T. McIntosh, Edts." Baton Rouge: Louisiana University Press, 1971. 8vo, cl, illus., chronology, Append., Index, xci, 594pp. Vol. II, 1841-1846, xxxix, 806pp. $35-y, $20, $15, $33. N.Y., Burt Franklin, 1972. "Research and source works series, American classics in historical and social science." $75.
..."The Papers of Jefferson Davis, Vol. 3, July 1946-December 1848. Edited by James T. McIntosh.
..."The Papers of Jefferson Davis, Vol. 4, 1849-1852. Edt: Lynda Lasswell Crist. Intro: Richard E. Beringer." Baton Rouge: Louisiana University Pr., 1983. 8vo, cl, dj, xxxix, 472pp. front, illus., maps, notes, append., sources, index. $37.50.
..."The Papers of Jefferson Davis, Vol. 5."Edt: Linda Lasswell Crist and Mary Seaton Dix. Baton Rouge: Louisiana State University Press, 1985. 8vo, cl, dj, xliii, 557pp. Intro: Robert M. Utley. $37.50.

244 ..."The Peace Commission-Letter from Ex-President Davis." In: SHSP, 1877, v.IV, p. 208-214. See: R.M.T. Hunter, reply, IV, p. 303.

245 ..."The peace conference of 1865, an unpublished letter from Jefferson Davis. With introductory note by J. William

Jones." In: Century, Nov. 1908, v.LXXVII, p. 67-69.

246 ..."Portrait of Jefferson Davis, engraved by William Sartain." Phila: Wm. Sartain, (old) $15. Plate: 9 3/8x11 1/8", overall: 15x19"

247 ..."Portrait (before the war) 16x20" hvy. paper." $4; mounted on cardboard, $4.50; 20x30 $7, mounted $7.50; 30x40" $10, mounted $10.50. Adv. in CV, v.40, p. 199.

248 ..."Portrait, three-quarter length, standing by W.B. Matthews, 1908. size: 6 3/4x4 3/8"

249 ..."Print of his last letter in color, written from his sick bed just five weeks before death. Shows Davis with three CSA battle flags by Hoen, of Richmond." 1896. 16x20 $12.50, $5.

250 ..."Jefferson Davis, privateer." In: SHSP, 1903, v.XXXI, p. 53-55. From: Savannah News, Dec. 1, 1903.

251 ..."Prison Life of Jefferson Davis." In: LWL, Aug. 1866. v.1, #4, p. 277-282. See: Lt. Col. John J. Craven.

252 ..."President Jefferson Davis." In: Blackwood's Edinburgh Magazine, Sept. 1862. v.92, p. 343-352.

253 ..."Proceedings incident to the celebration of the 100th anniversary of his birth." Montgomery Ala., 1908. 8vo, wraps, 8pp. $5.

254 ..."Relations of States. Speech of...of Mississippi, delivered in the Senate of U.S., May 7, 1860, on Resolution submitted by him on 1st March, 1860." Baltimore: John Murphy and Co., 1860. 8vo, wraps, 15pp. $12.50.

255 ..."Reviews of Jefferson Davis, Constitutionalist. His Letters, Papers, and Speeches. Jackson, Miss., 1924. 8vo, wraps, 11pp., tied with cord. $2.
...Do: 88pp., illus., $14-nc-'76.

256 ..."The Restoration of the name Jefferson Davis to Cabin John Bridge, Washington, D.C. Being the Official correspondence leading to this restoration." New Orleans, La., Confederate Southern Memorial Ass'n. of New Orleans. (1909) 8vo, orig. wraps, 24pp. $6.50.

257 ..."The Rise and Fall of the Confederate Government." N.Y., D. Appleton and Co., 1881. 8vo, gray cloth, 3/4 Mor., or full Mor., edition of superior paper and printing, fine set, $165. front(port), plates, ports, 13-maps, plans part folding, xx1, (1), 808pp. $75, $125.
...London, Longmans, Green and Co., $100, $125. also a 1912 edition. $35.
...Richmond, Va., (1938) Garrett and Massie. "United Daughters of the Confederacy Memorial Edition." 8vo, cl, fronts (ports), 1-illus., maps, 604, 675pp. $50, $30.
...Louisville, Ky., Lost Cause Pr., microcard, $9.27, v.II, $9.47.
...N.Y., Yoseloff, (1958) 2 vols., boxed, Full Mor., $75, $90, $125.
...Reprint, abridged for modern readers. Foreword: Earl Schenk Miers. N.Y., Collier Books (1961) $11.50, $9. Colliers Original Books, 12mo, cl, 573pp.
...Gulfport, Miss., Centennial Edition. Edt: Estelle T. Buchanan Heiss. 1st Edt. Mrs. John L. Heiss, 1963. 8vo, cl, front, illus., pt. 1, v.I,, Intro: Bell Wiley.

258 ..."A short history of the Confederate States of America." N.Y., Belford Co., 1890. 8vo, cl, port(front, xii, 505pp. $25, $35, $18.50, $22.50, $45, $75.

259 ..."Robert E. Lee." Edt: Col. Harold B. Simpson (Hillsboro, Texas) Hill Junior College. (1965) 8vo, cl, d/w, xx, 246pp., facsm., ports (incl. front) OP, $7.50, $12.

260 ..."Robert E. Lee." Hillsboro, Texas: Hill Junior College, 1966. 8vo, cl, d/w, p.xiii, 81. $30, $5. (1890, Jan.-North American Review) Civil War Centennial Edition Limited Edt: 100 copies $25.

261 ..."Robert E. Lee." In: (N.Y.) "North American Review." Jan, 1890, p. 12 (p.55-66) $3., $15.
...CV, 1931, v.39, p. 14-19.

262 ..."The Second Annual Message of his Excellency the President of the Confederate States to Congress, Jan. 12, 1863." London: 1863. 12mo, sewn, 38pp. (old) $5.

263 ..."Jefferson Davis, A Sketch of the Life and Character of the Pres. of the C.S.A." See: William T. Walthall.

264 ...BROADSIDE, 5 1/2x10" "Soldier's Address." "Old and battle-scarred comrades, we have met on this day to pay our humble respect to that brave and true and noble son Hon. Jefferson Davis...27 years ago we left our peaceful homes and gallantly went forth to fight thousands of Yankees, millions of lice, etc., winding up with "the most important thing to consider, where you get the best and most chewing tobacco for the smallest amount of money...Model Tobacco Works, Winston, N.C.", handed out to crowd listening to Davis." (c.1888) $20.

265 ..."Jefferson Davis".In: SHSP, See: Albert S. Johnston, Chs. M. Blackford, John W. Brown, Micajah H. Clark, John W. Daniel, George Davis, Mrs. Jefferson Davis, Thomas C. DeLeon, C.E. Fenner, Walter L. Fleming, Wade Hampton, Wm. P. Johnston, John W. Jones, Stephen D. Lee, Francis R. Lubbock, New Orleans Picayune, James H. Parker, Leslie J. Perry, Richmond, Va. Dispatch, Justus Scheibert, George Shea, Wm. H. Steward, W.T. Walthall.

266 ..."Some Civil War Documents, 1862-1864. Pope Pius IX and Jefferson Davis." In: Records of the Amer. Catholic Hist. Soc., v.XIV, 1903, p. 264, ff. Phila.

267 ..."Some post-war letters from J. Davis to his former aide-de-camp William Preston Johnston." Edt: Arthur Marvin Shaw. Richmond, Virginia Historical Society, 1943. Rep: Va. Mag. of Hist. and Biog., v.51, #2, April 1943, wraps, 9pp.

268 ..."Address on presentation of badges and Membership in Association Army of Tennessee." In: SHSP, 1889, v.17, p. 191-193.

269 ..."Beast Butler outlawed." In: SHSP, 1886, v.14, p. 470-475.

270 ..."Confederate Privateersmen." In: SHSP, 1883, v.11, p. 181-184.

271 ..."Correspondence between Governor Vance and President Davis." In: SHSP, 1896, v.24, p. 284-291.

272 ..."Extract from eulogy on Lee." In: SHSP, 1883, v.11, p. 428-429.

273 ..."A grand meeting in New Orleans, La., April 25, 1882, v.10, p. 223-244.

274 ..."Inaugural address...Feb. 1861." In: SHSP, 1876, v.1, p. 19-23.

275 ..."The Last Telegram of the Confederacy." In: SHSP, 1879, v.7, p. 127.

276 ..."Laying the Cornerstone of the Davis Monument." In: SHSP, 1896, v.24, p. 364-380.

277 ..."Letter correcting errors..." In: SHSP, 1883, v.14, p. 257-275.

278 ..."Letter in reply to General Sherman." In: SHSP, 1886, v.14, p. 257-275.

279 ..."Letter on States Rights, 1885." In: SHSP, 1886, p. 408-409.

280 ..."Letter relating to General Samuel Cooper. In: SHSP, 1877, v.3, p. 274-276.

281 ..."Letter to Confederate Veterans." In: SHSP, 1884, v.12, p. 334-336.

282 ..."Letter to General Lee declining to consider latter's resignation." In: SHSP, 1876, v.2, p. 55-56.

283 ..."Letter to Memorial Association...Macon, Ga." 1878, v.5, p. 302-304.

284 ..."Ladies of Petersburg, Va., petition for Mr. Davis' release." In: SHSP, 1896, v.24, p. 240-242.

285 ..."Reply to Mr. R.M.T. Hunter." In: SHSP, 1878, v.5, p. 222-227.

286 ..."Robert E. Lee." In: SHSP, 1889, v.12, p. 133-137, p. 362-372.

287 ..."Sabine Pass." In: SHSP, 1884, v.12, p. 133-137.

288 ..."Some war history never published." In: SHSP, 1906, v.34, p. 133-143. Conference at Centerville, question of invasion of the North was settled-Davis' version.

289 ..."Treatment of prisoners." In: SHSP, 1876, v.1, p. 113-120.

290 ..."Two addresses, 1863 and 1864." In: SHSP, 1886, v.14, p. 466-470.

291 ..."Some Post-War Observations of Jefferson Davis Concerning Early aspects of the Civil War." Edt: Arthur Shaw. (Baton Rouge, La.) JSH, May, 1944, v.X, #2, p. 207-211.

292 ..."Souvenir: Unveiling of the Jefferson Davis Monument at Jefferson Davis Parkway on Wed., Feb. 22, 1911, 15th anniv. inauguration of Davis as Pres. of C.S.A." New Orleans: Jefferson Davis Monument Association of New Orleans, 1911, 8vo, wraps, 40pp.

293 ..."Speech of the Hon. Jefferson Davis, of Mississippi on the Measures of Compromise. Delivered in the Senate of U.S., June 28, 1850." (Washington, DC) Tower Print. (1850). 8vo, folded uncut sheets, 16pp. $6. Admission of California, vis a vis Missouri Compromise and warns of impending civil war.

294 ..."Speech of President Davis." In: CV, 1902, v.10, p. 21-22.

295 ..."Speech of the Hon...., of Mississippi, delivered in the U.S. Senate, Jan. 10, 1861, upon the message of the President of the U.S. on the condition of things in South Carolina." Baltimore: J. Murphy and Co., 1861. 8vo, sewn, 16pp. $15, $22.50, $50, $125. Delivered a month before being president of the Confederacy. Asserts right of secession, denies coercion and urges withdrawal from Fort Sumter.

296 ..."Third Annual Message of President Davis." London, 1864. 8vo, wraps, p. 34.

297 ..."Two important letters by...discovered: they prove that he was in no way responsible for conditions at Andersonville military prison." In: SHSP, 1908, v.XXXVI, p. 8-12. See: Alf. James "Two Unpublish."

298 ..."An "Unseen Message" of President Davis'." In: CV, 1906, v.14, p. 364-371, ports. Appeared in "Rebellion Records", ser. 1, XLVII, pt. II, p. 1304, message not sent to Congress reappointment of Gen. J.E. Johnston to command Army of Tenn.

299 ..."An "Unseen message" of President Davis'. Concerning the military career of Gen. J.E. Johnston." In: CV, Aug. 1906, v.XIV, p. 364-371.

300 ..."Unveiling of the bust of Jefferson Davis, president of the Confederate States of America, presented by the state of Mississippi to the Commonwealth of Virginia and placed in Old Hall of the House of Delegates where the Congress of the C.S.A. met in the Capitol at Richmond, Va., June 25, 1952." (Richmond: Whittet and Shepperson, c.1952) 8vo, color decr. wraps, ports (incl. Davis as front), (7)pp.

301 ..."The Capture of Pres. Jefferson Davis by an Eyewitness." In: RKHS, Oct. 1966, v.64, #4, p. 270-276. Reprinted in "Tri-weekly Frankfort Kentucky Yeoman" (was living in Abbeville, S.C.)

302 ..."Jeff Davis since his capture. A full history of the life, conduct, etc., of Jeff Davis since his capture and imprisonment also, an account of his interviews with his wife, her efforts for his pardon, release, etc., togethr with many curious facts never before made public. This book is respectfully dedicated to General Grant." Phila: C.W. Alexander Pub., (1866) 8vo, wraps,

(17)-98 (i.e., 48)pp. illus. (incl. ports) Heading: "Popular Edition."

303 ..."Jefferson Davis and the Confederacy and treaties concluded by the Confederate States with Indian Tribes." Edited by Ronald Gibson. Dobbs Ferry, N.Y.: Oceana Publications, 1977. vii, 205pp., 24cm. Bibliography: p. 203-205.

304 ..."Lord Wolseley's Mistakes." In: NARev., 1889, v.149, p. 472-482. Re: Wolseley's "Amer. Civil War".

305 ..."Reply to the speech of Senator Douglas in the US Senate, May 16-17, 1760." Balt: Murphry Print, 1860. 8vo, sewn, 16pp., dbl. column. $30.

..."Inaugural address of Jefferson Davis." In: AHQ, 1943, v.5, #1, p. 7-11.

306 ..."The Jefferson Davis Recipe Book." Mableton, Ga., 1971, 8vo, wraps, illus., 32pp. $5-bmk.

307 ..."A letter from Jefferson Davis to Wm. L. Yancey." In: AHQ, v.2, #2, 1940, p. 258-261.

308 ..."More Yancey-Davis Letters." In: AHQ, 1940, v.2, #3, p. 334-341.

309 ..."President Jefferson Davis." In: Blackwood's Edinburgh Mag., v.XCII, July/-Dec., 1862, p. 343-352, dbl. column.

310 **DAVIS, John J.**
"The Mind of a Copperhead: Letters of John J. Davis on the Secession Crisis and Statehood Politics in West Virginia, 1860-1862. Edt: F. Gerald Ham." In: West Va. Hist., 1963, v.XXIV, p. 93-109.

311 **DAVIS, Joseph R., Brig-Gen.**
"General Davis' Report of Operations of Heth's Division. Hdq. Aug. 22, 1863." In: SHSP, 1880, v.VIII, p. 312-314; 320-322.

312 **DAVIS, Julia**
"Mount Up." New York: Harcourt, Brace and World, 1967. 8vo, cl, d/w, 199pp. Maj. E.A.H. McDonald, 11th Virginia Cavalry, unpublished memoirs. $3.75. ..."Mount Up; A True Story based on the Reminiscences of Major E. A. H. McDonald of the Confederate Cavalry." 1st Edt. N.Y., Harcourt, Brace & World (1967). 12mo, cl, 199p, map, plates (incl. ports). $25. Bibliog. p. 192.

313 ..."The Shenandoah." N.Y., Farrar and Rinehart (1945). 12mo, cl, dj, index, maps, vignettes, x, 374pp. $7.50. Confederacy, p. 135-294.

314 ..."Stonewall." N.Y., E.P. Dutton Co., (1931) $3. 12mo, cl, front, illus., ports, 255pp. For high school level. $10, $30-bmk-109.

...4th Edt. (1935) $2.50

...3rd Print (1931) $8.50. N.Y., E.P. Dutton Co., (1961) 8th edition.

315 **DAVIS, Leslie H.**
"The Capture of Beverly, W.Va." In: Confed. Vet., May 1913, XXI, p. 222-223. Rosser's Raid Jan. 11, 1865.

316 **DAVIS, Maggie**
"The far side of home." N.Y., Macmillan Co., 1963. 12mo, cl, 314pp. $7.50. Novel, on Battle of Jonesboro, Ga., Aug. 31-Sept. 1, 1864.

317 **DAVIS, Manton**
"The Alabama." In: CV, Sept., 1907, v.XV, p. 414-416.

318 **DAVIS, Mary Evelyn Moore**
"The Wire-Cutters." Boston: Houghton, Mifflin Co., 1899. 12mo, cl, 373pp. $10. Sugar plantation in La. war-times.

319 ..."In War Times at La Rose Blanche." Illus. by E.W. Kemble. Boston: D. Lothrop Co. (1888) $4, $12.50. 12mo, cl, vi, 11-257pp., front, plates. As above, fiction. In War-times.

320 **DAVIS, Mary Lamar**
"Floridians distinguished as lawyers and as soldiers: Brig-Gen. William G.M. Davis, CSA." In: Fla. Law. Jour., Feb. 1949, v.23, p. 36-40.

321 **DAVIS, Newton N.**
"Newton N. Davis Confederate Letters."

Ala. Hist. Quart., 1956, v.XVIII, p. 605-610.

322 **DAVIS, Nicholas A.**
"The Campaign from Texas to Maryland, by Rev. Nicholas A. Davis, Chaplain Fourth Texas." Richmond: Presbyterian Comm. of Pub., 1863. $2500-ob, $1500-bmk-110, $1500-jk-143. 12mo, cl, 165, (1)p. 2-ports, incl. front. Also issued in wraps. $450, $550.

...Louisville: Lost Cause Pr., micro-cd.

...Austin, Texas; The Steck Co., 1961. 12mo, boxed, (16), 168pp. 6-color pls. $40. "The Campaign from Texas to Maryland, with the Battle of Fredericksburg, etc."

..."The Campaign from Texas to Maryland; embracing a history and the adventures of the Fourth Texas Regiment, the battles it has fought and the laurels it has won; with notices of the First and Fifth Texas, biographical sketches of officers, incidents, etc." Houston, Texas: Richmond, Va., 1864, 1863. 12mo, wraps, 80pp. (E.H. Cushing?) 80pp. Raines, pg. 64 listing.

...2nd Edt; Houston, Texas: Telegraph Book and job establishment, 1863. 12mo, wraps, 87pp. Winkler-917.

323 ..."Chaplain Davis and Hood's Texas Brigade, being an expanded edition of the Reverend Nicholas A. Davis' the Campaign from Texas to Maryland, with the battle Fredericksburg, (Richmond, 1863) edited with an introduction by Donald E. Everett. San Antonio, Texas: Principia Press of Trinity University, 1962. 8vo, cl, dj, port on cover, xiii, 234pp. Muster Roll, p. 199-216. $12.50, $15-bmk-84, $25-bmk-105, $30.

324 **DAVIS, Nora Marshall**
"Jefferson Davis's route from Richmond, Va., to Irwinville, Ga., Apr. 2-May 10, 1865." In: "Proceedings of the S.C. Hist. Ass'n." 1941, p. 11-20.

325 ..."Military and Naval Operations in South Carolina, 1860-1865. A Chronological List, with References to Sources of Further Information." Columbia, S.C., Archives Dept. for S.C. Confed. War Centennial Comm., 1959. 8vo, wraps, (24)pp. $10, $1, $8-bmk-84.

326 **DAVIS, O.L. and Joan E.**
"Imported Yankee Textbooks for Confederate Texians." In: Jour. of the West, 1967, v.VI, p. 321-328.

327 **DAVIS, O.L., Jr.**
"The Educational Association of the C.S.A." In: CWH, March, 1964, v.X, #1, p. 67-79.

328 ..."E.H. Cushing: Textbooks in Confederate Texas." In: Library Chronicle (Texas University), 1966, v.VIII, ii, 46-50pp. $10-bmk.

329 ..."Textbooks for Virginia school children during the Civil War." In: Va. Journ. Education, 1965, v.LXIX, iii, 16-19pp.

330 **DAVIS, Paxton**
"Battle of New Market. A Story of Virginia Military Institute." Boston: Little, Brown and Co., (1963). 12mo, cl, color front, 145pp., map-ends. $8.50, $6.

331 ..."Three Days." N.Y., Atheneum (1980) 12mo, cl, 102pp., illus. Juvenile. Robert E. Lee at Gettysburg, 3 days.

332 **DAVIS, R.W.**
"Florida in the Days of Secession." In: Fla. Mag., 1902, v.5, p. 5-8.

333 **DAVIS, Reuben**
"Recollections of Mississippi and Mississippians by Reuben Davis." N.Y., Bost., Houghton, Mifflin, 1889. 8vo, cl, front(port), vi, 446pp. $17.50.

...Edts: 1890 and 1891. $20-bmk, $10. Final 3 chapters relates to the CSA.

334 ..."The Rights of the South-the course of the Black Republican Party. Speech of, on Relations of State, House Reps., June 6, 1860." Caption title, 16pp. $7.50

335 **DAVIS, Robert S.**
"Georgia suppliers to the Confederacy, 1861-1865." In: Ga. Geneal. Soc. Quart., 1985, v.21, #3, p. 144-148.
...Same. In: Cent. Ga. Geneal. Soc. Quart., 1985, v.7, #2, p. 64-69, 117-118.

336 ..."The Civil War: Amnesty and Pardons." In: Ancestoring, 1984, v.8, p. 13-27. Including list of those pardoned.

337 **DAVIS, Ruby Sellers**
"Howell Cobb, President of the Provincial Congress of the Confederacy." In: Ga. H.W., March, 1962, v.XLVI, #1, p. 20-33. $8.

338 **DAVIS, Sam**
"Sam Davis, a Southern Hero. Tribute to this martyr by Ella Wheeler Wilcox." In: SHSP, 1897, v.XXV, p. 231-134.

339 ..."Memories of martyr Sam Davis." In: Confed. Vet., 1901/1902, v.X, p. 205, illus. See: Wm. T. Richardson, Joshua Brown, Dr. Howard M. Hamill, Ella Wheeler Wilcox.

340 ..."Sam Davis home--a shrine." In: UDCM, May, 1948, v.11, #5, p. 21-22. port, view. Sam Davis Memorial Assn., acquires boyhood home, Smyrna, Tenn. "Sam Davis. The story of an old-fashioned boy." In: CV, 1909, v.17, p. 276-285, illus., ports.

341 **DAVIS, Samuel Boyer**
"Escape of a Confederate Officer From Prison. What he Saw at Andersonville, how he was sentenced to death and saved by the interposition of President Abraham Lincoln." Norfolk, Va., wraps, 72pp., 1892. Landmark Pub. Co. $250, $40, $50.

342 **DAVIS, Stephen**
"A Georgia Firebrand: Major General W.H.T. Walker, CSA." In: GHQ, Winter, 1979, v.LXIV, #4, p. 447-460.

343 ..."A Matter of Sensational Interest: The Century Battles and Leaders Series." In: CWH, Dec. 1981, v.27, #4, p. 338-349.

344 ..."Confederate Memorial Day in Atlanta: Old Times here are nearly forgotten." In: Atl. Hist. Jour., 1983, v.27, #1, p. 71-86.
..."A Confederate hospital: surgeon John Patterson & the Clayton during the Atlanta Campaign 1864." In: Jour. Med. Assn. of Georgia, 1986, vol. 75, #1, p.14-24.

345 ..."Empty Eyes, Marble Hand: The Confederate Monument and the South." In: Jour. of Popular Culture, 1982, v.XVI, #3, p. 2-21.

346 ..."Citizenship of General Lee." In: Lincoln Herald, Summer, 1979, p. 94-102.

347 **DAVIS, Stephen and Richard M. McMurry**
"A reader's guide to the Atlanta Campaign." In: AHJ, 1984, v.28, #3, p. 99-111.

348 **DAVIS, Steve**
"John Esten Cooke and Confederate Defeat." In: CWH, March 1978, v.24, #1, p. 66-.

349 ..."W.H.T. Walker and Patrick Cleburne's Emancipation proposal." In: CWTI, Dec. 1977, v.16, #8, p. 14-20, illus., ports.

350 **DAVIS, T. Frederick**
"Engagements at St. Johns Bluff, St. Johns River, Florida, Sept/Oct., 1862." In: Fla. Hist. Quart., 1936/1937, v.XV, p. 77-84.

351 **DAVIS, Varina Howell**
"Jefferson Davis, ex-president of the Confederate States of America; a Memoir by his wife..." N.Y., Belford Co. (1890). 8vo, cl, pls., ports, fldg. plans, facsms., (or, 3/4 Mor.), xvi, (1), 699, xxxii, 939pp. $17.50, $20, $27.50, $50-Mor-atg., $150-mcm-283, $100-mcm, $20, vil, $50-bmk.

352 ...Salesman's sample order book, with 1st chap., 23pp. plates, six prices, with samples of binding, $5, $6.50, $7.50, $8, $10, and $12, cloth, grained cloth, 1/2 Mor., 1/2 Russia, 1/2 calf., full Turkey Mor. See: Eron Opha Rowland's life of

Varina, Craddock Goins-Samuel Engle Burr.

353 ..."Mrs. Jefferson Davis at Fortress Monroe, Virginia. Edt: Arthur Marvin Shaw." In: JSH, Feb., 1950, v.16, p. 73-76. notes. Letters to Wm. Preston Johnston, Sept. 27, 1866, where she shared imprisonment with Jeff. Davis.

354 ..."Stonewall's Widow. Mrs. Jackson described by Mrs. Jefferson Davis." In: SHSP, 1893, v.XXI, p. 340-343.

355 ..."Prison Life of Jefferson Davis." In: SHSP, 1904, v.XXXII, p. 371-372. Writes to Savannah "Press", asking Gen. Nelson Miles to produce letter he claims she wrote thanking him to his treatment of husband.

356 ..."My Dearest Friend: A Letter from Mrs. Jefferson Davis, Edt: Arthur Marvin Shaw." In: SW Rev., Spring 1948, v.33, p. 137, Mill View(near Augusta, Ga.) Oct. 3, 1865.

357 ..."Jefferson Davis: ex-President of the Confederacy." 2 vols., 699-936p. Freeport, N.Y., Books for Libraries, 1980. $50.
...Salem, N.H., Select bibliographies, reprints. $95.

358 ..."White House of the Confederacy." In: Frank Leslie's Pop Monthly, May 1896, v.41, p. 509-520.

359 **DAVIS, W.B.**
"Southern Book. Origin of the Constitution. Incorporation of the General Government by the States, as National Public Agents in Trust, with no Sovereignty. History of the Puritans. Origin and Cause of Trouble between the North and South. Legal Mode of Redress." Wilmington, N.C., Dec. 1854, 8vo, cl, 184pp. Sabin 18896, Suppl: Wilmington, NC, 1856, 8vo, cl, 185-298pp.

360 ..."To the People of the South." (Wilmington, N.C., 1857?) 8vo, wraps, p.(303)-354. Caption title, collection of leaflets. Aug. 1856-Dec. 1857, suppl. to the "Southern Book." LC

361 **DAVIS, William C.**
"Battle of Bull Run a History of the First Major Campaign of the Civil War." Garden City, N.Y., Doubleday, 1977, OP, 12mo, cl, dj, ports, illus., maps, xiii, 298pp.
...Book Club Edt., $10, $15.

362 ..."The Battle New Market." Garden City, N.Y., Doubleday and Co., 1975, 8vo, cl, dj, illus., maps, bibliog., index, p.xxiii, 249, ports. $9-y.
...Book Club Edt, $10, $14-bmk, $20-bmk.

363 ..."Breckinridge: Statesman, Soldier, Symbol." Baton Rouge: Louisiana Univ. Pr., 1974. 8vo, cl, dj, illus., bibliog., xxii, 687pp. $17.50, $35-y, $40-y. Brig-Gen., in CSArmy, later Sect. War, served widely in field, except Trans-Miss.

364 ..."John C. Breckinridge." In: CWTI, June 1967, v.VI, #3, p. 11-18, illus., ports.

365 ..."Brother against Brother." Alexandria Va., Time-Life Books, 1983, 8vo, cl, 176pp. $13. Events and circumstances that led to Fort Sumter.

366 ..."The campaign to Appomattox." In: CWTI, Apr., 1975, #1, v.13, p. 50. Entire issue on campaign. facsms, drawings, illus., maps, ports.

367 ..."The conduct of "Mr. Thompson." In: CWTI, May 1970, v.IX, #2, p. 4-7, 43-47, facsm., ports. Corresp. of Jno. C. Breckinson and high CSA officials, all damning of Thompson. Recent and unpublished material.

368 ..."Shadows of the Storm. Vol. 1, The image of war, 1861-1865." Garden City, N.Y., Doubleday, 1981. 4to, cl, dj, 464pp., illus., $30.

369 ..."The South Besieged: Volume Five of the Image of War, 1861-1865, Edited by William C. Davis. Senior consulting editor Bell I. Wiley." Garden City, N.Y., Doub-

leday and Co., 1983, 8vo, cl, dj, illus., 461pp. $40.

370 ..."The Day at New Market(Va.) when an outnumbered scratch force of Confederates saved the Shenandoah and perhaps Lee's army and a corps of schoolboys created a lasting tradition." In: CWTI, July 1971, v.X, #4, p. 4-11, 43-48, illus., map, ports.

371 ..."The Deep Waters of the Proud: Volume 1 of the Imperiled Union: 1861-1865." Garden City, N.Y., Doubleday and Co., 1982, 8vo, cl, dj, illus., sviii, 316pp. notes, index. $20.

372 ..."Duel Between the First Ironclads." Garden City, N.Y., Doubleday, 1975. 12mo, fabricoid, dj, ports, illus., maps, x, 201pp. notes-index, p. 171-201. $9, $12.50-jk, $25-b.

373 ..."The Embattled Confederacy: Volume Three, The Image of War, 1861-1865. Edt: Wm. C. Davis." Garden City, N.Y., Doubleday and Co., 1982, 8vo, cl, dj, 464pp., illus., map, sources. $40.

374 ..."The Guns of '62. Vol. 2, The Image of War, 1861-1865." Garden City, N.Y., Doubleday, 1982. 4to, cl, dj, 460pp., illus. $30.

375 **DAVIS, William J.**
..."Letters by Wm. J. Davis, of Morgan's Cavalry, 1863. Edt: Otto A. Rothert." In: Filson Club Hist. Quart., 1935, v.IX, p. 191-195.

376 ..."A winter raid." In: South. Bivouac, NS, 1885/1886, v.1, p. 28-34.

377 **DAVIS, William L.**
"Frank Clement: the First Campaign." In: THQ, Spring 1976, v.35, #1, p. 83-91.

378 **DAVIS, William P.**
"A Confederate View of Southern Kentucky, 1861." Edt: Lowell H. Harrison." In: Reg. Ky. Hist. Soc., v.LXX, Oct., 1972, p. 163-178. Davis was in Co.B, 14th Miss. Reg.

379 **DAVIS, William Watson**
"The Civil War and Reconstruction in Florida." Studies in Hist., Economics, and Public Law. Edt: by the faculty of political science of Columbia University., v.LIII, whole #131. (heading) N.Y., Columbia University, Longmans Green and Co., 1913. tk. 8vo, cl, xxvi, 769, (5p-ads),pp. $50, Pres: $375-r, $150-bmk-105.
...Gainesville, Fla., Univ. of Florida Press, 1964. A facsimile reproduction of the 1913 edition with intro: Fletcher M. Green. Quadrecentennial Edition of Floridiana Facsimile and reprint series. 8vo, decr. fabric., color crest, 747, 20pp. $25.

380 ..."Flight Into Oblivion" by A.J. Hanna. A Review by..." In: FHQ, January, 1939, v.XVII, #3, p. 227-236.

381 **DAVIS, Winnie**
"Daughter of the Confederacy." In: Nat'l. Ass'n. Watch and Clock collectors Bul, Oct. 1957, v.7, p. 603-604. views. A watch presented to Winnie Davis, daughter of Jefferson Davis, by veterans of the CSA army, Macon, Ga., 1866. First printed in Galveston(Tex) Daily News, Apr. 1908.

382 **DAVIS, Z.M.**
"History of the siege of Vicksburg and maps of the Vicksburg National Military Park, showing the Confederate and Union lines, avenues and locations of all memorials, headquarters and camps, description of the National Cemetery and City of Vicksburg." 8vo, cover title, wraps, 32pp., illus., fldg. maps part in color. Vicksburg, Miss., Z.M. Davis, (1925?)

383 **"DAVIS-HOOD-JOHNSTON controversy of 1864, The"**
Mississippi Valley Historical Review, (offprint), v.11, #1, p. 54-84, sewn. $15.

384 **DAVISON, Nora F.**
"Confederate hospitals at Petersburg, Va." In: CV, Sept. 1921, v.XXIX, p. 338-339.

385 DAVISON, Stanley R. and Dale Tash
"Confederate Backwash in Montana Territory." In: Montana, 1967, v.XVII, iv, 50-58pp.

386 DAWES, E.C., Maj., Ohio Reg.
"The Confederate strength in the Atlanta Campaign." In: B & L, v.4, p. 281-283. Pl. "The Confederate Army", p. 289-292.

387 DAWKINS, Jo Cille
"Beauvoir Soldiers Home Cemetery." (Jackson, Miss.) Jour. Miss. Hist., Aug. 1970, v.XXXII, #3, p. 255-262. Roster of all buried there, CSA.

388 DAWSON, Francis Warrington
"Application for Admission to the Survivors Association of Charleston District, South Carolina." n.p., 1869. Sq. 8vo, 7pp. Turnbull, III, p. 455.

389 ..."Francis Warrington Dawson, Born May 17, 1840-Died March 12, 1889." He lives in fame that dies in virtue's cause. (Charleston) n.pub., 1889. 8vo, wraps, 28pp.

390 ..."In Memory of Francis Warrington Dawson. Born May 17, 1840. Died March 12, 1889. Editor, Soldier, Scholar, Statesman. A Grateful People hold his virtues and his work in abiding memory." Charleston, 1889. 8vo, wraps, 15pp. Turnbull, IV, p. 267.
..."Memoir of Francis W. Dawson of the News and Courier, Charleston, S.C." No imprint, (c.1889) cover title. 8vo, wraps, 15pp. Turnbull, IV, p. 270.

391 ..."Our Women in the War, an address by Capt. Francis W. Dawson, delivered Feb. 22, 1887, at the fifth annual reunion of the Association of the Maryland Line, at the Academy of Music, Baltimore, Md. Printed by order of the Association." Charleston, S.C., Walker, Evans and Cogswell Co., 1887. $45, $25-y, $10, $15, $17. 8vo, wraps. Husband to Sarah Morgan Dawson, an Englishman on Longstreet; staff.

392 ..."Reminiscences of Confederate Service, 1861-1865. By Capt. Francis W. Dawson, C.S.A." Charleston, S.C., News and Courier, 1882. 8vo, wraps, 180pp. (100 copies) $175, $150, $5000-bmk-105, $3500-g
...Reprint: Baton Rouge, La. Louisiana State University Press, 1979. Intro: Bell I Wiley, 8vo, cl, xv, 214pp., 1980. $15, $17.50.

393 DAWSON, Geo. W., Capt., CSA
"One Year at War: Letters of Capt. Geo. W. Dawson, C.S.A." In: M.H.R., Jan. 1979, v.LXXIII, #2, facsm., illus., ports, p. 165-197.

393a DAWSON, John Harper
"Wildcat Cavalry: A History of the 17th Virginia Cavalry." Dayton, Oh., Morningside Press, 1983. 8vo, cl, dj, 160p.

394 DAWSON, John P. and Frank E. Cooper
"The effect of inflation on private contracts; U.S., 1861-1879." In: Mich. Law Rev., 1935, v.XXXIII, p. 706-757, 852-922. Study of legal aspects of CSA inflation (1861-1865) and inflation of North (1862-1879).

395 DAWSON, Joseph G., III
"Army Generals and Reconstruction Louisiana, 1862-1877." Baton Rouge, La., State University Press, 1982, 8vo, cl, dj, 294pp., index, bibliog., appends. $25-cloth, $9-paper. Fourteen generals in fifteen years of rule and never mastered a solution to the dilemma. Finally grew tired of the whole concept.

396 DAWSON, Sarah Morgan
"A Confederate Girl's Diary, with introduction by Warrington Dawson, with illustrations." Boston and N.Y., Houghton Mifflin Co., 1913. 8vo, cl, xviii(1), 439, (3)pp. frontis, plates, ports, facsms. Life in Baton Rouge, New Orleans, etc. $20, $25, $7.50, $9, $35-nc, $17.50, $40, $50, $20-y, $75-jk-97.

397 ...London: William Heinemann, 1913. 8vo, cl, above, 1st. $5, $8.50, $10, $12.50, $60. Boston: Houghton, n.d., d/w, Louisville: Lost Cause Pr., micro-cd. $6.57. Bloomington: Indiana University Press (1960). Civil War Series, introduction by James I. Robertson. 8vo, cl, d/w, 473pp. $3, $22, $50-y, $7.50, $25, $30-bmk, $16-bmk.

...Westport, Conn., Greenwood Print (1972). 8vo, cl, port, xxxvi, 473pp. $17.50, $22.50-y.

..."Confed. Girl's Diary." 1913, annotated, reissue x $27.50.

...Do: Bos: (n.d.), $4, $6, $12.50.

398 **DAY, Carrie Cathcart**
"News from the front." In: SB, ns, v.II, 1886-1887, p. 485-488. Apprehension of the last days of the CSA.

399 **DAY, E.C.**
"Address...on Gen. Lee." Helena, Mont., 1903. 8vo, wraps, 13pp.

400 **DAY, James M.**
"Leon Smith: Confederate Mariner." In: ETHJ, March 1965, v.III, #1, p. 34-49, port, plate, notes, bibliog.

...Edt: "Senate Journal of 9th and 10th Legislature of the State of Texas." "House Journal of the 9th and 10th Legislature of the State of Texas." See: under above titles. 8vols. buckram, $150-jk-129.

401 **DAY, Samuel Phillips**
"Down South; or, An Englishman's experience at the seat of the American War. By Samuel Phillips Day, special correspondent of the Morning Herald." 2 vols. London: Hurst and Blackett, 1862. 12mo, cl, front(port), 328, 327pp. $40, $50, $300-ob.

...N.Y., Burt Franklin Press, 1971, "Research and source works, ser.#349." Most of 1861 spent in the South, camping with the Washington Artillery and Huger's cmd. $20, $35-y.

...Louisville, Ky., Lost Cause Pr., microcard, 1956.

402 **DAY, W.A.**
"Life among the bullets-the siege of Petersburg, Va." In: CV,Apr/June 1921, v.XXIX, p. 138-141, 173-175, 216-219. titles varies.

403 **DAY, W.A. (member Co.I)**
"A True History of Co.I; 49th Reg., N.C. Troops in the Great Civil War between the North and South." Newton, N.C., Enterprise Office, 1893, 8vo, wraps, 127pp.

..."Battle of Crater, July 30, 1864." In: CV, August 1903, v.XI, p. 355-356.

404 **DAY, Walter E. (pseud. "Miles")**
See: "Campaign Gettysburg."

405 **DAYTON, Ruth Woods**
"The Beginning-Philippi, 1861." (Lewisburg, W.Va. 1961) Printed for Civil War Cent. Comm. in Philippi (Va.) Reprinted from the West Virginia History Magazine, July 1952. Narrow 8vo, soft back, 11pp. Reprinted: Congressional Record, June 12, 1961, by Robt. C. Byrd, Sr.

406 ..."Samuel Woods and His Family." 1929. Private Print, not for sale. (Charleston, W.Va., Hood-Hiserman-Brodhag Co.) 8vo, cl, illus., ports, (vii), 170pp. Largely family letters, genealogical, but many (p.23-110) written during civil war. Confederate.

407 **DE BOW, James D.B., et al**
"The interest in slavery of the Southern Non-slaveholder. The right of peaceful Secession. Slavery in the Bible." 8vo, sewn, 30pp., Crandall-2886. $350-goodspeed.

408 **DE BRAY, X.B., Col.**
"A sketch of the history of DeBray's 26th Regiment of Texas Cavalry." Suffolk, Va., Robt. Hardy Pub., 1986. 8vo, wraps, 28pp.

409 **DE CAZENOVE, A.**
"Le Siege de Savannah. Extrait de la Revue du Midi." Nimes: Imprimerie de la

Revue du Midi, rue de la Madeleine, 1903. 8vo, wraps, 55pp. DeRenne, iii, 999.

410 **DE FONTAINE, Felix Gregory**
"American Abolitionism, from 1787 to 1861. A Compendium of historical facts, embracing legislation in Congress and agitation without. (originally published in the New York Herald)." N.Y., D. Appleton and Co., 1861. 8vo, wraps, 66pp. Also pub. under title:

411 ..."History of American Abolitionism: Its four great epochs, embracing narratives of the ordinance of 1787, Compromise of 1820, Annexation of Texas, Mexican War, Wilmot Proviso, Negro Insurrections, Abolition Riots, Slave Rescues, Compromise of 1850, Kansas Bill of 1854, John Brown Insurrection 1859, valuable statistics, &...together with a History of the Southern Confederacy. (Originally published in the New York Herald)." N.Y., D. Appleton and Co., 1861. 8vo, wraps, 66pp.

412 ..."Army Letters of "Personne"., F.G. Fontaine, war correspondent, etc., 1861-1865." Columbia, S.C., War Record Pub. Co., 1896-1897." 8vo, pict. wraps, (4), 51, (10), (2)-incl. covers (printer: State Co., Columbia, S.C.) #1-$50-bmk. v.2, (4), (61)-113pp. $22.50, $25, $65-j, $75-bmk, $100-bmk. Originally published in the Charleston Courier, 1861-1865.

413 ..."Marginalia; or, gleanings from an army notebook, by "Personne", army correspondent of the Charleston Courier, Press of F.G. DeFontaine Co., 1864." Tall 8vo, wraps, (6), iii, 248, (6)pp. ads (incl. wraps-covers). $50, $70, $75, $100, $125.

414 ..."Nothing to eat but raw bacon", letters of a war correspondent, 1862. Edt: James M. Merrill." In: Tenn. HQ, June 1958, v.XVII, p. 141-155. Letters from "Personne", correspondent of Charleston "Courier", Corinth, Miss., Apr 9-May 10, 1862.

415 ..."Personne goes to Georgia: Five Civil War Letters. Contributed by James M. Merrill." In: Ga. H.W., Sept. 1959, v.XLIII, #3, p. 202-211. $8. Fontaine was war correspondent for the "Charleston Courier", and in S.C. when Port Royal was fired on.

416 ..."Shoulder to shoulder, Reminiscences of Confederate camps and fields, by "personne". (Charleston, S.C.) issued in 4 parts, wraps. First appeared in "The XIX Century", v.I/II, p. 35-42, 85-91, 226-234, 297-304, 381-388, 439-450, 611-617. Some later issues had a sub-title "Reminiscences of the War".

417 ..."The first day of real war." In: (Louisville, Ky.) South. Bivouac, 1886-1887, ns, v.II, p. 73-79, illus. $10.

418 ..."The second day of the war." same above, p. 200-207, illus., $10.

419 **DE FOREST, John William**
"A Union Officer in Reconstruction." Edt: Jas. H. Croushore and David M. Potter, with Intro, and Notes. New Haven: Yale Univ. Press, 1948, 8vo, cl, dj, xxx, 211pp. Keen observer, skilled writer of the sturcture of Southern culture, the inferiority of the negro. Revealing acct. of this vast gov. agency. At Greenville, S.C.

420 ..."Chivalrous Southrons." In: New Eclectic, May/Oct. 1869, v.V, #4, p. 456-477, originally in Harper's Mag., Jan-Feb., 1869.

421 ..."Charleston under arms." In: Atl. Month. Mag., Apr, 1861, p. 488-505.

422 **DE GIVE, Laurent Marcellin Joseph**
"A Belgian consul on conditions in the South in 1860 and 1862. Trans/Edt: Paul Evans and Thomas P. Govan." In: JSH, 1937, v.III, p. 478-491. Text of two reports, 1861 and 1862, by consul at Atlanta, to Belgian Minister of Foreign Affairs. Re: conditions in the South and prospects in extending commerce to region.

423 **DE GRUMMOND, Lena Young and Lynn DeGrummond Delaune**
"Jeb Stuart." Phila: Lippincott and Co., (1962), 12mo, cl, illus., 160pp., bibliog. Juvenile. $3.25, $15-bmk-104.

424 …"Jeff Davis, Confederate Boy." Indianapolis: Bobbs-Merrill (1960). 12mo, cl, illus., 192pp. Juvenile fiction. (Childhood of Famous Americans)

425 **DE JARNETTE, Daniel Coleman**
"Secession of South Carolina. Speech of..., of Virginia, in the House of Representatives, Jan. 10, 1861." (Wash: Congressional Globe, 1861) 8vo, sewn, 7pp.

426 …"The Monroe Doctrine. Speech of..., of Virginia, in the Confederate House of Representatives, Jan. 30, 1865, pending negotiations for peace." (Richmond, 1865?) 12mo, sewn, caption title, 20pp. $15, $25, $65

427 **DE LEON, Edwin**
"Three Letters from a South Carolinian relating to Secession, Slavery and the Trent Case." London: Smith, Elder and Co., priv. print., 1862. 8vo, wraps, 22, (1)pp. Diplomat, early writer on "Southern Press", early interest in southern rights.

428 …"La Verite sur les Etats Confederes d'Amerique. Par Edwin De Leon." Paris: E. Dentu, 1862. 8vo, wraps, port, 32pp. $15, $25. Formerly diplomatic agent and consul general of the U.S., this pamphlet was used to gain French recognition of CSA while an agent in Paris.
…"Three Letters from a South Carolinian relating to Secession, Slavery and the Trent Case." London: Printed for private circulation by Smith, Elder and Co., 1862. 8vo, wraps, 22pp.

429 …"Thirty Years of my life on three continents…With a chapter on the life of women in the East, by Mrs. DeLeon." London: Ward and Downey, 1890. 8vo, cl, front(port) 2 vols.

430 …"Ruin and Reconstruction of Southern States." In: South. Mag., June, 1874, p. 562-590. $15-b

431 **DE LEON, Perry M.**
"Navies in the war and the Confederate Navy in the War Between the States; an address delivered before the Camp 171, United Confederate Veterans of Washington, D.C., Holmes Conrad, Commander, by Perry M. De Leon. Published by order of the Camp. Washington, D.C., Shaw Bros. (1910) 8vo, wraps, 46pp., plates, ports. (Bohl.) $50.

432 **DE LEON, Thomas Cooper**
"Belles, Beaux and Brains of the 60's." N.Y., G.W. Dillingham Co., (1907). 8vo, xi, (9), 9-464pp., front(port) illus. with 166 ports. $17.50, $30, $40.
…(1909) reprint, $12.75, $15, $25-bmk-119, $30, $50, $75.
…N.Y., Arno Press, 1974, 8vo, cl, illus., ix, 464pp. Rep: 1909 edt. $25-y. "Women in America from Colonial times to the Twentieth Century."

433 …"Crag-Nest. A romance of the days of Sheridan's ride." (quotes). Mobile, Ala., Gossip Print, 1897. 12mo, cl, 220pp. $6.50, $12.50.
…Same, (1910) $5, Louisville, Ky., Lost Cause Press, micro-cd. $3.25.

434 …(Confederate Souvenir), n.p., (1895). 8vo, wraps, 3-illus., (8)pp. (owens, p. 900)

435 …"Four years in Rebel capitals: an inside view of life in the Southern Confederacy, from birth to death. From original notes, collected in the years 1861 to 1865." Mobile, Ala., Gossip Print, 1890. 8vo, cl, 6, viii, (11)-376pp. $15, $17.50, $22.50, $75-bmk, $125, $100-bmk-109, $45-nc, $60.
…"Author's Autograph Edition", "With Biographical Sketch of the Author by Louis De V. Chaudron." Mobile: Gossip Print, 1892, tall 8vo, decr. cl, port(front) 12, 6, vii, (11)-376pp. $12.50, $15, $25,

$75-nc, $100.

...(West Salem, Wisc., Micro-card corp).

...Louisville: Lost Cause, Micro-card, (1956).

...N.Y., Collier Books (1960), paper-$1.50. 12mo, cl, 416pp. The Collier Bks, CW classics.

...Spartanburg, S.C., Reprint Co., 1975, $18.

436 ..."John Holden, unionist, a romance of the days of destruction and reconstruction in collaboration with Erwin Ledyard." St. Paul: The Price-McGill Co. (1893). 12mo, cl, front, pls, ix, (11)-338pp. $20-bmk.

...2nd Edt., N.Y., (1910), $40, $6.

437 ..."Joseph Wheeler, the man, the statesman, the soldier, seen in semi-biographical sketches by T.C. DeLeon." Atlanta, Byrd Print, 1899. reb-$200-full lt.-bmk-105, $150. 12mo, wraps, 142pp., illus., ports(frt). $10.

...Same, but 162pp., Dornbusch reports addl. text, to replace removed illus., Cover: "Searchlight Library, April, 1899, #1. $7.50.

...Kennesaw, Ga., Continental Books, 1960, 8vo, cl, 142pp., ports, illus., 1000 copies $6, $20-y, $15-nc.

438 ..."The real Jefferson Davis." In: SHSP, XXXVI, p. 74-85, 1908.

439 ..."Southern Women in the Civil War.", XXXII, SHSP, p. 146-150, 1904.

..."Remarkable Record of the Haskells of South Carolina. (from his "Town Topics", Nov. 1907) In: SHSP, 1907, v.XXXV, p. 151-154.

440 ..."South Songs: from the Lays of Later Days, collected and edited by T.C. DeLeon." N.Y., Blelock and Co., 1866. $7.50, $10, $75-bmk, $50-ginz-24. 12mo, cl, x, 1, lf, (15)-153pp., gilt edges.

441 ..."The rending of the solid South; a consideration." (quotes) Mobile, Ala., Gossip Print, 1895. Gossip Popular series, #3, 18mo, wraps, 35pp. (Owens, p. 900), $25 jk-122. 2nd edt., revised. Three edts. issued.

442 ..."The Soldier's Souvenir. Our National Guards in camp and drill, illustrated by historical sketches and full page illustrations of famous commands." Brentano's, Washington, D.C., (1887). Oblong 12mo, illus., 88pp. (1st edt., 1885) Sketches of: Mobile Rifle Co., Lomax Rifles, Montgomery Grays and "True Blues".

443 **DE LOZIER, Mary Jean**
"The Civil War and its aftermath in Putnam County." In: THQ, Winter, 1979, v.38, #3, p. 436-461.

444 **DE MORSE, Charles, Colonel**
"Indians for the Confederacy." Oklahoma City: Chron. Okla., Winter, 1972, v.L, #4, p. 474-478. Originally printed in Clarksville, Texas "Northern Standard", 1862.

445 **DE MOSS, John C.**
"A short history of the soldier-life, capture and death of William Francis Corbin, captain Fourth Kentucky Cavalry, C.S.A." (Midway, Ky., 1897) Cover title: A page of unwritten history. 8vo, wraps, port(front), 32pp. Louisville, Lost Cause Press, micro-cd. $3.50 $200-r.

446 **DE NOON, Charles E.**
"Charlie's Letters: The Correspondence of Charles E. DeNoon." Edt: Richard T. Couture. n.p., 1982, 8vo, wraps, 257pp. $20-bmk-128. Va., from Mar. 1862-Aug. 1864. Battle of Chancellorsville, etc. $25.

..."Charlies's Letters: The correspondence of Charles E. DeNoon by Richard T. Couture." (Cover title with contemporary port of Charlie (tin-type). 4to, stiff wraps, 257pp., port. $25-bmk. Edt: Richard T. Couture, sig: Bolling Island Plantation, June 12, 1982. Powhatan, Va.? Rosters.

447 **DE PEYSTER, John Watts**
"A Military Memoir of William Mahone Maj-Gen. in the Confederate Army." In:

Hist. Mag., Morrisania, 1870, VII, p. 390-406. Revised, with correspondence that occasioned the revision. In: Hist. Mag., (Morrisnia, 1871, v.X, p. 12-33.

448 DE RENNE, Wymberley Jones
"A short history of the Confederate Constitution of the CSA, 1861-1899." (Savannah, Ga., Morning News, 1909) 4to, wraps, photo of Davis taking oath office, (8)pp., fldg. facsm. of constitution, priv. print. $12.50. 150-copies, 100 on handmade paper.

449 DE ROSIER, Arthur H., Jr.
"The Confederates in Canada: A Survey." In: "Southern Quarterly, 1965, v.III, p. 312-324.

450 ..."Pioneers with Conflicting Ideals: Christianity and Slavery in the Choctaw Nation." (Jackson, Miss., Jour. Miss. Hist., July, 1959, v.XXI, #3, p. 174-189.

451 DE ROSSET, William L., Lt. Col.
"Third North Carolina around Richmond." In: OLOD, May 1875, v.2, #3, p. 293-294.

452 DE SAUSSURE, Nancy Bostick, Mrs.
"Old Plantation Days; being recollections of Southern Life before the Civil War." N.Y., Duffield and Co., 1909. atg-$36-nc, $50, $25-bmk, $17.50, $12.50. 8vo, cl, colored front, 123pp. Title actually misleading, for it contains much on the war, Sherman's March thru Georgia and So. Carolina.

453 DE VERGES, Edwin X., Mrs.
"Hon. John T. Monroe-The Confederate Mayor of New Orleans." New Orleans: LHQ, Jan. 1951, v.34, #1, p. 25-34.

454 DE WEES, Daniel S., Col. 19th Va. Regt.
"Recollections of a Lifetime." Eden, Calhoun County, W.Va., 1904 (Ghost-written by Aristotle Smith, Shetler, 194) Homefront, prison narr. 8vo, wraps, 72pp., illus. $20.

455 DE WITT, David Miller
"The Judicial Murder of Mary E. Surratt." Balt: John Murphy & Co., 1895. 12mo, cl, vi, 259pp. $22.50, $40, $100-mcm-248, $75-jk.

456 DE WOODY, Mary S.
"Life in the Sixties (1860)." In: Jefferson CHQ, #2, 1977, v.7, p. 14-20.

457 DEADERICK Chalmers
"Treatment of Southern commissioners." In: CV, Oct. 1914, v.XXII, p. 449-451. Comm. sent by South Carolina, right after secession, to Gov., re forts and other property in the state.

458 DEADERICK, Adeline Clifton McDowell
"Civil War Memoirs of...Edt: Anna Mary Moon." In: Tenn. HQ, Mar. 1949, v.VII, p. 52-71, written c.1898.

459 DEADRICK, Barron
"Battles of Shiloh and Memphis." (Memphis, Tenn., S.C. Toof Co., 1961) 16mo, stiff wraps, map verso wraps, (6), 26, (1)pp. atg. copy-$7.50, $10.

460 ..."Civil War Campaigns in Tennessee." W.Tenn. Hist. Soc., v.X, 1956, p. 53-77.

461 ..."Forrest", Wizard of the Saddle." (Memphis, Tenn., S.C. Toof Co., 1960) 12mo, wraps, cover title(illus.), 16pp. 1000 copies. $3.50

462 ..."Shiloh, Memphis and Vicksburg." Memphis, Tenn: West Tenn. Hist. Soc. (Press of S.C. Toof and co., 1960) 12mo, stiff wraps, 32pp. illus., verso cover. $3.50, $10.

463 ..."Strategy in the Civil War." Harrisburg, Military Service Pub. Co., 1946, $12, $10, $16-bmk, $25-bmk-109. 8vo, cl, ports, maps, plans, 200pp.
...Harrisburg, Pa., Stackpole Co., (1951) $6, $7.

464 ..."The Truth about Shiloh." (Memphis, Tenn., S.C. Toof Co., 1942) 12mo, stiff wraps, pl, maps, 36pp. inscribed copy-$10, $5, $20, $15-nc.

465 DEAN, Benjamin F.
"Letters of a Confederate soldier to his

wife in 1864. Contributed by H. Gresham Toole." In: W.Va. Hist., Oct. 1957, v.19, p. 69-70. From camp in Winchester, Va. 19 July 1864.

466 **DEAN, Earl**
"General James Green Martin (1819-1878) saved Petersburg (Va)." In: Pasquotank Hist. Soc. Yr. Bk., 1954, v.1, p. 105-106. Services in US and CSArmy, 1836-1865.

467 **DEAN, Henry Clay** "Crimes of the Civil War and Curse of the Funding System." Baltimore, 1868. 8vo, (8), 512pp., cl. $10, $17.50, $35-bmk, $25. Compilation of Union Army crimes.
...Rep. 1969, cl, (8), 539pp. $10.

468 **DEAN, L.Y., Capt.**
"A Memoir of the Life of..." n.p., n.d., port, 11pp. (Confed. Museum)

469 **DEANE, Francis H.**
"Address before the Pegram Battalion Ass'n., The Cavalry-"The Men who were always fighting." In: SHSP, 1886, v.XIV, p. 28-29.

470 **DEBO, Angie**
"The Site of the Battle of Round Mountain, 1861." (Okla. City) Chron. Okla., Summer 1949, v.XLI, #1, p. 70-104, map.

471 ..."Southern Refugees of the Cherokee Nation." In: SWHQ, Apr. 1932, v.XXXV, p. 255-266. Particularly Cherokees who broke with Union and followed the CSA.

472 **DEBRAY, Xavier Blanchard**
"Original photograph 11x9" (mounted stiff board, 17x14") with other CSA officers: Wm. M. (Buck) Walton, A.W. Terrell and other officers." Galveston, Texas: P.H. Rose, (c.1880) Debray commanded defenses at Galveston, 1862. $1000-jk-138.

473 ..."A Sketch of the History of Debray's 16th Regiment of Texas Cavalry." Austin, Texas: E. Von Boeckmann, 1884, 8vo, wraps, 26pp., $25, $75, $165, $225. Only 75 copies-(Libbey Auct.) $2500-g.
...Also: in Southern Historical Society Papers, xii (1884), p. 547-554. $350-brick row.

474 ...Waco, Texas: Waco Village Press, 1961, 8vo, stiff wraps (270-copies) (30-cloth) $10. (paper) $5, $10, $15. p.iv, 26. With introduction by Palmer Bradley, $40, $20-bmk.
...Pasadena, Texas: Abbotsford Press, June 1963. 8vo, stiff wraps, preface (1)p, 26pp. $5.

475 ...(Natchitoches, La., 1887) Debray's "History of the 9th Texas Partisan Rangers."

476 ..."A Sketch of Debray's Twenty-Sixth Regiment of Texas Cavalry." In: SHSP, 1884, v.XII, p. 547-554; v.XIII, 1885, p. 153-165. See: Thomas H. Edgar.

477 **DECATUR COUNTY, Georgia**
"Frank S. Jones': History of Decatur County, Georgia." Orig. pub., 1971"
...Spartanburg, S.C., Reprint Co., 1980. 420pp., new index $25. Decatur Co., in wars and monuments and historical markers, members of organizations and military companies, especially Civil War.

478 "**DECLARATION of Causes, A,**
which impel the state of Texas to secede from the Federal U." See: "Texas Secession"

479 "**DEDICATION of Monuments to Georgia** Confederate dead-Antietam National Battlefield Site-Gettysburg National Military Park. Presented by the State of Georgia to the U.S. Government. Sponsored by Centennial Hall of Fame Comm., Sept. 20-21, 1961." 8vo, wraps, ports, pl, 14pp. (2p list Georgia Units; both battles)

480 "**DEDICATION of Monument to Georgia** Confederate dead, Kennesaw Mt. Nat'l. Battlefield Park, presented by state of Georgia to U.S. Gov., sponsored Cent. Hall of Fame Comm., Aug. 16, 1963." 8vo, wraps, illus., facsms, ports, 16pp.

481 **"DEDICATION of Overlook** and Pavilion of 14 Georgia Confederate Generals who fought in the Battle of Kennesaw Mt., June 27, 1864. Kennesaw Mt. National Battlefield Park. Presented by the State of Georgia Cent. Hall of Fame Comm. to the U.S. Gov. sponsored Georgia Div. UDC and Georgia C.W. Cent. Comm. June 17, 1964." Atlanta, Ga., 1964. 8vo, wraps, illus., ports, 16pp.

482 **"DEDICATION of Soldiers and and Sailors** Monument, Richmond, Va., May 30, 1894. n.p., n.d., 8vo, wraps, 25pp. $30-bmk, $20-bmk, $12.50. See: R.C. Cave and "Unveiling of..."

483 **"DEDICATION of the Confederate** Monument at Greenwood Cemetery." New Orleans, La., 1874. 8vo, wraps.

484 **"DEDICATION of the Virginia Memorial** at Gettysburg, Friday, June 8, 1917." In: SHSP, Oct. 1917, v.XLII, p. 83-135. See: Leigh Robinson, address.

485 **"DEDICATION of the Virginia tablet** in the Vicksburg National Military Park. Friday evening, Nov. 22, 1907, exercises in the First Baptist Church, Vicksburg, Miss." (Vicksburg, Mississippi Print Co., 1907) 8vo, wraps, (25)pp. Dorn-II, 1897.

486 **"DEDICATION of the Double Equestrian** statue. General Robert E. Lee and Gen. Thomas J. Jackson(Stonewall), including explanatory text in program and address of the occasion, May 1, 1948." Baltimore, 1948. 4to, wraps, front, 27pp.

487 **"DEDICATION of tomb** of Army of Northern Virginia. Louisiana division and unveiling of statue of Stonewall Jackson at Metairie cemetery, New Orleans, May 10, 1881." New Orleans: M.F. Dunn and Bros., 1881, 8vo, wraps, front, illus.

488 **DEEMS, Clarence** "General Jackson's Shenandoah Valley Campaign, May/June, 1862." In: "Coast Artillery Journ.", 1926, v.LXV, p. 159-215.

489 **DEER CREEK Expedition** See: W.L. Ritter.

490 **DEERING, John Richard** "Lee and His Cause; or, the why and how of the War Between the States, by John R. Deering, once of the Claiborne Guards, Co.K, 12th Reg. Mississippi." N.Y. Neale Pub. Co., 1907. $50, $12.50, $75-bmk. 12mo, cl, 2-ports, incl. front, 183pp. $10. See: "View of the Constitution"-CHM.

491 **DEERING, Robert Waller** "Gen. Robert E. Lee." In: CV, Jan. 1915, v.XXIII, p. 17-20.

492 **"DEFAULTED debts of Southern states..."** See: "Corporate and Foreign bondholders."

493 **"DEFENDERS of Vicksburg, The** a monument to their memory unveiled at Vicksburg, Miss., April 25, 1893. Exercises on the occasion, with the addresses by Lt-Gen. Stephen D. Lee and Ex-Governor M.F. Lowry." In: SHSP, XXI, 1893, p. 183-206.

494 **"DEFENSE of Richmond, The** against the Federal Army, under Gen. McClellan. By a Prussian Officer in the Confederate Service." N.Y., Geo. F. Nesbitt and Co., 1863. 8vo, wraps, 16pp. Sabin-19241. $35, $75-b, $25-jenk. Trans: "Koelnisch Zeitung." From: Broadfoot Bookmark notes: "purportedly translated from a Cologne newspaper. It smacks of Bela Estvan's antics and is entirely too laudatory of the Federals. Plus the N.Y. imprint leads me to believe it fiction."

495 **DEITRICK, R.L.** "Deitrick's standard paper money catalogue: listing all Confederate Treasury Notes issued by the Confederate Government and all State Notes issued by the Confederate States during the Civil War. Reliable reference list. 20th edt., Lorraine,

Va., R.L.Deitrick, 1914. 12mo, wraps, 36pp. Swem-1409a.

496 **DEKLE, Peter**
"Peter Dekle's Letters. Edt: John K. Mahon." In: Civil War Hist., Mar. 1958, v.IV, p. 11-22. A Prvt., Co.F, 29th Ga., Vols Inf. to wife, Thomasville, Ga.

497 **DELANEY, Caldwell**
"Confederate Mobile; a Pictorial History." Mobile, Ala., Haunted Bookshop, 1971. 4to, cl, 360pp. (largely illus.) $25, $30.

498 **DELANEY, Norman C.**
"Charles Henry Foster and the Unionist of Eastern North Carolina." In: NCHR, July, 1960, v.XXXVII, p. 348-366. $8.

499 ..."Corpus Christi-the Vicksburg of Texas." In: CWTI, July 1977, v.16, #4, p. 4-9, 44-48, illus., map, ports.

500 ..."The Diary and Memoirs of Marshall Samuel Pierson, Company C, 17th Reg., Texas Cavalry, 1862-1865." In: Mil. Hist. Tex. and SoWest., 1977, v.XIII, #3, p. 23-38, Quarto.

501 ..."The End of the "Alabama"." In: Amer. Hertg., 1972, v.XXIII, iii, 58-69-102.

502 ..."Old Beeswax", Raphael Semmes of the Alabama." In: CWTI, Dec. 1973, v.XII, #8, p. 10-22, illus., ports.

503 ..."John McIntosh Kell: a Confederate Veteran in Politics." In: Ga.H.Q., Fall, 1973, v.LVII, #3, p. 376-389.
..."John McIntosh Kell of the Raider Alabama." University, Ala, University of Alabama Press, 1973. 8vo, cl, dj, x, 270pp. index, bibliog., $20, $25-y, $2.95, $8.50
..."Private Philip Cates Army of Tennessee." In: CV, ns, Jan.-Feb. 1988, v. 36, #1, p. 16-23, facsm, ports.

504 ..."The Raider and the Rascal. P.D. Haywood's "Cruise of the Alabama"." In: CWTI, May 1973, v.XII, #2, p. 16-22, illus., ports. John M. Kell exposes the fraud of Haywood's article claiming himself as "one of the crew". Century Mag., March 1887, announced that he was not a seaman on the ship. See also: CWTI, Oct. 1969, v.VIII, p. 4-9, 45-48. A reprint of Haywood's article in "Century".

505 ..."They fought until she sank beneath the waves." In: CV, ns, Mar./Apr. 1987, v.35, #2, p. 24-31, illus., incl. dbl. pg. color of the "Alabma", port Semmes on cover, map.

506 ..."Good ship "Hattaras" met death at Semme's hand." Apr.1979, v.18, #3, p. 22-27, illus., ports.

507 **DELANEY, Robert W.**
"Matamoros, Port for Texas during the Civil War." In: SwHQ, April, 1955, v.LVIII, #4, p. 473-387.

508 **DELANEY, Wayne Richard and Marie E. Bowery**
"The Seventeenth Virginia Volunteer Infantry Regiment, CSA." Washington, D.C., American Pr., (1961) 8vo, stiff wraps, (68)pp. $3.50, $5, $7.50, $20-bmk, $10-bmk-84. A history and muster roll. See: A. Herbert, A. Hunter, E. Warfield and Geo. Wise, and Marie E. Bowery.

509 ..."Muster roll of the Loudoun Guards taken from the Seventeenth Virginia Regiment, CSA." In: Bul. Loudoun Co. Hist. Soc., 1962, (6p) $10.

510 **DELAUTER, Roger U., Jr.**
"McNeill's Rangers." Lynchburg, Va., H.E. Howard. 8vo, cl, dj, (8), 130pp., maps, ports. 1000 copies, numbered, signed, bibliog.

511 ..."18th Virginia Cavalry." Lynchburg, Va., H.E. Howard, 1985. (J.P. Bell Print) Lim. Atg. Edt., 557. 8vo, cl, dj, (6), 105pp., illus., maps, ports, $17.50.
..."62nd Virginia Infantry." Lynchburg, Va, H. E. Howard, 1988. 8vo, cl, dj, (5), 121p, pl, ports, maps. 1,000 (#384) atg. copies.

512 **DELEHANT, John W.**
"Judah P. Benjamin (1811-1884): lawyer and statesman." In: Wyo. Law Jour., Fall,

1950, v.5, p. 10-23. On his public career, 1832-1865. CSA.

513 **DELERY, Charles Chauvin Boisclaire, Dr.**
"Le Dernier Chant du Guerrier Orateur; a la Memoire du Lieutenant-Colonel C. D. Dreux." (Nouvelle-Orleans, (La.), n.d. (1885?) 8vo, wraps, 6pp. Poem, written about 1861, commemorating a young officer slain early in war. Date of 1861 in error, as ads show telephone numbers!

514 **DELERY, Docteur Ch.**
"Confederes et federaux. Les Yankees fondateurs de l'esclavage aux Etats-Unis et initiateurs du droit de secession. Par le Docteur Ch. Delery." Paris: Librairie centrale, 1864. 8vo, wraps, 31pp. $8.50, $12.50.

515 **DEMBY, Josiah H., Maj.**
"Major Josiah H. Demby's History of Catterson's Militia. Edt: Ted. R. Worley." In: AHQ, 1957, v.XVI, p. 203-211. Ark. Reconstruction, Gen. Powell Clayton and the Ku Klux Klan.

516 **DEMUTH, David O.**
"The Burning of Hopefield." In: AHQ, Summer, 1977, v.XXXVI, #2, p. 123-129, plat.

517 ..."Federal Military Activity in Arkansas in the Fall of 1864 and Skirmish at Hurricane Creek." In: Ark. H.Q., Summer, 1979, v.38, #2, p. 131-145, map. notes.

518 **DENISON, Charles Wheeler**
"The Spy of the Shenandoah." In: Potter's Amer. Monthly, 1879, v.XIII, illus., p. 284-290.

519 **DENISON, Claude B., Engr. Serv. CSArmy**
"An address delivered in Raleigh, N.C., on Memorial Day, May 10, 1895, containing a memoir of the late Maj-Gen. William Chase Whiting, of the Confederate Army." Request of the Ladie's Memorial Ass'n. $45-bmk-99. Raleigh, N.C., Edwards and Broughton, 1895. 8vo, wraps, 56pp. also found in SHSP, xxvi, $22.50-y, p.129-181. Dornbusch-3168. (Confed. Museum)
...Wendell, N.C., Broadfoot's Bookmark, 1979, Lim. Edt. 500 copies, wraps, $5, $10.

520 ..."Address delivered before the State Chap. U.D.C., Raleigh, N.C., Oct. 10, 1900. Largely, Jefferson Davis. (Raleigh, N.C., 1900) 8vo, wraps, 20pp.

521 **DENMAN, Clarence Phillips**
"The Secession Movement in Alabama." Montgomery, Ala., State Dept. Archives and History, 1933. 12mo, cl, front, illus., maps, xiii, 190pp. $10, @12.50, $25, $15, $75.

522 **DENNY, Collins, Bishop**
"Memorial address at Arlington." In: SHSP, Oct., 1917, v.XLII, p. 181-188.

523 ..."Robert E. Lee, the Flower of the South." In: SHSP, Sept., 1916, XLI, p. 3-13. Aslo in: Meth. Qrt. Rev., April, 1910, v.LIX, p. 271-281.

524 **DENNY, George Hutcheson**
"Biographical sketch of Robert Edward Lee, with selections from his writings." Alderman Lib. South. Lit., 1909, v.7, p. 3145-4168.

525 **DENNY, George Taylor, Lt. Col.**
"Modern Cavalry; its organization, armament and employment in war. With an appendix containing letters from Generals Fitzhugh Lee, Stephen Lee and T.L. Rosser, of the Confederate States Cavalry and Col. Jenyn's system of nonpivot drill in use in the 13th hussars." London: T. Bosworth, 1868. 8vo, cl, xx, 376pp., incl. plan, 2-color pls (incl. front), 2-fldg. maps. $12.50.

526 ..."A History of Cavalry from the earliest times, with lessons for the future." London: Macmillan and Co., 1877. 8vo, cl, xxii, 567, (1)p., 2-fldg. maps, fldg. plan.
...2nd Edt., same, xxxi, 468pp., maps, plans, part fldg. London: 1913, $22.50-y

...Westport, Conn., Greenwood Press, 1968. A reprint of the 1877 edition. $24.50.

...Another printing, London: 1913.

527 **DENTISTRY in the Confederacy.**
See: Wm. N. Hodgkin.

528 **DEPARTMENT of Justice-CSA**
"Circular Letter to District Attorneys and to Receivers under the Sequestration Act. By Wade Keyes, Acting Attorney General. Department of Justice." Richmond, Va., October 22, 1862. Broadside: 9 3/4x7 3/4". $25. Not in Crand/Harw.

529 **DERRICK, Samuel Melanchthon**
"Centennial history of South Carolina railroad." Columbia, S.C., The State Co., 1930. 8vo, cl, x, 335pp., front, pl., ports, maps, facsms., part double. $60-bmk. One chap. on Civil War.

530 **DERRY, Joseph T.**
"Comments" by, in Century Magazine, 1891." v.XLII, p. 634-635.

531 ..."Battle of Shiloh. How the Federal advance in the West was crushed." In: SHSP, 1899, v.XXVII, p. 357-360.

532 ..."The aggressive vs. the defensive policy of the Confederate Army." In: CV, Oct. 1914, v.XXII, p. 465.

533 ..."Georgia." In: Evan's Confederate Military History, v.VI, Atlanta, GA., Confederate Pub. Co., 1899. 8vo, maps, ports, plates, vii, 461pp. Biog. (387-461). Reb-$30-b.

534 ...Biographical Suppl.-"Additional sketches illustrating the services of officers, privates and patriotic citizens." Tk.8vo, "Georgia", p.461; suppl., p. (463)-1069. $75-y.

535 ..."Memories of '64." (Atlanta, Ga., Franklin Print, 1901) 12mo, wraps, 24pp. (poem)

536 ..."The Siege of Atlanta. A Poem. Dedicated to the Confederate Veterans." Atlanta, Ga., Foote and Davies Co., 1898, 8vo, wraps, 16, (2)pp.

537 ..."A Southern View of the Question." Century Mag., v.XLIV, 1892, p. 956-957.

538 ..."The Strife of Brothers. Book First: The Gathering of the Hosts, a Poem." n.p., 1903. 8vo, wraps, 26pp.

539 ..."The Strife of Brothers a Poem." Atlanta, Ga., Franklin Print, 1904, 12mo, cl, port(front) illus., 160pp. $20-bmk, $5.

..."The Strife of Brothers. A Poem." N.Y., Neale Pub., 1906. 8vo, cl, illus., 164pp. $50-bmk, $20-bmk. Ex-Lib., stain, atg. pres. copy $10-bmk.

540 ..."The Story of the Confederate States: or, history of the war for Southern Independence. Embracing a brief but comprehensive sketch of the early settlement of the country, trouble with the Indians, the French Revolutionary and Mexican Wars, and a full complete and graphic account of the great four year's War Between the North and the South, its causes, effects, etc. By Joseph T. Derry, with an introduction by Gen. Clement A. Evans." Richmond, Va., B.F. Johnson Pub., 1895. 8vo, cl, illus., maps, ports, xvi, (19)-448pp. $15, $17.50, $35-Mor., $27.50.

...Richmond, Va., 1896, pp. 471. $17.50
...Same, 1898, (19)-552. $25.
...N.Y., Arno Press (1979). 8vo, bds, dj, 453pp. $17.50, $7.

541 ..."Story of the Confederate States, etc." Richmond: 1895. Salesman's sample, illus., abbreviated copy containing 24 names (mostly from Grimes County, Va., signed to buy copies). $12.

..."Georgia." v.VII. 8vo, cl, 1069pp., Wilmington, N.C., Broadfoot, 1987.

542 ..."The numerical strength of the Confederate Army." In: Cent., Oct. 1892, v.22, p. 956-959. rejoinder to Jos. T. Derry.

543 ..."Valor and skill in the Civil War." In: Cent., Oct. 1891, v.20, p. 634-635; reply of T.A. Dodge, p. 636.

544 **DES CHAMPS, Margaret B.**
"Benjamin Morgan Palmer, Orator Preacher of the Confederacy." Southern Speech Journal, September, 1953, v.XIX, p. 14-22.

545 **DES GEORGES, Herbert E.**
"The Battle of Glorieta Pass." In: Rio Grande History, 1976, v.6.

546 **"DESCRIPTIVE catalogue**
of Confederate Notes and Bonds for sale by John W. Haseltine, 1225 Chestnut St., Philadelphia. Price fifty-cents." Phila: Bavis and Pennypacker, 1876. 8vo, wraps, 36pp., insert price-list, 4pp.
...(reprint) ca. 1965? $2.50.

547 **"DESCRIPTIVE list of burial places, A,**
of the remains of Confederate soldiers, who fell in the battles of Antietam, South Mountain, Monocacy...in Washington and Frederick Counties Maryland." Hagerstown, Md., n.d. (c.1869) 8vo, wraps, 84pp. $75. Lists soldiers by name, company, regiment and state, remarks and locality. Later disinterred and buried in the Hagerstown Confederate Cemetery. $40-bmk.

548 **DESERTION-in the CSA.**
"Two special cases of desertion." In: SHSP, 1880, v.8, p. 28-31. Lee's clemency. See: Lucile Borgwald, Ella Lon, Bessie Martin.

549 **"DESTRUCTION of the City of Columbia, S.C.**
A Poem. By a Lady of Georgia(pseud)." Charleston: Joseph Walker, 1866. 12mo, wraps, 24pp. McKissick-607. Attributed to Elizabeth Dannelly. "because it appears in her Cactus, N.Y., Atlantic Pub. Co., 1879.

550 **DESVARREUX-LARPENTEUR, Raymond**
"Confederate Uniforms-Drawings by...; Text: Alfred B.C. Batson." Confederate series 1. Valley Forge, Pa., 1956. 4to, 4-color plates, sheets in portfolio, each pl. with a 12mo lf. description.

551 ..."Confederate Army Prints." Valley Forge, Pa., A.B.C. Batson(c.1956) (same description above).

552 ..."Revolutionary and Civil War Soldier's Uniforms." Drawings by Raymond Desvarreux-Larpenteur. Text on accompanying sheets by Alfred B.C. Batson. Valley Forge, pa., Alfred B.C. Batson, 1956. 4to, 12-color plates, in sheets, folder. Confederate Army and Navy uniforms.

553 **DEUPREE, J.G.**
"Reminiscences of Service with the First Mississippi Cavalry." In: 1903, (Oxford) Pub. Miss. Hist. Soc., v.VII, p. 85-100, Muster roll, Noxubee Cavalry at Union City, Tenn.

554 **DEUPREE, John G.**
"The Noxubee Squadron of First Mississippi Cavalry, CSA and McNeilly, J.S.-"War and Reconstruction in Mississippi, 1863-1890." (Jackson, Miss., 1918) 8vo, wraps, 124pp. Originally in Publications Mississippi Hist. Society, Centenary series, v.II, 1918, p. 12-143. $25.

555 ..."War Everters: Seward, Mallory, and Fort Pickens." In: FHQ, v.XLIX, January 1971, #3, p. 232-244.

556 **DEUTSCH, Eberhard P.**
"The Real Origin of the Secession Movement." In: Amer. Bar Assn. Jour., 1969, v.LV, p. 1134-1140.

557 **DEVEREUX, Thomas P.**
"From Petersburg to Appomattox." In: CV, June 1914, v.XXII, p. 257-261. Reminisc. of service in the ANV, 1864-1865.

558 **DEW, Aloma Williams**
"Between the hawk and the buzzard, Owensboro(Ky.) during the civil war." Winter, 1979, v.77, #1, p. 1-14.

559 **DEW, Charles B.**
"Ironmaker of the Confederacy: Joseph R. Anderson and The Tredegar Iron Works." New Haven, Conn: Yale University Press, 1966, 8vo, cl, d/w, xiv, 345pp., illus. $6, $10, $100-bmk, $50, $25, $20, $30.

560 ..."Who Won the Secession Election in Louisiana?" (Houston, Tex.) JSH, Feb., 1970. v.XXXVI, #1, p. 18-32. Tables. $10.

561 ..."The long lost returns: the candidates and their totals in Louisiana's Secession election." In: LaH, Fall, 1969, p. 353-369.

562 **DEYTON, Jason Basil**
"The Toe River Valley to 1865." In: NCHR, Oct., 1947, v.24, p. 423-466.

563 **D'HAMEL, E.B.**
"The Adventures of a Tenderfoot. A History of the 2nd Regt. Mounted Rifles and Co.G, 33rd Regt. and Capt. Coopwood's Spy Co., and 2nd Texas in Texas and New Mexico." 12mo, wraps, cover as title-page, n.p. (San Antonio, Texas, 1914) Only one known copy-R.H. Porter (Austin).
...Do: Reprint, by W.M. Morrison of Waco, Texas (1964) 8vo, stiff wraps, 24pp., port, 200 copies, 25 of which are specially bount. $3.50, $10-bmk-84.
"The adventures of a tenderfoot." Suffolk, Va., Robt. Hardy Pub., 1986, 8vo, wraps, 28pp., port.

564 **DIAL, Marshall**
"The Bootheel Swamp Struggle." Lilbourn, Mo., Lloyd Pubs., 1961. 8vo, decr. wrapsports, illus., (3), 62pp., $5, $10.

565 ..."Diary of a Virginia Schoolmistress, 1860-1865." Edt: Glenn Curtiss Smith. Harrisonburg, Va., Madison College, "The Madison Quarterly, v.IX, #2, March, 1949. Large 8vo, wraps, 58pp. $4.

566 **DIAMOND, George Washington**
"George Washington Diamond's Account of the Great Hanging at Gainesville, 1862." Austin: Texas State Historical Assoc., 1963, Tall 8vo, cl(or, wraps, $3.50) port-frontis, p. xvi, 103, index, color-map ends. $5, $15-b. Unionist "Peace Party Plot" against CSA, by largely border-state settlers who were against secession, later loyal to the CSA.
...First in SwHQ, January 1963, v.LXVI, #3, p. 331-414, ports. Edited by Sam Acheson and Julie Ann Hudson O'Connell.

567 **DIAMOND, William**
"Imports of the Confederate Government from Europe and Mexico." In: The Jour. of South. Hist., VI (1940) p. 470-403. $8.
...Offprint, wraps, 34pp., atg-$15-bmk.

568 **"DIARIES, LETTERS, and Recollections**
of the War Between the States. Printed by the Winchester-Frederick County Historical Society. Edt. Comm: Garland R. Quarles, Chm., Lewis N. Barton,C. Vernon Eddy, Mildred Lee Grove." Winchester: Winchester-Frederick Co. Historical Society, (Va.) 1955. 8vo, stiff wraps, 133pp. $20-bmk-105, $7.50, $25, $12-bmk.

569 **"DIARY of a Confederate Quartermaster."**
In: THQ, 1952. See: Charlotte Cleveland.

570 **"DIARY of a Confederate Boy, The"**
In: All the year round: a weekly journal. May 17, 1862. sm.4to, 7pp.(extract) $10.

571 **"DIARY of a Virginia Cavalry man,**
1863-1864, from the original manuscript." In: Hist. Mag., Morrisania, 1873, s 3 II, p. 210-215. "Probably 4th Sgt. Henry Corbin found on Fisher's Hill, Va., battlefield, Sept. 22, 1964."

572 **"DIARY of a Virginia Schoolmistress,**
1860-1865. Edt: Glenn Curtiss Smith." Harrisonburg, Va., Madison College, 1949. The Madison Quart., Mar. 1949, v.9, #2, p. 25-58. Kept by an unnamed teacher, Rockingham-Bath Counties, Va., and Ritchie Co., A. Va.

573 **"DIARY of a Pro-Union woman** of the Confederacy." p. 181-202. In: Harold Straubing's-"Civil War eyewitness reports", Hamden, Conn., Archon Bks. Excerpts from "Famous Adventures and Escapes of the Civil War." (Century, 1893) Written by a Mrs. H.L. who survived the battle of Vicksburg and ran out of writing material until Aug. 1863.

574 **DIBBLE, Ernest F.**
"Slave rentals to the Military Pensacola and the Gulf Coast." In: CWH, June 1977, v.23, #2, p. 101-113.

575 **DICKENS, Charles**
"A Waif from Dixie." Originally published Oct. 29, 1864, in-"All the Year Round", also in a bound volume XII, 1865. English reaction to Southern newspapers.

576 **DICKERT, D. Augustus**
"History of Kershaw's Brigade, with complete roll of companies, biographical sketches, incidents, anecdotes, etc." Newberry, S.C., Elbert H. Aull Co., 1899. 8vo, cl, ports (incl. front), 583, 5, 2pp. $75, $135, $200, $500-bmk-105, (atg)$225, $1000-b-144. First issued in wraps. Rosters: S.C. Regs: 2nd, 3rd, 7th, 8th, 3rd. Batt., 20th.
...(Dayton, Ohio) Morningside Bookshop, 1973. Facsimilie-13. Intro: Dr. Wm. Stanley Hoole, (4)pp., added. $20-y, $25-y, $15.
..."History of Kershaw's Brigade, with roll of companies, etc. . . . Dayton, Oh., Morningside Press, 1988. 8vo, cl, dj, 583p, ports, rosters. $30.

577 **DICKEY, Dallas C. and Donald C. Streeter**
"Lucius Q.C. Lamar. Speech Association of America, a history and criticism of American public addresses. (1955), v.3, p. 175-221, note bibliog. Relates to his public speaking, 1859-1887. Mainly in Miss., Confederacy and natl. politics.

578 **DICKEY, Thomas S. and Peter C. George**
"Field artillery projectiles of the American Civil War, including a selection of navy projectiles, hand grenades, rockets and land mines. Edt: Col. Floyd W. McRae, Jr." Atlanta, Ga., Arsenal Press, (1980). 4to, cl, dj, 505pp., (5)p. index, illus., sketches. Lim. signed copies to 2000 copies. $35.

579 **DICKINSON, A.G.**
"Memoirs of their son, A.G. Dickinson during and since the late war between the states. Collated by the Free Lance Frecksburg, Va." The Free Lance (1887)? 8vo, wraps, 23pp., front, ports. John W. Woltz, Edt. "Free Lance".

580 **DICKINSON, Henry Clay**
"Diary of Capt. Henry C. Dickinson, CSA, Morris Island 1864-1865." (Denver: Williamson-Haffner Co., 1888) 8vo, cl, pls., ports., facsms., 6pp., 15-189pp. t/p, text within ornamental borders, edt. complimentary, 225 copies (signed by Mrs. Anne D. Morris). $35, $15, $25, $350-bmk-105.

580a **DICKINSON, Jack**
"Confederate Soldiers of Western Virginia." Barboursville, Va., 1986. $17.50. 4to, wraps, 31 leaves, ills, maps, ports. CSA soldiers from west Va. counties & present day W. Va.

581 **DICKINSON, Jack L.**
"8th Virginia Cavalry." Lynchburg, Va., H.E. Howard, 1986. 8vo, cl, dj, (5), 119pp., illus., maps, ports. 1000 copies, numbered, signed.
..."Jenkins Led Vanguard into Pennsylvania." In: CV, ns, May/June 1988, v. 36, #3, p. 26-30, maps, ports (tinted). Excerpts from his "Jenkins of Greenbottom, a civil war saga."

582 **DICKINSON, L.T.**
"A Rebel in Yankee toils." In: B & G, 1893, v.1, p. 366-375, illus.

583 **DICKINSON, Mary**
"Dickinson and his men." Jacksonville, Fla., San Marco Bookstore, 1984. 8vo, cl, 261pp., illus. $17.

584 **DICKINSON, Sally Bruce**
"Confederate Leaders." Staunton, Va., McClure Print, (1937). 8vo, cl, port., facsm., 198pp. errata slip. $85, $50, $75, $10-bmk.

585 **DICKISON, J.J., Col.**
"Florida." v.XVI, 8vo, cl, 367pp., Wilmington, N.C., Broadfoot, 1987.

586 **DICKISON, John J., Col.**
"Military History of Florida." In: Evans Confederate Military History (Atlanta, Ga.), v.XI, combined with Military Hist. Texas. 8vo, cl, 3/4 calf, group port, front(port), fldg. map, 212pp., biogs: p. 195-212, vi-vii.
...Same, but added biographies: "Additonal sketches illustrating the services of officers and privates and patriotic citizens of Florida." Biogs: (213)-367pp. $85.
...In: CV, 1902, v.10, p.419-420, port.

587 **DICKISON, Mary Elizabeth**
"Dickison and His Men. Reminiscences of the War in Florida." Louisville, Ky.: Courier-Journal, 1890, 8vo, decr-gilt cloth, front, ports, illus., 266pp. $25, $35, $10, $15, $40, $350, $75-miami, $275-bmk-105, $150-nc'76, $175-dab.
...Facsimile reproduction of 1890 edition, Floridiana Facsimile and Reproduction Series; Intro: Saml. Proctor. Gainesville, Fla.: University Press, 1962, 8vo, fabr., xxiv, 266, 6pp. (index) ports, illus. printed on tan paper. $65-r, $15-b, $17.50-y, $6.

588 **DICKSON, Capers**
"John Ashton: A Story of the War Between the States." Atlanta, Ga., Foote & Davies, 1896, 8vo, cl, 179pp. $6.50, $10. Author a member of Cobb's Legion, Georgia Volunteers during war.

589 **DICKSON, Frederick S.**
"Blackwood's History of the U.S." Philadelphia: 1896. 8vo, wraps, 27pp., anti-Lincoln. $2.50.
...Tarrytown, N.Y., Wm. Abbott, 1925. Mag. of Hist., Notes and Queries, Ex. #109, "Rare Lincolniana #25- "Blackwood's Hist. of the U.S., etc." with other reprints.

590 **DIDIER, Eugene Lemoine**
"Some Southern War Songs and their authors." In: Blue & Gray (Phila) 1893. v.II, p. 464-468.

591 **DIETZ, Aug.**
"Confederate States Catalogue and handbook." Bay Harbor Islands, Florida: Bogg & Laurence Pub. Co., 1986. 8vo, cl, 280pp., illus., 8pp. in color. Large new sections added and completely reorganized, revised, expanded, supplemented, prices updated. Reg. edt. $75. Deluxe edt. $125.

592 **DIETZ, August**
"The Confederate States Post-Office Department its Stamps and Stationery. A Record of Achievement. A Handbook of the Daughters of the Confederacy." Richmond, Va., Dietz Press (1948). $300-bmk. 8vo, decr. wraps, illus.(part color) ports. 48pp. facsms. $20-bmk, $7.50. (1950: $5.50. Summary of 1929 edt.) $12-nc; (1956) wrps. $15; (1945) wrps. $30.

593 ..."The Capture of Holly Springs, Miss. Dec. 20, 1862." PMHS, v.IV, 1901, p. 49-61.

594 ..."Reminiscences of service with the 1st. Miss. Cavalry." In: PMHS, v.VII, 1903, p. 85-100.

595 ..."Dietz Confederate States Catalogue and Handbook of the postage stamps and envelopes of the Confederate States of America.. Comprising handstamped paids, postmaster provisionals, the general issues, official and semi-official envelopes,

prisoner-of-war and flag-of-truce covers, express companies and blockade-run covers, patriotic covers, college covers, packet and steamboat covers and markings, postmarks and cancellations, unusual usages, essays and proofs, fakes and counterfeits, Confederate stamp money, Confederate currency, historical date, and other pertinent information. 1959 Edition." Richmond, Va., Dietz Print, 1959. 8vo, cl, dj, front (port)illus., facsms, 282pp. $45, See: Frances B. Browin, $7.50, $15.

596 ..."Dietz Specialized Catalogue of the Postage Stamps of the Confederate States of America comprising the general issues of the Confederate government, provisional issues of the postmasters, and handstamped paids. Fully illustrated." Richmond, Va., Dietz Print, 1931, narrow 12mo, fabricoid, illus., 320pp. $80, $35-jenk, $15. Suppl., 1932. 2nd edt., 1937, cl, 8vo, 167pp. $10; 3rd edt., 1945, cl, 8vo, 231pp., $30, $15, $10, $20; 4th edt., 1959, cl, dj, completely revised.

597 ..."The Postal Service of the Confederate States of America." Richmond, Va., Dietz Print, 1929. Large 8vo, cl, or Mor., color front, map, illus., incl. facsms, color pl. diagr., xi, 439pp. $500-atg., $150-serv., $100-bmk, $75-bond, $15, $22.50; Deluxe-1/2 Mor., $300, $50.

598 ..."The South's "Way of Life". Random notes for the student of Confederates." N.Y., The Stamp Specialist (1944) vignette, p. 3-24.

599 **DIKET, A.L.**
"Wha hae vi' (Pender)...bled." N.Y., Vantage Press, 1979, 12mo, cl, 165pp. $7.50, $25-r. Gen. Wm. Dorsey Pender's letters to wife.

600 **DILL, Jacob S., Rev., D.D.**
"American Scientist who Chartered the Oceans-Pathfinder of the Seas. Life Story of Com. Matthew Fontaine Maury, etc." In: Jour. Amer. Hist., 1910, v.IV, #3, p. 319-337, (2), illus., ports.

601 **DILLAHUNTY, Albert**
"Shiloh National Military Park, Tennessee. By Albert Dillahunty." Wash: Nat'l. park Ser. Hist. Handbook, ser. #10, 1955 (reprint 1961). 8vo, pict. color stiff wraps, facsms, illus., maps, ports, (4), 47pp.

602 **DILLARD, Anthony W., Hon.**
"William Lowndes Yancey. The sincere and unfaltering advocate of Southern rights." In: SHSP, 1893, v.XXI, p. 151-159.

603 **DILLARD, Richard**
"The Civil War in Chowan County, N.C." n.p., 1916. 8vo, wraps, cover title, maps, 30pp.

..."The Civil War in Chowan County, North Carolina." Suffolk, Va., Robt. Hardy Pub., 1986, 8vo, wraps, 32pp., maps.

604 **DILLON, Edward, Colonel**
"A letter from Colonel Dillon, recollections of General Van Dorn." In: SHSP, 1891, v.XIX, p. 198-201.

605 ..."General Van Dorn's Operations between Columbia and Nashville in 1863." In: SHSP, 1879, v.VII, p. 144-146.

606 **DILLON, Merton Lyon**
"Jason W. James (1843-1933), frontier democrat." In: NMHR, April 1956, v.31, p. 89-101. Life as "CSA Cavalry Captain, KKK leader, Texas Ranger and SW cattleman, in Mo., La., Tex., N.Mex. His doctrine military preparedness, white and Nordic superioty, and "violence in the name of a worth cause." Expressed in his memoirs (1911, 1928).

607 ..."Ulrich Bonnell Phillips: Historian of the Old South." Baton Rouge: Louisiana State University Press, 1985. 8vo, cl, dj, xiii, 190pp., illus., notes $20. Reviewed: John David Smith.

608 **DILLON, Rodney E., Jr.**
"The Little Affair": the Southwest Florida Campaign, 1863-1864." In: FHQ, Jan.

1984, v.62, #3, p. 314-331.

...."South Florida in 1860." In: FHQ, April 1982, v.LX, #4, p. 440-454, notes.

610 **DIMICK, Howard T.**
"The Capture of Jefferson Davis." (Jackson, Miss., Jour. Miss. Hist., Oct., 1947, v.IX, #4, p. 238-254.

611 ...."Motives for the Burning of Oxford, Mississippi." (Jackson, Miss., Jour. Miss. Hist., July, p. 946, v.VIII, #3, p. 111-120. Lincoln's retribution for Ft. Pillow.

612 ...."The Mythical Confederate Treasure." (Jackson, Miss., Jour. Miss. Hist., Oct., 1949, v.XI, #4, p. 243-249.

613 ...."Peace Overtures of July, 1864." New Orleans: LHQ, October 1946, v.29, #4, p. 1241-1258.

614 **DIMITRY, Adelaide Stuart**
"War-Time Sketches Historical and Otherwise." "Historian" Stonewall Jackson Chapter of New Orleans, #1135, UDC, (1909-1911). New Orleans, La., Louisiana Print, (1911?) (a 1913 edt. reported?) 8vo, cl, (6), 92pp. $20, $27.50, $35, $250-b.

615 **DIMITRY, John Bull Smith**
"Louisiana." v.XIII, 8vo, cl, 631pp., Wilmington, N.C., Broadfoot, 1987.

...."Louisiana." (v.X, Evan's Confederate Military History, Atlanta, Ga., Confed. Pub. Co., 1899. Arkansas is in this vo.) 8vo, cl, front(port), dbl. pg. map, 2-pp. group port., v, 329pp. (p. 322-329, "Roster of Louisiana Troops, mustered into the Provisional Army, Confederate States.") $10, $15, Reb-$35-b.

...Do: "Louisiana and Additional sketches illustrating the services of officers, privates and patriotic citizens of Louisiana." Tk. 8vo, cl, 321pp., biographical suppl., p. (323)-631. $100.

616 ...."The battle of the handerchiefs." In: CV, May 1923, v.XXXI, p. 182-183. CSA women of New Orleans' fight on the levee, Feb. 20, 1863.

617 **DINKINS, James**
"Personal experiences and recollections: excerpts-"The Army arrives at the Chickahominy River", p. 52-61." In: Harold Straubing's Civil War eyewitness reports, Hamden, Conn., Archon Bks., 1985.

618 **DINKINS, James, Capt.**
"1861 to 1865, by an Old Johnnie. Personal recollections and experiences in the Confederate Army." ("Furl that Banner", poem, sketch, below title.) Cincinnati: Robert Clarke Co., 1897. 12mo, color decr. cl, illus., ports (incl. front) half title, xv, (17)-280, (2)pp. $30, $40, $55, $75, $300-g, $250-bmk-105, $200-bmk, $135-jk, $125-gins.

...(Dayton, Ohio) Morningside Press, 1975. 12mo, cl, facsimilie #24, (2)p. foreword by Kenneth L. Bandy. $15-y, $10.

619 ...."Address on Jefferson Davis Day, delivered by...at the presentation of crosses of honor, by Stonewall Jackson, Chapter $1135, UDC, at Memorial Hall, Friday, June 3, 1910, New Orleans, La." New Orleans, La., Picayune Print, 1910, 8vo, cover title, 10pp.

620 ...."The Balaclava of America, reminiscences of the Battle of Franklin, Nov. 30, 1864, by James Dinkins and Stephen D. Lee, New Orleans, La., Picayune Print, 1903. 8vo, wraps, cover title, 16pp. (dbl. column)

621 ...."Civil War Reminiscences." In: Illinois Central Magazine, Nov. 1914, v.III, p. 9-18 and cont'd. successive issues, May 1915.

622 ...."Griffith-Barksdale-Humphrey Mississippi Brigade and its campaigns." In: So. Hist. Soc. Pap., 1904, v.XXXII, p. 250-274.

623 ...."Barksdale, Mississippi Brigade at Fredericksburg, read at 17th Annual reunion. Louisiana Division, UCV, Monroe, La., Oct. 15, 1908." InSo. Hist. Soc. Pap., 1908, XXXIV, p. 17-25.

624 ..."An August Sunday Morning in Memphis." Reprinted in Robt. S. Henry's "As they saw Forrest.", pg. 251-268.

625 ..."The Battle of Malvern Hill." In: Confed. Vet., Nov. 1928, XXXVI, 410.

626 ..."Pursuit and Capture of Col. Streight." In: Confed. Vet., Jan. 1928, XXXVI, 15-18pp., v.XXXV, Dec. 1927, p. 452-454.

627 ..."Les We Forget-Ben Butler." In: So. His. Soc. Papr., 1902, XXX, p. 188-195.

628 ..."Forrest's wonderful achievements." In: Confed. Vet., Jan. 1927, XXXV, p. 10-13.

629 ..."How Forrest saved the Army of Tennessee." In: Confed. Vet., Feb./Mar., 1927, XXXV, p. 54-56, 94-96.

630 ..."The last campaign of Forrest's Cavalry." In: Confed. Vet., Apr/May, 1927, p. 136-139, 177-179.

631 ..."The Battle of Brice's Crossroads." In: Confed. Vet., Oct. 1925, XXXIII, p. 380-382.

632 ..."The Capture of Fort Pillow." In: Conf. Vet., Dec. 1925, XXXIII, p. 460-462.

633 ..."How Forrest destroyed Sherman's line of communication." In: Confed. Vet., Apr. 1926, XXXIV, p. 135-138.

634 ..."The Confederate Ram Albemarle." In: SHSP, 1902, v.XXX, p. 205-214.

635 ..."The Battle of Shiloh, April 6, 1862. From New Orleans "Picayune", Dec. 27, 1903 and Jan. 24, 1904." In: SHSP, 1903, v.XXXI, p. 298-320.

636 ..."The Battle of Chickamauga. Address before United Confederate Veterans in Baton Rouge, La., Sept. 1904." In: SHSP, 1904, v.XXXII, p. 299-310.

637 ..."Boy Soldiers. Capt. Dinkins asks each state to count her young heroes who went from schoolroom to War." In: SHSP, 1907, v.XXXV, p. 108-109. 205-214.

638 ..."The Capture of Memphis by General Nathan B. Forrest." In: SHSP, 1908, v.XXXVI, p. 180-196.

639 ..."The Last Tragedy of the War. Execution of Tom Martin at Cincinnati by Gen. Hooker." In: SHSP, 1902, v.XXX, p. 129-134.

640 ..."Pursuit an d capture of Colonel Streight." p. 452-454; cont'd. 1928, v.36, p. 15-18;

641 ..."Nathan Bedford Forrest." 1929, v.37, p. 339-342;

642 ..."Lieut. Gen. D.H. Hill." 1930, v.38, p. 218-221;

643 ..."Destroying Yankee Gunboats." p. 341-344.

644 ..."My old black mammy." In: CV, 1926, v.34, p. 20-22;

645 ..."How Forrest destroyed Sherman line of communications", p. 135-138;

646 ..."Destroying military stores and gunboats, p. 176-179, ports;

647 ..."With Forrest in middle Tennessee." p. 218-220, port.;

648 ..."Barksdale's Mississippi Brigade at Fredericksburg." p. 256-259, illus.;

649 ..."On writing history." p. 326-327.

650 "DIRECTORY of City of Montgomery (Alabama) and Historical Sketches of Alabama Soldiers." (Montgomery) Perry and Smith, Mar. 1866, 8vo, wraps, 112pp.

651 "DIRECTORY of Civil War Monuments and Memorials in Tennessee." Nashville: Tenn. Civil War Centennial. 1963, cover title in color, index, illus., 4to, 93pp.

652 "DISRUPTION of the Union. The," In: Black. Edn. Mag., July 1861, v.XC, p. 125-134. "Hopes the North will concede secession."

653 DITZEL, Paul
"The Fantastic Struggles of the Monitor and the Merrimac." In: "Amer. Legion Mag.", March 1969, illus., p. 30-34, 51-57.

654 DIVINE, John E.
"8th Virginia Infantry." Lynchburg, Va., H.E. Howard, 1984. (J.P. Bell Print) Lim.

Atg. Edt. 8vo, cl, dj, (7), 89pp., maps, ports, pls. $17.50.

655 ..."35th Battalion Virginia Cavalry." Lynchburg, Ca., H.E. Howard, 1985. (J.P. Bell Print) Lim. Atg. Edt. 8vo, cl, dj, (4), 112pp. map. $17.50.

656 **"DIXIE Calendar, The**
(1913), with a foreword by Matthew Page Andrews, Baltimore." N.Y., Dodge Publishing Co., (1912). 8vo, pict. stiff cover, silk-tied, (50)pp., in red-borders, printed on one side. 1st Edt., 1912. Day-by-day quotations made by Southern literary, military authors. At end a page of acknowledgements. Originally pub. title-"Dixie Book of Days."

657 **"DIXIE Date Book"**
Boston: Colonial Pub. Co., n.d. (1940's) Spriral-bound, 8vo, pict. wraps, boxed, unpaginated, 53 photos and portraits in color of CSA generals and battle sites. $7.50.

658 **"DIXIE Dates."**
St. Louis, Mo., U.D.C. (1912). St. Louis Chap. #624. 8vo, (70)pp., col. pl. Chronological Record, War dates. $.50, $15-bmk.

659 **"DIXIE Land Songster, The**
Published by Blackmar & Bros., Augusta Ga." Macon, Ga. Burke, Boykin & Co., 1863. 5 1/2" tall, 32pp. Crandall-3259. (wraps) $750-goodspeed. Albert Pike's version of Dixie and E. Young's song "Gilmer Blues" of Lexington.

660 **"DIXIE MAGAZINE, The**
Reunion Souvenir Historical Issue of Dixie Magazine, Mouthpiece of the South. Complimentary to the 36th Annual reunion United Confederate Veterans, Birmingham, Ala., May 18-21." 1926. (Little Rock, Ark., May, 1926. vol. III, #2, 4to, wraps, color flags, ports, illus., (4)pp. ads, (57), (19) ads, various authors, articles. $7.50.

661 **DIXON, Harry St. John**
"Recollections of a Rebel Private." In: The Sigma Chi Quart., 1886, v.V, p. 15-20, 71-77, 145-154, 195-207; 1887, v.VI, p. 141-149, 218-223.

662 **DIXON, Samuel H.**
"Robert Warren, the Texas Refugee..." Generally attributed to Dixon. See: Robert Warren

663 **DIXON, Thomas**
"The Victim; a Romance of the Real Jefferson Davis." N.Y., D. Appleton & Co., 1914. 12mo, cl, illus., front, 510pp. $7.50. Va. State Lib.-"professional fiction but atmosphere, many details for a comprehensive view of Davis' career.
...N.Y., Grossett & Dunlap (1916) plates, some in color.

664 ..."The Man in Gray: a Romance of North and South." N.Y., Lond: D. Appleton & Co., 1921. 12mo, cl, front, 5427pp. On Lee. $10-bmk.

665 **DOAR, Emma Catherine Burn**
"One family's life in wartime South." In: CWT, May, 1961, v.III, #2 (OS), p. 17-19, pl, port. Hardship, death and fright was lot on coastal South Carolina plantation.

666 **DOBIE, J. Frank**
"Old Bill, Confederate Ally." In: Atl. Monthly, Oct. 1943. $85-jk.

667 **DOBNEY, Frederick J.**
"From Denominationalism to Nationalism in the Civil War: a Case Study." In: Texana, 1971, v.IX, #4, p. 367-376, notes. Clergymen lead in secession, and morale in the CSA.

668 **"DOCUMENTAL and STATISTICAL Appendix**
to Clement Anselm Evans." "Confederate Military History." v.XII, p. 369-512. Index: 12vols. p. 513-551.

669 **"DOCUMENTS relating to Secession in Florida."**
In: FHQ, April, 1926, v.IV, p. 183-185.

670 **"DOCUMENTS relating to the Geneva Arbitration**
House Ex. Docs., No. 1, part 2 to 5, 42nd Cong., 3rd Sess., Vol. I. Containing the case of the U.S., the case of Great Britain, the counter case of the U.S. and additional documents, correspondence, and evidence laid before the tribunal of arbitration convened at Geneva under the treaty of Washington." 4 vols. Dec. 2, 1872. Covers the Alabama and Shenandoah. See: Ernest Scott and Jas. I. Waddell, Cornelius E. Hunt. Much of the Ex-Docs. (above) also found in "English Parliamentary Papers, 1866." Some identical.

670a **DODD, D. B.**
"Winston: an Antebellum & Civil War history of a hill county of North Alabama." Jasper, Ala., 1972. 8vo, cl, 319pp., ills, maps, ports. $25.

671 **DODD, David Owen**
"Letters of David O. Dodd with Biographical Sketch by Dallas T. Herndon." n.p., n.d. Large 8vo, wraps, 15, (1)p. $5, $16-bmk. Off-print, Ark. Hist. Ass'n., 1917, v.IV, p. (152)-169. Little Rock, Ark., Democrat Print. Also in Pub. Ark. Hist. Ass'n., IV, (1917), p. 140-151.

672 ..."The True Story of David Owen Dodd, presented to pupils of David O. Dodd School by Memorial Chapter #48, U.D.C., 1929." (Little Rock, Ark., Parke-Harper Co.). 32mo, wraps, port., illus., 12pp. See: Mrs. Myra Vaughan, LeRoy H. Fischer, Dallas T. Herndon, Col. W.C. Parham, Confed. Vet: Dec. 1905, v.XIII, #12-Roy D.Campbell, Mrs. J.T. Gray, Dec. 1922, v.XXX, #12, p. 477, Mrs. W.H. Walkup, Aug. 1931, v.XXXIX, #8, p. 294.

673 ..."Letters of David O. Dodd." In: Ark. Hist. Rev. 1934, v.I, #1, p. 44-64. Biog. sketch of Dodd who "was hanged at Little Rock, as a CSA spy, Jan. 8, 1864," text of letters written to sister and mother, 1862-1863.

674 **DODD, Dorothy**
"Florida in the War. 1861-1865." In: Fla. Handbook, 1959-1860. p. 1-90, facsms., maps, ports, views, notes.

675 ..."The Manufacture of Cotton in Florida before and during the Civil War." In: FHQ, July 1934, v.XIII, #1, p. (3)-15.

676 ..."The Secession Movement in Florida, 1850-1861." In: FHQ, July and Oct., 1933, v.XII, #1 and 2, p. (3)-24, p. (45)-66. See: Florida Secession.

677 **DODD, Ephraim Shelby**
"Diary of Ephraim Shelby Dodd Member of Co. D., Terry's Texas Rangers, Dec. 4, 1862-Jan. 1, 1864." Intro: E.W. Winkler, Austin, Texas: E.L. Steck Co., 1914, 8vo, wraps, 32pp., $15, $20, $25, $30, $40-y, $50, $75-jk-122, $125-bmk-105, $150-g. Terry's Rangers, See: C.C. Jeffries and L.B. Giles. 250 copies printed.

678 ..."Diary of E.S. Dodd and an account of his hanging as a Confederate spy, by R.F. Bunting." Austin, Texas: Ranger Press, 1979, 8vo, wraps, iv, 44pp. $6.50. Facsm. reprint of 1914 edt. Bunting's account first published in Houston Telegraph in 1865. An introduction by Tom Munnerlyn and an index added to both accounts. Dodd and Bunting were members of Terry's Texas Rangers and 8th Texas Cavalry.

679 **DODD, James M.**
"Civil War diary of James M. Dodd of the "Cooper Guards"." In: RKHS, Oct. 1961, v.59, #4, p. 343-349.

680 **DODD, John Morris**
"Autobiography of a surgeon." N.Y., Walter Neale, 1928. 8vo, cl, 323pp., front, illus., ports. $15.

681 **DODD, W.O., Capt.**
"Reminiscences of Hood's Tennessee Campaign." In: SHSP, 1881, v.IX, p. 518-524.

682 **DODD, William Edward**
"The Cotton Kingdom; a Chronicle of the Old South." New Haven: Yale Univ. Press (1919). Chronicles of America Series: XXVII, 8vo, cl, x, 161pp., plates, ports, fldg. map. "Abraham Lincoln Edt." $12.50.

683 ..."Jefferson Davis." Philadelphia: Geo. W.Jacobs (1907). 12mo, cl, front(port) 396pp. $3, $7, $7.50, $10.
...Reprint, N.Y., 1966, N.Y.-Russell & Russell. calf, $20, $10.50-y, $8.50.

684 ..."John Taylor, of Carolina, Prophet of Secession." (Lynchburg, Va., Randolph-Macon College) John P. Branch Hist. Papers, v.2, #3 and 4, June, 1908, p. (214)-252, Swem-1478.

685 ..."Lincoln or Lee; comparison and contrast of the two greatest leaders in the War Between the State, the narrow and accidental margins of success." New York: The Century Co., (1928). 12mo, cl, and bos, viii, 177pp., illus.(map)ports. $6, $12.50-7.
...Gloucester, Mass., P. Smith, 1964, $4.50.

686 ..."The Old South; Struggles for Democracy." New York: Macmillan Co., 1937. 8vo, cl, vii, ds, (4), 312pp., ports, maps. $9.50, $12.50, $18. 1st of 4 vols. Dodd planned; this period prior to 1690, on motives colonists brought, i.e., free homesteads, religion, trade and self-gov.

687 ..."Robert J. Walker." In: Bul. Randolph-Macon Woman's Col., v.1, #2, Jan. 1915. Vindicates Jeff Davis of Walkers' charges against Davis and Mississippi (Bond) repudiation.

688 ..."Statesmen of the Old South, or From Radicalism to Conservative Revolt." New York: The Macmillan Co., 1911. 12mo, cl, ix, 242pp. $6.50, $10.
...N.Y., Book League of America, 1929, as above, and 1926. $7.50, $9.50.

689 **DODGE, David**
"The Cave-dwellers of the Confederacy." In: Atlantic Monthly, 1891, v.LXVIII, p. 514-521.

690 ..."Domestic Economy in the Confederacy." In: Atlantic Monthly, Aug. 1886, v.58, p. 229-242.

691 **DODGE, David (pseud.)**
See: O(scar) W(illiam) Blacknall.

692 **DODGE, Theodore Ayrault, Colonel**
"The Battle of Chancellorsville. A lecture at Lowell Institute, Boston." In: SHSP, 1886, v.XIV, p. 276-292. See: William Allan.

693 **DODSON, A.R., Mrs.**
"The city of Chattanooga, Tenn." In: CV, Dec., 1928, v.XXXVI, p. 1461-462. Background hist., particularly Civil War.

694 ..."Tennessee in the Confederate Congresses." In: CV, Nov. 1927, v.XXXV, p. 424-425.

695 **DODSON, Clyde N.**
"The Battle of Brice's Crossroads." In: Military Review, 1964, v.XLIV-vi, p. 85-98.

696 **DODSON, William Carey**
"Campaigns of Wheeler and His Cavalry, 1862-1865, from material furnished by Gen. Joseph Wheeler, to which is added his concise and graphic account of the Santiago Campaign of 1898. Published under the auspices of Wheeler's Confederate Cavalry Association and edited by W.C. Dodson." Atlanta, Ga., Hudgins Pub., 1899. 8vo, cl, illus., ports, xxiv, 431, vi, (1), 78pp. (1/2 Mor.) $40, $17.50, $25, $30, $35, $60-bmk, $75-g, $100-db.

697 ..."Burning of Broad River Bridge." In: Confed. Vet., XVII, Sept. 1909, p. 462-465. Near Columbia, S.C., Feb. 16, 1865.

698 ..."Meeting of the Confederate Veterans at Memphis, Tennessee. Rejoiner to Bennett H. Young's address." In: SHSP, 1910, v.XXXVIII, p. 216-220.

699 **DOGGETT, David Seth, Rev.**
"A nation's Ebenezer. A discourse

delivered in the Broad St. Methodist Church, Richmond, Va., Thurs. Sept. 18, 1862: the day of public thanksgiving, appointed by the President of the Confederate States. Published by special request." Richmond, Va., Enquirer Print, 1862. 12mo, wraps, 18pp., $17.50, $20, $28, $35.

700 ..."The War and its Close. A discourse, delivered in Centenary Church, Richmond, Va., Friday, April 8, 1864, by..., pastor, on occasion of the National Fast. Pub. by the Soldier's Tract Ass'n., M.E. Church, South." Richmond, Va., MacFarlane & Fergusson, 1864. 16mo, wraps, 20pp.

701 **DOHERTY, Edward**
"Pursuit and death of John Wilkes Booth." In: Cent., Nov. 1889, v.17, p. 443-449.

702 **DOLES, George, General**
"Battle of Gettysburg-Report of General G. Doles, Hdq., July 10, 1863." In: SHSP, 1880, v.VIII, p.41-44.

703 **DOLL, Howard D.**
"John Hunt Morgan and the Soldier Printers." In: Filson Club Hist. Quart., 1973, v.XLVIII, p. 29-55.

704 **"DOLLIE and MOLLIE." (pseud.)**
"Our Own Heroes. A thrilling narrative. By Dollie and Mollie." v.1, 1863. Atlanta, Ga., Office of the Soldier's Friend. 12mo, cl, 128pp. (v.1, all published) $20.

705 **DONALD, David Herbert**
"The Confederate as a Fighting Man." (Lexington, Ky.) JSH, May, 1959, v.XXV, #2, p. 178-193. $8.

706 ..."The Southerner as a fighting man." In: Charles Grier Sellers, Jr., Edt-"Southerner as American." (Chapel Hill: Univ. of N.C. Press, (1960), p. 72-88, notes. "CSArmy an extraordinary democratic/aristocratic one, an admirable fighting man but a poor soldier."

707 ..."An excess of democracy: the American Civil War and the Social Process." Oxford: Clarendon Press, 1960. 8vo, wraps, 22, (1)pp.

708 ..."Why the North won the Civil War. Essays by Richard N. Current, et al." Baton Rouge, Louisiana State Univ. (1960). 8vo, cl, dj, 129pp., xv, $3.
...Reprint, (1973). $4.

709 **DONALD, William J.**
"Alabama Confederate Hospitals." In: "Ala. Review", 1962, v.XV, p. 271-281; 1963, v.XVI, p. 64-78.

710 ..."Confederate States Medicine-Alabama's Role." In: Med. Ass'n., Ala.-Journ., 1963, v.XXXIII, p. 69-73.

711 **DONALDSONVILLE Artillery**
See: R. Prosper Landry.

712 **DONNELLY, Ralph W.**
"The Bartow County Confederate Saltpetre Works." In:GHQ, Fall 1970, v. LIV, #3, p.305-19.

713 ..."Battle Honors & Services of Confederate Marines." In: Mil. Affairs, Spring, 1959, v.23, #1, p.37-40.

714 ..."Biographical Sketches of the Commissioned Officers of the Confederate States Marine Corps." (Alexandria, Va., 1973) (Richmond, Va., The Little Print Shop.) 4to, pict. stiff wraps, ports, vi, (6)pp. 24, ports, 68pp. $25-bmk, $6.
...1983 revised edition of the 1973 edition. 88pp. with 10pp. photos of all known CSA pixs of marine officers, introductory material of 21pp. a total of 88pp. $10.

715 ..."The Charlotte, N.C. Navy Yard, CSN." In: CWH, March, 1959, v.V, #1, p. 72-79.

716 ..."The Charlotte Mint: $.08 Balance." In: Numismatist, Nov. 1966, v.79, #11, p. 1484-1486.

717 ..."Confederate Copper." In: CWH, Dec., 1955, v.1, #4, p. 355-370.

718 ..."The Confederate Lead Mines of Wythe County, Va." In: CWH, Dec. 1959, v.V, #4, p. 402-414.

719 ..."The Confederate Marines at Drewry's Bluff." In: Va. Cavalcade, Autumn, 1966, v.XVI, #2, p. 42-47, ports, pls, map.

720 ..."Confederate Muster Rolls." In: Mil. Affairs, Fall, 1952, v.XVI, #3, p. 132-135.

721 ..."A Confederate Navy Forlorn Hope." In: Mil. Affairs, Summer, 1964, v.XXVIII, #2, p. 73-78.

722 ..."The Confederate States Marine Corps." In: UDC Mag., Dec. 1970, v.XXXIII, #12, p. 14-16; 22-23.

723 ..."District of Columbia Confederates." In: Mil. Affairs, Winter, 1959, v.XXIII, #4, p. 207-208. $4.

..."Gadfly on the Potomac (1861-1862), C.S.S. "George Page"." In: Amer. Neptune, April, 1983, p. 129-134.

724 ..."Georgia Uniforms of 1861." In: Mil. Coll. and Hist., Winter 1962, v.XIV, #4,.

725 ..."The History of the Confederate States Marine Corps." (Washington, N.C., the Author, 1976) (New Bern, N.C., Owen G. Dunn Co.) 4to, pict. stiff wraps, illus., ports, facsms. 3-fldg. tables, xi, (9)pp. pls., 275pp. $8.50, $40-b, atg.-$7-g. Essay on soures, p. 178-208; 223-260, index, 261-175. $16-cl.

726 ..."Local Defense in the Confederate Munitions Area." In: Mil. Affairs, Fall, 1954, v.XVIII, #3, p. 118-130.

..."Officers of the Revenue Marine Service in the Confederacy." In: Amer. Neptune, Oct. 1980, p. 298-304.

727 ..."Personnel of the Confederate Navy." In: CWTI, Jan. 1975, v.XIII, #9, p. 26-35.

..."Personnel records of the Confederate Sailor." In: CV, ns, Mar./Apr., 1987, v.35, #2, p. 18-21, 46-47, illus.

728 ..."Revenue Marine Service: The Nucleus of the Confederate Navy." In: Naval Inst. Proceedings.

729 ..."Rocket Batteries of the Civil War." In: Mil. Affairs, Summer, 1961, v.XXV, #2, p. 69-93. $15.

730 ..."Rocketry in the 1860's." In: Ordnance, May-June 1962, v.XLVI, #252, p. 767-769.

731 ..."Scientists of the Confederate Nitre and Mining Bureau." In: CWH, Dec. 1956, v.II, #4, p. 69-92. Also: reprint pamphlet.

732 ..."Spurious Confederate Marine Corps. Belt Buckles." In: Mil. Coll. and Hist., Spring, 1974, v.XXVI, #1, p. 37-39.

733 ..."Uniforms and Equipment of Confederate Marines." In: Mil. Coll. and Hist., Spring, 1957, v.IX, #1, 1.1-7.

734 DONNELL, F.S.
"The Confederate Territory of Arizona, as Compiled from Official Sources." (Albuquerque, N.M., New Mexico Historical Review, April, 1942, v.XVII, #2, p. 148-163.

735 ..."When Las Vegas was the Capital of New Mexico." Oct. 1933, New Mexico Hist. Rev., v.VIII, #4, p. 265-272, port. For a short time during the war, Vegas was capital, CSA forces held southern N.M. from Rio Grande to Fort Craig.

736 DONNELLY, Clarence Shirley
"David S. Creigh-The Greenbrier Martyr; A Tradegy of the Civil War." (Oak Hill, W.Va., The Author, 1950) 8vo, wraps, cover title, 11pp. See: Thomas Creigh.

737 ..."General "Tiger John" McCausland, the man who burned Chambersburg." In: W. Va. Hist., 1961, v.XXIII, p. 139-145.

738 ..."Historical Notes on Fayette County, W.Va." (Oak Hill, W.Va.) The Author, 1958. 8vo, cl, 178pp., facsm., map, ports, views. Much on CSA, M.W. Humphrey's "Mil. Opr. in Fayette Co., W.Va." is reprinted.

739 ..."The Thurmonds; a study in the genealogy and history of Philip Thurmond of Amherst County, Va., and his descendants. (And members of his family in the Confederate service). (Oak Hill, W.Va., 1939). tall 8vo, wraps, front, illus., (4),

47pp. $17.50. Lim. Edt. 125 copies, type destroyed.

740 DONNELLY, Shirley
"Tiger John" McCausland: the man who burned Chambersburg." In: WVaH., Jan. 1962, v.23, #2, p. 139-45.

741 DONNELLY, William J.
"Conspiracy or popular movement: the historiography of southern support for secession." In: NCHR, 1965, v.42, p. 70-84.

742 DONOHUE, John C.
"Fight at Front Royal." In: SHSP, 1896, v.XXIV, p. 131-138.

743 DONOVAN, Frank Robert
"The ironclads." N.Y., Barnes, (1961). 8vo, cl, illus., 125pp. "American History Series." Juvenile Lit.
..."Ironclads of the Civil War, by the Editors of American Heritage. Consultant Bruce Catton." N.Y., American Heritage Pub. Co., Harper & Row, (1964). "America Heritage Junior Library." Sm.4to, illus.(part color), maps (part color), ports (part color), 153pp. $6.

744 DOOLADY, Michael
"Jefferson Davis and Stonewall Jackson, Life and Public Service of both..." See under title "Jefferson Davis." Doolady appears under copyright.

745 DOOLEY, John Edward
"John Dooley, Confederate Soldier, his war journal." Edt: Joseph T. Durkin, S.J., with a foreword by Douglas Southall Freeman." (Washington, D.C.) Georgetown University Press, 1945. Sitterding Foundation. pres-$40-bmk-84, $20-bmk. 8vo, cl, front(port) facsm., xxiii, 244pp., index, map endsheets. $25-bmk. Dooley was an officer in 1st Va. Inf., Kemper's Brig., Pickett's Div. ANV.
...(Notre Dame, Ind.) Univ. Press, 1963, xix, 244pp., 12mo, wraps, $1.95, $3-y.

746 DOOLEY, Louis K.
"Little Sorrel: A War-horse for Stonewall." In: Army, 1975, v.XXV, p. iv, 34-39.

747 DORGAN, Howard
"The Doctrine of Victorious Defeat in the Rhetoric of Confederate Veterans." In: So. Speech Jour., 1972, v.XXXVIII, p. 119-130.

748 ..."Ringing Changes on the Southern Belles: The Cult of Southern Womanhood in the Ceremonial Oratory of Confederate."

749 DORMAN, J. Frederick
"General William Preston." At dedication of bronze bust of Gen. Preston, address. In: FCHQ, October, 1969, v.43, #4, p. 301-310.

750 DORMAN, James H.
"Thespis in Dixie. Professional Theater in Confederate Richmond." In: Virginia Cavalcade, Summer, 1978, v.XXVIII, #1, p. 4-13, facsms., illus(1-color), ports.

751 DORMAN, James Hervey
"In everything give thanks: a journal of the life and times of James Hervey Dorman." In: RKHS, Apr. 1962, v.60,, p. 85-106. Service in CSArmy, Owen County, Ky.

752 DORMAN, Lewy
"Part politics in Alabama from 1850 through 1960." Wetumpka, Ala., Wetumpka Print, 1935. 8vo, cl, 240pp., illus. (maps) Pub. of Alabama State Dept. Archives and History. Hist. and Patriotic ser. #13. Bibliog: P. 229-235.

753 DORNBUSCH, Charles E.
"Military Bibliography of the Civil War." Readex Books, Microprint Corp. (1975) 3 vols., 8vo, and sm. 4to, cloth.
..."Military Bibliography of the Civil War: Volume Four." Dayton, Oh., Morningside Press, 1987. Sm.4to, cl, xvii, 20-424p. $25.

754 DORNBUSCH, Charles Emil, Compiler
"Regimental Publications and Personal Narratives of the Civil War. A Checklist in 7-parts." N.Y., Public Library, 1961. sm

4to, pt. I-Illinois (46pp.); pt.II, N.Y., (73pp.); pt.III, New England States (107pp.); pt.IV-New Jersey and Pa. (72pp.); pt.V-Indiana and Ohio (88pp.); pt.VI-Iowa, Kan., Mich., Minn., Wisc. (93pp.); pt.VII-Index of names, (45pp.). Rep: 1971, $25.

...N.Y., 1967-"Regimental Publications and Personal Narratives: Southern, Border, and Western States and Territories; Federal Troops, Union and Confederate Biographies." xiii, 270pp., 1971,

...1971 reprint, $25-y.

...N.Y., 1972-vol.III, General References; Armed Forces; and Campaigns and Battles., xv, 224pp.,3 vo., cloth. Foregoing in wraps. $44,

...1983 reprint in 3 vols., $65., Vol.I-$25; Vol.II-$20; Vol.III-$20.

755 **DORR, James A.**
"Justice to the South! An address by..., a member of the New York Bar, Oct. 8, 1856." N.Y., n.d., 8vo, wraps, 12pp.

756 **DORRIS, Jonathan Truman**
"Pardoning John Cabell Breckenridge." In: Reg. Ky. Hist. Soc., Oct. 1958, v.56, p. 319-324. On his political status from 1860-1869.

757 ..."Pardoning the leaders of the Confederacy." In: MVHR, June 1928, v.XV, p. 3-21. $15-bmk. Archives holds 14,000-15,000 applications for a pardon, by officers who were excepted from clemency by Pres. Johnson. Many discussed in this study.

758 ..."Pardon and Amnesty during the Civil War and Reconstruction." Urbana, Ill., 1929. (abstract of thesis (phd)-University of Ill., 1926) 23pp.

759 ..."Pardon seekers and brokers; sequel to Appomattox." In: JSH, 1935, v.I, p. 276-292. (pardon brokerage business dev. by CSA "leaders".

760 ..."Pardon and Amnesty under Lincoln and Johnson: The Restoration of the Confederates to their rights and privileges, 1861-1898." Intro: J.G. Randall. Chapel Hill: Univ. of North Carolina, (1953) 8vo, cl, dj, bibliog., xxii, 459pp. $7.50, $14-bmk, $20.

761 ..."Pardon seekers and brokers: sequel to Appomattox." In: FCHQ, July 1963, v.37, #3, p. 210-226. (also: JSH, v.1, #3, p. 276-292) 1935.

762 ..."President Lincoln's treatment of Confederates." In: Filson Club Hist. Quart., April, 1959, v.33, p. 139-160.

763 ..."President Lincoln's treatment of Kentuckians." In: FCHQ, Jan. 1954, v.28, #1, p. 3-20.

764 ..."States Rights and Sectionalism. Address delivered by..., on Sept. 5, 1948, at the dedication of Monument to Three Unknown Confederate Soldiers (Morgan Raiders) buried in the cemetery at Old Washington, O., July, 1863." (Berea, 1949) 8vo, wraps, illus., 16pp. $5.

765 ..."Treatment of Confederates by Lincoln, Johnson and Congress, 1861-1898... Edt: Wayne C. Temple." (Richmond, Ky. ? 1960) 8vo, wraps, 32pp. See also: J.C. Chenault, Lincoln Herald, Spring, 1960.

766 **DORSEY, Frank**
"Wounding of Gen. J.E.B. Stuart." In: SHSP, 1902, v.30, p. 236-238.

767 ..."Gen. J.E.B. Stuart's last battle." In: CV, Feb. 1909, v.XVII, p. 76-77.

768 **DORSEY, Sarah Anne Ellis**
"Recollections of Henry Watkins Allen, Brigadier-General Confederate States Army Ex-Govenor of Louisiana." N.Y., M. Doolady and New Orleans, La. (1866). 12mo, cl, or 3/4 leather, port(front), 420pp. $15, $17.50, $20, $22.50, $27-nc, $25, $85-jk-121, $50-bmk.

769 ..."Lucia Dare: A Novel. by Filia." N.Y., M. Doolady, 1867. 8vo, cl, 138pp., dble-column. Wright-#777-778. Thru Civil War

period, author claims true to history, much of action around Natchez.

DORTCH, Hugh
"Lest We Forget: North Carolina's Commemoration of the War Between the States." In: NCHR, April, 1959, v.XXXVI, p. 163-164.

771 **DOSCH, Donald F.**
"The Hornet's Nest at Shiloh." In: THQ, Summer 1978, v.37, #2, p. 175-189.

772 **DOSTER, James F.**
"Were the Southern Railroads Destroyed by the Civil War?" In: CWH, September, 1961, v.VII, #3, p. 310-320.

773 **DOTSON, Susan Merle, Compl.**
"Who's Who of the Confederacy. A Symposium by the members of Albert Sidney Johnston, Chap. #2060, UDC." (San Antonio, Texas, Naylor Co., 1966) 8vo, cl, illus., ports, xvi, 368pp. $5-y, $20-bmk.

774 **DOTY, Franklin A.**
"Florida, Iowa, and the National "Balance of Power" in 1845." In: FHQ, July 1956, v.XXXV, #1, p. 30-59.

775 **DOUGAN, Michael B.**
"Confederate Arkansas: The People and Policies of a Frontier State in Wartime." University, Alabama: Univ. of Ala. Press, 1976, 8vo, cl, dj, vii, 165pp. $12-y, $8.50.

776 ..."The Little Rock Press goes to War, 1861-1865." In: AHQ, v.XXVIII, p. 14-27.

777 ..."Life in Confederate Arkansas." In: AHQ, 1972, v.XXXI, p. 15-35.
"Civil War years in Craighead County (Arkansas)." In: CrCHQ, Spring, 1975, v.13, p. 18-23.

778 ..."Two manuscript Folksongs from Civil War Arkansas and their background." In: Mid-South Folklore, Winter 1974, v.2, p. 83-88.

779 ..."An Ozark boy in the Confederate ranks: the soldier letters of W.V. Startk." In: Mid-South Folklore, Summer, 1978, v.6, p. 37-42.

780 **DOUGHERTY, William E., Capt.**
"An Eyewitness Account of second Bull Run." In: Amer. Hist., Dec. 1966, v.I, #8, p. 30-43, illus., ports, maps. Although Union soldier, a vivid acct. of how 48,000 CSA soldiers routes a Union force of 75,000 men.

781 **DOUGLAS, B.M. and B.H. Hughes**
"Catalogue of CSA and Southern States Currency with Historical Notes and Estimated values of Bradbeer's Varieties and Chase Types." Washington, D.C., 1955, 8vo, wraps, 31pp. $5.

782 **DOUGLAS, Beverly B.**
"Memorial Addresses on the Life and Character of..." Washington, 1879, 4to, cl, port, 42pp. $7.50. Representative from Va., served as a Major in the CSArmy.

783 **DOUGLAS, Clarence deWitt**
"Conscription and Writ of Habeas Corpus in North Carolina During Civil War." Durham, N.C., Duke University, 1922. 8vo, wraps, p. (5)-39. Historical Papers Trinity College Historical Society, Ser.XIV.

784 **DOUGLAS, Hamilton, Hon.**
"Lee Centennial Memorial Address." Atlanta, Ga., 1907 (100th Anniversary) 8vo, wraps, 12pp. $5.

785 **DOUGLAS, Henry Kyd, Col.**
"Stonewall Jackson in Maryland." In: B & L., v.2, p. 620-629, illus., ports.

786 **DOUGLAS, Henry Kyde**
"I Rode With Stonewall Being Chiefly the war experience of the youngest member of Jackson's staff from the John Brown Raid to the hanging of Mrs. Surratt." Chapel Hill: Univ. of N. Carolina (1940). $40-nc, $25-bmk, $16. 8vo, cl, dj, ports (incl. front)pls., fold. map, facsm, vii, 401pp. $8.50, $10, $20-bmk-84. (2nd, 3rd, 4th, 5th edts., 1940, also a London edt.; 6th(1941), (1943), (1945) and (1951) 10th Edt., 1968, 1980, $20, $12.50.

...."A Ride for Stonewall, a Confederate officer's wonderful record in Bank's rear." SHSP, v.XXI, p. 206-212, 1893.

787 ..."Stonewall Jackson, between his deathbed and his grave." p. 370-372. Balt: Southern Mag., 1874, v.XIV.

788 ..."Stonewall Jackson and His Men." Phila: 1879, p. 642-653.

789 ..."Stonewall Jackson in Maryland." In: "Battles and Leaders", II, p. 6290629.

790 ..."Stonewall Jackson's intentions at Harper's Ferry." (above) p. 617-718.

791 ..."Stonewall Jackson in Maryland." In: Cent., June 1886, ns, X, p. 285-295, illus., map.

792 **DOUGLAS, Henry Thompson, Colonel**
"A Famous Army and its Commander." In: SHSP, Oct., 1917, v.XLII, p. 189-198. Army of Peninsula and Gen. Magruder.

793 ..."Reminiscences of the Peninsula." In: CV, Dec. 1903, v.XI, p. 554-556.

794 **DOUGLAS, Lucia Rutherford, Edt.**
"Douglas's Texas, C.S.A." (Smith County Historical Society) (Waco, Texas: Texian Press) 8vo, cl, d/w, illus., append., ports, facsm., index, p. xiii, 238. 1000 copies, unit sketches, muster rolls, largely letters of Douglas to his wife. $20-atg., $12.50, $7.50.

795 **DOUGLAS, Stephen A.**
"The Montgomery address of Douglas. Edt: David R. Barbee and Milledge L. Bonham, Jr." In: JSH, v.5, #4, Nov. 1939, p. 527-552.

796 **DOUTHAT, Robert William**
"Gettysburg. A Battle Ode Descriptive of the Grand Charge of the third day, July 3, 1863. The Gettysburg Battle Lecture, one of Pickett's captains, and the only one of the ten captains in his regiment who came out of the charge unhurt!" N.Y., Neale Pub., 1905. 12mo, cl, 30pp., front. In Virginia Army. $750-b.

797 ..."Services with the Virginia Army." In: CV, Feb., 1928, v.XXXVI, p. 61-63.

798 **DOUTHIT, John M.**
"Johnny Reb's impression of Kentucky in the Fall of 1862. Edt: Nolan Fowler." In: Ky. Hist. Soc. Reg., 1950, v.XLVIII, p. 205-215. (near Rutledge, Tenn.) Oct. 28, 1862, by a pvt. of Carter Littlepage Stevenson's Div., of Gen. Kirby Smith's Army on recent operations in eastern Ky.

799 **DOW, J.C., Sr., Mrs.**
"The Blue and the Grey of After Many Days." Chicago: M.A. Donohue Co., (1904) 12mo, cl, ports, CSA generals, $5. Fiction.

800 **DOWD, Clement**
"Life of Zebulon B. Vance." Charlotte, N.C., Observer Print, 1897. 8vo, front, pls., ports, 493pp. $15, $20-reb., $25, $30(cl), 3/4 lt-$50-bmk.

801 **DOWD, W.F.**
"Lookout Mountain and Missionary Ridge." In: South. Bivouac, NS, 1885/1886, v.1, p. 397-399.

802 **DOWDEY, Clifford**
"Bugles Blow No More." Boston: Little, Brown & Co., 1937. 12mo, cl, d/w, 5pp., 1, (3)-497pp., map as endsheets. Better fiction, Richmond during war. $15, $12-bmk.
...Reprint, May, 1937. $5.
..."Reprint, 1942.
...N.Y., Rinehart & Co., (Feb. 1957). 8vo, cl, d/w, map-endsheets, 493pp. $5.
...N.Y., 1967 reprint, $10, $15, $30.

803 ..."Sellandra", Dunwoody, Georgia. Norman S. Berg Pub., 1971. 8vo, cl, dj. $18-y, $15.

804 ..."The Death of a Nation, the story of Lee and his men at Gettysburg." N.Y., Alfred Knopf, 1958. 8vo, cl, dj, front, 5-maps, ix, (1), 383pp. Bibliog., 353-374, index, ixp. $7.50, atg-$25, $30, $15-y. Also: "Civil War Book Club Edt." atg.
...1963, $15, $25, $10, $17.50-y.
...Baltimore: Butternut & Blue, 1988. 8vo, cl, 383p, plus 9p index. $27.

805 ..."Experiment in Rebellion." Garden City, N.Y., Doubleday Co., 1946. 8vo, cl, dj, ports, illus., map-incl. endsheets, xxi, (1), 455pp., bibliog.-index, p. 436-455., Rep: $19, $20-frayd op, $25-y. (1947) $9, (1950) $9, wraps $1.45), $10, $12.50-y, $40.
...N.Y., Arno Print, 1975, $26. "Essay Index Reprint Series."

806 ..."General Lee's unsolved problem." Amer. Heritage, 1955, v.VI, #3, p. 34-39. On limitations imposed by Pres. Davis on Lee's military authority.

807 ..."The Land they Fought for, the story of the South as the Confederacy, 1832-1865." Garden City: Doubleday Co., 1955. Half-title, "Mainstream of America Series, Lewis Gannett, Editor." 8vo, cl, dj, map-endsheets, viii, 438pp., $30, $25-bmk-84, $20-y, $17-mdj, $19, (1956) $6., $12, $7.50.
...Westport, Ct., Greenwood Pr., 1974., $24.50-y.

808 ..."Lee's Last Campaign, the story of Lee and his men against Grant, 1864." Boston: Little, Brown & Co., (1960). 8vo, cl, dj, maps (incl. endsheets), (v), 415pp., bibliog-index, 379-415. $7.50, 2nd edt., $15, $25, $11-nc.
...N.Y., Bonanza, n.d., $4, $12.50, $22.50.
...Wilmington, N.C., Broadfoot Pub., 1988. 8vo, cl, 415p. Reprint. $25.

809 ..."Lee." Boston: Little, Brown & Co., (1965). 8vo, cl, map-ends, 781pp., xiv, maps, ports, illus. $15, $17.50, $6.50, $12.50-b, $20. New material, period 1850-1876, Gro. Bolling Lee collection and others by one who worked with Freeman on the Richmond News Dispatch.
...N.Y., Bonanza. $6, $10.

810 ..."The Proud Retreat. A novel of the lost Confederate Treasure." N.Y., Doubleday Co., 1953. 8vo, cl, dj, map-endsheets, 319pp. $5, $20-bmk.

811 ..."The Seven Days. The Emergence of Lee." Boston: Little, Brown & Co. (1964) 1st Edt., 8vo, cl, d/w, v, 380pp., maps, $4, $15-y, $7.50, $30, $22.50-dabney.
...N.Y., Fairfax Press, 1978, dj, $10.
...Wilmington, N.C., Broadfoot Pub., 1988. 8vo, cl, 380p. Reprint. $25.

812 ..."In the Valley of Virginia." In: CWH, December, 1957, v.III, #4, p. 401-422.

813 ..."Where My Love Sleeps." Boston, 1945, Little, Brown & Co. 12mo, cl, dj, 298pp. $5. Novel of the war with historical background. 2nd print. $20.

814 ..."Wartime papers of R.E. Lee, edt: Cliff. Dowdey and Louis Manarin. See under: Robert Edward Lee., $20-y, $25-bmk, $30-bmk.

815 **DOWELL, W.A., Mrs.**
"The Job Neill Letters, CSA." In: Indp. Co. (Ark.) Chron., 1967, v.VIII, #1, p. 27-37.

816 **DOWIE, Menil Muriel, Edt.**
"Women Adventurers." London: T.F. Unwin, 1893. Half-title: Adventure Series #15. Reprint of four biographies, each with full t/p. "The woman in battle, a narr. of the exploits, adventures and travels of Madam Loreta Janeta Valazquez, edt. by C.J. Worthington, Hartford: Belknap, 1876. See also: L.J. Valazquez.

817 **DOWLING, R.L.**
"Shoulder arms of the Confederate Army." In: Antiques, Jan. 1951, v.59, p. 47. views.

818 **DOWLING, Richard W.**
"Dowling's victory at Sabine Pass." In: Front. Times, Sept., 1949, v.26, p. 304-308. Defense of Sabine Pass by Dowling and Capt. F.H. Odlum against Union attack under N.P. Banks. See: Aloysius M. Sullivan.

819 **DOWNER, Edward Thornton**
"Stonewall Jackson, a Living Memorial." (Richmond) Va. Cavl., Spring 1963, v.XII, #4, p. 23-31, ports, maps, dbl-pg. color and illus.

820 ..."Johnson's Island." In: CWH, June, 1962, v.VIII, #2, p. 202-217.

821 ..."Stonewall Jackson's Shenandoah Valley Campaign, 1862." Lexington, Va., Stonewall Jackson Memorial, Inc., 1959. 8vo, stiff wraps(port of Jackson cover, title, maps, 25pp. $2, $8-bmk-84, $15, $10-bmk-104.

822 **DOWNEY, Agnes M.**
"Thanks for the memory." In: Arlington HM, 1959, v.I, #3, p. 28-36, port, views, notes. Photos showing Arlington House during war and docs. useful in restoring to its former condition.

823 **DOWNEY, Fairfax**
"The guns at Gettysburg." Gaithersburg, Md., Butternut Press, 1985. 8vo, cl, illus., maps, 290pp. $25.

824 ..."Clash of Cavalry: the Battle of Brandy Station." Gaithersburg, Md., Butternut Press, 1985.

825 **DOWNEY, Fairfax Davis**
"Clash of Cavalry, The Battle of Brandy Station, June 9, 1863." New York: David McKay Co. (1959). 8vo, cl, d/w, maps, drawings, illus., ports, map end-sheets, xv, 238pp. Bibliog., 222-230, append., notes and references, p. 154-221. $5, $40, $30-bmk-99. Marks zenith of Amer. cavalry in Civil War. $30-b, $12.
..."The Blue, the Gray and the Red." In: CWTI, July, 1962, v.I, #2, p. 6-9, 26-30, illus., ports.
..."The Guns at Gettysburg." N.Y., D. McKay, (1958). 8vo, cl, dj, illus., 290pp. $9.50. Both CSA-Union artillerymen and commanders.

826 ..."A horse for General Lee; illustrated by Fred Chapmen." N.Y., Scribner, (1953) 12mo, cl, illus., 202pp., $20-bmk.

827 **DOWNING, Jack (pseud.)**
"Letters of Major Jack Downing, of the Downingville Militia, "the Constitution is a Dimmycratic machinery or it won't run at all!"-Major Jack Downing to Lincoln." N.Y., Bromley & Co., J.F. Feeks, 1864. 12mo, cl, front, plates, xiv, (15)-254pp. Humor, satire, cartoons, ridicules Lincoln's policies during the war. Appeared first in Copperhead newspapers. "not by Seba Smith or Chs. Aug. Davis." See Sabin-84179, many editions here in England.

828 **DOYLE, Elisabeth Joan**
"Greenbacks, Car Tickets, and the pot of gold. The effects of wartime occupation on the business life of New Orleans 1861-1865." In: CWH, December 1959, v.V, #4, p. 247-362. $10-bmk.

829 ..."Nurseries of Treason: Schools in Occupied New Orleans." (Lexington, Ky.) May, 1960, v.XXVI, #2, p. 161-179. JSH. $8.

830 **DOZIER, Orion Thoephilus**
"Foibles of Fancy and Rhymes of the Times." Birmingham, Ala., Dispatch Print, 1894. 12mo, cl, 4, 218pp., front(port), illus., color pl.

831 ..."A Galaxy of Southern Heroes and other poems by..., a compilation of many hitherto unpublished effusions of the author and a number of others which have appeared in sundry periodicals but largely a reprint of those appearing in the 1st and 2nd edition, "Foibles of Fancy Rhymes of the Times." issued by the writer in 1894." Birmingham: Dispathc Print, 1905. 12mo, cl, 4, 304pp., front(port)pls. (1-color) Confederate poetry. "Memorial Edition."
..."Poems and Prose of...5th Edt., includes selected poems and prose from former publications." Birmingham: Press of Birmingham Pub., (1927). $20-bmk. 12mo, cl, pl, ports (1-color), illus., 2pp., vii-xvi, 225pp.
..."Poems of...3rd Edt., including "A Galaxy of Southern Heroes" and other poems of former publications." N.Y., Neale Pub., 1905. 12mo, cl, xii, 13-272pp., front(port).

832 **DRAGO, Edward L.**
"How Sherman's March Through Georgia affected the Slaves." In: Ga. H.Q., Fall, 1973, v.LVII, #3, p. 361-375. $8.

833 **DRAKE, Edwin L., Lt. Col. C.S.A., Edt.**
"The Annals of the Army of Tennessee and Early Western History, including a chronological Summary of Battles and Engagements in the Western Armies of the Confederacy, including a summary of Lt. Gen. Joseph Wheeler's Cavalry engagements." Nashville: Austin D. Haynes Print, 1878- (suppl) Tavel, Eastman and Howell Pr., 1879, 8vo, v.I (all pub.) Apr-Dec., 1878, fldg. map, vi, 432, 99, (1)p-errata, $75, $87.50, $500-bmk-105.

834 ..."Chronological summary of battles and engagements of the Western Armies of the Confederate States, including summary of Lt. Gen. Joseph Wheeler's Cavalry engagements. Nashville, Tenn: Tavel, Eastman & Howell, 1879, 8vo, orig. wraps, 99, (1)pp. $75. Final part to this "Annals of Army of Tenn."

835 **DRAKE, H. Winbourne**
"Two letters of..., civil war refugee in Northwest Louisiana." In: LaH., 1966, v.7, p. 71-76.

836 **DRAKE, James Vaulx**
"Life of Gen. Robert Hatton, including his most important public speeches; together with much of his Washington and Army correspondence." Nashville, Tenn., Marshall & Bruce, 1867, tk 8vo, full gold-emb., Mor., e.g., front(port) xi, 458pp. $22.50, $50, $80-bmk, $175-g, $75, $225-b. Hatton died fighting for the CSA (7-Pines).

837 **DRAKE, Robert Y., Jr.**
"Two old juveniles." In: Ga. Rev., Winter, 1959, v.13, p. 443-453. On Frances Boyd Calhoun's "Miss. Minerva" and "Wm. Green Hill(1909)" and Thomas Nelson Page's "Two Little Confederates", novels about and for southern children.

838 **DRANE, Robert Brent**
"A sketch of the life of Tristrim Lowther Skinner, Major of First Regiment, North Carolina Volunteers, Confederate States Army, by Rev. Robert Brent Drane." (Edenton, N.C., 1931) 8vo, cover title, 10pp.

839 **DRANESVILLE, Battle of**
See: William S. Hammond.

840 **DREUX, Charles D., Col.**
"The Life and Military Services of Col. Charles D. Dreux. With Roll of the 1st Louisiana Battalion." Pub: A. Meynier, Jr. 1883, New Orleans, La: E.A. Brandao. 12mo, wraps, 36pp. $37.50. "1st Confed. Officer killed in late war", fell at Newport News, Va., July 5, 1861. A quarter of proceeds to be turned over to St. John's Fencing Club.

841 ..."Dreux-Rightor Louisiana Battalion, 1861-1911." n.p.,n.d., (1911). 8vo, wraps, cover title, with CSA flags, ports, 15, Tulane. See: "Sketch and rolls of Dreux's La. cavalry..."
..."Roster of Dreux's Battalion." In: West Tex. Geneal. Soc. Bul. (Abilene, Tx., Jan. 1961, v.3, #1, p. 2-3, 21-23, 35. Also: Grivot Guards, Shreveport Grays and La. Guards, Co. "C".

842 **DREWRY'S BLUFF, Battle of**
See: Wm. I. Clopton, Pierre G.T. Beauregard, August H. Drewry, Johnson Hagood, Robert F. Hoke, Chs. T. Loehr, John W. Sumpter.

843 **DREWRY, A.S.**
"The Purcell Battery from Richmond, Va., its gallant conduct at the Battle of Cedar Run." In: SHSP, 1899, v.XXVII, p. 89-92.

844 **DREWRY, Jones M.**
"The Double-Barrelled Cannon of Athens, Georgia." In: Ga.H.Q., Dec., 1964, v.XLVIII, #4, p. 442-450.

845 **DRINKWATER, John**
"John Drinkwater's poem about a Confed-

erate stamp. Edt: Van Dyk MacBride." In: Am. Philatelist, Dec., 1953, v.67, p. 182-184, 193. About a postage stamp pub. in 1931, mfg. for but never issued by the CSA. A $.01 yellow stamp.

..."Robert E. Lee. A Play." Bost., N.Y., Houghton Mifflin, 1923. 12mo, cl, (3), 128pp. (another edt., in) cloth and boards); 2nd impression. Aug. 4. $15-bmk.

...London: Sidgwick & Jackson, 1923. 12mo, cl, 95, (1)pp., wraps. $15, $4, $6, $15-bmk.

846 **DRISCOLL, Frederick**
"The Twelve Days' Campaign (in Virginia) An Impartial Account of the Final Campaign of the late War." Montreal: Longmore & Co., 1866. 8vo, cl, map, 103pp. Sabin-20954.

847 **DRIVER, Robert J., Jr.**
"52nd Virginia Infantry." Lynchburg, Va., H.E. Howard, 1986, 8vo, cl, dj, (5), 174pp., maps, ports. 1000 copies, numbered, signed.

..."The 1st & 2nd Rockbridge Artillery." 1st Edt. Lynchburg, Va., H.E. Howard, 1987. 8vo, cl, dj, (5), 153p, maps, ports. 1,000 copies, (#736) signed.

848 **DRYDEN, Charles**
"War in the midst of America, from a new point of view." London: Ackermann & Co., 1864. 11x15 1/2cm, cover title, 20 color fold-plates. Humors, characteritures, sketches on a continuous folded sheet over 35'. $1500-jk.

849 **DRYDEN, Charles (Map)**
"War in the Midst of America, from a new point of view." A British subject's rare "Panoramic History of the Civil War, in caricature, from outbreak and progress of war, numerous attached sheets, forming a panorama 18'x3 7/8", fold to, 12mo, cl, with pict. label. Strongly pro-Southern despite some of the first headings. London: Ackermann & Co. (c.1865) $75.

850 **DU BOIS, A.**
"Cold Harbor Salient. The Story told from the other side." In: SHSP, 1902, v.XXX, p. 276-279. DuBois, Co.F, 7th N.Y., Heavy Arty. Writes in response to SHSP, v.XXIX, p. 285.

851 **DU BOSE, Dudley McIver**
"The Fifteenth Georgia Regiment at Gettysburg, report of Col. D.M. DuBose." Rich: So. Hist. Soc. Papers, 1882, v.X, p. 179-183.

852 **DU BOSE, Henry Kershaw**
"The History of Company B, Twenty-first Regiment(infantry), South Carolina Volunteers, Confederate States Provisional Army." Columbia, S.C., R.L. Bryan Print, 1909. 8vo, cl, ports, 130pp. (old) $35, $500-g.

853 **DU BOSE, Joel Campbell**
"History of Alabama." Rich., Atlanta: B.F. Johnson Pub., (1908) 12mo, cl, front, illus., 432pp. CSA and Reconstruction, p. 131-227. Double pg. map.

854 **DU BOSE, John E.**
"Sermon to Capt. Parkhill's Company, "The Howell Guards", on the eve of their departure for the seat of war, Aug. 26, 1861." Tallahassee, Fla., Floridian and Journal, 1861. 8vo, wraps, cover title, 12pp.

855 **DU BOSE, John Witherspoon**
"Alabama-the relation of the state to the birth of the Southern Confederacy." In: CV, May 1916, v.XXIV, p. 201-208.

856 ..."Confederate Diplomacy. The opposition our representatives faced in Europe, reviews our failure." In: SHSP, 1902, v.XXXII, p. 102-116.

857 ..."Confederate Generals-their ability. Did General Lee counsel abandonment of Richmond after the Battle of Wilderness?" In: SHSP, 1899, v.XXVII, p. 290-293.

858 ..."The Fayetteville, N.C., road fight." In: CV, Feb., 1912, v.XX, p. 84-86. From his book on Jo Wheeler.

859 ..."Gen. Joseph Eggleston Johnston, CSA." In: CV, April 1914, v.XXII, p. 176-177.

860 ..."Ellison Capers." In: Sewanee Review, July, 1908, p. 368-373.

861 ..."A historian's tribute to Thomas Goode Jones, 1844-1914." In: Ala. Lawyer, Jan., 1953, v.14, p. 46-67. Reprint: Birmingham Age-Herald, 31 May, 1914. On Jones service in CSArmy, Alabama law and Politics.

...n.p., 1953, p. 23, (1), port., bound. In: Walter B. Jones' Huntly Cabin papers."

862 ..."The Life and Times of William Lowndes Yancey. A history of political parties in the United States, from 1834 to 1864; especially as to the origin of the Confederate States." Birmingham, Ala., Roberts & Co., 1892, 8vo, cl, (or, 3/4Mor.) ports, incl. front, xiv, (2), 752pp. $60, $75, $87.50, $125-bmk, $250-bmk. Most of the first edition was destroyed by fire.

...Louisville: Lost Cause Pr., micro-cd. $9.76.

...N.Y., Peter Smith, 1942. 8vo, same in 2 vols, $12, $17.50, $20-y, $50-bmk-94.

863 ..."William L. Yancey in History. Memorable debate on the slave trade at Montgomery, Alabama." In: SHSP, 1899, v.XXVII, p. 98-101.

864 ..."Yancey: a study." In: Gulf States Hist. Mag., Jan./Mar. 1903, v.I, #4/5, p. 239-252, 311-324. Montgomery, Ala.

865 ..."The tragedy of the commissariat." In: Gulf Mag., 1902, v.1, p. 27-32.

866 ..."Maj-Gen. Joseph Wheeler." In: CV, October, 1917, v.XXV, p. 460-463.

867 ..."General Joseph Wheeler and the Army of Tennessee." N.Y., Neale Pub., 1912. 8vo, cl, ports(incl. front), pl., 476pp. $22.50, $40, $45, $50, $60, $300-g, $250, $275-bmk-104.

868 ..."Wheeler's raid into Tennessee." In: CV, Jan. 1916, v.XXIV, p. 10-12.

869 **DU BOSE, William Porcher**
"Wade Hampton." In: Sewanee Rev., 1902, v.10, p. 364-368. See: B.J. Ramage.

870 **DU CHATEAU, Andre Paul**
"The Creek Nation on the Eve of the Civil War." (Oklahoma City) Chron. Okla., Fall, 1974, v.LII, #3, p. 290-315pp. ports, illus., map.

871 **DU PONT, Henry A., Col.**
"Address by Colonel duPont Upon the Unveiling of Maj. Gen. Stephen D. Ramseur's Monument." (Winterthur, 1920) Delaware. $5. His personal story of the death of CSA. Gen. Ramseur at Battle of Cedar Creek.

872 ..."A Crisis of Conscience: West Point Letters of..., Oct. 1860-June 1961." In: CWH, March 1979, v.25, #1, p. 55-65. Friendships and dividing loyalties.

873 **DU PREE, T.C., Capt.**
"Wartime Letters of Capt. T.C. DuPree, of the 2nd Ark. Cavalry, C.S.A." Fayetteville, Ark: Washington County Historical Society, 1953. Booklet series #2. op. 4to, soft back, (32)pp. Lim-50 copies. $10.

874 **DU SHANE, Jerome**
"Aboard a Blockade Runner: some Civil War experiences of Jerome DuShane." In: NCHR, 1967, v.44, p. 392-399.

875 **DUAINE, Carl L.**
"Dead Men Wore Boots. An Account of the 32nd. Texas Volunteer Cavalry, CSA. 1862-2865." Austin, Texas: San Felipe Press, 1966. 4to, cl, d/w, 126pp., ports, maps, charts, #323 of 500 Limited Edt. Autographed. $15-b, $10.

876 **DUBAY, Robert W.**
"Mississippi Political, Civilian, and Military Realities of 1861: a study in frustration and confusion." (Jackson) Jour. Miss.

Hist., Aug. 1974, v.XXXVI, #3, p. 215-241.

877 **DUDLEY, Edgar S., Col.**
"Was "Secession" taught at West Point? What the records show." In: Century Mag., Aug., 1909, v.LXXVIII, p. 629-635. $3.50.

878 **DUDLEY, G.W.**
"The battle of Corinth, Oct. 3-4, 1862. Including also the battle of Davis' Bridge, On Hatchie and skirmish at Tuscumbia, Oct. 5, 1862." Iuka, Miss., Vidette Press (1899). 8vo, wraps, cover-title, 2, (1), 24pp. illus., map, 2pls., 2 ports. double column. See: Monroe Cockrell, Lyla M. McDonald.

879 ..."The Lost Account of the Battle of Corinth and court-martial of Gen. Van Dorn. Intro. and essay on the battle by Monroe F. Cockrell." Jackson, Tann., McCowat-Mercer, 1955, 8vo, cl, illus., ports, fldg-map (pocket), 78pp. By "an unknown author". $7.50.

880 ..."The Battle of Iuka, fought Sept. 19, 1862. With map of the battlefield." 8vo, wraps, 16pp. port (Gen. Lewis Henry Little, who was killed in battle.) Iuka, Miss., Iuka Vidette, 1896.

881 **DUDLEY, Thomas U.**
"The Memory of Robert E. Lee. Address del. by..., at the 11th Annual Banquet of Confederate Veterans Camp of N.Y., Jan. 18, 1901." (N.Y., 1901) 8vo, wraps, cover title, 16pp. $5.

882 **DUES, Michael T.**
"Governor Beriah Magoffin of Kentucky: Sincere Neutral or Secret Secessionist?" In: FCHQ, January 1966, v.40, #1, p. 22-28.

883 ..."The Pro-secessionist Governor of Ky. Beriah Magoffin's credibility gap." In: RKHS, July 1969, v.67, #3, p. 221-231.

884 **DUFF, William Hiram**
"Terrors and horrors of prison life; or, six months a prisoner at Camp Chase, Ohio." (Lake Charles, La., Orphan Helper Pr., 1907) 12mo, wraps, front, pls., ports, (10), 37, 51pp. List of CSA soldiers buried at Camp Chase, p. 1-51.

885 ..."The Truth, a piano in Confederate trenches, PcPheely and his pioneers, a romantic story of the Siege of Jackson, Miss., July, 1863." (Monroe, La., 1913?) 12mo, wraps, cover title, port, plan, 19pp.

886 **DUFFEY, Jefferson Waite**
"McNeill's last charge; an account of a daring Confederate in the Civil War, by Rev. J.W. Duffey, D.D." (Winchester, Va., Geo. F. Norton, (1912) 17 1/2x13cm., cover title, illus., ports, 28pp. Muster roll, p. 26-27.
...Moorefield, W.Va., 1944 reprint.

887 **DUFFEY, Jefferson Waite, Rev.**
"Daring Capture by M'Neill's Rangers." In: Confed. Vet., v.XXVI, Aug. 1918, p. 350-352. Illus. of M'Neill's and Moorefield skirmish.

888 ..."Two Generals Kidnapped and a Race for a Prize. A Unique Incident in the War Between the States." (Moorefield, W.Va., 1944) 8vo, wraps, cover title, 22pp. $10.
...Wash., D.C., 1927, a 3rd edt., 18pp. McNeill's capture Gens. Geo Crook and Benj. Kelley. Includes roster: McNeill's Rangers, Co.F, 7th Va. Cav., Co. D, 11th Va. Cav., Shetler-209.
..."Capture of Generals Crook and Kelly." In: Confed. Vet., XXXIII, Nov. 1925, p. 420-423.

889 ..."McNeill's Last Charge, an account of a daring Confederate in the Civil War." (Winchester, Va., Geo. F. Norton, 1912). 12mo, wraps, ports, illus., 28pp. cover title.

890 **DUFFNER, Robert W.**
"Confederate Guerrilla victory at Centralia(Mo.) Sept. 27, 1864." In: Bull MoHS, April 1973, p. 131-144.

891 **DUFFY, John**
"Medical Practice in the Ante-Bellum South." (Lexington, KY.) JSH, Feb., 1959, v.XXV, #1, p. 53-72.

892 ..."Sectional Conflict and Medical Education in Louisiana." (Lexington, Ky.) JSH, Aug. 1957, v.XXIII, #3, p. 289-306.

893 ..."A note on Ante-Bellum Southern Nationalism and Medical Practice." In: JSH, 1968, v.XXXIV, p. 266-276.

894 **DUFOUR, Charles L.**
"Nine Men in Gray." Garden City, N.Y., Doubleday, 1963. 8vo, cl, dj, ports, xi, (2) 364pp. $10, $15, paper edt.-$1., pres-$30-bmk, $50-bmk.

895 ..."Gentle Tiger The Gallant Life of Roberdeau Wheat." Baton Rouge: La. Univ. Press (1957). 12mo, cl, dj, maps, facsms., ports (incl. front), xv, 232pp. notes-index, p. 201-232. $3.50, $7.50, $8.50, op $15, $75, $50-b, $25-bmk-105.

896 ..."The Night the War was Lost." Garden City, NY, Doubleday & Co., 1960. 8vo, cl, dj, illus., 427pp. $10, $12.50, $16, $25-b. Battle of New Orleans, 1862.
..."The night the war was lost. The fall of New Orleans: causes, consequences, culpability." In: La.H., 1961, v.2, p. 157-174.

897 **DUGAS, Vera Lea**
"The Ante-Bellum Career of Leonidas Polk." New Orleans: LHQ, April, 1949, v.32, #2, p. 245-356, bibliog.

898 ..."Texas Industry, 1860-1880." In: SwHQ, Oct. 1955, v.LIX, #2, p. 151-183, map.

899 **DUKE, Basil**
"John Morgan." In: B & L, v.4, p. 422-424.

900 ..."The last days of the Confederacy." In: B & L, v.4, p. 762-767. "Notes on the Union and Confederate Armies", p. 767-768.

901 **DUKE, Basil W., Brig.-Gen.**
"Morgan's cavalry during the Bragg invasion." In: B & L, v.3, p. 26-28, 30.

902 **DUKE, Basil Wilson**
"After the Fall of Richmond." In: South.Biv., 1887/1887, ns, v.II, p. 156-166. $10.

903 ..."Bragg's Campaign in Kentucky." In: South. Vib., ns, v.I, 1885-1886, ports, p. 161-167, 232-240. See: C.C. Gilbert. $10.

904 ..."The Battle of Hartsville." In: South. Biv., 1882-1883, v.I, p. 43-51.

905 ..."The Battle of Shiloh." In: South Biv., 1883-1884, v.II, p. 150-162; 201-216.

906 ..."The Confederate Career of General Albert Sidney Johnston. A review of the General's Memoirs." In: SHSP, 1878, v.VI, p. 133-141.

907 ..."History of Morgan's Cavalry." Cincinnati: Miami Print, 1867. tk.8vo, cl, front(port), vii, (9)-578pp., maps. $17.50, $20, $25, $30, $25-'73-nc, $75, $175.
...Bloomington: Indiana Univ. Pr., (1960), sm.8vo, cl, dj, xvii, (1), (9)-595pp. Intro: Cecil Fletcher Holland. $10, $17.50, $30-y, Mor.
...N.Y., Neale Pub., 1906, Revised, 8vo, cl, maps (9), ports(4), x, (11)-441pp. $15, $25, $150-b, $45-nc, $37.50.
...N.Y., Neal Pub., 1909, reprint of the revised edt.. $25.
...N.Y., Freeport, 1969 edition, $12.
...N.Y., Kraus Reprint, 1969. $50, $25.

908 ..."Last Days of the Confederacy." In: Batt. and Lead., v.IV, p. 762-767.

909 ..."Morgan's escape from prison." In: CV, Oct. 1916, v.24, #10, p. 449-453, pl., port. From a chapter in his "Morgan's Cavalry."

910 ..."Sketch of Gen. John H. Morgan." In: Confed. Vet., Dec. 1911, v.XIX, p. 565-570.

911 ...Sketch of Basil Duke's life. See: James W. Henning. (see: Dabney H. Smith)

912 ..."Reminiscences of General Basil W. Duke." Garden City, N.Y., Doubleday, Pag., 1911. 8vo, cl, front(port), xii, 512pp. $60, $75, $100. Also in: dj, $42.50, $50-y, $40-bmk.
...N.Y., Kraus reprint, 1969. "Civil War

Centennial series."

...N.Y., Arno Press, 1969, "Select Bibliographic Reprint Series." $21.75, $25, $30.50-y.

913 ..."The Romance of Morgan's Rough Riders, The Raid, The Capture and the Escape." In: Century Mag., Jan. 1891, illus., map, p. 403-425. Reprinted: (1955) Louisville: Book Nook. See: "The Great Indiana-Ohio Raid, etc."

914 ..."Morgan's cavalry during the Bragg invasion." In: B & L, III, p. 26-28.

...See: "Famous Adventures and Prison escapes." 70ps. article on Morgan's command.

915 ..."John Morgan in 1864." B & L, iv, p. 423-424.

..."A romance of Morgan's Rough-Riders, the raid, the capture and escape." In: "Famous Adventures and Prison Escapes of the Civil War." N.Y., Century Co., 1893, 12mo, cl, illus., 338pp. (Morgan article, p. 116-183) Reprinted, 1894, 1898, and 1915, 1855.

916 ..."Address at the reunion of Morgan's Men." In: South. Biv., v.I (1882-1883), p. 399-405.

917 ..."Address at reunion of Morgan's Men at Rich Pond, Warren Co., Ky., Oct. 27, 1883." In: South. Biv, v.II (1883-1884), p. 105-111.

918 ..."Morgan's Indiana & Ohio Raid." In: "Annals of the War", Phila: 1879, p. 241-256.

919 **DUKE, Basil and Orlando B. Wilcox and Thomas H. Hines**
"The romance of Morgan's Rough Riders-"The Raid", "the Capture", and the Escape"." In: Cent., Nov. 1890, v.19, p. 403-425, illus., map, ports.

920 **DUKE, Kevin**
"The Battle of Brice's Crossroads, Forrest's ultimate victory." In: CV (new) Sept. 1985, v.33, #5, p. 34-42, map, port (Forrest in color), p. 45-46 ports.

921 **DUKE, W. Sons & Co., Publishers**
"The Heroes of the Civil War." Litho: Knapp & Co., New York, n.d., 7x10 1/2", litho in full color, incl. pict. stiff covers. (60)pp. (c.1889) $25. Each page contains short biography of a Union and CSA general, continued on back of each page, with color port. and a battle scene. CSA: Lee, Longstreet, A.S. and J.E. Johnston, Semmes, Breckinridge, Bragg, Morgan, Forrest, Jackson, Hardee, Beauregard, Stuart, Hill, Kirby Smith, Wade Hampton, Price, Polk, Pemberton, Ewell, Hood, Early, Pickett, Grant-Lee, plate: Gettysburg and Merrimack-Monitor.

...Park Place, N.Y., 1888, Knapp & Co. 1 1/2 x 2 3/4" booklets, colored wraps, duplicate above ports, with battle scene on back, facsm. autograph verso front cover, i.e., "A Short History of Gen. R.E. Lee." 16pp. for each of the above 25 Generals, as for the Union, too. A note inside front cover mentions "Heroes of the Civil War" to be pub. Mar. 1, 1889." See: individual listings under each name. Probably these were given with Duke Cigarettes (?).

922 **DUKESHIRE, T.S.**
"Confederate Navy covers." In: Amer. Philatelist Cong. Book, 1958, v.24, p. 113-126, facsms.

923 ..."Early Confederate patriotic covers." In: Amer. Philatelist, Apr. 1959, v.72, p. 497-500. facsms.

924 ..."The Confederate Midshipmen and the treasure train." In: USN Inst. Proc., June 1957, v.83, p. 105-117. Special train that moved CSA gold/silver from CSN Adacemy.

925 ..."The Confederate Marine Corps." In: Weekly Philatelic Gossip, April 14, 1956, v.LXII, #7, whole #1796, p. 222-225.

926 ..."Found-A Confederate Marine Corps. Cover!" In: Confed. Philatelist, May 1962, v.7, #5, whole #71, p. 45-46, 48.

927 ..."The Confederate Midshipmen and the Treasure Train." In: US Naval Inst. Proc., June, 1957, p. 5. CSA Naval Academy guard gold/silver to Georgia, after Richmond's fall.

928 **DUMOND, Dwight Lowell**
"Antislavery origins of the Civil War in the United States." Ann Arbor: Univ. Michigan Press, 1939, 8vo, cl, vii, 143pp. $12.50-b, $25, $40.
...1956, $9, $6, $10.

929 ..."The Secession Movement 1860-1861." New York: Macmillan Co., 1931, 12mo, cl, vi, (1), 294pp. $5, $10, $15, $25-bmk, $40-b.
...Rep: 1963, N.Y., Octagon Books, (calf-20)
...Rep: 1964, $7.50, $13-y. Anti-slavery as a moral issue overlooks political aspects even before the constitution; New Eng's. bitter struggle over the South's use of slaves being added to the population and the 3/5 ration, etc.

930 ..."Southern Editorials of Secession." N.Y., Lond: Century Co., (1931). Title head: Amer. Hist. Ass'n. 8vo, decr. cl, xxxiii, 529pp. $20, $25, $50-bmk.
...Gloucester, P. Smith, 1964. $8.50, $12.50. See: Howard C. Perkins on North.

931 **DUNAWAY, Wayland Fuller, D.D., Rev.**
"Reminiscences of a Rebel." By Rev. Wayland Fuller Dunaway, formerly Captain of Co.I, 40th Va. Regt., Army of Northern Virginia. N.Y., Neale Pub. Co., 1913. 12mo, cl, 133pp. $15, $25, $60, $150-b, $85-dabney, $145, $90-bmk, $50-nc.
...Louisville: Lost Cause, micro-cd. $3.20 Coulter-138.

932 **DUNBAR, Mary Conway Shields**
"My Mother Used to Say: a Natchez Belle of the Sixties." Edt: Elizabeth Dunbar Murray. Boston: Christopher Pub. House (1959) 12mo, cl, d/w, ports (incl. front) view, 224pp. (largely CSA) $3.75. Mississippi plantation life, husband served in CSArmy, 1861-1863.

933 **DUNCAN, Alexander McC., Capt.**
"Roll of Officers and Members of the Georgia Hussars and of the Cavalry Companies, of which the Hussars are a Continuation. With Historical Sketch relating facts showing the origin and necessity of Rangers or Mounted Men in the Colony of Georgia from date of its founding." (Savannah, Ga., Morning News, 1907) 8vo, cl, ports, illus. (flag pl. in colors) $27.50. DeRenne's copy has pub. letter stating its printing in 1907, of 1000 copies for the Georgia Hussars. 560pp. 1906, Savannah, Ga. $400-boh, $300-bmk-120.

934 **DUNCAN, Bartlett Marshall and J.H. Utz**
"Biographical Sketches of the Bartlett Marshall Duncan and Henry Utz Families. Edited by W.H. Utz." St. Joseph, Mo., 1936. 8vo, cl, ports, incl. front.(2), 137pp. $65. Two early pioneer families, Platte Purchase and Buchanan Co., 1945-1860. Civil War condition in Missouri, letters relate to banishment of B.M. Duncan and narrow escape from hanging of J.H. Utz for making war within Federal lines.

935 **DUNCAN, Charles**
"Confederate Military Organization." In: Mil. Engineer, 1938, v.XXX, p. 441-445.

936 ..."Three cigars and a nation's fate." In: Mil. Engineer, 1938, v.XXX, p. 264-266. Battle of Antietam, deals with Lee's lost order (Special order #191) to Gen. Hill, which a Union soldier found wrapped around three cigars.

937 **DUNCAN, George Webster**
"John Archibald Campbell." Montgomery, Ala., 1905. 8vo, wraps, cover title, p. 107-151. Alabama Historical Society, Reprint

#33. From the Transactions, 1904, v.V, $7. Biog. Ass't. Secty. War for Confederacy.

938 DUNCAN, J.S.
"Martin Hart, Civil War Guerilla." In: TMH, 1973, v.XI, #2, p. 137-142. See: Wm. E. Sawyer, Alex Cameron.

939 ..."Alexander Cameron in the Louisiana Campaign, 1863-1865." In: MHT & S, 1975, v.XII, #4, p. 245-271, plates, v.XIII, #1, p. 37-57.

940 DUNCAN, John W.
"Letters of John W. Duncan, Captain Confederate States of America. Edt: Hubert L. Ferguson." In: Ark. Hist. Quart., 1950, v.IX, p. 298-312.

941 DUNCAN, Johnson K., Brig.-Gen.
"Bombardment of Forts Jackson and St. Philip." In: Confed. War. Jour., 1893, v.I, p. 181, 183-189.

942 DUNCAN, Norvin C., Rev.
"A Biographical sketch of Rev. Edmund Noah Joyner." Ashville, N.C., Inland Press, 1940. 12mo, wraps, 39pp. $25. Joyner enlisted in CSArmy at 17, serving in Co.D, 13th Battl. N.C. Light Artly. After war an Episcopal minister and chaplain in UC-Vets.

943 DUNCAN, Richard R.
"Marylanders and the Invasion of 1862." In: CWH, December 1965, v.XI, #4, p. 370-383.

..."Maryland's reaction to (Gen. Jubal) Early's raid July 1864-a summer of bitterness." In: MdHM, Fall 1969, p. 248-279.

944 DUNCAN, Robert Lipscomb
"Reluctant General. The Life and Times of Albert Pike." N.Y., E.P. Dutton (1961), 1st. 8vo, cl, d/w, 289pp. $50-r, $17.50-b, $15-b, $3.50, $5, $35-bmk, $25.

945 DUNCAN, Rose
"Why the Confederacy failed. Excessive issue of paper money, the policy of disersion and the neglect of the cavalry." In: Century, Nov./Apr., 1896-1897, v.31, n.s., p. 33-38, dbl. columns.

946 DUNCAN, Ruth Henley
"The Captain and Submarine CSS H.L. Hunley." (Memphis, Tenn., S.C. Toff & Co.) 1st Edt., Dec., 1965. sm.4to, cl, d/w, color flags and port of author(front), color photos other ports, 109pp. $12.50.

947 DUNCAN, Thomas D.
"Recollections of...A Confederate Soldier." Nashville, Tenn: McQuiddy Print, 1922. 12mo, stiff wraps, ports, 213pp., $8, $12.50, $20, $35-border, $100-y, $125-jk-151, lax wrap, $100-bmk.
...Louisville: Lost Cause Pr., micro-cd-$4.08.

948 DUNDAS, William Oswald
"Blockade running in the Civil War." In: Bellman, May 31, 1919, v.XXVI, p. 606-608.

949 ..."Blockade running during the War Between the States...compiled by F. De Sales Dundas. In: UDC Mag., Nov. 1952, v.15, #11, p. 5, 8-9, 12. port. reminisc. of a Confederate.

950 DUNFORD, A.H.
"The Gray Brigade" the success and failure of Confederate Arms in New Mexico." In: "The English Westerners Brand Book, v.II, Oct., 1959, map, 11, 1pp.

951 DUNKLE, John J.
"Prison Life During the Rebellion. Being a brief narrative of the miseries and sufferings of six-hundred Confederate prisoners sent from Fort Delaware to Morris Island to be punished. Written by Fritz Fuzzlebug (pseud.) one of their number. Pub. by the author." Singer's Glen, Va., J.Funk's Sons, 1869. 8vo, wraps, 49pp. $10, $12.50, $22.50, $75-o, $50-bmk, $40-c.hill, $35-nc, $65-jk-122. Louisville, Ky.: Lost Cause Press, micro card. $2.45.

952 DUNLOP, James Nathaniel
"Reply of...at banquet, Virginia Div:

A.N.V., Oct. 29, 1879, to the cavalry of Northern Va." (Richmond, Va., G.W. Gary Print, 1879) 8vo, wraps, 4pp.

953 ..."Address at the Annual Reunion of Pegram Battalion Association." In: SHSP, 1886, v.XIV, p. 23-26.

954 ..."The Cavalry-Remarks of Private James N. Dunlop, at A.N.V., Banquet, Oct. 19, 1879." In: SHSP, 1880, v.VIII, p. 15-17.

955 **DUNLOP, William S., Maj.**
"Lee's Sharpshooters; or, the Forefront of Battle. A story of Southern valor that has never been told." Little Rock, Ark., Tunnah & Pittard, 1899, 12mo, cl, front(color port), 488. (McM) $225, $200-bmk-full Mor., $100.
...Dayton, Oh., Morningside. Reprint, 1983. $30.
..."Lee's Sharpshooters; or, the forefront of Battle. A story of Southern Valor that never has been told." Little Rock, Ark., 1899. 8vo, wraps, 15pp. Promotional brochure for his book. $25.

956 **DUNN, Amanda Rucks**
"Some of the things that happened in our neighborhood during the war." In: Wash. Co. Hist. Soc. Paper, 1954, v.1910-1815, p. 227-230. Memoirs of the war in Greenville, Miss.

957 **DUNN, Ballard S.**
"Brazil the home for Southerners; or a practical account of what the author and others who visited that country for the same objects, saw and did while in that empire. By Rev. Ballard S. Dunn, Rector of St. Phillip's Church, New Orleans, and late of the Confederate Army." New York: C.B. Richardson, 1866. 8vo, cl, (2), iv, 272, (23)pp. front(port), large fldg. map, handcolored. $150-jk, $60.

958 **DUNN, Byron Archibald**
"General Nelson's Scout, a story of the Confederacy." Chicago: A.C. McClurg Print, 1898. 12mo, cl, front, pls., 320pp. (same, 1901)

959 ..."Raiding with Morgan." Chicago: A.C. McClurg Print, 1909. 12mo, cl, front, illus., 4th edt., fiction.
...Same: 1903, "Young Kentuckiens ser." 9-pls, p. (7)-334. 1913 (6th Edt.) $12.50.

960 ..."The Scout of Pea Ridge." Chicago: A.C. McClurg, 1911. "The Young Missourians ser." 12mo, cl, front, pls.,ix, 344pp.

961 **DUNN, Juanita Catherine**
"Names of Confederate soldiers who served in the Civil War from Fannin County, Tex., Houston, Tex., for the author, 1964." 4to, wraps, 62pp. typed. Houston, Texas: Pub. Lib., Gen. 976 4D.

962 **DUNN, Mathew Andres**
"Mathew Andrew Dunn Letters." Edt: Weymouth T. Jordan, Jackson, Miss. JMH. April 1939, v.1, #2, p. 110-127. Letters of a common soldier to his wife. Killed at Battle of Franklin, Tenn.

963 **DUNN, Nellie P.**
"General Lee in Grant's "Petersburg Progress"." In: So. Atl. Qrt., April, 1912, v.XII, p. 141-144. Extracts from Apr. 7th and 10th-issues of a newspaper printed at Petersburg by Union soldiers: Its attitude toward Gen. Lee.

964 **DUNN, Roy Sylvan**
"The K.G.C. in Texas 1860-1861." In: SWHQ, April, 1967, v.LXX, p. 543-573.
...Offprint, wraps, 30pp. $3.50.

965 **DUNN, William R.**
"Meem's Bottom." (Richmond) Va. Cavl., Autumn 1963, v.XIII, #2, p. 38-47, ports, map, illus., 1-color and dble-pg. cover (Mt. Jackson) Gen. Gilbert Meem, Turner Ashby and Shenandoah Co. during the war.

966 **DUNNING, William A.**
"Essays on the Civil War and Reconstruction." New York: Macmillan Co., 1897. 8vo, cl, 376pp. 2nd Revised Edt., 12mo, cl,

1904, p. 397. $5. 1898-$9. 3rd. 1921. $4, $5, 4th-$7.50, $8.50. 4th Edt. Harper's Torchbooks. The Academy Library, Harper & Row, (1965) Introduction by David Donald. p.xx, 397, ads-10. $1.95.

967 **DUNOVANT, Adelia A.**
"That Columbia College prize essay." In: CV, July 1912, v.XX, p. 341-344. Reply to Miss Kate DeRossett Meares on "Opposition to secession in the South." See under Miss. Meares.

968 **DUNOVANT, William**
"In Memory of R.E. Lee, an address before the R.E. Lee Chapter, UDC and the Dick Dowling Camp UCV, Houston, 1898." 8vo, wraps, 13pp. $65.

969 **DUNSTAN, William Edward, III**
"The Episcopal Church in the Confederacy." (Richmond) Va. Cavl., Spring 1970. v.XIX, #4, p. 4-15, ports, illus.(2-color).

970 **DUPUY, Trevor Nevitt**
"The First Book of Civil War Naval Action." N.Y., Franklin Watts, (1961). Sq.8vo, cl, maps, sketches, 95, (1)pp.

971 **DURDEN, Robert F.**
"The self-inflicted wound: Southern politics in the 19th Century." Lexington, University Press of Kentucky, 1985. 8vo, cl, dj, x, 150pp. $16.

972 **DUREN, C.M., Lt.**
"The Occupation of Jacksonville, Feb., 1864 and the Battle of Olustee. Letters of Lt. C.M. Duren, 54th Mass. Reg. USA." In: FHQ, April, 1954, v.XXXII, #4, p. 262-287, illus.

973 **DURHAM, Plato Tracy**
"Lee the American." Address on Lee delivered at Stone Mountain, Ga. In: Emory Univ. Quart., Dec. 1953, v.9, p. 241-249.

974 **DURHAM, Walter T.**
"Morgan at Gallatin." In: CV (new) Nov./Dec., 1986, v.34, #5, p. 6-11, illus. (1-color) map, ports. Based on his-"Rebellion Revisited."

975 ..."Nashville: the occupied city, the first seventeen months-Feb. 1862 to June, 1863." 8vo, cl, dj, xv, 307pp., illus., index, bibliog. $20. Nashville, Tennessee Historical Society 1985.

976 ..."Rebellion revisited: a history of Sumner County, Tenn., 1861-1870." Gallatin, Tenn., Sumner County Museum Association, 1982. 8vo, xiv, 362pp., paper-$10, Cl. $15.
..."Civil War letters to Wynnewood." In: THQ, Spring 1975, v.34, #1, p.32-47.

977 **DURKIN, Joseph T., SJ**
"The thought that caused the war: the compact theory in the North." In: MdHM, 1961, v.56, #1, p. 1-14.
..."Confederate Navy Chief: Stephen R. Mallory." Columbia, S.C., University Press, 1987. 8vo, cl, xi, 446p. $20. Reprint: 1954, Classic & Maritime Hist. Series. Edt: Wm. N. Still.

978 **DURKIN, Joseph Thomas**
"Armorer of the Confederacy, Secretary Mallory." N.Y., Benziger Bros., (1960) (Banner Books) 12mo, cl, illus., 196pp., juvenile. $15.

979 ..."Stephen R. Mallory: Confederate Navy Chief." Chapel Hill: Univ. N. Carolina Pr., 1954, 8vo, cl, dj, xi, 446pp., bibliog., index, p. 417-446. $7.50, $14, $16, $10, $12, $8.50. Durkin edited: "John Edward Dooley." $30-dabney.

980 **DURST, Charles Placide Bruno**
"A Confederate Letter (Texas): Bruno Durst to Jet Black." Contributed by Leon Durst." In: SwHQ, July 1953, v.LVII, #1, p. 94-96.

981 **DUTCHER, Salem**
"Address delivered by..., at Augusta, Ga., Memorial Day (Confederate) Apr. 26, 1898, by invitation of the Ladies' Memori-

al Ass'n." (n.p., 1898?) 8vo, wraps, caption title, 8pp.

982 ..."Williamsburg. A graphic story of the Battle of May 5, 1862, related by..., and endorsed by Gen. Longstreet. The Truth of History. May 20, 1890, from Augusta (Ga.) Chronicle." In: SHSP, 1889, XVII, p. 409-419.

983 ..."The South and the Constitution." In: CV, July, 1919, v.XXVII, p. 249-252. Denies the South fought to destroy the Const.

984 ..."In Honor Bound." In: Scott's Monthly Magazine, November 1866, v.II, p. 822-827.

985 **DUTY, Tony E.**
"The Home Front-McLennan County in the Civil War." In: Texana, 1874, v.XII, #3, p. 197-238.

986 **DUVAL, Capitaine**
"La combat de Mobile (5 aout 1864)." In: Rev. Maritime, n.s., #7, July 1920, p. 73-97.

987 **DWIGHT, Allan**
"Linn Dickson Confederate." N.Y., Macmillan Co., 1934, 12mo, cl, vignettes, 264pp. $3.50. A tale of the Civil War. $15-bmk.

988 **DWIGHT, Charles Stevens**
"A South Carolina Rebel's Recollections. Personal Reminiscences of the Evacuation of Richmond and the Battle of Sayler's Creek, April, 1865. Read before Camp Hampton's U.C>V., Columbia, S.C." Columbia, S.C., State Print, n.d. (1917). 8vo, wraps, 18pp. privately printed for friends, 150 copies. $25. Was Capt. Corps. Engrs. Gen. Kershaw's Brig.

989 **DWIGHT, Theodore F.**
"Critical Sketches of some of the Federal and Confederate Commanders." Boston: Houghton Mifflin Co., 1895. (Papers of the Military and Historical Society of Massachusetts, vol. 10), 8vo, cl, 3, 1, (ix)-x, 348pp. $10, $25, $50-bmk. Jno. C. Rope's "Gen. Beauregard." (reprint of At. Mon., Apr. 1884, p. 1-20; Maj-Gen. James Ewell Brown Stuart, from Atl. Mon., March 1886, p. 153-162.

990 **DWINNELL, Melvin**
"Letters of Melvin Dwinnell, Yankee Rebel. Edt: Virginia Griffin Bailey." In: Ga. H.Q., June 1963, v.XLVII, #2, p. 193-203. $10.
..."Vermonter in Gray, the story of Melvin Dwinell. Edt: Harold A. Dwinell." In: Vermont Hist., 1962, v.XXX, p. 220-237.

991 **DYE, Henry L.**
"The Journal of Henry L. Dye, Confederate Surgeon." Frederick J. Elsas. In: Surgery, 1968, v. 63, p.352-62.

992 **DYER, Brainerd**
"Confederate Naval and Privateering Activities in the Pacific." In: Pac. Hist. Rev., 1934, v.III, p. 433-443.

993 **DYER, Frederick H.**
"A Compendium of the war of the Rebellion. Compiled and arranged from official records of the Federal and Confederate armies. Reports of the Adjutant General of the several states, the Army Register and other reliable documents and sources." Desmoines, Dyer Pub. Co., 1908. Tk. 4to, cl, 1796pp.
...N.Y., Thos. Yoseloff (1954), 3 vols. With intro: Bell Wiley. illus., maps, ports (added to this edt.) paged continously, 1796pp.
...Dayton, Oh., Morningside Press, with The National Historical Society, Falls Church, Va. Facsm. #46, 1986. 2 vols., 4to, cl, 991, (997)-1796. $100.

994 **DYER, John Percy**
"The Civil War Career of Gen. Joseph Wheeler." Nashville, 1935, Vanderbilt Univ. thesis. 8vo, wraps, 32pp. $5. Reprint: Ga. Hist. Quart., v.XIX, #1, Mar., 1935, p. 17-46. Also Bul. Vanderbilt Univ.,

XXXIV, #9, p. 11-12. Abstract of theses. $8.

995 ..."Fighting Joe" Wheeler." University, La., La. State Univ., 1941. 8vo, cl, dj, maps, ports (incl. front), ill., pict. map endsheets, index, 417pp. $17.50, $125-r, $45-bmk, $25-y, $30.

996 ..."The Gallant Hood." Indianapolis: Bobbs-Merrill Co., (1950). 8vo, cl, dj, maps, ports (incl. front) 383pp. sources, index, 325-383pp. $55, $40-bmk-84, $25, $55, $22.50-y.

997 ..."From Shiloh to San Juan. The Life of "Fightin' Joe Wheeler." Baton Rouge: Louisiana State University Press (1961). Revised. 8vo, cl, d/w, ports, maps, 275pp. No new material than in the 1941 edition "Fightin' Joe" Wheeler. $2, $5, $35-atg., 1st edt. 1941, $20-bmk.

998 ..."Northern Relief for Savannah during Sherman's Occupation." (Lexington, Ky.) JSH, Nov. 1953, v.XIX, #4, p. 457-472. $8.

999 ..."Some aspects of cavalry operations in the Army of the Tennessee." In: Journ. South Hist., 1942, p. 210-225, v.VIII, $8.

1000 **DYER, John Will**
"Reminiscences; or, Four Years in the Confederate Army, a history of the experiences of the private soldier in camp hospital, prison, on the march, and on the battlefied, 1861 to 1865. Written by..., Pub. by Amelia W. Dyer." Evansville, Ind., Keller Print, 1898. 12mo, cl, illus., ports (1-color ill.) 323pp. $35, $65, $75, $400-bmk, $100, $250-g.

1001 **DYSON, B. Patricia**
"Contract stability in wartime: the example of the Confederacy." In: Amer. Jour. Legal Hist., 1975, v.XIX, p. 216-231.

E

1 **EADS, Leila Reeves**
"Defenders-A Confederate History of Henderson County, Texas." Athens, Texas: Henderson C. Historical Survey Comm.(1969). 4to, pict. wraps (stiff), illus., 42pp. $4, $25-jk.

2 **EAGLETON, Ethie M. and George E.**
"Stray Thoughts": the Civil War Diary of Ethie M. Foute Eagleton. Foreword by Ottis C. Skipper." In: E. Tenn. Hist. Soc. Pub., 1968 and 1969, v.40/41, p. 128-137, 116-128.

3 ..."The Tragic Dilemma of a Borderstate Moderate: The Rev. George E. Eagleton's views on Slavery and Secession." In: Tenn. Hist. Quart., Winter 1973, v.XXXII, p. 360-373.

4 **EARLE, Edward Meade**
"Egyptian cotton and the American Civil War." In: Pol. Sci. Quart., Dec. 1926, v.XLI, p. 520-545, off pr-$15.

5 **EARLE, Garet W.**
"Manse Jolly, a novel by Garet W. Earle." Anderson, S.C., Droke House/Hallux. (1973). 8vo, fabricoid, dj, port(front) 254pp. $8. Manson Sherrill Jolly, a guerrilla, or outlaw by the US Army, based on fact and legend, main characters are real.

6 **EARLE, Peter**
"Robert E. Lee." N.Y., Saturday Review Press (1973). sm.4to, cl, dj, illus., ports, incl. front, maps, facsms. (18 color illus.), 224pp. $25-b, $15, $12.50.

7 **EARLE-BUCHANAN Letters**
"The Earle-Buchanan Letters of 1861-1876." Edt: Robert E. Waterman and Thomas Rothrock. (Fayetteville, Ark.) Ark. Hist. Quar. Summer, '74, v.XXXIII, #2, p. 99-174. Ports, facsm., illus.

8 **EARLY, John Cabell**
"Steel Breast Plates. A defensive armor worn by Federal Troops in the War Between the States, 1861-1865." In: SHSP, 1904, v.XXXII, p. 221-222.

9 ..."A Southern boy's experience at Gettysburg." In: Jour. Mil. Ser. Inst., May 1911, v.XLVIII, p. 415-423. Author a nephew of Gen. Jubal A. Early.

..."A Southern Boy at Gettysburg." In: CWTI, June 1970, v.IX, #3, p. 35-58, illus., map, ports. Jubal's nephew, his service with uncle in '63. Originally published in: Jour. Mil. Serv. Inst., June 1911.

10 **EARLY, John M.**
"Early's Inferno. An epic poem of the Civil War. Edited by R.E. Stevenson and illustrated by Talbot O. Bateman." Little Rock, Ark., Allsop & Stevenson, 1896. 12mo, cl, plates, 1, (v)-vii, (1), 9-130pp. Confederate war poetry. $8, $10.

11 **EARLY, Jubal A., Lt.-Gen.**
"Early's march to Washington in 1864." In: B & L, v.4, p. 492-499, pl, maps.

12 ..."Winchester, Fisher's Hill, and Cedar Creek." In: B & L, v.4, p. 522-532., ports.

13 **EARLY, Jubal Anderson**
"The Advance upon Washington in July 1864." In: (Balt.) South. Mag., 1871, v.VIII, p. 750-763.

..."Advance on Washington, 1864." In: SHSP, v.IX, p. 74-76, 297-312.

..."Appeal for a Monument to Lee." In: SHSP, v.XVII, p. 188-189.

14 ..."Campaigns of Gen. Robert E. Lee. An address by..., before Washington & Lee University, Jan. 19, 1872." Balt: J. Murphy & Co., N.Y., E.J. Hale & Son, 1872. 1st edition. 8vo, wraps, 54pp. $25.

...Balt: J. Murphy & Co., 1872, 2nd revised edition, wraps, 47pp. $12.50, $75-bmk, $50-bmk.

15 ..."A correspondence between Generals Early and Mahone in regard to a military memoir of the latter." (Lynchburg, Va., 1871) 12mo, wraps, caption title, 19pp. $15, $35.

16 ..."Causes of Lee's defeat at Gettysburg." In: SHSP, v.IV, p. 50-66, IV, p. 241-281-302.

17 ..."Comments of Early the County of Paris." "Civil War in America." In: SHSP, v.III, p. 140-154.

18 ..."Discussion between J.A. Early, Chs. Marshall and Jos. E. Johnston, concerning strength of Lee's Army during the Seven Days Battle." In: SHSP, v.I, p. 408-424.

19 ..."General Barnard's report on defenses of Washington, July 1864." In: (Balt.) South. Mag., 1872, v.X, p. 716-724. $30-b.

20 ..."The Gettysburg Campaign. Report of Gen. J.A. Early." In: (Valt.) South. Mag., 1872, v.XI, p. 311-323, 385-393.

..."Gettysburg Campaign." In: SHSP, v.X, p. 529-555.

21 ..."An Interview with General Jubal A. Early in 1889." Edt: Martin F. Schmitt. (Baton Rouge, La.) JSH, Nov., 1945, v.XI, No.4, p. 547-563. $15.

22 ..."Jackson's Campaign against Pope in August 1862. An address before 1st annual meeting before the association of Maryland Line, together with proceedings at the 3rd annual banquet of the Society of Army and Navy of Confederate States in the state of Maryland." Cover title: "sold for relief of maimed and needy Confederate soldiers in Maryland.", printed in red, as heading. n.p., (c.1883) (Balt. Foley Bros.) 8vo, wraps, port of Early on both wraps and frontis, 52pp., bound in, with: "3rd Annual Banquet of the Society Army and Navy of Confederate States, in state of Maryland, held at Carrollton Hotel, Feb. 22, 1883." 8vo, front: Maj.-Gen. I.R. Trimble, p. 38. $10, $30, $40, $75, $150-r, $100bmk, (1932) $25, $150- bmk-105.

23 ..."Jubilee" General Jubal A. Early." In: CWTI, Dec., 1970, v.IX, No.8, p. 4-11, 43-48, illus., ports.

24 ..."Lee and Longstreet." In: So. Hist. Monthly, 1876, v.I, p. 184-219.

25 ..."A characteristic Letter of Gen. Jubal A. Early, disclaiming allegiance to Uncle Sam. Written just after the war by the old Confederate who never surrendered-facts concerning the bitter conquest." In: SHSP, 1896, v.XXIV, p. 176-182.

26 ..."Letter from Early on treatment of Federal prisoners in Confederate prisons, Gen. John H. Winder." In: So. Hist. Monthly, 1876, v.I, p. 173-183.

27 ..."Letter from Lieutenant-General J.A. Early asking further inquiry into the causes of the recent reverses in the Valley of Virginia." Senate Jan. 9, 1864. (Richmond, Va., 1965) 8vo, 4pp. folder (charges Early was drunk)

28 ..."Lieutenant General Jubal Anderson Early, C.S.A. Autobiographical sketch and narrative of the War Between the States, with notes by R.H. Early." Phila., Lond: J.B. Lippincott Co., 1912, 8vo, front, plates, ports, xxv, (1), 496pp. $60, $110, $150, $225-b.

...Bloomington: Indiana Univ. Pr., 1960, "War Memoirs: Autobiographical sketch and narrative of War Between the States." Edt: Frank Vandiver. 8vo, cl, dj, xlviii, 496pp. $17.50, $22.50, $40.

...N.Y., Krause reprint, 1969 (pub.$50) $25.

29 ..."Memorial of Gen. Jubal A. Early, an address: Hon. John W. Daniel, before Assn. ANV., Richmond, Dec. 13, 1894." In: SHSP, 1894, v.XXII, p. 281-335.

30 ..."A Memoir of the Last Year of the War for Independence in the Confederate States of America, containing an account

of the operations of his command in the years 1864 and 1865, by Lieutenant-Gen. Jubal A. Early, of the provisional army of the CSA." Toronto, Ca., Lovell & Gibson, 1866. 12mo, wraps, x, (2), (13)-144pp. 1st. edt. $85, $150, $250, $350-jk.

...Lynchburg, Va., Charles W. Button, 1867, 8vo, wraps, errata slip verso t.p., xii, (13)-135, (1)-index. 2nd edt. $60, $75, $120.

...New Orleans, La. (Blelock & Co.) 1867. 8vo, wraps, x, (1), (13)-112pp. $20, $25, $35. On cover-"Southern Edition". $130, $65, $100.

...Augusta, Ga., 1867, same. $12.50, $22. Early's "Memoir", revised and extended into his "Autobiographical Sketch". $40, $50, $75.

31 ..."Popular errors in regard to the battles of the war." In: Land We Love, 1868-1869, v.VI, p. 265-277.

32 ..."Proceedings of the third annual meeting of the Survivors Association of the State of South Carolina: and the annual address by Gen. Jubal A. Early." Charleston, S.C., Walker, Evans & Cogswell, 1872, wraps, 8vo, 38pp. $6.50, $100-r, $60- jk-122. Speech delivered Nov. 10, 1871. "Address", same, 24pp., wraps, $35-bmk.

33 ..."The Proceedings of the Southern Historical Convention, which assembled at the Montgomery White Sulphur Springs, Va., on the 14th of August, 1873; and of the Southern Historical Society as reorganized, with the address by Gen. Jubal A. Early." Baltimore: Turnbull Bros. (1873). 8vo, wraps, 44pp. $15, $45- jk-122.

34 ..."Relatives Numbers at Gettysburg... Letter from the Count of Paris, General Early's reply to the Count of Paris." In: SHSP, July 1878, v.VI, #1, p. 10-36.

..."Relative strength of the armies of Lee and Grant. Reply of Gen. Early to the letter of Gen. Badeau to the "London Standard." In: SHSP, July 1876, v.II, #1, p. 6-21. Also: separate pamphlet, 8vo, wraps, (1870) caption title, printed dbl-column. 8pp.

35 ..."Reminiscences of Gettysburg." In: Nation. Mag., July 1913, v.XXXVIII, p. 634-640. From his "Autobiography."

36 ..."Report of the operations of Early's Brigade in affair at Blackburn's Ford on Bull Run, July 18, 1861." In: So. Hist. Soc. Trans., 1875, v.II, p. 74-77.

..."Reply to Gen. Longstreet's second paper." In: SHSP, June 1878, v.V, #6, p. 270-287.

37 ..."A Short History of Gen. J.A. Early." Park Place, N.Y., Knapp & Co., 1888. 2 3/4x1 1/2" colored booklet, 16pp. facsm. signature. (packed in Duke's cigarettes) See: "Heroes of the C.W." and W. Duke Co.

38 ..."Stonewall Jackson at Fredericksburg, a letter from Early." In: Hist. Mag., Morrisania, 1870, v.VIII, p. 32-35.

39 ..."Stonewall Jackson, the story of his being an astrologer refuted. The manner in which he received his wound described by an eyewitness." In: South. Mag., 1873, v.XII, p. 537-555. SHSP, v.VI, 1878, p. 261-282.

40 ..."The Story of the attempted formation of a N.W. Confederacy, a letter from..." In: SHSP, April, 1882, Field Returns." In: SHSP, June/July, 1880, v.VIII, #6-7, p. 301-305.

41 ..."Unveiling of Valentine's recumbent figure of Lee at Lexington, Va., June 28, 1883, remarks of Gen. Early, etc." In: SHSP, Aug./Sept. 1883, #8-9, p. (336)-340, engr. of figure, front.

42 ..."Winchester and Fisher's Hill-Letter from Gen. Early to Gen. Lee." In: SHSP, Jan./Feb., 1882, v.X, #1 and 2, p. 78-81. Also: Battles and Leaders, v.4, p. 522-530. See: Vandiver's-"Jubal's Raid"; Bushong's

"Old Jube"; Jno. W. Daniel; W.B. Conway; G.L. Christian.

43 **EARNHART, T.M.**
"Surgical treatment in the Confederate Army." In: CV, Dec. 1918, v.XXVI, p. 528-529.

44 **EASBY-SMITH, Anne Mildred**
"William Russell Smith of Alabama, his Life and Works including the entire text of "The Uses of Solitude." Foreword by Geo. H. Denn." Philadelphia: Dolphin Press, 1931, 8vo, cl, dj, ports, pl, front, 298pp. $20-bmk, $7.50, $12-bmk. Author, Colonel, CSA, member CSA Congr. See also under subject's name. Wm. R. Smith.

45 **EASON, Thomas R.**
"Historic Institutional Change in the Mississippi Economy." (Jackson, Miss.) Jour. Miss. Hist., Nov. 1973, v.XXXV, #4, p. 345-359.

46 **"EAST TEXAS HISTORY.**
Selections from East Texas Historical Journal. Edited by Archie P. McDonald." Austin, Tex: Jenkins Pub. Co., 1978. See: Allan C. Ashcraft's- "ET Elect. 1860, and Ralph A. Wooster's-"Civil War East Tex."

47 **EAST, Charles, et al**
"Four Louisiana Civil War Stories." (Baton Rouge, La.) Pub. by La. Civil War Centennial Comm., 1961. 8vo, stiff wraps, 2-ports, 36pp.

48 **EAST, Omega G.**
"St. Augustine during the Civil War." In: Fla. Hist. Qrt., 1952, v.XXXI, p. 75-91.

49 **EASTIN, George B., Captain**
"The Killing of Colonel Dennis J. Halisey." In: SHSP, 1882, v.X, p. 513-518.

50 **EASTMAN, Mary Henderson, Mrs.**
"Aunt Phillis's Cabin; or, Life as it is." Phila: Lippincott, Grambo Co., 1852. 12mo, cl, front, illus. $17.50. Wife of Seth Eastman, born in Va., this is an answer to Mrs. Stowe's "Uncle Tom's Cabin."

51 **EASTWOOD, Bruce S.**
"Confederate Medical Problems in the Atlanta Campaign." In: Ga. H.Q., Sept., 1963, v.XLVII, #3, p. 276-292.

52 **EATON, Charles Edward**
"Robert E. Lee: an Ode." In: Ga. Rev., 1961, Summer, V.XV, No.2, p. 159-170. $8.

53 **EATON, Clement**
"A History of the Southern Confederacy." N.Y., Macmillan Co., 1954. N.Y., Macmillan Co., 1954. 8vo, cl, ix, (5), 351pp. notes, 303-335. $10, $20-bmk, dj, $15-nc. Editions, 1956 @ $3.75; N.Y. Free Press, (1965) paper, $2.45; (1966) 3rd print, $6; 1972, $10. Social, political and military hist. of South.

54 ..."Jefferson Davis." N.Y., Free Press (Macmillan Co.) (1977). Tall 8vo, bds-cl. spine, illus., ports, incl. front, facsm., xii, (1), 334pp. index, notes, (p. 277-319). $15, $13-y.

55 ..."The wanning of the Old South Civilization, 1860-1980's." Athens, Ga., University of Georgia Press (1968). 8vo, cl, dj, xii, 105pp. (Mercer University, Lamar Memorial Lectures, No.10.

56 **EATON, P.T.**
"Battle of Manassas. Plan of the Battlefield and Topographical Description." Broadside, folio, with text in four columns. New Orleans, La., 1861, not in Crandall or Harwell. $450-eberstadt

57 **EAVES, John J.**
"Record of an infantry company (33rd Inf., Co. C)." In: CV, 1908, v.XVI, p. 528.

58 **EBAUGH, David Chenoweth**
"David C. Ebaugh on the building of the "David"." In: S.C. Hist. Mag., Jan. 1953, 5pp. Reproduces letters recounting his role in building CSA submarine, 1864. p. 32-36.

59 **EBERT, Valerius**
"Letter from Mrs. Frietchie's Nephew

denying Whittier's "Facts"." In: SHSP, 1879, v.VII, p. 438-439.

60 **ECHENRODE, H.J. and Bryan Conrad, James Longstreet**
"Lee's war horse." Chapel Hill: University of North Carolina Press, 1985. New foreword by Gary W. Gallagher. 8vo, cl, dj, 420pp., 14-maps. $20.

61 **"ECHOES from the South**
Comprising the most important speeches, proclamations and public acts emanating from the South during the late war." N.Y., E.B. Treat; Balt., L.T. Palmer, 1866. 12mo, cl, vi, (7)-211pp. $12.50, $15, $20, $30, rep. $10.75-y. Nevins attributes to Ed. A. Pollard. Louisville: Lost Cause Pr., microcard.

62 **ECHOLS, John**
"Report of Brig.-Gen. Echols of the Battle of Droop Mountain. Published by order of Congress." Richmond, Va., R.M. Smith, 1864. 8vo, wraps, 16pp. Hdq. 1st Brig. Army Southwestern Va., Lewisburg, Nov. 19, 1863.

63 **ECHOLS, John Warnock**
"The man behind the gun"; an address by John Warnock Echols, before the historical of Fairfax County, Va., on the anniversary of Washington's birthday Feb. 22, 1917." Washington, DC, Judd & Detweiler, 1917. 8vo, wraps, 21pp. On Geo. Washington and Gen. Lee.

64 **ECHOLS, John, Gen.**
"Address on the Life and Character of Gen. John C. Breckinridge delivered at New Market, Va., May 15, 1877, and Memorial Eulogy on the Battle of New Market, May 15, 1864, by Joseph Salyards." New Market, Va., (1877). Tall 8vo, sewn, 13pp. $15.

65 ..."Reports to Gen. Lee after the war." In: Confed. Vet., 1901/1902, v.X, p. 305-308.

66 ..."Letter concerning General Lee." In: SHSP, v.XI, p. 451-454.

67 **ECKENRODE, Hamilton James**
"Jefferson Davis, President of the South." N.Y., Macmillan, 1923. 12mo, cl, (12), 371pp. $20-mcm, $8.50, $10, $18.
...Do: London (1924), Geo. Allen & Unwin, $10.
...Do: N.Y., 1930, 2nd Edt., $3, $15-y, $6.
..."Freeport, N.Y., Books for Libraries Press, (1971). $18.
...N.Y., Gordon Pr., $35-trade, $60-lib. bind.
...N.Y., Arno Press, 1978. $21. "Select bibliographies Reprint Series." $15.

68 ..."The Life of Nathan B. Forrest." Richmond, (1918). 12mo, cl, illus., maps, 186pp. $15. 5th Reader, very scarce. $30-bmk-104.

69 ...Eckenrode and Bryan Conrad. "James Longstreet Lee's War Horse." Chapel Hill: University of North Carolina, 1936, cl, d/w, 8vo, port(front), viii, 399pp. 14-maps. $6, $12.50, $15, $20, $25, $27.50, $30, $75-r, $60-bmk-104, $40-bmk.

70 ..."Negroes in Richmond in 1864." In: VaMH, 1928, v.XLVI, p. 193-200. Attitude of negroes during this year.

71 ..."The Political History of Virginia. During the Reconstruction." Baltimore: Johns Hopkins Press, 1904. University studies in historical and political science, Ser. 12, #6, 7, and 8. 8vo, cl, 128pp. $20-bmk-89.

72 **ECKERSON, Edmonds Augusta**
"Heroes of the South; address delivered under auspices of the U.D.C., Dept. of Missouri, at the Opera House, Warrensburg, Mo., Sept. 7, 1900." (St. Joseph, Mo., 1900?) 8vo, wraps, 16pp.

72a **ECKERT, Edward K.**
"Fiction Distorting Fact: The Prison Life Annotated by Jefferson Davis." Macon, Ga., Mercer University Press, 1987. 8vo, cl, dj, lxxii, 168p. append, index. $40.
See: Wm. Hanchett, John J. Craven.

73 **EDGAR, Thomas H.**
"History of De Bray's (26th) Regiment of Texas Cavalry, 1861-1898." Galveston, Texas, A.A. Finck & Co., 1898. 8vo, wraps, 64pp. (1940-$2.50) F. White, Jr., $1250. (1984). See: DeBray's 26th Texas Cavalry.

74 **EDGE, Frederick Milnes**
"The Alabama and the Kearsarge. An account of the Naval Engagement in the British Channel, on Sunday, June 19th, 1864, from information furnished to the writer by the wounded and paroled prisoners of the Confederate Privateer Alabama, the officers of the United States Sloop for War Kearsarge and citizens of Cherbourg." London, 1864. 16mo, wraps, 48pp. $25.
...N.Y., Anson D.F. Randolph, 1864, title. "An Englishman's View of the Battle between the Alabama and the Kearsarge..." 8vo, wraps, 48pp. Reprinted: N.Y., W. Abbatt, 1908. 8vo, wraps, 36pp. Mag. Hist. Notes and Queries, Ex. #2 (pt.1).

75 ..."The Alabama and the Kearsarge." Phil: King & Baird Print, 1868, 8vo, wraps, 64pp. $45.

76 **EDGEFIELD COUNTY, S.C.**
See: John A. Chapman. Spartanburg, S.C., Reprint Co., 1980.

77 **EDGINTON, T.B., Major**
"Major Edginton's Address (In Memoriam) of General Joseph Eggleston Johnston." In: SHSP, 1890, v.XVIII, p. 199-203.

78 ..."The Race Problem in the South-Was the Fifteenth Amendment a mistake?" In: SHSP, 1889, v.XVII, p. 23-23.

78a **EDMONDS, Amanda Virginia**
"Journal of Amanda Virginia Edmonds: Lass of the Mosby Confederacy, 1859-1867. Edt: Nancy Chappelear Baird." Stephens City, Va., 1984. 8vo, cl, 282p, ills. $30.

79 **EDMONDS, Dale**
"The saga of Louis Wetmore (died 1863)." In: Jr. Historian (Tex.) Dec. 1952, v.13, #3, p. 105. His services in CSArmy and Texas.

80 **EDMONDS, David C.**
"Surrender on the Bourbeaux: Honorable Defeat or Incompetency under Fire." In: La. Hist. 1978. V. 18, p. 63-86.

81 ..."The Guns of Port Hudson. Vol. 1, The River Campaign (Feb.-May, 1863)." Lafayette, La., Acadiana Press, 1983. 8vo, cl, 291pp., illus., index. $16. See: Edward Cunningham, Lt. Howard C. Wright. Port Hudson.
...Vol. 2: "The Investment, Siege and Reduction. 8vo, cl, xvi, 455pp., illus., index. $18.
..."Yankee Autumn in Acadiana; narrative of the Great Texas Overland expedition through Southwestern Louisiana, Oct.-Dec., 1863." Lafayette, La., Acadiana Press, 1988. 8vo, cl, 512p. $20.

82 **EDMONDS, George (pseud.)**
"Facts and Falsehoods." See: E.A. Meriweather.

83 **EDMONDSON, C.D.**
"The bombardment of Fort Sumter, Aug. 17-23, 1863." In: Quartermaster Rev., 1935, v.XV, p. 17-21.

84 **EDMONDSON, James K., Col.**
"My dear Emma, war letters of Col. James K. Edmondson, 1861-1865. Edt. by Charles W. Turner." Verona, Va., 1978. 8vo, cl, 151pp. $20. With the 27th Va. Inf., "Stonewall Brig."

85 **EDMONDSTON, Catherine Ann Devereux**
"Journal of a Secesh Lady", the Diary of Catherine Ann Devereux Edmondston 1860-1866. Edited by Beth G. Crabtree and James W. Patton." Raleigh (N.C.) Division of Archives and History Department of Cultural Resources, 1979.

Tk.sm.4to, cl, dj, facsms., illus.-incl. color front genealogical table, map liners, ports, 50pp. index, (2), xxxviii, (1)-850pp. $28.50.

..."The Journal of..., 1860-1866. Edt: Margaret Mackay Jones (Mrs. George Lyle Jones)." n.p., n.d. (1954) privately published in a lim. edt., 500 copies. 8vo, cl, map, illus., 111pp. $75, $50-bmk-84, $65-bmk-84. Diary kept on plantation owned by autho

86 EDMONDSTON, Patrick Muir
"Edmund Burke Haywood and Raleigh's Confederate Hospitals." In: NCHR, 1958, v.35, p. 153-166.

87 EDMONSON, Mary Sale, Mrs.
"This Old Book: the Civil War Diary of Mrs. Mary Sale Edmonson of Phillips County, Ark., R.P. Baker, Edt." In: PhCHQ, March, 1972, v.10, p. 1-14; Sept., p. 1-11; Dec., p. 1-8; Mar. 1973, v.11, p. 1-10; June, p. 1-10; Sept., p. 1-9; Dec., p. 1-10; Mar. 1974, v.11, p. 1-10; June, v.12, p. 2-10.

88 EDMUNDS, John B., Jr.
"Francis W. Pickens and the war begins." In: PSCHS, 1970, p. 21-29.

89 EDRINGTON, John Catesby
"Letters from John Catesby Edrington of Stafford (Va.) to his sisters, Misses Mary and Angelina Selden Edrington." In: North Neck Hist. Mag., Dec. 1954, v.4, p. 289-290. Dated Camp Lee, 22 Jan., 1862.

90 EDWARDS, Conley L., III
"The photographer of the Confederacy." In: CWTI, June 1974, v.13, #3, p. 26-33, illus., facsm., port.

91 EDWARDS, Dale
"Arkansas: Pea Ridge and State Division." In: Jour. of West, 1975, v.XIV, p. 167-184.

92 EDWARDS, Frank (i.e., John Frank)
"Army life of Frank Edwards, Confederate Veteran, Army of Northern Virginia, 1861-1865." (La Grange, Ga., 1911). $300-bmk-116. 12mo, wraps, cover title, 2-ports, 108pp. $15, $17.50. Cover-title: The Red Book; the life of Frank Edwards, Edt.: Earle E. Griggs.

93 EDWARDS, J. Griff, Mrs.
"Echoes from Dixie. A collection of Songs used in the South prior to and during the War Between the States." Portsmouth, Va., (1911). 4to, wraps, 80pp.

...(with) Matthew Page Andrews (comp. and edt.) N.Y., 1918. "Echoes from Dixie, Old Time Southern Songs." 8vo, wraps, 74pp. Largely Confederate and negro songs. $40-bmk-84, $20, Andrews atg.

94 EDWARDS, John
"My Escape in 1861." Oklahoma City: Chron. Okla. Spring, 1965, v.XLIII, #1, p. 60-89.

95 EDWARDS, John Ellis, Rev.
"The Confederate Soldier; being a memorial sketch of George N. and Bushrod W. Harris, privates in the Confederate Army." N.Y., Blelock & Co., 1868. 12mo, cl, vi, 139pp. Co. E., 19th Va. Inf. $17.50, $37.50, $150-bmk-105, $250-bmk-105.

...N.Y., same, 1888. $37.50.

96 EDWARDS, John Newman
"Biography, Memoirs, Reminiscences and Recollections; also a reprint of Shelby's Expedition to Mexico, an unwritten leaf of the War. Compiled by his wife, Jennie." Kansas City, Mo., Private Print, 1889. 12mo, cl, 428pp. Limited to 100 copies, numbered and signed. $30, $37.50, $75, $100.

97 ..."Noted Guerrillas; or, the warfare of the border, being a history of the lives and adventures of Quantrill, Bill Anderson, George Todd, Dave Poole, Fletcher Taylor, Peyton Long, Oll Shepherd, Arch Clements, John Maupin, Tuck and Woot Hill, Wm. Gregg, Thomas Maupin, the James Brothers, Younger Brothers, Author McCoy and numerous other well known guerrillas of the West." St. Louis: Bryan,

Brand & Co., 1877. 8vo, cl, xi, (13)-488pp. front, 15-pls, 2-adv. $35, $50, $60, $67.50, $85-mint, $100-jk. Reprinted: 1879, St. Louis: J.W. Marsh, 1880, 12mo, cl, illus., ports, $20. Dornbusch-III, 276-"a reprint thru first two lines of pg. 302 of the '77 edt. Two paragraph added closing text."
...Dayton, Oh., Morningside Press, 1976. $20.

98 ..."Shelby and His Men; or, the War in the West." $27.50, $30, $47.50, $65. Cinn., Miami Print, 1867. '73 aug, $27, $175, $60-bmk. 8vo, cl, front(port), fldg. map, ix, (10)-551pp.
...Kansas City, Mo., Hudson-Kimberly Co., 1897. $32.50. 12mo, cl, front(port), 461pp. $17.50, $27.50

99 ..."Shelby's Expedition to Mexico. An unwritten leaf of the War." Kansas City, Mo., Kansas City Times, 1872. 8vo, wraps, (or cl.), 139pp., dbl. columns. $75.
..."Shelby's expedition to Mexico; an unwritten leaf of the war." In: MoHR, Oct. 1919, v.XIV, pg. 111-144. Extracts from Edward's acct., pub. in 1872.
...Austin, Texas, The Steck Co., (1964). 8vo, cl, boxed, "a facsimile reproduction." with preface (3)pp., ports (front in color), 6-color illus., and others, map. $15.
..."Shelby's expedition to Mexico; an unwritten leaf of the war." In: MoHR, Jan./Apr. 1920, v.XIV, p. 246-264 (1919-pp. 111-144), 474-493; 1921, v.XV, p. 545-560, 707-720 (April/July), XVI, Oct., p. 146-157; July, p. 428-456. Extracts from Edward's acct., pub: 1872. Oct., 1922, v.XVII, p. 77-95; Jan./Apr., p. 187-197, 348-357; Jan./Feb., 1924, v.XVIII, p. 250-277, 438-453, Apr. 1925, v.XIX, p. 438-471.

100 **EDWARDS, L.R., Lieut.**
"Roll of Company E., Thirteenth Virginia Cavalry, and as to the Flag of the Regiment." In: SHSP, 1906, v.XXXIV, p. 210-211. See: "Roll of Brave Men."

101 **EDWARDS, W.H.**
"A Condensed History of Seventeenth Regiment, S.C.V., CSA, from its organization to the close of the war. Completed by Capt. Edwards, Fall, 1905." Columbia, S.C., R.L. Bryan Co., 1908. 12mo, wraps, 55pp. $18, $22.50.

102 **EDWARDS, Weldon Nathaniel**
"Memoir of Nathaniel Macon, of North Carolina." Raleigh: Register Steam Press, 1862, 12mo, wraps, 22pp. $125-jk, $150-bmk. See also-Nathaniel Macon.

103 **EDWARDS, William B.**
"Civil War Guns. The complete story of Federal and Confederate small arms: design, manufacture, identification, procurement, issue, employment, effectiveness and postwar disposal." Harrisburg, Pa., Stackpole Co., (1962) 4to, cl, d/w, color front, illus., 444pp. $15, $25-bmk, $18, $30.
...Secaucus, Castle Pr., 1962. $25, $7.95; (1972) $16.50.

104 ..."One-Man Armory: Col. J.H. Burton." (Richmond) Va. Cavl., Autumn, 1962, v.XII, #2, p. 28-33, illus., guns, made in Va., under direction of Gen. Gorgas.

105 **EDWARDS, William H.**
"A bit of history. (secession of Virginia)." In: W.Va.Mag., 1902, v.2.3, p. 59-66, port.

106 **EDWARDS, William L.**
"The William L. Edwards Letters, 1862. Edited: Ann Dempster and Dr. Homer L. Kerr." In: TMH, Spring, 1968, v.7, #1, p. 5-26.

107 **EDWARDS, William Walter**
"The invincible raider." In: Cav. Jour., Jan. 1930, v.XXXVIII, p.513-535. History of Forrest's operations during war.

108 ..."Stuart rides again." In: CAv. Jour., Jan., 1930, v.XXXVIII, p. 34-58. Acct. raids by Gen. Jeb Stuart in 1862.

109 ..."Turner Ashby, beau sabreur." In: Cav. Jour., Jan. 1922, v.XXI, p. 138-151. $25.

110 EFFORD, T.J.
"Yr. sincere friend." In: Chicago Hist., Winter, 1954, v.3, p. 315-317, port. Letter dated "Academy, Camp 3 miles above Rappahannock, 13 May, 1863. From a lieut. in CSArmy, to an unnamed person.

111 EGAN, Clifford L.
"Cuba, Spain and the American Civil War." In: Rocky Mountain Social Science Journal, Oct., 1968, v.5, p. 58-63. See: James W. Cortada.

112 EGGLESTON, Edmund T.
"Excerpts from the Civil War Diary of E.T. Eggleston, Edt: Edward Noyes." In: Tenn.HQ, Dec. 1958, v.XVII, p. 336-358. Records of Sgt. Eggleston, of 1st Miss. Regt. Artillery, Feb. 7-Dec., 1864, Ala., Ga., Tenn. and Miss.

113 ..."Captain Eggleston's Narrative of the Battle of the Merrimac." In: SHSP, 1916, v.41, p. 166-178.

114 EGGLESTON, Ethie M.
"Stray Thoughts": the Civil War diary of Ethie M. Eggleston. Edt: Elvie Eggleston Skipper and Ruth Gove." In: East TennHS, 1968, #40, p. 128-137; Pt. II, 1969, #41, p. 116-128.

115 EGGLESTON, George Cary
"American War Ballads and Lyrics; a collection of the songs and ballads of the Colonial Wars, the Revolution, the War of 1812-1815, the War with Mexico, and the Civil War. Edt: George Cary Eggleston." N.Y., Lond: G.P. Putnam's Sons (1889). 12mo, cl, front, illus., 2 vols. Civil War, V.I, p. 165-226. $15.

116 ..."A History of the Confederate War, its causes and its conduct; a narrative and critical history." N.Y., Sturgis & Walton Co., 1910, 8vo, cl, vi, 433, vi, 369pp. $15, $25, $27.50, $100- bmk, $85-bmk, $60-mcm, $50- mcm, $30. London: Heineman Print, 1910, $15, $20. Reprint: N.Y., London, 1926, $25-y, $27.50 y, $20.

117 ..."Notes on Cold Harbor." In: B & L, v.4, p. 230-232.

118 ..."The Master of Warlock a Virginia War Story." Boston: Lothrop Pub., Jan. 1903. 8vo, dec. cl., port on cover, illus., incl. front, 433pp. (2p. ads). $10, $6.50.
...N.Y., G.P. Putnam's Sons, 1878- $16.50, the 2nd edt., reprint: 1887; a 3rd, 1889-$35-bmk, 1897-$60-bmk, 4th edt., 1905, an added preface: 1xxv, 260pp. "Atlantic Monthly", 1874, xxxiii, p. 730-776; xxxiv, p. 94-101, 163-167, 333-340, 467-474, 594-602, 663-670. Where it first appeared.
...Bloomington, Indiana Univ. Press. (1959) 12mo, cl, dj, 187pp. Civil War Cent. Series. Intro: David Donald. $12.50, $17.50.
...N.Y., Kraus Reprints, 1969. $10.

119 ..."Recollections of a Varied Life." N.Y., Henry Holt Co., 1910. 8vo, cl, front(port), viii, 354, (6) -advs. Index. $12.50.

120 ..."Southern Soldier Stories, with illus., by R.F. Zogbaum." N.Y., Macmillan Co., 1898. 12mo, cl, front(port) illus., xi, 251pp. $12.50, $50-b, $35- bmk-104, $22-nc. Also pub. in wraps, 4-parts. Reprinted in July and Nov., 1898, a 2nd edt., 1909. $9.50.

121 EGGLESTON, George Cary, Sgt.-Maj.
"Notes on Cold Harbor." In: B & L, v.4, p. 230-232.

122 EGGLESTON, J.R.
"The Navy of the Confederate States." In: CV, Oct. 1907, v.XV, p. 449-453.

123 EGGLESTON, John Randolph, Mrs.
"The Women of the Confederacy. What they saw and suffered during the War." In: SHSP, 1906, v.XXXIV, p. 191-193.

124 EIDSON, William G.
"Louisville, Kentucky, during the First year of the Civil War." In: FCHQ, July, 1964, v.38, No.3, p. 224-238.

125 **"EIGHTEEN Hundred and Sixty Association, The"**
The 1860 Association." See: "The South alone should govern the South." See: John Townsend. Also: William D. Porter. Carolina Bks. No.10 (No. 320) observes- "Tract #2, advocates secession. Secret discussions among Charleston leaders in 1860. It was supported by some of the wealthiest, most influential men in S.C. Lowndes, Heywards, Middletons, Aikens, Wm. D. Porter. Most aggressive pubs. of secession pamphlets in the South in preparation for disunion."

126 **"EIGHTH ANNUAL REUNION Company "A",**
Second Texas Cavalry, C.S.A., held at Dallas, Texas, Oct. 4 and 5th, 1899." Waco, Texas. Kellner Print, 1899. 8vo, wraps, 12pp.

127 **"EIGHTH KENTUCKY, The**
at Pearl River." In: SB, 1885-1886, ns 1, p. 313. Signed A.B.

128 **"EIGHTH TENNESSEE Consolidation Association**
of Confederate Veterans. Annual Reunions. 18th (1899) at Petersburg, Va." In: CV, 1899, v.7, p. 395-396.

129 **"EIGHTH VIRGINIA'S Part**
in Second Manassas Col. N.B., tells of regiments victory over John Pope." In: SHSP, 1909, v.37, p. 313-316.

130 **EISENDRATH, Joseph L., Jr.**
"The Official Records--sixty-three years in the making." In: CWH, Mar. 1954, v.1, 89-94pp. The War of Rebellion Records of Union and CSArmies (128 vols., and Atlas, 1864-1927.
..."The Official Records-Sixty Years in the Making." In: CSH, Mar. 1955, v.1, No.1, p. 89-94.

131 **EISENSCHIML, Otto and E.B. Long**
"As Luck Would Have It Chance and Coincidence in the Civil War." Indianapolis, Ind: Bobbs-Merrill (1948), 8vo, cl, d/w, 285pp., maps. $8, $6, $25- bmk-84.

132 ..."Bragg's Headquarters." In: CWH, Mar. 1955, v.1, #1, p. 65-69.

133 ..."The Story of Shiloh." (Chicago, Ill., Norman Press, Apr., 1946) The Civil War Round Table. 8vo, decr. buck., ports, illus., 89pp. Limited Edt., sig: author and Monroe Cockrell. $15.

134 ..."Shiloh-the blunders and the blame." In: CWTI, Apr., 1963, v.II, No.1, p. 6-13, 30-34, illus., map, ports.

135 ..."Why Was Lincoln Murdered?" Boston: Little, Brown Co., 1937. 8vo, cl, illus., x, 503pp. Atg.-$25-y. Booth fired fatal ball as toll of Northern "radicals", led by Sect. Stanton.

136 **ELAM, W.C.**
"A sign in the heavens." In: B & G, 1894, v.III, p. 264. Re: Stonewall Jackson.

137 **ELDER, J.A., Printer**
"General T.J. Jackson." litho: 14x18", colored, from painting Corcoran Gallery (#3653) printed in Holland, New York Graphic Society.

138 ...Do: "General Robert E. Lee." (#3654)

139 **ELDER, William Henry**
"Civil War Diary (1862-1865) of Bishop Wm. Henry Elder, Bishop of Natchez." (Jackson, Miss., 1960) Pub. by Most Rev. R.O. Gerow, Bishop of Natchez and Jackson, Miss. Priv. Print. 8vo, cl, 125pp. OP, just after publication.

140 **ELDRIDGE, James W.**
"Catalogue of a remarkable collection of books, pamphlets, broadsides and manuscripts, formed by the late..., of Hartford, Conn., relating to the American Civil War from the Federal and Confederate sides, Lincolniana, John Brown, slavery, etc., Pt. 1. For sale by Wm. H. Murray. Hartford, Conn., n.d., 8vo, wraps, 106pp.

141 **"ELECTION, Wednesday, November 6, 1861.**
For President, Jefferson Davis." (Richmond, Va.?, 1861) Crandall-2735, Broadside-15 1/2x10cm. $200-bmk-114.

142 **"ELEVENTH Tennessee Infantry, The**
By John H. Ward." In: CV, 1908, v.xvi, p. 420.

143 ..."Reminiscences of Company A, 11th Tenn. Inf. By J.C. Alspaugh." In: CV, 1910, v.xviii, p. 506.

144 **ELIOT, Ellsworth**
"West Point in the Confederacy." N.Y., G.A. Baker & Co., 1941. 8vo, cl, dj, xxxii, 491pp. $15, $17.50, $75-b, $35-bmk, $22.50-y, $20-nc.

145 ..."Yale in the Civil War." New Haven: Yale Univ. Pr., 1932. 8vo, xiv, 222pp. Participation in war on both sides.

146 **ELIS, Lelia**
"Snapshots of the Civil War." n.p., n.d., Nantucket, Mass., (1929?) 8vo, wraps (cover title) 36pp. Per. narrative, Miss. in war, siege of Vicksburg.

147 **ELKHORN Campaign**
See: Dabney H. Maury, Paul C. Yates.

148 **ELLEN, John Calhoun, Jr.**
"Richard Yeadon, Confederate Patriot." In: S.C. Hist. Assoc., 1960. 8vo, wraps, 12pp. extract. $6.

149 **ELLERBE, J.E., Mrs.**
"Raphael Semmes." In: CV, May 1922, v.XXX, p. 178-180. Sketch: commander CSNavy "Alabama".

150 **ELLINGER, Esther Parker**
"Southern War Poetry of the Civil War." Phila: For the Author, 1918. (Hershey, Pa., Hershey Press) 8vo, cl, 192pp. Thesis: Univ. of Pa., Grad. school. $75.

151 **ELLIOTT, C.D.**
"A plea for the Tennessee Confederate Memorial and Historical Association." Nashville: C.R. & H.H. Hatch Pr., 1886. 8vo, wraps, 16pp. Elliott was Chaplain: Gen. Maney's Brig.

152 **ELLIOTT, Charles Grice**
"Kirkland's Brigade, Hoke's Division 1864-1865." (From Raleigh (N.C.) "State", Nov. 19, 1895) In: SHSP, 1895, v.XXIII, p. 165-174.

153 ..."Martin's Brigade, of Hoke's Division, 1863-1864." (From Raleigh, N.C. "State", Nov. 6, 1895) In: SHSP, 1895, v.XXIII, p. 189-198. Elliott: "Late Capt. and Ass't. Adj.-General."

154 **ELLIOTT, Charles, Rev.**
"History of the Great Secession from the Methodist Episcopal Church in the Year 1845. Eventuating in the organization of the New Church, entitled "Methodist Episcopal Church South". By the Rev. Dr. Elliott." Cincinnati, 1855, Royal 8vo, cl, 1143pp. $75. Much on Slavery. It is thought that this schism presaged the Civil War in the break between the North - South churches.

155 **ELLIOTT, Claude**
"Leathercoat; the life history of a Texas patriot...privately printed." San Antonio: Standard Printing Co., 1938. 8vo, cl, xiv, 2, (3), -315pp. front(port), pls. ports. $35. See: James Marten.

156 **ELLIOTT, Gilbert**
"The Ram "Albemarle"." In: Walter Clark's Hist. of Several Regs. and Batts. from N.C.", Vol. V, p. (1), 315-323.

157 **ELLIOTT, Gilbert, Her Builder.**
"The First battle of the Confederate Ram "Albemarle"." In: B & L, v.4, p. 625-627, pl, diagram, ports. Capt. A.F. Warley's "Note on the destruction of the "Albemarle"." p. 641-642.

158 **ELLIOTT, James Cantry**
"Lieutenant General Richard Heron Anderson: Lee's noble soldier." Dayton, Oh., Morningside House, 1985. 8vo, cl, 172pp.,

illus., bibliog., index, maps. $20. See: C. Irvine Walker.

159 **ELLIOTT, James Carson**
"The Southern Soldier Boy; a thousand shots for the Confederacy, by James Carson Elliott, Company F, 56 Regiment, N.C.T., CSA, 1861-1865...Historical incidents, reminiscences and personal experiences, covering the nine months siege of Petersburg and both prison pens, etc. Plain facts more interesting than fiction, all from the standpoint of a private soldier." Raleigh, N.C., Edwards & Broughton Pr. (1907) 8vo, front(port) 77, (1)pp. $125-r, $75-b.
...Wendell, N.C., Broadfoot's Bookmark, 1979, Lim. Edt., 500 copies, wraps, $5, $10.

160 **ELLIOTT, James Habersham**
"The Bloodless Victory. A sermon preached in St. Michael's Church, Charleston, S.C., on the occasion of the taking of Fort Sumter." Charleston, A.E. Miller, 1861. 12mo, wraps, 11pp. (McKissick-739)

161 **ELLIOTT, John, Lt.**
"Civil War Letters of Lieutenant John Elliott. Edited by John Barnwell." In: GaHQ, Fall, 1981, v.LXV, No.3, p. 203-239.

162 **ELLIOTT, M.A., Mrs.**
"The Garden of Memory; Stories of the Civil War as told by Veterans and Daughters of the Confederacy." Camden, Ark., Brown Printing Co., 1911, H.L. Grinstead Chap. U.D.C. sm.4to, cl, (1), (5), 98pp. ports, illus. cover, crossed CS flags- "1861-1865 They Bore the Flags of a Nations Trust." $15, $65.
...Camden, Ark., Hurley Co., 1976, p. 96, illus.

163 **ELLIOTT, Stephen, Bishop of Georgia**
"The Farewell Message and Obituary Notices of Bishop N.H. Cobbs." Montgomery, 1861. 8vo, sewn, 40pp. $10.

164 ..."Funeral services at the burial of the Right Rev. Leonidas Polk. Together with the sermon delivered in St. Paul's Church, Augusta, Ga., on June 19, 1864; being the feast of St. Peter the Apostle." Columbia: Evans & Cogswell, 1864. 8vo, wraps, 28pp.

165 ..."God's Presence with our army at Manassas: a sermon preached in Christ Church, Savannah, on Sunday, July 28th." Savannah, Ga., W. Thorne Williams, 1861, 8vo, wraps, 22pp.

166 ..."In Memoriam. Gen. Stephen Elliott." (Columbia, S.C., Julian A. Selby, 1866) Large 8vo, wraps, 29pp. South Carolina House of Representatives. Text in mourning borders. Also in: Southern Mag., 1870, v.6, p. 211-221.

167 ..."Sketch of Brigadier Gen. Stephen Elliott, CSA." In: LWL, April 1868, v.IV, No.6, p. 453-458. See: Wm. Henry Trescot, Maj. John A. Hamilton.

168 **ELLIS, A.T.**
"Returned Arkansas Confederate Flags." In: Ark.HAP, I, 1906, p. 187-190.

169 **ELLIS, Edward Sylvester**
"The Camp-fires of General Lee, from the Peninsula to Appomatox Court House, with reminiscences of the march, the camp, the bivouac and of personal adventure." Phila: Henry Harrison Co., (Feb. 1886) 12mo, cl, front, illus., 414, (2)pp. ads $10, $50-bmk, $40-bmk, $30-jk, $20, $16-bmk.

170 **ELLIS, Emily Caroline Searson**
"The flight of the clan: a diary of 1865, being an account of how the Ellis family of South Carolina, together with their kinsmen, the DeLoches, Hays and Framptons fled before Sherman's raiders...together with an introduction and historical notes by Frampton Erroll Ellis." Atlanta, 1954, 8vo, wraps, 14pp. $10-nc, $4.

171 **ELLIS, Henry G.**
"The influence of industrial and educational leaders on the secession of Vir-

ginia." In: So. Atl. Qrt., Oct. 1910, v.IX, p. 372-376.

172 **ELLIS, John H.**
"Henry Morton Woodson, Confederate Veteran, Historian, Memphian." In: W. Tenn. Hist. Soc. Papr., 1960, v.14, p. 74-90.

173 **ELLIS, John W., Gov. of N.C.**
"Governor's Message to the General Assembly, Nov. 20, 1860." (Raleigh: Spelman Print, 1860) 8vo, sewn, 32pp. $45. Recommends raising militia 110,000 men and 10,000 regulars. Likens Lincoln to George III.

174 ..."The North Carolina Forts." (Raleigh: Spelman, 17 Jan., 1860) 8vo, folded, 8pp. $45. Relative to premature seizure N.C. militia and citizenry Ft. Caswell-Johnston.

175 ..."Governor's Message to the General Assembly of North Carolina, May 1, 1861." (Raleigh, 1861) 8vo, sewn. $20. Use of military force to coerce a state to remain in union against Constitution, still less in principals on which our republic is based.

176 ..."Speech delivered before the Democratic State Convention in Raleigh, Mar. 9, 1860." Raleigh: Standard Office, 1860. 8vo, sewn, 15pp.

177 ..."The Papers of John Willis Ellis, Edt: Noble J. Tolbert." Raleigh, N.C., State Department of Archives and History, 1964. Tk.8vo, cl, dj, ports, illus., facsms., 2 vols., 340, (341)-918pp. $10, 2 vol. $20-bmk-84.

178 **ELLIS, Lewis E.**
"Reminiscences of the New Orleans, Jackson and Vicksburg, by a Louisiana Artilleryman." In: Confederate Annals, Aug. 1883, v.1, No.1, p. 47-55.

179 **ELLIS, Louis Tuffly**
"Maritime commerce on the far western Gulf, 1861-1865." (S.1: S N 1974?) offprint. 8vo, wraps, caption title, (169)-226pp. illus., map. Cover: SoWest Hist. Quart.

180 **ELLIS, Robert R.**
"The Confederate Corps of Engineers, 1861-1865." In: Mil. Engineer, Jan.-June, 1951, v.43: p. 36-40; 121-123; 187-191. ports, views, Nov.-Dec. 1950, v.42, p. 444-447.

181 ..."The Confederate Infantryman Officer 1861-1865." In: Inf. Jour., Nov. 1949, v.65, No.5, p. 16-19.
..."The Confederate Infantryman." In: Inf. Jour., Aug. 1949, v.65, #2, p. 25-28, view. On its org., discipline and achievements, CSA.

182 **ELLIS, Thomas Harding**
"The Richmond "Home Guard" of 1861." In: SHSP, 1891, v.XIX, p. 57-60.

183 **ELLIS, W.B.**
"Who lost Shiloh to the Confederacy?" In: CV, July 1914, v.XXII, p. 313-314.

183a **ELLISON, Burrell Marion & Benjamin Francis Emanuel**
"The Humane Hero of Fredericksburg, the Story of Richard Kirkland." Lancaster, S.C., The Carolina Museum, 1962. 4to, wraps, (3), (5)p. Roster, 2nd S.C. inf. See: Miss C. D. Kershaw's Rich. Kirkland & Joseph B. Kershaw's Rich. Kirkland.

184 **ELLISON, Joseph M.**
"Joseph M. Ellison: War Letters, 1862. Edt: Calvin J. Billman." In: Ga.H.Q., June 1964, v.XLVIII, No.2, p. 229-238.

185 **ELLISON, Mary**
"Support for Secession: Lanchashire and the American Civil War." Chicago, Univ. of Chicago Pr., 1972, 8vo, cl, dj, bibliog., ix, p. 259, maps. $10, $12-y.

186 **ELLISON, Rhoda Coleman**
"Huntingdon College, 1861-1865." In: AR, Jan. 1954, v.7, No.1, p. 3-21.
...Alabama: University of Alabama Press, 8vo, paper, xiii, 305pp. $4. 1954.

187 ELLSWORTH, Edward W.
"British Consuls in the Confederacy during 1862." In: Lincoln Herald, 1964, v.LXVI, p. 149-154.

188 ELLSWORTH, Eliot, Jr.
"West Point in the Confederacy." New York: G.A. Baker & Co., 1941, 8vo, cl, d/w, xxxii, 491pp. $6, $8.50, $10.

189 ELMIRA, N.Y., Prison
See: Marcus B. Toney, J.S. Hutchinson.

190 ELMORE, Albert Rhett
"Incidents of Service with the Charleston Light Dragoons." In: Confed. Vet., 1916, v.XXIV, p. 538-543.

191 ..."Testimony about burning of Columbia (S.C.)." In: CV, Mar. 1912, v.XX, p. 117-118.

192 ELMORE, Grace, Miss
"Diary of Miss. Grace Elmore, New York and Columbia, N.C., 1860-1870. Thomas Elmore (owner) Jacksonville, Florida." n.p., 1937. Copied by Historical Records Survey State Archives Survey, 1937." 4to, stiff boards, typed, (2), 26pp. $20.

193 ELSAS, Frederick J.
"The Journal of Henry L. Dye, Confederate Surgeon." In: Surgery, 1968, p. 352-362, v.LXIII.

194 ELSON, Henry W.
"The rise of Lee; Cedar Mountain-Pope's advance is checked." "The 2nd Battle of Bull Run." "Antietam-the invasion of the North." "Fredericksburg-disaster for a new Union leader." "Chancellorsville." In: Photo. Hist. CW, v.2, p. 13-128. Stephen D. Lee. "The first step in the war." In: B & L, v.1, p. 74-81, illus., ports.

195 ELTING, John R. and Michael J. McAfee, Edts.
"Long Endure: The Civil War Period, 1852-1867 Military Uniforms in America, Vol. III." Novato, Calif., Presidio Press, 1982. 8vo, cl, illus., index, 145pp. (color) $35. Third in a series, emphasis on Civil War. 64 colored illustrations, descriptive text, both Union and Confederate.

196 ELWELL, S.P.H.
"Recollections of war times. My Experiences in the West. By the Rev. S.P.H. Elwell, D.D., of the South Carolina Conference." Bamberg (S.C.) Herald Print, 1895. 12mo, wraps, illus., (4), 44pp. $37.50. Dornbusch: t.p., intro. on handpress, different paper than text.

197 ELZAS, Barnett Abraham
"Leaves from my Historical Scrap Book." (second series) Charleston, S.C., 1907. 8vo, (44)pp. Articles reprinted from Sunday News. Representative of Jewish community, its Rabbi.
...1908, second series, 12mo, wraps, (40)pp. as above.

198 ELZEY, Arnold, Maj.-Gen., of Maryland
Portrait: etched by Chas. B. Hall, folio. (New York: 1898). $5.

199 EMANUEL, Solomon
"An historical sketch of the Georgetown Rifle Guards and as Co.A of the Tenth Regiment, S.C. Volunteers, in the Army of the Confederate States, delivered at the dedication of the Company's armory, Georgetown, S.C., Nov. 17, 1909." n.p., n.d., 8vo, wraps, 32pp., cover title. $250-ob, $100-r.

200 EMERSON, Bettie Alder Calhoun, Mrs.
"Historic Southern Monuments; representative memorials of the heroic dead of the Southern Confederacy, compiled by..." N.Y., Wash., Neal Pub., 1911, 8vo, cl, illus., 466pp. $12.50, $25, $27.50, $85-ginz-34, $125-b, $100-bmk. See: Ralph W. Widener, Jr., "CSA Monuments."

201 EMERY, Russell Guy
"Robert E. Lee, 1807-1070." N.Y., Julian Messner, Inc., (1951). 8vo, cl, dj, port, (10), 176pp. $3.50.

202 EMMETT, Chris
"The general and the poet, Albert Sidney

Johnston and Sidney Lanier, a luminary follows a star." San Antonio, Texas, Naylor Co., 1937. 8vo, wraps, (8), 63pp. $40-atg., $150-m, $50-m, $50-jk. Shows the striking parallel of the two.

203 **EMMETT, Daniel Decatur**
"Dixie Land", Original score reprint, with Emmett's port on front cover and a facsm. letter, on back, from Emmett to Confederate Veteran Edt: S.A. Cunningham, n.p., n.d., 4to, 4pp., said to have been composed in 1859 (see Dichter, 105) $2.50.

204 ..."I Wish I Was in Dixie's Land." Written and composed expressly for Bryant's Minstrels. Arranged for the pianoforte: W.L. Hobbs. N.Y., Firth, Pond & Co., 1860. Folio, 6pp. $35, $7.50, $85-jk, $110-jk. 1st issue, printed from type. Adv. of music.

205 ..."How "Dixie" came to be written." In: SHSP, 1908, v.XXXVI, p. 369-370. See: John S. Mayfield, C.B. Galbreath.

206 ..."Helping Uncle Dan Emmett." In: CV, v.6, #2, p. 83, 6-illus., dbl. pg. spread, orig. score. Also: v.13, #3, port on cover. "Daniel Emmett and "Dixie's Land"." 1p.

207 ...Port and facsimilies of the original score of "Dixie", with a facsm. letter from Emmett to S.A. Cunningham, Edt. of CV, 1904, v.12, p. 432-435.

208 **"ENCOUNTER at Hanover:**
prelude to Gettysburg." Shippensburg, Pa., Beidel Print (1985). Historical Publication Commission at Hanover Chamber of Commerce. 8vo, cl, dj, xi, 274pp., illus., ports.

209 **ENDICOTT, William C.**
"Confederate Flags. Letter from the Secretary of War...calling for information relative to captured standards, flags and colors." Wash., Gov. Print. Off., 1888. 8vo, 20pp. Ex. Doc. 163. $17.50-y.

210 **ENGELSMAN, John Cornelius**
"The Freedmen's Bureau in Louisiana." New Orleans: LHQ, Jan. 1949, v.32, #1, p. 145-224.

211 **ENGINEERS: ,**
Getulius Kellersberger; James Lynn Nichols.

212 **ENGLEHARD, Joseph Adolphus, Major**
"Gettysburg. Report of Pender's Division." In: SHSP, 1880, v.VIII, p. 515-521.

213 **ENGLEHARDT, H.T.**
"A Note on the Death of John Bell Hood." In: SWHQ, July 1953, v.57, p. 91-93. Uncertain cause, probably yellow fever. Also offprint, wraps, 3pp. $3.

214 **ENGLERT, Kenneth E.**
"Raids by Reynolds." In: Westerners Brand Book (Denver), 1957, v.12, p. 149-173, views. Bibliog. On Jim Reynolds, with 8 accomplices, CSA raiders in Park and Jefferson counties, Colo., 1864. Six killed, others disappeared.

215 **ENGLISH OFFICER in CSArmy**
"The Battle of Gettysburg and the Campaign in Pennsylvania Diary of an English Officer in the Confederate Army." In: Edward A. Pollard's-"Second Year of the War." The Appendix, p. (326)-374. See: "A Month's Visit to the Confed. HDQ"

216 **ENN, C.C. (pseud.)**
"The Bloody First; or, Twelve Days with the 1st Pickaway throwing "Paw Paws" at John Morgan." (Circleville, Ohio: Circleville Democrat 1863) 12mo, wraps, 16pp. Author was C.C. Neibling, Co. E., 1st Pickaway Regiment.

217 **ENO, Clara B.**
"Activities of the Women of Arkansas during the War Between the States." In: AHQ, 1944, v.III, p. 5-27. port.

218 **"EPITAPH ,**
Here lie the mutilated and disjointed remains of the noblest form of government ever contrived by the wisdom of man..." (Charleston, S.C.) Harper & Calvo, 1860) Broadside: folio, black border. Crandall-

2738, Sabin-87821. $25.

..."Epitaph on the United States of America. Here lie the mutilated and disjointed remains of the noblest form of government ever contrived (At head of sheet) "printed for distribution amongst their friends by Evans and Cogswell, Charleston, S.C. (1860) Folio broadside, black border. Sabin-87822 notes: 50 copies edt., without heading, printed by I.D. Seabrook, according to a letter to Mass. His. Soc., Jan. 25, 1904. Original was printed on the day of secession.

219 **EPPES, Susan Bradford**
"Through Some Eventful Years." Author of the "Negro of the Old South", Tallahassee, Fla. Macon, Ga., Press of J.W. Burke Co., 1926. 8vo, cl, vi, 2, 11-378pp. color ports, 2-colored coat of arms (incl. front) On cover: A companion piece to Negro of the Old South. $40, $65, $75. War, Reconstruction and social life in N.C., Ga., and Fla., with excerpts from author's diary.
...Gainesville, Florida: University of Florida Press, 1968. A facsm. of 1926 edt., with introduction, index by Joseph D. Cushman, Jr. 8vo, decr. fabricoid, xxviii, (10), vi, (4)-378pp. 5pp.-index. Ports, crest, genealogical chart.

220 **EPPLE, Jess C.**
"Battle of Cabin Creek, Sept. 18, 19, 1864. Called 2nd Battle of Cabin Creek, Cherokee Nation, Indian Territory." 1000 copies. (Muskogee, Okla., Hoffman Print.) 1964. $25-jk-129, $3, $15, $7.50-borderland.

221 ..."Honey Springs Depot. Elm Creek, Creek Nation, Indian Territory." 1000 copies. (Muskogee, Okla., Hoffman Print) 1964. 8vo, wraps, 76pp., maps, ports, illus. $2. See: Chs. R. Freeman, $7.50 borderland.

221a **ERICSON, Carolyn Reeves & Terry Ingmire**
"Confederate Soldiers Buried at Vicksburg, Feb. 15, 1862-July 4, 1863." Vicksburg, Miss., Erickson Pub., 1981. 4to, wraps, 71p. $11.

222 **ERICKSON, Mary Wilson and Viola Parish Shackelford**
"The Yankees are Coming!!! An Historical three act play by... Arthur Manigault Chapter #63, United Daughters of the Confederacy." Georgetown, S.C., (June 6, 1966). 4to, wraps (cover title) memogr. one side (25)pp., variously paged. See: "For Love of a Rebel."

223 **ERNEST, Douglas J.**
"A "Needless Effusion of Blood": The Confederate Missouri Brigade and Hood's Invasion of Tennessee in 1864." In: MHR, Oct. 1983, v.LXXVIII, #1, p. 51-77, illus., map, ports.

224 **ERNUL, J.B.**
"Life of a Confederate Soldier in a Federal Prison." Vanceboro, N.C., n.d. $4. 16mo, wraps, cover title, 15pp.

225 **ERRICKSON, C. Stoctly**
"Life of General Robert Edward Lee, together with numerous anecdotes incidental to his career as a citizen and soldier. Edt: C. Stoctly Errickson." Phila: Barclay & Co. (c.1870) 8vo, wraps, port on cover, illus., 44pp.

226 **ERRICKSON, C. Stoctly, Edt.**
"Life of Gen. Robert Edmund Lee, together with numerous anecdotes incidental to his career as a citizen and soldier." Phila: Barclay & Co., (1870). $10. 8vo, decr. wraps, illus., port. on cover, 44pp. Dornb-I: 2927, cites variant with omission of paragraph following "closing years", pg. 37, which was an extract from McCabe's Life of Lee.

227 **ERSKINE, John, Judge**
"The Decision of Judge John Erskine. In

the Case Ex Parte William Law, under the "Attorney's Test Oath Act"." In: Ga.H.Q., Sept. 1919, v.III, #3, p. 101-130.

228 **ERWIN, Margaret Johnson**
"Like Some Green Laurel, Letters of ..., 1821-1863. Edt: John Seymour Erwin." Baton Rouge, 1981, LSU Press. $13, $10-bmk. 8vo, cl, dj, 154pp., illus., xxiip. Civil War letters from Mississippi.

229 **"ESCAPE from Johnson's Island, An"**
In: So.Mag., 1872, v.XI, p. 535-544. Dorn-II, 689.

230 **"ESCAPE of a Confederate Officer from Prison, An**
What he saw at Andersonville, etc." See: Samuel Boyer Davis.

231 **ESCHELMAN, B.F., Colonel**
"The Washington Artillery. Address of Colonel B.F. Eschelman at their Reunion." In: SHSP, 1883, v.XI, p. 247-248.

232 **ESCOTT, Paul D.**
"After Secession: Jefferson Davis and the Failure of Confederate Nationalism." Baton Rouge: Louisiana State University Press, 1978. 8vo, cl, dj, xiv, 295pp., bibliog. $17.50.

233 ..."The Context of Freedom: Georgia's Slaves during the Civil War." In: Ga. H.Q., Spring 1974, v.LVIII, #1, p. 79-104.

234 ..."The Cry of the Sufferers": The Problem of Welfare in the Confederacy." In: CWH, Sept., 1977, v.23, #3, p. 228-240. Also: Bell Wiley's "Plain People", Ramsdell's "Behind the Lines"; Emory Thomas' "CSA as Revolutionary Exp."; Mary E. Massey's "Ersatz in CSA".

235 ..."Jefferson Davis and Slavery in the Territories." In: JMH, May 1977, v.XXXIX, #2, p. 97-116.

236 ..."Joseph E. Brown, Jefferson Davis, and the Problem of Poverty in the Confederacy." In: Ga.H.Q., Spring, 1977, v.LXI, #1, p. 59-71. $8.

237 ..."Southern Yeomen and the Confederacy in 1861." In: La.Hist., Spring, 1978, v.19, p. 146-158.

238 "Poverty and government aid for the poor in Confederate North Carolina." In: NCHR, Oct. 1984, p. 462-480.

239 **ESKEW, Garnett Laidlaw**
"They Called Him "Town Burner": the story of the Confederate Gen. McCausland." In: W.Va.Rev., Nov., 1938, v.16, p. 40-43, 61-63.

240 **ESPOSITO, Vincent Joseph**
"The West Point Atlas of the Civil War, adapted from the West Point Atlas of American Wars, v.1. Compiled by the Dept. of Military Art and Engineering, the U.S. Military Academy. Chief Edt: Col. Vincent J. Esposito." N.Y., Frederick A. Praeger (1962). 4to, cl, maps (154) text facing. $30, $45-y, $100-bmk.

241 **"ESSAYS on the American Civil War."**
"Edts: William F. Holmes and Harold M. Hollingsworth. "Part of the Walter P. Webb Memorial Lectures." Austin, 1968, 8vo, cl, dj, 107pp. $10. Homer L. Kerr's "Battle of Elkhorn"; Martin H. Hall's "CSA Indian Policy"; Frank Vandiver's "Institutionalization force in CW, etc.".

242 **ESTAVILLE, Lawrence E., Jr.**
"A Small Contribution: Louisana's Short Rural Railroads in the Civil War." In: La. Hist. Winter, 1978, v.19, p. 87-103.

243 ..."A strategic railroad: the New Orleans, Jackson and Great Northern in the Civil War." In: LaH, 1973, v.14, p. 117-136.

244 **ESTES, Claud**
"List of field officers, regiments and battalions in the Confederate States Army, 1861-1865." Macon, Ga., J.W. Burke Co., 1912, 8vo, wraps, 137, 76pp. $12.50, $35-jk-122, $15, $150-bmk-105. See: Marcus J. Wright and Robt. K. Krick. Estes' reprint but Krick's annotated.

..."List of field officers, regiments and battalions in CSA..." Mattituck, N.Y., J.M. Carroll & Co., 1983. 8vo, xxii, 131, 1-91pp. wraps-#13; cl, $23. Intro: J.M. Carroll.

245 **ESTES, Thomas Jerome**
"Early Days and War Times in Northern Arkansas." Lubbock, Texas: Dow Print Co., 1928. 8vo, wraps, iii, 24pp. (Ark. Hist. Comm.)

246 **ESTVAN, Bela**
"War Pictures from the South. B. B. Estvan, Colonel of Cavalry in the Confederate Army. With illustrations." London: Routledge, Warne, Routledge, 1863, 12mo, cl, map, 10-pls., xiii, 310, x, 320pp. front(Davis), II-front (Jackson) $75, $175.
...N.Y., D. Appleton & Co., 1863, 12mo, cl, viii, 352pp. $50, $60. Same above, 1864. $10.
...Leipzig: F.A. Brockhaus, 1864. 12mo, cl, 2 vols., xxviii, 435pp. $12.50.
...Freeport, N.Y. "Books for libraries (1971) $21. Coulter-154, "some reason to believe Estvan was a fraud, since most of work a history and little personal experience; Howes-E203 flatly states-"This Hungarian impostor claims being a Confed. Cavalry Colonel, was a non-combatant hospital orderly."

247 **ETHEREDGE, William H.**
"Alexander Moseley Political editor extraordinaire." (Richmond) Va. Cavl., Winter 1969, v.XVIII, #3, p. 41-47.
..."Another Story of the Crater Battle." In: SHSP, 1909, v.XXXVII, p.203-7.

248 **"EVACUATION Night in Richmond."**
In: The Old Guard, April, 1867, v.V, #4, p. 267-272.

249 **EVANS, Augusta Jane**
See: Augusta Jane Wilson.

250 **EVANS, Clarence**
"Memoirs, Letters, and Dairy Entries of German Settlers in Northwest Arkansas, 1853-1863. Selected and translated by..." In: AHQ, 1947, v.VI, p. 225-249.

251 **EVANS, Clement Anselm**
Re: "Extended Editions." Dornbusch-#1384, points out that Dr. Freeman noticed these expanded biographical volumes in addition to the standard set, in his "South to Posterity", 1939, p. 186-187.
...Biographies of Confederate Soldiers, residing in the North." Vol. XIII, 8vo, cl, 297pp. (not an extended vol.) Wilmington, N.C., Broadfoot, 1987.
..."The Civil History of the Confederate States." Wilmington, N.C., Broadfoot, 1987, 8vo, cl, 737pp. (not an extended volume)
..."Confederate Military History..." Wilmington, N.C., Broadfoot's Bookmart, 1987. $450. The reprint of the "Extended Edition", 17 vols + 2 vol. index. 1200pp.

252 **EVANS, Clement Anselm, Edt.**
"Confederate Military History; a Library of Confederate States History, written by distinguished men of the South, Edt. by..." Atlanta, Ga., Confederate Pub. Co., 1899. 8vo, red.buck, 3/4 Red. calf., or black Mor., published in 13 Vols. (v.13 Biog. suppl.) Listed separately by state and the author, i.e., as follows:
..."The Civil History of the Confederate States." $10, $15. Vol. I, C.A. Evans' Confed. Mil. Hist., Atlanta, Ga., 1899, p. 247-570, port.
..."Biographies of Confederate Soldiers residing in the North." v.XIII of his Confederate Military History. Atlanta, Ga., Confederate Pub. Co., 1899, 8vo, 297pp. $150.
..."Biographical, officers of civil and military organizations." In: v.1, above. p. 571-737, ports. Sets in red cloth $50, $75-$100, $110, $125, $150, rebound-$500-bmk-95, orig. bnd.-$350.-bmk. Orig. 3/4 calf(red), or e/4 Levant in either red or black, $200, $275. 12 vols set, a rare set with 13 vols., "Biographical Supplement, Confederate soldiers residing in the North", p. 297.

Volumes are listed under author and state.

...N.Y., Yoseloff, 1962, reprint, 12 vols. with 4to, stiff wrap, atlas, (48)pp. $50, $125-nc.

..."Contributions of the South to the greatness of the American Union." An address by Gen. Clement A. Evans, of Atlanta, Georgia, delivered before the Association of Army of Northern Virginia, Oct. 10, 1895, Richmond, Virginia, with the proceedings of the Association on the occasion." In: SHSP, 1895, v.XXIII, p. 1-24. Also: in wraps, 24pp., Richmond, Va., Wm. Ellis Jones Print. $35-jk-122, $6.50.

..."An outline of Confederate Military History." v.XII, p. 195-265.

..."Confederate Military History; a Library of Confederate State Histories, written by distinguished men of the South and edited by Clement A. Evans." Blue & Gray Press, n.d. (c.1976) (Division of Book Sales, Secaucus, N.J.) 8vo, cl, 13-vols. (cheap paper edt.) $5.98 ea. $125-b, $75-set.

253 ..."Our Confederate Memorial Day." In: CV, July, 1896, v.IV, #7, p. 222-228, ports.

254 ..."Atlas to accompany Confederate Military History"-cover title. N.Y., Thos. Yoseloff (1962) 4to, decr. stiff wraps, (50)pp. color flags on back cover, 67 maps. Published for more easily reference than to the volumes individually.

..."Atlas to accompany The Campaigns of the Civil War." -cover title. N.Y., Thos. Yoseloff (A.S. Barnes Co., 1963) 4to, stiff wraps, (26)pp., 32 maps.

"Confederate Military History, Extended Edt., in 17 vols. Cumulative Index, Edt. Robert S. Bridgers. Vol. 1, A-H, Vol. 2, I-Z." Tk.8vo, cl, CLXII, 500p.-1159pp. Index set in double columns. Wilmington, N.C., Broadfoot Pub. Co., 1987.

...See following authors for contents of each volume: "Confederate Military Hist."

1.) J.L.M. Curry's "Legal Justification for Secession"; Wm. R. Garrett's "South as factor in Terr. Expansion"; Clement A. Evans' "Civil Hist. of Confederacy."; "Biographical officers of Civil and Military Organizations." 2.) Brig.-Gen. Bradley T. Johnson's "Maryland."; Col. Robert White's "West Virginia." 3.) Maj. Jed Hotchkiss' "Virginia." 4.) D.H. Hill-"North Carolina."; 5.) Brig.-Gen. Ellison Capers' "South Carolina." 6.)Joseph T. Derry's "Georgia." 7.) Lt. Gen. Joseph Wheeler's "Alabama."; Col. Charles E. Hooker's "Mississippi." 8.) James D. Porter's "Tennessee." 9.) Col. J. Stoddard Johnston's "Kentucky."; Col. John C. Moore's "Missouri." 10.) John Dimitry-"Louisiana."; Col. John M. Harrell's "Arkansas." 11.) Col. O.M. Roberts' "Texas."; Col. J.J. Dickison's "Military History of Florida." 12.) Capt. Wm. H. Parker's "Confederate States Navy."; J.Wm. Jones' "Morale of the Confed. Army"; Clement A. Evans' "Outline of CSA History."; Stephen D. Lee's "South Since the War."; "Documental and Statistical Append."

254a **EVANS, David**
"Wool, Women & War, Working Women Taken North." In: CWHI, Sept. 1987, v. 26, #5, p.38-42, ills. Woolen mill at Roswell, Ga., taken over by Sherman & workers sent to Nashville.

255 **EVANS, Edna H.**
"Sunstar and Pepper: scouting with Jeb Stuart." Chapel Hill: N.C. Press, 1947, 8vo, cl, juvenile $3.50.

256 **EVANS, Edward Steptoe**
"The Official Encyclopedic Guide to Richmond and vicinity, including battlefields." Richmond, Va., For the Official Guide Co., by the Richmond Press, 1906. 16mo, wraps, front, illus., fldg. map, 160pp. $30-bmk.

257 **EVANS, George Bird**
"Original copy of "Dixie" identified." In: CWT, Nov. 1961, v.III, #7, (OS), p. 12-15, facsms, illus., ports. See also Conf. Vet., Sept., 1895.

258 **EVANS, James W. and A. Wendell Keith, MD**
"Sam Hildebrand der Dick Turpin von Missouri. Von einem seiner Speissgellen." (St. Louis) 1870.
..."Autobiography of Samuel S. Hildebrand, the renowned Missouri "Bushwhacker" and unconquerable Rob Roy of America; being his complete confession recently made to the writers and carefully compiled by... of St. Francois County, Mo.; together with all the facts connected with his early history." Jefferson City, Mo., State Times, 1870, 12mo, cl, front and illus., 312pp. $85-jenk, $200-ob, $75-younger, $100-bmk, $50.

259 **EVANS, Marvin Davis**
"The Richmond Press on the Eve of the Civil War." In: Hist. Papers Randolph-Macon College, Jan. 1951. 8vo, wraps, 54pp. $12.

260 **EVANS, Moses F.T.**
"Dr. Evans and the War (1861-1865)." In: TQHGM, Jan. 1922, v.III, p. 157-163. Two letters by Dr. Evans, of 14th Va. Reg., Apr. 30/June 14, 1865.

261 **EVANS, Thomas R.**
"Tell Story of the Flying Machine of the Confederacy. Designated by Richmond Inventor, scheme to drop explosives from air on Washington." In: SHSP, 1909, v.XXXVII, p. 302-303.

262 **EVANS, W.A.**
"Jefferson Davis, His Diseases and his Doctors, and a biographical sketch of Dr. Ewing Fox Howard." Reprint: from The Mississippi Doctor, June 1942, 4to, wraps, 13pp.

263 ..."Jefferson Davis Shrine-Beauvoir House." (Jackson, Miss., Journ. of Miss. Hist. Oct., 1940, v.II, #4, p. 206-211.

264 **EVE, F. Edgeworth, Capt.**
"Address of... Confederate Survivors' Association, 17th Annual Meeting. Historian's Report by Charles E. Jones, with Gen. M.C. Butler's Narrative." Augusta, Ga., Chronicle Print, 1895, 8vo, wraps, 33, (1)pp. $22.50, $15. See also under "Confed. Surv. Ass'n.
...Augusta, Ga., 1896, wraps, 37pp. $7., $20-bmk-109.

265 ..."The Beau Sabreur of Georgia. A fitting tribute to the Gallant P.M.B. Young, CSA." Address to Confed. Survivors Ass'n. In: SHSP, 1897, v.XXV, p. 146-151.

266 **EVERETT, Edward George**
"Contraband and rebel sympathizers in Pennsylvania in 1861." In: W. Pa. Hist. Mag., Spring, 1958, v.41, p. 29-40, notes.

267 **EVERETT, Frank Edgar**
"Brierfield, Plantation Home of Jefferson Davis." Hattiesburg: Univ. and College Press of Mississippi, 1871. 8vo, cl, dj, xi, 153pp., illus., ends. $6. Reprint, 1979, $8.95.

268 ..."Delayed report of an important eyewitness to Gettysburg-Benjamin G. Hunphreys." In: JMH, Nov. 1984, v.XLVI, #4, 305-321. Humphrys' marginal notes on a copy of Col. Walter H. Taylor's "Four years with Gen. Lee." Defending Longstreet's action at Gettysburg.

269 **EVERETT, Lloyd Tilghman**
"The Case of Jefferson Davis: Why No Trial?" In: Tyler's Quart. Hist. and Geneal. Mag., Oct., 1947, v.XXIX, p. 94-116.

270 ..."Davis, Lincoln and the Kaiser. Some Comparisons Compared (National and International Ethics, 1861 and 1914) Ballston, Va., Yexid Pub., 1917, 12mo, wraps, 12pp. $10. South compelled to fight

for rights as laid down in Constitution and Decl. Indp.

..."Davis, Lincoln and the Kaiser, some comparisons compared." In: CV, Sept. 1917, v.25, #9, p. 405-408.

271 ..."Dixie's story in 5 books...a study of the rise and varying progress of the land we love; by a Southron; for Southrons and for all who love constitutional and living Confederate principals in sincerity and truth." In: TylerQHGM, July/Oct. 1950, v .32, p. 13-28, 111-120. notes. "Davis and democracy; constitutional rights and Southern independence, 1848-1865." Jan/Oct. 1951, v.32, p. 181-196, 275-281; v.33, p. 28-43, 107-113.

272 ..."Federal Initiative and Referendum." South Atl. Quart., Oct. 1912, p. 350-362. Rights of minorities in Nullification and Civil War periods.

273 ..."For Maryland's Honor; a Story of the War for Southern Independence." Bost: Christopher Pub. Hse., (1922) Fiction. 12mo, cl, color front, 229pp. $5.

274 ..."Living Confederate Principals a heritage for all time. An address delivered by... of Washington Camp #305, S.C.V. at the reception by the camp to the Confederate Veterans of Washington, D.C. and vicinity, Feb. 10, 1914; as revised and published in #40, Southern Historical Society Papers." Ballston, Va., Yexid Pub. Co., 1921. 8vo, wraps, cover title, 44pp. $7.50.
...Ballston, Va., Yexid Pub. Co., 1921. 8vo, wraps, 44pp. $5.

275 ..."Patrick R. Cleburne, Prophet." In: Tyler QHGMag. Jan. 1946, v.XXVIII, p. 15, $10.
...DeLand, Fla., Yexid Pub. Co., 1946, $10. 8vo, wraps, 15pp. reprint of Tyler's Quarterly.

276 ..."Was it Anti-slavery? Causes that led to the War Between the States." Ballston, Va., Yexid Pub., 1916, 8vo, wraps, 8pp. $4.

277 **EVERETT, Peter M., Capt.**
"Muster roll of Capt. P.M. Everett's Company (B) 1st Battalion Kentucky Mounted Rifles, Army of Confederate States of America, 1863." In: KyHSR, Jan. 1906, v.IV, p. 20.

278 **EVERHART, William C.**
"Vicksburg National Military Park, Mississippi, by William C. Everhart." Wash: Nat'l. Park Ser. Hist. Handbook Ser., #21, 1954, (reprint 1961). 8vo, pict. color stiff wraps, illus., maps, 1-dbl. pg., ports, (4), 60pp.

279 **EVIDENCE taken before the Committee**
of the House of Representatives appointed to inquire into the treatment of prisoners at Castle Thunder." Richmond, 1863, 8vo, sewn, 58pp. $125. See Harwell-138, a 6pp. doc. relating to same subject.

280 **"EVIDENCE that Abraham Lincoln**
was not born in lawful wedlock, or the Sad Story of Nancy Hanks."(Dallas, Texas, n.d., 1899?) Wm. M.C(oleman) Price $.25. 8vo, cl, caption title, 18pp. Evidence based on Lincoln-Enloe tradition.

281 **EVITTS, William J.**
"A Matter of Allegiance: Maryland from 1850-1861." Baltimore: Johns Hopkins Press, 1974. Studies in Historical and Political Science, 92nd Ser., #1, notes, index. $11. Breckenridge election a local issue and elct. not a matter of slavery, as such. See also: Jean H. Baker. More Southern than Northern. Md. forced into Union by military action.

282 **EWBANK, Louis W.**
"Morgan's Raid in Indiana." Ft. Wayne (Ind.): Public Library. Reprint Indiana Hist. Society Pubs., Vol. 7, #2, 8vo, stiff wraps, 59pp., illus., map. 1955. $18.50-y, $2.50. IHSP-for 1917, p. 51. Above pamphlet has "Louis W." on both cover and t.p./Louis B.

283 **EWELL, Alice Maude**
"A Virginia Scene, or, Life in Old Prince William. Lynchburg, Va., J.P. Bell Pub. (1931) 1st. 12mo, cl, d/w, port. illus, ix, 228pp. $10, $7.50. Contains Eleanor M.B. Ewell's "War Time at Dunblane." (50pp.)

284 **EWELL, Benjamin Stoddert**
"Generals Jackson and Ewell." In: SHSP, 1892, v.XX, p. 26-33; 1876, v.2, p. 26-33.

285 ..."Papers of Convention between Sherman and Johnston." In: SHSP, April, 1914, XXXIX, p. 45-62. Letters also from Beauregard and Gov. Joseph E. Brown.

286 ..."The college in the years 1861-1865." In: Wm. and Mary Quart., 2nd ser. Oct. 1923, v.III, p. 221-230. Report July 1865 on general and financial condition of the college. By Pres. Ewell.

287 **EWELL, Richard Stoddert, Gen.**
"Evacuation of Richmond. Report of General R.S. Ewell." In: SHSP, Jan. 1885, v.XIII, p.247-252.
..."Evacuation of Richmond. Reports of Generals Ewell and Kershaw." In: SHSTrans. 1874, v.I, p. 101-106.

288 ...Richard Stoddert Ewell and Pierre Gustave Toutant Beauregard. "The First Manassas. Correspondence between..., to which is added extracts from a letter of Gen. Fitz Lee." Nashville, Tenn., 1885- Wheeler, Osborn & Duckworth. 8vo, wraps, illus., map, (3), 8pp. $20-bmk, $10. Reprint: Louisville, Ky. R.N. Wathen, Jr. 1970. 8vo, 8pp., 100-copies (70 for sale). $7.50, $15-bmk.

289 ..."From the Rapidan to Spotsylvania Courthouse/Report of General R.S. Ewell." In: SHSP, Jan. 1885, v.XIII, p. 229-236.
...Also in: So. Hist. Soc. Trans., 1874, v.I, p. 107-123.

290 ..."General Ewell's Report of the Pennsylvania Campaign." In: SHSP, July 1882, v.X, p. 289-307.

291 ..."General Ewell to the High Private in the Rear." Contro: T. Harry Williams. (Richmond) Va. Mag. Hist. Biog., April, 1946, v.54, p. 157-160.
...Rep, wraps, 3pp. (on secession), $2-r, $10-bmk-86.

292 ..."The Making of a Soldier; letters of Gen. R.S. Ewell; arranged and edited by Captain Percy Gatling Hamlin." Richmond, Va., Whittet & Shepperson, 1935. 12mo, cl, and bds., dj, 2-ports, incl. front, pl. 161pp. $8.50, $12, $35-atg., $25-bmk, $15-y.

293 ...Portrait, lithographed by Kurz & Allison, Chicago, Ill., n.d., 18x23". $25.

294 ...Lithographic portrait, by J.L. Giles., N.Y., Geo. E. Perine Pub. (c.1864) 24x19" $15. Half-length, uniform, bearded.
...Same, tall folio, full wide margin, N.Y., Perine Pub. (c.1865) $7.50.

295 ..."Stonewall Jackson at Prayer (From the Lousiville "Courier-Journal", Oct. 19, 1891)" In: SHSP, Jan. 1891, v.XIX, p. 111-113. See also: Campbell, Brown, Jubal Early, B.S. Ewell, G.F. Harrison.

296 ..."Record in U.S. Army and C.S. Army." "Letter of General R.S. Ewell to Gen. Grany, April 16, 1865." In: SHSP, April 1914, v.XXXIX, p. 4-5. See: Thomas H. Carter's letter on Ewell.

297 ..."A Short History of Gen. R.S. Ewell." Park Place, N.Y., Knapp & Co., 1888. 2 3/4x1 1/2", colored booklet, 16pp. facsm. signature. (packed in Duke's cigarettes.) See: "Heroes of the C.W." and W. Duke Co.

298 **EWING, D.B., Rev., of Va.**
"Sketch of Gov. H.W. Allen (of Louisiana)." In: LWL, May 1867, v.III, #1, p. 43-47. See: H.W. Allen.

299 **EWING, Elbert William Robinson**
"Northern Rebellion and Southern Secession." Richmond, Va., J.L. Hill Co., 1904. 8vo, cl, 385pp., port, 1904. $7.50, $12.50,

$50, $60, errata slip. North rebels against laws, notably in Kan.-Neb.

300 ..."The Secession of 1861. Founded upon legal right." In: "The Gray Book", pub. by Sons of Confed. Vets., (10)pp.

301 **EWING, Floyd F., Jr.**
"Origins of Unionist sentiment on the West Texas frontier (1861)." In: W. Tex. Hist. Assn. Yr. Bk. Oct. 1956, v.32, p. 21-29. tables, notes.

302 ..."Suggestions for the observance in West Texas of the Civil War Centennial." In: W. Tex. HAYbook, 1960, v.36, p. 33-40, notes. "brief summary of the effects of the war on West Texas and "Informality" of the role West Texas played."

303 **EWING, George D.**
"The Battle of Blue Springs, Tenn." In: CV, FEb. 1922, v.XXX, p. 46-48.

304 ..."The Battle of Rogersville, or Big Creek Tenn." In: CV, Oct., 1922, v.XXX, p. 386-287.

305 ..."General Bragg's Kentucky Campaign." In: CV, June, 1926, v.XXXIV, p. 214-215.

306 ..."Missouri's trials at the beginning of the war." In: CV, July 1924, v.XXXII, p. 266-268.

307 ..."Morgan's last raid into Kentucky." In: CV, July 1923, v.XXXI, p. 254-256.

308 **EWING, Laura**
"The retreat from Little Rock (Arkansas) in 1863." In: Indp. Co. Chr., Oct. 1963, v.5, p. 3-17; also in Pulaski Co. HR, Dec. '63, v.11, p. 53-57.

309 **EWING, Tempe Berry, Mrs., Edt.**
"History of the Albemarle Chapter, United Daughters of the Confederacy from 1906-1922." (Albemarle, N.C., Press Pr.) 1932. 8vo, wraps, (4), 18pp.

310 **EX-BOY, by an...**
See: Royal W. Figg. "Report of the proceedings of various ass'n. Ex-CSA's.

311 **EX-CONFEDERATE ,**
"The First Shots." In: SB, ns, v.II, p. 66-67 (1886/1887) e.g., Fort Morris/Moultrie in reply to Hayne's Defense of Ft. Wagner.

312 **"EX-CONFEDERATE Missourians in Texas 1881."**
Austin, Tx., Genealogical Society Quarterly, Sept., 1975, v.16, #3, p. 69-81. roster.

313 **"EXCERCISES et manoeuvres**
de l'Infanterie. Ecole du soldat. Ecole de peloton. Ecole des guides. Service des places. Service en campagne." Nouvelle-Orleans, L. Marchand, impr., 1861. 12mo, wraps, 348pp. See Harwell-946. Thompson (pg.32) lists it under Alphonse Canonge. Crandall-2483, title:

314 ..."Theorie de l'art militaire. Exercise et monoeuvre de l'infanterie; ecole du soldat de peleton." Nouvelle-Orleans. Impr. de R.P. Theard, 1861, p. 223. Title head- "Confederation du Sud."

315 **"EXECUTIVE and Congressional**
Directory of the Confederate States, 1861-1865. Compiled from official records. Record and Pension Office." (Heading: "U.S. Record and Office.") 1899. (Washington, DC, Gov. Print Office) 1899. 8vo, sewn, 12pp. $125-r, $16-bmk.
...Tallahassee, Fla., 1899 reprint, 16pp. T.J. Appleyard Print. sewed.
...(n.p., 1960?) 13 lfs., 4to, reproduced from typewritten copy, by Bell I. Wiley.
...of the Confederate States of America, 1861-1865." In: Gulf SHM., Jan. 1903, v.I, p. 253-261. From official records of Record and Pension Offices.

316 **"EXECUTIVE Officers**
of the Confederate States 1861-1865." Congress of the Confederate States, n.p., 186-. Sheet 25x42 1/2cm fold to 25x14 1/2cm.

317 **"EXODUS, The" (caption title)**
8vo, 4p. folded sheet. n.p., n.d. (1861) $150-goodspeed. unrecorded. Verse celebrating flight of Federals from First Manassas.

318   **"EXOTIC Leaves gathered by a wanderer."**
London: W. Freeman, 1865. 12mo, cl, 78pp. Signed: "S.R." (Mrs. S. Richards) Copies of letters written to friends in the Confederacy.

319   **"EXPERIENCE of a Confederate States prisoner..."**
See: Beckwith West.

320   **"EXPORT duty on raw cotton, An**
and free trade in cotton fabrics the true policy of the Southern Confederacy." Charleston, S.C., 1861. 8vo, wraps, 19pp. Sig: "Cent-a-pound." copy: Cty.

321   **"EXTRACTS from an old "Order Book"**
of First Company Richmond Howitzers." In: Richmond Howitzers Batt., v.#4. Richmond, Va., Carlton McCarthy, 1886, p. 33-64.

322   **"EXTRACTS from the editorial columns**
of the New Orleans Picayune" (wrap. title) N.Y., 1861, wraps, 8vo. $6. Begins: "The Northern papers come freighted with threatenings to bring back the seceding states into the Union by force."

323   **"EYEWITNESS account of, An**
the occupation of Mt. Pleasant." In: SCHM, 1965, v.66, #1, p. 8-14.

324   **EZELL, John**
"Jefferson Davis Seeks Political Vindication, 1851-1857." (Jackson, Miss.) Jour. Miss. Hist. Nov. 1964, v.XXVI, #4, p. 307-321.

325   **EZZELL, S.R.**
"Bombardment and Battles of Galveston." n.p., n.d., (1862-1864) 8vo broadside. Many of Francis D. Allan's "Lone Star Ballads" were published at the Houston, Tx. Printing House during this period and later published in book form, 1874. See: Francis D. Allan.

F

1. **"FACSIMILE of the Constitution** for the Provisional Government of the Confederate States of America. Photo-Lithography from the Original parchment in the possession of F.G. de Fontaine, Esq." $125-ginz-30, $100-b, $65-jk-122. N.Y., Joseph Laing, Engraver and Publisher, 1883. 36 1/2x47cm, (11)pp. Doc. printed one side sheet. (Also printed on a sheet 10'x18", size of original on a wooden roller.) Oblong, stiff covers, cl. $50. See: "Constitution of Prov. Gov."

2. **"FACTS about the Civil War."** Lexington, Va., The Stonewall Jackson Memorial, Inc., n.d. (c.1961). 8vo, stiff wraps, cover title, 2-illus., flags, (2), 16, (2)pp. $1.50.

3. **FAGAN, W.L., Compiler** "Southern War Songs, Campfire, Patriotic and Sentimental." New York: M.T. Richardson, 1890. 8vo, cl, vi, 389, illus. $7.50, $15, $12.50, $100-b, $25-bmk. (same type 4to, full Mor., wide margins, color flags front. $8.50. Same: 1892, $7.50.

4. **FAHRNER, Alvin A.** "William "Extra Billy" Smith, Governor of Virginia-1864-1865: a pillar of the Confederacy." In: VMHB, Jan. 1966, v.74, #1, p. 68-107, port.

5. **FAIN, John Tyree** "Hergesheimer's Use of Historical Sources." (Lexington, Ky.) JSH, Nov., 1952, v.XVIII, #4, p. 497-504.

6. **FAIR, Stephen T.** "Three Civil War Letters. Edited by Mrs. Kate Beasley (daughter)." In: AHQ, 1944, v.III, p. 182-187.

7. **FAIRFAX COUNTY, Virginia** "Fairfax Monument, dedication at Fairfax Courthouse, Va., erected to the dead heroes from that county who fell in the Confederate States Army." In: SHSP, 1890, v.XVIII, p. 120-132. See: Wm. Smith's "Reminiscences of War."

8. **FAIRFAX COUNTY, Virginia, and the War Between the States.** "Fairfax Civil War Centennial Commission, 1961." Vienna, Va., Stenger Typographical Ser., sm.4to, pict. stiff wraps, 70pp., illus., ports, maps. $20.
...Fairfax, 1987 (reprint of 1961 edt.). 10 x 7", wraps, ills, maps, ports, 73p.

9. **FAIRFAX, L.** "The Elopement: A Tale of the Confederate States of America." London: Freeman Print, 1863. 12mo, cl, 176pp. $5, $15. Fiction.

10. **FALERO, Frank, Jr.** "Naval Engagements in Tampa Bay, 1862." In: FHQ, October, 1967, v.XLVI, No.2, p. 134-140.

11. **FALK, Stanley L.** "Jefferson Davis and Josiah Gorgas, an Appointment of Necessity." (Houston, Tex.) JSH, Feb., 1962, v.XXVIII, No.1, p. 84-86.

12. **FALKNER, Jefferson Manly** "Address at unveiling of Confederate monument at Montgomery, Alabama." In: SHSP, 1898, v.XXVI, p. 219-228.

13. **"FALL of Fort Sumter, The** or, Love and War in 1860-1861. By the Private Secretary to..." New York: Frederic A. Brady, (1867). 8vo, cl, iv, (5), 6-167pp., illus., front. $27.50. Printed dble-column, at head of cover title, "A Humorous Story." Depicts Washington politics at end of Buchannan's term, Wright-885, Turnbull, pg. 428 (III).

14. **"FALL of Port Royal, S.C., The** in 1861, with a sketch of subsequent

events to the present time." In: SoMag., 1873, v.XIII, p. 553-562.

15 **"FALL of Richmond, Va., The**
on the Night of April 2." N.Y., Currier & Ives, 1865. Colored Litho: 20x26" $25. Short descp. of scene below title.

16 **FALL, Albert Boult**
"Civil War Letters of..., gunner for the Confederacy." In: Ky.State Hist. Soc. Reg., 1961, v.LIX, p. 150-168.

17 **FALLER, Harold**
"A West Virginian, one of the two surviving Confederate generals." In: W.Va.Rev., Apr., 1926, v.3, p. 221-222, 245-247. Illus. McCausland.

18 **FALLIGANT, Robert, Judge**
"An address on Memorial Day, April 26, 1894, Parade Grounds, to Confed. Vets. Assn., Savannah, Ga., Pres. Annual Report, p. 41-49."

19 **"FALLING FLAG, The**
Evacuation of Richmond, etc., by an officer of the rear guard." pseud: Edward M. Boykin.

20 **FALLING WATERS, Battle of**
See: Henry Heth.

21 **"FAMOUS ADVENTURES**
and Prison Escapes of the Civil War." N.Y., The Century Co., 1893. $100 -ob, $75-bmk, $10. 12mo, cl, illus., front, x, 338pp. Mosby's Partizans, Morgan's Roughriders, Escape of Gen. Breckenridge.
...1917 edt., $35 -b.

22 **"FAMOUS WAR PRISONS and Escapes."**
From: Richmond Times Dispatch. In: CV, Nov. 1923, v.XXXI, p. 411-414. See: "Prison life in the Confed. War."

23 **FANE, Julian Henry Charles and Edward Robert Bulwer Lytton, 1st Earl.**
"Tannhauser; or, the Battle of the Bards. A Poem. By Neville Temple (pseud.) and Edward Trevor (pseud)." Mobile, Ala., S.H. Goetzel & Co., 1863. 8vo, wall-paper covers, bnd. in 3/4 lt., 125pp. $35, $50, $175 -ginz.26, $100.

24 **FARBER, James**
"Texas, C.S.A., a spotlight on disaster." N.Y., Jackson Co. (1947) $7.50. 8vo, cl, dj, map endsheets, xii, 265pp. front. $22 -bmk-84, $25 -bmk-84, $12.50, $15. Edt: 1000 numbered copies.

25 ..."Fort Worth in the Civil War as published in the Fort-Worth Star Telegram." Belton, Texas: Peter Hansbrough Bell Pr., 1960. 8vo, ports, illus., 58, (1)pp. (or wrap) $2.50, $10 -jc-145. Author's Edition, 200 copies, $7.50.

26 **FARIES, T.A., Capt. Comd. Batt. Mouton's Brig.**
"Official report of actions with Federal Gunboats, Ironclads and Vessels of US Navy in war, by officers Field Artillery P.A.C.S." In: SHSP, 1884, v.12, p. 54-59.

27 **FARINHOLT, Benjamin L.**
"The Staunton River Fight. Col. Farinholt replies to Gen. Dabney Maury-certain alleged errors corrected-another account of that famous engagement-to whom the honor of the victory is partly due-interesting details." (from: Richmond "Times", Nov. 22, 1891) In: SHSP, 1891, v.XIX, p. 201-207.

28 ..."The Gallant defense of Staunton River Bridge." (from: Richmond, Va., "Times Dispatch", Aug. 1889). In: SHSP, 1909, v.XXXVII, p. 321-325.

29 **FARLEY, M. Foster**
"Josiah Tattnall-Gallant American." In: Ga. H.Q. Suppl. 1974, v.LVIII, p. 172-180. $10.

30 **FARMER, H.H., M.D.**
"Virginia before and during the war." Henderson, Ky., The author, 1892, 8vo, wraps, 102pp. $15, $30. Fiction, based on facts.

31 **FARMER, James Ocsar, Jr.**
"The metaphysical Confederacy: James Henley Thornwell and the synthesis of

Southern values." Macon, Ga., Mercer Univ. Press, 1986, 8vo, cl, vii, 295pp. $29.

32 **FARMER, Margaret Pace**
"Record of Confederate Soldiers, 1861-1865. Pike County, Alabama." Troy, Ala., Troy Printing Co., 1962. 8vo, stiff wraps, 81pp., port. Roster of Pike Co., soldiers, with Index. $6.50. Official Publication Pike Co. Civil War Cent. Con.

33 **FARMINGTON, Mississippi, Battle of**
See: Daniel Ruggles.

34 **FARNELL, Earl W.**
"The Civil War Comes to Savannah." In: Ga.H.Q., Sept., 1959, v.XLIII, #3, p. 248-260.

35 **FARRAR, C.C.S., of Bolivar Co., Miss.**
"The War, its causes and consequences." Blelock & Co., Ill., Memphis, Tenn. and Paducah, Ky., 1864. $50-b, $20-c.hill. 12mo, cl, 260pp. $10, $12.50, $17.50. Deprecates war, slavery in no danger in 1860! States rights, criticizes democracy and secession and the South. Religious tone.

36 **FARRAR, Ferdinando R.**
"Johnny Reb, the Confederate: a lecture by... Delivered Apr. 18, 1866, for the first time. Dedicated to the survivors of the Army of Northern Virginia." Richmond: W.A.R. Nye Print, 1869. 8vo, wraps, 32pp. (old -$2.25, $3.50, $5.25)

37 ..."Rip Van Winkle, or the Virginian that slept ten years: a lecture by...delivered more than sixty times." Richmond: W.A.R. Nye, 1869. 8vo, wraps, 18pp.

38 **FARROW, Marion Humphreys**
"Troublesome Times in Texas." San Antonio, Texas: Naylor Co. (1959). 8vo, cl, dj, illus., ports, bibliog., ix, 106pp. $6. Largely reconstruction some CSA.

39 ...(San Antonio, Texas: The Clegg Co. (1957). 8vo, stiff wraps, ports, pl, v, 78pp. $12.50.

40 **FARWELL, Byron**
"The man who presumed: a biography of Henry (Morton) Stanley (1841-1904). NY, Henry Holt (1957). 8vo, cl, ix, (9), 334pp., maps, ports, views, bibliog., p. 321-326. Life of John Rowlands, an illegitimate child, as an English emigrant to to New Orleans, his adoption by Henry Morton Stanley, his service in CSArmy. Later newspaper reporter and explorations in Africa. See: Henry Morton Stanley.

41 **"FATHER ABRAHAM,**
we are needing our pay. A Joke...Appeal!" By "Billy R.M." (New Orleans, La., 1864). Broadside: 8.5x12:, written by "Billy R.M." Consists of 27 4-line stanzas verse, print in 3 columns, small type. Humorous complaint by a Union soldier to the Army and Uncle Sam, particularly to Lincoln. Has to barter clothes for food, plus other types of life in the city. Asks Lincoln for a 60 day furlough or payment. $250 -jk-142.

42 **FATHER JEROME**
"The Vatican and Southern Confed." St. Leo, Fla., Abbey, 1962. 12mo, wraps, 39pp., illus. $1.

43 **FAULK, Odie B.**
"Confederate Hero at Val Verde." (Albuquerque: New Mex. Hist. Rev., Oct., 1963, v.XXXVII, #4, p. 300-311.

44 ..."General Tom Green Fightin' Texas, with intro: Rupert N. Richardson." Waco, Texas: Texian Press, 1963. 8vo, pict. cl., color, illus., ports, ix, 77pp. $6.
..."General Tom Green, "A Fighting Texas"." San Angelo, Texas: Standard-Times, Sunday, December 30, 1962. $5. Folio extra-edition, 24pp., ports, illus., ads.

45 **FAULKNER, Charles J.**
"To the Public; as some recent criticisms have attracted public attention to my connexion with the Army of the Confederate States..." (Martinsburg: 1866) Broadside 19x12 3/8" printed 4-cols. Dated, signed:

Apr. 13, 1866. Reply to charges against Faulkner in the Charles Town "Spirit of Jefferson", and his view of the Test-oath. Shetler-238z.

47 **FAULKNER, William**
"The unvanquished." N.Y., New American Library (1958) 12mo, cl, 160pp. (A Signet Book).
...With foreword by Carvel Collins. 1959,, (A Signet Classic) 12mo, cl, xii, (13)-192pp.
...London: Chatto & Windus, 1960, 12mo, cl, 3pp., 319pp.
...2nd edt. (1960) N.Y., New American Library. (Signet Classics) $20. 12mo, cl, 192pp.

48 **FAUNTLEROY, Cornelius H.**
"The Constitutional right of Secession." In: CV, Feb./Mar., 1918, v.XXVI, p. 56-60, 109-112.

49 **FAUNTLEROY, James Henry**
"James H. Fauntleroy's Diary for the year 1862. Edt: Homer L. Calkin." In: Civ. War His., 1956, v.II, p. 7-43, map. "Elk Horn to Vicksburg." 1st Mo. Cavalry Rec., CSA.

50 **"FAUQUIER COUNTY,**
Virginia Historical Notes." Warrenton, Va., 1914. 8vo, stiff wraps, 45pp. $25. Biog. Eppa Hunton and other CSA material.

51 **FAUST, Drew Gilpin**
"James Henry Hammond and the old South: a design for mastery." Baton Rouge: Louisiana State Univ., 1982, 8vo, cl, dj, xviii, 407pp. $27.50.
..."Christian soldiers: the memory of Revivalism in the Confederate Army." In: JSH, Feb. 1987, v.53, #1, p. 63-90, notes. An excellent bibliography!

51a **FAUST, Patricia L., Editor**
"Historical Times Illustrated Encyclopedia of the Civil War." N.Y., Harper & Row, 1986. Tk.8vo, cl, 850pp. $40. 2,000 entries, 1,000 ills, 67 maps.

52 **FAY, Edwin Hedge**
"This Infernal War", the Confederate letters of Sgt. Edwin H. Fay. Edited by Bell irvin Wiley, with assistance of Lucy E. Fay." Austin: University of Texas Press (1958). 8vo, cl, dj, map end-sheets, front(port), viii, 474pp. op-$20-atg., $6, $10, $30, $25-bmk-89, atg-$50.

53 **FAY, John B.**
"With McNeil in Virginia." In: Confed. Vet., Sept., 1907, v.15, p. 408-410. His capture of 1st W.Va. Inf. camp at Moorefield.

54 **FAYETTE Artillery**
See: E.W. Gaines.

55 **FAYETTEVILLE Arsenal**
See: Matthew P. Taylor.

56 **FAYETTEVILLE, N.C.**
See: Graham Daves, Edward J. Hale, E.L. Wells

57 **FEARN, Frances Hewitt, Edt.**
"Diary of a Refugee, Edt: Frances Fearn. Illustrated by Rosalie Urquhart." N.Y., Moffat, Yard & Co., 1910. 12mo, cl, front, pls., ix, 149pp. $40-nc, $50-bmk, $12.50, $18.50, $20, $22.50, $25, $75-g. Edited from notes taken by the author from her mother.

58 **FEATHERS, Tom**
"The History of Military Activities in the vicinity of Fayetteville, Arkansas, including the Battle of Fayetteville and Siege of Fayetteville during the War Between the States." In: Wash. Co. Hist. Soc., "Flashback", April, 1953, v.III, #3, maps, 33pp.

59 **FEATHERSTON, John C., Capt., 8th Ala. Reg.**
"Extracts from a speech by...of Wilcox's Alabama Brigade, Feb. 6, 1913, in presenting a picture of Gen. Early to Garland-Rodes Camp, Confed. Veterans, Lynchburg, Va." In: CV, Oct. 1918, v.26, #10, p. 430-436, port of Gen. Jubal Early.

60 ..."Account of Battle of Crater. Charge of Wilcox Old Brigade under Gen. Saunders,

of Mahone's Division." In: SHSP, 1905, v.33, p. 358-374.

61 ..."Bloody Battle of Crater, Alabamians in Wilcox Brigade." In: SHSP, 1908, v.36, p. 161-173.

62 ..."The Battle of Crater as I saw it." In: CV, Jan. 1906, v.XIV, p. 23-26.

63 **FEATHERSTONE-POSEY-HARRIS Brigade**
See: E. Howard McCaleb.

64 **FEDERAL Personal Narratives**
See: George N. Bliss, New Haven Evening Register, St. Louis Globe-Democrat.

65 **"FEDERAL Raid on Tampa Bay."**
In: FHQ, January, 1926, v.IV, #3, p. 130-139. A report: Key West, Fla., Oct. 23, 1863, by "Phoenix". Another Oct. 24, by Theodorus Bailey.

66 **FEE, Robert Grand-Crawford**
"C.S.S. Alabama-C.S. Navy." (Norfolk?) n.d., 4to, mimeographed, illus., 18pp., 10-pls.

67 **FEHRENBACHER, Don E.**
"The South and Three Sectional Crises." Baton Rouge: Louisiana State University Pr., 198-, 8vo, cl, dj, xii, 81pp. $8.95.
3 sectional Crisis...NOTE. Missouri controversy, Wilmot Proviso resolved by the 1850 Compromise in the conflict over Kan. resulting in the South's isolation and resulting in secession.

68 **FEIBELMAN, Herbert U.**
"Edward Aylesworth Perry, Brig.-Gen. CSA, a former Governor of Florida." In: Fla. Law Journ., July 1949, v.23, p. 250-257, ports, view.

69 ..."Floridians distinguished at the bar and on the field of battle...Edward Aylsworth Perry, Brig.-Gen. CSA, and Governor of Florida." In: Fla. Law Jour., July 1949, v.22, p. 151-157. Port and plate.

70 ..."The Constitution of the Lost Cause." In: Commercial Law Jour., 1940, v.XLV, p. 47-49. Deals with the CSA constitution.

71 ..."Jesse Johnson Finley, Brig.-Gen., CSA." In: Fla. Law Jour., Apr., 1949, v.23, p. 133-137. Ports, notes.

72 **FELDMAN, Albert**
"The Strange Case of Simon Bolivar Buckner." In: CWH, June 1959, v.V, #2, p. 199-204.

73 **FELEN, W.H.**
"Life and character of General Robert E. Lee." Cartersville, Ga., 1870. 8vo, wraps, 22pp.

74 **FELGAR, Robert Pattison**
"The Ordnance Department of the Confederate States Army." In: Ala. Hist. Quart., 1946, v.VIII, p. 159-232, port.

75 **FELLOWS, Willis S., Maj.**
"Struggle for Atlanta." n.p., n.d. (Atlanta, Ga., 1967?) 4to, wraps, ports, illus., facsms, map. (20)pp. P.O. Box 11071. $3.

76 **FELMLY, Bradford K. and John C. Grady**
"The death of Private McDermott. His only crime was going home to care for family without official leave." In: CWTI, Dec., 1969, v.8, #9, p. 32-37, illus., ports.

77 ..."John C. Grady-Suffering in Silence, the 29th Texas Cavalry, CSA." With an introduction by Harold Simpson. Quanah, Texas, Nortex Print, 1975, 8vo, cl, dj, illus., photos, index, 243pp. $8.50, $10-y.
..."Suffering in silence: 29th Texas Cavalry CSA." (Quana, Texas, Nortex Press, 1975) 8vo, wraps, xii, 259pp. $8.50.

78 **FELT, Jeremy P.**
"Lucius B. Northrop and the Confederacy's Subsistence Department." In: Va. Mag. Hist. Biog., 1961, v.LXIX, p. 181-193.

79 **FELTON, Rebecca Latimer, Mrs.**
"My memoirs of Georgia politics, written and published by Mrs. William H. Felton after she had reached her 75th birthday." Atlanta, Ga., Index Print, 1911. 8vo, cl, illus., ports, viii, (5)-680pp.

80 ..."Country Life in Georgia during days of my youth." Also other addresses, etc...." Atlanta, Ga., 1919, Index Print. $50-jk, $20, $5(old), $12.50. 12mo, cl, port, 299, (3)pp. Slavery in South, Southern women in war.

81 **FENNER'S Louisiana Battery."**
In: CV, Nov. 1896, v.IV, #11, p. 372-373. Composite of 73 living members of Fenner's La. Bat., Sept. 1st, 1894. Out of enlistments during war of 265. Organized out of Dreux Batt. Mustered out of service at Yorktown, April, 1862. Last year with Johnston and Hood. See: Fannie Beers.

82 **FENNER, Charles E., Hon.**
"Ceremonies connected with the unveiling of the statue of General Robert E. Lee. At Lee Circle, New Orleans, La., Feb. 22, 1884. Oration by Hon. Chas. E. Fenner. Poem by H.F. Requier, Esq. Historical sketch of R.E. Lee Monumental Association." New Orleans, La., W.B. Stansbury, 1884. 8vo, wraps, 46pp. $3, $5, $27.50. Also in-SHSP, 1886, v.XIV, p. 62-102.

83 ..."The 93rd Anniversary of Birth of Pres. Jefferson Davis. Celebrated by various organizations of Southern women. At New Orleans, June 3, 1901. With an eloquent oration of Hon. Charles E. Fenner." In: SHSP, 1901, v.XXIX, p. 1-33. From the New Orleans "Picayune, June 4, 1901.

84 **FERGUSON, Edwin L.**
"Sumner County, Tennessee in the Civil War." (Thompkinsville, Ky.?) 1972. The author. 8vo, cl, illus., ports, 399pp. $16 Bmk-84, $30.

85 **FERGUSON, J.M.**
"The Battle of Scary, W.Va." In: Confed. Vet., Nov. 1917, v.25, p. 503.
FERGUSON, Janna
"Arkadelphia's contribution to the Civil War effort." In: ClarkCHQ (Arkansas), Winter, 1975, v.2, p. 23-30.

86 **FERGUSON, John Lewis**
"Arkansas and the Civil War." (Little Rock: Pioneer Press, 1965) Ark. Civil War Cent. Comm. Edt. 8vo, cl, dj, illus., color flags, ports, maps, charts, ix, 364pp. index. $14, $30, $20-bmk.

87 **FERGUSON, Samuel W., Gen.**
"Report: Sherman's campaign in Mississippi." In: SHSP, 1881, v.9, p. 338-340.

88 **FERGUSSON, James, Sir**
"A Report on Civil America: Sir James Fergusson's Five-week Visit." In: CWH, December 1966, v.XII, #4, p. 347-362.

89 **FERRELL, Charles Clifton**
"The Daughter of the Confederacy"-Her Life, Character and Writings." (Oxford, Miss., Publications of the Miss. Historical Society, 1899, v.II, p. 69-84. Winnie Davis, daughter of Pres. Davis and a writer in Miss.

90 **FERRIS, Norman B.**
"The Prince Consort", "The Times", and the "Trent Affair." In: CWH, June: 1960, v.VI, #2, p. 152-156.

91 ..."The Trent Affair, A Diplomatic crisis." Knoxville: University of Tenn. Press, 1977, 8vo, cl, 280pp., dj. $16.

92 **FERRY, Richard J., et. al.**
"The Battle of Olustee (or Ocean Pond), Feb. 20, 1864." In: Blue & Gray, Mar., 1986, v.III, #4, p. 6-16, 44-61, illus.(incl. color) maps, ports.

93 **FERTIG, James Walter**
"The Secession and reconstruction of Tennessee." Chicago: University of Chicago Pr., 1898, 8vo, cl, (7)-108pp. $10, $12.50, $25, $22.50-jk-97.

94 **FESLER, Mayo**
"Secret political societies in the North during the Civil War." In: Ind. Mag. Hist., Sept. 1918, v.XIV, p. 183-286. Contents: Origin Knights of Golden Circle, Order Amer. Knights and Sons of Liberty. Northwest Confederacy of 1864. Camp

Douglas Conspiracy, Treason Trials in Indiana.

95 ..."Knights of the Golden Circle." In: Amer. Hist. Rev., XLVII, p. 23-50.

96 **FETT, B.J.**
"Early Life of Richard Coke." In: Texana, 1972, v.X, #4, p. 310-320. Member Secession Convention and Capt. 1st Batt. Tex. Inf., known as "Speight's Battalion".

97 **FETZER,**
"Cap't. Fetzer's Co., CSA, Co.E, 45th Ark. Cavalry." In: Indp. Co. (Ark.) Chron., Jan. 1965, v.VI, #2, p. 34-44.

98 **"FEW HISTORICAL RECORDS, A**
of the Church in the Diocese of Texas during the Rebellion. Together with a correspondence between Right Rev. Alexander Gregg, D.D., and the Rev. Charles Gillette." N.Y., 1866, 8vo, cl, 131pp.

99 **FEWELL, L.R.,** Meridian, Miss
"Letters in War-Time." In: Southern Mag., June 1874, #4, p. 638-647. (starts: as II)

100 **FIDLER, William Perry**
"Augusta Jane Evans Wilson, 1835-1909; a biography." University, Ala., Univ. Press, 1951. 8vo, cl, facsms, ports, views, (notes: 228-239) (14), 251pp. On her life in Mobile, services to the CSA in her novels.
..."Augusta Evans Wilson as Confederate propagandist." In: Ala. Rev., Jan. 1949, v.2, p. 32-44. notes. Analyzes author Augusta Jane Evans of Mobile, Ala., 1859-1863.

101 **FIEBEGER, Gustave Joseph**
"Campaigns of the American Civil War." West Point, N.Y., U.S. Military Academy Print, 1914. 8vo, cl, (iv), 432pp., oblong 8vo, atlas. (1)p-index maps, 46 maps, printed one side (partly numbered), 6pp-chron. list of battles, at end. $20 (1910), 372pp., $20.

102 ..."The Campaign and Battle of Gettysburg from the Official Records of the Union and Confederate Armies. Prepared for the use of the cadets of the U.S. Mi. Acad." West Point, N.Y., U.S. Mil. Acad. Pr., 1915, 8vo, cl, (4), 116, (4)-append., 7-maps tip-in at back. $15-b, $10. Dornbusch-III, 2054, calls for fldg. maps.

103 ..."The Campaign of Gettysburg." (1902) 31, (2)pp. 5-maps, 1-fldg., cover title. "Prepared for visit of class '02, Mil. Acad. to Gettysburg, April, 1902, by Col. G.J. Fiebeger, Prof. Engrs. Dornbusch-2055. See: John Formby and Matthew F. Steel.

104 **FIEGEL, M.F.**
"The Baptist Church and the Confederate Cause." In: Okla. Acad. Science Proceed., 1968, v.XLVII, p. 314-318.

105 **"FIELD LETTERS from Head-quarters**
Second Corps., A.N.V. (A.S. Pendleton, Briscoe G. Baldwin)" In: SHSP, 1881, v.IX, p. 121-122.

106 **FIELD MANUAL for the use of officers on Ordnance Bureau."**
Richmond, Va., Ritchie & Dunnovant, 1862.

107 ..."New Material, Dean S. Thomas, Arendsville, Pa., 1984. 12mo, cl, dj, (4), 149, (34)pp. illus., ports.

108 **"FIELD TELEGRAMS,**
concerning operations around Richmond and Petersburg, in 1864." In: SHSP, 1877, v.III, p. 295-300; 1879, v.VII, p. 345-348; "Telegrams from General Lee's Hdq. Sept., 1864. 1880, v.IX, p. 332; v.IV, p. 189-191.

109 **"FIELD and FIRESIDE.**
Columbus, Ga. The Great or Broad Seal of the Confederate States of America. A brief history, 1863-1912." In: Ala. Hist. Quart., 1948, v.10:p.96-98, view.

110 **FIELD, Charles William, Maj.-Gen.**
"Campaign of 1864-1865, Narrative by." In: SHSP, 1886, v.17, p. 342-348.

111 ..."Bright Skies and Dark Shadows, with maps." N.Y., Charles Scribner's Sons, 1890. 21cm, cl, ii, (1), (9)-316pp. maps. $20, $65-jk-12, $35. Note: The green bind-

ing with "Scribners" at foot of spine: colored map of as front, an additional 3-maps (1-tinted) ports: Henry Grady, T.J. Jackson and recumbant fig. of Lee; another edition in green cl, with "Confed. Vet." foot of spine, has only 2-maps and front(port author); another edt. as the latter, 20cm, in light green cloth. $8.50, $10, $12.50. A long chap. on Battle of Franklin, Tenn.

112 ..."Blood is thicker than water; a few days among our southern brethren." N.Y., G. Munro, 1886. 12mo, wraps, viii, (11)-151pp., front. $10, $20.

113 ..."Stonewall Jackson." In: Harper's Mag., LXXXIII, 1891, illus., ports, 907-918pp.

114 ..."The battle of Franklin." In: His "Bright skies and dark shadows.", 1890, p. 209-256.

115 **FIELDER, Herbert, Esquire, of Georgia**
"The Disunionist: A Brief Treatise upon the Evils of the Union between the North and the South, and the Propriety of Separation and the Formation of a Southern United States." n.p., printed for author, 1858. 8vo, cl, 72pp. Sabin c.24299.

116 ..."A Sketch of the Life and Times of Joseph E. Brown. War Governor of Georgia, Georgia in Relation to the War, Reconstruction in Georgia, etc." Springfiled, Mass., 1883. 8vo, cl, 785pp., port. $5, $8.50, $10, $15, $30-bmk.

117 **FIELDS, Frank E., Jr.**
"28th Virginia Infantry." Lynchburg, Va., H.E. Howard, 1985. (J.P. Bell) Print, 1st Edt., Lim. Edt. Atg. 8vo, cl, dj, (3), 89pp., maps, ports. $17.50.

118 **FIELDS, Joseph E., Dr.**
"Robert E. Lee's Farewell Order." In: Autograph Collector's Jour., Jan./Oct., 1949, v.1, #2, p. 4-8; v.2, #1, p. 18-19. Facsm., notes, on Gen. Lee's Order #9, Hdq., ANV, Apr. 10, 1865. $12.

119 **FIFE, Iline**
"The Confederate Theatre, 1861-1865." South. Speech Jour., Spring 1955, v.20, p. 224-231. notes.

120 **FIGG, Royal W.**
"Where men only dare to go!" or, the story of a boy company. (C.S.A.) By an ex-boy." Richmond, Va., Whittet & Shepperson, 1885. 12mo, cl, front, port, viii, (17)-263pp. (Jk-142) about mint. $75-bmk, $125, $150-b, #200-r.

121 **FIGUERS, H.P.**
"A boy's impressions of the Battle of Franklin." In: CV, Jan. 1915, v.XXIII, p. 4-7.

122 **"FINAL REPLY to Westerner",**
from the Times-Dispatch of Sunday, Jan. 8, 1928." Caption title, n.p., 8vo, 19, (1)pp., reprints of letters to newspapers by Lincoln critics: Jno. T. Goolrick, Halpin Whitney, Peter J. White, L.M. Williams, M.D. Boland, Calude G. Bowers, Mary L. Rossilter and Giles B. Cooke. Managhan-3011. Also, an abbreviated ed. in FtwL, 8vo, (3)pp.

123 **FINANCES-CSA ,**
Judah P. Benjamin; Jno. G. Van Deusen; Richard C. Todd; Eugene Lerner; John C. Schwab; Rich. Lester.

124 **FINCH, Elizabeth Austin**
"Mary Gay, Confederate heroine." In: UDCM, May 1951, v.14, #5, p. 15, 18. Services in vicinity of Decatur, Ga., 1863-1864.

125 **"FINDING LIST of Military Biographies**
and other personal literature in the War Dept. Library." Wash: GPO, 1890, 2nd edt. 8vo, cl, 145pp. (subject catalogue #4) U.S., War Department Library.

126 **FINK, Harold S.**
"The East Tennessee campaign and Battle of Knoxville in 1863." In: East Tenn. Hist./Soc. Paper., 1957, v.XXIX, p. 79-117, view, maps, 1-fldg.

127 **FINK, Julia Dorothea**
"The story of the McGinty cannon." In: Jr. Hist. (Tex) Jan. 1954, v.14, #4, p. 1-1, 22. view CSA captures Union cannon near El Paso in 1863, stolen by Mexican re-volutionists in 1911 and again in 1915, now exhibited in El Paso.

128 **FINKE, Detmar H. and Lee A. Wallace**
"Virginia Military Forces, etc." See: Lee A. Wallace.

129 **FINKELMAN, Paul**
"Prigg vs. Pennsylvania and Northern State Courts: Anti-slavery use of a pro-slavery decision." In: CWH, March 1979, v.25, #1, p. 5-35, notes.

130 **FINLAY, Anne B.**
"One woman's experience, 1862-1865." In: Wash. Co. Hist. Soc., Papers, 1910-1915. (1954), p. 205-211, Reminisc. (1910) of war in Greenville, Miss.

131 **FINLEY, G.W.**
"With Pickett at Cemetery Ridge." Phila: Blue & Gray, v.IV, 1894, p. 37-40, illus.

132 **FINLEY, Luke W., Col., CSArmy**
"The Battle of Perryville. There was no ac-tion in the Civil War where the CSA soldier displayed more desperate courage-Bragg's men fought against overwhelming odds." In: SHSP, 1902, v.XXX, p. 238-150.

133 **FINNEGAN, Joseph**
"Report: Battle of Ocean Pond, Fla." In: SHSP, 1881, v.9, p. 16-20.

134 **FINNEY, William W., Col.**
"Presentation of the portrait of Lieut. Gen. Wade Hampton, C.S. Cavalry. To R.E. Lee Camp C.V., Richmond, Va., Sept. 15, 1904. Addresses of Col. W.W. Finney and Ex-Governor Charles T. O'-Ferral." (From "Times-Dispatch", Sept. 16, 1904) In: SHSP, 1904, v.XXXII, p. 134-142.

135 **"FIRST Land Battle**
of the Civil War Centennial Commemora-tion. Centennial Re-enactment, First Land Engagement of the Civil War, Philippi, West Virginia, June 3, 1861." (Philippi, W.Va., 1961. 8vo, wraps, (12)pp. Cols. E. Dumont and G.A. Porterfield's report.

136 **"FIRST Manassas (Bull Run)**
and the War Around it." Manassas, Vir-ginia., 1st Manassas Corp., (1961). 4to, color-Decr. wraps, 64pp., illus., ports, map. $2.

137 **"FIRST North Carolina Infantry**
of Confederate States Army, roster of its commissioned officers (& the song of the regiment")." In: SHSP, 1890, v.XVIII, p. 51-55.

138 **"FIRST North Carolina Volunteers**
and the Battle of Bethel." In: SHSP, 1891, v.19, p. 212-246. Signed "SYZ".

139 **"FIRST Secession Movement, The"**
In: N.C. Booklet, Oct. 1917, v.XVII, #2, p. 90-95. Letter from Dr. W.R. Wood to Walter Clark, with proceedings of first meeting declaring secession (in imitation of Mecklenburg Declaration) ever held. It antedated the S.C. Declaration more than two months. This was Oct. 14, 1860, that of S.C., Dec. 20th. $10, $15-bmk, $10-bmk-84.

140 **FIRST White House Association,**
Montgomery, Alabama. "Historical Souvenir of the opening of the First White House which in its present location is to be a permanent museum of Confederate History. Issued by the First White House Association." Montgomery, Ala., Paragon Press, 1921, 8vo, stiff cardboard wraps, illus., 20pp. $5. color pix, in open window of cover, port. "The First White House of the Confederacy." (Montgomery?) 1930. 8vo, wraps, illus. (incl. ports) color illus.-t/p, 16pp.
...Same (1940). See: Wilbur Jones. $1.75, $5. Reprints: 1936, 1948, 1951, 1956, 1958, 1962.

141 **FIRST Confederate Speller, The**
on a strictly philosophical and progressive plan, in which the 224 simple and compound sounds that form the words of the English language are presented in monosyllables and syllables; and in words of the same clan, of one, two, or more syllables are classed in tables, according to the peculiar terminations the number of words in each table varying in number according to the extend of the respective clans. By an association of Southern Teachers." Nashville, Tennessee, 1861. (John B. McFerrin, Agent) 17 1/2cm, sewn, (5)-p. 144pp. Mentioned in Oct. 1861 So. Lit. Mess., Crandall-4052.

142 **"FIRST Shot of the War**
was fired in the air. W.H. Gibbs, of South Carolina, aids in establishing the fact of who fired it." In: SHSP, 1903, v.XXXI, p. 73-39. From Richmond, Va., News-Leader, Aug. 14, 1893.

143 **FISCH, George, Rev.**
"Nine months in the United States during the Crisis by..., with an intro: Hon. Arthur Kinnaird, M.P., Preface: Rev. W. Arthur..." London: James Nesbit & Co., 1862. LC shows another edt., 1863, with (v, xvi, 166pp.) $125-ob. 12mo, cl, xvi, 166pp. Sabin-24416.
...Paris: Librarie E. Dentu, 1862. 12mo, cl, 238pp. Sabin-24415. $125-ob.

144 **FISCHER, LeRoy H.**
"Fort Washita, Confederate Headquarters in Indian Territory." In: UDC Magazine, FEb. 1966, #2, p. 33-39.

145 ..."Lee and Jackson-Kindred spirits." In: UDC Magazine, Mar. 1972, #3, p. 15, 18-19, 25.

146 ..."Western States in the Civil War." In: JW, Jan. 1975, v.14, #1, p. 1-184, 209-214.

147 ..."Western Territories in the Civil War." Manhattan, Kan., JW, 1977, p. 120. $9.

148 ..."Civil War Battles in the West." Manhattan, Kan., Sunflower University Press, 1981. 8vo, wraps, 112pp. Illus., notes, index. $9. Papers read at professional meetings:

149 ..." Oklahoma's Civil War Historical sites." Okla. Heritage Assn., Feb. 25, 1980.

150 ..."Civil War in Oklahoma." Pioneer Hist. Co., Ponca City, April 8, 1981.

151 ..."Historic Fort Gibson during the Civil War." Okla. Hist. Soc., April 9, 1983.

152 ..."New Interpretations of the Confederate War in Indian Territory." Sons of Conf. Vets., Okla. City, May 19, 1984.

153 ..."Unique features in the Civil War." Tulsa CWRT, Nov. 19, 1981.

154 ..."The War Between the States in Indian Territory, an overview." In: Confed. Vet., Mar./Apr., 1986, #2, p. 6-11, illus., ports, maps.

155 **FISCHER, LeRoy H. and Lary C. Rampp**
"Quantrill's Civil War Operations in Indian Territory." Oklahoma City: Okla. Hist. Society, 1968. wraps, 8vo, ports, maps $1.50, $5-nc, $10-b. Reprint: revised, Chronicles of Okla., Vol. XLVI, #2, p. 155-181.

156 **FISCHER, LeRoy H. and Wm. L. McMurry**
"Confederate Refugees from Indian Territory." In: Chr. Okla., Winter 1979, 1980, LVII, #4, p. 451-462. ports.

157 ..."Confederate Indian Forces Outside of Indian Territory." Oklahoma City, Okla. Hist. Society, 1969. Wraps, 8vo, maps, ports, 36pp. Reprint: revised from Chronicles of Okla., XLVI, #3, p. 249-284. $1.50, $3.50, $5-nc, $10.

158 ..."The Honey Springs National Battlefield Park Movement." Oklahoma City: Okla. Hist. Society, 1969. Wraps, 8vo, maps, illus., 16pp. Reprint: revised, Chronicles of Okla., Vol. XLVII, #1, p. 515-530. $.75.

159 ..."The Impact of the Civil War in Oklahoma: Death and Destruction." In: Okla. State Alumni Mag., Sept. 1964, v.V, p. 10-12.

160 ..."David O. Dodd: Folk Hero of Confederate Arkansas." In: Ark. HQ., Summer, 1978, v.XXXVII, #2, p. 130-146, illus., ports. See also under David O. Dodd.

161 **FISCHER, LeRoy H., Edt.**
"The Civil War Era in Indian Territory. Edited with introduction by LeRoy Fischer." Los Angeles: Lorrin L. Morrison, Pub., 1974, 8vo, cl, dj, illus., maps, index, xiv, 175pp. (Paper, $7) $13. In: Jour. of West, 1973, v.XII.

162 ..."Confederate Victory at Chusto-Talasha." Oklahoma City: Chron. Okla., Winter, 1971, '72, v.XLIX, #4, p. 452-476, ports, map., illus.

163 **FISCHER, Roger A.**
"The segregation struggle in Louisiana, 1862-1877." Urbana, Ill., University Press, 1974, 8vo, cl, xiv, 168pp. $7.

164 **FISH, Henry C.**
"The voice of our brother's blood: its source and its summons a discourse occasioned by the Sumner and Kansas outrages." Newark, 1856. 8vo, sewn, 16pp. $125-jk-142. Kansas-Missouri troubles, sack of Lawrence, etc. "If a man be found in Kansas, with the taint of Northern principals, he must be got rid of somehow-either by intimidation or abuse, or by the Bowie-knife and revolver."

165 **FISHBURNE, Charles C., Jr.**
"The Cedar Keys in the Civil War and Reconstruction, 1861-1876." (Cedar Key, Florida, Sea Hawke Pubs., 1982. 8vo, pict. stiff wraps, maps, vigs., pl., vii, 46pp. (Third in a series)

166 **FISHBURNE, Clement D.**
"Historical sketch of Rockbridge Artillery, CSArmy, by a member of the famous battery." In: SHSP, 1895, v.XXIII, p. 98-158. (roster, 5pp.)

167 ..."Stonewall Jackson-a Memoir." In: Amer. Hist., June 1967, v.II, #3, p. 31-37. illus., sketch, ports, incl. one of Jackson on back cover.

168 **FISHEL, Walter**
"More about Ship Island, Miss." In: Amer. Philatelist, July 1948, v.61, p. 789-803. facsms. On the post office at Ship Island, Feb. 7-Aug. 13, 1862.

169 **FISHER'S Hill, Battle of**
See: John H. Lane, James A Early, W.A. Conn.

170 **FISHER, Clyde Olin**
"The relief of soldier's families in North Carolina during the Civil War." In: So. Atl. Quart., Jan, 1917, v.XVI, p. 60-72.

171 **FISHER, George Adams**
"The Yankee Conscript; or, Eighteen Months in Dixie. With an introduction by Rev. William Dickson." Phila: J.W. Daughaday, 1864. 12mo, cl, front(port) illus.,chart, facsm. 151, (2-p. ads) pp. $15, $17.50, $22.50, $35-jk-122. An Ohioan sheepraiser in Texas, draft into CSArmy, escaped, redrafted but finally escaped in seond time, north.

172 **FISHER, Horace Newton**
"The Harris Letter" outlining Bragg's Plan of Campaign for the Invasion of Kentucky in 1862." (Dedham, Mass. ? 1953) 4to, 15 leaves, typed t.p., facsm. report. of author's undated mssc., CSA movements in Ky., spec. ref. to a supposed letter by Isham Green Harris.

173 **FISHER, John E.**
"Life on the common level: Inheritance, Conflict and Instruction." In: Tenn. HQ, 1967, v.XXVI, p. 304-322. concerns 11th Tenn. Cavl., CSA and life in Tenn.

174 **FISHER, Mike**
"Remember Poison Spring." In: MHR, April, 1980, v.LXXIV, #3, p. 323-342,

175 **FISHER, S.**
"The Amenities of War." In: Blue & Gray, Phil: 1893, v.I, p. 321-323.

176 **FISHWICK, Marshall William**
"Civil War II." In: Texas Quar., Summer, 1959, v.2(2), p. 109-128. On the North as "victor vanquished", in restitution of the Lost Cause by Southern writers and artists.

177 ..."Lee After the War." New York: Dodd, Mead & Co., (1963). 8vo, cl, d/w, ports, illus., 141pp. $1.50, $10-bmk, $4-prs.

178 ..."Robert E. Lee Churchman." Living History Series #2, 8vo, wraps, cover title, 27pp. (Diocese of Southwest Virginia.) In: Hist. Mag. Prot/Episc. Ch., Dec. 1961.

179 **FISHWICK, Marshall William and William M. Hollis**
"Preliminary checklist of writings about R.E. Lee." Charlottesville, Va., Bibliographical Society of the University of Virginia, 1951, 4to, 42 leaves, (538 items)

180 ..."General Lee's Photographer; the life and work of Michael Miley, 1841-1918." Chapel Hill: Univ. of North Carolina Pr. for Virginia Hist. Soc., 1954. 4to, cl, dj, ports (1-color), views (part color) notes, (12), 94pp. $4.50, $7.50, $35, $14-nc.

181 ...From: Rockbridge Hist. Soc. Pro., v.4, p. 13-15. An abridgement of an article in the American Quarterly, Fall, 1951. Life as a photographer in Lexington, Va., experiments in natural photog., particularly after 1865.

182 ..."Traveller: Virginia legend." In: Commonwealth (Va.), June 1954, v.21, p. 12-13. Port. Lore about Traveller (foaled 1857) Gen. Lee's horse.

183 ..."Virginians on Olympus: a cultural analysis of four great men." Richmond, Va., 1951. 8vo, wraps, view, notes, 74pp. Jno. Smith, Dan Boone, Geo. Washington, and Lee the Virginian as Confederate.

184 **FISHWICK, M.W.**
"Virginians on Olympus: II Robert E. Lee "Savier of the Lost Cause." In: Va. Mag., April 1950, v.58, #2, p. 163-181.

185 **FISHWICK, Marshall W.**
"Virginians on Olympus: II-Robert E. Lee: savior of the Lost Cause. #2, p. 163-180.

186 **FITCH, C. of Chariton, Iowa**
"Capture of Fort Pillow-Vindication of Gen. Chalmers by a Federal Officer." In: SHSP, 1879, v.7, p. 439-441.

187 **FITE, Emerson David**
"The Presidential Campaign of 1860." N.Y., Macmillan, 1911. 8vo, cl, xii, 356pp. $10, $16-bmk, $30.

188 **FITE, John A., Col.**
"Colonel John A. Fite's letters from prison, by Raymond D. White." In: THQ, 1973, v.32, p. 140-147.

189 **FITTS, Albert N.**
"The Confederate Convention." In: Ala. Rev., v.II, April 1949, p. 83-101, notes. "The Constitutional Debate.", v.II, July 1949, p. 189-210, notes.

190 **FITZ SIMONS, Theodore B., Jr.**
"The Camilla Riot." In: Ga.H.Q., June, 1951, v.XXXV, #2, p. 116-125. Struggle between native whites and radical Republicans.

191 **FITZGERALD, Elie Maury**
"Matthew Fontaine Maury, a Letter from his daughter Mrs. Corbin." (Richmond) Va. Mag. Hist. Biog., Jan. 1945, v.53, #1, p. 53-56.

192 **FITZGERALD, Oscar Penn**
"John B. McFerrin-A Biography." Nashville, Tenn., Methodist Pub. House, 1889 (another edt: 1888). 12mo, cl, front(port), 448pp. $22.50.
...only 1-chapter re CSA, chaplain Tenn.

193 **FITZGERALD, William S.**
"Did Nathan Bedford Forrest really rescue

194 FITZHUGH, Kester Newton, Comp'l., Edt.
"Cannon Smoke: the Letters of Capt. John J. Good, Good-Douglas Texas Battery, CSA." (Hillsboro, Texas: Hill Jr. College, 1971) 8vo, cl, d/w, ports, illus., facsms, ix, 209pp. $7.50, $25.
...Lim. 50 copies, signed. $75, $35, $30 Bmk-84.

195 ..."Little known Texas Confederates (military officers.)." In: Local Hist. and Genealog. Soc. Bul., March, 1958, v.3, #4, p. 3-6.

196 ..."Texas Batteries, battalions, regiments, commanders and field officers, Confederate States Army, 1861-1865." Midlothian, Texas: Mirrow Press, 1959. 8vo, stiff wraps, 33pp., $5, $6, $7.50, $10, atg-$17.50-jk, $20-bmi-105. Many copies destroyed by fire.

197 ..."Saluria, Ft. Esperanza, and military operations on the Texas Coast, 1861-1864." In: SWHQ, 1957, LXI, p. 66-100, maps.

198 ..."Texas forces in the Red River Campaign, Mar.-May, 1864. In: TMH, v.III, p. 15-22. fldg. map in pocket.

199 ..."Texas Colonels and Generals, CSA 1861-1865." n.p., 1964. Mimeo: 8 1/2x11" $5.

200 ..."Terry's Texas Rangers, 8th Texas Cavalry, CSA." An address by... Houston(Texas) Civil War Round Table, March 21, 1958. 8vo, cover title, soft cover, 22pp., vignettes, 1000 numbered copies @ $3., $5, $20-b, $10-mok, $12.50-y, $15, $30.

201 ..."Terry's Texas Rangers." (Waco, Texas: Texian Press, 1973). In: "Soldiers of Texas." 4to, pp. (71)-93. (1) color plate.

202 FITZHUGH, Robert H.
"R.E. Lee, an address to the United Daughters of the Confederacy, Lexington, Kentucky, Jan. 19, 1907." Lexington, Ky., 1910, U.D.C., 8vo, wraps, 21pp. $5.

203 FITZHUGH, St. George R.
"The Truth of History; a study in political development." Richmond, Va., Old Dominion Pr., 1926. 8vo, cl, 164pp. $35. Amer. Revo., Secession, CSA, etc.

204 FITZHUGH, William H., Mrs. and Mrs. R.E. Lee
"Funeral of Mrs. G.W.P. Custis and death of General R.E. Lee, described in contemporary letters, 1853, 1870." In: VaMH, Jan. 1927, v.XXXV, p. 22-26. Mrs. Lee describes her husband's death.

205 FITZPATRICK, L.A., Sr.
"Civil War Reminiscences." In: Phillips CHQ, Sept., 1967, v.5, p. 1-13.

206 FITZPATRICK, Marion Hill, Sgt.-Maj.
"Letters from Amanda and to his wife Amanda Olive Elizabeth White Fitzpatrick, from 1862-1865." Culloden, Ga., Mansel Hammock (c.1976) 4to, cl, 178pp., illus., Compiler: Henry Mansel Hammock.
FITZPATRICK, Marion, Sgt. Maj.
"Letters to Amanda from Sergeant Major Marion Hill Fitzpatrick...to his wife....1862-1865." Culloden, Ga., 1976. 8vo, wraps, 188pp. $20-bmk.

207 FIVE FORKS, Battle of
See: Geo. K. Griggs, J. Risque Hutter, Robert M. Stribling.

208 "FIVE POINTS in the Record
of North Carolina in the great war of 1861-1865. Report of the Committee appointed by the North Carolina Literary and Historical Association..1904." Goldsboro, N.C., Nash Bros, 1904. 8vo, wraps, 7-maps (4-dbl. pg.) 79pp. $12.50, $25-bmk, $35-bmk, $50-bmk. Same: for 1905. $25-bmk-105, $45-jk, $20-nc. "Rep. of Comm." (10pp.); Maj. E.J. Hale's -"1st at Bethel", (5pp.); Judge W.A. Montgomery's-"Carolina farthest front at Gettysburg", (13pp.); Lt. W.R. Bond's-"Longstreet's as-

sault at Gettysburg', (11pp.); Judge A.C. Avery's-"Farthest to the front at Chickamauge." (11pp.); Henry I. London's-"Last at Appomattox," (11pp.); E.J. Holt's-"Last capture of guns", (2pp.); Capt. S.A. Ashe's-"Numbers and losses of N.C. Troops," (7pp.). (See: N.C. in War Between States..."

209 ..."North Carolina in the War Between the States. Report of the Committee. (In: Literary and Historical Activities in North Carolina, 1900-1905. Publications of the Historical Commission." Raleigh, 1907. 8vo, wraps, v.1, p. 416-499, maps. $10. This is a reprint of "Five Points in the Record of N.C., in the Great War, etc." See: under title.

210 **FIVEASH, Joseph Gardner**
"The Virginia's Great Fight on Water. Her last challenge and why she was destroyed." In: SHSP, July 1906, v.XXXIV, p. 316-326.

211 ..."Virginia-(Merrimac) Monitor Engagement and a complete history of the operations of these two historic vessels in Hampton Roads and adjacent waters, C.S.A. Virginia, Mar. 8-May 11, 1862, U.S.S. Monitor, May 9, 1862-Jan. 2, 1863." Norfolk, Va., Fiveash Pub. Co., (c.1907) 8vo, wraps, 34pp., maps, ports, illus. $3, $7.50, $10.

212 **FLADELAND, Betty L.**
"Compensated Emancipation: A rejected alternative." In: JSH, May 1976, 18pp. $8.

213 **FLAGS of the Confederacy**
"Confederate States Flags. List of 544 of those of Virginia Troops and when captured." In: SHSP, 1904, v.32, p. 195-200.

214 ..."The Confederate Flag." In: SHSP, 1880, v.8, p. 155-161.
...See: Augusta, Ga. "Herald", Alice Baxter, Jno. C. Butler, Wm. L. Cabell, Leonard W. Colby, Bradley T. Johnson, John Lamb, Carleton McCarthy, Dabney H. Maury, Geo. H. Preble, Arthur L. Rogers, Alfred Romans.
...See: Glenn C. Allen. M. Jamison Chestney, Mary Lynn Conrad, Ellis L. Coulter, "Confederate Battle Flags Returned (Wisc.) Maynard Hill", "Last CSA flag on the Atlantic", Jessica Randolph Smith, Charles E. Ware.

215 **"FLAGS of the Confederate Armies, The**
Returned to the men who bore them by the United States Government, 1905." (St. Louis, Mo., Buxton & Skinner) sm.4to, pict. color wraps, port (Lee), 56pp. (39)pp. colored flags. $40-b, $25-bk, $15, $20. A souvenir booklet presented to veterans at their reunion, Louisville, June 14, 1905.
...Same, but 30pp. compliments of the Cotton-Belt Railroad. $10. See also: Mrs. W. B. Newell, Walter A. Montgomery, Peter Brannon, Mrs. W.R. Barnett, Jr.

216 ...Same: by Dunbar Rowland, Mississippi flags. Contained in the 4th Annual Report of the director of the Department of Archives and History of the State of Mississippi, 1904/1905. Nashville, Tenn., 1905. article of 7pp. (43pp.)

217 **"FLAGS of the Confederate States of America."**
By authority: United Confederate Veterans, Wm. E. Mickle, Adj. Gen. and Chief of Staff." New Orleans, (1900). 8vo, wraps, color-illus., 16mo, 10pp. $15-bmk, $1.50. 6pp.-1907, $8, $15-bmk.
By Authority of the United Confederate Veterans." (Baltimore: A. Hoen & Co., 1907) For sale by Wm. E. Mickle, Adj.-Gen. and Chief of Staff, New Orleans, La. 8vo, wraps (color flag on cover, (6)pp. $1, $15-bmk. Smaller-(10)pp. $15.

218 ...Marshall, Texas, Marshall Ordnance Depot Press, 1973. Spon: United Confed. Vets., 8vo, wraps, illus. (6)pp. $.25 reprint of 1907 edt.
...(Balt., 1907) UCV. Suffolk, Va., Robt.

Hardy Pub., 1986, 8vo, wraps, (8)pp. illus. ...Wallington, Surrey. Confederate States Print. House, 1976.

219 **FLAKE, Elijah Wilson**
"Battle Between the Merrimac and the Monitor." Polkton, N.C., The Author, 1914, 8vo, cl, port, 12pp., cover title. By the last survivor of Merrimack's crew.

220 **"FLANAGIN PAPERS, The"**
In: ClarkCHQ, Winter, 1975, v.2, p. 45-65. Includes wartime letters not given to Ark. Hist. Comm.

221 **FLANDERS, Bertram Holland**
"Bugle-horn of liberty: a Confederate humorous magazine (Griffin, Ga., nos. 1 and 2 and 3, Aug.-Oct. 1863." In: Emory Univ. Quart., June 1953, v.9, p. 79-85.

222 ..."Early Georgia Magazines: Literary Periodicals to 1865." Athens: Univ. of Georgia Press, 1944. 8vo, cl, dj, bibliog., xiv, 189pp.

223 **FLANNER, Henry G.**
"Flanner's N.C. Battery at the Battle of Crater." In: SHSP, 1878, v.V, p. 247-248.

224 **FLAT CREEK, Engagement at**
See: Arthur Herbert.

225 **FLEET, Benjamin Robert**
"Green Mount. A Virginia Plantation Family During the Civil War: Being the Journal of Benjamin Robert Fleet and Letters of His Family." Edt: Betsy Fleet and John D.P. Fuller. Lexington: University of Kentucky Press (1962). 8vo, cl, d/w, 374pp., vigs., decr. ends. $35, $30, $8.50, $5.25, $14-bmk, $25-bmk.

226 **FLEET, Betsy, Edt.**
"Green Mount after the war: the correspondence of Maria Louise Wacker Fleet and her family, 1865-1900." Charlottesville, University of Virginia Press, 1978. 8vo, cl, dj, 374pp. $15.

227 **FLEET, C.R.**
"The Fredericksburg Artillery, Captain Edward S. Marye. First appearance of the CSA flag with white field." In: SHSP, 1904, v.23, p. 240-242.

228 **FLEMING, Andrew Mangus**
"A Soldier of the Confederacy." Bost: Meador Pub., 1934. 12mo, cl, 345pp. (fiction) $17.50, $10, $15, $20.

229 **FLEMING, Berry**
"Autobiography of a City in Arms: Augusta, Georgia, 1861-1865. Compiled with a preface by Berry Fleming." Augusta, Ga., Richmond County Historical Society, 1976. 8vo, cl, maps, illus., xi, 165pp. $14.50. Paper-$6.50. $17-y

230 ...Originally in Richmond County History, Winter, 1975, v.7, p. 7-90.

231 **FLEMING, Francis Philip**
"Memoir of Capt. C. Seton Fleming of the Second Florida Infantry, CSA. Illustrative of the history of the Florida Troops in Virginia during the War Between the States. With an appendix of casualties." Jacksonville, Fla., Times-Union, 1884. 12mo, cl, ports (incl. front) xiv, (17)-124, (1)p. $22.50, $55, $60, $1000-ob.

232 ..."Gettysburg. The courageous part taken in the desperate conflict June 2-3, 1863, by the Florida Brigade (General E.A. Perry), there commanded by Colonel David Lang, with the serious casualties sustained (Taken from Fleming, Chap. VI, and append. G.)." In: SHSP, 1889, v.XXVII, p. 192-205.

233 ..."Francis P. Fleming in the War for Southern Independence. Soldiering with the 2nd Florida Regiment. Edt: Edward C. Williamson." In: Fla. Hist. Quart., 1949-1950, v.XXVII, p. 38-52, 143-155, 205-210. $8.

234 ..."Soldiering with the Second Florida Infantry Regiment. Edt: John P. Ingle, Jr., In: FHQ, Jan., 1981, v. LIX, #3, p. 335-339, notes.

..."Memoir of Capt. C. Seton Fleming of the 2nd Florida Infantry CSA." Alexandria, Va., Stonewall House, 1985. 12mo, cl,(port on cover), illus., xvii, (1), xiv, (2), (18)-124. Append-H (1)p; 1(33)p.; J (7)p. Index-(6)p. $20. Intro: Rodney E. Dillon, Jr.

235 **FLEMING, Julius J.**
"The Juhl Letters to the Charleston Courier. A View of the South, 1865-1871." Edited by John Hammond Moore." Athens, Ga., University Press(1974). sq. 12mo, cl, dj, viii, 391pp. $12.

236 **FLEMING, Mary Boyd**
"The last meeting of Lee and Jackson; the Southern painter, Julio, and his most celebrated work." In: Jour. Am. Hist. V, #3, p. 409-412.

237 **FLEMING, Mary Love Edwards**
"Dale County and its people during the Civil War." In: Ala. Hist. Quart., Spring 1957, v.19, p. 61-109. $10.

238 **FLEMING, Robert H.**
"The Confederate Naval Cadets and the Confederate Treasury: The Diary of Midshipman Robert H. Fleming. Edt: G. Melvin Herndon." In: Ga.H.Q., June 1965, v.L, #2, p. 207-216. $8.

239 **FLEMING, Vivian Minor**
"Battles of Fredericksburg and Chancellorsville, Virginia." Richmond, Va., W.C. Hill Pr., 1921, 8vo, wraps, 30pp. $50-bmk-105.

240 ..."Campaigns of the Army of Northern Virginia including the Jackson Valley Campaign, 1861-1865." Richmond, Va., William Byrd Pr. (1928). 16mo, cl, 2-fldg. maps (1-color) errata sheet, 167pp. $12.50, $18, $20, Pres. $100 and $75-bmk, $65, $50-bmk, $70.

241 ..."The Wilderness Campaign." Richmond, Va., W.C. Hill Pr., 1922, 8vo, wraps, 31pp. $30-y.

242 **FLEMING, Walter Lynwood**
"The Churches of Alabama during the Civil War and Reconstruction." Gulf Magazine, v.I, (1902), p. 103-127.

243 ..."Civil War and Reconstruction in Alabama (1861-1880)." N.Y., Columbia University Press and The Macmillan Co., agents, 1905. 8vo, cl, xxiii, 815pp., illus. (incl. maps) ports, plates, facsimilies. 850 copies. $50, $30, $37.50, $65, $75(macmillan), $150-nc-'76, $45, $250-b.bridgers (1906)
...Cleveland: Arthur H. Clark, 1911. $40.
...N.Y., Peter Smith, 1949, a Micro-off-set book, reproduced 4pp. to 1p. $10, $50-bwm, $25-nc.
...Spartanburg, S.C., The Reprint Co., 1978. 8vo, cl, index, illus., maps, 838pp. $30. With a new introduction.

244 ..."The Early Life of Jefferson Davis." Baton Rouge: Louisiana State University Pamphlet from University Bul., viii, #6. Reprinted from: Mississippi Valley Hist. Ass'n. Proceedings, April, 1917, v.ix, p. 151-176. (Cedar Rapids, Ia., 1917).

245 ..."Jefferson Davis first Marriage." University, Miss., 1912. Pamphlet, from Mississippi Historical Society Publications, v.12, p. 21-36. cov. title. $10-bmk.

246 ..."Home Life in Alabama During the War." In: "Southern History Association Publications." Washington, D.C., 1904, 8vo, v.8, pp.(81)-103.
...Also: So. Hist. Assn., 1904, v.VIII.

247 ..."Jefferson Davis at West Point." Reprint: Publications of Mississippi Historical Society, vo. 8. (University, Miss., c.1908). $10. 8vo, wraps, p. 247-267. Baton Rouge: LSU, 1910.

248 ..."Military Government in Alabama, 1865-1866." (Nashville, Tenn.) American Hist. Mag., Apr. 1903, v.VIII, #2 and 3, p. 163-179. "Mil. Gov. Ala., under Reconstruction Acts." (above) p. 222-251. $12.

249 ..."Peace Movement in Alabama During the Civil War." In: South Atlantic Quarterly, April-July, 1903, p. 114-124, 246-260.

250 ..."Religious Life of Jefferson Davis." Baltimore, 1910. tall 8vo, wraps, 18pp. (old) $2.25. Reprint from Methodist Review, Apr., 1910.
..."Religious Life of Jefferson Davis." Baton Rouge, La., Ortlieb Print Hse., 1910. Unvi. Bul., L.S.U., vol. 1, NS-#5. Reprint from Methodist Review, April, 1910.
..."Religious Life of Jefferson Davis." Baton Rouge: Louisiana Univ. Press, 1910. Pamphlet from University Bul. v.1, #5, p. 325-542. $2.50.

251 ..."Jefferson Davis and Andersonville." Pamphlet from Southern Historical Soc. Papers, v.36, p. 8-12. Shows conclusively he did not see report on prison conditions by Co. Chandler.

252 ..."The Sequel of Appomattox; a chronicle of the reunion of states." New Haven: Yale Univ. Press, 1919. half-title: Chronicles of America Ser. Allen Johnson, Edt., v.32, Abraham Lincoln Edt. 12mo, cl, ix, 322pp. front, ports. Reprints: 1920-"Graduate Edt.", 1921-"Roosevelt Edt." and "Text-book Edt."

253 ...Chicago: "The Dial: A Fortnightly Journal of Literary Criticism, Discussion and Info. 1904-1915, articles by Fleming in:

254 ..."The Seaboard Slave States." Oct. 1, 1904, XXXVII, #439, p. 203-205.

255 ..."Negro Slavery in Illinois." Nov. 16, 1904, XXXVII, #442, p. 307-310.

256 ..."A Woman's Reminiscences of Peace and War." Jan. 16, 1905. XXXVIII, #446, p. 43-44.

257 ..."Southern Life in War Time." May 16, 1905, XXXVIII, #454, p. 347-349.

258 ..."War-Time Memoirs of a Confederate Daughter." Nov. 1, 1905, XXXIX, #465, p. 269-270.

259 ..."After the War in Dixie." Nov. 1, 1906. XLI, #489, p. 274-276.

260 ..."War Memories of a Confederate Leader." June 1, 1907, XLII, #503, p. 332-335.

261 ..."The South Since the War." Nov. 1,1907, XLIII, #513, p. 281-282.

262 ..."The Negro Problem Viewed Across the Color Line: May 16, 1910, XLVIII, #574, p. 357-359.

263 ..."The Problem of the South: An English View." Sept. 1, 1910, XLIX, #581, p. 114-114.

264 ..."Slave Holding Indians in the Civil War." Sept. 16, 1915, LIX, #701, p. 216-218.

265 ..."Conscription and Exemption in Alabama during the Civil War, contained in the Gulf States Historical Magazine." Birmingham, Ala., 1904, wraps, 8vo, 16pp. $5.

266 **FLETCHER, Duncan U.**
"The cause was not entirely lost." In: CV, 1932, v.40, p. 8-13. Speech of Senator, US Congress (Florida) before UDC Convention at Jacksonville, Fla., Nov. 19, 1931.

267 **FLETCHER, Elliott H., Capt.**
"The Civil War Letters of...of Mill Bayou, Mississippi County, Arkansas. July-Dec., 1861." Transcribed and edited by J.H. Atkinson, 1963. Little Rock, Ark., Pulaski County Hist. Society. #5 Bulletin Series, April, 1963. 4to, cover title, memo, 37pp. $14-bmk, $.50. Also: Ar. Hist. Qurt.,1963, v.XXII, p. 48-54.

268 **FLETCHER, Henry Charles, Lt.-Col.**
"History of the American War." London: Richard Bentley, 1865-1866. 8vo, 3-vols: (16), 454; xi, (1), 446; xiii, (1), 549pp. 20-plates, 7-maps. Sabin-24722 differs from Howes in maps. ('61) E 7/10s.

269 **FLETCHER, Joshua C.**
"Complete roll of Company A, Seventh Virginia Cavalry, ANV." In: SHSP, 1907, v.35, p. 335-340. (from Richmond Times-Dispatch, July 8, 1906)

270 **FLETCHER, Susan**
"An Arkansas Lady in the Civil War. Reminiscences of Susan Fletcher. Edt. by Mary P. Fletcher." In: AHQ, 1943, v.II, p. 369-374.

271 **FLETCHER, William Andrew**
"Rebel Private Front and Rear, experiences and observations from the early fifties and through the Civil War by W.A. Fletcher." Beaumont, Texas: Greer Print, 1908. thin 8vo, decr., port, cl, 193pp. $50, $60, $75, $87.50. Many copies show smoke damage, others destroyed in fire. Author a member of Hood's Brigade. $1400-ob. $750-full leather, $250, $850, $1000-b.

...Austin, Texas, University of Texas Print, 1954. Preface: Bell I. Wiley. 8vo, cl, dj, 2-ports, xvii, 162pp. $25, $45.

...Louisv: Lost Cause Pr., micro-cd $3.86.

...Fletcher (Vallie)-"Biographical Sketch of William A. Fletcher, author of "Rebel Private." Beaumont, Texas: Lamp Print, 1950. 8vo, wraps, 27pp. $7.50.

272 **"FLIGHT at Pocotaligo, The"**
Circular, An answer by "A", to an article. In: Savannah Republican, Oct. 31, 1862, and relates the battle in which Henry Bauist, Capt. of Co. O, Abney's Battalion, takes offense for bringing his command in unfavorable notice. The Buist letter is printed at bottom and dates Bees Creek Hill, S.C., Nov. 11, 1862. 1pp. circular. not in Crandall $25. Note: Henry S. Tafft, late Cap., Signal Corps USA, relates this skirmish in Reminiscences "Soldiers and Sailors Hist. Soc., RI, 6th Ser. #3, in 1903.

273 **FLINT, Roy Kenneth**
"The Battle of Missionary Ridge." University, Alabama. 1960. Thesis, partial requirements MA Degree, Dept. History. 4to, soft back, maps, fldg. plan, print on ne side, mimeographed, 209pp. $10.

274 **FLIPPIN, Percy Scott**
"Herschel V. Johnson of Georgia State Rights Unionist." Richmond, Va., Dietz Print, 1931. 8vo, cl, xvi, 336pp. $30-bmk. Held high office in the Confederacy.

275 **FLOOD, Charles Bracelen**
"Lee the Last Years." Bost: Houghton-Mifflin Co., 1981. 8vo, cl, dj, x, (1), 308pp. notes, bibliog. (265-308) ports, illus. $15.

276 **FLORANCE, John E., Jr.**
"Morris Island: Victory or Blunder?" In: SCHM, July, 1955, v.LV, 10pp., p. 143-152. Argues Union forces should have moved on James Island approaching Charleston in 1863, or enter harbor by sea.

277 **FLORIDA ,**
"Constitution or form of government for the people of Florida, as revised and amended at a Convention of the people begun and holden at the City of Tallahassee Jan. 3, 1861, together with the ordinances adopted by said convention, Tallahassee: Office of Floridian and Journal. Printed by Dyke & Carlisle, 1861." 8vo, sewn, 68pp. $400-jk-127.

278 ..."Florida in the Civil War-1860 through Reconstruction. Edited: Alan J. Rick." Pensacola, Fla., Civil War Round Table 1961. 4to, wraps, illus., maps, 4, 66 leaves.

279 ..."Florida A Hundred Years Ago." Edt: Samuel Proctor. Coral Gables, Fla: Civil War Centennial Commission, 1960-1966. Dec. 1960, monthly thru June 1965, an Index, April 1966. 4to, punched for binder, average (4)pp. some (6) Index, (20)pp. total (238)pp.

280 **FLORIDA Brigade-Gettysburg.**
See: Francis P. Fleming.

281 **"FLORIDA Old Confederate Soldiers and Sailors Hom...Information and Facts."**
(Tallahassee, Fla., 1926) sm.4to, stiff wraps, (28)pp. Other copies in 1928 and 1929.

282 **"FLORIDA in War Times, Rosters of units..."**
See: Rowland H. Rerick. 2 vols.

283 **"FLORIDA in the Confederacy."**
In: Roland H. Rerick's "Memories of Florida." v.1, Chap. IX, p. 237-285. Edt: Francis P. Fleming. (most likely author.) See: Fleming, Atlanta, Ga., Southern Hist. Assn.

284 **FLORIDA-Secession Convention**
"Documents relating to Secession in Florida." (Jacksonville) Fla. Hist. Quart., April, 1926, v.IV, #4, p. 183-191. Sketch of John C. McGehee, pres. of the Fla. Secession Convention. See: Dorothy Dodd.

285 **FLORIDA: Acts**
"Acts and Resolutions adopted by the General Assembly at it's 10th Session." Tallahassee, Fla., 1861. 8vo, sewn, xiii, 242, xiv pp. $45. One act provides for "representation of this state in the Southern Confederacy". Not in Crandall.

286 **FLORY, Claude R.**
"The Odessey of John Calvin Peck: Georgia Yankee." In: Ga.Rev., Spring, 1961. 20pp. $8.

287 **FLOURNEY, H.W. Edt.**
"Calendar of Va. State Papers..." N.Y., Kraus Reprint Co., 1968.

288 **FLOURNOY, F.**
"Address on Lee Anniversary." Lexington, 1931. 8vo, wraps, 12pp.

289 **FLOURNOY, George M.**
"An unofficial account of the Battle of Wilson Creek, Aug. 10, 1861. Edt: Willard E. Wight." In: Ark. Hist. Quart., 1956, v.XV, p. 360-364.

290 **FLOURNOY, George, Col. CSA**
"Our beloved commander; tribute of respect to the memory of Col. G.F. by surviving officers and soldiers of his regiment." (Austin, Texas: s.n., 1889?) Broadside: 32cm. Sig: Will Lambert, Sec.

291 **FLOURNOY, Henry Wood**
"Address before Pegram Battalion Ass'n." In: SHSP, 1886, v.14, p. 26-28.

292 ..."Calendar of Virginia State Papers, and other misc., from Jan. 1, 1836-Arp. 15, 1869, preserved in the capitol at Virginia." Richmond: 1893. 4to, boards, vol. XI- (CSA, pp. 100-440)

293 **FLOURNOY, Mary H.**
"Essays: Historical and critical." Baltimore: The Norman, Remington Co. (1928). 8vo, cl, 96pp. $3, $4. Twin Patriots: Washington and Lee, Stratford Hall, Raphael Semmes, Mosby's Rangers, et al.

294 ..."Side lights on southern history." Richmond, Va., Dietz Press, 1939. 8vo, cl, plates, ports, (14), 259pp. $3, $6.50, $25, $15-nc. Largely of phases southern hist. before war.

295 ..."Twin Patriots: Washington and Lee." Baltimore: Norman Print, 1929. $4.50.

296 **FLOURNOY, William Cabell, Mrs.**
"The South's contribution to medical science." In: CV, 1931, v.39, p. 48-52.

297 **FLOWERS, George Washington, Lt.-Col.**
"The Thirty-eighth N.C. Regiment. Its history in the Civil War. Lieut.-Col. George W. Flowers, of this regiment, writes its splendid record in the Army of Northern Virginia-its officers-a carefully written and valuable addition to the State's War history. (From: Charlotte Observ., Mar. 31, 1895)." In: SHSP, 1897, v.XXV, p. 245-263.

298 **FLOWERS, Robert L.**
"Fort Hamby on the Yadkin." In: SHSP, 1895, v.23, p. 266-273.

299 **FLOYD, Dale E.**
"Paper in the Confederacy; or, the Soldier's Search for Stationery." "Prologue", Fall, 1972, p. 173-176.

300 **FLOYD, John Buchanan**
"The Battle of Ft. Donelson, a Report of General Floyd." In: Tenn. Hist. Mag.,

1919, v.V, p. 152-155. (From: Daily Natl. Patriot, Mar. 26, 1862.)

301 ..."Capture of Fort Donelson." In: Confed. War Jour., 1893, v.I, p. 116-117, 119-126, port, illus.

302 ..."Simon P. Buckner." In: Confed. War. Jour., 1893, v.I, p. 130-133, 135-138. See: R.F. Gross and T.J.Riddle.

303 **FLOYD, John Buchannan, Maj.-Gen.**
See: R.F. Gross, T.J. Riddle.

304 **FLOYD, Nicholas Jackson**
"The Last Cavaliers; or, The Phantom Peril. A historical romance with the cause and conduct of the war between the sections of American Union." New York: Broadway Pub. Co., (c.1904) 12mo, cl, xi, 427pp., front(port) plates. preface dated, Lynchburg. Swem-1787.

305 ..."Thorns in the Flesh. A romance of the war and Ku Klux periods. A voice of vindication from the South in answer to "A Fools Errand" and other slanders." Lynchburg, Va., J.P. Bell, 1884. 8vo, cl, front, 607pp. $6, $12.50, $15.

306 **FLOYD, Viola Caston**
"The Fall of Charleston." In: SCHM, 1965, v.66, #1, p. 1-7.

307 **FLUKER, Anne and Winifred**
"Confed'ric Gol." Macon, Ga., J.W. Burke Co., 1926, 12mo, decr. cl, front, xii, (13)-140pp. $5, $10.

308 ..."Confederate Gold. Intro: Richard Harwell." Macon, Ga., Tullous Books, 1984. 12mo, cl, dj, xii, (3)pp. facsms of 1926 edt. (2)pp., (9)-140pp. $11.
..."Confederate Gold." Macon, Ga., Tullous Books, 1984. 8vo, cl, 140pp. illus. $11.

309 **"FLUVANNA County Sketchbook, 1777-1963**
facts and fancies of Fluvanna County in the Commonwealth of Virginia. Dedicated to the citizens of the County of Fluvanna; a memorial to the past, a challenge to the present, a guide to the future. A project of Fluvanna Civil War Commission, 1961-1965." (Richmond: Whittet & Shepperson, 1963). 8vo, decr. stiff wraps, illus., maps, 111pp.

310 **FLYNT, Wayne**
"Southern Higher Education and the Civil War." In: CWH, September, 1968, v.XIV, #3, p. 211-225.

311 ..."The Texas Legion at Vicksburg." In: ETHJ, 1979, v.XVII, #1, p. 60-67.

312 **FOGEL, Robert W. and Stanley L. Engerman**
"Explaining the relative efficiency of slave agriculture in the Antebellum South." In: Amer. Eco. Rev., June, 1977, v.67, p. 275-296.

313 **FOLEY, Gardner P.H.**
"Adalbert Volck, dentist and artist (1828-1912)." In: Amer. College of Dentists, Jour., 16:60-16:66pp. June 1949. On his dentistry and painter in Baltimore, CSA cartoonist, his early life in Germany.

314 **FOLK, Winston**
"The Confederate States Naval Academy." In: USN Inst. Proc., 1934, v.LX, p. 1235-1240.

315 ..."A treasure hunt in reverse." In: USN Inst. Proc., 1937, v.LXIII, p. 380-386. Efforts of CSA officers and midshipmen to find a secure place for CSA Tres. gold, following evacuation of Richmond in '65.

316 **FOLKES, Joseph E.**
"The Confederate Grays." Richmond, Va., 1947. 8vo, wraps, 34pp. 25 copies printed. Intro: Kate Folkes Minor.

317 **FOLKES, Thomas M.**
"Mississippi Troops who served in Virginia 1861-1865." In: SHSP, 1907, v.35, p. 58-59.

318 **FOLMAR, John Kent**
"The war comes to Central Alabama, Ebenezer Church, April 1, 1865." In: AHQ, 1964, v.XXVI, p. 187-202, map.

319 **FOLSOM, James Madison**
"Heroes and Martyrs of Georgia. Georgia's Record in the Revolution of 1861." Macon, Ga., Burke, Boykin Co., 1864. 8vo, cl, 164pp., v.1 (all printed) Ga. Vols., 17 units at Petersburg, with short sketches.

320 **FOLSOM, Montgomery M.**
"Scraps of Songs and Southern Scenes, a collection of humorous poems and descriptive sketches of plantation life in the backwoods of Georgia." Atlanta: C.P. Byrd, 1889. 12mo, cl, iii, (2)-199pp., port, pl. LC $10.

321 **FOLSOM, William R.**
"Robert E. Lee: an appreciation. Vermonters in Battle and other papers." Montpelier: Vermont Historical Soc., 1953, p. 141-172.

322 **FONDE, Charles H.**
"An account of the great explosion of the U.S. Ordnance stores, which occurred (!) in Mobile, 25th May, 1865. Together with the proceedings of the principal sufferers and an appeal to the U.S. Gov., for indemnity." Mobile, Ala., H. Farrow & Co., 1869. 8vo, wraps, 12pp., 50, (2)pp. plan.

323 **FONER, Philip S.**
"Business and Slavery: The New York Merchants and the Irrepressible Conflict." Chapel Hill: Univ. of N.C. Press, 1941. 8vo, cl, dj, bibliog., ix, 356pp. $4, $15.

324 **FONERDEN, Clarence Albert**
"A brief history of the military career, Carpenter's Battery..." Gaithersburg, Md., Butternut Press, 1983. $15.
..."A Brief History of the Military Career of Carpenter's Battery, from its organization as a rifle company under the name of the Allegheny Roughs to the ending of the War Between the States." New Market, Va., Henkel Print, 1911. $350-bmk-111, $500-ob, $175-bmk. 12mo, wraps, 3-pls., 78pp. $65, $67.50, $75.
...Louisv: Lost Cause Pr., micro-card.

325 ..."Carpenter's Battery of the Stonewall Brigade." In: SHSP, 1900, v.XXVIII, p. 166-168.

326 **FONTAINE, Clement R., Colonel**
"A complete roster of the field and staff officers of the 57th Virginia Reg. of Infantry during the Civil War, including commissioned and non-commissioned officers." n.p., n.d., 8vo, wraps, cover title, 25pp.

327 ..."Resolutions adopted by the officers and men of the 57th Virginia regiment." (Richmond, Va.) House of Representatives, Jan. 30, 1865. 8vo, 2pp. folder.

328 **FONTAINE, Francis**
"Etowah. A Romance of the Confederacy." Atlanta, Ga., Francis Fontaine, 1887. 12mo, cl, viii, 522 (i.e., 524)pp. $10, $12, $15, $20.

329 **FONTAINE, Lamar**
"My Life and My Lectures." New York: Neale Pub. Co., 1908. 8vo, cl, port (front) 361pp. $18, $25, $27.50, $35, $45, $125-aldr., $50, $175-bmk-105, $225-b. Nearly all on the Confederacy.

330 ..."A Short Discourse on Causes of Lincoln Invasion and Bloody Conquest of the South." Lyon, Mass., 1909, 8vo, front, 30pp.

331 ..."The Prison life of Maj. Lamar Fontaine, one of the immortal six-hundred Confederate officers, prisoners of war, on prison ship Crescent City on Morris Island, Ft. Pulaski and Hilton Head, S.C., 1864-1865. Dedicated to Capt. J.W. Mathews, 25th Va. Inf. CSA." Clarksdale, Miss., Daily Register, 1910, 8vo, cl, port, 60pp.

332 **FONTAINE, William Winston**
"The descent of General R.E. Lee from King Robert the Bruce of Scotland." In: SHSP, 1881, v.9, p. 193-206.

333 **FONTANE, M. Marius**
"La Guerre d'Amerique recit d'un soldat du sud por..." 2 vols. Paris: Adrien le

Clerc, C. Dillet, n.d., 12mo, 1/2 lt., Marb. Bds., or/wraps (title on covers) Map (fldg.) at end, has date 1863, p. (3), 304, (2), 265. (8)pp. ads, at end. Also 2 vol. in I (1/2 Mor.) 2 vol. set (1860) and 1870) $20, $25, $28.50. Served under Lee. $100, $150-ob.

334 **FOOTE, Frank H.**
"A condensed report of the Annals of Claiborne County, Mississippi soldiers of the War 1861-1865." (n.p.) May 1, 1914. 8vo, wraps, cover title, 18pp.

335 ..."Recollections of Army Life with General Lee. (From: New Orleans Picayune, Sept. 20, 1903)." In: SHSP, 1903, v.31, p. 237-247.

336 ..."A roster of departed comrads, buried in the several cemeteries of Port Gibson, Claiborne County, State of Mississippi, from Apr. 1861 to date, May 1, 1917, and command in which they served." (n.p., 1917) 16mo, 12pp.

337 **FOOTE, Henry Stuart**
"Casket of Reminiscences." Washington, D.C., Chronicle Pub. Co., 1874. 8vo, decr., cl, 498pp. $20, $55, $150-bmk-105. As CSA senator, met many leading men and their impressions.

338 ..."War of the Rebellion; or, Scylla and Charybdis. Consisting of observations upon the causes, course, consequences of the late Civil War in the United States." N.Y., Harper & Bros., 1866. 12mo, xii, (13)-440pp., front(port).

339 **FOOTE, Shelby**
"The Civil War. A Narrative. Fort Sumter to Perryville." New York: Random House (1958). 1st. 8vo, cl, d/w, color endsheets (map), maps, 840pp. $4, $12.50, $10. 7th Printing. $20., v.II-"Fredericksburg to Meridian." Do. (1963), 988pp. $6, $12.50, $20. 3 vol., $60-nc, $25 ea., $15.

340 ..."Shiloh, a Novel." N.Y., Dial Press, 1952, 12mo, cl, dj, 226pp. $15, $8. See: James M. Cox.

341 **"FOR LOVE of a Rebel."**
Mrs. Viola Parish Olin, Chm., UDC, Arthur Manigault Chap. #63, Georgetown, S.C. (Charleston, S.C., Walker, Evans & Cogswell, 1964.) 8vo, cl, illus., part color, x, 212pp. $40. History of Georgetown during the war, muster rolls of their soldiers in several regiments, ANV, Wade Hampton, in west under Bragg and Hood. See: Mary W. Erickson.

342 **"FOR PRESIDENT, Jefferson Davis,**
of Mississippi. For Vice-President, A.H. Stephens, of Georgia." n.p., 1861, Crandall-2744. $125-jkn. Broadside-17.4x11.6cm. $200-bmk-114.

343 **FORBES, John Murray**
"Observations on affairs in the South in the Spring of 1865 (as given in a letter to his wife)." In: Gulf SHM, Jan. 1903, v.I, p. 285-287.

344 **FORD, Arthur P. and Marion Johnstone**
"Life in the Confederate Army; being personal experiences of a private soldier in the Confederate Army by A.P. Ford, an some experiences and sketches of Southern Life by Marion Johnstone Ford." N.Y. & Wash., Neale Pub. Co., 1905. 12mo, cl, 2-ports (incl. front) 136pp. $50-y, $75, $90, $150.

345 ..."The Last Battles of Hardee's Corps." In: SB, v.1, #3, 1885/1886, p. 140-143.

346 ..."Service on the Carolina Coast." In: SB, 1885/1886, v.1, #6, p. 325-327.

347 **FORD, Arthur Peronneau**
"The Last Battle of Hardee's Corp." In: So. Biv., 1885, ns, v.I, p. 140-143.

348 **FORD, Edsel**
"Return to Pea Ridge. Seven Poems." Rogers, Ark., May 31, 1963. 8vo, wraps, 16pp. (Lincoln, Ark., Leader.)

349 **FORD, Elizabeth Austin**
"Georgia churches and the War Between the States." In: UDCM, Jan. 1951, v.14, #1, p. 16, 18.

350 **FORD, Harvey S.**
"Van Dorn and the Pea Ridge Campaign." Amer. Mil. Inst. Journ., III (1939) maps, p. 222-236. Acct. of CSA Gen. Earl Van Dorn and Pea Ridge Campaign, 1862.

351 **FORD, John J., Jr.**
"The Confederate Cent." In: Coin Collectors Jour., Jan./Feb., 1851, v.18, p. 9-14. Facsms. A copper-nickel coin struck by Robt. Lovvett, Jr., Phila., 1861, but not adopted by CSA.

352 **FORD, John Salmon**
"Rip Ford's Texas. Edt: Stephen B. Oates." Austin, Texas: Univ. Press (1963). 8vo, cl, dj, port, illus., xlviii, 519pp. $7.50. p. (313)-407, relate to his services in the CSArmy.

353 **FORD, Lewis De Saussure, M.D., LL.D.**
"In Memoriam, 1801-1883. The Confederate Survivors' Association to their late Comrad..., Surgeon, C.S.A." Augusta, Ga., 1884. 8vo, wraps, 8pp. $10.

354 **FORD, Mark, Edt.**
"The Brandenburg Story, with particular reference to the John Hunt Morgan crossing of the Ohio, July 8, 1863. Prepared for the Centennial Celebration being held in Brandenburg, July, 1963. Prepared for the Centennial Celebration being held in Brandenburg, July 1963, by the Methodist Men's Club, Brandenburg, Ky." (Brandenburg, Ky., Centennial Booklet Committee, (1963). 8vo, wraps, port, illus., dbl-map, 22pp.

355 **FORD, Noah P.**
"Wade Hampton's Strategy. An attack on Richmond foiled. Kilpatrick and Dahlgren, with 4000 cavalry, were planning to take the almost defenseless city, burn it and kill the President and Cabinet." (From: Daily Charlotte, N.N., Observer, Apr. 7, 1895) In: SHSP, 1896, v.XXIV, p. 278-284. Ford was Capt. Co. F., 1st N.C. Cavalry.

356 **FORD, Sally Rochester**
"Raids and Romance of Morgan and His Men, by Sally Rochester Ford, author of "Grace Truman", "Mary Bunyan", etc. Reprinted from the Mobile Edition." N.Y., Chas. B. Richardson, 1864. 12mo, cl, port(front) 386pp., Appendix, (2), 389-417. $40-bmk, $20, $25.
...Same, Edts., 1865, 1866, $5 (old), $4, $75. The Mobile, 1864 edition, 332pp., wallpaper, wraps, verso "addenda", is supplement to 1st edt., imprisonment, escape of Morgan and is the 2nd Edt., since there is no known copy of the 1st (1863) of 319pp., also with wallpaper wraps. Harwell quotes review from "Southern Field and Fireside", n.s., I, (1863), 143. Copyright (Ala.), Apr. 13, 1863. Copies: Mobile, 1864, $30, $45, $87.50.

357 **FORD, W.S., Alabama**
See: "Compilation of Records Corresp., Muster Rolls." under title.

358 **FORE, James A., Mrs.**
"Cabinet Meeting in Charlotte." In: SHSP, 1916, v.41, p. 61-67. Davis authorizes Johnston to surrender.

359 **FOREIGN PUBLIC OPINION of the C.S.A.**
See: Percy Greg, Henri Martin.

360 **FOREIGN RELATIONS of the C.S.A.**
See: J.P. Benjamin, Jas. D. Bulloch, J.W. Du Bose, C.H. Giddings, R.M.T. Hunter, J.P. Holcome, James Lyons, Prince de Polignac.

361 **FOREIGN SUPPLIES, Bureau of. CSA**
"Report of the Bureau of Foreign Supplies CSA." In: SHSP, 1876, v.2, p. 103-105.

362 **FOREMAN, Carolyn Thomas**
"Lieutenant-General Theophilus Hunter Holmes, C.S.A. Founder of Fort Holmes."

Oklahoma City: Chron. Okla., Winter 1957, v.XXXV, #4, p. 425-534, port.

364 ..."John Gunter and his family." In: AHQ, 1949, v.9, #3, p. 412-452.

365 **FOREMAN, Grant**
"The Centennial of Fort Gibson." In: Ch. Okl., June 1924, v.II, p. 119-128. Descp. defenses and bldg. of fort during the Civil War.

366 ..."Fort Davis." In: Ch. Okl. June, 1939, v.XVII, p. 147-150. Existed only three years, relation of its activities during the war.

367 ..."The trial of Stand Watie." In: Chron. Ok., 1934, v.XII, p. 305-339. With article by Geo. W. Paschal on a trial (1843) of Watie, a Cherokee.

368 **FORMAN, Benjamin Rice**
"The Confederate Prisoners in Northern Prisons During the War." (n.p., n.d.), 189, wraps, 8vo, 19pp. also in Louisville, Ky: Lost Cause Press, Micro-card $2.45.

369 ..."The Confederate Prisoners in Northern Prisons During the War." n.p., 189-, 8vo, wraps, 19pp. See: Frances Terry Ingmire.

370 **FORMBY, John**
"The American Civil War. A concise history of its causes, progress and results." N.Y., Chas. Scribner's Sons, 1910. 8vo, cl, xiii, 1, (xv)-xvii, 520pp. Atlas: 2pl., 66 maps on 50 fold. pl.

371 **FORNELL, Earl**
"Sam Houston's defiance of the secessionists." In: Frontier Times, Oct./Dec., 1954, v.31, p. 433-438. On speech by Houston 19 Arp., 1861, at Galveston, with excerpts from Wm. Pitt Ballinger's diary of a conversation with Houston. (See: Guy M. Bryan)

372 **FORNELL, Earl Wesley**
"The Galveston Era-The Texas Crescent on the Eve of Secession." Austin: University of Texas Press, (1961). 8vo, cl, dj, decr. endsheets, xiv, 355pp. $35.

373 ..."Mobile During the Blockade." Ala. Hist. Quart., Spring, 1961. v.23, #1 and 2; p. 29-43, illus.

374 ..."Confederate Seaport Strategy." Civil War Hist., II-(Dec. 1956, p. 61-68.)

375 ..."The Civil War comes to Savannah." Ga. Hist. Quart., (Sept. 1959), p. 247-160.

376 **FORNEY, John H., Maj. Gen.**
"Historical data on Maj.-Gen. John H. Forney, CSA. Assembled by the Gen. John H. Forney Historical Society." v.I, (1961). n.p., n.d. (Anniston, Ala., Public Library?) 4to, stiff wraps, contents (1), (7)-Fifth Annual meeting at Vicksburg, (4)-program, (30), (1)-map, (46), ports, facsm., news articles, (89)pp. printed largely on one side sheet. $40. See: Annie Forney Daugette.

377 **FORREST, Douglas French**
"Odyssey in Gray: a diary of Confederate service, 1863-1865. Edt: Wm. M. Still, Jr." Richmond, Virginia State Library, 1979. 8vo, cl, xii, 352pp. $15.

378 **FORREST, Douglas French, CSN**
"An Odyssey in Gray, selections from a diary of Confederate naval life with the C.S.S. Rappahannock." In: VaCavl., Winter, 1980, v.XXIX, #3, p. 124-129, illus., ports.
..."Odyssey in Gray: a diary of Confederate Service, 1863-1865. Wm. N. Still, Jr., Editor." Richmond, Va., State Library, 1979, 8vo, cl, illus. ix, 352pp. $15.

379 **FORREST, Nathan Bedford**
"As General Forrest used to say..." In: Sewanee Review, April, 1944, v.52, p. 280-287. "Forrest's Own Words." In: Robt. S. Henry's-"As they saw Forrest", p. 286-299. Several Forrest letters (facsms.) and his farewell to his troops. (facsm.) with emphasis on his carthography.

380 ..."Short History of Gen. N.B. Forrest." Park Place, N.Y., Knapp & Co., 1888. 3/4x1 1/2" colored booklet, 16pp. facsm.

	signature. Packed in Duke's cigarettes.) See: "Heroes of the Civil War." and W. Duke & Sons.
381	..."Gunboats and Cavalry. A Story of Forrest's 1864 Johnsonville Campaign, as told to: J.P. Pryor and Thomas Jordan. Edt-reprinted: E.F. Williams, H.K. Humphreys. Memphis, Tenn: Nathan Bedford Forrest Trail Committee, 1965. 8vo, wraps, illus., maps, 24pp., port. $15-bmk-84, $2, $5, $8-bmk.
382	...Forrest Monument Association-"The Forrest Monument; its history and dedication; a memorial in art, oratory and literature." Memphis, Tenn., 1905. 8vo, wraps, 4pp. (13)-95pp., pl., 2 ports, incl. front.
383	..."How Forrest won over Streight." In: CV, Aug., 1912, v.20, p. 380-381.
384	..."Pursuit and capture of Col. Streight." In: CV, Jan. 1928, v.36, p. 15-18; v.35, Dec. 1927, p. 452-454. See: Dabney H. Maury, Rucker Agee, John A. Wyeth.
385	..."Lieutenant-General N.B. Forrest." In: LWL, Aug., 1866, v.1, #4, p. 268-275. Sig. at end "W.H.B."
386	..."Memorial Edition Print, issued by Sons of Confederate Veterans." 24x30". Signed on $20-Signed and numbered, $30-Proceeds from print sales to procure bronze bust of Forrest to be placed in state capitol.
387	...Lithographic portrait by J.L.Giles. N.Y., Geo. E. Perine Pub. (c.1864) Tinted, 23x17 1/2". $15. Half-length, uniform, bearded.
388	..."Portrait from an original oil by Joy Garner. 24x30, signed, $20-(numbered Edt., $30)-Nashville, Tenn., Forrest Bust Comm., to erect a bronze in State Capital, issued by Sons of CSA Veterans. Portrait, in color, reproduced from a Joy Garner's can vas. 24x30". Commissioned by the Gen. Joseph E. Johnston Camp #28, SCV, proceeds of which to erect a bronze statue of Forrest in the state capitol. Signed, $30.
389	..."Report of: operations against Smith and Grierson, 1864." In: SHSP, 1880, v.8, p. 567-568. (See: Leonidas Polk)
390	..."Report of operations in Dec. 1863." In: SHSP, 1880, v.8, p. 40-41.
391	..."Report of operations against W. Sooy Smith in Feb., 1864." v.8, p. 9-14. See: Dan W. Beard, Jas. R. Chalmers, James Denkins, Thos. F. Gailor, Dabney H. Maury, Jno. W. Morton, Viscount Wolseley., Rev. W.H. Whitsitt.
392	..."Maj.-Gen. N.B. Forrest's address to his command (caption title)." Tupelo, Miss., June 28, 1864. Broadside: 16 1/4x12". Goodspeed $2000. Unrecorded. Recounts victories: West Point. Fort Pillow and Brices Cross Roads.
393	**FORREST, Thomas Frank** "An Old Soldier's Career, his four long years experience, trials and sufferings in the bloody conflict of the sixties, between the states, as related by himself, by T. Frank Forrest, Confederate Veteran, Company "H", 14th N.C. Regiment." (Stewart, Miss., 1906). 8vo, wraps, caption title, (10)pp.
394	**FORRESTER, Izola** "This One Mad Act...The unknown story of John Wilkes Booth and his family, by his granddaughter Izola Forrester." Bost: Hal, Cushman & Flint, 1937. 8vo, cl, illus., ports (incl. front) xii, 500pp. $17.50, $20-bmk.
395	**FORRESTER, Rebel C.** "Glory and Tears Obion County, Tennessee, 1860-1870." Union City, Tenn., H.A. Lanzer Co. (1966). 12mo, cl, color front, illus., maps, ports, facsms., Muster Rolls, 222pp. $15, $30-bmk. Reprint: (p. 169-222) John Cavanaugh's Confederate Record, Hist. Sketch Obion Avalanche, Co. H, 9th Tenn. Inf., (see: author)

396 **FORSTER, Henry A.**
"Did the decision in the Dred Scott case lead to the Civil War?" In: Amer. Law Rev., Nov. 1918, v.LII, p. 875-884.

397 **FORSYTH, Charles**
"Official Report of Gettysburg." In: SHSP, 1885, v.13, p. 176-177. Was Lt. Col., 3rd. Ala. Reg.

398 **FORSYTH, Charles, Col.**
"History of the Third Alabama Regiment, CS. Introduction and Edited by William Stanley Hoole together with Pvt. Henry Hotze's Letters to the "Mobile Register", 1861 and a roster of the Third Regiment, 1861-1865." University, Ala., Confederate Pub. Co., 1987. Confederate Regiment Series, #12. 8vo, stiff wraps, 95pp. Forsyth's brief history was first published in Perry and Smith's Directory of the City of Montgomery, Ala., 1866, p. 56-63. Reprinted Montgomery Advertiser, June 19, 1902.

399 **FORT BEAUREGARD, Attack on**
See: Geo. Wm. Logan.

400 **FORT DELAWARE**
See: Wm. Owen, W.D. Reid.

401 **FORT DELAWARE, deaths of prisoners at...**
by B.F. Blackman." A list of Confederate dead between Sept. 9 and Oct. 24, 1863. In: CV, 1901, v.9, p. 545-547.

402 **FORT DONELSON**
"River Batteries at..., story of Terrific bombardment by Rev. Edward B. Ross and extracts from accounts by Gen. Lew Wallace." In: CV, Nov., 1896, v.IV, #11, p. 393-398. port, 2-plates.

403 **FORT DONELSON, Battle of**
See: H.L. Bedford, Richmond Dispatch

404 **FORT FISHER**
"Reunion of the survivors of Battles at the mouth of the Cape Fear-welcoming address of Maj. Devane and reply of Col. Lamb, etc." In: OLOD, Mar. 1876, v.4, #1, p. 100-107. See: Braxton Bragg and Col. Lamb.

405 **"FORT FISHER Restoration Committee.**
Colonel William Lamb Day, July 8, 1862-July 4, 1962." (Wilmington, N.C.), (1962) Confederate Centennial Committee. Large 8vo, cl, illus., maps, ports, 205pp.

406 **FORT FISHER, Battle of**
"A Yankee Account of the Battle of Fort Fisher, from Overland Monthly." In: OLOD, Dec. 1874, v.1, #4, p. 315-325. See: Braxton Bragg, William Lamb, Mrs. Wm. Lamb.

407 **FORT GILMER, Attack on**
See: Charles Johnston

408 **FORT GREGG, Battle of**
See: Napier Bartlett, Nathaniel H. Harris, A.K. Jones, James Henry Lane, New Orleans Picayune, Wm. Miller Owen, Geo. W. Richards, Cadmus M. Wilcox.
See: Napier Bartlett, Nathaniel H. Harris, A.K. Jones, Jas. Henry Lane, New Orleans Picayune, Wm. Miller Owen, Geo. W. Richards, Cadmus, Marcellus Wilcox.

409 **FORT HAMBY**
See: Robert L. Flowers.

410 **FORT HELL, Petersburg**
See under: "Story of Fort Hell, Fort Sedgwick."

411 **"FORT LA-FAYETTE LIFE."**
1863-1864, in extracts from the "Right flanker," a manuscript sheet circulating among the southern prisoners in Fort-la-Fayette, in 1863-1864." London, Simpson, Marshall & Col; Liverpool, E. Howell, 1865. 16mo, cl, g.e., v., (7)-102pp. fldg. facsm. paste in envp., with clipping from N.Y. Times, Oct. 7, 1861, giving names of prisoners. $22.50, $4, $5, $6, $7.50, $8.50, $18, $45-wantach, $200-bmk-105, $250-g.
...N.Y., Reprinted, W. Abbatt, 1911. The Magazine of History with notes and queries Extra number, no. 13, pt. 2. $20. Also found combined with Chs. C. Jones-

"Life and Services of Hon. Major-General Samuel Elbert, of Georgia, to which is added. Extracts from the Right Flanker, etc., etc., (37pp.) See also: John M. Brewer and Lawrence Sangston.

412 **FORT MCHENRY, Md.**
See: Thos. D. Witherspoon.

413 **"FORT MORGAN in the Confederacy."**
In: AHQ, 1946, v.7, #2, p. 254-268.

414 **FORT MORGAN, Attack on**
See: Richard L. Page.

415 **"FORT PILLOW revisited:**
new evidence about an old controversy. Edts: John Cimprich and Robert C. Mainfort, Jr." In: CWH, Dec. 1983, v.28, #4, p. (293)-306 notes. Largely Confederate soldier's letters about the encounter. See: Chs. W. Anderson, Albert Castel, James Ronald Chalmers, C. Fitch, Jno. L. Jordan, Thos. Jordan and Pryor's "Gen. Forrest."

416 **FORT PILLOW, Battle of**
See: C. Fitch.

417 **FORT PULASKI National Park**
See: Ralston B. Lattimore.

418 **"FORT STEADMAN'S Fall."**
In: CV, October 1914, v.XXII, p. 460-462. Reprint of article in Macon Georgia Telegraph, 1882.

419 **FORT STEDMAN, Assault on**
See: Jas. A. Walker.

420 **FORT SUMTER**
"Bombardment of Fort Sumter, Charleston Harbor." Lithograph 9x12. N.Y., Currier & Ives, 1861. Beauregard's bombardment of the Union Garrison, Oct. 12th. With, "Interior of Fort Sumter." $225.

421 **FORT SUMTER Memorial Commission,**
Charleston, S.C.-An Account of the Ft. Sumter Memorial." Charleston, S.C., The Commission, 1933. 8vo, wraps, 37pp., illus., ports. $5. Andrew B. Murray's bequest ($100) erect suitable monument to CSA dead.

422 **FORT SUMTER National Park**
See: Frank Barnes.

423 **FORT SUMTER, Capture of**
See: Charleston Courier, W.R. Davie, Wade Hampton Gibbes, Jno. A. Hamilton, Stephen Dill Lee, New York World, Richmond Times, Julian M. Ruffin, Iredell Jones.

424 **FORT TOWSON, Oklahoma**
"Final event of the Civil War Centennial. The surrender of Brig.-Gen. Stand Watie, CSA, June 23, 1865-June 23, 1965." (Durant, Okla., Southeastern State College) Fort Towson Commemoration Committee, Dorothy Orton. 12mo, stiff wraps, cover title, 19, (1)pp., double page plan.

425 **FORT, Dewitt Clinton**
"The Journal of a Civil War "Commando", Edt: Louis D. Bejach." In: W. Tenn. Hist. Soc. Pap., 1948, v.2, p. 5-32.

426 **FORT, John Porter**
"John Porter Fort, a memorial and personal reminiscences." N.Y., Knickerbocker Press, 1918. 12mo, cl, ports, facsms., 103pp. Rxp. as CSA soldier, p. 13-37, dictated to daughter, Martha.

427 **FORT, W.B.**
"First Submarine in the Confederate Navy." In: CV, Oct. 1918, v.XXVI, p. 459-460. Craft known as the "fish boat".

428 **FORTSON, Blanton**
"Robert E. Lee, the Soldier." In: Ga. Hist. Quart., 1926, v.X, p. 126-143. Review of Sir Fred. Maurice's Lee.

429 **FOSTER, G. Allen**
"Sunday in Centreville, the Battle of Bull Run, 1861." N.Y., David White, 1971. 8vo, cl, d/w, 166pp. $5.

429a **FOSTER, Gaines M.**
"Ghosts of the Confederacy: Defeat the Lost Cause, & the Emergence of the New South, 1865-1913." N.Y., Oxford University Press, 1987. 8vo, cl, dj, ills, 298pp. $30.

430 **FOSTER, Herbert Darling**
"Webster's seventh of March speech and the secession movement, 1850." In: Am. Hist. Rev., Jan. 1922, v.XXVII, p. 245-270. Reexams evidence of danger of secession and Webster's change of attitude and speech and its effects on attitude on the movement.

431 **FOSTER, Ira R.,** Quartermaster Gen., Georgia
"Annual Report for Fiscal Year ending Oct. 15, 1864." Milledgeville, Ga., Boughton, Nisbet, Barnes & Moore, 1864. 8vo, wraps, 23p. (cover title).

432 **FOSTER, John**
"Voyages of the Rebel "Alabama." In: Catholic Digest, 1864, v.XXVIII-viii, p. 97-101.

433 **FOSTER, John G.**
"The evacuation of Fort Moultrie, 1860. Edt: Frank F. White, Jr." In: SCHMag., Jan. 1952, v.53, p. 1-5, notes. Letter from capt. in charge to J.H.B. Latrobe, Jan. 10, 1861. Dated Ft. Sumter.

434 **FOSTER, John T.**
""Rebel Sea Raider Raphael Semmes." N.Y., W. Morrow Print, 1965. 8vo, cl, illus., 254pp., illus: Leonard E. Fisher. Juvenile Lit. $3.95.

435 **FOSTER, Samuel C.**
"We are prisoners of war. A Texan's account of the capture of Fort Hindman." In: CWTI, May 1977, v.16, #2, p. 24-33, illus., port.

436 **FOSTER, Samuel T.**
"One of Cleburne's Command: the Civil War Reminiscences and Diary of Capt. Samuel T. Foster, Granbury's Texas Brigade, C.S.A. Edt: Norman D. Brown." Austin, Texas, 1980, University of Texas Press. 8vo, cl, dj, Limited Edt., $15. xlvii, 192pp., illus., maps, drawings.

437 **FOSTER, William Lovelace**
"Vicksburg: Southern City under Siege." Edt: Kenneth Trist Urquhart. New Orleans, La., Historic New Orleans Collection, 1980. 8vo, cloth, 71pp. $15. Foster was pvt. Co. F., 35th Miss. Vols. Inf. Reg. While a Baptist preacher he did not become a chaplain until Feb. 1, 1863. Life of a CSA soldier in letters to his wife. (79pp. letter)

438 **FOUCHE, Rebecca S., Mrs. and I.D. Gaillard**
"Pen Pictures of Homes during and after the War." (Abbeville Distr., S.C., Saul and S.S. Marshall, Dr. J.P. Barrett) n.p., n.d. $6 (old). 8vo, stiff wraps, illus., 23pp., coat of arms.

439 **"FOUR ESSAYS on the right and propriety of Secession**
by Southern States by a Member of the Bar of Richmond, Virginia." pseud. Richmond: Ritch & Dunnavant, 1861. 8vo, wraps, 56pp., "printed before the secession of Virginia", Crandall-2783 gives author as James Lyons.

440 ...(Letters to the Enquirer, Sept., Oct., 1858, in regard to the political opinions of Stephen A. Douglas.) n.p., caption title, 8vo, sewn, 16pp.

441 **"FOURTH (4TH) ALABAMA Regiment, The**
at the Battle of Manassas." In: AHQ, 1961, v.XXIII, p. 208-210. From Huntsville Democrat, 7-31-61.

442 **FOUTE, Robert C., Rev.**
"Ministers, priests and chaplains of the Confederacy." In: UDCMag., Nov. 1952, v.15, #11, p. 18-19, port.

443 ..."The medical division of the CS War Dept." In: UDCMag. Oct., 1953, v.15, (10)pp., 21, 24, 34.

443a **FOWLER, John D.**
"Fowler the Soldier, Fowler the Marine, Edt. David M. Sullivan." In: CWTI, Feb. 1988, v. 26, #10, p.28-35, 44-45.

444 **FOWLER, Malcolm**
"Battle of Averasboro." oblong, decr. wraps, 12mo, illus., 18pp. N.C. Confed. Cent. Comm. on 100th Anniv. Battle of Averasboro, March 21, 1965.

445 **FOWLER, Nolan**
"Johnny Reb's impressions of Kentucky in the Fall of 1862." In: RKHS, Jan. 1950, v.48 (#164), p. 205-215.

446 **FOWLER, Robert H.**
"Jim Mundy, a novel of the American Civil War." N.Y., 1977, Harper & Row, (Hagerstown, etc.) 8vo, cl, dj, 470pp. Pbt. in 10th N.C. vols. $10, $15.

447 ..."Was Stanton behind Lincoln's murder?" In: CWT, Aug./Sept., 1961, v.III, #5, p. 4-23, illus., facsms., ports. The spy Baker left a coded message accused Stanton of the murder, poisoning him to keep him quiet. True? or a hoax?

448 **FOWLER, William Chauncy**
"The Sectional Controversy; Passages in the Political History of the U.S., including causes of the War Between the Sections, with certain results." New York: Charles Scribners, 1862. 8vo, cl, xii, 269pp. $17.50 O-MH, $6. Defends secession.
...Do: 1863-($2.50, $5, $12.50)
...Do: 1868-pp. 338 ($5.)

449 **FOX, Charles K., Edt.**
"Gettysburg." N.Y., 1969, 8vo, wraps, 89pp. $6-bmk-24. Reports of: Alexander Hunt and Inboden, excerpts from Fremantle's Diary.

450 **FOX, Frances Barton**
"Ridgeways, by Frances Renard (pseud.) N.Y. Stokes, 1934. 12mo, cl, 436pp. fiction. Three generations of Hardison family of Fairfax County, Ky., with Morgan.

451 **FOX, J.J.**
"The 27th North Carolina at Sharpsburg." Incl.-3rd Arkansas. Camden, S.C., The Author, 1985, 8vo, paper, 44pp., 5-maps.

452 **FOX, Joe**
"History of the Siege of Vicksburg and map of the Vicksburg National Military Park, showing Confederate and Union lines, avenue and locations of all memorials headquarters and camps." Vicksburg: Joe Fox, (1909) 16mo, wraps, cover title, fldg. map, 24pp.

453 **FOX, John A.**
"Public auction sale of Confederate Stamps and Covers, Oct. 29, 1949." 8vo, dec. wraps, 40pp., halftones illus., facsms. $7.50.

454 **FOX, John A., N.Y.**
"Auction of a stamp collection, Mar. 20, 1861." Charles F. Meroni, CSA stamps-8vo, illus., prices, 96, (4)pp.

455 **FOX, John Adam**
"The Capture of Jefferson Davis." (New York, 1964) cover title. Imp. 8vo, stiff wraps, ports, facsms, 40pp. $15-bmk. Story Davis' capture, papers: Benj. Pritchard.

456 **FOX, T.X.**
"Leaving West Virginia home for Dixie." In: Confed. Vet., May 1906, v.14, p. 215. Men from Harrison Co., join 17th Va. Cav.

457 **FOX, W.D.**
"Sam Davis: The Confederate Scout. A Drama." Nashville, Tenn., M.E. Church So., 1896. 16mo, cl, 88pp. $3.50

458 **"FRANCE-, LA**
Le Mexique et Les Etates Confederes." Paris: E. Dentu, 1863. Tall 8vo, wraps, 31pp. $50-jk-140. Sabin-25429.

459 **FRANCES, Mary (pseud.)**
See: Fanny Witherspoon Mason.

460 **FRANK Glenn**
"Being dead he yet speaks-Robert E. Lee, 1807-1870." In: Va. Jour. Educ., 1931, v.XXV, p. 211-215.

461 **FRANK, Fedora Small**
"Nashville Jewry during the Civil War." In: THQ.

462 **FRANK, Glenn**
"Being dead he yet speaks." In: Bul. Univ. Ga., v.31, #2a, 19pp.

463 **FRANK, John G.**
"Adolphus Heiman, architect and soldier." In: Tenn. Hist. Art., 1946, v.V, p. 35-37. $8-bmk.

464 **FRANK, Seymour J.**
"The Conspiracy to Implicate the Confederate Leaders in Lincoln's Assassination." (Cedar Rapids, Ia.) MVHR, March 1954. v.XL, #4, p. 629-656. $7.50

465 **FRANKE, Norman H.**
"Official and Industrial Aspects of Pharmacy in the Confederacy." In: Ga. H.Q., September 1958., V.XXXVII, #3, p. 175-187. ports.

466 ..."Pharmaceutical Conditions and Drug Supply in the Confederacy." Ga. H.Q., Dec. 1953, v.37, p. 287-298. $8.

467 ..."Medico-pharmaceutical conditions and drug supply in the Confederate States of America, 1861-1865." Ann Arbor: University Microfilms (17,311) 1956 (e.g., 1957) positive microfilm of typescript, xi, 287 lfs., facsms., ports, views, bibliog., Thesis-Univ. Wisconsin abstracted: Dissert. abstracts, v.17, p. 343-344. (Feb.)

468 ..."Pharmacy and Pharmacists in the Confederacy." In: Ga.H.Q., March 1954, v.XXXVIII, #1, p. 11-28. $8. See: E. Vernon Howell.

469 ..."Pharmaceutical Conditions and Drug Supply in the Confederacy." Madison, Wisconsin: American Institute of the History of Pharmacy, 1955. Contributions from the History of Pharmacy Department of the School of Pharmacy, University of Wisconsin, No. 3. 8vo, wraps, cover title, 2-ports, tables, favsm., 45, (3)pp. op $15.

470 **FRANKE, Norman H. and Laura Webb Stone**
"A History of the Association of Medical Officers of the Army and Navy of the Confederacy." In: Mil. Medicine, 1966, v.CXXXI, p. 321-334.

471 **FRANKLAND, Abraham Ephraim**
"Kronikals of the Times, Memphis, 1862. Edt: Maxwell Whiteman." In: Amer. Jew. Arch., Oct. 1957, v.IX, p. 83-127, ports, views, notes. Jew of Confed. sympathies.

472 **FRANKLIN, Charles H.**
"Study on Project of Publication, the War of the Rebellion." Wash., D.C., 1931. 8vo, cl, 485pp. $25-bmk. What pub. went thru to pub. War Rebell.

473 **FRANKLIN, John Hope**
"The Militant South, 1800-1861." Cambridge, Mass., Harvard University Press-Belknap Press, 1956. 8vo, cl, xvi, 317pp. Bibliog. $5.

474 **FRANKLIN, Robert M.**
"Battle of Galveston, Jan. 1, 1863." (Galveston, Tex: Galves News, 1911) 8vo, wraps, cover title, port, (2), 11pp. Address before Camp Magruder, UCV, Post 105, April 2, 1911. (100 copies) $20-y.

475 ...Galveston, Texas: San Luis Press, 1875. Introduction: Capt. Julius W. Jockusch, USN, (Ret.); Preface: Maury Darst, Galveston College. Limited, 750 copies, vi, 14pp. $4.50. Photos, illus., map. Intro: Capt. Julius W. Jackusch, preface: Maury Darst.

476 **FRANKLIN, Tenn.**
"Forty-fifth Anniversary at Franklin." In: CV, Jan. 1910, v.18, #1, p. 15-20, illus.

477 **FRANKLIN, Tennessee: Confederate Monument."**
In: CV, 1909, v.8, p. 5-15, ports, illus. Speech by Gen. John B. Gordon, Reminiscences by Capt. Henry H. Smith.

478 **FRANKS, Kenny A.**
"An Analysis of the Confederate Treaties with the Five Civilized Tribes." (Norman) Okla. Chronicles, Winter, 1972. v.XLIX, #4, p. 458-473.

479 ..."The Confederate States and the Five Civilized Tribes." July, 1973. Journal West, p. 439-454.

480 ..."The Implementation of the Confederate Treaties with the Five Civilized Tribes." (Norman) Chronicles of Okla., Spring, 1973, v.LI, #1, p. 21-33.

481 ..."Operations Against Opotheyahola, 1861." Mil. Hist. of Tex. and SoWest, v.X, #3, 1873, p. 187-196. Texas forces help keep Indian nation in the Confederacy's war on northern group.

482 ..."Stand Watie and the Agony of the Cherokee Nation." Mamphis, Tenn., State University Press, 1978, vii, (1979) $15. 8vo, cl, dj, photographs, 257pp. $13.
..."The career of Brigadier General Stand Watie." In: Confed. Vet., Mar./Apr., 1986, #2, p. 16-27, illus., map, ports (color port of Watie.

483 **FRANTZ, Mable Goode**
"Full many a name. The story of Sam Davis, Scout and Spy, C.S.A." Jackson, Tenn., Confederate House, 1961. (Jackson: McCowat-Mercer Press) 8vo, cl, endpapers, map, front, illus., 143pp. op-$10-y, $20-bmk, $3.95, $25.

484 **FRANZMAN, Tom**
"The final campaign. The Confederate offensive of 1864." In: CO, Fall, 1985, v.63, #3, p. 266-279, notes.
..."The Battle of Devil's Backbone Mountain." In: CO, Winter 1984/5, v.62, #4, p.420-8, map.

485 **FRASER, John**
"A Petition regarding the condition of the C.S.M. Prison at Columbia, S.C., addressed to the Confederate Authorities. Edited by George L. Anderson." Lawrence: University of Kansas Libraries, 1962. University of Kansas Publs., Library series 14. 8vo, wraps, illus., port, 57pp. The petition was addressed to Lieut.-Gen. Wm. J. Hardee, comm. offr., C.S.Military Department, S.C., Ga., and Fla.

486 **FRASSANITO, William A.**
"Grant and Lee: The Virginia Campaigns 1864-1865." N.Y., Charles Scribners Sons, 1983. 8vo, cl, dj, illus., maps, index, notes, 442pp. $25.

487 **FRAYSER'S FARM, Battle of-(Frazier's)**
See: David E. Johnston, John W. T. Leech.

488 **FRAYSER, Richard E., Capt.**
"Gen. J.E.B. Stuart. Capt. R.E. Frayser's tribute to his memory. Address prepared to be delivered at the dedication of the Stuart monument at Yellow Tavern-authentic biography of the great cavalry leader." In: SHSP, 1898, v.XXVI, p. 87-95.

489 ..."A narrative of Stuart's raid in the rear of the Army of the Potomac. By Richard E. Frayser, formerly Capt. on Gen. Stuart's staff and chief signal officer of the cavalry corps. A.N.V." In: SHSP, Nov. 1883, v.XI, #11, p. 505-517.

490 ..."Imprisoned Under Fire. Six hundred gallant Confederate officers on Morris Island, S.C., in reach of Confederate Guns. They were held in retaliation and two of them relate the experience of prison life stories of Capt. F.C. Barnes and Capt. R.E. Frayser. (From: Richmond, Va. "Times", Aug. 22, 1897) In: SHSP, 1897, v.XXV, p. 365-377, with roster of Va. members of the "Six Hundred".

491 **FREDERICK CITY**
"The Affair at Frederick City." In: SHSP, 1885, v.13, p. 417-419.

492 **FREDERICK J.W.**
"Reminiscences of the Civil War by J.W. Frederick. Edt.: Gerald J. Smith." In: Ga.H.Q., Suppl., 1975, v.LIX, p. 154-159.

493 **FREDERICKSBURG,**
and Adjacent National Battlefields Memorial Park Association of Va. "A few among the many reasons why there should be es-

tablished at or near Fredericksburg, in the State of Virginia, a national battlefield park, embracing the battlefields of Fredericksburg, Chancellorsville, Salem Church, Todd's Tavern, the Wilderness and Spotsylvania Court House." (Fredericksburg, Star Print, n.d., 18cm, 11pp., fldg. map. Dorn-II, 1660.

...and Adjacent Battlefields Memorial Association and Park Association." Fredericksburg, Va., The Free Lance, 1899. 8vo, wraps, cover title, 27pp., fldg. map. Lousiville, Ka: Lost Cause Press, microcards. $2.45.

494 **FREDERICKSBURG Battlefield**
"On Historic Spots. Visit to the Battlefield around Fredericksburg, Marye's Heights, Salem Church, Chancellorsville, Wilderness. (from Richmond Dispatch, July 23, 2899) In: SHSP, 1908, v.36, p. 197-209.

495 **"FREDERICKSBURG and Spotsylvania**
County National Military Park. Significance of the battles around Fredericksburg." Wash, D.C., U.S. National Park Service, (reprint, 1961) 4to, pict., wraps, 16pp., illus., ports, map.

496 **FREDERICKSBURG, Battle of and Artillery**
See: C.R. Fleet, Edward P. Alexander, James Dinkins, Benjamin G. Hunphreys, Jno. Lamb.

497 **FREDERICKSBURG, Va.**
See: John Critcher, Frances B. Goolrich, Bradley T. Johnson, Richmond "Dispatch".

498 **"FREE MASONRY and the War.**
Report of the Committee under the resolutions of 1862, Grand Lodge of Virginia, in reference to our relations as Masonic bodies and as Masons, in the North and South, growing out of the manner in which the present war has been prosecuted. Adopted by the Grand Lodge of Va., Dec. 12, 1864, and ordered to be published. John Dove, Grand Secretary." Richmond: Chas. H. Wynne Print, 1865. 8vo, wraps, cover title, 31pp. $7.50.

499 **FREEHLING, William W.**
"The Editorial Revolution, Virginia, and the Coming of the Civil War: A Review Essay." In: CWH, March, 1970, v.XVI, #1, p. 64-72.

500 ..."prelude to Civil War the Nullification Controversy in South Carolina, 1816-1836." N.Y., London: Harper and Row Print, 1965. 8vo, cl, dj, maps, xiii, 395pp. $17.50-bmk, $6, $22. N.Y. & Evanston, (1968), Harper's Torchbooks, 8vo, wraps, maps, xi, 395. $3.

501 **FREEMAN, Anne Hobson**
"A Cool Head in a Warm Climate." (Richmond) Va. Cavl., Winter 1962-1963. v.XII, #3, p. 9-17, illus., ports (1-color) Joseph Reid Anderson and the Tredegar Iron Works.

502 **FREEMAN, Benjamin H.**
"The Confederate Letters of Benjamin H. Freeman. Compiled and Edited by Stuart T. Wright." Hicksville, N.Y., Exposition Press (1974) 12mo, cl, dj, 109pp. $20, $10, $7, $5. Co. K, 44th N.C. Inf., Franklin Co., N.C. (op) $12.

503 **FREEMAN, Charles R.**
"The Battle of Honey Springs." In: Chr. Okla., 1935, v.XIII, p. 154-168. July, 17, 1865 in McIntosh Co., Okla. See: Jess C. Epple.

504 **FREEMAN, Douglas S.**
"When war came to Richmond." Richmond, Va., News Leader, 1981. 8vo, cl, 74pp. 500 copies $35. Originally published as part of the Bicentennial edition of the Richmond News Leader, Sept. 1937.

505 **FREEMAN, Douglas Southall**
"An address by..., April 1950, Appomattox Court House, Virginia." n.p., (1964, 8vo, wraps, 8pp. $9.50, $60-nc.

506 ..."Address-Memorial Exercises, May 10, 1916, Oakwood Cemetery, Richmond,

Va." In: SHSP, Sept., 1916, v.XLI, p. 14-19.

507 ..."Address before Civil War Round Tables, Richmond, 7 May, 1953. Civil War. Hist., Mar., v.1, p. 7-15. $20. On five difficulties a historian encounters, on the war of 1861-1865. An address shortly before his death.

508 ..."A Calendar of Confederate Papers, with a bibliography of some Confederate publications. Preliminary report of the Southern Historical Manuscripts Commission. Prepared under the direction of the Confederate Memorial Literary Society." Richmond, Va., Confederate Museum, 1908. Large 8vo, cl, 620pp., "Corrigenda", (1)pp. $35, $125. Edt: Limited to 1000 copies. $40, $75.
...N.Y. Kraus Reprints, 1968. $33.

509 ..."The Confederate Tradition of Richmond." In: CWHist., Dec. 1957, v.3, p. 369-373. From Richmond Mag., 1932.

510 ..."Lee's Dispatches Unpublished letters of General Robert E. Lee, CSA, to Jefferson Davis and the War Department of the Confederate States of America, 1862 to 1865. From the private collection of Wymberley Jones de Renne, of Wormsloe Georgia. Edt: with an Introduction and notes by Douglas Southall Freeman." N.Y., Lond: G.P. Putnam's Sons, 1915. 8vo, maroon cl, t.e.g., dj, front(port), pull out map, 400pp. $20, $25, $30, $50-nc-33, $60.
..."Second impression", $15, $20
...N.Y., G.P. Putnam's Sons (1957) New edt: with additional dispatches and foreword by Grady McWhiney. tk. 8vo, cl, dj, lxxi, 416pp. atg. spec. page. $35-bmk, $15-dj-84, $20-bk.

511 ..."R.E. Lee, a Biography." N.Y., Lond: Charles Scribner's Son, 1934/1935. 8vo, cl, ports (incl. front) illus., maps, facsms., $50, $60, $75. I-xviii, 647pp; II-xi, 621pp; xi, 559pp.; IV-viii, 594pp.; index: vols. II and IV. 1st fine-$225-jk-122.
...Same: 100 advanced, autographed copies $100 set., $100-1936-Pulitzer Prize Edt., * 1944, $150-fine, $80-y.
...This Edt: also in Morocco. $75. This edt., with added illus., ports.
...Other Edts: 1941, 1943, 1951, 1949.
..."Hudson River edition", reprint (1977) $90.

512 ..."Lee of Virginia." N.Y., Charles Scribner's Sons (1958) 8vo, cl, ports, views, xi, 243pp. Biography of Lee, written in 1944, now first published, intended as a condensed version of the author's earlier work on Lee. $20, $40.

513 ..."Lee, an abridgement in one volume, by Richard Harwell of the four-volume R.E. Lee by Douglas Southall Freeman." N.Y., Charles Scribner's Sons, (1961). 8vo, cl, maps, illus., ports, xvii, 601pp. $10, $15, $20-y.

514 ..."Freeman's Lee, reviewed" In: "Queen's Quart., 1938, v.XLV, p. 1-10pp. By Sir Andrew Macphail.

515 ..."R.E. Lee, a Biography." N.Y., Scribner's 1934. Salesman's dummy. Contains table of contents of each volume, part of first chapter, v.1, blank pages. Pub. prior to the set. $75-carolina bk.
...Salesman dummy-"Pulitzer Prize edition", N.Y., 1943, v.1 only (partial shown. $50-bmk.

516 ..."R.E. Lee One of the Best Soldiers of All Time...600 questions you will find the answers in the four beautiful volumes, published by..." N.Y., Charles Scribner's Sons, n.d., 8vo, wraps, port of Lee, 24pp. $10.

517 ..."Lee and the Ladies; unpublished letters of Robert E. Lee." In: Scribners, Oct.-Nov., 1925, v.LXXVII, p. 339-349, 459-471. $75.

518 ..."Lee y las mujeres; cartas ineditas de Robert E. Lee."In: Inter-America, Jan., 1926, v.IX, p. 450-460.

519 ..."Lee's Lieutenants: A Study in Command." I-Manassas to malvern Hill; II-Cedar Mountain to Chancellorsville; III-Gettysburg to Appomattox." N.Y., Charles Scribner's Sons, 1942-1945. 8vo, cl, ports, maps, I-Ivi, 733; II-xlvii, 862, Index: III-xlv, 760, index, fldg. map. $75, $95.
...Other Edts: 1945, 1946, 1949.
...1946-Arlington Edt., special blue binding, with extra illus., ports, as follows: I-Manassas to Malvern Hill":1vi, 773, (27)pp; II-"Cedar Mountain to Chancellorsville" xiv, 760, index, (26)pp.; III-"Gettysburg to Appomattox", xlvi, 410, (26)pp; IV -pt. 2, (8), (411)-862, index, fldg. map, (24pp. $40, $45, $50, $60, $75-y.
...Same: advanced, autographed sales, $50, $250-r.

520 ..."The Last Parade; an editorial by..., from the "Richmond News Leader", of Friday, June 24, 1932, the last day of the 42nd Annual Reunion of United Confederate Veterans." Richmond, Va., Whitter & Shepperson, 1932, 4to, stiff wraps, 20 lf, mounted front and pls. printed one side, 5pp-text. $17.50, $35, $175-al, $350-rowe. Lim. to 500 copies. Freeman's tribute to Armies of the CSA, on occasion of their last parade in Richmond. (rarest Freeman) $150-bmk-105.

521 ..."The Lengthening Shadow of Lee; an address before a joint session of the General Assembly of Virginia, in the hall of the House of Delegates, Jan. 20, 1936." Richmond: Div. of Purchase and Print, 1936. 8vo, wraps, front, 7pp. $75-r, $5. Va., Gen. Assembly, 1936, Senate Doc. 7.

522 ..."Robert E. Lee: is his military genius fact or fiction?" By Elbridge Colby and Douglas S. Freeman, in Current Hist., Oct. 1928, v.XXIX, p. 36-47. Freeman's view of Lee's achievements in spite of tremendous handicaps.

523 ..."Methods employed by General Lee to maintain morale in the Army of Northern Virginia. Lectuer, Army War College, Ft. Humphreys, D.C., 5 November 1936. Bound 1936-1937 lectures, 11pp.

524 ..."The South to Posterity. An introduction to the writing of Confederate history." N.Y., Charles Scribner's Sons, 1939. 8vo, cl, xii, (1), 235pp. index, notes. $40-bmk, dj, fine-$85.
...Same, reprint: $25-bmk, $50-bmk-105, $12.50, $125-r.
...Port Washington, NY, Kennikat Prss, (1964) $8.50.
...Wendell, N.C., 1983, Broadfoot Print. $25. Revised, with an introduction by Richard Harwell. 8vo, cl, xxxix, 235pp.

525 ..."The True Story of General Order #9, General Lee's farewell address to the Army of Northern Virginia." Lexington, Va., Lee Museum Comm., Washington and Lee University, 1928. 8vo, wraps, port, facsm. (6)pp.

526 ..."The causes and outbreak of the war between the States." Richmond, Va., Dep't. of Public Instruction, 1912. 8vo, wraps, 94pp., front of Lee. $50.

527 ..."An address, March 1955." In: CWH, v.1, #1, 9pp., (also an offprint) $15.

528 **FREEMAN, Walker Burford**
"Memoirs of Walker Burford Freeman, 1843-1935. Preface by John Stuart Bryan Richmond, Va., Private Print, 1925. (Richmond News Leader, Feb. 11, 1935) sq. 8vo, stiff wraps, (4), 58pp. $150. At the insistence of his father Dr. Douglas S. Freeman, penned these memoirs in 1919. Walter served in 58th Va. Inf. Reprinted 1970 for Rich. Round Table.

529 ..."Warren County Civil War Centennial Observance, Battle of Front Royal, Va., May 19-20, 1962 (quote) front. port of

Jackson." Front Royal, Va., Civil War Centennial Commission and Chamber of Commerce. 4to, pict. wraps, (24)pp. illus., maps, ports.

530 **FREEMANTLE, Arthur J.L., Sir**
"Three months in the Southern states...A portion of which was published in Blackwood's Edinburgh Magazine, v.94, Dec. 1863, p. 766-777.

531 **FRELIGHT, J.H.**
"The True Position, Interests and Policy of the South. Union or Secession: Which is best?" Memphis: Jan. 1861. 8vo, wraps, 35pp. $82.50-oh.

532 **FREMANTLE, Arthur James Lyon, Sir**
"Three months in the Southern states..." N.Y., Time-Life Books, 1984. 8vo, leather, gilt edges. $25. Collectors Library of the Civil War.
..."Three Months in the Southern States, April-June, 1863. By Lieut.-Col. Fremantle Coldstream Guards." Edinburgh: William Blackwood & Sons, 1863. 12mo, cl, front(port Jeff Davis), ix, 316pp. $200, $350, $125-autographed
...N.Y., John Bradburn, 1864. 12mo, 309pp. $25, $35.
...Mobile: S.H. Goetzel, 1864. 12mo, orig. printed wallpaper wraps, 158pp. $50, $67.50, $75, $110, $125, $385, $450, $127, $850-r.
...Bost: Little, Brown & Co., (Apr. 1954, reprinted twice, June 1954); London: Andre Deutxch Print, $12.50 (1956), $65-y-11. 12mo, cl, dj, ix, xv, 304pp. Edt: Walter Lord, $7.50, $8.50, $10, $20- jk-129. N.Y., Capricorn Books (#34) (1960) paper.

533 ..."The Battle of Gettysburg and the Campaign in Pennsylvania. Extract from the diary of an English Officer present with the Confederate Army." In: Blackwood Edinburgh Magazine, July-Dec., 1863, p. 29. First printing of diary? $8.50. A companion piece to Fitzgerald's "Visit to Cities and Camps in CSA.", which follows in Blackwoods.

534 ..."The Battle of Gettysburg. Sir Arthur J.L. Fremantle's View." In: "Two Views of Gettysburg by Sir Arthur J.L. Fremantle and Frank A. Haskell. Edt: Richard Harwell." Chicago: Lakeside Press, Christmas, 1964, 16mo, cl, map(front)ports, illus., xl, 3-92pp. Haskell, (1), 95-264, index. $20, $30.

535 **FRENCH, J.B.**
"A Southerner's letter describing the fall of Fort Sumter." In: Geneal. Mag., ns, III, Mar. 1916, p. 88-89. From Charleston, S.C., Apr. 19, 1861.

536 **FRENCH, Marcellus**
"Dispatch no. 2, from Grant to Lee." In: CV, Jan. 1911, v.XIX, p. 14-15.

537 **FRENCH, Samuel Bassett**
"Centennial Tales; memoirs of Colonel "Chester" S. Bassett French, extra aid-de-camp to Generals Lee and Jackson, the Army of Northern Virginia, 1861-1865." Compiled by Glenn C. Oldaker. N.Y., Carlton Press, 1962. (A Reflection Book) 12mo, cl, illus., 150pp. $15-bmk.

538 **FRENCH, Samuel Gibbs, Gen.**
"Two Wars: an Autobiography of Gen. Samuel G. French, an officer in the armies of the United States and Confederate States, a graduate from the U.S. Military Academy, West Point, 1843. Mexican War; War Between the States, a Diary; Reconstruction Period, his experience; incidents, Reminiscences, etc." Nashville, Tenn., Confederate Veteran, 1901. 8vo, color flags on cover, ports (incl. front), illus., maps, xv, (1), 404pp. errata slip. $20, $25, $35, $40, $60-nc, $75, $100-bmk, mint-$125-bmk, $120-bmk-84.
...Louisville: Lost Cause Pr., micro-cd, $6.18.

539 ..."General Joseph E. Johnston's Campaign in Georgia. Lt.-Gen. Leonidas Polk at Cassville. Criticisms of Gen. S.G. French." In: SHSP, 1894, v.XXII, p. 109.

540 ..."Kennesaw Mountain." In: SHSP, 1881, v.IX, p. 505-511; same, in-So.Vib., I, 1882-1883, 273-280.

541 ..."Movement against Allatoona-Letter from Gen. S.G. French." In: SHSP, 1882, v.X, p. 402-406.

542 ..."Autograph Letter, signed-to private secretary Jeff Davis, June 1863, Hdq. quarto pg. (Goodspeed, '73) $75. French defends action in burning cotton at Vicksburg.

543 FRENCH, Virginia
"The Beersheba Diary of L.Virginia French." In: ETexHS, 1981-1982. Pt. I, #52/53, p. 89-107. Pt. II-1982-1983, #53/55, p. 3-25. Edt: Herschel Gower. Diary: winter, spring, summer, 1864.

544 FRETWELL, Mark E.
"Rousseau's Alabama Raid." In: AHQ, 1956, v.XVIII, p. 526-550. See: Edwin Cole Bearss.

545 FREYTAG-LORINGHOVEN, Hogo Frederick Phillipp Johann, freiherr von
"Studien, uber Kriegfuhrung auf Grundlage des Nordmerikanischen sezessionskrieges in Virginien." Berlin: E.S. Mittler und Sohn, 1901-1903. 8vo, illus., maps, plans, (8-fldg. maps) 3 vols: part-1, maps, 1-4, p. 134; part-2, 1-3 (duplicates), map 5, p. 146; part-3, maps 1-2(duplicate) maps 6-8, p. 165. Issued in 3 parts, 1901-1903, with special title-pg. and contents, general title-pg. and contents inserted at end of 3rd part. Bull Run, 1861, Richmond, 1862, Manassas, 1862, Maryland, Fredericksburg, Chancellorsville 1863, Gettysburg, Atlanta, 1864, Spottsylvania, Petersburg. Savannah das ende.

546 FRIEDENWALD, Herbert
"The Pioneer of Secession." In: SHSP, 1900, v.28, p. 81-83.

547 FRIEDRICHS, Vic
"Have gun, had to travel to get it." In: Gun Rep., Sept., 1958, v.4, #4, p. 44-46, view. An 1860 army Colt, fluted cylinder, percussion revolver, originally owned by A.G. Dickinson Texas officer in the CSArmy, 1861-1865, now in author's possession.

548 FRIEND, Llerena B.
"The Texan of 1860." In: SwHQ, July, 1958, v.LXII, #1, p. 1-17. Re their military reputation, statistics of the state.

549 ..."A tentative bibliography of books on Texas and Texans in the Civil War." In: TMH, Fall 1964, v.4, #3, p. 197-211.

550 FRIERSON, W.H.
"The Confederate Soldier in the Perspective. Speech by...delivered before Confederate Gray Chapter #641, U.D.C. and Lake County Camp, U.C.V., at Leesburg, Fla., June 3, 1907." n.p., n.d. (1907). 8vo, stiff wraps, 7pp. $7.50.

551 FRIETCHIE, Barbara
See: Jubal Anderson Early, Valerius Ebert and William Gordon McCabe for the full story and refutation.

551a FRITZ, Donald T.
"Southern Leanings in Baltimore Prior to & During the War Between the States." In: CV, new, Nov./Dec. 1987, v. 36, #6, p.14-22, ills, port.

552 FRIZZELL, Robert W.
"Killed by Rebels": A Civil War Massacre and its Aftermath." In: Mo.H.R., July 1977, v.LXXI, #4, p. 369-395, illus., ports, map.

553 FROBEL, Anne S.
"The Civil War diary of Anne S. Frobel of Wilton Hill in Virginia. Intro. and Append. by Mary H. and Dallas M. Lancaster." Birmingham, Ala., Private Print, 1986. 8vo, wraps, 272pp., illus., front(facsm. and flag). $15.

554 FROBEL, B.W.
"Report of B.W. Frobel on the Battle of

555 Sharpsburg." In: Our Liv. and Dead, 1875, v.II, p. 26-29, Maj. of artillery.

555 ..."Report of B.W. Frobel, second battle of Manassas, Sept. 9, 1862." In: OLOD, 1875, v.II, p. 24-26. Camp near Frederick Maryland.

556 **FROHMAN, Charles E.**
"Rebels on Lake Erie." Columbus, Ohio: Ohio Historical Soc., 1965. 8vo, cl, facsms., illus., ports, v, 157pp. (plus 20pp. plates), maps. $5.50, $8.50. Acct., CSA officers at Johnson's Isle in Sandusky Bay.

557 ..."Rebels on Lake Erie: The Piracy, The Conspiracy, Prison Life." Columbus: Ohio Historical Society, 1975. Second printing, vi, 159pp. $6-y

558 **"FROM DIXIE:**
Original articles contributed by Southern Writers, etc."
See: Kate Pleasants Minor, Editor.

559 **FRONT ROYAL, Battle of**
See: John C. Donohoe.

560 **FROSSARD, Ed (48th Sale)**
"Collection of Confederate Currency and US Fractional Notes, coins, medals, etc." Dec. 1922, wraps, 52pp., 986 lots, 24cmx15. $25.

561 **FROST, Daniel Marsh**
"A Letter to Gen. Sterling Price, Accompanied by Official Documents." St. Louis: M.R. Cullen, 1865. Orig. printed wraps, 20cm, 16pp. waterstained. Apparently unrecorded (Streeter) From Jno. Henry Brown Library. $80-streeter.

562 **FROST, Griffin**
"Camp and Prison Journal, embracing scenes in camp, on the march and in prisons: Springfield, Gratiot St., St. Louis, and Macon City, Mo.; Ft. Delaware, Alton and Camp Douglas, Ill.; Camp Morton, Ind.; Camp Chase, Ohio. Also, scenes and incidents during a trip for exchange from St. Louis via Phila. to City Point, Va." Quincy, Ill., Herald Office Print, 1867. 8vo, calf, 303pp. (woodcuts) (Sabin-26020 gives vi, 393pp.) Frost states all but a handful of copies were destroyed at pub. office. $22.50, $30, $37.50, $100, $1500-g.

563 **FRY, A.F.**
"The defensive South." In: CV, Nov. 1919, v.XXVII, p. 422-425. The South was up to and during war between the States, on the defensive.

564 ..."The South and real Americanism." In: CV, Sept., 1919, v.XXVII, p. 325-328.

565 **FRY, Anna M. Gayle, Mrs.**
"Memories of Old Cahaba." Nashville, Tenn., Methodist Pub. Hse., 1908, 12mo, cl, illus., plates, 128pp. $100-b. References to 5th Ala. Reg., organized by Col. Robert E. Rodes. See also: Maj. Green Peyton's Sketch in Chas. D. Walker's "Biographical Sketches Grads. and Eleves of VMI, p. 440-457.

566 ..."Life in Dallas County, Ala., during the war." In: Mag. of Hist., Apr. 1916, v.XXII, p. 145-153.

567 **FRY, Birket Davenport**
"Pettigrew's charge at Gettysburg." In: SHSP, 1879, v.7, p. 91-93. See: Robt. A. Brock.

568 **FRY, H.W.**
"The influence of the V.M.I. upon the War Between the States." In: The Cadet, July, 1892-"Special Issue", illus., pict. wraps, Vol.ii, Virginia Military Institution.

569 **FRY, James B., Gen.**
"Lord Wolseley answered." In: NAR, 1889, v.149, p. 728-740. Re: An English view of the Civil War.

570 **FRY, James M.**
"The death of John H. Morgan and what led up to it." By an East Tennessee Confederate Scout." Wills Point, Texas: Chronicle, n.d. (1905). 8vo, wraps, 19, (2)pp. port, Pres. slip: $100.

571 ..."The Death of John Hunt Morgan, A Memoir of James M. Fry. Edited by W.A.

Smith and Wallace Milam." In: Tenn. H.Q., 1960, v.XIX, p. 54-64.

572 **FRYE, Dennis E.**
"2nd Virginia Infantry." Lynchburg, Va., 1984. H.E. Howard (J.P. Bell Print) Lim. Atg. Edt., 8vo, cl, dj, (5), 151pp., illus., maps, ports. $17.50.
..."12th Virginia Cavalry." Lynchburg, Va., H.E. Howard, 1988. 8vo, cl, dj, (9), 188pp, ports (incl. group). 1,000 (#385) atg. copies.

573 **FULHAM, George T.**
"Our Cruise in the Confederate States' War Steamer Alabama." (London, 1864), p. 61 (from footnote in American Neptune, Apr. 1962, #2, (p.98).

574 **FULKERSON, Abram**
"The Prison Experience of a Confederate Soldier. Narrative of the hardships, sufferings and hazzards of the six hundred officers of the CSA, who were prisoners from Aug. 16, 1864, to Mar. 4, 1865, and for six weeks on Morris Island, by Federal efforts, were under fire from Confederate Batteries. By Abram Fulkerson, late Col. 63rd Tenn. Inf., ANV. (From the "Briston Courier", Sept. 14, 1893.") In: SHSP, 1894, v.XXII, p. 127-146.

575 **FULKERSON, Horace S.**
"Random Recollections of Early Days in Mississippi." Vicksburg, Miss., Vicksburg Pub., 1885. 8vo, (paper, $.50, cl-$1), 158pp. $65, $150, $20, $250, $300.
...Baton Rouge, La., Otto Claitor, 1937. Intro: Percy L. Rainwater, "with a biographical sketch of the author." 8vo, cl, xi, 158pp. $12.50, $30.

576 ..."A civilian's recollections of the War Between the States." Edt: P.L. Rainwater. Baton Rouge, La., O. Claitor, 1939. 8vo, cl, (10), 253pp. 200 copies. $80, $25, $125.

577 ..."Excerpts from Fulkerson's "Recollections of the War Between the States." Edt: P.L. Rainwater. Miss. Valley Hist. Rev., XXIV, 1937, p. 351-373. Also a "separate", stapeled.

578 ..."Notes on Southern Personalities." Edt: P.L. Rainwater. (Baton Rouge, La.) JSH, May, 1938, v.IV, #2, p. 209-227. Unpublished Fulkerson notes on such Southern leaders: Govs. Moore, Allen and Pettus, DeBow, A.G. Brown, Judge Perkins, La., Yancey and "Mistress of Oakley".

579 **FULLAM, George Townley**
"Cruise of the Alabama from her departure from Liverpool until her arrival at the Cape of Good Hope. By an officer on board." Liverpool: Lee & Nightingale, W.H. Peat, 1863, 12mo, wraps, front(port), pl, 48pp. Pub. anon. Private journal of a boarding officer of the Alabama, period July 29, 1862 to Sept. 16, 1863. An article in Cornhill Magazine (new series) v.2 (1897)p.592-603, extracts are given from complete journal, erroneously stated that "this record...has never been printed in any shape or form, etc." in LC.

580 ..."The Cruise of the Alabama", Raphael Semmes, Commander, from her departure from Liverpool, July 29, 1862, by an officer on board, with gleanings from other sources". n.p., 1864. 8vo, wraps, 56pp. interleaved (see above note)

581 ..."Our Cruise on the Confederate States War Steamer Alabama-The Private Journal of an Officer." (London: Print by A. Schulze, 1863?) 8vo, wraps, 64pp. "from a supplement to the South African Advertiser and Mail, Capetown, Sat. Sept. 19, 1863.

582 ..."Cruise of the Alabama from her departure for Liverpool until her arrival at the Cape of Good Hope", by an Officer on Board." Liverpool, 1863, Lee & Nightingale, W.H. Peat, wraps, port, plate, tall 8vo, 48pp. $15, $24.50.
...London: 1864, p. 61.

583 ..."The Journal of George Townley Fullam, boarding officer of the Confederate Sea Raider "Alabama". Edt.: Charles G. Summersell." University: Univ. of Alabama Press, 1973. 8vo, cl, dj, illus., bibliog., index, 1iv, 229pp. $8, sig- 600 copies, lim. edt. $20, $75-bmk.

584 **FULLER, Claude E.**
"Confederate currency and stamps, 1861-1865: official acts of Congress authorizing their issue; historical data and official correspondence on the Confederate financial system including sketches on the coins, stamps, medals, seals, and flags." (Nashville: Parthenon Press, under auspices of the Tenn. Div., U.D.C., 1949) Large 8vo, cl, 236pp., facsms (part colored) ports views (part color) $40, $50, $75, $140(auction)
...Lawrence, Mass., Quarterman Pub. 1977 (35-)

585 ..."The Rifled Musket." Harrisburg, Pa., Stackpole Co., (1958) 4to, cl, dj, illus., facsms., 302pp. $25-nc.

586 ..."Firearms of the Confederacy." Lawrence, Mass., Quarterman Pub., (1980) 8vo, cl, xiv, 333pp. $25.
...1977 edt.
..."Firearms of the Confederacy; the shoulder Arms, pistols and revolvers of the Confederate soldier, including the regular United States models, the imported arms and those manufactured within the Confederacy. By Claude E. Fuller and Richard D. Steuart." Huntington, W.Va., Standard Pubs., 1944, 8vo, cl, dj, illus., plates, ports, facsms., 3pp., vi, (8)-333pp. $60, $75, $100-atg.

587 **FULLER, Ezra B.**
"Who fired the first shot at the Battle of Gettysburg?" In: Jour. USCav. Assoc., Mar. 1914, v.XXIV, p. 784-796.

588 **FULLER, Hiram**
"North and South by the White Republican." London: Chapman & Hall, 1863. 8vo, cl, (6), 336pp. $10.

589 ..."The Flag of Truce. Dedicated the Emperor of the French, by a White Republican." London: James Ridgway, 1862. 8vo, wraps, 52pp. Sabin-24644.

590 ..."The Times! or the Flag of Truce, dedicated to the cabinets at Washington and Richmond, by a White Republican." Richmond: Ritchie & Dunnavant, 1863. 12mo, wraps, cover title, 18pp. See Crandall-2746. $7.50 (old)

591 ..."Curiosity Visits to Southern Plantations by a Northern Man. 1863."

592 ..."Causes and Consequences of the Civil War in America." 1861. DAB-"Fuller was born in Mass., very pro-South, had to leave country for his utterances as war began. In London he started a weekly-"Cosmopolitan", to represent southern point of view, bankrupt, then wrote for "Fraser's Magazine", Sept. 1862-Feb. 1863, signed: White Republican.

593 **FULLER, John D.P.**
"Green Mount: A Virginia Plantation Family During the Civil War." Lexington, University of Kentucky Press, 1962. 8vo, cl, d/w, p. xxv, 374. $8.50.

594 **FULLER, John Frederick Charles, Maj.-Gen.**
"Grant and Lee. A Study in Personality and Generalship." London: Eyre & Spottiswoode, 1933. 8vo, cl, 323pp., illus., 11-fldg. maps. $4.50, $8.50, $16.
...N.Y., Scribner's, same above, (1938).
...London, Eyre & Spottieswoode (1959). Reprint, $6.95, $3.
...Bloomington, Ind., Indiana Univ. Press, Civil War Centennial Series, 1957. 1959-op. $5, $12.50.
...1982, p. 335 (paper $11) cloth $25.

595 ..."A study in mobility in the American Civil War." In: Army Quart., 1935, v.XXIX, p. 261-271.

596 **FULMORE, Z.T., Mrs.**
"Gen. Tom Green, an address before Texas Veterans in Dallas, Texas in behalf of the Tom Green monument." In: CV, 1907, v.15, p. 78-81, ports.

597 **FULTON COUNTY, Georgia**
"Official History of Fulton County, by Walter G. Cooper." Atlanta, Ga., Walter W. Brown Pub., 1934. 8vo, cl, xvi, 912pp., illus. Confederate soldiers from Fulton, p. 890-907.
...Spartanburg, S.C., Reprint Co., 1978, $35.

598 **FULTON, John**
See: pseud-S(amuel) M. Johnson

599 **FULTON, William Frierson**
"Family Record and War Reminiscences." n.p., n.d. (1910?) 8vo, cl, ports, fldg. chart, 183pp. Roster: North Sumter Rifles, Co. A., 5th, Alabama Battl. $750-g, $400-bmk.

600 **FULTON, William Frierson, II**
"The war reminiscences of William Frierson Fulton, II, 5th Alabama Battalion, Archer's's Brigade, A.P. Hill's Light Div., Gaithersburg: Butternut Press, 1986. 8vo, cl, 161pp. $27.50.
..."The war reminiscences of William Frierson Fulton, II. Fifth Alabama Battalion, Archer's Brigade, A.P. Hill's Light Division." Gaithersburg, Md., Butternut Press, 1986. 8vo, cl, dj, 161pp. $17.50.

601 **FUNK, Arville L.**
"The Morgan Raid in Indiana and Ohio (1863)." Mentore, Ind., Superior Print, 1978, 8vo, wraps, 68pp., illus. $5.

602 **FUNKHOUSER, Robert D.**
"From Manassas to Frazier's Farm. Recollections of a soldier in many battles." In: SHSP, 1907, v.XXXV, p. 366-369. (from "Times-Dispatch") Oct. 21, 1906.

603 ..."General Lee to the Rear Col. W.L. Goldsmith, of Miss., witnessed both events Gordon begging Lee to retire. Capt. Funkhouser's graphic description of the Ga. soldier persuading Gen. Lee to go to the rear and then leading the charge." In: SHS 79-82.

604 ..."Met His Death in Last Fight. John William Ashby is man who fell at Appomattox in Gordon's last assault. This question now settled once for all-also the last Federal soldier killed." In: SHSP, 1906, v.XXXIV, p. 218-221. From "Times Dispatch", July 29, 1906.

605 ..."The Warren Blues-Extra Billy's Men. Roll of officers and men of a famous band of veterans." In: SHSP, 1907, XXXV, p. 298-303. See: L.V. Hale and Phillips.

606 **FURNAS, J.C.**
"Goodby to Uncle Tom." N.Y., Wm. Sloan Assoc., 1956, 8vo, cl, dj, x, 435pp., illus., bibliog. $7.50. Debunking the many misconceptions and myths from Harriet B. Stowe to date about the negro and slavery.

607 **FURNESS, William Eliot**
"The Battle of Olustee, Florida, Feb. 20, 1864." In: Papers, Mil. Hist. Soc. Mass., 1904, v.IX, p. 233-263.

608 **FUTCH, Ovid L.**
"Andersonville Raiders." In: CWH, DEc. 1956, v.II, #4, p. 47-60. Small groups of cutthroats and thieves who were attracted by bounties for service in Union Army. Depredations on prisoners.

609 ..."History of Andersonville Prison, 1863-1865." Ann Arbor: University Microfilms, 1959 (1960). Positive microfilm of typescript, (245) leaves, Thesis-Emory Univ., Abstracted; dissert. 20:376 (March)

610 ..."Salmon P. Chase and Civil War Politics in Florida." In: FHQ, January, 1954, v.XXXII, #3, p. 163-188.

611 ..."History of Andersonville Prison." Gainesville: Univ. of Florida Press, 8vo, cl, 146pp., notes, index. $30, 1968.

612 **FUTRELL, Robert Frank**
"Federal Trade with the Confederate States 1861-1865; a study of governmental

policy." Ann Arbor, Mich., Univ. Microfilms. (#4395), 1950 (i.e., 1952) positive microfilm of 476 lf. typescript, bibliog., p. 466-476. Thesis: Vanderbilt Univ.

613 ..."Federal Military Government in the South, 1861-1865." In: Mil. Affairs, Winter, 1951, v.15:p. 181-191.

614 **FUZZLEBUG, Fritz (pseud.)**
"Prison Life Duirng the Rebellion." See: John H. Dunkle.

G

1 **G., A.M.**
"Pride of Mr. Laird." In: Blackwood's Magazine, 1963, v.CCXCIV, p. 213-224. On: C.S. Alabama.

2 **GABARD, William Montgomery**
"The Confederate Career of John Elliott Ward." In: Ga.H.Q. Summer, 1971, v.LV, #2, p. 177-207. $8.

3 **GACHE, Pere Louis-Hippolyte, S.J.**
"A Frenchman, A Chaplain, A Rebel: The war letters of Pere Louis-Hippolyte Gache. By Cornelius M. Buckley, S.J." Chicago: Loyola University Press, 1981. 8vo, cl, 288pp. $9.

4 **GADDY, David W.**
"Gray cloaks and daggers." In: CWTI, July 1975, v.13, #4, p. 20-27, facsms., illus., ports.

5 ..."William Norris and the Confederate Signal and Secret Service." In: Md. Hist. Mag., 1975, v.LII, p. 167-188.

6 **GADDY, David Winfred**
"William Morris and the Confederate Signal Secret Service." In: MdHM, Summer, 1965, v.70, #2, p. 167-188.

7 **GAGE, Larry Jay**
"The City of Austin on the Eve of the Civil War." In: SwHQ, Jan. 1960, v.LXIII, #3, p. 428-438, illus.

8 ..."The Texas Road to Secession and War. John Marshall and the Texas State Gazette, 1860-1861." In: SwHQ, October, 1958, v.LXII, #2, p. 191-226.

9 **GAILLARD, Edward Samuel**
"The Medical and Surgical Lessons of the Late War." (Baltimore) In: New Eclectic Magazine (Ext. of: "Land We Love"), v.IV, #6, 1869, p.705-718. $7.

10 **GAILOR, Frank M.**
"The Diary of a Confederate Quartermaster, Edt: Charlotte Cleveland and Robert Daniel." In: Tenn. Hist. Quart., 1952, v.XI, p. 78-85.

11 **GAILOR, Thomas Frank**
"General Nathan Bedford Forrest-summary of his remarkable achievements." In: SHSP, 1901, v.29, p.337-339.

12 ..."General Forrest." In: Sewanee Rev., Jan. 1901, v.9, p.1-12.

13 **GAINES' MILL, Battle of**
See: Joseph R. Anderson.

14 **GAINES, E.W.**
"Fayette Artillery, the movement on New Berne thirty-three years ago, a Richmond's better part. Both land and naval forces-a singular charge and a singular chase-quick surrender." (From Richmond "Dispatch, Mar. 28, 1897) In: SHSP, 1897, v.XXV, p. 288-297.

15 **GAINES, Francis Pendleton**
"Lee: the backgound of a great decision, August, 1865. An address to the officers and directors of the Robert E. Lee Memorial Foundation, Lee Chapel, Oct. 12, 1934." (Lexington, Va.) Washington and Lee University, 1934.) 8vo, wraps, front, (9)pp. $3.

16 ..."Lee, the Final Achievement, 1865-1870. Speeches by Dr. Francis Pendleton Gaines, Pres., Washington and Lee University, Lexington, Virginia." N.Y., The N.Y. Southern Society (1933). Limited Edition. $20-sig.np. $15, $20, $35-bmk. Tall 8vo, bds/cl., de, port(front) illus., 31pp. (1)p. (Roanoke, Va., Stone Printing, 1933).

17 **GAINES, George Towns**
"Fighting Tennesseeans." (Kingsport, Tenn., Kingsport Press, 1931) Privately printed. 8vo, cl, xiii, 127pp. $45-jk-122, $7.50, $12.50. Shiloh, Al. Sid. Johnston,

Murfreesboro, Chickamauga, N.B. Forrest, etc.

18 GAINES, J.M., Dr.
"Sick and wounded Confederate soldiers at Hagerstown and Williamsport." In: SHSP, 1899, v.27, p. 241-250.

19 GAINES, Samuel M., 1st Lt. Charlotte Cavalry, 14th Virginia.
"How General Lee saved the life of a Federal Officer." In: SHSP, 1905, v.33, p. 375-376.

20 GAINES, William H., Jr.
"Biographical Register of Members Virginia State Convention of 1861, First Session." Richmond: Virginia State Library, 1969. 8vo, wraps, 87pp. $6-jk, $1.

21 ..."From bullets to ballots: Confederate Veterans in postwar Virginia poliitcs." (Richmond) Va. Calv., Winter, 1953. v.III, #3, p. 12-16, ports, views.

22 GALBREATH, Charles Burleigh
"Daniel Decatur Emmett, Author of "Dixie." Columbus, Ohio: F.J. Heer Print, 1904. Tall 8vo, cl, illus., ports, 5, 66pp. $22. Privately printed, $45-jk.

23 GALES, Seaton
"Gen. George Burgwyn Anderson." In: Land We Love, 1867, v.III, p. 93-100. See: Our Liv. and Dead, 1875, III, p. 327-335, for same. port. Poem to: p. 345-346. See: Alfred Moore Waddell.

23a GALLAGHER, Gary, Dr.
"The Most Memorable Day of Our War." In: CWTI, May 1988, v. 27, #3, p.22-9, ills, ports, map. Spotsylvania, May 12, 1864. Saved Lee's army.

24 GALLAGHER, Gary W.
"Stephen Dodson Ramseur: Lee's gallant general." Chapel Hill: University of N.C. Press, 1983, 8vo, cl, 248pp., dj, 30 halftones, 18 maps. $22.50. See also: Stephen D. Ramseur.

25 "A widow and her soldier: LaSalle Corbell Pickett as author of the Geo. E. Pickett letters." In: VMHB, July, 1986, v.94, p. 329-344.

26 GALLAHER, DeWitt Clinton
"A Diary depicting the experiences of: in the War Between the States while serving in the Confederate Army." (n.p., Apr. 19, 1961) 12mo, wraps, 32pp. In 1919, Charleston, W.V., 1st edt. $45. In 1945, Charleston, W.Va., 31pp., $100-ob, $30-bmk-106.

27 ..."The battlefields around Fredericksburg, Va." In: CV, Nov. 1922, v.XXX, p. 406-408.

28 ..."Closing scenes of war in the Shenandoah Valley." In: CV, Jan. 1923, v.XXXImp. 12-14.

29 GALLAWAY, B.P., Edt.
"The Dark Corner of the Confederacy. Accounts of Civil War Texas as told by Contemporaries." Dubuque, Iowa: Wm. C. Brown Co.(1968) 8vo, pict. stiff bds., map, xvi, 188pp. $4.
...Dubuque, Iowa: Kendall-Hunt Co. (1972). same, xiii, 284pp. 2nd edt. $6.

30 ..."A Texas Farm Boy enlists in the 12th Cavalry." In: TMH, 1970, v.8, #2, p. 87-95. Subject: David C. Nance.

31 GALLAWAY, Rowena McCord
"The Southern Memorial Association, Washington County, Arkansas." (Fayetteville, Arkansas. 1956) Washington County Historical Society, Bul. #24, cover title, 4to, mimeo, 55pp., pls., ports, $4.50.

32 GALLOWAY, Charles Betts, Rev.
"Jefferson Davis, a judicial estimate; address delivered at the University of Mississippi, June 3, 1908." University of Mississippi, Bul. series: 6, #3, p.1-48, Aug., 1908. ports (front), wraps, 12mo, or, in suede.

33 ..."Jefferson Davis: his place in history." In: Meth. Qurt. Rev., Oct. 1910, v.LIX, p. 744-772.
...In: CV, June, 1925, v.XXXIII, p. 210-

217.

...Also: CV, July, 1908, v.16, p. 321-328, ports.

34 **GAMBLE MANSION**
"The Gamble Mansion." (Tallahassee, Fla., Board of Parks, n.d.) 4to, (4)pp. folder, illus., ports. Also designated: Judah P. Benjamin Memorial (UDC).

35 **GAMBRELL, Herbert P.**
"Rams versus gunboats." In: SW Rev., 1937, v.XXIII, p. 46-78.

36 **GAMMAGE, Washington Lafayette**
"The Camp, the Bivouac and the Battlefield, being a history of the 4th Arkansas Regiment, from its first organization down to the present date." Its campaigns and its battles, with an occasional reference to the current events of the times including biographical sketches of the field officers and others of the "Old Brigade". The whole interspersed here and there with descriptions of scenery, incidents of camp life, etc. By..., Brigade surgeon of McNair Brigade." Selma, Ala., Cooper & Kimball, Mississippian Book & Job Office, 1864. 8vo, cl, 164pp. $150.

...Little Rock, Ark., Southern Press, 1958. (Jackson, Tenn., McCowat-Mercer Press). 8vo, cl, illus., maps, 1-fldg., facsm., 150pp. Intro: Ted R. Worley. $12.50, $15, $30, $25-bmk, $90-bmk-105.

37 **GANAWAY, Loomis Morton**
"New Mexico and the Sectional Controversy, 1846-1861." Albuquerque: Univ. of N.M. Press, 1944. Historical Society of New Mexico Publications in History, v.XII. 8vo, wraps, illus., bibliog., x, 140pp.

...(Albuquerque, N.M., New Mexico) Historical Review, April, 1943, v.XVIII, #2, p. 113-147; #3, p. 205-246; #4, p. 325-348; Jan. 1944, v.XIX, #1, p. 55-79.

38 **GANAWAY, William T.**
"Trinity College in War Times." (North Carolina) In: Trinity Archive, May 1893, v.6, p. 324-329.

39 **GANNON, Michael V.**
"Rebel Bishop The Life and Era of Augustin Verot. With a foreword by John Tracy Ellis." Milwaukee: Bruce Pub. Co., (July 1964) 8vo, cl, dj, illus, map, ports, incl. front, xvii, (1), 267pp. $20-bmk-84, $25-bmk-123, $15-bmk, $20.

40 **GANTT, Edwart W.**
"Address of Brig. Gen. E.W. Gantt, C.S.A. First published October 7, 1863, at Little Rock, Arkansas." n.p., n.d. (Phil. 1863)? $85-bmk. 8vo, sewn, 29pp., cover title. $25. (Van Norman-#123(#14).

41 ..."Address of Hon. E.W. Gantt to the People of Arkansas, 1863." Little Rock, Ark., National Democrat Print (1893). 12mo, wraps, 24pp., Sabin-Hargrett-453. Attacks Albert Pike.

42 ..."Address of Brig. Gen. E.W. Gantt, CSA. First Published Oct. 7, 1863, at Little Rock, Arkansas." Union League of Philadelphia, #36, pt.2, n.d., 8vo, wraps, 29pp. Sabin-26543, $45. Appeal to Ex-Confederates of South, cease war. (Wantaugh-292) (#4).

43 ..."Address of Brig. Gen. E.W. Gantt, CSA. (To the people of Arkansas)." (Little Rock, 1863?) 8vo, printed wraps, sewn, 29pp. $65-jk-122. (Jenkins: variant of Sabin-26543).

44 ..."Loyal Publications Society of New York, #1-44. Loyal National League. Opinions of prominent men concerning the great questions of the times...on the anniversary of Sumter." N.Y., C.S. Wescott, 1863. #37, address of E.W. Gantt of Arkansas in favor of reunion 1863. See: also, Alex. H. Stephens "Prophecy and Fulfillment", N.Y., 1863, p.(23)-45. Gen. Gantt's apostacy took place following his capture and imprisonment by Union forces.

45 **GARAFALO, Robert and Mark Elrod**
"A pictorial history of Civil War era musical instruments and military bands." Charlestown, W.Va., Pictorial histories Pub. Co., 1985. 8vo, wraps, 124pp., illus(color, b/w) $10.

46 **GARBER, Alexander M., Jr.**
"Stonewall Jackson's Way, a sketch of the life and service, Maj. John A. Harmon, Chief Quartermaster, 2nd Corp., A.N.V. and Army of the Valley District, on staffs of Gens. Stonewall Jackson, Ewell and Early. Being a sketchy narrative of the war in Northern Virginia-containing many letters from Jackson and fresh anecdotes, never before published, as well as pen pictures of camp life, by an old comrad." Staunton, Va., "Spectator" Job Print, 1876, 8vo, wraps, 45pp. title and text within balck lines. Edt: "On Memoriam Sempiternam...

47 **GARBER, Asher Waterman**
"Artillery Work at Wilderness." In: SHSP, 1905, v.33, p. 341-343.

47a **GARBER, Hon. J. A., of Va.**
"Robert E. Lee, Speech of J. A. Garber in the House of Representatives, Jan. 20, 1930." Washington, 1930. 8vo, wraps, 7p.

48 **GARBER, Michael C., Jr.**
"Reminiscences of the burning of Columbia, South Carolina." In: Ind. Mag. Hist., Dec., 1915, v.XI, p. 285-300.
...In: Mag. of Hist., May 1916, v.XXII, p. 177-191.

49 **GARD, R. Max**
"The End of the Morgan Raid." (Lison, Ohio, Buckeye Pub. Co., July 1963) 8vo, stiff wraps, illus., port., dble-pg. map, 22pp.

50 ..."Morgan's Raid Into Ohio." Lisbon, Ohio: The Author, 1963. (Salem, Ohio: Lyle Print & Pub.) 8vo, cl, front(portrait) illus., 62pp. $4, $5. 1000 copies.

51 **GARDINER, Mabel and Ann Henshaw**
"Chronicles of Old Berkeley, a narrative history of a Virginia county from its beginning to 1926." Durham, N.C., Seeman Press, 1938. 8vo, cl, illus., map, ix, 323pp. Around Martinsburg, "Berkeley Border Guards, Co.D, 2nd Va. Inf., State Militia.

52 **GARDNER, Joseph L.**
"Bull Run Russell." In: Amer. Hert. June 1962, v.XII, #4, p. 59-61, 78-83, ports, illus., incl. dbl. pg. color scene. Wm. Howard Russell, British correspondent, London Times.

53 **GARDNER, Robert**
"A Tenth-Hour Apology for Slavery." (Lexington, Ky.) Aug., 1960, v.XXVI, #3, p. 352-367. Rev. John Leadly Dagg's "Elements of Moral Science." Pro-slave. Baptist split with North, 1845, Athens, Ga.

54 **GARLAND, John Lewis**
"Irish Soldiers of the American Confederacy." In: Irish Sword, v.I (Dublin, 1949/1953) p. 174-180. Dornbusch III-138.

55 **GARLAND, R.R., Col., 6th Tex. Inf.**
"Arkansas Post, its fall, Jan. 11, 1863." In: SHSP, 1894, at Washington, Arkansas." See: Claire N. Moody's Battle of Pea Ridge, p. 22-27.

56 **GARLAND, Robert R.**
"The Fall of Arkansas Post." In: SHSP, 1894, v.XXII, p. 10-13.

57 **GARLAND, Samuel**
"Report of the Battle of Seven Pines." In: SHSP, 1879, v.7, p. 113-122.

58 **GARLER, A.M., Jr.**
"Stonewall Jackson Way." Poetry, Staunton, Va., (1876). 8vo, wraps, 7pp.

59 **GARNER, Alto L. and Nathan Stott**
"William Lowndes Yancey: statesman of secession." In: AR, July 1962, v.15, #3, p. 190-202.

60 **GARNER, Bob**
"Let us be Patriots and Texans-a content analysis of the Secession rhetoric of Sam

Houston, 1854-1861." In: Texana, 1974, v.XII, #1, p. (1)-19.

61 **GARNER, James Wilford**
"The first struggle over secession in Mississippi." In: Pub. Miss. Hist. Soc., 1901, v.IV, p. (89)-104. Pub. as pamphlet, cover-title.

..."Reconstruction in Mississippi." N.Y., Lond: Macmillan Co., 1901. 8vo, cl, xiii, 422pp. $25, $35, $40, $50, $100-bmk-06.

...1902 edition, Thesis (PHd-Columbia University. Academic record.

63 **GARNER, Mabel C., compl.**
"A list of battles, actions, combats, skirmished, military events, etc. which did occur in Arkansas between the dates April 19, 1775-July 1, 1902, compiled for Arkansas History Commission. (Little Rock, Ark., 1960) cover title. 4to, (12)pp. compl. from F.B. Heitman, Hist. Register of U.A. Army, v.2.

64 **GARNER, William Wakefield**
"Letters of an Arkansas Confederate Soldier. Edt: D.D. McBrien." In: Ark. Hist. Quart., 1943, v.II, p. 58-70, 171-184, 268-286.

65 **GARNETT'S BRIGADE, at Gettysburg.**
See: Chs. S. Peyton.

66 **GARNETT, Alexander Yelverton Peyton**
"Burial ceremonies of Confederate dead. Oration of A.Y.P. Garnett, M.D., ode: by Rt. Rev. Wm. Pinkney, Dec. 11, 1874." Washington: S & R.O. Polkinhorn, 1875, 8vo, wraps, 16pp.

67 **GARNETT, James Mercer**
"Biographical sketch of Hon. Muscoe Russell Hunter Garnett (1821-1864) of "Elmwood", Essex Co., Va." (Williamsburg, 1909) 8vo, wraps, 76pp. $20. Reprint: July/Oct., 1909, Wm. and Mary Col. Quart. Mag.

68 ..."The Battle of Antietam or Sharpsburg. Reminiscences of Jackson's Old Division by Capt. Jas. M. Garnett and Alex. Hunter, with comments by Alex. Robert Chisholm. Numbers against Gen. Lee-an estimate that he had but 35,000 or 36,000 in the conflict-hungry men fought bravely." (From Baltimore, Md. "Sun", Sept. 16-Oct. 18, 1903." In: SHSP, 1903, v.XXXI, p. 32-37.

69 ..."Battle of Second Manassas, including Ox Hill. Ordnance Officer of Grime's (formerly Rhodes Div., 2nd Corps, ANV). In: SHSP, 1915, v.40, p. 224-229.

70 ..."Battle of Winchester. By..., formerly Capt. Confederate States Army and Ordnance officer of Gen. Rode's Division, A.N.Va., (From: Baltimore, Md., "Sun", Sept. 26, 1903." In: SHSP, 1903, v.XXXI, p. 61-68.

71 ..."Diary of Captain James M. Garnett. Ordnance officer Rode's Division, 2nd Corps. covering part of Gen. Early's Campaign in the Shenandoah Valley." In: SHSP, 1899, Jan.-Dec., v.XXVII, p. (1)-16.

..."Diary of Captain James M. Garnett. . ." In: SHSP, 1900, v. 28, p.58-71.

72 ..."Harper's Ferry and First Manassas. Extracts from the diary of Capt. James M. Garnett, in charge of General Reserve Ordnance Train, ANVa., from Jan. 1863 to Feb. 1864; and ordnance officer of Rode's (Later Grime's) division, 2nd Corp., ANVa. from Feb. 1864 to Apr. 9, 1865." In: SHSP, 1900, v.XXVIII, p. 58-71. Notes.

73 ..."Hon. James Mercer Garnett. Address by Prof. James Mercer Garnett, presenting the portrait of Hon. James M. Garnett in the courtroom at Tappahannock, Essex Co., Va., Judge Thos. R.B. Wright of the Circuit Court Presiding-June 20, 1898." In: SHSP, 1898, v.XXVI, p. 347-358.

74 ..."Ordnance Report of Grime's Division, 2nd Corps., ANVa., made at Appomattox

74 CH, Va., April 10, 1865. Report of Arms, etc." In: SHSP, 1899, v.XXVII, p. 177-179.

75 ..."Personal Reminiscences of Seven Days Battle Around Richmond. The Fortieth Anniversary." (From Baltimore "Sun", June 1902) In: SHSP, 1902, v.XXX, p. 147-151.

76 **GARNETT, John J., Col. Artillery, CSA**
"The battles of Fredericksburg, Dec. 13, 1862 and Chancellorsville, May 1863." In: Frank Leslie Pop. Monthly, Aug. 1896. vol. 42, p. 135-143, Aug., p. 261-271, Sept. '96.

77 ..."The great Confederate's part in the battle of Gettysburg, July 1863." In: Frank Leslie's Pop. Monthly, v.42, Aug. 1896, p.135-143; Sept. 1896, p. 261-271.

78 ..."The Seven Day's Campaign near Richmond." In:Frank Leslie's Pop. Monthly, v.41, June 1896, p. 611-623.

79 **GARNETT, John J., Col., Artly., CSA**
"The Artillery of the Gettysburg Campaign. Report of..." In: SHSP, 1882, v.10, p. 161-164.

80 **GARNETT, Muscoe Russell Hunter**
"Speech of...on the State of the Union, delivered in the House of Representatives, Jan. 16, 1861." Washington: McGill & Witherow, 1861. 8vo, wraps, 16pp. An eloquent orator, one of the most brilliant Southern statesmen, uncompromising defender of slavery, first able philosophical expression of relations of slavery to the Federal Government and challenges northern infringements of the constitutional rights of south. Advocated Virginia's secession (DAB). See: Jas. M. Garnett.

81 ..."The Union, Past and Future; How it Works, and How to Save it." by a Citizen of Virginia. Charleston: 1850. 8vo, wraps, 55pp. (old)-$4.

82 **GARNETT, Theodore Stanford**
"Address on M.R.H. Garnett." In: SHSP, 1899, v.27, p. 155-157.

83 ..."The Cruise of the Nashville." In: SHSP, 1884, v.12, p. 329-334.

84 ..."Tribute to General Lee." In: SHSP, 1894, v.22, p. 106-114.

85 ..."Address on presenting the portrait of R.M.T. Hunter." In: SHSP, 1899, v.XXVII, p. 151-155.

86 ..."The dashing Gen. J.E.B. Stuart." In: CV, Dec. 1911, v.XIX, p. 575-576.

87 ..."The Confederate Dead, Oration Memorial Day at Elmwood Cemetery, Norfolk, Va., under auspices Pickett-Buchanan Camp, Confederate Veterans, June 18, 1884." Norfolk, Va., Landmark Print(1884). 8vo, wraps, 19pp.

88 ..."J.E.B. Stuart(Major-General), an address at the unveiling of the equestrian statue of Gen. Stuart, at Richmond, Va., May 30, 1907, by...his Aide-de-camp." N.Y., Wash., Neale Pub. Co., 1907. 12mo, front(port)illus., 61pp. $20, $22.50, $18.50, $15, $17.50, $75-ns, $100-ob, $35-bmk, $45-bmk, $50-bmk.

89 ..."Glowing tribute to General R.E. Lee and a letter from Lord Wolseley." In: SHSP, 1900, v.28, p. 106-114.

90 **GARRETSON, Owen Albright**
"The Battle of Athens." In: Palimpsest, Oct., 1927, v.VIII, p. 138-149. CSA guerrilla attack on Athens, Mo., August, 1861.

91 **"GARRETT COUNTY Historical Society, Oakland Md."**
"The Glades Star", Civil War Cent., v.3, June 1961, illus. W.Va. border skirmishes and Roster Union and CSA men in county.

92 **GARRETT, David R.**
"The Civil War Letters of..., detailing the adventures of the 6th Texas Cavalry, 1861-1865. Edited by L. Col. Max Lale, U.S.A.R. with annotations and background material by Cdr. Hobart Jey, Jr., USNR(ret.) great-grandson of David Garrett." Marshall, Texas: Port Caddo Pre-

ss(Demmer Co., Inc., 1963). 4to, cl, ports(incl.front), illus., facsms (1-fldg.) 2-maps, xvii, 105pp., 300 copies. $15, $45-jk.

92a GARRETT, James Jackson
"Forty-fourth Alabama Regiment." In: AHST, 1897/8, v.II, p.34-8.

93 GARRETT, Jill K., Edt.
"Confederate Soldiers and Patriots of Maury County, Tenn." Columbia, Tenn., 1970, 8vo, stiff wraps, 381pp. $15-bmk-18, pt. 1.

94 GARRETT, Jill Knight
"The Civil War in Maury County, Tennessee, by Jill Knight Garrett and Marise P. Lightfoot." (Columbia, Tenn., 1966?) 4to, mimeographed, ports, 265pp. Collection of soldiers diaries, newspaper clippings, muster rolls, etc.

95 GARRETT, Richard B.
"End of a Manhunt." In: Amer. Hert. June, 1966, v.XVII, #4, p. 40-43, 105. ports, color pl. John Wilkes Booth hunt and capture.

96 GARRETT, Richard Baynham
"A chapter of unwritten history. Richard B. Garrett's account of the flight and death of John Wilkes Booth. Edt: Betsy Fleet." In: VMHB, Oct. 1963, v.71, #4, p. 387-407. + front(port), illus.

97 GARRETT, W.E.
"Strategy of New Creek Station." In: Confed. Vet., May 1905, v.XIII, p. 210.

98 GARRETT, William
"Reminiscences of public men in Alabama, for thirty years. With an Appendix. By Wm. Garrett, late secretary of State." Atlanta, Ga., Plantation Pub. Co., 1872. 8vo, cl, 809pp. $17.50, $22.50. Remin. in chronological form, covers the period of 1837-1868.

99 GARRETT, William H.
"True story of the capture of John Wilkes Booth." In: CV, April 1921, v.XXIX, p. 129-130.

100 GARRETT, William Robertson
"The Civil War from a Southern Standpoint, by the late William Robertson Garrett and Robert Ambrose Halley." Phila: Printed for subscribers only by G. Barrie & Sons (1905). 8vo, cl, col. front, plates, ports, maps, facsms., on Japan vellum, limited to 1000 copies, x, 383, xiiipp. $20, $35.

101 ...(1909), Phila: Geo. Barrie & Sons., v.XIV, "History of North America." 8vo, cl, ports, maps, pls, facsms., xxv, 553pp. $14.

102 ..."The South as a factor in the Territorial expansion of the United States." In: Clement Evans' Confed. Mil. Hist., v.1, p. 59-246.

GARRETT-ASBELL Letters
See: Lewis N. Wynne.

103 GARRISON, George P.
"Richard Montgomery Swearingen." In: SwHQ, 1905, v.VIII, p. 225-231.

104 GARRISON, L.R.
"Administrative Problems of the Confederate Post Office Department." In: QTSHA, Oct. 1915, v.XIX, #2, p. 111-141, #3, p. 232-250.

105 GARTH, David
"Gray Canaan." N.Y., G.P. Putnam (1947). 12mo, cl, dj, 3, 280pp. CSA novel. $15.

106 GARY, Eugene Blackburn
"Vindication of the South; address delivered at Abbeville, S.C., on Memorial Day, May 10, 1917, under auspices of United Daughters of the Confederacy." (Abbeville, S.C., Press & Banner, 1917). 12mo, wraps, 19pp. Atg.-$15, $10.

107 GARY, M.W.
"Remarks of...of Edgefield, S.C. in House Reps., Nov. 9, 1860. On Mr. Trenholm's Resolutions." n.p., 1860, sewn, 7pp. $8. Anti-Lincoln comments.

108 GASKELL, John Evan, Maj.
"Patriotic Songs, old and new." Ft. Worth,

Texas, J.E. Gaskell, (1917). 15cm, wraps, (39)pp. (without music), ports.

109 ..."Living Confederate Songs, by Lt. J.E. Gaskell. R.E. Lee Camp, Ft. Worth, Texas." Ft. Worth, Tex., n.d. 3 1/2"x6", wraps, 28pp. $5.
...Same, by Maj. J.E. Gaskell, n.d., stiff wraps, 36pp., n.d., Mor., $15.

110 **GASTON, A.P.**
"Partisan campaigns of Col. Lawrence M. Allen, commanding the 64th Reg. North Carolina Troops (State) during the late civil war." Raleigh, N.C., Edwards & Broughton, 1894. 8vo, wraps, 28pp. See also: John W. Moore's Roster N.C. Troops, v.IV; Walter Clark's v.III.

111 **GASTON, John Thomas**
"Confederate War Diary of John Thomas Gaston." Compiled by Alifaire (Allie) Gaston Walden." (Columbia, S.C., Vogue Press) 1960. 8vo, wraps, front(port), illus., ports, xvi, 22, (2)pp. pres. copy-$15, $30-bmk-105.

113 **GASTON, Robert H. and William H.**
"Tyler to Sharpsburg. The War Letters of...Co.H, First Texas Inf. Reg., Hood's Texas Brigade." Edt: Robert W. Glover. $3.50. Waco, Texas: W.M. Morrison, Texian Press, 1960. wraps, color-flag, port, facsm. letter, 22pp. 1000 copies. $15, $8-bmk, $2.

114 **GATES, Eva M.**
"Florida's Confederate Shrine. The Judah P. Benjamin Memorial. Gamble Mansion, Ellenton, Florida, on the Manatee River." n.p., Oct. 15, 1942. 8vo, illus., 15pp.

115 **GATES, Grace Hooten**
"The search for Semmes." In: AR, Apr. 1987, XL, #2, p. 83-94, facsms.

116 **GATES, Paul W.**
"Agriculture and The Civil War." N.Y., Alfred A. Knopf, 1965. 8vo, cl, d/w, pp.x, 383. $8.95, $35.

117 **GATLIN, Radford**
"The parentage, birth, nativity, and exploits of the immortal hero James Keelan, who defended successfully the bridge at Strawberry Plains, and alone, put to flight fifteen Lincolnites on the night of the eight of November, A.D., 1861, Atlanta, Ga., Daily Intelligencer Print, 1862." Knoxville: Stubley Print, 1932. 8vo, wraps, cover title, 13pp.

118 **GAUGHAN, T.J., Mrs., Edt.**
"Letters of a Confederate Surgeon, Junius Newport Bragg, 1861-1865." (Camden, Ark., Hurley Print, 1960. 8vo, cl, front(facsm.) (4), 276pp. 500 copies printed. $15-b, $10.

119 **GAUL, Gilbert**
"With the Confederate Colors, 1861-1865." (Nashville, Tenn.) Southern Art Pub. Co., 1907. Text: Thornwell Jacobs." Confederate War pictures, four-color, 20x30" (plate: 15x19"): "Between the Lines", "The Forager", "Faithful Unto Death", "Holding the Line at all Hazzards", "Leaving Home", "Picket", "Tidings from the Front", "Waiting for the Dawn". $10, $15. "Charging the Battery" (Storming?) Projected series of twelve lithographs.

120 ..."Series of Confederate scenes, enterprise of Southern Art Publishing Co." In: CV, 1907, v.15, p. 240(vii) and a short sketch of artist. Leather portfolio 7-pictures, $16.50 (1907).

121 **GAULDIE, Enid**
"The Effect of the American Civil War on Dundee's Trade." (London) Jour. Confed. Hist. Soc., Spring, 1968, v.6, #1, p. 26-30, pl.

122 **GAULTNEY, W.R., Rev.**
"Typical Guerillas of the war period." In: CV, April 1919, p. 132-136 dble-column. Eyewitness to the "Fort Hamby affair."

123 **GAUTIER, Ange Simon**
"Combat naval de Hampton-Roads (Etats-

Unis), 8 et 9 Mars, 1862." In: Revue Maritime et Coloniale, April 1862, v.VI, p. 806-819.

124 GAUTIER, George R.
"Harder than Death: The Life of George R. Gautier, an Old Texan, living at the Confederate Home, Austin, Texas. Written by himself." n.p., 1902. 8vo, wraps, 62pp., port, illus., $50. Cattle drives, adv. in war, imprisonment for manslaughter.

125 GAVIN, William G.
"Accoutrements plates, North and South, 1861-1865; an authorative reference with comparative values." Foreword: by Stephen V. Grancsay. Phila., Riling & Letz, 1963. 8vo, cl, illus., ports, xvii, 217pp. $25, $12. 2nd Edt: 1975, p. 367. New, enlarged, $20-y.

126 ..."Confederate belt buckles and cartridge box plates of the Confederacy." In: Mil. Collector and Hist., June 1954, v.6, p. 29-35, views.

127 GAY, Mary A.H.
"Life in Dixie during the war..." A chap. from..."Domestic life in the war-torn Dixie." In: Harold Straubig's-"Civil War eyewitness reports." Hamden, Conn., Archon Books, 1985. p. 203-219.

...Decatur, Ga., DeKalb Historical Society, Old Court House, 1985, 8vo, cl, 448pp. $20.

GAY, Mary Ann Harris
"Life in Dixie during the War. 1863-1864-1865." Atlanta, Ga: Constitution Office, 1892. 12mo, decr., cl, 255pp. $43-nc, $15.

...Atlanta, Ga., Foote & Davies, 1894. 1861-1862-1863-1864-1865." With an intro: Joel Chandler Harris. $30, $45-dab, $125-jk, $17.50. 12mo, decr., cl. (15), (16)-299pp.

...Atlanta, Ga., C.P. Byrd Print, 1897. 3rd edt., enlarged, 410pp., cl, or full decr. calf, $20, $175-jk-151, $25, $17.50, $75, $35-bmk, $50-bmk-105.

...Atlanta, Ga., 1901, edt. 4th, Tk. 12mo, cl, 404pp. $15, $90.

...Louisv: Lost Cause Pr., micro-cd. $6.

...Decatur, Ga., DeKalb Historical Society, 1982, Reprint of the 1904 edition. $18. See: Elizabeth Stevenson.

128 GAYARRE, Charles, Judge
"Review: Col. Alfred Romans "Military Operations of Beauregard." In: SHSP, 1884, v.12, p. 402-416, 432-447.

129 GAYARRE, Charles, La.
"Wm. H. Seward on Reconstruction." In: SB, ns, v.1, #9, p. 521-523, 1885/1886.

130 GAYLE, Richard H.
"Extracts from the diary of Richard H. Gayle, CSNavy, Edt: Frank E. Vandiver." In: TylerQHM, Oct. 1948, v.30, p. 85-92. Prisoner of war in Boston, Jan. 20-Apr. 3, 1865.

131 GEE, Boliver H., Maj., 49th Ga. Reg.
"Official Report of Gettysburg." In: SHSP, 1885, v.13, p. 196-197.

132 GEERLINGS, Gerald
"A temple of sacred memories in the breast of a granite mountain." n.p., Lyon-Young, n.d., (c.1910?) 4to, wraps, (24)pp. $20. Etchings, great artwork of Stone Mountain.

133 GEISE, William Royston
"Centennial Observance of the Establishment of Missouri's Confederate Capital at Marshall Texas." Reprint from Oct. 1962, Southwestern Historical Quarterly. 8vo, wraps, (24)pp. illus., facsm. $1. (Marshall, Texas: Caddo Press?, 1963)

134 ..."Decline and collapse, December, 1864-June, 1865." In: MHTSw, 1981, v.16, #2, p. 137-142.

135 ..."The Confederate Northwest, May-August, 1861. A study of Organization and Command in the Trans-Mississippi West." In: MHT & Sw, 1975, v.XIII, #1, p. 11-21; "Divided Command in the West August-September, 1961(sic)." #2, p. 47-54; Oc-

tober, 1861-January, 1862, #3, p. 49-57; "Texas-First Year of the War, April, 1861-April, 1862." #4, p. 29-43, map; "A New Command, Jan. 1862-May, 1862." v.XIV, #1, p. 33-44; "Hindman and Hebert Divide Command, pt. IV, June-July, 1862." #2, p. 107-119; "General Holmes Fails to Create a Department, August 1862-February 1863, Pt. VII'" #3, p. 169-178; "Holmes, Arkansas, and Defense of the Lower River, August 1862-February 1863, Pt. VIII, #4, p. 229-236"; "Isolation July-December 1863, Pt.X," v.XV, #2, p. 31-41"; "The Department Faces Total Isolation, February-July, 1863, Part IX." v.XV, #1, p. 35-47."

136 ..."Kirby Smith's War Department, 1864." In: MHTSw, 1980, v.XV, #3, p. 45-62.

137 ..."Kirby Smithdom, 1864." In: MHTSw, 1979, v.XV, #4, p. 17-35. notes.
..."Military Command and the Campaign of 1864, in the Trans-Mississippi Dept." In: MHT & Sw, 1980, v.16, #1, p. 55-76, notes.

138 ..."Missouri's Confederate Capital in Marshall, Texas." (Columbia, Mo., Mo. Hist. Review, Oct. 1963, v.LVIII-#1, p. 37-54, illus. 1st: Southwestern Hist. Quart., Oct. 1962, v.LXVI-#2, p. 193-207, illus.

139 **GELFANT, B.H.**
"Gone with the wind and the impossiblities of fiction." In: So. Lit. Jour., 1980, v.13, (1), p. 3-31.

140 **GENEALOGIES: ,**
See: Perry L. Blackshear, Bertram H. Groene, Samuel Ed Mays, Edmund Jennings Lee, Louise Parker Moore, Francis M. Purifoy, Thos. Keith Skinner, Lillian Reeves Wyatt, Katherine Wooten Springs.

141 **GENEALOGY: Civil War ancestor tracing.**
"Civil War Genealogy: 316pp. sources for tracing your ancestor. 1-The Civil War; 2-Archives; 3-National Publications; 4-State Publications; 5-Local Sources; 6-Military Unit Histories; 7-Civil War Events. Easley, S.C., Southern Hist. Press, 1962, 8vo, paper, 64pp. $8.

142 **"GENERAL CATECHISM**
of the Christian Doctrine on the basis adopted by the Plenary Council of Baltimore for the use of Catholics of Diocese of Savannah and Vicariate Apostolic of Florida, with slight additions and modifications ordered by the Right Rev. Augustin Verot, Bishop of Savannah, Adm. A. of Florida." Augusta, Ga., J.T. Paterson & Co., 1864. 16mo, wraps, 96pp. (unrecorded imprint) $20.

143 **"GENERAL OFFICERS, Union and Confederate-**
a complete Roster." In: Photo. Hist. C.W., v.10, p. 301-322, illus.

144 **"GENERALS in the Saddle.**
Famous men in both CSA and Union were good horsemen." In: SHSP, 1891, v.19, p. 167-175.

145 **GENERALS of the C.S.A.**
See: Joseph V. Bidgood, "Brooklyn Eagle", Wm. L. Cabell, John W. DuBose, "Generals in the Saddle.", Chs. C. Jones, Charles Edgeworth Jones, "Nashville Banner." "Richmond, Va. Dispatch.", "Virginia Generals in CSArmy."

146 **"GENERALS of the Confederate Army."**
Engraving by J. Rogers-Vannerson and Jones Photo Richmond, Va., n.d. 8x11", decorations around ovals of: Brax. Bragg, Longstreet, Johnston, Hood and Kirby Smith. $45.

147 **GENTRY, Claude**
"The Battle of Brice's Crossroads." Baldwyn, Miss., Magnolia Pub., (1963). 12mo, wraps, illus., map, 26pp. $1, $10, $20-b.
...1974, (5th Print.) $3.50-y, $5-y, $1.

148 ..."The Capture of Holly Springs." Baldwyn, Miss., Magnolia Pub., (1971). 12mo, stiff wraps, illus., (18)pp. $3.

149 ..."General Nathan Bedford Forrest, the Boy and the Man." Baldwyn, Miss., Magnolia Pub., (1972). 12mo, stiff wraps, 98pp. $15, $6.

150 ..."Private John Allen: Gentleman, Statesman, Sage, Prophet." (Baldwyn, Miss., 1951). 8vo, cl, facsms, ports, views, xviii, 189pp. $30-bmk, $5.50, $17.50-bond.

151 ..."Shiloh." Baldwyn, Mississippi(1966). 8vo, pict. stiff wraps, 38pp. cover illus. and fldg. map by author. $1, $10, $4-y.
..."The Battle of Corinth." Baldwyn, Miss., Magnolia Pub., 1976. 8vo, paper, 43pp.
..."The Battle of Harrisburg (Tupelo)." Baldwyn, Miss., Magnolia Pub., 1981. 8vo, paper, 38pp.

152 **GENTRY, Judith Fenner**
"A Confederate Success in Europe: The Erlanger Loan." In: JSH, May 1970, 32pp., v.XXXVI, p. 157-188. $8.

153 **GENTRY, Susie, Miss.**
"The Volunteer State(Tennessee) as a Seceder." (Raleigh, N.C., U.M. Uzzell 1903) 8vo, cover title, 14pp. In: N.C. Booklet, July, 1903, v.III, #3.

154 **GEOGHEGAN, William E., Thomas W. Green, Capt. R. Steensen, R.D.N., Frank J. Merli**
"The South's Scottish Sea Monster." Amer. Neptune, January 1969, Volume XXIX, #1, p. 5-29, plates (4).

155 **GEORG, Kathleen and John W. Busey**
"Nothing but Glory, Pickett's Division at Gettysburg." Hightstown, N.J., Longstreet House, 1987, 8vo, 600pp., illus.(30), maps, (7), index. $40.

156 **GEORGE, Charles E.**
"The Supreme Court of the Confederate States of America." In: Va. Law Rev., n.s., Dec. 1920, v.VI, p. 592-529.

157 **GEORGE, Henry**
"History of the 3rd, 7th, 8th, 12th, Kentucky, C.S.A." Louisville: C.T. Dearing Print, 1911. 8vo, cl, pl., ports, maps, facsm., 193pp. The 3-7-8th, were mounted Mar. '64, sometimes known as "Kentucky Brig." $22.50, $40, $55, $100-y, $175, $300-b, $100-ob, $20, $25-op, Reprint-$15.
...Lyndon, Ky., Mull-Wathen Press. (Dec. 1970) in a Limited Edt. 500 copies Tall 8vo, cl, exact litho-reproduced. $15, (border)$60, op-$30-y, $25.

158 **GEORGE, Joseph, Jr.**
"Abraham Africanus I": President Lincoln through the eyes of a Copperhead Editor." In: CWH, Sept., 1968, v.XIV, p. 226-239.

159 ..."A Catholic family newspaper" views the Lincoln Administration: John Mullaly's Copperhead Weekly." In: CWH, June 1978, v.24, #2, p. 112-132.

160 ..."Nature's first law: Louis J. Weichmann and Mrs. Surratt." In: CWH, June 1982, v.28, #2, p. 101-127. (see under: Weichmann)

161 **GEORGE, Robert H.**
"Brunonians in Confederate Ranks, 1861-1865." In: "Books at Brown", 1965, v.XX, p. 19-34.

162 **GEORGE, W.W.**
"In a Federal Prison." In: SHSP, 1901, v.29, p. 229-239.

163 **GEORGETOWN UNIVERSITY, Washington, D.C.-Alumni Association.**
"Blue & Gray: Georgetown University and the Civil War, Edt: James S. Ruby, Exec. Sect., Research Dir., Thos E. Prendergast." Washington, D.C., (1961). 8vo, cl, xv, 159pp., illus., ports. $15-bmk. A record of soldiers in Civil War, biographical sketches.

164 **GEORGIA ,**
"Index to 4th Georgia Cavalry, CSA." In: Ga. Genealog. Soc., v.2, #3, p. 8-28.

165   "GEORGIA CENTENNIAL TOURS, 7"
(Atlanta: Georgia Dept. of Commerce, 1961) 8vo, decr. color wraps, 24pp., cover title.

166   "GEORGIA Civil War Historical Markers."
Atlanta: Georgia Hist. Comm., (1964) $1. 8vo, wraps, 195pp., maps, index: (135)-195pp. Few descriptive lines to each marker, makes Ga. participation in war impressive.

167   GEORGIA HUSSARS, Savannah.
"Rules of the Georgia Hussars, of Savannah, Georgia. Company "A", Fifth Regiment Ga. Cavalry. Adopted Nov. 16, 1872. Revised and reprinted Dec. 1874...Apr. 12, 1883...Jan. 8, 1891." Savannah, Ga., Morning News, 1891, 24mo, 28pp., 3lf. wraps.
...Savannah, 1895. Revised and reprinted August 5, 1895. 24mo, cl, 34pp. 2 lfs.

168   ...Marcus Wright/Wm. F. Amann lists below: "Ga. Hussars, Co.A (Capt. J.F. Waring's Indp. Ga. Col; assigned Oct. 14, 1861, as Co. E, 6th Va. Cav.; relieved and assigned as Co.F, Jeff Davis Legion, Dec. 7, 1861. Ga. Hussar, Co. B(Capt. W.H. Wiltberger), Co. D, 2nd Battl., Georgia Cavalry." See: Alexander McC. Duncan.

169   GEORGIA MILITARY INSTITUTE
See: Robert L. Rodgers.

170   "GEORGIA MILITIA, General Orders, #24.
(Milledgeville, 1862) Dec. 27, 1862. Sm. Broadside 23 1/2x11cm. $150-bmk-114. Re: company strengths and furloughs. Not in Crandall/Harwell.

171   "GEORGIA POLITICS
(From the Augusta Constitutionalist)." n.p., 1860? 8vo, 10pp. DeRenne: II, p. 609.

172   "GEORGIA State Finance Committee:
Report of the Committee, appointed under resolution of the Convention on the financial operations of the Convention on the financial operations of the State of Georgia during the War." Milledgeville, Ga., Broughton Print., 1866. 8vo, stapled, fldg-table, 72pp. $22.50, $75-jk-122.

173   GEORGIA War Debt
"Some few considerations touching "The Georgia War Debt"." n.p., 1865, 8vo, wraps, 8pp. Argues against repudiation. (the act was passed Nov. 7, so this pamphlet was printed before this date) DeRenne-II, 675.

174   "GEORGIA Yesterday, Today, Tomorrow for Georgia Progress-
Centennial Commemoration Battle of Kennesaw Mt. June 27, 1864-1864, Official Souvenir Program." (Atlanta, Ga., Georgia Progress, 1964) 4to, wraps, color flags, illus., ports, 78pp. ads throughout text.

175   GEORGIA in the War
In: Walter G. Cooper's "Story of Georgia., N.Y., Amer. Hist. Soc., 1938. v.I-"Ga. on eve of war", p. 506 through 'Ga. Campaign 1864", p. 634; Finished in v.III, "Virginia Campaign", p. 1-89.

176   GEORGIA, In: SHSP
See: "Georgi'a Flag", Alice Baxter, Dudley M. DuBose, Gen. Johnston's campaign in..., Thomas Jordan, Armistead L. Long, "Twentieth Ga. at Chickamauga", Edward Willis.

177   GEORGIA-Broadside: ,
"Republic of Georgia, Ordinance of Secession passed Jan. 19, 1861, with the names of the signers. Jan. 21, 1861. Printed at Constitutuionalist Steam Pr., Augusta, Ga., 1861. Mounted on muslin. (Maj. Ed. Wills, of S.C., sale)

178   GEORGIA-Hdg.-Commissary General's Office.
To the Justices of Inferior Court. Macon, Ga., Oct. 1, 1864. Broadside: folio, 2-columns. $13.75. Instructions, how to apply for free salt.

179 **GEORGIA: 20th Regiment**
"Twentieth Georgia Regiment at Chickamauga." In: SHSP, 1888, v.16, p. 384-387.

180 **GEORGIA: Act to authorize convention.**
"An Act to authorize and require the Governor of the State of Georgia, to call a Convention of the people of this state; and for other purposes therein mentioned." In: Allen D. Candler's "CSA Records, II, 206-208.

181 **GEORGIA: Journal Secret Conv.**
"Journal of the Public and Secret Proceedings of the Convention of the People of Georgia held in Milledgeville and Savannah in 1861 together with the Ordinances adopted. Published by order of the Convention. Journal of the Convention held at Milledgeville in open session, Wednesday, Jan. 16, 1861." In: Allen D. Candler's "Confederate Records, v.1, p. (212)-751, appendix, index-p. 753-773.

182 **GEORGIA: Resolutions of counties.**
"Resolutions on Federal Relations, adopted by the People in the various counties of this State and presented by their representatives." In: Allen D. Candler's "Confederate Records", v.1, p. 58-156.

183 **"GEORGIA'S FLAG.**
Replaced Stars and Stripes before Sumter was fired on." In: SHSP, 1903, v.XXXI, p. 236-237.

184 **GERALD, G.B., Maj., 18th Miss. Reg.**
"Notes on the Battle of Cedar Creek." In: SHSP, 1888, v.16, p. 391-392.

185 **GERBER, John**
"Mark Twain's "Private Campaign"." In: C.W.H., Mar. 1855, v.1, #1, p. 37-60. See: Mark Twain's "Quintus Curtius Snodgrass."

186 **GERRISH, Theodore and Rev. John S. Hutchinson**
"The Blue and The Gray; a graphic history of the army of the Potomac and that of northern Virginia including the brilliant engagements of these forces from 1861-1865. The campaigns of the Shenandoah Valley and the Army of the James, together with reminiscences of tent and field...a complete roster of the two great armies by..." Gen. Fitzhugh Lee, Virginia. Bangor, Me., Brady, Mace & Co., 1884. 8vo, cl, 816pp., incl. maps (20). $5, $20-bmk, $11.
...1st Edt: Portland, Me., 1883 $30.

187 **GERSON, Armand J.**
"The inception of the Montgomery Convention." American Historical Ass'n., 1910 Annual Report, Washington, DC, 1912, p. 179-187.

188 **GERSTER, Patrick and Nicholas Cords**
"The Northern origins of Southern Mythology." In: JSH, Nov. 1977, v.43, #4, p. 567-582.

189 **GETTYSBURG ,**
"Historic views of America's greatest battlefield Gettysburg." Gettysburg, Pa., Pub. by Blocher's, n.d. (Chicago: Curt Teich & Co., n.d.) (c.1920) 22x27 1/2cm, stiff wraps, in color, pict., plates, ports, (44)pp. $7.50

190 **GETTYSBURG National Park**
See: Frederick Tilberg.

191 **"GETTYSBURG National Park.**
The Location of the Monuments and Markers and Tablets on the Battlefield of Gettysburg, 1907." 8vo, stiff wraps, 29pp. Confederate Troops, p. 21-29.

192 **"GETTYSBURG, A Complete Historical Narrative**
of the Battle of Gettysburg and the Campaign Preceding It." N.Y., Published for Patrons by J.M. Hill, Mgr. Cyclorama of the Battle of Gettysburg. (Brooklyn, N.Y., Eagle Pr., 1888. wraps, 12mo, 48pp. $75, $125-ob.

193 ..."Biographical sketch of Gen. Robert Edward Lee, with his reports of the Bat-

tles of Chancellorsville and Gettysburg compiled from memoirs of Gen. Lee by Gen. A.L. Long, Col. W.H. Taylor and John Esten Cooke and edited by...with program of the ceremonies of the unveiling of the equestrian statue at Richmond, Va., May 29, 1890." N.Y., 1890, 4to, wraps, port on cover, illus., 118pp. $10.

194 ..."Tribute to Gen. Robert E. Lee, by...-...delivered at the banquet of the Southern Auld Syne Society of Harlem, N.Y., on the anniversary of Gen. Lee's birthday, Jan. 20, 1890." N.Y., 1890. 12mo, wraps, 8pp.

195 **GETTYSBURG, Battle of**
Review of books on Gettysburg. In: Southern Review, April, 1869. $10-bmk. 8vo, wraps, 27pp. article.

196 **GETTYSBURG, Battle of. In: SHSP**
See: Edward P. Alexander, Wm. Allan, Rich. H. Anderson, Rich. S. Andrews, John P. Bane, Cullen A. Battle, Geo. W. Beale, Eugene Blackford, Robt. A. Bright, Jno. T. Brown, King Bryan, Henry C. Cabell, Jas. M. Campbell, Jas. McD. Carrington, Thos. H. Carter, Thomas E. Causby, Jas. F. Crocker, Junius Daniel, Joseph R. Davis, Geo. Doles, Dudley M. DuBose, Jubal A. Early, Joseph A. Englehard, Francis P. Fleming, Charles Forsyth, Birkett D. Fry, John J. Garnett, Boliver H. Gee, John Brown Gordon, Bryan Grimes, Wade Hampton, Harry T. Hays, Henry Heth, Martin W. Hazelwood, Ambrose P. Hill, Geo. Hillyer, Lamar Hollyday, Alfred Iverson, Bradley T. Johnson, Edward Johnson, Hilary P. Jones, John M. Jones, James H. Lane, J.W. Latimer, Fitzhugh Lee, Robt. E. Lee, J. Leslie, Chs. T. Loehr, "London Morning Advertiser", Armistead L. Long, Jas. Longstreet, Henry D. McDaniel, David D. McIntosh, Randolph H. McKim, Lafayette McLaws, Robt. C. Maffett, Wm. Mahone, P.J. Malone, Van H. Manning, Chs. Marshall, Rawley W. Martin, Joseph C. Mayo, Jacquelin M. Meridith, John S. Mosby, Jas. D. Nance, Wm. Nelson, New Haven Register, Wm. C. Oates, Louis P. d'O. Paris, Wm. N. Pendleton, Wm. F. Perry, Chas. S. Payton, Wm. T. Poague, Carnot Posey, Stephen D. Ramseur, Edward P. Reeve, Chs. Richardson, Robt E. Rodes, Jefferson C. Rogers, Justus Scheibert, Herman Schuricht, Lawrence H. Scruggs, W.J. Seymour, Jas. L. Sheffield, Wm. S. Shepherd, Jas. P. Smith, John H. Smith, Geo. H. Steuart, Robt. M. Stirbling, Jas. E.B. Stuart, Thos. M. R. Ralcott, Osmond B. Taylor, Walter H. Taylor, Edward L. Thomas, Geo. Thomas, Isaac R. Trimble, I.W. Waddell, Jas. A. Walker, Reuben L. Walker, Jas. B. Walton, Henry A. White, Cadmus M. Wilcox, Philip A. Work, Ambrose R. Wright, Wm. Youngblood, Wm. P. Zollinger.

197 **GETZENDANER, W.H. and A.M. Dechman**
"A brief and condensed history of Parson's Texas Cavalry Brigade composed of 12th, 19th, 21st, Morgan's Battalion, and Pratt's Battery pf Artillery of the Confederate States together with roster of the several commands as far as obtainable...some historical sketches General Orders and a memoranda of Parson's Brigade Association." Waxahachie, Texas: J.M. Flemister Pr., 1892. 8vo, wraps, 96pp. $85-oh.
...Waco, Texas: W.M. Morrison, 1962. 4to, cl/full leather, 96pp. (printed on-side) 100 copies (5 in leather.) $10.

198 **GHIOTO, Paul A.**
"The Centennial Celebration of the Battle of Horseshoe Bend." In: AHQ, 1978, v.40, #1 and 2, p. 78-85. (See: C.J. Coley)

199 ..."The storming of Mobile Bay. Edt: Richard D. Duncan." In: AHQ, 1978, v.40, #1 and 2, p. 6-19.

200 **GHOLSON, Thomas S.**
"Speech of Hon. Thos. S. Gholson, of Virginia on the policy of employing negro troops and the duty of all classes to aid in the persecution of the war...1-Feb., 1865." Rich: Geo. P. Evans & Co., 1865. 8vo, wraps, 20pp. Crand-2887, $250-jk.

201 **GIBBES, James Guiguard, Col.**
"Who Burnt Columbia?" $20. Newberry, S.C., Elbert H. Aull, 1902. 8vo, cl, ports, 137pp., iii-index. $17.50. See: August Conrad. $100-bmk-105.

202 ..."If we had the money. Col. Gibbes went to England to negotiate the cotton bonds." In: SHSP, 1907, v.35, p. 201-203.

203 **GIBBES, Robert Wilson**
"Memorial. To the honorable the Congress of the Confederate States of America." Columbia, S.C.?, 1864. 12mo, wraps, caption title, 4pp. Crandall-2749.

204 **GIBBES, Wade Hampton**
"First shot of the war was fired in the air, his father, Maj. Gibbes, fired the lanyard." In: SHSP, 1903, v.31, p. 73-79.

205 **GIBBON, John**
"Personal Recollection of Appomattox." In: Century, 1901-1902, v.63, p. 936-943.

206 **GIBBONS, Alfred Ringgold**
"The Recollections of an old Confederate Soldier." (Shelbyville, Mo., 1913) 12mo, stiff wraps, illus., ports, cover title, 31, (1)pp. $15.
...(Shelbyville, Mo., 1931) same. $12.50, $25-bmk-105, $40-b.

207 **GIBBONS, J.R., of Stuart's Cavalry**
"The Monument to Captain Henry Wirz. Mortality in CSA and Federal prison camps contrasted and causes explained." In: SHSP, 1908, v.36, p. 226-236.

208 **GIBBONS, James, Cardinal**
"Lee's Birthday." In: SHSP, 1889, v.17, p. 349.

209 **GIBBONS, Robert**
"Life at the Crossroads of the Confederacy: Atlanta, 1861-1865." In: Atl. Hist. Jour., 1979, v.23, p. 11-72.

210 **GIBBS, Frederick Waymouth, c.b.**
"Recognition. A chapter from the History of the North American and South American States." London: William Ridgway, 1863. 8vo, wraps, (2), 46pp. $15. CSA shouldn't be recognized until it wins, which it will! The world will gain from the overgrown US empire. Negro condition will gain under CSA. He disbelieves Lincoln's proclamation.

211 **GIBBS, George Alphonso**
"George Alphonso Gibb's Recollections of the Spring and Summer of 1861." Edt: Lawrence Lee. (Jackson, Miss.) Jour. Miss. Hist., Feb. 1964, v.XXVI, #1, p. 47-55. From Yazoo Co., Miss.

212 ..."With a Mississippi private in a little known part of the battle of First Bull Run and at Ball's Bluff, an eyewitness accounty by..." In: CWTI, April 1965, v.IV, #1, p. 42-49, illus., map. Append: by Col. W.S. Nye: Action North of Bull Run an often overlooked phase of the battle of First Manassas...described by Gibb.

212a **GIBBS, William E., Capt.**
Civil War Letters . . .
See: Charles H. Warner & McGinnis . . .

213 **GIBSON, A.M.**
"Confederates on the Great Plains: The Pike Mission to Wichita Agency." In: Great Plains Jour., 1964, v.IV, p. 7-16.

214 **GIBSON, Dennis A., Edt.**
"Index of Louisiana. Place names in ORec. War Rebellion Records." See title: "Index..."

215 **GIBSON, George, Captain**
"Captain George Gibson's Civil War Experiences, by Deanna Gibson." In: Washington Co. Historical Society "Flashback", Nov. 1978, v.28, #4, p. 7-14.

216 **GIBSON, J. Watt**
"Recollections of a Pioneer." (St. Joseph,

Ma., Nelson-Hanne Print, 1912) 12mo, cl, front(port), 216pp. War years, p. 106-170. Dornbusch II-2749.

217 **GIBSON, James Monroe**
"Memoirs of J.M. Gibson; terror of the Civil War and Reconstruction Days. Edt: James Gibson Alverson, Sr., and Jr." (San Gabriel, Calif., 1966?) (Houston, Tx.?) 8vo, cl, illus., coat of arms, maps, port., 108pp. $9, $25-atg.

218 **GIBSON, John Catlett and Dr. William W. Smith**
"The Battle of Spotsylvania Courthouse, May 12, 1864." "The Bloody Angle." "What the 49th Va. and Gen. Pegram's Brig. did. Episode of "Gen. Lee to the Rear"." Graphic Accounts by Col. Catlett and Smith." In: SHSP, 1904, v.XXXII, p. 200-215. See also: v.XXI, p. 228-254, for other accounts.

219 **GIBSON, John Mendinghall**
"Those 163 days; a Southern account of Sherman's March from Atlanta to Raleigh." N.Y., Coward-McCann (1961). 8vo, cl, dj, map endsheets, ports, illus., 317pp. $5.75(pub.), $7.50, $10, $12, $20.

220 **GIBSON, Moses**
"Valley Campaign of General Early." From SHSP: 1906, v.34, p. 212-217. (Richmond Times)

221 **GIBSON, Randall Lee**
"Correction of Gen. Patton Anderson. Report of the Battle of Jonesboro, Ga." In: SHSP, 1878, v.5, p. 132-133.

222 ..."Defence and fall of Spanish Fort." In: SHSP, 1877, v.IV, p. 215-223.

223 ..."Farewell address to Louisiana Brigade." In: SHSP, 1877, v.iv, p. 223-224.

224 ..."Official report of the Battle of Murfreesboro." In: SHSP, 1878, v.5, p. 216-221.

225 ..."Report of Operations in vicinity of Nashville." In: SHSP, 1877, v.iv, p. 140-143.

226 ..."Oration on Albert Sidney Johnston, Mentaire Cemetery, New Orleans, La., April 6, 1891. Address before the General Assembly of Louisiana, May 22, 1888." Washington, DC, Rufus H. Darby Pr., 1891. 8vo, wraps, cover title, 16pp. $5. How Civil War ammended the U.S. Constitution.

227 ...Bound-in address before the General Assembly of La., "How the Civil War amended the Constitution of the U.S." p. 9-16.

228 ..."Shiloh. Equestrian monument, erected by the veterans of the Army of Tennessee. Unveiled April 6, 1887, Metairie Cemetery, New Orleans, La. Oration by Randall Lee Gibson." New Orleans, La., Picayune Pr. (1887). 8vo, wraps, cover title, 9pp. $4.

229 **GIBSON, Ronald, Edt.**
"Jefferson Davis and the Confederacy." Dobbs Ferry, N.Y., Oceana Print, 1977. 8vo, cl, 205pp. $12.50. "Presidential Chronology Series." $15.

230 **GIDDENS, Paul H., Edt.**
"Benn Pitman on the trial of Lincoln's Assassin." In: Tylers QHGM, 1940, v.XXII.

231 **GIDDINGS, C.H.**
"Confederate Treaty-only one ever negotiated with a Foreign Power." In: SHSP, 1900, v.28, p.255-259.

232 **GIESE, William Royston**
"The Confederate Northwest, May-August 1861. A study of organization and command in the Trans-Mississippi West." In: Mil. Hist. Tex. & SoWest, 1976, v.XIII, #1, p. 11-21, quarto.

233 ..."Divided Command in the West, August-September 1961 (1861?)." In: above, 1976-1977, v.XIII, #2, p. 47-54, quarto.

..."Divided Command in the West, October, 1861-January, 1862." In: above, 1977, v.XIII, #3, p. 49-57. quarto.

234 **GIESECKE, Julius**
"The Diary of Julius Gieseck, 1861-1862."

Tran: Oscar Haas (New Braunfels, Tex.) Tex. Mil. Hist., 1963, v.III, p. 228-242; 1964, v.IV, p. 27-54.

235 ..."Civil War Diary of Captain Julius Giesecke 1861-1862, 1863-3865, Captain of Co. G, Fourth Tex. Cavalry." Trans: Oscar Haas. n.p., n.d. Mimeogr.

236 ...Tagebuch des Capt. Julius Giesecke wahrend des Burgerkrieges. Jahrbuch der Neu Braunfelser Zeitung." New Branfels, Texas: 1934, p. 37-60; 1935, p. 18-34.

237 **GIFT, George W.**
"The Story of the Arkansas." In: SHSP, 1884, v.12, p. 48-54, 115-119, 163-170, 205-212.

238 **GIGNILLIAT, John L.**
"A Historian's Dilemma: a Posthumous Footnote for Freeman's R.E. Lee." In: JSH, May, 1977, v.43, 20pp., p. 217-236. $8.

239 **GILBERT, Benjamin Franklin**
"The Confederate Raider "Shenandoah". The Elusive Destroyer in the Pacific and the Arctic." In: Jour. of the WEst, 1965, v.IV, p. 169-182.

240 ..."Confederate Warships off Brazil." Amer. Neptune, Oct. 1955, Vol. XV, #4, p. 287-302.

241 ..."The Salvador Pirates." In: CWH, June 1959, v.V, #3, p. 294-307.

242 ..."The "Shenandoah" down under: her Soujourn at Melbourne." In: Jour. of the West, 1966, v.V, p. 321-335.

243 ..."Kentucky Privateers in California." In: REg. Ky. Hist. Quart., July 1940, v.XXXVIII, p. 256-266.

244 ..."Rumours of Confederate Privateers. Operating in Victoria, Vancouver Island." In: British Columbia Hist. Quart., 1954, v.XVIII, p. 239-255.

245 ..."The Mythical Johnston Conspiracy." Offprint: California Hist. Soc. Quart., Vol. XXVIII, #2, stapeled, 165-174pp. Atg. copy to Gerald E. Cronin. $2.50.

246 ..."Life and writings of Hinton Rowan Helper." In: RKHS, Jan. 1955, v.53, p. 58-75.

247 **GILBERT, C.C.**
"Bragg's Invasion of Kentucky." In: So.-Biv., ns, v.I, 1885/1886, p. 217-222, 296-301, 336-342, 430-436, 465-477, 550-556. See: Basil W. Duke.

248 **GILBERT, C.E.**
"Two Presidents: Abraham Lincoln, Jefferson Davis. Origin, Cause and Conduct of War Between the States. The Truth of History Belongs to Posterity. As Much as Possible of Truth of History is Due the Patriots and Heroes who have gone before." 1927. (Houston, Texas: Trans-Mississippi Div., U.D.C.82pp.) Pro-Southern, the North couldn't make a tariff-war, so slavery was the pretext. $8, $12.50, $25, $8-jenk,

249 ..."San Antonio, Texas: The Naylor Co., 1973. 8vo, wraps, xxiii, 85pp. photos, index. $6.95. With introductions, highlights and explanations by Tom Hudson (author's nephew).

250 **GILBERT, John Warren**
"The Blue and the Gray; a history of the conflicts during Lee's invasion and Battle of Gettysburg, containing complete roster of the two armies, replete with incidents and maps; being for the most part contributions by Union and Confederate Officers condensed and arranged for popular reading." (Harrisburg, Pa., Evangelical Press) 1922. (Chicago: Curt Teich & Co., 1922) 8vo, illus. cover, in color, front, fldg. map, illus., ports, 166pp. $10, $15-bmk, $15. "Peoples pictorial edt." $15. See also author's Guides to the Battle of Gettysburg, several editions.

251 **GILBERT, Randal B.**
"The people of Tyler(Texas) are relieved of their fears-the building of the Camp Ford Stockade." In: Smith Co. HS, Winter,

1985, v.24, #2, p. 1-9, port, pl. (See: Camp Ford)

252 **GILBERT, Rensler R.**
"High Private's Confederate Letters, written for the Houston Telegraph, during the War of 1861-1865, with a short autobiographical sketch of the author..." Austin, Texas: Eugene von Boeckmann, 1890. 12mo, wraps, 74pp., ads. $15, $30. With 6th Texas Inf., medical discharge and with the Telegraph to end of war. See: "High Private's Second Edition, etc."

253 **GILCHRIST, Annie Somers**
"Katherine Somerville; or the Southland before and after the Civil War." Nashville Tenn., Marshall & Bruce, 1906. 12mo, cl, front, plates, 347pp. $8.50.

254 **GILCHRIST, Robert C., Maj.**
"The Confederate Defense of Morris Island Charleston Harbor, by the troops of South Carolina, Georgia and North Carolina, in the Late War Between the States. With a map of Morris and part of Folly Islands, and a plan of Fort Wagner- prepared from official reports and other sources by...a participant commanding Gist Guard Artillery in that defense." (Charleston, S.C., from the yearbook, 1884.) 8vo, wraps, fldg. map, fldg. plan of Wagner, 55pp. $350, $25, $12 (no map t.p.), $20.

255 **GILDERSLEEVE, Basil Lanneau**
"The Creed of the Old South, 1865-1915." Baltimore: Johns Hopkins Press, 1915. 12mo, cl, 126, (1), lf, (1)pp. ports. Appeared: Atlantic Monthly, Jan. 1892. Political view of the Southern cause. Author in 1st Va. Cavalry. $20-bmk, $40-b, $35-y, $12.50, $16.

256 **GILDERSLEEVE, John R., Dr.**
"History of Chimborazo Hospital, CSA." Abstract from address of..., Pres. Ass'n. of Medical Officers of the Army and Navy of the Confederacy, at Nashville, Tenn., June 14, 1904." In: SHSP, 1908, v.XXXVI, p. 86-94. (From the "News Leader", Jan. 7, 1909(?).

257 ..."History of Chimborazo Hospital, Richmond, Virginia and its Medical Officers during 1861-1865." (London) Jour. Confed. Hist. Soc., March 1965, v.III, #1, p. 16-21, pls-2.

258 ..."The Southern Guard and Sons of Liberty." In: Alumni Bul. Univ. of Va., April 1911. vo, wraps, 11pp. article. $15-bmk-84. Companies from the University of Va.

259 ..."Chimborazo hospital during the war, 1861-1865." In: CV, 1904, v.12, p. 577-579. Gildersleeve was Pres. Assoc. Medical Officer of the Army and Navy of the CSA.

260 **GILES, J.L.**
"Nathan Bedford Forrest, Litho Portrait, tinted, 23x17, halflength in uniform, bearded. NY (1874)" $25, $15. See: Ewell A. Phill.

261 ..."Joseph E. Johnston." Litho, tall, folio, NY, G.E. Perine (above) $7.50.

262 **GILES, Leonides Blanton**
"Terry's Texas Rangers." (Austin, Texas: Von Boeckmann-Jones c.1911) 12mo, cl, 105pp. $100, $125, $150, $1000-g, $750-jk-131, $500-114

...Louisv: Lost Cause Pr., micro-cd, $2.90.

...Austin, Tex: Pemberton Press, Brasada Reprint Series, 1967. 12mo, cl, dj, port(front) (10), 105, index (4)pp. (9)p-ads. $7.50.

263 **GILES, Valerius Cincinnatus**
"Rags and Hope, the Recollections of Val. C. Giles, four years with Hood's (Texas) Brigade, Fourth Texas Infantry, 1861-1865. Compiled and edited by Mary Lasswell." N.Y., Coward-McCann(1961), 8vo, cl, 280pp., dj. $30, $25-bmk-89, $40.

264 ..."The Tom Green Rifles." In: CV, Jan. 1918, v.XXVI, p. 20-23. Company B., 4th Texas Reg.

265 **GILL, John**
"Reminiscences of Four Years as a private soldier in the Confederate Army 1861-1865." Private print for author. Baltimore: Sun Print, 1904. 8vo, cl, front(port)xii, (13)-136pp. $350-b, $25, $47.50, $57.50, $60, $400-bmk, $125-ginsib.9.
...Louisv: Lost Cause micro-cd, $3.24.

265a **GILLELAND, William M.**
"Burial March of Maj. Gen. Tom Green. Inscribed to his old brigade & companions in arms." Austin, Texas, 1864. 8vo, 4pp, caption title. Winkler 1202.

266 **GILLESPIE, Mary Elise White, Mrs.**
"A Few Historic Records of the Church in the Diocese of Texas, during Rebellion. Together with a Correspondence between the Rt. Rev. Alexander Gregg...the Rev. Charles Gillette." N.Y., John A. Gray & Green, 1865. 8vo, cl, 131pp. (Ho.P.L.)

267 **GILLIAM, Robert C.**
"From Paraclifta to Mark's Mill, the Civil War correspondence of Lieutenant Robert C. Gilliam." In: Ark. Hist. Quart., 1958, v.XVIII, p. 222-302.

268 **GILLIG, John S.**
"Awful! Terrible! Grand! Gloomy! and Peculiar!" In: RKHS, Spring 1984, v.82, #2, p. 170-175, map, pl.

269 **GILLS, Mary Louise**
"It happened at Appomattox: the story of an historic Virginia village." Richmond: Dietz Press (1948). 8vo, wraps, map, views, (10), 42pp. Buildings and sites near Old Appomattox Courthouse, Va., historic by events of 1865 and on "famous men of Appomattox. $3, $7.50, 2nd Print('48). $20, $10-bmk-90, $5-nc.

270 **GILMAN, Bradley**
"Robert E. Lee." N.Y., Macmillan Co., 1915. "True stories of great Americans" 12mo, decr., cl, 2-ports, incl. front, ix, 205pp. $7.50.

271 **GILMAN, Carolina Howard**
"Letters of a Confederate mother; Charleston in the sixties." In: Atlantic, CXXXVII, April. 1926, p. 503-515. Reminisc: Mrs. Samuel Gilman of Charleston, S.C.

272 **GILMER, Jeremy Francis**
"Letter addressed to Hon. Wm. C. Rives, by John H. Gilmer, on the existing status of the Revolution, etc." (Richmond? 1864). Nov. 1, 1864. 8vo, sewn, caption title, 16pp.

273 ..."Southern Politics! What we are and what we will be. Considered in a letter from a Virginian to a New Yorker." Richmond: J. Wall Turner, 1867. 8vo, sewn, 18pp. Sabin-27443.

274 ..."War of Races. By whom it is sought to be brought about. Considered in two letters, with copious extracts from the recent work of Hilton (?, Hinton) R. Helper." Richmond, July 29, 1867. 8vo, sewn, 16pp. (old)$4.50, $6, $7.50, $75-gins.9

275 ..."Letter addressed to Wm. C. Rives, by John H. Gilmer, on the existing status of the Revolution, etc." Richmond, Nov. 1, 1864. 8vo, wraps, caption title, 16pp.

276 **GILMER, John A., Hon., N.C.**
"Speech of John A. Gilmer, of North Carolina, on the State of the Union, delivered in the House of Representatives, Jan. 26, 1861." Washington, 1861. 8vo, wraps, 8pp. $8.

277 **GILMER, Morgan S.**
"Shockley's Independent Escort Company. To the living members of this company and to the survivors of those who have answered the last roll call." (Montgomery, Ala., Woodruff Co., 1905) 8vo, wraps, cover title, 11pp. (roster)

278 ..."History of Shockley's Alabama Escort Company. Organized in 1864 by Cadets of the University of Alabama who served under Brig. Gen. Daniel W. Adams until

their surrender with Lt. Gen. Nathan Bedfort Forrest at Gainesville, Alabama, May 10, 1865." With Introduction and Edt. William Stanley Hoole. University, Ala. Confederate Pub. Co., 1983, 8vo, stiff wraps, 22pp. Confederate Regimental Series #3.

279 **GILMOR, Harry, Colonel**
"Four Years in the Saddle." N.Y., Harper & Bros., 1866. 12mo, cl, front, xii, (13)-291pp. Pres. copy. $15, $17.50, $20, $22.50, $25, $35, $85, $75-jk-137, $50-bmk-86, $40-nc, $60-bmk.
...London: Longmans, Green & Co., 1866, 8vo, cl, viii, 310pp. $30.

280 ..."Gilmor's field report of his raid in Baltimore County, July, 1864." In: Md. Hist. Mag., 1952, v.XLVII, p. 234-240.
GILMORE, Harry, Col.
"Four years in the saddle..." Balt: Butternut & Blue, 1987. 8vo, cl, dj, 291pp., illus. $25.

281 **GILSTRAP, Marguerite**
"Daniel Harvey Hill, Southern Propagandist." In: AHQ, March, 1943, v.II, #1, p. 43-50.

282 **GINDER, Henry**
"Letters." See: L. Moody Simms.

283 **GINGLES, Violet**
"Saline County, Arkansas First Infantry volunteers, CSA." In: Ark. Hist. Quart., 1959, v.XVII, p. 90-98.

284 **GINZBERG, Eli**
"The Economics of British Neutrality during the American Civil War." In: Agric. Hist. 1936, v.X, p. 147-156. "Northern wheat" counterbalanced "Southern Cotton", kept British from recongnizing CSA.

285 **GIPSON, Lawrence Henry**
"The Collapse of the Confederacy." In: MVHR, Mar. 1918, v.IV, p.437-458. Not only militarily but a psychological nature.

286 **GIRARD, Charles Frederic**
"Les Etats Confederes d'Amerique visites en 1863. Memoire adresse a S.M. Napoleon III. Paris: E. Dentu, 1864." 12mo, cl, fldg. map, viii, (9)-160pp. $12.50, $25, $85-r.

287 ..."A Visit to the Confederate States of America in 1863; Memoir addressed to His Majesty Napoleon III." Trans Edited: with an introduct. Wm. Stanley Hoole. Tuscaloosa, Ala: Confederate Pub. Co., 1962. 12mo, stiff wraps, port, map, facsms. 126pp. Limited 300 copies. Pro-Southern.
...Louisv" Lost Cause Pr., micro-cd, 1957. $30-b.

288 **GIRARDEAU, Claude, Mrs. and Mrs. Thornley Walker.**
"Catalogue of the Confederate Relic Room, Columbia, S.C." n.p., n.d. 12mo, wraps, 23pp. (McKissick-936)

289 **GIRARDEAU, John Lafayette Rev.**
"Confederate Memorial Day at Charleston, S.C.: Reinterment of the Carolina dead from Gettysburg." Charleston: William G. Mazyck, 1871. 8vo, wraps, 36pp. (McKissick-933)

290 **GIST, W.W.**
"The Battle of Franklin: the key to the last campaign in the West." In: TennHM, Jan. 1921, v.VI, p. 213-265.

291 ..."The other side at Franklin." In: CV, Jan. 1916, v.XXIV, p. 13-16. Written by a member of 26th Ohio Reg.

292 ..."The ages of the soldiers in the Civil War." In: Iowa Jour. Hist.

293 **GITTINGS, John G.**
"Personal Recollections of Stonewall Jackson, also sketches and stories." Cincinnati: Editor Pub. Co., 1899. $250-b. 12mo, cl, ports(incl. front), 3, 311pp. $30.

294 ..."Personal recollections of "Stonewall" Jackson." In: Blue & Gray, 1894, v.IV, p. 203-210, illus., ports.

295 **"GLANCE at the resources**
of the South in the event of separation and hostile collision with the North." Win-

nsboro, S.C., Herald Office, 1850. 8vo, wraps, 31pp. Turnbull-III, p. 92.

296 **GLASS, F.M.**
"Long Creek Rifles, a brief history. (Sallis) Long Creek Rifles Chapter, United Daughters of the Confederacy. n.p., 1910. 16mo, wraps, cover title, ports, (16)pp.

297 **GLASSELL, W.T., Comm. CSNavy**
"Reminiscences of Torpedo Service in Charleston Harbor." In: SHSP, 1877, v.4, p. 225-235.

298 ..."Torpedo service in Charleston Harbor." In: CV, Mar. 1917, v.XXV, p. 113-116.
..."W.T. Glassell & the Little Torpedo Boat "David." Los Angeles: Bruce McCallister at the Adcraft Press, 1937. 8vo, wraps, 30pp. $30 Bm.

299 **GLASSON, William H.**
"The South's Pension and Relief Provisions for the Soldiers of the Confederacy." In: N.C. Lit. & Hist. Ass'n. Proc., 1917, removed, bnd. stiff wraps, 12pp. $8.

300 **GLATTHAAR, Joseph T.**
"Sherman's army and total war: attitudes on destruction in the Savannah and Carolinas Campaign." In: AHJ, Spring 1985. 8vo, cl, xvi, 318pp., illus. $28.

301 **GLEASON, F.W. Foster**
"Two Chiefs of Ordnance (General Ripley, 1861-1863, and General Gorgas, C.S., 1861-1865)." In: Ordnance, 1963, v.XLVII, p. 438-440.

302 **GLENDALE, Battle of**
See: Frayser's Farm.

303 **GLENN, Audrey**
"A Vanderbilt at Greenwood: The "Star of the West"." (Jackson, Miss., Jour. Miss. Hist., Oct., 1954, v.XVI, #4, p. 258-267.

304 **GLENN, H.V.**
"The battle of St. Charles." In: Grand PrairieHB, Oct. 1961, v.4, p. 1-14.

305 **GLENN, John Foster**
"Brave Defence of the Cockade City." In: SHSP, 1907, v.35, p. 1-24. (Petersburg, Va.)

306 **"GLENN, L. Mell**
"The Story of a Sensational Trial." Greenville, S.C., Keys Print, 1965. 8vo, cl, (5), (49)-100pp. U.S. Trial of a CSA soldier.

307 **GLENN, William Wilkins**
"Between North and South: A Maryland Journalist Views the Civil War." Edt: Ellen Marks and Mark Norton Schatz, Rutherford, N.J., Fairleigh Dickinson University Press, 1976. 8vo, dj, 430pp. $25, $18. Glenn was strongly pro-Southern, he gives insight to changing moods of the Southerners in Baltimore.

308 **GLENNEY, Daniel W.**
(Sale of Federal Fleet) See: New Orleans Picayune.

309 **GLOVER, Gilbert Graffenreid**
"Immediate pre-Civil War compromise efforts." Nashville, Tenn., Geo. Peabody College for Teachers. (Contributions to education published under direction of Geo. Peabody College for Teachers. #131) 1934. 8vo, cl, x(i.e., xiii), 180pp. "Facts that led to and stood in way of an amicable adj. to sectional differences."

310 **GLOVER, P.J.**
"Proof of Simon Wheeler being a traitor, a liar and a scoundrel." Demopolis, Ala., P.J. Glover (1864). 8vo, wraps, 20pp. Local quarrel in Marengo Co., Ala.

311 **GLOVER, Robert**
"The Douglas Battery." In: Chron. Smith Co. (Texas)." v.1, #1, p. 14-19.

312 ..."The war letters of a Texas conscript in Arkansas." In: AHQ, v.20, p. 355-387.

313 **GODDIN, C. Hobson**
"Richmond, Virginia 1861-1865." Richmond: Civil War Cent. Comm. (Sept. 1961) 8vo, pict. wraps, ports, illus., 14pp. #8.

314 **GOEN, C.C.**
"Broken churches, broken nation:

denominational schisms and the coming of the American Civil War." Macon, Ga., Mercer University Press, 1985. 8vo, cl, dj, x, 198pp. $17.50.

315 **GOETCHINS, Henry R.**
"Robert E. Lee, gentleman, scholar, gallant soldier, great general and true christian. An address delivered in Columbus, Ga., Jan. 19, 1900-on the occasion of the celebration of the birthday of Gen. Robert E. Lee." Columbus, Ga., T. Gilbert, 1900. 8vo, wraps, 29pp.

316 **GOETCHIUS, Henry R.**
"Robert Edward Lee, gentleman, scholar, gallant soldier, great general and true Christian. An address delivered in Columbus, Ga., Jan. 19, 1900...on the occasion of the celebration of the birthday of Gen. Robert E. Lee." Columbus, Ga., T. Gilbert, 1900, 8vo, wraps, 29pp.

317 **GOFF, John S.**
"The Civil War Confiscation Cases in Arizona Territory." In: Amer. Jour. Legal Hist., October, 1970. v.14, p. 349-354. Laws permitted confiscation of land belonging to CSA sympathizers.

318 **GOFF, Reda C.**
"The Confederate Veteran Magazine." In: THQ, 1972, #1, p. 45-60, v.31.

319 **GOFF, Richard D.**
"Confederate Supply." Durham, N.C., Duke Univ. Pr., 1969, 8vo, cl, dj, xii, 275pp. (bibliog.253-265). $8.75. $10.75. $12.00. $20.00. $15.00-Bmk.

320 **GOFFE, Charles H.**
"The Old South in peace and war-confiscation of plantations." In: CV, Jan. 1921, v.XXIX, p. 16-18.

321 **GOGGIN, James M., Maj.**
"Report of Conner's South Carolina Brigade at Cedar Creek, Oct. 19, 1864." In: SHSP, 1883, v.11, p. 520-523.

322 ..."Chickamauga. A reply to Maj. Sykes." In: SHSP, 1884, v.12, p. 219-224.

323 **"GOING SOUTH in 1861."**
In: CV, Jan. 1921, v.XXIX, p. 13-14. Letter from a Marylander in the ANV. "Going South", an expression applied to men leaving MD to join the CSA.

324 **GOINS, Craddock**
"The Queen of the Confederacy." In: "Americana Illus." Apr. 1939, v.XXXIII, #2, p. 141-150. (Mrs. Jefferson Davis)

325 **GOLD, Thomas Daniel**
"History of Clarke County, Virginia, and its connection with the war between the states, with illustrations of colonial homes and of Confederate Officers." (Berryville, Va., C.R. Hughes) 1914. 8vo, cl, ports, illus., 337pp. small edt. $35., $3, $8.75, $15, $27.50, $175-bmk-123.

326 ...Reprint 1962. Berryville, Va: Chesapeake Book Co. Indexed edt. $10. Muster Rolls Co. "C" and "I", 2nd Va. Inf. and Co. D, 6th Va. Cavalry.

327 **GOLD, in the CSA**
See: Stanley W. Zamonski, Daniel Ellis Conner, Edt: Donald J. Berthrong.

328 **GOLDBERG, Mitchell S.**
"A Federal Naval Raid into Galveston Harbor, November 7-8, 1861: What Really Happened?" In: SwHQ, July 1972, v.LXXVI, #1, p. 58-70.

329 **GOLDBLATT, Kenneth A.**
"The Confederate Capture of Arizona." In: TMH, 1970, v.8, #2, p. 77-86.

330 **GOLDEN, James Lawrence**
"Hilliard vs Yancey: prelude to the Civil War." In: Quart. Jour. speech, Feb. 1956, v.42, p. 35-44. notes. Debates between the two in Alabama, 1851.

331 **GOLDMAN, Henry H.**
"Southern Sympathy in Southern California: 1860-1865." In: Jour. of the West, 1965, v.IV, p. 577-586.

332 **GOLDSBOROUGH, Edward Yerbury**
"Early's Great Raid. He advances through Maryland, the Union forces under Gen.

Lew Wallace stubbornly contest the field aginst overpowering numbers. Wallace retreats. Narrow escape from capture of Gen. E.B. Tyler and his staff and orderlies." (1898) (Frederick, Md.) $75-ob. 12mo, wraps, illus., plans, fldg. map, 35pp., Dornbusch-II, #494.

333 **GOLDSBOROUGH, W.W.**
"The Maryland line in the Confederacy." Gaithersburg, Md., Butternut Press, 1983, 8vo, cl, 404pp., illus., index. $35.

GOLDSBOROUGH, William Worthington
"The Maryland Line in the Confederate States Army." Baltimore: Kelly, Piet & Co., 1869. 12mo, cl, 9-ports, 357pp. $40, $75, $250-bmk, $200-bmk, $125-jk-97.

..."The Maryland Line in the Confederate Army. 1861-1865. Published for the benefit of the Maryland Line Confederate Soldier's Home, Pikesville, Md. under authority of the board of governors of the association of Md. Line." 1900. (Balt: Guggenheimer & Weil Co.) sm.4to, full Mor., ports, illus., front, (3), 371, (373-397, ads). $50.

...Port Washington: Kitticat Pr., 1972. 8vo, cl, 371, 74(index)pp. $30-y, $22.50.

334 ...Index: to 1900 edition, see Mrs. Chas. Lee Lewis, compiler. $15-bmk.

335 ..."Grants Change of Base. The horrors of the battle of Cold Harbor. From a soldier's note book. Sights which filled even veterans with horror-why McClellan failed-a mistake that cost many lives." (From: Phila. "Record", Apr. 7, 1901) In: SHSP, v.XXIX, p. 285-291.

336 ..."How Ashby was killed. A correspondent reviews the fighting before the battle of Cross Keys." (From: Phila. "Weekly Times", July 23, 1892) In: SHSP, 1893, v.XXI, p. 224-226.

...See: Winfield Peter's "Warrior-Hero."

337 **GOLDSMITH, Washington Lafayette**
"Cavalry versus Infantry." In: Blue & Gray, 1893, II, p. 214.

338 ..."General Lee to the Rear. Col. W. L. Goldsmith, of Mississippi, witnessed both events. Gordon begging Lee to retire. Capt. Funkhouser's graphic description of the Georgia soldier persuading Gen. Lee to go to the rear, and then leading the charge." In: SHSP, 1896, XXIV, p. 79-82.

339 ..."Stonewall" Jackson's last grand blow." In: Blue & Gray, 1893, v.II, ports, p. 302-303.

340 **GOLDTHORPE, George Weimer**
"The Battle of McDowell, Virginia." In: W.Va. Hist., 1952, v.XIII, p. 159-215.

341 **GOLLADAY, V. Dennis**
"Jubal Early's Last Stand." (Richmond) Va. Cavl., Summer 1970, v.XX, #1, p. 28-33, map, port, illus.

342 **GONE WITH THE WIND**
See: Herb Bridges, Richard Harwell, Darden Asbury Pyron, Margerete Mitchell.

343 **GONZALES, John E.**
"Henry Stuart Foote: Confederate Congressman and Exile." In: CWH, December 1965, v.XI, #4, p. 384-395.

..."Henry Stuart Foote in exile, 1865." In: JMH, April 1953, v.15, p. 90-98. notes. An unauthorized mission of peace in name of the CSA, his voyage to Europe, expelled from CSA congress and temporary exile from the U.S.

345 **GONZALES, William E.**
"Inscriptions for Memorial to Women of Confederacy." (from Richmond News-Leader) In: SHSP, 1910, v.38, p. 359-362.

346 **GOOCHLAND LIGHT ARTILLERY**
See: R.N. Allen, Thomas J. Riddle.

GOOCHLAND TROOPS
See: E.H. Lively, C.H. Powell.

347 **"GOOD WORK on foot. A,**
(caption title), Mr. H.W.R. Jackson, the

author of several volumes that have appeared during the war, recently set apart a certain percentage of his sales for a Free School for the orphans of deceased soldiers..." (Atlanta, GA., Atlanta Intelligencer, 1864. Broadside: 6x5" unrecorded. Gdsp. $75. Promotion for Jackson's "Southern woman" of the second American Revolution".

348 **GOOD, John J., Captain**
"Cannon Smoke: the Letters of Captain John J. Good, Good-Douglas Texas Battery, CSA. See: Lester Newton Fitzhugh, Compiler and Editor.

349 **GOODE, John**
"The Peace Conference in Hampton Roads. Errors corrected as to Gen. Lee in the breach to the finality of possible endeavor. Gen. Lee did not contemplate early surrender. Lincoln offered no terms-the veteran statesman denies that the Confederate Commissioners could have ended the war upon conditions that would have been satisfactory and creditable to the Southern people." From the Richmond, Va. "Times", Feb. 9, 1902. In: SHSP, 1901, v.XXIX, p. 177-193.

350 ..."The Confederate Soldier. An address by Hon. John Goode delivered at Manassas Virginia, June 3, 1903." Manassas, n.d. (c.1903). 12mo, wraps, port(front) 24pp. $7.50.

351 **GOODE, John, Hon., Va.**
"The Confederate Congress 1861-1865." In: "Conservative Review", v.IV, 1900. p. 97-112, colored plate. Excerpt, in 3/4 leather. $20.

352 **GOODE, John, Jr.**
"Personal Recollections of Peace Conference in Hampton Roads and Last meeting of Gen. R.E. Lee and Pres. Davis. Delivered before R.E. Lee Camp, #1, Confed. Veterans, Jan. 10, 1902." Richmond, Va., 1902. 8vo, wraps, 19pp. (McElroy bibliog.) Heading: "War History."

353 **GOODE, John, of Virginia.**
"Recollections of a Lifetime, by John Goode of Virginia." N.Y., Neale Print, 1906. 8vo, cl, port(front)x, (1), (13)-266pp. $12.50, $15, $17.50, $27.50, $32.50, $45-bmk, $75. Civil War in Va., in secession convention and CSA Congress. (50pp.)

354 **GOODHART, Briscoe**
"History of the Independent Loudoun Virginia Rangers." Gaithersburg, Md., Butternut Press, 1985. 8vo, cl, dj, xvi, vi, 243pp. illus. $25.

355 **GOODLETT, Emily Geiger**
"The Burning of Columbia by Gen. W.T. Sherman, Feb. 17, 1865." n.p., n.d. 2nd Edt. 8vo, wraps, 16pp. (McKissick-950)

356 **GOODLOE, Albert Theodore, Rev.**
"Rebel Relics from the seat of War." Nashville: Printed for Author, 1893. (Methodist Pub. Hse., Barber & Smith) 16mo, cl, front(port), 315pp. $35, $40. Goodloe was 1st Lt., Co.D, 35th Reg. Ala. Bal. Inf., CSA. full lt. $125-bmk, $250-jk.

357 ..."Confederate Echoes: a voice from the South in the days of secession and of the Southern Confederacy." Nashville, Tenn., Printed for Author, Pub. Hse., M.E. Church, South, Smith & Lamar, 1907. (Enlarged from his "Rebel Relics".) 12mo, cl, front, plates, ports, 452pp. $20, $25, $35, $40, $55, $150-bmk-105, $200-b.

358 ...Washington, DC, Zenger Pub. Co., 1983. 8vo, cl, illus., map+map endsheets, illus., index. $22. Includes portions of "Rebel Relics", left out in the "expanded edition", new index.

359 **GOODLOE, P.H.**
"Service in the Trans-Mississippi." In: CV, Jan. 1915, v.XXIII, p. 31-32.

360 **GOODMAN, Thomas M., Sergt.**
"A Thrilling Record founded on facts and observations obtained during ten day's ex-

perience with Col. Wm. T. Anderson the Notorious Guerrilla Chieftain, by...the only survivor of the inhuman massacre at Centralia, Mo., Sept. 27, 1864; and an eye-witness of the brutal and barbarous treatment by the guerrillas of the dead, wounded and captured of Maj. Johnson's Command. Edt., prepared for the press by Captain Harry A. Houston." Des Moines, Iowa: Mills & Co's Book, 1868, 12mo, stiff wraps, (9)-10-63pp. $5, $15-jk-122, $20.

361 **GOODNIGHT, Susan Pitman, (Mrs. T.H.)**
"War recollections." In: Va.MH, 1934, v.XLII, p. 224-228, 336-340; 1935, v.XLIII, p. 355-359. Brief sketches of writer's reminiscences as she remembered it in Virginia.

362 **GOODRICH, John T.**
"Gregg's Brigade in the Battle of Chickamauga." In: CV, June 1914, v.XXII, p. 264-265.

363 **GOODROW, Esther Marie, Sister**
"Mobile During the Civil War." Mobile: Historic Mobile Preservation Society, 1950. 8vo, stiff wraps, 68pp. Long OP, 150 copies.

363a **GOODSON, Joab**
"The letters of Captain Joab Goodson, 1862-1864. Edt: W. Stanley Hoole." In: Ala. Rev., Apr.-July, 1957, v.10, p. 126-153, 215-231. Captain in 44th Ala. Inf. Reg. to his niece Nannie Clements, Va. and Tenn., 14 Sept. 1862, 1 Jan. 1865.

364 **GOODWIN, A.T., Gen.**
"Memorial address of...Commdr. 1st Brigade U.C.V. Montgomery, Alabama, Apr. 26, 1926." cover title. (Montgomery, Ala, 1926) 8vo, wraps, 8pp. Emory

365 **GOODWIN, Martha**
"The Ram "Arkansas"." In: CV, July 1920, v.XXVIII, p. 263-264.

366 **GOODWIN, Robert Archer, Rev.**
"Memorial Sermon, in Old St. Johns Church "No fight for right and truth and honor was ever truly lost." (from Richmond Times-Dispatch, June 20, 1909) In: SHSP, 1909, v.37, p. 338-347.

367 **GOODWIN, Samuel A.**
"Oration on General Joseph E. Johnston." In: SHSP, 1890, v.18, p. 167-171.

368 ..."Why we should perpetuate the memory of the Confederate dead. An address by.-..of Savannah, Ga., Parade grounds, Memorial Day, April 26, 1893." In: Confed. Vets., Assn., Savannah, Ga., Pres. Annual Report, 1895, p. 5-11.

369 **GOODWYN, A.T., Gen.**
"Address: UCV at their 39th Reunion Charlotte, N.C., June 5, 1929." 8vo, wraps, cover title, 22pp., revised and published by request. (Montgomery, Ala. Beer's Print) $7.50, $12.50.

370 ..."Memorial address by..., commander First Brigade Confederate Veterans, Montgomery, Ala., April 26, 1926." 8vo, wraps, cover title, 8pp.

371 **GOODYEAR, Samuel M.**
"General Robert E. Lee's Invasion of Carlisle, 1863, a paper read before the Hamilton Library Association." (Carlisle, Pa., n.d.) 8vo, wraps, caption title, 7pp.

372 **GOOLRICK, Chester**
"He Didn't Like "Dixie"." (Richmond) Va. Cavl., Spring, 1960. v.IX, #4, p. 4-10, port, illus. (1-color) facsm. CSA bandmaster with A.N.V.

373 **GOOLRICK, Frances Bernard**
"Suffering in Fredericksburg. Refugee returned after Battle to find chaos in old city." In: SHSP, 1909, v.37, p. 355-359.

374 **GOOLSBY, John Cunningham**
"Crenshaw Battery, Pegram's Battalion, Confederate States Artillery. Graphic account of the effective career of this gallant organization. Highly interesting details. Hanging of Webster the spy. Battles of Mechanicsville, Gaines' Mill, Cold

Harbor, Malvern Hill Bristow Station, Centreville, Sharpsburg, Chancellorsville, Wilderness, Marye's Height, Gettysburg, Burgess's Mill, Hatcher's Run and Five Forks." In: sHSP, 1900, v.XXVIII, p. 336-377.

375 ..."The Crenshaw battery, its services during its return from Gettysburg at Falling Waters, Brandy station, Spotsylvania Courthouse, Jericho Ford, and Second Cold Harbor, reviews." In: SHSP, 1893, v.XXI, p. 368-374.

376 **GORBIN, Diana Fontaine Maury**
"Son of the South, Life and Services of Commodore Maury." (Proposed monument to Memory) In: SHSP, 1890, v.18, p. 365-371.

377 **GORDON, Armistead C.**
"Judge William McLaughlin; an address on the occasion of the presentation of his portrait to the trustees of Washington and Lee University, June 17, 1903." (Lexington, Va.? 1903?) 8vo, wraps, 12pp., (Carolina Bks.) $20. McLaughlin's service in Rockbridge Artillery, later command Artillery Batt. of Breckinridge's Div., Early's Corp. at Battle of Cold Harbor.
"Hard times in the Confederacy." In: Cent. Oct. 1888, p. 761-771.

378 **GORDON, Armistead Churchill**
"The Confederate Dead." A poem by...In: SHSP, 1897, v.XXV, p. 382-384.

379 ..."Jefferson Davis." New York: Charles Scribners, 1918. "Figures from American History." 12mo, cl, viii, 329pp. $4, $6, $10, $14, $25-b, $60-ob.

380 ..."Memories and Memorials of William Gordon McCabe." Richmond, Va., Old Dominion Press, 1925. 2 vols., cl, (10), 445, (4), 431pp. 8vo, ports (incl. front) facsm. $8.50, $15, $125-jk-122, $75-bmk, $40-bmk, $35-nc, $25-y. McCabe was an author and educator, served thruout war and wrote many well known Civil War poems.
...See also: Edwin A. Alderman, who he co-authored a biography of J.L.M. Curry.

381 ..."For Truth and Freedom. Poems of Commemoration." New York: Neale Pub., 1910. 12mo, cl, 73pp. $4.50.

382 ..."New Market Day at Virginia Military Institute." (from Richmond Times-Dispatch) In: SHSP, 1903, v.31, p. 173-185.

383 ..."William Gordon McCabe; a brief memoir." In: Va.MH, July 1920, v.XXVIII, p. 195-206. Also: offprint, 11pp., pres. copy. $25.

384 **GORDON, Carolina**
"None shall look back." N.Y., Scribner's 1937, 12mo, cl, 378pp. Fiction. Western Ky. the Allards from 1861-1864. Notes on Donelson, Chickamauga and Nathan B. Forrest.
...Reissued by Cooper Square Pub.

385 ..."Penhally." N.Y., Scribner's, 1931, fiction. 12mo, cl, 282pp. Llewellyn's of Penhally, Ky. Loyal to the South.

386 **GORDON, Caroline Lewis**
"Plantation Life with General John B. Gordon." In: Ga. Rev., Spring 1960, v.14, p. 17-34. $8. Excerpts from an unpublished book "De Gin'ral and Miss. Fanny."

387 **GORDON, E.C., Rev.**
"The Battle of Big Bethel." In: "Contributions to a History of Richmond Howitzers." v.I, p. 14-84, with "All Official Reports (C.S. and U.S.) Battle of Bethel. Richmond, Va., Carlton McCarthy, 1883.

388 **GORDON, G.I.**
"The Battle of Fort Fisher." In: Our Liv. and Dead, 1874, v.I, p. 313-315.

389 **GORDON, George Anderson**
"What will he do with it?" An essay delivered in Masonic Hall, Savannah, Thursday, Oct. 27, 1863, and again by special request, on Monday, Dec. 7, 1863, for the benefit of the Wayside Home in

Savannah, and repeated with slight alterations for similary objects in Augusta, Milledgeville, Macon, Atlanta, La Grange and Columbus by...63rd Reg. Ga. Vols. Published by request." Savannah, Ga., George N. Nichols Pr., 1863. 12mo, wraps, 28pp.

390 **GORDON, George W.**
"The famous snowball battle in the Confederate Army at Dalton, Ga., 1864. Suffolk, Va., Robt. Hardy Pub., 1986. 8vo, wraps, 12pp., port.

391 **GORDON, George W., General**
"General P.R. Cleburne. Dedication of a monument to his memory at Helena, Ark., May 10, 1891." In: SHSP, 1890, v.XVIII, p. 203-208.

392 ..."Memorial addresses delivered in the House of Representatives..." Washington, DC, 1913, GPO. 8vo, wraps, 97pp. $15-bmk, $20.

393 ..."General Joseph E. Johnston." In: SHSP, 1890, v.18, p. 203-208.

394 ..."General Patrick R. Cleburne." In: SHSP, 1890, v.18, p. 260-272.

395 **GORDON, J.F.**
"My first command and the outbreak of the war." In: Scribner's Mag., v.33, p. (515)-528. front, ports, illus. Known as "Raccoon Roughs".

396 **GORDON, James**
"The Battle and Retreat from Corinth." In: Miss. Hist. Soc. Pub., 1901, v.IV, p. 63-72.

397 **GORDON, John B.**
"Reminiscences..." Dayton, Oh., Morningside Press, 1981, Lim. Edt., 300 copies $35.
..."Reminiscences of the Civil War." Dayton, Oh., Morningside Press, 1985. Reprint of "Memorial Edition", with an Intro: Stephen D. Lee. $30.

398 **GORDON, John B., Gen.**
"Antietam and Chancellorsville." In: Scribner, 1903, v.33, p. 685-699, illus., port(Jackson).

399 ..."Gettysburg." In: Scribners, 1903, v.34, p. 2-24, illus., ports.

400 ..."My first command and the outbreak of the War." In: Scribner's, 1903, v.33, p. (514)-528, illus., ports.

401 **GORDON, John Brown, Gen.**
"Address of Gen. J.B. Gordon, in John W. Daniel's "Life and Reminiscences of Jeff. Davis". P. 269-273.

402 ..."Antietam and Chancellorsville." In: Scribner's June 1903, v.XXXIII, p. 685-699.

403 ..."Battle of Monocacy-Report of Gen. John B. Gordon." In: SHSP, 1879, v.VII, p. 173-176. (In: LWL, II, 1866/1877, p. 311-313)

404 ..."The Confederate Veterans." appeal for all to form camps and preserve traditions, etc. In: SHSP, 1891, v.XIX, p. 175-177.

405 ..."Defense of the South. Charges against Southern people answered. Speech of Hon. John B. Gordon, of Georgia, in the US Senate, Jan. 6, 1875." Washington: Gov. Print Off., 1875. 8vo, wraps, 12pp.

406 ..."The Gettysburg Campaign." In: SHSP, 1879, v.VII, p. 241-244. (This campaign in Scribner's Mag., July, 1903, v.XXXIV, #1)

407 ..."General J.B. Gordon's Report of Battle of Hatcher's Run." In: SHSP, 1880, v.VIII, p. 45.

408 ..."John B. Gordon Journal." Atlanta, Ga., John B. Gordon Camp. #46, Sons of Confederate Veterans. 4to, wraps-Gordon's port-illus., 6pp.

409 ..."The Last Days of the Confederacy, lecture of Gen. J.B. Gordon, given in various parts of the country, this, at Brooklyn, N.Y., Feb. 7, 1901." In: Modern Eloquence, Edt: Thos. B. Reed. Phila: John D. Davis Co., (1900) Also separate--Pamphlet, 8vo, wraps, cover title, p. 471-494.

410 ..."My First Command and the outbreak of war." In: Scribner's May 1903, v.XXXII, p. 515-528.

411 ..."The Old South, address delivered before the Confederate Survivors Ass'n in Augusta, Ga., on the occasion of its ninth reunion, on Memorial Day, April 26, 1887, by Governor John B. Gordon and Col. Charles C. Jones." Augusta, Ga., Chronicle Pub., 1887. 8vo, wraps, 23pp. (also under C.C. Jones)

412 ..."Reminiscences of the Civil War, by General John B. Gordon..." N.Y., Scribner's Sons, 1903. 8vo, cl, x, 1, xi-xiii, 474pp. 3 ports, incl. front. $30, $85, $75.
...London: 1904, $100-r, $30, $15. Editions: 1911 and 1913 (cheap)
...n.p., (1949) $12.
...Gettysburg, Pa., 1974. $15.
..."Memorial Edition", with an introduction by Gen. S.D. Lee, commander-in-chief of UCV. Memorial account by Frances Gordon Smith, illustrated." $17.50, $35, $75-fine. N.Y., Atlanta: Charles Scribner's Sons. The Martin and Hoyt Co., 1904. $30. Tk, 8vo, color flags(cover) ports (incl. front) illus., xxvii, (3), 474pp. (26 illus. and ports added, not numbered) index.
...Orig. pict. cl, 474pp. illus., near mint. With a 1890 letter, while governor of Georgia. $250-jk-169.
...N.Y., Charles Scribner's Sons, 1905. 8vo, cl, x, 41, 3-474pp. 3-ports. $15. DeRenne, p. 1027: 1st edt. shows minor text modifications, i.e., chp.xxvi, middle p. 385-394, certains passages omitted and new matter included.
...(Alexandria Va., 1981. Life-Time Books "Collector's Library of the Civil War" stamped on front cover. 8vo, emb. leather, g.e., marbled fly-leaves. $25.

413 ..."Report of the Gordon Commission." n.p., n.d. (Atlanta, Ga., 1907) 8vo, wraps, cover title, illus., ports, 65pp. DeRenne, p. 1336pb, notes: "not found". Relates the design, financing and unveiling of the Statue to Gordan, May 25, 1907. Solon H. Borglum, design and sculpt. See: Allen P. Tankersley's Biog. See: I.G. Bradwell's "Gordon Brigade after the Valley Campaign.

414 ..."They would mix on the picket line. Anecdotes of the war by Gen. Gordon." In: SHSP, 1882, v.X, p. 422-423.

415 ..."A Short History of Gen. J.B. Gordon." Park Place, N.Y., Knapp & Co., 1888. 2 3/4x1 1/2" colored booklet, 16pp. facsm. signature, (packed in Duke's cigarettes.) See: "Heroes of the C.W.", and W. Duke Co.

416 **GORDON, Ruth Nelson**
"Some young ladies of the Confederacy." In: Commonwealth, (Va.), Oct. 1950, v.17, (#10), p. 28, 30, views. Doll collection (1825-1865) now in CSA Museum.

417 **GORDON, W.F.**
"An episode of the war." In: So. Vib., 1885-1886, ns, v.I, p. 589-592.

418 ..."The Secession of Virginia. A poem by a Virginian." Louisa, Va., Press of News, 1897. 8vo, wraps, ports. (inc. front) illus., 30pp.

419 **GORE, Jesse P., Sgt.**
"Roster Co. "F", one of Col. John S. Mosby Companies." In: SHSP, 1899, v.27, p. 312-313. 43rd Batt. Cavalry.

420 **GOREE, Thomas Jewett, Capt., C.S.A.**
"A Young Texan goes to war-a collection of personal letters of Capt. Thomas Jewett Goree, CSA, aide-de-camp of Gen. James Longstreet." Edt: Henri Gerard Noordberg. (London) Jour. Confed. Hist. Soc., Winter, 1969, v.7, #4, p. 142-159; v.8, #1, p. 11-18, pl; v.8, #2, p. 30-42; v.8, #4, p. 106-116; v.9, #1-2, p. 35-47; v.9, #3, p. 75-89; v.9, #4, p. 124-133; v.10, #1, p. 27-

36; v.10, #2, p. 80-88; v.10, #3, p. 128-135; v.10, #4, p. 180-187.

421 ..."Five Goree Brothers, 1861-1865." Washington, D.C., n.d. (1970's). Oblong, 4to, spiral bound, (42)pp., unnumbered Xerox copies of service records of the five Gorees: Thos. Jewett, Robt. Daniel, Langston James, Edwin King, Pleasant Kittrell Goree.

422 ..."Thomas J. Goree Papers." University, La., 1950. Carbon copy, bound, 322pp. $50. Diary re: lot on Longstreet.

423 **GORGAS, Josiah**
Army Ordnance, XVI, p. 212-216; 283-288. Brig.-Gen. Gorgas' "Extracts from my notes written chiefly after close of the war." He was chief of ordnance of the CSA.

424 ..."The Civil War Diary of General Josiah Gorgas. Edited by Frank E. Vandiver." University: Univ. of Alabama Pr., 1947, 8vo, cl, dj, ports, xi, 208pp. $12.50, $16.50, $17.50, $20, $50-b.

425 ..."Contributions to the History of the Confederate Ordnance Department." In: SHSP, 1884, v.XII, p. 66-94.

426 ..."Notes on the Ordnance Department of the Confederate States of America." Ancon, Canal Zone, 1911. 8vo, wraps, 48pp.
...In: SHSP, 1884, v.12, p. 67-94.

427 ..."Ordnance Department of the Confederate Government." n.p., (c.1960's). 4to, mimeographed, 18pp. $15.

428 ..."The Ordnance Manual for the use of Officers of the Confederate States Army." Richmond: West & Johnston, 1863. Thick 12mo, cl, 546pp. 33plates at end, printed on-side. $120, $250.
...Dayton, Oh., Morningside Books, 1976. Intro: Sydney C. Kerksis, 620pp. $25.

429 ..."Report of Gen. J. Gorgas, Chief of Ordnance." In: SHSP, 1876, v.II, p. 58-63.

430 ..."A Sketch of the Life of Gen. Josiah Gorgas, Chief of Ordnance of the Confederate States." In: SHSP, 1885, v.XIII, port, p. 216-228.

431 ..."Sketch of..." In: 14th Reunion of Ass'n of Graduates of US Military Academy, June 12, 1883, p. 117-119. E. Saginaw, Mich. (1883)

432 **GORGAS, Mary Gayle**
"Captain Richard H. Gayle (1832-1873)." In: TylerQHGM, Jan. 1949, v.30, p. 206-207. Gayle as officer in CSNavy.

433 **GORHAM, George Congdon**
"General Johnston's surrender." In: SHSP, 1892, v.20, p. 205-212.

434 **GORMAN, George E.**
"Confederate accouterments." In: Gun Rep., April 1960, v.5, #11, p. 6-8, 49. views. On belts, buckles, cartridge boxes, holsters, cannisters, cap boxes, etc.

435 **GORMAN, John C., Capt.**
"Lee's Last Campaign. By Capt. J.C.G." Raleigh, N.C., Wm. B. Smith Pr., 1866. 12mo, wraps, 59pp. $200-ob.

436 ..."Lee's Last Campaign, with an accurate history of Stonewall Jackson's last wound, by Capt. J.C. Gorman." 2nd Edt., 10th thousand." Raleigh, N.C., Wm. B. Smith Co., 1866, 12mo, wraps, iv, (5)-71pp. $75.

437 **GORMAN, William R.**
In: OLOD, 1875, v.II, p. 18-24. Member of band who died of disease in 1863.

438 **GOSNELL, Harpur Allen**
"Guns on the Western Waters. The Story of River Gunboats in the Civil War." Baton Rouge: Louisiana State Univ. Pr. (1949). 8vo, cl, dj, illus(incl. front) maps, ports, xii, 273pp. $6.50 (pub) $7.50, $12.50, $20-jk, $15-bmk, $25, (dj).

439 ..."Rebel Raider, the cruise of Raphael Semmes' CSS Sumter, etc." under-"Semmes."

440 **GOSS, Lynn L.**
"Roster of Company E, Nineteenth Vir-

ginia Infantry." (from: SHSP, 1907, v.35, p. 312-319. Repeat: v.36, p. 237-244.

441 **GOTT, John Kenneth**
"A history of Marshall (formerly Salem), Fauquier County, Virginia (1797-1958)." (Middleburg?, Va., Denlinger? (1959?). 8vo, wraps, facsm., ports, tables, views. 94pp. Roster of Co. H., 6th Reg. Caval. Brig. CSA, Company B, 8th Reg. Va. Vals., CSA. The 1860 census of Salem Village and other Docs.

442 **GOURDIN, Robert N. and Robert Anderson**
"Robert N. Gourdin to Robert Anderson, 1861." In: SCHMag., Jan. 1959, v.60, p. 10-14. Letter dated FEb. 2, 1861, to Comm. Ft. Sumter why US forces should withdraw in peace, give fort back to S.C.

443 **GOVAN, Gilbert E. and James W. Livingood**
"Chattanooga under Military Occupation, 1863-1865." (Baton Rouge, La.) JHS, Feb., 1951, v.XVII, #1, p. 23-47.
...Issued, wraps, $10-b.

444 ..."A Different Valor. The Story of General Joseph E. Johnston, CSA." Indianapolis: Bobbs-Merrill Co. (1956). 8vo, cl, dj, maps, ports(incl. front) pl., 470pp. notes, bibliog., index (403-470) $20, $6(pub.), $10, $15, $17.50, $30. Also: "Civil War Book Club Edt., $40-bmk-84, $50, Atgs. $22.
...Westport, Ct., Greenwood Press (1973) $22.

445 **GOVAN, Gilbert Eaton**
"The Chattanooga Country, 1540-1951; from Tomahawks to TVA, by Gilbert Govan and James W. Livingood." N.Y. Dutton Print, 1952. 8vo, cl, dj, map liners, 500pp. (bibliog: 469-488) Chaps: ix-xiv, p. 159-311pp. relate to the war. Battle of Chickamauga, Under Stars and Bars, Peace to War, Under Military occupation, Road to reunion.

446 **GOW, June I.**
"Chiefs of staff in the Army of Tennessee under Braxton Bragg." In: THQ, 1968, v.27, p. 341-360.

447 ..."The Johnston and Brent Diaries: A Problem of Authorship." In: CWH, March 1968, v.XIV, #1, p. 46-50.

448 ..."Military Administration in the Confederate Army of Tennessee." (Houston, Tex.) JSH, May 1974, v.XL, #2, p. 183-198. $8.

449 ..."Theory and Practice in Confederate Administration." In: Mil. Affairs, Oct., 1975.

450 **GOWER, Herschel**
"Pen and Sword, the Life and Journals of Randal W. McGavock, Colonel, CSA. The Biography by Herschel Gower, Edt. The Journals, 1845-1851, Herschel Gower, Edt. The Political and Civil War Journals, 1853-1862, Jack Allen, Editor." Nashville: Tenn. Hist. Comm., 1959. 8vo, cl, dj, facsm. endsheets, illus., ports., 695pp. $6.50

451 **GOYNE, Minetta Altgelt**
"Lone Star and Double Eagle: Civil War letters of a German-Texas family." Fort Worth, Texas Christian University, 1982, 8vo, cl, dj, vi, 276pp., illus, ports, $15.

452 **GRABER, H(enry) W(illiam)**
"A Terry Texas Ranger, the Life Record of H.W. Graber. With introduction by Thomas W. Cutrer." Austin, Texas. State House Press, 1987. 8vo, cl, dj, xxxiii, 463pp. index. $20. Lim. Edt., 50 numbered copies, leather and cloth binding, slipcase. $60.
..."A Terry Texas Ranger: the Life Record of H.W. Graber (1841-1917)." Austin, Texas, State House Press, 1987. 8vo, cl, dj, 486p. Reprint: 1916 edition. $20. Lim.Edt. $60.

453 **GRABER, Henry William**
"The Life Record of H.W. Graber. A

Terry Texas Ranger, 1861-1865. Sixty-two Years in Texas." (Copyright 1916 by H.W. Graber), n.p., (Dallas, Texas) limited printing. $50, $75, $100, 3/4 lt., $500-bmk-105, $125, $750-jk-137. tk. 12mo, cl, port(front), 442pp.

...1st Edt., Dallas, Texas, "Times Herald", 3/4Mor., with 6x6" adv. "This book was written as a memento for Gen. Graber's descendants, and a limited edition only has been provided for the general public. There are now only 120 copies for distribution, and there will be no more printed." $750-jk-140.

..."Why Sherman did not go to Augusta." In: Confed. Vet., July 1914, v.XXII, p. 319-320.

454 **GRABILL, John H.**
"The Murder of David Getz. An instance of the brutality of Custer. His retributive fate." (From: Richmond, Va. "Dispatch", Feb. 18, 1900) In: SHSP, 1899, v.XXVII, p. 372-374. Also in: CV, 1907, v.XV, p. 120-121 (Johnson Isle.)

455 ..."Horrible deed by Federals in Virginia." In: CV, 1900, v.VIII, p. 537. Murder of David Getz.

456 **GRABILLE, John H.**
"Diary of a soldier of Stonewall Brigade (Woodtstock, Va., Shenandoah Herald.) c.1909. 8vo, wraps, 20pp. reprinted from the "Herald", in 8th, 15th, 22nd, 1909. Reprinted: 1969.

457 **GRACEY, Frank P., Capt.**
"The Capture of the "Mazeppa" (Federal steamer on the Tenn. River). Authentic History of how Capt. F.P. Gracey achieved it." n.p., n.d., 12mo, wraps, 24pp.

458 ..."Capture of the "Mazeppa." In: CV, 1905, v.13, p. 566-570, port. Julien F. Gracey corrects an injustice to his Father of an article in the CV.

459 **GRACIE, Archibald**
"The Truth about Chickamauga." Bost: Houghton Mifflin Co., 1911, 8vo, cl, dj, pls, ports, maps, plans, xxxii, (4), 462pp. $18, $30, #35, $100-ob, $45-nc, $40-y.

...Intro. Dr. W. G. Robertson. 8vo, cl, 402pp. Dayton, Oh., Morningside. $40.

460 ..."Gracie's Battalion at Williamsburg in 1862." In: Confed. Vet., 1911, Jan., XIX, p. 27-32, (11th Ala. Reg.)

461 **GRACY, David B., II**
"With Danger and Honor. Fight and Fall Back." In: Texana, Spring 1963, v.1, #2, p. 120-152, port, illus., v.1, #1, p. 1-19. Capt. Geo. Washington Littlefield, the Eighth Texas Cavalry, in Tennessee.

462 **GRADE, Rebecca Drake**
"Origin of the "Lost Cause" argument: analysis of Civil War letters." Southern Speech Communication Journal IL., 1984, p. 420-430.

463 **GRADY, Benjamin Franklin**
"Sectionalism and some of its fruits. Published by the Author." Goldsboro, N.C., Nash Bros. Print., 1909, 8vo, wraps, cover title, 40pp.

464 ..."The South's Burden; or, Curse of Sectionalism in the U.S." Goldsboro, N.C., Nash Print, 1906, 8vo, cl, 147pp.

465 ..."The Case of the South Against the North; or Historical Evidence Justifying the Southern States of the American Union in their long controversy with the Northern states..." Tall 8vo, cl, 345pp. (preface, xxix). Raleigh, N.C., 1899. Edwards & Broughton. $45-b, $7.50.

466 ..."A Review by William Walker." (from: New Orleans (La.) "Picayune", Dec. 30, 1900. In: SHSP, 1900, v.XXVIII, p. 156-166.

467 **GRADY, John C. and Bradford K. Felmly.**
"Suffering to Silence, 19th Texas Cavalry, CSA." Quanah, Texas: Nortex Press, 1975, 8vo, cl, dj, illus., maps, index, xi, 243pp. $15-bmk, $8.50.

468 **GRAF, LeRoy P.**
"Andrew Johnson and the Coming of the War." In: Tenn.HQ, 1960, v.XIX, p. 208-221. Position as Southerner, Unionist, Democrat.

469 **GRAF, William S.**
"The Origin of a Great Cavalryman, (Robert E. Lee)." In: Armor, 1963, v.LXXII-iv, p. 26-28.

470 **GRAHAM, H.C.**
"A Drum-head court martial." In: Blue & Gray, 1894, v.III, p. 57-59.

471 ..."How North Carolina went into the War." In: B & G, 1894, p. 282-286, illus., port.

472 ..."Richmond before and after the Seven-Days." In: B & G, 1895, v.V, p. 80-84.

473 ..."Sketch of J.J. Pettigrew." In: "Confed. Memorial Addresses of New Bern, N.C., p. 9-26.

474 **GRAHAM, Henry Tucker, D.D., L.L.D.**
"Some things for which the South did not fight, in the War Between the States." n.p., (Wadesboro, N.C., May 1946). 8vo, stiff wraps, 12pp. $3.50, $20.

475 **GRAHAM, James A.**
"The James A. Graham Papers, 1861-1884. Edt: H.M. Wagstaff." The James Sprunt Historical Studies, v.20, #2. Chapel Hill: Univ. North Carolina Pr., 1928. 8vo, wraps, (2), 91-324pp. $7.50, $12.50, $20, $15-bmk-84. Graham's war letters, Hist. of Orange Guards, Co.G., 27th Reg. N.C. Infr.

476 ..."Historical Sketch of the 27th Reg., North Carolina Infantry." In: Our Liv. and Our Dead, v.1, 1874, p. 97-122. See: John W. Moore's "Roster of N.C. Troops, v.2, p. 407-428, Co: A-K. Also: Walter Clark's Hist. of Several Reg.s, v.II, p. 425-563, written by Graham.

477 **GRAHAM, Phillip**
"A song was born: the South's "Dixie" (by Daniel Decatur Emmett, 1859)." In: Texas Quart., Spring 1958, v.1, #2, p. 51-54.

478 **GRAHAM, Stanley S.**
"Campaign for New Mexico 1861-1862." In: TMH, 1972, v.X, #1, p. 5-27.

479 **GRAHAM, William Alexander**
"The Papers of William Alexander Graham, vol. V: 1857-1863." Edt: Max R. Williams and J.G. de Roulhac Hamilton. Raleigh, North Carolina Archives and History, 1973. 8vo, cl, xxiv, 591pp. $15. Against secession, a moderate, five sons in CSA wrote many letters back home. See: Walter Clark.

480 ..."Speech of..., of Orange, in the Convention of North Carolina, Dec. 7, 1861, on the ordinance concerning test oaths and sedition." Raleigh, N.C., W.W. Holden, 1862, 8vo, wraps, cover title, 31pp. $40.

481 **GRAINGER, Gervis D.**
"Four years with the Boys in Gray. By Gervis D. Grainger, Co.I, Sixth Kentucky Infantry, Orphan-Brigade." Franklin, Ky., Favorite Office, 1902, 8vo, wraps, 45pp.
...Dayton, Oh., Morningside Bookshop, 1972. Facsimilie #8. $7.50-y, $15, $5. "Published originally in serial form in his home paper." (Gallatin, Tenn.?)

482 **GRAMP, W.E.H. (pseud.)**
"Journal of a Grandfather." See: Wm. Edgar Hughes.

483 **GRANBERRY, J.C.**
"Life Sketch of Captain Richard Irby, by Bishop J.C. Granberry." In: John P. Branch Hist. Papers, of Randolph-Macon College, June 1903, v.I, #3, p. 159-169. See also: Capt. Richard Irby.

484 ..."An address to the soldiers of the Southern Armies, by Rev. J.C. Granbery, Chaplain of the 11th Virginia Regiment." Raleigh, 186?, 8vo, sewn, 8pp. Crandall-4669. $65.

485 **GRAND ARMY of the Rupublic, Illinois-Columbia Post:**

"Ungenerous criticism of Dr. Cave." In: SHSP, 1894, v.22, p. 381-382. (Same) Mass. (from Richmond Times: "They honor a former foe.") In: SHSP, 1898, v.26, p. 308-312.

486 **GRAND CAMP Confederate Veterans-Virginia**
"Proceedings of the annual meeting of the Grand Camp Confederate Veterans, department of Virginia. (Richmond, Va., 18-) 8vo, wraps, color front. in one vol. 16th has impression: Pulaski, Va., 1904, 17th-18th, 1904-1905, issued together.

487 ..."Report of committee on ceremonies incident to the unveiling of the soldiers' and sailors' monument, at Richmond, Va., may 30, 1894." (Richmond, Va., 1894) 8vo, wraps, cover title, 21pp.

488 ..."Official Report of the History Committee..."

489 **"GRAND FEDERAL MENAGERIE!!**
Now on Exhibition! The Great Massachusetts Hyena, an extraordinary animal newly discovered, true to his traditional instincts he violates the grave!" n.p., n.d. (c.1862/1864) Lithograph 10x14" $50. CSA or Copperhead cartoon, shows Gen. Butler as a hyena digs at grave of Gen. Al. Sid. Johnston, monument of Washington Artillery, Col. Chs. Dreux skull and crossbones on ground dug from Dreux's grave.

490 **GRAND LODGE (Freemasons)**
of South Carolina: "Proceedings of the Most Worshipful Grand Lodge of Ancient Freemasons of South Carolina, at Five several Annual Communications, Nov. 5861, 5862, 5863, 5865. (A.D. 1861-1866) Charleston: Courier Job Press, 1866. 8vo, wraps, 87pp. McKissick-2062.

491 **GRAND LODGE (Masons)**
of Alabama, Proceedings, 1845-1888. Proceedings at Tuscaloosa, Ala. Contains: "Table of Grand Lodges of the Confederate States, of the US and Canada, p. xci. "Proceedings, Dec. 2, 1861, p. 47, lv." "Proceedings, Dec. 5, 1864, p. 58, xviii."

492 **"GRAND MAY PARTY!"**
Spring, 1863. To be given in Mr. M.T. Smith's Woods, Sat. 9th May. Maj. Wise's Celebrated Band in attendance, everybody invited. Queen, Miss. Sallie Smith, Maids, Seasons, etc. $15. 12mo, double-fold, printed on ruled paper, embossed "CS".

493 **"GRAND TORCHLIGHT Procession**
in honor of the Secession of Georgia in Dalton, Jan. 21, 1861." Broadside, folio. In: Henkel-#1118, Oct. 1914.

494 **"GRAND VARIETIES**
by the ladies of Austin, for the benefit of Sibley's Brigade, at Buaas' Hall, on Tuesday ev'g., Feb. 17th, 1863." (Austin, Texas, 1863) Broadside: 1p. 12.7x23.5cm. Winkler-#3915*.

495 **GRANDGUILLOT, Alcide Pierre**
"La reconnaissance du Sud. Par A. Grandguillot." Paris: E. Dentu, 1862. 8vo, wraps, 30pp. Carolina Book: "part 1, only, of 2." $10. Other sources list only 30pp.

496 ...Paris: Michel Levy Freres, 1861. 8vo, cl, 310, (1)p. Sabin-28271. Defends right of South to secede.

497 **GRANT, A.F., Major, (pseud.) Thos. C. Harbaugh**
"Loyal Ned; or, the last Cruise of the Alabama: a rattling romance of the famous Rebel Privateer." N.Y., Novelist Pub. Co., 1883. War Lib. Pocket Edition, v.I, #5, 12mo, illus., wraps, 96pp. $7.50.

498 ..."Fort Fisher; or, the thunder of siege guns. A story of the great bombardment." N.Y., Novelist Pub. Co., 1883." War Lib. Picket Edt., v.I, #10. 12mo, wraps, illus., 96pp.

499 ..."The War Detective; or, the plotters at Washington. A tale of Booth's conspiracy." N.Y., Novelist Pub., Co., 1883. War Lib. Pocket Edt., #1. 12mo, wraps, illus., 96pp.

500 **GRANT, Carl E.**
"Partisan warfare, model 1861-1865." In: Mil. Rev., Nov. 1958, v.38, #8, p. 42-56. On the South's partisan rangers.

501 **GRANT, Dorothy Fremont**
"Rose Greenhow, Confederate Secret Agent." N.Y., P.J. Kenedy & Son, (1961). American Background Books. 8vo, cl, 188pp.

502 **GRANT, Fred D., Gen.**
"Fred Grant as a boy with the army." In: CV, 1908, v.16, p. 10-14. Suppl. to his address on the Vicksburg campaign, to the Society of the Army of the Tenn. (in Dec. CV)

503 **GRANT, L.P., Col.**
"Col. L.P. Grant and the defenses of Atlanta." In: Atl. HB, Feb., 1932, v.1, #6, p. 32-35.

504 **GRANT, Lewis Addison**
"Review of Major-General Barlow's paper on the capture of the salient at Spottsylvania, May 12, 1864." In: Miss. Hist. Soc. Pub., 1881, v.IV, p. 263-271.

505 **GRANT, Parks**
"A Chamber Opera with a Civil War Plot." In: CWH, September 1958, v.IV, #3, p. 237-249. Musical scores. Re: Mississippi "University Grays".

506 **GRANT, Richard Southall**
"Captain William Sharp, of Norfolk, Va., U.S.N., C.S.N." (Richmond, Va. Mag. Hist. Biog. Jan. 1949, v.57, #1, p. 44-54.

507 **GRANT, Ulysses Simpson**
"Did Grant return Lee's sword?" See: Lee.

508 ..."Exchange of Prisoners." In: SHSP, 1889, v.17, p. 386-387.

509 ..."Letter concerning Confederate Soldiers' Home." In: SHSP, v.12, p. 238.

510 ..."A Northern view of Grant's generalship." In: SHSP, 1884, v.12, p. 20-22. (From NY Tribune) signed: "F.P.S."

511 ..."Grant and Lee in Virginia-May and June, 1864. Summary of the Campaign with sketch maps, to illustrate the operations and comments on the campaign." London: Forster Groom & Co., 1908. 12mo, cl, 63pp., 6-fldg. maps in pocket.
...See: Gen. R.E. Lee, W.W. Goldsborough, John William Jones, Dabney H. Maury, Leslie J. Perry, John Aaron Rawlins.

512 **"GRANVILLE GRAYS, The."**
In: OLOD, Aug., 1875, v.3, #2, p. 181-182. North Carolina Roster. Reorganized: Norfolk, Va.

513 **GRANVILLE, Earl**
"Earl Granville to C.A. Spring Rice." In: Mass. Hist. Soc. Proc., 1916, v.XLIX, p. 62. Letter written Apr. 10, 1887, re: attitude of British cabinet on recognition of the CSA.

514 **GRASSET, Ernest**
"La Guerre de Secession 1861-1865." Paris: Lib. Militaire de L. Baudoin, 1886, 2 vols. 12mo, 1/2 Mor., (old)$10. Pro-Jefferson Davis.

515 **GRATTAN, George D., Judge**
"The Battle of Boonsboro Gap, or South Mountain. An address delivered before R.E. Lee Camp, #1, on May 20, 1910." (Harrisonburg, Va., n.d.) 8vo, wraps, map, 11pp. $5, $12.50, $30-ob, Swem ref.2115 as "George C.G.
...Same, by..., Capt. and A.A.G. Staff of General Colquitt. In: SHSP, Apr. 1914, ns ser.#1, whole #XXXIX, p. 31-44.

516 **GRATTAN, Thomas Colley**
"England and the Disrupted States." London: Ridgway, 1861. 8vo, wraps, 42p.
...Do: Second Edt.
...Do: Third Edt., but 47pp. England and Confederacy bound incommon cause.

517 **GRATTEN, Peachy R.**
"Letter on the Constitutional Power of the General Assembly to extend the Boun-

daries of the City of Richmond..." Richmond, Va., H.K. Ellyson, 1861. 8vo, wraps, 14pp. Sabin-28337. $20.

518 **GRATZ, John**
"The Andersonville Prison Park." In: CV, March 1921, v.XXIX, p. 91-92.

519 **GRAVES of CSA Dead**
See: Burial of CSA dead.

520 **GRAVES, Charles A.**
"The Forged Letter of General Robert E. Lee. Paper read by Prof. Charles A. Graves of the Law School of the University of Virginia, before the Virginia State Bar Ass'n., at the Homestead Hotel, Hot Springs, Va., Aug. 4, 5, 6, 1914. Richmond, Va., Richmond Press, 1914. 8vo, wraps, 8vo, 40pp. cover title. $9-nc.
...Same: in Va. Bar. Assoc. Rep., 1914, v.XXVI, p. 176-215. Re: a letter in N.Y. Sun, Nov. 26, 1864, purported to be by Gen. Lee to his son, G.W. Custis Lee.

521 ..."Supplemental paper read before the Virginia State Bar Ass'n., White Sulphur Springs, W.Va., Aug. 4-6, 1915." Richmond, Va., Richmond Press (1915). 8vo, wraps, 17pp. Also in Report Va. St. Bar Ass'n., 1915. v.XXVIII, 1915.

522 ..."The Forged Letter of Gen. Lee." In: SHSP, ns, 1915, p. 101-148. The so-called "duty letter".
...Also in the Univ. of Va. Alumni Bul., 3rd ser., Jan.1916, v.IX, p. 92-102.

523 ..."The 'Duty' Letter and the Lloyd Letter, from the New York Times." In: SHSP, Oct., 1917, v.XLII, p. 234-236.

524 **GRAVES, Harrison A., Rev.**
"Andrew Jackson Potter, the fighting parson of the Texas frontier. Six years of Indian warfare in New Mexico and Arizona. Many wonderful events in the ministerial life of..., etc." Nashville, Tenn., Southern Methodist Pub., 1881. 12mo, cl, front(port) 471pp. $25-jk, $100-aldr. Pvt. in Capt. Stoke Home's Co., Wood's Reg., 32nd Texas Cavalry. (pg. 125-185) $250-jk-137.
...Same, 1883, Eberstd. #138 refers to "orig. edt." for the '83rd edt. (other; '82, '88, '90) $75, $135-d.david#6.

525 **GRAVES, Henry Lee**
"A Confederate Marine: a Sketch of Henry Lea Graves with excerpts from the Graves Family Correspondence, 1861-1865. Edited by Richard Harwell." Tuscaloosa, Ala., Confederate Pub. Co., 1963. 12mo, stiff wraps, facsm., front(port), 140pp. Index. $15-jk-122.

526 **GRAVES, John Temple, Edt.**
"Eloquent Sons of the South, a handbook of Southern Oratory." Boston: Chapple Pub. Co., 1909. 12mo, cl, 2 vols. Calhoun, Jeff Davis, R.E. Lee, A. Stephens, Rbt. Toombs, Henry Grady, etc.

527 ..."The Fighting South." N.Y., G.P. Putnam's Sons (1943) 8vo, cl, 4pp., 3-282pp. $5, $6.

528 **GRAVES, Joseph A.**
"The History of the Bedford Light Artillery, by Rev. Joseph A. Graves." Bedford City, (Va.) Democrat Print, 1903. 8vo, wraps, 83pp. $15, $30, $200-bmk. Gaithersburg, Md., 1983 reprint. $16.50, Butternut Press.

529 **GRAVES, Peter W., Rev.**
"Twenty-five Years on the Outside Row of the Northwest Texas Annual Conference. An Autobiography." Comanche, Texas: Exponent Steam Pr., 1892. 8vo, wraps, 67pp. $27.50(old) $175-jk. Describes Col. Allen's attack on negro camps in La., Battle of Milliken's Bend and leaving 1500 negroes and Yankee officers in ditches, accounts other bayonet charges.
..."Twenty-five Years on the Outside Row...Autobiography of..., with an introduction and notes by T.R. Havins James M. Day." Brownwood, Texas, 1966. 8vo, cl,

Lim. 1000 copies. $10, $5. Facsimilie: 1892 edt., only 3 copies known.

530 **GRAVES, William H.**
"Confederate Indian policy in the Southwest, interest, goals, attitudes." In: Mid-Amer., Oct. 1984, v.66, p. 111-119.

531 **GRAVES. L.H.**
"A Texas soldier of the Confederacy records his experiences in northwest Arkansas." In: Flashback, Aug. 1953, v.3, #5, p. 9-15. Diary kept from 1 May 1861-1 Apr., 1864.

532 **GRAY BOOK, The**
Published by the Gray Book Committee, S.C.V. by Authority and under auspices of the Sons of Confederate Veterans. n.p., n.d. (1920) A.H. Jennings, Chm., Lynchburg, Va. $10. 8vo, wraps (tied), 53, (1)pp. $5, $6.50, $7.50. Refutes Northern charges: Secession, slavery, prisoners, pensions, etc.

534 ...n.p., n.d.(c.1960's) Preface: Wm. D. McCain, Adj-in-chief, SCV, (Distr: Frank E. LaRue, Jr., Athens, Texas), 50pp. (omits last chap., Lyon G. Tyler's "South and Germany.")

535 ..."Confederate Gray Book-R.E. Lee Camp #158, UCV, Ft. Worth, Texas, 1908, added all presidents portraits to Theo. Roosevelt. $5.
..."Confederate Gray Book." Mobile, Ala., Raphael Semmes Camp, #11. 8vo, wraps, cover title, ports, ads in printed material, 52pp. (1912) United Conf. Vets.

536 **GRAY, Charles Martin**
"The Old Soldier's Story. Autobiography of Charles Martin Gray." Edgefield, S.C., Edgefield Advertiser, 1868, 8vo, wraps, 56pp. (McKissick-961).

537 **GRAY, Clayton**
"Conspiracy in Canada." Montreal: Atelier Press (1959). 8vo, cl, facsms., map, ports, views, bibliog. (p. 133-140), notes, 145, (2)pp. Lt. Bennett Young's raid on St. Albans from Montreal, the arrest, trial and release of participants; activities of J. Wilkes Booth as a CSAgent in Canada.

538 **GRAY, Edward H.**
"Narrative of a Confederate Prisoner of war, his capture at the battle of Chickamauga in Sept., 1863, his detention in a Federal prison and his escape from thence in Oct. 1864: with his subsequent wanderings and adventures." (London) Jour. Confed. Hist. Soc. Autumn, 1966, v.4, #3, p. 105-126, port. From an orig. mssc., in England.
...(Dublin), n.d., Printed for private circulation. 4to, wraps, cover title, 24pp. (old) $10. (Goodspeed's-393(#72).

538a **GRAY, Richard L.**
"Prison Diary of Lt. Richard L. Gray, in Diaries, Letters, & Recollections of the War between the States." In: Winchester-Frederick County Hist. Soc. papers. Winchester, Va., 1955, v.III, p.30-45.

539 **GRAY, Ricky Harold**
"Corona Female College (1857-1864)." In: JMH, May 1980, v.XLII, #2, p. 129-134.

540 **GRAY, Tom S., Jr.**
"The March to the Sea." In: Ga.H.Q., June, 1930, v.XIV, #2, p. 111-138. Sherman's campaign in Ga.

541 **GRAY, Virginia Davis**
"Life in Confederate Arkansas: the Diary of Virginia Davis Gray, 1863-1865. Part I, Edt: Carl H. Moneyhon." In: ArkHQm., Spring, 1983, v.XLII, #1, p. 47-85, map, notes. Part II, 1863-1866, Summer 1983, #2, p. 134-169.

542 **GRAY, William Fairfax**
"Edwin Fairfax Gray (1829-1884)." In: Jr. Hist. (Tex.) Nov. 1952, v.13, #2, p. 11-12. Services in Texas/US Navy, in CSArmy and as an engineer.

543 **GRAY, Wood**
"The Hidden Civil War; the Story of the Copperheads." N.Y., Viking Press, 1942.

8vo, cl, dj, illus. (maps), ports, facsms., 314pp. $12.50, $20, $25-bmk-84, $15. See: Frank L. Clement.

544 GRAYDON, Nell Saunders
"Main street's five colonels." In: UDCMag., May 1953, v.16, #5, p. 9, 24. CSA colonels from Abbeville, S.C.

545 "GRAY JACKETS, The
and how they lived, fought and died, for Dixie. With incidents and sketches of life in the Confederacy. Comprising narratives of personal adventure, army life, naval adventure, home life, partisan daring, life in the camp, field and hospital: together with the songs, ballads, anecdotes and humorous incidents of the war for Southern Independence, by a Confederate." Richmond, Atlanta, Phila., Cinn., St. Louis and Chicago. (1867) Jones Brothers & Co., Tk. 8vo, cl, pls, maps, ports (some fldg.) $20, $25, $35, $40, $125, $75-nc-reb., $90-bmk, $140-bmk, $150-bmk. Howes-6411 attributes authorship to Jas. D. McCabe(?) and also to John E. Cooke.
...copy, 3/4 Mor., raised bands, $150-bmk.

546 GRAYSON, F.L.
"Lambdlin P. Milligan-a Knight of the Golden Circle." In: Ind. Mag. of Hist., 1947, v.XL, p. 379-391.

547 GRAYSON, William John
"The autobiography of William John Grayson. Edt: Samuel Gaillard Stoney." In: SCHM Jan/Apr., 1950, v.51, p. 29-44, 103-117. notes. Editor and planter, largely 1860-1865.

548 ..."James Louis Petigru, of South Carolina. A Biographical Sketch." N.Y., Harper & Bros., 1866. 12mo, cl, port, 178pp. See: Thos. D. Jarrett. $50-bmk-109, $30-bmk, $40-bmk, $12.50, $17.50.

549 ..."Confederate Diary, Edt: Elmer J. Puryear." In: SCHM, July 1962, Oct., v.63, p. 137-149, 214-226, #3 and 4.

550 ..."Reply to Professor Hodge, on the "State of the Country"." Charleston, S.C., Evans & Cogswell, 1861. 8vo, sewn, 32pp., Sabin-28427, Crandall-#2760. Signed: Friends in Council. $11.50. One of first intellectual discussions, states Southern viewpoint.

551 "GREAT BATTLE of Pea Ridge,The. Confederate Generals who died there." In: Wash. Co. Hist. Soc. "Flashback", Feb. 1962, v.XII, #1, ports, facsms, map, illus., 40pp.

552 "GREAT BROAD SEAL of the Confederacy."
"The Great or Broad Seal of the Confederate States of America." In: AHQ, 1949, v.10, p. 96-98.

553 "GREAT CIVIL WAR HEROES
and their Battles. Edt: Walton Rawls." N.Y., Abbeville Press, 1985, Oblong 11x8 1/4", 304pp. $40. 195-illus., 158 color. See: W. Duke, Sons & Co., for basic edt. and "Short Histories of Confederate Generals." Miniature booklets issued in Duke's tobacco of 50 CSA and 50 Union generals which were published, all 100 in the basic volume mentioned above. This book seems to have added complete set of Kurtz and Allison color prints to the above Duke edition.

554 "GREAT DEBATES in American History..."
Edt: Marion Mills Miller. In 14 vols. N.Y., Current Lit. Pub. Co., 1913. "Slavery from 1790-1857." Edt. Chs. F. Adams. vol. IV. "States Rights", 1798-1861." vol. V, "Slavery, 1858-1861. Intro: E.D.Warfield" vol.VI, "The Civil War." Intro: Henry Watterson." VII.

555 "GREAT HANGING at Gainesville, Texas."
See: James Smallwood, James L. Clark, Thomas Barrett.

556 "GREAT ISSUE No. 19.
The Great Issue to be decided in Novem-

ber next! Shall the Constitution and the Union stand or fall, shall Sectionalism triumph? Lincoln and his supporters Behold the Record!" caption title. n.p., National Democratic Executive Committee, McGill & Witherow, printers, 1860. 8vo, sewn, 24pp. Monaghan, v.I, #39, variant FtwL has 1st line: "Breckinridge and Lane Campaign Document, No. 19 (propaganda showing Lincoln favored Negro equality.)

557 **"GREAT PANIC. The**
Being Incidents Connected With Two Weeks of the War in Tennessee." By Eye-Witness. (Mitchell's Tenn. Imprints) Nashville: Johnson & Whiting, 1862. 8vo, wraps, 36pp., (MHi, NjP, OCIWHi, MB, TKL.) $500-g, $50.

558 ...Nashville, Tenn., Elder - Sherbourne (1977) 12mo, color stiff wraps, (6), 36, (20)pp., illus., ports, intro: Hugh Walker. Author attributed to be John Miller McKee, in Drake's "Annals of Army of Tennessee." $8-bmk, $4.95-y, $3.

559 **GREAT SEAL of the Confederate States of America. The**
"The Great Seal of the Confederate States of America." Metal plaque: 13 1/2" diameter of original seal in Bronze of yellow brass, $20, or aluminum, $15.
..."Great seal found." In: Americana, July 1912, v.7, p. 699-701.
..."Great Seal of the Confederate States." Cast aluminum, 12 3/4" diam., antique gold finish. $22.95. Synehi Sale, 6 Hillrose Ave., Greenville, S.C. 29609.
...Minneapolis, Minn., Battlefield Guide Pub., 6012 Virginia Ave., So., 55424. Seal in full color, set in 6" ceramic plate, within 11" cast aluminum (30 oz.) plate, for hanging. $30.
..."Great Seal of the Confederacy." In: Chron. Okla., v.XXX, p. 309-311.
..."Great Seal of the Confederate States, 22 Feb., 1862, Deo Vindice. 18" diameter, in color, with statue of Washington in center. Framed in 22" frame. (gold, blue, red and green). $125. See: Annie Payne Pillow. Offered for sale 1915 in the Confederate Veteran, $1. Raising money to erect a statue to her father, Gen. Gideon J. Pillow. A 32pp. pamphlet offered for sale 1911-? in Confed. Vet., XIX, p. 367. See also CV, XXIV, #1. A review, p. 235, in v.XXIII, with port. See: Jno. T. Pickett, Mary B. Clark.

560 ..."Seal of the Southern Historical Society and Great Seal of the CSA." In: SHSP, v.16, p. 416-422, with spirited debate over the motto "Deo Vindice", the most complete description of the seal.
...CV, XX, #7, p. 307: Jno. T. Pickett, atty. in Washington, DC, authenticating seal in a letter Mar. 6, 1874. Made by J.S. and A.B. Wyon, London.
...Do: 376-379. Mrs. Mary B. Clark, Jackson, Tenn., writes of Seal being adopted by the CSA Congress at Montgomery, Ala., Apr. 30, 1862. Sent to Wyon firm by Hon. Jas. M. Mason, said to have been designed by Judah P. Benjamin.

561 ...Do: p. 471. R.M. Cheshire claims Herman Baumgarten designed it under direction of Benjamin, escaped thru blockade to Bermuda, London and Paris. In Journal of CSA Congress, Oct. 11, 1862, Baumgarten was paid in installments for its design.
...CV, XVIII, p. 366. The original seal adopted on Washington's birthday, Feb. 22, 1862, center of seal being Washington's statue in Richmond. E.A. Tyler, well known jeweler of New Orleans made several copies and destroyed the die. One copy given Washington Artillery and a stained glass window made for Memorial Hall, with a copy of the seal. Fate of original seal unknown July, 1910.
...CV, v.V, p. 99. Seal used on cover of CV

562 was given by Charley Herbst, a bronze seal owned by him, dated 1862.

562 ...CV, XXIX, p. 165. Refutes a common story that an old negro, James Jones claimed was entrusted to him by Pres. Jeff. Davis.

563 ...CV, XL, p. 412-414. Repeats story, it was first found in Bermuda, a history repeated in march 1932. "The Bermudian", being owned by a prominent family there, later sold with other papers from Richmond evacuation, now resting in the CSA Museum, Richmond.

564 ...Raphael P. Thian's "Documentary Hist. of the Flag and Seal of the CSA, 1861-1865". Wash., 1880 in rare bookroom of LC. Unpublished compilation. See: Wm. B. Smith, Paul P. Walsh, Allen P. Tankersley, Virginia Lee Jones, Mary B. Clark.

565 **"GREAT USURPATON. The**
The United States under the Confederate Senate and House of Representatives. An oligarchy." Washington: R.H. Darby, 1880, Doc. #10, 8vo, wraps, 16pp.

566 **"GREATEST Confederate Commander. The"**
(Washington, 1907?) 12mo, wraps, 38pp., 2nd edt. Replies received from 44 CSA officers, by Senator Charles A. Culberson (Texas), in answer to a circular letter dated Sept. 17, 1907, who is entitled to rank as the greatest commander on the Southern side of war? Col. M.L. Crimmins is collator of replies.
...1st edt., 36pp. (old) $7.50. See: Swem-2132.

567 **"GREELEY, BEECHER, GARRISON, Etc.,**
the Great Perversionists of the Constitution. Jeff Davis and the Rebels justified by the Friends of Freedom. The Constitution interpreted in Favor of Criminals and worst form of Opposition." (n.p., 1864) 8vo, p. 8, Sabin-28495.

568 **GREEMAN, Betty Dix**
"The Democratic Convention of 1860: Prelude to Secession." In: Md. Hist. Mag., 1972, v.LXVII, p. 225-253.

569 **GREEN, B.W., Col. of Little Rock, Ark.**
"Speech on Jefferson Davis delivered at the Reunion of United Confederate Veterans." Richmond, Va., June 1-3, 1915. n.p., 8vo, wraps, 24pp. N.O., 1915-orig. wraps, 148pp. $9.

570 ...Longstreet at Gettysburg." In: CV, Feb'y. 1919, v.XXVII, p. 55-56. Col. Benjamin William Green.

571 **GREEN, Beulah Gayle**
"Confederate Reporter 1861-1864." Austin, Texas: Burrell Print, 1962, 4to, soft wraps, 123, (4)pp. illus., largely from Richmond Dispatch and Petersburg, Va., Daily Express. $7.50.

572 **GREEN, Duff**
"Facts and suggestions relative to finance and currency. Addressed to the president of the Confederate States." Augusta, Ga., J.T. Paterson & Co., 1864, 8vo, wraps, 80pp.

573 ..."Some Famous Sea Fights." N.Y., The Century Co. (1927) 8vo, decr. cl, illus. (incl. front), maps, diagrams (2 fldg.), index, 346pp. "Mobile Bay", cahp. vi, p. 200-232.

574 **GREEN, Fletcher M.**
"Walter Lynwood Fleming: historian of Reconstruction." Journal of Southern History, v.II, p. 497-521. A survey of Fleming's works, one of the outstanding writers of southern history. Append: bibliography of his writings.

575 ..."Women of the Confederacy in War times." In: South. Mag., 1935, v.II, #6, p. 16-20, 47-48. Address: Agnes Lee Chapter UDC in Decatur, Ga.

576 ..."Studies in Confederate Leadership. An outline for individual and group study." Chapel Hill: University of N.C. Press (1930). Univ. of N.C. Extension Bul. X, #8, 8vo, wraps, 47pp. Bibliog., p. 3-40. Prepared for U.D.C. $4.
"George Davis, North Carolina Whig and Confederate statesman, 1820-1896." In: NCHR, Oct., 1946, v.23, p. 449-470.

577 **GREEN, Fletcher and J. Isaac Copeland**
"The Old South." Arlington Heights, Ill., AHM Pub. (1980) 8vo, cl, xvii, 173pp.

578 **GREEN, James W.**
"Memorial services, an address by J.W. Green, 100th anniversary of the Battle of Pea Ridge." In: AHA, v.21, p. 158-165.

579 **GREEN, John Uriah**
"Capture of the Federal Steamer "Maple Leaf", a bold dash for liberty." In: SHSP, 1896, v.24, p. 165-171.

580 **GREEN, John W.**
"General Nathan Bedford Forrest." 1944. 8vo, wraps, 16pp.?

581 **GREEN, John William**
"Johnny Green of Orphans Brigade, Jour. of a Confederate Soldier., etc." See: A.D. Kirwan, Edt. $35-ob.

582 **GREEN, Margaret**
"President of the Confederacy, Jefferson Davis." N.Y., Julian Messner (1963). 12mo, cl, d/w, 191pp. $3.25.

583 **GREEN, Michael Robert**
"...So Illy Provided..." Events leading to the creation of the Texas Military Board." In: TMH, 1972, v.X, #2, p. 115-125. Began 1862, disbanded April, 1864.

584 **GREEN, Paul**
"The Confederacy: A Symphonic Outdoor Drama based on the life of General Robert E. Lee." N.Y., Samuel French, 1959. 8vo, wraps, 123pp. $1.50.

585 **GREEN, Philip J.**
"Secession in Georgia, 1860-1861." In: No. Dak. Univ. Quart. Jour., Apr., 1927, v.XVII, p. 248-265.

586 **GREEN, S.S., Sgt.**
"Captured guns at Spotsylvania Courthouse." In: SHSP, 1879, v.7, p. 538-539. See: A.L. Long, R.C.M. Page, Thom. Carter.

587 **GREEN, Thomas W.**
"The Artillery of the Civil War." London: 1959. 4to, wraps, mimeographed, 15pp. $8. Civil War Round Table of London.

588 ..."Confederate Humor and Morale." (London) Jour. Confed. Hist. Soc., Spring, 1967, v.5, #1, p. 3-21; 35-37, pls(2)
...London-1958, wraps, 16pp. $8.

589 ..."Could the Laird Rams have lifted the Union Blockade?" In: CWTI, Apr. 1963, v.II, #1, p. 14-17, illus., diagram, port. By Thos. W. Green and Frank J. Jerli. The Federal government pressured England to deny the CSN delivery of two vessels that could have broken Union blockade.

590 ..."England's Confederate Research Club. Interest in the American Civil War draws group of Briton's together." In: CWT, Aug., 1960, v.II, #5, (OS), p. 7-8, illus., ports.

591 ..."Ironclads of the Sixties; address to members Confederate Research Club, Saturday, Jan. 31, 1959, Eccleston Hotel, Victoria, London." (London, 1959). 8vo, wraps, 12pp., from typed copy. $15-bmk.
..."Ironclads of the Sixties." (London) Jour. Confed. Hist. Soc., July 1962, v.I, #1, p. 8-(34), 2-pls. $15.

592 ..."Major Caleb Huse, C.S.A. A Memoir." London: 1966. Studies in Confederate History, #1. 4to, wraps, 45pp. $25-bmk.

593 ..."The Mission to Mexico." (London) Jour. Confed. Hist. Soc., Dec. 1963, v.II, #1, p. 3-10, map.

594 ..."Personnel Administration in the Confederate States Navy." (London) Jour.

Confed. Hist. Soc., June 1965, v.III, #2, p. 53-62, facsm., ports-2.

595 **GREEN, Thomas, Gen.**
"Battle of Atchafalaya River, Letter of...(to his wife)." In: SHSP, 1877, v.III, p. 62-63.

596 **GREEN, Wharton Jackson**
"Recollections and reflections, an auto of half a century and more." Raleigh: Edwards & Broughton, 1906. 8vo, illus., ports, cl, 349pp. $20, $45, $100, $75-bmk-105, $50-bmk-84.

597 ..."Prisoners of war and their treatment." In: So. Hist. Month., 1876, v.1, p. 148-156.
..."Second Battalion." In: W. Clarks "Several Regs.", v.IV, p. 243-260, 1-pl.

598 ..."General Bryan Grimes." In: Nor. Carolina Mag., ns, VIII, 1888, port., p. 185-209.

599 ..."Two Unknown Heroes." In: OLOD, May 1875, v.2, #3, p. 195-300.

600 **GREEN, William Mercer, Bishop**
"The Civil War Journal of Bishop William Mercer Green." Jackson, Miss., Jour. Miss. Hist., July, 1946, v.VIII, #3, p. 136-145.

601 **GREENBURG, Kenneth S.**
"The Civil War and the Redistribution of Land: Adams County, Mississippi, 1860-1870." In: Agricultural History, April, 1978, p. 292-307.

602 ..."Revolutionary Ideology and the Pro-slavery argument: The abolition of slavery in Antebellum South Carolina." In: JSH, 1976, v.XLII, p. 365-384.

602a **GREENE, A. Wilson**
"The Bloody Angle of Spotsylvania." In: CV, ns, Sept./Oct. 1988, v. 37, p.8-17, ills, ports.
..."Opportunity to the South: Meade versus Jackson at Fredericksburg." In: CWH, Dec. 1987, v.33, #4, p.295-314.

603 **GREENE, Nancy Lewis**
"Ye Olde Shaker Bells." Lexington, Ky. (Transylvania Print) 1930. wraps, 8vo, front, pls., 83pp. Background of Shaker Colony in Pleasanthill, Ky., Jan. 1856-Apr. 1865.

604 **GREENE, Talbot**
"The Bivouac; or, Life in the Central Army of Kentucky." (No. 1, all) Bowling-Green, Ky., 1861. 8vo, wraps, 40pp. Anti-Yankee propaganda. (Emory Un.)

605 **GREENHOW, Rose O'Neal**
"A blockade cover to Jefferson Davis from Rose O'Neal Greenhow, the famous Confederate woman spy. Edt: Van Dyk MacBride." In: Amer. Philatelist, Apr. 1956, v.69, p. 487-491. Facsms, ports, (Letters dated Charleston, 16 July, 1863, Wilmington 4 Aug., 1863, and St. George Bermuda, 19 Aug., 1863. On her forthcoming mission to England.)

606 ..."My Imprisonment and First Year of Abolition Rule at Washington." London: Richard Bentley, 1863. 12mo, cl, front(port), x, 352pp. $25, $50, ref-$80, bmk-84, Mor.$125. This Maryland woman, trusted friend of CSA.
...See: William Gilmore Beymer, Ishbel Ross, Harnet T. Kane, James D. Horan, Nash K. Burger.

607 **GREENVILLE Ladies Ass'n.**
"Minutes of proceedings of the G.L.A., in aid of the Volunteers of the Confederacy." Edt: Jos. Welch Patton. Hist. series, XXI, Durham, N.C., Duke Univ. Press, 1937. 8vo, wrps, 118pp. Hist. Papers Trinity College. $17.50-y.

608 **GREENVILLE(S.C.) Southern Enterprise**
"A Memory of May 5, 1865. Order published in paper announcing cessation of hostilities." In: SHSP, 1901, v.29, p. 279-281.

609 **GREENWELL, Dale**
"The Third Miss. Regt., CSA." (Pascagoula, Miss., Lewis Print, 1972) $35. 8vo, decr. fabricoid, ports, illus., maps, 144pp.

610 **GREER, Allen J.**
"Forrest: natural fighting leader of fighting men." In: Cavalry Jour., 1937, v.XLVI, p. 329-332.

611 ..."The Roaring Guns from the Seven Days to Cold Harbor." In: Field Artly. Jour., 1936, v.XXVI, p. 5-26. Comparative study artillery ANV and the Army/Potomac, June 26-July 1, 1862, to June 3, 1864.

612 **GREER, George H.T.**
"All thoughts are absorbed in the war." In: CWTI, Dec. 1978, v.17, #8, p.30-35, ill.,port.

613 **GREER, Hal W., Mrs.**
"Sabine Pass Battle (Texas)." In: SHSP, 1901, v.29, p. 314-319.

614 **GREER, James K.**
"Grand Prairie." Dallas, Tex., Tardy Pub., (1935) $150. 8vo, cl, dj, 284pp. (Cather-Brown) $100. Lengthy chapters on Civil War and reconst. at Grand Prairie, Tex.

615 **GREG, Percy**
"History of the United States from the foundation of Virginia to the reconstruction of the union." London: W.H. Allen & Co., 1887. 8vo, cl, maps, 2 vols., 380, 401pp. $15.
...Richmond, Va., West, Johnston & Co., 1892. 8vo, cl, 2 vols. in one. Strong Southern views, vol. 2 largely devoted to the Civil War (330pp.) Greg spent part of war in the South, contributed to the London "Standard", defends the CSA. Mine-$15, $10.

616 ..."Percy Greg's tribute to Confederate Heroes." In: SHSP, 1882, v.X, p. 562-564.

617 ..."The 9th of April, 1865." Poem. In: SHSP, 1900, v.XXVIII, p. 376-377.

618 ..."Interleaves in the work-day prose of Twenty-years." London: 1875, 16mo, cl, 124pp. Several poems of the CSA.

619 ..."Foreign Opinions of the Confederate Cause." In: SHSP, 1882, v.10, p. 562-564.

620 **GREGG, Alexander**
"The Present War", sermon preached at St. David's Church, Austin, Texas, April 12, 1861, by..., Bishop of Texas." n.p. (Austin, Texas, 1861) 8vo, wraps, p. 8-31pp. Removed from Journal of Diocese of Texas April, 1861, Bishop's 2nd Annual address.

621 ..."A Few Historic Records of the Church in the Diocese of Texas during rebellion. Together with correspondence between Rt. Rev. Alexander Gregg and Rev. Charles Gillette Rector of St. David's Church, Austin, Texas." N.Y., John A. Gray & Green, 1865. 8vo, wraps, 131pp. TSewU. $20-bmk, $75-mcm '74. See: Wilson Gregg.

622 **GREGG, Alexander, Rt. Rev.**
"Eulogy on the Hon. John Hemphill and Gen. Hugh McLeod delivered in the Capitol, Austin, Tex., Feb. 1, 1862." Houston, Tex. Teleg. Office, 1862. 8vo, wraps, 17pp. Bodies returned from Va.to Tex.

623 **GREGG, P.**
"The Rappahannock Incident." (London) Journ. Confed. Hist. Soc., Autumn, 1969, v.7, #3, p. 82-84, pl.

624 **GREGG, Parker**
"The Third Texas Cavalry, CSA." In: Jr. Hist. Tex. Hist. Soc., Mar. 1962, illus., v.XXII, p. 7-12.

625 **GREGG, Wilson**
"Alexander Gregg First Bishop of Texas, by his son..." Edt.: Rev. Arthur Howard Noll. Sewanee, Tenn., University Press (1912). 12mo, cl, front(port)x, (1), 138pp. $10, $25-bmk. In secession Gregg boldly declared "church must follow nationality" and withdrew from the National Diocese.

625a **GREGORY, Ival L.**
"The Battle of Prairie Grove, Ark., Dec. 7, 1872." In: Jour. West, Oct. 1980. p.63-75.

626 **GREGORY, William Henry**
"England and the Confederacy; a letter of

Sir William Henry Gregory. Edt: Nannie M. Tilley." In: Am. Hist. Rev., 1938, v.XLIV, p. 56-60. Letter to John Rutherford, of Va., in Eng. and CSA relations during war.

627 GREGSON, P. Barrow
"Incidents in the American Civil War." In: Chamber's Jour., 7th ser., Sept. 1912, v.II, p. 564-567. Notes on the CSA and its army.

628 GREMILLION, Nelson
"Company G, 1st Regiment Louisiana Cavalry, CSA." Lafayette, La., Center for Louisiana Studies, University of Southwestern La. 8vo, paper, illus., index, 77pp. 1987 $12. Capt. Fenelon Cannon's Co., later into 1st Reg. La. Cavalry. Avoyelles parish.

629 GRENFELL, George St. Leger, Col.
"Col. George St. Leger Grenfell, descendant presents Civil War Flag and transcripts of his letters, by Mabel Clare Weaks." In: FCHQ, Jan. 1960, v.34, #1, p. 5-23. See: US Congress, 39th, 2nd Sess. House Rep. Message from Pres. of US, in answer to resolution in House, Dec. 19th, transmitting papers relating to the case of G. St. Leger Grenfell, Jan. 21, 1867, Exec. Doc. 50, Wash: 1867." Atlantic Monthly, July 1865, v.XVI.

630 GRICE, Warren
"The Confederate States Court for Georgia." Savannah, Ga., Reprinted from June issue Georgia Historical Quarterly, 1925, v.9 #2. 8vo, stiff wraps, cover title, p. (131)-158. $25-r, $3.50, $6, $12-bmk.

631 GRIESE, Arthur A.
"A Louisville Tragedy, 1862." In: FCHQ, April 1952, v.26, #2, p. 133-154.

632 GRIEVES, Jefferson C.
"The First Valley Campaign." (London) Jour. Confed. Hist. Soc., Winter, 1968, v.6, #4, p. 162-174, map.

633 GRIFFIN'S BATTERY
See: N.B. Johnston.

634 GRIFFIN, Clarence W.
"History of old Tryon and Rutherford Counties, 1730-1936." Ashville, N.C., Miller Print, 1937. 8vo, cl, xv, 640pp., front, pls. Muster rolls, records of 1,734 men from these counties.

635 GRIFFIN, J. David
"Benevolence and Malevolence in Confederate Savannah." In: Ga.H.Q., Dec. 1965, v.XLIX, #4, p. 347-368. $10.

636 GRIFFIN, Pat
"The famous Tenth Tennessee." In: CV, 1905, v.13, p. 553-561. port. Paper read at a meeting of Frank Cheatham Camp, Nashville, about the famous Irish regiment.

637 GRIFFIN, Richard W.
"Problems of the Southern Cotton Planters after the Civil War." In: Ga.H.Q., June 1955, v.XXXIX, #2, p. 103-117. $8.

638 ..."Cotton frauds and confiscation in Alabama 1863-1866." In: Ala. Rev., Oct. 1954, v.7, p. 265-276.

639 ..."The Cotton Mill Campaign in Florida, 1828-1863." In: FHQ, January, 1962, v.XXXX, #3, p. 261-274.
"Cotton manufacture in Alabama to 1865." In: AHQ, 1956, v.18, #3, p. 289-308.

640 GRIFFITH, Harrison Patillo
"Personal Recollections of the Battle of Chancellorsville by P. Griffith, Captain, Company E, 14th South Carolina Vols." Gaffney, S.C., Ledger Print, 1897. 12mo, wraps, cover title, 15pp.

641 ..."Variosa. A collect. of sketches, essays and verses." n.p., 1911 (vivid acct. battle, Chancellorsville) 8vo, cl, 266pp., port. $15.

642 GRIFFITH, L.D.
"Confed...soldiers buried in Cross Roads Cemty., N.E. Paulding County, Ga., 1980."

In: NW Ga. Geneal. & Hist. Soc., Oct. 1980, v.12, #3, p. 25-34.

643 **GRIFFITH, Lucille**
"Mrs. Juliet Opie Hopkins and Alabama Hospitals." In: Ala. Review., VI, (1953), p. 99-120.

644 **GRIFFITH-BARKSDALE-HUMPHREY Brigade**
See: James Dinkins.

645 **GRIGGS, Edward Howard**
"Lee: the American warrior." In: his "American Statesmen", N.Y., Orchard Hill Press, 1927, p. 235-286.

646 **GRIGGS, George K., Col.**
"Memoranda of the 38th Va. Infantry, from the diary of..." In: SHSP, 1886, v.XIV, p. 250-257.

647 ..."The 38th Va. (Steuart's Brigade) at the Battle of Five Forks." In: SHSP, 1888, v.XVI, p. 230-231.

648 **GRIMBALL, John Berkley**
"Diary of..., 1858-1865. Edited by Anne King Gregoeir." In: SCHMag., 1956/1957: v.56, #1, 2, 3, 4, p. 8-30, 92-114, 157-177, 205-225; v.57, p. 28-50, 88-102. Business, Plantation and Milit. affairs near Charleston. $8-bmk, $16.

649 **GRIMBALL, John, Lieutenant, CSN**
"Career of the "Shenandoah". The terror of the Arctic Seas capt. 38 whalers and destroyed shipg. valued at nearly $7,000,000. A graphic account of the cruise of the great commerce destroyer, from the time of her fitting out near Funchal, Madeira, Oct. 1864, to her surrender to the British at Liverpool, Nov. 1865. With a summary by the Nav. Rec. Office." Rich: SHSP, 1897, xxv, p. 116-130.

650 **GRIMES' BATTERY**
"Centennial of Grimes' Battery. Portsmouth Artillery celebrates 100th Birthday of Organiz." (from Richmond News-Leader, Jan. 8, 1910) In: SHSP, 1909, v.37, p. 169-170. See: Portsmouth Arty.

651 **GRIMES, Absalom**
"Absalom Grimes Confed. Mail Runner. Edt: from Captain Grimes' own story by M.M. Quaife, of the Burton Hist. Collect." New Haven: Yale Univ. Press, 1926. 8vo, cl, port(front) pls., xii, 216pp. $15, $20, $40-nc-dj, $60-bmk-116, $730av, $32, $22.50-y, $30-b, $35-y. See: Jas. Bradley (Mo-Ark. CSA mailcarrier), Leonard V. Huber.

652 **GRIMES, Bryan, Maj.Gen.**
"Extract of Letters of Maj.Gen. Bryan Grimes, to his wife, written while in active service in the ANV. Together with some personal recollections of the war, written by him after its close, etc. Compiled from original mnscpts., by Pulaski Cowper of Raleigh, N.C." Raleigh, N.C., Alfred Williams Co., 1884, 8vo, wraps (cover head: "sold for the benefit of Oxford Orphan Asylum) 134pp. $50, $60, $250-ob, $125-bmk, $90.
...Raleigh, N.C., Edwards & Broughton Co., 1883, first edition. 137pp., 1p.-errata. $125, $500-bmk. ex-lib-$50, no covers $25-rebound, $90.

653 ..."Report of Colonel Grimes, of Fourth NC." In: SHSP, 1885, v.XIII, p. 175-176.

654 ..."The Surrender at Appomattox." In: SHSP, 1899, v.XXVII, p. 93-96. See: Jas. M. Garnett's "Ordnance Report." Henry A. London.

655 ..."Extracts of letters of..." New edition edited by Gary W. Gallagher, Wilmington, N.C., Broadfoot Pub., 1986, 8vo, 143pp., cl. $20.

656 **GRIMES, J.B., of N.C.**
"Speech of...at the unveiling of the Va.-NC Monument and Wyatt Monument at Bethel, Va., June 10, 1905." n.p., (c.1905) 8vo, wraps, cover title, 10pp.

657 **GRIMES, Maxyne Madden**
"Confed. Imprints and Civil War Newspapers on file in Miss. Dept. of Ar-

chives and History." Jackson: Journal of Miss. Hist., v.23, (1961) p. 231-154.

658 **GRIMM, Herbert L. and Paul L. Roy**
"Human Interest Stories of the three days Battles at Gettysburg." Gettysburg, Pa., Times & News Print, 1927. Quarto, color covers, ports, illus., map, 62, (2)pp. $3.50.

659 **GRIMSLEY, Daniel A.**
"Battles in Culpeper County, Va..." Orange, Va., Green Pub. Co., 8vo, stiff wraps, 56pp.

660 **GRIMSLEY, Daniel Amon**
"Battles in Culpeper County, Va., 1861-1865...and other articles by Maj. Daniel A. Grimsley of the Sixth Virginia Cavalry, compiled and published by Raleigh Travers Green, Culpeper, Va., 1900. (Culpeper, Va., Exponent Print.) 8vo, wraps, (3), 56pp. 500 copies print. $8.50, $10, $12.50, $15, $17.50, $22.50, $75-bmk-105, $65-bmk-89, $125-r, $35-jk-97.

660a **GRIMSLEY, Mark**
"A Legend of the South, 'Stonewall Jackson,' the Life of a Confederate Hero." In: CWTI, Apr. 1988, v. 27, #2, p.12-46, ills. b/w, color map, ports. Entire edition, Jackson.

661 **GRINNAN, Daniel**
"David Crockett Richardson. Mem." (Richmond, Va., 1930) 8vo, wraps, 11pp. $3.50. Reprint from Va. Hist. Mag., Jan. 1930, v.XXXVIII, p. 64-72. Richardson served with Parker's Battery in the ANV.

661a **GRISAMORE, Silas T.**
"Reminiscences of Uncle Silas: a History of the Eighteenth Louisiana Infantry Regiment." Edt: Arthur W. Bergeron, Jr. 4to, wraps, 302pp, ills. n.p., 1981. $65. Muster Rolls. Originally published in Weekly Thibodaux Sentinel. (Van Sickle)

662 **GRISCOM, George L.**
"Fighting with Ross' Tex. Cav. Brigade, C.S.A. The Diary of George L. Griscom, Adjt., 9th Tex. Cav. Regiment. Edt: Homer L. Kerr." Hillsboro, Tex.: Hill Jr. College, 1976, 8vo, cl, dj, facsm., index, maps, ports, xix, 255pp. $9.50. Rosters of 9th Tex. Cav.

663 **GRISSOM, Daniel M.**
"Claiborne F. Jackson (1807-1862)." In: MoHR, July 1926, v.X, p. 504-508. (CSA Gov. 1861) "Personal recollections of distinguished Missourians."

664 ..."Sterling Price." In: MoHR, Oct. 1925, v.XXXIII, p. 110-111.

665 **GRISWOLD, B. Howell, Jr.**
"The Spirit of Lee and Jackson." Balt: Norman, Remington Co., 1927, 8vo, decr. cl, illus., ports, 46pp. $5. Address before Balt. Chap. U.D.C. $40-bmk-128.

666 **GRIZZARD, Walter B.**
"War Prison experience of a Confed. soldier, Edt: W.J. Holmann, Jr." In: Tenn.HQ, June 1951, v.X, p. 149-160. Captured in Tenn. imprisoned: Columbus, Ky. and Alton, Ill. 1863-1865.

667 **GROCE, William W.**
"Major General John A. Wharton." In: SwHQ, 1916, v.XIX, p. 271-278.

668 **GROENE, Bertram Hawthorne**
"Alexander Hunter. Could any prison hold this elusive Rebel?" (Richmond) Va. Cavl., Spring 1970. v.XIX, #4, p. 22-29, ports, illus. (dbl. pg. color)

669 ..."Tracing Your Civil War Ancestor." Winston-Salem, N.C., 1973, 8vo, cl, 124pp. $9-bmk. Mssc. repositories, Natl. Archives, and State, historical societies, std. reference works and bibliographies.

670 **GROH, George W.**
"Last of the Rebel Raiders-CSN "Shenandoah"." In: Amer. Her., Dec. 1958, v.X, #1, p. 48-51, 126-127, port, color plate.

671 ..."The curious cruise of the Shenandoah." In: Ships and the Sea." Fall, 1956, v.6, #2, p. 42-45. On Waddell's cruise round the globe, many prizes taken by him, eluding capture until end of cruise at Liverpool.

672 **GROOVER, Robert L.**
"Margaret Mitchell, the Lady from Atlanta." In: Ga.H.Q., March, 1968, v.LII, #1, p. 53-69.

673 **GROSS, R.F.**
"Cavalry Raids in the War of Secession. Maj.Gen. John B. Floyd and the State Line, surrender at Fort Donelson." In: SHSP, 1908, v.36, p. 280-282. (From Richmond Times-Dispatch, Jan. 17, 1909) See: John Buchannan Floyd, T.J. Riddle.

674 **GROVE, James P.**
"Life and Reminiscences, with early sketches of John S. Moseby(sic). Late Lt.-Col. in the Rebel Army." (Urbana, Ohio, 1865?) 16mo, wraps, 32pp.

675 **GROVER, George S.**
"The Price Campaign of 1864." (Columbia, Mo., Mo.Hist. Review, July 1912, v.VI, #4, p. 167-181.

676 ..."Civil War in Missouri." In: MHR, Oct. 1913, v.8, p. 1-28.

677 ..."The Shelby Raid, 1863." (Columbia, Mo., Apr. 1912, v.VI, #3, p. 107-126. Read at Reunion at Clinton, Sept. 27, 1894. Reprint, in wraps, of above.

678 **GROVES, Malachi and Avline**
"With Pen in Hand: Letters of Malachi and Avline Groves (1860-1867)." (Jackson, Miss.) Jour. Miss. Hist. Aug. 1971, v.XXXIII, #3, p. 219-229.

679 **"GRUMBLE JONES-Brig. Gen. Wm. Edmondson Jones**
CS Cavalry. He is very apt to find fault!" In: CWTI, June 1968, v.VII, #3, p. 35-41, plate, ports.

680 **GRUMMOND, Lena Y. de, and L. De Grummond Delaune**
"Jeb Stuart." (juvenile). N.Y.-Phila., (1962) 12mo, cl, illus., 160pp., index, bibliog. Gretna, La., Pelican Pr., 1979, paper-$5., $3, dj-$40-b.

681 **GRUSS, Louis, Edt. and Trans.**
"Jose Julian Marti on Judah Philip Benjamin." New Orleans: LHQ, Jan. 1940, v.23, #1, p. 259-264.

682 ..."Judah Philip Benjamin." Louisiana Hist. Quart., XIX, 1936, p. 964-1068. Biograph. and to justify his flight to Europe after the war. See: Jose Julian Marti, his transl.

682a **GRZELAK, Jeff H.**
"Florida: History of Hernando, Pasco, & Citrus Counties during the Civil War." Orlando, Fla., U.A.D.F., 1987. 8vo, wraps, 60pp, ills, maps. $3.50. Hist. 3rd Fla. Infty., Co. C.

683 **GUDGER, J.C.L.**
"Muster Roll Comp'y I, 25th N.C. Troops, 1861." Ashville, N.C., Whiteside Pr., n.d. 12mo, wraps, cover title, 12pp. See: Walter Clark's-v.II, p. 291-301. John W. Moore's-v.II, p. 323-361.

684 **GUERNSEY, Alfred Hudson**
"The Campaigns of R.E. Lee." In: Galaxy, 1871, v.XI, p. 640-651, 818-826. Author edited "Harper's Pict. Hist. of the Civil War."

685 ..."The Seven Days Battle on the Peninsula." In: Harper's Dec./May 1865/1866, v.XXXII, p. 475-492, map.

686 **GUERRANT, Edward O., Rev.**
"Operations in East Tenn. and Southwest Va.." In: B & L, v.IV, p. 475-479. Author was ass't. Adj.Gen. to Gen. Humphrey Marshall, CSA.

"Operations in East Tenn. and Southwest Va." In: B & L, v.4, p. 475-479, pl, map, ports.

687 **GUERRILLAS,**
See: Young Ewing Allison, Aug. Appler, Carl W. Breihan, Rich. S. Brownlee, Jno. P. Burch, Albert E. Castel, Wm. E. Connelley, Kit Dalton, Jno. N. Edwards, Donald R. Hale, Dr. Robt. S. Holzman, Jno. McCorkle, Wm. E. Sawyer, Thurman Sesing, Hamp. B. Watts, Robert H. Williams, Guerrilla Chief Quantrill.

688 **GUERRY, Moultrei**
"Makers of Sewanee." (1. Leonidas Polk, Stephen Elliott, Charles Todd Quintard, Wm. Porcher DuBose.) In: Sewanee Rev., 1933, v.XLI, p. 80-90, 237-243, 365-373, 483-494. Famous in the CSA as well as founders of the Univ. of the South.

689 ..."Men Who Made Sewanee for Makers of Sewanee To-day Biographical Sketches." Sewanee, Tenn., Univ. of South, 1944, 8vo, wraps, ports, xv, 101pp. $5. Virtually a roster of CSA leaders. $15-bmk.

690 **GUESS, George W., Colonel**
"Civil War Letters of..., to Mrs. Sarah Horton Cockrell." n.p. (Chicago?) Spring, 1946. 8vo, cl, approx. 100pp., private edition of 12 copies, not for sale. Facsm. of letters from Col. Guess, a North Carolinian by birth, served in Dallas Light Arty., later in Sprights' Brigade, 31st Regt. Vol. Cavalry. $100-bmk.

691 **"GUIDE to Civil War Records**
in the NC State Archives." Raleigh: State Dept. Archives and History, 1966. 4to, cl(or wraps) 128pp. $6, $10.

692 **"GUIDE to the Civil War**
in Tenn." Nashville: Civil War Centennial Com. 1960, 4to, color pict. wraps and inside both covers, double fldg. map, illus., 32pp. $1.50.
...2nd Edition, 1961.

693 **"GUIDE to the Fortifications**
and Battlefields around Petersburg."
See: Philip Francis Brown.

694 **GUINN, Gilbert Sumter**
"Coastal defense of the Confed. Atlantic Seaboard states, 1861-1865. A study in political and military mobilization." n.p., c.1974. Thesis typescript, Univ. of South Carolina. (1973).

694a **GUNN, Ralph White**
"24th Virginia Infantry." 8vo, cl, dj, (4), 112pp, maps, ports. 1,000 copies, signed.

695 **GUY, John Henry**
"A Virginian at Fort Donelson: Excerpts from the prison diary of... Edt. B. Franklin Cooling." In: THQ, Summer, 1968, v.27, #2, p. 176-190.

H

1. **"H. HARK O'er the Southern Hills,** by a Southern Lady." Norfolk (Va.) Jan. 24, 1862, Broadside 10 x 6" Dbl. Column. Port of Jefferson Davis-title head. Signed "H" at bottom. (Jk-169) $200.00.

2. **HAAS, I.C.** "'Stonewall' Jackson's Death - Wounded by his own men, Last Order on the Battlefield." In: SHSP, 1904, v.32, p.94-98.

3. **HABERSHAM, Anna Wylly** "Journal of Anna Wylly Habersham." Darien, Ga., Ashantilly Press, 1961. 12mo., wraps, illus., port., 23pp. The Ashantilly Leaflets, ser. 2, Regional History, #2. "New Edition." Per. Narr., during the war, CSA.

4. **HABERSHAM, Barnard Elliott** "Some Letters of the Barnard Habersham Family, 1858-1868." Edt: Sarah Agnes Wallace (Charleston): So. Caro. Hist. & Genea. Mag., Oct., 1953, v.LIV, #4, p201-210; 1954, Jan. v.LV, #1, p.28-39, p.116-122; p.166-169.

5. **HABERSHAM, Josephine Clay** "Ebb Tide as seen through the Diary of Josephine Clay Habersham 1863. By Spencer Bidwell King, Jr., illustrations by William Etsel Snowden, Jr." Bmk $15.00. Athens: University of Georgia Press, 1958. 12mo., cl., dj., illus., map, xiii, (1), 129, index. $25.00.
...Macon, Ga., Mercer Univ. Press, 1987. Reprint, paper. $9.

6. **HABERSHAM, S.E., MD** "Observation upon Statistics of Chimborazo Hospital, with some remarks on Treatment of Various Diseases during the recent Civil War." Nashville: University Medical College, 1866. 8vo., wraps, 15pp.

7. ..."Remarks upon Compound Fractures of the Thigh, from Gun-shots." Nashville: University Medical College, W.H.F. Ligon, 1867. 8vo., wraps, 16pp. Reprint: Nashville: Journal of Medicine & Surgery.

8. **HACKLER, Rhoda E.A.** "The Civil War in Singapore." In: Foreign Serv. Journ., 1963, v.XL-vii, p.30-34. CSS Alabama anchored in Singapore in 1863.

9. **HACKLEY, William Beverley Randolph** "The Letters of William Beverley Randolph Hackley: Treasury Agent in West Tennessee 1863-1866. Edited by Walter Fraser, Jr., & Mrs. Pat C. Clark." In: W. Tenn. Hist. Soc. Papers, 1971, v.XXV, 17pp., wraps, limited to 500 copies. $10.00.

10. **HACKLEY, Woodford B.** "The Little Fork Rangers; a Sketch of Co. D. Fourth Virginia Cavalry." Richmond, Va., Dietz Print, 1927. 8vo., cl., 117pp., illus., plates. ($5.00, $10.00, $12.50), $15.00. Complete roster: p.107-117. $17.50, $23.50. 500 Copies pub.

11. **HADD, Donald R.** "The irony of Secession." In: FHQ, July, 1962, v.XLI, #1, p.22-28.

12. **HADEN, B.J.** "Reminiscences of J.E.B. Stuart's Cavalry, by Sergeant B.J. Haden, (Co. E) First Virginia Cavalry." Charlottesville, Va., Progress Pub., (190-?) 8vo, wraps, cover title, 46pp. $37.50.

13. **HADEN, Charles J.** "The Confederate Soldier...an address...Jan. 19, 1905, at Atlanta, Ga.," (Atlanta, Ga.) 1905, 8vo, wraps, 7 p. $15.00.

14. **HADEN, Charles J., of Atlanta Bar** "The Confederate Soldier. Address before Confederate Veterans & Daughters of the Confederacy, on the birthday of Robert E. Lee, Jan. 19, 1905 at Atlanta, Georgia."

(Atlanta, Ga., 1905) cover title, 8vo., wraps, 7pp., Emory.

14a **HAFENDORFER, Kenneth Allen**
"Perryville, Battle for Kentucky." Owensboro, Ky., McDowell Pubs., 1981. 8vo, cl, xx, 419pp, ills, maps, ports.

15 **HAFTER, Jerome C.**
"Letters from Private Richard C. Bridges, CSA: Their Social & Cultural Context." Jackson, Miss., J.M.H. Feb. 1973, v.XXXV, #1, p.75-81.

16 **HAGAN, H.H.**
"Judah P. Benjamin (1811-1884)" Amer. Law Review, XLVIII (May) 1914, p.365-389.

17 **HAGAN, Horace Henry**
"The Dred Scott Decision." In: Georgetown Law Journ., Jan. 1927, v.XV, p.95-114. Review "in light of new & illuminating historical data, e.g., letters from Justices Catron & Grier to Buchanan."

18 ..."The U.S. vs Jefferson Davis.: In: Sewanee Rev., Apr. 1917, v. XXV, p.220-225. Re 'treason trial' of Davis.

19 **HAGAN, John W.**
"The Confederate Letters of John W. Hagan, Ed: Bell I. Wiley." Athens: University of Georgia press, 1954, 12mo, wraps, front, 55 p. $25.00, served: GA. 29th Inf.
..."Confederate Letters of John W. Hagan, Edt: Bell Irvin Wiley." Athens: Univ. of Ga., Press (1954). 8vo., wraps, front(port), 55pp. $3.00. Served with 29th GA. Vol. Infty. In: Ga. Hist. Quart., 1954, v.38, p.170-200, 268-290.

20 **HAGENAH, De Witt**
"Le Mat & the Rebel Grapeshot Pistols." In: Muzzle Blasts, July 1955, v.16, #11, p.14-15. Arms patented by Jean A.F. La Mat & Mfg. for Cs army & Navy 1856-1865.

21 **HAGERMAN, Edgar**
"The Tactical Thought of R.E. Lee & the Origins of Trench Warfare in the American Civil War, 1861-1862." In: Historian, 1975, v.XXXVIII, p.21-38.

22 **HAGERSTOWN HOSPITAL**
See: Dr. J.M. Gaines.

23 **HAGOOD, James R., Col., 1st S.C. Vols.**
"Report: of the Campaign of 1864." In: SHSP, 1885, v.13, p.434-438.

24 **HAGOOD, Johnson, Brig.-Gen.**
"Battle of Drewry's Bluff, report of Gen. Johnson Hagood." In: SHSP, 1884, v.XII, p.229-232.

25 ..."Battle of Secessionville report of Col. Johnson Hagood." In: SHSP, 1884, v.XII, p.63-65.

26 ..."Gen. P.G.T. Beauregard. His comprehensive & aggressive strategy. Drewry's Bluff & Petersburg. Address of Gen. Johnson Hagood at the Beauregard Memorial Meeting at Charleston, S.C., Dec. 1, 1894." In: SHSP, 1900, v. XXVIII, p.318-336.

27 ..."Hagood's Brigade. Its services in the trenches of Petersburg, Va., 1864." In: SHSP, 1888, v.XVI, p.395-416

28 ..."Letter from Johnson Hagood to Thos. Wentworth Higginson.: In: Mass. Hist. Soc. Proc., 1914, v. XLVII, p.341-343. Re burial of Col. R.G. Shaw at Battery Wagner, July 19, 1863.

29 ..."Letter from General Hagood on recapture of a Flag." In: SHSP, 1885, v.XIII, p.423-427.

30 ..."Memoirs of the War of Secession from the original manuscripts,
I-Hagood's 1st 12 Months S.C.V.
II-Hagood's Brigade."
Columbia, S.C., State Co., 1910. 8vo., cl., port(front), maps (1-dble.pg), illus., index, (3), (8), (9), -496pp. $35.00. $15.00 - $20.00 -$22.50 -$25.00 -$60.00 -NC 76.

31 ..."Operations before Petersburg, May 6-11, 1864. Report of Johnson Hagood." In: SHSP, 1884, v.XII, p.119-123, 321-323, 459-462.

Hagood was governor S.C., after war & his material also in Wm. Izler's 'Edisto Rifles'. See U.R. Brooks 'Memoirs', also from orig. mssc. of J. Hagood.

32 **HAGUE, Parthenia Antoinette Vardaman, Mrs.**
"A Blockaded Family: Life in Southern Alabama during the Civil War." Boston & N.Y., Houghton, Mifflin Co., (1888). 12mo., cl., V, 176pp. (micro-cd.,$3.43) ($7.50, $10.00, $12.00, $17.50, $22.50) Do: 1890, as above, ($12.50 & $22.50). 1889 edt., $22.50.N.Y. Arno Press, "Black Heritage Library Collection Series." (c.1974) $14.00, $17.00-y.

33 **HAGY, P.S.**
"The Cheat Mountain Campaign." In: Confed. Vet., Mar. 1915, v.23, p.122-123.

34 ..."The Laurel Hill Retreat in 1861" In: Confed. Vet., Apr. 1916, v.24, p.169-173. Glade Spring Rifle Co., Abingdon, Va., & as Co. F, 37th Va. at Corricks Ford.

35 ..."Jackson's Winter Campaign in 1862." In:CV, Feb., 1917, v.XXV, p.76-78.

36 ..."Military Operations of the lower Trans-Mississippi Dept., 1863-1864." In: CV, Dec. 1916, v.XXIV, p.545-549.

37 **HAHN, George W.**
"Catawba Soldiers of the Civil War." Hickory, N.C. (1978) reprint. Handsome reprint, lim. edt. numbered $25.00
"The Catawba Soldier of the Civil War. A sketch of every soldier from Catawba County, N.C., with the photograph, biographical sketch, & reminiscences of many of them together with a sketch of Catawba County from 1860 to 1911, a complete history of these valiant men in war & peace." Hickory, N.C., Clay Print., 1911. 8vo., cl., ports., 385pp.(11pp.-ads) $38.00, $60.00. About 1,500 men, sketches & photos. Many copies destroyed by fire & scarce.

38 **HAIGHT, William R. & Zed H. Burns**
"Confederate Generals, Parts I, II, & III." In: Jo.M.H., 1977/1978, v.XXXIX/XL, #3,4. p.227-238; 363-375; XL-#1, p.61-72.

39 **HAIL, S.A.**
"A Short Story of my Long Life, Batesville, Ark., May 1912." In: Indsp. Co. Chron., July 1979, v.XX, #4, p.4-37. Civil War with 7th Reg. Ark. Vols.

40 **HAILEY, Daniel M., Maj.Gen.**
"Records of the Confederate Veterans of the State of Oklahoma." (McAlester, Okl., 1913, ports, 148, 110 p.; 1914, 4th ed.; 1917, 89 pp.

40a ..."Confederate Veterans Association of the State of Oklahoma by Maj.-Gen. Daniel M. Hailey, Commanding the Oklahoma Division." McAlester, Okla., News-Capital, 1911. Oblong 8vo, wraps, 151,(2)p.

41 **HAINES, Randall A.**
"The Wartime Adventures & Heroic Death of Acting Master John Yates Beall, CSN." In: CV, ns. Mar/Apr. 1987, v.35, #2, p.6-12, illus., port.

42 **HALDEMAN, Walter N.**
"Chancellorsville." An address before the Wilson Club, Jan. 9, 1961. In: FCHQ, July 1962, v.36, #3, p.222-231.

43 **HALE, Donald R.**
"We Rode with Quantrill: Quantrill & the Guerrilla War as told by the men & women who were with him. With a true sketch of Quantrill's Life." Clinton, Missouri: The Printery (1975) $3.00. 12mo., stiff wraps, ports., illus., facsms., 197pp.

44 ..."They Called him Bloody Bill. The life of William Anderson Missouri Guerrilla." Clinton, Missouri: The printery (1975). $3.00. 12mo., stiff wraps, illus., ports., (1), iv, (1), 118pp. (Cover adds: "The Missouri Badman who taught Jesse James outlawry.")

45 **HALE, Douglas**
"One man's war: Captain Joseph H. Bruton, 1861-1865." In: ETHA, Fall 1982, v.XX, #2, p.28-45, map, ports. (2)

46 **HALE, Edward Joseph**
"Sherman's Bummers" & some of their work. In: SHSP, 1884, v.12, p.427-429.

47 **HALE, G.W.B.**
"Recollections of Malvern Hill." In: CV, Sept. 1922, v.XXX, p.332-333.

48 **HALE, Jonathan D.**
"Champ Ferguson: a sketch of the war in East Tennessee detailing some of the awful murders on the border, & describing one of the leading spirits of the rebellion." Cincinnati, 1862. 12mo., wraps, 20pp. Biased, sensational type.

49 ..."The Bloody Shirt." Wash., DC. (1888), cover title, fldg. facsm., 51pp. See-Thurman Sensing.

50 **HALE, Laura V.**
"Four Valiant Years..." reprint 1986. Front Royal, Va., Hathaway Pub. Co. $45.00.

51 **HALE, Laura Virginia**
"Battle of Wapping Heights (Warren Co., Va. 1863)" In: UDC Mag., June 1949, v.12, #6, p.15-18. Includes excerpts: Diary of Charles Eckardt & Lucy Buck of Front Royal.

52 ..."Four Valiant Years in the Lower Shenandoah Valley 1861-1865." tk 4to, Buck, illus., ports, facsms, set in IBM554 pp., index., 1st edt., 1,000 copies. $15.00, 2nd edt., 500 copies. $30.00.

53 ..."Memorials in Marble. The Story of the Four Confederate Monuments at Front Royal, Va." (Front Royal, Va., Warren Press)(1956) 4to, wraps, (32)pp., illus., ports. 10-bmk $1.00

54 ..."Belle Boyd Southern Spy of the Shenandoah." Front Royal, Va., Warren Rifles Chap. UDC, n.d., 8vo, color decr-wraps, (16)pp., illus., ads thru $0.25, bmk $12.00.

55 ..."Warren County Civil War Centennial Commemoration: Battle of Front Royal, May 19-20, 1962" (Front Royal, Va., Warren Co. Civil War Cent. Comm., 1962) 4to, wraps, (24)pp., illus., ports $0.50.

56 **HALE, Laura Virginia & S.S. Phillips**
"History of the Forty-ninth Virginia Infantry, CSA," Extra Billy Smith's Boys." Lanham, Md., S.S. Phillips & Assoc., 1981, 8vo, cl, 367 p., ills., index $20.00, based on Capt. Robert Daniel Funkhouser, 'Warren Blues', Co. D, See R.D. Funkhouser.

57 **HALE, Will T. & Dixon L. Merritt**
"A History of Tennessee & Tennesseeans Leaders and Representative Men, etc." Chicago, N.Y., Lewis Pub. Co., 1913, 4to, cl, 8 vol. set, illus., pls. ports, edt:1933 civil War, v.iii, p.529-849. $20.00

58 **HALE, William Thomas**
"History of DeKalb County, Tennessee." Nashville: P.Hunter, 1915, 8vo, cl, front, pls., ports, xii, 254pp.

59 ..."McMinnville, Tenn., Ben Lomond, 1969 about half book on the war, Wheeler's Cavalry, Morgan, etc. bmk $10.00.

60 **HALL, Alvin L.**
"Charles Csaky De Nordendorf, Soldier-Songster of the Confederacy." In: Va. Cavl. Summer, 1974, v.XXIV, #1, p.40-47, illus., facsms, port.

61 **HALL, Charles Bryan, Engraver**
"1861-1865 Military Records of General Officers of the Confederate States of America. Commander-in-Chief, Generals, Lieutenant Generals and Major Generals arranged in order of their rank, with their military records in the Confederate Army & previous records in the US Army, of all those who graduated from the US Military Academy at West Point or were appointed from civil life. With one hundred and eight portraits most of which are now published for the first time etched or engraved on copper or steel. Compiled &

illustrated by Charles B. Hall." N.Y., Charles B. Hall, 1898 (Lockwood Press), 4to ports. on white paper, facing biographical sketches (cream paper), inserted in solander case, 3/4 dark blue morocco, gilt. 12x16 inches, front etching, xiii, 108pp.(i.e. 216pp.) only the biographical pages are numbered. $2,500.00 bmk, $1,500.

62 **HALL, Courtney Robert**
"Confederate Medicine; caring for the Confederate Soldier. An introduction to the history of the medical corps of the Confederate army in the war between states." N.Y., Froben Print, 1935, Half-title: "Medical Life", v.42, #9, Sept. 1935, Confederate Medicine No., bibliog. 505-508pp., 8vo, wraps, (445)-508 pp. $40.00, $20.00 bmk.

63 ..."The influence of the medical department upon Confederate war operations." In: Amer. Mil. Hist. Found. Journ., 1937, v.1, p.46-54.

64 ..."The Confederate Medical Department, its influence upon war operations." In: Army Ordnance, 1936, v.XVII, p.33-35.

65 **HALL, Elizabeth Calbert**
"Bowling Green & the Civil War, written in 1894." In: FCHQ, October, 1937, v.11, #4, p.241-251.

66 **HALL, Ellen Young & Della Tyler Key**
"Confederate Veterans in Potter County (Texas)" Amarillo, Texas: M.F. Maury Chap. UDC, 1959 typescript.

67 **HALL, Everatd**
Camp Life, with a few reflections incident thereto." In: Our Liv. & Dead, 1875, v.II, pp.157-164..

68 **HALL, Frances, Mrs.**
"Major Hall's Wife. A thrilling story of the life of a southern wife & mother, while a refugee in the Confederacy, during the late struggle-written by herself." Syracuse, N.Y., Weed & Co., 1884, 8vo, wraps, 49pp., was wife of Maj. Geoffrey Hall, La., C.S.A.

69 **HALL, Granville Davisson**
"Lee's Invasion of Northwest Virginia, 1861" (Chicago: Press of Mayer & Miller, 1907) 12mo, cl, 3p., 1, 9-164pp. $8.50, $10.00. $20.00.
...1911 reprint + (2)p. ads. $15.00

70 ..."The Rending of Virginia, A History." (Chicago: Mayer & Miller) 1902, 12 mo, 3p., 1, (11)-630, illus., ports. $7.50 $10.00 $12.50 Separation of Va. & W.Va., slavery in Va--Civil War period.

71 **HALL, Harry K.**
"A Johnny Reb Band from Salem: The Pride of Tarheelia." N.C. Confederate Centennial Comm., Raleigh, 1963, 8vo, wraps, facsm, maps, illus., xi, (1), 118pp. $40.00.
...N.Y., Da Capo Press, 1980, Reprint: 1963 edition.

72 **HALL, Howard**
"Franklin County in the Secession Crisis, 1861." In: Tenn. HQ, Mar. 1958, v.XVII, p.37-44.

73 **HALL, James Edmond**
"The Diary of a Confederate Soldier..." Edt.-Ruth Woods Dayton, n.p., (Charleston, WV) (1961) 12mo, cl, port-front, 141pp., Education Foundation, Inc. $4.00, $14.00 bmk, (25) $20.00 bmk 105.

74 **HALL, Jno. Lesslie**
"Half-hours in the Southern History." Richmond, Atlanta, Dallas: B.F. Johnson Pub. Co., 1907, 12mo, cl, ports (incl. front), 320pp. $10.00; 1908, 2nd edt., $7.50.

75 **HALL, Kermit L.**
"(Judge) West H. Humphreys & the Crisis of the Union." In: Tenn. Hist. Quart., 1975, v.XXXIV, p.48-69.

76 **HALL, Mark**
"Alexander H. Stephens & Joseph E. Brown & the Georgia Resolution for

Peace." In: GA. HQ, Spring 1980, v.LXIV, #1, p. 50-63. $8.00.

77 **HALL, Martin Hardwick**
"An appraisal of the 1862 New Mexico Campaign: A Confederate Officer's Letter to Nacogdoches." In: NMHR, Oct. 1976, v.LI, #4, p.329-335. Capt. William Lee Alexander's Co. H., 4th Reg. Tex. Cav., criticizes Sibley & the New Mexico Campaign.

78 ..."The Baylor-Kelley Fight, a Civil-war incident in old Mesilla." In: Password of the El Paso Hist. Soc., 1960, v.V, p.83-90. See under: George W. Baylor.

79 ..."The Confederate Army of New Mexico" Austin, Texas: Presidio Press, 1978, sm.4to, cl, dj, illus., one color, maps(5), 422pp., Deluxe copies(35), signed, full calf $40.00jk, $17.50 cloth, jk146 $100.00.

80 ..."The Court-martial of Arthur Pendleton Bagby, CSA." In: ETHJ, Fall 1981, v.XIX, #2, p.60-67, port, notes.

81 ..."Col. James Reiley's Diplomatic Missions to Chihuahua & Sonora." (Albuquerque, New Mexico, Historical Review) July, 1956, v.XXXI, #3, p.232-242. Sibley's Campaign into New Mexico & Arizona.

82 ..."The Formation of Sibley's Brigade and the March to New Mexico." In: So. West. Hist. Quart., 1957/1958, p.383-405.

83 ..."Sibley's New Mexico Campaign" Austin: Univ. of Texas Press (1960) 8vo, cl, dj, ports (incl. front), facsms., illus., maps, sv, 366pp. op $6.00 $7.50. $30.00 bmk 96. See also: Gertrude Harris. Muster Rolls, p.227-329.

84 ..."The Skirmish at Mesilla, July 25, 1861." In:Ariz. & West., 1959, port, v.I, pp.343-351.

85 ..."The Skirmish at Picacho." In: Civ. War. Hist., 1958, v.IV, p. 27-36. See: Simeon Hart.

86 ..."Albert Sidney Johnston's First Confederate Command." In: McNeese Rev. v.XIII, pp.3-12., 1962

87 ..."Ragsdale's Company, Co. D, 5th Tex. Mounted Vols." In: MHT & Sw, 1974 v.XII, #4, pp.301-307.

88 ..."Capt. Thomas J. Mastin's Arizona Guards, CSA" (Albuquerque) NMHR, April 1974, v.XLIX, #2, p.143-151. Roster.

89 ..."A Nacogdoches Company in the Confederate Army of New Mexico." In: ETJH, Fall, 1974, v.XII, #2, p.45-50.

90 ..."Capt. John G. Phillips...." In: TMH, 1973, v.XI, #2, pp.131-135.

91 ..."The Grimes County Rangers", Co. C, 5th Reg. Texas Mounted Vols." In: MHT & Sw, 1974, v.XII, #3, p. 203-211, port., Roster.

92 ..."The Mesilla Times: A Journal of Confederate Arizona." In: Amer. West. Winter, 1963, v.5, p.337-351.

93 ..."Etched & Engraved Portraits of Confederate Generals prominent in (here various CSA states, Campaign, is listed below). N.Y., Charles B. Hall, H.B. Hall's Sons, (1898), folio sheets, with a composite of those generals of a particular state. This follows a similar plan of a publication, 1898, "General of the Confederate States Army," in which 108 portraits were individually printed, with a page biography. $750.00

94 ..."Antietam Campaign" (4)R.E. Lee, J.B. Hood, Lt.Gen. Early & Jackson.

95 ..."Florida." (10) Beauregard, Bragg, Clayton, Forney, Saml. Jones, Mahone, Pemberton, M.L. Smith, W.H.T. Walker, others associated with Fla. battles.

96 ..."Kentucky." (13) Six officially associated with Ky., others officially designated as of Ky. or commanded armies.

97 ..."North Carolina." (10 etch., 5 engr.) (9) NC-Grimes, J.B. Gordon, D.H. Hill,

Hoke, T.H. Holmes, Pender, Ramseur, Matt W. & Robert J. Ransom.

98 ..."Tennessee." (18 etch., 9 engr.) Bate, J.C. Brown, Cheatham, Donelson, Forrest, Hames, B.R. Johnson, McCown, Stewart, Wilcox, Tenn. & Va., Chief battle grounds and accounts for a fourth of Gens.

99 ..."Texas." Maj.Gen. Sam Bell Maxey of. Etched port. CSA Supt. Indian affairs in Ind. Terr., Comm. CSA Distr. Ind. Terr., Dec. 1861-Mar. 1862; Dec. '63-Mar. '65.

100 ..."Virginia." (15) Saml. Cooper, J.F. Gilmer, H. Heth, J.L. Kemper, Fitzhugh/G.W.C./R.E./ & W.H.F. Lee, L.L. Lomax, Wm. Mahone, J. Pegram, J.C. Pemberton, Wm. Smith, C.L. Stevenson, W.B. Taliaferro.
..."Virginia." (12) Saml. Cooper, Heth, Hill, Kemper, Fitz/G.W.C./& W.H.F. Lee, Lomas, PEgram, Wm. Smith, Jeb Stuart.
...Individual Portraits, folio, J.E.B. Stuart, A.P. Hill & R.S. Ewell.

101 ...Austin, Texas: The Steck Co., 1963, 31cm, alphabetical list, (1)p at end reprint of the 1898 edition, in slip case. $100.00, $50.00.

102 **HALL, Rowland M., Capt.**
"Would to God that war was rendered impossible"; letters of Capt. Rowland M. Hall, Apr/July 1864." In Va. MHB, Oct. 1981, p. 448-466. Edt: Edward G. Longacre.

103 **HALL, Thomas O.**
"The Key to Vicksburg." In: SB, 1883-1884, v.II, p.393-396.

104 **HALL, Wade H.**
"Reflections of the Civil War in Southern Humor." Gainesville: University of Florida Press U/F Monographs Humanities, #10, Spring 1962, 8vo, wraps, (8), 82pp. $1.25 $2.00.

105 **HALL, William A., Rev.**
"The Historic Significance of the Southern Revolution. A lecture delivered by invitation in Petersburg, Va., Mar. 14 & Apr. 29, 1864. And, in Richmond, Va., April 7th & 21st, 1862. By Rev. William A. Hall of New Orleans Battalion Washington Artillery." Petersburg, Va., A.F. Crutchfield Co., 1864, 12mo, wraps, 45pp. $150.00.

106 **HALL, William Thomas**
"Religion in the Army of the Tennessee." In: LWL, 1867/68, v.IV, p.127-131.

107 **HALL, Wilmer L.**
"A Bibliography of Virginia, pt. IV-Three series of Sessional Documents of the House of Delegates: Extra Session, Jan. 7-April 4, 1861; Called Session, Sept. 15-Oct. 6, 1862; and Adjourned Session, Jan. 7-March 31, 1863." Asst. State Librarian. Richmond, Va., Purchase & Printing, 1932, Bull. Va. State Library, vol.XVIII, #2-June, 1932., 8vo, wraps, p.(57)-96, incl. t/p. intro.

108 **HALL, Winchester**
"Story of the 26th Louisiana Regiment." Gaithersburg, Md., Butternut Press, 1984. Intro: Ed Bearss. $28.00.
The Story of the 26th Louisiana Infantry in the Service of the Confederate States." n.p., n.d. (c.1890) 8vo, cl, plan, 4p, 1., 228, (2)pp. $35.00 $75.00 bmk $750.

109 **HALLEY, Robert Ambrose**
"A Rebel Newspaper War Story; Being a Narrative of the war history of the Memphis Appeal." Nashville, 1903. Amer. Hist. Mag. & Tenn. Hist. Quart., vol. 8, #2, April, 8vo, wraps, 31pp. $6.00. See also as co-author with William Robertson Garrett "Civil War, etc.

110 **HALLMAN, Henderson, Hon.**
"Give us Back the Constitution of our Fathers. Address of...to the UCV, the Sons of Confederate Veterans & the Confederate Southern Memorial Assn. delivered before the joint assembly of these bodies held in Memphis, Je. 3,

111 **HALLOCK, Charles**
"A complete biographical sketch of "Stonewall" Jackson: giving a full & accurate account of the leading events of his military career, his dying moments, & the obsequies at Richmond & Lexington." Augusta, Ga., Steam Power Press Chronicle & Sentinel, 1863, 8vo, cover title, 38, (1), iipp. Crandall-2578, Howes-4438.
...Halifax, Canada, 1863, "First Life of Jackson."
..."Sketches of "Stonewall Jackson", giving the leading events of his life & military career, his dying moments, & obsequis at Richmond & Lexington. From the English edition." Montreal, John Lovell, 1863, 8vo, wraps, 50pp.
...Halifax, N.S., 1863. sm.8vo, wraps, 56pp.

112 **HALLUM, John**
"Reminiscences of the Civil War." Little Rock, Ark., Tunnah & Pittard, 1903 TK., 8vo, 400pp., vol. 1 (all pub.) $45.00. At end: "This vol. will be followed at an early date by a vol.-"Three years in the secret service of Gen. Forrest, then another-"Reminiscences of Civil War."

113 ...(Specimen advance sheets of 'Reminiscences of the Civil War.') Little Rock, Ark., 1903, 8vo, printed wraps, 34pp. salesmen's copy with subscription slips bound-in. Text relate to N.B. Forrest Cavalry. $35.00.

114 **HALSELL, Willie D.**
"The Friendship of L.Q.C. Lamar & Jefferson Davis." (Jackson, Miss., Journ. Miss. Hist., July 1944 v.VI, #3, pp.131-144.

"1924." n.p., narrow 8vo, wraps, 18pp., printed, distributed by S.C.V. reproduced from Manufacturers Record, with intro. letter by the comm.-in-chief Etheridge of S.C.V., editorial by Richard H. Edmonds.

115 ..."The Oxford Hospital, 1862." (Jackson, Miss., Journ. Miss. Hist., Jan. 1946, v.VIII, #1, pp.36-44.

116 **HALSEY, Ashley, Jr.**
"Who Fired the First Shot? And Other Untold Stories of the Civil War." New York: Hawthorne Books, 1963 ($5.00) 8vo, cl d/w, ports, illus., 224pp. ($2.50)

117 ..."South Carolina began preparing for war in 1851." In: CWTI, Apr. 1962, v.1, #1, p.3-13, illus., map, facsms.

118 ..."The Last Duel in the Confederacy." In: CWTI, Nov. 1962, v.1, #7, p.6-8, 31, illus.

119 **HALSEY, Don P., Capt, CSA**
"Captain Don P. Halsey, CSA. A gallant officer, accomplished scholar and able lawyer." In: SHSP, 1903, XXXI, p.193-207. By Don Peters Halsey, Jr.

120 ..."Robert Edward Lee. The speech of Hon. Don P. Halsey, on the Bill to provide a statue of Robert Edward Lee to be placed in Statutory hall in the capitol at Washington, Delivered in the Senate of Virginia, Feb. 6, 1903." In: SHSP, 1903 v.XXXI, p.81-99. Also separate, wraps. $15.00.

121 ..."A sketch of the life of Capt. Don P. Halsey of the Confederate States Army, patriot, scholar & counselor at law." Richmond, Va., W. Ellis Jones pr., 1904. 8vo., wraps, 17pp. cover title. Reprint: SHSP, 1904, v.XXXI, p.193-207. $25.00, $35.00.

122 ..."The Loyalty of Robert E. Lee." In: Outlook July 11, 1903, V.LXXIV, p.646-648.

123 ..."The Patriotism of General Lee." In: Outlook, Aug. 8, 1903, v.LXXIV, p.881-883.

124 ..."Historic & Heroic Lynchburg." Lynchburg, Va., J.P. Bell Co., 1935, 8vo., cl., vii, 166pp. $6.00. Compilation of speeches on people & deeds re Lynchburg.

125 **HALSTEAD, Murat**
"Historic illustrations of the Confederacy." n.p., August, 1890, 8vo, wraps, 12 p.

126 ..."Reports of the Caucuses of 1860, etc." See under Wm. B. Hesseltine, edt.

127 **HALSTED, George Bruce**
"Washington, the Ideal of the South; Resurgent in Lee & Ross. Address before the Charles Broadway Rouss Camp Sons of Confederate Veterans. February 21, 1899." Austin: Ben C. Jones & Co., 1899. 12mo., wraps, 20pp. $7.50.

128 **HAM, Edward B.**
"Amnesty (for Confederates) & Blaine of Maine (1876)." In: New Eng. Quart., June 1955, v.28, p.255-258, notes.

129 **HAMBY, William R., Compiler**
"Glory of Hood's Texas Brigade." In: Confed. Vet., Dec. 1910, v.XVIII, p.563-566.
..."Incomplete Rolls First Regiment Texas Infantry., CSA. Fourth Regiment Texas Infantry, CSA. Fifth Regiment Infantry, CSA., Hood's Texas Brigade, Army of Northern Virginia, 1861-1865." A vol. of 135 typewritten pages, presented to Texas State Library. A review by E.W. Winkler in: QTSHA, April 1913, v.XVI, #4, p.434-435. See: Hood's Texas Brigade & Col. Harold B. Simpson.

130 ..."Fourth Texas in Battle of Gaines' Mill." In: CV, April. 1906, v.XIV, p.183-185.

131 **HAMER, Philip May**
"The Secession Movement in South Carolina in 1847-1852." Allentown, Pa., H.R. Haas Co., 1918, 8vo., cl., v., 152pp. Thesis, Univ. of Pa., 1918.
...NY, Da Capo pr., 1971. 15-y. $9.50.

132 **HAMIL, Howard Melancthom, Dr.**
"Sam Davis. A true story of a Confederate soldier who was hanged because he would not betray a secret of his commander." Griffin, Ga., (c.1912) 8vo., wraps, 32pp. Bmk(117) 75. $35.00
...Kennesaw, Ga., Continental Book, 1959. 8vo., stiff wraps, 32pp. 500 copies. $7.50, $10.00
..."Sam Davis; the Story of an Old-fashioned Boy." (Pub., J.F. Thompson, Griffin, Ga., Mills Print, 189?)
...Same, Compliments of the Confederate Veteran. (Atlanta, Ga., 1908) 12mo., wraps, cover title, illus. (incl. ports.) 16pp.

133 ..."The Old South; a Monograph." Nashville, Tenn., Dallas, Texas, Smith & Lamar, agents Publishing House M.E. Church, South. (c.1905) 16mo., wraps (or bds., cl. spine), illus. & 6-ports., cinl. front., 79pp. $5.00.
...Nashville, Tenn., Confederate Veteran, 1905. 16mo., wraps, 79pp. $4.00
...Dallas, Texas: Pub. Hse. M.E. Church South (1913)

134 **HAMILTON, Charles Granville**
"The Flag was Flame above a sea of Gray." (Aberdeen, Miss., Gregg-Hamilton Pub.) c.1975 (s.i., s.n.) 8vo., wraps, 189pp. Epic poem of CSA.

135 **HAMILTON, D.H.**
"History of Company M, First Texas Volunteer Infantry, Hood's Brigade, Longstreet Corps, Army of the Confederate States of America, by D.H. Hamilton, Sergeant Company M, 1st Texas V.I.C.S.A." (Groveton, Tex.) 1925. 12mo., wraps, 91pp. roster. $75.00.
...Waco, Texas: W.M. Morrison, 1962, 8vo., cl., 91pp. (print one side) $5.00 $15.00. Bmk. 84. 40 Bmk. 105. 250 copies.

136 **HAMILTON, David Twiggs, Col., Ga.**
"Presidency of the Confederacy Offered Stephens & Refused." In: SHSP, 1908, v.XXXVI, p.141-145.

137 **HAMILTON, Frank E.**
"Chicora, a Blockade Runner that came to the Lakes." In: Steamboat Bill of Facts, Sept. 1954, v.12, p.49-52, 57. views, Built in England for the Cs navy in 1864 & sunk in Toronto in 1919.

138 **HAMILTON, H.S.**
"The Dixie Jacket." n.p., 1935, 8vo., wraps, 14pp. (bmk) $20.00. Sketch of the CSA.

139 **HAMILTON, Holman**
"The Cave of the Winds & the Compromise of 1850." (Lexington, Ky.) JSH, Aug., 1957, v.XXIII, #3, p331-353.

140 ..."Democratic Senate Leadership & the Compromise of 1850." (Cedar Rapids, Ia.) MVHR, Dec. 1954, v.XLI, #3, p.403-418.

141 ..."The Three Kentucky Presidents: Lincoln, Taylor, Davis." Lexington: Ky. Univ. Pr., 1978. 8vo., cl., dj., xvi, 70pp. $5.00

142 ..."Three Kentucky Presidents, Lincoln, Taylor & Davis." University Press of Kentucky. Bicentennial Bookshelf (1978). 12mo., wraps, xv, 69, (1), (4)lfs, illus. $5.00.

143 ..."Prologue to Conflict: The Crisis & Compromises of 1850." Lexington: Univ. of Ky. Press, 1750 JK, 1964, 8vo., cl., dj, viii, 236 pp., maps. $7.50.
...N.Y., W.W. Norton (1966) reprint softback, N-345. $1.75.

144 **HAMILTON, James Allen**
"The Civil War Diary of James Allen Hamilton. 1861-1864. Edited by Alwyn Barr." In: Texana, Summer 1964, v.II, #2, p.132-145.

145 **HAMILTON, James J.**
"The Battle of Fort Donelson." N.Y., Thos. Yoseloff (19680. 8vo., cl., d/w, maps, 378pp. $8.50. 10 Bmk, 25 Bmk, 50 5.

146 **HAMILTON, John A., Maj.**
"General Stephen Elliott." In: SHSP 1881, v.IX, p.476-479.

147 ..."General Stephen Elliott, Lieut. John A. Hamilton & Elliott's Torpedoes." In: SHSP, 1882, v.X, p.183-186.

148 ..."Anecdotes of the War." In:SHSP, 1883, v.XI, p.318-319. See: Mrs. Sarah K. Rowe.

149 **HAMILTON, Joseph Gredoire de Roulhac**
"The Heroes of America." In: South. Hist. Ass'n. Pub., Jan. 1907, p.10-19. On secret political society, which came into existence during the Civil War in S.C., because of conditions at time but later a factor in Reconstruction.

150 ..."Southern Policy of Andrew Johnson." In: N.C. Lit. & Hist. Assn. Proc., 1916, v.XVI, p.65-80.

151 ..."Lincoln's Election an Immediate Menace to Slavery in the States?" Reprint: American Historical Review, vol.XXVII-#4, July 1932. Large 8vo., wraps, cover title, p(700) -11.

152 ..."State Courts & the Confederate Constitution." Reprint: Journal of Southern History, vol.IV-#4, Nov. 1938. Large 8vo., wraps, cover title, p(425) -48. 10 Bmk 84.

153 ..."The Life of Robert E. Lee For Boys & Girls." Boston: Houghton Mifflin Co. (Oct. 1917) 8vo., cl., ports., XI (2), 209pp. ($1.50, $2.50, $3.75) 5-10.

154 ..."North Carolina since 1860." In: History of North Carolina. Chicago: Lewis Pub. Co., 1919. (in 6 vols.) v.III, vi, 434pp., illus., maps, $100.00.
...Spartanburg, S.C., the Reprint Co., 1973, $18.00. $25.00. About half v.III devoted to Civil War & Reconstruction.

155 ..."The Prison Experiences of Randolph Shotwell." In: No. Car. Hist. Rev., 1925, v.II, p.147-161, 332-350, 559-574. See: also under Shotwell (Hamilton, edt.). Also edt: Thomas Ruffin Papers. Convicted on false evidence, complicity in Ku Klux Conspiracy.

156 ..."North Carolina Courts & the Confederacy." In: N. Car. Hist. Rev., Oct. 1927, v.IV, p.366-403. #10 Bmk 86.

157 **HAMILTON, Peter Joseph**
"Lee & the Confederacy." In: So. Hist. Ass'n., September 1900, v.IV, #5, p.317-334.

158 ..."A Little Boy in Confederate Mobile." (Mobile, Ala.) Colonial Mobile Book

Shop (1947) Arr. for Pub., Rachel-Duke Hamilton Cannon; illus. William Bush. 12mo., 1/2 cl. & boards, front (port.)s. sketches, pl, (3), 31, (1) pp. $5.00. 30 Bmk. 500 Copies by Gill Printing Co., 18-Bmk, 40-Bmk.

159 ..."Lee & the Confederacy." In: Southern History Ass'n. Publication, v.4, 1900, p.316-334. Also published as a pamphlet, 18pp., wraps.

160 **HAMILTON, Sylla Withers Thomas, Mrs., of Ga.**
"Forsaking all others; a story of Sherman's March through Georgia." NY - Wash., Neale Print., 1905. 12mo., cl., 197pp. (fiction based facts) $50.00. Southern suffering, brutality of Sherman.

161 **HAMILTON, W.F.**
"Military Annals of Carroll County. Sketches of the companies that were organized in Carroll County for service in the Confederate Armies from 1861 to 1865. By W.F. Hamilton, a member of Co. K, 11th Mississippi Reg." Carrollton (Miss.) Conservative Print., 1906, 12mo., wraps, cover title, (2), 76pp. $25.00, $75.00.

162 **HAMLIN, Myra Sawyer**
"Recollections of my Childhood in the '60s." Cambridge, Priv. Print, 1913. 16mo., boards, 62pp. Impressions of a little girl of northern parents, in Charleston during war & part Reconstruction.

163 **HAMLIN, Percy Gatling, Capt.**
"Old Bald Head" (General R.S. Ewell) the Portrait of a Soldier." Strasburg, Va., Shenandoah Pub. House, 1940. 8vo., cl., dj., maps, x, 216pp. $10.00, $12.00, $15.00, $22.50. See also: under Gen. R.S. Ewell. 40 -Bmk, 100 - Bmk.

164 ..."Richard S. Ewell: His Humanity & Humor." (Richmond) Va. Cavl., Autumn 1971, v.XXI, #2, p.4-11, facsm, pl., ports., 1 color.

164a ..."Old Bald Head (Gen. R. S. Ewell) Portrait of a Soldier" plus "The Making of a Soldier: Letters of General R. S. Ewell. With new introduction by Gary W. Gallagher." (Two books combined). Gauthersburg, Md., Ron R. Van Sickle, 1987. 8vo, cl,

165 **HAMMER, Bette Barber**
"Vicksburg, Gibralter of the Confederacy." N.Y., L. Kintner, 1954. 8vo., wraps, views, 32pp. pictorial.

166 **HAMMERS, Clyde C.**
"The Pea Ridge Battle/A Keetsville Skirmish and Blockade Hollow." Pub. on Occasion of 100th Anniv. Battle of Pea Ridge, Mar. 7-8, 1962. Kansas City, Mo., Westport Printing Co. (1962), 8vo., wraps, 25pp., 2 maps. $3.50.

167 **HAMMETT, Hugh B.**
"Reconstruction history before Dunning, Hilary Herbert & the South's victory of the books." In: Ala. rev., July 1974. pp. 185-196. Impact of "Why the solid South?"
..."Hilary Abner Herbert: a Southerner Returns to the Union." Phila:American Philosophical Society, 1976. "Memoirs Series, #110." 8vo., wraps, 264pp. $8.00. Co. Commander 8th Ala., experiences in Reconstruction.

168 **HAMMOCK, John C.**
"With Honor Untarnished, the story of the First Arkansas Infantry Regiment Confederate States Army. Intro: Dr. John L. Ferguson." (Little Rock, Ark., Pioneer Press, 1961) 8vo., cl., dj., illus., ports., xxiv, 164pp., map, endsheets. $5.00, $7.50, $15.00

169 **HAMMOND, Paul F.**
"Campaign of E. Kirby Smith in Ky., in 1862." In: SHSP, 1881, v.9, p.225-233, 246-254, 289-297, 445-462; 1882, v.10, p.70-76, 158-161.

170 **HAMMOND, W.R.**
"Was the Confederate Soldier a Rebel?"

(Answered by Bushrod C. Washington) In: SHSP, 1900, v.28, p.247-250.

171 **HAMMOND, William S.**
"The Battle of Dranesville, Va., First Federal Victory South of Potomac." In: SHSP, 1907, v.35, p.69-78.

172 **HAMNER, James H. & Musadora Caledonia (Scales Hamner) Stacy**
"Civil War Letters of a Mother & Son. Edited: by Wilena Robart Bejach." In: W. Tenn. Hist. Soc. Papr., 1950, v.4, p.50-71. Letters of a CSA officer in Ky., Tenn., Miss. to mother in Lowndes Co., Tenn. 1861-1865. $8.00.

173 **HAMPSHIRE COUNTY**
Expedition to, See: Jubal A. Early.

174 **HAMPTON ROADS CONFERENCE**
See: Jefferson Davis, John Goode, Robert M.T. Hunter, Bradley T. Johnson, John H. Reagan.

175 ..."Truth of the Hampton Roads Conference." In: CV, June 1916, v.XXIV, p.249-256. Peace conference held at Hampton Roads Feb. 3, 1865, between Lincoln, Seward & commissioners for the CSA. See: Julian S. Carr, John H. Reagan.

176 **HAMPTON ROADS, Battle of**
See: Franklin Buchanan, Wm. E. Cameron, Robert C. Foute.

177 **"HAMPTON'S CAVALRY, Sketches of...**
1861. 62-63. "Being reprint of a pamphlet pub.: Columbia, 1864, author unknown, printing press & pamphlets destroyed by Sherman Army, copy loaned by J.H. White of Graham, N.C., pp. (67)-128. Note: D.B. Rea's "Sketches from Hampton's Cavalry, embracing principal exploits of cavalry in campaign of 1862-1863. Columbia, SC, 1864, wraps, 158 pp. (In U.R. Brooks-"Stories of the Confed." See: Wells (E.D.L.)

178 **HAMPTON, Noah Jasper**
"An Eye Witness to Dark Days of 1861-1865; or, a private soldier's adventures & hardships during the war." Nashville, Tenn., Private Print, 1898, 12mo., wraps, front(port.) 80pp., illus., ports., col.pl. (Ark. Hist. Comm.) Tenn. Inftry., 18th Reg. CSA.

179 **HAMPTON, Sally Baxter**
"A Divided Heart. Letters of Sally Baxter Hampton, 1853-1862. Edt: Ann Fripp Hampton." Spartanburg, S.C., The Reprint Co., 1980. 8vo., cl., illus., xlii, 146pp., index. $20.00 v.4, The South Carolinian Series: Bibliographical & Textual, James B. Meriwether Ser., edt. Life on S.C. Plantation during war, from New York, married Wade Hampton's brother.

180 **HAMPTON, Wade**
"Acceptance & Unveiling of the Statue of Wade Hampton. Presented by the State of South Carolina, Proceedings in the Congress & in Statuary Hall, United States Capitol." Wash: US Gov. Print. Off., 1929. 8vo., wraps, 55pp. Bmk $15.00, $25.00.

181 ..."Reception of Gen. Wade Hampton, Speech of, & those of W.W. Gordon & Chs. Olmstead, April 27, 1892." In: Confed. Vets. Ass'n., Pres. Annual Report, Savannah, Ga., 1895, p.97-114.

182 ..."Address on the Life & Character of Gen. Robert E. Lee, Oct. 12, 1871, before Society of Confederate Soldiers & Sailors in Maryland." by Lt.-Gen. Wade Hampton. Baltimore: J. Murphy & Co., 1871. 8vo., wraps, 54pp. ($6.00, $10.00, $17.50) 65-JK 97 -122, 40 NC, 20-Bmk.

183 ..."An Effort to Rescue Jefferson Davis Statement of Gen. Wade Hampton as to the Connection of Himself & Command Therewith." In: SHSP, 1899, v.XXVII, p.132-136.

184 ..."Attempt of Kilpatrick & Dahlgren to Capture Richmond, from report of Lt.-Gen. Wade Hampton." In: SHSP, 1874, v.1, p.150-154.

185 ..."Battle of Bentonville." In: Cent. Mag., Oct. 1887, v.XXXIV, p.939-945, illus. Also: B & L, v.IV, p.700-705.

186 ..."Cavalry Scouts (George D.) Shadbourne." In: Land We Love, 1867, v.III, p.348-351. See also authors: W.R. Brooks, D. Cardwell, Wm. W. Finney, N.P. Ford, T.J. Mackey & Edward L. Wells.

187 ..."Correspondence Concerning the Campaign of 1864." In: SHSP, 1879, v.VII, p.291-292.

188 ..."Engagement at Sappony Church - report of Gen. Wade Hampton." In: SHSP, 1879, v.VII, p.168-171;LWL, v.II, #2, p.77-79.

189 ...Extracts from Gen. Wade Hampton's report of cavalry operations in Fall of 1864. In: SHSP, 1874, v.1, p.72-80.

190 ..."Family Letters of the Three Wade Hamptons, 1782-1901. Edt: Charles Edward Cauthen." Columbia: Univ. of South Carolina Press, 1953. 8vo., facsms, ports., views, notes, xix, 181pp. (1067 Bmk 30) $15.00. South Carolina: Sesquincentennial series, #4. Deals with plantations, nat'l. politics, civil war, p.73-114.

191 ..."Final Report on the Commission to Provide a Monument to the Memory of Wade Hampton." $2.50. Columbia, S.C., 1906. wraps, 8vo., 37pp.

192 ..."Gettysburg Campaign - report of Brig-Gen. Wade Hampton." In: SHSP, 1879, v.VII, p.245-246

193 ..."General Hampton's Report of the Battle of Trevilian's Depot & Subsequent Operations." In: SHSP, 1879, v.VII, p.147-151.

194 ..."General Hampton's Report." In: LWL, Nov. 1866, v.II, #1, p.1-4.

195 ..."General Robert E. Lee." In: SHSP, Sept. 1915, v.XL, p.335-336. Retrospect of Lee's decision on the service to the Confederacy.

196 ..."Hart's South Carolina Battery, its War Guidon - addresses of Maj Hart & Governor Hampton." In: SHSP, 1878, v.VI, p.128-132.

197 ..."Letter from General Wade Hampton on the Burning of Columbia." In: SHSP, 1879, v.VII, p.156-158. Also: under title "Burning of Columbia."

198 ..."Night Attack on the 1st & 2nd N. Carolina Cavalry upon Kilpatrick's Division (Atlee, Va., Mar. 1, 1864) In: Our Liv. & Dead, 1875, v.II, p.166-170.

199 ...(and others)"The Respectful Remonstrance, on Behalf of White People of South Carolina, Against the Constitution of the Late Convention of that State, now submitted to Congress for Ratification." Columbia, S.C., 1868. 8vo., wraps, 14pp. (above, old) $12.50.

200 ..."A Short History of Gen. Wade Hampton." Park Place, N.Y., Knapp & Co., 1888. 2 3/4 X 1 1/2" colored booklet, 16pp., facsm., signature. (packed in Duke's cigarettes). See: "Heroes of the C.W." & W. Duke Co.

201 ..."To His Excellency, Andrew Johnson, President of the United States. Letter from a distinguished southern General...The Freedman's Bureau & Negro Garrisons." (Southern Printing, 186?) Broadside folio. (Heartman, cat. #120)

202 **HAMPTON, Wade, Lt.-Gen.**
"The Battle of Bentonville.: In: B & L, v.4, p. 700-705, map, port.

203 **HANCE, Charles Hewitt**
"Reminiscences of one who Suffered in the Lost Cause. Dedicated to friends & relatives, by..." (Los Angeles, Kingsley, Mason & Collins Co., 1915) 8vo., wraps, front (port.), 37pp. Native of Missouri (Randolph Co.). Overland trade to Colorado, served under Porter.

204 **HANCHETT, William**
"Reconstruction & the Rehabilitation of

Jefferson Davis: Charles G. Halpine's 'Prison Life'." Journal of American History (1969) p.280-289. Real authorship of Craven's volume & Davis' marginal comment.

205 **HANCOCK, Marvin J.**
"The Second Battle of Cabin Creek, 1864." Oklahoma City: Chron. Okla., Winter, 1961-1962, v.XXXIX, #4, p.414-426.

206 **HANCOCK, Mary Alice**
"Four Brothers in Gray." Wilkesboro, N.C., Wilkes Community College, 1975. 4to, wraps, 53 leaves. 126 letters from the ANV, by Andrew, Harrison, Alfred & Calvin Proffit.

207 **HANCOCK, Richard R.**
"Hancock's Diary; or, a History of the Second Tennessee Cavalry, with sketches of First & Seventh battalions also portraits & biographical sketches. Nashville, Tenn., Brandon Print, 1887. 8vo., cl., ports., xii, (17), 644pp. $50.00, $100.00, $115.00, $125.00. 250 - Bmk 105.

208 **HANDER, Wilhelm**
"Excerpts from the Hander Diary." Edt: (Trans.) Leonard B. Plummer. A Texan (1st) at Vicksburg.

208a **HANDKERCHIEF, CSA**
as printed flag, colored. See:Confederate Flag - seven star flag.

209 **HANDLIN, William Wallace**
"American Politics, a moral & political work, treating of the causes of the Civil War, the nature of government, & the necessity for reform." New Orleans, La., Isaac T. Hinton, 1864. 12mo., cl., 108pp. 125. $97.50. Objective, a little known work the usual causes as slavery, politics & the press.

210 **HANDS, John Arthur**
"Address: Atlanta, United Confederate Veterans, Daughters. June 3, 1904. In the Hall, House of Representatives., Atlanta, Ga., on the Life & Character of Jefferson Davis." (Atlanta, Ga., 1904?) 8vo, wraps, 20pp.

211 ..."The Hypodermic Syringe. First used in the Confederate States Army." From 'Chattanooga News', Feb. 10, 1904. Used in the Army of Tennessee." In: SHSP 1903, v.XXXI, p. 372.

212 ..."I'll Take My Stand. The South & The Agrarian Tradition." by 12 Southerners. New York: Harper & Bros., 1930. 8vo, cl, d/w, xx, 359 pp. 1st Edt.
...Reprint: New York: Harper Torchbooks. The Academy Library, (1962). 8vo, soft-back, p. xxx, 385. $2.25

213 ..."Illustrated Guide to Richmond, the Confederate Capital. A Facsimile reprint of the City Intelligencer of 1862 with contemporary prints." Richmond, Va., The Confederate Museum-The Valentine Museum (1960) William Byrd Press). Oblong 8vo, stiff colored wraps, illus., incl. endsheets, (56) pp., with bound insert. "City Intelligencer of Stranger's Guide.", 24 pp.

214 ..."Illustrated London News" 1861-1865. Folio, 10 vols, 1/2 Leather. $850.00. Extensive drawings & articles relating to the Confederacy by artist-correspondent, Frank Vizetelly.

215 ..."Illinois division, United Daughters of the Confederacy, 1909-1913." (Chicago, Ill.? 1914?) 12mo, wraps, 37 pp. Includes list of officers, 1909-13; abbreviated minutes of the 1st-3rd & minutes of the 4th annual convention, 1910-1913; constitution & by-laws. no more printed.

216 ...Reports of 1914-1918, incl. in abbreviated minutes of the annual convention, Illinois div. UDC.

217 ..."Yearbook of the Stonewall chapter, #1038, United Daughters of the Confederacy, Illinois Division." (Chicago, 19- 12mo, wraps, Report of the 1915-1918 included in abbreviated minutes of the an-

nual convention, Illinois Div., UDC, 1914-1918.

218 **HANDY, Isaac William Ker, Rev.**
"United States Bonds; or, Duress by Federal Authority. Journal of Current Events During an imprisonment of 15 months at Ft. Delaware by I.W.K.H., of Augusta Co., Va." Baltimore: Turnbull Bros., 1874. 8vo., cl., front., pls., ports., xxviii, 670pp. append has 600 CSA officers removed from Morris Island, S.C., by Capt. J.L. Cantwell. $12.50, $17.50, $35.00, $45.00. 65 -, $50.00, 75-R. Prison journal Rev. Handy, of Augusta Co., Va.

219 ..."Our National Sins. A Sermon,... Portsmouth, Va. On the Day of Fasting... Jan.4, 1861." Portsmouth, Va., 1861. 8vo., print-wraps, 20pp. Bmk 20. $37.50. "fearfully threatened by gen. revolution."

220 **HANEY, John Hancock**
"Bragg's Kentucky Campaign: a Confederate Soldier's Account. Edt: Frank Steely & Orville W. Taylor." In: Reg. Ky. Hist. Soc., 1959, v.LVII, p.49-55

221 **HANFORD, Stanley Wing**
"Again the Alabama." In: U.S. Naval Inst. Proc., 1964, v. XC - vi, p.172-174.

222 ..."David Herbert Llewellyn: Surgeon to the Confederate War Steamer 'Alabama'." In: Mil. Medicine, 1965, v.CXXX, p.229-233. An English physician.

223 **HANKINS, Samuel W.**
"Simple Story of a Soldier." Nashville, Tenn: Confed. Veteran, (1912) Arkansas History Comm. 12mo., wraps, port., 63pp.

224 ...Also serially in Confed. Veteran 1912, p.442-443, 457-459, 536-537, 571-572. Vol.XX.

225 **HANKS, Carlos C.**
"The Last Confederate Raider." In: U.S. Naval Inst. Procd., LXVII (1941) p.21-24.

226 ..."The Confederacy's only Foreign War." In: U.S. Naval Inst. Procd., ibid, p.534-538.

227 ..."A Commerce Raider off New York." In: USN Inst. Procd., 1940, v.LXVI, p.1237-1240. A CSN raider destroys ships in NY harbor in 1864.

228 **HANKS, O.T.**
"History of Captains B.F. Benton's Company, Hood's Texas Brigade, 1861-1865. Reminiscences of an East Texas Company." Edt. Richard Morrison, Austin, Texas, 1984, 8vo, wraps, 54 p., lim. 300 copies. $17.50

229 **HANLEITER, Cornelius Redding, Col.**
"Reminiscences of the life of one of Atlanta's Pioneers." In: Atlanta Hist. Bul., 1936, v.II, #9, p.49-55.

230 ..."Extracts from the Diary of..." In: Atl. Hist. Bul., Dec. 1930, v.I, p.39-43. Served in Joe Thompson artillery. $18.00 Bmk.

231 **HANLY, Thomas B.**
"Letters of Thomas B. Hanly. 1863-1864, edited by William E. Wight." In: AHQ, 1956, v.XV, p.161-171. Was in the CSA House Representatives & delegate to the CSA Convention.

232 **HANNA, Alfred Jackson & Kathryn Abbey**
"Confederate Exiles in Venezuela." Tuscaloosa, Ala.: Confed. Pub. Co., 1960. Confederate Centennial Studies, #15. 12mo., stiff wraps, 149pp. Lim. Edt., 450 copies. $5.00. Bmk -20.

233 ..."A Confederate Newspaper in Mexico." (Baton Rouge, La.) JSH, Feb. 1946, v.XII, #1, p.67-83.

234 ..."The Escape of Confederate Secretary of War, John Cabell Breckinridge as revealed in his diary." In: KyHSR, 1939, v.XXXVII, p.323-333.

235 ..."Flight into Oblivion." (Richmond, Va.) Johnson Pub. Co., (1938) sm. 8vo., decr. cl., map endsheets, front. 30-35. illus., maps, xiii, 306pp. $10.00, $15.00, $20.00.
...Same, 2nd edt., $15.00, $20.00.
..."Bloomington, Ind., (1959) (Civil War

236 ..."Confed. Baggage Train, flight to Fla. See: Tench Francis Tilghman. 18 Bmk 84.

237 **HANNA, Ebenezer**
"The Journal of Ebenezer Hanna. Edited by Marin H. Hall." In: 'Password', v.III, p.14-29.

238 **HANNA, J. Marshall**
"The Acts of Kings: a Biblical Narrative of the acts of the first & second Kings of the First Province once Virginia. Including the doings of the first & second Tycoons of the city of Richmond, from the surrender to the present time. By J. Marshall Hanna, Associate Editor of the 'Southern Opinion'." N.Y., G.W. Carleton Pub.,1868. 16mo., decr. stiff wraps, sketches, 74pp. (10) ads. Satire on carpetbaggers, with negro satraps in full command in Richmond.

239 **HANNA, Kathryn Abbey**
"Incidents of the Confederate Blockade." (Baton Rouge, La.) JSH, May 1945, v.XI, #2, p.214-229. $10.00.

240 ..."The Roles of the South in the French Intervention in Mexico." (Lexington, Ky.)JSH, Feb. 1954, v.XX, #1, p.3-21.

241 **HANNAH, Howard Malcolm**
"Confederate Action in Franklin Co., Tenn." Sewanee, Tenn.: Franklin Co. Civil War Cent. Sewanee University Press, 1963. 12mo., cl., fldg-map(front), vii, 69pp. 35-13. $5.00.

242 **"HANNIBAL ANTE PERTAS"**
In: Old Dartmouth Hist. Soc. Bul., Summer 1961. p.1-4. Depredations of 20 men detached from the CSS "Florida", using 4 vessels against Union ships from Brazil to Maine, May-June 1863.

243 **"HANOVER COUNTY HEROES**
Partial list of soldiers from Hanover County who perished in the War of 1861-1865. (From the Richmond, Va.'Dispatch', Oct. 15, 1899)" in: SHSP, 1899, v.XXVII, p.85-89.

244 **"HANOVER GRAYS**
A roll of this gallant organization - a long death list." In: SHSP, 1907, v.XXXV, p.363-365. Roll of Co. I, 15th Virginia Infantry.

245 **HANSEL, William Uhler**
"Robert E. Lee as a Citizen, Soldier, & Statesman." In: Cliosophic Society, Lancaster, Pa., Jan. 11, 1909. 8vo., wraps, 43pp.

246 **HANSEN, Vagn K.**
"Jefferson Davis & the Repudiation of Mississippi Bonds: the Development of a Political Myth." (Jackson, Miss.) Journ. Miss. Hist. May, 1971, v.XXXIII, #2, p.105-132.

247 **HANSON, Burton**
"Judah Phillip Benjamin." In: Am. Law Rev. May/June, 1906, v.XL, p.331-339.

248 **HANSON, E. Hunn**
"Forrest's Defeat of Sturgis at Brice's Crossroads, June 10, 1864." In: B & L. v.IV, p.421-422.

249 **HANSON, E. Hunn, 4th Mo. Cav. US**
"Forrest's defeat of Sturgis at Brice's Cross-Roads, June 10, 1864." In:B & L. v.4, p. 419-421.

250 **HANSON, E.W.**
"An Episode." In: UU navy Inst. Proc., Sept. 1930, v.LVI, p.843-844. CSA raids on US commerce off coast Brazil.

251 **HANSON, G.A.**
"Minor Incidents of the Late War, as seen & Chronicled by an Eye-Witness. Actual occurrences, truly related just as they transpired. By one of the participants." Bartow, Florida: Sessions, Berker & Kilpatrick, 1887. 12mo., wraps, 97pp. Rode with Bedford Forrest.

252 **HANSON, John F.**
"A memorial Address Delivered by...of Macon, Ga., at Andersonville, Ga.

Saturday May 30, 1891." Macon, Ga., News Print, 1891. 8vo., wraps, cover title, 24pp. $10.00, $15.00.

253 **HANSON, Joseph Mills**
"Bull Run Remembers...the history, traditions & landmarks of the Manassas (Bull Run) Campaigns before Washington 1861-1862." Manassas, Va., National Capitol Pub., 1953. 8vo., colored stiff wraps (CSA flag), illus., maps, tables, ix, 194pp. (2nd edt:1957) 10.
...(same) 3rd Edt., 1961 "Centennial Edt." on cover (CSA flag dropped from 1st edt.)

254 ..."John Pelham", In: Field Artly. Journ. 1932, v.XXII, p.161-177.

255 ..."A Stolen March: Cold Harbor to Petersburg." In: Am. Mil. Hist. Found. Journ., 1937, v.I, p.139-150. See: Co-Edt: Cyrus Asbury Peterson.

256 ..."Joseph Orville Shelby (1830-1897)." Cavalry Journal (U.S. Cavalry Ass'n., Washington, D.C.) Sept.-Oct., 1933, v.XLII, p.12-18. Ablest Southern cavalry leader west of the Mississippi, Brig-Gen., CSA.

257 ..."Wade Hampton." In: Cavalry Journal, XLIII, #185, 1934. p.30-37. His military career in Confederate Army.

258 ..."Thomas Lafayette Rosser." In: Cavalry Journal, XLIII, #182, 1934, p.21-29. Biog. study Gen. Rosser (1836-1910) with emphasis on activities in CS army.

259 **HANSON, Maynard J.**
"Battle of Pea Ridge, Ark., Mar. 6/8, 1862, "InJour West, Oct. 1980, p. 39-50.

260 **HAPPEL, Ralph**
"Appomattox Court House National Historic Park, Virginia." (Wash: US Dept. of Interior, National Park Service, 1961. (reprint, 1961) 4to., pict., wraps, facsm., illus., ports., map, 15, (1)pp.

261 **HARBAUGH, Thomas Chalmers**
"Lyrics of the Gray for Southern Hearts & Southern Homes." (Casstown, Ohio), n.d., (1904) 8vo., wraps, cover title, front(port.), 56pp. $10.00.
...n.p., 1890? port. on cover. See: Maj. A.F. Grant (pseud.)

262 **HARBAUGH, Thomas Chalmers, (pseud.),Maj. A.F. Grant**
"Morgan's Rough Riders." NY, 1883 (War Library, v.2, #40...NY, 1885 (War Library v.6, #157)? Prolific writer of dime-novels, juvenile.

263 **HARBORD, James Guthrie**
"The History of the Cavalry of the Army of Northern Virginia." In: JUSCA, 1904, v.XIV, 423-503. Dorn-II, 837B.

264 **HARBY, Lee C.**
"Hart's Battery...dedicated to the survivors of Hart's Battery, in memory of my only brother, Dr. Marx E. Cohen, a member of the company who fell at the Battle of Bentonville, Mar. 19, 1865." 12 mo, wraps, cover title, no imprint, 8 pp. Poem.
..."Hart's Battery by Lee C. Harby." Dedicated to the survivors of Hart's Battery, in memory of my only brother, Dr. Marx E. Cohen, a member of the company who fell at the Battle of Bentonville, March 19, 1865. (Charleston, 1898?) 12mo., wraps, cover title, 8pp. Poetry. "Charleston reunion April 27, 1898." See: Jas. Franklin Hart.

265 **HARCOURT, A.P.**
"Terry's Texas Rangers." In: SB, v.I(os) p.89-97.

266 **HARCOURT, William George G., Sir**
"Historical Sketch of the Savannah Volunteer Guards Battalion, Chatham Artillery Centennial, May 1886. Reprinted from the 'Morning News'." Savannah, Ga., Morning News, 1886. 8vo, wraps, fldg. pl., ports, 24 pp.

267 ..."Historical Sketch of the Third Conquest of Florida, Capt. LeDiable." Port Royal, S.C., 1864. 12mo, wraps, 19 pp. Sabin 24866, $300- Satire of operations Union

army when it occupied Florida. not in Crand-Harw.

268 ..."Historical sketch of the volunteers of Norfolk & Portsmouth, Virginia: Norfolk Light Infantry Blues, Norfolk City Guards, Lee Rifles, Jackson Light Infantry, Grime's Battery, Old Dominion Guards, Portsmouth Rifle Company." Norfolk, Va., 1898 4to, stiff wraps, illus. $50-

269 ..."Historical sketches of Alabama soldiers, Edt. Fronk L. Smith." In: Directory of the City of Montgomery, & historical sketches of Alabama soldiers." (Montgomery), Perry & Smith, 1866 12mo, wraps, 112 pp. The 1st, 3rd, 26th Ala.Inf. & Cant'y brigade.

270 ..."Historic Vicksburg The Story of the Campaign in Siege & Defence of Vicksburg & of the commands, Union & Confederae, engaged therein. Compiled from tablet inscriptions in the Vicksburg National Military Park." Sq 8vo, caption title, map, illus. 96 pp.(i.e. 48) dble-column, folded to narrow 8vo. Edt. 1909 distributed by Illinois Central RRy.

271 ..."Historical Vicksburg & her part in the great drama, a succinct account of the great campaign for the possession of Vicksburg during the Civil War. The number of the troops engaged. Something of the National military park which will commemorate the heroic valor displayed by the American soldier on both sides during that great conflict for possession of the city." n.p., 1901 8vo, folder, (4) p. map. caption title.

272 ..."History of Company B. (Originally Pickens Planters) 40th Regiment--Alabama, Confederate States Army.
See: Willett (Capt. E.D.)

273 ..."History of the confederated memorial association of the South. Published by the Confederated Southern Memorial Association. Rev. & authorized edition." (New Orleans, La., The Graham press, 1904) $30-Bmk 8vo, pls. ports, 318 pp. (1903, p. 229)
Foreword: M. Louise Benton Graham, Daisy M.L. Hodgson, Virginia Frazer Boyle, Comm.

274 ..."Minutes of the annual meeting of the Confederated Southern Memorial Association New Orleans (Graham press?) 1900-

275 ..."History of Co. E., 20th N.C. Regiment, 1861-1865. Confederate Greys." Goldsboro, N.C., Nash Bros., 1905 8vo, wraps, 23 pp. Written largely by B.B. Carr, one of a comm. to prepare this sketch.
See: Jno. W. Moore's Roster N.C. Troops v.2, p. 143-174, comp's. A thru K. & Walter Clark's 'Several Regs.', v. II, p. 111-127 by Brig. Gen. Thos. F. Toon.

276 ..."A History of the Origin of Memorial Day as adpted by the Ladie's Memorial Association of Columbus, Georgia-Presented to Lizzie Rutherford Chapter. Daughters of the Confederacy, under whose direction it is now published." Columbus, Ga., Thos. Gil bert print, 1898 12mo, decr.cl, 40, (2)pp.

277 ..."History of the Quitman Rifles. Historic command, organized in 1859, composed of Pike County's Pride." In: SHSP, 1906 v.XXXIV, p. 239-242.

278 ..."History of Scotland Neck Mounted Riflemen, Co.G., 3rd N.C. Cavalry." Scotland Neck, N.C., dn.d. 8vo, wraps, 4pp.
See: Walter Clark's "Several Regiments" v.II, p. 767-787, Sgt. Joshua B. Hill.

279 ..."History of Tennessee from earliest time to present, together with history of biography sketches from 25 to 30 counties of East Tennessee." Chicago, Nashville: Goodspeed Pub., 1886/7. Tk, 8vo, plates, ports, maps, viii, (13)-1317 p., CSA, p. 513-617 in all editions as follows: 1886 (p. 930); 1886 (1232pp.); 1886 (1402 pp.);

1887 (971 pp.); 1887 (1087 pp.); 1887 (1217 pp, above.

280 **HARCOURT, William George Granville Venable V., Sir**
"American Neutrality: by Historicus, pseud. N.Y., 1865. Reprinted from the London Times of Dec. 22, 1864." 8vo., wraps, 11pp. Defends British neutrality.
..."Belligerent right of Maritime Capture, by Historicus, pseud." Liverpool: Webb & Hunt, 1863. Blockade, neutral trade, contraband with CSA.

281 ..."Letters by Historicus on some questions of International Law, Reprinted from 'The Times' with considerable additions." London (Cambridge), Macmillan Co., 1863. 8vo., cl., xiii, (2), 212pp. WH $27.50.

282 **"HARD TACK"**
Vol.1, #1. Atlanta, Ga., 1864. 4to., wraps, 8pp. An illustrated comic sheet with jokes, verse & quips on the war refers to Lincoln as "a lewd fellow of the baser sort." (Henkel-cat. #1090, May 1913)

283 **HARD, Julia E.**
"Old Canoochee-Ogeechee Chronicles 'War Time & After'." In: Ga. H.Q. Dec., 1932, v.XVI, #4, p.298-312.

284 **HARDAWAY, Robert A.**
"Correction in Organization of the Army of Northern Virginia." In: SHSP, 1884, v.12, p.240.

285 **HARDAWAY, Roger D.**
"Tennesseans at the Confederate Constitutional Convention." In: THQ, Spring 1984, v.43, #1, p. 44-48.

286 **HARDEE, Charles Seton Henry**
"Reminiscences of Charles Seton Henry Hardee. Edt: Martha Gallaudet Waring." In: Ga.H.Q., June-Sept.-Dec., 1928, v.XII, #2, #3, & #4., p.158-176 ($10.00 war period), 254-288, 353-389, v.XIII, #1, p.13-49.

287 ..."Recollections of Old Savannah, Edited by Martha Gallaudet Waring. Part II, incidents of the War Between the States." In: Ga. Hist. Quart., 1929, v.XIII, p.13-30.

288 ..."Reminiscences & Recollections of Old Savannah." Savannah, Ga., n.d. (1928). Tall 8vo., stiff wraps, illus., 131pp. $20.00. Limited edition, 500 copies. Author was 2nd Lt., Tattnall Guards, considerable section on CSA.

289 ..."Reminiscences of Charles Seton Henry Hardee, Edt: Martha Gallaudet Waring." In: Ga. Hist. Quart., June/Dec., 1928, v.XII, p.158-176, 255-288, 353-389; Mar. 1929, v.XIII, p.13-49.

290 **HARDEE, William Joseph**
"Rifle & Light Infantry Tactics; for the exercise & manoeuvers of troops when acting as light infantry or riflemen. Prepared under the direction of the War Dept., v.I -'Schools of the soldier & Co.; instruction for skirmishes. v.II - School for the battalion." First edition. Phila: Lippincott, Grambo, 1855. 1860 $40.00, 2vols. 12mo., cl., pls., diagrs., (part fold), front. 250, t.p., 5-232pp. Preface sig: Jeff. Davis, sec't war & officially adopted. Frequently reprinted both North & South.
...Phila: J.B. Lippincott, 1861, same.

291 ...(Mobile, Ala., 1861) Broadside, 16mo., Fort Morgan, June 18, 1861: Notice. So many editions of my "Infantry & Rifle Tactics" having lately been published, I think it due to both the public & publishers to state: that the copyright edt. of my infantry & rifle tactics, pub. by S.H. Goetzel Co., in Mobile, is the only complete, correct & revised edt." (below)
...Mobile: S.H. Goetzel & Co., "First Year of the Confederacy", (1861) "The only copyright edition", at head, & repeats "Notice", above. 21cm., same: in 12cm.
...Same (1861) 2nd. Edt., 2vols, 21cm. & another edt., 13cm. v.1 only 75 BMK $50.00
...Same, revised & improved, 5th Edt.,

13cm., 1/2 leather & boards. $35.00

...Same, 1863, 7th Edt.

...Same, 1863, 8th Edt., 13cm., 228, (2), 232pp. $27.50.

...Same, 1863, 9th Edt., 13cm. $35.00, $50.00. v.I-32pls., v.II-37pls. 228, 232pp. 500 Bmk. Wallpaper.

..."Rifle & Infantry Tactics - Infantry Tactics; or rules of the exercise & manoeuvers of Infantry." Raleigh, N.C., 1862. 8vo., cl., 210pp. 2 vols in 1. bmk $400.00. Differs from Crandall in pagination & co-author Scott.

293 ...Raleigh, John Spelman, by order of the Gov. of North Carolina for their troops, 21cm., 144, iv, pp. (bound in with W. Scotts Infantry Tactics. 1862. 150 $85.00.

...(Memphis, Tenn: E.C. Kirk & Co., 1861. Complete in one volume, 84pp.

...Jackson, Miss., Power & Cadwallader Print, 1861. Two vols. in one, 110pp., 19cm., Another copy, 112pp, 21cm.

...Memphis: Southern Pub. House, Hutton & Freligh, 1861. 2 vols. in one. 21cm, 202pp. $50.00, $100.00. I (1) 88pp.; v.II (89) 195; index, (197) - 202.

...Nashville, Tenn., J.O. Griffith & Co., Union & American office, 1861. 14cm., 2 vols. $45.00, $50.00, $90.00.

...Louisville: J.W. Tompkins Co., 1861. 24mo., 250, 232pp. $38.50 MOB 75. Includes 'Manual of the Piece', v.1 & 'Manual of Colt's Pistol', v.II

...New Orleans, La., H.P. Lathrop, 1861. 21cm., 98, xcix-cii pp.pls.

...Richmond, Va., J.W. Randolph, 1861. 13cm., 202pp., 2 vols. in one. pls., $50.00 -100. Crandall -2436 reports Emory's copy is without plates.

...Little Rock, Ark., True Democrat, 1862. 22cm., 73, (1), ivpp.

...Houston, Texas: Texas Printing House E.W. Cave, 1863. 2 vols. in one. 16cm., 108pp. this is also in wallpaper covers.

$125.00. By order of Kirby-Smith for use of the Trans-Miss., Dept., CSA.

...New Orleans, La., H.P. Lathrop Print, 1861. 67p. 22cm., cover title, "The Soldier's Manual of Hardee's Rifle & Light Infantry Drill", used in the Army of the CSA. Also military terms & their definitions.

294 ..."Biographical sketch of Major-General Patrick R. Cleburne." In: SHSP, 1903, XXXI, p.151-163.

295 ..."Memorial to the Congress of the Confederate States." Mobile, Ala., Dec. 14, 1863. 8v., sewn, caption title, 6pp. $22.50 $25.00

..."Glendale, N.Y., Benchmark Pub., 1970. Reprint of 'Rifle & Infty. Tactics', Memphis 1861 edt., 2 vols. in one, 202pp. $7.00, $18.00.

...Westport, Conn., Greenwood Pub. (1971) "West Point Military Library." same. 32. 25 Y. Biographies of Hardee: see: Col. T.B. Roy, Nathan C. Hughes, W.J. Milner; Wm. P. Snow "Southern Generals", p.458-465, port., & his "Lee & His Generals", p.485-4 92.

296 ..."Battle of Shiloh & Pittsburg Landing." In: Confed. War Journ., 1893, v.I, p.165-171.

297 ..."General William J. Hardee & Confederate Publication Rights." Edt: Thomas Conn Bryan. (Baton Rouge, La.) JSH, May, 1946. v.XII, #2, p.263-274.

...See: W.J. Milner

298 ..."A Short History of Gen. W.J. Hardee." Park Place, N.Y., Knapp & Co., 1888. 2 3/4 X 1 1/2" colored booklet, 16pp. facsm., signature. (packed in Duke's cigarettes) See: "Heroes of the C.W." & W. Duke Co.

299 **HARDEMAN, Nicholas P.**
"The Bloody Battle that almost Happened: William Clarke Quantrill & Peter Hardeman on the Western Border." In: CWH,

Sept., 1977, v.23, #3, p.251-258. Was in Co. A, of John R. Baylor's 2nd Reg. Mounted Rifles.

300 ..."Bushwhacker Activity on the Missouri Border. Letters to Dr. Glen O. Hardeman 1862-1865." (Columbia, Mo., Mo. Hist. Review, April 1964, v.LVIII, #3, p.265-277. illus., ports.

301 **HARDEMAN, Thomas, Col.**
"Unveiling the Confederate Monument. Address of..., Oct. 29, 1879." Macon, Ga., J.W. Burke & Co., (1879) 8vo., cover title, 8pp.

302 **HARDEN, William**
"Recollections of a Long & Satisfactory Life." Savannah, Ga., Review print (1934) 8vo., cl., dj., port(front), illus., 150, viipp. $20.00 Served in Oglethorpe Light Infty., CSA 150.

303 ..."Recollections of a Private in the Signal Corps, Jan. 1863 - Apr. 1865." In: Addresses delivered before the Confederate Veterans Ass'n., of Savannah, Ga., Braid & Hutton print, 1898. 8vo., wraps, speech: p.15-42.

304 ..."The Capture of the US Steamer 'Water Witch' in Ossabaw Sound, Georgia, June 2-3, 1864, by the Editor." In: Ga.H.Q., March 1919, v.III, #1, p.11-27. 15

305 **HARDER, William**
"Confederates who are Congressmen." In: CV, Aug. 1911, v.XIX, p.378-379.

305a **HARDIN, Bayless**
"Brigadier General John Hunt Morgan of Kentucky." Frankfurt, Ky., Ky. State Hist. Soc. (1938) 8vo., stiff boards, illus., map, 12pp. $15.00 Bmk 20.

306 **HARDIN, Elizabeth Pendleton**
"The Private War of Lizzie Hardin: a Kentucky Confederate girl's Diary of the Civil War in Kentucky, Virginia, Tennessee, Alabama & Georgia. Edited by G. Glenn Clift." Frankfort, Ky., Ky. Hist. Society, 1963. 8vo., cl., dj., port(front), xxiii, 306pp. $10.00.

307 **HARDIN, Lizzie**
"Address at Flag Presentation...1861." In: SHSP, 1892, v.20, p.55-56.

308 **HARDIN, S.H., Mrs.**
"Diary of S.T. Anderson, Confederate Prisoner of War 1864-1865." 1st Lt. Co. D, 1st Reg. S.C. Cavalry 1861-1865. (Chester, S.C., Nov. 20, 1908) 12mo., wraps, 16pp. CM

309 **HARDING, R.J., Capt., 1st Tex. Reg.**
"Report: Battle of Chickamauga." In: SHSP, 1885, v.13, p.416-417. In battles of 19-20th Sept., 1863.

310 **HARDING, Aaron, of Ky.**
"Speech of..., on the President's Proclamation & the Two Rebellions. Del. in Hse. Reps., in Congress, Jan. 21, 1863." Washington: M'Gill & Witherow, 1863. 8vo., cover title, Monaghan - 185. p.15 Opposes emancipation, writ habeas corpus.

311 ..."Speech: in which President Lincoln & his administration are arraigned & tried on their own testimony, & by their own acts. Mar. 26-Washington, D.C., 1864. 8vo., sewed, 12pp. $16.50.

312 **HARDING, Samuel Bannister, Prof.**
"Missouri Party Struggles in the Civil War Period." In: AHA, Annual report for 1900, v.1, p.85-103.

313 **HARDING, T. Sherman**
Warriors in Gray: A survey of Confederates in the Collection of T. Sherman Harding. IN: Mil. Images, Sept./Oct., 1981, v.3, $2.00, p. 16-23, ports.

314 **HARDING, Ursula & James F.**
"The Guns of the 'Keokuk'." In: CWTI, Nov. 1962, v.1, #7, p.22-25, illus. Federals gave up salvage but CSN recovered & turned on the Federals.

315 **HARDINGE, B.**
"Belle Boyd, in Camp & Prison. With an intro., by a friend to the South." 1867 40

Bmk, 1968 Bmk $15.00. 150. See: Belle Boyd.

316 **HARDWAY, Roger D.**
"The Confederate Constitution: a legal & historical examination." In: AlaHQ, 1982, v.XLII, #1, & #2, p.18-31.

317 **HARDY COUNTY**
"Early's Expedition to Hardy County." In: SHSP, 1881, v.9, p.267-269.

318 **HARDY, John**
"The Rise & Fall of Selma, Alabama." In: CV, Nov. 1918, p.480-482. From author's History of Selma, & its providing materials to army & navy.

319 **HARGIS, O.P.**
"Thrilling Experiences of a First Georgia Cavalryman in the Civil War." Atlanta, Ga., n.d., (c.1900) 16mo., wraps, 43pp.
...Washington: Neale Pub. (1905) 16mo., wraps, 43pp.

320 ..."We Came very near Capturing Gen. Wilder. By a Georgia Farmboy with Wheeler's Cavalry" In: CWTI, Nov. 1968, v.VII, #8, p.37-42. illus., ports.

321 ..."We Kept Fighting & Falling Back." In: CWTI Dec. 1968, v.VII, #8, p.37-42, illus., map, port.

322 **HARGIS, Samuel H.**
"Anecdotes & Reminiscences of the Civil War." Ardmore, I.T., 1894. 8vo., cl., port(front), 123pp. $75.00.

323 **HARGIS, William J.**
"The Pathfinder & the Civil War." (Matthew Fontaine Maury) Commonwealth, Mag. of Virginia, June 1962.

324 **HARGRETT, Lester**
"An Unrivaled Collection of Confederate Louisiana Session Laws, Legislative Journals & Related Documents." Tallahassee, Fla., n.d. $20.00. 4to., wraps, 11pp. Bmk. 114.

325 **HARKNESS, David James**
"Heroines of the Blue & Gray." A Civil War Centennial Program Manual. The University of Tenn. Newsletter, XXXIX, #4. Aug. 1960. Knoxville, Tenn. 8vo., wraps, 14pp. B -Bmk 84.

326 **HARLESTON, Francis Huger**
See: Ellison Capers, Claudine Rhett.

327 **HARLESTON, John**
"Battery Wagner on Morris Island." In: SCHM Jan. 1956, v.57, #1. p.1-13. Recoll. by a private in Charleston Light Dragoons.

328 **HARLEY, Al. B., Jr., M.D.**
"The South Carolina Military Academy & the War Between the States." (London) Journ. Confed. Hist. Soc., Winter 1973, v.10, #4, p.176-179.

329 **HARLEY, James A.**
"The Battle of Olustee." In: CV, October 1914, v.XXII, p.456-457.

330 **HARLOW, William F.**
"James Madison Hudson, CSA Soldier." Canyon, Texas: West Texas State University, 1964. 4to., wraps, 130pp. mimeographed. Thesis.

331 **HARLOW, William F., Jr.**
"James Madison Hudson: Confederate Soldier" In: Jefferson CHQ, 1979, #2, v.8, p. 14-35; 1980, #3, p. 4-25; #4, p. 17-44.

332 **HARMAN, Asher Waterman**
"The Valley After Kernstown." In: SHSP, 1891, v.19, p.318-323.

333 **HARMAN, M.G., Col.**
"Notice to Members of the 52nd Reg. Va. Vols., with Casualty Lists for June 8-9, 1862." Staunton, Va., June 22, 1862. Broadside.

334 ..."Notice to members of the 52nd Reg. Virginia Vols.! I am authorized to state to members of my regiment who are absent without leave that all those who report themselves to me in my residence at Staunton within five days after this date will be allowed to join their regiment without punishment...Staunton, June 22, 1862." Broadside 19 X 38cm. 'We append a list of

the killed & wounded in the battles of Port Republic, June 8-9, 1862'.

335 **HARMON, George D.**
"Confederate Migrations to Mexico." Bethlehem, Pa., Lehigh Univ. (1938). The Institute of Research, Cir. #137, Studies in the Humanities, #18. v.XII, #2, pp. (2), 459-487. Reprinted from: Hispanic American Hist. Review, v.XVII, #4, Nov. 1937.

336 ..."Letters of Luther Rice Mills - a Confederate Soldier." (Raleigh) NCHRev., July 1927, v.IV, #3, p.285-310. Bmk $12.00.

337 ..."Military Experiences of James A. Peifer, 1861-1865." In: NCHR, July 1955, v.32, p.385-409; Oct., p.544-572.

338 **HARMON, S.L., Col.**
"Ptocowa, a Strange, Sad Story of Fifteen Years in Dixie, as told in a Single Night." Rochester, N.Y., John P. Smith, 1887. 8vo., cl., port. of author, vi, 267pp. $75.00 Howes locates Huntington copy. A Ku Klux Klan novel.

339 **HARNETT COUNTY (N.C.)**
in the Civil War: See: Malcolm Fowler's "The Passed this way, a personal narrative of Harnett Co. History. "Centennial, Inc. (1955) n.p., 8vo., stiff wraps, ports., illus., (4), 167pp. Chap.X "Harnett Co. in the War Between the States" (p.73-95 plus 20pp. unnumbered plates) Chap. XI 'Battle of Averasboro', p.95-100.

340 **HAROLDSON, John**
"The Lay of John Haroldson." Phila., 1866. 12mo., wraps, 16pp. Ltd. 63 copies. Bmk-$100.00. The famous chamberpot poem, widely circulated.

341 ...Broadside 4 X 9", printed on heavy green paper (n.p., n.d., c.1880s?) See: Major MacKnight.

342 **HARPENDING, Asbury**
"The Great Diamond Hoax & Other Stirring Incidents in the Life of Asbury Harpending. Edt. by James H. Wilkins." San Francisco: the James H. Barry Co., 1913. 8vo., cl., 283pp., illus. (Carolina Bk) $75.00. 'Southern sympathizer in California tries to have the state secede from the Union. Travels across Mexico & on a blockader to Charleston. On to Richmond to present a plan to Jeff. Davis to intercept gold bound for California. Was commissioned a capt. in CS navy, back to California to outfit a ship to attack Union shipping. This "Chapmen Affair" failed, he was tried for treason & imprisoned." (Carolin Bks.)

...Norman: University of Okla. Press, 1958, 8vo., cl., dj., 211pp. $15.00 Foreword: Glen Dawson. "The Western Frontier Library" series.

343 **HARPER'S FERRY**
"Correspondence relative to the Insurrection at Harper's Ferry, 17th October, 1859." Annapolis: B.H. Richardson, 1860. 8vo., wraps, 79pp. $50.00. In Maryland Senate, lim. to 500 copies.

344 ..."Report of the Select Committee of the Senate appointed to inquire into the late Invasion & seizure of the Public Property at Harper's Ferry." Washington, 1860. 8vo., cl., 255, (1)pp. Sabin-30450.

345 ..."Rise & Progress of the Bloody Outbreak at Harper's Ferry, published by direction of the New York Democratic Vigilant Association." N.Y., John F. Trow (1860) 8vo., wraps, 20pp. Sabin-30451.

346 ..."Report of the Select Committee of the Senate 'The late invasion & seizure of the public property at Harper's Ferry'." Washington 1860. 8vo., cl., 225, (1)pp. Jk-152 $85.00. Reports of: Jeff Davis, J.M. Mason, Col. R. E. Lee, Comdt. Testimony: Jan/May 1860.

347 ..."Harper's Ferry 1859." In: VaCavl. Autumn 1959, v.IX, #2, p.23-33, facsms., ports., illus., incl. dbl. pg. color. See: Jas. M. Garnett, Richmond Times Dispatch, A.D. Warwick.

348 **HARPER'S WEEKLY**
Individual issues, unbound, 1858-1864 unbroken run. Bmk -109 $3,000.

349 **HARPER, Alan D.**
"William A. Dunning: The Historian as Nemesis." In: CSH, March 1964, v.X, #1, p.54-66.

350 **HARPER, Annie**
"Annie Harper's Journal: a Southern Mother's Legacy. Edt. with notes, Jeannie Marie Deen." Denton, (Miss.?) Flower Mound Writing Co. (1983). 8vo., stiff wraps, ix, 76pp., facsms., illus., ports.

351 **HARPER, George Washington Finley**
"Reminiscences of Caldwell County, N.C., in the Great War 1861-1865." compiled by G.W.F. Harper, whose war experience was not altogether unlike that of our, etc. Cover title: "Sketch of the 58th Regiment (Inf.) North Carolina Troops." (Lenoir, N.C., 1901. 8vo., wraps, 23pp. 2pp. ports. (Confed. Museum) 100.

352 ..."Sketch of the 58th Reg., Inf. North Carolina Troops." (Clark's Hist., III, p.431-445 (Lenoir, N.C., 1901) 8vo., wraps, cover title, 2 pls, ports., 23pp. Dornsbusch - 835. 15. $28.50.

353 ..."Reminiscences of Caldwell County, North Carolina in the Great War, 1861-1865." Lenoir, N.C., 1913. 8vo., wraps, ports., 59pp. (Duke) $35.00. See: author in Walter Clark's 'Several Regs.', v.III, p.431-445; Bailey's p.447-454, Jno. W. Moore's Roster: v.3, p.633-652.

354 **HARRELL, Isaac Samuel**
"Loyalism in Virginia..." Durham, N.c., Duke University, 1926. 8vo., cl., x, 203pp. boards, cl-back. $7.50.

355 **HARRELL, John M., Col.**
"Arkansas." v.XIV. 8vo., cl., 605pp. Wilmington, N.C., Broadfoot, 1987.
..."Arkansas." In: Clement Evan's "Confed. Mil. Hist." X. 8vo., 2 maps (1 dble), ports. (2 group), 419pp. Append: Medical Officers, Trans-Mississippi Dept., p.377-387.
...Biographical extension edition: "Additional sketches illustrating the services of officers & privates & patriotic citizens." p.(389)-605.

356 **HARRILL, Lawson**
"Reminiscences, 1861-1865. Lawson Harrill, Capt., Company I, 56th Regiment, North Carolina Troops, General M.W. Ransom's Brigade." Statesville, N.C., Brady print, 1910. 8vo., stiff wraps, 50, (1)pp. roster. $15.00 200 Bmk 105.

357 **HARRINGTON, Fred Harvey**
"Arkansas Defends the Mississippi." In: AHQ, 1945, v.IV, p.109-117, from 'Official Records'." Best Northern acct. by R.B. Irwin's Hist. 19th Army Corps. Best CSA acct., by Howard C. Wright in New Orleans 'True Delta.' See under Wright (Howard C.)

358 ..."A Peace Mission of 1863." In: Am. Hist. Rev., 1940, v.XLVI, p.76-86. Series of letters by Issachar Zacharie, a Jewish chiropodist, acting as a spy, under Lincoln's orders visited Richmond & conferred with CSA cabinets.

359 **HARRINGTON, George F.**
"Inside: A Chronicle of Secession." Illus. by Thomas Nast. New York: Harper & Bros., 1866 120. 8vo., cl., 223pp. Bmk 50. $28.75. oh-$26.50.

360 **HARRINGTON, Zeb D. & Martha**
"To Bear Arms: Civil War Information from local Folks Chatham County & Adjacent Counties." Moncure, N.C., The Author, 1984. 8vo., wraps, 308pp. $16.50.

361 **HARRIS, Abner, Compl., Edt.**
"Report of the Adj-Gen. State of Kentucky. Confederate Kentucky Volunteers in the War, 1861-1865." J. Tandy Ellis, Adj-Gen. (Frankfurt, Ky., State Journal Co., 1915) 4to., cl., (6), 749pp. Late Capt. 4th Va. Cav., ANVa.

362 **HARRIS, Alexander**
"A Review of the Political Conflict in America, from the commencement of the anti-slavery agitation to the close of Southern Reconstruction; comprising also a resume of the career of Thaddeus Stevens: being a survey of the struggle of parties, which destroyed the republic & virtually monarchized its government." N.Y., T.H. Pollock Pub., Rep 22.50Y. 1876. Large 8vo., cl., vii, (9) -517pp. $15.00. Fanatical abolitionists gained power with Lincoln, made war on South under pretense of defending the Union.

363 ..."The Cause of the War Shown; or, inquiries: Who are responsible for the civil War in America, & what are the designs of its authors? Answered." Philadelphia, 1863, 8vo., wraps, 86pp. $12.50 "an unconstitutional war, carried on in pretense of restoring Union; whereas real design is emancipation of negroes.

364 **HARRIS, Charles**
"State Sovereignty - Forgotten Testimony" In: SHSP, 1881, v.9, p.433-454.
..."Newport'd News." In: SHSP, 1882, v.10, p.489-503.

365 **HARRIS, Cicero Willis**
"The Sectional Struggle; an account of troubles between the North & South, from earlier times to the close of the Civil War." Philadelphia: Lippincott, 1902, 8vo., cl., 343pp. $10.00.

366 **HARRIS, D.W., & B.M. Hulse**
"The History of Claiborne Parish, Louisiana, from its incorporation in 1828 to the close of the year 1885, with sketches of pioneer life in north Louisiana...also the Muster & Death rolls of her sons in the late bloody war...Comp. by..." New Orleans, La., W.B. Stansbury, 1886, 16mo., cl., 4p, 1., (7)-263, (19)pp. War period: p.173-255.

367 **HARRIS, David Bullock**
"Sketch of his Life." In: SHSP, 1892, v.20, p.395-398.

368 **HARRIS, Gertrude**
"A Tale of Men who knew not fear. Dedicated to the memory of the brave men who went with Sibley's Brigade & to the lonely trench graves in New Mexico where Texas boys lie buried." (San Antonio, Texas: Alamo Print (1935). 8vo., cl., port., illus., 97, (2)pp. $20.00, $50.00. Cover adds: "Sibley's Campaign of 1862 & Robt. E. Lee in Texas." 35-ATG

369 **HARRIS, Harry**
"The Death of John H. Morgan." In: Wilson Club Hist., 1965, v.XXXIX, p.46-51.

370 **HARRIS, Helena J., Mrs.**
"Southern Sketches. Cecil Gray; or, The soldier's Revenge. Rosa Sherwood; or, the Avenger." New orleans, la., Crescent Job Print, 1866, 8vo., printed wraps, 20pp. $50.00. Deeply southern in tone, time of civil war.

371 **HARRIS, Isham G., Gov. of Tenn.**
"Message to the general assembly of Connessee(sic)." 8vo., wraps, 12pp. Nashville, 25 April 1861. $60.00 Not in Crandall/Harwell. Gov. urges gen. assembly to establish state as a "separate sovereignty" from union. "memorial addresses, life & character". -15.

372 **HARRIS, James Morrison, Hon.**
"A Reminiscence of the troublous times of April, 1861, based upon interviews with the authorities at Washington, touching the movement of troops through Baltimore, a paper read before the Maryland Historical Society, March 9, 1891." Baltimore, 1891. 8vo., half-title, 25pp. $35.00.

373 **HARRIS, James Sidney**
"Historical Sketches of the Seventh Regiment North Carolina Troops by J.S. Harris, Capt. Co. B, 7th N.C.T., Lanes Bri-

gade, Hill's Corps, A.N.V., 1861-1865." Mooresville, N.C.: Mooresville pr(1893) 8vo., wraps, cover title, 70pp. $75.00.

...See: Walter Clark's "Several Regs." v.I, p.361-386, by Capt. Harris.

374 **HARRIS, Joel Chandler**
"On the Wings of Occasions Being the authorized version of certain curious episodes of the late Civil War, including the hitherto suppressed narrative of the kidnapping of President Lincoln." N.Y., Doubleday, Page Co., 1900, 12mo, decr. cl., illus. (incl. front), vii, 310pp. $30.00.

...Same, 1902 edt. $10.00 $15.00.

375 ..."On the Plantation: a story of a Georgia Boy's Adventures during the War."N.Y., D. Appleton & Co., 1892. 12mo., decr. cl., dj., port (front), Kemble illus., xii, 233pp., (10)pp ads. $15.00.

...Same, (1903) $6.50.

...Athens: University of Ga., pr. 1979 Brown B. Thrasher paperback ser., $5.00 -15.

376 ..."Tales of the Home Folks in Peace & War." Bost., N.Y., Houghton, Mifflin Co., 1898, 12mo., cl., front, illus., 5pp., 1, 417, (1)p. $7.50.

...Same, London edt. $5.00.

377 ..."Women of the South." In: SHSP, 1890, v.xviii, p.277-281.

378 **HARRIS, John H., Capt.**
"Diary of..." In: Raynor Hubbell's Confederate stamps, old letters & history. Append: p.2-13. Muster rolls, see: Hubbell.

379 **HARRIS, John W., Dr.**
"The Gold of the Confederate States Treasury Guarded to Atlanta, Ga., by Naval Cadets." In: SHSP, 1904, v.32, p.157-163. See: SHSP: v.IX, p.542 et seq., v.XXVI, p.94.

380 **HARRIS, Nathaniel Edwin**
"Autobiography The Story of an old Man's Life with Reminiscences of Seventy-five Years." Macon, Ga., J.W. Burke Co., 1925. 12mo., cl., ports., incl. front, illus., 550pp. In Co. D, 63rd Tenn. Regt., later on governor of Ga. $15.00 JK, $17.50. 20 Bmk 84. 45-CH.

...Louis: Lost Cause, micro-cd. $7.79.

381 ..."The Civil War, its results, & lessons, an address delivered at Louisville, Ky., to the Confederate Veterans in reunion, June 15, 1905." Macon, Ga., J.W. Burke Co., 1906. 8vo., wraps, ports., pls., 34pp. $10.00.

382 **HARRIS, Nathaniel H., Gen.**
"Defense of Battery Gregg." In: SHSP, 1880, v.8, p.475-488.

382a **HARRIS, Scott H.**
"And the Band Played On . . . 'Stonewall Brigade Band' & its 125 years in service to Staunton, Va., & the nation." In: Augusta Hist. Bul. 17, #1, Spring 1981, p.10-19.

383 **HARRIS, Sheldon H.**
"John L. O'Sullivan Serves the Confederacy." In: CWH, September 1964. v.X, #3, p.275-290.

384 **HARRIS, W.M.**
"Movements of the Confederate Army in Virginia & part taken by the 19th Mississippi Regiment...from the diary of Gen. Nathaniel H. Harris." Duncansby, Miss., 1901. 8vo., wrap, 45pp. See: Thos. M. Folkes on the 19th Miss. Emmet Duvergne Cavett.

385 **HARRIS, Wade Hampton**
"My Schooldays, Reconstruction Experience in the South." N.Y., Neale Print, 1914. $8.50. 12mo., cl., front, pls., ports., 57pp.

386 **HARRIS, Walter Alexander**
"I knew him, Horatio." In: Ga. Bar Ass'n., Feb 1958, v.20, p.333-349. The invasion of St. Albans by CSA forces from Canada under Bennett Young, 1864, arrest in Canada & trials there & in England in connection with demands of US for extradition.

387 ..."By Right of Conquest: the Confederate Laboratory at Macon (Ga.) 1864-1877." In: Ga. Bar Journ., May 1948, v.10, p.428-436.

388 **HARRIS, William Alexander**
"The Record of Fort Sumter, from its occupation by Major Anderson, to its reduction by South Carolina Troops, during the Administration of Governor Pickens, compiled by W.A. Harris." Columbia, S.C., South Carolinian pr, 1862, 8vo., wraps, addendum tip-in, p.13. $25.00, $42.00, $65.00. $100.00 Bmk. 200 Ginsberg.

389 **HARRIS, William C.**
"The Southern Unionist critique of the Civil War." IN: ArkHQ, Spring 1985, v.XLIV, p. 39-56. Northern agression against constitutional right and Southern way of life caused the sectional confrontation.

390 ..."Leroy Pope Walker: Confederate Secretary of War." Tuscaloosa, Ala.: Confederate Pub. Co., 1962. Confederate Centennial Studies, #20, 12mo, stiff wraps, 141pp. port. Lim. 450 copies 15-$5.00.

390a ..."Lincoln & Wartime Reconstruction in North Carolina, 1861-3." In: NCHR, 1986, v.63, #2, p.149-68.

391 **HARRIS, William L., Hon.**
"Address of..., Commissioner from the State of Mississippi, delivered before the General Assembly of the State of Georgia on Monday, Dec. 17, 1860." Milledgeville, Ga., 1860. 8vo., wraps, 8pp. $15.00. As violent as Yancey, on secession.

392 **HARRISON, Burton N.**
"Some unpublished letters of Burton N. Harrison." by James Elliott Walmsley. In: Pub. Miss. Hist. Soc., Oxford, Miss., 1904, v.VIII, p.81-85. Re: Pres. Davis' imprisonment.

393 **HARRISON, Burton N., Col., CSA**
"Capture of Jefferson Davis, article in: Century, v. V, p. 130-145. Harrison was one of Davis's party.

394 **HARRISON, Burton, Mrs. (Constance Cary)**
"The Carlyles; a story of the fall of the Confederacy." N.Y., Appleton's, 1905 & (1906) 12mo., cl., 283, (4)pp. $4.50, $8.00.

395 ..."Richmond Scenes in '62." In: B & L, v.II, p.439-448.
..."Virginia Scenes in '61." In: B & L, v.I, p.160-166.

396 ..."Flower de Hundred; the story of a Virginia Plantation, by Mrs. Burton Harrison." N.Y., Cassell Pub., (1890) 12mo., cl., 4pp., 301pp. Life before & during the war.

397 ..."Recollections Grave & Gay." New York: Chs. Scribner's, 1911. 8vo., cl., 386pp. ($6.00 - $9.00 - $10.00 - $14.50) $17.50, $20.00. 35 JK, 40 - 25. Do: 1912 & 1916 ($6.00 & $12.50) $15.00. Burton Harrison was priv. sect. to Jeff Davis. This, domestic life in CSA.

398 **HARRISON, Constance Cary (Mrs. Burton)**
"Lee after the war.: In:Cent., 1879, v. 16. p. 271-276.

399 ..."Richmond Scenes in '62." In:B & L, v. 2, p. 439-448, illus.
..."Virginia Scenes in '61." In:B & L, v. 1, p. 160-166, illus., facsm.

400 ..."A Virginia Girl in the First Year of the War." In:Century, Aug. 1885, v. 30, #4, p. 606-614.

401 **HARRISON, Dabney Carr, Rev.**
"Fort Donelson. Reminiscences of the Fifteenth Virginia Infantry - death of Captain Dabney Carr Harrison - the Virginia State Flag." (from Richmond 'Dispatch', June 7, 1891) In: SHSP, 1891, v.XIX, p.372-373.

402 **HARRISON, Fairfax, Edt.**
"Aris Sonis Focisque, being Memoirs American Family 'Harrisons of Skimimo',

particularly Jesse Burton & Burton Norvell Harrison." From material of Francis Burton H., privately printed by them 1910. cloth, 413pp. (Rep.: Cent. Mag., Nov. 1883) $27.50. Fine acc't., with letters of Burton H., priv. sect. to Jeff. Davis, with account of his capture, with previous unpublished annotations by J. Davis. 35.

403 **HARRISON, George F., Capt.**
"Ewell at First Manassas." In: SHSP, 1886, v.XIV, p.356-359.

404 **HARRISON, George Paul, Jr., Gen.**
"The Youngest General of the Confederate Army." (from Opelika, Ala. 'Post') In: SHSP, 1907, v.35, p.55-58.

405 ..."Report: Battle of Ocean Pond, Fla." In: SHSP, 1881, v.9, p.23-26.

406 ..."Battle of Olustee." In: CV, Aug. 1916, v.XXIV, p.344-347.

407 **HARRISON, George T.**
"Memorial Sketch of James Lawrence Cabell." n.p., (c.1889) 8vo., wraps, 5pp. Cabell was head of CSA hospital in Charlottesville, Va. Military Hosp.

408 **HARRISON, Ida Withers, Mrs.**
"Memoirs of William Temple Withers, (1825-1889)." By his daughter. Boston: Christopher Pub. House, 1924. 50 - B. $23.00 WL. 8vo., cl., port., 155pp.

409 ..."Beyond the Battle's Rim. A Story of the Confederate Refugees." N.Y., Neale Pub. Co., 1918. 8vo., cl., port., 247pp. $7.50 50-$20.00, 30 Bmk - 40.

410 **HARRISON, Jeanne V.**
"Matthew Leeper, Confederate Agent at the Wichita Agency, Indian Territory." Oklahoma City: Chron. Okla., Autumn, 1969, v.XLVII, #3, p.242-257, ports.

411 **HARRISON, John M.**
"William Barnes, CSA, Capt. Leyden's Battery, ninth Georgia Batt. Artly." In: Atlanta Hist. Bul. Jan. 1947, v.VIII, p.100-104. See: Mecaslin Letters - Editor of. $10.00

412 **HARRISON, Jon P.**
"Tenth Texas Cavalry, CSA." In: MHT & Sw, 1974, v.XII, #2, p.93-107, maps, plate; #2, p.171-183.

413 **HARRISON, Lowell**
"The civil war in Kentucky: some persistent questions." In:KY HS, Jan. 1979, p. 1-21.

414 ..."The Diary of an average Confederate Soldier." In:THQ, 1970, v.29, p.256-271.

415 ..."George W. Johnson & Richard Hawes, The Governors of Civil War Kentucky." In:RKHS, Winter 1981, p.3-39.

416 ..."Gen. Basil W. Duke, CSA." In:Filson Club HQ., Jan. 1980, p.5-36.

417 ..."Battle Beyond Knoxville. Confederates Turn & Fight at Bean's Station." In: CWTI, May 1987, v.26, #3, p.16-21, 46-47, illus., maps, ports.

418 ..."A Confederate View of Southern Ky., 1861." In: RKHS, July 1972, v.70, #3, p.163-178.

419 ...Kentucky born Generals in the Civil War." In: RKHS, Apr. 1966, v.64, #2, p.129-160.

420 ..."Gov. Magoffin & the Secession Crisis." In: RKHS, Apr. 1974, v,72, #2, p.91-110.

421 ..."The Civil War in Kentucky: Some persistent questions." In: RKHS, Jan. 1978, v.76, #1, p.1-21.

422 ..."George W. Johnson & Richard Hames: the Governors of Confederate Kentucky." In: RKHS, Winter 1981, v.79, #1, p.3-39.

424 **HARRISON, Lowell H.**
"John C. Breckinridge: Nationalist, Confederate, Kentuckian." In: Wilson Club Hist. Quart., 1973, v.XLVII, p.125-144.

425 ..."The Civil War in Kentucky." (Lexington, Ky.) University of Kentucky Press (1975) 12mo., cl., scene on cover, illus., maps, ix, (1), 115, (1)pp. $4.25.

426 ..."The Diary of an 'Average' Confederate Soldier." In:THQ, 1970, v.29, p.256-271.

427 ..."Conscription in the Confederacy." In: CWTI, July 1970, v.IX, #4, p.10-19, illus., ports. See: Ella Lonn, Albert B. Moore.

428 ..."Confederate Kentucky - the state that almost was." In: CWTI, April 1973, v.12, #1, p.12-21, cartoon, map, ports.

429 ..."A Confederate View of Southern Kentucky, 1861." In: Kentucky Historical Society Register, v.LXX, p.163-178, Lt. William P. Davis, of 14th Miss.

430 ..."The C.S.S. Shenandoah. In its thirteen month cruise this steamer captured 38 ships, 1,053 prisoners & inflicted over $6 million in direct damage." In: CWTI, July 1976, v.XV, #4, p.4-9, 44-47, ports., illus.

431 ..."How the Southern generals rated their leaders. In 1907 a Texas senator questioned 43 former CSA generals, who was the greatest commander" In: CWTI, Oct. 1966, Oct. 1966, v.5, #6, p.27-35. illus.

432 ..."Memories of Slavery Days in Kentucky." In: FCHQ, July, 1973, v.47, #3, p.242-257.

433 ..."A Federal Officer Pursues John Hunt Morgan." In: FCHQ, April 1974, v.48, #2, p.129-143. Samuel McDowell Starling of Hopkinsville, Ky. pursues Morgan.

434 ..."Thomas Roderick Dew: Philosopher of the Old South." In: VMHB, Oct. 1949, v.LVII, p.390-404.

435 ..."Simon Bolivar Buckner: a Profile." In: CWTI Feb. 1978, v.16, #10, p.36-45. Facsm., illus., ports., 'The most perfect gentleman in the Cs army.'

436 ..."Should I Surrender? A Civil War Incident." In: FCHQ, October 1966, v.40, #4, p.297-306.

437 **HARRISON, M. Clifford**
"Petersburg's Ninth of June. Not without reason does the Cockade City celebrate Memorial Day each year ten days later than the rest of the nation." (Richmond) Va. Cavl., Summer 1958. v.VIII, #1, p.10-15, ports., illus. (1 -color)

438 ..."A Fighting Confederate Chaplain Spy." (Richmond) Va. Cavl., Spring 1963. v.XII, #4, p.18-22, ports., illus. Thomas Nelson Conrad, capt. in CSA.

439 ..."Soldier, Scholar, Gentleman." (Richmond) Va. Cavl., Spring 1965, v.XIV, #4, p.20-31, ports, illus., 3 page, 1 dbl.p. color plates. Cap't. William Gordon McCabe, D.D.

440 **HARRISON, Peleg Dennis**
"The Stars & Stripes & other American Flags, including their origin & history, army & navy regulations concerning the national standard & ensign, flag making, salutes improvised, unique, & combination flags, flag legislation, & many associations of American flags, including the origin of the name "Old Glory", with songs & their origin." Boston: Little, Brown & Co., 1906, 8vo., cl., xii, 419pp., 8 color pls.(front). CSA fully covered. (Edts: 1914 & 1918, p.431)

441 **HARRISON, R.S.**
"The Thirteenth Regiment of Virginia Cavalry in Gen. J.E.B. Stuart's Raid into Pennsylvania." In: So.Biv., 1882, v.I, p.203-208.

442 **HARRISON, Royden**
"British Labour & the Confederacy." In: International Rev. Soc. Hist., 1951, p.78-105.

443 **HARRISON, W.H., Capt.**
"Capt. W.H. Harrison shows that Cooper's History does not do the South Justice." (Atlanta, Ga., 1898) 8vo., wraps, 5pp. Dorn - II, 119. "I was appointed to prepare & submit a written criticism of the school history recently written by Profs: Cooper, Estill & Lemon, of Texas, & pub. by Ginn & Co. Boston, Mass." from cover title.

444 **HARRISON, Walter Hamilton**
"Pickett's Men; a Fragment of War Hist."

Gaithersburg, Md., Butternut Press 1984 $24.00.

..."Pickett's Men, a fragment of War History." New York: D. Van Nostrand, 1870. 12mo., cl., 2-fronts(port. & illus.) 202pp. $8.50, $10.00, $12.00, $20.00, & $22.50. 35 - appl. 50-Gins., 40 Bmk. 75 Bmk. '73 AVG $22.00. A.A. & Insp-Gen., Pickett's Div., ANV.

445 **HARRISON, William Henry, Capt.**
"Letters of Wm. Henry Harrison." In: Helen Eliza Terrill 'Stewart Co., Ga.', p.270-275.

445a **"HARRISONBURG, Va.,**
Diary of a Citizen from May 9, 1862-Aug. 22, 1864. Local Events during the Civil War." Harrisonburg, Va., E.R. Grymes Heneberger, Nov.15, 1961. 4to., stiff pict. wraps, 150pp. 100 copies made.

446 **HART, Freeman H.**
"Numerical strength of the Confederate Army." In: Current Hist., Oct. 1926, v.XXV, p.91-96.

447 **HART, H.O.**
"A Boy's Recollections of the War Between the States." In: LaHQ, Apr. 1928, v.XI, p.253-260.

448 **HART, Henry**
"Hart's South Carolina Battery - Its War Guidon - addresses by Maj. Hart & Governor Hampton." In: SHSP, 1878, v.VI, p.128-132.

449 **HART, James F., Maj.**
"Record of Hart's Battery from its organization to the end of the war. When & where it was formed." In: U.R. Brook's 'Stories of the Confederacy.' ports., illus., p.246-273. See: Lee C. Harby, Henry Hart.

450 **HART, Scott**
"Eight April Days." N.Y. Coward-McCann (1949). 12mo., cl., 188pp., map (on lining paper) $15.00. Fiction. The story of Old Pine, CSA woman at Sayler's Creek.

..."From Sayler's Creek to Appomattox. Last Desperate Days." (Farmville, Va., Randolph House, Inc., 1961. $10.00) 4to., Decr. color wraps, 42pp., illus., map, ports.

451 **HART, Semeon**
"Sibley's Brigade", in letters from Hart - In: Texana, Fall 1968, v.VI, #3, p.288-292. See: Martin H. Hall, Geo. W. Baylor.

452 **HART, W.O. & Y.R. LeMonnier**
"The Confederate Die for the Coinage of Silver Half Dollars." In: La. Hist. Quart. v.V, Oct. 1914, p.505-508.

453 **HART, William Octave**
"A Boy's Recollection of the War." Reprint from Pub. of Miss. Hist. Soc. v.12, 14pp., wraps. n.p., n.d. $2.50.

..."A Boy's Recollection of the War." (Oxford, Miss., Pub. Miss. Hist. Soc. 1912), v.XII, p.148-154.

454 ..."When Jefferson Davis was Freed." In: CV June, 1923, v.XXXI, p.208-209.

455 **HARTER, Eugene C.**
"The Lost Colony of the Confederacy" Jackson: University Press of Mississippi, 1985, 8vo, cl, dj, xiv, 141 pp. illus. $15.00. See: Lawrence F. Hill, Blanche Henry Clark Weaver, Frank B. Goldman.

456 **HARTJE, Robert G.**
"A Confederate Dilemma Across the Mississippi." In: AHQ, 1958, v.XVII, p.119-131.

457 ..."Van Dorn Conducts a Raid on Holly Springs & enters Tennessee." In: Tenn. HQ June 1959, v.XVIII, p.120-133. Cavalry raid in north Miss., Dec. 1862.

458 **HARTJE, Robert George**
"Maj-Gen. Earl Van Dorn (1820-1863)." Ann Arbor: University microfilms, 1955. typescript, iii, 312 leaves, maps. Thesis Vanderbilt Univ., abstracted Dissert., 15:1381. US/Cs army, 1842-1863.

459 ..."Van Dorn, The Life & Times of a Confederate General." Nashville, Tenn.: Vanderbilt Univ. 1967. Bmk 30. 8vo., cl., d/w,

pp.xiii, 359, maps. $8.95. 14. 20-DAR, OP.$12.50Y Port(front.), $5.00

460 ..."The Gray Dragoon Wins his Final Victory." In: THQ, 1964, v.23, p.38-58.

461 **HARTMAN, Peter S.**
"Civil War Reminiscences." In: Mennonite Qrt. Rev., July 1929, v.III, p.203-219. Mennonite conscientious objector's experience under CSA government in Richmond, Va.

462 **HARTSELL, Henry F.**
"Battle of Cane Hill, Arkansas, Nov. 28, 1862." In:Jour. West. Oct. 1980, p.51-62.

463 **HARTZ, Asa**
"Letter from Johnson's Island, Dec. 25, 1863." In: So. Biv., 1882, v.I, p.251-155.

464 **HARTZ, Louis**
"The reactionary enlightenment: Southern political thought before the civil war." In: West Pol. Quart., March 1952, v.5, p.31-50. On conservative reaction in Southern political theory, 1850-1863.

464a **HARTZLER, Daniel David**
"Medical Doctors of Marland in the CSA." Funkstown, Md., 1979. 4to, wraps, 98pp, ills. Dornb-IV(1822).
..."Marylanders in the Confederacy." Silver Springs, Md., Family Line Pubs., 1986. Sm.4to, cl, dj, 416pp. $25. Alphabetical list of approx. 12,000 names of command groups, & names units, highest rank, residence, etc.

465 **HARVEY, Paul, Jr.**
"Old Tige: General William L. Cabell C.S.A." (Hillsboro, Texas) Hill Junior College Monograph, #4, 1970. 8vo., stiff wraps, ports., illus., ix, 89pp. $4.00, $12.50 JK 122, 25, 7.

466 **HARVIE, E.J.**
"Gen. Joseph E. Johnston." In: CV, Nov. 1910, v.XVIII, p.521-523.

467 **HARWELL, J.D.**
"In & Around Vicksburg." In: CV, Sept. 1922, v.XXX, p.333-334.

468 **HARWELL, Richard Barksdale**
"A Military Tourist; Colonel Fremantle and his Confederate Travels." Chicago. Abraham Lincoln Books, 195, 8vo, wraps, 13 pp. $10.00. Reprinted from Emory University Quarterly, v. X, #1, March 1954. Titled: "Col. Freemantle and his Confederate Travels."
..."Atlanta Publications of the Civil War." In: At. Hist. Soc. Bul., July 1941, v.6, #25. Bmk 20. 36pp.

469 ..."A Brief Calendar of the Jefferson Davis Papers in the Keith M. Read Confederate Collection of the Emory University Library." (Jackson, Miss., Journ. of Miss. Hist., Jan. 1942, v.IV, #1, p.20-30.

470 ..."Brief Candle: The confederate Theatre." Worchester, Mass., American Antiquarian Society, 1971. Reprinted from "Proceedings of the American Antiquarian Society for April 1971. 8vo., wraps, pp. unnumbered, 41-160. facsimiles. Deals only with the theatre in Richmond, Va. 1141 Bmk $25.00. $12.50.

471 ..."The Cause that Refreshes: reading, 'riting & rebellion." In: College & Research Lib., July 1959, v.20, p.281-288. Bmk 10. On literature pub. both North & South during war & interest by collectors, since 1865, in such pubs.

472 ..."Civilian Life in Atlanta in 1862." In: Atl. Hist. Soc. Bul., Oct. 1944, v.7, #29.

473 ..."Civil War Collecting." In: Stechert-Hafner Book News, May 1960. 3pp. $20.00

474 ..."Confederate Anti-Lincoln Literature." Lincoln Herald, v.52, #3, Fall, 1951, p.22-27, 37, cartoons, facsm. $7.00 15 (7pp.)

475 ..."Confederate Belles-Lettres a Bibliographical & a finding list of the fiction, poetry, drama, songsters & a miscellaneous literature published in the Confederate States of America, with a foreword by Robert H. Woody." Hat-

tiesburg, Miss., The Book Farm, 1941. 8vo., wraps, 79pp. Heartman's Hist. Ser. #56. 199 copies printed. $5.00, $7.50, $35.00Y 75.

...N.Y., Gordon Press (Lib. bnd.) $70.00.

476 ..."Confederate Carousel: Southern Songs of the Sixties." Chicago: Civil War Round Table (1950) 8vo., wraps, notes, 19pp. Reprint: Emory Univ. Quart., June v.6, p.84-100. $10.00. On "some of the more than 600 songs pub. during the Confederacy, & their composers."

477 ..."The Confederate Constitution." Athens: University of Georgia Press, 1979, 8vo., wraps, xii, 22pp. $15.00. Facsm.: 1861 at Milledgeville's Printing.

478 ..."A Confederate Diary of the Retreat from Petersburg, April 3-20, 1865, Edited by R.B.H." Atlanta, Ga., The Library, Emory Univ., publications, Sources & Reprints, Ser. 8, #1. 1953. 15-Bmk 84, 10-25-. 8vo., wraps, bibliog. 8-9, p.23. $5.00, $7.50. Appomattox Campaign, incorrectly identified as Samuel Howard Gray.

479 ..."Colonel Fremantle & His Confederate Travels." In: Emory Univ. Quart., Mar. 1954, v.10, p.21-31. On Col. Fremantle's "Three Months in Southern States." recently reprinted.

..."Chicago, Ill., Abraham Lincoln Bookstore, 1954. 8vo., wraps, port., notes, 13pp. $8.00 Bmk.

480 ..."The Confederate Hundred. A bibliophilic selection of Confederate books." (Urbana, Ill.) Beta Phi Mu, 1964. Tall 8vo., wraps, xxiii, 58pp. illus., facsms. chapbook #7 (1M copies) 40. $50.00 - Bmk 114. $7.50.

...Wendell, N.C., reprint, 1982. 2nd edt., with new preface, stiff wraps, $15.00. Bound copies, signed (100 copies) $25.00. 500 copies printed.

481 ..."A Confederate Marine: A Sketch of Henry Lea Graves with Excerpts from the Graves Family Correspondence, 1861-1865." Tuscaloosa, Ala.: Confed. Pub. co., 1963. Confederate Centennial Studies, #24. 12mo., stiff wraps, 140pp. port., facsm., $5.00. Lim. Edt., 450 copies. 15.

482 ..."Confederate Music." Chapel Hill: Univ. of N.C. Press (1950) 30-, 20. 8vo., cl., dj., facsm (front), viii, (2), 184pp. $15.00. bibliog-index, p.165-184. $5.00, $7.50, $10.00. See: also in Marjorie Crandall's "Confederate Imprints", v.II; Harwell's "More Confederate Imprints." 20- 30-Bmk 114.

483 ..."Confederate Imprints" In: Stechert-Hafner Book News, Apr. 1954. 3pp. $20.00 Bmk.

484 ..."Confederate Imprints in the University of Georgia Libraries." Univ. of Georgia Libraries Misc. Pub. #5. Athens, Ga., Univ. of Ga. Press, 1964. 8vo., stiff wraps, facsms (incl. front.) xi, 49pp. $3.50. 5. Includes a numerical list of Harwell numbers in Crandall's Confederate Imprints.

485 ..."Gone With the Wind: as book & film." Columbia, S.C., University of S.C., 1983. 8vo., cl., dj., xxi, 274pp., illus., notes, index. $20.00.

486 ..."Jefferson Davis in song." In: Lincoln Herald, Oct. 1948, v.50, #3, p.23-27. facsms., includes checklist of Davis' songs. 1861-1867.

487 ..."Robert E. Lee." Civil War History (1957) v.3, p.362-368, 376 (Dec.), port. Letters from Lee to Davis.

488 ..."Lincoln & 'Dixie': The Yankee Conversion of some Southern Songs, 1859-1865." The Lincoln Herald, v.53, #1, Spring of 1951, p.22-27, cartoons, facsm.

489 ..."Propaganda for Secession: the 1860 Association & the Secession Convention of 1860." The Lincoln Herald, v.54, #4, winter 1952. p.27-41. Facsms & a list of

490 ..."The Richmond Stage." In: CWH, June 1955, v.1, #2, p.295-304.

491 ..."Songs of the Confederacy." N.Y., Broadcast Music (1951) (Dj) 100-. 40-Bmk. 4to., cl., facsms., 112pp. 75 - $12.50. Consists largely of 38 facsimiles, printed between 1861-1865, with historical text.

492 ..."In Tall Cotton. The 200 Most Important Books in the Reader, Researcher & Collector. With preface: E. Merton Coulter." Austin (Texas), Jenkins Publishing Co., & Frontier America Corporation. 1978. Half-title:"Contribution to Bibliography III, John H. Jenkins, Wm. S. Reese, editors. sm. 4to., decr. boards, facsms., xi, 82pp. Afterword, index. 40 - $19.50.

493 ..."The War They Fought." N.Y., Longmans, Green, 1960. tk. 8vo., cl., illus., 380, 362pp., dj. Full-Ca/F $30.00 Bmk 109. Reprint of his "Confederate" & "Union" Reader of 1957 & 1958.

494 **HARWELL, Thomas Fletcher**
"Confederate Biography. Brief histories of the lives of Members of Camp Ben McCulloch, United Confederate Veterans, Camp #946. Also a few other Ex-Confederates..." Kyle, Texas, 1923. 8vo., decr. wraps, illus., 58pp. 100 copies. $35.00. (Jenkins catalogue lists a copy with 88pp.)

495 ..."Eight Years under the Stars & Bars. Including biographical sketches of "100 Confederate Soldiers I have known", information concerning the organization of the United Confederate Veterans. Organization & History of Camp Ben McCulloch, United Confederate Veterans near Driftwood, Hays County, Texas. Contains lots of pictures fully illustrated by Thomas F. Harwell, Historian General, U.C.V. (General Organization), is doubtless the only book of its kind published, price propaganda pamphlets. 1953 wraps, 15pp. $15.00.

$1.00." (Kyle, Texas, c.1947) $12.50, $25.00. 8vo., decr. wraps, color, illus., ports., 108pp.

496 **HASELTINE, John W.**
"Descriptive Catalogue of Confederate Notes & Bonds, for sale by..." Philadelphia, Pa., Bavis & Pennypacker, 1876, @ $.50 or "a few copies printed on extra large & fine paper @ $1.00 each." 8vo., wraps, 36pp. (4pp. insert, price list.)...n.p., n.d., reprint $1.00.

497 **HASKELL, John Cheves**
"The Haskell Memoirs/John Cheves Haskell. Edt: Gilbert E. Govan & James W. Livingood." N.Y., G.P. Putnam's Sons (1960) 20, 15-Bmk $12.50Y. 12mo., cl., dj., front. (port.), xiv, (1), 176pp. $10.00.

498 ..."Remarkable Record of the Haskells of South Carolina. (T.C. DeLeon, in 'Town Topics', Nov. 1907)" In: SHSP, 1907, v.XXXV, p.151-154.

499 **HASKINS, W.W.**
"General Lee's Last Camp." In: SHSP, 1909, v.37, p.208-209.

500 **HASS, Bruce S.**
"Beauregard and the Image of Napoleon." In: LaH., 1964, v.5, p.179-186.

501 **HASSKARL, Robert A.**
"Waul's Texas Legion 1862-1865." Ada, Oklahoma, Book Bindery, 1976. 4to., wraps, 103pp., illus. See: Laura Simmons.

502 **HASSLER, Frederick W.B.**
"The Campaign in W. Virginia, 1861-1862." In: Hist. Mag., VI, Morrisania, 1869, p.355-358.

503 ..."A Military View of Passing Events from Inside the Confederacy; I, the Campaign in W. Virginia 1861-1862." (See: Carlisle Barracks -210) LC, not here.

504 **HASSLER, Warren W., Dr.**
"How the Confederates Controlled Blockade Running." In: CWTI, Oct., 1963, v.II, #6, p.43-49, illus., port.

505 **HASSLER, William Woods**
"A.P. Hill, Lee's Forgotten General." Richmond, Va., Garrett & Massie (1957) 8vo., cl., dj., illus., maps, plans, ports., xiv, Pres-25. 249pp. $20.00, Pres. copy, $35.00.
...Revised reprint (1962) $16.00.
...Reprint, 1979. $12.00.

506 ..."A.P. Hill, Mystery Man of the Confederacy." In: CWTI, Oct. 1977, v.16, #6, p.4-10, 40-42. illus., ports.

507 ..."The Hill-McClellan-Marcy Triangle" In: Ga. Rev., Fall 1958, v.XII, p.252-265. Rivalry for hand of Ellen Marcy, breaks engagement with Hill, who remains good friend with McClellan during War.

508 ..."The Hill-Jackson Feud." In: CWTI, May 1965, v.IV, #2, p.36-42, illus., ports. Tragic death of Jackson spared Lee the scandal of a double court-martial of two of his most trusted generals.

509 ..."Lee's Hard-luck General Harry Heth." In: CWTI, July 1966, v.5, #4, p.12-20, illus., port.

510 ..."The Davis-Stephens Feud." In: CWTI, April 1964, v.III, #1, p.42-49, illus., ports. President Davis & his V-Pres. at loggerhead during most of the war.

511 ..."Fighting Dick Anderson." In: CWTI, Feb. 1974, v.12, #10, p.4-10, 40-43, illus., port.

512 ..."Stonewall of the West, Maj-Gen. Patrick R. Cleburne, commander of the Army of Tennessee." In: CWTI, Feb. 1972, v.10, #10, p.4-9, 44-47, facsm.,ports.

513 ..."The 'Ghost' of General Longstreet." In: GHQ, Spring 1981, v.LXV, #1, p.22-27, note.

514 ..."Dr. Hunter Holmes McGuire. Surgeon to Stonewall Jackson, the Confederacy, & the nation." In: Va. Cavalcade, Autumn 1982, v.32, #2, p.52-61, ports., views, color port.: McGuire.

515 ..."'Willie' Pegram General Lee's Brilliant Young Virginia Artillerist." (Richmond) Va. Cavl., Autumn 1973, v.XXIII, #2, p.12-19, map, ports., illus.

516 ..."Colonel John Pelham Lee's Boy Artillerist." Richmond, Va., Garrett & Massie, (1960) (1979) $12.00 Bmk 20, Bmk 30, 15. 12mo., cl., dj., ports., incl. front., maps & other illus. by Sidney E. King, xiii, 185, (1)pp. $12.50.

517 ..."John Pelham of the Horse Artillery." In: CWTI, Aug. 1964, v.III, #5, p.10-14, illus., ports.

518 ..."Scrappy Little 'Billy' Mahone." In: CWTI, Apr. 1963, v.II, #1, p.18-22, illus., port.

519 ..."'Extra Billy' Smith." In: CWTI, Dec. 1963, v.II, #8, p.38-41, illus., port.

520 ..."Dorsey Pender." In: CWTI, Oct. 1962, v.I, #6, p.18-22. He disliked Jackson & mistrusted Stuart. From unpublished letters to wife. Lee's favorite young general. Illus., ports.

521 ..."The Religious Conversion of General W. Dorsey Pender, CSA." In: Hist. Mag. of Protest. Episcopal Church, 1964, v.XXXIII, p.171-178.

522 **HASTINGS, Earl C. & David S.**
"Encounter in the Rain, the Battle of Williamsburg, 1862." (Richmond) Va. Cavl., Winter 1973, v.XXII, #3, p.20-27, maps, illus. (color)

523 **HATCHER'S RUN, Battle of**
Lee, Robert E., "Battle of Hatcher's Run." In: SHSP, 1881, v.9, p.81-82. Telegram.
See: John Brown Gordon.

524 **HATTAWAY, Herman**
"Clio's Southern Soldiers: The United Confederates and History." In: LaH., 1971, v.12, p.213-242.

525 ..."The United Confederate Veterans in Louisiana." In: LaH, 1975, v.16, p.5-37.
..."Confederate Myth Making: Top Command & the Chickasaw Bayou Campaign." (Jackson, Miss.) Journ. Miss. Hist., Nov. 1970, v.XXXII, #4, p.311-326.

526 ..."General Stephen D. Lee." Jackson: University Press of Mississippi, 1976. 8vo., cl., dj., facsm., illus., maps, ports., xi, 283pp. Notes, index, bibliog., p.235-283. $35.00.

527 ..."Stephen Dill Lee - a personality profile." In: CWTI, Aug. 1969, v.VIII, #5, p.16-25, illus., ports.

528 ..."Via Confederate Post." In: CWTI, April 1976, v.15, #1, p.22-29, facsms., port.

528a HATTAWAY, Herman & Lloyd A. Hunter
"Which Side Are You On, God? The War inside the Church." In: CWHI, Jan. 1988, v.26, #9, p.28-33, ills, port.

529 HATTON, Clarence R.
"The Great Battle of Cedar Creek - Early's Thin Gray Line." (from: Richmond, Va. Times Dispatch, Nov. 11, 1906) In: SHSP, 1906, v.34, p.194-199.

530 ..."Gen. Archibald Campbell Godwin." In: CV, April 1920, v.XXVIII, p.133-136.

531 ..."The Valley Campaign of 1864." In: CV, May 1919, v.XXVII, p.168-172, 197.

532 HATTON, Robert, Brig.-Gen.
Portrait: mezzotint by Samuel Sartain on small folio sheet, with msc. biographical sketch in ink. (Philadelphia, c. 1900) $5.00.

533 HATTON, Roy O.
"Camille de Polignac: a Prince among the Confederates." In: RKHS, Jan. 1968, v.66, #1, p.65-74.

534 ..."The Prince of the Confederacy." In: CWTI, Aug. 1980, v.19, #5, p.8-18, illus., ports. Diary: pt.II, Oct. 1980, #6, p.34-41. illus., ports. Camille Polignac's Services.
..."Prince Camille de Polignac & the American Civil War, 1863-1865." In: Louisiana Studies, 1964, v.III, p.163-195. Frenchman serving in Cs army.

535 ..."Camille de Polignac: A Prince Among Confederates." Jan. 1968, Ky. Hist. Society (Register) p.65-74.

536 HATTON, Roy, Dr.
"A Damn frog-eating Frenchman, Prince Polignac & the Texas Confederates." In: CV (new), May/June 1986, v.34, #3, p.(12)-21, map, ports.

537 HAULMAN, C.A.
"Changes in the Economic Power Structure in Duval County, Florida, during the Civil War & Reconstruction." In: FHQ, October, 1973, LU #2, p.175-184, tables.

538 HAUNTON, Richard H.
"Law & Order in Savannah, 1850-1860" IN: Ga. H.Q., Spring 1972, v.LVI, #1, p.1-24.

539 HAUT, Marc de
"La Crise Americaine, ses Causes, ses Resultats probables, ses Rapports avec l'Europe et la France." (American Crisis, its causes, probable results & its ties with Europe & France). paris: E. Dentu, Lib. Edt., 1862. 8vo., cl., pp.(7), 168.

540 HAVARD, William C.
"The Florida Executive Council. An experiment in Civil War Administration." In: FHQ, October, 1954. v.XXXIII, #3, p.77-96.

541 HAVENS, Edwin R.
"How Mosby Destroyed our Train." In: Mich. Hist. Mag., Apr. 1930, v.XIV, p.294-298.

542 HAVINS, Thomas Robert
"Administration of the Sequestration act in the Confederate District Court for the Western District of Texas, 1862-1865." In: SwHQ, Jan. 1940, v.XLIII, #3, p.294-322.

543 ..."The Texas Mounted Regiment at Camp Colorado." In: TMH, Summer, 1964, v.4, #2, p.67-79.

544 HAW, Joseph R.
"The Battle of Haw's Shop, Va.," In: CV, Oct. 1925, v.XXXIII, p. 373-376.

545 ..."The Burning of Hampton, Va." In: CV. Oct. 1924, v.XXXII, p.389-390.

546 ..."The Last of C.S. Ordnance Department." In: CV, Dec. 1926, v.XXXIV, p.450-452.

547 **HAWES, George Percy**
"The Battle of Cedar Creek." In: CV, May 1923, v.XXXI, p.169-170.

548 ..."The last Days of the Army of Northern Virginia; a Courier's Recollections of the last ten days of the war." In: CV, Sept. 1919, v.XXVII, p.341-344.

549 **HAWK, Emory Qwinter**
"Economic History of the South. Foreword by Tipton R. Snavely." N.Y., Prentice Hall History Ser., 1934. 8vo., cl., dj., illus., (maps), diagrs., xvii, 557pp. About a third relates to the war. $20.00

550 **HAWKS, Esther Hill, Dr.**
"A woman doctor's civil war, Esther Hill Hawks' diary. Edt: Gerald Schwartz." Columbia: University of South Carolina Press, 1984, 8vo, cl, dj, x, 301 pp. $18.00.

551 **HAWN, William**
"All Around the Civil War, or - Before & After." N.Y., Wynkoop Hallenbeck Crawford (1908), 8vo., cl., 58pp. ($5.00, $8.50, $10.00, $12.50) with 7th La. Reg., CSA 50-30. Why South seceded.

552 **HAWTHORNE, Hildegarde**
"Matthew Fontaine Maury Trail Maker of the Seas." N.Y., Toronto: Longmans, Green Co., 1943, 12mo., cl., dj., v., (2)226pp. $8.50.

553 **HAWTHORNE, J.B., Rev.**
"The Courage of the Confederate Soldier." In: SHSP, 1881, v.9, p.36-38.

554 **HAY, David & Joan**
"The Last of the Confederate Privateers." (N.Y.) Crescent Books-Division of Crown Pub. Co., (1977)(Scolar Press, Ilkley - G.B.) 8vo., cl., facsms., illus., maps, ports., incl. front., x, 178pp. $6.00. (Dj) 15, Bmk III 20, 25-Bmk.

555 **HAY, Thomas Robson**
"The Atlanta Campaign." in Ga. Hist. Quart., Mar. & June, 1923, v.VII, p.19-43, 99-118, map. $6.50.

556 ..."The Battle of Spring Hill." In: Tenn. Hist. Mag., VII, #2, July 1921, (issued May 1923) p.74-91. Briefed from his "ts Hood's Tenn. Campaign." 8.

557 ..."Davis, Bragg, & Johnston in the Atlanta Campaign." In Ga. Hist. Quart. v.8, #1, Mar. 1924, p.38-48. $6.00 10. Also: as a separate pamphlet, wraps. cover title, $7.50.

558 ..."The Battle of Chattanooga." In Ga. Hist. Quart., VIII, #2, June 1924, p.121-141. Also: 8vo., wraps, 21pp. pamphlet $7.50. 15.

559 ..."Braxton Bragg & the Southern Confederacy." as contained in Savannah: Ga. Hist. Quart., Dec. 1925, v.9, #4, 44pp., p.267-316. $6.00
..."Published also as an off-print. $25.00

560 ..."The Campaign & Battle of Chickamauga." as contained in Ga. Hist. Quart., Sept. 1923. p.213-250. p.38. 8-15. $6.00.

561 ..."The Cavalry at Spring Hill." In: Ga. Hist. Quart., VIII, #2, June 1924, p.121-141. Also: 8vo., wraps, 21pp. pamphlet $7.50. 15.

562 ..."The Confederate Leadership at Vicksburg." In: Miss. Valley Hist. Rev., March 1925, v.XI, p.543-560 (off print 15-)

563 ..."The Davis-Hood-Johnston Controversy of 1864." In: Miss. Valley Hist. Review, XI, June 1924, p.54-84.

564 ..."Gazaway Bugg Lamar, Confederate Banker & Business Man." In: Ga.H.Q., June 1953, v.XXXVII, #2, p.89-128, port.

565 ..."Hood's Tennessee Campaign." N.Y., Walter Neale, 1929, 8vo., cl., maps (front., 2-fldg.) xv, (17) -272pp. $18.50, $22.50, 30, 40. 200-Pres. 125, 100 Bmk 123, 105. 75 Bmk 84, $17.50 20Y Dayton: Morningside, 1976. Rec'd. Johnson Mil. prize by AHA as outstanding work.

566 ..."Jefferson Davis once more." In: South Atlan. Quart., Oct. 1924, p.362-276.

567 ..."Joseph Emerson Brown, Governor of Georgia, 1857-1865." In: Ga. Hist. Quart., June 1929, v.XIII, p.89-109. Bmk $8.00.

...Co-author, see under following: Buck (Irving Ashby -"Cleburne & his Command.", Sanger (Donald Bridgman) -"Jas. Longstreet."

568 ..."Lucius B. Northrop: Commissary General of the Confederacy." In: CWH, March 1963, v.IX, #1, p.5-23, vign.

569 ..."The South & the Arming of Slaves." In: Miss. Valley Hist. Rev. June, 1919, v.VI, p.34-73.

570 **HAY, W.C., Pvt.**
"Reminiscences of the War by... in letters to the children of Cuthbert, Ga." and,

571 ..."Story of the Soldier's Home" by Hugh H. Colquitt. (Atlanta, Ga.?) 1920. 12mo., wraps (port. on cover) same as t/p, 44pp, ports., illus.

572 **HAYDEN, Clara Ryder**
"Confederate Postwar Organizations & history of Anna Jackson Chapter, UDC." (Tallahassee, 1896-1947) In: Apalachee, 1948-1950, p.71-79.

573 **HAYDEN, Horace Edwin**
"A Refutation of Charges made against the CSA having authorized use of explosives & poisoned musket & rifle balls during the late civil war, 1861-1865." Richmond, Va., G.W. Gary Print, 1879, 8vo., wraps, 13pp. 45-OB

574 ..."Explosive or poisoned musket or rifle balls - were they authorized & used by the Cs army, or by the Us army during the civil war? A slander refuted." In: SHSP, 1880, v.VIII, p.18-28.

575 ..."The First Maryland Cavalry, CSA." In: SHSP, 1878, v.V, p251-253.

576 ..."How Many Confederate Towns did the enemy burn during the war?" In: SHSP, 1882, v.X, p.92-93.

577 ..."The Maryland Line." In: SHSP, 1881, v.IX, p.254-257

578 **HAYDN, Ruff**
"Pine Mountain Americans." N.Y., Hobson Book Print, 1947, Tall 8vo., cl., illus., map, 110pp. $12.50y. Acct. of "Ballard Gang" in Pine Mt., district, Faulkner Co., Ark. in the war.

579 **HAYDON, Frederick S.**
"Aeronautics in the Union & Confederate Armies." N.Y., Arno Pub., 1980 reprint. $45.00.

580 **HAYDON, Frederocl Stansbury**
"Aeronautics in the Union & Confederate Armies. With a survey of military Aeronautics prior to 1861." Balt.: Johns Hopkins Pr., 1941. 8vo., cl., illus., ports. (45 pls) 421pp. v.1 (all pub.) $15.00, $20.00, $22.50. 125- 100- 75-Bmk. 45.

581 ..."First attempts at Military Aeronautics in the U.S." In: Amer. Mil. Hist. Found. Journ., 1938, v.II, p.131-138. Largely period of 1835-1861.

582 ..."Confederate Railroad Battery at Jacksonville, Fla., Mar. 1863, not the first use of railroad ordnance in U.S." In: Amer. Mil. Hist. Found. Journ., 1938, v.II, p.229-234.

583 **HAYES, A.A. (Augustus Allen)**
"The New Mexican Campaign of 1862." Magazine of American History, Feb. 1886, p.171-184.

584 **HAYES, D.J.**
"Civil War Military & Naval Engagements in the State of Texas." Houseton: (D.J. Hayes), 1961, wraps, 8vo., p.8, map.

585 **HAYES, J.D.**
"Lee Against the Sea." In: "Shipmates", June 1957, p.9. Influence of naval in Peninsula Campaign. See also, Robt. W. Daly's "Merrimac".

586 **HAYES, Merwin A.**
"William L. Yancey presents the Southern Case to the North: 1860." In: Southern Speech Journ., 1964, v.XXIX, p.194-208.

587 **HAYNE, Isaac William**
"To the People of the South, Senator Hammond, & the Tribune, Tract #3." 24., 8vo., cover. Turnbull attributes this to Hayne, see v.III, p.306. Sabin-97064, to Hammond (James Hamilton - should be Jas. Henry). a more likely candidate. Another edition has title, but without imprint or date. 10.

588 ..."Correspondence between Isaac W. Hayne & the President, relating to Fort Sumter." Charleston: Evans & Cogswell, 1861, 8vo., wraps, 17pp. (McKissick - 1103)

589 **HAYNE, Paul Hamilton**
"The Defense of Fort Wagner." In: South. Bivouac., Mar. 1886, p.599-608.

590 ..."My Impression of General Robert Edward Lee." In: SB, ns, v.1, #9, p.535-542, port. Largely impressions by Henry W. Cleveland of notes dictated by him, while governor of Georgia. Never previously published.

591 ..."The Broken Battalions.: (Baltimore, Md., 1885) 16mo., wraps, 4p., 1, 5-9 numb.1. Composed for the Confederate relief bazaar of Maryland. Baltimore April 7 to 11, 1885. In verse.

592 ..."Confederate War Songs." In: SB, ns, v.1, 1885/1886. p.35-43.

593 ..."M.M.S. of volume first of work entitled "Politics of South Carolina, F.W. Pickens' Speeches, reports, etc." (Columbia, S.C., c.1865) 8vo., sheets (unbound), uncut, (1), 104pp., (CSA imprint, 1864) incomplete? $85.00.

594 ..."The Southern Dilemma: two unpublished letters of...Edt: Richard Beale Davis." In: JSH, Feb. 1951. v.17:64-70pp. Notes. To: Horatio Woodman, 5 July, 1860 & Daniel J. Wilkinson, 1 Aug., 1878.

595 ..."A Southern Genteelist: Letters by Paul Hamilton to Julia C(aroline) R(ipley) Dorr." Edt.: Charles Duffy. (Charleston: So. Caro. Hist. & Genea. Mag. April, 1951-Jan. 1952), v.LII, p.65-73; 154-165, 207-217; v.LIII, p.19-30.

596 ..."A Confederate View of the Southern Poets." Edt: Richard Barksdale Harwell. Amer. Lit., Mar., 1952, v.XXIV, p.51-61. 12.

597 **HAYNES, Draughton Stith**
"The Field Diary of a Confederate Soldier..., while serving with the army of Northern Virginia, CSA." Darien, Ga., Ashantilly press, 1963, 12mo, cl, front (mounted port), ill. maps, xx, 44, (1) pp. (Ashantilly leaflets, ser. II, regional history #3. $10 - Edition of 400 copies.

598 **HAYNIE, Mariam**
"The trunk. "In: Va. & the Va. county, Aug. 1953 v.7, #8, p. 14, 37-38. Two letters to her from R. Morris Dawson, CS Army, in Va., 1862/1863. From Maryland to Amanda Bell Leonard.

599 **HAYS, Harry T., Brig.Gen.**
"Report: The Gettysburg Campaign." In: SHSP, 1880, v. 8, p. 230-234....Original photograph. New Orleans: Washburn (c.1865) CDV albumen print. (Jk-169) $450

600 ..."Gettysburg." In: SHSP, 1880, v. 8, p. 230-234.

601 **HAYS, John Bowen**
"An incident of the battle of Shiloh." In: Tenn. Hist. Mag., 1925, v. IX, p. 264-265.

602 **HAYS, Will S.**
"I'm Looking For Him Home." A Beautiful Ballad Written, Composed by Will S. Hays. Louisville, Ky., (1862) One of many ballads of little popularity and soon forgotten.

603 **HAYTHORNTHWAITE, Philip J.**
"Uniforms of the Civil War 1861-1865. Color illustrations by Michael Chappell. (heading: 'Macmillan Color Series.) N.Y., Macmillan pub. (1975) printed Great

Britain, 1st American Edt (1976), 12 mo, dj, 192 pp., 64 color pls. 1/2 CDS, $7.

604 HAYWARD, W. Stephen
"The Black Angel: a Tale of the American Civil War." London: n.d., (c. 1871) 12 mo, pict. boards, 404 p. $7.50 $15-

605 ..."Star of the South: a sequel to the "Black Angel", by the author of "The Black Angel", etc. London: n.d., (c. 1865) - 360 pp. 12 mo, pict. boards, 308 pp. $15-
... Same, New Edt., London: Bryce, 1862 Confederate fiction. (also: 1864, p. iv, 380.

606 ..."Fiery Cross. A Tale of the Great American War." London: C.H. Clarke (1862) (1868) 12 mo, cl, vi, 340 pp.

607 ..."The Rebel Privateer; or, the last cruise of the Black Angel." London: C.H. Clarke (1874)? 12 mo. cl, vi 340 pp.

608 HAYWARD, Walter Brownell
"Civil war incidents. "In: Seven Seas, April, 1916, v. II, p. 21-22. Piratical operations of CSA: John C. Braine & his company of adventurers who captured 2 Amer. passenger ships, taking to British ports.

609 HAYWOOD, Philip Drayton
"The Cruise of the Alabama. With Notes from historical authorities...by One of the Crew. Riverside paper series - #20 Boston: Houghton Mifflin, 1886. 12 mo, decr. wraps, map, fldg - map, ill. Riverside Paper Series #20, June 26, 1886. 150 pp., 12 pp. - ads ($30 -) $7.50
Do: Liverpool, 1863. Cl, 8vo, 48 pp. port wraps. Howe - 4696 $28.50
Do: "Our Cruise in the Confederate States War Steamer Alabama. The Private Journal of an Officer." Capetown (Africa) 1863. 8vo, 64 pp, Sabin 57916.
Do: reprint, n.p., 1864. Cl, 8vo, 56 pp.

610 ..."Aboard the Alabama." In: CWTI, Oct. 1969, v. VIII, #6, p. 4-9, 45-48, ill. map. A reprint of Century Mag., March 1887 and later disallowed by the editor, after book was declared a hoax by Jno. M. Kell. See: Norman C. Delaney.

611 HAZELTON, John W.
"Descriptive Catalogue of Confederate Notes & Bonds, for sale by..." Philadelphia, Pa., 1876. 8vo, wraps, priced, 36 pp. $3.50

612 HAZELWOOD, Martin William, Capt.
"The Gettysburg Charge." In: SHSP, 1895 v. 23, p. 229-237.

613 ..."The Roll of Co.A., 15th Virginia Regt. In: SHSP, 1894, v. 22, p. 48-54

614 HAZLETT, James C.
"The Confederate Napoleon Gun." In: Mil. Coll. & Hist., 1964. p. 104-110.

615 HAZLETT, James C. - Edwin Olmstead & M. Hume Parks
"Field artillery weapons of the Civil War. With foreword by Harold L. Peterson." Newark: University of Delaware pr, (1983) 4to, cl, dj, 322 pp., drawings, ill. $20-

616 HAZZARD, William Miles, Capt.
"Raid on St. Simon's Island." In: SHSP, 1881, v. 9, p. 282-283.

617 HEAD, J.D.
"Albert Pike," In: So. Mag., Winter 1935-1936, v. II, #4, p. 16-19, 46-47. Biog. sketch.

618 HEAD, Thomas Anthony
"Campaigns & battles of the Sixteenth regiment, Tennessee Volunteers, in the War Between the States, with incidental sketches of the part performed by other Tennessee troops in the same war, 1861-1865." 12 mo, cl, ill., ports, 488 pp. 12 mo, cl, ill. ports, 488 pp., errata slip. Nashville: Cumberland Presbyterian Publ. House, 1885 $27.50, $35.00, $45.00
...McMinnville, Ten: Womack Pr., 1961, reprint, with Intro: Stanley F. Horn. 8vo, cl, (5), 488 pp., ill. on endsheets, pls. ports.

619 **HEADLEY, John W.**
"The Secret Service of the Confederacy." In: Photo. Hist. C.W., v.8, p.285-304., illus., ports.

620 **HEADLEY, John William**
"Confederate Operations in Canada & New York." Wash., N.Y., Neale pub., 1906. 8vo, cl, ports, incl. front, xv, (19)-480 pp. $25, $35, $40, $45, $75, $80, $125.

621 ..."Headquarters-Department of Texas. General Order No. 2. Houston, January 13, 1862." Houston (1862) 8vo, 1 p. broadside Undescribed CSA Imprint. $12.50.

622 **HEADSPETH, William Carroll**
"Halifax Volunteers in the Confederate Army. News Ferry & Clover Troops at Rich Mountain. Original Muster rolls of eleven Halifax Companies. (Virginia)" "Westbury? Long Island, N.Y., 1939?) 8vo, wraps, cover title, ill. port, map, 28 pp.

622a ..."Halifax Volunteers . . ." South Boston, Va., The Author, 1982. 8vo, wraps, 56pp, ills. $10. Brief unit histories & co. rosters. (Rowe).

623 ..."The Battle of Staunton River Bridge." South Boston, Va., 1949. 8vo, wraps, ill. 30 pp. Bmk-104 $25-

624 **HEAGNEY, Anne**
"Charity goes to war." Milwaukee: Bruce Pub., (1961) 12 mo, cl, dj, sketches, vii, (1) 145 pp. Sister Euphemia of Emmitsburg, Md., ministers to wounded, on both sides, during war. Fiction based on facts.

625 **HEAGNEY, H.J.**
"Blockade Runner, a Tale of Adventure aboard the Robert E. Lee." N.Y., Toronto, Longmans, Green, 1939 12 mo, cl, ill. 187, (1) p. "Some historical Sources," 1st. edt. Fict. Reprint (1943); & 1952 (wraps)

626 ..."Chaplain in Gray Abram Ryan. Poet-Priest of the Confederacy." N.Y., P.J. Kennedy (1958) 12 mo, cl, d/w, 190 pp. ill., fiction $2.50

627 ..."Recollections of Father Ryan." In: Cath. World, Jan. 1928, v. CXXVI, p. 497-504.

628 **HEARD, G.D.**
"Confederate dead, Cemetery, Covington, Ga." In: CV, v. 6, p. 9-10. plate.

629 **HEARD, George Alexander**
"St. Simons Island during the War Between the States." In: Ga. H.W., Sept., 1938, #3, p. 249-272. $8-

630 **HEARD, S.S., Col.**
"Letter from: Battle of Shiloh." In: SHSP, 1879, v. 7, p. 44-45.

631 **HEARTMAN, Charles F.**
"What Constitutes a Confederate Imprint? Preliminary Suggestions for Bibliographers & Catalogers." Hattiesburg, Miss., The Book Farm, Jan., 1939. 250 copies printed. Large 8vo, cover title, 8 pp. 50-Bmk-105 $3-

632 **HEARTSILL, William Williston**
"Fourteen hundred & 91 days in the Confederate Army, a journal kept by W.W. Heartsill, for four years, one month, & one day, or, camp life, day by day of the W.P. Lane Rangers, from April 19, 1861, to May 20th, 1865." (Marshall, Texas, 1876) $7500-G, JK(140-976) $6500 8vo, cl, (5), 264, (1) pp. mounted cabinet photos, unnumbered, in addition to pgs. 65 photos. (number may vary) $1,800-, $225, $275, $1,000 (Mor.) $10,000-bmk.
...Louisv: Lost Cause pr, micro-cd (1957)
...Jackson, Tenn., McCowat-Mercer., 1954, cl, dj, xxiv, 332-336, $40.00y

633 ...Wilmington, NC, 1988. 336 pages. Limited MS Edition. Original MS page tipped in.
...Review by Robert B. Brown, in papers Bibliog. Soc. of Amer., 1950, v. 41, p. 373-8, Rev: So. West. Hist. Quart., LVIII, p. 571 See: John H. Jenkins and Arthur M. Shaw.

634 **HEASLET, J.G.**
"Civil War Experiences of a Benton

County Youth." In: Benton CP, Jan. 1958, v.3, p.3-9.

635 **HEATER, Jacob**
"Battle of the Wilderness." In: CV, June 1906, v. XIV, p. 262-264.

636 **HEATH, Allan W.**
"Lieut.Gen. James Longstreet" In: NGJ, 1984, Summer v.1, p.52-59.
..."Lieut-Gen. James Longstreet." In: GL, v.4, #3, p.15-16+.

637 **HEATH, Gary N.**
"The First Federal Invasion of Indian Territory." Oklahoma City: Chron. Okla. Winter 1966-1967, v. XLIV, #4, p. 409-419
See: William J. Willey.

638 **HEATHCOTE, Charles William**
"The decade of compromise (1850-60) West Chester, Pa., State teachers college, Dept. Social Studies (1940) 8vo, cl, 106 pp.

639 **"HEBE SKIRMISH Centennial**
And the Fort Fisher Visitor Center-Museum ground-breaking program, Aug. 24, 1963, The." 8vo, wraps, ill., port, (20) pp. Hebe (steamship), naval operations, shipwrecks, excavations archaeology.

641 **HEBRON, Ellen E.**
"Songs of the South." Baltimore: Eugene R. Smith, 1875
16 mo, cl, 245 pp., (1) errata. Longest poem: "Cornelia-Romance of the War." (119 pp. Mar. 1868) $10-

642 **HECHT, Arthur**
"Confederate Postal Records in the National Archives." In: Ga. H.Q., June 1961, v. XLV, #2, p. 186-189.

643 **HECK, Frank H.**
"John C. Breckinridge in the Crisis of 1860-1861." (Lexington, Ky.) JSH, August 1955, v. XXI, #3, p. 316-346.

644 **HECK, John H.**
"Proud Kentuckian: John C. Breckinridge, 1821-1875." Louisville: University Press of Kentucky, Bicentennial Bookshelf Series, 1976 8vo, cl, dj, 172 pp. 5- $4.00

645 **HEFFERNAN, John B.**
"The Blockade of the Southern Confederacy: 1861-1865." In: Smithsonian Jour. Hist., 1967-1968, v. II, p. iv, 23-44.

646 **HEFLIN, John A., Jr.**
"Postal System of the Confederate States Army." (London) Jour. Confed. Hist. Soc., Summer, 1966, v. 4, #2, p. 54-74, pl.

647 **HEFLIN, John L., Jr.**
"Postmaster General John Reagan." (London) Jour. Confed. Hist. Soc., Dec. 1964, v. II, #4, p. 163-166, port.

648 **HEFLIN, W.P.**
"Blind man on the warpath" Co. D., Mississippi regiment. n.p., n.d. (Chicago: Stern & co, 1902) 8vo, wraps, ill., ports, 96 pp. "Dictated by the author, written by Miss. Annette Batson."

649 **HEGARTY, Lela Whitton**
"Father Wore Gray." San Antonio, Texas: Naylor co. (1963)
8vo, cl, dj, xii, (12), 205 pp., ill., ports, facsm. $7.50

650 **HEIDT, Amelia Arnold**
"Abram J. Ryan (1838-1886), poet-patriot of the South." In: UDC Mag. Dec. 1948, v. 11, #12, p. 16-18. view. Largely on poems concerning the war.

651 **HEITE, Edward F.**
"Captain Robert B. Pegram: Hero Under Four Flags." (Richmond) Va. Cavl., Autumn 1965, v. XV, #2, p. 38-43, ports, ill.

652 ..."Extra Billy Smith a beloved & eccentric governor met difficult challenges with unusual solutions." (Richmond) Va. Cavl., Winter 1966, v. XV, #3, p. 4-13, ports, diagr., ill., 1-color, facsm. Subject-Gen. William Smith in CSA. See: Memoirs by Bell (Jno. W.)

653 ..."Judge Robert Ould, his struggle for justice continued long after war was over."

(Richmond) Va. Cavl., Spring 1965, v. XIV, #4, p. 10-19, ports, ill. (1-color) Held respect of both Union & CSA.

654 **HELENA, ARKANSAS**
"The Attack on Helena, 4th of July battle to save Vicksburg. reported in the New York Sun, July 1896." In: SHSP, 1896, v. 24, p. 197-200.

655 **HELM, Benjamin Hardin, Gen.**
"Sketch of B.H. Helm." In: Land We Love, 1867, v. III, p. 163-167. By: --Bedford, KY.

656 **HELM, Charles J.**
"Letter on the Blodkade(sic) & Rights of Neutrals, to his Excellency the Captain General, Don Francisco Serrono, Superior Governor of Cuba." n.p., n.d. (Havana, December 5, 1861) 8vo, wraps, 15 pp. (Sabin-3259 give pages as 19) Helm was Cs agent in Havana & giver here a survey of International law concerning neutrals *present conflict to Spanish, English & Danish possessions in the West Indies.

657 **HELMS, Roy**
"Essays on Robert E. Lee & 'Stonewall' Jackson." Amelia, Va., Oct. 1933. 4to., 35 mimeographed sheets.

658 **HEMELRYCK, P.E.J.**
"Forty years reminiscences of the cotton market; the American war time & after." Liverpool, Eng., Rockliff Bros., 1916 8vo, wraps, 28 pp.
Writer, a member of Liverpool cotton ass'n.

659 **HEMMER, Joseph J., Jr.**
"The Charleston, S.C., platform debate of the 1860 Democratic National Convention in rhetorical-historical perspective." In: Quart. Jour. Speech, Dec. 1970, p.406-416.

660 **HEMMING, Charles C.**
"Biographical Sketch of..." In: SHSP. 1899, v. 27, p. 129-131.
..."A Confederate Odyssey (Jacksonville reference) In: Amer. Heritage, Dec. 1984, v.36, p.60-85.

661 **HEMPHILL, M. Clifford**
"Dead, but Sceptered Sovereigns. Confederate Virginians who died on Johnson's Island, Lake Erie, 1862-1865." (Richmond) Va. Cavl., Summer, 1958 v. VIII, #1, p. 36-41, ill. (1-color).

662 **HEMPHILL, W. Edwin**
"Bibles through the blockade." In: Commonwealth (Va.) Aug. 1949, v. 16, #8, p. 9-12, 30-32. bibliog., (Reprint: Presby. sur., Dec. 1949, v. 549-551, 581-582. Rev. Wm. James Hoge moves bibles from England to CSA forces, 1861-1863. Photos of 11 gravestones of Virginians.

663 **HEMPHILL, W.A., Col.**
"Colonel W.A. Hemphill." In: CV, 1902, v. 10, p. 373-374, port. Confederate officer & journalist.

663a **"HEMPSTEAD County** in the Civil War. 1861-1865, part 1." In: Hempstead Co. Hist. Soc., v.11, Spring 1987. Entire issue, p.1-40, illus, ports, facsms. Roster Hempstead Rifles. 4to, stiff wraps. Largely letters: Arkansas. $6.

664 **HENAGAN, Mary Rhodes**
"Reminiscences of Mary Rhodes Henagan." Suffolk, Va., Robt. Hardy Pub., 1986. 8vo., wraps, 8pp.

665 **HENDERSON, Daniel Sullivan**
"A call to the Confederate Survivors & to their descendants! Annual address before the Confederates' reunion of the South, delivered at Chattanooga, Tenn., May 22, 1913, by Daniel S. Henderson." n.p., (1913) 8vo, wraps, cover title, 19 pp.

666 ..."Address of..., at the unveiling of the Palmetto monument at the national park, Chickamauga, May 17, 1901."
Aiken, S.C., Journal & Review press, 1901 8vo, wraps, 12 pp.

667 ..."Aftermath of the Confederacy & Duty of the South. An address delivered at Greenwood, S.C., at the reunion of Confederate veterans of South Carolina, July

25, 1919.
n.p., (1919) 12 mo, wraps, 11 pp/ Turnbull-V, 182

668 **HENDERSON, Don E., Judge**
"General Hood's Brigade." In: SHSP, 1901, v. XXXIX, p. 185-200.

669 **HENDERSON, Edward Prioleau**
"Autobiography of Arab." (Columbia, S.C., R.L. Bryan co, 1901) 12 mo, cl, front.port, 170 pp. (Dorn-II) (Turnbull-IV, p. 425, gives 210 pp, 8vo)

670 **HENDERSON, G.F.R.**
"The Campaign of Fredericksburg, Nov.-Dec., 1862, a tactical study for officers." Falls Church, Va., Confederate printers. $17.00.

671 ..."Review of Gen. James Longstreet's Book" n.p., n.d., 1896? 8vo., wraps, 12pp. $50.00-ob.

672 **HENDERSON, George Francis Robert, Lt.Col.**
"First Lecture on the American Civil War, 1861-1865. The composition, organization, system, & tactics of the Federal & Confederate Armies." (Aldershot Military Society, #XXXVI, Feb. 9, 1892.) London: Gale & Polden, 1892.

673 ..."Second lecture on the American Civil War, 1861-1865. A resume of some of the principal events of the war, illustrative of the strategy & tactics of the belligerents." (Aldershot Military Society, #XXXVII, Feb. 16, 1892)
London: Gale & Polden, 1892

674 ..."The Science of War A collection of essays & lectures 1891-1903. By the late ..., Edt: Capt. Neill Malcolm, DSO. With a Memoir of the Author by Field Marshal Earl Roberts, VC. with a portrait, 4-maps N.Y., Bombay., Longmans, Green co, 1905, xxxvii, 442 pp., 8vo, cl, 65-JK129, 125-B $17.50
pp. 187-337 devoted to the civil war.

675 ...Same, 1906, 2nd impression. $12.00 (1909, 25-Bmk, $10-); Other edts: 1908-$60; 1912-$26; 1913, 1916 & 1919-$12.

676 ..."The Civil War: a Soldier's View. A collection of Civil War writings., edited by Jay Luvaas." Chicago, 1958, Univ. of Chicago pr. 8vo, cl, dg, illus., maps (1-fld) plans, xi, 323 Pub: $6, $8.50; $10-, $13.50Y, $17.50, $25 Bmk

677 ..."The Campaign of Fredericksburg, Nov-Dec., 1862. A tactical study for officers." By a Staff Officer. London: Keagan print, 1886 (1st Edt) 12 mo, cl, fldg. maps, xx, 145 pp. $65, $75, Bmk-105 $150

678 ..."Campaign of Fredericksburg. A study for officers of volunteers, by a Line Officer." 2nd edt.
London: 1888 $100-Bmk, $125-Bmk, $90-KC
...London: Chatham, Gale & Polden, (1891) 3rd Edt., with colored maps. 12 mo, cl, 2-pls, 4-maps (part fold), xviii, 145 pp. G.F.R. Henderson has name and 82 pp.-ads & indes on t.p. with the 3rd edt. $90-Bmk.
Same; 1892, 3rd edt. $40.00
...(Aldershot, n.d. (c. 1905), 147 pp., $38.50; with 3rd edt.
Note: a copy reported as having 145 pp. with an additional 36 pp., $60.00 A 3rd edt., $38.50 & $45.00

679 ..."Letter from Col. Henderson to Capt. Fred. M. Colston." In: SHSP, 1915, v. 40, p. 305-306. Re Henderson's review of Longstreet's book, "From Manassas to Appomattox." In: SHSP, April, 1914, v. XXXIX, p. 104-117

680 ..."Stonewall Jackson & the American Civil War. By Lt.Col. G.F.R. Henderson, Major, the York & Lancaster Regiment; Professor of Military Art & History, the Staff College author-: The Battle of Spicheren, "A Tactical Study", & "The Campaign of Fredericksburg", in Two

Volumes." London, N.Y., Bombay: Longmans, Green & co., Spottiswoode print, 1898 Large 8vo, cl, ports, maps, illus., I-xiv, 550, 32(ads); II-4, 641 pp. 21-fldg. maps $30, $35-cloth, $37.50, 3/4 Mor. $50.00 Fine 80-Y $50

...April 1899, 2nd Edt., with added 14 pp. introduction by Field Marshal-the Right Hon. Viscount Wolseley $20.00

...2 vol.Crown 8vo, editions: Apr. 1900, Oct. 1902, $65-B, Mar. 1903, Mar. 1904, Jan. 1905, Sept. 1906 $40-$35 Bmk-84, 1906: 3/4 MOR-Nevin-sic(owned) 250 JK

...Aug. 1909, New Impression. 33 maps, (5-fold) $10, $15- $20.00

...Edts:July 1911/1913($17.50), Apr. 1927 ($12.50), June 1932.

...1936, "Authorized American Edition" in One Volume., xxiv, 737 pp., maps in text, with 5-maps in pocket. Same for 1927, 1943.

...n.d., Grosset & Dunlap, xix, 737 pp.

...June 1949, "History Book Club Edt." and same for 1955.

...Jan.1961, "Civil War Centennial War Edition", with a preface by Walter Bedell Smith, General U.S. Army, RTD. xxv, 737, 28-maps in text, 6-maps pocket.

...Greenwich, Conn., Fawcett Pubs., 1962 The Civil War in paperbacks, $.75

...Gloucester, Mass., P. Smith, 1968 Into: E.B. Long (abridged. Maps(5) in pocket. $10-, $12-

681 ..."The Campaign in the Wilderness of Virginia." Jan. 24, 1894. London: H.Rees ltd., 1908 12 mo, cl, 4-fldg. maps, 40 pp. JK(142) $65-, Bmk(105) $150- One of a lecture(the other on Gettysburg) in his "Science of war." chap. XI, p. 307-37.

682 **HENDERSON, Harry McCorry, Col.**
"Texas in the Confederacy." San Antonio, Texas: Naylor co, (1955) 12 mo, cl, dj, xv, 166 pp. $7.50, $8.75, $37.50, $20-Bmk, $25-Bmk, $90-Bmk.

683 ..."History of the 141st infantry, 36th infantry, Texas National Guard." San Antonio, Texas: Naylor co, (1950), 8vo, cl, fldg.pl, facsm, color front, x, 71 pp. The 1st & 2nd Texas Inf., in civil war.

684 ..."Hood's Texas Brigade."
(Houston, Texas, Civil War Round Table. Address Feb. 2, 1955 8 1/2X11, heavy paper covers, folded to 8vo., 10pp. Also: p. 1-50 pp., 'Tex. in the CSA.'

685 ..."Walker's Texas division." In: his 'Tex. in the CSA." San Antonio: Naylor Co, 1955. p. 51-68

686 ..."26th Texas Cavalry(DeBray's regiment) In: Tex. in CSA...

687 **HENDERSON, Henry Ebenezer**
"Yankee in Gray, the Civil War Memoirs of Henry E. Henderson, with a selection of his wartime letters. A biographical introduction by Clyde Lottridge Crummer." (Cleveland) Western Reserve Univ. (1962) tall 8co., cl., dj., front (port.), facsm., port., vii, 132pp. $6.50, $10.00. 30 - Bmk 97 $12.50.

688 **HENDERSON, Lillian**
"Roster of the Confederate Soldiers of Georgia 1861-1865." 6 volumes. (Hapeville, Ga., Longino & Porter, 1959-1964.) compiled for the State of Georgia by Lillian Henderson, Dir. Confederate Pension & Record Department.
v. 1, 1st-9th Regiments x, 1068 pp.
v. 2, 10th-23rd " xi, 1082 pp.
v. 3, 24th-36th " xi, 1013 pp.
v. 4, 37th-46th " xi, 1026 pp.
v. 5, 47th-57th " xi, 1023 pp.
v. 6, 59th-66th " x, 818 pp.
Note: The 58th Reg. Ga. Inf., failed to complete organization. See: Allan D. Canner & report Ga. Soldiers. $50.00 $125.00 Bmk. Index volume, 532 pp. $30-
Spartanburg, SC, The Reprint Co., 1983
Roster of CSA Soldiers of Ga., 1861-1865. Easley, S.C., Southern Hist. Pub. 1964,

8vo., 6vols., $17.50 ea. Index:1982, $30.00. Author, Juanita S. Brightwell.

689 **HENDERSON, Lindsey P., Jr.**
"The Oglethorpe Light Infantry-A Military History-Confederate War Series-The Civil War Centennial Commission of Savannah & Chatham County." n.p.(c.1961) (Savannah, Ga.?) 8vo, wraps, illus., ports, front, 57, (1) pp. ATG $20-, $15- Bmk.

690 **HENDERSON, Lizzie George**
"Private Letters of Mrs. Humphreys, written immediately before & after the ejection of her husband from the executive mansion." (Oxford, Miss., Miss. Hist. Soc. Pubs. 1900, v.III, pp. 99-106. (Reconstruction)

691 **HENDERSON, Mildred Lee**
"January's 'Stonewall' Jackson". In: W. Va. Rev., Jan., 1939, p. 123. Org. in 1895, of record-keeping Stonewall Brigade members, orig. officers Allegheny Rifles, Co. A, 27th Regiment.

692 **HENDERSON, Paul**
"The Confederate blockade runners." In: USN Inst. Proc., 1933, v. LIX, p. 506-512.

693 **HENDERSON, W.O.**
"The Lancashire Cotton Famine, 1861-5" Manchester, Eng.: University pr., 1934 8vo., cl, xiv, 128 pp. Economic Hist. Ser., #IX. The famine not entirely caused by civil war but an overproduction in 1859-1860.

694 **HENDERSON, William**
"Family record of Henderson & Whidden families & their descendants with a Muster Roll of Co.G.; 14th Ga. Reg. Co. F., 57th Ga. Reg; Co. B., 10th Ga. batt., Co. F: 49th Ga. Reg., Co. A., 61st Ga. Reg. Co. F., 10th Ga. State Troops." (Ark. Univ.) Atlanta, Ga., Byrd Press, 1926 8vo, cl, 2p, 1(3), 314 pp. front(port)

695 **HENDERSON, William D.**
"12th Virginia Infantry." Lynchburg, Va., H.E. Howard, 1984, (J.P. Bell print) 1st, Atg. Lim. Edt., 857, 8vo., cl., dj. (3), 174pp., maps, ports. $17.50.

696 ..."41st Virginia Infantry." Lynchburg, Va., H.E. Howard, 1986. 8vo., cl., dj., (4), 154pp. 1,000 copies, numbered, signed.

697 **HENDRICK, Burton Jesse**
"The Lees of Virginia; Biography of a Family." Boston:Little, Brown co., 1935. $40-B 8vo, cl, front, pl, ports. fldg. geneal. table (v), xii, (8), 455 pp. 300 copies, autographed. ...N.Y., Halcyon House, (1937) $10.00

698 ..."Statesmen of the Lost Cause; Jefferson Davis & His Cabinet." Boston: Little, Brown co., 1939, Nov., 1st. 8vo, cl, dj, illus., incl. front, ports, xvii, 452 pp. $5 $7.50 $10.00 $20.00 Bmk ...N.Y., Literary Guild of Amer., (1939) ...Boston, (1944) $3.00 $5.00

699 **HENDRICKS, Sam**
"Military Operations in Jefferson County, Va. & W. Virginia, 1861-1865." n.p., 1911 Tall 8vo, cl, index, 43 pp. $5, $15-

700 ..."Memorial to Confederate Soldiers, Elmwood Cemetery, Shepherdstown, W. Va., unveiled Sept. 18, 1937." 8vo, wraps, cover title, illus., group port, color illus. on cover, 27 pp.

701 **HENDRICKS, Thomas Wayman**
"Cherished letters of..., compiled by Josie Armstrong McLaughlin." (Birmingham, Ala., 1947., Birmingham pub.co.,) 100 copies 8vo, plastic spiral-bound, facsm., 2-ports 104 pp. (Letters to wife, army-life, etc.) Co. "B", 12th Ala. Reg. of Cvlry. $45-OB, $14- GH, $12-

702 **HENKELS, Stan V.**
"Rare Confederate Books & Pamphlets & publications on Confederate History, to be sold May 16, 1913." Phila: Samuel T. Freeman & co, auctions. sm.4to, wraps(color flags) 41 pp., 2-pls, incl. front. $25- B'See: Jas. T. Mitchell.

702a **HENNESSY, John**
"The Fight for Henry Hill, Manassas, Va., July 21, 1861." In: Morningside Bookshop Catalogue #20, p.3-15, dbl. column, 4to. "The field manual for the use of the officer on ordnance duty. Prepared by the Ordnance Bureau." Richmond: Ritchie & Dunnavant,
...Dayton, Oh., Morningside Press, 1982. 8vo, cl, 176pp (incl. 32p photo suppl. index).

703 **HENNING, James W.**
"Basil Wilson Duke, 1838-1916, one of the founders of the Filson Club." In: FCHQ, April 1940, v. 14, #2, pp. 59-64, ports.

704 **HENRY, J. Milton**
"The Revolution in Tennessee, Feb. 1861 to June 1861." In: Tenn. HQ, June 1959, v. XVIII, pp. 99-119. notes.

705 **HENRY, Patrick**
"Adam's brigade in the Battle of Franklin." In: CV, Feb. 1913, v. XXI, p. 76-77

706 **HENRY, Robert S.**
"First with the most, Forrest..." $35.00. Westport, Ct., Greenwood Press, 1974.

707 **HENRY, Robert Selph**
"Chattanooga & the War." In: Tenn. Hist. Quart., 1960, v. XIX, pp. 222-230.

708 ..."As They Saw Forrest; some recollections & comments of contemporaries." Jackson, Tenn., McCowat-Mercer pr, 1956, 8vo, cl, dj, illus. ports, maps, facsms, xvi, 306 pp. $7.50, $15.00, $10- op, $50-B, $75-, Civil War Book Club-Atg. copy. Contains Witherspoon's "Reminsc. of Scout. Hubbard (J.M.), Dinkins (Jas.), Morton (J.W.), Rambaut (G.V.), Hughes (E)

709 ..."First With the Most" Forrest." Indianapolis, N.Y., Bobbs-Merrill co. (1944) 8vo, cl, dj, front, illus, ports, facsms, maps 558 pp. "First Edt." verso t/p. $10, $15, $22.50 $30-, $25, $40
...Sam: "Bedford Edition", on half-title, Lim & Signed by author, $75-, $40- Bmk, $37.50, $50, $25-, $60-
...1969 reprint, same, Jackson, Tenn., McM, New reprint, corrected, pict. sect of 24 pp. $27.50, $40-

710 ..."Railroads & the Confederacy." In: Railway & Locomotive Hist. Soc. Bul. #40, 1936, pp. 46-52. Also in: Ala. Rev., Jan. 1953, v. VI, pp. 3-13, notes. ATC $10-

711 ..."Story of the Confederacy." Indianapolis: Bobbs-Merrill (1931) "First Edt." 8vo, cl, dj, map endsheets, maps, ports (incl. frt.), illus. 514 pp. $47.50 ATC $15.00
...N.Y., Indp., Bobbs-Merrill co (1931-1936) Revised Edt. with a foreword by Douglas Southall Freeman." (8), 514 pp., (front port Lee, younger man than standing portrait of 1st Edt.) $25-
...Editions: 1943-"new & revised", & 1957. JK $122
...Gloucester, Mass., 1970 edt.
...Garden City, N.Y., Garden City Pub. Co, n.d. 8vo, cl, front(Lee) (dbl-pg. CSA uniforms)(6) pp, index, 11-514 pp.

712 **HENRY, Will (pseud.), Henry Allen**
"Journey to Shiloh." N.Y., Random House (1960)
12 mo, cl, 242 pp. (fiction) Texas recruits in the CsArmy.

713 **HENRY, William Wirt**
"Kenner's mission to Europe." In: Wm. & Mary Quar., July 1916, v. XXV, p. 9-12. Mssc. in LC, Henry reporting conversation with Duncan F. Kenner & his acct. of mission to England & France, in 1864-5, as special envoy from Jefferson Davis.

714 **HENSEL, William Uhler**
"Robert E. Lee, as a Citizen, soldier & statesman." Lancaster, Pa., New Era Print, 1909 8vo, wraps, 44 pp. bmk-$15.

715 **HENSHAW, F.R.**
"Stonewall Jackson & the engineers." In: Cana Defence Quart., Oct. 1925, v. III, p. 66-70.

716 **HENTY, G.A.**
"With Lee in Virginia: a story of the American Civil War."
London: Blackie & son; N.Y., Charles Scribner's sons. (1893) 12 mo, decr. gilt cl, illus. 4-maps (1-dbl.) vi, (2), (9) -384 pp.-ads. $10.00 Other edt: 1921, 1918, 1898.

717 **HERALD, A.M., Mrs.**
"Shiloh-the first great battle." In: CV, Sept. 1928, v. XXXVI, p. 335-337.

718 **HERBERT, Arthur**
"An address delivered by..., on the 15th Anniversary of the occupation of Alexandria by the Federal troops, May 24, 1861" (Washington, DC/.1911?) 8vo, wraps, cover title, 12 pp.

719 ..."The Seventeenth Virginia Infantry at Flat Creek & Drewry's Bluff." In: SHSP, v. XII, pp. 289-294.
..."Sketches & incidents of movements of the Seventeenth Virginia infantry, read before the R.E. Lee camp, C.V., Alexandria, Va., Washington, DC (1909?) 8vo, wraps, cover title, (2), 41 pp. Append: Gen. W. Merritt's Offic. Rep. of Manassas Gap fight; Extracts from Gen. Kautz's Rep. of Opr. on Richmond & Danville Rwy; Gen. Spear's Rep. of Flat Creek fight.

720 **HERBERT, Hilary Abner**
"Address at unveiling of Confederate Monument at Montgomery Alabama, on Capitol Hill, Dec. 7, 1898." In: SHSP, 1898 v. XXVI, pp. 215-219.

721 ...""History of the Arlington Confederate Monument by..., chairman of executive comm., of the Ass'n. c. U.D.C."
(Wash., D.C., B.S. Adams print, 1914) 8vo, cl, ports, illus, vii, (9) - 79 pp. $5.00
"History of the Eighth Alabama Volunteer Regiment, C.S.A. Edt: Maurice S. Fortin." In:AHQ, 1977, v.39, #1-4. 321pp.

722 **HERBERT, P.T.**
"A Card-Simeon Hart, of El Paso, Texas." April 28, 1862.
Attached Hart, horse-whipped in the street. Broadside. (Mor.) $175.00

723 **HERBERT, Walter**
"The Opening Guns of the Civil War." (Houston, Texas) Civil War Round Table. Address Nov. 3, 1954. 8 1/2x11, heavy paper covers, folded to 8vo, 9 pp.

724 **HEREFORD, Elizabeth J.**
"Rebel Rhymes & other poems." N.Y., Lond: G.P. Putnam's, 1888 12 mo, cl, vi, 78 pp. Dedicated to A.N. Va. $3.50

725 **HERGESHEIMER, Joseph**
"Swords & Roses." N.Y., Lond: Alfred A. Knopf, 1929 8vo, cl, dj, (7), (3) -327, (2) pp.
...Limited Edt., Japan Vellum, $75- $15- copies, boxed, signed $35.00
...(1931) edition, same trade edt.
...1972 edition $20-Y
...N.Y., Arno print, 1970 $19- "Essay Index Reprint Series."

726 **HERKLOTZ, Hildegarde Rose**
"Jayhawkers in Missouri, 1858-1863." (Columbia, Mo., Mo. Hist. Review, v. XVII, Apr.-July, 1923, pp. 266-284; 505-513; Oct. XVIII, pp. 64-101.

727 **HERMAN, Hortense**
"Rank & file of the Confederate armies. " In" CV, May 1914, v. XXII, p. 201-205.

728 **HERMANN, Isaac**
"A hard-hitting private in the War Between the States." Jacob Rader Marcus, Edt: Memoirs of American Jews., Phila: Jewish Pub. Soc. of Amer., 3 vols (1955) v. 3, p. 236-268. port, view. His service in Cs army, 1861-1865.

729 ..."Memoirs of a Veteran who served as a private in the '60's in the War Between the states. Personal incidents, experiences & observations, written by Capt...., who served in three branches of the Confederate Army." Atlanta, Ga., Byrd print, 1911. 8vo, cl, front(port), illus, 285 pp. $22.50,

$37-, $175-

...Louisv: Lost Cause pr., micro-cd, $4.88 Roster: Washington Rifles, Co. E, 1st, Ga. OP $15-

...Lakemont, Ga., (1974) CSA Press. 8vo, gray gilt stamp cl, dj, illus. $25-

...Atlanta, Ga., Educational Supply co., 1975 8vo, cl, 1,000 copies. $20-

730 **HERNDON, Dallas Tabor**
"Letters of David O. Dodd with Biographical Sketch." In: Pub. Ark. Hist. Assn., v. IV, 1917, pp. 152-169.

...(Little Rock: Arkansas Historical Comm.) sm. 4to, wraps, cover title, 16pp. reprint above.

731 ..."The Kie Oldham Papers. Documents." In: AHQ, Mar. 1942, v. 1, #1, p. 63-73. War period in Ark., Secession & War.

732 **HERNDON, George Melvin**
"The Confederate States Naval Academy" In: VMHB, July 1961, v.69, #3, p.300-323.

..."The Confederate States Naval Academy 1862-1865. In: VaMHB, July 1861, v. 69, p. 300-323, port, view rosters.

733 **HERNDON, John G.**
"Infantry & cavalry service." In: CV, May 1922, v. 30, #5, p. 172-177.

734 **HERNON, Joseph M., Jr.**
"British Sympathies in the American Civil War: A Reconsideration." (Houston, TEx.) JSH, Aug. 1967 v.XXXIII, #3, pp. 354-367. $8-

735 ..."Celts, Catholics & Copperheads: Ireland Views the American Civil War." Columbus: Ohio State University Press, 1968 8vo, cl, d/w, viii, 150 pp. Largest foreign class of both armies, their fears abolition would largely affect their economic well-being. The moderate nationalist supported secession, even a strong pro-south among unionist.

736 ..."The Irish Nationalists & Southern Secession." In: CWH, March 1966, v. XII, #1, p. 43-53.

737 ..."The Heroes of the Civil War, 1861-1865", Pub.: W. Duke Sons & Co.
See: Under publisher's name
See: Under Short History of..."

738 ..."Heroism & Adventure in the Nineteenth Century: as exemplified in the American Civil War." "H.S. April 1866 With numerous anecdotes, a map, & portraits. London: Warne & Co., 1867 12 mo, cl, g/e, viii, 264 pp. fldg. map, ports, frontis., sympathetic to South.

739 **HERRICK, Sophia Bledsoe**
"Personal recollections of my father, Albert Taylor Bledsoe, & Mr. Lincoln & Mr. Davis." In: Meth. Quar. Rev., Oct. 1915, v. LXIV, p. 665-679.

740 ..."Heroism of a Widow. General Schofield's Recognition of the bravery of a Southern woman." In: SHSP, 1895, v. XXIII, p. 328-329

741 **HERRING, Ethel & Carolee Williams**
"Fort Caswell in war & peace." Wendell, NC, Broadfoot's Bookmark 8vo, cl, illus, maps, charts, x, 148 pp. $15- On the lower Cape Fear, NC, civil war pp. 25-54.

742 **HERRINGTON, W.D.**
"The Deserter's Daughter." By W.D. Herrington, 3rd NC Cavalry, author. "The Refugee's Niece", "The Deserter's Daughter", etc., Raleigh, NC, William B. Smith, 1865, Southern Field & Fireside novelette, #3, New Series.

12 mo, wraps, 27 pp., plus ads. $25, $37.50

743 ..."The Captain's Bride, a tale of the War, by W.D. Herrington, 3rd NC Cavalry, author: "The Refugee's Niece, "The Deserter's Daughter", etc." Raleigh, NC, William B. Smith, 1864. Illustrated Mercury, Novelette, #1. 8vo, wraps, 22 pp.

...2nd Edt: Raleigh, 1865, "Southern Field & Fireside Novelette, #3, New Series. 12 mo, wraps, (above)

744 **HERRIOT, Robert**
"At Greensboro, N.C., in April 1865." In: CV, Mar. 1922, v. XXX, p. 101-102.

745 **HERZBERG, Heyman**
"Civil war adventure of a Georgia merchant Edt: Jacob Rader Marcus, in: Memoirs of Am Jews. Phila: Jewish Pub. soc. amer., 3 vols., 1955., v.3, p. 115-131 views. His brief service in Cs army, escape North, return to Ga., with smuggled goods, 2nd. escape North, with family, 1861-1863.

746 **HESS, Earl J.**
"Civilians at war: the Georgia Militia in the Atlanta Campaign." In: GHQ, Fall 1982, v. LXVI, #3, p. 332-345, notes.

747 ..."Confiscation & the Northern War Effort: the Army of the Southwest at Helena." In: ArkHQ, Spring 1985, v.XLIV, #1. p. 56-75.

748 **HESS, George**
"Battle-field Guide of the Battles of South Mountain & Antietam, Md. The Maryland Campaign from Sept. 1st to Sept. 20th, 1862. History & explanation of the battles of South Mountain, Md. Giving a brief account of the most important engagements of the Maryland Campaign; also an estimate of the forces engaged, & losses in the above-named battles. Compiled, written & illustrated by George Hess, Supt. Antietam National Cemetery, late of Co. I, 28th Regt., Pa Vet. Vol. Inf., 1890." Hagerstown: Globe Job Print, 1890. 8vo., wraps, 67, (3)pp., 2 fronts (ports.) illus., ports...Suffolk, Va., Robt. Hardy, 1986 (Cs & Fed. Report).

749 **HESSELTINE, William Best**
"Civil War Prisons; a study in war psychology." Columbus, Ohio: Ohio State univ, 1930 Contributions in Hist. & Pol. Sc, #12 8vo, cl, xi, 290 pp. NY 1978 $15, $50

750 ..."Arkansas' Confederate Leaders after the war," In: Ark. HQ, 1950, v. IX, p. (259)-269.

751 ..."Andersonville Revisited." In: GaHQ Spring, 1956, v. 10, pp. 91-100. Exaggerations of horrors of war & the "atrocity propagandists." by former prisoners with failing memories & irresponsible novelists. $10-

752 ..."Andersonville, Feb. 1864 - May 1865." In: Ga Rev., Spring, 1949, v. 3, p. 103-14.

753 ..."Confederate Leaders in the New South." (The Walter Lynwood Fleming Lectures in Southern History.) Baton Rouge: Louisiana Univ. pr. (1950) 12 mo, cl, dj, xi, 146, (1) pp.
...Westport, Conn., Greenwood pr (1970) reprint.
..."Confederate leaders in post-war Alabama." In: Ala. Rev., Jan 1951, v. 4, p. 5-21, notes.
..."Georgia's Confederate Leaders after Appomattox." In: Ga. H.Q., Mar. 1951, v. XXXV, #1, pp. 1-15. $10-

754 ..."Lyman Draper & the South." (Lexington, Ky.) JSH, Feb. 1953, v. XIX, #1, pp. 20-31.

755 ..."Mississippi's Confederate Leaders After the War." (Jackson, Miss., Jour. Miss. Hist., April, 1951, v. XIII, #2, pp. 88-100.

756 ..."The Propaganda Literature of Confederate Prisons." (Baton Rouge, La.) JSH., Feb., 1935, v. 1, #1. pp. 56-66. $8-

757 ..."Sherman Burns the Libraries." (Charleston: So. Caro. Hist. & Genea. Mag., July, 1954, v. LV, #3, pp. 137-142.

758 ..."Some new aspects of the pro-slavery argument." In: Journ. Negro Hist., 1936, v. XXI, p. 1-14. Contention that abolition movement in North precipitated South's turn to defend slavery.

759 ..."The South in American History." 2nd Edt. Englewood Cliffs, N.J., Prentice-Hall

(Feb. 1960) 2nd Printing, Feb., 1961. 8vo, cl, pp. X, 630. illus. ports, Originally published as: Hesseltine (William B.) - "A History of the South 1607-1936." (mostly on civil war, reconstruction. N.Y., Prentice-Hall (1936) 8vo, cl, xiii, 748 pp. A single volume synthesis of southern development, designed as manual for students. 1943 Edition, as above.

760 ..."Three Against Lincoln. Murat Halstead reports the Caucuses of 1860. Edt. with & into: by William B. Hesseltine." Baton Rouge: Louisiana State Univ. (1960) 8vo, cl, dj, xxxi, 321 pp. Reports Republican & Democratic conventions (& dissidents) Caucus system was inadequate, corrupt, dishonest & bribery rampant.

761 ..."The Tragic Conflict; the Civil War & Reconstruction. Selected & edited by Wm. B. Hesseltine." Intro. & notes. N.Y., G. Braziller, 1962 8vo, cl, 528 pp.

762 **HESSLEIN, Bernhard**
"Jefferson Davis, ein Socialpolitischer Roman aus dem Amerikanischen Burgerkriege." Leipzig, G.J. Purfurst, 1866-1867. 12mo., cl., 3vol. in one. fiction. Pseud: J. Retcliffe.

763 **HESTER, Earl Randolph**
"Muster Roll of Company H, 28th Inf., 1862-1863." Arcadia, La., 1960 4to, mimeo., 71fs (7) leaves.

764 **HETH, Henry**
"Letter on causes of Lee's Defeat at Gettysburg." In: SHSP, 1877, v. IV, pp. 151-160.

765 ..."Report: Gettysburg Campaign." In: SHSP, 1878, v. VI, p. 258-261.

766 ..."The Memoirs of Henry Heth. Edited by: James L. Morrison, Jr." In: Civil War Hist. 1962, v. VIII, p. 1-24, 300-326, ports.
..."The Memoirs of Henry Heth. Edt: James L. Morrison." Westport, Conn., Greenwood Press, 1974 8vo, cl, lxxxvi, 303 pp. It is said Lee addressed Heth, of all officers!, by his first name. Bmk $25-

767 ..."The Heth Papers." In: SHSP, 1923, ns, VI, Whole: XLIV, p. 232-240. Corresp: Gen. Henry Heth, CSA.

768 **HETH, Henry, Maj.-Gen.**
"Report of the Affair at Falling Waters." In: SHSP, 1879, v.7,p.196-199.

769 **HEWETT, John Hill**
"King Linkum, the First, A Musical Burletta as performed at the Concert Hall, Augusta, Ga., Feb. 23, 1863. Edited by Richard B. Harwell." Emory University Sources & reprints, ser.IV, #1. (Atlanta, Ga.) Emory University, 1947 8vo, wraps, 32 pp. $10.00

770 ..."War: a poem, with copious notes, founded on the revolution of 1861-1862, (up to the Battles before Richmond, inclusive)." Richmond, Va., West & Johnston, 1862 sm. 8vo, wraps, vi(7)-85 pp. $35-

771 ..."Give our Flag to the breeze! A new national song, written & composed by..." (Richmond, 1861)Broadside: 8 1/2 x 16 cm. Crandall-3172.

772 **HEWITT, J.E.**
"The Battle of Mansfield." In: Confed. Vet., May 1925, p. 172-173, p. 198. Commemorates dedication of monument to Generals Richard Taylor & de Polignac, April 25.
..."Mansfield, La., Enterprise Pub. co, 1925 8vo, wraps, ills. 19pp. $40-
See: "Battle of Mansfield" Plummer (A)
..."Battle of Mansfield, Mansfield, La. Fought April 8, 1864. Gen. Richard Taylor Commander Confederate Forces, Gen. N.P. Banks, Commander Federal Forces." Pub. on 61st Anniv. of Battle & Unveiling of Monuments to Gen. Taylor & Polignac. (Logansport, La., Interstate Progress) 1949 8vo, wraps, ports, illus., map, 20 pp. $27.50

772a **HEWITT, Lawrence Lee**
"Port Hudson, Confederate Bastion on the Mississippi." Baton Rouge: Louisiana State University Press, 1985. 8vo, cl, dj, 232pp, ills. $20.

773 **HEWITT, Lawrence L. & Arthur W. Gergeron**
"Post Hospital Ledger, Port Hudson, La., 1862-1863 Baton Rouge, Le Comite des Archives de la Louisiane, (1981) sm. 4to, pict. wraps, illus., 132 pp. $15- List of patients at hospital, CSA & Union. Indexed by name, state, branch of service & unit. (Carolina Bks.)

774 **HEYSINGER, Isaac Winter**
"Antietam & the Maryland & Virginia Campaigns of 1862 from the government records - Union & Confederate - mostly unknown & which now first disclosed the truth; approved by the War department, by New York: Neale Pub. Co., 1912 12 mo, cl, 322 pp. $75-, $90-
..."Antietam & the Maryland & Virginia Campaigns of 1862." Gaithersburg, Md., Old Soldier Books, 1988. Reprint. 8vo, cl, 322pp, Neale reprint. $30.

775 **HEYWARD, DuBose & Herbert Ravenel Sass**
"Fort Sumter." New York: Farrar & Rinehart (1938) 12 mo, cl, XI, 109 pp. Currier ends. 2nd Edt., adapted from H.R. Sass's - "Look Back to Glory", also DuBose Heyward's "Peter Ashley." $20- C. Hill

776 ..."Peter Ashley." N.Y. Farrar & Rinehart (1932) 12 mo, cl, illus. liners, 316 pp. bmk $20- Novel of Charleston during the war.

777 **HEYWARD, T.S.**
"The Confederate Oak: random poems." (Savannah, Ga., Braid & Hutton, 1929) 8vo., wraps, 15pp., illus.

778 **HIBBARD, Clarence Addison, Edt.**
"Stories of the South, old & new., with an introduction, biographical notes & bibliography." Chapel Hill: Univ. of North Carolina Press, 1931) 8vo, cl, xvii, 520 pp. $17.50 JK122 $15-

779 **HIBBARD, James & Albert Castel**
"(Brig-Gen. Judson) Kilpatrick's Jonesboro (Georgia) Raid, Aug. 18-22, 1864."In:Atl. HJ, Summer 1985, v.29, p.31-45.

780 **HICKERSON, Thomas Felix**
"Echoes of Happy Valley Letters & Diaries Family Life in the South Civil War History." (CW-pp. 58-120) Chapel Hill, N.C., The Author (1962) Distrib: Bull's Head Bookshop. Sm.4to, cl, x, 245, (2)pp, facsms. fldg. chart, ports, illus. scene on rear end sheets, index, genealogical tables $30-B $20-

781 **HICKLING, R.A., Dr.**
"In Memory: David Herbert Llewellyn, Surg: CSS "Alabama." (London) Jour. Confed. Hist. Soc. March 1963, v.I, #3, pp. 71-78, port. Appeared in Feb. 1958, v. 56, #1 - "Charing Cross Hospital Gazette. Also in: Ala. hist. quart., winter 1958, v. 20, p. 630-635. Surgeon to the CSS Alabama, & his death when vessel sank, 1864. Also some account of early life in England. Hickman Co., Tenn. See: W.J.D. Spence

782 **HICKMAN, John P.**
"Confederate Generals of Tennessee." In: CV, 1910, v. XVIII, p. 170-172.

783 **HICKS, Irl Roger**
"The Prisoners farewell to Johnson's Island; or, Valedictory address to the Young Men's Christian Association of Johnson's Island, Ohio - a Poem." St. Louis(Mo.) Southwest Book, pr., 1872 12 mo, wraps, 29 pp. $100-G

784 **HICKS, Jimmie**
"Texas & Separate Independence, 1860-1861." In: ETHJ, October 1966 v. IV, #2, pp. 85-106, bibliog.

785 ..."Some letters concerning the knights of the Golden Circle in Texas, 1860-1861." In: SwHQ, July 1961, v. LXV, #1, pp. 80-86.

786 **HIDEN, J.C.**
"Death of Willie Abel." In: SHSP, 1883, v. 11, p. 184-185.

787 ..."Stonewall Jackson." In: SHSP, 1892, v. 20, p. 307-311.

788 **HIGDON, Hal**
"The Union vs Dr. Mudd." Chicago, Ill: Follett pub. co, 1964 8vo, cl, dj, ports(incl. front) illus., map. (9), 235, (1) (16) pp. illus unnumbered.

789 **HIGDON, Robert G.**
"The cause of the war between the states." dIn: CV Oct. 1921, v. XXIX, p. 383-384.

790 **HIGGINBOTHAM, Don**
"A Raider Refuels: Diplomatic Repercussions." In: CWH, June 1958, v. IV, #2, pp. 129-141. CSN-"Florida" refuels in Barbados & embroils Britain.

791 **HIGGINBOTHAM, W.R.**
"The Arkansas Rats." (Batesville, Ark., Jan. 1978 12 mo, still wraps, 38 pp. Entire issue #2, v. XIX, "Independence County Chronicle", Northeast Arkansas, along the White River called "river rats", Arkansas Confederates. Roster.

792 **HIGGINS, Frances Caldwell**
"Life on the Southern plantation during the War Between the States." In: CV, April 1912 v. XXI, p. 161-166.

793 **HIGGINS, W. Robert**
"The Geographical Origins of Negro Slaves in Colonial South Carolina." In: So. Atl. Quar. 1971, v. LXX, p. 34-47.

794 ..."High Privates, Second Edition of Confederate Letters written for the Houston Telegraph during the late war, with the addition of the Secrets of Success, or business advice to the young men of the South. Revised & enlarged." Austin, Texas, 1894, Eugene von Boeckmann. 8vo, wraps, 75 pp.(R.R. Gilbert) author- $22.50 $25.00

795 **HIGHSMITH, William E.**
"Some Aspects of Reconstruction in the Heart of Louisiana." (Baton Rouge, La.) JSH, Nov. 1947, v. XIII, #4, pp. 460-491. Tables.

796 ..."Louisiana land-holding during war & Reconstruction (1860-1880)" In: LHQ, Jan. 1955, v. 38, #1, p. 39-54. notes.

797 **HIGHTOWER, Harvey Judson**
"Letters from..., a Confederate Soldier, 1862-1864." Edt: Dewey W. Grantham, jr. In: Ga. Hist. Quart., June 1956, v. XL, p. 174-189. Letters (14) from a pvt. in 20th Ga. Reg. Vols., served: Va. & Ga. to his sister, Martha S. Hightower.

798 **HILDEBRAND, Samuel S.**
See: James W. Evans & A. Wendell Keith. Jefferson City, Mo., 1870 $100-

798a **HILL COLLEGE MONOGRAPHS**
in Texas and Confederate History:
..."General Lee and Hood's Texas Brigade at the Battle of the Wilderness." Dayton Kelley.
..."Fraudulent Finance: Counterfeiting and the Confederate States, 1861-1865." By Judith Ann Benner.
..."Old Tige" General William L. Cabell, CSA." By Paul Harvey, Jr.
..."Colonel John Robert Baylor: Texas Indian Fighter and Confederate Soldier." By Jerry Don Thompson.
..."West of the Mississippi with Waller's 13th Texas Cavalry Battalion, CSA." Compiled and Edited by Charles Spurlin.

798b **HILL COLLEGE PRESS BOOKS**
Robert E. Lee. By Jefferson Davis and Alexander Stephens.
...Touched With Valor. Edited and with a Biography of General Jerome B. Robertson by Colonel Harold B. Simpson.
...Pat Cleburne, Confederate General. A Definitive Biography by Howell and

Elizabeth Purdue.

...Robert E. Lee. By Jefferson Davis. Edited and with an Introduction and Notes by Colonel Harold B. Simpson.

...Campaigning With Parson's Texas Cavalry, CSA. Edited by John Q. Anderson.

...Cry Comanche. By Harold B. Simpson.

...Red Granite For Gray Heroes. By Harold B. Simpson.

...Hood's Texas Brigade: A Compendium. By Harold B. Simpson.

...Hood's Texas Brigade in Reunion and Memory. By Harold B. Simpson.

...Bood's Texas Brigade in Poetry and Song. By Harold B. Simpson.

...Ten More Texans in Gray. By Dr. W. C. Nunn.

...Ten Texans in Gray. By Dr. W. C. Nunn.

...Texas in the War, 1861-1865. By Wright and Simpson.

...The Civil War Letters of General Frank "Bull" Paxton. Edited by John Gallatin Paxton and Introduced by Harold B. Simpson.

...Cannon Smoke. Edited by Lester Newton Fitzhugh.

...Fighting With Ross' Texas Cavalry Brigade, CSA. Edited by Homer L. Kerr.

...Texas in the Confederacy. Bill Winsor. Introduction Harold B. Simpson.

799 **HILL, Ambrose Powell, Gen.**
"Souvenir Hill Monument Unveiling May 30, 1892." (Richmond, Va., 1892?) Oblong 8vo, pict. wraps in color, 41 pp. Contains sketch of Gen. A. P. Hill's Life.
See also Geo. S. Bernard.

800 ..."A Short History of Gen. A.P. Hill." Park Place, N.Y., Knapp & Co., 1888 2 3/4x1 1/2" colored booklet, 16 pp. facsm signature, (packed in Duke's cigarettes.) See: "Heroes of the C.W." & W. Duke & co.

801 ...Lithographic portrait by J.L. Giles. N.Y., Geo. E. Perine pub., (1865) Tall folio, wide margins

802 ...Portrait: litho on yellow-tint background by J.L. Giles. wide margins. tall folio New York: G.E. Perine (c. 1870) $25.00

803 ..."Lieutenant-General A.P. Hill. Some reminiscences of the famous Virginia commander-curious mistakes growing out of the absence of his insignia of rank-teamsters' blundurs reported with vigor-the first burial of his remains." (From: Richmond 'Dispatch', July 26/Aug. 2, 1891) In: SHSP, 1891, v. XIX, p. 178-183, by "D.F.C."

804 ..."Sketch of Gen. A.P. Hill."In: Land we Love, 1867, v. II, p. 287-279.

805 ..."Hill Monument Ass'n., Richmond, Va., Souvenir Hill Monument unveiling, May 30, 1892." (Richmond, Va., J.L. Hill print, 1892) 8vo, wraps, illus., ports, cover in colors, some ads., (48) pp.

806 ..."Unveiling of the Statue of Gen. A.P. Hill", In: SHSP, 1892, v. XX, p. 352-395, from the Richmond 'Dispatch'.

807 ..."Presentation of the Statue of A.P. Hill, from the Petersburg 'Index-Appeal' In: SHSP, 1892, v. XX, p. 184-205.

808 ..."General A.P. Hill's Report of Battle of Gettysburg". (from his Atg. Mssc.) In: SHSP, 1876, v. II, p. 222-226.

809 ..."Further details of the death of General A.P. Hill, 'Letter from a Courier', & from Col. Charles S. Venable." In: SHSP, 1884, v. XII, p. 183-187.
See also: W.E. Cameron, Jno. W. Hauk, G. Powell Hill, W.W. Hassler, Jas. P. Matthews Martin Schenck & G.W.W. Tucker.

810 **HILL, Andrew Malone**
"Personal recollections of..." In: AHQ, 1958, v. XX, p. 85-91. 16th Reg. Alabama Infty.

811 **HILL, Benjamin Harvey, Senator**
"Address on Jefferson Davis, delivered before the Georgia branch of the Southern Historical Society, at Atlanta, Ga., Feb. 18, 1874." Pamphlet from the So. Hist.

Soc.P. 8vo, wraps, pp. 485-505. (Richmond, Va.?) Highly critical of the homefront in its prosecution of the war. Jeff. Davis agrees.

812 ..."Exchange of Prisoners(Andersonville) In: SHSP, 1886, v. 14, p. 387-388.

813 ..."Memorial Addresses of the Life & Character of...del. in Senate & House Representatives, 47th Congress, 2nd Session, Jan. 25, 1883 Washington: Government Printing Office, 1883. Sm.4to, cl, port(front) 101 pp. $4.

814 ..."Speech on the Condition of the Country, delivered in City of Atlanta, July 16, 1867, & Letter of Ex-Gov. Hers'l. V. Johnson." Augusta, Ga., 1867 (Chronicle & Sentinel) 8vo, wraps, 16 pp. (old) $6.00

815 ..."Notes on the Situation, as published in the Chronicle & Sentinel." Augusta, Ga., 1867 8vo, wraps, 47 pp. (old) $7.50
See: Joseph E. Brown Reply.

816 ..."Speech on the means of success, sources of danger & consequences of failure in the Confederate struggle for Independence, deliv: Sterling Hall, La Grange, Ga., Mar. 11, 1865." Atlanta, Ga: Economical Book & Job Pr. 1874. (LC-no other descp.) 8vo, 32 pp. $75-jk 122 First opposed secession, later signed as a member of comm. Orator for Southern cause.
See: Pearce (H.J.)" Benj. H. Hill, Secession & Reconstruction".

817 ..."Senator Benjamin H. Hill of Georgia-His Life, speeches & writings, compiled by his son, Benjamin H. Hill, Jr. Also Memorial addresses, tributes of the press, both North & South and exercises attending the unveiling of a statue to his memory." Atlanta: H.C. Hudgins & Co., 1891 8vo, cl, iii, ix, (11)-823 pp. pls, ports $12.50 ($6, $9-) $25.00 $45-JK
Do:Atlanta: T.H.P. Bloodworth, 1893
Do:Louisville, Ky:Lost Cause Press, micro-card.
See: Wm. H. Bailey. Reprint: $35.00 See: John C. Reed

818 ..."We are in our Father's House." Speech of...of Georgia, on the General Amnesty Bill. Delivered in the House of Representatives, Jan. 11, 1876." Washington: Cunningham & Brashears, 1876 8vo, sewn, 16 pp.
see also in Jefferson Davis "Amnesty".

819 **HILL, D.H.**
"North Carolina." v.V. 8vo., cl., 813pp. Wilmington, N.C., Broadfoot, 1987.

820 **HILL, Daniel H., Lt.-Gen.**
"The Battle of South Mountain, or Boonsboro. Fighting for time at Turner's & Fox's Gaps." In: B & L., v.2, p.559-590, illus. ports, map.

821 ..."Chickamauga - the Great Battle of the West." In: B & L., v.3, p.638-665, illus., maps, ports. Also: Gen. Polk at Chickamauga & Gates P. Thruston's Crisis at Chickamauga.

822 ..."Lee's Attack North of Chickahominy." In: B & L., v.2, p.347-362, illus.+ E.M. Law.

823 "On the Confederate Right at Gaines Mill." p62-65.

824 ..."McClellan's Change of Base & Malvern Hill." In: B & L., v.2, p.383-395, illus., maps, port.

825 **HILL, Daniel Harvey**
"Address: at Unveiling of monument to N.C. Women, etc."
See: Robt. D.W. Connor.

826 ..."Address Reunion of the Virginia division: A.N.V." In: SHSP, 1885, v. XIII, p. 259-276.

827 ..."Address before the Mecklenburg, N.C., Historical Society." In: SHSP, 1876 v. 1, p. 389-398.

828 ..."Avery (Alphonso C., life of Hill, see under author's name.

829   ..."Battle of Bethel. First engagement of the War Between the States. Barely mentioned in History. Of sufficient importance to be recorded on its pages-Men engaged in it on both sides who afterwards became famous." (From Richmond, Va., 'Dispatch', Oct. 13, 1901 In: SHSP, 1901, v. XXXIX, p. 197-207.

830   ..."Folio sheet, advertising" "Land We Love", signed "D.H.Hill". $25.00 Magazine was edited by D.H.Hill.

831   ..."Bethel To Sharpsburg." Half-title: A History of North Carolina In the War Between the States." $200-B $150-Bmk 105 Raleigh(N.C.) Edwards & Broughton, 1926 8vo, cl, 1-vols, xvi, 436 pp. 457. ($12.50, 15.00, 21.50, 28.50, 45.00)

832   ..."The Battle of Gaines' Mill." In: Century, May & Oct., 1885, v. XXX, pp. 294-309.

833   ..."Chickamauga, the great battle of the West." In: B & L, v.III, p. 638-662.

834   ..."Gen'l D.H. Hill's report of the battle of Chickamauga." In: OLOD, 1874-5, v.1, p. 205-217.

835   ..."Confederate ordnance department." In: N.C. Lit. & Hist. Assoc. Proc., 1922, XX-XXI, ann.sess., p. 80-91. Bmk $20.

836   ..."The Confederate Soldier in the Ranks. An Address by...at Richmond, Va. Oct. 22, 1885" Richmond, Va., Wm. Ellis Jones, 1885 8vo, wraps, 28 pp.

837   ..."Elements of Algebra." First book published in response for books of Southern interest against slanted books from the North. Several examples offered herein reflect on Northern soldier's patriotism & Yankee duplicity.

838   ..."Historic Parallels." In: N.C. Lit. & Hist. Assoc. Proc., 1918, v. XVIII, pp. 44-51. Conditions in South during CSA.

839   ..."Lee's attack north of the Chickahominy." In: B & L, v. 2, pp. 347-362.

840   ..."The Battle of South Mountain, or Boonsboro. Fighting for time, at Turner's & Fox's Gaps." In: Cent., May 1886, ns-X, p. 137-152. ports, illus., map. Also: B & L, v. II, p. 559-581 Bmk $25-

841   ..."The Lost Dispatch-Letter from General D.H. Hill." In: SHSP, 1885, XIII, pp. 420-423, LWL, 1867/8, v. IV, p. 270-284.

842   ..."North Carolina." In: Vol. IV, Evan's Confederate Military History. Atlanta: Confederate Pub. Co., 1899 8vo, cl, 813 pp. ports, maps (1-fldg) plans. Biographical: pp. 287-354; Additional biographical sketches illustrating services of officers & privates & political citizens of North Carolina, pp. 355-813 $75.00

843   ..."North Carolina." v. IV, Evan's Confed. Mil. Hist." Regular edt., in 12 vol. set. port, 3-pls. composite ports, 6-maps, 1-fld. 8vo, 354 pp. Biog. suppl. pp.(287)-354. $15.

844   ..."The Old South. An Address: delivered by Lt.Gen. D.H.Hill at Ford's grand opera house, on Memorial Day, June 6, 1887, before the Society of the Army & Navy of the Confederate States in the State of Maryland." Baltimore:Andrew J. Conlon, 1887 8vo, wraps, 23 pp. also micro-cards,--Louisville, Ky: Lost Cause Press, $2.45 In:SHSP, v. 16, pp. 423-443.

845   ..."Offprint, wraps, $50 $85.bmk.

846   ..."Official Report of Col. Hill, Battle of Bethel Church." (Raleigh, N.C., 1861) 8vo, caption head, 8 pp. State Convention 1861.

847   ..."The real Stonewall Jackson", In: Century Mag., 1893/1894, v.XLVII, p. 623-628. (Hill, a brother-in-law of Jackson)

848   ..."General D.H. Hill's Report of the Battle of Chickamauga." In: OLOD, 1874/5, v. 1, p. 205-217.

849   ..."Report of the Battle of Chickamauga." In: LWL, Sept. 1866, v. 1, #5, p. 305-309; v. 1, #6, pp. 393-404.

See: Marguerite Gilstrap, Alphonso C. Avery, Joseph M. Hill.

850 **HILL, David Bennett**
"Number of North Carolina Troops in the Confederate States Army." In: SHSP, 1901, v.29, p. 295-296.

851 **HILL, Frederick Stanhope**
"Twenty-six historic ships; the story of certain famous vessels of war & of their successors in the navies of the U.S. & the Confederate States of America from 1775 to 1902, with introduction by Rear-Admiral George Eugene Belknap." N.Y. Putnam's, 1903 (1902) 8vo, cl, 16 pls., 16 ports, xlix, 515 pp.

852 **HILL, Frederick Trevor**
"On the trail of Grant & Lee; a narrative history of the boyhood and manhood of two great Americans, based upon their own writings, official records, & other authoritative information." N.Y., London: D. Appleton co, 1911 8vo, cl, xiv, 305 pp., color pls., illus., facsms., maps. (National Holiday Series)

853 ..."The 'Alabama' arbitration. An international lawsuit." In: Harper's, Jan. 1907, v. CXIV, p. 191-201.

854 **HILL, G. Powell**
"First Burial of General Hill's Remains." In: SHSP, 1891, v. XIX, p. 183-187.

855 ..."Lieutenant-General A.P. Hill-the first burial of his remains." In:SHSP, 1891, v. 19, p. 178-186.

856 **HILL, G.W.**
"Palmer's Brigade in the Carolinas." In: CV, 1910, v.XVIII, p. 332.
See: John B. Palmer.

857 **HILL, James D.**
"The Burning of Columbia reconsidered." So.Atlan. Quart., v. XXV (1926), p. 269-282. wraps $8.00

858 ..."Charles W. Read, Confederate von Lucknen. In: So. Atl. Quart., Oct. 1929, v.XXXVIII, p. 390-405.

859 ..."Some economic aspects of slavery, 1850-1860. "In: So. Atl. Quart., Apr., 1927, v.XXVI, p. 161-177.

860 **HILL, James Ewing**
"Addresses of Hon. James E. Hill & Judge J.M. Crosson at the Confederate Monument unveiling, Livingston, Texas October 10, 1901." Livingston, Texas: T.M. McClure (1901) 8vo, wraps, 14 pp.-dbl. column.

861 ...(and) J.M. Alexander & T.F. Meece: "Historical Polk County, Texas. Companies & soldiers organized & enrolled in the Confederate Army & Navy." Livingston, Texas: Polk Co. Enterprise, (1901). 8vo, wraps, 66 pp. $50.00 $100.00
See: "Historical Polk Co. Texas." (1965 edt.)

862 **HILL, Jim Dan**
"Sea Dogs of the Sixties. Farragut & seven contemporaries." Minneapolis, Minn: Univ. of Minn, pr, 1935, 8vo, cl, dj, ports (incl.front) illus, maps, xiv, 265 pp. Bmk $35-, $10.00 CSN: Wilkinson, Bulloch, Read, Waddell.
...NY, A.S. Barnes, 1961. pict. wrp. $5-

863 **HILL, Joseph M.**
"Biography of Daniel Harvey Hill, Lt-Gen., Confederate States of America, educator, author, editor, by his son." Little Rock, Arkansas History Commission, n.d. 8vo., wraps, 37pp., port.

864 **HILL, Lawrence Francis**
"The Confederate Exodus to Latin America.: (Austin, Texas ?)1936 8vo, wraps, 94 pp. Except for minor changes, same as found in Tex. (So.West) Hist. Soc., Oct., Jan., Apr., 1935/1936; SwHQ, Oct. 1935, v.XXXIX, #2, p. 100-134. #3, p. 161-199, #4, p. 309-326.

865 ..."Confederate exiles in Brazil." In: Hisp. Am. Hist. Rev., May, 1928, v.VII, p. 192-210.

866 **HILL, Louise Biles**
"Joseph E. Brown & the Confederacy." Chapel Hill: Univ. of North Carolina, 1939 8vo, cl, dj, viii, 360 pp. $15- $20.00 Gov. Brown of Georgia during war. $25- Bmk Reprint: (1972) Westport, Conn: Greenwood pr.

867 ..."Governor Brown & the Confederacy." (Nashville) 1958, summary of thesis (PhD) Vanderbilt University, 1936.8vo, wraps, (2), 54 pp. Private Edition, dist. Joint University libraries, Nashville, Tenn. Reprinted: from Ga. Hist. Quart., Sept-Dec., 1937, v. XXI, #3 & 4. pp. 239-264; 345-372. $12-

868 ..."State Socialism in the Confederate States of America.: Charlottesville, Va., Historical pub., 1936 8vo, wraps, 31 pp. Southern Sketches, #9, 1st ser., Edt: Dr. J.D. Eggleston. $417.50-JK $14-Bmk Brief study of CSA to control commerce between CSA & Europe, 1864-5.

869 ..."Report: Battle of Chickamauga." In: SHSP, 1885, v. 13, p. 367-372.

870 ..."Report of Maj.Gen. Hindman, of his Operations in the Trans-Mississippi District. Publ. by Order of Congress." Richmond: R.M. Smith, 1864. 23cm, bound in Mor., 26 pp. Pertains to operations in Ark., and what is now Okla., detailed difficulties of Hindman with Albert Pike. $40- (Streeter $100) $175-Gdsp.

871 ..."Vignette etched portrait, mounted on small folio sheet. By A.B. Hall., n.p., n.d. (c. 1898)

872 **HILL, Mary S.**
"A British subject's Recollections of the Confederacy, while a visitor & attendant in its hospitals & camps." Tall 8vo, wraps, 114 pp. $175-OB Baltimore: Turnbull bros, 1875.

873 ..."Florence Nightingale of the Army of Northern Virginia." In: Confed. Vet., 1902, v.X, port, p. 124.

874 **HILL, Richard Taylor & William Edward Anthony**
"Confederate Longarms & Pistols. A Pictorial Study." Charlotte, N.C., The Authors. (Dallas, Texas. Taylor Pub. Co., 1978, 4to, fabricoid, gilt), illus. 304 pp. $30-, 5000 copies.

875 **HILLDRUP, Robert Leroy**
"The romance of a man in gray, including the love letters of Capt. James S. Perry, Forty-fifth Virginia infantry regiment, CSA." In: WVaH, Jan/Apr/July 1961, v. 22, p. 83-116, 217-239. Cross Lanes, Camp Gauley & Fayette Co. & the Kanawha Valley in 1862/1863.

876 ..."Cold war against the Yankees in the antebellum literature of Southern women (Novelists, 1827-1860) In: NCHR, July 1954, v. 31, p. 370-384., notes.

877 **HILLMAN, Benjamin J.**
"Monuments to Memories. Virginia's Civil War Heritage in Bronze & Stone." (Richomnd, Va.) Virginia Civil War Comm., n.d., 8vo, pict. wraps, 48 pp., illus.

878 ..."Virginia's Decision. The Story of the Secession Convention of 1861." (Richomnd, Va.)Virginia Civil War (Centennial) Commission. (1964) 8vo, stiff wraps (illus. on cover), ports, 23 pp.

879 ..."A letter written by General Thomas C. Hindman in Mexico, Edt. Ted. R. Worley." In: AHW, 1956, v.XV, p. 365-368.

880 **HILLS, Alfred C.**
"MacPherson, the Great Confederate Philosopher & Southern Blower. A record of his philosophy, his career as a warrior, traveller, clergyman, poet & newspaper publisher, his death, resuscitation, & subsequent election to the office as governor of Louisiana. By Alfred C. Hills, editor of the New Orleans Era." N.Y., James Miller, 1864 12mo, cl, 209 (6-advs.)pp. $126- Ginz(35) Satire, wartime Gov. of La.,

881 ..."Emancipation in Louisiana. Speech of Alfred C. Hills in the Constitutional Convention of Louisiana, May 4-5th, 1864." New Orleans, La., 1864. 8vo, sewn, 21 pp. Sabin-31906
...(New Orleans, n.d.) 8vo, 4pp.
..."Yankees made Southerners..Speech of Alfred C. Hills, Nov. 28, 1863."

882 **HILLYER, George**
"Battle of Gettysburg. Address before the Walton county, Georgia Confederate Veterans, August 2, 1904. From the Walton Tribune." (Monroe, Ga.?) Walton Tribune, 1904? 8vo, wraps, 16 pp. $25.00

883 ..."Report of Captain Hillyer, Ninth Georgia Regiment." In: SHSP, 1885, XIII, p. 204-206.

884 **HINCHMAN, Walter**
"Sketches & Poems, 1845-1920." n.p., n.d. (1920?) 8vo. cl., 253pp., illus., drawings, maps. $12.00. Served with Gen. Hunter in Virginia, 1864.

885 ..."History of the 49th Virginia Infantry." See: Laura Virginia Hale...

886 **HINDMAN, Briscoe**
"Maj. Gen. Thomas Carmichael Hindman, CSA, by his son." In: CV, 1930, v. 38, p. 97-104.

887 ..."General Pat. Cleburne. Thrilling story of a street fight at Helena (Ark.) in which he was desperately wounded." In: SHSP, 1903, v.XXXI, p. 163-165.

888 **HINDMAN, Thomas Carmichael, Maj.Gen.**
"Battle of Prairie Grove." Report of...(Fort Smith? 1862) Broadside: 22.5cm. text in 3 columns, both sides. Hdq. 1st Corps, Trans-Miss. Army, Camp near Fort Smith, Dec. 25, 1862. to: Lt. Col. S.S. Anderson, A.A. Gen'l. (Hargrett)

889 ..."CSArmy-Trans-Mississippi District, L.R.
Orders of..., organizing the Provost Marshal's department. General Order #17 HDQ-Trans-Miss.Distr., Little Rock., June 17, 1862." Broadsheet 21x23cm.text 3-columns.

890 ..."Stonewall Jackson at Chancellorsville." In: CV, 1905, v.13, p. 229-233. Also an account by Col. W.H. Palmer. Reprint of the first account in July, 1866, LWL, published by Hill, with repro of Jackson & his staff.

891 **HINDS, William Green Dudley**
"Exciting episodes: true stories of adventure of the Civil War." (McAlester, Oklahoma, News Office, 1908) private print. 8vo,(20)pp, cover title, explanatory notes tipped-in. (Ark. Univ.) 1st pub: Conf. Vet., XXXIII, May, 25, pg. 172-173
...reprinted in Ark.Hist.Quart., 1954. XIII, p. 329-37. plates, illus., port.

892 ..."A True Story of the Civil War." In: "Flashback", Washington Co. Hist. Soc., Fayetteville, Ark., May 1977, v.27, #2, p. 1-8 pp. Reccol. of WGD Hinds of McAlester, Okla., Mar. 1, 1908.
Also: ArkHQ, 1954, v. 13, p. 325-337. (1st edt. 1908)

893 **HINES, ---**
"Thrilling Narrative of the Escape of Gen. John H. Morgan from the Ohio Penitentiary." Intro: glimpse of the interior arraingement of the prison." (Columbus, Ohio., O.P. Print, 1887 12mo, wraps, 38 pp., front(port) (Ark. Univ.)
...Southern Bivouac, NS, 1(1885) illus., map, port, p. 49-59.
...(Century Mag., Jan. 1891)
...Louis., Ky. Lost Cause, micro-cd.

894 ..."The Northwestern Conspiracy." In: SB, ns, 1886/1887, v.II, p. 437-445, 500-510, 567-574, 699-704.
See: Editor's Table, p. 390 & 452.

895 **HINKINS, Virginia**
"Stonewall's Courier-the Story of Charles Randolph & General Jackson." N.Y., Whittlesey House, McGraw-Hill (1959)

896 **HINKLE, Joseph A.**
"The odyssey of Priv. Hinkle, captured at Fort Donelson, in prison in Indiana, a Tennessee rebel escapes & through Yandeedom to his home." In: CWTI, Dec. 1969, v.8, #9, p. 24-31, illus., map port.

897 **HINSDALE, H.**
"Confederate Gray; the Story of Traveller Gen. Robert E. Lee's Favorite Horse." Peterborough, N.H., Rich. R. Smith (1963) 8vo, cl, d/w, 102 pp. group ports, map $4-

898 **HINSDALE, John Wetmore, Col.**
"History of the Seventy-second regiment of North Carolina Troops in the War Between the States, 1861-1865." Goldsboro, N.C., Nash bros pr. (1901) Tall 8vo, wraps, ports, facsm., maps, 32, (1)pp.

899 **HINSON, William G.**
"The Diary of...during the War of Secession, Pt. 1., Edt: Joseph Ioor Waring." In: SCHM, 1974, v.75, #1, p. 14-23, Pt.II, #2, p. 111-120

900 **HINTON, Isaac T.**
"Historical Sketch of the Quitman Guards, Co. E., 16th Mississippi Regiment, Harris Brigade from the organization in Holmsville, 21st Apr., 1861 to the surrender of the A.N.V., 9th of April, 1865, by one of the Quitman Guards." New Orleans, La., Isaac T. Hinton, 1866 8vo, wraps, xv, 77 pp. (Last 5pp missing in copy: Miss. Archives, War Dept. Library shows a copy of 70 pp.)

901 **HINTON, James W.**
"The late Col. James W. Hinton, from Norfolk, Va." In: OLOD, Mar. 1875, v.2, #1, p. 34-36.

902 **HIPPEN, James C.**
"The influence of geographical conditions upon Civil War strategy in the Mississippi delta, 1861-1865." In: Okla. Acad. Science Proc., 1958, v.38, p. 128-131, bibliog.

903 ..."Historic Beauvoir-Souvenir Booklet of Beauvoir-on-the-Gulf, Harrison County Mississippi." Designed & edited-Mrs. Wilbur Moore Jones, state historian UDC, Hattiesburg, Miss., American Commercial print (Nov. 1921) 4to, stiff wraps-flags on cover, front, illus. ports, fldg-plate, 110, (1) pp.

904 ..."Historic flag of the Confederacy returned to Tennessee by Illinois." In: Jour. Ill. state hist. soc., 1915, v.VIII, p. 327-336.

905 ..."Historical Polk County, Texas. Companies & Soldiers Organized in & Enrolled From Said County in Confederate States Army & Navy-1861-1865." (Livingston, Texas: Polk Co. Enterprise) Organization Ike Turner Camp, U.C.V., Unveiling, etc., 1965. 8vo, wraps, 68 pp. op $20- 1st ed., See: Jas. E. Hill

906 ..."Historic Pulaski, birthplace of the Ku Klux Klan, scene of the execution of Sam Davis." Nashville: Methodist Pub. House(1913) 12mo, cl, illus(facsms)pls., 7-108 pp. Based on information furnished by R.J. Brunson. Joshua Brown's "Sam Davis, p. 102-108

907 ..."Historical Sketch of the Confederate Home & College. Charleston, S.C., 1967-1921." Charleston, S.C., Walker, Evans & Cogswell, 1921. 8vo, wraps, front., 32 pp.

908 ..."Historical Sketch explanatory of Memorial or certificate of membership in the United Confederate Veterans..." (New Orleans, La., Hopkin's print, 1897.) 8vo, wraps, 32pp.

909 ..."Historical Sketch of the Quitman Guards Company E, Sixteenth Mississippi regiment, Harris' Brigade, from its organization in Holmesville, 21st April, 1861, to the surrender of the Army of Northern Virginia, 9th April, 1865, by one of the

Quitman Guards." New Orleans, La., Isaac T. Hinton, 1866 12mo, wraps, xv, 77 pp. errata slip insert.

..."Historicus", pseud.

910 **HIRSCH, Charles B.**
"Gunboat personnel in the Western waters, 1861-1862." In: Mid-Amer., Apr. 1952, v. 34, p. 75-86, notes.

910a **HISTORY OF Crater** & ten months siege of Petersburg, Va.," n.p. (Monument unveiled June 20, 1908). 8vo, wraps, 16pp, ills, cover map & title. See: Crater, attle of..."

911 **"HISTORY OF THE 7th Alabama**
Cavalry Regiment including Capt. Charles P. Storrs' Troop of University Cadet Volunteers. Author Unknown. With Introduction & Edited by William Stanley Hoole." University, Ala., Confederate Pub. Co., 1984. 8vo., stiff wraps, 21 pp., plate.

912 **"HISTORY OF THE 8th Regiment**
of Alabama Volunteers (Infantry) Author Unknown. Introduction & Edited by William Stanley Hoole, with a Roster of the Regiment." University, Ala., Confederate Pub. Co., 1985. Confederate Regimental Series, #10. 8vo., stiff wraps, 39pp., port. This article first published in Perry & Smith Directory of City of Montgomery (Alabama) 1866, pp.87-91.

913 **HITCH, Robert M.**
"Address before Francis B. Bartow camp #93, U.S.C.V. (sic) at Chatham Artillery Hall, Wed., Jan. 21, 1903."(half-title:"The Georgia Secession Convention of 1861 & its Causes." Savannah, Ga., Bycks Print, 1903
8vo, wraps, 26 pp.

914 **HITCHCOCK, Bert**
"The Alabama-Bierce Connections." In: AR, July 1985, v.38, p.222-238, port.

915 **HITCHCOCK, Reuben**
"Letters from the Washington Peace Conference of 1861." Edt: Robert Gray Gunderson. (Baton Rouge, La.) JSH, Aug. 1951 v.XVII, #3, p. 382-392.

916 **HITCHCOCK, William S.**
"Southern Moderates & Secession: Senator Robert M.T. Hunter's Call for Union." In: Journ. Amer. Hist., 1973 v.LIX, p. 871-884.

917 **HITE, Cornelius Baldwin**
"The Confederate army." In: CV, June 1923, v.XXXI, p. 221-222 Re number of troops in the CSArmy.

918 **HITNER, John K.**
"Memories of Stonewall Jackson." In: CV, Dec., 1924, v. XXXII, p. 468-470.

919 **HITZ, Alex M.**
"The Origin of & Distinction between the two Protestant Episcopal Churches known as St. Luke's Church, Atlanta." In: Ga.H.Q., March 1950, v. XXXIV, #1, p. 1-7.

920 **HOAR, Jay S.**
"Louisiana's Last Boys in Gray." In: LaH. 1978, v.19, p.336-352.

..."The South's Last Boys in Gray - an Epic Prose Elegy Substudy of Sunset & Dusk of the Blue & Gray." Bowling Green (Ky) State University, 1986. 'Popular Press' 8vo., cl., dj., 605pp., ills, ports. (paper, $20) $40. Biographies of 170 CVets over 100

921 **HOBART-HAMPDEN, Augustus Charles**
"Hobert Pasha. Blockade-Running, slaver-hunting, & war & sport in Turkey." Edt.: Horace Kephart. Outing Adventure Library (at head) N.Y., Outing publishing co, 1915. 12mo, decr.cl, 285 pp.(2)p-adv. $10-, $40- bmk

...Oyster Bay, N.Y., Nelson Doubleday (1915), same above, but on thinner paper, no adv. in back.

922 ...Captain Roberts-running the blockade." In: CWTI, Dec. 1967, v.VI, #8, p. 10-15. illus. map. First chapter of a reprint by the 'Blockade Runners Museum.

923 ..."Never Caught. Personal Adventures connected with Twelve successful trips in Blockade-running during the American Civil War, 1863-4. By Captain Roberts." London: J.C. Hotten, 1867 $400-g, $118- (Bmk-105 $250- Fcap.8vo, (4), 123 pp.(32 pp. ads)

...Reprint: "Magazine of History", #3, Extra number, 75 copies., 4to, 65 pp., n.y., 1908, William Abbatt. $35- Bk-86

...Carolina Beach, N.C., Blockade Runner Museum, 1967. 8vo, stiff wraps, pl, vii, (1)-59 pp. $2.50

924 ..."Sketches from my life. By the late Admiral Hobart Pasha." London: Longmans, Green co, 1886 12mo, cl, front(port), (8), 282 pp. $70-nc A reprint, with additions, of "Never Caught". A 2nd edition issued 1886. $150-

...London: 1887, Longman's 8vo, cl, port, (6), 282 pp. Bmk $100-

...N.Y., D. Appleton & co., 1887 8vo, cl, 276 pp.

...Leipzig, 1887 Edition in German.

925 **HOBBS, Thomas Hubbard**
"The Journals of Thomas Hubbard Hobbs: A Contemporary Record of an Aristocrat from Athens, Alabama, written between 1840, when the diarist was fourteen years old, & 1862 when he died serving the Confederate States of America." Edt. by Faye Acton Axford. University: Alabama Press, 1976 8vo, cl, illus, x, 272, (2) pp pls. Bibliog. 255-260. $18.50 y

926 **HOBEIKA, John Elias**
"An appreciation of the character & career of Lyon Gardiner Tyler & of his writings on Abraham Lincoln & War Between the States. 'The Sage of Lion's Den' N.Y., Exposition press (1948) 12mo, cl, dj, 64 pp.

927 ..."The Fratricidal strife-through New England eyes." In: Tyler Quart. Hist & Geneal. Mag., 1935, v.XVII, p. 16-22. "South's position re civil war, shows how, out of New England's writers, her position completely vindicated."

928 ..."Lyon Gardiner Tyler The Sage of Lion's Den." In: Tyler Quart. Hist. & Genealog. Mag., 1937, v. XVIII, p. 193-231.

929 ..."Lee, the Soul of Honor. An appreciation by an Orientalist, with additional facts. With a foreword by Lyon Gardiner Tyler." Boston: Christopher pub.hse., 1932 8vo, cl, illus., ports, 303 pp. $15-

930 ..."A Tribute to the Confederate Soldier; Address Before Anne Fulmore Harllee Chap. United Daughters of the Confederacy, Dillon, S.C.: Introduction by Oliver Orr. (Dillon, S.C., Herald Pub. Co., 1930) 8vo, stiff wraps, 28 pp. ($3) $15-

931 **HOBSON, Annie J.W.**
"Memorial of the Unveiling of the Lee Statue, Richmond, Va., May 29, 1890." Richmond, Va., Wm. Ellis Jones, 1890 8vo, wraps, in colors, 15 pp. (2nd edt.)

...(Same) "Dedication by Annie J.W. Hobson (daughter of Gen. Henry A. Wise) Richmond, Va., 1890 8vo, wraps, 8 pp. (1st edt)

932 **HOBSON, Edwin La Fayette**
See: Cullen Andrews Battle.

933 **HOBSON, Fred**
"Tell about the South: the Southern Rage to Explain." Baton Rouge: Louisiana State Univ. Pr., 8vo., cl., dj., xii, 391pp., index. $35.00. 1983.

934 **HOBSON, Henry S.**
"The Famous Cruise of the Kearsarge. An authentic account in verse of the battle with the Alabama off Cherbourge, France on Sunday June 19, 1864; concluding with a brief history of the famous ship, together with interesting information concerning her officers during the civil war, to the date of her wreck on Roncador Reef in the Caribbean Sea, Feb. 2, 1894. By H.S. Hobson, one of her original crew." Bonds

Village, Mass., The Author, 1894. 12mo., cl., 167, (3), 5 pl., 2 ports (front). $100.00.

935 **HOBSON, Nancy**
"Samuel Bell Maxcey as Confederate Commander of Indian Territory." In: Jour. of West., 1973, v.XII, p. 424-438.

936 **HOCHMUTH, C. Arthur**
"A Yankee Invasion Thwarted." In: Mont. MWH, v.XII, p. 34-37. Apr. 1962 In Texas.
..."A Yankee Invasion Thwarted." In: Montana, Spring 1962, p.34-37, facsms., illus., ports.

937 **HOCKERSMITH, Hubert Holman**
"Thirtieth Tennessee regiment." In: So. Vib., 1883, v.II, p. 407-409.

938 **HOCKERSMITH, Lorenzo D.**
"Morgan's Escape. A thrilling story of war times. A true history of the raid of General Morgan & his men through Kentucky, Indiana & Ohio."$350-, $750-R Madisonville, Ky., Glenn's graphic print, 1903 8vo, port, plans, wraps, iv, 54 pp. Louisville: Lost Cause pr, micro-cd $3.95

939 **HODGE, George Baird**
"Report of Brig-Gen. George B. Hodge, CSA of the operations of his command, Sept. 9, 1863." (n.p., 188-) 8vo, fold, (4)p. Dorn-II, 2985.

940 ..."Sketch of the First Kentucky Brigade, by its Adjutant General G.B. Hodge." Frankfort, Ky: Kentucky Yeoman Office, Major & Johnston, 1874. 8vo,wraps,31pp. Louisville, Ky: Lost Cause Print, micro-card $2.45 (see also: Orphan Brigade)
...Also in "Land We Love." v.4, (97)-104; (177)-181; (265)-268; (393)-401. diagrs. (11) Bmk 20-

941 **HODGE, John**
"Memoirs of a C.S.A. treasury note lithographer. Edt: L. Miles Raisig." In: Numismatist Aug. 1951, v.64, p.838-842, facsms. Eng.lithographer in Charleston & Columbia, S.C., 1862-1865.

941a **HODGE, Robert A.**
"A Death Roster of the Confederate General Hospital at Culpeper, Va." Fredericksburg, Va., The Author, 1977. 4to, wraps, 127pp.

942 **HODGES, James Gregory**
See: James Francis Crocker.

943 **HODGKIN, James B.**
"Southland Stories." Manassas, Va., Journal Press, 1903, 16mo,cl,(5), 175 pp. Background of war stories.

944 **HODGKIN, William N.**
"Dentistry in the Confederacy." In: Amer. Dental Ass'n. Jour., June 1955, v.50, p. 647-655. Facsm., tables, views, notes on CSA particularly in Va., 1864-5. Reprint, wraps, 10 pp. $8.00

945 **HODGKINS, N.M., Maj.**
"The Macon Light Artillery at Fredericksburg." In: SHSP, 1883, v.XI, p. 138-139.

946 **HODGKINS, William Henry**
"Catalogue of the extensive private library of the late Major Wm. H. Hodgkins of Somerville, comprising large collections of books & pamphlets relating to the Civil War, slavery & Confederate States." Boston, 1906/1907., C.F.Libbie & co (auctions) 8vo,cl, 2 vols.

947 **HODGSON, Joseph**
"The cradle of the Confederacy; or, the times of Troup, Quitman, & Yancey. A sketch of southwestern political history from the formation of the federal government to a.d. 1861." Mobile, Ala., Register publishing off., 1876 8vo,cl,4, (xiii)-xv, 528 pp. $75- $125- Maintains that Northern leaders drove the SW states to secession. Between 1850-1860.
...Spartanburg, S.C., Reprint Co., 1975. $25.

948 ..."The Confederate vivandiere; or, the Battle of Leesburg, a military drama in three acts; as performed at the Montgomery (Alabama)Theatre, by an amateur

company, for the benefit of the First Regiment of Alabama Cavalry." Montgomery, J.M.Floyd, 186 2 12mo, wraps, cover title, 20 pp. Cradnll-3227

949 **HODGSON, Matthew**
"Hampton of Hampton's Legion; an Informal Study of Confederate Command." In: CWII, June 1960, v.VI, #2, p. 157-169, pl.

950 **(HODGSON, TELFAIR, MRS.)**
"Ante-Bellum & War Memoirs of Mrs. Telfair Hodgson. Edt: Sarah Hodgson Torian." In: Ga.H.Q., Dec. 1943, v.XXVII, #4, p. 350-356. $8-

951 **HODGSON, W.I.**
"Historical sketch of the R.E. Lee Monument Association of New Orleans." In: SHSP, 1886, v. 14, p. 96-102.

952 **HOEHLING, Adolph A.**
"The Day Richmond Died." N.Y., A.S. Barnes (1981) 8vo,cl,dj,facsm. illus., map, ports, xvii, 270 p.

953 ..."Last Train from Atlanta." N.Y., Lond: Thomas Yoseloff(1958) "Frist printing, signed by author", on spec. half-title. Large 8vo,cl,ports, illus., facsms, map, 558 pp. bibliog, no index. $10- $15- atg $30 B $26- B Note: 1st. edt. black cloth Variants: Navy blue & dark gray.
...N.Y., Bonanza (1975) $7- $12.50

954 ..."Thunder at Hampton Roads." Englewood Cliffs, N.J., Prentice-Hall, 1976 8vo,cl,dj,xvi,232 pp. $15- $10- "Monitor" & "Merrimack."

955 ...Vicksburg: 47 Days of Siege." Englewood Cliffs, N.J., Prentice-Hall. (1969) Map endsheets, illus., ports, facsm. 8vo,cl,x,386 pp. $30- Dabney $14- Bmk.

956 **HOEHLING, Adolph A. & Mary**
"The Last Days of the Confederacy." N.Y., Fairfax Press, (1986). 8vo., cl., dj., xv, 270pp., illus. Originally published as "The Day Richmond Died." (1981)

957 **HOFFERT, Sylvia D.**
"Madame Loretta Valasquez; heroine or hooker?" In: CWTI, June 1978, v.17, #3, p. 24-31, illus, ports.

958 **HOFFMANN, John**
"The Confederate Collapse at the Battle of Missionary Ridge; the Reports of James Patton Anderson & his Brigade Commanders." Dayton, Oh., Morningside Press, 1985. 8vo., wraps, 92pp. $15.00.

959 **HOGAN, George H.**
"Parson's brigade of Texas Cavalry." In: CV, Jan. 1925, v.XXXIII, p. 17-20.
See: author's under "Parson's Texas Cavalry."

960 **HOGAN, Wilber Fisk**
"The Story of Sixty Years, by 'Ino'. Birmingham, Ala., 1902 (c. 1908 by W.F. Hogan) 8vo,wraps (color), 112 pp.
Birmingham & Jefferson Co., Alabama.

961 **HOGANE, James T., Maj.**
"Reminiscences of the Siege of Vicksburg, by Major J.T. Hogane of the Engineer corps." In: SHSP, Nov. 1883, v.XI, p. 223-227, 291-297, 484-489.

962 **HOGE, John Milton**
"A Journal by...., 1862-1865; Containing Some of the most particular incidents that occurred during his enlistment as a soldier in the Confederate Army. Written by himself, at Guest Station, Wise Co., Va., Aug., 1865." (stamped: Cincinnati, M.H. Bruce, 1961) 8vo,43pp., wraps, illus. bibliog., 8th Reg.Va.Cav.CSA.

963 **HOGE, Moses D., Rev.**
"Inauguration of Jackson Statue, Tuesday Oct. 26, 1875. Gov. Kemper's Address. Oration by Rev. Moses D. Hoge." Suffolk, Va., Robt. Hardy Pub., 1986. 8vo., wraps, 20pp., facsm., port.

964 **HOGE, Moses Drury, Rev.**
"Inauguration of the Jackson Statue. Introductory Address of Gov. Kemper & Oration by Rev. Moses D. Hoge, D.D. on

Tues. Oct. 26, 1876." Richmond, Va., R.F. Walker, 1875 8vo, wraps, 23 pp. $35-OB

...Do: Richmond: Wm. Ellis Jones, 1885 8vo,wraps, 30pp.

...Do: "Oration by Rev. Moses D. Hoge, D.D. (Inauguration of the Jackson Statue) (n.p., 1875?) 8vo, wraps, 14 pp.

See: Peyton H. Hoge.

965 ..."Lee's Birthday" In: SHSP, 1889, v.XVII, p. 353.

966 ..."Oration at the unveiling of Stonewall Jackson's Statue." In: SHSP, 1875, v.XIII, p. 314-335.

See also: Robt. Alonzo Brock.

967 **HOGE, Peyton Harrison**
"Moses Drury Hoge: Life & Letters. By his nephew Peyton Harrison Hoge Richmond, Va., Presbyterian Comm. of publicaiton, (1899) $75-B $50- 8vo, cl, front(port), ports, ix, 518 pp. Carolina Bk. #10, interesting comments.

968 **HOGE, William James**
"Sketch of Dabney Carr Harrison, minister of the gospel & Captain in the army of the Confederate States of America." Richmond, Va., Presbyterian Committee of publication, of the Confederate States 1863." Crandall-2582. 16mo, wraps, 48 pp.

See: Dabney C. Harrison.

969 **HOGG, Thomas E.**
"The Fate of Marvin & other Poems." Houston, Texas: E.H. Cushing print, 1873 (Lange, Little & Hillman, printers, N.Y.) 12mo,cl,274 pp.

...(Houston, Texas: Press of Premier Sept., 1973. Centennial Edt. 1873-1973) 12mo, stiff wraps, (7), 8-186, front, port CSA soldier in uniform. Blank verse.

970 **HOGG, Tom**
"Reminiscences of the War; the Last Day at Corinth (1862)" In: E.Tex.HJ, Spring 1982, p.48-53. Robert C. Cotner, Edt.

971 **HOIG, Stan**
"War for Survival-the Wichita Indians during the Civil War." In: CO, Fall 1984, v. LXII, #3, p. 266-283, ports, plates, notes.

972 **HOKE, Robert F.**
"Battle of Drewry's Bluff, 1864." In: SHSP, 1884, v.XII, p. 227-229.

973 ..."Last Address." In: SHSP, 1893, v.XXI, p. 297-299.

974 ..."Operations against Newbern in 1864." In: SHSP, 1881, v.IX, p. 4-7.

975 ..."Operations in front of Petersburg." In: SHSP, 1884, v.XII, p. 462-465.

976 ..."Gen. Hoke's farewell address to his division." In: LWL, 1866, v.II, #1, p. 56-57.

977 **HOKE, William J.**
"Sketch of the 38th regiment, N.C. troops." In: Our Liv. & Dead, 1874, v.I, p. 545-551.

978 ..."Company G, 38th regiment, N.C. troops." In: Our Liv. & Dead, 1875, v.III, 180 pp(i.e., 1p) correction by John E. Rheim.

979 ..."What Lincoln County did in the Late War." In: OLOD, Jan. 1875, v.1, #5, p. 429-434. Roster.

979a **HOLBROOK, Francis X.**
"A Mosby or an Quantrill? The Civil War Career (1861-6) of John Clibbon Braine." In: Amer. Neptune, July 1973, p.199-211.

980 **HOLCOMBE GUARDS -**
See: W.A. Parrott.

981 **HOLCOMBE, James Philemon, Judge**
"Official Correspondence-Confederate State Department(Mission to Canada.) Letters from: J.P. Holcombe, Jacob Thompson, J.P. Benjamin, W. J. Almon. In: SHSP, 1879, v.7, p. 99-106, 132-139, 293-294; 1886, v.14, p. 410.

982 **HOLCOMBE, Return I. & Adams**
"An Account of the Battle of Wilson's Creek, or Oak Hills, fought between the Union Troops, commanded by Gen. N. Lyons, & the Southern, or Confederate Troops, under the command of Gens. McCulloch & Price, on Sat. Aug. 10, 1861

in Greene County, Missouri." Springfield, Mo., Dow & Adams, 1883. 8vo,cl,2-ports, 104 pp. $125- Bmk

Do: Centennial Edt. Pub. by Springfield Public Library & Green Co. Hist. Soc., 1961 8vo,cl,xii, 111 pp. (indexed) OP $25-$30-

983 **HOLCOMBE, William Henry, M.D.**
"The Alternative; a separate nationality or, the Africanization of the South." New Orleans, La., Delta Mammoth, 1860 8vo,wraps, cover title, 15 pp. Slavery & secession.

984 ..."Southern Voices; Poems by Wm. H. Holcombe." Phila: J.P. Lippincott co, 1872 12mo, cl, 164 pp. A La. physician, contains many poems on the CSA.

985 **HOLCROFT, F.**
"The Lancashire Cotton Famine." (London) Journ. Confed. Hist. Soc. Dec. 1965, v. III, #4, p. 127-132, pls.-2.

986 ..."Public Opinion & Propaganda in Lancashire, 1859-1865." (London) Jour.Confed. Hist. Soc., Autumn, 1967, v. 5, #3, p. 90-101.

987 ..."The Terrible Nightmare." (London) Jour. Confed. Hist. Soc., Autumn 1966, v. 4, #3, p. 98-101. Lancashire cotton famine.

988 **HOLDEN, Benedict M.**
"Colonel Charles H. Olmstead & Connecticut." In: Ga. H.Q., June 1961, v.XLV, #2, p. 128-136.
See also under Col. Chs. H. Olmstead.

989 **HOLDEN, Edgar**
"Journey of a Confederate Mother." In: WTHSP 1965, v. 19, p. 36-57.

990 **HOLDEN, Joseph William**
"Hatteras, & other poems." Raleigh, N.C., Edwards & Broughton, 12 mo, wraps, xi, 51 pp. front (port). $25- alternate pp. blank. Brief biographical sketch of Holden, who served with 31st N.C., captured at Roanoke Island. Pix in CSA uniform.

991 **HOLDEN, W.C.**
"Frontier Defense in Texas during the Civil War." (Abilene, Tex.) West Tex. Hist. Assn. Yr. Bk., 1928, v.IV, p. 16.

992 **HOLDEN, William Woods**
"Memoirs of W. W. Holden." Durham, N.C., Seeman print, 1911 $104- Bmk $40- 12mo, cl, viii, 199 pp. Head: "The John Lawson Monographs of Trinity College Historical Soc.", v. 2 Large: politics, little of war, reconstruction remainder.

992a **HOLIEN, Kim Bernard**
"Battle of Ball's Bluff." Orange, Va., Moss Publications, 1985. 8vo, cl, 166pp, ills, index. $25.

993 **HOLIFIELD, M.B.**
"The Secession of Southern States did not constitute a rebellion or an insurrection against the United States because they legally exercised their reserve powers."
In: FCHQ, July 1954, v. 28, #3, p. 215-232. By the Asst. Atty-Gen. of Kentucky.

994 ..."Secession...a right reserved by the states (1787-1868). "In: Ky. state bar jour., Sept. 1954, v. 18, p. 160-173. notes.
Also: Ala. Lawyer. Jan, 1955, v. 16, p. 76-99. notes.

995 **HOLLADAY, Florence E.**
"The Powers of the Commander of the Confederate Trans-Mississippi Dep't." In: SWHQ, Jan. 1918, v.XXI, p. 279-298, 333-359.

996 **HOLLAND, Annie Jefferson**
"The Refugees: a sequel to "Uncle Tom's Cabin" Austin, Texas., The Author, 1892. 12mo, cl, printed wraps, 179 pp. (jk-129) $35- Fictional apologia for slavery.

997 **HOLLAND, Cecil Fletcher**
"Morgan & his Raiders, a biography of the Confederate General." N.Y., Macmillan co, 1942 8vo,cl,dj,map,facsms, illus. ports,

xiii (2), 373 pp. ATG $27.50 $50-B $30-
...same, 1943? $30-Dabney

998 **HOLLAND, Lynwood M.**
"Georgia Military Institute, the West Point of Georgia, 1851-1864" In: Ga. H.Q., Sept. 1959, v. XLIII, #3, p. 225-247. $8-

999 ..."Pierce M.B. Young, the Warwick of the South."
Athens: 1964 8vo,cl,259 pp. Youngest Maj-Gen. of CSA, cavalryman (Stuart)

1000 **HOLLIDAY, F.W.M., Col.**
"In Memoriam General Robert E. Lee, Ceremonies at Winchester, Va., Jan. 19, 1871. Oration by..., Poem by Daniel B. Lucas, Esq." Winchester, Va., Times Office, 1871 8vo, wraps, 60 pp. $40- Bmk 106

1001 **HOLLINGSWORTH, Alan M.**
"The Third Day at Gettysburg: Pickett's Charge, by Alan M. Hollingsworth & James M. Cox." N.Y., Henry Holt & co., (1959) 8vo, cl, dj, maps, plans, vii, 162 pp. Largely from Official Records.

1001a **HOLLINGSWORTH, Annie Mae**
"Theodore O'Hara." In: AHQ, 1947, v.7, #3, p.416-424.

1002 **HOLLINS, George Nichols**
"The Capture of the Steamer Saint Nicholas: In: SHSP, 1896, v. 24, p. 88-91.

1003 **HOLLISTER, Ovando James**
"History of the First Regiment of Colorado Volunteers." Denver, Col., Thos. Gibson & co, 1863 12mo, wraps, 178 pp. (Eberst, 163) $2500- Valuable in adversary role to Gen. Sibley's Texans at Glorieta Pass.

1004 ..."Boldly They Rode, a history of the First Colorado Regiment of Volunteers, with an introduction: William M. Raine." Lakewood, Colo: Golden Press, 1949 12mo, cl, dj, (8), 190 pp. $35-

1005 ..."Colorado Volunteers in New Mexico 1862. Edt: Richard Harwell." Chicago, Ill., Lakeside Press, 1962. 16mo, cl, front(port), illus., 309 pp.
..."Lakeside Classics, #60."

1005a **HOLLOWAY, W. R.**
"The Camp Morton Controbersy, Comments on Dr. Wyeth's Rejoinder; & Conclusion by Dr. Wyeth." In: Cent., Nov. 1891, p.475-7. See: Dr. Wyeth's rejoinder in Cent., Oct. 1891, v.20, p.771-5.

1006 **HOLLOWELL, J.M.**
"War-Time Reminiscences & Other Sketches." (Goldsboro, N.C.) Goldsboro Herald, June 1939. 8vo, wraps, (2), 53, (1)pp., port, illus., printed in double-columns. About half on CSA. $20-Bmk $50-Bmk-105

1007 **HOLLYDAY, Henry**
"Running the Blockade: Henry Hollyday joins the Confederacy. Edt: Frederic B.M. Hollyday." In: Md. Hist. Mag. 1946, v.XLI, p. 1-10
...Separate, wraps. 10pp. $15- Bmk.
..."Running the Blockade." In: CV, Mar. 1921, v.XXIX, p. 93-96.

1008 **HOLLYDAY, Lamar**
"Gen. George H. Steuart's Brigade at the Battle of Gettysburg.: In: SHSP, 1876, v.II, p. 105-107.

1009 ..."Maryland Troops in the Confederate Service." In: SHSP, 1877, v.III, p. 130-139.

1010 ..."The Virginia & the Monitor." In: CV, Oct. 1922, v.XXX, p.380-382. Sets Northern accounts to right.

1011 **HOLLYWOOD MEMORIAL ASSOCIATION**
"Appeal for a Monument to Lee, by the Hollywood Memorial Association." In: SHSP, 1886, v.14, p. 188-194.

1012 **HOLMAN, Dwayne & Henry Keatts**
"The Coldest Day. The activities of a Confederate Boy Spy-David O. Dodd." In: TMH, 1971, v.IX, #4, p. 281-288.

1013 **HOLMAN, W.J., Jr.**
"War experience of a Confederate Offi-

cer." In: THQ, 1951, v.10, p. 149-160. See: Sam L. Clark, Jr.

1014 **HOLMES, Alester G. & George R. Sherrill**
"Thomas Green Clemson, His Life & Work." Richmond, Va., Garrett & Massie, 1937 8vo, cl, illus., bibliog., xvii, 212 pp. A Northern man who chose to live in South, serve the CSA & help reconstruct after war.

1015 **HOLMES, Anne Middleton**
"The New York Ladies' Southern Relief Association, 1866-1867; an account of the relief furnished by citizens of New York City to the inhabitants of the devastated regions of the South immediately after the Civil War." N.Y., Mary Mildred Sullivan Chapted UDC 1926. 8vo, wraps, 113 pp. $12.00

1016 **HOLMES, Clayton Wood**
"The Elmira Prison Camp; a history of the military prison at Elmira, N.Y., July 6, 1864 to July 10, 1865; with an appendix, containing names of the Confederate prisoners buried in Woodlawn Cemetery." N.Y., Lond: G.P. Putnam's, 1912 Tall, 8vo, cl, illus.(62), plates, ports, xvii, 465 pp. $15-, $20-, $25- $80- OB Many letters from CSA prisoners. Roll-377-461

1017 **HOLMES, Emma E.**
"The Charleston Fire of 1861 as described in her Diary..Edt: John F. Marszalek, Jr." In: SCHM, 1975, v.76, #2, p. 60-67

1018 ..."The Diary of Miss Emma Holmes, 1861-1866." Edited with introduction by John F. Marszalek. Baton Rouge: Louisiana State University Press, 1979. "Library of Southern Civilization" 8vo, cl, dj, xxv, 496 pp. $35- $37.50 See: Eliz. Stevenson

1019 **HOLMES, George Frederick**
"Uncle Tom's Cabin, a Review". In: Southern Literary Messenger, Dec. 1852, v. XVIII, p. 721-731.

1019a **HOLMES, Henry McCall**
"Diary of Henry McCall Holmes, Army of Tennessee, Asst. Surg., Florida Troops, with related documents . . ." State College, Miss., 1968. 8vo, 99pp, facsms, ills. Errata sheet.

1020 **HOLMES, Jack David Lazarus**
"Forrest's 1864 raid on Memphis." In: Tenn. HQ, Dec. 1959, v. XVIII, p. 295-321

1021 ..."Joseph A. Gronauer, 1830-1911 & the Civil War in Memphis." In: W. Tenn. HSP. 1959, v.14, p. 148-158. Notes, war & business in Memphis, Tenn.

1022 ..."The Not-so-Gentle Louisiana Tigers." In: CWTI, May 1963, #2, p. 22-25, illus. Highly regarded by Stonewall Jackson.

1023 ..."The battle of Sabine Crossroads." In: CWTI, No. 1962, v. 1, #7, p. 14-19, illus., map, ports.

1024 ..."The Mississippi county that 'seceded' from the Confederate States of America." In: CWTI, Feb. 1965, v. 3, #10, p. 45-50. illus.

1025 **HOLMES, James G., Edt.**
"Memorials to the Memory of Mrs. Mary Amarinthia Snowden offered by Societies, Associations & Confederate Camps. Published by the Ladies Memorial Association of Charleston, S.C. A Tribute to its founder. Edited by James G. Holmes." Charleston, S.C., Walker, Evans & Cogswell Co., printers, 1898. 8vo, wraps, p. (3)-4, 46. Was active in hospital work during the War.

1026 **HOLMES, Robert Masten, CSA**
"Kemper County Rebel: The Civil War Diary of Robert Masten Holmes, CSA. Edited by Frank Allen Dennis; foreword by Thomas L. Connelly." Jackson: University & College Press of Mississippi, (1973) 12mo, cl, dj, xix, 115 pp., index $25-B

1027 **HOLMES, Sarah Katherine (Stone)**
"Brokenburn, The Journal of Kate Stone

1861-1868. Edt: John Q. Anderson." Baton Rouge: Louisiana State Univ. Press (1955) 2nd printing (1956). 8vo, cl-boards, dj, port(front)map endsheet, xxii, (1), (3)-400 pp. index. $20- Civil War girl's diary in La. & Texas.

1028 **HOLMES, T.H., Lt. Gen.**
"General Orders #15: All employees of the QM & subsistence depts. in Dist. of Arkansas will be enrolled, assigned to companies, then regularly detailed for their present duties, by-" Hdg. Dist. of Ark., Little Rock, Apr. 28, 1863. Broadside: 18x27cm.(not in Crand-Harw) $50.00

1029 **HOLMES, Tomie**
"Thomas Stonehouse (1830-1920)." In: Jr. historian (Tex.) Mar. 1952, v. 12, #5, p. 17-19. Services in CSArmy, life in Kinney & Tom Green counties, Texas.

1030 **HOLT, Hiram Talbert**
"An Alabama Confederate Soldier's report to his wife, Edt: Robert Partin." In: Jan. 1950, Ala. Rev., v. III, p. 22-35. Pvt. in Suggsville Greys, later 38th Ala. Reg. to Angelina Caroline (DeWitt) Holt.

1031 ..."A Confederate Sergeant's report to his wife during the bombardment of Ft. Pillow, by Robert Love Partin." In: Tenn. Hist. Quart., Sept. 1956, v. XV, p. 243-252. 4 letters from Sgt. Holt, in Tenn. Apr. '62.
..."(same) during the campaign from Tullahoma to Dalton." In: Tenn. Hist. Quar. Dec. 1953, v.XII, p. 291-308. Letters while in Tenn. & Georgia, 1863-1864.

1032 ..."Momentous Events" of the civil war as reported by a Confederate private-sergeant." In: Tenn. Hist. Quart., March 1959, v. XVIII, p. 69-86. Letters based on Sgt. Holt (who died in '64) Ala. Greys, Co. D., 2nd Inf. Reg., Ala. Vols, later Co. I, 38 th Inf. Reg., from Apr. 1861-Feb. 1864. Refers to a collection of 138 letters from Holt, 1861-1864, edt. by Partin as an unpublished typescript of 498 leaves.

1033 **HOLT, Joseph, Hon.**
"Report of the Judge Advocate General on the "Order of American Knights" or, "Sons of Liberty." A Western Conspiracy in aide of the Southern Rebellion." $100- JK Washington: G.P.O., 1864, wraps, 8vo, 16 pp., (Do: another copy carries imprint of the Washington Chronicle.)

1033a **HOLT, Thad, Jr.**
"The Organization of the Confederate Navy." In: AHQ, 1947, v.7, #4, p.537-41.

1034 **HOLT, Thad, Jr., Edt.**
"Miss Waring's Journal: 1863 & 1865. Being the Diary of Miss Mary Waring of Mobile, during the final days of the War Between the States." Chicago: The Wyvern Press of S.F.E., Inc., Mobile, Alabama, Graphics, Inc. (1964) Tall 8vo, pict. wraps, illus., 17 pp.

1035 **HOLZER, Harold - Gabor S. Boritt & Mark E. Neely, Jr.**
"Images of Peace. Every Picture Tells a Different Story Showing Lee's Surrender." In: CWTI, May 1987, v.26, #3, p.22-29, illus., facsms. Prints perpetuating the myth of the signing in an apple orchard, not at McLean's house.

1036 **HOLZMAN, Robert S.**
"Adapt or Perish: The Life of General Roger A. Pryor, C.S.A." Hamden, Conn., Archon Books, 1976 8vo, cl, dj, 209 pp. $15-Y

1037 **HOLZMAN, Robert S., Dr.**
"The soldier with two sexes-both as "Sue Mundy"/Jerome Clarke." In: CWTI, Jan. 1964, v.III, #9, p. 12-14. illus. A Kentuckian: Marcus Jerome Clarke, at 16 became a spy & guerrilla most of the war, hung March 15, 1864.

1038 **HOME, Marshall**
"The MacGregors." Chicago: Scroll pub., 1901 12mo, decr.cl, illus., incl. front, 285 pp. $7.50 Fiction, based on 1st hand accounts & scrapbook, laid in Missouri.

Author: Mrs. Virginia Yates McCanne of Moberly, Mo., Atg. inscription to Maj. E.C. Lewis on fly-leaf.

1039 "HOMES FOR Confederate Veterans. Hearings before sub-committee on S. 643, to provide homes for Confederate Veterans of the Civil War., statement of Perry M. deLeon, 1916." Military Affairs Committee, Senate. Wash., DC., p.ii, 3-14 pp.

1040 "HOMES FOR the mothers, widows & daughters of Confederate Soldiers, Charleston, S.C.". Charleston, S.C., News & Courier press, 1875. Seventh Annual Report. Tall, 8vo, wraps, 10pp.

1040a HOMES FOR the mothers, widows, daughters of Confederate soldiers, Charleston, S.C." Charleston, S.C., News & Courier Press, 1872. Proceedings of Fourth Anniversary, with Addresses: Dr. Girardeau, Winkler & Rev. Bowman. 8vo, wraps, 18pp. $1

...Same, 6th Anniversary, addresses of Judge Aldrich & Gen. Chestnut. 8vo, wraps, 10pp. $15.

1041 HOMES, Mary Sophie [Shaw] Rogers, Mrs.
"Progression; or, the South Defended, by Millie Mayfield (pseud) of New Orleans." Cinncinnati: Applegate & co., 1860 12mo, cl, 226 pp. Defends South, re Uncle Tom's Cabin.

1042 HONEWELL, Roy J., Col.
"Men of God in Uniform." In: CWTI, Aug. 1967, v.VI, #5, p. 30-37, illus., ports. Dr. Quintard & j. Wm. Jones, (2 of 4)

1043 ..."Honor Roll of Confederate Veterans of Chester County from 1861-1865." Chester, S.C., W.A. Bowles, n.d. 8vo, wraps, 20 pp. (McKissick-1204)

1043a HONEY, Michael K.
"The War within the Confederacy: White Unionists of North Carolina." In: Prologue, 1986, v.18, #2, p.75-93.

1044 HONIG, Lawrence E.
"John Henry Brown, Texian Journalist, 1820-1895." El Paso, Texas. Texas Western Press, 1973. Southwest studies, monogram #36. 8vo., wraps, 55pp., illus. Brown was with W.W. Heartsill at Pea Ridge, edited the "War Bulletin", see: also under Jno. H. Brown.

1045 HOOBER, Richard T.
"Enigma of the Confederate cent (minted by Robert Lovett, Jr., Philadelphia, 1861)." In: Numismatist, Sept. 1956, v. 69, p. 989, coins.

1045a HOOBLER, James A.
"Cities under the Gun: Images of Occupied Nashville & Chattanooga." In: CV, Sept./Oct. 1987, ns, v.35, #5, p.24-29, ills, port, map.

..."Cities under the Gun: Images of Occupied Nashville & Chattanooga." 8vo, 224pp. $40. Nashville, Tenn., Rutledge Press.

1046 HOOD, B.H., Mrs. & Mrs. W.S. Dozier
"Records & Reminiscences of Confederate Soldiers in Terrell Count." (Dawson, Ga., News Print, 1914) Edts" Mrs. Jas. M. Griggs, historian, Mary Brantley chap., U.D.C. 2nd title-page: "Muster Roll of Terrell Co. Men in War Between the States, 1861-1865." Record of Confederate soldiers taken from tax receiver's books & pension lists in ordinary's office-Dawson, Terrell Co., Ga. 8vo, wraps, 152, (9) pp. Bmk-$250- Separate title pages listed as follows: Mrs. B.H. Hood "Reminiscences of Confederate Soldiers 1861-1865." Dawson, Ga., Sept. 22, 1915 (p. 25); Dozier-Hood-"Reminiscences of Confederate Soldiers 1861-5", 1914 (p. 36) Mrs. B.H. Hood-"History of Memorial Day & Confederate Flags." Dawson, Ga., Sept. 22, 1915.(p. 69), "Records of the Mary Brantley Chap. UDC & the Mildred Rutherford Chap. Children of the Confed-

eracy."(p. 103) ; "Records of Confederate Soldiers taken from Tax Receiver's Book & Pension lists in Ordinary's Office- Dawson, Terrell County, Ga." (p. 152)

1047 **HOOD, Emma Nelson, Mrs.**
"Bob Dean, or 'Our Other Boarder'." Phila: E. Claxton/Austin: A.K. Hawkes, 1882. 12 mo., cl., 1pp., vii-xii, 13-370pp. Opens while Texas a Republic, closes at end of civil war.

1048 **HOOD, Fred**
"Twilight of the Confederacy in Indian Territory." Oklahoma City: Chron. Okla. Winter 1963-1964, v.XLI, #4, pp. 425-441.

1049 **HOOD, Ida Richardson**
"In Memory of General J.B. Hood." In: SHSP, 1904, v. XXXII, p. 151-156.

1050 **HOOD, John B.**
"Advance & Retreat..." Secaucus, N.J., Blue & Gray Press, 1985.
...Nashville, Tenn., Blue & Gray Press, 1985. 8vo, cl, dj. $13.50.

1050a ..."Hood's Brigade Historical Papers." n.p., n.d. (1880s ?). 8vo, wraps, 34p. cover title. Casualty lists, war correspondence.

1051 **HOOD, John Bell**
"Advance & Retreat. Personal experiences in the United States & Confederate States Armies." New Orleans, La., 1880. Published for the Hood orphan memorial fund, G.T. Beauregard. (Phila: Press of Burke & M'Fetridge.) 8vo, (gray cl., full sheep, full emboss) Pres. Bind $300- Mor., 3/4 Mor., marbled boards Rebound 2-ports (incl. front), 4-maps (1-fldg.) $50-$75-. 358 pp. $20-, $25-, $32-.50 Full Mor., edges gilt. $50-, $75- $173 Avc $22- $80- Bmk-84 3/4 Lt.
..."Bloomington: Indiana Univ. press, (1959), Edt., with Intro., notes by Richard N. Current. 12mo, cl, dj, xiv, (2), 376 pp., front(port) 4-maps, 1-double."Civil War Cent. Series."... OP $25-Y
...Millwood, N.Y., Kraus Reprint, Kraus-Thomson, 1969. Pub. #33-
See: F.B. Chilton, T.G. Dabney, Nicholas A. Davis, W.O. Dodd, Jno. P. Dyer, Wm. A. Fletcher, Val. C. Giles, Thos. Robson Hay, Don Henderson, Ida R. Hood, Jas. H. M'Neilly, Rich. O'Connor, Joe. B. Polley, Jerome B. Robertson, Harold B. Simpson, Jno. C. West, Mrs. A.V. Winkler, Wm. R. Hamby (Rolls)

1052 ..."The defense of Atlanta." In: B & L, v.IV, p. 336-344.(from 'advance & retreat.

1053 ..."The invasion of Tennessee." In: B & L, v.IV, p. 425-437.

1054 ..."Hood's Nashville Campaign, the Full Story of Franklin & Nashville, Cavalry Operations, Human Interest Stories by Leading Experts-lavishly illustrated." Special Nashville Campaign Edition of "Civil War Times Illustrated), 1964 (Gettysburg, Pa.) 4to, decr. colored wraps, illus., maps, 50 pp.(20)pp-Commemoration Program Battle of Nashville Centennial, Dec. 11-13, 1964. (inserted in center)
Note: Regular issue of Vol. 3, #8, Dec. 1964 was issued, 50 pp., without commemoration program, issued in center (20)p.

1055 ..."Letter from, on causes of Lee's defeat at Gettysburg." In: SHSP, 1877, v.iv, p. 145-150.

1056 ..."Proceedings of the Annual meeting of the Survivors Association of the State of South Carolina, & oration of Jno. B. Hood." Charleston: Walker, Evans & Cogswell, 1873. Address December 12, 1872. 8vo, wraps, 19p. (McKissick-1205)

1057 ..."A Short History of John B. Hood." Park Place, N.Y., Knapp & co, 1888. 2 3/4x1 1/2", colored booklet, 16pp. facsm. signature.(packed in Duke's cigarettes) See: "Heroes of the C.W.", & W. Duke co.

1058 **HOOD, John Bell, Mrs.**
"Hood's Texas Brigade, 53rd. Reunion,

Bryan, Texas, 1924." (Bryan, Texas, 1924 ?) 8vo, wraps, 16pp.

1058a **HOOGERWERF, Frank W.**
Confederate Sheet-Music Imprints." Brooklyn, N.Y., Institute for Studies in American Music. Brooklyn College of CUNY [SAM monograph #21]. 1984. 8vo, wraps, xxix, 158, ills, incl. frontisp, bibliog. & indexes. $12. Consolidates and updates, with new ent

1059 **HOOKER, Charles E., Col.**
"Mississippi." v.IX. 8vo., cl, 515pp. Wilmington, N.C., Broadfoot, 1987.
..."Mississippi." v.IX, Extended Edition. Wilmington, N.C., Broadfoot Pub., 1987. 8vo, cl, 515pp. ills, ports, fldg. map.

1060 **HOOKER, Charles Edward, Col.**
"Albert Sidney Johnston." In: SB, 1882/1883. v.1, p. 319-330.

1061 ..."Mississippi." In: Clement Evans'sonfed. Mil. Hist." VII, 8vo, 4-maps(2-fldg), ports (3-groups), 278 pp.
...Biographical extension edition: "Additional sketches illustrating the services of officers & private & patriotic citizens." p. (279)-515.

1062 ..."Address of...Laying the corner stone of the monument tomb of the Army of Tenn. assn. New Orleans. (Statue of Gen. Albert S. Johnston. In: SHSP, 1883, v.XI, p. 257-269. Also in: S.B., 1882-3, v.I, p. 319-330.

1063 **HOOLE, William Stanley**
"Alabama Tories, The First Alabama Cavalry, U.S.A., 1862-1865." Tuscaloosa, Ala: Confed. Pub. Co., 1960. Confederate Centennial Studies, #16. 12mo, stiff wraps, 141 pp. Lim. edt., 450 copies $20- Bmk, $30- Bmk

1064 ..."Charleston Theatricals During the Tragic Decade, 1860-1869." (Baton Rouge, La.) JSH, Nov. 1945, v.XI, #4, p. 538-547.

1065 ..."The Confederate Armory at Tallassee, Alabama 1864-1865." In: Alabama Review, v.XXV, p. 3-29.

1066 ..."Alabama-built submarine was first to send a battleship." In: Birmingham (Ala News Magazine, Dec. 13, 1953, p. 12-13.

1067 ..."Four Years in the Confederate Navy: The Career of Captain John Low on the C.S.S. Fingal, Florida, Alabama, Tuscaloosa, & Ajax." Athens: Univ. of Georgia pr, 1964. 8vo, cl, dj, map, illus., ports, facsms bibliog., xiv, 147 pp. OP. $20-Bmk $40.

1068 ..."Lawley Covers the Confederacy." Tuscaloosa, Ala: Confed. Pub. Co., 1964 12mo, stiff wraps, port, 132 pp. Lim. Edt: 300 copies

1069 ..."Letters from a Georgia Midshipman on the S.S.S. 'Alabama.'" In: Ga. H.Q. Winter, 1975, v.LIX, #4, p. 416-432.

1070 ..."Alias Simon Suggs: The Life & Times of Johnson Jones Hooper." (Tuscaloosa) Univ. of Ala., press, 1952 8vo, cl, dj, front, bibliog. xxv, 283 pp. Leading Southern humorist, secessionist with DeBow in efforts to develop an econimically strong South. Se: J.J. Hooper.

1071 ..."William L. Yancey's European Diary, March-June, 1861." In: Alabama Review V.XXV, p. 143-142.

1072 ..."Vizetelly Covers the Confederacy." Tuscaloosa, Ala: Conf. Pub. Co., 1957. Confederate Centennial Studies, #4 12 mo, stiff wraps, 173 pp., port, illus. Lim. Edt. 450 copies $20- Bmk.

1073 ..."Historical Sketch of the Fifth Alabama Infantry Regiment, CSA. With a partial Roster of the Regiment." University, Ala., Confederate Pub. Co., 1985. Confederate Regimental Series, #11. 8vo., stiff wraps, 32pp. port.

1073a ..."History of Shockley's Alabama Escort Co.," Edt. See: Morgan S. Gilmer.
..."History of 7th Alabama Cavalry Regmt." See under title.

1073b ..."John W. Mallet & the Confederate Ordnance laboratories, May 1862-65." In:

Ala. Rev., Jan. 1973, p.33-72.

..."The log of bark 'Virginia,' sunk by CSS 'Alabama' (Aug. 26, 1862)." In: Ame Neptune, 1973, #1, p.52-62.

1073c ..."Admiral on Horseback: the Diary of Brig. Gen. Raphael Semmes, Feb./May 1865." In: A. Rev., Apr. 1975, v.28, #2, p.129-50.

..."The Confederate Armory at Tallassee, Ala., 1864-5." In: A. Rev., Jan. 1973, v.25, #1, p.3-29.

..."The CSS "Alabama" at Capetown: Centennial Celebration 1863-1963." In: A. Rev., July 1964, v.17, #3, p.228-35.

HOOLE, William Stanley & Addie Shirley
"Alabama's Boy Generals." University, Alabama, Confederate Pub. Co., 1984. 8vo, wraps, 40pp. ports. Generals John Herbert Kelly & John Caldwell Calhoun Sanders.

1074 **HOOLE, William Stanley & Elizabeth Hoole McArthur**
"The Yankee Invasion of West Alabama, Mar.-Apr. 1865. Including the Battle of Trion (Vance), the Battle of Tuscaloosa, Burning of the University, & the Battle of Romulus." University, Ala., Confederate Pub. Co., 1985. 8vo., stiff wraps, 88pp., illus., ports, map.

1074a ..."The Battle of Resaca, Georgia, May 14-15, 1864." University, Alabama Confederate Pub. Co., 1983. 12mo, wraps, 21pp. maps.

1074b **HOOPER, George**
"Col. Jo Shelby also raids Humansville, Mo. in 1863." In: Polk Co. Historama, Jan. 1980.

1075 **HOOPER, Johnson Jones**
"Simon Suggs' Adventures. Late of the Tallapoosa Volunteers. Together with "Taking the Census", and other Alabama Sketches. With a portrait of Captain Simon Suggs. By Johnson J. Hooper, with ten illustrations by Darley." Phila: T.B. Peterson & bros., (1881) 12mo, cl, illus., front, 2, 17-217 pp.

...Chapel Hill: Univ. N.C. Press, 1969 12mo, wraps, 207 pp. Ala. newspaperman, helped form CSA & popular among leaders of the South. See: Stanley Hoole.

1076 ..."Some Adventures of Capt. Simon Suggs Upper Saddle River, N.J., Literature Hse., 1970. 8vo, cl, illus., 201 pp.

1077 **HOOVER, Sallie Wellford Scott, Hist. UDC.**
See: "Confed. Soldiers Randolph Co." under title

1078 ..."Colonal John Augustine Washington, CSA" In: Mag. Hist. & Biog., 1926, v.III, p. 19-28. Lee's Aide at Elkwater, Randolph co.

1079 **HOPE, James Barron, Capt.**
"Mahone's Brigade. A metrical address recited on the anniversary of the Battle of Crater, before surviving officers & men of Mahone's Brigade." n.p., n.d., 8vo, wraps, cover title, 8pp. $10-

1080 **HOPKINS, Abner C.**
"Letter, with enclosures concerning John Brown at Harper's Ferry." In: SHSP, 1885, v.13, p. 337-342.

1081 **HOPKINS, Garland Evans, F.I.A.G.**
"The First Battle of Modern Naval History." Richmond, Va., House of Dietz, 1943 $10- 8vo, fabricoid, dj, woodcuts(incl. front) 34 pp. Lim. Edt., 199 copies (#2), atgd. $75-, $124-, $100-, Bmk-104 $60-

1082 **HOPKINS, George**
"Imprisoned under fire." In: SHSP, 1897 v. 25, p. 377.

1083 **HOPKINS, John Baker**
"The Fall of the Confederacy." London: William Freeman(1867) 12 mo, wraps, 96 pp. $175-DB Sabin, 32923: Hopkin's Introduction to Hon. James Williams' - "The South Vindicated, etc." London: 186-, 8vo, p. xii, 40.

1084 ..."Peace or War? An Unbiassed View of the American Crisis." London: Diprose & Bateman, 1861, 8vo, wraps, 15pp., Sabin, 32925

1085 **HOPKINS, Luther Wesley**
"From Bull Run to Appomattox; a boy's view, by L.W. Hopkins of Gen. J.E.B. Stuart's Cavalry, 6th Virginia regiment, C.S.A." Baltimore: Fleet-McGinley co, (1908) 12mo, cl, front, pls., ports, fldg. map in pocket, $15-, $17.50, $22.50 $95-, $70-, $55-, $84
...(2nd Edt.) (1908) contains five add'l. chapters, 311 pp.

1086 ...3rd Edt., Jan. 1911-1915, fldg. map & plan, plates, facsm., ports, 1-color pl. $75-, $60- Bmk-111, $70- Insert song: "Good Old Rebel war song between p. 238-239.
...Another Edt. (1918)

1087 **HOPLEY, Catherine Cooper**
"Life in the South; from the commencement of the War. By a Blockaded British Subject Being a Social History of those who took part in the Battles, from a personal acquaintance with them in their homes. From the Spring of 1800 to August 1862." By S.L.J. London: Chapman & Hall, 1863. $50-, $80-, $125- Gin2, $200- MKM, $250- Bkm, $300- 12mo, cl, xvi, 427, viii, 404 pp. fldg. map of the Battle of Bethel Church(not in all books). Variously attributed to Sarah L. Jones but definitely Miss Hopley, whose personal copy in the Va. Hist. Soc., with marginal notes. See next item. (Hopley)
...N.Y., Da Capo Press, 1968 reprint. Also: Louisville: Lost Cause Press, microcard.
...N.Y., Da Capo Press, 1974. "American Scene Series." N.Y. Kelley Pr., 1979 $40-, $49.50

1088 ..."Catherine Cooper Hopley." (Richmond) Va. Mag. Hist. Biog., Jan. 1949, v.57, #1, p. 77-78. The London, 1863 edition can also be found in 1 vol., $37.50
See: "Stonewall Jackson", late Gen.,...under title

1089 **HOPSON, Ella Lord, Edt. by wife**
"Memoirs of Dr. Winthrop Harlty Hopson." Cincinnati: Standard Pub. Co., 1887 8vo, cl, xiii, 239, frontis(port) Experiences Cambellite minister in Missouri. Incarcerated as southern sympathizer during war, then served under Jno. Morgan as chaplain.

1090 **HORAN, James David**
"Confederate Agent A Discovery in History." New York: Crown Pub., (1954 8vo, cl, map end-sheets, fron(port)ports, illus., facsms. xxii, (5), 326 pp., d/w $117 Bmk-25, $15 ok
...(1954)a (1960) reprint, differs: stiffer paper, blacker face type, orange color covers instead of gray (1st. Edt.) all edges trimmed, while 1st has one edge uncut.
See: Elizabeth Coombs' detailed corrections of facts in volume: Ky. Hist. Soc., Oct. 1954, v. 52, p. 360-365
...Fairfax Press (Crown Pub. Co., 1977)

1091 ..."Desperate Women." N.Y., G.P. Putnam's sons (1952) 8vo, cl, dj, ports, illus., facsms, xi, (1), 336 pp. Greenhow, Belle Boyd. $20-

1092 ..."Seek Out & Destroy." N.Y., Crown pub., (1958) 8vo, cl, dj, 302 pp. Fiction, about "Shenandoah," a famous raider of the CSA navy.

1093 **HORD, Ben M'Culloch**
"Forty hours in a dungeon at Rock Island." In: CV, 1904, v. 12, p. 385-389, port, Hord was in Dobbin's Regiment, Walker's brigade of Arkansas cavalry.

1094 **HORN, Stanley Fitzgerald**
"The Army of Tennessee A Military History. by Stanley F. Horn." Indianapolis-N.Y., Bobbs-Merrill (1941). Tk. 8vo, cl, dj, ports, incl. front, facsms., maps, views, bibliog(483-487), notes (431-79) xiii, 503 pp. $15-, $20-, $26-, $30-, $75- MM

...Norman: Univ. of Oklahoma pr. (1952), (1953) $25- B, $40-, (1955), (1968) $25- $20- Y, OP, $85- JK, $75- MM
...Tennessee Edt., Lim. 1000 copies (1941 atg. by author $100-

1095 ..."The Boy's Life of Robert E. Lee." N.Y., Harper's., 1935 12mo, cl, dj, illus., ports, maps, ix, 328 pp. $435- Y(15)
...N.Y., Grossett & Dunlap (1935)

1096 ..."The Decisive Battle of Nashville." Baton Rouge: Louisiana Univ. pr. (1956) 12mo, bds., illus., ports, 2-maps, xiii, (2), 181 pp. $7.50, $10-, $20- Y, $35- B
...Same: "Civil War Book Club," Atg. by author for members. special t/p. gray dj, (trade edt: pink dj.)
...Same(Revised, March 1957)
...3rd Edt.(Nov. 1968) Knoxville: Univ. Tennessee press $20- Y
...(In Print, 1983) 200 pp., illus.

1097 ..."Gallant Rebel The Fabulous Cruise of the C.S.S. 'Shenandoah'." New Brunswick, N.J., Rutgers Univ, 1947 12mo, cl, dj, map-endsheets, viii, (1), 292 pp. $20- Y (Atg.) $20- $25-

1098 ...The Robert E. Lee Reader, Edited by Stanley F. Horn." Indianapolis, N.Y., Bobbs-Merrill (1949) 8vo, cl, dj, illus., ports, incl. front, facsimilie letter, inserted. $30- Bmk-84, $20- Bmk

1099 ..."Robert E. Lee: a defeated soldier plucks the flower of fame from the thistle of failure." In: Am. heritage, Winter 1952, v.3, #2., p. 16-17, 81, 84. Port, view. On Lee's presidency of Wash. & Lee College, 1865-1870.

1100 ..."Nashville During the War." In: Tenn. HQ, 1945, v. IV, p. 3-22. Reprinted in "Tenn. Old & New." II, p. 223-241.

1101 ..."Dr. John Rolfe Hudson & the Confederate underground in Nashville." In: Tenn. HQ, 1963, v.XXII, p. 38-52.

1102 ..."Perryville-Bragg's invasion of Kentucky brought no laurels to either side." In: CWTI Feb. 1966, v.4, #10, p. 4-11, 42-47, illus., map ports.

1103 ..."The Spring Hill Legend-the Nashville Campaign." In: CWTI, April 1969, v.XIII, #1, p. 20-32, illus., maps, ports.

1104 ..."Tennessee's War 1861-1865 described by participants. Compiled & edited by..." Nashville: Tennessee Civil War Centennial Commission (1965) 4to, cl, dj, map endsheets, 364 pp. $30-, $40-
See: as chairman of C.W. Cent. Comm's.
..."Tennesseans in the Civil War." 2 vols. - 1980 $19-

1105 **HORNADY, Henry Carr**
"How to be saved." Macon, Ga., n.d. (186?) 12mo, sewn, 4pp. CSA Tract. bmk- $150-
Pastor of Atlanta's Baptist Church

1106 **HORNBECK, Betty Dutton**
"Upshur Brothers of the Blue & Gray." (Buckhannon: The Republican-Delta, 1962) 8vo, cl, ports, illus., maps, 259 pp. OP Bmk $35-

1107 **HORNER, Dave**
"The Blockade Runners, True Tales of Running the Yankee Blockade of the Confederate Coast." New York: Dodd, Meade & Co. (1968) $35- Bmk-84 8vo, cl, d/w, illus., 241 pp.

1107a **HORRY, Harriott Pinckney**
"A Colonial Plantation Cookbook: The receipt book of Harriott Pinckney Horry, 1770. Edt. with intro. by Richard J. Hooker." Columbia, University of South Carolina Press, 1984. 8vo, paper, 157pp, ills, front, index. $15.

1108 **HORSLEY, Reginald Ernest**
"Stonewall's Scout: a Story of the American Civil War." London: Sampson, Low, Marston, 1896. 12mo, cl., vi, 372pp.
Juvenile about Stonewall Jackson.

1109 **HORST, Samuel L.**
"Mennonites in the Confederacy: A Study in Civil War Pacifism." Scottdale, Pa.,

Herald Press, 1967 8vo, cl, d/w, p. 148, illus., fld. map. $10- Bmk.

1110 HORTON, Louise
"Gen. Sam Bell Maxey Prepares for the Invasion of Kentucky Fall 1862." In: RKHS Spring 1981, v.79, #2, p.122-135, ports (3)

1111 HORTON, Louise W.
"Sam Bell Maxey. A biography." Austin, Texas: Univ. of Tex., (1974) 8vo, cl, dj, illus., xii, 222 pp. bibliog. (197)-211.

1112 ..."General Sam Bell Maxey: His defense of North Texas & the Indian Territory." In: SwHQ, April 1971, v. LXXIV, #4, p. 507-524, maps.

1113 HORTON, R.G.
"A Youth's History of the Great Civil War in the United States from 1861-1865." New York: Van Evrie, Horton & Co., 1866 12mo, cl, illus.(incl. front) ports, (xiv)-383 pp. (8) pp. ads. $35-
...1866, also, 2nd edt.
1867 (45th Edt.) as above $25- NC
...1868 edition, Sabin 33078
...1925 New & revised edition, Mary D. Carter & Lloyd T. Everett, edts. Dallas, Texas: Southern Pub. Co. 12mo, cl, d/j, xxii, 298 pp. Diatribe against Lincoln, Republican party & abolitionists, not juvenile. Northern Man, a copperhead, against Lincoln.

1114 HOSFORD, John W., Lt.
"A Florida soldier in the Army of Northern Virginia: The Hosford Letters." Edt.: Knox Mellon, Jr. In: FHQ, v.XLVI, #3, p. 243-271.

1115 HOSLETT, Schuyler Dean
"Southern expectations of British intervention in the civil war, as reflected in the newspapers of Richmond, Va." In: Tyler's QHGMag., Oct. 1940, v.XXII, p. 19.

1116 ..."The Richmond daily press on British intervention in the civil war." In: Wm. & Mary Quart., 2nd ser., 1940, v.XX, p. 79-83.

1117 ..."Hospital Regulations-with additional rules." Broadside 10x7.
Signed: E.W. McCrary, Surgeon-in-Charge, 1st Arkansas Hospital. Fort Gaines, Ga., Aug. 22, 1864. Cuthbert, Ga., Byrd's Job Office. Not in Crandall/Harwell.(Ark. Hist. Com.)

1118 HOTCHKISS, Jed, Maj.
"Virginia", v. IV, 8vo., cl., 1293pp. Wilmington, N.C., Broadfoot, 1987.

1118a HOTCHKISS, Jedediah, Mapmaker See: Under Wm. Allan, Archie McDonald.

1119 HOTCHKISS, Jedediah
"The Battlefields of Virginia. Chancellorsville; embracing the operations of the Army of Northern Virginia, from the first Battle of Fredericksburg to the death of Lieut. General Jackson. By Jed Hotchkiss & Wm. Allan." N.Y., D. Van Nostrand; London: Trubner & co., 1867 8vo, cl, front(port), fldg. maps, 152 pp. Includes H. McGuire's "Last days of Jackson." p. 118-31. Bmk(105) $175-, $200- DB, Atg. $300- B
...and William Allan: Baltimore, Butternut & Blue, 1984. 8vo, dj, fldg. map in color, 152pp. Limited to 600 copies. $40.

1120 ..."The Hotchkiss map collection; a list of manuscript maps, many of the civil war period, prepared by Maj. Jed Hotchkiss, & other manuscript & annotated maps in his possession, compiled by Clara Egli LeGear with a foreword by Willard Webb." Wash: Lib. Congr., Map Div., 1951 8vo, wraps, 67 pp. (341 maps).

1121 ...Make me a Map of the Valley: The Civil War Journal of Jackson's Topographer. Edt.: Archie P. McDonald. Dallas, Texas: Southern Methodist Univ. press, 1973. 8vo, cl, dj, xxxvii, 352 pp. Bmk $30-, $40-, $50-

1122 ..."Virginia". In: C.A. Evans "Confederate Military History." $15- $18- Atlanta, Ga., Confederate pub. co., 1899. 8vo, cl, port, group ports, 11-maps, some fold, v.III
...Same, extended-"additional sketches illustrating services of officers, privates & patriotic citizens." 1295 pp. $100-
...(Dayton, Ohio) Morningside Bookshop, 1975. Tk. 8vo, cl, facsimilie #23. $50- $40- Y
See:Arch. P. McDonald & Everard Meade

1123 **HOTZE, Henry**
"Three Months in the Confederate Army, printed in facsimilie from the London Index, 1862. Intro. & notes by Richard Barksdale Harwell." University: Univ. Ala. press 1952 8vo, wraps, 38pp. $20- Bmk $30- Bmk 97

1124 ..."The creed of a propagandist; letter from a Confederate editor. Edt: Richard Barksdale Harwell. In: Journalism qurt. Spring, 1951, v. 28, p. 213-218. notes. To John George Witt, London: 11th Aug., 1864 on "The Index", edited by Hotze for CSA.

1124a **HOUCK, Peter W.** "A Prototype of a Confederate Hospital Center in Lynchburg, Va." Lynchburg, Va., Warwick House Pub., 1986. 8vo, cl, 228pp, ills (some color), facsms, biblg., index. Pres. copy. $20.

1125 **HOUGHTON, Mitchell Bennett**
"From the beginning until now." (Birmingham, Al., 1912/1914?) 8vo, cl, illus., 2-ports, 276 pp.(old) $150- In: 15th Ala. Inf.

1126 **HOUGHTON, William Robert & M.B.**
"Two Boys in the Civil War & after." Montgomery, Ala., Paragon pr, 1912 8vo, cl, front, 2-ports, 242 pp. Atg. (M.B.) $125-, $350--G, $225-R

1127 **HOUK, Eliza Phillips [Thurston], Mrs.**
"A tribute to General Gates Phillips Thruston." (Dayton, Ohio, United Brethern Publishing House, 1914. 8vo, cl, illus., incl. ports, 129 pp. See also: Gen. Gates P. Thruston.

1128 **"HOUSE JOURNAL of the 9th Legislature,**
Regular Session of the State of Texas." Nov. 4, 1861-Jan. 14, 1862." Edt: James M. Day. (400 copies, Waco: Texian Press.) Austin: Texas State Library, 1964. 8vo, gray buck, front, ports, index, 166 pp.
..."House Journal of the 9th Legislature, First Called Session of the State of Texas. Feb. 1, 1863-Mar. 7, 1863." Edt: James M. Day. (400 copies, Waco: Texian Press.) Austin: Texas State Library, 1963 8vo, gray buck, front, ports, 253 pp., index.
..."House Journal of the Tenth Legislature, Regular Session of State of Texas. Nov. 3- Dec. 16, 1863." Edt: James M. Day.(400 copies, Waco, Texian Press) Austin: Texas State Library, 1965. 8vo, gray buck, front, index, ports, 288 pp.
See also: Senate/Senate & House Journals Texas.

1129 **HOUSE, Albert V., Jr.**
"Northern Congressional Democrats as defenders of the South during Reconstruction." In: JSH, Feb. 1940, v.vi, p. 46-71. $8-
..."Deterioration of a Georgia Rice plantation during four years of Civil War." Edt. by Avery V. House, Jr. In: JSH, 1943, v.9, #1, p.98-112.

1129a **HOUSE BILL #411** A Bill to be entitled "An Act Relating to Kansas," Sept. 13, 1863 8vo, 2pp. $8- Kansas equitably belongs to the CSA.

1130 **HOUSE, Boyce**
"Confederate Navy Hero put the flag back in place!" In: Tenn. HQ, June 1960, v.XIX, p. 172-175. Dabney M. Scales daring conduct while aboard CSS Arkansas at Vicksburg.

1131 **HOUSTON, A.M., Mrs.**
"The evacuation of Richmond." In: CV, Apr. 1916, v. XXIV, p. 165-166.

1132 **HOUSTON, David Franklin**
"Ordinances of Secession & other documents, 1860-1861." Edt: A.B. Hart & E. Channing. (Amer. Hist. Leaflets, #12, Nov., 1893) Print. Supvr., David F. Houston. 16mo, wrap, 22 pp. N.Y. A. Lovell & co., 1896. N.Y., P.O. Simmons co.(c.1917) Reprint. 8vo, wraps, cover title, 22 pp.

1133 ..."A critical study of Nullification in South Carolina." Harvard Historical Studies, v.III, The Henry Warren Torrey Fund. N.Y., Longamns, Green & co., 1896 $30- Roy sm.8vo, cl, ix, 169 pp.

1134 **HOUSTON, Mollie H.**
"President Davis & General Johnston." In: Confed. Vet. Je/Ag. 1919, v.XXVII, p. 216-18, 256-8, 302-304.

1135 ..."The Misrepresentation of Jefferson Davis in History & Fiction.: In: C.V., July 1918, v.XXVI, p. 289-291.

1136 ..."Jefferson Davis, the sublime martyr of all ages." In: CV, Jan. 1921, v.XXIX< p. 14-15.

1137 ..."The unanimity of the choice of Mr. Davis." In: CV, Mar. 1921, v.XXIX, p. 88-89.

1138 **HOUSTON, R.M.**
"The Confederacy after July 4, 1863." In: CV June 1914, v.XXII, p. 262-264.

1139 **HOUSTON, Sam**
"Message of Gov. Sam Houston, on the South Carolina Resolution." Austin: John Marshall & co, 1860 8vo, sewn, 16pp. $250- Houston exhorts Texas not to secede, resulting in his retirement.

1140 **HOUSTON, Sam - Senate, Texas**
"Resolution." Jan. 14, 1850 $30- Washington, DC. Senate Doc. 27, 1p. "Congress has no power over negro slavery in the U.S., Slavery in Southern, Western states no conflict as admission to union.

1141 ..."Letter From Sam Houston on "The Crisis." Huntsville, Texas, Nov. 14, 1860. (Galveston, Texas: Daily Civilian Steam Press) 8vo, sewed, 4pp. printed two columns. Comm. asking Houston's opinion on secession.

1142 ..."Proclamation Feb. 9, 1861." Broadside 23 1/2X50 1/2 cm. (Austin, 1861) Crandall-2195. Reprint: Waco, Texas: Morrison's (c.1964) Calling election, for-/against secession. $4500 (Reuben-27)

1143 ..."Proclamation by the Governor." Broadside, 14x17", Austin, Texas. Sept. 19, 1860. $2250-Jenkins, 1978.
Calls for general election (Lincoln elected) Texas secedes from Union.

1144 ..."Sam Houston's Speech at Independence Texas, May 10, 1861." In: Texana, 1972, v.X, p. 191-195. Supports cause of secession, now the people of Texas have spoken.

1145 ..."To the People of Texas." Broadside Austin, Tex., March 16, 1861. 17x42cm. Declares secession invalid, he will remain Gov. of Texas, refuses to take oath of allegiance to CSA. Houston was ousted next day. jk-127 $3000- Winkler locates four copies.

1146 ..."Civil war letters of Sam Houston. Edt: David P. Smith.: In: SWHQ, Apr. 1978, v.LXXX1, #4, p. 416-426.

1167 **HOUSTON, Samuel, Jr.**
"Shiloh Shadows." In: So. W. Hist. Quart. 1930, v.XXXIV, p. 329-333.

1168 **HOUSTON, TEXAS-"CHRONICLE"-**
"The First Ironclad, constructed & commanded by a Texan(C.W. Austin)" In: SHSP, 1902, v.30, p. 196-204. It was the "Enoch Train", rebuilt in New Orleans.

1169 **HOUSTON, TEXAS: Civil War Round Table.**
See: Dr. A.Q. Cato; Monroe Covkrell, Lester N. Fitzhugh, Harry McCorry Henderson, Walter Herbert, Dan O'Flaherty,

J.W. Petty, Jr., Ezra W. Warner, T. Harry Williams.

1169a **HOUZEAU, Jean-Charles**
"My Passage at the New Orleans Tribune. A Memoir of the Civil War Era. Edt: David C. Rankin; Trans: Gerald F. Denault." Baton Rouge, Louisiana State Univ., Pr. 1984.

1170 **HOVEY, Carl**
"Stonewall Jackson." Bost: Small, Maynard co., 1900. 'The Beacon Biographies.' 16mo, cl, front(port)xi, 131 pp. --1908 Bmk $25- Bmk $40-

1171 **"HOW THE CONFEDERACY Armed Its Soldiers."**
In: CV, Jan. 1922, v.XXX, p. 10-11. Development & mfg. firearms & munitions.

1172 **"HOW THE SEVEN DAYS' BATTLE Around Richmond Began."**
In: SHSP, 1900, v.XXVIII, p. 99-97. Signed: J.B.M.

1173 **"HOW WE FAILED TO WIN."**
In: SHSP, 1902, v.30, p. 368-371.

1174 **HOWARD, Annie Hornaday & Florine Harden Smith**
"Intimate Glimpses into the Life of Alexander Hamilton Stephens." In: GHQ, 1921, v.XVI, p. 38-46.

1175 **HOWARD, Charles Wallace, Rev.**
"The Women of the late war. An address delivered in Hibernian Hall, Charleston, S.C., Feb. 11, 1874, in behalf of the Confederate Home, Charleston." Charleston, S.C., A.J. Burke, 1875 8vo, wraps, 17pp.

1176 **HOWARD, D.R.**
"General Steuart's Brigade at Gettysburg." In: SHSP, 1876, v.2, p. 105-107.

1177 **HOWARD, Frances Thomas**
"In & Out of the Lines. An accurate account of incidents during the occupation of Georgia by Federal troops in 1864-1865." N.Y., Neale pub., 1905 12mo, cl, 4,(5)-238 pp. Bmk-105 $100- Written in 1870, exp. of southern family.

1178 **HOWARD, Frank Key**
"Fourteen Months in American Bastiles." Balt: Kelly, Hedian & Piet,, 1863 8vo, wraps, 89 pp., three editions. $18-, $25-, $75- G, $50- Ginz
...Lond: Henry F. Mackintosh, 1863 8vo, wraps, 84 pp.
An influential news editor, imprisoned by Lincoln at Ft. Monroe, with other leading Md. legislators.

1179 **HOWARD, James L.**
"Hope of Glory. A tale of Shiloh & the Civil War." NY, Pageant press (1961) 12mo, cl, dj, 239. Based on authentic documents fictionalized, border state KY.

1180 **HOWARD, James McHenry**
"Recollections of a Maryland Confederate soldier & staff officer under Johnston, Jackson & Lee." Balt: Williams & Wilkins, 1914. Tall 8vo, front, illus. pls., fldg. map, facsms. 423 pp. Errata sheet is rare. $225 $175 Bmk $200
...Louisv: Lost Cause pr., micro-cd., $6.39
...Dayton, Ohio: Morningside Press, 1975. 8vo, cl, illus, facsms., illus, maps, (2), xx, 483 pp. map lines, $20 Introduction, corrections & notes by James I. Robertson, Jr., Head History Department, Virginia Polytechnic Institute & State University. (Intro: xxpp, Notes & Corrections, p. 424-483.)

1181 ..."Closing scenes of the war about Richmond. Retreat of Custis Lee's Div. & Battle of Sailor's Creek. By Capt. McHenry Howard of Balt., Ass't. Inspec. Gen., CSA, Gen. Custis Lee's Division." From New Orleans' Picayune, Oct. 4-11, 1903. In: SHSP, 1903, v.XXXI, pp. 129-145.

1182 ..."Notes & recollections of the opening of the Campaign of 1864." In: Mil. Hist. Soc. Mass Papr..Bost: 1905, v. IV, pp. 81-116.

1183 ..."Retreat of Custis Lee's division & battle of Sailor's Creek." In: SHST, 1874, v.I, p. 61-72 See: "Unveiling of Confederate Monument, May 2 Address by McHenry Howard. under title. See: Tunstall Smith Memoir.

1184 ..."Recollections & Opinions Concerning the Events which Immediately Preceded & Followed the Outbreak of the War Between the Northern & Southern States." Balt: Sun Book & Job Print, 1922. 8vo., wraps, 46pp. $150.00 ob. 'A fragment left by Howard, who had been a student at Univ. of Va. & volunteered for service in the Confed. States. Priv. print for friends.

1185 **HOWARD, John**
"The Evacuation of Richmond, April 3, 1865 & disastrous conflagration, etc." In: SHSP, 1895, , p. 175-181.

1186 **HOWARD, Milo B., Jr.**
"Alabama State Currency, 1861-1865." In: Ala. Hist. Quart., Spring-Summer 1963, v. 25, #1 & 2, pp. 70-98, facsms.

1186a **HOWARD, Oliver Otis**
"General Robert E. Lee." In: Frank Leslie Pop. Monthly, Dec. 1896, v.42, p.641-8

1187 **HOWARD, Robert Milton**
"Reminiscences." Columbus, Ga., Gilbert print, 1912 12mo, cl, ports (incl. front), (5), 346 pp. Author in 2nd S.C. Reg., $16.50, $45-, $75 ob

1188 **HOWARD, Victor B.**
"The Kentucky Press & the Black Suffrage Controversy, 1865-1872."
In: FCHQ, July 1973, v. 47, #3, pp. 215-237.

1189 ..."John Brown's Raid at Harper's Ferry & the Sectional Crisis in North Carolina." In: NCHR, Oct. 1978, v.55, #4, p.396-420. Facsm. map, ports.

1190 **HOWARD, Wilcy C.**
"Sketch of Cobb Legion Cavalry & Some Incidents & Scenes Remembered." Suffolk, Va., Robt. Hardy, 1986. 8vo., wraps, 24pp., port.

1191 **HOWARD, Wiley C. of Company C.**
"Sketch of Cobb Legion Cavalry & some incidents & scenes remembered." Prepared & read under appointment of Atlanta camp 159, UCV, Aug. 19, 1901." (Atlanta, 1901) 8vo, wraps, port on cover, 20 pp., $50, $175-ob DeRene-III, 981, reports their 2nd copy "same, but with portrait of author on the cover." With clipping laid in, with Capt. Eve's April 30, 1893 address on "Cobb's Legion," from "Athens Banner."
...Facsimile reprint, n.p., n.d., 8vo, pict. wraps, 22 pp. $20-, Atlanta(recent reprint), Bmk $20

1192 **HOWE, Daniel Dunbar**
"Listen to the mockingbird: the life & times of a pioneer Virginia family." Boyce, Va., Carr pub. co., 1961, 8vo, cl, 373 pp. illus., 1000 copies. Family life during civil war & reconstruction. John Howe Capt., Co. E., 4th Va.

1193 **HOWE, J.L.**
"Confederate postage stamps. " In: CV, Cugust 1914, v. XXII, p. 347-348.

1194 **HOWELL, Alfred Thomas**
"A Texan in the Civil War. Edts: William E. Sawyer & Neal A. Baker, jr." In: Tex. Mil. Hist., 1962, v. IV, p. 275-278. In the 34th & 22nd Texas Cavalry.

1195 **HOWELL, Clark**
The Aftermath of Reconstruction; how the South found itself." In: Century, Apr. 1913, v. LXXXV, pp. 844-853. Southern view of Reconstruction.

1196 **HOWELL, D.S.**
"Along the Texas frontier during the Civil War." (Abilene, Texas) West Tex. Hist. Assoc. Yr. Bk., 1937, v.XIII, pp. 82-95.

1197 **HOWELL, E. Vernon**
"Medical & Pharmaceutical Conditions in the Confederacy." In: N.C. Lit. & Hist. As-

soc. Proceedings, 1917. 33 pp. $15-Bmk. See also: Norman H. Franke.

1198 **HOWELL, Elmo**
"William Faulkner & the Andrews Raid in Georgia, 1862." In: Ga. H.Q. June 1965, v. XLIX, #2, p. 187-192.

1199 **HOWELL, Gertrude Jenkins**
"What Fort Fisher meant to the Confederacy." In: CV, 1930, v. 38, p. 226-230.

1200 **HOWELL, H. Grady, Jr.**
"Going to meet the Yankees, a history of the 'Bloody Sixth' Mississippi Infantry. CSA Jackson, Miss., Chickasaw Bayou Press, 8vo, cl. illus., index, 388 pp. $30- 1981. Complete muster roll of each company.

1201 **HOWELL, R.H.**
Lithograph: "The First Flag of Independence Raised in the South, by the Citizens of Savannah Georgia, Nov. 8, 1960 Savannah, Ga., (after Henry Cleenewerck.)

1202 **HOWISON, Robert Reid**
"History of the War." In: South. Lit. Mess., Richmond, Va., 1834-64. v. 36 (i.e., 34) 1862: p. 172-188, (209)-228, (273)-288, (335)-352, (401)-425, (513)-530, (593)-613, v. 37 (i.e., 35) 1863: p. (1)-14, (65)-78, (129)-147, (193)-206, (257)-270, (321)-337, (385)-397, (449)-462, (513)-527, (577)-589, (641)-654, v. 38 (i.e. 36) 1864, p. 15-27, (65)-77, (129)-138, (193)-205, (257)-269, (321)-333. From LC. Campaigns: Cheat Mt., E. Panhandle, Kanawha & Tygart Mts.

1203 **HOWLETT HOUSE, Capture of...**
"A Desperate Dash-Capture & reoccupation of the Howlett House in 1864." In: SHSP, 1893 v. 21, p. 177-183. See Morrison (Emmett M.)

1203 **HOWRY, Charles B.**
"Responsibility for the war." In: CV, Mar., 1923, v. XXXI, p. 90-93.

1204 **HOWSLEY, Marilynne**
"Forting up on the Texas Frontier during the Civil War." (Abilene, Tex.) West. Tex. Hist. Assoc. Yr. Bk., 1941, v. XVIII, p. 71- 76.

1205 **HOY, Patrick Crawford**
"Brief History of Bradford's Battery Confederate Guards Artillery of Pontotoc County, Miss., Personal Recollections of Lt. P.C. Hoy." (Petersburg, Va., 1903) 8vo, cover title, 32, (1) pp. (Miss. Archives shows: (Pontotoc, Miss. Advocate Print, 1903), as (1), 33 pp.)
...2nd, (Pontotoc, Miss. E.T. Winston, 1932, wraps, 8vo, pp. 254-76. $150-
...Also, in E.T. Winston-"Story of Pontotoc, part 1-III." (Pontotoc, Miss., Pontotoc progress print, 1931. 8vo, cl, 192, (6), 203-319 (4) pp. part III-"War & Reocnstruction."
...Dornbusch-557 records MOLLUS-Mich., II, p. 153-166. "Personal Recollections of the Siege of Petersburg by Confederate Officer (P.C. Hay) (sic)

1206 **HOYT, James Alfred**
"The Palmetto Rifleman. Co. B, Fourth regiment S.C. Vols. Co. C, Palmetto Sharpshooters. Historical Sketch. An address delivered by James A. Hoyt on 21st. July, 1885. Together with a roll of the company & other information." (Greenville,S.C., Hoyt & Keys pr, 1886) 12mo, wraps, 59 pp.

1207 ..."The Confederate Archives & Felix Gregory de Fontaine." In: SCHMag., Oct. 1956, v.57, #4, p. 199-203. Rescues Richmond (CSA) records to Chester, S.C., later selling most of them.

1208 **HOYT, William D., Jr., Edt.**
"To Coosawhatchie in December 1861." (Charleston: So.Caro. Hist. & Genea. Mag. Jan. 1952, v.LIII, #1, p. 6-12. Letters of Joseph W. Turner (Virginia) with Turner's Artillery., in protection of Carolinas.
..."New Light on General Jubal A. Early after Appomattox. Edt: Wm. D. Hoyt." In:

JSH, 1943, v.9, #1, p.113-17.

..."Some Personal Letters of Robert E. Lee 1850-8." In: JSH, v.12, #4, Nov. 1946.

1209 **HUBARD, R.T., Adj., 3rd. Va. Cavalry**
"Operations of Gen. Stuart before Chacellorsville." In: SHSP, 1880, v.8, p. 249-254.

1210 **HUBBARD, Henry Clyde**
"Pro-Southern" influences in the free West 1840-1865." In: MVHR, 1933, v.XX, p. 45-62.

1211 **HUBBARD, J. Milton**
"Notes of a Private." Boliver, Tenn., R.P. Shackelford, 1973. 8vo., 207pp., front port. 'Souvenir Edition.'

1212 **HUBBARD, John Milton**
"Notes of a Private, by John Milton Hubbard, Co. E, 7th Tenn. Reg." Memphis: E.H. Clark*bro, 1909. 12mo, cl, front(port), illus., 189 pp. $25.00, $30.00, $32.50, $200.00, Ex-Lib $125.00 Bmk, JK(142) $100.00

...Louisv: Lost Cause, micro-cd $3.83

...St. Louis, Mo., Nixon-Jones, 1911 12mo, cl, port(front), illus., 207 pp. $35.00, $100.00 JC Souvenir Edt., $17.50, $27.50, $30.00

...Same, 1913 edition, "Memorial Edt." 212 pp.

...Same, 1915 edition, $105.00 Boston

1213 ..."Notes of a Private," reprinted in Robt. S. Henry's "As they saw Forrest," chaps: 1-12, but omits II, III, IV, V, the non-Forrest period, See p. 135-223.

1214 **HUBBELL, Finley L.**
"Diary of Lieut. Col. Hubbell, of 3d. regiment Missouri Infantry, CSA." In: LWL, Dec. 1868, v. VI, #2, p. 97-105 Sig: M.F.P., Carrollton, Mo.

1215 **HUBBELL, Jay Broadus**
"The Last Years of Henry Timrod, 1864-1867, including letters of Timrod to Paul Hayne & Letters about Timrod by William Gilmore Simms, John R. Thompson, John Greenleaf Whittier, & others. With four uncollected poems & several uncollected prose pieces. Drawn chiefly from the Paul Hamilton Haynes collection in the Duke University Library. Edited by Jay B. Hubbell." Durham, N.C., Duke University pr., 1941, 12mo, cl, xi, 184 pp. Wartime letters from Columbia, S.C. See: Henry Timrod & Paul Hayne.

1215a ..."Southern Life in Fiction." Athens: University of Ga. Press, (1960). 8vo., wraps, 99pp. (Eugenia Dorothy Blount Lamar Memorial Lectures. 1959)

1216 **HUBBELL, John T.**
"Three Georgia Unionists & the Compromise of 1850." In: Ga. H.Q., Sept. 1967, v. LI, #3, p. 307-323.

1217 **HUBBELL, Raynor**
"Confederate Stamps, Old Letters, & History. A story of three score years & ten of stamp collecting. What it has done for me & what it could do for you whatever may be your age." $50-Bmk, $60- Pres. Griffin, Ga.: Confederate Hdq. (c. 1958), 4to, cl, facsms, illus., ports, , 67, (1)-22 pp. Append: 'Diary Capt. John H. Harris,' Muster rolls: Co. I, 44th Ga: Co. E, Morgan & Henry Volunteers(counties)

1218 **HUBBERT, Mike M.**
"The travels of the 13th Mississippi Regiment: excerpts from the diary of Mike M. Hubbert of Attala County (1861-1862.)" Edt: John E. Fisher." In: JMH, Nov. 1983, v. XLV, #4, p. 288-313.

1219 **HUBER, Leonard Victor**
"The Battle of the Handkerchiefs." In: CWH, March 1962, v. VIII, #1, P. 48-53, pls.

1220 ..."Blockade-run mail from New Orleans, 1862-1864." In: Am. Philatelist, Feb. 1951, v. 64, p. 337-348. Facsms, views, notes. Letters to Emile Reynes from Polyxene & Joseph Reynes.

1221 ..."Confederate mail forwarders, 1863-1864: the Louisiana Relief Committee at

Mobile." In: Am. philatelist, Mar/Apr., 1953, v. 66, p. 451-458, 505-511, facsms, views.

1222 ..."Confederate mail packets on the lower Mississippi: a short history of their relation to the organization & first year of operation of the Confederate States Post Office Dep't. March 1861-March 1862." In: Amer. philatelist Sept. 1956, v.69, p. 857-866. facsma, port, views, notes.

1223 ..."The saga of Captain Absalom Grimes, CSA mail carrier extraordinary." In: Am. philatelist, July 1952, v.65, p. 761-767. port, views. Delivery of mail between Mo/Miss., 1862-1863.

1224 **HUBNER, Charles William**
"War Poets of the South & Confederate Camp-fire Songs." (Atlanta, Ga., c. 1896?) (C.P. Byrd press) 12mo, wraps, vii, illus., 176 pp., N.Y. Neale Pub., 1906.
...same, cloth, viii, illus. & facsm., (17)-207 pp., p. 177-207 largely "notes." This title is listed on t/p of the 1906 Neale publication of his "Representative Southern Poets." $30-

1225 **HUCKABY, Leander**
"A Mississippian in Lee's Army: The Letters of Leander Huckaby." pt. I Edt: Donald E. Reynolds. (Jackson, Miss.) Jour. Miss. Hist. Feb. 1974, v. XXXVI, #1, p. 53-67, May 1974, V. XXXVI, #2, p. 165-78., Aug. 1974, V. XXXVI, #3, p. 273-288.

1226 **HUDDLESTON, Ed**
"The Civil War in Middle Tennessee." pt. 1(1861-1862); pt. II (1863); pt. III (1864); pt. IV (Nov. 1864-Apr. (, 1865) p. 36, 36, 36, & 48. sm. folio, profusely illustrated color covers, maps, ports, facsms. Nashivlle, Tenn., Banner. Also in hard covers @ $5-, $40-(JK131)

1227 **HUDGINS, F.L.**
"With the 38th Georgia Regiment." In: C.V., April, 1918, v. XXVI, p. 161-163.

1228 **HUDNALL, Henry, Capt.**
"Organization of First Company & John Brown Raid." In: 'Contributions to a History of Richmond Howitzers.' Richmond, Va., Calton McCarthy, 1883 p. 3-10, v.I

1229 **HUDSON, Eduard M.**
"Der Zweite Unabhangigkeits-Krieg in Amerika. Von E.M. Hudson." Berlin: A Charisius, 1862. 8vo, cl, vii, (1), 99, (1) p. Sabin-33487. Howes reports same with 78, (2) pp. with 2nd edt., same imprint, (8), 100 pp.

1230 ..."The Second War of Independence in America. Trans. by author from second revised edt. (German) with Intro: Bolling A. Pope." London: Longmans, Green, Longman, 1863. 8vo, cl, 177 pp. (2nd edt., viii, 132 pp. $15-

1231 **HUDSON, George**
"Message of the Principal Chief of the Choctaw Nation." (Boggy Depot, 1861) 8vo, plain wraps, 8pp. Mor. case $750-. In no reference works, Eberstadt sale. Resolutions to form a new government, to join with Arkansas & Texas if a dissolution made of Amer. Union.

1232 **HUDSON, James G.**
"A Story of Co. D, 4th Alabama Infantry Regiment, CSA. by Chaplain & Treasurer." In: Ala. Hist. Quart., Spring 1961, v. 23, #1 & 2, p. 139-179.

1233 **HUDSON, James Madison**
"Memoirs of James Madison Hudson. Edt: by Walter C. Hudson." In: AHQ, 1860, v. XIX, p. 271-279. With Hindman in Co. G, 2nd Ark. Inf.

1234 **HUDSON, Joshua Hilary**
"Sketches & Reminiscences." Columbia, S.C., State co, 1903, 8vo, cl, front (port) facsm, illus., 190 pp. Hudson was Lieut-Col. 26th S.C. Reg. Inf. Battle of Crater. $150-OB, $75-B

1235 **HUDSON, Robert S., Judge**
"The Breakdown of Morale in Central Mississippi in 1864: Letters of Judge Robert S. Hudson." (Jackson, Miss., Jour Miss. Hist. April, 1954, v. XVI, #2, p. 99-120.

1236 **HUDSON, Travis**
"Soldier Boys in Gray: a history of the 59th Georgia Volunteer Infantry Regiment." In: Atl. Hist. Jour., Spring 1979, v. 23, p. 45-70

1237 ..."The Charleston & Knoxville Campaigns." History of the 59th Georgia Infantry Volunteer Regiment, Part II." In: Atlanta Hist. Journ. 1981, v. 25, #3, p. 45-66.

1238 ..."Cold Harbor to Richmond: a history of the 59th Georgia Volunteer Regiment(Infantry) pt. IV," In: Atl. Hist. Jour., 1983, v. 27, #3, p. 31-45.

1239 ..."Pursuit to Appomattox: history of the 59th. Georgia Infantry Volunteers Regiment, pt.V, v. 27, #4, p. 5-25.

1240 ..."A History of the 59th Georgia Volunteer Infantry Regiment." Issued in five pamphlets, AJH, 1985-1986 as:
1."Soldier Boys in Gray." v.23, #1, p.45-70.
2."The Charleston & Knoxville Campaign." v.25, #3, p.45-66.
3."The Wilderness & Cold Harbor." v.26, #4, p.19-30.
4."Cold Harbor to Richmond." v.27, #3, p.31-45.
5."Pursuit to Appomattox." v.27, #4, p.5-25. $3.00 each, or 1 vol. $15.00.

1241 **HUEY, Mattie McAdory**
"History of the Alabama Division: United Daughters of the Confederacy." Opelika, Ala., Post Pub. Co., 1937 8vo, cl, illus. ports, 400 pp. See: McDowell(Carolina Dent), vo. II 2 vos. - $45-

1242 **HUFF, C.L.**
"EXTRA! EXTRA!" "Eye witness Account, Battle of Prairie Grove, as recorded in the Civil War diary of Lt. C.L. Huff, whose brother Barney Huff, was a casualty of the battle, & is buried in the National Cemetery At Fayetteville." Van Buren, Ark., Press Argus, n.d. Broadside 57X45, folded to 23x15 (portfolio)

1243 **HUFF, Lawrence**
"Joseph Addison Turner: Southern Editor During the Civil War." (Houston, Texas.) JSH, Nov. 1963, v. XXIX, #4, p. 469-485. $8-

1244 **HUFF, Leo E.**
"The Martial Law Controversy in Arkansas 1861-1865. A case history of internal Confederate conflict." In: Ark. HQ, Summer 1978, v.XXXVII, #2, p. 147-167.

1245 ..."The Military Board in Confederate Arkansas." In: AHQ, 1967, v. XXVI, p. 75-95.

1246 ..."The Marmaduke-Walker Duel: The Last Duel in Arkansas." (Fayetteville: Ark. Hist. Quart. Spring 1964. v.XXIII, #1, p. 36-49. Ports.
...Reprint: Mo. Hist. Rev., July 1964, v.LVIII, #4, p. 452-463, illus., ports, vigs.

1247 ..."The Union Expedition against Little Rock, August-September 1863. In: AHQ, 1963, v.XXII, p. 223-237, plate, 4 ports, maps, 2.

1248 ..."The Memphis & Little Rock Railroad during the Civil War." In: AHQ, 1964, v. XXIII, p. 260-270, map.

1249 ..."Guerrillas, Jayhawkers & Bushwhackers in Northern Arkansas during the Civil War." In: AHQ, 1965, v. XXIV, pp. 126-148, 3 plates.

1249a ..."Confederate Cavalry Charge at the Battle of Wilson's Creek." In: Green Co. Hist. Bul., Dec. 1979/Jan. 1980. Springfield, Mo.

1250 **HUFFMAN, James**
"Prisoner of war." In: Atl. Mo., 1939, v. CLXIII, p. 542-548. Acct. selected from a longer mssc., written during later years of his life.

1251 ..."Ups & Downs of a Confederate Soldier. N.Y., William E. Rudge's sons, 1940. By James Huffman, 10th Va. Infty." 12mo, cl, label, mounted illus., facsms, ports, 175 pp. 600 copies. privately printed. $60-, $75-R

1252 **HUFFSTAT, Robert S.**
"The brief, glorious career of the CSS Arkansas." In: CWTI, July 1968, v. VII, #4, p. 20-27, illus., map, port.

1253 **HUFHAM, James Dunn**
"Memoir of Rev. John L. Prichard, late pastor of the First Baptist Church, Wilmington, N.C., by Rev. J.D. Hufham." Raleigh, N.C., Hufham & Hughes, 1867. 12mo, cl, 2pp., (vii,-viii), (9), 182 pp. Lynchburg, Va., later in Wilmington, N.C. ministering to wounded during the war. Based on Prichard's diary.

1254 **HUGHES, James B., Jr.**
"Confederate Gun Makers, Armories & Arsenals." Southern Edition. n.p., 1961. 4to, stiff wraps, stapled, 24 pp., mimeographed one-side. $10.00

1255 **HUGHES, John, Maj. of New Berne, N.C.**
"Lawrence O'Brian Branch-an oration, delivered at Raleigh, May 10, 1884." (Raleigh, c. 1884) 8vo, wraps, port, 14 pp. Branch fought with Jackson, was Brig-Gen 33rd N.C., command around New Berne.

1255a **HUGHES, Michael A.**
"Wartime Gristmill Destruction in Northwest Arkansas & Military-farm Colonies." In: AHQ, Summer 1987, v.46, #2, p.167-86.

1256 **HUGHES, Nathaniel Cheirs, Jr.**
"The Civil War comes to Dade County" (Chattanooga, Tenn.) Private print, 1975 8vo, cl, dj, vii, 203 pp. stiff wraps

1257 ..."Hardee's Defense of Savannah." In: Ga. H.Q., March 1963, v. XLVII, #1, p. 43-67. $8-

1258 ..."General William J. Hardee: Old Reliable." Baton Rouge: Louisiana State University Press (1965) p. ix, 329, 8vo, cl, dj, port $30-

1258a ..."General William J. Hardee: Old Reliable." Wilmington, N.C., Broadfoot, 1987. 8vo, cl, 351pp, index, front, 11 new maps. $30.

1259 ..."William Joseph Hardee, CSA, 1861-1865." ANN Arbor: University microfilms, 1959. Positive microfilm from typescript, ii, 636 pp. leaves, maps, port. bibliog -592-636 pp. thesis, University of North Carolina, 20:2253, Dec.

1260 **HUGHES, Nicholas Collin**
"Hendersonville in Civil War Times 1860-1865 written in the memory of a very small child. Hendersonville, N.C., Blue Ridge Specialty Print, 1936. 8vo, wraps, cover title, illus, port, 30 pp. $10-

1261 **HUGHES, Robert Morton**
"Civil War" &/or "War Between the States." In: Wm. & Mary Quart., 1935, v. XV, p. 40-44, 2nd series.

1262 ..."Floyd's resignation from Buchannan's Cabinet." In: Tyler Quart. Hist. & Genl. Mag., Oct. 1923, v.V, #2, p. (73)-95. Buchannan's sect. war & Sumter.

1263 ..."General Johnston." N.Y., D. Appleton & Co., 1893. 12mo, cl (or, 1/2 Roan) port (front), ix, (2), 353pp. maps (1-fldg.) $10, $17.50, $75-Bmk 105. Half-title: Great Commanders-General Johnston "Army & Navy Edition."1897 Editions: 1895; 1897, 1898.

...1st Edt: Large paper edition, limited to 1000 copies, numbered, signed, cloth issued prior to the trade edition. $100-Bmk.

1264 ..."Joseph Eggleston Johnston, soldier & man, address by..., at unveiling of bust of Gen. Johnston in the Old Hall of the House of Delegates of Virginia, Feb. 3, 1933." In: Wm. & Mary Col. Hist. Mag., 1933, v.XIII, p. 63-84.

1265 ..."The Monitor defeated the Merrimac-myth." In: Tyler's Quart. Hist. & Geneal. Mag., July, 1926, v.VIII, p. 30-36. Also edited (see under Joseph E. Johnston "Letters." $15-Bmk.

1266 **HUGHES, Thomas**
"A Boy's Experience in the Civil War, 1860-1865." (Baltimore: Daily Record co.) 1904 Privately printed. 12mo, cl, 55pp.

1267 **HUGHES, William Edgar**
"The Journal of a Grandfather." (St. Louis, Mo., Privately printed, Nixon-Jones print co., 1912) 8vo, front, plates, prots, 239 pp. $50-, Dedication: W.E.H. Gramp (i.e., grandfather) Served in 1st Texas artillery, Col. of 16th CSA Cavalry.

1268 **HUGHES, William J.**
"Rebellious Ranger; Rip Ford & the Old Southwest." Norman, Univ. of Okla. press, (1964) 8vo, cl, dj, illus., ports, map, xi, 300 pp. More well known as a Texas Ranger. CSA p. 187-244. Secession & Rio Grande Exp. Force $95-R.

1269 **HUGO, Hammar**
"The Monitor & the Merrimac." Trans: from the Swedish by Lt. A.D.W. Moore, R.N. Mariner's Mirrow, 1940, 1940, v.XXVI, p. 163-184. Re design, building, their historic engagement at Hampton Roads.

1270 **HUHNER, Leon**
"David L. Yulee, Florida's first senator." In: Am. Jew. Hist. Soc. Pub., 1917, v.XXV, p. 1-29. Yulee was 1st Jew elected to US Senate. Served in CSA congress throughout war. In prison at Ft. Pulaski, later released. See also Yulee (C. Wickliffe).

1271 **HULET, C.C.**
Federal Defense at Spring Hill." In: Confed. Vet., Apr. 1919, v.XXVII, p. 138-140.

1272 **HULING, Polly**
"Missourians at Vicksburg." (Columbia, Mo., Mo. Hist. Review, Oct. 1955, v.L, #1, p. 1-16., illus.

1273 **HULL, Augustus Longstreet**
"The Campaigns of the Confederate Army, by..., Sect. Univ. of Ga." Atlanta, Ga., Foote & Davies co, 1901. 12mo, decr. bds., pl, 2-maps (1-fldg.) 107 pp. (cloth edt. cheaper, thicker paper) $85 Bmk-127, Pres copy $150-ob.

1274 ..."The Making of the Confederate Constitution." In: Pubs. So. Hist. Ass'n., Wash., DC, Sept., 1905, v.9, p. 272-292.

1274a ..."Annals of Athens, Georgia, 1801-1901 with an intro by Dr. Henry Hull." Athens, Banner Job Office, 1906. 8vo, cl, ills, 495pp. $75. Much on Athen's war service, with some rosters & a history of a dbl-barrelled cannon developed at Athens.

1275 **HULL, Susan Rebecca [Thompson], Mrs.**
"Boy Soldiers of the Confederacy, collated by Susan R. Hull." N.Y., Neal pub., 1905. 12mo, cl, illus., front, pls, ports, 256 pp. $150-Bmk-105. Hist. records of boys, 11-18, who served in CSArmies.

1276 **HULLIHEN, Walter Q.**
"The prayer offered at the unveiling of the equestrian statue of Gen. J.E.B. Stuart." Richmond, Va., 1907. 8vo, wraps, 6 pp. bmk $8-

1277 **HULSTON, John K. & James W. Goodrich**
"John Trousdale Coffee: Lawyer, Politician, Confederate." In: MoHR, April 1983, v.LXXVII, #3, p. 272-295, ports, illus., facs.

1278 ..."West Point & Wilson's Creek." In: CWH, Dec. 1955, v.1, #4, p. 333-354. Known also as "Springfield," or "Oak Hills" by Confederates.

1279 **HUME, Edgar Erskine, Maj.**
"Nicola Marschall (1829-1917) the German Artist who designed the Confederate Flag & Uniform." Amer.-German Rev., VI, 1940 #6, p. 6-9, 39.

1280 ..."Peter Johnston, Junior Virginia Soldier & Jurist." in Southern Sketches #4, First Series. Charlottesville, Va., Historical Pub. co., 1935. 8vo, wraps, 13 pp.

1281 ..."Colonel Theodore O'Hara author of the Bivouac of the Dead." In: Southern Sketches, #6, First Series. Charlottesville, Va., Historical Pub. co. 1936. 8vo, wraps, front(port), 57 pp. JK-122 $35-

1282 ..."Colonel Heros von Borcke a Famous Prussian Volunteer in the Confederate States Army." In: Southern Sketches #2, First Series. 1935. Charlottesville, Va., Historical Pub. co., 8vo, wraps, 24, (1) pp. Bmk-$25-

1283 ..."Chimborazo Hospital, Confederate States Army-America's largest military hospital." In: Mil. Surgeon, 1934 at unveiling of bronze tablet at site of hopsital at Richmond, Va.

1284 ..."The Confederate medal of honor & the Kentuckians who won it." In: KyHSR, Sept., 1927, v.XXV, p. 270-292.

1285 **HUME, Frank**
"A scouting expedition during the Civil War" In: Arlington hist. mag., Oct. 1960, v. 1, #4, p. 50-53. Undated recollections, apparently fragmentary, or author's movement as a CSA spy, across Potomac in Va., as far as Marlborough.

1285a **HUMPHREY, Charles**
"The Civil War Diary of Charles Humphrey." In: Wagon Wheels, Winter 1981, v.1, p.16-25. Arkansas.

1286 **HUMPHREYS, Andrew Atkinson**
"Unveiling the Monument at Fredericksburg to Humphreys' Division." (from Richmond Times-Dispatch, Nov. 12, 1908) In: SHSP, 1908, v.36, p. 174-179.

1287 **HUMPHREYS, Benjamin Grubb**
"Battle of Chickamauga." In: SHSP, 1885, v. 13, p. 387-388. See: Frank E. Everett, Jr. for Humphrey's marginal notes on a copy of Taylor's 'Four Years with Lee.'

1288 ..."Recollections of Fredericksburg from the monring of 19th April to the 6th of May, 1863." In: LWL, Oct. 1867, v.III, $6, p. 443-460. map. Also in: SHSP, 1886. v. 14, p. 415-428.

1289 **HUMPHREYS, David, Maj.**
"Heroes & Spies of the Civil War, by..., of the original 'Stonewall' Brigade, & later Captain in Ashby's Cavalry." Wash: Neale pub., 1903. 12mo, cl, port(front), 223 pp. $100 Bmk

1290 **HUMPHREYS, Milton Wylie**
"A History of the Lynchburg Campaign by Milton W. Humphreys, member King's Artillery, CSA." Charlottesville, Va., Michie print, 1924 8vo, wraps, 74 pp. $30-

1291 ..."Last Days of the Army in Southwest Virginia." In:SHSP, 1905, v.XXXIII, p. 344, 350 pp.

1292 ..."Military Operations, 1861-1863, Fayetteville, W.Va., by..., Bryan's Battery, King's Artillery, CSA." Fayetteville, Priv. Print., Chas. A. Goddard 1926. 8vo, wraps, illus., (iv), 31 pp.
..."Military Operations, 1861-1864, Fayetteville, West Virginia, & the lynchburg Campaign, by...etc." Fayetteville: Priv. Prin., Charles A. Goddard 1926. (Edt: 50 copies.) 8vo, wraps, (iv), 38 pp. (Shetler-362, has an additional p. (39-40) in his copy. 2nd ?issue.
...Same, 74 pp., Shetler-363, as 3rd. issue?
...Same, 1ax map, lists corrections, p. (75)
...Same title, adds: "Battle of Carnifex Ferry by Roy Bird Cook." Fayetteville: Priv. Prin., Charles A. Goddard (1931?), (ii), (40) pp., 5th issue? See: Shetler #361-64a, details of various diff. points. $200-B

1293 **HUNDLEY, George Jefferson**
"Beginning & Ending. Reminiscences of the First & Last days of the war. Interesting personal observations. The thrilling & exciting times immediately preceding the war-First battle of Manassas." (from

Richmond 'Times' Feb. 2, 1896) In: SHSP, 1895, v.XXIII, p. 294-313.

1294 **HUNDLY, Daniel Robinson, 31st. Ala. Infty.**
"Prison Echoes of the Great Rebellion." by D.R. Hundley, late of the C.S.A. New York: S.W. Green, 1874. 12mo, cl, 235 pp. Prison life: Johnson's Isle, Lake Erie.

1295 ..."Social Relations in Our Southern States." New York: Henry B. Price, 1860. 12mo, cl, vi, (7)-367 pp. Sabin-33831; Howes 5115 says: the ablest answer to abolition propaganda, but too late for effectiveness & most copies burned before distribution. $100- Jk-135 $40-Bmk (119) $75-Bmk.

...Baton Rouge: Louisiana State University Press, 1979. 8vo, cl, dj, 416 pp. Edited, with introduction by William J. Cooper, Jr.

1296 **HUNSAKER, William J.**
"Lansford W. Hastings' project for the invasion & conquest of Arizona & New Mexico for the Southern Confederacy." In: AriHR., 1931, v.IV, #2, p. 5-12, port.

1297 **HUNSICKER, Neva Ingram**
"Rayburn the Raider." In: AHQ, 1948, v.VII, p. 87-91. Parson's Brigade of Texans.

1298 **HUNT, Bernard C., Mrs.**
"The Confederate home of Missouri." In: CV, Aug., 1928, v.XXXVI, p. 299-301.

1299 **HUNT, Cornelius E.**
"The Shenandoah; or the Last Confederate Cruiser." by One of her officers. N.Y., G.W. Carleton & Co., 1867. 12mo, cl, front, 273 pp. (2) pp. ads, $125-Bmk.

...Albany, N.Y., W. Abbott, 1910 reprint: Magazine of History-Notes & Queries, ex. #12, pl. (6), 135 pp.

1300 **HUNT, Gaillard**
"John C. Calhoun" Phila:Geo. W. Jacobs co (1908) American Crisis Biographies. 12mo, cl, pp.(5)-335.

1301 **HUNT, Grace Lea**
"Some Old Southern Letters." (Wilkes-Barre, Pa., The Raeder Co., 1924) 8vo, cl, illus., cover-title, (48) pp. Federal occupation of New Orleans.

1302 **HUNT, Livingston**
"The Southern letters of marque." In: Harv. Grad. Mag., 1932, v.XL, p. 345-354. Commissioning of privateers by the CSA gov. during war.

1302a **HUNT, O. E.**
"Defending the Citadel of the Confederacy." In: Photo. Hist. CW, v.5, p.303-21, ills, port, map.

1303 **HUNT, Robert**
"A Daring Deed. Paper read before the Confed. Vets. Assn.), Savannah, Ga., Pres. Annual Report, 1895. p. 51-56.

1304 **HUNTEN, F., C.S.A.**
Improved Hunten's Instruction for the Piano-Forte, part II, Richmond, Va., George Dunn & C., 4th Nov. 1863. cover title, 9 1/2x11 3/4. Similar to Crandall-#3161 (which sold for $450.00) $150.00

1305 **HUNTER, Alexander**
"Johnny Reb & Billy Yank, Illustrated by Harold Macdonald & R.O. Tolman." N.Y., Wash., The Neale co, 1905. Tk. 8vo, cl, front(port, illus., sketches, 720 pp. $22.50, $28.50, $30, $35, $40, $200-Bmk-105, $75-fine, $300-NC 33, $350-Bmk-105.

1306 ..."A High Private's account of the Battle of Sharpsburg. (From 'Four years in the ranks', (now in press) by..." In: SHSP, 1882, v.X, p. 503-12; 1883, v.XI, p. 10-21.

1307 ..."Battle of Antietam." In: SHSP, 1903, v.XXXI, p. 37-43.

1308 ..."The Women of the Debatable Land." Washington, DC, Cobden pub., 1912. 12mo, cl, illus, ports, fldg. map, viii, (4), 261 pp. $12.50, $20, $22.50, $25.00, $100-Bmk.

1309 ..."The Women of Mosby's Confederacy." In: CV, 1907, v. 15, p. 257-262, plate.

1310 HUNTER, Charles M.
"Apache Fox." In: True West, Nov/Dec, 1958, v.6, #2, p. 22-23. views. Killing of Lt. Robert Mayes, CSA & all but one of the men in his detachment by Mescalero Apaches under Chief Gian-na-tah, about 20 miles south of Alpine, Texas, in 1862.

1311 HUNTER, David
"Hunter's Raid, 1864. Charge through Harrisonburg." (from Richmond Dispatch, July 8, 1900) In: SHSP, 1908, v.36, p. 95-103. See: Henrietta E. Lee, J. Scott Moore, Mrs. F.H. Smith.

1312 HUNTER, J. Marvin
"Battle of Dove Creek." (Abilene, Tex.) West Tex. Hist. Assn. Yr. Bk., 1934. v.X, p. 74-87.

1313 ..."Texas during the civil war." In: Frontr. Times, Mar. 1950, v. 27, p. 170-173.

1314 ..."Last battle of the Civil War(White's Ranch, near Brownsville, Texas, 12 May, 1865." In: Frontier Times, July/Sept, 1954, v.31, p. 348-350.

1315 HUNTER, James T., Capt.
"Battle of Chickamauga." In SHSP 1888, v.XVI, p. 380-381.

1316 ...Lieut. Gen. John B. Hood." In: Confed. Vet., June 1916, v.XXIV, p. 257-258.

1317 ..."At Yorktown in 1862 & what followed." In:CV, Feb/Mar, 1918, v.XXVI, p. 66-8, 112-115.

1318 HUNTER, John Warren
"Heel-Fly Time in Texas, a Story of the Civil War Period." Bandera, Texas: Frontier Times (1947) 4to, wraps, 47 pp. (double column) $25- Reminiscences of author, chased by "Heel-flys", young home guards, often gangs who terrorized unprotected civilians, even returned soldiers.

1319 ...Bandera, Texas: Frontier Times, 1936. 12mo, wraps, 123 pp., 3rd edt. Originally run serially in the Times in 1924, v.I, #7 (p. 33-48); #8 (p. 33-48; #9 (p. 33-47, dbl. colmn). The first edition of 1924 was of 300 copies.
...Same: 2nd edt., Feb. 1932, of 156 pp. $750-G Originally written in 1911 by Hunter & published Anon., in "Hunter's Magazine," but as a pamphlet, first in 1924.

1320 HUNTER, Martha T.
"A Memoir of Robert M.T. Hunter by Martha T. Hunter (his daughter), with an address on his life by Col. L Quinton Washington (prepared for the Hunter Monument Association." Washington: Neale pub., 1903, 12mo, cl, front(port), 166 pp. $80-B. Hunter served as Sect. of State, CSA during part of the war. See also under Hunter's name.

1321 HUNTER, Robert Mercer Taliaferro
"Correspondence of Robert M.T. Hunter, 1826-1876. Edt: Charles Henry Ambler." Wash: GPO-Amer. Hist. Ass'n., Report for 1916, v.II, 1918. 8vo, cl, 383 pp.
...N.Y., Da Capo press, 1971. Hunter was a prominent Va. states rights Democrat, US Senator, 1847-1861.

1322 ..."Instructions to Hon. James M. Mason, Letter from R.M.T. Hunter, Sect. State, CSA." In: SHSP, 1879, v. VII, p. 231-241.

1323 ..."Letter of Instructions to Hon. John Slidell." In: SHSP, 1885, v.XIII, p. 455-466.

1324 ..."Origin of the Late War.: In: SHSP, Jan. 1876, v.I, #1, p. (1)-13.

1325 ..."The Peace Commission of 1865." In: SHSP, 1877, v.III, p. 168-76, IV, p. 303-318.

1326 ..."The Republic of Republics" (Review) In: SHSP, 1885, v.XIII, p. 342-355. See: Sage, Bernard J. See also: Jefferson Davis, Theo. Garnett, Henry H. Simms, L.Q. Washington, Martha T. Hunter, D.R. Anderson

1327 ..."Speech of Hon. R.M.T. Hunter of Virginia, on Invasion of States. Delivered in the Senate of the United States, Jan. 30,

1860." (Washington) L. Towers print(1860). 8vo, sewn, 16pp.
..."Speech, Jan. 31" (same) 8 pp., $10-

1328 ..."Speech...on the resolution proposing to retrocede the forts, dockyards, etc. to the States applying for the same. Delivered in the Senate of the United States, January 11, 1861." Washington: Lemuel Towers, 1861. 8vo, wraps, 16pp.

1329 **HUNTER, Robert W., Maj.**
"Fitzhugh Lee, address delivered at the Jamestown Exposition." In: SHSP, 1907, v.XXXV, p. 132-145.

1330 ...Major-General (Edward) Johnson at Spotsylvania." In: SHSP, 1905, v.XXXIII, p. 335-340.

1331 ..."Men of Virginia at Ball's Bluff." In: SHSP, 1906, v.XXXIV, p. 254-274. Honors brave men from Miss., famous 8th Va. Inf., cavalry & Richmond Howitzers, numbers engaged on both sides.

1332 ...Generals in the Confederate States Army from Virginia." In: SHSP, 1908, v.XXXVI, p. 105-120.

1333 ..."Virginia in the Confederacy, 1861-1865 (with a bibliography)." In: The South in the Building of a Nation, v.I, p. 113-126.

1334 **HUNTINGTON, Henry, Mrs.**
"Escape from Atlanta: The HUNTINGTON Memoir." In: CWH, June 1965, v. XI, p. 160-177.

1335 **HUNTON, Eppa**
"Autobiography of Eppa Hunton." Richmond, Va., William Byrd pr, 1933. 8vo, cl, ports, xx, 268 pp. $18, $70, $100- Edition of 100 copies. Subject a Va. lawyer, fought in CSArmy, after-three terms in Congress. $1500, $3500-Bmk, $4000 (D.J.)

1336 ..."General Eppa Hunton at the Battle of Bull Run, July 21, 1861. Statement that he saved the CSArmy from defeat." In: SHSP, 1904, v.XXXII, p. 143-145. See: Fauquier Co. Va.

1337 ..."Gaines Mill, Gen. Eppa Hunton writes to the Virginians there." In: CV, 1899, v.7, p. 223-228. ports.

1338 **HURD, William B.**
"Alexandria, Virginia 1861-1865." Alexandria, Va., 1970 sm. 4to, pict wraps, 80 p. index. (Carolina Bks.)

1339 **HURLEY, Meromora Kingsley**
"Robert E. Lee, -acomposite paradox." In: CV, May, 1910, v.XVIII, p. 209-213.

1340 **HURST, John**
"Archer's Brigade at Chancellorsville." In: CV, July 1920, v.XXVIII, p. 261-262.

1341 **HURST, M.B.**
"History of the Fourteenth Regiment, Alabama Volunteers, with a list of the names of every man that ever belonged to the Regiment, by..., Chief Musician, 14th Regiment." Richmond, Va., 1863. 16mo, wraps, cover title, 48 pp. $125.00

1342 ...Dadeville, Alabama, Spot Cash press (n.d.), 32 pp.
"History of the Fourteenth Regiment Alabama Volunteers with a list of the names of every man that ever belonged to the regiment, by M.B. Hurst, Chief Lusician. 14th Regiment Alabama Volunteers. Edited with an introduction by William Stanley Hoole." University, Ala., Confederate Pub. Co., 1982. Confederate Regimental Series #1, 8vo., stiff wraps, 42pp.

1343 **HURST, T.M.**
"The Battle of Shiloh", In: Amer. Hist. Mag., 1902, v.7, p. 22-37.

1344 ..."Battle of Shiloh." In: Tenn. H. Mag., July 1919, v. 5, p. 81-96. $8.00

1345 **HUSE, Caleb**
"The Supplies of the Confederate Army how they were obtained in Europe & how paid for. Personal reminiscences & unpublished history, by Caleb Huse) Major & purchasing agent, CSA." 8vo, wraps, front(port)facsm., 36 pp., Boston: T.R.

Marvin & son, 1904. See also: Saml. B. Thompson. $100-G, $75-JK137.

...Houston, Texas: Deep River Armory, 1970, illus. wraps, 36, (3)p. $20-

...Dayton, Oh., Morningside press, 1976. 12mo, wraps, 36 pp.

1345a ..."Major Caleb Huse, CSA, a Memoir & an Appreciation, being a reprint of the Huse pamphlet of 1904, with an appreciation & two appendices, by Thomas W. Green." London, Confederate Historical Society, 1966. (Studies in Confederate history #1)

1346 **HUSLEY, Val**
"Men of Virginia-Men of Kanawha-To Arms! A History of the Twenty-second Virginia Volunteer Infantry Regiment, CSA" In: W.Va. Hist., 1974, v.XXV, p. 220-236.

1347 **HUSTED & NENNING**
"Map of the Confederate States of America Richmond, Va., A/Morris Pub., 1861. Drawn & colored by Husted & Nenning. 48 1/2x70cm. $1000-Bmk

1348 **HUTCHESON, Joseph C., Jr.**
"We March but we Remember." Houston, Texas: Anson Jones pr., 1941. 12mo, cl, (1), 36 pp. Cover: "Stratford MemorialAddress." On Freeman's "Lee."

1349 **HUTCHINS, Edward Ridgeway**
"The War of the Sixties, compiled by E.R. Hutchins." N.Y., Neale pub., 1912. 8vo, cl, 490 pp. Sketches of the war by both Union & Confederate writers. $100-Bmk-105.

1350 **HUTCHINS, William J.**
"To the Senators & Representatives in Congress from the State of Texas." (Houston, Texas) 'News Print' (1864) 12mo., wraps, 19pp., caption title. Financing the Army of CSA by sale of cotton in Texas.

1351 **HUTCHINSON, John S., Rev.**
"The Blue & the Gray; a true history of the Army of the Potomac & that of Northern Virginia, etc." co-edited with, see: Theodore Gerrish.

1352 ..."Two Witnesses on Prison Mortality at Elmira." In: SHSP, 1883, v.XI, p. 524-526.

1353 **HUTCHINSON, R.R.**
"Albert Sidney Johnston at Shiloh." In: CV, 1898. v.6, p. 311-314, illus., port, map.

1354 **HUTCHISON, John Russell**
"The Texas Dead of Hood's Brigade & Battle of Franklin, Tenn." In: Reminiscences, Sketches & Addresses During a Ministry of 45 Years in Mississippi, Louisiana & Texas." Houston: E.H. Cushing, 1874. 12mo, cl, 262 pp.(CSA, p. 216-218.) $75.00

1355 **HUTTER, J. Risque, Col.**
"The Eleventh at Five Forks Fight. Graphic story of daring deeds performed on hopeless field of battle.' Had Pickett been there'-the sad story of Five Forks told for the first time." (From Richmond 'Times Dispatch', July 1, 1906) In: SHSP, 1907, v.XXXV, p. 357-362.

1355a **HUTTON, A. W.**
"Address delivered before Robert E. Lee chapter U.D.C. at Y.M.C.A. Hall, Los Angeles, Cal., June 3, 1902." Los Angeles, 1903. 8vo, wraps, 11p.

1356 **HUTTON, James V., Jr.**
"The One-armed Hero of the Shenandoah." (Richmond) Va. Cavl., Summer 1969. v.XIX (misnumbered XVIII) #1 (misnumber #5) p. 4-11. illus., ports (1-color).

1357 **HYDE, Anne Bachman**
"The battle of Shiloh." In: CV, April 1923, v.XXXI, p. 129-132.

1358 ..."Early efforts to supress the slave trade & abolish slavery in the South." In: CV, Mar. 1919., v. XXVII, p. 83-86.

1359 **HYMAN, Harold M.**
"Deceit in Dixie." In: CWH, Mar. 1957, v.III, #1, p. 65-82.

1360 ..."Era of the Oath: Northern Loyalty Tests during the Civil War & Reconstruction." Phila: Univ. of Pa. press, 1954. 8vo, cl, dj, illus., bibliog., xiv, 229 pp.

1361 ..."New Frontiers of the American Reconstruction." Urbana: Univ. of Illinois pr, 1966. 8vo, cl, x, 156 pp. North as race-conscious as South.

I

1 **IKARD, Robert W.**
"Lieut. (James Turner Sanford) Thompson reports (by letter, Oct. 8, 1863) on Chickamauga; a Comparison of Immediate & Historical Perspectives of the Battle." In: THQ, Winter 1985, v.44, p.417-38.

IMBODEN RAID
See: John A. McNeil.

1a **IMBODEN, George W.**
"Distinguished Soldier & Citizen." In: Confederate Vet., v.XXX, 1922, p. 125. Sketch of Col. Imboden's life, who died Jan. 8, 1922 at Ansted.

2 **IMBODEN, John Daniel, Brig-Gen.**
"The Battle of New Market, May 15, 1864." In: B & L, v.4, p. 480-486.

3 ..."Battle of Piedmont", In: Confed. Vet., Dec., 1923, v.XXXI, p. 459-461; Jan. 1924, vXXXII, p. 18-20.

4 ..."Confederate Retreat from Gettysburg." In: B & L, v.III, p. 420-429.

5 ..."Fire, Sword, & the Halter." In: Phila: Annals of War, 1879, p. 169-183.

6 ..."Imboden's dash into Charleston. a war incident in which the 9th Maryland Federal Regiment figured-an act of kindness that was remembered." from Balt: "Sunday Sun" Sug. 30, 1903) In: SHSP, 1903, v.XXXI, 11-19.

7 ..."Incidents of the First Bull Run." In: B & L., v.1, p. 229-239.

8 ..."Jackson at Harper's Ferry in 1861." In: B & L., v. 1 pp. 111-125.

9 ..."Stonewall Jackson in the Shenandoah" In: B & L., v. 1, p. 282-298.

10 ..."Lee at Gettysburg." In: "Galaxy", 1871, v.XI, p. 507-513.

11 ..."Reminiscences of Lee & Jackson." In: "Galaxy", Nov. 1871, v.XII, p. 627-634.

12 ..."Treatment of Prisoners of War-statement of General J.D. Imboden." In: SHSP, 1876, v.1, p. 187-196. See: Cary Ingram Crockett's "Battery that saved the day." & Festus P. Summers'-"Jones Imboden Raid."

13 ..."Famous Pennsylvania-Germans, General John D. Imboden." In: 'Pennsylvania-German', 1934, v.V, p. 3-7, port. See: Haviland H. Abbot.

14 ..."Organized & Authorized Partisan Rangers!" (Staunton, Va., 1862?) Broadside: 10 1/2x7 1/4" Authorized by act of congress, Apr. 21, 1862.

15 ..."Reminiscences of Lee & Jackson" In: Galaxy Nov. 1861. 8 p.

16 ..."Immortal 600." In: Confed. Vet., July 1899, v.VII, p. 321. Listing W. Va. officers, units & home towns.

16a **INCIDENTS OF LIFE** in a Southern City during the War. A Series of Sketches Written for the Rutland Herald by a Vermont Gentleman, who was for many years a prominent merchant in Mobile. Printed for private distribution." (Rutland, Vt., 1880s).

17 **"IN MEMORIAM SEMPITERNAM.**
Edited by Mrs. A.W. Garber." Richmond, Va., Confederate Museum, 1896. 12mo, half boards, front, illus. 98 pp. Occasion laying corner-stone of monument to Jefferson Davis. Action of each state on seceeding.

18 **"IN MEMORIAM, Seventh Tennessee Cavalry, CSA."**
Introduction by Mrs. A. Aden. In: W. Tenn. Hist. Soc. Paper, 1963, v. XVII, #1, p. 118-117. See: J.M. Hubbard, J.P. Young.

19 **"IN MEMORIAM. The dead of the Otey battery**

20 **"IN MEMORY of the Heroes in Gray."** Published by Confederate Soldier's Home of Georgia (1861-1928)" n.p., (c. 1928) cover title. 4to, stiff decr. color wraps, 96 pp. ports illus., with ads. See: "Confederate Soldier's Home."

of the 13th Virginia Artillery, Army of Northern Virginia, CSA. Published by the committees." Richmond, Va., West, Johnston co, 1887. 4to, wraps, 22pp.

21 **"INDEX for applications** for Texas Confederate pensions." Revised edition, archives division Texas State Library, Austin, Texas. $5-, 1st Edition, 1899 approved 52,094 pensioners. 9,212 turned down. Old list of original plus 1,100 additonal, corrected names. Contains name, birthplace, length of service, company, widow's birthplace, date & place of marriage.

22 **"INDEX of Louisiana place names** mentioned in the War of the Rebellion, a compilation of Official Records of Union & Confederate armies. Edt: Dennis A. Gibson, indexed by Jeffrey Baker (Lafayette, La., University of Southwest La., 1975. 4to, cl, illus, vii, 383 pp.

23 **"INDEX of compiled service records** of Confederate soldiers who served in organizations from the state of Florida." Wash: National Archives, 1955. Positive microfilm, 9 rolls (733') #225. Card index giving name, rank & unit.

24 **"INDEX to Louisiana place names** mentioned in the War of the Rebellion Records, a compilation of the Official Records of the Union & Confederate Armies. Edt., Dennis A. Gibson. Index by Jeffrey a Baker, et, al." (Lafayette, La., University Southwest La., 1975, 4to, cl, illus., vii, 383 pp.

25 **"INDEX to Questionnaires** of Civil War Veterans." (i.e., CSA only 3pp. Union) Nashville, Tenn., State Library & Archives Div., 1962. Mimeo, 4to, wraps, 33, (1) p. supl.

26 **"INDEX to compiled service record** of Confederate soldiers who served in organization from the state of Georgia." Wash: National Archives, 1955. Positive microfilm. 67 rolls (5,171') #226. Card index of name, rank & unit.

27 **"INDEX to compiled service records** of Confederate Soldiers who served in organizations from the State of Mississippi." Wash.: National Archives, 1956. Positive microfilm. 45 rolls, 3,481, pub. 232

28 ...State of North Carolina, 43 rolls, 4,585' Micro. pub. #230.

29 ...State of Tennessee, 24 rolls, 4029', Natl. Archives Micro. pub. #23.

30 ..."Index to compiled service records of Confederate soldiers who served in organizations from the State of Texas." Wash: National Archives, 1955. Positive microfilm. 41 rolls (3,216'. #227. Card index: name, rank & unit.

31 **"INDEX to the Records of Proceedings** of the Advisory Council of Virginia- containing names of all appointments of officers in the Provisional Army of Virginia, "advised", or "rejected" from April 21 to June 10, 1861." n.p., n.d. (c.1881). 8vo, stapled, 20 pp. Printed around the time as the "Official Records, War of Rebellion."

32 **"INDEX Guide** to the Southern Historical Society Papers, An." See: Southern Historical Society Papers.

33 **"INDEX. A Weekly Journal, (The)** ...Devoted to the Exposition of the Mutual Interests, political & Commercial, of Great Britain & the Confederate States of America." London: 1862-1864. 4 Vols., folio, May 1, 1862 to May 1, 1864 (40.5 cm) Suppl. to v. 4 (#135, Nov. 24, 1864 not pub'd.) v. 5 has t/p for v. 4, with cor-

rections. Publication financed by Confederacy, managed by Henry Hotze. $500; $1500.

INDIANOLA (Ironclad) Capture - U.S.N.
See: Joseph L. Brent, Wm. L. Ritter.

34 **INDIANS IN THE CONFEDERACY**
Chronicles of Oklahoma: Caddo Indians:XIV, p. 144; XV, p. 25; XVI, p. 420. Cherokees: XV, p. 263; XVI, p. 320, 323, 342; XVII, p. 146, 182; XVIII, p. 101, 144; XX, p. 397; XXX, p. 115; XXXIV, p. 353; XXII, p. 397. Chickasaw: XV, p. 381; XVIII, p. 99, 142, 351; XXXII, p. 327. Choctaw: XVII, p. 192, 203; XVIII, p. 99, 142, 357; XIX, p. 318. Creeks: XV, p. 168-169, 171, 173-174, 177-178, 181; xvi, p. 402; XVIII, p. 143. Seminoles: SVIII, p. 144; XXXIV, p. 266, 285. Cherokee Nation: XV, p. 58, 62; SVI, p. 179, 318. Chickasaw Nation: SVI, p. 226; XXXIV, p. 412n. Choctaw Nation: XVI, p. 238. Indian Territory: XIV, p. 28, 32; XVI, p. 413-414; XVII, p. 59; XXXII, p. 128; XXXIV, p. 393; XXXVI, p. 32; Indians in: XIV, p. 5; XXXV, p. 430. Ohland Morton's 'Five Civilized Tribes', XXXI, p. 189-204, 299-322; AlaHQ-V, p. 59-65.

35 ..."Indian Cavalry in Confederate Service. Being a brief account of Confederate organization & operation of Indian troops in Indian Territory, 1861-1865, containing excerpts from official records of Gen. Albert Pike." American Scene Magazine: Thomas Gilcrease Institute of American History & Art. Tulsa, Okla., 1965. 4to, Decr. wraps, illus., (16) pp.

36 **INGENTHRON, Elmo**
"Borderland Rebellion; Civil War in the Ark.-Mo. 'No-man's land.' Branson, Mo., Mountaineer Bookshop, Rt. 3, Box 868, Branson, Mo. 65616. Cl $16. Paper $11.
..."Bosterland Rebellion; a history of the Civil War on the Missouri-Arkansas border. Edt: Kathleen van Buskirk." Branson, Mo., Ozark Mountaineer, 1980. Ozark Regional History series #3. 8vo, cl, 393pp, ill, ports.

37 **INGERSOLL, Charles**
"Letter to a friend in a slave state, by A Citizen of Pennsylvania. (Charles Ingersoll) Phila: John Campbell, 1862. 8vo, wraps, 60pp. Sabin-34726). "The mail difficulty lies with the North ruled by the Abolitionists." Who would scrap the constitution for political power. Peace is possible for them.

38 **INGLESBY, Charles**
"Historical Sketch of the First Regiment of South Carolina Artillery (Regulars)". Charleston: Walker, Evans & Cogswell (1896). 8vo, wraps, 28 pp.

38a **INGMIRE, Frances Terry**
"Confederate POWs: Soldiers & Sailors who died in Federal Prisons & Military Hospitals in the North." Nacogdoches, Texas: Erickson books, 1984. 8vo, cl, 500pp. $32.50. Reprint: National Archives War Dept., 1912.
See: Benj. Rice Forman.
..."Confederate Pension Applications of Fannin County, Texas." St. Louis, F.T. Ingmire, 1981. 4to, wraps, 81pp, index.
...Same for Trinity County, Texas. 4to, wraps, 37pp.

38b **INGMIRE, Frances Terry & Robert Lee Thompson**
"Johnny Rebs of Hunt County, Texas." Author, St. Louis, Mo., 63136, 10166 Clairmont Dr. 8vo, cl, 133pp. $7.35. CSA soldiers buried in Hunt Co., Tex. Diary of Fountain E. Pitts Harrel.

39 **INGRAHAM, Alfred, Mrs.**
"The Vicksburg Diary of Mrs. Alfred Ingraham (May 2-June 13, 1863). Edt.: W. Maury Darst." In: JHM, May 1982, v. XLIV, #2, p. 148-179.

40 **INGRAHAM, Prentiss, Col.**
"The Two Flags; or, Love for the Blue,

Duty for the Gray. A War Romance." N.Y., Beadle & Adams, 1897. 'Beadle's New York Dime Library, #968. sm. 4to, wraps, 28pp. $50-Bm-106.

...N.Y., The Banner Weekly, III, #133. May 30, 1885. Illus.(3). Johannsen. Date: 1859 & during civil war, Texas, New Orleans & Mississippi river, West Point.

40a **INGRAM, George W.**
"Hurrah for the Texans: the Civil War Letters of George W. Ingram. Edt. by Charles R. Schltz." College Station, Texas, A & M College Press, 1974. 4to, wraps, 25pp, ills. $110. 150 copies.

41 **INKSTER, Tom H.**
"Waddell's War on the Whalers." In: Hist. Today, 1966, v.XVI, p. 627-632. Reply by A.B. Cross, 729 p. (Commander of CSS 'Shenandoah.'

41a "**INTERESTING LOVE STORY** found in a Rebel Camp Ground, An. Written by a Southern soldier, drafter in the Rebel Army, whose sympathies were with the North." New York, 1863. 16mo, wraps, 12pp. (Wright II-1322).

42 **INZER, John W.**
"How the news of the assassination of President Lincoln was received by the Confederate prisoners on Johnson's Island, in April 1965." In: Gulf Mag., v.1, 1902; p. 194-198.

43 ..."Alabama's secession convention, 1861." In: CV, Jan. 1923, v.XXXI, p. 7-9. Scenes & incidents remembered by Col. John W. Inzer, notes dictated to grandson John Inzer Freeman.

43a **INZER, John Washington**
"Diary of a Confederate Soldier: John Washington Inzer. Edt: Mattie Lou Teague Crow." Huntsville, Ala., Strode Pub., 1877. 8vo, cl, ills, map, bibliog-index. 191pp. $8.

44 **IOBST, Richard W.**
"Battle of New Bern." Raleigh, North Carolina Centennial Commission, (1962). 12mo, wraps, pl, plan, 14 pp.

45 ..."Battle of Roanoke Island, Feb. 7-8, 1862. Copy of address at Centennial observance of the battle...Manteo High School Auditorium, Feb. 8, 1962, under auspieces of Dare Co., Civil War Centennial Comm." Manteo, Dare Co. Tourist Bureau (1962). 4to, wraps, 4pp.

46 ..."The Bloody Sixth. The Sixth North Carolina Regiment, Confederate States of America. By Richard W. Iobst. Roster by Louis H. Manarin. With a narrative of the reactivation regiment, by Wade Lewis. (Raleigh, North Carolina Confederate Centennial Commission, c. 1965). 8vo, cl, front, illus., ports, xv, 493 pp. $75-

..."The Bloody Sixth, N.C. Regiment . . ." Gaithersburg, Ma., Butternut Press, 1987. $35.

47 **IRBY, James A.**
"Backdoor at Bagdad: the Civil War on the Rio Grande." El Paso, Texas: Western press, 1977. 8vo, wraps, facs., maps, 64 pp. Trade along the international border, naval blockade, etc.

48 **IRBY, Richard, Capt.**
"Historical sketch of the Nottoway Grays afterwards Co. G, 18th Virginia Reg., ANVa; prepared at the request of the surviving members of the company at their first reunion at Bellefont church, July 21, 1877." Richmond: J.W. Fergusson & son, 1878. 8vo, wraps, illus., tip-in photos, 48, (1)p. $18.50, $22.50, $37.50, $50.00, $65.00 $150-G, $100-Bmk TENN 124, $80-Bmk.

...Gaithersburg, MD., (1983?) reprint, 1st Maryland Campaign.

49 ..."A Brilliant Record. The Nottoway Grays Co. G, 18th Va. Reg., Pickett's Division." In: SHSP, 1896, v. XXIV, p. 237-240.

50 ..."Early days of the war." In: CV, 1902, v. 10, p. 257-258.

51 ..."First Manassas. July 21, 1861.

52 ...The Captain Remembers, the papers of Capt....Edt: Virginia Fitzgerald Jordan." Blackstone, Va., 1975. 8vo, wraps, front, illus, 124 pp.

53 ...Invalid Pensions Committee. Claims of Confederate Soldier, hearings on HR 478, pay to Confederate soldier $500 & $30 a month during remainder of their lives." (Wash., DC) June 19, 1916. 16 pp. sewn.

53a IRELAND - Capston's Mission to . . . See: Judan P. Benjamin.

54 IREY, Henry Tillinghast
See: Wm. D. McCain & Charlotte Capers

55 "IRISH VOLUNTEERS, The
Memorial Meeting & Military Hall Festival, October-November 1877." Charleston, S.C., News & Courier pr, 1878. 12mo, wraps, 35, (4) p. (dbl. col.).

56 IRONS, George Vernon
"Howard College as a Confederate military hospital (Marion, Ala., 1863-4). In: Ala. rev. Jan. 1956, v. 9, p. 22-32, notes. Studies largely diagnoses & treatments.

57 IRVINE, Dallas D.
"The Genesis of the 'Official Records." (Cedar Rapids, Ia.) MVHR, Sept. 1937. v.XXIV, #2, p. 221-229.

58 ISLAR, William Valmore
"A Sketch of the War Record of the Edisto Rifles, 1861-1865, by..., Company "A", 1st Regiment S.C.V. Infantry Colonel Johnson Hagood Provisional Army of the Confederate States 1861-1862. Company "G", 25th Regiment S.C.V. Infantry Colonel Charles H. Simonton Confederate States Army 1862-1865. Published by August Kohn." Columbia, S.C., State Co., 1914. 12mo, cl, ports (18), 168 pp. $100- Bmk-105 $125-G

...Louiv: Lost Cause, micro-cd, $3.59.

59 "ISSUE Fairly Presented, The.
The Senate bill for the admission of Kansas as a state. Democracy, Law, Order, & the will of the majority of the whole people of the territory, against Black Republicanism, Usurpation, Revolution, Anarchy, & the will of a meagre Minority." Washington: Union Office, 1856. 8vo, wraps, 30pp. (Jk-142) $30- Supports Kan-Neb Act, charges Republicans with leaving "Bleeding Kansas" to anarchy in a catch-phrase during approaching election.

59a "ITINERARY OF THE FOURTH VIRGINIA Cavalry. Mar. 27-Apr. 9th, 1865." In: SHSP, 1889, v.XVII, p.376-8. By W. B. Wooldridge.

59b IVERSON, Alfred
"Gettysburg." In: SHSP, 1880, v.8, pp.136-39.

60 IVES, Cora Semmes, Mrs.
"Princess of the Moon; a Confederate Fairy Story, written by a lady of Warrenton, Va." Warrenton, Va., 1869. 16mo, front, wraps, 72 pp.

61 IVES, Washington (4th Florida)
"Civil War Journal & Letters . . . See: Jim Cabanis.

J

1 **JACKMAN, John S.**
"Vicksburg in 1862." In: SB, 1884-5, v. III, p. 1-8.

2 ..."From Dalton to Atlanta." In: SB, 1881-2, v. 1, p. 319-328, 414-420, 451-459.

3 ..."The Jack Morgan Songster. Compiled by a Capt. in Gen. Lee's Army." Raleigh, N.C., Branson & Farrar, 1864. 16mo, calf(wraps bound-in), 64 pp. (Thomas Branson) $300-Bmk-114.

4 ..."Jack Sterry, the Jessie Scout...by a Confederate soldier. See: John Cussons.

5 **JACKSON CLARION-LEDGER**
"See Cover of the Confederacy, famous Boy Company of Richmond, Capt. W.W. Parker." In: SHSP, 1907, v. 35, p. 102-107.

6 **JACKSON, A.T.**
"Confederate gunpowder." In: Frontier Time Nov. 1950, v. 28, p. 32-43. view. Mfg. gunpowder in Texas, 1862-1865.

7 **JACKSON, Alto Loftin, Edt.**
"So morns the dove; a confederate infantryman & his family..." See: Benjamin Franklin Jackson.

8 **JACKSON, Andrew B.**
"The panic at Washington after the firing on Fort Sumter." In: Wis. Mag. Hist., Dec. 1919, v.III, p. 244-245. Letter written from D.C., April 18, 1861.

9 **JACKSON, Benjamin Franklin**
"So Mourns the Dove; Letters of a Confederate Infantryman & his Family." Edt: Alto Loftin Jackson. N.Y., Exposition Press (1965) An Exposition-Lochinvar Book. sm. 8vo, cl, 92 pp. 33rd Ala. Inf. Rec. $25-B.

10 **JACKSON, C.L.**
"The officer who rode the gray horse." (in: New Orleans, La., Picayune) In: SHSP, 1893, v. 23, p. 301-304.

11 **JACKSON, Crawford M.**
"An account of the occupation of Port Hudson La. 1863." In: Ala. HQ, winter 1956, v. 18, p. 474-485. Reminisc. of a CSA sergeant.

12 **JACKSON, Edgar Allan**
"Letters of Edgar Allan Jackson. Sept. 7, 1860-Apr. 15, 1863." (Franklin, Va., June, 1929) (News Pub. Co.?) Large 4 1/2x10 3/4" 8vo, 22 pp. stiff cover title. 50 copies. Member of N.C. Inf., 1st Reg. Co. F. $250-OB Reprint: 1955-"Three Rebels Write Home."

13 ..."Three Rebels Write Home, Including the Letters of Edgar Allan Jackson, Sept. 7, 1860-Apr. 15, 1863; James Fenton Bryant, June 20, 1861-Dec. 30, 1866; Irvin Cross Wills, Apr. 9, 1862-July 29, 1863 & Miscellaneous Items, April, 1955." (Franklin, Va: News Publishing Co.) 8vo, stiff wraps, 102, (3) pp. 150 copies 1st Edt., pub. 1939, in an edt. of 50 copies, titled: "Letters of Edgar Allan Jackson." $75-Bmk-105, $50-Bmk.
...Franklin, Va., News Pub. Co., 1955. 8vo, stiff wraps, stapled, (2), 155, (2) pp. Limited to 150 copies. $50-Bmk.

14 **JACKSON, Henry Melville**
"Address to Pegram Battalion Association" In: SHSP, 1888, v. 16, p. 195-207.
..."Our Cause in History." In: SHSP, 1883, v.11, p. 26-30.

15 **JACKSON, Henry R.**
"The Crisis-What is Resistance?" Letters from H.R. Jackson to Hon. Alex H. Stephens." Savannah: John M. Cooper & Co., 1860. 8vo, wraps, 31 pp. cover title. CM

16 ..."Letter from Jackson to Ex-Senator Allen G. Thurman, with explanatory papers." (Atlanta, V.P. Sisson Prt., 1887)

17 **JACKSON, Henry W.R.**
"Letters to Hon. Alex H. Stephens." Savannah, Ga., John M. Cooper, 1860.

18 ..."Confederate monitor & patriot's friend. Containing sketches of numerous important & thrilling events of the present revolution, together with several interesting chapters of history concerning Gen. Stonewall Jackson, Gen. Morgan & other great men of a new nation her armor & salvation..." Atlanta, Ga: Franklin Print, J.J. Toon & Co, 1862. 12mo, 120 pp. Crandall-2632

19 ..."Historical Register, and Confederate assistant to national independence. Containing a discovery for the preservation of butter, together with other valuable recipes & important information for the soldier, & the people in general throughout CSA." Augusta, Ga: Constitutionalist, 1862. 12mo, wraps, 48 pp. Crandall-2633.

20 ..."The Southern women of the second American revolution. Their trials, etc., Yankee barbarity illustrated. Our naval victories & exploits of Confederate war steamers. Capture Yankee gunboats." Atlanta, Ga: Intelligencer Press, 1863. $300-Carolina. 12mo, wraps, 120 pp.(2)-index. Crandall-2634. Do: Louisville: Lost Cause Pr., micro-cd, $3.81.

21 ...(?) "Poems of the Confederate States." Aiken, S.C., title of a work on cover of above book.

22 **JACKSON, Jacob Beeson**
"Stonewall Jackson frightened." In: SHSP, 1882, v.10, p. 190-191.

22a **JACKSON, James W.**
"Life of James W. Jackson, the Alexandria hero, the slayer of Ellsworth, the first martyr of Southern independence; containing a full account of the circumstances of his heroic death, & the many remarkable incidents of his eventful life, constituting a

...With Intro by Walton H. Owen, II, Limited Edition. Falls Church, Va., Confederate Printers, 1985. 500 numbered copies. 8vo, stiff wraps, tied, 46,(3)p, ills, port. on cover.

23 **JACKSON, John King, General**
"Report: Lookout Mountain." In: SHSP, 1880, v. 8, p. 387-396.

23a **JACKSON, Lawerence**
"The Battle of Olustee--as I remember it." Jan. 17, 1929, Tampa, Fla. (Tampa ?), Frank Jamon Press, 1973. 8vo, pict. wraps, map, 8pp.

24 **JACKSON, Mary Ann**
"Stonewall Jackson." In: Hearst's Magazine, Aug/Sept/Oct/Nov, 1913, illus. Titles: "Memories of my warrior soldier," "With Stonewall Jackson in camp." "Stonewall Jackson the Campaigner." "Some wartime letters of Stonewall Jackson." p. 9, 10.

25 ..."Life & Letters of Gen. Thomas J. Jackson (Stonewall Jackson)." By his wife, Mary Ann Jackson, with Introduction by Rev. Henry M. Field, D.D. N.Y., Harper's (c. 1891) $32-173AVC. 8vo, cl, illus., plates, prots, xviii, 479 pp.
...1892-$60-MM.242, $50-Bmk., $75-, Fine 125-B.
...Do: "Memoirs of Stonewall Jackson by his widow Mary Ann Jackson. With Intro by Lt. Gen. John B. Gordon & Rev. Henry M. Field, Sketches by Lee, French, Laws, et. al." Louisville, Ky: Prentice Press (c. 1895) sm. 4to, decr. cl, front (ports) illus., pls. xxiv., 647 pp. Pres-$175-, V.G. $125-, $100-Bmk.
...Dayton, Ohio, Morningside print, 1976. sm. 4to, decr., gilt cl, same size as original 704 pp. $50-, $25-, $35-Y, 1985.
..."Mrs. Jefferson Davis." "Stonewall Jack-

8vo, wraps, 16 pp. cover title. Argument over whether Secession is dead. $20-Bmk.

son's Widow." In: SHSP, 1893, v. 21, p. 340-343.

25a **JACKSON, Mary Anna**
"Memoirs of Stonewall Jackson . . ." Dayton, Oh., Morningside Press, 1985. Sm.8vo, decr. cover, 657pp, ills, map, ports. With intro by Lowell Reidenbaugh. $50.

25b ..."Julia Jackson Christian." Charlotte, N.C., Stone & Barringer, 1910. 8vo, boards, 57pp, ills. $75.

26 **JACKSON, Mary Anna Morrison**
"Life & Letters of General Thomas J. Jackson (Stonewall Jackson), by his wife Mary Anna Jackson. With an introduction by Henry M. Field." N.Y., Harper & bro., 1892.JNCL $50-. 12mo, cl, front (port), illus., ports, xviii, 479 pp.
...1st Edt., 1891, same.
..."Memoirs of Stonewall Jackson by his widow Mary Anna Jackosn. With introduction by Lieut. Gen. John B. Gordon & Rev. Henry M. Field & sketches by Generals Fitzhugh Lee, S.G. French, Lafayette McLaws, M.C. Butler, Bradley T. Johnson, James H. Lane, William B. Taliaferro, Samuel G. McGowan, Henry Heth, Basil W. Duke, Ex-Gov. F.W.M. Holliday, Revs. J.W. Jones & J.R. Graham, Col. Augustua C. Hamlin, Capt. Joseph S. Morrison & Viscount (General) Wolseley, Commander-in-chief of the Armies of Great Britain, & Col. G.F.R. Henderson, Professor in the British Staff College, Camberly, Surrey, England." Louisville, KY., Prentice Press, Courier-Journal, Job printing (1895). 4to, decr. gold port of Jackson, cover. ports, incl. front, illus., incl. map, facsm. xxiv, 647 p.
...Dayton, Oh., Morningside press, 1976. Reproduction of orig., & cover, 704 pp.

27 ..."Recollections of Mrs. Stonewall Jackson." In: Confed. Vet., Apr. 1922, v. XXX, p. 412-414.

28 ...Memories of my warrior husband "Stonewall Jackson", C.S.A." In: Hearst's Mag., July Nov., 1912. v. XXIV, pp. 188-197; 386-394; 565-573; 762-770. Title headings vary.

29 ..."Memoir of Julia Jackson Christian, daughter of "Stonewall Jackson." 16mo, cl, illus., 57 pp. Ports/Stone & Barringer Pr., Charlotte, N.C., (1910). $25-Bmk-111

30 **JACKSON, T.J. (STONEWALL)**
"Autograph letter, signed." Near Gordonsville,", July 25, 1862. Gdsp(11-'82) $2,600.00 Cautioning to watch his flank & not let Pope with superior forces get in his rear.

31 ...Broadside: 7 1/2x10 1/4" Two Continents, Both Friend & Foe Mourn Premature Death of Gen. Jackson, etc." eminent sculptor J.H. Foley has undertaken to execute a marble statue, heroic size, for 1000 lbs. With list of committee names. $50-

32 ...(Jackson, Gen. Stonewall) Statue "Inauguration of the Jackson statue. Se: Rev. Moses D. Hoge address.
...Ceremony of Laying the Corner-stone for the Equestrian Statue of...Richmond, June 3, 1915...12pp. Print. wraps, Port., bordered text. Richmond, 1915.

33 ..."Portrait, standing. Color 18x27", by J.M. Garner. Oil, signed, numbered copies. Sponsored by SCV, (Remarqued, $90-. Washington, DC, Southern Heritage, 1974.

34 ...Engraving by J. Rogers: "From ambertype by Brady expressly for this work." 8 1/4x11", heavy engraved decorations around oval of "Stonewall Jackson Mortally Wounded." small battle scene below engraving. $45-

35 ..."Jackson, Johnston & Lee. Engraving 18x24" on panel 27x32". Showing Stonewall Jackson, hat in hand. Gen. Joe Johnston(center), right arm on hip & Gen. Lee,

right arm extended with left hand on sword. Standing figures.

36 ..Engraved full-length portrait, before a tent, in full uniform, sitting. NY, Johnson Fry & co., 1865. 10 1/2x8".

37 ..."A Federal Soldier's opinion of Gen. Stonewall Jackson." In: SHSP, 1882, v.X, p. 334-335.

38 ..."Grave of Stonewall Jackson, Lexington Va., from a sketch by a General Officer of the CSA, made during the war. Balt: E. Sachse & Co., n.d. Hand-colored litho 12 1/2x9 1/4" plus margins. $65.00. Grave with CSA flag, soldier standing at grave with rifle resting on ground.

39 ...Print 24x30", black & white. Full-length on horseback, holding field-glasses, broken cannon in front (left), with three members of staff in left background. Baltimore: Smith & Holden, 1866.

40 ..."Jackson's religious views." In: CV, Sept. 1922. v.XXX, p. 326-327. See: Henry Churchill Semple.

41 ..."Our Fallen Braves," large-scale port. flanked by eight prominent CSA generals who died in battle. Below are scenes of Chancellorsville, where Jackson fell, and Johnston's death at Shiloh. New York: Haasis & Lubrecht, 1867. Size 33x26" (Nebenz #11) $285.00

42 ...Jackson (Gen. Stonewall) Original colored lithograph, issued 1871 to raise money for erection of a monument honoring him at V.M.I. 19x24" (plate), full margins, 28x34" $500-. Matching lithographs same as with Lee. (Bmk.90)

43 ..."Daily Richmond Examiner-EXTRA Edition, May 10, 1866. Richmond, Va., 1866. Folio, 4pp. printed mourning border third anniversary of his death. Memorial Association benefit of Confederate dead. Entirely devoted to Stonewall Jackson.

44 ..."Jackson is Dead, by Rebel." n.p.n.d., handbill, 5x10", 56 lines on his death. $100-. See: Elizabeth Dabney Coleman.

45 ..."Portrait-10 1/4x27", lithograph. Chicago: Kurtz & Allison Art Studion, n.d. Jackson mounted on fine charger, with two mounted officers in background. All in plummed hats. $50-.

46 ..."The man who killed Stonewall Jackson by Shalimar." In: Blackwood's Magazine (Great Britain) October, 1930. 22pp.

47 ...Lithograph of Stonewall Jackson, by 'Fabronius.' Boston: L. Prang & Co., n.d. 11x13 1/2", of Jackson as a young man in the uniform of the U.S. Army. $25-

48 ..."Inauguration of the Jackson statue, Tues., Oct. 26, 1875." Richmond, Va., R.F. Walker, 1875. 8vo, wraps, 23 pp.
...October 26, 1876...Richmond, Wm. Ellis Jones, 1889. 8vo, wraps, 30 pp. Published by J.Wm. Jones of Southern historical society to meet continuing demands of the society.

49 ...Portrait: From a photograph from life. New York: C.B. Richardson, 1864. Oval on sheet 17x21", creased $50-

50 ...Lieut. Gen. Thos. J. Jackson & his family." Mezzotint by Wm. Sartain. 14x19 plus margin. Phila: Wm. Sartain litho., 1866. oblong folio, proof copy. $35-. With wife & child. Portrait of Lee, busts of Washington & Calhoun in background, bible under general's hand, on table.

51 ..."The Life of Stonewall Jackson. From official papers, cotemporary(sic) narratives, & personal acquaintance. By a Virginian." Richmond, Ayres & Wade, Illustrated News Steam Presses, 1863. 12mo, wraps (with engraved portrait) port, 305 pp., with 6pp. pub. advts. at end. Front. port of Jackson by E. Crehen of Richmond. Author: John Esten Cooke, who wrote book "In the intervals of campaigning."

52 ..."A Short History of T.J. Jackson." N.Y. Knapp & co, 1888. Booklets, colored, 2 3/4x1 1/2", 16 pp. See: W. Duke & sons & co, pub., $25-. See: W. Duke & Sons., (Packed in Duke's cigarettes.)

53 ..."Stonewall Jackson." N.p., 1928 published by John (Boston Hancock Mutual Life Ins., Co.) 12mo, decr. wraps, 16 pp.

54 ..."Stonewall Jackson's First Confederate Command." In: SB, Jan. 1883, v. 1, p. 184-6. At Harper's Ferry, April, 1861.

55 ..."Stonewall Cemetery for soldiers." In: Armchair Researcher, 1980. v.1, #3, p. 157-165. Spalding county, Ga., (genealogical)

56 ..."Life & Military Career of "Stonewall Jackson." London: Bacon & Co., (1863) 8vo, wraps, 15 pp.

57 ..."Prospectus for a Statue of the late Gen. Thos. J. "Stonewall" Jackson." London, 1863. 4to. Statue erected Sept. 1875.

58 ..."Report of Lt. Gen. Jackson of Operations from 5th to 27th September, 1862." In: OLOD, Sept., 1874, v. 1, #1, p. 22-28.

59 ..."Sketches of General Jackson." In: LWL, Sept. 1866. v. 1, #5, p. 310-314.

60 ...(Jackson, Thomas Jonathan "Stonewall") "Unveiling of Bust & Tablet for...in the auditorium of library of N.Y. University, University Heights, N.Y., May 19, 1957. 3:00 pm." n.p., n.d. 8vo, wraps, 16pp., illus., facsms., ports, map, programe.

61 ..."Wounding of Lieutenant-General T.J. Jackson." In: LWL, July 1866, v.1, #3, p. 179.

62 ...Unveiling of statue of Stonewall Jackson...New Orleans, La. See: "Dedication of tomb of ANV..."

63 ..."Stonewall Jackson, late general of the Confederate Army, a biographical sketch & an outline of his Virginian campaigns. By the author of "Life in the South." (Catherine Cooper Hopley) London: Chapman & Hall, 1863. 12mo, boards (Jackson port. on cover), fldg. map, xiv, 178 pp. $500-OB, $200-G

...2nd same above & a 3rd edt., same. See: Catherine Cooper Hopley & note, authorship.

64 ..."With Stonewall Jackson. Illustrations by Allen C. Redwood." In: Scribner's, June 1879. 14 pp., in stapled binder.

65 ..."Stonewall Jackson's Valley campaign." In: Anl. of War, p. 724-749.

66 ...Jackson (Thomas Jonathan, "Stonewall.") SHSP. See: Wm. Allan, Samuel Z. Ammen, Randolph S. Barton, A.R. Boteler, Joseph Bryan, Robert L. Dabney, J.D. Davidson, Jubal A. Early, Benj. S. Ewell, I.C. Haas, Asher W. Harman, J.C. Hiden, Moses D. Hoge, "B.M.I.", Jacob B. Jackson, John W. Jones, Jas. L. Kemper, Benj. W. Leigh, "Louisville Christian Observer." Louisville Courier-Journal, "G.H.M." Hunter H. McGuire, Dabney H. Maury, Marcellus N. Moorman, Thomas T. Munford, Wm. A. Obenchain, John W. Palmer, John M. Patton, Wm. F. Randolph, Reidsville(N.C.) Times, Wm. M. Robins, W.P. St. John, Mary A. Townsend, Rufus R. Wilson, John H. Worsham. "Field Notes", SHSP, 1883, v.11, p. 137.

66a ..."Civil War Times, Illustrated." April 1988. Entire issue devoted to Jackson, illustrated with many b/w & color ills, ports on front & back covers in color. 50pp. See: Mark Grimsley.

66b ..."Stonewall Jackson March" composed by John Pridham. 4to, lithograph in color on cover of music. Mounted on prancing horse, with flowing cape, holding small scope, plume in hat, a pose like Stuart. Printed in England, Brewer & Co.

66c ..."Report of the Battle of Port Republic." n.p., (1963). 8vo, wraps, 15pp. facsm. $20. Geo. Markham, Jr.

66d ...Print: 'Stonewall Jackson, Bull Run, Aug. 17, 1861.' From painting by H.A.

Ogden. $22.50. Double-page print (removed) 10 x 12 3/4.

66e **JACKSON, Thomas J., et.al.**
"Anecdotes for Our Soldiers. #3." (Caption title). Charleston, 186?. Goodspeed $200. 16mo, sewn, 8pp. Crandall-4565.

67 **JACKSON, William H., Gen.**
"Sherman's advance on Meridian (Report) In: SHSP, 1881, v. 9, p. 156-159.

68 ..."The Battle of Crater." In: Am. Mil. Hist. Found. Journ., 1938, v.II, p. 3-25. "Glance" at '64 campaign, general situation leading to Crater, near Petersburg, Va., Jly. 30.

69 ..."General Joseph Eggleston Johnston, storm center of the Confederate Army." In: MVHR, Dec., 1927, v.XIV, p. 342-359. $20-

70 ..."Jefferson Davis & his generals: a study in the breakdown of unity of command in the Confederacy." In: Univ. Chicago, Abstract of theses, Humanistic ser. v.III, Chi. Univ. press., 1927, p. 191-198.

71 ...Two unpublished letters of Jefferson Davis. Edt: Alfred P. James." In: MVHR, v.XXV, p. 539-542, (1939). Letters to Mrs. S.A. Ayers in 1872-1874.

72 **JACOB, Thaddeus Ovander**
"Reminiscences of the Army of Northern Virginia-(45th Georgia Regiment)." Forsyth, Ga., 1871. 8vo, wraps, cover title, 32 pp. $200-OB One known copy? Lillian Henderson's Roster of CSA soldiers of Georgia, v.IV, p. 868. lists as priv. Mar 4, 1862; 1st Lt., Sept. 10, 1862; Capt., Dec. 25, 1862. Resigned Jan. 23, 1865.

72a **JACOBS, Charles & Marian W.**
"A Biography of Col. W. V. White." Pub: Montgomery County Md., Historical Society, in two parts: Nov. 1978/Feb. 1979. See also: Elijah Veirs White.

73 **JACOBS, Eloise Tyler**
"Commodore Montgomery, a Confederate Naval hero, & his adventures." In: CV, Jan. 1917, v.XXV, p. 26-27.

74 **JACOBS, Joseph, Phar. M. SC. D.**
"Some of the drug conditions during the War Between the States, 1861-65." In: Ga. H.Q., Sept. 1926, v.X, #3, p. 200-222.
..."Some of the drug conditions during the War Between the States, 1861-1865. Paper read before the American Pharmaceutical Ass'n., in Baltimore, Aug. 1898." In: SHSP, 1905, v. 33, p. 161-187.

74a **JACOBS, Thornwell**
"Red Lanterns on St. Michael's." N.Y., E.P. Dutton Co., 1940. 12mo, cl, front, ills, 670pp. Fiction: Charleston siege, 1863.

74b ..."With the Confederate Colors." n.p., Southern Art Pub. Co., 1907. Color lithos of Gilbert Gaul.

75 **JACOBSON, Gabe**
"Judah P. Benjamin; lawyer & statesman." Mississippi Law Journal, VII, pp. 483-491. Biog. sketch of CSA Sec't. State.

76 **JAGER, Ronald**
"Houston, Texas Fights the Civil War." In: Texana, 1973, v.XI, #1, p. 30-51, notes.

77 **JAHNS, Patricia**
"Matthew Fontaine Maury & Joseph Henry: Scientists of Civil War." N.Y., Hastings House (1961) 8vo, cl, d/w, 308 pp. $20- Bmk-111.

77a **JAMBORSKY, William Eric**
"Confederate Leadership & Defeat in the West." In: Lincoln Herald, 1984 (Summer) p.50-77.

78 **JAMES CITY CAVALRY**
See: James H. Allen.

79 **JAMES, Alfred P.**
"The strategy of concentration of the Confederate forces in the Mississippi Valley in the spring of 1862." Reprint: Amer. Hist. Assn., for 1919, v.1, p. 365-374. In: MVHR, Ext.
Nov. 1921. p. 363-372.

80 **JAMES, C.F.**
"Battle of Sailor's Creek. Part taken by Hunter's Brigade." In: SHSP, 1896, v. 24,

p. 83-88. James was Capt., Co. F., 8th Va. Inft.

81 **JAMES, D. Clayton**
"Mississippi Agriculture, 1861-1865." (Jackson, Miss.), Jour. Miss. Hist. July, 1962, v. XXIV, , #3, p. 129-141.

82 **JAMES, G. Watson, Dr., Co. G, 3rd Bat.**
"Dahlgren's Raid." In: SHSP, Apr. 1914., v. XXXIX, p. 63-72. Raid before the Fall of Richmond to free prisoners.

83 ...An historic broadcast." In: Virginia record June 1958, v. 80, #6, p. 13-14, 36. port, view. An NBC broadcast of the last United Confederate Veteran's reunion, Richmond, 1932. Arrainged by the author, et.al.

84 **JAMES, Jason W.**
"Memorable Events in the Life of Captain Jason W. James." n.p. (Roswell, N.Mex.) 1911. 12mo, wraps, front(port), 150 pp., CSA Cavalry Capt. KKK leader, Texas Ranger & So. West cattleman.

85 ..."Memories & Viewpoints." (Roswell, N.Mex., 1928) no front, 183 pp. $50-. See also: M.L. Dillon sketch, N.M. Hist. Review, April 1956.

86 **JAMES, John G.**
"The Southern Student's Hand-book of Selections for Reading & Oratory." N.Y., A.S. Barnes & Co., 1879. 8vo, decr. cl, xi, 407 pp. Much CSA authors & subject matter.

87 **JAMES, Martha Elizabeth McArthur, Mrs.**
"A Mixed Up Family, a Sampson County Autobiography 1852-1868." Clinton, N.C., 1955. 8vo, wraps, illus., 35 pp. About half on the war.

88 **JAMES, Westwood, Corporal, MD**
"The Diary of Corporal Westwood James, Edt. by Michael Musick." In: CWTI, Oct. 1978, v.17, #6, p. 34-42, illus., port.

89 **JAMESON, J. Franklin, Dr.**
"The London Expenditures of the Confederate Secret Service." Amer. Hist. Rev., (1920), v.XXV, p. 811-824.

90 **JAMESTOWN (Gunboat) C.S.N.**
See: Robert Wright.

91 **JAMISON, Alma Hill**
"The Cyclorama of the Battle of Atlanta." In: (Ga.)Atl. Hist. Bul., II, 1937, #10, p. 58-75. Painted in 1885, purchased by Atlanta, 1892. See: Wilbur G. Kurtz.

92 **JAMISON, David Flavel**
"The Life & Times of Bertrand Du Guesclin: a History of the Fourteenth Century." Charleston, S.C., John Russell, 1864. 8vo, cl, port, 287, 314 pp. $175-B

93 **JAMISON, Henry Downs, Jr. and Margierote Jamison McTigue**
"Letters & Recollections of a Confederate Soldier 1860-1865." (printed one side) Nashville, Tenn. 1964. 4to, soft cover, ports, (8)185, (5) pp, Jamison & Spain genealogy in back. Distributed free to family & friends. pp. 139-185: "Reminiscences of a Tennessee Confederate Veteran," by Prf. R.D. Jamison. First run weekly in the Noxubee (Mississippi) County Review, c. 1908.

94 **JARMAN, Robert A.**
"A Mississippian at Nashville. One soldier's view of the last great Confederate offensive in the West. Edt: Richard M. McMurry." In: CWTI, May 1973, v.XII, #2, p. 8-11, 14-15, illus., ports, map.

95 **JARVIS, Rupert Charles**
"The Alabama & the Law. Address given before members of Confederate Research Club, on the 5th annual Confederate dinner, Saturday, Mar. 28, 1959, Eccleston Hotel." (London? 1959). 8vo, wraps, 11 pp., reproduced from typed copy.

96 **JAYNES, R.T.**
"Address: "The Confederate Character." Quarterly meeting, Norton Camp, United Daughters of the Confederacy. May 4,

1939. Walhalla, S.C., (1939?) 8vo, wraps, 8pp.

97 **JEFFERSON COUNTY, GEORGIA**
Mrs. Z.V. Thomas' "History of Jefferson County." Macon, Ga., 1927. $55-
...Spartanburg, S.C., Reprint Co, 1978. New index, illus. 144 pp. Jefferson Co., in the war, with CSA companies "Jefferson Co., in the war, with CSA companies "Jefferson Co. Guards', "Jeff Grays", "Battey Guards," "Jefferson Volunteers," and "Grubbs Hussars."

98 ..."Jefferson Davis" (Privateer), C.S.N.
See: Savannah News

99 **JEFFERSON, George C.**
"Lee's retreat, 1865." In: Tyler Quart. Hist. & Gean. Mag., July 1922, v. IV, p. 70-71. A personal reminiscence.

100 **JEFFREY, Robert W.**
"Virginia Military Institute (founded 1840)" In: Commonwealth(Va.), Apr. 1954, v. 21, #4, p. 17-19, 44-46, ports, views. See: John S. Wise & Jennings C. Wise.

101 **JEFFREY, William H.**
"Richmond Prisons 1861-1862, compiled from original records kept by the Confederate government; journals kept by Union prisoners of war, together with the name, rank, company, regiment & state of the four thousand who were confined there." St. Johnsbury (Vt.) Republican press (1893) $60- 12mo, cl, illus., ports, facsms, 271 pp.

102 **JEFFREYS, Thomas D., Capt., 56th Va.**
"The 'Red Badge' Explained." (from Richmond Times-Dispatch, May 20, 1906) In: SHSP, 1908 v. 36, p. 248-249.

103 **JEFFRIES, C.C.**
"Terry's Rangers." New York: Vantage Press (1961), 8vo, cl, d/w & 139 pp.

104 ..."The Character of Terry's Texas Rangers." In: SwHQ, April, 1961, v.LXIV, #4, p. 454-462.

105 **JEFFRIES, Clarence**
"Running the blockade on the Mississippi." In: CV, Jan. 1914, v. XXII, p. 22-23. At mouth of Red River by CSN ram 'Webb.'

106 **JEFFRIES, Joseph A.**
"The Night Attack at Fairfax Court House." In: So. Mag., Sept. 1899, wraps 5 pp., Manassas, Va., 1899.

107 **JENKINS BRIGADE**
See: Hermann Schuricht.

108 **JENKINS, A.G., W. Va.**
"Brigadier-General A.G. Jenkins." In: LWL, July 1866, v. 1, #3, pp. 183.

109 **JENKINS, Ann**
"The day in St. Albans." In: New Eng. teacher, April 1958, v. 5, #4, p. 12, 14-15, 18. Robbery of Franklin Co., Bank at St. Albans, Vt. by CSA soldiers, 19 Oct., 1864.

110 **JENKINS, Brian**
"Frank Lawley & the Confederacy." In: CWH, June 1977, v. 23, #2, p. 144-160. See also Wm. S. Hoole.

111 **JENKINS, Charles J.**
"Authorship of the Georgia Platform of 1850: A Letter by Charles J. Jenkins Edt: Royce McCrary." In: Ga. H.W., Winter 1970, v. LIV, #4, p. 585-590.

112 **JENKINS, Coleman W.**
"Robert E. Lee. An example of leadership." In: Mil. Engineer, Jan. 1930, v. XXII, p. 32-38.

113 **JENKINS, Dan**
"Confederate & union Buttons of the Gulf Coast, 1861-1865" Mobile, Ala., Museum of the City of Mobile, 1983. (Museum Publication No. 7.) 12 mo, stiff wraps, 58 pp. facsms, index.

114 **JENKINS, E. Courtney**
"John Carrell Jenkins, color bearer, Company B, 21st Virginia infantry, in Memoriam Army of CSA." n.p., 190-?) 12mo, wraps, xl, 2pls, ports. $250-R.

115 **JENKINS, John Carrell**
"In Memoriam: Color Bearer, Co. B., 21st Va.Inf., CSA." (Richmond, Va., 1883) 24mo, wraps, illus., 40pp.

116 **JENKINS, John H.**
"W.W. Heartsill Diary. The most remarkable Texas book: an essay on W.W. Heartsill's Fourteen hundred & 91 days in the Confederate army." Austin, Texas, Jenkins Pub., co. 1980. 4to, cl & leather spine, with an original leaf from the original book, in pocket. Lim. Edt. 64 numbered & atg. copies. Facsm. title-pg. (Copy with 4-orig. photos, $400-) $125-

117 **JENKINS, Paul B.**
"The Battle of Westport, Oct. 21-23, 1864 & the movement of the Missouri Valley Historical Society of Kansas City to make a memorial park out of a part of the battlefield." (cover title) An address before the Knife & Fork club of Kansas City, Oct. 23, 1923, the 59th Anniversary of the battle." n.p., (c. 1923) 8vo, wraps, 50pp. ports, map.(Ark.Univ.) See: H.H. Crittenden

118 ..."The Battle of Westport." Kansas City, Mo., Franklin Hudson Pr., 1906. sm.8vo, cl, d/w, 193 pp. maps, index. Author refers to it as Gettysburg of West. $55-Bmk.

119 **JENKINS, Thomas E.**
"Gettysburg in war & in peace, a brief & historical review of interesting historical facts & incidents relative to the famous three days." Baltimore: Passenger Dept., Western Maryland Railroad (Press of John Cox's sons, 1890. 8vo, wraps, illus., fold. illus, map, 9, 92 pp. Roster of the ANV, (8) p. "The old Tape worm rail road,' now Gettysburg short line of the Western Maryland Rry, p. 61-80. Dorn-II, 2269.
...1898 reprinting, 2nd Souvenir Edt., 116 pp.

120 **JENKINS, Weston**
"The unponderable in an estimate of the situation: as illustrated by Stonewall Jackson's valley campaign." In: Inf. Journ., 1932, v. XXXIX, p. 361-367.

121 **JENNINGS, Arthur H.**
"Appomattox after sixty-two years." In: Curr. Hist., Apr. 1927, v.XXVI, p. 1-6.
..."Confederate Forces in the Civil War." In: Curr. Hist., Apr. 1924, v.XX, p. 113-115.

122 ..."Jefferson Davis's pre-war statesmanship." In: Curr. Hist., Nov. 1926, v.XXV, p. 210-213.

123 ..."The South not responsible for slavery." In: Confed. Vet., Jan. 1918, v.XXVI, p. 24-25. (Also in "The Gray Book", p. 11-17.)

124 ..."A view of Rutledge's 'Lincoln'" a Southern view." In: Confed. Vet., Apr. 1925, v.XXXIII, p. 129-130. (See: Rutledge). Chm: 'The Gray Book Comm., Sons.C.Vet.

125 **JENNINGS, Roscoe Greene**
"Downeasters in Arkansas: Letters of Roscoe G. Jennings to his brother. Edt. by Eugene A. Nolte." In: AHQ, 1959, v.XVIII, p. 3-25. His brother, Orville, was a native of Maine. From various camps of the 12th Ark. Vols., CSA writer was regimental surgeon.

126 **JENNINGS, Thelma**
David Potter - 'The Empending Crisis', 1848-1861." In: THW, 1976, v.XXXV, p. 329-352.

126a ..."Nashville Convention: Southern Movement for Unity, 1848-51." Memphis: Tenn. State University Press, 1980. 8vo, cl, dj, x, 309pp. $17. The South would concede much to save the union if the north would accept a few fundamental Southern right

126b ..."Tennessee & the Nashville Convention of 1850." In: THQ, 1971, v.30, p,70-82.

127 **JENSEN, Billie Barnes**
"Confederate sentiment in Colorado,

1861-1865." In: West. brand book (Denver) 1958, v. 13, p. 85-117. fldg. map, port, views, notes.

127a **JEROME, Father**
"The Vatican & the Southern Confederacy." St. Leo, Florida: Abbey Press, 1962. 12mo, stiff wraps, ports, ills, 39pp.

127b **JERVEY, Susan Ravenel**
"Extracts from a Journal kept by Susan R. Jervey at Northampton Plantation." Suffolk, Va., Robt. Hardy Pub., 1986. 8vo, wraps, 28pp.
See: Charlotte St.J. Ravenel.

128 **JERVEY, Susan Ravenel & Charlotte St. Julien Ravenel**
"Two Diaries from Middle St. John's, Berkeley, South Carolina, Feb-May, 1865. Journals kept by Miss Susan R. Jervey & Miss Charlotte St. J. Ravenel, at Northampton & Pooshee Plantations, & reminiscences of Mrs. (Waring) Henagan. With two contemporary reports from federal officials." (Pinopolis, S.C.) St. John's Hunting Club, 1921. (300 copies, limited edition) 8vo, stiff wraps, 56 pp. $35-Bmk-90.

129 **JERVEY, Theodore Dehon**
"Charleston During the Civil War." Washington: Amer. Hist. Ass'n., 1915. Reprint: wraps, AHA Annual report, v. 1 for 1913., p. 167-176.

130 ..."The Railroad, the conqueror, blockade running." Columbia, S.C., The State co., 1913. 8vo, wraps, plates, 44pp. $35-Bmk-90. Economic conditions in South 1820- until Civil War, influence of railroads in development of industries & slave labor. Louisville, Cincinnati & Charleston RRy.

131 ..."Robert Y. Hayne & His Times." N.Y., Macmillan, 1909. 8vo, cl, ports, xix, 555pp. Half-title: 'Hayne & his times; hist. sketch of So. Carolina in first five decades of the constitution & political influence of state on the union of that period.'

132 **JETTON, Robert H.**
"Sue Ella a Historical Romance founded on incidents of the War Between the States by Robt. H. Jetton, Oakwood, Texas. Illustrated by Thos. B. Woodburn. A Texas Novel by a Texas Editor." (Oakwood, Texas, The Author, 1915). 12mo, cl, illus., incl. front, (8), 160 pp. $50-. Historical background, N.Mex. & Texas based on actual facts. Notes on Tom Green's Tex. Brig.

133 **JEWELL, Carey C.**
"Harvest of Death: a Detailed Account of the Army of Tennessee at the Battle of Franklin." Hicksville, N.Y., Exposition Press, 1976. 8vo, cl, dj, 87 pp.

134 ..."The Jews of the Confederacy," with an Intor: Dr. Bertram W. Korn. In: Amer. Jewish Archives, April 1961, v. XIII, #1, Civil War Centennial Southern Issue. 8vo, stiff wraps, ports, illus., (3)-90 pp.

135 **JOHANNSEN, Robert W.**
"Stephen A. Douglas & the South." In: JSH, Feb. 1967, (25)pp.

135a ..."The Mind of a Secessionist: Social Conservatism or Romantic Adventure?" In: Rev. in Amer. Hist., Sept. 1986, v.14, p.354-60.

136 **JOHN, Evan (pseud.)**
See: Simpson, Evan John, Col.

137 **JOHN, Samuel Will**
"War records of Alabama." In: Report of Alabama History Comm. to Gov. of Ala. Dec. 1, 1900. Edt: Thos. McAdory Owen. Montgomery, Ala., Brown pr., 1901. Part iv., Pub. Ala. Hist. Soc. Mssc.coll., v.1, p. 319-353.

138 ..."Alabama corps of cadets, 1860-1865." In: CV, Jan. 1917, v.XXV, p. 12-14.

139 **JOHNS, Frank S. & Anne Page**
"Chimborazo Hospital & J.B. McCaw, Surgeon-in-Chief." (Richmond) Va. Mag. Hist. Biog., April 1954, v. 62, #2, p. 190-200, facsm.s, 1-foldg. This was the largest

military hospital in the world, crude as it was, mortality of only 9%. The complete records were found, intact(in Nat'l. Archives) where every patient can be found. 168 mssc. volumes may be read!

140 **JOHNS, John**
"Wilmington during the Blockade," by a late Confederate officer." In: Harper's June/Nov., 1867, v.XXXV, p. 497-503.

141 **JOHNS, John E.**
"Florida During the Civil War." Gainesville: University of Florida Pr, 1963. 8vo, cl, dj, illus., ports, maps, incl. liners, ix, 265 pp., notes, bibliog. index (p. 216-265) $55-$15-25-Bmk-105

142 ..."Florida in the Confederacy." Ann Arbor: University Microfilms, 1959 (1960). Positive microfilm of typescript, 460 leaves, bibliog(425-460). Thesis--University N.C. Abstracted, dissert., 20:3270 Feb.

143 **JOHNS, John, Bishop**
"A Bishop's Visitation in the Field of War, an address: St. Paul's Church Richmond, Va., Sept. 20, 1865." In: SHSP, April 1914, v.XXXIX, p. 137-143.

144 **JOHNSON'S BATTERY**
See: Wm. W. Parker.

145 **JOHNSON'S ISLAND, LAKE ERIE**
"Autographs of Confederate Officers on Johnson's Island, 1864."
...do., dated, 1865. Albums owned by A.O.P. Nicholson, Jr., Columbia, Tenn. Article in CV, Dec. 1896, v.IV, #12, p. 437-438, Plate, from a prisoner's drawing, Johnson's Island in 1864-1865.

146 ...Johnson's Island, Ohio, Lake Erie, 1863-1865: Autograph Album of Confed Officers Imprisoned at......." n.p., n.d., (c. 1940) wraps, mimogr. 123 pp, repro. of album, names of officers, units, place of capture & several poems, composed there. $25-

147 ..."Johnson's Island autograph album." In: UDCM July 1952, v. 15, #7, p. 3, 38. Describes a vol. autographs of prisoners CSA, 1864-5 acquired by Sandusky Pub. Lib.

148 ..."Johnson's Island, Lake Erie, Ohio." U.S. Military Prison" Photo on cardboard mount 6 1/2x8 3/4" drawn by Maj. Smith of St. Louis in autograph album of Col. C.W. Frayser in 1864, who was pres. Southern Hist. Assn., Memphis. Copied in 1897 by Hilliard of Memphis.

149 ..."Johnson's Island, prison for Confederate soldiers." In: South. Mag., 1935, v.II, #1 p. 20-21, 41. a CSA officers' prison during war.

150 ...Johnson's Island, Sandusky Bay, Lake Erie. "Officers prisoners on Johnson's island. In: CV, 1900, v.8, p. 305-307, with a list of CSA dead buried there.

151 ...(Johnson's Island) "Johnson's Island. Thrilling story a visit thereto recalls. Thompson Conspiracy," Maj. C.H. Cole, etc. In: SHSP, 1902, v.XXX, p. 256-265. Partial roster of 100 recognized names for a stone marker.

152 ...(Johnsons Island Prison) Lithograph: Depot Prisoners of War on Johnson's Island. Sketched by Edwd. Gould, Co. B 128 Regt. OVI." 18x24 1/2" Cincinnati: Middleton, Strobridge & Co Prison for CSA Officers. $35-

153 ...Johnson's Island, Lake Erie, Ohio. See: L.W. Allen, W.H.H. Blackman, Robert A. Brock, Cincinnati Commercial Gazette, Robert Dabney Minor, Wm. S. Pierson.

154 **JOHNSON, Adam Rankin**
"The Partisan Rangers of the Confederate States Army, Edt: William J. Davis." Louisville, Ky., Geo. G. Fetter, 1904. 8vo, cl(or, 3/4 Lt.), plan, illus., ports, xii, 476 pp. mcm-248, $250-Bmk-105. Louisville: Lost Cause pr, micro-cd $6.98.
...Evansville, Ind., Unigraphic pr., 1971. 8vo, buckram, reprint. $22.50Y

155 ...Hartford, Ky., Cook & McDowell pub (1979). 8vo, cl, illus., new index, xii, 516 pp.(65)lfs. plates

156 **JOHNSON, Albert Sidney, Dr.**
"The Confederate Cause Yesterday & Today." Speech by..., at First Presbyterian Church, Jackson, Miss., March 1, 1951, Distributed by Irbia Warren Windham, of Jefferson Davis Camp, #635, Sons of Confederate Veterans of Jackson, Miss.

157 ..."Gen. Albert Sidney Johnson." In CV, March 1895, v.III, #3, p. 81-87, illus., maps, port.

158 ..."Northern men in the Confederate Army." In: CV, Feb. 1928, v.XXXVI, p. 48-49.

159 **JOHNSON, Andrew**
See: LeRoy Graf, Gregg Phifer, Ralph Joseph Roske.

160 **JOHNSON, Andrew, of Tenn.**
"The Constitutionality & Rightfulness of Secession." Speech of... in Senate of U.S. Tues. & Wed., Dec. 18 & 19, 1860. (caption title) 23 pp, sewed, n.p., n.d., (Wash. 1860)

161 ..."Letters from North Carolina to Andrew Johnson." Edt: Elizabeth Gregory McPherson. (Raleigh) NCHRev., Jan. 1951, v.XXVIII, #1, p. 63-87.

162 ..."Letters from North Carolina to Andrew Johnson." v.XXVII, #3, (Raleigh) NCHRev., July 1950, p. 336-363.

163 ..."Message...Transmitting Final Report of the Names of Persons Engaged in Rebellion Who Have Been Pardoned." Washington: GPO, 1867. 8vo, sewed, 147 pp. Lists 7,000 Confederates by name, rank, date & recommendation. Famous pardon list issued just before Johnson retired.

164 **JOHNSON, Boyd W.**
"The Civil War in Ouachita County." (Camden, Arkansas. Ouachita County Historical Society, n.d., (1968). 4to, soft back-photo on cover, illus. ports, (3) maps, (8) pp., 63, (2) pp.

165 ..."Cullen Montgomery Baker the Arkansas-Texas Desperado." In: AHQ 1966, v.XXV, p. 229-239, map. See: Ed Bartholomew, Thos. Orr,

166 **JOHNSON, Bradley Tyler, Gen.**
"Address Before the Association of Confederate Soldiers & Sailors of Maryland, June 10, 1874." Baltimore, 1874- *"The Lost Cause?" 8vo, orig. wraps, 11 pp. Brief acct. Maryland's part for south.

167 ..."Address on 1st Maryland campaign at the reunion of the ANV." In: SHSP, 1884, v.12, p. 500-537.

168 ..."Address delivered at dedication of the Confederate memorial hall at Richmond, Va., Feb. 22, 1896." Richmond, Va., Wm. Ellis Jones, 1896. 8vo, wraps, 16 pp.

169 ..."Address delivered by..., before the Society of the Army & Navy of the Confederate States & the Association of the Maryland Line, at Maryland Hall Baltimore, MD., Nov. 16, 1886." Baltimore (1886). 8vo, wraps, 8pp. Cover title: "Cause of the Confederate States."

170 ..."The Cause of the Confederate States. Address...to Society of Army & Navy of Confederate States, in the State of Maryland & the Association of the Maryland Line, at Maryland Hall, Baltimore, Md. Nov. 16, 1886." n.p., cover title, 8 pp., wraps.

171 ..."The Confederate Flag." In: SHSP 1896, v. 24, p. 117-119.

172 ..."Confederate States Supreme Court." In: SHSP, 1899, v. 27, p. 307-311.

173 ..."The Confederate States A Government De Facto, and the effects of the War on existing contracts. Argument before the Court of Appeals of Maryland in John et US vs Robertson." (n.p., n.d., c. 1868) 8vo, sewed, 22pp.

174 ..."The Constitution of the Confederate States, Montgomery, 1861. Address by Gen'l. Bradley T. Johnson, delivered June 10, 1891 at the dedication of the Confederate monument at Fredericksburg, Va. Printed by order of the Society of the Army & Navy of the Confederate States, in the State of Maryland." Baltimore: William H. Mules & Co., 1891. 8vo, wraps, 16pp.

175 ..."Dedication of the South's Museum." In: SHSP, 1895, v. 23, p. 364-372.

176 ..."Colonel Asa S. Morgan-soldier, orator, civic leader, civil war letter writer." In: Ouachita CHQ, Mar. 1973, v.4, p. 1-10.

177 ..."The First Maryland Campaign. Address by Gen. Bradley T. Johnson, of Maryland, before the Association of the Army of Northern Virginia, at Richmond, Va., Thursday evening, Oct. 23, 1884. Pub. by order of the Ass'n." Richmond: William Ellis Jones, 1884. Tall 8vo, wraps, 39 pp. $65-R $45-Bmk.

178 ..."The First Maryland Campaign. An Address by..., delivered at the 4th Annual Reunion of the Association of the Maryland Line, at Baltimore, Md., on Feb. 22, 1886. At Oratorio Hall." Baltimore: Andrew J. Conlon, 1886. 8vo, wraps, 41 pp. $45-Bmk $50-

179 ..."MARYLAND." (Atlanta: Confederate Pub. Co., 1899) v. 2, in Clement Evans' Confederate Military History. 8vo, cl, ports, illus., map, iv, 184 pp.

...Do: Biographical supplement, same above, addl. p. 185-447. $75-

179a ..."Maryland." Vol. 2. Wilmington, N.C., Broadfoot, 1987. 8vo, cl, 447p.

180 ..."To the people of Maryland! After sixteen months of oppression more galling than the Austrian tyranny, the victorious Army of the South brings freedom to your doors..." signed Bradley T. Johnson, Col. C.S.A." (n.p., 1862) Broadside. 36x30 cm. Sept. 8, 1862 (Harwell-#981)

181 ..."The Maryland Confederates, address to Confederate Society of St. Mary's at Leonardtown, March 1894." Baltimore: J. Harry Drechsler print (1894). 8vo, wraps, 9, (1) pp. $45-G

182 ..."The Maryland Confederate Monument at Gettysburg. An address by..." SHSP, 1886, v. 14, p. 429-436.

183 ..."The Maryland Line in the Confederate Army." In: SHSP, 1883, v. 11, p. 21-26.

184 ..."Memoir of Jane C. Johnson." In: SHSP 1901, v. 29, p. 33-45.

185 ..."Memoir of First Maryland Regiment." In: SHSP, 1881, v. 9, p. 344-353, 481-488, v. 10, 1882, p. 46-56, 97-109, 145-153, 214-223.

186 ..."Stonewall Jackson's intentions at Harper's Ferry." In: B & L, II, p. 614-616.

187 ...Monument to Confederate Dead at Fredericksburg." In: SHSP, 1890, v. 18, p. 397-406.

188 ..."Official Report of Gettysburg." In: SHSP, 1885, v.13, p. 173-175.

189 ..."The Peace Conference." In: SHSP, 1899, v. 27, p. 374-377.

190 ..."Tarheel's thin gray line." In: SHSP 1899, v. 27, p. 170-174.
See: David Waldhauer, R.D. Stewart.

191 ..."A Memoir of the Life & Public Service of Joseph E. Johnston, once the quartermaster General of the Army of the U.S. & a General in the Army of the C.S.A. Edt: Bradley T. Johnson, formerly a soldier in the Army of Northern Virginia." Baltimore: R.H. Woodward & co, 1891. 12mo, cl, ports (incl. front), illus., viii, 362 p. 1894. $50- $35-Bmk $50-G

192 ...(other editions have bound-in with:) "Life & Reminiscences of Jefferson Davis by Distinguished Men of His Time, Introduction by John W. Daniel." Baltimore: R.H. Woodward., 12mo, cl, xviii, 308 pp.

	$35.00 Note: This separate volume is 23 1/2cm with 490 pp. See also under Davis (J.).
193	..."My ride around Baltimore in 1864." In: U.S. Cavalry Assn. Journ., p. 250-260. Ft. Leavenworth, 1889, wraps. ...In: SHSP, 1902, v. 30, p. 215-225.
194	..."Second Maryland Cavalry." In: Goldsborough (W.W.) Maryland Line.." 1900 edt., p. 241-248. Roster.
195	..."A striking war incident." In: SHSP, v. 19, 1901, p. 227-229. How Jeb Stuart lost his life capturing a Md. Battery.
196	..."Reports of cases decided by Chief Justice Chase in the Circuit Court of the US for the 4th circuit, during the years 1865-1869, in the district of Md., Va., N.C. & S.C. Revised corrected by the chief justice. Containing an Appendix with the Constitution of the CSA, and the conscription, impressment & sequestration acts of that government by Bradley T. Johnson, of the Va. Bar." N.Y., Diossy & co, 1876. 8vo, cl, xx, 737 pp.
197	..."Why the Confederate States of America had no Supreme Court. A Symposium by Bradley T. Johnson, John V. Wright, J.A. Orr & L.Q. Washington.: In: Publications of the Southern History Association." March 1900, wraps, 21 pp.
198	**JOHNSON, Bushrod Rust, Gen.** "Battle of Chickamauga." In: SHSP, v.14, 1885, p. 393-415.
199	..."Report: Operations from May 6/11, 1864. In: SHSP, 1884, v. 12, p. 274-282.
200	**JOHNSON, E. Polk** "Some Generals I've Known." In: SB, 1885/1886, v. 1, #2, p. 120-122.
201	..."Were you scared?" "A soldier & afraid!" In: SB, 1885/1886, v. 1, #6, p. 374-376.
202	..."Secession, North & South." In: CV, May, 1919, v.XXVII, p. 173-176.
203	**JOHNSON, Edward, Gen.** "From the Rapidan to Spotsylvania Courthouse." In: SHSP, v.13, p. 240-241; also-SHST, v. 1, p. 140-141.
204	..."Official Report: Gettysburg Campaign." In: SHSP, 1878, v. 6, p. 254-257.
205	..."Report of the capture of Winchester." I: SHSP, 1879, v. 7, p. 200-204. See: R.W. Hunter.
206	**JOHNSON, Ella H.** "Granny Remembers." Macon, Ga., 1928. 12mo, cl, wraps, 86 pp. CSA in SW Ky., area largely CSA sentiment.
206a	**JOHNSON, Evans C.** "Henry W. Hilliard & the Civil War Years." in: AR, Apr. 1964, v.17, #2, p.102-12.
207	**JOHNSON, Flora Smith** "The Civil War Record of Albert Gallatin Jenkins, CSA." In: W.Va. Hist. July 1947, v. 8, p. 392-404.
207a	**JOHNSON, George W.** "Letters of the Provisional Governor of Kentucky under the Confederacy." In: RKHS, Jan. 1942, (#133), v. 40, p.336-52, front(port).
208	**JOHNSON, Gerald White** "The Secession of the Southern States." N.Y., G.P. Putnam's sons, 1933. 12mo, cl, ills. incl. front., ports, 176 pp. "Great Occasions" series.
209	..."The Undefeated." N.Y., Minton, Balch & Co, 1927. 12mo, cl, 4, 120 pp., front. Stone Mt. memorial & Borglum.
210	**JOHNSON, J.R.** "Morgan's Men." In: Marine Corps. gaz. June 1953, v. 37, #6, p. 36-39. views. On the Partisans in Morgan's Cav., in Ky & Tenn., 1862-1864.
211	**JOHNSON, James Ralph (Alfred Hoyt Bill)** "Horseman Blue & Gray: a Pictorial History." N.Y., Oxford press, 1960. 4to, cl, d/w, viii, 236 pp., illus., maps.
212	**JOHNSON, Jane Claudia** See: Bradley T. Johnson.

213 **JOHNSON, Jemmy Grant, Mrs.**
"The University War Hospital." (Oxford, Miss., Pub. Miss. Hist. Soc. 1912, v.XII, pp. 94-106, ports(3)

214 **JOHNSON, John**
"Calendar of events in the defense of Charleston, S.C. (1861-1865)." In the Charleston Yearbook, 1888. p. i-xx.

215 ..."The Defense of Charleston Harbor, including Fort Sumter & the Adjacent Islands. 1863-1865, by..., formerly Maj. of engineers in the service of the Confederate States. With original papers in Appen., full official reports, maps & illustrations." Charleston, S.C., Walker, Evans & Cogswell, 1890. Tall 8vo, cl, crest, ports, illus (some faded), sketches, diagrams, 5-fldg. maps at end, 176, clxxxvipp. $20-, $30-, $35-, $125-$150-, $100-bmk.

216 ..."The Confederate Defense of Fort Sumter." In: Batt. & Lead, IV, p. 23-26. See: Ellison Capers "Last Commander."
"Defense of Charleston Harbor." Freeport, N.Y., Books for Libraries (1970).
...N.Y., Arno press, Bibliographical Reprint Series, 1973. Intro: H.W. Feilden $30-

217 ..."Proceedings of a special meeting of the Survivors Association of Charleston district, July 25, 1890. The Defense of Charleston Harbor." (Columbia, Ga. ?) 1890. 8vo, wraps, 19pp.

218 ..."Story of the Confederate Armored Ram Arkansas." In: SHSP, 1905, v. 33, p. 1-15.

219 ...Views of Fort Sumter as it was during the War of Secession showing the effects of the Bombardment of 1863-1865. By Maj. Jno. Johnson, Engineer at Fort Sumter." Charleston, S.C., Walker, Evans & Cogswell, 1899. 16mo, wraps, 30, (1) pp. illus. $25-

220 **JOHNSON, John Lipscomb, Rev.**
"The University memorial; biographical sketches of alumni of the University of Virginia who fell in the Confederate war; five volumes in one, by..." Baltimore: Turnbull Bros., 1871. 8vo, cl, front, ports, illus. 765 pp. $75- $100-

221 ..."Jefferson Davis-an Address delivered at Winchester, Tenn., Dec. 11, 1889 to Turney Bivouac #13." (Nashville, Tenn., Marshall & Bruce, 1890) 8vo, wraps, 15pp.

222 ..."Autobiographical Notes, Aug. 12, 1835, March 1, 1915." (Boulder, Colo.) Priv. Print., 1958 8vo, cl, pls., facsms, map endsheets, 388 pp. Author Confed. chaplain, Capt. cavalry. Edt: 500 copies, d/j. $35- $50-

222a **JOHNSON, Kenneth R.**
"Confederate Defenses & Union Gunboats on the Tennessee River: a Federal Raid into Northwest Alabama." In: AHQ, 1968, v.30, #2, p,39-60.

222b **JOHNSON, Lucetta A.**
"Johnson's Civil War Book Prices." 1962. 8vo, cl, I-1457; II-1485; III-1140.

223 **JOHNSON, Ludwell H.**
"Beverley Tucker's Canadian Mission, 1864-1865." (Houston, Tex.) JSH, Feb. 1963, v. XXIX, #1, p. 88-99.

224 ..."Civil War Military History: A Few Revisions in Need of Revising." In: CWH, June 1971, v. XVII, #2, p. 115-130.

225 ..."Contraband Trade during the Last Year of the Civil War." (Cedar Rapids, Ia.) MVHR, March, 1963, v. XLIX, #4, p. 635-652.

226 ..."Fort Sumter & Confederate Diplomacy." (Lexington, Ky.) JSH, Nov., 1960, v. XXVI, #4, p. 441-477. From standpoint of Davis & CSA Gov. $8-

227 ..."Jefferson Davis & Abraham Lincoln as war presidents: nothing succeeds like success." In: CWH, Mar., 1981, v. 27, #1, P. 49-63.

228 ..."The Louis A. Welton Affair: A Confederate Attempt to buy supplies in the North." In: CWH, March 1969, v. XV, #1, p. 30-38.

229 ..."Northern Profit & Profiteers: The Cotton Rings of 1864-1865." In: CWH, June 1966, #2, p. 101-115.

230 ..."Red River Campaign: Politics & Cotton in the Civil War." Baltimore: Johns Hopkins press, 1958 8vo, cl, maps, 317 pp. $20-Bmk-84.

230a ..."The Confederacy: What was it? The view from the Federal Courts." In: CWH, March 1986, v.32, #1, p.5-22.

230b ..."Trading with the Union: the Evolution of Confederate Policy." In: VMHB, July 1970, v.78, #3, p.308-25.

231 **JOHNSON, Michael P.**
"A new look at the popular vote for delegates to the Georgia Secession Convention." In: Ga. H.Q., Summer, 1972, v. LVI, #2, p. 259-275.

232 ..."Toward a Patriarchial Republic; the Secession of Georgia." Baton Rouge: Louisiana State University press, 1977. 8vo, cl, dj, xxiv, 244 pp.

232a ..."Mary Boykin Chesnut's Autobiography & Biography: a Review Essay." In: JSH, Nov. 1981, v.47, #4, p.585-92.

233 **JOHNSON, Monroe**
"Taney & Lincoln." Speech before the American Bar Ass'n., August 1930. In: CV 1931, v. 39, p. 377-382. From the Amer. Bar Journal, Aug. 1930.

234 **JOHNSON, Polk G.**
"Clarksville (Tenn.) Boys of 1861." n.p., 1887 8vo, wraps, 16 pp. CM

235 **JOHNSON, Robert U. & Clarence C. Buel**
See: "Battles & Leaders of the Civil War."

236 **JOHNSON, Samuel M. (pseud?)**
"Southern Rights' & 'Union' Parties in Maryland contrasted." Balt: W.M. Innes, 1863 8vo, wraps, 30pp. Sabin-88479 (36318) "Probably John Fulton who wrote under pseud-S.M. Johnson, tho Cushing attributes to Richard Malcolm Johnston. Pro CSA-" its time that something more is said about the struggle made by Southern men of Border States for the preservation of their rights.

237 ..."The Dual Revolution. Anti-slavery & Pro-slavery." By S.M. Johnson. Balt: W.M. Innes, 1863. 8vo, wraps, 48pp.

238 ..."The Constitution & the Reconstruction Laws: the policy, economy, and justice of Reconstruction, etc." Wash: 1868 8vo, wraps, 48pp. Not in Sabin or LC. Reconstructions laws unconstitutional, since falsely claim ten sovereign sttes have forfeited their rights as states. (Jk-122) $50.00

239 **JOHNSON, Sidney Smith**
"Texans Who Wore the Gray, by Sid S. Johnson, Capt. 3rd Texas Cavlary, Ross Brigade, CSA., & Brigadier general Texas brigade, Forrest's Cavalry, UCV." (quote) 'copyright secured, volume one (all printed) (Tyler, Texas., c. 1907) 8vo, cl, ports, (15), (5)-407pp. $250-Bmk-84 $400-JK-137

239a **JOHNSON, Swofford**
"Great Battles of the Confederacy." N.Y., W.H. Smith, Gallery Books, 1985. 4to, cl, dj, 192pp, ports, ills (part color).

240 **JOHNSON, Thomas Clary**
"The Life & letters of Benjamin Morgan Palmer." Richmond, Va., Presbyterian Comm. of publication, (1906) 8vo, cl, front, ports, pls, fldg. genealog. table, 3, (v)-x, 688 pp. Life before, during & after the war. $30-Bmk

241 ...Sketch, in: "Lib. South. Lit., 1909, v.9, p. 3907-3933.

242 ..."The Life & Letters of Robert Lewis Dabney." Richmond, Va., Presbyterian Com of Pub(1903) 8vo, cl, xvi, 585 pp, pls., ports (incl. front) geneal. tables, Dabney served on Stonewall's staff. $100-B

242a **JOHNSON, Timothy D.**
"Benjamin Franklin Cheatham at Belmont." In: MoHR, Jan. 1987, v.81, #2, p.159-72, ills, ports, map.

243 **JOHNSON, V.M.**
"Barbara Frietchie." In: Nat'l. tribune scrap book, v.1, p. 3-20.

244 **JOHNSONVILLE, TENN., Battle of...**
See: John W. Morton.

245 **JOHNSTON, Adelia A.**
"Two sides of a shield; a story of civil War." (Cleveland, Oh., Penton press, 1911) 12mo, wraps, illus., 43pp., 300 copies. Secret service in the C.S.A.

246 **JOHNSTON, Albert Sidney**
"Correspondence between Johnston & Gov. Isham G. Harris (Gov. Tenn.)" In: SHSP, 1877, v.IV, p. 185-188.

247 ..."Letter, Oct. 17, 1861." In: SHSP, 1877, v.3, p. 128-129.

248 ..."A Tributary epitaph." In: SHSP 1908, v. 36, p. 104.
See: Jeff Davis, Basil Duke, Charles E. Hooker, Chas. P. Roland, Avery C. Moore, Wm. Preston Johnston.

249 ..."Portrait: Engraved, stipple & line, by Geor. E. Perine. tall folio (New Orleans) Jas. A. Hummel, 1867, 23x17 1/2" Jk, 122 $125- $25-

250 ..."Original carte de Visite photograph by E. Anthoney, 1862, CSA univorm. jk-127 $45-

251 ..."Portrait: from the etching by Jacques Reich of a photograph taken at Camp Floyd, 1859, in US uniform, with open lapels, bust. 11x14", black & white.

252 ..."Capt. Beirne Chapman & Chapman's Battery: An Historical Sketch." Union (Camp Beirne Chapman #148, United Sons of Confederate Veterans) 1903. 8vo, wraps, 54 pp. cover-title. Roll Chapman Bat., p. 7-9; org. of Bat., Greenbrier, Monroe counties, Apr. 1862, short sketches of major engagements. (Shetler-387) $375-G

253 ..."Albert Sidney Johnston Journal." Houston, Texas: Pub. by Albert Sidney Johnston Camp 67 Sons of Confederate Veterans, V.I, #1, Sept. 1964, Pub., Sept., Dec., Mar., & June each year. 4to, mimeogr., stapled covers, (7) p. print on one side, port Johnston cover. (#3, p.10)

254 ..."Letter, October 17, 1861." In: SHSP 1877, v.III, p. 128-129.

255 ..."General Albert Sidney Johnston." In: SB, ns, v.II, p. 320-325. 1886/1887 signed-"W"

256 ..."The Confederate cause yesterday & today." In: UDC mag., June 1949, v.12, #6, p. 23-26. "History has not dealt fairly with the Southern Confederacy."

257 ..."A Short History of A.S. Johnston." Park Place, N.Y., Knapp*Co, 1888. 2 3/4x1 1/2" colored booklet, 16pp. facsm. signature.(packed in Duke's cigarettes) See: "Heroes of the C.W. " & W. Duke co.

258 ..."The Diary of Eliza (Mrs. Albert Sidney) Johnston. The Second Cavalry comes to Texas. Edited by Charles P. Roland & Richard C. Robins." In: SwHQ, April, 1957, v.LX, #4, p. 463-500, may, facsm.

259 ..."Gen. Johnston in Texas, letters to relatives in Kentucky, 1847-60. Edt: Arthur Marvin Shaw." In: RKHS, Jan. 1942, v.40 (#132), p.290-317.

259a ..."Soldiers of the Army of the Mississippi." Sm. broadside, 3 1/2 x 5 1/4". Corinth, Miss., Hdq. Army of the Mississippi, April 3, 1862. Gdsp $1,250. Unrecorded.

260 **JOHNSTON, Andrew**
"Correction in reference to Gen. Pickett." In: SHSP, 1876, v.1, p. 387-388.

260a ..."The American Constitution & the Impeachment of the President." In: Blackwoods, June 1968, v.103, p.707-27.

261 **JOHNSTON, Angus James, II**
"Disloyalty on Confederate railroads in Virginia." In: Va. mag. hist. biog., Oct. 1955, v.62, p. 410-426. notes.

262 ..."Lee's Last Lifeline: The Richmond & Danville." In: CWH, September 1961, v.VII, #3, p. 288-297, tables.

263 ..."Virginia Railroads in April 1861." (Lexington, Ky.) JSH, Aug., 1957. v.XXIII, #3, p. 307-330, map, talbes.

264 ...Virginia Railroads in the Civil War." For Virginia Historical Society by the Chapel Hill: Univ. of N.C. Press, 1961. 8vo, cl, d/w, illus., maps, xiv, 336 pp. $35-Bmk

265 **JOHNSTON, Charles**
"Attack on Fort Gilmer, September 29, 1864." In: SHSP, 1876, v.1, p. 438-442. 44th Inf. See: R.G. Cross, G.W.D. Porter.
...See also in: Annals Army of Tenn. & early western hist., 1878, v.1, p. 130-134.

266 **JOHNSTON, David Emmons**
"Charge of Kemper's Brigade at Frazier's Farm." In: SHSP, 1890, v. 18, p. 391-393.

267 ..."Confederates in West Virginia." In: CV, Nov. 1897, v.5, p. 579-580. Mercer Co., CSA Vets.

268 ...Four Years a Soldier, By David E. Johnston, a member of Company D Seventh Virginia Infantry, & Sergeant Major of the Regiment." Princeton, W.Va., 1887. 16mo, cl, 437, ixpp. $50-

269 ..."A History of the Middle New River Settlement & Contiguous Territory." Huntington, W. Va., Standard print, 1906. Tk. 8vo, decr. cl, plates, ports, incl. front 500, xxxipp. CSA, p. 185-319; regiments p. 462-500. $75- $80-Bmk-84.
...Bridgewater, Va., C.J. Carrier, 1969, reprint.

270 ..."The Story of a Confederate Boy in the Civil War, by David E. Johnston of the 7th Virginia Infantry. With an introduction by Rev., C. E. Cline. (Portland, Or., Glass & Prudhomme, 1914). 8vo, cl, ports, incl. front, xiv, 379 pp. $75-, $150-Bmk-105.
...2nd Edition, revised.
..."Rewriting & publishing of his "Four Years a Soldier." By a member of 7th Va. Inf.

271 **JOHNSTON, Frank**
"The Vicksburg Campaign." Oxford, Miss., PMHS, v.X, 1909. p. 63-90.
...See: PMHS, 1902, v. 6, p. 65-67.

272 **JOHNSTON, Frontis W.**
"Zebulon Baird Vance: A Personality Sketch." In: NCHR, April, 1953, v.XXX, p. 178-190. $8-

273 **JOHNSTON, George Burke**
"A Book for General Lee." In: Va. Cavalcade, Autumn, 1980, v.XXX, #2, p. 88-95, ports, illus., facsm, color pl. Geo. Long's 'Aurelius', with dedication to Lee but pirated by Ticknor & Fields, changing dedication to Emerson. Long's answer.
...See: James Henry Lane.

274 **JOHNSTON, Ida Lee**
"Over the stone wall at Gettysburg." In: CV July 1923, v.XXXI, p. 248-249. Sketch of Lt. John A. I. Lee, Co. C., 28th Va. Reg. First man in Pickett's div. to cross stone wall in charge at Gettysburg.

275 **JOHNSTON, J. Ambler**
"Echoes of 1861-1961." n.p., Private print, 1970. 4to, cl, maps, illus., (7), 111pp. printed one-side.

275a ..."The Civil War 1861-1865 in Arkansas & Missouri. Notes on the April 1967 trip to the Chicago Civil War Round Table." (Richmond?) Virginia State Penitentiary, July 1967. Released March, 1968. Sm.4to, wraps, 43pp. $40-Bm. Johnston was an Hono

275b ..."The Civil War 1861-1865 in Arkansas & Missouri. Notes on the April, 1967 trip of the Chicago Civil War Round Table." n.p., Virginia State Penitentiary, July 1967. 4to, wraps, maps, 43pp. $5.

276 **JOHNSTON, James D. Comm.**
"Report: Fight in Mobile Bay." In: SHSP, 1878, v.VI, p. 224-227; 1881, v.9, p. 471-476.

276a ..."The Ram "Tennessee" at Mobile Bay." In: B&L, v.4, p,401-6, ills, port.

277 **JOHNSTON, James Steptoe, Rev.**
"A Reminiscence of Sharpsburg." In: SHSP, 1880, v.8, p. 526-529.

278 **JOHNSTON, John**
"The Civil War Reminiscences of John Johnston, 1861-1865. Edt: Wm. T. Alderson." In: Tenn. HQ, 1955, v.XIII, p. 65-82, 156-178, 244-276, 329-354; v.XIV, p. 43-81, 142-175, Mar. 1954/June 1955, Dbl. map. Service as private in Co. K, 6th Tenn. Inf., 7th & 14th Cav., of Forrest.

279 ..."Forrest's march out of West Tennessee. December 1863: Recollections (1902?) of a private." In W. TennHSP, 1958, v.12, p. 38-48, map.

279a **JOHNSTON, John Thomas Morris**
"General Robert E. Lee." p. 211-37 in his 'World Patriots.' N.Y., 1917 (3rd, 1924).

280 **JOHNSTON, Joseph Eggleston, Gen.**
Autographed, signed letter, June 8, 1874, thanx for sending copy of Sherman's Memoirs. framed with hand-colored engraving. $175-

281 ..."The Battle of Atlanta." In: Cent. Mag., Aug. 1887.

282 ..."The Battle of Bull Run, an important letter from..." In: Hist. Mag., 1867, v.II, p. 232-237.
See: Drury L. Armistead, J.A. Early, Chs. Marshall.

283 ..."Confederate loss at Seven Pines Letter from Gen. J.E. Johnston." In: SHSP, 1877, v.IV, p. 42.

284 ..."Discussion between J.A. Early, Chas. Marshall & Jos. E. Johnston concerning strength of Lee's Army during the Seven Days Battles." In: SHSP, 1876, v.1, p. 407-424.

285 ..."The Dalton-Atlanta operations". In: AW, p. 330-341.

286 ..."General Joseph E. Johnston's Campaign in Georgia. Some letters by him that have never been published." In: SHSP, 1893, v.XXI, p. 314-321. From the New Orleans 'Times Picaynune.'

287 ..."On the Georgia Campaign in 1864." In: N.Y. Bul. 6(1902) p. 170.

288 ..."General Order #32, Dec. 4, 1863." Meridian, Miss., Broadside, quarto, 1p. Court martials of S.C. & Ark. soldiers.

289 ..."General Polk's Death. Gen. Johnston describes how he was killed." In: SHSP, 1890, v.XVIII, p. 380-381

290 ..."In Memoriam", General Joseph Eggleston Johnston." In: SHSP, 1890, v.XVIII, p. 158-66. (66-217) cont'd.

291 ..."Jefferson Davis & the Mississippi campaign." In: N. Amer. Rev., 1886, v.CXLIII, p. 585-598.

292 ..."Letter from General J.E. Johnston(correcting statements concerning the 'Seven Days Battle'.) In: SHSP, 1876, v. 1, 89-90.

293 ..."Manassas to Seven Pines." In: B & L, v.II, p. 202-218. Re Davis' Rise & Fall of Confed.", above battles.

294 ..."Memorial Services in Memphis, Tenn., Mar. 31, 1891." In: SHSP, 1890, v.XVIII, p. 189-199.

295 ..."My negotiations with Gen. Sherman." In: N.Amer. Rev., 1886, v. CXLIII, p. 183-197; SHSP, v. 39, 1914, p. 45-59. "Ewell Papers"

296 ..."Narratives of Military Operations, directed, during the late war between the states, by Joseph E. Johnston, General, C.S.A." N.Y., D. Appleton & Co., 1874. Tk. 8vo, decr. cl, (Sheep, or 3/4 Mor.) 6-maps (1-fldg), 15-engraved ports, incl/front, 602 pp. Fine $80-Bmk, Fine $150-Bmk.
..."Bloomington: Indiana University press Civil War Centennial Series, 1959. Tk.

12mo, cl, dj, xxxi, 621 pp., index. With an introduction by Frank E. Vandiver, (p. vii-xxxi), $20-, $36-Y
...N.Y., Kraus reprint, 1969, $57-
...Louisv., Lost Cause micro-cd. $9-

297 ..."Official Report of General Johnston of the Battle of Seven Pines." In: SHSP, 1890, v.XVIII, p. 182-185.

298 ..."Official Report of General Johnston of the Battle of 'Seven Pines', or "Fair Oaks." In: SHSP, 1880, v.VIII, p. 235-238.

299 ..."Official Report of Gen. Joseph E. Johnston, Vineville, Ga., Oct. 20, 1864." (Richmond, Va., 1865) (Crandall 1216) 8vo, sewn, caption title, 14pp.

300 ..."Opposing Sherman's Advance to Atlanta." In: B & L., v. IV, p. 260-277.
...Also: Cent. mag., Aug. 1887, v.XXXIV, p. 584-596. illus., maps.

301 ...Portrait: 21 1/2x26 1/2-1872 by Brady, after photo. Cincinnati: Bostwick Co., engr. A.B. Walter. Bust in uniform. color, 22 1/2x18", mounted, India Proof. $25-

302 ...Do: Portrait, on horseback, in uniform, holding a sword. Battle in background. Baltimore: 1867, Smith & Holden, 20 1/4x26. $22.50

303 ..."Portrait, in uniform." engraved by A.B. Campbell. N.Y., n.d., bust, facing forward in oval. Tall folio.

304 ...Phila: Engraved & published by Wm. Sartain, n.d. (1870). 12x15" bust in uniform, in oval. Engr: "Johnson" in title.

305 ...Portrait: from the etching by Frederick Dielman, Pres. N.Y. Academy of Design. 11/x4", black & white.

306 ...Mezzotint 17 1/4x13 5/8", dark oval tint within a slight darker area, shows three-stars general. Philadelphia, engr. & pub., Wm. Sartain, no date. $20-

307 ...Lithograph portrait, bust, ***General, double-row buttons. 14 3/4x12 1/4". NY, Geo. E. Perine, n.d. (c. 1870) Light tint, wide margins. Litho by J.L. Giles.
...(1865) same but no tint.

308 ..."Proclamation of Thanks for the conduct of the Army of Tennessee at the Battle of Murfreesboro." Headquarters, Chattanooga, Jan. 28, 1863. Broadside 5x8"

309 ..."Report of Gen. Johnston, the Battle of Manassas." In: LWL, 1866/7, v.II, p. 155-163. Also: Confed. War. Journal-I-1893, p. 58-60.
..."Suppressed part... p. 259-260.

310 ..."Report of General Joseph E. Johnston of operations in the Department of Mississippi & East Louisiana, together with Lieut. General Pemberton's Report of the battles of Port Gibson, Baker's Creek, & the siege of Vicksburg. Published by order of Congress." Richmond, Va., R.M. Smith, Pr., 1864. 8vo, cl, 213 pp. Crandall-1418. $60-

311 ..."Sketch of the career of General Joseph E. Johnston, 'The very God of war.' From the Richmond, Va. Times-Dispatch, Feb. 19, 1911. (Col. Edwin J. Harvie). In: SHSP, 1910, v.XXXVIII, p. 340-347.

312 ..."Some war letters of General Joseph E. Johnston; Edt. by Robert M. Hughes." In: Jour. Mil. Ser. Inst., May 1912, v. L, p. 318-328. (Written in 1863/1864).

313 ..."Two letters concerning General Joseph E. Johnston. Edited by Percy G. Hamlin, MD. In: VMHB, July 1948, v.56, #3, p. 299-303.

314 ..."A Short History of Genl. J.E. Johnston." Park Place, NY, Knapp & Co., 1888. 2 3/4 x 1 1/2" colored booklet, 16 pp. (packed in Duke's cigarettes) Facsm. signature, $20-

314a ..."Johnston's Last Stand - Bentonville (N.C.)." In: NCHR, 1956, v.33, p.332-58.

314b ..."Responsibilities of the First Bull Run." In: B&L, v.1, p,240-61, ports.
...See: W. Duke & Sons, & "Heroes of the C.W." "Joseph E. Johnston Papers: Earl G. Swem.

315 ...See: Jeff Davis' "Unseen message", concerns military career of J.E. Johnston.

316 ...See: Marshall, T.B. Edgington, W.S. Walker, Samuel A. Goodwin, Geo. W. Gordon, Geo. C. Gorham, Dabney H. Maury, Jas. M. Mullen, New Orleans Picayune, Benj. M. Palmer, Leslie J. Perry, Leigh Robinson, D.M. Sadler, Richmond Times Dispatch.

317 **JOHNSTON, Joseph Forney, Senator**
"Memorial addresses del. in Senate & House of US 63 Congr., 3rd sess." Wash: GPO, 1915. Imp. 8vo, cl, port, 98 pp. Senate Doc. 991 Served in the 18th Alabama. Gov. of Ala.

318 **JOHNSTON, Josiah Stoddard, Colonel**
"Kentucky." In: v.IX-Clement Evan's 'Confed. Mil. Hist." ports, maps (1-fldg.), viii, 257 pp. REB $35-
...Biographical extension: "Additional sketches illustrating the services of officers & privates & patriotic citizens." p. (259)-592.

318a ..."Kentucky." v. XI. 8vo, cl, 592pp. Wilmington, N.C., Broadfoot, 1987.

319 ..."Sketches of Operations of General John C. Breckinridge-from Dalton Georgia to Hanover Junction, Va." In: SHSP, 1879, v. VII, p. 257-262; p. 317-323; p. 385-392.

320 ..."Sketch of Theodore O'Hara (1820-67)" In: Ky. Hist. Soc. Reg., Sept. 1912, v.XI, p. 65-72. See: sketch by Al. G. Brackett.

320a **JOHNSTON, Mrs. Maria Isabella (Barnett)**
"The Siege of Vicksburg." Boston: Pratt Brothers, 1869. 16mo, cl, 4p. (13)-330p. Fiction.

321 **JOHNSTON, Marianne C. (Howe)**
"The Young Chaplain...(by his mother)" N.Y., N. Tibbals & sons, 1876. 12mo, cl, front (photo), ip, 1-1f, 138 pp. Sketch of-life: William Curtis Johnston, Chaplain of the 13th Ky. vols.

322 **JOHNSTON, Mary**
"Address read at Vicksburg upon the occasion of the unveiling of a tablet commemorating the services to the South of the Botetourt artillery," Cambridge, Riverside press, 1897. 12mo, wraps, 28, (1) p. $40-

323 ..."Address by...Dedication of a bronze tablet in honor of Botetourt Battery, in Vicksburg National Park, Nov. 23, 1907." In: SHSP, 1907, v.XXXV, p. 29-52, roster.

324 ..."Cease Firing." With illus. in color by N.C. Wyeth. (500 copies, atg. Edt., $33.00) Bost-N.Y., Houghton Mifflin co, 1912. 12mo, decr. cl, map as endsheets, 457 pp.

325 ..."The Long Roll." Illus. by N.C. Wyeth. Bost-N.Y., 1911, 12mo, decr. cl, 683 pp. Hist. novel on Jackson atg $25-, $20-

326 ...Boston (1911/12) Matching pair of "Long Roll & Cease Firing," Special autographed edition, Lim. Edt., 500 copies, paper label, uncut copies $100-

327 **JOHNSTON, Mary Tabb & Elizabeth Johnston Lipscomb**
"Amelia Gayle Gorgas: A Biography." University: Univ. Alabama pr, 1978. 8vo, cl, dj, xiv, 168 pp. Amelia spent entire war years in Richmond, while Gen. Gorgas was chief Ordnance for the CSA.

328 **JOHNSTON, N.B.**
"What Confederate Battery fired the last shot?" In: SHSP, 1881, v.9, p. 429-430.

329 **JOHNSTON, Richard Malcolm & William Hand Browne**
"Life of Alexander H. Stephens." Philadelphia: J.B. Lippincott & Co., 1878. Large 8vo, cl, port & facing home front, 619 pp. $50- $20-
...New & Revised Edt: 1883, (above) 635 pp.
...Edt: 1884, (above) 708 pp.
...Louisville: Lost Cause Press, m-card, $8.48

330 ..."Travis & Major Jonathan Wilby." In: Cent. ns, v.XVIII, p. 125-134, illus.

331 **JOHNSTON, Richard Malcomb**
"Autobiography of Col..." New York: Neale Co., 1900. 8vo, cl, front(port) 190 pp. $50-
...2nd Edt., 1901.
...Washington: Neale Pub. Co., 1910, 12mo, cl, 190 pp., illus, port. Confederate politics. See also: Crandall #3097, Wright-1361-2

331a ..."Lee as a Soldier." p. 256-310. In: "Leading American Soldiers." N.Y., 1907. 371p.

332 **JOHNSTON, Robert Matteson**
"Bull Run; its strategy & tactics." Bost: Houghton Mifflin, 1912. 8vo, cl, xiv, (2), 293 pp. fldg. maps. $50-B

333 **JOHNSTON, W.F.**
"The Second Rockbridge Battery, its Roster & Career." In: SHSP, 1897, v. 25, p. 281-284.

334 **JOHNSTON, William**
"An Address on the aspects of National Affairs & the right of Secession." Cincinnati: Rickey & Carroll, 1861. 8vo, wraps, 42 pp. also in-micro-card, Lousiville: Lost Cause Press, $2.45

335 **JOHNSTON, William Preston, Col.**
"The Army of Tennessee." In: SHSP, 1883, v.XIII, p. 40-42.

336 ..."The Capture of Jefferson Davis, Letter from Col. Wm. Preston Johnston, late aide to President Davis." In: SHSP, 1878, v.V, p. 118-121.

337 ..."William Preston Johnston, soldier scholar, poet & educator. Article from New Orleans 'Times-Democrat', July 17, 1899." (Re Johnston's death) In: SHSP, 1899, v.XXVII, p. 294-302.

338 ..."The Life of Gen. Albert Sidney Johnston embracing his services in the Armies of the United States, the Republic of Texas, & the Confederate States. By William Preston Johnston (his son), with illustrations on steel & wood." NY, D. Appleton & Co., 1878. 8vo, cl, (or 3/4 Mor., full calf), front (port), illus., maps, sviii, 755 pp., index. $25, $35, $40, $250, $200-JK $50-

339 ..."General William N. Pendleton." In: SB, 1882/3, v.I, p. 294-301.

340 ..."Zagonyi's Charge with Fremont's body-guard-a picturesque fol-de-rol." In: SHSP, 1877, v.III, p. 195-196. See: Avery C. Moore & Chas. P. Roland 'Life of Albert Sidney Johnston.'

341 ..."A War Letter from William Preston Johnston, Aide-de-Camp of Jefferson Davis August 24, 1862." Edt: Arthur Marvin Shaw. (Jackson, Miss., Jour. of Miss. Hist., Jan. 1942, v.IV, #1, p. 43-46.

341a ..."Reminiscences of General Robert E. Lee." In: Belford Mag., June 1890, v.V, #25, p.84-91.

341b ..."Albert Sidney Johnston at Shiloh, by his son." In: B&L, v.1, p.540-68, ills, ports, maps.

342 **JOHNSTON, William R.**
"Sketches of some of the battles & Operations around Kennesaw Mountain in 1864." (London) Jour. Confed. Hist. Soc., Summer 1968, v.6, #2, p. 48-71, maps (6)

343 **JOHNSTONE, H.W.**
"Truth of the War Conspiracy of 1861. 'Everyone should do all in his power to collect & disseminate the truth.' W.E. Lee, Dec. 3, 1865." Copy-right, 1921. H.W. Johnstone, Curryville, Ga. (Atlanta: Foote & Davies.) 8vo, wraps, 40 pp. (A variant has Idylwide, Ga., imprint, 38 pp. Johnstone served with 5th Georgia Vols.

344 **JOHNSTONE, J.E.**
"Opposing Gen. Sherman's advance to Atlanta." In: Century Mag., c. 1887. 11 pp. in stapeled binder. bmk. $10-

345 **JOHNSTONE, William Jackson**
"Robert E. Lee, the Christian." N.Y.,

Cinn., Abingdon press, 1933. 8vo, cl, port, pls., 301 pp. $40-B

346 **"JOINT HISTORY Committee of the Confederate Veterans Organization of Alabama."** (Montgomery, Ala., 1902. 8vo, wraps, 2 no. caption title: "The comm. is especially desirous of obtaining information as to what histories are in use in the various schools & colleges of the state." (e.g., civil war & teaching.)

347 **JONAS, Benjamin Franklin**
"Address of Hon. B.F. Jonas, at the laying of the cornerstone of the monument to the memory of Confederate dead at Baton Rouge Feb. 22, 1886." New Orleans, La., Hopkins print, 1886. 8vo, wraps, 19pp.

348 **JONAS, S.A.**
"Lines on the back of a Confederate Note." (Richmond, Va., n.d.) 4to, heavy gray paper, folder ready to frame. Genuine CSA note tipped-in over the famous poem-" representing nothing on God's earth. See: CV 1905, v. 13, p. 246.

349 **JONES, A.C.**
"The Mountain Campaign Failure." In: CV, July/Aug., 1914, v. 22, p. 305-6, 368. CSAccount of Cheat Mt. Campaign.

350 ..."Longstreet at Gettysburg." In: CV, Dec. 1915, v.XXIII, p. 551-551.

351 **JONES, A.K., Capt.**
"The Battle of Fort Gregg." In: SHSP, v. 31, 1903, p. 56-60. (See: ante XXIII, p. 74.

352 **JONES, Alexander H.**
"Knocking at the door. Alexander H. Jones, member-elect to Congress: His course before the war. Adventures & escapes." Washington: McGill & Witherow, 1866. 8vo, wraps, 38 pp. Southern refugees, N.C. politics & government during the war.

353 **JONES, Allen W.**
"A Georgia Confederate soldier visits Montgomery, Alabama, 1862-63." In: Ala. Hist. Quart., Spring-Summer, 1963, v. 25, #1 & 2, p. 99-113.

354 ..."A Federal Raid into Southeast Alabama." In: Ala. Rev., Oct. 1961, v. 14, p. 259-268. Capture of CSN "Bloomer" on Choctawhatchee River, Dec. 1862.

355 ..."Military Events in Arkansas during the Civil War, 1861-1865. By Allen W. Jones & Virginia Ann Buttry. In: AHQ, 1963, v.XXII, p. 124-170.

356 ..."Military Events in Florida during the Civil War, 1861-1865." In: FHQ, July 1960, v.XXXIX, #1, p. 42-45, chronological.

357 ..."Military Events in Texas during the Civil War, 1861-1865." In: SwHQ, July 1960, v.LXIV, #1, p. 64-70, chron. list events.

357a ..."Military Events in Louisiana during the Civil War, 1861-1865." In: LaH., 1961, v.2, p,301-21.

358 **JONES, Anna Clark**
"The Mountain campaign failure." In: CV, July Aug., 1914, v.XXII, p. 305-306, 368. Known as Cheat Mountain expedition in 1861.

359 **JONES, Archer**
"Confederate Strategy from Shiloh to Vicksburg." Baton Rouge: Louisiana State University Press, (1961). 8vo, cl, dj, 3-maps at end, xxi, 258 pp. $25-, op-$10-

360 ...In: JMH, July 1962, v.XXIV, #3, p. 158-167.

361 ...Ann Arbor: University microfilms, 1958. Positive microfilm of typescript, vii, 290 leaves, fldg. maps, bibliog. 280-290. Thesis-Univ. of Va. dist. abstr. 19: 1355.

362 ..."The Gettysburg decision." In: VaMHB. July 1960, v.68, p. 331-343. notes. CSA strategy Feb/May 1863, involving Davis Lee & Jas. A. Seddon, Sect. War.

363 ..."Secretary Randolph & Confederate Strategy." (Richmond) Va. Mag. Hist. Biog. Jan. 1953, v. 61, p. 45-59. Geo.

364 ..."Some aspects of George W. Randolph's Service as Confederate Secretary of War." (Lexington, Ky.) JSH, Aug., 1960, v.XXVI, #3, p. 299-314. Wythe Randolph, sect. war, 1862, "responsibility without authority."

365 ..."Tennessee & Mississippi: Joe Johnston's strategic problem." In: Tenn. Hist. Quart., 1959, v. 18, p. 134-147. June, notes. $6.00. Reprint, wraps, 13pp.

366 ..."The Vicksburg Campaign." (Jackson, Miss.) Jour. Miss. Hist. Feb. 1967, v.XXIX, #1, p. 12-27.

367 **JONES, Benjamin Washington**
"Under the stars & bars; a history of the Surry light artillery; recollections of a private soldier in the war between the states." Richmond: Everett Waddey Co., 1909. 12mo, xiii, 297 pp. cl $375-G, $300-Bmk-105, $450-OB

...Do: Louisville: Lost Cause Pr., micro-cd. $5.01

...(Dayton, Ohio) Morningside Bookshop, 1975. 12mo, cl, map endsheets, (2) xii, xiii, 425 pp. Facsimilie, #22. Intro., notes, Roster & Index by Lee A. WAllace, Jr., p. (298)-412, index (413)-425 $20.00

368 ..."Battle Roll of Surry County, Va., in the war between the states, with historical & personal notes. Richmond: Everett Waddey Co., 1913. 8vo, wraps, front, 70 pp. Swem-1866.

369 **JONES, Buehring H.**
"Memorial of the Federal Prison on Johnson's Island, Lake Erie, 1862-1864, containing a list of prisoners of war. from the Confederate States Army & of the deaths among them; with 'prison lays' by distinguished officer." In: Va. Hist. Soc. Coll. n.s., Richmond, Va., v. 6, p. 233-345, illus., 1887/

370 ..."The Sunny Land; or, Prison Prose & Poetry, containing the productions of the ablest writers in the South, & prison lays of distinguished Confederate officers by Col. Buehring H. Jones...Ed., with a preface, biographies, sketches & stories by J.A. Houston." Baltimore: (Innes & Co., print) 1868. Tk. 12mo, cl, errata slip, viii, 540 pp. $45-, copy-$25-

371 **JONES, C.W.**
"In Prison at Point Lookout, by C.W. Jones of Martinsville, Private Company H. Twenty-fourth Va. cavalry." (Martinsville, Bulletin print, n.d.) c. 1890. 8vo, wraps, port on cover, 9pp. (Wantg) $75-

...Martinsville, Va., Bulletin Print & Pub. (c. 1915) narrow 8vo, port on cover, 9pp. $45- (Wantg)

372 **JONES, Catesby ap Roger**
"The First Confederate Iron-Clad the 'Virginia' formerly the US steam frigate 'Merrimac'," In: South. Mag., Dec. 1874, v.XV, p. 200-207. Also: SHSP, Jan. 1883, v.XI, p. 65-75, United Ser. June 1883, v.VIII, p. 660-668.

373 ..."Services of the "Virginia" (Merrimac) In: SHSP, 1876, v.I, p. 90-91; 1883, v.11, p. 65-75. Also in Confed. War Jour., v. 1, illus., p. 98-101.

374 **JONES, Charles Colcock, Jr.**
"An Address delivered before the Confederate Survivors Association, in Augusta, Ga., at its First Annual Meeting, on Memorial Day, Apr. 26, 1879." By...(cut of flag) Augusta, Ga., Jowitt & Shaver, 1879. 8vo, wraps, 8pp.

375 ...Second Annual Meeting, Apr. 26, 1880. Augusta Ga., M.M. Hill & Co., 1880 Opera House Arcade. 8vo, wraps, 9pp. $35-

376 ...Third Annual Meeting, Apr. 26, 1881 8vo, wraps, 11 pp. $25-Bmk.

377 ...Fourth Annual Meeting, Apr. 26, 1882. Augusta, Ga., Jas. L. Gow, 1882. 8vo, wraps, 7pp. (see: Rains, Geo. Washington - address)

378 ...Fifth Annual Meeting, Apr. 26, 1883. "Military Lessons inculcated on the coast of Georgia during the Confederate War." August, Ga., Chronicle War." Augusta, Ga., Chronicle Print, 1883. 8vo, wraps, 15pp. $40-, $30-Bmk-84.

379 ...Sixth Annual Meeting, Apr. 26, 1884. "Gen. Sherman's March from Atlanta to the Coast." Augusta, Ga., Chronicle Print, 1884. 8vo, wraps, 19pp.

380 ...Seventh Annual Meeting, Apr. 27, 1885. "The Battle of Honey-Hill." Augusta, Ga., Chronicle Print, 1885. 8vo, wraps, 16pp. $20-Bmk. (see: also, in Southern Historical Society Papers. Richmond: 1885, v.13, p. 365-377.) $35-

381 ...Eighth Annual Meeting, Apr. 26, 1886. "Brigadier General Robert Toombs." Augusta, Ga., Chronicle Office, 1886. 8vo, wraps, 17pp. ($2.25, $3.00, $4.00, $6.00) $45-Jk-151. (see: also, in Southern Historical Society Papers. Richmond: 1886, v. 14, p. 293-304.
...Atlanta, Ga. (1970) Reprint.

382 ..."At its Quarterly Meeting, Aug. 2d, 1887. "Hon. R.M.T. Hunter. Post-Bellum Mortality Among Confederates." Augusta, Ga., Chronicle Pub., 1887. 8vo, wraps, 9pp. $30-OB, $20-JK

383 ...Ninth Annual Reunion, Apr. 26, 1887. "The Old South", by His Excellency, Gov. John B. Gordon. Augusta, Ga., Chronicle Pub., 1887. 8vo, wraps, 23 pp. $30-. See: also, Gen. John Brown Gordon.

384 ..."An Address delivered before the Confederate Survivors Association, in Augusta, Georgia, on Memorial Day, Apr. 26, 1888." By... "The Evacuation of Battery Wagner, and the Battle of Ocean Pond." Tenth Annual Meeting. Augusta, Ga., Chronicle Pub., 1888. 8vo, wraps, 20 pp. $50-R (See: also, 14th Annual Meeting) (See: Also, SHSP Rich: 1888).

385 ...Eleventh Annual Reunion, Apr. 26, 1889. "Georgians during the War between the States." Augusta Ga., Chronicle Print, 1889. 8vo, wraps, 34, (1) pp.

386 ...Twelfth Annual Reunion, Apr. 26, 1890. "The Siege & Evacuation of Savannah, Ga. in December, 1864." Augusta, Ga., Chronicle Pub., 1890. 8vo, wraps, 30, (1) pp. $50-, $40Bmk-84.

387 ...Thirteenth Annual Reunion, Apr. 27, 1891. "Sons of Confederate Veterans." Augusta, Ga., Chronicle Pub., 1891. 8 vo, wraps, 9, 1, (1) pp. $25-

388 ...Fourteenth Annual Reunion, Apr. 26, 1892. "Defense of Battery Wagner, July 18, 1863." by Hon. Lieut. Col. H.D.D. Twiggs, member of the Association; and by Captain F. Edgeworth Eve, First Vice President of the Association." Augusta, Ga., Chronicle Pub., 1892. 8vo, wraps, 30, (1) p. Only intro. remarks, pp. (3)-6, by C.C. Jones. (See: also 10th Annual Meeting.) $75-R

389 ...Fifteenth Annual Reunion, Apr. 26, 1893. "Military Operations in Georgia during the War Between the States." etc., & Chickamauga by Col. Joseph B. Cumming, a member of the Association." Augusta, Ga., Chronicle Job Print, 1893. 8vo, wraps, 32, (1) p. $30-Bmk-84, $40-Bmk-94.

390 ..."Bombardment & Capture of Ft. McAllister." (New York, 1885) excerpt: "Magazine of American History, v.XIV, #5, Nov. 1885. 8vo, wraps, (501)-508 pp.

391 ..."Bibliography of the Writings of Charles C. Jones, Jr., compiled by Paul Leicester Ford." In: Amer. Hist. Assn., Annual Report for year 1889." Washington: GPO, 1890. p. 287-293, with original covers. DeRenne II, p. 885, "Mr. Ford was probably assisted by Col. Jones himself in preparation." See" Barbara Ann Byrne.

392 ..."Celebration of the Seventy-fifth anniversary of the Chatham artillery of Savannah, May 1, 1861." Savannah, Ga., John M. Cooper, 1861. 8vo, wraps, 65 pp. Crandall-2500 p. 9-62.

393 ..."Funeral Oration pronounced in the Opera House, in Augusta, Georgia, Dec. 11, 1889, upon the occasion of Memorial Services, in honor of President Jefferson Davis." Augusta, Ga., Chronicle Print, 1889. 8vo, wraps, 18pp, port of Davis. $30-Bmk. Confed. Surv. Ass'n-Augusta-16th R., See: Col. Joseph B. Cumming-16th Annual Reunion.

394 ..."Historical Sketch of Chatham Artillery during the Confederate Struggle for Independence." Albany, N.Y., Joel Munsell, 1867. 8vo, (some 3/4 Mor.) also bound in paper. Large copies 10 5/8x7", 240 pp. 3 maps. (50 copies in the large paper $150-Bmk-105.

395 ..."In Memoriam. Col. Charles C. Jones, Jr. Historian, Biographer & Archaeologist. 1813-93." by Charles Edgeworth Jones. Augusta, Ga., Chronicle Job Print, 1893. 8vo, wraps, 13 pp.

396 ..."Col. Charles C. Jones, late of Augusta, Ga." by Charles Edgeworth Jones. (In: Gulf States Historical Magazine, v. 1, #5. Montgomery, Ala., 1903. 8vo, wraps, p. (302)-310. port. See: Jas. C. Bonner. Rob't M. Myers.

397 ..."Oration on the Occasion: Unveiling & Dedication of the Confederate Monument. Erected by the Ladies Memorial Ass'n., Augusta, Ga., Oct. 31, 1878." cover title, (Augusta, Ga.) Reprinted from Augusta Evening Sentinel (1878). 8vo, wraps, 9pp. See: Ceremonies Unveiling...

398 ..."Roster of General Officers, heads of departments, senators, representatives, military organizations, etc., in Confederate service during the War Between the States." Richmond: Southern Historical Society, 1876. Issued as a Supplement to the Sout hern Historical Society Papers, v. 1-3, 1876-1877, detached from first set of that publication for separate binding. Separate pagination at end of each vol: v. 1-31pp.; v.2-(32)-101; v.3-(102-135 pp.

399 ...Richmond, Va., Southern Historical Society, 1876. Cloth 8vo, 125 pp. (De Renne, II, pg. 760: says, the work was in "Monthly papers" of Southern Historical Society, Richmond, Va., the present reprint was made up from the same type, accounting for number of blank pages. Col. Jones wrote that he'd planned this printing thru Appleton but Gen. Early prevailed upon him to deliver to the SHS, where no reading of proof was made & therefore many errors.

400 ...Also in: "The Banner of the South & Planter's Journal," Augusta, Ga., Chronicle Print, Nov. 12, 1870-March 4, 1871. Weekly.

401 ..."A Roster of General Officers of the Confederate States of America (giving dates of their commision.)" in The Collector; a Monthly Magazine for Autograph Collectors. New York: Walter R. Benjamin, 1889. v.II-#17-8, Jan-Feb., 1889, p. 67-9, 92-94.

402 ..."The Life & Services of Commodore Josiah Tattnall." Savannah: Morning News Print, 1878. 8vo, cl, ix, 255, 4pp. port (front) From its sale hoped to erect monument at Bonaventure. $60-, $125-bmk.

403 ..."The Seizure & Reduction of Ft. Pulaski. (New York, 1885) excerpt:"Mag. Amer. Hist., v.XIV, #1, July 1885. 8vo, wraps, p. 53-57.

404 ...The Siege of Savannah in Dec., 1864, and the Confederate Operations in Georgia & the Third Military District of South Carolina during General Sherman's March from Atlanta to the Sea." By...late Lieut. Col. Artillery, CSA & Chief of Ar-

tillery during the Siege. Albany: Joel Munsell, 1874 for the author. 4to, cl, x, 184 pp. errata slip, large paper, only 10 copies so issued, original blue covers. The small in green; both 8 1/2" tall, the large paper 6 1/2" wide, the small only 6". wraps bound in. Small copies: MCVT $75-Bmk.

404a ..."The Siege & Evacuation of Savannah, Georgia, in December, 1864." Suffolk, Va., Robt. Hardy Pub., 1986. 8vo, wraps, 32pp.

404b ..."Military Operations in Georgia during the War between the States." Suffolk, Va., Robt. Hardy Pub., 1986. 8vo, wraps, 32pp.

405 ..."The Third South Carolina cavalry." In: U.R. Brooks-'Stories of the Confederacy' p. 219-233.

406 ..."Negro Slaves during the Civil War. Their Relations to the Confederate Government." New York: Magazine of American History, 1886. excerpt, v. XVI, #2, Aug. 1886. p. (168)-175.

406a ..."Letter of Gen. Robert E. Lee, tendering to the President of the Confederate States his resignation of the command of the Army of Northern Virginia, with explanatory remarks." 8vo, wraps, 12lfs, author's mssc. of an article appeared as a "p

406b ..."Military & Naval roster of the Confederate States." Augusta, Ga., Chronicle Pub. Co., 1870. 4to, wraps, 19pp. (detached from "Banner of the South & Planter's Journal," 1870.

406c ..."A Roster of Confederate Generals & their Commands, 1861-65." Washington: 1880. 12mo, wraps, no pagination.

406d ..."A Roster of General Officers, heads of Departments, Senators, Representatives, military organizations, etc. in Confederate service during the War between the States." Richmond, Va., Southern Historical Society, 1876. 8vo, wraps, 17pp.

...An edt. issued as a suppl. to SHSP, v. 1-3, 1876-7. 12mo, wraps, 130pp.

...Another suppl. of 135pp. 8vo, detached for binding.

406e **JONES, Charles E.**
"Report submitted to the Confederate Survivors Association of Augusta, Ga., 19th Annual Reunion, April 26th, 1897. Historian of the Assn. Augusta, Ga., 1897. 8vo, wraps, 12p. $15.

407 **JONES, Charles Edgeworth**
"Confederate Generals." In: SHSP, 1895. v.XXIII, p. 335. See: Col. Chas. C. Jones "In Memoriam."

408 ..."General officers of the regular C.S. Army." In: CV, Jan. 1908, v. 16, p. 45-48. With stte & date of rank.

409 ..."Georgia in the War 1861-1865, by Chas. Edgeworth Jones of Augusta, Ga. price $1, Formerly, Historian Camp #435, U.C.V." (Atlanta, Ga., Foote & Davies) (1909) 12mo, wraps, (4)-5-167 pp. Entire book on units from Georgia, field officers, local designations of troops. CSA $75-

410 ..."In Memoriam - Col. Charles C. Jones, Jr. Historian, Geographer & Archaeologist, 1831-1893." Augusta, Ga., Augusta Chronicle, 1893. 8vo, wraps, port, 13pp. CM. Text & Title in mourning border.

411 ..."Twelfth annual report as submitted in Richmond Co. Court House, to Camp 435, UCV of Augusta, Georgia, on Memorial Day, April 26, 1905. By Charles Edgeworth Jones Historian of the Association." (Augusta, 1905?) 8vo, wraps, 8pp.

412 **JONES, Charles T., Jr.**
"Five Confederates: The Sons of Bolling Hall in Civil War." Theses for M.A., at Texas University, Feb. 1961. (Montgomery, Ala.) State Dept. Archives & History, 1962. 8vo, wraps, Vol. 24-#2, 3, & 4. (132)-221 pp. Compelte issue.

413 **JONES, David Rumph**
"Report of Maj-Gen. D.R. Jones, of

second battle of Manassas & operations in Maryland." In: SHST. 1874, v.1, p. 56-60.

414 **JONES, Dorsey D.**
"He taught near Eudora, Arkansas in the early '60s." In: AHQ, v.18, p. 237-279.

415 **JONES, Douglas C.**
"Elkhorn Tavern." N.Y. Holt, Rinehart & Winston, 1980. Tall 8vo, c1211p.dj. Battle of Pea Ridge, Ark.

416 **JONES, Freeman W.**
"A daring expedition." In: Geo. Barnard's 'War Talks" p. 231-234.

416a ..."A Daring Expedition. An Address before A.P. Hill Camp, Confederate Veterans, Petersburg, Virginia, Jan. 2, 1890." Suffolk, Va., Robt. Hardy Pub., 1986. 8vo, wraps, 12pp.

417 ..."Experience at Point Lookout about the close of the War." In: (above), p. 83-86.

417a **JONES, George W., Maj.** Controlling & Quartermaster of Alabama. "Circular - Marion, Alabama. August 15, 1864. Broadside: 15 x 21 cm., printed in ornate script. (re: tax & cotton tithe). Unlisted, G. Hendershott. $250.

418 **JONES, Hamilton Chamberlain**
"Cases in Equity, Dec/1860-June 1863. 8vo, full calf, lt. label, vi, (1), 412 pp. Salisbury, N.C., J.J. Bruner, 1862/63. $100

419 ..."History of the 57th North Carolina Regiment." United Confederate Veterans-North Carolina Division: North Carolina Confederate Monuments & Memorials." Raleigh, N.C. 1941. 4to, cl, 131 pp. See also: Clark, v.III, p. 409-29. $20-

420 ..."Reports of Cases in Law, argued & determined in the Supreme Court of Carolina" June Term, 1862, Vol. VIII; p. viii, 532. $250-B

421 ..."Reports of cases at law, argued & determined in the Supreme Court of North Carolina June & August terms, 1861. Vol. VIII, by Hamilton C. Jones, reporter." Salisbury, N.C., J.J. Bruner print, 1861. 8vo, cl, cover title, (317-419pp.) Title head: No. 2, Vol. 8. Harwell-756(1862-4).

422 ..."Reports of cases at law, argued & determined in the Supreme Court of North Carolina June term." n.p., 1863/1864. 8vo, cl, 2vols, index. Bookmark-144 $250-

423 **JONES, Herbert S.P. Leland**
"Decision at Shiloh." St. Joseph, Mo., Platte Purchase Enterprise, 1961. 8vo, cl, illus., plates, ports, maps, xviii, 137pp.

424 **JONES, Hilary P.**
"Report of Gettysburg Battle of..." In: SHSP, 1882, v. 10, p. 64.

425 **JONES, Houston G.**
"Bedford Brown: State Rights Unionist." (Raleigh) NCHRev., July 1955. v.XXXII, #3, p. 321-345. port. $120

426 ...Carrollton, Ga., 1955. 8vo, wraps, facsm., port, view notes, (2) 54pp. Activities in N. Carolina & national politics.

427 **JONES, Iredell, Capt.**
"The South Carolina College Cadets." See: Yates Snowden's Bull. of S.C. Univ.

428 ...Carolina Cadets." In: SHSP, 1902, v. 30, p. 138-141.

429 ..."Letters from Fort Sumter." In: SHSP, 1884, v. 12, p. 5-7, 137-139, 160-162, 212-215, 253-258, 543-546.

430 **JONES, J.H.**
"The Rank & File at Vicksburg." In: (Oxford), 1903, Pub. Miss. Hist. Soc., v. VII, p. 17-31.

431 **JONES, James Dunwody**
"A Guard at Andersonville." In: CWTI, Feb. 1964, v.II, #10, p. 24-29, illus., port.

432 **JONES, James Pickett**
"Lincoln's Courier: John L. Worden's Mission to Fort Pickens." In: FHQ, October 1962, v.XLI, #2, p. 145-153.

433 ..."John L. Worden & the Fort Pickens Mission: the Confederacy's first prisoner of war." In: Ala. Rev., April 1968, v.21, p. 112-132. Sent originally by Gideon Welles

to Fort Pickens, captured, released & later became Comm. ironclad "Monitor."

434 ..."Wilson's Raiders reach Georgia: the Fall of Columbus, 1865." In: Ga. H.Q. Fall, 1975, v. LIX, #3, p. 313-329. $8-

434a ..."Yankee Blitzkrieg, Wilson's Raid through Alabama & Georgia." Athens, University of Georgia Press, 1976. 8vo, cl, dj, xiv, 256pp. front(port)ills, port.

435 **JONES, Jesse H.**
"General Robert E. Lee. Address of Jesse H. Jones, chairman of Reconstruction finance corp., at the unveiling of the Robert E. Lee statue by President Roosevelt, Dallas, Texas. Friday June 12, 1936." (Washington, D.C.?) 1936. 8vo, wraps, 11 pp. Also issued in mimeographed form.

436 **JONES, John Beauchamp**
"Secession, Coercion & Civil War. A Story of 1861." Philadelphia: T.B. Peterson Bros, (1861) 12mo, cl, 502 pp. Baltimore: Armstrong & Berry, 1861.

437 ..."The Rebel War Clerk's Diary at the Confederate States Capital. By J.B. Jones Clerk in the War Department of the Confederate States Government; author of "Wild Western Scenes, etc. etc." Phila: J.B. Lippincott & Co., 1866. 12mo, cl, xii, (13)-392, 480 pp. Also, 2vols in I, $225-, $250-Bmk-105, $45-(v. 1 only).

...N.Y., Old Hickory Bookshop, 1935. "A new & enlarged edition edited with an introduction & historical notes by Howar Swiggett." Tall 8vo, cl(pict), index, XII, (1), (14)-403, 490pp. $50-

...N.Y., Sagamore Press(1958) "Condensed, edited, & annotated by Earl Schenck Miers, complete in one volume" Tk, 8vo, cl, dj, index, xiv, 545 pp. op

...N.Y., A.S. Barnes-"A Perpetual Bk." 8vo, wraps.

...N.Y., Encore Library of Civil War." (1961) paper.

438 ..."Border War: a Tale of Disunion." N.Y., Rudd & Carlton, 1859.

...Phila: T.B. Peterson (1859).

439 ..."Wild Southern Scenes: a Tale of Disunion." 12mo, cl,front,x,(11)-502 pp.

440 ...Also titled-"Secession, Coercion & Civil War. The Story of 1861." By Peterson. Also published in Baltimore: Armstrong & Berry 1861. See Wright's Amer. Fiction, #1370; Sabin: 78704. Predicts war between the states, Britain going South.

441 **JONES, John Marshall**
"Report: Battle of Gettysburg." In: SHSP 1880, v.8, 171-173.

442 **JONES, John William, Rev.**
"Action of R.E. Lee Camp. #1, Sons of Confederate veterans..., in regard to Barne's brief history of the U.S." Richmond, Va., 1895. 8vo, wraps, 14pp.

443 ..."Army of Northern Virginia, Memorial Vol. by...At the request of the Virginia Division of Army of Northern Virginia Association." Richmond: J.W. Randolph & English, 1880($100) Tall 8vo, cl, 347 pp. Incl. proceedings of Lee Memorial meeting & Annual meetings, reminiscences 1st to 9th Va. Division A.N.V. Ass'n., roster ANV, p. 334-342.

...Dayton, Oh., Morningside press, 1976. Intro: Dr. James I. Robertson, Jr., 352 pp., $17.50

444 ..."Christ in Camp: or, Religion in Lee's Army; Intro: by Rev. J.C. Granberry, Bishop M.E. Church South." ($6, $10-) Richmond: B.F. Johnson & Co., 1887. 8vo, cl, 528 pp. front (port), illus., pls.

..."Christ in Camp: or, Religion in Lee's Army...Supplemented by a sketch of the work in the other Confederate armies with an Intro: Rev. J.C. Granberry, Bishop of M.E. Church South." Richmond: B.F. Johnson & Co, (1888). 8vo, cl, color front, illus., col. pls., 624 pp. Append. #2, The work of grace in other armies of the Confederacy, p. 535-624. $50-

...New Edition: Atlanta: Martin & Hoyt (1904). Append: 'Letters from our army workers.' p. 465-534.

...Louisville: Lost Cause Press, micro-cd. $7.30

445 ...Broadside, 12x17" Adv. printed both sides, 3-illus. from book (cl. $2.50 with gilt edges-$3.00) Amer. Mor., gilt edges

...6pp. folder, Advertising for above.

446 ..."Confederate View of the Treatment of Prisoners. Compiled from Official Records & Other Documents." comprising Vol. I, #3 & 4, Southern Historical Society Papers." Richmond, 1876. first edt. in book form. 8vo, cl, p. 113-330. (March & April 1876) $75-G.

..."Treatment of prisoners during the war." In: CV, 1905, v. 13, p. 401-405.

447 ..."The Career of Stonewall Jackson." In: SHSP, 1907, v. 35, p. 79-98.

448 ..."Concerning Lee's official report of Gettysburg." In: SHSP, 1880, v.8, p. 192.

449 ..."Confederate Generals are passing away." In SHSP, 1903, v.31, p. 189-192.

450 ..."Correspondence between J.W. Jones & Comte de Paris." In: SHSP, 1876, v.1, p. 253-256.

451 ..."Review: Eclectic History of the U.S.". In: SHSP, 1884, v.12, p. 283-287, 421-426.

452 ..."The Friendship between Lee & Scott." In: SHSP, 1883, v.11, p. 417-426.

453 ..."General Grant's Tabletalk." In: SHSP 1878, v.6, p. 142-144.

454 ..."The Historic Appletree at Appomattox." In: SHSP, 1884, v.12, p. 429-430.

455 ..."The Kilpatrick-Dahlgren raid upon Richmond." In: SHSP, 1885, v.12, p. 515-560.

456 ..."Long's Memoir of Gen. R.E. Lee." In: SHSP, 1886, v.14, p. 563-569.

457 ..."The Longstreet-Gettysburg controversy." In: SHSP, 1886, v.14, p. 563-568.

458 ..."Reminiscences of the Army of Northern Virginia." In: SHSP, 1881, v.9, p. 90-95, 129-134, 185-189, 233-280, 426-429, 557-570, 1881, v.10, p. 81-90.

459 ..."The Morale of General Lee's Army." In: AW, p. 191-204.

460 ..."Appomattox, the true story of the Surrender." In: Hist. Mag., Morrisania, 1873, p. 235-239, v.31.

461 ..."Review-Rise & Fall of CSA Government." In: SHSP, 1881, v. 9, p. 285-288.

462 ..."The Secession of Virginia." In: SHSP, 1886, v. 14, p. 359-364.

463 ..."Several incidents of Christ in Camp." In: SHSP, 1886, v.14, p. 370-375.

464 ..."Sketch of the Lee Memorial Association." In: SHSP, 1883, v. 11, p. 388-417.

465 ..."Stonewall Jackson." In: SHSP, 1891, v. 19, p. 145-164.

466 ..."The Davis Memorial Volume; or, Our Dead President Jefferson Davis, and the World's Tribute to his Memory." Richmond: B.F. Johnson & Co., 1890. 8vo, cl(or sheep), xxiii, (27)-672 pp., $40-Bmk, illus., plates, ports (incl. front. engr.) facsm. Pub lished by authority of Mrs. Davis. Some copies have crossed flags on cover.

...Waco, Texas, 1890 (above). $45-Jk-122

...Dallas, Texas, 1890 (above) W.M. Cornett & Co.

...Atlanta, Ga., 1890 (above)

467 ..."Extracts from 'Christ in Camp' to be used in arranging programs for 1937. Prepared by the Historian-General Mrs. Walter D. Lamar." (note at end: "This document available through courtesy of May Kennedy Hall (Mrs. J. E. Hall) Macon, Ga.) 1937? 8vo, cover title, 20 pp.

468 ..."Jefferson Davis." In CV, 1901, v. 9, p. 118-121. Address: Southern Historical Society in New Orleans.

469 ..."General Lee to the Rear." In: Southern Historical Society Papers, Richmond, 1880, v. 8, p. 31-36; 105-110.

470 ..."Morale of the Confederate Army." In: Evans Confederate Military History, Atlanta, 1899. v. 12, p. 117-193. port.

471 ..."Virginia's Next Governor: Gen. Fitzhugh Lee." New York: Cheap Pub. Co., (1885) 12mo, 31 pp., port on cover, wraps.

472 ..."Life & Letters of Robert Edward Lee, Soldier & Man." New York: Neale Pub., 1906. 8vo, cl, 9, (xi)-xii-(13)-486 pp., front, ports. $100-B, $150-B. $60-NC
...Harrisonburg, 1978. Reprint $16-

473 ..."Personal Reminiscences & Anecdotes, Letters of Robert E. Lee Published by authority Lee Family & Faculty of Washington & Lee University." New York: D. Appleton & Co., 1874. 8vo, cl, xvi, 509 pp., front, pl., illus-ports. $75-G, $45
...1875 edition, ports, calf, 1/2 mor $75-, $50-
...1876 edition, ports

474 ..."Biographical Sketch of Jefferson Davis with selections from his writings." In: E.A. Alderman Library of Southern Literature, 1909. v. 3, p. 1243-1271.

475 ..."Why the Confederacy Failed, with a Bibliography." In: South in the Building of a Nation., v 4, p. 544-552.

476 ..."Partial sketch of Gen. A.P. Hill, of his thrilling career." In: CV, Aug. 1893, v. 1, #8, p. 233-236, port.

477 ..."Record of Confed. Armies in possession of the Southern Historical Society at Richmond, Va. (Printed from catalogue furnished by Rev. J.W. Jones). Washington: War Records Pub., 1880. 8vo, wraps, cover title, xxxiii, (3), 58 pp.

478 ..."A Reminiscence of an official interview with Gen. R.E. Lee." In: SHSP, 1882, v. 10, p. 91-122.

479 ..."School History of the United States." Revised edt., (first pub: 1896) N.Y., New Orleans, University Pub. Co., 1898. 12mo, cl, xxi, 475 pp. front, illus., maps.
...New Orleans, 1901. (above) 456 pp. "written as a Southerner, for Southern schools I have treated more fully than I have seen elsewhere many matters of especial interest to south.

480 ..."A Slander refuted (concerning Gen. Carter Stevenson's Divison." In: SHSP 1877, v.4, p. 43-44.

481 ..."Thomas & Lee-historical facts." In: CV, Nov. 1903, v. XI, p. 559-560. "Gen. Thomas was a strong secessionist."

482 ..."The Truth of History." In: SHSP, 1891, v. 19, p. 376-379.

483 ..."Unveiling of the statue of Stonewall Jackson at New Orleans." In SHSP, 1881, v. 9, p. 212-219.

484 ..."A Visit to Beauvoir." In: SHSP, 1886, v. 14, p. 447-454.

484a ..."What Louisa Did in the War between the States." In: Louisa Co. Hist. Mag., Summer 1971, v.9.

485 **JONES, Joseph**
"Agricultural Resources of Georgia. An Address before the Cotton Planters Convention of Georgia, at Macon, Dec. 13, 1860. By Joseph Jones, M.D. chemist of the association, & professor of medical chemistry in the Medical College of Georgia, at Augusta, Ga."August, Ga., Chronical & Sentinel, 1861, 8vo, wraps, 13 pp. Sabin-36575; Crandall-2918. Deals with political situation, independence & secession. "Ga. the Empire State of South, with resources to maintain indp. & form herself an Empire."

486 ..."Andersonville. The relations of the Confederate Government to Federal prisoners. Letter of Prof. Joseph Jones Md, of New Orleans, to Hon. B.H. Hill. Letter of Gen. R.E. Lee on Federal & Confederate prisons." n.p., 1876.

487 ..."Correspondence between Dr. Jones & Gen. Samuel Cooper concerning Confederate losses during the war." In: SHSP, 1879, v. 7, p. 287-290.

488 ..."Investigation upon the nature, causes & treatment of hospital gangrene, as it prevailed in the Confederate Armies, 1861-5." New Orleans, La., "Bronze Pen" book print. 1869. 8vo, wraps, 60pp. Also in "US Sanitary Comm., Surgical memoirs of War of Rebellion (N.Y. 1871) II-p. 143-570.

489 ..."Medical & Surgical Memoirs; containing investigations on the geographical distribution, cause, nature, relations & treatment of various diseases..." New Orleans, La., Clark & Hofeline, 1876, 1890. Printed for the Author. Imp. 8vo, cl, 3vol. in 4 Front (v. 3, pt. 2) illus., plates (part col. fldg. maps, plans, charts, tables. About 1/2 of v. 1 pertain to CSA soldiers medical problems. $600-ob. Vol. 1 pub. in 1876, other two vols in 1887 & 1890. The hard-to-find v. 1 was mainly presented to his friends nearly all inscribed. Other vols. were remaindered to Tulane Medical sch. for distribution. Many chromo-lithos maps, charts, tables & engravings.

490 ..."Medical history of Confederate states." In: SHSP, 1892, v. 20, p. 109-166.

491 ..."Medical officers of Army of Tennessee." In: SHSP, 1894, v. 22, p. 165-280.

492 ..."Organization of Medical Corps, UCV." In: SHSP, 1894, v. 22, p. 14-17.

493 ..."Observations upon the losses of the Confederate armies from battles, wounds, & disease during the Americal civil war, 1861-1875." Article in Richmond Medical Journal, Oct., 1869, p. 19.

494 ..."Official Report of..., New Orleans, Surg-Gen., UCV, concerning the medical department of the Confederate Army & Navy, June 30, 1890."

II. "Brief report of proceedings of reunion of survivors of the Medical Corps-Confederate Army & Navy, July 2, 1890. At Nathan Bedford Forrest Camp, Chattanooga, Tenn. Address of Joseph Jones containing war statistics of the armies of Mississippi & Tennessee, 1861-5; also results of Great Battles of Tenn., Miss., La., and Ga."

III-"Official correspondence 1890-2, Joseph Jones in reference to forces & losses of individual Southern states during war 1861-1865, with reference to number & condition of surviving Confederate soldiers who were disabled by wounds & diseases." New Orleans, La., Sur-Gen. UCV, 1892. 8vo, wraps, illus. tables, 34 pp.

495 ..."Quinine as a Prophylactic against Malarial Fever." Nashville, 1867. 8vo, wraps, 34 pp., Append. to 3rd report on Typhoid & Malarial Fever, del. to the Confed. Gen., Aug. 1864.

496 ..."Researches upon 'Spurious Vaccinations' or the abnormal phenomena accompanying & following vaccination in the Confederate Army during the recent civil war, 1861-1865." Nashville, Ten., University Medical print, 1867, from Nashville Journal of Medicine & Surgery. 2nd ser., v. 1, #s. 1-6. 8vo, cl, 136 pp.
...Nashville, 1867, wraps, 164 pp. atg., $200-G, $350-(Ginz)

497 ..."Roster of the medical officers of the Army of Tennessee, during the civil war." In: SHSP, 1893, v. XXII, p. 165-180.

498 ..."Treatment of Prisoners." In: SHSP, 1876, v. 1, p. 170-178.

499 ..."United Confederate Veterans." In: SHSP 1893, v. 21, p. 1-14.

500 **JONES, Katherine M.**
"Heroines of Dixie; Confederate Women Tell their Story of the War." Indianapolis, Ind., Bobbs-Merrill (1955). 8vo, cl, dj, xiv, 430 pp. (15)pp. 'Gallery of Confederate

Ladies.'

...(1955) "Lost Cause edition", atg. by editor for 'Civil War Book Club.' $20-, $30-Bmk, $35-

...(1955) "Stars & Bars," 1st Edt. signed, Limited Edt.

...Westport, Ct., Greenwood press, 1973, Library binding, $25.50Y "Mockingbird Books," paper, 1974.

501 ..."Ladies of Richmond. Confederate Capital." With introduction by Clifford Dowdey. Indianapolis, Ind: Bobbs-Merrill (1962) 8vo, cl, bds., dj, illus., ports, 365 pp. atg-$40-b

502 ..."New Confederate Short Stories." Columbia: University of South Carolina Press, 1954. 8vo, cl, dj, 202pp. Thirteen stories, modern writers, reappraising the meaning of the CSA. A 2nd edition printed. 1958.

503 ..."The Plantation South." Indianapolis, Ind: Bobbs-Merrill (1957). 8vo, cl, dj, xv, 412 pp. (14)pp. 'Selection of Plantation Houses of the Ante-Bellum South.' Bmk-$25

504 ..."Southern Heritage Edition," Limited & Signed Edition.

505 ..."When Sherman Came: Southern Women & the "Great March." Indianapolis, Ind: Bobbs-Merrill(1964). 8vo, cl, dj, xiv, 353 pp. Bibliog-notes, p. 325-340. Atg. $25-

505a **JONES, Kenneth W.**
"The Fourth Alabama Infantry: First Blood." In: AHQ, 1974, v.36, #1, p.35-53.

505b ..."The Fourth Alabama Infantry: a Fighting Legion." In: AHQ, 1976, v.38, #3, p.171-203.

506 **JONES, Lewis Pinckney**
"Ambrosio Jose Gonzales (1818-1893) a Cuban patriot in Carolina." In SCHM, Apr. 1955, v. 56, p. 67-76. Filibustering activities in US & service in the CSA Army.

507 ..."William Elliott, South Carolina Non-conformist." (Baton Rouge, La.) JSH, Aug. 1951, v. XVII, #3, p. 361-381.

508 **JONES, Margaret Belle**
"Bastrop (Texas); a compilation of material relating to the history of the town of Bastrop, with letters written by Terry Rangers." Bastrop, Texas. 1936. 8vo, cl, illus., 75 pp. See: L.B. Giles, Lester N. Fitzhugh, JKP Blackburn

509 **JONES, Mary Sharpe & Mary Jones Mallard**
"Yankees A'Coming. One Month;s Experience During the Invasion of Liberty County, Georgia 1864-1865." Lim. Edt. 450 copies. Tuscaloosa, Ala: Confederate Pub. Co., 1959. Confederate Centennial Studies, #12. 12mo, stiff wraps, port, map, illus., 102 pp. $35-

510 **JONES, Maryus**
"Colonel William Todd Robins, Confederae Hero." In: SHSP, 1906, v. 34, p. 275-279.

511 **JONES, P.R.**
"Recollections of the battle of Murfreesboro." In: CV, Sept. 1923, v. XXXI, p. 341-342.

512 **JONES, R.Y.**
"An Alabama Heroine-Miss. Emma Sansone." In: SHSP, 1897, v. 25, p. 45-54. See: Mary Bankhead Owen.

513 **JONES, Richard Watson**
"Confederate Cemeteries & Monuments in Mississippi." In: Pub. Miss. Hist. Soc., Oxford, Miss., 1904, v. VIII, p. 87-119.

514 **JONES, Robert A.**
"Aftermath of an Ironclad." In: CWTI, Oct. 1972, v. XI, #6, p. 21-25, illus.

515 **JONES, Robert Hunn**
"The American Civil War in the British Sessional Papers: catalogue & commentary." N.Y., Readex Microprint Corp., (1964?) 4to, cover title, wraps, 12pp. From

Proceedings American Philosophical Society, v. 107, #5, Oct., 1963.

516 **JONES, Robert M.**
"The 'Kentucky Rifle' of Robert M. Jones, Choctaw Delegate to the Confederate Congress at Richmond, Virginia." Oklahoma City: Chron. Okla., Autumn, 1963, v. XLI, #3, p. 323-327, plate.

517 **JONES, Samuel, Formerly Maj-Gen. C.S.Army**
"The Battle of Prairie Grove, Dec. 7, 1862." (Louisville, Ky.?)(1885) wraps, 32mo, 38 pp. From the Southern Bivouac (N.S., v. 1, p. 203-211)
Reprint: August 1965 (Fayetteville, Ark.) annotated: Elsa Vaught, port, (3) pp., 38 pp., (2) pp., tied red ribbon. $25-

518 ..."The Battle of Olustee, or Ocean Pond, Florida." In: B & L, v. IV, p. 76-79.

519 ..."Joseph R. Hawley's Comments on Gen. Jones' paper." In: B & L, v. IV, p. 79-80.

520 ..."The Battle of Prairie Grove, Dec. 7, 1862." In: SB, 1885/6, v. 1, ns, p. 203-211.(also: wraps, 12mo, cover t/p, 38 pp., (1910?) (1965) rep.

521 ..."Capture of General Scammon" In: SHSP, 1881, v. IX, p. 82-84.

522 ..."Defense of Charleston from July 1-July 10, 1864." In: SHSP, 1876, v. II, p. 192-196.

523 ..."Letters on the Treatment & Exchange of Prisoners." In: SHSP, 1877, v. III, p. 77-81.

524 ..."Report of Maj-Gen. Samuel Jones of Operations at Charleston, South Carolina, from Dec. 5th to 27th, 1864." In: SHSP, 1877, v. III, p. 261-268.

525 ..."The Siege of Charleston & the Operations on the South Atlantic Coast in the War among the States, by Saml. Jones formerly Major-General, CSA." N.Y., Wash., Neale Pub., 1911, 8vo, cl, front(port), 195 pp. $300-B-150-11

526 **JONES, Sarah L., Miss**
"Governor Milton & his Family. A contemporary picture of life in Florida during the war, by an English Tutor." In: FHQ, July 1909, v. II, #2, p. 42-50. An extract from her "Life in the South, etc."

527 **JONES, Spencer Cone**
"Address of...delivered, Winchester, Va., June 5, 1880 on the unveiling of monument erected to memory of Maryland Confederate dead." Published by Society of Army & Navy Confederate States in state of Maryland." Baltimore: King Bros. Print, 1880. 8vo, wraps, cover title, 16pp.

528 **JONES, T. Catesby**
"The Iron-Clad Virginia." (Richmond) Va. Mag. Hist. Biog., Oct., 1941, v. XLIX, #4, p. 296-303, illus.

529 ..."The Merrimack & her Big Guns." (Richmond) Va. Mag. Hist., Biog. Jan, 1942, v. L, #1, p. 13-37.

529a **JONES, Terry L.**
"Lee's Tigers: the Louisiana Infantry in the Army of Northern Virginia." 1987. Baton Rouge, Louisiana State University. 8vo, cl, dj, 274pp, ills, maps. $22.50. See: Alison Moore.

529b ..."Shreveport (La.) goes to War: Soldier's Views." In: LaH., 1984, v.25, p.391-401.

529c ..."Wharf-rats, cutthroats & thieves: the Louisiana Tigers, 1861-2." In: LH, Spring 1986, v.27, #2, p.147-65. See: Chs. Dufour, Francis C. Kajencki, Alison Moore.

530 **JONES, Thomas A.**
"Running the Confederate mails across the Potomac river. Edt: Van Dyk MacBride. In: Armer. philatelist, Oct. 1955, v. 69, p. 27-30. port, view, (from the author's "J. Wilkes Booth Chicago, 1893. On his signal & mail service from his house on a Potomac bluff in south. Md, 1862-1865."

531 **JONES, Thomas A. J.**
"J. Wilkes Booth. An Account of his Sojourn in Southern Maryland after Assassination of A. Lincoln, his Passage across the Potomac, & His Death in Virginia. By Thos. A. Jones, the Only living man who can tell the story." Chicago: Laird & Lee, 1893. 12mo, cl, 126 pp., illus. Monaghan: An account by a regenerated Confed. sympathizer. $200-
...Also In: Amateur book collector, Sept/Nov. monthly installments, 1954, v. 5, p. 1-3. facsm. ports, views, reprint of the 1893 edt.Chicago: n.d. $20-

532 **JONES, Thomas G., of Alabama**
"Memorial tribute to Gen. John B. Gordon. In: CV, 1904, v. 12, p. 329-333, port.

533 **JONES, Thomas Goode, Gov., Va.**
"Address at Unveiling of the Confederate Monument at Montgomery, Alabama." In: SHSP, 1898, v. XXVI, p. 186-209.

534 ..."The Last Days of the Army of Northern Virginia. An address before the Division of the Ass'n. ANV, Oct. 12, 1893." In: SHSP, v. XXI, p. 57-103. Offprint, wraps, 46pp. (Bmk-105) $125-

535 ..."Speech...at the complimentary dinner given in his honor, published in pursuance of a resolution of the meeting, Oct. 1, 1875. J.T. Hite." n.p., n.d., (1875) 8vo, wraps, p. 8. "The mission of the Northern & Southern soldiery." text of speech.

536 ..."Memorial oration delivered before the Ladies Memorial Ass'n., in Confederate Cemetery at Montgomery, Ala., Apr. 17, 1874." n.p., n.d., 8vo, wraps, p. 8.

537 **JONES, Thomas Laurens**
"Amnesty & the Jefferson Davis Amendment. Speech in the House of Representatives, Jan. 13, 1876." Washington, 1876. 8vo, sewn, 6pp.

537a **JONES, Virgil C.**
"First Manassas-the Story of the Bull Run Campaign." In: CWTI, July 1980, v.19, #4, p.50 (complete issue), ills, maps, sketches.

538 **JONES, Virgil Carrington**
"The Battle of Galveston, New Years day 1863, Confederates brake Union blockade." In: CWTI, Feb. 1967, v. 5, #10, p. 28-38, illus., map, ports.

539 ..."How the Confederacy created its Navy." In: CWTI, July 1969, v. VIII, #4, p. 4-9, 42-6, illus., ports.

540 ..."Construction, fighting career & destruction of the 'Albemarle.'" In: CWTI, June 1962, v. 1, #3, p. 6-11, 43-46. illus., map, ports. Built under direction of a teenager, threatens Federal control of N.C. sound until destroyed.

541 ..."The Civil War at Sea. January 1861, March 1862. 'The Blockaders' v. I, Foreword by Admiral E.M. Eller, Director of Naval History." N.Y., Holt, Rinehart, Winston (1960). tk. 12mo, cl, dj, illus., ports, maps, xxvi, 483 pp. map liners. $20-bmk
Vol. II - "The River War." (1961). Tk, 12mo, cl, dj, illus., ports, map, xx, 490pp. map liners. OP
Vol. III - "The Final Effort, July 1863-November, 1865." (1962) maps, illus., bibliog., xxii, 456 pp. 3vols. calf $65-Bmk. OP $100

542 ..."Eight Hours Before Richmond. Introduction: Col. Robert Selph Henry." N.Y. Henry Holt & Co., (1957) 8vo, cl, dj, illus., ports, maps, facsm. x, (1), 180 pp., map liners $30-bmk-99

543 ..."Gray Ghosts & Rebel Raiders, Intro: Bruce Catton." N.Y., Henry Holt & Co., (1956) Tk. 8vo, cl, dj, illus., ports, map liners xiv, (2), 431 pp. notes, p. 373-415, index. $25- 1956: Limited ATG. Edt., for Civil War Book Club members, Edts: 2nd print(1956); 3rd print., FEb. '58-1959. 1976 Georgia, wrap $3-

544 ..."The problem of writing about the Guerillas." In: Mil. Affairs (Spring) 1957, v. 21, p. 21-25. Problems author had in writing "Gray Ghosts."

545 ..."Ranger Mosby." Chapel Hill: University of North Carolina Press, 1944 (four printings 1944). 8vo, cl, dj, illus., ports, incl. front, xiii, 347 pp. map liners, $10- Printing, 1969. atg. $35-, $10-Bmk-106.
...11th 1976-

546 **JONES, Virginia Lee**
"The Confederate Great Seal & its replicas." In: Spinning wheel, Sept., 1960, v. 16, #9, p.24, seals. Designed by Judah Benjamin & the 1,000 replicas made by Jno. J. Pickett in 1873.

547 **JONES, Walter Burgwyn**
"The Alabama state memorial at Vicksburg." In: AlaHQ. 1952, v. XIV, p. 135-139.

548 ..."Alabama Secedes from the Union; an address by Walter B. Jones before the Brannon historical society of the womans College of Alabama, Montgomery." Montgomery, The Paragon Press (1929) 8vo, wraps, illus, 16 pp.
...(Also: CV, 1931, v. 39, p. 168-178.

549 ..."The Alabama State Memorial at Vicksburg." In: AHQ, 1952, v. XIV, p. 135-139.

550 ..."Anectodes (sic) about Gov. Thomas G. Jones 1844-1914." In: Ala. lawyer, July 1956, v. 17, p. 188-304. Author's father as officer in the CSArmy & lawyer, political leader in Alabama.

551 ..."The Confederate Dead." Montgomery, Ala., 1951. 6pp. (Bound-in with 'Huntly- Cabin Papers."

552 ..."In Memoriam: Thomas Goode Jones, 1844-1914 & Georgena Bird Jones, 1846- 1921." Montgomery, Ala., Thomas Goode Jones Camp, Sons of Confederate Veterans, 1956, 8vo, wraps, illus., ports, 55pp.

553 ..."One of Lee's flags of truce." In: Ala.HW, 1940, v. II, p. 36-43. Lee sent to Union lines at the surrender at Appomattox.

554 ..."The Confederate Veteran, an address." Montgomery, Ala., 1944. 8vo, wraps, 13 pp.

555 ..."The Great Cannoneer: an address on the life & military genius of Maj. John Pelham, CSA...upon the occasion of the presentation of the State of Alabama of the sword of Maj. Pelham, Hall of the House of Representatives. State Capitol, Montgomery, Dec. 3, 1929. Montgomery, Ala., 1929. 8vo, wraps, p. 11, port.

556 ..."War Poems of the Southern Confederacy...an address by...Oct. 7, 1946." Before the 56th annual reunion United Confederate Vets., Banquet Hall, Edgewater Gulf Hotel." n.p., printed by United Confed. Vets. 8vo, wraps, color flags, port, pls, 63 pp.
...Montgomery, Ala., 1959, stiff decr. wraps, 77 pp., 1000 copies.
...Reprint, 1961.

556a ..."The Last Confederate Reunion." In: AHQ, 1944, v.6, #1, p.7-11.

557 **JONES, Wilbur Devereux**
"The Confederate Rams at Birkenhead: A Chapter in Anglo-American Relations." Tuscaloosa, Ala: Confed. Pub. Co., 1961. Confederate Centennial Studies, #19. 12mo, stiff wraps, 124 pp., illus. Lim. Edt. 450 copies $15-bmk

558 ..."The British conservatives & the American Civil War." In: Am. Hist. Rev., Apr. 1953, v. 58, p. 527-543, notes.

559 **JONES, Wilbur Moore, Mrs., Edt.**
"Jefferson Davis. Historic Beauvoir- Souvenir Booklet of Beauvoir on the Gulf, Harrison County, Miss." U.D.C. Hattiesburg, Miss., American Commercial print, (Nov. 1921) 4to, stiff decr. wraps,

crossed-flags, illus., fldg. pl., 110 pp. See: "First White House."

560 **JONES, William Edmondson, Gen.**
"Summer campaign of 1863. (Report) In: SHSP, 1881, v. 9, p. 115-119.

561 **JONES, William F.**
"Elbert County in Our Country's Wars." Atlanta, Ga., Cherokee Pub., 1981. 8vo, cl, dj, illus, index, xix, 373 pp. Biog. sketches, lists, muster rolls, & rosters of service men in all wars from Revolution to the present. $25-

561a **JONES, William M.**
"A Report on the Site of Camp Finegan." In: FHQ, April, 1961, v.XXXIX, #4, p.366-73, map.

562 **JONESBORO, Battle of...**
See: Ellison Capers, Henry DeL. Clayton, Randall L. Gibson, Stephen D. Lee.

563 **JORDAN, A.L.**
"General Joseph E. Johnston, a collection of sketches showing the injustice of the Confederate government's attitude toward him. Also a few brief opinions of Gen. Johnston's military ability by A.L. Jordan, Company F, 54th Virginia regiment (Pulaski, R. Smith & bros print, 1924. 8vo, wraps, 33pp., front(port)illus, ports.

563a **JORDAN, Charles Edward**
"A Letter from Charles Edward Jordan to his Family and Friends." (Charlottesville, Va.) The Author, 1932. 8vo, wraps, 47pp (Cather & Brown) $200. About half CSA, Prince Edward Rifles, 17th Va. Inf.

564 **JORDAN, Cornelia Jane Matthews, Mrs.**
"Corinth, & Other Poems of the War, By Cornelia J.M. Jordan." Lynchburg, (Va) Johnson & Schaffter (1865) 12mo, wraps, 31pp. (Gen. Terry ordered them burned, publicly, as objectionable & incendiary.

565 ..."Echoes from the Connon. Edited by Theresa J. Ambler." Buffalo (N.Y.), C.W. Moulton, 1899. 12mo, cl, 4, (v)-vii, 9-207 pp. front (port) Poetry of the Confederacy.

566 ..."In Memoriam. The death of the young partizan...John T. Waller, of Lynchburg, Va., Company A., Mosby's command, killed Mar. 14th, 1865, aged 19 years, seven months & 20 days." 8vo, wraps, caption title, dated Elk Hill, Bedford Co., Va., Mar. 31, 1865. Crandall, 3143.

567 ..."Richmond: her glory & her graves. A Poem, in two parts." Richmond, Va., Richmond Medical Journal print, 1867. 8vo, xxxixpp. CSA poetry, $10-, $75-jk

568 ...Richmond, Va., 1886, Medical Journal print. 8vo, wraps, 8pp.

569 **JORDAN, Donaldson**
"Europe & the American civil war, by Donaldson Jordan & Edwin J. Pratt with introduction by Samuel Eliot Morrison." Bost., NY, Houghton Miflin co, 1931. 8vo, cl, front, illus., xii, (1) p. $25-bmk

569a **JORDAN, Ervin, Jr. & Herbert A. Thomas**
"19th Virginia Infantry." Lynchburg, Va., H.E. Howard, 1987. 8vo, cl, dj, (5), 112pp, maps, ports, groups. 1,000 copies, signed.

570 **JORDAN, Holman D.**
"The Military career of Henry Delamar Clayton (officer in the CSArmy, 1861-1865) In: Ala. rev., April 1960, v. 13, p. 127-134 notes.

571 **JORDAN, John L.**
"Was there a massacre at Fort Pillow?" In: Tenn. HQ 1947, v.VI, p. 99-133.

572 **JORDAN, Mary**
"Diary of a Citizen from May 9, 1862 to August 22, 1864." Harrisonburg, 1961. 4to, mimeographed, 149 pp. Homelife during civil war.

573 **JORDAN, Thomas G.**
"The Thomas G. Jordan Family during the War Between the States." Edt: Max W. White. In: Ga. H.Q., Suppl., 1975, v.LIX, pp. 134-140.

574 **JORDAN, Thomas, General**
"Battle of Shiloh." In: SHSP, 1888, v.XVI, p. 297-318; 1907, v.XXXV, p. 204-230.

575 ..."Beginnings of the Civil War in America." In: Mag. Amer. Hist., 1885, v.XIV, p. 113-137, 269-287. facsms, illus., plan, ports.

576 ..."Campaign & Battle of Shiloh." In: US, 1885, v. XII, p. 262-280, 393-410. 1904, v.VI, 430-450, 576-595.

577 ..."The Campaigns of Lieut-Gen. N.B. Forrest & of Forrest's Cavalry by General Thomas Jordan & J.P. Pryor." New Orleans, La., Blelock & co, 1868. 8vo, cl, maps (3-fldg) ports, xiv, (17)-704 pp. 3/4 Mor., marbled bds. $175-B $200-ob

578 ..."Campaign of N.B. Forrest & Forrest Cavalry Cincinnatti & St. Louis: J.P. Miller & co, 1868. 12mo, 704 pp., ports, maps (partly folded.) $140-
...(Dayton, Ohio) Morningside Bookshop, 1973. Facsmilie #14. Introduction to new edition by Exra J. Warner. 8vo, cl, mapliners, maps, ports, 704pp. $27.50-y

579 ..."Jefferson Davis," In Harpers Mag., October 1865.

580 ..."Recollections of Gen. Beauregard Service in West Tennessee in Spring 1862." In: SHSP, 1880, v.VIII, p. 404-417.

581 ..."Seacoast defences of South Carolina & Georgia." In: SHSP, 1876, v. 1, p. 403-407.

582 ..."The Vicksburg Campaign in 1862-1863." In: US, 1885, v.XIII, p. 22-33.

582a ..."Notes on a Confederate Staff-officer at Shiloh." In: B&L, v.1, p.594-603, ills.

582b **JORDAN, Thomas, Gen. & J. Pryor**
"The Campaigns of Lieut. N. B. Forrest & of Forrest's Cavalry." Dayton, Oh., Morningside Press, 1988. 8vo, cl, dj, 735pp, maps, ports. $35.

582c **JORDAN, Weymouth T., Jr.**
"North Carolina Troops 1861-65, a Roster Vol. IX Infantry 32nd to 35th & 37th Regiments." Raleigh, N.C., Division of Archives & History, 1983. 8vo, cl, dj, ills, county maps. 658pp. $25.

582d ... "System of Farming at Beaver Bend, Alabama, 1862. Edt.: WTJ." In: JSH, 1941, v.7, #1, p.76-83.

582e ..."North Carolina Troops 1861-65. A Roster, vol. X. Raleigh, N.C., Archives & History, 1985. 8vo, cl, 549, ills, map. $22.

583 **JORDAN, William C.**
"Some Events & Incidents of the Civil War, by Wm. C. Jordan, Co. B, 15th Ala. Reg., C.S.A." Montgomery, Ala., Paragon Press, 1909. tall 8vo, wraps, 142 pp.

584 **"JOURNAL of Both Sessions**
of the Convention of the State of Arkansas, Which Were Begun & Held in the Capitol, in the City of Little Rock. Published by Authority." Little Rock, Ark., Johnson & Yerkes, 1861. sm 8vo, wraps/cl., 509pp. Append: with extracts from proceeding of the conventions in South Carolina & Georgia. "The Secession" convention.
...Do., March 4, 1861. 144pp.

585 **"JOURNAL of a Milledgeville Girl, 1861-67."**
See: Cook (Anna Maria Green)

586 **"JOURNAL of Southern History."**
Baton Rouge, La., The Southern Historical Association, v.I, Feb. 1935...Quarterly. Editors: W.H. Stephenson, et. al. vols. 1-48(1977) 8vo, wraps, JK, 122 $875-

587 **"JOURNAL of the Committee**
of Thirty-three on the Disturbed Condition of the Country." Washington, DC, HR-31, 1861. 8vo, sewn, 101pp. Comm. met from Dec. 4, 1860-Jan. 14, 1861 to avoid civil war, one from each state. Proposed several laws on slavery & fugitive slave laws, all in vain.

588 **"JOURNAL of the Confederate**
Historical Society." Editor: M.A. Rich. Sect: K.M. Broughton. Leigh on Sea, Essex., v.1-#1, July 1962; #4, Je. 1963. Quar-

terly, continuously paged, 165 pp. not including pages illustrated, (#1,(2)pp; #2(5)pp; #3()pp; #4(9)pp. v.II-#1, Dec. 1963, p. 57(12) v.III-#1, 1966.

589 **"JOURNAL of the Congress**
of the Confederate States of America, 1861-1865." Washington: Government Print. off., 1904-1905. 58th Cong., 2nd Sess., Senate, Doc. #234. 7 Volumes, Gen. Index, p. 847-966. 8vo, cl.(or. red. Mor.) $300-(bmk), $40-ea.. $350- 105-bmk$250. v.I, v.II, v.III, v.IV, 797, v.V.606, v.VI, v.VII, 964, $400-bmk.
...1969 reprint, 7vols., 602-cl. 2 vol. set., $175.00

"JOURNAL of the Convention
of the People of South Carolina, Held in 1860, 1861. Together with the Reports, Resolutions, etc. Published by Order of the Convention." Charleston: Evans & Cogswell print, 1861. 8vo, cl, 420, (1)p. jk-137 $250-

590 **"JOURNAL of the House of Delegates,**
of the State of Virginia, for the Session of 1864-5." Alexandria, Va., 1865. 8vo, orig. blue wraps, 83pp. (Jk.122) $150. Sess. Dec. 1864 thru Mar. 1865. Pierpont (Gov., Va.) "Condition of the Commonwealth is deplorable, etc."

591 **"JOURNAL of the Proceedings**
of the Convention of the People of Florida, Begun & Held at the Capitol in the City of Tallassee(sic), on Thursday, Jan. 3, A.D. 1861." Tallahassee: Floridian & Journal, 1861." 8vo, sewn, 112pp. Crandall-1499. (Bound in with).."Proceeding of the Convention of the people of Florida, at Called Sessions, begun & held at the Capitol in Tallahassee, on Tuesday, Feb. 16th, & Thursday, April 18th, 1861." (Tallahassee, 1861) 12mo, wraps, 70pp. Crandall-1502.

592 ...Jacksonville, Fla., 1928. H & W B. Drew 8vo, wraps, 124, 77pp.

of the Convention of the People of Florida, Begun & Held at the Capitol in the City of Tallahassee, Thursday Jan. 3, 1861." Tallahassee: Floridian & Journal, 1861. Reprint: 1928, Jackson, Florida: H. & W.B. Drew. 8vo, wraps, 124pp.

of the General Council of the Protestant Episcopal Church in the Confederate States of America, Held in St. Paul's Church, Augusta, Ga., from Nov. 12 to Nov. 22, Inclusive in the Year of our Lord, 1862. Edt: Wm. A. Clebsch." facsms. Austin, Texas: Church Historical Society, 1962. 8vo, cl, 216, 15, xiii, (3), 59, viii, (2)pp.

593 ...Augusta, Ga., Chronicle & Sentinel, 1863. 1st Edt., Crandall-4519 $50-

of the House of Representatives of Florida at its Tenth Session." Tallahassee, 1860. 8vo, sewn, 390pp. Gov. urgent message, Nov. 26, "crisis has come. Election of Lincoln & Hamilton aught to extinguish any desire of the Southern people to prolong their connection..." Not in Imprints Inventory.

594 **"JOURNAL of the Public Proceedings**
of the Convention of the People of South Carolina Held in 1860-61. Together with the Ordinances. Published by Order of the Convention." Charleston: Evans & Cogswell, 1860. 8vo, cl, 170pp. Turnbull (III)-310

595 **"JOURNAL of the Secession Convention**
of Texas, 1861. Edited from the Original in the Department of State by Ernest Wm. Winkler, State Librarian." Head: Texas Library & Historical Commission The State Library. Austin, (Texas), Austin Print co., 1912. 8vo, cl(or, wraps.) fldg. facsm. signers of Document, 469, (1)p-errata. Jk-127 $125.

596 **"JOURNAL of the South Carolina**
Executive Council of 1861 & 1862."

Edited: Charles E. Cauthen. See: "South Carolina, Executive Council"

597 **"JOURNAL of the Southern Confederacy."** Jasper, Florida., (1971) illus. ports, maps. v.1, #1-4, pp. 36-42 each, quarterly. v.2, #1-4, 1972/3; p. 42,62,62,82. $75-bmk-127

598 **"JOURNAL of the State Convention** & Ordinances, Resolutions, Adopted Jan. 1861, with an Appendix." (Jackson, Miss., Hederman Bros, 1962) Appendix: "An Address on the Declaration of Immediate Causes to induce & justify Secession of Mississippi from the Federal Union, and Ordinances of Secession." 98pp. Jackson, Miss., Mississippian Book & Job Print, 1861.
...Jackson, Miss., Civil War Centennial, 1962. 8vo, wraps, 102pp.

599 **"JOURNALS of the Protestant Episcopal Church** in the Confederate States of America: Centenary Edition in Facmilile." Edt: William A. Clebsch. Austin, Texas: Church Historical Society, 1962. 9vo, cl, pp. xvi, 28, 47, 315, 50. Reissue of the proceedings Southern Episcopal clergy in Montgomery, July 3-6, 1861, adjourned to Columbia, Oct. 16-24, 1861. Together with the Journals of the general councils in Augusta, Nov. 12-22, 1862, & Nov. 8-10, 1865.

600 **"JOURNALS of the State Convention** of South Carolina, Together with the Resolution & Ordinance." Columbia, S.C., Johnston & Cavis, 1852. 8vo, wraps, 45pp. Prelude to secession.

601 **JOUROLMON, Leon, Jr.** "Robert Edward Lee." In: Univ. Tenn. Mag., Dec. 1919, v.L, 97-107.

602 **JOYCE, David D.** "Pro-Confederate Sympathy in the British Parliament." In: Social Science 1969, v. XLIV, p. 95-100.

603 **JOYCE, Frederick** "Orphan Brigade at Chickamauga." In: SB, 1884-5, v.III, p. 19-32.

604 **JOYCE, John A., Col.** "Jewels of Memory." Washington: Gibson bros., 1895. 12mo, cl, front(port) 245 pp. (a 2nd edt. 1896, same above. Author a Kentuckian, sketches: Stonewall Jackson, Jno. Breckenridge, Forrest.

605 **JOYCE, W.J.** "Life of W.J. Joyce, written by himself: The History of a Long, Laborious & Happy Life of 57 Years in the Ministry in Texas." San Marcos, Texas., 1913. 8vo, cl, 126pp. $250- Served under John S. "Rip" Ford in the 2nd Texas Mounted Rifles in the CSA in South Texas, Indian fighting after war & served as chaplain of Texas Legislature.

606 **JOYNER, Fred B.** "A brief Calendar of Jefferson Davis Papers in the Samuel Richey Confederate Collection of Miami University Library, Oxford, Ohio." (Jackson, Miss) Jour. Miss. Hist., Jan. 1963, v.XXV, #1, pp. 15-32.

607 **JOYNER, Sara Porter** "The last chapter of the Confederacy." (Jacksonville, Fla., Evergreen Press, 1959) 8vo, wraps, ports, views, 20pp. Life of Davis from fall of Richmond till his death, 1865-1899, some monuments to him.

608 **JOYNES, Edward Satchell** "General Robert E. Lee as college president, reminiscences of his work in Lexington, Va." In" SHSP, 1900, v.28, p. 243-246.

609 **JUDD, H.O.** "Look within for facts & fiction consisting of instructing sketches, & thrilling narratives. By H.O. Judd." Macon, Ga., For the Author, 1864. 16mo, wraps, 204pp. Fiction.

610 **JUERGENSEN, Hans** "Historic Fort McAllister (Georgia)" n.p.,

March 20, 1958 Programe... 12mo, wraps- color flag, *(8) pp.

611 ..."Fort Pulaski." In: CWTI, May 1970, v.IX, #2, p. 8-21, facsms, map, diagram, ports.

612 **"JUHL LETTERS, THE**
to the Charleston Courier, A View of the South, 1865-71. Edt: John Hammond Moore." Athens, Ga., University Press, (1974) 12mo, cl, dj, vii, 391pp.

613 **"JUNIUS TERTIUS."**
"Kennesaw Mountain." In: Ga. H.Q. Dec. 1935. v.XIX, #4, p. 313-324. Yankees roasted crisp.

614 **JURIDICUS (pseud.)**
"The recognition of the confederate states considered in a reply to the letters of "Historicus" in the London Times. By Juridicus." Charleston, S.C., Evans & Cogswell, 1863. 8vo, wraps, 11pp. South should be recognized by Europeans.

K

1   **"K.G.C." (HIATT, J.M., Dr.)**
"An Authentic Exposition of the Origin, Objects, & Secret Work of the Organization known as the Knights of the Golden Circle." U.S. National, U.C., Feb. 1862. wraps, 8vo, p. 16. Also: "A Full Exposure of the Southern Traitors: The Knights of the Golden Circle." Boston: E.H. Bullard(1861) 8vo, wraps, p. 8. (Entered, cropyright-Kentucky, 1862)

..."An Authentic Exposition of the "K.G.C." Knights of the Golden Circle: A History of Secession from 1834-1861, by a Member of the Order." (Indianapolis, 1861) 80pp. wrps. Gen. Bickley later ridiculed this expose & denied its authorship, which Dr. Hiatt had attributed to him. $450- Morrison copy 88pp. secret rituals & codes (814) 125- See: Curtis Hugh Morrow. Eberstaut attributed to C.D. Perrine (#163) $75- See: Bethania M. Smith

..."An Authentic Exposition of the "K.G.C.," Knights of the Golden Circle;" or, A History of the Secession from 1834 to 1861 by a member of the order." Indianapolis, Ind., (1864) C.O. Perrine Pr. 12mo, printed wraps, 88pp. In fine, cl slipcase ($450-) $50-wh $85-jk.

2   ..."A Full Exposure of the Southern Traitors; the Knights of the Golden Circle..." Boston: E.H. Bullard & Co (1861) 8vo, wraps, 8pp, Sabin 36968.

3   ..."K.G.C. First, or Military Degree." n.p., n.d. 32mo, 13pp. wraps. Copy at TU

4   ..."Knights of the Golden Circle." See" Report of the Judge Advocate General, on the Order of American Knights, or "Sons of Liberty, etc."

...See: Ollinger Crenshaw, Jimmie Hicks, C.A. Bridges, Roy S. Dunn, Mayo Fisler.

..."An Authentic Exposition of the "K.G.C." "Knights of the Golden Circle;" or a History of Secession from 1834 to 1861..." Indianapolis, Ind.: C.O. Perrine, 1861. 8vo, wraps, 88pp. Sabin-38132 differs from other quoted sources & included here. Eberstadt copy-#163(cat.) 12mo, pict. wraps, plates, 80pp. $85- $75-

..."An Authentic Exposition of the KGC or a History of Secession. By a member of the order." Indianapolis, 1861. 12mo, printed wraps, 88pp. 1st edt. with dated t.p.

..."K.G.C. An authentic Exposition of the Origin, Objects & Secret Work of the Organization known as the Knights of the Golden Circle." U.S. National, U.C., Feb. 1862. (Louisville, Ky., 1862). 8vo, sewn, 16pp. Rare earliest U(nion) C(lubs) publication, which was organized in Louisville, May 1861 for express purpose of saving Ky. from secession. Implacable foes of KGC.

5   ..."Proceedings of the State U.C. of Ohio." (Cincinnati, 1862) 8vo, orig. blank wraps, 16pp. Extension into Ohio to combat KGC. See: C.A. Bridges.

6   ...Knights of the Golden Circle: Engraved certificates(sheet of four 8 1/2x13 1/4" each: 3 1/8x8 1/2" signed by Geo. Bickley, Comm. in Chief & R.C. Tyler, Reg. colonel, dated in pen May 20, 1859. Top is a seal of "Mexico Union;" cert. is a receipt for $1, repayable in bonds of the "City of Andalusia" at 20% per annum at 20% $75-. This brilliant medical teacher, Cincinnati. Dr. George (W.L) Bickley, was founder of this subversive organization. As early as 1855 supposed to have been active in the South, in support of Southern Rights Clubs, organizing Castles

of his K.G.C. As early as May 1861 he boasted of 8,000 Knights in every county of Ky. Altho it was rumored to overthrow Mexican Gov., its likely this was a cover in extension of the cause in the North, these notes being membership cards. This is earliest known documentary proof of the order. (note by Ernest Wessen)

7 **KAHN, Edgar M.**
"Judah P. Benjamin in California." In: Calif. Hist. Soc. Quart., 1968, v.XLVII, p. 157-173.

8 **KANE, G.A.**
"Music & Words of Dixie. Dan Emmett the author & N.Y., the place of production." In: SHSP, 1893, v.XXI, p. 212-214.

9 **KANE, Harnett Thomas**
"Bride of Fortune; a novel based on the life of Mrs. Jefferson Davis." Garden City: Doubleday, 1948. 12mo., cl, dj, 301pp. Atg.

10 ..."The Gallant Mrs. Stonewall; a novel based on the lives of General & Mrs. Stonewall Jackson." Garden City, N.Y., Doubleday, 1957. 12mo, cl, dj, illus., 320pp. fiction.

11 ..."The Lady of Arlington, a novel based on the life of Mrs. Robert E. Lee" Garden City, N.Y., Doubleday, 1953. 12mo, cl, dj, 288pp. bibliog.

12 ..."The Smiling Rebel; a novel based on the life of Belle Boyd." Garden City, N.Y., Doubleday, 1955. 12mo, cl, dj, 314pp. fiction.

13 ..."Spies for the Blue & Gray." Garden City, N.Y., Hanover House(1954) 8vo, cl, dj, 311 pp. bibliog-index. (291-311) "Southern Edition," Atg. $30- $25-Bmk.

14 ..."A Picture Story of the Confederacy." Illustrated: William R. Lohse. New York: Lothrop, Lee & Shepard (1965) sm. 4to, cl, d/w, illus, 128pp.

15 **KANTOR, Mackinley**
"If the South Had Won the Civil War." N.Y., Bantom Books (1961) 12mo, cl, 112 pp. ficiton.

15a **KASER, David**
"Books & Libraries in Camp & Battle; the Civil War Experience." Westport, Conn., Greenwood Press, 1984. 8vo, cl, 141p, ills. $28. Soldiers were avid readers, since 90% Union and 70% CSA were literate. Reading everything they could scrunge.

15b **KATCHER, Philip R. N.**
"American Civil War Armies: Confederate Artillery, Cavalry, & Infantry." London: Osprey Print, 1986. Narrow 8vo, stiff wraps, 48pp, ills, color pls. Clothing, army accoutrements provided by the CSArmy.

15c ..."The Army of Northern Virginia. Color by Michael Youens." Reading (England): Osprey Print, 1975. 'Men at Arms series.' Narrow 8vo, stiff wraps, 40pp, ills (some in color, ports. $17.50.

16 **KATES, Charles O.**
"Hardtack & hominy." In: Quartermaster Rev. 1938, v.XVII, #4, p. 29-32, 63. Difficulty encountered by both US & CSA governments in feeding troops.

17 **KAUFMANN, Wilhelm**
"Dir Deutschen im Amerikanischen Burgerkriege (Sezessionskreig 1861-65)" Munchen & Berlin, 1911.

17a **KAY, William Kennon**
"Drewy's Bluff or Fort Darling." In: VMHB, Apr. 1969, v.77, #2, p.191-200.

18 **KAYLOR, P.C.**
"The Killing of Lieutenant Meigs, 1864." p. 187-196. In: John W. Wayland's 'Virginia Valley Records Strasburg, Va.', Shenandoah Pub., 1930.

19 **KAZAR, John D., Jr.**
"The Canadian View of the Confederate Raid on St. Albans." In: Vermont Hist., 1965, v.XXXIII, p. 255-273.

20 **KEADY, William G., Rev.**
"Incidents of Prison Life at Camp Douglas

Experience of Corp. J.G. Blanchard." In: SHSP, 1884, v.XII, p. 269-273.

21 **KEAN, Robert Garlick Hill**
"Inside the Confederate Government, The Diary of Robert Garlick Hill Kean, head of the Bureau of War. Edited by: Edward Younger." (8.50, 12- $15-) N.Y., Oxford University press, 1957. 12mo, cl, dj. port(front,xxxvi, 241pp. "Civil War Book Club Edition, Atg. $395 25-
...Westport, Conn., Greenwood pr., 1974.

22 ..."Resources of the Confederacy in February, 1865, Letter from Colonel R.G.H. Kean," In: SHSP, 1876, v.II, p. 56-58.

23 ..."Treatment of prisoners during the war. Letter of Hon. R.G.H. Kean, Chief Clerk of the Confederate War Department, Lynchburg, Va., Sept. 11, 1876." In: SHSP, 1876, v.1, p. 199-203.

24 **KEARSEY, A. Alexander Horace Cyril**
"A study of the strategy & tactics of the Shenandoah Valley Campaign 1861-1862, with six maps, illustrating the Principals of War Battles Described by..., late Lieutenant Colonel General Staff." Aldershot, London, etc., Gale & Polden (1930) 8vo, stiff wraps, (6), 70pp. 6-fldg maps at end.
...Same, (1952) vi, 66pp., 6-fldg. maps. $45-

25 **KEATLEY, John H.,Col.**
"Letters confirming Col. Baldwin's account of interview with Lincoln & documents lost in battle." In: SHSP, 1881, v.IX, p. 88-89.

26 ..."Opinion of a U.S. officer of the depopulation of Atlanta." In: SHSP, 1881, v.IX, p. 272-273.

27 **KEELER, John Wells**
"Civil War Chronicle." (Denver, 1966) 38cm, illus., maps, ports, (10), 118pp. Cover Titel: "News of the Civil War! A History of the Civil War in modern newspaper style; Civil War Chronicle." Acknowledgements 1st 7pp. Newspapers both North & South.

28 **KEELIN, James**
"A modern Horatius. Defence of a bridge by one Confederate against forty Federals." In: SHSP, 1893, v.XXI, p. 294-297.

29 **KEEN, Nancy Travis**
"Confederate Prisoners of War at Ft. Delaware (Pea Patch Island in Delaware River, April 1862 to Jan. 1866)." April, 1968, p. 1-27.

30 **KEEN, Newton Asbury**
"Such is War.: The Confederate Memoirs of Newton Asbury Keen. Edited by William Clyde Billingsley." In: TMH, Winter 1967. v.6, #4, p. 238-252, port, facsm. maps., pt. 2: v.7, #1, p. 44-70; pt. 3, v.7, #2, p. 103-119; pt. 4:v.7, #3, p. 176-194.

30a ..."Living & Fighting with the Texas 6th Cavalry." Gaithersburg, Md., Butternut Press, 1986. 8vo, cl, 101p. $18.50.

31 **KEENE, Jesse L.**
"The Peace Convention of 1861." Tuscaloosa, Ala: Confed. Pub., 1961. Confederate Centennial Studies, #18. 12mo, stiff wraps, 141 pp. Lim. Edt., 450 copies. $15- bmk.

32 ..."Sectionalism in the Peace Convention of 1861." In: FHQ, July 1961, v.XXXX, #1, p. 53-81.

33 **KEGLEY, Tracy M.**
"Bushrod Rust Johnson, soldier & teacher." In: TennHQ, 1948, v.7, p. 249-258. See: E. Polk Johnson.

34 **KEIDEL, George C.**
"Colonel Magnus Thompson's Little Confederate museum, Leesburg, Va.," In: Wm. & Mry. Quart., 2nd ser., 1934, v.XIV, p. 171-172. Brief descp. some of contents of museum.

35 ..."Jeb Stuart in Maryland. June, 1863.." In: Md. HM, 1939, v.XXXIV, p. 161-164. Stuart in Md., after Gettysburg, 1863.

36 **KEILEY, Anthony M.**
"In Vinculis; or, the Prisoner of War. Being the Experience of a Rebel in Two Federal Pens, interspersed with Reminiscences of the Late War; Anecdotes of Southern Generals, etc." By a Virginia Confederate. N.Y., Blelock & Co., 1866. 12mo, cl, (2), 216pp. Swem shows imprint of Petersburg, Va., 1866. Sabin-37168. notes others have author's name on t/p, "a well written, interesting, amusing narr.

37 ..."The Model Infantryman". In: Rev. J.W. Jones's ANV Memorial Vol." p. 261-292, with Wm. Allan's Jax. Valley Campaing.'..."Our Fallen Heroes, address on Memorial day at Loudon Park." In SHSP, 1879, v.VII, p. 373-384.

38 ..."Prison-Pens North." In: SHSP, 1890, v.XVIII, p. 333-340. Experiences of Keiley in Northern prisons.

39 ..."Prisoner of War, or five months among the Yankees. Being a narrative of the crosses, calamities & consolations of a Petersburg militiaman during an enforced summer resident north. By A Rifleman, Esq. Gent." Ricmond, Va., West & Johnston, (1865). 8vo, cl, 120pp. jk-137 $100-
..."1866 edt. pub. in N.Y., authors name. The 1865 edt. was largely destroyed by fire at the capture of Richmond.

40 ..."Treatment of Prisoners." In: SHSP, 1876. v.I, p. 259-270. Review of Keiley's book. But part of an entire article, p. 225-327.

40a ..."Our Dead. An Address delivered at Loudon Cemetery, near Baltimore, June 5, 1870, at the Confederate Graves." Richmond, Va., Geo. W. Gary, 1879. 8vo, wraps, 14pp. $42.50.

41 **KEILEY, Benjamin J.**
"McClellan for Peace." In: SHSP, 1903, v.31, p. 45-48.

41a **KEIM, Dr. Lon. W.**
"Confederate General Service Accoutrement Plates." Omaha, NE, The Author, 1985. 4to, cl, 300pp. (500 specimens). $37.50. Deluxe $50.

42 **KEITH, Harold Verne**
"Rifles for Watie." N.Y., Crowell & co (1957). 12mo, cl, illus., 332pp. (fiction) The Indian General Stand Watie, CSA.

43 **KEITH, James, Judge**
"Unveiling statue to William Smith, Governor William Smith & Major-General CSArmy, hero & patriot." (from Richmond Times-Dispatch, May 30, 1906) In: SHSP, 1906, v.34, p. 222-238. See: Gen. Wm. Smith.

44 **KEITH, K.D.**
"Military Operations: Sabine Pass, 1861-1863. In: Burke's Texas Almanac, 1883. p. 65-69.
...Reprint in Tex. State Hist. Ass'n. program, 67th annual meeting, Apr. 26-27, 1963. Austin, Texas, (5)pp. $5.00

45 **KEITH, Katherine Isham**
"The record of the Black Horse troop." In: Fauquier (Va) Hist. Soc. Bul. 1924, v.IV, p. 435-460.

46 **KEITT, Laurence Massillon & Sue Sparks**
"Letters from the Provisional Congress of the Confederacy, 1861. Edt: Elmer Don Herd, Jr." In: SCHMag. Jan. 1960, v.61, p. 19-25, notes. Letters to Jas. H. Hammond & Susan Sparks Keitt, from Montgomery Feb. 13, May 15, 1861 & Richmond, Aug. 20, 1861. Sue Sparks Keitt to a Northern friend, Mar. 4, 1861. Edt: Elmer Don Herd, Jr., In: SCHM, v.62, #1, 1961.

47 **KELEHER, William A.**
"The Confederate invasion of New Mexico.: In: his 'Turmoil in New Mexico,' Sante Fe, Rydal press, 1952. p. (141)-210.

48 **KELL, John McIntosh**
"Recollections of a Naval Life, Including the Cruises of the Confederate States Steamers "Sumter" & "Alabama." Wash-

49 ..."Story of the Sinking of Alabama. Given to Alfred Iverson Branham, forty-six years ago, June 1883." (Atlanta, Ga., Cornell print, 1930) 8vo, wraps, 16pp.

49a ..."Century Mag., April 1886. Kell accuses Philip d. Haywood's 'Cruise of the Ala. by one of the crew' an imposter. In this issue three articles on Haywood, who answers Kell in the July 1886 issue. Century Mag., March 1887 announces Haywood as a fraud.
See: Norman Dalaney's CWTI articles reprinting this expose from Century.

49b ..."Cruise & Combats of the "Alabama." In: B&L, v.4, p.600-14, ills, maps, ports.

50 **KELLER, Allan**
"Morgan's Raid." Indianapolis & N.Y., Bobbs-Merrill (1961). 8vo, cl, d/w, 272pp. ports, illus., map.$35-bmk.

51 ..."Canada & the Civil War." In: CWTI, Nov. 1964. v.III, #7, p. 49-54, illus.

52 ..."A 'Thunderbolt' out of the South." In: CWTI, June 1963, v.II, #3, p. 6-9, 34-37, illus., map, port. John Hunt Morgan led 3,400 Southern horsemen across Ohio river on raids.

53 ..."Johnston vs Sherman-on the road to Atlanta." In: CWTI, Dec. 1962, v.1, #8, p. 18-22, 32-35, illus., ports, map.

54 ..."Queen Varina." In: CWTI, June 1962, v.1, #3, p. 18-21, pl., ports. Jefferson Davis secretary & wife.

54a **KELLER, Mark**
"Alabama Plantation Life in 1860 - Gov. Benjamin Fitzpatrick's 'Oak Grove.'" In: AHQ, 1976, v.38, #3, p.218-27.

55 **KELLER, Martha Carolina**
"Love & rebellion, a story of the civil war & Reconstruction." N.Y., J.S. Ogilvie, (1891). The sunnyside series, no. 26. 12mo, cl, 235 pp. Includes the seige of Vicksburg.

56 ..."Severed at Gettysburg." Chicago: J.S. Ogilvie & Co., (1887). "The fireside series." 12mo, cl, 256pp. Miss Keller lived at Leesburg, Fla. Both books received glowing reviews in the Confederate Veteran.

57 **KELLERSBERGER, Gertulius**
"Erlebnisse eines schweizerischen in Californien, Mexico und Texas zur Zeit des amerikanischen Burgerkrieges, 1861-1865, von G. Kellersberger." Zurich: Buchdruckerei Juchli & Beck, 1896. 8vo, cl, 196 (1), front (port).

58 ..."Memoirs of an engineer in the Confederate Army in Texas." Translated from German by Helen S. Sundstrom (Zurich: Juchli & Beck, 1896) Austin, Texas: Privately printed for University of Texas Library, 1957. (Hereford, Texas: A.J. Schroeter, 1964) Reprint. 8vo, 48pp.

59 ..."The First (and last) Rocket Battery of the Confederate Army in Texas." In: CWTI June 1963, v.II, #3, p. 26-27, plate.

60 **KELLN, Albert L.**
"Confederate Submarines." (Richmond) Va. Mag. Hist. Biob. July 1953, v.61, #3, p. 293-303.

60a **KELLY, Dennis P.**
"Battle of Shepherdstown." In: CWTI, Nov. 1981, v.20, #7, p.8-15, 32-5, ills, map, ports.

61 **KELLY, Henry B.**
"Port Republic, by Henry B. Kelly, Colonel C.S.A. (8th Louisiana)." Phila: J.B. Lippincott co, 1886. 8vo, wraps, front(map), 27pp. $200-R. One battle in Stonewall's Valley Campaign.

61a **KELLY, James**
"Bibliography of the writings of Stanley F. Horn." In: THQ, Winter 1981, v.40, #4, p.395-400.

61b **KELLY, Maud McClure**
"Gen. John Herbert Kelly, the Boy General of the Confederacy." In: AHQ, 1947, v.9, #1, p.9-114.

62 **KELLY, Thomas**
"Jefferson Davis & His Cabinet, with Gen. Lee in the Council Chamber at Richmond." New York, Thomas Kelley, 1866.

62a **KELLY, William Milner**
"A History of the Thirtieth Alabama Volunteers (Infantry), Confederate States Army." In: AHQ, 1947, v.9, #1, p.115-167.

63 **KELSEY, Albert Warren**
"Autobiographical notes & memoranda by Albert Warren Kelsey, 1840-1910." (For private circulation only.) (Baltimore, Munder-Thomsen press, 1911) 8vo, cl, front(port), 129, (1)pp. $100-B $75- 200 numbered copies. On cover: "On the Blockade, 1861 to 1863. Cotton planting in the Confederacy."

64 **KELSEY, D.M.**
"Deeds of daring by both blue & gray; thrilling narratives of personal adventure...on each side the line during the great civil war." Phil: & St. Louis: Scammell & co., 1883. 8vo, cl, illus., including front, xxi, (i), 23-608pp.
...Bost: D.L. Guernsey, 1884.
...Phila: Scammel & co, 1890, New revised, enlarged & illus. edt., xxi, 23-672. illus., ports.
...Chicago: Werner & co., 1898.
...NY, Saalifield pub., 1907. "The Blue & Gray. The Amer. Soldier, North & South."

65 **KELSEY, Jasper**
"The Battle of Shiloh." In: CV, Feb. 1917. v.XXV, p. 71-74.

65a **KEMP, Kathryn W.**
"Dear Asa Hartz (pseud. of CSA Maj. George McKnight)." Rhymed political satire on exchange on Union & Confederate prisoners of war, from a Confederate pen (Spring 1864)." In: Atl. HJ, Fall 1985, v.29, p.47-54.

66 **KEMP, Robert, Mrs.**
"When Sherman Paid us a Visit." Gulfport, Miss., n.d. Connell Pr., 19--. wraps, 21pp.
...New Orleans: Garcia Stationery-n.d., 39pp.

67 **KEMP, Vernon E.**
"The Lee Memorial Fund." In: S.R.Va. Quart. Mag., July 1922, v.I, p. 19-21.

68 **KEMPER, James Lawson, Gov., Va.**
"Inauguration of the Jackson Statue, Tuesday, Oct. 26, 1875. Gov. Kemper's address & the Oration by Rev. Moses D. Hoge, D.D. (Richmond?) 1875. 8vo, wraps, 15pp. In: SHSP-1885, v.13, p. 311-314 (See-Mose Hoge)

69 **KENAN, Thomas S., Col.**
"Sketch of the Forty-third regiment North Carolina Troops (infantry)." (Raleigh, 1895) 8vo, wraps, cover title, 26pp.+12pp. Confed. Museum. "prepared in 1895 by officers & men who were participants in its movements." $35-
...Recent reprint, n.p. (c. 1967), n.d. See: Jno. W. Moore's "Roster N.C. Troops" III, p. 196-223. Forty-third Inf., Company A thru K. Also: Walter Clark's "Several Regiments," v.III, p. 1-20 reprint.

70 **KENDALL, George E.**
"An humble belisarius; or, the life of a 'Johnny Reb,' by 'Sonander"...Richmond, Va., Ware, Duke & Taylor, 1887. 12mo, wraps, 26pp. $90-ob.
...Richmond, Ware & Duke printers, 1892. 12mo, wraps, 24pp. Dorn-II, 1151 1/2.
...Suffolk, Va., Robt. Hardy Pub., 1986. 8vo, wraps, 26pp.

71 **KENDALL, John Smith**
"Recollections of a Confederate Officer." Louisiana Historical Quarterly, vol. 19-1946, p. 1041-1228. Narrative of John Irwin Kendall, father, with additional material from his assocs.

72   **KENDALL, John Smith, Edt.**
"Muster Rolls of the Fourth Louisiana Regiment of Volunteers, CSA." New Orleans: LHQ, April, 1947, v.30, #2, p. 481-522.

73   **KENDALL, Lane C.**
"The Interregnum in Louisiana in 1861." New Orleans: LHQ, Apr. 1933, v.XVI, p. 175-208; July, p. 375-408; Oct. p. 639-669; XVII, 1934, p. 124-138; p. 339-348; p. 524-536.

73a **KENEALLY, Thomas**
"The Confederates." N.Y., Harper-Row Pub., 1980. 8vo, cl, 440p. $13.
...N.Y., G.P.Putnam's Berkley Pub. Corp., 1983. 8vo, paper, 448p. $5.
Said to be the finest novel since Crane's "Red Badge of Courage."

74   **KENNAWAY, John Henry, Sir, Baronet**
"On Sherman's track; or, the South after the war." London: Seeley, Jackson & Halliday, 1867. 12mo, cl, front, pls., x, 320pp. (jk1142) $85.

74a **KENNEDY, Chester**
"A look at an Arkansas Civil War unit & some of its members. " In: Carroll CHQ, Summer 1980, v.5, p.43-55.

75   **KENNEDY, Edward**
"Last work of Wheeler's Special Confederate Scouts." In: CV, Feb. 1924, v.XXXII, p. 60-61.

76   **KENNEDY, John Pendleton**
"Slavery the mere pretext for the rebellion not its cause. Andrew Jackson's prophecy in 1833. His last will & testament in 1843. Bequests of his three swords. Picture of the conspiracy. Drawn in 1863 by a Southern man." Phila: C. Sherman son & co., 1863. cover title, 8vo, 16pp. Signed: Paul Ambrose (pseud) From the National Intelligencer, Washington, March 1863.

77   **KENNEDY, Joseph Camp Griffith**
"The United States on the Eve of the Civil War. As described in the 1860 Census." Wash: US Civil War Centennial Commission, 1963 (1964). 8vo, pict. stiff wraps, facsm. illus., port, statistical tables, vii, 73pp.

78   ..."Preliminary report on the eighth Census, 1860, by Jos. C.G. Kennedy, Superintendent." Wash: Gov. Print. off., 1862. 8bo, cl, xvi, 294 pp. See: Sabin- #37425-32. The reprint is a condensation of Kennedy's report on the conditions of the country on eve of the conflict.

79   **KENNEDY, Kemble K., Mrs.**
"Report of the War Between the States com. In: UDCMag., May 1948, v.11, #5, p. 10-2. Proper designation of a series of military events between 1861-1865.

80   **KENNEDY, Philip W.**
"Union & Confederate Relations with Mexico." In: Duquesne Rev., 1966, v.XI, p. 47-63.

81   **KENNEDY, Robert Cobb**
"The Hotel Burners. The confessions of Robert Cobb Kennedy, the rebel incendiary. Ft. Lafayette (N.Y.) March 25, 1865-1866 A.M., etc." Folded 12mo sheet, unopened, pp. 6 (N.Y., 1865) (with) Case of Robert C. Kennedy. Head-Quarters, Department of East. N.Y. City, Mar. 20, 1865, etc. Folded 12mo sheet, pp. 4. (N.Y., 1865) Escaped from Johnson's Island, to Canada. Met a number of confederates. Sent with eight men to N.Y., to set fire to a number of public buildings, in retailiation for Sheridan's pillage. Sentenced to be hung for his arson.

81a **KENNEDY, Roger G.**
"Mourning a National Casualty." In: SWTI, March 1988, v.27, #1, p.34-39, 45-6, ills, some in color.

82   **KENNEDY, William V.**
"The cavalry battle of Brandy Station (Culpepper Co., Va., 9 June, 1863." In: Armor, Jan/Feb 1956, v.65, #1, p. 27-31.

port. See: Von Borcke (Heros), Fairfax Downey.

83 **KENNER, Duncan F.**
"Kenner's mission to Europe." In: Tyler Hist. Quart. Genea. Mag., July 1922, v.IV, p. 23-27. His mission to Europe from CS gov., 1865. Copied from the Brent-Kenner family book.
..."The Last Effort: the Secret Mission of the Confederate Diplomat Duncan F. Kenner." In: LH, v.22, p.67-95, 1981.

84 **KENNERLY, Samuel Jackson**
"The Story of Sam Tag, age from ten to fifteen from 1860-1865."N.Y., The Cosmopolitan press, 1911. 12mo, cl, 184pp. Boy's life on a plantation in Tennessee Valley during the War.

85 **KENNERLY, Sarah Law**
"Confederate juvenile imprints; children's books & periodicals published in the CSA 1861-1865." Ann Arbor: University microfilms, 1957 ('59). Positive microfilm of typescript, viii, 485 leaves. (bibliog. leaves 477-485). Thesis-University of Michigan: abstracted April, 18: 1441-1442, includes "classified bibliography of CSA juvenile imprints," (leaves 346-455.)

86 **"KENNESAW MOUNTAIN**
National Battlefield Park & The Atlanta Campaign, Georgia." (Wash: US Dept. of Interior, National Park Service, 1961. (reprint, 1961) 4to, pict. wraps, illus., maps, ports, 12, (4)pp.
..."Kennesaw Mountain National Battlefield Park, Georgia." (Chicago: Gunthorp-Warren print, Mar. 1946) US Dept. of Interior, Nat'l. Park Serv. 8vo, 6pp. folder, illus., map, insert fldg. map. See: "Junius Tertius."

87 **KENNESAW MOUNTAIN, Battle of.**
See: Samuel G. French, Maney's Brigade

88 **KENNETT, Lee**
"Strange Career of the (CSS) Stonewall." In: US Naval Inst. Proceed., 1968, v.XCIV, ii, 74-85pp.

89 **KENNON, Beverley**
"Fighting Farragut below New Orleans, by the Commander of the "Governor Moore," In: Cent., July 1886, n.s., v.X, illus., maps, port, p. 444-454. See: Marion Baker.

90 **KENNON, L.W.V.**
"The Valley Campaign of 1864; a Military Study." In: CV, Dec. 1918, v.XXVI, p. 517-523.

91 **KENNY, Thomas Moore**
"Two Graves, or: The Blue & the Gray, & other poems by Thomas Moore Kenny." Baltimore: Cusbing(sic) & Co., 1902. 12mo, cl, front(port), 160pp. Lim. Edt. $15.

92 **"KENTUCKIANS, To Arms!!!"**
Louisville, Ky., 1861. Broadsheet 7 1/4x3 1/2" (Jk-145) $250-. Six four-line stanzas, CSA patriotic fervor.

92a **KENTUCKY - Adjutant-General Report.**
"Report: Confederate Ky. Vols. 1861-5." Utica, Ky., McDowell Pubs., 1980. Reprint, 2 vols. $100.

93 **KENTUCKY Civil War Commission**
"Kentucky Remembers, Civil War Centennial manual for use of county committees, schools, newspapers, tourists, civic & patriotic organizations & Kentuckians at large." Lexington, KY., 1961. 8vo, wraps, fldg. map, 24pp.

93a **"KENTUCKY: Civil War Letters."** In: RKHS, July 1974, v.72, #3, p.262-75.

94 **"KENTUCKY Confederate Congress:**
Resolution of Congress in Kentucky 1861." Reprint. Lyndon, Kentucky. 1970, Mull-Wathen His't. Press. 8vo, stiff wraps, 34pp.(orig, 20, (1)pp. $10-. Contains: "President's Message," "Ordinance of the Kentucky Convention" (with list of names of those attending the convention) & "Communication of the Gov. of Ken-

tucky." Reprint: Robert Emmett McDowell introduction.

95 **KENTUCKY Confederates**
Buried at Camp Douglas, Illinois. In: Reg. KyHS, 1949, v.XLVI, p. 404-09. Dorn-II-62.

96 **KENTUCKY, Eighth,**
"The Eighth Kentucky at Pearl River" sign, "A.B." In: SB, ns, 1885-86, v.1, no. 5, p. 312.
"History of the State, etc, etc... By See: J.H. Battle, et. al.

97 ..."The Kentucky Invasion of 1862." In: CV, Sept. 1915, v.XXIII, p. 408-10.

97a **KENTUCKY in the Civil War:**
"History of the War, Edts: Wm. E. Connelley & E. M. Coulter. Chicago: Amer. Hist. Soc., 1922, v.II, Chap. LX, p.842-921, ills, ports.

98 **KENTUCKY Senate;**
"Joint resolutions. January 25, 1861. Special order for Saturday January 26. (Frankfurt), 1861. Folio bill, 2pp. (jk-142) $250. Responding to Virginia's call for a compromise over issue of secession, Senate appoint. Crittendon, Powell, Hawes, Bell, Wickliffe at comm., attend Peace Conference, Feb. 4, 1861 in Washington, DC, adequate guarantees of security to slave-holding states.

99 **KENTUCKY, TENNESSEE Reunion,**
Confederate Veterans, October 14-15, 1896. "The Sun Shines Bright," In: CV, Oct., 1896, v.IV, no. 10, p. 325-330. Ports. Officers of the First Kentucky "Orphan Brigade," 2pp. 20 ports.

100 **KENTUCKY (In SHSP)**
See: Braxton Bragg, Anderson C. Quisenberry, John H. Weller.

101 **KENTUCKY,**
"Declaration of Independence & Constitution of the Provisional Government of the State of Ky., with Message of the Governor." Bowling Green, 1861. W.N. Haldeman, State Printer. 8vo, wraps, 16pp. (Sabin-37503) Henkel Cat. no. 1090, May 1912: Rare memento, one of most curious political pretense in Hist. Late in 1861, a small region of Ky. came in possession of a CSA force. It's thought Col. G.W. Johnson, a Ky. CSA. called a "sovereignty convention." Delegates self-appointed or chosen by troops. It sat three days, passed above & went to Congress in Richmond. On Dec. 9, Ky. was admitted to Confed. Later in war this delegation held the capitol of state for one hour. Installed government & as inaugural began, city was recaptured.
..."Kentucky, a history of the state in Nine Editions (Volumes) Orig. Pub. 1885-8." W.H. Perrin, J.H. Battle, G.C. Kniffin. Easley, S.C., Southern Hist. Pub., 1978 & 1979 editions. $25 to $37.50 each.
Note: Each vol. contains a history of the state & ties with early Virginia and a listing of both CSA & Union troops in service from Kentucky.

102 **KENTUCKY: Adjutant General Report**
"Report of the Adjutant General of the State of Kentucky; Confederate Kentucky Volunteers War of 1861-1865. Printed by authority of the Legislature of Kentucky." (Frankfort, KY., Yeoman Office, T.H. Harney) 4to, cl, 1vols., vii, 985pp-1866; (2), 981, 178pp. Append., 1867. Dorn, 372A.
...(Frankfort, Ky., State Journal Co. Dec. 14, 1918 Vol. II, 4to, cl, color-flag Ky., 433pp.
...(Frankfort, Ky., State Journal co, 1915) 8vo, cl, (6), 749 pp. Comp: Abner Harris(slip verso front cover).

103 **KENTUCKY: Confederate Pensions Dept.,**
"List of Persons Receiving Pensions under Confederate Pensions Act. State of Kentucky. W.J. Stone, Commissioner."

104 **KERBY, Joseph Orten**
"Fort Pickens from the Confederate side." In: Relief of Fort Pickens, Florida. (1st expedition, 2nd Expedition by L.L. Langdon; Henry J. Hunt." In: Jour. Mil. Ser. Inst. Sept. 1909, v.XLV, p. 267-296.

Frankfort, Ky., State Journal, 1920? 8vo, wraps, 66pp.

105 **KERBY, Robert Lee**
"The Confederate invasion of New Mexico & Arizona, 1861-1862." Los Angeles, Calif., Westernlore pr, 1958. 12mo, cl, dj, illus., facsms, maps, ports, xix, (1), 23-159pp. Lim. Edt., 850 copies. Vol. 13 of Westernlore's Great West & Indian Series. Sibley plan to take California. $75.

106 **KERKSIS, Stanley**
"Confederate States buttons (or Army & Navy 1861-1865." In: Mil. collector & hist., winter 1960, v.12, p. 103-106. facsm., views notes.

107 **KERKSIS, Sydney C.**
"The bogus $20 Confederate note (25 July 1861)", In: Numismatist, May 1951, v.64, pp.507-13, facsm., bibliog.

108 ..."A dangerous counterfeit note (2 Sept. 1861) In: Numismatist, Nov. 1951, v. 64, 1179.

109 ..."Johnny Reb & His Buttons." In: Natl. Button Bul., Sept. 1957, p. 1-7, v.16, p.289-91. CS Army buttons, 1861-65.

110 ..."Enigmatical Confederate Currency issues." In: Numismatist, March 1951. v.64, 255-62p., facsm., bibliog. On "essay" Notes of $10 & $20s & a $10 note, all dated 2 Sept., 1862.

111 ..."Field Artillery Projectiles of the Civil War, 1861-65." Atlanta (Kennesaw ?) Ga., Phoenix 30 Bmk Press, (1968) 3rd printing, (1970) 4to, cl, dj, 307pp., 233 photos, 24 drawings, append., bibliog., index, & gloss. Lim. 500 copies. $40-B.

112 ..."Heavy Artillery Projectiles of the Civil War, 1861, by Sydney C. Kerksis & Thomas S. Dickey." Kennesaw, Ga., Phoenix Press (1972) 4to, cl, dj, ills., 277 pp. Edt.: 500 Copies. $35.

113 ..."A newly discovered Confederate Treasury note: the $10 manouvrier." In: Numismatist, Sept. 1952, v.65, p.870-76, facsms., corresp., C.G. Memminger, Sect. CS Treasury, 1861.

114 ..."Plates & Buckles of the American Military, 1795-1874." Kennesaw, Ga. The Gilgal Press, 1974. op. 4to, cl, dj, 568pp. illus. $40-B

115 ..."State of Georgia Treasury notes." In: Numismatist, Feb., 1951, v.64, p. 130-140, facsms, Checklist, 1862-1865."

116 ..."State of Georgia Treasury Notes (1862): addenda & classification revisions." In: Numismatist, Nov. 1953, v. 66, p. 1157-1163. facsms. Article with: L. Miles Raisig.

117 ..."A mystery of the Confederate Currency solved." In: Numismatist, July 1950, v. 63, p. 412-419. facsms. On the $100 CSTreas. note issue Feb. 17, 1864.

117a ..."The Atlanta Papers, compiled & arranged with notes by Sydney C. Kerksis. Biographical sketches of the authors by Lee A. Wallace, Jr., Index by Margie Riddle Bearss." Dayton, Oh., Morningside Press, 1980. 8vo, cl, 900p., ills, ports, maps (end sheets).

118 **KERN, Albert**
"Bullets used in the Civil War." In: CV, July 1916, v.XXIV, p. 310-311.

119 **KERR, Homer, Dr., Edt.**
"Fighting with Ross' Texas Cavalry Brigade, CSA." Hillsboro, Texas, Hill Junior College pr., 1976. 8vo, cl, dj, illus., maps, index, 275pp. Special Cavalry Edt., Leather, 25copies. $55. Complete Roster of 9th Tex. Cav. Reg., also the 3rd, 6th & 27th Tex. Cav.

119a **KERR, Homer Lee**
"Battle of Elkhorn, the Gettysburg of the

Trans-Mississippi West." See: 'Essays on the American Civil War.' 1968. pp.32-44.

120 **KERR, John Leeds**
"The Story of a Southern Carrier, the Louisville & Nashville, which revealed to the world the military value of the railroad, prospered during the war of secession & later played a recognized part in the industrial reconstruciton of the South." N.Y., Young & Ottley, 1933. tall 8vo, cl, (8), 67pp.

121 **KERR, W.J.W.**
"Execution of Capt. Henry Wirz." In: CV, Sept. 1903, v.XI, p. 412-413.

122 **KERR, William Schomberg Robert**
See: Lothian, Marquis of.

123 **KERSHAW, C.D., Miss**
"Richard Kirkland, c.s.a." Compiled by Miss. C.D. Kershaw at the request of the John D. Kennedy Chapter, U.D.C." (Camden, S.C., 1910) News Print. 9vo, wraps, 32pp., illus., port. $25.

124 **KERSHAW, John, Rev.**
"Address delivered before the Ladies' Memorial Association & Citizens of Charleston, on Memorial Day, March 10, 1893." Charleston, S.C. 1893. 8vo, wraps, 8pp. On the nature of the Southern Soldier.

125 **KERSHAW, Joseph Brevard, Gen.**
"Battle of Chickamauga." In SHSP, 1885, v.13, p. 388-393.

126 ..."Kershaw's Brigade at Gettysburg." In: B & L, v.III, p. 331-338.

127 ..."Operations of Kershaw's Division(in the Battle of Wilderness)" In: SHSP, 1878, v.6, p. 80-82.

128 ..."Report of...Battle of Gettysburg. In: SHSP, 1877, v.IV, p. 178-184.

129 ..."Richard Kirkland, the humane hero of Fredericksburg." In: SHSP, 1880, v.8, p. 186-188.

130 ..."Kershaw's brigade at Fredericksburg." In: B & L, v.III, p.95. Gen. Kershaw corrects an error by Ransom's 'Narrative,' Dec. 6th, 1887."

131 **KERSHAW, T. Bentley**
"The Truth of the American Question, being a reply to the prize essay of Mr. Rowan." Manchester, Eng., Southern Independence ass'n., (1864) 8vo, wraps, 32pp.

132 **KERWOOD, John Richard**
"Turner Ashby-his daring was proverbial." In: CWTI, Aug. 1968, v.VII, #5, p. 18-25, 28-30. illus., ports.

133 **KETCHEY, John A.**
"Life, adventures & suffering of J.A. Ketchey, written by himself." Salisbury, N.C., Author, 1874. 8vo, wraps, 91pp., port on t.p., Civil war, 8-15pp. Dorn-II, 768.

133a **KETTELL, T. P.**
"Southern Wealth & Northern Profits, intro: Fletcher Green." University: Alabama Press, 1965. 8vo, cl, dj, 181pp. tables. index. $25.

134 **KEY, Thomas J.**
"Two Soldiers..." See: Wirt A. Cate, Edt.

135 **KEY, William**
"The Battle of Atlanta & the Georgia Campaign." N.Y., Twayne Pub., (1958) 8vo, cl, dj, illus., sketches, front, 91, (3)pp. $12.50jk-122
...Atlanta, Ga., Peachtree Pub. (1981) 2nd edition, revised, xiv, 96pp.

135a **KEYES, Francis Parkinson (Wheeler)**
"Madame Castel's lodger." N.Y., Farrar, Straus & Cudahy, 1962. 8vo, cl, 471pp, ills, bibliog. front. $25. Novel of P. G. T. Beauregard.

136 **KEYS, Thomas Bland**
"The Federal Pillage of Anderson, South Carolina: Brown's Raid." In: S. Car. Hist. Mag., 1975, v.LXXVI, p. 80-86.

136a ..."Tarheel Cossack, W. P. Roberts, youngest Confederate General." Orlando, Fla., The Author, 1983. 8vo, wraps, 103pp. $6.

137 **KEYSVILLE GUARDS-**
"Economic factors & British Neutrality 1861-1865." In: "The Historian," Aug. 1963, v.XXV, #4, p. 451-465, notes.

138 **KIBBY, Leo P.**
"Book Review Reference for a Decade of Civil War Books, 1950-1960." San Jose, California, State College, Jan. 1961. Spartan Bookstore. 4to, decr. stiff wraps, vii, 64pp. 1960-Supplement, 13pp.

139 **KIBLER, Forrest, Mrs.**
"First Confederat cemetery---established by Mary Green of Georgia." In: UDCMag., June 1952, v.15, #6, p. 5, 8-9, 12, views. 1865. On the Resaca CSA cemetery, Ga., estb. 186-

140 **KIBLER, James Allen**
"Letters from a Confederate Soldier." In: Tyler QHGMag., Oct. 1949, v.XXXI, p. 120-127. A Corp. in Co. F., 10th Va. Reg. May 9, 1861-Mar. 31, 1863.

141 **KIBLER, Lillian Adele**
"Benjamin F. Perry South Carolina Unionist." Durham, N.C., Duke University pr (1946) 8vo, cl, dj, facsm, pl, ports, incl. front, xiii, (2), 562pp. bibliog-index, (523)-562. Opposed secession but loyal to CSA in the war.

142 ..."Unionist Sentiment in South Carolina in 1860." (Baton Rouge, La.) JSH, Aug. 1939. v.IV, #3, p. 346-366. Bmk $10-

142a **KIDD, Jack Russell**
"Echoes of the War Between the States." Gaffney, S.C., 1971, Southern Renaissance Press. 8vo, pict. wraps, 27pp.

143 **KILLEBREW, J.B.**
"Every inch a Hero." In: SB, ns, 1886/7, v.II, p. 771-772. Sam Davis.

144 ..."The Hanging of Sam Davis, by Col. J.B. Killebrew." In: Annals of Tennessee," 1878, p. 294-298. Also in John B. Lindsley's "Military Annals of Tennessee," p. 168-171.

145 **KILLGORE, Gabriel M.**
"Vicksburg Diary: the Journal of Gabriel M. Killgore." In: CWH, March 1964, v.X, #1, p. 33-53.

146 **KILLIN, Hugh Edward**
"The Texans & the California column." Lubbock, Tex., (Thesis (MA) Texas technological college, 1931. 4to, mimeographed, viii, 127 leaves. Gen. Albert Sidney Johnston & Gen. James H. Carleton in military phase of the civil war in the Southwest.

KILPATRICK-DAHLGREN Raid Against Richmond.
See: Cavalry raid by Custer, Wade Hampton, G. Watson James, Jno. Wm. Jones, Virgil C. Jones.

147 **KILPATRICK, Emmett**
"Le departement executif des Etats Confeders d'Amerique, 1861-1865." Paris: E. De Boccard, 1924. 8vo, cl, 3p, 1f, 339pp.

148 **KILPATRICK, Hugh J.**
See: Edward L. Wells.

149 **KILPATRICK, James Jackson**
"The Sovereign States. Notes of a Citizen of Virginia. Chicago: Henry Regnery Co., 1957. 8vo, cl, xi, 347pp.

150 **KIMBALL, William Joseph, Edt.**
"The Bread Riots in Richmond, 1863." In: CWH, June 1961, v.VII, #2, p. 149-154.

151 ..."As a Confederate viewed the attack by Burnside." In: CWTI, Dec. 1862, v.1, #8, p. 30-35, illus., map, ports.

152 ..."Richmond in Time of War." Boston: Houghton Mifflin (1960) "Research Series, 5." $8-. 8vo, cl, (or, wraps), x, 166pp. table, bibliog. (p. 1v) excerpts diaries, newspapers, reminiscences.

153 ..."Starve or Fall: Richmond & its People, 1861-1865." Ann Arbor: University Microfilms Int. Monogr. Pub. on Demand, vi, 214pp. $13.50

154 ..."Richmond Begins the Work of War." (Richmond) Va. Cavl., Spring 1961. v.X, #4, p. 13-18. ports, illus.

155 ..."As Richmond girded for war in Spring of 1861." In: CWTI, Nov. 1963, v.II, #7, p. 36-40, illus.

156 ..."Ransom's North Carolina Brigade served the Confederacy bravely." In: CWTI, May, 1962, v.1, #2, p. 45-47, illus., ports. Malvern Hill to Five Forks.

157 ..."Richmond 1865: The Final Three Months." (Richmond) Va. Cavl., Summer 1969. v.XIX(misnumbered XVIII) #1(misnumbered-#5) p. 38-47. Illus., ports(1-color).

158 ..."War-Time Richmond." (Richmond Va. Cavl., Spring 1962, v.XI, #4, p. 33-40, facsms, color portrait Jeff. Davis.

159 **KIMBLE, June, Capt.**
"Tennesseeans at Gettysburg-The Retreat." In: CV, 1910, v.XVIII, p. 460-

160 **KIMMEL, Stanley Preston**
"The Mad Booths of Maryland." Indianapolis: Bobbs-Merrill (1940), 9vo, cl, dj, illus., 400pp. $40-B, $15-

161 ..."Mr. Davis's Richmond." N.Y., Coward-McCann(1958).4to, cl, dj, illus., ports, maps, facsms, 214pp. N.Y., Bramhall House, 1958) dj-bmk $25-

...N.Y., Dover publications, 1970 8vo, stiff wraps, front, illus., 418 pp. 2nd revised & enlarged edition with 83 illus. atg-$40-. Stranger than fiction, best on Booth.

162 **KINCHELOE, David H.**
"The Life & Character of Jefferson Davis." In: CV, June 1917, v.XXV, p. 254-257.

163 **KINCHEN, Oscar A.**
"Confederate Operations in Canada & the North: A Little-Known Phase of the American Civil War." North Quincy, Mass., Christopher Pub., 1970. 8vo, cl, d/w, 254pp. dj $20-bmk

164 ..."Daredevils of the Confederate Army. The Story of the St. Albans Raiders." Boston: Christopher Pub. House (1959) 23mo, cl, d/w, 171pp. $25-

165 ..."Some Unpublished Documents on the St. Albans Raid." In: Vermont History, 1964, v.XXXII, p. 179-183.

166 ..."Women Who Spied for the Blue & Gray." Phila Dorrance & Co., 1972. 9vo, cl, dj, bibliog., ix, 165pp. OP, CSA (14) the Union (7).

166a ..."General Bennett H. Young: Confederate Raider & a Man of Many Adventures." West Hanover, Mass., Christopher Pub., 1981. 8vo, paper, 163p., ills., bibliog. $9.

167 **KING WILLIAM ARTILLERY**
"Roster of King William Artillery." In: SHSP, 1896, v.24, p. 156-157.

168 **KING, Alexander C.**
"On Georgia's Influence on the Secession Movement." Savannah, Ga., Morning News print, 1917, 9vo, wraps, 66pp. An address in "Proceedings of the 78th Annual Meeting of Georgia Historical Society."

169 **KING, Alvy L.**
"Louis T. Wigfall: Southern Fire-eater." Baton Rouge: La. State Univ. Pr., 1970. 8vo, cl, d/w, ix, 259pp. $20-b

170 **KING, C. Richard**
"Col. John Sidney Thrasher: Superintendent of the Confederate Press Association.: In: Texana, Spring 1968, v.VI, #1, p. 56-86.

171 ..."The Shadow & the Glory." The Neill Family." In: Texana, 1971, v.IX, #2, p. 87-134, Confederate Letters.

171a **KING, H.C.**
"General Lee's Last Campaign, April 1865." In: Frank Leslie's Pop. Monthly, Oct. 1896, v.42, pp.378-86.

171b **KING, Henry T.**
"Sketches of Pitt County, a brief history of the county." Raleigh, N.C., Edwards &

Broughton, 1911. 8vo, cl, ports, ills, CSA. pp.118-68. $50.

172 **KING, J. Wayne**
"Death camp at Florence." In: CWTI, Jan. 1974. v.12, #9, p. 34-42, illus.

173 **KING, Jerlena**
"Jackson Lewis of the Confederate Creek Regiment." Oklahoma City: Chron. Okla. Spring, 1963, v.XLI, #1, p. 66-69, port.

174 **KING, John H., MD**
"Three Hundred Days in Yankee Prison. Reminiscences of War Life Captivity Imprisonment at Camp Chase, Ohio, by John H. King, MD. Surgeon Confederate Soldiers Home. Atlanta, Ga., 1904." (Jas. P. Daves, Atlanta, Ga.) 12mo, stiff wraps, port, 114pp. full lt. $200-bmk-105.
...Kennesaw, Ga., Continental Book, 1959, 12mo, cl, front(port), 114pp.

175 **KING, John Rufus**
"My Experience in the Confederate Army & in Northern Prisons, written from memory by John R. King. Stonewall Jackson chapter No. 1333, United Daughters of Confederacy." Clarksburg, W.Va., c. 1917. 8vo, front (port), 52pp.

176 **KING, Joseph Edward**
"Shoulder Straps for Aesculapius: The Vicksburg Campaign of 1863." Military Surgeon, March 1954, v.CXIV, p. 216-226.

177 **KING, Spencer Bidwell, Jr.**
"April in Macon (Ga.)" In: Ga. rev., summer 1960, v.14, p. 143-155. On the Union occupation of Macon under Bvt. Maj. Gen. Jas. Harrison Wilson, 20 Apr. 11th May, 1865 & his incompletely successful efforts to prevent looting & debauchery.

178 ..."Darien, the death & rebirth of a Southern town." Macon, Ga., Mercer University pr (1981) 8vo, cl, 112pp., illus., bibliog., index. Union officers directs negro troops to burn & sack the town, June 11, 1863.

179 ..."Impact of Impressment on North West Georgia, as seen in a petition of Floyd County Citizens, 1863." In: Ga. H.Q., December 1959, v.XLIII, #4, p. 411-418.

180 ..."Sound of drums: selected writings of Spencer B. King from his Civil War Centennial column appearing in the Macon(Georgia) Telegraph News, 1960-1965. Foreword by Henry Y. Warnock, Macon, Ga., Mercer University press, 1984. 8vo, cl, dj, xi, 543 pp. $33-

181 **KING, William B.**
"Gladiator" cotton claims. Statement...before the Committee on war claims, House of representatives. 63rd. Congr., 2nd. sess., HR6066, a bill for the relief of owners of certain cotton taken by the US authorities in Adams Co., Miss., in 1863 & shipped away on the steamer "Gladiator." Wash: GPO 8vo, sewn, 17pp.

182 **KING, William H.**
"Forrest's attack on Murfreesboro, July 13, 1862." In: CV, Nov. 1924, v.XXXII, p. 430-431, 437.

183 **KINGSBURY, Gilbert**
"Covington (Ky) in the war between the states." In: Christopher Gist HSP, 1949-1950, 113-129 leaves.

184 **KINGSBURY, T.B.**
"Chivalry." In: OLOD, Nov. 1975, v.3, #5, p. 659-674. Contrast between "Beast" Butler & Gen. Lee's Gen. Ord. #73.

185 ..."North Carolina Generals." In: OLOD, Dec. 1875, v.3, #6, p. 749-752.

186 ..."Did Gen. Lee offer to lead two brigades?" In: OLOD, Mar. 1875, v.2, #1, p. 46-51.

187 ..."Appomattox." p. 51-55.

188 ..."History Perverted," In: OLOD, April 1875, v.2 #2, p. 170-175.

189 ..."'The South must write its own histories." In: OLOD, May 1875, v.2, #3, p. 300-305.

190 …"The number of troops furnished by North Carolina: In: OLOD, June 1875, v.2 #4, p. 431-434.

191 …"North Carolina at the Gettysburg." In: OLOD, Nov. 1874, v.1, #3, p. 193-
…"Another Witness-Gettysburg." In: OLOD, Oct. 1975, v.3, #4, p. 457-463.

192 **KINNEY, John M., Compiler**
"Index to Applications for Texas Confederate Pensions." (65,000 vets) Austin: Archives Division Texas State Library, 1975. 4to, stiff wraps, VII, 354pp. Facsm, cover.

192a **KINNIER, B.J., Mrs.**
"Personal Sketches & Reminiscences of a Long Life." Richmond, Va., 1904. 12mo, cl, port, 92pp. $4.50.

192b **KINSLAND, William S.**
"The Civil War comes to Limpkin County." In: NGJ, 1984, v.1, summer, p.21-6.

192c …"The Dahlonega Mint, a Civil War Mystery." In: NGJ, Summer, 1984, v.1, p.39-46.

193 **KINSOLVING, Roberta Cary Corbin**
"Stonewall Jackson in winter quarters; memories of Moss Neck in the winter of 1862-1863." In: CV, Jan. 1912, v.XX, p. 24-26.

194 **"KINSTON, WHITEHALL & GOLDSBORO**
(North Carolina) Expedition, December 1862." N.Y., W.W. Howe, 1890, & Editor. 12mo, cl, 4-fldg. pls, port, 92, xiip. Anon. diary of New York Herald corresp. from New Berne, N.C. & member of Gen. J.G. Foster's command. Extracts from a contemporary newspaper, arrainged to form a consecutive narrative. Some copies contained no illus. (111) bmk-100-

195 **"KIRBY SMITH'S Confederacy:**
The Trans-Mississippi South, 1863-1865." New York: Columbia University press, 1972. 8vo, cl, dj, viii, 529pp. maps, index

196 …"Why the Confederacy Lost." In: Rev. of Politics, 1973, v.XXXV, p. 326-345.

197 **KIRBY, Eleanor G. Kirby**
"General Edmund Kirby Smith." In: CV, Sept. 1924, v.XXXII, p. 340-341.

197a **KIRBY, WALTER J.**
"Roll Call: The Civil War in Kent County, Maryland." Decorah, IA, 1985. 8vo, cl, 181pp, ills. A divided country as of a monument with both Union & CSA soldiers.

198 **KIRKLAND, Richard**
See: Joseph B. Kershaw.

199 **KIRKPATRICK, Arthur Roy, Maj.**
"Missouri's Delegation in the Confederate Congress." In: CWH, June 1959, v.V, #2, p. 188-198.

200 …"Missouri on the Eve of Civil War." (Columbia, Mo., Mo. Hist. Review, Jan., 1961, v.LV, #2, p. 99-108. illus.

201 …"Missouri in the Early Months of the Civil War." (Columbia, Mo., Mo. Hist. Review, April 1961, v.LV, #3, p. 235-266. illus, ports.

202 …"The Admission of Missouri to the Confederacy." (Columbia, Mo., Mo. Hist. Review, July 1961, v.LV, #4, p. 366-386. illus., ports.

203 …"Missouri, the twelfth Confederate State. Ann Arbor: University Microfilms, 1955. Typescript, 2, 372 leaves. ports. Thesis Univ. of Mo., abstracted: Dissert. abstracts, v. 15, p. 109. (Jan. 1955).

204 …"Missouri Secessionist Government 1861-5." In: Missouri Historical Review, Jan. 1951, Vol. XLV, #2, p. 124-137, illus.

205 **KIRWAN, Albert D.**
"The Confederacy." N.Y., Meridian Books (1959) Meridian Documents of American History. 12mo, cl, d/w, 320pp. Reprint: World Pub., wraps, $1.45

206 …"Johnny Green of the Orphan Brigade the Journal of a Confederate Soldier." (Lexington) University of Kentucky (1956) 8vo, cl, xxviii, 217pp. ports, maps, map as endsheets. ($2.50, 3.50) $5.00.

North Ky. Reg., 1st Brig. Ky. Inf. CSA $35-

...Civil War Book Club Ed't. Atg.

206a **KITCHENS, Ben Earl**
"Gunboats & Cavalry: a History of Eastport, Mississippi; with special emphasis on events of the War between the States." Florence, Alabama: Thornwood Books, 1985. 8vo, cl, dj, iii, 198pp, ills, index.

207 **KLAUS, Samuel, Edt.**
"The Milligan Case." N.Y. Alfred Knopf, 1929. 8vo, cl, 476 p. "American Trial series." $25- "Civil liberties guaranteed by the Constitution to be safeguarded in war or peace. Milligan was jailed as a Copperhead. See: Lambdin P. Milligan.

208 **KLAXON (------)**
"Stout hearts." In: Blackwood's, 1935, v.CCXXXVII, p. 540-550. Use by South of latest naval inventions to break naval blockade.

209 **KLEIN, Frederic S.**
"Man on a Tightrope." In: Amer. Hist. April 1966, v.1, #2, p. 12-24. ports, illus. Role of James Buchanan. (couldn't necessarily prevent the civil war)

210 ...The Great Copperhead Conspiracy." In: CWTI, June 1965, v.IV, #3, p. 21-26, illus., facm. port. They lacked leadership & clear-cut aims. Otherwise it may have crippled the Union.

211 **KLEIN, Maury**
"Edward Porter Alexander." Athens: University of Georgia Press, (1971). 9vo, cl, dj, xii, 279 pp. $30-r. front, port.

212 ..."E.P. Alexander-a personality profile." In: CWTI, June 1969, v.VIII, #3, p. 4-12, illus., map, ports. "One of the most able in Lee's army, most reliable memoir written by a Confederate."

..."E.P. Alexander," reprint: N.Y., Burt Franklin, 1972 (Resource & source works series American classics in hist. & SS.)

213 ..."Copperhead Secret Societies in Illinois during the Civil War." In: Journ. Ill. State Hist. Soc., Summer, 1955, v.XLVIII, p. 152-180.

214 ..."Phineas C. Wright, the Order of American Knights, & the Sanderson Expose." In: CWH, March 1972, v.XVIII, #1, p. 5-23.

215 ..."The state between the war: the L & N in wartime, 1861-5." In his "History of L & N Railway," a chapter, p. 27-44. N.Y., Macmillan (1972) Louisville & Nashville Railway.

216 **KLEMENT, Frank L.**
"(Henry B.) Carrington & the Golden Circle Legend in Indiana during the Civil War." In: Ind. Mag. Hist., 1965, v.LXI, p. 31-52.

217 ..."The Copperheads in the Middle West." Chicago: Univ. of Chicago press (1960) 8vo, cl, dj, ports, facsms, xiii, 341pp. See: Gray Wood, with whom he differs. $20- bmkIII

218 ..."Copperheads & Copperheadism in Wisconson: Democratic opposition to the Lincoln administration." In: Wis. Mag., hist. Spring, 1959, v.42, p. 182-188, view, notes.

219 ..."Middle Western Copperheadism & the genesis of the Granger Movement, 1860-63." In: MVHR, Mar. 1952, v.38, p. 679-694. notes.

220 ..."The Limits of Dissent: Clement L. Vallandigham & the Civil War." Lexington: Ky. Univ. Press., 1970 8vo, cl, d/w, xii, 351pp.

221 ..."Rumors of Golden Circle Activity in Iowa during the Civil War Years." In: Annals of Iowa, 1965, v.XXXVII, p. 523-536.

222 ..."Clement L. Vallandigham's Exile in the Confederacy, May 25-June 17, 1863." (Houston, Tex.) JSH, May, 1965. v.XXXI, #2, p. 149-163. 8-

222a ..."Dark Lanterns: Secret Political Societies, Conspiracies, & Treason Trails in the Civil War." Baton Rouge: Louisiana University Press, 1984. 8vo, cl, dj, xii, 263pp, ills, bibliog. $25. Sums up his work on dissidents during the war as myth

223 **KLINE, P.W.**
"With Flash of Steel Amid Hearts of Oak; a description of the first battle between modern ironclads; the memorable battles of the Confederate ram Virginia, otherwise known as the Merrimac, & the Federal fleet, including the Monitor in Hampton Roads, Virginia, Mar. 8 & 9, 1862." Newport News, Va., (c. 1904) 8vo, wraps, cover title, 22pp. Kline was aboard Merrimac during battle. David R. Smith, #54.

224 **KLINE, Sherman J.**
"General Stand Watie, a great soldier-statesman of the Cherokee Nation (1806-1871). In: Americana, Oct. 1929, v.XXIII, p. 421-426.

225 **KLOSS, Gerald**
"Was Dr. Mudd guilty? Historians disagree about his involvement in the assassination of Abraham Lincoln." In: CWT, July 1960, v.II, #4(OS) p. 7-8, illus., ports.

226 **KNAPP, David, Jr.**
"The Confederate Horsemen." N.Y., Vantage Press (1966) 8vo, cl, d/w, illus., 302pp. $6-b

227 ..."Magnificent Rebel." Mobile, Ala., Gill Print & Stationery(1967) 8vo, illus., stiff wraps, 236pp.

228 ..."A New Source on the Confederate Exodus to Mexico: the Two Republics." (Lexington, Ky.) JSH, Aug. 1953, v.XIX, #3, p. 364-373.

229 **KNAUS, W.H., Col.**
"Honor roll of Confederate dead in Ohio." In: CV, v.6, p. 3-8, 168-169.

230 **KNAUSS, William H.**
"The Story of Camp Chase a History of the Prison & its Cemetery, together with other cemeteries where Confederate Prisoners are buried, etc." Nashville, Tenn. Methodist Episcopal Church, South. Smith & Lamar, 1906. Tall 8vo, cl, facsms, illus., incl. front, ports, fold. table, xx, 407pp. Append., list of the Confederate dead buried at Camp Chase, p. 345-404. $100-ob

231 ..."The Story of Camp Chase," In: Ohio Mag., 1906, v.I, p. 233-240, illus.

231a **KNIFFIN, Thomas Henderson**
"Kentucky of Kentucky; a romance of the blue grass region." N.Y. Cochrane Pub., 1909. 12mo, cl, 163p. Fiction. The Morris family of Lexington & Georgetown, before & during the war. In Alabama.

232 **KNIGHT, Edgar W.**
"The Influence of the Civil War on Education in North Carolina." In: N.C. Lit. & Hi. Assoc. Proc., 1918, v.XVIII,

233 **KNIGHT, Ethel**
"The Echo of the Black Horn. An authentic tale of "The Governor" of "The Free State of Jones(Miss.)" (Parthenon Press, on spine, Nashville Ten.? 1951) 8vo, cl, dj, sketches, ports(1), 328pp. Knight Family of Jones Co., Miss." The characters are real people, not a fictitious name in the book."

234 **KNIGHT, Lucian Lamar & Mrs. Horace M. Holden**
"Alexander H. Stephens The Sage of Liberty Hall. Georgia's Great Commoner" (Athens, Ga., McGregor print, 1928) 8vo, cl, illus., ports, v, 169, (1), (8)pp. ads. $25-b. Parts II & III compiled by Mrs. Horace M. Holden (Mary Corry Holden)
...n.p., 1930 edition, reprint..... bmk $25-
...Athens, Ga., McGregor print, 1960. 1960 reprint.

235 ..."Memorials of Dixie-Land, Orations, Essays, Sketches & Poems on topics Historical, Commemorative, Literary & Patriotic." Atlanta, Ga., Byrd print, 1919.

8vo, cl, illus., incl. front, xii, 604pp. index $50-

236 ..."Indigent Confederate Veterans in Georgia, 1894." In: Ga. Genealog. Soc. Quart., 1981, v.17, #1, p. 43-59.

237 ..."Reminiscences of Famous Georgians, embracing episodes & incidents in the lives of the Great Men of the State, also an appendix devoted to extracts from speeches & addresses." Atlanta, Ga., Franklin-Turner co, 1907-08. 12mo, 1/2 Lt., xxi, (1), 763;II, xviii, 723 pp. errata slip (v.I), 33 illus. $45-

238 ..."Stone Mountain; or, the Lay of the Gray Minstrel; an epic poem in twenty-four parts commemorative of the South's Confederate, pre-historic, colonial, revolutionary & world-war days, to which are added a number of other poems, patriotic, humorous & occasional, besides a few prose selections. Atlanta, Ga., Johnson-Dallis co, 1928. 12mo, cl, front, illus., ports, xvi, 277 pp.

239 **KNIGHT, Mac, Major**
"The Real Jefferson Davis." Battle Creek, Mich., Pilgrim Magazine Co., 1904. 12mo, cl, 203pp. Jk-$20

240 ..."John Haroldson." Broadfoot attributes Knight as author of this famous ditty, while prisoner of war at Johnson's Island. After seeing the advertisement for "chamber lye," in the Selma, Alabama Gazette.

241 **KNOLES, George Harmon, Edt.**
"The Crisis of the Union, 1860-61." Baton Rouge, Louisiana State Univ. Press, 1965. 8vo, cl, viii, 115pp.

242 **KNOX, Dudley W.**
"General Index: Official Records of Union & Confederate Navies in War of Rebellion." New York, Antiquarian Press, 1964. Tk, 8vo, cl, 457pp.

243 **KNOXVILLE (Tenn.) Seige of...**
See: James D. Nance, Benjamin F. Wyly.

244 **KOENIG, Louis W.**
"The Most Unpopular man in the North." In: Amer. Hert., Feb. 1964, v.XV, #2, p. 12-15, 81-88, port, cartoons, color pl.

245 **KOLLOCK, Macartan Campbell**
"The Confederate Song Book, by a Confederate Veteran, containing the old war songs familiar to the soldiers of our Southland-also appendix giving dates of principal battles & other important events." Savannah, Ga., (Braid & Hutton) 1899. 12mo, cl, 5p., 60pp. (Tenn. State Lib.)

...(Greenwood, S.C., Drinkard Press, 1873. 8vo, wraps, 60pp., reprint.

246 ..."The Defenses of Charleston Harbor in 1863. A paper read before Confederate Veterans Association, April 16, 1893." In: CVAss'n. Savannah, Ga. Annual Report, 1895. Savannah: Geo. Nicols, 1895, p. 13-19.

247 **KOLLOCK, Susan M., Edt.**
"Letters of the Kollock & Allied Families, 1826-1884. Part IV, H.C. McDonnell to George J. Kollock, Jr., VMI, Lexington, Va., Part V, Mrs. Geo. J. Kollock to W.W. Kollock, Marietta Institute, Marietta, Ga." In: Ga. H.Q. Sept-Dec. 1950, v.XXXIV, #3 & 4, p. 227-257; 313-327.

248 **KONDERT, Nancy T.**
"The Romance & Reality of Defeat: Southern Women in 1865." (Jackson, Miss.) Jour. Miss. Hist., May, 1973, v.XXXV, #2, p. 141-152.

249 **KORN, Bertram Wallace**
"Jews & Negro Slavery in the Old South 1789-1865." Elkins Park, Pa., 1961. 8vo, wraps, illus., 68pp. Delivered as the presidential address at the 59th Annual meeting of Jewish Historical Society, Feb. 18, 1961 & reprinted from March 1961 issue of its quarterly publication. Reform Congregation Keneseth Israel, 1961.

250 ..."Judah P. Benjamin as a Jew." In: Amer. Jew. Hist. Soc. Pub., Mar. 1949, v.38, p. 153-171 notes. Benjamin as lawyer & military officer in CSA, resident of England.

251 ..."Was there a Confederate Jewish Chaplain?" In: Amer. Jew. Hist. Quart., 1963, v.LIII, p. 63-69/after war.

252 **KOUNTZ, John S.**
"Record of organizations engaged in the campaign, siege & defense of Vicksburg. Compiled from Official Records by..., secretary & historian of the commission." Washington: Gov. print. off., 1901. 8vo, wraps, fldg. map, 72pp. $30-bmk.

253 **KRANTZ, John Christian, Jr.**
"The implications of the medical history of General (Robert E.) Lee (from 1839-1870)." In: USArmed forces med. jour., March 1960, v.11, p. 329-337. ports, From: Va. Med. Monthly, June, 1959.

253a **KRAUS REPRINT**
Dept. RO2, Millwood, N.Y.
..."A History of Morgan's Cavalry" by Basil W. Duke. Ed. with introduction and notes by Cecil F. Holland. Bloomington, Ind., 1960, cl. $50.
..."War Memoirs: Autobiographical Sketch and Narrative of the War Between the States." by Jubal A. Early. Ed. with an introduction by Frank E. Vandiver. Bloomington, Ind., 1960, cl. $47.
..."Advance and Retreat; Personal Experiences in the United States & Confederate States Armies" by John Bell Hood. Ed. with an introd. and notes by Richard N. Current. Bloomington, Ind., 1959, cl. $33.
..."Narrative of Military Operations Directed During the Late War Between the States" by Joseph Eggleston Johnston. Introd. by Frank E. Vandiver. Bloomington, Ind., 1959, cl. $57.
...Reprinted again 1981.
..."Lee and Longstreet at High Tide; Gettysburg in the Light of the Official Records" by Helen (Dortch) Longstreet. Gainesville, Ga., 1904, cl. $31.
..."From Manassas to Appomattox, Memoirs of the Civil War in America" by James Longstreet. Ed. with an introd. and notes by James I. Robertson Jr. Bloomington, Ind., 1960, cl. $63.
..."I Rode with Jeb Stuart; the Life and Campaigns of Major General J.E.B. Stuart" by Henry Brainerd McClellan. Introd. and notes by Burke Davis. Bloomington, Ind., 1958, cl. $40.
..."Memoirs" by John S. Mosby. Ed. by Charles Wells Russell, preface by Virgil C. Jones. Bloomington, Ind., 1959, cl. $37.

254 **"KRAUSS' SOUTHERNER;**
A Monthly Magazine, Edt: Miss Daisy Turney Krauss." New Orleans: May 1906. Large 8vo, wraps, 32pp. (only issue?) Ports Southern heroes, a story of the war, a sketch or two, verse.(only copy at Howard Tilton?)

255 **KREPELA, Rick**
"The Twilight of the Confederacy." Reply with a rejoinder by I.M. Hamilton." In: History Today, 1964, v.XIV, p. 542-549, 651.

255a **KREYLING, Michael**
"Lee Agonistes: the Southern hero in the 'mid-passage.'" in: So. Atl. Quart., Autumn, 1985, v.84, p.401-18.

256 **KRICK, Robert K.**
"The Gettysburg Death Roster: The Confederate dead at Gettysburg." Dayton, Oh., Morningside print, 1981. 4to, wraps, 96pp. 'Pres. copy.' $30-

256a ..."The Confederate Dead at Gettysburg. ." Dayton, Oh., Morningside Press, 1986. 4to, decr. cl, 128pp, 2nd edt., completely revised.

256b ..."The Fredericksburg Artillery." Lynchburg, Va., H.E. Howard, 1986. 8vo,

257 ..."Maxcy Gregg: Political Extremist & Confederate General." In: CWH, December 1973, v.XIX, #4, p. 293-313.
...Reprint, 1973. 8vo, wraps, 23pp. 8vo, stiff wraps, port, 23pp. OP $25-r, $15-, $2.00

258 ..."Lee's Colonels, a biographical register of the Field Officers of the Army of Northern Virginia." Dayton, Ohio., Morningside press, 1979, 2nd edt-1984. 8vo, cl, xxiv, 415pp. endpapers chart. $30-. Good statistical additons, annotations. See: Marcus Wrights's original & a reprint by Claud Estes (1912); a 1983 reprint by Mattituck, N.Y.; as well as a listing under title: "List of Field Officers Staff Officers.

258a ..."Lee's Colonels . . . 2nd Edt., revised." Dayton, Oh., Morningside Press, 1984. 8vo, cl, 462pp, ports.

259 ..."Parker's Virginia Battery, C.S.A. layout & maps by Stuart A. Vogt." Berryville, Va., Virginia Book Co. 1975. 8vo, illus., 408pp. $40-b Bibiog., pp. 387-393.

260 ..."Roster of the Confederate Dead in the Fredericksburg Confederate Cemetery." Fredericksburg: (Va.) 1974. 8vo, stiff wraps, ports on cover, (20) pp.

260a ..."9th Virginia Cavalry." Lynchburg, Va., H.E. Howard, 1982. (J.P. Bell Print.) Lim. Atg. Edt. 8vo, cl, dj, (4), 128pp, maps, prots. $17.50.

261 ..."30th Virginia Infantry." Lynchburg, Va., H.E. Howard, 1983) 8vo, stiff wraps, ports on cover, (20)pp.

262 ..."30th Virginia Infantry." Lynchburg, Va., H.E. Howard, 1983) 8vo, cl, 143pp., illus., maps, 1000 copies signed. Muster roll, bibliography. $15-

262a ..."40th Virginia Infantry." Lynchburg, Va., H.E. Howard, 1985. (J.P. Bell Print.) Lim. Atg. Edt. $17.50. 8vo, cl, dj, (2), 108pp. Maps, ill, ports.

cl, dj, (4), 119pp. maps, ports. 1,000 copies, numbered, signed. Bibliog.

263 **KRUMAN, Marc W.**
"Dissent in the Confederacy: the North Carolina Experience." In: CWH, Dec. 1981, v.27, #4, p. 294-313pp.

264 ..."Parties & politics in North Carolina, 1836-1865." Baton Rouge: Louisiana State Univ. press, 8vo, cl, dj, xx, 304pp. 1983. $37.50

265 **KURTZ, Henry I.**
"Arms for the South. Sometimes better armed than Federal troops." In CWTI, April 1967, v.6, #1, p. 12-19. illus. port.

266 ..."The Blue & the Gray fought at Palmetto Ranch a month after Appomattox." In: CWTI, Apr. 1963, v.1, #1, p. 32-33, map, port. Maj. John S. (Rip) Ford, led the 2nd Tex. Cav. in the last armed clash of the civil war.

267 **KURTZ, Lucy Fitzhugh & Benny Ritter**
"A Roster of Confederate Soldiers Buried in Stonewall Cemetery, Winchester, Virginia." (Winchester, Va.) Farmers & Merchants Nat'l. Bank. 1962, wraps, 8vo, 70pp. $15-

267a ..."A Roster of Confederate Soldiers buried in Stonewall Cemetery, Winchester, Va." Winchester, Va., Farmer & Merchants Natl. Bank, 1984. 8vo, wraps, 70pp. $12.50.

268 **KURTZ, Wilbur G.**
"The Atlanta cyclorama, the story of the famed battle of Atlanta. Compiled & written by...Published by the City of Atlanta, Georgia (Atlanta, Ga., Higgins-McArthur co, 1954) 8vo, 32pp., illus, some color., maps, ports. See: Alma Hill Jamison.

269 ..."The Death of Major General W.H.T. Walker, July 22, 1864." In: CWH, June 1960, v.VI, #2, p. 174-179, map, plate.

270 ..."The murder of Tom Terry, a sensational crime of the summer of 1861, that ocurred in Atlanta during the period of rejoicing that followed the first battle of

Manassas." In: Atl. Hist. Bul, II, #9, p. 39-49.

271 ..."Map of the Battle of Atlanta, 1864. By Wilbur Kurtz, with Key." In: Atl. Hist. Bul., II, #8, Sept. 1934.

272 **KURTZ & ALLISON Prints-**
See under title-"Battles of the Civil War."

273 **KUYKENDALL, Rhea**
"Dr. Arthur R. Barry." In: CV, June 1926, v.XXXIV, p. 209-210. Surgeons of the Confederacy.

274 **KYLE, David J.**
"The Last Hour with Stonewall Jackson (His guide's story)." In: CV, Sept. 1896, v.IV, #9.

L

1 **LA BREE, Benjamin**
"Camp Fires of the Confederacy; a volume of humorous anecdotes, reminiscences, deeds of heroism, thrilling narratives, campaigns, hand-to-hand fights, bold dashes, terrible hardships endured, imprisonments, etc. Confederate Poems & selected songs. Edt. by Ben LaBree." Louisville, Ky: Courier-Journal pr., 1898. sm. 4to, cl, illus, 560pp. (or, 1/2 Mor.) $75, $100-bmk. Half-title: The Battle Abbey or Memorial Edition.
...Same, 1899.
...N.Y., Pageant Pr. 1959.
..."The Confederate Soldier in the Civil War, 1861-1865. Prefaced by a eulogy by Maj-Gen. Fitzhugh Lee. A complete history of the foundation & formation of the Confederacy & the secession of the Southern States & prominent parts taken by Hon. Jefferson Davis & others. Campaigns, battles, sieges, charges, skirmished, by General Robert E. Lee (57 names), et.al. The Confederate States Navy, by Admiral Franklin Buchanan (12 names) Edited by Ben La Bree." Louisville: Courier-Journal pr, 1895. Folio, gilt decr. cl, color front, illus., 480pp. facsms, maps, ports, 1-p color flags. $100-fine. $200-bohl.
...Louisville: The Prentice Press, (Courier-Journal Press) 1897. Reprint of the 1895 edition $65. Text, both edts, three columns.
...Paterson, N.J., Pageant Pr. (1959) $45. 480pp. $35-bmk.
...N.Y., Fairfax Print (Div: Crown Pub., N.D., 1977?) $50.
...Louisv: Lost Cause, micro-cd. $4.

2 ..."The Pictorial Battles of the Civil War, illustrated by upwards of 1,000 engravings from sketches by Thos. Nast, Waud, Schell, etc., With an introduction by L.G. Wunder. The U.S. Navy & the part it took in the civil war, by Adm. David D. Porter. An historical sketch by Hon. W.C. Carrington. A comprehensive history of the civil war & the events leading thereto. Edt. by Benjamin LaBree." N.Y., Sherman Pub. Co., 1885. Folio, cl, 2 Vols. illus., ports, maps, fldg. pls. Gen. Marcus Wright's Gen. Officers CSArmy. Bmk-117 $100.

3 ..."Interesting war statistics. Compilation of men in service, the fatalities of various commands during the war." In: CV, Dec. 1896. v, IV, #12, p. 432-434. tables.

4 **LA FAUCHEUR, L.J.**
"The fight between the Merrimac & Monitor. Account by a Confederate Spectator." In: Belford Mag., Dec. 1890, v.VI, p. 104-112.

5 **LABADIE, Cecelia**
"Cecilia Labadie: Diary Fragment Jan. 19, Feb. 3, 1863. Edited by Mrs. Marjorie Logan Williams." In Texana, 1972, v.X, #3, p. 273-283, footnotes.

6 **LABOULAYE, Edourd**
"Les Etats-Unis et La France." Paris: E.-Dentu, 1862. 8vo, wraps, 72pp.

7 **LACK, Paul**
"Law & disorder in Confederate Atlanta." In: GaHQ, Summer 1982, v.LXVI, #2, p. 171-195, tables, notes.

8 **LACY, Benjamin T.**
"Address of the Chaplain of the Second Corps Stonewall Jackson's ANV." In: SHSP, 1886, v.14, p. 348-356.

9 **LACY, J. Horace**
"Lee at Fredericksburg." In: Cent., Aug. 1886, n.s., v.X, p. 605-608, illus.

10 **LACY, James B., Sgt-Maj.**
"The Fifteenth Virginia, composed of Richmond, Henrico & Hanover Boys." In: SHSP, 1899, v.27, p. 48-51.

10a **LACY, Wray T.**
"History of the Byrd Rifles of Goochland County Virginia." In: Goochland Co. Hist. Soc. Mag., 1983, v.15, p.35-9.

11 **LADIE'S BENEVOLENT Association of Louisiana...**
"Dedication of the Confederate Monument at Greenwood Cemetery, Friday, April 10, 1874." New Orleans: Jas. A. Gresham, 1874, 8vo, wraps, 26pp.

12 ..."Semi-Centennial of the Organization of the Ladies' Benevolent Association of Louisiana. (Ladies' Confederate Memorial Association.) Wednesday, May 10, 1916, 8 P.M., 1866-1916. Memorial Hall." New Orleans, La., 1916. 8vo, wraps.

13 **"LADIES HOLLYWOOD Memorial Association: Richmond"**
See: "Our Confederate Dead, etc." "Register of Confederate Dead."

14 **"LADIES MEMORIAL ASSOCIATION.**
Confederate Memorial Addresses. Monday May 11th, 1885. New Bern, N.C." Richmond, Va., Whittet & Shepperson. 1886. 8vo, wraps, 32pp. sketch Gen. Pettigrew $20-nc.

15 **"LADIES VOLUNTEER AID ASSOCIATION**
of Sandersville, Washington County, Georgia 1861-1862." In: Ga. H.Q., March 1968. v.LII, #1, p. 78-95. Edt: Kenneth Coleman.

16 **"LADIES' MEMORIAL ASSOCIATION**
of New Bern, N.C., Sketch of, by L.C. Vass." In: "Confederate Memorial Addresses of New Bern, N.C., May 11, 1885." p. 5-7.

17 **"LADIES' MEMORIAL ASSOCIATION, Charleston S.C.**
"A Brief History of the Ladies' Memorial Association of Charleston, S.C., from its organization in 1865 to April 1, 1880. Together with a Roster of the Confederate Dead, interred at Magnolia & the various city church-yards." Charleston: H.P. Cooke & co, 1880. 8vo, wraps, 42pp. Compiler: Prof. F.A. Porcher.

18 ..."Confederate Memorial Day at Charleston, S.C. Reinterment of the Carolina dead from Gettysburg. Addresses of Rev. Dr. Girardeau, odes, etc." Charleston, S.C. W.G. Mazyck or, 1871. 8vo, wraps, 36pp. Names listed p. 32-36.

19 ..."Memorials. To the memory of Mrs. Mary Amarinthia Snowden, offered by societies, associations & Confederate Camps. Published by the Ladies Memorial Association of Charleston, S.C., Ed. by James G. Holmes." 1898. Charleston: Walker, Evans & Cogswell, 8vo, wraps, front(port), 46pp.

20 **LADY OF GEORGIA (pseud.)**
"Destruction of the City of Columbia, S.C. A Poem. A True Statement of Fact. By A Lady of Georgia." Charleston, S.C., Joseph Walker, 1866. 12mo, wraps, 24pp. Turnbull (III), pg. 412.

21 **LADY OF GEORGIA, A**
See: "Destruction of the City of Columbia."

21a **LADY OF VIRGINIA, A**
Author of "Gen. Lee, the Christian Soldier."
See: McGuire, Judith White (Brockenbrough) Mrs. John P. McGuire.

22 **"LADY OF WARRENTON, VA., A (pseud.)**
See: Mrs. Cora Semmes Ives.

23 **LAFARGUE, Andre**
"The Manuscript of General Richard Taylor's 'Destruction & Reconstruction.'" In: La. Hist. Quar., Jan, 1930, v.XIII, p. 46-58.

24 **LAFFERTY, John Aker**
"Civil war reminiscences of...Edt: W.T. Lafferty." In RKHS, 1961, v.LIX, p. 1-28. Unit roster, Co.K., p. 3-4.

25 **LAGARD, Garald**
"Leaps the Live Thunder." N.Y., Morrow print, 1955. 12mo, cl, 256pp. On Bedford Forrest, fiction.

26 ..."Scarlet Cockerel." N.Y., W. Morrow, 1948. 12mo, cl, 441pp. On John S. Mosby, fiction.

27 **LAGRANGE, GEORGIA**
Light Guard-Muster Roll. In: "Out of Our Past," 1981, v.1, #1, p. 36-38.

28 **LAKE, Thomas W.S.**
"A midnight ride with the enemy." In: CV, Nov. 1928, v.XXXVI, p. 416-417. Campaign in Va., July 1864 by a member of the Va. cavalry.

29 **LALE, Max S.**
"Albert Sidney Johnston's Cruel Uncertainy." In: ETHJ, 1977, v.XV, #2, p. 18-28, notes.

30 ..."The Military Occupation of Marshall Texas by the 8th Illinois Volunteer Infantry, USA, 1865." In: MHT & Sw, 1975, v.XIII, #3, p. 39-47.

31 ..."The Boy-Bugler of the Third Texas Cavalry: the A.B.Blocker Narrative, Pt. I. In: MHT & Sw, 1976, v.XIV, #2, p. 71-92; pt. 2, #3, p. 147-167, facsm. Pt. 3, #4, p. 215-227; Pt. IV, v.XV, #1, 1977, p. 21-34.

32 ..."Robert W. Loughery: Rebel Editor." In: ETHA 1983, v.XXI, #2, p. 3-15. Politics in Marshall, Texas & Harrison Co., Secession & the war.

33 **LAMAR COUNTY, GEORGIA**
"History of Lamar County, Ga., sponsored by Willie Hunt Smith chapter, UDC. Mrs. Augusta Lambdin, editor, Mrs. Edward A. Fish, mng. editor." (Barnesville, Ga.) The Barnesville news-gazette, 1932. 8vo, illus., maps, 516pp.

34 **"LAMAR RIFLES.**
A History of Co.G., Eleventh Mississippi Regiment, CSA. With the official Rolls, giving each man's record from time of enlistment to 19th March, 1865. Individual & company sketches, May 1861 to Apr. 1865." n.p., n.d. (Roanoke, Va., Stone print. 1902?) 8vo, wraps, illus, front, 93pp. Sig. of Thos H. Chilton, member of historical Com., who prepared book. See: Thos. P. Burford.

35 **LAMAR, Gazaway B.**
"The activities & attitudes of a Confederate business man: G.B.L. In: JSH, 1943, v.IX, p. 3-36.

36 **LAMAR, Joseph Rucker**
"Biographical notes on the life of Hon. Howell Cobb, 1815-1868." In: Chr. Okl., Autumn 1956, v.34, p. 344-349, port. Activities in Ga., Natl., & Confed. politics. Also: in Wm. J. Northen's "Men of Mark in Ga.", v.III, p. 566-581.

37 ..."The Private Soldier of the Confederacy." Address of...delivered Memorial day, Apr. 1902 at Athens, Ga., now reprinted by request of N.Y. City friends, with Intro: by Albert Shaw." (Brooklyn, N.Y., Eagle print) 1902. 12mo, wraps, 48pp., cover title $75-bmk-105.

..."The Private Soldier of the Confederacy Patriotism is but one of the many names of Duty. Address before Ladies' Memorial Associaiton, of Athens, Ga., Apr. 26, 1902." Augusta, Ga., Chronicle print, 1902. 8vo, 18pp., wraps. 1st edt. cover title & caption-"The Private Soldier of the Confederacy."

38 **LAMAR, Lucius Quintus Cincinnatus**
"L.Q.C. Lamar's Letters to Edward Donaldson Clark, 1868-1885, pt. I: 1868-1873." Edt: James H. Stone. (Jackson, Miss.) Jour. Miss. Hist. Feb. 1973, v.XXXV,, #1 p. 65-73.

39 ..."Speech of., The Slavery Question, in-House of Reps., Feb. 21, 1860." caption title. n.p., n.d., (T. McGill).

40 ..."Letter, in reply to Hon. P.F. Liddell of Carrollton Miss., 12pp., wraps, Wash., 1860? $30. How South might oppose Fed. Gov.

41 ..."Why Lamar Eulogized Sumner." Edt: Mattie Russell. (Lexington, Ky.) JSH, Aug. 1955. v, XXI, #3, p. 374-378.

41a ..."Speech of...of Miss., on the State of the Country Delivered in the Atheneum, Atlanta, Ga., Thursday evening April 14, 1864. Reported by A. E. Marshall. Published by request." Atlanta, Ga., J.J. Toon Co., 1864. 12mo, wraps, 30p. Crandall 278

42 **LAMB, John, Hon.**
"Address: 12th Annual Reunion of Neff-Rice Camp, UCV, #1194, near New Market, Va., August 19, 1910." In: SHSP, 1910., v.XXXVIII, p. 298-308.

43 ..."Address on Memorial Day, May 26, 1906 at Ashland, Va." In: SHSP, 1906, v.XXXIV, p. 57-68.

44 ..."Battle of Fredericksburg, details of the mighty conflict." In: SHSP, 1899, v.XXVII, p. 231-240.

45 ..."Character & Services of the Confederate Soldier, an address by..." In: SHSP, 1915, v.XL, p. 230-239.

46 ..."The Confederate Cavalry, its wants trials, & heroism, an address by John Lamb, late Capt. of Cavalry, address by." In: SHSP, 1898, v.XXVI, p. 359-365.

47 ..."Malvern Hill, July 1st. 1862. Address delivered before Picket Camp, Confederate Veterans, Richmond, Va., on March 8th, 1897, by John Lamb." Richmond, Va., James E. Goode pr, 1897. 8vo, wraps, 21pp. Also: SHSP, 1897, v.XXV, p. 208-221.

48 ..."Returning Confederate Flags." In: SHSP, 1905, v.XXXIII, p. 300-305.

49 ..."Remarks of Capt. John Lamb on Mar. 24, 1899, at Richmond, in the Hall of R.E. Lee Camp #1, C.V., accepting portrait of Gen. Thomas T. Munford, CS Cavalry." In: SHSP, 1904, v.XXXII, p. 1-12.

49a ..."Presentation of Portrait of Gen. Thomas T. Munford. C.S. Cavalry, March 24, 1899." Richmond, 1905. 8vo, wraps, 14p. $60-ob.

50 **LAMB, Sarah Anne Chaffee**
"Letters from the Colonel's lady: correspondence of Mrs. (Col.) William Lamb written from Fort Fisher, N.C., CSA to her parents in Providence, R.I., USA Dec. 1861-Jan. 1865. from the Lamb collection in the Library of William & Mary College." Edt" Cornelius M. Dickinson Thomas. (Winnabow, N.C., Charles Towne Preservation Trust, 1965) (Clarendon imprint, #7) 8vo, wraps, xxii, 97pp., illus., facsms, map, ports. 1nd Edt., corrected in msc. to 1st edt. on verso t.p.

51 **LAMB, William, Col.**
"Defence of Fort Fisher, North Carolina." In: Mil. Hist. Soc., Mass., Papers, Bost: 1912, v.IX, p. 347-388 read Feb. 4, 1896.

52 ..."Account of Col. Lamb on Defence & Fall of Fort Fisher." In: SHSP, 1882, v.10, p. 350-368; 1893, v.21, p. 257-290.
...B & L, p. 642-654.

53 ..."The Battle of Fort Fisher, N.C." Wilmington, N.C., Chamber of Commerce. (Harris print & adv. 1946) 8vo, wraps, illus., 12pp. Rep: "Battles & Leaders."

54 ..."Fight with Blockaders." In: Walter Clark's Hist. of Several Regs. & Batt.s from N.C.", Vol. V, p. (1), 351-352.

55 ..."Colonel Lamb's Story of Fort Fisher The battles fought here in 1864-1865. An interesting address by..., written at the request of Cape Fear Camp, U.C.V. of Wilmington." Carolina Beach, N.C., Blockade Runner Museum 1966 (Wilmington Printing Co.) From the Wilmington Messenger,

June 15, 1893. 8vo, stiff wraps, vii, 40pp., front (port) map & Illus. by Richard Frye. ...Also in Southern Historical Society Papers 1892, XXI, p. 257-290, maps (2).

56 **LAMB, William, Mrs.**
"The Heroine of Confederate Point." In: SHSP 1892, v.20, p. 301-306.

57 **LAMBDIN, Milton Bennett**
"A boy of the Old Dominion during the war between the states." In: CV, 1929, v.37, p. 332-335, 378-381, 420-425.

58 **LAMBERT, Harold**
"He swapped his uniform for a pen." In: W.Va. State Mag., April 1958, v.9, p. 6. "Shriver Grays, CSA., organized Wheeling & sketch of commander Capt. Bob McEldowney. Shell-425.

59 **LAMBERT, Samuel**
"A Record of the Late Fourth Louisiana Reg't, C.S.A. It's Service, Etc." Edited by Mark T. Carleton." In: JLSA, Summer, 1969, v.X, #3, p. 255-260.

60 **LAMBRIGHT, J.T.**
"History of the Liberty Independent Troop during the Civil War, 1862-1865." Brunswick, Ga., Glover Bros., (1910?) 8vo, wraps, 8leaves. Dedication dated June 1, 1910, Brunswick, Ga., DeRenneIII, 1097.

61 **LAMPKIN'S BATTERY...**
See: Fletcher T. Massie.

61a **LANCEY, S. Herbert**
"Military Flotsam & Jetsam." In: Unit S, June 1903, v.XLI, p.1275-8. War dept of CSA.

62 **LAND, Bessie Mell**
"Dear Bet. The Carter Letters: 1861-1863." Greenville, S.C., Keys Print, 1978. 8vo, cl, illus., map, append, index, xxv, 165pp. Lt. Sidney Carter, Co. A, 14th Reg., S.C. Vols., Gregg's-McGowan's Brig., CSA.

63 **"LAND WE LOVE, The**
A Monthly Magazine Devoted To Literature, Military History, & Agriculture. Vol. 1, May--October, 1866." Charlotte, N.C., Jas. P. Irwin & D.H. Hill v.1, (446pp.); II, (476 pp.); III, (514pp.), map; IV, (542 pp.), 2-ports; V, (548 pp.), 2-ports; VI, (436 pp.), plate. Each issues (6), final vol. 5 issues., index iv to vi, each vol. In wraps, bound vols., in cloth or 3/4Mor. $35-$50-/vols., $300 set. Vols II-V, 4vols. $450-bmk (grimes sig.) See: Ray M. Atchison, Mott-Amer. Mags. Rebound set, 6vols, $450-jk, $20-ea issue-Carolina; vi, #6 Set-$500 $1000ob

64 **LANDER, Ernest M., Jr.**
"A Confederate Girl (Floride Clemson) Visits Pennsylvania, July-September, 1863." In: W. Penna. Hist. Mag., 1966, v.XLIX, p. 111-126; 197-211.

65 **LANDERS, Emmet M.**
"Some observations concerning Confederate ordnance during 1861." In: SoW. Soc. Sci. Qrt. 1936, v.XVII, p. 38-48. Supply & maintenance of arms & ammo. of CSArmy during early period.

66 **LANDERS, H.L.**
"Wet Sand & Cotton-Bank's Red River Campaign." In: LHQ, 1936, v.XIX, p. 150-195. Scandals in connection with cotton speculations during the expedition.

67 **LANDIS, C.E., Mrs.**
"The siege & fall of Selma, Ala." In: CV, Mar. 1923, v.XXXI, p. 96-97.

68 **LANDON, Fred**
"Ulrich Bonnell Phillips: Historian of the South." (Baton Rouge, La.) JSH., Aug. 1939. v.V, #3, p. 364-371.

69 ..."Canadian opinion of Southern Secession, 1860-1." In: Cand. Hist. Rev., Sept. 1920, v.I, p. 246-254.

70 **LANDRETH, David**
"A plea for compromise. Letter from David Landreth, on the crisis." n.p., n.d. (Bloomsdale, Pa., 1861) 8vo, 4pp. folder, wraps. A pro-Confederate pamphlet by a "Yankee."

71 **LANDRUM, J.B.O., Dr.**
"History of Spartanburg County, S.C." Atlanta, Ga., Franklin Pr., 1900. Reprint Co., 1960. $75- See: Spartanburg County.

72 **LANDRY, R. Prosper**
"The Donaldsonville Artillery at the Battle of Fredericksburg (From: New Orleans Picayune, Jan. 26, 1896.)" In: SHSP, 1895, v.23, p. 198-202.

73 **LANE, James Henry**
"Report on a Bill to set apart a portion of the State of Texas for the use of persons of African descent." Committee on Territories. Washington, DC., Senate report #8 of 38th Cong. 1st sess. 8vo, sewn, 4pp. To establish a black republic in South Texas, to be called "Territory of the Rio Grand," to be separated from Texas as reparations for its joining the Confederacy. jk 127 $45-

74 ..."Vindication of the policy of the administration. Speech of Lane, of Kansas, inthe US Senate FEb. 16, 1864, special order, Senate bill #45, to set apart a portion of the State of Texas for use of persons of African descent." Washington, D., D.C. Gibson Bros, 1864, 8vo, sewn, 16pp.

75 ..."Speech: in Cooper Institute, N.Y., & Gen. Neal Dow, in the New City Hall, Portland, Thursday evening, Mar. 24, 1861(sic) on his return from captivity in a Rebel Prison." Washington, D.C., Wm. H. Moore pr. 1864, 12mo, wraps, 16pp.

76 ..."The Truth of History." In: SHSP, 1890, v.18, p. 71-80.

77 ..."The Twenth-eighth North Carolina Inf. In: SHSP, 1896, v.24, p. 324-339.

78 ..."Letter on "Causes of Lee's Defeat at Gettysburg." In: SHSP, 1877, v.V, p. 38-46.

79 ..."Defence of Ft. Gregg." In: SHSP, 1877, v.3, p. 19-28; v.9, p. 102-107. See: reply to Gen. Harris, Mar. 1881, v.9, p. 102-107.

80 ..."First North Carolina Infantry, CSA." In: SHSP, 1890, v.18, p. 51-54, 1891, v.19, p. 212. Roster of Com. officers.

81 ..."Glimpses of Army Life in 1864. In: SHSP, 1890, v. 18, p. 406-422. Extracts from letters written by Brig-Gen. J.H. Lane.

82 ..."History of Lane's North Carolina brigade." In: SHSP, 1879-1882. VII, p. 513-522; VIII, p. 1-8, 67-76, 97-104, 145-154, 192-202, 241-8, 396-403, 489-496, IX, p. 29-35, 71-73, 124-129, 145-156, 241-246, 353-361, 489-496; X, p. 57-59, 206-213, 241-248.

83 ..."How Stonewall Jackson met his death an interesting authentic statement from Gen. James H. Lane." In: OLOD, 1875, v.III, p. 33-36.

84 ..."Lane's Corps of Sharpshooters." In: SHSP, 1900, v.28, p. 1-8.

85 ..."Note on George Burgwyn Johnston, Capt., CSA." In: SHSP, 1890, v.18, p. 132-133.

86 ..."Pollard's new book. (Lee & his Lieutenants)." In: OLOD, Mar. 1876, v.4, #1, p. 22-25.

87 ..."Lane's Report of the Battle of Chancellorsville." In: OLOD, Aug. 1875, v.3, #2, p. 183-187.

88 ..."Report of engagement, Sept. 30, 1864. Casualties in Lane's Brigade, campaigns 1862-1864." In: Southern Hist. Monthly, 1876, v.1, p. 247-252.

89 ..."Report of the First Maryland campaign from the Battle of Cedar Run to Sheperdstown." In: OLOD, 1874-1875, p. 16-21.

90 ..."Report of the Battle of Gettysburg." In: OLOD, Sept. 1875, v.3, #3, p. 321-326. Also: SHSP, 1878, v.5, p. 38-46.

91 ..."Report of the Battle of Fredericksburg." In: OLOD, Nov. 1874, v.1, #3, p. 197-203.

92 ..."Report of the Battle of Jericho's Ford." In: OLOD, Mar. 1876, v.4, #1, p. 19-21.

93 ..."Roster & Song of the First N.C. Inf." In: SHSP, 1890, v.18, p. 51-55. See: Wm. Ruffin Cox.

94 **LANE, John H.**
"The Battle of Fisher's Hill." In: SHSP, 1891, v.19, p. 289-295. Sept. 22, 1864.

95 **LANE, Mills, Edt.**
"Dear Mother: Don't Grieve about me. If I get killed, I'll only be dead." Savannah, Ga., Beehive Press, 1977. Sm. 4to, cl, illus., xxxi, 353pp. Mssc. letters from Georgia soldiers at war.

96 **LANE, Walter Paye**
"The Adventures & Recollections of Gen. Walter P. Lane, a San Jacinto Veteran, containing sketches of the Texian, Mexican, & late wars, with several Indian fights thrown in." Marshall, Texas: Tri-Weekly Herald, 1887. 12mo, wraps, 114pp, front(port) $175, $1500, $1250-jk-137, $750-ob.
...Marshall, Texas: News Messenger, (1928) 12mo, cl, 180pp, front(port) with addend, by Mary Jane Lane. $45-bmk-84.
...Austin, Texas & N.Y. Pemberton Press, 1970.

97 **LANEY, Clara**
"Union County (N.C.) Cemeteries 1710-1914 & Roster of Confederate & Revolutionary Soldiers." (Monroe, N.C.?) 1958, N. Carolina Hist. Survey. 4to, memeo. 223pp.(one side) indexed. CSA(145 182)
...1982 Reprint-spiral bound $45.

98 **LANG, David, Colonel**
"Civil War Letters of Colonel David Lang." Edt: Bertram H. Groene. In: Fla. Hist. Quart., 1976, v.LIV, #3, p. 340-366, ports.

99 **LANG, Herbert H.**
"J.F.H. Claiborne at "Laurel Wood" Plantation, 1853-1870." (Jackson, Miss., Jour. Miss. Hist., Jan., 1956, v.XVIII, #1, p. 1-17.

100 **LANG, Theodore F.**
"Captain A.J. Smith's sketch." In: Loyal W. Va. from 1861-1865. Baltimore, 1895). p. 54-57. On the organization of Co. C, 31st Va. in Clarksburg.

101 **LANG, Winfield S.**
"Career of Lt. Col. D.B. Lang." In: CV, Mar. 1905, v.13, port, 129-130pp. Maj. 62nd. Va. Inf. written by his son.

101a **LANGDON, C. C.**
"Reply to the Twenty-seven, by the editor of the Mobile Daily Advertiser." Mobile, 1850. 8vo, wraps, 1850. Goodspeed (599) "Mayor of Mobile & editor of the leading Whig newspaper, who was pro-slavery but anti-session. Answers letter signed by 27 Mobil

102 **LANGHEIN, Eric**
"Jefferson Davis: Patriot, a biography, 1808-1865." N.Y., Vantage press (1962) 12mo, cl, 101 pp. bibliog. $20-ll.

103 **LANGSDORF, Edgar**
"Price's Raid & the Battle of Mine Creek." In: Kansas Hist. Quart., 1964, v.XXX, p. 281-306. Separate wraps, 30pp. $10-b.

103a **LANKIEWICZ, Donald**
"Journey to asylum, a secretary of state runs for his life." In: CWTI, Dec. 1987. p. 16-21, 44-5, ills. Judah Benjamin.

104 **LANIER, Richard Nunn**
"The Angel of Marye's Heights." Fredericksburg, Va., Fredericksburg press, 1961. 8vo, wraps, 20pp. Heroism of Sgt. Richard Kirkland of Kershaw Co., S.C. at the Battle of Fredericksburg.

105 **LANIS, Edward Stanley**
"Allen Pinkerton & the Baltimore "assassination" plot against Lincoln (1861)." In: MdHM., Mar. 1950, v.45, p. 1-13, cartoon, notes.

106 **LANNEUA, John F., Lieut. Engineers**
"Personal contacts with R.E. Lee." (Wake Forest, N.C., "Biblical Recorder." cover

title, paper read before the Wake Forest literary club, Jan. 19, 1906. 7, (1)p.

107 **LANUX, Pierre de**
"Sud." Paris: Plon, 1932. (pres. to wiley) $75-. 12mo, pict. battle-flag wraps, illus., map, 4p, 1, iii, 278pp., fldg. map, bibliog. (273)-274. On Lee, Beauregard Pelham, Hampton, etc. Sympathetic study of South during war.
...Le roman du Sud; tableaux de l'Amerique en guerre, 1861-1865." In: Rev. Hebdomadaire, XL ann., #31, p. 13-28; #32, p. 176-196; #33, p. 315-331; #34, p. 456-480. (1931).

107a **LAPOINTE, Patricia M.**
Military Hospitals in Memphis, 1861-65." In: THQ, Winter 1983, v.42, #4, p.325-42.

107b **LARGENT, Robert J.**
"Virginia Takes the Road to Secession." In: WVa.H., Jan. 1941.

108 **LARIOS, Avila**
"Brownsville-Matamoros: Confederate life-line (1861-1865)." In: Mid-Amer., April 1958, v.40, p. 67-91, map, notes.

109 **LARKIN, J.L.**
"Battle of Santa Rosa Island." In: FHQ, January-April, 1959, v.XXXVII, #3/4, p. 372-376, plates(2).

110 **LARRICK, Herbert S.**
"The True Jefferson Davis, address by..." (of the Winchester, Va. Bar) before Gen. Turner Ashby Camp. U.C.V., Mar. 9, 1903." (Winchester, Va., Henry Print) 8vo, wraps, 14pp.

111 **LARSON, Norman C.**
"The North Carolina Confederate Centennial Commission." (Raleigh) NCHRev., April 1961. v.XXXVIII, #2, p. 194-198.

111a ..."Report of the North Carolina Confederate Centennial Commission." 1965, v.42, p.216-23.

112 **LARTER, Harry**
"Fifth Company, Washington Artillery of New Orleans, CSA, 1862." In: MC & H., 1953, p. 101-102, illus., incl. color plate.

113 ..."Terry's Texas Rangers (8th Texas cavalry), CSA." In: Mil. coll. & hist. 1954, v.V, p. 15-16, col. pl. illus.

114 **LARY, Samuel D.**
"Sam Lary's "scraps from my knapsack." Edt: W.E. Wight." In: Ala. HQ, winter 1956, v.18, p. 499-525, notes. Nine sketches of the 15th Ala. Inf. Reg. CSA, by a pvt. in Co. B, deals with activities in Va. 1861. Reprinted from Daily Columbus enquir. Columbus, Ga., 23 Mar.-1 May 1864.

115 **LASH, Jeffrey N.**
"Joseph E. Johnston's Grenada Blunder A Failure in Command." In: CWH, June, 1977, v.23, #2, p. 114-128.

116 ..."Major George Whitfield & Confederate Railway Policy, 1863-1865." In: JMH, Aug. 1980, v.XLII, #3, p. 172-193, notes.

117 **LASHLEY, Tommy G.**
"Oklahoma's Confederate Veterans Home." In: Chron. Okla., 1977, v.LV, #1, p. 34-55, port, illus., map.

117a **LASKA, Lewis L.**
"Mr. Justice Sanford & the Fourteenth Amendment." In: THQ, Summer 1974, v.33, #2, p.210-27.

118 **LASSITER, Charles T., Hon.**
"Tribute of Love to her Noble Dead-services in Old Blandford (Cemetery)." (from Richmond Times-Dispatch, July 31, 1908). In: SHSP, 1908, v.36, p. 125-132.

119 **LASSITER, Mabel S, et al**
See: "Confederate Memoirs: Alamance co.

120 **"LAST BATTLE of the Civil War"**
Charles Jewell Smith. Claim: "Battle at Palmetto Ranch, Texas. May 12, 1865, a CSA victory. Author:
"LAST BATTLE of the War
Palmetto Ranch Resca Chica, Texas. Mouth of the Rio Grande, The." In: SHSP, 1893, v.21, p. 226-227. See: Louis

J. Schuler, James E. Slaughter. Luther Conyers version.

121 "**LAST BATTLE of the War,**
by W.J. Slatter of Winchester, Tenn." In: CV, Nov. 1896, v.IV, #11, p. 381-382. See: Reply to Slatter in Dec. '96, #12, p. 416, by Luther Conyer of San Diego, Texas. The real last battle being at Palmetto Ranch, on the Rio Grande, near Brownsville, Texas, May 13, 1865 between the negro troops of 62nd. US under Col. T.H. Barrett & CSA's Benanide's Reg., under Rip Ford, etc.

122 "**LAST CONFEDERATE FLAG**
on the Atlantic." In: South Mag., July 1875, v.X, #1, 14pp. pt. II, Aug. 1875, v.X, #2, 15pp.

123 "**LAST CONFEDERATE Payroll,**
Letters of Lewis Shepherd, W.E.R. Byrne, Joseph M. Brown & the Confederate Military History, The." In: SHSP, April 1914, v.XXXIX, p. 23-30.

124 ..."The Last Days of the Southern Confederacy. Scenes in streets of Richmond-fabulous prices." In: SHSP, 1891, v.19, p. 329-333.

125 ..."Last Capital of the Confederacy." In: SHSP, 1903,v. 31. pg. 80, (both titles from N.Y. Herald.)

126 "**LAST MAN KILLED in the Civil War,**
from the Baltimore American." In: SHSP, 1906, v.34, p. 221. John Jefferson Williams.

127 "**LAST OFFICER--April 1865, The**
Edt: John Hammond Moore." In: SCHM, 1966, v. 67, #1, p. 1-14.

128 **LATANE, John H.**
"Brunswick guard, a detailed account of its fine record, its marches fights & roll of members." In: SHSP, 1900, v.28, p. 8-14.

128a **LATANE, Lucy Temple**
"A Short Sketch of James Allen Latane." Richmond, 1949. Whittet & Shepperson. 8vo, 100pp, ills, ports. $25. Latane was a secessionist Episcopal bishop, partially on civil war, on Va. during war.

129 **LATANE, William**
See: Richmond, Va., Dispatch.

130 **LATANE, William, Capt.**
"Burial of Latane." In: SHSP, v.24, p. 190-194. From the Richmond Times Dispatch. ...Also in: CV, Feb. 1897, v.V, #2, p. 49-54. Illus., ports. See: Col. Wilbur S. Nye.

131 **LATHROP, Barnes F.**
"A Confederate Artilleryman at Shiloh." In: CWH, December 1962, v.VIII, #4, p. 373-385.

132 ..."Disaffection in Louisiana: The Case of William Hyman." (Lexington, Ky.) JSH, Aug. 1958. v.XXIV, #3, p. 308-318. $10-

133 ..."Essays on Southern History written in honor of Barnes F. Lathrop. Edt: Gary W. Gallagher, Austin, Texas: University of Texas press, 1982. The General Libraries, 8vo, cl, dj, 182 pp., 800 copies, $25-. Stephen B. Oates on Lincoln & slavery; Frank Vandiver on Jeff Davis; Ralph Wooster on "Wealthy Southerners on eve of the civil war.

134 ..."The Lafourche District in 1861-1862: a problem in local defense." In: La. hist, spring 1960, v.1, p. 99-129. map. War in the swampy area of the Atchafalaya & Gulf to the Mississippi.

..."The Lafourche district in 1862: Confederate revival." In: La. hist., fall 1960, v.1, p. 300-319, notes.

..."The Lafourche district in 1862: militia & partisan rangers." In: La. hist., summer 1960, v.1, p. 230-244 notes. Includes excerpts from CSA-correspondence.

..."The Lafourche District in 1862: Invasion." In: LaH., 1961, v.2, p,175-201.

134a **LATHROP, George Parsons**
"The Bailing of Jefferson Davis" In: Cent., Jan. 1887, v.33, #3, p.636-44, facsm.

135 **LATHROP, H.P.**
"Plan of the Western Seat of War. Pub-

lished by H.P. Lathrop." N.O., J. Manouvrier & co, Litho. (186-?) Map 22X14 1/2" CR-3053 (JK-126) $1000.

136 **LATIMER, G.W., Compl. of Richmond, Va.**
"The Confederate Souvenir." (Atlanta, Ga: Sudden & Son, n.d.) 8vo, wraps, ports (CS Generals) illus. many ads, (20)pp. printed pink paper.

137 **LATIMER, J.W., Maj.**
"The Artillery of the Gettysburg Campaign." SHSP, 1882, v.10, p.130-134.

138 **LATTIMORE, Ralston B.**
"Fort Pulaski National Monument, Georgia." Wash: Nat'l. Park Ser. Hist. Handbook, #18, 1954, (reprint, 1961). 8vo, pict. color stiff wraps, facsms, illus., ports, (4), 55, (1)pp.
...See: Robert E. Lee, "Story of..." Editor.

139 **LAUGHLIN, Patrick, Maj.**
"Rebel Marines." In: Marine Corps Gaz. Nov. 1953, v.37, #11, p. 52-55.

140 **LAUGHTON, John E.**
"The sharpshooters of Mahone's brigade., some account of this gallant organization." In: SHSP, 1894, v.XXII, p. 98-105.

141 **LAUGHTON, John E., Capt.**
"The Sharpshooters of Mahone's Brigade." In: SHSP, 1894, v.22, p. 98-105.

142 **LAVENDER, John W., Capt.**
"The War Memoirs of Captain John W. Lavender, C.S.A., Edt: Ted. R. Worley." Pine Bluff, Ark., W.M. Hackett & D.R. Perdue, Pub., Southern Press, (1956). 12mo, pict. cl, (3), iii, (2), 158pp. Story of Co. F, Fourth Arkansas, Inf., CSA (originally known as the Montgomery Hunters) Muster Roll. $40.

143 **LAW, Agnes, Mrs.**
"The Burning of Columbia-Affidavit of Mrs. Agnes Law." In: SHSP, v.XII, 1884, p. 233-234.

144 **LAW, Evander McIvor, Maj-Gen.**
Portrait, etched by Chas. B. Hall. N.Y., 1898.

145 ..."The Confederate Revolution. Address of...at annual reunion of the Association of the Army of Northern Virginia." In: SHSP, 1889, v.XVII, p. 85-112. May 28, 1890. Reprinted: 8vo, wraps, 29pp.

146 ..."Lookout Valley, Oct. 28, 1863." In: SHSP, 1880, v.VIII, p. 500-506. Wm. Ellis Jones Pr.

147 ..."The fight for Richmond in 1862." In: SB, ns, vII, 1886/7, p. 649-660. maps, p. 713-723.

148 ..."From the Wilderness to Cold Harbor. In: B & L, v.iv, p. 118-144.

149 ..."On the Confederate right at Gaines' Mill." In: B & L, v.II, p. 363-365.

150 ..."The struggle for "Round Top." In: B & L, v. III, p. 318-330.

150a ..."Round Top" & the Confederate right at Gettysburg." In: Cent., Dec. 1886, v.33, #2, p.296-305, ills, port.

151 **LAW, John G., Rev.**
"Diary of a Confederate Soldier." In: SHSP, 1882, v.10, p. 378-381, 564-569; 1883, v.11, p. 175-181, 297-303, 460-465; 1884, v.12, p. 22-28, 215-219, 390-395, 538-543.

152 **LAW, Sallie Chapman Gordon, Mrs.**
"A Mother of the Confederacy." (Memphis Tenn: Appeal-Avalanche)." In: SHSP, 1894, v.22, p. 63-64.

153 **LAW, Thomas Hart**
"Citidel Cadets. The Journal of Cadet Tom Law. Published from the original manuscript & edited with explanatory notes about the persons mentioned." Clinton, S.C., P.C. Press, (1942). Edited by John Adger Law. 4to, (3), vii, 346pp. Additional pages of illus., not numbered. Schoolboy life of South Carolinians who became heroes of the CSA.

154 **LAWRENCE, Alexander A.**
"Johnny Leber & the Confederate Major." Illustrated by William G. Haynes, Jr. Darien, Georgia-Ashantilly Pr., 1962. 8vo, boards-paper label, illus., map. (4), 59, (3)pp. 500 copies printed. Hardee & 8th Tex. Cav. $30-bmk.

155 ..."The night Lt. Pelot was killed aboard the "Water Witch." In: Ga. Rev., Fall 1950, v.4, p. 174-176. Death of Thomas Postell Pelot, CSNavy while boarding the USS Water Witch in Ossabaw Sound, Jan. 2, 1864.

156 ..."A Present for Mr. Lincoln, the Story of Savannah from Secession to Sherman." Macon, Ga., Ardivian press, 1961. 8vo, cl, xii, 321pp. Illus.

157 ..."James Moore Wayne Southern Unionist." Chapel Hill: University of NC Press, 1943. 8vo, cl, d/w, ports, illus., 250pp. $25.

158 **LAWRENCE, F. Lee & Robert W. Glover**
"Camp Ford, C.S.A. The Story of Union Prisoners in Texas." Austin, Texas: Texas Civil War Centennial Advisory Committee(1964). (El Paso, Texas: Carl Hertzog). 8vo, cl, ports, facsms, illus.(incl. front), map endsheets, xi, (1), 99pp. 550 copies $45-jk.
...Some copies with full page sketch by Jose Cisneros of CSA soldiers, presentation by author. $275.

159 **LAWRENCE, George Alfred**
"Border & Bastile. By the author of "Guy Livingston." London: Tinsley Bros., 1863. 8vo, cl(or, 1/2 calf), xii, 277pp. Editions: 2nd, 3rd; "New Edt." 1864; N.Y., W.I. Pooley & Co. (1863), 12mo, cl, xii, 291pp.
...Leipzig: Bernhard Tauchnitz, 1863. 12mo, cl, x, (4), 266pp.

160 **LAWRENCE, Jessie**
"Historical work in schools." In: UDCMag., Sept. 1948, v.11, #9, p. 14-15. Promote CSA studies in schools.

161 **LAWRENCE, R. De T.**
"On the retreat from Charleston." In: CV, Mar. 1921, v.XXIX, p. 90-91. Retreat from Sherman's army.

162 **"LAWS & JOINT RESOLUTIONS**
of the Last Session of the Confederate Congress (Nov. 7, 1864-March 18, 1865) Together with the Secret Acts of Previous Congresses, with an Introduction & a Bibliographical Note, by Charles W. Ramsdell, Editor." Durham, N.C., Duke University Press (1941) 8vo, cl, front, illus.(facsms.), xxvii, 183pp. $40-bmk-84.
...N.Y., AMS press (1965) reprint. "Contains a nearly complete set of the hitherto unpublished laws of the CSA."

163 **"LAWS THAT UNITED**
Choctaw & Chickasaw Indians with the Confederacy." In: CV, Oct. 1903, v.XI, p. 448-458. With sketch of Gen. Albert Pike.

164 **LAWSON, Albert**
"War anecdotes & incidents of army life, reminiscences from both sides of the conflict between North & South." Cincinnati, Albert Lawson, 1888. 8vo, cl, 152, (2)p. Dorn-II, 462.

164a **LAWSON, Lewis A.**
"Wheeler's last raid." Greenwood, Fla., Penkeville Pub., 1986. 8vo, cl, xix, 446p. $25.

165 **LAWTON, Alexander Robert**
"A Brief Record of the Proceedings of the Corporation & People of Savannah in honor of the late General Robert Edward Lee, together with a Eulogy on his life, character & services." Savannah, Ga., Geo. N. Nichols' print, 1871. 8vo, wraps, (or leather), 52pp. $50-ob.

166 ..."Resources of the Confederacy in Feb. 1865." In: SHSP, 1876, v.II, p. 113-122. See: other reports, v.II, p. 85-103.

167 **"LAY OF THE LAST REBEL." Songsheet**
(Savannah, Ga., c. 1866) 9x4". Amusing

verse by unreconstructed Rebel. See: James Randolph.

168 **LAY, Henry C., Right Rev.**
"Sherman in Georgia: Notes of a Confederate Bishop." In: Atlantic Monthly, Feb. 1932, p. 166-173.

169 ..."Grant before Appomattox. Notes of a Confederate Bishop." Excerpts from Atl. Monthly, March, 1932. p. 333-340. Parts of the diary of a CSA missionary in the armies, 1864. See: Henry T. Shanks.

170 **LAY, John Fitzhugh**
"Address of Hon. John Fitzhugh Lay, late Colonel of Cavalry, Confederate States Army." In: SHSP, 1888, v.XVI, p. 207-213. Before Pegram Battalion Association.

171 ..."Reminiscences of the Powhatan Troop of Cavalry in 1861." In: SHSP, 1880, v.VIII, p. 418-426.

172 **"LAYING OF THE CORNER-STONE** of a Confederate Monument at Madison, Va., by Linn Banks Lodge, Sept. 19, 1900." n.p., n.d., 8vo, 6p. folder.

173 **"LAYS OF THE SOUTH:** Verses Relative to the War Between the Two Sections of the American States." (Liverpool) Printed for the Liverpool Bazaar, in aid of the Southern prisoner's relief fund, 1864." 12mo, wraps, 2, 83pp.

173a **LAYTON, Edwin**
"Colin McRae & the Selma Arsenal." In: AR, Apr. 1966, v.19, #2, p.125-36.

174 **LE CATO, Nathaniel James Walter**
"Theodora." N.Y., 1872 & Balt: F.A. Hanzache, 1871. 12mo, orig. wraps, 61pp. Poem of 1st battle of civil war on Eastern shores of Virginia.

175 ..."Tom Burton: or, the Days of '61. A Virginia Story of the Stirring Days of '61." Chicago, (1888) Belford, Clarke & co. 12mo, 235pp.

175a **LE CONTE, John**
"How to make salt from sea-water. By professor John LeConte. Published by the Governor & Council of South Carolina." Columbia, S. C., Charles P. Pelham, State Printer, 1862. 12mo, wraps, 10p. Crandall-2923.

176 **L'ECLAIR ,**
"Lenare; a Story of the Southern Revolution & Other Poems." New Orleans, La., Bouvain & Lewis, 1866. 12mo, cl, 107pp. Dated Vicksburg, Oct 30, 1866. $20-nc.

176a **L'ESTRANGE, Capt. W. D.**
"Under Fourteen Flags - Life & adventures of Brig. Gen. Maciver soldier of fortune." London: Tinsley Print, 1884. 12mo, cl, 2 vols., 260, 251p.
...1888, viii, 344pp.

176b **LE GAL, Eugene**
"School of the Guides, or the practical soldier; designed for the use of the militia of the Confederate States. (Illustrations in text)." New Orleans: Bloomfield & Steel, 1861. 14cm, (61)p, limp cloth. Crandall-2450. Goodspeed-$650.

177 **LE GEAR, Clara Egli**
"The Hotchkiss Map Collection: a list of manuscript maps, many of the Civil War period, prepared by Major Jedediah Hotchkiss (1828-99) & other manuscript & annotated maps in his possession." Washington: GPO, 1951. (5)lfs, 67, (13)pp. List of 341 entries arranged topically, comprising maps of the Civil War (#1-199), some as late, 1853.

178 ...Also: Lib. Cong. Quart. Jour., Nov. 1948, v.6, #1, p. 16-20. Relates largely to Va., & W.Va., 1861-1865. Made & acquired by Maj. Hotchkiss.

178a ..."Hotchkiss Map Collection . . . reprint." Falls Church, Va., Sterling Press, 1977.

179 **LE GRAND, Julia Ellen**
"Journal of..." See: Waitz (Julia Ellen LeGrand).

180 **LE MONNIER, Yves Rene, Dr.**
"General Beauregard at Shiloh, Sunday. April 6, 1862, by..., ex-Private, Co. "B,"

Crescent Reg., Louisiana Inf...Pond's Brig., Ruggles Div., Bragg's Corp. Army of Miss." New Orleans, La. Graham pr., 1913. 8vo, wraps, 32pp.

181 ..."Who lost Shiloh to the Confederacy?" In: Confed. Vet., Sept. 1914, v.XXII, 415-416.

182 ..."Beauregard at Shiloh," also in Neal's III(Feb. 1914) p. 147-165. See: as co-author, W.O. Hart.

183 ..."Gen. Leonidas Polk at Chickamauga." In: CV, Jan. 1916, v.XXIV, p. 17-19.

184 **LEA, H.J.**
"With the Fourth Louisiana battalion." In: CV Sept., 1919, v.XXVII, p. 339-340.

185 ..."The Fourth Louisiana battalion at the Battle of Secessionville, S.C." In: CV, Jan. 1923, v.XXXI, p. 14-16.

186 **LEA, Reba F., Compiler**
"Nesson County, Virginia. Civil War Soldiers." Wraps, 22pp., n.d. (Livingston, Va.) co. st. 4-2-67.

186a **LEA, Tom**
"The Confederacy's Back door, 1861-65." In: his 'The King Ranch,' v.1. Kingsville, Texas: Printed for the King Ranch, 1957. pp.175-235.

187 **LEACH, Richard H.**
"John Archibald Campbell & the Alston letter." In: Ala. rev., Jan 1958, v.11, p. 64-75. Notes. Reasons for imprisonment of a former Assc. Justice Supreme Court(US) & CSA Asst. Sect. War., 1865; letter from Lt. W. Alston to Pres. CSA (Nov. 9, 1864) offering services to "rid my country of some of her deadliest enemies by striking at the very heart of those who seek to en-chain her in slavery."

188 **LEAF, William N.**
"War in the second New Orleans district." In: Mil. Engineer, 1938, v.XXX, p. 195-203. "Battles & skirmishes" about N.O., in war.

189 **LEAKE, Walter D.**
"Heroism of James Pleasants of the Goochland County Cavalry." In: SHSP, 1888, v.16, p. 222-223.

190 **LEARY, William M., Jr.**
"Alabama versus Kearsarge: A Diplomatic View." Amer. Neptune, July 1969, Volume XXIX, #3, p. 167-173.

191 **LEAVELL, George W.**
"Battle of Franklin. Reminiscences." In: CV 1901/2, v.10, p. 500-503, ports.

192 **LEBBY, Robert**
"The First Shot on Fort Sumter." South Carolina Historical & Genealogical Magazine, XII, July, 1911, p. 141-145.

192a **LEBERGOTT, Stanley**
"Why the South Lost: Commercial Purpose in the Confederacy." In: Jour. Amer. Hist., June 1983, v.LXX, pp.58-74.

192b ..."Through the Blockade; the profitability & extent of the cottom-smuggling 1861-1865." In: Jour. Econ. Hist., Dec. 1981, p.867-88.

193 **LEBLEU, Susanne**
"Corpus Christi (Texas) during the Civil War." In: Jr. Hist., (Texas), May 1957, v.17, #6, p. 5-7, 23.

194 **LECONTE, Emma**
"When the World Ended. The Diary of Emma LeConte. Edited by Earl Schenck Miers." N.Y., Oxford University press, 1957. 12mo, cl, dj, port(front) xviii, 124pp. Columbia S.C., Jan-Aug, 1865.

195 **LECONTE, Joseph**
"The Autobiography of Joseph LeConte; Edited by William Dallam Armes." N.Y., D. Appleton & Co., 1902, 12mo, cl, front, illus., ports xvii, 337pp. $75-bmk-105.

..."Ware Sherman, a Journal of three months' personal experience in the last days of the Confederacy. With an introductory reminiscences by his daughter Carolina LeConte." Berkeley, California, University of California press, 1937.

12mo, bds, illus., front(port), xxxi, 146. Acct. Sherman's March thru Ga. 2nd Edition, 1938. $40.

196 **LEDBETTER, Barbara Neal**
"Civil War Days in Young County, Texas, 1861-1865." (Newcastle, Texas; For Author (1965) 8vo, stiff wraps, illus., 20pp. Chiefly court records, muster rolls.

197 **LEDBETTER, M.T.**
"With Archer's Brigade, Battle of Gaine's Mill & Mechanicsville Well described." In: SHSP, 1901, v.29, p. 349-354.

199 **LEDFORD, Preston Lafayette**
"Reminiscences of the Civil War, 1861-1865." Thomasville, N.C., News Printing House, 1909. price $.25. 12mo, wraps, 104pp., N.C. Inf., 14th Reg. $150- $360-ob.
...1961 reprint, Wade H. Phillips.

200 **LEE & STONEWALL JACKSON (Lithograph)**
"The Last Meeting-Generals Lee & Jackson." By artist: E.F.D. Julio, 1869 with engraver Fred. Halperin (co. 1873). Litho 26 1/2 x 20 3/4", plus margins, hand colored, engraver's proof, before letters, signed by artist in pencil. $125- Both Lee, pointing to right, and Jackson are on horses, with three mounted soldiers in background.

201 ..."Carte-de-Visite photography of Lee." Lexington, Va. Boude & Miley (c. 1866) Signed in ink by Lee, front. $450-jk100.

202 ...Engraving by J. Rogers. 8 1/4x11", lower left corner, as roof-top with white flag. $45.

203 ...Photogravure, half length, standing. 8x6", full sheet 22 1/8x15", large paper impress. One of 25 copies, privately printed for Mrs. G.W.J. DeRenne, Savannah, Ga., 1883. Also as front: Jno. W. Daniel's "Robert E. Lee an oration, Savannah, Ga., 1883.

204 **LEE MEMORIAL ASSOCIATION**
"Sketch of the Lee Memorial Association." In: SHSP, 1883, v.11, p. 388-417. By Rev. John William Jones.

205 ..."Lee Memorial Number," of the Southern Collegian. Pub. by the literary societies of Washington & Lee University, Lexington, Va., Summer Bul., 1907. Bul. n.s., v. 6, #3, July 1907. 8vo, wraps, 91, (2)p. front (port) pls. ports.
...v.39, #3. March 1900. 82pp. See: Death of Lee.

206 ..."In memoriam: Winchester, Va. 1-18-71." See: Col. F.W.M. Holliday.
See: "Ceremonies connected with the inauguration of the mausoleum..." John Warwick Daniel.
Do: "Historical Sketch of the Association," by Wm. Allan, p. (3)-19.
See: Chs. E. Fenner.

207 ..."Official souvenier of the dedication of the monument to General Robert E. Lee containing a full & complete history of the Monument association, together with the order of exercises and other matter..." Richmond, R. Newton Moon & co, 1890. 8vo, wraps, illus., ports, 31pp. jk-$25. With brief sketch of Gen. Lee.

208 ..."The Proposed Memorial to General Robt. Edward Lee in the Washington Cathedral." (Richmond) Va. Mag. Hist. Biog., July 1949, v.57, #3, p. 301-306, illus.

209 ...Lee Monument Association, Ceremonies connected with the unveiling of statue of R.E. Lee-See: Charles Fenner.

210 ..."Order of Procession in the Funeral of." 8x10" black bordered broadside, Oct. 15, 1870, n.p., (Washington College & WMI (Lexington, Va.) $100.
...(Washington College announces Lee's death) "The Southern Collegian," Oct. 15, 1970. 4pp. mourning banner, entire publication devoted to stories life, accomplishments & pending funeral. Hostick $125-
See: Lee Memorial.

211 ..."Organization of the Lee Monument Association & the Association of the Army of Northern Virginia." Richmond, Va., Nov. 3-4, 1870." Richmond, Va., J.W. Randolph & English, 1871. 8vo, 3/4 calf, marbled bds. port, 52pp.

212 ...Lee Monument Association. "Souvenier Lee Monument Unveiling." Richmond, Va., 1890. 8vo, wraps, color pictorial. 96pp., illus., bmk-$30.

213 ..."The Lee Museum, Washington & Lee University (Lexington, Va., Committee on the Lee Museum, Washington & Lee University, (c. 1928). 8vo, wraps, illus., (8)pp.

214 ...Robert E. Lee General-In-Chief. Confederate States Army- "Lest We Forget." Ambrose Lee, Williamsbridge, New York City, (1907), stiff cardboard, given with subscriptions to Confed. Veteran Magazine.

215 ..."Robert E. Lee The Beloved General." Boston, Mass., John Hancock Life Ins. (1926), 16mo, color wraps, illus.(incl. front), 16, (1)pp. $5.
...Do: 1956.

216 ...(Lee, Robert E.) Camp Soldier's Home. "Report of the Board of visitors, Lee Camp Soldier's Home, Richmond, Va. Dec. 31, 1916. Richmond, Va., (J.W.Ferguson sons) 1917. 8vo, wraps, 24pp. Reports above for years: 1916-1925, incl.

217 ..."Robert E. Lee to Albert Sidney Johnston, 1857." Edt: Marilyn McAdams Sibley. (Houston, Tex.) JSH, FEb. 1963. v.XXIX, #1, p. 100-107.

218 ...PLAQUE, 10" in diameter, cast aluminum, gilt finish, mounted on wood. Adam Pietz, sculptor.

219 ..."Report of..., & subordinate reports of the battle of Chancellorsville; also, reports of Maj. Gen. JEB Stuart & Brig.-Gen. Fitz Lee, of cavalry engagements at Kelleysville. Also report of Gen. W.H.F. Lee, & subordinates, of cavalry operations of the 14th/15th April 1863. Published by order of Congress." Richmond, Va., R.M. Smith, 1864. 8vo, cl, 144, (5)pp. Crandall-1419 $75.

220 ..."Report of..., of operations at Rappahannock Bridge; also report of Lt.-Gen. E.K. Smith, of operations in lower Louisiana, & report of Maj.-Gen. Jones, of engagments at Rogersville, Ten. Published by order of Congress." Richmond, Va., R.M. Smith, 1861. 8vo, cl, 61pp. Also in Lee's "Reports of ANV, from June 1862, includes battle of Fredericksburg, Dec. 13, 1862. In 2 vols. Richmond, Va., R.M. Smith, 1864. (Jk) $450., Bk-$250. (v.1-602pp. v.2-627pp.)

221 ...Paperweights, Baccarat Crystal, Cameo (sulphide) 2 1/2" x 1 1/2" tall. Sept. 1955. 913 copies made. Atlanta, Ga., Maier & Berkele.

222 ..."Report to General Lee after the war." In: CV, 1902, v.10, p. 305-308.

223 ..."General Lee on Sewell Mountain," In: So. Biv., Jan. 1883, v.1, p. 181-184. A commentary on Lee's inactivity.

224 ..."Gen. R.E. Lee at Cheat Mountain." In: Conf. Vet., Mar. 1899, v.7, p. 116-117.

225 ...(Lee, General Robert E. Lee) "A Short History of Gen. R.E. Lee." Park Place, N.Y., Knapp & co., 1888. 2 3/4 x 1 1/2". colored booklet, 16pp. facsm. signature.(packed in Duke cigarettes) See: "Heroes of the C.W." & W.Duke Co.

226 ..."The Seven Day's Battles before Richmond Va." In: Confed. War Journ., 1894, v.II, #1, p. 5, p. 7-11.

227 ..."Lee's Lieutenants. Names of surviving generals of the Confederate Army-a valuable roster. Personal notes about a number of the leading military men on our side." Richmond Dispatch, May 19, 1890." In: SHSP, 1889, v.XVII, p. 419-428.

228 ..."Robert E. Lee, Soldier, Patriot, Educator with special reference to his life & services at Washington & Lee Universi-

ty, Lexington, Va., Published for the Lee Memorial Fund." (Philadelphia: Patterson & White, 1921) Tall 8vo, wraps(port on cover), facsm., illus., ports, (31)pp. $20-b.

229 ..."Lee's Surrender. The room in McLean House, at Appomattox, Gen. Lee's surrender to Gen. Grant, portraits of 5-CSA & 12-Union officers, as grouped. Boston, n.d., Ambertype, Forbes & Co., Litho: 21 3/8" x 25".

230 ..."EXTRA DISPATCH. Lee's Surrender! Full particulars, correspondence between Gens. Grant & Lee. The Army of Northern Virginia Surrendered!!" Head: "Glory to God in the Highest: Peace on Earth, Good will amongst men." (device) eagle & ribbon. Two columns of text, at end: "Full particulars in first edition Evening Dispatch." Broadside, long folio, 1p. April 9, 1865/ Unrecorded? $485-jk100.

231 **LEE RANGERS**
"The famous Lee Rangers, the organization service & roster of this Company." In: SHSP, 1895, v.23, p. 290-292.

232 **LEE, Baker P.**
"Confederate Memorial Address, delivered at Elmwood Cemetery, Norfolk, Va., May 19, 1887 by Major Baker P. Lee, on invitation of Pickett-Buchanan Camp." Richmond, Va., G.R. Tenser, 1887. 8vo, wraps, 8pp. cover title. $30.

233 ..."Re-union of Confederate Veterans at Gloucester C.H., Va., September 8, 1886. Address of Maj. Baker P. Lee by invitation of the Gloucester monument association." Richmond, Va., G.R. Tenser, 1886. 8vo, wraps, 8pp, covr title. $5.

234 ..."Magruder's Peninsula Campaign, 1862." In: SHSP, 1891, v. 19, p. 60-65.

235 **LEE, Cassius Francis**
"Correspondence of General R.E. Lee, showing the spirit of 1861." In: SHSP, 1878, v6. p.91-94.

236 **LEE, Cazenove Gardner**
"Lee Chronicle, studies of the early generations of the Lees of Virginia. Compiled & edited by Dorothy Mills Parker." N.Y., New York University press, 1957. Large 8vo, cl, illus., incl. front, ports, maps, coats of arms, geneal. tables. $25.

237 ..."Relative numbers of the U.S. & Confederate States Armies." In: SHSP, 1904, v.32, p. 46-50.

237a **LEE, Charles Henry**
"The Judge Advocate's Vade Mecum; embracing a general view of military law & a practice before courts martial, with an apitome of the law of evidence, as applicable to military trials." Richmond, Va., West & Johnston, 1863. 8vo, cl, (or wraps), 251p. $
...2nd edt., revised & enlarged, 1864. 308pp. 12mo. Crandall-2441/2.

238 **LEE, Charles Robert**
"The Confederate Constitution." Chapel Hill: N.C. University (1963). 8vo, cl, d/w, viii, 225pp. $6.
...Westport, Conn., Greenwood Pr., 1974. Lib-bind-$45.

239 **LEE, Edmund Jennings, Edt.**
"Lee of Virginia, 1642-1892. Biographical & genealogical sketches of the descendants of Colonel Richard Lee. With brief notices of the related families of Allerton Armistead..." Phila., Edmund Jennings Lee, 1895. Tk. 4to, 586pp., 60 illus., incl. color front & 1 fldg. pl., indexed. $75-

240 **LEE, F.D. & J.L. Agnew**
"Historical Record of the City of Savannah." Savannah, Ga., J.H. Estill, 1869. 12mo, cl, pp. xii, 200. Maps(3) Pls(3). p. 80-128, relate to war with Savannah's "Roll of Honor."

241 **LEE, Fitzhugh**
"Account of a Tour of the South in behalf of the SHS.: In: SHSP, 1882, v.X, p. 569-74; v.XI, 1883, p. 228-238.

242 ..."Causes of Lee's Defeat at Gettysburg." In: SHSP, 1877, v.IV, p. 69-76.

243 ..."Chancellorsville, an address of Gen. Fitzhugh Lee, before the Virginia Division, ANV, at their annual meeting, held in the capitol in Richmond, Va., Oct. 29, 1879." Richmond, Va., Geo. W. Cary, 1879. 12mo, wraps, 44pp. $60-. Also in SHSP, 1879, v.VII, p. 545-585.

244 ..."General Lee." N.Y., D. Appleton & Co., 1894 ($16) 12mo, front(port), 2-fldg. maps, 433pp. Heading: "Great Commanders" series. Also: Large paper edition of 1,000 copies, 1/2 Lt. ($75-bmk), $125. Editions: 1897 & 1901, 1895, 1899, 1907.
...N.Y., J.A. Hill, 1904 in cloth or 1/2 Lt., "Makers of American History," series.

245 ..."Reply to General Longstreet." In: SHSP, 1878, v.V, p. 162-194.

246 ..."Report of the Cavalry Corps, A.N.V. from Mar. 28 to Apr. 9, 1865. In: SHSP, 1884, v.XII, p. 367-376. Also in: SHST, 1875, v.II, p. 77-85.

247 ..."Sketch of the late General Samuel Cooper." In: SHSP, 1877, v.III.

248 ..."Speech on Oct. 28, 1875, urging erection of a monument to J.E.B. Stuart." In: SHSP, 1876, v.1, p. 99-103. See also: Robert W. Hunter.

249 ..."The Second Virginia Regiment of Cavalry." In: SHSP, 1888, v.16, p. 354-356.

250 ..."Virginia's Next Governor, Gen. Fitzhugh Lee." New York: Cheap Publishing Co., (c.1885) 8vo, wraps, 32pp. Good CSA material, Lee went in as governor waving the CSA flag. Preface states it was written by one of Va. eminent divines but his modesty kept name anon.

251 **LEE, Floride Clemson**
"A Rebel Comes Home; the diary of Floride Clemson tells of her wartime adventures in Yankeeland, 1863-1864, her trip home to South Carolina, & life in the South during the last few months of the Civil War & the year following. Edts: Charles M. McGee, Jr., Ernest M. Lander, Jr." Columbia: Univ. of South Carolina pr, 1961. 8vo, cl, dj, illus. 153pp.

252 **LEE, George Taylor**
"Reminiscences of General Robert E. Lee. 1865-1868." In: So. Atl. Quart., July 1927, v.XX, V.XXVI, p. 236-251.

253 **LEE, George Washington Custis**
"The Evacuation of Richmond." In: SHSP, 1885, v.13, p. 255-259.

254 ..."Report of General G.W.C. Lee from 1nd to 6th of April, 1865." In: SHSTrans. 1874, v.1, p. 118-121. See: W. Gordon McCabe.

255 **LEE, Guy Carleton**
"Tribute to Gen. J.H. Morgan." In: CV, Dec. 1911, v.XIX, p. 570-571.

256 **LEE, Henrietta E.**
"Letter to Gen. David Hunter on the burning of her house." In: SHSP, 1880, v.8, p. 215-216.

257 **LEE, James Kendall**
"The volunteers handbook: containing an abridgement of Hardee's infantry tactics, adapted to the use of the percussion musket in squad & company excercises, manual of arms for riflemen, & U.S. Army regulations as to parades, reiews, inspections, guard mounting, etc. By James K. Lee, of the First regiment Virginia Volunteers." Richmond: West & Johnston, 1860. 16mo, limp pict.cl, 111pp. (jk) $80.
...Richmond: 1861, third thousand.
...Richmond: 1861, seventh thousand $50.
...Richmond: 1861, (2), ii, (5)-96pp. Twentieth thousand.
...Richmond: 1861, twenty-fifth thousand.
...Richmond: 3rd Edt. 111 pp. $65.
...Raleigh, N.C., Institute for Deaf & Dumb & the Blind, 1861. 16mo, cl, 96, iipp. Printed before secession of N.C.

258 **LEE, John F.**
"John Sappington Marmaduke (1833-

1887)." In: Mo. Hist. Soc. Coll. II, July 1906, p. 26-40. Marmaduke was Gov. of Missouri after war in 1885-1887.

259 **LEE, Keun Sang**
"The capture of the "J.R. Williams." In: Chron. Okl., Spring, 1982, v.LX, #1, p. 22-33, ports. See: James D. Morrison.

260 **LEE, Laura Elizabeth**
"For-Get-Me-Nots." See: Battle (Laura E. Lee).

261 **LEE, Mary Charlton Greenhow (1819-1906)**
"An extract from the journal of Mrs. Hugh H. (Holmes) Lee of Winchester, Va., May 23-31, 1862. Edt: C.A. Porter Hopkins." In: Md.HM. Dec. 1958, v.53, p. 380-393, notes. Observations onconduct of Yankee & Rebel forces in the streets & in her house.

261a **LEE, R. M.**
"General Lee's City: an Illustrated Guide to the Historic Sites of Confederate Richmond." McLean, 1987. 11 x 8 1/2", wraps, 184pp, ills(150), maps(15). $18.

262 **LEE, Richard Henry, Col.**
"The Causes of the war." In: CV, July 1893, v.1, p. 200-205. Address at dedication of CSA monument at Old Chapel, Clarke Co., Va. (Port, sketch, p. 226) Col. R.H. Lee.

263 **LEE, Robert E. & U.S. Grant: Surrender**
"Headquarters Middle Military Division. The following correspondence which took place between Generals Grant & Lee previous to the surrender of the Army of Northern Virginia." Winchester, Va., April 11, 1865. Quarto, 3pp. "This circular published for the information of the people in the vicinity of the lines." jk-128 $300. Nine letters, beginning with Grant's pointing out "hopelessness" of continuing resistance.

264 ...Lee(Robert E.) & U.S. Grant- Signatures: "Signatures of U.S. Grant, Lt.-Gen. USA & R.E. Lee, Matted with woodcut of surrender at Appomattox, bold sigs. (bmk-95) $600.

265 ..."Statue of Gen. Robert E. Lee. Committee on the Library. Report. To accompany H.J. Res. 142, 75th Congr., 1st sess., Senate Report 1143." U.S. Congress. House (head) (Washington: US Gov. print off., 1937) 8vo, fold, 3pp. See: "Acceptance of statue of Wash/Lee."

266 ..."The Story of Robert E. Lee as told in his own words & those of his contemporaries." (Washington, D.C., Colortone Press, 1964) in cooperation with Eastern National Park and Monument Association. Source Book Series, #1. 4to, cl, color wraps, color ports & crest of Lee. 96pp. viii, ports, illus., facsms $20.

267 ..."Suggestions for the celebration of the one-hundredth anniversary of the birth of Gen. Robert E. Lee, Jan. 19, 1907. Issued by the Confederate Association of New Orleans, La." (New Orleans, La., 1907) 8vo, wraps, (7)pp. title vignette(port).

268 ..."The Tomb of Lee, Lexington, Virginia." n.p., n.d. (c. 1879). 24mo, wraps, 14pp.

269 ..."The wartime papers of R.E. Lee." Clifford Dowdey, Edt; Louis H. Manarin, assoc. Edt., with connective narratives by Clifford Dowdey & maps by Samuel H. Bryant." Virginia Civil War Comm. Boston: Little, Brown, (1961) $30- 8vo, dj, facsm., maps, xiv, 994pp. 2nd edt. $25.
...N.Y., Bramhall House (1961) reprint. (Crown Pub. Co., nd.) tk. 8v., cl, dj, 998pp.

270 ..."Tributes to General Lee." In: South. mag. 1871, v.8, p. 1-46.

271 ..."Washington & Lee University. Summer Bulletin, 1907." Special Lee Centennial number, with much on Lee. Lexington, Va., wraps, illus., 91pp.

272 ..."Gen. Lee at the Wilderness." by R.C. _____, of Hood's Texas Brigade." In: LWL, Oct. 1868. v.V, #6, p. 481-486.

273 ..."Letter to Miss. Mary Meade, 12th Oct., 1870." In: Va. Mag. Hist. Biog., Jan. 1927 (Richmond) v. XXXV, #1, p. 23-26. Letter written day Lee died, background.

274 ..."Lee & His Generals." Lithograph in color-27-16". By Geo B. Matthews. $25-N.Y., National Print & Exhib. co(1907)
...Richmond, Va., Bell Book co(1907) same but 24x12" $30.

275 ..."General Robert E. Lee." Lithograph, (lightly tinted) 12x15". Chicago: Rice & Allen, Chicago Lithographing Co., 1866. Lee in uniform, three-star, top of sword showing in half length pose.(plate mark curved only at top).

276 ..."General Robert E. Lee.", Collection of the Corcoran Galley of Art, by J.A. Elder. Printed in Holland. New York Graphic Society, #3654, n.d. Three quarter length pose, arms folded, three-star uniform with belt & sash, hat on table, with gloves & map, sword. Full color.

277 ..."Colored mezzotint protrait 22x18". Briston, Eng., T.Hamilton Crawford, 1939. Signed proof of Lee as a Lieut-General in uniform, with his home in background. $40.

278 ...Mezzotint protrait, after photo by A.B. Walter, colored. Sold by authority of Lee Memorial Ass'n. for the erection of a monument at his tomb. (Lexington, Va., c. 1870) 18x15 1/2" oval, with black rectang. border, bust in uniform. $20.

279 ...Same, by Charles P. Augustus Tholey Philadelphia: John Smith (1867) Tinted litho: 20x24" (see also: "Album of Amer. Battle Art."

280 ...Corpus Christi, Texas: Bill Pledger, 1977 3840 S. Padre Isle Dr., 78415. 17x26" duotone Litho., reprint.

281 **LEE, Robert E. (portrait)**
N.Y., W.G. Jackman; Blelock & Co., n.d. 8x10" color steel engraving, a 3/4 full figure, sword, sash & glover (3-stars).

282 ..."Portrait, vignetted oval, civilian suit, bow tie, frontal-left side, facsm. signature. n.p., n.d., 24"x29". Matching one of Jackson.

283 ..."Original oval photo, signed on the mount, "R.E.Lee". Framed in oval mahogany "OG" frame. Approx. 8x10" frame: 11/13", light foxing. gdsp. $1000-. Lee sitting in arm-chair photo from right side. Dressed in black, small bow tie, clock on table at left-hand.

284 ..."Lee-A new look at the General." April 1971, v.10, p. 22-23, port + first time a new group port. CWTI.

285 ...Portrait (bust) civilian clothes, 16x20" full margins, 20x24". color portrai from Robert Karr canvas, 2500 signed copies. Hopkinsville, Ky., Southern Galleries, 1975. $30-

286 ..."Colored portrait (facing left), after a portrait, from life, engraved by A.B. Walter." Washington (1870) 24 1/2 x 30".
...Color restrike, 28 x 22" $30.

287 ..."Mezzotint portrait by Wm. Sartain." Philadelphia: Wm. Sartain, pub. & engr. (c. 1867-1870). Litho: 11/13", bust, facing left, in the uniform he appeared at close of war.

288 ..."General Lee at the Grave of Stonewall Jackson." n.p., copy entered by act of congress, A.D., 1862, altho Jackson was killed 1863. Drawn by G.G. White, engraved & pub. by John C. McRae. Colored steel engr. 12 1/2 x 13".
..."N.Y., 1867, same 18x23" $25.

289 ..."Portrait, engraved by P. Giradet. India paper proof, mounted, folio. N.Y. (Paris) (c. 1890) Bust port., in uniform.

290 ..."Portrait, etched by W.H.W. Bicknell mounted, on India paper. Signed, artist." Boston: John A. Lowell BN Co., 1906. Tall folio., Also issued: (1) unsigned proof, (2) normal issue. Lithograph, after an orig. photo. Handcolored, 12 1/2 x 10" (paper:

	17 1/2 x 13") Bost: E.F. Ackermann, n.d. $50-. Full uniform, boots, hat-in-hand, holding sword, sitting on camp stool at edge of tent, with cannon background, leaning slightly to the right, full face.
291	...Gen. Robert E. Lee-1867-engraving by J.C. McRae, after a Brady photo. N.Y., T. Kelly $150. 23 1/2 x 18, plus wide margins, hand-color., standing in full-uniform, holding hat, left hand resting on sword, at edge of tent & an open map spread over a stool, flag in front of tents(3) background.
292	...Engraving in copper, G. O'Conner, a plate size 9 1/2 x 6 1/2" $385. After a Brady photo, but the seated Lee in Victorian chair, civilian clothes & partly opened vest, Lee holds a scroll instead of hat (Brady). Lee faces right. Original colored lithograph. Issued to raise maney for erection of a monument honoring them, at Washington & Lee University. 1870 (bmk.90) 19x24" (plate) full margins, 28x34" $500. See: Stonewall Jackson-matching port.
293	..."Gen. R.E. Lee on 'Traveller.'" Lithograph of a painting by Mrs. L. Kirby-Parrish, of Nashville, Ten., 20x24" & 12x15", mount on wide margin white card, for framing.
294	...Photograph, bust, 11x14" mounted on heavy photograph board. (copy. 1907) Edward B. Eaton of Hartford, Conn.
295	..."CSA-State Department." Correspondence concerning campaign of 1864." In: SHSP, 1879. v7, p. 291-292.
295a	..."Congressional testimony of . . . before the Congressional Committee (Reconstruction)." 8vo, wraps, 23pp. N.Y., Baker & Godwin Print, 1866. $50-bm.
296	..."Correspondence & Orders concerning the Army of Northern Virginia, May to June, 1862. In: SHSP, 1882, v.10, p. 272-279.
297	..."Description (Lee) of his horse "Traveller." In: SHSP, 1913, v.41, p. 158-159. See: T.L. Brown.
298	..."Did Grant return Lee's sword at Appomatox?" In: SHSP, 1881, v.9, p. 139-140.
299	..."Farewell address to his army." In: SHSP 1883, v.11, p. 428.
300	..."Field Telegrams, May & June 1864." In: SHSP, 1877, v.3, p. 295-300; v.4, p. 189-191; 1879, v.7, p. 345-348; 1886, v.14, p. 569-573; 1888, v.16, p. 261-270.
301	..."First Observance of Lee's Birthday as a legal holiday." In: SHSP, 1890, v.18, p. 133-158.
302	..."Second Observance Lee's Birthday." In: SHSP, 1891, v.19, p. 389-406; 1900, v.28, p. 228-243. B.M. Palmer's Characterization.
303	..."General Lee's horse "Lucy Long." In: SHSP, 1890, v.18, p. 388-391; 1891, v.19, p. 333-335.
304	..."General Order (concerning observance of Sunday), Feb. 7, 1864." In: SHSP, 1882, v.10, p. 91.
305	..."Laying the cornerstone of Lexington Mausoleum." In: SHSP, 1879, v.7, p. 48.
306	..."Letter concerning "Offensive Policy" in the Campaign of 1864." In: SHSP, 1881, v.9, p. 137-138.
307	..."Letter concerning his campaign (invasion north of the Potomac)." In: SHSP, 1879, v.7, p. 445-446.
308	..."Letter to Cassius Lee, April 1861." In: SHSP, 1878, v.6, p. 94.
309	..."Letter to Gen. W.N. Pendleton." In: SHSP, 1888, v.16, p. 228-229.
310	..."Letter to President Davis, July 19, 1863." In: SHSP, 1884, v.12, p. 267-268.
311	..."Letter to President Davis (offering to resign) Aug. 8, 1863." In: SHSP, 1876, v.1, p. 53-54.
312	..."Letters...1862-1865." In: SHSP, 1889, v.17, p. 335-341.

313 ..."Letters on the "situation," Sept. 14, 1863." In: SHSP, 1884, p. 323-326.

314 ..."Letters to W.W. Corcoran." In: SHSP, v.7, p. 152-155, 1879.

315 ..."Lee & Stuart at Harper's Ferry," from Richmond Times Dispatch." In: SHSP, 1910, p. 372-387.

316 ..."Monument to General Lee." In: SHSP, 1889, v.17, p. 187-335.

317 ..."Natal day of General Lee." New Orleans U.D.C." In: SHSP, 1900, v.28, p. 228-243.

317a ..."A Postbellum visit with Lee: A Letter. Edt: Marshall Scott Legan." 3pp. In: GHQ, Winter, 1973. $7.50.

318 ..."Reminiscences of Lee & Gordon at Appomattox Courthouse." In: SHSP, 1880, v.8, p. 37-39.

319 ..."Report of the Battle of Chancellorsville." In: SHSP, 1877, v.3, p. 230-243.

320 ..."Report of the Bristoe Campaign." In: SHSP, 1879, v.7, p. 250-252.

321 ..."Report of the Pennsylvania campaign & Battle of Gettysburg." In: SHSP, 1876, v.2, p. 33-49.

322 ..."Treatment of Prisoners." In: SHSP, 1876, v.1, p. 120-122.

322a ..."Recumbent Figure of General R. E. Lee, by Edward V. Valentine." Washington, D.C., 1875 (sold for the benefit of the Lee Memorial Association). Photographed by M. Miley, Lexington, Va. 12 1/2 x 8 3/4" mounted. $125.

323 ..."Tributes of eminent men to Lee." In: SHSP, 1889, v.17, p. 348-357. (from Richmond "State") Schfield (J.M.), Porter (D.D.), Campbell (J.E.), Reagan (J.H.), Gibbons (Jas.), Dana (C.A.), Bayard (T.F.), Warner (C.D.), Daniel (J.W.),Watterson (Henry), Stringfellow (Frank), Hoge, (M.D.), Randolph (A.M.), Wilson (W.L.), White (J.J.), Milburn (W.H.), McClure (A.K.), Palmer (B.M.), Stone (D.M.), Dudley (T.U.), Minor (J.B.), Newton (J.B.).

See: Charles F. Adams, W. Allan, Archer Anderson, Chs. Anderson, Walter B. Barker, T.F. Bayard, W.W. Blackford, T.L. Brown, Thos. W. Bullitt, David S.G. Cabell, Wm. E. Cameron, J.E. Campbell, Jno. H. Charmberlayne, J.H. Claiborne, W.B. Conway, Jabez L.M. Curry, C.A. Dana, Jno. W. Daniel, Jefferson Davis, T.U. Dudley, Jubal A. Early, Jno. Echols, Cha. E. Fenner, Henry M. Field, W.W. Fontaine, R.D. Funkhouser, Saml. M. Gaines, Theo. S. Garnett, Jas. Cardinal Gibbons, Washington L. Goldsmith, Don P. Halsey, Jr., W.W. Haskins, W.I. Hodgson, M.D. Hoge, Hollywood Memorial Ass'n., Jno Wm. Jones, Edward S. Joynes, Cassius F. Lee, F. Mangold, Charles Marshall, T.E. Moberly. W.H. Milburn, J.B. Minor, T.C. Morton, J.B. Newton, Chs. T. O'Ferrall, B.M. Palmer, Wm. H. Palmer, R.S. Parks, Leslie J. Perry, D.D. Porter, Geo. Henry Ray, A.M. Randolph, J.H. Reagan, H.F. Requier, Abram J. Ryan, J. Scheibert, Jas. P. Smith, J.M. Shofield, Wm. W. Smith, Henry Thompson Staunton, D.M. Stone, C.S. Stringfellow, Frank Stringfellow, Thomas M. Talcott, Walter H. Taylor, John R. Thompson, Mary A. Townsend, Miss. S.B. Valentine, C.D. Warner, Henry Watterson, Jas. J. White, C.M. Wilcox, Joseph P.B. Wilmer, W.L. Wilson, Viscount Wolseley.

323a **LEE, Robert Edward**
"Program: 'Ceremonies unveiling of the statue of Robert Edward Lee, under the auspacies of the Governor & the general assembly of Virginia Old Hall of the House of Delegates, Tuesday, Jan. 19, 1932, 12:15 p.m. Ports, 4to, stiff wraps, embossed, silk-ti

323b ..."Secession is Nothing but Revolution," a letter of Robert E. Lee to his son

"Rooney." Edt. Wm. M. E. Rachael." in: VMHB, Jan. 1961, v.69, #1, p.3-6.

324 ..."Acceptance of the Statues of George Washington & Robert E. Lee." Washington, DC, GPO, 1934. 8vo, cl, (or 3/4 Mor.,) 63pp.

325 ..."Robert E. Lee." In: Frank Leslie's Pop. Monthly, May 1896, v.41, p. 490-507.

326 ..."Address of...to the Veterans. Delivered during the Confederate Reunion held at Richmond, Va., 1907." n.p., n.d., 8vo, wraps, 8pp.

327 ...Appointed commander-in-chief of all Confederate armies. See: Gen. Samuel Cooper.

328 ..."The autographed field letters of R.E. Lee, Gen. Edt: Van Dyk MacBride. In: "Amer. Philatelist, Dec. 1951, v.65: p. 172-179. Facsms., dated in Va., Mar. 26, May 21, 1863; Nov. 14, 1864, editorial account of their postal covers.

329 ..."Blockade Runner (CSS "Letter" B) to Coal Barge." In: Detroit Hist. Soc. Bul., 1971, v.XXVII, iv, 11.

...Lee, Camp- See: J.C. Shields.

330 ..."Ceremonies at the Unveiling of the statue of General Lee, Old Hall of the House of Delegates. Tuesday, January 19, 1932." Richmond: Division of pruchase & printing, General Assembly, 1932. House, Doc. 6. 8vo, ports, wraps, 19pp. Also: in wraps, tied, 8pp. $10.

331 ..."Centennial Celebration of his birth, held under the auspices of the University of South Carolina on 19th of January, 1907." Columbia, S.C., Stateco., 1907. 8vo, wraps, ports, 36pp. Address: Maj. Henry Ed Young-" Lee the Soldier;" Ed. S. Joynes-" Lee, the College President."

332 ..."General Robert E. Lee, the Christian Soldier..published for the City missionary association of the Protestant Episcopal Church of Richmond, Va." Phila: Claxton, Remsen & Haffelfinger; Richmond: Woodhouse & Parham, 1873. 12mo, cl, (viii-xii) 12-198pp.

333 ..."Ceremonies connected with the Innauguration of the Mausoleum & Unveiling of the Recombent figure of General Robert Edward Lee.: See: under John W. Daniel, his oration.

334 ..."Ceremonies in celebration of the one hundredth anniversary of the birth of Robert E. Lee, under the auspices of the Confederate organizations of New Orleans." (New Orleans, J.G. Hauser, 1907) 8vo, wraps, illus., 8pp. Life of Lee & tributes from various sources. $20.

335 ..."The Closing Scene-Letter from General Lee to Jeff Davis, on his surrender." In: OLOD, August 1875, v.3, #2, p. 200-202.

336 ..."Gen. R.E. Lee at Cheat Mountain." In: Conf. Vet., Mar 1899, v.VII, p. 116-117.

337 ..."Lee's conduct in the Wilderness campaign." In: Amer. Hist. Ass'n. Report, 1908, v.1, p. 235-243.

338 ..."R.E. Lee Camp, C.V., Protest against relief of Confederates by National appropriation, the P.J. Otey's Bill." In: SHSP, 1895, v.23, p. 337-341.

339 ..."Lee Camp Soldier's Home, Richmond, Va. (in Richmond Dispatch)." In: SHSP, 1892, v.20, p. 315-324.

340 ..."The Death of General Lee." from Washington College, Va., "Southern Collegian," half sheet Extra, v.III, #1. Lexington, Va., Oct. 15, 1870. Sm. folio, (4)pp., lined in black. Facsm. (The Meriden Gravure Co., 1955).

341 ...Atlanta, Ga., The Library, Emory Univ., (Emory Univ. publications. Sources & reprints ser. #3. 1955. Intro: Richard Barksdale Harwell. 8vo, wraps, fold-facsm., 11, (1), (4)pp. notes. $8.

342 ..."Lee's Dispatches; unpublished letters of General Robert E. Lee, CSA, to Jefferson Davis & the War Department of the Confederate States of America, 1862-1865.

From the private collection of Wymberley Jones de Renne, of Wormsloe, Georgia. Edited with an intro. & notes by Douglas Southall Freeman. New edition. With additional dispatches & foreword by Grady McWhiney." N.Y., Putnam's (1957). 8vo, cl, ports, fldg. color map, lxxi, 416pp.

...N.Y. & London, G.P. Putnam's sons, 1915. 1st Edition, lxiii, 400pp. front(port), fldg. map, 1nd Edt. (above) contains an additional ten dispatches. $45.

"DuPont presents "The Cavalcade of America starring Philip Mersivale in Robert E. Lee." Richmond, Va., Tuesday, April 12, 1940. Script of radio program prepared & produced by Batten, Barton, Durstine & Osborn, Inc.

343 ..."Lee's Farewell: fine mssc. of General Order No. 9 (Headquarters of the Army of Northern Virginia, 10, April, 1865) signed by General Robert E. Lee." In: Month at Goodspeed's, Nov/Dec. 1957, v.19, p. 35-38. facsm. (Boston: Goodspeed's Bookstore).

344 ..."Lee's Farewell to Texas February 9, 1861." In: MHT & Sw, 1978l, v.XIV, #4, p. 244-245.

345 ..."General Lee's Final Report of the Pennsylvania Campaign & the Battle of Gettysburg." (From the Southern Mag. August, 1872.) In: Southern Hist. Monthly Jan, 1876, v. 1, #1, p. 36-56; also OLOD, Mar. 1876, v.4, #1, p. 33-53.

...Also in: SHSP, 1876, v.II, p. 33-49.

...In: Hist. Mag., s 2, V(Morrisania 1869) p. 97-105.

346 ..."Funeral of General R.E. Lee." In: SHSP, 1916, v.41, p.188-191. Incident relocation of a casket for Lee.

347 ..."The Incident with Harris' Mississippi Brigade." In: SHSP, 1880, v. 8, p. 105-10. N.H. Harris & Col. C.S. Venable corrects Jno. Esten Cooke's version. (W.W. Smith).

348 ..."Lee's General Order Number Nine." Chicago, Ill., The Lakeside Press, n.d.(1955?) R.R. Donnelley & Sons, "Deeptone Offset Reproduction." Folio, heavy gray paper, facsimile of Lee's holograph letter, inserted loosely, 7p. 35 1/2 x 13cm, notes. $40-bmk

349 ..."Fredericksburg, Va., Finnegan's Press, 17 Blair Rd., 22401. 1980. Fake parchment, wide border.

350 ..."The Fundamental Creed of Robert E. Lee. A selection from Lee's writings & papers. Arranged & annotated by Earl Schench Miers. Woodcuts by Antonio Frasconi." (NY, Spiral Press) Newark, Del., Printed for friends of the Curtis Paper Co., 1958. 8vo, cl, illus., 33, (1)p. "Fifth annual pub. in a series of Americana commissioned by the Curtis Paper Co., of Newark, Delaware."

351 ..."Faces from the Past--II." In: Amer. Hert. June 1961, v.XII, #4, p. 28-29. port of Lee. After Appomattox, Lee returns to Richmond.

352 ..."Robert Edward Lee, 1807-1870; Jefferson Davis, 1808-1889." (Charleston, S.C., 1891) 12mo, wraps, 8pp. Limited to edt. 250. Printed for benefit of the Confederate Home. Two poems about Lee & tribute to Davis.

353 ..."A Robert E. Lee letter on abandoning the South after the War. Edt: William Tate." In: Ga. H.Q., September 1953, v.XXXVII, #3, p. 255-256.

354 ..."A Lee Letter on the "Lost Dispatch" & the Maryland Campaign of 1862." n.p., wraps, 6pp. reprint from, $4-. In: Va. Mag. Hist. & Biog., Apr. 1958, v.66, p. 161-166. Letter to Gen. Daniel Harvey Hill, Lexington, Va. 1/21/1868.

355 ..."A Letter of General R.E. Lee to Mr. Robert Beverley." (Richmond) Va. Mag. Hist. Biog. July 1951, v.59, #3, p. 353-355, (2)p. facsm.

356 ..."Some Personal Letters of Robert E. Lee, 1850-1858.: (Baton Rouge, La.) JSH, Nov. 1946, v.XII, #4, p. 557-570.

357 ..."Map of the Battlefield of Fredericksburg, explained from official reports; also Lee's report of the battle." Lynchburg, Va., 1866. 8vo, marbled wraps, 33pp., map. (Copy, with no map, $25).

358 ..."To Markie;" the letters of Robert E. Lee to Martha Custis Williams from the originals in the Huntington Library." Edt. & Intro: Avery O. Craven. Cambridge: Harvard Univ. Press, 1933. 8vo, cl, d/w, port, facsm., vii, 91pp.
...2nd edt. 1934...$30.

359 ..."General Lee & two of his hitherto unpublished letters, Edt: Amos R. Koontz. In: Military Medicine, 1964, v.CXXIX, p. 61-66.

360 ..."Lee Miscellany." In: VaMHB, 1925, v.33, p. 371-382.

361 ..."Monument to General R.E. Lee. The Undersigned connected with the Hollywood Memorial Association of Richmond, Va.(requests contributions for an equestrian bronze statue of Lee to be put in Hollywood Cemetery) signed: Mrs. Wm. H. McFarland, et, al. Richmond, Va., Oct. 19, 1870. Broadside: 23x15cm.

362 ..."To the survivors of the Army of Northern Virginia. Comrads: The Lee Monumental Association...has been organized...(to solicit subscriptions for a monument in Richmond to Robert E. Lee. Richmond, August 12, 1871. Broadside: 28x22cm.

363 ..."To the survivors of the Army & Navy of the Confederate States & to all the admirers of the character of the late Robert E. Lee, wherever they may reside." (a letter from Jubal Early soliciting funds for the project & report on the "resolution adopted at the meeting of Nov. 3, 1870." Broadside: Quarto. (Goodspeed cat. 592.)

364 ..."Robert E. Lee. In Memoriam. A tribute of respect offered by the citizens of Louisville. (quote)." Louisville: John P. Morton Co., 1870. Sq. 8vo, cl-gold design, embossed, plate port(front) 45pp. $30.

364a ..."The Confederate Army." In: B&L, v.4, p.751-3; 'Farewell address to his Army,' p. 747, pl; 'Lee's report of the Surrender at Appomattox,' p. 724.

364b ..."Lee's Surrender at Appomattox." In: AHQ, 1946, v.7, #1, p.128-34.

364c ..."Three Competitions for a design for a monument to Gen. R. E. Lee, 1877-87. A protest & a review." Richmond: Whittet & Shepperson, 1887. 8vo, wraps, 27pp.

364d ..."Reports of the Operations of the Army of Northern Virginia, from June 1862, to & including the battle of Fredericksburg, Dec. 13, 1862. In two vols." Richmond: R.M. Smith, 1864. 8vo, wraps, 627, 602pp. Crand-1435. $450-jk. $400-McM. 1/4 lt

364e **LEE, Robert E., Gen. & Wm. P. Johnston**
"Memoranda of conversations between Lee & Johnston, May 7, 1868-Mar. 18, 1870. Edt: W.G. Bean." In: VMHB, Oct. 1965, v.73, #4, p.474-84.

365 **LEE, Robert Edward, Jr., Capt.**
"Recollections & Letters of General Robert E. Lee by his son Captain Robert E. Lee, with photogravure portraits." N.Y., Doubleday, Page & co, 1904. 8vo, decr. cl, color flag, pl, ports, incl. front, xii, (1), 461 pp. $8.50, $10. Copy in Mor., $15, $20. Editions: 1905 ($27.50); 1909 ($16); Westminster, 1904-First English Edt.
..."Recollections & Letters of General Robert E. Lee." Reprint. Wilmington, N.C., Broadfoot Pub., 1988. $25.
..."Recollections of General Lee." In: Frank Leslie's Pop. Monthly, Aug/Oct. 1900, v.50, p. 399-414.
..."Recollections & letters of General Robert E. Lee, by his son, Captain Robert E. Lee; introduction by Gamaliel Brad-

ford...concluding with new & previously unpublished material gathered by Dr. William Taylor Thom." Garden City, N.Y., Doubleday, Page, 1924. 8vo, cl, front, pl ports, xix, 471pp. $20-bmk.
...1926.

366 ..."My Father, General Lee. A new edition of "Recollections & Letters of General Robert E. Lee by his son Robt. E. Lee, Jr., CSA. With a new introduction & Lee chronology by Phillip Van Doren Stern." Garden City, N.Y., Doubleday & co, 1960. 8vo, cl, dj, facsms, illus., ports, incl. front. xxv, 453, (21)-index. Bmk $15-. "Star Reprint series."

367 **LEE, S.L., Miss**
"War Time in Alexandria, Virginia." In: So. Atl. Quart., July 1905, v.IV, #3.

368 **LEE, Stephen Dill, Lieut.-Gen.**
"Address at Nashville, 1904." In: SHSP, 1904, v.32, p. 178-182.

369 ..."Address at unveiling of monument to defenders of Vicksburg." In: SHSP, 1893, v.21, p. 189-200.

370 ..."Gen. Stephen D. Lee's account of the Battle of Harrisburg(Miss.), read before the Mississippi State Historical Society, differing in many respects from version generally accepted." (n.p., 19--). 8vo, wraps, caption title, 15pp.

371 ..."Battle of Harrisburg, or Tupelo." In: PMHS, v.VI, p. 39-52.

372 ..."Battle of Brice's Cross-roads, or Tishimingo creek, June 2-12th, 1864." In: Pub. Miss. Hist. Soc., 1906, v.VI, p. 27-37.

373 ..."Battle of Tupelo, or Harrisburg, July 14, 1863." In: Pub. Miss. Hist. Soc., 1902, v.VI, p. 39-52, plan.

374 ..."The Campaign of Vicksburg, Miss., in 1863-From April 15 to & including the Battle of Champion Hills, or Baker's Creek, May 16, 1863." (Oxford, Miss., Pub. Miss. Hist. Soc., 1900, v.III, p. 21-53, fldg. map.

375 ..."The Siege of Vicksburg." (above) p. 55-71. Rep: wraps $20-y.

376 ..."Campaigns of Generals Grant & Sherman against Vicksburg, Dec. 1862 & Jan. 1863, the "Chickasaw Bayou Campaign." reprint from the Mississippi Historical Society Publications, v.4, (1901) p. 15-36. wraps, fldg. map, 36pp. $17.50

377 ..."Corps Commander reports of the Battle of Nashville Dec. 15/16, 1864." In: CV, 1904, v.12, p. 269-274; Append: p. 274-277. Gen. George H. Thomas, for the South.

378 ..."Correction of General Patton Anderson's report of the Battle of Jonesboro, Ga." In: SHSP, 1878, v.5, p. 130-131.

379 ..."Dedication of the Statue of the late Park Commissioner..., Commander-in-Chief, UCV in the Vicksburg National Military Park, Friday, June 11, 1909." (Vicksburg, Mississippi Printing co, 1909) 8vo, stiff wraps, front(port), plate, 38pp. See: Jas. Dinkins.

380 ..."Details of important work by two Confederate telegraph operators Christmas Eve, 1862, which prevented the almost complete surprise of the Confederate Army at Vicksburg." In: Pub. Miss. Hist. Soc., Oxford, Miss., 1904, v.VIII, p. 51-55.

381 ..."Index to Campaigns, Battles, & Skirmishes. Series I, in Mississippi from 1861 to 1865." In: Pub. Miss Hist. Society., Oxford, Miss. 1904, v.VIII, p. 23-32.

382 ..."Johnson's Division in the Battle of Franklin." In: (Oxford, 1903, Pub. of Miss. Hist. Soc., v.VII, p. 75-83.

383 ..."Operations of the cavalry in Mississippi." In: SHSP, 1881, v.9, p. 97-102.

384 ..."Report of the Battle of Chickasaw Bayou." In: SHSP, 1878, v.6, p. 49-53.

385 ..."Report of the Siege of Vicksburg." In: SHSP, 1877, v.4, p. 14-18.

386 ..."Report of the Tennessee Campaign." In: SHSP, 1877, v.3, p. 64-71. Sept. 29, 1864.

387 ..."The Second battle of Manassas, A reply to Gen. Longstreet." In: SHSP, 1878, v.6, p. 59-70, 250-254.

388 ..."Sherman's expedition from Vicksburg to Meridian...1864." In: SHSP, v. 32, p. 310-319. 1904.

389 ..."Speech at the laying of cornerstone of Davis Monument." In: SHSP, 1896, v.24, p. 366-380.

390 ..."Speeches at Richmond reunion May 30 to June 3, 1907, of Gen. Stephen D. Lee, Comm. in chief UCV., Col. Robert E. Lee, Jr., & Col. J.W. Daniel." (Richmond, Va., 1907). 8vo, wraps, 23pp.

391 ..."Sherman's Meridian Expedition & Sooy Smith's raid at West Point(Miss.)-a review by Gen. S.D. Lee." period: Feb. 3-Mar. 6, 1863. In: SHSP. 1880, v.VIII, p. 49-61. (In: PMHS, iv, p. 37-47.

392 ..."Speech at Richmond reunion, May 30 to June 3, 1907 of Gen. Stephen D. Lee Commander-in-chief U.C.V., Col. Robt. E. Lee, Jr., & Col. J.W. Daniel." (Richmond, 1907) 8vo, wraps, 23pp., Swem-3093. In: Illinois Cent. Mag., April 1916, v.4, #10, p. 11-21, illus., ports.

393 ..."Lieutenant General Stephen D. Lee." In: LWL, March 1867, v.II, #5, p. 324-329, #6, p. 407-413.

394 ..."Stephen D. Lee (Gen.); his life character & services." by Dabney Lipscomb in Miss. Hist. Soc. Pub., v.X, p. 13-33.

395 ..."The South Since the War." In: v.12, Evan's Confederate Military Hist. Atlanta, Ga., 1899. Port(front), p. (267)-368.

396 ..."Vicksburg Confederate Hill." In: Jour. Miss. Hist., 1944, v.VI, p. 3-29.

397 ..."The War in Mississippi after the Fall of Vicksburg, July 4, 1863." PMHS. Oxford, Miss., 1909, v.X, p. 47-62.

398 ..."Who fired the first gun at Sumter?" In: SHSP, 1883, v.11, p. 501-502. See: Defenders of Vicksburg.

399 **LEE, Susan Pendleton**
"Memoirs of William Nelson Pendleton, by his daughter...(Brig-Gen., ANV, chf. artly) Phila: J.B. Lippincott co, 1893. 8vo, cl, front(port), 490pp. civil war, 131-407. $150- nl-33 + 80. $300-bmk-106.

400 **LEE, William**
"The Currency of the Confederate States of America. A description of the various notes, their dates of issue, varities, series, subseries, letters, numbers, etc.; accompanied with photographs of the distinctions of each issue." Washington, DC., 1875. 9vo, wraps, 27pp. & atlas of vii (e.g., 10) pl. (mounted photos) 22x35cm.

401 **LEE, William Henry Fitzhugh**
"Memoranda...General Stoneman's Raid into Virginia, April 29, 1863." In: SHSp, 1891, v.19, p. 271-272. See: Ass'n. ANV-Gen. Lee & Long.

402 ..."Memorial addresses on the Life & Character of William Henry Fitzhugh Lee, delivered in the house of Representatives." Washington, DC, GPO, 1892. 8vo, cl, 107pp. front. Lee was Maj-Gen. Cavalry, wounded at Brandy Station, captured.

403 **LEE, William Mack**
"History of the Life of Rev. Wm. Mack Lee, body servant of General Robert E. Lee, through the civil war, cook from 1861 to 1865; still living under the protection of the Southern States." (Norfolk, Va., Smith Print, 1918) 8vo, wraps, cover title, (10)p., incl. illus., port. Note: Bookmark Books, reports a 28pp. with pictorial wraps, (#104) Bmk $50.

404 **LEECH, John W.T., Co. C. 14th Reg. La. Inf.**
"The Battle of Frazier's Farm. Part taken by Louisiana Troops." In: SHSP, 1893, v.21, p. 160-165.

405 **LEEMHUIS, Roger P.**
"James L. Orr & the Sectional Conflict." Washington: University Press of America,

1979. 9vo, cl, dj, v., 218pp. Helped draft S.C. Ordnance of Secession.

406 **LEEPER, Wesley Thurman**
"Rebels Valiant, Second Arkansas Mounted Rifles (Dismounted)." (Little Rock, Ark., Pioneer Press, 1964) 8vo, cl, d/w, port, 328pp. 850 copies. $30.

407 **LEFLER, Hugh T.**
"Thomas Atkinson, Third Bishop of North Carolina." (Garrison, N.Y.)-Hist. Mag. of Protestant Episcopal Church, Vol. XVII-#4, Dec. 1948. p. 422-434 (Church affairs in N.C. in War.)

407a ..."Hinton Rowan Helper, advocate of a "White America." Charlottesville, Va., 1935, Southern Sketches, no. 1. 8vo, stiff blue wraps, 45pp. $20.

408 **LEFTWICH, George J.**
"Reconstruction in Monroe County." (Oxford, Miss., Pub. Miss. Hist. Soc. 1906, v.IX, p. 53-84.

409 **LEFTWICH, William G., Jr.**
"The Battle of Brice's Cross Roads." In: WTHSP, 1966, v.20, p. 5-19.

410 **LEFTWICH, William M., Rev.**
"Martyrdom in Missouri A History of religious proscription, the seizure of churches & the persecution of ministers of the gospel, in the state of Missouri during the late Civil War & under the "Test Oath" of the New Constitution." Saint Louis: Southwestern Book pub., 1870, 12mo, cl, port, p. 436-445. Atg: $75-jk Methodist Episcopal Church, South in Missouri during the war. Pro South.

411 **LEGERGOTT, Stanley**
"Why the South lost: commercial purpose in the Confederacy. 1861-1865." In: JOUR. Amer. Hist., 1983, v.70, #1, p. 58-74.

412 **LEGION FRANCAISE, New Orleans, La.**
"Legion Francaise. Counseil d'administration..." (Nouvelle Orleans, 1861) 8vo, wraps, 48pp. cover title. Proceedings of the 15th-19th meetings. Oct. 18-Nov. 13, 1861. The Legion Francaise, composed of French citizens residing in New Orleans, was organized for the defense of the city only.

413 ..."Ordre du jour." (Nouvelle Orleans, 1861) caption title. 8vo, 7pp. Signed: Albin Rochereau, chef de bataillon: dated Nouvelle Orleans, 2 Dec., 1861.

414 ..."Reglements de la Legion Francaise a la Nouvelle Orleans le 26 avril 1861. 12mo, wraps, cover title, 24pp. Above in La. Union Cat. 1, p. 440.

415 ..."Dissensions in organization & relations to the C.S.A. Authorities." Dated 2, December, 1864. In: Henkel's catalogue.

416 **LEHMAN, Howard**
"Confederate States: the two cent green stamp (1862)." In: Collectors Club philatelist, Jan. 1952, v.31, p. (3-25). facsms. Describes all known survivors of issue.

417 ..."Confederate States: further information on the two cent green stamp (1862ff)." In: Collectors Club Philatelist, July 1953, v.32, p. 171-181. facsms.

418 **LEIGH, Benjamin Watkins, Maj.**
"The wounding of Stonewall Jackson." In: SHSP, 1878, v.VI, p. 230-234.

418a **LEIGH, Egbert G., Jr.**
An appreciation of Col. Archer Anderson late president of the Tredgar Company for the records of the Tredgar Company December 1918. Sm4to, wraps, $40.

419 **LEIGH, Townes Randolph, Mrs.**
"The Confederate Southern Memorial Association." In: Confed. Vet., Sept. 1928, v.XXXVI, p. 342-344.

420 ..."The Jews in the Confederacy." In: SHSP, April 1914, v.XXXIX, p. 177-180.

421 ..."The City of Pensacola, Florida." In: CV, July 1928, v.XXXVI, p. 252-253. Hist. acct., particularly during the war.

422 **LEINBACK, Julius Augustus**
"Regiment Bank of Twenty-sixth North Carolina." Edt: Don M. McCorkle. Winston-Salem, N.C. 1958. Reprint: Civil War Hist., Sept. 1958, v.IV, #3, p. 225-236. Moravian Music Foundation, pub. #5.

423 **LEITER, Levi Ziegler**
"The Leiter Library: A Catalogue of Books, Manuscripts & Maps relating principally to America collected by the late Levi Ziegler Leiter." Washington, Privately Printed, 1907. 8vo, cl, front, facsms. (20), xiii, 533 pp. Lim. Edt., 100 copies. Edt: Hugh Alexander Morrison. CSA-p. 241-341. $100.

424 **LELAND, Charles Godfrey**
"Ye Book of Copperheads." Phila: Frederick Leypoldt, 1863. 8vo, cl, (2), 24, (6)pp. Sabin-39962. Satirical limerick's directed against Lincoln & the "Copperheads" those Northerners sympathetic to the Southern cause during the war.

425 ..."Centralization or "States Rights". N.Y., C.T. Evans, 1863. 8vo, wraps, 14pp. Sabin-39963, et al.
...N.Y., 1863-"Spirit of the Times," 23 limericks "Nursery Rhymes of the Army," signed L.L.D., initials which likely represents Leland's name with vowels omitted, according to Gershon Legman.

426 **LEMKE, W.J.**
"The Hindman Family Portraits." In: AHQ, 1955, v.XIV, p. 102-8. General T.C. Hindman & family, 4pp. 12-ports, illus.

427 ..."Prisoner of war diary. In: AHQ, 1953, v.XII, p. 333-339.

428 **LEMLEY, Harry J., Judge**
"Historic Letters of General Ben McCulloch & Chief John Ross in the Civil War." Oklahoma City" Chron. Okla. Summer, 1962. v.XL, #2, p. 286-294.

429 **LEMMON, George**
"Letter to Fitzhugh Lee concerning episode of Chancellorsville." In: SHSP, 1881, v.XIX, p. 141-142.

430 **LEMMONDS, C.Q., Esq.**
"Speech of...on the Convention Bill, delivered in the House of Commons, Jan. 17, 1861." Raleigh, N.C., 1861. 8vo, sewn, 16pp. Favoring of calling a convention. e.g., "popular liberty," according to one of the secessionists.

431 **LEMONNIER, Leon**
"La Guerre de Secession." (Paris: Gallimard pr., 1943) 8vo, cl, 3, (9)-364pp. illus. (map). Civil War & Reconstruction.

432 **LENDT, David L.**
"Iowa & the Copperhead Movement." In: Annals of Iowa. 3rd. ser., 1970, v.XL, p. 412-427.

433 ..."Early love & Copperhead Journalism." In: An. Iowa, Summer 1972. v. 41, p. 994-1006.

434 **LENNON, George H., Mrs.**
"The thirty wives of 26 Confederate governors." In: UDCMag., Sept/Dec. 1953. v.16, #9, p. 6, 25; #10, p. 42, 50-51. Biographical sketches.

435 **LENNOX, Mary, (pseud.)**
"Memoirs of a Missouri Confederaet Soldier." Bowen's Division. (Texarkana, Texas) 1906. 8vo, wraps, cover title, 58pp. $75. "Personal Memoirs of a Mo. Confed. soldier & his commentaries on the race & liquor question," Dornbusch, #703 (Comments: (31)-58pp.

436 **LEON, Louis**
"Diary of a Tar Heel Confederate soldier, by L. Leon." Charlotte, N.C., Stone print (1913). 12mo, wraps, front(port), illus. 87pp. (17)pp. ads at end, $150-c Pict. cover, another copy. Louisv., Lost Cause pr. micro-cd. $3.

437 ..."Tarheel veteran." In: Jacob Rader Marcus' "Memoirs of Amer. Jews." Phila: Jewish pub. soc. Amer., 3 vols., 1955, v. 3, p. 197-225. Excerpts from author's printed

reminisc., 1913, of his service as a private in the 1st & 53rd N.C. Reg., later a prisoner of war in NY, & MD. 1861-1865.

438 **LEPOTIER, Adolphe Auguste Marie**
"Les Corsaires du Sud et le pavillon etoile de l'Alabama a l'Emden. Preface du vice-amiral Castex." Paris: Societe d'editions geographiques, maritimes et coloniales., 1936. 8vo, cl, illus., 202pp. Based on OR, ser.I vols. I-III. $30-b.

439 **LERCHE, Charles O., Jr.**
"Congressional Interpretations of the Guarantee of a Republican Form of Government during Reconstruction." (Baton Rouge, La.) JSH, May, 1949. v.XV, #2, p. 192-211. $8.

440 **LERNER, Eugene**
"The Monetary & Fiscal Programs of the Confederate Government." In: Journ. Political Economy, 1954, v.LXII, p. 506-522.

441 ..."Money, Prices & Wages in the Confederacy." In: JPE, 1955, v.LXIII, p. 20-40. A dissert. for PHd., Univ. Chicago, June 1954, also in hectographic copy.

442 ..."Inflation in the Confederacy, 1861-1865." In: Studies in the quantity theory of money. Edt. Milton Friedman. Chicago, Ill., Univ. of Chicago press, 1956, p. 161-175.

443 **LESH, Ulysses Samuel**
"A Knight of the Golden Circle." Boston: R.G. Badger print, 1911. 12mo, cl, 282pp. Indiana fiction.

444 ...Library of Fort Wayne & Allen Co., 1956. p. (6), 9 ports., from the Michigan alumnus 26 July, 1947. Original speech before CWRT of Chicago 1945. Case of Lambdin P. Milligan, of Ohio, involving validity of military trial of civilian when civil courts are available, 1865.

445 **LESLIE'S NEWSPAPER**
"Frank Leslie's Illustrated Newspaper." v.11, Nov. 24, 186-, v.15, Sept. 1863 (Sept. 19) Approx. 150 issues, unbroken run, rebound. Full page & double-page, & 4p. folding supplements (150 dbl. pgs.) (bmk-116) $600 1 single vol. Sept. 23, 1865-Sept. 15, 1866. $150.

446 **LESLIE, J.**
"General Lee & the Battle of Gettysburg." In: SHSP, 1895, v.23, p. 253-259.

447 **LESLIE, William R.**
"The Confederate Constitution." In: Mich. Quart. Rev., 1963, v.II, p. 153-165.

448 ..."The Constitutional Significance of Indian's Statute of 1824 on Fugitives from Labor." (Baton Rouge, La.) JSH, August, 1947, v.XIII, #3, p. 338-353.

449 ..."The Lesson & Legacy. A special issue commemorating the Centennial of the U.S. Army in the Civil War 1861-1865." (Alexandria, Va., Cameron Station) "Official Army Information Digest, August 1961. U.S. Army Magazine." 8vo, color wraps, illus., map, ports, 128pp. Various authors, phases of army in combat.

449a **LESSOFF, Howard**
"The Civil War with 'Punch.'" Wendell, N.C., Broadfoot, 1984. 4to, small 4to pict/wraps, 18, (132)p.

450 **LESTER, Richard I.**
"Confederate Finance & Purchasing in Great Britain." Charlottesville: University press of Virginia, 1975. 8vo, cl, dj, front, facsm. illus., tables, index, xii, (1), 267pp.

451 ..."Construction & purchase of Confederate Cruisers in Great Britain during the American civil war." In: Mariner's Mirror, London, Feb. 1977, wraps, 22pp.

452 **LESTER, William Wharton**
"A Digest of Military & Naval Laws of the Confederate States, from the commencement of the Provisional Congress to the end of the First Congress under the permanent constitution. Analytically arranged by Capt. W.W. Lester & Wm. J. Bromwell." Columbia (S.C., Evans & Cogswell,

1864. 12mo, cl, vii, 1, (11)-329, (1)p. $150, $250. Not in Crandall/Harwell, Sabin.
...Also in VaMHB, 1912, v.XX, #4, p. 428.

453 **LETCHER, John, Gov. of Virginia**
"Governor's Message to the General Assembly of the State of Virginia, January 7, 1861." Richmond, Va., 1861. 8vo, sewn, 54pp. (Jk.122) $125. Va. seceded April 17. Urges preparation for war, the North to bear the blame.

454 ..."Official Correspondence of Governor Letcher, of Virginia." In: SHSP, 1876, v.1, p. 455-462. See: E.B. Prettyman.

455 ..."Letters of John Letcher to J. Hierholzer, 1864-1865." In: Wm. MO., 2nd ser. Apr. 1928, v.VIII, p. 137-140. (Describes war conditions).

456 **LETFORD, William & Allen E. Jones**
"Location & classification & dates of Military events in Alabama, 1861-1865." Reprint: Spring issue, 1961, Alabama Historical Quarterly, by Alabama Civil War Centennial Commission, Sept. 1961. 8vo, wraps, (187)-206pp. fldg. map. $20.
...1971 Reprint: Ala. Hist.Quart., v.23-#1 & 2. "Military & Naval Activities in Alabama from 1861-1865, together with a location map." cover title. Caption title- "Actions, affairs, attacks, battles, bombardments, campaigns, captures, demonstrations, engagements, evacuations, expeditions, investments, occupations, reconnsissances, scouts, sieges & skirmished in Alabama from: 1861-1865."

456a "LETTERA di un misionario sulla schiavitu domestica degli stati Confedera ti di America." Roma, 1864, Tipografia di Giovanni Cesaretti. 8vo, full leather, 83pp. $75-ob.

456b **LETTER OF THE SECRETARY OF WAR** communicating, in compliance with resolutions of the Senate, Dec. 14, 1870, information relative to an alleged unlawful traffic with the Rebels in the State of Texas during the late war, intered into by the War Dep't." Washington, GPO, 1871. 8vo, cl, 4
See: Jas. W. Daddysman's "Matamoros Trade, etc."

457 **"LETTER RELATING to Confederate** Cemetery Lands, June 3rd, 1878. George W. McCrary, Secretary." Wash: Senate Ex-Docs., #93, 45th Congress 2nd Session, v.II, p. 4.

458 **LETTER RELATING to Purchase** of Certain Papers, Dec. 9, 1880. Senator Alexander. Wash: Senate Ex-Docs, #6, 46th Congress 3rd Session, vol. 1, 53pp. Pertains to negotiations with estate of Generals Bragg & Polk (deceased), relating to the late war.

459 **"LETTER TO HIS EXCELLENCY Whitemarsh B. Seabrook..."**
See: Wm. J. Grayson.

460 **"LETTERS BY TERRY RANGERS"**
In: Margaret Belle Jones' Bastrop, a compl. of material...1936, p. 41-71.

461 **"LETTERS FROM COLUMBIA (Arkansas)**
County Confederate Soldiers, Edt. by Ted R. Worley." In: AHQ, 1956, v.XV, p. 172-175.

461a **"LETTERS FROM THE BATTLE** of Lexington." 1861. (Columbia, Mo., Mo. Hist. Review, Oct. 1961, v. LVI-#1, pp.53-8, ills.

462 **"LETTERS FROM THE DIOCESE** of Little Rock 1861-1865. Edt: Willard E. Wight." In: AHQ, 1959, v.XVIII, p. 366-374. Letters of Archbishop to New Orleans from Bshp. Andrew Byrne, Laurence Smythe & Patrick R. Reilly, priests.

463 **"LETTERS FROM THE Secretary of Treasury,**
relating to persons who sold cotton to the Confederate States Government." Washington: Government print, 1912. 62nd Cong., 2nd sess., House Doc. 449, 8vo, sewn, 3pp.

464 …"Letter from the secretary of the treasury transmitting in accordance with a resolution of the Senate of April 22, 1912, a report of sales of cotton to the Confederate States." Washington: Government print, 1913. 62nd Congr., 2nd sess., Sen. Doc. #987. $40.

465 "LETTERS OF A CONFEDERATE OFFICER to his Family in Europe, etc."
See: Richard W. Corbin…

465a "LETTERS OF A CONFEDERATE SOLDIER:
the Andrew J. Fogle Collection. Edt: Howard L. Meredith & James L. Nichols.' In: TU-Library Chronicle, Spring 1965, p.34-9. Subject in the 9th Texas Infty. Of interest in dialect of a semi-literate soldier.

466 "LETTERS OF THE SOUTHERN SPY in Wash. & Elsewhere"
See: Edward A. Pollard.

467 "LETTERS SENT (Letters Received, V.1) by the Confederate States War Dept. in Relation to the war of the Rebellion, 1860-1865." Washington, DC: Adj-Gen. print off. 1876. 8vo, 2vol. in 1, paged continuously, xiii, 465pp. Herein is explained project, developing program for publication of the Official Records of the Civil War. Note: see-"Correspondence & orders..."

468 "LETTERS--OLD & NEW"
In: UDCMag., Mar. 1948, Sept. 1949. Scattered issues, letters from: O.T. Plummer, Cleburne, Texas, 1884, names members Co. A, 48th Reg. Tenn. Infty; Philip McKendree Miller to Harriet Frances Miller(3) Tenn., 1861-1865." Wasington, D C., U.S. Department State. Microfilm: 57 rolls, 1967.

469 LEVENSON, Dorothy
"The First Book of the Confederacy." New York: Franklin Watts Co. (1968). 8vl, cl, illus., photo-covers, 80pp. Illus: orig. Civil War drawings, photos. Juv. Rev. Edt.

470 LEVENTHORPE, Collett, Gen.
"Services held in the Chapel of rest, Yadkin valley, NC, at the burial of the late Gen. Collett Leventhorpe, with the sermon by the Rev. James A. Weston, rector of the parish, & sketch of the life of the deceased." n.p., 1890. 8vo, wraps, 15pp.

470a LEVERETT, Rudy H.
"Legend of the Free State of Jones." Jackson, University of Miss. Press, 1984. 8vo, wraps, xii, 131pp. $8.

471 LEVIN, Alexandra Lee
"Why have you burned my house?" Henrietta Lee & the burning of Bedford. In: Virginia Cavalcade, Fall 1978, vol. XXVIII, #2, p. 84-95, illus., incl. color, map ports.

471a …"The Canada Contact, Edwin Gray Lee." In: CWTI, Apr. 1979, v.18, #3, p.4-8, 42-7. Facsms, ports.

471b …"This Awful Drama: General Edwin Gray Lee, CSA, & his family." N.Y., 1987. 8vo, cl, dj, 248pp. $15. Cousin of Lee's, col. in 33rd Va.

472 LEVY, Eugene Henry
"Appomattox: prelude & postlude." Jacob Rader Marcus' Memoirs of Amer. Jews. Phila: Jewish Pub. Soc. of Amer., 3vols, 1955, v.3, p. 299-323. Mssc. diary of a CSA private in Va., May '64, Apr. 1865.

473 LEWINSVILLE, AFFAIR AT…
See: Jeb Stuart. "Correspondence at…"

473a LEWIS, Arthur J.
"Problems of the Selma Post Office, 1861-1865." In: AR, Oct. 1966, v.19, #4, p.277-82.

474 LEWIS, Charles Lee, Mrs.
"The Confederate Ironclad Virginia." In: South. Mag., June 1935, v.II, p. 12-13, 48-49.

475 …"Index to The Maryland Line in the Confederate Army 1861-1865." State of

Maryland: Hall of Records Comm. #3(1944) 8vo, wraps, 74pp. From the 1900 edt: W.W. Goldsborough "Maryland Line in the Confederate Army."

476 ..."The Marines of the Confederate States of America." In: UDC Mag., Jan. 1944, v.7, #1, p. 14-15.

477 ..."Admiral Franklin Buchanan Fearless Man of Action." Baltimore: Norman Remington Co., 1929, 8vo, cl, facsms, illus., ports, incl. color front, map liners, xvi, (1)285pp. index.

478 ..."Matthew Fontaine Maury, the Pathfinder of the Sea." Annapolis: U.S. Naval Institute, 1927. $35-bmk 8vo, cl, illus., ports, xvii, 264pp., index $18. (C.W.-40pp.)

479 ...Matthew Fontain Maury." In CV, Sept. 1925, v.XXXIII, p. 296-318.

480 ..."Admiral Franklin Buchanan." In: CV, 1929v. 37, p. 414-419.

481 **LEWIS, Elsie M.**
"Robert Ward Johnson: Militant Spokesman of the Old-South-West." In: AHQ, v.1954, v.XIII, p. 16-30.

482 ..."Economic conditions in Ante-Bellum Arkansas-1850-1861." In: AHQ, 1947, v.VI, p. 256-274.

483 **LEWIS, Elsie Rhett**
"Fort Sumter: The Key of Charleston." (Charleston, S.C., Lucas & Richardson) (1896) 8vo, wraps(tied), illus., 16pp.

483a **LEWIS, Gordon**
"Ninth Virginia Cavalry." In" Northern Neck of Virginia Historical Magazine." 1963, v.13, p.1172-8.

484 **LEWIS, J.W., Capt.**
"Wilson's defeat at Staunton River Bridge, 1864." In: SHSP, 1891, v.19, p. 56-57.

485 **LEWIS, John Howard**
"Recollections from 1860 to 1865. With incidents of camp life, descriptions of battles, the life of the Southern soldier, his hardships & sufferings, & the life of a prisoner of war in the northern prisons." Washington, DC, D.C. Peake & Co., 1895. 16mo, wraps, cover title, front(port), 92pp. $750 Bmk-105, $600 Bmk-105. At Ft. Delaware & Johnson's Island.

..."Recollections 1860-5." Dayton: Morningside, 1983. Facsm #74.

486 **LEWIS, Lloyd**
"Propaganda & the Kansas-Missouri War." Columbia, Missouri Hist. Review, Oct. 1939. Vol. XXXIV, #1, p. 3-17. Background for understanding the volatile nature of Abolitionists methods undermining the law & order in Mo-Kan conflict.

487 ..."Rivers of blood." In Am. Mercury, 1931, v.XXIII, p. 62-73. Battle of Shiloh, 1862.

488 **LEWIS, Marion Brunson**
"Sherman & the Burning of Columbia." College Station: Texas A & M Press, 1976. 8vo, cl, dj, illus., 188pp.

489 **LEWIS, Mort Reis**
"The Civil War Horse an Equine Saga." Richmond, Va., Civil War Centennial Committee, Official pub. #10, (1961) 8vo, plate, (4)p. folder. humor.

490 **LEWIS, Oscar**
"The war in the Far West, 1861-1865." Garden City, N.Y., Doubleday Co., 1961. 12mo, cl, dj, 163pp. $35-B.

491 **LEWIS, R.A., MD**
"The Search." In: CWTI, July 1970, v.IX, #4, p. 39-vignettes. A three year hunt for the father of a lost girl of a dead mother, by the author.

492 **LEWIS, Richard Welbourne**
"Aunt Emily or a Black Woman with a White Heart." (A Mississippi-Memphis Story of the "Old South Plantation Life.") (Memphis, 1931) Siloam Springs, Ark., Good Books Co., c. 1931, 8vo, wraps, 60pp. During & immediately following the Civil War period.

493 **LEWIS, Richard, Lt.**
"Camp Life of a Confederate boy, of Brat-

ton's Brigade, Longstreet's Corp, CSA. Letters written by...of Walker's regiment, to his mother, during the war. Facts & inspiration of camp life, marches, etc." Charleston, S.C., News & Courier Press, 1883. 8vo, cl, 113pp. $750. $500-ob.
...Gaithersburg, MD., 1983 reprint, $18.50.

494 **LEWIS, Samuel E., Dr.**
"The Treatment of Prisoners-of-War 1861-1865. Over 12% Confederate soldiers died in Northern prisons. Less than 9% Federal (Unionist) prisoners died in Southern prisons. The North held 220,000 Confederate prisoners, the South held 270,000 Federal (Unionist) soldiers as prisoners-of-war." Washington, DC., Samuel E. Lewis, MD, Late Ass't. surgeon, CSArmy. Richmond, Va., Wm. Ellis Jones, 1910. 8vo, wraps, 16pp. $40-, $75-ob. Head: The Confederate Memorial Literary Society, Richmond, Va.

495 ..."Biographical sketch of Samuel Preston Moore, Surgeon-General CSA." In: SHSP, 1901, v.29, p. 273-279.

496 ..."Jackson & McGuire at Winchester in 1862." In: South. Hist. Assn. Pub., 1902, v.30, p. 226-236.

497 ..."Treatment of Prisoners of War." (London) Jour. Confed. Hist. Soc., Summer 1972, v.10, #2, p. 63-76, pl. Extracts from his pamphlet.

498 **LEWIS, Warner, Colonel**
"An Ill-Fated Expedition: The Experiences of Colonel Warner Lewis." Intro: Merle Woods. (Okla. City.) Chron. Okla., Fall, 1973, v.I, #3, p. 280-284, port.

498a **LEWIS, William Terrell**
"Centennial History of Winston County, Mississippi." Pasadena, Texas: Globe Publishers International, (1972). 8vo, cl, 216pp, ills. $15. Largely civil war/complete rosters.

499 **LEXINGTON HISTORICAL SOCIETY**
"The Battle of Lexington, fought in & around the city of Lexington, Missouri, onSept. 18-20th, 1861, by the forces under command of Col. James A. Mulligan & Gen. Sterling Price. The Official Records of both parties to the conflict, to which is added memoirs of participants with maps & cuts. Printed for the Lexington Historical Society." (Lexington, Mo.) Intelligencer print, 1903. 12mo, wraps, illus., plans, ports, fldg. map, 68pp.

500 **"LIBBY PRISON Richomnd, Virginia."**
Richmond Civil War Centennial Committee, official pub. #12. (1961) 8vo, illus., (6)pp., bibliog. See: Rev. J.L. Burrows. W.S. Sclater & "Walls that Talk..."

501 **"LIBBY PRISON, A View of, Richmond, Va."**
Richmond, Va., A Hoen & Co., Litho, 1882. Oblong 4to, tinted litho., from a 1863 photo. By J.L. Barlow?, prison, tents, many figures.

502 **"LIBERTY HALL VOLUNTEERS-**
Papers relating to article contained in Washington & Lee University Historical Papers #6." Lynchburg, Va., 1904. 8vo, wraps, 25pp. $18.50-b See: W.G. Bean, Givens Brown Strickler, A.T. Barclay.
..."Washington & Lee University, Lexington, Virginia. Historical papers, #6, 1904. Part 2: Papers relating to the Liberty Hall Volunteers (Company I, Fourth Virginia Infantry). Lynchburg, Va., J.P. Bell Print, 1904. 8vo, cl, 136p. $125 bm.
See: Liberty Hall Volunteers.

503 **LIDDELL HART, Basil H.**
"The psychology of a commander." In: Army Quart., 1935, v.XXX, p. 50-58, 206-216. Review of Douglas Freeman's Lee.

504 **LIDDELL, St. John R., La.**
"Liddell's Record of the Civil War." In: SB, ns, 1885/1886, v.1, #7 & 9, p. 411-420, p. 529-535, port.

505 ..."Trans-Mississippi & Spanish Fort." In: SB, ns, v.II, 1886/1887, p. 736-740.

505a ..."Liddell's Record. Edt: Dr. Nathaniel Hughes." Dayton, Oh., Morningside Press, 1985. 8vo, cl, 216pp, maps, photo. $20. Liddell commanded Cleburne's Ark. Brig. unit of Army of Tenn.

506 **"LIFE & PUBLIC SERVICES of an Army Straggler"**
Macon, Ga., J.W. Burke & Co., 1865. 8vo, wraps, 90pp. Only known copy at University of Georgia. See: Kittrell J. Warren, author.

506a **"LIFE OF JAMES W. JACKSON,**
See: Jackson, James W.

507 **"LIFE IN BATTERY WAGNER."**
In: LWL, 1866-1887, v. II, p. 351-355.

508 **"LIFE IN THE SOUTH**
from the Commencement of the War, by a Blockaded British Subject, etc." See: Catherine Hopley.

508a **LIGHTFOOT, Henry W.**
"In Memoriam of General Samuel B. Maxey: read before the Association of the graduates of the US Military Academy, June 11, 1896. n.p., 1896? 8vo, wraps, 13p. port.

509 **LIGHTFOOT, James N., Thomas R. & William E.**
"Letters of three Lightfoot Brothers 1861-1864. Contributed by Edmund Cody Burnett." In: Ga. H.Q., Dec. 1941, v.XXV, #4, p. 371-401; Mar. 1942, v.XXVI, #1, p. 65-90. Born, Blakely, Ga., cousins of the Cody brothers. $20.

510 **LIGHTFOOT, William B., Mrs.**
"The evacuation of Richmond." In: Va. MH, 1933, v.XLI, p. 215-222. Account of evacuation of Richmond & entrance of Federal troops, for her children, 1865.

511 **LIGHTSEY, Ada Christine**
"The Veteran's Story by Ada Christine Lightsey, dedicated to the Heroes, Who Wore the Gray." Meridian News (Mississippi) Apr. 3, 1899) 8vo, cl, 51pp. Roster of Company F, 16th Mississippi.

512 **LIGON, Cornelia Barrett**
"Legend of the South-a Southern Woman's Memoir of a by-gone era." In: Amer. Hert., June 1956, v.VII, #4, p. 52-53, 108-111. sketches.

513 **"LINCOLN & ANDERSONVILLE."**
In: Tyler Quar. Hist. & Geneal. Mag., 1934, v.XV, p. 209-220. Study of the question of exchange prisoners from Off. Rec., Ser.II, v.VIII.

514 **"LINCOLN & FORT SUMTER."**
In: Wm. & Mary Quar., Oct. 1915, v.XXIV, p. 75-84. Evacuation, secret hist. by Gov. Pickens, from Daily Examiner, Richmond, Va. Aug. 8, 1861., p. 78-84.

515 **"LINCOLN & LEE."**
In: So. Atl. Quar., Jan. 1927, v.26, p. 4-21. Author a North Carolinian remains anon.

516 **"LINCOLN & THE BALTIMORE PLOT 1861,**
from Pinkerton Records & related papers. Edt: Norma B. Cuthbert." San Marino, Calif: Huntington Library, 1949. 8vo, cl, dj, front, xxii, 161pp.

517 **"LINCOLN & THE EVACUATION of Fort Sumter."**
In: Tyler QHGM, 1932, v.XIV, p. 77-81.

518 **"LINCOLN CATECHISM, The**
wherein the Eccentricities & Beauties of Despotism are fully set forth. A Guide to the Presidential Election of 1864." N.Y., J.F. Feeks (1864) 12mo, 46pp. Strongly opposed to Lincoln election.

519 **LINCOLN COUNTY, N.C.**
"Roster of Confederate Soldiers in the War Between the States Furnished by...1861-1865." Published by W.J. Hoke Camp Confederate Veterans. A. Nixon (& others) Comm. Pubs. Lincolnton, N.C., Journal Print, 1905. 8vo, wraps, 64pp.

520 **"LINCOLN EULOGIES,**
in Richmond Times-Dispatch, Feb. 23, 1928. Lincoln Eulogies Merely "Facet of Herd Psychology," to The Editor of the

Times Dispatch: Sir:" caption title, n.p., 8vo, 4pp folder. Monaghan-3040. Three letters by John T. Goolrick, M.D. Boland & Claude G. Bowers, disparaging Lincoln, Republican Party, "As a smoke screen to cover up their schemes." These letters found in "Final Reply to Westerner," also.

521 **"LINCOLN'S Place in History, Abraham"**
In: "The Old Guard," 1867, v.V, p. 207-217. Quotes Lincoln, compares speech, statements of crimes committed against Constitution.

522 **LINCOLN, Abraham in SHSP**
See: J.A. Campbell, W.W. Cleary, Mrs. B.G. Clifford, Robert Lewis Dabney, Charles L.C. Minor.

523 **"LINCOLN, as seen by the 'London Punch.'"**
In: CWT, June 1960, v.1, #3, p. 12-13. illus. by John Tenniel, whose satirical cartoons reflected the upper-class English attitude toward Abe Lincoln, until Lincoln's death.

524 **LINCOLN: ,**
"Trial of Abraham Lincoln by the Great Statemen of the Republic. A Council of the Past on the Tyranny of the Present. The Spirit of the Constitutuion on the Bench-Abraham Lincoln, Prisoner at the Bar, his own Counsel." New York: Metropolitan Record, 1863. 8vo, wraps, 32pp. $75, $40.
...Same above, but 29pp.
...Monaghan (252) shows two variants, one 1867, "all orig. pub. 1863 in "Metropolitan Record," a Catholic family paper, edt. by John Mullaly. Quotations from Lincoln & others, selected to discredit administration.
..."Trial of Abraham Lincoln by the Great Statesmen of the Republic. A council of the past on the tyranny of the present. The Spirit of the Constitution on the Bench-Abraham Lincoln, Prisoner at the Bar, His Own Counsel 1863." Caption title, Monaghan (251). 8vo, sewn, 8pp.

524a **LINDEMAN, Jack, Edt.**
"The Conflict of convictions, American writers report the CW. A selection & arrangement from the Journals, correspondence & articles of the major men & women of letters who lived thru the war." Philadelphia, (1968), Chilton Book Co. 8vo, cl, xiv, 308pp.Bmk-109 $15.

525 **LINDER, Ethel**
"Patrick Cleburne, Hero from Helena." In: AHQ, 1945, v.IV, p. 307-314.

526 **LINDSAY, Morn**
"Confederate soldiers in Tallapoosa county Alabama, 1907." In: Ga. Geneal. Mag., 1980. v.#75-76, p. 107-114. Including many born in Georgia.

527 **LINDSEY, D.**
"St. Albans has been surprised: Confederate Raid on St. Albans, Vermont, 1864." In: Amer. Hist. illus., 1976, v.X, p. ix, 14-22.

528 **LINDSEY, David**
"A. Lincoln/Jefferson Davis: the House divided." Cleveland: H. Allen (1960) 8vo, cl, (12), 186, (1)p. ports, bibliog. 185-6. "Men & Issues in American History." Comparison of ideas & beliefs concerning society & Gov., their treatment of 11 "problems & issues," 1860-1865.

529 **LINDSEY, John R.**
"Lindseys from Georgia who volunteered as Confederate Soldiers in the Civil War." In Ancestoring V, p. 22-25.

530 **LINDSEY, John W.**
"Third Ga. regiment, history of its campaigns, from April 26th, 1861 to Apr. 9th, 1865. By J.W. Lindsey, Sgt. Co. I & C.H. Andrews, Co. D." In: Madisonian, Madison, Ga., in the '90's. Subject: Conclusions of Gettysburg & back into Va." Dorn-II, 251.

531 **LINDSLEY, John Berrien**
"The Military Annals of Tennessee, Confederate. First Series, embracing a review of military operations, with regimental histories & memorial rolls, compiled from original & official sources, & edited by John Berrien Lindsley. Printed for subscribers." Nashville, Tenn: J.M. Lindsley & Co., 1886. Tk 8vo, cl (or, 3/4 Mor.) 36-plates (20 have from 3 to 8 ports), 910pp. $140, $140 Bmk-105.
...1974 reprint: Spartanburg, S.C. The Reprint Co. $32.50.

532 **LINES, Amelia Akehurst**
"To raise myself a little. The diaries & letters of Jennie, a Georgia teacher, 1851-1886." Edt: Thomas Dyer. Athens: University of Georgia press, 1982. 12mo, cl, dj, 188pp. $10. In & around Atlanta, the latter when it burned. Much about society during the war.

533 **LINING, Charles**
"The cruise of the Confederate steamship "Shenandoah." In: TennHM, July 1924, v.VIII, p. 102-111.

534 ..."War History of the Old First Virginia Infantry regiment, Army of Northern Virginia, by...at request of the Old 1st Virginia association." Richmond: Wm. Ellis Jones, 1884. 8vo, cl, 87pp. list of members. $500 Bmk-105.
...Dayton, Ohio, Morningside Bookshop 1970. Intro: Lee A. Wallace, Jr. Limited edt: 500 copies, prot, 98pp.

535 **LINK, Samuel Albert**
Nashville Tenn., Pub., M.E. Church, south., (c.1899) 1911 vol. 1; vol. 2, (c. 1900), 1903. 16mo, cl, 284, (285)-599pp. Curiously, v.1 dated 1911, but v. 2 is 1903 (copyright, above).

536 **LINNEY, C.B.**
"Distinguished Men of Albemarle & Orange County, of the Colonial & Civil War period." Charlottesville, Va., (c. 1928). 8vo, wraps, illus., 49pp.

537 **LIPSCOMB, Dabney**
"General Stephen D. Lee; his Life, Character & services." In: PMHS, 1909, v.X, p. 14-33.

538 **LIPSCOMB, Oscar Hugh**
"The Administration of John Quinlan, Second Bishop of Mobile (La.), 1859-83." (Philadelphia, Pa., 1967). Records of the American Catholic Historical Society of Philadelphia. Vol. LXXVIII, #1-4, Mar-Dec., 1967. Wraps, 8vo, 163pp.

538a ..."Some unpublished poems of Abram J. Ryan." In: ARev., July 1972, v.25, #5, p.163-77.

539 **LIST OF CONFEDERATE**
Soldiers in the General Assembly of North Carolina, 1874-1875." In: OLOD, April 1875, v.2, #2, p. 180-183.

540 ...Officers, Prisoners, Who Were Held by Federal Authority on Morris Island, S.C., under Confederate Fire from Sept. 7 to October 21, 1864, A." In: SHSP, 1889, XVII, p. 34-46.

541 **"LIST OF FIELD Officers,**
Regiments & Battalions in the Confederate States Army, 1861-1865." Washington, DC (1881). Tall 8vo, wraps, 131, 91pp. $200-r, $150 Bmk-84.
...Macon, Ga., 1912, Claud Estes, compl. 8vo, 138, 76pp., paper or cloth. Pub: J.W. Burke & Co.

542 **"LIST OF MAIMED**
Confederate Soldiers who Lost Limbs in the Service & to Whom Payments Have Been Made for the Period from 1883 to Sept. 1, 1886. Executive Department State of Georgia." Atlanta, Ga., Jas. P. Harrison print, 1886. 8vo, wraps, 47pp. DeRennell, 846.

543 ...Soldiers & Widows of Confederate Soldiers to Whom Warrants Were Issued under Act, Feb. 28, 1889, for Their Re-

lief." In: Annual report (auditor), 1889, p. xli. (Alabama) arranged by counties: Autauga to Winston. See: "Payment of needy CSA soldiers...

544 **"LIST OF NAMES**
of Citizens of Louisiana from Whom the United States Direct Tax Was Collected in 1865. Together with the Amounts Paid by Each." n.p., 1892, 8vo, cl, 354pp.

545 **"LIST OF OFFICERS,**
Regiments & Battalions (Texas) in the Confederate Army." Washington, D.C., War Dep't., 1892, 8vo, wraps, 91pp. Separate printing of above (91pp.)

546 **"LIST OF RELICS**
Alabama Room Confederate Museum" Richmond, Va., June 1922. 8vo, wraps, (8)pp.

547 **"LIST OF STAFF OFFICERS**
of the Confederate States Army, 1861-1865. Together with List of Field Officers, Regiments & Battalions in the Confederate States Army, 1861-65." Washington, D.C., 1891, GPO. Tall 8vo, orig. wraps, two pamphlets bound 186, 131, 91pp. $350-bohl.

548 ..."List of Field Officers, Regiments & Battalions in the Confederate States Army, 1861-65." (Washington, D.C., 1891?) 8vo, cl, 131pp. 91pp.
...Mattituck, N.Y., 1983, reprint $23.
Note: see also, Marcus J. Wright's "Roster of Confederate General Officers & their Commands' Wash: 1880.
Note: see also, "Memorandum relative to General Officers appointed by the President in Armies of the Confed. States."

548a ..."List of Staff Officers of Confederate States Army, 1861-1865." Washington, GPO, 1891. 8vo, wraps, 186pp. $200-ob.

549 **"LIST OF THE ARTILLERY**
Organizations in the Confederate States Service, A" (Washington, DC, 18--?) 8vo, cl, 186, 37pp. Arranged alphabetically, synonyms & state organizations. With Rosters. Ink corrections. Title variant (inked in)-"Artillery organizations of the Confederate States, 1861-1865. Compiled in the Rebel Archives Div., War Dept., Washington, 1889." Note: See Marcus J. Wright's "List of Artillery Officers, C.S.A." binder's title, this has precisely the same pg. numbers; Tex. Univ. copy interleaved with 49pp. mssc. See also: "Memorandum relative to General Officers appointed by the president in Armies of the Confed. States, 1861-1865."

550 **"LIST OF Virginia Chaplains,**
Army of Northern Virginia." In: SHSP, 1906, v.XXXIV, p. 313-315. In the 1st, 2nd, 3rd, & 4th Corp.

551 **"LIST SHOWING HEADSTONES**
for Confederate Soldiers & Sailors Who, While Prisoners of War, Died at Camp Butler, Illinois & Were Buried There." n.p., n.d., 8vo, wraps, 18pp.

552 **"LIST SHOWING INSCRIPTIONS**
on Headstones for Confederate Soldiers & Sailors, who While Prisoners of War, Died at Columbus & Camp Dennison, Ohio & Were Buried in Camp Chase Confederate Cemetery, Those Dying at Camp Dennison Having Been Thense Removed." Washington: Gov. Print. Office, 1907. 8vo, sewn, 54pp.

553 ...on Headstones for Confederate Soldiers & Sailors Who, While Prisoners of War, Died at St. Louis, Missouri & Buried in Jefferson Barracks, Mo." Washington: Gov. Print Office, 1907. 8vo, sewn, 19pp.

554 ...on Headstones for Confederate Soldiers & Sailors Who, While Prisoners of War, Died at Alton, Ill. Buried in North Alton Confederate Cemetary & on Small Pox Island." Washington: Gov. Print Office, 1907. 8vo, sewn, 28pp.

555 ...on Headstones for Confederate Soldiers & Sailors Who, While Prisoners of War,

556 ...on Headstones for Confederate Soldiers & Sailors who, While Prisoners of War, Died at Camp Douglas, Chicago, Ill., & Were Buried but Subsequently Removed, either to Their Respective Homes, or to the Confederate Mound Oak Woods Cemetery, Chicago." Washington: Gov. Print. Office, 1907, 8vo, sewn, 89pp.

556 ...on Headstones for Confederate Soldiers & Sailors who, While Prisoners of War, Died at Camp Morton, Indianapolis, Indiana & Were Buried in Green Lawn Cemetery." Washington: Gov. Print Office, 1907, 8vo, sewn, 33pp.

557 ...on Headstones for Confederate Soldiers & Sailors who, While Prisoners of War, Died at Fort Delaware, Del., & Were Buried in Finn's Point, N.J. National Cemetery, Near Salem, N.J." Washington: Gov. Print. Office, 1907, 8vo, sewn, 49pp.

558 ...on Headstones for Confederate Soldiers & Sailors who, While Prisoners of War, Died at Point Lookout, Md. & There Buried, but Subsequently Removed, Either to the Point Lookout Confederate Cemetery, or to Their Respective Homes." Washington: Gov. Print Office, 1907, 8vo, sewn, 69pp.

559 ...on Headstones for Confederate Soldiers & Sailors who, While Prisoners of War, Died on Rock Island Illinois & Buried." Washington: Gov. Print. Office, 1907, 8vo, sewn, 39pp.

560 ...on Headstones for Confederate Soldiers & Sailors who, While Prisoners of War, Died at Elmira, NY & Were Buried in Woodlawn National Cemetery." Washington: Gov. Print. Office, 1907. 8vo, sewn, 54pp.

561 **"LITERARY & HISTORICAL Activities** in North Carolina 1900-1905." Vol. 1 (all published) Raleigh, N.C., 1907 (W.J. Peele, edt.) 8vo, cl, 623pp. Contains 83pp. (9 articles) re: War Between the States.

562 **LITTLE, George & James R. Maxwell** "A History of Lumsden's Battery, C.S.A. Published by R.E. Rhones Chapter U.D.C." Tuscaloosa, Alabama. (c. 1905). 8vo, stiff wraps, front(group photo). 70pp, (4)pp. unit roster inserted at p. 67(not in all copies $75-bmk-106. $85-jk-137. "written from memory in 1905, by Dr. Maxwell, Oct. 15, 1863, with help of a diary kept by Dr. James T. Searcy." 2nd Ala. Bat. Co. F., CSA 1/2 case $150.

563 **LITTLE, Henry, Gen., CSA** "The Diary of General Henry Little, C.S.A." Edt: Albert Castel. In: CWTI, Oct. 1972, v.XI, #6, p. 4-11, 41-47. ports, illus.

564 **LITTLE, Robert D.** "General Hardee & the Atlanta Campaign." March 1945, v.XXIX, #1, p. 1-22.

565 ..."Southern Historians & the downfall of the Confederacy (Part 1)." In: Ala. Rev., Oct. 1950, v.3, p. 243-262; Jan. 1951, v.4, p. 38-54 (Pt. 2) A Study "anayses of defeat." 1866ff.

566 **LITTLE, Robert Henry** "A Year of Starvation Amid Plenty, or How a Confederate Soldier Suffered from Hunger & Cruelty in a Prison of War During the Awful Days of the 60's." Belton, Texas, n.d., 16mo., reprinted from local newspaper, 1891. $300.

...Do: Reprint 1966 (Waco, Texas: Texian Pr. 16mo, cl, 40pp. op.

567 **LITTLEJOHN, Elbridge** "The Civil War Letters of Elbridge Littlejohn. Edited by Vicki Betts." In: Chron. Smith Co., Tex., Winter, 1978.

..."Civil War letters. Edt. Vicki Betts." Pt. II. Summer, 1979, v.18, #1, p.11-51.

568 **LITTLEPAGE, Hardin Beverly** "A midshipman aboard the Virginia." In: CWTI, April 1974, v.13, #1, p. 4-11, 42-47, Part 1, Part II-May 1974, #2, p. 36-43. Part III-June, #3, p. 19-26. illus., ports, sketch.

569 **LIVELY, E.H.**
"Roster of Goochland Co. Troops." In: SHSP 1901, v.29, p. 223-226.

570 ..."Williamsburg Junior Guards." In: SHSP 1901, v.29, p. 175-177.

571 **LIVELY, Robert A.**
"Fiction Fights the Civil War: an Unfinished Chapter in the Literary History of the American People." Chapel Hill: Univ. of N.C. pr (1957) 8vo, cl, dj, viii, 230pp. $35-bmk.

572 ..."The novelist as historian of the Civil War." In: Univ. Of N.C. "Research in Progress," 1951, v.29, p. 166-167. An abstract of thesis, surveying 512 novels 1862-1948.

573 **LIVERMORE, Thomas Leonard**
"Numbers & losses in the Civil War in America, 1861-1865." Bost., N.Y., Houghton, Mifflin., 1900 8vo, cl, iv, 150pp.
...2nd Edt., 1901.
...Bloomington: Indiana Univ. Pr., 1957, 12mo, cl, dj, xi, (4) 150pp. Introduction: Edward E. Barthell, Jr.

574 **LIVERMORE, William Roscoe**
"Lee's conduct of the Wilderness Campaign." In: Amer. Hist. Assoc. Rep., 1908, v.I, p. 235-243.

574a **LIVINGOOD, James W.**
"Chattanooga 'Rebel.'" In: East TennHS, 1967, #39, p.42-55.

574b **"LLEWELLYN, 1864."**
In: AHQ, Winter 1958, v.20, #4, p.630-5.

575 **LLOYD, J.C.**
"The battles of Fredericksburg." In: CV, Nov., 1915, v.XXIII, p. 500-502.

576 **LLOYD, John Uri**
"Felix Moses, the beloved Jew of Stringtown on the pike; pages from the life experiences of a unique character. A man whose romantic record challenges imagination." Cincinnati, OH., printed for author by Caxton press, (1930). 8vo, cl, xxix, 354pp., front, illus., incl. map, music, plates, ports, facsm., diagr. liner-paper map. $75-b.
...2nd printing, 1000 copies, Nov. 1930. Moses, with 9th CS cavalry.

576a ..."Warwick of the Knobs; a story of Gtringtown County, Ky." N.Y., Dodd, Mead, 1901. Fiction. 12mo, cl, 305pp. CSA Sympathizers, Warwick gives three sons to Morgan.

577 **"LOCAL DESIGNATIONS**
of Confederate Troops." n.p., n.d., (Washington, D.C., 189-?) 8vo, cl, 169pp. Attributed to Marcus J. Wright, Copy in Confederate Museum has 152pp.

578 **LOCHRIDGE, Thomas Henry**
"Letters Home: from Private Thomas Henry Lochridge, 1961-1962." Edt: Tommy R. Thompson. (Fayetteville, Ark.) Ark. Hist. Quart. 1974. Autumn, v.XXXIII, #3, p. 239-251.

579 **LOCKETT, S.H., Col.**
"The defense of Vicksburg." In: B & L, v. III, p. 482-492. CSA engineer.

579a **LOCKHART, Paul D.**
"The Confederate Navy Squadron at Charleston & the failure of Naval Harbor Defense." In: Amer. Neptune, Fall 1984, p.257-75.

580 **LOCKRIDGE, Dora Jeanne Smith**
"Reminiscences." In: UDCMag., Oct. 1953, v.16, #10, p. 28-29, 32-36. On burning of Cassville, Ga., 1864.

581 **LODOR, John A.**
"An address delivered by...before the Grand Lodge of the State of Alabama, Dec. 3, 1861." Montgomery, Ala., Advertiser, 1862. 8vo, wraps, 16pp.

582 **LOEHR, Charles Theodore**
"Battle of Drewry's Bluff." In: SHSP, 1891, v.19, p. 100-111.

583 ..."The Battle of Milford Station: address before Pickett Camp, UCV, Aug. 31, 1896." In: SHSP, 1898, v.26, p. 110-115, plan.

584 ..."The First Virginia Infantry in the Peninsula Campaign, reminiscences of..." In: SHSP, 1893, v.21, p. 104-110.

585 ..."The Old First Virginia at Gettysburg." In: SHSP, 1904, v.32, p. 33-40.

586 ..."Point Lookout, address to Pickett Camp Cvets, Oct. 1, 1890." In: SHSP, 1890, v.18, p. 113-120.

586a ..."War History of the Old First Virginia Inf." Dayton, Oh., Morningside, (1970). 8vo, wraps, Lim. Edt. Reprint #1.
...Reissue, same 1978. $12.50.

586b ..." War History of the Old First Virginia Infantry Regiment, ANV. Published by request of the Old first Virginia ass'n." Richmond, Va., Wm. Ellis Jones, 1884. 8vo, wraps, 87pp. Pres-750-cb.

586c **LOGAN COUNTY, ARKANSAS**
"Civil War in Logan County, Arkansas." Paris, Ark., Logan County Historical Society, Summer 1981 issue.
..."Civil War in Logan County, Arkansas," In: Wagon Wheels, Summer, 1981, v.1, pp.6-66.

587 **LOGAN, Frenise A.**
"India-Britain's Substitute for American cotton in 1861-1865." (Lexington, Ky.) JSH, v.XXIV, #3, Nov., 1958, p. 472-480.

588 **LOGAN, George William, Col.**
"Report: Engagement between Federal Gunboats & Fort Beauregard May 10/11, 1863." In: SHSP, 1883, v.11, p. 497-501.

589 **LOGAN, Herschel C.**
"Buckskin & satin: the life of Texas Jack (J.B. Omohundro) buckskin clad scout, indian fighter, plainsman, cowboy, hunter, guide & actor, etc. Harrisburg, Pa., Stackpole Co, (1954) 8vo, cl, facsms, maps, ports, views, xiv, 218pp. (1846-1880) in Va. services in CSArmy, the west later with Buffalo Bill, etc.

590 ..."The Confederate LeMat revolver." In: Amer. rifleman, Nov., 1960, v.108, #11, p. 35-36, diagr. table, view. Gun patented by Dr. Jean Alexandre Francois Le Mat, of New Orleans, in 1856 for the CSA.

591 **LOGAN, India Washington Peddicord**
"Kelion Franklin Peddicord of Quirk's Scouts Morgan's Kentucky Cavalry, CSA. Biographical & Autobiographical, together with a general biographical outline of the Peddicord family." N.Y., Neale Pub., 1908. $500-ob, $250-bmk-105. 12mo, cl, 4-ports, incl. front, 170pp.
...Louisv., Lost Cause Press, micro-ed.

592 **LOGAN, Kevin J.**
"My Confederate Girlhood; the Memoirs of Kate Virginia Cox Logan, edited by her daughter, Lily Logan Morrill." Richmond, Va., Garrett & Massie, 1932. 8vo, cl, plates, ports, xv, 150pp. $45-B, $35-bmk-111.

593 ..."The Bee-Hive Newspaper & British Working Class Attitudes toward the American Civil War." In: CWH, Dec. 1976, v.22, #4, p. 337-348.

594 **LOGAN, Robert R.**
"Arkansas Confederates Among the Immortal Six Hundred." (Fayetteville) Arkansas Historical Quarterly, Spring issue, 1957. reprint, cover title, 8vo, wraps, (5)pp.

595 ..."Confederates among the Immortal Six Hundred." cover title Rep: Arkansas Hist. Quart., 16:91-5, 8vo, wraps, Spring 1957.

596 ..."Battle of Prairie Grove," Dec. 1862. From Arkansas Hist. Quart., Autumn, 1957; v.16:258-67, notes. Append: p. 267-280. Contributions of several persons on Prairie Grove Battlefield Park, estb. at site 1906.

597 ..."Dedication of Prairie Grove Monument. Address: Dec. 7, 1956." Fayetteville, Ark., 1956. 8vo, wraps, 24pp. In: Ar. HQ, 1957, v.XVI, p. 257-280, illus., map.

598 **LOGAN, Thomas Muldrup**
"Oration delivered by Gen. T.M. Logan at the Reunion of the Hampton Legion, in

Columbus, S.C., 21st July, 1875. Published by his friends in Charleston." Charleston, S.C., Walker, Evans, Cogswell, 1875. 8vo, wraps, 28pp. $17.50-jk.

599 ..."Reception of General T.M. Logan, Ex-captain, W.L.I. Volunteers, Co. A. Hampton Legion Infantry at the Hibernian Hall, Charleston, S.C., July 26, 1875, by his comrades of the Washington Light Infantry." Charleston: News & Courier print, 1875. 8vo, wraps, 16pp.

600 **LOGUE, John Alan**
"A Texan (Nathaniel Alexander Morgan) views the civil war." In: TSHA, Jr. Hist., 1961, v.XXII, p. 17-18, 21. Morgan, Ass't. surgeon, 1st CSA inf.

601 **LOKKE, Carl L.**
"The captured Confederate records under Francis Lieber." In: Am. Archivist, Oct. 1946, v.9, p. 277-319. Stanton & Lieber had political goals but when no evidence was found to indict Jeff Davis, they lost interest.

602 **LOMAX, Elizabeth Lindsay**
"Leaves from Old Washington Diary 1954-1963." (New York) Books, Inc., E.P. Dutton 1943-first edition. $20-. 12mo, cl, d/w, 256pp. Edt: Lindsay Lomax Wood, granddaughter.

603 **LOMAX, Virginia (Mattie Virginia Sarah Lindsay Lomax)**
"The Old Capitol & Its Inmates. By a Lady, who enjoyed the hospitalities of the Government for a "season." N.Y., E.J. Hale & Son, 1867. 12mo, cl, 226pp. (3)pp. ads of "Southern School Books."

604 **LONDON INDEX.**
"General J.E.B. Stuart." In: SHSP, 1895, v.23, p. 202-205.

605 **LONDON MORNING ADVITISER-**
"Within a stone's throw of Independence." In: SHSP, 1884, v.12, p. 111-112.

606 **"(LONDON) TIMES & The American Civil War, The"**
(London) Journ. Confed. Hist. Soc., July 1962, v.I, #1thru v.VIII, #3, p.99-102., #4, p. 142-144, v.II, #1, p. 40-44, #3, p. 126-131, plate, #4, p. 167-171; v.III, #1, p. 32-35, #2, p.65-68, #3, p.103-107, #4, p.142-147, v.IV, #1, p. 30-35, plate, #2, p.79-84, #3, p. 126-130, #4, p. 167-171, v.V, #1, p.26-30, #2, p.69-73, #3, p.106-110, #4, p.157-161; v.VI, #1, p.31-35, #2, p.86-90, #4, p.178-83, v.VII, #1, p.33-38, #2, p.74-78, #3, p.112-118.

607 **LONDON, Henry Armand**
"Memorial address on the life & services of Bryan Grimes, a Major-General in the provisional army of the Confederate states delivered on Memorial Day, May 10, 1886, at Raleigh, N.C." Raleigh, E.M. Uzzell print, 1886. $100-r, $75-bmk-104. 8vo, wraps, 22pp.

608 ..."Appomattox Echo. The Last Volley of the memorable field, etc." In: SHSP, 1899, v.XXVII, p. 92-93.

609 ..."The university during the war." In: Univ. N.C. Record, June 1911, #93, (15pp.) Including a "list of members of Civil War classes & their records."

610 **LONDON, Lawrence Foushee**
"Confederate Literature & its publishers." In James Sprunt Studies in History & Political Science, v.39, p. (82)-96. 1957.

611 ...The Literature of the Church in the Confederate States 1861-1865." Reprint: Protestant Episcopal Church, 1948. Garrison, N.Y., 11pp.
See also: Edgar Legare Pennington (same issue)

612 ..."Bishop Joseph Blount Cheshire, his Life & Work." Chapel Hill: N.C. University, 1941. 8vo, cl, front(port), illus., viii, 140pp. See also under Chesire (Jos. B.)

612a **LONG, A. L.**
"Memoirs of Robert E. Lee . . ." Secaucus, N.J., Book Sales Inc., 1983. Blue & Grey Press.

613 **LONG, Alexander, Hon., of Ohio**
"Present condition & future prospects of the Country." April 8, 1864.(n.p., n.d.) 8vo, 20pp. "Speech April 7, 1864 (on the state of the Union." n.p., n.d., 8vo, 7pp. Long favored abandoning the war & recognizing the Southern Confederacy.

614 **LONG, Andrew Davidson, Co.A, 5th, Va. Reg.**
"Stonewall's Foot Cavalryman." (Austin, Texas: The Steck Co., 1965) Priv. Prt., ATG., by Walter E. Long. Front., illus. 8vo, cl, 37, (2)pp. Not for sale. $30.

615 **LONG, Armistead Lindsay, Gen.**
"Army of Northern Virginia., Assoc. of...General Lee & Long." In: SHSP, 1891, v.19, p. 271-273.

616 ..."Captured Guns at Spotsylvania Court House." In: SHSP, 1879, v.7, p. 539.

617 ..."Causes of Lee's Defeat at Gettysburg." In: SHSP, 1877, v.4, p.66-68, 118-123.

618 ..."From Rapidan to Spotsylvania Court House." In: SHSP, 1885, v.13, p. 241-247.

619 ..."Gen. Early's Valley Campaign." In: SHSP, 1877, v.3, p. 112-122, 1890, v.18, p. 80-91.

620 ..."Memoir of Gen. John B. Magruder." 1884, v.12, p. 105-110.

621 ..."Lee's W. Virginia Campaign." In: AW, p. 82-94.

622 ..."Report of Brig-Gen. A.L. Long, artillery, Second Corps, from 4th to 31st. May, 1864." In: SHST, 1874, v.1, p. 113-118.

623 ..."Seacoast Defences of South Carolina & Georgia." In: SHSP, 1876, v.1, p. 103-107, v.2, p. 239-240. (See: Gen. Thomas Jordan).

624 ..."Memoirs of Robert E. Lee his Military & Personal History embracing a large amount of information hitherto unpublished, by A.L. Long formerly military secretary to General Lee, afterwards Brig-Gen. & Chief of Artillery, Second Corps, A.N.V., together with incidents relating to his private life subsequent to the war, collected & edited with the assistance of Marcus J. Wright. Formerly Brig-Gen., Army of Tennessee & Agent of the U.S. for the collection of Confederate Records." N.Y., Phila., Wash: J.M. Stoddart co, 1886. Tk. 8vo, cl, (full sheep, or full Mor., with raised bands) ports, incl. front, pls., large fldg. map & 7-facsms. Lee's field-maps. (3), 707 pp. Append: p. 503-699, Official reports of Lee's operations, ANV to the War Dept., Richmond, 1887 edition, same. $40-bmk $60-bmk.

..."Memoirs of Robert E. Lee . . ." N.Y., J.M. Stoddart, 1887 (2nd printing). Steve Rowe reports the 2nd print contains 12 Wm. L. Sheppard prints not found in the 1st ed. $150.

625 **LONG, Daniel Albright**
"Jefferson Davis: Address delivered at Concord, N.C., June 3, 1921." Raleigh, NC, 1923 (Edwards & Brought) 8vo, stiff wraps, 20pp.

626 ..."Jefferson Davis." in North Carolina Booklet, XXI, 1922, p. 3-20.

626a **LONG, Durwood**
"Economics & politics in the 1860 presidential election in Alabama." In: AHQ, 1965, v.27, #1 & 2, p.43-58.

626b ..."Political Parties & propaganda in Alabama in the presidential election of 1860." In: AHQ, 1963, v.25, #1 & 2, p.120-35.

626c **LONG, E. B.**
"The Paducah (Ky.) affair: Bloodless action that altered the Civil War in the Mississippi Valley." In: RKHS, Oct. 1972, v.70, #4, p.253-76.

627 **LONG, Edward John**
"When railroading went to war." In: Trains, Jan. 1956, v.16 #3, p.22-26. views. On tactical use of RRy by Union & CSArmy.

628 **LONG, J.M.**
A seventeen year old Texas boy at Shiloh." In: B & G, 1893, v.1, p.278-279.

629 **LONG, Jack**
"General James Longstreet-"Old Pete"- In: Marine Corp. Gazette, 1938, v.XXII, #2, p.54-56, 78. Anecdote concerns Longstreet 2nd day battle of Chickamauga.

630 **LONG, John S.**
"Carved in brass & marble." In: Southern Hist. Monthly, Jan. 1876, v.1, #1, p.78-82. Also: OLOD, Dec. 1875, v.3, #6, p. 789-793.

631 **LONG, John Sherman**
"The Gosport Affair, 1861."(Lexington, Ky.) JSH, May, 1957, v.XXIII, #2, p. 155-172. $8.

632 **LONG, Melvin Durward**
"Alabama & the formation of the Confederacy Ann Arbor: University microfilms, 1959. Positive microfilm typscript, 226 leaves, Thesis--Univ. Fla. Dissrt. abstract: 20:279-80. Local politics in Ala., votes in presidential election, selection of delegates to the convention 1860-1861.

633 ..."Unanimity & Disloyalty in Secessionist Alabama." In: CWH, September 1965, v.XI, #3, p. 257-273.

634 ..."Alabama's Secession Commissioners." In: CWH, March 1963, v.IX, #1, p.55-66.

635 **LONG, N.M.**
"Address on Robert E. Lee, delivered at Goodwyn Institute." Memphis, Ten., 1920. 8vo, wraps, 16pp.

635a **LONG, Roger**
"Uncle Dan & 'Dixie'. Music that moved the South." In: CWTI, Apr. 1981, v.20, #1, p.12-17, ills, facsms, port, pl. Facm. back cover.

636 **LONGACRE, Edward G.**
"Three Brothers face the baptism of battle, July 1961." In: FHQ, Summer, 1977, v.LXI, #2, p.156-168. John, Sanford & Hamilton Brach, in the Georgia 8th Infantry.

637 ..."Target: Winchester, Virginia." In: CWTI, June 1976, v.15, p. 22-31, illus., maps, ports.

638 ..."Mounted Raids of the Civil War." N.Y., South Brunswick, A.S. Barnes co., London: Yoseloff & co., (1975). 8vo, cl, dj, illus., ports, 348pp., index, bibliog., 325-337. CSA: Stuart, Van Dorn, Jones-Imboden, Morgan, Wheeler & Forrest. $20-bmk

639 ..."The Battle of Brandy Station A Shock that made the earth tremble." In: VaCavl. Winter, 1976, v.XXV, #3, p. 136-143, illus., ports.

640 ..."Stuart's Dumfries Raid." In: CWTI, July 1976, v.XV, #4, p. 18-26, illus., ports, map.

640a ..."Inspired blundering: Union operations against Richmond during the Gettysburg Campaign." In: CWH, March 1986, v.32, #1, p.23-43.

640b **LONGSTREET, Augustus Baldwin, Rev.**
"Valuable Suggestions addressed to the Soldiers of the Confederate States." n.p., n.d. (c. 1864). Albert Castel has unearthed a pamphlet (although no copy has been located) in an article in: CWT, June 1987, v.33, #2, p. 103-114. When the war was going badly for CS Rev. Longstreet published this pamphlet & distributed it among the soldiers to boost their morale. It was reprinted in a slightly abridged form in the 'Cincinnati Commercial,' July 19, 1864, with an editorial noting the pamphlet was picked up at Marietta (Ga.) by one of their correspondents. An apparently completed version appeared in Frank Moore, Edt. "Rebellion Record." 12 vols. Reprint: NY, Arno Press, 1977, Vol. 8, p.433-37.

640c **LONGSTREET, Edward**
"Down to earth, 50 prosettes (rhymed prose editorials, Martial style) by the

rhyming Maretian, a cosmic astronaut whose Martian grandfather interviewed Robert E. Lee & James Longstreet one hundred years ago, Comprising 13 original prosettes on civil rights for blacks & whites, 1 to 13;37 prosettes on civil sense & moral recompense, 14 to 50 (one for each star in the American flag) plus an appendix for the District of Columbia, entitled Cosmic death of a nation. This book is a declaration of independence for American whites, an answer to Uncle Tom's Cabin." Lakemont, Ga., Georgia Free Press, 1964. Sm4to, 54pp,. port. reproduced from typewritten copy. Edward Longstreet, retired reporter.

641 **LONGSTREET, Helen Dortch**
"Lee & Longstreet at High Tide, Gettysburg in the light of the Official Records." Gainesville, Ga., Published by the Author, 1904. (Phila: J.B.Lippincott) 8vo, cl, facsms. illus., ports, incl. front. 346pp. $80, $150-b, $85, $75, $80.
..."Second Edition." 1905.
...NY, Kraus reprint, 1969.

642 ..."In the Path of Lee's Old War Horse." (Atlanta, Ga., 1917) cl. Entire edition was burned, except for two copies, handwritten copy was used for copyright.

643 ...The great American Gen. James Longstreet." In: Mark Twain quart., 1953, v.9, #3, p. 5-10. Defends his activities in the Civil War.

644 **LONGSTREET, James**
"Battle of Chickamauga, Report of Gen. Longstreet, Hdq. near Chattanooga, Oct. 1862." In: SHSP, 1883, v.XI, p. 171-175.

645 ..."Battle of Fredericksburg." In: B & L, v.III, p. 70-85.

646 ..."Battle of Fredericksburg, report of Lieut-Gen. Longstreet." In: SHST, 1874, v.I, p. 42-48.

647 ..."Battle of Fredericksburg." In: Cent. Mag., Aug. 1886, ns, v.X, illus., map, ports, p. 609-626.

648 ..."Gen. Lee's right wing at Gettysburg." In: B & L, v.III, p. 339.

649 ..."Causes of Lee's defeat at Gettysburg, Gen. Longstreet's account of the campaign & battle." In: SHSP, 1878, v.V, p.54-86, 171-175, 257-287.

650 ..."General Longstreet's report on the Pennsylvania campaign." In: SHST, 1874, v.I, p. 49-55.

651 ..."Gen. Lee in Pennsylvania." In: AW, p. 414-446.

652 ..."Gen. Lee's Invasion of Pennsylvania." In: B & L, v.III, p. 244-251.

653 ..."The Invasion of Maryland." In: B & L, v.II, p. 663-674.

654 ..."Lee's Invasion of Pennsylvania." In: Cent. Feb. 1887, v.34, p. 622-635.

655 ..."The Invasion of Maryland." In: Cent. Mag., June 1886, ns, v.X, illus., ports, p. 309-315.

656 ..."Report of Affair of Oct. 27, 1864., Hdq., ANV." In: SHSP, 1879, v.VII, p.541-543.

657 ..."Report of the Battle of Seven Pines." In: SHSP, 1877, v.III, p. 277-280.

658 ..."Report of the Battle of Wilderness." In: SHSP, 1878, v.VI, p. 78-80. Hdq. 1st/Army Corps., Mar. 23, 1865.

659 ..."Report of the Pennsylvania Campaign." In: SHSP, 1882, v.X, p. 337-345. Hdq., 1st Army Corp., Dept. N.Va., July 27, 1863.

660 ..."Second Battle of Manassas-Reply to General S.D.Lee. The Artillery of Manassas." In: SHSP, 1878, v.VI, p.215-217.

661 ..."Report of Operations of part of the 1st Corp., ANV, in East Tennessee, Nov. & Dec., 1863." In: SHST, 1875, v.II, P. 85-98.

662 ..."The Seven Days." including Frayser's Farm." In B & L, v.II, p. 396-405.
See also: Ed. Porter Alexander, Gamaliel Bradford, Sears W. Cabell, Jubal A. Early, Jno. W. Jones, Fitzhugh Lee, S.D. Lee, Lt.

Richard Lewis, Helen D. Longstreet, Wm. A. McClendon, Frank M. Mixson, Donald B. Sanger, Gilbert M. Sorrell, Walter H. Taylor, Jack Long.

663 ..."The Longstreet-Gettysburg Controversy." In: SHSP, 1895, v.23, p.342-348.

664 ..."From Manassas to Appomattox, Memoirs of the Civil War in America. By James Longstreet, Lieutenant-General Confederate Army." Phila: J.B. Lippincott & co, 1896. 8vo, cl, illus., maps, ports, incl front, xxii, 690pp. (sheep); (full Mor) $175-bmk-123 $100-mcm.
...2nd Edt., revised, 1903. 8vo, decr. cl, xxii, 698pp. facsms, illus., maps (color coded), ports, incl front. $60.
...same, for 1908 $45.
...Louisv: Lost Cause pr, micro-cd, $9.
...Bloomington: Indiana University press (1960), Civil War Centennial Series, Edt. with intro & notes, James I. Robertson, Jr., 12mo, cl, dj, xxix, (1), (13)-692pp. $60.
...N.Y., Kraus pr, (reprint) 1969. $45.
...Millwood, N.Y., 1976 reprint.

665 ..."Mistakes at Gettysburg," In: AW, P. 619-633.

666 ..."Operations about Lookout Mountain." In: SHSP, 1880, v.VIII, P. 266-269.

667 ..."Our March against Pope." In: B & L, v.II, p. 512-526.

668 ..."Plan of Campaign for 1864." In: LWL, 1868, v.I, p. 170-171, Petersburg, Mar. 15, 1864.

669 ..."A Short History of J. Longstreet." Park Place, N.Y., Knapp & co, 1888. 2 3/4x1 1/2" colored booklet, 16pp. facsm. signature, (Packed in Duke's cigarettes) See: "Heroes of the C.W." & W. Duke Co.

669a ..."Manassas to Appomattox." Phil: Lippincott, 1896. 3/4 leather, special bound, autographed edition, Lim. 250 copies signed by J.L. $400-r.

669b ..."Manassas to Appomattox." Secaucus, N.J., Blue & Gray Press, 1984. $17.50. $20.

See: Wm. L. Richter "Gen. Longstreet during Reconstruction." In: LaH., 1970, v.11, p.215-30.

670 **LONN, Ella**
"Desertion during the Civil War." N.Y., Lond: Century co., 1928. 8vo, front (fldg. map), vii, 251pp. $75-ob.
...Gloucester, Peter Smith, 1966. 12mo, cl, vii, 251pp. $8, $10.

671 ..."Foreigners in the Confederacy." Chapel Hill: Univ. of N.C. pr., 1940 $100-b 8vo, cl, photolith repro.

672 ..."Salt as a Factor in the Confederacy." N.Y., Wash: Neale pr., 1933. $100-bmk-108 $100-r 8vo, cl, map, 324pp. $15, $25.
...University: Alabama Univ. Pr(1965) 12mo, cl, dj, map liners, viii, (1), (13)-324. "Southern History Publications #4."

673 ..."The Extent & Importance of Federal Naval Raids on salt-making in Florida, 1862-1865." In: FHQ, Apr. 1932, v.X, p.(167)-184.

674 ..."Reconciliation between the North & the South." In: JSH, Feb. 1947, 24pp. $8.

675 **LOOKOUT MOUNTAIN, Battle of...**
See: Braxton Bragg, John Bratton, John Calvin Brown, John King Jackson, Evander McIver Law, James Longstreet, Edmund Winston Pettus, James L. Sheffield, Carter L. Stevenson, Edward Cary Walthall.

676 **LOONEY, Morgan H.**
"Eulogy on Gen. R.E. Lee, delivered in the Seminary Hall at Gilmer, Texas." N.Y., 1871, 8vo, wraps, 16pp. Jk $45.

676a **LORCH, Fred W.**
"Mark Twain & the "Campaign that failed." In: Amer. Lit., Mar. 1940, v.12, p.454-70.
See: cent., Dec. 1885, v.31.

677 **LORD, Daniel**
"The Effect of Secession upon the Commercial Relations between the North & the South & upon each section..." N.Y.,

1861, 12mo, map, 72pp. sewn. $37.50.
...2nd Edt., 1861.
...London: 1861, 8vo, above.

678 **LORD, Francis Alfred**
"Analysis of photos of dead show equipment of Confederates in 1864." In: CWTI, Apr. 1966, v.5, #1, p. 18-21, illus.

679 ..."Civil War Collector's Encyclopedia: Arms, Uniforms, & equipment of Union & the Confederacy." Harrisburg, Pa., Stackpole co. (1963) 8vo, cl, illus (some color) facsm, 360pp.
...Bonanza Reprint, 1965.
...West Columbia, S.C., 1969. vo. 3, illus., 207pp. $20-y.
...n.p., 1975, vol. 2.

680 ..."Confederate Cavalrymen found revolvers better than sabers or rifles." In: cWTI, Jan. 1963, v.1, #9, p. 46-47, illus.

681 ..."The Mississippi rifle." In: CWTI, FEb. 1965, v.3, #10, p. 36-38, illus.

682 ...Uniforms of the Civil War." Illus: by Arthur Wise. N.Y., Thos. Yoseloff(1970) 4to, cl, dj, plates, sketches facsms., 174pp. $18-bmk.

683 ...Civil War Sutlers & their wares." N.Y., Thomas Yoseloff, 1969. 8vo, cl, dj, illus., 161pp. append, bibliog. index.

684 ..."That "Wonderful solace," Virginia Tobacco in the Civil War." (Richmond) Va. Cavl. Spring 1971. v.XX, #4, p. 36-47. sketches, illus., (1-color) Gilbert Gaul, A.C. Redwood sketch CSA soldiers in respose.

684a ..."Civil War collector's encyclopedia of Arms, Uniforms & equipment . . ." v.1. Seacaucus, N.J., Blue & Gray Press, 1974.
...Columbia, S.C., 1975. v.II. $25.
...Columbia, S.C., 1979. v.III. $25.
...Columbia, S.C., 1984. v.IV. $25.
..."Civil War Collector's Encyclopedia; v.II" West Columbia, S.C., Lord Americana & Research, 1975. 8vo, cl, 214pp, ills. $20.
...Vol. III, 207pp. ills., 1979. $20.
..."Civil War Collector's Encyclopedia, Vol. IV." West Columbia, S.C., Lord Americana & Research, 1985. 8vo, cl, 218pp, ills, index. $25.

685 **LORD, John**
"Robert E. Lee," in the "Southern Confederacy." In: Beacon lights of history ser. NY, 1885, v.12, p.321-354.

686 **LORD, William Wing**
"A child at the siege of Vicksburg." In: Harper's, Dec. 1908, v.CXVIII, p. 44-53. Personal reminisc. of the siege.

687 ..."In the path of Sherman." In: Harper's Feb. 1910, v.CXX, p. 438-446.

688 ..."Report of Maj-Gen. Loring. Of Battle of Baker's Creek, & subsequent movements of his command. Pub. by order of Congress." Richmond, R.M. Smith, print, 1864. 8vo, wraps, 29pp. Crandall, 1423-jk $150.

689 ..."To the people of Western Virginia. The Army of the Confederate States has come among you to expel the enemy, to rescue the people from the despotism of the counterfeit State Government imposed on you by the Northern bayonets & to restore the country once more to its natural allegiance to the State." (Gdsp-592) $400. Broadside, 13x6 1/2" (Charleston, W.Va. 1862) Crandall-749 & 2552; Norona-330; Harwell's CSA in Univ. Ga. (Jk, with Alsg) $100. A forgery: in sixth line "intend to," the "to," 1900 carried to line 7. (jk-122, $325) A variant printing is at the Univ. of Ga.

689a **LOSSON, Christopher**
"Major-General Benjamin Franklin Cheatham & the Battle of Stone's River." In: THQ, Fall 1982, v.41, #3, p.279-92.

690 **"LOST CAUSE Press Microcard Catalogue."**
Louisville, Ky., Lost Cause pr, 1962, 8vo, wraps, vi, 198pp. Coulter's Travels in the

CSA; Clark Travels in Old South; Southern Lit. Messenger; Wagner's Plains & the Rockies; Kentucky histories, etc.

691 **"LOST CAUSE,**
A Monthly Illustrated Journal of History, devoted to the collection & preservation of the Records of the Confederacy, The." Louisville, Ky., 1902.

692 **"LOST CAUSE, The" Lithograph, colored.**
(Copy) J.B. Wilson, 1872. $250. 20 1/4 x 26", five CSA generals above & below emblem of CSA, surrounded by 8 Confed. bank notes (real old ones, paste-on) 4-vignettes each corner.

693 **"LOST CAUSE: a Confederate War Record, The"**
v. 1-10; June 1898-April 1904. Louisville, Ky: Courier-Journal, 1898; 1902; Mrs. Basil W. Duke, Florence Barlow, Sept. 1902. April 1904. Vol. 8 one vol. only, Feb. 1903. No more published, see: LC card. Vol. 6, #3, p. 129-143, largely CSA Reunion Dallas, Tex., Apr. 22-25.
(Taken over by the Daughters of the Confederacy).

694 **"LOST DISPATCH, The"**
Galesburg (Ill), 1889. 12mo, cl, p. 115. Fiction based on Lee's Special order #191, graphically described. Secret service, Battle of Antietam.
See: under title, Daniel H. Hill & D. J. Sobol.

695 **LOTHIAN, Marquis of**
(William Schomberg Robert Kerr) "The Confederate Secession." Edinburgh: William Blackwood Sons, 1864. Post 8vo, vi, (2), 226pp. $250-ob $150-Jk-135.

696 **"LOUDOUN COUNTY**
& the Civil War; a History & guide. Text by John Divine, et. al. edited by Fitzhugh Turner, with foreword by Geo. A. Horkam, Jr." (Leesburg, 1961) Civil War Centennial Commission, County of Loudoun, Commonwealth of Virginia. 8vo, stiff colored wraps, colored endsheets, prots, illus., maps, index 80pp. $30-b.
..."The Bulletin of...", v.III, 1962. Leesburg, Va., The Society, 1962. 8vo, wraps, 61pp. "Centennial ceremony of the Battle of Ball's Bluff, Oct. 21, 1961." "The economics of slavery & the coming of the Civil War."; Muster roll-Loudoun Guards, the men who served with Co. C, 17th Va. Inf., CSA.

697 **LOUGHBOROUGH, James M., Mrs.**
"My Cave Life in Vicksburg with letters of Trial & Travel." St. Louis: R.P. Studley & Co. 1882. 16mo, cl, 196pp. a reprint of the N.Y., D. Appleton & Co., 1864. $75-ob $40, $50-bmk.
...Little Rock, Ark., 1882. 2nd Edition. Issued in wraps & cloth.
...Spartanburg, S.C., 1976.

698 **LOUGHERY, E.M., Mrs.**
"War & Reconstruction times in Texas, 1861-1865." Nacogdoches, Texas., Plain-dealer, 1897, 8vo, 40pp.
...Austin, Texas, Von Boechmann-Jones, 1914. 2nd edt. $45.

699 ..."Memoir of the life, character & services of the late Col. R.W. Loughery "the father of Texas democracy," the well remembered veteran journalist & stainless patriot...etc." Nacoghoches, Texas, Plain-dealer, 1986. An arden "secesh."

700 **"LOUISA COUNTY**
& the War Between the States, 1861-1865." (various authors) (Charlottesville, Va., Wayside press, nd) (c. 1961) Louisa County Centennial Comm. 8vo, stiff, colored wraps, dbl. fldg. map. sketch, plate, (3), 16pp.

701 **"LOUISIANA BRIGADE"**
See: R.L. Gibson

702 **LOUISIANA SOLDIER'S HOME**
"Act establishing Louisiana Soldier's Home." In: SHSP, 1883, v.11, p. 477-479.

703 **LOUISIANA:,**
LOUISIANA-CSA LAWS
"Acts passed by the Twenty-seventh legislature of the State of Louisiana in extra session at Opelousas, December, 1862 & January 1863. Pub. by Authority." Natchitoches, La., "Times" office, L. Dupleix, 1864. 8vo, wraps, 2p, 1, (1), 4-40, 3, 3, 4, 4p. English & French opposite pages, French t.p., Crandall-1620.
...New Orleans, J.G. Hause, 1910. Reprint, 48pp.
...Ann Arbor, Mich., Xerox Process, microfilms ?(c.1960's)? 100 copies.

704 ..."Official Journal of the House of Representatives, State of Louisiana. Extra Session of 1863. 8vo, printed wraps, 60, 64pp. English/French. Not in Crandall/Harwell. Only known copy, Hargrett.

705 ..."To the People of Louisiana, Texas, Arkansas & Missouri, & the Allied Indian Nations." Broadside: 30x14 cm. Shreveport, La., Off of the South-Western. Dated: Marshall, Texas August 18, 1863. Signed: Tho. O. Moore, Gov. La., F.R. Lubbock, Gov. Texas, Harris Flanagin, Gov. Ark., Thos. C. Reynolds, Gov. Mo. Hargrett: "only known copy."

706 ..."Official Journal of the House of Representatives, & Senate of Louisiana. Seventh Legislature-Session of 1864." Shreveport, La., News Office-John Dickinson, 8vo, wraps title, 75, 76, 8pp. In English. Hargrett: not in Crandall/Harwell. Only known.

707 ..."Louisiana in the Civil War-a bibliography." Compiled under the direction of Edith T. Atkinson, Librarian, Louisiana State Library Baton Rouge, La., (1961) Louisiana Civil War Centennial Commission. tall 8vo, decr. wraps, (20) pp. $10-pp.

708 ..."Louisiana 1861-1961." narrow, 8vo, illus., ports, (12)pp. chronological list civil war events in La., folded 18x22. map, colored, location of battles or events.

709 ..."Louisiana: Confederate States Court Records, 1862, filed in the U.S. Land Office at Baton Rouge, Louisiana." (New Orleans, La., Survey of Federal Archives in Louisiana, 1940) 4to, soft back, 3p, 74.

710 ...Louisiana: "Debates in the Convention for Revision & Ammendment to the Constitution of Louisiana." New Orleans, 1864, 8vo, cl, 643pp.

711 ...Louisiana: Governor Henry W. Allen-"Official report relative to the conduct of Federal Troops, etc." See: under title: "Official report, etc."

712 **LOUISIANA HISTORICAL ASSOCIATION**
"Calendar of the Jefferson Davis postwar manuscripts in the LHA collection, Confederate Memorial Hall, New Orleans, La." New Orleans, 1943. 8vo, 1p.

713 ..."Confederate Memorial Hall, Museum of Confederate Relics." New Orleans, 1891. 8vo, wraps, 7pp.

714 ..."Catalogue of the La. Hist. Ass'n. Relics, maps, protraits, & documents pertaining to the civil war & to the old South, 1889-1935." New Orleans, 1935. 9vo, wraps, cover title, 48pp.

715 ..."Dedication of the Monument" "Providential Aspect & Salutary Tendency of the Existing Crisis." New Orleans: Picayune Office, 1861. 8vo, printed wraps. Undescribed CSA imprint.

716 ...Louisiana: Commissioner of Military Records. "Appointed by the governor under act 156, 1908. the commissioner was directed to collect & preserve all muster-rolls, records & other facts & materials, showing names of men enlisted in the military, marine & naval service of the Confederacy from the state of La. He was required to compile from this material military records of the state, & to publish

them in book form, for free distribution to schools, etc. a short history of Louisiana troops in the confederacy..an annual report to the Governor, act 73 states to cease in 1916, reports were issued to 1922." See: Andrew B. Booth, for set in question.

...(Letter to Confederate veterans in an effort to secure rolls of all commands) New Orleans (1908?) (4)pp.

717 ...Louisiana: "The Roll of Honor. Roster of the Citizens Soldiery who saved Louisiana. Revised & Complete." (New Orleans, 1877) 16mo, sewn, or wraps, 70pp. Members of the White League.

718 ..."Louisiana soldier's relief association & hospital, in the city of Richmond, Va." Richmond, Va., Tyler, Wise, Allegre & Smith, 1862. 12mo, wraps, 38pp.

Louisiana Tigers-See: Alison Moore.

719 ..."Louisiana-Vicksburg Park Memorial Commission, Report of...to Governor." Baton Rouge, La., Ramires-Jones print, 1922. 8vo, wraps, 32pp. includes Siege of Vicksburg, La. commands in that campaign.

720 ..."Louisiana's Vote of Thanks to Virginia." In: SHSP, 1884, v.12, p. 377-378. See: W.T. Walshe & New Orleans Picayune.

721 **LOUISVILLE CHRISTIAN OBSERVER** "Stonewall Jackson's most dreaded foe." In: SHSP, 1895, p. 333-334.

722 **LOUISVILLE COURIER-JOURNAL** "A Modern Horatious: defence of a bridge by one Confederate against 40 Federals." In: SHSP, 1893, v. 21, p. 294-297.

723 ..."Stonewall Jackson at Prayer." In: SHSP 1891, v.19, p. 111-113.

724 **"LOVE & WAR:** A Photograph of the Confederate War in the United States Taken from Kentucky." A monument to one who died to be free. novel. London: Victoria Press, 1875. 8vo, cl, 288pp. 100 copies (30 for private distr.).

725 **LOVE, D.C.** "The Prairie Guards, a history of their organization, their heroism, their battles & their triumphs." n.p., n.d. (Columbus, Ga., 1890) 8vo, wraps, 19pp. Author used Sgt. A.J. Halbert's material for publication in Columbus Dispatch, as as authorized by survivors.

726 **LOVE, William A.** "General Jackson's Military Road" In: Miss. Hist. Soc. Pub., 1910, v.XI, p. 403-417.

727 ..."Garibaldi & the war against secession." In: CV, Sept., 1923, v.XXXI, p. 328-329.

728 ..."Mississippi at Gettysburg." Oxford, Miss., Publ. Miss. Hist. Soc. 1906, v.IX, p. 25-51. Offprint, wraps, $50.

728a ..."Mississippi at Gettysburg." In: "Gettysburg Sources, Vol. 1." Balt: Butternut Press, 1986. p.122-150.

729 ..."Surgeons & Chaplains of Mississippi Troops, CSA." In: Conf. Vet., Nov. 1924, v.XXXII, p. 428-429.

730 ..."Reminiscences of the closing days of the War of Secession." In: Miss. Hist. Soc. Pub., Cent. Ser., 1921, v.IV, p. 258-267.

731 ..."Twin Confederate Disasters." In: Conf. Vet., Aug. 1925, v.XXXIII, p. 292-295. Refers to both Gettysburg & Vicksburg campaigns.

732 **LOVEL, Mansfield, Gen.** "Confederate Army Order...Dept. 1. General Order, No. 17...Camp Moore, La., May 3, 1862." Broadsheet 4x10, blue paper.(Jk-151) $450. Printed on army field press. Exhorts citizens destroy all cotton, depriving north of needed supplies. Issued only a few days after fall of New Orleans.

733 ..."The Fall of New Orleans, La." In: Conf. War Jour., 1894, v.II, #1, p. 2-4. Portrait:

etched by Chas. B. Hall. (New York, 1898) folio.

734 **LOVELL, R.I.**
"The case for the "Alabama." In: Queen's Qur. (London), 1935, v.XLII, p. 515-522. Reconsideration of the justness of the verdict in the "Alabama" case. 1862-1871.

735 **LOVETT, Howard Meriwether**
"Grandmother stories from the land of used-to-be." Atlanta, Ga., A.B. Caldwell, 1913. 8vo, cl, 254, (6)p., front, illus., plates, ports. Juvenile, many CSA stories.

736 ..."Macon(Ga.) in the war between the states." In: CV, Jan/Feb., 1924, v.XXXII, p. 20-2, 51-54.

737 ..."Georgia's intellectual center in the sixties." In: CV, Mar. 1924, v.XXXII, p. 97-98.

738 ..."Planters of the old South." In: CV, July 1918, v.XVII, p. 300-301.

739 **LOVING, Oliver**
"Loving proposed expedition against Indians & Denver." In: Colo. mag., July 1957, v.34, p. 203-206. notes. 2 letters to Gov. Lubbock of Texas. One from Weatherford, Tx., 16 April 1862, proposes a CSA invasion of Colorado.

740 **LOW, John, Lieutenant, C.S.N.**
"The Logs of the C.S.S. Alabama & the C.S.S. Tuscaloosa, 1862-1863." University, Ala. (Tuscaloosa), 1972, 4to, mimeograph, cd. wraps, x, 94pp. 350 copies. Intro: W. Stanley Hoole

741 **LOWE, E. Louis**
"Ex-Governor Lowe's letter to the Virginia Legislature." Dated Ashland Va., December 16, 1861. n.p., n.d., 8vo, 4p. folder. Sabin-42413 gives pamphlet as 16pp.

742 ..."Communication from E. Louis Lowe Esq. Ex-Governor of Maryland." n.p., 1861. 8vo, sewn, 8pp. relates to secession.

743 **LOWE, R.G., Col.**
"Magruder's defense of the Peninsula." In: CV, 1900, v.8, p. 105-108, ports.

744 **LOWREY, Lawrence Tyndale**
"Northern opinion of approaching Secession, October 1859-November 1960." Northampton, Mass., Smith College Dept. Hist., Studies, v.III, #4, 1918. Pub. also as thesis, 1917 at Columbia Univ., 8vo, wraps, 191-257.

745 **LOWRY, Lucile Cary**
"The origin of Memorial Day (Columbus, Ga., 1866). In: UDC mag., Apr. 1949, v.12, #4, p. 10-12.

746 **LOWRY, Mark P.**
"Address: Unveiling of monument to defenders of Vicksburg." In: SHSP. 1893, v.21, p. 203-205.

747 ...An Autobiography." In: SHSP, 1888. v.16, p. 365-376.

748 ..."Report: Battle of Taylor's Ridge in SHSP, 1881, v.9, p. 63-65.

749 **LOWRY, Samuel Catawba**
"Diary of..., the War for Independence, North & South, Edited: Vaughan Camp, Jr." In: S.C.H.S.M., July 1978, v.79, p. 17. $8- See: C.V., v.35, p. 132, p. 182-197.

750 **LOWRY, Terry**
"The Battle of Scary Creek." Charleston, W.Va., Pictorial Pub. Co., 1982. 8vo, stiff wraps, illus., index, 192 pp. Kanawha Co., part of Va., later into W.Va., scene of bitter fighting early in war. From a Southern view but objective.

750a ..."September Blood: the Battle of Carnifex Ferry." Charleston, W.Va., Pictorial Histories Pub. Co., 1985. 8vo, wraps, 168pp. ills, bibliog. $10.

750b ..."The Sewell Mountain Campaign Wise vs. Floyd." In: CV (new), Nov. 1985, v.33, #6, p.12-17, color map, ports (1 color).

751 **LOYALL, B.P., (Benjamin P.)**
"Capture of the 'Underwriter,' New Bern, N.C., 2 Feb. 1864." In: Walter Clark's

"Hist. of Several Regs & Batts. of N.C." Vol. V, p. 325-333. In: SHSP, 1899, v.27, p. 136-144.

752 **LUBBOCK, Francis Richard**
"Address before the Twenty-second Legislature on presenting to the Senate in behalf of the donors, the portrait of Jefferson Davis. March 7, 1891." Austin, 1891 from Raines, p. 141. See also under Jeff Davis, presumably a separately printed pamphlet.

753 ...Broadside, General Order #34-Transfer of state troops to Confederate command. Signed Adj-Gen. J.Y. Dashiell. 8vo. Not in Crand/Harw. $35.

754 ..."Capture of Jefferson Davis." In: SHSP, 1878, v.5, p. 122-124.

755 ..."In Memoriam: Jefferson Davis." Austin, Texas: Henry Hutchings, 1891. 8vo, 1/2 Mor., 59pp. $150-. Davis' Memoir, 40pp., some personal corresp. of Lubbock-Davis, & recollections of the CSA. Presentation of a protrait, unveiled by Miss Ima Hogg. Raines cites it as only copy he saw.

756 ..."Six Decades in Texas: or, Memoira of...Gov. of Texas in War Times 1861-1863, A Personal experience in business, war & politics." Edt: C.W. Raines. Austin, Texas: B.C. Jones & Co., 1900. 8vo, cl, 3/4 Lt., xvi-685pp. illus., pls, ports, facsms., ($20 & $30) $200 $125-bmk-100.
Do: Austin, Texas: Pemberton Press, 1968. 8vo, cl, d/w, 718pp.

757 ..."To the People of Texas, Louisiana, Arkansas, & Missouri, & the Allied Indian Nations.(Signed): Tho. O. Moore, Harris Flanagan, F.R. Lubbock & Thos. C. Reynolds." Broadside: 45x32cm. Marshall, Texas, August 18, 1863. (Dorman David, cat. #6) $400.

758 **LUCAS, Daniel Bedinger**
"Memoir of John Yates Beall; his Life, Trial, correspondence, diary & private manuscript found among his papers, including his own account of the raid on Lake Erie." Montreal: John Lovell, 1865. 8vo, cl, front(mounted port), vi, (1), 297pp. $500-g $300-bmk-105. Private in Stonewall's Brig.
...Louisv: Lost Cause pr, micro cd. '62.

759 ..."Speech at the Reunion of Va. Div. ANV Association." In: SHSP, 1885, v.XIII, p. 278-284.

760 ..."On the death of Stonewall Jackson." In: So. Atl. Quar., July 1917, v.XVI, p. 227-235.

761 ..."Stonewall Jackson: the Christian warrior." In: So. Atl. Quar., Jan. 1917, v.XVI, p. 44-55.

762 **LUCAS, Marion Brunson**
"Sherman & the Burning of Columbia." College Station, Texas: Texas A & M University Press, 1976. 8vo, cl, dj, 188pp., illus., maps, index.

763 ..."Civil War Career of Colonel George Washington Scott." In: FHQ, October, 1979, v.LVIII, #2, p. 129-149. See: Katherine J. Willis.

764 **LUCE, Stephen B.**
"The story of the Monitor." Read Jan. 7, 1896. No place. p. 127-154. stitched, in printed wraps, pres. copy by author. Offprint from unstated source. $22.

765 **LUCKETT, William W.**
"Bedford Forrest in the Battle of Brice's Cross Roads." In: Tenn. HQ, June 1956, v.15, p. 99-110. notes, fldg. map. In NE Miss., June 1864.

765a **LUKE, Clive John**
"The Marshall Powder Mill site; the 1973-4 excavation by Clive John Luke." Auston, Texas: State Dept. Highways & Pub. Transportation Hwy. Design Div., 1978. 4to, cl, x, 147p, ill. Pub. in Archaeology, Rep. #11. CSA Army Ordnance & ordnance Stores.

765b **LUKER, Lady E.**
"Chronilogical History of the Civil War in

Jackson Coutny (Arkansas)." In: 'Stream of History.' April 1963, v.3, append. p.1-10.

...."Civil War Letters." In: SH, July 1970. v.8, p.28-36.

...."List of Confederate Soldiers found in Old Ledger." In: SH, April 1967, v.5, p.23-30.

766 **LUMPKIN, Ben Gray**
"The Happy Land of Canaan." Unpublished Civil War Song. Reprint: Civil War History, v.XI, #1, March, 1965. Stapled, 44-57pp.

767 **LUMPKIN, Katherine Dupre**
"The Making of a Southerner." New York: Alfred A. Knopf, 1947. 8vo, cl, d/w, 248pp. Some CSA, largely reconstruction.

768 **LUNDEBERG, Olav K.**
"Mosby's Men thundered through Upperville; prelude & variations on a theme from Northern Virginia." In: So. Atl. Quart., 1937, v.XXXVI, p. 289-301.

768a **LUNT, George**
"The Origin of the Late War: traced from the beginning of the Constitution to the revolt of the Southern States." N.Y., D. Appleton, 1866 (also 1867). 12mo, cl, xiv, 491pp. $25. $35. Conservative, pro Southern account. "Slavery not in reality the cause! Northern politicians made use of slavery as an avenue to power & forced war on South, as a means to maintain power. Lunt was a conservative Mass. Whig turned to the Democrats & opposed abolitionists.

769 **LUNT, James**
"Jeb Stuart: Cavalier of the Confederacy." (London): History Today, Aug. 1961, illus., 11pp. article.

770 **LURAGHI, Raimondo**
"The Civil War & the Modernization of American Society: Social Structure & Industrial Revolution in the Old South before & during the War." (Ken, Ohio., Civil War History, v.18, #3, Sept. 1972, p. 230-250.

771 ...."The Confederate Raider "Alabama": a Journal by its boarding officer." In: GHQ, Winter, 1977, v.LXI, #4, p. 347-353. $8.

772 ...."Storia della guerra civile Americana." Torino (Italy) Guilio Einaudi editore, 1966. Tk. 8vo, cl, xlii, 1395pp. (L.8000) Outstanding foreign work of an author sympathetic to the Southern point of view. The clash, a result of aggressive North with a static Southern culture. Rich bibliog.: p. 1295-1350.

773 **LURIA, Albert Moses**
"Albert Moses Luria, gallant young Confederate (excerpts from diary)." In: Amer. Jewish Archives, 1955, v.VII, p. 90-103. Co. I, 23rd. Reg. NC Vols. served in Va., Aug. 19, 1861 - Jan. 1962.

774 **LUSTYIK, Andrew F.**
"Civil War Carbines. From Service to Sentiment." (Aledo, Ill., World-Wide Gun Reports, 1962) 8vo, wraps, illus., 65pp.

775 **LUVAAS, Jay**
"Bentonville-last chance to stop Sherman." In: CWTI, Oct., 1963, v.II, #6, p. 6-9, 38-42, illus., maps, ports.

776 ....Joseph E. Johnston." In: CWTI, Jan. 1966, v.4, #9, p. 4-7, 28-32, illus., ports.

777 ...."G.F.R. Henderson & the American Civil War." In: Mil. Affairs, Fall 1956, v.20, p. 139-153. On Fredericksburg, a tactical study & Stonewall, a strategical study, its influence on british military education.

778 ...."Johnston's Last Stand-Bentonville." In: NCHR, July 1956, v.33, p. 332-358. March 18, 1865. atg. $10.

779 ...."The Military Legacy of the Civil War. The European Inheritance." The University of Chicago Press (1959). 8vo, cl, d/w, xi, 253pp. illus. $35.

780 ...."A Prussian Observer with Lee." Reprint: Military Affairs, vol. XXI, #3, Fall 1957. sm. 4to, cover title, stiff wraps, p.

105-117. (Capt. Justus Scheibert). Bmk-$10.

781 **LYKES, Richard Wayne**
"Campaign for Petersburg." National Park Service History Series. Wash., D.C., Nat'l. Park Service (1970) 8vo, pict. color stiff wraps, illus., maps, ports, (4), 56pp.

782 ..."The Great Civil War Beef Raid." In: CWTI Feb. 1967, v.5, #10, p. 4-13, 47-49. illus., map, ports. Biggest cattle rustling operation took place in Virginia, 1864, when 2,000 seized from the Union forces.

783 **LYLE, Royster, Jr. & Matthew W. Paxton, Jr.**
"The V.M.I. Barracks." In: VaCav., Winter, 1974, v.XXIII, #3, p. 14-29, facsms, illus.(2 color), ports.

784 **LYMAN, E.S.**
"Robert E. Lee, an address to Sam H. Gist Camp No. 1481, U.C.V., Calera, Alabama, Jan. 1915." Calera, Ala., 1915. 8vo, wraps.

785 **LYNCH, James Daniel**
"Robert E. Lee, or Heroes of the South. A Poem." West Point, Miss., 1876, G.W. Reed, print. 8vo, wraps, 31pp.

786 ..."Kemper County Vindicated & a Peep at Radical Rule in Mississippi." N.Y., E.J. Hale & Son, 1878. 12mo, cl, 420pp.

787 ...1879 edition of 416pp. $15.

788 ..."James D. Lynch in war & peace. Edt. James A. Carpenter." In: AlaHQ, Spring 1958, v.20, p. 71-84. Letters from a captain in Armistead's Cav. Reg., to his wife in Miss., from Mar. 1862-Mar. 1865, the last one from Vicksburg.

789 **LYNCH, Patrick Niesen, Bishop**
"Reports of Bishop Lynch of Charleston, S.C., Commissioner of the Confederate States...." In: Amer. Catholic Quart. Rev., July 1905. See: Leo Francis Stock.

790 ..."Some Wartime Letters of Bishop Lynch." Edt: William E. Wight. Catholic Hist. Rev., April, 1957, v.XLIII, p. 20-37. Letters of Bishop of Charleston, et al, on ecclesiastical, political & military affairs in South & Catholicism there.

790a **LYNCH, William O.**
"The Westward flow of Southern colonists before 1861.: In: JSH, 1943, v.9, #3, p.303-327.

791 **LYNCHBURG, Battle of...**
See: Charles Minor Blackford.

791a **LYNCHBURG, VA.**
Soldiers of Virginia who fought in her defense in the War between the States 1861-65; muster rolls, troops of cavalry, companies, companies of Artillery & companies of infantry, organized, recruited or enlisted, in whole or in part, in the city of Lync

792 **LYON, Hylan Benton**
"Memoirs of Hylan B. Lyon, Brig. Gen. C.S.A., Edited by Edward M. Coffman." In: Tenn. HQ, Mar. 1959, v.18, p. 35-53. See: B.L. Roberson.

793 **LYON, Mattie Harris**
"My Memories of the War Between the States." n.p., 1960. 4to, wraps, spiral-bound, 21pp. War & Reconstruction in Marietta, Ga. $25-bmk-115.

794 **LYON, Ralph M.**
"Moses Waddel & the Willington Academy." (Raleigh) NCHRev., July, 1931, v.VIII, #3, p. 284-299. Influence of an outstanding teacher on future leaders of the country.

795 **LYON, William H.**
"Claiborne Fox Jackson & the Secession Crisis in Missouri." (Columbia, Mo., Mo. Hist. Review, July 1963, v.LVIII, #4, p. 422-441, illus., ports.

796 **LYONS, James**
"Foreign recognition of the Confederacy Letter from Hon. James Lyons." In: SHSP, Aug., 1879, v.VII, #8, p. 353-359. See also: Four Essays...etc."

797 **LYTLE, Andrew Nelson**
"Bedford Forrest & His Critter Com-

pany." N.Y., Minton, Balch & Co., 1931. 8vo, cl decr. paste-on front cover, ports, incl. front, illus., maps. $26-, ix, 402pp. tall copy $50-bmk-90. $75-n, $35-n, $45.

...N.Y., G.P. Putnam's Sons (1931) 4th Impression (cheaper paper).

...London Edt., 1939.

...Reprinted: 1947, A (1958) edt.

...N.Y., McDowell, Obolensky (1960) $35-pab.

798 ..."Bedford Forrest & His Critter Company." New York: McDowell, Obolensky, 1960. 8vo, cl, d/w, illus., maps, p. xvii, 403. $50-b.

...Seminole, Fla., Green Key Press $16- Penkevill Pub. Co., Greenwood, Fla. 1984.

799 ..."R.E. Lee," a review of Freeman in South. Rev., I, p. 411-422.

800 ..."A hero & the doctrinaires of defeat." In: Ga. rev., winter 1956, v.10, p. 453-467. On the issue of states rights within the CSA as a cause of its military failure.

801 **LYTLE, William Haynes, Gen.**
See: Douglass West.

NORTH CAROLINA ROOM
NEW HANOVER COUNTY PUBLIC LIBRARY

NCr

COMPENDIUM
OF THE
CONFEDERACY

AN ANNOTATED BIBLIOGRAPHY

Books • Pamphlets • Serials

Compiled by
JOHN H. WRIGHT

Volume II
M-Z

BROADFOOT PUBLISHING COMPANY
Wilmington, North Carolina
1989

BROADFOOT PUBLISHING COMPANY
CIVIL WAR BOOKS
Route 4, Box 508-C
Wilmington, North Carolina 28405

Catalog Upon Request

THIS VOLUME IS PRINTED ON ACID-FREE PAPER

Copyright © 1989
FRIENDS OF FONDREN LIBRARY
Rice University
ISBN 0-916107-74-4

BROADFOOT PUBLISHING COMPANY
Route 4, Box 508-C
Wilmington, North Carolina 28405

M

1. **M. (C.S.), Surgeon, CSA**
"The Battle of Cedar Creek. By a Surgeon of the Confederate Army (Richmond Dispatch, Dec. 27, 1888)." In: SHSP, 1888, v.16, p. 443-446.

2. **"M.G.H." signed**
"Stonewall Jackson in Lexington, Va." In: SHSP, v.9, p.41-45.

3. **MacBRIDE, Dorothy**
"Lieutenant Jefferson Davis." In: Palimpsest, Oct. 1923, v.IV, p.346-357.

4. **MacBRIDE, Robert**
"Civil War Ironclads: The Dawn of Naval Armor." Phila: Chilton Books, (1962) 8vo, cl, illus., bibliog. xi, 185pp.

5. **MacBRIDE, Van Dyk**
"An addenda(sic) to a bibliography of books & articles on Confederate stamps & postal history (Apr. 1, 1954-Apr. 1, 1956)" In: Philatelic hist. rev., 1956, v.6, p.65-69 (2nd quart.)

6. ..."The Autograph Field Letters of Gen. Robert E. Lee." N.Y., The Stamp Specialist (1946) Port, facsms, fldg-pl., p. 2025.

7. ..."A bibliography of books & articles on Confederate stamps & postal history." In: Philatelic Lit. Rev., Fall 1950, Spring 1951, March 1952, v.1, p.5-15, 33, v.2, p. 17-20, Apr, 1954, v.4, p.23-27.

8. ..."Camp Shenandoah, Va., a Confederate Postal Mystery." N.Y., The Stamp Specialist (1947), facsms, p. 103-108.

9. ..."Captain Absolom Grimes the Confederate Mail Carrier." N.Y., The Stamp Specialist (1944), ports, facsms., p. 106-144.

10. ..."Camp Shenandoah, Va.: were there two?" In: The stamp specialist, forest green book. N.Y., H.L. Lindquist, 1948, p.64-70, facsms, map. Evidence that a CSA camp of this name exists in Augusta Co., & Rockingham Co., both in Apr. 1862.

11. ..."Confederate Patriotic Covers, including a check list of all known designs." Federalsburg, Md., 1943, 8vo, wraps, illus., 64pp.

12. ..."The Confederate Postal Proclamation & some of its effects & results." In: Amer. Philatelist, Aug., 1951, v.64:871-3, facsm. Proclamation of Jno. Reagan, PMG of CSA.

13. ..."Confederate postmasters: appointments & commissions." In: Amer. philatelist, Aug. 1956, v.69, p. 787-789, facsms. On the forms & language of these documents.

14. ..."A Sequel to the Autograph Field Letters of Gen. Robert E. Lee." N.Y., The Stamp Specialist (1948). facsms., p. 112-122.

15. ..."Some major varieties in Confederate stamps." In: S.P.A. journ., Jan/June 1952, v.14, p.237-238, 499-501, facsm. On typographed stamps & engraved stamps.

16. ..."A unique Robert E. Lee cover." In: Amr. Philatelist, Jan. 1957, v.70, p.269-270. facsm. Envelope by Lee to daughter-in-law Charlotte (Wickham) Lee, mailed with copy of CSA 5 cent green, 1861 issue stamp (#1) cancel. Richmond, Va., Apr. 27, 1862.

17. **MacCABE, John C. of Forrest's Cavalry**
"President of the Confederacy." In: CV, 1901, v.9, p.401-403, ports.

18. **MacCORKEL, William Alexander**
"The White Sulphur Springs; the traditions, history, & Social Life of the Greenbriar White Sulphur Springs." N.Y., Neale Pub., 1916. 8vo, cl, front, pls, port,

maps, facsms., x, -410pp. Includes Battle of White Sulphur Springs, $75-

19 **MACKALL, Leonard Leopold**
"American Forgeries in Print. The Spurious A.H. Stephens Speech against Secession." In: New York Herald Tribune, "Books," Notes for Bibliophiles, Nov. 9-16, 1924." 4to, (2)pp. DeRenne, III, p. 1325.

20 **MacDONALD, Rose Mortimer Ellzey**
"Mrs. Robert E. Lee (1809-1873)." Boston, New York, Ginn & Co., (1939) xxvi, 309pp., illus., ports. Juvenile.

21 **MacFARLAND, Elinor B., Edt.**
"W.T. Glassell & the Little Torpedo Boat "David." Los Angeles, Cal., Private print, 1937. Glassell commanded CSA Navy torpedo Boat "David," which attempted to blow up the New Ironsides in Charleston Harbor.

22 **MacLEAN, Malcolm**
"The Short Cruise of the C.S.S. "Atlanta." In: Ga. H.Q., June 1956, v.XL, #2, p. 130-143.
...Reprint, cardboard wraps, 16pp.

23 **MacMULLEN, Jerry**
"San Diego war vessel alerted!" In: San Diego Hist. Quart., April 1961, v.7, p. 27-29. Interception of "J.M. Chapmen", secretly acquired by Asbury Harpending (Capt. of CSNavy, served as raider by USS "Cyane," & San Franciso police dept., Mar. 14, 1863. Only action by CSSNavy in California waters.

24 **MacPHAIL, Andrew, Sir**
"Robert Edward Lee." In: Queen's Quart. 1938, v.XLV, 1-10. Reviews Freeman's "R.E. Lee."

25 **MacPHERSON, Ernest**
"Gettysburg & its effect upon the fortunes of the Confederacy." In: CV, FEb. 1915, v.XXIII, p. 75-77.

26 **MacRAE, David, Rev.**
"America revisited & men I have met." Glasgow, J. Smith & son, 1908. 12mo., cl, 325, (1)p.

27 ..."The Americans at home: Pen-&-ink sketches of American men, manners & institutions." Edinburgh: Edmonston & Douglas, 1870. 12mo, cl, illus(music). 2vols.
...Glasgow: J.S. Marr & sons, 1875, 12mo, cl, vi, (viii)-488 pp. revised edt.
...Glasgow: J. Smith & son, 1908, 12mo, cl, 2vols., Uniform edt."

28 ...N.Y., E.P. Dutton, 1952, 12mo, cl, 606pp. $25- Carolina Bk:"Journey thru the South, on war & its aftermath, talking to both Union & CSA leaders, e.g., Lee, Grant, Semmes, Beauregard, Maffitt, Vance & D.H. Hill. Two chaps. on Stonewall Jackson when he was given Jackson's bloodstained coat wore when fatally wounded."

29 **MacRAE, James C.**
"Address under the auspices of the Johnston Pettigrew chapter, U.D.C., in the hall of the House of Representatives, Raleigh, N.C., Jan. 19, 1907. Durham, N.C., 1907. 8vo, wraps, 21pp.

30 ..."Fayetteville Independent light infantry." In: NC Booklet, Apr. 1908, v.VII, p. 248-266. $12-

31 **MACKALL, T.B., Lieut.**
"Journal, in Official Records Union & CSArmies. Series I, v.XXXVIII, pt. 3, p. 978-991. See: Richard M. McMurray's review of its authenticity in CWH, Dec. 1974, v.20, #4, p. 311-328.

32 **MACKALL, William W.**
"A son's recollections of his father." N.Y., E.P. Dutton & Co., (1930) 8vo, cl, xvi, 2lfs, 3-236pp., front, illus., ports. 200 copies for private distribution. $250-b.

33 **MACKAY, Charles**
"The History of the United States of America. With a continuation, including the Presidencies of Pierce & Buchanan." (And the Southern Secession.) London:

Virtue & co (c.1863) 2vols. 8vo, cl, (or, 1/2 calf) maps (1-colored), ports views, (4), iv, 816; (2), vi, 772pp. (old) $40-. Sympathetic to the CSA, including a 27pp. supplement - "twenty million white Northern men exist under a despotism, attack state sovereignty, all the world looks on with sympathy & wonder."

34 **MACKEY, Alice Hurley**
"Father Murrow; civil war period." In: Chron. Okl., 1934, v.XII, p. 55-65. Father a CSAgent for Seminoles & other Indian tribes for CSA refugees.

35 **MACKEY, T.J.**
"A Lady of Arcadia, the doomed garrison of Pilot Knob & how it was saved, by T.J. Mackey, late Captain engineers, CSA." In: Home & Country, 1895-1896, v.XI, p.319-329, illus., map, ports. Dorn-II, 3286.

36 ..."The True Story of the battle between the Monitor & the Merrimac, by T.J. Mackey, late Captain of engineers, CSA." In: Home & Country, 1897, v.14, p.138-146, illus.

37 **MACKEY, Thomas Jefferson**
"Hampton's Duel, on the field of Gettysburg with a Federal Soldier." In: SHSP, 1894, v.22, p.122-126.

38 **MACON COUNTY, GEORGIA**
(Hays, Louise Frederick). "History of Macon County, Georgia." Atlanta, Ga., Stein Press, 1933, 8vo, illus., maps, 803, (21)pp. Roster of CSA vets: (686)-730pp.

39 **MACON, Emma Cassandra Riley & Reuben Conway Macon**
"Reminiscences of the Civil War." Cedar Rapids, Iowa, 1911, Priv. Pr., 8vo, cl, front, port, pl, 158, (2)pp. $10.00. The Torch Press, Macon was adj. in the 13th Va. Infty, Ewell's Div. of Stonewall's Corps. LC. $75.00.

39a **"MACON, GEORGIA for 1912**
The most central city in the Confederate States." Macon, Ga., Burke Print, 1911. 8vo, wraps, 8pp. $35. Promotion book prepared for the Confed. Vet. Reunion.

40 **MACON, Nathaniel**
"Letters to Charles O'Conor. The Destruction of the Union is Emancipation, The Status of Slavery. The Rights of the States and Territories." Philadelphia: John Campbell, 1862, 8vo, wraps, 38pp. JK-129, #65; Nine latters, dated Montgomery, Ala., Aug. 24-Oct. 5, 1860, signed Nathaniel Macon.

41 ..."The Rights of the States & Territories." By Nathaniel Macon. Montgomery, Ala. 1860, Sabin 43618. See Weldon N. Edwards.

42 **MACON, Thomas Jospeh**
"Life Gleanings compiled by T.J. Macon, Richmond, Va." Richmond, W.H. Adams, Pub. 1913, thin 8vo, cl, 101pp. $50.00. $75.00-Bmk84. Was private in 1st Co. Richmond Howitzers.

43 ..."Reminiscences of the First Company of Richmond Howitzers, by T.J. Macon." Richmond, Whittet & Shepperson, 1909, 8vo, wraps, 126pp. $125.00-OB. $90.00-Bmk.

44 **MADAUS, Howard Michael**
"The Battle Flags of the Confederate Army of Tennessee." Milwaukee, Wisc., Milwaukee Public Museum, 1976, 8vo, cl, dj, illus. color flags, 152pp.

44a **MADDEN, David**
"Unionist Resistance to Confederate Occupation. The Bridge-Burners of East Tennessee." In: ETHS Pub. 1980-81, p.22-39.

45 **MADDEX, Jack P., Jr.**
"Pollard's 'The Lost Cause Regained'; A Mask for Southern Accommodation." In: JSH, Nov., 1974, (18) pp., v.xl, p. 595-612. $8.00.

45a ..."The Reconstruction of Edward A. Pollard: a rebel's conversion to post-bellum Unionism." Chapel Hill, University of

N.C. Press, 1974. The James Sprunt Studies in history & political science, vol. 54. 8vo, wraps, (x), 110p. $5.

46 **MADDOX, George T.**
"Hard Trials & Tribulations of an old Confederate Soldier." Van Buren, Ark., Argus Office, 1897, 12mo, wraps, front(port), 82pp., Early campaigns in Missouri.

47 **MADUS, Howard Michael**
"The Battle Flags of the Confederate Army of Tennessee." Milwaukee, Wisc., Milwaukee Public Museum, 1976, 8vo, cl, dj, illus., color flags, 152pp. $20.00-B.

48 **MAFFETT, Robert C., Maj., 3rd S.C. Regt.**
"Official Report of Gettysburg." In: SHAP, 1885, v.13, p.206-209.

49 **MAFFITT, Emma Martin, Mrs.**
"The Life and Services of John Newland Maffitt, by Emma Martin Maffitt (his widow)." N.Y., Neale Pub., 1906, 8vo, cl, pl, 6 ports. (incl. front), 436 pp., bmk, 105 (95), 202 (105), $250.00. See: Josephus Daniels.
..."The Confederate Navy." In: CV, Apr/Jly 1917, v.XXV, p. 157-160, 217-221, 264-267, 315-317. See: Duncan Rose.

50 **MAFFITT, John N., Capt.**
"Portrait engraved by J.E. Baker, of Commander of Rebel Steamer "Florida". Plate: 10 1/2 x 7 1/2," Maffit stands on deck gazing off to sea. $35.00. See: Jas. Sprunt.

50a **MAFFITT, John Newland, Jr.**
Life & Services of Raphael Semmes." In: South Atlantic, Wilmington, N.C., Nov./Dec., 1877.

50b ..."Reminiscences of the Confederate Navy." In: United Service, Philadelphia, Oct. 1880.

50c ..."Blockade Running." Ibid., June/July, 1882. v.7, ns, #2, p.147-73 (1892).

51 **MAGAZINE OF Albermarle County,**
The, History, Civil War Issue. v. Twenty-two 1963-1964. Albemarle County Historical Society." (Charlottesville, Va., The Michie Co., 1964) 8vo, stiff wraps, facsm., ports, pls. (-1 fld) 210, (2)pp.

52 **MAGEE, Warren G.**
"The Confederate Letters of Warren G. Magee.: Edt: Bell Irvin Wiley. (Jackson, Miss., Jour. Miss. Hist., Oct., 1943, v.V, #4, p. 204-213. Port Hudson & Johnson Isle, Ohio.

53 **MAGILL, Mary Tucker**
"Stories from Virginia History for the Young." Lynchburg, Va., J.P. Bell, (1897), 12mo, cl, illus., 217pp. $7.50. Author lived in Winchester, Va., when taken by Union troops. Lengthy sketches of Lee, Jackson, Turner Ashby, Jeb Stuart & the Beverly Raid.

54 ..."Women, or Chronicles of the Late War." Baltimore: Turnbull Bros., 1871, 12mo, cl, xvii, 393, (1)ads, pp. facsm-letter from T.J. Jackson. $25.00. Women's work in re the war, laid around Winchester-Richmond.

55 **MAGILL, Robert M.**
"Magill Family Record." Richmond, Va., R.E. Magill, Pub. 1907, 8vo, cl, front., illus., crests, 244pp. $25.00. CSA remin. pp.171-244. 50-Y of Co.F, 39th Ga. Inf.

56 **MAGLENN, James**
"The Steamer Ad-Vance." In: Walter Clark's 'Hist. of Several Regs & Batts. from N.C.' v.V, pp.(1), 335-340. (Cont's pp.341-344 with Moses Hoge).

57 **MAGNOLIA, THE**
A Southern Home Magazine Richmond, VA., v.1-3, #19; Oct. 4,1862-April1, 1865." (Crandall-5210) "To nurture Southern writers & shun those of the North." Jas.D. McCabe, Jr., became third editor 20 June 1863. His serialized novel, 'The Aid-de-Camp, appeared in book form after

readers demanded reprint Renamed 'The Magnolia Weekly, v.II, Mar. 12, 1864. See: Sketch by Carlton P. Brooks.

58 **MAGNUS, Charles**
Playing Card Portraits of Famous Confederate Personalities. 24 separate port. engraved in red & black, 2 1/2 x 3 1/2" (New York, 186-?) $65.00. Thought smuggled into CSA, near end of war, for lack of facilities there. Back of each card a port. of some CS Gen. Lee, Jackson, Bragg, Price, Davis, Stephens, Beauregard, etc., front blank to avoid a tax by writing in playing-cd numerals. 28 1/2 x 48 cm: sheet.

59 ..."Western (Eastern) Territory of the Present War." Colored lithograph. N.Y., Charles Magnus, n.d.(1861). 23 x40 1/2" map in two sections, with 33 vignette portraits of Union & Confederate Officers, with inset map of country between Fortress Monroe & Richmond.

60 ..."Magnue' Historical War Map. One Hundred Fifty Miles around Richmond." N.Y., n.d. (c.1864). Mounted in linen folder (10 1/4 x 7") Map 25 1/2 x 20 1/2", shows portraits Lee & Grant, oprs. by Maj.Gen. Canby/Sherman. $50.00. N.Y. Lithographer.
See: "Confederate Generals."

61 **MAGOFFIN, Beriah, Gov. of Ky.**
"Message of Gov. Magoffin to the General Assembly of Kentucky at Regular Session, Sept., 1861." Frankfort, Ky., 1861. 8vo, wraps, 36pp (Henkel, cat.1090, May 1913). His relations with both U.S. & CSA, corresp. both sides. Refused Lincoln's call for troops, tho opposing secession, he resigned after the Leg., passed, over his veto, occupation of Ky. by the CSA.

62 **MAGRUDER MONUMENTAL ASSOCIATION:**
"Honor to the Memory of Gen. J. Bankhead Magruder. Circular letter...(Call for local organizations to collect funds to erect in Galveston a monument to perpetuate the heroic career of Gen. J. Bankhead Magruder." Headq'rs Magruder Monumental Ass'n., Galveston, Texas, Jan. 1, 1876. Thos. M. Jack, X.B. Debray, Braxton Bragg, O.M. Watson, C.M. Mason, comm., n.p. Broadside, 16 1/2x28cm. Winkler-3796.

63 **MAGRUDER, Henry C.**
"Three Years in the Saddle, Life & Confessions of..., the Original "Sue Munday" The Scourge of Kentucky, written by self." Louisville, Published by his captor Major Cyrus J. Wilson, 1865. 15cm, wraps, vi, 124, (1)pp. 2-front(ports). Member of "Buckner Guards" (Gen.S.B.) Confederate guerillas in Civil War, Ky. (In Tenn.State Lib.) $50.00. ABC-'45 - $70.00 - Parke-Bernet sale: 631.

MAGRUDER, John Bankhead
"See: Baker P. Lee, Armistead L. Long, P. G. Robert"

64 ..."Battles of Sabine Pass: Citation of the Defenders." Hdq. Dist. Texas, New Mexico & Arizona. Confederate (Late U.S.) Steamer Clifton, Sabine Pass, Sept, 13, 1863... Broadside sheet, 2pp. $200.00. Dowling's 40 men defeat 15,000 assault on fort. Not in Crandall.

65 ..."General Order #16." Houston, Headquarters District of Texas. Dec. 11, 1862. Broadside, 1p. small quarto, Setting up his command in Houston, Texas.

66 ..."A Short History of J.B. Magruder." Park Place, N.Y., Knapp & Co., 1888. 2 3/4 x 1 1/2" colored booklet, 16pp. fascm. signature, (packed in Duke's cigarettes).
See: "Heroes in the C.W." & W. Duke Co., Thos. M. Settles.

67 **MAGRUDER, John Bowie**
See: William Henry Stewart.

68 **MAGUIRE, Thomas Miller**
"The Campaigns in Virginia, 1861-62."

London: W.H. Allen & Co., 1891, 8vo, cl(or, decr. calf), 5 maps, incl. fldg. front., 70pp. $125.00.

69 ..."The Campaign in Virginia, May & June, 1864." London: 1908, William Clowed & Sons, 8vo, cl, 6-fldg. maps, ix, 88 pp.

70 ..."Jackson's Campaign in Virginia, 1861-62." London, W. Clowes & Sons, 1913. 8vo, cl, vi, (2), 62pp., maps.

71 **MAHAN, Bruce E.**
"A Confederate Spy." In: Palimpsest, Feb., 1923, v.IV, p.33-52. Incidents in career of John Yates Beall.

72 **MAHAN, Dennis Hart**
"An Elementary Treatise on Advance-Guard, Out-Post & Detachment Service of Troops." New Orleans: Bloomfield & Steel, 1861, 16mo, cloth, 143 p. (Crandall-2454) Gdsp: $600.

73 **MAHAN, Harold E.**
"The Arsenal of History: The Official Records of the War of the Rebellion." In: CWH, March 1983, v.29, #1, p.5-27.

74 ..."The Search for Arkansas Civil War Records 1892." In: ArkHQ, Autumn, 1982, v.XLI, #3, p.253-257, port.

74a ..."The Final Battle, the Southern Historical Society (organized 1869) & Confederate hopes for history." In: South. Hist., Spring 1984, v.5, p.27-37.

75 **MAHER, Edward R., Jr.**
"Sam Houston & Secession." In: SwHQ, April 1952, v.LV, #4, p.448-458, port.

76 **MAHONE, William, Maj.-Gen. ("Little Billy")**
"Memoir. (Military memoir of Maj.Gen. Wm. Mahone-running title). n.p., n.d. (c.1890), 8vo, sewn, 16pp.(incomplete?). Had been read & approved by Mahone, in red ink on first page "strictly confidential, burn when read as it is suppressed."

77 ..."On the Road to Appomattox, Edt. Wm.C. Davis. In: CWTI, Jan. 1971, v.IX, #9, p.4-11, 42-49, illus., ports.

78 ..."Mahone's Brigade. Second Reunion..held on the Anniversary of the Battle of Crater, Norfold, Va., July 31, 1876. Report of the Norfolk Landmark." Norfolk, Va., 1876, 8vo, wraps, 13pp. Lee made him Maj.-Gen. on-the-spot, for his renown as best shock-troops of war. Composed of: 6th, 12th, 16th, 41st, 61st, Reg. Va. Inf.

79 ..."Report of Brigadier-General William Mahone. Battle of Gettysburg." In: SHSP, 1880, v.VIII, p.324.

80 ..."Report of the Battle of Wilderness" In: SHSP, 1878, v.VI, p.84-85.

81 ..."The Sharpshooters of Mahone's Old Brigade at the Crater." In: SHSP, 1900, v. XXVIII, p.307-308.

82 See: Nelson Morehouse Blake, Geo. Smith Bernard, John E. Laughton, John R. Turner, "Battle of Crater," H.A. Minor.

82a **MAHONE, William & Lt. J. J. Chase**
"Two views of a Battle: The Crater, Petersburg, Va., July 30, 1864." Collingswood, 1988. Reprint of Mahone's 12pp pamphlet. J.J. Chase's "The charge at Daybreak: Scenes & incidents at the battle of the Mine Explosion, near Petersburg, Va., July 30, 1864." Lewiston, 1875. Wraps, 32pp. $7.

83 **MAHONEY, D.A.**
"The Prisoner of State." New York, Carleton, 1863, 12mo, cl, 414 pp.

84 ..."Political Opinions in 1776 & 1863: a Letter to a Victim of Arbitrary Arrests & "American Bastiles." New York, Anson D.F. Randolph, 1863, 12mo, wraps, 19pp. Sabin-43877. Mahony was senior edt: Dubuque Herald, put in jail for Copperhead activities.

85 **MAHONEY, Ella V.**
"Sketches of Tudoe Hall & the Booth Family, by Ella V. Mahoney." Belair, Md., 1925, 12mo, wraps, illus., ports, 59pp. $35.00.

86 **MAIL CARRIERS**
See: Absolem Grimes, James Bradley (Missouri), Mrs. W.A. Mitchell.

86a **MAINFORT, Robert C., Jr.**
"Archaelogical Investigations at Fort Pillow State Historical Area: 1976-78." Nashville: Tennessee Department of Conservation, Division of Archaeology, 1980. 8vo, wraps, 198pp, ills. $8.

87 **"MAJORITY REPORT**
of the Committee on Commissioner from Georgia..." March, 1861. (St. Louis? 1861) 8vo, wraps, caption title, 20pp. Title head: Missouri State Convention. (on Federal relations) Sig: John B. Henderson, Chm.

88 ..."Minority Report of Committee on Federal relations, Missouri State Convention, Mar. 11, 1861 (St. Louis, 1861) 8vo, wraps, 8pp. Sig: John T. Redd, H. Hough.
..."Resolutions in Missouri State Convention, March 7, 1861." (St. Louis? 1861) 8vo, wraps, 10pp.

89 **MALET, William Wyndham, Rev.**
"An Errand to the South in the Summer of 1862." London: Richard Bentley, 1863, 12mo, cl, front., viii, 312 pp. $250.00. Largely on a S.C. plantation with his sister.

89a **MALLET, J. W. & E. O. Hunt**
"The Ordnance of the Confederacy." In: Photo Hist. C.W., v.5, p.155-70, ills, ports.

90 **MALLETT, John William**
"How the South got Chemicals during the War, Resourcefulness of the CSA during Blockade." In: SHSP, 1903, v.31, p.100-102.

91 ..."Work of the Ordnance Bureau of War Dept., 1861-1865. By Ex.-Lt.Col. of Artillery Supt. CS Ordnance Labs." In: SHSP, 1909, v.37, p.1-20.
..."Work of the Ordnance Bureau." In: SHSP, 1909, v.XXXVII, p.1-20.

92 **MALLORY, Stephen Russell**
"The Flight from Richmond," Part 1. In: CWTI, April, 1972, v.11, #1, p.24-31, illus., Part II, June, 1972, p.28-36, illus., maps, ports.

93 ..."Letters July 19, 1866 & Aug. 18th to his wife Andela, edited by Occie Clubbs." In: Pensacola Hist. Soc. Quart., July 19, 1966, v.2, #3, p.1-6.

94 ..."Letter of Stephen R. Mallory, 1861." In: Am.Hist.Rev., Oct., 1906, v.XII, p.103-108.

95 ..."Mallory Waltz. Composed by Miss. Modeste Hargin, Pensacola, Florida." New Orleans, La., Louis Grunewald Co., (1980), 35cm, 5pp. sheet music. Heading: "Dedicated to the Hon. Stephen R. Mallory." UWF.

96 ..."Stephen R. Mallory Secretary of the Navy Confederate States of America." (Pensacola, Fla., Pensacola Home & Savings Association, 1969) cover title, 8vo, wraps, illus., (24)pp. (based on a masters' thesis by Miss Occie Clubbs).

97 ..."Unpublished Chapters of History. Last Days of the Confederate Government. From Papers left by Stephen R. Mallory, Sect. of the Navy in the Confederate Cabinet. Intro; his daughter - Ruby Mallory Kennedy." In: McClure's Mag., Dec., 1900, v.16, p.99-107.

98 ..."Stephen Russell Mallory (late Senator from Florida) Memorial Addresses, 60th Congress, First Session, Senate of the U.S., May 2, 1908. House of Representatives May 3, 1908. Comp. under direction of the Joint Comm. on Printing." Washington, Gov. Print Off., 1909 (60th Cong., 2nd Sess. Senate Doc. 762) 8vo, wraps, 86pp.

99 **MALONE, Bartlett Yancey**
"The Diary of Barltett Yancey Malone, Edt: William Whatley Pierson, Jr." Chapel

Hill, N.C., James Sprunt Hist. Pub., of North Carolina Hist. Soc., 1919, v.16, pp.3-59. Served in 6th N.C. & A.N.V. 75-Bmk 105.

100 ..."Whipt 'em Everytime; the Diary of Bartlett Yancey Malone." Jackson, Tenn., McCowat-Mercer Press, 1960, 12mo, cl, dj, illus., 131 pp., ports., facsm. pl., facsm, liners. $27.50.
...Edt. W. W. Pierson, Jr., Gen. Edt. Bell I. Wiley. Wilmington, N.C., Broadfoot Pub., 1987. 8vo, cl, dj, 131pp, ills, ports, roster. $20.

100a **MALONE, DUMAS**
"The Pen of Douglas Southall Freeman. And prefatory note by Mary Wells Ashworth. Printed from the original plates as they appear in vol. 6 of George Washington. Presented by Charles Scribner's Sons through J. Ambler Johnston to the Chicago Civil War Round Table on the occasion of Lee's 150th Birthday (Jan. 19) & Freeman as his Biographer." n.p., 8vo, wraps, xlvp. 1957. $40.

101 **MALONE, Henry Thompson**
"The Charleston Daily Courier Standard-Bearer of the Confederacy." Minneapolis, Minn., 14; Reprint: Summer, 1952, Journalism Quarterly, v.29, p.307-315, 8vo, stapled, caption title, (9)pp.

102 ..."Atlanta (Ga.) Journalism during the Confederacy." In: Ga.HQ, Sept, 1953, v.37, p.210-219, notes.

103 ..."The 'Weekly Atlanta Intelligencer,' as a Secessionist Journal.: In: Ga., H.Q., December, 1953, v.XXXVII, #4, p.278-286.

104 **MALONE, Joseph S.**
"Guided & Guarded; or, Some Incidents in the Life of a Minister-Soldier." New York, The Abbey Press (1901), 12mo, cl, 221 pp. CSA(fiction?).

105 **MALONE, P.J.**
"Charge of Black's Cavalry Regiment at Gettysburg." In: SHSP, 1888, v.16, p.224-228.

106 **MALONE, Thomas H., 1st Tenn. Infty.**
"Memoir of Thomas H. Malone, an Autobiography written for his Children." Intro: J.M.Dickinson, (Nashville: Baird-Ward Print) 1928, lim edt. 100 copies. 150-Bmk, 8vo, cl, vii, 227pp. front(port.), 1st Tenn.Infty., prison: Johnson's Isle. CSA pp.89-200.

106a **MALONE, Wallace**
"Vicksburg." In; AHQ, 1949, v.9, #3, p.341-351.

107 **MALONEY, Eugene A.**
"A History of Buckingham County (Va.)" Waynesboro, Va., 1976, 8vo, cl, dj, 119p/. port., illus., maps, roster, Pub: Bicentennial Commission.

108 **MALPASS, George N.**
"Alexandria in the Civil War." In: Collector Club Philatelist, May 1950, v.29, p.135-140, facsms., map, views. Designs commemorating events (1861) there.

109 ..."Anti-Lincoln Patriotic Envelopes." In: Amer. Philatelist, Feb., 1959, v.72, p.349-352, facsms. notes, detailed descriptions of 13 examples, 1860-1862.

110 ..."A Checklist of Uncataloged Envelopes bearing Patriotic Designs of Southern Sentiment." New York, The Stamp Specialist (1948), facsms., pp.40-64.

111 ..."The Confederate Privateers." In: Am.Philatelist, Oct., 1952, v.66, p.37-44. Facsms. On Engraved envelopes representing or caricaturing these vessels.

112 ..."A Confederate or Union Patriotic Design?" In: S.P.A. Jour., May, 1952, v.14, p.455-456. facsm. Patriotic envelope print by Saml. C. Upham, sent from Lynchburg, Va., to a Georgia address sometime during the war.

113 ..."The Jefferson Davis Postage Stamp Issues of the Confederacy." In: Handbook #6-Society of Philatelic Americas.

114 ..."The Jefferson Davis Postage Stamp Issues of the Confederacy their Production & Use, including Related Biographical & Historical Material." n.p., n.d., S.P.A. Handbook #6, revised edt. Pub: Society of Philatelic Americans. 8vo, stiff wraps(pl), facsms., port. Davis on wraps, 24pp.

115 ..."An Early Collector of Confederates." In: Amer. Philatelist, Aug., 1949, v.62, p.897-899. Port. Activities Jno. Boyd, Maj-Gen., CSA, as collector of CSA stamps, covers, currency, buttons, etc., 1865-1925.

116 ..."Patriotics: "Anti-Confederate" Overprints, 1860-1861." In: Amer. Philatelist, July, 1955, v.68, p.723-726, facsms, notes.

117 ..."Three Confederate Covers of Historic Interest, 1862, 1864." In: S.P.A. Joun., Oct., 1951, v.14, p.65-68, facsms.

118 ..."Jefferson Davis, Champion of Southern Independence." In: S.P.A. Jour., Aug./Oct., 1954, v.16, p.607-614, v.17, p.7-13, 59-66, facsms. Representations of Davis on CSA stamps.

119 ..."Unusual Dates on Confederate Covers." In: S.P.A. Journ., Mar., 1959, v.21, p.323-325, facsms, on mail stamped on "historic days e.g., 12, April 1861, the day the 'shooting war' began."

120 **MALTBY, Mary Breckinridge**
"Recollection of Civil War Times in Ky." In: RKHS, July 1947, v.45(#152), p. 225-234.

121 **MALVERN HILL, Battle of**
See: George Smith Bernard, James Francis Crocker, John Lamb, Josiah Staunton Moore.

122 **MANAKEE, Harold Randall**
"Omenhausser's Confederate Prisoners of War Sketch." In: Md.HR., June, 1958, v.53, p.177-179, view. Confederate prison life at Point Lookout, one of 46 water colors made in 1865 by John T. Omenhausser, a prisoner.

122a ..."Maryland in the Civil War." Baltimore, Md., 1961. 8vo, cl, 173p, ills, maps, dj. $55.

123 **MANARIN, Louis H.**
"Richmond Volunteers; the Volunteer Companies of the City of Richmond & Henrico County, Va., 1861-1865. By Louis H. Manarin & Lee A. Wallace, Jr." Richmond, Va., Westover Print, 1969, 8vo, cl, dj, illus., ports., maps, xiii(1), 296pp.(2). Richmond Civil War Centennial Commission official publication #26. 30-Bmk 105.

124 ..."North Carolina Troops, 1861-1865, A Roster," Vol.1-Artillery. Large ivo, illus., map on lining paper, muster rolls, 619pp., Raleigh, N.C., State Dept. Archives & History, 1966. op Bmk 84 $50.00.
...Do: 1968, Vol.II-Cavalry. Large 8vo, cl, dj, 789pp. op ($175.00).
...Do: 1971, Vol.III-Infantry. Large 8vo, cl,dj,663pp.
...Do: 1973, Vol.IV-Infantry. Large 8vo, cl, dj, 687pp.
...Do: 1975, Vol.V-Infantry. Large 8vo, cl, dj,678pp.

125 ...Do: 1977, A Roster. 16th-18th & 20th-21st Regiments. Compiled by Weymouth T. Jordan, Jr. Large 8vo, cl,dj,712pp.

126 ...Do: 1979, v.VII-Infantry Rosters, 22nd-26th Regiments, Edt: Weymouth T. Jordan. Large 8vo, cl, dj, 662pp. index (Vols 1-8, Bmk. $500.00-$600.00.

127 ..."North Carolina troops, 1861-1865: A Roster." Compiled by Weymouth T. Jordan, Jr. Unit Histories by Louis H. Manarin." Raleigh, N.C., Division of Archives & History, 1981, 8vo, cl, pp, xiv, 566, index.

128 ..."North Carolina Troops, 1861-1865: A Roster. Raleigh: State Dept. Archives & History, 1966, pp.xvii, 691.

129 **MANARIN, Louis H. & Robert W. Waitt, Jr.**
"Directory of Officials 1861-1865 Richmond, Va. and Confederate." Richmond:

Civil War Cent. Comm. (Mar., 1963), 8vo, ports., (6)pp. #15...."A Guide to Military Organizations & Installations in North Carolina, 1861-1865." (Raleigh) North Carolina Confed. Cent. Comm. (Sept, 1961), 4to, stiff wraps, mimeograph, (2), 43, 30, 3, 7, (1)pp. Bmk.-20. Cloth 25-B.

130 ..."Richmond at War: The Minutes of the City Council, 1861-1865." Chapel Hill: Univ. of N.C. Press, 1966, pp.xii, 645, cl, d/w, op. $30.00.

131 ..."Lee in Command." In: VaCavl. Spring, 1976, v.XXV, #4, pp.164-175, illus., incl. dbl. pg. color, ports., map.

132 "**MANASSAS BATTLEFIELD, THE** Confederate Park (Inc.)-Prince William Co., Va. near Manassas, Warrenton, Fairfax County Court-house & about 35 miles from Leesburg, Mt. Vernon, Washington City & Arlington. The South's Proposed Memorial to Volunteers & in the Interest of American History." Washington, D.C., revised edt.(1921), 8vo, wraps, cover title, map, illus., ports., 20pp.

133 **MANASSAS (BULL RUN) PARK**
See: Francis B. Wilshin

134 **MANASSAS (IRONCLAD), C.S.N.**
See: Houston, Texas 'Chronicle,', 1st Ironclad.

135 "**MANASSAS NATIONAL BATTLEFIELD** Park, Va." By Raleigh C. Taylor. Washington, D.C., Nat'l Park Service, n.d., 4to, wraps, Jackson statue on cover, map, prot., illus., sketches, 15pp.

136 **MANASSAS, FIRST Battle of...**
See: Campbell Brown, Daniel B. Conrad, Arthur C. Cummings, John Warwick Daniel, J.M. Garnett, Gen. Hunton at Bull Run, G.F. Harrison, Thomas Taylor Mumford, Winfield Peters, William F. Randolph, Richmond Dispatch, William Smith.

MANASSAS, SECOND Battle of...
See: William Allan, Montgomery D. Corse, 'Eighth Virginia,' Stephen Dill Lee, James Longstreet, Edward McCrady, Robert M. Mayo, John H. Worsham.

137 **MANESS, Lonnie E.**
"Forrest & the Battle of Trenton." In: WTenn. HSP, 1975, #29, p.121-29.
..."A Ruse that Worked: The Capture of Union City, 1864." In: WTennHSP, 1976, #30, p.91-103.

138 ..."The Fort Pillow Massacre; Fact or Fiction." In: THQ, Winter, 1986, v.xlv, #4, p.287-315, illus., map, ports.

139 ..."Forrest & the Battle of Parker's Crossroads." In: Tenn. Hist. Quart., 1975, v.XXXIV, p.154-167.

139a ..."Fort Pillow under Confederate & Union control." In: W. Tenn. HSP, Dec., 1984, v.38, p.84-98.

140 **MANEY'S BRIGADE** at Kennesaw Mt. Battle. "The Battle of Kennesaw Mountain...the part borne by the First & Twenty-seventh Consolidated Tennessee Regiments, Maney's Brigade. By a member of the Rock City Guards." In; Annals of Tenn., & early western history.. Nashville, Tenn., 1878, v.1, p.109-117. See: Samuel G. French, W.M. Pollard.

141 ..."Maney's Brigade after the Battle of Missionary Ridge." In: SB, 1883-1884, v.II, p.345-348. Sig: Private Rock City Guards.

142 **MANGOLD, F.**
"Letter Concerning Lee's Course." In-:SHSP, 1878, v.VI, p.190-191.

143 **MANGUM, Adolphus Williamson**
"Salisbury (N.C.) Confederate Prison." In: Pub. So. Hist. Ass'n., v.III, 1899. p.307-336

144 ..."Memorial Sketch of William R. Gorman." In: OLOD, Mar. 1875, v.2, #1, p.18-24. In band of 4th N.C. Reg.

145 **MANGUM, Willie Person**
The Papers of....Edt.: Henry Thomas Shanks. v.5 (1847-1894), tk 8vo, cl., ports. incl. front. xxxiv, (2), illus, 812pp., facsms. Raleigh: State Dept. Archives & History, 1956.

146 **MANIGAULT, Arthur Middleton, Brig-Gen.**
"A Carolinian Goes to War: The Civil War Narrative of Arthur Middleton Manigault, Brigidier General, CSA. Edt.:R. Lockwood Tower. Foreword: Thomas L. Connelly" Columbia, S.C., University of South Carolina Press, 1983. 8vo., cl., xvi, 344pp. illus. (21), maps (10).

147 **MANIGAULT, Gabriel Edward, Dr.**
"General George Izard's Military Career; a reply to Mr. Henry Adams." In: Amer. Hist. Mag., 1891, p.457-462.

148 ..."The U.S. Unmasked. A search into the causes of the rise & progress of these states, & an exposure of their present material & moral conditions. With additions & corrections by the author." London: E. Stanford, 1879, 12mo, cl., 168pp. Adjutant, 4th S.C. Cavalry.

149 ..."The Military Career of General George Izard." In: Mag. Amer. Hist., June 1888, p. 462-478.

150 ..."Suggestions as to Arming the States." Charleston, S.C., Evans & Cogswell, 1860. 8vo., wraps, 12pp. Turnbull -III, p.313. A Catalogue gives Manigault as author, 1860 Association publication. $100.00

151 ..."The Signs of the Times." By G. Manignault(sic), of South Carolina. N.Y., Blelock & Co. (n.d.) 8vo, wraps, 60pp. Sabin-44295 (see:93461)

152 **MANIGAULT, Louis**
"Letter from an Eyewitness at Andersonville Prison, 1864.: Edt.: Spencer B. King, Jr., In: Ga. H.Q., March 1954, v.XXXVIII, #1, p.82-85.

152a **MANIGAULT, T.E.**
"Siege Train, the journal of a Confederate Artilleryman in the defense of Charleston. Edt: Warren Ripley." Columbia, 1986, Univ. of S.C. Press. 8vo, cl, dj, 364pp, ills, fldg. maps.

153 **MANLY, Basil, Dr.**
"The Diary of Dr. Basil Manly, 1858-1867, Edt: Wm. Stanley Hoole." In: Ala. Rev., Apr. 1951-Apr. 1952. v.4: 127-149, 221-236, 270-289; v.5: 61-74, 142-155, notes. On his Baptist ministry in Montgomery (Ala.) CSA politics & plantation in Lowndes County.

154 **MANLY, Marline (pseud.)**
See: St. George Rathborne.

155 **MANN, A. Dudley**
"A Dudley Mann's Mission in Europe, 1863-1864; an Unpublished letter to Jefferson Davis. Edt: Joseph O. Baylen & Wm. W. White." In: VMHB, July 1961, v. 69, #3, p.324-328.

156 ..."My Ever Dearest Friend. The Letters of A. Dudley Mann to Jefferson Davis, 1869-1889." Tuscaloosa, Ala.: Confederate Pub. Co., 1960, Confederate Centennial Studies, #14. 12mo., stiff wraps, 114pp. Lim. Edt. 450 copies, Edt.: John Preston Moore. 25-Bmk.

157 **MANN, J.T., Rev.**
"Hanged as a Spy at Barrancas, Florida, During the Civil War. Had a Narrow Escape, Rev. J.T. Mann, of Fitzgerald, Ga., who is now in Pensacola, relates story of his experience..." Pensacola, (Fla.) Pensacola Journal, 1906. 12mo., wraps, 14, (1)p. Was with Co. C Third Louisiana Bat., from Pensacola Journal, June 26, 1906.

158 ..."A Spy in the Service of the Confederacy; how it feels to be hung by the neck & die, by Rev. J.T. Mann..." (Atlanta, Ga., 1908?) (Pensacola, Fla.?) 16mo, wraps, cover title, 15pp. Copy: NYPL.

159 **MANN, Justine**
"John Archibald Campbell: Assistant Secretary of War, CSA." In: At. HJ, v.26, #4, p.53-63.

160 **MANNING, Van H., Col., 3rd Ark. Reg.**
"Official Report of Gettysburg." In: SHSP, 1885, v.13, p.195-196.

161 **MANOUVRIER, J. & Co.**
"Map of the Present Seat of war in Missouri New Orleans, La., J. Manouvier (1861)? 26 X 20 1/2cm. Bmk $400.00.

162 **MANSFIELD, Battle of:**
See: Hewitt (Jno. Edmong), Plummer (Alonzo H.) "Red River Campaign."

163 **MANSUR, W.H.**
"Diary of Lieut. W.H. Mansur (in Georgia & Alabama, 1864) Edt.: Mary R. Ellis." In: UDCM Dec. 1948, v.11, #12, p.9-10.

164 **"MANUAL OF MILITARY SURGERY**
Prepared for the use of the Confederate States Army. By Order of the Surgeon-General." Richmond, Va., Ayers & Wade, 1863. 12mo., cl., 297pp., 30pp. plates. (Baldwin's book farm) $350.00 Sabin-44410. 750-R, 13-650.

165 **MANUCY, Albert C.**
"An Autobiography of Samuel Arnold, a Lincoln Conspirator." In: FHQ, October 1943, v.XXII, #2, p.92-102. See also under Sam Arnold.

166 **"MANUFACTURING HISTORY."**
Who runs the machine? Army & Navy Journal accuses South of literary conspiracy. In: SHSP, 1881, v.IX, p.378-380.

167 **"MAP OF PRESENT RICHMOND**
Showing important battlegrounds, fortifications, roads & points of historical interest within w twenty-five mile area." City of Richmond, Va., (1961) 25 X 34" colored map with references to Important Battles. Richmond Civil War Centennial Committee.

168 **MAP OF THE BATTLE FIELD OF FREDERICKSBURG...**
See: Carter M. Braxton

169 **"MAP OF THE CITY OF RICHMOND, VIRGINIA 1861-1865."**
Richmond: Civil War Cent. Comm., by Confederate Museum, the Valentine Museum, City of Richmond Dept. of Public Works (1961) 25 X 34", colored, Table of References, cartouches.

170 **MAP OF THE CONFEDERACY**
Ettling (T.)
"The United States of North America." Federal area in red; Border States, orange, Confederate States, in green." London: Weekly Dispatch, 1863. 2-sheets, each 19 1/2 X 13 1/2", issued as supplements, two issues of a Sunday newspaper. The "Dispatch Atlas" (Phillips 839), made up of similar sheets, contained only the normal 4-sheet map of the U.S. Litho: E. Weller.

171 **"MAP OF THE VICINITY OF RICHMOND**
& Part of the Peninsula From Surveys Made Under the direction of A.H. Campbell, Capt. P.E., CSA in charge Topograph'l. Dept. D.N.V." Maj-Gen. J.F. Gilmer, Chief Engineer. (Richmond) 1864. Sanxay & Gilbert Patent. Linen mounted, 37 X 40", folded to 6 1/4 X 10". Unrecorded map. $35.00.

172 **"MAP OF VIRGINIA,**
The Principal Towns, Railroads, Rivers, Canals & Other Internal Improvements..." 26x37", folded in original stiff paper covers, Richmond: West & Johnston, 1862. Crandall-3067. Goodspeed $1,000.

172a **MAP: "Military Map**
of Northeast Virginia & Vicinity of Washington. Compiled by Topographical Engineers office at Division Headquarters of Gen. Irvin McDowell, Arlington, Jan. 1st, 1862 corrected from recent surveys & re-

connaissances under Dir. Bur. Topographical Engrs. A

...''Map of 1st District, Campbell County, Ga. South of the Cherokee Boundry Line. Compiled under Dir. Capt. W. E. Merrill, Chief Topl. Engr. D.C., Sgt. Finegan, from notes of a captured rebel engr. & State map (south of Chatahooche River) scale: 2" to

...''Map of the Battlefield of Fredericksburg, extracts from OR: also Gen. Lee's Report of the Battle." Lynchburg, Va. Power Press, 1966. Map by C. L. Blackford. 22cm, 24pp. Map 33pp. Gen Lee's Report, Adv. to p.44. Entered, 1866, by Carter M. Braxton.

173 **"MAPLE LEAF"**
Federal Steamer Captured, See: John Uriah Green.

174 **MAPP, Alf J., Jr.**
"Frock Coats & Epaulets." N.Y., London: Thomas Yoseloff (1963) 8vo., cl., dj., ports., 501pp. Character studies of six CSA leaders, Davis, Lee, Jackson, Benjamin, Stuart, & Joseph E. Johnston.

..."Frock Coats & Epaulets: Psychological Portraits of Confederate Military & Political Leaders." Lanham, Md., Hamilton Press. 8vo, soft, 501pp. $10.

175 **MAPS,**
Sheppard (Edwin), Paterson (Jas. T.), Bethel, Battle of "Seat of War...", Manouvrier (J.), Husted & Nenning, West & Johnston - Map of Va., Bufford (J.H.), Dryden (Charles).

175a **MARCH, Bryan**
"Confederate Letters of Bryan March 1862-3." In: Chron. Smith Co., Texas (Tyler, Texas). Winter, 1975. $9. v.14, facsm, p. 43-55.

176 **MARCHAND, Sidney A.**
"Forgotten Fighters 1861-1865." Donaldsonville, Louisiana. 1966. 8vo., decr. cl., ports., illus., 172pp. 15- Bmk. Largely Ascension Parish regiments from Gen. a.B. Booth's La. CSA History.

177 **"MARGINALIA,**
or, Gleanings from an Army Notebook." By Personne, Army Correspondent, etc. See: under Felix Gregory (De Fontaine).

178 **MARION, Alan P.**
"Marines for the Confederacy." In: CWTI, Nov. 1978, v.17, #7, p.28-36, facsm., illus., ports.

179 **MARKELL, Catherine Susannah Thomas**
"Frederick Diary: Sept. 5-14, 1862." In: MdHM, June 1965, v.60, p.132-8.

180 **MARKENS, Isaac**
"Last Days of John Yates Beall." In: CV, Nov. 1922, v.XXX, p.426-428. Beall a CSA, executed as a spy by Federals Feb. 1865.

181 ..."President Lincoln & the Case of John Y. Beall." N.Y., printed for the Author, 1911, 8vo., wraps, port., 11pp. Also in: Americana, May 1911, v.VI, p.425-435.

182 ..."John Wilkes Booth; the True Story of his Death & Buriel." In: CV, Apr., 1925, v.XXXIII, p.135-136.

183 **MARKHAM, Jerald H.**
"The Botetourt Artillery." Lynchburg, Va., H.E. Howard, 1986, 8vo, cl, dj, (6), 95p., port., group ports., 1,000 copies, numbered, signed, bibliog.

184 **MARKHAM, Thomas R., Rev. Dr.**
"A Tribute to the Army of Tennessee. In: SHSP, 1880, v8, p.511-15.

185 ..."Tribute to the Confederate Dead. In: SHSP, 1882, v10, p. 174-8.

186 **MARKING OF GRAVES**
Of Confederate Dead. "Confederate Mound, Oakwood Cemetery, Chicago, Illinois. Suplemental estimate of appropriations required by the War Dept., for the year 1917." Feb. 15, 1916. Quartermaster Gen. of Army, 64th Congress, 1st Session, Hse. Doc. 701, v.148; 7102 Wash., DC, 2pp.

187 ..."Report of the Committee on Confederate Graves. Marking Confederate Graves with Recommendations for further continuance of said act & reasons thereof, Feb. 25, 1916." 64th Congress, 1st session, Hse. Doc. 795, in v.144; 7098. 6pp. Wash., DC, War Department.

188 ..."Locating & Marking Confederate Graves. Report accomp. Hse. Joint Res. 171. (To continue in effect providing act Mar. 9, 1906) Soldiers & sailors of Confederate Army & Navy who died in Northern Prisons. Submitted by Mr. Hay, Mar. 7, 1916. 64th Congress, 1st session, Hse. Report #306, v.1, 6903. 5pp. Hse. Mil. Affairs Com.

189 ..."Report to accompany S. 5044 (to continue in effect provisions of act. Mar. 9, 1906) Submitted by Mr. Chamberlain, Mar. 24, 1916. 5pp. 64th Cong., 1st Session S. Rep. 292, v.2, 6898.

190 ..."House Joint Resolution 171, public resolution 14, Approved Apr. 17, 1916. Also in Statutes at Large, v.39, pt.1, p.52-53. 1pp.

191 ..."Marking the Graves of Confederate Dead." Report to accompany S.J. 125 U.S. Congr. Senate Committee on Military Affairs. 61st Congr., 3rd Sess. Senate Report 928. (Washington, DC, GPO 1910?) 8vo, sewn, 7pp. submitted by Mr. Warren.

192 ...(Same) (Washington, 1903) 5th Congr. 2nd Sess., senate report 25. Calendar 140. 8vo sewn, 25 pp. submitted: Mr. Foraker.

193 ...(Same) (Washington: GPO, 1905) to accompany S. 1234) 59th Congr., 1st Sess. Senate report 25) Calendar #19, (12/20/05) 8vo, sewn, 25pp. submitted: Mr. Foraker. See: Jas. H. Berry. Title: "A Bill to Provide for the appropriate marking of the graves of the soldiers of the Confederate Army & Navy, & for other purposes." (copy, bound, 17pp.)

194 ...Report (to accompany S.J., res., 125." Wash: Gov. print off, 1910. 61st Cong., 3rd Sess. Senate, Rep. 928, 8vo, wraps, 7pp. submitted by Mr. Warren.

195 ..."Marking of graves of soldiers of the Confederate Army & Navy." House Rep. #2533. (Washington, 1903) 58th Cong., 2nd Sess. Senate Report 25 submitted by Mr. Foraker. 8vo, wraps, 25pp.

196 ..."Do: Report (to accompany S. 1234) 59th Congr., 1st Sess. Senate, Rep. 25. Calendar #19. 8vo, wraps, 256pp. prepared by Samuel E. Lewis. Data relating to location & condition of graves of CSA dead, in federal prisons, military hospitals & buried near place of confinement.

197 **"MARKING THE GRAVES**
of the Soldiers of the Confederate Army & Navy: Report from the Committee on Military Affairs." 57th Congress, 2nd Session, House Report-#3389. 8vo., sewed, 25pp., Washington, 1903. Report #2589, p.17, same $17.50Y.

198 **MARLIN, Lloyd Garrison**
"The History of Cherokee County, By Rev. Lloyd G. Marlin." Atlanta, Ga. Walter W. Brown Pub. 1932, 8vo, cl, illus., incl. ports & maps, V-xiii, 289 pp. bmk-112 $75.00. 17p. chap. on CSA, 20pp. roster Cherokee Co. soldiers.

199 **MARMADUKE, John Sappington, Gen.**
"Campaign against Steele in 1864." In: SHSP, 1883, v.11, p.75-83.

200 ..."General Marmaduke's campaign against Maj.Gen. Steele." In:SM, 1872, V.X, p.445-452.

201 ..."Expedition against Pine Bluff." In::SHSP, 1881, v.9, p.238. See: John F. Lee.

202 **MARMONT, Auguste Frederic Louis Viesse De, Duc De Raguse**
"The spirit of military institutions...a new version of Gen. Jomini's 35th chap. Treatise on grand military operations, by Frank Schaller, Col. 22nd Reg. Miss. In-

fantry, CSA." Columbia, SC, Evans & Cogswell, 1864 12mo, 3/4 leather, raised bands. Pub. presentation copy to R.E. Lee, with special bookplate. (Broadfoot) $1,500.00. Other copies $400.00.

203 ..."Louis Viesse de....duc de Raguse. "The Spirit of Military Institutions, by... Translated from the last Paris edition (1859) & augmented by biographical, historical, topographical, & military notes; with a new version of Gen. Jomini's celebrated 35th chap., part 1, of Treatise on grand military operations. By Frank Schaller, Col. 22d Regiment Mississippi Inf., CSArmy." (Albert Sid. Johnston life, 237-259) Columbia, S.C., Evans & Cogswell, 1864. 16mo, cl, 278pp. $75.00.

204 **MAROUBY, G.**
"Robert Lee, generalissime des Etats Confederes du Sud (1807-1870)." Paris, Imp. P. Feron-Vrau, le gerant E. Petithenery, 1896. Imp. 8vo, 16p. illus., maps, port. captain title, signed: G. Marouby. (Les contemporains 424).

205 **MARRINER, W.M.**
"Chickamauga, the opening." In: SB, 1884-1885, v.III, p.8-11.

206 **MARSCHALL, Nicola**
"Alabama Legislature declares Nicola Marschall designer first Confederate Flag, Stars & Bars, supported by affidavits of Marshcall's contemporaries & others, including "The True Story of the First Confederate Flag", by Mrs. Chappell Cory." Publications Historical & Patriotic Series, #12. 8vo, wraps, illus., 71pp. cover in colors. See also: Egar Erskine Hume. See: Virginia Clare's Life of Rutherford.

207 **MARSHALL TEXAS POWDER MILL.**
"Civil War Post Revived" In: Texas Highways, August 1974, Evacuation of Marshall Texas Powder Mill.

207a **MARSHALL, Alexander J.**
Five chapters of an unpublished "Book for the timers;" giving a Virginia view of the causes of the Revolution in the border slave states. And demonstrating who were the true authors of the Civil War." Richmond, Va., James E. Goode, 1863, 8vo, wraps, 40

208 **MARSHALL, Charles**
"An Aide-de-camp of Lee, being the papers of Colonel Charles Marshall, sometimes aide-de-camp, military secretary, and assistant adjutant general on the staff of Robert E. Lee, 1862, 1865. Edited by Major General Sir Frederick Maurice." Boston: Little, Brown & Co., 1927, 8vo, cl, maps (some fold), ports, facsms, xix, 287 pp. $18.00.

209 ..."Address delivered before the Lee Monument Association, at Richmond, Va., Oct. 27, 1887 on the occasion of laying the corner-stone of the monument to General Robert E. Lee." Boston: John Murphy & Co., 1888, 8vo, wraps, 59pp.

210 ..."Address of...on the Monument to General Robert E. Lee." In: SHSP, 1889, v.XVII, p. 215-245. (entire article p.187, 235, "Lee Monument Memorial Vol.).

211 ..."Address of..(formerly private secretary & ADC to Gen. Robert E. Lee of Baltimore, before the Virginia division of the Army of Northern Virginia at their annual meeting, held at the capitol at Richmond, Va., Oct. 29, 1874, Richmond, Va., Gary's print, 1875, 8vo, wraps, 23pp. "Strategic Value Richmond".

212 ..."Appomattox Courthouse, incidents of the surrender of Gen. Lee...address of...on Observance of Anniversary of Lee's Birthday, at Baltimore, Jan. 19, 1894." In: SHSP, 1893, v.XXI, p.353-360.

..."Appomattox. An address delivered before the Society of the Army & Navy of the Confederate States, in the state of Maryland, on Jan. 19, 1894, at the Academy of Music, Baltimore, Md." Baltimore: Guggenheimer, Weil, 1894. 8vo, wraps, port (front), 22pp. $35.00.

213 ..."Events leading on to the battle of Gettysburg. Address of...before the Confederate Veterans Association of Washington, DC (Celebrate Lee's birthday) In: SHSP, 1895, v.XXIII, p.205-229.

214 ..."The Last Days of Lee's Army" In: Cent., 1901-1902, v.63, p.935-935.

215 ..."Lee's farewell address to his army." In: B & L, v.4, p.747.

216 ..."Strength of Gen'l. Lee's Army during the Seven Days Battles--Extract from an address of Col. Charles Marshall, before the Virginia division of the A.N.V." In: SHSP, 1876, v.1, p.407-424.

217 ..."The Surrender of General Lee." In: Confed. Vet., Aug. 1924, v.XXXII, p.298-300.

218 ..."The Sword of Lee. It was not offered to Gen. Grant at Appomattox. Col. Marshall's testimony corrects an oft-repeated misstatement." In: SHSP, 1901, v.XXIX, p.269-272.

219 ..."When Forrest Captured Franklin" In: Confed. Vet., Sept. 1924, v.XXXII, p.342.

220 ..."Occurrences at Lee's Surrender."In: CV, Feb. 1894, v.II, #2, p.42-46. Address at Baltimore Jan. 19, 1894.

221 **MARSHALL, David**
"A Civilian Fort on the Confederate Frontier: Samuel & Susan Newcomb at Ft. Davis (Tex.) on the Clear Folk on the Brazos." In: W.Tex.HAssn. 1985, v.lxi, p.74-77, notes.

222 **MARSHALL, F.R.D.**
"Southern Banners." (London) Journ. Confed. Hist. Soc. v.I, #2, p.49-55, plate-flags. pt. 2, #2, p. 90-98, plate.

223 ...(London) JOUR. CONFED. Hist. Soc. Dec. 1963, v.II, #1, p. 10-17, pl. -1. Dec. 1965, v.III, #4, p.133-142, pl. -1.

224 ..."Southern Banners." (London) Jour. Confed. Hist. Soc., Dec. 1965, v.III, #4, p.133-142, pl-1.

225 **MARSHALL, Fielding Lewis**
"Recollections & Reflections of...a Virginian gentleman of the old school. Compiled by Maris Newton Marshall n.p., n.d., (Orange, 1911?) 8vo, cl, front (port), 176pp.

226 **MARSHALL, H. Snowden**
"Address delivered at the opening of the building of the Confederate Memorial Institute of Richmond, May 3, 1921." Richmond, 1921 (Dietz Pr.) 2nd. 1925, 8vo, wraps, 16pp. On origins of the war between the states. $25.00.

227 ..."(Address at the) dedication of the South's "Battle Abbey." In: CV, June 1921, v.XXIX, p.208-212.

228 **MARSHALL, John L.**
"A biographical sketch of the military life of the late Col. T.W. Thompson." In: SB, 1882-3, v.1, p.11-14.

229 **MARSHALL, Mary Louise**
"Nurse Heroines of the Confederacy." Reprint: Bul. Medical Library Assn., v.45, #3, July 1957, cover title. 8vo, wraps, ports, bibliog., pp. 319-336.

230 ..."Plantation Medicine." In: Bul. of Med. Lib. Assn., 1938, v.XXVI, p.115-128.

231 **MARSHALL, Park**
"Artillery in the Battle of Franklin." In: Confed. Vet., March 1915, v.XXIII, p.100-102.

232 ..."The Life of William B. Bate, Citizen, Soldier & Statesman. With Memorial Addresses...& Orations." Nashville, Tenn., 1908, Cumberland Press, 12mo, cl, ports, 363pp. Bate was CSA General during war. 75 bmk-105 150-R.

233 ..."Hood's Failure at Spring Hill." In: CV, Jan. 1914, v.22, #1, p.14-15, 58-60. Rebuttal to J.D. Remington's article in CV, December 1913, V.21, p. 569-571. See: Re-

mington's Answer, CV, v.22, p.234. See also: J.P. Young's article, v.22, p.126 & in Jan. 1908, v.16, p.25-41.

234 **MARSHALL, Robert A.**
"When Missouri went into the war." In: CV, Jan. 1920, v.XXVII, p.18-19.

235 **MARSHALL, W.F.**
"James Daniel Moore, 1846-1905. A collection of obituary matter which was variously published upon his death." Raleigh, NC, Edwards & Broughton, 1907. 8vo, wraps, 60p., illus., ports.

236 **MARSZALEK, John F., Jr.**
"The Charleston Fire of 1861 as described in the Emma Holmes Diary." In: So. Car. Hist. Mag., 1975, v.LXXVI, p.60-67.

237 **MARTEL, Glenn G.**
"The Escape of Capt. Joe & Lt. Dock Daniel." In: AHQ, 1947, v.VI, p.302-343.

237a **MARTEN, James**
"The Lamentations of a Whig; James Throckmorton writes a letter." In: CWH, June 1985, v.31, #2, p.163-70.
See: Claude Elliott.

238 **MARTI, Jose Julian**
"Jose Julian Martin, on Judah Philip Benjamin (1811-1884). Ed. & Translated by Louis Gruss. Louisiana Hist. Quart., XXIII, 1940, p. 256-264.

239 **"MARTIAL LAW."**
n.p., 1861, 8vo, wraps, 18pp. (Jk-163) $65.00. "Lambastes Lincoln administration's use of martial law, justified by suspension of habeas corpus & other measures at beginning of war."

239 **MARTIN'S BRIGADE.**
See: Charles G. Elliott.

240 **MARTIN, Abbott C.**
"Chancellorsville, a soldier's letter." In: VA MHB, 1929, v.XXXVII, p.221-228.

241 **MARTIN, Bessie**
"Desertion of Alabama Troops from the Confederate Army; a study in sectionalism." N.Y., Columbia Univ. Press; London, P.S. King & Son, 1932. Columbia Univ. Studies #378. Tall, 8vo, cl, illus. (maps), 7-281pp.

242 **MARTIN, Charles L.**
"The Red River Campaign" In: CV, May 1925, v.XXXIII, p. 169-170.

243 **MARTIN, David, Dr.**
"Confederate Monuments at Gettysburg, the Gettysburg Battle Monuments." Vol. 1. Baltimore: Butternut Press, 1986. 8vo, cl, dj, 297pp, ills, map. 100 monuments, location, text.
..."Confederate Monuments at Gettysburg." In: CV (new), July/Aug. 1986, v.34, #4, p.25-31, ills.

244 **MARTIN, Edwin**
"Mr. Davis' Citizenship." In: SB, ns, v.II, 1886/1887, p. 262-262.

245 **MARTIN, Fred R.**
"Pelham, of Alabama." In: CV, Jan. 1921, v.XXIX, p.9-10. Story of "Gallant John Pelham".

246 **MARTIN, G.W.**
"The Killing of Lt. Meigs, of Sheridan staff-proof it was done in fair combat. In: SHSP, 1881, v.9, p.77-79.

247 **MARTIN, Henri**
"Foreign Opinions of the Confederate Cause." In: SHSP, 1882, v.10, p.560-562.

248 **MARTIN, Howard N.**
"Texas Redskins in Confederate Gray." In: SWHQ, April 1967, v.LXX, #4, p. 586-592.

249 **MARTIN, John Henry**
"Columbus, Georgia, from its selection as a 'trading town' in 1827, to its partial destruction by Wilson's Raid, 1865. History, incident, personality, compiled by John H. Martin." 150-. Columbus, Ga., T. Gilbert, 1874-1875, 12mo, cl, 2vol. in 1, 169; cl xxiv, 196pp. Martin was editor: Columbus Enquirer.
..."Address of Maj.Gen. J.H. Martin at the reunion of the Georgia Div. UCV at Co-

lumbus, Ga., Oct. 19, 1910." Atlanta: Charles P. Boyd, 1911, 8vo, wraps, cover-title, port(front) 30pp.

250 ..."Longstreet's forces at Chickamauga." In: CV, Dec. 1912, v.XX, p.564-565.

251 **MARTIN, Micajah D.**
"Chancellorsville." In: Va. Mag. Hist., July 1929, v.XXXVII, p.221-228. Letters from Virginia in 1863 by Sgt. Martin, Co. D, 2nd Georgia Bat., his brigade's action. Also: as Excerpt, 8vo, wraps.

252 **MARTIN, Patricia**
"Jefferson Davis." N.Y., G.P. Putnam's Sons (1966), 12mo, decr., cl, d/w, 62pp. illus. juvenile.

252a **MARTIN, Richard A. & Daniel L. Schafer**
"Jacksonville's Ordeal by Fire." Jacksonville: Florida Pub. Co., 1984. 8vo, cl, 304pp, ills, bibliog., index. $15.

253 **MARTIN, R., Capt.**
"Muster Roll of Capt. R. Martin's Company Light Artillery, Army of Confederate States of America, from 28th Feb. 1863, when last mustered to 30th day of April, 1863." In: Ga. G.Q., v.1, #1, Mar. 1917, p.57-59.

254 **MARTIN, Rawley White, Col.**
"The Battle of Gettysburg, & the charge of Pickett's Division." In: SHSP, v.XXXII, 1904, p.183-189.

255 ..."Armistead at the Battle of Gettysburg. Extracts from letters by Dr. R.W. Martin to Rev. James Poindexter." In: SHSP, April 1914, v.XXXIX, p.186-187. See: Rev. James E. Poindexter.

256 **MARTIN, Richard A.**
"Defeat in Victory: Yankee Experience in early Civil War Jacksonville." In: Fla. Hist. Quart., July 1974, v.LII, #1, p.1-32, port, illus.

257 ..."Henry's Raid Set Stage for Olustee Battle" In: Jacksonville (Fla.), v.XIX, 1982, Jan/Feb. p.55-63.

258 **MARTIN, Robert Hugh**
"A Boy of Old Shenandoah. Edt: Carolyn Martin Rutherford." Parsons, A. Va., 1977, 12mo, cl, illus., dj., 125pp., Boy's view of the war.

259 **MARTIN, Sidney Walter**
"Charles Frederick Crisp (1845-1896), speaker of the house." In: GA Rev., Summer 1954, v.8, p.167-177. Services in CSArmy in Ga., & national politics.

260 ..."Origins of the name 'War Between the States'. In: UDC Mag., May 1951, v.14, #5, p. 3,30.

261 **MARTIN, Thomas H.**
"Atlanta and its Builders, a Comprehensive History of the Gate City of the South." (Atlanta, Ga.) Century Memorial Pub., 1902, Tk. 4to, cl, 718; v.2, 723 pp. illus., ports, $65.00. Vol. 1 largely civil war operations in and around Atlanta, pp.154-709, drawn on the "Official Records".

262 ..."The Advent of William Gregg & the Granitville Company." (Baton Rouge, La.) JSH, Aug., 1945, v.XI, #3, pp.389-423.

263 **MARTIN, Thomas Ricaud**
"The Great Parliamentary Battle & Farewell Addresses of the Civil War." N.Y., Wash., Neale Pub. Co., 1905, 12mo, cl, 255pp. 100-JK-138.

264 **MARTIN, Vincent F.**
"Story of Brook's Battalion". In: Brooks 'Story of the Confederacy', Columbia, SC, State Co. 1912, p. 313-327.

265 **MARTIN, William C.**
"Memorial address of...of Natchez, Miss. Delivered at "Mt. Airy" In Adams County, Miss., home of the late Capt. Wm., H. Wilson, CSA on occation of the 118th anniversary birthday of Jefferson Davis, one-time president of the CSA." (n.p., 1926?) 8vo, wraps, 16pp.

266 **MARTIN, William E.**
"The South; its dangers & its resources; an address delivered at the celebration of the

Battle of Fort Moultrie, June 28, 1850." Charleston, SC, Edward C. Councell, 1850, 8vo, wraps, 12pp., Oration of North's efforts to make the South "the Ireland of America.", through economic dominance & abolition of slaves.

267 **MARTIN, William J.**
"The Eleventh North Carolina Regiment, successor of the First N.C. Volunteers (The Bethel Regiment)."In: SHSP, 1895, v.23, p.42-56.

268 **MARTIN, William T., Gen.**
"A Defence of General Bragg's conduct at Chickamauga." In: SHSP, 1883, v.11, p.201-206.

269 **MARVIN, David P., Lt. Comm.**
"The Harriet Lane." In: SWHQ, July, 1935, v.XXXIX, #1, p.14-20, illus. See: Trexler (H.A., Tucker, P.C., 3d. CSNavy takes ship in Galveston Harbor in 1862 as prize from Federals.

270 **MARX, Rudolph**
"The Fifth Column at the Battle of Gettysburg." In: Surgery, gynecol., & obstet., Mar. 1958, v.106, p.375-378. On dysentery in armies & question whether it weakened judgment of Gen. Lee.

271 **MARYE, John L.**
"The First Gun at Gettysburg with the Confederate Advance Guard." In: Amer. Hist. Reg., 1895, v.II, p.1225-1232.

272 **MARYLAND CAMPAIGN:**
See: William Allan, 'Richmond Dispatch.' Bradley T. Johnson.

273 **MARYLAND CONFEDERATE SOLDIER'S HOME**
See: Winfield Peters.

274 "**MARYLAND LINE**
Confederate Soldier's Home." Baltimore, 1889, 8vo, wraps, 20pp. bmk-$20.00.

275 **MARYLAND SOCIETY ARMY & NAVY, CSA**
"Reunion & Banquet." In: SHSP, 1882, v.X, p.94-95.

276 **MARYLAND,**
See: Horace E. Hayden, Henry May, Lamar Hollyday, Bradley Tyler Johnson, Edward H. McDonald, Winfield Peters, William L. Ritter, J.R. Stonebraker, Isaac Ridgeway Trimble, Geo. Thomas, Mrs. Daniel Giraud Wright.

277 ..."The Charge of the First Maryland Regiment at the death of Ashby." Print: litho by Hoen, 20x28 Baltimore (c. 1870) $25.00.

278 ..."An Earnest Appeal of the people of Maryland upon the important issues of the times...issued by the State Democratic Executive Committee, Baltimore City, October 8, 1860." Baltimore, J.B. Rose & Co., 1860, 8vo, sewn, 16pp.

279 ..."Message of the Governor of Maryland to the General Assembly in Extra Session 1861." Frederick, Beale H. Richardson, 1861, 8vo, wraps, 24pp. $30.00. Relates to the murder of Union troops and turmoil caused by Southerners (below).

280 ..."Report of the Commissioners appointed to wait on the President of the US, to the General Assembly of Maryland, Extra Session 1861." Frederick, Beale H. Richardson, 1861, 8vo, sewn, 4pp. $25.00.

281 ..."Report of the Committee on Federal Relations in regard to the calling of a Sovereign Convention." Frederick, Beale H. Richardson, 1861, 8vo, wraps, 22pp. $20.00. Protests to Federal Gov. of military measures against Confederacy, recognizing the CSA & sympathy with secession movement.

282 ..."Report of the Peace Commissioners appointed to wait on Presidents Lincoln & Davis, by the General Assembly, 1861." Annapolis, Md., 1861.

283 ..."Report of the committee on Federal relations in regard to the calling of a sovereign convention. Frederick, Md., E.S.

Riley Print, 1861, 8vo, wraps, 22pp. (Doc.F.) $25.00. Title head: By the House of Delegates, May 9, 1861. Read & 10,000 copies ordered printed. Mssc. note on cover: "The greater part of this issue was siezed and destroyed by the Gov." Sabin 45358- "Very rare; consisting of letters from prominent Union men in Maryland, giving information regarding Southern sympathizers; which letters were captured by Stonewall Jackson from Gen. Banks." Called in proposition to the Governor's acquiescence in honoring Lincoln's call for state militia to suppress rebellion. Calls for recognition of CSA. Largely Southern sympathizers, protesting Lincoln's asking states to raise a 75,000 militia.

284 ..."Report of the Committee on Federal Relations upon the Messages of the Governor, in regard to the arbitrary Proceedings of the United States Authorities, and the Governor's Correspondence with the United States Government." Frederick: Elihu S. Riley, 1861, 8vo, wraps, 8pp. (Doc-H).

285 ..."Communications from the Mayor of Baltimore." Frederick: 1861, 8vo, wraps, 9pp. $25.00.

286 ..."Report & Resolutions of the Joint Committee of the Senate & House of Delegates of Maryland upon the Reports and Memorials of the Police Commissioners and the Mayor & City Council of Baltimore." Frederick: 1861, 8vo, wraps, 26pp.

287 ..."Journal of Proceedings of the Senate of Maryland, in Extra Session, April 1861. Frederick: Beale H. Richardson, 1861, 8vo, cl, 365, Secret Proceedings, 6, rules, 8.

288 ..."Address & Resolutions adopted at the meeting of the Southern Rights Convention of Maryland, held in...Baltimore, Feb., 1861." Baltimore, Md., J.B. Rose & Co., 1861, 8vo, wraps, 14pp. Sabin-45049.

289 ..."Letters to Gov. Bradford by a Marylander." Baltimore, 1863, 8vo, sewn, 21pp. Attacks Gov. because of his support, Lincoln.

MARYLANDER

290 "Poem: On L----n's, Proclamation of April 1, 1863, by a Marylander." n.p., n.d. (c. 1863) Broadside. 8-stanzas of treason (?) beginning. "We have read the tyrant's order and the signet to the rule, and thought the kingly jester meant to make an April fool, for we knew that nothing better than a joke in such a strain, could e'r be made to emanate from his degraded brain...."

291 **MASKED LADY, THE**
of the White House: or the Ku Klux Klan. A Most Startling Exposure of the Doings of this Extensive Secret Band, Whose Mysterious Lodges Exists in every City & County in the Land." Phila., C.W. Alexander (1868), 8vo, wraps, 19-62p. illus.

292 **MASLOWSKI, Peter**
"Treason must be made odius: Military Occupation & Wartime Reconstruction in Nashville, Tennessee, 1862-1865." Millwood, NY, KTO Press, 1978, 8vo, cl, dj, xiii, 164pp. $18.95.

293 **MASON & SLIDELL AFFAIR**
"Correspondence relative to the Case of Messrs. Mason & Slidell." Washington, 1862. 8vo, wraps, 15pp., The Trent Affair. $30.00-Bmk.

294 ..."A Legal View of the Seisure of Messers Mason & Slidell." New York, 1861, 8vo, wraps, 27pp. A view, their capture of Southern comm. not justified by international law.
See: Walter L. Fleming's Memoirs, Jas. Murray Mason & Louis M. Sears.

295 **"MASON SMITH Family Letters."**
See: Smith, Daniel E. Huger.

296 **MASON, E.C.**
"Old Copperheads & New." In: Wis. Mag.

Hist., Dec.1917, v.I, p.202-203. Activities of anti-war group during war in Wisconsin.

296a **MASON, Edward G.**
"A Visit to South Carolina in 1860." In: Atl. Monthly, 1884, v.53, p.241-50.

297 **MASON, Emily Virginia**
"Popular Life of Gen. Robert Edward Lee. Dedicated by permission of Mrs. Lee. Illustrated with 17 original designs by Professor Volck." Baltimore: J. Murphy & Co., 1872, 12mo, decr., gilt cl, illus., ports, incl. front, xi, (13)-432pp. 35-M.

298 ...2nd Revised edition. 1872; on cover, Premium Library.

299 ...2nd Revised edition. 1874, also an 1877 edition.

300 ..."Memories of a Hospital Matron." In: Atlanta Monthly, 1902, v.XC, p.305-318, 475-485.

301 ..."Journal of a Young Lady of Virginia 1782." Baltimore: Printed and published for benefit of Lee Memorial Association of Richmond, 1871, 8vo, wraps, 56pp. From an old manuscript of a country place in Maryland.

302 ..."The Southern Poems of the War. Collected & Arrainged by Miss Emily V. Mason." Baltimore: J. Murphy & Co., 1867, 16mo, cl, 456pp. 40- 75-.
...2nd Revised and enlarged edition, front, 524pp.
...3rd Revised and enlarged edition, front, 524pp.
...4th Revised and enlarged edition, front, 524pp.

303 **MASON, Fanny Witherspoon**
"Daddy Dave. By Mary Frances (pseud.)" N.Y., Funk & Wagnells, 1886, 12mo, cl, vi, (7)-116pp. A tribute to a faithful family servant during & after the war.

304 **MASON, Francis Van Wyck**
"Proud New Flags.: Phila, Lippincott Press, 1951, 8vo, xiii, 493pp.; Historical novel of the CSA Navy.

305 ..."Our Valiant Few." Baltimore: Little, Brown Co. 1956, 1st, 8vo, cl, illus., maps, xii, 436pp. South's efforts to break blockage around Charleston.

306 **MASON, Harley Norton, Jr.**
"The Official Flags of the Confederate States." In: Commonwealth, Va. 1951, 18(#12), 10-13pp., 80, dec. col. flags, port.

307 **MASON, James Monroe**
"Confederate soldiers used covered bridge as block-house in 1862." In: Covered Bridge Topics, Fall 1953, v.11, #3, p.1-2. Flint River Bridge 12 miles, Huntsville, Ala. in 1862.

308 **MASON, James Murray**
"Correspondence with Mr. Mason respecting Blockade, & Recognition of the Confederate States." London: British Parliament, 1863. Folio, 17p., JK $125.00 Corresp: PM Russell & Mason.

309 **MASON, James Murray ("Mason & Slidell")**
See: R.M.T. Hunter, Henry A. Wise, Virginia Mason, "Mason & Slidell."

310 **MASON, John**
"Three Years in the Army; or, the life & adventures of a Rebel soldier." (Warren, Ohio?), c.1950, 4to, 32 leafs, 1861-1864.

311 **MASON, Sara Elizabeth, Lucile Crutcher & Sarah A. Verner**
"Confederate Imprints in the University of Alabama Library. Foreword: Wm. Stanley Hoole University, Ala., 1961, 4to, stiff wraps, III, 158pp. Bmk-$25.00.

312 **MASON, Virginia**
"The Public Life & Diplomatic Correspondence of James M. Mason with some personal history by Virginia Mason, his daughter." Roanoke, Va., Stone Print, 1903, 8vo, cl, front(port), ix, 603pp.
...N.Y., Neale Pub. Co., 1906, 8vo, cl, ix,

603pp., front $50.00. Subject was CSA commissioner to Great Britain.

313 **MASSEY, Annie G.**
"The Secession of Arkansas." In: CV, 1931, v.39, p.414-418.

313a **MASSEY, J. M.**
"The Exploits of Gen. Jo O. Shelby in Phillips County." In: PhCHQ, Sept. 1973. v.11, p.22-32.
..."The Lost Weapon--Truth or Legend." In: PhCHQ, v.7, p.10-4. Sept. 1969; Mar. 1970, v.7, p.1-6. Civil War tale.

314 **MASSEY, John**
"Reminiscences, giving sketches of scenes through which the author has passed & pen pictures of people who have modified his life." Nashville, Tenn., M.E. Church South, Smith & Lamar, Agents (Dallas), 1916, 8vo, cl, ports., incl. front., 330pp. Author was in Alabama Legion, afterwards Gracie's Brigade. R-$250.00.

315 **MASSEY, John Edward, Rev.**
"Autobiography of John E. Massey; Edt. by Elizabeth H. Hancock." N.Y., Neale Print, 1909, 8vo, cl, port., 312pp. $35.00-Bmk. Baptist minister, ardent supporter of CSA & political affairs in Va., Reconstruction.

316 **MASSEY, Mary Elizabeth**
"Confederate Refugees flock to the cities." In: CWTI, Nov. 1971, v.10, #7, p.14-24, illus., port.

317 ..."Confederate Refugees in North Carolina." In: NCHR, Spring, 1963, v.XL, pp.158-182.

318 ..."Ersatz in the Confederacy." Columbia, University of South Carolina Press, 1952, 8vo, cl, dj, illus., xii, 233pp. $60.00.

319 ..."Frustration, homesickness the lot of the average Southern Refugee..." In: CWTI, May 1964, v.III, #2, p.42-48, illus. From author's 'Refugee life in the CSA.'

320 ..."Home Management in the Confederacy." In: The New Index, January 1957, 8vo, wraps, 10pp. $6.00.

321 ..."The Effect of Shortages on the Confederate Homefront." In: AHQ, 1950, v.IX, pp.172-193.

322 ..."The Making of a Feminist." Taken from Ella Gertrude Clanton Thomas's Diary (at Duke University) of 41 years, in 13 vols., from the Civil War Generation. Houston, Tex., JSH, Feb. 1973, v.XXXIX, #1, pp.3-23.

323 ..."Refugee Life in the Confederacy." Baton Rouge, Louisiana Univ. Press, 1964, 8vo, cl, dj, illus, xii, 327pp. $10.00. $8.00. $35.00.

324 ..."Southern Refugee Life During the Civil War." In: NCHRev., Jan 1943, x.XX, #1, p.1-21, #2, April, p.132-156.

325 **MASSIE, Fletcher T., Lt., 2nd Lt., Lampkin's Bat.**
"From Petersburg to Appomattox. Lampkin's Battery of Artillery." From Richmond, Va. Times-Dispatch, Oct. 28, 1906 In: SHSP, 1906 v.34, p.243-248.

326 **MASTERS, Edgar Lee**
"Lee, A Dramatic Poem." N.Y., Macmillan Co., 1926, 8vo, cl, 6, 1, 139pp. 250 signed, lim. edt. SK122 $55.00.
...12mo, cl, 139pp. Trade Edition.

327 ..."Stephen A. Douglas." In: Am.Mercury, 1931, v.XXII, p.11-23. "Douglas was superior to Lincoln in genius, in strength of mind, & in moral character."

328 **MASTIN, Claudius Henry**
"The Medical Profession in the War." In: SHSP, 1885, v.13, p.476-480.

328a **MATHER, Fred**
"Request for Recovery of his Sword." In: SHSP, 1881, v.IX, p.431-2.

329 **MATHERS, Augustus Henry**
"The Civil War Letters of Augustus Henry Mathers, Assistant Surgeon, Forth Florida

Regiment, C.S.A." In: FHQ, October 1957, v.XXXVI, #2, p.94-124, port.

330 **MATHES, James Harvey, Capt.**
"General Forrest." New York, D. Appleton & Co., 1902, Great Commanders Series, 12mo, cl, front, pl, port., maps, facsm, illus., ix, 395pp. $75.00-Bmk105. $50.00-Bmk.
...Deluxe Edt. (Large Paper) 1,000 copies, numbered. $75.00.
...Memphis, Tenn., Burke's Book Store, 1979, reprint 1902 edt. $23.50. 12mo, cl, 395pp.
...Gaithersburg, Md., Olde Soldiers Books, 1988 reprint. 8vo, cl, 395pp. $30.
..."The Old Guard in Gray-Researches in Annals of the Confederate Historical Association, Sketches of Memphis Veterans who upheld her standard in the war & of other Confederate Worthies." Memphis, Tenn., S.C. Toof Co., 1897, tall 8vo, cl, regular edt., 292pp., illus., ports.(incl. front).
...(Same) Enlarged Edt., 298, 148pp. $125.00-Bmk86. $75.00-Y.
...Marceline, Mo., Walsworth Pub. Co., 1975, 2 vols in one, 298, 248pp.

331 **MATHES, Valerie L.**
"Chief John Ross." In:'The Masterkey', Apr/June 1980. Ross's role in Cherokee CSA alliance.

332 **MATHEWS, Alfred E.**
"Interesting Narrative: Being a Journal of a Flight of Alfred E. Mathews of Stark Co., Ohio. From the State of Texas, on 20th April & His Arrival Chicago on the 28th of May, after travelling on foot & alone a distance of 800 miles across the State of Louisiana, Arkansas & Missouri, by the most unfrequent routes; together with intresting descriptions of men & things; of what he saw & heard; appearance of the country, habits of the people, etc, etc." n.p., 1861, wraps, (7)-34, (1)p. Streeter $550.00. Northerner from Carthage, Texas to Ironton, Mo., nearly hanged as a northerner, local sentiment on secession, etc.

332a **MATHIS, Ray**
"John Horry Deant: South Carolina Aristocrat on the Alabama Frontier." University: Alabama Univ. Press, 1979. 8vo, cl, dj, ills, xiv, 267pp. $17.50. Microcosm of Plantation South, replaces myth & prejudices of South.

333 **MATHIS, Ray & Douglas C. Purcell, Edts.**
"In the Land of the Living: Wartime Letters of Confederates from the Chattahooche Valley of Alabama & Georgia." Troy, Ala., Historic Chattahoochee Commission, Troy State University, 1981, 9x12, cl, dj, illus., 16 maps, color coded, ix, 131pp., 500 copies. 200 letters by about 30 men from SW Ga., South Alabama & Pensacola, Fla. serving in the ANV & Army of Tenn.

334 **MATHIS, Robert Neil**
"Freedom of the Press in the Confederacy: a Reality." In: Historian, 1975, v.XXXVII, pp.633-648.
..."The Ordeal of Confiscation: The Post Civil War Trials of Gazaway Bugg Lamar." In: GHQ, Fall 1979, v.LXIV, #3, pp.339-353, notes.

335 **MATTAM, Henry Clay**
"Civil War Memoirs of the First Maryland Cavalry, CSA." Edt: Samuel H. Miller. In: MHM, 1963, v.LVIII, p.137-170, port.

336 **MATTESON, Maurice**
"Southrons All: A Music Drama of the Confederacy..1861-1865." Beaufort, N.C., Centennial Souvenir Edition 1961. 8vo, wraps, 90p. Script & Music of the play.

337 **MATTHEWS, Albert**
"Origin of Butternut & Copperhead." Colonial Society of Massachusetts, 1920, v.XX, pp.205-37.
..."A Last Word on "Copperhead." Nation, 1918, June 29, pp.758, v.CVI.

338 **MATTHEWS, Church M.**
"John Hunt Morgan 1825-1864." In: Confed. Vet., May 1928, v.XXXVI, p.177-178.

338a **MATTHEWS, H. H.**
"Major John Pelham, Confederate Hero, Lee called him the "Gallant Pelham." In: SHSP, 1902, v.30, p.379-84.
..."Recollections of Maj. James Breathed, A Maryland Confederate, by a member of the Battery." In: SHSP, 1902, v.30, p.346-8.

339 **MATTHEWS, J.E.F.**
"Address delivered at unveiling of Confederate Monument Thomaston, Ga., May, 1908. Roster of Companies going to war from Upson County." Roster pp. (11)-32, 8vo, wraps, cover title, 32pp.

340 **MATTHEWS, James M., Edt.**
"Constitution of the Confederate States. Quotations from Statutes at large of the Confederate States of America." Washington, Gov. Print, 1913, 63rd Congress, 1st Sess. Senate Doc. 181, 8vo, sewn, 23pp.
See: "Statutes at Large of the CSA."
"Acts & Joint Resolutions..."
"Public Laws of the Confederate States of Amer..."
"Statutes at Large of the Provisional Government..."

341 **MATTHEWS, James P.**
"How General A.P. Hill met his fate. Comprehending the statements of sergt. Geo. W. Tucker, CSA & John H. Mauk, US Army. With some notice of their lives. Also an account of the death of Maj.Gen. John Sedgwick, US Army." In: SHSP, 1899, v.XXVII, p.26-38, port.

342 **MATTHEWS, Sidney T.**
"Control of the Baltimore Press during the Civil War." In: MdHM, June 1941, v.XXXVI, 21pp. Bmk-115 $10.00.

342a **MATTHEWS, William H., Jr.**
"Geography & Southern Sectionalism in the Civil War." In: Phila. Geo. Soc. Bul., Oct. 1928, v.XXVI, pp.255-78.
Also separate, 8vo, wraps, cover title, maps, p.(19)-39.

342b **MATTISON, J. W., Co. G.**
"Orr's South Carolina Rifles, brief sketch of the Regiment." In: SHSP, 1899, v.27, p.157-65.

343 **MATTSON, J. Stanley**
"Twain's Last Months on the Mississippi." Columbia, Mo., Mo. Hist. Review, July, 1968, v.LXII, #4, pp.398-409, port, illus. Correst details of Twain's CSArmy enlistment with later material than his "Letters of Quintus Snodgrass."
..."Mark Twain on War & Peace: the Missouri Rebel & the 'campaign that failed.'" In: Amer. Quart., 1968, v.20, p. 783-94.
See: Allan Bates & Claude S. Brinegar.

343a **MAUK, John W.**
"Who Killed Gen. A. P. Hill?" In: SHSP, 1892, v.XX, p.349-51.

344 **MAURER, Oscar Edward**
"Punch" on slavery & Civil War in America, 1841-1865." In: Victorian Studies, Sept. 1957, v.1, p.5-28, cartoons, notes. On satirical comments by Douglas Jerrold satirical verses by Shirley Brooks, cartoons by Sir John Tenniel, expressing prevailing pro-Southern & anti-Lincoln attitudes in "Punch."

345 **MAURICE, Frederick**
"Aide-de-Camp of Lee."
See: Chs. Marshall.

346 **MAURICE, Frederick Barton, Maj-Gen. Sir**
"An Aide-de-Camp of Lee, being papers of Col. Charles Marshall, etc." Edited by Maj-Gen. Maurice.
See: Under: Col. Charles Marshall.
..."Freeman's Lee, a Review by Maj.Gen. Maurice." In: Va.Quart.Rev., 1935, v.XI, p.435-440.
..."Robert E. Lee, the Soldier," review by Blanton Fortson in Ga.Hist.Quart.
See: Fortson.

..."Robert E. Lee the Soldier." Boston, N.Y., Houghton Mifflin Co, 1925, 8vo, cl, port.(front), facsm., maps (2 fldg). $25.00. Editions: 1925 three impressions; 1926 4th impression; Boston 1928; London 1925 & 1930; N.Y., Bonanza, n.d.(1976).

...Statesmen & Soldiers of the Civil War, a Study of the Conduct of the War." Boston, Little, Brown & Co., 1926, 8vo, cl, d/w, pp.xi, front prots., 173, illus $25.00. The Lee-Knowles Lectures for 1925-1926, Trinity College, Cambridge. Later published Atlantic Monthly (one lecture in the 'Forum.')

..."Governments & War; A Study of the Conduct of War." London, W. Heineman Co., 1926, American edition, 8vo, cl, 171pp., Boston, Little, Brown, 1926. Relations between statesmen & soldiers in prolonged war. Jeff Davis & J.E. Johnston, Davis & Lee.

..."Soldiers & Statesmen in the Civil War." In: Atlantic, July - Aug., 1926, v. CXXXVIII, p.52-61, 224-236. Prs. Davis & J.E. Johnston, Lincoln & Grant.

346a **MAURY COUNTY, TENN.**
"Confederate Soldiers & Patriots of Maury County, Tennessee." Original publication 1970. Easley, S.C., Southern Hist. Pub., 1985. 8vo, paper, 8 1/2 x 11, xii, 386pp. Capt. James Midison Sparkman Chap., UDC, Maury Co., Tenn., sent 29 companies to CSA. Contains names of 3,483 soldiers & local guards.

347 **MAURY, Anne Fontaine, Edt.**
"Intimate Virginiana; a Century of Maury Travels by land & Sea." Richmond, Va., Dietz Press, 1941, 8vo, pict. cl., illus., 342pp. $45.00. Carolina Bks: "Two chapters (43p.) letters by Maury family during war, especially on home conditions during war."

348 **MAURY, Betty Herndon**
"The Confederate Diary of...daughter of Lt.Comm. M.F. Maury...1861-1863." Edt.: Alice Maury Parmelee. Washington, D.C., Private Print, 1938, 8vo, cl, front(port.)2, 102pp. For presentation 25 copies printed. Mssc. in L.C. $100.00.

349 **MAURY, Dabney Herndon**
"Address at Reunion of Confederate Reunion, Maury Camp, #2, Fredericksburg, Va., Aug. 23, 1883." In: SHSP, 1883, v.XI, pp.544-51.

..."Americans as Fighters." In: SHSP, 1891, v.XIX, p.386-89.

...Autograph: Holograph letter to an Atg. Collector, L.J. Cist, Dec. 3, 1866. $35.00.

..."Defense of Mobile in 1865." In: SM, 1873, v.XII, p.288-95.

..."The Defence of Mobile in 1865." In: SHSP, 1877, v.III, p.1-13.

..."Did Gen. G.H. Thomas have any purpose of fighting on the side of Va. his native state, at the commencement of the late war?" In: SHSP, 1882, v.X, p.524-25.

..."Exploits of the Torpedo-Boat St. Patrick, Gen. Maury's Report: Hdq. Dist. of Gulf, Mobile, Feb. 3, 1865." In: SHSP, 1881, v.IX, p.81.

..."Grant as a Soldier & Civilian." In: SHSP, v.V, 1878, p.227-39.

..."Grant's Campaign in N. Miss., 1862." In" SoMag, 1873, v.XIII, p.410-17.

..."How the Confederacy changed Naval Warfare, Ironclads & Torpedoes." In: SHSP, 1894, v.XXII, p.75-81.

..."Incidents in the remarkable career of General T.J. "Stonewall" Jackson." In: SHSP, 1897, v.XXV, p.309-16.

..."Interesting Reminiscences of General Johnston." In: SHSP, v.XVIII, p.171-81.

..."McClellan & Lee at Sharpsburg (Antietam). A review of Mr. Curtis' article in the North American Review." In: SHSP, 1880, v.VIII, p.261-66.

..."Maury on Longstreet, by W.B. McGroarty." In: Tyler's Q.Hist. & Geneal.

Mag., 1936, v.XVIII, p.5-7.

..."Merrimac & Monitor, letter, Gen. Maury." In:SHSP, 1883, v.XI, pp.31-32.

..."Recollections of Campaign against Grant in North Mississippi in 1862-1863." In: SHSP, v.XIII, p.285-311.

..."Recollections of the campaign in N. Miss. in 1862-63 of Gens. Van Dorn & Price against Grant." In: SoMag, 1872, p.607-12.

..."Recollections of a Virginian, Mex., Indian, & Civil War." N.Y., Scribner's Sons, 1894, 12mo, decr. cl, front(port.), xi, 279pp. $27.50. $35.00. (Mor.Copy) $37.50. $150-Jenk. London, 1894; N.Y., 1894 ($20); 2nd Edt., $15.; N.Y., 1897 ($10).

..."Recollections of General Earl Van Dorn." In: SHSP, 1891, v.XIX, p.191-201.

..."Van Dorn, the Hero of Mississippi." In: AW, 1879, p.460-66.

..."Recollections of the Elkhorn Campaign." In: SHSP, 1876, v.II, p.180-92.

..."Review, Chap. Van Horne, Army of Cumberland." In:SHSP, 1876, v.I, p.424-30.

..."Return of a Conf. Flag to its Orig. Owner." In: SHSP, 1891, v.XIX, p.263-66.

..."Sketch of D.H. Maury, Maj.Gen." In: SHSP, 1899, v. XXVII, p.335-49.

..."Sketch of General Richard Taylor," In: SHSP, 1879, v.VII, p.343-45.

..."Spanish Fort defence, comments on P.D. Stephenson's article." In: SHSP, Arpil 1914, v.XXXIX, p.130-136.

..."The Surrender of Colonel Streight." In: SHSP, 1897, v.XXV, p.54-55.

..."West Point & Secession." In: SHSP, 1878, v.VI, p.249.

..."Wilson's Defeat, Staunton R. Bridge, 1864." In: SHSP, 1891, v.XIX, p.51-54.

..."Woman's Devotion", Winchester Heroine." In:SHSP, 1878, v.VI, p.218-19. (See: Betty H. Maury.)

350 **MAURY, Matthew-Fontaine**
"Appreciation of M.F. Maury (by A.B. Chandler, Jr.); 'Maury & the Conf. Navy' (by E. Lee Trinkle). In: State Normal School for Women, Fredericksburg, Va., 1923, Bul., V.VIII, #5, Jan. 192?, pp.23, (1), 8vo, wrap.

..."Capt. Maury's Letter on American Affairs." Baltimore, "The South" Office, 1862, 8vo, wraps, 10pp., caption title.

..."Matthew Fontaine Maury, 1806-1873." In: CV, Feb. 1918, v.XXVI, p.54-56.

..."Letter to Maury from Constantine Grand Admiral of Russia & Maury's reply." In: SHSP, 1876, v.II, p.51-53.

..."In Memoriam: M.F. Maury, LL.D. Univ. Cambridge, England. Proceedings of the academic board of the VMI, on the occasion of the death of Comdr. M.F. Maury. LL.D., prof. of physics, in the VMI, 1873." n.p., (Lexington, Va.?), 8vo, wraps, 32pp., Swen-6109. (See: J.A. Coke.)

..."A Vindication of Virginia & the South." In: SHSP, 1876, v.1, p.48-61.

See also under: Brown, Ralph Minthrone - Bibliography; Blair, Miss Marie; Caskie, Jaquelin Ambler; Chandler, Algernon Bertrand; Corbin, Diana Fontaine (Maury); Coke, John A.; Jahns, Patricia; Lewis, Charles Lee; Maury, Betty Herndon; Maury, Richard Lancelot; Wayland, John Walter; Williams, Frances Leigh; Tillman, G.N.; Wickham, Julia Porcher.

351 **MAURY, Richard L., Col.**
"The Battle of Williamsburg & the Charge of the 24th Virginia of Early's Brigade." Suffolk, Va., Robt., Hardy Pub., 1986. 8vo, wraps, 24 p.

..."A Brief Sketch of the Work of Matthew Fontaine Maury during the War 1861-1865. by his son Richard L. Maury, Richmond." Richmond, Va., Whittet & Shepperson, 1915, 12mo, stiff wraps, 36pp.

..."The Battle of Williamsburg & the Charge of the 24th Virginia of Early's Brigade by Col. Richard L. Maury." (quote) Richmond, Va., Johns & Goolsby, 1880, 8vo, wraps, cover title, 20, (1)p. $75.00. $100.00-Bmk124. $125.00.

...A Reprint (above) from: SHSP, 1880, VIII, pp.281-300. (1962 reprint, n.p.,n.d.) $8.00-Bmk.

..."Battle of Williamsburg, Va., June 1, 1862, a paper read before Pickett Camp Confed. Vets. by Col. Richard L. Maury." In: SHSP, 1894, v.XXII, p.106-122. Offprint $175.00. Basically, same as foregoing. $200.00-Bmk105.

...(Williamsburg?, 1970s?), 8vo, wraps, 20pp.

..."The First Marine Torpedoes were made in Richmond, Va., & used in James River." In: SHSP, 1903, v.XXXI, p.326-333.

..."In Memorian. Richard L. Maury. Ex-member Ex-Comm., Life Member. Wilfred E. Cutshaw." In: SHSP, 1907, v.XXXV, p.371-372.

352 **MAXEY, Sam Bell, Maj.Gen.**
"Address before the Texas Veteran Ass'n. Paris, Tex., April 21, 1884." 8vo, wraps, 23p.
See: Louise Horton.

353 **MAXWELL, C.W.**
"Tommy Woods - Scout. A Story of Randolph Co. in the days of the Civil War." In: W.Va., Reb., Aug., 1928, v.5, p.434,444, illus, Tommy Woods CSA Scout (for Gen. Lee at Mingo) From Randolph Co. Hist. Soc. 4th Annual, 1927.

354 **MAXWELL, David Elwell**
"Some Letters to his parents by a Floridian in the Confederate Army. Transcribed by Gilbert Wright." In: FHG, April, 1958, v.XXXVI, #4, p.353-372, portrait sketch.

355 **MAXWELL, Hu**
"History of Barbour County, W.Va., from the Earliest Exploration & Settlement to Present." Morgantown, Acme Pub., 1899, 517pp. 'Sketch Union & CSA positions at Philipi,' Rich Mt., Muster Rolls, Barbour Greys (CSA), Capt. W.K. Jenkins' Barbour Co., Cavalry CSA.

..."History of Monongalia Co.," n.p.,n.d., 17-480pp. contains Confederate Rosters of men from this county.

..."History of Hampshire Co., W.Va., with H.L. Swisher. Morgantown, Brown Boughner, 1897, 744pp., CSA Va. Units: Grassy Lick Militia (114th Va. Militia), Capt Pile's Co., Co. K, Imbodens Cav. Brig.; McMackin's Militia Co. I, 18th Cavly. Co. C., 18th Cav.; Co. E, 23rd Cav.; Frontier Riflemen, Co. I, 13th Inf.; Hampshire Guards, Co. K, 13th Inf.; Co. D, 11th Cav.; Co. C., 23rd Cav; Co. A., 33rd Inf.; Potomac Guards; Co. F, 18th Cavalry. Shetler-493.

..."Retreat of General Robert S. Garnett." In: Transallegheny Hist.Mag., April, 1902, v.1,pp.225-233.

356 **MAXWELL, James Robert, Dr.**
"Autobiography of James Robert Maxwell of Tuscaloosa, Alabama." N.Y., Greenberg Print, 1926, 12mo, cl, illus., ports, viii, (1), 325pp. $35.00. Note: Maxwell & Little wrote "Lumsden's Battery." See under George Little.

356a **MAXWELL, Jerry H.**
"A Knight & His Scoundrels: Rob Wheat & tghe Louisiana Tigers." In: Lincold Herald, Summer 1981, p.631-40.

357 **MAXWELL, Louise Wisnton**
"The Secession of South Carolina." In: CV, Dec. 1915, v.XXIII, pp.553-556.

358 **MAXWELL, Mary Elizabeth, Mrs (Braddon)**
"John Marchmont's Legacy; a Novel." Richmond, Va., 1865, 8vo, cl, 168pp. not in

Crand/Harwell.

..."Eleanor's Victory." Richmond, Va., 1864, 12mo, cl, 180pp.

..."Aurora Floyd." A Novel. Richmond, Va., 1863, 12mo, cl, 198pp.

..."David Markham; or Captain of the "Volture." Richmond, Va., 1863, 12mo, cl, 138pp., CSA Novel.

359 **MAY, C. Welles**
"Sequel to the Squalus." In: So.Lit.Mess., 1940, v.II, p.48-52. Account of USS 'Housatonic' sinking by an innamed CSN submarine in Charleston harbor Feb. 17, 1864.

360 **MAY, Henry of Md.**
"Speech of the Hon...., of Maryland, delivered in the House Representatives at 3rd Session 37th Congress." Baltimore, Kelly, Hedian, 1863, 8vo, wraps, 45pp. Against war & arming negroes.

..."Speech...against the War & Arming Negroes, & for Peace & Recognition, Feb. 2, 1863." n.p., n.d., 8vo, 700. Sabin-47067.

...Same, Feb. 20, 1863, Baltimore, Kelly, 1863, 8vo, pp.18, Sabin-477067.

..."Speeches of...del. in House Representatives, 3rd Sess. of 37th Congress on death of Senator Pearce, speech against War & Arming Negroes & for Peace & Recognition; against Indemnifying Executive Writ of Habeas Corpus, append. of proceedings of Congress interesting to Mdy." Baltimore, Kelly, Hedian & Piet, 1863, 8vo, wraps, 45pp.

360a **MAY, James**
"Correspondence of General R. E. Lee showing the spirit of 1861." In: SHSP, 1878, v.VI, p.91-4.

..."Letter urging peace, April 22, 1861." In: SHSP, 1878, v.VI, p.91-4.

360b **MAY, John Amasa - Joan Reynolds Faunt**
"South Carolina Secedes. With Biographical Sketches of Members of South Carolina's Secession Convention." Columbia, Univ. of South Carolina Pr., 1960, 8vo, cl, dj, illus., ports., XV, 231pp. About one third abridges "Journal of the People of S.C., held in 1860-1862, together with Ordinances, Reports, Resolutions, etc." $25.00.

361 **MAY, Robert E.**
"The Southern Dream of a Caribbean Empire, 1854-1861." Baton Rouge: Louisiana State U. Pr., 1973, 8vo, cl, dj, 286pp., index, bibliog. Filibusters expd. to Nicaragua, Mexico & Cuba, to extend slavery brought added strain between North & South.

..."Gone With the Wind as Southern History A Reappraisal." In: South. Quart.: Jour. of Arts in the South., Fall, 1978, v.XVII, p.51-64.

..."Dixie's Martial Image: a Continuing Historiographical Enigma." In: 'Historian', February, 1978.

...John A. Quitman: Old South Crusader." Baton Rouge: Louisiana State Univ. Press, 1985. 8vo, cl, xviii, 465p. $40 (paper $20).

362 **MAYER, Brantz**
"The emancipation problem in Maryland" (Baltimore, 1862) 8vo, caption title, 4p., bmk $25.00. 'Contributed originally to the Baltimore American.' "It's not so much emancipation which is to be feared in Maryland as the emancipated."

362a **MAYER, Henry**
"A Leaven of Disunion: The Growth Secessionist Faction in Alabama 1847-1851." In: AR, Apr., 1969, v.22, #2, p.83-116.

363 **MAYES, Edward**
"Lucius Q. C. Lamar: His Life, Times & Speeches, 1825-1893." Nashville, Tenn., Pub. House, Methodist Episcopal Church South, 1896. 4to, cl, ills., ports., incl. front., index, 820pp. $37.50Y.

...2nd Edition, same date, etc.

...Louisv.: Lost Cause, micro-cd.
...Reprint, $37.50.
Lamar was member CSA congress, Lt.-Col., 19th Miss. Reg.

363a **MAYFIELD, John S.**
"A Note on "Dixie"; Old-Time Minstrel Man tells of Dan Emmett & his famous song." In: "Bunker's Monthly," Ft. Worth, Texas, May, 1928, v.1, #5, pp.718-714.

364 **MAYHALL, Mildred P.**
"Camp Cooper-First Federal Fort in Texas to fall, 1861, & events preceding its fall." In: Texana, Winter, 1967, v.V, #4, pp.317-343, notes, plate.

364a **MAYNARD, Douglas H.**
"The Escape of the 'Florida'." In: Pa.Mag. of Hist. & Biog., April, 1953, 17pp. Circumstances in which the future CSA raider slipped out of Eng. as the "Oreto" in 1862. v.77, p.181-197.
..."The Confederacy's Super-"Alabama." In: CWH, March 1959, v.V, #1, p.80-95.
..."Plotting the Escape of the "Alabama." Lexington, Ky., JSH, May 1954, v.XX, #2, pp.197-209. $8.00.
..."Union Efforts to Prevent the Escape of the "Alabama." Cedar Rapids, Ia., MVHR, June 1954, v.XLI, #1, pp.41-60.

365 **MAYO, C.B.**
"Stonewall Jackson from a naval viewpoint." In: U.S.N. Inst. Proc., Dec. 1917, v.XLIII, pp. 2893-2896.

365a **MAYO, Joseph, Col., 3rd Va. Inf.**
"Pickett's Charge at Gettysburg." In: SHSP, 1906, v.34, p.327-35.

365b **MAYO, Lida**
"John Yates Beall: The Southern John Brown." Richmond, Va., Cavl., Spring 1965, v.XIV, #4, pp.4-9, map, port., illus.

365c **MAYO, Robert M.**
"The Second Battle of Manassas." In: SHSP, 1879, v.7, p.122-125.

365d **MAYS, Samuel Elias**
"Famous Battles as a Confederate Private saw them." In: Tyler's Quart. Hist. & Ceneal. Mag., Apr. 1923, v.IV, p.388-405.

366 **McAFEE, John J.**
"General John H. Morgan, his capture & death." In: JMH, November, 1977, v.XXXIX, #4, p. 357-361.

366a **McALISTER, Jesse Monroe**
"A Rebel Yell: a compendium of slightly biased historical data." (Columbia?, S.C.) 1951. 12mo, wraps, 16pp. Chronology of CSA arranged by months, days, with years ignored.

366b **McALISTER, W.M.**
"Alleghany Roughs, or Carpenter's Battery." (Co. A, of the 27th Reg. Va. Vols, Stonewall's Brigade was known as the "Alleghany Light Infantry," by the boys as "Alleghany Roughs," later on as Carpenter's Battery.") In: CV, 1905, v.13, p. 365-366, muster roll, July 1, 1861.

366c **McALLISTER, James Gray**
"Sketch of Captain Thompson McAllister, Co. A, 27th Virginia Regiment. For private distribution." Petersburg, Va., Fenn & Owen print, 1896. 8vo, stiff wraps, port(front) 39pp. $75-bmk.
..."Family records. Compiled for the descendants of Abraham Addams McAllister & his wife Julia Ellen (Stratton) McAllister, of Covington, Va., containing a sketch of A.A. McAllister, prepared & published by the conspiracy & cooperation of his sons and related data, which will answer some of the questions our grandchildren are sure to ask." November 1912. (Easton, Pa., Chemical pub. co., 1912) 8vo, wraps, front(port) illus., 88pp. Abraham was Sergt. Bryan's Battery, 12th Batt., Va. Artillery, extracts from his war diary.

366d **McALLISTER, James Gray & G.O. Guerrant**
"Edward O. Guerrant: Apostle of the Southern Highlanders." Richmond, Va.,

Richmond Press, 1950. 8vo, wraps, viii, 238p, ills, ports. $40.

367 **McALLISTER, W.E., Maj.**
"Confederate Veterans Annual Yearbook 1861-1927. Some photographs of the few remaining survivors ("The Thin Gray Line.")." n.p., (c.1927). 8vo, wraps, 52pp. History, poetry, etc.

367a **McALMONT FAMILY**
"The McAlmont Family of Little Rock views the Civil War." By Martha Bridges. In: Pulaski Co. HS, Ark., Sept, 1979, v.26, p. 43-55.

367b **McALPINE, Newton**
"Sketch of Company I, 61st Virginia Infantry Mahone's Brigade, CSA." In: SHSP, 1896, v.24, p.89-108. Roster.

367c **McALWEE, G. W.**
"A Good Shot exploded the boiler." SHSP, 1909, v.37, p.354.

367d **McANERNY, John**
"Dahlgren's raid on Richmond." In: CV, Jan. 1921, v.XXIX, p. 20-21.

367e **McBARRON, Hugh Charles & Frederick Porter Todd**
"Citadel cadet battery, Morris Island, 1861." In: Mil. coll. & hist., 1957, v.IX, p. 74-75, col. plate, illus.

367f **McBLAIR, Charles H.**
"Historical Sketch of the Confederate Navy." In: United Ser., Nov. 1880, v.III, p. 588-613." Also: Do: 3rd ser. III, May 1903, p.1155-1183.
..."The Confederacy's First Shot." In: CWH, March 1968, v.XIV, #1, p. 5-14.
..."Controversy in Kentucky: Braxton Bragg Campaign of 1862." In: CWH, March 1960, v.VI, #1, p. 5-42.
..."Grant, Lee, Lincoln & the Radicals; essays on Civil War leadership." N.Y., Harper & Rowe Colophon books (1964). 12mo, stiff colored wraps, vi, (1), (3)-117, (1)p. Authors: Bruce Catton, Charles P. Roland, David Donald & T. Harry Williams.
..."Jefferson Davis & the art of war." In: CWH, June 1975, v.21, #2, p.101-112.
..."Jefferson Davis-The Unforgiven." In: JMH, May 1980, v.XLII, #2, p.113-127. See: Robert Penn Warren.
..."Who Whipped Whom? Confederate defeat Re-examined." In: CWH, March 1965, v.XI, #1, p. 5-26.

367g **McBRIDE, Robert M.**
"The "Confederate Sins" of Major Cheairs." In: Tenn. HQ, 1964, v.XXIII, p.121-135.

368 **McBRIEN, Joe Bennett**
"The Tennessee Brigade." Chattanooga, Tenn., Hudson Printing & Litho. co., 1977, 8vo, cl, 117pp. Archer's Brigade, A.P. Hill Co., rp., A.N.V. Largely from OR. See also: Henry Heth, Div. Commander.

368a **McBRYDE, John Lauren**
"An eyewitness to history." In: CWTI, Jan. 1964, v.II, #9, p.37-41, illus. First Confederate death, the firing on Ft. Sumter, Fairfax Court House & last meeting of Confederate Cabinet-all recollections of.
..."Random recollections of an octogenarian." In: Sawanee rev., 1923, v.31, p. 50-59.

368b **McBRYDE, Randell W.**
"The Historic "General," a thrilling episode of the Civil War..." Chattanooga: MacGowan & Cooke (1904). 12mo, color wraps, illus., map, ports, 55pp. (1st edt., 10,000 copies). At end, sketches of Wm. A. Fuller & Capt. W.J. Whitsett, CSA.

368c **McCABE, James Dabney, Jr.**
"The Aid-de-camp; a romance of the war by James D. McCabe, Jr." Richmond, Va., W.A.J. Smith, 1863." 8vo, cl or wraps, 113pp. Orig. pub. in the "Magnolia Weekly." $125-bmk-114.
..."Confederate Literature in the Sixties." In: SHSP, October 1917, v.XLII, p.199-203.

..."Fanaticism & its results; or, Facts versus fancies. By a Southerner." Baltimore: Joseph Robinson, 1860. 8vo, wraps, 36pp. Swem-3260.

..."The Guerillas: an original domestic drama, in three acts. By James D. McCabe, Jr. With cast of characters, stage business costumes, relative positions, etc., by R.D.'Orsey Ogden, acting & stage manager of Richmond Varities & New Richmond Theatre." Richmond, Va., West & Johnston, 1863, 12mo, wraps, 44pp. "First orig. drama pub. in the CSA."

..."The Life of Lieut. Gen. T.J. Jackson. By an Ex-cadet." Richmond, Va., James E. Goode, 1863. 12mo, cl, or wraps, 128pp. $75.

...2nd Edt., revised & enlarged by the author, 196pp. 1864. $300-ob.

..."Life & Campaigns of General Robert E. Lee." National Pub. Co., Atlanta, Phila., Cinn., St. Louis; N.Y., Blelock & Co., (1866). 8vo, cl, port(front) by G.E. Perine, (coat unbuttoned, 3-star, differs from 1870 edt., 6-fldg. maps, 717pp. (1p. adv) $75 bmk-99.

...N.Y., Blelock & co, 1867. (1870) Publication same as '66 edt., but N.Y., Blelock & co dropped from title. Front port of Lee differs, buttoned coat, 3fldg. maps, 11-pg. maps, (4p-adv) 732pp.

369 **McCABE, William Gordon**
"Address at unveiling of soldier's monument in Petersburg." In: SHSP, 1889, v.XVII, p. 394-403.

..."A brief sketch of Andrew Reid Venable, Jr., formerly A.A. & Inspector General Cavalry corps, A.N.V." Richmond: Wm. Ellis Jones print, 1909. 8vo, wraps, 15pp. Reprint from SHSP, 1909, v.XXXVII, p. 61-73. Port.

..."Address: Annual Reunion of Pegram Battalion Association in the Hall of House of Delegates, Richmond, Va. May 21, 1886." In: SHSP, 1886, v.XIV, p. 5-21. (Note: also in same program: Maj. Thomas A. Brander & Judge H.W. Flournoy's addresses, p. 21-34.)

..."Admirer of Lost Cause, Battleflag of the South flies on English lawn." In: SHSP, 1907, v.XXXVII, p. 125-126.

..."Defense of Petersburg. Address of Capt. W. Gordon McCabe (formerly Adjutant of Pegram's battalion of artillery, Third corps, ANV.) Before the Virginia division of the Army of Northern Virginia at their annual meeting, held in the Capitol at Richmond, Va., Nov. 1st, 1876. Richmond: Geo. W. Gary print, 1876. 8vo, wraps, 52pp. Reprint: from SHSP, 1876, v.II, p. 256-306.

..."Joseph Bryan, a brief Memoir." In: Va. MH, Apr. 1909, v.xvii, p. 1-xxix. Bryan served with Mosby. Offprint: 29pp. full leather, $50-bmk-105.

..."Graduates of the United States Military Academy at West Point, N.Y., who served in the Confederate States Army, with the highest commission & highest command attained." In: SHSP, 1902, p. 34-76, v.XXX.

..."The Hon. Theodore S. Garnett, address before the Virginia Historical Society." In: SHSP, 1916, v.XLI, p. 68-81.

...Same, as separate, n.p., n.d., tall 8vo, wraps, cover title, 16pp. signed.

..."Major-General George Washington Custis Lee." In: SHSP, 1914, v.XXXIX, p. 167-176. See: G.W.A. Lee. Also as offprint, 9pp., Va. His. 1914.

370 ..."Memories & Memorials of McCabe, see: Armistead C. Gordon.

371 ..."Our Dead." In: "Contribution to History of Richmond Howitzers." Richmond, Va., Calton McCarthy, 1883, p. 11-13, v.I.

372 ..."The Real Barbara Fritchie." In: SHSP, 1899, v.XXVII, p. 187-189.

373 ..."Resolutions submitted by McCabe on tribute to Gen. Early." In: SHSP, 1894, v.XXII, p. 332-335.

374 ..."Speech of Capt. W. Gordon McCabe, delivered before the New England society, New York city, at the Waldorf Astoria, on Dec. 22, 1899." Nashville, Tenn., Brandon print, (1900). 12mo, wraps, 14pp.

375 ..."The War Between the States." In: Sat. Rev., May 7, 1910, p. 590-591.

376 ..."The Original Confederate Constitutuion." In: SHSP, Sept. 1916, v.XLI, p. 34-36.

377 ..."Maj-Gen. George Washington Custis Lee." In: SHSP, 1914, v.39, p. 167-176.
..."Capt. Robert E. Lee." Richmond, 1915. 8vo, wraps, 15pp. bmk-24. $10. $25.

378 **McCAFFREY, J.M.**
"This Band of Heroes, Granbury's Texas Brigade, C.S.A." Austin, Texas: Eakin Press, 1985, 8vo, cl, dj, 262pp., illus., roster.

379 **McCAIN, William D.**
"Nathan Bedford Forrest: An Evaluation." (Jackson, Miss., Jour. Miss. Hist., Oct., 1962, v.XXIV, #4, p. 203-225.

379a **McCAIN, William D. & Charlotte Capers, Eds.**
"Memoirs of Henry Tillinghast Ireys; papers of the Washington County Historical Society 1910-15." Jackson, Miss., Miss. Dept. of Archives- Mississippi Historical Society, 1954. 8vo, stiff wraps, 423pp. Port, index. $15.
See: Capt. J. M. Montgomery, 1st Miss. Cav.

380 **McCALEB, D.**
"Lenare; A Story of the Southern Revolution, & Other Poems." New Orleans, La., 1866. 8vo, cl, 107pp. $75-jk-129. Written during the war, in Mobile, Vicksburg, and Montebello, Ala.

381 **McCALEB, E. Howard**
"Address delivered by E. Howard McCaleb, of New Orleans, (Late Adjutant 12th Mississippi Infantry Regiment & Captain commanding President's escort) at the Reunion of the surviving veterans Harris' Mississippi Brigade, Army of Northern Virginia, held at Port Gibson, Claiborne Co., Mississippi November 13th, 1879." New Orleans, La., A.W. Hyatt pr. (1879) 8vo, wraps, cover title, 18pp.
..."Featherstone-Posey-Harris Mississippi Brigade." In: SHSP, 1904, v.XXXII, p. 329-337.

382 **McCALEB, Walter Flavius**
"The Organization of the Post Office Department of the Confederacy." In: Amer. Hist. Rev., Oct. 1906, v.12, #1, p. 66-74, McCaleb edt: Jno. H. Reagan.

383 **McCALLIE, Elizabeth Hanleiter**
"The Atlanta Campaign." (Atlanta, Ga., Franklin Print, c. 1929) 12mo, stiff decr. wraps, 31pp., maps-1-fldg., Read at a meeting of Atlanta Historical Society, Feb. 26, 1938.

384 **McCALLUM, James H., Dr.**
"Martin County, N.C., During the Civil War." Williamston, N.C., Enterprise Pub. (1971), 8vo, wraps, 188pp.

385 **McCANN, James M.**
"Scouting in West Virginia." In: CV, July 1894, v.2, p. 214-215. Scouts & as mail carriers.

386 **McCANNE, Virginia Yates, Mrs.**
"The McGregors by Marshall Home." Chi: Scroll pub., 1901, Pseud: see Marshall Home.

387 **McCANTS, Dorothea Olga, Sister**
"They Came to Louisiana: Letters of a Catholic Mission, 1854-1882." Baton Rouge: La. State Univ. press, 1970. 8vo, cl, d/w, xxiii, 263pp. Social customs, economic conditions in central La. during the Civil War & Reconstruction, in a series of letters within the mission.

388 **McCANTS, Elliott Crayton**
"One of the Gray Jackets & other stories." Columbia, S.C., The State Co., 1908. 12mo, cl, 160pp. Full leather, $50.

389 **McCARDELL, John**
"The Idea of a Southern Nation and Southern Nationalism 1830-1860." N.Y., Lond.: W.W. Norton (1979), 8vo, cl, xii, 394pp.

390 **McCARDLE, William H.**
"William H. McCardle's Account of the Great War Between the States." (Jackson, Miss., Jour. Miss. Hist. July, 1947, v.IX, #3, P. 174-181.

390a **McCARLEY, J. Britt**
"Atlanta is ours & fairly won: a driving tour of Atlanta's areas principal Civil War battlefields." In: AHJ, 1984, v.28(3), p.5-32. 'Battle of Peachtree Creek & Atlanta.' Maps for Atlanta battlefield, battle of Ezra Church, battle of Jonesboro, etc.

391 **McCARTER, James**
"The Burning of Columbia, Again." Answer to Nicholas by a Columbia native." In: Harper's, June/Nov. 1867. p. 642-647, v.XXXV

392 **McCARTHY, Carleton**
"Camp fires of the boys in gray, by Private Carlton McCarthy, Richmond Howitzers." In: SHSP, 1876, v.1, p. 76-89.

393 ..."Detailed Minutiae of Soldier Life in the Army of Northern Virginia 1861-1865. By Carlton McCarthy, privae second company Richmond Howitzers, Cutshaw's Battalion Artillery, second corps, A.N.V., With illustrations by Wm. L. Sheppard, lieutenant second company Richmond Howitzers A.N.V." Richmond: Carlton McCarthy co., 1882. 12mo, cl, front, illus., vi, 224pp. $25., $30., (3/4 Mor.) $45. bmk, $80., $100.
Editions: $65. 1884; 1888($20.) $100.; 1889($15.); 1899
...First pub. in SHSP, 1876, v.II, p. 129-135, 226-232; v. III (1877), p. 13-19; 1878, v.VI, p. 1-9, 193-214; v.7, p. 176-185.

394 ..."Origin of the Confederate Battle Flag." In: SHSP, 1880, v.VIII, p. 497-499.

395 ..."Soldier Life in the Army of Northern Virginia, 1861-1865. By Carlton McCarthy, private second company, Richmond Howitzers, Cutshaw's Battalion artillery, second corp., A.N.V., with pen & ink illustrations by Wm. L. Sheppard, Esq., Lieutenant second company Richmond Howitzers, ANV." Richmond: B.F. Johnson pub. (1882, 1908) 12mo, decr. cl, illus., front(color flag), vi, (7)-230pp. $25. Reprinted in Philip Van Doren Stern's "Soldier Life in Union & Confederate Army." See: "Richmond Howitzers," Edt. "Contributions to a History of the Richmond Howitzer Battalion."
..."Walks about Richmond. A story for boys & a guide to persons visiting the city, desiring to see the principal points of interest, with an index showing the exact location of each point mentioned..." Richmond, Va., McCarthy & Ellyson, 1870. 12mo, cl, vii, 9-175. 4-plates, incl. front, with mounted portrait of Lee tipped-in. $125-bmk. Last 40pp. a detailed account of Lee's death & several memorial statements of former officers.
..."Detailed minutiae of Soldiers Life..." N.Y., Time-Life Books, 1984, 8vo, leather, gilt edges, lim. edt. $25.00, Collector's Library of the Civil War.

396 **McCARTHY, Henry**
"The Bonnie Blue Flag." (n.p., n.d.) ornamental borders. Broadside, 23x9cm. $150 bmk-114. Not in Crandall/Harwell.

397 **McCARTY, Burke**
"The Suppressed Truth about the Assassination of Abraham Lincoln. Written & Compiled by Burke McCarty, Ex-Romaist."N.Y., Chedney Press, n.d. (at end: "Made in Taiwan.") 12mo, boards,

dj(port of Lincoln) 255pp. Monaghan, II, p. 140): Washington, D.C. 1922, cl, $20-$150- wraps, $1.00, illus, 272pp. Also variant, Phila. 1924, p. 255. "The alleged Jesuit Plot."

398 **McCASH, William B.**
"Thomas R. R. Cobb & the "Better Terms" Argument." In: Ga. H.Q., Spring 1976, v.LX, #1, p. 49-53. Advocated immediate, permanent separation of the sections & no compromise!
..."Thomas R. R. Cobb, the making of a Southern Nationalist." Macon, Ga., Mercer Univ. press, 1977, 8vo, cl, dj, 344pp. $19.
...1983, p. xi, 356

399 **McCASLAN, R.H., Capt., et al**
"Addresses delivered before Camp J. Foster Marshall, at Ninety-Six, S.C., Oct. 17, 1897, by Capt. R.H. McCaslan, Col. J.Q. Marshall & Rev. F.O.S. Curtis, on the presentation of a portrait of Col. Foster.
...Marshall to the camp." Columbia, S.C., N.D.(c. 1897) 12mo, stiff wraps, 23pp.

400 **McCAUSLAND, John**
"The Burning of Chambersburg, Pa." In: SHSP, 1903, v.XXXI, p. 266-270. See also in Annals of War, p. 770-774. See: Clarence Shirley Donnelly.

401 **McCAUSLAND, Susan A. Arnold, Mrs.**
"The Battle of Lexington as seen by a Woman." (Columbia, Mo., Apr. 1912, v.VI, #3, p. 127-135; CV, May 1912, v.XX, p. 223-226. Author gave an orig. painting, made at time of battle, to M. Hist. Society. Reprint, in wraps, of above.

402 **McCHESNEY, James Z.**
"Herd Fighting in West Virginia." In: CV, Jan. 1918, v.26, p. 12, illus. at Oldfields.

403 ..."Scouting on Hunter's Raid to Lynchburg, Va." In: CV, May, 1920, v.28, p. 173-176. 14th Va Cavalry.

404 ..."On the Chambersburg-burning of during CS raid of 1864." In: CWTI, Nov. 1971, v.10, #7, p. 10-13, illus.

405 **McCLARY, Ben H.**
"The Pathfinder of the Seas, Matthew Fontaine Maury." In: CWTI, June 1963, v.II, #3, p. 10-17, illus., ports.

406 **McCLATCHEY, Minerva Leah Rowles**
"A Georgia Woman's Civil War Diary: the Journal of Minerva Leah Rowles McClatchey, 1864-1865. Edt: T. Conn Bryan." In: Ga. H.Q., June 1967, v.LI, #2, p. 197-216.

407 **McCLELLAN, George B., Gen.**
"General McClellan." In: Black. Edn. mag., Nov. 1864, v.XCVI, p. 619-644.
See: Banjamin Keiley, Leslie J. Perry, Wm. Allan's Review of McClellan's Campaign.

408 **McCLELLAN, Henry B.**
"The Life and Campaigns of Major General J.E.B. Stuart." Little Rock, Ark., Eagle Press, 1987, 8vo, cl, dj, 468pp., illus., port, maps $40.00.

409 **McCLELLAN, Henry Brainerd**
"The Life & Campaigns of Major-General J.E.B. Stuart, commander of the Cavalry of the Army of Northern Virginia, by..., late major, assistant adjutant-general, & chief of staff of the Cavalry corps, Army of Northern Virginia." Boston-N.Y., Houghton, Mifflin; Richmond Va., J.W. Randolph & English, 1885. Large 8vo, cl, front(port) errata slip, 7-fldg. maps (some in rear pocket, & colored), xv, 468pp. $200-ob, $175., Rolls of the 2nd & 3rd Reg., Co. B.,E.,F.,K., 1st Reg. Virginia Cavalry, p. (423)-468.

410 ..."Address of Major H.B. McClellan, of Lexington, Ky., on the Life, Campaigns & Character of Gen'l. J.E.B. Stuart. Tenth Annual Reunion of the Virginia Division, Army of Northern Virginia." In: SHSP, 1880, v.VIII, p. 431-456.

...Same: issued separate, 8vo, wraps, 28pp. $75-ob.

411 ..."I Rode with Jeb Stuart. The Life & Campaigns of Major General J.E.B. Stuart, by H.B. McClellan, with an introduction & notes by Burke Davis." Bloomington: Indiana University Press (1958) Civil War Centennial Series. Tk. 12mo, cl, dj, front(port differs from that of the 1st edt.) 4-page maps, drawn for this edition, xv, (2), 454pp. $40-B.
...N.Y., Kraus reprint, 1969, $40- $23-

412 ..."Battle of Fleetwood." In: Annals War, pg. 392-402.

413 ..."The Gallant Pelham" & His Guns at Fredericksburg." In: SHSP, 1884, p.466-470.

414 **McCLELLAND, Margaret Greenway**
"Old Ike's Memories." Richmond, Va., West, Johnson & co, 1884. 12mo, wraps, 16pp. Negro dialect recollections of civil war in poetical form.

415 **McCLENDON, R. Earle**
"Status of the ex-Confederate states as seen in the readmission of the United States senators." In: Am. Hist. Rev., 1936, v.XLI, p. 703-709. e.g., filling vacant seats instead of elections of a new position, a process of regarding the states as having never been out of union.

416 **McCLENDON, William Augustus**
"Recollections of war times, by an old veteran, while under Stonewall Jackson & Lieutenant General James Longstreet; how I got in, & how I got out." Montgomery, Ala., Paragon Press, 1909. 8vo, cl, front(port), 238pp. $50.
...San Bernardino, Calif. 1973

417 **McCLINTON, Oliver Wood**
"The Career of the Confederate States Ram "Arkansas." In: AHQ, 1948, v.VII, p. 329-333.

417a **McCLUNG, Maj. J. W.**
"A Confederate Who Led a Federal Charge." In: SHSP, 1891, v.19, 1.297-8.

418 **McCLURE, Alexander Kelly, Col.**
"Annals of the war, written by leading participants, North & South. Originally published in the Philadelphia Weekly Times." Phila: Weekly Times, 1879. tk. 8vo, cl, illus., 800pp. $50.
...Gettysburg, Pa., Civil War Times Illustrated, 1974, reprint.

419 ..."The lesson of our civil war. Address delivered before the literary societies of Washington & Lee University at Lexington, Va., June 16, 1886." Phila: McLaughlin Bros., 1886. 8vo, wraps, 36pp. (Dorn-1989).

420 ..."The proposed equestrian statue to Lee at Gettysburg. Arguments presented before the Committee of the Legislature in favor of the bill providing that Pennsylvania & Virginia shall unite to erect an equestrian statue to Lee on Seminary hill at Gettysburg." n.p., (1903). 8vo, wraps, caption title, 13pp.

421 ..."Recollections of Half a Century." Salem, Mass., Salem press, (1902) 8vo, cl, plates, ports(incl. front) viii, 502pp., index. uncommon. Altho Union, it contains following on CSA: Lincoln & Jeff Davis; Robert E. Lee, one of the Great Commanders of the century; Alex A. Stephens, one of the ablest & most unique Southern leaders; Wade Hampton, chivalric soldier, statesman.

421a ..."Lee's Birthday." In: SHSP, 1888, v.XVII, p.354.

422 **McCLURE, C.B.**
"The Battle of Adobe Walls." In: Panhandle Plains Hist. Rev., 1948, v.XXI, p. 18-65.

423 **McCLURE, Lela**
"Capt. Rosborough & the Confederate Memorial." This article is a Civic Project

of Texarkana Chap. 568 UDC. A short history. (Texarkana, Texas) n.d. (1960's) 4to, memogr., 10, (1)p.

424 **McCLURG, Alexander C.**
"The Last Chance of the Confederacy (Battle of Averasboro & Bentonsville N.C.)" In: Atl. Monthly, Sept. 1882, v.1, p. 389-400.

425 **McCOLLEY, Robert**
"Lincoln & Davis." In: The Old Guard, Nov. 1867, V, #11, p. 844-847.

426 **McCOLLOM, Albert O.**
"The War-time Letters of Albert O. McCollom." Edt: W.J. Lemke, Civil War Centennial series, Fayetteville, Ark., Washington Co. Hist. Soc. May 1961. stiff wraps(port), 4to, memo (one side) facsm. envelopes, (40)pp., 32-letters & rosters. $14-bmk.

427 **McCOLLUM, Duncan**
"The Diary of Captain Duncan McCollum Co. A, 4th Mississippi Cavalry, 1865. By J.K. McCollum, Sr. & J.K. McCollum, Jr. (San Bernardino, Calif.) 1964. 4to, (2), ii, 17lf, maps.

428 ..."Duncan McCollum's Diary 1861. Edt. by Kinlock McCollum." n.p. (1940?) 8vo, wraps, 83pp. $50.

429 **McCOMB, William**
"The Battles in front of Richmond, 1862." In: CV, April 1915, v.XXIII, p. 161-162. Part taken by the Tenn. brigade.

430 ..."Tennesseans in the Mountain Campaign, 1861." In: CV, May 1914, v.XXII, p. 210-212.

431 **McCONNELL, Newton Whitfield**
"Autobiographical Sketch." In: his "Genealogical History of the Families of McConnells, Martins, Barbers, Wilson Bairds, McCalls & Morris. The Histories of the Scotch-Irish & of the Presbyterians in the Revolutionary War. The Battles of King's Mountain & the Cowpens, together with an Autogiographical Sketch by..." n.p., n.d., (c. 1913). 8vo, cl, ports(incl. front) illus., 399pp. $35-. Autogiog. sketch, p. 291-299, errata slip (4)pp. index. Largely his experiences in Johnston's army, later Morgan's Men & prison in Ft. Deleware, Johnson's Isle, escaped to Canada. Reconstruction.

432 **McCORKLE, John**
"Three Years with Quantrill; a true story, told by his scout John McCorkle, written by O.S. Barton." Armstrong, Mo., Armstrong Herald, 1914. 8vo, cl, ports, 157pp. $17.50, $25., $110.(wraps) $150. ginz, $300. jk-137.
...N.Y., Buffalo-Head press, 1966. Same, reprint
...N.Y. 1970. Buffalo Head, Pr. 1966 $25.

433 **McCORMACK, John F., Jr.**
"Sabine Pass." In: CWTI, Dec. 1973, v.XII, #8, p.4-9, 34-37. ports, illus., diagram, map.

434 **McCORMICK, John Gilchrist**
"Personnel of the Convention of 1861." Battle (Kemp Plummer) "Legislation of the Convention of 1861." Chapel Hill, N.C., 1900. University of North Carolina Publications, James Sprunt Historical Monographs #1. 8vo, sewed, 144pp. $15-bmk. See: Kemp P. Battle, joint author.

435 **McCORVEY, Thomas Chalmers**
"Alabama Historical Sketches." 1960 Charlottesville, University of Virginia press. 8vo, cl, xiii, 254pp. About half on the war. $20.
...2nd print, 1971 $15.

436 ..."A one-sided naval battle on Alabama waters. "Alabama historical sketches." Edt: George Burk Johnston. Charlottesville, Va., University of Va. press, 1960. p. 136-142. notes. From the Montgomery advertiser 3 April 1910. An attack by US-Naval vessels on a flatboat of Joseph B. Packer, near Monroeville, in belief Packer was Jefferson Davis, 26 April 1865.

437 ..."An unheralded battle," Do: "sketches." p. 143-56, also from Montgomery advertiser 10 Sept. 1911. On an engagement between CS regiment 15th (mounted) under Lt. Co.. Thos. J. Myers & the Separate Cavalry Brigade under Gen. T.J. Lucas, near Mt. Pleasant, Monroe Co., Ala. 11 April 1865. Recollections by author.

438 ..."Raphael Semmes (1809-1877) & the Confederate Navy ... T.C. McCorvey, Alabama historical sketches. Edt: George Burke Johnston." Charlottesville, Va.: University of Va., 1960, p. 117-35. Unpublished lectures 16 June 1813, on his service in US/CSNavy, 1826-1865.

439 ..."Southern Cadets in Action. A short sketch of the capture of Tuscaloosa & the burning of the University of Alabama by Federal Troops in April, 1865." In: Century Mag., Nov. 1889, v.XXXIX, pp. Reprint in part "Destruction of the Univ. of Ala., in 1865." in the "Corolla," Ala. Univ., 1893, p. 90-93. (Owens Ala. Bibliog.).

440 ..."The War Poetry of the South, 1861-1865., T.C. McCorvey," Alabama historical sketches." Edt: George Burke Johnston. (Charlottesville, Va., University of Va. Press, 1960, p. 223-45. From the New Orleans Times-Democrat, 28 Dec., 1884.

441 **McCOWAT-MERCER Press**
Jackson, Tenn.
A LIFE FOR THE CONFEDERACY - War Diary of Robert A. Moore. Wilmington, NC, 1987, reprint by Broadfoot.
A SOUTHERN WOMAN'S STORY - Phoebe Pember. Wilmington, NC, Broadfoot reprint, 1987.
AS THEY SAW FORREST - Robert S. Henry. Wilmington, NC, Broadfoot reprint, 1987.
CLEBURNE AND HIS COMMAND - Capt. Irving A. Buck. Wilmington, NC, Broadfoot reprint, 1987.
FOUR YEARS ON THE FIRING LINE - James Cooper Nesbit. Wilmington, NC, Broadfoot reprint, 1987.
FULL MANY A NAME - The Story of Sam Davis - Mabel Frantz. Wilmington, NC, Broadfoot reprint, 1987.
GUNNER WITH STONEWALL - William Thomas Poague. Wilmington, NC, Broadfoot reprint, 1987.
KENTUCKY CAVALIERS IN DIXIE - George Dallas Mosgrove. Wilmington, NC, Broadfoot reprint, 1987.
RECOLLECTIONS OF A CONFEDERATE STAFF OFFICER - G. Moxley Sorrell. Wilmington, NC, Broadfoot reprint, 1987.
REMINISCENCES OF BIG I - William N. Wood. Wilmington, NC, Broadfoot reprint, 1987.
THE ROAD TO APPOMATTOX - Bell I. Wiley. Wilmington, NC, Broadfoot reprint, 1987.
THE STORY OF THE CONFEDERACY - Robert Selph Henry. Wilmington, NC, Broadfoot reprint, 1987.
WHIPT 'EM EVERYTIME - The Diary of Bartlet Yancey Malone. Wilmington, NC, Broadfoot reprint, 1987.
ONE OF JACKSON'S FOOT CAVALRY - John H. Worsham. Wilmington, NC, Broadfoot reprint, 1987.
THE CAMP, THE BIVOUAC AND THE BATTLEFIELD - W.L. Gammage. Wilmington, NC, Broadfoot reprint, 1987.
FIRST WITH THE MOST FORREST - Robert S. Henry. Wilmington, NC, Broadfoot reprint, 1987.
COMPANY AYTCH - Sam R. Watkins. Wilmington, NC, Broadfoot reprint, 1987.
FOURTEEN HUNDRED & NINETY-ONE DAYS IN CONF. ARMY-W.W. Heartsill. Wilmington, NC, Broadfoot reprint, 1987.

REMINISCENCES OF NEWTON CANNON, 1ST SGT. 11TH TN - Newton Cannon.

442 **McCOWN, James L.**
"The memoirs of James L. McCown, CSA." Edt: Albert McCown." In: Rockbridge hist. soc. Proc., 1954, v.4, 24. Excerpts, 11 May, 1 Aug. 1864. His participation in battles near Spotsylvania CH & his confinement Ft. Deleware.

443 **McCOY, Raymond**
"Confederate cannon." In: New Mex. Mag., 1953, v.XXXI, p. 18, 49-51.

444 ..."The Battle of Glorieta Pass, N.M., 1862. In: NMMag., Aug. 1951, v.29, #8, p. 24-5, 47, 49, 51, 53, map, view.
Also: UDCMag., Feb. 1952, v.15, #2, p.13, 23.

445 ..."The Battle of Valverde, N.M. mag., Sept. 1952, v.30, #90, p. 24-25, 51-53, map, ports, views.

446 ..."Arizona: Early Confederate Territory." In: Montana, April 1962, p. 16-20, facsm., map, port.

446a **McCRACKEN, Walter M.**
"The Augusta County Militia." In: Augusta Hist. Bul. 18, #1, Spring 1982, p.6-14.

447 **McCRADY, Edward, Jr., Lt.-Col.**
"Address of...before Company A. (Greggs Regiment), First South Carolina Volunteers at the Reunion at Williston, Barnwell Co., S.C., 14th July, 1882." Charleston, S.C., News & Courier pr., 1882, 8vo, wraps, 10pp. Turnbull, IV, p. 142.
...Same: SHSP, 1888, v.XVI, p. 246-261. (see below, "Gregg's Brigade.")

448 ..."Address of...at Reunion of Virginia Division, A.N.V. Association." In: SHSP, 1886, v.XIV, p. 183-222. (Also, a separate.)

449 ..."Formation, organization, discipline & characteristics of the Army of Northern Virginia," an address delivered in the Hall of the House of Delegates, Richmond, Va., Thursday Oct. 21, 1886. Published by order of the Association." Richmond, Va., Wm. Ellis Jones pr, 1886. 8vo, wraps, 41pp. cover title. $65.

450 ..."The Boy Heroes of Cold Harbor. How Taylor, Hayne, Pinckney & Gadsden Holmes died. Colonel Edward McCrady, after consultation with Captains Armstrong, Kelly, Hasell, Hutson & Dr. Frost, tells the story of the heroism of the four young South Carolinians who fell at Cold Harbor supporting the colors of the First Regiment, S.C.V. - The gallant Dominick Spellman, of the Irish Volunteers." In: SHSP, 1897, v.XXV, p. 234-239.

451 ..."Gregg's Brigade of South Carolinians in the Second battle of Manassas, an address before the survivors of the Twelfth regiment South Carolina Volunteers, by...Lt. Col., 1st S.C. Vols., At Walhalla, South Carolina Volunteers, August 21, 1884." Richmond, Va., Wm. Ellis Jones, pr. 1885. 8vo, wraps, cover title, 40pp. $75-bmk.
Also: SHSP, 1885, v.XIII, p. 3-40.

452 ..."Heroes of the old Camden District, South Carolina, 1776-1861. An address to the survivors of Fairfield County, delivered at Winnsboro, S.C., Sept. 1, 1888." In: SHSP, 1888, v.XVI, p. (3)-35. Contains review of both the "Twelfth" & "Seventeenth" Regiments, p. 18-25. See: Louis De B. McCrady.

453 ..."The Sixth regiment (South Carolina)." In: SHSP, 1888, v.XVI, p. 15-18.

454 ..."The Twelfth regiment." In: SHSP, 1888, v.XVI, p. 18-22.
..."Seventeenth Regt." p. 22-25.

455 **McCRADY, Louis De B.**
"General Edward McCrady & some of the incidents in his career." By His Brother, at the request of the Mayor for the City Year Book (1904) Charleston, S.C.,

Yearbook for 1904. Cation title, 8vo, p. 43-80. $15.

456 **McCREARY, James Bennett**
"The journal of my soldier life. By James Bennett McCreary, CSA. Contributed by his grandchildren, Robert N. McCreary, of Chicago & Mrs. Gatewood Gay, of Lexington, Ky." In: KyHSR, 1935, v.XXXIII, p. 97-117, 191-211. Jour. of a former Gov. of Ky., while in CSArm. Aug. 30, 1862-Nov. 19, 1863.

457 **McCREERY, J.V.L.**
"That Hog-Hole," an impromptu banquet speech by..." In: "Contributions to a History of Richmond Howitzers." Richmond, Va., J.W. Randolph & English, 1886, v.4, p. 28-33.

458 **McCREERY, J.V.S.**
"Richmond Howitzers, at Harper's Ferry, October, 1859. The First Howitzers." In: SHSP, 1896, v.24, p.110-111.

459 **McCULLOCH, Ben & Chief John Ross**
"Historic Letters of General Ben. McCulloch & Chief John Ross in the Civil War." by Harry J. Lemley. (Okla. City) Chron. Okla., Autumn 1962, v.XL, #3, p. 286-294.

460 ..."Ben McCulloch Letters. Edited by Edward M. Coffman." In: SwHQ, July 1956, v.LX, #1, p. 118-122. See: Victor Rose.

461 ..."The Military Operations in Missouri in the Summer & Autumn of 1861." Morrisania, N.Y., Henry B. Dawson, March 1872, third series, Vol. 1, #3. The Historical Magazine & Notes & Queries Concerning the Antiquities, History & Biography of America.
...(Columbia, Mo., Mo. Hist. Review, July, 1932, v.XXVI, #4, p. 354-367. See: Jack W. Gunn

462 **McCULLOCH, Henry E., Brig.Gen.**
"Life Sketch of...in L.E. Daniel's Personnel of Tex. State Govmt. 1887."
...(broadside) "Fellow soldiers of the First Regiment Texas Mounted Riflemen." San Antonio, Texas. Apr. 8, 1862. Not in Crandall or Harwell, varies from Winkler #307 $87.50 Announces supposed appointment as General, encourages their re-inlisting & their use as cavalry in the east.

463 **McCULLOCH, Hugh, Hon.**
"Confederate Property in Europe." Washington, DC., House Ex-Doc. 304, 1868, wraps, 8vo, 13pp.

464 **McCULLOCH, Robert**
"The "High Tide at Gettysburg." In: CV, Oct. 1913, v.XXI, p. 473-476.

465 **McDANIEL, George White**
"A Memorial Wreath." Dallas, Texas: Baptist Standard pr. 1921. 12mo, wraps, 4pp. (7)-94pp.
...Richmond, Va., 1921.
..."A Memorial Wreath to Lee's Veterans & Others." 12mo, wraps, 94pp.

466 **McDANIEL, H. Pleasants**
"War Poems 1861-1865." New York: Abbey Press (1901). 12mo, decr. cl (color flags on cover) 110pp. $25-bmk.

467 **McDANIEL, Henry D.**
"With Unabated Trust: Major Henry McDaniels love letters from Confederate Battlefields as treasured in Hester McDaniel's bonnet-box. Edt: Anita Sams Monroe (Ga.): Walton County Historical Society, 1980 (1977), 8vo, cl, svii, 276pp., illus.(6)pls.
..."Official Report of Gettysburg." In: SHSP, 1885, v.13, p.202-3.

468 **McDANIEL, J.J.**
"Diary of battles, marches, & incidents of the 7th South Carolina Regiment, by J.J. McDaniel of Co. "M". n.p., n.d. (1862?) 12mo, wraps, 19pp.

469 **McDANIEL, Robert W.**
"Forgotten Heritage: the Battle of Hatchie

	Bridge." In: West Tenn. Hist. Soc. Paper., Fall, 1978.	480	..."We knew we could overpower the guard & sieze the boat." In: CWTI, May 1967, v.VI, #2, p. 45-49, illus., port.
470	**McDAVID, Peter A., Capt.** "With the Palmetto Riflemen." In: CV, 1929, v.37, p. 262-265, 298-300, 342-344.	481	..."We drove them from the field." Nov. 1967, v.VI, #7, p. 28-35, illus.
471	**McDONALD, Archie P.** "Jedediah Hotchkiss: Confederate Map Maker." In: Mil. Engineer, 1968, v.L, #394, p. 121-123. See: J Hotchkiss.	482	..."I saw an immense colum of Yankee cavalry." In: CWTI, Feb. 1968, v.VI, #10, p. 42-47, illus., port.
472	..."Youth & the Confederacy." (London) Journ. Confed. Hist. Soc., Autumn, 1971, v.9, #3, p. 65-75, tables.	483	..."McDonald Memoirs, pt. 6." In: CWTI, June 1968, v.VII, #3, p. 28-34, illus., port.
473	..."List of Men enrolled for Camps, 1862-64." In: TMH, Summer 1965, v.5, #2, p. 79-89.	484	..."Hard times of an ex-Confederate." In: CWTI, Oct. 1968, v.VII, #6, p. 37-42, illus., Final number.
474	..."The Illusive Commission of 'Maj.' Jedediah Hothkiss." In: VMHB, Apr. 1967, v.75, #2, p.181-217.	484a	..."How Virginia supplied Maryland with Arms." Lee refuses to occupy Baltimore." In: SHSP, 1901, v.29, p.163-6.
474a	**McDONALD, Archie P., Edt.** "Make my a Map of the Valley." See: under Jed Hotchkiss.	485	**McDONALD, Harold L.** "The Battle of Jenkins' Ferry." In: AHQ, 1948, v.VII, p. 57-67.
475	**McDONALD, Cornelia, Mrs.** "A Diary with Reminiscences of the War & Refugee Life in the Shenandoah Valley, 1860-1865. Mrs. Cornelia McDonald, Louisville, Ky., 1875. Annotated & supplemented by Hunter McDonald, Nashville, Tenn., 1934." Nashville: Cullom & Ghertner co., 1934. Tk. 8vo, cl, color flags front, illus. & ports, part color, facsms, 3-fldg. maps, xvi, 540pp. index $75-b	486	**McDONALD, Helen G.** "Canadian Public Opinion on the American Civil War." N.Y., Columbia University press, 1926. Studies in History, Economics & Public Law. Vol. CXXIV, #2, whole #273. 8vo, wraps, 237pp. ads at end, (24)pp. $25-bmk. ...N.Y., Kraus reprint, 1969. nc $20. 1974 printing.
476	**McDONALD, E.H.M.** "The young color-bearer (James M. Watkins)." In: SB, 1882, v. 1, pp. 23-27.	487	**McDONALD, Hunter** "General Robert E. Lee after Appomattox." In: Tenn. Hist. Mag., July 1925 (uused May 1927), v.IX, p. 87-101. See: Cornelia McDonald, suppl. $8.
477	**McDONALD, E.P.** "General Lee on Sewell mountain." In: SB 1882/1883, v.1, p. 181-184.	488	**McDONALD, John W.** "Longstreet at Blackburn's Ford, July 18, 1861." In: Hist. soc. Fairfax Co., Va., yr. bk. 1954, v.3, p. 9-13, notes.
478	**McDONALD, Edward H., Maj.** "Memoirs: "Fighting under Ashby in the Shenandoah." In: CWTI, July 1966, v.5, #4, p. 28-35, illus., map, ports.	489	..."Story of the Battle of Fairfax Court hse. (1861). In: Hist. soc. Fairfax Co., Va., yr. bk. 1951, v.1, p. 42-56. ...Append: letters from Hannah Moore to her mother: Mrs. Jacob Morris; Mary Custis Lee to Mildred Lee, 6 June, 19 June, 1861.
479	..."Laurel Brigade raid across northern Virginia." In: CWTI, Nov, 1966, v.5, #7, p. 44-48, illus., ports.		

490 ..."Skirmished near Bailey's Cross Roads, Fairfax, Va. Aug. 25-Sept. 1, 1861." In: Hist. Soc. Fairfax Co., Va. Yr. Bak., 1953, v.2, p. 23-27.

490a ..."Soldier of Fortune. Life & Adventures of Gen. Henry Ronald Maciver." N.Y., 1888. pub----. 12mo, cl, 331pp. On Jackson's staff. $20.

491 **McDONALD, Lyla Merrill**
"Iuka's history embodying Dudley's battle of Iuka." (Corinth, Miss., Rankin printery, 1923). 12mo, wraps, plate, 32pp. (Civil war, p. 12-22. Unit roster Co. K, 2nd Miss. inf., 12-13.

491a **McDONALD, William C.**
"The True Gentleman: on Robert E. Lee's Definition of the Gentleman." In: CWH, June 1986, v.32, #2, p.119-38.

492 **McDONALD, William Lindsey**
"Colonel James Jackson's raid in Lauderdale county (Ala.) April 11, 1864." In: N.Ala. Hist. association Bul., v.5, p. 10-13, port, bibliog.

493 **McDONALD, William Naylor**
"A History of the Laurel Brigade, originally the Ashby Cavalry of ANV & Chew's Battery, by the late Captain William N. McDonald, Ordnance officer of the Brigade, edited by Bushrod C. Washington. Published by Mrs. Kate S. McDonald." Balt: Sun job print 1907. 8vo, ports, illus., 499pp. $50., $55., $75., $97.50, $300-g, $250 bmk-90.
...(Arlington, Va., Beatty print, 1969) 8vo, cl, ports, 499pp. $40-
...Gaithersburg, Md., Olde Soldier Books. 1988 reprint. 8vo, cl, 499pp. $30.

494 ..."Battle of Lookout Mountain." In: So.-Biv., 1883-1884, map, p. 97-105.

495 ..."Battle of Missionary Ridge." In: So. Biv., 1883-1884, map, p. 193-201.

496 ..."Battle of Wilson's Creek." In: So. Biv., 1884-1885, v.III, p. 49-54.

497 ..."Capture of Lexington, Missouri by Price's Army." In: So. Biv., 1884-1885, III, p. 105-110.

498 ..."Cavalry versus Infantry." In: So. Biv., I, 1882-1883, p. 160-167.

499 ..."Confederate Dead in Stonewall Cemetery, Winchester, Va. Memorial services, June 6, 1894. Eulogy by Capt. Wm. N. McDonald, on Major James W. Thompson, CSArtillery. Career of Chews Battery." In: SHSP, 1894, v.XXII, p. 41-48. (From Winchester, Va. "News," June 13, 1894.

500 ..."Sketch of Lieutenant-General N.B. Forrest." In: So. Biv., 1883-1884, v.II, p. 289-198, 337-245, port.

501 ..."Sketch of Lieutenant-General Joseph Wheeler." In: So. Biv., 1883-1884, v.II, port, p. 241-146.

502 ..."Lee's Retreat." In: So. Biv. 1882-1883, v.I, p. 28-34.

503 ..."The Two Rebellions; or, Treason Unmasked, by A Virginia." Richmond: Smith, Bailey & co., 1865, 12mo, cl, 144pp. Jno. Brown's outbreak at the Ferry was 1st rebellion, the 2nd plotted for a long time, probably organized by Seward, Greeley & co at Chicago the following year. Sabin-100584 attributes to Angus W. McD.

504 ..."A school history of the United States of America from the earliest discoveries to the present time by W.N. McDonald & J(ohn) S. Blackburn." Southern view. Baltimore: G. Lycett, 1869. 12mo, cl, viii, 507pp. $25.

505 ..."Hampton's Cattle Raid." In: CV, March 1923, v.XXXI, p. 94-86.

505a **McDONNELL, Laurence T.**
"Struggle against Suicide: Joseph H. Hammond & the Secession of South Carolina." In: So. Stud., Summer 1983, p.109-37.

506 **McDONOUGH, James Lee**
"Chattanooga, a Death Grip on the Confederacy." Knoxville, Tenn., University of

	Tennessee Press, 1984. 8vo, cl, dj, xviii, 198pp. $20.
507	..."Five Tragic Hours-- the Battle of Franklin." Knoxville, University of Tennessee press, 1983. 8vo, cl, dj, illus., 5-maps, xiii, 217pp.
508	..."Shiloh-- In Hell Before Night." Knoxville, Tenn., University of Tennessee Press, 1977, 8vo, cl, dj, illus., maps, bibliog. & index, xii, 260pp. $15.50y.
509	..."Stones River-- Bloody Winter in Tennessee." Knoxville: University of Tennessee pr., 1980. 8vo, cl, dj, maps, illus., xiv, 271pp. Index & bibliography. $17.50. From a Union point of view, see Alexander F. Stevenson account, Bost: Osgood, 1884.
510	..."West Point classmates, eleven years later: some observations on the Spring Hill-Franklin campaign." In: THQ, 1969, v.18, p. 182-196.
511	..."Shiloh: the Hornet's nest." In:CV (new), Jan/Feb. 1987, v.35, #1, p.14-18., illus.
511a	..."Bayonets & Blunders: Confederate tactics against the hornet's nest (Battle of Shiloh)." In: W.Tenn.HSP, 1979, p.5-19.
511b	..."Glory can not Atone: Shiloh-April 6, 7, 1862." In: THQ, Fall 1976, v.35, #3, p.279-95.
511c	..."The Last Day at Stones River-- Experiences of a Yank & Reb." In: THQ, Spring 1981, v.40, #1, p.3-12.
511d	**McDONOUGH, James & Thomas Connelly** "Prelude to Disaster. The Spring Hill Affair sets the stage for Franklin." Special Edition: Battle of Franklin. In: Confederate Veteran (new), Dec. 1985, 48pp, ills (many in color), maps, ports. Vol.XXXIII, #7.
511e	**McDONOUGH, Thomas** See: George W. Campbell.
512	**McDOWELL, Armanda** "Fiddles in the Cumberlands." See: Armanda McD. Burns.
513	**McDOWELL, Carolina Dent and Mollie Hollifield Jones, Compilers** "History of the Alabama Division: United Daughters of the Confederacy." Opelika, Ala., Post Pub. Co., 1952, v.II, 8vo, cl, illus., ports, 174pp. See: Huey (Mattie McAdory) for vol. I.
514	**McDOWELL, F.C.** "William Dorsey Pender." Durham, NC, Trinity College, 1894. 8vo, wraps, 6pp. Part II, of "Trinity Archive." covering war career of Pender.
515	**McDOWELL, John E. & William C. Davis** "Joe writes his own praise." In: CWTI, Feb. 1970, v.VIII, #10, p. 36-39, illus., ports. Re: Joseph Kershaw & Beauregard, other Generals who wrote to let others know who they were.
516	**McDOWELL, Robert Emmett** "City of Conflict, Louisville in the Civil War 1861-1865." Intro: Barry Bingham. Kingsport, Tenn., Kingsport Press, the Louisville Civil War Round Table, 1962, 8vo, cl, dj, front, illus., notes bibliog., index, xiii, 259pp. $10-bmk.
517	**McELREATH, Walter** "Robert E. Lee, the man, the gentleman & the American." Atlanta, Ga., 1926. 8vo, wraps, 14pp.
518	**McELROY, Cyrus Decatur** "The diary of a Confederate volunteer." San Antonio, Texas, Southern Literary Institute, 1935. 12mo, wraps, 16pp. Edt: Russell Edward Bellinger.
519	**McELROY, J.C., Capt.** "The Battle of Chickamauga. Historical Map & Guide Book." (cover title) 16mo, soft cl, ports, (1), 18pp. Large fldg. map, color coded. $10.
520	**McELROY, John** "The Struggle for Missouri." Washington:

National Tribune, 1909. 8vo, cl, illus., col. pl., ports, maps, ix, 342pp. $10.
...1913 Reprint, wraps, 193pp.

521 **McELROY, Robert**
"Jefferson Davis, the Unreal & the Real." N.Y., London: Harper & bros, 1937. 8vo, cl, ports (incl. fronts), xiii, (1), 368; II-(5), (369)-783pp. index, critical bibliog. p. 699-759. $50.
...N.Y., Kraus reprints, 1969. $30.
...N.Y., Burt Franklin, 1972. "Research & source works series, American classics in historical & social science." 2vols. in 1., Pub. $30.

522 ..."A new Davis letter." In: Tyler's Quar. Hist. & Geneag. Mag., 1935, v.XVII, p. 22-24. Edts., with historical intro, Mrs. Davis' letter to Mrs. President Tyler asking help getting her children to Canada, while she was in prison.

523 ..."Jefferson Davis, Note: Mentions (pg. 759) a book by 'B.W.' which was the best on Davis' career and secession but never located it. He refers to a letter written by L.B. Northrop to Davis (see: Rowland v.IX, p.469) in which Mr. Benjamin Williams of Miss.(sic) "Mass." can be found in SHSP, v.XIV, p.119 titled "Died for their State."

524 **McENTEE, Girard Lindsey**
"Confederate munitions area & its influence on Federal strategy (1861-1865)." In: St. John's Univ., Abstracts of dissert., 1950, v.4, p. 21-22.

524a **McEVOY, Joseph A., Dr.**
"Contested Crown: Debate of the Seasons." n.p., 1864. (New Orleans ?). 8vo, sewn, 60pp. Written for the St. Joseph School of New Orleans.

525 **McFADDEN, Marguerite**
"Colonel John Thompson Drew: Cherokee Cavalier." In: OHS, Spring 1981, v.LIX, #1, p.30-53. facsm, illus., ports. Relations with Stand Watie, CSA & his salt works.

526 **McFARLAND, Baxter**
"Casualties of the 11th Miss. Reg. at Gettysburg." In: CV, Sept. 1916, v.XXUV, p. 410-411.

527 ..."The Eleventh Mississippi regiment at Gettysburg." In: Miss. Hist. Soc. Pub. Cent. Ser., II, p. 549-568. $15-

528 ..."A Forgotten Expedition to Pensacola in January, 1861." (Oxford, Miss., Pub. Miss. Hist. Soc., 1906, v.IX, p. 15-23. Member of "Chickasaw Guards."

529 ..."Losses of the Eleventh Mississippi Regiment at Gettysburg." In: Confed. Vet. July 1923, v.XXXI, p. 258-260.

530 **McFARLAND, Louis Burchette**
"Address of...of Memphis, Tennessee at reunion of H.S. Bradford Camp. UCV Brownsville, Tenn., July 15, 1907. 8vo, wraps, cover title, 17pp.

531 ..."Address of L.B. McFarland of Memphis, at Re-union United Confederate Veterans, Macon Ga., May 8, 1912." (New Orleans, La.?) n.p., n.d. 8vo, stiff wraps, 16pp. On Gen. George W. Gordon.

532 ..."Maney's Brigade at the Battle of Perryville." In: Confed. Vet., Dec. 1922, v.XXX, p. 467-469.

533 ..."The Battle of West Point(Georgia)." In: Confed. Vet., Aug. 1915, v.XXIII, p. 353-355.

533a ..."Memoirs & Addresses." n.p., (1922), privately printed for family. 8vo, cl-leather label. Gdsp. $250.

534 **McFARLAND, R.W.**
"The Morgan Raid in Ohio." In: Oh. Archeo. & Hist. Soc. Pub., July 1908, v.XVII, p. 243-246.

535 **McFERRIN, John Berry**
"Religion in the Army of Tennessee." In: The Home Monthly, April/June, 1868, p. 161-162, 211-213, 281,285.

536 **McGANN, Will Spencer**
"The old Carter House at Franklin, Ten-

nessee." In: TennHM, 2nd ser., 1932, v.III, p. 40-44.

537 **McGARITY, Abner Embry, Dr.**
"Letters of a Confederate Surgeon, 1862-1865." Notes: Edmund Cody Burnett. Athens, Ga., 1946. reprint from Ga. Hist. Qrt. XXIX-#2,3,4; XXX-#1, Je., Sept., Dec. 1945, Mar., 1946. wraps, 8vo, 141pp. Ga. Hist. Quart., XXIX (1945), p. 76-114; 159-190; 222-253; v.XXX(1946), p. 35-70. McGarity served with Ga., Ala., & N.C. $15.

538 **McGAVOCK, Randal W.**
"Pen & Sword: the Life & Journals of Randal W. McGavock, Edt: Herschel Gower & Jack Allen." Nashville, Tennessee Hist. Comm. 1959, 8vo, cl, dj, illus., 695pp. p. 582-675. CW Jour. $35.

539 **McGEHEE, Harney M.**
"The right of secession." In: CV, Nov. 1922, v.XXX, p. 416-421.

540 **McGEHEE, Jacob Owen**
"Causes that led to the War Between the States, by...53rd Va. Reg., Armistead's brig., Pickett's Div., Longstreets Corp., A.N.V." Atlanta, Ga., A.B. Caldwell Co., 1915. 12mo, cl, 108, (4)pp-index, errata slip, ports, bibliog-p. 105-108.

541 **McGEHEE, John C.**
"Address of John C. McGehee before the Southern Rights Association of Madison County, June 7, 1851." In: FHQ, October 1926, v.V, #2, p. (66)-87, port. "The right of secession is clear, no possibility of doubt & a "duty" absolute & unavoidable." NOTES: p. 116-118. See: "Documents relating to secession in Florida."

542 **McGEHEE, Valentine Merriwether, Captain**
"Diary-with Introduction by General Joseph A. Reeves, Camden, Arkansas, "Arkansas Brigade," & Howard M. Ingham, Rector St. John's Episcopal Church, Camden, Arkansas." In: Pub. Ark. Hist. Assn., v.IV, 1917, p. 140-151.

543 **McGETTIGAN, James William, Jr.**
"Boone County (Mo.) Slaves: Sales, Estate Divisions & Families, 1820-1865." In: Mo. H. Rev., Jan. 1978, v.LXXII, #2, p. 176-197. Part I, charts, illus. Part II, #3, April 1978, p. 271-295.

544 **McGIFFIN, Lee**
"Swords, Stars & Bars." N.Y., E.P. Dutton, 1958, 12mo, cl, 160pp., illus. CSA Cavalry Generals $20-bmk.

545 **McGILL, Daniel**
"Eulogy on the life & character of General Robert Edward Lee." Bainbridge, Ga., 1871. 8vo, wraps, 14pp.

546 **McGILL, John, Bishop of Richmond.**
"War Letters of the Bishop of Richmond. Edt.: Willard E. Wight." In: Va. Mag. Hist. Biog., July 1959, v.67, p. 259-270. ports, notes. Letters to Patrick N. Lynch, Catholic Bishop of Charleston, Apr.,1861-Dec., 1963. See: Willard E. Wight.

547 **McGINNIS, A.C.**
"Skirmish at Buck Horn (Arkansas)." In: Indp. Co. (Ark) Chron., Jan. 1963, vol.IV, #2, p. 31-39.

547a ..."Occupation of Batesville in 1864." In: Indp. Co. Chron., Jan 1964, v.5, p.25-34.

548 **McGINTY, Brian**
"A Shining Presence Rebel Poet Lanier Goes to War.: In: CWTI, May, 1980, V.19, #2, p.24-31, illus., ports, facsms.
..."I will call a traitor a traitor, A.S. Johnston, Col., US Army" In: CWTI, June 1981, V.20, #3, p. 24-31, illus., ports.

549 **McGLASHAN, Peter Alexander Selkirk**
"The Battle of Cedar Creek." In: Addresses delivered before the Confederate veterans association of Savannah, Ga., 1893, p.49-55.

550 ..."Battle of Salem Church, May 3, 1863." In: Addresses delivered before the Con-

federate association of Savannah, Ga., 1893. p. 89-94.

551 ..."Longstreet's charge at Gettysburg, July 2, 1893." In: Addresses delivered before Confederate veteran's association of Savannah, Ga., 1898-1902, p. 20-25.

..."Our Last Retreat. An address of, delivered at the Savannah Volunteer Guard Armory, Dec. 5, 1894." In: Pres. Annual Report, 1895, p. 57-65.

..."Recollections of Petersburg, Va., June 1864." In: Above Report, p. 67-69.

552 **McGLONE, John E., III**
"The Lost Corps: The Confederate States Marines." In: U.S. Naval Inst. Proc., Nov. 1972, v.98, #11, p. 68-73.

McGOODWIN, Bessie Ware
"War-Time Memoirs of the Southland by a Lady of Selma, Alabama." n.p., n.d. 12mo, wraps, 88pp. $20. Pres-$35.

553 **McGOWAN, Daniel A.**
"Report: Battles of the Wilderness & Spotsylvania Courthouse." In: SHSP, 1878, v.VI, p. 145-150.

...See: "An account of the celebration 34th Anniversary, Washington Artly...

553a **McGRATH, John, Gen.**
"Organization of the 13th Louisiana Infantry. Camp Mandeville, the Avegno Zouaves, Reg. formed at Camp Moore." In: SHSP, 1903, v.31, p.103-120.

554 **McGREGOR, James C.**
"The Disruption of Virginia." N.Y., Macmillan Co., 1922. 12mo, cl, fldg. map, xiv, 328pp. $25. Unbiased acct., strange course of events from election Lincoln to June 1863, when W. Va. was admitted to Union. See: "Virginia Joins the Confederacy. Bev. B. Munford, Henry T. Shanks.

555 **McGUIRE, Hunter Holmes, Dr.**
"Address of Dr. Hunter McGuire, Medical director Second Army Corps (Stonewall Jackson, Army of Northern Virginia delivered on 23rd day of June, 1897, at Virginia Military Institute, in the presence of a vast audience, upon the occasion of the inauguration of the Stonewall Jackson Memorial building, published by the Va. Military Institute." Lynchburg, Va., J.P. Bell Co., 1897, 8vo, wraps, 22pp.

556 ..."An address: General T.J. ("Stonewall") Jackson, CSArmy, his career & character. In: SHSP, 1897, v.XXV, p. 91-112.

..."An address: Stonewall Jackson, at the dedication of the Jackson Memorial Hall, Virginia Military Institute & repeated before R.E. Lee Camp, #1, Confederate Veterans, Richmond, Va., July 9th, 1897." (Richmond, Va.) R.E. Lee Camp, #1, 1897, 8vo, wraps, 24pp. $22.50

...Same: (Richmond, Va., 1899, wraps, cover title, 17pp.

..."The memory of "Stonewall" Jackson delivered by Hunter McGuire, at the eighth annual banquet of the Confederate Veteran camp of New York at the St. Dennis Hotel, Jan. 22, 1898." n.p., 12mo, wraps, 15, (1)pp.

..."General Thomas J. Jackson. Reminiscences of the famous leader." In: SHSP, 1891, v.XIX, p. 298-318.

..."Death of Stonewall Jackson's Corp." In: SHSP. 1886, v.XIV, p. 154-163.

..."The Confederate Cause & Conduct inthe War Between the States, as set forth in the reports of the history committee of the Grand Camp, C.V. of Virginia & other Confederate Papers by Hunter McGuire & Hon. George L. Christian of Richmond, Va. With an introduction by Rev. James Power Smith, D.D., last survivor of the staff of "Stonewall" Jackson." Richmond, Va., L.H. Jenkins (1907), 8vo, cl, 2-ports, incl. front, xi, 229pp. $30-bmk; $25.; $40.- bmk; $60-c.

...2nd Edt. (1909), Addenda, 48pp., an address delivered before R.E. Lee Camp #1, Oct. 29, 1909.

...."Ceremonies & addresses attending the presentation of a statue of Hunter Holmes McGuire by the Hunter McGuire memorial association & its acceptance by the state at Richmond, Va., Jan. 7, 1904. Published under auspices of R.E. Lee Camp, #1, Confederate Vetrans, Richmond, Va." n.p., plate, large 8vo, wraps, 3-30pp.

557 ..."Official report of the history committee of the Grand Camp, C.V., department of Virginia, Oct. 12, 1899." Richmond, Va., J.L. Hill print. 1899, 8vo, wraps, cover title, 16pp. $15-bmk.

558 ..."Gun-shot & other wounds of the peritoneum...read before the Medical Society of Virginia, Nov. 12, 1873." 8vo, wraps, 12pp.

559 ..."Progress of Medicine in the South." In: SHSP, 1889, v.XVII, p. 3-12.

560 ..."Surgeons of the Confederacy." In: Confed. Vet., Apr. 1926, v.XXXIV, p. 140-143.

561 ..."Sketch of the Life & Career of Hunter Holmes McGuire, M.D., surgeon, physician, teacher & patriot." In: SHSP. 1900, v.XXVIII, p. 267-279.

562 ..."Unveiling a statue in the capitol square, Richmond, Va., Jan. 7, 1904 to Hunter Holmes McGuire." In: SHSP, 1903, v.XXXI, p. 248-266. See: Stuart McGuire's Sketch... Wm. W. Hassler.

563 **McGUIRE, Judith White Brockenbrough, (Mrs. John P. McGuire)**
"Diary of a Southern Refugee during the War. By a Lady of Virginia." N.Y., E.J. Hale & son, 1867. 12mo, cl, 360pp. (3pp-adv) $75.
...2nd Edt., same
...3rd Edt., Richmond, Va., J.W. Randolph & English, 1889. "with corrections & additions." 372pp. $50-b.

564 ...N.Y., Arno's "American Women Series Images & Realities." 1972 $22-y.

565 ..."General Robert E. Lee, the christian soldier. Published for the City missionary association of the Protestant Episcopal church of Richmond, Va." Phila: Claxton, Remsen & Haffelfinger, 1873. 16mo, cl, xii, 13-198pp. Dornbusch II $35.

566 ..."The Burial of Latane." Edt: Blake Tyler Newton." In: North. Neck Va. Hist. Mag., Dec. 1954, v.4, p. 287-288. Excerpts from a diary of a Southern Refugee 14/15 Aug. 1862, describing the burial of a CSA captain, acct. of an anon. painting of the scene.

567 **McGUIRE, Peter S.**
"The Railroads of Georgia 1860-1880." In: Ga. H.Q., Sept. 1932, v.XVI, #3, p. 179-213, map.

568 **McGUIRE, Stuart**
"Hunter Holmes McGuire (1835-1900) M.D." In: Ann. Med. Hist., ns, X 1938, p. 1-14, 136-161.
...offprint, 8vo, wraps, 40pp. $25-mbk-106.

569 **McHENRY, George**
"The Cotton Trade: its bearing upon the Prosperity of Great Britain & Commerce of the American Republics considered in connection with the System of Negro Slavery in Confederate States." London: Saunders, Otley & Co., 1863. 8vo, cl, iii-lxix, (2), 292. $125-b.
...2nd Edt., same

570 ...N.Y., Negro University press, 1969, Written to influence British recognition of the Confederacy re: cotton.

571 ..."The Cotton Supply of the United States of America." 2nd edt. with additional remarks. London: Spottiswoode & co., 1865. 8vo, wraps, 66pp., Sabin-43303. See, also: John Elliott Cairnes.

572 ..."Why Pennsylvania Should Become one of the Confederate States of America. By a Native Pennsylvania." London: J. Wilson, 1862, 8vo, wraps, 15pp. $7.50
...N.P., 1861, wraps, 8vo, with fldg. map.

572a ..."A Paper Containing a Statement of Facts relating to the Approaching Cotton Crisis." Richmond, Dec. 31, 1865. 8vo, 87pp. House of Representatives. Secret session. Head: Cotton crisis. Crandall-2927.

572b **McILVAINE, Charles Pettit**
"Leonidas Polk. The Bishop-General who died for the South." In: SHSP, v.18, p.371-9.

573 **McILWAINE, Bess Blakeney**
"Lee the Famous." (Translated into Japanese by Jiro Suzuki.) Tokyo? n.d., (1930's?) 12mo, 135pp. pict. boards, map, illus. $35- Text in Japanese. A biography of Lee written by a Presbyterian missionary, born in Japan. (Carolina bk.)

574 **McILWAINE, H.R.**
"Substance of the Laws in Reference to Confederate States Government Publications." In: Bibliog. Soc. Am. Proc., 1909, v.iii, p.85-91.

575 **McILWAINE, Richard**
"Memories of three score years & ten." N.Y., Wash., Neale pub., 1908. 8vo, cl, front, ports, xiv, (11)-383pp. Served in the Amelia Minute Men, afterwards known as Co. H, 44th Va. Vals. during war. $20-$22.50 $47--bmk- $125-ob

576 **McINTOSH, David Gregg, Col.**
"The Artillery on the Gettysburg Campaign, Report of Major McIntosh." In: SHSP, 1882, v.X, p. 134-137.

577 ..."The Life & Letters of John Hay." In: SHSP, Sept., 1916, v.XLI, p. 194-221. Rather unfriendly toward the South.

578 ..."Lectures of Charles Francis Adams on "Our American Civil War." In: SHSP, April 1914, v.XXXIX, p. 153-166.

579 ..."The Campaign of Chancellorsville." Richmond: Wm. Ellis Jones Sons, 1915. 8vo, wraps, t/p-cover title, 54pp. Pres copy $150 bmk-90.
...In: SHSP, 1915, xl, p. 44-100.

579a ..."Review of the Gettysburg Campaign." Falls Church, Va., Confederate Printers, 1984. 8vo, cl, 83pp, maps, Lim. Edt. of 485 copies. $14.

580 ..."Review of the Gettysburg Campaign." n.p., n.d. (1909) 8vo, wraps, maps, 83pp., atg. copy. In: SHSP, V.XXXVII, p. 74-143.

580a ..."The Confederate Artillery--its organization & development." In: Photo.Hist. CW, V.5, p.55-70, ills, ports.

581 **McINTOSH, J.R., Chairman**
"The South's Battle Abbey." (New Orleans, La.? 1895?) 12mo, decr. color wraps, dbl. column, newsprint(fragile) 32pp.

582 **McINTOSH, W.H., Rev.**
"James C. Sumner, the young soldier ready for death." Marion, Ala., Rev. W.H. McIntosh, n.d. 12mo, wraps, no t.p. Was member 41st Regt. Ala. Vols. (Owens).

583 **McINVALE, Morton R.**
"All that Devils could wish for: The Griswoldville Campaign, Nov. 1864." In: Ga. H.Q., Summer, 1976, v.LX, #2, p. 116-130. $8.

584 ..."That Thing of Infamy, Macon's Camp Oglethorpe during the Civil War." In: GHQ Summer 1979, v.LXIII, #2, p. 279-291, notes. $8.

585 ..."The Battle of Pickett's Mill: Foredoomed to Oblivion." Atlanta: Department of Natural Resources, Office of Planning and Research, Historical Preservation Section (1977), 4to, cl, 175pp. (10)leaves of plates, illus., bibliog., p.169-175.

586 **McIVER, George W.**
"North Carolinians at West Point Before the Civil War." (Raleigh) NCHRev., January 1930, v.VII, #1, p. 15-45, roster.

586a **McIVER, Stuart**
"The Murder of a Scalawag." In: CWHI,

April 1973, v.VIII, p.12-18. John Stephens of N.C., as revealed by one of the men.

587 **McKEE, George A.**
"Boyhood Impressions of the Lexington Missouri, Area, 1858-1863." (Columbia, Mo., Mo. Hist. Review, Oct. 1957, v.LII-#1, p. 16-24, illus.

588 **McKEE, Howard I.**
"The "Swamp Fox," Meriwether Jeff Thompson (1826-1876)." In: Mo. Hist. Soc. Bul, Jan. 1957, v.13, p. 118-34. Activities in Mo. & Ark., merchant & engin'r officer in CSArmy, 1861-1865.

589 **McKEE, James Cooper, Major**
"Narrative of the Surrender of a command of U.S. Forces at Fort Filmore, N.M., in July, A.D. 1861, at the breaking out of the Civil War, between the North & the South." Prescott, A.T., 1878. 12mo, wraps, cover title, 15pp. $90- "printed & distributed among army friends only."
...New York, 1881. Second edition, revised & corrected. cover title. 16mo, wraps, cover title, 30pp. $62.50
...Boston: John A. Lovell, 1886. 4to, wraps, map (front), fldg. map, 32pp. Index, 3rd edt., 300 copies for private circulation. $50.00
...Houston, Texas: Stagecoach Press, 1960. 12mo, cl, dj, viii, 64, (1)pp., map(front) fldg. map, 550 copies. Added title- "by Major James Cooper McKee, surgeon, U.S. Army. With related reports by John R. Baylor, CSA, & others." Read with: A.F.H. Armstrong's, "The Case of Major Isaac Lynde." In: New Mex. Hist. Rev., Jan. 1961, v.XXXVI, #1, p. 1-35. Martin H. Hall's- "Sibley's New Mexico Campaign." Robert Lee Kerby's "CSA Invasion of New Mexico." Charles S. Walker, William Waldrip, Ralph Emerson Twitchell, Trevanion T. Teel, George H. Pettis, Mrs. Carolina Baldwin Darrow, Hank Smith.

590 **McKEE, James W., Jr.**
"William Barksdale & the Congressional Election of 1853 in Mississippi." (Jackson, Miss.) Jour. Miss. Hist. May, 1972, v.XXXIV, #2, p. 129-158

591 ..."Felix K. Zollicoffer (1812-1862) Confederate Defender of East Tennessee." East Tenn. Hist. Soc. Pub., #43. (1971), pt. I, p. 34-58; 1972, v.44, p. 17-40.

591a **McKEE, John Miller**
"The Great Panic . . ." (see under title, anon.) Goodspeed (599) "Previously unknown author identifies himself to J. Berrien Lindsley, author of 'Mil.Annals Tenn.,' with marginal notes by Lindsley...." Gdsp $500.

591b **McKENZIE, Belle H.**
"McKenzie Letters." In: Phillips CHQ, Mar. 1970, v.8, p.16-22.

591c **McKENZIE, Robert H.**
"The Economic Impact of Federal Operations in Alabama during the Civil War." In: AHQ, 1976, v.38, #1, p.51-68.

592 **McKIM, Randolph Harrison**
"The Campaign & Battle of Gettysburg." In: Unit. Ser. Mag., Aug. 1913, v.CCXXII, p. 569-571.

593 ..."The Confederate Cavalry in the Gettysburg Campaign." In: Jour. Mil. Ser. Inst., May 1910, v.XLVI, p. 414-427.
..."Injustice to the South." In: "The Gray Book," pub. by Sons of Confed. Vets., (6)pp.

594 ..."The Confederate Armies; not more than 700,000 men served with the colors." In: Confed. Vet., June 1912, v.XX, p. 223-226.
..."The Confederate Soldier, address at Nashville reunion." In: CV, 1905, v.13, p. 113-121. port.

595 ..."Echoes of Christian Truth, from the Life of Gen. Robert E. Lee." Balt: George Lycett, 1871. 12mo, wraps, pl., 36pp.

596 ..."The Gettysburg Campaign." In: SHSP, 1915, XL, p. 253-300.

..."Glimpses of the Confederate Army." In: Rev. of Rev., April 1911, p. 431-437.

596a ..."Glimpses of the Confederate Army." In: Photo. Hist. C.W., v.8, p.105-36, ports, ills.

597 ...In Memoriam. Good men a nation's strength, a sermon preached on the occasion of the death of Gen. Robert E. Lee, in Christ Church, Alexandria, Va., Oct. 16, 1870, by the Rector, Rev. Randolph McKim Baltimore: John Murphy & co., 1870. 8vo, wraps, 16pp.

...Baltimore: George Lycett, 1870. 8vo, wraps, 15, text: black borders.

598 ..."Lee, the Christian Hero, a sermon delivered in the Lee Memorial Church, Lexington, Va., Sunday, Jan. 20, 1907 on the invitation of the Rector & Vestry." Wash: Brentano's, 1907. 8vo, wraps, front(port), 22pp.

..."A Soldier's Recollections: Leaves from the diary of a young Confederate." Washington, DC. Zenger Pub. co., 1982. 8vo, cl, dj, illus., new index, maps, 332pp. Intro: Michael E. Schnitter $20.

599 ..."The Soul of Lee, by one of his soldiers." N.Y. Longmans, Green co., (1917) 8vo, cl, port, xii, 258pp. Same, 1918. $35 bmk-99.

..."Steuart's Brigade at the Battle of Gettysburg-A narrative by Rev. Rand. H. McKim, late 1st Lt. & Aide-de-Camp Confederate Army." In: SHSP, 1878, v.V, p. 291-300.

600 ..."General J.E.B. Stuart in the Gettysburg Campaign. A reply to Col. John S. Mosby, by..." In: SHSP, 1909, v.XXXVII, p. 210-231. (reprint below)

...Richmond: Wm. Ellis Jones Print, 1909. 8vo, wraps, 24pp.

..."Motives & Aims of the Soldiers of the South in the Civil War. Oration delivered before the United Confederate Veterans at their fourteenth annual reunion at Nashville, Tenn., June 14, 1904. n.p., stitched, 8vo, 34pp. Note: Bound also as Appendix to the 14th annual meet., U.C.V. $50-b also issued, with wraps, cover title: "The Confederate Soldier his motives & aims." $50 bmk-104 $25 bmk-1904.

601 ..."The Numerical Strength of the Confederate Army; an examination of the arguments of the Hon. Charles Francis Adams & others, by Randolph H. McKim." N.Y., Neale pub., 1912. 12mo, cl, 71, (1)pp. $10.;- $90.; 150 bmk-105; $12.

Refutes Adams's claim of 1,200,000 men in the CSArmy by McKim-late 1st Lieut & A.D.C., 3rd Brigade, A.N.V.

602 ..."An oration on the 2nd Maryland infantry, delivered at Annapolis, Md., May 7, 1909. n.p., n.d. 8vo, wraps, 28pp.

603 ..."The Second Maryland Infantry, oration delivered in the State House at Annapolis, Md., Friday, May 7, 1909, upon the occasion of the presentation of one of its battle flags to the Governor of the State. By Rev. Randolph H. McKim, formerly 1st Lieut. & ADC Third Brigade, Army of Northern Virginia." (N.Y., Neale pub., 1909) 12mo, wraps, 28pp. $250-ob.

..."A Soldier's Recollection; leaves from the diary of a young Confederate, with an oration on the motives & aims of the soldiers of the South." N.Y., Longmans, Green co., 1910. 8vo, cl, front, 5-ports, xvii, 362pp. $150-ob Do: 1911 Edt., $75- 1912 Edt., $150- 1921 Edt., $50- p. 133-208, Gettysburg campaign, special reference to Mosby's "Stuarts cavalry."

...Louisv: Lost Cause, micro-cd., $5.72.

604 ..."Colonel Winston's Correction Corrected." In: SHSP, 1879, v.VII, p. 315-316, chart.

605 **McKINNEY, William Fortunatus, Capt.**
"The Camp Ford Diary of Capt. Wm. F. McKinney., Preface: Howard O. Pollan,

606 **McKITTRICK, Samuel, Captain**
"A Confederate Officer's Letters on Sherman's March to Atlanta. Contributed by Donals W. Lewis." In: Ga. H.Q., Dec. 1967, v.LI, #4, p. 491-494. Of Co. I, 16th S.C. Regiment, Gist's Brigade, Walder's Div. of Tenn. to his wife Mary. Killed near Atlanta. with introduction: Randal B. Gilbert." In: Smith Co. HS, Summer, 1986, v.25, #1, p.15-26, port., Carter Letters, p. 27-31.

606a **McLANE, Bobbie Jones**
"Montgomery Owen Campbell: Confederate & Union Veterans." In: The Record, 1970, v.11, p.20-29, Includes Remins. Campbell.

607 **McLAUGHLIN, Jack**
"Gettysburg" The Long Encampment. The Battle, the men, the memories." New York: Appleton-Century (1963) 4to, cl, d/w, ix, 244pp. illus., ports, facsms. plans(endsheets)

608 **McLAUGHLIN, James Fairfax**
"The American Cyclops, the hero of New Orleans & the Spoiler of silver spoons." dubbed LL.d., by Pasquino (i.e., Benj. Butler) Baltimore: Kelly & Piet, 1868. 8vo, wraps, 27pp., 12plates (inc. front). In verse, printed on one side, illus. are by Dr. A.J. Volk, see also under "Volk." Satiric couplets on Gen. B.F. Butler & dams all Yankees with him.

609 **McLAUGHLIN, William**
"Ceremonies connected with the unveiling of the bronze statue of Gen. Thomas J. (Stonewall) Jackson, at Lexington, Va. July 21st, 1891. By William McLaughlin, a member of the executive committee of the Jackson Memorial Association." Baltimore, John Murphy & co., 1891. 8vo, wraps, front(port), 65pp. illus. Address by Gen. Jubal Early. $45-ob

610 **McLAWS, Lafayette, Gen.**
"The Battle of Fredericksburg." In: Confed. Vets. Assn., Savannah, Ga., Pres. Annual Report, 1895, p. 71-93.

611 ..."The Confederate left at Fredericksburg." In: B & L, v.III, p. 86-94.

612 ..."After Chickamauga. Address before Confederate Veterans association of Savannah, Ga." Savannah, Ga., Braid & Hutton, 1898. 8vo, p. 49-72.

613 ..."Battle of Gettysburg. Address to CVAS.: Savannah, Ga., Braid & Hutton, 1896. 8vo, wraps, p. 57-97.

614 ..."Gettysburg." In: SHSP, 1879, v.7, p. 64-90.

614a **McLEAN, Clara D., Mrs.**
"The Last Raid--from a Journal kept from 1859-1871." In: SHSP, 1885, v.13, p.466-476.
..."Return of a Refugee." In: SHSP, 1885, v.13, p.502-15.

615 **McLEAN, Eugene, Mrs.**
"When the states seceded; from the diary of Mrs. Eugene McLean." In: Harper's Jan. 1914, v.CXXVIII, p. 282-8.

616 ..."A Northern woman in the Confederacy; from the diary of Mrs. Eugene McLean." In: Harper's, Feb. 1914, v.CXXVIII, p. 440-451. Written at Washington, events Nov. 1860 to April 1861.

617 **McLEAN, Guy**
"The Georgian Affair: An Incident in the American Civil War." The Canadian Historical Review, XLII, 1961, p. 133-44. Jacob Thompson's activities in Canada (CSA commissioner to Canada.) See: David Rankin Barbee, P.L. Rainwater.

617a **McLEAN, Harvard W. & Donald A. Pribble**
"Could the South Have Won the Civil War? Maps & military strategy." In: Soc.Studies, Nov/Dec. 1980, p.274-282.

617b **McLEAN, JOHN**
"The McLean Story." John Bruce Constantine." Bangor, Me., 1969. Remover: Husson College Review. 46pp, 1-color pl. $10.

618 **McLEARY, A.C.**
"Humorous Incidents of the Civil War." n.p., n.d. (Humboldt, Tenn., 1902?) $75-ob 8vo, wraps, ports, 23pp. Exper. of a young private in Co. G., 12th Tenn. Cavlary under Forrest.

619 **McLEARY, J.H.**
"Green's Brigade." In: Dudley G. Wooten's "Comprehensive History of Texas." v.II, p. 695-740.

620 **McLEOD, Martha Norriss, Edt.**
"Brother warriors; the reminisences(sic) of Union & Confederate veterans, ed., with an introduction, notes, & maps." Washington, DC, Darling print., 1940 $50-g 8vo, cl, ports, maps, (16), 358pp. Most stories recorded by author at last meet between "Blue & Grays," 75th anniversary of battle of Gettysburg, held in June/July, 1938. Some in their homes & others by corresp.

621 **McLOUGHLIN, Emmett**
"An inquiry into the assassination of Abraham Lincoln." N.Y., Lyle Stuart, Inc., (1963) 12mo, cl, dj, illus., 190pp., index. Roman Catholic Church related to the conspiracy.

622 **McMAHON, C.W., Mrs.**
"Cause & Contrast: an Essay on the American Crisis by T.W. McMahon." Richmond, Va., West & Johnston, 1862. 8vo, wraps (pasted on endsheets, front/back, for binding), xv, 192pp., adv. back cover. $325 jk-109; $150-b.

633 **McMASTER, Fitz William, Col.**
"The Battle of Crater, July 30, 1864." In: SHSP, 1882, v.X, p. 119-123.

..."Col. McMaster's rejoiner to Brig. Gen. Evans." (Wilmington, N.C., 1864) 8vo, wraps, 26pp. Crandall-2522.

634 ..."Elliott's Brigade how it held the Crater & saved Petersburg, a story of the bloodiest hand-to-hand conflict of the war, as told by Col. McMaster. Laying & firing the mine by Charles Pinckney Elliott." (Savannah, Ga., Review print, nd.d) 8vo, wraps, 46pp.

635 ..."Proceedings in a general court martial in the case of Col. F.W. McMaster, 17th Regiment S.C.V., held at Wilmington, N.C., March 30, 1863." Greenville, S.C., E. Elford's pr., 1864. 12mo, wraps, cover title, 72pp.

636 ...Columbia, S.C., South Carolinian Steam press, 1863. 12mo, wraps, 92pp. Crandall-2523/4.

...Same, with 88pp., Turnbull, III, p. 375. Was pub. by McMaster who had been charged with cowardice, mutinous conduct, etc.

637 ..."Speech before the 8th Annual Meeting of Survivors' Association of Ex-Confederate Surgeons." Yorkville, S.C., 1895. 8vo, wraps, 16pp. See: Dr. F.P. Porcher's (CSA Surgeons)

638 **McMASTER, Richard Keith & George Ruhlen**
"The Guns of Valverde." In: "Password," Jan. 1960, v.5, p. 20-34. Map, ports, view, notes. Guns used by both Union & CSArmies in the Battle of Valverde, N.M., FEb. 1862. For comment by Martin H. Hall, see p. 79-80.

639 ..."Light Artillery at the Pass of the North." In: "Password," v.II, p. 87-90.

..."The Saga of Captain McRae." In: "Password," v.III, p. 76-78.

..."Canby's Captains of the Southwest, 1860-1862." In: "Password", v.VI, p. 79-95, 123-140.

640 **McMASTERS, Elizabeth Waring**
"The Girls of the Sixties-This Memorial Vol. is lovingly dedicated to: Malvina Sarah Waring (Mrs. Clark Waring) by her daughter." Columbia, S.C., 1937 (The State Co) 8vo, cl, prots, 175pp. $20.

641 **McMEEKIN, Isabel McLennan**
"Robert Edward Lee (1807-1870); knight

of the South." NY, Dodd, Mead. 1950 12mo., cl, ports, views, bibliog. (233-234), viii, (2), 238pp. semifictional in style.

642 **McMICHAEL, J.R.**
"Autograph & Diary of...Book bought July 15, 1864, at Fort Delaware, Del." n.p., n.d. (Dec. 1938) stiff wraps. 4to, mimeo. (one side 34, 18pp. (append.)
..."Diary of Captain J.R. McMichael, prisoner of war, 1864-1865." (Atlanta, ? 194-?) $40- 4to, 2pp., 3-34. Caption title, reproduced from type written copy.
..."Diary of Captain J.R. McMichael." Augusta, Ga., March 1945. Bulletin of the University Hospital, wraps.

643 **McMILLAN, Malcolm Cook**
"The Alabama Confederate Reader." University, Ala., University Ala., (1963). 8vo, cl, dj, illus., 468pp. Pres. $30. $45.

644 ..."The Selection of Montgomery as Alabama's Capital." In: Ala. Rev., April 1948, v.I, p. 79-90, notes.

645 ..."William L. Yancey & the Historians: One Hundred Years." In Ala. Rev., 1967, v.XX, p. 163-186.

646 ..."The Disintegration of a Confederate State: Three Governors & Alabama's Wartime Home Front, 1861-1865." Macon, GQ., Mercer University Press, 1986. 8vo, cl,dj,ix,152pp., illus., maps/index.

647 **McMILLEN, James Adelbert**
"A Rare Confederate Louisiana state document & its History." (New Orleans, 1944). 8vo, wraps, 4pp. Reprint: Louisiana Historical Quarterly, v.27, #4, Oct. 1944. p. 1226-1228.

648 **McMILLIN, Lamar**
"Historical notes & speculations on the activities of six sons of David McMillin during the civil war." In: (Louisville, Miss.? 1954?) 13, (3)p. ports. On Leroy, William, John, Sam Jim, & David, of Winston co., Miss. 8vo, wraps.

649 **McMORRIES, Edward Young**
"History of the First Regiment Alabama Volunteer Infantry, CSA. By Edward Young McMorries, Phd. A private in the Perote Guards, Co. G., 1862-1865; and an original member of both the company & Regiment." Montgomery, Ala., Brown print, 1904. State of Alabama Dept. of Archives & History. Thos. M. Owen, Dir., Bul. 2 8vo, stiff gray wraps, 142pp. State Archives issue, no plates, maps, ports, etc. 16x24 1/2cm. uncut. $175-, 150-3 lt, jk 100 -(29).
...Same, with front, plates, ports, maps (1pfldg.), plan facsm. cloth bind., $135- See Coulter-312 detailed dscp.
...Same, in full leather, (c. 1902) Priv. print by same printer above in a lim. edition. $600-r $125.
...Louisv: Lost Cause micro-cd, $3.30
...N.Y., Arno pr., 1976. "Select bibliographic series reprints.

650 **McMULLAN, M.J., Capt.**
"Muster Roll of Captain M.J. McMullans Company of the Wise Guards from 31st day of Aug., to 31st. Oct. 1862, stationed at Camp Jasper, near Savannah." In: GHQ, v.1, #2, June 1917, 106-107pp.

651 **McMULLEN COUNTY (Texas)**
Civil War Centennial Commemoration, April 25, 1964." Tilden, Texas. 1964. sq. 8vo, stiff wraps, cord-tied, 18pp. mimeogr., muster rolls.

652 **McMURRAY, William Josiah**
"History of the Twentieth Tennessee Regiment Volunteer Infantry, C.S.A., by W.J. McMurray. Published by the Publication Committee, consisting of W.J. McMurray, Deering J. Roberts & Ralph J. Neel." Nashville, Tenn., 1904. 8vo, cl, ports, incl. front, 520pp., index. $150-g $100-bmk.
...Nashville, reprint, 1976. C. Elder. $25-
..."Canby's Captains of the Southwest,

1860-1862." In: "Password", v.VI, p. 79-95, 123-140.

653 **McMURRY, Richard M.**
"Confederate Morale in the Atlanta Campaign of 1864." In: Ga. H.Q., Summer, 1970, v.LIV, #1, p. 26-43.

654 ..."The Enemy at Richmond.": Joseph E. Johnston & the Confederate Government." In: CWH, Mar., 1981, v.27, #1, p. 5-31.

655 ..."Resaca: A heap of hard fiten"...the opening of the Atlanta campaign determining ultimate victor in Georgia." In: CWTI, Nov. 1970, v.IX, #7. illus., maps, ports. p. 4-20.

656 ..."Kennesaw Mountain." In: CWTI, Jan. 1970, v.VIII, #9, p. 19-34. illus., maps, ports.

657 ..."Joseph E. Brown of Georgia." In: CWTI, Nov. 1971, #9, p. 19-34, illus., maps, ports.

658 ..."Joseph E. Brown of Georgia." In: CWTI, Nov. 1971, v.10, #7, p. 30-39, illus., maps, ports.

659 ..."The Death of Leonidas Polk, CSA." (London) Jour. Confed. Hist. Soc. Autumn, 1967, v.5, #3, p. 83-87.

660 ..."Disappointment in History: The Papers of John Bell Hood." In: Prologue, 1972, v.IV, p. 161-4.

661 ..."John Bell Hood & the war for Southern Independence." Lexington, KY. University press, 1982, 8vo, cl, dj, illus., maps, xi, 239pp. front(port) Bibliog., 228-231. $20.

662 ..."The Mackall Journal & its Antecedents." In: CWH, Dec. 1974, v.20, #4, p. 311-328. The Journal of Lieut. T.B. Mackall, aide-de-camp to Brig. Gen. W.W. Mackall (his cousin) to Gen. J.E.Johnston Pub. in ORser. I, v.XXXVIII, pt. 3, p. 978-991, is now questioned as to authenticity/forged? Offprint Press.

663 ..."Negroes at New Market Bridge." (London) Jour. Confed. Hist. Soc., Spring, 1968, v.6, #1, p. 3-6.

664 ..."On the road to the sea: Sherman's Savannah Campaign." In: CWTI, 1983, v.27, #2, p. 5-24.

665 ..."The President's Tenth & the Battle of Olustee." In: CWTI, Jan. 1978, v.16, #9, p. 12-24, illus., ports. "Political aspirations as well as control of Florida, in the balance."

666 ..."The Road Past Kennesaw. The Atlanta Campaign of 1864." Wash: Nat'l. Park Serv., 1972. 8vo, wrap, ports, illus., sketches, 8vo, wrap, ports, illus., sketches, color maps, (3), iv, (2), 71, (1) p. Foreword-Bell Wiley. $1.

667 ..."Western Battlefields-Fort Donelson." (London) Jour. Confed. Hist. Soc. Dec., 1964, v.II, #4, p. 143-160, map, pl-1.

668 ..."Western Battlefields (pt. 2) Shiloh." (London) Jour. Confed. Hist. Soc. Spring, 1966, v.4, #1, p. 11-24, map.

669 ..."Western Battlefields-Kentucky, pt. 4." (London) Jour. Confed. Hist. Soc., Summer, 1969, v.7, #2, p. 62-71, pl.

669a ..."The Opening Phase of the 1864 Campaign in the West." In: Atl.Hist. Jour., Summer, 1983, p.5-24.

669b **McMURTREY, James Addison**
"Letters to Lucinda, 1862-4." Huntsville, Ala., 1985. 4to, wraps, iii, 72pp. port.

670 **McMURTRY, R. Gerald**
"Ben Hardin Helm, "Rebel" brother-in-law of Abraham Lincoln-with a biographical sketch of his wife & an account of the Todd Family of Kentucky." Chicago, Ill., Privately printed for Civil War Round Table, 1943. 12mo, cl, illus., 72pp. Limited edition 250 copies. $22.50
...(Madison, Wisconsin) 1959. Condensation of the original study. 8vo, wraps, 18, (1)p., ports. (Lincoln Fellowship of Wisconsin, Historical bul. 17.) Also in: FCHQ, Oct., 1958, v.32, p. 311-328.

671 …"Zollicoffer & the Battle of Mill Springs." In: FCHQ, Oct. 1955, v.29, #4, p. 303-319. An address delivered before the Filson Club, Louisville, Ky., Dec. 6, 1954.

672 …"Confederate Gen. Ben Hardin Helm: KY Brother-in-law of Abraham Lincoln." In: FCHQ, Oct. 1958, v.32, p.311-328.

673 **McNAMARA, J.H.**
"My knapsack." In: LWL, 1868-1869, v.VI, p. 316-319, Seizure of CSA forces at Camp Jackson..." Gen. Sterling Price's report of battle of Oak Hills." In: SoMag., 1869, v.II, p. 99-104. 1st pub., Springfield, Mo. "Mirrow", Aug. 12, 1861.

673a **McNAMARA, M.**
"Lieutenant Pierce's attempt to escape from Prison (Johnson's Isle)." In: SHSP, 1880, v.8, p.61-7.

674 **McNEEL, John A.**
"Confederate Treaties with the Tribes of Indian Territory." Oklahoma City: Chron. Okla., Winter, 1964-1965. v.XLII, #4, p. 408-420.

674a **McNEIL, John A.**
"Famous Retreat from Philippi--one of the earliest battles of the war." In: SHSP, 1906, v.34, p.280-93.
…"The Imboden Raid & its effects." In: SHSP, 1906, v.34, p.294-312.

675 **McNEILL, Charles D. W.**
"Three days battle showing who were the victors in front of Atlanta, Georgia. Campaign, or Gingercrack Charlie, the boy who successfully wore the Gray. Presented by C.D.W. McNeill, Commander of Sutton camp #1404, Texas division, U.C.V., Port Lavaca, Texas." (Port Lavaca, Texas, n.d., c.1904?) 8vo, wraps, cover title, ports, pl., 52pp.

676 **McNEILL, John Hanson**
"McNeill the Partisan." In: SB, Jan. 1885, v.3, p. 204-206. On death of Capt. John Hanson McNeill.

677 **McNEILL, William J.**
"A survey of Confederate Soldier Morale during Sherman's Campaign through Georgia & the Carolinas." In: Ga. H.Q., Spring 1971, v.LV, #1, p. 1-25.

678 **McNEILLY, J.S.**
"War & Reconstruction in Mississippi 1863-1890." In: MHSP, Cent.Ser., v.II, p.165-535.
…Offprint, 8vo, wraps. $10.00.

679 **McNEILLY, J.S., Capt.**
"Battle of Cedar Creek, Oct. 19, 1864. (Tactics employed by General Early)." In: SHSP, 1904, v.XXXII, p. 223-239.

680 …"Barksdale's Mississippi Brigade at Gettysburg." Most maginificent charge of the war." In: Pub. Miss. Hist. Soc., 1914, v.XIV, p. 231-265. $10.
…Gaithersburg, Md., Butternut Press, 1987. 8vo, pict. wraps, 35pp.
…"A Mississippi Brigade in the Last Days of the Confederacy." In: (Oxford) Pub. Miss. Hist. Soc., v.VII, p. 33-55. 1903. See: 1902, v.6, p. 129-140.

681 **McNEILLY, James H., Rev.**
"Andersonville & Maj. Henry Wirz." In: CV, 1907, v.15, p. 14-19, port. Incl: Location of Wirz monument, excerpts from others, as A.H. Stephens, Davis, Hill.

682 …"The Battle of The Alamance." In: Confed. Vet., Oct. 1921, v.XXIX, p. 376-378.

683 …"Capture of Generals Kell(e)y & Crook." In: CV, Sept., 1906, v.14, p. 410-413. port, maps. See: W.D. Vandiver. John Hanson.

684 …"Characteristics of the Old South." In: Confed. Vet., Apr., 1919, v.XXVII, p. 136-138.
…"Conduct of the War, 1861-1865." In: Confed. Vet., Mar. 1921, v.XXIX, p. 96-100.

685 …"Colonel Ashbel Smith of Texas (1805-1886): In: Confed. Vet., Dec. 1919, v.XXVII, p. 463-465.
…"Efforts of Confederacy for Peace." In:

Confed. Vet., Nov., 1921, v.XXIX, p. 418-420.

686 ..."End of Vicksburg Campaign." In: Confed. Vet., Mar. 1920, v.XXVIII, p. 96-99.

687 ..."The Failure of the Confederacy-was it a blessing?" Nashville, Tenn: Confederate Veteran (1912) 8vo, wraps, port, 47pp.
..."Failure of the Confederacy-was it a blessing?"In: SHSP, Sept. 1916,v.XLI, p. 115-144. In: Confed. Vet., Apr. 1916, v.XXIV, 65-68, p. 112-116; 160-165.

688 ..."Jefferson Davis." In: Confed. Vet., FEb. 1922, v.XXX, p. 58-59.

689 ..."John Yates Beall (1835-1865): his thrilling career for the South." In: Jefferson Co. hist. soc. mag., Dec. 9,1953, v.19, p. 38-48. Services to CSArmy & Navy & his execution in N.Y., reprint from CV, 1899, v.7, p. 66-69, 110-111, port, pl.

690 ..."General Joseph E. Johnston." In: Confed. Vet., Dec. 1917, v.XXV, p. 554-556.

691 ..."General Johnston's campaign for the relief of Vicksburg." In: Confed. Vet., Feb. 1920, v.XXVIII, p. 58-60.
..."A Great Game of Strategy." In: Confed. Vet., Oct. 1919, v.XXVII, p. 377-384. Sherman march to sea, 1864, campaign N. Georgia.

692 ..."Religion in the Confederate Armies." May 1913, v.XXI, p. 230-231.

693 ..."The Retreat from Tennessee." In: Confed. Vet., July 1918, v.XXVI, p. 303-307.

694 ..."Under fire at Port Hudson." In: Confed. Vet., Sept. 1919, v.XXVII, p. 336-339.

695 ..."Virginia-a Tribute." In: Confed. Vet., Mar. 1919, v.XXVII, p. 94-96. To service of country in every crisis.
..."What caused the War?" In: Confed. Vet., Aug. 1909, v.XVII, p. 404-407.

696 ..."Roster of McNeill's Rangers." furnished by Corp. D.M. Parson, one of the rangers. In: SHSP, v.XXXV, 1907. p. 323-325. See: Rev. J.W. Duffey, Simeon M. Bright.
..."Sudden change in Northern sentiment as to coercion in 1861." In: Confed. Vet., Oct. 1916, v.XXIV, p. 446-448.

697 ..."In Winter Quarters at Dalton, Georgia." In: Confed. Vet., April 1920, v.XXVIII, p. 130-132.
..."With Hood before Nashville." In: Confed. Vet., June 1918, v.XXVI, p. 251-154.

697a ..."The Enforcement Act of 1871 & the Ku Klux Klan in Mississippi." In: MHSP, 1906, v.IX, p,109-71.

697b **McPEEK, Allie, Mrs.**
"Heroism of a Widow, from the 'Atlanta Constitution.' In: SHSP, 1895, v.23, p.328-9.

697c **McPHAIL, John B., Maj.**
"Wilson's defeat at Staunton River Bridge, 1864." In: SHSP, 1891, v.19, p.54-6.

698 **McPHERSON, MISSISSIPPI**
See: Pinckney (Susanna Shulrick Hayne), daughter: Jno. M. Pinckney, Congressman from Texas, a CSA soldier.

699 **McRAE, A.T., CSA**
"Map of the Battleground of Greenbrier River, drawn & published by..., Quitman Guards, First Reg't. Ga. Vol's. Engraved by J. Baumgarten. Richmond, Va., Gary Printer, (1861?) bmk $300., Map-11x15 5/8". Stutler/Shetler.

700 **McRAE, Duncan K.**
"Battle of Williamsburg, Va., May 1862." In: Wm & M. Q., July 1922, v.II, 2nd ser., p. 195-197. Report of Col. D.K, McRae, 5th NC reg., May 10, 1862.
..."Battle of Williamsburg-Reply to Col. Bratton." In: SHSP, 1879, v.7, p. 360-72.

701 **McRAE, James C. & Charles Maney Busbee**
"The "bloody fifth." In: Southland", Greenville, N.C., 1898. p. 180-189.

702 **McRAE, John J.**
"A "Repentant Rebel." :Letter from John J. McRae to William L. Sharkey." (Jackson, Miss., Journ. Miss. Hist., Oct., 1956, v.XVIII, #4, p. 302-306.

703 ..."Address delivered by..., to the Fayette Independent Light Infantry Co., on the occasion of its 81st Anniversary. In: OLOD, Sept., 1874, v.1, #1, p. 32-38.

704 **McRAE, Walter G.**
"Confederate prisoners at Morris Island." In: CV, May 1921, v.XXIX, p. 178-179. Exp. of CSA officer in prison there.

705 **McRAVEN, David Olando & Amanda Nantz**
"The correspondence of...1864-1865. Edt: Louis A. Brown." In: NCHR, Jan. 1949, v.26, p. 41-98, notes. David was a pvt., Co. G. 1nd NC Regt. of reserves, guarding Union prisoners at Salisbury, writing his wife.

706 **McSWAIN, Eleanor D.**
"Crumbling Defenses or Memoirs & Reminiscences of John Logan Black, Colonel C.S.A." Macon, Georgia: The Author (1960) $50. (Atlanta, Ga., J.W. Burke Co.) 8vo, cl, 133pp., facsms (1-fldg.) map, port.

707 **McSWAIN, John Jackson**
"The Causes of Secession, an essay prepared by J.J. McSwain in 1896 while a student at South Carolina College." Greenville, S.C., 1917. 10 1/2cm, xi, 40--. (LC) McKissick-1624-copy has 27pp.

707a **McVICAR, Charles W.** "Chew's Battery. Reunion of October 1890." In: SHSP, 1890, v.18, p.281-6.

708 **McWHINEY, Grady**
"Braxton Bragg & Confederate Defeat. Field Command." N.Y., Columbia Univ. press, 1969. 8vo, cl, dj, illus., maps, bibliog. xviii, 421pp. Vol. 1-"Field Command." Bmk-1/2 $100- Bmk-$20.

709 ..."Braxton Bragg at Shiloh." In: Tenn. HQ, 1962, v.XXI, p. 19-30.

710 ..."Braxton Bragg." In: CWTI, April 1972, v.11, #1, p. 4-7, 42-48, illus., ports.

..."A lady of Arcadia, the doomed garrison of Pilot Knob & how it was saved, by T.J. Mackey, late Captain engineers, CSA." In: Home & Country, 1895-1896, v.XI, p. 319-329, illus., map ports. Dorn-II, 3286.

711 ..."The true story of the battle between the Monitor & the Merrimac, by T.J. Mackey late Captain of engineers, CSA." In: Home & country, 1897, v.14, p. 138-146, illus.

711a ..."General Beauregard's "Complete Victory" at Shiloh: an interpretation." In: SH, Aug. 1983, v.49, #3, p.421-34.

711b ..."Grant, Lee, Lincoln & the Radicals. Essays on Civil War leadership by Bruce Catton." Evanston, Ill., Northwest University Press., 1964. 12mo, cl, vi, (4), 3-117pp. $30.

711c ..."Jefferson Davis - the unforgiven." In: JMH, May 1980, v.42, p.113-27.

712 **McWHINEY, Grady & Perry D. Jamieson**
"Attack & Die, Civil War Military tactics & the Southern Heritage." University, Alabama. University Press (1982) 8vo, cl, dj, xv, (2), (3)-209pp. maps, tables, index, sources (192)-201. $18-

712a **McWHINEY, H. Grady & Grancis B. Simkins** "The Ghostly Legend & the Ku Klux Klan." In: NHB, Feb. 1951, v.XIV, p.109-12. Disguises & frightening the negro.

713 **McWHORTER, Virginia L.M. (Mrs. J.K.)**
"Caring for the soldiers in the sixties." In: CV, Nov. 1921, v.XXIX, p.409-411.

714 **MEAD, Everard Kidder**
"Maps & other papers of Maj. Jedediah Hotchkiss, CSA." In: Clarke Co., Hist. Assoc. Proc. 1948/49, v.8, p. 56-66, maps, describes maps, diaries, corresp., 1861-1865, mainly war in Va.

MEADE, George Gordon, Gen.
See: Leslie J. Perry.

715 **MEADE, Robert Douthat**
"Some Neglected Aspects of the American Civil War: Recollections of John C. Wade." In: W&MQHS, July, 1936, v.16, #3, p.408-413.

716 ..."Judah P. Benjamin Confederate Statesman." N.Y., Oxford University Press, 1943 8vo, cl, pl. ports, incl. front., ix, (2), 432pp. Editions: 2nd Edt., 1943, 4th print (1944) ($7.50); London, 1943, $5.00.

717 ..."Judah P. Benjamin." In: CWTI, June 1971, v.X, #3, p.10-20, illus., map, ports. See: J.P. Benjamin, Pierce Butler.

718 ..."The relations between Judah P. Benjamin & Jefferson Davis: Some new light on the working of the Confederat emachine." Journ. Southern Hist., V, 1939, pp.468-478. $8.00.

719 **MEADOR, L.E.**
"Souvenir program of Battle of Wilson Creek, Seventy-Seventh anniversary, Aug. 10-11, 1938. History of the Battle of Wilson Creek." (Springfield, MO) 1938, 8vo, wraps, 35pp.

720 **MEANEY, Peter J., OSB**
"The Prison Ministry of Father Whelan Georgia Priest & Confederate Chaplain." In: GHQ, Spring, 1987, v.71, #1, p.1-14, illus., facsms., ports.

721 ..."Valiant Chaplain of the Bloody Tenth". In: Tenn. HQ, Spring 1982, v.XLI, #1, p. 37-47.

722 ..."The Civil War Engagement at Cool Spring, July 18, 1864. (The largest battle ever fought in Clarke County, Virginia.)" (Morristown, N.J., St. Mary's Abbey, July 18, 1979), 8vo, stiff pict. wraps, illus., maps, 71pp Index and Bibliography. "Chap 4 thru 8, appear in Pro. Clark Co. Hist. Assn., 1979/80, Berryville, Va.

722a ..."Valiant Chaplain of the Bloody Tenth." In: THQ, Spring 1982, v.41, #1, p.37-47. Medical & Sanitary Affairs of the C.S. Army....
See: Joseph Jacobs, Joseph Jones, Samuel E. Lewis, Hunter Holmes McGuire, C.H. Mastin, George Moorman, Francis Peyre Porcher.

723 **MEANS, Alexander**
"Diary for 1861 by Alexander Means. Edt: Ross H. McLean, Prof. of History." Atlanta, Ga., Emory University Library 1949. Emory University Publications, Sources & Reprints Ser. VI, #1, 8vo, stiff wraps, 46pp. Secession member of Ga. convention.

724 **MEANY, Edmond Stephen**
"Name of the American War of 1861-1865." (Seattle, 1910.) 8vo, sewn, caption title pp. 3-18, reproduced from Congressional record, p. 929-933. Debate in the US Senate Jan. 11, 1907. See: Ellis Merton Coulter.

725 **MEARES, Gaston, Mrs.**
"Address: ...Presentation of Cross of Honor to Veterans of the Confederate Army of Cape Fear Chap., Daughters of the Confederacy, Jan. 19, 1901." 8vo, wraps, 7pp. wood-textured wraps.

726 **MEARS, Kate De Rossett**
"Opposition to secession in the South." In: CV, April 1912, v.20, #4, p.161-167, bibliog.

727 **MEBANE, John**
"Books relating to the Civil War; a priced checklist, including regimental histories, Lincolniana & Confederate Imprints." N.Y., T. Yoseloff (1963), 8vo, cl, dj, 144pp.

728 **MECASLIN, John M. & Mary Ann**
"Mecaslin Letters, 1964-1865." In: Atlanta Hist. Bul., 1938, v.III, p.127-139. Written after Atlanta's fall, Sept. 2, 1964, plight of citizens forced to leave city.
..."(same) In: Atl. Hist. Bul., pp. 120-139. Biogr. notes on John M., letters of Ann on fall of Atlanta, appended.

729 **MECHLING, W.T., Maj.**
"Regulations of the Army of the Confederate States, 1862; Containing a complete set of forms for the Quartermaster's, subsistence Ordnance & Medical Departments of the army; Articles of war; forms

also for general regimental & garrison courts martial. Pub. by authority of Gen. P.O. Hebert, commanding camp Trans-Mississippi District. By Major W.T. Mechling, commanding camp of instruction, near Austin, (Tex.)" Austin, Tex., State Gazette Office, 1862. 8vo, clo, 306, vip, plans, Crand-1410 $950.00

730 **MECHLING, William T.**
"William T. Mechling's Journel of the Red River Campaign, April 7-May 10, 1864. Edited by Alwyn Barr." In: Texana Fall 1963, v.i, #4, pp.363-379, notes.

731 **MECKLIN, Robert W.**
"The Mecklin Letters, written in 1863-1864 at Mt. Comfort, by...founder of Ozark Institute." Edt: W.J. Lempke (Fayetteville) Washington County Historical Society, Bul. Ser. #10. 1955, 4to, mimeo, 44pp.

732 **MEDALS OF THE CONFEDERACY-**
See: Bauman L. Belden.

733 **MEDFORD, H.C.**
"The Diary of H.C. Medford, Confederate Soldier, 1864. Edt: Rebecca W. Smith & Marion Mullins." In: SWHQ, Oct. 1930, v.XXXIV, #2 & 3, p. 106-140. 203-230.

734 **MEDICAL SOCIETY**
Of the State of North Carolina, Confederates Comm. "Provisional Record of Confederate Medical Officers." n.p. 1890., 8vo, wraps, cover title, 57pp.

735 **MEEGAN, Beatrice Van Court**
"P.G. Toutant de Beauregard, General C.S.A." Washington (D.C.) The Sudwarth Co., 1914, 8vo, wraps, port, col. illus., 16pp. Printed under auspices: Beauregard chap. #1102, UDC of the Dictrict of Columbia.
..."Causes of Secession." In: CV, Feb. 1923, v.XXXI, p.58-59.

736 **MEEHAN, Patrick**
"A Soldier's story of the American Civil War" In: Irish Sword, 1952/3, v.1, pp.348-352. Letter 30, July 1865, to the mother of Patrick McGuire, a soldier of CSArmy reviewing his service (& that of the writer) from May 1861 till his death of wounds in June 1864, with a "list of battles he was in."

737 **MEEK, Samuel M.**
"Address of...& Lt.Commander W.H. Sims on Jan. 20, 1890 at the presentation ceremony of the portrait of Col. Isham Harrison, to Isham Harrison Camp, #3, Confederate Veterans." Columbus, Miss., n.d., 8vo, cover title, 10p. While Col. of 6th Miss. Cavalry was killed July 14, 1864 at battle of Harrisburg, Lee Co., Miss.

738 **MEERS, Andrew Jackson**
"Souvenir Poems by Capt. Meers-"The Dying Confederacy; or, Through the Congress Halls." Austin, Texas. (1910). 8vo, wrps, 30p. Title head: 'Confederate Home, Austin, Tx.'

739 **"MEETING OF GENERALS GRANT**
& Lee Preparatory to the Surrender of General Lee and his entire army to U.S. Grant, April 9, 1864." Published by Joseph Hoover...Phila: 1866. P.S. Duval & Son, Phila., Litho. Folio: 22x28" good margins, hand-color. $300.00

740 **MEIER, Neal**
"Battlefield Analysis Study & Tactical Exercise without Troops: Shenandoah Valley Guide to Maj.Gen. T.J. Jackson "Stonewall Shenandoah Valley Campaign." n.p., n.d. 8vo, wraps, maps, 51p. $35.00 Not produced for purchase.

740a **MEIGS, John Rodgers**
See: G. W. Martin.

741 **MEINERS, Fredericka**
"The Texas Border Cotton Trade, 1862-1863." In: CWH, Dec. 1977, v.23, #4, p.293-306.
..."Hamilton P. Bee in the Red River Campaign of 1864." in: SwHQ, July 1974, v.LXXVIII, #1, p.21-44. Maps, port.

742 **MEINUNG, Alexander**
"Sketches from the field." In: CWH, 1958, v.4, following p.398. (2 leaves engr. both sides). Four Va. drawings by a member of the 26th N.C. Reg., 1863.

743 **MELL, Patrick Hues**
"Life of Patrick Hues Mell, by his son, P.H. Mell, Jr." Louisville, KY, Baptist Book Concern, 1895, 12mo, cl, front (port), viii, (9)-258pp. Commander of Mell's Riflemen during war.

744 **MELLTOWN, Bennie Catherine**
"Memories of a Pre-Civil War Community" (Birmingham, Alabama, 1950) Private print. 8vo, wraps, facsm., views, notes, ix, 67pp. On Crumly's Chapel, Ala., Based on old stories retold by her mother. Large section on Civil War & reconstruction.

745 **MELTON, Maurice**
"Cruise of the Rebel Sea Wolf Sumter: Her Career & Triumph." In: CWTI, Jan 1982, v.20, #9, p.16-25, illus (1-color), port.
..."Bringing in the (CSS) Fingal". In: CWTI, 1972, XI, v, 16-25pp.

746 ..."The Confederate Ironclads." New York, London: Yoseloff (1968) 8vo, cl, d/w, ports, illus., 319pp. $12.50.

747 ..."A Grand Assemblage", George W. Rains & the Augusta Powder Works." in: CWTI, Jan. 1973, v.XI, #9, p. 28-37, diagrams, illus., ports.

748 ..."Disloyal Confederates- 'Men of Bad Character" In: CWTI, Aug. 1977, v.16, #5, p.12-19, illus., facsms., ports.

749 ..."First and Last Cruise of the CSS Atlanta." In: CWTI, Nov. 1971, v.10, p.4-9, 44-46, illus., map, ports.

750 ..."The Selma Naval Ordnance Works." In: CWTI, Dec. 1975, v.14, #8, p.18-31, illus., ports.

751 **MELTON, Wightman Fletcher**
"'Fighting Joe'" Wheeler." In: Nat. Mag., April 1906, v.XXIV, p.61-71.

752 **MELVIN, Philip**
"Stephen Russell Mallory, Southern Naval Statesman." (Baton Rouge, La.) JSH, May, 1944, v.X, #2, pp.137-160.

753 **MELZER, Dorothy Garrett**
"Mr. Breckinridge Accepts: In: RKHS, Jly 1958, v.56, #3, p.217-232. Note: Jonathon T. Dorris' Pardoning Jno. Cabell Breckinridge,' Oct. 1958, v.56, #4, p.319-324.

754 **MEMMINGER, Charles Gustavus**
"Address of the Hon.... special commissioner from the state of South Carolina, before the assembled authorities of the state of Virginia, Jan. 19, 1860." 8vo, wraps, 43pp. Swem-3642 $75.00jk. From Virginia-Gen. Assembly, Annual report officers, boards, etc. Doc. LVIII.

755 ..."Lecture delivered before the Young Mens' Library Association, of Augusta, Apr. 10, 1851. Showing African Slavery to be consistent with the moral & physical progress of a nation by Memminger of Charleston, S.C. Pub. by request of the Ass'n." Augusta, Ga., W.S. Jones, 1851, 8vo, wraps, 25pp. DeRenne-II, p.541.

756 ..."The Mission of South Carolina to Virginia." Baltimore, J. Lucas & Son, 1860?, 8vo, wraps, 34pp. Swem-3643. $75.00jk. Reprint: DeBow's Review, Dec. 1860.

757 ...Also in Virginia General Assembly, as Doc #58, series 1859-1860. "Address delivered before the Gen. Assembly of Virginia, Jan. 19, 1860, by CGM, special Comm. from the state of South Carolina." 43pp.

758 ..."Southern Rights & Cooperation Doc. #7. Speech of Mr. Memminger at a public meeting of the Friends of Co-operation in the cause of Southern Rights, helf in Charleston, Sept. 23, 1895, for the purpose of nominating delegates to the Southern

Congress." Charleston, S.C., Walker & James Print, 1851, 8vo, wraps, 23pp.

758a **MEMMINGER, R. W., Major**
"The Surrender of Vicksburg--A Defence of General Pemberton." In: SHSP, 1884, v.12, p.352-60.

759 **"MEMOIRS & real Confederate Receipts,** by real daughters." United Daughters of the Confederacy. Florida Division, Southern Cross Chap. #796, Miami, Florida." 1960. (Miami, Fla., 1961) 8vo, wraps, 67pp.

760 **"MEMOIRS OF GEORGIA;** containing historical accounts of the state's civil, military, industrial & professional interests, & personal sketches of many of its people." Atlanta, Ga., Southern Hist. Assn., 1895 tk. 4to, cl, illus., ports (150p) bmk-$150. Around 2,000 sketches, most of whom served in the war, their service emphasized.

761 **"MEMORANDA of facts** bearing on the Kentucky Campaign." (Re: Braxton Bragg) n.p. 1862? 8vo, 4pp. LC notes #2 in a vol. of pamphlets with binder's title: CSA pamphlets, v.1, 1861-1866.

762 **"MEMORANDUM OF FIELD OFFICERS** and regiments in the Confederate States Army, 1861-1865." (Washington, DC 18--), 4to, cl, 133pp.

763 ..."Memorandum of engineer officers of the regular & provisional corps for Aug., 1864 - Confederate States of America." (Washington, DC, 1882), 8vo, sewn, 8p.

764 ..."Memorandum of officers in the Commissary-General's Dept., June 6 and July 14, 1864 (Washington, DC 1882), 8vo, sewn, 13p.

765 ..."Memorandum of Officers in the Quartermaster's Dept. for June 30, 1864." (Washington, DC, 1882) 8vo, wraps, 28pp. Dorn-II, 1016.

766 **"MEMORANDUM of Armies,** Corps, & Geographical Commands in the Confederate States, 1861-1865." Washington, D.C., 1876, 8vo, caption title, pp. (1)(173)-376. Attributed to Marcus Wright. Reprint by William Frayne Amann, Edt. N.Y. Yoseloff, 1961. This & three copies of the War Dept. known to exist, of 25 copies made.
See also 'Local designations of Confed. organizations...', & Marcus Wright. "Organizatio of ANV."

767 **"MEMORANDUM of Artillery Officers** in the Confederate States Service." (Washington, 18--), 8vo, cl, 140, 2, 141-164pp., Roster of Officers; page 3-63; organizations: p.(65)-140, 2, 141-146.

768 **"MEMORANDUM of information** as to Battles, etc., in the year 1864, called for by the Honorable Secretary of War." In: SHSP, 1876, v.II, p.22-25.

769 **"MEMORANDUM relative to General Officers** appointed by the president in Armies of the Confederate States, 1861-1865." Compiled from Official Records. 60th Cong. 1st Sess-Senate Doc. #244, Feb. 11, 1908. Military Secretary Department. Washington: Gov. Print, 1908, 8vo, wraps, cover title, 41pp. 1905 $50.

770 **"MEMORIAL & BIOGRAPHICAL HISTORY** of Johnson & Hill County, TX. Chicago, Ill: Lewis Pub. Co., 1892. 4to, tk. dbl. column; Contains: Co A & B, 12th and 19th Texas Cavalry, Parson's Brigade, Dea's. Brig., Hillsboro Guard, pp. 117, 122, 254-269.

771 **"MEMORIAL DAY ANNUAL, 1912.** The causes and outbreak of the war between the states, 1861-1865. For use as a source book of contemporary authors. Published by the Department of Public Instruction at the request of the Confeder-

ate Memorial Literary Soc." (Richmond, Va., Press) 1912, 8vo, wraps, front, port, 94pp.
H.J. Eckenrode's 'Right of Secession', H.R. McIllwaine's 'Maintenance of the Doctrine of Secession', Edwin P. Cox' 'Virginia's Position in 1861-views of all sections of the state. George L. Christian's 'Fort Sumter, et, all.

772 "MEMORIAL History
of John Bowie Strange Camp UCV." Charlottesville, Va., 1920, 8vo, cl, illus., 330pp., Charlottesville & Albemarle during war.

773 "MEMORIAL Services
at Pea Ridge, March 11, 1962." In: ARHQ, 1962, v.XXI, illus., ports, p.158-165. "Pea Ridge Memorial Association, Mrs. W.W. Vaught, Pres."

774 "MEMORIAL of the Association
of the Maryland Line to the Legislature of the State of Maryland, Baltimore, Feb. 8, 1888." 12mo, wraps, cover title, 15p.; State should pay the pensions.

775 "MEMORIAL of the Congress
of the Confederate States." Mobile, 1863, wraps, 8vo, 6pp. Decision on copyright, Hardee Infantry Tactics.

776 "MEMORIAL of the unveiling
of the monument to the unknown confederate dead, May 19, 1887." Hopkinsville, Ky. The Story of a Monument by SCM, portraits, 8vo, cl, New York, 1888.

777 "MEMORIAL pamphlet.
Confederate Soldiers who died in the service of their country & are buried in Columbia, SC, 1861-1865." Columbia, SC, United Daughters of the Confederacy, 1924, 12mo, wraps, 32pp.

778 "MEMORIAL to Confederate Soldiers,
Elmwood Cemetery, Shepherdstown, Wa. Va." 1937, 8vo, wraps, illus., 27pp. Erected by Henry Kyd Douglas Camp, Sons of CV of Shepherdstown. Reg. & Co. Officers 2nd VA Inf., Rosters of Co.'s B & H, 2nd VA INF., Co.F, 1st Va. Cav., Co. D, 12th Va. Cav.

779 "MEMORIALS - Col. Richard Owen,
the Good Samaritan of Camp Morton. Sam Davis the Boy Hero of Tennessee." n.p., n.d. (c. 1913) 12mo, wraps, cover title, 47, (1)pp, ports, illus., CSA Tribute to comdr. of prisoners for kind treatment by Owen. Sponsored by S.A. Cunningham of Confederate Veteran.

780 "MEMORIALS of Three Great Virginians,
Maury, Lee & Jackson." etc.
See: John A. Coke, et.al.

780a MEMORIALS To Men
Who Fell at Spotsylvania, monument unveiled by Bloody Angle & Salem Church." (fron Richmond Times-Dispatch, May 13, 1909). In: SHSP, 1909, v.37, p.164-8.

781 "MEMORIES of the Confederacy-
Flowers & Songs." n.p.n.d. (c.1899) (Baltimore: Apr. 11, 1898-pub. for the Confederate Relief Bazaar by the collector of flowers, ? B.E.J.G. (Gwathmey?) Sq. 12mo, stiff boards, tied, 24pp. poems, various authors, opposite a pressed flower, picked from the field of that battle, i.e., Manassas, Crater, etc.

781a MEMPHIS APPEAL-AVALANCHE-
"Monument to the Defenders of Vicksburg, Address Stephen D. Lee." In: SHSP, 1893, v.21, pp.183-206.
..."A Mother of the Confederacy." In: SHSP, 1894, v.22, p.63-64.

781b MEMPHIS, TENN., Capture of
See: James Dinkins "Forrest Captures... "

782 "MEN WHO MARCHED and fought well;
list of officers and Roster of Company E, nineteenth Virginia Infantry." In: SHSP, 1908, v.XXXVI, p.237-244.

782a "MEN WHO WORE THE GRAY"
See: Abram J. Ryan. (poem).

783 MENDENHALL, Willard Hall
"Life is uncertain..." Willard Hall Menden-

hall's 1862 Civil War Diary. Edt: Margaret Mendenhall Frazier & James W. Goodrich." Part 1. In: MoHR, July 1984, v.LXXVIII, #4, p.428-452, facsms, illus., port. October 1984, v.LXXIX, #1, p.65-88, pt. II.

783a ..."Missouri Ordeal, 1862-4: Diaries of William Hall Mendenhall. Transcribed by Margaret Mendenhall Frazier." Newhall, Calif., Carl Boyer, III. 1985. 8vo, cl, 219pp, ills, index. $22. Southern sympathies, his father in medical dep't. with Price in Missouri, but he remained civilian. Diary reflects all troubles as a border state.

784 **MERCER, Philip**
"The Life of the Gallant Pelham." Macon, Ga., J.W. Burke Co., 1929, 12mo, cl, pls., ports, incl., front, map.
..."Kennesaw, Ga., Continental Book Co., 1958., 12mo, cl, map, ports, views (2), 180pp.
See: Fred Martin.

785 **MERCER, S.C.**
"The Two Kentuckians", read by Mrs. Irwin Dugan before the Filson Club, Louisville, Ky. Louisville, Ky.: S.T. Copeland, 1901, 8vo, cover title, 8p. illus., Monaghan 1350. Poem on Jeff Davis and Lincoln plus another "After the Reunion."

786 **MERCER, Walter C., Compl.**
"Confederate Reunion Song Book, Richmond, Va., June 1-3, 1915." Richmond, Va., Confederate Reunion 8vo, wraps, 23pp.

787 **MERCER, Oliver E., Lt. & Sara Elizabeth**
See: Lillian (Reeves) Wyatt's Reever, Mercer Kirk families of North Carolina. Lt. Oliver E. Mercer's CSArmy career & Sara Elizabeth's 1863 letters.

788 **MERCHANT, S.W.**
"A Raft Voyage Down the Rio Grande." In: Frontier Times, Nov. 1951, v.29, p.33-40. Capt. Bethel Coopwood's "Arizona Spy Company", CSA rangers & prisoner of war in New Mexico on a raft to an unnamed point in 1861-1862.

788a **MEREDITH, Jaquelin Marshall**
"General Harry Heth's First Day at Gettysburg, who opened the Battle." In: SHSP, 1896, v.24, p.182-7.

789 **MEREDITH, Roy**
"Storm over Sumter; the opening engagement of the Civil War." N.Y., Simon & Schuster, 1957, 8vo, cl, dj, map, ports (1-dble), (8), 214 (1)p. Bombardment, Capture by CSA forces.

790 ..."The Face of Robert E. Lee: in Life and in Legend." N.Y., London: Charles Scribner's, 1947, 4to, dl, dj, 143pp., illus., ports (100) 35- 30--.

790a **MERIDIAN, Battle of . . .**
See: William H. Jackson, Stephen Dill Lee, Robert V. Richardson, Peter B. Starke.

790b **MERING, John Vollmer**
"Persistent Whiggery in the Confederate South: a Reconsideration." In: So. Atl. Quart., Winter 1970, p.124-43.

791 **MERIWETHER, Colyer**
"Raphael Semmes." Phila: Jacobs print (1913), 12mo, cl, port (front), 367 pp. American Crisis Biographies.

792 **MERIWETHER, Edward B.**
"Excerpts from an address given at the Confederate Cemetery in Fayetteville, Arkansas on June 2, 1940." in: AHQ, 1944, v.III, pp.351-355.

793 **MERIWETHER, Elizabeth Avery**
"Facts and Falsehoods concerning the war on the South, 1861-1865, by George Edmonds (pseud.)" Memphis, Tenn., A.R. Taylor Co., (1904), 8vo, cl, (or wraps), vii, (1), 271pp. $40.; $45. Bitter attack on Lincoln and other Union leaders, opinions in 'factual form'.

794 ..."Recollections of 92 Years, 1824-1916" Nashville, Tenn., Tennessee Historical Commission (1958), 8vo, cl, ill., 2 ports,

xii, 249pp. Tenn, SC, during war and reconstruction.

794a ..."The Ku Klux Klan; or, the Carpetbagger in New Orleans." Memphis, Tenn., Southern Baptist Pub., 1877. 8vo, cl, 51pp. (Tulane).

795 **MERIWETHER, Lee, Miss**
"My Yesteryears: An Autobiography." Webster Grove, Mo., International Mark Twain Society, 1942, 8vo, cl, front, pls., ports, 440pp, chaps. on Jeff Davis, Prisons, etc.

796 ..."Address on Jefferson Davis at reunion of United Sons of Confederate Veterans, June 10, 1908." Birmingham, Ala., 1908, 8vo, wraps, (8) pp.

797 **MERIWETHER, Walter Scott**
"The Paul Jones of the Confederacy; the brilliant but forgotten exploits of Captain Charles W. Read of Mississippi." In: Munsey's July 1916, v.LVIII, p.264-277.

798 **MERLI, Frank**
"Crown versus Cruiser: The Curious Case of the Alexandra." In: CWH, v.IX, #2, p.167-177.

799 ..."The South on the Seas-Strengths & Weaknesses of Confederate Sea Strategy." In: CWTI, Nov. 1972, v.11, #7, p.4-8, 39-45, cartoons, illus., ports.

799a **MERLI, Frank J., Edt.**
"Alternative to Appomattox: a Virginia's vision of an Anglo-Confederate Colony on the Amazon." In; VMHB, April 1986, v.94, p.210-9.

800 **MERLI, Frank J. & Theodore A. Wilson**"
The British Cabinet & the Confederacy Autumn 1862." In: Md. Hist. Mag., 1970, v.LXV, p.239-262.

801 **MERLI, Frank J. & Thomas W. Green**
"Great Britain & the Confederate Navy, 1861-1865." Bloomington, Indiana Univ. Press, 1970, 8vo, cl, d/w, xvi, 342pp., illus., Reply by A.H. McClelland, in 'History Today, 1964, v.XIV, p.687-695, 871.

802 **MERRICK, Carolina Elizabeth Thomas, Mrs.**
"Old Times in Dixie Land; a Southern matron's memoirs, by Carolina E. Merrick." N.Y., Grafton Press, 1901, 12mo, cl, illus., front(port), 241pp. $20.00. Life in old South, before, during and after the Civil War (Louisiana).

802a **MERRILL, C. E.**
"Old Mose." A Gettysburg Incident. Epic Poem." n.p., n.d. Colonel of a Georgia Regiment to his body servant. Port of "Mose," colored Confederate flag, 12mo, wraps, 4pp.

803 **MERRILL, James M.**
"Confederate Shipbuilding in New Orleans." (Houston, TX) JSH, Feb., 1962, v.XXVIII, #1, pp.87-93.

804 ..."The Hatteras Expedition, Aug. 1861." In: NCHR, April 1952, v.XXIX, p.204-219.

805 ..."Nothing to Eat but Raw Bacon--Letters from a war correspondent 1862." In: THQ, 1958, v.1958, v.17, p.141-155.

805a ..."Battle Flags South: The Story of the Civil War Navies on Western Waters." Rutherford, 1970. 8vo, cl, 334pp, index. $25.

805b **MERRILL, James Milford**
See: Morris Redwing, pseud.

806 **MERRILL, Louis Taylor**
"General Benjamin F. Butler & the Widow Mumford." New Orleans: LHQ, April, 1946, v.29, #2, pp.341-354.

807 **"MERRIMAC & MONITOR, The"**
In: SHSP, 1883, v.11, p. 32-34.

808 ..."Merrimac vs Monitor, a midshipmen's account of the battle with the "Cheese Box," in Wm. C. King & W.P. Derby Camp-Fire Sketches & Battlefield Echows of 1861-1865." Springfield, Mass: King, Richardson, 1888. p. 333-337. CS Navyman's account of plans to sink the "Monitor."

809 ...In: SHSP, Jan. 1883, v.XI, p.31-40. Crew of Monitor do not deserve prize money. See: Gentleman's Mag., May 1862, v.CCXII, p.631-635.

810 ..."Officially, there's a 'K' in Merrimac." In: CWH, Mar. 1961, v.VII, p.89.
..."Wonderful Career of the Merrimac." In: CV, July, 1907, v.XV, p.310-313. By the engineer, serving on Merrimac.

811 ..."Battle between the Monitor and Merrimac, fought Mar. 9, 1862 at Hampton Roads, near Norfolk, Va." Chicago: Kurtz & Allison, 1889, Color litho, 20 1/2 x 27 1/2" $35.00. "Minnesota" burns in left foreground, with Union soldiers, edge of fort, observes it.

812 ...Reprint, 1960, Little Rock, Ark., Pioneer Press. Included in complete set K & A's.

813 ..."Fight between the 'Merrimac' & 'Monitor', March 9, 1862." N. Y., Currier & Ives, 1862, From a sketch by F. Newman, Norfolk, Virginia. Lithographed in color, 8" x 12 1/2". (plate) $50.00.

814 ..."Merrimac & Monitor Engagement." Baltimore, n.d., The Baltimore Cyclorama. 8vo, wraps, front, illus., maps, 16pp.

815 ..."The Great Fight Between the Merrimac & Monitor. Mar. 9, 1962, color, 8 1/4 x 12 1/4 plus wide margins, Currier/Ives: $50.00. Merrimac at left front. F. Newman sketch.

816 ..."The Sinking of the 'Cumberland' by the Iron Clad 'Merrimac' off Newport News, Va., March 8, 1862." N.Y., Currier & Ives, 1862. Sm. folio lithograph, hand colored, $50.00. Sinking Cumberland foreground, seamen abandoning ship, Merrimac in background.

817 ..."Terrific Engagement between the Monitor, 2 guns, & Merrimac, 10 guns, in Hampton Roads, Mar. 9, 1862. First fight between iron clad ships of war." N.Y., Currier & Ives, by F.F. Palmer. 16 x 22 1/4", plus margins, color, $250.00

818 ..."Terrific Combat between 'Monitor', 2 guns, & Merrimac, 11 guns, in Hampton Roads, Mar. 9, 1862. N.Y., Currier & Ives, 8 1/2 x 12 1/2", plus wide margins, colored 65-$50.00. A rare variant, both ships center, with 2" open water foreground.

819 ...The Merrimac (The Virginia), "US Steam Frigate Merrimac (Virginia) Sectional View, (drawn in 1857) by G.G. Pook, Lithographed (Julius Bien, 24 Vesey.)N.Y., D. Van Nostrand Pub., n.d., folio 30x45 3/4", good margins, b/w. Before she became the CSA ironclad "Virginia" $225.00.

820 ..."U.S. Auxiliary Screw Steam Frigate 'Merrimac', 60 Guns, off the entrance to New York Harbour." London, Day & Son, lithographer, n.d. After T.G. Dutton, 15 3/4" x 23 1/4", plus margins, colored $250.00. Ship siezed by CSA, rebuilt with slope sides, iron plate & destroyed Northern shipping, later engaged the 'Monitor.'

821 ...Merrimac (ironclad) colored lithograph- "Last of the wooden Navy. Battle between the Merrimac (Virginia) & the US fleet in Hampton Roads, March 8, 1862." Wash., DC, A.B. Graham Co., litho. Painted by G.B. Matthews, from a drawing made by Lieut. H.B. Littlepage of the Merrimac. (1907). "G.B. Matthews, 1906 appears lower right. DeRenne III, 1277.

821a ..."Report of the Committee on Naval Affairs." In: SHSP, 1885. v.13, p.90-119. (Hse. Reps., 48th Congr., 1st sess., Reprot #1725. (application for bounty).

822 **MERRIMAC ,**
"The Old Merrimack" Lithograph, 16 x 23", n.p., n.d. As she was before conversion to the Confederate ironclad. A contemporary litho, probably Southern origin, in Henkel #1090, May 1913.

823 **MERRIT, Elizabeth**
"James Henry Hammond, 1807-1864" Baltimore, Johns Hopkins Univ. Press, Studies Ser. XLI, #4, 1923, 8vo, cl, 151pp. 30-. Study to show a distinct public body in South Carolina, public opinion from nullification in '32 to secession in '60, for a united South, a Southern nation.

824 **MERTINS, Gustave, Mrs. & Walter B. Jones**
"The Secession of Alabama." In: CV, 1931, v.39. In: CV, 1931, v.39, p.168-178, illus., port.

824a **MERTZ, Gregory A.**
"Chancellorsville: the Zenith of a Relationship." In: CV, ns, July/Aug. 1987, v.35, #4, p.24-9, 34-5, ills, incl. cover, map.

825 **MESSAGE From the Army of the Valley of Virginia**
Feb. 10, 1865, n.p., 1865. Camp of Smith's Brigade, 8vo, (1)p broadside, caption title. Crandall-698. Facsm. Henkel's cat. 1090, May 1913.

826 **MESSAGE Of the President**
In response to a Senate resolution inquiring whether any state of the U.S. had intimated a desire to make overtures for peace. Nov. 21, 1864. (Richmond, Va., 1864) 8vo, 2pp. $12.50.

827 **MESSAGE Of the President**
Richmond, Dec. 23, 1863, covering Gen. Lee's report of Operations of Army of N.Va., from date of assumption of command to the including Battle of Fredericksburg, Dec. 13, 1862. lacks title and last 3pp., 623 pp. (one of 2 vols., Crandall #1435??)

828 **MESSAGE Of the President**
Feb. 6, 1864. Richmond, paper, 8vo, p. 3.
..."Act to protect rights of owners of slaves taken by, or employed in army." Do: Feb. 8, 1864, Richmond, p. 3, stitch.

829 ..."Report of Maj. E. Griswold, relative to passport system. Do: Feb. 12, 1864, p. 10, stitch. Richmond. "trial & convict - W.E. Coffman, Mil. Court. (Above three, not in Crandall?)

830 **MESSAGE Of the President (of C.S.A.)**
Feb. 12, 1864...relative to the trial and conviction of W.E. Coffman by a military court, and the interposition of the Circuit Court of Rockingham County, Va., by Habeas Corpus, to prevent the execution of Coffman. Sabin 48146, n.p., n.d., 8vo, wraps, p. 10.
..Feb. 15, 1864, transmitting copies of charges & specifications in Case of Maj. H.C. Guerin. CSA." n.p., n.d., 8vo, wraps, pp. 41. Sabin 48146.

831 **MESSAGE Of the President, & report**
Of Albert Pike, Commissioner of the Confederate States to the Indian Nation west of Arkansas, of the results of his mission. Richmond: Enquirer, 1861, 8vo, wraps, 38pp., Crandall 614.
...(Washington, DC, Scottish Rite, 1968.)

832 **MESSMER, Charles K.**
"Louisville & the Confederate invasion of 1862." In: KYHSR, Oct. 1957, v.55, p.299-324.
..."Louisville on the Eve of the Civil War." In: FCHQ, July, 1976, v.50, #3, p. 249-289.

833 **METHODIST QUARTERLY REVIEW-**
Nashville, Tenn., v.1-79. Jan. 1847-Oct. 1930, or to date. Early issues break with north? During CSA? See: Rev. Charles Elliott. William Pope Harrison, John N. Norwood, A schism within the Methodist church, c.1845 presages a more serious break nationwide in '61.

834 **METHVIN, T.W.**
"In the Wilderness Campaign." In: CV, Oct. 1915, v.XXIII, p.454-456.

835 **METTS, James I.**
"Longstreet's Charge at Gettysburg, Pa. Pickett's, Pettigrew's & Trimble's division. Historical Essay, by James I. Metts, Capt.

Co. G, 3d NC Infantry, & Asst. Insp. Gen'l. Bryan Grimes' staff. Wilmington (N.C.) Morning Star Press (1899), 12mo, wraps, 18pp. dbl. column. Dornbusch II, 765 has date (c. 1899) altho LC fails to list until 1958.

836 **MEXICO ,**
"Notas diplomaticas, ultimas cambiadas entre Ministerio de relaciones esteriores de la republica Mexicana, y las legaciones estrangeras." Mexico, 1862, 4to, wraps, 43pp., Sabin 55942.

837 **MEYER, Duane**
"The Heritage of Missouri- a History." Hazelwood, Mo., State Pub. Co. (1963) (1970) 4th revised edition, 8vo, cl, dj, facsms., illus., maps, bibliog (5)pp. Chap. X - The Growing Conflict, p. 307-347. XI - The Civil War" p.348-404.

838 **MEYER, Milton M.**
"The Postal Service of the Confederacy." (Richmond) Va. Cavl., Winter, 1959, v.IX, #3, p. 4-9, illus., 1-color & cover.

839 **MEYERS, Lewis, Capt.**
"Greyclad Marines." In: Marine Corp. Gazette, Mar. 1947, v.31, #3, p.26-29.

840 **MEYNARDIE, Elias J., Rev.**
"The Siege of Charleston; its History and Progress. A discourse delivered in Bethel Church, Charleston, SC, November 19, 1863 (Thanksgiving Day)." Columbia, SC, Evans & Cogswell, 1864, 8vo, wraps, 15pp. 300.

841 **MEYNIER, Arthur, Jr.**
See: "Confederate Knapsack" Col. Charles D. Dreux. Editor of above works.

842 **MICHIE, Peter S., Capt.**
"Richmond, Virginia 1865." Two part: Map 49 x 58", a larger version of same map published in Atlas to Accompany the Official Records of the Union & Confederate Armies, 1861-1865. Originally on a scale of 3/4" - 1 mile, this map is 8" to 1 mile. The original is found in National Archives. Richmond: Civil War Centennial Comm., 1965 Detailed description, cartouche.

842a **MICHIGAN POST & TRIBUNE**
"Concerning Prisoners at Andersonville." In: SHSP, 1882, v.10, p.285-6.

843 **MICKLER, William English**
"Report of...Adj.Gen. & Chief of Staff, from the date of his appointment by Gen. John B. Gordon, Jan. 19, 1903 to Dec. 31, 1907." New Orleans, La., United Confederate Vets., 8vo, wraps, pamphlets bound, p. 12,30,33, (4), 35, 9, (4), 35, (4).

844 ..."Well known Confederate Veterans & their War Records. Arranged alphabetically." New Orleans, La., The Author, 1907, 4to, cl. (vol. 1, all pub.) illus., ports, front., 74, xxxixpp.
...Same, 1915, cl, 8vo, 205pp. $25.00.

845 ..."Well known Confederate Veterans and their war records." New Orleans, La., The Author, 1915, 8vo, cl, illus., plates, ports, 205pp. Brief Biographies of CSA vets.

846 **MIDDLETON, Arthur**
"Middleton Correspondence, 1861-1865. Edited by Isabella Middleton Leland." In: SCHM, 1962. 1963-1964, v.63, Jan., p.33-41, April, p.61-70, July, p.164-174, October, P.204-210; Jan. 1963, v.64, p.28-38, April, p.95-104, July, p.158-168, October, p. 212-219; Jan. 1964, v.65, p. 33-44, April, p. 98-109.

847 ..."A Midnight Ride from Petersburg." In: South Mag., December 1871, 8vo, wraps, 7pp. article. $10-bmk.

848 **MIERS, Earl Schenck**
"Robert E. Lee, A Great Life In Brief" N.Y., Alfred A. Knopf, 1967, 12mo, cl, d/w, (2), dbl-pg. map, 203, Index, viii, (1)p. 5th - (1967).

849 ..."1st Edt., April 16, 1956, p. 199-200, reprinted three times.

850 **MIKELL, Isaac Jenkins**
"Rumblings of the Chariot Wheels."

Columbia, S.C., The State Company, 1923, 12mo, cl, front, (10) 273pp. 25-; Barefoot boy's life on a Southern Plantation, Charleston & Aiken, SC, before, during and after the war.

850a **MILBURN, William Henry**
"Lee's Birthday." In: SHSP, 1889, v.XVII, p.354.

851 **MILES, Dudley**
"The Civil War as a Unifier." In: Sewanee Rev., April 1913, v.XXI, p. 188-197.

851a **MILES, J.**
"Georgia Civil War Sites: a comprehensive guide to 300 Civil War battlefields, forts, museum & cemeteries in Georgia." Warner Robins, 1987. 8vo, wraps, 1389, ills, index. $8. Signed by author.

852 **MILES, J. Tom**
"Abraham J. Ryan." In: South Mag., 1936, v.II, 11, p.3-5, #12, p.15-18; v.III, #1, p.21-25, #2, p.11-13. First installment by Andrew Wyatt Miles.

853 **MILES, Susan & Mary Bain Spence**
"Major Ben Ficklin (Benjamin Franklin Ficklin.)" In: W. Tex. Hist. Assoc. Yr. Bk. 1951, v.27: 58-77pp., notes, port. Life as cadet at VMI, officer in CSArmy, teacher, operator stage line in Ala. & the West.

854 **MILES, Thomas Jefferson**
"To all whom it may concern", "The Conspiracy of leading men of the Republican Party to destroy the American Union proved by their words and acts antecedent and subsequent to the rebellion." N.Y., J. Walter & Co., 1864, 8vo, wraps, 35pp., Lincoln and his party torn constitution to shreds.

855 **MILES, William Porcher**
"Speech of..., of South Carolina, on the organization of the House, Jan. 6, 1860." n.p., n.d., c.1860, 8vo, wraps, 8pp. $12.00. Makes plea for states rights.

855a **MILEY, Herbert F.**
"Complete Roll of Muhlenburg Rifles, of Co. F., Tenth Virginia Regiment." SHSP, 1900, v.28, p.115-24.

855b **MILFORD STATION, Battle of ...**
See: Charles T. Loehr.

856 **MILHAM, Charles G.**
"Gallant Pelham: American Extraordinaire." Gaithersburg, Md., Butternut Press, 1985. $25.00

857 ..."Gallant Pelham American Extraordinary. Intro: Maj.Gen., U.S. Grant, 3rd." Washington, DC, Public Affairs Press 1959, 8vo, cl, dj, sketches, ix, (1), 250pp. $80.

858 **MILHOLLEN, Hirst Dillon**
"Horsemen, Blue & Gray: a Pictorial History. Text by James Ralph Johnson & Alfred Hoyt Bill." N.Y., Oxford University Press, 1960, 4to, cl, facsms., maps, music, ports, views, bibliog.

858a **MILITARY ANALYSIS of the Civil War:**
An Anthology be the editors of 'Military Affairs.' Millwood, KTO Press, 1977. 8vo, cl, 414pp. $15. Both Union & CSA contributions.

859 **"MILITARY HISTORY of Kentucky,**
chronologically arranged, written by workers of the Federal Writer's Project of the Works Progress Administration for the State of Kentucky." (Frankfort, Ky.) (State Journal, 1939) (American Guide Series.) 8vo, cl, plates, ports, viii, 493pp. 100pp. on Civil War.

860 **"MILITARY LAWS of the Confederate States;**
embracing all the legislation of Congress appertaining to military affairs, from the first to the last session inclusive, with a copious index." Richmond, 1863; 12mo, paper.

861 **"MILITARY OPERATIONS in Jefferson Co.,**
Virginia (and W. Va.) 1861-1865." United Confederate Veterans, Virginia Div. (Charles Town, W.Va.) Farmers Advocate

862 Print, 1911, 8vo, boards, map, 43pp. 75 bmk-124.

862 ..."Ranson, W.Va., Whitney & White Print, 1960. Reprint, 45pp. DLC author was Roger Preston Chew. U.C.V., Va., Div., Jefferson Co. Camp #123.

862a **MILITARY OPERATIONS of the Civil War:**
A Guide-Index of the Official Records of the Union & Confederate Armies, 1861-65. Compiled by Dallas D. Irvine, et. al, v.IV-Main Western Theatre of Operations except Gulf Approach (1861-63). v.V Trans-Mississippi & Pacific Coast Theatres of Operations." Washington: National Archives & Records Service, GSA, 1980. 4to, soft back, pp.v, 189, v, 205. $6. each, GPO.
...Vol. II - Main Eastern Theatre of Operations. Washington, D.C., National Archives, 1968/9. Pub. 1970. 4to, wraps, 76, 77-172. May 1971, vol. II, pt. 2, pp.173-252. 1971-2, p.253-332, p.333-428.
...Vol. III - Lower Seaboard Theatre of Operations & Gulf approach, 1861-3 - Main Western Theatre. Washington, 1977. pp.vi, 92; viii, 71. ($2.30).

862b **"MILITIA ENROLLMENT Lists,**
Butts County, Ga. Act. 14th Dec., 1863." In: D.A.R. Typescripts 1984 (#270), p.69-73.

863 **"MILITIA LAWS of the State of Arkansas;**
published by direction of the Commander-in-Chief of the Army of the State of Arkansas, & of the militia thereof." Little Rock, Ark., Johnson & Yerkes, 1860, sm. 8vo, wraps, 68pp.

864 **"THE MILITIA & PATROL LAWS of South Carolina,**
to Dec. 1859. Published by resolution of the General Assembly, Columbia, SC, R.W. Gibbes Print, 1860, 8vo, cl, 158pp. (Uniforms of Militia, p. 135-158.)

864a **MILL SPRINGS, Battle of . . .**
See: Bennett H. Young.

865 **MILLAR, Alexander, Mrs.**
"Our own beloved Jackson." In: Va. Jour. Educ. 1935, v.XXVIII, p.176-179. Written for elementary schools.

866 **MILLAR, J.S.R.**
"Memorial sketch of Adjutant 1st Reg. NC Troops, by T.D.B. of Hertford Co., NC." In: OLOD, Mar. 1875, v.2, #1, pp.30-33.

867 **MILLARD, Flora**
"The Foreign Policy of the Confederate States." In: CV, June 1918, v.XXVI, pp. 241-246.

868 **MILLER, Charles F.**
"Capture of Wagon Train by McNeill's Men." In: CV, Jan. 1913, v.21, p.20, Nov. 16, 1863.

869 **MILLER, Darlis A.**
"Hispanos and the Civil War in New Mexico: a Reconsideration." In: NMHR, April 1979, v.54, #2, p.105-123, notes.

870 ..."Military supply in Civil War New Mexico." In: Mil. Hist. Tex. & SW., v.16, #3, p.177-197, notes, map.

871 **MILLER, Edmund Thornton**
"The State Finances of Texas During the Civil War." n.p., n.d., 1910, Texas State Historical Assn., Vol. XIV, #1, p. 23. $10.00. Reprint, cover title.
...Part 2, same, #2, p. (26) $10.00.
..."Repudiation of state debt in Texas since 1861." (Austin)-Southw. Hist. Assn. Quart. 1912, v.xvi (Oct.), p. 169-183.

872 **MILLER, Edward**
"Bound for Hampton Roads." In: CWTI, July 1981, v.20, #4, p.22-31, illus., ports., map.

873 **MILLER, Francis Trevelyan, Edt. Chief**
"The Photographic History of the Civil War. Robert S. Lanier, Mgr. Edt. Thousands of scenes photographed 1861-1865 with text by many special authorities. N.Y., Review of Reviews, 1911, 4to, cl,

	ports, illus., (most by Brady), maps. $325, $250, $135, $175-y $100.00
874	..."Semi-Centennial Memorial Edition." Printed on special paper, first impressions of new plates, 1,000 sets (#339), 4to, full Mor., gilt, spec. Title-page, color. $185, $200.
	...Same, bound 3/4 Mor., heavy gilt, but no limitation. $150.
	...N.Y., T. Yoseloff (1957), 10 volumes in 5. With an introduction by Henry Steele Commager, issued in a case bmk-100.
	...N.Y., Castle Books (1957) (T. Yoseloff) 4to, boards, dj, cheap paper edt., $10/vol. Contents: I-The Opening Battles, 368 (1); II, Two Years of Grim War, 352, (i); III - The Decisive Battles, 346, (6), The Cavalry, IV, p.336, (1) V-Forts & Artillery, 322pp.; VI-The Navies, 332; VII-Soldier Life & Secret Service, 382, (1)p.; IX-Poetry & Eliquence of Blue & Gray, 352, (1)p.; X-Armies & Leaders, 358pp. Index, p.323-358.
874a	**MILLER, H. J.** "The Roll of Company "G", Forty-Ninth Virginia Infantry." In: SHSP, 1896, v.24, p.171-2.
875	**MILLER, Helen Toppong** "Christmas with Robert E. Lee." N.Y., Longmans, Green co, 1958, 8vo, wraps, 79pp.
876	**MILLER, J.M.** "Recollections of a Pine Knot in the Lost Cause: Campaigns of West Virginia, Kentucky, Fort Donaldson, Battle of Corinth, Siege of Fort Pemberton, All Campaigns Western & North Mississippi & Atlanta, or 100 Days Campaign from Dalton to Lovejoy; Hood's Famous Campaign to Nashville; Greensboro, North Carolina." Greenwood: Commonwealth Pub. co., n.d. (1899). Large 8vo, wraps, 56pp.
877	**MILLER, James H.** "History of Summers County." (Hinton?) 1908, pp.838. Lists CSA & Union soldiers from county. Also account of Thurmond Rangers, CSA. (Shelter-501)
878	**MILLER, Raymond O.** "A stupendous failure. " In: Mil. rev., July 1960, v.40, #4, p.31-44. Maps, views, Battle of Crater, 27 July, 1864
879	**MILLER, Rex** "The Forgotten Regiment. A Day-by-Day Account of the 55th Alabama Infantry Regiment CSA, 1861-65." (Williamsville, N.Y., Patrex Press, 1984) Sq.8vo, front(port.)x, 303p., illus., facsm., ports., maps, rosters, revised edt., 2nd print. $40.00
880	**MILLER, Robert E.** "Proud Confederate: Thomas Lowndes Snead of Missouri." In: MoHR, Jan., 1985 v.79, #2, p.167-189, illus., ports, notes.
880a	..."General Mosby M. Parsons Missouri Secessionist." In: MHR, Oct. 1985, v.80, #1, p.33-57, ports, ills.
880b	..."One of the Ruling Class" Thomas Caute Reynolds: second Confederate Governor of Missouri." In: MHR, July 1986, v.80, #4, p.422-48, ills, facsms, ports.
881	**MILLER, Robert Henry** "Letters of Liet. Robert H. Miller to his family, 1861-1862. Edt: Forrest P. Connor. "In: Va. MHB, 1962, v.LXX, p. 62-91, pl, facm, port.
881a	**MILLER, Samuel, Edt.** "Civil War Memoirs of the First Maryland Cavalry." In: MdHM, June 1963, p.137-69. $40. Reminiscences of Henry Clay Mettham, 1st Md. Cav., CSA.
882	**MILLER, Samuel H.** "Yellow Tavern." In: CWH, March 1956 v.II, #1, p.57-81, maps. Action around Yellow Tavern & death of Jeb Stuart. See: David Herr Coblentz.
883	**MILLER, Stephen Franks** "Ahab Lincoln: A tragedy of the Potomac." (Milledgeville, Ga., 1861 ?) 8vo,

sewn, 6pp. CSA mock poem.
...With an introduction by Richard Harwell. Chicago: Civil War Round Table, 1958. 12mo, wraps, 21, (1)p. $10. Orig. pub. Milledgeville, Ga., 1861.

884 **MILLER, Thomas L.**
"Texas Land Grants To Confederate Veterans & Widows." In: SwHQ, July 1965, v.LXXIX, #1, pp.59-65.

885 **MILLER, W.C.**
"List of officers and privates who volunteered in Confedetate States service from Wilkinson county, Miss., 1861-1865." Woodville, Miss. (Zoller's job pr.) 1903 8vo, cover title, 16pp.

886 **MILLER, Walter L.**
"Life & Character of James Louis Petigru." In: SHSP, 1897, v. XXV, pp.55-60.
..."The last meeting of the Confederate Cabinet." In:South. mag., 1899, August. 8vo, wraps, 13pp.article bmk $15.00

886a **MILLIGAN, James C.**
"Fort McCulloch, Indian Territory: Gray command on the Blue." In: Red River Val. His't. Rev., Spring 1982, p.17-27.

887 **MILLIGAN, John D.**
"The First American Ironclads. The Evolution of a Design." In: Bul. MHS, Oct. 1965, v.22, #1, p.1-13.

888 **MILLIGAN, Lambdin P.**
Copperhead- "Decision of the US Supreme Court on Military Commissions. Case, Ex parte Lambdin P. Milligan, et a;. December Term, 1866." Washington: W.H. & O.H. Morrison, 1867 8vo, sewed, 23pp. Sabin-49087. 25.

889 ...This elicited- "Review of the Decision of the US Supreme Court, in the case of L.P. Milligan, et al, the Indiana Conspirators." (Washington, DC) 1867 8vo, 24pp.

890 ..."Knight of the Golden Circle.: In: Ind. Mag. Hist., 1947, v.XL, p.379-391.

891 **MILLIGAN, Leo, Capt.**
"Gilleland's Double Barrelled Cannon." (London) Jour. Conf. Historical Society, March 1965, v.III, #1, p.14-16, pl-1.

892 **MILLING, Chapman L.**
"Illium in flames." In: CV, Apr/June 1928, v.xxxvi, pp.135-138, 179-183, 212-216. Burning of Columbia, S.C. in 1865.

893 **MILLS, Gary B.**
"Patriotism Frustated the Native Guards of Confederate Natchitoches
In: La. Hist., Fall, 1978.p.437-451.

893a ..."Alexandria, Louisiana, a Confederate City at War with itself." In: Red River Val. Hist. Rev., Winter 1980, p.23-36.

894 **MILLS, Laurens Tenney**
"A South Carolina Family: Mills-Smith & related lines. By Laurens Tenney Mills. With addenda by Lilla Mills Hawes & Sarah Mills Norton." Columbia, S.C., 1960. Privately printed, for sale by Mrs. W.L. Norton, Walhalla, S.C. 8vo, cl, maps, charts. Sect.III, "Manuscripts", memoirs & much Civil War data given.

895 **MILLS, Luther Rice**
"Letters from the Trenches", In: Wake Forrest Student, 1911, v.XXXI, p.261-295.
..."Letters of Luther Rice Mills, a Confederate soldier." In: N. Caro. Hist. Rev., July 1927, p.285-310. Edt: George D. Harmon, vol. IV. bmk-12-.
..."Letters of a Confederate Soldier." See: George D. Harmon.

896 **MILNER, W.J.**
"The Battle of Santa Rosa Island." In: CV, Jan. 1903, v.XI, p. 20-21.
..."Lieut. Gen. William Joseph Hardee." In: Confed. Vet., Aug. 1914, p. 360-364.

897 **MILTON, George Fort**
"The Eve of Conflict. Stephen A. Douglas & the Needless War." Boston: Houghton Mifflin Co., 1934, large 8vo, cl, dj, ports, incl. front, facsm., xii, (2), 608pp. bibliog.,

index.
...N.Y., 1963 reprint.

898 ..."The Age of Hate; Andrew Johnson & the Radicals." N.Y., Coward-McCann, 1930, 8vo, cl, front, facsms., illus., ports, xi, 787 pp., Hamden, Ct., Archon Books (1965).

899 **MIMS, Edwin**
"General Lee's place in history." In: Outlook, Dec. 22, 1906, v.LXXXIV, p.978-982. See: Henry Shepherd's criticism (following).

900 ..."Poets of the Civil War, II-The South." In: Cambridge History American Literature." N.Y.: Putnam's University Press, 1918.

901 **MIMS, Livingston**
"Address on-" The Life & Works of Jefferson Davis." Delivered in the Hall of the House of Representatives State Capitol of Georgia, before the Daughters of the Confederacy and the Confederate Veterans, June 3, 1902, 8vo, caption title, 22pp., n.p., n.d. (c.1902).

902 **MIMS, Wilbur F., Capt.**
"War History of the Prattville Dragoons compiled by Capt. Wilbur F. Mims, Co. H Third Alabama Cavalry. Prattville, Ala., Autauga County 1861-1865." Thurber, Texas: Journal Printery (n.d.) $100, 12mo, wraps, 15, (1)pp., (20cm).
...Reprint, n.p., n.d., green stiff wraps, 21cm. (1950s?)

902a **MINES, John F.**
"Life in a Richmond Prison." In: SHSP, 1882. v.X, p.333-4.

903 **MINNICH, J.W. of Grand Isle, La.**
"Inside of Rock Island Prison, from Dec. 1863-June 1865." Suppl. with a sketch. Nashville, Tenn., Methodist Episcopal Church, South, 1908, 12mo, wraps, port(front), view of prison, 59pp. Includes Mrs. K.E. Perry-Mosher history, p. 41-59.

904 ..."The Sixth Georgia Cavalry." In: C.V., April 1918, v.XXVI, p. 156-157.

905 ..."The Cavalry at Knoxville." In: CV, Jan. 1924, v.XXXII. p. 10-13. Longstreet's tactics in Knoxville campaign in 1863.

906 ..."Incidents in the Peninsula Campaign." In: CV, Feb. 1922, v.XXX, p. 53-56.

907 **MINNINGERODE, Charles, Rev.**
"Jefferson Davis. A Memorial address delivered in St. Paul's Church, Richmond, Va., Dec. 11, 1889." (McElroy biblio) Richmond, Va., Baughman Bros., 1890, 8vo, wraps, 20pp.

908 ..."Jefferson Davis Not a Traitor." Winchester, Va., Geo. F. Norton, 1904, 8vo, wraps, 15pp. (McElroy bibliog.)

909 ..."Jefferson Davis and the Southern People were not traitors, nor rebels. They were patriots who loved the Constitution and obeyed the laws made for the protection of all American citizens...A short story of the Confederate soldier, the ideal soldier of the world." Manassas, Va., Manassas Democratic Press, 1911, wraps, 8vo, 48pp. (McElroy bibliog).

910 ..."Three Stories in One: "The Statesman"; "The Confederate Soldier, the Ideal Soldier of the World"; "The South's Peerless Women of the World." (McElroy bibliog.) Pamphlet, privately printed, 1915, p.65.

911 **MINOGUE, Anna Catherine**
"Cardone; a Romance of Kentucky." N.Y., P.F. Collier, 1904. 12mo, cl,306p., fiction. Service of Hal Todd & H. Clay Powell with Morgan, escapes from Columbus, Ohio.

912 **MINOR, Benjamin Blake**
"Jeb Stuart." In: SHSP, 1908, v.36, p.267-270.

913 ..."Judge William Brockenbrough." In: SHSP, 1899, v.27, p.350-365.

914 **MINOR, Berkeley**
"Lincoln. For the Spectator: Staunton, Va.

March 19, 1909, caption title, signed Berkeley Minor, sometime private in Rockbridge Artillery Stonewall Brigade, 8vo, wraps (4)p. folder. Monaghan (1820) states a variant in text at Lincoln Nat'l. Life (Ft. Wayne).

915 ..."If Lee Could Have Stood at the Helm." caption title, from "Times Dispatch" Jan. 15, 1911, 8vo, (4)pp. folder, n.p., (Richmond?) $4.00.
..."The South & the Union." In: SHSP, 1902, v.30, p.332-338.

916 **MINOR, Charles Landon Carter**
"The Real Lincoln..., with article by Lyon G. Tyler. Edt: Kate Mason Rowland author of "Life of George Mason, etc." Richmond, Va., Everett Waddey, 1901, 12mo, wraps, 66pp. Shows Lincoln forced war, north against emancipation. Monaghan-1351.

917 ..."The Real Lincoln from the testimony of his contemporaries. 2nd Edt. revised & enlarged." Richmond, Va., Everett Waddey Co., 1904, 16mo, cl, front(port) 230pp.
...(Prospectus, & comments by historians) "Ready Feb. 20 Fourth Edt., revised & enlarged of the Real Lincoln from the testimony of his contemporaries by...(Edt. M.D. Carter). Startling but little known facts about the life & administration of the great Civil War President . From your book dealer or from the publishers Atkins-Rankin Co., Gastonia, N.C., 12mo, (8)p. double folder.
..."The Real Lincoln from the testimony of his contemporaries." 4th Edt: revised, enlarged Edt: M.D. Carter., Gastonia, NC, Atkins-Rankin Co., 1928, 8vo, cl, 273pp.
..."The Old System of Slavery, compensations & contrasts with present labor conditions." In: SHSP, 1902, v.30, p.125-9.
..."President Lincoln, his character & opinions discussed." In: SHSP, 1899, v.27, p.165-70, 365-71.

918 **MINOR, H.A.**
"Surrender of Mahone's division." In: CV, July 1914, v.XXII, p.312-313. Surrender: Mahone's Div., ANV, Appomattox.

919 **MINOR, Hubbard Taylor**
"I am getting a good education" In: CWTI, March 1975, v.13, #7, p.24-32, illus., ports; April, #8, p.24-36, illus., dble.-pg., ports. From an unpublished diary by a cadet in the CS Navy Academy.

919a **MINOR, John Brokenbrough**
"Lee's Birthday." In: SHSP, 1889, v. XVII, p.356.

920 **MINOR, Kate Pleasants, Mrs.**
"An Author and Subject Index to the Southern Historical Society Papers, Vols. 1-38. Compiled by Mrs. Kate Pleasants Minor, Reference Librarian, under the direction of Earl G. Swem, Assistant Librarian." Richmond: Davis Bottom, 1913. Virginia State Library Bulletin, July, October Vol. 6, Nos. 3,4, 8vo, wraps, 139pp. $35.00.

921 ..."Dayton, Ohio, Morningside Press (1970), facs., #2, 500 copies. See: James I. Robertson, Jr. Index Guide bmk 20-.

922 ..."From Dixie Original articles contributed by Southern writers for publication as a Souvenir of the Memorial Bazaar for the benefit of the Monument to the Private Soldiers & Sailors of the Confederacy and the establishment of the Museum for Confederate Relics, with heretofore unpublished poems, by some who have "crossed over the river." Richmond, Va., West Johnston & Co, 1893, cl, 12mo, 167pp. 30-bmk-96.

923 ..."Minor (Kate Pleasants & Susie B. Harrison.) "A list of newspapers in the Virginia State Library, Confederate Museum and Valentine Museum." Under Dir. of Earl G. Swem. Richmond, Va., Virginia State Library. Bul. V, #4, p. (6), 285-425 $20.00.

923a **MINOR, Robert Dabney**
"Plan to rescue Johnson's Island prisoners." In: SHSP, 1895, v.23, p.283-90. ..."Some notes on the Confederate Navy." In: SHSP, 1900, v.28, p.305-7.

923b **MINTER, Winfred P.**
"Confederate Military Supply Policy." In: Social Science, June 1959. v.34, #3, p.163-71.

924 **MINUTES of the Annual Convention, Florida Division**
United Daughters of the Confederacy, (1st) 1896-19-- (St. Augustine, etc., 1897-19.), 12mo, 8vo, wraps; titles vary: (1896) Formation of Florida division United Daughters of the Confederacy, imprint from Daily Florida Citizen of July 15, 1896." 1897: Proceedings of the Florida State division. 1898-1904: Proceedings of the annual state conv.; 1905-1907: Proceedings of the annual state conv.; 1909: Minutes of the annual convention; 1901 was the 4th Annual; 1902-the 7th annual.

925 **MINUTES of the Annual Convention, Georgia Division**
United Daughters of the Confederacy. Rome, Ga., 1890-1919, 8vo, wraps, fldg. table, cover title: "1918-"Report of the years work (24th), Georgia Division United Daughters of the Confederacy; convention to have been held in Atlanta, Ga., Oct. 22/5, 1918, called off account of influenca epidemic varies titles for other years.

925a **MINUTES of the General Assembly**
of the Presbyterian Church in the Confederate States of America: with an appendix. Vol. 1, A.D. 1864." Columbia, S.C., Evans & Cogswell, 1864. 8vo, wraps, pp.239-342. Yates Snowden notes: 'Although ammounc'd as "Vol. 1," this exceeding rare Confederate

926 **MINUTES of the meeting-Society of Immortal 600**
Held annually in Mobile, Alabama, Apr. 26-28, 1910. (Mobile, Ala., Manassas Democrat Press, 1910) wraps, 8vo, cover title, 34pp., Roll of survivors, Shetler #725.

926a **MINUTES of the Proceedings**
Greenville Ladies Ass'n (S.C.) . . .
See under Jas. W. Patton.

927 **MINUTES of the Proceedings of the Reunion, of the Hampton Legion Survivors**
Held in Columbia, SC, on the 21st day of July, 1875, Charleston, SC, Walker, Evans & Cogswell, 1875, 8vo, stiff wraps, 47pp., almost entirely addresses: Gen. Wade Hampton, T.M. Logan & M.W. Gary.

928 **MINUTES of the Proceedings of Ass'n. Survivors**
Of Ross', Ector's, Grandberry Brigades, U.C.V., held at Garland, Texas, Oct. 8 and 9, 1899." $37.50. Orig. wraps, 29pp., incl. report and roster, last campaigns Ross' Texas cavalry, by L.S. Ross, at Corinth, Miss., Jan. 12, 1865, Sulphur Springs, Tex: McDaniel Print. See: United Confederate Veterans, Tex. "Minutes of the 46th Reunion-First Texas Div., etc.

928a **"MINUTES of the Third Annual Meeting**
& Reunion of the Unified Confederate Veterans, April 8 & 9, 1892." New Orleans, La., 1892. 8vo, cl, 172pp. $20.

929 **MINUTES, U.C.V. Camp 941**
Wilson County, Tennessee, 1897-1928. Compiled, edited by Thomas E. Partlow. Baltimore: Gateway Print, 1975, 8vo, wraps, 181pp. index.

930 **MISCELLANEOUS Correspondence**
And orders of the Adjutant and inspector general's office, and correspondence of the quartermaster general's ordanance, and engineer bureaus, of the Confederate states, 1861. Washington, DC, 1876., 8vo, cl, xxx, 278pp. See: Special Orders, Adj. and Insp. Gen.

930a **"MISSING RECORDS**
of the Confederate Cabinet Apr. 1, 1861-Mar. 24, 1865. Embracing legal history of the Southern Confederacy from adoption of its constitution to close, CW Officially written by attys. Gens., Judah P. Benjamin, Wade Keyes, Jr., Thomas Bragg, Thomas H. Watts & Geo. Davis." Verso front wrap, F.G. deFontain's "Army Letters." 1896.
See: Ga. Hist. Quar., v.II, June 1918, p.74, note.

931 **MISSION of South Carolina to Virginia**
Baltimore (1860) see Chs. G. Memmeminger. Touching the subject of Southern wrongs and the proper remedy for them.

932 **MISSIONARY RIDGE**
"Descriptive catalogue of the Cyclorama: Storming of Missionary Ridge and Battle above the Clouds." Atlanta, Ga., Paul M. Atkinson, Mgr. Atlanta, Ga., J.A. McCown Print, 1891, 12mo, wraps, 15, (1)p. 4, lf. ads in back.

932a **MISSIONARY RIDGE, Battle of . . .**
See: Braxton Bragg, Irving Ashley Buck.

933 **MISSISSIPPI Centennial Commission**
War Between the States, to honor our Confederate Heroes, to tell the true story of Mississippi's role in the conflict, to dramatize the great ideals that are a basis of our freedom and tradition." (Jackson, Miss.) Commission on War between the States, 8vo, wraps-colored, 48pp.

MISSISSIPPI Civil War & Ante-bellum Historical Sites
And points of interest. (Jackson, Miss., 1962) Mississippi CW Centennial Commission, 8vo, wraps, illus., maps, 37pp., dbl. fld. map, color illus.

933a **"MISSISSIPPI Convention of May 1861.**
The People of Mississippi in Convention assembled do declare & ordain as follows . . ." (collecting taxes for military funds for defense of State & military purposes, loans by Gov., etc.). folio, 2pp. $75.

934 **MISSISSIPPI in the War between the States**
Booklet of facts for Information of Mississippi in Connection with Observance of the Civil War Centennial 1961-1965." (Jackson, Miss.) C.W. Centennial on War between States 4to, wraps, 36pp. (OP).

935 **MISSISSIPPI Historical Society**
"Publications of the Mississippi Historical Society..." v.1-14, Oxford, Miss., etc., The Society, 1898, 1914, Tk., 8vo, cl, illus., pls., ports, maps (part fldg.) facsms., bmk $25-$30 ea.

936 ...Publications, centenary series, v.1, Jackson, Miss., The Society, 1916, v.2, 1918, v.3, 1920; v.IV, 1921., vol. I, II, III, 35.

937 **"MISSISSIPPI EXTRA**
(Caption title above CSA Flag & Firing Cannon) Monday, April 7, 1862-12M...VICTORY! VICTORY! Broadside 12 3/4 x 4", Jackson, Miss., 1862. Unrecorded. Goodspeed-601 $650.00 News from first day at Shiloh. Enemy routed, driven into Tenn. River, Sidney Johnson (sic) killed.

938 **MISSISSIPPI IN THE WAR**
McLemore (Richard Aubrey) Edt: A History of Mississippi, vol. 1, See under authors: Glover Moore, Edwin C. Bearss, John K. Bettersworth, William C. Harris.

939 **MISSISSIPPI: LAWS**
"Laws of the State of Mississippi passed at a called session-held in Jackson, Nov., 1860." Jackson, Miss., E. Barksdale (1860), 8vo, wraps, 48pp., considers relations between U.S. & Miss., declares secession a proper action for the southern states.

939a **MISSISSIPPI**
See: W. Adams, A. F. Brown, Confederate Dead (Miss.), James Dinkins, S.W. Ferguson, Thomas M. Folkes, Dabney H. Maury.

940 **"MISSOURI ARMY ARGUS, THE"**
A 4pp., 3 column Confederate paper, printed by Wm. F. Wiseley, edited: Joseph W. Tucker "Deacon Tucker", a Southern Methodist minister, edited Missouri State Journal St. Louis, but imprisoned after criticism of Federal gov., escaped to join Gen. Price's army. With state money printed: Neosho, Mo., Oct. 28, 1861, vol. 1-#1 contained proceedings of "Rebel Legislature"; Cassville, Mo., Nov. 6, 1861, #2; Greenfield, Dade Co., Nov. 22, 1861, #3-& Sterling Price's address to army, his proclamation to people of Central & North Missouri, corresp. on exchange prisoners, acts of Leg., & poem by Albert G. Pike. (The #3 issue owned by State Hist. Society the only know copy, no others known.) North Missouri, Dec. 18, 1861, #4; Camp Des Arc, Apr. 14, 1862 on sheet foolscap size; last number at Camp Churchill Clark, near Corinth, Ark. (From: Mo. Hist. Rev., v.IV, #4, p.291.)

941 ..."A Missouri Confederate in the Civil War, the Journal of Henry Martyn Cheavens, 1862-1863." Edt: James E. Moss. (Columbia, Mo., Mo. Hist. Review, Oct. 1962, v.XVII, #1, p. 16-52, illus., port.

942 **"MISSOURI CONFEDERATE**
Souvenir Program - 'Battle of Wilson's Creek', 7th Anniversary, August 10, 1938." Springfield, Mo., n.d., 8vo, pict. wraps, 36pp.

943 **MISSOURI EX-CONFEDERATE PENSIONERS**
"Missouri Adj-Gen. Biennial Report, Jefferson City, 1915, 8vo, wraps, Contains the names of all ex-Confederate pensioners enrolled under the act approved Apr. 23, 1913 and those deceased since enrollment. MISSOURI: Annual Report of the Adj.-General (Confederate) (G.A. Parsons) Jan. 18, 1861. In: Appendix to the Journal of the House of Representatives of the State of Missouri at the First Session of the Twenty-first General Assembly." Jefferson City, Mo., 1861, 8vo, sewn, p. (645)-657.

944 **"MISSOURI TROOPS**
In Service During the Civil War. Letter from the Secretary of War in Response to the Senate's Resolution passed on June 14, 1902, transmitting a paper prepared by the chief of Record and pension office of the War Department, showing various classes of Missouri volunteers, militia, and home guards in service during the civil war, and the laws, etc., under which they were raised; also what classes of such are recognized by the War Dept., as being in the military service of the US, what classes are not recognized, June 18, 1902. Laid on the table and ordered to be printed." Washington: GPO, 1902, 8vo, cl, 335, (1)pp. (57th Congr., 1st Session, Senate Doc. #412. CSA: "Introductory Remarks" p.239. "Missouri Volunteers, Confederate Service, p.283-319; "Lists of Confederate Organizations', p.327-336. See: Arthur Roy Kirkpatrick's Missouri's Secessionist Government, 1861-1865." In: MHR, Jan. 1951, p. 124-137.

...Missouri Historical Review, Jan. 1908, v.II, #2. The war department compiled a complete roster of Confederate soldiers of Missouri and Capt. James W. Allen sent 3,000 documents from which the lists were made.

...Organization and Status of Missouri Troops (Union and Confederate) in Service during the Civil War." Washington: Gov. Print. Off., 1902, 8vo, wraps, 242pp.

945 **MISSOURI-KANSAS STRUGGLE**
James M. Breckenridge, Bibliography, MISSOURI:
Anderson (Ephraim McD.); Bevier, (Robt.S.); Bradley,(James)

Breihan, (Carl W.); Brownlee, (Rich.S.)
Edwards, (Jno. N.); Hildebrand, (Sam'l. S.)
Holcombe, (Return I.); Leftwich, (Wm. M.)
Maddox, (Geo. T.); McElroy, (Jno.)
"Missouri Troops in War"
Monaghan, (Jas.); Monks, (Wm.)
Mudd, (Joseph A.); Parrish, (Wm. E.)
Peterson, (Cyrus A.); Reminisc. Women of Mo.
Ryle., (Walter H.); Schrantz, (Ward L.)
Smith, (Edward C.); Snead, (Thos. L.)
Tunnard, (Wm. H.); Woodruff, (Wm. E.)

946 **MISSOURI ,**
"Journal of the Senate, Extra Session of the Rebel Legislature called together by a Proclamation of C.F. Jackson, begun and held at Neosho, Newton County, Missouri, on the twenty-first of October, 1861." Jefferson City: Emory S. Foster, Public Press 1865. 8vo, wraps, cover title, 45pp. $45.00. Sabin 49602, lists: n.p., n.d. $100.00. See also: Arthur Roy Kirkpatrick's "Mo. Secessionist Government." These proceedings captured by the 49th. Missouri Vols. in Alabama and printed. A certain sect. of Mo. seceded from Union.

947 MISSOURI: Ray County. "History of Ray County, Missouri."
St. Louis: 1881. Missouri Hist. Co., 4to, 818pp. front, ports., Civil War and lists of Union and CSA soldiers, p.281-324.
..."Civil War in Missouri." Civil War Centennial Comm., 196? Missouri Historical Society, 16pp.
See: Sterling Price, Lawrence S. Ross.

948 **MISSOURI: Governor Claiborne Fox Jackson**
"Inaugural Address Jan. 2, 1861." In: Journal of House of Representatives at 1st Session of the 21st General Assembly." Jefferson City, Mo., 1861, 8vo, sewn, p.45-53.
...Do: Message Jan. 18, 1861. p.113-114.
...Do: Message Jan. 29, 1861. p.153-159.
...Do: Message Feb. 16, 1861. p. 326. Calls out the Militia.
...Do: "Special Message. Mar. 7, 1861. p.755-762.
...Do: Message May 3, 1861. p. 13-16.
...Do: Message May 3, 1861. p.7-10.

949 ..."Message of R.M. Stewart, Jan. 3, 1861. p. 20-44. Jackson, a native Virginian, moved to Missouri and in Mo. legislature 1836-1848, speaker of House, member state convention, senator 1848-1849. Helped found banking system. Elect3ed Gov., 1860. After SC seceded, declared a secessionist but fails with legislature. Confrontation with Federals at St. Louis and later withdraws to become a Brig.Gen. in CSA until death Dec. 1862.

949a **MITCHAM, Samuel W., Jr.**
"Fort Beauregard, Louisiana: Confederate Stronghold on the Ouachita." In: La. H/1981, v.22, p.183-7.

950 **MITCHEL, Cora**
"Reminiscences of the Civil War." Providence (R.I.?) Snow & Farnham, 1916?, 16mo, wraps, 43pp., war-time experiences in Apalachicola, Fla., & Columbia, Ga., daughter of Thos. Leeds Mitchel of Conn., cotton merchant.

951 **MITCHELL, A.L., Mrs., Comp.**
"Songs of the Confederacy & Plantation Melodies" Cincinnati, Oh., 1901, 8vo, wraps, 46pp. bmk-106 $30.00.

952 **MITCHELL, Adele**
"Jackson's engineer Capt. James K. Boswell" In: CWTI, June 1968, v.VII, #3, p.12-17, pl, port.

MITCHELL, Betty L.
"Superflous lags the veteran on stage", the death of Confederate Edmund Ruffin." in: Va., Caval., Winter 1983, v.32, #3, p.126-133., views, ports, facsms.

953 **MITCHELL, Broadus**
"William Gregg (1800-1867) factory master of the Old South." (note: dividends in gold during war) Chapel Hill: University Press of N.C., 1928, 8vo,cl, port, pl, facsm., xi, 331pp.

954 **MITCHELL, Enoch L.**
"Nathan Bedford Forrest accepts counsel." In: Tenn. HQ, 1963, v.22, p.382-383.

955 ..."The roll of Gen. George Washington Gordon in the Ku Klux Klan." In: W. Tenn. HSP., 1947, v.1, p.73-80.

956 **MITCHELL, Frances Letcher**
"Georgia Land and People." Atlanta, Ga., (Franklin Press, 1900) 12mo, cl, xxvii, 495pp. $50.00.
...Spartanburg, SC, Reprint Co., 1974, More than a third on CSA. $18.00.

956a **MITCHELL, George E.**
"The Brunswick Guards - a Roll of the Officers & Privates - a List of the Dead." In: SHSP, 1903, v.31, p.120-4.
See: Richmond Dispatch.

957 **MITCHELL, James Madison**
"A Confederate Soldier's Letter, Contributed and edited by George W. Clower." In: GaHQ, 1952, v.XXX, p.286-288. Biographical note, see: XV, p.293.

958 **MITCHELL, James Tyndale, Hon.**
An extraordinary collection of engraved portraits and views relating to the civil war in America belonging to the..." Phila: Stan V. Henkels, Samuel T. Freeman auction cat.#944, part ix, Nov. 4, 1910, 8vo, wraps, color flags of US & CSA, 46pp. $25.00.

959 **MITCHELL, James and Sara**
"Civil War Letters from James Mitchell to his wife, Sarah Elizabeth Latta Mitchell, Edt. by Frances Mitchell Ross." In: AHQ, Winter 1978, v.XXXVII, #4, p.306-317, ports.

960 **MITCHELL, John Broadus**
"Exchange of Civil War Prisoners." In: CV, July 1911, v.XIX, p.340-343.

MITCHELL, John C.
See: Claudine Rhett.

960a **MITCHELL, John K.**
"Operations of Confederate States Navy." In: SHSP, 1876, v.II, p.240-4.

961 **MITCHELL, Joseph B., Lt.Col.**
"Decisive Battles of the Civil War." N.Y., G.P. Putnam's Sons, 1955, 8vo, cl, dj, maps, bibliog., 226pp., Lee, Jackson & Forrest treated well here. Pro-south throughout.

961a ..."The Generalship of Robert E. Lee." In: CV (new) July/Aug. 1986, v.34, #4, p.12-22, ills (color), maps, facsm, ports.

962 **MITCHELL, Kirkwood**
"Lee and the Bullet of the Civil War." In: Wm. and Mary Quart., 2nd Ser., 1936, v.XVI, p.26-37. A reply to Liddell Hart's "Why Lee Lost at Gettysburg." (Sat. Rev. Lit., Mar. 23, 1935. A review of Freeman's 'Lee.'

962a **MITCHELL, Laurence M.**
"The Engagement at Blackburn's Ford." In: Fairfax Co. Hist. Bul. 1969, v.X, p.59-91.
See: Jubal Early's 'Blackburn's Ford.'

963 **MITCHELL, Leon, Jr.**
"Camp Ford Confederate Military Prison." In: SWHQ, July 1962, v.LXVI, #1, p. 1-16, facsm., map.

964 ..."Camp Groce Confederate Military Prison." In: SWHQ, July, 1963, v.LXVII, #1, p.15-21.

965 **MITCHELL, Margaret**
Special, In: AHJ, winter 1985, v.29, #4, p.4-60.

966 ..."Margaret Mitchell Memorial Issue" Atlanta Historical Bulletin, May 1950, illus., 8vo, wraps, 150pp. bmk-$20.00.
..."Gone With the Wind." N.Y., 1936, (1037p.) first edition, first issue with dust jacket, mint copy (Jk-169) $750.00.
..."Gone With the Wind." N.Y., The Macmillan Co., 1936, Tk., 8vo, cl, 4, 3-1087pp.

Published June 1936. 1st Edt. 500-ds, 600-u.

...1st issue with slip, "Compliments of the Author.", May, 1936. 1,250-jk.

...1939, the first two-volume edition issued Dec. 1, 1939, limited to 1,000 copies."

...1939, The Motion Picture edition 8vo, cl, colored pls., 4,391 pp.

..."Borte med blaesten, paa dansk ved Erik Friesleben." Kobenhavn, S. Hasselbalch, 1937, 8vo, cl, front, pls., map, 1070pp.

..."Tatt av vinden, oversatt av Ben Horne og Charles Kent." Oslo, H. Aschehoug Co., (W. Nygaard) 1937, 12mo, in 3 vols.

..."Vom winde verweht (Gone With the Wind) roman." Hamburg, Leipzig, H. Goverts, 1937, 8vo, cl, 1007 (1)pp.

..."Deutsch von Martin Beheim-Schwarzbach."

..."(N.Y. 1939) "Gone With the Wind" booklet sold in theatres, on its first run. Review of actors. Edt: Howard Dietz, 4to, pict. wraps, 18pp. color and b/w. $25.00-jk.

...N.Y., Macmillan, 1975 "75th Anniversary Edition," $15.00; a 2 vol. Deluxe boxed, 1 2 vol. large-print edt. $15.00, Garden City, N.Y., International Collectors Library (1968), 8vo, cl, 733pp.

...N.Y., Heritage Press (1968), Intro: Henry Steele Commager, illus.: John Groth, 4to, boxed, illus., port(color), 593pp.

...N.Y., Limited Editions Club, 1968, 4to, deluxe slipcase, 2 vols., illus., port(color).

...N.Y., MacMillan Co. (1968, c.1964), 8vo, tk cl, 1037pp.

967 **MITCHELL, Martha Carolyn**
"Health and the Medical Profession in the Lower South, 1845-1860." (Baton Rouge, La.) JSH, Nov., 1944, #4, p. 424-446.

968 **MITCHELL, Mary**
"Divided Town." Barre, Mass., Barre Pub., 1968, 8vo, cl, dj, x, 193pp., illus., ports, maps, Georgetown, DC, largely Southern, war experiences there.

969 **MITCHELL, Mary H.**
"Hollywood Cemetery: The History of a Southern Shrine." Richmond: State Library, 1985, 8vo, cl, xvi, 194p., color plates, black/white, (66)plates, some color, $25.00
See: Burial of Confederate Dead.

970 **MITCHELL, Memory F.**
"Legal Aspects of Conscription & Exemption in North Carolina, 1861-1865." Chapel Hill: University of North Carolina Press, 1965. Cl, 8vo, d/w, James Sprunt studies in Hist. and political science, p. 103 bmk-84.

971 **MITCHELL, Peggy**
"Georgia Generals for Stone Mountain Memorial (accounts of John Brown Gordon, Pierce Butler, Young Thos. R.R. cobb, Ambrose R. Wright, Henry Lewis Benning." In: Atl. Hist. Soc. Bul. May, 1950, v.9, #34.

..."Georgia Generals for Stone Mountain Memorial." In: Atlanta Hist. Bul. #34 (May 1950), p. 67-99. Reprint from Atlanta Journal Sunday Mag. Nov. 29-Dec. 13, 1925. Generals: J.B. Gordon, Pierce M. Butler, Thos. R.R. Cobb, Henry Benning and Ambrose R. Wright. Dorn-II, 32. Author: Margaret Mitchell Marsh.

972 **MITCHELL, Tandy Key, Sr., Dr.**
"Autobiography of...Lawrenceville, Gwinnett County, Georgia, Nov. 25, 1912." Atlanta, Ga., 1914. Priv. Print. 8vo, wraps, 2-ports, 15pp. Brief acct., service with 24th Reg. Ga. Inf.

973 **MITCHELL, W.A., Mrs.**
"The Confederate Mail Carrier." In: CV, Dec. 1914, v.XXII, p.549-551. Re: Absalom's (Grimes) carrying mail from camps to homes in Mo. & Ky. troops.

973a **MITCHELL, W. H., Rev.**
"Letters of Rev. W. H. Mitchell, Jan. 1861.

Edt: Virginia K. Jones." In: AHQ, 1961, v.23, #1 & 2, p.180-8.

974 **MITCHELL, William H.**
"Muster Roll Company A, 38th Georgia Regiment." (Dunwoody, Ga., 1920)8vo, wraps, cover title, (4)pp.

975 **"MIXED COMMISSION**
On American & British Claims. Wood, George J. & Heyworth, J. and Lawrence vs. United States...No. 103; Caroline Gravely vs. United States. No. 292. Depositions for defence. (Washington: Judd & Detweiler, 1872, 8vo, cl, 392pp. marbled boards, 3/4 Lt., bmk-$40.00- Depredation of Sherman's Troops in S.C., Columbia, burning of cotton belonging to England. See "Burning of Columbia."
...Washington, D.C., 1872?. 8vo, cl, 329pp. Bmk-$50. Sherman's depredations in Ga. & S.C., with American and British claims resulting. Burning of Columbia, etc.
See: "Who Burnt Columbia?"

MIXSON, Frank M.
"Reminiscences of a Private. By Frank M. Mixson, Company E", 1st SC Vols. (Hagood's) Jenkin's Brigade 1861. Lee's Army 1865. Columbia, SC, The State Co., 1910, 12mo, ports, 130pp. 275-bmk, 200-bmk, 350-013.
..."Louisv. Lost Cause Press, Micro-cd. $3.17.

975a **MOBERLY, T. E.**
"Robert E. Lee. The estimate of the Southern leader by a Canadian." In: SHSP, 1889, v.17, pp.373-6.

MOBILE BAY, Battle of ...
See: Franklin Buchannan, James D. Johnston.

MOBILE IN 1861-1865:
Companion volumes (3) see under the author's (editor's) name: Sidney Adair Smith; C. Carter Smith, Jr. "Two Naval Journals"; Thad Holt, Jr., "Miss. Waring's Journal".

976 **MOBILE, ALABAMA**
"The Explosion of the US Magazine at Mobile, May 25, 1865." Drawn by J.S. Young, an eyewitness." Madison, Eisc., S.W. Martin, N.D., Colored lithograph, 10x16 1/4" lithographed by L. Lipman, Milwaukee. $135.00. An unrecorded print. An indemnity was made to US Gov., by Mobile for carelessly handled ammunition.

976a **MOBILE REGISTER**
"The Gallant Pelham." In: SHSP, 1902, v.30, p.338-45.

MOBILE, Seige of ...
See: Dabney H. Maury.

976b **MOBLEY, Joe A.**
"The Siege of Mobile, August, 1864-April 1865.: In: AHQ, 1976, v.38, #4, p.250-70.

977 **MOBLEY, Margery Magruder**
"Prairie Grove Remembered." In: 'Flash Back', Wash. Co. Hist. Soc., Fayetteville, Ark., v.25, #2, 1975, p. 1-15, ports, pl, from Noble L. Prentis' 'Kansas Miscellany.'

977a **MOCKLER, William E.**
"The Source of "Ku Klux." In: Names, March 1955, v.III, p.14-18. Derivation of KKK.

978 **MOEHRING, Eugene P.**
See: "The Charleston Mercury and N.Y. Times."

979 **MOFFAT, Charles H.**
"Conflicting Interpretations as to the Causes of the Civil War." In. W.Va., H., Oct, 1961, v.23, #1, p.5-14.

979a **MOFFATT, Josiah**
"The Yomanry of Dixie." In: So. Atl. Quart., 1937, v.XXXVI, p.85-95. Type of men who make up rank & file of the CSArmy during the war.

980 **MOFFETT, George H.**
"The Jones Raid through West Virginia." In: CV, October 1905, v.13, p.449-451. The 11th Virginia Cavalry.

..."Battle of Brandy Station." In: CV, Feb. 1906, v.XIV, p.74-75.

..."War Prison Experiences." In: CV, 1905, v.13, p.105-110.

981 **MOFFETT, W.L.**
"The Last Charge of the 14th Virginia Cavalry at Appomattox Courthouse, Apr. 9, 1865." In: SHSP, 1908, v.36, p.13-16.

982 **MOFFITT, E.E., Mrs., Comp.**
"Biographical Sketches: Captain Edmund Jones, compiled & edited by Mrs. E.E. Moffitt." In: N.C. Booklet, October 1916, v.XVI, #2, p.103-105.

983 **MOGER, Allen W.**
"General Lee's Unwritten History of the A.N.V." In: VMHB, July 1963, v.71, #3, p. 341-363.

"The Value of a Portrait." In:CWH, December 1957, v.III, #4, p.435-437. John Marshall portrait given Wash. College for tuition of his grandson.

984 **MOHR, Clarence L.**
"On the Threshold of Freedom: Masters & Slaves in Civil War Georgia." Athens: University of Georgia Press, 1986, 8vo, cl, dj, 296p., illus., index. $35.00.

985 **MOLEN, Dayle H.**
"Decision at La Glorieta Pass." In: Montana, Spring, 1962. p.20-32, fascms., illus., maps, ports.

"Decision at La Glorieta Pass." In: Mont. MWH, v.XII, p.20-33. Apr. 1962.

986 **MOLINEAUX, Emily E.**
"Lifetime Recollections." San Francisco, Cal., C.W. Gordon Print., 1902, 8vo, cl, 98pp. $60.00-Jk117. Life in Southern states before & during the War, incidents in the bombardment of Atlanta, Ga.

987 **MONAGHAN, Jay**
"Civil War on the Western Border, 1854-1865." Boston, Little, Brown Co., 1955, 8vo, cl, d/w, x, 454pp., index. Believes Civil War began with Kansas struggle; Indians, guerillas, politics. N.Y. Bonanza (1975?) Reprint.

988 ..."Swamp Fox of the Confederacy. The Life & Military Services of M. Jeff Thompson." Tuscaloosa, Ala., Confederate Pub. Co., 1956, 12mo, stiff wraps, 123pp., Lim. Edt. 450 copies. Confederate Centennial Studies, #2. $40.00-B.

989 **MONCURE, Eustace Conway**
"Reminiscences of the Civil War, by Judge E.C. Moncure of Carolina County, Va." n.p., (1914?), 12mo, wraps, 31pp. $100.00. Two known copies.

...Richmond, Va., Virginia State Library, Bul.#2/3, v.XVI, July 1927.

See: W.W. Scott, Edt., reprint, p.49-76.

990 **MONETT, Howard N.**
"The Origin of the Confederate Invasion of Missouri, 1864." In: BHMS, 1961, v.XVIII, p.37-48.

991 ..."The Confederate advance to Lexington, 1864." In: BHMS, 1962-1963, v.XIX, p.260-272.

MONEY of the Confederate States...
See: Baumgartner, Julius B., "Charlotte Observer." Confederate Currency.

991a **MONEYHON, Carl H.**
"The Civil War in Phillips County, Arkansas." In: PhCHQ, June/Sept., 1981, v.19, p.18-36.

..."The Civil War & Social-economic in Jackson County, Arkansas." In: 'Stream of History,' Nov. 1979, v.18, p.21-6.

992 **MONITOR -**
"Who planned the Monitor? A letter from America." In: Black. Edn. Mag., June 1862, v.XCI, p.787-789. Claims plan was first published in Blackwood Edinburg Mag., Nov./Dec. 1860, viii, p.616-649. "Ironclad ships of war" in Dec., p.644 was three diagrams of the invention. Capt. Erricsson must have seen the article."

MONITOR (Ironclad), USNavy
See: H. B. Littlepage, Dabney H. Maury,

Wm. H. Parker, "Officers & Crew (Monitor)."

993 **"MONITOR AND THE MERRIMAC, THE"**
See: David R. Smith Bibliography---Nicholas J. Adts, Greville Bathe, H.B. Littlepage, John L. Porter, St. George T. Brooke, Anna Semmes Bryan, Mrs. A.A. Campbell, Raleigh E. Colston, Col. Baron de Suarce, Joe G. Fiveash, Ange S. Gautier, Lamar Hollyday, Catesby ap. R. Jones, L.J. La Faugheur, Chs. Lee Lewis, Charles H. McBlair, John W.H. Porter, Robt. L. Preston, H. Ashton Ramsey, J.F. Shipp, Arthur Sinclair, Elliot Snow, Lyon G. Tyler, 'Virginia-Merrimac' Henry L. Walker, John T. Wood.

994 **MONKS, William**
"A History of Southern Missouri & Northern Arkansas; being an account of the early settlements, the Civil War, the Ku Klux, & times of peace." West Plains, Mo., Journal Co., 1909, 12mo, cl, front, illus., ports., 247pp. Guerrillas & division between Union & CSA. Civil War, p.40-185.

995 **MONNETT, Howard N.**
"Action Before Westport 1864." Kansas City, Mo., Westport Historical Society, 1964. Paintings & maps by George Barnett. 8vo, cl, d/w, front, xxi, 190pp., illus., ports, page, maps. $30.00-Bmk84.

MONOCACY, Battle of
See: John Brown Gordon.

996 **MONROE, Haskell**
"Men without Law: Federal Raiding in Liberty County, Georgia." In: Ga.H.Q., June 1960, v.XLIV, #2, p.154-171. $10.00.

997 ..."South Carolinians & the Formation of the Presbyterian Church in the Confederate States of America." In: Jour. of Presby. Hist., 1964, v.XLII, p.219-243.

998 ..."Southern Presbyterian & the Secession Crisis." In: CWH, Dec. 1960, v.VI, #4, p.351-360.

..."Early Confederate Political Patronage." In: Ala. Rev., Jan. 1967, 17pp., v.XX, p.45-61. $7.00.

999 **MONSELL, Helen A.**
"Boy of Old Virginia, Robert E. Lee. Illustrations: Clotilde Embree Funk." Indianapolis, Bobbs-Merrell, 1937, 8vo, cl, map, 165pp., juvenile.

1000 ..."Young Stonewall, Tom Jackson. By Helen Albee Monsell, illustrated by Charles John." Indianapolis, Ind., Bobbs-Merrill Co., 1942, 12mo, cl, illus., vii, 1, 9-177pp. "Boyhood of famous Americans series." Juvenile. 1953 - $12.50.

1001 **MONTAGU, Robert, Lord**
"A Mirror in America." London, Saunders, Otley & Co., 1861, 12mo, cl, 108pp. Attacks North. Against British interests.

1002 **MONTAGUE, Ludwell Lee**
"Gloucester County, (Va.) in the Civil War." Gloucester, Va., De Hardit Press, 1965, 4to, wraps, ix, 97pp., ports, maps, incl. front. $15.00.

1003 **MONTEIRO, Aristides**
"War Reminiscences of the Surgeon..." Gathersburg, Md., Butternut Press, 1984. $25.00.

1004 ..."Was Reminiscences, by the Surgeon of Mosby's Command." Richmond, Va., Everett Waddey, 1890, 12mo, cl, (or wraps), front(port), vii, (9)-208pp. $250.00-OB. $150.00. Full Lt. $175.00.

1005 ...Richmond, Va., 1890 (printer's name omitted), 12mo, cl, viii, (9)-236, (1)errata notes errors remain in 2nd edt. Chaps. XXIII-XXV added: "Sketches of Prison Life by a Guerrilla." $100.00.
See: Dannette, G.L.

1006 **MONTEIRO, Margaret Kean**
"The presidential election of 1860 in Virginia." In: Richmond Coll. Hist. Pap., 1916, v.1, #2, p.222-258.

1007 **MONTFORT, Theodorick Winfield**
"Another letter from "The Rebel Lawyer Montfort. Edt: Richard M. McMurry." In: Ga.H.Q., June 1968, v.LII, #2, p.220-222.

1008 ..."Excerpts from letters of T.W. Montfort of Oglethorpe, Georgia, 1st Lieut. Co. K, 25th Reg. Georgia Vol. Infy." Wise Guards. In: Louise F. Hays' Hist. Macon Co., Ga., 1933, p.262-276.

1009 ..."Rebel Lawyer: The Letters of Lt. Theodorick W. Montfort, 1861-1862. Edt: Spencer Bidwell King, Jr." In: Ga.H.Q., Sept. 1964, v.XLVIII, #3, p.313-333. Pt.II, #4, p.451-471; Pt.III, Mar. 1965, #1, p.82-97; Pt.IV, #2, p.200-216; Pt.V, #3, p.324-334. $25.00.

1010 ..."Rebel Lawyer: Letters of Throdorick W. Montfort, 1861-1862. Edt: Spencer B. King, Jr." Athens, University of Ga., 1965, 8vo, wraps, IV, 84pp. $20.00-B.

1011 **"MONTGOMERY (Alabama)**
as the Confederate Capital: View of a New Nation. Edited with an Introductory Chapter by James P. Jones & William Warren Rogers." 8vo, wraps, 125pp., illus.(front), atg. copy. $10.00. Entire issue, Alabama Historical Quart., v.26, #1, Spring 1964. State Dept. Archives & History. Largely a compilation of reports printed in the Charleston, S.C. 'Courier'.
See: J.M. Falkner, H.A. Herbert, T.G. Jones, J.W.A. Sanford, B.H. Screws.

1012 **"MONTGOMERY Advertiser**
Confederate Centennial Edition, The." Feb. 19, 1961, folio, fine. $15.00.
..."Unveiling Confederate Monument at Montgomery, Alabama." In: SHSP, 1898, v.26, p.181-232.

1012a **MONTGOMERY COUNTY, Alabama**
In: CSA. In: AHQ, 1956, V.18, #1, as follows: 'Montgomery Rifles, Army of Alabama, 1861' (p.66-8), 'Montgomery True Blues,' (p.62-3), 'Capt. Rush Elmore's Company' (p.64-5), 'Capt. Troy's Company' (p,69-71), 'First White House of the Confederacy.'

1013 **"MONTGOMERY Greys Under Two Flags.**
Montgomery Greys retired corps, organized December 27, 1906. Constitution & Roster, Surrendered at Appomattox, 1865." Montgomery, Ala., Brown Print, 1907, 16mo, wraps, 47pp.

1014 ..."Montgomery Greys under two Flags. Montgomery greys retired corps. Organized Dec. 27, 1906. Constitution & roster. Montgomery, Ala., 1908, 16mo, wraps, 62pp., 2-col. pls., 4p. insert.

1014a **MONTGOMERY, Elizabeth R.**
"Poem to Defenders of Vicksburg." In: SHSP, 1893, v.21, p.205-6.

1015 **MONTGOMERY, Frank Alexander**
"Reminiscences of a Mississippian in Peace & War, by Frank A. Montgomery, Lieutenant Colonel First Mississippi Cavalry." Cincinnati, Robert Clarke Co., 1901, 8vo, decr. cl., ports, xv, 305pp. $100.00. $75.00-Bmk90.
...Louisv., Lost Cause Pr., micro-cd.

1016 **MONTGOMERY, Goode**
"Alleged Secession of Jones County." In: Pub. Miss.Hist.Soc., Oxford, Miss., 1904, v.VIII, p.(13)-22.
See: Alex. L. Bondurant.

1017 **MONTGOMERY, Horace**
"Howell Cobb's Confederate Career." Tuscaloosa, Ala., Confed. Pub. Co., 1959, Confederate Centennial Studies, #10, stiff covers, 12mo, 144pp., port. Lim. Edt. 450 copies. $30.00-B.

1018 ..."Johnny Cobb: Confederate Aristocrat." Athens, University of Georgia Pr., 1964, University of Georgia Monographs, #11, 12mo, stiff wraps, ports, viii, 104pp., Alexandria, Va., Durant Pr. 1981.

1019 ..."The Two Howell Cobbs: A Case of Mistaken Identity." Houston, Tex., JSH, Aug., 1962, v.XXVIII, #3, p.348-355.

1020 **MONTGOMERY, J.M.**
"Reminiscences of a cavalryman." In: Wash. Co. Hist. Soc. Papers, 1910-1915, p.171-204. Author's services in 1st Miss. Cavalry, 1861-1865 with exchange letters with Frank Armstrong (Gen.), Victor Montgomery on reminiscences. $20.00-Bmk. Jackson, Miss., 1954, Dept. Archives & Hist.

1021 **MONTGOMERY, Joseph E.**
"Commodore J.E. Montgomery." In: CV, 1902, v.10, p.416-417, port.

1022 ..."Death of Commodore Joseph E. Montgomery." In: Gulf Mag., 1902, v.1, p.154-156.

1023 **MONTGOMERY, Walter Alexander**
"Address & Poem, delivered at unveiling of monument to the Confederate dead of Warren County, N.C., Aug. 27, 1903." Raleigh, Edwards & Broughton, 1906, 8vo, wraps, 20pp. Thornton-8840.

1024 ..."Flags of the Confederacy." In: CV, May 1916, v.XXIV, p.196-198.

1025 ..."W.A. Montgomery's Record of the Raymond Fencibles." Edt: P.L. Rainwater, Jackson, Miss., Jour. Miss. Hist., April, 1944, v.VI, #2, p.113-118. Roster.

1026 ..."Memorial Address, May 26, 1940, Auspices of Albermarle Chapter UDC." Charlottesville, Va., 1940?, 8vo, wraps, 10pp. Thornton-8843.

1027 ..."Memorial Address on the Life & Character of Maj.-Gen. William D. Pender. Delivered before the Ladies' Memorial Ass'n., in Raleigh, May 10, 1894." Raleigh, N.C., News & Observer, May 15, 1894, Edwards & Proughton Print, 8vo, wraps, 27pp.

1028 ..."Relations between the Confederate States government & the government of North Carolina." (Raleigh?), N.C. State Literary & Historical Society Proceedings, XIV, p.35-55. $15.00.

1029 ..."The Days of old & the years that are past." by... 2nd Lt., Co. F, 12th N.C. Infty." n.p., n.d. (Charlottesville, Va., Priv. Pr., 1939?). 8vo, wraps, 67pp., facsm. Dornbusch-784. $100.00-OB. $65.00.

1030 ..."Appomattox & Return Home." by... 2nd Lt., Co. F., 12th N.C. Infty. Charlottesville, Va., Wm. A. Montgomery, Jr., 1937, 8vo, wraps, 13pp. reprint from Walter A. Clark's "Hist. of Several N.C. Regiments."

1031 **"MONTH with the "Rebels," A."**
In: Black. EDn. Mag., Dec. 1861, v.XC, p.755-767.

1032 **"MONTH'S VISIT, A**
To the Confederate Headquarters, by an English officer." In: Blackwoods, Jan., 1863, v.93, p.1-29.

1033 **"MONTH'S Visit to the Confederate Headquarters,**
by an English Officer, A." In: Blackwood's Edinburgh Magazine, Jan.-June 1863, p.29.

1034 **"MONTHLY Return**
of the Department of Northern Virginia, Commanded by Gen. Robert E. Lee, March 31, 1863." (Washington, DC, 1878), Broadside, 22 1/2 x 72cm.

1035 ..."Monthly return of the Army of Northern Virginia, commanded by Gen. Robert E. Lee, May 31, 1863." (Washington, DC, 1878), Broadside 23 1/2 x 70cm.

1035a **"MONUMENT to Confederates**
at Point Lookout." In: SHSP, 1910, v.38, p.431-5.

1036 **"MONUMENT to Our Women**
- Report of Committee of Atlanta Camp #159, Oct. 19, 1903." Confederate Woman's Monument Association - Georgia Confederate Veterans. Atlanta, Ga., Geo. W. Harrison, Franklin Print, 8vo, wraps, (4)pp.

1037 **MOODY, Claire N.**
"Battle of Pea Ridge or Elkhorn Tavern." Little Rock, Arkansas Valley Press, 1956,

8vo, wraps, illus., map, port., VII, 39pp. $12.50.

1038 **MOON, Anna Mary, Edt.**
"A Southern Woman in 1897, remembers the Civil War." ETHSP, 1949, v.21, p.111-115.
See: Adeline Deaderick.

1039 **MOON, William Arthur**
"Hist. Significance of Brown's Gap in the War Between the States." Waynesboro News-Virginian, reprint, Jan. 13-16, 1937. 8vo, wraps, 18pp. $12.00-Bmk.

1040 **MOONEY, C.P.J.**
"The Confederacy after July 4, 1863." Memphis, Tenn., Convention Division Business Men's Club, 1913, 8vo, wraps, 15pp.
Also: Confederate Veteran, XXII, Mar., p.113-116.

1041 **MOONEY, Sue F. Dromgoole, Mrs.**
"My Moving Tent." Nashville, Tenn., M.E. Church, South, 1903, 12mo, cl, ports(2), 300 pp. $35.00-Bmk. Several chapters on CSA, minutes of Gen. Assoc., chaplains & missionaries of Army of Tenn.

1042 **MOORE, A.H.**
"Heth's Division at Gettysburg." In: SB, 1884-1885, v.III, p.383-395.

1043 **MOORE, Albert Burton**
"Conscription & Conflict in the Confederacy." N.Y., The Macmillan Co., 1924, 8vo, cl, ix, 2, 367pp. $20.00-$25.00, $30.00. $50.00-ATG-Bmk.
...Same, 1963. $36.00-$40.00.
...N.Y., Hillary House, 1963.

1044 ...(University Alabama) Civil War Centennial Commission, 1965. "A New Nation, a War, a Young Hero, & a Surrender." 8vo, wraps, 49pp.

1045 ..."Prologue to the Great American Tragedy." University Alabama, Civil War Centennial Commission, 1964, 8vo, wraps, 15pp. "Each of these essays was published in a daily newspaper in Alabama, & revised for this publication."

1046 ...University Alabama, Civil War Centennial Comm., 1963, "Reasons for the national centennial celebration, commemorating the Civil War: its basic objectives & potential values." 8vo, wraps, 11pp.

1047 ..."History of Alabama & Her People." Chicago, N.Y., American Hist. Soc., 1927, tk8vo, cl, CSA section: 'Plantation Times', 'Slavery', 'Secession', 'Organization & preparation for war,' 'Four Years War,' p.413-562.

1048 **MOORE, Alison**
"The Louisiana Tigers or the Two Louisiana Brigades of the Army of Northern Virginia, 1861-1865." Baton Rouge, La., Ortlieb Pr., 1961, 8vo, cl, illus., ports, (3) 183pp.fldg. map. $75.00-B. $50.00-B.

1049 ..."Old Bob Wheat, High Private." Baton Rouge, La., Ortlieb Pr., 1957, 8vo, cl, port, 219pp.

1050 **MOORE, Andrew B.**
"A.B. Moore correspondence relating to Secession (Alabama)." In: Alabama Historical Quarterly, Spring 1961, vol. 23, #1 & 2, 27pp. Between Gill Shorter, I.W. Garrott, E.W. Pettus & S.D. Cabaniss. Ports.

1051 **MOORE, Avery C.**
"Destiny's Soldier (General Albert Sidney Johnston) The Thrilling story of one of the Confederacy's great leaders." San Francisco, Calif., Fearon Pub., 1958, 8vo, decr. color wraps, port, 197pp. $30.00. $8.00-Bmk.

1052 ..."Confederate California, by Avery C. Moore." Sonora, Calif., Mother Lode Press, 1956, 8vo, pict. wraps, port, 29pp. $16.00-Bmk.

1053 **MOORE, C. Moffett, Comp.**
"Nathan Bedford Forrest & the Civil War in Memphis. A Selective Bibliography of Books & Other References." Memphis,

Tenn., Memphis Public Library, 1961, 4to, illus., mimeographed, 42pp.

1054 **MOORE, Charrie Adair**
"William Penn Adair." In: Ch.Okl., Spring, 1951, v.XXIX, p.32-41. Adiar's relative writes of his Civil War activities in it.

1055 **MOORE, Claude Hunter**
"Thomas Overton Moore, a Confederate Governor." Clinton, N.C., Commercial Printing Co., 1960, 8vo, wraps, 78pp., port, plates. O.P. $30.00-B.

1056 **MOORE, E. Walton**
"Two Virginia citizens were considered for president Lincoln's cabinet, & one of them offered an appointment." In: TylerQHGM, 1932, v.XIV, p.1-7. Robert E. Scott of Fauquier Co., James Barbour of Culpeper Co., Scott to the Navy.

1057 **MOORE, Edward Alexander**
"The Story of a Cannonneer under Stonewall Jackson, in which is told the part taken by the Rockbridge Artillery in the Army of Northern Virginia by Edward A. Moore, of the Rockbridge Artillery. With introduction by Capt. Robert E. Lee, Jr., & Hon. Henry St. George Tucker. Fully illustrated by portraits." N.Y., Wash., Neale Pub. Co., 1907, 8vo, cl, facsm., illus., ports., incl. front, 315pp. $25.00, $40.00-$80.00.
...Lynchburg, Va.,J.P. Bell, 1910. Same, but 315pp. $200.00-Bmk105. $125.00.
...Louisv., Lost Cause Pr., micro-card, $5.10.
...N.Y. Arno's 'Select Bibliographies.' Reprint series, 1971. $20.00-Y.
...N.Y., Time-Life Series, 1983. 12mo, full leather, t.e.g., Civil War Collectors Library. $25.

1057a **MOORE, Edwin G., Co. A, 24th N.C. Reg.**
"Ransom's Brigade, gallant conduct in the Capture of Plymouth." (from Richmond Dispatch, Feb. 25, 1901). In: SHSP, 1908, v.36, p.363-67.

1058 **MOORE, Frank**
"Anecdotes, poetry & incidents of the War: North & South, 1860-1865." N.Y., Pub. Office, Bible House, 1867, 12mo, cl, front, port, 560pp. $20.00-Bmk.

1059 ..."The Civil War in Song & Story, 1860-1865. Collected & arrainged by Frank Moore." N.Y., P.F. Collier, 1889, 8vo, cl, 560pp., front port. Earlier editions, 1866-1867 issued as "Civil War in Song & Story."

1060 ...N.Y., Johnson reprint 'Rediscovering America Series', 1970. Reprint of the 1882 edition. Lib. Bnd. $35.00.

1061 ..."Rebel Rhymes & Rhapsodies, collected & edited by Frank Moore." N.Y., G.P. Putnam, 1864, 16mo, cl, xiv, 299pp. $16.00, $18.00, $20.00. Half roan $35.00.
..."Rebel Rhymes & Rhapsodies." (Confederate series). N.Y., Boling Green Sta., Gordon Pub. Co., 1976, Library binding. $60.
...Do: 1980, $35.

1062 ..."Songs & Ballads of the Southern People, 1861-1865. Collected & edited by Frank Moore." N.Y., D. Appleton & Co., 1886, 16mo, cl, 324pp.
...Reprint, N.Y., 1971. Burt Franklin Pr., Research & Source Works Ser 767.
...Reprint, N.Y., 1976. $35.00.

1063 **MOORE, George E.**
"A Banner in the Hills/West Virginia's Statehood." New York, Appleton-Century-Crofts, 1963, 8vo, cl, d/w, xii, 256pp., maps, pict. ends. Va. politics, secession, sectional controversy.

1064 ..."Slavery as a factor in thr formation of West Virginia, 1620-1865." In: W.Va. Hist., Oct. 1956, v.18, p.5-89, notes.

1065 **MOORE, Glover**
"William Jemison Mims, Soldier & Squire." Birmingham, Ala., Bmg. Print, 1966, 8vo, cl, front, xvi, 134pp. CSA, p.31-56.

1066 **MOORE, Guy Will**
"The Case of Mrs. Surratt: her controversial trial & execution for conspiracy in the Lincoln assassination." Norman, Univ. of Oklahoma, 1954, 8vo, cl, d/w, xi, 142, (2)pp. facsms, maps, ports. Her trial & activities of son.

1066a **MOORE, J.B.**
"A Recollection of Pelham." In: SHSP, 1989, v.26, p.306-08.
..."Battle of Sharpsburg." In: SHSP, 1899, v.27, p.210-9.

1067 **MOORE, J.H.**
"Fredericksburg." In: SB, ns, v.II, p.179-184, map, 1886-1887.
..."With Jackson at Hamilton's Crossing." In: B&L, v.3, p.139-41, 46-7.

1068 **MOORE, J. Preston**
"Jefferson Davis & Ambrose Dudley Mann." In: Jour. Miss. Hist., July 1957, (Jackson) v.XIX, #3, p.137-153.

1068a **MOORE, J. Scott**
"Southern Account of the Burning of Chambersburg - unwritten history." In: SHSP, 1897, v.25, p.315-22.
..."General Hunter's Raid - burning of the Institute." In: SHSP, 1897, v.27, p.179-91.
..."The Rockbridge Second Dragoons, short history of the company & its Roll." In: SHSP 1897, v.25, p.177-80; 1899, v.27, p.377-9

1069 **MOORE, James O.**
"Custer's Raid into Albemarle County, Va., The Skirmish at Rio Hill, Feb. 29, 1864." In: VMHB, July, 1971, v.79, #3, p.338-348, maps, plates.

1069a **MOORE, James Tice**
"Men in Crisis, Virginia's Civil War Governors." In: Va. Cavl., Spring 1986, v.35, #4, p.148-61, facsms, ills, incl. color, ports.
..."Secession & the States: a Review Essay." In: VMHB, 1986, v.94, #1, p.60-76.

1070 **MOORE, Jessie Randolph**
"The Five Great Indian Nations. Cherokee, Choctaw, Chickasaw, Seminole & Creek: The part they played in behalf of the Confederacy in the War between the States." Oklahoma City, Chron. Okla., Autumn, 1951, v.XXIX, #3, p.324-336. First appeared in "The Southern Magazine," v.III, #2, Aug.-Sept. 1936.

1071 **MOORE, John**
"Letters from Johnson's Island Prison, 1864. Edt: Wm. Stanley Hoole." In: Ala. Rev., July 1959, v.12, p.222-233. Notes. Officer of 40th Ala. reg. to Prof. S.S. Sherman of Milwaukee, 6 July-6 Nov., 1864.

1072 **MOORE, John C., Col.**
"Missouri." v.XII, 8vo, co, 451p. Wilmington, N.C., Broadfoot, 1987.
"Missouri." In: IX-Clement Evan's 'Conf. Mil. Hist.', ports, maps (1-fldg), 225pp.

1073 ..."Biographical extention: 'Additional sketches illustrating the services of officers & privates & patriotic citizens.'" p.227-451.

1074 ..."Shiloh issues again." In: Confed. Vet., 1902, v.X, p.316-317.

1075 ..."Early's Strength at Winchester." In: Confed. Vet., Sept. 1903, v.XI, p.396.

1076 ..."Battle of Lookout Mountain." In: CV, 1898, v.6, p.426-429, illus.

1077 **MOORE, John G.**
"The Battle of Chantilly (Va.)." In: Military Affairs, Summer 1964, v.XXXVIII, #2, p.49-63.

1078 **MOORE, John H.**
"The Jefferson Davis Monument." Richmond, Va. Cavl., Spring, 1961, v.X, #4, p.28-34, ports, illus., 1 color.

1079 **MOORE, John H., Mrs. (Sallie Alexander)**
"Memories of a Long Life in Virginia, by Mrs. John H. Moore." Staunton, Va., McClure Print, 1930, 12mo, cl, illus., ports,

183pp. Much on CSA, knew Lee & Jackson.

1079a **MOORE, John Henry**
"A Study in States Rights, by John H. Moore, a Virginia minister." N.Y., Neale Pub., 1911. 12mo, cl, 227p. Krick-329. $75-ob.

1080 **MOORE, John Trotwood**
"Tom's Last Forage." Nashville, Tenn., Cokesbury Pr., 1926, 12mo, wraps, vi, 36pp. Story of an old negro & master during & after the war.

1080a **MOORE, John Trotwood, Compiler**
Colleen Morse Elliott & Louise Armstrong Moxley, Editors. "Tenn. Civil War Questionaires...."
See: under title.

1081 **MOORE, John Wheeler**
"Roster of North Carolina Troops in the War Between the States. Prepared, by order of Legislature of 1881, by John W. Moore, late major commanding third battalion, light artillery." Raleigh, N.C., Ashe & Gatling, 1882, tk8vo, cl(gilt design), vol. 1, p.x, 581; v.II, p.4, 743; v.III, p.4-741; v.IV, vii, 458. Set: $1,200.00-Bmk136. v.III, $75.00.

1082 **MOORE, Joseph Hampton**
"Baker at Balls Bluff." Philadelphia, Pa.?, 8vo, wraps, cover title, 7pp. Address at reunion of the 71st Pa. (California) Reg., GAR, & Confederate Veterans at Balls Bluff, Potomac River, Virginia, on the 50th Anniversary of the Battle, October 21, 1911.

1083 **MOORE, Josiah Stuanton**
"An address...at the 50th Reunion of the Fifteenth Virginia Regiment, at Williamsburg, Va., May 24, 1911." n.p., n.d., 8vo, wrasp, 13pp.

1084 ..."Malvern Hill, some reminisc. of one of the survivors." In: SHSP, 1907, v.XXXV, p.121-124.

1085 ..."Reminiscences, Letters, Poetry & Miscellanies." Richmond, Va., O.E. Flanhart Pr., 1903, 12mo, cl, front(port), viii, 785pp. $25.00. First 91pp. letters of Prv. Moore, CSA. Roll of Va. Life Guards, Co.B, 15th Va. Inf.

1086 **MOORE, Louis Toomer**
"Why are there 13 stars in the Confederate flag?" In: UDC Mag., Sept 1951/Feb. 1952, v.14(9), p.8-9; v.15, #2, p.16-17.

1087 **MOORE, Louise Parker**
"Descendants of Corporal Nicholas Parker, Civil War Company B, 51st infantry N.C., of Duplin County." n.p., n.d. (1978), 73pp., blue wraps. $10.00.

1088 ..."Descendants of Larkin Newby Parker Civil War Company B, 51st Infantry, Duplin County, N.C." Bethesda, Md., The Author, 1978, 4to, wraps, 97pp.

1088a **MOORE, M. J.**
"Longest March in shortest time - Suffold to Gettysburg." In: SHSP, 1906, v.34, p.248-9. Of: Co. E., 18th Va. Reg., Bunton's Brigade, Pickett's Div., Longstreet's Corps.

1089 **MOORE, Marinda Branson, Mrs.**
"The Dixie Speller. To follow the First Dixie Reader. By Mrs. M.B. Moore, author of the Dixie Series." Raleigh, N.C., Branson & Farrar, 1864, 12mo, cl, illus., 120pp. Crandall-4067.

1090 ..."The First Dixie Reader; designed to follow the Dixie Primer." 12mo, cl, 62, (1)p. $135.00-Jk. $175.00.

1091 ..."The First Dixie Reader; designed to follow the Dixie Primer." Raleigh, N.C. Branson, Farrar & Co., 1863, cover title, 2nd edt., 1864. Crandall-4069.

1092 ..."The Geographical Reader, for the Dixie Children." Raleigh, N.C., Branson, Farrar & Co., 1863, 12mo, wraps, maps, 48pp. $100.00-Jk. $1,500.00

1093 ..."Primary Geography, arranged as a reading book for common schools., with questions & answers attached. 2nd edt." Raleigh, N.C., Branson & Garrar, 1864, 12mo, wraps, maps, 47, (1)pp. Crandall 4071.

See also under "Text Books."

1094 **MOORE, Martin V.**
"The Crossing of the Potomac by the Confederate Cavalry." In; So.Hist.Monthly, 1876, v.1, p.73-78.

1095 ..."Gen. Stuart in Pennsylvania. The Great Cavalry Expedition of 1862." In: SHST, 1874, v.1, p.121-134.

1096 ..."A Staff Officer's Recollections of Gen. Lee." In: Frank Leslie's Pop. Monthly, Sept., 1896, v.42, p.272-283.

1097 **MOORE, Nancy E.**
"The Journal of Eldress Nancy, kept at South Union, Ky. Shaker Colony, Aug. 15, 1861 - Sept. 4, 1864." edited with an introduction & glossary by Mary Julia Neal. Sold by the Shakers, Auburn, Ky. Nashville, Tenn., Parthenon Press, 1963, 8vo, cl, illus., xii, 256pp.

1098 **MOORE, R. Walton**
"The Southern Confederacy & its Constitution." in Proceedings 41st Annual meeting of Virginia state Bar Ass'n., held at...Old Point Comfort, Va., Aug. 6, 7, 8, 1930." Richmond, 1930, Press Print, 8vo, wraps, p.403-421.

1099 **MOORE, Robert Augustus**
"The diary of a Confederate veteran. Edt: Jas. W. Silver." In: La.HQ, July 1956, v.39, p.245-374. Record: Service of Co. G, 17th Miss. Reg. in Miss., Va., Gettysburg. 27 Mya 1861-19 Sept. 1863.

1100 ..."A Life for the Confederacy. As recorded in the pocket diaries of..." Co. G, 17th Miss. Reg. Confederate Guards, Holly Springs, Mississippi. Edt: James W. Silver; foreword Bell Irwin Wiley. Jackson, Tenn., McCowat-Mercer Press, 1959, 8vo, cl, d/w, 182pp., illus., ports(incl. front), Special Atg. Edt. $35.00. First published in LHQ, July 1956, v.XXXIX, p.237-374. ...Wilmington, N.C., Broadfoot Pub., 1987. 8vo, cl, dj, 182pp. $20.

1100a **MOORE, Robert C.**
"To the Members of the Seven Generals Chapter of the U.D.C., from Robert C. Moore." In: Phillips CHQ, June 1971, v.9, p.21-8; Sept. p.18-26. Civil War remembrances.

1101 **MOORE, Robert T.**
"Letter of...Aug. 22, 1861; & a letter of Wm. T. Moore, April 21, 1862." In: AHQ, 1961, v.XXIII, p.300-302.

1102 **MOORE, Ross H.**
"The Vicksburg Campaign of 1863." Jackson, Miss., Jour. of Miss. Hist., July 1939, v.1, #3, p.151-168.

1103 **MOORE, S. McD.**
"Substance of a speech delivered by S. McD. Moore of Rockbridge in the convention of Virginia, on his resolutions on federal relations, on the 24th of Feb. 1861." Richmond, Va., Whig Book & Job Off., 1861, 8vo, wraps, 24pp., Crandall-2789. Printed before secession convention.

1104 **MOORE, Sallie Alexander, Mrs. John H.**
"Memories of a long life in Virginia." Staunton, Va., The McClure Co., 1920, 12mo, 183pp. signed pres. copy. $50.00. Carolina Bk - 'about 50pp. relates to war. Knew Jackson before war & the Lees afterwards.'

1105 **MOORE, Samuel Preston, Surg.-Gen.**
"Surgeon-General Samuel Preston Moore & the officers of the Medical Department of the Confederate States." by E.R. Wiese. Atlanta, Ga., C.1912, 8vo, wraps, cover title, 8pp., illus. Proposed monument to Moore. $35.00-Bmk104.

..."Resources of the Confederacy." In: SHSP, 1876, v.II, p.125-128.
See: Sam'l E. Lewis's Life.

1106 ..."Samuel Preston Moore - Surgeon-Gen. of the C.S.A." A resolution to erect a monument to the memory of...adopted by the ass'n. of medical officers of the Army & Navy of the Confederacy-Memphis, Tenn., June 9, 1909, cover title. Washington, D.C., Samuel E. Lewis, M.D., chairman, June 1, 1910.

1107 ..."Life & Times of...Sug.-Gen. C.S.A." by E.R. Wiese. In the Southern Medical Journal, XXIII, Oct. 1930, p.916-921.

1108 ..."Samuel Preston Moore's letters to Wm. E. Woodruff. By John W. Payne." In: ArkHQ, Autumn, 1956, v.15, p.228-248. Notes. Letters from a medical officer in both US & CS Armies, 1846-1871.

1109 ..."Samuel Preston Moore, Md., Surgeon-General of the Confederate States of America." Washington, Press of Judd & Detweiler, n.d., 8vo, wraps, unnumbered pp. (McKissick-2305).

1110 **MOORE, T.V.**
"Memorial Discourse on the Death of Gen. Robert E. Lee." Nashville, Tenn., 1870, 8vo, wraps, 19pp.

1111 **MOORE, Thomas O., Gov.**
"Letters to & from Gov. Thomas O. Moore, 1863, concerning Loyalty of Slaves in north Louisiana, 1863. Edt: John H. Randsell." In: LHQ, Oct., 1931, v.14, #4, p.487-502.

1112 **MOORE, Thomas Overton**
"Anecdotes of General Cleburne." In: SHSP, 1893, v.XXI, p.299-301.
..."Governor Moore's Proclamation converning General Butler's infamous order. May 24, 1862." In: SHSP, 1878, v.VI, p.228-229.
..."Gov. Thomas Overton Moore's inaugural address (1860)." In: LaH., 1960, v.1, p.380-94.

1113 **MOORE, Waldo W.**
"The defense of Shrevesport, La. the Confederacy's last redoubt (1864)." In: Mil. Affairs, Summer 1953, v.17, p.72-82, notes.

1114 **MOORE, William D.**
"The life & works of Col. Henry Hughes, a funeral sermon preached in the Methodist Episcopal Church, Port Gibson, Miss., Oct. 26, 1862." Mobile, Ala., Farrow & Bennett, 1863, 8vo, wraps, 40pp.

1115 ...List of battles & casualties of the Claiborne Guards, Co. K, 12th Miss., & those companies furnished by Claiborne County.

1116 ..."The New Confederate Flag Song Book, No. 1." Mobile, Ala., H.C. Clarke, 1864, 16mo, wraps, 78, iipp. Crandall-3264. Another copy with 4th edition, on wraps. 1st edt(?), 13cm, 62, iipp., index. $200.00-Bmk114.

1117 **MOORMAN, George, Gen.**
"Gen. George Moorman died in harness, right arm of Confederate Veteran Association." In: CV, 1903, v.11, p.8-11.
..."Circular: ReOrganization of Medical Corps UCV." In: SHSP, 1894, v.22, p.17-19.
See: Joseph Jones.

1117a **MOORMAN, Marcellus N., Maj.**
"The Wounding of General T. J. (Stonewall) Jackson, by Maj. Moorman, Stuart's Horse artillery corps, ANV." In: SHSP, 1902, v.30, p.110-16.
..."Recollections of Cedar Creek & Fisher's Hill, Oct. 19, 1864." In: SHSP, 1902, v.30, p.371-2.
See: Capt. Saml. Buck, ante, p.104.

1117b **MOREAU, M. Henry**
"La Politique Francaise en Amerique 1861-64." Paris: E. Dentu, 1864. 8vo, cl, 176pp. Listed for the French point of view which was largely Union.

1118 **MOREHEAD, Charles B.**
"Southern Confederation, an historical summary. A speech by..." Liverpool, 1862, 8vo, wraps, 30pp. No: LC, Sabin.

1119 **MORELAND, Thomas W.**
"Robert E. Lee." In: Edwin DuBois Shur-

ter, Edt. "Representative College Orations." N.Y., Macmillan, 1909, p.90-95.

1120 **"MORGAN COUNTY (GA.)**
Confederate Roster." In: Ga. Armchair Researcher, 1983, v.4, #4, p.182-188." Roll of the 'Home Guards' from Madison Co., later known as Co. D. Third Regiment Georgia Volunteers (infantry).
...Historical Roll of the 'Home Guard' (Co. D, Third Regiment, Georgia Volunteer Infantry." In: Armchair Reseracher, v.3, #4, p.163-169.

1121 **MORGAN, George H.**
"Experiences in the enemy's lines." In: CV, May 1909, v.XVII, p.216-219.

1122 **MORGAN, George P. & Stephen A.**
"A Confederate Journal." Edt: George E. Moore. In: W.Va. Hist., July 1961, v.22, p.201-216. Diary: July 8, 1861-Sept. 15; cont'd. by Stephen, Oct. 3-Dec.26, 1861.

1122a **MORGAN, Henrietta H., Mrs.**
"Death of a Mother of Soldiers." (from the Louisville Courier Journal, Sept. 9, 1891). In: SHSP, 1891, v.19, p267-8.

1123 **MORGAN, Henry T.**
"Letters of a North Louisiana Private to his wife, 1862-1865. Edt: John A. Cawthon." In: MVHR, 1944, v.XXX, p.533-550.

1124 **MORGAN, James F.**
"The Choctaw Warrents of 1863." In: Chron. Okl., Spring, 1979, Vol. LVII, #1, p.55-66, facms, ports, map.

1125 ..."The Cherokee Script Issuance of 1862." In: Okla. Hist. Chronicles, 1976, v.LIV, #3, p.393-400, facsm.

1125a ..."Graybacks & Gold: Confederate Monetary Policy." Pensacola, Fla., Perdido Bay Press, 1985. 8vo, hard cover, 230pp, ills, tables, index, bibliography. $20.

1125b ..."The Lost Opportunity: the Confederate Invasion of New Mexico." In: CV, ns, May-June 1987, v.35, #3, p.24-9, ports, map, ills. incl. color cover.

1125c **MORGAN, James L.**
"A Brief History of the 45th Arkansas Cavalry Reg., CSA." In: 'Stream of Hist.,' Oct. 1978, v.16, p.3-10, 19-25.
..."Early History of the Tom Hindman Camp, #318, U.C.V. In: SH, v.16, p.27-40.

1126 **MORGAN, James Morris, Dr.**
"A Mystery of the Seas." In: USN Inst. Proc., June 1921, XL, p.909-915. Story of CS 'Shenandoah'-"alias Sea King," built in England in 1864.

1127 ..."The St. Lawrence & the 'Petrel'." in: USN Inst. Proc., Aug. 1920, XLVI, p.1219-1221. Sketch of engagement between St. Lawrence & CS cruiser 'Petrel', belonging to S.C. navy off Atlantic Coast, after outbreak of war.

1128 **MORGAN, James Morris**
"The Last Blockade Run of the Sumter, 1863. Communication by..." In: Mass. Hist. Soc., Proc., 1911, v.XLIV, p.283-296.

1129 ..."The Confederate Cruiser 'Florida'." In: U.S.N. Inst. Proc., Sept. 1916, v.XLII, p.1581-1588.

1130 ..."A Realistic War College." In: USN, Inst. Proc., March, 1916, v.XLII, p.543-554. Account of CSA Naval Academy.

1131 ..."Recollections of a Rebel Reefer." Boston, Houghton, Mifflin Co., 1917, 8vo, cl, front., pls., port., xix, (1)491, (1)p.60-95.
...Same, in special edition, limited to 200 copies. $150.00. $75.00-Bmk105.
...London, Constable & Co., 1917, 8vo, cl, CSA flag on cover, no plates, xiv, 372pp. $20.00. $27.50.
...London, 1918.
Sketch of, see: Milledge L. Bonham. Jr.

1132 ..."Recollections of a Rebel Reefer." In: Atlantic, Jan.-Mar., 1917, v.CXIX, p.1-11, 153-162, 338-348. Titles vary & all included in his book of same title.

1133 ..."The Lost Cause." In: Atlantic, April 1917, v.CXIX, p.500-508. Remin. of serv.

at 'Battery Semmes,' on James River near Richmond.

1134 ..."Confederate Commerce-destroyer "The Confederacy's Only Foreign War." in: Cent. Mag., 1898, v.LVI, p.594-610, illus., map.

1135 ..."A Rebel reefer rights the record, by Doris H. Hamilton." In: Hobbies, Jan. 1958, v.62, #11, p.106-107. A Morgan letter to an unnamed person, Pittsburg, 26 June 1917, recalling engagement between CSNavy 'Manassas" & USS 'Richmond' in the Miss. Delta; & sinking of USS 'Housatonic' by CSA submarine Hunley, 1864.

1136 **MORGAN, John H.**
"Escape of... & Capt. Thos. H. Hines from the Ohio Penitentiary, Nov. 27, 1863. From manuscript written Jan. 1864, by one of the Confederate officers confined in penitentiary. Frankfort, Ky., Capital Print, n.d., cover title, (14)pp., wraps.
Louisville, Lost Cause Press, micro-cd, $2.45.
See also: Hines, T.H., Sam C. Reid.

1137 ..."The Great Indiana-Ohio Raid by Brig. Gen. John Hunt Morgan & His Men, July 1863. An authentic account of the most spectacular Confederate Cavalry Raid into Union territory during the War Between the States. The capture & subsequent escape of Brig-Gen. Morgan, as seen & told by Brig.-Gen. Basil W. Duke (CSA), Brig.-Gen. Orlando B. Willcox (USA) & Capt. Thomas H. Hines (CSA) each of whom was an active participant in the various phases of the event." Intro: Don D. John. with maps, illus., Louisville, Ky., Book Nook Press, n.d. (1955), small 4to, wraps(in color), 32pp., double columns, reprint: "Brandenburg Story," see: Mark Ford. $25.00-Bmk.

1138 ..."The Romance of Morgan's Rough Riders. The Raid, the Capture & the Escape." In: Cent. Mag., 1891, v.XLI, p.403-425, illus., port, map. Seen by: B. Duke, O.B. Willcox & T.H. Hines.

1139 ..."The Capture & wonderful escape of Gen. John H. Morgan, etc...."
See: Reid, Samuel Chester, Jr.
Atlanta, Ga., Emory Univ., reprint 1864 edt.

1140 ..."John Morgan Raid in Ohio." In: Ohio Arch. & Hist. Pub., 1908, v.XVII, p.48-59. By a vet. living in Bayton Soldier's Home. See Also: L.J. Weber, Maj. Geo. Rue.

1141 ..."Morgan's Raid & First Ohio Invasion." n.p., reprint, Ohio Handbook of Civil War (1961) for Ohio Civil War Centennial Comm., 8vo, decr. wraps, cover title, dble-pg. map, port of Morgan, illus., 12pp.

1142 **MORGAN, John Hunt**
"Camp Charity," "Hidden Sabre," & "Reunion in Kentucky." Articles In: Confed. Annals, Aug. 1883, v.1, #2, p.72-78.

1143 ..."History of the Forty-Sixth Regiment Indiana Volunteers, September, 1861-September, 1865: compiled by order of the Regimental Association." Logansport, Ind., Wilson, Humphreys & Co., 1888, 8vo, cl, vi, (7)-220pp. Official reports covering largely Hunt's Indiana Raids.

1144 ..."Humors of the Morgan Raid into Indiana & Ohio." In: LWL, Apr. 1867, v.II, #6, p.405-407, May 1867, v.III, #1, p.36-37, 233-236. April 1868, v.IV, p.535-538. Final article by J. Parish Steele.

1145 ..."The John Morgan Raid in Ohio (1863)." In: Ohio Arch.& Hist. Soc. Pub., Jan. 1908, v.XVII, p.48-59.

1146 ..."The John Morgan Raid in Ohio." In: Magazine of History, April 1910, v.XI, p.209-219. Written by a Civil War veteran.

1147 ..."Last Night & Last day of John Morgan's raid." (East Liverpool, Ohio, J.H. Simms).

1148 ..."How far did Morgan get?" In: Confed. Vet., May 1923, v.XXXI, p.170-172. Ar-

1149 ..."Morgan's disastrous raid through Indiana & Ohio, with extracts from official records, Jno. Morgan's escapes, last raid, & death." In: "Two Great Raids," e.g., with Col. Grierson. Washington, National Tribune, 1897, 12mo, cl, front, illus., maps, ports, 320pp. 'Old Glory Library, #8.'

1150 ..."A Short History of General John Morgan." Park Place, N.Y., Knapp & Co., 1888, 2 3/4 x 1 1/2", colored booklet, 16pp. facsm. signature (packed in Duke's cigarettes).
See: "Heroes of the C.W." & W. Duke Co.

1151 ..."Report of the Commissioners of Morgan Raid Claims to the Governor of the State of Ohio, Dec. 15, 1864." Columbus, Richard Nevins Print, 1865, 8vo, cl, 453pp. County by county breakdown, list of towns of claimants. Most accurate route available of Hunt's raids there.

1152 ..."Burial of John Hunt Morgan." Signed: "Howard." In: LWL, June 1868, v.V, #3, p.184/185.

1153 ..."Morgan's Death." In: Univ. NC Mag., Oct. 1902, wraps, 7pp. $15.00-Bmk.

1153a ..."Proclamation--to the inhabitants of Kentucky! Fellow Countrymen--I have kept my promise. Young men of Kentucky flock to my standard . . . ." Broadside 16 x 41 cm, unlisted. $1,250. G. Hindershott. At bottom: 'Morgan's Press Print, Aug. 22, 1862.' (Morgan's own press).
..."The Vidette 'Extra.'" Hartsville, Tenn., Aug. 17, 1862. Broadside: 30.5 x 48.2 cm, print on pink paper, unrecorded. (G. Hindershott) $2,000. Atg: 'Respects Gen. Jno. H. Morgan.'
See Authors:
J.H. Battle, James B. Benedict, John L. Blair, Margarette Boyer, Lorine L. Butler, Mary Cone, Basil Duke, C.C. Enn, Louis B. Ewbank, Mark Ford, Ronald M. Gard, Allen Keller, Anderson C. Quisenberry, Samuel C. Reid, Faunt LeRoy Senour, Flora E. Simmons, Jeremiah H. Simms, John S. Still, R.W. McFarland, Lois Purcell Noel, Geo. D. Mosgrove, Jas. Wall Scully, 'Richmond Times,' Henry Lane Stone, J.Eberle West, Jas. M. Fry.

1154 **MORGAN, John Tyler**
"Address at the unveiling of a monument to the unknown Confederate dead, at Winchester, Va., June 6, 1879." Washington, D.C., Globe Pr., 1879, 8vo, wraps, cover title, 24pp. $15.00-Flk.
..."Address to the Southern Historical Society, Oct. 31, 1877." In: SHSP, 1877, v.V, p.1-33, Re doctrines of the "Federal War Party," war on the Constitution by the Radical Party.

1155 ..."Political alliance of the South with West." In: N. Amer. Rev., Mar./Apr., 1878, p.309-322.

1156 **MORGAN, Julia "Mrs. Irby Morgan"**
"How it was; four years among the rebels By Mrs. Irby Morgan." Nashville, Tenn., Printed for the author, Methodist Episcopal Church South, 1892, 12mo, cl, front, ports, 204pp. CSA, Georgia, Tenn., Jno. Hunt Morgan. $75.00-Bmk112. $250.00-Jk.

1157 **MORGAN, Marshall**
"Battle of Franklin." Franklin, Tenn., Press of News, c.1931, 8vo, wraps, 22pp., incl. ads.

1157a **MORGAN, Michael R.**
"Feeding General Lee's Army - surrender at Appomattox." In: SHSP, 1893, v.21, p.360.

1158 **MORGAN, Murray C.**
"Dixie Raider; the Saga of the C.S.S. Shenandoah." N.Y., E.P. Dutton, 1948, 8vo, cl, illus., map, ports, map liners, 36pp. $30.00.

1159 **MORGAN, Stephen A.**
"The Civil War Journal of S.A.M." In: W.Va.H., 1960/1961, v.22, p.207-216.

1160 **MORGAN, William Henry**
"Personal Reminiscences of the War of 1861-1865, in camp, in bivouac, on the march, on picket, on the skirmish line, on the battlefield, & in prison." Lynchburg, Va., J.P. Bell Co., 1911, 12mo, cl, front(port.), 4pp. 1,7-286. $75.00-Bmk. Unit Roster, Co. C, 11th Va. Companies A, E, G, H. Author in Clifton Grays.
...N.Y., Libraries Press, 1971.
...Louisville, Ky., Lost Cause Pr., Micro-cd, $4.96.

1160a **MORGAN'S MEN**
"Reunion of Morgan's Men." In: SHSP, 1883, v.11, p.430-2.

1160b **MORGAN'S Raid in Indiana-Ohio, 1863.'**
Corydon, Ind., Alfco Pubs., 1980. 8vo, wraps, 70pp, maps, ills. $3.50.

1161 **MORRILL, Lily Logan**
"A Builder of the New South, Notes on the Career of Thomas M. Logan." Boston, Christopher Print, 1940, 12mo, cl, plates, ports., 255pp. $30.00-Bmk. Brig.-Gen. Logan commanded Butler's Brigade, N.C. & Va., Columbia defense. Lily L. Morrill edited 'Memoirs of Kate Virginia Cox Logan'.

1162 **MORRIS ISLAND, S.C. - PRISON**
See: F.C. Barnes, Richard E. Frayser, George Hopkins, Claudine Rhett, "List of Confederate Prisoners," John Odgen Murray, Col. Abram Fulkerson.

1163 **MORRIS, George R.**
"The Battle of Bayou des Allemands." In: CV, Jan. 1926, v.XXXIV, p.14-16.

1163a **MORRIS, George & Susan Foutz**
"Lynchburg in the Civil War. The City - the People - the Battle." Lynchburg, Va., H.E. Howard, 1984 (2nd edt). 12mo, cl, dj, 118pp. maps, ills. 1,000 copies, Atg. numbered.

1164 **MORRIS, Jerome F.**
"The Brief belligerence of Fort Macon." Raleigh, N.C., Confederate Centennial Commission, c. 1962, 8vo, wraps, illus., map, 12pp, photocopy.

1164a **MORRIS, Mary Blackburn, Mrs.**
"Notice of her death & services." In: SHSP, 1884, v.12, p.431.

1165 **MORRIS, Scott, Jr.**
"Confederate Poets Physician & Priest, Francis Orray Ticknor; Abram Joesph Ryan." Macon, Ga., Southern Press, 1963, 12mo, stiff wraps, 51pp, OP.

1166 ..."John Thomas Pound Confederate Soldier." Macon, Ga., Southern Press, 1964, 12mo, cl, 45pp.

1167 **MORRIS, Wentworth Seymour**
"The Civil War & Virginia Politics as reflected in the Papers of Jonathan McCally Bennett." Morgantown, 1936, 4to, stiff wraps, 108 leaves. Pro-Southern sentiment on military/ civilian affairs in W.Va., letters received by Bennett from first auditor of Va., at Richmond. (Shetler).

1168 **MORRIS, William S.**
"Statement of..., president of Southern Telegraph Companies, to Hon. J.H. Reagan, Postmaster General, CSA, in regard to the difficulties & troubles of the company in carrying on its services to the Confederacy, May 19, 1862." n.p., without title, probably priv. print, 8vo, sewn, 27pp. (Henkel, cat. #1090, May 1913). Unable to locate in any references.

1169 **MORRISON, Alfred J.**
"Remarks on the Civil War." In: TQHGM, July 1921, v.III, p.14-16. "Editorial comment," p.16-19.

1170 **MORRISON, Alice S.**
"Jefferson Davis Historical Essay." Washington, D.C., Law Reporter Print, n.d., Stonewall Jackson Chap. #20, United Daughters of the Confederacy, 12mo, wraps(tied), port., medals, (12)pp.

1170a MORRISON, Emmett M.
"Capture of the Howlett House." In: SHSP, 1894, v.22, p.20-4.
..."The Fifteenth virginia Infantry at Sharpsburg." In: SHSP, 1895, v.23, p.99-110.
See: Richmond, Va., Dispatch "Desperate Dash. 'Capture of Howlett House.'"

1171 MORRISON, F.W.
"The Confederate Navy." In: Univ. N.C. Mag., Nov. 1911, wraps, 8pp. $15.00-Bmk.

1172 MORRISON, Hugh Alexander
"Bibliography of the Official Publications of the Confederate States of America." In: Bibliographical Society of America, Proceedings & Papers, 1908. N.Y., 1909, v.3, 8vo, wraps, p.92-132.

1173 MORRISON, James D.
"Capture of the Steamboat (Federal) "J.R. Williams," on the Arkansas River." Centennial Commemoration of the Civil War..." Oklahoma City, Chron. Okla., Summer, 1964, v.XLII, #2, p.105-108.
See: Kenn S. Lee.

1174 MORRISON, John Franklin
"The Battle of Shiloh. A Sketch of the Battle of Shiloh, in the war Between the States (Civil War), fought April 6 & 7, 1862, at Pittsburg Landing, in Hardin County, Tennessee, & of military events both prior to & after the Battle." Lawrenceburg, Lawrence Co. Hist. Soc., 1962, 23 leaves.

1175 MORRISON, William Brown
"Fort Towson," In: Ch. Okl., June 1930, v.VIII, p.226-232. CSA activity there during war & its surrender, 1865.

1176 ..."Fort Washita," In: Ch. Okl., June 1927, v.V, p.256-258. Part it played in Civil War in IT.

1177 ..."A Visit to old Fort Washita." In: Ch. Okl., June 1929, v.VII, p.175-179.

1178 MORRISON, William Morrison, Jr
"Drewry's Bluff: Naval Defense of Richmond, 1862." In: CWH, June 1961, v.VII, #2, p.167-175, pls.

1179 MORRISSETT, William Harrison
"A Confederate Soldier's Eye-witness account of the 'Merrimack' Battle." In: Ga.H.Q., Fall 1970, v.LIV, #3, p.430-432.

1180 MORROW, Curtis Hugh
"Politico-military societies of the Northwest, 1860-1865." Knights of the Golden Circle, Worcester, Mass., 1929, 8vo, cl, (4), 92pp., maps, diagrs., thesis(Phd), Clark University, 1927. Pub: Social Science, v.IV, 1928-1929. KGC-rise & development, why concentrated in the NW (especially Ill. & Ind.).

1181 MORROW, Decatur Franklin
"Then & Now; reminiscences & historical romance, 1856-1865." Macon, Ga., J.W. Burke Co., 1926, 12mo, cl, front, ports, illus., 346pp. Rutherford Co., N.C. fictionalized to protect identities of those mentioned.
...Copy in wraps.

1182 MORROW, H.P., Henry Preston
"Reminiscing from 1861 to 1865. an "Ex Confed." H.P. Morrow. Edt: James L. Nichols." In: ETHJ, March 1971, v.IX, #1, p.5-19, notes.

1183 MORROW, John P., Jr.
"Confederate Generals from Arkansas." In: AHQ, 1962, v.XXI, p.231-246, plate of four generals.

1184 MORROW, John Patterson
"Forrest the Man & the Soldier."

1185 ..."North by West. The Story of John A. Wyeth, M.D., & his three years on White River (Arkansas)."

1186 ..."Brice's Cross Roads, 1864, Impressions in 1954."

1187 ..."Skirmish at Tarpley's Shop. A sequel to Brice's Cross Road."

1188 ..."Forrest's Last Campaign: Wilson's Raid on Selma, Alabama."

1189 ..."The Ku Klux Klan (so called) by Robert G. Shaver."
Articles in entire edition: Independence County Chronicle, Batesville, Ark., July 1978, v.XIX, #4, pl, 2 ports, facsms, 70, (5)pp.

1190 ..."Confederate Generals from Arkansas." In: AHQ, v.21, p.231-246, ports.

1191 **MORROW, Maude**
"Recollections of the Civil War." Lockland, Oh., 1901, 8vo, stiff wraps, illus., 48pp. $22.00. Sketches, largely of a Union girl in Jackson, Miss.
See: Maude Morrow Brown.

1192 **MORSE, Howard Newcomb**
"A Study in the legality of the doctrines of nullification & secession (1794-1867)." In: Fed. Bar. Jour., Jan. 1951, v.12, p.174-194.

1193 ..."Gen. Beauregard & the Colonel Rhett Controversy." In: SCHM, 1977, v.78, #3, p.184-190.

1194 **MORSE, William Eugene**
"The Fight of Jefferson Davis over the will of his brother, Joseph E. Davis, for his home, "Brierfield." Jackson, Miss., Jour. Miss. Hist., May, 1971, v.XXXIII, #2, p.141-148.

1195 **MORTINER, J.**
"La Secession aux Etats-Unis et son origine Par un Journaliste Americain." Paris, E. Dentu, 1861, 8vo, wraps, 30pp. Sabin-34749. Statement on origin of war, entirely on slavery, proved by quotes by Crittenden Compromise, Cameron's letter to Butler & Washington's Farewell Addr., signed: J.M.(ortimer).

1196 **MORTON, C. Brinkley**
"The Later Life of Jefferson Davis." Jackson, Miss., Jour. Miss. Hist., July 1946, v.VIII, #3, p.129-135.

MORTON, Camp
See: Thomas E. Spotswood.

1197 **MORTON, Frederic**
"The Story of Winchester in Virginia."
See: Oren Frederic.

1198 **MORTON, G. Nash**
"From the Rapidan to Richmond." In: CV, June 1924, v.XXXII, p.215-217. Reviews Wm. M. Dame's book of same title.

1199 ..."The Richmond Howitzers & the battle of Ball's Bluff." In: CV, Jan. 1924, v.XXXII, p.13-15.

1199a **MORTON, Howard**
"The Newmarket Charge." In: SHSP, 1896, v.24, p.302-3; 1908, v.36, p.282-4. (same).
See: Virginia Military Institute.

1200 **MORTON, Jennie C.**
"Colonel B.G. Slaughter, sketch of his life." In: RKHS, 1904, v.II, p.87-95, port.

1201 **MORTON, John Watson**
"The Artillery of Nathan Bedford Forrest's Cavalry. "The Wizard of the Saddle." By John Watson Morton, chief of artillery." Nashville, Tenn., Pub. House, M.E. Church South, 1909, 8vo, cl, facsms, ports, incl. front, fldg. pl., 374pp. $85.00 Atg. $250.00-B124. Full lt., $150.00-Bmk105.

1202 ...Kennesaw, Ga., Continental Book, 1962, 8vo, cl, Lim.Edt. 200 copies.

1203 ...Louisv., Lost Cause, micro-cd. $5.57.

1204 ..."Battle of Johnsonville." In: SHSP, 1882, v.X, p.471-488.

1205 ..."Raid of Forrest's Cavalry on the Tennessee River in 1864." In: SHSP, 1882, v.X, p.261-268.

1206 ..."A Soldier Sums Up." In: Robt. S. Henry's "As They Saw Forrest," Morton's estimate of Forrest from his "Artillery of Forrest." p.269-281.

1207 ..."Battle of Tishomingo or Brice's crossroads." In: SB, 1882-1883, v.1, p.366-383.

1208 **MORTON, Marmaduke B.**
"The Battle of Nashville." In: CV, Jan. 1909, v.XVII, p.17-21, map.

1209 **MORTON, Ohland**
"Confederate Government Relations with the Five Civilized Tribes." Oklahoma City, Chron. Okla., Summer, 1953, v.XXXI, #2, p.189-204, append. pt. II, Autumn, 1953, #3, p.299-322.

1210 **MORTON, Oren Frederic**
"A History of Monroe County, W. Virginia." Staunton, Va., McClure, 1916, 8vo, cl, 509pp. $40.00. Monroe Co. men in: Bryan's Battery; Burdette's Co.; Chapman's Battery; Edgar's Battalion; Fleshman's Co.: Co. F, 26th Va. Cav., Monroe Guards; Lowery's battery; Monroe Sharpshooters; Rocky Point Greys; Thurmond's Rangers; Vawter Co., p.422-460. Shetler-575.

1211 ..."A History of Pendleton Co., W.Virginia." Franklin, W.Va., The Author, 1910, 8vo, cl, 493pp. CSA Reg., of Pendleton men, p.402-429. Interstate war 170-116. Shetler-576. $60.00.

1212 ..."A History of Preston Co., W. Va." Kingwood, W.Va., Journal, 1914, 2 vols., List of CSA & Union men, v.1, p.488-522. Shetler-577. $60.00.

1213 ..."The Story of Winchester in Virginia, the oldest town in the Shenandoah Valley." Strasburg, Va., Shenandoah Pub., 1925, 8vo, cl, illus., incl. front, index, 336pp. Three chapters on the war. (55pp.) Carolina. $40.00.

1214 **MORTON, R.L.**
"Virginia since 1861." In: History of Virginia, v.III."
See: Virginia, History of

1214a **MORTON, Thomas (Capt. T.C. Morton)**
"Anecdotes of General R. E. Lee." In: SHSP, 1883, v.11, p.517-20.
..."Incidents of the skirmish at Totopotomoy Creek, Hanover Co., Va., May 30, 1864." In: SHSP, 1888, v.16, p.47-56. With 26th Virginia Battalion.

1215 **MOSBY, John Singleton**
"An appraisal of John S. Mosby, by the staff of the Civil War times, Illustrated." In: CWTI, Nov. 1965, v.IV, #7, p.4-7, 49-54, illus., map, ports.

1216 ..."Cause of the Loss of Gettysburg: Longstreet & Stuart. A Review by Mosby." In: SHSP, 1895, v.XXIII, p.238-247.

1217 ..."A Bit of Partisan Service." In: B&L, v.III, p.148-153.

1218 ..."The Confederate Cavalry in the Gettysburg campaign." In. B&L, v.III, p.251-252.

1219 ..."The Letters of John S. Mosby." Carlisle, Pa., Stuart Mosby Historical Society, 1986. Edited by Adele Mitchell. 8vo, cl,dj,xiv, 294pp., 28pp. illus., LimEdt. 500. 200 to & from Mosby. $27.00

1220 ..."Heth intended to cover his error." In: SHSP, 1909, v.XXXVII, p.369-372.

1221 ..."Longstreet & Stuart, highly interesting review by Col. John S. Mosby." In: SHSP, 1905, v.23, p.238-247.

1222 ..."A Horror of the War. How General Custer hung some of Mosby's Men." In: SHSP, 1897, v.XXV, p.239-244.

1223 ..."Hanging of Mosby's Men in 1864." In: SHSP, 1896, v.XXIV, p.108-109.

1224 ..."John S. Mosby." In: Hist. Soc., Fairfax, Va. Co. Yr. Bk, 1951, v.1, p.23-37, facsm., ports, view. Letter from Mosby to Thos. Keith, 20 Aug. 1900 denies he & Antonia Ford acted as CSA spies in winter of 1861-1862.

1225 ..."The Memoirs of Colonel John S. Mosby, edited by Charles Wells Russell." Boston, Little, Brown & Co., 1917, 12mo, cl, fldg-map, ports, xxi, 414pp. $125.00-Bmik90. $175.00-Bmk105.

1226 ..."A Photographic reproduction, with preface by Virgil Carrington Jones." Bloomington, Indiana University Press, Civil War Centennial Series, 1959, map liners, 12mo, cl, dj, front(port), xxviii,

414pp.

...N.Y., Kraus Reprint, 1969.

..."Reprint, 1975.

1227 ..."Monument to Mosby's Men, ceremonies at the unveiling, Sept. 23, 1899, Speech of Mosby, et al." In: SHSP, 1899, v.XXVII, p.250-287.

1228 ..."Mosby's War Reminiscences & Stuart's Cavalry Campaigns by John S. Mosby, late Colonel C.S.A. (quote)." Boston, Geo. A. Jones Co., 1887, 12mo, cl(or wraps), cloth edt. has two ports (incl front), Atg., 256pp. yellow wraps, with ports. $25.00. $35.00. $50.00. First edition.

...N.Y., Dodd, Meade & Co., 1887, 12mo, cl/or wraps, 256pp. $150.00-Bmk106. $75.00-Bmk.

...N.Y., Dodd, Mead & Co., 1898, 12mo, cl/or wraps, 264pp. most copies Atg., of an unauthorized edt. in 1887, of 264pp. a decr. color cloth & cheaper, thicker paper. $125.00-B. A "regular edt." N.Y., Dodd, 1887, having 256pp.

...N.Y., Pageant Book Co., 1958, 12mo, cl, dj, 264pp. $25.00-B.

..."Mosby's War Reminiscences." Falls Church, Va., Confederate Printers, 1984. Old Dominion Edt., Limt. Edt., 485 copies. $24. $35.

..."Stuart's Cavalry in the Gettysburg Campaign." Falls Church, Va., Confederate Printers, 1984. Old Dominion Edt., Limited Edt., 485 copies. $23. $35.

..."Stonewall Jackson." In: Munsey's Mag. June, 1912, v.47, p.333-8.

1229 ..."A Participant in the most brilliant battle fought by Mosby's Command." In: SHSP, 1909, v.XXXVII, p.348.

1230 ..."Personal Recollections of Gen. J.E.B. Stuart." In: Munsay's Mag., Apr., 1913, v.XLIX, p.35-41. $12.00-Bmk.

1231 ..."Personal Recollections of Gen. Lee." In: Munsay's Mag., Apr. 1911, v.XLIX, p.65-69.

1232 ..."Retaliation, the execution of seven prisoners." In: SHSP, 1899, v.XXVII, p.314-322.

1233 ..."The Ride Around Gen. McClellan, Colonel John Mosby tells about Gen. Stuart's brilliant feat of war." In: SHSP, 1898, v.XXVI, p.246-254.

1234 ..."Stuart's Cavalry in the Gettysburg Campaign." Excerpts from: Belford's Magazine, where it first appeared. N.Y., 1891, v.VII, ns, v.1, Oct./Nov., p.149-163, 261-275, map.

...Gaithersburg, Md., Butternut, 1987. 8vo, cl, dj, fldg map, 222pp. $25.

1235 ..."General Stuart & the Battle of Gettysburg." In: JMSI, Nov. 1908, v.XLIII, p.476-483.

1236 ..."Stuart in the Gettysburg Campaign, a defense of a cavalry commander." In: USCAJr., 1910, v.XX, p.1150-1162.

...Same, in SHSP, 1910, v.XXXVIII, p.184-196.

1237 ..."Stuart & Gettysburg." In: SHSP, 1895, v.XXIII, p.348-353.

1238 ..."Stuart's Cavalry in the Gettysburg Campaign, by John S. Mosby." N.Y., Moffat, Yard & Co., 1908, tk. 12mo, cl, fldg. map, ports., (2)incl. front., xxxiii, 222pp. $100.00-B.

1239 ...A revised edt., 1908. $35.00. See: Col. T.M.R. Talcott's review of "Stuart's Cavalry Camp." In: SHSP, 1909, v.XXXVII, p.21-37; v.XXXVIII, p.197-210.

See also: John H. Alexander, J. Marshall Crawford, Mary H. Flournay, Jesse P. Gore, Edwin R. Havens, Olan K. Lundeberg, Randolph H. McKim, Jno. W. Munson, Frank I. Rahm, Adolph Edwards Richards, Maj. John Scott, Percy Cross Standing, W.C. Waller, Jas. J. Williamson, James G. Wiltshire.

1240 ..."Mosby, the Guerilla." In: Nation, June 8, 1916, v.CII, p.611-612. An editorial acct.

MOSBY'S BATTALION
See: Jesse P. Gore.

1240a **MOSELEY, Frank Ruffner**
"A Mountineer in Grey." Radford, Va., 1972. 8vo, wraps, 136pp, ills, maps. $35. Masters thesis from Radford College.

1241 **MOSER, Harold D.**
"Reaction of North Carolina to Emancipation Proclamation." In: NCHR, 1967, v.LXXV, p.331-348.

1242 **MOSES, Armida**
"The Confederate Navy." In: CV, May 1920, v.XXVIII, p.181-182.

1243 **MOSES, Belle**
"The Gray Knight; the Story of Robert E. Lee." N.Y., London, Appleton-Century, 1936, 12mo, cl, illus., xiii, 268pp. Juvenile.

1244 **MOSES, Franklin J., Jr.**
"How South Carolina Seceded, by the private secretary of Gov. Pickens of S.C." Boston, The Mickell Magazine, December, 1897, p.345-351.

1245 **MOSES, Raphael Jacob**
"A Southern romantic." In: Jacob Rader Marcus 'Memoirs of Amer. Jews,' Philadelphia, Jewish Pub. Soc. Amer., 3 vols., 1955, v.1, p.146-202, views. In Charleston, S.C., Columbus, Ga., & officer in CSArmy.

1246 **MOSGROVE, George Dallas**
"Kentucky Cavaliers in Dixie; Or the Reminiscences of a Confederate Cavalryman...embracing much of the history of General Humphrey Marshall & his "army" & of "Morgan & his men," Colonel Henry L. Gilmore & his cavalry brigade, & history of the Fourth Kentucky cavalry regiment recollections of Generals John C. Breckinridge, Wm. Preston, "Cerro Gordo" Williams, S.B. Buckner, Jubal A. Early in the Shenandoah Valley; pen portraits of officers & men; life in tent & field; battles, cavalry raids, songs, incidents & anecdotes; characteristics of the Confederate Soldier; intersting miscellany, etc." Louisville, Ky., Courier-Journal Pr., 1895, 12mo, cl, illus., ports(20), incl. front, errata slip, plan, 265pp. $250.00-G. $450.00-OB. Muster Roll. Fourth Ky. Cavalry. $90.00.

1247 ..."Kentucky Cavaliers in Dixie. Reminiscences of a Confederate Cavalryman." Edited by Bell Irvin Wiley." Monographs, Sources & Reprints in Southern History, Jackson, Tenn, McCowat-Mercer, 1957, 12mo, cl, dj, xxvi, (16)pp(ports, pls. unnumbered), 281, pp. index.
...Wilmington, N.C., Broadfoot Pub., 1987. 8vo, cl, 281pp. $30.
See: John C. DeMoss; 4th Ky. Cavalry.

1248 ..."Following Morgan's plume through Indiana & Ohio." In: SHSP, 1907, v.XXXV, p.110-120.

1249 **MOSHER, Kate E. Perry**
"History of Rock Island, Ill., 1863." In: CV, Jan. 1906, v.XIV, p.27-32.

1250 **MOSLEY, Edward, Dr.**
"The Pre-Civil War Attitude of the Arkansas Gazette Toward Slavery." Batesville, Ark., Independence County Chronicle, July 1973, v.XIV, #4, p.2-20.

1251 **MOSS, A. Hugh**
"The diary of A. Hugh Moss, Coulie Croche St. Landry Parish, La." Lake Charles, La.?, 1948, 8vo, wraps, (4),56pp. Reminisc. & diary of a vol. CSArmy in La. & Miss., Mar. 1862-July 1863, including the siege of Vicksburg.

1252 ..."The Diary of A. Hugh Moss, Coulie Croche St. Landry Parish, Louisiana, Stationed at Vicksburg, Miss., April 25, 1863, mustered in the service of Lt. Millett, Washington, La., Mar, 22, 1862; a diary or cursory sketch of events transpiring to my knowledge during the war between the Confederate States of America. A daily account of the last siege of Vicksburg, beginning May 18 & ending July 4th,

1863." Lake Charles, La., 1948, 12mo, wraps, (4),56pp. Dornb-II, 3015: (N.Y., Scribner Press, 1948).

1253 **MOSS, Margarete Anne**
"Miss Millie Rutherford, Southerner." In: Ga.Rev., Spring, 1953, v.6, p.57-66, port. On Mildred Lewis Rutherford, officer of United Daughter of the Confederacy & a prolific writer on the CSA.

1254 **MOULTON, Gary E.**
"Chief John Ross During the Civil War." In: CWH, December 1973, v.XIX, #4, p.314-333.

1254a **MOUNT JACKSON, Va.**
"Rest at Mount Jackson Confederate Dead in Shenandoah Cemetery." In: SHSP, 1901, v.29, p.321-8.

1255 **MOUSSON, Albert**
"Erlebniss des Zurchers Albert Mousson wahrend des Sezessionkrieges. Edited by George Mousson. In Zurcher Taschenbuch, nf 83. (1963), 140-157, plate (illus). 'To be continued, full name: Johann David Albrecht Mousson. Dorn-II, 3016.

1256 **MOUTON, Eugenie**
"Josephine Joseph: Texas sketches." Cincinnati, Editor Pub. Co., 1900, 12mo, cl, 234pp. $65.00-Carolina Bk. Last 80pp. on Civil War, factual history of the 'Battle of Galveston,' Hood's Texas Brigade.

1257 **MOYER, Henry S.**
"Where were General Lee's headquarters at Gettysburg?" In: Pa.-German, May 1907, v.VIII, p.210-214.

1258 ..."Gen. Lee's Hdq. at Gettysburg, Pa." Allentown, c.1911, (4)p. illus., maps, 8vo, wraps.

1259 **MRUCK, Armin E.**
"The Role of Railroads in the Atlanta Campaign." In: CWH, September 1961, v.VII, #3, p.264-271.

1260 **MUDD, Joseph Aloysius**
"With Porter in Missouri. A Chapter in the History of the War Between the States." Washington, D.C., National Pub. Co., 1909, 8vo, cl, ports, incl. front, 452pp. With the 9th Missouri Infantry. $75.00. $100.00-OB.

1261 ..."What I Saw at Wilson's Creek." (Columbia, Mo., Jan. 1913, v.VII, #2, pp.89-105. One of the Confederate decisive wins. Reprint in wraps, above.

1262 **MUDD, Nettie**
"The Life of Dr. Samuel A. Mudd..." Linden, Tenn., Continental Book Co., 1975, ivo, cl, 378, (3)pp. New chapters and new illus., and fold-out Michigan Legislature's House Concurrent Resolution #126. p.378 extended 383pp.

1263 **MUDD, Samuel Alexander, Dr.**
"The Life of Dr. Samuel A. Mudd containing his letters from Fort Jefferson, Dry Tortugas Island, where he was imprisoned four years for alleged complicity in the assassination of Abraham Lincoln with statements of Mrs. Samuel A. Mudd, Dr. Samuel A. Mudd, & Edward Spangler regarding the assassination & the argument of General Ewing on the question of the jurisdiction of the military commission & on the law & facts of the case also "Diary: of John Wilkes Booth. Edited by his daughter Nettie Mudd with a preface by D. Eldridge Monroe of the Baltimore Bar." N.Y., Washington, Neale Pub. Co., 1906, 8vo, cl, illus., ports, incl. front, 326pp. $175.00-OB. $90.00.

1264 ...Marietta, Ga., Continental Book Co., 1955, 12mo, cl, 2-illus., added, pp.(1), (327)-363pp. added material. $22.50.

1265 ...Saginaw, Mich., Priv. Pub., R.D. Mudd, 1962, 8vo, cl, illus., ports, 363pp. reprint of same material as the above Marietta, Ga. $25.00.

1266 ...Linden, Tenn., 1975, reprint of the 1906 edition.
Three new chapters & an addenda. Letters from Dr. Mudd not previously

printed, 4 new illustrations.
...Georgia reprint, 1975.

1267 ..."Testimony for the prosecution & the defence in the case of Dr. Samuel A. Mudd charged with conspiracy to assassinate the President of the United States, etc. Tried before a military commission, of which Maj.-Gen. David Hunter is president, May & June 1865, published for the accused, from the verbatim official report of the 'National Intelligencer.' Washington, Polkinhorn & Son, 1865, 12mo, cl, cover title, 311pp.

1268 **MUELLER-KRANEFELDT, ----**
"Stuarts Kavallerie im amerikanischen Sezessionskriege." In: Militar-Wochenblatt, Jahrg., 2.Bd.Nov. 19, 1912, p.3388-3390.

1268a **MUGRIDGE, Donald H.**
"The American Civil War." Washington, D.C., Library of Congress, 1960. 4to, wraps, 24pp. $7.50. Gen. reference & bibliographical Div.

MUHLENBURG RIFLES
See: Herbert F. Miley.

1269 **MUHLENFELD, Elizabeth**
"Mary Boykin Chesnut: A Biography, with an Introduction by C. Vann Woodward." Baton Rouge; State University Press, 1981, 8vo, cl, dj, xv, 271pp., index, sources.

1270 **MUIR, Andrew Forest**
"Dick Dowling & the Battle of Sabine Pass." In: CWH, December 1958, v.IV, #4, p.399-428.

1271 ..."Sam Houston & the Civil War." In: Texana, Fall, 1968, v.VI, #3, p.282-287.

MUIR, Dorothy Troth
"Presence of a lady; Mount Vernon 1861-1868." Washington, Mount Vernon Pub., 1946, 8vo, cl, front, plates (1 dbl.) 90pp.

1272 **MUIR, E.C.**
"A Cause celebre." In: Brant HSP, 1930, p.9-19. Confederates tried in Canada, 1864 for their raids on Vermont.

1273 **MULDOWNY, John**
"Jefferson Davis: The Postwar Years." In: Miss. Quart., 1970, v.XXIII, p.17-33.

1274 **MULLEN, James M.**
"Last Days of Johnston's Army. An Address before A.P. Hill Camp, Confederate Veterans, Petersburg, Virginia, Nov. 25, 1890." Suffolk, Va., Robt. Hardy Pub., 1986. 8vo, wraps, 20pp., port.
...In: SHSP, 1890, v.18, p.97-113.

1275 **MULLEN, Jay Carlton**
"Pope's New Madrid (Mo.) & Island Number 10 Campaigns." Columbia, Mo., Mo. Hist. Review, April, 1965, v.LIX, #3, p.325-343, map, illus.

1276 **MULLER, William F.**
"War Papers of the Confederacy. Authentic reproductions of Official Orders. Telegrams, Letters, Pictures & Memoranda of the Civil War." Charlottesville, Va., M&M Co., c.1961, 4to, wraps, crossed color flags, cover title, & color flags, seal, on back cover, illus., facsms, ports, & in groups, (32)pp. $15.00-Bmk.

1277 **MULVIHILL, Michael J.**
"First Mississippi Regiment: its foundation, organization & record. By Col. M.J. Mulvihill, Sr." Vicksburg, Miss., Van Norman Print, 1931, 8vo, stiff wraps, in color, port, 62pp. $35.00.

1278 **MULVIHILL, Michael J., Compl.**
"Vicksburg & Warren County, Mississippi, Tunica Indians, Quebec missionaries, Civil War veterans. Published by authority of the Mayor & Aldermen of the city of Vicksburg & Board of supervisors of Warren County." Vicksburg, Miss., Van Norman Print, 1931, 8vo, color wraps, illus., maps, ports, 80pp. Civil War in Vicksburg & Yazoo River, Fort Snyder, C.S. Ram Arkansas & Battle of Chickasaw Bayou, p.22-80, all CSA.

1279 **MUNDY, Sue (pseud.) of Ky.**
See: L.L Valentine, July '64 Ky.'Register'.

Young Ewing Allison; Dr. Robert S. Holzman; Henry Magruder's "Three Years in the Saddle."

1280 **MUNFORD, Beverly Bland**
"Random Recollections." N.Y., Priv. Print, The De Vinne Press, 1905, 12mo, cl, 5pp. 1,(3)-238pp. Memories Richmond Bar, politics & Civil War.

1281 ..."Virginia's Attitude toward Slavery & Secession." N.Y., etc, Longmans, Green Co., 1909, 8vo, cl, xiii, (1),329pp. errata slip. $10.00. $12.00. $30.00.

1282 ..."New Edition," 1910. 2nd Edt. 12mo, cl, xiii, (1), 330pp. (vipp. comments by press). $15.00.

1283 ...N.Y., 1969 reprint of 1909 edt. Westport, Conn., Greenwood Pr. Other Editions: N.Y., 1914; N.Y., n.d.; & Richmond, Va., n.d. (1915).

1284 ...Other editions: "School Edition, July 1911; School Edition, 2nd Edt., July 1914; school edition, 3rd edt., Nov. 1915. 12mo, cl, xx, (1),330pp. Richmond, Va., L.H. Jenkins Print, 1915.

1284a ..."A Vindication of the South--Right of Secession." In: SHSP, 1899, v.27, p.60-84.

1285 **MUNFORD, George Wythe**
"The Jewels of Virginia; a lecture delivered by invitation of the Hollywood Memorial Association in Richmond, Jan. 18, 1867...Pub. for the benefit of the association." Richmond, Va., Gary & Clemmitt, 1867, 8vo, wraps, 50pp. Partially on the War. $30.00.

1286 **MUNFORD, Thomas Taylor, Gen. CSA**
"The amenities of war." In: JMSIUS, 1911, v.xlix, p.419-420.

1287 ..."Closing Scenes of 1st Manassas." In: SHSP, 1895, v.23, p.264-266.

1288 ..."A Confederate Officer's Reminiscences." In: JUSCA, 1891, v.IV, p.276-288; 1892, v.V, p.65-75.

1289 ..."Reminiscences of cavalry operations." In: SHSP, 1884, v.XII, p.342-350, 447-459; 1885, v.XIII, p.133-144.

1290 ..."Reminiscences of Jackson's Valley Campaign." In: SHSP, 1879, v.7, p.523-534. See: John Lamb.
MUNFORD'S MARYLANDERS
See: John R. Stonebraker.
MUNFORDSVILLE, Battle of
See: Edward T. Sykes.

1291 **MUNHALL, B.D.**
"The Cofer Revolver." In: Amer. Rifleman, 1950, Aug., v.98, #8, p.30-32. Invented by Thomas W. Cofer & patented by the CSA, Aug. 12, 1861.

1292 **MUNSON, John William**
"Reminiscences of a Mosby Guerrilla." N.Y., Moffat, Yard & Co., 1906, 8vo, cl, facsm, illus., ports, incl. front, x, (3), 277pp. $125.00-B. $50.00-McM251.

1293 ..."Recollections of a Mosby Guerrilla." Extract: Munsey's Magazine for Sept., Oct., Nov. & Dec., 1904 & 1905 (Jan.), 8vo, illus., bound sheets. $85.00-Bmk106. Pub. a year before his "Reminiscences."

1294 ..."Reminiscences of a Mosby Guerrilla." Washington, D.C., Zenger Pub. Co., 1983, 8vo, cl, new index, end-paper map, biog. sketch of Munson, 284pp., dj. $20.00.
MURDAUGH, William Henry
See: J. Davis Reed.

1295 **MURDOCK, William D.C. of Maryland**
"An address to the Democratic Party on the present crisis & the next presidential election." Washington, 1864, 8vo, stitched, 28pp. $25.00. Anti-Lincoln, note verso title by author saying this was to have been printed in National Intelligencer but never printed owing to difference of opinion concerning emancipation.

1296 **MURFIN, James V.**
"The Gleam of Bayonets, The Battle of Antietam & the Maryland Campaign of 1862." Intro: James I. Robertson, Jr., J.D.

Bowlby maps. N.Y.-London, Thomas Yoseloff, 1965, 8vo, cl, d/w, illus., facsms, ports, maps, 451pp. $30.00.

...2nd Print, April 1968. Only change, cheaper binding in reprint. (5,000 in 1st, 3,000 in 2nd).

...3rd Print, July 1970.

...Atlanta, Ga., Mockingbird Books, 1976, 8vo, paper, 319pp.

...N.Y., Bonanza, Reprint (c.1975). $7.50-Y.

1297 ..."How Stonewall got his name." In: CWTI, July 1962, v.1, #4, p.39-40, port. From Gen. Barnard Bee at First Manassas.

1298 ..."The Lost Orders." In: CWTI, Aug. 1962, v.1, #5, p.28-31, map. Federals found Lee's detailed marching order. Who lost them? Why didn't McClellan take advantage & move faster?

1299 **MURFREE, James T.**
"The University cadet corps." In: AHQ, 1943, v.V, p.55-58. Explaining war record of Univ. cadets to E.N.C. Snow's inquery, June 24, 1903.

MURFREESBORO, Battle of
See: Jouh Cabell Breckinridge, Randall Lee Gibson.

1300 **MURPHEY, George S.**
"Nuggets of Gold from the Southland." Macon, 1936, J.W. Burke Co., 8vo, cl, wraps, 142pp., illus., front. CSA history. $10.00.

1301 **MURPHREE, Joel Dyer**
"Autobiography & Civil War Letters of Joel Murphree of Troy, Alabama, 1864-1865. Introduction: H.E. Sterkx." In: AHQ, Spring, 1957, v.XIX, p.170-207. Extract. $7.00. Letters of quartermaster sergeant, 57th Reg., Ala. Inf., Apr. 28, 1864-Apr. 17, 1865.

1302 **MURPHREE, Thomas Marion**
"Record of Confederate Soldiers 1861-1865, Pike County Alabama, compiled from the Records of Thomas Marion Murphree, etc."
See under: Margaret Pace Farmer.

1303 **MURPHRY, James**
"Justice John Archibald Campbell, on Secession." In" AR, Jan, 1975, v.28, #1, p48-57.

1303a **MURPHY, Anthony**
"Helped capture engine "General," a wild race during the Civil War." (from Richmond Times-Dispatch, Dec. 29, 1909). In: SHSP, 1909, v.37, p.264-5.

1304 **MURPHY, D.F.**
"The Jeff Davis Piracy Case."
See: William Smith, Confederate Seaman.

1305 **MURPHY, DuBose**
"The Spirit of a Primitive Fellowship: the Reunion of the Church." Garrison, N.Y., Hist. Mag. of Protestant Episcopal Church, vol. XVII-#4, Dec. 1948, p.435-448.

1306 ..."The Protestant Episcopal Church in Texas during the Civil War." In: P.E., Ch. Hist. Mag., 1932, v.i, p.90-101.

1307 **MURPHY, James B., Edt.**
"A Confederate Soldier's View of Johnson's Island Prison." In: Ohio Hist., 1970, v.LXXIX, p.101-111. The 28th North Carolina.

1308 **MURPHY, James L.**
"Alabama & the Charleston Convention of 1860 (Secession)." Montgomery, 1905, Reprint of Alabama Historical Society Transactions, 1904--, vol. V, #36, wraps, 8vo, p.239-266. $7.50.

1309 ..."L.Q.C. Lamar Pragmatic Patriot." Baton Rouge, Louisiana State University Press, 1973, 8vo, cl, dj, front(port.), (5),294pp. $12.00.

1310 ...N.Y., Burt Franklin, 197(?). 'Research & Source works series, American classics in Historical & Social Science." 22.50.

1311 **MURPHY, John M.**
"Confederate Carbines & Musketoons."

(Dallas, Texas, Taylor Pub., Co., 1986) 4to, cl, 248pp., illus., color front., CSA gold embossed seal on cover. $55.00.

1311a **MURRAH, P., Gov.**
"To the People of Texas, April 27, 1865. Austin, Texas." Broadside: 17 1/2 x 27.5 cm. $1,000. Unlisted, G. Hendershott. Call for troops to defend Texas against impending invasion.

1312 **MURRAY, Alton J.**
"South Georgia Rebels, the True Wartime Experiences of the 26th Regiment Georgia Volunteer Infantry Lawton-Gordon-Evans Brigade Confederate States Army 1861-1865." St. Marys, Georgia, Alton J. Murray, 1976, 8vo, cl, dj, end-sheets, index, 326pp. $40.00. $35.00-B. Complete roster: officers & men, list also Appomattox Roster, & casualty units & added & corrections to the 26th of Lillian Henderson 'Roster of the CSA Soldiers of Ga.'

1313 **MURRAY, Elizabeth Dunbar**
"My Mother Used to Say." Boston, Christopher Pub. Hse., 1959, 8vo, cl, 224pp. Natchez in the 1860s, letters back home from the war front. Federal occupation.

1314 **MURRAY, J. Odgen, Maj.**
"The Immortal Six Hundred." Little Rock, Ark., Eagle Press, 1986, 8vo, cl, 355pp. $25.00.

1315 **MURRAY, J.J.**
"Like a Stone Wall." In: Presbyt. survey, Oct. 1957, v.47, #10, p.10-11, 28, port, views. Religious convictions of Gen. Jackson, who was admitted to Presbyterian Church, 1851, Lexington, Va.

1316 **MURRAY, John Ogden**
"First Soldier Killed in the War." In: CV, October 1908, v.16, p.494. Bailey Brown, killed May 22, 1861 at Fetterman.

..."Jefferson Davis & the Southern People were not traitors, nor rebels. They were Patriots who loved the constitution & obeyed the laws made for the protection of all American citizens. A short story of the Confederate Soldier, the ideal soldier of the world 1911. By J. Ogden Murray, a soldier of 1861-1865, CSA." Manassas, Manassas Democrat Press, 1911, 8vo, wraps, port, 48, (1)pp.

1317 ..."The Immortal Six Hundred; a story of cruelty to Confederate prisoners of war, by Major J. Ogden Murray, one of the six-hundred." Winchester, Va., Eddy Press, 1905, 12mo, cl, ports, incl. front, 274pp. $135.00. $75.00-Bmk105.

1318 ...Roanoke, Va., Stone Print, 1911, 12mo, cl, ports, 355pp., enlarged 2nd edt., with a diary of Campt. A.M. Bedford, 3rd Miss. Cav. $60.00. $100.00.
See: "Claims of certain Confederate Officers & statement of J. Ogden Murray."

1319 ..."Jefferson Davis not a traitor. The Confederate Soldier the ideal soldier of the world. By J. Ogden Murray." Winchester, Va., Geo. F. Norton Pr., 1904, 8vo, wraps, cover title, 15, (1)pp. $10.00.

1320 ...Manassas, Manassas Deomcrat, 1911, 8vo, wraps, 48pp.

1321 ..."Three Stories in One: The Statesman: The Confederate Soldier, The Ideal Soldier of the world: The South's peerless women of the world, by Maj. J. Ogden Murray." Richmond, Va., Whittet & Shepperson, 1915, 8vo, wraps, 2-ports, 65 (1)pp. From three separate addresses. $25.00.

1322 **MURRAY, R.W.**
"Life & character of General Robert E. Lee." Warrington, Eng., 1877, 8vo, cl, 169pp.

1323 **MURRAY, R.W., Esq.**
"Life & Character of General Robert E. Lee, 13th Jan. 1877." Suffolk, Va., Robt. Hardy Pub., 1986, 8vo, wraps, 28pp., facsm. cover. Talk by a former CSA

soldier to an English audience at the Warrington Literary & Philosophical Society.

1324 **MURRAY, Robert B.**
"The Condemnation of the C.S.S. Georgia." In: Ga.H.Q., September, 1968, v.LII, #3, p.277-284.

1325 ..."The Padelford Claim." In: Ga.H.Q., Sept., 1967, v.LI, #3, p.324-330. Bonds first issued by CSA, politics of Supreme Ct., Federal policy on claims.

1326 **MURRELL, Cornelia Randolph, (Mrs. D.G.)**
"The White Castle of Louisiana." Louisville, Ky., J.P. Morton & Co., 1903, 8vo, cl, viii, 264pp. front, 3pl, port. Before, during & after war, on a Louisiana plantation.

1327 **MUSCALUS, John Anthony**
"Parish Script; issued in Louisiana, by John A. Muscalus." Bridgeport, Pa., Historical paper money research Institute, (1966) 8vo, wraps, 32pp. (chiefly illus.) facsms. $25.00.

1328 **MUSE, Will D.**
"Brig. Gen. John Adams in His Heroic Ride at the Battle of Franklin, Nov. 30, 1864." Broadside, poem, double column, port, n.p. (Memphis, Tenn.?), n.d.

1329 **MUSHKAT, Jerome**
"Ben Wood's 'Fort Lafayette'; a source for studying the 'Peace Democrats.'" In: CWH, June 1975, v.21, #2, p.160-171.

1330 **MUSIC (Confederate)**
"Listen to the Mocking Bird, with variations Chs. Grobe. Op.603 (Gems from Ch. Grobe). New Orleans, 186-, 4to, 7pp. $15.00.

1331 ..."Remembrance of Camp Lewis Polka March, composed & dedicated to Col. Aug. Reichard, & the officers & members of Lowell's Rifle Regiment, by J. Kirschenheiter." New Orleans, La., Werlein & Halsey, 1861, 4to, 5pp, ads on back. $60.00.

1332 **MUSIC OF THE CONFEDERACY**
EMI/Columbia 33sX1325, Civil War Almanac, vol. 2 - Rebels. Sung by the 'Cumberland Three.'

1333 ...EMI/Mercury MMC 14088/MC 20634, Songs of the Blue & Gray. Sung by the 'Wayfarer Trio.'

1334 ...RCA/Decca Mono. R.D. 27226. Songs of Billy Yank & Johnny Reb. Sung by Jimmy Driftwood.

1335 ...Mercury Stereo LPS 2-901/Mono LPS 2-501. The Civil War. (side 2) Confederate Bank Music. Camp Garrison & field calls, narration - Sounds of conflict, Ft. Sumter to Gettysburg.

1336 ...Columbia DL 220. The Confederacy. The National Gallery Orchestra & Cantata Choir of Lutheran Church of the Reformation, Washington. The Rise & Fall of the Confederacy. Issued as a record, also in a cloth-bound book describing origin & presentation of the music. Illustrated & has essays by Bruce Catton & Clifford Dowdey.

1337 ...Whitehall Stereo WHS 40022 - The Sound of the Confederacy. Played by Col. Beauregard Johnson & the Volunteers.

1338 ...Decca DL 8093 - Songs of the North & South. Sung by Frank Luther & Zora Layman with the Century Quartet (17 Confederate tracks, 19 Union).

1339 ...Capitol T1539 - Civil War Songs of the South sung by Tennessee Ernie Ford, of lesser known songs.

1340 ...Folkways - 2187/2188 - Ballads of the Civil War. With guitar accompaniment folk-singer: Hermes Nye, i.e., "I'm a Good Old Rebel", "Roll Alabama Roll."

MUSKET BALLS
See: Horace E. Hayden.

1341 **MUSSER, Richard H.**
"The War in Missouri." In: SB, n.s., v.1, 1885/1886, port, map, p.678-685, 745-782; n.s., v.II, 1886/1887, p.43-48, 102-107.

1342 **M.(USSON), E.(ugene)**
"Lettre a Napoleon III sur l'esclavage aux etats du Sud, par un creole de la Louisiane." (sig: Eugene Musson). Paris, E.-Dentu, 1862, 8vo, cl, vii, 160pp.

1343 ..."Letter to Napoleon III on the slavery in the Southern States, by a Creole of Louisiana. Tr. from the French." London, W.S. Kirkland & Co., 1862, 12mo, cl, 2p, 1, 128pp (jk. 122) $125.00. "Extracts from speeches on the slavery question, del. by John C. Calhoun in the US Senate from 1836 to 1850. Defense of economic, religious & social grounds.

1344 **MUSTER & Pay-roll**
of Company, Jo Thompson Artillery...
See: Jo Thompson.

1345 **MUSTER ROLL**
...Of Co. A, B, F, G, H, 11th Cavalry, Kentucky vols., CSArmy. In: Jno. C. Chenault's 'Old Cane Springs,' 1936, p.232-240.

1346 ...Of Company B, First Missouri Cavalry, Trans-Mississippi Department, CSA. In: MoHR, 1908-1909, v.III, p.161-163.

1347 ...Of Co. E, 31st Reg. Ga. Vols. Infty, Evans; Brigade, Gordons Division, CSA, Steward Co., Georgia. Bartow Guards Time enlistment, Nov. 13, 1861, p.251-253. In: Helen Eliz Terrill's 'Stewart Co. Ga.'

1348 ...Of Co. F, 2nd Reg. Ga. Cav., Clayton County. In: Ancestors Unlimited, 1981, v.3, #2, p.63-70.

1349 ...Of a Company of Confederate state troops. In: Ga.HQ, Mar./Sept., 1917, v.I, p.57-59, 106-107, 266-269. Muster rolls of Capt. R. Martin's Co. Lt. Inf., 1863; Capt. M.J. McMullan's Co. Wise Guards, 1862; Co. Chestatee Artillery, 1862; Jo Thomas Artillery, 1862.
Capt. R. Martin's Co.
See: Capt. R. Martin.

1350 ...of First Regiment Georgia Volunteers, 1861. Atlanta, Ga., W.J. Campbell, 1890, 8vo, wraps, 36pp. Ramsey's Reg. (Goodspeed-#393) $80.00-Bmk.

1351 ...Of Fourth Louisiana Regiment of Vols., CSA...
See: Jno. Smith Kendall, Edt.

1351a ...of the Confederate Army for 1862, 1863, & 1864." In: Historical Magazine, August 1867, 12pp. From the New York Tribune.

1351b ...of the Thirtieth Alabama Volunteers from the files of the Military Division, Alabama Department of Archives & History."

"MY CAVE Life in Vicksburg, etc."
See: Mrs. James Loughborough.

1352 **MY PAROLE.**
Written in the Interval between the Surrender of General Lee & General Johnston. By an Old Soldier. 25x22cm, two-column verse within dec. borders, Columbia Phoenix Print (S.C.?). A Rev. Richard Johnson letter is pasted on same folder, with a published poem by 'Ecclesia' & his signature beside it, from the "Carolinian." Date: Feb. 22, 1867.

1353 **MYERS, Frank M.**
"The Comanches: Hist. White's Brig... " Gaithersburg, Md., Butternut Press, 1987. $35.00. Intro: Lee A. Wallace, Jr. with new illus.

1354 ..."The Comanches: a History of White's Battalion, Virginia Cavalry, Laurel Brig., Hampton Div., A.N.V. by Frank M. Myers, late capt. Co. A, 35th Va. Cav., Approved by all the officers of the battalion." Baltimore, Kelly, Piet & Co., 1871, 12mo, cl, 400pp. $1,000.00-OB. $750.00-Bmk105. $225.00-Y111.

1355 ...Marietta, Ga., Continental Book Co., 1956, 8vo, buck, 400pp. $45.00-B. $35.00-Y.

1356 **MYERS, Gustavus A.**
"Abraham Lincoln in Richmond." In: VaMH, 1933, v.XLI, p.318-322. Myers was British consul during war, this mem. writ-

ten in early April 1865 describe meeting with Lincoln in Richmond.

1356a **MYERS, H. Melville, Jr.**
"The Stay-Law, & all its Ammendments. The Tax Act for 1866. An Ordinance of the Convention. Freedman's Code. New Constitution of the State of South Carolina." Charleston: Steward & Rhodes, 1866. 8vo, printed boards, 63pp. jk-128. $385. Black Code to control negro labor, table of debasement of CSA currency.

1357 **MYERS, Henry**
"Cruising with the Sumter." In: CV, Dec. 1923, v.XXXI, p.452-454.

1358 **MYERS, Raymond E.**
"The Zollie Tree, with a foreword by Robert Emmett McDowell." (Quote). Louisville, Ky., Filson Club Press, 1964, Filson Club Publication Second Series, 8vo, cl, dj, ports, incl. front, illus., maps, facsm, xiii, (2),200pp., facsm endsheets. $20.00-Bmk84.

1359 **MYERS, Robert Manson, Edt.**
"The Children of Pride A True Story of Georgia & the Civil War." New Haven, Yale Univ. Pr., 1972, 8vo, cl, d/w, xxv, 1, 845pp. $35.00-Bmk96.
...(1973) New Edt: N.Y., Popular Library, 12mo, 3 vols., stiff wraps, boxed.

1360 ...New Haven, Ct., Yale University, 1984, 8vo, cl, dj, xiv, 671pp., maps, illus. $25.00. Reduced from 1,845pp to 700. Omits index, 'Who's Who,' & letters predating Civil War.
See: Charles C. Jones, Jr.

1361 **MYERS, Thomas J.**
"How they made South Carolina "Howl." Letter from one of "Sherman's Bummers." In: SHSP, v.XII, 1884, p.113-114.

N

1 **NABORS, W.A.**
"Active Service of a Texas Command." In: CV, Feb. 1916, v.XXIV, p.69-72.

2 **NACKMAN, Mark E.**
"The Making of the Texas Citizen Soldier, 1835-1860." In: SwHQ, January 1975, v.LXXVIII, #3, p.231-253.

3 **NAISAWALS, Louis Van Loan**
"The Battle of Bristoe Station." (Richmond) Va.Cavl., Autumn 1968, v.XVIII, #2, pp.39-45, illus., map, ports., 1 color. Lee:"Let us say no more about it."

4 ..."The Little Church at Sudley, Va." In: Va. Caval., Winter, 1958, v.8, #3, p. 40-47, facsms, map, ports., views. M.E. Church at Sudley, used as CSA hospital, after Battle of Manassas. Nearby Pvt. John L. Rice was found abandoned as dead by Amos & Marg. Benson & nursed back to health. Later a fund was collected by Rice at New Hampshire in 1886, for a new church on the same site.

5 ..."Little Devils with the White Flag." In: Feb. 1962, CWT, III, #10(OS), p.6-8, 23-24, illus., map, ports. Charge of VMI Cadets at New Market.

6 ..."The Manassas Gap Railroad." (Richmond) Va. Cavl., Spring 1970, v.XIX, #4, pp.30-41, ports., illus., 1 color.

7 ..."Stuart as a Cavalryman's Cavalryman." In: CWTI, Feb. 1963, v.1, #10, p.6-9, 42-47, illus., incl. front cover, color, maps, ports.

8 ..."Why Confederates crossed Potomac." In: CWTI, Aug. 1962, v.1, #5, p.18-23, illus, map. Foreign recognition, supplies, forage, Maryland support & other major victory.

9 **NALTY, Bernard C.**
"Blue & Gray." In: Leatherneck, Nov. 1960, v.XLIII, #11, p.54-57; reprinted in same: Nov. 1971, v.LIV, #11, p.50-53.

10 ..."Names of Officers of the Ordnance Bureau of the Confederate States, Serving under orders of the Chief of Ordnance." n.p., n.d., 8vo, wraps, 4pp.
See: "Memoranda of...(likely printed under others in 1880's)

11 ..."Names of Six Hundred Confederate Officers who were subjected to severest prison fare & placed under fire of Confederate Cannon in Charleston Harbor." (Nashville, 189-?), The Confederate Veteran, 4to, wraps, cover-title, (8)pp., double column. Residence, regiment & place of capture. Dorn-II, 602.

12 **NANCE, James D., Col. 3rd S.C. Reg.**
"Supplementary Report of Operations of 3rd S.C. Reg., at Gettysburg." In: SHSP, 1885, v.13, p.209-210.

13 ..."Official Report of Chickamauga." In: SHSP, 1888, v.16, p.377-379.

14 ..."The Siege of Knoxville." In: SHSP, 1888, v.16, p.387-390.

15 **NANCE, Rosa Ayleene**
"Captain James E(lisha) Reynolds (1837-1920). In: Ch.Okla., Spring 1954, v.32, p.2-17, port., table, views, notes.
Service in Miss. Inf. CSArmy. Text of his reminisc., 1862-1863.

15a **NAPIER, Cameron Freeman**
"The Struggle to Preserve the First White House of the Confederacy." In: Ala. Rev., Jan. 1983, p.3-17.

16 **NAPIER, John H., III**
"Lower Pearl's Civil War Losses." (Jackson, Miss.) Jour. Miss. Hist., April 1961, v.XXIII, #2, pp.94-103.

17 **NAPIER, John Hawkins, III**
"The Militant South Revisited: Myths &

Realities." In: Ala. Rev., Oct. 1980, v.XXXIII, p.243-265.

18 **NAROLL, Raoul S.**
"Lincoln & the Sherman Peace Fiasco Another Fable?" (Lexington, KY.) JSH, Nov. 1954, v.XX, #4, pp.459-483.

19 ..."Narrative of the Cruise of the Alabama, & a list of her Officers & Men. By One of her Crew." London, 1864, 8vo, wraps, 116pp. Sabin-577.

20 ..."A Narrative of the Leading Incidents of the Organization of the First Popular Movement in Virginia in 1865 to Re-establish Peaceful Relations between the Northern & Southern States & of Subsequent Efforts of the Committee of Nine in 1869 to secure the restoration of Virginia to the Union." Richmond, 1888, 8vo, orig. wraps, 72pp. $30.00.

"**NARRATIVE of the Battle of Bull Run** and Manassas Junction, July 18th & 21st, 1861. Accounts of the Advance of Both Armies, the battles, and the defeat & rout of the enemy. Compiled chiefly from the detailed reports of the Virginia & South Carolina Press." Charleston, S.C., Evans & Cogswell, 1861. 8vo, cover title, 32p. Yates Snowden remarks: 'The graphic "Northern Accounts of the Great Rout" here republished is that of the correspondent of the New York World, Edmund Clarence Stedman, later & banker & poet, although his name is not given in the "Narrative." It agrees substantially with the report sent to the London Times by its correspondent, W. H. Russell.

Note: Stedman's 'Battle of Bull Run' was published in NY (Rudd & Carleton, 1861) in a pamphlet of 42pp.

21 **NASH, Charles Edward**
"Biographical Sketches of Gen. Pat Cleburne & Gen. T.C. Hindman, together with humorous anecdotes & reminiscences of the late Civil War, by Charles Edward Nash. Dedicated to the Confederate Veterans & their children." Little Rock, Ark., Tunnah & Pittard, 1898, 12mo, cl., illus., ports., incl. front, 300pp. $400.00.

22 ...Dayton, Ohio: Morningside Press, 1977. Facsimile-39. 12mo, cl, illus., ports., incl. front, (3), 300pp.(8), unnumbered pp. ports & illus.

23 **NASH, E.**
"Jackson's Strategy, a Lecture Delivered by E. Nash, Oct. 21, 1904, in Ballroom of Hotel Victoria, Aldershot." London: Kegen Paul, Trench Trubner Co., 1904 (a 2nd edt., 1905), 12mo, wraps, 32pp. A former lecturer & prof. military history RMC, Kingston, Canada.

24 **NASH, Herbert M.**
"Some Reminiscences of a Confederate Surgeon." In: Trans. College of Physic. of Phila., 1906, 3rd Ser., v.XXVIII, pp.122-144.

25 **NASH, Howard Pervear**
"The CSS Alabama: Roving Terror of the Sea." In: CWTI, Aug. 1963, v.II, #5, p.6-9, 34-39, illus., map, port.

26 ..."A Civil War Legend Examined." In: Amer. Neptune, July 1963, v.XXIII, #3, pp.197-203. Examines the construction of Monitor, Ericsson's difficulties with Wash., in light of the Merrimack's threat.

27 ..."The Ignominious Stone Fleet." In: CWTI, v.III, #3, p.44-49, illus., port. CSA sunk old ships, filled with stones, to prevent ships of Union from entering harbor three months before the war began.

28 ..."Ironclads, Tinclads, & Cottonclads." In: 'Tradition', Oct. 1960, v.3, illus., 11pp. $10.00.

29 **NASH, Howard R.**
"Naval Hist. of Civil War, Union & Confederate." New York, 1973, 8vo, cl., 2nd pr. $15.00.

30 **NASHVILLE Banner**
"Rank in the U.S. & C.S. Armies." In: SHSP 1903, v.31, p.369-370.
NASHVILLE, Battle of
See: Henry De Lamar Clayton.
NASHVILLE, Steamer, CSNavy
See: Theodore S. Garnett, William Conway Whittle.

31 **NASHVILLE, the C.S.S.**
"The Union Iron Clad Monitor "Montauk" destroying the Rebel Steamship "Nashville:, in the Ogeechee River near Savannah, GA., Feb. 27, 1863." N.Y., Currier & Ives, color lithograph, 8 x 12 1/2:, plus margins. $35.00.
Montauk foreground, "Nashville" in background close to shore.

31a **NASHVILLE'S Greeting**
to the Confederate Veterans, Richmond, Va., 1896. Extending an invitation to the U.C.V., to hold their Reunion of 1897 at the Capital of Tennessee." 8vo, wraps, ills. $3.50.

32 **NAST, F.A.**
"History of Confederate Stamps." In: CV, Mar. 1894, v.II, #3, p.77-78, facsms. CV notes that Nast was one of a committee preparing a book on CSA stamps.

33 **NATCHEZ, Mississippi**
See: Mrs. G. Griffing Wilcox.

34 **NATIONS' Most Historic Airport, The:**
Richard E. Byrd Flying Field (City of Richmond Municipal Airport) Site of Three Civil War Battles: Fair Oaks, Oak Grove, etc., 8vo, wraps, (6)pp. ports. illus.

35 **"NATIVE Mexican**
Relations in Confederate Arizona." In: Jour. Ariz. Hist., Autumn 1967, v.8, p.171-178.
NAVAL Architecture: C.S.A. Navy.
See: "Contributions of the CSA to...

36 **NAVAL ENGAGEMENT**
Between the Kearsarge & the Alabama. Fought on the 19th June, 1864 nine miles off Cherbourg. Paris: F. Sinnett; N.Y., W. Schauss, 1864, folio: 17 3/4" x 23 1/2", ('58) $75. Hand- colored. Louis Lebretin (Le Breton).
NAVY of the Confederate States
See: Confederate States Navy.

36a **NEAGLE, James C.**
"Confederate Research Sources: A Guide to Archives Collections." Salt Lake City: Ancestry Pub., 1986. 8vo, cl, 286pp, ills, notes, append, index, bibliog. Paper $13. Cl $17. Guide for those doing genealogical research for Confederate veterans.

37 **NEAL Julia**
"South Union Shakers during War Years." In: FCHQ, April 1965, v.39, #2, p.147-150.

38 **NEAL, Basil Llewellin McKeen Green**
"A Son of the American Revolution; being the Life & Reminiscences of...." Washington, Ga., Washington Reporter Print, 1914. 12mo, cl, illus., ports., 135,(1)pp. $50.00. Genealogy, p.119-130. Misleading title, it pertains almost exclusively to the CSA. Author was 2nd Sgt., Co. D., 12th Ga. Bat. Evans Brig.

39 **NEAL, Lois S., Compiler**
"A Personal Name Index to the Expanded Edition of Jedediah Hotchkiss' Virginia, v.3 of Confederate Military History in 12 vols., Gen. Clement A. Evans., Gen. Edt." Raleigh, N.C., The Author, 1976, 12mo, stiff wraps, (3)-122pp.

40 ..."Genealogical Index to D.H. Hill's North Carolina, v.4 of Confederate Military Hist., in 12 vols., Clement A. Evans. Gen. Edt." Raleigh, N.C., The Author, 1975, 12mo, stiff wraps, (2)-65pp.

41 **NEAL, Mary Julia, Editor**
"The Journal of Eldress Nancy." Nashville, Tenn.: Parthenon Press, 8vo, cl, maps, illus., xii, 256. Shaker colony of South Union, Ky. civilian acct. of war kept by Eldress Nancy Moore.

42 **NEALE, Walter**
"The Sovereignty of the States, an oration. Address to the Survivors of the Eighth Virginia Regiment, while they were gathered about the graves of their fallen comrads, on the battleground of Manassas July 21, 1910." N.Y., Wash., Neale Pul., 1910, 12mo, cl, (5), 143pp. $300.00-Bmk. $125.00-$150.00.

..."Life of Ambrose Bierce." N.Y., Walter Neale, 1929. 8vo, cl, 489pp, ports, incl. front.

43 **NEBLETT, Thomas R.**
"Major Edward C. Anderson & the C.S.S. 'Fingal'". In: Ga. H.Q., June 1968, v.LII, #2, pp.132-158.

44 ..."The Yacht America: A New Account Pertaining to Her Confederate Operations. In: Amer. Neptune, Oct. 1967, Vol.XXVII, #4, pp.233-253.

45 ..."The Necessity for Improved Military Defences considered...."In Time of Peace Prepare for War." Charleston: Walker, Evans Co., 1859, 8vo, wraps, 28pp, vignette, port. Sabin-52210 (Henkel-#1118, part of title).

45a **NEELY, Mark E., Jr., Harold Holzer & Gabor S. Boritt**
"The Confederate Image: Prints of the Lost Cause." Chapel Hill: North Carolina University Press, 1987. 8vo, cl, dj, 274pp, ills. $32.50. Lithos & engravings of the CSA after the war.

46 **NEELY, Rufus Polk**
"General Rufus Polk Neely," In: Illinois Cent. Mag., Nov. 1915, v.4, #5, p.9-16.

47 **NEESE, George Michael**
"Three Years in the Confederate Horse Artillery by George M. Neese a gunner in Chew's Battery, Stuart's horse artillery Army of Northern Virginia." N.Y., Wash., Neale Pub., 1911, 12mo, cl, (2), 362pp. $350.00-c $250.00.

...Dayton: Morningside Press, 1983 $27.50. Intro: Lee A. Wallace, Jr., 8vo, cl., illus., maps, index, 396pp.
...1988. $35.
...Louisville: Lost Cause pr., micro-cd. $5.72.

48 **NEET, J. Frederick, Jr.**
"Stand Watie; Confederate General in the Cherokee Nation." Fall, 1966, Greta Plains Journal, pp.36-51, illus.

49 **NEFF, Ray A.**
"Stonewall Jackson's 'Drunkard Colonel.'" In: CWT, Feb. 1962, v.III, #10(OS), p.16-17, port.

50 **NEIGHBORS, Kenneth F.**
"Elm Creek Raid in Young County Texas in 1864." Abilene, Texas, 1964, West.Tex.Hist.Assoc.Yr.Bk., v.XXXX, p. 83-89.

51 **NEILL, A., Lt. Col.**
"Attention, Partizan Rangers!" Broadside. Washington, Ark., Aug. 15, 1862, Large 4to. $125.00. Companies organized by Col. W.P. Lane, report to Maj. Burns, urgent marching ord. Rondo for Ft. Gibson. "We are not to be dismounted." Not in Crand/Harw/Hargrett.

52 ..."Andrew Neill's Galveston Letters by C. Richard King." In: Texana, Fall 1965, v.III, #3, p.203-217.

53 **NEILSON, Eliza Lucy Irion**
"Lucy's Journal." Greenwood, Miss., Baff Print, 1967, 8vo, cl, illus., ports., 108pp. $25.00. Columbus, Miss., during the war, & Neilson-Irion families.

54 **NEILSON, Thomas H.**
"Fight at Beverly, W.Va." In: CV, August 1907, v.15, p.357-359.

55 ..."Thrilling Experiences of Lieut. Col. Lang." In: CV, November 1905, v.13, p. 497-498. Lang was Sgt., Co. D., 62nd Virginia.

56 **NEIMAN, Simon I.**
"Judah Benjamin. With a foreword by Otto Eisenschiml." Indianapolis, Bobbs-

Merrill 1963, 12mo, cl, 220pp. $40.00. "Mystery man of the Confederacy."

57 **NELLIGAN, Murray H(omer)**
"Curtis-Lee Mansion: The Robert E. Lee Memorial, Virginia. Wash.: US National Park Service, 1950, revised 1956. Historical handbook ser. 6, 8vo, pict. wraps, facsm, fld-map, plans, ports., views, bibliog., (4),48pp. Arlington House built 1802 by Lee's father-in-law.

58 **NELSON, Bernard Hamilton**
"Confederate Slave Impressment Legislation 1861-65." Washington: Journal of Negro History, XXXI-#4, October 1946, pp.392-410.

59 ..."Some Aspects of Negro Life in North Carolina during the Civil War." In: NCHR April 1948, v.XXV, pp.143-166. Bmk- $10.00.

60 ..."Legislative Control of the Southern Free Negro, 1861-1865." In: Catholic Hist.Rev., April 1946, v.XXXII, pp.28-45.

61 **NELSON County, Virginia Civil War Soldiers,**
Lovingston, Va., Nelson County, 1963?. Signed: Austin Embrey, Clerk of Circuit Court of Nelson County, at end: Reba F. Lea, publisher. 8vo, stiff wraps, cover title, 23pp. Lamkins & Ruives Batt., Nelson Lt. Artly, Booker's Batt., Co. B, 8th, Va. Inf., Co. D, 56th, Co. E, 51st, Co. D,19th, Co. H, 49th, Va. Co. J(or i), 5th Va. Cavalry.

62 **NELSON, George W.**
"Treatment of Prisoners." In: SHSP, 1876, v.1, p.243-258.

62a **NELSON, Grace B.**
"Arkadelphia: a Confederate Arsenal Center." In: Clark-CHQ, Winter 1975, v.2, p.10-16.
..."The Federal Invasion of Clark Co." In: CkCHQ, Winter 1975, v.2, p.1-9.

63 **NELSON, Guy, Jr.**
"Baylor University at Independence. The War Years: 1861-1865." In: Texana, Summer, 1964, v.II, #2, p.87-111.

64 **NELSON, Horatio**
"If I'm Killed on this Trip, I Want My Horse Kept by my Brother." The Diary of..." Va. 4th Cavalry, n.p., 1980, 8vo, wraps, ports., illus., maps, 23pp. Manassas Chap: U.D.C. Bmk-106. $10.00.

65 **NELSON, James Poyntz**
"Reminiscences of General Robert E. Lee as president of Washington College now Washington & Lee University." In: Va. Hour. Educ., Jan. 1925, v.XVIII, p.189-192.

66 **NELSON, Larry E.**
"Bullets, Ballots & Rhetoric. Confederate policy for the United States Presidential Contest of 1864." University, Ala., University of Alabama Press, 1980, 8vo, cl, dj, xii, (1), 235p. bibliog: (217)-230 $17.50.

67 ..."Independence or Fight." In: CWTI, June 1976, vo.15, #3, p.10, pl., port.

68 **NELSON, William, Lieut.-Col.**
"Report: The Gettysburg Campaign." In: SHSP, 1882, v. 10, p.62-64.

69 **"NEMO" (pseud.)**
"Remarks on the Policy of Recognizing the Independence of the Southern States." London: William Brown Co., 1863, 24mo, sewn, 48pp. Sabin-52327.

70 ..."Remarks on the Policy of Recognizing the Independence of the Southern States of North America, & on the Struggle in that Continent, by Nemo." Price sixpence. London: Effingham Wilson, 1863, 8vo, sewn, 31,(1)p. Favors recognition of CSA, repudiates the "Times"-"Historicus." Sir Wm. George Granville Venables Vernon Harcourt has compiled "Letters of Historicus."

71 ..."A Few Thoughts on the Confiscation Act, by "Nemo." Augusta, Ga., Office of Constitutionalist 1861, 8vo, wraps, 16pp. DeRenne & Crandall.

72 **NEPTUNE, Daisy C.**
"Flag of the Nighthawk Rangers." In: CV, August 1932, v.40, p.292. Re: Co. F, 17th Va. Cavalry.

73 **NEPVEUX, Ethel Trenholm Seabrook**
"George Alfred Trenholm - The Company that went to War 1861-1865." Charleston, S.C., Comprint, 1973, 8vo, clo, ports., illus., (1),123pp. facsms. $35.00-m. $20.00-Bmk.

73a **NESBIT, James Cooper**
"Four Years on the Firing Line. Edt. Bell Irvin Wiley." Wilmington, N.C., Broadfoot Pub., 1987. 8vo, cl, dj, 276pp, ills (reprint 1914). $30.

74 **NESS, George T., Jr.**
"Georgia's Confederate Dead in Frederick, Maryland Cemetery." In: Ga.H.Q., Dec. 1941, v.XXV, #4, p.364-370.

75 ...Georgia's Early Graduates of West Point.: In: Ga.H.Q., June 1944, v.XXVIII, #2, p.80-92.

76 ..."Louisiana Officers of the Confederate Navy." Reprint: Louisian Historical Quarterly, v.27, #2, April 1944. New Orleans, La., 1944, 8vo, wraps, 10pp.

77 ..."Missouri at West Point, Her Graduates through the Civil War Years." Columbia, Mo., Mo.Hist.Review, Jan. 1944, v.XXXVIII, #2, pp.162-169. About half in the CSA.

78 **NEVILLE, H. Clay**
"Wilson's Creek. Monument to be erected to heroes who fell there." In: SHSP, 1910, v.CCCVIII, p.363-372.

79 **NEVINS, Allan**
"The Needless Conflict. If Buchannan had met the Kansas problem firmly, we might have avoided Civil War." In: Ameri.Hert., Aug. 1956, v.VII, #5, p.4-9, 88-90, facsm, port., illus., incl. color.

80 ..."The Statesmanship of the Civil War." N.Y., Macmillan, 1953, 8vo, cl, (10), 82pp. The Page-Barbour lectures, University of Va., 1951. On the personalities & political doctrines of Lincoln & Jeff Davis, & their relations with their congresses & cabinets.

81 **NEVINS, Allan, James I. ROBERTSON, Jr.**
"Civil War Books, a Critical Bibliography." Baton Rouge, Louisiana State University Press., Pub. for the US Civil War Centennial Commission, 1969, 4to, cl, ix, 278, ix, 326pp., index. $65.00. Vol. 1, second printing, 1970. Vol. 2, o.p.
...Wendell, N.C., Broadfoot, 1980. 2 vols. Vol. I - $20.00. Vol. II - $25.00.

82 **NEW BERN, N.C., Battle**
Barton, J.M.
"Acct. of the Battle."
Hoke, Robt. F.
Iobst, Rich. W.
Pickett, Geo. Edward

83 **NEW HAMPSHIRE Peace Democracy: The**
Clement L. Vallandigham & Frank Pierce, their true relation & objects - Vallandigham - he is endorsed. They denounce Gen. A.E. Burnside & Hon. H.H. Leavitt & the President of the U.S. No censure of rebels." n.p., n.d.(1863), 8vo, caption title, sewn, 7pp.

84 **NEW HAVEN Evening Register**
"An Anecdote (incident) at Gettysburg." In: SHSP, 1885, v.13, p.427-430.

85 **"NEW INDEX, THE**
Journal of the Confederate Research Club, vol. 1, June 1955, Portsmouth, England."

86 **NEW MADRID, Missouri**
Junior Chamber of Commerce. "Centennial Re-enactment, New Madrid, Missouri." New Madrid: Junior Chamber of Commerce, 1962, 8vo, wraps, 76pp. ads in back. Battle of Island #10, Siege of New Madrid, April, 1862; Generals Jno. Pope (Union) & M.Jeff Thompson.

87 **NEW MARKET Cadets:**
Cocke, Preston
Couper, Wm.
Imboden, Jno. D.
Salyards, Joseph
Short, James R.
Stanard, Beverly
Turner, Edward R.
"Official report of Commandant..."
Wise, John S.
Bruce, D.H.
Holmes, Conrad
Morton, Howard
Richmond Times Dispatch
Virginia Military Institute
Echols, Gen. John
Wayland, John W.

88 **NEW MARKET Day at V.M.I.**
Celebrating the 39th Anniversary of the Battle of New Market & Unveiling of Ezekiel's Statue: Virginia mourning her dead. Virginia Military Institute, Lexington Alumni Assn., Roanoke, Va., Stone Print, 1903. 8vo, wraps, 84pp. illus., ports., $125.00-R. Addresses by J.N. Upshur, H. Conrad & John S. Wise.

88a **NEW ORLEANS (LA) 'Picayune'**
"Andersonville Prison." In: SHSP, 1908, v.36, p.1-7.
..."Attempted Sale of the Federal Fleet." In: SHSP, 1904, v.32, p.58-67.
..."The Battle of Fort Gregg." In: SHSP, 1900, v.28, p.265-7.
..."The Battle of Chickamauga." In: SHSP, 1902, v.30, p.178-88.
..."Butler's Investment of New Orleans." In: SHSP, 1895, v.23, p.182-8.
..."Colonel Eugene Waggaman." In: SHSP, 1888, v.16, p.446-51.
..."Sketch of Eugene Waggaman." In: SHSP, 1897, v.25, p.180-6.
..."Gen. Johnston's campaign in Georgia." In: SHSP, 1893, v.21, p.314-21.
..."History of Quitman Rifles." In: SHSP, 1906, v.34, p.239-42.
..."Ninety-third Anniversary of the Birth of Jefferson Davis." In: SHSP, 1901, v.29, p.1-33.
..."Hon. Thos. J. Semmes." In: SHSP, 1897, v.25, p.317-33.
..."The Officer Who Rode the Gray Horse." In: SHSP, 1893, v.21, p.301-4.
..."Palmer, B.M. Address at New Orleans." In: SHSP, 1882, v.10, p.250-4.
..."Two Cavalry Chieftans." In: SHSP, 1888, v.16, p.451-4.
..."Why We Failed to Win. Inquiry into Causes of CSA defeat." In: SHSP, 1902, v.30, p.368-71.

NEW ORLEANS R.E. Lee Monument Association
See: W. I. Hodgson.

89 **NEW ORLEANS:**
United Daughters of the Confederacy. "The Natal Day of General Lee." In: SHSP, 1900, v.28, p.228-243.

90 **"THE NEW SOUTH & the Old South.**
Myths & Mythmakers." In: Tyler's Quart.Hist. & Genea. Mag., July 1925, v.VII, #1, p.145-154. Tyler reviews Judge Robert W. Winston's 'Rebirth of the Southern States.'

90a **"NEW TESTAMENT."**
Nashville, Tenn. Graves, Marks Co., 1861. 5 1/8" cl. Crandall-4213. Gdsp. $750.

91 **"NEW TEXAS Grammer, The."**
1864, 24pp., James C.G.R. Patton Announced as "Now ready for delivery," Houston: TWT, Dec. 12, 1864.

92 **"NEW TEXAS Primary Reader**
for the use of Primary Schools, The." Houston: E.H. Cushing book & job print, 1863, 12mo, stiff boards, 96pp. Crandall-4074, Heading: 'New Texas Series.'

93 **"NEW TEXAS Primary Speller, The,"**
1863, (50?)pp., announced as "Now out & for sale," Houston: TWT, May 27, 1863.

94 ..."The New Texas Primary Speller." 40pp., Second Edt., 1864, stiff paper wraps, announced as "now out," Houston: TWT, Nov. 4, 1864.

95 **"NEW TEXAS Primer, The."**
1863, 24pp., wraps, announced for sale in Houston 'Tri-Weekly Telegraph,' May 13, 1863. 'Fourth Edt. just out,' Nov. 19, 1864.

96 **"NEW TEXAS Primers, Spelling Books."**
List prepared by O.L. Davis, Jr. for Texas University: Library Chronicle: The following list, known as "Ghosts," while no copy is known to exist, there is reasonable evidence they did exist.

97 **"NEW TEXAS Reader,**
designed for the use of schools in Texas, The," Houston, Texas: E.H. Cushing, 1864, 16mo, boards, vii, (1), 184pp. (jk-$850.00) $350.00-Mor. $750.00 David. Much on Civil War battles, history. At head: 'The New Texas Series.'

98 **"NEW TEXAS Spelling Book, The,"**
96pp., printed boards, announced as, "Now Published," Houston: TWT, Aug. 3, 1863.

99 ..."The New Texas Spelling Book." 96pp. Second Edt., 1864, announced as "Just Published," Houston: TWT, August 17, 1864.

100 ...Houston: Telegraph Print, 1863, 12mo, pict. boards, 95,(1)pp. $100.00. One of the many by E.H. Cushing. Harwell-4074-2, gives an 1865 edition of 145pp.

101 **NEW YORK WORLD**
"Who fired the first gun at Fort Sumter?" In: SHSP, 1892, v.20, p.61-63.

102 **NEWBERRY, Thomas Jefferson**
"The Civil War Letters of Thomas Jefferson Newberry." Jackson, Miss., Jour. Miss., Hist., Jan. 1948, v.X, #1, pp.44-80. Priv.: 29th Miss. Reg. 1862-1864.

103 **NEWBOLT, Henry John, Sir**
"The Book of the Thin Red Line, with 8 colored plates & 38 illustrations in black & white by Stanley L. Wood." London, N.Y., Longmans, Green, 1915, 12mo, cl, col. front & others, illus., xii, 308pp. Final chap. devoted to adventures of Thos. (Stonewall) Jackson.

104 **NEWCOMB, James Pearson**
"Address of Hon. James P. Newcomb, delivered at Comfort, Texas on the 10th of August 1887, the 25th anniversary of the Nueces Massacre." San Antonio, Texas, Johnson Bros., 1887, 12mo, wraps, cover title, 10p.
See: Jno. W. Sansom, Robert W. Shook, Robert H. Williams.

105 ..."Sketch of Secession times in Texas & Journal of Travel through Texas to California, including a history of "Box Colony." by..., formerly editor of the "Alamo Express," San Antonio, Texas." San Francisco, California, August, 1863, 8vo, wraps, 2p.1., 12pp., 1. 33pp., Vandale. Union Refuge in Texas (TWS-$650).

106 **NEWCOMER, Lee Nathaniel**
"The Battle of Memphis, 1862." In: WTHSP, 1958, v. 12, p.40-57, notes.

107 ..."The Battle of the Rams." Amer.Neptune, April 1965, vol.XXV, #2, pp.128-139.

108 **NEWELL, Robert R.**
"Capture & Burning of the ship Anna F. Schmidt by Alabama." In: Amer.Neptune, Jan. 1965, vol. XXV, #1, pp.18-28.

109 **NEWELL, W.B., Mrs.**
"Flags of the Confederate States of America, 1861-1865.: Richmond, Va., n.d., 12mo, wraps, illus. in full color, 12pp. Story of the creation & adaption of the designs of the CSA flags.

109a **NEWHALL, F.C.**
"The Battle of Beverly Ford." In: "Annals of War." Philadelphia: Times Pub. Co., 1879, p.134-46.

110 **NEWMAN, Harry Wright**
"Maryland & the Confederacy." Annapolis, Md., 1976, 8vo, cl, dj, 396pp.,

limited edition of 600, #50. Unit sketch each Md. CSA regiment.

111 **NEWMAN, Ralph & E.B. LONG**
"The Civil War Digest. (New & enlarged edition of 'The Civil War: The Picture Chronicle') Intro: Allan Nevins, maps by Barbara Long." N.Y., The Universal Library, Grosset & Dunlap, 1956, 1960, 12mo, cl & bds., facsms, illus., maps, ports., front, xiii, (1), 274pp.

112 **NEWMAN, S.H., Mrs.**
"Admiral Raphael Semmes: His Services to the Southern Confederacy." In: CV, Oct. 1927, v. XXXV, p. 376-378.

NEWPORT NEWS, Virginia
See: Charles Harris.

112a **NEWTON, James K.**
"The Siege of Mobile." In: AHQ, Winter 1958, v.20, #4, p.595-600.

113 **NEWTON, John Brockenbrough**
"Lee's Birthday." In: SHSP, 1889, v.17, pp.356-357.

114 **NEWTON, Virginius**
"The Confederate Navy." In: SHSP, 1894, v.22, p.87-98.

115 ..."The Merrimac or Virginia." In: SHSP 1892, v.20, p.1-26.

116 ..."The Confederate States Ram, Merrimac or Virginia. The History of her plan, construction & her engagements with the U.S. Fleet, Mar. 8 & 9, 1862." Reprint, SHSP, v.XX, 1892, pp.26. $25.00-B. Richmond "Dispatch" originally printed.
...Richmond: Hermitage Press, 1907, 8vo, wraps, 34pp. $16.00-Bmk.
...Richmond: William Ellis Jones, 1892, 8vo, wraps, 28pp.

116a **NICHOLAS, Samuel Smith**
See: under title "South Carolina, Disunion & a Miss. Valley Confederacy."...
..."Conservative essays, legal & political." Phila: J.B. Lippincott, 1863-9, (in 4 vols). Above title in 'Essays.' p.116-44 in Vol. 1.

117 **NICHOLS, George W.**
"A Soldier's Story of his Regiment (61st Georgia) & Incidentally of the Lawton-Gordon-Evans Brigade, Army of Northern Virginia by Private G.W. Nichols." Jesup, Ga., 1898, 12mo, wraps, ports., xi,(1), (13)-291, (2), illus., atg. copy dated 1899. $750.00-ATG. $1,000.00-OB. $500.00-Bmk 106.
...Kennesaw, Ga., Continental Book, 1961, 12mo, cl, ports., x, (13)-291, (2)p. $21.25.

118 **NICHOLS, J.H.**
"Experiences in battle of Murfreesboro, Tenn." In: CV, 1902, v. 10, p.162-163. Battle: Dec. 31, 1862 - Jan. 3, 1863.

119 **NICHOLS, James L.**
"Confederate Engineers." Tuscaloosa, Ala.: Confed. Pub. Co., 1957, Confederate Centennial Studies, #5, 12mo, stiff wraps, port, 122 pp., Lim. Edt., 450 copies. $25.00-Bmk.
..."Confederate Engineers." Gaithersburg, Md., Olde Soldier Books. 1988 reprint. 8vo, wraps, 122pp.

120 ..."Confederate Engineers & the Defense of Mobile, 1861-1865." In: Ala. Rev., July 1959, v.12, p.180-195, map, table notes.

121 ..."The Confederate Quartermaster in the Trans-Mississippi." Austin: University of Texas Press, 1964, 8vo, cl, d/w, pp.vii, 126, illus. $30.00-Bmk.

122 ..."Confederate Map Supply." In: Mil.Engineer, Jan./Feb., 1954, v.XLVI, p.28-32.

123 ..."The Tax-in-Kind in the Department of the Trans-Mississippi." In: CWH, Dec., 1959, v.V, #4, p.382-389.

124 **NICHOLS, James Wilson**
"Now you Hear My Horn. The Journal of James Wilson Nichols 1820-1887. Edited by Catherine W. McDowell, illustrated by Eldridge Hardie." Austin & London: University of Texas Press, 1967, Daughters of the Republic of Texas, Charles Hertzog typography, 8vo, cl, dj, facsms, illus,

sketches, port., maps, inclu. liners, xvi, (5), 212pp.

125 **NICHOLS, Roy F.**
"1461-1861: The American Civil War in Perspective." Baton Rouge, La., JSH, May, 1950, v.XVI, #2, pp.143-160.

126 ..."A Hundred Years Later: Perspectives on the Civil War." Houston, Tex., JSH, May 1967, v.XXXIII, #2, pp.153-162. Unresolved questions remaining on key points, from secession thru war. $8.00.

127 ..."The Operation of American Democracy, 1861-1865: Some Questions." Lexington, Ky., JSH, Feb., 1959, v.XXV, #1, pp.31-52.

128 ..."The Stakes of Power 1845-1877." New York: Hill & Wang, 1961, "The Makers of America," General Editor: David Donald. 8vo, cl, d/w, 246pp., maps. A contest of power by north to break dominance of power in congress of South.

129 ..."United States vs. Jefferson Davis, 1865-1869." Amer.Hist.Rev., January 1926, v.XXXI, p.266-283.

130 **NICHOLS, Wesley**
"Autobiography & Civil War recollections of...Wesley Nichols, Leesville, S.C." Leesville, S.C., Twin-county print, 1915, 12mo, cover title, 27pp.

131 **NICHOLS, William H.**
"The siege & capture of Harper's Ferry by the Confederates, September 1862. By William H. Nichols, 3rd, (late corporal Co.A, Seventh squadron Rhode Island cavalry), Providence, The Society, 1889, 12mo, wraps, illus., maps, 250 copies, 48pp. $25.00. Papers read before the Rhode Island soldiers & sailors society, 4th ser., #2.

132 **NICHOLSON, James William**
"Stories of Dixie." N.Y., American Book Co., 1915, 12mo, cl, front, illus., ports., pl., 242pp., Life in N. Louisiana before Civil War & his exp. as a CSA soldier.

...Baton Rouge, La., Claitor's Book Store 1966 Reprint, 12mo, decr. cl., illus., 247pp., port.(front) CSA chaps: VI-IX, p.133-235. $4.00.

133 **NICHOLSON, John**
"To Mock My Maker" A Civil War Letter on Freedom of Conscience." In: Hist.Mag.Protest.Episc., Church 1972, v.XLI, p.67-76.

134 **NICHOLSON, John Page**
Catalogue of the Library of Lt.Col. John Page Nicholson relating to the War of the Rebellion." Philadelphia: Private print, 1914, J.T. Palmer, tall 8vo, cl, front, 3,1,5-1022pp. $300.00

135 **NICHOLSON, William A.**
"The Burning of Columbia." Columbia, S.C., Wm. Sloane pr., 1895, 12mo, wraps, 12pp., Turnbull-IV.

136 **NICKELSON, B.C.**
"A Brief Sketch of the Life of a Confederate Soldier & the Ups & Downs during Pioneer & Indian Warfare in Texas." Dallas, Tex., Stellmacher & Clark, 1928, 16mo, wraps, port, 16pp., $25.00. Print of 1932 on portrait page. Some copies spell author B.C. Nicholson.

136a **NICKERSON, Edmond A.**
"Heroes of the South: Address delivered under auspices of the UCV, department of Missouri, at the Opera House, Wattenbury, Missouri, Sept. 27, 1900." (St. Joseph ? 1900 ?). 8vo, wraps, 16pp.

137 **NICKERSON, Hoffman**
"Grant & Lee." In: Amer.Rev., 1934, v.4, p.67-83. Reviews 'Grant & Lee', by J.F.C. Fuller.

137a **NICOLAY, John G. & John Hay**
"Jackson's Valley Campaign & Seven Day Battles (in Abraham Lincoln, A History)." In: Cent., Nov. 1888, v.15, p.130-48.

138 **NIELSEN, J.V., Jr.**
"Post Confederate Finance in South Caro-

NIEMEYER, William Frederick
See: Wm. Henry Stewart.

139 **NIGHTINGALE, Florence**
"Directions for cooking by troops in camp & hospital, prepared for the Army of Virginia & published by order of the Surgeon General: with essays on "taking food" & "what food." Richmond, Va., J.W., Randolph, 1861, 12mo, wraps, 35, (5)pp.

140 **NINETEENTH CENTURY**
"What the Alabama Did." In: SHSP, 1896, v.24, p.249-250.

141 **"XIX CENTURY, THE."**
Charleston, S.C., 1869, 8 3/4 x 5 1/2", 3/4 calf, vii, 496pp. vol.1, June 1869-#6, Nov. 1869, complete in one vol., scarce monthly. Contains: 'Confederate Blockade Runner,' 'Shoulder to Shoulder,' in 4 parts, 'Reminiscences CSA Camp & Field,' in six installments. v.2 #6, $18.00. Note: Felix G. de Fontaine wrote & reprinted "Shoulder to Shoulder."

142 **NIPPERT, Alfred K.**
"Lucius Quintus Cincinnatus Lamar, an Appreciation." n.p., n.d., (Oxford, Miss.?), 12mo, wraps, (11)pp., port(front), color illus.(front), printed in sepia ink. Author's subject Lamar was assoc. Justice, US Supreme Ct., founder Miss. Gamma Chap. Sigma Alpha Epsilon.

143 **NISBET, James Cooper**
"Four Years on the Firing Line, by Col. James Cooper Nisbet." Chattanooga, Tenn., Imperial pr, 1914, 12mo, cl, front.(port), 445pp., 3/4 lt, Bmk105-$400.00. $750.00-OB. Bmk112-$500.00.
...Jackson, Tenn., McCowat-Mercer pr., 1963, Edt.: Bell I. Wiley, 8vo, cl, dj, illus., facsm., ports., incl. front, xxi, (1), 267pp., index. $40.00.
...Louisville: Lost Cause, micro-cd. $6.64.

144 **NIST, John A.**
"Dulce et decorum. Book one & two. An epic of the American Civil War. Book one: The Peninsula Campaign, (2) The Second Manassas. Battle biography (in poetry) of Stonewall Jackson some men under his command." Beloit, Wisc., 1960, 8vo, wraps, 88, 56pp.
...Beloit, Wisc., 1958, The Beloit Poetry Journal, v.9, #1/2, fall, winter 1958, 8vo, wraps, port, 88pp., "The Peninsula Campaign," Book 1.

145 **NIVEN, Alexander C.**
"Joseph E. Brown, Confederate Obstructionist." In: Ga.H.Q., Sept., 1958, v.XLII, #3, pp. 233-257. $8.00.

146 ..."German military literature & the Confederacy" In: Amer.-German Rev., Feb./Mar., 1959, v.25, p.31-33. Comments on: Justus Schiebert, Heros von Borcke, & Hugo Fred. Phil. Johan.

147 ..."The Private Papers of Dr. William M. McPheeters." London, Jour. Confed.Hist.Soc., Spring 1966, v.4, #1, p.24-30.

148 **NIX, Bennie E.**
"Compiled List of Confederate Soldiers of Shelby County Texas." Center, Texas: J.B. Sanders Offset Press, 1965, 4to, wraps, illus., 31pp. $35.00-Bmk.

149 **NIXON, Alfred**
"Address: Confederate Memorial Hall, Lincolnton, N.C., Aug. 27, 1908." Lincolnton, N.C., News print, 1908, Southern States Chap., U.D.C., 8vo, wraps, 22pp. $15.00.

150 ..."Roster, Ex-Confederate Soldiers living in Lincoln County, with address of A. Nixon before the U.D.C. & the Confederate Veterans in the court house Lincolnton, N.C., Memorial Day, May 10, 1907." Lincolnton, N.C., News print, 1907, 8vo, wraps, 19pp.

lina." In: SCHMag., April 1955, v.56, #2, p.85-91.

151 **NIXON, Alfred, et al**
"Roster of Confederate soldiers in the War Between the States furnished by Lincoln County, N.C., 1861-1865. Published by order of W.J. Hoke Camp, Confederate Veterans." Lincolnton, N.C., Journal Print, 1905, tall 8vo, wraps, 64pp. $100.00.-Carolina Bks. $125.00.

152 **NIXON, Herman Clarence & John T.**
"The Old South Today." In: Va.Q.Rev., 1955, v.31, p.265-275, Spring. $8.00. Characteristics of South in '50s & extent they survive.

153 ..."The Confederate Constitution (1861) Today." In: Ga.Rev., Winter, 1955, v.9, p.369-376. $8.00. Modern merits of the CSA constitution & public philosophy.

154 **NIXON, J.R. (Joseph Robert)**
"Exercises of Lee & Jackson Day, Lincolnton, N.C., Jan. 23, 1915." n.p., wraps, 15pp.

155 **NIXON, Liberty Independence**
"An Alabamian at Shiloh: The Diary of Liberty Independence Nixon. Edt.: Hugh C. Bailey." In: Ala.HQ, April 1958, v.11, p.144-155, notes. Records of Pvt. in 26th Ala. Inf., 24 Feb.-6 Apr. 1862.

156 **NOEL, E.F., Governor**
"Life & Services of David Warren Sanders." Autobiographical Sketch, Univ.Miss., PMHS, p.331-343, 1910. Sanders was with Hood's Brigade.

157 **NOEL, Lois Purcell**
"John Hunt Morgan." Paducah, Ky., The Author, 1933, 12mo, wraps, 51pp. $35.00.

158 **NOEL, Theophilus**
"Circular. Prospectus..., a work history of the War in the Trans-Mississippi Department of the Campaigns in the State of Texas, New Mexico, Arizona, Arkansas, Louisiana, Missouri, & the Indian Territory." "At Present or intentions are of publishing an octavo volume of 450 pages, to be illustrated." Asks for data. Theo. Noel, author of "A Campaign from Santa Fe," etc. Houston, March 20th, 1865. Broadside, 1p., 21.3 x 26.5cm. Winkler-1379. TU

159 ..."Autobiography & Reminiscences of Theophilus Noel." Chicago: Theo. Noel Co., Print, 1904, 8vo, cl, illus., port(front), 348,(1)p. $80.00. $100.00-B. $200.00-G.

160 ..."A Campaign from Santa Fe to the Mississippi, being a history of the Old Sibley Brigade, from its first organization to the present time, its Campaigns in New Mexico, Arizona, Texas, Louisiana & Arkansas, in the year of 1861-1862-1863-1864, by Theo. Noel, 4th Texas Cavalry." Shreveport, La., Shreveport News Pr., John Dickinson, propr., 1865, 8vo, cl, front (fldg. table), 152pp. (Copy sold '54 in Texas, $1,150.00).
...Raleigh, N.C., C.R. Sanders, Jr., 1961, Large 8vo, clo, (17)p., (152p.facsms), (2)pp. Introduction by Neal Austin.
...Houston, Texas, Stagecoach Press, 1961, 8vo, cl, dj, xxvii, 183p. maps. $40.00. Newly edited with an intro: Martin Hardwick Hall & Edwin Adams Davis, reset type, limited edt., 7000 copies. Dornb-II, notes "p.98-126 of original pub. are omitted."
...Louisville: Lost Cause Pr., micro-cd., 1957.

161 **NOELL, John W.**
"Emancipation of the Slaves of Rebels: View of the Minority on the Bill for Emancipation of the Slaves of Rebels." Washington, 1862. House report 120, 37th Congress, 2nd Session, 8vo, 3pp. folder (opposes emancipation). (old) $2.00.

162 **NOLAN, Jeannette Covert**
"Belle Boyd, Secret Agent." N.Y., Messner Print, 1967, 8vo, cl, 191pp., juvenile fiction.
..."Spy for the Confederacy: Rose O'Neal Greenhow." N.Y., J. Messner Print, 1960, 8vo, cl, 192pp, bibliog., a juvenile lit.

162a **NOLAN, Lewis Edward, Captain**
"Cavalry; its History & Tactics, by Captain L. E. Nolan, 15th Hussars. First American from the second London edition." Columbia, S.C., Evans & Cogswell, 1864. 12mo, cl, xii, 202p. $100. Crandall-2454. Yates Snowden notes: 'was the one who gave the unfortunate command to the 'Light Brigade' at Balaklava.
...Columbia, S.C., Evans & Cogswell, 1864. 16mo, cl-boards, xii, 202p. Crandall-2464. Goodspeed $750.

163 **NOLAN, Terence H. & Jerrell H. Shafner**
"A Reckless, Unthinking Adventurer-George St. Leger Grenfell." In: CWTI, Jan. 1971, v.IX, #9, p.29-39, illus., ports.

164 **NOLL, Arthur Howard, Rev.**
"General Kirby-Smith." Sewanee, Tenn., University Press at the University of the South, 1907, 12mo, cl, front(port), vi, (1), 293pp. ($27.50, $125.00, $140.00-Bmk.) $200.00-Bmk105 $300.00, $250.00-OB
See: Rev. Charles Todd Quintard, CSA. Edt., extended by Rev. Noll.

165 **NORMAN, William M.**
"A Portion of My Life; being of short & imperfect history written while a prisoner of war on Johnson's Island, 1864." Winston-Salem, N.C., J.F. Blair print, 1959, 8vo, cl, dj, illus., incl., liners, 242pp.

166 **NORONA, Delf & Charles Shetler**
"West Virginia Imprints, 1790-1863. A checklist of books, newspapers, periodicals & broadsides. Publication #1." 1958, Moundsville: West Virginia Library Assn., 8vo, cl, facsms, 316pp.

167 **NORRIS, William R.**
"The Boggstown Resolutions." In: Ind.Mag.His., Dec. 1954, v.50, p.381-388. Account (first printed in 1887) of meeting 16 Feb. 1861, in which citizens of Sugar Creek Township, Shelby Co., Ind., expressed wish to "be attached to the Southern Confederacy: if the union should be divided.

168 **NORRIS, William, Col.**
"Story of the Confederate States Ship "Virginia", (once Merrimac). Her Victory over the Monitor. Born March 7. Died May 10th, 1862. Sic Iter Ad Astra." Baltimore, 1879. 8vo, wraps, 25pp. $50.00. Col. Norris was Chief of Signal Corps & Secret Service Bureau, CSArmy. Notes SHSP item was republished from the one copy surviving the destruction of the edition.
...In: SHSP, n.s., #4, whole No.XLII, Oct. 1917, p.204-233. Norris' reply to an article in Mary & Navy Journal-"The Monitor & the Merrimac, of June 13th. Its "manufactured history".
..."Col. William Norris & the Confederate Signal & Secret Service." In: MdHM, Summer 1975, p.22. $20.

169 **NORTH CAROLINA**
"Executive & Legislative Documents, Session 1860-1861. Total 42 separately paged documents." Raleigh, 1861, Tk8vo. $150.00. $200.00-Ginz. Gov. message, communications from Commissioners to Alabama & Miss., & from Gov. of Texas; Alabama sess. Ordinance & Tenn. Resolutions.
...In the Confederate Congress." In: NCHR, 1952, v.29, p.359-378.

170 ...In the War Between the States. Report of the Comm. Lit. & Hist. Activities in N.C., etc."
See: Five Points in the Record of N.C. in the Great War.

171 ..."Public & Private Laws of the State of North Carolina passed by the General Assembly at its regular session 1864-1865. Adjourned session of 1865 & Acts & Resolutions, Secret Session." Raleigh, N.C., 1865, 8vo, cl, 130, 75pp.

172 ..."State Guard. Turn on the Lights." Testimony of two old soldiers who wore the gray, when there was some danger in doing so..., Wilmington, N.C., 1891, 8vo, wraps, 14pp., (C.Hill) $15.00. Spirited controversy over gray vs. blue uniforms.

173 **NORTH CAROLINA - In: SHSP:**
See: Kemp Plummer Battle, Wm.H.S. Burgwyn, Geo.L. Christian, Graham Daves, "1st N.C. Vols.," H.G. Flanner, Geo. W. Glowers, Daniel Harvey Hill, Jr., Bradley T. Johnson, James Henry Lane, Wm. J. Martin, F.A. Olds, Thos. R. Roulhac, Chs. M. Stedman, R.D. Stewart, Matthew F. Taylor, Zeb Baird Vance, H.C. Wall, Stepehn B. Weeks, 'Wilmington, N.C. Messenger.'

174 **NORTH CAROLINA Civil War Documentary,**
Edts: W.Buck Yearns & John G. Barrett. Chapel Hill: University of North Carolina, 1980, 8vo, cl, dj, map-liners, illus., port, xvi, (1), 365pp., index, bibliog., (343)-49.

175 **NORTH CAROLINA Confederate Veteran,**
1898. Entire issue devoted to North Carolina, v.6, #5, pp.195-234, cont'd., #6, p.257-269, illus., ports.

175a **NORTH CAROLINA General Assembly**
"An Act for the Relief of Certain Soldiers of the late War between the States." Raleigh, 1889. 8vo, wraps, 4p. (Rowe). $35.

176 **NORTH CAROLINA Legislature**
"A Bill to be entitled the Revenue Act." N.C. House Bill, Sess. 1864-1865." Raleigh. N.C.?, 1865?, 8vo, sewn, wraps, 42pp. $20.00. Not in Crandall/Harwell.

177 **NORTH CAROLINA Soldiers**
at Appomattox. In: SHSP, 1896, v.24, p.254-255, From 'Wilmington N.C., Messenger.'

178 **"NORTH CAROLINA at Gettysburg."**
Published on the occasion of the rededication of the North Carolina Monument at Gettysburg National Military Park, July 1, 1963. Raleigh, N.C., 1963, North Carolina Confederate Centennial Commission, 15x21cm, illus., ports., wraps, 27pp.

179 **"NORTH CAROLINA in the Civil War."**
Washington, D.C., Pub.South.Hist.Assn., July 1902, v.VI, #4, pp.328-334. Review of works on Civil War in N.C.

180 **NORTH CAROLINA:**
Confederate & State Securities in the Treasury. Report of the Secretary of State & Comptroller concerning...." Raleigh, N.C., 1867?, Ex.Doc.#16, Sess. 1866-67, 8vo, wraps, 7pp. Note: except for 3 examples of each, all bonds & notes were burned. Bmk-111. $25.00.

180a **NORTH CAROLINA TROOPS** 1861-5, a Roster.
See: Louis H. Manarin & Weymouth T. Jordan, Jr.

181 **NORTH, Nancy**
"The Boy Gunners of Lee." In: CV, Feb. 1924, v.XXXII, p.59-60.

182 **NORTH, Robert W.**
"An Independent Scout." In: SHSP, 1886, v.14, p.241-245.

183 ..."Visit of a Confederate Cavalryman to a Federal General's Headquarters." In: SHSP, 1880, v.8, p.535-537.

183a **NORTH, Thomas**
"Five Years in Texas: or, what you did not hear during the war from January 1861 to January 1865. A narrative of his travel experiences, & observations in Texas & Mexico." Cincinnati, Elm Street Print, 1870. 12mo, cl, viii, (90-231p. 1st. gdsp $300.
...1871 Edt.

184 **NORTHERN MAN**
with Southern Principles, & the Southern Man with American Principles; or, a View of the Comparative Claims of W.H. Harrison, & M. Van Buren...to the Support of Citizens of the Southern States. Washing-

ton, 1940, Peter Force, 8vo. Candidates for President, heading: Republican Committee of Seventy-six. (copy: Carlisle Barracks Library).

185 **NORTHERN PRISON Life:**
Lee's Army in Pennsylvania - Battle of Gettysburg. In: LWL, v.II, 1866-1867, pp.39-44, 102-107, 172-179, Sig: "Sigma Chi, Fayetteville, N.C., May 8, 1866.

186 **"NORTHERN Robbery"**
(South Carolina) Oldham (England) Hirst & Rennie, print., "Chronicle" office., (186-?), Small broadside, Sabin-87901.

187 **NORTHERN Voice**
for the Dissolution of the Union, A. Sabin-55835. n.p., 1860-(1861?), 8vo.

188 **NORTHERN, Robert Nixon**
"The Raw Confederate of April, 1861." In: SHSP, 1893, v.21, p.346-352.

189 **NORTHERN, William J., Edt.**
"Men of Mark in Georgia. A Complete & Elaborate History of the state from its settlement to the present time, chiefly told in Biographies & Autobiographies of the most eminent men in each of Georgia's progress & development." Atlanta, Ga., A.B. Caldwell Pub., 1907-1912, 7 vols., v.III, vi, 581pp. (CSA vol.) $50.00.
...Spartanburg, S.C., The Reprint Co., 1974. $25.00.

190 **NORTHROP, Claudian Bird**
"Political Remarks by "N". Numbers IX, X, XI." Charleston, S.C., Evans & Cogswell, 1861, 8vo, wraps, 31pp. Dated Charleston 26th Dec., 1860. Originally pub. in Charleston Courier, #s I-IX, only in newspapers.

191 ..."Southern Odes by the Outcast. A Gentleman of South Carolina. Published for the benefit of the Ladies Fuel Society." Charleston, S.C., Harper & Calvo, 1861, 8vo, wraps, 40pp.

192 **NORTHROP, Lucius Bellinger**
"Report of Commissary General Northrop CSA-Subsistence Department, Feb. 9, 1865." In: SHSP, 1876, v.II, p.86-103.

193 ..."Some Letters of...1860-1865. Edt.: Willard E. Wight." In: VMHB, Oct. 1960, v.68, p.456-477, offprint, wraps, 22pp. $10.00.

194 **NORTHROP, Theodore F.**
"Other Side of the Fayetteville Road Fight." In: CV, Sept., 1912, v.XX, p.423.

195 **NORTHUMBERLAND Historical Society, Va.**
"Bulletin of the Northumberland Historical Society - Civil War Centennial Issue, v.1, #1, n.p., 1965, v. II, #1, 84pp. With a brief sketch of the 37th Regiment, Infantry, Virginia. $8.00 each.

NORTHWESTERN Confederacy:
See: Jubal A. Early.

196 **NORTON, Andre (pseud.) Mary Alice Norton**
"Rebel Spurs." Cleveland, World Pub., 1962, 12mo, cl, 224pp., juvenile fiction.

197 ..."Ride Proud, Rebel!" Cleveland, World Publ, 1961, 12mo, cl, 255pp., juvenile fiction. Novel of scout for Forrest.

198 **NORTON, Anthony Banning**
"Speech of Hon. A.B. Norton, in vindication of History & the Constitution of the Union, in the Texas Legislature, Jan. 24, 1860." Austin, Texas, Southern intelligencer print, 1860, 8vo, caption title, 16pp.
See: Texas Secession.

199 ..."Vindication of A.B. Norton, from attacks of his enemies." Made in the Texas Legislature April 6, 1861, n.p., 1861, 8vo, yellow wraps, 8pp. Marginal notes by John Henry Brown, his copy.

200 **NORTON, Frank Henry**
"The Life of Alexander H. Stephens." N.Y., John B. Alden, pub., 1886, 16mo, cl, port(front), 1-illus., 88, (4,ads)pp.

201 **NORTON, Herman**
"Rebel Religion-The Story of the Confederate Chaplains." St. Louis, Mo., Bethany

Press, 1961, 12mo, cl, dj, illus, sketches, 144pp. Roster of CSA Chaplains, bibliog., pp.135-144. Op $40.00.

202 ..."The Organization & Function of the Confederate Military Chaplaincy 1861-1865." Ann Arbor, University Microfilm, Pub. 20,032, 1956 (e.g. 1957), micro/-typescript, 360lfs. Vanderblt.

203 ..."Revivalism in the Confederate Armies." In" CWH, December, 1960, v.VI, #4, p.410-424.

204 **NORTON, Wesley**
"The Role of a Religious Newspaper in Georgia During the Civil War." In: Ga.H.Q., June 1964, v.XLVIII, #2, pp.125-146.

205 ..."The Methodist Episcopal Church & the Civil Disturbances in North Texas in 1859 & 1860." In: SwHQ, January 1965, v.LXVIII, #3, pp.317-341.

206 **NORVELL, James R.**
"The Supreme Court of Texas under the Confederacy - 1861-1865." In: Houston Law Rev., 1966, v.IV, p.46-61.

207 ..."The Reconstruction Courts of Texas, 1867-1873." In: SwHQ, October, 1958, v.LXII, #2, pp.141-163.

208 **NORWOOD, John Nelson**
"The Schism in the Methodist Episcopal Church, 1844: A Study of Slavery & Ecclesiastical Politics." Alfred, N.Y., Alfred University, 1923, 8vo, cl, map, 225pp. (Alfred University Studies, #1).
See: Methodist Quarterly Review.

209 **NORWOOD, Thomas Manson, Judge**
"An Appeal to men & women of the South to build a Christian Pantheon in honor of our Confederate Heroes." also, cover title. Savannah, Ga., Grizell & Alleyn Pr., 1906?, 8vo, wraps, 16pp. Emory.

210 ..."A True Vindication of the South." Savannah, Ga., 1917, tall 8vo, cl, 451pp., $20.00. Former senator from Ga., extremely bitter in his denunciation of the North.

211 ..."Notes on Secession in Tallahassee & Leon County." In: FHQ, October, 1925, v.IV, #2, pp.62-67.

212 **NOTICE!**,
The Republicans of Macon City, Missouri, requested by an assemblage of Southern citizens, to settle their business as soon as possible, & Withdraw from the confines of the Honorable state of Missouri, & travel to parts better suited to their Abolition views, on or before the 4th March, 1861. We are determined & resolved to rid ourselves of Black Republicanism. Beware the time is close at hand! True Southerners. Broadside, pg.365, Mo.Hist.Rev. LI-#4.

NOTTOWAY GRAYS
See: Capt. Richard Irby.

212a **NOURSE, Margaret Tilloston Kemble**
"Strangers & Pilgrims," the diary of Margaret Tilloston Kemble Nourse, 4 April - Nov. 11, 1862. Edt: Edward C. Campbell, Jr." In: VMHB, Oct. 1983, v.91, #4, p.440-508. Map, port, pl. On a plantation outside Washington.

213 **NOWLIN, S.H.**
"Capture & Escape of S.H. Nowlin, Private, Fifth Virginia Cavalry." In: SB, 1883-1884, v.II, p.70-73.

214 **NUERMBERGER, Ruth Ketring**
"The Clays of Alabama: A Planter-Lawyer-Politician Family." Lexington, University of Ky. Press, 1958, 8vo, cl, dj, bibliog., x, 342pp. $7.50. Clement C. Clay in CSA, Senate, his wife wrote "Belle of the Fifties." Chap. 8-10 Road to Secession, CSA Senator, p.150-237.

215 **NUGENT, William L. & Eleanor Smith**
"My Dear Nellie: The Civil War Letters of William L. Nugent to Eleanor Smith Nugent. Edited by William M. Cash & Lucy Somerville Howorth." Jackson, Uni-

versity Press of Mississippi, 1977, 8vo, cl, dj, xii, 247pp.

215a **NULTY, William H.**
"The Seymour Decision: an Appraisal of the Olustee Campaign." In: FHQ, Jan. 1987, v.65, #3, p.298-316. Map.

216 **NUMISMATIC ,**
Haseltine, Jno. W.
Hart, W.O., et al
Criswell, Grover C.
Belden, Baumen L.
Baumgarten, Julias B.
Bradbeer, Wm. W.
Chase, Philip H.
Lee, Wm.
Thian, Raphael P.
Harris, J.W.
Parker, Wm. H.
Wheless, John F.
Clark, Micajah H.
Confederate Currency
Todd, Richard C.
Werlich, Robert
Affleck, C.J. & B.M. Douglas
Bachtel, C.H.
Massmor, G.W.
"Register of Issues of CSA State currency Treasury Notes."
Fuller, Claude E.
Douglas, B.M. & B.H. Hughes
Slabough, Arlie R.
Bieciuk, Hank & Corbin
Frossard, Ed
Allen, H.D.
'Coins connected with CSA'
Ford, John J., Jr.
Breen, Walter
Randall, J. Calvin & Haseltine
Raisig, L. Miles
Philpott, W.A.
Hoober, Richard T.
Reinfeld, Fred
Curto, James J.
Beer, William
Drowne, Dr. M.S.
"Paper Money of the Confederate States of America...."

217 **NUNN, W.C., Dr., Edt.**
"Ten Texans in Gray. John Robert Baylor, Edward Clark, Richard W. "Dick" Dowling, John Bell Hood, Francis Richard Lubbock, John Bankhead Magruder, Pendleton Murrah, Williamson Simpson Oldham, John H. Reagan, Louis T. Wigfall." Hillsboro, Texas, Hill Junior College, 1968, Waco, Texas, Texian Press, 8vo, cl, d/w, xii, (1),229pp., ports. $10.00. Lim. sig. edt. 50 copies $50.00.

218 ..."Ten More Texans in Gray. Edt.: Dr. W.C. Nunn." Hillsboro, Texas, Hill Junior College, 1980, 8vo, cl, dj, illus, notes, xii, 216pp. $12.50.

219 **NUTT, Laetitia Lafon Ashmore**
"Courageous Journey. The Civil War Journal of Laetitia Lafon Ahsemore Nutt. Edited with a foreword by Florance Ashemore Cowles Hamlett Martin." Miami, Fla., E.A. Seeman Pub., 1975, 12mo, fabricoid, front(port.), illus., 88pp.

220 **NYE, Wilbur Sturtevant**
"The Battle that was fought on the Fort Bragg Reservation." In: Field Artillery Journal, 1932, v.XXII, p.67-92. Called battle of Monroe's Cross Roads, N.C., 1865.

221 ..."The Burial of Latane" & how it moved Southern Hearts." In: CWTI, Jan. 1964, v.II, #9, p.26-28, plate. Death & burial of a Va. cavalry officer.

222 ..."How Stuart got back across the Potomac." In: CWTI, Jan. 1966, v.4, #9, p.45-48, illus.

223 ..."Here Comes the Rebels - Story of Lee's Invasion of Pennsylvania." Baton Rouge, La. State Univ., 1965, 8vo, cl, d/w, maps, xvi, 412pp. $30.00.
...Dayton, Oh., Morningside, 1984. 8vo, cl, 366pp, notes, maps, index. $25.
...Dayton, Oh., Morningside, 1988. $25.

224 ..."The Prelude to Gettysburg," In: CWTI, July 1963, v.II, #4, p.14-19, illus., port.' A special map portfolio - the Gettysburg Campaign', p.53-56, color coded.

225 ..."The First Battle of Gettysburg." In: CWTI, Aug. 1965, v.4, #5, p.12-18, illus., map, port.

O

1 **O'BRIEN, George W., Capt.**
"The Diary of Captain George W. O'Brien, 1863. Edited by Cooper K. Ragan." In: SWHQ, July, 1963, v.LXVII, #1, 2 &3, pp.28-54, 235-246, 413-433, port., maps, roster.

2 **O'BRIEN, Jean Getman**
"The Last Days of Jackson." In: CWTI, Dec. 1963, v.II, #8, p.31-35, illus., ports.

3 **O'BRIEN, Matthew C.**
"William Faulkner & the Civil War in Oxford, Mississippi." Jackson, Miss., Jour. Miss. Hist., May, 1973, v.XXXV, #2, pp.167-174.

4 **O'BRIEN, Robert Alfred**
"Three Relics of Lee's Surrender (1865)" Appomattox ?, Va., 1950, 8vo, wraps, 35pp. Describes an apple tree, poplar tree & the McLean house.

5 **O'CONNOR, Florence J.**
"The Heroine of the Confederacy; or, Truth & Justice. By Miss Florence J. O'-Connor." London, Harrison Print, 1866, 8vo, cl, 432pp.
...New Orleans, La., A. Eyrich, 1869, 8vo, cl, 408pp.

6 **O'CONNOR, John R.**
"John Cabell Breckinridge's Personal Secession: A Rhetorical Insight." In: Filson Club Hist. Quart., 1969, v.XLIII, p345-352.

7 **O'CONNOR, Richard**
"Hood: Cavalier General." New York, Prentice-Hall, 1949, 8vo, cl, dj, maps, front(port.), x,(2), 316pp. $40.00-B.

8 ..."Robert E. Lee: the Southern Saint (1861-1870)." In: Amer. Mercury, May 1949, v.68, p.578-586.

9 **O'CONNOR, Thomas H.**
"Lincoln & the Cotton Trade." In: CWH, March 1961, v.VII, #1, p.20-35.

..."Lords of the Loom: The Cotton Whigs & the Coming of the Civil War." New York, Chs. Schribner's, 1968, 8vo, cl, d/w, pp.ix,214.

10 **O'DELL, Samuel W.**
"The lives & campaigns of Grant & Lee. A comparison & contrast of the deeds & characters of the two great leaders in the Civil War." With intro + reminiscences by Maj.Gen. Oliver O. Howard & Bishop John P. Newman." Chicago, Star Pub., 1895, 8vo, cl, 5p, 1, (7)-602, illus., front(port.), maps, ports.

10a **O'DONNELL, J. H.**
"The "Accidental" Explosion at City Point, Aug. 9, 1864." In: VMHB, July 1964, v.72, #3, p.356-60.

10b **O'DONNELL, William W.**
"The Civil War Quadrennium, a Narrative History of Day-to-Day Life in Little Rock, Arkansas during the American War between the States, 1861-1865." North Little Rock, Ark., Horton Bros., 1985. 8vo, stiff wraps, 100pp. $10.

11 **O'FERRALL, Charles Triplett**
"Forty Years of Active Service, being some history of the war between the Confederacy & the Union & of the events leading up to it, with reminiscences of the struggle & accounts of the author's experiences of four years from private to Lieutenant-Colonel, & acting Colonel in the Cavalry of the Army of Northern Virginia, also much of the history of Virginia & the nation in which the author took part for many years in political conventions & on the hustings & as lawyer, member of the legislature of Virginia, judge, member of the House of Representatives of the United States & Governor of Virginia." (third thousand) New York, Neale Pub.,

1904, 8vo, decr. cl., front (port.), 367pp. $35.00. $125.00-McM. $75.00.

12 ..."Lee's Birthday." In: SHSP, 1891, v.XIX, pp.402-405.

13 **O'FLAHERTY, Daniel**
"General Jo Shelby Undefeated Rebel." Chapel Hill, University of N.Carolina Pr., 1954, 8vo, cl, dj, front(port.), map, xiv, (2), 437pp. notes, index, (p.403-437). $32.50.

14 ..."The Blockade that failed - not until Civil War was about over did the US Navy manage to halt the South's imports." In: Amer. Hert., Aug. 1955, VI, #5, p.38-41, 104-105, illus. (1 color).

15 ..."General Jo Shelby, Undefeated Rebel." Houston, Texas, Civil War Round Table, Address Mar. 15, 1955, 81/2 x 11", heavy paper covers, folded to 8vo, 7pp. 3pp. questions & answers.

16 **O'HARA, Theodore, Colonel**
"Bivouac of the Dead." Aiken, S.C., Ye Palmetto Press, 1900, 16mo, wraps, 14pp. title in red-black, within ornamental borders.
See: Albert G. Brackett, Annie Mae Hollingsworth.

17 **O'KEEFE, Matthew, Chap.**
"Chaplain Matthew O'Keefe of Mahone's Brigade." In: SHSP, 1907, v.35, p.176-182.

17a **O'NEALL, John Belton & John A. Chapman**
"The Annals of Newberry in Two Parts." Newberry, S.C., Aull & Houseal, 1892. 8vo, cl, 823p, ills, index. $125. Biogs. Newberry CSA, County at war. (Rowe).

18 **O'NEIL, Charles**
"Engagement between the 'Cumberland' & 'Merrimack.'" In: USN. Inst. Proc.,June 1922, v.XLVIII, p.863-893.

19 **O'QUINLIVAN, Michael & Rowland P. Gill**
"An Annotated Bibliography of the United States Marines in the Civil War." Washington, D.C., 1963. Historical Branch, G-3 Division Headquarters, U.S. Marines Corps, Revised, 1968. 4to, stiff wraps, (2), 15pp. Cover Head: "Marine Corps Historical Reference Bibliographies."

19a **O'REILLY, Noel S., David C. Bosse & Robert W. Karrow, Jr.**
"Civil War Maps A Graphic Index to the Atlas to accompany the official records of the Union & Confederate Armies." Chicago: Newberry Library, 1987. 4to, stiff wraps, 68pp. (55 maps). The Hermon Dunlop Smith center for the History fo Cartography occasional publication #1.

20 **O'SULLIVAN, Daniel E.**
"Theodore O'Hara." In: SB, ns, v.II, 1886/7, p.489-494, port., plate.

21 **O'SULLIVAN, John L.**
"Union, Disunion & Reunion. A Letter to Gen. Franklin Pierce, ex-president of the United States." London, Richard Bentley, 1862, 8vo, wraps, 122pp.

22 ...Recognition; Its International Legality, Its Justice & Its Policy. A Letter to Lord Palmerston." London, Waterloo & Sons, 1863, 8vo, wraps, 30pp. McElvoy Bibliog., states, "a not very convincing plea for recognition of CSA by England."

23 ..."Peace, the Sole Chance Now Left for Reunion. A Letter to Prof. S.F.B. Morse." London, Wm. Brown & Co., 1863. McElroy - "Argument for peace with amicable separation & trust funds investment in Southern war debt."

24 **OAKHILL Cemetery**
Confederate Soldiers Section, Jefferson Street, Newnan, Georgia. In: Cent. Ga. G.

25 **OATES, Stephen Berry**
"Cavalry fight at Cane Hill." In: ArkHQ, v.20, p.65-73.

26 ..."Confederate Cavalry West of the River." Austin: University of Texas Press, 1961, 8vo, cl, d/w, 234pp., maps, ports. $30.00-JK129.

27 ..."Confederate Cavalrymen of the Trans-Mississippi." In CWH, March, 1961, v.VII, #1, p.13-19.

28 ..."Henry Hotze: Confederate Agent Abroad." In: Historian, 1965, v.XXVII, p.131-154.

29 ..."John S. 'Rip' Ford prudent Cavalryman, C.S.A." In SwHQ, January, 1961, v.LXIV, #3, p.289-314, port., map.

30 ..."Marmaduke's Cape Girardeau Expedition, 1863." Columbia, Mo., Mo. Hist. Review, Apr. 1963, v.LVII, #3, pp.237-247, map, illus., port.

31 ..."Marmaduke's first Missouri Raid." In: BHMS, 1961, v.XVII, p.147-153.

32 ..."Nathaniel Lyon." In: CWTI, Feb., 1968, v.VI, #10, p.14-25, illus., maps, ports.

33 ..."The Prairie Grove Campaign, 1862." In: AHQ, 1960, v.XIX, pp.119-141, 2p. map Mil. operations in NW Arkansas.

34 ..."Recruiting Confederate Cavalry in Texas." In: SWHQ, April 1961, v.LXVI, p.463-477.

35 ..."Supply for Confederate Cavalry in the Trans-Mississippi." In: Mil. Affairs, v.XXV, pp.94-99, Summer, 1961.

36 ..."Shelby's Great Raid, 1863." In: BHMS, 1961, v.XVII, p.337-345.

37 ..."Texas Under the Secessionists." In: SwHQ, October 1963, v.LXVII, #2, p.167-212.

38 **OATES, William Calvin**
"Oates' Regiment." Series in Montgomery Ala. Advertiser:
Co. B, of Bullock Co., May 30, 1897; Co. C, Macon Co., June 20, 1897; Co. F., "Fort Browder Roughs," of Barbour Co., July 4, 1897; Co. A, Russell Co., July 25, 1897; Co. K, Jan. 23, 1898; Co. L., Feb. 6, 1898; Field & Staff, 15th Regt., Feb. 20, 1898; "True Blues," Feb. 23, 1898, "Summary," Feb. 27, 1898. Owens.

39 ..."The War between the Union & the Confederacy & its lost opportunities with a History of the 15th Alabama Regiment & the forty-eight battles in which it was engaged. Being an account of the author's experiences in the greatest conflict of modern times...& the author's observations & experiences as Brigadier-General in the War Between the United States & Spain, etc, etc." New York, Washington, Neale Pub., 1905, Fifth Thousand, tk8vo, decr. cl., color flags on cover, facsm., illus., ports., incl. front, xxiv, (25) -808pp. $200.00. $300.00G $250.00-Bmk105.

40 ...Dayton, Ohio: Morningside Print, 1974, Facsimilie #17, introduction to the new edition by Robert K. Krick. 8vo, cl, illus., ports., (29), vii-viii-xxiv, (25)-26-808pp.(3)pp. $35.00 O.P.

41 ..."Gettysburg, the battle on the right." In: SHSP, 1878, v.VI, p.172-182; "Official Report of Gettysburg," SHSP, 1885, v.XIII, pp.180-181.

41a ..."Gettysburg, July 2, 1863. Col. Wm. C. Oates Comm. 15th Reg. Alabama Reg., to Col. Homer R. Stoughton, Comm. 2nd Reg. U.S. Sharpshooters. 1888." 12mo, 3p.
...Dayton, Oh., Morningside Books, 1974. Reprint plus (23)p. Intro: Robert K. Krick.

42 ..."Speech of Gov. William C. Oates of Alabama, delivered at Chattanooga, Tenn., Sept. 20, 1895, on the Battle of Chickamauga & Chattanooga. Dedication of the National Park." Montgomery, Ala., Roemer Print, 1895, 8vo, wraps, cover-title, 18pp. $30.00B.

43 **OBENCHAIN, William A.**
"Stonewall Jackson's Scabbard Speech." In: SHSP, 1888, v.16, p.36-47.

44 **OBER, Warren U.**
"Noise in the Guard Room." Richmond, Va. Cavl., Winter, 1959, v.IX, #3, pp.38-47, facsms, ports., (1-color). Rougish boys at V.M.I., left imprint on ledger pages & on to glory in gallant roles in the CSA.

44a **"OBITUARIES of Georgia's Confederate Soldiers.** In: Ga. Armchair Researcher, 1984, v.5(1), p.19-26.

45 **OCCUPIED Beaufort, 1863**
A War Correspondent's View, Edt: P.J. Staudenraus. In: SCHM, 1963, v.64.

46 **OCEAN POND, Battle of (Battle of Olustee, Fla.)**
See: Pierre G.T. Beauregard, Alfred Holt Colquitt, Joseph Finnegan, Geo. P. Harison, Caraway Smith. See under Olustee, Fla.

47 **ODIN, Jean Marie, Bishop**
"A Letter from the Archbishop of New Orleans, 1862. Edited by Willard W. Wight." In: J.L.H.A., Spring, 1962, v.III, #2, pp.129-132, notes.

47a **ODOM, Ellen Payne & Nell Arnold Gammage**
"Confederate Soldiers in Colquitt County, Georgia." Moultrie, Georgia, Moultrie McNeill Chapter #661, U.D.C., 1980. 8vo, stiff wraps, iii, 46pp. Roster (p.4-46) from Lillian Henderson's Ga. soldiers, v.5, p.347.

48 **ODOM, Van D.**
"The Political Career of Thomas Overton Moore, Secession Governor of Louisiana." New Orleans, LHQ, October 1943, v.26, #4, pp.975-1054, offprint, wraps.
See: G.P. Whittington.

49 **OEMLER, Marie Conway**
"Johnny Reb. A Story of South Carolina." New York, London, The Century Co., 1929, 12mo, cl, dj, vii, 433pp.

50 **"OFFICERS & Crew**
(Monitor), application for bounty." In: SHSP, 1885, v.13, p.90-119.
See: Virginia (Ironclad), CSA.

51 **OFFICERS ,**
In the Confederate States Navy, 1861-1865." Washington, GPO, 1898, 8vo, wraps, 157pp. $45.00Bmk.
See revision: "Register of Officers...."

51a **'OFFICIAL Atlas**
Of the Civil War. Intro: Henry Steele Commager." N.Y., T. Yoseloff, 1958. $125. Folio (45cm), (8)p, facsm: 29pp, 175 plates, incl. ills, part color, maps (part color), plans.

52 **OFFICIAL Documents**
Of the Post Office Department of the Confederate States of America. A reprint, compiled by Theron Wierenga. Holland, Mich., Theron Wierenga, 1979, 8vo, 2 vols., tables, (16)p. inserted.
Head: Confederate States of Amer.-Post office department.

53 **OFFICIAL Guide**
Of the Confederate Government from 1861 to 1865 at Richmond. Showing the location of the public buildings & offices of the Confederate, State & City Governments, Residences of the principal Officers, etc. Price $.10, 12mo, wraps, cover title(woodcut), 32, (1)pp. Richmond, 1907?, Swem-4016. $15.00. First issued as "The Official Guide to the Confederate Government during the Civil War."

54 **OFFICIAL Intelligence.**
Appointments & promotions in the Provisional Army of the Confederate States of America, since the adjournment of Congress, Feb. 18, 1864. In: Smith & Barrow's Monthly Mag., May 1864, v.1, p.78-96. Dorn-II, 883.

55 **OFFICIAL Journal**
Of the Convention of the State of Louisiana. New Orleans, La., 1861, 8vo, wraps, 63pp., dbl. columns. Not in Crandall. See #1613/1614 similar entries in both English & French, with more pages.

56 ...Of the Proceedings of the Convention of the State of Louisiana. By Authority." New Orleans, J.O. Nixon, 1861, 8vo, cl, 292pp. Crandall-1613.

57 ...Reprint: New Orleans, Louisiana History, Journal of the Louisiana Historical

58 ...Ass'n. whole issue Winter, 1961, vol.II, #1 from one of only three known copies, pp. 101. English only, dbl. columns.

58 ..."Journal of the State Convention. Secret Session." (continued) pp.(103), 1, (105)-111. Signed: J.T. Wheat, Sec'y. dbl. column, English only.

59 ..."Ordinances passed by the Convention of the State of Louisiana during its session commencing on the 2nd of January & ending on the 26th of March, 1861. Official." New Orleans, J.O. Nixon, Printer to the Convention, 1861. (228), 1,(229)-292. Signed A. Mouton. English version only, dbl. columns. Facsimilie & pagination preserved in lieu of the excised French portion. JLHA number 151pp. total.

60 **OFFICIAL Records**
"The War of the Rebellion: a compilation of the Official Records of the Union & Confederate Armies. Published under the Direction of the Secretary of War." Washington, GPO, 1880-1901. Thick 8vo, cl, 3/4 mor., 3/4 calf, 70 vols. in 128. Found also in House Mssc.Docs., 52nd-56th Congress. Special index in each vol., additional corrections, etc. Vols. 112-113 have not been published (v.54,55), black cloth, $1.250.00 index & atlas. $1,500.00-Bmk. $1,875.00 Senator's edt., 3/4mor, index, atlas, index: original. $2,000.00-Bmk117. Atlas: original $750.00, wraps, $290.00.

61 ..."Official Records of the Union & Confederate Navies in the War of the Rebellion. Ser. I, v.1-27; Ser.II, v.1-3." Washington, GPO, 1894-1922. Tk8vo, cl, 3/4 mor, of calf, illus., ports., maps, part folding, 30 vols., $350.00. $550.00. $700.00-B. $800.00 Rebound.

62 ..."Official Records of the Union & Confederate Navies. Circular. Washington, DC, 1903, caption title, 8vo, wraps, 3pp.
...Washington, 1927, Gov.Print.Off., "General Index," 457pp. 594-Y.

63 ...Of Confederate War - Archives Bureau at Washington." In: SHSP, 1878, v.5, p.255-256; 1878, v.6, p.239-240.
...New York, Antiquarian Press, 1961, Index with a new introduction by Philip Van Doren Stern, tk8vo, cl, xviii, 457pp.

64 ...Atlas, set 3 vols., slip-case (Bmk) $800.00
Same: (y)$1,000. Complete set Official Records, incl, Navy series & orig. maps, $2,400.00.

65 ..."Official Military Atlas of the Civil War." By Maj. George B. Davis, Leslie J. Perry, Joseph W. Kirkley. Compiled by Capt. Calvin D. Cowles, introduction by Richard Sommers. New York, Crown Pub., 1978, folio, cl, 821 maps, 106 engravings, 209 drawings, indices. Set 128 vols., rebound, fabricoid $3,000.00-Bmk.

66 ..."Official Records of the Union & Confederate Navies in the War of the Rebellion. Pub. under direction of The Hon. Curtis D. Wilbur, Secretary of the Navy by Dudley W. Knox, Capt., U.S. Navy, retired. Officer in charge, Office of Naval Records & Library, By authority of an act of Congress approved July 31, 1894. General Index." Washington, U.S. Gov.Print.Off., 1927, 8vo, cl, (1), 457pp.
...New York, Antiquarian Press, 1961, Tk8vo, cl, xviii, 457pp. With a new introduction by Philip Van Doren Stern.

67 ..."Official Records of the Union & Confederate Armies War of the Rebellion. Pub. under direction of The Hon. Elihu Root, Secretary of War, by Brig.-Gen., Fred C. Ainsworth, Chief of the Record & Pension Office, War Dept., & Mr. Joseph W. Kirkley. G eneral Index & Additions & Corrections - Mr. John S. Moodey, Indexer." Washington, Government Printing Off., 1901, Tk8vo, cl, LI, 1242pp. $75.00.
...Reprint $67.50.

68 ..."Official Records of the Union & Confederate Armies, 1861-1865, Circular. Washington, 1902. 8vo, sewn, caption title, 10pp.
See: Harold E. Mahan, Marcus Wright.

68a **OFFICIAL Register**
Of the South Carolina Military Academy, April 1861." Columbia, S.C., 1861. Bmk-$60. 12mo, wraps. In 1842 two military academies established 'The Citadel' at Charleston & 'Arsenal Academy' at Columbia. Later on were combined, then closed in 1865. Reopened in 1882. The 'South Carolina Military Academy, in 1911, changed to 'The Citadel.'
See: John P. Thomas' sketch of SCMA.

69 **OFFICIAL Report**
Of Battles, Published by Order of Congress." Richmond, Va., Enquirer Book Pr., 1862, 8vo, cl/wraps, 571pp. $275.00. Edt: 1864, with 562pp. Other reports in Crandall-1372-81.
...New York, Chas. B. Richardson, 1863, 8vo, cl/calf, port, 578pp. $150.00. Edt: 1864. Also as v.4 in Ed.A. Pollard "Southern History of the War." First published in N.Y., in 2 vols., 298, 294pp.

70 ...New York, Chas. B. Richardson, 1863, 8vo, wraps/or cl, 578pp. (2 vols. in one) $35.00. Also: published as "Southern History of the War," v.4, of Pollard's 1st, 2nd & 3rd Year of the War. From the original Richmond edition. Sabin-56786; Howes: 9664/7529-35. 2 vols. $200.00. Pt.I 298pp. $160.00-Bmk84.
...Of Battles, 1863." N.Y., Kraus Reprint Co., 1970.

71 ...Of the Commandant of Cadets (Virginia Military Institute) of the Battle of New Market." Richmond, Va., 1865, 8vo, wraps, 14p.

72 ...Head: Doc #XXV. (Doc. called session, 1864-65 by Supt. Francis H. Smith, Jan. 11, 1865, reporting the faculty casualties of the war.

73 ...Report: July 4, 1864, Lt.Col. S. Ship, Comm. of Cadets.
See: John S. Wise's Memorial address.

74 ...Of the History Committee of the Grand Camp, Confederate Veteran Dep't. of Virginia...." Richmond, Va., 1901, 8vo, wraps, 32pp. jk $20.00. Veteran's comments on conduct of Sherman & Sheridan during the war.

75 ...Relative to the conduct of Federal Troops in Western Louisiana, during the invasion of 1863-1864. Compiled from sworn testimony, under direction of Gov. Henry W. Allen. Shreveport, Apr. 1865. (cover title omits place & date). Shreveport, La., News Printing Estb., John Dickinson, Propr., 1865, 8vo, wraps, 89pp. Crandall-1638. (Baton Rouge, 1939) tall 8vo, cl, 89pp. Lim.Edt. of 75 copies.

76 **OFFICIAL Reports**
Of Actions with Federal Gunboats. Ironclads & Vessels of the U.S. Navy, during the war between the states, by Officers of Field Artillery, P.A.C.S. First Brigade Infantry, (Mouton's) Forces South of Red River, Bayou Teche, La., Nov. 10, 1862. In: SHSP, 1884, v.XII, p.54-59.

76a **OFFICIAL Reports**
Of Battles, Evacuations & Retreats, incl. all reports of officers of Army & Navy of the Confed., from the highest to the lowest that has been ordered to make a report, with appropriate commentaries on same by most disting. commanders of Land & Sea service. Pub. by patronage of congress. Edt: John Poynter McMillan, of the Missouri Army. Richmond, 1864 (two). Reported Va. Mag. Hist. & Biog., v.XX, #4, 1912, p.426. Notes.

77 **OFFICIAL Reports (Confederate)**
Relating to the Gettysburg Campaign,

1863. Washington, 1883, 8vo, cl, 492p. Preliminary printing of Official Records.

78 **OGDEN, H.A. (Artist)**
"Pickett at Gettysburg," "Stuart's Raid," Chambersburg. Two only CSA hand-color plates (4-Union subjects) 10 1/4 x 13", fold to 8 1/2 x 10 3/4". n.p., Jones Pub. Co., c.1900.

79 **OGLESBY, T.K. (Thaddeus Kosciusko)**
"Alexander Hamilton Stephens, born Feb. 11, 1812; died March 4, 1883. A Sketch. (2 quotes) n.p., n.d. (Footnote: written for the "Union & Recorder," Milledgeville, Ga., pub. Apr. 10-1883). Subtitle: "Sage, Patriot, Statesman & Philanthropist." 8vo, printed wraps, 18pp.

80 ..."The Britannica Answered, & the South Vindicated...And A Criticism of that Work. Montgomery, Ala., 1891, 8vo, wraps, 60pp. $20.00-Bmk94. Reason for South leaving Union.

81 ..."Some Truths of History. A Vindication of the South against the Encyclopedia Brittannica & Other Maligners." Atlanta, Ga., Byrd Print, 1903, 12mo, cl, 263pp.

82 ..."Captor & Captive; the Shackler & the Shackled - The Truth of History as to the Shackling of Jefferson Davis." Read before Atlanta Camp, Confederate Veterans. Atlanta, Ga., Franklin Print, 1899, 8vo, wraps, 17pp.

83 **OLANETA, Don Jose Antonio de, Capt.**
"Guerra de los Estados-Unidos. Estudios sobre artilleria, fortification y marina malitar." Madrid, Impr. del Memorial de Ingelieros, 1868, 8vo, cl, 19-pls., fld. map (Charleston Bay), diagrams, 332pp. $42.50. Study for the Span. Army, on coast artillery & fortifications.

"OLD Capitol & Its Inmates, etc, The."
By a Lady.
See: Lomax, Virginia.

84 **OLD Dominion,**
A Monthly Magazine of Literature, Science & Art. Richmond, Va., M.W. Hazelwood, 1870-1872. April 15, 1870 contains DePeyster's Stonewall Jackson at Chancellorsville & Death of Gen. T.J. Jackson; Nov. 15, 1870 contains Death of Gen. Lee & Gen. Lee & Washington College.

85 **OLD Dominion Dragoons -**
From the Richmond Dispatch. In: SHSP, 1896, v.24, p.187-189.

86 **"OLD Gray Mare, The"**
In: Cattleman, Sept, 1953, v.40, #4, p.74,76,78,80. Music. On tune & words composed by Gus Bailey, showman enlisted in Hood's Texas Brigade, near Manassas, ca. 1862. Revived by R. Wright Armstrong & his Old Gray Mare Band.

87 **"OLD Guard.**
A Monthly Journal, Devoted to the Principals of 1776 & 1787, The." Edt: C. Chauncey Burr. Pamphlets of 24pp. each, 1863 & 1864.
Do: "The Old Guard, a Monthly Magazine Devoted to Literature, Science & Art & the Political Principals of 1776 & 1778." Pub: New York, Van Evrie, Horton & Co., between 1865-1870. After the war the size was enlarged & published at Richmond, with many pictures of southern military leaders, into more of a literary magazine. Vol.1-1862 (three issues, then a decision to begin in 1863, so that the Mar.-Sept. should be #3-9, vo Vol. 1) Vol.II-1863 (Jan. & Feb. are #1 & 2) From Vol. II-VIII, a regular annual volume of 12 monthly issues (Mott) Burr defends slavery, right of secession, attacked Lincoln violently in every issue & urged cessation of war. Even after the war, he attacked the memory of Lincoln & defended the Confederate States. I, II, IV, V, VI (#5,7,9-12) $100.00. Vol. I-VI, 1863-1868, 3/4 mor. $350.00.
See: Joseph George, Jr., Wm. W. Rogers.

Note: V.4 contains steel ports. of: Lee, Jackson, J.E. Johnston, Beaureguard, Ewell, Longstreet, Wade Hampton, Polk, Sterling Price, G.W. Smith, Jeb Stuart, & A.P. Hill. I, 1863, 288pp.; II, 1864, 284pp.; III, 1865, 572pp.; IV, 1866, 768pp.; V, 1867, 956pp. $65.00-Bmk117.

88 **"OLD Jack" & his Foot-Cavalry;**
or a Virginian Boy's Progress to Renown. A Story of the War in the Old Dominion." New York, John Bradburn, 1864, 12mo, clo, 4-plates, iv, 300pp. $60.00. A revised reprint of the Anon. "Jefferson Davis & "Stonewall Jackson," life & public services of each, etc." M.Addey.

89 **OLD STARS & STRIPES**
Of the Richmond "Grays" in the Confederate Army. Boston, GAR Massachusetts Dept., John A. Andrews Post #15, 8vo, wraps, 12 leaves, 'Memorial report, 100 copies.'

90 **OLD SOUTH & the Crucible of War**
Harry P. Owens & James J. Cooke, editors. Jackson, University of Mississippi Press, 1983, 8vo, cl, dj, x, 110p. Outgrowth of a 7th Annual Chancellor's Symposium at Miss. U., Emory Thomas, Paul D. Escott, Leon Litwack, Thomas B. Alexander.

91 **OLD TEXAS BRIGADE**
Memorial Stone to their heroism at Wilderness. In: SHSP, 1891, v.19, p.122-124.

92 **OLD, William W., Capt.**
"Trees whittled down at Horseshoe, "Bloody Angle," battle near Spotsylvania CH." In: SHSP, 1905, v.33, p.16-24.

93 **OLDAKER, Glenn C., Compiler**
"Centennial Tales, Memoirs of Col. "Chester" S. Bassett French...."
See: under Sam B. French.

94 **OLDHAM, W.B., Mrs.**
"War Between the States in New Mexico." In: UDCMag., Apr. 1953, v.16, p.9, 29, 32. Facsm.

95 **OLDHAM, W.S.**
"Colonel John Marshall." In: SwHQ, 1916, v.XX, pp.132-138.

96 **OLDROYD, Osborn Hamiline**
"A Soldier's Story of the Siege of Vicksburg. From the Diary of Osborn H. Oldroyd...With Confederate accounts from authentic sources & an introduction by Brevet Maj.-Gen. M.F. Force." Springfield, Ill., For the Author, 1885, 8vo, cl, port., map, illus., viii, 200pp. $45.00. Append: Army Corps Badges, p.181-194, Tunnard's Reminiscences & Houston's Hist. of Vaughn's Confed. Brig., etc. Author was in the 20th Ohio Vols.

97 **OLDS, Fred A.**
"Brave Carolinians fell at Gettysburg." In: SHSP, 1907, v.35, p.320-322. (same, in v.36, p.245-247).

98 ..."North Carolina Troops - how they were armed during the war." In: SHSP, 1901, v.29, p.144-151.

99 **OLIPHANT (Mary C. Simms)**
EAVES (T.C. Duncan)
"The Letters of William G. Simms, v. IV (1858-1866)." Columbia, Univ. So. Carolina Pr., 1955, pp.xxv,643.

100 **OLIPHANT, William J.**
"Arkansas Post." In: SB(ns), v.1, 1885, pp.736-739.

100a **OLIVER, David L.**
"The Contribution of Kentucky to Lincoln Fourth of July session of Congress, 1861." In: RKHS, Apr. 1962, v.60, #2, p.134-42.

101 **OLIVER, James McCarty**
"The Battle of Franklin. The Little Girl at Spanish Fort & other Poems." Philadelphia, J.B. Lippincott & Co., 1870, 12mo, cl, 118pp.

102 **OLIVER, Thaddeus**
"All Quiet along the Potomac Tonight, proof that it was written by Thaddeus Oliver, of Twiggs Co., Ga." In: SHSP,

1880, v.8, p.255-256, by Frank Daves. See: John D. Ashton.

103 **OLMSTEAD, Charles Hart**
"Fort Pulaski." In: Ga.H.Q., v.1, #2, June 1917, p.98-105, dbl. pg. facsm. map.

104 ..."Reminiscences of Service in Charleston Harbor in 1863." SHSP, 1883, v.XI, pp.118-125, pt. 2, p.158-171.

105 ..."Two Unknown Heroes of the Ranks." In: SHSP, 1883, v.XI, p.139-140.

106 ..."The Memoirs of Charles H. Olmstead. Edt: Lilla Mills Hawes." In: Ga.H.Q., Dec. 1958, v.XLII, #4, part I, p.389-408; v.XLIII, #1, p.60-73; #2, p.170-185; #3, p.261-280, #4, p.378-390. Complete in 5 parts.

107 ...Savannah, Ga., 1964. Collections of Georgia Historical Society, v.XIV, 8vo, cl, 192pp. Reprint of GHQ.

108 ..."Reminiscences of Service with the First Volunteer Regiment of Georgia, Charleston Harbor, in 1863. An address delivered before the Georgia Historical Society, Mar. 3, 1879." Savannah, Ga., Morning News, 1879, 8vo, sewn, 15pp, cover title, running title - "Annals of the War." $100.00-Bmk.
...Also in SHSP, 1883, v.XI, p.118-125, 158-171.

109 ..."Memoirs of Col. Charles H. Olmstead." Savannah, Georgia Historical Society, 1964, 8vo, cl, illus., 192pp. in Hist. Collections, v.14.

110 **OLSBERG, R. Nicholas**
"Archives News." In: SCHMag., July/Oct. 1971, v.72, #3/4, pp.198-205, 254-258. South Carolina Archives movement to escape Sherman's Army, as well as CSA archives.

111 **OLSEN, Theodore V.**
"There was a season; a biographical novel of Jefferson Davis." Garden City, N.Y., Doubleday, 1972, 12mo, cl, dj, 444p.

111a **OLSON, Kenneth E., Dr.**
"Music & Musket; bands & Bandsmen of the American Civil War. Contributions oto the study of Music & Dance, #1." Westport, Conn., Greenwood Press, 1981. 8vo, cl, dj, ii, xxii, 299pp. $27.50
..."Strike up the Band: the bands of the Confederate Army." In: CV, (new) Jan/Feb., 1986, v.34, #1, p.40-7, ills (groups) facsm.

112 **OLUSTEE (Florida), Battle of**
Also under "Ocean Pond, Battle of--
See: Geo. F. Baltzell, P.G.T. Beauregard, Ruth Cole, Alfred Holt Colquitt, Joseph Finnegan, Geo. P. Harrison, James A. Harley, J.G. Rice, Caraway Smith, Wm. Furness, Richard J. Ferry.

113 **ONESIMUS SECUNDUS**
"The true interpretation of the American Civil War & of England's Cotton difficulty' or, Slavery, from a different point of view, showing the relative responsibilities of America & Great Britain. By Onesimus Secundus." London, Trubner & Co., 1863, 12mo, cl, iv, (5)-47pp. Sabin-57351.

114 **ONSLOW, Walton**
"America's first fifth column: the Northwest Conspiracy." London, Jour. Confed. Hist. Soc., Winter 1970, v.8, #4, p.83-105, port.

115 **OPELIKA POST, The (Opelika, Ala.)**
"The Youngest Confederate General." In: SHSP, 1907, v.35, p.55-58.

116 **"Operations of Confederate States Navy**
In Defence of New Orleans." In: SHSP, v.II, 1876, pp.240-244.

117 **OPIE, John Newton, Maj.**
"How Major J.N. Opie led a charge." In: SHSP, 1891, v.19, p.251-253.

118 ..."A Rebel Cavalryman with Lee, Stuart & Jackson, by John N. Opie." Chicago, W.B. Conkey Co., 1899, 12mo, cl, illus., drawings, ports, incl, front, 336pp. $25.00.

$200.00G. $125.00. $175.00-Bmk.
...Dayton, Ohio, Morningside Bookshop, 1972, Facsimile-10, 12mo, cl, ills, ports. incl. front, 336pp.

119 **OPPOSING Forces at Pea Ridge, Ark., March 7th & 8th, 1862.**
The composition & losses as here stated give the gist of all the data available in the Official Records. Robert, Ark., Pea Ridge National Park Association, 1926. Broadside 32 x 21 1/2 cm.

119a **ORANGE in the Civil War,**
1861-5--1961-5. Orange, Va., Orange County Civil War Centennial Commission, 1965." Orange, Va., Orange Review. Reprinted, Jan. 1979. 8vo, colored pict. stiff wraps, (1)p. 46pp, port, ills.

120 **ORANGE COUNTY, Virginia**
"Orange County in the war & roster of Confederate Troops." Chapter on... In: W.W. Scott's History of Orange County, Richmond, Va., 1907, pp.292. $40.00-b.

121 **ORDINANCE to dissolve the union**
Between the state of South Carolina & other states united with her under the compact entitled: "The Constitution of the United States of America, An. Charleston, Evans & Cogswell Print., 1860, Broadside 12x24 1/2", mounted on board. (2 copies sold in 1977 for $1,500 ea.)

122 **ORDINANCE to dissolve the union**
Between the State of Alabama & the other states. Baltimore, 1861, folio, 1st separate printing.
See: Crandall-1452, longer title.

123 **ORDINANCE & Resolutions**
Recommended by a Conference Committee & passed by the State Convention, Wed., Mar. 20, 1861. Little Rock, Ark., True Democrat Pr., 1861, Broadside, 32 cm., Hargrett.

124 **ORDINANCES of the State Convention**
Which convened in Little Rock, May 6, 1861. Little Rock, Ark., Johnson & Yerkes, 1861, sm.8vo, wraps, 128pp. (Allen #406 & 9).

125 **ORDNANCE Instructions**
For the Confederate States Navy relating to preparation of war for battle, to the duty of officers & others when at quarters, to ordnance & ordnance stores, & to gunnery. London, Saunders, Otley & Co., 1864, 8vo, cl, xix, 171, cixpp.21-plates.

126 **ORDNANCE Manual**
For the Officers of the C.S.Army. 2nd Edition. Richmond, Va., 1861. 12mo, cl, charts, 475pp. $200.00-R. $150.00y. Since the U.S. Army Manual, published by West & Johnston (see Crandall-2487) has same number pages, same date, etc. this seems to be just a new t.p. Also see Crandall-1382/3, the Gorgas edition seems a revised (546pp.) edt. of 1863.
...Charleston, S.C., 1863, p.546 (Reb. $200.00).
...Dayton, Oh., Morningside Pr., 1976. $25.00. With introduction by Sydney Kerksis. 620pp. Reprint of the Charleston Edt.

127 **ORGAIN, Kate Alma**
"A Waif from Texas." Austin, Texas, Ben C. Jones, 1901, 12mo, cl, 238pp. Ante-Bellum recollections of life on plantation slaves, in Texas Panhandle after war.

127a **ORGANIZATION and Administration**
Of the Medical Department of the Confederate Army." In: NCHR, 1954, v.31, p.385-409.

128 **ORGANIZATION of Armies**
..."Organization of the Army of Northern Virginia, July 23, 1862." Washington, D.C., 1881, 8vo, sewn, 7p.

129 ...(General R.E. Lee commanding), August 28 to Sept. 1, 1862." Washington, D.C., 1882, 8vo, sewn, 6p.

130 ...Organization of the Second army corps of the Army of Northern Virginia, Dec.

20, 1862, Washington, D.C., 1881, 8vo, sewn, 6p.

131 ..."Organization of the First & Second army corps of the Army of Northern Virginia, June 22, 1863." Washington, D.C., 1881, 8vo, sewn, 5p.

132 ..."Organization of the Army of Northern Virginia, (commanded by Gen. Robert E. Lee), July 31, 1863." Washington, D.C., 1882, 8vo, sewn, 7p.

133 ...August 31, 1863." Washington, D.C., 1882, 8vo, sewn, 7p.

134 ...January 31, 1864." Washington, D.C., 1881, 8vo, sewn, 8p.

135 ..."And forces in the Richmond & Petersburg lines (under General G.T. Beauregard) early in May 1864." Washington, D.C., War Records office, 1888, 8vo, sewn, 12p.

136 ..."August, 1864." Washington, D.C., 1881, 8vo, sewn, 7p.

137 ..."August 31, 1864." Washington, D.C., War Records office, 1883, 8vo, sewn, 8p.

138 ...(Commanded by General Robert E. Lee) January, 1865." Washington, D.C., 1881, 8vo, sewn, 9p.

139 ..."Organization of the Army of the Valley District, August 20, 1864." Washington, War Records Bureau, 1883, 8vo, sewn, (3)p.

140 ..."Organization of the Army of Tennessee, Gen. Braxton Bragg, Confederate States Army, Commanding, at the Battle of Chickamauga." In: SHSP, 1884, v.XII, p.145-160. From War-Records office, roster of officers in all units.

141 ..."Organization of the Army of the Valley District August 20, 1864." In: SHSP, 1884, v.XII, p.326-327. From War-Records (above) p.8-20.

142 ..."Organization of the Army of Northern Virginia (General R.E. Lee commanding) August 28 to September 1, 1862." In: SHSP, 1882, v.X, p.555-560. Roster of officers.

143 ...Washington, D.C., War Records Office, 1882, 8vo, wraps, offprint, 6p.
...Washington, D.C., 1883, 8vo, wraps, 7p.

144 ..."Organization of the Army of Tennessee (commanded by General Braxton Bragg), August 31, 1863." Washington, D.C., 1881, 8vo, sewn, 6p.

145 ..."November 20, 1863." Washington, D.C., 1884, 8vo, sewn, 9p.

146 ..."Organization of the Army of Tennessee, November 23, 1863." Washington, D.C., 1881. 8vo, sewn, 6p.

147 ..."Organization of the Army of Tennessee (commanded by General John B. Hood) for the period ending December 10, 1864." Washington, D.C., 1885, 8vo, sewn, 6p.

148 ..."Organization of the cavalry of Army of Tennessee, August 15, 1863." Washington, D.C., 1881, 8vo, sewn, (3)p.

149 ..."Organization of the Confederate Army of Vicksburg (Lieut.-Gen. John C. Pemberton commanding), July 4, 1863." Washington, War Records Office, 1885, 8vo, sewn, 4p.

150 ..."Organization of the Confederate armies, 1863-1864." Washington, D.C., 1881, 8vo, wraps, 18pp. Dorn-II, 1150.

151 ..."Organization of the Army of the Department of Mississippi & East Louisiana (Lieut.-Gen. W.J. Hardee, CSArmy, commanding, July 30, 1863," Washington, D..C., War Records Office, 1885, 8vo, sewn, 4p.

152 ..."Organization of the troops of the Department of Mississippi & E. Louisiana, (Lieut.-Gen. J.C. Pemberton, commanding.) April 1863." Washington, D.C., 1881, 8vo, sewn, 7p.

153 ..."Organization of the troops in the Department of Mississippi & E. Louisiana (Gen. Joseph E. Johnston commanding),

Nob. 20, 1863." Washington, D.C., 1881, 8vo, sewn, 5p. Dorn-II, 1151-1153.

154 ..."Organization of the Army of the Mississippi, April 6th & 7th, 1862." Washington, D.C., 1881, 8vo, sewn, 4p., caption title. Sig.: Braxton Bragg, Gen. Commd., Dept. #2, Tupelo, Miss., June 20, 1862.

154a **ORIGINAL Interments**
At Cahaba Cemetery now interred at Mareitta National Cemetery." In: NCHR, 1954, v.25, #1 & 2, p.192 & 9.

155 **ORPHAN BRIGADE**
"First Annual Reunion of the First Kentucky Orphan Brigade, C.S.A., Cynthiana, Ky., Aug. 18th, 1886." Frankfort, Ky., Western Argus, 1887, 8vo, wraps, 36pp. also in micro-card, Louisville, Lost Cause Press, $2.45.
See: Hodge, G.B.

156 ..."Reunion of the "Orphan Brigade," at Paris, Ky., Sept. 28, 1892. Souvenir Confederate Edition, Illustrated Kentuckian, Vol. I, #6." Lexington, October 1892, 17x11" printed four columns, pict. wraps, (18)pp. Contains Ed. Porter Thompson's sketch of Orphans Brigade, see his book.
See: Lot D. Young
Ed. Porter Thompson
Jno. Wm. Green

ORR'S South Carolina Rifles
See: J.W. Mattison.

157 **ORR, Dorothy**
"Gustavus John Orr, 1819-1887." In: Atlanta Hist. Bull., Fall/Winter, 1971, wraps, 269pp. Partially on war in Georgia (tax collector).

158 **ORR, James Lawrence**
"Address...delivered before the Legislature of South Carolina, Nov. 29, 1865." Columbia, Julian A. Selby, 1865, 8vo, sewn, 7p. McKissick-1866.

159 ..."Agreement between the US Government & South Carolina as to "preserving the Status" of the Forts at Charleston." In: SHSP, 1884, v.XII, pp.60-63.

160 ..."Southern Rights Documents. Speech of James L. Orr before the convention of the Southern Rights Association, May 1951." n.p., caption title, 8vo, wraps, 16pp.

161 ..."Address of the Confederate Congress to the people of the Confederate States." n.p., n.d., (Richmond, 1864), 8vo, sewn, 16pp. (Crandall-74)

162 ..."James L. Orr on Congressional Reconstruction." Edt: Martin Abbott. Charleston, So. Caro. Hist. & Genea. Mag., July 1953, v.LIV, #3, pp.141-142.

163 **ORR, Thomas, Edt.**
"Life of the notorious desperado, Cullen Baker, from his childhood to his death, with a full account of all the murders he committed." Little Rock, Ark., Price & Barton, 1870, 16mo, wraps, 49pp. Only known copy in LC?

164 **ORTH, Michael**
"The CSS Stonewall." In: CWTI, April 1966, v.5, #1, p.44-48, illus., port.

165 **ORVIN, Maxwell Clayton**
"In South Carolina Waters, 1861-1865." Charleston, S.C., ?1961, Nelsons Print., 8vo, cl, dj, pls., 196, (1 errata pg.). $30.00- Bmk105.

166 **OSBORN, George C.**
"The Atlanta Campaign, 1864." In: Ga.H.Q., December 1950, v.XXXIV, #4, pp.271-287. $8.00.

167 **OSBORNE, D.F.**
"The last hope of the South - to establish a principal." In: Ga.H.Q., September, 1931, v.XV, #3, p.223-251.

168 **OSBORNE, Hampden**
"The Struggle for Fort Mahone." In: CV, May 1917, v.XXV, p.226-229.

169 **OSBORNE, Hampden, Mrs.**
"Echoes from Dixie." New Edition, New York, Noble & Noble, (c. 1924), Edt:

Matthew Page Andrews. (Adv., CV, Jan. 1925, v.33, #1.)

170 **OSBORNE, Henry J.**
"Augusta, Georgia, 1860-1861: as seen in three letters. Edt: John Kent Folmar." In: Ga.H.Q., Dec. 1969, v.LIII, #4, p.523-528.

171 **OSGOODE, J.A.**
"Confederate Fire-Eaters, William L. Yancey." In: The Libertarian, Jan. 1924, 8vo, wraps, 9pp.

172 ..."The First Confederate Captial; its present & past." In: C.Vet., Mar. 1920, v.XXVIII, pp.88-90.

172a **OSTERHOUT, Charles Hotchkiss**
"A Johnny Reb from Windsor, N.Y.," In: "Courier Mag." Jan. 1955, p.20-1.

172b **OSTERHOUT, Charles Hotchkiss, Edt.**
"Stonewall Jackson's map-maker, excerpts from his letters & papers." (1977). 12mo, wraps, 128pp, ills.

173 **OSTERHOUT, J.P., Edt.**
"Handbook of Songs & Rhymes for the Annual Reunions of Texas Camps of United Confederate Veterans. Dedicated to Mrs. Lavinia Porter Talley of Temple Texas." Temple, Texas, c. 1908, 12mo, wraps, 30pp. cover title.

174 **OSTERWEIS, Rollin G.**
"The Myth of the Lost Cause, 1865-1900." Hamden, Conn., Archon Books, 1973, 8vo, cl, dj, xii, 188pp. $8.50.

175 ..."Will Success Spoil Jeff Davis? The Last Book About the Civil War." N.Y., McGraw-Hill, 1963, 12mo, cl, decr. d/w, illus., 143pp. ($1) $3.95.

176 **OSTERWEIS, Rollin Gustav**
"Judah P. Benjamin, Statesman of the Lost Cause. Foreword by Horace D. Taft." N.Y., Putnam's 1933, 8vo, cl, illus., 205pp, index. $50.00. Publication withdrawn, it infringed on Pierce Butler's biog. of 1906, all remaining books were destroyed.

177 ..."Romanticism & Nationalism in the Old South (1815-1861)" New Haven, Yale University Press, 1949, Yale Historical Publication, Misscellany, 49, 8vo, cl, 275pp.(x), illus.

178 ..."The Myth of the Lost Cause." Hamden, Conn., Archon Books, 1973, 8vo, cl, dj, notes, index, 188pp. $8.50.

179 ..."Treat it Gently - It is Holy." N.Y., Burt Franklin, 1973 (Resource & source works series).

180 **OTEY BATTERY**
"In Memoriam. The dead of the Otey Battery, of the Thirteenth Battalion, Va. artillery, ANV., CSA. Published by the committee." Richmond, Va., 1887, 8vo, wraps, 22pp.

181 ..."Reunion of the Otey battery, CSA." Richmond, Va., Feb. 22, 1876, 8vo, wraps, 6p. cover title
See: George Savage.

182 **OTEY, Mercer, Maj. (of San Francisco)**
"Story of our great war." In: CV, 1899, v.7, p.120-125, port. + p.213-216, 262-265, 549-551, 366-367, + v. 8, p.129-130, 342-343; v.9, p.107-110, 153-155.

182a **OTIS, George Alexander**
A Report of Surgical Cases Treated in the Army of the U.S., from 1865-71." Washington: GPO, 1871. 4to, wraps, 296pp, ills, iv pl. US Surg-Gen. office, circular #8.

..."A Report on a plan for transporting wounded soldiers by railway in time of war with descriptions of various methods employed for this purpose on different occasions." Washington, D.C., Surg-Gen. office, 1875. 8vo, wraps, 56pp, ills. Bibliog. of RRy hospital transport, 54-56.

..."A report on amputations at the hip-joint in military surgery." Washington, GPO, 1867. 8vo, wraps, 87, (1), incl. tables, 9 pls, partly colored. War Dept., Surg-Gen. Office, circular #7.

..."A report on excisions of the head of the femur for gunshot injury." Washington: GPO, 1869. 29 x 23 cm, wraps, 141pp, incl.

ills, tables, bibliog: 138-41. Bmk $75. War Dept., Surg-Gen office, circular #2.

..."A report to the Surg.-Gen. on the transport of sick & wounded by pack animals." Washington, GPO, 1877. 4to, 2p, 1, 32pp, ills. US Surg-Gen. office, circular #9.

..."Report on the extent & nature of the materials available for the preparation of a medical & surgical history of the Rebellion." Philadelphia: J.B. Lippincott, for the Surg-Gen. office, 1865. 4to, 1p, 1, 165pp, incl. ills, tables, diagrs, col. plates. Circular #6. Prepared by Geo. A. Otis & J. J. Woodward. Undoubtedly portends a 6 vol. work by Jos. K. Barnes' 'Medical & Surgical History.'

183 **OTTEN, James T.**
"Disloyalty in the Upper Districts of S.C. during the CW." In: SCHM, 1974, v.75, #2, p.95-110.

184 **OULD, Robert**
"Argument in the four salt cases before the Court of Appeals of Virginia." n.p., n.d. (c. 1866), 8vo, wraps, 25pp. $25.00-Bmk.

185 ..."Capt. Irving & the Steamer Convoy." In: SHSP, 1882, v.10, p.320-328.

186 ..."The Exchange of Prisoners." In: AW, p.32-59.

187 ..."Letter (concerning exchange of prisoners)." In: SHSP, 1877, v. iv, pp.93-94.
..."Treatment of Prisoners." In: SHSP, 1876, v.1, p.125-131.

188 **"OUR Battle Flag.**
The Star Gem'd Azure Cross. To the Confederate Army." New Orleans, La., 1862, words by Clinton, music by Charles Young, quarto, 5pp. CSA flag in color as front cover.

189 **"OUR Confederate Dead.**
This Souvenir is authorized by the Ladie's Hollywood Memorial Association of Richmond, Va., Price 10 cents, 1896." Richmond, Va., Whittet & Shepperson. 2$20.00. 12mo, wraps, color-flag front., illus., (20)p.

...Richmond, Whittet & Shepperson, 1916, 16mo, wraps, 2-pls, incl, front, 24pp.

190 **"OUR Cruise**
in the Confederate States. War Steamer Alabama. The Private Journal of an Officer. From a Supplement to the South African Advitiser,..." Cape Town (South Africa), Sept. 19, 1863, 8vo, sewn, 64pp. Sabin-57916. $25.00. London, 1863.

191 **"OUR Dead at Shepherdstown, W.Va.,"**
In: CV, April 1905, v.13, p.170. Buried in Elmwood Cemetery by Shepherdstown Southern Memorial Association. Shelter-611.

192 **"OUR Flags.**
Souvenir of Solid South Booth. Confederate Bazaar. April 1903." n.p., (c.1903), 8vo, color wraps, color illus., (12)pp.

193 ..."Our Flags, Souvenir of Solid South Room, Confederate Museum." Richmond, Va., 1910, 2nd edt., 12mo, wraps, (14)pp. incl. color illus.

194 **"OUR Heroes & Our Flag."**
An engraving (on silk) 19x19" of Lee, Jackson & Beauregard, in full-dress uniform. Four CSA flags in each corner. $50.00.

195 **"OUR Heroes & Our Flags,"**
Engraving 19x24", n.p., Tarr & Ross, 1895. Around decr. border are 18 CSA generals with facsm. autographs below. Lee is in center, with his statue below. This was given free with renewal of the "Confederate Veteran," plus two others.

...(Do) but shows Lee, Jackson, Beauregard standing, Lee's hand on sword, Jackson holds his hat.

196 **"OUR Living & Our Dead.**
Devoted to North Carolina - Her Past, Her Present & Her Future. S.D. Pook, Editor." The official organ of the N.C.

branch of the Southern Historical Society. Newbern, N.C., (with new numbering) v.1-#1, Sept., 1874-#6, Feb. 1875. $50.00. Vo. II-Mar. 1875-June. (#1-4) $35.00. Vol. III-July-Dec. 1875 (#1-6) $50.00. Vol. IV-#1,-March 1876, pp.128, discont'd. Note: While there was no issues for Jan. & Feb. 1876 (v.IV) an issue Vol. 1-#1, January 1876 was issued with exact cover design & Edt. S.D. Pool as "Southern Historical Monthly." There was a different cover design for Sept. 1874 (v.1-#1) on which table of contents was placed, but most all issues were printed with standard design thru '76. Pages for each issues vary 100 to 130.
See: Ray M. Atchison, NCHR, XL(1963), p.423-433.

196a "OUR Neutrality."
In: Blackwoods, Apr. 1864, v.95, p.447-61.

197 "OUR Rancarous "Cousins."
In: Black. Edn. Mag., Nov. 1863, v.XCIV, p.636-652. "North persists in efforts to enslave South as a 'Battle for freedom.' The abolitionists Christian aspirations to exterminate the South, impudence pure & simple!"

198 "OUR Refugee Household."
N.Y., Blelock & Co., 1866, 12mo, cl, 226pp. Refugees from Sherman's march & return home with their experiences while away.

198a "OUR Soldiers in the Civil War."
In: 'Wagon Wheels.' Fall 1981, v.1, p.7-39.

199 "OUR Women in the War."
The Lives they lived; the deaths they died. From the 'Weekly News & Courier, Charleston, S.C.(quote)." Charleston, S.C., News & Courier, 1885, 8vo, cl, xii, 482-double column. $100.00B. Women tell their stories of the war, thru columns of the local news.

200 OUTERBRIDGE, T.L.
"Imprisoned for blockade running, 1863-4." In: Bermuda Hist. Quart., Apr./June, 1949, v.6, p.105-107. Author's imprisonment in Va., after capture on the 'Robert E. Lee,' off Wilmington, N.C.

201 OUTWEST, Oliver (pseud.)
"Adventures of Lena Rouden, a "Southern Letter Carrier," or rebel spy; a story of the Late War." Chicago, Horton & Leonard Pr., 1872, 8vo, wraps, 69pp. Wright-1830. Laid in Tenn.

202 OVERLEY, Milford
"Kentucky in the Southern Confederacy." In: CV, August, 1906, v.XIV, p.358-360.

203 OVERTON, Walter Alexander
"Excerpts from the Diary of Walter Alexander Overton, 1860-1862." Jackson, Miss., Jour. Miss. Hist., July, 1955, v.XVII, #3, pp.191-204.

203a OWEN, A. L., Mrs.
"Elmwood" during the war & my old Battered Canteen." Richmond, Va., 1896. 8vo, blue paper covers, cover title. The Brock Collection, Oct. 1922.
...(Richmond, Va., 1896?). 8vo, wraps, 15pp. (Goodspeeds-599). $50.

204 OWEN, Allison, Maj.
"History of the Washington Artillery." New Orleans, La., La. Hist. Society Publications, 1918, v.X, pp.46-59, with review by Dr. Joseph Holt, pp.64-67.

205 ..."Record of an old Artillery organization." In: Field Artly. Jour., 1914, v.IV, illus., 5-18pp.

206 OWEN, Dock
"Campfire Stories & Reminiscences, by Dock Owen, Co.F, Holcomb Legion, CSA." Greenwood, S.C., Index Pub. Co., n.d. (c.1885?). $50.00.

207 OWEN, Edward
"Reminiscences of Washington Artillery of New Orleans." In: B.&G., 1893, v.II, pp.43-44.

208 …"The Confederate Veteran Camp of New York." In; National Mag., 1892, v.XVI, p.455-467.
209 **OWEN, Kathryn**
"Civil War Days in Clark County, Ky." n.p., n.d., 8vo, wraps, color flags (cover), 87pp. (Lexington, Ky., 1863. Edt. of 200 copies) author. Keystone Printers. $20.00-B.
210 **OWEN, Mary Bankhead**
"Emma Sansone." In: SHSP, 1910, v.38, p.350-358.
…"Raising the first Confederate Flag." In: CV, May,1916, v.XXIV, p.199.
211 **OWEN, Narcissa Chisholm**
"Memoirs of Narcissa Owen, 1831-1907." Washington, D.C., 1907?, 8vo, cl, illus., ports, 126pp. $60.00-Bmk86. While largely on Cherokees, lived in Lynchburg during the war, made CSA uniforms, describes Hunter's Raid, etc.
212 **OWEN, Thomas, Compiler**
"Minutes of the 11th Annual reunion of the United Sons of Confederate Veterans, New Orleans, La., April, 1926." Nashville, Tenn., 1907, 8vo, wraps or cloth, 357p. $25.00.
212a **OWEN, Thomas M.**
"Proceedings of the First Annual Reunion of the Alabama division, United Sons of Confederate Veterans." Montgomery, Ala., 1902. 8vo, wraps, 32pp. $30.
213 **OWEN, Urban G.**
"Letters of a Confederate Surgeon in the Army of Tennessee to his wife. Edt: Enoch L. Mitchell." In: Tenn.HQ, 1945, v.IV, p.341-353; 1946, v.V, p.60-81, 142-181. Offprint, wraps, 73pp.
214 **OWEN, William Miller**
"The Artillery defenders of Fort Gregg." In: SHSP, 1891, v.XIX, p.65-71.
215 …"Correction," in: SHSP, 1892, v.XX, p.33.
216 …"A Hot Day on Marye's Heights." In: B&L, v.III, p.97-99.
217 …"In Camp & Battle with the Washington Artillery of New Orleans, a narrative of events during the late Civil War, from Bull Run to Appomattox & Spanish Fort. Compiled by the Adjutant from his diary & from authentic documents & orders. By William Miller Owen, 1st Lieutenant & Adjutant B.W.A." Boston, Ticknor & Co., 1885, 8vo, cl, gold seal on cover, illus, color-code, maps, xv, (1), 467pp. Rosters. $119.00, $125.00. $300-G, $175-Ginz, $200-NC, $225.00.
218 …New Orleans, La., Pelican Pub., 1964, XXXIII, 467pp. An exact reproduction of original, with three added illus., list of present-day officers & an introduction by Kenneth Urquhart.(op).
…Gaithersburg, Md., 1983. Reprint.
219 …"Prison Pastimes." In: SHSP, 1891, v.XIX, p.35-47.
220 …"Recollections of the third day at Gettysburg." In: US, 1885, v.XIII, p.148-151.
221 …"The Washington Artillery." In: SHSP, 1883, v.XI, p.248-254.
222 **OWENS, Harry P. & James J. Cooke, Edts.**
"The Old South & the Crucible of War." Jackson, Miss., University Press, 1983, 8vo, cl, dj, x, 110p. notes.
223 **OWSLEY, F.L., Jr.**
"The Capture of the CSS Florida." Amer. Neptune, Jan. 1962, Vol. XXII, #1, pp.45-54, pls. 2.
224 …"The C.S.S. Florida: Her Building and Operations." Philadelphia, University of Pa. Press, 1965, pp.208, cl, illus. $20.00.
…"The C.S.S. Florida's Tour de Force at Mobile Bay." In: AR, Oct. 1962, v.15, #4, p.262-70.
…University: Alabama Press, 1987. 8vo, cl, 209pp. ills, bibliog., index. $16. Reprint: 1965 edt.

225 ..."The Pattern of Migration & Settlement on the Southern Frontier." Baton Rouge, La., JSH, May, 1945, v.XI, #2, pp.147-176.

226 ..."Plain Folk of the Old South." Baton Rouge, La., State Univ., 1949, 8vo, cl, dj, maps, tables, xxii, 235pp.

227 ..."The South: Old & New Essays of Frank Lawrence Owsley." Edt: Harriet Chappell Owsley. Athens, University of Georgia Press, 1970, 8vo, cl, xix, 284pp.

228 **OWSLEY, Frank Lawrence**
"America & the freedom of the seas, 1861-1865." In: 'Essays in honor of Wm. E. Dodd, by his former students at the University of Chicago; Edt. by Avery Craven." Chicago, Univ. of Chicago Pr., 1935, pp.194-256.

229 ..."The American Triangle." In: VaQR, 1935, v.XI, p.113-119. Reviewing Jas. T. Adams' "Amer. Tragedy" & Geo. F. Milton's "Eve of Conflict."

230 ..."Defeatism in the Confederacy." Raleigh, N.C., Edwards & Broughton Co., 1926, 8vo, wraps, 13pp., reprinted from the N.C. Hist. Rev., July, 1926.

231 ..."The Economic Basis of Society in the late ante-bellum South. By Frank L. & Harriet Owsley." In: Jour.Sou.Hist., 1940, v.VI, p.24-45.

232 ..."The fundamental cause of the Civil War, egocentric sectionalism." Reprint: Jour. South. Hist., Feb. 1941, v.VII, #1, p.3-17, 8vo, wraps, 18pp.

233 ..."Jefferson Davis." In: South. Rev. 1938, v.III, p.762-768. A review of McElroy's "Jefferson Davis."

234 ..."King Cotton diplomacy; foreign relations of the Confederate States of America." Chicago, University of Chicago Pr., 1931, 8vo, cl, xi, 617pp. bibliog., pp.579-591.
...2nd Edt., Revised by Harriet Chappell Owsley, 1959, 1969. $30.00-Bmk94. 8vo, cl, dj, xxiii, 614pp. $10.00

235 ..."Local Defense & the Overthrow of the Confederacy; a study in state rights.: In: Miss. Val. Hist. Rev., Mar. 1925, v.XI, p.490-525. Bmk-$10.00.

236 ..."The Old South & the New." In: Amer. Rev., 1936, v.VI, p.475-485. A review of B.B. Kendrick's 'The South looks at its past.'

237 ..."The Soldier who walked with God." In: Amer. Rev., 1935, v.IV, p.435-459; v.V, p.62-74.

238 ..."A Southerner's View of Abraham Lincoln." In: Ga.Rev., Spring 1958, v.12, p.5-17. $8.00.

239 ..."State Rights in the Confederacy." Chicago, University of Chicago Press., 1925, 12mo, cl, ix, 289, (1)pp. $20.00.
...Reprinted in 1931. $40.00.
...Gloucester, Mass., Peter Smith, 1961.

240 ..."States' rights & the downfall of the Confederacy." In: Univ. of Chi., abstracts of theses. Humanistic Ser., v.II, p.187-192. Abstract from his larger book.

241 **OWSLEY, Harriet Fason Chappell**
"Peace & the Presidential Election of 1864." In: Tenn.HQ, Mar. 1959, v.XVIII, p.3-19, port., notes.

241a **OXLEY, James McDonald**
"Baffling the Blockade." London, 1896. Bmk(115) $30. 12mo, pict. cover, ills, 375pp, (novel).

242 **OZANNE, T.D., Rev.**
"The South as it is, or Twenty-one years experience in the Southern States of America." London, Saunders, Otley & Co., 1863, 12mo, cl, v, (i) 306pp. $125.00-jk.

P

1 **PABST, Loraine Beatrice**
"The Sack & Occupation of Athens, Ala. 1862-1865." In: North Ala. Hist. Assn. Bul., 1959, v.4, p.11-22. Notes.

2 **PABST, Warren E.**
"The Great Parrott Hunt." London, Jour. Confed. Hist. Soc., Spring, 1967, v.5, !1, p.21-26, pl.
See letter: v.5, #3, p.114-116.

3 **PACKARD, Joseph**
"The Retreat from Petersburg to Appomattox - Personal Recollections." 1918. In: Md. Hist. Mag., Mar. 1918, v.XIII, p.1-19.

4 **PACKARD, Joseph D.D.**
"Recollections of a Long Life. 1812-1902." Edt.: Rev. Thomas J. Packard. Washington, DC, Byron S. Adams, 1902, 8vo, cl, illus., ports(incl. front), 364pp. War years: p.264-285, relations with leading southern families, life in Virginia.

5 **PAGE, James Madison**
"The True Story of Andersonville Prison; a defense of Major Henry Wirz, by James Madison Page, late 2nd lieut. Co. A, Sixth Michigan Cavalry, in collaboration with M.J. Haley. With portraits." N.Y., Wash, Neale Pub. Co., 1908, 12mo, cl, front, ports., 248pp. $100.00-OB.

6 ..."Union Prisoners at Andersonville." In: CV, May 1908, #5, v.16, p.217-222. Captured at Battle of Liberty Mills, Va., Sept. 21, 1864. Defends Major Wirz.

7 **PAGE, John Randolph**
"Report on the history, symptoms & diagnosis of glanders & farcy in horses. Being a series of investigations made by request of Maj. Jas. G. Paxton, Q.M. at Lynchburg, with a view to eradicate these diseases from the horses of the Confederate States Army. By Jno. R. Page, PACS, J.J. Terrell, Asst. Surg., PACS, Lynchburg, Pub-Johnson & Schaffter, 1864." 12mo, wraps, 16pp. Crandall-3038. Rep: with additions & modifications, at Charlottesville, Va., Chronicle, 1876 (32pp).

8 **PAGE, John W.**
"Uncle Robin, in his Cabin in Virginia & Tom without one in Boston." Richmond, J.W. Randolph, 1853, 12mo, cl, 299pp. plate. Sabin-58154 calls for 2nd Edt. Pro-slavery.
See: "Uncle Tom's Cabin."

9 **PAGE, Richard Channing Moore**
"Diary of Maj. R.C.M. Page, Chief of CS Artillery, Dept. Douthwest Va. & East Tenn., from Oct. 1864 to May 1865." N.Y., 1888. 8vo, cover title, 12pp.
Also in: SHSP, 1888, v.16, p.58-68.

10 ..."Sketch of Page's Battery; or, Morris Artillery, 2nd Corps, Army Northern Virginia, by one of the Company." N.Y., Thomas Smeltzer, Print, 1885, 16mo, wraps, 82, (1)p., 200 copies printed. Notice signed by Dr. R.C.M. Page. $425.00-R.

11 ..."Captured guns at Spotsylvania Courthouse-Correction of Gen. Ewell's Report." In: SHSP, 1879, v.7, p.535-538.
See: S.S. Green, A.L. Long, Thom. Carter.

12 **PAGE, Richard Lucian**
"Defence of Fort Morgan - Report of." In: SHSP, 1877, v.III, p.37-42.
Also: B&L, v.iv, p.408-410.

13 **PAGE, Rosewell**
"The Iliads of the South; an epic of the War Between the States." Richmond, Garrett & Massie, 1932, sm. 4to, cl, xiii, 1, 206pp.

14 ..."Thomas Nelson Page: a Memoir of a Virginia Gentleman, by his brother, Rosewell Page." N.Y., C.Scribner's Sons,

14 1923, 12mo, cl, front(port), vi, 1, 210pp., ATG. $35.00-Bmk.

15 ..."Hanover County its History & Legends." Richmond, Va., 1926, 12mo, cl, front, pls., ports, 4p. 153pp. $75.00. $60.00. Partially on Civil War, with rosters.

16 **PAGE, Thomas Jefferson, Capt.**
"The Career of the Confederate Cruiser "Stonewall." In: SHSP, 1879, v.7, p.263-280.
See: Richmond Times.

17 **PAGE, Thomas Nelson**
"Among the Camps; or Young People's Stories of the War." N.Y., C. Scribner's Sons, 1891, 12mo, cl, illus., incl. front, 7, 163pp. Editions: 1902. [1920 Edt. $15.00].

18 ..."The Burial of the Guns." N.Y., C. Scribner's Sons, 1894, London, 1894, 12mo, cl, 3, 258pp. Editions: 1900. In: Scribner's Mag., Apr. 1894, v.16, p.410-422.

19 ..."Robert E. Lee, Man & Soldier." London, Laurie Print, 1909, 12mo, cl, 326pp.

20 ..."Robert E. Lee, Man & Soldier." N.Y., C. Scribner's Sons, 1911, 8vo, cl, front(port), 9-maps (2 fldg), xviii, 734pp.

21 ...1912, Edition in 2 vols., 12mo, cl, index, 488, 427pp. Vols. XVII & XVIII from the "Works of Thomas Nelson Page."; 1926 in 1 vol. $10.00.

22 ..."Robert E. Lee the Southerner." N.Y., C. Scribner's Sons, 1908, 12mo, cl, front(port), xiii, 312pp. $20.00. Editions: 1909 & 1910.

23 ..."Lee in Defeat." In. So. Atl. Quart., Jan. 1907, v.6, p.1-26. Also as a pamphlet. $5.00.
See: Rosewell Page's memoir of his brother.

24 ..."Gen. Lee & the Confederate Government." In: Scribner's, Nov. 1911, v.L, p.581-592.

25 ..."Meh Lady; a Story of the War." N.Y., C. Scribner's Sons, 1901, 12mo, cl, illus., incl. front., 70pp. $20.00-Bmk. Aslo 'Cent.', XXXII, 1886, p.187-205.

26 **PAGE, Thomas Nelson & Roswell Page**
"The Red Riders." N.Y., Scribner's, 1924, 12mo, c1338pp. Civil War & Reconstruction, set in S.C. Published posthumously & finished by the author's brother.

27 ..."Two Little Confederates." N.Y., C. Scribner's Sons, 1888, sq.8vo, decr. cl., illus., incl. front, 4, 156pp. (8)pp. ads. $30.00-Bmk.
See: Robert Y. Drake.
Editions: 1889, 1892, 1907, 1932; 8vo, cl, 190pp. Reprint (1960).

28 ..."Two Little Confederates." N.Y., Scribner's, 1925, 8vo, cl, 169pp., illus. $40.00- Carolina Bks. Based on boyhood experiences of Page & his brother Roswell. Sig. pres. copy.
...Edts - 1940, 1950 & 1956; 190pp.

29 **PAINTER, Henry M., Rev.**
"Brief Narrative of Incidents in the War of Missouri, & of the Personal Experience of one who has Suffered." Boston, Press of Daily Courier, 1863, 8vo, wraps, 28pp., C.S.A. $35.00. Southern Sympathizers murder by Union Troops.

30 **PAISLEY, Clifton**
"Tallahassee through the Storybooks War Clouds & War, 1860-1863." In: FHQ, July 1972, v.LI, #1, p.37-51, pl.

30a **PAISLEY, Emma Butler & William**
"Tulip Evermore: Emma Butler & William Paisley, their lives in letters, 1857-1887. Edited by Elizabeth Pailey Huckaby & Ethel C. Simpson, with introduction by Ethel C. Simpson." Fayetteville: University of Arkansas, 1985. Sm4to, 480p (paper $18) $39. Southern Arkansas during & after war.

31 **PALFREY, Ed. A., Col.**
"Some of the Secret History of Gettysburg." In: SHSP, 1880, v.8, p.521-526.

32 **PALMER, Benjamin Morgan**
"Address delivered at the funeral of General Maxcy Gregg, in the Presbyterian Church, Columbia, S.C., December 20, 1862 by B.M. Palmer, D.D." Columbia, S.C., Southern Guardian, 1863, 8vo, wraps, 11pp.

33 ..."Discourse at New Orleans, La., on the occasion of the (Gen. Jos. E.) Johnston Memorial services..." In: SHSP, 1890, v.XVIII, p.210-217.

34 ..."A Discourse before the General Assembly of South Carolina, on Dec. 10, 1863, appointed by the Legislature as a day of fasting, humiliation & prayer." Columbia, S.C., C.P. Pelham Print., 1864, 8vo, wraps, 24pp.

35 ..."A Discourse Commemorative of the life, Character, & genius of the late Rev. J.H. Thornwell." Columbia, Southern Guardian Press, 1862, 8vo, wraps, 57pp. McKissick-1889.

36 ..."The Life & Letters of James Henley Thornwell." Richmond, Whittet & Shepperson, 1875, 8vo, cl, 614pp.
Do: Louisville, Lost Cause Press, $8.24. $27.50. Palmer was active in founding the Presbyterian Church, CSA, ardent defender slavery & advocated secession. Thornwell's pamphlets circulated among SC Soldiers; was firm defender southern point of view.

37 ..."The Natal Day of Gen. R.E. Lee." In: SHSP, 1900, v.XXVIII, p.240-243.

38 ..."National Responsibility before God. A discourse, delivered on the day of fasting, humiliation & prayer, appointed by the President of the Confederate States of America, June 13, 1861, by B.M. Palmer, D.D., pastor of the First Presbyterian Church, New Orleans, La. published by request of the Confederate Guards Companies "A" & "B". New Orleans, Price-Current Print, 1861, 8vo, wraps, 28pp.

39 ..."The Oath of Allegiance to the United States, discussed in its moral & political bearings. By Rev. B.M. Palmer, D.D. late of New Orleans. Published by the Soldiers' Tract Association, M.E. Church South." Richmond, Macfarlane & Fergusson, 1863, 16mo, wraps, cover title, 22pp.

40 ..."Oath of Allegiance." Columbia, S.C., 1863, 8vo, sewn, 16pp. old Ebrst $10.00. variant Crandall-2804: "The Oath of Allegiance to the United States," 32pp. (n.p., 1863?) Letter addressed to Hon. John Perkins, dates Columbia, S.C., Feb. 10, 1863. $30.00. Commends citizen of La. for refusing to take oath of allegiance to U.S.

41 ..."The Present Crisis & its issues. An address delivered before the literary societies of Washington & Lee University, Lexington, Va., 27th June, 1872. Pub. at request of the board of trustees of the University." Baltimore, J. Murphy & Co., 1872, 8vo, wraps, 28pp. (Reconstruction).

42 ..."The Rights of the South defended in the pulpits by B.M. Palmer, D.D. & W.T. Leacock, D.D., of New Orleans." Mobile, Ala., J.Y., Thompson, 1860, 8vo, cover title, 16pp. $150.00-G.

43 ..."The South; Her Peril & her Duty." A Discourse...Delivered in the 1st Presbyterian Church, New Orleans, Nov. 29, 1860." New Orleans, True Witness & Sentinel, 8vo, wraps, 16pp. $100.00-Ginz(35).
Do: Milledgeville, Ga., 1860.
Do: New York, 1861, p.20.

44 ..."A Vindication of Secession & the South from the Scriptures of Rev. R.J. Breckinridge in the Danville Quarterly Review. By. B.M. Palmer, New Orleans, La. (From the Southern Presbyterian Review for April, 1861). Columbia, S.C., Southern Guardian Pr., 1861, 8vo, wraps, 46pp.

44a ..."Secessionist become Nationlist." In: LH, 1977, v.18, p.287-301.

44b ..."Thanksgiving address of . . . (1860)." In: LaH., 1963, v.4, p.105-18.

45 **PALMER, Donald Mc.N.**
"Four Weeks in the Rebel Army." New London, D.S. Ruddock, 1865, 8vo, wraps, 40pp. ATG $500.00-G. Dornbusch (3029) Captured in engagement at Potosi, Sept. 27, 1864, conscripted by South.

46 **PALMER, J.W.**
"Stonewall Jackson's Way. By J.W. Palmer. The manuscript from which this is printed was written by the author for Edmund Clarence Stedman & is now privately printed for the firends of the present owner." William K. Bixby, St. Louis, Mo., MCMXV, 4to, wraps, 7p., 200 copies printed at Torch Press, Cedar Rapids, Iowa. $50.00-B.

46a ..."Stonewall Jackson's Way" a Song by JWP." In: SHSP, 1883, v.11, p.136-7.

47 **PALMER, John B.**
"The 58th North Carolina at the Battle of Chickamauga." In: OLOD, Oct. 1975, v.3, #4, p.454-455.
See: G.W. Hill.

47a **PALMER, Jonathan W.**
"The Southern Soldier's Prize Songster Martial & Patriotic Pieces (chiefly original) applicable to the present war." Mobile, Ala., Wisely print, 1864.

48 **PALMER, Joseph**
"Corrections concerning the Battle of Chickamauga." In: SHSP, 1884, v.12, p.239-240.

48a **PALMER, Mary**
"The Gallant Pelham." In: AHQ, 1947, v.7, #4, p.542-46.

48b **PALMER, T. W., Dr. & E. F. Ellsberry**
"War Classes of Univ. Ala., 1861-65." Tuscaloosa, Ala., 1907. 8vo, wraps, 24pp.

49 **PALMER, William H., Col.**
"Correspondence of Gen. Robt. E. Lee. Chancellorsville to Gettysburg, March to August, 1863." In: SHSP, 1900, v.28, p.148-155.

50 **PALMETTO RANCH, Battle of**
See: Luther Conyer's 'Last Battle of War.' SHSP, 1893, v.21, p.226-227.
See: Louis J. Schuler.

51 **PALMYRA (Mo.) Confederate Monument Association**
"The Palmyra massacre, a short but concise true history of the execution of ten Confederate soldiers, at Palmyra, Mo., Oct. 18, 1862. Written, published & circulated by the Palmyra Confederate Monument Association." Palmyra, Sosey Bros., Print, (c. 1903), 8vo, wraps, 15, (1)pp.

52 ..."Origin of an Ironclad; how the Merrimac came to be transformed - the original plan still in existence." In: CV, May 1915, v. XXIII, p. 219-221. By the son of the designer.

53 ..."The Confederate States Navy & a brief history of what became of it." In: SHSP, 1900, v.28, p.125-134.

53a **PALO, Rani-Villem**
"(Nathan Bedford) Forrest & Okolona (Miss.) victory (Feb. 22, 1864)." In: CWTI, Apr, 1985, v.24, p.32-9.

54 **PALUDAN, Philip Shaw**
"Victims, a true story of the Civil War." Knoxville, University of Tennessee Pr., 8vo, cl, dj, xvi, 144pp. CSA Troops supress Union guerrillas in N.C.

55 ..."Paper Money in the Confederate States of America... A descriptive History of..." In: 'The Numismatist', Baltimore, Md., beginning June 1917. (Adv. in CV, June 1917, v. 25, p.289.). Every bill issued by the CSA, 1861-1864, with a full history of the design & biographical sketch of all Southern men & women whose pictures appear on same.

55a **PAPPAS, James D.**
"Organization of the Confederate States

Navy." In: AHQ, 1952, v.14, #1 & 2, p.122-124.

56 **PARAMORE, J.B., Col.**
"Florida Confederate Officer, 1840-1902." In: CV, 1902, v.10, p.269.

57 **PARHAM, Benjamin M.**
"The Battle of Cold Harbor & the touching death of Clarence Warwick." In: SHSP, 1895, v.23, p.79-82.

58 **PARHAM, John T., 32nd Va. Inf.**
"Thirty-second at Sharpsburg, forty-five percent loss." In: SHSP, 1906, v.32, p.250-253.

59 **PARHAM, W.C., Col.**
"David O. Dodd, The Nathan Hale of Arkansas." In: Pub. Ark. Hist. Assn., v.II, 1908, p.531-535. Executed as a spy by Steele's army.
See: Dallas T. Herndon.
Also: SHSP, 1883, v.11, p.310-313.

60 **PARIS, John**
"A Sermon preached before Brig.-Gen. Hoke's brigade, at Kinston, N.C., on the 28th of Feb., 1864 by John Paris, chaplain 54th Reg., N.C. Troops, upon the death of twenty-two men, who had been executed in the presence of the brigade for the crime of desertion." Greensborough, N.C., A.W. Ingold, 1864, 12mo, wraps, 15pp. Crandall-4177.

61 ..."The Soldier's History of the War, containing a narrative of events, campaigns & battles." In: OLOD, 1874-1876: v.I, p.289-303, 401-418, 529-545; v.II, p.1-18, 131-152, 259-279, 389-406; v.III, p.1-20, 147-161, 291-311, 435-448, 577-592; v. IV, p.3-18.

62 ..."Causes which produced the War between the States. From "the Soldier's History of the War." In: Southern Hist. Monthly, Jan, 1876, v.1, #1, p.(3)-20. ('to be continued').

63 **PARIS, Louis Philippe Albert d'Orleans, comte de**
"Causes of Lee's defeat at Gettysburg." In: SHSP, 1878, v.V, p.88-89.

64 ..."Correspondence between J.W. Jones & Comte de Paris." In: SHSP, 1876, v.II, p.253-256.

65 ..."Strength of both armies at Gettysburg." In: SHSP, v.V, p.204-207; v.VI, p.10-12.
See: Wm. Baird, Jubal A. Early.

66 **PARK, Clyde W.**
"Morgan the Unpredictable." Cincinnati, Ohio, Christmas gift of the Krehbeil (C.J.) Co., 1959, 12mo, decr. fabricoid, front (port.), illus, 40pp., double-page map. $40.00-Bmk104.

67 **PARK, Hugh, Edt.**
"Pea Ridge: The Place Where the South Lost the Civil War." published on occasion 99th Anniversary Memorial Service at Pea Ridge, Arkansas, Sunday, March 5, 1961." Van Buren, Ark., Press-Argus Printers, Arkansas Historical Series #11, 8vo, stiff wraps, 23pp.(1)p. ad., pt.II-J.S. Sweet, "Battle of Pea Ridge." Gen. research Div.; Library Congress, May 28, 1955.

68 **PARK, Lemuel Madison**
"The "Rebel Prison Pen" at Andersonville, Georgia." In: South Mag., 1874, v.XIV, p.528-537. bm$20.00. Park a member of Co. G, 1st (Fannin's) Ga. Inf. reserves.

69 **PARK, Robert Emory**
"War Diary of Capt. Robert Emory Park, Twelfth Alabama Regiment, Jan. 28, 1863-Jan. 27, 1864." In: SHSP, Jan. 1898, v.XXVI, p.1-31.

70 ..."Diary of Robert E. Parks, Macon, Georgia, late Captain Twelfth Alabama Regiment, CSA." June 6-15th, 1864-1865, p.370-386, p.430-437, p.78-85, p.172-180, p.232-239, p.306-315; v.III, 1877, p.43-46, p.55-61, p.123-127, p.183-189, p.244-254.

71 ..."Sketch of the Twelfth Alabama Infantry of Battle's Brigade, Rode's Division, Early's Corps, of the Army of Northern Virginia, by Robert Emory Park, of

Macon, Georgia, late Captain, Company F, 12th Alabama Regiment. (Reprinted from Southern Historical Society Papers, v. XXXIII)." Richmond, Wm. Ellis Jones, 1906, 8vo, wraps, 106pp. $275.00. $350.00. $450.00.
...SHSP, 1905, v.XXXIII, p.193-296.

72 ..."Rode's Brigade at Seven Pines." In: LWL, 1867, v.IV, p.389-391.

73 **PARK, Ruie Ann Smith, Compl., Edt.**
Dear Parents-- Civil War Letters of the Shibley Brothers of Van Buren, Arkansas." Fayetteville, Ark., Washington Co. Hist. Soc. In Observance of Civil War Centennial, Feb. 1963, 4to, stiff wraps, mimeo, ports., illus., 19pp.,(67) of 46 letters (largely printed on one side). $12.00-Bmk.

74 **PARKER, Daisy**
"John Milton, Governor of Florida/A Loyal Confederate." In: FHQ, April, 1942, v.XX, #4, pp.346-361.

75 ..."Battle flags of Florida troops in Confederate service." In: Apapache, 1948-50, p.1-10.

76 **PARKER, David B.**
"Bill Arp & blacks: The forgotten Letters." In: GaHQ, Fall 1983, v.LXVII, #3, p.336-349.
See: Chas. H. Smith.

77 **PARKER, Elmer Oris**
"Captain Lyle: Forgotten Hero of the Confederacy." In: Prologue, v.IV, pp.165-172. Fall, 1972.

78 ..."Confederate Army Muster Rolls." In; Military Affairs, 1964, v.XXVIII, p.79-82.

79 **PARKER, Francis L. Le Jau**
"Battle of Fort Sumter as seen from Morris Island." In: SCHM, 1961, v.62, #2, p.65-71. Diary of ass't. surgeon, CSA, Apr. 11-13, 1861.

79a **PARKER, Henry Gillam**
"The History of a Confederate Casualty." n.p., (1981) (Skyland, N.C.). 8vo, stiff wraps, port on cover, facsms, ills, ports, 18pp, (9)p., (19)-31, (3)p. Home-life before & during war, eastern Carolinas.

80 **PARKER, J. W., Mrs., Historian**
"Prize Essays presented by the N.C. division U.D.C." Raleigh, N.C., Edwards & Broughton, 1936, numerous essays, various authors on those prominent in C.S.A., 8vo, cl, front(port), 178pp.

81 **PARKER, James H.**
"The Capture of Mr. Jefferson Davis, President of Confederate States." In: SHSP, 1877, v.IV, p.91-92. Union man refutes Davis wore dress, as one of those of his capture.

82 **PARKER, Parson**
"Sufferings of the Twelfth Georgia Reg't in the Mountains of Virginia." n.p., 1862(?), Shetler-615. Broadside 23x8 1/2".

83 **PARKER, Prescott A.**
"Story of the Tensaw, Blakely, Spanish Fort, Jackson Oaks, Fort Mims." Montrose, Ala., Author, (1922?), 8vo, cl, 19, (11)pp., front., illus. Story of the Siege of Mobile, 1865. The organization of Union forces, Mar. 17, Apr. 12, 1865; C.S. Army, Mar. 10, 1865.

83a **PARKER, Price**
"From Alabama to Appomattox, the history of the 9th Infantry, pictures, complete muster roll by Price Parker." Athens, Alabama, 1970. 8vo, cl, 160pp, ills.

84 **PARKER, Tom**
"Soldiers of the Confederate States of America." Hartsdale, N.Y., Rampart House, 1958. Four authentic uniforms (4-color) 5"x7", 1st Virginia Wash. Artlly., 3rd S.C., Terry's Rangers.

85 **PARKER, W. W.**
"Seed cover of the Confederacy, the famous boy company of Richmond, commanded by Captain W.W. Parker." In: SHSP, 1907, v.XXXV, p.102-107.
See: Royal W. Figg.

86	**PARKER, William Harwar** "Recollections of a Naval Officer, 1841-1865." N.Y. Charles Scribner's Sons, 1883, 12mo, cl, xv, 372pp. $50.00. ...Annapolis, Md., 1985. $22.	93	**PARKS, Edd Winfield** "John Jacob Zollicoffer." In: THQ, 1953, v.11, p.346-355. Dec. Activities in Tenn. Journalism, politics & CSArmy.
87	..."The Confederate States Navy." v.XII Clement Evans' "Confed. Mil. Hist." pp. 1-115, Port(front), composite ports.	94	**PARKS, James H.** "A Confederate Trade Center under Federal Occupation: Memphis, 1862 to 1865." In: Jour. of South. Hist., VII, 1941, p.289-314. $10.00-Bmk.
88	..."The Gold & Silver in the Confederate States Treasury. What Became of it. The account of Captain William H. Parker, Confederate States Navy, who had it in charge in its transportation South." In: SHSP, 1893, v.XXI, p.304-313.	95	**PARKS, Joseph Howard** "Joseph E. Brown of Georgia." Baton Rouge, Louisiana State University Press, 1977, 8vo, cl, dj, illus., bibliog., 578 p. $35.00. In Print $40.00.
89	..."The Merrimac & Monitor," Letter from Captain Parker." In: SHSP, 1883, v.XI, p.34-40.	96	..."Memphis under military rule, 1862-1965." In: ETHSP, 1942, v.14, p.31-58.
89a	..."Confederate States Navy." v.XVII. 8vo, cl, 515pp. (not an extended volume). Wilmington, N.C., Broadfoot, 1987.	97	..."General Leonidas Polk, C.S.A. the Fighting Bishop." Baton Rouge, Louisiana State University Press, 1962, Kingsport, Tenn., Kingsport Press, 8vo, cl, dj, illus., maps, ports, incl, front, (5) 408pp. $25.00-Bmk. $45.00-OP.
89b	..."Elements of Seamanship. Prepared as a text book for the midshipmen of the C.S. Navy. By Wm. H. Parker commanding C.S. School-ship 'Patrick Henry.'" Richmond, Va., Macfarlane & Fergusson, 1864. 12mo, cl, xi, 189p. Crandall-2466.	98	...First Edition, Baton Rouge; Louisiana State University Press, 1954, 8vo, cl, dj, viii, (4), 537pp., maps, ports, views, bibliog., notes, p.510-515. $20.00.
89c	..."Instruction for naval light artillery, afloat & ashore, prepared & arranged by William H. Parker." Newport, J. Atkinson Print, 1862. 8vo, 3p, 1, (3)-67. 19 plates. ...2nd Edt., 'revised for US Naval Acad. N.Y., D. Van Nostrand, 1862. 8vo, 120p, 22 plates, including diagrams. $75.	99	..."General Edmund Kirby Smith, C.S.A." Baton Rouge, Louisiana State University Press, 1954, 8vo, cl, dj, pls, maps, port(front), viii, (2) 537pp. index. $30.00-Bmk.
90	**PARKER, William Watts, Dr.** "How the Southern Soldiers kept house during the war." In: SHSP, 1895, v.23, p.318-328, plate.	100	...1962, second printing (slightly larger), 8vo, Atg., $23.00.
91	..."What Confederate fired the last shot?" In: SHSP, 1881, v.9, p.381. The experience of Dr. W.W. Parker, Major of Artillery.	101	..."States Rights in a Crisis: Governor Joseph E. Brown vs. President Jefferson Davis." In: JSH, Feb. 1966, 22pp., v.32, #1, p.3-24. $8.00.
92	**PARKS, Aileen W.** "Bedford Forrest, boy on horseback." Indianapolis, Bobbs-Merrill, 1952, 12mo, cl, dj. $10.00.	102	..."The Tennessee Whigs & the Kansas-Nebraska Bill." Baton Rouge, La., JSH, Aug., 1944, v.X, #3, pp.308-330.
		102a	..."John Bell & Secession." In: East Tenn HS, 1944. #19, p.30-47.

102b ..."A Confederate Trade Center Under Federal Occupation: Memphis 1862-65." In: JSH, Aug. 1941, v.7, #3, p.289-314.

103 **PARKS, Ken**
"The Civil War in Mississippi, 1861-1865." Bolton, Miss., Ken Parks Associates, 1959, 4to, decr. wraps (in color), fldg. map, (28)pp.

103a **PARKS, Leighton**
"What a Boy Saw of the Civil War with Glimpses of Gen. Lee." In: Cent. Mag., June 1905, v.70, p.258-64.

104 **PARKS, Louise Wiseman**
"Captain Wiseman: a bit of family history." McAllen, Texas, 1950, 8vo, wraps, (4), 65, (7), 17p. port. Planters in N.C., S.C., & Texas. Covers William Henderson Wiseman (1829-1911), an officer in CSArmy: "Life as I found it; memoirs of eighty years of living, as told to Louise Parks.

105 **PARKS, R.S.**
"Anniversary of General Lee's Birthday." In: SHSP, 1897, v.25, p.354-364.

106 **PARKS, Thomas**
"The Confederate Roll of Honor." Oklahoma City: Chron. Okla., Summer 1956, v.XXXIV, #2, pp.234-238, plate.

107 **PARKS, Virginia, Alan Rick & Norman Simons.**
"Pensacola in the Civil War." In: Pensacola Hist. Soc. Qrt., Spring, 1978. p.1-44. Reprint: 1983.

108 **PARKS, W.M.**
"Building a war ship in the Southern Confederacy." In: USN Inst. Proc., Aug. 1923, v.XLIX, p.1299-1307.

109 ..."Paroles of the Army of Northern Va., R.E. Lee, Gen. C.S.A., Commanding, surrendered at Appomattox C.H., Va., April 9, 1865, to Lt.-Gen. U.S. Grant commanding armies of the U.S., now first printed from the duplicate originals in the archives of Southern Historical Society, edt. with Intro: R.A. Brock, Sect., SHSP." x.XV. Richmond, Va., Pub. by Society, 1887, Wm. Ellis Jones, Print., Tall 8vo, wraps, xxvii, 508pp., index, p. 489-508. $45.00-Folk. Rep. 1962 $60.00-Is.

110 ..."Paroles of the Army of Northern Virginia." In: SHSP, v.15, xxvii, 508pp., v.16, p.386-388; v.32, p.51-57; v.18, p.386.

110a **PARMELEE, L. R.**
"Helena & West Helena--a Civil War Engineers Reminiscences." In: Phillips CHQ, Dec. 1962, v.1, p.1-25.

111 **PARRAMORE, Thomas C.**
"The Burning of Winton in 1862." Raleigh, NCHRev., Winter, 1962, v.XXIX, #1, pp.18-31, port., pl.

112 **PARRAMORE, Thomas C., F. Roy Johnson & E. Frank Stephenson, Jr., Edts.**
"Before the Rebel Flag Fell. Five viewpoints of the Civil War by: Annie B. Darden, Richard Barnes, Thomas D. Boone, Media Evans & Jno. W. Moore." Murfreesboro, N.C., Johnson Pub., 1965, 8vo, decr. fabricoid, (16), 132pp. $25.00-B.

113 **PARRISH, Randall**
"My Lady of the South; a Story of the Civil War." Chicago, A.C. McClurg Co., 1909, 12mo, cl, color illus., incl. front, 361pp.

113a **PARRISH, T. Michael & R. M. Willingham, Jr.**
"Confederate Imprints, a bibliography of Southern Publications from Secession to Surrenter. (Expanding & Revising the earlier works of Marjorie Crandall & Richard Harwell)." Austin, Texas, Jenkins Pub. Co., 1987. Tk4to, cl, dj, 991pp, (150) facsms. $95. Approx. 10,000 entries, books, pamphlets, maps, sheet music, etc.

113b **PARRISH, T. Z.**
"The Saga of the Confederate Ram 'Arkansas;' the Mississippi Valley Campaign, 1862. Intro: Harold B. Simpson."

Hillsboro, Texas, Junior College, 1987. 8vo, cl, dj, ills, maps, ports, index, 237pp.

113c **PARRISH, William E.**
"Turbulent Partnership, Missouri & the Union, 1861-65." Columbia, University of Missouri Pr., 1963. 12-Bmk. 8vo, cl, d/w, 242pp, indexed. $5.50. Believed in states rights but stayed in Union in troubled times.

114 **PARROTT, W.A.**
"Muster Roll of the Holcombe Guards." In: SHSP, 1896, v.24, p.115-116.

115 **PARRY, Roger William**
"John Hunt Morgan (1825-1864) - Gentleman - General." In: Christopher Gist Hist. Soc. Paper, 1955-1956, leaves 93-102.

116 **"PARSON'S Texas Cavalry"**
See: Anderson, John Q.
W.H. Getzendaner
W.H. Parsons
Geo. H. Hogan.

117 **PARSON, W.H.**
"Condensed History of Parsons Texas Cavalry Brigade, 1861-1865. Together with inside history & heretofore unwritten chapters of the Red River Campaign of 1864. By Gen. W.H. Parsons." Corsicana, Sun-light Pub. Co., 1903, 8vo, wraps, 106pp.
See: Geo. H. Hogan.

118 **PARSONS' Texas Brigade Associaiton**
"A Brief & Condensed History of Parson's Texas Cavalry Brigade, composed of Twelfth, Nineteenth, Twenty-first, Morgan's Battalion, & Pratt's Battery of Artillery of the Confederate States. Together with roster of the several commands, as far as obtainable some historical sketches, General orders & a memoranda of Parson's Brigade Association." Waxahachie, Texas, J.M. Fleming Pr., 1892, 8vo, wraps, 96pp.

119 ...Waco, Texas, W.M. Morrison, 1962, 4to, cl, facsm, t/p, 96pp., print on one side, mimeogr., Lim.Edt. 100 copies. $32.00-Bmk84. At end is a note," To Parson's Texas Cavalry Brigade; written at Kaufman, Aug. 7th, 1889, by Mrs. G.W. Farris, Huntsville, Texas."

120 ..."A Partial list of Confederate Soldiers buried in Confederate Cemetery, Fayetteville, Arkansas." In: AHQ, 1946, v.V, p,406-410. Soldiers from Arkansas, Texas & Missouri.

121 **PARSONS, Henry S.**
"Wall-paper editions of the Vicksburg "Daily Citizen." in: Antiques, 1934, XXV, p.97-98. On the edition July 2, 1863.

121a **PART My Country**
Played in the Confederacy, The." In: AHQ, 1943, v.5, #2, p.124-47.

122 **PARTIN, Robert**
"The Money Matters of a Confederate Soldier." In: Ala. Hist. Quart., Spring-Summer, 1963, v.25, #1&2, p.49-69.

123 ..."The Sustaining Faith of an Alabama Soldier." In: CWH, December 1960, v.VI, #4, p.425-438.

124 ..."A Confederate Sergeant's Report to his wife during the Campaign from Tullahoma to Dalton." In: Tenn.HQ, 1953, v.XII, p.291-308, extract. $8.00.

125 ...(cont'd).."during the Bombardment of Fort Pillow." In: Tenn.HQ, Sept. 1956, v.XV, p243-252. Sgt. Hiram Talbert Holt.

126 ..."The Momentous events of the Civil War as reported by a Confederate private-sergeant." In: Tenn.HQ, Mar. 1959, p.69-86. Based on letters from Sgt. Hiram Talbert Holt (died 1864) of Ala. Greys, Co. D, 2nd Inf. Reft. Ala. Vols. later Co. I, 38th Inf. Regt. to his wife Angeline, at Choctaw Corner, Ala. Apr 1861-Feb. 1864. Collection of 138 letters edited by Partin, from a typescript 498lf.

127 ..."The Wartime Experiences of Margaret McCalla: Confederate Refugee from East Tennessee." In: Tenn.HQ, 1965, v.XXIV, p.39-53.

128 ..."The Civil War in East Tennessee as reported by a Confederate Railroad builder." In:THQ, 1963, v.22, p.238-258.

128a ..."An Alabama Confederate Soldier's Report to his Wife." In: AR, v.3, p.22-35.

128b ..."Report of a Corporal of the Alabama First Infantry." In: AHQ, 1958, v.20, #4, p.583-94.

129 **PARTIN, Robert Love**
"The Secession Movement in Tennessee." Nashville, Tenn., George Peabody College for Teachers, 1935. Abstracts of Contribution to Education, #153, 8vo, wraps, (2), 8pp. (also pub. with series incorrectly numbered "156" on t.p. & cover).

130 **PARTRIDGE, M.F.**
"The last official CSA war order, 9 Apr. '65." In: UDCMag., June 1953, v.16, #6, p.3,38, facsm.
See: Article, same title, signed: E.A.W. in some issue, p.26-27.
...In: Autograph Coll. Jour., Winter, 1953, v.5, #2, p.28-30, facsms.

131 **PASCOE, W.H.**
"Confederate Cavalry around Port Hudson." In: SHSP, 1905, v.33, p.83-96.

132 **PASHA, Admiral Hobart (pseud.)**
See: Hobart-Hampden, Augustus Charles, "Sketches from my Life'" ! "Never Caught," etc.

132a **PASKOFF, Paul F. & Daniel J. Wilson**
"The Cause of the South; Selections from De Bows Reveiw, 1846-67." Baton Rouge, Louisiana Univ. Press, 1982. 8vo, cl, dj, XIV, 306pp, (wrp #9) $27.50.

133 **PASQUINO, (pseud.)**
See: McLaughlin, J.F.

134 **PATCH, Charles A.**
"Valor & Skill in the Civil War. Was either the better soldier? Which was the better army?" In: Cent., ns, SVIII, 1890, p.144-150, Tables.

135 ..."At the "death angle", May 12, 1864." In: Mag. Amer. Hist., 1886, v.XVI, p.176-179.

136 **PATCH, Joseph Dorst, Gen.**
"The Battle of Ball's Bluff. Edt: Fitzhugh Turner, with an introduction by Virgil Carrington Jones." Leesburg, Va., Potomac Press, 1958, 8vo, stiff decr. color wraps (or cloth), map end-sheets, ports., illus., 123pp. $6.50. Wraps, 30-B. Contemporary news account & those of both Northern & Southern officers.

137 **PATE, Henry Clay**
"Proceesings of the General Court Martial in the case of Lt.-Col. H. Clay Pate, 5th Va. Cavlary." Richmond, Va., 1863, 8vo, wraps, caption title, 126, (1)p. Crandall-2535.

138 **PATE, O.K.**
"The Character of Stonewall Jackson, a lecture delivered in the hall of the House of Delegates, at Richmond, Virginia, Jan. 28, 1865." Richmond, Va., Republished in the "Southern Star" office, 1865, 12mo, wraps, 12pp. Dorn-II, 2849.

138a **PATON, James E.**
"Civil War Journal of James E. Paton, Edt: Wade Hampton Whitley." In: RKHS, July 1963, v.61, #3, p.220-31.

139 **PATRICK, Rembert W.**
"The Fall of Richmond." Baton Rouge, Louisiana State University Press, 1960, 12mo, cl, dj, facsm, illus., incl. dbl-page t/p, ports, index, 144pp.

140 ..."Jefferson Davis & his Cabinet." Baton Rouge, Louisiana State University Press, 1944, 8vo, cl, dj, c, 401pp., index, bibliog., p.369-401. $25.00. $20.00-Bmk84.
...Reprint, 1961. $20.00-Bmk.

141 ..."Opinions of the Confederate Attorneys Generals." See: "Confederate States of America - Dept. of Justice." Edited by Patrick.

142 ..."Race relations in the South (1800-1957), 8vo, wraps, ii, 21p.

143 **PATRICK, Robert Draughon**
"Reluctant Rebel. The Secret Diary of Robert Patrick, 1861-1865." Baton Rouge, Louisiana State University Press, 1959, 8vo, cl, dj, facsms, illus, sketches, maps, incl. liners, xiii, 271pp., 2nd ptg, 1961. $35.00.
See: Foster Jay Taylor.

144 **"PATRIOTIC Letters of Confederate Leaders."**
In: SHSP, 1876, v.II, p.49-56. Lee, Davis, Maury, Constantine of Russia.

145 **PATTERSON, Camm, Capt.**
"Company D, Fifth Virginia. Roster of the famous "Buckingham Yancey Guard," in the front at Gettysburg." In: SHSP, 1902, v.30, p.154-160.

146 **PATTERSON, Caroline**
"The Secession of Georgia." In: CV, 1931, v.39, p.207-212, illus.

147 **PATTERSON, Edmund De Witt**
"Yankee Rebel: The Civil War Journal of Edmund De Witt Patterson. Edited with introduction by John G. Barrett. Biographical essay by Edmund Brooks Patterson." Chapel Hill, Univ. of North Carolina, 1966, 8vo, cl, xx, 207pp., facsm, endsht. An Ohioan, became enamored with the South, fought in CSArmy, prisoner of war at Johnson's Island. $30.00-Bmk.

148 **PATTERSON, Gerard**
"Allegheny Johnson." In: CWTI, Jan. 1967, v.V, #9, p.12-19, illus., ports. Maj.-Gen. Edward Johnson, eccentric but a tough & able commander.

149 ..."John Bell Hood." In: CWTI, Feb. 1971, v.IX, #10, p.12-21, illus., ports.

150 ..."George E. Pickett, graduates at bottom of class at West Point, where does he belong among Confederate generals?" In: CWTI, Oct. 1968, v. VII, #6, p.4-10, 43-47, illus., maps, plan, ports.

151 **PATTERSON, H.K.W.**
"War Memories of Fort Monroe & Vicinity. Containing an account of the memorable battle between the "Merrimac" & "Monitor", the incarceration of Jefferson C(!) Davis & other topics..." Fort Monroe, Va., Pool & Deuschle, 1885, 12mo, cl, 3p, 1, 102pp. Swem-4167; Smith-78. Author served in 3rd Va. Artly.

152 **PATTERSON, I. Frank**
"Day Book of I. Frank Patterson, July 22, 1864-April 30, 1865. Edt: Mildred Patterson Putnam." n.p., 1962, wraps(spiral) 97pp. $26.00-Bmk. From Cabarrus Co., N.C., (Concord, N.C.)

153 **PATTERSON, Josiah Blair**
"Irrepressible Optimism of a Georgia Confederate in 1864: a Letter. Edited Martin Abbott." In: Ga.H.Q., Dec. 1953, v.XXXVII, #4, p.348-350.

154 **PATTON, James Welch, Edt.**
"Minutes of the proceedings of the Greenville ladies ass'n. in aid of the volunteers of the Confederate Army." Durham, N.C., Duke University Press, 1937, Hist. Papers of Trinity College Historical Society, series XXI, 8vo, wraps, 118pp. $15.00.

155 ..."Unionism & Reconstruction in Tennessee, 1860-1869." Chapel Hill, Univ. of N.C. Press, 1934, 8vo, cl, xii, 267pp. More the political history of last state to seceed & first to rejoin the Union.

156 ..."The Work of Soldier's aid societies in South Carolina during the Civil War." In: S.C. Hist. Ass'n. Proc., 1937, p.3-12.

157 **PATTON, John Mercer**
"Reminiscences of Jackson's Infantry." In: SHSP, 1880, v.8, p.139-142.

158 **PAUL, James C.N.**
"Rift in Democracy." Philadelphia, Univ. of Pa. Press, 1951, 8vo, cl, dj, 200pp. Largely from misc. sources, thesis: political disputes in Democratic party in 1844

over annexation of Texas led to the Civil War.

159 **PAULLIN, Charles Oscar**
"The Naval Administration of the Southern States during the Revolution." In: Sewanee Rev., 1902, v.10, p.418-428.

160 **PAXTON, Alexander Gallatin**
"The Vicksburg Campaign, a Story of Perserverance, by A.G. Pacton, Colonel 114th F.A. Mississippi National Guard." Grenada, Miss., 1959, 21cm, wraps, 17pp. Dorn-II, 2861.

161 ..."The Vicksburg campaign, a story of perseverance." 2nd ed., Greenville, Miss., 1959, 22cm, maps, 18pp. $15.00-B.

162 **PAXTON, Alexander S.**
"Private Ailstock, a Confederate hero." In: B & G, 1984, v.III, p.37-38.

163 ..."Sherman's Bummers." In: SHSP, 1907, v.32, p.89-93.

164 **PAXTON, Elisha Franklin**
"The Civil War Letters of General Frank "Bull" Paxton, CSA: A Lieutenant of Lee & Jackson, edited by John Gallatin Paxton (son), Introduction: Harold B. Simpson." Hillsboro, Texas, Hill Junior College, 1978, 8vo, cl, v-viii, 102pp.

165 ..."Memoir & Memorials Elisha Franklin Paxton, Brigadier-General, CSA, composed of his letters from camp & field while an officer in the Confederate Army, with an introductory & connecting narrative collected & arranged by his son, John Gallatin Paxton...printed not published." N.Y., De Vinne Press, 1905, 8vo, cl, vi, 114pp. front(port.) $450.00-OB.

166 ...N.Y., Neale Pub., Aug. 5, 1907 with permission of Mr. Paxton, exactly as the original. $45.00.
Note: One listed copy shows a 1905 edt. as Washington: Plimpton Press, Private Printing for Family. Morningside #7 (#352) gives a 1st of 1905 N.P. (Independence, Missouri). $100.00-y. $325.00 $300.00-Bmk.

166a **PAXTON, William Edwards**
"The Civil War Letters of William Edwards Paxton." In: LaH., 1979, v.20, p.169-96.

167 **"PAYMENTS to Needy Confederate soldiers**
& widows, (with a list of)". In: Auditor's Annual Report, 1893, pp.124-153. See also Reports for 1894/5 & 1890. (Alabama.) Owens (p.860).
See: "List of Maimed Soldiers..."

168 **PAYNE, James E.**
"Missouri Troops in the Vicksburg Campaign." In: CV, Aug./Oct., 1928, v.XXXVI, pp.302-303, 340-341, 377-379.

169 ..."The Sixth Missouri at Corinth." In: CV, Dec. 1928, v.XXXVI, p.462-465.

170 **PAYNE, Louis Douglass**
"With the Orphan Brigade of Kentucky." In: CV, Dec. 1927, v.35, #12, p.456-460.

171 **PAYNE, Peter & Frank J. Merli**
"A Blockade-Running Charter: Spring: 1862." In: Amer. Neptune, April, 1966, Vol. XXVI, #2, pp.134-137.

172 **PAYNE, Thomas J.**
"The Life of the Common Arkansas Civil War soldier. Edt: Mary Means." In: Pulaski Co. Hist. Rev., Dec. 1953, v.1, #3, p.13-16. Two letters from a capt. in CSArmy, in Tenn., Mr. 23 & Apr. 30, 1862. to wife.

173 **PAYNE, William Henry Fitzhugh**
See: Leigh Robinson, Thomas Smith.

174 **PAYTON, Charles S.**
"Garnett's Brigade at Gettysburg." In: SHSP, 1877, v.3, p.215-218.

175 **PAYTON, John Lewis**
"The American Crisis; or, pages from the notebook of a state agent during the Civil War." London, Saunders, Otley & Co., 1867, 12mo, cl, front, port, xii, 340, vi, 329pp. $175.00-McM. Lewis served as

agent of the state of North Carolina in England. $150.-B. 2 vol. in 1, $150.00.

176 ..."Memoir of William Madison Peyton of Roanoke, together with some of his speeches in the House of Delegates of Virginia & his letters in reference to Secession & the threatened Civil War in the United States, etc." London, J. Wilson, 1873, 8vo, cl, vii, 392pp. ATG-150-Jk137. See: Bezer Blundell's review of...

177 **PEA RIDGE Battle**
"A Look at the Battle of Pea Ridge." In: Benton Co. Pioneer, Siloam Springs, Arkansas, Spring, 1979, v.24, #2, p.30-36, ports, illus., map.

178 **PEA RIDGE: See--**
"Battle of...," "Battlefield of...," Bearrs, Edwin C.; Benton Co. Pioneer; Baxter, Wm.; Bond, John W.; Brown, Walter L.; Cathey, Clyde; Clifford, Roy A.; Ford, Harvey S.; Logan, Robert R; Maury, Dabney; "Memorial Services at..."; Moody, Claire N.; "The Opposing Forces at.."; Park, Hugh; Stewart, Faye L.; Willett, John T.; Brown, Dee Alex; Great Battle of Pea Ridge, J.S. Sweet.

179 **"PEA Ridge Memorial Association**
Organized Jan. 8, 1961. Siloam Springs, Ark., 1st Day of the Centennial Observance." Reports of Historical Marker Program, Mar. 10, 1963. Rogers, AR, Press Pub. Co., 4to, wraps, ills., 24pp., map back cover. 50 cents.

180 **"PEA Ridge National Military Park, Arkansas"**
Washington, G.P.O., 1971, reprint, 1971, tall 8vo, (10)p. folder, illus., maps.

181 **PEACE Commission, 1865.**
See: Jefferson Davis, John Goode, Robert M.T. Hunter, Bradley T. Johnson, John H. Reagan.

182 **PEACOCK, G.J.**
"The Surrender at Appomattox Courthouse." In: SHSP, 1891, v.19, p.268-270.

183 **PEACOCK, Jane B., Edt.**
"A Georgian's View of War in Virginia." In: Atl. Hist. Bull., 1979, v.23, p.91-136. Letters of Arthur B. Simms, Covington, Ga.

184 ..."A Wartime Story: The Davidson Letters, 1862-1865." In: Atl.Hist.Bul., 1975, #1, p.9-121.

184a ..."Arthur Benjamin Simms, Aug. 7, 1861- Mar. 21, 1865." In: Atl. HJ, Summer, 1979. p.91-136.

185 **PEARCE, H.D.**
"126 Biographical Sketches of Confederate Soldiers taken in Central Texas from 1885 to 1896." Robert Lee, Coke County, Texas, Sept. 1910, 8vo, wraps, 56pp. $100.00.
See: D.M. Ray, who refers to a roll made by Pearce about 20 years ago, July 20, 1907. (c.1887?).

186 **PEARCE, Haywood J., Jr.**
"Benjamin H. Hill-Secession & Reconstruction." 12mo, cl, ix, 330pp. $25.00. Chicago, University of Chicago Press, 1928.
See also under Benj. H. Hill by his son.

187 ...University of Chicago, Abstracts of theses. Humanistic series, v.VI, p.219-226. ...Westport, Ct., Negro Univ. Pr., 1974, $13.00.

188 ..."Longstreet's Responsibility on the second day at Gettysburg." In: Ga.H.Q., March 1926, v.X, #1, pp.26-45.

189 **PEARCE, Nicholas B., Gen.**
"Price's Campaign of 1861." In: Pub.Ark.Hist. Assn., v.IV, 1917, p.332-351.

190 ..."Arkansas Troops in the Battle of Wilson's Creek." In: B&L, v.1, p.298-303.

191 ..."Reminiscences of...(late) Brig. Gen. commanding 1st Div. Army of Arkansas, C.S.A., covering events transpiring in NW Arkansas & SW Missouri in 1861, culminating in the Battle of Oak Hills, (Wilson's Creek) Missouri. Written by

Nicholas B. Pearce of Gainesville, Texas in 1892 at the request of Kie Oldham of Little Rock, Arkansas." 8vo, wraps, 37pp. in Oldham collection, Arkansas Historical Comm.

191a **PEARCE, T. H.**
"The Immortal Six Hundred." In: CV (new), Jan/Feb., 1986, v.34, #1, p.6-12, 11 pp. unnumbered, map, ills, ports. Roster for each state, colored ills.

192 **PEARCE, Thilbert H.**
"They Fought, by... The story of Franklin County men in the years 1861-1865." Franklinton, N.C., 1969, Adams Pr., 8vo, cl, d/w, vi, 366pp. Roster, p.282-366.
...Reprint, Limited 500 copies. $20.00.

193 **PEARL, Cyril**
"Rebel down Under; when the Shenandoah shook Melbourne, 1865." Melbourne, Australia, Heinemans, 1970, 8vo, cl, dj, illus, maps, 199pp. $20.00-Bmk.
See under 'Shenandoah.'

193a **PEARL, Louisa Brown**
"The Civil War Diary of Louisa Brown Pearl. Edt: James A. Hoobler." In: THQ, Winter 1979, v.38, #3, p.308-21.

194 **PEARSON, Alden B., Jr.**
"A Middle-class, Border-state Family during the Civil War." In: CWH, Dec. 1976, v.22, #4, p.318-336. Principals: George Ewing Eagleton & Ethelinda Foute.
See also under Eagleton, George E. & Ethie M. Foute Eagleton.

194a ..."The Tragic Dilemma of a Border-state moderate: the Rev. George E. Eagleton's views on slavery & secession." In: THQ, 1973, v.32, #4, p.360-73.

195 **PEARSON, Elizabeth Ware, Edt.**
"Letters from Port Royal written at the time of the Civil War." Boston, W.B. Clarke Co., 1906, 12mo, W.B. Clarke Co., 1906, 12mo, cl, dbl. pg. map, ix, 345, (1)p. Some letters from Edward S. Philbrick.

196 **PEARSON, I. Everett**
"Stuart in Westminster, a narrative of events in Westminster, Carroll County, Md. during the week of the war in which took place the battle of Gettysburg." In: SHSP, 1875, v.II, p.17-27. Dorn-II, 2000.

196a **PEASE, Louise McNeill**
"The Prison Notebook (1863-5) of Capt. James M. McNeill, CSA." In: W.Va.H. April 1970, p.180-4.

197 **PEAVY, James Dudley, Edt.**
"Confederate Scout, Virginia's Frank Stringfellow." Onancock, Va., Eastern Shore Print, 1956, 8vo, wraps, front(port), 3,62p.(even number on recto). $12.50 $25.00(cloth). Adventures under command Gen. Jeb Stuart.
See: Frank Stringfellow (Lim.Edt. 1,000).

198 **PEAY, Austin**
"The Battle of Dug Gap, Ga." May 8-11, 1864." In: CV, May 1921, v.XXIX, p.182-183.

199 **PECK, Mamie Downard, Mrs.**
"Poems of the South." Corsicana, Texas, Stokes Print, 1925, 8vo, wraps, cover title, 35, (1)pp. Largely Confederate poems.

200 **PECK, Rufus H.**
"Reminiscences of a Confederate soldier of Co. C, 2nd Va. cavalry, by R.H. Peck." Fincastle, Va., 1913, 12mo, wraps, cover title, 2 ports (the author), 73pp. Private Printing of 250 copies. 250-R.

201 **PECK, William Henry**
"The Confederate Flag on the Ocean: A Tale of the Cruises of Sumter & Alabama..." N.Y., Van Evrie, Horton & Co., 1868, 18mo, wraps, 96pp.
...Louisville, Lost Cause micro-cd.

202 ..."The conspirators of New Orleans; or, the might of the battle." Greenville, Ga., Peck & Wells, 1963, 8vo, cl, 192pp. Crandall-3107, Wright-1867, gives Emory copy as 132pp.

203 ..."The M'Donalds; or, The Ashes of Southern Homes: A Tale of Sherman's March." N.Y., Metropolitan Record Office, 1867, 12mo, cl, 192pp.

204 ..."The Phanton." C.S.A., Greenville, Ga., 1862, Peck & Wells, ?.

205 **PECKHAM, Stephen Farnum**
"John Tyler's Plan to prevent the catastrophe of the Civil War." In: Jour. Amer.Hist., 1912, v.VI, #1, p.73-86.

206 **PECQUET, Paul Du Bellet**
"The Diplomacy of the Confederate Cabinet of Richmond & Its Agents Abroad: being Memorandum Notes taken in Paris during the Rebellion of Southern States, 1861-1865." Tuscaloosa, Ala., Confed. Pub. Co., 1963, Confederate Centennial Studies, #23, 12mo, stiff wraps, 130pp., Lim. 450 copies.

207 ..."Lettre a L'empereur de la Reconnaissance des Etats Confederes D'Amerique." Paris, n.d. (1865, E.Dentu?), 8vo, sewn, 14pp. Concerns effects of war on French commerce.

208 ..."La Revolution Americaine devoilee." Paris, E.Dentu, 1861, 8vo, wraps, 31pp., Civil War on the French public opinion, politics & Govnm.

209 **PEDDY, George W., Dr. & Kate F.**
"Saddle Bag & Spinning Wheel: being the Civil War letters of George W. Peddy, MD & his wife Kate F. Peddy, Edited by George Peddy Cuttino." Macon, Ga., Mercer University Press, 1981, 8vo, cl, dj, illus., genealogical chart, index, XII, 332pp.

209a **PEEBLES, Ruth**
"Polk County, Texas, in the war between the States." Livingston, Texas, The Author, 1987. 8vo, cl, 648pp, ills. $26. 1,500 service records, diaries, letters.

209b **PEEL Confederate Letters, The.**
In: AHQ, 1947, v.8, #1, p.81-104.

210 **PEELE, William Joseph**
"Lives of distinguished North Carolinians, with illustrations & speeches..." Raleigh, The North Carolina Pub. Society, 1898, 8vo, cl, front, port, 605pp. $50.00. Sketches of 15 famous NC men, e.g., Walter Clark, Z. Vance, Wm. A. Graham, Cornelia Spencer. About a third of book on Civil War generals. Thornton-10591.
See: Literary & Historical activities in NC...

211 **PEERCE, John T.**
"Capture of a Railroad Train." In: SB, April 1884, v.2, p.352-355. Destroys shops at Piedmont, captures train at Bloomington in '64. Shelter-618.

212 **PEGRAM Battalion Association.**
"Address delivered by Rev. H. Melville Jackson & John Fitzhugh Lay, on occasion of the dedication of a memorial window, & depositing a register of the dead, May 31, 1887." In: SHSP, v. XVI, p.194-214.

213 ..."Annual Reunion of... in the Hall of House of Delegates, Richmond, Va., May 21, 1886." In: SHSP, 1886, v.XIV, pp.(5)-33. Also: Richmond, Va., Wm. Ellis Jones, 1886, 8vo, wraps, 32pp. $125.00-Bmk105. Addresses: T.A. Brander, J.N. Dunlop, H.W. Flournoy, F.H. Deane, W.G. McCabe, C.S. Stringfellow.
See: H.M. Jackson & J.F. Lay addresses.

214 **PEGRAM, Robert B., Lt., CSN**
"The Cruist of the CSS Nashville/Report of Lieutenant Robert B. Pegram, CSN." Richmond, Va. Mag. Hist. Biog., July 1958, v.66, #3, p.345-350, port. plate. $8.00.

215 **PEGRAM, William M.**
"An Historical Identification. John Wilkes Booth - What became of him? In: Md.H.M., Dec. 1913, v.VIII, p.327-331.

216 **PEISSNER, Elias**
"The American Question in its National Aspect. Being also an Incidental Reply to

	Mr. H.R. Helper's "Compendium on the Impending Crisis of the South." N.Y., H.H.Lloyd & Co., 1861, 12mo, cl, 164pp.
217	**PELHAM'S Battery** See: Winfield Peters. Stuart Horse Artillery.
218	**PELHAM, John** "Alabama's Heroes: Pelham & Wheeler." See: E.P. Cox. "The Gallant Pelham & his Gun. See: Henry B. McClellan. See: H.H. Matthews' Pelham.
219	..."The Gallant Pelham. Jeb Stuart's "Boy Artillerist," from Alabama." In: SHSP, 1902, v.30, p.338-345. (from: Mobile Register).
220	..."Roll & Roster of Pelham's, afterward - Breathed's Battalion, Famous Battery, Stuart's Horse Artillery Battalion, Cavalry Corps, ANV. In: SHSP, 1902, v.30, p.348-355. See: H.H. Matthews, J.B. Morre, Winfield Peters, Stuart's Horse Artillery.
220a	**PELZER, John & Linda** "Cotton, Cotton Everywhere--Running the Blockade through Nassau." In: CWTI, Jan. 1981, v.19, #9, p.10-17, ills, port.
221	**PEMBER, Phoebe Yates Levy** "A Southern Woman's Story." N.Y., G.W. Carleton & Co., 1879, 16mo, decr. cl, (7)-192pp. $37.50. Her exper. as sup't. in Southern Hospital during the war. $125.00-Bmk124.
222	..."A Southern Woman's Story: life in Confederate Richmond..including unpublished letters written from the Chimborazo Hospital." Edt: Bell I. Wiley, Jackson, Tenn., McCowat-Mercer Press, 1959, cl, 8vo, (8), 199pp. port., views. $40.00.
223	**PEMBERTON, John Clifford, Gen.** "A Short History of Gen. J.C. Pemberton." Park Place, N.Y., Knapp & Co., 1888, 2 3/4 x 1 1/2" colored booklet, 16pp. facsm. signature (packed in Duke's cigarettes). See: "Heroes of the C.W. & W. Duke Co.
224	..."Pemberton Defender of Vicksburg. With an foreword by Douglas Southall Freeman." Chapel Hill, University of N.Carolina Press, 1942. 8vo, cl, dj, illus., maps, ports, incl, front., xiv, (2), 350pp. notes & index (p.321-350). $10.00. $20.00. 75-R. ...2nd edt. (1945), same above, $12.50. $15.00.
225	..."Terms of Surrender at Vicksburg. Gen. Pemberton replies to Gen. Badean." In: SHSP, 1882, v.10, p.406-410.
226	**PENDER'S Division** See: J.A. Englehard.
227	**PENDER, William Dorsey, Gen.** "The Civil War Letters of Gen. William Dorsey Pender to his Wife." Edt: William W. Hassler. In: Ga. Rev., Spring 1963, 19pp. $8.00.
228	..."The General to His Lady: The Civil War Letters of William Dorsey Pender to Fanny Pender." Edt: Wm. W. Hassler. Chapel Hill, Univ. of N.C. Press, 1965, 8vo, cl, d/w, pp.xiii, 271. ...New Introduction by Kent Masterson Brown. Gaithersburg, Md., Ron R. Van Sickle, 1987. 8vo, cl, dj, 271pp, ills.
229	..."Sketch of Maj.Gen. William Dorsey Pender, CSA." In: South Atlantic, Jan. 1878, pp.228-235. See: F.C. McDowell.
230	**PENDLETON, George Cassety** "Some Facts of History. Speech delivered Speech delivered at the Confed. Reunion." Belton, Tex., Journal-Reporter, 1908, 12mo, wraps, cover title, 10pp.
231	**PENDLETON, George Hunt** "But, sir, armies, money, blood cannot maintain this Union - justice, reason, peace may. Speech of Hon. George H. Pendleton, of Ohio, on the state of the union. Delivered in the House of repres.,

Jan. 18, 1861." Wash., L.Towers, 1861, 8vo, caption title, 8pp.

232 ..."The Copperhead candidate for Vice-President. His hostility to the American Republic, illustrated by his record as a repres. in Congress of the U.S., from the State of Ohio." Wash., 1864, 8vo, folded sheet, 8pp.

233 ..."Hear Hon. Geo. H. Pendleton, speech at N.Y. hotel, October 24, 1864. Lincoln the Rebel candidate. From the Richmond Inquirer, Sept. 5, & Richmond Examiner, Oct. 17." n.p., n.d. (Richmond, 1864?), 8vo, caption title, 8pp.

234 ..."Speech of...on the state of the Union, Jan. 18, 1861." n.p., n.d., 8vo, caption title, 8pp.

235 **PENDLETON, Louis Beauregard**
"In the Okefenokee, a story of war time & the great Ga. swamp." Boston, Roberts Bros., 1895, 12mo, cl, front, pls., vi, 182pp. novel.

236 ..."Alexander H. Stephens." Philadephia, Geo. W. Jacobs Co., 1908, 12mo, cl, or, 3/4 Mor., port, 406pp., 1/2 title-American Crisis Biographies. $30.00.

237 **PENDLETON, Rose Page**
"Gen. David Hunter's Sack of Lexington, Va., 10-14, 1864. Account by Rose Page Pendleton. Edt: Charles W. Turner." In: VMHB, April 1975, v.83, p.173-183.

237a **PENDLETON, Sandie (Alexander Swift)**
"Sandie Pendleton Stonewall Jackson's aide." In: Va. Cavl., Spring 1987, v.36, #4, p.158-69. Facsm, ports, ills (some in color).
..."The Valley Campaign of 1862, as revealed in letters of Sandie Pendleton. Edt: W. G. Bean." In: VaMHB, July 1970, p.326-364. Letters between Sandie & his wife Mrs. Alexander Swift Pendleton (Kate Corbin).

238 **PENDLETON, W.F., Capt.**
"Confederate Diary...Jan. to Apr. 1865. From the original in the possession of the Pendleton family, Pendle House, Bryn Athyn, Pennsylvania, 1957." Private Print, for members of the family, 8vo, stiff wraps, 21pp. $25.00-Bmk.

239 ..."Confederate Memoirs Early Life & Family History William Frederic Pendleton, Mary Lawson Young Pendleton." Edited by: Constance Pendleton. Suppl. by Amena Pendle Haines." Bryn Athyn, Pa., 1958, Private Pt., 12mo, cl, front(port), ports., coat-of-arms, geneaology, 181pp. Distributed free by family. 100-R.

240 **PENDLETON, William Cecil**
"History of Tazewell County & Southwest Va." Richmond, Va., 1920, 700pp. illus. About 100pp. on Civil War. Bmk.

241 ..."Political History of Appalachian Virginia, 1776-1927." Dayton, Va., Shenandoah Press, 1927, 8vo, cl, xiv, 1, 613pp. illus., ports, much on the war.

241a **PENDLETON, William G.**
"The Character of Robert Edward Lee." Winchester, Va., Farmers & Merchants National Bank, 1962. Winchester-Frederick County Historical Society. 8vo, wraps, cover title, (5)p.
"This booklet is a publication of the Winchester-Frederick County Historical Society."

242 **PENDLETON, William Nelson**
"Artillery of the Army of N. Va. & last campaign at surrender." In: SHSP, 1878, v.9, p.418-424.

243 ..."Official report of the Battle of Gettysburg." In: SHSP, 1878, v.V, p.194-201.
See: Susan P. Lee
Lee's Letter to Pendleton.

244 ..."Personal Recollect. of Gen. Lee, an address delivered at Washington & Lee Univ., at the request of the Univ. authorities, on Gen. Lee's birthday, Jan.

19, 1873." In: South. Mag., 1874, v.15, p.603-636. $45.00.

245 **PENHOAT, Captaine**
"Kearsarge & Alabama: French official report, 1864." In: Am.Hist. Rev., Oct. 1917, v.XXIII, p.119-123. Report to prefet maritime of Cherbourg, by Capt. of the 'Couronne,' a French ironclad present at the fight.

246 **PENICK, Charles Clifton, D.D., Rev.**
"Our Dead: Our Memories: Our Lessons; Our Duties; an Oration of the Decoration of Confed. Graves, Louisville, May 26, 1888." 12mo, wraps, 11pp.

247 **PENINSULAR Campaign**
See: William Allan, Baker P. Lee.

248 **PENNINGTON, Edgar Legare**
"The Battle of Sewanee.", Sewanee, Tenn., Archives Dept., Univ. of the South, c.1950?, 8vo, cover title, 29pp.
...Reprint: Tenn.Hist.Quart., vol.IX, #3, Sept. 1950, 29pp. Large 8vo, wraps, cover title. p.217-246.

249 ..."Bishop Stephen Elliott & the Confederate Episcopal Church." Reprint: Ga. Review, vol.IV, #3, Fall 1950, large 8vo, wraps, cover title, pp.(231)-247.

250 ..."The Confederate Episcopal Church, 1863." Charleston, S.C. Hist. & Genea. Mag., Jan. 1951, v.LII, #1, pp.5-16.

251 ..."The Literature of the Church in the Confederate States." Reprint: Hist. Magazine of Episc. Church, Garrison, N.Y., vol.XVII, 8vo, wraps, cover title, pp.345-355.

252 ..."Organization of the Protestant Episcopal Church in the CSA." Garrison, N.Y., n.d., cover title, 8vo, 31pp. Reprint from the Hist. Magazine of Episc. Church, xvii, pp.308-338.
See: Rich. H. Smith, same subject.

253 ..."The Church in the Confederate States." Garrison, N.Y., Historical Magazine of the Protestant Episcopal Church, Vol. XVII, #4, Dec. 1948. Entire issue devoted to the church in CSA. 8vo, wraps, pp.(307)-448. Index of Vol. XVII, pp.xiv, (4)pp. ads.
See listed authors, other than Pennington, G. MacLaren Brydon; Lawrence F. London; Nelson Waite Rightmyer; Hugh T. Lefler & DuBose Murphy.

254 ..."The Confederate Episcopal Church & the Southern Soldiers." Garrison, N.Y., Hist. Mag. of Protestant Episcopal Church, vol. XVII, #4, Dec. 1948, p.356-383.
...Reprint, wraps, 8vo, 27 (1)pp.

254a **PENNINGTON, Estill Curtis**
"The Last Meeting's Lost Cause." Spartanburg, S.C., 1987. 8vo, paper, 84pp, ills. $22. Lee & Jackson.

255 **PENNSYLVANIA ,**
See: J.H. Bassler, R.S. Ewell, Jeb Stuart.

256 **"PENSACOLA'S Navy Yard 1528-1911."**
Pensacola, Fla., The Pensacola Home & Sav. Assn., Dec. 1967, 8vo, stiff wraps, cover title, illus., ports, maps, (24)pp.

257 **"PENSACOLA," Confederate Poem,**
Written for the Constitutionalist, Augusta, Oct. 14, 1861." Signed: Mrs. Jane Kerrick, with printed initials: H.C.B., 4x9" page. Not in Crandall.

258 **PENSIONS ,**
"Pensioning Confed. Soldiers by the U.S." In: SHSP, 1898, v.26, p.312-315.

259 ..."R.E. Lee Camp, C. Vets, 'Protect against relief of Confederates by the U.S." In: SHSP, 1895, v.23, p.337-341.

260 ..."The Southern States & their Vet. Soldiers." In: SHSP, v.19, p.336-337.

261 **PEOPLES, Morgan**
"The Scapegoat of Andersonville: Union execution of Confed. Captain Henry Wirtz." In: No. La. Hist. Assn. Jour., 1980, v.II, #4, p.3-18.

261a **PEPLE, W. L.**
"Hunter Holmes McGuire." Chicago: Sur-

gery, Gynecology & Obstretrics, 1923. 4to, 5p extract, port, ills. A brief biographical sketch.

261b PERDUE, David R.
"The Battle of Pine Bluff." In: Jefferson CHQ, Spring 1962, v.1, p.14-19.

262 PERENYI, Eleanor
"The Bright Sword." N.Y., Rinehart, 1955, 12mo, cl, 309pp. Historical novel on Gen. Hood, in N. Ga., 1863.

263 PEREYRA, Lillian A.
"James Lusk Alcorn: Persistent Whig." Baton Rouge, Louisiana State Univ., 1966, 8vo, cl, dj, illus., xv, 237pp.

264 PERKERSON, Elizabeth
"A Civil War Letter on the Capture of Atlanta." Edt: Medora Field Perkerson. In" Ga.H.Q., Dec. 1944, v.XXVIII, #4, p.251-269, illus., ports.

265 PERKINS, Howard Cecil, Edt.
"Northern Editorials on Secession." Published by the Amer. Hist. Assn. N.Y., D. Appleton & Co., 1942, 8vo, cl, v.I, xxxiv, 538; v.II, xxviii, 569p. Index. A companion vol. by D.L. Dumond for the South.

266 PERKINS, J.R.
"Jefferson Davis & Gen. Sterling Price." In: C.Vet., October, 1911, v.19, p.473-477.

267 PERKINS, Lee N.
"Personal Reminiscences of the War, 1861-1865." C.S.A. Boone, N.C., 1910, "Watauga Democrat: in 12 installments. Perkins was in Co. A, 3rd Ky. Cavalry.

268 PERRIN, Abner M.
"A Little more light on Gettysburg." In: Miss. Val. Hist. Rev., 1948, v.XXVI, p.519-525. A letter to Gov. Milledge Bonham, S.C., July 29, 1863 describing military operations. Perrin a Col. in CSA.

268a PERRIN, William E., Jr.
"Civil War Military Operations in & around Ponchatoula, La." In: LaH., 1971, v.12, p.123-36.

269 PERRINE, David P.
"Battle of Val Verde, New Mexico Terr. Feb. 21, 1862." In: Jour. West., p.26-38.

270 PERRY, Edward Aylsworth, Brig.-Gen.
"Report of, Battle of Chancellorsville." In: SHSP, 1877, v.IV, p.203-207.
See: Herbert U. Feibelman.

271 PERRY, Eugene O.
"Whip the Devil & His Hosts, the Civil War Letters of Private Eugene O. Perry of Hood's Texas Brigade." In: Chronicles of Smith Co., Texas, Tyler Texas, Fall, 1967, illus., Edt: Col. Harold B. Simpson.

272 PERRY, Flavius W., Lt.
"The Letters of Lt. Flavius W. Perry 17th Tex. Cav., 1862-63. Edited: Joe R. Wise, MD." In: MHT & Sw, 1975, v.XIII, #2, p.11-37.

273 PERRY, "Flintlock"
"Memorial Poem." Charleston, ?, n.d., Broadside 8 x 3 1/2". Shelter-619-A, Verse on CSA soldiers from Charleston, W.Va.

274 PERRY, Herman H.
"Surrender at Appomattox Crt. House." In: SHSP, 1892, v.20, p.56-61.

275 PERRY, Leslie J.
"Battle of Wills Valley, Tenn." In: CV, Apr. 1915, v.XXIII, p.162-163.

276 ..."Buckner & McClellan. How the former clearly outwitted the latter." In: SHSP, 1896, v.24, p.295-301.

277 ..."Davis & Johnston." In: SHSP, 1892, v.20, p.95-108.

278 ..."Gen. Lee & the Battle of Gettysburg, he planned to fight there." In: SHSP, 1895, v.23, p.253-259.

279 ..."Gen. Meade's Temper - made him an enigma." In: SHSP, 1895, v.23, p.247-253.

280 ..."A Parrallel for Grant's Action, compares Campaign of 1864 to Lee's Campaign in 1862." In: SHSP, 1896, v.24, p.138-145.

281 PERRY, Madison Starke
"Governor's Message, transmitted to the

Legislature of Florida, November 26, 1860." Tallahassee, Fla., 1860, 8vo, sewn, 7pp. $60.00jk. Calls for immediate secession.

282 **PERRY, Milton F.**
"Infernal Machines: The Story of Confederate Submarine & Mine Warfare." Baton Rouge, La., State Univ. Press, 1965, 8vo, cl, d/w, maps, xiii, 232pp., illus. $35.00-Bmk.

283 **PERRY, William Flake**
"Official Report of Gettysburg," In: SHSP, 1885, v.13, p.185-186.

284 ..."Reminiscences of the Campaign of 1864 in Virginia." In: SHSP, 1879, v.7, p.49-63.

285 **PERRY-MOSHER, Kate E.**
"The Rock Island P.O.W. Camp. Account of a girl rebel, served as a link in a Confederate Underground to this Federal prison." In: CWTI, July, 1969, v.VIII, #4, p.28-36, illus., facsm.
See: J.W. Minnich's Rock Island Prison.

286 **PERRYVILLE, Battle of**
See: Luke W. Finley.

287 **PERSON County, N.C.**
See: Stuart T. Wright.

288 **PERSONAL Narratives in SHSP**
See: Samuel Z. Ammen, Launcelot Minor Blackford, Thos. Ballard Blake, U.R. Brooks, J.H. Carter, Thos. R.R. Cobb, Fred M. Colston, J. Churchill Cooke, S.A. Cunningham, Henry G. Damon, Henry Kid Douglas, Frank H. Foote, Robert D. Funkhouser, James M. Garnett, John B. Gordon, John U. Green, John A. Hamilton, Geo. N. Hollins, Geo. J. Hundley, Iredell Jones, James H. Lane, John G. Law, M.T. Ledbetter, J.W. McClung, John McGrath, Clara D. Maclean, Dabney H. Maury, Robert W. North, Robert Nixon Northen, Charles H. Olmstead, John N. Opie, Richard C.M. Page, Banjamin M. Parham, Robert Emory Park, Wm. W. Parker, Alex S. Paxton, Geo. A. Porterfield, S.F. Power, John G. Pressley, Mrs. Robert C. Randolph, Warren D. Reid, Richmond 'Dispatch' & 'Times', David M. Sadler, W.F. Shippey, Mrs. Kate Cummings Starritt, Harry C. Townsend, E.L. Welles, Henry M. White, W.S. White, Mrs. G. Griffing Wilcox.

289 **PETER, Frances Dallam**
"Window on the War. Frances Dallam Peter's Lexington Civil War Diary. Edt: John David Smith & William Cooper, Jr., Lexington, Ky., Fayette County Historic Commission, 1976. 8vo, pict. wraps, facsms, ports, illus., pen & ink sketches, plat, (6), 53pp.

290 **PETERKIN, George William**
"An address by Bishop Peterkin before Camp Jenkins, Parkersburg, W.Va., in the celebration of the birthdays of Generals Lee & Jackson, Jan. 20, 1905." n.p., 1905?, 8vo, wraps, cover title, 12p. dbl. column.

291 ..."The disparity in numbers & resources in the War between the States. An address before the Daughters of the Confederacy, Patkersburg, W.V., on the annual Lee & Jackson celebration, January 20, 1911." n.p., n.d., 1911, 8vo, wraps, 19pp.

292 ..."In Memoriam - an address in memory of Confederate dead buried at Valley Mt., 1861." n.p., n.d., 8vo, wraps, 12pp.

293 **PETERKIN, Joshua**
"Andersonville prison (poem)." In: SHSP, 1891, v.19, p.188-191.

294 **PETERKIN, W.G.**
"Stonewall Jackson's Corps." In: CV, Apr. 1925, v.33, #4, p.131-132.

295 **PETERS, Steve**
"The Murder of Col. Joesph M. Bounds, Eleventh Texas Cavalry, Young's Regiment CSA." In: Texana, 1974, v.XII, #1, p.56-60.

296 **PETERS, William Elisha**
"Refused to Burn it." Col. Peters disobeys

orders at Chambersburg, Pa." In: SHSP, 1902, v.30, p.266-269.

297 **PETERS, Winfield**
"Confederates who fell in battle re-interred in Maryland." In: SHSP, 1910, v.38, p.288-289.

298 ..."First Battle of Manassas." In: SHSP, 1906, v.34, p.170-178.

299 ..."The lost sword of Gen. R.B. Garnett." In: SHSP, 1905, v.33, p.26-31.

300 ..."Maryland Confederates." In: SHSP, 1901, v.29, p.132-138.

301 ..."Maryland Confederate Soldier's Home." In: SHSP, 1910, v.38, p.289-290.

302 ..."A Maryland warrior & Hero." In: SHSP 1901, v.29, p.243-250.

304 ..."Roll & Roster of Pegram's Battery." In: SHSP, 1902, v.30, p.348-354.

305 ..."A Maryland Warrior & Hero. Death of Maj. William W. Goldsborough, of the famous Maryland Line, VSA. Military funerat in Baltimore-sketch of his eventful life & distinguished services-soldier, journalist, historian. By..., Lt.-Col., etc. UDC Md. member Hist. Com., UCV." In: SHSP, 1901, v.XXIX, p.243-250.

306 **PETERSBURG,**
"A Guide to Fortifications & Battlefields Around Petersburg." with a splendid map. Petersburg, Va., 1866, wraps, 33pp. $30.00.

307 **PETERSBURG Grays**
See: James C. Birdsong.

308 **PETERSBURG Ladies Memorial Association**
See: Charles Trotter Lassiter.

309 **PETERSBURG Nat'l Park**
See: Richard W. Lykes
"Story of Fort Hell, etc."

310 "**PETERSBURG National Military Park, Virginia.**" Wash., US Dept. of Interior, Nat'l. Park Service, 194
...July, 1941, 8vo, (6)p. folder, illus., map. See: "Story of Fort Hell (Fort Sedgwick)."

311 **PETERSBURG, Virginia**
See: Charles F. Collier, John Foster Glenn, Johnson Hagood, Robert F. Hoke, Wm. Gordon McCabe, William M. Thomas. 'Unveiling of Soldier's Monument in Petersburg.'

312 **PETERSBURG, Virginia, Ladies of**
"Petition for Mr. Davis, release." In: SHSP, 1896, v.24, p.240-242.

313 **PETERSON, Cyrus Asbury & Joseph Mills Hanson**
"Pilot Knob, the Thermopylae of the West." New York, Neale Pub., 1914, 8vo, cl, 324pp., map endsheets. 100-Bohl. $80.00.

314 ...Cape Girardeau, Mo., Ramfre Print, 1964. Sept 27, 1864. CSA under Price repulsed in his first raid into Missouri.

315 **PETERSON, Harold L.**
"Notes on Ordnance of the American Civil War. Illus. Robert L. Miller." Wash., American Ordnance Assoc., 1959. 4to, wraps, illus., tables, (16)pp. $15.00.

315a ..."The Apex of the Muzzle-loader, 1836-65. Chap. IV in: 'Round Shot & Rammers.'" N.Y., Bonanza, 1968. pp.83-128, index, ills, bibliog.

316 **PETERSON, James T.**
"North & South Carolina." Augusta, S.C., James T. Paterson, 1863?, 39x56 1/2cm. (B/W or color) color $125.00. Cover-title: "Map of the seat of war in North & South Carolina."

317 **PETERSON, Owen Maurice**
"Yancey's Speech Education." In: South. Speech Jour., 1967, v.XXXIII, p.93-107.

318 ..."Judah P. Benjamin's Senate speeches on slavery & secession (1856-61)." In: South. Speech Jour., Fall, 1957, v.23, p.10-20. Notes.

318a **PETICOLAS, A. B.**
"Rebels on the Rio Grande. The Civil War Journal of A. B. Peticolas." Edt: Don E. Alberts. Albuquerque: University of New

Mexico Press 1984. 8vo, wraps, 187p, ills, bibliog., index. $10.

319 **PETIGRU, James Louis**
"Memorial of the late James Louis Petigru. Proceedings of the Bar of Charleston, S.C., March 25, 1863." N.Y., Richardson & Co., 1866, 8vo, wraps, 43pp. $35.00. Considerable on CSA & Petigru's position on Union vs. CSA.
See: Walter L. Miller's Life of...
J. Rion McKissick.

320 **PETRIE, George**
"What will be the final estimate of Yancey?" Montgomery, Ala., 1904, Alabama Historical Society, Montgomery, Reprint #14, from Transactions 1899-1903, vol.IV, 8vo, wraps, (307)-312pp.

321 **PETTIGREW, James Johnston, Brig.-Gen.**
"Gen. James Johnston Pettigrew, C.S.A." In: CV, Nov. 1920, v.XXVIII, p.413-415.
...In: NC Univ. Monthly, June 1883, wraps, 9pp. $20.00-Bmk.

322 **PETTIGREW, James Johnston, Brig.-Gen., C.S.A.**
See: Wm. H. Trescott
Louis G. Young
H.C. Graham
Wm. S. Pettigrew
W.R. Bond

323 **PETTIGREW, William S.**
"Sketch of James Johnston Pettigrew." In: N.C. Univ. Mag., V.VI, 1886-1887, p.43-50, port. $20.00-Bmk.

324 **PETTIS, George H., Brevet Captain**
"The Confederate Invasion of New Mexico & Arizona." In: B&L, 1887, v.II, p.103-111.

325 **PETTUS, Edmund Winston, Brig.-Gen.**
"Report: Operations at Lookout Mountain." In: SHSP, 1884, v.12, p.224-226.

326 **PETTUS, Maia**
"Princess of Glenndale a Story of the South." Washington, Neale Pub., 1901, 12mo, cl, 314pp. War, slavery & politics.

327 **PETTY, Elijah P.**
"Journal to Pleasant Hill, the Civil War letters of Elijah P. Petty, Walker's Texas Division." Edt: Norman D. Brown. San Antonio, Texas, 1982, University of Texas, 8vo, cl, XX, 471pp., 28 color pls., 100 drawings, 7 maps, 17th Infantry, Boxed 'Collector's Edition,' 2 vols., Lim: 500 sets. $75.00.

328 **PETTY, J.W., Jr.**
"Confederate Campaign in New Mexico, 1862 Sibley's Campaign into New Mexico." Houston, Texas Civil War Round Table, Address: Nov. 30, 1955, 8 1/2 x 11", heavy paper covers, folded to 8vo, 15pp.

329 **PFADENHAUER, Ruby M.**
"Why Sherman by-passed Augusta." In: Richmond Co. Hist., 1983, v.15, #2, pp.17-23..

330 **PFANZ, Harry W.**
"The Surrender Negotiations between General Joseph E. Johnston & General Sherman, April 1865." In: Mil. Affairs, Summer 1952, v.16, p.61-70, Notes.
..."Gettysburg - the Second Day." Chapel Hill: University of North Carolina Press, 1986. 8vo, cl, dj, 610pp, 60 ills, 13 maps. $35.

330a **PFOHL, Bernard J.**
"The Salem Band." Winston-Salem, 1953. Privately printed. 8vo, wraps, 85p, ills.
See: Julius Leinbach's 26th N.C. Regimental Band, pub. herein as an append.

331 **PHALEN, James M.**
"Surgeon La Fayette Guild (1825-1870), Medical Director of the Army of Northern Virginia." Mil. Surgeon, 1940, LXXXVII, pp.174-176.

332 **PHARMACEUTICALS in CSA**
See: E. Vernon Howell, Norman H. Franke, Joseph Jacobs, Joseph P. Cullen, Harris D. Riley.

333 **PHARR, Walter W.**
"A Short History of the Life, Character & Death of Capt. John B. Andrews, by Rev. Walter W. Pharr, of N.C." n.p., 1862?, 12mo wraps, 4p. caption title, #78. Crandall-4798.

334 **PHI GAMMA DELTA**
See: James M. Wells.

335 **PHILATELY,**
Allen, H.D.
Ashbrook, Stanley
Antrim, Earl (CSA Stampless covers)
Bennett, L.
Booth, Jno. Wilkes (covers)
Calman, H.C.
Collins, H.
'Confederate Postal History'
'Confederates Untangled'
Dietz, August
Donnelly, Ralph W.
Drinkwater, John
Dukeshire, T.S.
Fox, John A.
Fuller, Claude
Greenhow, Rose O'Neal
Howe, J.L.
Huber, Leonard V.
Jones, Thomas A.
Lehman, Howard
Macbride, Van Dyk
Malpass, George N.
Nast, F.A.
Phillips, Chas. J.
Raisig, L. Miles
Shenfield, Lawrence L.
Sheppard, Harvey E.
Spelman, Henry M.
Weatherly, Earl
Wilkinson, Raymond Moore

336 **PHILIPS, Martin W., Dr.**
"Diary of a Mississippi Planter, Jan. 1, 1840-Apr. 1863." By Franklin L. Riley. Oxford, Miss., PMHS, v.X, 1909, p.305-481.

337 **PHILIPPI, Battle of**
See: John A. McNeil, Eva M. Carnes, Philip M. Conley, Betty Hornbeck, Hu Maxwell, Ruth Woods Dayton, 'First Land Battle of Civil War...', J.N. Potts., D.B. Stewart.

337a **PHILLIPS County, Arkansas**
"Civil War & Reconstruction in . . ." In: Phillip CoHQ, June 1978, v.16, p.1-23.

337b **"PHILLIPS County Soldiers"**
In: PhCHQ, December 1978, v.17, p.12-17.

338 **PHILLIPS, C. D., Col.**
"Report of... Confederate Memorial Board." Atlanta, Ga., Franklin Print., 1905, 8vo, wraps, 24pp. fldg. map, plans.

339 **PHILLIPS, Charles J.**
"Phillips' Specialized Priced Catalogue of Confederate States General Issues. Price $1.00 Post Free." N.Y., Charles JH. Phillips, 1928, 16mo, stiff wraps, illus., 31pp.(8-ads), Richmond, Va., Dietz Press. $5.00.

340 **PHILLIPS, Dinwiddie Brazier**
"The Career of the Iron-Clad Virginia (Formerly the Merrimac), Confederate States Navy, Mar.-May, 1862." From Collections of the Virginia Historical Society, n.s., v.VI, 1887, p.193-231. In: SB, ns, v.II, 1886/1887, p.598-608; B&L, Civil War.

341 **PHILLIPS, Edward Hamilton**
"The Shenandoah Valley in 1864: An Episode in the History of Warfare." Charleston, S.C., The Citadel Monagraph Series, No. V., 1965, 8vo, wraps, 36pp., distributed free.

342 ..."The Lower Shenandoah Valley during the Civil War: impact of war upon the Civilian Population & upon Civil Institutions." Ann Arbor, University microfilms, 1958, i.e., 1959. Positive microfilm of typescript, 439 leaves, bibliog: 419-439. Thesis: Univ. N.C. Abstr. Disst., 19:2592 April.

343 **PHILLIPS, Edwin D.**
"Texas & Its Late Military Occupation by

an Officer of the Army." N.Y., D.Van Nostrand, 1862, 8vo, wraps, 35pp. 350-G. Tried to save Federal property, when siezed by Texas State forces.

343a PHILLIPS, Elizabeth Byford
"Matthew Fontaine Maury." N.Y., (s.n.), 1921. 8vo, wraps, 15pp. Read at the regular monthly meeting of the Mary Mildred Sullivan Chap. UDC, N.Y. City, April 4, 1921.

344 PHILLIPS, Eugenia Levy
"Defiant Rebel." In: Jacob Rader Marcus' 'Memoirs of American Jews." Phila.: Jewish Pub. Soc. of Amer., 3 vols., 1955, v.3, p.161-196. Author's imprisonment in Wash. & Ship Island, Miss., as a spy, 1861-1862, recorded in her diary & reminisc.

345 PHILLIPS, Harry David
"Phillips Family History; a brief History of the Phillips Family, beginning with the emigration from Wales & a detailed geneaology of the descendants of John & Benjamin Phillips, pioneer citizens of Wilson County, Tenn." Lebanon, Tenn., Lebanon Democrat, 1935, 8vo, cl, illus., (6), 242, xixpp. Includes Diary of David Phillips, a CSA soldier.

345a PHILLIPS, Herb
"Champion Hill." Edwards, Miss., 1984. 8vo, wraps, ills, 40p, maps. $6. Vicksburg campaign.

345b PHILLIPS, John Wilson
"Civil War Diary of John Wilson Phillips." In: VMHB, Jan. 1954, v.62, p.95-123.

346 PHILLIPS, S. K.
"Immortelles & Other Memorial Poems." Chattanooga, Tenn., MacGowan & Cooke, 1890, 12mo, wraps, 47pp. Poetry dedicated to the Confederacy.

346a PHILLIPS, Stanley S.
"Excavated Artifacts from battlefields & campsites of the Civil War, 1861-5." Lanham, Md., 1974 & 1977. 4to, cl, 199p, 18p, Lim. Edt.. 1,500 photos.

347 PHILLIPS, Ulrich Bonnell
"The Course of the South to Secession." an interpretation by...with intro: E. Merton Coulter. Head of title-Amer. Hist. Ass'n., from Albert J. Beveridge Memorial Fund., N.Y., D. Appleton & Co., 1939, 8vo, wraps, port., xi, 176pp. Reprint: Gloucester, 1959. P. Smith. N.Y., Hill & Wang, 1964, Amer. Cent. Series. Lectures at Northwestern Univ. were printed in Georgia Hist. Quart., Dec. 1936 - March 1938, after Phillips death. First of six chapts. completed by Phillips as companion vol. to "Life & Labors in the Old South." GHQ: XXI, 1937, p.1-49, 113-141, 217-238, 309-344, v.XXII, 1938, p.41-71. See: Sam E. Salem, John Herbert Roper.

348 ..."The Literary Movement for Secession." N.Y., Columbia Univ. Press, 1914, Reprint from 'Studies in Southern History & politics' - inscribed to Wm. A. Dunning, 8vo, wraps, p.33-60.

348a ..."The economic & political essays of the ante-bellum South." Richmond, Va., Southern Pub. Soc., 1909. Reprint: South in Building of Nation, v.VII. 8vo, wraps, (2), (173)-199.

349 PHILPOT, G.B.
"A Maryland Boy in the Confederate Army." In: CV, July, 1916, v.24, #7, p.312-315, 361-363.

350 PHILPOTT, William A.
"Word 'Dixie' derives from the old bank note." In: Numismatist, May 1952, v.65, p.450-452, facsms. On the "dix" note ($10 bill) of the Citizen Bank of La., 1845-1862.

351 ..."A Unique(?) Confederate Half-dollar restrike (1878, dates 1861)." In: Numismatist, Apr. 1950, v.63, p.189-193, views.

352 PHILPOTT, William Bledsoe, Edt.
"The Sponsor Souvenir Album & History of the United Confederate Veterans' Reunion, 1895. Patriotic Poems, war songs, romantic incidents, biographical & histori-

cal sketches." Houston, Texas, Sponsor Souvenir Co., 1895, large 8vo, cl, illus., ports., color front., 241, (124) pp. $90.00- Bmk. $150.00

353 **"PHOTOGRAPHIC History**
of Union & Confederate Cavalry in the Civil War, 1861-1865." Edts: Theophilus F. Rodenbough, et al, Glendale, N.Y., Benchmark Pub. Co., 1970, small 4to, 336pp., illus., ports, Reprint: Springfield, 1911 Edt.

354 **PHUL, Frank von**
"General Little's Burial." In: SHSP, 1901, v.29, p.212-215. Gen. Henry Little of Iuka, Miss.

355 **PICKARD, William Lowndes**
"Under the War Flags of 1861. A Romance of the South." Louisville, Ky., Chas. T. Dearing, 1895, 12mo, cl, color flags on cover, 372pp. The characters herein depicted are real, only their names are fictitious.

356 **PICKENS County, Georgia**
Luke E. Tate's "History of Pickens County, Georgia." Atlanta, Ga., 1935, Spartanburg, S.C., Reprint Co., 1978, index, illus., 322pp. $15.00. Military activity in Pickens Co., during war, CSA military rosters by company, muster roll of county militia.

356a **PICKENS, Kel N.**
"Battle of Wilsons Creek, Mo., Aug. 10, 1861." In: Jour. West. Oct. 1980, p.10-25.

357 **PICKERING, W.A.**
"The Washington Artillery of Augusta, Ga." In: CV, Jan. 1909, v.XVII, p.24-26.

358 **PICKETT'S & Hood's Charges**
At Gettysburg. In: SB, 1884-1885, v.III, p.748. Hood's Charge by: Private Co. H., 5th Tex. Reg.

359 **PICKETT, A.St.J.**
"The Sublime Tragedy of the Lost Cause. A Tragic Poem of the War." Columbus, O., The Westbote Print., 1884, 12mo, cl, 238, (2)pp. $75.00. An old Confederate tells story of secession, war & slavery.

359a **PICKETT, Charles Edward**
"The Existing Revolution; its causes & results." Sacramento (Calif.), 1861. 8vo, wraps, 24pp. "second edition." $150. Gdsp: "by a pro-Southern Virginia-born Californian."

360 **PICKETT, George Edward**
"The Heart of a Soldier, as revealed in the intimate letters of General George E. Pickett, CSA." N.Y., Seth Moyle, 1913, 8vo, cl, illus., (7), 215pp. Atg. copies. $35.00. Contains two less letters than in his "Soldier of the South."

361 ..."Soldier of the South. General Pickett's War Letters to his wife. Edited by Arthur Crew Inman." Boston, N.Y., Houghton Mifflin, 1928, 12mo, cl/bds, facsm, ports, incl. color front, xii, (2), 157, (1)pp. Pub. 1913 as "Heart of a Soldier." $30.00- Bmk84. $25.00-Jk122.

362 ..."Operations against Newbern 1864, Report of General Pickett, Hdq. Dept., N.C., Feb. 15, 1864." In: SHSP, 1881, v.IX, p.1-4. See: Walter Clark, Jas. C. Beckel, R.A. Bright, Fred E. Brooks, Andrew Johnston, J.C. Mayo.

363 ..."An Echo of War-times; letters of Gen'l. George E. Pickett written fifty years ago from the great battlefields of the Confederacy." In: Americana, Feb. 1913, v.VIII, p.107-112. Extracts from letters from his 'Heart of a Soldier.' Litho: Pickett.
See: H.A. Ogden.

364 ..."A Short History of Gen'l. G.E. Pickett." Park Place, N.Y., Knapp & Co., 1888, 2 3/4 x 1 1/2" colored booklet, 16pp. facsm signature, packed in Duke's cigarettes.
See: "Heroes of the C.W." & W. Duke Co.

364a ..."Love Letters (1863) to bethrothed La Salle Corbell." In: W. Tenn. HSP, p.143-8.

365 **PICKETT, John Thomas**
"Sigillogia. Being some account of the

Great or Broad Seal of the Confederate States of America. A Monograph. (Cut of Seal) Non omnis moriar. Dedicated to the sacred memory of the "gallant cavaliers who died in vain, for those who knew not to reign or reign." By Joannes Didymus Archaeologos. (Honi soit qui mal y pense!). Price $.25. Washington, D.C., Kercand & Towers, print by Powell & Ginck, 1873, 8vo, wraps, 23pp. $35.00-Bmk.

366 ..."Letter from Colonel John T. Pickett, of the Southern Confederacy, to Senor Don Manuel de Zamacona, minister of foreign affairs, Mexico. Intro: Mary Wilhelmine Williams." In: Hispanic Am. Hist. Rev., Nov. 1919, v.II, p.611-617. Pickett sent to Mexico in early 1861, as a diplomatic agent of CSA. This letter written in Sept. 16, 1861.

367 **PICKETT, LaSalle Corbell (Mrs. G.E. Pickett)**
"The Bugles of Gettysburg, by LaSalle Corbell Pickett (Mrs. General George E. Pickett). Chicago, F.G. Browne & Co., 1913, 12mo, cl, front, 163pp. $20.00-Bmk95.

368 ..."General George E. Pickett, a letter from his widow." In: SHSP, 1896, v.XXIV, p.151-154.

369 ..."Across my Path: Memories of People I Have Known." N.Y., Brentano's, 1916, 12mo, cl, ix, 148pp. $40.00-B. About five women connected with CSA.

370 ..."Pickett & His Men." Atlanta, Ga., Foote & Davies, 1899, 12mo, cl, front(port), xiii, 439pp, index. $15.00-$25.00-(Atg.) $35.00.
...2nd Edt., Atlanta, 1900, with an introduction by James Longstreet, p.xi, xiii added" pl., facsm, prot to the 1st edt. $30.00-Bmk.
...Phila., London, J.B. Lippincott, 1913, with 16 illus., front, plates, ports, xi, 313pp.

371 ..."The War-time Story of General Pickett." In: Cosmopol., Nov. 1913, LV, p.752-760, Dec. LVI, p.33-42; Jan/May, p.178-185, 332-339, 473-481, 611-622, 762-769; June/Aug., LVII, p.35-43, 196-205, 369-377.

372 ..."What Happened to Me." N.Y., Brentano's, 1917, 12mo, front, plates, ports, vi, 366pp. $40.00-McM251.

373 ..."Personal Memories of Robert E. Lee." In: Lippincott's Jan. 1907, v.LXXXIX, p.52-59.

373a ..."My Soldier (Geo. S. Pickett)." n.p., n.d. 8vo, wraps, 9pp.

374 **PICKETT, Thomas Edward**
"A Soldier of the Civil War, by a member of the Virginia Historical Society (quote)" Cleveland, Ohio, Burrows Bros. Co., 1900, "A limited number privately printed for the author," 8vo, stiff wraps, tied with silk ribbon, front port, maps, x, (11)-62, (1)pp. $25.00. Reprint of newspaper review of 'Pickett & His Men,' by his wife LaSalle.

375 **PICKETT, William D.**
"Reminiscences of Murfreesboro." In: CV, Sept., 1908, v.XVI, p.449-454.

376 ..."Why General Sherman's name is detested." In: CV, July 1906, c.XIV, p.295-298.

376a ..."Sketch of the Military Career of Gen. William J. Hardee, CSA." Lexington, Ky., 1910. 8vo, wraps, 51pp. $12.50.

377 **PICKETT-BUCHANAN Camp, Norfolk, Va.,**
"Pensioning of the Confederate Soldier by the United States, protest against." In: SHSP, 1898, v.26, p.312-315.

378 **"PICTURE Story of the Port Hudson**
Battlefield 1863 & other Louisiana Civil War Scenes, The." n.p., n.d. (Baton Rouge, La., Kennedy Print Shop, 1962?). Folio folder, with loose sheets, 43cm (12) & (2) dble-pg. sheets 43x54 1/2cm. Each with note: "Reproduced by Committee for Pre-

servation of the Port Hudson Battlefield." From Harper's Weekly.
See: Edward Cunningham, "Battle of Baton Rouge," for which some are duplicates.

379 **PIEDMONT GUARDS**
See. Lynn L. Goss

380 **PIERCE, Charles Hatch**
See. McNamara, M.

381 **PIERCE, Franklin, President**
"A Northern Gentleman & a Northern Politician." In: Tyler's Quart. Hist. & Gen. Mag., July 1925, v.VII, #1, p.1-8. The North re-writes Southern history.

382 **PIERCE, John E.**
"Jackson, Garnett & the "unfortunate breach." In: CWTI, Oct, 1973, v.12, #6, p.32-40, pl. map, port.

383 **PIERCE, Thomas Lovick**
"Their Last Battle, fight at Bentonville, N.C. between Sherman & Johnston, some persoanl observations." In: SHS, 1901, v.XXIX, p.215-222.

384 **PIERCE, Wendell E., Dr.**
"The Acadia A Blockade Runner 1865." Houston, Texas, Center Post Pub., March 1973, 8vo, decr. color wraps, illus., ports, map endsheets, 39pp.

385 ..."The Blockade Runner 'Acadia.' London Jour. Confed. Hist. Soc., Winte, 1972, v.10, #4, p.147-168, pl.

386 **PIERREPONT, Alice V.D.**
"Reuben Vaughan Kidd Soldier of the Confederacy." Petersburg, Va., Private Print, 1947, tk 8vo, cl, dj, facsms, illus., ports., incl. front., map, xii, 462pp. index. $100.00-OB. Kidd was Capt. Co. A. 4th Ala. Reg. Hood's Brig., ANV. (300 copies) $150.00-Bmk.

387 **PIERSON, Marshall Samuel**
"The Diary & Memoirs of Marshall Samuel Pierson, Company C. 17th Reg. Texas Cavalry, 1862-1865. Edited by Norman C. Delaney." In: MHT, Sw, 1975, v.XIII, #3, p.23-38.

388 **PIERSON, William S.**
"Report of Commandant of Johnson's Island 1862-1864." In: SHSP, 1890, v.18, p.289.

389 **PIERSON, William Whatley, Jr.**
"Texas versus White, a Study in Legal History." Durham, N.C., 1916, 8vo, wraps, 103pp. bibliog. State sovereignty after Civil War and reconstruction. First Appeared in: QTSHA, April 1915, v.XVIII, #4, p.341-367; July 1915, v.XIX, #1, p.1-36, #2, p.142-158.

390 **PIKE, Albert**
"Address: To the Senators & Representatives of the State of Arkansas in the Congress of the Confederate States." Louisiana, 1863, caption title, 8vo, 20pp.

391 ..."Charges & Specifications preferred Aug. 23, 1862, by Brig.-Gen. Albert Pike, against Maj.-Gen. Thos. C. Hindman." Richmond, Va., Smith, Bailey & Co., 1863, 8vo, sewed, 13pp.

392 ..."To the chiefs & people of the Cherokees, Seminoles, Chickasaws, & Choctaws." Fort McCulloch, 1862, Broadside, large 8vo, text in two columns. (Streeter) $2,000.00. Pike resigns command of Ind. Terr., goes to Richmond to protect their rights.
See: Jas. U. Vincent.

393 ...Confederate States of America. ARMY. Dept. INDIAN Terr. Collection of eight unnumbered General Orders of Gen. Al Pike, issued by Fayette Hewitt as Adjutant General, dated Headquarters, Dept., Ind. Ter., Fort McCulloch, May 14, 19, 24, 29; June 17, 30; & July 4, 17, 1862, and order #122, June 16, 1862. (Streeter) $1,500.00. Broadsides: Hargrett #205, 206, 207, 208, 210, 211, 214, 216 & 217.

394 ..."Confederate States of America. Treaties, 1861. Treaty with the Cherokees.

Oct. 7, 1861." Richmond?, 1862?, caption title, 26pp. 8vo, sewed. Streeter $1,700.00.

395 ..."Confederate Treaty with the Creek Nation, 1861." Notes & Documents. Chron. Okla. Summer, 1984, v.62, #2, p.207-209.

396 ..."Draught of a declaration of independence, proposed to the convention of the State of Arkansas, & withdrawn from its consideration." Little Rock, R.S. Yerkes & Co., 1861, 8vo, sewed, 13pp. (Streeter auction) $250.00.
...Do: Reprint, 25 copies, rag paper.

397 ..."Indian Troops Wanted! Hdq. Department Indian Territory, 10th June, 1862." (Fort McCulloch, 1862) Broadside, sq 8vo, By Order: Brig.-Gen. Albert Pike, Comm. Dept. Indian Territory. Fayette Hewitt, Asst. Adj.-Gen. Streeter $1,750.00.

398 ..."Laws that united Choctaw & Chickasaw Indians with the Confederacy." In: CV, Oct, 1903, c.XI, p.448-458. With Sketch of Gen. Albert Pike.

399 ..."Albert Pike's Letter addressed to Maj.-Gen. Holmes." Dec. 30, 1862. Little Rock, 1862, caption title, 8vo, sewed, 8pp. text, 2 columns. Atend: J.D. Butler, Print. Streeter.
...Do: Broadside (above) printed wallpaper, 4to, 5 columns.

400 ..."Second letter to Lieut.-Gen. Theophilus H. Holmes." caption title, Richmond? 1863, dated Apr. 30, 1863, 8vo, 20pp. H-1083.

401 ..."Albert Pike's Letter addressed to Maj.-Gen. Holmes." Dec. 30, 1862. Little Rock, 1862, caption title, sm. 8vo, sewed, 700. 2 column.

402 ..."Letter to the chief magistrate of the Confederacy calling his attention to the enclosed orders of Maj.-Gen. Hindman, commanding the Trans-Mississippi District." Fort McCulloch, Choctaw Nation, July 3, 1862, 8vo, sewed, (3)pp. (Streeter) $1,700.00.

403 ..."Message of the President & Report of... Commissioner of the Confederat States to the Indian Nations West of Arkansas, of the Results of his Mission." Dec. 12, 1861, Richmond, Enquirer Book & Job Press, 1861, Tyler, Wise, Allegre & Smith, 8vo, sewed, 38pp. (Streeter) $950.00.
See: "Laws that United..."

404 ..."Report of Albert Pike on Mission to the Indian Nations. Richmond, 1861." Washington, D.C., Supreme Council, 33 Ancient & Accepted Scottish Rite, Southern Jurisdiction, U.S.A." 1968, Caption cover title, a facsimilie reprint of the Richmond, Va., 1861, "Message of the President & Report of Albert Pike, etc.", 8vo, wraps, (1) front(port), 38pp.

405 ..."State or province? Bond or Free?" The vital principal of equality, which cements the union of the States. "Madison. Addressed particularly to the people of Arkansas." (Little Rock? 1861), large 8vo, printed wraps, 40pp., Pike's name not on wraps. Boyden - $21.00, cites 23pp. appendix. Urges Arkansas to secede before Lincoln elected. Louisville, Lost Cause Press $1.93. $75.00.

406 ..."In the Supreme Court of the U.S.: The State of Texas vs. White: Argument for the Defendant." Washington, D.C., 1868, 8vo, wraps, 96pp. jk-128 $250.00. Texas, having seceded, had status/right to sue in the US Supreme Ct., The court held the Union was indestructable, repudiating the doctrine of state sovereignty.

407 **PIKE, James Shepherd**
"First Blows of the Civil War, the ten years of preliminary conflict in the U.S. from 1850 to 1860. A contemporaneous exposition Progress of the struggle shown by public records & private correspondence. With letters, now first published."

N.Y., American News Co., 1879, 8vo, cl, xiv, 526pp.

407a **PILCHER, John M.**
"The Early Days of the War. An Address before A.P. Hill Camp, Confederate Veterans, Petersburg, Virginia, Apr. 4, 1889." Suffolk, Va., Robt. Hardy Pub., 1986. 8vo, wraps, 12p.

408 **PILCHER, Joseph Mitchell**
"Judah Philip Benjamin (1811-1884) or, Jewish Prophecy fulfilled." Louisiana Hist. Quar., III (Oct.), 1920, p.278-485.

409 ..."The early days of the war." In: Geo. Barnard 'War talks of Confed. Veterans.' 1892. p.1-7.

410 **PILLAR, James J., O.M.I.**
"The Catholic Church in Mississippi, 1837-1865." New Orleans, La., Hauser Pr., 1964, 8vo, cl, XX, 380pp. Near three-fourths of book to work of Bishop Elder & Civil War.

411 **PILLOW, Annie Payne**
"The Great Seal of the Confederate States of America, 1861-1865." n.p. (Washington, DC?) 1911/1912, 4to, wraps, facsms, ports, cover title(seal), 32pp, sold c/o War Dept., Washington, D.C. $1.00.

412 **PINCKNEY, Susanna Shulrick Hayne**
"Douglas; Tender & True. By Miss McPherson, St. Louis, Mixon-Jones Print, 1892, 12mo, cl, 210pp. jk-129 $35.00. Plantation life during war, a Southern belle in love with a soldier in Hood's Texas Brigade.

413 **PINE BLUFF, Expedition Against**
See: John Sap. Marmaduke.

414 **PINER, Howell Lake**
"Ruth; a Romance of the Civil War." Van Alstyne, Texas, Leader Pub., 1895, 12mo, cl, 2p. 1,(7)-172pp. (Carolina Bk.) 'Based on a true story of Ruth Montaye, set in Memphis, Tenn. during war.' Inscription from author, July 1899. $75.00.

415 **PINKOWSKI, Edward**
"Pills, Pens & Politics, the Story of General Leon Jastremski, a CSA officer at eighteen." Wilmington, Del., Captain Stanislaus Mlothowski Memmorial Brigade Society, 1843-1907, 1974, 8vo, cl, illus., ports, 172, (7)p. pls.

416 **"PIONEER Banner, The"**
a Confederate Camp Newspaper. Edited: Peter A. Brannon. In: AHQ, Fall/Winter, 1961, v.23, p.211-219. Facimiles of only two known issues of a mmsc. 1st Ala. Vols., Ft. Barrancas, Feb. 23, & April 20, 1861. UWF.

417 **PIRTLE, John B. Maj.**
"Defense of Vicksburg in 1861 - The Battle of Baton Rouge." In: SHSP, 1880, v.8, p.324-332.

418 **PISANI, Ferri**
"Lettres sur les Etats-Unis d'Amerique Par le Lieutenant-Colonel Ferri Pisani.." Paris, L. Hachette et Cie, 1862, 16mo, cl, (4), 455pp.

418a **PISTON, W. G.**
"Lee's tarnished lieutenant: James Longstreet & his place in Southern history." Athens, Ga., University, 1987. 8vo, cl, dj, maps, port. 252p. $25.

419 **PITMAN, Benn, Edt.**
"The Trials for Treason (of Harrison H. Dodd, Wm. A Bowles & others) at Indianapolis, disclosing the plans for establishing a North-Western Confederacy..." Cincinnati, Morre, Wilstack & Baldwin, 1865, 8vo, cl, p.339, frontis. group ports, plates, 16pp. ads. jk-130 $150.00. Official trails of leaders: Golden Circle, Circle of Honor, Order of Amer. Knights, sons of Liberty, Conspiracy to form a Western Confederacy.

PITT COUNTY, North Carolina
See: Henry T. King's History.

420 **PITTARD, Pen Lile & W.C. Watts**
"Alexander County Confederates." n.p.,

n.d., mimeo (one side), spiral bound, 67pp. Roster 47pp., c. 1960, 100 copies. OP $50.00.

420a **PITTMAN, Walter E., Jr.**
"Gen. Nathan Bedford Forrest & Military Leadership." In: W. Tenn.HSP, Oct. 1981, p.51-62.

..."Richard P. Hobson & the sinking of the 'Merrimac.'" In: AHQ, 1976, v.38, #2, p.101-111.

421 **PITTMAN, William Edward**
"The Pittmans Family in the Civil War. Part 1 - Brothers in Battle." In: "Flaskback," Washington Co. Hist. Soc., Aug. 1977, v.27, #3, p.(16)-26, plate, Fayetteville, Ark., Part II - A Civil War Journey M. Dallas Pittman Hinds, pp.27-34, ports.

422 **PITTS, Charles F.**
"Chaplains in Gray the Confederate Chaplain's Story." Nashville, Tenn., Broadman Pr., 1957, 12mo, cl, dj, xv, 166pp. Roster of Confederate Chaplains. $20.00-Bmk84.

423 **PITTS, John Abram**
"Personal & Professional Reminiscences of an old Lawyer." Kingsport, Tenn., Southern Pub., 1930, 12mo, cl, front(port), xxii, 381pp. Five chaps. on Civil War & reconstruct. in Tennessee. $15.00.

424 **PITTS, Joseph J.**
"A Methodist Circuit Rider between the lines: the Private Journal of Joseph J. Pitts 1862-1864." In: Tenn. HQ, Sept, 1960, v.XIX, pp.252-259. Work in Smith's Fork Circuit in presence of both Union & CSA soldiers.

425 **PITTS, Lulie**
"History of Gordon County, Georgia." Calhoun, Ga., Calhoun Times, 1933, 8vo, cl, illus., ports, ix, (2), 12-480pp. "War between the States," Chap. III, p.131-171. Entirely made up of the various Rosters made up from Gordon County, plus Confed. Pensioners.

426 **PLAISANCE, Aloysius, O.S.B.**
"Emmeran Bliemel, O.S.B., Heroic Confederate Chaplain." In: American Benedictine Review, 1966, v.XVII, p.209-216.

427 **PLANCK, D.A., Rev.**
"Life & Character of ex-Governor B.G. Humphreys of Mississippi, Eulogy at Port Gibson, Dec. 27, 1882." In: SHSP, 1883, v.11, p.241-247.

428 **PLANE, William Fisher**
"Letters of William Fisher Plane C.S.A., to his wife." In: Ga.H.Q., June 1964, c.XLVIII, #2, p.215-228. Edt: S. Joseph Lewis Jr.

429 **PLAYING CARDS - Confederate**
London, Goodall & Son, 1862. Backs show the Confederate flags & seal of the CSA; Catherine Perry Hargrave's "Hist. of Playing Cards" gives another example - "The Game of Battles" going thru several editions, as a box was lettered 'Second Series', North & South, 1861-1862-1863. At the top of each of 52 cards, is either the Stars & Stripes or the Confederate flag. Below is the name of battle in which the followers of the flag were victorious, the date and statistics.

430 **PLEASANT HILL, Battle of**
See: Hamilton P. Bee.

431 **PLEASANTS, H.R., Va.**
"Character of the Southern People as established by the events of the late war." In: LWL, Jan. 1868, IV, #3, p.243-248.

432 **PLEASANTS, James**
See: Walter D. Leake.

433 **PLEASANTS, Reuben B., 2nd Co.**
"The First Detachment at Fredericksburg." In: 'Contributions to a History of the Richmond Howitzers,' v.3, p.58-61, Richmond, Va., Carlton McCarthy, 1884.

434 **PLECKER, Adam H.**
"Roster of the Botetourt Battery." In: SHSP, 1907, v.35, p.50-52.
See: Mary Johnston.

435 **PLOWDEN, John Covert, Pvt.**
"Letters of Pvt. John Coverty Plowden, 1862-1865. Edt: Henry B. Rollins." Sumter, S.C., 1970 (Manning, S.C.), J.C. Daniels (1970), 12mo, wraps, 164pp.

436 **PLUM, William Rattle**
"The Military Telegraph during the Civil War in the U.S., with an exposition of ancient & Modern means of Communication & of the Federal & Confederate cipher systems, also a running account of the War Between the States." Chicago, Jensen, McClurg Co., 1882, 8vo, cl, front, illus., maps, facsms, 2 vols. $200.00-OB.

437 ..."The Sword & the Soul." N.Y., Neale Pub., 1917, 12mo, cl, 446pp., illus. Novel of the war. $50.00-Bmk127.

438 **PLUMMER, Alonzo H.**
"Confederate Victory at Mansfield. Including Federal advance from & retreat to Natchitoches." Mansfield, La., Ideal Print, 1969. Pub: Kate Beard Chap. 397, U.D.C., sm. 4to, soft back, illus., facsms, maps, 56pp., printed covers.

439 ..."Chronology of events in Federal & Confederate forces during Red River Campaign from the approach of the Main Federal forces to Natchitoches & Grand Encore on Mar. 30, to the arrival at that point on the retreat on Apr. 11-12, 1864." Mansfield Battle Park (c.1968), Louisiana State Parks & Recreation Comm., 8vo, printed wraps, illus., map, 12pp.

440 ..."Mansfield Battle Park Museum." n.p., n.d. (c.1968), 8vo, wraps, illus., maps.
See: Jno. E. Hewitt, Battle of Mansfield.

441 **PLUMMER, Mark A.**
"Missouri & Kansas & the Capture of General Marmaduke." Columbia, Mo, Mo. Hist. Review, Oct. 1964, v.LVIV, #1, p.90-104, ports, illus., maps.

441a **POAGUE, William Thomas**
"Gunner with Stonewall, reminiscences of William Thomas Poague...a memoir written for his children in 1903. Edited by Monroe F. Cockrell. With an introduction by Bell Irvin Wiley." Jackson, Tenn., McCowat-Mercer Pr., 1957, 8vo, cl, dj, facsms, illus., ports, plan, xxii, 181pp. full calf. $40.00-OP. Civil War Book Club Edition $60.00. $50.00-B.
...Wilmington, N.C., Broadfoot Pub., 1987. 8vo, cl, dj, 176pp, ills. $30.
..."Report: Battle of Gettysburg." In: SHSP, 1880, v.8, p.429-430.

442 **POCHE, Felix Pierre**
"A Louisiana Confederate: Diary of Felix Pierre Poche." Natchitoches, Louisiana Studies Inst. of Northwestern State University, 1972, 8vo, cl, 352pp. O.P. $25.00-B.

443 **POE, Clarence**
"True Tales of the South at War; how soldiers fought & families lived, 1861-1865. Collected & edited by Clarence Poe." Chapel Hill, University of North Carolina Press, 1961, 12mo, cl, dj, xiii, (1), 208pp. $20.00-Bmk.

444 ..."Special Edition," Decr. endsheets & bound in gray cloth. "Confederate Descendants' Edition," with cover device & special endsheets, gray buck.

445 **POE, Clarence H.**
"The Tragedy of Jefferson Davis." In: Outlook, June 1908, v.LXXXIX, p.333-336.

446 **POE, David**
"Personal Reminiscences of the Civil War, by Capt. David Poe." Charleston, W.Va., News-Mail Pub., 1908, 8vo, wraps, 81pp. (John on t.p., corrected to "David". Dornbusch II-1269B. 200 - 300-R.

447 ...Buckhannon, W.Va., Upshur Republican, 1911, 8vo, wraps, 96pp. Roster Co.

A, 20th Va. Cavalry; Co. A, 25th Va. Inf. Shetler-630.

448 **POE, J.C., Edt.**
"The Raving Foe the Civil War Diary of Maj.James T. Poe, C.S.A. & the 11th Arkansas Volunteers. And a complete List of Prisoners." Eastland, Texas, Longhorn Press, 1967, 12mo, cl, half-title, (xii), post, 72pp, (11)p., illus., facsms, (42)pp - "Alphabetical listing of 1,253 Confederate Prisoners on Johnson's Island, Ohio." map, coat-of-arms. $35.00-B.

449 **POEM (By W. Gordon McCabe)**
& address (By James Barron Hope) delivered on the first annual meeting of the Society of the "Old Boys of Hampton Academy," July 1860." Printed by order of the Society, Richmond, Va., W.H. Clemmitt, 1861, 8vo, wraps, 22pp.

450 **POEMS: in SHSP**
See: J.E. Battaile, R.E. Colston, J.E. Cooke, A.C. Gordon, Percy Greg, Paul Hayne, Ida R. Hood, 'Light Artillery,' Fannie H. Marr, E.R. Montgomery, James H. Lane, J.W. Palmer, J. Peterkin, J.R. Randall, H.F. Requier, S.N. Roach, A.H. Ryan, W.H.Seymour, Mrs. F.H. Smith, H.T. Staunton, J.R. Thompson, Mary A. Townsend, S.B. Valentine, J.G. Walker, E.W. Wilcox, P.S. Worsley.

451 **POFFINBERGER, Moses**
"A Descriptive List of the burial places of the remains of Confederate Soldiers, who fell in the Battles of Antietam, South Mountain, Monocacy, & other points in Washington & Frederick Counties, in the State of Maryland." Hagerstown, Md., (c.1868?), 8vo, wraps, 84pp. $250.00-Bmk106.

452 **POHORESKY, William L.**
"Newport, North Carolina during the Civil War." Havelock, N.C., The Print Shop, 1985. 4to, wraps, typescript, 175pp. maps, ills. Parts of 17th & 42nd NC regs. in action Feb. 2, 1864.

454 **POINDEXTER, Charles**
"Richmond: An illustrated hand-book & guide with notices of the battle-fields." Richmond, J.L. Hill Print, 1896, 16mo, wraps, illus., pl. map, 112pp. Swem-4308.

455 ..."Richmond: an illustrated hand-book of the city & battle fields, with historic sketch & maps." 16mo, stiff wraps, 2-fldg. maps, illus., ports, 126pp. Richmond, Hermitage Press, 1907.
See: Also under - Richmond, illustrated...

456 ..."Richmond Howitzers. Facts about the Battery during the Appomattox Campaign." In: SHSP, 1899, v.XXVII, p.322-334.

457 ..."Major J. Scheibert (of the Prussian Army) on Confederate History." Review in: SHSP, 1890, v.XVIII, p.422-428.

458 **POINDEXTER, James E., Rev.**
"Address on the life & services of Gen. Lewis A. Armistead before R.E. Lee camp #1, Confederate Veterans, Jan. 29, 1909." Richmond, Va., 1909, 8vo, wraps, 8pp. $7.50. $75.00-Bmk99. $100.00. Late Capt, in 38th Virginia Regiment, Armistead's Brigade, Pickett's Division, Jas. E. Poindexter.

459 ..."General Armistead's Portrait presented an address delivered befroe R.E. Lee Camp #1, C.V., Richmond, Va., Jan. 29, 1909. By Rev. James E. Poindexter, Late Captain in 38th Va. Reg., Armistead's Brigade, Pickett's Division." In: SHSP, 1909, v.XXXVII, p.144-151. (offprint, wrp. atg). $75.00.

460 ..."Richmond, Va., Hdq. First Corps Area, 1927." 4to, 5lfs, mimeogr., 50 copies repro.

460a ..."Lewis A. Armistead: An Address before Lee Camp, Confederate Veterans, Richmond, Va., 1909." Suffolk, Va., Robt. Hardy Pub., 1986. 8vo, wraps, 16pp.

461 **POINDEXTER, William B.**
"A Midnight Charge & Death of J.E.B. Stuart." In: SHSP, 1904, v.32, p.117-121.

462 **POINT LOOKOUT, MD.**
See: Chs. T. Loehr, "Monuments to Confederates at Point Lookout," J.B. Traywick.

463 **POISON SPRING, Arkansas, Battle**
See: Bearss - "Steele's Retreat from Camden, Jenkins Ferry."

464 **POISONED Rifle Balls**
See: H.E. Hayden.

465 **POLIGNAC, Camille Armand Jules Marie, prince de**
"Polignac's Mission. Defence of President Davis." In: SHSP, 1904, v.32, p.364-371; 1907, v.35, p.326-334; 1910, v.38, p.241-242.

466 ..."L'Union Americaine apres la guerre; par le Prince Camille de Polignac, ex-general de division, etats Confederes." Paris, E. Dentu, 1866, thin large 8vo, wraps, 48pp.
See: Alwyn Barr-'Polignac's Tex. Brig.'

467 ..."The Political Right of Secession a Reserved Power under the Constitution Printed for Personal Friends." N.Y., 1862, 8vo, wraps, 16pp. Drake Wills, author inserts atg. L. Oct. 1862, "to destroy pamphlet I sent & accept a revised copy, etc."

468 **POLK COUNTY, Texas:**
Companies & Soldiers organized in:
See: "Historical Polk Co..."

469 **POLK, J.M., Capt.**
"Memories of the Lost Cause, stories & adventures of a Confederate Soldier in General R.E. Lee's Army, 1861-1865, & ten years in South American, its resources, trade & commerce, & business & social intercourse with other countries." Austin, Texas, 1905, 8vo, wraps, front(port), 46pp. $75.00-Ginsb. First pub. in the weekly mag. "State Topics," Austin, Texas. Jeff McLemore, editor. Mar. 27 - May 8, 1904 (7 installm.) Polk a member of Hood's Brigade, lists members Co. I, 4th Tex. Inf., vivid descp. Seven Pines, Gaines' Mill.

470 ..."Memories of the Lost Cause & Ten Years in South America." Austin, Texas, J.P. Polk, 1907, Sam T. Hill Print., 2nd edt., 8vo, wraps, port., illus. (incl. front.), 47pp. 150-OM. $30.00.

471 ..."The Confederate Soldier & Ten Years in South America." 3rd Edt., Austin, Texas, Von Boeckmann-Jones, 1910, 8vo, wraps, illus., port(front), 57pp, (3p.ads). $15.00.

472 ..."The North & South American Review. Austin, Texas, Von Boeckmann-Jones, 1912, 4th Edt., 8vo, wraps, port., illus., 64pp. $45.00-White. $75.00.

473 ...Same: 1914, with addition of fldg. map colored, Texas. With a large fldg. genealogical Tree of Polk family (date: 1849). $40.00-Bmk. $75.00-Ginsb. $12.50. $15.00.

474 ..."Memories of a Lost Cause." In: Tex. Mil. Hist., Feb. 1962, v.2, #1, p.23-43, port-Polk.

475 **POLK, Leonidas, Gen.**
"The Career of General Leonidas Polk. The soldier who abandoned the Army for the Church." The New York Tribune's review of Dr. Wm. M. Polk's book. In: SHSP, 1893, v.21, p.321-326.

476 ..."General Forrest's Operations against Smith & Grierson." In: SHSP, 1880, v.8, p.566-568 (See: Gen. Forrest).

477 ..."General Polk's Report of the Battle of Belmont." Hdq. West. Dept., Columbus, Ky., 1861 (Nov. 10), 12mo, 8pp. Crandall 1352.

478 ..."Order on assuming command in Mississippi." In: SHSP, 1888, v.16, p.329-230.

479 ..."Funeral Service at the Burial of..., Bishop of Louisiana, Together with the Sermon by Rt. Reb. Stephen Elliott, in

Augusta, Ga., June 29, 1864." New Orleans, La., Isaac T. Hinton, 1866, 8vo, wraps, 32pp. Sabin-63846.

...Columbia, S.C., Evans & Cogswell, 1864, wraps, 8vo, 28pp.

...Do: 1865.

480 ..."God's Presence with out Army at Manassas: A Sermon preached in Christ Church, Savannah, on Sunday, July 28th.: Savannah, Ga., W. Thorne Williams, 1861, 12mo, wraps, 22pp. McKissick-747.

481 ..."General Polk's Report of the Battle of Belmont." Nov. 10, 1861. Columbus, Ky., 1861, 12mo, sewn, 8pp. Crandall-1352.

482 ..."Leonidas Polk, Bishop & General, Apr. 10, 1806 - June 14, 1864." In: P.E. Church Hist. Mag., 1938, v.VII, p.324-418.

See: Moultrie Guerry, Joseph H. Parks, Wm. M. Polk.

483 ..."A Short History of Gen. Leonidas Polk." Park Place, N.Y., Knapp & Co., 1888, 2 3/4 x 1 1/2" colored booklet, 16pp. facsm signature (packed in Duke's cigarettes).

See: "Heroes of the C.W.," & W. Duke Co.

484 ..."Battle of Shiloh or Pittsburg Landing." In: Confed. War Jour., 1893, v.1, p.162-165.

See: Samuel G. French, Joseph E. Johnston, Charles P. McIlvaine.

485 **POLK, Lucius Eugene**
"Report of the Battle of Taylor's Ridge." In: SHSP, 1879, v.7, p.590-591.

486 **POLK, William Mecklenburg**
"Leonidas Polk, Bishop & General." In: CV, 1899, v.7, p.218-220, ports.

487 ..."Army of the Mississippi before Shiloh." In: SHSP, 1880, v.VIII, p.457-463.

488 ..."The Battle of Chickamauga." In: SHSP, 1882, v.X, p.1-25, v.XII, p.378-390.

489 ..."General Polk at Chickamauga." In: B&L, v.III, p.662-663.

490 ..."Leonidas Polk Bishop & General." N.Y., etc., Longmans, Green Co., 1893, 12mo, cl, illus.(some fldg), maps, ports., incl. front., 349, 442pp. $50.00.

...1894 Edition, Pres. copy. $50.00.

...1915 New Edition, x, 385; viii, 464p. $25.00. $27.50. 150-Bmk. ATG-$100.00.

491 ..."Roster of Troops at Chickamauga." In: SHSP, 1882/1884, v.X & XII, p.236-238, p.378-390.

See: Joseph H. Parks biog.

492 ..."Concentration before Shiloh - reply Gen. Ruggles." In: SHSP, 1881, v.9, p.178-185.

492a ..."Gen. Polk & the battle of Belmont, by his son." In: B&L, v.1, p.348-57, ills, ports, map.

493 **POLLARD, Edward Alfred**
"The First Year of the War." Richmond, Va., West & Johnston, 1862, 8vo, cl, or wraps, viii, (17)-374pp., 1st issue, yellow wraps. 185-Jk129. 150-Bk.

494 ...Corrected & Improved edition, Richmond, West & Johnston, 1862, 8vo, cl, xvi, (17)-406pp.

...Same, 2nd Edition, 8vo, cl, port, map, 389pp. $50.00-Jk137.

...Same, 3rd Edition, Richmond, West & Johnston, 1863, 8vo, cl, viii, (17)-406pp. $75.00.

Note: Reprinted in N.Y. As follows:

495 ..."Southern History of the War. The First Year of the War. Reprinted from the Richmond Corrected Edition." N.Y., Charles B. Richardson, 1863, 8vo, cl, (6), 360pp. 2 maps, 3 ports, 3/4 leather, 1863-1866. $450.00.

...Same: (6), 389pp. map, 4 ports, 1864.

...Same: 1965 bust of Jackson added.

Note: Sabin-63856, above title followed by a reprint of the Richmond edition. Some copies of the 1863 contain map, 4 port some in paper covers. Cloth covers have gilt CSA flag. 1863 Edt. carries errata slip, as enlarged edt., with higher price. Pollard's position as editor of the Richmond Examiner placed within his reach a mass of authentic material which was not accessible to any other Southern writer.

496 ..."The First Year of the War...The Second Northern from the Second Southern Edition, enlarged, with the addition of portraits of Davis, Lee, Beauregard, & Stonewall Jackson; with a map." London, Henry Stevens, June 10, 1863, 8vo, cl, (10), 360, Append., 367--368. This N.Y. edition with extra t.p. & preface by H. Stevens. $25.00-Bmk. N.Y., 1864, 389pp, rebound, N.Y., 1863. $20.00.
...London, George Philip & Son, 1863, 8vo, cl, xvi, 354pp. Reprinted from the last corrected & revised Richmond Edition. $100.00-G.

497 ...Toronto, P.R. Randall, 1863, titled "Southern History of the Great Civil War in the United States, by Edward A. Pollard, Member of the Confederate Congress." Title on cover reads "A Voice from Richmond. The Southern History of the War in the United States." 8vo, wraps, 383pp. $60.00-Bmk.
...A rare mezzotint portraits of Lincoln by A.B. Walker, R.E. Lee by Sartain, Jefferson Davis, etc. Unusual edition, containing the first year of the war.
...N.Y., Fairfax Press, Crown Pub., 1917, 2 vols. in 1, tk. 8vo, cl, dj, 657, 598, (2). $65.00-Y.

498 ..."Southern Hist. of the War." 4 vols., N.Y., 1863-1866, calf 3/4, raised bds., very good sound set. $450.00-Bmk86.

499 ..."The Second Year of the War." Richmond, Va., West & Johnston, 1863, 8vo, cl, (2), x, xvii, 326pp. $150.00.
Reprinted in N.Y. as follows:

500 ..."Southern History of the War. The Second Year of the War." N.Y., Charles B. Richardson, 1863, 8vo, cl, 5 ports, incl, front, fldg. map, (5), 10, (17)-386pp.
...Same Coll., for 1864 & 1865.

501 ..."The Third Year of the War." (Southern History of the War), N.Y., Charles B. Richardson, 1864, 8vo, cl, 5 ports, incl. front., 391pp.
...Same: for 1865 & 1866.
Note: First issued in London, Saunders Otley & Co., 1865, republished above in New York, In 1866 it was titled "The War in America, 1863-1864." See under this title.

502 ..."Southern History of the War. The Last Year of the War." N.Y., Charles R. Richardson, 1866, 8vo, cl, 4 ports, incl, front, (2), 5-363pp. Scarce, only a small edition was printed & bound separately. $35.00.
Note: This title may also be found in the 2 vol. set (following) from chap xiv, p.309-644.

503 ..."Southern History of the War." N.Y., Charles B. Richardson, 1866, 8vo, 2 vols., p.676, 644, ports (20).

504 ..."Southern History of the War." N.Y., Charles B. Richardson, 1866, tk. 8vo, p.657; (2), 5-598, leaf pg. 1258. $75.00.
Note: to "Southern History of the War." N.Y., Chas. B. Richardson, 1866, 2 vols., leaf of errata at end, p.1257-1258, is identical with p.405-406 of "corrected & improved Edition" of Pollard's "First Year of the War," Richmond, 1862.

505 ..."The Lost Cause, a new Southern history of the war of the Confederates. Comprising a full & authentic account of the rise & Progress of the late Southern Confederacy - the campaigns, battles, incidents, & adventures of the most gigantic struggle of the world's history. Drawn from official sources & approved by the most distinguished Confederate leaders. With numerous splendid steel portraits. N.Y., E.B. Treat & Co., 1867.

506 ...Condensed Version of 4 vol. edt., 1st ptg., 1866. $55.00. Tk. 8vo, cl. (or full calf; 1/2 Mor.), plates (6 containing 24 ports), xxx, (1), (33)-752pp. (i.e. 740). Error in paging: nos. 730-741 omitted.
...New & Enlarged edition, Baltimore, E.B. Treat (N.Y.) & J.S. Morrow (Baltimore), 1867. xxx, (33)-762, map & 6 plates.
...Same above, 1868. $32.50.
...Louisville, Lost Cause Press, micro cards, 1962.
...Freeport, N.Y., Books for Libraries, 1970, Rep. 1866 edt., 740pp. $20.00.
...Bonanza Reprint (c.1974). $15.00-Jk. $5.98.
...N.Y. Arno's "Select Bibliographies Reprint Series." 1974. $30.50.
Note: The Lost Cause is a condensed version of his Southern History of War.
...N.Y., Jack Brussel, Blue & Gray Press, 1960, 12mo, cl, reprint in 4 vols.

507 ..."La Cause Perdue, historie de la Guerre des Confederes..." Nouvelle Orleans, Publiee par la Renaissance Louisianise, 1867, 4to, 420, (3)pp., 8 ports, 3 maps, in pocket at rear, 1/2 Mor., as issued in 34 separate parts, wraps, in varying colors, paper & quality, as reflected in wartime conditions. (Listed in Jenkins-152...$950.00). $750.00.

508 ..."La Cause Perdue, histoire de la guerre des Confederes d'apres des rapports officiels et des documents authentiques, par Edward A. Pollard. Traduction francaise de Jules Noblom. Edition illustree et augmentee de notes et de renseignements complimentaires concernant La Louisiane." New Orleans, La., La Renaissance Louisianaise, 1867, sm. 4to, cl, front, ports (some mounted), 3 maps, plans, 420, (3)pp. text double columns. $75.00-Bmk127. $150-B. Portrait of Lee and his staff found in some copies.
...N.Y., 1970 edt., cl, 578pp.
...N.Y., Arno's 'Select Bibliography Reprint Series, 1979, set: 2 vols., v.1 & v.2, "Southern History of the War." $54.00.
...N.Y., Fairfax Press, 1977, tk. 8vo, cl, dj, 657, 598, (2)pp.

509 ..."The Lost Cause Regained." N.Y., G.W. Carleton & Co., 1868, 12mo, cl, 214pp.
...Freeport, N.Y., Books for Libraries, 1970, reprint, 1868 edition.
...N.Y. Arno's 'Select Bibliographies Reprint Series.' 1978. $13.75.
...AMS reprint (1868 edt).
Reconstruction, the Negro question, etc.

510 ..."Stonewall Jackson, an Historical study." In: 'Putnam's Mag.' ns, v.II, p.733-740.

511 ..."Jail Journal of the author in Fort Warren, etc." In: Pollard's 3rd Year of War, append: p.(323)-386.
Also: under his title - "Observations in the North, etc."

512 ..."The Key to the Ku Klux. Individual reports & Revelations, by Edward A. Pollard, on the Condition of the South." 12mo, wraps, n.p., n.d., 32pp.

513 ..."Lee & His Lieutenants; comprising the Early Life, Public Services, & Campaigns of General Robert E. Lee, & his companions in arms, with a record of their campaigns & heroic deeds." N.Y., E.B. Treat & Co., 1867, 8vo, cl, illus., ports, incl, front, vi, (1), (9) 851pp., 7 plates. Bmk125.
...Same: 1868, also 1870 with 6 plates.

514 ..."Early Life & Campaigns & Public Services of Robert E. Lee, with a record of the campaigns & heroic deeds of his companions in arms, by a distinguished Southern Journalist." N.Y., E.B. Treat & Co., New Orleans, La., J.H. Hummel, etc., 1870, 8vo, cl, (9)-26, (33)-851, ports, incl. front(added t.p., vignette: conflagration of Richmond) pub. 1867 as "Lee & His Lieutenants." 6 plates.

...N.Y., 1871, 3/4 Mor., same as above. $45.00.

515 ..."Memoir of the assassination of Henry Rives Pollard. Prepared by his brother, Edward A. Pollard." Lynchburg, Va., Schaffter & Bryant Printers, 1869, 8vo, wraps, 32pp.

516 ..."Observations in the North: Eight Months in Prison & on parole." Richmond, Va., E.W. Ayres, 1865, 12mo, cl, or, wrps, vii, (9)-142pp. $40.00. $60.00. $125.00. $150.00 $200.00. $300.00-Jk122. One of the last books pub. in the CSA. In Harwell's "Confed. 100" identifies a 2nd print, pg. 136, the numeral "6" below its proper place. Attached to front wraps a note - "relic of the Rebellion." Most copies taken by the editor of the NY "Times."

517 ..."Recollections of Appomattox Court-House." In: "Old & New," v.IV, 1871-1872, p.166-175.

518 ..."The Rival Administration : Richmond & Washington in December, 1863." Richmond, The Author, 1864, 8vo, wraps, (8), 31, (1)pp. $20.00 $75.00. Sabin-63862 notes: Rare pamphlet, printed on coarse paper, only a portion of "Third Year of War," printed in Richmond. Acct. scarcity paper, was pub. in N.Y. as the "Southern History of the War" attacks both Lincoln & Pres. Davis.
See: Alex. St. Clair Abrams' Review of Pollard's "Rival Administration."

519 ..."The Second Battle of Manassas, with Sketches of the recent campaign in Northern Virginia & on the upper Potomac. Prepared from special materials, by the author of "The First Year of the War." Richmond, West & Johnston, 1862, 8vo, wraps, 48pp. $75.00.

520 ..."The Seven Days' Battle in front of Richmond. An outline narrative of the series of engagements which opened at Mechanicsville, near Richmond, on Thursday, June 26, 1862, & resulted in the defeat & retreat of the Northern Army under Major-General McClellan. Compiled from the detailed accounts of the newspaper press." Richmond, West & Johnston, 1862, 8vo, wraps, 45pp. Crandall-2654. 375-OB.
...Charleston, S.C., Evans & Cogswell Print, 1862, same.
...Columbia, S.C., Townsend & North Print, 1862, same.

521 ..."The Southern Spy, or Curiosities of Slavery in the South. Letters from a Southerner to a Northern Friend." Washington, Henry Polkinhorn Pr., 1859, 12mo, wraps, 72pp.
Note: Published under author's name as "Black Diamonds gathered in Darkey Homes of the South." Enlarged.

522 ..."The Weekly Southern Spy, an account of the events, progress & spirit of the American War." Baltimore, published every Saturday by E.A. Pollard & Co., June 29, 1861, vol.1, no.1, discontinued. Pollard also edited "Echoes from the South," see under that title (below).

523 ..."Echoes from the South. Comprising the most important speeches, proclamations, & public acts emanating from the South during the late war. N.Y., E.B. Treat & Co., Baltimore, Md., L.T.Palmer & Co., etc., 1866, 12mo, cl, vi, (7)-211pp.
...Westport, Ct., Negro Univ., 1974, 1979.
...Louisv., Lost Cause Pr., micro/card.

524 ..."A Letter on the State of the War, by one recently returned from the enemy's country." Richmond, Va., 1865, 12mo, caption title, 8pp.

525 ..."Letters of the Southern Spy, in Washington & elsewhere." Baltimore, 1861, Pub. anon., 12mo, wraps, 92, (3), append. prospectus (3)p. of the 'Southern Spy,' to be issued weekly in Baltimore. Sabin - 63870 states, 'erroneously attributed to

526　…W.S. Umbaugh. Reprinted, with 3 additional letters, as:

526　…"The Southern Spy. Letters on the Policy & Inauguration of the Lincoln War. Written anonymously in Washington & elsewhere. By Edward A. Pollard, Richmond, Va., West & Johnston, 1861, 12mo, wraps, 103, ivpp. $85.00jk. First edition, Baltimore, 1861, under title "Letters of the Southern Spy," "Notices of the Press," ivpp. at end, 91pp. $100.00-OB.
…Richmond, Va., West & Johnston, 3rd edition, 1862, 16mo, wraps, 118pp.

526a　…"The Weekly Southern Spy; an Account of the events, progress & spirit of the American War." v.1, #1, June 29, 1861. Baltimore, 1861. 8vo, sewn as issued, 20pp. Gdsp. $300. Goodspeed (599)-- "Only 2 known numbers pub., the 2nd July 6, 1861; a 3rd supposed to have been issued but unrecorded. Union lists only 5 copies of this number (only 3 of the 2nd)."

527　…"Life of Jefferson Davis, with a secret history of the Southern Confederacy gathered 'behind the scenes in Richmond.' Containing curious & extraordinary information on the principal connection with President Davis & in relation to the various intrigues of his administration." Phila., Chi., etc., National Pub., 1869, 8vo, cl, front(port), viii, 536pp. $65.00-Jk137.
…N.Y., Arno's 'Select Bibliographies Reprint Series,' 1975.

528　…"Two Nations; a Key to the History of the American War." Richmond, Ayres & Wade, 1864, 8vo, wraps, 16pp. $30.00.

529　…"The War in America, 1863-1864." Author's Edition, London, Saunders, Otley & Co., 1866, 8vo, cl, xv, 407pp. $30.00
Other editions in 1865; 1864 (354pp).
See: Jack P. Maddex, Jr.

530　**POLLARD, Ernest C.**
"Grandfather of Patton lead West Virginia in Reb Army." In: W.Va. State Mag., Dec. 1953, v.5, p.9, 35, 40. On Col. Geo. S. Patton & 22nd Va. Inf. in the Kanawha Valley. Shetler-634.

531　**POLLARD, Henry Robinson**
"Address delivered before Oakwood Memorial Association, Saturday, May 7, 1910. Richmond, Va." Richmond, Va., Whittet & Shepperson, 1910, 8vo, wraps, 16pp. A private in Co. E, 24th Va. Cavalry, Gary's Brigade, A.N.V.

532　…"Addresses delivered at the unveiling of a monument to the memory of Edward Bagby (1842-1864) at Bruington Church, King & Queen County, Virginia, Aug. 8, 1912." Richmond, Va., Everett Waddey Co., 1912, 8vo, wraps, 53pp. (Battle of Petersburg Crater).
See: Confed. Vet., XXVII (Dec.), p.453-458.

533　…"Memoirs & Sketches of the Life of... An Autobiography." Richmond, Va., Lewis Print, 1923, 8vo, cl, xiv, 443pp., pls., tables. Top engr. of C.S.A., p.95-136 CS Service.

534　**POLLARD, W.M.**
"Brief History of the First Tennessee. (Maney's)." In: CV, 1909, v.xvii, p.543-544.

535　**POLLEY, Joseph Benjamin**
"Hood's Texas Brigade, its Marches, its Battles, its Achievements." N.Y., Wash., Neale Pub., 1910, 8vo, cl, pl, ports, incl. front, 347pp. $600.00-Bmk105. $750.00-Bmk.
…Dayton, Oh., Morningside, 1976. Introduction: Richard M. McMurry. $22.50-Y.
…Dayton, Oh., Morningside, 1988. 8vo, cl, 347pp, ills, ports, roster. $30.

536　…"A Soldier's Letters to Charming Nellie." N.Y., Wash., Neale Pub., 1908, 12mo, cl, ports(18), incl. front, vi, (i), (9)-317pp. $450.00-G.
…Louisv., Lost Cause Pr., micro-cd. $5.56. $350.00-Bmk105.

...Baltimore: Butternut Press, 1984. 8vo, cl, dj, 326p. $32.50.

536a **POLSTON, Mike**
"Allison Nelson (1822-62): Atlanta Mayor, Texas hero, Confederate general." In: SHJ, Fall 1985, v.29, p.19-25. [AHJ]

536b **POLSTON, Michael D.**
"Little Rock Did Herself Proud: a History of the 1911 United Confederate Veterans Reunion." In: Pulaski CHR, Summer 1981, v.29, p.22-32.
See: also under UCV-Arkansas.

537 **POMEROY, Earl S.**
"French Substitutes for American Cotton, 1861-1865." Baton Rouge, La., JSH, Nov. 1943, v.IX, #4, p.555-560.

538 **POMFREY, J.W.**
"A True Disclosure & Exposition of the Knights of the Golden Circle, including the secret signs, Grips, & Charges, of the Three Degrees, as Practiced by the Order." Cincinnati, 1861, Privately Printed for Author, v, (6)-47pp., illus., 12mo. Has been attributed to William Henry Smith. Louisville, Lost Cause Pr., micro-cd, $3.95.

539 **POMPEY, Sherman Lee**
"A Brief History of the Independent Arizona Territory Confederate States Battalions in Arizona Territory, 1861-1862." Kingsburg, Calif., Pacific Specialties, Nov. 1971, 4to, 1, (1)-7 lfs.

540 ..."Genealogical Records of the American South." Fresno, Calif., 1968, 4to, 99lfs. Compiled from tax records, US Census, military unit histories, Southern States & CSA." 4to, 28, (71), 1p.

541 ..."An Honor Roll of the members of the First Alabama-Mississippi-Tennessee Infantry, buried at Oakwood Cemetery, Chicago, Ill." Fresno, Calif., c. 1968, 4to, 4 lfs.

542 ..."Muster list of the Alabama Confederate troops." Independence, Calif., Hist. & Geneal. Pub., 1968, 4to, 3 vols.
Vol. 1 - Capt. Goldsmith's Independent Co. Ala. Vol. Inf.; Capt. Gorff's Co. Mobile Pulaski Ala. Rifles; Capt. Gueringer's Co. Ala. Mil., Hardy's Co., Eufala Ala., Minute Men; Capt. Charles A. Hert's Co., Mobile Ala, Infty.
Vol. 2 - Capt. Thomas Hunt's Ala. Militia; Capt. Lee Jr.'s Co. Ala. Vols.; Capt. L.I. Lockett's Co. Ala. City Guards; Capt. Meador's Co. Ala. Vols.
Vol. 3 - John Oden's Co. Ala. Vols.; Capt. Orr's Co. Morgan Alabama Defenders; Capt. Palmers Co., Ala. State Reserves; Capt. Young's Co. Ala. Nitre & Mining Corps.

543 ..."Muster List of Arkansas Confederate Troops, Independence, Calif., Hist. & Geneal. Pub., 1965, 4to, 2 vols.,
Vol. 1 - Capt. Ballard's Co. Ark. Infty; Clear Lake Indp. Guards Ark Infty, Capt. Perry Clayton's Co. Ark. Infty.; Capt. Ernest's Co. Ark., Capt. Hutchinson's Co. Davis Blues Ark., Infty.
Vol. 2 - Keykendall's Co. Ark. Infty.; G.W. Louis Co., Ark. Militia; Spark's Ark. Infty: Capt. Willett's Co., Little Rock Provost Guards.

544 ..."Burial Lists of the Independent Arkansas Confederate Regiments." Kingsburg, Calif., Pacific Specialists, 1972, 4to, 6 lfs.

545 ..."Burial lists of the Miscellaneous Arkansas independent Cavalry Regiments, CSA. Kingsburg, Calif., Pacific Specialists, 1972, 4to, 5 lfs.

546 ..."Some Civil War Veterans buried in Arkansas." Fresno, Calif., c. 1969, 4to, 10 lfs.

547 ..."Burial List of the members of the First Arkansas Cav., CSA. Kingsburg, Calif., Pacific Specialties, 1972, 4to, 3 lfs.

548 ...Burial list of the members of the First (Crawford's Arkansas Cavalry), CSA. Kingsburg, Calif., Pacific Specialties, 1972, 4to, 3 lfs.

549 ..."Burial members of the members of the 1st (Dobbins') Arkansas Cavalry, CSA." Kingsburg, Calif., Pacific Specialties, 1972, 4to, 2 lfs.

550 ..."Burial List of the members of the 1st (Monroe's) Arkansas Cavalry, CSA." Kingsburg, Calif., 1972, 4to, 2 lfs.

551 ..."Burial list of the members of the 7th (Hill's) Arkansas Cavalry, CSA." Kingsburg, Calif., 1972, 4to, 2 lfs.

552 ..."Burial List of members of the 1st Arkansas Infantry, CSA." Kingsburg, Calif. Pacific Specialties, 1972, 4to, 3 lfs.

553 ..."Burial List of members of the 2nd Arkansas Infantry, CSA." Kingsburg, Calif., Pacific Specialties, 1972, 4to, 2 lfs.

554 ..."Burial List of members of the 8th Arkansas infantry, CSA." Kingsburg, Calif., Pacific Specialties, 1972, 4to, 2 lfs.

555 ..."Burial List of members of the 10th Arkansas Infantry, CSA." Kingsburg, Calif., Pacific Specialties, 1972, 4to, 2 lfs.

556 ..."Burial List of members of the 11th Arkansas Infantry, CSA." Kingsburg, Calif., Pacific Specialties, 1972, 4to, 2 lfs.

557 ..."Burial List of members of the 12th Arkansas Infantry, CSA." Kingsburg, Calif., Pacific Specialties, 1972, 4to, 2 lfs.

558 ..."Burial List of members of the 15th (Johnson's) Arkansas Infantry, CSA." Kingsburg, Calif., Pacific Specialties, 1972, 4to, 4 lfs.

559 ..."Burial List of members of the 19th Arkansas Infantry, CSA." Kingsburg, Calif., Pacific Specialties, 1972, 4to, 6 lfs.

560 ..."Burial List of members of the 24th Arkansas Infantry, CSA." Kingsburg, Calif., Pacific Specialties, 1972, 4to, 3 lfs.

561 ..."Burial List of the members of the 36th (Glenn's) Arkansas Infantry, CSA." Kingsburg, Calif., Pacific Specialties, 1972, 4to, 2 lfs.

562 ..."Burial List of the members of the 37th (Bell's) Arkansas Infantry, CSA." Kingsburg, Calif., Pacific Specialties, 1972, 4to, 3 lfs.

563 ..."Muster List of the American rifles of Maryland, Baltimore Artly, Maryland Guerilla Zouaves & Capt. Walter's Co. Maryland Zarvona Zouaves of the Confederacy." Independence, Calif., Hist. & Geneal. Pub., 1965, 4to, 4 lfs.

564 ..."Muster list of Cherokee Confederate Indians." Independence, Calif., Hist. & Geneal. Pub., 1965, 4to, 3 lfs.

565 ..."Muster List of the Creek & other Confederate Indains." Bakersfield, Calif., Hist. & Geneal. Pub., 1966, 4to, 9 lfs.

566 ..."Burial Lists of the Confederate government Infantry Regiments." Kingsburg, Calif., Pacific Specialists, 1972, 4to, 4 lfs.

567 ..."Burial List of the 2,436 Confederate Soldiers, mostly taken prisoners of war at the Battle of Gettysburg, Pa., interned as prisoners of war at Fort Delaware on Pea Patch Island, & interred in Finn's Point National Cemetery, near Salem, N.J." Harrisburg, Ore., Pacific Specialties, 1975, 4to, 53 folios.

568 ..."Civil War veteran burial listings. Long Beach, California, Southern California Genealogical Society, 1965, 12 vols., 4to. V.4: Covering men in regiments of the Cherokee Indians (Confederate States), Dakotas, Neb. & Tex. V. 9: Covering men in regiments from Missouri Union & Confederates Infantry, state militia. V.11: Covering men in regiments from Ark. & La. V.12: Covering Confederates, regiments unknown.

569 ..."Civil War veteran burials: Confederate Government Troops." Clovis, Calif., 1970, 4to, cover title, 5 lfs.

570 ..."Confederate Soldiers buried in Colorado." Independence, Calif., Historical & Genealogical Pub. Co., c.1965, 4to, cover title, 19 lfs.

571 ..."Confederates buried in Illinois." Clovis, Calif., 1970. Vol. 1: Louisiana; Vol. 2: South Carolina.

572 ..."Col. P.T. Herbert's Battalion, Arizona Cavalry, CSA." Independence, Calif., Hist. & Genealog. Pub., 1965, 4to, 6 lfs.

573 ..."Civil War Veteran Burials from Florida." Fresno, Calif., c. 1968, 4to, 12 lfs.

574 ..."Cross Reference of local Florida Confederate units & their Regimental Designations." Kingsburg, Calif., Pacific Specialties, December, 1971, 4to, (1). (1)-3 lfs.

575 ..."Civil War Veterans Burials of Georgia Confederate Regiments." n.p., 1970, 4to, iii, 20 lfs.

576 ..."Some Mississippi Civil War Veteran's Burials." Clovis, Calif., 1970, 4to, 2 lfs.

577 ..."Burial List of Missouri Confederate Artillerymen." Kingsburg, Calif., Pacific Specialties, January, 1972, 4to, (2) lfs.

578 ..."Burial List of members of the 1st Missouri Cavalry, CSA." Kingsburg, Calif., Pacific Specialties, January 1972, 4to, (1), (1)-2 lfs.

579 ..."Burial List of members of the 1st Northeast Missouri Cavalry, CSA." Kingsburg, Calif., Pacific Specialties, January 1972, 4to, (2) lfs.

580 ..."Burial List of members of the 2nd Missouri Cavalry, CSA." Kingsburg, Calif., Pacific Specialties, January 1972, 4to, (2) lfs.

581 ..."Burial List of members of the 3rd Missouri Cavalry, CSA." Kingsburg, Calif., Pacific Specialties, January 1972, 4to, (1), (1)-2 lfs.

582 ..."Burial List of members of the 4th Missouri Cavalry, CSA." Kingsburg, Calif., Pacific Specialties, January 1972, 4to, (2) lfs.

583 ..."Burial List of members of the Independent Missouri Cavalry Regiments, CSA." Kingsburg, Calif., Pacific Specialties, February 1972, 4to, (4) lfs.

584 ..."Burial List of members of Poindexter's Missouri Cavalry, CSA." Kingsburg, Calif., Pacific Specialties, January 1971, 4to, (2) lfs.

585 ..."Burial List of members of Porter's Missouri Cavalry, CSA." Kingsburg, Calif., Pacific Specialties, January 1972, 4to, (2) lfs.

586 ..."Muster list of the Missouri Confederates." Independence, Calif., Hist. & Geneal. Pub., 1965, (Vols. 5-9 have Bakersfield imprint), 4to, 9 vols.
Vol. 1 - Capt. Moses Beck's Co. Mo. Cav.; Capt. John N. Hick's Co. Mo. Cav.; Capt. J. S. Hibb's Co. Mo. Cav. (Franklin's Reg.); Capt. Wm. C. Quantrill's Mo. Cav. Scouts.
Vol. 2 - Capt. D.R. Stallard's Co. Mo. Cavalry.
Vol. 3 - Capt. Barrett's Co. Mo. Light Artilly.; Capt. Lowe's Co. (Jackson Batt.) Mo. Artlly.
Vol. 4 - Hunter's Mo. Cav.; Jackson's Mo. Cav.; Lawther's Mo. Partisan Rangers; Lt. Hamilton Prairie Gun Batt., Mo. Light Artlly.
Vol. 5 - Capt. E.W. Price's Co. Mo. State Guards, Capt. T.H. Walton's Co. Mo. State Guards; Capt. W.S. Richardson's Co. Mo. State Guards; Capt. W.S. Richardson's Co. Mo. State Guards; Mo. Border Guards Co. Mo. State Guards. Marion Artillery Mo. State Guards; Silver Greys Co. Mo. State Guards; Capt. James W. Kneisley's Co. Mo. State Guards; Capt. Feagan's Co. Mo. State Guards; Capt. Lycurgus James' Co. Mo. State Guards; Capt. Wm. B. Brown's Co. Mo. State Guards;
Vol. 6 - Capt. C.M. Johnson's Co. Mo. State Guards; Capt. Hiram Bledsoe's Batt. Mo. State Guards; Capt. James Synnamon's Co. Mo. State Guards; Capt. James E. Withers' Co. Mo. State Guards; Capt. Robert Ruxton's Co. Mo. State

Guards, Capt. Edward J. Brown's Co. Mo. State Guards.

Vol. 7 - Capt. F.M. Cockrell's Co. Mo. State Guards; Capt. O.A. Waddell's Co. Mo. State Guards; Capt. H. Mile's Co. Mo. State Guards; Capt. Mack Newton's Co. Mo. State Guards; Capt. Leonidas St. Clair (Dick) Campbell's Co. Mo. State Guards; Capt. John Sappington Marmaduke's Co. Saline Jackson Guards Mo. State Guards; Capt. T.W.B. Crew's Co.

Vol. 8 - Capt. Thomas Flood's Co. Mo. State Guards; Capt. Ben Eli Guthrie's Co. Mo. State Guards; Capt. Masten G. Corlew Co. Mo. State Guards; Capt. S.J. Talbot's Co. Mo. State Guards; Capt. Robert J. Williams Co. Mo. State Guards; Capt. Kelsey McDowell's Co. Mo. State Guards; Capt. W.W. Williams Co. Moniteau Rangers Mo. State Guards.

Vol. 9 - Capt. Charles Haggerty's Mo. State Guards; Vernon County Batt. Mo. State Guards; Capt. George William Sandusky's Co. Mo. State Guards; Capt. Joseph Moreland's Co. Mo. State Guards; Capt. George Butler's Co. Mo. State Guards; Capt. R.J. Wickersham's Co. Mo. State Guards; Capt. V.B. Hill's Mo. State Guards, Capt. W.L. Jeffer's Co. Mo. State Guards; Capt. E.T. Wingo's Co. Mo. State Guards.

587 ..."Some Civil War Veterans burials in North Carolina." Fresno, Calif., c.1969, 4to, 26lfs.

588 ..."A List of Confederate Civil War Veterans buried in Cabarrus County, N.C." W. Sacramento, Calif., Pacific Specialties, November, 1972, 4to, (1), (1)-6lfs.

589 ..."Some Civil War Veterans buried in Cleveland, Davidson, Davie, Gaston, Henderson, Iredell, Stanly & Stokes Counties, N.C." W. Sacramento, Calif., Pacific Specialties, November, 1972, 4to, (1)-lfs.

590 ..."Tennessee Confederates buried in Illinois." Clovis, Calif., 1970, 4to, 9lfs.

591 ..."Burial Lists of the Members of the 1st through 14th Texas Cavalry, CSA." Kingsburg, Calif., Pacific Specialists, 1972, 4to, 4lfs.

592 ..."Burial Lists of the Members of the 1st through 5th Texas Infantry, CSA." Kingsburg, Calif., Pacific Specialties, 1972, 4to, 3lfs.

593 ..."Burial Lists of the Members of the 6th Texas Infantry, CSA, who died as Union Prisoners of War & were buried in Camp Butler National Cemetery, Springfield, Illinois." Kingsburg, Calif., Pacific Specialties, 1972, 4to, 3lfs.

594 ..."Burial List of the Members of the 7th Texas Infantry, CSA, who died as Union prisoners of war buried in Oakwood Cemetery, Chicago, Illinois." Kingsbury, Calif., Pacific Specialties, April, 1972, 4to, (1), (1)-3lfs.

595 ..."Burial List of Members of the 8th & 9th Texas Infantry, CSA, who died as Union Prisoners of War & buried in Oakwood Cemetery, Chicago, Illinois." Kingsburg, Calif.,m Pacific Specialties, April, 1972, 4to, 3lfs.

596 ..."Burial List of Members of the 10th Texas Infantry, CSA, who died as Union Prisoners of War & buried in Oakwood Cemetery, Chicago, Illinois." Kingsburg, Calif., Pacific Specialties, April 1972, 4to, (1), (1)-3lfs.

597 ..."Burial List of Members of the 11th-14th Texas Infantry, CSA, who died as Union Prisoners of war & buried in Oakwood Cemetery, Chicago, Illinois." Kingsburg, Calif., Pacific Specialties, April 1972, 4to, (1), (1)-2lfs.

598 ..."Burial List of the Members of the 15th Texas Cavalry, CSA, who died as Union Prisoners of War & were buried at Oakwood Cemetery, Chicago, Illinois."

	Kingsburg, Calif., Pacific Specialties, 1972, 4to, 4lfs.
599	..."Burial Lists of the members of the 16th Texas Cavalry, CSA, who died as Union Prisoners of War & were buried in Oakwood Cemetery, Chicago, Illinois." Kingsburg, Calif., Pacific Specialties, 1972, 4to, 2lfs.
600	..."Burial List of the members of the 17th Texas Cavalry, CSA, who died as Union Prisoners of War & were buried in Oakwood Cemetery, Chicago, Illinois." Kingsburg, Calif., Pacific Specialties, 1972, 4to, 4lfs.
601	..."Burial List of members of the 18th Texas Cavalry, CSA, who dies as Union Prisoners of War & were buried in Oakwood Cemetery, Chicago, Illinois." Kingsburg, Calif., Pacific Specialties, April 1972, 4to, (1), (1)-3, (1)lfs., 1p. addl. - "19th Texas Cavalry, Co.D."
602	..."Organization of Brigadier General Henry Hopkins Sibley's Texas Brigade, CSA, in the Arizona Territory, 1861-1862." Kingsburg, Calif., Pacific Specialties, December 1971, 4to.
603	..."Muster List of the Texas Confederate Troops." Independence, Calif., Hist. & Geneal. Pub., 4to, 8 vols., 1966. Vol. 1 - Capt. Coopwood's Spy Co. Texas Cav.; Capt. Bone's Co. Texas Cav.; Capt. Doughty's Co. Texas State Cav. (Refugio Spies); Capt. Durant's Co. Texas Cav.; Capt. Lilly's Co. Texas Cavalry. Vol. 2 - Capt. Samuel J. McDowell's Texas State Guards Cav.; Capt. Nolan's Mounted Co. Texas Cav.' Capt. Pearson's Co. Texas Partisan Rangers; Capt. Ragsdale's Co. Texas Cav.; Capt. W.H. Randolph's Co. Texas Cav.; Capt. J.F. Spear's Lavaca Co. Minute Men Texas Cavalry. Vol. 3 - Capt. Sutton's Co. Texas Cav.; Capt. Terry's Mounted Co. Texas State Troops Cav.; Capt. Thomas' Co. Texas Partisan Rangers; Capt. Justo Trevino's Squad Texas Partisan Rangers; Capt. Upton Co. Texas Cavalry. Vol. 4 - Carter's Austin City Texas Light Infty.; Capt. Maxey's Co. Texas Light Infty. & Riflemen (lamar Rifles); Capt, McMinn's Co., Collin Co. Texas Local Defense Infty.; Capt. McNeel's Co. Texas Coast Guard Defense Troops; Capt. Merriman's Orange Co. Coast Guard Troops Local Defense Troops. Vol. 5 - Capt. Patrick Perry's Fort Bend Scouts Texas Local Defense; Capt. Raineys Co. Anderson Co. Invincibles Texas Vols., Capt. Rutherford's Co. Texas Infty.; Capt. Simm's Co. Texas Home Guards Infty. Vol. 6 - Capt. Edgar's Co. Alamo City State Guards Texas Infty.; Capt. Gould's Texas State Troops Infty. (Clarksville Light Infty.); Capt. Graham's Co. Mounted Coast Guards Texas State Troops; Capt. Hampton's Co. Texas State Troops (Victoria Blues); Capt. Killough's Co. Wheelock Texas Home Guards. Vol. 7 - Capt. Cotton's Co. Sabine Texas Vol. Infty.; Capt. Ed H. Cunningham's Texas Infty.; Capt. Currie's Co. Texas Infty. Vol. 8 - Capt. Arnold's Co. Texas Militia Riflemen; Capt. Charles Atkin's Co. Texas State Troops; Capt. Benton's Co. Texas Vol. Brazoria Co. Minute Men; Capt. Watt Cameron's Co. Texas Infantry.
604	..."Burial List of Members of 24th Texas Cavalry, CSA, who died as Union Prisoners of War & buried in Camp Butler National Cemetery, Springfield, Illinois." Kingsburg, Calif., Pacific Specialties, 1972, 4to, (1), (1)-4lfs.
605	..."Burial List of the members of the 25th Texas Cavalry, CSA, who died as Union Prisoners of War & who were buried in

Camp Butler National Cemetery, Springfield, Illinois." Kingsburg, Calif., Pacific Specialties, 1972, 4to, 5lfs.

606 ..."Burial Lists of the Miscellaneous Local Texas Confederate Regiments who died as Union Prisoners of war & were duried in Oakwood Cemetery, Chicago, Illinois." Kingsburg, Calif., Pacific Specialties, 1972, 4to, 3lfs.

607 ..."Register of the Civil War dead; Virginia Confederate Regiments." Clovis, Calif., 1970, 4to, 15lfs.

608 **POND, Cornelia Jones**
"Life on a Liberty County Plantation, The Journal of..., Edited by Josephine Bacon Martin." Darien, Ga., 1974, Ashantilley Press, 8vo, 146pp., lim., 1,000 copies. Georgia during the Civil War.

609 **POND, George Edward**
"Review of W. Allan's 'Shenandoah Valley in 1864.' In: SHSP, 1883,v.11, p.270-282.

610 **POOL, William C.**
"The Battle of Dove Creek." In: SwHQ, April 1950, v.LIII, #4, p.367-385, roster. Controversal conflict between CSA troops and the Kickapoos.

611 **POOLMAN, Kenneth**
"The Alabama Incident." London, William Kimber, 1958, 8vo, cl, d/w, illus., 203pp. (5)pp. ads.

611a **POPE and the Confederacy, The ...**
See: Jefferson Davis, Judge Robert L. Rodgers, Father Jerome.

612 **POPE, Edith**
"Sam Davis Tennessee's Boy Hero of the Sixties (quote) The home of Sam Davis at Smyrna, Tennessee near Nashville. The two-story colonial house & grounds are a state shrine. Under management of the Sam Davis Memorial Association, Smyrna, Tenn." (Nahsville, Tenn.?), n.d. (c.1930), small 4to, wraps, cover title (illus.), plates, 13, (1).

613 ..."The Necessity of preserving Southern Historical Material." In: Tenn. Hist. Mag., ser. 2, 1935, v.III, p.152-159.

614 **POPPENHEIM, Mary Barnett, et al**
"History of the United Daughters of the Confederacy." Maude Blake Merchant, Ruth Jennings Lawton, Chm., by authority granted in convention at Hot Springs, Ark., 1925, Richmond, Va., Garrett & Massie, 1938, 8vo, cl, xi, 226pp., illus. $20.00-Bmk84.

615 ..."History of the United Daughters of the Confederacy, 1894-1955." Ruth Jennings Lawton, v. 2, Mrs. Albert Lee Thompson. Raleigh, N.C., Edwards & Broughton, 1956, 8vo, cl, (18), 226, (10), 227-391pp. 2 vol. in 1. 30-B. $20.00-Bmk84.

616 **POPULAR Confederate War Songs.**
Dedicated to the Armies of the South." Richmond, Va., Whittet & Shepperson, 1907, 12mo, stiff wraps (color flag), 24, (1)p. $10.00.

617 **PORCHER, Frederick Adolphus, Prof.**
"Address before the Association of Survivors of the Confederate Surgeons, of South Carolina, at the Annual Meeting held at Columbia, S.C., Nobember, 1889. by... Surgeon of the Holcombe Legion, to the Confederate Hospital, Ft. Nelson, Norfolk Harbor, & the South Carolina Hospital, Petersburg, Va." Charleston, S.C., Walker, Evans & Cogswell, 1890, 8vo, wraps, 14pp. From: SHSP, 1889, v. XVII, p.12-21.

618 ..."A Brief History of the Ladies' Memorial Association of Charleston, from its beginning in 1865 to April 1, 1890. Together with a roster of the Confederate dead, interred at Magnolia & the various city churchyards." Charleston, S.C., H.P. Cooke Co., 1880, 8vo, wraps, 42pp. Reprinted: Charleston Yeqrbook for 1944. Notes: Mary A. Sparkman, p. 203-215. See: Samuel G. Stoney 'Memoirs."

619 …"Resources of Southern Fields & Forests, Medical, Economical, & Agricultural. Being also a medical botany of the Confederate States; with practical information on the useful properties of the trees, plants & shrubs. Prepared & published by order of the Surgeon-General. Richmond, Va." Charleston, Evans & Cogswell, 1863, 8vo, cl, xxv, 601pp. $37.50. $100.00. $950.00-Jk135.
…Richmond, Va., West & Johnston, 1863, 8vo, cl, xxv, 594pp. $1,500.00 - $1,000.00-Carolina NR.

620 …"Prospectus broadsheet on Southern Fields & Forests," issued by publisher, sq. 4to, p.3, 1869.
…Another folio broadside, with reviews & comments, 1869.
See: Jonathan M. Townsend.
…New York, reprint edition by Arno Press, 1970, 8vo, cl, dj, xxv, 601pp. $46.50. Porcher was generally accurate taxonomically. Still practical & applicable.

621 **PORT HUDSON**
See: Howard C. Wright
Milledge Bonham
James H. M'Neilly
Preston, Francis W.
W.H. Pascoe, Marshall
J. Smith, et al

622 **PORT ROYAL FERRY, S.C.**
"Report of Affair at Port Royal Ferry on 1st January, 1862, J.C. Pemberton, Brigadier-General, commanding." n.p., (1862?), 8vo, sewn, 21pp. (Henkel #1090, May 1913).

623 **PORTER, Anthony Toomer, Rev.**
"Led on! Step by Step, scenes from clerical, military, educational & plantation life in the South, 1828-1898, an autobiography." N.Y., C.P. Putnam's Sons, 1898, 8vo, cl, illus., ports., xv, 462pp. $30.00. $60.00.
…Same, 1899.
…Charleston, S.C., Porter-Gaud Books, 1969, Limited Edt., 100th Anniversary.

624 …"In Memoriam Gen. Joseph E. Johnston Services by Request of the Survivors Association of Charleston District at the Church of the Holy Communion, Sunday evening, April 26, 1891. Sermon by Rev. A.T. Porter." Charelston, Walker, Evans & Cogswell, 1891, 8vo, wraps, 26pp.

625 …"A History of a work of faith & love in Charleston, S.C., which grew out of the Calamities of the late Civil War, & is a record of God's wonderful providence. Institution founded by Rev. A. Toomer Porter, 1868, 3rd edition brought down to October 1, 1880." N.Y., D. Appleton & Co., 1881, 8vo, cl, 200pp. Contains a good account of the burning of Columbia, S.C., by Federals.

626 **PORTER, Charles**
"Charles Porter's Account of the Confed. Attempt to Seize Arizona & New Mexico." Edt.: Alwyn Barr, Austin, Texas, Pemberton Press, 1964, 8vo, cl, 33pp., OP. $9.50. U.S. Inf., acct. of Sibley's raid, Scurry.

627 **PORTER, D.S., Edt.**
"Three Unpublished Conversations with Nassau Senior." In: Bodleian Lib. Record, 1964, v.VII, p.122-133. (Conversations with the British economist with three Americans on the course of the war & the future of the C.S.A.

628 **PORTER, David Dixon**
"Lee's Birthday." In: SHSP, 1889, v.17, p.349.

629 **PORTER, Duval**
"The Lost Cause, & Other Poems." Danville, Va., Blair & Boatwright, 1897, 8vo, wraps, 96pp. (Swem).

630 …"Lyrics of the Lost Cause." (Danville, Va., 1914), J.T. Townes Print, 12mo, cl, 150pp., #25. $40.00.

631 **PORTER, G.W.D.**
"Nine Months in a Northern Prison." In: Annals Army of Tenn., Early Western Hist., 1878, v.1, p.157-162.

632 **PORTER, George Alexander, Jr.**
"General Robert E. Lee of the Confederacy; a condensation of the life of Robert E. Lee." Pembroke, Mass., 1961, Porter's Civil War Museum, 8vo, wraps, illus., 72pp.

633 **PORTER, Horace**
"Incidents of the Surrender (Appomattox)." In: CV, Oct. 1923, v.XXXI, p.373-375.

634 ..."Lee's Surrender at Appomattox." In: Outlook, Dec. 22, 1906, v.LXXXIV, p.970-976.

635 **PORTER, I. M., Miss (of Ala.)**
"Brigadier General John Herbert Kelly, Sketch of." In: LWL, March, 1868, v.IV, #5, p.373-377.

636 **PORTER, James Davis**
"An Address Delivered at the inveiling of Henry County Confederate Monument, Paris, Tennessee, Sat. Oct. 13, 1900." Paris, Tenn., Post Intelligencer Print, 1900, 12mo, wraps, 24pp., incl. front(port), Tenn. State Library.

637 ..."Tennessee, by James D. Porter." Atlanta, Ga., Confederate Publishing Co., 1899, 8vo, cl, or 3/4lt., maps (1-fldg), plans (1-dbl), ports., iv, 348pp., v.VIII. Extended Edt: Additional Biographical sketches & portraits, 487pp. $125.00-Bmk. $100.00.
..."Tennessee." v.X. 8vo, cl, 806pp. Wilmington, N.C., Broadfoot, 1987.
..."Tennessee. Confederate Military History." n.p., 1970s. Blue & Gray Press. 8vo, cl, dj, 348pp. $10.
..."Tennessee." v.X Extended Edition. Wilmington, N.C., Broadfoot Pub., 1987. 8vo, cl, 806pp, ills, ports, fldg. map.

638 ..."Correspondence between Gov. Porter & Major Sykes concerning Reynolds Brigade." In: SHSP, 1884, v.XII, p.45-48.

639 ..."A Sketch of the life & Services of Gen. B.F. Cheatham." In: SB, 1883/1884, v.II, port. p.145-150.

640 **PORTER, John Luke**
"Plan & Construction of the 'Merrimac.'" In: B&L, N.Y., Century, 1887, v.I, p.716-717. CS Naval officer who built the ship.

641 **PORTER, John W.H.**
"A Record of Events in Norfolk County, Va., from Apr. 19, 1861, to May 10, 1862, with a history of the soldiers & sailors of Norfolk County, Norfolk City & Portsmouth, who served in the Confederate States Army & Navy, by..., a comrade of Stonewall camp, Confederate veteran, of Portsmouth, Va." Portsmouth, Va., W.A. Fiske Print, 1892, 8vo, cl, 366pp. $130.00. $100.00-Bmk.

642 ..."The Confederate Soldier." In: CV, Oct. 1916, v.XXIV, p.460-461.

643 **PORTER, Kenneth W.**
"Billy Bowlegs (Holata Micco) in the Civil War." In: FHQ, April 1967, v.XLV, #4, p.391-401.

643a **PORTER, M. E., Mrs.**
"The Novel of the Century. Captain Trueman's last prisoner, a tale of the sixties." Chicago: John N. Reynolds (1909). 12mo, cl, 1p,(5)-135p. Mrs. Porter also wrote a New Southern cookery book . . . (1871).

644 **PORTER, Mel-Inda Jennie, Mrs.**
"Valkyria, or, Chaplets of Mars." N.Y., W.B. Smith Co., 1881, 12mo, wraps, 3pp., (5)-133pp. Epic of a fallen South.

644a **PORTER, Patrick G.**
"Advertising in the Early Cigarette Industry: W. Duke & Sons, Co., Durham (N.C.)" In: NCHR, Winter 1971, v.48, #1, p.31-43. Collection at Duke University,

645 **PORTER, R.R.**
"Maj. John R. McDonald (Alabama Confederate Officer)" In: CV, 1902, v.10, p.122-123, port.

646 **PORTER, Rufus Kilpatrick**
"Sketch of General T.R.R. Cobb." In: LWL, v.III, July 1867, p.183-197.

647 **PORTER, Thomas Kennedy**
"Capture of the Confederate Steamer Florida by US Steamer Wachusett." In: SHSP, 1884, v.12, p.39-45.

648 **PORTER, W.C.**
"War Diary of W.C. Porter. Edited by J.V. Frederick." In: AHQ, 1952, v.XI, pp. 286-314.

649 **PORTER, William Denison**
"An Account of the Revival of the Co." See under "Washington Light Inf. of Charl."

650 ..."Oration delivered at the Academy of Music, on the occasion of the sixty-sixth Anniversary of the Washington Light infantry Rifle Club, Feb. 22, 1873." Charleston, Walker, Evans, & Cogswell, 1873, 8vo, wraps, 35pp. 98pp. O'Brien Copy $75.00.

651 ..."Mr. Douglas & the doctrine of coercion. Together with letters from Hon. Herschel V. Johnson, formerly Secretary of the Navy." Charleston, 1860, 8vo, sewn, 24pp. Sig: "Rutledge," pub. anon., head: "1860 Association Tract #2."

652 ..."Separate State Secession, practically discussed, in a series of articles published originally in the Edgefield Advertiser by "Rutledge"." Edgefield, S.C., Advertiser Print, 1851, 8vo, sewn, 42pp. Turnbull-III, p.131.

653 ...Edgefield Court House, S.C., Advertiser Print, 1860, 8vo, sewn, 38pp, Turnbull-III, p.316.

1,700 loose advertising premiums. Ills, facsms. See: W. Duke.

654 ..."State Sovereignty & the Doctrine of Coercion, by the Hon. Wm. D. Porter together with a letter from Hon. J.K. Pualding, former Sec. of Navy. The Right to Secede, by "States." Read & send to your neighbor." Head: "1860 Association Tract, #2." Charleston, S.C., Evans & Cogswell, 1860. $20.00. 8vo, 36pp. $65.00-Jk122. $100.00-G.
...Another edition, 1860, pp.34. The Tract warns "well nigh certain elect: Lincoln will force a war of extermination, urges Southern states secede & fight."

655 ..."In Memoriam William Denison Porter born Nov. 24, 1810. Died Jan. 5, 1883." Charleston, S.C., News & Courier, 1883, 8vo, wraps, 37pp. Special order #1, & proceedings of a meeting Washington Light Infantry, Feb. 5, 1883. Turnbull IV - p.157.

656 ..."Proceedings of the Washington Light Infantry on the death of Wm. D. Porter." Charleston, S.C., News & Courier, 1883, 100 copies for Mr. William A. Courtenay. Turnbull IV-p.162.

657 ..."Ceremonies at unveiling of the bronze bust of Wm. Gilmore Simms at White Point Garden, Charleston, S.C., June 11, 1879. Address of Hon. W.D. Porter. Charleston, News & Courier, 1879, 37pp.

658 **PORTERFIELD, George Alexander**
"A Narrative of the Service of Colonel Geo. A. Porterfield in Northwestern Virginia in 1861-1862." In: SHSP, 1888, v.16, p.82-91.

659 **PORTIS, John C.**
"Resaca's Bloody Field. Interesting Reminiscences of a Confederate Soldier." n.p., 1896, 8vo, wraps, p.4. Owen's Miss. p.787.

660 **PORTSMOUTH ARTILLERY**
"Shaft to the Portsmouth Artillery." In: SHSP, 1906, v.34, p.144-161, Portsmouth, Va., 'Star.'
See: Capt. John H. Thompson.

661 **PORTSMOUTH, Virginia, Trinity Church**
"The Memorial Window in Trinity Church, Portsmouth, Virginia." In: SHSP, 1891, v.19, p.207-212.

662 **POSEY, Carnot, Gen.**
"Report: Battle of Gettysburg." In: SHSP, 1880, v.8, p.322-323.

663 **POST, John Eager Howard**
"Letter to his mother, June 17, 1862." In: MHM, 1945, v.XL, p.290-294.

664 **POSTAGE STAMPS**
See: Julius B. Baumgarten.
Or: Philately.

665 **POSTER ,**
Recruiting Office Poster, Knoxville, Tenn., Nov. 16, 1863 to the Enrolling Office-District- County. Adjutant & Inspector General's Office Richmond, Nov. 8, 1862, Gen. Ord. #82. The following Acts of Congress & Regulations are Published for the information of all concerned." 1-page, folio.

666 **POTTER, David M.**
"The South & the Sectional Conflict." Baton Rouge, La. State Univ. Print, 1968, 8vo, cl, d/w, xvi, 322pp.

667 ..."On Understanding the South: A Review Article." Houston, Tex., JSH, Nov. 1964, v.XXX, #4, p.451-462.

668 ..."Jefferson Davis & the political factors in Confederate defeat." In: David Donald's "Why the North Won the Civil War." Baton Rouge, Louisiana University Press, 1960, p.91-114.

668a **POTTER, Jerry O'Neil**
"The First West Tennessee Raid of Nathan Bedford Forrest." In: WTennHSP, 1974, #26, p.55-74.

669 **POTTS, Eugenia Dunlap, Mrs.**
"Historic papers on the causes of the Civil War. Read before the Lexington Chapter UDC, Feb. 14, 1909." Lexington, Ky., Ashland Print, 1909, 8vo, wraps, cover title, (37)pp.

670 **POTTS, Frank**
"The Death of the Confederacy; the last week of the Army of Northern Virginia as set forth in a letter of April 1865, by Frank Potts, Captain Confederate States Army, staff of Lieut.-Gen. James Longstreet. Edt: with foreword by Douglas Southall Freeman." Richmond, Va., Private print for A. Potts, 1928, 8vo, wraps, 15pp. $300.00-Rowe. $150.00-Bmk105. New facts regarding details of surrender at Appomattox.

671 **POTTS, J.N.**
"Hard Fighting Virginians." In: CV, July 1905, v.13, p.306. Death of Col. D.B. Land, 62nd Virginia.

672 ..."That Battle at Philippi." In: CV, September, 1898, v.6, p.424.

673 **POULAIN, Ernest**
"La Crise Americaine. Recueil de Documents pouvant servir a l'Histoire de la Guerre des Etats-Unis, 1859, 1860, 1862. Le Nord et le Sud." paris, E. Dentu, 1863, 8vo, cl, 174pp.

674 ...Deuxieme Edition, Paris, G. Guerin, 1863.

675 **POUNCING on Pickets,**
bold dash of a detachment of the 9th Virginia Cavalry." In: SHSP, 1896, v.XXIV, p.213-218.

676 **POWE, James Harrington**
"Reminiscences & Sketches of Confederate Times. by one who lived through them. Edited by Harriet Powe Lynch, Cheraw, S.C., Columbia, S.C., R.L. Bryan, 1909, tall 8vo, wraps, 44pp.

677 **POWELL, C.H., Co. F., 4th Va.Cav.**
"Goochland Light Dragoons, organization & first outpost experience, the Roll." In: SHSP, 1896, v.24, p.359-361.

678 **POWELL, Edward Payson**
"Nullification & Secession in the United

States. A History of the Six Attempts During the First Century of the Republic." N.Y., G.P. Putnams Sons, 1897, small 8vo, cl, xi, 461pp. $17.50. "It is time to deal justly by the South."

679 POWELL, Junius L.
"A Memory of our Great War." In: Jour. Mil. Ser. Inst., Jan. 1911, v.XLVIII, p.87-99. CSA Officer at Battle of Deep Bottom, Aug. 16, 1864.

680 POWELL, Lawrence N.
"New Masters: Northern Planters during the Civil War & Reconstruction." New Haven, Conn., Yale University Pr., 1980, 8vo, cl, dj, xiv, 253pp. $22.50.

681 POWELL, Morgan A.
"Col. Thomas J. Morgan - Country's highest ranking Confederate soldier." In: Indp. Co. (Ark. Chron.), 1966, v.VII, #2, p.2-15.

682 POWELL, Morgan Allen
"Cotton for the Relief of Confederate Prisoners." In: CWH, Marck, 1963, v.IV, #1, p.24-35.

682a POWER, J. Tracy
"Edward Willis Young & full of promise." In: CWTI, Apr, 1979, v.18, #1, ills, ports, p.22-7.

683 POWER, William H., Col.
"A Memoir of Colonel William H. Power." In: SHSP, 1928, v.46, p.v-xii.

683a POWERS, John M.
"That Terrible First Day (Shiloh)." In: Mil. Hist., Oct. 1984, p.38-43.

684 POWERS, John Wesley
"Report of a corporal of the Alabama First infantry on talk & fighting along Mississippi, 1862-1863. Edt: Robert Partin." In: AlaHQ, Winter 1958, v.20, p.583-594. Notes. Excerpts & paraphrases of 5 letters to Linn B. Sanders of Auburn, Ala., Holly Springs & Port Hudson, 20 Oct. 1862 - 17 March 1863.

684a POWERS, Nick
"Civil War cookbook from Booger Hollow Confederate recipes, civil war facts & humor of Mountain folks." Rome, Ga., Rome Printing Co., 1972. 8vo, wraps, 32pp. $5.

685 POWERS, S.F.
"The Last Battle of the late war, personal reminiscences." In: SHSP, 1895, v.23, p.38-41.
See: 'The Last Battle of War.' Luther Conyer.

686 POWHATAN Troop of Cavalry
See: John Fitzhugh Lay.

687 POYAS, Cathering Gendron
"Year of Grief & other Poems." Charleston, S.C., Walker, Evans & Cogswell, 12mo, cl, viii, 242pp., 1869. Poems growing out of the late war, pt. 2.

688 PRATT, Edwin J.
"Spanish Opinion of the North American Civil War." In: Hisp. Am. Hist. Rev., Feb. 1930, v.X, p.14-25. Six leading newspapers in Spain, opinions by three ministerial & three democratic.

689 PRATT, Fletcher
"Civil War on Western Waters." N.Y., Henry Holt & Co., 1956, 12mo, cl, dj, illus., ports., maps, 255pp. $20.00-Bmk89.

690 ..."The Military Genius of Robert E. Lee (1861-1865)." In: Pac. Spectator, 1948, v.2, p.79-82.

691 ..."The Monitor & the Merrimac; illustrated by John O'Hara Cosgrave." N.Y., Random House, 1951, Landmark Books, 16, 8vo, cl, illus., 185pp.

692 PRATT, Harry E.
"Albert Taylor Bledsoe: Critic of Lincoln." In: Illinois State Hist. Soc. Trans., 1934, p.153-183. A biog. sketch, asst. sect. war & founder & edt., "Southern Review."

693 PRATT, John C. & Jabez D.
"Brother against Brother." Unpublished letters show how one family was bitterly

split. In: Amer. Hert., April 1961, v.11, #3, p.4-7, 89-93, plates, 1 color. Boston, April 19, 1861. Northern troops fire on local citizens.

693a **PRATT, N. A., Rev.**
"Perils of a Dissolution of the Union, a disclosure delivered in the Presbyterian Church of Rosell, on the day of public Thanksgiving, Nov. 20, 1856." Atlanta, Ga., C.R. Hanletter Co., 1856. 8vo, wraps, 21pp.

694 **PRATT, Thomas H.**
"The Postmaster's Provisionals of Memphis, Tenn." Richmond, Va., Dietz Press, 1929, 8vo, wraps, illus., facsms, 43pp. Col. Matthew C. Gallaway, postmstr.

695 **PRAUS, Alexis A.**
"Confederate Soldiers, Sailors & Civilians who died as prisoners of war at Camp Douglas, Chicago, Illinois, 1862-1865." Kalamazoo, Mich., E.Gray Pub., 1968, 4to, wraps.
See: under title.
..."Confederate Soldiers & Sailors who died as prisoners of war at Camp Butler, Illinois, 1862-5." Kalamazoo, Michigan, Edgar Gray Pub., n.d. 4to, wraps, 51p. (from typed copy). Also under title.

696 **PRAY, May M. Brewer (Mrs. R.F. Pray)**
"Dick Dowling's Battle. An account of the War Between the States in the Eastern Gulf Coast Region of Texas." San Antonio, Texas, The Naylor Co., 1936, 12mo, cl, dj, 2-ports, incl. front, xii, 143pp., map. $50.00-OB. Hist of Lt. Richard W. Dowling's part in the war.
See: Frank X. Tolbert, Jo Young, Frances R. Sackett, Robt. M. Franklin.

697 **PRAYERS & other devotions**
For the use of the soldiers of the Army of the Confederate States. Published for the Female Bible, Prayer Book & Tract Society." Charleston, Evans & Cogswell, n.d. (1863), 16mo, wraps, 12pp. Turnbull-III 375. $75.00-B.

698 **PREBLE, George Henry**
"The Flag of the Confederate States of America, extracted from Preble's History of the Flag of the USA." In: SHSP, 1904, v.32, p.243-261.

699 **PREISSER, Thomas M.**
"The Virginia Decision to Use Negro Soldiers in the Civil War, 1864-1865." In: Va. Mag. Hist. & Biog., 1975, v.LXXXIII, p.98-113.

700 **PRENCE, Katherine**
"The Confederate mines - 1862-1865." In: Mag. of Hist., Jan. 1909, v.IX, p.13-16.

701 **PRENTIS, Noble Lovely**
"Battle Corners," i.e., Battles of Wilsons Creek, Pea Ridge & Prairie Grove. In his first chapter - "Kansas Miscellanies," Topeka Kansas., 1889, 12mo, cl, 218pp.
See: also Margery Magruder Mobley.

702 **PRENTISS, Sergeant Smith**
See: John G. Baldwin.

703 **PRESBYTERIAN Church, South Carolina**
"Report of the Provisional Committee on Foreign Missions presented to the General Assembly of the Presbyterian Church in the Confederate States of America." Columbia, S.C., 1862, 8vo, wraps, cover title, (Hook cat-#30, 1940).

704 **PRESS Association of the Confederate States of America**
"The Press Association of the CSA. Introduction, Organization, Constitution, Minutes of Directors, Rules. Minutes of Directors 2nd Session, Report of Supt., General Instructions." Title heading: "Private". Griffin, Ga., Hill & Swayze's, 1863, 8vo, 56pp. Covers first two sessions.

705 ..."Minutes of the Board of Directors of the Press Association embracing Quarterly Report of the Superintendant. Third Session. Augusta, Ga., July 8, 1863." Grif-

fin, Ga., 1863, 8vo, 34pp. Title heading: "Private".

706 ..."Minutes of the Board of Directors of the Press Association embracing the Quarterly Reports of the Superintendant October & January (Fourth & Fifth Sessions)." Atlanta, Ga., Franklin Steam Press, 1864, 8vo, 62pp. Title heading: "Private".

707 ..."First Annual Meeting of the Press Association, Augusta, Ga., April 6, 1864 with minutes of the Board of Directors & Quarterly Report of the Superintendant." Montgomery, Ala., Memphis Appeal Pr., 1864, 8vo, 34pp. Title heading: "Private". 4-parts, one vol. 1/2 leather. $225.00. Personal copy of organizer, John Grame, with his signature & note, "bound together for preservation & has reason to believe no similar volume is extant." De Renne p.657; Crandall-3283-4 does not list the 3rd session (above).

708 **PRESSLEY, Benjamin C.**
"Reasons for the Dissolution of the Union, being a reply to the letter of the Hon. W.J. Grayson & to his answer to 'One of the People.'" Charleston, S.C., A.J. Burke Pr., 1850, 12mo, wraps, caption title, 18pp.

709 **PRESSLEY, John G.**
"Extracts from the Diary, July 22, 1862-July 18, 1863, of JGP, of 25th S.C. Vols." In: SHSP, 1886, v.14, p.35-62.

710 ..."The Wee Nee Volunteers of Williamsburg District, S.C., in the First (Gregg's) Regiment - Siege & Capture of Fort Sumter." In: SHSP, 1885, v.13, p.480-496; 1886, v.16, p.116-194.

711 **PRESSLY, Thomas J.**
"Americans Interpret their Civil War." Princeton, University Press, 1954, 8vo, cl, dj, xvi, 347pp., bibliog. 329-334.
...N.Y., Collier Books, 1962, 18cm, 384pp. with a new intro by author. A rebellion? War between the States? A revolution or an irrepressible conflict?

712 **PRESTON, Anna Jackson, Miss**
"Stonewall Jackson. Sketch of the Life of Stonewall Jackson, by... & Presented to the Senate on May 10, 1928, by Hon. Cole L. Blease senator from South Carolina." Washington, D.C., GPO, 1929, 8vo, leaflet, 4pp., 70th Congress, 2nd Session, Senate Doc. #173. $25.00-Bmk.
See: Anna Jackson (Preston) Shaffer.

713 **PRESTON, Anthony**
"The Raiders that Never Made It." In: US Naval Inst. Proceed., 1968, v.XCIV, iii, 140-141pp. (CSS 'Rappahannock').

714 **PRESTON, E.R.**
"Lee at Lexington. An address." Charlottesville, Va., 1923, 8vo, wraps, 15pp.
Note: A reported address in Ancon, Canal Zone, 1935/1936.

715 **PRESTON, Francis W.**
"Port Hudson; a history of the investment siege & capture...Rebel opinion of the attack on the 27th of May, as given by a correspondent, July 14, 1863, with the partial experience by the author during three years in the march, camp, field & hospitals, 19th army corps, department of the Gulf. With illustrations." Brooklyn, N.Y., Published & for sale by Comrade F.W. Preston, 1892, 12mo, wraps, illus., 71, (1)p. Personal narratives, Union but also from a Confederate view of battle.

716 **PRESTON, John Smith**
"Address before the Survivors' Association of South Carolina, at their Annual Meeting in Columbia, Nov. 10, 1870." n.p., (c.1870), 8vo, wraps, 13pp.

717 ..."Address delivered before the Virginia State Convention by John S. Preston, Commissioner from South Carolina, Feb. 1861." Richmond, Va., Elliott Print, 1861, 8vo, wraps, 64pp. Urges Va. to secession

718 ..."The South Carolina Monument Association & the oration of Gen. John S. Preston." Charleston, News & Courier Press, 1879, 8vo, front, (5), 6, 70pp. with S.C.
See: "Proceedings of 1st & 2nd Meeting.."
See: under title for full description.

719 **PRESTON, Julia Jackson Christian**
"Stonewall's Widow." by her grandaughter. Winston-Salem, N.C., 1961, 12mo(?), 44pp., wraps, illus., gray pict. wraps. Biog. sketch: Mary Anna (Morrison) Jackson, widow of Stonewall, resided in Charlotte from the end of war 'til death in 1915.

719a **PRESTON, Madge**
"A Private War: Letters & Diaries of Madge Preston. 1862-1867. Edt. Virginia Walcott Beauchamp." New Brunswick, N.J., Rutgers University Press, 1987. 8vo, cl, dj, 374 p. index.

720 **PRESTON, Margaret Junkin, Mrs.**
"Beechenbrook; a Rhyme of the War." Richmond, Va., J.W. Randolph, 1865, 16mo, cl, or wraps, 64pp. $200.00-Bmk114.
...Baltimore, Kelly & Piet, 1866, 12mo, cl, 94pp.
...Baltimore, John B. Piet (c.1866), 16mo, decr-gilt cl, iv, (1), 106pp. $15.00. 7th thousand.
...Boston, Kelly & Piet, 1867 (5,000), 8vo, cl, front, 5-pls, 3,9-106pp.
...Edt. 1868, same, 9th thousand.
...1868 - "Illustrated Edition," 4to, cl.
...1868 - "Rockbridge Edition".
...1868 - "Peoples Edition"; 1872 Edt.
...Louisv., Lost Cause, micro-cd, $2.50.
In Mrs. Preston's Journal, Col. Preston paid $2,600 for 2,000 copies of the pamphlet, about 50 sent out of Richmond the remainder burned at evacuation.
See: Eliza. Preston Allen's Life & Letters of Mrs. Preston, & Life in Lexington.

721 ..."Lee after the war, a friend & neighbor." In: CWTI, Jan, 1969, v.VII, #9, p.4-9, 47-48, illus., port, group port.

722 ..."Personal Reminiscences of Stonewall Jackson." In: Century, Oct. 1886, p.927-936, port. (Sister-in-law of Jackson).

723 ..."Paul Hamilton Hayne." In: SB, ns, v.II, 1886-1887, p.222-231.

724 ..."Semi-centennial ode for the Virginia Military Institute, Lexington, Virginia, 1839-1889. Written at the request of the board of visitors." N.Y., G.P. Putnam's Sons, 1889, 12mo, wraps, 26 numb. lfs. $25.00-Bmk106.

725 **PRESTON, Robert L.**
"Did the 'Monitor,' or 'Merrimac' revolutionize naval warfare?" In: Wm. & M.W., July 1915, v.XXIV, p.58-66.

726 **PRESTON, Walter Creigh**
"Lee, West Point & Lexington." Yellow Springs, Ohio, Antioch Press, 1934, 8vo, cl, (12), 116pp.

727 **PRESTON, William, Brig.-Gen.**
"Report: Battle of Chickamauga." In: SHSP, 1884, v.12, p.558-568.

728 **PRETTYMAN, E.B.**
"John Letcher (1813-1884)." In: Branch Hist. Pap. III, #4, 1912, p.314-349. Political affairs in Va., as Gov., 1860-1864.

729 **PRICE, Beulah M. D'Olive**
"The Corinth War Eagle." Jackson, Miss., Jour. Miss. Hist., Oct. 1958, v.XX, #4, p.244-250.

730 ..."The Rev. John Baptist Mouton: Confederate Chaplain." Jackson, Miss., Jour. Miss. Hist., April, 1962, v.XXIV, #2, p.102-106.

730a ..."The Civil War & Battles of Corinth & Shiloh." Corinth, Miss., Corinth Civil War Centennial Commission, 1961 ('Daily Corinthian.'). 4to, wraps, 96pp, ills.

731 **PRICE, C.B.**
"Company C, Thirty-seventh Va. Infantry.

732 **PRICE, Channing**
"Stuart's Chambersburg raid - an eyewitness account." In: CWTI, Jan. 1966, v.4, #9, p.8-15, 42-44, illus., maps, ports.

733 **PRICE, Charles L.**
"North Carolina Railroads During the Civil War." In: CWH, September, 1961, v.VII, #3, p.298-309.

734 ..."Shock & Assault in the First Battle of Fort Fisher." In: NCHR, Jan. 1970, 16pp. $8.00.

735 **PRICE, Henry M., Dr., Co. K, 44th Va. Vols.**
"Rich Mountain in 1861 - campaign & how Gen. Garnett was killed." In: SHSP, 1899, v.27, p.38-44.

736 **PRICE, Marcus W.**
"Additional notes on 'Ella & Annie'." In: Am. Neptune, Jan. 1854, v.14, p.61-63. Notes. Evidence that a CSN blockade-runner of this name was built at Wilmington, Del., by Wm. G. Hughes.

737 ..."Blockade Running as a Business in South Carolina during the War Between the States, 1861-1865." In: Amer. Neptune, Jan. 1949, Volume IX, #1, p.31-62.

738 ..."Ella & Annie," Amer. Neptune, Jan. 1954, Vol.XIV, #1, p.61-63.

739 ..."Four from Bristol." In: Amer. Neptune, 1957, v.17, p.249-261 (Oct.), notes. Four British ships from England running Union blockade to CSA, 1862-1864.

740 ..."Ships that tested the blockade of the Carolina ports, 1861-1865." In: Amer. Nep. July 1958, v.8, p.196-237, p.215-237 table of ships, each year, name & type, crew, place, date capture, etc. Also successfuls.

741 ..."Ships that tested the blockade in the Gulf ports, 1861-1865." In: Am. Neptune, Oct., 1951, July 1952, v.11, p.262-290; v.12, p.52-59, 154-161, 229-238, map, view, bibliog., notes. Tabulated info. for each vessel, type tunnage, number of crew, place & date of capture & other successful runs.

742 ..."Ships that Tested the Blockade of the Georgia & East Florida Ports in 1861-1865." In: Amr. Neptune, April, 1955, Vol.XV, #2, p.97-132.

743 ..."Masters & Pilots who tested the Blockade of the Confederate Ports, 1861-1865." In: Amer. Neptune, April, 1961, Vol. XXI, #2, p.79-106, illus., ports.

744 **PRICE, Sterling**
"Engraved Portrait, 21x16". Bust in an oval - with wide margins. N.Y., Perine & Co., c.1865. $25.00.

745 ..."Missouri Miniatures." Columbia, Mo., Mo. Hist. Review, July 1941, v.XXXV, #4, p.578-587, bibliog.

746 ..."A Short History of Gen. Sterling Price." Park Place, N.Y., Knapp & Co., 1888, 2 3/4 x 1 1/2" colored booklet, 16pp. facsm. signature, packed in Duke's cigarettes. See: "Heroes of the C.W." & W. Duke Co.

747 ..."Sketch of Maj. Gen. Sterling Price." In: LWL, Sept. 1866, v.1, #5, p.364-374.

748 ..."Gen. Price's report of the Missouri Campaign, 1864." In: LWL, September 1868, v.V, #5, p.379-397.
...Also in SHSP, 1879, v.7, p.209-231.

749 ..."Price's raid into Missouri." In: CV, Aug. 1903, v.XI, p.359-362.

750 **PRICE, William H.**
"The Civil War Centennial Handbook." Arlington, Va., Prince Litho., 1961, 8vo, decr. wraps, 72pp., illus., color-uniforms, map. Fairfax, Va., reprint.

751 ..."Civil War Centennial Handbook." Vienna, Va., C.W. Research Associates.

752 **PRICE, William Thomas**
"Guerrilla Warfare; the Ambush on Greenbrier River in which seven troopers wre killed." In: W.Va. Hist. Mag. Qrt., July 1904, v.4, p.241-249. Pro-Southern guerrilla activity on Cheat Mt., following Rich

Mt., by one of the scouts (E. Devier Shetler-647).

753 ..."Historical Sketches of Pocahontas County, W.Va." Marlinton, W.Va., Price Bros., 1901, 8vo, cl, 622pp. Union & CSA soldiers. p.582-585.

754 ..."Memorials of Edward Herndon Scott, M.D." Wytheville, Va., Jim Presgraves, 1974, 8vo, wraps, 29pp. Reprint of 1873 pamphlet. Concerns Dr. Scott in Missouri, with 1st Mo. Cavl. & service at Battle of New Market.

755 ..."On to Grafton: An Account of One of the First Campaigns of the Civil War, May 1861." Marlington, 1901 (O'Hare shows as 1902; Canner also has 1902 imprint), W.Va., 8vo, wraps, port., 68pp. Shetler, 649. $35.00. Valuable diary of Tygart Valley & W.Va., camp by Wm. T. Price, Osborne Wilson & Chs. Lewis Campbell, Highland Co., Va. members of 31st Virginia Infantry. Roster of Highlanders. Grafton was an important cross-road & staginf area of CSA.

756 **PRICHARD, Walter**
"The Effects of the Civil War on the Louisiana Sugar Industry." Baton Rouge, La., JSH, Aug., 1939, v.V, #3, p.315-332.
See: Daniel Thompson.

757 **PRIM, G. Clinton, Jr.**
"Revivals in the Armies of Mississippi during the Civil War." In: JMH, August 1982, v.XLIV, #3, p.227-234.
..."Southern Methodism in the Confederacy." In: Methodist Hist., July 1985, v.24, p.240-9.

758 **PRINCE William Cavalry**
See: Mrs. M.R. Barlow.

759 **PRINCE, Sigsbee C., Jr.**
"Edward A. Perry, Yankee General of the Florida Brigade.: In: FHQ, January, 1951, v.XXIX, #3, p.197-205. Pensacola Rifle Rangers, became Co. A, 2nd Fla. Inf., ANV. Perry was Col., later Brig.-Gen. 2nd Fla.

759a **"PRINCESS of the Moon.**
A Confederate fairy story. Written by a Lady of Warrenton, Va." Printed at the Sun Book & Job Print., Baltimore, Md., 1969. Copyright: R. W. Payne. 16mo, wraps, 72p, front.

759b **"PRINCIPLES & Issues**
of the American Struggle, The." In: Blackwood, July, 1866, v.100, p.17-34.

760 **PRINGLE, Elizabeth Waties Allston**
"Chronicles of Chicora Wood." N.Y., C. Scribner's Sons, 1922, 12mo, cl, front, illus., ports, ix, 366pp. $35.00.
...Boston, Christopher Pub., 1940, 12mo, cl, front, illus., ports, xii, 366pp. Considerable section on desolate latter days of the Confederacy.
...Atlanta, Ga., 1976, reprint, 369pp.

761 **PRIOR, Leon O.**
"Lewis Payne, pawn of John Wilkes Booth." In: FHQ, July 1964, v.XLIII, #1, p.1-20, facsm., port.

762 **PRISON Life in the Confederate War**
See: Judah P. Benjamin, Benj. F. Butler, Albert S. Caison, Geo. L. Christian, Jas. F. Crocker, Richard H. Dabney, Abram Fulkerson, W.W. George, Ulysses S. Grant, Benj. H. Hill, John W. Jones, Saml. Jones, Anthony M. Keiley, John F. Mines, Robert Ould, Ruth Rodgers, George T. Smith, James T. Wells, John Allen Wyeth.
See: Andersonville, Camp Douglas, Camp Morton, Elmira, Fort Delaware, Fort McHenry, Libby Prison, Johnson's Island, Morris Island, "Famous War prisons..."

763 **"PRISONER OF WAR,**
Five Months among Yankees."
Under: Anthony Keiley.

764 **"PRISONER OF WAR, A."**
by 'High Private'. In: The XIX century I/II, Charleston, 1869-1894. Dorn-II, 684.

765 **PRISONER, A (pseud.)**
"Two Months in Fort Lafayette...by A Prisoner." N.Y., The Author, 1862, 18mo, wraps, 53pp.

766 **"PRIVATE Co. H., Fifth Texas Regiment,**
"Pickett's & Hood's Charges at Gettysburg." In: SB(os), v.III, 1884, p.75-78.

767 **"PRIVATE Correspondence,"**
cover title. To: E. Kirby Smith, Poem, 14pp. signed: N.P. Banks. To: Corp. N.P. Banks - Commander so-called U.S. Forces, 2pp. signed: E. Kirby Smith. n.p., n.d. (1864?), 32mo, wraps. Satire poem.

768 **PRIVATEERS ,**
See: David Hay.

769 **"PROCEEDINGS & Memorial**
of a Conference of Confederate Roster Commissioners of Atlanta, Ga., July 20, 1903." Montgomery, Ala., Alabama Print, 1903, 8vo, wraps, 16pp. $20.00.

770 **"PROCEEDINGS at the Unveiling**
of the Monument to the Charleston Light Dragoons, Charleston, May 10, 1886. Oration of Generals M.C. Butler & B.H. Rutledge." 8vo, wraps, 30pp.
See: Matthew C. Butler.

771 **"PROCEEDINGS of First Confederate**
Congress. End of Second Session, third Session in part." In: SHSP, Dec. 1930, v.XLVII, pp.(2), (1)-229.

772 ..."Proceedings of the First Confederate Congress third session in part. Jan. 29 - March 19, 1863." In: SHSP, September, 1941, v.LXVIII, p.vi, (1)-329.

773 ..."Proceedings of the First Confederate Congress. Third Session in part. March 20 - May 1, 1863." In: SHSP, May 1943, v.XLIX, p.vi, (1)-274.

774 ..."Proceedings of the First Confederate Congress, Fourth Session. 7 December 1863 - 18 February 1864. Edited: Frank E. Vandiver." In: SHSP, December 1943, v.L, p.viii, (1)-463.

775 ..."Proceedings of the Second Confederate Congress, First Session, Second Session in part. 2 May - 14 June 1864. 7 November - 14 December 1864. Edt: Frank E. Vandiver." In: SHSP, March 1959, v.LI, p.xi, (1)-475.

776 ..."Proceedings of the Second Confederate Congress, Second Session in part. December 15, 1864 - March 18, 1865. Edt: Frank E. Vandiver." In: SHSP, July 1959, v.LII, p.xx, (1)-500.

777 ..."Proceedings of the First Confederate Congress - First Session, in part." In: SHSP, June 1923, v.XLIV, (3), (6)-206pp.
See: "Journal of the Congress of the Confederate States of America 1861-1865, v.II, Wash., GPO, 1904. Senate Doc. #234.

778 ..."Proceedings of First Confederate Congress First Session completed Second Session in part." In: SHSP, May 1925, v.XLV, p.286.

779 ..."Proceedings of First Confederate Congress Second Session in part.: In: SHSP, January 1928, v.XLVI, p.(1)-256.

780 **"PROCEEDINGS of Ross' Texas Brigade**
Association of Ex-Confederate had at its Reunions Sulpher Springs '81-'82; Terrell (Tex.), '82 McKinney (Tex.) '83; Together with combined items connected with combined reunions of Old Pioneers, Veterans, Ex-Confederates, Ex-Union soldiers held at last named place." McKinney (Texas), Enquirer Job Print, 1884, 8vo, wraps, 98pp. (advs verso front/back wrp).
e.g. Gen. Lawrence Sullivan Ross.

781 ..."Proceedings of the Annual Meeting of Ross' Brigade at Dallas, Texas, Aug. 17th, 18th & 19th, 1887." Denison, Texas, Murray's Print, 1887, 12mo, stiff wraps, 8pp.

782 **"PROCEEDINGS of a Mass Meeting**
in Accordance with the Call Issued on the 8th Inst. The People of Travis County assembled in Mass Meeting, at the Court

House, in Austin, on Saturday, the 13th Dec., 1862 at 11:00 o'clock, when the following Proceedings were had...(caption title). Broadside: 35.6 x 12.7cm, n.p., n.d. Brickrow $150.00. Meet called by Col. A.R. Crozier & Judge S.G. Sneed, elected Pres. Purpose to show inadequacies of militia & call for all capable persons to organize against Yankee invasion.

783   **"PROCEEDINGS of a meeting**
of officers & men of the 154th Sr. Tenn. Regiment. (Dalton, Ga.) 1864." 8vo, titlehead, 2p. Crandall-399. Hse. Reps., Jan. 26, 1864. Dated Camp 154th Sr. Reg. Tenn. Vols., near Dalton, Ga., Jan. 14, 1864. Sig: M. Mageveney, Jr. chm., W.R. Lucas, sect.
See: Marcus J. Wright, "Proceed. of meet. of offic."

783a   **"PROCEEDINGS of the Bank Convention**
of the Confederate States, held at Richmond, Va., July 24th, 25th & 26th, 1861. Charleston, S.C., Walker, Evans & Cogswell, 1861. 8vo, wraps, 14pp.

784   **"PROCEEDINGS of the Ceremony**
of unveiling of the monument erected by the people of Mobile & of the South to the memory of the Rev. E.C. de la Moriniere." Mobile, W.B. Delchamps Print, 1913, 8vo, wraps, plate, 28pp.

785   **"PROCEEDINGS of the Chamber of Commerce**
of New York State, on the continued Piracies of Vessels fitted out in Great Britain upon American Commerce." N.Y., 1863, wraps, 27pp. $20.00.
See: "The Alabama".
of the State of New York, on the burning of the ship 'Brilliant', by the Rebel Pirate 'Alabama', Tuesday, October 21, 1862." N.Y., 1862, 8vo, wraps, 22pp. Smith 1772. $50.00.

786   **"PROCEEDINGS of the Conventions**
at Charleston & Baltimore. Published by order of the National Democratic Convention, (Maryland Institute, Baltimore) and under the Supervision of the National Democratic Executive Committee." Washington, August, 1860, 8vo, cl, 255pp. Sabin-65837.
...Cleveland, 1860. Sabin-65840.

787   **"PROCEEDINGS of the Court of Inquiry,**
relative to the Fall of New Orleans. Published by order of Congress." Richmond, Va., R.M. Smith Print., 1864, 8vo, cl, (or, sewn), pp.(5), 206. $125.00.

788   **"PROCEEDINGS of the First**
Confederate Congress - First Session." 8vo, (Offprint) Southern Historical Society Papers, n.s., #6, June 1923, 240pp.

789   **"PROCEEDINGS of the First &**
Second Annual Meeting of the Survivors Association of the State of South Carolina, & Oration of General John S. Preston. Delivered before the Association, Nov. 10, 1870." Charleston, Walker, Evans & Cogswell, 1870, 8vo, wraps, pp.(4)-5-63.
See: John S. Preston.

790   **"PROCEEDINGS of the Louisiana**
State Convention, together with the ordinances passed by said convention & the Constitution of the State as ammended." New Orleans, 1861, (in English & French), 8vo, cl, 330pp.

790a   **PROCEEDINGS of the Second**
Annual Session, Association of Medical Officers of the Confederate States of America Army & Navy. Held in Richmond, Va., Oct. 19-20, 1875. Together with an alphabetical register of members. Richmond, Va., Ferguson Print, 1875. 8vo, wraps, 16pp.
...Do: 'Samuel Preston Moore, Md., Sur-Gen. of the Confederate States of Amer." Washington: Judd & Detweiler, 1910. 8vo, wraps, 12pp.

791   **"PROCEEDINGS of the Virginia**
State Convention of 1861...Feb. 13-May1."

4 volumes, boxed. Richmond, Va., Virginia State Library, 1965. Imp. 8vo, cl, v.1-xxiv, 796pp.; v.2-x, 768pp.; v.3-ix, 784pp.; v.4-xi, 807pp. $60.00. Editor: George H. Reese.

792 "PROCEEDINGS of the meeting of delegates
from the Southern Rights Association of South Carolina. Held at Charleston, May, 1851." Columbia, S.C., Johnston & Cavis, 1851, 8vo, wraps, 31pp.
See: Robt. W. Barnwell, Ed. B. Bryan, Wm. F. Colcock, James L. Orr, "Meeting of Students of South Carolina College.

793 PROCTER, Ben H.
"John H. Reagan & the Confederate Post Office." In: Ga. Rev., Winter 1957, v.11: p.387-399. $8.00.

794 ..."Not Without Honor. The Life of John H. Reagan." Austin, University of Texas Pr., 1962, 8vo, cl, dj, pl. ports, incl. front, xii, (2) 361pp. Bibliog-index p.303-361. Paper, illus., 375pp.

795 PROCTOR, Samuel
"Jacksonville During the Civil War." Jacksonville, Fla., Florida Historical Quarterly, April, 1963, v.XLI, #4, p.343-355, illus., port.

796 ..."The Call to Arms, Secession from a feminine point of view." In: FHQ, Jan. 1957, v.35, p.266-270.

797 ..."Saltmaking along Florida's Gulf Coast profitable but vulnerable CW business." In: CWTI, Nov. 1962, v.1, #7, p.46-48, plate.

797a ..."Florida Commemorates the Civil War Centennial, 1861-5; a Manual for the Observance of the Civil War in the Counties & cities of the State of Florida." Coral Gables, Florida Civil War Centennial Commission, 1962? 8vo, wraps, cover title, 24pp, fld. map.

798 PROGRAM of the Confederate
Veterans entertainment, for the benefit of Battle Abbey, at Theater Vendome, Tuesday nite June 2, 1896. Nashville, Tenn., Paul & Baylies, 1896, 8vo, cover title, 32pp.

799 PROPAGANDA, C.S.A.
"Southern Propaganda printed inside envelopes." In: CWH, September 1959, v.V, #3, p.312-314.

800 PROSSER, W.F.
"A remarkable episode of the late Civil War." In: 'United Ser.' Phila., 1889, v.II, ns, p.615-632. Col. Wm. O. Williams & Lt. Walter G. Peter executed as CS spies, June 1863.

801 "PROTEST against Provincialism,
Report of Sons of Confederate Veterans. 37th Annual Convention." Richmond, Va., 1932, 8vo, wraps, 29pp. Protests treatment of Civil War Text books.

802 "PROTEST of New Jersey."
In: Tyler QHGM, 1931, v.XIII, p.80-84. Protest against Lincoln's conduct of war, adopted March 18, 1863.

803 PROTESTANT Episcopal Church in the Confederate States of America
Pastoral Letter from Bishops of P.E.C., to the clergy & laity of the church in the C.S.A. delivered before the General Council, in St. Paul's Church, Augusta, Sat., Nov. 22, 1862." Augusta, Ga., Chronicle & Sentinel, 1862, 8vo, wraps, cover title, 15pp.
...Baltimore, Md., 1863.
Reprinted in Centenary Edt., P.E.C. of C.S.A. included in Journal of General Council, 1862. Paged separately, following page 216, with same title page.

804 ..."Journals. Centenary Ed. in facsimilie. Edited by William A. Clebsch." Austin, Texas, Church Historical Society, 1962, Publications, new series: sources #1, 8vo, cl, facsms, various paginations.
e.g. Proceedings: bishops, clergymen, laymen, July 3, 1861; Proceed. adjourned

convention, Oct. 16/24, 1861; Pro. Gen. Council, Nov. 12/22, 1862, with constitution & a digest of church canons, Pro. General Council 8/10 Nov., 1865.

805 **PROTESTANT Episcopal Church of Virginia**
"The Army & Navy Prayer Book. Diocesan Missionary Society of the Protestant Episcopal Church of Virginia." $75.00. Richmond, Va., 1865, wraps, 32mo, 95pp.
See: Wm. Edward Dunstan
Lawrence L. Pennington
Lawrence F. London.

806 **PROTESTANT Episcopal Church,**
Diocese of Alabama, "To Churchmen: Memorial to the General Council of the Protestant Episcopal Church in the Confederate States of America." Montgomery, Ala., Advertiser Book & Job Office, 1862, Nov. 22nd, 8vo, wraps, 8pp. Not in Crandall.

807 **PROVISIONAL & Permanent Constitution,**
Together with the Acts & Resolutions of the Three Sessions of the Provisional Congress of the Confederate States. Richmond, Tyler, Wise, Allegre & Smith, 1861, 12mo, yellow printed wraps, 159, 119, 94pp., errata. $650.00. Crandall-14 copy covers only thru 'Acts & Resolutions.' Signature: "James H. Nash, C.S.Senate." Nash being Sect. of the Senate.

808 **PROVISIONAL Record**
of Confederate Medical Officers. n.p. (Wilmington, N.C.?), n.d. (c.1890), 8vo, sewn, 57pp. Broadfoot: "Approximately 300 N.C., CSA medical officers, some with full information, others just name, rank & regiment. Mailed by Surg. Thos. Wood to medical officers for review & information."

809 **PROWELL, George R.**
"The invasion of Pennsylvania by the Confederates, under Gen. Robert E. Lee, & its effect upon Lancaster & York Counties." In: Lancaster Co. HSP, Apr. 1925, v.XXIX, #4, p.41-53.

809a **PRUETT, Jakie L. & Scott Black**
"Civil War Letters, 1861-65." Austin, Texas, Eakin Press, 1985. 8vo, cl, VII, 95pp, ills, dj, facsms, 1M copies, 500 deluxe, boxed. $16, $30.

810 **PRUSSIAN Officer in C.S.Army**
"The Seven Days' Contests, June 25-July 1, 1862. By a Prussian Officer in the Confederate Army." In: Edward A. Pollard's "Second Year of the War." In Appendix, p.(309)-325.

811 **PRYOR, Roger Atkinson**
"The Capture of Gen. Roger A. Pryor." New York, 1889, 8vo, caption title, 12pp.

812 ..."Essays & Addresses, with explanatory notes, by Roger Pryor." N.Y., Neale Pub. Co., 1912, 12mo, cl, front(port), 6, 11-262pp. $25.00. Pryor was a member of CSA Congress, Brig.-Gen. in the army, a prisoner of war during the last year of the war.

813 ..."Independence of the South. Speech of Hon. Roger A. Pryor, of Virginia, on the resolutions reported by the committee of Thirty-three." Washington, Henry Polkinhorn, 1861, 8vo, sewn, 8pp.

814 **PYROR, Sara Agnes Rice (Mrs. R.A. Pryor)**
"My Day; Reminiscences of a long life by Mrs. Roger A. Pryor." N.Y., Macmillan Co., 1909, 12mo, cl, front, pls., ports., ix, 454pp. $25.00-Bmk89. $30.00.

815 ..."Reminiscences of Peace & War." N.Y., Lond, Macmillan Co., 1904, 12mo, cl, 1-illus., ports, incl. front, xiv, 2,3-402pp. $50.00.
...Revised & enlarged edition, 1905, dbl-pg. map, xviii, 418pp. $10.00.
Editions: 1924 ($12.50); 1970; 1909 ($25.00).

See also: Robt. A. Brock, essays on Lee. ...N.Y., Arno Pr., "Select Bibliographic Reprint Series." 1970.

816 **PRYOR, Shepherd Green**
"Action at Camp Bartow, October 4, 1861. Letter describing---" In: Ga. Rev., Spring 1961, v.15, p.3-5. Member 12th Ga. Reg.

817 **PUBLIC Ceremonies**
in Connections with the war memorials of the Washington Light Infantry, with orations by Gen. Wade Hampton...
See: "Washington Light Infty...."

818 **PUBLIC Laws**
Of the CSA, passed at the 1st Session, 1st Congress, 1st Session, of 2nd Congress, 1862-1864. Carefully collated with original at Richmond, Va., Edt: James M. Matthews. Richmond, Va., R.M. Smith, 1862-1864. Holmes Beach, Fla., W.W. Gaunt, 1970. Spine: Conf. States Acts, 1st & 2nd Congress, 1862/1864. Each vol. has Private Laws of the Conf. States of America, passed during that session of Congress.
Note: Part of Crandall-24, public & private laws, 288, 18pp., 8vo, cl, 5 v. in 1.

819 **PUGH, Eliza Lofton Phillips, Mrs.**
"In a Crucible: A Novel." Phila., Claxton, Remsen & Haffelfinger, New Orleans, J.A. Gresham, 1872, 12mo, 389pp. La. during the War.

820 **PUGH, Maud**
"Capon Valley, It's Pioneers & their Descendants 1698-1940." Capon Bridge, c.1946-1948, 2 vols., W.Va. Roster Co. F, 18th Virginia Cavalry, Imboden's Brigade, v.1, p.252-263. Shetler-653.

821 **PULASKI County (Arkansas) Historical Review**
"Seizure of the U.S. Arsenal February, 1861." In: v.V, #1, Mar. 1957, p.1-16. Made up of Gen. Orders, reports, broadsides; v.XI, #2, June 1963: letters, Little Rock, Trip to Richmond, last days of CSA; v.X, #2, June 1962: Battle of Shiloh & letters around Little Rock.

822 **PULASKI County 1861-1865 Arkansas**
Letters from in the Confederacy, Edt: Ted R. Worley. (See under Editor.) "At Home in Confederate Arkansas."

822a **PULASKI County, Missouri**
Civil War Centennial, sponsored by the Waynesville Chamber of Commerce. June 5-10, 1961.
..."Under Two Flags," a pageant, Centennial booklet, celebration, June 5-10, 1961.

823 **PULASKI Guards**
J.B. Caddall, John W. Daniel.

824 **PUMPHREY, Wm. F.**
"Catalogue of valuable & rare collection of Confederate miscellany. Wm. F. Pumphrey. Richmond, Va." 8vo, wraps, (Richmond, Va.,?) 187-), 8pp. Early list CSA books. $60.00-Bmk114.

825 **PURCELL Battery**
"The Purcell Battery, in the Seven Days Battles before Richmond." In: SHSP, 1893, v.21, p.362-365.
See: A.S. Drewry.

825a **PURCELL, Douglas Clare**
"Joseph Barbiere: Confederate (Tenn.) in Alabama (1961-5)". In: Ala.Rev., Oct. 1982, p.243-59.
..."Joseph Barbiere: Tennessee Confederate in Alabama." In: AR, Oct. 1982, v.35, #4, p.243-59.
..."Military Conscription in Alabama during the Civil War (1862-65)." In: Ala.-Rev., April 1981, p.94-106.

826 **PURDUE, Howell & Elizabeth**
"Pat Cleburne Confederate General. A Definitive Biography by..." Hillsboro, Texas, Hill Jr. College, 1973, 8vo, cl, dj, ports, incl. front., illus., maps, crest, xv, (1), 498, (1)pp. map-endsheets. Bibliog. 462-480, index. Pres. $30.00. OP
...Tuscaloosa, Ala., Portals Pr., 1977, Reprint. $35.00.

...Gaithersburg, Md., Butternut Press, 1987. 8vo, cl, dj, 499pp. Reprint of 1973 edt. $30.

827 **PURDUE, Ida Pace**
"Papers Pertaining to the Confederacy." compiled by her son, Howell Purdue. Foreword: Robert Selph Henry. Cover title, n.p. (Washington, D.C., July 19, 1960), 8vo, wraps, 39pp, 2-ports, very limited edition, distributed to family & friends. $10.00.

828 **PURIFOY, Francis Marion**
"Descendants of John Purifoy who were Confederate Soldiers." Montgomery, Alabama, 1904. Alabama Historical Society, Montgomery Reprint #20, (from: Transactions, 1899-1903, vol.IV), 8vo, wraps, p.441-444.

829 **PURIFOY, John**
"The Artillery at Gettysburg." In: CV, 1924, Nov. v.XXXII, p.424-427, 466-468.

830 ..."Assault on Anderson's Division, July 2, 1863, Oct. 1923, v.XXXI, p.377-378. In: CV.

831 ..."Back to Rapidan." In: CV, Feb. 1926, v.XXXIV, p.55-56, the ANV, July 1863.

832 ..."In Battle array at Williamsport & Hagerstown." In: CV, Oct. 1925, v.XXXIII, p.371-373.

833 ..."The Battle of Gettysburg." In: CV, Jan. 1924, v.XXXII, p.16-18. On July 3, 1863. Also 1925, Jan.-Apr., June-July, Sept.-Dec., p.13-16, 53-55, 95-97, 132-135, 224-225, 254-255, 338-340, 371-373, 414-416. Title varies. (Below, cont'd.)

834 ..."The Captured Dispatches." In: CV, Oct. 1924, v.XXXII, p.390-392. Davis to Lee at Hagerstown, taken to Meade.

835 ..."Cavalry action near Fairfield, Pa., July 3, 1863." In: CV, Sept. 1924, v.XXXII, p.345-346.

836 ..."Cavalry assault (at Gettysburg), July 3, 1863." In: CV, May-June, 1924, v.XXXII, p.178-181, 226-229.

837 ..."Ewell's attack at Gettysburg, July 2, 1863." In: CV, Dec. 1923, v.XXXI, p.454-456.

838 ..."Farnsworth's charge & death at Gettysburg." In: CV, Aug. 1924, v.XXXII, p.307-309.

839 ..."Gen. Robert E. Lee, the peerless soldier." In: CV, Aug. 1926, v.XXXIV, p.302-305, 337-340, 420-423, 458-461. "Letters," p.100-103.

840 ..."Jackson's last battle." In: CV, Mar. 1920, v.XXVIII, p.93-96. Battle of Chancellorsville, Va., May 1863.

841 ..."Jefferson Davis, the Artillery at Bloody Angle." In: CV, v.XXIV, p.222-224, May 1916. Also: v.XXXI, Sept. 1923, p.331-333. At Spotsylvania Courthouse May 12, 1864.

842 ..."Lieut. Dwight E. Bates, Jeff Davis Artillery CSA." In: CV, May 1925, v.XXXIII, p. 174-176.

843 ..."Longstreet's attack at Gettysburg, July 2, 1863." In: CV, Aug. 1923, v.XXXI, p.292-294. Gettysburg, July 3, 1863: CV, Feb.-Apr., 1924, v.XXXII, p.54-56, 100-102, 178-181.

844 ..."The Lost opportunity at Gettysburg." In: CV, June 1923, v.XXXI, p.214-218.

845 ..."The Splendid valor shown at Gettysburg, July 2, 1863." In: CV, Jan. 1926, v.XXXIV, p.17-19.

846 ..."Stuart's Cavalry at Gettysburg, July 3, 1863." In: CV, July 1924, v.XXXII, p.260-263.

847 ..."Stuart's ride through enemy's country." In: CV, Feb. 1923, v.XXXI, p.55-56.

848 ..."West Virginia Campaigns, Letters on the:" In: CV, June 1926, v.XXXIV, p.216-218.

849 ..."With Ewell & Rodes in Pennsylvania." In: CV, Dec. 1922, v.XXX, p.462-464.

850 ..."With Jackson in the Valley." In: CV, Oct.-Nov. 1922, v.XXX, p.383-385, 421-422.

851 ..."Battle of Gettysburg, July 1, 1863." In: CV, Jan.-Apr., 1923, v.XXXI, p.22-25, 138-142; July 2, 1863 in July-Nov., p.252-253, 416-419.

852 **PURSLEY, William**
"William Pursley Letters, 1863. Contributed by J.D. Howard." In: TMH, Fall 1964, v.4, #3, p.193-195.

852a **PURVIS, Joseph Edward**
"A Confederate View of Prison Life; a Virginian (Joseph Edward Purvis) in Fort Delaware, 1863." In: Del.Hist., Fall/winter 1979, p.226-35.

853 **PUTNAM, Elizabeth Whitney**
"The Peace Convention of 1861." In: CV, Aug., 1918, v.XXVI, p.345-350.

854 **PUTNAM, Sallie A. Brock (Mrs. Richard)**
"Richmond During the War; Four Years of Personal Observation." New York, G.W. Carleton & Co., 1867, 12mo, cl, viii-xiv, (15)-389, (6)ads. $125.00-Ginz. $50.00-Bmk.
...Louisville, Lost Cause Press, micro-cd.
...N.Y., Robert M. McBride Co., 1961. "In Richmond During the Confederacy." Intro: Willard Webb, (2)pp. addition. With: By a Lady of Richmond (Sallie A. Putnam).
...N.Y., Time-Life Books, 1983. 'Collectors library of the civil war.' 8vo, Kivar binding, gilt edges, marbled endsheets. $27.

855 **PYE, Edward Arell**
"Letters from the Conf. Medical Serv. in Texas, 1863-1865. Intro: E.C. Barker, notes by F.E. Vandiver." In: SwHQ, Jan. 1952, v.LV, #3, p.378-393; #4, p.459-474.

856 **PYLE, Howard**
"The Battle of Nashville." In: Amer. Hist. Ill., v.1, #1, April 1966, (4)pp. double page color panorama.

857 **PYRON, Darden Asbury**
"The Inner War of Southern History." In: South. Studies, Sprint, 1981, v.XX, p.5-19.

858 **PYRON, Darden Asbury, Edt.**
"Recasting: Gone With the Wind, in American culture." Gainesville, Univ. Press of Fla., 1983, 8vo, cl, dj, x, 232p. $18.25.

Q

1   **QUAD, M., of Detroit Free Press**
"Sherman's March to the Sea, as seen by a Northern Soldier." In: SHSP, 1882, v.10, p.410-415. "Terms of Surrender at Vicksburg"

2   **QUANTRILL, the Guerrilla Chieftain**
From his own diary. (n.p., 189-?), 12 mo, wraps, 59pp. Fictitious narrative, Dorn-II, 264.

2a **QUARLES, Garland Redd**
"Diaries, letters & recollections of the war between the States." Winchester, Va., prepared for Farmers & Merchants National Bank, 1955. 8vo, wraps, 133pp. $30.
..."Occupied Winchester, 1861-65." Winchester, Va., prepared for Farmers & Merchants National Bank, 1976. 8vo, wraps, ills, 142pp. $15.

3   **QUARTERMASTER ,**
Frank M. Gailor

4   **QUARTERMASTER General, C.S.A.**
"Report, Feb.16, 1865." In: SHSP, v.2, 1876, p.113-122.

5   **QUATTLEBAUM, Isabel**
"Twelve Women in the First Days of the Confederacy." In: CWH, December 1961, v. VII, #4, p.370-385, ports.

6   **QUEENER, Verton M.**
"East Tennessee sentiment & the secession movement, Nov., 1860-June 1861. " In: East THS 1948, v.20, p.59-83, notes.

7   **"QUELQUES Considerations**
sur la Defense de l'Etat de la Louisiane et sur l'Organisation de ses Milices."
pp.58, wraps, 8vo. N.O. 1861.

8   **QUENZEL, Carroll H.**
"Edgar Snowden, Sr., Virginia Journalist & Civic Leader."
Charlottesville, Va., Bibliographical Society of University of Virginia, 1954, 16 mo, unbound, 59, (1) pp.

9   ..."Gen. Henry Hopkins Sibley (1816-): military inventor. In: Va MHB, Apr. 1956, v.64, p. 166-176. notes. On his tent (1856) & stove (1861) both adopted by US Army, which failed to pay royalty after his entry into the CS Army.

10 **QUILLIN, Martha A., Miss**
"A letter on Sherman's March through Georgia. Edt.: George W. Clower. " In: Ga. H.Q., June 1953 v. XXXVII, #2, pp.160-162

11 **QUINN, Silvanus Jackson**
"The History of Fredericksburg, Virginia. Prepared & printed by authority of the Common council thereof, under the direction of its committee on publication consisting of the following councilmen: H.B. Lane, Wm. E. Bradley & S.W. Somerville, S.J. Quinn, historian." Richmond, Va., Hermitage Press, 1908. 8vo, cl, 6, (2), 7-349p., front, plates, ports. Much on CSA. Bmk- $75.00.

12 **QUINTARD, Charles Todd, Rev.**
"Doctor Quintard Chaplain, C.S.A. & Second Bishop of Tennessee, Being his Story of the War, 1861-1865. Edited & extended by the Rev. Arthur Howard Noll." (Sewanee, Tenn.) The University of the South Press, 1905. 12mo, decr. cl, front (port), (5), 1, 183, (1)-vi., (also in wraps) $25.00, 200- Bmk- 105, 105- Bmk-95.

13 ..."B.F. Cheatham, Maj.-Gen., C.S.A., Tribute to his Memory." In: SHSP, 1888, v.XVI, p.349-354.

14 ..."Balm for the Weary & the Wounded. By Rev. C.T. Quintard, Chaplain 1st Tenn. Regt. CSA." Columbia, S.C., Evans & Cogswell, 1864. 14cm, 85pp., cover title. Crandall- 4234.

15 ..."The Confederate Soldier's Pocket Manual of Devotions. Compiled by Rev.

C.T. Quintard, Chaplain 1st Tenn. Regiment." Charleston: Evans & Cogswell, 1863, 11 1/2cm, 80pp. Crandall- 4235.

16 ..."Charles Todd Quintard (1824- 1898) by Hiram K. Douglas." In: Am. Church Mo., Feb. 1930, v.XXVI, p. 142-147. (sketch 2nd. Bishop of Tenn.)

17 **QUIRK'S SCOUTS, CSA**
"Roll of Quirk's scouts, CSA, at Camp Liberty, Tenn., Jan. 1863, after the Christman raid." In: RKHS, 1904, v.II, p.35-36.

18 **QUISENBERRY, Anderson Chenault**
"The Eleventh Kentucky Cavalry, CSA." In: SHSP, 1907, v.XXXV, p.259-289.

19 ..."Morgan's Men in Ohio." In: SHSP, April 1914, v. XXXIX, p.91-99.

20 ..."The Battle of Richmond, Kentucky, September, 1862; A Reminiscence." In: Ky. Hist. Soc. Reg., Sept. 1918, v.XVI, p.9-24. (Battles of Big Hill & Richmond.)

21 ..."The Confederate Campaign in Kentucky, 1862; the Battle of Perryville." In: Ky. Hist. Soc. Reg., Jan. 1919, v.XVII, p. 31-38.

22 ..."History of Morgan's Men." In: Ky. Hist. Soc. Reg., Sept.1917, v.XV, pp.23-46.

23 ..."The Alleged Secession of Kentucky." In: Ky. HSR., May 1917, v.XV, p.15-32.

24 ..."Kentucky's Neutrality in 1861." In: Ky. HSR, Jan. 1917, v.XV, p.9-21.

25 **QUITMAN RIFLES**
"History of Quitman Rifles, organized 1859, composed of Pike County's Pride." (from New Orleans, La. Picayune, April 22, 1906) In: SHSP 1906, v.34, p.239-242.

26 **QUYNN, Russell Hoover**
"The Constitutions of Abraham Lincoln & Jefferson Davis." N.Y., Exposition Press, 1959. 8vo, cl, 304pp. Judicial review of 13, 14, 15th amendments, not constitutionally ratified by 3/4th states, when the white voters kept from polls & negroes voted to enfranchise themselves.

R

1 **RABLE, George C.**
"Anatomy of a Unionist: Andrew Johnson in the Secession Crisis." In: THQ, 1973, v.32, p.332-54.

1a **RABUN, James Z.**
"Alexander H. Stephens & Jefferson Davis." American Historical Review, v. LVIII, Jan., 1953, pp. 290-321.

2 ..."Alexander H. Stephens & the Confederacy, 1861-1865. "In: Emory Univ. Quart., June 1950, v. 6, pp. 129-146.

3 **RACHAL, William M.E.**
"The Burning of Richmond, 1865." (Richmond, Va., Cavalcade, Spring, 1952, v. 1, #4.pp. 23-28. map, views.

4 ..."Christmas Dinner for Lee's army: cooked in one of Richmond's finest hotels, the feast was eaten in field." Richmond, Va., Cavalcade, Winter, 1951, v. I, #3, pp. 11-15, views, cartoons, partly colored.

5 ..."Salt the South Could Not Savor." In: Va., Cavalcade, Autumn, 1953, v. 3, #2, p. 4-7. Facsms., views. On salt works at Saltville, Va., poor distribution to other CSA states, 1861-1864.

6 **RAE, R.N.**
"A Mississippi Soldier of the Confederacy." In: CV, July/ Aug., 1922, v. XXX, p. 262-265, 287-289. Per reminisc., member 13th Miss. reg. CSA.

7 **RAEUBER, Charles A.**
"The Index: A Weekly Journal of Politics, Literature & News- First Published in London, May 1, 1862." London, May 1, 1862." London Jour. Confed. Hist. Soc., Winter 1966, v. 4, #4, p. 173-176, life Henry Hotze.

8 **RAGAN, Cooper K.**
"Tyler County Goes to War." Woodville, Texas: Tyler County Dogwood Festival, March 25, 1961. Sm. 4to, decr. wraps, ills., 107 pp. An 11 pp. article in a special edition.

..."Tyler County Goes to War- 1861: Company F, First Texas Regiment, CSA." In: Tx. Mil. Hist. Nov., 1961, v. 1, #3, p.1-11, roster.

9 ..."Josephus Somerville Irvine, 1819- 1876, the Worthy Citizen: Address delivered at the dedication of the Josephus Somerville Irvine Monument, Wilson's Chapel, Newton county, Texas, April 21, 1963." Houston, Texas, 1963, cover title. 4to, wraps, 46 pp. bibliog., 34-39.

10 **RAHM, Frank Henry**
"Reminiscences of his capture and escape from prison and adventure within the Federal lines, by a member of Mosby's command, with a narrative by a C.S. Naval officer." Richmond, Daniel Murphy Print, 1895. 8vo, wraps, 48pp. cover title. $350-g. Narrative of Lt. Edward Archer, p.23-43. Dorn-II, 1295.

11 **RAINES, L.H., Mrs.**
"United Daughters of the Confederacy. Origin, history, and growth of the organization." In: CV, 1898, v.6, p.451-462, ports.

12 **RAINEY, Isaac Nelson**
"Experiences of I.N. Rainey in the Confederate Army." (Columbia?, Tenn., 1965) 4to, wraps, 107pp. (rep. from typed copy)

13 **RAINS, Gabriel James**
"Torpedoes, by the Chief of Confederate Torpedo Service." In: SHSP, 1877, v.3, p.255-260.

14 **RAINS, George Washington**
"History of the Confederate Powder Works. Address delivered by invitation before the Confederate Survivors Association at its fourth annual meeting, on Memorial Day, April 26, 1882." $250-r, Pres:

$150-r. Augusta, Ga., Chronical. and Constitutionalist Print, 1882, wraps, 8vo, 30pp. (micro-cd, $3.)

...Newburgh, N.Y., Newburgh Daily News, (1900's) (1884)-$250., 1882. 8vo, wraps, 29pp.

...Wendell, N.C., Broadfoot's Bookmark, 1979, 8vo, wraps (stiff), 29pp. $10.

15 ..."Notes on making saltpetre from the earth of the caves. By Maj. Geo. W. Rains, corps. of artillery and ordnance, in charge of the Gunpowder Dept., CSA, late of the USA, and former asst.-prof. chemistry, etc., USMA." Augusta, Ga., Chronicle and Sentinel, 1861. 8vo, wraps, 12pp.

...Richmond: Chas. H. Wynne Pr. 1862. 8vo, wraps, 15pp.

16 **RAINWATER, Percy Lee**
"An analysis of the secession controversy in Mississippi, 1854-1861." In: Miss. Valley Hist. Rev., 1937, v.XXIV, p.35-42. $7.50.

17 ..."An Economic Interpretation of Secession: Opinions in Mississippi in the 1850's." (Baton Rouge, La.) JSH, Nov. 1935, v.I, #4, p.18.

...Reprint: in printed wraps (Franklin Press) Baton Rouge, La., 18pp.

..."Excerpts from Fulkerson's "Recollections of the War Between the States." In: Miss. Val. Hist. Rev., 1937, v.XXIV, p.351-373. Published also as loose extract.

18 ..."The Presidential Canvass of 1860 in Mississippi." In: Miss. Law Jour., Aug. 1933, v.V, #4, p.267-291. Other articles, in this series under title:-

19 ..."Mississippi storm center of secession, 1856-1861." Baton Rouge, La., O. Claitor, 1938. 8vo, cl, illus., maps, xi, (2), 248pp. 300 copies. $125-bmk-96.

...Baton Rouge, La., Louisiana University Press, 1985. 8vo, cl, dj, 266p. $32.50.

20 ..."Notes on Southern Personalities." In: Jour. South. Hist., 1938, v.IV, p.209-227. Leading personalities of Civil War period. Govs. Clark and Pettus (Miss.) Henry W. Allen, J.D.B. DeBow, Al. G. Brown, Judge Jno. Perkins (La.), Wm. L. Yancey, etc.

21 ..."Letters to and from Jacob Thompson." (Baton Rouge, La.) JSH, 1940, v.VI, p.95-111.

22 **RAISIG, Lewis Miles**
"The Confederate $20 Diana note (1861)." In: Numismatic Scrapbook, May, 1960, v.26, p.1249-1255. facsm., view, bibliog.

23 ..."Confederate treasury notes; new views on old vignettes...the CSA $20 clipper ship notes of 1861." In: Numismatist, July 1956, v.69, v.69, p.739-741, facsms.

24 ..."Confederate Treasury Notes: new views on old vignettes (1864)." In: Numismatist, April, 1953, v.66, p.338-343. facsm., port.

25 ..."The CSA $1 paddle steamer notes of 1862." In: Numismatic Scrapbook, April 1959, v.25, p.823-827, facsm., view, bibliog.

26 ..."Currier's Express-train and legal tender." In: Antiques, Sept. 1954, v.66, p.210-211. views facsms. 20 types of American bank notes and CSA currency, c.1855-1865.

27 ..."The hammer cancellation of Confederate treasury notes." In: Numismatic Scrapbook, May 1958, v.24, p.921-925, facsms., view.

28 ..."Postmarks on interest-bearing CSA Treasury notes, 1862-1863." In: Numismatist, May, 1952, v.65, p.484-487, facsms.

29 **RALEIGH NEWS AND OBSERVER**
"What might have been. Incident in financial history of the CSA." In: SHSP, 1896, v.24, p.230-231.

30 **RAMAGE, B.J.**
"Wade Hampton." In: Sewanee Rev., 1902, v.10, p.368-373. See: Wm. P. DuBose.

31 **RAMAGE, C.J.**
"Robert Toombs." In: Va. Law Reg., ns, June, 1923, v.IX, p.104-107.

32 ..."Sketch of Howell Cobb (1816-1886)." In: Va. Law Reg., ns, Nov. 1922, v.VIII, p.486-491.

32a **RAMAGE, James A.**
"John Hunt Morgan: Folk Hero of the Confederacy." In: CV (new) Nov/Dec. 1986, v.34, #5, p.14-19, plate, ports.
..."Rebel Raider: the Life of General John Hunt Morgan." Lexington: University of Ky. Press, 1985. 8vo, cl, dj, 328pp, ills. plus 16 p. ills. $25.

33 **RAMEY, Emily G. and Marshall John K. Gott**
"The Years of Anguish/Fauquier County, Virginia, 1861-1865." Collected and compiled for the Fauquier County Civil War Centennial Committee. (Warrenton, Va., 1965) Fauquier Democrat. 8vo, cl, engr. endsheets, ports, illus., facsms., 201, xxxi, (233)-(2)pp., i.e., 235pp. $45.

34 ..."Confederate Indian Sinking of the J.R. Williams, June, 1864." "Journal West", Jan. 1972, p.43-50., v.XI.

35 ..."The Phillips Expedition. The abortive Federal Invasion of Texas, January-February, 1864. By Lary C. and Donald L. Rampp." In: TMH, 1971, v.IX, #1, p.22-33, fldg. map.

36 **RAMPP, Lary C.**
"Civil War Battle of Barren Creek Indian Territory, 1863." Oklahoma City: Chron. Okla., Spring, 1970, v.XLVIII, #1, p.74-82, illus.

37 **RAMPP, Lary C. and Donald L.**
"The Civil War in the Indian Territory." Austin, Texas: Presidial Press, 1975. 8vo, cl, dj, maps (2-fldg.) ports, vii, (1),, 210pp. map liners, bibliog., 181-201. $10.

38 ..."William C. Quantrill's Civil War Activities in Texas, 1861-1863." In: TMH, 1970, v.8, #4, p.221-231.

39 ..."The Civil War in the Indian Territory. The Confederate advantage, 1861-1862." In: TMH, 1972, v.X, #1, p.29-41.

40 ..."The Civil War in the Indian Territory. Blunt's Pursuit." In: TMH, 1972, v.X, #4, p.249-272, fldg. map.

41 ..."The Civil War in the Indian Territory. The Phillips' Expedition and Stalemate." In: TMH, 1973, v.XI, #2, p.77-108.

42 ..."The Civil War in the Indian Territory. Confederate Guerrilla Operations Intensify." In: TMH, 1973, v.XI, #3, p.173-195.
..."The Civil War in Indian Territory. Confederate Guerrilla Operations End." In: TMH, 1973, v.XI, #4, p.251-280.

43 **RAMSAY, H. Ashton**
"The most famous of sea duels." In: Harpers Wk., Feb. 10, 1912, v.LVI, p.11-12, v.LVI, p.11-12.

44 ..."Wonderful career of the Merrimac." In: CV, June-July, 1907, v.XV, p.310-313.
"Monitor and Merrimac." See: John Lorimer Worden

45 **RAMSAY, T.N.**
"Sketches of the great Battles in 1861, in the Confederate States of America. Sumter, Bethel, Manassas, Springfield, Hatteras, Lexington, Leesburg, Port Royal, Columbus or Belmont. Also sketches of Jefferson Davis and A.H. Stephens." Salisbury, N.C., J.J. Bruner Print, 1861, 8vo, wraps, 32pp. Cover: "Sketches of the American Revolution of 1861."

46 **RAMSDELL, Charles William**
"Behind the Lines in the Southern Confederacy. Edited with a foreword by Wendell H. Stephenson." Baton Rouge, Louisiana State University Press, 1944. 12mo, cl, dj, front(port), cloth, xxi, (1), 136pp. $40.
...(1969) Greenwood Press, Reprint.

47 ..."The Changing Interpretations of the Civil War." Reprint: Journal of Southern History. $8. V.III-#1, Feb., 1937, wraps, 25pp., p.3-27.

48 ..."The Control of Manufacturing by the Confederate Government." n.p., 1921, Offprint, wraps, 19pp. From: MVHR, Dec. 1921, v.VIII, #3, p.(231)-249.

49 ..."Confederate Government and the Railway." In: Amer. Hist. Rev., July 1917, v.XXII, #4, p.794-810. $15.

50 ..."The Frontier and Secession." Reprinted: from "Studies in Southern History and Politics." Columbia University, New York, 1914. 8vo, wraps, cover title, 1/2-title. (61)-79pp.

51 ..."Last hope of the Confederacy-John Tyler to the Governor and Authorities of Texas." In: QTSHA, 1910/1911, v.XIV, p.129-145.

52 ..."Laws and Joint Resolutions of the Last Session of CSA Congress." Edt., see as title. $40.

53 ..."Gen. R.E. Lee's Horse Supply, 1862-1865." (Lancaster, Pa. Press, 1930) 8vo, wraps, cover title, p.758-777, reprint Amer. Hist. Review, XXXV, July 1930, #4.

54 ..."Lincoln and Ft. Sumter." Journal of Southern History, Vol.III (Aug. 1937), 259-288.
...Do: "Some Problems Involved in Writing Hist. of the Confederacy." ibid, II (May 1936, 133-147)

55 ..."Lincoln and the South." Baton Rouge: Louisiana State University Press, 1946. 12mo, cl, facsms., ports, viii, (2), 161pp.

56 ..."Materials for research in the Agricultural History of the Confederacy." In: Agricultural Hist., Jan. 1930, v.IV, p. 18-22.

57 ..."Some problems involved in writing the history of the Confederacy." In: JSH, 1936, v.II, p.142-157.

58 ..."Texas in the Confederacy, 1861-1865." In: "The South in the Building of Nation." 13vols. (Richmond: So. Hist. Pub. Soc., 1909-1913, v.III, p.402-417.

59 ..."Texas from the Fall of the Confederacy to the Beginning of Reconstruction." In: TSHA, 1907/1908, v.XI, p.199-219.

60 ..."The Texas State Military Board, 1862-1865." In: SWHQ, 1923/1924, p.253-275, v.XXVII.

61 ...See Wendell H. Stephenson's sketch of Ramsdell as historian of the CSA.

62 **RAMSEUR, Stephen Dodson, Major, CSA**
"The Fight between the two iron monsters, the Monitor versus the Virginia as described by Maj. Stephen Dodson Ramseur, CSA." In: CVH, Sept. 1984, v.30, #3, p.268-271. Edt: Gary Gallagher. See: Gary Gallagher, (new biography of Ramseur.

63 ..."Gettysburg." In: SHSP, 1880, v.8, p.310-312. See: Gary W. Gallagher.

64 ..."Sketch of Maj. Gen. S.D. Ramseur." In: LWL, May 1968, v.V, #1, p.1-10.

65 ..."From Rapidan to Spotsylvania Court House." In: SHSP, 1885, v.13, p.236-239. See: Wm. Ruffin Cox.

66 ..."Maj.Gen. S.D. Ramseur's report of operations, from 4th-27th May 1864." In: SHST, 1874, v.1, p.138-140.

67 **RAMSEY, Frank H.**
"Confederate Marines." In: Leatherneck, Nov. 1955, v.38, #11, p.38-39.

68 **RAMSEY, Grover C.**
"Confederate Postmasters in Texas, 1861-1865." Waco, Texas, W.M. Morrison, 1963. 8vo, stiff wraps, (71)pp. $25-b, 200 copies printed.

69 **RAMSEY, J.G.M., Dr.**
"Autobiography and Letters of..." Edited: William B. Hesseltine, Nashville: Tenn. Hist. Comm., 1954. 8vo, cl, port(front), illus., xvi, (1), 367pp. CSA surgeon and Confederate Treasury Agent. $20.

70 **RAMSEY, James Verlin**
"God's Way in the Sanctuary remembered. A sermon preached Dec. 23, 1860, before the congregations of the 1st and 2nd Pre-

sbyterian Churches of Lynchburg, assembled together in commemoration of the first meeting of the General Assembly of the Church of Scotland, on Dec. 20, 1860." Lynchburg: 1861. 8vo, wraps, undescribed CSA Imprint.

71 ..."True Eminence founded on holiness. A discourse occasioned by the death of Lt. Gen. T.J. Jackson. Preached in the First Presbyterian Church of Lynchburg, May 24, 1863. By Rev. James B. Ramsey." Lynchburg: Virginian "Water Power Pr." 1863, cover title. 8vo, wraps, 57pp. $60.

72 **RANCK, George Washington**
"The Bivouac of the Dead and its author." Cincinnati: The R. Clarke Co., 1898, 12mo, cl, pl. port, 73pp. $45. Contains text of the poem.

73 ..."O'Hara and his elegies." Baltimore: Turnbull Bros., 1875. 16mo, cl, 41pp. Text of "Bivouac of the Dead." See: Gen. Albert G. Brackett and T. O'Hara.

74 **RAND, Clayton**
"Sons of the South." Portraits by Dalton Shourds, Harry Coughlin and Constance Joan Naar. New York: Holt, Rinehart and Winston. (1961) 4to, cl, 212pp. ports. Rise and Fall of the Confed., p.97-151.

75 **RANDALL, J. Calvin and John W. Haseltine.**
"Circular to collectors." In: Numismatist, Feb., 1952, v.65, p.129, facsm. of broadside (Phila. Apr. 2, 1874) on restrike of dies made for CSA cents but not adopted by the CSA.

76 **RANDALL, James Garfield**
"The Civil War and Reconstruction." Bost., N.Y., D.C. Heath Co. (1937) 8vo, cl, illus., ports, maps, facsms., diagrs., Bibliog/notes, 881-924, xvii, 959pp. The whole period of conflict and readjustments, political factors as well as a cultural background.

77 ..."The Civil War and Reconstruction with supplementary bibliography." xvii, 971pp.
...Bost: D.C. Heath and Co., 1961, Second edition, revised. Large 8vo, cl, illus., maps, notes, bibliog., xvi, 820pp. Basically same as 1937 edt., but five chap. titles altered, follows a more "liberal" turn, less "southern" i.e., more critical of slavery issue; more pro-Lincoln's handling of the Sumter engagement; sees reconstruction in a "revisionist" light.
...1973 Reprint.

78 ..."The Divided Union." Bost: D.C. Heath Co., (1961), 3rd., xvi, 572pp. Identical to 1961, except for chapters on Reconstruction omitted.
...1969, p.838, $10.50

79 ..."Lincoln and the South." Baton Rouge: Louisiana State University Press, 1946. 12mo, cl, dj, facsms., ports, viii, 161pp.

80 ..."Lincoln in the role of a dictator." In: So. Atl. Quart., July 1929, v.XXVIII, p.236-252. The liberal statesman Lincoln approached a dictatorship more closely than any Amer. President.

81 ..."The Unpopular Mr. Lincoln." Abraham Lincoln Quarterly, June 1943, reprint, v.II, #6, p.255-280.

82 ..."The War Restudied." (Baton Rouge, La.) JSH, Nov. 1940, v.VI, #4, p.439-457. Separate reprint, printed wraps. $4.

83 ..."Some legal aspects of the confiscation acts of the Civil War." In: Am. Hist. Rev., Oct. 1912, v.XVIII, p.79-96.

84 ..."When war came in 1861." In: Abe Lincoln Qrt., 1940, v.1, p.3-42. Incidents and factors in 1860/1861, involved in Lincoln's decision to declare war.

85 **RANDALL, James Ryder**
"Maryland. Air-"My Normandy." n.p., n.d., 1p. $225-bmk. "Unrecorded CSA imprint." Handcolored in green and yellow, central illus. in red.
..."Maryland." (Savannah, 1862?) Broad-

side. 32x11cm. $150-bmk. Crandáll-3202.

..."Maryland, my Maryland and there's life in the old land yet, by J.R. Randall, late of Baltimore. Respectfully dedicated to the Army of the Potomac, by the ladies of Richmond." Richmond: MacFarland and Ferguson, 1862. 12mo, wraps, 8pp. Crandall-3151.

..."Maryland, my Maryland and other poems by James Ryder Randall." Balt., N.Y., J. Murphy Co. (1908) 12mo, cl, 180pp., incl. front(port)

86 ..."The poems of James Ryder Randall." Edt., with Intro. by Matthew Page Andrews. N.Y., Tandy-Thomas Co.,1910. 12mo, c, x, 221pp., facsm., front (port) plates, facsm.

..."Maryland, my Maryland." Broadside, 1p. narrow folio. n.p., n.d., (1861?) One of the earliest printings, identified by misspelling author's name "Randal" and of misprint "touch" for "torch" in 3rd line. $150.

..."My Maryland." Richmond, 186?. Broadside 24x14cm. Harwell-1245 + 3202.

..."Maryland, My Maryland. Crescite et Multiplicamini. Written by a Baltimorean in Louisiana. Music adapted and arranged by C.E." Baltimore: Miller and Beacham, 1861. Folio, 5pp. (Dichter and Shapiro, p.113.

..."Maryland, My Maryland. Sheet music Randall was in Louisiana when he learned the Southern states had seceded. That night he was inspired to write MMM. The next day he mailed a copy to a friend in Baltimore, where it was immediately published without his knowledge. This is a prior issue without advertisements on page 6. Due to fact the printing was rushed, its unlikely a long list of music would have been printed on final leaf.

87 ..."The Gallant Pelham. Jeb Stuart's "Boy Artillerist", from Alabama." In: SHSP, 1902, v.XXX, p.338-339. Poem.

88 ..."General W.H.C. Whiting. A Chevalier of the Lost Cause." In: SHSP, 1896, v.XXIV, p.274-277.

89 ..."We Sleep, but We are not dead." Patriotic song, illus. with Maryland coat of arms on front cover." Baltimore: 1862. 4to, 6pp.

90 ..."Maryland. Air-"My Normandy"." n.p., n.d. Not in Crandall/Harwell. Broadside: 24 1/2x20cm. Central illus., in red. Colored geren and yellow. $225-bmk-114.

90a **RANDALL, Ruth**
"I Varina: a biography of the girl who married Jefferson Davis." Boston: Little, Brown, 1962. 8vo, cl, 243p, ills, ports. $20.

91 **RANDOLPH COUNTY, Virginia**
"Roster of Confederate Veterans from Randolph County." Randolph County Historical Society. In: Mag. Hist. and Biog., April 1961, v.12, p.76-85. Monuments: Elkwater, Mt. Iser, Beverly, Mingo Flats and Mace Mts.

92 **"RANDOLPH Guard (Virginia),**
Brief History of the Company. Muster Roll of the Company as it left Farmville, June 11, 1861. Comm. by Capt. N. Cobb, 44th Va. Reg." In: SHSP, 1895, v.XXIII, p.94-98.

93 **RANDOLPH, Alfred Magill**
"Lee's Birthday." In: SHSP, 1889, v.17, p.352.

94 **RANDOLPH, Bessie Carter**
"Foreign Bondholders and the Repudiated debts of the Southern States." (Concord, N.H., 1931) Reprint: American Journal International Law, v.25, #1, Jan. 1931. p.63-82. 8vo, wraps. Still outstanding bonds for: N.C., S.C., Fla., Ala., Miss., La., Ark.

94a **RANDOLPH, Forrest**
"Ride beyond Glory." N.Y., Kingston Pub.

Co., 1984. 12mo, paper, 253pp. Zebra Books. Series: 'The Confederate,' #2. Division: Simon & Schuster.

95 **RANDOLPH, Hollins Nicholas**
"Address delivered at the annual convention United Daughters of the Confederacy by...president Stone Mountain Confederate Monument Association, at Savannah, Ga., Wednesday, Nov. 19, 1924." (Savannah?) 1924. 8vo, wraps, cover-title, 11pp. $20-bmk-121. A plea for contributions to SMCMA.

96 **RANDOLPH, Innes**
"Poems." Edt: Harold Randolph. Baltimore: Williams and Wilkins (1898) 12mo, wraps, front(port) (vii), 13-17pp. See: Curtis Carroll Davis.

97 ..."The good rebel." Edt: George H. Callcott. In: South. Folklore Jour., Sept. 1954, v.18, p.175-176. Oral text of a ballad composed and printed in 1866, represents sentiment of Confed. soldier after the war.

98 **RANDOLPH, Isham**
"Gleanings from a harvest of Memoirs." Columbia, Mo., Privately printed for author by E.W. Stephens, 1937. Confed. memoirs by a Virginia., 8vo, cl, ports, 5-84pp. $50.

99 **RANDOLPH, J.W. and Co.**
"Catalogue of scarce Confederate publications (new and second-hand books) and books relating to the War Between the States. For Sale." J.W. Randolph and Co., Richmond, Va., July 1893. 8vo, wraps, 15pp. $35-bmk-114.

100 **RANDOLPH, James**
"The Lay of the Last Rebel." (Poem) (Savannah, Ga., 1867) 12mo, 3pp. No imprint. Dated at end: Savannah, Mar. 1867. Written by James Randolph. DeRenne-II, 697. See: under title.

101 **RANDOLPH, Norman Vincent**
"Address delivered by Comrad N.V. Randolph before R.E. Lee Camp, #1, Confed. Vets., Dec. 3, 1886." Richmond: Johns and Co., 1887. 8vo, wraps, 15pp. Origin, growth, present cond. Lee #1. $25.

102 **RANDOLPH, Nowlin**
"Judge William Pinckney Hill aids the Confederate War effort." In: SwHQ, July 1964, v.LXVIII, #1, p.14-28.

103 **RANDOLPH, Robert C., Mrs.**
"Letter from a Virginia Lady to the Federal Commander at Winchester, Va." In: SHSP, 1880, v.8, p.124-132.

104 **RANDOLPH, Sarah Nicholas**
"The Life of Gen. Thomas J. Jackson ("Stonewall Jackson")." Phila: J.B. Lippincott and Co., 1876. tk.12mo, cl, front(port), 363pp., illus. $90-bmk.

105 **RANDOLPH, W.F., Capt.**
"Manner of Stonewall Jackson's death." In: CV, 1903, v.11, p.545-547, plate. Randolph was Capt. of Jackson's bodyguard.

106 **RANDOLPH, William Fitzhugh**
"Chancellorsville-the flank movement that routed the Yankees, Gen. Jackson's mortal wound and how he received it, by Capt. W.F. Randolph." In: SHSP, 1901, v.XXIX, p.329-337.

107 ..."First Manassas. The closing scenes of battle." In: SHSP, 1895, v.XXIII, p.259-264.

108 ..."With Stonewall Jackson at Chancellorsville, by W.F. Randolph, Captain of Jackson bodygurad." n.p., n.d., 12mo, wraps, (12)pp. $65.

109 **"RANK and File:**
Civil War Essays in Honor of Bell Irwin Wiley. Edited: James I. Robertson and Richard M. McMurry." San Rafael, Cal., Presidio Press (1976) 8vo, cl, 164pp., bibliog., 157-164. $10-bmk.

110 **"RANK, respectively,**
in the United States and Confederate States Armies." Nashville Banner, Feb. 1904. In: SHSP, 1903, v.XXXI, p.369-370. See: ante, p.190 for a list, CSA.

110a **RANKIN, Thomas M.**
"23rd Virginia Infantry." Lynchburg, Va., H.E. Howard, 1985. J.P. Bell Print, Lim. Atg. Edt, 646. 8vo, cl, (3), 141p, maps, ports. $17.50.
..."37th Virginia Infantry." Lynchburg, Va., H.E. Howard, 1987. 8vo, cl, dj, (4), 150p, maps, port. 1,000 copies, signed.

111 **RANKINS, Walter**
"Morgan's Cavalry and the Home Guards at Augusta, Kentucky. An account of the Attack of a detachment of Morgan's Cavalry, on the home guard at Augusta, Ky., Sept. 27, 1862." p.308-320. Louisville, Ky: Standard Print Co., 1953. Reprint: Filson Club Hist. Quart., v.27, #4, Oct. 1953. $30-ob. 8vo, wraps, 15pp. (said: 100 copies)

112 **RANSOM'S Brigade**
See: Edwin G. Moore.

113 **RANSOM, Matt Whitaker**
"Addresses at the unveiling of the bust of Matt. W. Ransom." Raleigh, N.C., 1911, Edwards and Broughton. 8vo, wraps, port, 55pp. CSA General from Northampton Co., N.C. Pub. N.C. Hist. Comm., Bul. #10. Statue in the Rotunda, State Capitol at Raleigh.

114 **RANSON, A.R.H.**
"General Lee as I knew him." In: Harpers Monthly Mag., Feb. 1911. 15pp. colored print. $40.

115 ..."Reminiscences of the Civil War, by a Confederate Staff Officer." In: Sewanee Review, 1913, v.XXI, p.428-447; 1914, v.XXII, p.1-23, 129-150, 298-318, 444-457; XXIII, Jan. 1915, p.75-83. Early part of war in Va., Army of Tenn., Battle of Wilderness, Petersburg Campgn. Also: So. Atl. Qrt., Oct., 1913, v.XII, p.291-301.
n.p., n.d., wraps, 122pp. "Privately printed for relatives and friends of Major A.H. Ranson." $40.

116 ..."New stories of Lee and Jackson." In: So. Atl. Quart., Oct., 1913, v.12, p.291-301.

117 **RAPER, Horace W.**
"William W. Holden the Peace Movement in North Carolina." In: NCHR, Oct. 1954, v.XXXI, p.493-516. $8.
..."William W. Holden: North Carolina's Political enigma." Chapel Hill: University of North Carolina Press, 1985. 8vo, cl, xvi, 376pp, $30.

118 **RAPHAEL, Morris**
"The Battle in the Bayou Country and beginning of chapters by Chester Harrington Minvielle." Detroit, Mich., Harlo Print (1975). 8vo, cl, dj, illus., maps, 199pp.

119 **RAPIER, Regina (title)**
"Felix Senac:...Saga of Felix Senac, being the Legend and Biography of a Confederate Agent in Europe." (Atlanta) Social Circle, Ga., 1972. 12mo, cl, illus., index, 216pp. Author, "Bulletin of Art and History", v.11, #1.

120 **RAPP, Wilhelm**
"Baltimore, 1861: we want Rapp. A letter, trans. and edt., Alice H. Finchk." In: Soc. Hist. Germans in Md., Rep. Describes secession riots in Balt., and author's flight from the city.

121 **"RARE Confederate Books**
and Pamphlets and Publications on Confederate History. The result of 40 years research by a diligent collector. Sold Tuesday afternoon, May 6, 1913. A catalogue sale conducted by Stan V. Henkels/Samuel T. Freeman, Phila." sm.4to, wraps, color flags, front, facsm., plate, 41pp., 352 items.

122 **RASCHE, Dennis T.**
"Fortalice 88." In: Glades Star (Oakland, Md.) June 1956, v.2, p.317-319. views. Fortification protecting B & O Bridge 88, across Youghiogheny River, Garrett Co., captured by Confederates 26, April 1863.

123 **RATCHFORD, James Wylie**
"Some Reminiscences of persons and incidents of the Civil War, by...Asst. Adj-Gen. of the CSA." Richmond, Va., Whittet and Shepperson, 1909. 8vo, wraps, 69, (1)p. errata. $40-bmk.
...(Austin, Texas: Shoal Creek Pub., 1971. 8vo, cl, boxed, xxi, 69, (1)pp. Mor., $30. 2-ports, preface: Dr. Bluford B. Hestir. $25 bmk-84...1972.

124 **RATHBORNE, St. George**
"Battle Smoke; or, the War Correspondent among guerrillas. A thrilling tale of Perryville and Stone River. By Hugh Allen (pseud)." N.Y., Novelist Pub. Co., 1883. War Library, pocket edition, v.1, #2. 12mo, pict. wraps, 111pp.

125 ..."The Old Knapsack, or Longstreet's Mad Charge at Knoxville." By Marline Many (pseud)." War Library, v.7, #257. 4to, pict. wraps, 24pp. $40-bmk.

126 **RATLIFF, Mary**
"The City of Vicksburg." In: CV, Oct. 1928, v.XXXVI, p.385-398. Historical items re city during the war.

127 **RATTERMANN, Heinrich Armin**
"General Johann Andreas Wagner, eine biographische Skizze, von H.A. Rattermann." Cincinnati, Druck von Mecklenborg and Rosenthal, 1877. Dornb-II, 3145. 8vo, wraps, front(port), 30pp.

128 **"RATTLESNAKE. The,"**
Richmond, Va., Service Press, 1923-1940. v.1-18 (#2): April 1923-Feb. 1940, bound 18 vols. in 5. Illus., part colored, music, plates, some colored, folded, ports, maps (some fldg.) facsimilies. Official publication, Virginia Division Sons of Confederate Veterans, 1934-1940, authorized publication Veterans Corp., 1st Va. Infantry. Edt: Capt. John C. Weckert. Titles vary, v.1-7, #7, April 1923-July 1929. "The Stars and Bars."; afterwards, "Rattlesnake."

128a **RAVENEL, Charlotte St. J.**
"Journal letter kept by Charlotte St. J. Ravenel of Pooshee Plantation for Miss. Meta Heyward." Suffolk, Va., Robt. Hardy Pub., 1986. 8vo, wraps, 24pp.
See: Susan R. Jervey.

129 **RAVENEL, Henry William**
"The Private Journal of Henry William Ravenel, 1859-1887. Edited by Arney Robinson Childs." Columbia: University of South Carolina Press, 1947. (The R.L. Bryan Co.) 8vo, cl, dj, front(port), sketches, facsm. liners, xxi, (1), 428pp., index. $35-b.

130 ..."Recollections of southern plantation life." In: Yale Rev., n.s., 1936, v.XXV, p.748-777. (Planter, botanist and writer. Set down in Feb. 1876, describes negro slave.

131 **RAVENEL, Samuel W.**
"The boy brigade of South Carolina." In: CV, Nov. 1921, v.XXIX, p.417-418.

132 **RAWLE, William**
See: Dabney Herndon Maury.

133 **RAWLEY, James A.**
"Race and Politics", "Bleeding Kansas", and the "coming of the Civil War." Phila: Lippincott, 1969. 8vo, cl, 304pp.

134 **RAWLINS, John Aaron**
"General Grant's Censor-Rawlins warns he must stop drinking." In: SHSP, 1896, v.24, p.154-155.

135 **RAWLS, John L.**
"The spar torpedo in the War Between the States (1864)." In: Mil. Collect. and Hist., 1957, v.9, p.70-72 (Fall) diagr., notes.

136 **RAY, Benjamin L., Dr.**
"Diary of Dr. Benjamin L. Ray, Army Corps in Virginia and Pennsylvania, June 12, 1861 to April 27, 1865. Owner Mrs. Lulu Mobley, Dade City, Florida." Copies by Historical Records Survey, State Archives Survey, 1937. 4to, stiff boards, (1), 9pp. $20.

137 **RAY, D.M.**
"Roster of the 16th Texas Cavalry (dismounted) C.S.A." Whitewright, Texas, private print, July 29, 1907. (See: H.D. Pearce) 8vo, stiff wraps, 24pp. Lists officers and enlistees of regiment and location after War. North Central Texas, rendezvoused at Clarksville and disbanded at Hempstead in 1865.

138 **RAY, Frederic**
"The Art of Gilbert Gaul." In: CWTI, April 1963, v.II, #1, p.24-30, illus. This artist was only 10 at war's end, but his talent was exhibited in many sympathetic drawings of the Confederacy.

139 ..."As an illustrator from England saw the South and its people, Frank Vizetelly." In: CWTI, May 1965, v.IV, #2, p.12-16, illus., port. British correspondent for the Illustrated London News.

140 ..."Chambersburg, Pa., war came three times to this Northern town." In: CWT, May 1960, v.II, #2, (OS) p.12-14, illus., maps, port.

141 ..."Forgotten artist of the Confederacy. Allen C. Redwood." In: CWTI, June 1964, v.III, #3, p.40-43, illus.

142 ..."Frenchman painted Confederate masterpieces." In: CWT, May 1961, v.III, #2 (OS), p.12-13. Charles Hoffbauer made four murals for the Memorial Institute, "Battle Abbey." In 1913-1920, four seasons: Spring: foot cavalry of Stonewall Jackson; Summer: Lee and his generals; Autumn: J.E.B. Stuart and a group of cavalrymen on a foray; Winter: battery of artillery struggle accross a snowy field.

143 **RAY, George Henry**
"Oration on Lee." In: SHSP, 1891, v.19, p.392-400.

144 **RAY, Lavender**
"The Attack upon Cheat Mountain. Death of Thomas Y. Brown." Noonan, Ga. (1880) Galley Proff. (Stutler/Shetler-663.) The 1st Ga. Reg. in Cheat Mt. Campaign, Sept. 12-13, 1861.

145 **RAY, Neill W.**
"Sketch of the Sixth Regiment, North Carolina State Troops (Infantry)." (n.p., d. 1901?) 8vo, wraps (cover title), 1p., lf, 44pp., lf. Dedication signed: N.W. Ray, Capt. Co. "D", "6th" N.C. State Troops.

146 **RAYBURN, Larry**
"Wherever the Fight is Thickest": General James Patton Anderson of Florida." In: FHQ, January 1982, v.LX, #3, p.313-336, (2)pp. ports. See also Gen. Jas. Patton Anderson Letters, Henry D. Clayton.

147 **RAYMOND, Robert Rossiter**
"Fort Sumter." In: Coast Guard Art. Jour., Aug. 1929, v.LXXI, p.136-142. Operations leading to bombardment of Fort from official records Union/CSA armies.

148 **RAYNER, Juan Timoleon**
"An eyewitness account of Forrest's raid on Memphis (1863)." In: West THSP, 1958, v.12, p.134-137. Letter to sister Louisa Rayner Hodges, from Pueblo, Colo, 25 July 1926.

149 **REA, D.B.**
"Cavalry incidents of the Maryland Campaign." In: Maine Bugle, 1895, v.II, p.117-123.

150 ..."Sketches from Hampton's Cavalry, in the Summer, Fall and Winter Campaigns of '62, including Stuart's Raid into Pennsylvania and also, in Burnside's rear, by a Private." Raleigh: Strother and Co., 1863. 12mo, wraps, cover title, 72pp. (Duke)

151 ..."Sketches from Hampton's Cavalry, embracing the principal exploits of the cavalry in the campaign of 1862 and 1863." Columbia: South Carolinian Steam Pr., 1864. 12mo, wraps, cover title, 158pp. $85. Crandall-2658; Dornb-II 747/749.

..."Sketches from Hampton's Cavalry, 1861-1862-1863, being a reprint of a pamphlet published in Columbia later part of '64 author unknown." From U.R. Brooks' "Stories of the Confederacy", 1912. p.67-218. See: Edward L. Wells.

152 **REA, H.C.**
"An immortal son of the South. Address at Gen. James H. Lane Chapter, UDC, Jan. 8, 1943." Charlotte, N.C., 1943. 8vo, wraps, 12pp.

153 **REA, R.N., Capt.**
"A Mississippi soldier of the Confederacy." In: CV, July 1922, v.30, #7, p.262-265, 287-289.

154 **REA, Ralph R.**
"Sterling Price, the Lee of the West." Little Rock, Ark., Pioneer Press (1959) 8vo, cl, dj, illus., maps, ports., map liners, xii, (1), 229pp. op $15-r.

154a **REA, Reba F.**
"Nelson County Civil War Soldiers."
See: under title.

155 **READ, Charles W.**
"Reminiscences of the Confederate States Navy." In: SHSP, 1876, v.1, p.331-362.

156 **READER, Samuel James**
"The First Day's Battle at Hickory Point." Kan. State Hist. Soc., 1931, v.I, #1, p.28-49. Edt. from diary of Reader by George A. Root, Battle, Sept. 13-14, 1856, with Jim Lane's Free-State men and Kickapoo Rangers or "Border Ruffians (pro-slave party). One of the first conflicts precipitating the Civil War between states.

157 **REAGAN, James W. and James Mitchell**
"More about the fight at Brocks Crossroads." In: CV, May 1910, v.XVIII, p.228-230.

158 **REAGAN, John Henninger**
"An Account of the Organization and Operations of the Post Office Department of the Confederate States of America, 1861-1865." In: So. Hist. Assn. Pubs., Wash., D.C., 1902, v.6, p.(314)-327.

159 ...Autograph: signature, framed with port. of the CSA Postmaster-General. $50.

160 ..."The cause of the war." In: CV, May 1894, v.II, #5, p.146-149.

161 ..."The Real Cause of the War." In: CV, 1902, v.10, p.209-211, port.
...also, Mar. 1896, v.IV, #3, p.75-79, ports.

162 ..."Why the South seceded." In: CV, May 1903, v.XI, p.215-217.

163 ..."A conversation with Governor Houston." In: QTSHA, April 1900, v.III, #4, p.279-281. Secession, English and French reasons for a war and building up their respective sources of cotton in India and Algeria.

164 ..."Flight and capture of Jefferson Davis." In: Ann. War, p.147-159.

165 ..."John Reagan's courage." In: CV, March 1903, v.XI, p.119-120.

166 ..."Lee's Birthday." In: sHSP, 1889, v.XVII, p.349.

167 ..."Memoirs With Special Reference to Secession and the Civil War." N.Y., Neale Pub. Co., 1906. 8vo, buck, port(front)ports, illus., 351pp. $150-bmk-105, $200-bohl.
...Do: Austin, Texas: Pemberton Press, 1968. 8vo, cl, d/w, new intro-index, 382pp. $9.50.
...n.v., Ams. Press, 1973.

168 ..."Reasons against a trial of Jefferson Davis." In: South Hist. Assn. Pub., 1902, v.6, p.422-427.

169 ..."Selections from the Reagan Papers: The Butler-Reagan Ticket of 1884." Edt: Gerald Nash. (Lexington, Ky.) JSH, Aug., 1955, v.XXI, #3, p.379-386.

170 ..."Southern Political Views, 1865. Letter to Pres. Johnson." In: South Hist. Assn. Pub., 1902, v.6, p.132-142, 210-219.

171 ..."Speech of Judge Reagan, 1897." In: SHSP, 1915, v.40, p.312-314. States rights, women of the CSA.

172 ..."Speech of Hon. John H. Reagan of Texas in the House of Representatives, Feb. 29, 1860." (slavery and secession).

Wash., T.McGill, printer (1860) 8vo, sewn, 15pp. Caption title.

173 ..."State of the Union. Speech of the Hon. John H. Reagan, of Texas. Delivered in the House of Representatives, January 15, 1861." (Wash., W.H. Moore, Print, 1861.) 8vo, sewn, 15pp., caption title.

174 ..."The Truth of History. Judge Reagan on the Hampton Roads Conference. Reply to Watterson." In: SHSP, 1897, v.XXV, p.68-77.

175 ..."That Hampton Roads Conference." In: CV, 1901, v.9, p.168-170.

176 **REAMS'S STATION, Battle of**
See: Charles M. Stedman, Williams Carter Wickham.

177 **REARDON, Patrick**
"Confederate Small Arms." (London) Jour. Confed. Hist. Soc., June 1963, v.I, #4, p.131-142, ports (2)pls: 4, Dec. 1963, II, #1, p.27-40. Plates (6).

177a **REAVES, Jordan B.**
"The Long Arm at Honey Springs." In: Con. Vet., Mar/Apr., 1986, #2, p.32-6, ill, map, ports.

178 **"REBEL Bull Session**
on guns as reported by "An English Combatant who fought for the South, A. by T.E.C. From the 1864 edition of "Battlefields of the South." In: CWTI, Aug. 1967, v.VI, #5, p.26-29, illus.

179 **"REBEL Gunpowder."**
Broadside. n.p., c.1865. 8x3 3/4", decr. borders, with several other bawdy verses. $35.

180 **"REBEL Officers."**
Engraving (5 1/2x9") by H.Wright Smith. A composite of Beauregard, Johnston, Lee, Davis, Johnson, Bragg, Buckner and Hollins, all in Federal uniforms. $25.

181 ...Same, Price, Stuart, Polk, Pemberton, Jackson, Magruder, Ewell, Longstreet and A.P. Hill, all in Federal Univorm, in ovals. Small engr. below of a negro leaning on a bale of cotton, with "CSA" and a CSA flag. $25.

182 **"REBEL, The,"**
(Columbia) Jan. 28, 1863. In: SCHM, Jan. 1963, v.64, #1, p.13-15.

183 **REBELLE, A Young, (pseud.)**
"Abram. A military poem, by a Young Rebelle, Esq., of the army." Richmond: Macfarlane and Fergusson, 1863. 12mo, wraps, 63pp. (auction '64) $50.

184 **"REBELLION in the North!!**
Extraordinary disclosures! Vallandigham's plan to overthrow the government! The peace party plot! Full details of the organization. Its declaration, oaths, charges, signa, signals, passwords, grips, etc., etc." (Richmond? 1864) 8vo, caption title, 16pp. Order of American Knights, Order of the Sons of Liberty.

185 **"RECOGNITION of the Confederate States**
considered in a reply to the letter of "Historicus" in the London Times. By Juridicus. Originally published in the Charleston Courier." Charleston, S.C., Evans and Cogswell, 1863, (Crandall-2741) 12mo, wraps, 41pp. (Millard Fillmore)

186 **"RECOGNITION of the Southern Confederacy.**
Indispensible for resolving the American Question." London: William Ridgway, 1863. 8vo, sewn, 7pp., front(fldg. map)

187 **"RECORD of Company G,**
originally Co. M, of the 6th Regiment, Alabama Infantry Volunteers, from 2nd day of June, 1861, to 31st day December, 1864." n.p., n.d. 8vo, wraps, cover title, 13pp.

188 **"RECORD of organizations**
engaged in the campaign, siege and defense of Vicksburg. Compiled from the Official Records by John S. Kountz, Sect.

and Historian of the Commission." Wash: GPO, 1901. 8vo, wraps, fldg. map, 72pp.

189 **"RECORD of the Lynchburg Home Guards,**
organized Nov. 8, 1859. Mustered into the C.S. service April 24, 1861. Reorganized April 22, 1871." Lynchburg, Va., Bell, Browne and Co., 1877. 8vo, wraps, 30, (2)p. and roster.

190 **"RECORDS in the National Archives**
relating to Confederate soldiers." Washington, D.C. (1959) 8vo folder (8)pp., its publication 60-10.

190a **RECORDS of the Confederate Armies**
in possession of Southern Historical Society, Richmond, Va. (cover title). Wash.: War Records Pub. Offices, 1880. 8vo, 1/2 Mor., xxxiii, 58pp. Head: Southern Historical Society.

191a **"RECORDS of the Confederate Military**
Commission in San Antonio, July 2- October 10, 1862. Edited by Alwyn Barr." In: SwHQ, July 1966, v.LXX, #1, 2, and 4, p.93-109, 289-313, 623-644, Oct. 1967, v.LXXI, #2, p.247-277; July 1969, v.LXXIII, #1, p.83-104; Oct. 1969, v.LXXIII, #3, p.243-274.

192 **RECTOR, Charles R.**
"Morgan "Goes a-Raiding" and Views West Virginia." In: W.Va. Rev., May 1929, v.6, p.310-311, 322. illus.

193 **RECTOR, Henry M. and J.R. Kannaday**
"Letters of Henry M. Rector and J.R. Cannaday to John Ross of the Cherokee Nation." By Harry J. Lemley. Oklahoma City: Chron. Okla., Autumn, 1964. v.XLII, #3, p.320-329. Biographical notes.

194 **RECTOR, Henry Massey, Gov. Arkansas**
"Special Message of the Governor on Federal Relations." title head: (House Doc.) (Little Rock, Ark.) Johnson and Yerkes, 1860. sm.8vo, sewn, 7, 7pp. 13th Session. See: Elias Nelson Conway.

195 ..."Message of the Governor to the State Convention, Marcy 4, 1861." Little Rock, Ark., True Democrat Pr., 1861. 8vo, wraps, 7pp.

196 ..."Message of the Governor to the State Convention, May 6, 1861." Little Rock: Johnson and Yerkes, 1861. sm.8vo, wraps, 13pp. text in double column. Also in: Jour. both sessions of convt., #406. "Best exclude these papers from gen. circul."

197 ..."Message from the Governor to the General Assembly of Arkansas, in extra session, Nov. 6, 1861." Little Rock: Johnson and Yerkes, 1861. 8vo, wraps, 32pp.

198 ..."Message to the Senate. Executive Office, Little Rock, Nov. 11, 1861." caption title, no imprint. (Little Rock, Ark., 1861) 12mo, sewn, 3pp.

199 ..."Message of the Governor of Arkansas and other documents on Federal Relations." Little Rock, Ark., Johnson and Yerkes, 1861. 8vo, wraps, 35pp. See: Elias N. Conway.

200 ..."Rules and articles for the government of the Army of Arkansas. Office of the Military Board, Little Rock, June 1861." Little Rock, Ark., Johnson and Yerkes, 1861. 8vo, wraps, 39pp. Half-title: "Articles of war of Arkansas and the Confederate States." (Allen, 1860-1861.)

201 **RED BADGES**
See: Thomas D. Jeffreys.

202 **"RED RIVER CAMPAIGN.**
Centennial Commemoration Center, Texas-Mansfield, Louisiana April 4, 1964. Battle of Mansfield." n.p., (1964) (The publication and distribution of this booklet to the libraries of Texas has been made possible by: El Paso Natural Gas Company, El Paso, Texas) 8vo, stiff decr. wraps, cover title, map, ports, plate, 36pp. (various authors) See: Chs. L. Martin.

203 **RED RIVER CAMPAIGN:**
Battle of Mansfield; Alwyn Barr; William

Byrd; Lester Fitzhugh; Jno. E. Hewitt; Alonzo H. Plummer; Red River Campaign; Charles L. Martin.

204 **REDD, Richard Menefee**
"Reminiscences of Richard Menefee Redd, better known as Colonel "Dick" Redd, from childhood to old age..." Lexington, Ky., Clay Print, 1929. 8vo, wraps, p.62, (2), front(port). "War record", 20-23. Dorn-II, 3073.

205 **REDDICK, Glenn Eugene**
"When the Southern Senators said farewell." In: South. Speech Jour., Mar. 1950, v.15, p.169-197. Form and contents of their farewell speeches in the Senate Jan./Feb., 1861.

206 **REDDICK, Henry W.**
"Seventy-seven years in Dixie; the Boys in Gray of 61-65. By H.W. Reddick. Santa Rosa, Washington County, Florida." (Freeport, Fla., Observer Pr.) Published by H.W. Reddick, 1910. 8vo, wraps, 3lf., (9)-48pp. Intro: A.P. Bjorklund, Sept. 1910. Reddick enlisted in "Walton Guards".
...Reprinted, 1963.

207 **REDFIELD, Horace V.**
"Death of General John H. Morgan." In: AW, 1879, p.614-618.

208 **REDPATH, James**
"Neither Traitor Nor Rebel." Denver, Colo., Commonwealth Pub., 1890. Reprint: "The Commonwealth", vol. II, #4, Jan. 1890, wraps, 8vo, p.385-392. Jeff Davis. (Widener Lib.)

209 **REDWAY, George William, Major**
"Fredericksburg, a Study in War." London: S. Sonnenschein and Co., N.Y., Macmillan Company, 1906. 16mo, cl, xvi, 297, (1)p. incl. map., 5-fldg. maps, (in pocket) Special Campaign Series #3.

210 ..."The War of Secession, 1861-1862. Bull Run to Malvern Hill." London: Swan Sonnenschein and Co., 1910. 12mo, cl, viii, 392pp. 14-fldg. maps in pocket. Special Campaign Series #11.

211 ..."The American Civil War; a Reply..." In: Unit. Ser. Mag., ns, Mar. 1911, v.XLII, p.636-641. A reply to his critics.

212 **REDWAY, Maurine Whorton**
"Marks of Lee on our Land." San Antonio, Tex: Naylor Co., 1972. 8vo, cl, dj, illus., xvi, 180pp. $25-bmk.

212a **REDWING, Morris (pseud.) Jas. Milford Merrill**
"Freedom's Sons; or, the Palmetto Rifles of Carolina." N.Y.(?), The War Library, v.6, #66. Wraps, ills, 24pp. (Bmk-26) $14.
..."Mosby's Trail; or, Guerillas of the Potomac. By Morris Redwing." N.Y., 1883, Beadle War Library #196, vol. 6. 8vo, wraps, 23pp.
...N.Y., 1883. 8vo, wraps, 21pp, vol. 3, #55.

212b **REDWOOD, A. C. (Allen?)**
Sketches of CSA Soldiers during Rest Periods. In Va. State Library, shown on pp.40, 41, 42 in Va. Cavalcade, XX, #4. Spring 1971.

213 **REDWOOD, Allen C.**
"Following Stuart's Feather." In: Jour. Mil. Ser. Inst., XLIX (July), p.111-121. 1911. Member Cav. Corp., ANV, under Stuart.

214 ..."With Stonewall Jackson." In: Scribner's Monthly, June 1879. 8vo, sewn, extract 14pp. illus.

215 ..."Chancellorsville Revisited." In: Jour. Mil. Ser. Inst., Jan. 1909, v.XLIV, p.91-95. Re: Chancellorsville Campaign."

216 ..."Cover Picture: Allen C. Redwood, Confederate Illustrator." In: Md. Hist. Mag., 1959, v.54, p.293-294. By Richard Walsh and C.A. Porter Hopkins.

217 ..."Jackson's "Foot Cavalry" at the second Bull Run." In: B & L, v.II, p.530-538, illus.
...Also: CWTI, Dec. 1965, v.4, p.42-

218 ..."A Boy in Gray." In: Scribner's Monthly, 1881, v.22, p.641-650.

219 ..."The cook of the Confederate Army." In: Scribner's Monthly, 1879, v.18, p.560-568, illus.

220 ..."The fortunes and misfortunes of Co. "C"." In: Scribner's Monthly, 1878/1879, v.17, p.528-536, illus.

221 ..."Johnny Reb at play." In: Scribner's Monthly, 1878/1879, v.17, p.33-37, illus.

222 ..."The horsemen in Gray." In: CWTI, June 1970, v.IX, #3, p.4-8, 45-48, illus., ports. Memoir of a Va. cavalryman and success of the CSA horse.

222a ..."The Confederate of '61." In: Photo.Hist. C.W., v.8, p. 137-54, ills.

..."The Confederate in the Field." In: Photo.Hist. C.W., v.8, p.155-78, ills.

222b ..."Stonewall Jackson." In: Photo.Hist. CW, v.10, p.97-116. Ports, incl. composite.

223 **REED, D.W., Compl.**
"The Battle of Shiloh and the organization engaged. Compiled from official records...under authority of the Commission." 1902 revised. Washington, D.C., GPO, 1909. 8vo, wraps, fold. maps, 122pp. $70-bmk. Head: "Shiloh National Military Park Comm."

224 ..."The Death of General Albert Sidney Johnston on the Battlefield of Shiloh." In: La. Jour. Hist., April, 1918, v.XVI, p.275-281. Maj. Reed was Sect., Historian Shiloh Mil. Park.

225 **REED, J. Davis**
"Capt. William Henry Murdaugh, Naval Career and Reminiscences." In: SHSP, 1909, v.37, p.38-51.

226 **REED, John Calvin**
"The Brothers' War." Boston: Little, Brown Co., 1905. 12mo, cl, xviii, 456pp., index. $15.

...Same, 1906. Defense of South and KKK.

227 ..."Reminiscences of Ben Hill." In: So. Atl. Quart., April 1906, v.V, p.134-149. Senator Benjamin H. Hill of Georgia.

227a **REED, Lida Lord**
"A Woman's Experiences during the Siege of Vicksburg." In: Cent. Mag/Apr. 1901. (v.39) NS, p.922-8.

228 **REED, Thomas Benton**
"A Private in Gray, by Thomas Benton Reed." Ninth Louisiana Infantry. Camden, Ark., T.B. Reed, 1905. 12mo, 2-ports, incl. front, 128pp. (brittle) Cloth or wraps. Rare. $300-ob.

229 **REED, Wallace Putnam**
"History of Atlanta, Georgia, with illustrations and biographical sketches of some of its prominent men and pioneers. Edited by Wallace P. Reed." Syracuse, N.Y., D. Mason and Co., 1889. sm.4to, ports, (5)-491, 211pp. Civil War period, p.83-217.

230 ..."Last forlorn hope of the Confederacy, in Trans-Mississippi Department." In: SHSP, 1902, v.30, p.117-121.

..."Last forlorn hope of the Confederacy." In: SHSP, 1902, v.30, p.117-121.

231 **REEDER, Red, Colonel**
"The Southern Generals." N.Y., Duell, Sloan and Pearce (1965). 8vo, cl, d/w, xiii, 237pp., maps, ports.

232 **REESE, Gussie**
"This They Remembered. The history of the four companies who went from Oglethorpe County to serve the War Between the States. The Gilmer Blues, Oglethorpe Rifles, Tom Cobb Infty., Echols Artillery." (Washington, Ga., Publishing Co., Jan. 17, 1965) 8vo, cl, 200pp., illus., ports, facsms., map. $40-b.

233 **REESE, James ("Edney Grays")**
"Private soldier life-humorous features." In: CV, April 1908, v.16, p.161-166.

233a **REESE, Michael II**
"Autographs of the Confederacy, a collection of handwriting of the men who led the Confederacy." Yonkers, N.Y., a Cohasco Pub., 1984. 4to, xxvi, 224pp, dj. Regular $48. Atg. $90.

234 **REESE, Thomas H.**
"Robert Edward Lee-No Citizen He." In: Mil. Law Rev., 1970, v.L, p.141-147.

235 **REEVE, Edward Payson**
"Casualties in the Old First at Gettysburg." In: SHSP, v.17, p.407-409.

236 **REEVES, Bennie Leronius**
"Lucius Quintus Cincinnatus Lamar: Reluctant Secessionist and Spokesman for the South, 1860-1885." Chapel Hill, N.C., University Press, 1973. 8vo, cl, v. 147 lfs. typescript, dissertation. Ann Arbor, Mich., University Micro., 1974.

236a **"REGISTER of Issues**
of Confederate States Treasury Notes." Dearborn, Mich., Dearborn Press, 1951. 8vo, iv, 189pp.
...Washington, D.C., GPO, (1900?) 8vo, cl, 190pp.

236b **"REGISTER of Names**
of Men Buried in the Confederate Cemetery, Spottsylvania Court House, Va. War 1861 to 1864." n.p., n.d. 12mo, wraps, 20pp. Reprint, 1966.

237 **"REGISTER of North Carolina Troops, 1861."**
Raleigh, N.C., Adjutant General's Office, Nov. 1, 1861. 12mo, wraps, 26, (1)pp. Crandall-1858.

238 **"REGISTER of officers**
of the Confederate States Navy, 1861-1865. As compiled and revised by the Office of Naval Records and Library, United States Navy Department, 1931, from all available data." Washington, GPO, 1931. 8vo, wraps, ii, 220pp.
...Mattituck, N.Y., 1983 reprint. $23. Jim Carroll and Co., 8vo, cl, intro, 220pp.
...Mattituck, N.Y., J.M. Carroll & Co., 1983. 8vo, xxvi, 220pp. Wraps $13. Cl $23. Intro: J. M. Carroll.

239 **"REGISTER of the Confederate dead**
interred in Hollywood Cemetery, Richmond, Va., Hollywood Memorial Association of Richmond, Richmond, Va." Gary, Clemmitt and Jones, 1869. Tall 8vo, wraps, 58pp.

240 **"REGISTER of the commissioned**
and warrant officers of the Navy of the Confederate States, to January 1, 1863." Richmond: Macfarlane and Fergusson, 1862. 8vo, (1), 38pp.
...(Richmond, Va., 1863?) 8vo, 14pp.
...Richmond: Macfarlane and Fergusson, 1864. 8vo, wraps, 16pp. Sewn as issued, not an imprint.

240a **"REGULATIONS**
for the Army of the CSA, 1863." Harrisburg, Pa., 1980 reprint. Bmk-$25. National Historical Society. 8vo, lc, 1420pp.

241 **"REGULATIONS for the government**
of the forces of the Confederate States, in the Department of Indian Territory. Promulgated at Fort McCulloch, May 1862." (Fort McCulloch, 1862) 8vo, orig. marbled paper wraps, 26, 14pp. Final 14pp. contains 21 general orders, presumably adopted by Albert Pike for Indian Territory. Streeter-$7000.
of the forces of the Confederate States in Dept. of Indian Territory. Part II-Respecting the rights, duties and business of the officer and soldier. Promulgated at Fort McCulloch, 1st July 1862." (Fort McCulloch, 1862) Streeter-$2000. 8vo, marbled paper wraps, 36pp.

242 **REID, Bill G.**
"Confederate Opponents of Arming the Slaves, 1861-1865." (Jackson, Miss.) Jour. Miss. Hist., Oct., 1960, v.XXII, #4, p.249-270.

243 **REID, George E.**
"Thrilling Reminiscences, Facts and Experiences of..., Company F, 23rd Regiment Alabama Volunteers in the Civil War from 1861-1865." Greenville, Alabama, (1900) 8vo, wraps, 28pp.

244 **REID, H.J., Miss**
"Sketch of Black Hawk Rifles, by Col. H.J. Reid." n.p., n.d., 8vo, wraps, cover title, 8pp.

245 **REID, Hugo**
"The American Question in a Nutshell; or, why we should recognize the Confederates." London: R. Hardwicke, 1862. 12mo, wraps, 31pp.

246 ..."Sketches in America with some account of the slavery question." London: Longmans, Green and Roberts, 1861. 12mo, cl, vi, (9)-320pp.
...Reprint: "American Crisis", Lond: 1862. Favored Eng. recognizing the CSA.

247 **REID, James E., et al**
"Richmond Grays' Flag. Ante Bellum. The Grays in the Confederate Army." Boston, Mass., 1887, (cover title) 8vo, gray cl, 100 copies (Carolina Bk)-$75. Members of Boston's GAR Post were presented the original "Stars and Stripes" by the Richmond Grays. To honor gift, 200 copies of booklet were given to members of the GAR Post and various members and officials in Mass. and Va. The sketch was given by Miles T. Phillips of Richmond. No recorded copy.

248 **REID, Jesse Walton**
"History of the Fourth Regiment of S.C. Volunteers, from the commencement of the war until Lee's surrender. Giving a full account of all its movements, fights and hardships of all kinds. Also a very correct account of the travels and fights of the Army of Northern Virginia during the same period. This book is a copy of the letters written in Virginia at the time by the author and sent home to his family. Containing an account of the author's services in the First Regiment of Engineer troops in the latter part of the war. With a short sketch of the life of the author. By J.W. Reid, private in Co. C., 4th Reg. S.C. Vols., afterwards Sgt. Co. K, 1st. Reg. Engineer troops." Greenville, S.C., Shannon and Co., 1892, 1/2lt, slip-case. $200-bmk-105.
...Dayton, Oh., Morningside, 1975, $12.50. 8vo, wraps, front(port), vi, (7)-143pp. $60-bmk.

249 ..."Honor Roll of Confederate Veterans of Chester County, S.C." Chester, S.C., n.d., 12mo, wraps, 20--.

250 ..."The Fourth Regiment of South Carolina Confederate Infantry." In: "Maine Bugle", 1897, v.IV, p.111-131. Letters to his wife.

251 **REID, Richard**
"A test case of "Crying evil"; desertion among North Carolina Troops during the Civil War." In: NCHR, Summer, 1981, wraps, 29pp.

252 **REID, Samuel Chester, Jr.**
"The Capture and Wonderful Escape of Gen. John H. Morgan, as reported by...of the Atlanta "Intelligencer". Edt: Joseph J. Mathews." Atlanta, Ga., Library of Emory Univ., 1947. Emory University Publications Sources and Reprints, Series IV. 8vo, wraps, 20pp., facsm., 350 copies. See also: T.H. Hines, J.H. Morgan. $30.

253 ..."A full account of the capture and wonderful escape of Gen. John H. Morgan with Captain T. Henry; thrilling and interesting incidents by 190." Atlanta, Intelligencer Presses, 1864. 8vo, wraps, 16pp.

254 ..."The Great Battle of Chickamauga." (Rebel Report) by S.C. Reed, ("Ora") Correspondent of the Mobile Tribune." Chattanooga (Tenn.) Reprinted for private circulation, 1864. 16mo, wraps, 14pp. (Mitchell-256)
..."Great Battle of Chickamauga, a concise history of events from the evacuation of Chattanooga to the evacuation of Chattanooga to the defeat of the enemy. Full details of the battle, incidents, etc., by S.C.

Reid, "Ora" of the Mobile Tribune." Mobile: F. Titcomb, 1863. 12mo, wraps, 16pp. Crandall 2660.

255 **REID, Sarah Robinson**
"Immortelles-A Tribute to the "Old South"." Little Rock, Ark: Brown Print, 1896. 12mo, cl, ix, (11)-295pp., (i), V-index, front. Much CSA-Mo. and Ark., port of J. Davis.

256 **REID, Warren D.**
"Escape from Fort Delaware-A Mississippi Confederate tells of his escape." (from the Richmond Dispatch, Aug. 19, 1900) In: SHSP, 1908, v.36, p.271-279.

257 **REID, William G.**
"Confederate opponents of arming of slaves, 1861-1865." In: JMH, 1960, v.XXII, p.249-270. See: Thos. R. Hay, Edward Spender.

257a **REIDENBAUGH, Lowell**
"33rd Virginia Infantry." Lynchburg, Va., H.E. Howard, 1987. 8vo, cl, dj, (3), 151p., maps, ports. 1,000 copies, signed.

258 **"REIDSVILLE (N.C.) Times."**
"Stonewall Jackson's Death." In: SHSP, 1882, v.10, p.143.

259 **REIGER, John F.**
"Deprivation, Disaffection and Desertion in Confederate Florida." In: FHQ, January, 1970, v.XLVIII, #3, p.279-298.
"Florida after Secession: Abandonment by the Confederacy and its consequences." In: FHQ, October 1971, v.L, #2, p.128-142.

260 ..."Secession of Florida from the Union. A Minority Decision?" In: FHQ, v.XLVI, #4, p.358-368.

261 **REIN, Otto**
"Aus meinem Leben wahrend der Gefangenschaft unter· den Confoderierten in Texas." In: Deutsch-Am. Geschichtsblatter, 1928, v.XXVIII, p.120-164.

261a **REINDERS, Robert C., Edt.**
"Two Letters of English Soldiers in Louisiana Confederate Regiments." In: LaH., 1967, v.8, p.260-4.

262 **REINFELD, Fred**
"The Story of Civil War Money." New York, Sterling Pub. Co., 1959, 8vo, wraps, illus., 93pp. $50-b. Short cat., Civil War money, Union, and CSA, currency and coins. 157 plates.

263 **REINHARDT, Victor**
"A Drummer Boy at Shiloh, by Vic Reinhardt." Terrell, Texas, 1910. 8vo, wraps, 12pp. $50. Append. as note: "Boy from Alabama at Shiloh."

264 **"RELATIVE strength of the two armies."**
In: CV, 1905, v.13, p.60. See: Gen. J.A. Early, in SHSP. Gen. Samuel Cooper, Randolph H. McKim.

265 **RELIGION in the CSArmy-SHSP**
See: Rev. John W. Jones, Benj. T. Lacy.

265a **"REMARKABLE Trials & Executions**
in the Confed. Serv., both in Army & Navy, with appropriate commentaries. By an exper. prosecutor & Judge Advocate, Confed. Army. With such reflections as may be suffester by expr. in regard the Mil. law, trials & executions of the army & Navy service." In 1. vol. Pub. under the patronage of Congress, Richmond, 1864. Richmond, 1864. Entered by John Poynter McMillan, Jan. 12, 1864.
Notes: v.XX, #4, p.428, Va. Mag. Hist. Mag.

266 **"REMARKS on Mr. Motley's Letter**
in the London Times on the War in America." Charleston: Evans and Cogswell, 1861. 8vo, wraps, 23pp. Sabin-69420 does not identify author (Wm. John Grayson) Author refutes Motley's "Causes of the Civil War" which made Motley ambassador to Vienna. See: Sabin-51103 for Motley's "Causes."

267 **"REMARKS on the manufacture**
of bank notes and other promises to pay. Addressed to bankers of the Southern

Confederacy." Columbia, S.C., F.G. DeFontaine and Co., 1864. 8vo, wraps, front, 31pp.

268 **"REMINISCENCE of fifty years ago. A,"**
In: "Nation", Feb. 16, 1911, v.XCII, p.178-179. Story of how formation of the CSA was received in community at large and point of view of finance.

269 **"REMINISCENCES of Confederate Cavalry Service."**
In: SB, ns, v.1, #10, p.609-613, 1885/1886. By a "soldier in the ranks, from Huntsville, Ala." Gen. Bragg's march into Ky., headed by Forrest, who commissioned Frank B. Burley.

270 **"REMINISCENCES of the Women**
of Missouri during the Sixties. Gathered, compiled and published by Missouri Division, United Daughters of the Confederacy." (Jefferson City, Mo., Hugh Stephens, n.d.) (1913). $65-g, $50-bmk-105. 8vo, cl, 311pp.

271 **RENFREW, Andrew W.**
"The Lake Erie Conspiracy." In: Detroit Hist. Soc. Bul., Mar. 1953, v.9, #6, p.5-9. CSA plot to seize steamer "Michigan", 1864.

272 **RENFROE, John J.D.**
"A Model Confederate Soldier, being a brief sketch of the Rev. Nathaniel D. Renfroe, Lieutenant of a company in the Fifth Alabama Battalion, of Gen. A.P. Hill Division, who fell in the Battle of Fredericksburg, December 13th, 1862." 13cm, 16pp., n.p., n.d., (1863?) Reprinted from "South Western Baptist" and from "Religious Herald." Issued as a Tract. (Thos. Owen)

273 ..."The Battle is God's." A sermon preached before Wilcox's Brigade, on fast day, the 21st August, 1863, near Orange Court House, Va., by J.J.D. Renfroe, chaplain 10th Alabama Regiment." Richmond, Va., Macfarlane and Fergusson, 1863. 8vo, wraps, cover title, 27pp. Crandall-4186.

274 **RENNOLDS, Edwin Hansford**
"A History of the Henry County Commands which served in the Confederate States Army, including rosters of the various companies enlisted in Henry County, Tenn. By Lieut. Edwin H. Rennolds, Company "K" Fifth Tennessee Infantry." Jacksonville, Fla., Sun Pub. Co., 1904. 12mo, cl, pl., ports, incl. front, 301pp. $300-g, $500.
...Kennesaw, Ga., Continental Book Co., 1961. 12mo, cl, reprint above. $25.

275 **RENSHAW, James A.**
"Major John B. Prodos, a Confederate Officer." In: LaHQ, 1927, v.X, p.241-248.

276 **RENTZ, William Oliphant**
"The Confederate States Ship "Georgia"." In: Georgia Hist. Quart., v.LVI, p.307-317. $8.

277 **"REPLY to a Critique**
on "Uncle John's Cabin", A, which appeared in the "Dundee Advertiser", April 1, 1865. By the author of "The attempt of the North to subdue the Southerners, etc." London: Simkins, Marshall Co., Liverpool, Edward Howell, 1865. 12mo, wraps, 45pp. Sabin-69680. See: "Attempt of the North, etc."

278 **"REPORT and Resolutions**
from the Committee on Relations with the Slaveholding States, providing for Commissioners to such states. Adopted in Convention, Monday, December 31, 1860." Charleston: Evans and Cogswell, 1861. 8vo, wraps, 7pp. Heading: "Convention of South Carolina."

279 **"REPORT of Commissioner**
for marking Confederate Graves. Letters from the Secretary of War transmitting final report of the Commissioner appointed to continue the work of locating and marking the graves of Confederate

dead." Washington: Government Print., Doc. 1105, 62nd Cong., 3rd Sess. House. 1912. 8vo, sewn, 28pp. Jas. H. Berry, Comm.

280 **"REPORT of Evidence**
taken before a Joint Special Committee of both Houses of the Confederate Congress, to investigate the Affairs of the Navy Department." P. Kean, reporter. Richmond, Va., Geo. P. Evans Co. (1863) 8vo, half-calf, 472pp.

280a **"REPORT of Georgia Soldier**
Roster Comm. submitted to the Legislature, July 2, 1906. Atlanta, Ga., Granklin print, 1906. 8vo, cl.
...Atlanta, Ga., G. W. Harrison, 1904. 1st Report issued. 6pp.
See: Allen D. Candler & Lillian Henderson.

281 **"REPORT of Military Operations**
(Confederate) during the Rebellion, 1861-1865." Washington: War Record Publication Office, 1878-1882?. 20 vols in 21 and supplement, fldg. maps. 8vo, "Prepared under direction of War Dept. of US, forms a part of preliminary edition "War of the Rebellion", a compilation of the official records of the Union and Confederate Armies." See also: "Miscellaneous Correspondence and Orders of Adj. and Insp. Gen. Office..."

282 **REPORT of Secretary of War:**
Exchange of Prisoners-Mar. 17, 1862 to the Confederate Congress. (Richmond, Va., 1862) 8vo, wraps, 27pp. (Henkels-1090, May 13) Besides Secty. report, letters and docs. of both Federal and Confederate officials of details and agreements of exchange.

283 **"REPORT of proceedings**
of various associations of ex-Confederates held at Dallas, Aug. 6-9, 1884." Dallas, Texas: Herald Print, 1884. $75. 8vo, wraps, 302, (1)pp. index. Includes history of Gano, Polignac and Ross Brigades, in Missouri, Tenn. and Ark.

284 ..."Report of proceedings of the various associations of ex-Confederates of Missouri, 1881." Dallas, Texas: Dallas Herald, 1881.
...2nd Meeting held in 1883 (Caxton Press)

285 **"REPORT of the Chief**
of the Department of the Military of South Carolina to His Excellency Governor Pickens." Columbia, S.C., Charles P. Pelham, 1862. 8vo, yellow wraps, 64pp. $35. (James Chestnut)

286 **"REPORT of the Committee**
on Federal relations in regard to the calling of a Sovereign Convention." Frederick, Md., E.S. Riley, 1861. 8vo, wraps, 22pp. Cover heading (Document F) by the House of Delegates, May 9, 1861. Condemns Federals for declaring war on Va., and the CSA and not taking sides. See: "Resolutions of the Comm. on Federal relations..."
...of the Free Market of New Orleans. Established for the Benefit of the Families of our Absent Volunteers, Aug. 16-Dec. 31, 1861." New Orleans, 1862, wraps, 8vo, 66pp.
...of Two Hundred Citizens appointed at a meeting of the resident population of New Orleans, on 12th December, 1872." New Orleans, La., 1873. 8vo, wraps, 27pp. $125. Led by Thomas A. Adams, protesting actions by the Pinchback government's radical reconstruction.

287 **"REPORT of the Committee,**
appointed under resolution of the Convention of the Financial Operations of the State of Georgia during the War." Milledgeville, Ga., Boughton Print, 1866. 8vo, stapled, fldg. table, 72pp.

288 **"REPORT of the Georgia**
Soldier Roster Commission, submitted to the Legislature July 2, 1906." Atlanta, Ga., Franklin Print, 1906, 8vo, wraps, pp.___.

...Atlanta, Ga., G.W. Harrison Print, 1904, 1st report issued, 6p.

289 **"REPORT of the Georgia Civil War** Centennial Commission Commemorating the War Between the States 1959-1965." (Atlanta: Georgia Civil War Cent. Comm., 1963) 8vo, stiff wraps, cover title, illus., 24pp.

290 **"REPORT of the Georgia State** Memorial Board of Monuments and Markers erected on Chickamauga Battlefield... Gen. J. McIntosh Kell, Chairman, et al." Atlanta: Franklin Print, 1899. 8vo, wraps, 58pp., illus(front) Emory.

291 **"REPORT of the Historian** of the Confederate Records to the General Assembly of South Carolina." Columbia, S.C., The State Co., 1898. 8vo, p.280-294. Evidently a preliminary report to following:

292 ..."Report of the Historian of the Confederate Records to the General Assembly of South Carolina." 5 vols. (Wm. J. Rivers, comp.) Columbia, S.C., The Bryan Print, 1898-1900. 8vo, cl, tables.
...Do: 1900, 89pp. (McKissick-2156)

293 ..."A List of Official publications of the CSA Government of Virginia." See: Earl G. Swem.

294 **"REPORT of the Joint Committee** of the General Assembly of Virginia on the Harper's Ferry outrages, Jan. 26, 1860." Doc: XXXI, Richmond, Va., 1860. 8vo, sewn, 24pp. $75-Carolina Book.

294a **"REPORT of the Joint Select Committee** appointed to investigate the condition & treatment of prisoners of war." Richmond, Va., 1865. 8vo, sewn, 17pp, caption title. House of representatives, March 3, 1865. Confederate States, House of Representatives.

295 **"REPORT of the Judge Advocate General** on "The Order of American Knights" alias "The Sons of Liberty", a Western Conspiracy in aid of the Southern rebellion." Washington, D.C., Chronicle Print, 1864. 8vo, wraps, 16pp.

296 ..."Sons of Liberty." (Indianapolis? 1864) 8vo, wraps, 10pp. $20. Secret Ritual of Sons of Liberty.

297 **"REPORT of the Proceedings** of Ross' Texas Brigade Association, at its sixth annual reunion, held in the city of Greenville, Texas, in conjunction with Ector's and Granbury's Brigades, Maxey's Brigade, Eleventh Texas and many unattached ex-Confederates, Wednesday and Thursday, Aug. 5 and 6, 1885." Dallas, Texas: Carter and Gibson Print, 1886. 14x22cm, 57pp. $30.
...of the Society of the Army of Tennessee at the 37th Meeting, held at Vicksburg, Miss., Nov. 7/8, 1907." Tall 8vo, decr. cl, front. in color, 232pp. Cincinnati, Oh., 1908.

298 **"REPORT of the Secretary of the Navy;** Messages and Documents, 1864-1865." Wash: GPO, 1864. Tk.8vo, cl, 1259pp. diagrams, maps. $50. Much on Naval operations, Blockade-running off coast of N.C. (around 150pp.)

299 **"REPORT of the Special Committee,** on the Recent Military Disaster at Forts Henry and Donelson and the evacuation of Nashville. Hon. H.S. Foote, Chm. H.C. McLaughlin, clerk." Richmond: Enquirer Book and Job Press, Tyler Wise, Allegre and Smith, 1862. 12mo, wraps, 178pp. $150-bmk.
...N.Y., Arno, 1972, "Confederate Imprints Collection Series."

300 **"REPORT of the Special Joint Committee** in regard to certain public property on hand at the Evacuation of Columbia and the Surrender of General Johnston's Army." Columbia, S.C., F.G. DeFontaine, 1866. 8vo, wraps, 31pp. Sabin-87496.

301 **"REPORT of the Stars and Bars** Committee, United Confederate Veterans, Richmond Reunion, June 1 to 3, 1915." (n.p., 1915) 12mo, wraps, 16pp.

302 **"REPORT on Lee's School History. The,** Defended by Georgia Society Committee. Some unwritten history about the Mission of the steamer "Star of the West". The exchange of prisoners responsibility for refusal to exchange placed upon the North. Lee's history defended in toto by Committee's Report. From the Chattanooga (Tenn.) Sunday Times, Nov. 6, 1899." (Chattanooga, 1899) 8vo, wraps, 8pp. DeRenne III, 964.

303 **"REPORT on Publication** of the Official History of the Rebellion. May 18, 1866." Wash: Senate Missc. Docs., #102, 39th Congress, 1st Sess., Vol. 1, p.2. Senator Wilson recommends passage of this joint resolution.

304 **"REPORT on the address** of a portion of the members of the General Assembly of Georgia. Printed by order of the convention." Charleston, S.C., Evans and Cogswell, 1860. 8vo, wraps, 6pp. Signed: William G. DeSassure. Printed also in Journals of the Convention 1860-1861. An answer to the address of a portion of the members of the General Assembly of Georgia against State action.

305 **"REPORT on the reburial** of Confederate Dead in Arlington Cemetery and attention called to the care required for the graves of Confederate soldiers who died in Federal prisons and military hospitals now buried in Northern States." Washington, 1901. 8vo, wraps, fldg. plates and plans and large map. United Confederate Veterans. Washington, D.C. Division. Charles Broadway Rouss Camp, #1199.

306 **"REPORTS of Federal** and Confederate officers, including account of the Battles at Lewisburg, West Virginia, May 24, 1862, and the Battle of Dry Creek (White Sulphur Springs), W.Va., Aug. 26, 1863. These copies of reports were recently furnished by Col. J.M. Schoonmaker who commanded the 14th Pa. Regiment in the Battle of Dry Creek." (White Sulphur Springs, 1915) 12mo, wraps, 19pp.

307 **"REPORTS of the First,** Seventh and Seventeenth Virginia Regiments in 1862." In: SHSP, 1910, v.38, p.262-267.

307a **"REPORTS of the Operations** of the Army of Northern Virginia, from June 1862 to & including the Battle of Fredericksburg, Dec. 13, 1862. In 2 vols." Richmond, R. M. Smith, 1864. 8vo, cl, v.I, 602pp, v.II, 627pp. (Jk-$450). Bmk-$250. (Wm. Allan $400).

308 **"REPORTS of the Special Committee** on the recent military disasters at Forts Henry and Donelson and the evacuation of Nashville." Richmond, 1862. Congress, Hse. Reps., Special Comm. on recent military disasters. 8vo, cl, 178pp. Hon. Henry Stuart Foote, Chm.

309 **REQUIER, H.F.D.**
"Lee, a Poem." In: SHSP, 1886, v.14, p.62-63.

309a **RERICK, Roland H.**
"Memories of Florida; embracing a gene history of the province, territory, & state." Atlanta, Ga., Southern Historical Ass'n, 1902. 4to, cl. 2 vols, ports. Vol. 1, contains events in wartime Florida & rosters of various units.

310 **"RESACA, Ga. Centennial Program** May 16, 1964. Calhoun, Georgia. Resaca Confederate Cemetery 1864-1964." Large 8vo, stiff wraps, stapled in a 16mo, (16)pp. roster of CSA dead, dble. pg. map, battle, etc.

311 "RESERVATIONS of right of secession in adopting the Constitution." In: Am. Law Rev., Nov. 1903, v.XXXVII, p.945-946.

311a "RESOLUTION Adopted by Humphrey's Mississippi Brigade, Army of Northern Virginia (caption title)." Richmond, 1865. Crand:537. 8vo, broadside. Gdsp. $100.

312 "RESOLUTION of Company B, 20th Artillery Batt., Alabama Volunteers to re-enlist for the war." n.p., 1864. Broadside 24x15cm. Crandall 406. Hse. Reps., Feb. 8, 1864, Decatur, Ga., Jan. 27, 1864, Decatur, Ga., Jan. 27, 1864. T.J. Flake, Pres. See: Maj. Elbert Willett, John H. Curry.

313 "RESOLUTION of the Texas Brigade. 1st, 4th and 5th Texas Regiments, "Field's Division", Longstreet's Corps., Army of Northern Va." Camp Texas, Jan. 24, 1865. $100-0b. 8vo, 4pp. sewed.

314 "RESOLUTION passed at a meeting of the 9th Virginia Infantry, Jan. 25, 1865." Richmond, Va., House of Representatives, Jan. 30, 1865. 8vo, 2pp. folder, Thos. H. Williams, Pres.

315 "RESOLUTION passed by the Convention of the People of Arkansas, on Mar. 20, 1861." Little Rock, Ark., True Democrat Pr. (1861) Broadside, 34cm, text in 3-column. (Hargrett)

315a "RESOLUTIONS adopted by Company "H", "I", & "K", 13th Virginia Infantry, Jan. 28, 1865." Richmond, 1865. Crand: 536. 8vo, 2p. caption title. Dgsp. $100.

316 "RESOLUTIONS adopted by Sturdivant's Artillery Battalion, ANV, expressive of their determination to continue their efforts for independence." Broadside, 24 1/2x15 1/2cm, 1865. Head: Hse. of Reps., March 7, 1865. Crandall-558. $150.

317 "RESOLUTIONS expressive of the determination of Georgia to prosecute the present war..." Richmond, Va., 1864. 8vo, sewn, caption title, 2pp. House of Representatives, Jan. 11, 1864.

318 "RESOLUTIONS of the Committee on Federal relations of the House of Delegates of Maryland, with Senate Ammendments. Extra Session, 1861." Frederick, Md., B.H. Richardson Print, 1861. 8vo, wraps, 4pp. (Doc.I) By the Senate, May 14, 1861. See: Report of the Comm. on Fed. Relations.

318a "RESOLUTIONS of Wise's Brigade." Hdq. Wise's Brig., trenches near Petersburg, Va., Feb. 1, 1865. 8vo, wraps, 3p. (Crandall-2377) $75-Bmk.

319 "RESOLUTIONS passed at a meeting of the 14th Virginia Infantry, Jan. 24, 1865." Richmond, Va., House of Representatives Jan. 30, 1865. caption title. 8vo, 2pp folder. $150-r.

320 RESOURCES of the Confederacy in Feb. '65. "Confederate States of America, War Dept. Engineer Bureau. Richmond, Va., 16th Feb. 1865 and the Surgeon-General's Office." In: SHSP, 1876, v.II, p.123-125; 56-63; 85-105; 113-128; v.III, p.97-111.

321 "RESOURCES of the Confederacy." See: Robert G.H. Kean, Lucius B. Northrup, Sam'l P. Moore, Alex. R. Lawton, Jeremy F. Gilmer, I.M. St. John.

322 "RESTORATION of the name Jefferson Davis to the Cabin John Bridge, Washington, D.C. ...Reprint in: SHSP, 1910, v.XXXVIII, p.41-155.

323 "RETURN to the State of Louisiana of the flag of tenth Louisiana Regiment which was captured by the 11th Connecticut Regiment during the War Between the States in 1864. By the Grand Army of the Republic. Connecticut Dep. n.p.,

(1925) 12mo, wraps, cover title, (8)pp. Program. Dorn-II, 462.

324 **"RETURNED Battleflags**
of the Virginia Regiments in the War Between the States. The," (cover title adds: "with a history of the Confederate Memorial Institute, n.d. (1939). 12mo, wraps, 24pp. cover title. $15-bmk. In:Print $7.50

324a **"RETURNED Battle Flags**
presented to the Confederates at their reunion, Louisville, Ky., June 14, 1905." St. Louis: Buxton & Skinner, 1905. $75. Compliments of the Passenger Dept. "Cotton Belt Route" 8vo, buckram, (60)p., numerous flag color plates. Flags of the CSArmy, returned to the men who bore them by the US Government, 1905.
..."Returned Battle Flags to Virginia by the Secretary of War, Mar. 28th, 1905. Richmond, Va., Whittet & Shepperson, 1907?, 12mo, wraps, 30pp. $50-Bm.

325 **"REUNION of Company D,**
First Regiment Virginia Cavalry, CSA, held at Abingdon, Va., July 4, 1892." In: SHSP, 1892, v.XX, p.39-55.

326 **"REUNION of Confederate Veterans.**
Proceedings of the 27th Annual Reunion of the Confederate Southern Memorial Association and 22nd Annual Reunion of the Confederate Veterans held in Washington, D.C., June 4, 5, 6, and 7, 1917. Referred to committee on printing." Washington, D.C., GPO, 1918. 65th Congr., 1st Sess., Senate Doc. 117. 8vo, cl, 101pp.

327 **"REUNION of the West Virginia**
Div., Confederate Veterans and Sons of Confed. Vets, Hinton, W.Va. Speech of Hon. John T. McGraw of Grafton, W.Va." (Charleston, W.Va., 1911?) 8vo, wraps, 25pp. On cover-"Supplement" illus., Comp: Maj. J. Coleman Alderson.

328 ..."Reunion W. Virginia Div-Confederate Veterans and Sons of Veterans." Charleston, W.Va., News-mail (1912?) 8vo, wraps, 42pp. many illus.-monuments and generals. Held at Hinton, W.Va., Oct. 4-5, 1911. Shetler-$783.

329 **"REVELATIONS: a Companion**
to the "New Gospel of Peace", according to Abraham." New York: M. Doolady, 1863, 12mo, wraps, 36pp. Satire on Lincoln Administration, in a Biblical format. (Richard Grant White)
...Copy: with NY-Feeks and Bancker
...Copy: with Doolady on t.p., and cover.
...Copy: by J. Abbott in "New Gospel of Peace", #256.

330 **REYNOLDS, Albert, Capt.**
"Chancellorsville, retrospective glance at the Battlefield." In: SHSP, 1896, v.24, p.205-210.

331 **REYNOLDS, Alexander Welch**
"Correspondence between Governor Porter and Major Sykes concerning Reynold's Brigade." In: SHSP, 1884, v.12, p.45-48.

332 **REYNOLDS, Cedric Okell**
"The Postal System of the Southern Confederacy." In: W.Va. Hist., Apr. 1951. v.12: 200-279, notes. M.A. Thesis, W.Va. University.

333 **REYNOLDS, Donald E.**
"Editors Make War: Southern Newspapers in the Secession Crisis." Nashville: Vanderbilt Univ. Press, 1970, 8vo, cl, d/w, xi, 304pp. o.p.

334 **REYNOLDS, George**
"Sewanee and the Cumberland Plateau in the Civil War." (Sewanee, Tenn., Archives Dept., University of the South, c.1961) 8vo, wraps, cover title, 16pp.

335 **REYNOLDS, Henry Clay, Capt.**
"A Warrior and His Wife. Historical Narrative of the First President of Alabama College." Compl., Henry Bruce Rogan (Montevallo, Alabama, Times Print., 1962) 8vo, wraps, 51pp. 500 copies.

336 **REYNOLDS, John Hugh**
"Official Orders of Governor Harris Flanagin, Commander in Chief of the Militia of Arkansas." July 20, 1863, to Nov. 10, 1864. In: Pub. Ark. Hist. Assn., v.II, 1908, p.362-423.

336a **REYNOLDS, Thomas C.**
"CIRCULAR Sir: Each county & parish should form a voluntary Confederate association, to cooperate with the Trans-Mississippi committee of Public Safety & the corresponding committee. . . ." Marshall, Texas: 20th Aug., 1863. Broadside: 11 x 8.5", 2p printed both sides in bdl. column. Winkler-903. $950. Exiled Gov. Missouri.

337 **REYNOLDS, William Clark**
"The Diary of William Clark Reynolds, 1860-1861." In: Christopher Gist Hist. Soc., Papers, 1955-1956. Leaves 52-70. A sale merchant of Lexington, Mo., near Charleston, W.Va., Jan, 1860-Jan. 1862, with his CSA service with W.Va. troops as far as Lynchburg.

338 **RHETT, Claudine**
"Frank H. Harleston. A Hero of Fort Sumter." In: SHSP, 1882, v.10, p.307-320.

339 ..."Morris Island." In: SHSP, 1884, v.12, p.336-342.

340 ..."Sketch of John C. Mitchel, of Ireland killed whilst in command of Ft. Sumter." In: SHSP, 1882, v.10, p.268-272.

341 **RHETT, R. Barnwell**
"The destroyers of the late Confederacy." In: South. Mag., July/Dec., 1874, v.XV, 12pp.

..."The Confederate Government at Montgomery." By Edt. 'Charleston Mercury, 1860-2.' In: B&L, v.1, p.99-110, ports, ills.

342 **RHINESMITH, W. Donald**
"Traveller. Just the horse for General Lee." In: Va. Caval., Summer, 1983, v.XXXIII, #1, p.38-47. illus., ports+group port., seal. Back/front a cover (color) of Lee and his generals, Summer mural by Charles Hoffbauer.

342a **RHOADES, Jeffrey L.**
"Scapegoat General: the Story of Maj.-Gen. Benjamin Huger, CSA. Hamden, Conn., Shoestring Press, 1985. 8vo, cl, dj, 164pp, ills, maps, notes, bibliog. $17.50.

343 **RHODES, Charles Dudley**
"Partisan Rangers of the Confederacy." In: "Photographic Hist. of Civil War." v.4, N.Y., 1911, p.165-180. Reprint: Glendale, Calif., 1970.

344 ..."Robert E. Lee the West Pointer, including Stratford Hall by Mrs. Robert Scott Spilman and The Lineage and Career of Robert E. Lee, by George S. Wallace. Illustrations by J.F. DeYoung." (Richmond, Va., Garrett and Massie, 1932) The West Virginia Division of the Robt. E. Lee Memorial Foundation. 4to, decr. boards, color, ports, vi, 42pp. vignettes thru text. $40-bmk.

345 **RHODES, James Ford**
"Who Burned Columbia?" In: Amer. Hist. Rev., v.VII, 1902, p.485-493.

346 **RICARDS, Sherman L. and Geo. M. Blackburn**
"A Demographic History of Slavery: Georgetown County, S.C., 1850." In: SCHM, 1975, v.76, #4, p.215-224.

347 **RICE, De Long, Supt. Nat'l. Park**
"The Story of Shiloh." (Nashville, Tenn: Brandon Print, 1919) Stiff wraps, 8vo, 64pp. illus.

...Do: 1920 edt.

...Do: (Jackson, Tenn: McCowat-Mercer) 1924, stiff wrap, illus., 70pp.

348 **RICE, Harvey Mitchell**
"The Life of Jonathan M. Bennett, a study of the Virginias in transition." Chapel Hill, North Carolina University Press, 1943. $25-bmk-84. 8vo, cl, facsm., front(port), xiii, 300pp. Bennett was Confederate State Auditor in Richmond, during the war, his

influence advanced Stonewall Jackson in rank.

349 **RICE, J.G.**
"The Battle of Olustee." In: CV, June 1914, v.XXII, p.244-255.

350 **RICE, Jessie Pearl**
"J.L.M. Curry: Southerner, Statesman and Educator." N.Y., King's Crown Press, 1949. 8vo, xii, 242, (1)pp. bibliog: 231-8. Thesis Columbia Univ., on Jabez Lamar Monroe Curry (1825-1903) officer CSA.

350a **RICE, John H.**
"A System of Modern Geography, compiled from various sources & adapted to the present condition of the world; expressly for the schools & academies in the Confederate States of America. In which the political & physical condition of the states comprising the Confederate States of America are fully treated of, & their progress in commerce, education, agriculture, internal improvements & mechanic arts, prominently set forth." Atlanta, Ga., Franklin Printing House, Wood, Hanleiter, Rice & Co., 1861. 4to, wraps, 91p.

350b **RICE, Turner**
"The adventurous career of the C.S.S. 'Dunbar'." In: Ala. Rev., Oct. 1985, v.38, p.280-8.

351 **RICH MOUNTAIN, Battle of**
See: C.T. Allen, Henry M. Price.

352 **"RICH'S Commemorates**
the Civil War Cent. 1861-1865." n.p., n.d., (Atlanta, Ga.) 12mo, wraps-decr., (16)pp., ports generals in red, on gray paper.

353 **RICH, Doris**
"Fort Morgan and the Battle of Mobile Bay." n.p., 1973. 8vo, wraps, illus., 65pp., spiral bound.
...(Foley, Ala., Underwood Print, 1982) 2nd print., illus., photos, illus., 65pp. wraps.

354 **RICH, Edward Robins**
"Comrads! By Edward R. Rich, during the Civil War a member of Company E, First Maryland Cavalry, Confederate States' Army." (Easton, Md., S.E. Whitman, 1898) 12mo, wraps, illus., front, vi, 168pp. $50. One of only 50 copies printed.
...Wash., Neale Print, 1907. "Comrades Four!" 16mo, wraps, 230pp. $450-ob, $350-bmk-105.

355 **RICH, Joseph W.**
"A descriptive list of Confederate flags in the possession of the State Historical Society of Iowa." Iowa City, Ia., State Historical Society of Iowa. 1918. 8vo, wraps, plate, 6pp. $15.

356 **RICH, M.A., Edt.**
"Southern Cadet Corps. in the Civil War." (London) Jour. Confed. Hist. Soc., June 1965, v.III, #2, p.48-52, pl-1.

357 **RICHARD, J. Fraise**
"The Florence Nightingale of the Southern Army-Experiences of Mrs. Ella K. Newsom-Trader, Confederate Nurse in the great war, 1861-1865." (Mrs. Ella King Trader) New York: Broadway Pub. Co.(1914)$35-bmk. 12mo, decr.-cl (port on cover) d/e, v, 101pp., port.

358 **RICHARDS, Adolphus E., Maj.**
"Mosby and his men-the seven martyrs." In: CV, 1899, v.7, p.510-513, port.

359 **RICHARDS, Adolphus Edwards**
"The capture of Gen. Stoughton, March, 1863." In: SB, ns, v.1, #4, p.251-253.

360 ..."General Turner Ashby." In: SB, ns, v.1, 1885/1886, p.753-760; v.II, p.60-65.

361 ..."Monument unveiled, Sept. 23, 1899, at Front Royal, Va., in memory of seven of Mosby's Men who were executed after surrendering. Oration by Maj. Richards of Mosby's Command. Subsequent correspondence." (Richmond, 1899) cover title. 8vo, wraps, 19pp. Also in SHSP, v.27, 1899, p.253-262.

362 ..."Mosby's Partizan Rangers." In: "Famous adventures and prison escapes of the Civil War, p.102-115."

362a **RICHARDS, Amable Peltier**
"The Saint Helena (Parish) Rifles." Edt. Randall Shoemaker. Houston, 1968. 8vo, pict. wraps, 43p., ports. $50. Muster roll, 4th La. Inf.

363 **RICHARDS, George W.**
"Fort Gregg Again. A surgeon's defense of the garrison." In: SHSP, 1903, v.31, p.370-372.

364 **RICHARDS, Ira Don**
"The Battle of Poison Spring." In: AHQ, 1959, v.VIII, p.338-349, maps, 2pp. Near Camden, Ark., Apr. 1864.

365 ..."The Engagement at Marks' Mills." In: AHQ, 1960, v.XIX, p.51-60, pg. map. Between Camden and Pine Bluff, Apr. 25, 1864.

366 ..."The Battle of Jenkins' Ferry." In: AHQ, 1961, v.XX, p.3-16, map.

367 ..."Little Rock on the road to reunion, 1865-1880." In: AHQ, 1966, v.XXV, p.312-335, illus.

368 **RICHARDSON GUARD**
..."Richardson Guards, muster roll of this Madison County Regiment." In: SHSP, 1896, v.24, p.361-363.
See: Catlett Conway.

369 **RICHARDSON, C.A.**
"Judah P. Benjamin, recollections of the CSA, Sect. State." In: SHSP, 1904, v.32, p.169-173.

370 **RICHARDSON, Charles**
"The Chancellorsville Campaign. Fredericksburg to Salem Church." N.Y., Neale Print, 1907. 12mo, cl, 124pp. $110.

371 ..."Tales of a Warrior. Sansuine but not Sanguinary for Old-time People." N.Y., Neale Print, 1907, 12m, cl, 224pp. dialect.

372 ..."Operations of detachment from Cashtown to Williamsport-a report of Gettysburg." In: SHSP, 1885, v.13, p.211-213.

372a **RICHARDSON, Dr.**
"Memoranda of facts bearing on the Kentucky Campaign. . ." Goodspeed $500.
See: Under title, notes. Crandall-2528.

373 **RICHARDSON, E. Ramsay (Mrs. Eudora)**
"Little Aleck a Life of Alexander H. Stephens the Fighting Vice-President of the Confederacy." Indianapolis: Bobbs-Merrill Co. (1932) 8vo, cl, dj, illus., ports, incl. front, xiv, (2), (17)-359pp., index. $25-atg., $20.
...Grosset and Dunlop, n.d.

374 **RICHARDSON, Frank L.**
"War as I saw it, 1861-1865." Louisiana Historical Quarterly, 1923. Jan. (pp. 86-106); Apr. (p.223-254) Reminiscences of a Confederate soldier.

375 ..."Repulse of Wilson at West Point, Georgia." In: SB,, ns, 1885/1886, v.1, #5, p.313-314.

376 **RICHARDSON, George W.**
"Speech of..., of Hanover, in Committee of the whole. On the report of the Committee on Federal Relations, in Convention of Virginia, April 4, 1861." Richmond, Whig Book and Job Office, 1862. 8vo, 32pp. $150-jk. Crandall-2831. "probably printed before secession of Va."

376a **RICHARDSON, George & William**
"For my country, the Richardson Letters, 1861-65. Compiled & edited by Gordon C. Jones." Wendell, N.C., Broadfoot Pub., 1983. 8vo, wraps, 195pp, ills, index. $15.

377 **RICHARDSON, J.M.**
"Confederate Re-Union Song." Daingerfield, Texas: News Job Print, n.d. 8vo, wraps, port on cover, (4)pp. Author was edt. local news and a poet.

378 **RICHARDSON, James D.**
"A Compilation of the Messages and Papers of the Confederacy. Including the Diplomatic Correspondence 1861-1865. Published by permission of Congress." In two

volumes. Nashville, Tenn., United States Pub. 1905. 8vo, cl, (or, 3/4 Mor.) pls., ports, xv, 643, v, 760pp. index to both vols. $50-bmk-116, $100.

...Nashville, 1905 edition.

...N.Y., Chelsea House-R, Hector, 1966. $75. A new edition with an introduction by Allan Nevins-"The Embattled Confederacy. Its Tasks and Leadership." (22)pp. $45-y.

...1981, paper, $30.

379 **RICHARDSON, Joe M.**
"Some Civil War Letters of a Mississippi Private." In: JMH, Feb. 1976, v.XXXVIII, #1, p.69-74.

380 **RICHARDSON, John**
"Five Civil War vignettes. Drawings by Charles Hargens, with an assist in editing from Matthew Imrie." New Hope, Pa., 1964. 8vo, cl, illus., 55pp. Belle Boyd, Leonidas Polk, etc.

381 **RICHARDSON, John Anderson**
"Richardson's Defense of the South." Atlanta, Ga., A.B. Caldwell, 1914. 8vo, cl, front(port), 598pp. errata. $20.

382 **RICHARDSON, Ralph**
"The Choice of Jefferson Davis as Confederate President." (Jackson, Miss., Jour. Miss. Hist., July 1955, v.XVII, #3, p.161-176.

383 **RICHARDSON, Ralph E.**
"The rhetorical death rattle of the Confederacy." In: South. Speech Jour., Winter 1954, v.20, p.109-116, notes. On Confederate speeches in Richmond, Feb. 1865.

384 ..."The Speaking and Speeches of Jefferson Davis, from 1845 to his death, 1889." Northwestern Univ., Summaries of doctoral dissert., 18: 157-161.

385 **RICHARDSON, Robert V., Gen.**
"Report: Sherman's advance on Meridian." In: SHSP, 1881, v.9, p.159-163. See: Wm. H. Jackson, Col. Peter B. Starke.

386 **RICHARDSON, Rufus Bryan**
"The Prison Question again (on Andersonville)." In: SHSP, 1880, v.8, p.569-572.

387 **RICHARDSON, Simon Peter**
"The Lights and Shadows of itinerant life; an Autobiography of Rev. Simon Peter Richardson, North Georgia Conference. With an introduction by Rev. John B. Robins." Nashville, Tenn., Barbee and Smith, 1901. 12mo, cl, ports, xix, 288pp. A Major in the CSArmy.

388 **RICHARDSON, Vivian**
"Belle Boyd-Spy. Something of the career of the Confederacy's most famous woman secret agent." Ft. Worth: Texas Monthly, Nov. 1929, v.IV, #4, p.475-480.

389 **RICHARDSON, Willard, and Geo. Ware Fulton**
"A Manual of Infantry and Rifle Tactics, with honors paid by the troops, Inspections, Reviews, etc." Richmond: A Morris Print, 1861. 16mo, 1/2 lt. 360pp. pl. $200. Ginz-$300. Crandall-2471.

390 **RICHEY, Homer**
"Memorial History of John Bowie Strange Camp, U.C.V. Sketches of Albermarle Chapter of U.D.C. and R.T.W. Duke Camp, Sons of Confederate Veterans." Charlottesville, Va., Michie Print, 1920. 8vo, cl, front, ports, viii, 330pp. $50-bmk-84.

391 **RICHMOND,**
"Ten days in Richmond." In: Black. Edn. Mag., Oct. 1862, v.XCII, p.391-402. Gen. McClellan's flank movement, public opinions in South and the Northern government.

392 **RICHMOND Civil War Centennial Commission:**
"The American Civil War. A selected reading list-the Richmond Public Library." #3, 8vo, 8pp. pamphlet, cover title.

393 ..."A selected reading list for Young People." RCWCC-#5. 8vo, (4)pp. pamphlet,

cover title. #3 (April, 1961), #5 (May 1961).

..."Map of Richmond." See: "Map of..."

394 **"RICHMOND Civil War Centennial Memorial Ceremony,**
The 100th Anniversary of the Resumption of Academic Duties of the Corps of Cadets of Virginia Military Institute at the Almshouse, Richmond. Dec. 28, 1864." Richmond, Va., Russell Cary Montague Chapel-Richmond Nursing Home, Dep't. Public Welfare. Dec. 28, 1964. 4to, stiff wraps, (6), 20, (9)pp. printed one side, including: Francis H. Smith, Supt. VMI, "Introductions, Lecture read before the Corps of Cadets on the Resumption of Academic Duties of Virginia Military Institute at the Alms House, Richmond, Va., Dec. 28, 1864." Richmond: Macfarland and Fergusson, 1865. (reprint of the above (9)pp. in the program, part of the above).

395 **"RICHMOND Daily Dispatch."**
Apr. 13, 1861-Ft. Sumter, the War Begins; July 22, 1861-1st. Manassas; July 7, 1863-Battle of Gettysburg; and Jan. 30, 1865-April 1, 1865, War's Edn. Four facsm. newspapers (4)pp. each, in envp.

396 **RICHMOND Examiner**
"Death of General J.E.B. Stuart." In: SHSP, 1879, v.7, p.107-110, 140-144.

397 **RICHMOND Home Guard**
See: Thomas Harding Ellis.

398 **"RICHMOND Howitzer Battalion"**
See: "Contributions to a History of the Richmond Howitzer Battalion." Richmond, Va., Carlton McCarthy and Co., 1883-1886. $850-r, $400-bmk-105-1/2lt. case. $250-bmk, $50. Pamphlets: #1, #2, #3, #4. Indexed under the individual authors: #1: Capt. Henry Hudnall's "1st Co."; Capt. W. Gordon McCabe's-"Our Dead." Rev. E.C. Gordon's-"Battle of Bethel.", "Official Reports (C.S. and US) Sect. War., J.B. Magruder, D.H. Hill, Wm. D. Stuart, G.W. Randolph, E.B. Montague and Gen. W.H. Werth." p.62-84. #2: William S. White's-"Diary of the War" and "Rolls and Record-Third Company, Richmond Howitzers." p.287-304. #3: T. Roberts Baker's Diary; Creed T. Davis Diary; John Waldrop and William Y. Mordecai Diaries; Reuben B. Pleasants First Detachment at Fredericksburg; William S. White's Diary, corrected; "Roll of Second Company, etc." #4: Creed T. Davis Diary (2nd Co.); J.V.L. McCreery-"That Hog Hole."; "Extracts from an Old Order Book of First Company, Richmond Howitzers. See also: Andrew Jackson Andrews, Geo. L. Christian, Wm. M. Dame, Fred S. Daniel, Carlton McCarthy, Thos. J. Macon, Charles Poindexter, Robert Stiles, Henry C. Tinsley, Harry C. Townsend, "Sketch of the Richmond Howitzers." Muster Rolls, Rosters, 1861-1865 in "Confederate Memorial Literary Society" Yearbook. L. Manarin's "Richmond Volunteers." ..."Richmond Howitzers, facts about the battery during the Appomattox Campaign extracts from official records..." In: SHSP, 1899, v.XXVI, p.322-334.

399 ..."The Richmond Howitzers at Harpers Ferry, Oct. 1859." In: SHSP, 1896, v.XXIV, p.110-111. Sig: J.V.S. M'Creery. See also: "Souvenir of unveiling of R.H.

400 **RICHMOND Howitzers**
"Extracts from an old "Order Book" of First Company Richmond Howitzers." Richmond, Va., J.W. Randolph and English, v.4, 1886, p.33-64.

401 ..."Rolls of Third Co., Richmond Howitzers as Mustered in and as Surrendered." In: V.2, "Contributions to a History of Richmond Howitzers Battalion." Richmond, Va., Carlton McCarthy, 1883. p.287-304.

402 ..."Roll of Second Company, as mustered in and as surrendered, April 9, 1865." Richmond, Va., Carlton McCarthy, 1884. v.3, p.62-64. See: "A Souvenir of Unveiling of Richmond Howitzers.

403 **RICHMOND LADY, A**
See: Sallie A. Putnam (Brock)

404 **RICHMOND Light Dragoons**
See: Charles M. Wallace.

405 **RICHMOND Nat'l. Battle Park**
See: Joseph P. Cullen, Jas. R. Sullivan.

406 **RICHMOND State**
"Tributes from eminent men to Lee." SHSP, 1889, v.17, p.348-357.

407 **RICHMOND Times-Dispatch**
"Battle of New Market." In: SHSP, 1907, v.35, p.231-234.

408 ..."The Confederate States Navy." In: SHSP, 1907, v.35, p.290-297.

409 ..."The First Memorial Day." In: SHSP, 1907, v.35, p.369-370.

410 ..."Helped Capture engine "General"." In: SHSP, 1909, v.37, p.264-265.

411 ..."The Honor Roll of the University of Virginia." In: SHSP, 1905, v.33, p.43-56.

412 ..."Lee and Stuart at Harper's Ferry." In: SHSP, v.38, 1910, p.372-387.

413 ..."New Market Day at Va. Military Institute." In: SHSP, 1903, v.31, p.173-185.

414 ..."Origin of Memorial Day." In: SHSP, 1909, v.37, p.368.

415 ..."Roster of Co.G., 18th Virginia Cavalry." In: SHSP, 1907, v.35, p.161-165.

416 ..."Roster of McNeil's Rangers." In: SHSP, 1907, v.35, p.323-325.

417 ..."Roster of Officers of City Battalion." In: SHSP, 1903, v.31, p.323-325.

418 ..."Sketch of Gen. Joseph E. Johnston." In: SHSP, 1910, v.38, p.340-347.

419 ..."The Spotsylvania Memorials." In: SHSP, v.37, p.164-168.

420 ..."Unveiling Monument to Humphrey's Division." In: SHSP, 1908, v.36, p.174-179.

421 ..."Unveiling Statue of Governor Smith." In: SHSP, 1906, v.34, p.222-238.

422 **"RICHMOND and Washington During the War."**
From: Cornhill Magazine, Jan./June 1863, extract, 9pp.

423 **"RICHMOND, Illustrated Guide**
to the Confederate Capital. With a facsimilie reprint of the "City Intelligencer" of 1862." Oblong 8vo, wraps, 56, 24pp. Richmond, Va., 1960. See also: "City Intelligencer", "Stranger's Guide", C. Poindexter.

423a **"RICHMOND, Va., Medical Journal, The.**
Vol. I, Jan. 1866, Vol. II, July 1866. Much on treatment of wounds/sutures during the Civil War. One article on last wound of Stonewall by Hunter McGuire. (O"Brien) $200.

424 **RICHMOND, Va. "Sentinel".**
"War Time Story of Dahlgren's Raid." In: SHSP, 1909, v.37, p.198-202. See: Ulric Dahlgren, John Wilder Atkinson, Dahlgren's Raid.

425 **RICHMOND, Va., "Times."**
See: Battle of Cedar Run, Black Horse Troops, Capt. Thos. Jefferson Page, A Central Confederacy, A Confederate Veteran, First Gun at Sumter, The Last Blood Shed, Monument to Mosby's Men, Morgan's famous raid, Running the Blockade, Seven days battle around Richmond, They Honor a former foe.

426 **"RICHMOND, Va., Civil War**
Panoramic Photograph." Richmond, Va., Apr. 1962, Richmond Camera Shop. 5x19" and 8x37"

427 **RICHMOND, Virginia**
"City of Richmond." Detailed street plan of the Confederate Capital during the war. Important buildings are identified. (Washington), Lindenkohl and Krebs, 1864. Black and white, 18x20 (plate size) $85.

428 ...Black and white print, 18x20" (1973) $85.

429 ..."The Nation's most historic airport, Richard E. Byrd Flying Field (City of Richmond Municipal Airport) Site of three Civil War Battles: "Seven Pines", "French's Field", and "Williamsburg Rd." "Richmond: Civil War Centennial Committee, 1961-1965." 8vo, (6)pp. folder, ports, illus.

430 ..."The Stranger's guide and Official Directory for the City of Richmond. Showing the location of the Public Buildings and officers of the Confederate, State and City Governments, Residences of the Principal Officers, etc." Vol. 1, #1-October. (Richmond): Geo. P. Evans and Co., 1863. 12mo, wraps, cover title, 31pp. Crandall-2676, Sabin-71210.
...1863 reprint. Crandall-"woodcut on title and typography differs from above."

431 ..."Visitor's Guide to Richmond and Vicinity; embracing a Sketch of the City, Social Statistics and Notices of all Places and about the City of Interest to Tourist." (By M.P. Handy and W.H. Pleasants?) Richmond, Va., Benj. Bates, 1871. 18mo, wraps, 4-pls., map, 50pp. Sabin-71211. See: Chas. Poindexter.

432 ..."The City Intelligencer; or, Stranger's Guide. By V and C. Richmond, Va., Macfarlane and Fergusson, 1862. Crandall-2667, Sabin-71171. 16mo, wraps, 24pp.

433 **RICHMOND, Virginia "Dispatch."**
See: Battle of Sailor's Creek, Brunswick Blues, Brunswick Guard, Burial of Latane, Capture of Howlett House, Charlotte Rifles, Co. G. 26th Virginia Regiment, The Confederate Army, Confederate Dead, Arlington Cemetery, Cumberland Grays, First Federals entering Richmond, First Manassas, Fort Donelson, Gen. D.H. Maury, Hanover Co. Heroes, Hunter Holmes McGuire, Hunter's Raid, Jefferson Davis House, Lee's Lieutenants, Lt.-Gen. A.P. Hill, Mahone's Old Brigade at Crater, Maryland Campaign, Old Dominion Dragoons, On Historic Spots, Pouncing on Pickets, Refused to burn it, Rest at Mount Jackson, Richmond Ambulance Corps, Roll Co. B 9th Va. Cavalry, Roster and Services of Lee Rangers, Soldier's Home-Richmond, Stuart's Raid on Catlett's, Unveiling Howitzer Monument, Unveiling Statue Gen. A.P. Hill, Virginia Battlefield park, Washington Artillery heroes, Wilson's Creek, Yancy and Hill.

434 **RICHMOND, Virginia "News Leader."**
See: "Battle of Crater/C. Edward Berkely Brothers."; "Grimes Battery, Centennial."; "Confederate Constitution"; "Battle Abbey-Location"; Henry W. Wyatt (Monument).

435 **RICHMOND, Virginia Guide Books.**
See under:
"Illustrated Guide to Richmond, etc."; "Stranger's Guide and Official Directory..."; "Visitors Guide to Richmond and Vicinity."; Wm. D. Chesterman; Edward S. Evans; Charles Poindexter and "City Intelligencer."; Charles A. Vanfelson.

436 **RICHMOND, Virginia-SHSP:**
See: Edward M. Alfriend, J.H. Averill, Horation W. Bruce, W.P. Cabell, J.A. Campbell, R.C. Cave, Richard T.W. Duke, Richard S. Ewell, John Howard, Joseph B. Kewshaw, George W.C. Lee, New York Herald, Richmond Dispatch, Edward H. Ripley, Richmond Times Dispatch, Dallas Tucker.

437 **RICHTER, William L.**
"Spread-Eagle Eccentricities: Military Civilian Relations in Reconstruction Texas." In: Texana, 1970, v.VIII, #4, p.311-327.

438 ..."The Army and the Negro during Texas Reconstruction, 1865-1870." In: ETHJ, Spring, 1972, v.X, #1, p.7-17, notes.

439 ..."Outside my Profession", the Army and Civil Affairs in Texas Reconstruction." In: TMH, 1971, v.IX, #1, p.5-21.

440 ..."Texas Politics and the United States Army, 1866-1867." In: TMH, 1972, v.X, #3, p.159-186.

441 ..."A Better Time is in Store for Us." An analysis of the Reconstruction attitudes of George Armstrong Custer." In: TMH, 1973, v.XI, #1, p.31-50.

441a ..."James Longstreet: from Rebel to Scalawag." In: La.H., 1970, v.11, p.215-30.

442 **RICK, Alan John**
"Pensacola in the Civil War." In: Pensacola Hist. Soc. Quart., April 1969, v.5, #1, p.1-16. Military units serving in area, Roster Co.K, 1st Fla. Infty., Co.A, 2nd Fla. Inf.

443 ..."Florida's Activities in CW-Reconstr." C.W. Round Table, P.O. Box 2397, Pensacola.

443a **RICKER, Eli S., Cpl. (1985)**
"We left a black track in South Carolina, letters of Corp. Eli. S. Ricker. Edt: Edward G. Longacre." In: SCHM, July 1981, p.210-24.

444 **RICKS, Robert Henry**
"Some reminiscences of service in the Confederate Army." In: Univ. N.C. Mag., 1917-1918, v.XLVII, p.136-141. Served in 1st (Bethel) Reg. Inf., later 3rd Reg. Artly., thence 1st Reg. Artly., Oct. 4, 1862.

445 **RIDDELL, William Renwick**
"A court martial fifty years ago." In: Amer. Law Rev., Jan. 1916, v.L, p.15-20. Acct. trial of John Yates Beall, of CSArmy in 1864, convicted as spy and executed.

446 **RIDDLE, Thomas J., Dr.**
"The Goochland Light Artillery." In: SHSP, 1896, v.24, p.316-323.

447 ..."Reminiscences of Floyd's Operations in West Virginia in 1861." In: SHSP, 1883, v.11, p.92-98.

448 **RIDDLEBERGER, Patrick W.**
"1866: The Critical Years Revisited." Carbondale, Southern Illinois University Pr., 1979. 8vo, cl, dj, illus., append., notes, bibliog., index, xiii, 287pp. See: Howard K. Beale, Hans S. Trefousse, Albert Castel, James Sefton, Eric McKitrick.

449 **RIDGELY, Nicholas Greenberry (Broadside Verse)**
"A Voice from the old Maryland Line Air: "Maryland, My Maryland". Written under the influence of the excitement prevalent in Baltimore when the news was received that the Confederates had crossed the Potomac at Port Tobacco and cut Gen. Sickles Brigade to pieces." Baltimore, Oct. 27, 1861. Broadside verse 4.25x16.5" Border of double rules. Cut flag of Maryland.

450 **RIDLEY, Bromfield Lewis**
"Battles and Sketches of the Army of the Tennessee, by Bromfield L. Ridley, Lieut.-Gen. A.P. Stewart's Staff." Mexico, Mo., Missouri Print and Pub., 1906. 8vo, cl, xvi, (17)-662pp. (10)pp. index, color flag, illus., map, ports, incl. front errata slip at end. $250-g, $200-bmk-105.
...Morningside Bookshop, 1979. 8vo, cl, 672pp. $30. Intro: Dr. Robert J. Womack. $35-y.

451 ..."Echoes from the Battle of Murfreesboro." In: CV, Feb. 1903, v.XI, p.65-68. (Federals designated as Stone Rive.)

452 ..."Champ Ferguson." In: CV, 1899, v.7, p.442-443.

453 ..."Southern side at Chickamauga." In: CV, 1898, v.6, p.407-409, 514-517, 556-558. illus., ports.

454 **RIEGEL, R.E.**
"Federal operation of the Southern railroads during the Civil War." In: MVHR, Sept. 1922, v.IX, p.126-138.

455 **RIETTI, John C.**
"History of the Mississippi Rifles, 10th

Mississippi Regiment, compiled from Company Official Records by J.C. Rietti Glasgow, printed by W.Anderson Eadie." n.d., 12mo, 15pp. See also: Lamar Fontaine of 10th Miss.

456 ..."Military Annals of Mississippi. Military organizations which entered the service of the Confederate States of America, from the State of Mississippi Regiment, Jackson, Miss. To the memory of the Confederate dead, of Mississippi that host of heroes of the Lost Cause, who with them, have passed over the river, this memento is inscribed to the Private Soldier", Vol. 1, price 50 cents. 12mo, cl, 196pp., errata sheet, cover title, brittle paper. (only vol. published) $87.50.

...Spartanburg, S.C., The Reprint Co., 1976, "with an index by the staff of Mississippi Collection, University of Mississippi Library Oxford." 12mo, cl, (2), 196pp. facsm. repro., index: p.197-245.

457 ..."History of the organization, military service, and a record of battles and marches, of the Mississippi Rifles, Co. "A" and "D", 10th Regt. Miss. Vols. Gen. J.R. Chalmer's "high-pressure Mississippi Brigade", CSA from the organization of the company at Jackson, Miss., Jan. 1858, to the surrender of Gen. Johnston's Army, Apr. 26, 1865." Compiled by J.C. Rietti, O.S. Jackson, J.C. Rietti (n.d.) (1872?) cover title, 8vo, wraps, 8pp., text double column, within border lines. Dornbusch, 575, pagination as "14 folios".

458 **RIFLEMAN, A. (pseud.)**
"Prisoner of War, five months among." See: Anthony M. Keiley.

459 **RIGBY, William T.**
"Confederate Dead in Vicksburg Cemetery." In: SHSP, 1907, v.35, p.53-54.

460 **RIGGS, B.F., Louisville, Ky.**
"Capture of the "J.H. Miller". Account of the wonderful achievement of three boys (Johnny Jones, Church Price, Bennie Riggs) on the Arkansas River." In: CV, 1907, v.15, p.73-77, ports.

461 **RIGGS, David F.**
"Stonewall Jackson's raincoat." In: CWTI, July, 1977, v.16, p.36-41, illus., ports.

..."Put the Boys In." In. CWTI, Jan. 1980, v.18, #9, p.24-32, ills, ports. Re: VMI Cadets.

..."Robert Young Conrad & the Ordeal of Secession." In: VMHS, July 1978, v.86, #3, p.259-74, port.

..."7th Virginia Infantry." Lynchburg, Va., H.E. Howard, 1982. J.P. Bell print, Lim. Atg. Edt. 8vo, cl, dj, (4), 107pp, ill, maps, ports. $17.50.

462 **RIGGS, Joseph Howard**
"A study of the rhetorical events in the West Virginia Statehood movement." In: W.Va. Hist., Apr. 1956, v.17, p.191-251, notes. Speeches and debates in W.Va., Va., and Wash., 1860-1862.

463 **RIGGS, Robert L.**
"The Roads to Gettysburg", an address before the Filson Club, Oct. 2, 1961." In: FCHQ, July 1962, v.36, #3, p.232-241.

464 **"RIGHT Shall Make Might."**
An account of the celebration of the Thirty-Fourth Anniversary of the Washington Artillery with oration of General Samuel McGowan of Abbeville, S.C. and the transfer and reception of the War Guidon of Hart's Battery, at Charleston, S.C., Washington's Day, Feb. 22, 1878." Charleston, S.C., News and Courier, 1878, 8vo, wraps, 48pp.

465 **"RIGHT of Recognition;**
a sketch of the present policy of the Confederate States. By a Recent Tourist." London: R. Hardwick, 1862. 12mo, wraps, 30pp. Author: Leslie Stephens?

466 **"RIGHT of Suffrage**
and the condition of the South. The," In:

The Old Guard, July 1867, V, #7, p.526-532.

467 **RIGHT, Edmund (pseud.)**
"Narrative of Edmund Wright: his adventure with an escape from the Knights of the Golden Circle." Cincinnati: J.R. Hawley, 1864. 12mo, cl, 150pp., illus. (Wright-II, 2802)

468 **RIGHTMYER, Nelson Waite**
"The Church in a Border State-Maryland." (Garrison, N.Y.) Hist. Mag. Protestant Episcopal Church, Vol. XVII-#4, Dec. 1948, p.411-421. (church problems during War.)

469 **RIGHTS, Douglas LeTell**
"Salem in the War Between the States." (Raleigh) NCHRev., July 1950. v.XXVII, #3, p.277-288.

470 **RILEY, Benjamin Franklin**
"Conecuh Guards. Company E, Fourth Alabama Regiment." In: author's book, "History of Conecuh County, Alabama." Append. II, p.225-233. Also Chap: XXI and XXIII, War Record and Reconstruction. Columbus, Ga., Thos. Gilbert, 1881, 16mo, cl, xi, (13)-233pp.

471 **RILEY, Edward M.**
"Historic Fort Moultrie in Charleston Harbor." (Charleston: So. Caro. Hist. and Genea. Mag., April, 1950, v.LI, #2, p.63-74.

472 **RILEY, Elihu Samuel**
"Stonewall Jackson", a thesaurus of anecdotes of and incidents in the life of Lieut-General Thomas Jonathan Jackson, C.S.A." Annapolis, Md., privately printed, 1920. 8vo, cl, port, 203pp.

473 **RILEY, Franklin Lafayette**
"General Robert E. Lee after Appomattox. Edited by Franklin L. Riley." N.Y., Macmillan and Co., 1922. 12mo, cl, dj, illus., ports, incl. front, xiv, 250pp.
...1930 edition, $30-bmk-105, $40-bmk-105.

474 ..."Life of Col. J.F.H. Claiborne." (Oxford, Miss., 1903) Reprinted from Publications of Mississippi Historical Society, v.VII, p.217-244. front(port), 8vo, wraps, cover title.

475 **RILEY, Harris D.**
"Medicine in the Confederacy." In: Military Medicine, 1956, v.CXVII, p.53-63, 145-153. Reprint, n.p., 1956, wraps, 8vo, 21pp. $10.

475a **RILEY, Harris D., Jr.**
"Jefferson Davis & his Health. Part 1: June 1808-December 1860." In: JMH, August 1987, #3, v.49, p.179-202. Part II: January 1861-December 1889. pp.261-87.
..."Robert E. Lee's Battle with Diseases." In: CWTI, 1979, v.18, #8, p.12-22, ills, ports.

476 **RILEY, James**
"The Shenandoah-exploits in the Pacific Ocean after the sturggle of 1861-1865." In: SHSP, 1893, v.21, p.165-176.

477 **RILEY, Susan B.**
"The Hazards of Periodical Publishing in the South during the Nineteenth Century." In: Tenn. HQ, 1962, v.XXI, p.365-376.

478 **RILING, Ray**
"Uniform and dress of the Army and Navy of the CSA..." See under title.

479 **RINGGOLD GAP, Battle of**
See: Patrick R. Cleburne.

480 **RINGOLD, May Spencer**
"James Lusk Alcorn." (Jackson, Miss.) Jour. Miss. Hist., Jan, 1964, v.XXV, #1, p.1-14. Heads state troops during war and Gov., during Reconstruction.

481 ..."The Role of the State Legislatures in the Confederacy." Athens: University of Georgia, 1967. 8vo, cl, d/w, p.viii, 141pp. $20. Also: G.H.Q., Sept. 1964, p.255-270.
...Ann Arbor: University Microfilms, 1956, (i.e., 1959) positive microfilm of typescript (251) leaves, thesis--Emory Univ., abstract 19: 2594, April.

482 ..."Wm. Gourdin Young and the Wigfall Mission Fort Sumter, April 13, 1861." In: SCHM, 1972, v.73, #1, p.27-36.

483 ..."Robert Mewman Gourdin and the "1869 Association"." In: Ga. H.Q., Winter, 1971, v.LV, #4, p.501-509.

484 **RIO GRANDE (Texas), Operations on**
See: Wm. R. Scurry.

485 **RIPLEY, Edward Hastings, Col.**
"The Burning of Richmond, April 3, 1865." In: SHSP, 1904, v.32, p.73-76.

486 **RIPLEY, Elizabeth McHatton**
"Capture of Richmond." N.Y., 1907, 8vo, wraps, 31pp. (Howes-8637)

487 ..."Social Life in Old New Orleans, Being Recollections of My Girlhood." N.Y., Lond: Appleton and Co., 1912, 8vo, cl, (12)-331pp. illus., plates, ports. Social life, plantation, N.O. during War. P ep: "Times". $12.50, $22.50.

488 ..."From Flag to Flag, a woman's adventures and Experiences in the South during the War, in Mexico and in Cuba." New York: D.Appleton and Co., 1889. 12mo, cl, 296pp. $75-bmk. First part chiefly life in La.

489 **RIPLEY, Roswell Sabine**
"Correspondence relating to fortifications of Morris Island and operations of Engineers, Charleston, S.C., 1863." N.Y., John J. Canlon Co., 1878. 8vo, wraps, (3), 4-43pp. Corresp. between Beauregard, Ripley and others in the Department.

490 ..."The Fortifications and Line of Defense Around Charleston, 1860-1865." Charleston, S.C., Yearbook of City, 1885. 8vo, cl, 392pp. (23pp. is above) large fldg. map shows battlefield.

491 **RIPLEY, Warren**
"Artillery and Ammunition of the Civil War." N.Y., etc., Van Nostrand Reinhold Co. (1970). 4to, cl, dj, diagrams, illus., facsms., outline sketches, tables, index, 384pp. $45-b.

..."The Battle of Chapmen's Fort, May 26, 1864." Green Poind, S.C., Asherpoo Plantation, 1978. Privately printed. 12mo, cl, 108p, fascms, ills, maps, some colored. 1,500 copies at Lakeside Press of R. R. Donnelley Co., Chicago, Ill.

492 **RIPPE, Peter**
"Lee's Wartime Home." (London) Jour. Confed. Hist. Soc., Autumn, 1967, v.5, #3, p.87-90, pl.

493 **RIPPLE, Ezra H.**
"A Civil and sometimes Uncivil War. Edt: and Intro: Bruce Catton." In: Amer. Hert. Oct. 1964, v.XV, #6, p.50-60, color pls. (18) while Union (Pa.) it remains a vivid acct. related more as a newspaper man than confined.

494 **RIPPY, J. Fred**
"Mexican projects of the Confederacy." In: SwHQ, April, 1919, v.XXII, #4, p.291-317.

494a **RISE & Fall of the Confederacy,**
historical pageant, presented at Charlotte, N.C. June 5, 1929. Program. 8vo, wraps, 8pp. self wrap. $12.50.

495 **RISK, T.F.**
"A view of the impending political crisis, from a Western standpoint. An address before the St. Louis Literary and Philosophical Association, Jan. 6, 1861." (St. Louis?, 1861) 8vo, wraps, 7pp. Notes on TFR, in MHR: 28:282, 2:244.

496 **RISTER, Carl Coke**
"Robert E. Lee in Texas." Norman: Univ. Oklahoma Pr., 1946, 12mo, cl, dj, illus., ports, map, xiii, 183pp. Atg. copy.
...750 copies "Texas Edt." $35.

497 ..."Carlota, a Confederate Colony in Mexico." (Baton Rouge, La. Feb., 1945, v.XI, #1, p.33-50. $25-bmk-105.

498 **RITTENHOUSE, Jack D.**
"Found: Original Copy of an 1862 Confederate Handbill." In: El Palacio, 1967, v.LXXIV, i, 5-9pp.

499 ..."New Mexico Civil War Bibliography 1861-1865. An annotated checklist of books and pamphlets." Houston, Texas: Stagecoach Press, 1961. 8vo, cl, dj, 36pp., 400 copies. (Enlarged edition)

500 ..."Maverick Tales. True Stories of Early Texas." (N.Y.) Winchester Press (1971). 8vo, cl, dj, (7), 248pp. CSA, p.79-134: "Confederate on the Rio Grande", "Black Day for the Navy", "Confederate Victory After Appomattox".

501 **RITTER, Ben**
"Jackson's first war-time portrait-widow's favorite." In: CWTI, Feb. 1979, v.17, #10, p.36-39, illus., ports.

502 **RITTER, William L., Capt.**
"An incident of the Deer Creek Expedition of 1863." In: SHSP, 1881, v.IX, p.280-281.

503 ..."History of the Third Maryland Artillery." (Balt: Guggenheimer and Weil, 1900) 8vo, wraps, cover title, 23pp. Also in: W.W. Goldsborough, "Md. Line, etc.", 1900 edt., p.296-318.

504 ..."Biographical Memoir and Sketch of the Third Battery of Maryland Artillery." Baltimore: 1902, 8vo, full Lt., 23pp. $50. Waviant of Dornb. #509.

505 ..."Letter from Capt. W.L. Ritter." In: SHSP, May 1876, v.I, #5, p.362-363. (Add'l. info on capture: Indianola.)

506 ..."Operations of a section of the 3rd Maryland Battery on the Mississippi in the Spring of 1863." In: SHSP, May, 1879, v.VII, #5, p.247-249.

507 ..."Sketch of the Third Battery of Maryland Artillery." In: SHSP, June 1882, v.X, #6, p.328-332; 392-401, "For Vicksburg, Miss."; 464-471, "To the East."; Feb.-Mar., 1883, v.XI, #2/3, p.113-118; 186-193; 433-442; 537-544, "The disastrous expedition to Sherman's Rear."; Apr., 1884, v.XII, #4, p.170-172, "Retreat from Nashville."; 1894, XXII, p.19-20, "Its history in brief, and its commanders."

508 **RIVERS, William James**
"River's Account of the Raising of Troops in South Carolina for Confederate and State Service. Pub. for revision and ammendment." Columbia, S.C., Bryan Print, 1899. 8vo, wraps, 42pp. Thornton, IV-p.401, notes John P. Thomas State Historian of Confederate Records was concerned with this work although name was not used. (5th vol. in series "Annual Report")

509 **RIVES, William Cabell**
"Letter from the Hon...., to a friend, on the important questions of the day. (Castle Hill, Jan. 27, 1860)" Richmond: Whig Book and Job Office, 1860, 8vo, sewn, 16pp. Essay on secession. Rives was a member to Peace Conf., later on Davis' cabinet.

510 ..."Correspondence, Albemarle Co., Va., 1861, sewn, 8vo, 3pp. T.J. Wertenbaker and 553 others request Rives represent them, secession convt.

511 ..."Letter of Hon. Wm. C. Rives to Mr. Beteler of the House of Representatives, on the National Crisis." Castle Hill (Va.), 8 Dec. 1860. 4to Broadside, 3 columns. See division of states into a Northern, West and South, hopes Union can be saved along Southern terms. S.C., irreconciliable; Pa., N.Y., and N.J. could be expected to go with the South.

512 **RIZK, Estelle Smith**
"No more muffled hoofbeats." Phila: Dorrance (1960) 8vo, cl, vii, (5), 80pp. map. On Civil War in Carter Co., Ky., 1861-1865. $20.

512a **ROACH, S. Fred**
"The Untold Story of J.C.B. Davis' contributions to the London Times pre-civil war attitudes toward the United States." In: Atl. HJ, Spring 1979, p.71-80.

513 **ROACH, Sallie Neill, Mrs.**
"Theon, A tale of the American Civil War." Phila: J.B. Lippincott and Co., 1882. 12mo, cl, 220pp. in 22 cantos. CSA Civil War poetry.

514 **ROARK, Bertha E.**
"The siege of Vicksburg as told by a Mississippian." In: Jour. Am. Hist., 1933, v.XXVII, p.177-183.

515 **ROARK, Garland**
"The Outlawed Banner." Garden City: Doubleday, 1956. 12mo, cl, dj, 379pp. Novel of two friends, a Northerner and a Southerner; Northerner becomes a Union officer on "Kearsarge", the Alabamian on the CS raider "Alabama". Action in Mobile Bay and destruction of Selma." (Carolina Bk.)

516 **ROBARDS, Charles L.**
"Synopsis of the decisions of the Supreme Court of the State of Texas, rendered, upon application for write of habeas corpus, original and upon appeal, arising from restraints by conscript and other military authorities, during the terms in 1862, 1863, and 1864, and the Galveston term, 1865." Austin: Brown and Foster, 1865. 8vo, wraps, 40pp.

517 ...New York: Baker, Voorhis and Co., 1935.

518 ...Photo reproduction, Arkansas Law Library, Dennis and Co., 1935.

519 ..."Synopsis of Texas Reports. Habeas Corpus Cases." Austin, Texas: Dixie Bookstore (1938?)

520 **ROBBINS, John B.**
"The Confederacy and the Writ of Habeas Corpus." In: Ga.H.Q., Spring 1971, v.LV, #1, p.83-101.
...Offprint (19)pp. $10.

520a **ROBBINS, Lois Brown**
"The South's Finest Hour, essays on the War between the States." N.Y., American Press, 1965. 12mo, cl, 166pp, ills, 10 ports.

521 **ROBBINS, Peggy**
"Jim Limber and the Davises." In: CWTI, Nov. 1978, v.17, #7, p.22-27, illus., ports.

522 ..."When the Yankees held Memphis." In: CWTI, Jan. 1978, v.16, #9, p.26-37, illus., map, ports.

523 ..."Dr. Samuel Mudd's attempt to escape from Fort Jefferson." In: CWTI, Feb. 1978, #10, p.10-16, illus., ports.

524 **ROBBINS, William Mack**
"Historic Gettysburg." (Selma, Ala., 1903) Broadside 38x29 1/2cm. 4-column text, from Selma Journal. Corrects W.R. Houghton's aspersions on CSA soldiers valor.

525 ..."Gettysburg." (Selma, Ala., 1904). Broadside 32x25cm, 3-column text. More of same.

526 **ROBERSON, B.L.**
"The Courthouse Burnin'est General." In: THQ, 1964, v.23, p.372-378. Story of Hylan B. Lyon, CSA general. See: Hylan Benton Lyon.

527 **ROBERT, Joseph C.**
"Lee the Farmer." In: JSH, 1937, v.III, p.422-440.

528 **ROBERT, Patrick Gibson**
"Letter of-"Justice to Gen. Magruder." In: SHSP, 1878, v.V, p.249-250.

529 **ROBERTS, A. Sellew**
"The Federal Government and Confederate Cotton." N.Y., Amer. Hist. Rev., Jan. 1927, v.XXXII, p.262-275.

530 ..."High prices and the Blockade in the Confederacy." In: So. Atl. Qrt., April, 1925, v.XXIV, p.154-163. $10.

531 ..."The Peace Movement in North Carolina." In: MVHR, 1924, v.11, p.190-199.

532 **ROBERTS, A., Capt., (pseud)**
"Never Caught, etc." See: Augustus C. Hobart-Hampden, various titles.

533 **ROBERTS, Albert Hubbard**
"Wilkinson Call, Soldier and Senator." In: FHQ, Jan./Apr., 1934, Vol. XII, #3 and 4,

p.95-113, 179-197. Capt. Call was in Co. A, 6th Fla. Reg. and 5th Fla. Cav., Act. Asst. Adj-Gen. of Fla., participated in Battle of Olustee.

534 **ROBERTS, Allen E.**
"House Undivided, the Story of Freemasonry in the Civil War." N.Y., Macay Pub. and Masonic Supply Co., (1961). 8vo, cl, d/w, front, xviii, 356pp., maps and map endsheets.
...Reprinted (1964) Richmond, 1976.

535 **ROBERTS, B.A.**
"The Keysville Guards." In: SHSP, 1908, v.36, p.146-151. Roll of members.

536 **ROBERTS, Bobby L.**
"General T.C. Hindman and the Trans-Mississippi District." In: AHQ, 1973, v.XXXII, p.297-311, port.

ROBERTS, Deering J., Surg., CSA
"Medical Service of the Confederacy." In: Photo. Hist. C.W., v.7, p.237-50, ills, ports.
..."The Surgeon in the Field." In: Photo. Hist. CW, V.7, p.251-72.
..."Permanent & General Hospitals." In: same, p.273-96.
..."Organization & personnel of the Medical Dept. of the Confederacy." In: same, Append. D, p. 349-52.

537 **ROBERTS, Derrell**
"The University of Georgia and Georgia's Civil War G.I. Bill." In: Ga. H.Q., Dec. 1965, v.XLIX, #4, p.418-423.

538 **ROBERTS, E.E., Rear-Adm., USN**
"How mosquitoes prevented capture of Farragut." (from Richmond Times-Dispatch, Dec. 23, 1907) In: SHSP, 1907, v.35, p.174-175.

539 **ROBERTS, F.C., Mrs.**
"Historical Incidents; What "Our Women in the War" did and suffered." Beaufort, N.C., St. Paul's School Print, 1909, wraps, 8vo, 14pp.

540 **ROBERTS, James Walter**
"The Wilderness and Spottsylvania, May 4-12, 1864." In: FHQ, October 1932, v.XI, #2, p.58-76. Diary of an Alabamian during this campaign. Moved to Fla. after war.

541 **ROBERTS, Joseph, Capt.**
"The Handbook of Artillery, by Capt. Joseph Roberts, Fourth Regt. Artillery, U.S. Army." Richmond: Ritchie and Dunnavant, 1861. 16mo, wraps, 168pp.

542 ..."The handbook of artillery, for the service of the United States. (Army and Militia) By Capt. Joseph Roberts, 4th Regt. Art. U.S. Army. Second Edition." Charleston, S.C., Evans and Cogswell, 1861.
...Richmond, Va., West and Johnston, 1862. Second edition, revised and enlarged. 16mo, wraps, illus., 192pp. (Hill) $90.
..."The hand-book of artillery." Richmond: Ritchie & Dunnavant, 1861. 16mo, wraps, 137p, ills. (Crandall-2472). Goodspeed-$650.
...2nd Edt., revised & enlarged. 16mo, limp cl., 192pp, ills. Richmond: West & Johnston, 1862. Crandall-2475. Goodspeed-$600.

543 **ROBERTS, Kate Quintard Noble**
"A war time foundry: a story of a Confederate foundry at the present Anniston." In: AlaHQ, Winter, 1956, v.18, p.463-467. Iron works estb. by Noble Bros. in Cherokee Co., Ala. 1861-1864.
..."Samuel Noble." In: AHQ, 1956, v.18, #4, p.466-73.

544 **ROBERTS, Maria Yandell**
"David W. Yandell, MD, LLd." In: CV, July 1926, v.XXXIV, p.254-256. Surgeons of the Confederacy.

545 **ROBERTS, Oran Milo, Judge**
"Our Federal Relations from a Southern view of them." Austin, Tex., E.Von Boeckmann, 1892. $125-jk-127. 8vo, 1/2 sheep, cl, 175, 23, 16pp. Append: "The use and misuse of the principal in the expression:

all men are created equal...", "The history of the evolution of the government of the U.S."

546 ..."Texas. By Col. O.M. Roberts." (Atlanta, Ga., Confederate Pub. Co., 1892) 8vo, cl, map, port, vii, 268pp. $50-jk. In: C.A. Evans, Edt.: "Confederate Military History", v.11.
...v.XV. Wilmington, N.C., Broadfoot, 1987.

547 ..."The Experiences of an unrecognized Senator." In: QTSHA, Oct. 1908, v.XII, #2, p.87-147. (Robert's vain journey to Wash., 1866-1867, but Senator's seat denied him. Was Chm. Session Convention, Chief Justice and later Gov. of Texas.

548 ..."Speech of..., of the Supreme Court of Texas, at the Capitol, on 1st of Dec., 1860, upon the "Impending crisis." sewed. (Austin, Texas, 1860) 8vo, 32pp. $60.

549 **ROBERTS, Walter Adolphe**
"Semmes of the Alabama." Indianapolis: Bobbs-Merrill (1938) 8vo, cl, dj, illus., 320pp. Career of Semmes on "Sumter" and "Alabama". ports, incl. front, facsms., dj, $50-bmk.
..."Hartford & the Tennessee in Mobile Bay (in the War between the States)." In: 'US Navy fights,' NY: Bobs-Merrill, 1942. p.139-53. front, plates, ports.

550 **ROBERTS, William Paul**
"James Dunwoody Bulloch and the Confederate Navy." In: NCHR, July 1947, v.XXIV, p.315-366.

551 ..."Paroles of the Army of Northern Virginia." In: SHSP, 1890, v.18, p.386-388.

552 **ROBERTSON, Alexander Farish**
"Alexander Hugh Holmes Stuart, 1807-1891, a biography by Alexander F. Robertson." Richmond, Va., Wm. Byrd Pr. (1925) 8vo, cl, front, pl, ports, xix, 484pp. $35-bmk. Member Va. Convention of 1861. See also under Stuart.

553 **ROBERTSON, Archibald Thomas, Rev.**
"Life and letters of John Albert Broadus." Phila: American Baptist Pub., Society, 1901, 12mo, clxiv, 462pp., ports(3), 2fldg. facsms., $40-bmk. Much of interest in CSA chaplaincy, preaching in camps, visited 13th Va., corresp: J. Wm. Jones.

554 **ROBERTSON, Constance**
"The Unterrified." N.Y., Holt, Pub., 1946. 12mo, cl, dj, 503pp. N.York City's Copperheads.

555 **ROBERTSON, Felix, Brig.-Gen.**
"Life Story of Brig.-Gen. Felix Robertson, from an interview conducted by Helen Pool Baldwin and intro: Dr. Jas. H. Colgin." (Waco, Texas) reprinted from Texana, vol.VIII, 1970. 8vo, wraps, 1/2 title, p.(153)-182.

556 ..."On Wheeler's last raid in middle Tennessee." In: CV, September 1922, v.XXX, p.334-335.

557 ..."Sherman and Augusta." In: CV, Sept. 1914, v.XXII, p.407. See: Dr. James Thomas Searcy.

558 **ROBERTSON, Fred L., Compl.**
"Soldiers of Florida in the Seminole Indian, Civil and Spanish-American Wars." See under title.

559 **ROBERTSON, George F.**
"A small boy's recollections of the Civil War (War Between the States)." Clover, S.C., G.F. Robertson, 1932. 12mo, cl, front(port), illus., 122pp. $35.

560 **ROBERTSON, J. Barr**
"The Confederate Debt and Private Southern Debts." London: 1884, Waterlow and Sons. 4to, marbled bds., lt. spine, iv, 38pp. $75. Pro-southern tract, by an Englishman for consumption abroad.

560a **ROBERTSON, James I.**
"General A. P. Hill: The Story of a Confederate Warrier." N.Y., 1987. 8vo, cl, dj, 382pp, ills, maps.
..."Civil War sites in Virginia: A Tour

Guide." Charlottesville, Va., University Press, 1982. 8vo, wraps, 108pp, ills, maps. $5. $20-Bm.

..."18th Virginia Infantry." Lynchburg, Va., H.E. Howard, 1984. J.P. Bell Print, Lim. Atg. Edt., 944. 8vo, cl, dj, (3), 88pp., maps, ports. $17.50.

..." Stonewall in the Shenandoah--the Valley Campaign of 1862--Special edition by Edts." May 1972, v.11, #2, CWTI, 50pp, ills, maps, ports.

561 **ROBERTSON, James Irvin, Jr.**
"The Civil War." Washington, D.C., U.S. Civil War Cent. Comm. 1963. 8vo, pict. wraps, 64pp., illus., ports, map. Objective, but a bit more CSA than northern in pict. content.

562 ..."The Continuing Battle of Gettysburg: an Essay Review." In: Ga. H.Q., Summer, 1974, v.LVIII, #2, p.278-282.

563 ..."The Council of Three Advisors to Governor "Honest John" Letcher." In: Va.-Cavl., Spring, 1977, v.XXVI, #4, p.176-183, ports, illus.

564 ..."Am. Index-Guide to the Southern Historical Society Papers, 1876-1959. Edt. by James I. Robertson, Jr." Millwood, N.Y., Kraus International, 1980. 8vo, cl, 2 vols., v.1, xx, 498pp., v.II, 614pp. $95.

565 ..."Jackson's stone wall: a history of the Stonewall Brigade." Ann Arbor: University Microfilms (1959) (1960). Positive microfilm of typescript (364) leaves, Thesis-Emory Univ. Abstr., dissert., v.20: 3274-3275 (Feb.) Forces serving under Jackson.

566 ..."The Right Arm of Lee and Jackson." In: CWH, December 1957, v.III, #4, p.423-434.

567 ..."The Scourge of Elmira." In: CWH, June 1962, v.VIII, #2, p.184-201.

568 ..."The Human Battle of Franklin." In: Tenn. HQ, 1965, v.XXIV, p.20-30.

569 ..."The Stonewall Brigade." Baton Rouge: Louisiana State University Press (1963) 8vo, cl, dj, illus., ports, xiii, 271pp. index. ...1979 reprint, $20, $100, paper, 288pp.

570 ..."The Stonewall Brigade: they marched to glory." In: CWTI, Dec., 1963, v.II, #8, p.6-8, 24-30, illus., port.

571 ..."4th Virginia Infantry." (Lynchburg, Va., H.E. Howard, 1982) 8vo, cl, (6), 83pp., maps, ports, 600 copies numbered, signed. $16.

572 ..."Virginia 1861-1865. Iron Gate to the Confederacy." Richmond: Virginia Civil War Comm., (1963) 2nd prt. 8vo, decr-color wraps, 64pp., illus., maps, ports. 1st Edt. 1961, $15.

572a ..."Danville under Military Occupation, 1865." In: VMHB, July 1967, v.75, #3, p.331-48.

572b ..."English Views of the Civil War - A Unique Excursion to Virginia April 2-8, 1863." In: VMHB 1969, v.77, p.201-12 plus (8)p. plates, notes.

..."English views of the Civil War: A unique excursion to Virginia, April 2-8, 1865." In: VaMHB, April 1969, p.201-12.

573 **ROBERTSON, James Rood**
"Sectionalism in Kentucky from 1855-1865." Washington: Amer. Hist. Ass'n., 1917. Annual Report, p.49-63; also in Miss. Val. Hist. Soc., IV, June 1917. A separate reprint (1916).

574 **ROBERTSON, Jerome Bonaparte and Felix Huston**
"Dedication of a memorial honoring Confederate Generals..., the only father-son generals to serve in the Civil War except for Robert E. Lee and his two sons. Oakwood Cemetery, Waco, Texas, Sunday, Apr. 11, 1965. 4:00 pm." (Hillsboro, Texas: Hill Junior College Research Center; Memorial presented by...) 8vo, (8)pp. folder, 2-ports and sketches. See: Helen Pool Baldwin.

575 ..."Hood's Brigade Casualties and Historical Papers, Edited by Brigadier General

Jerome B. Robertson." n.p., n.d., (Hillsboro, Texas: Hill Junior College Press, 1965?) 4to, (1), 34pp. photolith. In preface to Robertson's "Touched with Valor", notes that Hood's Texas Brigade. Association meeting at Brenham, Texas, June 22, 1881, authorized publication of casualty list. H. Castle of San Antonio, later on, submitted proofs to Robertson for correction and nothing further happened. In 1962 the proofs were discovered and herewith reproduced.

576 ..."Official Report of the Battle of Gettysburg." In: SHSP, 1877, v.IV, p.161-165.

577 ..."Report: Battle of Chickamauga." In: SHSP, 1885, v.13, p.384-386.

578 ..."Touched With Valor. Civil War Papers and Casualty Reports of Hood's Texas Brigade." Edt: Col. Harold B. Simpson. Hllsboro, Texas: Hill Junior College Press. (1964) Lim: 750 copies, 8vo, cl, d/w, ports, 126pp. op. $30-r.

579 **ROBERTSON, M.E., Mrs.**
"President Davis' Last Official Meeting. The last meeting of President Davis with his officers and those of his cabinet remaining with him, in the "Old State Bank Building" at Washington, Georgia." Washington: Southern History Assn., Publications, v.5, 1901, p.9

580 **ROBERTSON, Margaret B.S.**
"My Childhood Recollections of the War." In: SHSP, June 1923, v.XLIV, p.215-222.

581 **ROBERTSON, Middleton**
"Recollections of Morgan's Raid." In: Ind. Mag. of Hist., 1938, v.XXXIV, p.188-194. Boyhood reminiscences of raid in Jefferson Co., Ind.

582 **ROBERTSON, Thomas Chinn**
"Battle of Shiloh from a Southern Standpoint. A letter witten to his mother when a soldier boy." Baton Rouge, La., 1912. 12mo, wraps, cover title, CSA flag, 10pp.

583 **ROBERTSON, W. Glenn**
"The Siege of Suffolk, 1863, another name for futility?" In: VaCavl., Spring, 1978, v.XXVII, #4, p.164-173. illus., incl. dbl. pg. color ports, maps.

584 **ROBERTSON, W.B., Mrs.**
"The brave young life of J.E.B. Stuart." In: CV, Mar. 1919, v.XXVII, p.97-98.

585 **ROBINETT, Paul M.**
"Marmaduke's Expedition into Missouri." In: Armor., 1963, v.LXXII-iv, p.49-54.
"Marmaduke's Expedition into Missouri: The Battles of Springfield and Hartville, January, 1863." (Columbia, Mo., Mo. Hist. Review, Jan. 1964, v.LVIII, #2, p.151-173. Maps, ports, illus.

586 **ROBINS, H.M.**
"Sherman's March through North Carolina." In: N.C. Univ. Mag., March 1902, p.4.

587 **ROBINS, Sallie Nelson, Mrs.**
"Aftermath (A sketch of Gen. R.E. Lee)." In: Taylor Trotwood Mag., Jan. 1909, p.321-334.

588 ..."General Robert E. Lee." In: Frank Leslie's Pop. Monthly, Nov. 1896, v.42, p.503-516.

589 **ROBINS, William M.**
"The Soubriquet "Stonewall", how it was acquired." In: SHSP, 1891, v.19, p.164-167.

590 **ROBINS, William Todd**
See: Maryus Jones.
..."Stuart's ride around McClellan." In: B & L, v.II, p.271-275.

591 **ROBINSON, Benjamin**
"Dolores: a tale of disappointment and distress. Compiled. Arranged and edited from the journal, letters and other mss. of Roland Vernon, Esq. and from contributions by a conversations with the Vernon family of Rushbrook, in Carolina (North Carolina)." N.Y., E.J. Hale and Sons, 1868. 8vo, cl, 180pp-dbl. columns. $50. Partially on the Civil War. $50.

592 ROBINSON, Felix G.
"Two big ones that didn't get away." In: Glades Star, Mar. 1959, v.2, p.499-503. McNeill's Rangers capture Union Generals Benj. F. Kelley and George Crook in midst of Union occupied Cumberland.

593 ROBINSON, H.W.
"Winchester kind to living and the dead." In: SHSP, 1896, v.24, p.275-277.

594 ROBINSON, Harwood G.
"The Wrongs of the South has endured and the issues before us. Addressed to the people of Arkansas...Little Rock, 1861." n.p., Sabin-72080 title.

595 ROBINSON, John Enders, Mrs., Edt.,
See title: "Restoration of name Jeff. Davis, Cabin J. Bridge.

596 ROBINSON, Leigh
"Address: Dedication of the Virginia Memorial at Gettysburg, Friday, June 8, 1917. p.97-135. Invocation by Rev. Jas. Power Smith; Address of His Excellency Henry Carter Stuart, Gov. of Virginia; and an address by Hon. William M. Ingraham, Asst.-Sect. War. History of the monument. "Eulogy on Gen. W.H. Payne, address of Leigh Robinson, Lee Camp Confederate Veterans, Lee Hall, Richmond, Dec. 18, 1908." In: SHSP, 1908, XXXVI, p.293-353. Rep: wraps.

597 ..."Address (above), in acceptance of the portrait of General William H. Payne." Richmond, Va., Wm. Ellis Jones, 1909, 8vo, wraps, 64pp.

598 ..."Address of..., with rolls of the three companies and lists of battles. "A souvenir of the unveiling of the Richmond Howitzer Monument at Richmond, Va., Dec. 13, 1892." Richmond, Va., J.L. Hill Pr., 1893. 8vo, front, 98pp. $75, $60-bmk, $15. Also in: SHSP, 1892, v.XX, p.259-300.

599 ..."Joseph E. Johnston, an address delivered before the Association of ex-Confederate soldiers and sailors of Washington, D.C., by ..., May 12, 1891, at the memorial service held in Mt. Vernon M.E. Church, South and the proceedings of the occasion." Wash: R.O. Polihorn, 1891. 8vo, wraps, 61pp. Also in: SHSP, 1891, v.XIX, p.337-370. $75-ob.

600 ..."The soul of Lee." In: CV, Aug. 1919, v.XXVII, p.293-299.

601 ..."The South before and at the Battle of Wilderness. Address of...(formerly of the Richmond Howitzers) of Washington, D.C., before the Virginia Division of Army of Northern Virginia at the annual meeting, held in the Capitol in Richmond, Va., Nov. 1, 1877." Richmond: James E. Goode Pr., 1878. 8vo, wraps, vi, (1) errata, 111pp. $100-g, $50-bmk-104.

602 ROBINSON, Madeline Russell
"An introduction to the Papers of the New York Prize Court, 1861-1865." N.Y., Columbia University Pr., 1945. 8vo, cl, 203pp. Much on CSA and letters carried to and from abroad, captured with boats.

603 ROBINSON, Mary Fisher
"Sketch of James Lush Alcorn (1816-1894)." In: Jour. Miss. Hist., Jan. 1950, v.12, p.28-45. US Senate, Miss. Gov., planter and officer in CSArmy.

604 ROBINSON, Morgan Poitaux
"Concerning the Boyson essay and its defense; prepared, 1909, by... at the request, under supervison of Mrs. J. Enders Robinson, Hist.-General, United Daughters of the Confederacy." (Richmond, Va.?) 1909. Concerns Gen. Lee. 8vo, wraps, 46pp., tables, 1000 copies.

605 ROBINSON, Raymond V.
"Confederate Copyright Entries." In: Wm. and M. Q., 2nd ser., 1936, v.XVI, p.248-266. List: copyrights reg. (May 4, 1861-Mar. 30, 1865) In: Ala., Ga., Miss., N.C., 19pp., removed, stapeled. $15.

606 **ROBINSON, W.F.**
"Last battle before surrender." In: CV, Dec. 1924, v.XXXII, p.470-471. Appomattox, April 8, 1865.

607 **ROBINSON, W.P.**
"Artillery in the Battle of Crater." In: CV, Apr. 1911, v.XIX, p.164-166.

608 ..."The Battle of Cloyd's Farm." In: CV, Mar. 1925, v.XXXIII, p.97-100. Five miles from Dublin, Va., May 8, 1864.

609 **ROBINSON, William J., Capt.**
"Civil War Diary of..." n.p., 1975, 8vo, wraps, 65pp. Capt., 10th Tenn. Cavl., under Forrest.

610 **ROBINSON, William Morrison, Jr.**
"Admiralty in 1861. The Confederate States District Court for the division of Pamlico of the district of North Carolina." (Raleigh) NCHRev., April 1940, v.XVII, #2, p.132-138.

611 ..."The Alabama-Kearsarge Battle; a Study in Original Sources." Salem, Mass., Essex Institute, 1924. 8vo, wraps, map, 34pp., reprint from Essex Inst. Hist. Coll., LX(Apr.-Jly.) 1924, p.97-120, 209-218.

612 ..."The Confederate Privateers." New Haven: Yale University Pr., 1928. Tall 8vo, illus., facsms., xvi, 372pp. $85, $100.

613 ..."The Confederate Engineers." (Washington, D.C.: Military Engineer, 1930, July-Nov., v.XXII-297-305; 410-419; 512-517)

614 ..."The Confederate District Courts in Admiralty." South Atlantic Quarterly, 1930. v.XXIX, April, p.190-199.

615 ..."Justice in Gray; a history of the judicial system of the Confederate States of America." Cambridge, Mass., Harvard Univ. Pr., 1941. Published with the aid of a grant from the American Council of Learned Societies. Index of cases, bibliog., notes, 8vo, cl, dbl-map, xxi, 713pp. 1st history Judicial system CSA., In dj-$100.
...N.Y., Russell & Russell, Athaneum House, 1958. Bmk $25.

616 ..."Legal System of the Confederate States." In: JSH, Nov. 1936, v.II, p.453-467.

617 ..."The Second Congress of the Confederate States: enactments at its second and last session." In: Am. Hist. Rev., 1936, v.XLI, p.306-317.

618 ..."A new deal in constitutions." In: JSH, 1938, v.IV, p.449-461. The provisional and permanent constitutions of the CSA contrasted with the US and how it departs from the model.

619 ..."Prohibition in the Confederacy." Amer. Hist. Review, XXXVII, #1, Oct., 1931, p.50-58.

620 **ROBISON, Daniel M.**
"The Carter House Focus of the Battle of Franklin." (Nashville) Reprint Tennessee Historical Quarterly, March 1963, vol.XXII-#1, wraps, 8vo, decr. red illus., 20pp. $10-b.

621 ..."The Whigs in the politics of the Confederacy." In: E. Tenn. HSP, #11, 1940, p.3-10.

622 **ROBISON, Hugh Harris**
"Hugh Harris Robison letters." In: Jour. Miss. Hist., 1939, v.I, p.53-59. Edt: Weymouth T. Jordan. Six letters written while in CSArmy and as a prisoner at Columbus, Ohio.

623 **ROBSON, John S.**
"How a one legged Rebel lives; or, a history of the 52nd Virginia Regiment. Incidents in the life of the writer, during and since the close of the war. Concluding with a biographical sketch of John (i.e., William) Randolph Barbee, the distinguished Virginia sculptor." Richmond, W.H. Wade and Co., 1876. 16mo, wraps, vi, 138pp. $60.
...Charlottesville, Va., 1888. $60.

624 ..."How a one-legged Rebel lives, reminiscences of the Civil War, the story of the campaigns of Stonewall Jackson, as told by a high Private in the "Foot Cavlary". From

the Alleghany mountains to Chancellorsville. With the complete Regimental Roster of both the great armies at Gettysburg. Concluding with a trip from Catlettsburg, to Pike, Ky." Charlottesville, Va., Chronicle Pr., 1891. 16mo, wraps, 148pp. $90-bmk-105, Rec. $75-bmk. (another copy, 140pp., without 8pp. ads.)
..."How a one legged Rebel lives, reminiscences of the Civil War, the story of the campaigns of Stonewall Jackson, as told by a high Private in the "foot cavalry". From Alleghany mountains to Chancellorsville, with the complete Regimental roster of both the great armies at Gettysburg, by John S. Robson, late of the 52nd Regiment, Virginia Infantry." (Durham, N.C., Educator Press, 1898) 16mo, wraps (ports on cover), 192pp. (6pp. ads) $75, $60.
...Gaithersburg, Md., Butternut Press, 1984. $25.

625 **ROBUCK, J.E.**
"My own personal experience and observation as a soldier in the Confederate Army during the Civil War, 1861-1865, also during the period of Reconstruction. Appending a history of the Origin, Rise, Career and Disbanding of the famous Ku Klux Klan, or Invisible Empire. Exactly why, when and where it originated. By J.E. Robuck, once of Company A, 29th Mississippi Regiment, General E.C. Walthall's Brigade, C.S.A." (Birmingham, Ala., Leslie Print, 1911) 8vo, wraps, front(port), 136pp. $100. See: Edward Sykes.
...Memphis, Tenn., Burke's Book Store, 1979. 8vo, cl, 136pp. reprint of (1911) edt. $20.

626 **ROCHELLE, James Henry, Capt.**
"The Confederate Steamship "Patrick Henry"." In: SHSP, 1886, v.14, p.126-136.
ROCKBRIDGE ARTILLERY-Battery
See: Clement D. Fishburne, W.F. Johnston, Calvin Wilson, Edward Alex. Moore, Philip Slaughter.

627 **ROCKBRIDGE Battery**
"Roll of the Rockbridge Battery of Artillery, April 10, 1865." In: SHSP, 1888, v.XVI, p.277-280.

628 **ROCKBRIDGE Dragoons**
See: J. Scott Moore, "Staunton Daily News".

629 **ROCKWELL, William S.**
"The Oglethorpe Light Infantry of Savannah, in peace and in war. A brief sketch of its Two C Companies: "A" Company, known in the Confederate States Army as Co. B., 8th Regt. Ga. Vols. and "B" Company, known as Co. H., 1st Volunteer Regt. of Ga. Written by Capt. W.S. Rockwell. Published in aid of the Monument to Gen. Francis S. Bartow." Savannah: Printed for and presented to the Monument Association by J.H. Estill, a member of the corps. 1894. 8vo, wraps, 36pp. port of Gen. Bartow. Slip of "Omissions" inserted. DeRenne III, 921.

630 **RODENBAUGH, Theo. F.**
"Some Cavalry Leaders (Federal and Confederate." In: "Photographic Hist. of the Civil War." v.4, N.Y., 1911, p.262-288. Reprint: Glendale, Calif., 1970. Rodenbaugh was Gen. Edt. Cavalry Sect.
..."Photograph Hist. of Civil War--Cavalry." N.Y., Fairfax Press, 1983. $15.

631 **RODES, Robert Emmett**
"Report of the Battle of Chancellorsville." In: SHSP, 1876, v.II, p.161-172.

632 ..."Report of the Battle of Gettysburg." In: SHSP, 1876, v.II, p.135-158. See: Maj. Green Peyton's Sketch in Chs. D. Walker's "Biog. Sketches Grads and Eleves of VMI." p.440-457. Rodes was Col., organized 5th Ala. Regt. Chief Engr., NE/SW Ala. RRy. See: Anna M. Fry's "Memories of Old Cahaba." Rosa Faulkner Yancey's "Lynchburg and its neighbors." p.99-110.

633 **RODGERS, Robert L., Judge**
"The Cadet Battalion-Georgia Military Institute." (London) Jour. Confed. Hist. Soc., Spring, 1972, v.10, #1, p.5-15, port. Extracts from his pamphlet.

634 ..."The Confederate States Organized Arizona in 1862." In: SHSP, 1900, v.XXVIII, p.222-227.

635 ..."Jeff" Davis and the Pope. A Sketch of Confederate History." Aurora, Missouri, Parker Pub., (1925). 12mo, stiff wraps, 91, (2 pads) $50.

636 ...(see also, Father Jerome-"Vatican and the Southern Confederacy)

637 ..."Roster of the Battalion of the Georgia Military Institute Cadets." In: SHSP, 1905, v.XXXIII, p.306-319.

638 ..."What is a Confederate Veteran?" In: SHSP, 1900, v.XXVIII, p.316-317.

639 ..."A Historical Sketch of the Georgia Military Institute, Marietta, Ga.", "G.M.I. Cadet's in War Service-Maj. F.W. Capers"; "Military Reports-Gen. Henry C. Wayne"; "Surrender of Vicksburg and Battle of Chickamauga-Capt. Frank T. Ryan"; "The Joe Thompson Artillery-Recollections of Capt. C.R. Hanleiter." Atlanta, Ga., Kimsey's Book Shop, 1956, 8vo, wraps, cover title, (48)pp., i.e., (75)-98; (49)-74.

640 ..."History of the Confederate Veterans Association of Fulton County, Georgia." n.p., n.d.(Atlanta, Ga., c.1890) 8vo, color flags on wraps, ads, 198, (8)pp. Includes a sketch of Ga. Mil. Inst., it's Cadet Battalion service in the War. See: Rob't H. Rogers.

641 ..."Report of..., historian to Atlanta Camp #159, U.C.V., on the capture of De Gress Battery, and Battery A., 1st Ill. Light Artillery, in the Battle of Atlanta, July 22, 1864, with other papers bearing thereon. Pub. by some of the survivors of Manigault's Brigade." n.p., n.d. (Atlanta, Ga., 1896) 8vo, wraps, 47pp.

642 **RODGERS, Ruth, Miss**
"Secessionist Strength in Missouri." In: Mo.HR, July 1978, v.LXXII, #4, p.412-423, illus., ports, map, chart.

643 **ROGAN, Lafayette**
"A Confederate Prisoner at Rock Island. The Diary of... Edited by John H. Hauberg." In: Jour. Ill. State Hist. Soc., 1941, v.XXXIV, illus., p.26-49. Also: Springfiled, Ill., offprint, wraps.

643a ..."Diary of Lafayette Rogan, CSA prisoner of War at Rock Island Prison Barracks." n.p., 1938. 4to, pict. wraps, 94pp, ills. $65. Five copies for the family. Reprinted in Jour. Ill. State Hist. Soc. 1941, v.34. From Alabama.

644 **ROGERS, Albert A.**
"Lee as cavalier and soldier." In: Wm. and Mary Quart., 1935, v.XV, 2nd Ser., p.123-125, 267-270. Reviews Douglas Freeman's Lee.

645 **ROGERS, Andrew J.**
"A Daring Deed. A True Story of the Confederacy. Written by an Eye Witness." Richmond, Va., R.C. Gulley, 1915. 12mo, wraps, illus., each page print within borders, 20, (1)pp. signed in facsm., at end, A.J. Rogers. Altho fictional in form, founded on facts.

646 **ROGERS, Arthur Lee, Maj.**
"History of the Confederate Flag." In: SHSP, 1900, v.28, p.89-90.

..."The Wounding & Death of Stonewall Jackson." In: CV, new ser., Sept/Oct. 1988, v.37, #2, p.4-6, port. Letter to Gen. Asa Rogers about death.

647 **ROGERS, Charles Kaufman**
"Beleagured Charleston: Letters from the City, 1860-1864." Edited by Martin Abbott and Elmer L. Puryear." 8vo, wraps, 14pp. From SC Hist. Soc. Rec., April/Oct. 1960, v.61, p.61-74; 164-175; 210-217. Notes.

Letters to author's sister, Emeline Rogers Divver.

648 **ROGERS, George A. and R.F. Saunders, Jr.**
"The Scourge of Sherman's Men in Liberty County, Georgia." In: Ga.H.Q., Winter, 1976, v.LX, #4, p.356-369.

649 ..."Camp Lawton Stockade, Millen, Georgia, CSA." In: Atlanta Hist. Jour., 1981, v.25, #4, p.80-94. On the site of a prisoner of war camp in Ga.

650 **ROGERS, Hugh Cuthbert Basset**
"The Confederates and Federals at War." London: Allan Press, 1973. 8vo, cl, illus., ports, maps, 184, (32)pp. bibliog., index. N.Y., Burt Franklin's "Hippocrene Bks.", 1975.

651 **ROGERS, J.H.**
"The South Vindicated-reunion oration at New Orleans, May 19/22, 1903." In: CV, 1903, v.11, p.252-263, port.

ROGERS, J. Rowan
651a "What I saw & knew of J. Johnston Pettigrew." July 10, 1925." 12mo, wraps, 16p. cover title.

652 **ROGERS, James Webb**
"Madame Surratt; a drama in five acts, by J.W. Rogers." Wash., D.C.,T.J. brashears Pr., 1879. 12mo, cl, 148pp.
...N.Y., William Abbatt, 1912. $75-g. Magazine of History with Notes and Queries Extra #20. sm.4to, wraps, cover title, 161pp.
...Wash., D.C., Judd and Detweiler (1926) 8vo, wraps, front(port), 135pp. 4th Edt. written by a clergyman, served in CSArmy.

653 **ROGERS, Jefferson C., Maj., 5th Tex. Reg.**
"Official Report of Gettysburg." In: SHSP, 1885, v.13, p.193-195.

654 **ROGERS, John H., Judge**
"The South Vindicated. Reunion address by..." The 13th Annual reunion, held in New Orleans, May 19-22, 1903, Confederate Veterans. Nashville: S.A. Cunningham, n.d. (c.1903) 8vo, wraps, 40pp., illus. Also: Confed. Vet., v.XI, 1903, p.252-263, ports.

655 **ROGERS, Robert L.**
"Roster of the Battalion of the Georgia Military Institute Cadets in the Confederate Army Service in the Civil War, from May 10, 1864 to May 20th, 1865." In: SHSP, 1905, v.XXXIII, p.306-319. See: Francis W. Capers, Robt. L. Rodgers.

656 **ROGERS, W. McDowell**
"Seizure of United States' Lands by Seceding States." In: Ga. H.Q., Sept., 1934, v.XVIII, #3, p.264-269.

657 **ROGERS, William J.**
"William J. Rogers Memorandum Book." In: West Tenn. Soc. Papers, 1955, v.9, p.59-92. Diary of an officer, 13th Tenn. Reg. CSA. 2 June 1862-25 May, 1863.

658 **ROGERS, William P., Col.**
"The Diary and Letters of William P. Rogers, 1846-1862. Edt: Elanor Damon Pace." In: SwHQ, April 1929, v.XXXII, #4, p.285-299. (The Civil War period only)

659 **ROGERS, William Warren**
"C. Chauncey Burr and the "Old Guard"." In: N.J. Hist. Soc. Proc., July 1955, v.73, p.168-181. Notes. Edited a pro-Democratic and Southern Magazine, violently anti-Lincoln and criticizing North during the War. See: Joseph George, Jr.

660 ..."A soldier's odyssey: Henry Francis Jones and the Civil War." In: GaHQ, Winter 1982, v.LXVI, #4, p.450-466.

661 ..."Thomas County During the Civil War." Tallahassee: Florida State University, 1964, Fla. State Univ. Studies #41 (2nd printing) 8vo, cl, d/w, map, illus., ports, 112pp. $30-b.

661a ..."A Great Stirring in the Land: Tallahassee & Leon County in 1860." In: FHQ, Oct. 1985, v.LXIV, #2, p.148-60.

662 **ROGGE, Edward**
"Accommodating Theory to Necessity: The Confederate Congress and Conscription." In: South. Speech Jour., 1963, v.XXIX, p.115-124.

663 **ROHRABACHER, L.E.C., Mrs.**
"Prose, Poetry and Song of the Southern Confederacy, comprising the traditions, manners, and customs of the South. Biographical sketches of its statesmen, Generals, and authors. The Battles of the Civil War, with its thrilling incidents, its daring adventures and its romantic reminiscences; its flags, its music, and its minstrelsy. Edited by Mrs. L.E.C. Rohrabacher. " Galveston, Texas: M. Strickland and Co. (1884) 33 1/2 cm, plates (5-ports to the plate) 192pp. Issued in 8-parts, numbered by hand, wraps, some in bound volumes, double columns. Originally to have been in 40 parts, but only known copies (TU and Rosenberg Lib., Galveston) has in 8 pts., #8. $75. Four issues had only the one portrait as: Jeff Davis, Lee and Jackson, Benjamin and Maxcey. Four with composit ports.

664 **ROLAND, Charles P.**
"Albert Sidney Johnston and the Loss of Forts Henry and Donelson." (Lexington, Ky.) JSH, Feb., 1957, v.XXIII, #1, p.45-69, map. duo-offprint pamph. 35pp.

665 ..."The Confederacy." Chicago: University Press (1960) 8vo, cl, d/w, ports, maps, illus. ix, 218pp. $25. Series: History of American People.
...1968.

666 ..."Albert Sidney Johnston and the Shiloh Campaign." In: CWH, December 1958, v.IV, #4, p.355-382.

667 ..."Albert Sidney Johnston, Soldier of Three Republics." Austin: University of Texas Press, (1964), 302, 8vo, cl, d/w, port, maps, 384pp., xvi.

668 ..."The Generalship of Robert E. Lee." In: Grady McWhiney's "Grant, Lee, Lincoln and the Radicals."

669 ..."Louisiana Sugar Plantations During the American Civil War." c.1957. Leiden, Netherlands, 1957. Pub. first as a PhD LSU in 1951. $20-bmk.

670 ..."Difficulties of Civil War sugar planting in Louisiana." In: LHQ, Oct. 1955, v.38, #4, p.40-62, notes.

670a ..."Louisiana & Secession." In: LaH., 1978, v.19, p.389-99.

671 **ROLFE, Moro O., (pseud)-"Col. Oram Eflor."**
"Chain-Shot; or, Mosby and his men." N.Y., The War Library, 1883, v.2, #35, 4to, wraps, 23pp. $100.

672 **"ROLL and Brief Historical Sketch**
of Company C., Nineteenth Alabama Regiment, Infantry." n.p., 1904, 12mo, wraps, 10pp. See: J.H. Savage.

673 **"ROLL and Record-Third Company,**
Richmond Howitzers." In: Richmond Howitzers Batt., v.2, p.287-304. Richmond, Va., Carlton McCarthy, 1884.

674 **"ROLL of Company B,**
Ninth Virginia Cavalry, from the Richmond Dispatch." In: SHSP, 1895, v.XXIII, p.292-294.

675 **"ROLL of Company I,**
Thirteenth Regiment of Virginia Cavalry (1861)." In: SHSP, 1906, v.XXXIV, p.278-279.

676 **"ROLL of Honor, The North Carolina.**
Account of its inception, preparations, etc." In: OLOD, Mar. 1876, v.4, #1, p.25-32. The mssc. roll is preserved at the State Library, Raleigh.

677 **"ROLL of brave men, Company I,**
Thirteenth Regiment of Virginia Cavalry." In: SHSP, 1906, v.XXIV, p.278-279. See: Lt. L.R. Edwards.

678 **"ROLL of officers and members**
of the Georgia Hussars and the Cavalry

Companies of which the Hussars are a continuation, with a historical sketch relating facts showing the origin and necessity of rangers or mounted men in the Colony of Georgia from the date of its founding." (Savannah, Ga., Morning News, 1906?) 8vo, cl, front, illus., pls (1 color) ports, 560pp. $300-bmk. Preface: A. McC. Duncan. They entered war as 6th Va. Cavalry, Co. E, shortly afterward transferred: Jeff Davis Legion of Cavalry, Co.F.

679 "ROLL of the Association of the Army of Tennessee, Louisiana Division, Camp #2, U.C.V., from its organization in May, 1877, to date April 1st, 1902." (New Orleans, La., 1902) 12mo, cl, caption title, 38pp. errata sheet in back. (Compiler? Mrs. John Dimitry, a copy inscribed "Comps. Assn. Army of Tenn. Camp #2, UCV, May 13th, 1902.

680 ROLLE, Andrew F.
"The Lost Cause. The Confederate Exodus to Mexico, with a Foreword by A.L. Rowse." Norman: University of Oklahoma Pr., (1965) 1st edition. 8vo, cl, dj, map, illus., ports, xv, 248pp. op($5.95)

681 ROLLER, A.H.
"Roanoke Grays-Muster Roll of the Company and some of its casualties." In: SHSP, 1896, v.26, p.291-294.

682 ROLLER, John E., Gen.
"Address: Our Heroes, the Leaders of a new reformation. From the "Shenandoah Valley", New Market, Virginia. Delivered Jan 19, 1907. Celebration of birthday of Robert E. Lee." 8vo, sewn, 15pp., dbl. column. $30. Inserted: atg. letter from Roller and Capt. F.A. Daingerfield.

683 ..."Gen. Robert E. Lee-Birthday. Celebration Thursday Jan. 19, 1905." Harrisonburg, Va., 1905, 8vo, wraps, 8pp. $25-b.

684 ROLLINGS, Robert C.
"Fort Myer: old home of the cavalry." In: Commonwealth (Va.) Oct. 1956, v.23, #10, p.15-17, views. On a post estb. in Arlington Co., as Fort Whipple in 1863.

685 "ROLLS of Company B, E, F, and K, First Regiment Virginia Cavalry." In: McClellan's "Life of Jeb Stuart", p.461-468.

686 ..."Roll of 2nd Reg., Va. Cavl., p.423-444. See: "The Second Va. Reg. of Cavalry..."

687 ..."Roll of 3rd. Va. Cavl." p.446-460.

688 "ROLLS of Several Military Organizations which entered the service of the C.S.A., from the City of Natchez and Adams County, Mississippi. Compl. from archives of their successors, the Adam Light Infantry, together with a complete roll of the latter company from the date of organization to the present time." John Harper, et al. (Natchez, Miss., c.1890) n.p., n.d. Democrat Print. 8vo, wraps, 86pp. slip case, full lt., $350-bmk-105. cover title: Memorial Souvenir, Adams Light Infty.

689 ROLPH, G.V. and Noel Clark
"The Civil War Soldier." Washington, D.C., Historical Impressions Co., 1961. 8vo, wraps, 24pp., illus. His dress and equipment.

690 ROMAN, Alfred
"The Military Operations of General Beauregard, in the War Between the States, 1861 to 1865, including a brief personal sketch and a narrative of his services in the War with Mexico, 1846-1848. By Alfred Roman, formerly Colonel of the 18th Louisiana Volunteers, afterwards Aide-de-camp and Inspector General on the staff of General Beauregard." $175-bmk-124, $100-bmk-99, 2 vols. 1st-1883, $125-bmk. N.Y., Harper and Bros., 1884. Tk. 8vo, cl (or full calf), fronts (ports). $75. xvii, (1), 594, errata slip; xvi, 691, errata slip, 12pp. ads, 1-pl, 1-map.

691 ...Reviews of Roman's "Mil. Oper." by Col. Wm. Allan, p.258-266; Judge Charles Gayarre, p.402-416, 433-447. In: SHSP, 1884, v.XII.

692 ..."Judge Roman's address." Flag presentation to the Washington Artillery." In: SHSP, 1884, v.XII, p.28-32.

693 ..."A letter by..., Shiloh-the Causes of a failure." (London) Jour. Confed. Hist. Soc., Autumn, 1970, v.8, #3, p.61-64.

694 **"ROMANCE of Blockade Running. The,"** In: Chamb. Jour., 6th Ser., Nov. 1903, v.VI, p.727-729.

695 **ROMERO, Sidney J.**
"The Confederate Chaplain." In: CWH, June 1955, v.1, #2, p.127-140. Offprint-$15.

696 ..."Religion in the Rebel ranks." In: La. State Univ., Abstracts of Dissert., 1954, v.16, p.74-75. On work of chaplains, ministers, and distr. of religious tracts in CSArmy and "Great Revival" of 1861-1865.

697 ..."Religion in the Rebel Ranks." Washington, D.C., University Press of America, 1983. 8vo, cl, x, 214pp.

697a ..."Louisiana clergy & the Confederate Army." In: LAH, 1961, v.2, p.277-300.

698 **ROMIG, Edna Davis**
"Marse Lee." Phila: Dorrance and Co., (1930). 12mo, cl, 80pp. Half-title: Contemporary poets of Dorrance, 94.

699 **ROMILLY, Henry**
"Letters on the Civil War in America." London: Henry Hansard and Son, 1889. 12mo, cl, 171pp. (CSA, p.52-151) Emory. Pro-south.

700 **ROMINE, William Bethel, Mr. and Mrs.**
"A Story of the Original Ku Klux Klan." Pulaski, Tenn: Citizen, 1924. 12mo, wraps, plates, port, 30pp. Do: revised, 1934, wraps, 8vo, pls., ports, 29pp.

701 ..."The Story of Sam Davis." by W.B. Romine. $35. (Pulaski, Tenn: Citizen, 1928) 8vo, wraps, (15)pp., illus.

702 **RONEY, Henry Clay**
"Reminiscences of the Experiences of a Boy Soldier in the War Between the States by Henry Clay Roney." Edt: Carl T. Sutherland. In: Richmond County History, 1979, v.11(1), p.20-25. Warren was from Warren Co., later on judge of the Augusta Circuit.

703 **ROONEY, William E.**
"The first "incident" of secession: seizure of the New Orleans Marine Hospital, Jan. 11, 1861." In: LaHQ, Apr. 1951, v.34, p.135-142.

703a **ROPER, John Herbert**
"U.B. Phillips: A Southern Mind." Macon, Ga., Mercer Univ. Press, 1984. 8vo, cl, dj, vi, 198pp, ills, incl. front., notes, sources, bibliog., index. $17.

704 **ROPES, John C.**
"Beauregard" and "Jeb. Stuart". See under Theo F. Dwight's "Critical Sketches", collection.

705 **ROPPOLO, Joseph Patrick**
"Uncle Tom in New Orleans: three lost plays." In: New Eng. Quart., June 1954, v.27, p.213-226. On "Uncle Tom's Cabin; or, life in the South as it is (by Joseph M. Field); "Uncle Tom's Cabin in Louisiana. (by Dr. Wm. T. Leonard) and "The Old Plantation; or, Uncle Tom as he is (by Geo. Jamison), 1854. Opposing the anti-slavery views of Harriet Beecher Stowe.

706 **"ROSALE Guards March, dedicated to:**
G.M. Miller, 1st Lt. Rosale Guards, 11th Reg. La. Val. by Miss. S. O'Connor. Composed by A. Cardona, Prof. of Music, Orleans Female Academy." New Orleans: A.E. Blackmar and Bro. 91861) N.O., W.H. Leeson, Printer. 4to, 5pp. not in Crand/Harwell. $75.

707 **ROSCOE, Theodore**
"The Web of Conspiracy. The Complete Story of the men who murdered Abraham Lincoln." Englewood Cliffs, N.J., Prentice-Hall, 1959. 8vo, cl, dj, front, illus., maps, xvi, 562pp. See: Dr. Otto Eisenschiml.

708 **ROSCOE, Theodore and Fred Freeman**
"Picture History of the U.S. Navy, the Old Navy to New, 1776-1897." N.Y., Scribner's Sons, 1956. 4to, cl, (384)pp. facsms., illus., ports, maps, drawings.
...N.Y., Bonanza Books (1956) Chap. VII (100pp.) major scenes, ports, ships and men for US and CSNavies.

709 **"ROSE Cottage.**
A real incident of the War, by M.J.H." In: LWL, Feb. 1869, v.VI, #4, p.279-292.

710 **ROSE, Duncan**
"Romantic career of a naval officer, Federal and Confederate: Captain Maffitt of the USS Crusader and the CSS Florida." (Spray, N.C.) The Author, 1935. 8vo, stiff boards, port, 68pp. See: Emma M. Maffitt.
..."Why the Confederacy failed." Fayetteville, N.C., 1896. 8vo, wraps, 34pp. Reprint from Cent. Mag., Nov. 1896. Paper money, neglect of cavalry and defense of too many points.

711 **ROSE, F.P.**
"The Confederate Ram, Arkansas." In: AHQ, 1953, v.XII, p.333-339. See: Oliver Wood McClinton.

711a **ROSE, Nelson Peabody**
"Robert E. Lee of Virginia, the anguish of conflicting loyalties." Cleveland, Oh., Academy Graphic Communication, 1986. 8vo, cl, dj, xiv, 255pp, ports.

712 **ROSE, U.M. of Arkansas**
"Jefferson Davis." In: Adresses of U.M. Rose. Chicago: G.I. Jones, 1914, p.171-192.

713 **ROSE, Victor M.**
"The Life and Services of Gen. Ben McCulloch, by Victor M. Rose." Phila: Pictorial Bureau of the Press, 1888. 8vo, cl, 2 ports, 2pp., 1, (25)-260pp. $1000-white, $850-jk, $125-(1/sMor.), $650, mint copy-jk. $1250-ginz-35.
...Austin, Texas: The Steck Co., (1958) 8vo, cl, (boxed), 5-color illus., incl. front ports, incl. 3-new ports, at end, Ill. (3), (3), (25)-260, (4)pp.

714 ..."Ross' Texas Brigade, being narratives of events connected with its service in the late War Between the States." Louisville: Courier-Journal Pr., 1881. 12mo, cl, 5-ports, incl. front, 185pp. $650-jk-mint copy. $900-r, $1250, $1000-bmk-105.
..."Kennesaw, Ga., Continental Book, 1960. 8vo, ports, 185pp. Facsm. reprint. $25 Bmk-84. See also: A.W. Sparks "Recollections", a great part of which was reprinted from Rose's "Ross' Texas Brigade".

715 ..."Celeste Valcoeur. A Legend of Dixie." Laredo, Texas. Printed for author, Jan. 1886. (Phila: Pictorial Bureau of the Press) 12mo, stiff boards (or cloth) 35pp. Epic poem of the Civil War. $120.

716 **ROSEBOOM, Eugene H.**
"Southern Ohio and the Union in 1863." (Cedar Rapids, Ia.) MVHR, June 1952, v.XXXIX, #1, p.29-44. Re: Southern settlers, Copperheads, Vallandigham.

717 **ROSENBLOOM, Joseph R., Dr.**
"Rebecca Gratz-example of conflicting sectional loyalties during the Civil War." In: FCHQ, Jan. 1961, v.35, #1, p.5-10.

718 **ROSS, Beverly**
"Letter of a Confederate soldier." In: Tyler QHGM, 1933, v.XIV, p.233-237. At camp near Dutch Gap, Va., Feb. 8, 1865.

719 **ROSS, Caleb**
"The Destruction of Louisville." In: SB, ns, v.II, p.49-58. (1886/1887)

720 **ROSS, FitzGerald**
"A Visit to the Cities and Camps of the

Confederate States, 1863-1864." Blackwood's Edinburgh Magazine, Vol. XCVI, July-Dec., 1864. American Edt., vol. LVIII, N.Y., Leonard Scott and Co., 1864. p.645-670; XCVII (1865), p.26-48; p.151-175. Remainder of narrative published in book form. $75-bmk-105.
...Edinburgh: William Blackwood and Sons, 1865. 8vo, cl, map, x, 300pp. $400-r.
...(Urbana, Ill.: University of Illinois Press (1958) Edt: Richard Barksdale Harwell) 12mo, cl, facsm. endsheets, illus., ports, xxii, 262pp., index. $25-r, $30-bmk-84. Harwell points out this work as a sequel to Col. A.J.L. Fremantle's "Three Months in the Southern States." Atg.-$25-bmk.

721 **ROSS, Ishbell**
"First Lady of the South. The Life of Mrs. Jefferson Davis." N.Y., Harper and Bros. (1958) $30-b. 8vo, cl, dj, facsms., illus., ports, xii, 475pp. Notes, bibliog., index, p.421-475.

722 ..."Rebel Rose; Life of Rose O'Neal Greenhow, Confederate Spy." N.Y., Harper and Bros., (1954) 8vo, cl, dj, illus., facsms., ports, xiii, 294, (1)pp. Bibliog. p.275-281. $20-bmk-84.

723 **ROSS, John**
"Correspondence" (Tahlequah, (IT), 1861. Broadside, 28cm, (Gilcrease-Hargrett) Corresp: Jno. Ross, Gen. Ben McCulloch and CSA Indian Comm.-David Hubbard on Cherokee neutrality. Only known copy.

724 ..."Proclamation to the Cherokee People" (Tahlequat (IT), 1861) Folio broadside. Append: to corresp. on the Cherokee neutrality between Ross, Arkansas, Texas, and CSA officials. Only known copy.

724a **ROSS, John DeHart, Col., CSA**
"Harper's Ferry to the fall of Richmond. Letters of Col. John DeHart Ross, CSA." Edt: Richard W. Oram. In: W.Va.History, 1984, p.159-74.

725 **ROSS, Lawrence Sullivan, Gen.**
"Sherman's campaign in Mississippi in Winter of 1864." In: SHSP, 1881, v.9, p.332-337. See: Victor Rose, J.A. Creager, "Proceedings of Ross' Texas Brigade.

725a **ROSS, Margaret S.**
"Seisure of the U.S. Arsenal, Feb. 1861." In: Pulaski CHR, March 1957, v.5, p.1-16.

726 **ROSSER, Thomas Lafayette**
"The Cavalry, A.N.V. Address by... at the Annual Reunion of the Assoc. of Maryland Line, Academy of Music, Baltimore, Md., Feb. 22, 1889." Baltimore, Md., Sun Book Pr., 1889, 8vo, wraps, front(port), 43pp. $500.

727 ..."Address of..., at 7th Annual Reunion of the Ass'n., of Maryland Line, Academy of Music, Baltimore, Md., Feb. 22, 1889, on Memorial Day, Staunton, Va., June 8, 1889." New York: L.A. Williams Pr., 1889, 8vo, wraps, front(port) 49pp.

728 ..."Report: Expedition to Hardy and Hampshire." In: SHSP, 1881, v.9, p.269-271.

729 ..."Report: of the fight at Aldie." In: SHSP, 1881, v.9, p.119-121. See: Wm. C. Wickham.

730 ..."General Robert E. Lee: Personal Traits of General Lee." In: Frank Leslie's Pop. Monthly, Jan. 1897, v.43, p.12-16.

731 **"ROSTER and Historical Sketch**
of A.P. Hill Camp, Confederate Veterans, #6, Virginia." n.p., n.d. (c.1915). 8vo, wraps, 63pp. $25.

731a **"ROSTER & Sketches**
of the several military companies which were in regular service of the Confederate States during the Civil War from Yazoo County, Miss. collected from the Muster Rolls & authentic sources of reliable men." Yazoo City, Miss., Waller print, 1905. 8vo, wraps, 21pp. $200. Cather & Brown notes one known copy.

732 "ROSTER of Confederate Pensioners of Virginia 1917." 1912. Richmond, 1917. 1914. 8vo, wraps, 106pp. 1920. $20. ...Same, 1926, 106pp.

732a "ROSTER of Confederate Soldiers of Georgia, 1861-65. INDEX. Spartenburg, S.C., Prepared by Lake Brackshear Regional Library, 1982. Americus, Ga. 8vo, cl, 513pp. $35. 100,000 entires. See: Lillian Henderson.

733 "ROSTER of Crenshaw's Battery, Pegrams Artillery Battalion, 3rd Corps, ANV, of Richmond, Va." Richmond, Va., Johns and Goolsby, 1884. 8vo, wraps, 8pp.

734 "ROSTER of Departed Comrads Buried in the Several Cemeteries of Port Gibson, Claiborne County, State of Mississippi, from April, 1861, to date, May 1, 1917, and Command in which they served. A," n.p., n.d. (1917) 8vo, wraps, 12pp.

735 "ROSTER of First Texas Battery, Good's Brigade." In: West Tex. Geneal. Soc. Bul. (Abilene, Tx.) Jan. 1961, v.3, #1, p.67-70. July 1986, #1, v.27, p.21-23.

736 "ROSTER of Goochland County Troops." SHSP, 1901, v.XXIX, p.223-226. By E.H. Lively.

737 "ROSTER of Officers and Members of R.E. Lee Camp, #1, Confederate Veterans, Richmond, Va., Will Roll of deceased members." (Richmond, Va., 1913) 8vo, pict. wraps, 30pp. $20-b.

738 "ROSTER of R.E. Lee Camp, No. 2, Confederate Veterans of Alexandria, Va." n.p., n.d. 8vo, wraps, 18pp. $20. Short biographical sketches.

739 "ROSTER of the Army of Northern Virginia: "Seven Days' Battle", p.334-337. "June 1st, 1863", p.338-342. In: Rev. J.W. Jone's Army of Northern Va. Memorial Vol."

740 "ROSTER of the Field and Staff Officers of the 7th Reg., Ga. Vol. Inf., CSA." n.p., n.d. (Hapeville, Ga., Longino and Porter, 1959-1964?) Offprint. 8vo, wraps, 66pp.

741 "ROSTER of the general officers of the Confederate States of America." In: Collector, Dec. 1906, v.XX, p.16-17, Jan., Mar., Apr., p.28-29, 52-53, 63-65.

742 "ROSTER, Company A, 9th Georgia Battalion Artillery, C.S.A." n.p., 1904, 8vo, wraps, 12pp. cover title. Account of reunions 1898-1904. Dorn-II, 213.

743 "ROSTER, of Rangers, 10th Kentucky Cavalry." In: Adam R. Rankins's "Partisan Rangers of the CSA," p.308-333.

744 "ROSTER. Louisiana Division Army of Northern Virginia, Camp #1, U.C.V." New Orleans, La., La. Review Print, 1893, 8vo, wraps (cover title) 11pp. $3.50, $6. Edwin Marks, Comm., Jno. S. Mioton, Sect. With many corrections, additions and date changed to 1894.

745 ROTHER, Otto A. "Browsing in our Archives: Letter by William J. Davis of Morgan's Cavalry, 1863." In: FCHQ, v.9, #3, p.191-195. The club has 150 letters written during the War by Maj. Wm. J. Davis, Southern soldier to his sweetheart, Francis Cunningham of Springfield, Ky.

746 ROTHSCHILD, Salomon de "A Casual View of America. The Home Letters of Salomon de Rothschild, 1859-1861." Translated and edited: Sigmund Diamond. Stanford: University Press, 1961. 8vo, cl, viii, 136pp. Conservative aristocrat, saw in the Abolitionist an insidious campaign to disposses the South, confiscate their property.

747 ROULHAC, Thomas R., 1st Lieut., Co. D. "The Forty-Ninth North Carolina Infantry, CSA." In: SHSP, 1895, v.23, p.58-78.

748 ROUND, Harold F. "The Handwriting on the Wall." (Richmond) Va. Cavl., Spring 1962, v.XI, #4,

p.41-44, illus. War around Massaponax left many words scratched on church walls by both sides of the conflict.

749 ROUNDTREE, Benjamin
"Letters from a Confederate Soldier, Angus McDermid." In: Ga. Rev., Fall 1964, (30)pp. $8.

750 ROUNTREE, John Asa, Mrs. (Maude McIver)
"The Cross of Military Service ("C.M.S.") History and records of men of lineal Confederate descent who served honorably in the Army, Navy or Marine Corps. of the United States or its allies during the period of the World War (April 6, 1917-November 11, 1918). Edited and Compiled for the United Daughters of the Confederacy by Mrs. J.A. Rountree, Chairman (Maude McIver Rountree) World War Insignia Committee." Volume 1, 1927. (Birmingham, Ala., UDC, 1927) 8vo, cl, 311pp., front (Cross) errata slip.

751 ROUSE, Milton, Capt.
"Statement in regard the charge that he violated parole." In: SHSP, 1888, v.16, p.35-36.

752 ROUSE, Parke, Jr.
"Keeping body and soul together-at Newport News Point on the Peninsula." In: CWTI, Dec. 1978, v.17, #8, p.18-28, illus., ports.

753 ROUSS, Charles Broadway
"A National Repository for the records and relics of the Southern cause." In: SHSP, 1894, v.22, p.387-389.

754 ROWE, George Henry Clay
"Fredericksburg's political hostages: the Old Capitol Journal of George Henry Clay Rowe. Edt: Lucille Griffith." In: VMHB, oct. 1964, v.72, #4, p.395-429.

755 ROWE, Sarah K., Mrs.
See: Maj. John A. Hamilton.

756 ROWELL, Adelaide Corinne
"On Jordan's stormy banks, a novel of Sam Davis, the Confederate Scout." Indianapolis: Bobbs-Merrill Co. (1948) 8vo, cl, dj, 368pp. $12.50.

757 ROWELL, Red
"A Soldier's Adventures." In: SB, v.1, #2, 1885/1886, p.88-98.

758 ROWLAND, Dunbar
"Catalogue of Confederate War Records of State of Mississippi." Jackson, Miss., 1903. 8vo, wraps, cover title, 16pp. $25.

759 ...Gulf Mag., 1902, v.1, p.147-149.

760 ..."Jefferson's Davis in History as revealed in his letters, papers, and speeches. By Dunbar Rowland, State Historian of Mississippi. (Jackson, Miss., Torgerson Press, 1923) 8vo, wraps, 16pp. Miss. Dept. Archives and History. $15.

761 ..."Private and Official Papers of Jefferson Davis." In: Harper's Magazine, Dec., 1911, v.124, p.97-104.

762 ..."The Dictionary of American Biography. A partisan, sectional, political publication, a protest." Jackson, Miss., 1931. 8vo, wraps, 16pp.

763 ..."A library of Mississippi History the Heart of the South. Publications of the Mississippi Department of Archives and History and Publications of the Mississippi Historical Society, 1898-1925." Jackson, Miss., 1929. 8vo, wraps, cover title, 18pp.

764 ..."Jefferson Davis Constitutionalist." n.p., n.d. (c.1923) 8vo, wraps, tied, port(tip-in) 11pp. adv. folder of quotes of prominent men.

765 ..."Military History of Mississippi, 1803-1898." In: "Official and Statistical Register of the State of Mississippi, 1908. 383-947. Jackson, Miss., Dept. Archives and History. Tk. 8vo, cl, fldg. maps, Civil War Period: p.420-947. $85-y.
...Spartanburg, S.C., The Reprint Co., 1978, 8vo, cl, 704pp. New Intro., Index. $32.50.

766 ..."Mississippi Official and Statistical Register." Jackson, Miss. Dept. of Archives and History. 1904 (pub. every four years thereafter)" CSA-1908: pt.V, "Military History of Mississippi. Nashville-1908. 1803-1898. "p.385-947..."Civil War, 1861-1865." p.420-943. fld. maps, $85-y, $50-jk. 1912: "Roster of Mississippi Soldiers, Army of Northern Virginia, Paroled at Appomattox." p.190-203. 4th Annual Report, see "Flags of Confederate..."

767 ..."Second Annual Report of the Director of the Department of Archives and History of the State of Mississippi, from Oct. 1, 1902 to Oct. 1, 1903." Nashville, Tenn: Brandon Print, 1904. 8vo, stiff wraps, 61pp. $10. CSA records, rosters on file in Miss.

768 ..."Speech of acceptance upon the presentation of a portrait of Jefferson Davis to the State of Mississippi by the Daughters of the Confederacy, Mississippi Division." Nashville, Tenn., 1905. 8vo, wraps, 8pp. (McElroy bibliog.)

769 **ROWLAND, Eron Opha Moore**
"Varina Howell, wife of Jefferson Davis. By Eron Rowland (Mrs. Dunbar Rowland)." N.Y., The Macmillan Co., 1927-1931. 12mo, cl, front, pl., ports, 499, 583pp. $30-bmk. II only $10.

770 **ROWLAND, Kate Mason**
"The English Friends of the Southern Confederacy." A Paper read on the Third Historical Evening, Richmond, Va., Nov. 9, 1911." (McElroy bibliog.) Pamphlet, privately printed, 10pp. In: CV, May 1917, v.XXV, p.198-202.

771 ..."Kate Rowland." In: SHSP, 1916, v.41, p.113-114. Sketch of life, died June 28, 1916, Richmond, Va.

772 **ROWLAND, Thomas, Major**
"Letters of a Virginia cadet at West Point, 1859-1861. By Maj. Thomas Rowland, CSA. Intro: Kate Mason Rowland." In: So. Atl. Quar. July/Oct., 1915, v.XIV, p.201-219, 330-347, v.XV, Jan/July, 1916, p.1-17, 142-156, 201-215. Containing letters between 1860-1861.

773 ..."Letters of Major Thomas Rowland, CSA, from North Carolina, 1861 and 1862." In: "Wm. and Mary Quar.", Oct. 1916, v.XXV, p.73-82.

774 ..."Letters of Major Thomas Rowland, CSA, from the camps at Ashland and Richmond, Virginia, 1861." In: Wm. and Mary Quar., Jan. Apr., 1916, v.XXIV, p.145-153, 232-238.

775 ..."Letters of Major Thomas Rowland, CSA (1862)." In: Wm. and Mary Quar., April 1917, p.225-235, v.XXV.

776 **ROWLEY, Henry M.**
"Sketch of Thomas F. Marshall." In: SHSP, 1890, v.18, p.38-51.

777 **ROY, Paul L.**
"The last reunion of the Blue and Gray." (Gettysburg, Pa., The Bookmart, 1950) 8vo, wraps, illus., ports, ix, 150pp.

778 **ROY, T.B., Colonel**
"General Hardee and the Military Operations around Atlanta." In: SHSP, 1880, v.VIII, p.337-387. Late of Gen. Hardee's staff.

779 **ROYAL Gazette, Hamilton, Bermuda.**
"Passing of the Monitor "Scorpion", built in England for the CSNavy." In: SHSP, 1903, v.31, p.71-72.

780 **ROYALL, William Lawrence**
"Some Reminiscences." N.Y., Wash, Neale Pr., 1909. 12mo, cl, 210pp. $100-bmk. Served: Co.A, 9th Va. Cavalry.

..."Reply to (Tourgee's) "A Fool's Errand, by one of the Fools.", N.Y., 1880, $8.95, $50-bmk., N.Y., 1881, complete 3rd edt. 8vo, wraps, 160--. Va. CSA Vet., edt-"Commonwealth", Richmond, 1880. Southern view of Reconstruction, with two additional rejoinders to Judge Tourgee.

781 **ROYCE, Edmund H.**
"St. Albans Raid October 19, 1864." Centennial Edition. (1964) (St. Albans, Vt., North Country Press) (26)pp. 8vo, pict. wraps, illus., ports, dble. pg. map. Editions: 1953, 1954, 1957, 1958, 1959, 1961, 1962, 1964. Distributed gratis by Franklin Co. Bank, also 1966, 1968. (1953, p.20) (1958, p.(2) 22pp.) See also: John Branch, Robert Ashley, L.N., B.C.L. Benjamin, John W. Headly, "St. Albans Raid."

782 **ROZWENC, Edwin Charles, Edt.**
"The Causes of the American Civil War." Boston: D.C. Heath and Co. (1961) "Problems in American Civilization." 2nd: (1965) 8vo, cl, viii, (3), 233pp. CSA: Jeff Davis, E.A. Pollard, Alex Stephens, Frank Owsley, Chs. Ramsdell, A. Craven.

783 **RUBIN, Louis D., Jr.**
"Lee's Surgeon's Horse: A Plea for Historiography." In: CWH, Dec. 1957, v.III, #4, p.385-399.

784 **RUBIN, Louis Decimus, Jr.**
"The imagine of an army: the Civil War in Southern Fiction (since the 1860's)." In: Va. in Hist., and Tradition (Farmville, Va., 1958) Longwood College, Institute of Southern Culture. Edt: Rinaldo C. Simonini, Jr., p.22-42. Also: In, Tex. Quart., Spring, 1958, v.1, #2, p.17-34.

785 **RUBY, Barbara C.**
"General Patrick Cleburne's Proposal to arm Southern Slaves." In: AHQ, 1971, v.XXX, p.193-212, ports.

786 **RUBY, James S. and Thomas E. Prendergast**
"Blue and Gray: Georgetown University and the Civil War." Edited by Ruby-Prendergast. Washington: Georgetown University Alumni Association, 1961. 8vo, cl, dj, 159pp., ports, roster, CSA (925) and Union (216). $25.

787 **RUDOLPH, Earle Leighton**
"Confederate Broadside Verse; a bibliography and finding list of Confederate Broadside Ballads and Songs." New Braunfels, Texas: Book Farm, 1950. (Heartman's Historical Series, #76) 8vo, stiff wraps, facsms., 118pp. Limited edition of 199 copies.

788 **RUE, George W., Maj.**
"Celebration of the Surrender of General John H. Morgan." In: Ohio Arch. and Hist. Pub., 1911, v.XX, p.368-277, ports, plate.

789 **RUFFIN, Edmund**
..."Edmund Ruffin's Account of the Florida Secession Convention, 1861." In: FHQ, October 1933, v.XII, #2, p.67-76.

790 ..."Extracts from the Diary of Edmund Ruffin." In: Wm. and Mary Quar., Jan-/Apr. 1915, v.XXIII, p.154-171, 240-258. Feb. 13, 1861-Dec. 13, 1864, Jan. 18-Feb. 19, 1857.

791 ..."Anticipations of the future, to serve as lessons for the present time. In the form of extracts of letters from an English resident in the U.S., to the London Times, from 1864 to 1870. With an appendix, on the causes and consequences of the Independence of the South." Richmond: J.W. Randolph, 1860. 8vo, cl, ix, 416pp. $250-jk. Ardent secessionist, fired 1st shot Sumter.

792 ..."The Diary of Edmund Ruffin. Vol. 1. "Toward Independence, October 1956-April, 1861. Edt., with introduction and notes by William Kauffman Scarborough with a Foreword by Avery Craven." Baton Rouge: Louisiana State Univ. Press, 1972. tk 8vo, cl, dj, port(front), xlviii, 664pp.
...Vol.II, 1976: "The Years of Hope, April 1861-June, 1863." p.xxxv, 706. $35.

793 ..."Extracts from the Diary of Edmund Ruffin." In: Wm. and Mary Quart., April, 1913, v.XXI, p.224-232. Pres. Davis and retaliation, Federal devastion Lincoln's war policy, exchange of prisoners.

794 ..."The First Shot at Fort Sumter." In: Wm. and Mary Quart., Oct. 1911, v.XX, p.69-101. Extract from unpub. diary.

795 RUFFIN, Julian M.
"Who fired the first gun at Sumter?" In: SHSP, 1883, v.11, p.502-504.

RUFFIN, Margaret Ellen Henry, Mrs. F.G.
"John Gildart, an Heroic Poem." N.Y., Wm. H. Young andCo., etc., 1901, sq.8vo, decr. cl, illus., front(port) print on one side only, 78pp. a 2nd edt. noted in LC. Soldier deserts to care for family need but returns to regiment, was shot for desertion.

796 RUFFIN, P.G.
"A Chapter of Confederate History." In: N.Amer. Rev., Jan. 1882. 14pp. removed, in binded. $10.

797 RUFFIN, Thomas
"The Constitution and the Union. Speech of the Hon. Thomas Ruffin, of North Carolina, upon the next presidential elections, etc., delivered in the House of Representatives, Aug. 2, 1856." Washington: Congressional Globe, 1856. 8vo, sewed, 8pp. Democratic Campaign Lit.

798 ..."The Papers of Thomas Ruffin, collected and edited by J.G. De Roulhac Hamilton." 4vol. Raleigh, N.C., Edwards and Broughton, 1918-1920. 8vo, cl, port(front), 541. (c.630), index. North Carolina Historical Commission Pub., Vol. 3, covers the Confederacy. Ruffin was for secession and a CSA Commissioner from N.C. 4vol-$100, $150, $75.

799 ..."State Rights and State Equality. Speech of Hon. Thomas Ruffin, of North Carolina, delivered in the House of Representatives, Feb. 20, 1861." (Washington: H. Polkinborn's Steam Pr., 1861) 8vo, sewed, 8pp. Caption title.

800 RUFFNER, Joseph
"The Tables Turned." In: W.Va. Hist. Mag., Oct. 1901, v.1, p.63-66. Capture in Clay Co. six furloughed Kanawha Valley soldiers of 22nd Va. Reg., then Yankee captors made prisoners of the CSA. (Shetler-689.

801 RUFFNER, Kevin Conley
"From Aquia to Appomattox: the history of the 30th Virginia Infantry Regiment, 1861-1865." (See: Robt. Krick) (s.1) n.p., the author, 1980. 8vo, 42, 4, 4, (11)leaves.

801a ..."44th Virginia Infantry." 1st Edition. Lynchburg, Va., H.E. Howard, 1987. 8vo, cl, dj, (6), 121pp, ills, ports, maps. 1,000 copies (#360) signed.

802 RUFFNER, S.T., Capt.
"Sketch of First Missouri Battery, CSA." In: CV, Sept., 1912, v.20, #9, p.417-420.

803 RUGELEY, H.J.H., Edt.
"Batchelor-Turner Letters 1861-1864. Written by Two of Terry's Texas Rangers." (Austin, Texas: The Steck Co., 1961) $12.50-jenk, $14. 8vo, stiff wraps, ports, facsms., 99pp.

804 RUGGLES, Daniel
"The military orders of Daniel Ruggles, Dept. of Fredericksburg, Apr. 22-June 5, 1861. Edt: Meriwether Stuart." In: VMHB, April 1961, v.69, #2, p.149-180.

805 RUGGLES, Daniel, Gen.
"General Orders #7, Hq. 1st District, Dept. #1, Tangipahea, La., July 14, 1862." 1p. relates to conscripts not in Crandall/Harwell.

806 ..."Gen. Order #5, Hdq. 1st Distr., Dept. 1, Tangipahoa, La., July 10, 1862." 8vo, blue paper, 1p. Relative to taking measures to prevent trespassing on the community, wives, etc.

807 ..."Amended report of the Battle of Shiloh." In: SHSP, 1879, v.7, p.35-47.

808 ..."The Battle of Cane-Brake." In: SHSP, 1880, v.8, p.529-535.

809 ..."The concentration before Shiloh." In: SHSP, 1881, v.9, p.49-63.

810	..."Fight with Gunboats at Mathias Point." In: SHSP, 1881, v.9, p.496-500.		Petersburg, Va., from "War Talks of Confederate Veterans.", Geo. S. Bernard, Edt., J.M. Pilcher, W.E. Cameron, etc. 8vo, caption title, 14pp.
811	..."Report of the Battle of Farmington." In: SHSP, 1879, v.7, p.330-333.	819a	RUSHING, Anthony "Cleburne the Stonewall Jackson of the West." In: CV (new) May/June 1986, v.34, #3, p.38-46, ports, crest (color), maps.
812	"RULES and articles for the government of the Army of Virginia." Richmond, Va., Wyatt M. Elliott, 1861, 8vo, wraps, 29pp. Dorn-II, 922. $400-ob.	820	RUSS, William A. "Disfranchisement in Louisiana, 1862-1870." In: LHQ, July 1935, v.18, #3, p.557-581.
813	"RULES of the House and Joint Rules of Both Houses of the (Confederate) Legislature of Texas." Austin, Texas, 1863. 8vo, 12pp., 1/2Mor. $200. Not in Crand-Harwell, Winkler, others.	821	RUSSELL, Don "Jeb Stuart's other Indian fight." In: CWTI, Jan. 1974, v.12, #9, p.10-17, illus., ports.
814	RUMBOUGH, George P.C. "From Dust to Ashes-a Romance of the Confederacy." Little Rock, Ark., Brown Print Co., 1895. 12mo,cl, illus., color flags on half-title., 193pp.	822	..."Jeb Stuart on the frontier." In: CWTI, Apr. 1974, v.13, #1, p.12-17, pl., ports.
815	RUMPH, Langdon Leslie "Letters of a Teenage Confederate. Edt: Henry Eugene Sterkx and Brooks Thompson." In: FHQ, April, 1960, v.XXXVIII, #4, p.339-346.	823	RUSSELL, E.L., Col. "Address at the reunion of veterans in Birmingham, Ala." In: CV, July 1908, v.16, p.315-320.
816	RUNNELS, Hardin R., Hon. "Message of...Gov. of Texas. Printed by order of the eighth Legislature." Austin: John Marshall and Co., 1859. (Senate Journal, p.15-41; House, 25-51pp. "Equality and security in Union or Independence outside it, should be motto of every Southern state." $100.	824	RUSSELL, H.G. "Devil Dogs of Dixie." In: Adventure, Dec. 1942, p.65-71, p.6, 8, and 118.
		825	RUSSELL, J.W., Mrs. "Mrs. Russell and the Battle of Raymond, Miss." Edt: Allan C. Ashcraft. (Jackson, Miss.) Jour. Miss. Hist., Jan. 1963, v.XXV, #1, p.38-40.
817	"RUNNING the Blockade. Daring exploits at Charleston in War Times." In: SHSP, 1906, v.XXIV, p.225-229.	826	RUSSELL, John S., Lt. "An unrecorded tale of the war. He was one of Mosby's Battalion of Cavalry. (Appleland Bks., $10)" In: Proceedings of Clarke Co. Hist. Assn., v.V, 1945, Berryville, Va., 68pp.
818	RUOFF, John C. "Frivolity to Consumption: Or, Southern Womanhood in Antebellum Literature." (Kent, Ohio, Civil War History, v.18, #3, 1972 Sept., p.213-229.	827	RUSSELL, Lenie See: Dabney Maury's "Woman's devotion."
819	"RURAL Messenger---(heading) Biographical Sketches (Petersburg, Va., 1892) Printed in columns of the Rural Messenger, weekly newspaper in	828	RUSSELL, Lyman Brightman "Granddad's Autobiography." Comanche, Texas, Privately printed. (c.1926/1930) (Commanche Pub., n.d. (1930) 8vo, stiff wraps, 30pp. Lim. Edt., 300 (addenda

829 **RUSSELL, Mattie, Edt.**
"The Bill of Fare of the Hotel de Vicksburg-1863." (Jackson, Miss., Jour. Miss. Hist., October 1955, v.XVII, #4, p.282-285. Soldier's humorous recall of bed and board in devestated Vicksburg.

830 **RUSSELL, Mildred Brewer**
"Lowndes Court House. A Chronicle of Hayneville an Alabama Black-Belt Village, 1820-1900." Montgomery, Ala., Paragon Pr., (1951) 8vo, cl, dj, port, 293pp. "Lowndes Answers the Call to Arms C.S.A., p.99-125 (32) Rosters: Hayneville Guards, Lowndesboro Guards, Lowndes Beauregards and Moore Guards.

831 **RUSSELL, Orpha**
"Ekvn-Hv'lwuce Site of Oklahoma's First Civil War Battle." Oklahoma City: Chron. Okla., Winter, 1951-1952, v.XXIX, #4, p.401-407, map, pl.

832 **RUSSELL, Phillips**
"The woman who rang the bell; the story of Cornelia Phillips Spencer." Chapel Hill: University of North Carolina Press, (1949). 8vo, cl, xi, 293pp., illus., ports. $25. Full name: Charles Phillips Russell. Biography of the author who wrote-"The last ninety days of the war in North Carolina." See also under Cornelia P. Spencer.

833 **RUSSELL, William Hepburn**
"Jefferson Davis; address delivered at the thirteenth annual banquet of the Confederate Veteran Camp of New York, at the Waldorf-Astoria, Jan. 26, 1903." N.Y., 1903, Private Print. 8vo, wraps, 15pp. (McElroy's bibliog. gives it as 9pp.)

834 **RUSSELL, William Howard**
"The Battle of Bull Run." N.Y., Rudd and Carleton, 1861. 12mo, cl, (2), 5-30pp.

835 ..."The Civil War in America: By William Howard Russell, Special Correspondent of the London Times." Bost: Gardner A Fuller; London: Trubner and Co., (1861). 12mo, cl, 189pp.

836 ...Boston: G.A. Fuller (1961) "Fuller's Modern Age, #1.) 12mo, cl, 189pp. A series of letters, Mar. 29-June 19, 1861, written for London Times, the first three in Wash., remainder in various Southern points. Except for first five letters, first appeared as "Pictures of Southern Life, social, political and military.

837 ..."My Diary, North and South." London: Bradbury and Evans, 1863. 8vo, cl, 2 vols., xvi, 424, xi, 442pp. map. $125, $250. Represented London Times, which was favorable to south. Before he left states, turned favorable to North.
...Boston: T.O.H.P. Burnham, 1863, 12mo, cl, xxii, 602pp.
...N.Y., Harpers and Bros., 1863. 12mo, cl, (or wraps) front, viii, 225pp. $50-nc.
...Toronto, same.
...N.Y., O.S. Felt Print, 1863. 12mo, cl, xxii, 602pp.
...N.Y. Harper and Bro., (1954) 2nd. 12mo, cl, d/w, front(port) illus., xiii, 268pp. Intro: Fletcher Pratt. $25.

838 ..."Pictures of Southern Life, Social Political and Military. Written for the London Times." N.Y. James G. Gregory, 1861. 12mo, cl, 143pp. Written from several places in the south, Apr. 30-June 23, 1861. With five additional letters from Washington, Mar. 29-Apr. 9 under title-"The Civil War in America." Boston: Gardner A. Fuller (1861) 12mo, 189pp. See: Jno. Black Atkins.

839 ..."The London Times' American correspondent in 1861; unpublished letters of Wm. H. Russell in the first year of the Civil War." In: Hist. Outlook, Oct. 1925, v.XVI, p.251-257. Edt: Louis M. Sears.

840 **RUST, Albert, of Ark.**
"Speech of Hon. Albert Rust, of Arkansas, on the State of the Union. Delivered in

the House of Representatives, 24 Jan. 1861." Wash: Lemuel Towers (1861) 8vo, sewn, 16pp. Native of Va., resigned congress in March, became a Brig.-Gen., CSA.

841 ..."State-Rights and National Union. Speech of Hon. Albert Rust, of Arkansas, on the Organization of the House. Delivered Dec. 28, 1859." Wash: Lemuel Towers (1860) 8vo, sewn, 16pp.

842 **RUST, Bushrod**
"Met his death in last fight." In: SHSO, 1906, v.34, p.219-220.

843 **RUST, Jeanne**
"Portrait of Laura Ratcliffe." (Richmond) Va. Cavl., Winter 1962, v.XII, #3, p.34-39, ports, illus. (1-color) Spy for the CSA and friend of many generals of the CSA.

844 **RUTHERFORD, John C. of Goochland**
"Speech of...in House of Delegates of Virginia, 21 Feb., 1860, in Favor of Proposed Conference of Southern States." Richmond: Wm. H. Clemmitt Printer, 1860. 8vo, sewn, 27pp. $50-ginz(24). Early call for Secession.

845 **RUTHERFORD, Mildred Lewis**
"Address delivered by..., New Willard Hotel, Washington, D.C., Thurs., Nov. 19, 1912." (Athens, Ga.) 1912. 8vo, wraps, 20pp. Author: Historian Generl U.D.C.

846 ..."Battles and Leaders. The Surrender and Results." Scrapbook, #10, October. Athens, Ga., 1923. 8vo, wraps, 20pp. (4)pp. $10-bmk.

847 ..."The Causes that led to the War Between the States." Scrapbook, #1, Jan., Athens, Ga., 1923.

848 ..."Jefferson Davis, president of CSA, Abraham Lincoln, president USA, 1861-1865, by...State Hist., Ga. Div. UDC." (Richmond, Va., Virginia Stationery Co.) 1916. 8vo, cl/or wraps, 48pp. $10-bmk.

849 ..."Contrasted Lives of Jefferson Davis and Abraham Lincoln-Miss. Rutherford's Hist. Notes (formerly "Scrap Book.") Vol. 1, Jan. 1927. Athens, Ga. 40pp. $12.50, $10.

850 ..."Contrasted Lives of Jefferson Davis and Abraham Lincoln-The Wise Politician and Statesman, The Shrewd Politician and Statesman." Vol.II, Athens, Ga., Feb. 1927. 8vo, wraps, cover title, 20pp.

851 ..."Contrasted Lives of Jefferson Davis and Abraham Lincoln-Jefferson Davis Attitude to Slavery, Lincoln's Attitude to Slavery." Vol. III, Athens, Ga., March, 1927, 24pp. $10-bmk. 8vo, wraps, cover title, errata slip.

852 ..."Contrasted Lives of Jefferson Davis and Abraham Lincoln: Policy of Parties Electing Them." Vol.IV, Athens, Ga., April 1927. 8vo, wraps, cover title, 32pp. $10-bmk-86.

853 ..."Contrasted Lives of Jefferson Davis and Abraham Lincoln-Jefferson Davis: The Peacemaker, Abraham Lincoln: The Warmaker." Vol. V, Athens, Ga., May 1927, 8vo, wraps, cover title, 20pp.

854 ..."Contrasted Lives of Jefferson Davis and Abraham Lincoln. Jefferson Davis: The Home of a Christian Gentleman, Abraham Lincoln: The Home of an Unbeliever." Vol. VI, Athens, Ga., June 1927. 8vo, wraps, cover title, 20pp. $8.

855 ..."Facts and Figures vs Myths and Misrepresentations: Henry Wirz and Andersonville." Athens, Ga., Jan. 1921. $12.50-y. Tall 8vo, wraps, cover title, 52, (3)pp-index.

856 ..."Formation of the Southern Confederacy." Scrapbook, #3, March. Athens, Ga., 1923. 8vo, wraps, 19pp. (5)pp. $10.

857 ..."Four Addresses by...Hist-Gen. UDC, 1911-1916. Author of, etc., etc." Birmingham, Ala., Mildred Rutherford Historical Circle. (1916) 8vo, cl, 119pp. Portrait (in color) includes (1) South in Building of Nation, (2) Thirteen Periods of U.S. History, (3) Wrongs of History Righted, and

(4) Historical Sins of Omission and Commission. $12.

858 ..."Historical Sins of Omission and Commission-address by...Hist.-Gen. UDC." In: San Francisco, Cal., Friday, Oct. 22, 1915, Civic Auditorium." (Athens, Ga., McGregor Print, 1915) 8vo, wraps, 36pp.

859 ..."History of the Ladies Memorial Associations: Monuments to the Confederate Soldiers." Scrapbook, #4, April, Athens, Ga., 1924. $10-bmk-89. 8vo, wraps, 22, (2)pp.

860 ..."The History of Stone Mt. Memorial." (Athens, Ga.? 1924) 8vo, illus. (ports), 15pp., t/p, illus. of unfinished memorial.

861 ..."Origin of the Daughters of the Confederacy History of the Cross of Honor." Scrapbook, #7, July, Athens, Ga., 1924. $10-bmk.

862 ..."Organization of the United Confederate Veterans. Sons of Confederate Veterans; Children of the confederacy." Scrapbook, #8, August. Athens, Ga., 1924. 8vo, wraps, 23pp. $10-bmk.

863 ..."Memorial Day Orations. The Meaning of Memorial Day. Heroes and Heroines of 1861-1865." Scrapbook, #3, April. Athens, Ga., 1925. 8vo, wraps, 20pp. $10.

864 ..."A measuring rod to test text books and reference books in schools, colleges and libraries." Athens, Ga., (c.1919) 8vo, wraps, 23pp. $7.50. UCV starts movement to disseminate the truth of Confederate history.

865 ..."Secession Was Not Rebellion." Scrapbook, #2, Feb., Athens, Ga., 1923. 8vo, wraps, 24pp. (4)pp. $10-bmk.

866 ..."The South in the Building of a Nation. Thirteen Periods of US History. Two addresses delivered at Washington, D.C. and New Orleans, La., by...Historian Gen. UDC, Athens, Ga." (Athens, 1913) 1st Edt. DeRenne III, 12mo, wraps, cover title, 40pp. see above.

867 ..."The South's Greatest Vindication. Stone Mountain Memorial." Scrapbook, #10, October, 1924. (Athens, Ga., The McGregor Co.) 8vo, wraps, (color flags) illus., ports, music, 46, (2)pp-ads. $15-bmk.

868 ..."The South in History and Literature: a Handbook of Southern Authors from the settlement of Jamestown, 1607, to living writers...by...Chair of Literature, Lucy Cobb Institute, Athens, Ga." (Atlanta, Ga., Franklin-Turner Co., 1907) 8vo, cl, xxxviii, 866pp. $17.50.

869 ..."The South Must Have Her Rightful Place in History (quotation from Jeff Davis)." Athens, Ga., March 1923. $10. 8vo, wraps, cover title, 50pp. $2.50. Textbooks unfair to South, should be ruled out of schools and libraries.

870 ..."Surgeons and Chaplains." Scrapbook, #9, September. Athens, Ga., 1923. 8vo, wraps, 17pp. (3)pp. ads. $10-bmk.

871 ..."Thirteen periods of US History; the South's part in making history-address of...historian general. UDC, Grunewald Hotel, New Orleans, la., Thurs. Nov. 13, 1913, n.p., wraps, 31pp. $6.50. Note: DeRenne (III-1149) gives Athens, Ga. 1913 as 1st edt., with "South in Building of the Nation", printed under one cover. (Birmingham, Ala., Mildred Rutherford Hist. Circle, 1916) 8vo, wraps 29pp. DeRenne III, 1148 notes a variations in t/p with cover and error of date repeated, i.e., Thurs. should be Friday, Nov. 21, 1913. Printed, same type, but continuous type, in her "Four Addresses."

872 ..."Truths of History presented by...A Fair, Unbiased, Impartial, Unprejudiced and Conscientious Study of History. Object: To Secure a Peaceful Settlement of the Many Perplexing Questions Now Causing

Contention Between North and South." cover title-authorities, pl. 1-13. (Athens, Ga., Jan. 1920) 8vo, wraps, 13, 114pp. xi, $12.

873 ..."Valuable Information About the South: The Assassination of Abraham Lincoln." Athens, Ga., Jan. 1924, Vol.II. 8vo, wraps, cover title, 25pp. Evidence shown Booth was never caught. Miss. Rutherford's Scrap Book, gen-title.

874 ..."Was Coercion Constitutional?" In: Mrs. Rutherford's Scrap Book, June 1923, v.VI, wraps, 15pp., v.6. Mildred L. Rutherford Sketch, see Margaret Anne Moss.

875 ..."What the South May Claim; or, Where the South Leads." Athens, Ga., McGregor Print (1916?) Tall 8vo, 1, 42pp. (ads, p.39-42)

876 ..."Where the South Leads and Where Georgia Leads." (Athens, Ga., 1917?) sm.4to, wraps, 1, 45pp. CSA and Ga. history.

877 ..."Henry Wirz and the Andersonville Prison." Athens (1921) 8vo, wraps, index, 52pp.

878 ..."Henry Wirz. The True History of Andersonville." Scrapbook, #6, June. Athens, Ga., 1924. 8vo, wraps, 24pp. $10-bmk-86.

879 ..."Woman's War Work, 1861-1865." Scrapbook, #8, August. Athens, Ga., 1923. 8vo, wraps, 17pp. $9.

880 ..."Wrongs of History Righted. Address by...Historian General UDC, at--Savannah, Ga., Friday, Nov. 13, 1914." (Athens, Ga., McGregor Co.) 8vo, wraps, cover title, 34, (1)pp. $10-bmk-86. Causes of CW, slavery, Davis and Lincoln. Barbara Fritchie myth. prisons, N and S. Index: v.1-5, op. "Scrapbook", 8pp., wraps.

881 **RUTHERFORD, Phillip**
"The Great Gainesville (Texas) Hanging." In: CWTI, April 1978, v.17, #1, p.12-20, illus.

882 **RUTHERFORD, Phillip R.**
"Texas leaves the Union." In: CWTI, June 1981, v.20, #3, p.12-23, illus., ports.
..."The New Bern Raid." In: CWTI, Jan. 1982, v.20, #9, p.8-15, illus (2-color) map, port.

883 **RUTLAND, Robert Allen**
"The Copperheads of Iowa: a re-examination (1861-1865)." In: Iowa Jour. Hist., 1954, LII, p.1-54, table, notes.

884 **RUTLEDGE, (pseud.)**
"Mr. Douglas and the Doctrine of Coercion, together with Letters from Herschel V. Johnson, of Georgia, and Hon. J.K. Paulding." (n.p., 1860) Tract #2. 8vo, sewed, 24pp.

885 ..."Separate State Secession Practically discussed. In a Series of Articles published originally in the Edgefield Advitiser, by Rutledge." Edgefield Court House, S.C., Advitiser Print(1860?) 8vo, sewd, 38pp. Sabin-74480-1.

886 **RUTLEDGE, Archibald Hamilton**
"My Colonel and his lady." N.Y., Indianapolis: Bobbs-Merrill Co. (1937) 12mo, cl, illus.-lining papers, 189pp.
...1945 edt., dj, signed. $25. Tribute to parents. Father was youngest colonel in CSArmy, served in 25th N.C. Reg., anecdotes about Lee, Jackson and Pickett.

887 ..."A Southerner views Lincoln." In: Scribner's Feb. 1928, v.LXXXIII, p.204-213.

888 ..."Abraham Lincoln fights the battle of Fort Sumter." In: So. Atl. Quart., 1935, v.XXXIV, p.368-383. Lincoln's strategy in handling Sumter episode. See: A.H. Jennings.

889 ..."Lincoln, a Southern view." Chapel Hill, N.C., (c.1925) 8vo, wraps, cover title, 16pp. $25.

890 **RUTMAN, Darrett B.**
"The War Crimes and Trial of Henry Wirz." In: CWH, June 1960, v.VI, #2,

p.117-133. Illus., port. Sympathetic treatment.

891 **RYALS, John Vincent**
"Yankee Doodle Dixie; or, Love the light of life. A historical romance, illustrative of life and love in an old Virginia country home, and also an explanatory account of the passions, prejudices and opinions which culminated in the Civil War." Richmond, Va., Waddey Co., 1890. 12mo, cl, vii, 1, (9)-532pp. $10.

892 **RYAN, Abram Joseph, Father**
"Father Ryan, Poet-Priest of the Confederacy." Columbia, Mo., Mo. Hist. Review, Oct. 1941, v.XXXVI-#1, p.61-66.

893 ..."Father Ryan's Poems. (quote)." Mobile (Ala.), John L. Rapier, 1879, 8vo, cl, front(port), pl. (flag), 262, (1)p. $75.
...Baltimore: J.B. Piet, 1880, 12mo, cl, front(port) 3-pls, xiv, 347, (1)p. Edts: 1881, 1888-Edt. 12, p.456; 1892; 1895 (p.464) with introduction by Rev. John Talbot Smith; 1896, p.361; 1897; 1908-contains his posthumous poems.

894 ...Oration; delivered before the members of St. Mary's Orphan Association, July 4th, 1866, by Rev. A.J. Rayn...to which is appended a history of the asylum; a list of members and principal contributors; the Conquered Banner by Sir Henry Haughton, bart.; "The Sword of Lee' by Rev. A.J. Ryan." Nashville: Printed for St. Mary's Orphan Association, at the Nashville Gazette Book and Job Office, 1866. 12mo, wraps, 43pp.

895 ..."The Sword of Lee, by Abram J. Rayn, (Father Ryan). Poses and directions for pantomiming and reciting by Cozette Keller." (N.Y., E.S. Werner and Co, 1911) 8vo, loose fold, sheet (part color), 8pp. Illustrations on sheet 56x71 1/2 cm. $20.
...In: NC Univ. Monthly, Feb. 1884, wraps, 4pp.

896 ..."Selected Poems of Father Ryan. Edt: by Gordon Weaver." Jackson: University and College Press of Mississippi, 1973. 8vo, cl, xiii, 122pp. See: J. Tom Miles.

897 ..."The Men who wore the Gray (poem)." In: SHSP, 1882, v.10, p.279-283.
..."Robert E. Lee (poem)." In: SHSP, 1883, v.11, p.429.
..."The Southern Soldier Boy. (poem)." In: SHSP, 1882, v.10, p.186.

900 ..."Judah Benjamin: unsung Rebel prince." Ashville, N.C., Stephens Press, 1948, 8vo, wraps, 112pp. $25-nc.
...Harriman, Tenn., Pioneer Press, $50. (195?) reprint.

901 **RYAN, Carmelita S., Compl.**
"Preliminary Inventory of the Treasury Department Collection of Confederate Records." Washington: 1967 (Record Group 365) Pub. #68-3-Preliminary Inv. #169. Large 8vo, wraps, ix, 65pp.

902 **RYAN, Frank T.**
"The Kentucky Campaign and Battle of Richmond." In: CV, April 1918, v.XXVI, p.158-160.

903 **RYAN, Ignatius L., C.P., M.A.**
"Confederate Agents in Ireland." N.Y., United States Catholic Historical Society, 1936 in v.XXVI, Historical Records and Studies, p.40-98. Robert Dowling, Jas. L. Capston, John Bannon, with a biogarphy of latter, bibliography.

904 **RYCKMAN, W.G.**
"Clash of cavalry at Trevilians." In: VMHB, Oct. 1967, v.75, #4, p.443-458, pl. maps.

905 **RYDER, William Henry**
"A Calendar of the Ryder Collection of Confederate Archives at Tufts College. Prepared by the Historical Records Surv. Div: professional and service projects, WPA." Boston: Historical Records Survey, 1940, 4to, stiff wraps, 168pp. reproduced from typescript.

906 **RYLE, Walter Harrington**
"Missouri: Union or Secession." Nashville, Tenn., George Peabody College for Teachers, 1931. 8vo, cl, (8), 247pp. (Contributions to Education, #82) A 1930 thesis, political and economic study during 1850s, leading to the decision to stay in union.

907 **RYWELL, Martin**
"Confederate Guns and Their Current Prices. Illustrated handbook that lists, describes and gives up-to-date values of all the known hand guns and shoulder firearms made and used by the Confederacy in the War Between the States. Plus Directory of Confederate Edged Weapons-Swords, Sabres, Bayonets, Bowie Knives-Makers, Dealers, Importers." Harriman, Tenn: Pioneer Press (1962) 10th Edt. 8vo, stiff wraps, 55, (4)pp. illus.
...Do: 1952, stiff wraps, 54pp. $25-bmk. (130-151, 40pp.)
...Do: 1955-1957, Edt. "2nd", $1(paper) cl, $15.
...Do: 1974, 55pp., 1950-$15.

S

1 **SABIN, Edwin L., Edt.**
"Vicksburg and after; being the experience of a Southern merchant and non-combatant during the sixties. Arranged by Edward L. Sabin." In: Sewanee Rev., Oct., 1907, v.XV, p. 485-496.

2 **SABINE PASS (Texas), Battle of**
"Commemorating the battle of Sabine Pass." In: CV, Dec. 1924, v.XXXII, p. 456-457.
..."Battle of Sabine Pass-a view from both sides." In: CV, Dec. 1928, v.XXXVI, p. 453-454.
See: Frank Tolbert, Mrs. R.F. Pray, Frances R. Sackett, Jefferson Davis, Mrs. Hal W. Greer, Frederick Speed. In: SHSP, 1884, v.12, p. 130-137.

3 **SABINE, David B.**
"Blue and Gray Chemistry." In: CWTI, October, 1969, v.VIII, #6, p. 22-29, illus., facsms., ports. "New ways of killing men invented during war but so was dehydrated vegetables, condensed milk and various medicinal substitutes.

4 ..."Ironmonger to the South-famous Tredegar works of Richmond was efficient and productive." In: CWTI, Oct., 1966, v.V, #6, p. 12-21, illus., facsm., port.

5 ..."The midnight ride of Millie Tynes." In: CWT, Aug., 1964, v.III, #5, p. 36-37, illus., map, port. A Virginia girl rides miles to save a vital salt works from Yankee raiders.

6 ..."Resources compared: North vs South." In: CWTI, Feb., 1968, illus., map. "The North could not fail to win, but the South had enough resources to wage war, plus its military talent."

7 ..."Captain Sally Tompkins." In: CWTI, Nov., 1965, v.IV, #7, p. 36-39, port. Founder and supervisor of best hospital at Richmond, only woman with Army Commission.

8 **"SACK and Destruction of the City of Columbia."**
See: Wm. Gilmore Simms

9 **SACKETT, Frances Robertson**
"Dick Dowling." Houston, Texas: Gulf Pub. Co., (1937). 12mo, cl, front(port) xiv, 80pp. Defender of Sabine Pass, Texas, during the War. $45, $35-b. See: Mrs. R.F. Pray, Frank Tolbert.

10 **SADLER, David M.**
"Johnston's Last Volley, experience in Durham at close of the war." In: SHSP, 1902, v.30, p. 174-178.

11 **SAGE, Bernard Janin**
"Davis and Lee; a protest against the attempt of the Yankee radicals to have them and the other Confederate chiefs murdered; a vindication of the Southern states, citizens, and rights by the Federal Constitution and its makers; and an exposure of the perversions of the said Constitution, and the falsifications of historical records, by the Massachusetts expounders; also (incidentally) President Johnson's Southern and States Rights principals. By P.C. Centz, barrister (pseud)." London: C. Mitchell and Co., 1865, 12mo, wraps, 80pp. (See variation in title, N.Y., 1866).
..."Davis and Lee; a vindication of the Southern States, citizens, and rights by the Federal Constitution and its makers, , and an exposure of the perversions of the said constitution, and the falsifications of historical records, by the Massachusetts expounders. By P.C. Centz, barrister, (pseud.)." London, Eng., N.Y., Van Evrie, Horton & Co., 1866. (also a N.Y., 1865, above) 8vo, wraps, (7)-80pp.

12 ...N.Y., Van Evrie, Horton & Co., 1861, 8vo, wraps, 80pp. Sabin-11691.

..."The Republic of Republics...an attempt to ascertain from the Federal Constitution, etc., sovereignty and treason and the reason why the trial of the Confederate Chiefs was evaded. By one of the Counsel in the Case of Jefferson Davis." Phila: The Author, 1878. 8vo, cl, 603pp. (enlarged, and best edition).

..."The Republic of Republics: a retrospect of our century of Federal liberty. An attempt to ascertain from the federal constitution, from the acts of the pre-existent states, and from the contemporaneous exposition of the fathers, the sovereignty, citizenship allegiance and treason of the United States; the obligations of the president's constitutional oath; and the reasons why the trial of the Confederate Chiefs was evaded. By one of the counsel in the Case of Jefferson Davis. 3rd edt., carefully revised and greatly amplified. With a very large appendix, containing much opposite matter now out of print. Philadelphia: W.W. Harding, 1878, 8vo, cl, illus., pl, xxiii, 453, (135)pp.

..."The Republic of Republics; or, American Federal Liberty. By P.C. Centz, barrister, (pseud.) 4th edition. Boston: Little, Brown & Co., 1881. 8vo, cl, diagrams, xxvii, 606pp.

13 ..."Some great Constitutional Questions-Corrections of Errors." In: SHSP, 1884, v.12, p. 485-499. See: Robert M.T. Hunter review.

14 **SAGER, Carl**
"A boy in the Confederate Cavalry." In: CV, Oct. 1928, v.XXXVI, p. 374-376. Exp. of the late B.F. Nelson of Minneapolis, Minn., written by son-in-law Carl Sager, as described by him.

15 **SAHW, W.T.**
"The Red River campaign." In: CV, Mar. 1917, v.XXV, p. 116-118.

16 **SAILOR'S CREEK, Battle of**
See: C.F. James, Richmond Dispatch.

17 **SAINT ALBAN'S RAID**
See: John Branch; Oscar A. Kinchen; Robin W. Winks; Edmund H. Royce; L.N. Benjamin; St. Alban's Raid, title; Roland Franklyn Andrews; Walter Alexander Harris; Ann Jenkins.

18 ..."The Saint Alban's Raid. Investigation by the Police Committee and the City Council of Montreal, into the charges preferred by the Councilor B. Devlin, against Guillaume Lamothe, Esq., Chief of Police; and proceedings of the Council in reference thereto." Montreal: Owler and Stevenson, 1864. 8vo, wraps, 78pp. Sabin-74983.

19 ..."The Hit and Run Raid." In: Amer. Hert., Aug., 1961, v.XII, #5, p. 28-31, 90-93, illus. By Charles Morrow Wilson.

20 **SAINT AMAND, Jeanette Cox, Mrs.**
"A Roster of Confederate Troops from New Hanover and Pender counties, which includes names of pensioners from those counties and a roster of Cape Fear Camp, UCV." Wilmington, N.C., 1960, large 8vo, wraps, 142pp.

20a **SAINT CLAIR, Kenneth E.**
"Judicial Machinery in North Carolina in 1865." In: NCHR, July 1953, v.30, p.415-39.

21 **SAINT JOHN, Isaac Monroe, Gen., Comm. Gen.**
"Report: Resources of the Confederacy in 1865." In: SHSP, 1877, v.3, p. 97-111.

22 **SAINT JOHN, W.P.**
"One who "was out with Old Stonewall"-the moral influence of Gen. Jackson." In: SHSP, 1891, v.19, p. 370-371.

23 **SAINT LOUIS GLOBE-Democrat-**
"The Bond of Heroism." In: SHSP, 1894, v.22, p. 67-69.

24 **"SAINT MARY'S CAMP...**
Quarters of Maryland Line, near Hanover Junction, Va., Jan. 1864." N.Y., Brett Co. Lithograph. Drawn on stone by one of the Line. Lith: 19x24", with a list of officers, Bradley Johnson, Commanding Brig. Hdq., Church, Guard Mounting, etc. $50.

25 **SAINT NICHOLAS (Steamboat)**
"Capture of steamer, St. Nicholas." In: SHSP, 1896, v.24, p. 88-91.

SAINT PATRICK (Torpedo Boat), C.S. Navy
See: Dabney H. Maury.

26 **SAINT SIMON'S ISLAND, Raid on**
See: Wm. Miles Hazzard.

27 **SAINT-AMAND, Mary Scott**
"A Balcony in Charleston, with a foreword by Archibald Rutledge." Richmond, Va., Garrett and Massie (1941). 8vo, cl, front(port), pls, facsm., xii, 157pp. Letters of life and times of Caroline Gilman, experiences of a "Confederate Mother", during Civil War, to her sister in the North and to her daughter, the wife of Jas. Russell Lowell.

28 **SALA, George Augustus**
"My Diary in America in midst of War." London: Tinsley Bros., 1865. 8vo, cl, (10), 424, vi, 425pp. $100-b.
...2nd Edt., revised, 1865, 2 vols.

29 **SALEM, Sam E.**
"U.B. Phillips and the Scientific Tradition." In: Ga.H.Q., June 1960, v.XLIV, #2, p. 172-185.

30 **SALISBURY PRISON, N.C.**
See: Louis A. Brown; J.Wm. Jones; Adolphus W. Mangum; "Bird's Eye View...".

31 **SALLEY, Alexander Samuel**
"South Carolina Troops in Confederate Service." 3 vols. $500-ob, $250-bmk-105, I and III, $75. 8vo, cl, flags on cover, xv, 783pp. index. 1st Reg. S.C. Inf. (regulars) Haygood's and Gregg's Regs., SCV. Columbia, S.C., The State Co., v.2, 743pp., index. (2nd, 3rd, and 4th Regs.) Columbia, S.C., printed for the Historical Comm. of S.C., by the State Co., 1930. thin, 8vo, 341pp., index. The 5th Reg. $175-bmk.

32 ..."Journals of the Commons House of Assembly, for the Four Sessions of 1863, Edited by A.S. Salley, Jr. Columbia, S.C., Historical Comm., 1907, 8vo, wraps, 41pp.

33 ..."Tentative Roster of the 3rd. Regiment South Carolina Volunteers, Confederate States Provisional Army." Columbia, S.C., The State Co., for the Historical Commission of S.C., 1908, 8vo, wraps (or,cl.), 129pp. See also: Wm. J. Rivers.

34 **SALLEY, Marion**
"The Edisto Rifles." In: CV, Nov. 1924, v.XXXII, p. 420-422.

35 ..."Errors and Omissions in text-books on American History." n.p. (Athens, Ga.?) 1929. 8vo, wraps, 8pp. Much on Secession, War, and Reconstruction.

36 **SALMON, Emily J.**
"The Burial of Latane. Symbol of the Lost Cause." In: Va.Cavl., Winter, 1979, v.XXVIII, #3, p. 118-129, facsms., illus., incl. dbl. pg. color, ports.

37 **SALMON, Emily J. and John S.**
"General Lee's Photographer, Michael Miley of Lexington (Va.)." In: Va. Cavalcade, Autumn, 1983, v.XXXIII, #2, p. 86-95, illus.

37a **SALTUS, J. Sanford**
"Flags & Insignia of the Confed. States of Amer." In: Amer. Numismatic & Archaeological Society." N.Y., 1899, large 8vo, wraps, 67pp. (1 of 3 articles).

38 **SALYARDS, Joseph**
"Memorial Eulogy of the Battle of New Market." (New Market, Va., Henkel,

Calvert & Co.?) See: pamphlet-under John Echols.

39 **SAMUEL, Bunford**
"Secession and Constitutional Liberty. In which is shown the right of a nation to secede from a compact of federation and that such right is necessary to constitutional liberty and a surety of union. (quote)." N.Y. Neale Pub. Co. (1920). 2vols. 8vo, cl, 403, 435pp., index. $100-b.

40 **SANBORN, Margaret**
"Robert E. Lee: A Portrait, 1807-1861." Philadelphia: J.B. Lippincott, (1966). 8vo, cl, d/w, pp.xii, 353, vol. I, illus., ports. $20-b. Different, in the sense of being a very warm, humorous, infinitely patient man, as revealed in his letters.

41 ..."The complete man, 1861-1870." Phila: Lippincott, 1967. 8vo, illus., ports, bibliog., p. 399-412. 2 vols, 1st edts. $40-bmk. v.2, port, xiv, (2), 430pp., illus., endsheets.

42 **SANDBO, Anna Irene**
"Beginnings of the Secession movement in Texas." Southwestern Hist. Quart., XVIII-July 1914, p. 41-73.

43 ..."The First Session of the Secession Convention in Texas." Southwestern Hist. Quart., Oct. 1914, p. 162-194.

44 **SANDEFER, H.L., Lt. and Archie P. McDonald**
"Sabine Pass: David and Goliath." In: Texana, 1969, v.VII, #3, p. 177-188.

45 **SANDERLIN, Walter S.**
"The Vicissitudes of the Chesapeake and Ohio Canal During the Civil War." (Baton Rouge, La.) FEb. 1945, JSH, v.XI, #1, p. 51-67.

46 **SANDERS, C.C., Col., 24th Ga. Reg.**
"Chancellorsville." In: SHSP, 1901, v.29, p. 166-172.

47 **SANDERS, David W.**
"Hood's Tennessee Campaign." In: Confed. Vet., Sept. 1907, p. 401-404. Address before Southern Historical Society, April, 1881. Also: SB, V.II, 1884/1885, p. 97-104, 145-153, 193-203, 241-252, 289-294, 350-366; SB, ns, v.1, 1885/1886, p. 6-13, 110-115, 168-176, 244-251, ports, plate(map).

48 **SANDERS, Lee Baber and Nola Green**
"Sarah Jane; Reminiscences of a Family and a Community by Lee Sanders and Nola Green." n.p., 1961? (Jacksonville, Ark.?) 12mo, cl, illus., 191pp. Sarah Jane Nelson Baber, 1852-1942.

49 **SANDERS, Robert W.**
"Efforts to capture Charleston, S.C., and evacuation of the city." In: CV, Apr., 1925, v.XXXIII, p. 142-143.

50 **SANDERS, Samuel D., Dr.**
"If Fortune Should Fail." Civil War Letter by Walter Rundell, Jr." In: SCHM, 1964, v.65, p.129-144, #4, p. 143-151.

51 **SANDIDGE, L.D., Capt.**
"Letter from: Battle of Shiloh." In: SHSP, 1879, v.7, p. 43-44.

..."The Battle of Shiloh." In: SHSP, 1880, v.8, p. 173-177.

52 **SANFORD, A.**
"Treason Unmasked. An Exposition of the Origin, Objects and Principals of the Knights of the Golden Circle, whose sole and only object is to overthrow the American Gov., and establish a Southern Confederacy, upon the basis of slavery." Albion, N.Y., John Marsh, Bruner Bro., 1863, 12mo, print-wraps, 42pp. $150.

53 **SANFORD, John W.A.**
"Address at unveiling of Confederate Monument at Montgomery (Ala.)." In: SHSP, 1898, v.26, p. 209-212.

54 **SANFORD, Orlin M.**
"A Virginian's diary in Civil War days." In: Americana, Oct., 1924, v.XVIII, p. 353-368. Edward Carter Turner's diary, on Kinloch, Fauquier Co., Va., Aug.-Dec., 1862.

55 **SANGER, Donald Bridgman**
"General James Longstreet and the Civil

War. Part of a dissertation submitted to the faculty of the division of Social Science in candidacy for the degree PHd, Dept. of History, 1934." Chicago, Ill., University Library. Privately edited and distributed, 1937, 8vo, wraps, (2), 25pp. photolithograph.

56 ..."A brief survey of the growth of nullification and its relation to secession." Tyler's Quart. Hist. and General Mag., XIX(1938), p. 195-214; XX(1938), p. 13-52.

57 ..."James Longstreet. I. Soldier, by Donald Bridgman Sanger. II. Politician, Officeholder, and Writer, by Thomas Robson Hay." Baton Rouge: Louisiana University Pr., (1952) (Vail-Ballou Pr., Binghamton, N.Y.) 8vo, cl, dj, facsm., maps, ports, viii, (2), 460pp., index. $60, $40.

...Gloucester, Mass., Peter Smith, 1968 reprint.

58 ..."Was Longstreet a scape-goat?" In: Infty. Jour., 1936, v.45, p. 39-45, Rich., Va.

59 ..."Three Letters." In: Infantry Jour., June, 1930, v.XXXVI, p. 632-635. Lee to Jeff Davis, resigning command, Aug. 8, 1863, Davis' reply and Lee's counter reply.

60 ..."Red River mercantile expedition." In: TylerQHGM, 1935, v.XVII, p. 70-81. Bank's expedition to Red River, not so much military as political and speculation in cotton.

61 ..."Some problems facing Joseph E. Johnston." In: "Essays Honoring Wm. E. Dodd by his former students." Chicago University Press, p. 257-290. Career from command of the West, Nov. 1862, to Fall of Vicksburg, July 4, 1863.

62 **SANGSTON, Laurence**
"The Bastiles of the North, by a Member of the Maryland Legislature." Baltimore: Kelly, Hedian & Piet, 1863. 8vo, wraps, 136pp. Sabin-76521. $50. See also: J.M. Brewer.

63 **SANSOM, John W.**
"Battle of Nueces River in Kinney County, August 10th, 1862, as seen and reported by John W. Sansom." (San Antonio, Texas, 1905). 8vo, wraps, cover title, port. 24pp. $100.

64 ...Bandera, Texas, Frontier Times, n.d., sm.4to, wraps, 36pp., 1954. See: Robt. H. Williams' "Border Ruffians." Also: Frontier Times, Oct./Dec., 1953, v.30, p. 439-452. Remins.(1911) of the Civil War.

65 **SANTEE, J.F.**
"The battle of La Glorieta Pass." In: New MexHR, 1931, v.VI, p. 66-75. March, 1862, battle of frustrated CSA plans on the far West.

66 **SAPPONY CHURCH, Battle of**
See: Wade Hampton.

67 **SASS, Herbert Ravenel**
"Look back to glory." Indianapolis: Bobbs-Merrill, 1933. 12mo, cl, 360pp. Laid in Charleston during the war. Fiction.

68 **SATCHER, Buford**
"Louisiana: Six Hundred Engagements." In: Jour. of West, 1975, v.XIV, p. 149-166.

69 **SATCHWELL, S.S., M.D., 1873**
"Medico-Chirurgical Lessons of the Late War from Southern standpoints." (London) Jour. Confed. Hist. Soc., June, 1965, v.III, #2, p. 63-68.

70 **SATTERFIELD, Paul H.**
"Recreation of soldiers (C.S. Army) 1861-1865." In: AlaHQ, Winter, 1958, v.20, p. 601-610. Notes, bibliog.

71 **SAUERS, Richard Allen**
"The Gettysburg Campaign, June 3-August 1, 1863. A comprehensive, selectively annotated bibliography. Foreword: Warren W. Hassler, Jr." West Port, Conn., Greenwood Press (1982) 8vo, cl, dj, xvi, 277pp. (1).

72 **SAUM, Lewis O.**
"Schlesinger and the "State Rights Fetish": a note." In: CWH, Dec. 1978, v.24, #4, p. 351-359.

73 **SAUNDERS, W.J.**
"Governor Zebulon B. Vance." In: SHSP, 1904, v.32, p. 164-168.

74 **SAUNDERS, William**
See: Alfred Moore Waddell.

75 **SAUSSY, Clement, Savannah, GA.**
"With Wheaton's Battery in the War. Reminiscences, humorous and pathetic of a private soldier in Camp, in action and on the march." In: CV, 1906, v.14, p. 209-213.

76 **SAUSSY, George Nolan, Col.**
"Campaigning with Jeb Stuart" (5pp.); "Some reminiscences from men on the firing line." (4pp.). In: Watson's Jeffersonian Magazine, August 1911. Pict. wraps, Chap. XIII.

77 ..."Lee's Army, an address...in addresses delivered before the Confederate Veterans Association of Savannah, Ga., 1893, p. 67-88.

78 ..."The night of New Year's Eve, a leaf from the autobiography of a Confederate soldier who was prisoner for eighteen months, same addresses (above) 1899-1902. p. 62-71.

79 ..."Some heroic and strenuous rides with Jeb Stuart." In: Watson's Jeffersonian Mag., May and June 1910, v.IV, p. 426-429, 483-488.

80 ..."Upperville's cavalry battle." In: WJM (above) April, 1910, v.IV, p. 332-336.

81 **SAVAGE, George**
"An address delivered by Private George Savage at the Annual Reunion of the Survivors of the Otey Battery, Thirteenth Battalion Virginia Artillery, CSA, at James River Brewer Park, near Richmond, Va., June 10, 1878. Published by the survivors." Richmond, Baughman Bros., 1878, 12mo, wraps, cover title, 11pp. $150-ob.

82 **SAVAGE, Henry, Jr.**
"Seeds of Time: The Background of Southern Thinking." N.Y., Henry Holt, 1959, 8vo, cl, viii, 312pp.

83 **SAVAGE, John Houston**
"Company Roll and a brief historical War Record, Company I, 19th Regiment Alabama Volunteers." n.p., n.d. (1905?) 8vo, wraps, 12pp. Signed: J.H. Savage. $100. See: "Roll and Brief Hist. Sketch Co. C., 19th."

84 ..."The Life of..., Citizen, Soldier, Lawyer and Congressman, written by himself." Nashville, Tenn., Printed for Author, 1903, 12mo, cl, front(port), 200pp. Served in Mexican War, Col. 16th Tenn. Reg., 1861-1863. CSA. $750-g

85 **SAVANNAH NEWS**
"Jefferson Davis(Privateer), C.S. Navy." In: SHSP, v.31, (1903), p. 53-55.

86 **SAVANNAH, Georgia**
See: Charles Colcock Jones.

87 **SAWYER, Elbert Henry**
"The National Military Park, established by the Government to commemorate the gallant deeds of the Federal and Confederate Armies in the four major battles, Fredericksburg, Chancellorsville, Wilderness, and Spottsylvania, Va. The story is prefaced by the condensed statement of an interview given by General Clem, chairman of the Park Commission and the detailed account of the battles by Col. E.H. Sawyer." (Chickasha, Okl.) 73pp.

88 **SAWYER, William E.**
"The Martin Hart Conspiracy." In: AHQ, 1964, v.XXIII, p. 154-165. plate. A Texas organized "Greenville Guards" later joined Union forces, renegade or hero?

89 ..."Martin Hart, Civil War Guerrilla." In: TMH, Fall, 1963, v.3, #3, p. 146-153. See: J.S. Duncan

90 **SAXON, Elizabeth Lyle, Mrs.**
"A Southern Woman's War-time Reminis-

cences." (Memphis, Tenn., Pilcher Print, 1905) 12mo, cl, 3, (9)-72pp. Benefit of Shiloh Monument Fund.

91 **SAYLES, John**
"The Constitution of the State of Texas, the Reconstruction Acts and the Confederate Constitution, annotated." St. Louis, Mo., 1888. tk 8vo, cl, (or, calf) 657pp. $125.

91a **SCAIFE, William R.**
"Atlas of Atlanta area Civil War Battles." Atlanta, The Author, 1982. 8vo, wraps, 61pp, ills, maps. $12.
"The Campaign for Atlanta." Atlanta, Ga., The Author, 1985. 8vo, cl, 149p., ills, bibliog., 27p, maps. $29.00. Enlarged & improved version of his Atlas.

92 **SCALES, Alfred Moore**
"The Battle of Fredericksburg, address by Alfred M. Scales, before the Association of the Virginia Division, ANV, at Richmond, Nov. 1, 1883." Washington: R.O. Polkinhorn Pr., 1884, 8vo, wraps, 23pp. $50-b, $125-r. Also: SHSP, 1915, v.XL, p. 195-223. See: Rob't W. Connor.

93 **SCALES, Cordelia Lewis**
"The Civil War Letters of Cordelia Scales." Edt: Percy L. Rainwater. (Jackson, Miss., Jour. of Miss. Hist., p. 169-181, v.VI, 1939.

94 ..."Dear Darling Loulie", Letters of Cordelia Lewis Scales to Loulie W. Irby During War Between the States." Edt: Martha Neville Lumpkin. Boulder, Colo., Ben Gray Lumpkin, 1955, 4to, boards, mimograph, 151pp., ports. Privately printed, o.p. $75.

95 ...Clarksville, Tenn., August, 1972, 4to, stiff wraps, memogr., 157pp. ports. Note: "Dear Darling Loulie." 275 copies of 1st edition. 12 had bound, the remainder in gray stiff wraps. A few sent to schools, remainder to the family. 25 copies to a bookseller in Va. (Ben Gray Lumpkin).

96 **SCALF, Henry P.**
"The Battle of Ivy Mountain." In: RKHS, Jan. 1958, v.56, #1, p.11-26.

97 **SCAMMON, Eliakim Parker**
See: Samuel Jones.

98 **SCAPEL, M.D.**
See: Edward H. Dixon

98a **SCARBORO, David D.**
"North Carolina & the Confederacy: the weakness of states rights during the War." In: NCHR, Spring 1979, p.133-49.

99 **SCARBOROUGH, Rabun**
"The Civil War Letters of Rabun Scarborough,, Apalachicola, Florida, 1861-1862." In: Magnolia Monthly, Sept., 1975, v.13, #9, p. 17-20. Letters from Camp Retrieve.

100 **SCARBOROUGH, Ruth**
"Belle Boyd: Siren of the South." Macon, Ga., Mercer University Pr., 1983. 8vo, cl, xxi, 212pp., front, illus., notes.

101 **SCARBOROUGH, William K.**
"Edmund Ruffin at Seven Pines." In: CWTI, Dec., 1976, v.17, #8, p. 32-39, illus., ports.

102 **SCHAFF, Morris (See: Eban Swift)**
"The Battle of the Wilderness." Bost., N.Y., Houghton Mifflin (1910). 12mo, cl, maps (2-dbl. pg.) incl. front, (8), 345, (1)pp. First in Atlantic Monthly, ciii-v. July/Dec., 1909, v.CIV, p. 34-45, 183-194, 374-389, 476-488, 632-643, 721-723, 808-817.

103 ..."Jefferson Davis, his Life and Personality." Bost: John W. Luce & Co. (1922). 12mo, cl, (8), 277pp.

104 ..."The Sunset of the Confederacy." Bost: John W. Luce & Co., (1912). 12mo, cl, (8), 277pp.
..."The Sunset of the Confederacy." Bost: John W. Luce & Co., (1912). 12mo, cl, maps, incl. fldg. front, (4), 302pp.
...Baltimore, Md., Butternut Press, 1986, (30). $35-b.

105 **SCHARF, J. Thomas, Col.**
"History of the Confederate States Navy from its organization to the surrender of its last vessel. Its stupendous struggle with the great navy of the U.S.; the engagements fought in the rivers and harbors of the South, and upon the high seas; blockade-running, first use of iron-clads and torpedoes and privateer history." New York: Rogers & Sherwood; San Francisco, A.L. Bancroft, etc., 1887. Fine-$175. 8vo, decr. dl, (also in full sheep or boards), x, (11)-824pp., front, illus. (incl. plans, diagrs., plates and ports) $100, Fine-$85.
...Louisville, Ky., Lost Cause micro-cd, $11.
...Albany, N.Y., Joseph McDonough, 1894, 2 vols.
...Freeport, N.Y., Books for Libraries Print., (1969) Select Bibliographies reprint series. 2 vols., 824pp., illus., maps, ports, 8vo, cloth.
...Fairfax Press, (c.1977), (Crown Pub. Co.), $35, $42-y
...2 vols. Salem, N.H., 'Select Bibliographies Reprint Series,' 1980. $40.

106 ..."History of Western Maryland. Being a History of Frederick, Montgomery, Carroll, Washington, Allegheny and Garrett counties; biographical sketches of representative men." Phila: L.H. Everts Pr., 1882, 2 vols. 4to, cl, illus., pls.(incl. illus., ports, col. map) Civil War: list of Union and CSA commands; Maryland volunteers, Union and CSA, p. 194-340.

107 **SCHAUB, J.L.**
"Fourth and Fourteenth North Carolina." In: CV, 1902, v.10, p. 537, port.

108 **SCHEIBER, Harry N.**
"The Pay of Confederate Troops and Problems of Demoralization: A Case of Administrative Failure." In: CWH, September, 1969, v.XV, #3, p. 226-236.

109 ..."The Pay of Troops and Confederate Morale." In: AHQ, 1959, v.XVIII, p. 350-365, notes. See: Paul P. Van Riper.

110 **SCHEIBERT, Justus, Major**
"Causes of Lee's Defeat at Gettysburg, Letter from Maj. Scheibert, of the Prussian Royal Engineers." In: SHSP, 1878, v.V, p. 90-93.

111 ..."Der Burgerkrieg in den Nordamerikanischen Staaten: Militarisch beleuchette fur den deutschen Offizier. Mit 1 Karte von Virginien und 3 Planen." Berlin: Ernst-Siegfried-Mittler und Sohn, 1874. 8vo, wraps, 2-fldg. maps, (4)pp. $50. Analysis of Naval affairs along the Mississippi.

112 ..."La Guerre civile aux Etats-Unis d'Amerique (guerre de la Secession) consideree au point de vue militaire pour les officiers de l'armee Allenmandre. Traduit par J. Bornecque." Paris: Lib. Militaire de J. Dumaine, 1876. Head: "Publication de la Reunion des Officers." 8vo, full leather, 4-fldg. maps, 3pls., 278pp.
...Same, with (2), 315, (4)pp.
...Sabin-77534 copy: vi, 320pp., map, 3-pls.

113 ..."Jefferson Davis. President of the late Confederate States." In: SHSP, 1891, v.XIX, p. 406-416.

114 ..."Stonewall Jackson's Way." St. Louis: W.K. Bixby, 1915 (Cedar Rapids: The Torch Press). 8vo, boards, 7pp. Priv. Print for the author for friends. Only 200 copies.

115 ..."Sieben Monate in den Rebellen-Staaten wahrend des nordamerikanischen Kriegs 1863 von Scheibert. Hierzu vier Gefechts- und Situationsplane." Stettin: Verlag von Th. von der Nahmer, 1868. 12mo, wraps, vi, 126, maps (4)-fldg. $50. (Howes gives 2-maps; LC, 4-fldg. plans)

116 ..."Seven months in the rebel states, during the North American War, 1863, by Captain Justus Scheibert. Translated from

the German by Joseph C. Hayes. Edited with an introduction by Wm. Stanley Hoole Tuscaloosa, Ala., Confederate Pub. Co., 1958, 12mo, stiff wraps, front(port), 4-maps, 166pp. Lim. edt., 450 copies. Confederate Centennial studies, #9.

117 ..."Work of the Southern Historical Society in Europe." In: SHSP, 1881, v.9, p. 570-572. See: Chs. Poindexter, Chs. Scott Venable. Review-"Valley Camp." SHSP, v.11, p. 327-328.

118 **SCHELIHA, Viktor Ernst Karl Rudolph von**
"A Treatise on Coast-Defense: based on the experience gained by...Engineers of Army of the Confederate States, and compiled from Official Reports of Officers of the Navy of the United States, 1861-1862." By Von Scheliha. London: E. & F. N. Spon, 1868. 8vo, cl, p. xviii, 326. Plates (12) 2 vols. one vol. maps. Sabin 77540. $175. color front, engraved added titlepage. $175, $225. Westport, Conn., 1971.

119 **SCHENCK, Martin**
"Up Came Hill; the story of the Light Division and its Leaders." (Harrisburg, Pa., Stackpole Co. (1958) 8vo, cl, illus., xi, 344pp., maps, ports. $17.50, $50-b. "Civil War Campaigns."
...Gaithersburg, Md., Butternut Press, 1985. 8vo, cl, 344p., ills, maps, index. $25.

120 **SCHENE, Michael G.**
"The daring escape of Judah P. Benjamin." In: Tampa Bay History" (Fla.) Spring/Summer, 1982, v.IV, p. 69-73.

121 **SCHILDT, John W.**
"Stonewall Jackson day by day." Chewsville, Md., 1980? 8vo, wraps, illus.
...Chewsville, Md., Antietam Pub., 1980. 8vo, wraps, 135pp, ills, bibliog. $7.50.

122 ..."September Echoes, the Maryland Campaign of 1862, the places, the battles, the results by John W. Schildt." (Middletown, Md., Valley Register, 1960) 8vo, cl, illus., ports, plans, viii, 140pp.
...(Hagerstown, Md., Hagerstown Book Print, 3rd printing) Study of Lee's Maryland campaign, 1862. Lee's first northern invasion, culminating in the Battle of Antietam, or Sharpsburg.
..."Hunter Holmes McGuire; Doctor in Gray." Chewsville, Va., The Author, 1986, 8vo, cl, 135pp., illus.
..."Roads to Gettysburg." Parsons, W.Va., McClain Print, 1978. 8vo, cl, 582pp, ills, maps. $18.

123 **SCHIRMER DIARY, South Carolina**
"Extracts from the Schirmer Diary, April-December, 1860, Jan./Mar., 1861." In: SCHM, 1961, v.62, #1, p. 54, 113-114, #2, 3, and 4, p. 162, 182, 232-237.

124 **SCHMANDT, Raymond H. and Josephine H. Schulte**
"Civil War Chaplains-A document from a Jesuit Community." In: Rec. Amer. Catholic Hist. Soc. of Phila., 1962, v.LXXIII, p. 58-64. Memo from Spring Hill College, Mobile, Ala. of chaplains who served.

125 ..."Spring Hill College Diary." In: Ala. Rev., 1962, v.XV, p. 213-226. Diary at the college detailing life in college during the war.

126 **SCHMIDT, Louis Bernard**
"The Influence of Wheat and Cotton on Anglo-American relations during the Civil War." In: La. Jour. Hist., July, 1918, v.XVI, p. 400-439.

127 **SCHMITT, William A.**
"The last days of the Lost Cause: capture imprisonment and trial of President Jefferson Davis." Clarksdale, Miss: Delta Press (1949) 8vo, wraps, 59pp., map, ports, views. $25-bmk Retreat of Davis from Richmond to Irwinville, Ga., imprisonment at Fortress Monroe, Va., release on bail and trial.

128 **SCHOFIELD, John McAllister**
"Lee's Birthday." In: SHSP, 1889, v.17, p. 348.

129 **SCHOOL BOOKS**
See: Text Books

130 **SCHOOL BOOKS on the Confederate War**
See: Wm. Allan's Eclectic Hist., J.W. Jones's review of...

131 **SCHOONOVER, Thomas**
"Confederate Diplomacy and the Texas-Mexican Border, 1861-1865." In: ETHJ, Spring, 1973, v.XI, #1, p. 33-39, notes.
..."Documents concerning Lemuel Dale Evans' plan to keep Texas in the Union in 1861." In: ETHJ, Spring, 1974, v.XII, #1, p. 35-38, notes.

132 **SCHRANTZ, Ward L.**
"The Battle of Carthage(Missouri)." (Columbia, Mo., Mo. Hist. Review. Jan. 1937, v.XXXI-#2, p. 140-149. CSA checks Sigel's forces in retreat.

133 ..."Jasper County, Missouri, in the Civil War." Carthage, Mo., Carthage Press, 1923, 12mo, cl, front(map), illus., xxi, (23)-269pp. Missouri Guerrillas, Price's and Shelby's Raids, etc.

134 **SCHREINER, Hermann L.**
"The Beauregard Songster, being a selection of patriotic, sentimental and comic songs, the most popular of the day." Macon and Savannah, Ga., J.C. Schreiner, 1864, 16mo, wraps, 36pp.

135 ..."The General Lee Songster, being a collection of the most popular, sentimental, patriotic and comic songs." Macon and Savannah, Ga., Schreiner & Hewill, Augusta, Ga., 1865. 16mo, wraps, cover title, 36pp.

135a **SCHROEDER, Glenna R.**
"We will support the Govt. to the bitter end: The Augusta office of the Confederate Nitre & mining Bureau." In: GaHQ, Summer 1986, v.70, #2, p.288-305, ports, notes.

136 **SCHROEDER, L.E.**
"The Battle of Wilson's Creek and its Effect Upon Missouri." In: MHR, Jan., 1977, v.LXXI, #2, p. 156-173, ports, illus.

137 **SCHULER, Louis J.**
"The Last Battle in the War Between the States, May 13, 1865. Louis J. Schuler Confederate force of 300 defeats 1700 Federals near Brownsville, Texas." (Brownsville, Tex: Springman-King (1960) 12mo, stiff wraps, color flag, port, illus., map, facsm., v, (1), 30pp. See: "Last Battle of the War."

138 **SCHULLER, Frank**
"General Albert Sidney Johnston." In: Southern Review, v.X, p. 78-109.

139 **SCHULTZ, Harold Seesel**
"Nationalism and Sectionalism in South Carolina, 1852-1860; a study of the movement for Southern independence." Durham, N.C., Duke University Press, 1950, cl, x, 259pp. diagrams, maps. N.Y., Rep: Da Capo, 1969, $15.

140 **SCHURICHT, Hermann, 14th Virginia Cavalry**
"Jenkins' Brigade in the Gettysburg campaign, extracts from the diary of Lieut. Hermann Schuricht of the 14th Va. Cavl." In: SHSP, 1896, v.24, p. 339-351.

141 **SCHWAB, John Christopher**
"The Confederate States of America 1861-1865. A Financial and Industrial History of the South During the Civil War." $15, $17.50, $25, $35, $28.50. N.Y., Charles Scribner's, 1901. 8vo, cl, xi, 332pp., fold. tabl. half-title. "Yale Bicentennial Publications." $60-ob.
...N.Y., Scribners-1904, 2nd Edt.
...New Haven: Yale University, 1913, $100. 8vo, xii, 332pp., fldg. table, $17.50, $20. Bibliog. foreign books in CS finance.
...N.Y., Burt Franklin (1968) Burt Franklin

Research and Source Works Series. American classics in history and social science. Reprint of the 1901 edition. ...N.Y., Gordon Pr., $60.

142 ..."The Confederate Foreign Loan; an episode in the Financial History of the Civil War." In: Yale Review, 1892, v.1, p. 175-186.

143 ..."The South during the War (1861-1865)." In: Camb. Modern Hist., 1903, v.VII, p. 603-621.

143a **SCHWABE, Edward, Jr.**
"Sherman's march through Georgia: a reappraisel of the right wing." In: GHQ, Winter 1985, v.69, #4, p.522-35, maps.

144 **SCHWARZ, Ted**
"Counterfeit Confederate-in order to topple the CS economy." In: CWTI, May 1977, v.16, #2, p. 34-39, facsms, port.

144a **SCHWIEKART, Larry**
"Secession & Southern Banks." IN: CWH, June 1985, v.31, #2, p.111-25, charts.

145 **SCLATER, W.S**
"A complete and authentic history of Libby Prison, compiled by W.S. Sclater." Richmond, Va., Southern Art Emporium. 1894. Dorn-II, 668. 8vo, wraps, 28, (1)p., J.C. Weckert Print.

146 **SCORPION (Monitor), C.S. Navy**
"Passing of the Monitor Scorpion." In: Royal Gazette, Hamilton, Bermuda." In: SHSP, 1903, v.31, p. 71-72.

147 **SCOTT'S CATALOGUE**
of United States Stamps, specialized; Includes the Confederate States." N.Y., Scott's Pub., 32nd edt., (c.1953). CSA, p. 473-500.

148 **SCOTT'S MONTHLY MAGAZINE**
v.1, Dec. 1865-Dec. 1869. Edts: Rev. Wm. J. Scott (W.H. Wylly, the final number) Atlanta, Ga., J.J. Toon (1865-1869) Many war incidents and campaigns, e.g., B.W. Frobel's "Field and Camp" series. Many engravings: Lee, Johnston, Davis, Stephens by Geo. Perine.

149 ..."Scott's Monthly Magazine. A Georgia Post-Bellum Periodical of Literature and Military History. By Ray M. Atchison." In: Ga.H.Q., September 1965, v.LXIX, #3, p. 294-305.

..."Scott's Monthly Magazine--Wm. J. Scott, Edt., 1865/9. "The Georgia Campaign; or a South-side view of Sherman's march to the Sea." Feb./Mar. 1868.

..."W.S.B."--(v.1) "Battle of Gettysburg (Jan-Apr. 1865)--6 accts: Battle of Chancellorsville, Shiloh, Ft. Donelson & 2nd Manassas."

..."Field & Camp, during the late four years war." Sept. 1866-Dec. 1867. D. W. Frobel.

..."Steel engravings by Geo. E. Perine, N.Y., Generals: Andrew Johnson (June 1866), Lee (Jan. 1867), Joseph E. Johnston (Mar. 1867), J. Davis (Feb. 1867), Alex Stephens (Apr. 1867), Stephen Elliott (June 1867).

149a **SCOTT, Carole E.**
"Coping with inflation: Atlanta, 1860-65." In: GHQ, Winter 1985, v.69, #4, p.536-56. Charts, notes.

150 **SCOTT, D.M.**
"Selma and Dallas County, Alabama. (During the Civil War)." In: CV, May 1916, v.XXIV, p. 214-222.

151 **SCOTT, Edward Herndon, MD.**
"Memorials of Edward Herndon Scott, Md." (Singer's Glen, Rockingham, Va., 1873) Ruebush, Kieffer & Co., Pub. by attached Friends. 12mo, stitched, 29pp. Title in mourning borders. Brock Collection, Oct. 1922.

152 ..."Memorials of Edward Herndon Scott..." Wytheville, Va., (1974) Jim Presgraves. 8vo, wraps, 29pp. Scott served with Hughes Batt., 6th Missouri, 1st Missouri Cavalry and with Rosser.

153 **SCOTT, Edwin J.**
"Random Recollections of a Long Life 1806-1876." Columbia, S.C., Chs. A. Calvo, 1884, 12mo, cl, vi, (3)-216pp. Life in S.C., principally in Columbia and Lexington.

153a **SCOTT, Ernest**
"The Shenandoah Incident, 1865." Melbourne, Australia University. In: The Victorian Historical Magazine, Sept. 1926, v.XI, #2, p.55-75, 270-3. With suppl: John A. Gurner.
See: Jas. I. Waddell, Cornelius Hunt, "Executive Docs. US House Reps." "Shenandoah." "Historical Magazine" Oct. 1867, p.248.

154 **SCOTT, George W., Colonel**
"How to escape the Yankees: Major Scott's Letter to his wife at Tallahassee, March 1864. Edited: Clifton Paisley." In: FHQ, July, 1971, v.L, #1, p. 53-61, port, sketch.
See: Marion B. Lucas

155 **SCOTT, J.L.**
"36th and 37th Battalions Virginia Cavalry." Lynchburg, Va., H.E. Howard, 1986, 8vo, cl, dj, (5), 104pp., illus., maps, ports. 1000 numbered, signed copies.
..."36th Virginia Infantry." 1st Edition. Lynchburg, Va., H.E. Howard, 1987. 8vo, cl, dj, (5), 116pp, ills, ports, diagram. 1,000 copies (#432) signed.

156 **SCOTT, Joe M.**
"Four Years Service in the Southern Army." Fayetteville, Ark: Washington County Historical Society, 1959. Booklet series #33. 4to, soft backs, 50pp. Reprint of the rare 1897 Mulberry, Ark. Booklet.

157 ....Mulberry, Ark., Leader Office Pr., 1897. 12mo, wraps, front(port), 74pp. $2000-bmk-105.

158 ..."Joseph M. Scott, Sr.'s. reminiscences of Civil War." In: "The Heritage", Crawford County Hist. Soc., 1961, v.IV, p. 14-17.

159 **SCOTT, Joe T.**
"A Georgia Confederate soldier visits Montgomery, Alabama, 1862-1863. Edt: Allen W. Jones." In: AHQ, 1963, v.XXV, p. 99-113.

160 **SCOTT, John**
"The Black Horse Cavalry." In: AQ, p. 590-613.
..."A ruse of war." In: AW, p. 380-383.

161 "Lost principals or sectional equilibrium..." Westport, Conn., Negro Univ. Press.

162 **SCOTT, John O.**
"Aftermath of Hartsville(Tenn.)." In: CV, 1902, v.10, p. 29-30, port. Civil War action, Dec. 7, 1862.

163 **SCOTT, John, of Fauquier (Va.), C.S. Army**
"Letters to an Officer in the Army, proposing Constitutional Reform in the Confederate Government after the close of the present War. A Supplement to "The Lost Principal"." Richmond, Va., A. Morris, 1864. 8vo, cl, iv, (5)-82pp. $75.

164 ..."The Lost Principal; or the Sectional Equilibrium: How it was created-How destroyed-How it may be restored." by "Barbarossa." Richmond, Va., James Woodhouse & Co., 1860. 8vo, cl, viii(9)-266pp. $50, $60.

165 ..."Partisan Life of Col. John S. Mosby." New York: Harper & Bros., 1867. Large 8vo, cl, ports, facsm., fldg. map, illus., vii-xvi, (19)-492pp. $10, $17.50, $20, $27, $150, $125.
...Do: London, Sampson Low, 1867, as above(autographed).
...Gaithersburg, Md., Butternut Press, 1984. $30.

166 ..."During the War and After the War." Warrenton, Va., Caldwell and Frank (1897?) 8vo, cl, 59-113pp. pt. 2-"Coupon Controversy" (above LC copy, but the Virginia State Library copy addl. "21"pp. may be referring to size).
...Do: 2nd Edt. on cover. Warrenton, Va.,

The True Index (1900?) 8vo, port, 5, 99pp., facsms. $100.

167 **SCOTT, Paul R.**
"Shannon's Scouts combat reconnaissance detachment of Terry's Texas Rangers." In: MHTSw, v.XV, #3, 1980, p. 5-23, port.

168 **SCOTT, Sutton Selwyn**
"Southbooke." Columbus, Ga., Thos. Gilbert Pr., 1880, 12mo, cl, 5, 259pp. Much on CSA. $65.

169 ..."Conditions of Indians West of Arkansas, 1863. Intro: Mark Lea "Beau" Cantrell." In: CO, Fall, 1984, v.LXII, #3, p. 325-333.

170 ..."Some account of Confederate Indian affairs." In: Gulf States Hist. Mag., Nov. 1903, v.II, #3, p. 137-154. (Scott, Comm. Indian Affairs, CSA)

170a **SCOTT, William J., Rev.**
"South Side Views. Dr. Whedon & the fathers. Also Dr. Haygood's "Brothers in Black." Atlanta, Ga., J.P. Harrison & Co., 1883. 8vo, wraps, 80pp. Book reviews steeped in pro-slavery arguments.

171 **SCOTT, William Wallace**
"Some fugitive rhymes by an Old Confederate Soldier." Richmond, Va., Printed for author by Everett Waddey & Co., 1914. 12mo, wraps, 34pp.

172 ...(& W.G. Stanard) "The Capitol of Virginia and the Confederate States: being a descriptive and historical catalogue of the public square and buildings and of the statuary, paintings and curios therein." Richmond: James E. Goode, Printer, 1894. sm.4to, stiff decr. wraps, 23pp. dbl. column.

173 ..."Some personal memories of General Robert E. Lee." In: Wm. & M. Quart., Oct., 1926, v.VI, ser. 2, p. 277-288.

174 ..."Two Confederate Items." Richmond, Va., Davis Bottom, 1927, Bull. of the Virginia State Library, v.XVI, #2 and 3, July 1927. $20. 8vo, wraps, 76pp. Diary of Capt. H.W. Wingfield and Reminiscences of the Civil War, by Judge E. C. Moncure. See: Orange County

175 **SCOTT, Winfield**
See: Thomas W. Bullitt, John Wm. Jones.

176 **SCREWS, Benjamin H.**
"Address at unveiling of Confederate Monument at Montgomery, Alabama." In: SHSP, 1898, v.26, p. 212-215.

177 **SCRIBNER, Robert Leslie**
"Belle Isle." Richmond (Va.) Calv., Winter, 1955. v.V, #3, p. 8-14. views (part colored) Seats of iron mfg., Civil War Prison.

178 ..."Born of Battle." In: Va. Cavalcade, Winter, 1953, v.3, #3, p. 24-32. facsm., ports (part col) views (part col.) Chs. Hoffbauer's murals in CSA Memorial Institute: Richmond, 1913/1914, 1919/1921. Scenes of the Civil War on walls of Battle Abbey and transfer to the Va. Hist. Soc. ...Spring, 1954, v.5, #3, p. 32-40.

179 ..."The Battle of Fredericksburg, 1862." In: Va. Cavalcade, Winter, 1956, v.6, #3, p. 20-35. Map, views (part col., 1 dble.)

180 ..."Inflation in the "good old days"." In: Va. Cavalcade, Summer, 1954, v.4, #1, p. 14-19. Facsms., port, views. Inflation in the CSA.

181 ..."The final maneuvers: retreat and surrender (at Appomattox), Apr. 2-9, 1865." In: Va. Cavalcade, Jan. 1955, v.4, #4, p. 20-26. map, views (1 dble-col.)

182 ..."Petersburg nightmare, 1864-1865." In: Va. Cavalcade, Autumn, 1956, v.6, #2, p. 4-9. ports, views (1 co.) Civilian life during the siege.

183 ..."The second siege (of Yorktown, Apr. 1862)." In: Va. Cavalcade, Autumn, 1957, v.7, #2, p. 27-30. ports, views.

184 ..."The Stonewall Brigade of a Band of Heroes their Commanders." Lexington, Va., Stonewall Jackson Memorial, ports, views (1-dbl. col.). Reprint: "Virginia

Cavalcade", Spring, 1956, tall, 8vo, 8pp. (Spring, 1956, v.5(4), p. 22-28.)

185 ..."Submission, coercion, or secession?" (Richmond) Va. Calv., Autumn, 1953, v.III, #2, p. 43-47, facsm., ports.

186 ..."The White House of the Confederacy." (Richmond) Va. Cavl., Winter, 1952, v.II, #3, p. 4-6, ports, views.

187 **SCROGGS, Jack B. and Donald E. Reynolds**
"Arkansas and the Vicksburg Campaign." In: CWH, December, 1959, v.V, #4, p. 390-401.

188 ..."Arkansas in the Secession Crisis." In: AHQ, 1953, v.XII, p. 179-224.

189 **SCRUGGS, Lawrence H., Col., of 4th Alabama**
"Official Report of Gettysburg." In: SHSP, 1885, v.13, p. 182-183.

190 **SCRUGHAM, Mary, Dr.**
"The peaceable Americans of 1860-1861; a study in public opinion." 8vo, 2p, 1, 7-127pp. Thesis, Phd, Columbia University, 1921.
...N.Y., Columbia University, 1921. 8vo, 125pp. "Studies in History, economics and public law. By the faculty of political science, Vol. xcvi, #3, whole #219.

191 ..."Force or consent as the basis of American Government." Lexington, Ky., United Daughters of the Confederacy, (1923). 8vo, wraps, 32pp. See: C.V. Vet., 1924, v.32, #10, p. 396-398.

192 **SCULLY, Everett Graham**
"The Story of Robert E. Lee." Portland, Maine, L.H. Nelson Co., 1905, 25x20 1/2cm, front(port)illus., 32pp. Juvenile. $30-bmk.

193 **SCULLY, James Wall**
"Gen. John Morgan, the celebrated Confederate Cavalry Leader." In: SHSP, 1903, v.31, p. 125-128.

194 **SCURRY, William R., Lt.-Col., 4th Reg. Tex. Mt. Vol.**
"Operations on the Rio Grande, Feb. 21, 1862." In: SHSP, 1890, v.18, p. 318-321.

195 **SEA, Sophie Fox, Mrs.**
"Confederate dead buried in Kentucky." In: CV, 1905, v.13, p. 74-77.

196 ..."Secession of Kentucky, replies to an article by J. Randolph Smith." In: CV, 1904, v.12, p. 288-291; also: Mrs. Henrietta Morgan Duke, Illus.

196a ..."Requiem Bells. A Memorial Poem, read at Decoration of Graves of Confed. Dead, Cave Hill Cemetery, Louisville, Ky., May 25, 1889. n.p.,n.d. 4to, wraps. $2.50. Ills. by Nicola Marschall.

197 **SEABOURNE, J. Gay, Col.**
"The Battle of Cedar Mountain. Stonewall wins victory over smaller Union force in opening engagement in 2nd Manassas Campaign." In: CWTI, Dec. 1966, v.5, #8, p. 28-41, illus., maps, ports.

198 **SEABROOK, Phoebe Hamilton**
"A Daughter of the Confederacy. A Story of the Old South and the New." N.Y., Neale Pub., 1906. 12mo, cl, 290pp. Southern life in South during the War.

199 **"SEAL of the Confederacy."**
See: "Great Seal of the Confederate States"; John T. Pickett, Mary B. Clark, Annie P. Pillow.

200 **SEALS of CSA**
See: Julius B. Baumgarten, Thomas J. Semmes.

201 **SEARCHER, Victor**
"An Arkansas Druggist Defeats a Famous General." In: AHQ, 1954, v.XIII, p. 249-263. Pat Cleburne defeats Sherman at Missionary Ridge.

202 **SEARCY, James Thomas, Dr.**
"Service of Dr. James Thomas Searcy." In: CV, July 1920, v.XXVIII, p. 250-252. With Lumden's battery by Jas. R. Maxwell. His service with reserve artillery, by Felix I. Robertson.

203 **SEARS, Louis Martin**
"A Confederate Diplomat at the Court of Napoleon, III." In: Amer. Hist. Rev., Jan. 1921, v.XXVI, p. 255-281.
..."John Slidell, by Louis Martin Sears." Durham, N.C., Duke University Pr., 1925, 12mo, cl, front(port), ports, 4, 252pp. $50. CSA Commissioner to France.
..."John Slidell, forgotten leader in a lost cause." In: So. Atl. Quart., July 1924, v.XXIII, p. 225-241. See: Wm. H. Russell.

203a **SEARS, Stephen W.**
"Landscape turned red: The Battle of Antietam." New Haven, Tucknor & Fields, 1983. 8vo, cl, ills, 448p, maps, index. $18.
SEARS, Stephen W., et. al.
"Fire on the Mountain: the Battle of South Mountain, Sept. 14, 1862." In: Blue & Gray Mag., 1986, v.4, #3, p.4-15, 18-22,48-63.

203b **"SEAT of War Manassas and its vicinity."**
(Richmond, printed by the Richmond Inquirer 1861) Map 12x15". Engraved by Baumgarten. 4-columns text at bottom. Crandall-3063. $450.

204 **"SEAT of War in Virginia. Sheet 3."**
(London), 1862. Map, 19x14", showing area from Richmond and Petersburg north and westward to Staunton and Lynchburg. Blind-stamped in margin: "Suppl. to the Weekly Dispatch of Sunday, Dec. 14, 1862." Edward Well, lithographer. $75-jk

205 **SEAT, W.H., Rev.**
"The Confederate States of America in Prophecy. By the Rev. W.H. Seat, of the Texas Conference." Nashville, Tenn., Printed for the author, at the Southern Methodist Pub. House, 1861, 16mo, bds-lt. spine, vi, 7-144pp. $25, $37.50, $150. Attempts to apply prophesies of Book of Daniel to the CSA.

206 **SEATON, Benjamin M.**
"The Bugle Softly Blows, the Confederate Diary of Benjamin M. Seaton, Edited by Col. Harold B. Simpson." Waco, Texas: Texian Press, 1965, 8vo, cl, dj, illus., map, ports, facsm. of diary as liners, xxv, 117pp. index. $17.50

207 **SEAY, C.C.**
"The arsenal of Selma, Alabama." In: CV, May 1928, v.XXXVI, p. 185-186.

208 **SEAY, Samuel**
"A Private at Stone River." In: SB, ns, v.1, #3, 1885/1886, p. 156-160.

209 **SECESSION ,**
13 Articles in CV, v.39.
See: John A. Campbell; W.R. Hammond; John Wm. Jones; Dabney H. Maury; Beverley B. Munford; Bernard J. Sage; Frederick W. Sims; Benjamin J. Williams; Herbert Friedenwald.

209a **"SECESSION & Coercion;**
the relation between the state & Federal governments." Sacramento, Cal., 1861. 8vo, wraps, 15p. $20. Pro-Southern pamphlets, to the democrats of California. See: Jno. B. Jones, similar title.

210 **"SECESSION Spirit (1861) in Illinois."**
In: CV, 1901, v.9, p. 5-6. Judge J.M. Dickinson of Tenn., refers to historical events in Williamson Co., Ill. by Erwin's history of the county.

211 **"SECESSION in Florida.**
Pensacola on its own." In: FHQ, April 1948, v.XXVI, #4, p. 283-299. Documents, letters and other papers. A list of signers.

212 **"SECESSION of the Whole South, The**
an Existing Fact. A Peaceable Separation the True Course. Its Effect on Peace and Trade Between the Sections." (Cincinnati, 1861) 8vo, sewd, 15, (1)pp. Sabin-78709. Rep: from "Cincinnati Daily Press."

213 **"SECESSION'S Mailbag."**
In: Amer. Hert., April, 1962, v.XIII, #3, p. 66-67, with color illus., 8-CSA patriotic envelopes.

214 **"SECESSION, Coercion and Civil War.**
The Story of 1861." See under author: John Beauchamp Jones.

215 **"SECESSION: considered as right**
in the states composing the late American Union of states and as to the grounds of justification of the Southern states in exercising the right. By a gentleman of Mississippi." Jackson, Miss., South-Western Confederate Printing House, 1863. 12mo, wraps, 45pp.

..."Secession: conversational opinions of the leaders of Secession-a monograph." In: Atlantic Monthly, July, 1862, v.X, p. 613-623.

216 **SECESSIONVILLE, Battle of**
See: Johnson Hagood.

217 **"SECOND Tennessee Regiment**
at Chickamauga, The." In: Annl. Army, Tenn., 1878, v.1, p. 52-62. Sig: Vieux seconde. Dorn-II, 1004.

218 **"SECOND Virginia Cavalry, CSA. The**
A tribute to its discipline and efficiency and defiant resolutions passed by it, Feb. 28, 1865." In: SHSP, 1888, v.XVI, p. 354-356.

219 **"SECRET RITUAL of Knights of Golden Circle."**
no title, n.p., n.d., blank wrappers, 7pp. 5 1/2 x 3 3/4". (Indianapolis?, 1864)

220 **SECRETARY of the Navy, C.S.A.**
"Report of the Secretary of the Navy, March 29, 1862." Monitor and Merrimac Fight. (Richmond, Va., 1862)" 8vo, sewn, 4pp. (Henkel #1090, May, 1913) Detailed acct. reconstruction of "Merrimac" into ironclad vessel, CSN-"Virginia".

..."Message of the President Executive Dept., April 10, 1862." I herewith transmit to Congress a communication of Secty. Navy, of detailed report of Flag Officer Buchanan, brilliant triumph of his squadron over vastly superior forces, Hampton Roads, on 8th and 9th march last- Jefferson Davis." (Richmond, 1862) 8vo, wraps, 13pp. (Henkel sale #1090) Official report of commd. "Merrimac" renamed "Virginia", giving details of naval duels revolutionizing naval warfare.

221 **SECRIST, Philip L.**
"The role of Cavalry in the Atlanta Campaign, 1864." In: Ga.H.Q., Winter, 1972, v.LVI, #4, p. 510-528. $8.

..."Life in Atlanta." In: CWTI, July 1970, v.IX, #4, p. 30-38, illus. Daily life much like any other Southern city, from prosperity to destitution.

..."Resaca: for Sherman a moment of truth." In: Atl. HJ, Sprint 1979, p.9-41.

222 **SEDBERRY, William R.**
"Fellow Citizens: of the Sixtieth Representative District, composed of the Counties of McLennan and Bosque." (Waco, Tex.?) June 13, 1861. Broadside: 15z10", printed 3 columns. Running for Hse. Reps., promises to defend the Constitution of CSA. Unrecorded, Jenkins (cat. 197) $1250.

223 **SEDDON, James A.**
"Letter from Secretary of War Seddon to General J.E. Johnston, April 5, 1863: to relieve the Army of disqualified and incompetent officers." n.p., n.d. (1963) sheet: 5x8"

224 **SEDDON, Sallie Bruce**
See: Wm. P. Cabell.

225 **SEGAR, Joseph Eggleston**
"Speech of..., of the York District, delivered in the House of Delegates of Virginia March 30, 1861, on the resolutions of the Senate, directing the Governor of Virginia to seize, by military force, the U.S. guns at Bellona Arsenal, and on the secession of Virginia." (Richmond, 1861?) 12mo, wraps, 23pp. (Crandall-2840) $125.

..."To the voters of Accomac and Northampton." (n.p.) 1863, 8vo, wraps, 3pp.

226 **SEIBERT, Mary Frances**
"Zulma", a story of the old South." Natchez, Miss., Natches Print, 1897, 8vo, cl, 310pp. On plantation in Pointe Coupee Parish before and during Civil War, faithfulness of a slave girl.

227 **SEIBERT, Shirley**
"Land of tommorrow; a Legend of Kentucky". N.Y., M.S. Mill Print, 1937. 12mo, cl, 320pp. fiction.

228 **SEIFERT, Shirley**
"Farewell, my General." Philadelphia: Lippincott (1954) 12mo, cl, 315pp. $30-b. Historical novel on Jeb Stuart.

229 **SEIP, Terry L.**
"The South returns to Congress: Men, economic measures and intersectional relationships, 1868-1879." Baton Rouge: Louisiana State Univ., 1983, 8vo, cl, dj, xii, 322pp. $25.

230 **SEITZ, Don Carlos**
"Braxton Bragg, General of the Confederacy." Columbia, S.C., The State Co., 1924. $100-bmk-105, $135-jk. Tk, 8vo, cl, front(port)544pp. Dornbusch notes (v.2) Errata slip. In the NcD copy there's a 2nd t/p, with pub. date 1923, verso, c.1923.

231 **SEIZURE of Forts, Arsenals,**
Revenue Cutters and other property of the United States. Washington, D.C., GPO, 1861. 36th Congress, 2nd Session, House of Representative, Report #91. 8vo, sewn, 94pp. Concerns seizures by Confederates at outbreak of hostilities.

232 **SELBY, John Millin**
"The Stonewall Brigade. Color plates by Michael Roffe." Reading, Osprey Print, 1971-"Men at Arms Ser." 8vo(narrow), stiff color wraps, illus., some colored maps, plans, ports, 40, p., (8)p. pls.
...N.Y., Hippocrene Books, 1971 (c.1970) same.
..."Stonewall Jackson as Military Commander." London: Batsford; Princeton, N.J., Van Nostrand 1968, Norwich: Jarrold & Son (1970). 8vo, cl, illus., maps(some colored), plans, ports, illus., 251pp. (27)plates. dj. $35.

233 **SELBY, Julian**
"Memorabilia and Anecdotal of Columbia, S.C. and Incidents Connected Therewith." Columbia, S.C., R.L.Bryan,1905. 8vo, cl, front(port), 200pp. Includes: Simm's "Sack and Destruction of Columbia." p. 154-196. n.p., 1970 reprint. See: "A Checkered Life." Library of Congress lists as Julian A. Selby. A photocopy, without comment.
..."The Countess Pourtales." (Columbia, S.C., S & H Pub. Co., 1915) 8vo, wraps, 64pp. Reprint with new introduction of the 1878 edition of "A Checkered Life".

234 **"SELECTED Civil War**
State Historical Markers, Virginia." (Richmond, Va., 1961) Virginia Civil War Centennial Commission. 12mo, wraps, cover title, 48pp.

235 **SELLERS, James L.**
"The economic incidence of the Civil War in the South." In: MVHR, Sept., 1927, v.14, p. 179-191. Sherman's premeditated economic chaos in his march to the sea.

236 **SELLERS, Tom**
"The raising of the 'Muscogee.' In: CWT, Jan. 1962, v.III, #9, (OS) p. 6-8, illus., drawing. CSN armored gunboat-scuttled in 1865, found in 1960-object of salvaging operation.

237 **SELLERS, William W.**
"History of Marion County, S.C. from earliest time to present, 1901." Columbia, S.C., R.L. Bryan Co., 1902. 8vo, cl, front(port), ix, 647pp. Rolls various CSA orgs: p. 572-646.

238 **SELPH, Fannie Eoline**
"The Confederate Navy." In her: "South in Amer. Hist." Nashville: 1928, p. (185)-253.
..."Drinkwater's 'Lincoln' and history." In:

CV, Dec. 1920, v.28, #12, p. 461-465.

..."The Emancipation Proclamation. Was it the instrument by which the slaves were emancipated?" In: CV, Dec. 1915, v.23, #12, p. 545-548.

..."The South in American Life and History. An effort at the Nashville Chapters of the United Daughters of the Confederacy, approved by the Tennessee Division, to present the true spirit and achievements of the South's civilization through the different periods of her history, that the South may be understood and justly judged, through the author and representative." Nashville, Tenn., McQuiddy Print, 1928. 8vo, cl, pl, ports, incl. front, 297pp. $60. More than half pertains to Confederacy.

..."Texas or the broken link in the chain of family honors. A romance of the Civil War." West Nashville, Tenn.(Cumberland Press, 1905) 16mo, cl, illus., incl. front, 245pp.

239 **SEMMES, Raphael**
See: S. Spencer Semmes.

240 **SEMMES, Raphael, Admiral**
"A Short History of Adml. Semmes." Park Place, N.Y., Knapp & Co., 1888. 2 3/4x1 1/2" colored booklet, 16pp. facsm. signature. (packed in Duke's cigarettes) See: "Heroes of the C.W. & W. Duke Co., Mrs. J.E. Ellerbe, Mrs. S.H. Newman.

241 **SEMMES, Raphael, Brig.Gen.**
"Admiral on Horseback: the Diary of Brigadier General Raphael Semmes, Feb.-May, 1865. Edited by W. Stanley Hoole." In: Ala. Rev., 1975, v.XXVIII, p. 129-150.

..."Centennial of the Birth of Admiral Semmes, Charles County, Md., Sept. 27, 1809. Address of Prof. Henry E. Shepherd. Monograph of his son, Capt. S. Spencer Semmes." In: SHSP, 1910, v.XXXVIII, p. 22-40.

..."Civil War Song sheets, one of the collections of the Maryland Historical Society." In: MHM, 1943, v.XXXVIII, 205-229, facsms(2).

..."The Cruise of the Alabama and the Sumter. From the private Journals and other papers of Commander R. Semmes, CSN and other officers." In two vols. London: Saunders, Otley & Co., 1864. 12mo, cl, 7-pls., xiv, (1), 410, (1), xii, 436pp. First edition. 3/4 lt. $250-bmk-105. Same, 2nd Edt., 1864.

...London: Saunders, Otley & Co. Richmond West & Johnson (sic), 1864. 8vo, cl, xii, 338p. Harwell notes that "only two copies of it are presently (1978) known to exist, one at the Confederate Museum, Richmond, & the other at Western Reserve Historical Society, Cleveland."

...N.Y., Carleton & Co., 1864. 12mo, cl, 328pp., 2vol. in 1, 2nd Edt. $65.

..."Croisieres de l'Alabama et du Sumter, livre de bord et journal particulier du commandant R. Semmes et des autres officiers de son etat-major." Paris: E. Dentu, 1864, wraps, 12mo, cl, 471pp. (or, 1/2 lt.)

..."The Confederate Raider "Alabama", selections from "Memories of Service Afloat During the War Between the States by Her Commander Raphael Semmes, Edt. with an introduction by Philip Van Doren Stern." Bloomington: Indiana University Press, $35-dj. Civil War Centennial Series, (1962). Tk.12mo, cl, dj, illus., incl. front, ports, facsms., maps, xxii, 23-464pp.

...Greenwich, Conn., Fawcett Pub. (1962). ("A premier Civil War Classic.") (T-146) Also a London Edt., paper. Also: Ann Arbor, Mich: University Microfilm (positive), 1961. American Culture Series, 169:12, of Semmes' Cruise of Ala. and Sumter" N.Y., Carleton, 1864 edition.

..."Kuristogten van de Alabama en de Sumter. Scheep Journaal van de Kapitein." Zwolle (Holland), 1864-1865.

8vo, cl, 2 vols.

..."Eleven letters of Raphael Semmes, 1866-1888. Edt: Elizabeth Joan Doyle." In: Ala. Rev., July, 1952, v.5, p. 222-232. notes. To Col. David French Boyd, Supt., LaState Seminary, on his personal activities in Ala. and Tenn.

242 ..."Georgians in the Naval Service of the Confederacy." In: Gulf Mag., 1902, v.1, p. 139-140.

243 ..."Celebration of the 100th Anniversary of the Birth of Admiral Raphael Semmes, C.S.N." Montgomery, Ala., Sept. 27, 1909. 8vo, wraps, 4pp. n.p., n.d. $40.

244 ..."Captain Raphael Semmes & the C.S.S. Alabama." (Washington, D.C., Naval Historical Foundation, August, 1968. Series 3-#10. 8vo, decr. stiff wraps, head: "Naval Historical Publication", map, ports, illus., facsm., 26pp.

245 ...Lithograph of Capt. Semmes "Of the Pirate Alabama." 11x13 1/2". Boston: L. Prang & Co., n.d.

246 ..."The Log of the Alabama and the Sumter. From the Private Journals and other papers of Commander R. Semmes, CSN, and other officers. Abridged from the library edition." London: Saunders, Otley & Co., 1864, 12mo, cl, xi, 297pp.
...Same, 1865.

247 ..."Memoirs of Service Afloat, during the War Between the States. By Admiral Raphael Semmes, of the late Confederate States Navy." Baltimore: Kelly, Piet & Co., 1869. Tk.8vo, cl, 7-pls, 3-ports, 1-map, vi, xi, 833pp. Other Edts: N.Y., n.d.; N.Y., 1887; N.Y., 1896. $65.
...Same: 1903 edt.-color plates.
...Secaucus, N.Y., 1987. 8vo, cl, dj, 833p, port. $11.
..."My Adventures Afloat: A Personal Memoir of my Cruises & Services in the "Sumter" and "Alabama". By Admiral Raphael Semmes, of the late Confederate States Navy." London: Richard Bentley, 1869. Tk. 8vo, cl, 9-plates (6 in color), port, map. 2 vols. in one, vi, xi-444; (2), 445-833. $65, $150-g.

248 ..."The Prison Diary of Raphael Semmes, Edt: Elizabeth Bethel." (Lexington, KY) JSH, Nov., 1956, v.XXII, #4, p. 498-509.

249 ..."Raphael Semmes, Rear Admiral, Confederate States Navy, Brig.-Gen. Confederate States Army: Documents pertaining to the charges preferred against him by the U.S. Government, with a pictorial history of his voyages of the "Sumter" and "Alabama". Claims commission. Edited with an introduction by Caldwell Delaney." Mobile, Ala., Museum of the City of Mobile, 1978. #5, 4to, wraps, illus., (82)pp.

250 ..."Rebel Raider. Being an account of Raphael Semmes' Cruise in the C.S.S. Sumter. Composed in large part of extracts from Semmes' "Memoir of Service Afloat" written in the year 1869. Selected and supplemented by Harpur Allen Gosnell, Lieut.-Commander USNR." Chapel Hill: University of North Carolina Press, 1948. 8vo, cl, dj, illus., maps, ports, incl. front, vii, (2), 218pp. $30.

251 ..."Service Afloat; or, the remarkable career of the Confederate Cruisers Sumter and Alabama, during the War Between the States. By Admiral Raphael Semmes, of the late Confederate States Navy, author of "Service Afloat and Ashore during the Mexican War." Illustrated with steel engraved portraits and eight engravings from original designs, printed in Chromo-tints." Baltimore: Baltimore Pub. Co., 1887. Tk 8vo, decr. gilt covers, front(port) xvi, (17)-833pp.
...Same, "Publishers Dummy", pict. cl, ports, 8-color pls.
...Louisv: Lost Cause, micro-cd. edt.
Same: 1887 edt., N.Y., 1900.

...N.Y., P.J. Kenedy, 1903. Tk.8vo, cl, front(port) 2-pls, composite of 7-ports each. Calls for color pls. but none seem to have been included.

252 ..."Semmes the Pirate. By Lieut-Col. ....." N.Y., T.R. Dawley, 1865. 12mo, cl, p. 13-105. Sabin-79084.

253 **SEMMES, Thomas Jenkins, Hon.**
"Sketch of...in New Orleans Picayune, Jan. 23, 1898." In: SHSP, 1897, v.25, p. 317-333.

..."Seal of the Confederate States." In: SHSP, 1888, v.16, p. 416-422.

255 **SEMPLE, Henry Churchill**
"The spirituality of Stonewall Jackson and Catholic influence." In: Cath. World, Dec. 1922, v.CXVI, p. 349-356. See: "Jackson's religious views."

...In: AHQ, 1956, v.18, #4, p.551-63.

256 **SENATE JOURNAL**
Of the 9th Legislature of the State of Texas, Nov. 4, 1861-Jan. 14, 1862. Edt: James M. Day. (400 copies, Waco: Texian Pr.) Austin, Texas: State Library, 1963. 8vo, gray buck, ports, 339pp., front, index.

257 ...Of the 9th Legislature, 1st Called Session of the State of Texas. Feb. 2, 1863-Mar. 7, 1863. Edt: James M. Day. (400 copies, Waco: Texian Pr.) Austin: Texas State Library, 1963. 8vo, gray buck, illus., ports, 212pp., index, front. $30.

...Of the 10th Legislature, Regular Session, State of Texas, Nov. 3, 1863-Dec.-16, 1863." Edt: James M. Day. (400 copies, Waco: Texian Press) Austin: Texas State Library, 1964. 8vo, gray buck, illus., ports, 214pp., index, front.

258 **SENATE and HOUSE JOURNALS**
Of the 10th Legislature, First Called Session of the State of Texas, May 9, 1864-May 28. Edt: James M. Day. (400 copies, Waco: Texian Press) Austin: Texas State Library, 1965. 8vo, gray cl, buck, front, ports, 244pp., index.

259 ...Of the 10th Legislature, Second Called Session of the State of Texas. Oct. 19-Nov. 15, 1864. Edt: James M. Day. (400 copies, Waco: Texian Press) Austin: Texas State Library, 1966. 8vo, gray buck, ports, front, 162pp., index. See also: "House Journals of 9-10th Leg."

260 **SENOUR, Faunt Le Roy**
"Morgan and his Captors." Cincinnati: C.F. Vent & Co., 1965. 12mo, cl, front(port), x, (11)-389pp. Pro-Union.

261 **SENSING, Thurman**
"Champ Ferguson, Confederate Guerrilla, by Thurman Sensing." Nashville: Vanderbilt University Press, 1942. 8vo, cl, front(port), map, xi, 256pp. Also served Morgan and Wheeler. Copy: presentation, $75-bmk.

...Champaign, Ill., University Press, 1985 for Vanderbilt University. 8vo, cl, 256p. $15.

262 **SERGENT, Mary Elizabeth**
"A Surplus of Lees." In: CWH, Mar., 1958, v.IV, #1, p. 69-72.

263 **SETTLES, Thomas Michael**
"The Military Career of John Bankhead Magruder." (Ft. Worth, Texas, Texas Christian College, 1972) Thesis, Phd., TCU, 330 folios.

...Ann Arbor, Mich., University Microfilms Int., 4to, 343pp., soft-back.

264 **"SEVEN DAYS BATTLES around Richmond."**
"Article from the Richmond Times on the Seven Days Battle." In: SHSP, 1900, v.28, p. 90-97.

264a ..."Strength of Lee's Army in the Seven Days." In: SHSP, v.1, p. 407-424. See: E.P. Alexander, James Mercer Garnett, Joseph E. Johnston.

265 **"SEVEN Fateful Days of 1865.**
The story of General Robert E. Lee's retreat from Petersburg to Appomattox, Va., April 2-9, 1865. Reprinted from a

special section published Arpil 7, 1962, from the Farmville Herald & the Times-Virginian of Appomattox." Farmville, Va., 'Herald,' 1962. 8vo, wraps, 32pp, ills, port. Map shows retreat of Lee from Richmond & Petersburg. Information compl. by Wilmer R. Turner.

266 SEVEN PINES, Battle of
See: John Bratton, W.P. Carter, Samuel Garland, Joseph P. Johnston, James Longstreet, Cadmus Marcellus Wilcox.

267 SEVENTEEN INFANTRY, Company A, Tennessee
"Remarkable survival of company officers. By J.H. Hastings." In: CV, 1910, v.XVIII, p. 577.

268 SEVERIN, John Powers and Lee A. Wallace
"Battalion of Washington Artillery of New Orleans, 1861." In: Mil. Coll. and Hist., 1958, p. 71-72, col. pl, illus.

269 SEVERIN, John Powers and Milton F. Perry
"Guilford Grays, North Carolina Militia, 1860." In: Mil. Coll. and Hist., 1956, v.VIII, p. 106-107, col. pl., illus.

270 SEWARD, Simon
"An Escape from Point Lookout." From: Geo. Barnard's "War Talks", p.77-83.
"An escape from Point Lookout. Address before A.P. Hill Camp, Confederate Veterans, Petersburg, Virginia, Sept. 5, 1889. Suffolk, Va., Robt. Hardy Pub., 1986. 8vo, wraps, 12pp., port.

271 SEWARD, William H., Sect. State
"The correspondence between Mr. Seward and the Confederate Commissioners." In: Southern Hist. Monthly, Jan. 1876, v.1, #1, p. 21-35.

272 SEWARD, William Henry
See: L.W. Wise.

273 SEXTON, Franklin Barlow
"Diary of a Confederate Congressman, 1862-1863. Edt. by Mary S. Estille." In: SoWest. Hist. Quart., Apr.-July, 1935, XXXVIII, 270-301, XXXIX, 33-65. Some material on secret sessions. $25-bmk.

274 SEYMOUR, Digby Gordon
"Divided Loyalties. Fort Sanders and the Civil War in East Tennessee." Knoxville: University of Tennessee Press (1963) 4to, cl, d/w, xi, 244pp., illus., ports, maps. "An impartial Civil War book by an unreconstructed rebel." Largely CSA, many illus., ports.
...1982 Reprint, 310pp., $25.

275 SEYMOUR, Trueman
"Letter concerning Major Warley." In: SHSP, 1882, v.10, p. 239.

276 SEYMOUR, W.H.
"The Battle of the handkerchiefs, (poem)." In: SHSP, 1903, v.31, p. 320-333.

277 SEYMOUR, W.J.
"Secret history of Gettysburg." In: SHSP, 1880, v.8, p. 521-526, 1881, v.9, p. 47.

278 SHACKLEFORD, Thomas L.
"The principals of the Confederacy." In: CV, Nov., 1924, v.XXXII, p. 417-419.

279 SHADGETT, Olive Hall
"Charles Jones Jenkins, Jr., 1805-1883. Edt: Horace Montgomery. "Georgians in profile: historical essays in honor of Ellis Merton Coulter." Athens: University of Georgia Press, 1958. 8vo, cl, p. 220-244, 367-370, notes. On his activities in Ga. and national politics, 1830-1877. Including his service as justice of the Supreme Court of Georgia, 1860-1865.

280 ..."James Johnson, Provisional Governor of Georgia (1865)." In: GaHQ, 1952, v.36, p. 1-21.

280 SHAFFER, Anna Jackson Preston
"Mrs. Emil Shaffer." "Stonewall Jackson. Sketch of the Life of Stonewall Jackson written by Mrs. Emil Shaffer, nee Miss. Anna Jackson Preston, and presented to the Senate on May 10, 1928, by Hon. Cole L. Blease, senator from South Carolina."

Washington: US GPO, 1936, U.S. 74th Cong., 2nd Sess., Senate Doc. 148. 8vo, (2), 4pp folder, reprint Sen. Doc. 173. See also: Anna Jackson Preston.

282 **SHAFFNER, John Francis**
"Diary of Dr. J.F. Shaffner, Sr., commencing Sept. 13, 1863, ending Feb. 5, 1865." (Winston Salem, N.C., 1936?) Priv. Print., Edt: by daughter, C.L. Shaffner. 8vo, wraps, cover title, 67pp. $250-r.

283 **SHAFFNER, Louis, Edt.**
"A Civil War Surgeon's Diary." In: N.C. Med. Jour., 1966, v.XXVII, p. 409-415 (J.F. Shaffner, surgeon to 33rd and 4th N.C., CSA.)

284 **SHAFFNER, Taliaferro Preston**
"The War in America: being an historical and political account of the Southern and Northern States: showing the origin and cause of the present secession war. With a large map of the U.S., eng. on steel." London: Hamilton & Adams Co., (1862). 16mo, cl, front(fldg. map)vi, 418pp. Pro-South Theories of Causes. $200-g.

285 **SHALER, Nathaniel Southgate**
"From Old Fields Poems of the Civil War." (quote) Bost., N.Y., Houghton Mifflin, 1906. 8vo, cl, bds, x-308pp. Altho a Kentucky Unionist (volunteers) wrote these stirring poems of those who fought for the CSA Kentuckians.

286 **SHALHOPE, Robert E.**
"Sterling Price Portrait of a Southerner." Columbia, University of Missouri Pr. (1971) 8vo, cl, dj, maps, xii, 311pp. $20.

287 **SHANAHAN, Frank E., Jr.**
"L.Q.C. Lamar: An Evaluation." (Jackson, Miss.) Jour. Miss. Hist., May, 1964, v.XXVI, #2, p. 91-222.

288 **SHANK, George Kline, Jr.**
"Meridian: A Mississippi City at Birth, During the Civil War and in Reconstruction." (Jackson, Miss.) Jour. Miss. Hist., Nov., 1964, v.XXVI, #4, p. 275-282.

289 **SHANKMAN, Arnold**
"William B. Reed (Pennsylvania Copperhead) and the Civil War." In: Penna. Hist., 1972, v.XXXIX, p. 455-468.

290 **SHANKS, Henry Thomas**
"Documents relating to the diocese of Arkansas, 1861-1865, and Bishop Henry C. Lay Papers." P.E. Church Hist. Mag., 1939, v.VIII, p. 67-90. Organization of church following outbreak of war in CSA and diocese of Ark.

291 ..."The Secession Movement in Virginia, 1847-1861, by Henry T. Shanks." Richmond, Va., Garrett & Massie (1934). $30. 8vo, cl, front, maps, xi, 296pp.
...N.Y., A.M.S. Press (1965-1969)
...N.Y., Da Capo Press, 1970. $29.50-y, 8vo, cl, (iv), xiv, 296pp. See: Beverly B. Munford, Jas. Clyde McGreg., "Va. Joins the Confederacy."

292 ..."Disloyalty to the Confederacy in Southwestern Virginia, 1861-1865." In: NCHR, April, 1944, v.XXI, p. 118-135.

293 ..."Conservative Constitutional Tendencies of the Virginia Secession Convention." In: "Essays in Southern History presented to J.G. De Roulhac Hamilton (Chapel Hill, 1949) Edt: Fletcher Green.

294 **SHANNON, Isaac N.**
"Sharpshooters with Hood's Army." In: CV, 1907, v.15, p. 123-127, ports.

294a **SHAPIRO, Edward S.**
"Frank L. Owsley & the defense of Southern identy." In: THQ, 1977, v.36, #1, p.75-94.

295 **SHAPIRO, Henry D.**
"Confiscation of Confederate Property in the North." Ithaca, N.Y., Cornell Unvi. Press (1962) Cornell studies in American History, Literature and Folklore, #VII. 8vo, stiff wraps, x, (1), 58pp.

296 **SHARKEY, Clay**
"My Confederate History-Clay Sharkey." Edt: George C. Osborn. (Jackson, Miss.,

Jour. of Miss. Hist., Oct. 1942, v.IV, #4, p. 225-232.) See: Geo. C. Osborn.

297 **SHARKEY, H. Clay**
"Confederate Floating Mines." In: CV, April, 1905, v.XXIII, p. 167-168.

298 **SHARKEY, William L., Judge**
"Judge Sharkey Papers." In: MVHR, 1933, v.XX, p. 75-90. Edt: F. Garvin Davenport. Judge Sharkey of Missouri, agreement with his overseer, Jan. 1, 1842 and two essays on martial law (CSA), and "The Crisis", explains CSA reverses, c.1863.

299 ..."The essay on "habeas corpus", in the Judge Sharkey Papers." In: MVHR, 1936, v.XXIII, p. 243-246. Protests bill in CSA house, authorizing the president to suspend the writ.

300 **SHARP, Myron B., Edt.**
"The Confederate Raid at Morgantown, W.Va." In: W.Penna. Hist. Mag., 1967, v.L, p. 335-338.

301 **SHARPE, John Allen**
"Diary of a Confederate Refugee." By: J.A.S. Durham, N.C., Duke University, 1899, 8vo, wraps, p. 8-16. Historical Papers Trinity College Historical Society, Ser.III.

302 **SHARPSBURG, Battle of**
See: Wm. Allan, Henry Lewis Benning, Alex. Robert Chisholm, A.S. Cutts, John W. Daniel, James M. Garnett, Alexander Hunter, James Steptoe Johnston, Dabney H. Maury, J.B. Moore, Emmett M. Morrison, John T. Parham, Walter Herron Taylor.

303 **SHAVER, Lewellyn Adolphus**
"A History of the Sixtieth Alabama Regiment, Gracie's Alabama Brigade, by Lewellyn A. Shaver.(quotation)." Montgomery, Ala, Barrett & Brown, 1867. 8vo, cl(or wraps), 111pp. $600-ob. Cloth bound copies had a photo(front) of Brig.-Gen. A. Gracie. No rosters.

...Gaithersburg, Md., Butternut Press, 1985. $15.

304 **SHAVIN, Norman**
"The Atlanta Century, a non-partisan account of events of this week 100 years ago (March, 1860-May, 1865) written by Norman Shavin and Mike Edwards of the Atlanta Journal-Constitution, c.1960. Historical advisor: Martin Abbott." (Atlanta, Ga., c.1965) caption title, 272pp. originally appeared in the Atlanta Journal-Constitution, March 1960-May 1965.

305 ..."The Atlanta Century--March 1860-May 1865. Atlanta, Ga., I/D Pub. Co., c.1966, 2nd Edt. Folio, unpaged, illus. $22.50

306 ..."Old Atlanta." (Atlanta, Ga., Century House, 1969) 4to, stiff pict. wraps, illus., 40pp. $1.25. Battle for Atlanta, destruction largely from newspapers, old photos, p. 14-25.

307 **SHAW, Arthur Marvin**
"A letter by Jefferson Davis relating to events preceding his capture." In: Ga.H.Q., Mar. 1947, v.XXXI, #1, p. 30-33.

308 ..."The Personal Goods of General Albert Sidney Johnston at Corinth." (Jackson, Miss., Jour. Miss. Hist., Oct., 1949, v.XI, #4, p. 250-251)

309 ..."General Albert Sidney Johnston's Horses at Shiloh." In: Ark. HQ, 1949, v.VIII, p. (206)-210.

310 ..."General Albert Sidney Johnston: a man on horseback." In: McNeese Rev., Spring 1953, v.5, p. 99-107. His Texas, USArmy and CSArmy career.

311 ..."A Texas Ranger Company at the Battle of Arkansas Post." In: Ark. HQ, 1950, v.IX, p. (270)-197. Largely from W.W. Heartsill Diary. See also: Walter P. Lane, "Adventures, etc."

312 ..."William Preston Johnston, a transitional figure of the Confederacy." Baton Rouge: Louisiana University Pr., 1943.

8vo, cl, illus., ports, incl.front, xv, 299pp. ...Gloucester: P. Smith Reprint. $40-bmk.

313 ..."Centenary College goes to war in 1861." Shreveport, La., Centenary College, 1940. 8vo, wraps, illus. (facsms.) 14pp.

..."The Family Sorrows of Jefferson Davis." In: AHQ, 1949, #3, p.400-04.

313a **SHAW, Horace T. & James H. Rogers**
"Thine is the Kingdom Forever, love-story letters 1861." Athens, Ga., McGregor Print, 1974. 8vo, cl, 123pp.

314 **SHAW, William L.**
"The Confederate Conscription and Exemption Acts." In: Amer. Jour. Legal Hist., Oct., 1962, p. 368-405.

315 **SHEA, George, Hon. (one of his counsel)**
"Jefferson Davis: a statement concerning imputed causes of his long imprisonment by the government of the U.S. and his tardy release by due process of law. Contained in a letter from George Shea. Reprinted from the N.Y. Tribune of Jan. 24, 1876." London: Edward Stanford, 1877. 12mo, sewn, 20pp.

...Richmond: South. Hist. Soc. Papers, v.37, p. 243-252.

316 ..."A statement of the facts concerning the imprisonment and TREATMENT of Jefferson Davis while a military prisoner at Fort Monroe, Virginia, in 1865 and 1866." Washington, 1902. 8vo, wraps, 12pp.

...Louisville: Lost Cause Pr., micro-cd.

317 **SHEA, John C., Edt.**
"The Only True History of Quantrill's Raid ever published. Reminiscences of Quantrill's Raid upon the City of Lawrence, Kan. Thrilling narratives by living eye-witnesses." Kansas City, Mo., 1879. 8vo, wraps, 27pp. $175-whm.

318 **SHEA, William L.**
"Battle at Ditch Bayou." In: Arkansas HQ, Autumn 1980, v.XXXIX, #3, p. 195-207, plan. The Red River Campaign.

319 ..."The Camden Fortifications." In: ArkHQ, Winter 1982, v.XLI, #4, map, plate, p. 318-326. CSA retreats from Union occupation of Little Rock to Camden. See: Edwin C. Bearss.

320 **SHEEHAN, John Louis**
"Thomas Jonathan (Stonewall) Jackson." In: Jour. Irish-Amer. Hist. Soc., 1910, v.9, p. 183-196.

321 **SHEERAN, James B., Rev.**
"Confederate Chaplain, a War Journal of Rev. James B. Sheeran, CSA, 14th Louisiana, CSA. Edited by Rev. Joseph T. Durkin. With a preface by Bruce Catton." Milwaukee, Bruce Pub. Co., (1960) 8vo, cl, dj, facsm., illus., map, port., xiii, (1), 168pp. $25.

322 **SHEFFIELD, James L., Col.**
"Report: Lookout Valley." In: SHSP, 1880, v.8, p. 505-508.

..."Official report of Gettysburg." In: SHSP, 1885, v.13, p. 183-184.

324 **SHEILD, Conway H., Mrs.**
"Roll of Company "I", York Rangers, 32nd Regiment, Hunter's Brigade, Virginia Volunteers in the Army of the Confederate States of America. Copied from Yorktown Clerk's Office, May 1934." In: Am. & Mary Quart., 2nd ser., v.XIV, p. 235-237.

325 **SHELBY, Jo. O., Gen., Brig-Gen Commanding**
"Address of Gen. J.O. Shelby to his division (Pittsburg, Texas, April 26, 1865) Broadside, printed on wall-paper. Flowery speech, vowing to fight, "we will all hang together". Reprinted St. Louis Missouri Democrat & Columbia Missouri Statesman, July 14, 1865. Text found also in Missouri Historical Review, Oct., 1939, v.XXXIV, #1, p. 134.

326 **SHELBYVILLE, Tennessee, Monument**
"Confederate Monument, Shelbyville, Tennessee." In: CV, 1899, v.VII, p. 496-499.

327 **SHELDON, James R.**
"Last march of the Army of Lee." In: An address before Confederate Veterans Association of Savannah, Ga., 1898-1902, p. 84-94.

328 **SHELLENBERGER, John K.**
"The Battle of Franklin. Paper read before the Minnesota Commandery of the Loyal Legion U.S., Dec. 9, 1902." (Minneapolis?, 1902) 8vo, wraps, 29pp.

329 ..."The Battle of Franklin Tenn., Nov. 30, 1864; a statement of the erroneous claims made by Gen. Schofield, and an exposition of the blunder which opened the battle." Cleveland, Oh., The Author(Arthur H. Clark) 8vo, wraps, 42pp.

330 ..."Federal blunders at Franklin (Tenn.)." In: CV, Oct./Nov., 1928, v.XXXVI, p. 380-384, 419-422. The Battle of Franklin.

331 ..."The Battle of Spring Hill, Tennessee." n.p., 1907, Title head: "Military Order of the Loyal Legion of U.S., Commandry of the State of Missouri." 8vo, wraps, 26pp.

332 ..."The Fighting at Spring Hill, Tenn." In: Confed. Vet., Mar.-May, 1928, v.XXXVI, p. 100-103; 140-143; 188.

333 **SHELTON, Horace H., Maj.**
"Sea Battles in Texas Waters between Confederates & Federals." In: Under Texas Skies, Austin, Texas, May 1951, v.II, #1, port, p. 2-9.

334 ..."Dick Dowling's Great Victory." In: Under Texas Skies, Austin, Texas, May 1951, v.II, #1, illus., p. 10-12.

335 ..."Texas service of General Lee was invaluable in tempering his for high command." In: "Under Texas Skies", Austin, Tex., Feb. 1952, v.II, #10, p. 7-18, pix. Lee, cover.

336 **SHELTON, Phillip M.**
"Camp Beauregard Graves County, Ky." In: RKHS, Apr. 1962,

337 **SHELTON, Vernon**
"Mask for Treason-the Lincoln Murder Trial." Harrisburg, Pa., Stackpole Books (1965) 8vo, cl, illus., 480pp., ports, facsms, map.

338 **SHELTON, William J.**
"Confederate Poems." Lynchburg, Va., Virginia Pwr. Pr., 1862. 16mo, wraps, 28, (4)pp.

339 ..."The Downfall of Burnside. (Tune)-"The Rose Tree." Lynchburg, Va., Johnson & Schaffter (1862) Broadside: 25 1/2x19cm.

340 ..."Fighting Joe Hooker" (Tune). "Old Dan Tucker". (Lynchburg, Va., 1863?) Broadside: 26 1/2x19cm.

341 **SHENANDOAH (Privateer), C.S. Navy**
See: John Grimball, James Riley, James I. Waddell, Wm. Conway Whittle, Ernest Scott, Shanandoah Valley, William Allan, Stonewall Jackson.
See: Hist. Mag., Oct. 1867, p.248. Officer of Shenandoah denounces Cornelius Hunt's "Shenandoah."

342 **"SHENANDOAH, The**
by An Officer Thereof." In: Walter Clark's "Hist. of Several Regs. and Batts. of N.C.) Vol. V, p. (1), 345-350.

343 ..."The Private War of the CSS "Shenandoah." N.Y., The Atlantic Co., "Cargoes", #37. June, 8pp., (49 Wall St., NYC, 05) 1956.

344 ..."The Surrender of the C.S.S. Shenandoah." (London) Jour. Confed. Hist. Soc., DEc., 1965, v.III, #4, p. 123-127, pl-1.
..."The Confederate Cruiser . . . Insurance against capture, & the Geneva award. No author. N.Y., Powers, McGowan & Slipper, 1873. 8vo, 13, (1)p. $75-Bmk.

345 **SHENFIELD, Lawrence L.**
"C.S.A.; The Special Postal Routes." New York, 1961. (Collector's Club Handbook #10) Auspices of Theo. E. Steinway Memorial Publishing Fund of Collector's Club. 8vo, cl, facsms, tables, 101pp.

346 ..."Confederate States Trans-Mississippi Express Mail." In: Am. Philatelist, Mar.

1952, v.65, p. 423-430. facsms. CS service between Meridian or Bravdon, Miss., and Shrevesport/Alexandria, 1863-1864.

347 ..."The Confederate States of America: The Trans-Mississippi Express Mail... latest analysis of all known covers which travelled this secret route to avoid Federal gunboats and patrols (1863-1865)." In: Collectors Club Philatel., Sept., 1956, v.35, p. 283-288, 316, facsms, tables.

348 ..."Confederate States of America the Special Postal Routes." N.Y., Collector's Club (1961) thin 8vo, illus., 101pp.

349 ..."Confederate States of America: the essay die proofs and proofs of issued stamps, printed in Richmond, the "specimen" overprints of the De La Rue printing (1861)." In: Collectors Club Philatelist, July 1957, v.36, p. 161-166, 173-174, facsms.

350 ..."Confederate States of America: the $.10 blue 1863 die B, date of issue and earliest color." In: Collectors Club Phil., May 1956, v.35, p. 162, facsm., 174.

351 ..."The imprint of the Confederate $.05 Mobile provisional." In: Am. Philatelist, Oct. 1951, v.65, p. 5-11. On William R. Robertson as print/engraver in Mobile, 1850-1861.

352 ..."The $.10 Uniontown, Ala.: census of a rare postmaster provisional." In: Collector's Club Philatelist, Jan. 1951, v.30, p. 42-48. On seven known examples of this stamp, '61/'62.

353 **SHEPARD, Charles U.**
"Reporter. Opinions of the Judges of the Supreme Court of Alabama, in the "conscript case"; involving the question, whether State Courts and Judicial Officers have jurisdiction on "habeas corpus", to discharge conscripts from custody of enrolling officer of Confederate States. Reported by J.W. Shepherd, reporter of Supreme Court." Montgomery, Ala, Mail Book Office, 1863, 8vo, wraps, 31pp. Owen. State courts held to have no jurisdiction.

354 ..."Select cases argued and determined in the Supreme Court of Alabama, during the years 1861-1862-1863. Reported by John W. Shepherd, State Reporter, Vol. 1." Montgomery, Ala., Advitiser, 1864. 8vo, cl, 792pp. (no other pub.) Owen.

355 **SHEPARD, Frederick J.**
"The Johnson's Island Plot, an historical narrative of the conspiracy of the Confederates, in 1864, to capture the U.S. Steamship Michigan on Lake Erie, and release the prisoners of war in Sandusky Bay." In Publications of the Buffalo Historical Society, IX (1906) 51pp.

356 **SHEPARD, John**
"Religion in the Army of Northern Virginia." In: NCHR, July 1948, v.XXV, p. 341-376,notes.

357 **SHEPHERD, Henry Elliot**
"Narrative of Prison Life at Baltimore and Johnson's Island, Ohio." Baltimore: Commercial Print, 1917. 12mo, wraps (or, 3/4 Mor.) front (port) 1p., (5)-22pp. (Md. CSA officer)

358 ..."Life of Robert Edward Lee." N.Y., Neale Pub. Co., 1906. 8vo, cl, front, pls., ports, 280pp. $150-jk.

359 ..."In defense of Southern Poets." (critic of Edwin Mims (see: article in Cambridge edt., Southern Poets.) In: CV, 1921, v.XXIX, 18/19.

360 ..."Comments on Gordon's biography of Jefferson Davis." In: CV, Mar. 1920, v.XVIII, p. 87-88. Re: Armistead Gordon's Life of Davis.

361 ..."Gen. D.H. Hill: a character study." In: CV, July/Sept., 1917, v.XXV, p. 306-308, 366-367, 411-413.

362 ..."Recollections of Frederick, Md." In: CV, May 1919, v.XXVII, p. 167-168. Mainly of Civil War period.

363 SHEPHERD, Joseph H.
"Company D, Clarke Cavalry, History and Roster." In: SHSP, 1896, v.24, p. 145-151.

364 SHEPHERD, Lewis
"The Confederate Treasure Train." In: CV, June, 1917, v.XXV, p. 257-259.

365 SHEPHERD, William Biddle, Hon.
"Speech on the right of secession, revolution, etc." Raleigh, N.C., Wm. W. Holden, 1851, 8vo, wraps, 32pp. Del. in N.C. Senate, 31 Jan., 1951.

365a SHEPHERD, W. F.
"Palmyra Soldier: Diary & Letters of ..." In: Bul. Fluvanna Co. Hist. Soc., Oct. 1984, v.38, p.5-41. Edt: David W. C. Bearr.

366 SHEPHERD, William G.
"Shattering the myth of John Wilkes Booth's escape." In: Harpers, Nov. 1924, v.CXLIX, p. 702-719.

367 SHEPHERD, William S., Col., 2nd Ga. Reg.
"Official Report of Gettysburg." In: SHSP, 1885, v.13, p. 197-199.

368 SHEPPARD, Edwin
"Map showing the battle grounds of the Chickahominy and the positions of the subsequent engagements in the retreat of the Federal Army towards James River and all the other points of interest in connection with the siege of Richmond from the most reliable information to be obtained." Richmond, Va., Hoyer & Ludwig, 1862?, 41 1/2x51cm. Eberst.

369 SHEPPARD, Eric William, Maj.
"The American Civil War 1864-1865." Aldershot: Gale & Polden, Ltd., n.d., 8vo, boards, xviii, 171pp., 12 fldg. maps (2 in pocket, at end) (c.1938) A book to help officers in their Army Promotion Examinations. $100-bmk-105.

370 ..."Bedford Forrest the Confederacy's Greatest Cavalryman." London: H.F. & G. Witherby (1930). $150-b. tk 8vo, cl, port(front) ports, page sketch maps, fldg. maps, 320pp., index.
...N.Y., L. MacVeagh, The Dial Press; Toronto: Longsmans, Green, 1930 (same)
...Dayton, Oh., Morningside, 1981.

371 ..."The Legend of the Shenandoah Valley." Army Quarterly, XXIII, p. 48-60. The campaign of Stonewall Jackson, 1862.

372 ..."The Campaign in Virginia & Maryland, June 26th to Sept. 20th, 1862, Cedar Run, Manassas and Sharpsburg." London: Allen & Co., N.Y., Macmillan, 1911. Special Campaign series, #14. 8vo, cl, illus., 7-maps (in pocket), xv, 306pp.

373 ..."Generals of the American Civil War." Pt.I: the Northern Generals; part II: The Southern Generals." In: Army Quarterly and Defense Journal, 1963, v.LXXXVI, p. 171-181; LXXXVII, p. 61-71.

374 SHEPPARD, George
"A Canadian view of parties and issues on the eve of the Civil War. Edt: James J. Talman." In: JSH, 1939, v.V, p. 245-253. Extracts from letters: Geo. Sheppard, a news corresp., in Wash., to Chs. Clark in Ontario 1860-1861. Reveals business depression in DC, indicating a partisan's leaning toward the principals of Breckinridge's party.

375 SHEPPARD, Harvey E.
"The Confederate postmaster's provisional in the (Thomas K.) Tapling collection (bequeathed to the British Museum)." In: Amer. Philatelic Congr., "Congress Book, 1960, v.26, p. 111-129, facsms.

376 ..."The Confederacy & West Virginia." In: Confed. Philatelist, August 1961, v.6, p. 97-100, 103. Postal Service in W. Va.
...Also in Weekly Philatelic Gossip, Feb. 5, 1955, v.59, p. 730, 732, illus.

377 ..."Confederate Postal History in Virginia; things to watch out for!" In: Weekly Philatelic Gossip, Feb. 11, 1956, v.61, p. 678-682, illus.

378 ..."Collecting Confederate Covers: it pays to know your history and your troops." In: Weekly, Philatelic Gossip, July 9, 1960; Jan. 7, 1961; Jan. 14, 1961, p. 466, 468, 470; 472-474; 496-497, illus. CSA Postal History and Military Activities in W. Va.

379 ..."Lewisburgh, Va., CSA." In: Weekly Philatelic Gossip, Feb. 20, 1954, v.57, p. 799, illus. Postal history at Lewisburgh.

380 ..."The Mails and the War in Virginia, 1861-1865." In: Weekly Philatelic Gossip, Feb. 2, 1957, p. 717-719, 722.

381 ..."Postal History in Confederate Virginia. A Research Study." In: Amer. Philatelist, April 1962, v.75, p. 505-510, illus.

382 ..."Traveller's Repose" In: Confederate Philatelist, Oct. 1960, v.5, p.(81)-82, 87, illus. PO at Camp Bartow, Aug.-Oct., 1861. Shetler-701-3A.

383 **SHEPPARD, Peggy**
"Andersonville, Georgia, U.S.A." Leslie, Ga., Private Print(1973) 8vo, decr. wraps, front(map), illus., ports, 95pp.

384 **SHEPPARD, William Ludwell**
"Virginia, 1864." Lithograph. Boston: Photogravue Co., n.d. Lithograph, 20x26", a spirited battle scene, horses rearing while pulling an ammunition cart to gun in foreground, men and cavalry in action. Note: See also his illustrations in McCarthy's "Detailed Minutiae of Soldier Life in Army of ANV."

385 ..."Three Branches of the Confederate Army: The Artillery, Cavalryman & Infantryman", four-color lithographs, 12x18", from original paintings in the Confederate Museum. $125. Rich: Confed. Museum, (n.d.) These pictures were sold for the benefit of the Jefferson Davis monument. The set sold for $1, Size: 10 1/2"x17", mount on board 15x20", ready to frame.

386 ..."The First Gun in Virginia in 1861." In: Blue & Gray (phil.) 1894, v.IV, 15-17. See: Ulrich Troubetzkoy.

387 **SHEPPERSON, William G., Dr.**
"War Songs of the South. Edited by "Bohemian", correspondent Richmond Dispatch..." Crandall-3154. Richmond: West & Johnson, 1862, 16mo, wraps, 216pp.

388 **SHERIDAN'S RAID**
See: N.M. Burkholder

389 **SHERIDAN, Philip Henry**
See: New Orleans Picayune, A.S. Paxton.

390 **SHERIDAN, Richard C.**
"Brig.-Gen. James Deshler, Professional Soldier." In: "Ala. Hist. Quart." 1964, v.XXVI, facsm., illus., port, p. 203-216.
..."Alabama Chemists in the Civil War." In: AHQ, 1975, v.37, #4, p.265-74.

391 **SHERMAN, Sidney, Gen.**
"In: W.N. Bate's - "General Sidney Sherman Texas Soldier, Statesman & Builder." Waco, Texas: Texian Press, 1974. CSA, Galveston, Texas, p. 259-277. Better known in Battle of San Jacinto during Republic of Texas days.

392 **SHERMAN, William Tecumseh**
See: W. Adams, "Army and Navy Journal", A.R. Chisholm, Jefferson Davis, S.W. Ferguson, W.T. Sherman, W.H. Jackson, Stephen D. Lee, M. Quad, Lawrence S. Ross.

393 ..."Grant, Thomas, Lee." In: No. Amer. Rev., 1887, v.144, p. 437-450.

394 ...Sherman's March to the Sea. See: Alex R. Chisholm, E.J. Hale, Charles Colcock Jones, Charles B. Lewis.

395 ..."Sherman's Occupation of Savannah. Two letters contributed by Mrs. Homer H. Berger. Commenced Savannah, Feby. 28, 1865, finished April 3rd." In: Ga.HQ, March, 1966, v.L, #1, p. 109-115.

396 **SHERRILL, Miles O.**
"A Soldier's Story. Prison life and other incidents in the War of 1861-1865." (Raleigh, N.C., 1904) 8vo, wraps, 20pp. $250-r.

397 ...Raleigh, N.C., Edwards & Broughton (1911). 8vo, wraps, front (port), 23, (1)p. Ode- "Carolina." Sherrill from Catawba Co., served in 12th N.C. Inf.

398 SHERRILL, Samuel Wells
"Heroes in Gray." Nashville, Tenn., C.J. Bell, (1909) 12mo, wraps, 170pp. $50.

399 SHERWOOD, Adiel
"Conversation in a Tent." Macon, Ga., n.d., (c.1860's) 8vo, wraps, 4pp. Concerns soldiers and religion, Jackson and Beauregard. Prominent clergyman, pub. "Gazetteer of Georgia", "Notes on New Testament".

400 SHETLER, Charles
"West Virginia Civil War Literature, an Annotated Bibliography." Morgantown: W.Va. University Library, 1963. 8vo, cl (or wraps), illus., xii, (1), 184pp. $30. Excellent review, C.W. contents, Co. History.

401 SHIELDS, John C.
"The Old Camp Lee-story of the camp's formation, Inf., Cav., Artillery, conscripts." In: SHSP, 1898, v.26, p. 241-246.

402 SHIELDS, Samuel Jackson
"A Chevalier of Dixie." N.Y.-Wash., Neale Pub., 1907, 12mo, cl, 226pp. Novel of the CSA.

403 SHILOH NATIONAL PARK
See: Albert Dillahunty.

404 SHILOH, Battle of
See: J.A. Chalaron, Joseph T. Derry, James Dinkins, Thomas Jordan, Wm. M. Polk, Daniel Ruggles, L.D. Sandidge, Joseph Wheeler, Marcus Wright.

405 SHILOH: Battle, April 6-7, 1862.
"Misfortune to Southern arms at Shiloh." In: CV, 1902, v.10, p. 106-108. See: John C. Moore.

406 SHINGLETON, Royce Gordon
"Cruise of the CSS Tallahassee." In: CWTI, May, 1976, v.15, #2, p. 30-40, facsm., illus., map.

407 ..."John Taylor Wood, Sea Ghost of the Confederacy." Athens, Ga., University Press (c.1979) 8vo, cl, dj, illus., xiv, 242pp. bibliog. (225)-229. $20. See also: John Taylor Wood.

408 SHIPLEY, Charles L.
"The Old Confederate Soldier's Home." n.p., 1944. 8vo, wraps, 29pp., illus. $20. Illustrated history of Home at Pikesville, Md.

409 SHIPMAN, Lemuel
"Recollections of the prison life of Jefferson Davis at Fortress Monroe, Virginia." In: Americana, June 1913, v.VIII, p. 505-511.

410 SHIPP, J.F.
"The famous battle of Hampton Roads." In: CV, July 1916, v.XXIV, p. 305-207. CSA soldier in 4th Ga. Reg., observes battle.

411 ..."The famous battle of Hampton Roads." In: CV, ns, Mar./Apr., 1987, v.35, #2, p.14-17, color illus.

412 SHIPPEY, W.F.
"A leaf from my log-book." In: SHSP, 1884, v.12, p. 416-421.

413 ..."A Reminiscence of Christmas of 1861." In: SHSP, 1883, v.11, p. 255-257.

414 SHIRAS, Frances
"Major Wolfe and Abraham Lincoln. An Episode of the Civil War." In: AHQ, 1943, v.II, p. 353-358, 369-374.

415 SHIRK, George H.
"Confederate Postal System in the Indian Territory." Oklahoma City: Chron. Okla. Summer, 1963, v.XLI, #2, p. 160-218, facsms., ports, map.

416 ..."The Great Seal of the Confederacy." Oklahoma City: Chron. Okla. Autumn, 1952, v.XXX, #3, p. 309-311, plate.

..."The Place of Indian Territory in the Command Structure of the Civil War." Oklahoma City: Chron. Okla. Winter,

1967-1868, v.XLV, #4, p. 464-471. Both the Union and Confederates.

418 **SHIRLEY, Franklin Ray**
"The rhetoric of Zebulon B(aird) Vance (1830-1894): Tarheel spokesman." Ann Arbor: University Microfilm, 1959(1960). Positive microfilm of typescript, (411) leaves. Thesis--University of Florida, Abstr. Dissrt., 20:2963, Jan.

419 **SHIVERS, John**
"Dance Brothers Confederate revolvers." In: Jr. Historian (Texas), Nov. 1958, v.19, p. 1-2, 30. James H. George P. & David Dance (Marion, Texas), Blacksmiths and Farm inpl. mfg., 1862-1863, probably totaling 324 pieces, of which only 20 are known to survive.

420 **SHOEMAKER, Arthur**
"The Battle of Chustenahlah." Oklahoma City: Chron. Okla., Summer, 1960, v.XXXVIII, #2, p. 180-184, map, pl. Col. Jas. McIntosh defeats Opothleyohola Union forces and cuts off Cherokee Creek, joining the upper Indian territory.

421 **SHOEMAKER, Floyd C.**
"Missouri-Heir of Southern Tradition and Individuality." (Columbia, Mo., Mo. Hist. Review, July, 1942, v.XXXVI, #4, p. 435-446. Largely on the Confederacy.

422 ..."The Story of the Civil War in Northeast Missouri. Missouri a Border State." (Columbus, Mo., Jan.-Apr., 1913, v.VII, #2 and 3, p. 63-75; p. 113-131. Vital and little known statistics relating to Missouri's participation in war. Reprint, in wraps, of above.

423 **SHOEMAKER, John J.**
"Shoemaker's Battery, Stuart's Horse Artillery, Pelham's Battalion, afterwards commanded by Col. R.P. Chew, Army of Northern Virginia." (Memphis, Tenn., S.C. Toof & Co., 1908) 12mo, cl, 2-ports, 108pp. Roster. $1400, $1800-bmk.

...Gaithersburg, Md., Butternut Press, 1985. $22.

424 **SHOFNER, Jerrell H. and William Warren Rogers**
"Confederate Railroad Construction. The Live Oak to Lawton Connector." In: FHQ, Jan. 1965, v.XLIII, #3, p. 217-228.

425 ..."Montgomery to Richmond: The Confederacy Selects a Capital." In: CWH, June, 1964, v.X, #2, p. 155-166.

426 ..."Textile Manufacturing in Florida during the Civil War." In: Textile History Review, 1963, v.IV, p. 118-125.

427 **SHONERT, Genevieve Hancock**
"A page of unwritten history." In: Christopher Gist. Hist. Soc. Papers, 1954-1955, leaves 90-98. A Conviction and execution of Capt. Wm. Francis Corbin and Jefferson McGraw as CSA recruiting officers in Pendleton Co., Ky.

428 **SHOOK, Robert W.**
"The Federal Military in Texas, 1865-1870." In: TMH, Spring 1967, v.6, #1, p. 3-53, maps, charts.

429 ..."Custer's Texas Command, 1865-1866." (Reconstruction) In: TMH, 1971, v.IX, #1, p. 49-54, port.

430 ..."Military Activities in Victoria, 1865-1866." In: Texana, Winter, 1965, v.III, #4, p. 347-352. Reconstruction.

431 ..."The Battle of Nueces, August 10, 1862." In: SwHQ, July, 1962, v.LXVI, #1, p. 31-42, illus., map.

432 **"SHORT HISTORIES**
of Confederate Generals." (Packed in Duke's Cigarettes) (New York: Park Place, NY-Knapp & Co., 1888) 1 1/2x2 3/4", color port on stiff wraps, with facsm. signature inside, each with 15pp. short history, and list of 50 Union and Confederate Generals on back cover: Beauregard, Bragg, Breckinridge, Early, Ewell, Forrest, Gordon, Hampton, Hardee, Hill, Hood, Jackson, Johnston, G. A.S. & J.E., Lee,

Longstreet, Morgan, Pemberton, Pickett, Polk, Price, Magruder, Semmes, Kirby Smith, Stuart, CSA. See: "Heroes of the Civil War."

433 **SHORT, D.M.**
"Reminiscences...of a "Blue Hen's Chicken"." n.p., c.1901. 8vo, pict. wraps, 8pp. $125. "Left Delaware in '42 to Texas to Marshall, Tx., raised a company for CSA in Texas.

434 **SHORT, James R.**
"Citizen soldiers at Spangler's Woods, Va." In: Va. Cavalcade, Summer, 1955, v.5, #1, p. 44-47, view(1 col.) Monument at Gettysburg to Va. Veterans who had fought there. Designed by F. William Sievers in 1910, unveiled-1917.

435 ..."Field of Honor." In: Va. Cavalcade, Spring, 1954, v.3, #4, p. 30-35, maps, ports, views (one color) A corp. of VMI cadets at the Battle of New Market, May 1864.

436 **SHORTER, John Gill, Gov.**
"Gov. John Gill Shorter, 1861-1863. Part 1, Edt: Anne Kindrick Walker." In: AR, July, 1958, v.11, #3, p.208-232; Pt. II, Oct., 1958, #4, p.267-285.

437 **SHORTER, John Gill, Gov. Alabama**
"Governor John Gill Shorter, Executive Papers. Edt: Milo B. Howard, Jr." In:AHQ, 1961, v.23, #3 and 4, p. 278-288.

438 **SHORTRIDGE, Wilson Porter**
"Kentucky neutrality in 1861." In: MVHR, Mar. 1923, v.IX, p. 283-301.

439 **SHOTWELL, Randolph Abbott**
"The Papers of Randolph Abbott Shotwell. Edt: J.G. De Roulhac Hamilton and Rebecca Cameron." In 3 vols. Raleigh, N.C., N. Carolina Hist. Comm., 1929, 1931, 1936. 8vo, cl, front(port), xxv, 511, x 581, 466pp. I-Biog. as soldier in CSA; II-"Three years in Battle and three in Federal Prison."
...Louisv: Lost Cause, micro-cd: $5.74 ea.

440 ..."Virginia and North Carolina in the Battle of Gettysburg." In: So. Hist. Monthly, 1876, v.I, p. 101-118.
...Also in: Our Liv. and Dead, Mar. 1876, v.IV, #1, p. 80-97.

441 **SHOUP, F.A., Gen., Francis A.**
"How we went to Shiloh. Ludicrous stories of official blunders in the great battle." In: CV, May 1894, v.II, #5, p. 137-140.

442 **SHOWELL, Margaret Letcher**
"Ex-Governor Letcher's Home. How it was burned during the war." In: SHSP, 1890, v.18, p. 393-397.

443 **SHRYOCK, Richard Harrison**
"Medical Practice in the Old South." In: South Atl. Quart., XXIX, (1930), p. 160-178.

444 **SHUEY, Mary Willis**
"Young Stanley: Arkansas Episode." In: AHQ, 1944, v.III, p. 356-366. Reprint: Southwest Review, Winter, 1942. See also under Henry M. Stanley.

445 **SHUFFLER, R. Henderson**
"Decimus et Ultimus Barziza." In: SwHQ, April, 1963, v.LXVI, #4, p. 501-512, port. See under: Barziza.

446 **SHUGG, Roger Wallace**
"A suppressed Co-operationist protest against secession." In: LHQ, 1936, v.XIX, p. 199-203. Attempt to suppress the minority views.

447 ..."Prophet of the deep: the "H.L. Hunley"." Feb. 1973, v.11, #10, p. 4-10, 44-47, facsm.,diagrams, illus., port, color cover. CWHI.

448 **SHUMATE, Madge Bocock and Annie V. Mann**
"Thomas S. Bocock: only Speaker of the Confederate Congress." Prize-winning essay in 1939, Virginia Div. United Daughters of Confederacy Contest. Richmond, Va., 1940, wraps, 21pp.

449 **SHURTER, Edwin DuBois**
"Oratory of the South. From the Civil War

to the present." N.Y., Neale Pub. Co., 1908, 8vo, cl, 336pp. See: Henry W. Grady. $45-jk-129.

450 **SIBLEY'S BRIGADE**
See: "Grand Varieties by the Ladies of Austin, Texas."

451 **SIBLEY, Henry H., Maj. Gen.**
"Reminiscences." In: NMHR, July, 1930, v.V, #3, p. 315-324.

452 ..."Expelling Federal Troops from New Mexico." 1931, v.V, #1, p. 68-71, 75.

453 **SICKLES, D.E., Hon., of N.Y.**
"Remarks of...on relations of the North and South and the duty of the North in the present crisis." Washington?, 1860. 8vo, sewed, 16pp. A pro-Southern speech.

453a "SIDELIGHTS on Little Rock (Arkansas) in the last days of Confederate control." In: Pulaski CHR, June 1963, v.11, p.17-22.

453b **SIDES, S. D.**
"Women & Slaves: an interpretation based on writings of Southern Women." Ann Arbor, Mich., Xerox'd. 8vo, wraps, 281pp. Bmk-$10.

454 "**SIEGE of New Berne, N.C.,**
from Feb. 1st to 4th, 1864." (n.p., n.d.) 8vo, sewn, 15pp.

455 **SIEPEL, Kevin H.**
"Rebel: The Life and Times of John Singleton Mosby." N.Y., St. Martin's Press, 1983, 8vo, cl, dj, xx, 346pp., illus.

456 **SIGAUD, Louis A.**
"When Belle Boyd wrote Lincoln." n.p., n.d. (Richmond, 1948) 8vo, wraps, 8pp. Reprint: Lincoln Herald. v.50, #1, p. 15-22.

457 ..."Belle Boyd Confederate Spy." Richmond, Va., Dietz Press (1944) 8vo, cl, dj, facsm., illus., ports, (13), (vii)-254pp. index, sources, dj, $30.
...2nd Edt., January 1945, $20-bmk.

458 ..."Mrs. Greenhow and the Rebel Spy Ring." In: Maryland Historical Magazine, Sept., 1946, v.XLI, #3, p. 173-198, notes.

459 "**SIGILLOGIA, Being Some Account**
Of the great or broad seal of CSA." See: John T. Pickett. $25.

460 **SIGNAL CORPS, C.S. Army**
See: E.H. Cummins, A.W. Taft.

461 **SIKES, Enoch Walter**
"The Confederate States Congress." Raleigh, N.C., Edwards & Broughton, 1903, 8vo, wraps, 29pp.

462 **SILBEY, Joel H.**
"The Civil War Synthesis in American Political History." In: CWH, June 1964, v.X, #2, p. 130-140.
..."A respectable minority: the Deomcratic party in the Civil War era." N.Y., W.W. Norton, 1977. 8vo, cl, dj, xviii, 267pp. $11.

463 **SILL, Edward**
"Who is responsible for the destruction of the City of Columbia, S.C., on the night of 17th February, 1865?" In: LWL, v.IV, 1867/1868, p. 361-369.

464 **SILVER, James W.**
"Confederate Morale and Church Propaganda." Tuscaloosa, Ala: Confederate Pub. Co., 1957. Confederate Centennial Studies #3, 12mo, stiff wraps, 120pp. Lim. Edt. 450 copies. Rep: Gloucester, Mass., P. Smith, 1964. Norton Pr., 167, paper.

465 ..."The Confederate Preacher goes to war." In: NCHR, Oct. 1956, v.XXXIII, p. 499-509.

466 ..."Mississippi in the Confederacy. As seen in retrospect." Jackson, Miss., Dept. Archives and History. Louisiana State Univ. Press, (1961). Pres. copy, $25-bmk. 8vo, cl, dj, illus., ports, facsm., xx, 319pp. See: John K. Bettersworth, vol. 1, also Kraus reprint note to v.1.

467 ..."Propaganda in the Confederacy." (Baton Rouge, La.) JSH, Nov. 1945, v.XI, #4, p. 487-503. $8.

467a **SILVERMAN, Jason H.**
"Confederate ambitions for the Southwest

a new perspective." In: Red River H. Rev., Winter 1979, p.62-71.

468 SILVERTHORNE, Elizabeth
"Ashbel Smith of Texas. Pioneer, Patriot, Statesman, 1805-1886." College Station: Texas A & M Univ. Pr., 1982, 8vo, cl, illus., 280pp. $24.50. Surg.-Gen., Texian Army (Republic), Mexican War and Capt. of Bayland Guards, CSA. Col. of 2nd Texas Inf. Later Bvt.Brig.-Gen. forces protecting Gulf Coast and defense Galveston Island.
"Once right in the eyes of God. The amazing career of Ashbel Smith." In: CWTI, Dec. 1980, v.19, #8, p.18-25, illus., port, maps.

469 SIMKINS, Francis Butler and Jas. Welch Patton
"The Women of the Confederacy." Richmond: Garrett and Massie, 1936. $40. 8vo, cl, d/w, xiii, 306pp., illus.
...N.Y., Scholarly Reprints, 1971.

470 ..."The Work of Southern women among the sick and wounded of Confederate armies." Journal of Southern History, I, p. 476-496. $8.

471 SIMMES, James P., Col.
"Report: Operations from June 2, 1864, to Dec., 1864." In: SHSP, 1885, v.13, p. 496-501.

472 SIMMONS, Sampson Sanders
"Memoirs of Sampson Sanders Simmons, a Confederate Veteran." Pasadena, California, 1954. 8vo, wraps, 66pp. Xerox copy, bound. Va. 8th Cavalry.

473 SIMMONS, Flora E.
"A complete account of the John Morgan raid through Kentucky, Indiana and Ohio, in July 1863." (Louisville, Ky.) Flora E. Simmons, 1863, 16mo, 94pp.
...1863 Edt. of 108pp.

474 SIMMONS, J.W.
"Conscripting Atlanta theatre in 1863." In: CV, June 1903, v.XI, p. 279.

475 SIMMONS, John
"The Confederate letters of John Simmons. Edt.: Jon Harrison." In: Smith Co. HS, 1975, v.14, #1, p.25-57, illus., ports. (4to)

476 SIMMONS, Laura
"Waul's Legion from Texas to Mississippi." (Waco, Texas: Texian Press, 1969) Offprint from "Texana", VII-#1, Spring '69. 8vo, cl, 16pp. 50 copies. $9.50.

477 SIMMONS, Lois L.
"The First Mrs. Jefferson Davis." In: East and West Baton Rouge Hist. Soc. Proc. 1917, v.1, p. 33-36. Sarah Knox Taylor Davis.

478 SIMMS, Arthur B.
Covington, Ga. See: Jane B. Peacock.

479 SIMMS, Henry Harrison
"A Decade of Sectional Controversy, 1851-1861." Chapel Hill: Univ. of N.C. Press, 1942. 8vo, cl, d/w, xi, 284pp.
...Westport, Conn: Greenwood Pr., 1978. $18.75.

480 ..."The Life of Robert M.T. Hunter. Study in Sectionalism and Secession." Richmond: William Byrd Press, (1935). 8vo, cl, 5pp. 3-234pp. front(port). Served sect-state for CSA, part of war.

481 ..."Life of John Taylor; the story of a brilliant leader in early Virginia State Rights School." Richmond: William Byrd Press, 1932. 8vo, cl, viii, 234pp., illus., front(port)

482 SIMMS, Jeremiah H.
"Morgan's Raid and Capture, the story from its inception to the last night and last camp at Bergholz, formerly, "Old Nebo", chronicled by J.H. Simms, of East Liverpool Morning Tribune." (East Liverpool, Ohio, Morning Tribune, c.1913) 4to, wraps, illus, ports, 40pp. (three columns) caption title. Note: A 1st edition in 1911, typed.

483 ..."Last Night and Last Day of John Morgan's Raid." (East Liverpool, Oh., J.H.

Simms Print, 1913) 8vo, wraps, cover title, illus., ports, 40pp. Reprint of Morgan's Raid with new title. Edition: 1917.
...1963, reprint, wraps, ads, 76pp.

484 **SIMMS, L. Moody, Jr.**
"Conrad Wise Chapman, a Virginia Expatriate Painter." (Richmond) Va. Cavl., Spring, 1971, v.XX, #4, p. 12-27, ports, illus., dbl. page, 1-color. In Wise's Brigade, painted many CSA scenes, spent last years in Mexico.

485 ..."John A. Elder: Memorial Artist of the Confederacy." Lincoln Herald, v.LXXIV, p. 29-33, 34-40. 1972.

486 ..."A Virginia Sculptor, following the Civil War, Edward Virginius Valentine preserved in marble the great Confederate heroes." In: VaCav., Summer, 1970, v.XX, #1, p. 20-27, illus., ports, 2p. color illus.

487 **SIMMS, William Gilmore**
"Sack and Destruction of the City of Columbia, S.C. To which is added a list of the property destroyed." Columbia, Press of Daily Phoenix, 1865, 12mo, wraps, 76pp. Crandall-2661. $125. Streeter sale, $200 (500 copies made) Note: A special edition was printed on bank-note paper, interleaved, Henkel sale, 1118, very rare.
...Atlanta, Ga., Oglethorpe University Press, 1937, 2nd Edt., Edited with notes by A.S. Salley. 8vo, cl, 2p., vii-xx, (2), 25-106pp.
...N.Y. Arno's "Select Bibliographies reprint series." 1978.
...Freeport, N.Y., Books for libraries (1971).

488 ..."The Destruction of Columbia, S.C." In: S.C. State Mag., #3 and 4, Mar/Apr., 1911. Aiken, S.C., Palmetto Pub. Co., 25cm.

489 ...The Letters of William Gilmore Simms." Collected and edited by Mary C. Simms Oliphant, Alfred Taylor Odell and T.C. Duncan Eaves. (Columbia: University of South Carolina Press, 1955. Vol.IV, 1858-1866. 8vo, cl, pp.xxvi, 643, illus., ports, front. See: Wm. P. Trent.

490 ..."War Poetry of the South. Edited by William Gilmore Simms." N.Y., Richardson & Co., 1866. 1st Edt., 12mo, cl, 482pp.
...N.Y., 1867, 2nd Edt. $30. Review 5pp., in "Old Guard", N.Y., 1867, v.V, p. 202-206.
...N.Y. Arno's "The Romantic tradition in American literature Ser." 1972. $32-y.

491 **SIMON, John Y.**
"Civil War: Confederate Letters at Washington University." "Manuscripts" (Manuscript Society) Winter, 1971, v.XXIII, p. 60-62.

492 **SIMONS, James**
"Sketch of Bachman's Battery." In: U.R. Brook's "Stories of the Confederacy." p.276-283.

493 **SIMONS, M.K.**
"The Vicksburg Diary of M.K. Simons, 1863. Edited by Walter H. Mays." In: TMH, Spring 1965, v.5, #1, p.21-38.

494 **SIMONTON, Charles H.**
"Address...on the unveiling of the Washington Light Infantry Monument, July 21, 1891." In: The Charleston Yearbook, 1891, 11pp. article.

494a **SIMPSON, Amos E.**
"The wartime adiminstration of Governor Henry W. Allen." In: LaH, 1964, v.5, p.257-69.

495 **SIMPSON, Amos E. and Vaughan Baker**
"Michael Hahn: Steady Patriot." Louisiana History, v.XIII, p. 229-252.

495a **SIMPSON, Craig M.**
"A Good Southerner: the life of Henry A. Wise of Virginia." Chapel Hill: University of North Carolina Press, 1985. 8vo, cl, dj, xviii, 450pp. $28.

496 **SIMPSON, Evan John, Col.**
"Atlantic Impact, 1861." N.Y., G.P. Putnam's Sons (1952). 12mo, cl, dj, ports, illus., incl. front, color endsheets, x, 296pp.

index. Motives, personalities of Trent Affair, US and England.
...London: Heinemann (1952)

497 SIMPSON, George Lee, Jr.
"The Cokers of Carolina: A Social Biography of a Family." Chapel Hill: Univ. of N.C. Press, 1956. 8vo, cl, illus., bibliog., viii, 327pp. S.C. family, plantation thru Civil War. Hannah Lide married Coker.

498 SIMPSON, Harold B., Dr.
"Robert E. Lee, the Texas years, resignation from the army, 1855-1861." p. 70-117. Proceedings, 1986, Confederate States symposium, Hill College, Hillsboro, Texas. 1986. 4to, hardback, 129pp., maps, #53 of 75 copies. +Grady McWhiney's "Shiloh: a Confederate Disaster, Apr. 6/7, 1862."

499 ..."Hood's Texans at Chickamauga." In: CV(new) Jan./Feb. 1987, v.35, #1, p.6-12, illus. (1-color)mpa, ports.

500 SIMPSON, Harold B., Col.
"Brawling Brass North and South. The most famous quarrels of the Civil War involving Stonewall Jackson and A.P. Hill, Jos. Johnston and Jno. B. Hood, Robert E. Lee and Jas. Longstreet, Geo. Meade and Dan Sickles, Phil Sheridan and Governor K. Warren, Jno. Pope and Fitz-John Porter. (Waco, Texas, Texian Press, 1960) 8vo, color-pict. wraps, (6), 78pp. 1000 copies.

501 ..."Cry Comanche: The 2nd Cavalry in Texas, 1855-1861." Hillsboro, Texas: Hill Jr. College, 1979. 8vo, stiff wraps, xii, 185pp.

502 ..."Foraging with Hood's Brigade from Texas to Pennsylvania." Reprint: Texana, Summer 1963, v.1, #3, 8vo, wraps, 2-illus., p.(257)-276. $3.50.

503 ..."The recruiting, training and camp life of a company of Hood's Brigade in Texas, 1861." Reprint: Texas Military History, Aug. 1962, v.2, #3, p.171-192, plastic spiral.

504 ..."Gaines' Mill to Appomattox. Waco and McLennan County, in Hood's Texas Brigade." Waco, Texas: Texian Press, 1963. 8vo, cl, dj, facms., illus., maps, ports, xii, 294pp. (50-copies, full Lt.) $50-b.

505 ..."Hood's Texas Brigade." (Waco, Texas: Texian Press, 1973) In: "Soldiers of Texas." p.(43), (1) color plate, p.47-69. 4to. OP

506 ..."Hood's Texas Brigade: Lee's Grenadier Guard." Waco, Texas: Texian Press, 1970. op, $40. Tk.8vo, cl, d/w, xv, 512pp., illus., ports, maps, facsms. (bibliog-15pp.) index, map endsheet.

507 ..."Hood's Texas Brigade in Reunion and Memory." Lim. Edt., 25 copies, lt. $125. Hillsboro, Texas: Hill Junior College, 1974, 8vo, cl, dj, xviii, 369pp.

508 ..."Hood's Texas Brigade in Poetry and Song. Intro: William E. Bard." (Hillsboro, Texas, Hill Junior College) (Waco, Texas: Texian Press, 1968) 8vo, cl, dj, facsms, illus., ports, incl. front. Music. (3), xii, (2), 296pp. op,

508a ..."Hood's Texas Brigade at Gettysburg." In: CV, ns, May/June 1988, v.36, #3, p.8-19, pl, maps, ports (tinted). From his book on Hood, excerpts.

509 ..."General John Bell Hood, Southern Thunderbolt." n.p., 1956. 4to, wraps, (i), 52 lfs. bibliog., p. 52. Address before CWRT of Wiesbaden, Ger. at Officer's Club, Air Base, 12 Mar., 1956.

510 ..."Hoods's Texas Brigade: a Compendium." Hillsboro, Texas: Hill Jr. College, 1977. Tk.8vo, cl, dj, illus., index, ports, tables, xii, (1), 614pp. (Lim. Edt., 25 copies, $125) Rosters: 1st, 4th, 5th, Tex. Inf., 3rd Ark., 18th Ga., Hampton's S.C. Legion and Rowan Artillery.

511 ..."Hood's Texas Brigade at Appomattox." In: Texana, Spring 1965, v.III, #1, p. 1-19, port, illus., members of Hood's Brigade paroled at Appomattox.

512 ..."East Texas Companies in Hood's Brigade." In: ETHJ, March 1965, v.III, #1, p. 5-17.

513 ..."The Marshall Guards/Harrison County's Contribution to Hood's Texas Brigade." Marshall, Texas: Caddo Press (1967). Harrison Co. Historical Society. $20. 8vo, wraps, viipp., 26pp. port.

514 ..."Maj.-Gen. James Lawson Kemper, soldier and statesman." (Presentation of Col. Harold B. Simpson before the Civil War Round Table of Wiesbaden, Germany, on Monday, 21 May, 1956.) n.p., 4to, 24 lfs., mimeogr. See: Marcus Wright's "Texas in the War."

515 ..."No one ever sees the backsides of my Texans." In: CWTI, Oct. 1965, v.IV, #6, p. 34-39, illus., ports. "Except for their depredations on the hog and chicken population of Virginia, Hood's Texas Brigade."

516 ..."Red Granite for Gray Heroes. The Monuments to Hood's Texas Brigade on Eastern Battlefields. Texas Remembers the Valor and Devotion of Her Sons." Intro: Hon. Ralph W. Yarborough. (Hillsboro, Texas: Hill Junior College Press, 1969.) 8vo, cl, boxed, ix, (2), 25, (5), (1)p. illus., maps. Special Limited Edition, 25 copies, box, $25, the regular edition. OP. $60-bmk.

517 ..."West Pointers in the Texas Confederate Army." In: TMH, Spring, 1967, v.6, #1, p.55-88, ports.

517a **SIMPSON, John A.**
"The cult of the "Lost Cause." In: THQ, Winter 1975, v.34, #4, p.350-61.

518 **SIMPSON, John Eddins**
"Howell Cobb: The Politics of Ambition." Chicago: Adams Press, 1973. 8vo, stiff wraps, vi, 198pp. See: David E. Meerse's Review in CWH, June 1974, v.20, #2. That Simpson was completely wrong about Cobb.

519 ..."Howell Cobb's bid for the presidency in 1860." In: Ga.H.Q., Spring 1971, v.LV, #1, p.102-113.

520 ..."Prelude to Compromise: Howell Cobb and the House Speakership Battle, 1849." In: Ga.H.Q., Winter, 1974, v.LVIII, #4, p.389-399.

521 **SIMPSON, W.A.C.**
"Britain and the Blockade-in Theory." (London) Jour. Confed. Hist. Soc., Spring, 1968, v.6, #1, p.6-26, maps(2), plates (2).

522 **SIMPSON, William Dunlap**
"Some letters of Wm. Dunlap Simpson, 1860-1863. Edt: Willard E. Wight." In: SCHMag., Oct. 1956, v.57(Oct.) p.204-222. Activities as officer in CSArmy, member CSA Congress.

523 **SIMS, Frederick Wilmer**
"The Right of Secession-a review of Bledsoe, "Is Davis a Traitor?" Views of Webster, Calhoun and other statesmen." In: SHSP, 1907, v.35, p.166-173.

524 **SIMS, James Marion, Dr.**
"Story of My Life." New York: D. Appleton, 1884, 12mo, cl, 471pp.
...Editions in 1885, 1886, 1889, +port.

525 **SIMS, Lydel**
"The Submarine that wouldn't come up." In: Amer. Hert., April 1958, v.IX, #3, p.48-51, 107-111, illus., incl. color. Refers to CSN "Hunley".

526 **SINCLAIR, Arthur**
"How the 'Merrimac' fought the 'Monitor.'" In: Hearst Mag., Dec. 1913, v.XXIV, p. 884-894. Served on board the "Merrimac".

527 ..."Two Years on the Alabama, by Arthur Sinclair...with over thirty illustration." Boston: Lee & Shepard, 1895. 8vo, decr. cl, illus., incl. front, ports, facsm., $200-Dabney., vi, 344pp., Reb.-$40.
...2nd Edt., 1896, $75; 3rd Edt., 1896 (352pp.)

528 **SINCLAIR, G. Terry**
"The Eventful Cruise of the "Florida"." In: Cent. Mag., 1898, v.LVI, p. 417-427. ports, illus. Formerly midshipman, CSN.

529 **SINGLETON, Otis A. and James I. Robertson, J. Vincent P. DeSantis and Thomas D. Clark**
"Four Southern Historians, memorial tributes to: T. Harry Williams, Bell I. Wiley, Holman Hamilton and Clement Eaton." In: RKHS, Spring, 1982, v.80, #2, p.119-150.

529a **SINGLETON, Theresa A., Edt.**
"The archaeology of slavery & plantation life." Orlando, Fla., Academic Press, 1985. 8vo, cl, dj, xvii, 338pp, ills, maps, notes, index. $65.

530 **SINGLEY, Frederick J., Jr.**
"Denial of Habeas Corpus: a contrast in Blue and Gray." In: Amer. Bar. Assn. Jour., 1963, v.XLIX, p. 172-175.

531 **"SINKING of the "Cumberland", The**
by the Ironclad "Merrimac", off Newport News, Virginia, March 8, 1862, sketched by F. Newman, Newport News." N.Y., Currier & Ives, 1862. Small folio, litho uncolored.

532 **SISLER, George**
"The arrest of a "Memphis Daily Appeal" war correspondent on charges of treason." In: W.Tenn. Hist. Soc. Paper, 1957, v.XI, #1, p.76-92. Gen. Braxton Bragg against John H. Linebaugh, '63.

533 **SISTLER, Byron**
"1890 Civil War Veterans Census, Tennesseans in Texas." Evanston, Ill., Byron and Barbara Sistler, 1978. 4to, viii, 22 leaves, cover title.

534 **SITTERSON, Joseph Carlyle**
"The Secession Movement in North Carolina." Chapel Hill: University North Carolina, 1939. 8vo, wraps, vii, (1), 285pp., maps, bibliog., 250-272, index. James Sprunt Studies in History and Political Science, v.23, #2.

535 **SITUATION in America. The"**
In: Blackwoods, Feb. 1977, v.121, p.196-220. Using negroes to infranchise themselves and keep Republicans in power and control.

536 **"SITUATION, The**
what the South has not lost by the War." In: The Old Guard, Nov. 1867, V, #12, p.881-886.

537 **"SIX HUNDRED Confederate Officers, The**
placed under fire of Confederate cannon in retaliation." In: CV, 1899, v.7, p.313-321, p.255. Listed alphabetically by states.

538 **SKETCH of Major Chatham Roberdeau Wheat**
In: SB, 1883-1884, v.II, p. 385-392. port, illus.

539 **SKETCH and ROLLS**
Of Dreux's Louisiana Cavalry, CSA. Prepared by a Committee of the survivors of Dreux's Louisiana cavalry. n.p., (1901). 12mo, wraps, cover title, 18p.front, port. See also: Col. Chas. D. Dreux.

540 **SKETCH of 12 Months Service, A**
In the Mobile Rifle Co., by an Unidentified Member. Co.I, 3rd Ala. Inf. Regt., Louis T. Woodruff, Capt. In: Ala. Hist. Quart., Spring-Summer, 1963, v.25, #1 and 2, p.149-189. There's no other archival roster of this group.

541 **SKETCH of Page's Battery**
Morris Artillery, 2nd Corp ANV, by One of the Comp. See: Richard Channing, Moore Page, Pub. anon.

542 **SKETCH of the Duplin Rifles.**
Prepared in 1895 by Participants in its movements. Company C, 2nd Regiment, N.C. Volunteers. Roll of Campany A, 43rd N.C. Infantry. n.p., n.d. (Raleigh, N.C.? 1895?) 8vo, 12pp. caption title.

543 **SKETCH of the Forty-third Regiment**
North Carolina Troops, Infantry.
See: under Thos. S. Kenan.

544 **SKETCH of the Richmond Howitzers, A**
And their historic home. Organized November 9, 1859. Reorganized April 10, 1871. Published by the Richmond Howitzers, 1903. (Presses of J.L. Hill Print, Richmond, Va.) Tall 8vo, wraps, illus., 40pp.

545 **SKETCHES of the History**
Of the Washington artillery, by Col. J.B. Walton, Capt. J.A. Chaleron, Col. B.F. Exchelman, Col. W.M. Owen. In: SHSP, 1883, v.XI, p.210-222, 247-254.

546 **SKIDMORE, Joe**
"The Copperhead Press and the Civil War." (Minneapolis, Minn., Journalism Quarterly, XVI, 1939, p.345-355. Study of the opposition press from 1861-1864.

547 **SKINKER, Thomas Keith**
"Samuel Skinker and his descendants; and account of the Skinker family and all their kindred who have the blood of Samuel Skinker in their veins." n.p., The Author, 1923 (St. Louis, Mo.) 8vo, cl, 6p, 1298pp., front, illus. (coat of Arms) ports. $100-bmk. List of corrections inserted between p.2/3 preliminary leaves. Blank pages for notes at end. Info: on Capt. James K. Boswell, Gen. R.L.T. Beale and members of the Skinker clan who served in the CSArmy. Also a transcription of Capt. Boswell's war diary, kept while an engineer on Jackson's staff. (Broadfoot)

548 **SKINNER, Woodward B.**
"The Civil War's Influence on Pensacola." Pensacola (Fla.) Escarosa Humanities Center (1970). 4to, (i), 15 leaves.

549 ..."Pensacola's Exiled Government." In: FHQ, January 1961, v.XXXIX, #3, p.270-276.

550 **SKIPPER, Otis Clark**
"J(ames) D(unwoody) B(rownston) De Bow (1820-1867), Magazinist of the Old South." Athens: Univ. of Georgia Pr.(1958). 8vo, cl, d/w, facsm., port, tables, bibliog. (p.248-261), notes (p.225-247), x, 269pp. Life in Charleston, pub. Review, in New Orleans, Dir: CSA states Produce Loan Agency. See: W.D. Weatherford, also.

551 **SKIPWITH, P.H.**
"How many Confederate towns were burned?" In: SHSP, 1882, v.10, p.189-190.

552 **SLABAUGH, Arlie R.**
"Confederate States Paper Money. A type catalogue of the paper money issued by the Confederate States during the Civil War 1861-1865." Racine, Wisconsin: Whitman Pub. Co. (1958) 12mo, soft fabricord, illus., 48pp.
...2nd Edt. (1959)
...3rd Edt. Centennial Edt. (1961) 64pp. Title addition: "Part 1-Catalogue; Part II-Historical Data. CSA flag added: cover.
..."Confederate States of America Paper Money." Hewitt's Numismatic Information Series-4th Edt., Racine, Wisc., 1871. 8vo, wraps, illus., value. 1st through 3rd editions.

553 **SLACK, W.Y., Gen.**
"The reinterment of General Slack." In: "Flashback" June/July 1951, v.1, #4, p.19-20. From: Fayetteville (Ark.) Weekly Democrat. 29 May, 1880. On the death of Gen. Slack, wounded at the battle of Pea Ridge, removed from an unmarked burial place to the CSA cemetery in Fayetteville, Ark.

554 ..."A sketch of General W.Y. Slack, of Missouri." In: LWL, March 1869, v.VI, #5, p.357-360.

555 **SLAUGHTER'S MOUNTAIN, Battle of**
See: Cedar Mountain, Battle of

556 **SLAUGHTER, Frank Gill**
"Storm Haven." Garden City, N.Y., Doubleday, 1953. 8vo, cl, 282pp. Novel of a

Florida cattle-drive during War Between the States.

557 ..."The Stonewall Brigade." Garden City, N.Y., Doubleday, 1975. 8vo, cl, 456pp. novel.

558 **SLAUGHTER, J.E.**
"General Orders, #12. Western Sub-District of Texas. Brownsville, Texas, Dec. 9, 1864." Broadside: 4.5x7" $200. Brownsville area open ports to export cotton, any other shipping open to confiscation.

559 ..."The Last Battle of the War." In: SHSP, 1893, v.21, p.226-227. (see under title)

560 **SLAUGHTER, Philip**
"A sketch of the life of Randolph Fairfax, a private in the ranks of the Rockbridge Artillery, attached to "Stonewall Brigade" subsequently to the 1st Regt. Va. Light Artillery, 2nd Corps, Army of Northern Virginia; including a brief account of Jackson's celebrated Valley Campaign." Richmond, Va., Tyler, Allegre and McDaniel 1864." (head of title: Second Edition)
...1st Edt. 1863, Howes suggests it may have been in a periodical. 12mo, wraps, 48pp.
...3rd Edt. (Baltimore: Innes & Co.), 1878. $100. 12mo, cl, x, 72pp. front(port. $150-b
...4th Edt., Richmond, Va. Wm. E. Jones, 1902. Reprint from 1878 Edt., 8vo, wraps, 46pp.

561 ..."Coercion and Conciliation. A Sermon, preached in camp, at Centreville, Virginia, by the Rev. P. Slaughter, Chaplain of the 19th Regiment Virginia Volunteers. Condensed by request, into a tract for the times." Richmond, Va., Macfarlane & Ferguson, n.d., 8vo, wraps, 7pp.

562 **"SLAVE TRADE**
in the Southern Congress"; and L.W. Spratt, "The Philosophy of Secession". A protest from the South Carolina against a decision of the Southern Congress." In: Living Age, March 1861, p.801-810. See: L.W. Spratt.

563 **"SLAVERY and its contradictions."**
In: Tyler QHGM, July 1929, v.XI, p.67-68. Concerns provision in CSA Constitution prohibiting slave trade.

564 **"SLAVERY the mere pretext for the rebellion..."**
See: John Pendleton Kennedy

565 **SLIDELL, John**
See: Robert M.T. Hunter.

566 **SLIGER, J.E.**
"How General Taylor fought the Battle of Mansfield, La." In: Confed. Veteran, March 1923, v.XXXI, p.456-458.

567 **SLINGLUFF, Fielder C.**
"The Burning of Chambersburg." In: CV, Nov. 1909, v.XVII, p. 559-561. Also: "Pa.-German", July 1909, v.X, p. 324-330. In: SHSP, 1909, v.37, p.152-163.

568 **SLOAN, Benjamin**
"The Merrimac and the Monitor." Columbia: Bul., University of South Carolina, #189, 1926. 8vo, wraps, front(port), 16pp. Author was Major on staff of Maj. Gen. Benjamin Huger, CSA.

569 **SLOAN, John Alexander, Capt.**
"North Carolina in the War Between the States." Washington: Rufus H. Darby, 1883. 8vo, wraps, front, 2-ports, two parts in one, paged continuously, pt. I, 1-90, vi; pt. 2, 91-170, vii-xxiipp. $250, $400. N.C. Legislature authorized publication but it was never done. Note: In: Pub. South. Hist. Assn., v.III, #2, p.152, "This was really the work of Hon. William Macon Coleman of N.C., later of Washington, D.C."

570 ..."Reminiscences of the Guilford Grays, Co.B, 27th N.C. Regiment, by John A. Sloan." Washington: R.O. Polkinhorn Pr., 1883. 12mo, wraps, iv, 129, (1)pp. Fine-$250, $125. The Grays, 1861-1865. Roster, $175-bmk-'72.
...Wendell, N.C., Broadfoot's Bookmark,

Reprint, 1978, 12mo, cl, (2), iv, (1)(3)-128pp. (1)(1)p. adv. 500 copies.

570a **SMALL, Pompey**
"A small contribution: Louisiana's short rural railroads in the Civil War." In: LaH, 1977, v.18, p.87-103.

571 **SMALLWOOD, James**
"Disaffection in Confederate Texas: The Great Hanging at Gainesville." In: CWH, Dec. 1976, v.22, #4, p.349-360.

572 **SMEDES, Susan Dabney**
"Memorials of a Southern Planter." Baltimore: Cushing & Bailey, 1887, 12mo, cl, port, 341pp.
...Balt: 1888, edts. 2nd, 3rd.
...London: John Murray, 1889. "A Southern Planter." 12mo, cl, x, (1)p-addendum.
...N.Y., James Pott & Co., 1890. "Memorials of a Southern Planter." 12mo, cl, front(port), 342pp. $75.
...N.Y., 1899 (7th edition) J.Pott Co.
...1900, N.Y., James Pott & Co. "A Southern Planter; social life in the Old South." 12mo, decr. cl, 342pp., illus.
...1906 edition. A Southern Planter." 342ppl.
...N.Y., Alfred A. Knopf, 1965. "Memorials of a Southern Planter." Edt: Fletcher M. Green. 8vo, cl, dj, facsm., genealogical table, illus., port, 1xx, 337pp. "Memorials of Thomas Smith Gregory Dabney, born in King and Queen Co., Va., Jan. 1798. Plantation, slave life before, during and after the War."
...Jackson, Miss., University Press, 1981.

573 **SMEDES, William C., Esq.**
"Speech of..., at Vicksburg, Miss. on 27th October, 1860, upon the Right of a State to secede from the Union. And other political topics." Vicksburg, Miss., M. Shannon Print, 1860. 8vo, sewn, 40pp. Sabin-82246.

574 ..."Letter of..., of Vicksburg, Miss., in vindication of the Southern Confederacy." Jackson, Miss., Power & Cadwalader, 1861. 8vo, sewn, 13pp. Sabin-82245.

575 **SMILEY, David L.**
"Revolutionary origins of the South's Constitutional Defenses." In: NCHR, 1967, v.XLIV, p. 256-269.

576 **SMILEY, Thomas M.**
"The Muster Roll of Company D, Fifth Virginia Regiment, Stonewall Brigade." In: SHSP, 1893, v.21, p.50-57.

577 **SMIRNOFF, Alexander**
"General Robert E. Lee and Napoleon." In: Army Quart., Apr. 1927, v.XIV, #1, p.121-129. Influence of Napoleon on Lee.

578 **"SMITH BRIGGS" (Gunboat), USNavy.**
See: R.S. Thomas.

579 **SMITH, A. Morton**
"The Great Hanging." In: Naylor's Epic-Century Mag., April, 1955, v.22, #2. p.17-19, 24, illus. Excerpts from author's "The First Hundred Years in Cooke County." See: Dr. Thomas Barrett.

580 **SMITH, Alan Cornwall**
"The "Monitor-Merrimac" legend." In: USN Inst. Proc., 1940, v.LXVI, p.385-389.

581 **SMITH, Albion, Edt.**
"The Franklin Guard Report." In: "Password", v.IV, p.79-81.

582 **SMITH, Alfred Glaze, Jr.**
"Economic Readjustment of an Old Cotton State: South Carolina, 1820-1860." Columbia: Univ. South Carolina Pr., 1958. 8vo, cl, dj, bibliog., viii, 239pp.

583 **SMITH, Alice R. Huger**
See: Herbert Ravenel Sall, Daniel Elliott Huger Smith.

584 **SMITH, Anna, M.D.**
"Lieut.-Colonel Francis W. Smith, CSA." In: SHSP, 1896, v.24, p.39-40.

585 **SMITH, Bethania Meradith**
"Civil War subversives." In: ISHS Jour., Autumn, 1952, v.45, p.220-240. Knights of

Golden Circle, Sons of Liberty in Ohio, Ind., illus. 1854-1864.

586 **SMITH, Blanche Lucas**
"North Carolina's Confederate Monuments and Memorials, compiled by..." (Raleigh, 1941) United Daughters of Confederacy, Div.-N.C. 8vo, cl, front, plates, ports, 131pp.

587 **SMITH, Byron**
"Reminiscences of a Confederate Prisoner. Scott's Cavalry composed of 1st Georgia, 1st Louisiana and 3rd Tennessee Regiments. A True story full of interesting events." (Jackson, Miss., Baptist Orphanage Pr., 1910) 12mo, wraps, 42pp. $100. Very crude print, probably by inmates.

588 **SMITH, C. Alphonso**
"Matthew Fontaine Maury (1806-1873)." (Charlottesville?, Va.) Reprint from the Alumni Bul., Univ. of Va., 3rd Ser. XVII, #1, January 1924. 8vo, wraps, 10pp.

589 **SMITH, C. Carter, Jr., Edt.**
"Two Naval Journals: 1864. The Journal of Mr. John C. O'Connell, CSN, on C.S.S. Tennessee, and The Journal of Pvt. Charles Brother, USMC on the U.S.S. Hartford at the Battle of Mobile Bay." Chicago: The Wyvern Press of S.F.E., Inc. Mobile, Alabama, Graphics, Inc. (1964). Tall 8vo, pict. wraps, ports, illus., 51pp.

590 **SMITH, Cabell, Mrs.**
"Down Memory Lane; gleanings from the Confederate Veteran." In: UDCMag., Mar. 1953, v.16, #3, p.12, 32. Re: a periodical founded by Sumner A. Cunningham, 1892-1932.

591 ..."Some sidelights on the restoration of Arlington." In: UDCMag., July/Aug. 1948, v.1, #7, p.26-27; #8, p.14-17. Largely letters to the Edt., 1921-1924, 1945 by Sophie C. Richardson and Frances Parkinson Keyes, on efforts of UDC to restore Lee's mansion.

592 **SMITH, Caraway, Colonel**
"Report: Battle of Ocean Pond, Fla." In: SHSP, 1881, v.9, p.27-28.

593 **SMITH, Carrie Weaver**
"Andrew's Raid. A Ballad and Selected Poems." (Cullowhee, N.C., Dec. 1943) copy-1944. 8vo, decr. color-wraps, 57pp. some description of the Raid. CSA flag on wrap.

594 **SMITH, Charles Forster**
"Reminiscences and Sketches." Nashville: M.E. Church South, 1908. 12mo, cl, 448pp. Contains sketches Lee, Lanier and many others.

595 ..."Robert E. Lee once more." In: So.Atl. Quart., Oct. 1908, v.VII, p. 359-369.

596 **SMITH, Charles Henry**
"Bill Arp, from the Uncivil War to Date. 1861-1903. Memorial Edition." Atlanta, Ga., Hudgins Pub. Co., 1903. Tall 8vo, cl, illus., ports, incl. front, 378pp. See: Charles Henry/Bill Arp.

597 ..."Bill Arp, so called; a side-show of the Southern side of the War." N.Y., Metropolitan Record Office, 1866, (v) $100.16mo, cl, port, 204pp., illus.
...Same, 1867, with illus. by M.A. Sullivan.
...Same, Edt-1869 (Hodgkins sale-1906 by C.F. Libbie, notes: very rare, only 200 copies ever printed(doubtful). "The Record office was torn down by a mob for pub. this book." Sub-title-"I'm a good Union man, so-called but I'll bet on Dixie as long as I've got a dollar."

598 ..."The Farm and Fireside: Sketches of Domestic Life in War and Peace. Written and published for the entertainment of people at home, and dedicated especially to mothers and children." Atlanta, Ga., Constitution Pub. Co., 1891, 8vo, cl, illus., 345pp. DeRenne-II, 894. See: Jas. C. Austin, 1892 Edition.

599 **SMITH, Coleman**
"Capture of the gunboat "Queen City." In:

CV, March 1914, v.XXII, p. 120-121. Captured by Shelby's Brigade at Clarendon, Ark., June 24, 1864.

600 **SMITH, Dabney Howard**
"D. Howard Smith letter, 1867: corrections on "History of Morgan Cavalry"." In: KyHSR, Apr. 1954, v.52, p.114-124. Letter, 15 Feb. 1867, to Gen. B.W. Duke, auth. of the history.

601 ..."The killing of Gen. John H. Morgan." In: SB, 1882/1883, v.1, p.447-451.

602 **SMITH, Daniel E. Huger, Alice R. and Arney R. Childs, Editors**
"Mason Smith Family Letters, 1860-1868." Columbia: Univ. of South Carolina Press, 1950. Large 8vo, xxiv, 292pp. ports. $40-b. Letters largely by or to Eliza Carolina Middleton (Huger) Smith. Charleston.

603 **SMITH, Daniel Elliott Huger**
"A Charlestonian's Recollections, 1846-1913." Charleston, S.C., Carolina Art Ass'n., (1950) 8vo, cl, (6), 162pp. CSA Service (p.81-114) Charleston Lwyr. to '77.

604 **SMITH, Daniel P.**
"Company K, First Alabama Regiment; or, Three Years in the Confederate Service." Prattville, Alabama, Published by the Survivors, 1885. (Phila: Burk & McFetridge) 12mo, cl, 135, (10)pp. Append. of Roster, Roll and index. Roll of Co.K, 1st Ala. Reg. Said to be only 25 copies printed. $100, $600.
"Co. K., First Alabama regiment..." Gaithersburg, Md., Butternut Press, 1984. $18.50.

605 **SMITH, David C.**
"Lilly in the Valley: Civil War at Mossy Creek." New Market, Tenn., The Author, 1986, 8vo, wraps, 105pp. bibliog. notes. $10. Jas. Longstreet's stay, 1863-1864.

606 **SMITH, David R.**
"The Monitor and the Merrimac a Bibliography." Los Angeles: University of California Library, 1968. UCLA Library occasional papers, #15. 4to, stiff wraps, front, illus., ports, map, 35pp.

607 ..."The Beast of New Orleans, as the South Remembers." In: CWTI, Oct. 1969, v.VIII, #6, p.10-21, illus., facsm., ports.

608 **SMITH, Dean**
"Shoot out at Picacho Pass." In: CWTI, 1980, v.18, #6, p.4-9, 40-47, illus., map, ports.

609 **SMITH, Duane Allan**
"The Confederate Cause in the Colorado Territory, 1861-1865." In: CWH, March 1961, v.VII, #1, p.71-80.

610 **SMITH, Edmund Kirby, Gen.**
"Campaigns of Gen. E. Kirby Smith." In: SHSP, 1881, v.9, p.225-233, 246-254, 289-297, 455-462,; v.7(1879), p.442; 1882, v.10, p.70-76, 158-161.

611 ..."The Last Battle of the War." See title.

612 ..."The defense of the Red River." In: B & L, v.IV, p.369-374.

613 ...Smith, E. Kirby, Gen. and Gen. Ben McCulloch. Texas-Confederate Broadside. Gen. Ord:45. Shrevesport, La., Sept. 16, 1863. 8vo. Declares treasonable not to accept CSA money for supplies. Not in Crand/Har.

614 ..."A Short History of Gen. E. Kirby Smith." Park Place, N.Y., Knapp & Co., 1888. 2 3/4x1 1/2" colored booklet, 16pp. facsm. signature, (packed in Duke's cigarettes) See: "Heroes of the Civil War", and W. Duke. Paul F. Hammond.
...See: Arthur H. Noll, Joseph H. Parks, Eleanor G. Kirby.

615 **SMITH, Edward A., Rev.**
"Records of Walthall's Brigade of Mississippians, compiled by Rev. E.A. Smith, Co. A, 29th, Miss." Brewton, Ala., 1904. $97.50. 8vo, wraps, 89, (1)p.errata, roster: 14-65. See: E.T. Sykes, Gen. E.C. Walthall.

616 **SMITH, Edward Conrad**
"The Borderland in the Civil War." N.Y., Macmillan Co., 1927. 8vo, cl, maps, (7), 412pp. index.
...N.Y., A.M.S. Press, 1969.

617 ..."Thomas Jonathan Jackson, 1824-1863, A Sketch." Weston, W.Va., Society of Historical Engravings (1920) (Private distribution) 8vo, boards, port (front) (38)pp., print in decr. borders. $75.

618 **SMITH, Emma Frances Lee**
"Personal recollections of a nobel man, (Hilary A. Herbert)." In: Confed. Vet., 1919, v.XXVII, July, p.246-248.

619 **SMITH, Emmett W.**
"Abraham Lincoln as he was-Abraham Lincoln of Illinois-John Brown of Kansas. Two hearts beat as one. Dedicated to the Sons & Daughters of the Confederacy." n.p. (Waco, Texas?) n.d. 8vo, wraps, port on cover, 12pp. $.10 copy. "Lincoln could have stopped war", anti-Lincoln.

620 **SMITH, Ernest Ashton**
"The History of the Confederate Treasury. A dissertation presented to the board of University Studies of the Johns Hopkins University for the degree of Doctor of Philosophy." (From publications of the Southern History Association for Jan., Mar., May, 1901)(Press of Harrisburg Pub.)(Penn.) 8vo, wraps, (2), (1)-126pp., v.V, #1, (34p), #2, p.99-150, #3, p.188-227.

621 **SMITH, Essie Wade Butler, Edt. (Mrs. Cabell Smith)**
"The English inscription on the Arlington Confederate Monument." In: UDCMag. Oct. 1948, v.11, #10, p.18-19. Inscrip. composed by Rev. Randolph H. McKim.

622 ..."Forty years with the Virginia Division, United Daughters of the Confederacy." (n.p., 1935?) 8vo, wraps, 22pp.
...Southern Magazine, 1935, v.II, #3, p.29-35.

623 **SMITH, Francis H.**
"The Virginia Military Institute; its building and rebuilding." Lynchburg, Ca., J.P. Bell Co., 1912, 8vo, cl, illus., port, 227pp. Acct. of Institute before and after the War.

624 **SMITH, Francis Henney**
"Discourse on the Life and Character of Lt. Gen. Thos. J. Jackson, (CSA), late Professor of Natural and Experimental Philosophy in the Virginia Military Institute. By Francis H. Smith, A.M., Superintendent of the Virginia Military Institute. Read before the board of visitors, faculty and cadets, July 1, 1863. With proceedings of the institution, in honor of the illustrious deceased. (Published by order of the board of visitors.)" Richmond, Va., Ritchie & Dunnavant, 1863, 12mo, wraps, 23pp.

625 ..." Introductory lecture read before the Corps of Cadets, on the resumption of the academic duties of the Virginia Military Institute, at the Alms House, Richmond, Va., December 28, 1864. By Francis H. Smith. Published by order of the Board of Visitors." Richmond, Va., MacFarlane & Fergusson, 1865. 12mo, wraps, 8pp.
...1866, p 21.

626 ..."General Hunter's Raid, (poem)." In: SHSP, 1899, v.27, p.184-185.

627 **SMITH, Francis Henry**
"Biographical sketch of Matthew Fontaine Maury, with selections from his writings." In: E.A. Alderman-Library of Southern Literature, 1909, v.8, p.3435-3457.

628 **SMITH, Francis Williamson**
See: Anna M.D. Smith.

629 **SMITH, Frank H.**
"The Forrest-Gould Affair. An eyewitness account of the fatal encounter between Forrest and an aggrieved Lieut. of his command." In: CWTI, Nov. 1970, v.IX, p.32-27, illus., port., diagram.

629a **SMITH, Gene**
"Lee & Grant: a dual biography." N.Y., McGraw Hill books, 1984. 8vo, cl, 412p. ills, index, bibliog. $18.

630 **SMITH, George Gilman**
"The Boy in Gray. A Story of the War." Macon, Ga., Macon Pub. Co., 1895. 12mo, decr. cl, 267pp. 1st Edt., 1894. Other editions: 1896 and 1903. Nashville, Tenn., Epworth Era Pub., 1907, 12mo, cl, 266pp. Smith was chaplain of Phillips Legion, Georgia Volunteers.

631 ..."History of Methodism in Georgia and Florida from 1785-1865. By Geo. G. Smith of North Georgia Conference." Macon, Ga., Jno. W. Burke & Co., 1877, 12m0, cl, ports(11), 530pp.

632 ...Atlanta: A.B. Caldwell, 1913, 8vo, cl, illus., ports, 430pp.

633 ..."The Life and Times of George Foster Pierce, Bishop of the M.E. Church, South Sparta, Ga., Hancock Print, 1888. 8vo, cl, illus., ports, xiv, 688pp.

634 **SMITH, George H.**
"More of the Battle of New Market." In: CV, Nov. 1908, v.XVI, p.569-572.

634a ..."The positions & movements of the troops in the Battle of New Market, fought May 15, 1864. By Col. Smith, of the 62nd Va. Reg. written for distribution, with the good wishes & affectionate regards of the author, among the surviving men & officers of Imboden's Brigade, & other participating in the battle." n.p., n.d. George F. Markham, Jr. 8vo, stiff wraps, 58pp. $175-Bmk.

635 **SMITH, George T., Rev.**
"Prison experience of a Northern Soldier." In: SHSP, 1883, v.11, p.330-335.

636 **SMITH, George Winston**
"Ante-Bellum Attempts of Northern Business Interests to "Redeem" the Upper South." (Baton Rouge, La.) JSH, May, 1945, v.XI, #2, p.177-213.

637 ..."Cotton from Savannah in 1865." (Lexington, Ky.) JSH, Nov. 1955, v.XXI, #4, p.495-512.

638 ..."Henry C. Carey and American Sectional Conflict." Albuquerque: Univ. of New Mexico Press, 1951. Publications in History #3. 8vo, cl, 127pp.

639 ..."Some Northern Wartime Attitudes toward the Post-Civil War South." (Baton Rouge, La.) JSH, Aug. 1944, v.X, #3, p.253-274. Greed to siphon off the wealth of the South, dominate its politics, fueled Reconstruction policies.

640 **SMITH, Gerald J.**
"Reminiscences of the Civil War by J.W. Frederick." In: Ga. Hist. Quart., 1975, v.LIX, p.154-159.

641 **SMITH, Gerrit**
"Gerrit Smith on Bailing of Jefferson Davis." Sabin-82613. n.p. (Peterboro?) (1864) (1867, June 6) $125. Folio, p.(3) Defends Davis' bail.

642 ..."No Treason in Civil War (speech). "N.Y., June 8, 1865." N.Y., American News Co., 1865. 8vo, wraps, 25pp., Sabin-82651. "Was folly to try Davis for treason."

643 ..."No More Punishment of the South, Gerrit Smith to Prof. Lewis, Nov. 6, 1866." n.p., Folio, p.(4) Sabin-82648.

644 **SMITH, Glenn Curtiss, Edt.**
"Diary of a Virginia Schoolmistress, 1860-1865." Harrisonburg, Va., Madison Quart. (College) 1949. Vol.IX, #2, March. Entire issue. p.35-58.

645 **SMITH, Goldwin**
"The Confederate Cruisers." In: Independent, N.Y., 1902, v.54, p.849-851.

646 ..."England and the War of Secession." In: Atlantic, 1902, v.89, p.303-311.

647 **SMITH, Gustavus Woodson**
"The Battle of Seven Pines. By Gustavus W. Smith, formerly Major-General, Confederate States Army." N.Y., C.G. Crawford Print, 1891. Tall 8vo, cl, maps,

facsms., 202pp. $150-slip case, $100-bmk-105.

...Dayton, Oh., Morningside (1975) Map end-sheets added. $15.

648 ..."Confederate War Papers. Fairfax Court House, New Orleans, Seven Pines, Richmond and North Carolina. By Gustavus W. Smith, late Major General Confederate States Army." N.Y., Atlantic Pub. & Engr., 1884. 12mo, cl, port(front), fldg. maps, (2), 381pp. $30, $85, $70-g,
...Do: second edition. $200-r.

649 ..."The Georgia Militia about Atlanta." In: B & L, IV, p.331-335.

650 ..."The Georgia Militia during Sherman's march to the sea." In: B & L, IV, p.667.

651 ..."General J.E. Johnston and G.T. Beauregard at the Battle of Manassas, July, 1861." N.Y., C.G. Crawford, 1892. 8vo, wraps, fldg. map, iv, (6)-48pp. $125-ob.

652 ..."A "Great Captain" at the Battle of Seven Pines." N.Y., 1894. 81 typescript legal leafs. $500, $800. An unpublished mssc., in which Smith critizes Johnston in a review of this action (Seven Pines). After criticisms in both Johnston's and Smith's books.

653 ..."Memoranda on Longstreet and Chickamauga." Original typed mssc., 4to, 47pp., c.1885. With handwritten corrections in Smith's hand. Critical of Longstreet. $125.

654 ..."Two days battle at Seven Pines, (Fair Oaks)." In: B & L, II, p.220-263.

655 ..."Some war history never published." In: SHSP, 1906, v.XXXIV, p.128-143. Extensive letters by Jeff Davis.

656 ..."Report of the operations of the militia, from Oct. 13, 1864 to Feb. 11, 1865, by Maj-Generals G.W. Smith and Wayne, together with memoranda by Gen. Smith, for the improvement of the State military organization." Macon, Ga., Boughton, Nesbit, Barnes and Moore State Printers, (1965). 8vo, wraps, 29pp. Harwell-464. $275-ob.

657 **SMITH, H.A.**
"The author of "Dixie". From Taylor's Mag." In: CV, 1932, v.40, p.17-20.

658 **SMITH, Hampden Harrison**
"Jefferson Davis. A Character Sketch." Blackstone, Va., n.d., 32mo, port on wraps, 40pp. $20.

659 ..."Stonewall Jackson. A Character Sketch." Blackstone, Va., n.d. (c.1920) 32mo, port on wraps, 48pp.

660 ..."Robert E. Lee. A Character Sketch." Blackstone, Va., n.d. 32mo, port on wraps, 48pp.

661 ..."J.E.B. Stuart. A Character Sketch." (Richmond, Va., Williams Ptg. Co., 1932) 32mo, port on wraps, 32pp.

662 ..."Gen. N.B. Forrest. A Character Sketch." p.29-33.

663 **SMITH, Hank**
"Mining and Indian Fighting in Arizona and New Mexico, 1858-1861: Memoirs of Hank Smith." Edt. Hattie M. Anderson. (Canyon, Texas: Panhandle Plains Historical Review) 1928, v.1, #1, p.67-115. Maps. Recounts affair at Fort Fillmore.

664 ..."With the Confederates in New Mexico. Memoirs of Hank Smith. Edited by Hattie M. Anderson." In: PPHR, v.II, p.65-97. (1929)

665 **SMITH, Hannis S.**
"The futile "Star of the West"." In: JMH, Jan. 1952, v.14, p.63-66. The career in merchant service and CSNavy, 1855-1863.

666 **SMITH, Harold**
"Leonidas Polk, Bishop and General." In: Churchman, ns, Jan. 1918, v.XXXII, p.35-39. Bishop of Louisiana and General in the CSA.

667 **SMITH, Harold F.**
"The 1861 Struggle for Lexington, Missouri." In: CWH, June 1961, v.VII, #2, p.155-166, port, pl.

668 **SMITH, Harold T.**
"The Know Nothings in Arkansas." In: Ark. Hist. Quart., Winter, 1975, v.XXXIV, #4, p.291-303.

669 **SMITH, Harry Allen**
"The Rebel Yell: being a carpetbagger's attempt to establish the truth concerning the screech of the Confederate soldier plus lesser matters appertaining to the peculiar habits of the South." N.Y., Garden City, Doubleday, 1954, 8vo, cl, 124pp. Humorous.

670 **SMITH, Henry King, Jr.**
Some Encounters With General Forrest." n.p., n.d. (c.1956). 8vo, stiff wraps, illus. 10pp. Johnsonville Battle of 1864. Several battles in West Tennessee.

670a **SMITH, Isaac Noyes**
"A Virginian's dilemma (the Civil War diary of Isaac Noyes Smith in which he describes the activities of the 22nd regiment of Virginia Volunteers, Sept. to Nov. 1861." Edt: William C. Childers. In: W.Va. Hist. 1966, v.27, p.173-200.

671 **SMITH, J. Calvin**
"Maps of the Southern States, covering the Civil War Period." Cincinnati, Ohio: Kag Industries, 1967. A reprint edition of 300 copies (9-maps) Pub. in Germany, Spring, 1861. 15 1/2x19" fldg. Flat-$7.

672 **SMITH, James Harmon**
"The State of Georgia showing major campaigns areas and engagements sites on War Between the States 1861-1865." Atlanta, Ga., Georgia Department of Commerce, 1961. Color map 73x61cm., (80) numbered sites.

673 **SMITH, James Power**
"Battlefield markers-Spotsylvania and Jefferson Counties." In: SHSP, Sept. 1916, v.XLI, p.145-146. Also: Apr. 1914, v.XXXIX, p.100-101.

674 ..."Stonewall Jackson at Chancellorsville. A paper read before the Military Historical Society of Massachusetts, on the first of March, 1904." Read Mar.4, 1904, at MHSM, in V.5, p.351-376. Richmond, Va., Pub. by R.E. Lee Camp #1, Confederate Veterans, (1904). 8vo, wraps, 23pp.

675 ..."Stonewall Jackson's Last Battle." In: B & L, v.III, p.204-214.
...In: Cent., Oct., 1886, illus., p.921-926.

676 ..."With Stonewall Jackson in the Army of Northern Virginia by James Power Smith, Capt. and A.D.C., an artillery corporal and the General's Aide." In: SHSP, Sept., 1920, v.XLIII, (3), (1)-110pp.
...Same, 8vo, cl, 110pp. and Allan's (185pp.). $40.

677 ...Also: issued with Wm. Allan's "Hist. of the Campaign of Gen. T.J. (Stonewall) Jackson in the Shenandoah Valley of Virginia." as No.5, Sept. 1920, issue of SHSP. 295pp., (6) fold-out color maps of battles and troop movements. $75-bmk-161.
...Gaithersburg, MD, 1982 reprint.

678 ..."Stonewall Jackson-his character." In: CV, Oct. 1911, v.XIX, p.496-498.

679 ..."The Religious Character of Stonewall Jackson, an address delivered at the Inauguration of the Stonewall Jackson Memorial Building, Virginia Military Institute, June 23, 1897." Lexington, Va., Stonewall Jackson Memorial Inc., n.d., (1950's?) 8vo, wraps, (16)pp. (Smith was Capt., A.D.C., staff of Gen. Jackson)

680 ..."Mrs. "Stonewall" Jackson." In: SHSP, Sept. 1915, p.323-324. Smith was on Jackson's staff.

681 ..."General Lee at Gettysburg. A paper read before the Military Historical Society of Massachusetts, on the Fourth of April, 1905. By James Power Smith, Captain and A.D.C., to Gen. Ewell." Richmond, Va., Pub. by R.E. Lee Camp #1, Confederate Veterans, (1905). 8vo, wraps, 19pp. (Wm. Ellis Jones Print). $75-b.
...Same: In: SHSP, 1905, v.XXXIII, p.135-

160. (& PMHSM, V, p.377-410) 1905.
...Dayton, Oh., Morningside Bk., 1978.
...In: "Gettysburg Sources," Vol.1. Baltimore: Butternut Press, 1986. p.28-56.

682 **SMITH, James West**
"A Confederate soldier's diary, Vicksburg in 1863." In: SoWest Rev., 1943, v.XXVIII, p.293-327.

683 **SMITH, Jessica Randolph**
"About design of the First Flag." In: CV, 1905, v.13, p.509-510, port., plate.

684 **SMITH, Jodie Arnold**
"Battle Grounds and Soldiers of Arkansas, 1861-1865." In: AHQ, 1947, v.VI, p.180-185.

684a **SMITH, John David**
"Life & Labor of Ulrich Bonnell Phillips." In: GaHQ, Summer, 1986, v.70, #2, p.254-72, port, notes.

685 **SMITH, John Holmes**
"The Battle of Gettysburg." In: SHSP, 1904, v.32, p.189-195.

686 **SMITH, John Julius Pringle**
"The War Between the States, its causes and consequences as now described by Northern expositors. Also, a refutation of calumnies from the same quarter, and a vindication, sustained by documentary evidence, of the South and Southern character, against the slanders upon them." Charleston, S.C., J.D. Parry, 1880. 8vo, wraps, 68pp. Dorn-II 123.

687 **SMITH, Kenneth L.**
"Edmund Ruffin and the Raid on Harper's Ferry." (Richmond) Va. Cavl., Autumn, 1972, v.XXII, #2, p.28-37, ports, illus., color, dbl. pg. cover (color) Harper's Fy.

688 **SMITH, Kennon**
"Virginia Military Institute during the War Between the States." (Richmond, Va.?) 1938?) 8vo, wraps, 5pp. High School essay, Virginia Division of the United Daughters of Confederacy.

689 **SMITH, Lucille**
"The Confederate-Capt. Delagnel (DeLaguel)." Randolph Co. Hist. Soc., Mag. Hist. & Biog., 1942, v.10, p.50-52. Capt. DeLagnel wounded at Rich Mt., recovery at Frank White home. Shetler-721.

689a **SMITH, Malcolm R.**
"Flags of the Confederacy." St. Louis, Mo., River City Pub., 1976. 12mo, wraps, (40)p.

690 **SMITH, Marian Caroline**
"I Remember." Emory, n.p., n.d. (gift of author. 1932) 8vo, wraps, d/e, 27pp. A daughter's remembrances of father in CSA.

691 **SMITH, Marion O.**
"The Sauta Cave Confederate Niter Works." In: CWH, DEc. 1983, v.29, #4, p.293-315.
..."Confederate Saltpetre Mining in Northern Alabama." In: AHQ, 1980, v.42, #1-2, p.72-86.

692 **SMITH, Marshall J., et al**
"Fortification and Siege of Port Hudson." In: SHSP, 1886, v.14, p.305-348.

693 **SMITH, Mary, Capt., Mrs., Mobile, Ala.**
"A Souvenir of the Confederate Veterans Reunion at Chattanooga, Tenn., July 3, 1890; Jackson, Miss., June 2, 1891; New Orleans, La., Apr. 8/9, 1892; Birmingham, Ala., Apr.25/26, 1894; Houston, Tex., May 22/23/24, 1895; Richmond, Va., June 30 and July 1/2, 1896; Nashville, Tenn., June 22-24, 1897; Atlanta, Ga., July 20-23, 1898; Charleston, S.C., May 20-13, 1899; Louisville, Ky., 1900." 16mo, stiff wraps, color-flag: 10th S.C., title: "Mementoes of Dixie by Capt. (Mrs.) Mary Smith, Mobile, Ala., Aid-de-camp, U.C.V., Oklahoma Division." port(front), 43pp. (Charleston, S.C., Walker, Evans & Cogswell Print, 1900) (4th Edition, 1899.)

694 ..."Souvenir of the Confederate Veterans Reunion, Chattanooga, Tenn., July 3, 1890, etc." (n.p., Mrs. Mary Smith, 1898)

Poems. 16mo, wraps-"Mementoes of Dixie", (28)pp.

695 **SMITH, Mason Philip**
"Confederates Downeast." Portland, Maine. Provincial Press, $12. 8vo, cl, 232pp., illus., maps, index. Confederate operations in and around Maine.

696 **SMITH, Minnie E.**
"A Sassy Little Rebel." In: CV, Sept., 1919, v.27, p.333-336. CSA sympathies of little girl in Parkersburg.

697 **SMITH, Mitchell**
"The "neutral" Matamoros trade (with the Confederate states, 1861-1865)." In: SWRev., Autumn, 1952, v.37, p.319-324.

698 **SMITH, Myron J., Jr.**
"Gunboats in a ditch: The Steele's Bayou Expedition, 1863." In: Jour. Miss. Hist., 1975, v.XXXVII, #2, p.165-188. See: Richard S. West, Jr. "Yazoo Pass".

699 **SMITH, N.H., Lt.**
"N.H. Smith's Letters from Sabine Pass, 1863. Edt.: Alwyn Barr." In: ETHJ, October, 1966, v.IV, #2, p.140-143.

700 **SMITH, Nannie Davis, Miss.**
"Reminiscences of Jefferson Davis." In: CV, 1930, v.38, p.178-182, port.

701 **SMITH, Norfleet S.**
"History of the Scotland Neck Mounted Riflemen, later Co.G, 3rd North Carolina Calvary(sic) 41st Reg., C.S.A." Scotland Neck, N.C., n.d. 12mo, wraps, 4pp. With Roster.

702 **SMITH, Ophia Delilah (Smith)**
"The incorrigible "Miss. Ginger"." In: West Tenn.HSP, 1955, v.9, p.93-118. notes. On Virginia Bethel Moon (born 1844), native of Ohio and resident of Memphis, CSA spy and courier.

703 **SMITH, Orren Randolph**
"The dedication and unveiling of the Memorial to..., 1827-1913, who in February 1861 designed the Stars and Bars, the first official flag of the Confederacy, adopted by the Confederate States Congress, Mar. 4, 1861. Under auspices of N.C. Division UDC at Cavalry Episcopal Church, Fletcher, N.C., Sunday afternoon, Nov. 16, 1930." (Fletcher?, N.C., 1930) 8vo, wraps, (4)pp.

704 ..."History of the Stars and Bars." Designed by..., Feb. 1861, at Louisburg, N.C. Adopted by CSA at Montgomery, Ala., Mar. 4, 1861. Raleigh, N.C., Edwards & Broughton Pr., 1913. 8vo, wraps with color flag, tied color ribbons, port, 30pp., illus. of flags, atg. T.M. Pittman, one of contributors-"Stars and Bars, Who Designed It?"

705 ..."The Stars and Bars. A speech by..." 8vo, wraps, port, 13pp. Report: Stars and Bars Comm. Confed. Southern Memorial Ass'n. Richmond, 1915. Joint-Resolution #21 of Gen. Assembly, North Carolina, 1917. Report of "Stars and Bars" Comm. U.C.V., Tulsa Reunion, 1918. $16.50.

706 **SMITH, Paul S.**
"First use of the term "Copperhead." In: Am. Hist. Rev., July 1927, v.XXXII, p.799-800.

707 **SMITH, Ralph J.**
"Reminiscences of the Civil War and other Sketches, by Ralph J. Smith." (San Marcos, Texas? 1911) 8vo, wraps, cover title, front(port) 26pp. (Co. K, 2nd Tex. Inf.)

708 ...Waco, Texas, W.M. Morrison, 1962. Sm.4to, cl, mimeogr., one side, front(port) (3), 50pp. Lim. Edt. 250 copies.

SMITH, Richard H.
"Organization of the Protestant Episcopal Church of Confederate States, AD 1861 and its reunion with the Protestant Episcopal Church in the U.S., AD, 1865." Weldon, N.C., Harrell's Cheap Bk. Job. Print, 1882. 8vo, wraps, cover title, 11pp. Lay Deputy from Diocese of N.C. See: Lawrence L. Pennington's title.

709 **SMITH, Robert Alexander**
"Robert Alexander Smith, a Southern Son. Edt. William Robert Stevenson." In: AlaHQ, Spring, 1958, v.20, p.35-58, notes. Letters from soldier in 3rd Ala. Cav. to wife Eliza Spencer Smith, from Ala., Ga., Tenn., 30 Aug. 1863-1869, Naj. 1864.
...See: Edward Turner Sykes
..."Letters to Robert Smith." In: AHQ, Winter 1958, v.20, #4, p.623-9.

710 **SMITH, Robert B.**
"3300 Federal Prisoners and I"-A Confederate officer recalls a wartime novelty." In: CWTI, Dec. 1975, v.14, #8, p.40-43, illus., port.

711 **SMITH, Robert Freeman**
"John R. Eakin: Confederate Propagandist." In: AHQ, 1953, v.XII, p.316-326.

712 ..."The Confederate attempt to counteract reunion propaganda in Arkansas: 1863-1865." In: AHQ, 1957, v.XVI, p.54-62.

713 **SMITH, Robert Hardy**
"An address to the citizens of Alabama, on the Constitution and Laws of the C.S.A. at Temperance Hall, Mar. 30, 1861." Mobile (Ala.), Daily Register Print, 1861, 8vo, wraps, 24pp.

714 **SMITH, Robert Ross**
"Ox Hill, the most neglected battle of the Civil War, Sept. 1862." Fairfax, Va., Civil War Centennial Commission, Fairfax County and War Between the States. (Vienna, Va., 1961) 8vo, wraps, maps, ports, views, notes, p.18-64.

715 **SMITH, S.L., Mrs. (Blanche Lucas)**
"North Carolina's Confederate Monuments and Memorials." compiled by..., N.C. Div. U.D.C. (Raleigh, N.C., 1941) 8vo, wraps, front, pls., ports, 131pp.

715a **SMITH, Sarah Margaret**
"General Albert Sidney Johnston." In: AHQ, 1947, v.7, #4, p.574-5.

716 **SMITH, Sidney Adair and C. Carter Smith, Jr., Edts.**
"Mobile: 1861-1865. Notes and a Bibliography." Chicago: The Wyvern Press of S.F.E., Inc., Mobile, Alabama, Graphics, Inc. (1964). Tall 8vo, pict. wraps, port, illus., map, 52pp.

717 **SMITH, Susan E.D., Mrs.**
"The soldier's friend; being a thrilling narrative of Grandmaw Smith's four years experience, as matron, in the hospitals of the South, during the late disastrous conflict in America. Revised by Rev. John Little and dedicated to the Rebel Soldiers." Memphis, Tenn., Bulletin Pub. Co., 1867. 12mo, cl, port front, 300pp. about 100pp. of letters from CSA soldiers. $100-g, $200-ob.

718 **SMITH, Sydney K.**
"Life, army record and public services of D. Howard Smith, by Sydney K. Smith." Louisville, Ky., Bradley and Gilbert Co., 1890. 8vo, front(port), 211pp. With Morgan's command. $300-ob.

719 **SMITH, Thomas Burton, Gen.**
"Twentieth Tennessee Regiment." In: CV, 1910, v.XVIIII, p.577.

720 **SMITH, Thomas C.**
"Here's Yer Mule. The Diary of Thomas C. Smith, 3rd Sergeant, Company "G", Wood's Regiment, 32nd Texas Cavalry, C.S.A. March 30, 1862-December 31, 1862." Waco, Texas, The Little Texas Press, W.M. Morrison Pub., 1958 (The Midlothian Mirror, Midlothian, Texas) Thin, 8vo, cl, facsm., music score, 40pp. Lim. Edt., 150 copies, in leather.
...Waco, Texas: The Little Texan Press, W. M. Morrison, 1958. 8vo, (10), 40pp. Lim. Edt. $100. $40-Bm. DeLuxe: 3/4 leather, lim. edt. 100 copies.

721 **SMITH, Thomas H.**
"Crawford County 'Es Trooly Dimecratic: A Study in Midwestern Copperheadism." In: Ohio Hist., 1967, v.LXXVI, p. 33-53.

722 **SMITH, Thomas, Col.**
"Eulogy on Gen. W.H. Payne from good old Rebels." (From Richmond News-Leader, Jan. 28, 1909) In: SHSP, 1908, v.36, p.285-293. Other speakers: Leigh Robinson, p.293-353.

723 **SMITH, Tom**
"The true description of the fight between the "Merrimac" and "Monitor" in Hampton Roads, Sunday Mar. 9, 1862. as witnessed by Capt. Tom Smith." Suffolk, Va., Robt. Hardy Pub., 1986, 8vo, wraps, 12pp.

724 **SMITH, Treadwell**
"Treadwell Smith's Diary of the Civil War, Oct. 17, 1859-April 20, 1865." Berryville, Virginia-Civil War Centennial Comm., Berryville & Clarke Co. Chamber of Commerce, n.d., 12mo, wraps, 18pp.

725 **SMITH, Tunstall, Edt.**
"Richard Snowden Andrews, Lieutenant-Colonel the First Maryland Artillery (Andrew's Battalion) Confederate States Army; a Memoir, Edt. by Tunstall Smith." Baltimore: Press of Sun Print, 1910. 8vo, cl, colored front, facsms, pls, ports, 151pp.

726 ..."James McHenry Howard. A Memoir." Baltimore: Privately Printed, 1916. 8vo, bds., ports, 27pp. Howard served with Co. C, 1st Md. Infty. $175.
...1915. Bmk $75.00.

727 **SMITH, W. Angie, Rev.**
"Robert E. Lee. An Appreciation." An address by..., to members of the Dallas Southern Memorial Association, on their Annual Robert E. Lee Day, Jan. 15, 1941." n.p., 12mo, stiff wraps (color flag), 133, (1)p.

728 **SMITH, W. Wayne**
"An Experiment in Counterinsurgency: The Assessment of Confederate Sympathizers in Missouri." (Houston, Tex.) JSH, Aug. 1969. v.XXXV, #3, p.361-380. $8.

729 **SMITH, William (Confederate Seaman)**
"The Jeff Davis Piracy Case. Full report of the trial of...for piracy, as one of the crew of the Confederate privateer, the Jeff Davis. Before Judge Grier and Cadwalader in the circuit court of the U.S., eastern district of Penna., held at Phildelphia, Oct., 1861." By D.F. Murphy of the Phila. Bar. Phila: King & Baird Print, 1861 (Sabin-84728) 8vo, wraps (and cover title), (2), 7-100pp., dbl-column, 160pp.(?)

730 **SMITH, William Alexander**
"The Anson Guards, Company C, Fourteenth Regiment North Carolina Volunteers 1861-1865." Charlotte, N.C., Stone Pub. Co., 1914. 12mo, cl, (8), 368pp., ports, incl. front. $500-ob, $400-b. Unit Rosters. Sabin-84734. See: Preston L. Ledford; Thos. F. Forrest.
...(Wendell, N.C., Broadfoot's Bookmark, 1978 Reprint. 500 copies)

731 ..."First Secession Flag. The raising and taking down of the flag at Ansonville in February, 1861." In: N.C. Booklet, April, 1917, XVI, #4, p.219-226. (pamphlet)

732 **SMITH, William B.**
"Recovery of the Great Seal of the Confederacy." In: SHSP, 1916, v.41, p.20-33.

733 **SMITH, William Henry**
"With Sibley in New Mexico: The Journal of William Henry Smith. Edt. Walter A. Faulkner." In: WTHAYB, v.XXVII, p.111-142. (Hank Smith Memoirs?)

734 **SMITH, William Russell**
"An address to the people of the Second Congressional District of the State of Alabama." Richmond, Jan. 20, 1865. Broadside: 10 1/2x6 1/2"

735 ..."The history and debates of the Convention of the People of Alabama, begun and held in the City of Montgomery, on the 7th day of Janauary, 1861; in which is preserved the speeches of the secret sessions and many valuable state papers. By Wil-

liam R. Smith, one of the Delegates from Tuscaloosa." Montgomery: White, Pfister & Co.; Tuscaloosa: D. Woodruff; Atlanta: Wood, Hanleiter, Rice & Co., 1861. 8vo, cl, viii, 464, xii, $325., $400.

...Spartanburg, S.C., Reprint Co., 1975. See: Easby-Smith (Mildred) $25.

736 ..."Reminiscences of a long life; historical, political, personal and literary." Vol. 1, Washington: W.R. Smith, Sr. (1889). 12mo, cl, 375, (1)p., 8-ports, incl. front. $200-cather-brown. Historical and biographical sketches, principally in Tuscaloosa, Ala. No others published.

737 ..."The Royal Ape: a dramatic poem." Richmond: West & Johnston, 1863. Story of Washington life at time of battle of Bull Run. Owen. Satire against Lincoln, 8vo, wraps, 85pp.

738 ..."The Secession Convention." This and three following items: Owen, p.1162.

739 ..."Circular to the voters of the counties of Tuscaloosa, Fayette, Marion, Winston, Walker, Blout and Jefferson. Issued from "Camp of Instruction", Tuscumbia, October 17, 1861." Broadside: 9x6". Smith was Col. of 26th Ala. Reg. Inf. CSA was elected to CSA Congress at this election.

740 ..."Circular, to the citizens of Tuscaloosa County, with resolutiona and appealing for support of candidates, R. Jemison, Jr., and William R. Smith, to election to the Secession Convention of 1861." Broadside: 9x7"

741 **SMITH, William Waugh**
"Battle of Spotsylvania Courthouse." In: SHSP, 1904, v.32, p.210-215.

742 ..."General Lee to the Rear." In: SHSP, 1880, v.8, p.562-566.

743 **SMITH, William, General**
"Reminiscences of First Manassas." In: SHSP, 1882, v.10, p.433-444.

744 ..."Reminiscences of the War. Skirmish at Fairfax Courthouse, May 31, 1861." In: SHSP, 1882, v.10, p.368-379.

..."An Eye-witness Account of the Skirmish at Fairfax Courthouse." Fairfax County & the War between the States, p.1-10. Vienna, Va., Fairfax County Civil War Centennial Comm., 1961. Smith corrects Union reports of skirmish.

745 ..."Unveiling statue to Gov. Smith (Richmond Times-Dispatch)." 1906, v.34, p.222-238. See: Judge Jas. Keith.

746 **SMYRL, Frank H.**
"Texans in the Union Army, 1861-1865." In: SwHQ, October 1961, v.LXV, #2, p.234-250.

747 ..."Unionism in Texas, 1856-1861." In: SwHQ, October, 1964, v.LXVIII, #2, p.172-195.

748 **SMYTH BLUES**
See: John S. Apperson

749 **SMYTH COUNTY, Va.**
"Smyth County, Families and History." Pulaski, Va., B.D. Smith, 1974. 8vo, stiff wraps, illus., maps, index, 70pp. Annotated roster of Confederates from county, taken from "Hardesty's Historical and Geographical Encyclopedia."

750 **SMYTH, Clifford**
"Robert E. Lee, who brought the South back to the Nation." New York-London: Funk & Wagnells, 1931, v.XX-Builders of America set. 12mo, fabricoid, 172pp.

751 **SMYTH, Thomas, Rev.**
"Autobiographical notes, letters and reflections. Edited by his granddaughter Louisa Cheves Stoney." Charleston, S.C., Walker, Evans & Cogswell, 1914. 8vo, cl, illus., (ports, coat-of-arms) 784pp. For 40 years minister 2nd Church, (Presbyterian) Charleston, S.C. Relates to secession and the war, 1860-1865. p.547-675. Smith genealogy, 743-751.

752 ..."The Sin and the Curse; or, the Union, the true source of disunion and our present duty in the present crisis. A discourse

preached on the occasion of the day of humiliation and prayer appointed by the governor of South Carolina, on Nov. 21, 1860, in the Second Presbyterian Church, Charleston, S.C., pub. by request." Charleston: Evans & Cogswell, 1860. 8vo, wraps, 24pp. Sabin-85324.

753 ..."The War of the South vindicated and the war against the South Condemned. A discourse preached on the occasion of the appointment of the now sectionalized General Assembly of the O.S. Presbyterian Church of the 4th of July as a Day of Prayer for the Lincoln usurpation." (Charleston?, 1861?) Sabin-85339- "possibly never printed until appears": "Southern Presbyterian Review", April, 1863, v.15, p.479-514.

754 **SMYTHE, Augustine T., Jr.**
"History of the United Daughters." In: CV, Feb. 1911, v.XIX, p.61-62.

755 ..."Torpedo and Submarine attacks on the Federal Blockading Fleet off Charleston during the War of Secession." Charleston, S.C., 1908. In: Yearbook fo the City of Charleston. 8vo, p.53-64.
...(Virginia, 1907) Charlottesville, Va. Univ.. 8vo, wraps, 14pp.

756 **SMYTHE, David Porter**
"Some Civil War letters of David Porter Smythe. Edt: John Thomas Duncan." In: WTHA Year Book, 1961, v.37, p.147-176. Twelve letters of surgeon, 1st Tex. Reg. mounted rifles to his wife, April 21-Dec. 6, 1861.

757 **SMYTHE, Gerald**
See: Wm. Gordon McCabe.

758 **SMYTHE, H. Gerald**
"Robert E. Lee; a retrospect and an appreciation." In: CV, Jan. 1921, v.XXIX, p.6-8.

759 **SMYTHE, James M.**
"Ethel Somers; or, the Fate of the Union, by a Southerner." Augusta, Ga., H.D. Norell, 1857. 12mo, cl, 382pp. (Wright II-2281) On slavery and States Rights.

759a **SNAIR, Dale S.**
"Lt. Thomas P. Bell, CSN, & the action at Trent's Reach." In: Blue & Gray Mag., 1986, v.3, #4, p.23-8.

760 **SNEAD, Claiborne**
"Address by Col. Claiborne Snead at the Reunion of the Third Georgia Regiment, at Union Point, on the 31st July, 1874. History of the Third Georgia Regiment and the career of its first command, Gen. Ambrose R. Wright." Augusta, Ga., Chronicle & Sentinel Pr., 1874. sm.8vo, wraps, 11pp. (dbl. col.)
...Savannah, Ga., 1874, wraps, 68pp. From: "State Participation in C.W."

761 **SNEAD, Thomas L(owndes)**
"The fight for Missouri. From the election of Lincoln to the death of Lyon. By Thomas L. Snead, A.D.C. of the Governor; acting Adjutant-General of the Missouri State Guards; Chief of Staff of the Army of the West; Member of the Confederate Congress. With maps." N.Y., Charles Scribner's Sons, 1886. 12mo, cl, viii, 322pp. Advs.(6), 2-maps (1-fldg.) Same for 1888.

762 ..."The Conquest of Arkansas." In: B & L, v.3, p.441-461.

763 ..."First Year of the War in Missouri." In: B & L, v.1, p.262-277.

764 ..."With Price East of the Mississippi." In: B & L, v.2, p.1-9.

765 **SNIDER, Denton Jaques**
"The American Ten Years War, 1855-1865." St. Louis, Mo., Sigma Pub. Co., 1906. 12mo, cl, 527pp.

766 **SNOW, Elliot**
"The Metamorphosis of the "Merrimac." In: USNIP, Nov. 1931, v.LVII, p.1518-1521.

767 **SNOW, William Parker, Capt.**
"Lee and his generals..." N.Y., Fairfax Press, (Crown Pub. Co., 1982)

...."Southern Generals, who they are and what they have done." N.Y., Charles B. Richardson, 1865. 8vo, cl, (or full calf), 18 engravings, incl. front, for each of the biographies (3)-473pp. $50.

...Pub. anonymously, republished in 1867 as "Lee and His Generals." 1/2 lt. $75-bmk.

768 ...Southern Generals, their lives and campaigns, by William Parker Snow." N.Y.,Charles B. Richardson, 1866. 8vo, cl, ports, 500pp. (6), 9-500, maps(3).

...London: Sampson, Low & Sons, 1865. 8vo, cl, 17 ports, (6), 9-473pp. Ads, (3).

..."Lee and His Generals, by Capt. Wm. P. Snow." N.Y., Richardson & Co., 1867. 8vo, cl, ports, 500pp. (2), v-vi, (2), 9-500, + ads(2). Copy: 3/4 calf.

769 **SNOWDEN, Yates, Edt.**
"Bulletin of the University of South Carolina, part II, No.VIII: War Records." (Columbia, S.C., R.L. Bryan Co., 1907) 8vo, wraps, 48pp. South Carolina College's role in the war, including Capt. Iredell Jones'-"The South Carolina College Cadets." (12pp.)

770 ..."Charleston in War-Time, 1861-1865." Caption title. (Charleston, S.C., 1909) In: Yearbook of the City of Charleston for 1908. Sig. "Y.S." 8vo, p.41-58, Appendix.

771 ..."Confederate Books. The titles of many of them and how they were made." Charleston, S.C., Daggett Print, 1903. 8vo, cover title, 8pp.

772 ..."War-Time Publications (1861-1865). From the Press of Walker, Evans & Cogswell Co. An addendum to "One Hundred Years of Wecco", by Yates Snowden." Charleston, S.C., Walker, Evans and Cogswell, 1922. 12mo, wraps, 30pp. $65. From the (Columbia) State, Jan.30, 1921, revised and enlarged.

773 ..."Marching with Sherman. A review...of the Letters and Campaign Diaries of Henry Hitchcock, Maj., Asst.-Adjt. Gen. of Volunteers." Columbia, S.C., The State, 1929, 8vo, wraps, p.(5)-6-58. Reprint of Yale Press.

774 **SNYDER, Ann E., Mrs.**
"The Civil War from a Southern Standpoint." Nashville, Tenn., M.E. Church South Pub., 1890. 12mo, cl, illus., incl. front, maps, 308pp.

...Editions: 1891, (360pp.); 1893-"Revised and arranged for use in schools and colleges", 356pp.

775 ..."A Narrative of the Civil War for schools and colleges (a supplementary reader) abridgment of the author's larger volume, "The Civil War", 1890." Nahville, Tenn: Barbee & Smith, 1899. $25. 12mo, cl, and bds., color flag front, illus., 192pp.

776 **SNYDER, J.F.**
"The Capture of Lexington." (Columbia, Mo., Oct., 1912, v.VII, #1, p.9. With Gen. Price in the battle. Reprint, in wraps, of above

777 ..."The Democratic State Convention in Missouri in 1860." Columbia, Missouri: Hist. Review, Jan. 1908, vol.II-#2, p.112-130. Missouri troubles preceeding the Secession Convention.

778 **SNYDER, Perry A.**
"Shreveport, Louisiana, 1861-1865: From Secession to Surrender." In: Louisiana Studies, v.XI, p.50-70.

779 **SOBOL, Donald J.**
"The Lost Dispatch; a story of Antietam." N.Y., F. Watts, (1958) 12mo, cl, 173pp., illus., map. Fiction, based on historic facts. $20. See also under title.

780 **SOCIETY of Philatelic Americans**
Series of Confederate notables engraved plates with biographical note on leaf, 250 copies each, e.g., Robert E. Lee, Jefferson Davis, Jeb Stuart, Judah P. Benjamin, Stonewall Jackson, John Hunt Morgan, Beauregard, Braxton Bragg, Joseph E.

Johnston, John Slidell, John N. Maffitt. $1 each. See: Geo. N. Malpass

781 **"SOCIETY of the "Old Boys**
of Hampton Academy." First Annual Meeting; an address by J.B. Hope and Poem by W.G. McCabe. Richmond, 1861, 8vo, wraps.

782 **"SOCIETY of the Army and Navy**
of the Confederate States in the State of Maryland. Roster of officers and members of the Society of the Army and Navy of the Confederate States in the State of Maryland, with Constitution and By-laws." Baltimore: Sun Job Print, 1883. 8vo, wraps, 43pp. Name, rank, branch of service and address.
...Same, for 1888, with 36pp. See: W.W. Goldsborough.

783 **"SOCIETY of the Ex-Confederate**
Soldiers in Hampshire County (W.Va.) Constitution." (cover title) (Romney, W.Va., 1883?) 8vo, wraps, 8pp. "In answer to a call in the "South Branch Intelligencer", a number of ex-Confed. soldiers, Hampshire Co. met in court-house 31st July, 1883..."

784 **SOHLBERG, Oscar Nathaniel**
"Joseph Eggleston Johnston (1807-1891)." In: Professional Memoirs, Corps. of Engineers, U.S. Army and Engineering Dept.-at-large." Washington Engineer School, Washington Barracks, v.IX, #44, p.204-206. 1917.

785 **"SOLDIER in Our Civil War, The.**
Abridged Edt.-Famous War Pictures illustrating the Valor of the Soldiers as Displayed on Battlefields. Sketched on the spot by Famous War Artists." New York: Stanley-Bradley Pub. Co. (1894) Oblong folio, 256pp., orig. plates: Frank Leslie Illustrated Newspaper, 1861-1865. Only description is under each plate. 256 plates.

786 **SOLDIER'S HOMES**
See: "Southern States and Veterans Soldiers." U.S. Grant's letter concerning CS homes, Richmond Dispatch.

787 **"SOLDIER'S NEWS LETTER. v.I, #1."**
Ship Island, Harrison Co., Miss., May 9, 1862. 8vo, 4pp. Edt: A.W. Eastman. Contains report of the Battle of New Orleans.

788 **SOLDIERS AND SAILORS' Monument at Richmond, Virginia.**
See: "Dedication of...", "Unveiling of..." and Robt. C. Cave.

789 **SOLDIERS of Florida**
In the Seminole Indian, Civil and Spanish-American Wars. Prepared and published under the supervision of the Board and State Institutions, as authorized by Chapter 2203 Laws of Florida, approved May 14, 1903. Live Oak, Florida. Democrat and Job Print, (1903?) 8vo, wraps, or marb. bds., sheep spine, 368pp. Almost entirely (p.36-338) pertaining to the Confederacy, muster rolls of various Florida Regiments, short historical sketches, military organizations and biographical. $150. Compiled by Fred L. Robertson.
...Macclenny, Fla., Richard J. Ferry, 1983.

789a **SOLEY, James Russell, Prof., USN**
"The Confederate Cruisers." In: B&L, v.4, p.595-9, ports.

790 **SOME ACCOUNT**
Of both sides of the American War. In: Black Edn. Mag., Dec. 1861, v.XC, p.768-779.

791 **SOME CONFEDERATE LETTERS:**
Alabama, Georgia and Tennessee. Contributed by Edmund Cody Burnett. In: Ga. H.Q., June 1937, v.XXI, #2, p.188-203. $8.

792 **SOME FLORIDA heroes**
At second Battle of Cold Harbor. In: CV, Aug. 1903, v.XI, p.363-365.

792a **"SOME Interesting Old Letters.**
In: Benton Co. Pioneer, April 1967, v.12, p.36-47.

793 **"SOME WAR HISTORY never published..."**
See: Gustavus Woodson Smith.

793a **SOMERS, Dale A.**
"New Orleans at War: a merchant's view." In: LaH., 1973, v.14, p.48-68.

794 **SOMERSET, Edward Adolphus Seymour, 12th Duke**
"Speech: The Monitor and Merrimac. Parliament by First Lord of the Admiralty." In: SHSP, 1888, v.16, p.218-222.

795 **SOMMERS, Richard**
"Fury at Fort Harrison." In: CWTI, Oct., 1980, v.19, #6, p.12-28, illus., ports, maps.

796 **SOMMERS, Richard J.**
"The Dutch Gap Affair: Military Atrocities and rights of negro soldiers." In: CWH, March, 1975, v.XXI, #1, p.51-64.

797 ..."Richmond Redeemed-the Siege at Petersburg. Foreword: Frank E. Vandiver."
Garden City, N.Y., Doubleday Co., 1981. Tk.8vo, cl, dj, xxii, (2), 670pp. Bibliog. (591)-628, index, maps, ports, illus.

798 **"SONANDER" (pseud.)**
George E. Kendall-"An humble belisarius."

798a **"SONG of the Trinity**
Air--'Rock of Ages.'" Augusta, Ga., Dec. 30, 1864. Broadside 22 x 15 cm., decr. borders. $200. Title-head from the Baptist Banner. Bmk-'unrecorded.'

799 **"SONGS OF THE SOUTH."**
Richmond, Va., 1864. 12mo, wraps, 70, iipp. Goodspeed $650. Unrecorded by Gdsp. but a variant from Crandall-3270/3271.

800 **"SONGS from Georgia."**
Atlanta, The Grand Commandry Knights Templar of Georgia, 1916. (Atlanta, 1916?) 8vo, wraps, cover-title, illus.-cover, 16pp. Civil War poetry, Confederacy.

801 **SONGS between the States.**
Expressions of the independent spirit and deep emotional sentiment of our people-Songs of the Blue and the Gray, sung at home, in camp, on the march, in prison, 1861-1865. Washington, D.C., 1946. (Judd & Detweiler, Dec. 1946) (Design and Director, Lester Douglas.) 12mo, wraps, 41, (1)p. printed in pict. blue and red.

802 **SONGS of Dixie.**
A Collection of Camp Songs, Home Songs, Marching Songs, Plantation Songs, by Favorite Authors. N.Y., Chicago, S. Brainard's Sons, 1890. sm.4to, stiff wraps-cl. spine, 142 songs. "Here's Your Mule", "Lee's Address", (also his "Farewell Address"), "Goober Peas", "Southern Marseillaise", "Bonnie Blue Flag", etc.

803 **SONGS of the South**
And Other Poems By Kentucky. "Dedicated to Kentucky's Dead, who lie on every Southern battlefield and in the graveyard of every U.S. prison; to those sworn into the Confederate service who have been foully murdered as guerillas; and to those who have been shot on their way to the C.S.A." Backstrip lettered, "War Lyrics, etc." (London, 1865?) 16mo. See: Crandall-3270/3271, Richmond, Va., J.W. Randolph, 1862/1863, p.71. See: "War Lyrics and Songs of the South."

804 **SONNICHSIN, Charles Leland**
"Major McMullen's invasion of New Mexico." In: Password of El Paso Hist. Soc., 1957, v.II, p.38-43.

805 **SONS OF LIBERTY**
"Proceedings of the Grand Council of the State of Indiana, at their meeting, held on the 16th and 17th of Feb., 1864." (Indianapolis, Ind.) 1864. 8vo, wraps, 9pp.

806 **SONS of Confederate Veterans (United Sons of CV)**
"Constitution of United Sons of Confederate Veterans. Revised and adopted by the Seventh Annual Convention, Dallas, Texas, April 22-25, 1902." St. Louis, Mo.,

	W.F. Rower & Co., 1902. 16mo, wraps, 28pp. Originally adopted July, 1896.
807	..."Minutes of the Sons of Confederate Veterans Annual Reunion." Waco, Texas, ports, wraps, 8vo, 1914 the Society was changed from "United" to "Sons" of Confederate Veterans.
808	..."The Gray Book; published by the Gray Book Committee S.C.V., by authority and under the auspices of the Sons of Confederate Veterans." (n.p., 1920) (sig) "A.H. Jennings, Chrm." 8vo, wraps, cover title, 53, (1)pp. See also under title. (Lynchburg, Va.) 1920. Reprinted by various chapters: Corsicana, Texas, Ft. Worth, Texas, Athens, Texas, Mobile, Ala.
809	..."Report of the Monument Committee, Annual Reunion, Convention, United Sons of Confederate Veterans." Nashville, Tenn. 8vo, wraps, reprinted from minutes of Annual Meet.
810	..."Report of Camp Beauregard, #130, USCV, by W.O. Hart, retiring Comm., Jan. 12, 1910." (New Orleans?, 1910) 8vo, cover title, illus., ports, 13, (1)pp. Port on cover.
811	..."By-laws of Harry Burgwyn Camp, #166, United Sons of Confederate Veterans." Raleigh, N.C., Alford, Bynum and Christopher, 1900. (verso t.p., "Camp Publication No.1) 16mo, wraps, 13pp.
812	..."Charter Members of Harry Burgwyn Camp, #166, United Sons of Confederate Veterans, Raleigh, N.C., including records of ancestors through whom they derive eligibility." Raleigh, N.C., Alford, Bynum & Christopher, 1900. (verso t.p., "Camp Publication #2") 16mo, wraps, 14pp.
813	..."Souvenir Program, 57th Annual Convention, Jackson, Miss., June 3-6, 1952." 4to, wraps, 40pp.
814	..."The Stars & Bars, January, 1924." v.2, #1, 8vo, wraps, 10pp.
814a	..."Alabama Division, 1896-1996." Florence, Ala., Dallas M. & Mary H. Lancaster. 8vo, stiff wraps, 197p. $17.50.
815	**SONS of Confederate Veterans,** Camp Beauregard #130. (brief history of the group) (New Orleans, La., (c.1907), n.d. 8vo, wraps, 20pp.
816	**SONS of Confederate Veterans:** "Report of the "Stars & Bars" Committee." Washington, 1917. 8vo, wraps, 28pp. $30. Detailed study of the origin of the Stars & Bars Battle Flag, concludes that Maj. Orren R. Smith of N.C., sent design to CSA Congress Feb. 1861, and it was accepted over three others, thus refuting the claim of Nicola Marschall. See: Orren R. Smith, Nocola Marschall, Fannie R. Williams, Albert L. Cox, Maj. Edgar E. Hume, Charles C. Jones.
817	**SONS of Confederate Veterans: S.C.** "Minutes of the Fourth Annual Re-Union, United Sons of Confederate Veterans." Charleston: Walker, Evans & Cogswell, 1899, 8vo, wraps, 35pp.
818	**SONS of the South** "S.S. (sideways on front wrappers surrounded by decorative printer's ornaments)." n.p., (1862?) Goodspeeds-601 $2000. 8vo, 16pp. blue wraps. Unrecorded. "to perpetuate Gov. of CSA, preserving white race purity, lectuer on slavery, etc."
819	**SORREL, Gilbert Moxley** "Recollections of a Confederate Staff Officer by Gen. G. Moxley Sorrel, Lieutenant-Colonel and Chief of Staff, Longstreet's 1st Army Corps; Brig.-Gen. Commanding Sorrell's Brigade, A.P. Hill's 3rd Army Corps, ANV, with introduction by Senator John W. Daniel." N.Y., Wash., Neale Print, 1905. $200-jk-138, $150-bmk-105. 12mo, cl, front(port), 315pp., N.Y., Wash.-1917, p.309, port. ...Jackson, Tenn: McCowat-Mercer Press, 1958. Edited by Bell Irvin Wiley. 8vo, cl,

dj, xxii, illus., ports, facsm., not in original edt. Index and append at end. "Civil War Book Club. Edt."

...N.Y., Wash., Neale Pr., 1917, 12mo, cl, port, 309pp. $50, $100-b.

...Dayton, Oh., Morningside Books, 1977, 12mo, cl, front(port), 333pp. Intro: Edwin C. Bearss.

...Wilmington, N.C., Broadfoot Pub. Co., 1987. 8vo, cl, dj, 322, ills. $30.

820 **SOSEY, Frank H.**
"Robert Devoy, a Tale of the Palmyra Massacre." Souvenir Edition. (Palmyra, Mo., Sosey Bros. (1903) (1920). 8vo, boards and cl. spine, decr. endsheets, plates (incl. front) xvi, 157pp. History, not fiction, about execution of ten CSA prisoners. Book originally in serial form in "Palmyra Spector" by the Sosey family. An earlier account can be found in E.F. Perkins-"History of Marion County." 1884, which author used in the account above.

...1st Edition (1903) of 6pp., lf, 172pp., front, 4-plates, 12mo, cl. 2nd and 3rd edts. same year, 1903.

821 **SOSNOWSKI, Sophie**
"The Burning of Columbia." In: Georgia Hist. Quart. (1924), p.195-214. $10.

822 **SOUND of the Confederacy. The**
Col. Beauregard, Johnson and the Volunteers. Playing Dixie's Land, Short Rations, Maryland My Maryland, Bonnie Blue Flag and Others. New York: Westminster Recording Co., n.d. (1960's) Color battle scene of CSA on cover.

822a **SOUTH Alone,**
Should govern the South & African slavery should be controlled by those only who are friendly to it." Charleston, S.C., 1860. 8vo, sewn, 60pp. $25. $100-g.

...3rd Edt., Charleston, S.C., Evans & Cogswell, 1860. 8vo, warps, 60, (2). Sabin 96379.

...4th Edt. same above, heading "Tract I." Originally pub. in Charleston Mercury. See: John Townsend, "Troup", James Henry Hammond.

823 **"SOUTH AND SECESSION. The"**
In: Tyler Quart., Jan., 1932, (9)pp. $8.

824 **SOUTH CAROLINA**
"Acts of the General Assembly of the State of South Carolina, passed in Dec. 1864. Printed by order of the Legislature in conformity with the Statutes at Large & designed to form a part of the thirteenth volume, commencing with the Acts of 1861." Columbia, S.C., Evans & Cogswell, 1865. 8vo, cl, pp.iv, 231-281, vi. Sabin: "All but 25 copies were destroyed in the burning of Evans & Cogswell." Yates Snowden: "In 1866 this was reprinted by the then state printer, Julian Selby, a committee having reported that when Sherman's army reached Columbia the Acts of 1864 had been printed & but 50 copies distributed & the rest burned." The Selby print of 1866 has pp.(2), ii, ii, 231-370, iv, xv.

..."Declaration of the causes which justify the Secession of South Carolina from the Federal Union." Wash: Lester Hargrett, 1843. Facsimile, 7pp. of the 1860 original CSA imprint. One of Hargrett's "Legal Reprints series, Lim. 33 copies. cloth. $65-jk.

825 **SOUTH CAROLINA (pseud.)**
"In the Back-country of South Carolina 1862-1864." In: "Mag. of Hist." 1909, v.IX, p.33-40. Sig: "Carolina South"

826 **SOUTH CAROLINA -Broadside**
"The Union is Dissolved." Charleston Mercury-EXTRA. Passed unanimously at 1:15 o'clock P.M., Dec. 20, 1860, an ordinance to Dissolve the Union between the State of South Carolina and the other States United with her under the compact entitled: "The Constitution of the United

States of America." Folio (Maj. Ed., Willis sale)

827 **SOUTH CAROLINA Cadets**
See: Iredell Jones.

828 **SOUTH CAROLINA DISUNION**
And a Mississippi Valley Confederacy. (Louisville?, 1860?) 8vo, sewn, 15pp. Reprint: Phila., 1863, "Conservative Essays", vol.1, p.116-144. Antecedents of "South Carolina Declaration of Independence", in a Miss. Val. Confed. See: Saml. Smith Nicholas-"Conservative Essays, Legal and Political."

829 **SOUTH CAROLINA UNIVERSITY**
"War Records." (Columbia, S.C., The University, 1908) 12mo, co, 54pp. (contd. from #viii, pt.II) University of South Carolina Bul. #XII. Contains: W.A. Clark's "S.C. College Cadets in the War; Minutes of the Board of Trustee of the S.C. College, 1861-1865; Alumni of the S.C. College who died in service of the CSA.

830 **"SOUTH CAROLINA WOMEN**
in the Confederacy. Records collected by Mrs. A.T. Smythe, Miss M.B. Poppenheim and Mrs. Thomas Taylor. Edt. and published by Mrs. Thomas Taylor, Chairman, Mrs. Smythe, Mrs. August Kohn, Miss. Poppenheim, Miss. Martha B. Washington, State Comm. Daughters of the Confederacy." Columbia, S.C., State Co., 1903-1907. v.I $60, $125. 8vo, cl, ports, incl. front, 2 vols. (2), 413. $40. v.2, edt. and pub. by Mrs. James Conner, Mrs. Thomas Taylor, et al. 243pp.

831 **SOUTH CAROLINA-Chickamauga Commission**
"Ceremonies at the unveiling of South Carolina Monument on the Chickamauga Battlefield, May 27, 1901, together with record of the Commission who suggested and were instrumental in securing and erecting the monument, etc." (n.p., 1901) 8vo, wraps, 50pp.

832 **SOUTH CAROLINA:**
Executive Council Chm. Columbia, Mar.6, 1862. Resolutions outlining details C.S. Military service, Board Examiners, draft system, exemptions, etc., with Docs: by F.J. Moses and S.R. Gist.

833 "Declaration of Independence of the State of South Carolina in Convention at the City of Charleston, December 20, 1860. An Ordinance to dissolve the Union between the State of South Carolina and other states united with her under the Compact entitled "The Constitution of the United States of America." (Charleston, S.C., Evans & Cogswell, (1860) Folio Broadside, 17x24"

834 ...Charleston, S.C., The Ravenel Agency, Inc., Civil War Centennial Commission, reprinting on the 100th Anniversary of the Ordinance of Dec. 20, 1860. Parchment Broadside, folio.

835 ...Executive Council. "Journals of the South Carolina Executive Councils of 1861 and 1862. Edited by Charles E. Cauthen. Heading: The State Records of South Carolina. Columbia: South Carolina Archives Department, 1956. 4to, cl, dj, front (facsm.) (2), xv, 336pp.

836 ...South Carolina Executive Council Chamber: "Circular, Columbia March 6, 1862...Resolution of the Governor and Council by which to raise the quota of 12,500 men between ages of 18 and 45." 8vo, sewn, 4pp. (not in Crandall)

837 ..."Journal of the State Convention: together with the Resolution and Ordinance." Columbia: Johnston and Cavis, 1852. 8vo, wraps, 45pp. $200. State had right to secede from Union but expedience demanded unity.

838 ..."The South Carolina Monument Association. Origin, History and Work, with an account of the Proceedings at the Unveiling of the Monument to the Confeder-

ate Dead and the oration of Gen. John S. Preston at Columbia, S.C., May 13, 1879. Edited by the Recording Sect. of the Association and published through the courtesy of the Proprietor of the News and Courier, Charleston." Charleston, S.C., News and Courier, 1879. 8vo, wraps, front, (5), 6-70pp. See: Joseph Blyth Allston.

839 ...South Carolina: Secession-Broadside. "The Union is Dissolved, Charleston Mercury Extra, passed unanimously at 1:15 o'clock PM, Dec. 20, 1860, an ordinance to Dissolve the Union between the State of South Carolina and the other States United with her under the compact entitled "The Constitution of the United States of America." Folio. Henkel cat. 1118, Oct., 1914.

840 ..."The Charleston Mercury Extra, Sunday morning, Dec. 30, 1860. The News from Washington! Peace or War! The Opinions of the Cabinet, a General Break-Up anticipated. Majority of the cabinet opposed to withdrawing the Troops from Ft. Sumter." 4to, Broadside. Henkel, (above).

...Another copy, later imprint. (above)

841 ..."Attention Southern Men! Down with the Abolition Press! Meet at Schneider's, at 8 o'clock, this night, Dec. 26, 1860." Broadside, 4to, mounted. (above)

842 ..."Four Ordinances. An Ordinance to establish a Patrol. An Ordinance to alter the time of Ringing the Four Bells and to establish a Special Patrol, etc." Anderson, S.C., Dec. 27, 1860. 4to, Broadside. (above)

843 ...South Carolina: Secession and War. Lithographs relating to the First Year of War, from election of Lincoln to Battles around Port Royal, Jan. 1862. Largely Folio. Evacuation of Fort Moultrie by Union troops 25 Dec., 1860; Scene on floating battery in Charleston Harbor during bombardment of Ft. Sumter; Guard of Confederate Boats in Charleston Harbor; General View of Charleston Harbor and City; Castle Pinckney; Fort Sumter Before Bombardment; Bombardment of Fort Sumter; Floating Battery at Charleston with Dr. DeVega's Hospital; General View of Bombardment from Morris Island; Arsenal at Charleston; View of the Interior of the Confed. Ft. Walker during the Bombardment of the National Fleet; Retreat of the Confederate Garrison from Ft. Walker; Birdseye View of Hilton Head Island; Bombardment and Capture of Fts. Walker and Beauregard; View of Beaufort; View of Interior of Ft. Beauregard; Entrance of Steven's Brigade into Beaufort.

844 ..."South Carolina Speaks" These addresses of prominent South Carolinians speaking on South Carolina's participation in the Centennial of the Confederate War Centennial Commission, 1961. 8vo, stiff wraps, color flags, (3), 43pp.

845 ..."The War of Secession, 1861-1865." See: David Duncan Wallace.

846 **SOUTH CAROLINA: Adjutant General** "General Orders, #4: Headquarters. (Signed): R.G.M. Dunovant, Adjt. and Inspector General." Charleston, (S.C.) Dec. 27th, 1860. 1p, 14x8 1/2", in folder. $500. (Parke-Bernet, #2698, May 8, 1968) One week after secession, Anderson moved soldiers to Fort Sumter, S.C., felt Buchanan broke promise and so this was a call for volunteers.

847 **SOUTH CAROLINA: Confederate States of America.**
District Courts-"The Sequestration cases, before the Hon. A.G. Magrath. Reported by-J. Woodruff. (Charleston-1861) 8vo, wraps, 3pp. 1, 5-67, (1)p. Louisville: Lost Cause Press, micro-cd.

848 …"Declaration of the immediate causes which induce and justify the secession of South Carolina from the Federal Union; and the Ordinance of Secession. Printed by order of the Convention." Charleston: Evans & Cogswell, printers to the Convention, 1860. $600-jk-135, $300. 8vo, wraps, 13pp. Cover title has "cause" for "causes" and "streets" for "Street".

…(same), a third variant of Crandall-1873, with both "causes" and "Streets" on wraps. $200. See: Eberstadt, cat-163(#189). Crandall points out: "on other pamphlets than above, "printers to the convention" has been dropped to: "Evans & Cogswell"."

…(same) (the counterfeit at Americus, Ga., (1925), but 12mo, wraps. Both wraps and t.p. have same erros as on the 1st edt.

849 **SOUTH CAROLINA: in SHSP**
See: Wm. A. Courtenay, Wade Hampton, Henry Hart, J.W. Mattison, Thomas Jordan, Armistead L. Long, T.J. Myers, J.L. Orr, Francis A. Porcher, Wm. Wallace.

850 **SOUTH CAROLINIAN, A. (pseud)**
"The Confederate. By a South Carolinian "Respice Finem"." Mobile, Ala., S.H. Goetzel and Co., 1863. (cover title)- Farrow and Dennett, print. 12mo, stiff wraps, 102pp. (1)-list books. In twelve numbers, last is signed "H". $450-jk, $500-bmk.

851 …"Economical Causes of Slavery in the United States and Obstacles to Abolition. By a South Carolinian." See: H. Middleton.

852 **"SOUTH'S BATTLE ABBEY, The."**
Atlanta, Ga., Respess Co.(1896) 12mo, wraps, cover title, 32pp.

853 **SOUTH'S MUSEUM. The**
Davis Mansion thrown open for reception of relics. Battle Abbey of the CSA. Oration by Bradley T. Johnson. In: SHSP, 1895, v.23, p.354-381, ports.

854 **"SOUTH, The**
Newspaper published: Baltimore Complete File, #1, Apr.22, 1861 to #123, Sept. 13, 1861. Folio (old-Harper cat. #105, 1904) Not in Crandall. Federal officers broke into office of Edt: Thos. W. Hall, Jr., who was imprisoned at Ft. McHenry. Files seized, presumably destroyed.

855 **SOUTH, The:**
History and Literature, 1861-1865. Confederate Imprints Collection. N.Y., Arno Press, 1972. 8vo, wraps, 48pp. Prospectus for reprinting CSA Imprints, which was never done.

856 **SOUTHARD, John W., Capt.**
"Capt. Montague: Confederate Free Lance…a strange tale of the Virginia Peninsula." N.Y., Novilist Pub. Co., 1886. War Library, v.7, 220. 4to, wraps, 24pp.

857 **"SOUTHERN BATTLEFIELDS.**
A list of battlefields on and near lines of the Nashville, Chattanooga and St. Louis Ry. and Western and Atlantic Ry., and a brief description of more important battles fought along these lines; also information about Lookout Mountain, Chickamauga Park and the famous engine "General." Nashville: Marshall and Bruce, (1906?) 12mo, wraps, illus., maps, ports, 47pp. Editions: A copy with no place, nor date.

858 **"SOUTHERN BAZAAR, The**
held in St. George's Hall, Liverpool, October 1864. Report of the Proceedings." London: Richard Bentley and Liverpool: Webb and Hunt, n.d. (1864). 12mo, wraps, 51pp. Contributors at end. Money collected for relief of Southern prisoners of war.

859 **"SOUTHERN BIVOUAC."**
Louisville, Ky., E.H. and W.N. McDonald, Publishers, 1882-1885. Vol.I, Sept. 1882-

Sept., 1883, p.iv, 472. Vol.II, Sept. 1883-Sept. 1884, p.iv, 572. Vol.III, Sept. 1884-May 1885, p.(4), 426. In June 1885, B.F. Avery and Sons, pubs. of "Home and Farm", became publishers. Subtitles: "A Monthly Literary and Historical Magazine. Conducted by Basil W. Duke and R.W. Knott. New Series: Louisville, Ky., B.F. Avery and Sons, 1886/1887. Vol. I, June 1885 to May, 1886. N.S. iv, 772pp. Vol.II, June 1886 to May, 1887, iv, 776pp. N.S. volumes sm.4to, cl or full sheep. Facsms, illus., maps (2 color keyed) ports, first 3 vols (old series) few illus. or prts. Vol. I(1883) $125-y.

860 "SOUTHERN BOUQUET, The
A Selection... (Don't Forget My Name) N'Qoubliez Pas Mon Nom, Caprice de Salon, Op. 20, by A Cardona." New Orleans: L. Grunewald, 1864. 9, (1)p., with catalogue of new and popular music pub. by Louis Grunewald.

861 "SOUTHERN CAUSE, The
and Its Prospects. Reprinted from "The Oldham Chronicle" of August 29, 1863." (Oldham: Hirst and Rennie Print) Folio Broadside. Sabin-88316.

862 "SOUTHERN CHIVALRY;
the Adventures of G. Whillikens, CSA. Knights of the Golden Circle; and of Guinea Pete, his negro squire. An epic-doggeral in six books. By a Citizen of the Cotton Country." Philadelphia, (c.1861). 12mo, stitched, 78pp.

863 "SOUTHERN ENTERPRISE EXTRA, The"
Greenville, S.C., Friday May 5, 1865. A Memory of May 5, 1865. Orders Pub. in a paper announcing cessation of hostilities." In: SHSP, 1901, v.XXIX, p.279-281.

864 "SOUTHERN EXPRESS COMPANY (of Georgia)"
Successor to Adams Express Co. Printed receipt forms as published in oblong 8vo. book, bound in boards, cloth back. Names of shippers and receivers and amounts of money sent being filled in with pen and receipts dated from Nov. 25, 1861-Jan. 29, 1862. Richmond Va.

865 ..."To the members of the advisory board, sitting at (Morganton, N.C.)" (Augusta, 1864) July 13, 1864. 21 1/2cm, 4pp. Crandall-2940.

866 "SOUTHERN FIELD
and Fireside Novelette, #1, The." containing "Myra Bruce; or, True Love running roughly", with illustrations; "Riverlands", a charming story of Southern life; and "Five chapters of a history: A Georgia court, forty years ago." Augusta, Ga., James Gardner (1863) 12mo, cl, illus., 35, 41, 19pp. Crandall-3109. (v.1, #1, May 28, 1859, folio, 8pp., 1865?)
...Raleigh, N.C, 1865, New series, wrap Novelette #2. Edward C. Edgeville.

867 SOUTHERN HISTORICAL Assn. Proceesings
of the South. Hist. Convention, August, 1873.
See: Gen. Jubal A. Early "Proceedings, a speech."

868 "SOUTHERN HISTORICAL MONTHLY."
Raleigh, N.C., S.D. Pool, Edt., vol. 1, #1 & 2, Jan.-Feb. 1876. 8vo, wraps, 254pp. Supercedes "Our Living and Our Dead." Only two issues, discontinued after Feb., 1876.

869 SOUTHERN HISTORICAL SOCIETY
See: Annual Meeting, Robert A. Brock, Grand Meeting in N.O., B.H. Hill, Benjamin M. Palmer, Justus Scheibert, "Sketch of the Origin, hist., etc."
"Transactions of the Southern Historical Society, v.1, (2), Jan. 1874 (June, 1875)." Baltimore: Turnbull Bros., 1874-1875. 8vo, cl, 116pp. $75. Running head: Southern Historical Society. v.2, incomplete, ends in

mid-sentence p.116. Cont'd., So. Hist. Soc. Papers, v.1, Jan. 1876, p.61. Pub. as suppl. to the Southern Magazine Jan. 1874-June 1975. (Entry in LC)

870 **SOUTHERN HISTORICAL SOCIETY PAPERS**
"An Index-Guide to the Southern Historical Society Papers. Edt. James I. Robertson, Jr., et al. Millwood, N.Y., Kraus International Publications, (1980). $130. tk. 8vo, cl, v.1, xxii, 498; v.II, viii, 1114pp. Richmond, Va., Civil War Centennial Committee sponsored the project.
...Dayton, Oh., Morningside Bookshop, 1988. 52 vols, plus 2 vol. index. $2,236.00.

871 **"SOUTHERN HISTORICAL SOCIETY PAPERS."**
Richmond, Va., (1876)-1959. 8vo, wraps/cloth, 3/4Mor., 52 vols. 52 Bound volumes $1250-bmk. From 1876-1878, issued 2 vols, per year. 1879 on/ 1 vol. a year. Proceedings of the 1st Confed. Congress vols. XLIV-LII. Paroles of the Army of Northern Va. is v.XV. Rosters of General Officers, etc., etc. is a suppl. at end of v.1, p.(5), (6)-31. Also as a separate of 135pp., See: Chas. Colcock Jones and notes to title. Confederate view of treatment of prisoners at Andersonville by J. Wm. Jones, an offprint, p.(113)-330, 1876. Memorials of Gen. Edward Willis, 1890, offprint from v.XVII. Robert Emory Park's Sketch of the 12th Ala. Inf., 1906, an offprint that ran in serial in SHSP. Index compiled by Mrs. Kate Pleasants Minor, 1913, of vols. 1-38. Complete Index: (See: Jas. I. Robertson) Reprint(about half orig.) Bound set 1,143. Rep-52 vol. set, $1000.

872 ..."Proceedings of the 2nd Annual Meeting of the Southern Historical Society held in Richmond." Richmond, Va., Southern Hist. Soc., 1874, 8vo, wraps, 20pp.
...Proceedings of the Second Annual Meeting, held in the city of Richmond 27th October, 1874." Richmond, Va., James E. Goode, 1874. 8vo, wraps, 20pp. $30.
...Millwood, N.Y., Kraus Reprint, 1980, 1-52 vols, cloth. $2150.

873 ...Gettysburg, Pa., National Historical Society with Civil War Times Illustrated, reprint $16 per vol.

874 **"SOUTHERN HISTORICAL SOCIETY, The"**
from DeBow's Rev. In: New Eclectic (LWL) Oct. 1869, v.5, #4, p.443-446.

875 **SOUTHERN HISTORY ASSOCIATION.**
"Publications of the Southern History Association. Colyer Meriwether, editor." Washington, DC, 1897-1907. 8vo, in 11 vols., map, tab. Quarterly, 1897, 1899, bimonthly, 1900-1907. (v.3-11) $175.

876 **"SOUTHERN HISTORY of the War.**
Official Reports of Battles, as published by order of the Confederate States of America at Richmond, Va." N.Y., Richardson Print, 1863.
...N.Y., Kraus Reprint Co., 1970. 8vo, cl, front(port), 578pp. Author: Edward Alfred Pollard, see under his name.

877 **"SOUTHERN INDEPENDENCE ASSOCIATION,**
London Southern Independence Association of Lond." (Lond, 1863) 8vo, caption title, 3pp.

878 ..."Southern Independence Association, Manchester, Eng., Papers for the People No.IV. Issued by the Southern Independence Association. Central Office, Manchester." (Hyde, 1863?) 8vo, caption title, 4pp. Sabin-88377-"Probably pub. 1863-1864. Nos. 4-8, caption title only, 4pp. each; #9, has 8pp. "Papers of the People", issued by SIA. Tariffs, taxation and causes of the dissolution of the American Union. Hyde: R. Higham and Co., (1864?) Alex-

ander James Beresford B. Hope, Chairman of the S.I.A.

879 **A SOUTHERN LADY**
See: H. Hark! O'er Southrn Hills. Norfolk, Va., Jan. 24, 1862.

880 **"SOUTHERN MAGAZINE, The."**
v.1-17, Jan. 1868-Dec. 1875. Baltimore: Turnbull and Murlock. Vol. 8-17 called also (new ser., v.1-10. Official organ of the Southern Historical Society, from 1874-June 1875. Titles varies: 1868 (v.1-3) The New Eclectic; a monthly magazine of select literature. 1869-1870(v.4-7) The New Electic Magazine. 1871-1875(v.8-17) The Southern Magzine, W.H. Browne, Edt., 1870-1875. Absorbed "The Land We Love", April 1869. No more published. (L.C.) Many articles on the CSA.

881 **SOUTHERN MISCELLANY:**
Essays in History in honor of Glover Moore. Edt: Frank Allen Dennis. Jackson: University of Mississippi, 1981, 8vo, cl, dj, xiii, 202pp. covers largely the Civil War period as represented by Frank Owsley, J.D. B. DeBaow's Review, Wm. Barksdale, Frank Dennis' Shiloh (Beauregard and Johnston), Fabian Val Husley's Miss. troops in ANV.

882 **SOUTHERN MONTHLY COLLECTION**
Of Patriotic Songs and Heroic Poems. Memphis, Tenn: Hutton & Freligh. 1862. wraps, 18mo, 80pp. Sabin-88418.

883 **SOUTHERN PHILATELIST;**
An exponent of advanced philately. Richmond, Va., Dietz Press, 1924. Monthly, vol. 1, November 1924. 8vo, decr. wraps, illus., incl. ports. Largely Confederate stamps, covers. See: "Confederate Stamp Album", "Confederate Philatelist", T.W. Crigler, Jr., states: "The first pub. of the "Confederate Stamp Alliance was the "Confederate Bulletin," Edt. August Dietz of Richmond Va., at irregular intervals from 1942 to 1952, a total of 27 issues. Pub. renamed "Confederate Stamp Album", from Jan. 1956 to Dec. 1959, for a total of 42 issues. Beginning Jan. 1960 it was further renamed "The Confederate Philatelist". It continues to present every quarterly.

884 **SOUTHERN PROPAGANDA**
Printed inside envelope. In: CWH, Sept., 1959, v.5, p.312-314. Includes an example (1862?) addressed to "soldiers of the northwest", signed "South".

885 **SOUTHERN RELIEF FUND OF EUROPE**
"Committee. Charles Atkinson, Charleston (S.C.), Chairman. To Southern States Citizens in Europe and to generous European Friends who sympathise with the Cause of the South." Caption title "confidential". (Liverpool? 1863) 4to, wraps, 7, (1)pp.-Sabin-88469. Letters of appeal dated 1862-1863, send to J.H. Ashbridge, Treas. #56 Brown's Bldg. Liverpool Exchange.

886 **"SOUTHERN REVIEW, The"**
Baltimore: Bledsoe and Browne, 1867. Pub., v.1, #1, 1867 to v.13, #28, 1873. 8vo, cloth, (2), 503pp. $300. Edt: A.T. Bledsoe, quarterly from '67 to 1879. After 1870, Methodist Episcopal Church, South. Pub. at St. Louis from July 1871, to Jan. 1875.

887 **"SOUTHERN RIGHTS"**
And "Union" Parties in Maryland Contrasted." Balt: W.M. Innes, 1863. 8vo, wraps, 30pp. See: S.M. Johnson. $70.

888 **"SOUTHERN RIGHTS" and Yankee Humor.**
A Confederate-Federal Jacksonville Newspaper." In: FHQ, July 1955, v.XXXIV, #1, p.30-35, facsms.

889 **"SOUTHERN SKETCHES."**
Gen. Edt: Dr. J.D. Eggleston, Charleston, Va., Historical Pub. Co. Following authors, as listed: Hugh Talmage Lefler, Maj. Edgar Erskine Hume, W.D.

Weatherford, Edward A. Wyatt, IV, Col. Wm. Couper, Louis B. Hill, Robert H. Woody, Harvey Wish.

890 **SOUTHERN SOCIETY:**
Exponent of Southern Literature, Society and Art. Conducted by Eugene Didier, William M'Clellan, and Porter Morse. Published weekly. Baltimore: Oct. 5, 1867-April 4, 1868. Complete file of 22 issues and supplement. 8pp per number, 4 columns per page. Folio, original boards, papers label. $100. Mott, p.47-"contains valuable record of the war, literary and historical articles by noted Southern contributors, local scenes.

891 **SOUTHERN SOLDIER'S**
Prize Songster, containing Martial and Patriotic Pieces (chiefly original), applicable to the present war. Mobile, Ala., W.F. Wisely, 1864. 16mo, cl, 104pp. Jonathan W. Palmer, M.D.? Crandall-3272.

892 **SOUTHERN STATES**
See: Wm. C.P. Breckinridge, Matthew C. Butler, Clement A. Evans, Daniel H. Hill, Robert L. Taylor, John S. Williams, Wm. Walker.
...And Their Veteran Soldiers. The. In: SHSP, 1891, v.19, p.336-337.

892a **"SOUTHERN WAGON, The.**
Broadside 4 1/2 x 8", n.p., n.d. (c. May 1861). Cohasco-25. $150. A song exhorting Southern States to jump on the 'dissolution wagon,' secession is our watchword. Jeff Davis is pres. & Stevens (sic) by his side. All states had seceded but Mo., N.C., & Ark., finally seceded May 6, 1861.

893 **SOUTHWOOD, Marion**
"Beauty and Booty", a Watchword of New Orleans. By Marion Southwood, a Landy of New Orleans. N.Y., Published for the Author, by M. Doolady, 1867. 12mo, cl, front, 303pp.(7)p. ads. Acct. pf atrocities in New Orleans in New Orleans during the war.

894 ..."A Souvenir of the Unveiling of the Richmond Howitzer Monument at Richmond, Va., Dec. 13, 1892. Address of Mr. Leigh Robinson, with Rolls of Three Companies and Lists of Battles, 1893." $75. See: Leigh Robinson.

895 **SOUVENIR PROGRAM-Dedication:**
Louisiana Monument, Stonewall Cemetery, Winchester Virginia. July 4, 1896. A Roster of Sons of Louisiana Who Fell in defense of principals on the soil of Virginia, Louisiana Division Army of Northern Virginia. n.p., 12mo, wraps (color flags) (4)p. folder.

896 **SOUVENIR Unveiling Soldiers**
And Sailors Monument. Richmond, Va., May 30, 1894. Dedication address: Robert C. Cave. Richmond, Va., J.L. Hill Print, (1894) $30. 12mo, wraps, illus., (25)pp.

897 **"SOUVENIR of the Confederacy."**
(Augusta, Ga., New Orleans, La., etc. Blackmar, 186?) v.p., t/p missing. 30cm, collection of Confederate songs. La. Union cat., suppl. 1963-1967. Not in Crandall/Harwell, DeRenne.

898 **SOUVENIR of the General Convention**
Of the United Daughters of the Confederacy. Held Nov. 16-22, 1930, at the George Vanderbilt Hotel. Asheville, N.C. (Ashville, N.C., 1930) sm.4to, wraps, 47pp. Many views and local ads.

899 **"SOUVENIR",**
(Charleston, S.C., c.1891) (?1899) 5 3/4X9 1/2", oblong, cord tied, 5-color, CSA flags, ports: Davis, Lee, Jackson, Johnston, Beauregard and Wade Hampton. (14)pp., (1)p. ads. View of Charleston, no descriptive matter. Possible that this souvenir was distributed at 1899 Confed. Vets meeting in Charleston.

900 **SOWELL, Andrew Jackson**
"Cap't. John F(iles) Tom, a Biography." n.p., (c. 1906) 12mo, wraps, 12pp. Joined Stephen F. Austin in Revolution of Tex.

later with Sam Houston in retreat to San Jacinto. During Civil War, organized ranger company for frontier protection. Died 1906.

901 **SOWLE, Patrick**
"Quaker conscript in Confederate North Carolina." In: Quaker Hist., 1967. v.LVI, p.90-105.

902 ..."The trials of a Virginia Unionist: Wm. Cabell Rives and the secession crisis, 1860-1861." In: VMHB, Jan. 1972, v.80, #1, p.3-20.

903 **SOWLES, Edward A., Hon.**
"History of the St. Albans Raid. Annual address delivered at Montpelier, Vt., Tues, Eve. Oct. 17, 1876." St. Albans, Vt., 1876. 8vo, wraps, 48pp. $15-ob.

904 **SPAIN, Rufus Buin**
"Robert Boyte Crawford Howell: Nashville Baptist leader in the Civil War Period." In: Tenn. HQ, 1955, v.XIV, p. 323-340; 99-119; 195-226. notes.

905 **SPALDING, William Basil**
"The Confederate raid on Cumberland in 1865." In: Md.HM, 1941, v.36, p.33-38.

906 **SPANISH FORT, Attack on**
See: Randall Lee Gibson.

907 **SPARKS, A.W.**
"War Between the States as I saw it, Reminiscences, Historical and Personal, by A.W. Sparks." Tyler, Texas: Lee and Burnett, 1901. 8vo, cl, front(port) 393pp. Cover title: "Recollections of the Great War." $250. The 1st, 3rd, and 9th Texas. A great part of book is a reprint of Victor Rose-"Ross' Texas Brigade."

..."Recollections of the great war or the war between the states, as I saw it." Longview, Texas, D&D Pub. Co., 1987. 8vo, cl, 400p. $25. 3rd, 6th, 9th Texas Cavalry Regiments, Ross' Texas Cavalry Brigade. A greater part being a reprint of Rose's Ross Texas Brigade.

908 **SPARKS, Randy J.**
"John P. Osterhout Yankee, Rebel, Republican." In: SWHQ, Oct. 1986, v.xc, #2, p.111-138.

909 **SPARTANBURG COUNTY, South Carolina:**
"List of names of soldiers from Spartanburg County, S.C., who were enlisted in the Confederate Army, including those listed in S.C. State Militia, State Reserves and Cadet Corps during the years 1861-1865 inclusive." In: Dr. J.B.O. Landrums's Hist. Spartanburg, Co., S.C., p. 495-539. Many CSA biographies, with ports, among the many biographies making up the entire book. Reprint Co., S.C.

910 **SPAULDING, Branch**
"Eyes that saw not." In: Inf. Jour., 1940, v.XLVII, p.249-259. Battle of the Wilderness, 1864.

911 ..."Jackson's Fredericksburg tactics." In: Am. Mil. Inst. Jour., 1939, v.III, p. 39-42. During battle Dec. 13, 1862.

912 **SPAULDING, Oliver Lyman**
"The Bombardment of Fort Sumter, 1861." In: Amer. Hist. Ass'n., annual report, 1913, p.177-203. Also: reprinted in wraps.

913 **"SPECIAL ORDERS of the Adjutant**
and Inspector Generals Office, Confederate States, (March 7) 1861-April 1, 1865."Wash: GPO, 1876. 8vo, 5 volumes. (I-324pp. and II-306pp. $200-b) (III-310pp.) (IV-310pp.) (V-78pp.) See: "Miscellaneous Corresp. and orders."

914 **SPEED, Frederic**
"A Federal account of the Battle of Sabine Pass (Texas)." In: SHSP, 1884, v.12, p.130-133.

915 **SPEED, Thomas, Ky.**
"Who Fought the Battle. Strength of the Union and Confederate Forces Compared." Address by Capt. Thos. Speed before the Army Corps Society of Louisville, Ky., Jan. 26, 1904. Louisville, Ky: F.G.

Nunemacher, 1904. cover title, 8vo, wraps, 31pp. Lousiville: Lost Cause Press, micro-cd.-$3.95.

916 ..."Battle of Bean's station, East Tennessee." In: SB, 1883-1884, v.II, p. 112-118.

917 **SPEER, Emory**
"Joseph E. Brown of Georgia. Baccalaureate address commencement of Mercer University, Macon, Ga., June 17, 1905. (Atlanta, Ga., 1905?) 8vo, wraps, 77pp.

918 ..."Lincoln, Lee, Grant & other biographical addresses." N.Y., Wash., Neale Print, 1909. $65. 8vo, cl, ports, 269pp. (Also Gov. Joseph E. Brown.)

919 **SPEER, William A.**
"The sub with six lives." In: S.C. Mag., Feb., 1948, v.11, (#2), p. 12-13. On the sub "Hunley", 1863-1864. See: Submarine Hunley.

920 **SPEER, William H. A.**
"A Confederate Soldier's View of Johnson's Island Prison. Edt: James B. Murphy." In: Ohio Hist. 1970, v.79, p.101-111.

921 **SPELL, Lota M.**
"Music in Texas." In: CWH, Sept., 1958, v.IV, #3, p.301-306.

922 **SPELMAN, Henry M., III and Harvey E. Sheppard**
"A Through the Lines Cover." In: Confederate Philatelist, June 1960, v.5, p.(41)-43, illus. Postmark at Shepherdstown.

923 **SPENCE, Emmit Leslie**
"Reports of the First, Seventh and Seventeenth Virginia Regiments in 1862." In: SHSP, 1910, v.38, p.262-267.

924 **SPENCE, James**
"The American Union; its effect on National character and policy, with an inquiry into Secession as a Constitutional Right and the Causes of the Disruption." London: Richard Bentley, 1861. 8vo, cl, xvi, 366pp. Pres. copy. Edts: 2nd (1862) and 3rd, same imprint. (1866). 272pp. 4th and Revised Edt., xvi, 391pp.

925 ...Richmond, Va., West and Johnston, 1863, 1st Amer. Edt., from 4th Revised Lond. Edt. Spence was a Liverpool cotton merchant and strongly espoused Southern cause, arranged cotton loans to the South.
...N.Y., Kraus Rep., (1969), (Rev. 4th)

925a ..."Die amerikanische Union; ihre Einwirkung auf National-Charakter und Politik. Nebst Erorterungen uber Secession, Deutsch von A.P. Wetter." Barmen: M. Langeweische, 1863. 8vo, cl, 272pp. Sabin-89280.

926 ..."On the Recognition of the Southern Confederation. By James Spence, author of "The American Union", and the S. letters to the "Times" on American Affairs." London: Richard Bentley, 1862 and 2nd Edt. 8vo, wraps, 48pp. Eds: 2nd and 3rd, same date, imprint.
...Louisv: Lost Cause Pr., Micro-cd. $2.45.

927 ..."Southern Independence: an address delivered at a public meeting, in the City Hall, Glasgow, by James Spence, 26th November, 1863." London: Richard Bentley, 1863. 8vo, wraps, 39pp. Sabin-89282. Liverpool, 1863 edt., same imprint date.

928 ..."L'Union Americaine. Ses effets sur le caractere national et la politique, causes de la dissolution et etude du droit constitutionel de separation traduit de l'anglais de James Spence." Paris: Michel Levy Freres, 1862. 8vo, cl, 434pp.

929 ..."Spencer's American Union." In: Black Edn. Mag., Apr. 1862, v.XCI, p. 514-536. "No true advantage to any section in subjugation of the South."

930 **SPENCE, W. Jerome D.**
"A history of Hickman County, Tennessee, by W. Jerome D. and David L. Spence." Nashville, Tenn., Gospel Advocate Pub., 1900. 12mo, cl, front, port, 509pp.

931 **SPENCER, C.R., Jr.**
"The morale of the Confederate soldier." In: CV, Feb. 1919, v.XXVII, p. 49-52.

932 **SPENCER, Carrie Esther (Samuels), Bernard Samuels and Walter Berry Samuels, Editors**
"A Civil War Marriage in Virginia: Reminiscences and Letters, collected by the three surviving children." (Boyce, Va., Carr Pub. Co., (1956) 8vo, cl, dj, facsms, maps, incl. map liners, ports, views, notes, vi, (2), 267-(214)-index. Letters while in service in CSArmy. Family in Front Royal, Va., Woodstock, Va.

933 **SPENCER, Cornelia Phillips, Mrs.**
"The Last Ninety Days of the War in North Carolina." New York: Watchman Pub. Co., 1866, $175-g. 12mo, cl, 287pp. Do: 2nd Thousand. Preface: was originally published in the New York Watchman. Louisville: Lost Cause Pr., micro-cd. $4.65. (See: H.S. Chamberlain's-"Old Days in Chapel Hill; being the Life and Letters of Cornelia Phillips Spencer." See also: Chs. Phillips Russell.)

934 **SPENCER, I.J.**
"A Memorial Sermon of Festus and Elizabeth B. Dickinson and letters concerning them... from distinguished Virginian, Fredericksburg, Va., n.d." 8vo, wraps.

935 **SPENCER, John**
"Terrell's Texas Cavalry: wild horsemen of the Plains in the Civil War." Austin, Tex., Eakin Press, 1986. 8vo, 208pp. $13.

936 **SPENCER, John W.**
"Terrell's Texas Cavalry." Burnett, Texas: Eakin Press, 1982. 8vo, cl, dj, 199pp. bibliog., index, append. Trans Mississippi with the 34th Vol. Texas Cavalry/Terrell's Texas Cavalry. Largely from East Texas. Red River Campaign.

937 ..."From Corsicana to Appomattox. Story of the "Corsicana Invincibles" and "Navarro Rifles." Corsicana, Texas, Texas Press, 1984. A sesquincentennial History. 8vo, cl, dj, viii, 199pp., illus. $16.50

..."The Confederate Guns of Navarro County (Texas)." Corsicana, Tex., Texas Press, 1986. 8vo, cl, dj, 152pp, ills, rosters, index. #20. 500 numbered, signed copies.

937a **SPENCER, Samuel**
"In memoriam Samuel Spencer. Exercises at the unveiling of the monument erected by the employees of the Southern railway company." Atlanta, Ga., 1910. 8vo, wraps, 55pp, ills, port.

938 **SPENCER, Warren F.**
"The Confederate Navy in Europe." University: University of Alabama Pr., 1983. 8vo, cl, dj, xiii, 268pp. notes, bibliog. index.

939 ..."French tobacco in Richmond during the Civil War." In: VMHB, April 1963, v.71, #2, p.185-202.

940 ..."The French view of the Fall of Richmond: Alfred Paul's report to Drouyn de Llys, April 11, 1865." In: VMHB, Apr. 1965, v.73, #2, p.178-188. See: Col. Christopher Thompkins.

941 **SPENDER, Edward**
"Confederate negro enlistments." In: Annl. War., p.536-553.

942 **SPIES ,**
A bibliography in Davis' "Belle Boyd", append: p.401-414.

943 **SPIRES, Charles W.**
"Boy Officer" of the Washington Artillery." In: CWTI, May 1975, v.13, #2, p.10-23, part 1. Part II-"My artillery fire was very destructive." June, 1975, #3, p.18-29, illus., ports.

944 **SPOTSWOOD, Thomas E., Dr.**
"Horrors of Camp Morton." In: SHSP, 1890, v.18, p.327-333. See: Jno. Allen Wyeth.

945 **SPOTSYLVANIA COURT HOUSE, Battle of**

See: David W. Anderson, Wm. S. Archer, Thos. Henry Carter, Wilfred E. Cutshaw, Jno. Catlett Gibson, S.S. Green, Robert W. Hunter, Wm. W. Old, Richard Channing M. Page, Wm. W. Smith, M.S. Stringfellow, Richmond Times Dispatch, Jas. Alex. Walker, "Memorials to Men...".

946 **SPRAGGINS, Tinsley Lee**
"Mobilization of Negro Labor for the Department of Virginia and North Carolina, 1861-1865." (Raleigh) NCHRev., April, 1947. v.XXIV, #2, p.160-197, fld. map, tables. $8-bmk.

946a **SPRAGUE, John Titcomb**
"The treachery in Texas, the secession of Texas & the arrest of the US officers & soldiers serving in Texas. Read before the N.Y. Historical Society, June 25, 1861." N.Y., Printed for the Society, 1862. Large 8vo, 1p, 1,p(109)-142. $40 $60-g. An officer seized & paroled by Texas forces & charged with treason.

947 **SPRATT, Barnett**
"Miss Betty of Bonnet Rock School, 1864-1865." N.Y., Hastings House, 1965, 8vo, pict. cl, dj, illus., 125pp. Civil War novel based on reminiscences of Elizabeth Killian, a Chester Co., S.C., school teacher.

948 **SPRATT, L.W., Hon.**
"The philosophy of secession; a Southern view presented in a letter addressed to the Hon. Mr. Perkins of Louisiana, in criticism on the Provisional Constitution adopted by the Southern Congress at Montgomery, Alabama." n.p., (1861), 8vo, sewn, 8p.

949 ..."The foreign slave trade and the source of political power-of material progress of social integrity, and of social emancipation to the South." Charleston, S.C., Walker, Evans and Co., 1858, 8vo, wraps, 31pp. In: columns of "Charleston Standard" and "New Orleans Delta."

950 **"SPRING HILL, Alabama College Diary, 1861-1865."**
Edt: Raymond Schmandt and Josephine H. Schulte. In: AR, July 1962, v.15, #3, p.213-225.

951 **SPRING HILL, Tennessee, Battle of**
See: Benj. Franklin Cheatham.

952 **SPRINGER, Francis W.**
"February: American Myth Month." Greenville, N.C., Pace Pub., 1973. 8vo, stiff wraps, 62pp. Misconceptions: abolition, slavery, Lincoln, the Union and secession.

953 **SPRINGS, Katherine Wooten**
"The Squires of Springfield." Charlotte, N.C., William Loftin, 1965. 8vo, cl, illus., chart index, 350pp. Civil War section (61pp.), Reconstruction (34pp.). Wartime letters, home front, securing supplies to the army. (Carolina Bks.)

954 **SPRUILL, Frank S., Hon.**
"Gen. William Ruffin Cox." Address in presenting portrait of the distinguished Confederate officer, to the State." In: N.C. Booklet, Oct. 20, Jan-Apr. 1921, v.XX, #2, 3, 4, p.159-170.

955 **SPRUNT, James**
"Blockade Running." In: Walter Clark's "Hist. of Several Regs. and Batts. from N.C." Vol.V, p.353-451, ports and illus., Included in a section-"N.C. in the Navy", p.293-451.

956 ..."Chronicles of the Cape Fear River; being some account of historic events on the Cape Fear River." Raleigh, N.C., Edwards and Broughton, 1914, 8vo, cl, xiv, 594pp. $250-bmk-128.
..."Chronicle of the Cape Fear River, 1660-1916." 2nd Edt., orig. 1/2lt. Raleigh, N.C., Edwards and Broughton, 1916. 8vo, cl, fldg. plans, maps(part fldg.), xi, 732pp, 3/4 Mor. $250, $175-bmk-105. Blockade running, p.387-500. Harbor was last one closed during war, mine of information on

blockade running, naval history about this strategic point.
...Spartanburg, S.C., The Reprint Co., 1973. Half of book relates to the CSA. op.

957 ..."Derelicts. An account of ships lost at sea in general commercial traffic and a brief history of Blockade Runners stranded along the North Carolina coast 1861-1865." Wilmington, N.C., private print (1920). 8vo, front, cl, xii, 304pp. $200, $175-bmk-84.

958 ..."George Davis." In: N.C. Lit. and Hist. Assoc. Proc., 19th Ann. Sess., 1919, p.15-21. Davis was Atty-Gen. of CSA, died in 1896.

959 ..."Running of the Blockade-a Sketch of Captain Maffitt." In: SHSP, 1896, v.24, p.157-165.

960 ..."Tales of the Cape Fear Blockade, being a turn of the century account of blockade running with editorial map showing lower Cape Fear and coast of Brunswick Co., with plantations, places, fortifications and wrecks of blockading-runners 1861-1865." Edt: Cornelius M.D. Thomas. Wilmington, N.C., J.E. Hicks Print for the Charles Towne Preservation Trust, 1960, 12mo, wraps, illus., 134pp. (Clarendon Imprint #4).
..."Tales of the Cape Fear Blockade." Raleigh, N.C., Capitol Print, 1902. North Carolina Booklet, v.1, #10. 12mo, cl, front, 112pp. By the purser of CSN "Lillian".
...Reprint, Wilmington, N.C., 1960. 12mo, cl, 134pp.

961 ..."Tales and Traditions of the Lower Cape Fear 1661-1896." Wilmington, N.C., LeGwin Bros., 1896. 12mo, cl, front, illus., xii, 215pp. $150.
...Spartanburg, S.C., Reprint Co., 1973, 8vo, cl, 215, lxivpp. $15.

962 **SPURLIN, Charles, Edt.**
"West of the Mississippi with Waller's 13th Texas Cavalry Battalion, CSA." (Hillsboro, Texas) A Hill Jr. College Monograph #6, 1971. 8vo, stiff wraps, ports, illus., fldg-map, x, (1), 99pp., index, bibliog. $20-b.

963 **SQUIRES, William H.T.**
"The Land of Decision." Portsmouth, Va., Printcraft, 1931. $100-b. 8vo, cl, illus., ma[s, xiv, 402pp., lim. edt. Virginia in the Confederacy.

964 ..."A Confederate Anthology, gathered from newspapers, magazines and other sources, many contemporary and presented to the State Library of Virginia, by..." Norfolk, Va., 1946. 4to, cl, illus. (1-color) ports, facsm., music coats-of-arm, (3)-85 (i.e., 87)pp.

965 **SRYGLEY, Fletcher Douglas**
"Seventy Years in Dixie, Recollections Sermons and Sayings of T.W. Casky, et al." Nashville, Tenn: Gospel Advocate Pub., 1891, 8vo, cl, illus., 400pp.
...Reprint, 1954.

966 **ST. PAUL, Henry**
"Our home and foreign policy." 8vo, sewn, 23pp. Crandall-2835. (Mobile: Dailey Register, 1863) Gdsp-$400.

967 **STACKPOLE, Edward James**
"Harrisburg the objective of Lee's invasion of Pennsylvania, June 1863: the setting the stage for Gettysburg campaign." In: Dauphin Co. HR, Dec. 1958, v.6, p.13-22.

968 ..."Chancellorsville, Lee's greatest battle." Harrisburg: Stackpole Co., (1958) 8vo, cl, dj, 384pp., illus., maps (including endsheet plans and prots). NY, Bonanza, n.d.

969 ..."Stonewall Jackson in the Shenandoah." In: CWTI, Nov. 1964, v.III, #7, p.4-11, 36-41, illus., maps, ports.

970 **STAFFORD, George Mason Graham**
"General Leroy Augustus Stafford, his forebears and descendants; a genealogy compiled by grandson, Dr. G.M.G. Stafford." New Orleans: Pelican Pub., (1943).

8vo, cl, 4, 474, (35)pp. frontis, facsms, diagr.

971 **STALHOPE, Robert E.**
"Sterling Price: Portrait of a Southerner." Columbia, Mo., Univ. of Missouri Press, 1871. 8vo, cl, d/w, 311pp., index, bibliog.

972 **STAMP, J.B.**
"Ten months experience in Northern prisons (Point Lookout and Elmira, 1864-1865)." In: AlaHQ, winter, 1956, v.18, p.486-498. Reminisc. of a CSA sergeant.

973 **STAMPP, Kenneth Milton, Edt.**
"The causes of the Civil War." Englewood Cliffs, N.J., 1959. 8vo, cl, dj, x, 181pp. 91 articles, speeches, chapters from books, reprinted from primary sources and secondary works, 1798-1953.

974 ..."Lincoln and the Strategy of Defense in the Crisis of 1861." (Baton Rouge, La.) JSH, Aug., 1945, v.XI, #3, p.297-323.

975 ..."And the War Came: The North and the Secession Crisis, 1860-1861." Baton Rouge: Louisiana State Univ. Press., 1950. 8vo, cl, dj, illus., bibliog., xi, 331pp., 1967. Balanced account of sectional difference.
..."The imperiled Union: essays on the background of the Civil War." N.Y., Oxford University Press, 1980. 8vo, cl, dj, xvi, 320p. $16.

976 **STANARD, Beverly**
"Letters of a New Market Cadet Beverly Stanard. Edited by John G. Barrett and Robert K. Turner, Jr." Chapel Hill: University of North Carolina Press (1961) (Van Rees Press, N.Y.) 8vo, cl, dj, color front, xxiv, 70pp.

977 **STANARD, Mary Newton**
"John Brockenbrough Newton. A Biographical Sketch." (cover title) (Richmond, Va., 1924) n.p., n.d. Rep: Virginia Churchman, private distr., 8vo, pls, ports, 61pp. $40.

978 ..."Richmond, its people and its story." Phila., Lond: Lippincott and Co., 1923. 8vo, cl, pls., ports, map, facsm., xix, 238pp. Contains a full acct. of the war in and around Richmond.

979 **STANARD, Robert C., Mrs.**
"A Confederate woman's kind act finely told...hospitality to two Confederates." In: SHSP, 1910, v.XXXVIII, p.309-312.

980 **STANDARD, Diffee William**
"Columbus, Georgia, in the Confederacy. The social and industrial life of the Chattahoochee River port, by Diffee William Standard, head of the English Department Tennessee Military Institute." N.Y., William-Frederick Press, 1954. 12mo, stiff wraps, 77pp. $25-atg. 12mo, stiff wraps, 77pp. See: Chattahoochee Valley Hist. Society.

981 **STANDING, Percy Cross**
"Guerilla leaders of the world." London: S. Paul and Co., (1912) 8vo, cl, pls., ports, maps, 294pp.
...Bost., Houghton Mifflin, 1913. Chapters on Mosby, Morgan & Forrest. p.173-211.

982 ..."A Woman's Life of Stonewall Jackson." In: Unit. Ser. Mag., n.s., Jan. 1918, v.LXVI, p.305-310. Refers to Chatherine Cooper Hopley, pub. anon in London, 1863.

983 ..."The greatest living guerrilla." In: Cham. Jour., 7th ser., Apr. 1915, v.V, p.222-224. Sketch of Gen. John S. Mosby.

984 ..."Two Confederate Colonels (Turner Ashby and Richard Ashby.)." In: Unit. Ser. Mag., n.s., LXVI, March 1918, p.464-466.

985 **STANFORD, Edward, Pub.**
"Stanford"-map of the seat of war in America." London: Edward Stanford, Pub., Oct. 1, 1861. Large fold. map 44 1/2x2x52:, mounted on linen, slip case. (Bohling) $850. Colored, slave states in blue, rail lines in red.

986 ..."Stanford's New Hand-map of the United States...showing the boundry of the seceding states." London, 1861. Colored

19x25" linen-backed, folded into cloth covers. Only those states seceded by April 1861. Ala., Fla., Ga., La., Miss., NC, Tex., and Va.

987 **STANLEY, Caroline Abbott**
"Order No. 11, a tale of the border." N.Y., Century Co., 1904. 12mo, cl, front, plates, viii, 420pp.
...1921 reprint. Border conflict Missouri-Kansas, 1860-1865. Plantation life during the war at "Keswick". Fiction based on facts.

988 **STANLEY, Francis Louis Crocchiola**
"The Civil War in New Mexico." Denver, Colorado: World Press (1960) 8vo, cl, xiii, 508pp.

989 **STANLEY, Henry Morton, Sir**
"The Autobiography of Sir Henry Morton Stanley. Edt. by his wife, Dorothy Stanley." Boston: Houghton Mifflin Co., (Oct. 1909) 8vo, cl, facsm., illus., ports, incl. front, fldg. color map, xvii, 551pp. Editions: a 1911 edition. Served with the "Dixie Grays", during war attached to the 6th Ark. Reg., CSA, p.140-224.

990 ..."Henry M. Stanley in Arkansas and the Dixie Grays." Document. In: AHQ, 1942, v.1, p.244-263. See: Mary Willis Shuey, Byron Farwell.

991 **STANLEY, J. Randall**
"History of Jackson County." (Florida) Jackson County Historical Society (1950) (Marianna, Fla?) 8vo, cl, 281pp. Chaps: 15-21: Secession, Civil War, War-Years in Jackson Co., Battle of Marianna, chaos follows war, Second Rebellion-Reconstruction, End of Carpetbag rule, p.151-217.

991a **STANLEY, Lebergott**
"Why the South lost: commerical purpose in the Confederacy, 1861-5." In: Jour. Am. Hist., June 1983, p.58-74.

992 **STANLEY, Vara Smith**
"A History of Appomattox County. Past, Present, Future. 1845-1965." Appomattox, Va., Times-Virginian (1965) 8vo, wraps, front (color coat-arms) ports, illus., map, 92pp., facsms, roster of men in CSA, from county. Appomattox Civil War Centennial, Apr. 9, 1965.

992a **STANLEY, William M.**
"To the Memory of . . . , whose soldier's grave is unmarked by shaft or stone." Tyler, Tx., 1965. (54th Ala. Inf.) 8vo, wraps, 65pp, lim. edt. 100 copies. $16.

993 **STANTON, C.L.**
"Submarines and torpedo boats." In: CV, Sept. 1914, v.XXII, p. 398-399. Acct: CSN ship "Fishboat", in Charleston harbor in 1864.

994 **STANTON, Donald J., Goodwin F. Berquist, Jr., and Paul C. Bowers**
"Missouri's Forgotten General: M. Jeff Thompson and the Civil War." In: MHRev., April 1976, v.LXX, #3, p.237-258, ports, illus.

995 ..."General M. Jeff Thompson: Soldier Rhetorician." In: Mo. Hist. Rev., Oct. 1976, v.LXXI, #1, p.44-58, port, illus.

996 **STANTON, Frank Lebby**
"Songs From Dixieland." Indianapolis (1900) Bowen-Merrill Co. Illus. by W.H. Gallaway, plates, front. 12mo, cl, xi-xiv, 239pp.

997 **STANTON, Henry Thompson**
"Poems of the Confederate States of America. Being selections from the writings of Maj. Henry Stanton of Kentucky." Louisville, Ky., J.P. Morton and Co., 1900, 8vo, wraps, 46pp., front (port.)

998 **STAPLES, Thomas S.**
"The Arkansas Secession Convention of 1861." In: SW Pol and Soc. Sci. Ass'n, Pro of 5th ann. conv., Ft. Worth, Tx., Mar 24-26, 1924, p.54-77.

999 **STARK, Alexander W.**
"Instructions for Field Artillery..." Rich-

mond: A Morris, 1864. 12mo, limp bds., 264pp. Crandall-2482. Goodspeed $650.

1000 **STARK, Richard Boles and Janet C.**
"Surgical care of the Confederate States Army, 1861-1865." In: U.S. Armed Forces Med. Jour., Jan. 1959, v.10: p.50-68, diagr., facsm., ports, views, notes. From Bull. N.Y. Acad. Med., June 1958. Reprint, wrap, 24pp. Also in: Va. Med. Monthly, May 1960.
..."Surgeons and Surgical Care of the Confederate States Army." (London) Jour. Confed. Hist. Soc., Sept. 1964, v.II, #3, p.98-113, ports-2, plates-3. Also: Va. Med. Monthly, May 1960.

1000a **STARK, W. V., Letters**
See: Michael B. Dougan.

1001 **STARKE, Peter B., Col.**
"Report: Sherman's advance on Meridian." In: SHSP, 1881, v.9, p.163-168.

1002 **STARKEY, Larry**
"Wilkes Booth Came to Washington." N.Y., Random House, 1976. 8vo, cl, dj, xiii, 209pp. Theory about fomenting war between Canada/England and the U.S., on the side of the Confederacy.

1003 **STARNES, James W.**
"Battle of Douglass's Church." In: CV, Oct. 1921, v.XXIX, p. 369-371. Off. rep., Col. Starnes hdq. camp near Spring Hill, Tenn., Apr. 13, 1863.

1004 **STARNES, Lucy Gaylord**
"Girl Spy of the Valley." (Richmond) Va. Cavl., Autumn 1963, v.XIII, #2, p.32-37, ports, illus.(1-color) John Esten Cooke, who took part in many events of which he wrote.

1005 **STARR, Douglas P.**
"Secession Speeches of Four Deep South Governors Who Would Rather Fight Than Switch." In: Southern Speech Communication Journal, XXXVIII, p. 131-141.

1006 **STARR, Frank**
"New Mexico Campaign Letters of Frank Starr, 1861-1862. Edited by David B. Gracey, II." In: TMH, Fall, 1964, v.4, #3, p.169-188.

1007 **STARR, Michael I.**
"A pack of Indians and cowards. Federals besieged at Ft. Gibson." In: CWTI, June 1980, v.19, #3, p.38-46, illus., ports, map, facsm.

1008 **STARR, R.F.S.**
"A Prussian for Virginia. Heros Von Borcke." In: CWTI, FEb. 1981, v.19, $10, p.32-39, illus., ports.

1009 **STARR, Stephen Z.**
"Colonel George St. Leger Grenfell: His Pre-Civil War Career." (Houston, Tex.) JSH, Aug. 1964, v.XXX, #3, p.278-297. Lt. Col. Grenfell, a professional British soldier, did a tour of duty with John Hunt Morgan, June to Dec., 1862. Colorful soldier. See: under Col. Grenfell.

1010 ..."Colonel Grenfell's Wars. The Life of a Soldier of Fortune." Baton Rouge: Louisiana State University Press, (1971). 8vo, cl, dj, front(port), vii, 352pp. index, bibliography. $20-bmk.

1011 ..."Was there a Northwest Conspiracy?" In: Filson Club Hist. Quart., 1964, v.XXXVIII, p. 323-339.

1012 **STARRETT, Vincent**
"Renfrew the Silent: an uncompleted research." In: New Colophon, 1950 (#3), p.105-109. On the legend or fiction of Henry Clay Renfrew of Ky., an officer in CSArmy, invented by Col. Theodore F. Allen, c.1900.

1013 **STARRITT, Kate Cumming, Mrs.**
"A Refugee Story. How a Rebel gave the Yankees the slip." In: SHSP, 1908, v.36, p.210-212.

1013a **"STARS & BARS,"**
Virginia Division of Sons of Confederate

Veterans. Official organ., later called "Rattlesnake." April 1923-July 1929.

1014 **STATE DEPARTMENT, C.S.A.-**
See: C.C. Clay, Jr., Jas. P. Holcombe, Judah P. Benjamin, L. Quinton Washington.

1015 ..."Correspondence concerning the Campaign of 1864." In: SHSP, 1879, v.7, p.291-292.

1016 **"STATE MILITIA of Alabama**
during the administration of Lewis E. Parsons, Provisional Governor, June 21, 1865 to Dec. 18, 1865." In: AlaHQ, v.14, p.301-330. Includes muster rolls and corresp.

1017 **"STATE OF GEORGIA**
Civil War Centennial, 1864 showing the major campaign areas and engagement sites of the Union and Confederate Armies, The." Folded map, 22x34" (Atlanta) State Highway Dept. of Georgia. Route of Wilson's Raiders, Davis' attempted escape and Sherman's main force.

1018 **"STATE OF PLANTER'S BANK**
of Tennessee and Branches, June 29, 1861.(caption title)." (Wash.? 1917. 8vo, wraps, 14pp., illus., maps. Reprinted from June 1917-"Sea Power". Stewart was editor of the Official Records of the Union and CSANavy.

1018a **STATE PAPERS &**
Public Documents of the Confed. States from the Foundation of the Confed. in 1860, exhibiting a complete view of our foreign relations since that time. Pub. under patronage of Congress. Incl. confidential corresp., now pub. for 1st time, embracing a full acct. of causes which led to withdrawal of Southern States & the formation of the Confed." Edt., Pub., John Poynter McMillan, of the Missouri Army, Richmond, 1864. 5 vols (reported in notes), p. 426. Va. Mag. Hist., Biog., v.XX, #4, 1912.

1019 **STATE RIGHTS-**
See: Jefferson Davis, Charles Harris, "Secession".

1020 **"STATEMENT OF RECORDS**
relating to the Confederacy." In: Biennial report, Alabama Adjutant General. Montgomery: Brown Print, 1894. 8vo, wraps, p.200-224.

1021 **"STATES" (pseud.)**
"The Right to Secede. State Sovereignty and the doctrine of coercion." Charleston, 1860. 8vo, sewd, 36pp. See: Wm. D. Porter.

1022 **STATISTICS of the Confederate States-**
See: Wm. F. Fox, J.F. Gilmer, Chs. C. Jones, Joseph Jones, Robert G.H. Kean, A.R. Lawton, C.G. Lee, S.P. Moore, L.B. Northrup, Richmond Dispatch, I.M. St. John, J.S. Ward.

1023 **STATON, Kate Elony, Mrs.**
"Old Southern Songs of the Period; of the Confederacy; the Dixie Trophy Collection." New York and London, 1926, S. French. 8vo, wraps, 146pp. $75. Of Tarboro, N.C. In 1923 a "Dixie loving cup" offered for the best compilation of "Old Southern Songs of the CSA period", Won by Mrs. Staton.

1024 **"STATUES in stamped copper and bronze,**
the W.H. Mullins Co., Salem, Ohio." Cleveland: The Caxton Co., 1913 (compiler) 8vo, pict. boards, 79pp., illus. Statuary company catalogue of specimens of Union and CSA courthouse statues and battlefield monuments.

1025 **"STATUTES at Large**
of the Provisional Government of the Confederate States of America, from the institution of the Government, February 8, 1861, to its termination, February 18, 1862, inclusive. Arranged in chronological order. Together with the Constitution for the Provisional Government and the per-

manent Constitution of the Confederate States and the Treaties concluded by the Confederate States with Indian Tribes. Edited by James M(uscoe) Matthews, Attorney at Law and law clerk in the Department of Justice." Richmond, Va., R.M. Smith, printer, 1864. Tk.8vo, full sheep, xv, (1), 411, xlviii pp. (index) $140, $150-bmk. Crandall-19. $1250-jk-137. (Bound in: Public/Private Laws of the CSA, 2nd sess., 1st Cong., 1862; 3rd sess., 1st Cong. 1863; 3rd and 4th sess., 1st Congr. 1863-1864; 1st and 2nd Congr., 1864. Total of 950pp. See: under Public/Private Laws of CSA. Continued as Crandall's #20 thru 24.

1026 ..."Statutes at large of the Provisional Government of the Confederate States of America...Crandall #19." (Holmes Beach, Florida, W.W. Gaunt Photo Reproduction, D & S Publishers, Indian Rocks Beach, Florida, 1970) 8vo, cl, 411, xivii. Spine: "Statutes at Large, Confederate States, 1861-1862."

1027 "STATUTES at Large of South Carolina. Vol. XIII, containing the Acts from Dec. 1861 to Dec. 1866. Arranged chronologically, pub. under authority of Legislature." Columbia, S.C., Reprinted by Republican Printing Co., State Printers, 1875. Tall 8vo, orig. wraps, xviii, 488, 22pp.-index.

1028 **STAUDENRAUS, P.J., Edt.**
"The Secession Crisis, 1860-1861." Chicago, Ill., Rand McNally (1963) 12mo, stiff wraps, 60pp.

1029 **STAUFFER, William H.**
"What the Civil War Centennial should mean to Virginia, by..., Virginia Civil War Centennial Corporation." Heading: The University of Virginia News Letter, pub. semi-monthly by the Bureau of Public Administration. Charlottesville, Va., April 1, 1958. v.XXXIV, #13, Edt: Weldon Cooper. Broadside sheet: 19 1/2x12 1/2", fold.

1029a **STAUFFER, William H., Dr. et al.**
"Seven fateful days in 1865, retreat of Lee's Army of Northern Virginia from Petersburg to Appomattox, April 2-9, 1865." Farmville, Va., Farmville Herald, 1962. 8vo, wraps, 32pp, ills. $22.50 With Wilmer R. Turner's Map showing roads used by Lee in retreat from Richmond & Petersburg & Gen. Grant's advance on Appomattox folded in.

1030 **STAUNTON DAILY NEWS-**
"Reunion of Rockbridge Dragoons." In: SHSP, 1894, v.22, p.73-75.

1031 **STAUNTON RIVER, Battle of**
See: Benjamin L. Farinholt, J.W. Lewis, John B. McPahil, Dabney H. Maury.

1032 **STEADMAN, J.M.**
"Wade Hampton, soldier and Statesman." In: Meth. Quar. Rev., July 1917, v.LXVI, p. 502-513.

1033 **"STEAM FRIGATE, New Ironsides. The"**
In: Charleston Yearbook, 1888, p.xxi-xxxv.

1034 **STEDMAN, Charles Manly**
"Battle at Ream's Station, extract from the "Memorial address, delivered May 10, 1890, at Wilmington, N.C., by Charles M. Steadman." In: SHSP, 1890, v.XIX, p.113-120.

1035 ..."Historical sketch of the Forty-Fourth N.C. Infantry." In: SHSP, 1897, v.XXV, p.334-345.

1036 ..."General Stephen Dodson Ramseur (1837-1864)." In: Confed. Vet., Dec. 1920, v.XXVIII, p. 453-457.

1037 ..."Memorial address delivered May 10, 1890, at Wilmington, N.C., by... A sketch of the life and character of General William McRae, with an account of the battle of Ream's Station." Wilmington, N.C., Wm. L. DeRosset, 1890. 8vo, wraps, 27pp.

1038 ..."Memorial services held in the House of Representatives of the U.S. together with remarks presented in eulogy of Charles M. Stedman, late a representative from

North Carolina." 71st Cong., 3rd sess. Hse. Doc. 807. Wash: Gov. Print Off., 1931. 8vo, cl, port, 56pp.

1039 **STEDMAN, George Clinton**
"Amid the strife: further correspondence of George Clinton Stedman. Edt.: Jurt F. Leidecker." In: KyHSR, July 1953, v.51, p.191-216. facsm., port, notes. Services in CSArmy, court-reporter in St. Louis and Jefferson City, 1858-1864.

1040 **STEDMAN, W. Ellsworth**
"The Confederate Spy; a Military Drama in fave acts, by W. Ellsworth Stedman." N.Y., S. French and Son (etc., etc., 1887) 12mo, stiff wraps, 51pp. (reprint 1915) Frenche's standard drama. The acting edition, #401.

1041 **STEEL, Edward M., Jr.**
"T. Butler King of Georgia." Athens, University of Georgia Press (1964) 8vo, cl, dj, port, viii, 204pp. Biography of a Confederate diplomat.

1042 **STEEL, S.S.**
"Albert Taylor Bledsoe: sometime editor of this review." (1809-1877) In: Meth. Quar. Rev., Apr. 1915, v.LXIV, p. 211-228.

1043 **STEEL, Samuel Augustus**
"Explaining the Objection to "Rebel"." Richmond, Va., Confederate Museum, 1913, wraps, 8vo, 10pp.

1044 ..."The Sunny Road, Home Life in Dixie During the War." n.p., n.d., (Mansfield, La.? c.1924) 12mo, printed wraps, 160pp.
...Same, (Memphis, Tenn., Latsch and Arnold, c.1925) (In Ark. Univ.) 12mo, front(port) v.2, 185pp.

1045 ..."Lee: The Passing of the Old South." (Atlanta) Emory University, Ga., Banner Press, 1932. 8vo, wraps, port, 62pp. (Verse Craft Series) pt.1, causes of war; pt.-2, battles of 1864-1865; pt.-3, the new South.

1046 ..."Lee at Appomattox." In: Methodist Quarterly Review, LXIX (April) 1920, 8vo, wraps, p.317-332.

1047 ..."The South Was Right." Columbia, S.C., R.L. Bryan Co., 1914. 8vo, wraps, 67pp. South's right to secede.

1048 **STEELE, James Columbus**
"Sketches of the Civil War, especially of Companies A, C, and H. From Iredell County, N.C. and the 4th Regimental Band." Statesville, N.C., Brady Print, 1921. 8vo, wraps, slip. (Copy: Mitchell College Lib., Statesville, N.C. 100 copies.

1049 **STEELE, Matthew Forney, Maj. U.S. Cav.**
"American Campaigns." (head)-War Dept. Office of Chief of Staff, 2nd sect., General staff, #13." Washington: Byron S. Admas, 1909. War Dept. Doc. #324, Off. Chief of Staff. 8vo, 3/4Mor., 2 vols., viii, (1), 731pp., v.II-Maps: xii, 311 (largely printed one side), many double page, color coded. $60-nc. In v.I, append: "Union and Confederate Commanders in some of the principal campaigns and battles of the Civil War." p.628-672; index to v.I, p.673-731. See also: John Formby and G.J. Fiebeger. Other Edts: same, 1922 and 3rd print, 1931.

1050 ..."Atlas to accompany Steele's American Campaign. Edited by Vincent J. Esposito." West Point, N.Y., Military Academy, 1945. 28x37cm., 136-color coded maps. $75. 1956 Edition, with 158 maps. "In the present edition additional maps have been added so as to provide a complete atlas for Steele's book."

1050a **STEELE, Nimrod Hunter**
"The Nimrod Hunter Steele Diary & Letter. In: 'Diaries, letters & recollections of the war between the states.' In: Winchester County Hist. Soc. Papers." Winchester, Va., 1955, v.III, p.48-57.

1051 **STEELE, William, General, CSA**
"A Civil War Letter of General William

Steele, CSA. Edited: Allan C. Ashcraft." In: AHQ, 1963, v.XXII, p. 278-281.

1052 **STEEN, Ralph W.**
"Texas Newspapers and Lincoln." In: SwHQ, January 1948, v.LI, #3, p.199-212.

1053 **STEERE, Edward**
"The Wilderness Campaign." Harrisburg, Pa., Stackpole Co., 1960, 8vo, cl, maps, 552pp.
...Gaithersburg, Md., Butternut, 1987. 8vo, cl, dj, 522pp. $30.

1054 **STEFFEN, Randy and Ronald E. Youngquist**
"1st special battalion, Louisiana infantry (Wheat's Tigers), 1861-1862." In: Mil. Coll. and Hist., 1959, v.XI, p.10, col. pl.

1055 **STEGEMAN, John F.**
"These Men She Gave; Civil War Diary of Athens, Georgia." Athens: University of Ga., (1964) 8vo, cl, dj, illus., ports, maps, viii, 179pp. See also: "Athens, Ga., 1861-1865."

1056 ..."Athens men at Gettysburg." In: Ga. Rev., Summer. 1963, (11), 11pp. $8.

1057 **STEGMAIER, Mark Joseph**
"The Kidnapping of Generals Crook and Kelley by the McNeill Rangers, Feb. 21, 1865." In: W.Va.Hist., 1967, v.XXIX, p.13-47.
..."Zachary Taylor versus the South." In: CWH, v.33, #3, Sept. 1987, p.218-41. Re: Alex Stephens & Robt. Tooms. Western territories admission to union & slavery.
..."Intensifying the sectional conflict: William Seward vs. James Hammond in the Lecompton debate of 1858." In: CWH, Spt. 1985, v.31, #3, p.197-221. Seward outlines North's plan for ruling the South as a "conquered province," excluding the South from power. Hammond-Seward debates brought a sharper focus in the coming of the war.

1058 **STEIN, Peter**
"State Rights and the South, 1850-1860." In: British Assn. for Amer. Studies, Bul., n.s., #11, 1965, p.3-12.

1059 **STEINBERG, Alfred**
"Fire-eating farmer of the Confederate States-at Sumter Edmund Ruffin unwittingly pushed toward ruin the region whose agricultural economy he had revived." In: Amer. Hert., Dec. 1957, v.IX, #3, p.22-25, 114-117, facsms., pl, port.

1060 **STEINER, Paul Eby**
"Medical-Military Portraits of Union and Confederate Generals." Phila: Whitmore Pub. Co., 1968, 8vo, cl, dj, vii, 342pp.

1061 ..."Brig. Gen. James Johnston Pettigrew." In: Mil. Medicine, 1965, v.CXXX, p.225-228.

1062 ..."Maj. Gen. Stephen D. Ramseur, CSA." In: Mil. Medicine, 1965, v.CXXX, p.1016-1022. (Ellis' Artillery and 49th North Carolina)

1063 ..."Brig. Gen. William R. Terrill, USV, and Brig. Gen. James B. Terrill, CSA." In: Mil. Medicine, 1966, v.CXXXI, p.178-183.

1064 ..."Major General Thomas L. Rosser, CSA." In: Mil. Medicine, 1966, CXXXI, p.72-80.

1065 **STELL, John D.**
"A letter from the Texas Secession Convention. Edited by Willard E. Wight." In: SwHQ, Oct. 1956, v.LX, #2, p.289-291.

1066 **STENNIS, John**
"The Image of Jefferson Davis." (Jackson, Miss.) Jour. Miss. Hist., Apr. 1960, v.XXII, #2, p.123-127. Unveiling of a statue of Davis in Wash.

1067 **STEPHEN, Leslie, Sir**
"The "Times" on the American War; a historical study." London: W. Ridgway, 1865. N.Y., W. Abbatt (The Magazine of History with notes and queries, Extra number #37, 1915. sm.4to, wraps, 104pp.

1068 **STEPHEN, Walter Willisson**
"The Brooke guns from Selma (Ala.)." In: Ala.HQ, Fall 1958, v.20, p.462-475. Can-

nons mfg. in Selma naval foundry, 1863-1864.

..."The Sunken Guns of the Chattahoochee River." In: AHQ, Winter 1958, v.20, #4, p.618-22.

1069 **STEPHENS, Alexander Hamilton**
Autograph: note on small paper, on Dec. 10, 1866.

1070 ..."A.L. Sig." 4to, 1p. Crawfordville, Georgia, 1842, V-Pres. of the CSA.

1071 ..."Acceptance and unveiling of the statue of Alexander Hamilton Stephens. Presented to the State of Georgia. Proceedings in the Congress and in Statuary Hall, United States Capitol." Washington: Gov. Print Office, 1929. 70th Cong., 2nd Sess. Senate Doc. 179. 8vo, cl, port, front, 63pp.

1072 ..."Assertions of a Secessionist: from the speech of A.H. Stephens, of Georgia, November 14, 1864." N.Y., Loyal Publication Society, 1864. 8vo, sewn, 8pp. DeRenne II, p.671, notes a same copy with no imprint of printer's name on last page.

1073 ..."A Compendium of the History of the United States from the earliest settlement to 1872. Designed to answer the purpose of a text-book in schools and colleges as well as to meet the wants of general readers. By..., author of "Constitutional View of the Late War between the States" and professor elect of History and Political Science in the University of Georgia. New Edition. Revised." N.Y., E.J. Hale & Sons, 1874. 8vo, cl, illus., 513pp.

1074 ..."A Comprehensive and Popular History of the United States, embracing a full account of the discovery and settlement of the country, the history of the Colonies until their union as States; the French and Indian Wars; the War of the Revolution; the War of 1812; the long period of peace; the Mexican War; the Great War between the North and South and its results; the Centennial of our Independence; the Assassination of President Garfield; and events down to the present time. E, bellished with more than 360 fine historical engravings and portraits." Baltimore: C. McGarvey (1882) 8vo, cl, portraits, illus., maps, 5-6, vii-xxv, 17-1048pp. See: Isaac Avery, G. Bradford, Rich. H. Clark, Henry Cleveland, D.T. Hamilton, Henry R. Jackson, Rich. M. Johnston, L.L. Mackall, Frank H. Norton, L.B. Pendleton, E.R. Richardson, Jas. A. Stewart, Robt. A. Toombs, R.R. Von Abele, U.B. Phillips.

1075 ..."Confederate Memorial address at Talbottom, Ga., Apr. 26, 1906." 8vo, wraps, 16pp. Atlanta: Parthonon Press (1906).

..."A Constitutional View of the Late War Between the States; its Causes, Character, Conduct and Results presented in a Series of Colloquies at Liberty. (quote)." National Publishing Co., Phila., Cinn., Atlanta, Zeigler, McCurdy Co., Chi., St. Louis, 1868-1870. 8vo, cl,(or, full sheep, 3/4 calf, etc.) map, ports, front, facsm., v.1 (655pp.); II-827. $125.

1076 ...Salesman's Dummy, various paging, illus., ports, list of subscribers at end, with various types bindings.
...Same, 2 vols in one, 654, xii, 827pp. Thick 8vo, 3/4Calf, marbled boards. $75.
...Louisv., Lost Cause Pr., micro-cd. $17.75.
...N.Y., 1970, H.P. Kraus Reprint.

1077 ..."A Letter from Alexander H. Stephens to Dr. George W. Bagby." In: Wm. & Mary Quart., 1936, v.XVI, p.359-361. Friendship with the famous humorist.

1078 ..."A Letter for Posterity Alex Stephens to his Brother Linton, June 3, 1864." Edt: James Z. Rabun. Atlanta, Ga., Library of Emory University 1954; University Publications, Sources and Reprints, series VIII-#3. 8vo, stiff wraps, 24pp. See: Jas. D. Waddell.

1079 ..."Meredith Poindexter Gentry. 1809-1867." In: Confed. Vet., 1906, v.XIV, p.257-261.

1080 ..."My impression of General Robert Edward Lee." In: SB, Feb. 1886, wraps, 7pp.

1081 ...Portrait; Engraving...22x28" overall. By Marshall. N.Y., J. Howard Brown, pub., n.d.

1082 ...Portrait from original painting by Chappel, signature in facsmilie, full length, seated, to left. N.Y., Johnson, Fry and Co., 1867. 7 1/4x5 1/2" engr. surface. DeRenne III.

1083 ..."Prison life of Vice President A.H. Stephens." In: Confed. Vet., April 1906, v.XIV, p.169-173. Extracts from diary.

1084 ..."Recollections of..., His Diary kept when a Prisoner at Fort Warren, Boston Harbour, 1865; giving incidents and reflections of his Prison Life and some Letters and Reminiscences/Edited by Myrta Lockett Avary, with a biographical study." N.Y., Doubleday, Page & Co., 1910. 8vo, port, cloth, xii, 572pp.
...Da Capo Press Reprint, 1971.

1085 ..."The Reviewers Reviewed; a supplement to the "War Between the States", etc. with an appendix in review of "Reconstruction", so called." N.Y., D. Appleton & Co., 1872. 8vo, cl, 273pp. $35.
...Louisv., Lost Cause Pr., micro-cd. $4.50. Stephens answer to bitter reviews of his "Constitutional View". Special chap. where he repudiates his "forged" speech, given in the Ga. Convention.

1086 ..."The Rebuke of Secession Doctrines by Southern Statesmen." Phila: Printed for gratuitous distribution, 1863. 8vo, sewn, 16pp. Also includes the forged speech, p.6.

1087 ..."Prophecy and Fulfillment Speech of A.H. Stephens, of Georgia, (Vice-President of the so-called Confederate States) in opposition to Secession in 1860. Address of E.W. Gantt, of Arkansas, (Brig.-Gen. in the Confederate Army) in favor of Reunion in 1863. (cut of Loyal Publication Society seal), #36. N.Y., Holman Print, 1863. 8vo, wraps, 45pp. (H.P. 1865) Speech of Stephens of Nov. 14, 1860 and that of Gantt. DeRenne, II, p.660 reports issue of N.Y., 1865, Stephens speech only, 22pp.

1088 ..."A Campaign Tract for 1864." Extract from A.H. Stephens' Speech in Georgia, Jan. 1861." n.p. (1864) 12mo, caption title, sewn, 16pp. Another forged speech printing.

1089 ..."Prophecy and Fulfillment. Part I. Speech of A.H. Stephens, of Georgia, (Vice-president of so-called Confederate States) in opposition to Secession, Delivered November 14, 1860." (Loyal Publication Society, tract 36.) (N.Y., 1865) 8vo, caption title, 22pp. This is the genuine speech, DeRenneIII, p.1317. While containing a note on cover title: "Part II. Address of E.W. Gantt, is not contained in this printing. NOTE: Many others used this "forged" speech: Edward Everett "Address at Faneuil Hall, Oct. 19, 1864. John Minor Botts-"Great Rebellion". John William Draper's "Hist. of American Civil War."

1090 ..."A Remarkable Relic of the Confederacy." Letter addressed to Judge Thos. J. Semmes, dated: Crawfordsville, Ga., Nov. 5, 1864. Read before the Louisiana Historical Society on Feb. 20, 1895. New Orleans, La., L. Graham and Son 1895, v.I, pt. II, p.25-36. Publications. See: Ulrich B. Phillips (Edt.) "Corresp. Robert Toombs, Alex H. Stephens and Howell Cobb."

1091 ..."Reminiscences of Alexander H. Stephens vs those of Gen. Richard Taylor." By Hon. Alexander H. Stephens, Late Vice-President of the Southern Confederacy." Excerpt--New York: The International Review, The A.S. Barnes Co., 1878. 8vo, sewn, p.145-154. V.5, #2, March-April.

1092 ..."Speech of Hon. Alex. H. Stevens(sic), delivered at City Hall Park, Augusta, Georgia, on Saturday Evening, Sept. 1, 1860." caption title. Indianapolis: Bingham & Doughty (1860). 8vo, sewn, p.11.
...(Wash.?) Lemuel Towers, n.d., $1000. 8vo, sewn, 16pp.

1093 ..."Speech for the Union, by Alexander H. Stephens, now Vice-President of the Southern Confederacy, delivered at Milledgeville, Georgia, in Nov. 1860, before the members of the Georgia Legislature." Delivered Nov. 14th. Baltimore: John W. Woods, (1861?) 8vo, sewn, 8pp. DeRenne, II, p.637.
...Reprint: in Allen D. Candler's "Confederate Records", v.1, p.183-205.

1094 ..."Speech of Hon. Alex H. Stephens, delivered before the Georgia Legislature on Wednesday night, March 16, 1864. Reported for the Atlanta Intelligencer by A.E. Marshall and revised by himself." Atlanta, Ga., Intelligencer Press, 1864, 8vo, sewn, 28pp. Attacks government policies.

1095 ..."The Great Speech of..., delivered before the Georgia Legislature, on Wednesday night, March 16, 1864, to which is added extracts from Gov. Brown's message to the Georgia Legislature." n.p. (1864) caption title. (Milledgeville) 8vo, sewn, 32pp.

1096 ..."The Great Union Speech of Hon. Alexander H. Stephens, Vice-President of the Southern Confederacy." n.p. (1894?) folio broadside 19x11 1/2". Another issue of the forged speech used in political camp.

1097 ..."Extract from a Speech by Alexander H. Stephens, Vice-President of the Confederate States, Delivered in the Secession Convention of Georgia, January, 1861." n.p. (1863?) (Boston: Rifley Print) 3pp., 12mo, 4pp. folder. See DeRenne, III, p.1315. Extensive notes on forgery, v.II, p.660. It being used in the campaign of 1864 but repudiated by Stephens, as well as by L.L. Mackall in N.Y. Herald Tribune, Nov. 9 and 16, 1924 in "Books".

1098 ..."Some Lincoln correspondence with Southern leaders before the outbreak of the Civil War, from the collection of Judd Stewart." (N.Y.?) 1909. wraps, 19pp. Corresp: Lincoln, Stephens & Crittenden.

1099 ..."Who is Responsible for the War? Who Accountable for its horrors and Desolation? Extract from a Speech by Alexander H. Stephens (now Vice-President of the Confederate States, delivered in the Secession Convention of Georgia, on the 31st day of January, 1861." n.p., 1864? 4to Broadside, 9x11". Another example of the "forged" speech.

1100 **STEPHENS, Bertha**
"The Rebel Cousins; or, Life and Love in Secessia, the Autobiography of the beautiful Bertha Stephens, the accomplished niece of the Hon. Alexander H. Stephens, Vice President of the Southern Confederacy; the terrible trials of imprisonment and severe sufferings she endured, etc., written by herself." Edt: Alfreda Eva Bell. Philadelphia, Barclay & Co., 1864. 8vo, wraps, (19)-48pp. 4-pls (inc. frt.)

1100a **STEPHENS, J. W.**
"Special report on Confedeate Pension Law." Austin, Tx., 1908. 8vo, wraps, 6pp.

1101 **STEPHENS, John**
"Confederate salt works." In: Jr. Hist., Texas, Jan. 1951, v.11, (#4), p.1-2, 22. View. On Swenson's Salines, Lampasas, Tex. (Co.)

1102 **STEPHENS, Linton**
"Biographical Sketches of...(Late Assoc. Justice of Supreme Court of Georgia) containing a selection of his Letters, Speeches, State Papers, etc., Edt: James

D. Waddell, Atlanta, Ga., Dodson & Scott, 1877. 8vo, cl, 4pp., 434pp. port, atg. Stephens. $150.

1103 **STEPHENS, Robert G.**
"Georgia's part in the War Between the States." In: CV, Sept. 1925, v.XXXIII, p.334-337.

1104 **STEPHENS, Robert W.**
"August Buchel: Texas Soldier of Fortune." (Com. 1st Tex. Cavalry) Dallas, Tex., 1970. 8vo, wraps, 7pp., 200 copies.

1105 **STEPHENS, Winston J.T. and Octavia**
"Rogues and Black Hearted Scamps"; Civil War letters of Winston and Octavia Stephens 1862-1863. Edited by Ellen E. Hodges and Stephen Kerber." In: Fla.HQ, July 1977, July 1978, v.LVI/LVII, p.45-74, 54-82.

1106 **STEPHENSON, Nathaniel Wright**
"The Day of the Confederacy; a chronicle of the embattled South." New Haven: Yale Univ. Press, Chronicles of America Series, Allen Johnson, Edt., v.XXX, 1919. 8vo, decr. cl, pl, ports, front, xi, 214pp. Edt: 1920, same.

1107 ..."The Confederacy, fifty years after." In: Atlantic, CXXIII, June 1919, p.750-755.

1108 ..."A theory of Jefferson Davis." In: Amer. Hist. Rev., Oct., 1915, v.21, p.73-90.

1109 ..."Davis and the validity of Sectionalism." In: Lectures on Typical Americans and their problems..." Claremont, Cal., Scripps College, 1919. Scripps College papers, III, p.39-56.

1110 ..."The Question of Arming the Slaves." In: Am. Hist. Rev., Jan. 1913, v.XVIII, p.295-308. Reprint, wraps, 14pp., Atg.

1111 **STEPHENSON, P.D., Rev.**
"Defense of Spanish Fort. On Mobil Bay- Last Great Battle of the War. By P.D. Stephenson, Fifth Co., Washington Artly., New Orleans, La., (Piece Four)." In: SHSP, April 1914, v.XXXIX, p.118-129.

(Comments of Dabney Maury, in SHSP, p.130-136, above issue.

1112 ..."Missionary Ridge, by P.D. Stephenson, Priv. First, Co.K, 13th Ark. Inf. 2nd, of 5th Co., Washington Artly. A paper read before R.E. Lee Camp, #1, of Richmond, Va., Feb. 21, 1913." (Richmond? 1913) 8vo, cover title, 14pp.
...Also: SHSP, April 1914, v.XXXIX, p.8-22.
...In: Confed. Vet., Nov. 1913, v.XXI, p.540-541.

1113 ..."Reminiscences of the Last Campaign of the Army of Tennessee, from May 1864 to January 1865, by P.D. Stephenson, Pvt. Piece 4, Sgt. Thomas C. Allen, 5th Co., Washington Artillery, Capt. C.H. Slocomb, Commanding." In: SHSP, 1884, v.XII, p.32-39.

1114 **STEPHENSON, Richard W.**
"Civil War Maps An Annotated List of Maps and Atlasas in Map Collections of the Library of Congress." Washington, D.C., Map Division, Reference Department, Library of Congress, 1961. sm.4to, stiff decr. wraps, v, 138pp. Index.

1115 ...Falls Church, Va., Civil War Press, 1977, reprint. $5.95. Maps listed here, do not include those in Clara Egli Le Gear's Hotchkiss Collection, (Washington, 1951). See: Civil War Maps in National Archives."

1116 **STEPHENSON, Wendell Holmes**
"Civil War, Cold War, Modern War: Thirty Volumes in Review." (Lexington, KY) JSH, August 1959, v.XXV, #3, p.287-305.

1117 ..."Charles W. Ramsdell: Historian of the Confederacy." (Lexington, Ky.) JSH, Nov., 1960, v.XXVI, #4, p.501-525, extract. Reprint: wraps, 30pp.

1118 **STEPP, John W.**
"Mirror of War. The Washington Star reports the Civil War. By John W. Stepp,

compiler and editor, Star Staff writer and I. William Hill, feature editor, the Star." Englewood Cliffs, N.J., Prentice-Hall, 1961, 4to, cl, dj, facsms, illus., ports, index, vi, 378pp. Also published in "The Sunday Star Magazine" beginning Jan. 8, 1961-1965, serially.

1119 **STERKX, H. E.**
"Partners in Rebellion: Alabama Women in the Civil War." Cranbury, N.J., Associated University Presses, 1970. 8vo, cl, d/w, 238pp. illus., bibliog., (Rutherford: Fairlie Dickison Univ. Press.)

1120 ..."Some Notable Alabama Women During the Civil war." (University, Ala.) Alabama Civil War Centennial Comm., 1962. 8vo, wraps, ports, 70pp.

1120a **STERKX, H. E., Edt.**
"A Patriotic Confederate Woman's Diary 1862-63." In: AHQ, Winter 1958, v.20, #4, p.611-17.

1121 **STERN, Philip Van Doren**
"The Confederate Navy, a Pictorial History." Garden City, N.Y., Doubleday, 1962, 4to, cl, dj, illus., map-liners, 252pp.
...N.Y., Bonanza Reprint.

1122 ..."Robert E. Lee. The Man and the Soldier. A Pictorial Biography by..." N.Y., McGraw-Hill Book Co. (1963) 4to, cl, dj, illus., facsms, ports, maps, genealogical chart, 256pp., index.
...N.Y., Bonanza Books (1963).

1123 ..."The Man Who Killed Lincoln. The Story of John Wilkes Booth and his part in the assassination." New York: Random House, 1939. 8vo, cl, port(front)vii, 376pp., map endsheets, pocket at end contains 32pp. pamphlet: "Afterword", in which the author discusses the sources used in writing this book, tells what happened to some of the people who were involved in the assassination and comments on the still-unsolved mysteries surrounding the murder of Abraham Lincoln, together with a bibliography." Fictionalized account of the murder. Ports, ill.

1124 ..."Prologue to Sumter. The Beginnings of the Civil War from the John Brown Raid to the Surrender of Fort Sumter. Woven into a continuous narrative." Bloomington: Indiana University Press, Civil War Centennial Series, (1961). Tk. 12mo, cl, dj, illus., incl. front, ports, maps, xvi, (1), (17)-57pp. index.
...Greenwich, Conn: Fawcett Pub. (1961) "A premier Civil war Classic", paper.

1125 ..."Secret Missions of the Civil War. First hand accounts by men and women who risked their lives in underground activities for the North and the South, woven into a continuous narrative by..." Chicago: Rand McNally and Co. (Feb. 1959) 12mo, cl, dj, illus., 320pp. 2nd (1960).
...N.Y., Bonanza Books (1959).

1126 ..."Soldier Life in the Union and Confederate Armies. Edited with an introduction and notes by Philip Van Doren Stern. From "Hardtack & Coffee", by John D. Billings and "Detailed Minutiae of Soldier Life in the Army of Northern Virginia by Carlton McCarthy, original sketches by Charles W. Reed and William L. Sheppard." Bloomington: Indiana University Press, Civil War Centennial Series, (1961). 12mo, cl, dj, ix, (1), (13)-400pp. index. (See also: Carleton McCarthy)
...Greenwich, Conn., Fawcett Pub. (1961) "A premier Civil War Classic", paper.

1127 ..."They Were There. The Civil War in Action as seen by its Combat Artists. With six poems by Walt Whitman." N.Y., Crown Publishers, (1959) 4to, cl/bds., illus., b/w, 6pp. in color, ports, 166, (2)pp. index. Both Union and CSA. $35.

1129 ..."When the Guns Roared; World Aspects of the American Civil War." Garden City, N.Y., Doubleday, 1965. 8vo, cl, dj, illus., map(on liners), ports, xxii, 385pp. Notes, bibliog., p.(353)-372. Foreign relations and public opinion, CSA and U.S.

1130 **STEUART, George Hume**
"Battle of Gettysburg." In: SHSP, 1880, v.8, p.132-136.

1131 ..."Operations around Winchester." In: SHSP, 1881, v.9, p.330-332. See: Lamar Hollyday, Stephen D. Thruston, W.P. Zollinger.

1132 **STEUART, Richard Dennis**
"The Story of the Confederate Colt-to the memory of E. Barkley Bowie." 1934: Army Ordnance, XV, p.83-92. See: Wm. A. Albaugh, in colab. with.

1133 ..."The Long Arm of the Confederacy." In: CV, July 1927, v.XXXV, p.250-253. Cannons used, where obtained and the various types.

1134 ..."How Johnny got his gun." In: CV, May 1924, v.XXXII, p.166-169.

1135 ..."Firearms of the CSA, 1861-1865." In: Mag. of Antique Firearms, Dec. 1911. Athens, Tenn., Jno. N. Clements.

1136 ..."Confederate buttons." In: Natl. Button Bul., Jan./May 1960, v.19, p.22-27, 54-55, 131-133. views. From the Essex Inst. Hist. Col. July 1943. On types and mfgs. CS military buttons.

1137 **STEVENS, Atherton H., Maj.**
"The First Federal to enter Richmond." In: SHSP, 1902, v.30, p.152-153.

1138 **STEVENS, Flora E.**
"Lee: an Epic." Kansas City, Mo., Burton Pub., (c.1917) 12mo, wraps, 80pp. incl. front.

1138a **STEVENS, Hawley**
"C.S.S. 'Georgia;' memory & history." In: Amer. Neptune, Summer, 1985, v.45, p.191-8.

1139 **STEVENS, J.H.**
"The Artillery at Williamsburg-May 4/5, 1862." In: Field Artlly. Jour., Jan. 1913, v.III, p.85-95.

1140 **STEVENS, John W., Judge**
"Reminiscences of the Civil War. By Judge Jno. W. Stevens, a soldier in Hood's Texas Brigade, Army of Northern Virginia." Hillsboro, Texas: Hillsboro Mirror Print., 1902. 8vo, wraps, front(port), 213pp. $650.
...Powhatan, Va., 1982, Rep. $400-bmk-105.
...Gaithersburg, Md., Butternut Press, 1982. $22.

STEVENS, Tillman H.
1141 "The "Other Side" in the Battle of Franklin." In: Confed. Vet., April, 1903, v.XI, p.165-168.

1142 **STEVENS, Walter B.**
"The home coming of Shelby's men." In: Mo.HR, July 1925, v.XIX, p.604-610. Return of Missourians of CSA sympathies, with Gen. Shelby from Mexico and 1st reunion of ex-Missourians of ex-CSAs at Roanoke in 1871.

1143 **STEVENSON, Carter L., Maj.-Gen.**
"Operations about Lookout Mountain." In: SHSP, 1880, v.8, p.270-275.

1144 ..."Report of...from beginning of the Dalton-Atlanta campaign to May 30, 1864." In: SHSP, 1877, v.3, p.225-229.

1145 ..."Report of the Tennessee Campaign." In: SHSP, 1877, v.3, p.161-167. See: John Wm. Jones.

1145 **STEVENSON, Elizabeth**
"Surviving the Civil War Years." In: GaHQ, Spring 1980, v.LXIV, #1, p.85-91. Contrasts Mary Gay's Dixie During War and Diary of Emma Holmes.

1147 **STEVENSON, Laura Agnes, Mrs.**
"The Ladies Benevolent and Industrial Sallymog Society, being a series of comic chapters, taken from an unpublished novel written by L.S. Charlottetown, Prince Edward Island. Also a condensed account of Southern Campaign, written by the late S. Wentworth Stevenson, formerly of H.B.

Majesty's service, 6th Dragoon Guards, Carbiniers, subsequently of the Confederate Army, America." Charlottetown, Prince Edward Island: W.H. Bremmer, 1868. $50. 12mo, cl, xi, (1), (13)-131pp. (Ark. Univ.)

1148 **STEVENSON, Reston**
"Wilmington and the Blockade Runners of the Civil War." In: Univ. NCMag., March 1902. 6pp.

1149 **STEVENSON, Richard Randolph**
"The Southern Side; or, Andersonville Prison, compiled from official documents by R. Randolph Stevenson...together with an examination of the Wirz Trial. A comparison of the mortality in northern prisons and Southern. Remarks on the Exchange Bureau, etc. An Appendix, showing the number of prisoners that died at Andersonville and the causes of death. Classified lists of all that died in stockade and hospitals, etc. By the Chief Surgeon of Confederate Military Prison Hospitals." Baltimore: Turnbull Bros., 1876. 8vo, decr. cl, front (fldg. diagr.) plates, fldg. facsm., 488pp. $100-ob.

1150 ..."Prospectus of a book entitled: "The Southern Side; or, Andersonville Prison." Halifax, Nova Scotia, 1874. 8vo, wraps, 10pp. inscribed by author.

1151 **STEVENSON, Samuel Wentworth**
"Sketch of a Southern Campaign, by S. Wentworth Stevenson, formerly of H.M.S. 6th Dragoon Guards." p.(103)-131. See: Mrs. Laura Agnes Stevenson.

1152 **STEVENSON, William G.**
"Thirteen months in the Rebel Army, being a narrative of personal adventure in the infantry, ordnance, cavalry, courier and hospital services, with an exhibition of the power, purposes, earnestness, military despotism and demoralization of the South, by an impressed New Yorker." N.Y., A.S. Barnes & Burr, 1862 (London) 16mo, cl, illus., front, 232pp. Editions: 1863, 1864. $60.

1153 ..."Treize mois dans l'armee des rebelles, aventures d'un engage volontaire malgre lui, par William G. Stevenson." Geneva, Imprimerie Ramboz et Schuchardt, 1863. 16mo, cl, 181, (1)p.
...N.Y., A.S. Barnes & Co. (1959) 16mo, cl, dj, front(illus.), 160pp. $75.

1154 **STEVENSON, William Grafton, Capt., CSA**
"Diary of Wm. Grafton Stevenson, Capt., C.S.A." In: Ala. Hist. Quart., Spring, 1961, v.23, #1 and 2, p.45-71.

1155 **STEWART, Alexander Peter**
"General Stewart's report, April 3, 1865, operations of his corps on 29th Nov., 1864." In: SB, 1882-1883, p.199-201, v.1. J.B. Hood denies any intention of reflection on Stewart's conduct.

1155a **STEWART, Charles West**
"The Blockade & the Cruisers of the Confederacy." cover title. Wash., ? 1917. 8vo, wraps, 14pp, ills, maps. Reprint of the June 1917-'Sea Power.' Stewart was editor of the Official Records Union & CSA Navy.

1156 **STEWART, D.B.**
"First Infantry Fight of the War." In: CV, Oct. 1909, v.17, p.500. CSAccount of Battle of Philippi.

1157 **STEWART, Earl**
"Alexander Stephens." In: Edwin DuBois Shurter's "Representative college orations." N.Y., Macmillan's, 1909, p.236-241.

1158 **STEWART, Faye L.**
"Battle of Pea Ridge." In: MHR, Jan. 1928, v.XXII, p.187-192.

1159 **STEWART, George Rippey**
"Pickett's Charge, a microhistory of the final attack at Gettysburg, July 3, 1863." Boston: Houghton, Mifflin Co., 1959. 8vo, cl, dj, xii, 354pp., plans, ports, illus. $35.

...Dayton, Oh., Morningside, 1986, $20.
...Dayton, Oh., Morningside, 1980. $15.

1160 **STEWART, James A.**
"Conservative Views. The Government of the United States: What is it? Comprising a correspondence with Hon. Alexander H. Stephens, eliciting views touching the nature and character of the government of the United States, the impolicy of secession, the evils of disunion and the means of restoration." Atlanta, Ga., Franklin Print., J.J. Toon, Prop., 1869. DeRenne, II-714. 8vo, cl, covers bound-in, 92pp.

1161 **STEWART, Joseph Spencer and Lucian L. Knight**
"Georgia oratory, containing selections from Georgians arranged in chronological groupings to illustrate outstanding epocs in Georgia history. Designed for special use of high schools and colleges." (Athens, Ga., McGregor Co., 1933. 12mo, cl, 111pp. (CSA, p.18-60.)

1162 **STEWART, Kensey Johns**
"A Geography for Beginners. By the Rev. K.J. Stewart. Palmetto Series. Illustrated with maps and engravings." Richmond, Va., J.W. Randolph, 1864. 16mo, cl, illus., maps, vii, 223pp. Maps with imprint: George Philip and Son, London and Liverpool.

1163 **STEWART, Miller J.**
"For Them, No Medals or Crowns." In: "Horseman", March 1974. Horse supply situation of CSA and Union Armies.

1164 **STEWART, O. Sidney**
"The Capture and Escape of James L. and Dr. Jesse M. Stewart, Co.C., 41st Tenn. C.S.A. by their brother O. Sidney Stewart. Published by their nephew, S.W. Dandridge." Fayetteville (Tenn.) Pylant's Press. (192?) cover title, 8vo, (28)pp.

1165 **STEWART, R.D.**
"Tarheel's thin gray line." In: SHSP, 1899, v.27, p.174-176. See: Bradley T. Johnson's title.

1166 **STEWART, William C.**
"Bill Anderson: Guerrilla. Was he killed in 1864? Or did he live near Brownwood, Texas, until two years ago?" Ft. Worth: Texas Monthly, April, 1929, v.III, #4, p.455-462. Chief henchman of Wm. Quantrill.

1167 **STEWART, William H.**
"Description of the Battle of Crater. Recollections of the Recapture of the lines." Suffolk, VA., Robt. Hardy Pub., 1986. 8vo, wraps, 20pp., facsm., port. 61st Va. Inf.

1168 **STEWART, William Henry**
"Appomattox." In: B & L, 1893, v.1, illus., port, p.293-295.

1169 ..."Beleagured Petersburg." In: B & L, 1893, v.II, port, p.172-174.

1170 ..."Biographical sketch of Lieut.-Col. William Frederick Niemeyer, of the sixty-first Virginia Infantry, by Col. Wm. H. Stewart." Portsmouth, Va., (190?) 8vo, wraps, 7pp.
...Same, In: SHSP, 1900, v.XXVIII, p.84-88.

1171 ..."The Charge of the Crater. A graphic account of the memorable action." In: SHSP, 1897, v.XXV, p.77-90; v.XXXIII, 1905, p.353-357.

1172 ..."Colonel John Bowie Magruder, an historical sketch of his life." In: SHSP, 1899, p.205-210, v.27.

1173 ..."Confederate Valor and Devotion (from the Spartansburg, S.C., Spartan." In: SHSP, 1899, v.27, p.383-384.

1174 ..."Description of the Battle of Crater, recollections of the recapture of the lines." Norfolk, Va., Landmark Office, 1876, 16mo, wraps, 16pp.

1175 ..."The last victory of the Lost Cause." In: B & G, 1894, v.IV, ports, p.20-21.

1176 …"The "No Name" Battle." In: B & G, 1895, v.V, p.29-32 (CSA side; followed by that of the union)

1177 …"Our March to Gettysburg." In: B & G, 1893, v.II, p.300-301.

1178 …"A Pair of Blankets, war-time history in letters to the young people of the South." $200, $150. N.Y., Broadway Pub. Co., (1911) 12mo, decr. cl, photo on cover, 2-ports, incl. front, 217pp.

1179 …"Prison Life of Jefferson Davis." In: SHSP, 1904, v.XXXII, p.338-346.

1180 …"Shaft of Historic Old Portsmouth Artillery-"The Patriotism of Peace", a speech by Col. Stewart." In: SHSP, 1906, v.XXXIV, p.155-161.

1181 …"The Spirit of the South; orations, essays and lectuers by Col. Stewart." N.Y., Neale Pub., 1908. 12mo, cl, 238pp. $75. Chaps: Lee, Jackson, Davis, Army of N.Va.

1182 …"Spirit of the South" contains many articles, e.g., Eulogy/Birthday of Lee, Battle Spottsylvania Hist. Crater, Life of/Port. of Matthew F. Maury, Women of the South, Army Northern Virginia, Mahone's Brigade, Fitzhugh Lee, Stonewall Jax, Jeff Davis and Appomattox.

1183 …"The Typical Hero of the South." In: SHSP, 1892, v.XX, p.311-314.

1183a **STICK, David**
"The Civil War: a history of Smith Isle and Cape Fear, (N.C.)." A chapter in his 'Bald Head--History of Smith Island & Cape Fear.' p.43-49, ills, port, map. Wendell, N.C., Broadfoot Pub., 1985.

1184 **STICKLES, Arndt M.**
"A Confederate Fort and Historical Marker on the Campus of Western Kentucky State College." In: FCHQ, Oct. 1965, v.39, #4, p.326-330.

1185 …"Simon Bolivar Buckner; Borderland Knight." Chapel Hill: Univ. of N.C. Press, 1940, 8vo, cl, xi, 446pp., ports, illus. Brig.-Gen. thru war in CSA, later was Gov. of Ky. Lifelong friend of Grant. $55.

1186 **STICKLEY, E.E.**
"Battle of Sharpsburg." In: CV, Feb. 1914, v.XXII, p.66-67.

1187 …"Stonewall Brigade at second Manassas." In: CV, May 1914, v.XXII, p.231-232.

1188 **STIDGER, Felix G., Edt.**
"Treason History of the Order of Sons of Liberty, formerly Circle of Honor, succeeded by Knights of the Golden Circle, afterward Order of American Knights. The Most gigantic treasonable conspiracy the world has ever known. Chicago: 1903, for the author. 8vo, cl, 246, 30pp., front, illus., ports. $100, $125.

1189 **STILES, John C.**
"For distinguished valor and skill." In: CV, Aug.-Sept., 1924, v.XXXII, p.310-311, 348-349, CSA and Navy list of promotions.
…"In the year 1861." In: CV, 1917, v.25, p.80-82, from OR, v.I-III; p.120-121 (v.IV) "In the year 1861-1862." p.317-319 (v.V); "In the Year 1862", p.368-369; p.414-416; "In the Years of War", 1862, p.464-465.

1190 **STILES, Joseph Clay, Rev.**
"Capt. Thomas E. King; or, A word to the Army and the country." Charleston, S.C., South Carolina Tract Society, 1864. 16mo, wraps, cover title, 56pp.

1191 …"National Rectitude the only true basis of national prosperity; an appeal to the Confederate States." Petersburg, Va., Evangelical Tract Society 1863. 12mo, wraps, 45pp.

1192 **STILES, Kenneth L.**
"4th Virginia Cavalry." Lynchburg, Va., H.E. Howard, 1985. 8vo, cl, dj, (6), 154pp., illus., maps, ports, sketches.

1193 …"Selma and the Confederate States Navy." In: AR, Jan. 1962, v.15, #1, p.19-37.

1194 **STILES, Robert**
"Address at the dedication of the Monument to the Confederate dead, University

of Virginia, June 7, 1893." Richmond, Va., Taylor and Taylor, 1893, 8vo, wraps, 28pp. Also in: SHSP, 1893, v.XXI, p.15-37.

1195 ..."Address before Washington and Lee University on Jan. 19th, 1875, the fifth anniversary celebration of the birth of General R.E. Lee." In: SHST, 1875, v.II, p.41-52.

1196 ..."Four Years Under Marse Robert by Robert Stiles, Major of artillery in the Army of Northern Virginia." N.Y., Neale Pub., 1903. $125, $100-b. 8vo, cl, illus. on cover, front(port), xvi, (17)-368pp.
...2nd Edt., 1903.
...3rd Edt., 1904, eighth thousand, 1905 Edt., 1910.
...Dayton, Ohio: Morningside Press, 1977. With introduction and index by Robert K. Krick, p.xvi, 378.
...Dayton, Oh., Morningside Press, 1988. 8vo, cl, 368pp. $20.

1197 ..."It was obedience even unto death. Jas. H. Beers came South to fight with us." In: SHSP, 1899, v.XXVII, p.17-25.

1198 **STILL, John S.**
"Blitzkreig, 1863; Morgan's Raid and Rout." In: CWH, September 1957, v.III, #3, p.291-306, map.

1199 **STILL, William N., Jr.**
"Confederate behemoth-the CSS Louisiana." In: CWTI, Nov. 1977, v. 16, #7, p.20-25, illus., ports.

1200 ..."Confederate Naval Strategy: The Ironclad." (Houston, Tex.) JSH, Aug., 1961, v.XXVII, #3, p.330-343. $8.

1201 ..."The Confederate States Navy at Mobile, (Nov.) 1861 to August 1864." In: AHQ, Fall-Winter 1968, p.127-144.

1202 ..."The Career of the Confederate Ironclad "Neuse"." In: NCHR, Jan. 1966, 13pp. $8.

1203 ..."Confederate Shipbuilding." Athens, Ga., Univ. of Ga. Press, 1969. 8vo, wraps, xii, 110pp.
...Columbia, 1987. 8vo, cl, dj, ills, 132pp. $18.

1204 ..."Confederate Shipbuilding in Mississippi." (Jackson, Miss., Jour. Miss. Hist.) Nov. 1968, v.XXX, #4, p.291-303.

1205 ..."Confederate Naval Policy and the Ironclads." In: CWH, June 1963, v.IX, #2, p.145-158.

1206 ..."Facilities for the Construction of War Vessels in the Confederacy." (Houston, Tex.) JSH, Aug. 1965, v.XXXI, #3, p.285-304.

1207 ..."Iron Afloat. The Story of Confederate Armorclads." (Nashville, Tenn.) Vanderbilt University Press, 1971. 8vo, x, 260pp., sketch maps, facsms., illus. cross-sect. ship as endsheet.
...Columbia: University of South Carolina Press, 1985. 8vo, cl, 262p,. ills, index. $18.
..."The Iron Rebel Navy - the birth of the armored Confederate fleet." In: CWTI, June 1980, v.19, #3, p.22-31, ills, ports.
..."Selma & the Confederate States Navy." In: AR, Jan. 1962, v.15, #1, p.19-37.

1208 **STILLWELL, Lucille**
"John Cabell Breckinridge...(heading "Born to be a Statesman.")." Caldwell, Idaho: Caxton Print, 1936. 12mo, cl, facsm., illus., ports, incl. front (5)-196pp. map inside cover, bibliog., index, 183-196.

1209 **STINSON, Byron**
"The Battle of Tupelo." In: CWTI, July, 1972, v.11, #4, p.4-9, 46-48, illus., maps, port.

1210 **STINSON, Dwight E.**
"The bloodiest atrocity of the Civil War." In: CWTI, Dec. 1963, v.II, #8, p.42-46, illus., map, ports.

1211 **STINSON, J.B., Dr.**
"The Last Reville. A Memorial Ode with several other poems by..." cover title. (Sherman, Texas, Democrat Press) 1903, 8vo, wraps, port, 8pp., (1)p. music. Emory.

1211a **STIRMAN, Ras**
"In Fine Spirits; the Civil War letters of Ras Stirman." Fayetteville, Ark., Washington County Historical Society, 1986. 8vo, paper, 83pp. $10. Confederate Arkansas.

1212 **STOCK, Leo Francis**
"Catholic Participation in the Diplomacy of the Southern Confederacy." In: Catholic Historical Review, XVI, 1930. Apr. p.1-18. Account of Father Bannon of St. Louis and Bishop Lynch of Charleston, for sympathy of Ireland for the Southern cause. Reprint: wraps, 18pp.

1213 **STOCKHAM, Richard**
"Alabama iron for the Confederacy." In: AR, July 1968, v.21, #3, p.163-172.

1213a **STOCKTON, Will & Ju.**
"The correspondence of Will & Ju Stockton, 1845-69. Annotated by Herman Ulmer, Jr. Jacksonville, Fla. 4to, wraps, xii, 312pp, port, facsm. $25. Three-fourth of 150 letters written in civil war days; including 19 from Col. Stockton while in Federal prison: Johnson's Island in Lake Erie.

1214 **STOKER, William Elisha**
"The War Letters of a Texas Conscript in Arkansas. Edt: Robert W. Glover." In: AHQ, 1961, v.XX, p.355-387.

1215 **STOKES, J.W.**
"The retreat from Laurel Hill, W.Va." In: SB, Sept./Oct., 1884, v.3, p.11-16, 61-66. Jim Parsons leads 1st. Ga. Vols., under Maj. G. Harvey Thompson around Corricks Ford on the retreat.

1216 **STOKES, John Lemacks**
"Eldon Drayton; or crises intellectual and Moral. By Reginald May (pseud.)." Nashville, Tenn., Southern Methodist Pub. House, 1886. 16mo, cl, 205pp. Moralistic tale set in Charleston during war.

1217 **STOKES, Marcus B.**
"A long march to battle." In: Cavalry Jour., 1931, v.XL, p.38-39, 64. A 469 mile march of a cavalry reg. from S.C. to Virginia during war, taken from Journal of Col. William Stokes.

1218 **STONE RIVER, Battle of**
See: S.N. Roach

1219 **STONE, Alfred Holt**
"Fact and Tradition in Southern History." (Jackson, Miss., Jour. Miss. Hist., Jan. 1955, v.XVII, #1, p.1-23.

1220 ..."Post Bellum Reconstruction an American Experience." (Jackson, Miss., Journal of Miss. Hist., July, 1941, v.III, #3, p.227-246.) Much about secession, constitutional.
"The early slave laws of Mississippi. Being some brief observations thereon in a paper read before the Mississippi Historical Society, a meeting held in Natchez, Apr. 20, 1899. (cover title)" (Oxford, Miss., 1899) reprint from Pub. MHS, v.2, p.133-145.

1221 ..."Mississippi Constitution and statements in reference to freedmen and their alleged relations to Reconstruction acts and war amendments." In: MHSP, 1901, v.iv, p.143-226, Oct. 1901.

1222 **STONE, Benjamin**
"My Love to them all: Letters of Pvt. Benjamin Stone, CSA, to his Sister." In: Miss. Quart., 1970, v.XXIII, 1. 175-179. (The 3rd Miss.)

1213 **STONE, Cornelia Branch**
"Catechism for Children. Arranged for the Veuve Jefferson Davis Chap. U.D.C., Galveston, Texas. 1904" 12mo, wraps. See: Becca Lamar West.

1224 **STONE, David Marvin**
"Lee's Birthday." In: SHSP, 1889, v.17, p.355.

1225 **STONE, Henry**
"General Sherman's method of making war." In: SHSP, 1885, v.13, p.439-441.

1226 ..."Hood's invasion of Tennessee." In: Cent., Aug. 1887, #4, p.597-616. illus., ports, maps.

1227 **STONE, Henry Lane**
"Morgan's men escape from prison, etc. Paper read at quarterly meeting of the George B. Eastin Camp, 803, UCV, April 1901, Louisville, Ky." In: CV, 1906, v.14, p.188-192. port.
..."Morgan's Men", a narrative of personal experiences delivered before George B. Eastin Camp #803, UCV-Free Public Library, Louisville, Ky., April 8, 1919." (Louisville, Ky., Westerfield-Bonte Co.) 1919. 8vo, wraps, port, 36pp.

1228 ..."Reminiscences of Morgan's Men." In: SB, 1882/1883, v.I, p.406-414.
"Morgan's Men", a narrative of personal experiences by Henry Lane Stone delivered before George B. Eastin Camp #803, UCV. at the Free Public Library, Louisville, Ky., April 8, 1919." Suffolk, Va., Robt. Hardy Pub., 1986. 8vo, wraps, 40pp. front(port)

1229 **STONE, James H.**
"General Absalom Madden West and the Civil War in Mississippi." In: JMH, May, 1980, v.XLII, #2, p.135-144.
STONE, Kate Brokenburn
See: Sarah Katherine Stone Holmes.

1230 **STONE, W.J., Capt.**
"Argument of...Examiner of Confederate Pensions before the Court of Appeals, June 30, 1913." Frankfort, Ky., 1913. 8vo, wraps, 20pp. A legal first. First layman with a case, not his own, before appeals court.

1231 **STONEBRAKER, J. Clarence**
"The Unwritten South. Cause, progress and result of the Civil War. Relics of hidden truth, after forty years." Hagerstown, Md., Bookbinding and Pr. (1903) 12mo, cl and boards, 193, (1)pp.
...(1903) with illus., 212pp.
...(1908) n.p., ports, color front., 224pp., (1)pp., 12mo, cl. This is the 3rd Edt.
...(1908) n.p., 4th Ed.t 209pp.
...(1908) n.p., 6th Edt.

1232 **STONEBRAKER, John R.**
"A Rebel of '61." New York and Albany: Wynkoop, Hallenbeck, Crawford Co., 1899, 8vo, cl, 116pp., front, illus. (facsms.), plates, ports, fldg. genealogical table, with Co.C, 1st. Md. Cavalry, A.N.V. $650-ob, $250-b, Pres-$500.

1233 **STONEMAN'S RAID into Virginia**
See: Wm. Henry Fitz Lee.

1234 **STONESIFER, Roy P., Jr.**
"Gideon J. Pillow: a study in egotism." In: THQ, 1966, v.25, p.340-350.
STONEWALL (Ironclad) C.S.N.
See: Thomas Jefferson Page.

1235 **STONEWALL BRIGADE**
"Battles of the Stonewall Brigade." From: Rockingham Register, Nov. 10, 1895. In: SHSP, 1895, v.23, p.56-57. See: C.A. Fonerden, Wm. Terry, E.E. Stickley.

1236 **"STONEWALL JACKSON'S WAY."** (song)
See: John Williamson Palmer. Title: (Book) See: John Walter Wayland.

1236 **"STONEWALL SONG BOOK, The**
Being a Collection of patriotic, sentimental and comic songs." Fourth edition (head of title) Richmond, Va. 1983 (West & Johnston?) 5 3/4" tall, 72pp. Pict. wraps. Goodspeed notes Crandall-3274 (1865) as a 11th Edt., revised.

1238 **STONEY, John Safford, Dr.**
"Recollections of John Safford Stoney, Confederate Surgeon. Edt: Samuel G. Stoney." In: SCHMag., Oct. 1959, v.60, p.208-220. notes. Medical service in CSArmy. Early life.

1239 **STONEY, Samuel Gaillard**
"The Memoirs of Frederick Adolphus Porcher. Edited by Samuel G. Stoney." In:

S.C. Hist. & Geneal. Mag., 1943, #2, v.XVIV.

1240 **STONY CREEK, Battle of**
See: W.R. Brooks

1241 **STOREY, L.J.**
"The story of the great war." In: CV, 1902, v.10, p.17-21.

1242 **STOREY, Leonidas Jefferson, Hon.**
"Address of Hon. L. J. Storey at the celebration of the 99th anniversary of the birth of Jefferson Davis, held at Lockhart, Texas, under auspices of the Geo. E. Pickett Camp, Confederate Veterans, the X.B. Debray Chap. UDC." (Lockhart, Texas) 1907. 8vo, wraps, 19pp.

1242a **"STORIES of the Civil War."**
Falls Church, Va., 1965. Sterling Press. Bmk(94)-$10. Folio newspaper type, with ills, 52pp.

1243 **STORMONT, John W.**
"The Economics of Secession and Coercion 1861." Victoria, Texas: Advocate Pub., 1957, 8vo, cl, 148pp.

1244 **STORRS, George S.**
"Kennesaw Mountain." In: SB, 1882-1883, v.1, p.135-140.

1245 **"STORY of "General" 1862."**
(Nashville, Tenn.) Nashville, Chattanooga and St. Louis RRy., n.d., 32mo, wraps, illus., ports, (c.1935).

1246 **"STORY of Fort Hell (Fort Sedgewick), The**
Constructed during the siege of Petersburg, 1864-1865." Petersburg, Va., Fort Hell Battlefield, box 43. 8vo, pict. stiff wraps, illus., ports, dbl-pg. map 12pp.

1247 **"STORY of a Monument, The**
Memorial of the unveiling of the monument to the unknown Confederate dead, May 19, 1887 at Hopkinsville, Ky. and address of Hon. Jos. Breathitt, Rev. Chs. F. Deems and Hon. W.C.P. Breckinridge." N.Y., Dennison and Brown, 1888. 8vo, wraps, 70pp., illus., ports, pls. By-S.C.M.

1248 **"STORY of the Confederate**
States Ship "Virginia" (once Merrimac), etc.
See: under Col. Wm. Norris.

1249 **"STORY of the Great War."**
In: CV, 1902, v.10, p.17-20.

1249a **STORY, James Osgood Andrew**
"Pocket diary for 1861. Edt: Dr. Llerena Friend." In: AHQ, 1966, v.28, #1 & 2, p.51-121.

1250 **STOUT, Joe A., Jr.**
"The Erstwhile Duke of Sonora." In: Mil. Hist. of Tex. and SoWest, v.X, #3, 1972. p.197-208pp. Wm. McK. Gwin, as ex-Calif. senator's scheme to establish a new country with himself as "Duke", where Southern institutions could flourish. Maximilian uncooperative.

1251 **STOUT, L.H.**
"Reminiscences of General Braxton Bragg." Hattiesburg, Miss., The Book Farm, 1942, Heartman's Historical Series, no. 63. 8vo, wraps, 23pp. Lim. Edt. 99 copies.

1252 **STOUT, Samuel Hollingsworth, Dr.**
"Outline of the Organization of the Medical Department of the Confederate Army and Department of Tennessee. Edited by Sam. L. Clark and H.D. Riley, Jr." In: Tenn. H.Q., v.XVI, p.55-140. Reminisc. (1897) by former "Medical Dir. of Gen. Hospitals of CSArmy and Dept. of Tenn.

1253 ..."Some facts of the History of the Organization of the Medical Service of the Confederate Armies and Hospitals." Southern Practitioner, XXV, (Sept., 1903), p. 517-526.

1254 **STOUTAMIRE, Albert**
"Music of the Old South: Colony of Confederacy." Rutherford, Madison and Teaneck: Fairleigh Dickinson Univ. Pr., 1972. 8vo, cl, dj, 349pp. Colonial Williamsburg, Richmond Theatre, concerts, 1797-1865.

1255 **"STOVALL'S BRIGADE** at Jackson, Mississippi, July 12, 1863." Editor of the "Land We Love. In: LWL, Sept. 1867, v.III, #5, p.365-367.

1256 **STOVALL, Pleasant A.**
"Robert Toombs, Statesman, Speaker, Soldier, Sage. His career in Congress and on the hustings-his work in the courts-his record with the army-his life at home." N.Y., Cassell Pub. Co., (1892) 8vo, cl, viii, 396pp., ports (incl. front) $10, $12.50, $15 Toombs was Sec. State in CSA, later Brig.-Gen. in active service. $75.

1257 **STOVER, John F.**
"The Ruined Railroads of the Confederacy." In: Ga. H.Q., Dec. 1958, v.XLII, #4, p.376-388. $8.

1258 **STRAIGHT, William M., Edt.**
"The Pensacola Campaign through a nurse's eye." In: Fla. Med. Assn. Jour., Aug. 1969, v.56, p.632-636. Undated letter of a nun of Cornette Sisters, Emmitsburg, Md., period Aug. 12, 1861.-March 1962. Orig. pub. in Pensacola Hist. Quart., July, 1967, v.3, #3.

1259 ..."Florida Medicine and the War Between the States." In: Jour. Fla. Med. Assn., August, 1980, p.748-760.

1260 **STRAIT, Newton Allen**
"An Alphabetical List of the Battles of the Rebellion with dates, from Fort Sumter, S.C., April 12, 1861, to Kirby Smith's surrender, May 26, 1865. Compiled from the Official Records of the offices of the Adjutant-General and the surgeon-General, USA. Also the battles of the War of Independence, war with Northwest Indians, 1790 to 1795 & a chronological history of the late war and the War with Mexico, from 1845 to 1848; and a list of the presidents and vice-presidents of the United States, from Washington to Arthur." Washington, DC, N.A. Strait, 1883. 8vo, cl, 107pp.; 1882 Edt., 320pp. $45.

1261 ..."Alphabetical List of Battles, 1754-1900, War of the Rebellion, Spanish-American War. Phillipine Insurrection and all Old Wars with dates. Summary of events of the War of the Rebellion 1860-1865. Spanish-American War, Phillipine Insurrection, 1898-1900. Troubles in China, 1900 with other valuable information in regard to the various wars. Compiled from official records by Newton A. Strait." Washington, DC: 1900; also 1905. 8vo, decr. cl, (2), 252pp. (CSA-Union, p.3-170. ...1909 Edt.

1262 **STRALEY, W.**
"Soldiers and their Deeds, compiled by W. Straley." Hico, Texas. Hico Print, 1913. 12mo, wraps, maps, ports-1 fldg.) 25pp. ...1915 Edition, 58pp.

1263 **STRANGE, Mildred Lindsey**
"Mobile's Confederate Generals." In: UDCMag., July 1948, v.11, #7, p.18-19.

1264 **"STRANGER'S GUIDE and Official Directory**
for the City of Richmond. Showing the location of the public buildings and offices of the Confederate, State, and City Government, Residences of the principal oficers, etc." (Richmond, Va.), Geo. P. Evans Co., 1863, 16mo, wraps (cover: Oct., Vol. I, #1), 31pp. price $.50, woodcut on t/p.
...Same, another copy, slightly smaller and type reset. Seal of Va., on cover, Reprinted several times.

1265 **"STRATEGIC POINTS,**
their value in War Between the States and how they fiercely fought for." In: SHSP, 1893, v.21, p. 376-383.

1266 **STRATHEDEN, William Frederick Campbell**
"Speech of Lord Campbell in the House of Lords, on the right of neutral powers to acknowledge the Southern Confederacy, March 23, 1863." London: James Ridgway,

1863. 12mo, wraps, 28pp. Grt. Britain and France should recognize CSA Ind.

1267 **STRATTON, J. Taylor**
"Portrait Gallery and Library of R.E. Lee Camp, No. 1. Compiled by J. Taylor Stratton, Richmond, Va., 1913." 8vo, wraps, 11pp.

1268 **STRATTON, Robert Burcher**
"A Father's Talks with his children about three great characters, by a Confederate Soldier." Lynchburg, Va., J.P. Bell Print, 1892. 8vo, wraps, 36pp. Preface signed by R.B. Stratton. Three: Lee, Jackson and Stuart.

1269 ..."Heroes in Gray, by a Confederate Soldier." Lynchburg, Va., Gregory Bros., 1894, 8vo, cl, 140pp. $200-g. Stratton was with the 2nd Va. Cav.

1270 **STRAUS, Isidor**
"A Young Confederate Businessman." In: Jacob Rader Marcus' "Memories of Amer. Jews." Phila.: Jewish Pub. Soc. Amer., 1955 (3 vol.) v.2, p.301-319. Excerpts from a mssc. autobiog. (1911) of author's experience in Columbus, GA., 1862-1866.

1271 **STRAYHORN, Thomas Jackson**
"Letters of Thomas Jackson Strayhorn, Edt: Henry McGilbert Wagstaff." In: NCHR, 1936, v.XIII, p.310-334. A Lt.-Col. in the CSArmy, 1863-1864.

1272 **STREET, James Howell**
"The Civil War: an unvarnished account of the late but still lively hostilities." N.Y., Dial Press (1953) 8vo, cl, 144pp. A Mississippian's point of view.

1273 ..."The Civil War as Told by James Street." N.Y., Dial Press, 1953. 8vo, cl, 144pp.

1274 ..."By Valour and Arms." N.Y., Dial Press, 1944, 8vo, cl, dj, 538pp. Defense of Vicksburg, building the "Arkansas".

1275 ..."Captain Little Ax." Phila: Lippincott, 1956. 8vo, cl, 377pp. Confederate soldier from Mississippi.

1276 **STREIGHT, Colonel**
See: Dabney H. Maury.

1277 **"STRENGTH of the Infantry and Cavalry** Army of Northern Virginia as shown by the inspection reports, February 24-28, 1865." (Washington, DC, 1886) 8vo, sewn, 5pp. See: "Organization of the ANV", "Monthly return of the Dept. of ANV", "Memorandum of Armies, etc."

1278 **STRIBLING, Robert Mackey**
"Causes of Gettysburg Failure." In: SHSP, 1897, v.XXV, p.60-67.

1279 ..."Gettysburg Campaign and Campaigns of 1864 and 1865 in Virginia. By Robert M. Stribling, Lieut. Col. of Artillery, CSA." Petersburg, Va., Franklin Press, 1905. $85-g 12mo, cl, x, (11)-308pp. $97.50.

1280 ..."Story of the Battle of Five Forks and other events of the last days of the Confederacy. The Appomattox Surrender." In: SHSP, 1909, v.XXXVII, p.172-178.

1281 **STRICKLAND, Alice**
"Blockade Runners." In: FHQ, Oct., 1957, v.XXXVI, #2, p.85-93, Plate, port.

1282 **STRICKLER, Givens Brown, Dr.**
"Liberty Hall Volunteers, Co.I, 4th Va. Infty." Lynchburg, Va., J.P. Bell, 1904. p.111-122, composite ports. In: "Historical Papers", #6-Washington and Lee University, Lexington, Va. See: A.T. Barclay, W.G. Bean. $75.

1283 **STRICKLER, Theodore D., Compl.**
"When and Where we met each other on shore and afloat; battles, engagements, actions, skirmishes and expeditions during the Civil War, 1861-1866, to which is added concise date concerning the army corps and legends of the army corps badges; compiled from official and other authentic sources..." Washington, DC, National Tribune (1899) 12mo, cl, 219, (1)pp. Lists engagements by states.

1284 **STRIDER, Robert Edward Lee**
"The Life and Work of George William

Peterkin." Phila: G.W. Jacobs and Co., (1929) 12mo, cl, front, ports, xii, 1, 331pp. Co.F, 21st Va. Inf., under both Lee and Jackson at Cheat Mt. and Valley Campaign. See: also under G.W. Peterkin.

1285 **STRINGFELLOW, Charles Simeon**
"Address before Pegram Battalion Assn." In: SHSP, 1886, v.14, p.29-33.

1286 ..."Infantry of the Army of Northern Virginia." In: SHSP, 1881, v.9, p.500-504.

1287 ..."Reply to ungenerous criticism of R.C. Cave." In: SHSP, 1894, v.22, p.383-386.

1288 ..."Robert Edward Lee." In: SHSP, 1890, v.18, p.136-142.

1289 **STRINGFELLOW, Frank, Rev.**
"War Reminiscences. The Life of a Confederate Scout inside the enemy's line." (n.p., n.d.) (1892). 8vo, wraps, 12pp.
..."War Reminiscences by Rev. Frank Stringfellow of Virginia." n.p., n.d. (1892) 8vo, (4)pp. endorsements by J.W. Daniel, Fitzhugh Lee, Wade Hampdon, H.B. McClellan. See: Geo. F. Stringfellow, Jas. D. Peaney.

1290 ..."Lee's Birthday." In: SHSP, 1889, v.XVII, p.351.

1291 **STRINGFELLOW, George F.**
"Some incidents in the Life of Frank Stringfellow, famous Confederate soldier and scout." In: Wm. & M. Quart., 1934, 2nd ser., v.XIV, p.230-234.

1292 **STRINGFELLOW, M.S.**
"The Bloody Angle." In: SHSP, 1893, v.XXI, p.244-251.

1293 ..."The 13th Virginia Infantry and It's Part in the Confederate Service." Phila., 1886. 8vo, wraps, 18pp. See: Emma C.R. Macon.

1294 **STRINGFIELD, W.W., Capt., CSA, Broadside**
"Martial Law: As Deputy Provost Marshall, for the District, composed of the counties of Carter and Johnson, it is my duty to enforce martial law to the full extent proclaimed by the Maj. General commanding this dept., Regulations... All proclamations issued by Pres. Davis and Commanders of this dept., must be respected. Confed. money must be acknowledged as currency..." Elizabeth Tenn., 1862. 10x9", crudely printed, not in Crandall/Harwell.

1295 **"STROBHART-SAVED BY A WOMAN"**
See: Whitemarsh B. Seabrook.

1296 **STRODE, Hudson**
"Jefferson Davis' Private Letters, 1823-1889." Selected and edited by... New York: Harcourt, Brace and World, (1966) 8vo, cl, d/w, xxi, 580pp., port, as frontis.

1297 ..."Jefferson Davis, American Patriot, 1808-1861." N.Y., Harcourt, Brace and Co. (1955) 8vo, cl, dj, ports, incl. color front, xx, 460pp. "Montgomery Edition" atg.
..."Jefferson Davis, Conf. President." N.Y., Harcourt, Brace and Co., (1959). 8vo, cl, dj, front(port) map liners, xvii, 556pp.
..."Jefferson Davis, Tragic Hero, the last twenty-five years, 1864-1889." N.Y., 1964. 8vo, cl, dj, 556pp.
...N.Y., 1955-1964, 3 vols, (1st edts.) All 1st., dj, $100-bmk, $50-bmk.
"The next and most fatal April." In: VMHB, April, 1964, v.72, #2, p.131-140. Port of Davis.

1298 **STRONG, Edwin, Thomas Buckley and Annetta St. Clair.**
"The Odyssey of the CSS "Stonewall"." In: CWH, Dec. 1984, v.30, #4, p.306-323.

1299 **STRONG, Henry**
"U.S. Grant and Robert E. Lee. A comparison by a Northern Soldier." In: SB, ns, v.II, 1886/1887. p.279-283.

1300 **STRONG, Leah A., Edt.**
"The Daughter of the Confederacy. (Varina A. Davis)." In: Miss. Quart., 1967, v.XX, p.234-239.

1301 **STROTHER, A.E.**
"Battle and capture of Fort Gregg." In: CV, Nov. 1921, v.XXIX, p.425-526.

1301a **STROTHER, David**
"An eye-witness account of the Battle of Lynchburg by Porte Crayon." In: Iron Worker, Spring 1960, v.24, p.26-32.

1302 **STROTHER, David Boyd**
"John Bright, the devil's advocate." In: South. Speech Jour., Summer 1959, v.24, p.201-209. On his influence preventing "British armed intervention on behalf of the South in 1861".

1303 **STROTHER, David H.**
"The last hours of the John Brown Raid-Narrative of David H. Strother. Edt: Cecil D. Eby." In: VMHB, April, 1965, v.73, #2, p.169-177.

1304 **STROUPE, Henry Smith**
"The Religious Press in the South Atlantic States, 1802-1865; an Annotated Bibliography with Historical Introduction and Notes." Durham, N.C., Duke University Press, 1956, 8vo, wraps, x, 172pp. Historical Papers of the Trinity College Historical Society.

1305 **STROYER, Jacob**
"Sketches of My Life in the South." Salem, Mass., Salem Press, 1879, 8vo, p.16 L, 51. (Turnbull V, 103) A slave in Singleton family of S.C.
...Salem, Mass., Observer Pr., 1885, 12mo, wraps, 83pp. third edt.
...Same, New and enlarged edt. 1891, 12mo, wraps, front, 83pp.
...Salem, Mass: Newcom and Gross, 1898, 12mo, cl, 100pp. $750, $65. Account of capture of Fort Sumter by the Union forces. Worked for CSA inside fort, when taken.

1306 **"STRUGGLE for Vicksburg;**
the battle and siege that decided the Civil War, from the editors of Civil War Times, Illustrated." Harrisburg, Pa., Stackpole Print (1967) 4to, hard cover, illus. (some color) maps, ports, (some color), 66pp. Reprint of July, 1967 issue.

1307 **STUART, Albert Rhett, Rev.**
"The Confederate Soldier and the Southern Cause. Address delivered by..., under the auspices of the Confederate Veterans Association, D.C., over the Unknown Confederate Dead in Grace Churchyard, Woodside, Md. May thirtieth, 1901. This address was delivered without notes and subsequently recalled and published by request." Washington, DC: Gibson Bros., 1901, 12mo, stiff wraps, 24pp.
...1902 edt.

1308 **STUART, Alexander Hugh Holmes**
"A narrative of leading incidents of the organization of the first popular movement in Virginia in 1865 to reestablish peaceful relations between the northern and southern states and subsequent efforts of the "committee of nine", in 1869 to secure the restoration of Virginia to the union." Richmond, Va., W.E. Jones, 1888. 8vo, wraps, 72pp.
...Raleigh, N.C., Edwards & Broughton Co., 1948, 8vo, cl, 69pp. "For J. Bailey Owen, Henderson, N.C."

1308 ..."To the People of Augusta County." (n.p., 1861?) Broadside, 37 1/2x22 cm. Crandall-2851.
"The recent revolution; its causes and its consequences, and the duties and responsibilities which it has imposed on the people and especially the young men, of the south." An address of...delivered before the Literary Societies of the University of Virginia, June 29, 1866. 8vo, wraps, 26pp., Swem 5363. See: Alex F. Robertson

1310 **STUART, James Ewell Brown, Gen.**
"Stuart's raid on Chambersburg, Pa." Chambersburg, Pa., Civil War Centennial

Comm., 1962. 8vo, wraps, 12pp., illus., maps.

1311 ..."Military genius portrayed by General J(ames) E(well) B(rown) Stuart, 1833-1864." In: UDCMag. Apr. 1953, v.16, #4, p.31, 34-35. Accomplished as the "foremost cavalry leader of the world."

1312 ... "Cavalry operations in May, 1863." In: SHSP, 1877, v.3, p.177-180.

1313 ..."Cavalry operations on First Maryland campaign, Aug. 30-Sept. 18, 1862, Report of..." In: SHSP, 1877, v.3, p.281-294.

1314 ..."Cavalry Expedition into Pennsylvania in Oct., 1862. Report of..." In: SHSP, 1877, v.3, p.72-76.

1315 ..."J.E.B. Stuart, Cavalry Leader, for Stuart exhibit: Virginia Civil War Centennial Commission, Richmond, Mar. 15-June 15, 1964." (Richmond, Va., 1964.) 8vo, wraps, illus., port., map, (8)pp.

1316 ..."Commission to study proper location of the J.E.B. Stuart Monument." Richmond: Div. of Purchase & Print, Commonwealth of Va., 1953. (Va. Gen. Assembly, 1954. Senate Doc. 12, p.7. Proposes to move monument commemorating CSA forces, commanded by Stuart, to the Yellow Tavern Battlefield, near Richmond.

1317 ..."Correspondence at Lewinsville, 1861." In: SHSP, 1881, v.9, p.191.

1318 ..."The Death of General J.E.B. Stuart. By a private in the 6th Virginia Cavalry." In: Southern Bivouac, v.III, 1st ser. 1884, p.33-34. Reprinted in Battles and Leaders, v.4, p.194. See: SHSP, v.7, p.107-110, 140-144.

1319 ..."Field Letters from Stuart's head quarters." In: SHSP, 1877, v.3, p.190-194.

1320 ..."Field notes at Chancellorsville." In: SHSP, 1883, v.11, p.137-138.

1321 ..."Full report of Gettysburg Campaign." In: SHSP, v.7, 1879, p.401-434.

1322 ..."Letters of General J.E.B. Stuart to His Wife, 1861." Edt: Bingham Duncan. Atlanta, Ga., Emory University, 1943, 8vo, wraps, 30pp. 300 copies. Series #1, Emory Univ. Pubs. Series, Sources and Reprints. $75-ob.

..."Jeb Stuart's letters to his Hairston kin." In: NCHR, 1974, p.261-333.

1323 ..."Official reports on the expedition into Pennsylvania." In: SHSP, 1886, v.14, p.477-484.

1324 ..."PORTRAIT, by Everett R. Garrison." North Middletown, Ky., 40357. Thatchers Mill Historic Prints, 1980. 17x22 1/2" (image size) Lim. Edt., 1000 prints signed and numbered by artist. $30.

1325 ..."Report of the Battle of Chancellorsville." In: SHSP, 1877, v.4, p.9-14.

1326 ..."Report of the Battle of Kelleysville by Stuart and Fitz Lee." In: SHSP, 1877, v.4, p.1-2; Lee's report, p.4-7.

1327 ..."Report of operations after Gettysburg." In: SHSP, 1876, v.2, p.65-78.

1328 ..."Stuart's Last Dispatch." In: SHSP, 1881, v.9, p.138-139.

1329 ..."Roll of the Stuart Horse Artillery." In: SHSP, 1891, v.19, p.281-283. (McGregor's Battery, ANV.) See: Pelham Battery.

1330 ..."A Short History of Gen. J.E.B. Stuart." Park Place, N.Y., Knapp & Co., 1888, 2 3/4x1 1/2" colored booklet, 16pp. facsm. signature. (Packed in Duke's cigarettes.) See: "Heroes of the Civil War", and W.Duke & Sons.

1331 ...Sketch by John C. Ropes, in Theo. F. Dwights's "Critical Sketches" See: W.W. Burgess, Frank Dorsey, Rich. E. Frayser, R.T. Hubard, Bradley Tyler Johnson, Fitz Lee, London Index, Henry B. McClellan, Ralph H. McKim, Benj. B. Minor, John S. Mosby, New Orleans Picayune, Richmond Dispatch, Rich. Examiner, Thos. M.R. Talcott, Richmond Times-Dispatch, Geo. W. Beale, Wm. W. Blackford, Heros von Borcke, Burke Davis, Luther W. Hopkins,

Jno. N. Opie, Jno. W. Thomason, Mueller-Kranefeldt.

1332 **STUART, Meriweather**
"Samuel Ruth and Gen. R.E. Lee. Disloyalty and the line of supply to Fredericksburg, 1862-1863." In: VMHB, Jan. 1963, v.71, #1, p.35-109, facsms, maps, ports.

1333 ..."Col. Ulric Dahlgren and Richmond's Union underground, April 1864." In: VMHB, April, 1964, v.72, #2, p.152-216, ports.

1334 ..."Operation Sanders wherein old frinds and ardent Southerners prove to be Union secret agents." In: VMHB, Apr. 1973, v.81, #2, p.157-216.

1335 ..."Of spies and borrowed names. The indentity of Union operatives in Richmond known as "The Phillipses discovered." In: VMHB, July 1981, v.89, #3, p.308-317.

1336 **STUART, Meriwether**
"The Military Orders of Daniel Ruggles, Department of Fredericksburg, Apr. 22-June 5, 1861." Reprint: Va. Mag. Hist. Biog., April 1961, v.LXIX, #2, p.149-180.

1337 ..."Samuel Ruth and General R.E. Lee, disloyalty and the line of supply to Fredericksburg, 1862-1863." In: Va. Mag. Hist. Biog., 1963, v.LXXI, facsm., illus., map, p.35-109.
...Reprint, wraps, 190pp.

1337a ..."The Record of Virginia Forces, a study in the compilation of Civil War Records." n.p., 1960. 8vo, wraps, fldg. chart, 57pp.

1338 ..."The Record of Virginia Forces. A Study in the compilation of Civil War Records." (Richmond) Va. Mag. Hist. Biog., January 1960, v.68, #1, p.3-57, large fldg. Reg. $8.

1339 **STUART, Reginald C.**
"Cavalry raids in the West: case studies of Civil War cavalry raids." In: THQ, 1971, v.30, p.259-276.

1340 **STUART, W.A.**
"A North Carolina Boy hero (Wilson M. Kher)." In: OLOD, 1875, v.III, p.182-183.

1341 **STUBBS, Jane**
"Virginians Run the Sea Blockade." (Richmond) Va. Cavl., Spring 1960, v.IX, p.17-22, ports, views.

1342 **"STUDIES in Southern History and Politics;**
inscribed to William Archibald Dunning, Lieber professor history and political philosophy in Columbia University, by his former pupils, the authors." N.Y. Columbia Univ. Press, 1914, 8vo, cl, viii, 394pp. $30. i.e., W.L. Fleming, U.B. Phillips, C.W. Ramsdell, M.L. Bonham, Jr., J.G. de R. Hamilton, etc. Sid. D. Brummer.

1343 **STURGES, E.E.**
"Recollections of Jefferson Davis." In: Ky. Hist. Soc. Reg., May, 1912, v.X, p.9-19.

1344 **STURGILL, Claude C. and Charles L. Price**
"McCabe's Impression of the Bombardment of Charleston, 1863." In: SCHM, 1970, v.71, #4, p.266-269.
..."Shock & Assault in the first battle of Fort Fisher (N.C., Dec. 1864)." In: NCHR, Winter 1970, p.24-39.

1345 **STURTEVANT, Wilbur**
"Here Comes the Rebels!" Baton Rouge, La., State University Press, 1965. 8vo, cl, p.xvi, 412.

1346 **STUTLER, Boyd B.**
"West Virginia in the Civil War." A series of sketches by Education Foundation, for distribution to West Virginia newspapers. (Charleston, W.Va., 1958-1962) These releases of around 5pp. typed leaves for BBS or PC, dated, illustrated, following are numbers of CSA interest:
(1)-(107);

1347 (5) Death of John Augustine Washington, Colonel CSA, at Elkwater; on the shooting of Gen. Lee's aide-de-camp by a detachment of 17th. Ind. Inf. near Elkwater Bridge, Sept. 13, 1861. (BBS, 11-30-58);

1348 (11) "First action Kanawha Valley. On the org. of Confed. companies and estb. of camps under Col. Christopher Q. Tomkins and Gen. Henry A. Wise, occupation of Charleston and the beginning of CSA withdrawal from upper valley after action: Scary Creek, July 17, 1861. (BBS, 1-18-59);

1349 (12) CSA rally to control western Va. On the Confed. strategy, July/Aug. 1861 under Gen. W.W. Loring. (PC, 1-18-59);

1350 (13) Preparing the Battle of Kanawha, CSA movements around Charleston, lower Valley, June/July, 1861. (BBS, 1-25-59);

1351 (17) Wise retreats from Kanawha Valley, July/Sept. 861. (BBS, 2-22-59);

1352 (21) Lee fails in mountain campaign. On Lee in W.Va. Aug/Oct. 1861. (BBS, 3-22-59);

1353 (47) W.Va. generals in gray. (BBS, 11-1-59);

1354 (53) Morgan's Men raid across W.Va. July, 1863. (BBS, 1-10-60);

1355 (54) McNeill Rangers capture two generals (BBS, 1-24-60);

1356 (55) The thirty day raid of Jones and Imboden. (BBS, 2-7-60);

1357 (57) Belle Boyd, Confederate Spy. (BBS, 3-6-60) "West Virginia in the Civil War."

1358 (65) John Yates Beall and the Johnson's Isle raid. (BBS, 6-26-60);

1359 (72) The Boy colonel of 25th Inf. CSA. John Higginbotham of Buckhannon, recruits a company at 18 and becomes colonel at age 20. (BBS, 10-2-60)

1360 (93) Charleston man, Capt. Joseph N. Broun made last CSA payroll. (BBS, 8-13-61);

1361 (96) Tuckwiller's Hill skirmish. Col. Geo. Edgar's 26th Bat. Va. Inf. defeats Col. Jno C. Paxton's 2nd W.Va. Cav., Lewisburg, May 2, 1863. (BBS, 9-24-61);

1362 (97) Georgia troops first to aid Va. 1st and 12th Ga. Reg. in W.Va., 1861-1862. (BBS, 10-22-61);

1363 (101) Stonewall Jackson resigns when Richmond meddles with his army. (BBS, 12-31-61);

1364 (102) CSA postal service in W.Va. (BBS 12-17-61);

1365 (103) Robt. Augustus Baily org. Fayetteville Rifles first from Fayette, unit becomes Co.K, 22nd Va. Inf. under Col. Geo S. Patton. (BBS, 12-31-61);

1366 (104) CSA diary: Jas. Edmond Hall of Barbour Greys, later Co.H, 31st Va. Inf. (BBS, 1-14-62) Shetler-220.

1367 ...Charleston, W.Va., Education Found. 1963, Edt: 2nd, 1966. 8vo, cl,dj, illus., maps, vii, 304pp. Based on above 107 parts.
...2nd Edition, with illus. $25., 1966.

1368 ..."The Hanging of John Brown." In: Amer. Hert. Feb. 1955, VI, p.4-9. Unpublished report of D.H. Struthers (Porte Crayon). Facsm. pl., color port.

1369 ..."Annals of the Mountain State." In: W.Va., Rev., Jan. 1930, v.7, p.107-108, 124. Hays family, Peregrine Hays in Moccasin Rangers (Co.A, 19th Va. Cav.) from Calhoun Co. and Henry A. Wise, soldier. Shetler-747.

1370 ..."The Civil War in W.Va." In: W.Va. Hist., Jan. 1961, v.22, p.(76)-82. CSA and Union manpower, formation of regiments and rise of general officers. Shetler-750.

1371 ..."The Confederate Postal Service in West Virginia." In: W.Va. Hist., Oct. 1962, v.24, p.32-41, illus.

1372 ..."Death of Col. John Augustine Washington, CSA." In: Randolph Co. Hist. Soc.,

Mag. Hist. & Biog., 1954, v.11, p.11-18. Shetler-752.

1373 ..."Imboden Raids in Central West Virginia." In: Randolph Co. Hist. Soc., Mag. Hist. and Biog., April, 1961, v.12, p.53-57, illus., ports.

1374 ..."Lee fails in Mountain Campaign." In: Randolph Co. Hist. Soc., Mag. Hist. & Biog., April 1961, v.12, p.40-44. Lee's Cheat Mt. Camp.

1375 ..."White Sulphur Springs: "Battle for law books." In: CWT, June 1961, v.III, #3, (OS)p.17-19, illus., map, port. Profile: George S. Patton. This lesser known action, also known as: Rocky Gap, Dry Creek Howard's Creek and White Sulphur Springs. The Union under Brig.-Gen. Wm. W. Averell ordered troops to seize and carry away the law library at Lewisburg, which belonged to W.Va. anyway. The judges needed them.

1376 **SUARCE, Baron de, Colonel**
"Le Monitor et le Merrimac." Paris: N. Chaix, 1862. 8vo, wraps, 23pp. Favors the CSN

1377 **SUBLETT, Charles W.**
"57th Virginia Infantry." Lynchburg, Va., H.E. Howard, 1985, 8vo, cl, dj, (5), 94pp. maps, ports. 1000 numbered, signed copies

1378 **SUBMARINE "HUNLEY" (Dr. Berry Bownam)**
"The "Hunley"-Ill-fated Confederate Submarine." In: CWH, September 1959, v.V, #3, p.315-319. Harry Von Kolnitz. See: Wm. A. Speer, C.L. Stanton

1379 **SUBSISTENCE DEPARTMENT of C.S. Army**
"Report of Feb. 9, 1865." In: SHSP, 1876, v.2, p.86-103.

1380 **SUDDATH, James Butler**
"From Sumter to the Wilderness: Letters of Sgt. JBS, Co.E., 7th Reg. S.C.V., Edited by Frank B. Williams, Jr. In: SCHM, 1962, v.63, #1, p.1-11.

1380a **SUDEROW, Bryce A.**
"Thunder in Arcadia Valley: Price's defeat, Sept. 27, 1864." Cape Girardeau, Mo., Center for regional history & cultural heritage, Southeast Missouri State University, 1986. 8vo, 176pp.

1381 **"SUGGESTIONS as to Arming the States."**
See: Gabriel Manigault's (author?) South Carolina 1860 Assn. Pub.

1382 **SULIVANE, Clement, Col.**
"Who was last soldier to leave burning city." In: SHSP, 1909, v.37, p.317-318. Signed: "XX".
..."The Fall of Richmond - The Evacuation." In: B&L, v.4, p725-8, ills. 'The Occupation' by Thomas Thatcher Graves.

1383 **SULLINS, David**
"Recollections of an Old Man. Seventy Years in Dixie, 1827-1897. By D. Sullins Cleveland, Tenn., Second Edition." Bristol, Tenn., King Printing Co., 1910. 8vo, cl, illus., ports, incl. front, 426pp. $65. Sullins was Chaplain in 19th Tenn. Reg., 2nd Edt. seems to have been printed in the same year as the First.

1384 **SULLIVAN, Aloysius Michael**
"The ballad of Dick Dowling, a Texas incident, of the War Between the States." N.Y., Amer. Irish Hist. Soc., 1954, 12mo, wraps, (12)pp, plan, port.

1385 **SULLIVAN, David M.**
"The Confederate States Marine Corps in Georgia, 1861-1865." In: AHJ, 1985-1986, v.29, #4, p.75-94.
..."The Confederate States Marine Corps in South Carolina, 1861-5." In: SCHM, Apr., 1985, v.86, p.113-27.

1386 ..."Tennessee's Confederate Marines: Memphis' detachment." In: THQ, Summer, 1986, v.xlv, #2, p.152-168, pl, ports.
..."Baptism of fire (burning of Confederate

schooner 'Judah in Pensacola, 1861." In: Pensacola Hist. Illust., v.1, 1984. p.9-14.

..."John Albert Pearson, Jr.: Arkansas soldier & Confederate Marine." In: AHQ, Autumn, 1986, v.XLV, #3, p.250-60, plate, port.

1387 **SULLIVAN, James R.**
"Chickamauga and Chattanooga Battlefields, Chickamauga and Chattanooga National Military Park, Georgia-Tennessee." Wash: Nat'l. Park Ser. Hist. Handbook Ser., #25." 1956 (reprint 1961). 8vo, pict. color stiff wraps, illus., ports, map, 3-dbl. pg., (4), 60pp.

1388 **SULLIVAN, Mary Mildred**
Broadside: 9x18", n.p., 1927 Christmas. Verse: "The Blue and the Gray", by Francis Miles Finch of Ithica, N.Y., presented to United Daughters of Confederacy Chapter.

1389 **SUMMER, Andrew J.**
"War spirit at the Virginia Military Institute (1861)." In: CV, June 1914, v.XXII, p.261-262.

1390 **SUMMERS, Festus P., Edt.**
"A Borderland Confederate." Pittsburg: University of Pittsburg Press. (1962) Cl, 8vo, 138pp. Letters of Wm. L. Wilson, 12th Va. Cavl.

1391 ..."The Jones-Imboden Raid." In: W.Va. Hist., 1939, v.1, p.15-39.

1392 ..."William L. Wilson and Tariff Reform." New Brunswick, N.J., Rutgers Univ. Press, 1953. "Three years in the saddle", p.17-33, on Wilson's service with Co.B, 12th Va. Cav. in W.Va., and Shenandoah Valley. Shetler-762.

1393 **SUMMERSELL, Charles Grayson**
"The Cruise of C.S.S. Sumter." Tuscaloosa, Ala.: Confed. Pub. Co., 1965, 12mo, stiff wraps, 187pp, port, illus. Lim. 450 copies. Confederate Centennial Studies #27.

..."C.S.S. Alabama: builder, captain & plans." University: Alabama Press, 1985. 8vo, cl, dj, xi, 135p., ills, incl. fold-out plans, ills, ports, notes. $40. Masterful.

1394 **SUMNER, F.W.**
"Written by F.W. Sumner of Texas during the Civil war 1860-1865." sq. 8vo, wraps, cover title, 10, (1)p., typed, stapled.

1395 **SUMNER, John Osborne**
"Materials for the History of the Government of the Southern Confederacy." N.Y., G.P. Putnam's, October, 1890, in Papers of the American Historical Association, v.IV, part 4, p.5-19, wraps, 8vo.

1396 **SUMPTER, John U., Capt., Co.G, 11th Va. Inf.**
"Fighting that was close by us, one who was there tells about the Battle of Drewry's Bluff, errors corrected." In: SHSP, 1909, v.37, p.179-183. Intro: Jno. W. Daniel.

1397 **"SUMTER", Verses, etc.**
See: Joseph Blyth Allston.

1398 **SUNDAY OBSERVANCE**
See: Robert Edward Lee, "General Order, concerning the observance of Sunday." In: SHSP, 1882, v.10, p.91.

1399 **SUNDERLAND, Glenn W.**
"The Battle of Corinth." In: CWTI, Apr. 1967, v.6, #1, p.28-37, illus., map, port.

..."Lightening at Hoover's Gap. The Story of Welder's Brigade." N.Y., 1969. 8vo, cl, dj, 237pp, ills, maps. $17.50. Ky. CSA under Morgan.

1400 **SUPREME COURT of Confederate States**
"Report of Feb. 9, 1865." In: SHSP, v.10, p.125-128, 1876. See: Francis P. Porcher, surgeon.

1401 **SURRATT, John H.**
"A remarkable lecture-John H. Surratt tells his story." In: Lincoln Herald, Dec. 1949, v.51, #4, p.20-33, 39. ports, fasms. Lecture delivered Dec. 6, 1870, at Rockville, Md., on his part in the conspiracy to assassinate Lincoln.

1402 **SURRATT, Mary E., Mrs.**
"Trial of Mrs. Surratt; or, contracts of the past and present." Amator Justitae. Washington, DC, June 5, 1865, caption title, 8vo, 4pp. folder, an appeal for Mrs. Surratt Monaghan I-784.
See: James W. Rogers, Trial of Mrs. Surratt.

1403 **"SURVIVING Confederate Pensioners."**
In: AlaHQ, 1940, v.II, p.208-216.

1404 **SURVIVORS ASSOCIATION**
of the State of South Carolina. "Proceedings of the first and second annual meeting of the..., and oration of Gen. John S. Preston, delivered before the association, Nov. 10, 1870." Charleston, S.C., Walker, Evans, Cogswell. 8vo, wraps, 63pp. 1870.

1405 ..."Proceedings of the third annual meeting of the... and the annual address by Gen. Jubal A. Early, delivered before the association, Nov. 10, 1871." Charleston: Walker, Evans and Cogswell, 1872, 8vo, wraps, 38pp. Dorn-II, 807/807.

1406 ..."Proceedings of the Annual Meeting of the Survivors Association of the State of South Carolina and oration of Gen. J.B. Hood, delivered before the Association, Dec. 12, 1872." Charleston, S.C., Walker, Evans and Cogswell, 1873, 8vo, wraps, 19pp.

1407 **"SUSSEX COUNTY, Va., a tale of three centuries."**
Richmond, Va., WPA workers, 1942, 4to, stiff wraps, 324pp., illus., Rosters. $30.

1408 **SUSSEX LIGHT DRAGOONS,**
A Complete Roster. In: SHSP, 1899, v.XXVII, p.97-98. From: Petersburg Express. See: Wm. M. Blow.

1409 **SUTHERLAND, Daniel E.**
"Former Confederates in the Post Civil War North: an unexplored aspect of Reconstruction History." In: JSH, August, 1981, v.XLVII, p.393-410.

1409a ..."Exiles, emigrants, & sojourners: post Civil War Confederate exodus in perspective." In: CWH, Sept. 1985, v.31, #3, p.237-56. Good bibliography notes.

1409b ..."Looking for a Home: Louisiana's emigrants during the Civil War & Reconstruction." In: LaH., 1980, v.21, p.341-59.

1410 **SUTHERLAND, Elihu Jasper and J.H.T.**
"Dickenson County in War Time. A Community History." Clintwood, Va., 1955, 8vo, wraps, 30pp.

1411 **SUTTON, E.H.**
"Personal Recollections of the Civil war." Demorest, Ga., Banner Print, 1910, 12mo, wraps, front(port) 78pp. cover title: "Grand Pa's War Stories."

1412 ..."Civil War Stories, written by E.H. Sutton. Demorist, Banner Print Co. (1910) 12mo, 78pp. port. Unit roster Co.K, 76-78pp. Dornbusch-p.29, #281, v.2, cover, as above.

1413 **SUTTON, Francena Lavinia Martin**
"A Civil War Experience of some Arkansas Women in Indian Territory." In: Chron. Okl. Summer, 1979, v.LVII, #2, p.137-163, illus., ports.

1414 **SWAIN, Margie P.**
"Mara: or, a romance of the war. A Poem by Miss. M.P.S., of Sunny-Side." Selma, Ala., Mississippian Steam Bk., 1864, 12mo, wraps, 80, (2)pp.

1415 **SWALLOW, Jane Frances**
"A Romance of the Siege of Vicksburg." Boston: Chapple Pub. Co., 1925, 12mo, cl, port, 126pp. Fiction based on fact by author. $30.

1416 **SWALLOW, William H.**
"From Fredericksburg to Gettysburg." In: Southern Bivouac, 1885/1886, ns, v.1, p.352-266.

1417 ..."The First(-third) day at Gettysburg." Sou. Biv., 1885/1886, ns, v.1, p.436-444, 490-499, 562-572, port, map.

1418 ..."Retreat of the Confederate Government from Richmond to the Gulf." In: Mag. Amer. Hist., June 1886, p.596-611. See: Jno. D. Vautier and W.G. Waller.

1419 **SWAN, Samuel Alexander Ramsey**
"A Tennessean at the Siege of Vicksburg: the Diary of Samuel Swan, May-July, 1863." In: Tenn. HQ, Dec. 1955, v.XIV, p.353-372, notes. Edt.: George C. Osborn.

1420 **SWANBERG, W.A.**
"First Blood. The Story of Fort Sumter." N.Y., Charles Scribner's Sons (1957) 8vo, cl, dj, cartoons, facsms, maps, ports, views, index, bibliog., viii, (2), 373pp.

1421 ..."Was the Secretary of War a Traitor?" In: Amer. Hert., Feb. 1963, v.XIV, #2, p.34-37, 96, 7, port, group port.

1422 **SWANN, John S.**
"Excerpts from Swann's "Prison Life at Fort Delaware." Edt: Elizabeth Cometti." In: W.Va. Hist., Jan. 1941, p.22.

1423 **SWANSON, Claude A., Gov. of Va.**
"Proclamation of...on the One Hundredth Anniversary of the birth of General Robert E. Lee." n.p., Jan. 19, 1907. 8vo, wraps, 4pp. Engraved port. Lee on cover.

1423a **SWANSON, Guy R. & Timothy D. Johnson**
"Conflict in East Tennessee: Generals Law, Jenkins, & Longstreet." In: CWH, June 1985, v.31, #2, p.101-10.

1424 **SWEENEY, Talbot**
"A Vindication from a Northern standpoint of General Robert E. Lee and his fellow officers who left the United States Army and Navy in 1861, from the Northern charge of treason and perjury." Richmond, Va., J.L. Hill Co., 1890. 8vo, wraps, 48pp.

1424a **SWEENEY, William M**
"Maj-Gen. Patrick R. Cleburne, CSA." In: Jour. Irish-Amer. Hist. Soc., 1930/1, v.29, p.157-06.

1425 **SWEET, J.S.**
"The Battle of Pea Ridge." Report of: History and general research division of Library of Congress, May 28, 1855. See: Hugh Park, Edt., "Pea Ridge."

1426 **SWEET, Leonard I.**
"The Reaction of the Protestant Episcopal Church in Virginia to the Secession Crisis: October 1859 to May 1861." In: Hist. Mag. Protestant Episc. Ch." 1972, v.XLI, p.137-151.

1427 **SWEET, William Warren**
"The Methodist Episcopal Church and the Civil War." Cincinnati, Oh., Methodist Book, 1912, 8vo, cl, 228pp. Thesis, Univ. Pa., 1912, Preachers in CSArmy, p.219-225.

1428 **SWEET, Zelia Wilson**
"New Smyrna, Florida in the Civil War. Assembled by..., with the help of friends New Smyrna Florida. 1963." A Volusia County Historical Commission Publication, n.p. 8vo, stiff wraps, ports, illus., facsm. (24)pp.

1429 **SWEM, Earl Gregg**
"A list of official publications of the Confederate States government in the Virginia State Library and the Library of the Confederate Memorial Literary Society." Richmond, Va., 1911. Bulletin of the Virginia State Library, v.4, #1, January 1911, 8vo, wraps, 72pp.

1430 ..."Joseph E. Johnston Papers--John Marshall Papers in the Library of William and Mary College, Williamsburg, Va., Wm. & Mary College Bul., 1939, 8vo, wraps, 19pp.

1431 **SWIFT CREEK, Battle of**
See: George C. Cabell.

1432 **SWIFT, Charles Jewett**
"The Last Battle of the Civil War, paper read by..., at the organizing or first meeting of the Columbus Historical Society, Wednesday night, Feb. 10th, 1915." (quote) Columbus, Ga., Gilbert Print,

(1915). $75. 8vo, stiff wraps, port, illus. (incl. front) 33pp. Capture of Columbus by the Union, Apr. 16, '85.

1433 ...Journal of the Military service institution of the U.S., 1915, v.LVI, p.359-375.

1434 **SWIFT, Eben**
"The Military Education of Robert E. Lee." n.p., 1926. 8vo, limp leather, illus., maps, 160pp. $75. Signed, mimeogr. copies used to secure a copyright. War college lectures, 1926-1927 session.
...In: Va. Mag. Hist., Apr. 1927, XXXV, p.97-160. Large part concerns Lee's strategy in the Civil War, p.109-160.

1435 ..."The Bull Run Campaign in Virginia, 1861...compiled by Capt. Eben Swift, 5th Cavalry." (n.p., n.d.) 12mo, wraps, caption title, 4pp.

1436 ..."The Wilderness Campaign. The Wilderness campaign from our present point of view." In: Amer. Hist. Assn., Annual Report for 1908, v.1, p.244-247. See: Morris Schaff.

1437 **SWIFT, Lester L.**
"Col. Jaquess' First Peace Mission." In: FCHQ, January 1967, v.41, #1, p.26-34. Rev. Jaquess was a member of the convention in dividing the Methodist Church, North and South. His efforts thru the church in this peace mission.

1438 **SWIGGETT, Howard**
"The Rebel Raider. A Life of John Hunt Morgan." Indianapolis, Ind., Bobbs-Merrill Co. (1934). 8vo, cl, dj, facsms., illus., incl. front, ports, map liners, 341pp. $30.
...Garden City, N.Y., Garden City Pub., (1937) reprint, above. Edition omits illus.

1439 **SWINDELL, Anna Tillman**
"The Burning of Columbia." Prize essay of Wade Hampton Chapter Daughters of the Confederacy." n.p., 1924, by the U.D.C.

1440 **SWINDELL, David E., III**
"Archaeological Excavations of Gun Emplacement Number 17 (8Es 126): A suspected Confederate Battery at Pensacola, Florida." In: "Bur. of Hist. Sites and Properties, Bul. #5, Div. of Archives and Records Management." Fla. Dept. of State, Tallahassee, Fla. 1976, 4to, p.1-14, illus., drawings.

1441 **SWINDLER, Henry O.**
"The last stroke of a master." In: Am. Mercury, Nov. 1929, v.XVIII, p.321-330. Early's campaign against Washington in June and July, 1864.

1442 **SWINDLER, William F.**
"The Southern Press in Missouri, 1861-1864." (Columbia, Mo., Mo. Hist. Review, Apr. 1941, v.XXXV, #3, p.394-400.

1443 **SWINT, Henry Lee**
"The Northern Teacher in the South, 1862-1870." Nashville, Tenn., Vanderbilt Univ., 1941, Tall 8vo, cl, dj, 221pp.
...N.Y., Octagon Press, 1969, 8vo, cl, reprint.

1444 ..."Dear Ones at Home; letters from Contraband Camps. Selected and edited by Henry L. Swint." Nashville, Tenn., Vanderbilt Univ., 1966, Large 8vo, cl, dj, map, 274pp.

1445 **SWORD, Wiley**
"The Battle of Shiloh." Entire Edition. In: CWTI, May 1978, v.17, #2, 50pp., illus., maps, ports.

1446 ..."Cavalry on trial at Kelley's Ford." In: CWTI, April 1974, v.13, #1, p.32-40, illus., map, ports.

1447 ..."Shiloh: Bloody April." N.Y., Morrow Pub., 1974, 8vo, cl, illus., maps, xx, 519pp. Bibliog., p.463-470. o.p., $45.
...Dayton: Morningside Print, 1983. $35.

1448 ..."Classic of the Civil War." In: Gun Rep., Mar. 1959, v.4, #10, p.16-17, view. On Griswold and Grier revolvers, mfg. for the CSA at Griswoldville, Ga., 1862-1864.
"Shiloh: bloody April." N.Y., William Morrow (1974) 8vo, paper, 430pp., index. $30.

Uncorrected advanced proof. This edt. preceeded the bound 1st edition.

1449 ..."Firearms from abroad. The Confederate Enfield and LeMat revolver with new data on a variety of Confederate small arms. Lincoln, R.E., Andrew Mobray, (1986)." sm. 4to, cl, dj, 110pp. $20. "Man at arms monograph series, #2.

1450 **SYKES' "Walthall's Brigade" adv.**
Nov. 1928, Confed. Vet., p.402. Order: Miss. Augusta Sykes, Columbus, Miss.

1451 **SYKES, Edward Turner, Maj.**
"Correspondence between Gov. Porter and Maj. Sykes, concerning Reynolds Brigade." In: SHSP, 1884, v.12, p.45-48.

1452 ..."General Bragg's Campaigns." In: SHSP, 1883, v.11, p.304-310, 466-474, 490-497; 1884, v.12, p.1-5.

1453 ..."The Monument at Munfordville." In: SHSP, 1884, v.12, p.470-485.

1454 ..."A cursory sketch of Gen. Bragg's campaigns." In: SHSP, 1883, v.XI, p.304-310, 466-474, 490-497; 1884, v.XII, p.1-5.

1455 ..."An incident in the Battle of Munfordville, Ky., Sept. 14, 1862." (1918) (Jackson, Miss., Miss. Hist. Soc. Pub., Centenard Series, vol.II, p.536-548. Author: Capt. in 10th Miss. Inf. Army Tenn., also-Offprint, 8vo, 13pp.

1456 ..."Walthall's Brigade. A Cursory Sketch with personal experiences of Walthall's Brigade, Army of Tennessee, CSA 1862-2865." by E.T. Sykes, Late Adj-Gen. Walthall's Brigade. (Jackson, Miss., 1916 Miss. Hist. Society) 8vo, cl, front (Walthall) and port of Sykes, (1), (479)-623pp. Index, uniform binding with the Miss. Hist. Society. Offprint. $150-b.
...Same above, in "Publications of the Miss. Hist. Soc.-Centenary Series, vol. 1." p.479-623. Jackson, Miss., Printed for Society, 1916. See: Early Life of Walthall in Jour. of Miss. Hist., Jan. 1944, v.VI, #1, p.30-38. See: E.A. Smith, J.E. Robuck.

1457 **SYKES, Eugene Lanier**
"General R.E. Lee, Commemorate, address before R.E. Lee Chap., UDC, Aberdeen, Miss. on the anniversary of the great commander's birth, Jan. 19, 1887." n.p., n.d. (Aberdeen Miss? 1908?) 12mo, wraps, cover title, (3)-12pp.

1458 **SYLVIA, Stephen W. & Michale J. O'Donnell**
"The Illustrated History of American Civil War Relics." Orange, Va., Moss Pubs., 1978. 8vo, cl, ills, 319pp. $35.
..."Civil War Canteens." Orange, Va., Moss Publications, 1983. 8vo, wraps, 120pp, ills. $12.50.

T

1. **TABB, Jennie Masters**
"Father Tabb, his life and his work; a memorial by his niece. Introduction by Dr. Charles Alphonso Smith." Boston: Stratford Co., 1921. 8vo, cl, illus., (4), xi, 174pp. Served on the "Robert E. Lee", ran the Blockade at Wilmington, N.C., 21 times.

2. **TABER, Fred R.**
"Taber Collection (Letters); Calendars of Manuscripts Collections in Louisiana, #1." (Baton Rouge, La.) Louisiana State University, 1938. Prepared by Historical records survey. Works Progress Adm., Series 1. Department of Archives, #1. 4to, 12pp., a series of 19 letters to his family while in the CSArmy, 1861-1862.

3. **TACONEY (Privateer), C.S. Navy**
See: Robert H. Woods.

4. **TAFT, A.W.**
"The Signal Service Corps-address before Camp Sumter, CV, Charleston, S.C., May 1, 1897." In: SHSP, 1897, v.25, p.130-131.

5. **TALCOTT, Thomas Mann Randolph**
"From Petersburg to Appomattox." In: SHSP, 1904, v.XXXII, p.67-72. Was Colonel, Engineer troops, ANV.

6. ..."Officers of Gen. R.E. Lee's Staff." In: SHSP, 1907, v.XXXV, p.25-28.

7. ..."General Lee's Strategy at the Battle of Chancellorsville." In: SHSP, 1906, v.XXXIX, p.(1)-27.

8. ..."Stuart's Cavalry in the Gettysburg Campaign. A reply to the Letter of Col. John S. Mosby, pub. in Richmond, Va., Times-Dispatch, Jan. 30, 1910." In: SHSP, 1910, v.XXXVIII, p.197-210, map.

9. ...(Mosby's answer to Col. Talcott)-"Stuart in the Gettysburg Campaign. A defense of the Cavalry Commander." In: SHSP, 1910, v.XXXVIII, p.184-196.

10. ..."Parole List of Engineer Troops, ANV, surrendered at Appomattox, Apr. 9, 1865." In: SHSP, 1904, v.XXXII, p.51-57.

11. ..."Stuart's Cavalry in the Gettysburg Campaign, a Review by Col. Talcott." In: SHSP, 1909, v.XXXVII, p.21-37. Offprint, $75-bmk.

12. ..."The Third day at Gettysburg." In: SHSP, 1916, v.XLI, p.37-48.
..."Reminiscences of the Confederate Engineer Service." In: Photo. Hist., CW, v.5, p.255-70, ills, ports.

13. **TALIAFERRO, Alexander Galt**
"Gen. Galt Taliaferro." In: CV, Apr., 1921, v.XXIX, p.126-129. Statement of service in the CSA, prepared by Gen. Taliaferro in 1878.

14. **TALIAFERRO, Harriotte Lee, Mrs.**
"Memoir of Mrs. Harriotte Lee Taliaferro. Concerning events in Virginia, Apr. 11-12, 1861. Intro. Notes: Ludwell L. Montague." (Richmond) Va. Mag. Hist. Biog., Oct., 1949, v.57, #4, p.416-420.

15. **TALIAFERRO, William Booth**
"Defense of Charleston from July 1st to July 10th, 1864." In: SHSP, 1876, v.II, p.196-204.

16. ..."Report of the Battle of Averasboro, N.C." In: SHSP, 1879, v.7, p.31-34, 195.

17. ..."Jackson's raid around Pope." In: B & L, v.II, p.501-511.

18. **TALMADGE, John Erwin**
"Joseph E. Brown and Missing Correspondence." In: Ga. H.Q., Dec. 1960, v.XLIV, #4, p.411-418.

19. ..."Peace movement activities in Civil War Georgia." In: Ga. Rev., Autumn, 1953, v.6, p.190-203. Efforts of Alex Stephens, Joe E. Brown, Henry W. Cleveland and Nathan S. Morse, 1864-1865.

20 **TAMKE, Alexander R.**
"Basil Duke Lee: The Confederate F. Scott Fitzgerald." In: Miss. Quart., 1967, v.XX, p.231-233.

21 **TANCIG, W.J., Compiler**
"Confederate Military Land Units 1861-1865." New York: Thomas Yoseloff (1967) 12mo, cl, d/w, 109pp. $40-dj. List, by states, units, regiments and battalions and companies the CSA land forces.

22 **TANKERSLEY, Allen P.**
"John B. Gordon: a Study in Gallantry." Atlanta, Ga., Whitehall Press, 1955. 8vo, cl, dj, facsm., illus., ports, incl. front. xii, 400pp., bibliog., index (p.377-400). $50.

23 ..."Address to the convention of the United Daughters of the Confederacy, 1948." In: UDC Jour., Feb. 1949, v.12, #2, p.12-14. On historiography of the Civil War.

24 ..."Mrs. Joseph E(merson) Brown, wife of Georgia's war governor." In: UDCMag., Oct., 1952, v.15, #10, p.11, 22-23, 26-27, ports. On Elizabeth (Grisham) Brown.

25 ..."Mrs. John B. Gordon: heroine of the Confederacy." In: UDCM, May 1952, v.15, #5, p.6-7, 10, 31, notes, ports. On Fanny (Haralson) Gordon, a Georgian.

26 ..."Sallie Chapman Gordon Law (1804-1894), mother of the Confederacy." In: UDCM, July 1952, v.15, #7, p.6-7, 11, 37, ports. Life in Memphis, work as a nurse during war.

27 ..."The Great Seal of the Confederate States of America (1864 ff)." In: UDCMag., May/June, 1953, v.15, #5, p.3; #6, p.13, 16.

28 ..."How the U.D.C. got its name (1886-1896)." In: UDCMag., Nov. 1952, v.15, #11, p.20-21, 28, port, bibliog. anecdotes of Atlanta.

29 ..."When Sherman visited Georgia's war capital (Milledgeville, 1864)." In: UDCM, Aug. 1952, v.15, #8, p.6-8, 25-26, port, views, bibliog.

30 **TANNER, Robert G.**
"Stonewall in the Valley. Thomas J. "Stonewall" Jackson's Shenandoah Valley Campaign, Spring of 1862." Garden City, N.Y., Doubleday and Co., 1976, 8vo, cl, dj, illus., ports, maps, xix, 436pp.

31 ..."We are in for it-Jackson saves the Valley." In: CWTI, Nov. 1976, v.17, #7, p.16-28, illus., maps, ports.

32 **TANNER, William R.**
"Reminiscences of the War Between the States, by W.R. Tanner, Sr." (Cowpens, S.C.) 1931. 12mo, wraps, port, 26pp. $175-ob. Roll of Co.C and Reg. officers, 22-26. Dorn-II, 917.

33 **TANSILL, Charles C.**
"Jefferson Davis, ardent American." In: Tyler QHGM, Apr. 1949, v.30, p.243-251. Reprint, Ala. Lawyer, v.8, #4(Oct., 1947) on Davis' literary and military career, 1845-1861.

34 **TANSILL, Robert**
"A free and impartial exposition of the causes which led to the failure of the Confederate States to establish their independence." By Col. Robert Tansill, of late Confederate States Army. Washington, D.C.: 1865. $250-g. 8vo, wraps, 24pp., also micro-card, Do: Louisville: Lost Cause Press.

..."Great struggle for Richmond in 1862, by a Confederate Officer." Washington, n.d. Wraps, 20pp. Not LC, Sabin, Crandall, Nevin, Dornb.

35 **TAPP, Hambleton**
"The Assassination of General Wm. Nelson, September 29, 1862 and its ramifications." In: FCHQ, October 1945, v.19, #4, p.195-207.

36 ..."The Battle of Perryville. Confederate Monument, Perryville Battlefield State Park, Perryville, Ky." caption cover. (Perryville, Ky: Lions Club and American

	Legion, Battlefield Post #301) 8vo, wraps (blue paper thruout) ports, (12)pp., illus.
37	..."The Battle of Perryville, 1862. An address before the Filson Club, Feb. 4, 1935." In: FCHQ, July 1935, v.9, #3, p.158-181, map.
38	..."Confederate Invasion of Kentucky, 1862, and the Battle of Perryville, Oct. 8, 1862." (Lexington, Ky., 1962?) 8vo, large 8vo, wraps, cover title, map, bibliog. footnotes, 47 leaves.
39	..."Report of the Kentucky Civil War Centennial Commission, from June 7 thru Dec. 31, 1962." n.p., n.d., 4to, mimeo. (14) sheets, print one-side. ...Do: Jan. 1, 1963-Aug. 1, 1963, p.8, in blue stiff wraps.
40	..."A sketch of the early life and services in the Confederate army of Dr. John A. Lewis of Georgetown, Ky." In: RKHS, April 1977, v.75, #2, p.121-140, (2) maps.
41	TARBELL, Ida M. "Disbanding the Confederate Army." In: CWTI, Jan. 1968, v.VI, #9, p.10-19, illus.
41a	TARLETON, Robert "The Civil War letters of Robert Tarleton. Edt: William N. Still, Jr." In: AHQ, 1970, v.32, #1 & 2, p.21-80.
42	TATE, Allen "Stonewall Jackson the Good Soldier, a Narrative by Allen Tate." N.Y., Minton, Balch and Co., 1928, (J.J. Little and Co., N.Y.) atg.-$45. 12mo, cl, paper labels, illus., maps, ports, incl. front, viii, (1), 322pp. ...(Second printing, April, 1928) same but for thicker paper. ...London, etc., Cassell & Co., (printed by J.J. Little & Co., N.Y.) (1st Pub. 1930). ...(Ann Arbor) University of Michigan Press (1957, c.1856) Ann Arbor paperback. (Edt: 1965, cloth)
43	..."Jefferson Davis: His Rise and Fall. A Bibliographical narrative." N.Y., Minton, Balch & Co., 1929, 12mo, cl, ports, 311pp. $35-jk-122. ...Second printing, 1929. ...N.Y., Kraus reprint, 1969.
44	..."Ode to the Confederate Dead, being the revised and final version of a poem previously published on several occasions to which are added Message from abroad and the cross, by Allen Tate." N.Y., Published for the Author by Minton, Balch & Co., 1930. 19x15cm, (20)pp. Cover title: "Three Poems. A Private edition of 125 copies, of which 25 are numbered and signed by author.
45	..."The Southern Vanguard." N.Y., Prentice-Hall (1947) 12mo, cl, x, 331pp.
46	TATE, Michael L. "The Frontier of Northwest Texas during the Civil War." (Okla. City) Chron. Okla., Summer, 1972, v.L, #2, p.177-189, port. Also: Great Plains Jour., 1972, v.XI.
47	TATUM, Edith Brittain (Crenshaw), Mrs. "Disloyalty and disloyal organizations in the Confederacy." Nashville, Tenn., Vanderbilt University Bul., v.XXXIII, #9, 1933. Abstract of thesis, 8vo, wraps, p.20-21.
48	..."Disloyalty in the Confederacy." Chapel Hill: Univ. of N. Carolina Pr., 1934, 8vo, cl, dj, xi, 176pp. $40-bmk-105. ...N.Y., AMS print(1969), reprint. ...N.Y., AMS print, 1977.
49	TAYLOR'S RIDGE, Battle of See: Mark P. Lowry, Lucius E. Polk.
49a	TAYLOR, A. Reed "The War History of Two Soldiers. John F. Bropst & W. Anderson Stephens: a two-sided view of the Civil War." In: Ala. Rev., April 1970, p.83-109.
50	TAYLOR, Allan and Lois Dwight Cole (pseud) See: Allan Dwight, "Linn Dickson, Confederate", fiction.

51 **TAYLOR, Charles E., Dr.**
"The Signal and Secret Service of the Confederate States by Dr. Chas. E. Taylor." Hamlet, N.C., Capital Print, 1903. 16mo, wraps, 24pp. $35-b. North Carolina Booklet, vol.II, #11, March, 1903. Also: Ed. H. Cummins, CV, 1932, v.40, p.302-305, 338-342.
...Hermons, Md., Toomey Press, 1986. 8vo, wraps, 36pp. $7. Intro. notes: David Winfrey Gaddy.

51a **TAYLOR, Clarence**
"Vignettes of the Civil War in Pine Bluff." In: Jefferson CHQ, Summer, 1963, v.2, p.8-17.

51b **TAYLOR, Ethel**
"Discontent in Confederate Louisiana." In: LaH., 1961, v.2, p.410-28.

52 **TAYLOR, Foster Jay**
"Reluctant rebel." In: La. Lib. Assoc., Bul. Fall, 1959, v.22, p.79-82, 94. Civil War journal of Robert Patrick. See: Robt. Patrick.

53 **TAYLOR, Grace N.**
"The Blair family in the Civil War." In: RKHS, Oct., 1940, v.38, (#125), p.380-394. (#126) p.47-57; (#127) p.138-156.

54 **TAYLOR, H.L.**
"The Indian Battle of Chustenahlah." In: CV, Mar. 1916, v.XXIV, p.122-123. Battle between CSA Reg. and Creeks, Choctaw Indians, in Arkansas, Dec. 25, 1861.

55 **TAYLOR, John Dykes, Sgt.**
"History of the 48th Alabama Volunteer Infantry Regiment, CSA. Edt: William Stanley Hoole, with a partial roster of the regiment." University Ala., Confederate Pub. Co., 1985, Confederate Regimental Series, #7. 8vo, stiff wraps, 42pp. First pub. in the "Montgomery Advertiser, Marcy 9, 1902. This being the first edition separately.

56 **TAYLOR, John S.**
"Sixteenth South Carolina Regiment CSA. From Greenville County, S.C." (Greenville, S.C.) John S. Taylor, 1964. 8vo, color-decr. wraps, flags, ports, 52pp. Pres-$25.

56a **TAYLOR, Lenette Sengel**
"Polemics & partisanship: the Arkansas Press in the 1860 election." In: AHQ, Winter 1985, v.XLIV, #4, p.314-35, map.

57 **TAYLOR, Matthew P.**
"Fayetteville Arsenal, history of the 6th (N.C.) Battalion Armory Guards." In: SHSP, 1896, v.24, p.231-237.

58 **TAYLOR, Milam**
"The Taylor Letters: Confederate Correspondence from Fort Bliss, 1861. Edited by Martin Hardwick Hall." In: MHT and SW, 1979, v.XV, #2, p.53-60.

59 **TAYLOR, Morris F.**
"Confederate Guerrillas in Southern Colorado." In: Colo. Mag., 1969, v.XLVI, p.304-323.

60 **TAYLOR, Osmond B., Capt.**
"Official Report of Gettysburg." In: SHSP, 1885, v.13, p.213-216. Of: Alexander's Battalion Artillery.

61 **TAYLOR, Richard, Lt.-Gen.**
"Advance sheets of Reminiscences of Secession, War and Reconstruction." In: SHSP, 1878, v.V, p.136-140.

62 ..."A chapter of history-his meeting with General Canby." In: SHSP, 1903, v.XXXI, p.48-52.

63 ..."Destruction and Reconstruction, personal experiences in the late war, by Richard Taylor, Lieut-General in the Confederate Army." $75. N.Y., D. Appleton and Co., 1879. 8vo, cl, 274pp. $125-g. Editions: Edinburgh and London, 1879, 8vo, cl, 369pp. (copy 3/4 calf) 2nd Edt: N.Y., 1896 and 1897; N.Y. 1903, a reprinting; London, 1912.
..."Destruction and Reconstruction." N.Y., Time-Life Books, 1982. 8vo, leather. Collectors Lib. of Civil War.
...N.Y., Longmans, Green Co., 1955, Edt:

Richard B. Harwell, xxxii, 380pp. Notes: p.333-369, $15; 2nd reprint, 1959; 1974, Harrisburg, Pa., 1974, Gettysburg, Pa. ...Waltham, Mass., Blaisdell Print, (1968) "Primary sources in American History", stiff wraps, 12mo, xiii, 274pp. The book first appeared in the North American Review, Jan. 1878 to April.

64 ..."The Last Confederate Surrender." In: SHSP, 1877, v.III, p.155-158. Also in: AW, p.67-71.

65 ..."Operations in the Trans-Mississippi Department in June 1863." In: SHSP, 1879, v.VII, p.442-444; 497-502.

66 ..."Reminiscences of the Civil War." In: North Amer. Rev., 1878, v.cxxv, p.77-96.

67 ..."Stonewall Jackson and the Valley Campaign." In: North Amer. Rev., 1878, v.LXXVI, p.238-261. March and April.

68 ..."Terms of capitulation of the command of Lieut-Gen. Richard Taylor." In: SHSP, 1888, v.XVI, p.215-218. See also: D.F. Boyd, Jackson Beauregard Davis, J.E. Hewett, Andre Lafargue, Dabney H. Maury, J.E. Sliger.

69 ..."Walter H. Taylor." (From: Richmond News-Leader) In: SHSP, 1916, v.41, p.82-87.

70 **TAYLOR, Robert A.**
"Cow Cavalry: Munnerlyn's Battalion in Florida, 1864-1865." In: FHQ, Oct. 1986, v.65, #2, p.196-214. facsm.

71 ..."Rebel beef: Florida cattle and the Confederacy, 1861-1865." Thesis: M.A., Tampa University of South Florida. August, 1985, 4to, stiff wraps, vi, 181pp.

72 **TAYLOR, Robert Love**
"The Land of Dixie, extract from a reunion speech by Gov. Love." In: SHSP, 1901, v.29, p.361-364.

73 ..."Robert Edward Lee." Nashville, Tenn., Taylor-Trotwood Magazine, Jan. 1907, p.8.

74 **TAYLOR, Rosser Howard**
"Letters dealing with the Secession Movement in South Carolina." In: Bulletin of Furman University, Greenville, S.C., Dec. 1934. 8vo, wraps, 12pp.

75 **TAYLOR, Thomas E.**
"Running the Blockade. A personal narrative of adventures, risks and escapes during the American Civil War. With an introduction by Julian Corbett, 1896. 12mo, cl, illus., incl. front, port, fldg. map, xxii, 1, 180pp. $50, $75 Bmk105, $100 Bmk106. London: John Murray, 1896. Editions: N.Y., 1896 (2nd); London, John Murray, 1897 (3rd); London, 1912, 4th Edt.' Freeport, N.Y., Books for Libraries (1971).
...N.Y., Arno's "Select Bibliographies Reprint Series." 1979.

75a **TAYLOR, Thomas J., Capt., CSA**
"An extraordinary perseverance, the Journal of . . . Edt. Lilian Taylor Wall & Robert M. McBride." In: THQ, Winter 1972, v.31, #4, p.328-59.

76 **TAYLOR, Walter Herron**
"The Battle of Sharpsburg." (From the "Norfolk Landmark".) In: SHSP, 1896, v.XXIV, p.267-274.

77 ..."Campaign in Penna." In: Annals of War, Phila: 1879, p.305-318.

78 ..."Causes of Lee's Defeat at Gettysburg, "Memorandum by Col. Walter H. Taylor, of Gen. Lee's Staff"." In: SHSP, Aug. 1877, v.IV, #2, p.80-87, 124-139.

79 ..."Four Years with General Lee, being a summary of the more important events touching the career of General Robert E. Lee, in the War Between the States, together with an authoritative statement of the strength of the army which he commanded in the field, by Walter H. Taylor, of his staff." Sig. $225-r, slipcase-$100-b, Mint-$150-jk-137, $65. N.Y., D. Appleton Co., 1877. 8vo, cl, front(port), 199pp. "Ad-

dress on character of Lee by Cap't. John Hampden Chamberlayne", p.190-199.
...Same, 1878.
...Bloomington: Indiana University Press (1962) With a new introduction, index and notes by James I. Robertson, Jr., "Civil War Centennial Series". 12mo, cl, dj, pls, incl. front, xi, 218pp.
...N.Y., Bonanza Reprint, 1972.
...N.Y., Appleton, 1978. 2nd edt. $125-bm.

80 ..."General Lee, his campaigns in Virginia, 1861-1865, with personal reminiscences, by Walter H. Taylor, Adj-Gen. of ANV, CSA." (Brooklyn, N.Y., Braunworth Co., 1906) Norfolk, Va., Nusbaum Book Co., 8vo, cl, fldg. maps, x, 314pp. $150, $275-r.
...(Dayton, Ohio) Morningside Bookshop, 1975. Facsimile #25. 328pp., 9p fldg. color maps.

81 ..."Lee and Longstreet (from the Richmond Tiems, June 14, 1896)." In: SHSP, 1896, XXIV, p.73-79.

82 ..."Numerical strength of the armies at Gettysburg." In: SHSP, May 1878, v.V, #5, p.239-246. See: Cadmus M. Wilcox's review of W.H. Taylor's "Four Years With Lee".

83 ..."Colonel Walter Herron Taylor, A.A.G." In: SHSP, 1916, v.40, p.82-87.

84 ..."Col. Taylor's reply to the Count of Paris." In: SHSP, 1878, v.V, p.242-246.

85 **TAYLOR, William Henry**
"Some Experiences of a Confederate Assistant Surgeon." Philadelphia, 1906. Printed for the College, v.28, third series. 8vo, wraps, 30pp. From: Transactions of the College of Physicians of Philadelphia, v.28, 3rd. series, p.91-121.

86 ..."De Quibus; discourses and essays by; (Human Surgery in the field.)" Richmond, Va., Bell Book Co., 1908, 8vo, 380pp. Contains above essay-"Some experiences of a CSA surgeon." Taylor served with Garnett's Brigade.

87 **TAYLOR, William Rogers, Admiral**
"Rejoinder to Gen. Beauregard..." See: P.G.T. Beauregard's "Mistakes of Adm. Taylor."
"Cavalier & Yankee, the Old South & American National character." N.Y., George Braziller, 1961. 12mo, cl, 384pp. $30-bm.

88 **TEAGUE, B.H.**
"Why Gen. Sherman did not come to Augusta." In: CV, May 1914, v.XXII, p.209.

89 **TEBAULT, Christopher Hamilton**
"Address by the Surgeon General UCV." In: CV, 1900, v.8, p.362-367, port.

90 ..."History of the Association of Medical Officers of the Army and Navy of the Confederacy...read at the meeting of the Association in Mobile, Alabama, April 26, 1910. (20th Annual Meeting of U.C.V.) 8vo, wraps, cover title, (9)pp. reprinted from Aug. 1910 "Southern Practitioner."

91 ..."Official report of C.H. Tebault, Surgeon-General United Confederate Veterans. From minutes of the 12th Annual meeting, held at Dallas, Texas. April 22-25, 1902." New Orleans, La., Palfrey-Dameron (1902) 8vo, wraps, cover title, 31pp.

92 ..."Surgeon General Tebault's report for the 8th Annual Reunion United Confederate Veterans, 1898. 12mo, wraps, caption title, 13pp. Andersonville soldier treatment.

93 ..."Treatment of prisoners during the War Between the States, 1861-1865." n.p., (1905) 8vo, wraps, cover title, 15pp. Reprint from "Southern Practioner", June 1905. Read at meeting of medical officers Army and Navy of the Confederacy June 1904. The 7th Annual Meeting.

94 ..."Surgeon General Tebault's report on Treatment of President of the Southern Confederacy. Jefferson Davis, as a

Federal prisoner and how he was finally released." (New Orleans, La., 1910?). 8vo, wraps, cover title, 40pp. At Annual Meeting of U.C.V., held at Mobile, Ala., April 26-28, 1910-20th Annual Meeting.
..."Official History Report, by Surgeon General U.C.V.--"Who was responsible for the war between the states?" New Orleans, La., 1901. 8vo, wraps, 36p. $30-ob.

95 **TEEL, Trevanion T., Captain, CSA**
"Sibley's New Mexican Campaign-its objects and the cause of its failure." In: B & L, 1887, v.II, p.700.

96 **TEETOR, Paul R.**
"A matter of hours: treason at Harper's Ferry." Rutherford, N.J., Fairleigh Dickinson University Press, 1982. 8vo, cl, dj, 309pp.

97 **TEGO, Heyl G.**
"Confederate pikes (1862-1865)." In: Gun Rep. June 1958, v.4, #1, p.34-35, views, notes.

98 **"TELEGRAMS Received**
by the Confederate War Department and Adjutant and Inspector General's office, in relation to the War of the Rebellion, 1860-1865." Washington, D.C.: Adj-Gen. Print Off., 1876. 8vo, 1 vol. in 2 parts, paged continuously 3/4 Mor., 554pp.

99 ..."Telegrams Sent by the Confederate War Department, in relation to the War of the Rebellion, 1860-1865." Washington, D.C.: Adj-Gen. Print Off., 1876, 8vo, See: Wm. R. Plum

100 **"TELEGRAPH. Direct! By, Natchez Courier Natchez, Mississippi**
Wednesday, June 4, -10, 1/2 a.m. Later news further from Richmond. Killed and wounded, "Natchez Fencibles" (caption title.) Broadside 7x4 5/8" printed blue. Natchez, Miss., (1862) Goodspeed $400. Unrecorded. About Fair Oaks and Seven Pines in Peninsula Campaign.

101 **TELFAIR COUNTY, Georgia**
"Floris Perkins Mann's History of Telfair County, Georgia, from 1812-1949." Macon, Ga., 1949.
...Spartanburg, S.C., Reprint Co., 1978, New index, illus., xviii, 204pp., illus. Rosters for the Civil War and letters from the troops of the period.

102 **TEMPLE, Neville and Ed Trevor**
"Tannhauser; Battle of Bards." See: Chs. Julian

103 **TEMPLE, Oliver Perry**
"East Tennessee and the Civil War." Cincinnati: R. Clarke Co., 1899, 8vo, cl, xvi, 588pp., ports, fldg. map.

104 **TEMPLE, Sarah Blackwell Gober**
"The First Hundred Years; a short history of Cobb County, Ga." Atlanta, Ga., W.W. Brown Pub., 1935. Tk. 8vo, cl, illus., map, xiii, 901pp. 4-chapts., 175pp., on war around Marietta and Atlanta. $125.

105 **"TEN DAYS in Richmond."**
In: Blackwood. Oct. 1862, v.xcii, p.391-402.

106 **TENKOTTE, Paul Allen**
"A note on regional allegiances during the Civil War: Kenton County, Ky. A test case." In: RKHS, Summer, 1981, v.79, #3, p.211-218.

107 **TENNANT, Charles**
"The American Question and how to settle it." London: S. Low, Son & Co., 1863. 12mo, cl, 313pp. France and England should intervene and force a final division between North and South.

108 **TENNESSEE (Ironclad), C.S.Navy**
See: R.C. Bowles, Daniel B. Conrad.

109 **TENNESSEE CONFEDERATE MEMORIAL**
and Historical Association. "Charter and By-laws of... Adopted Jan. 9, 1886." Nashville, Tenn., 1886. 8vo, wraps, 12pp.

110 **"TENNESSEE CONFEDERATE PENSION**
APPLICATIONS, An Index to..." (Nash-

ville, Tenn., 1964) Tennessee State Library and Archives." 4to, stiff wraps, plastic spiral bound, viii, 323pp.

111 **TENNESSEE Civil War Centennial Comm.**
"Directory of Civil War Monuments and Memorials in Tennessee." Nashville: 1963. 4to, wraps, illus., 93pp.

112 ..."Guide to the Civil War in Tennessee." Nashville (Tenn.) Division of Information Dep't. of Conservation, 1960." 4to, color-ill. front cover and endsheets, illus. fldg. map, 32pp. 1st edition.
...Nashville, 1961, 2nd edition.

113 ..."Outline of Unit Work on the Civil War. Prepared jointly by the Tennessee Civil War Centennial Comm. and the State Dept. of Education." Nashville: State Dept. of Education, 1960, 4to, 6 lf, 10pp.
...See also: "Tenn. in the Civil War, a Military History, etc." 2 vols.

114 ..."Tennessee in the Civil War." n.p., 1962, 8vo, wraps, 8pp. Script used in conjunction with a filmstrip.

115 ..."Tennessee in the Civil War. A Military History of Confederate and Union Units with Available Rosters of Personnel." 2 vols. Nashville: Civil War Centennial Comm. 1964-1965. 4to, fabricoid, viii, 471, 608pp. (CSA 313pp.) (471) and 450pp. (of 608) second vol. entirely Index. op. Pub: $17.50, vol. 1, now $25 (roster). Pub: gray cl, reprinted, black cl, vol. II, reprint, 1981, Univ. of Tenn., $60.

115a **"TENNESSEE Civil War Questionnaires."** Original compilers (1914-15) Dr. Gus Dyer & in 1920 by John Trotwood Moore. Edt.: Colleen Morse Elliott & Louise Armstrong Moxley." In 5 vols., Easley, S.C., Southern Historic Press, 1985. $250. 5 vols., as follows:
V.1 - Federal soldiers (Acuff-wood) 161 veterans. CSA (Abbott-Byrne) 204 vets. index, 472pp.
V.2 - CSA soldiers (Caldwell-Fuston) 307 vets. 479pp.
V.3 - CSA (Gailbraith-Kyle) 325 vets. 487pp.
V.4 - CSA (Lackey-Quarles) 317 vets. 510pp.
V.5 - CSA (Rainey-Young) 372 vets. 525pp.

116 **TENNESSEE INFANTRY (C.S.A.)**
"154th Regiment. Camp 154th of Tennessee Regiment near Dalton, Georgia, Jan. 14, 1864. Edt: Buford C. Utley." In: W. Tenn. Hist. Soc. Pap., 1960, v.14, p.124-125. "Minutes of a meeting of all officers and men of the regiment offering to continue without regard to enlistment or date and remain as a unit if ever reorganized. See: Maj. Jack C. Vaughan.

117 **TENNESSEE in the Civil War:**
Stanley J. Folmsbee's "History of Tenn." N.Y., Lewis Pub. Co., 1960, v.1, p.1-69.

118 **TENNESSEE- In SHSP**
See: Dan W. Beard, John Bell Hood "Tenn. Camp.", Stephen D. Lee.

119 **TENNESSEE-Hdq. Army of**
"Headquarters, Army of Tennessee, General Orders, No. 5." General Johnston, at end. Dalton, Ga. 8vo, sewn, 7pp, unrecorded CSA Imprint.

120 **TENNESSEE**
"Action of Tennessee Legislature, May 6, 1861. Military League between the State of Tennessee and the Confederate States. (certified at end). J.E. Ray, Secretary of State." Broadside, two column, closely printed text, 8x19". (Nashville, May 7, 1861?) Official publication, with message of Gov. Isham G. Harris, to enter into a Mil. league with CSA. Transcript of agreement, joint resolution of Leg., ratification and Decl. of Indp., of Tenn., submit to vote, etc. Not in Crand/Harw. $250.

121 ..."House Journal 1861-1862 of the first Session of the 34th General Assembly of

the State of Tennessee, convened at Nashville, First Monday, Oct. 1961, adjourned Memphis, March 20, 1862." Nashville: Tennessee Hist. Comm., 1957. 8vo, cl, d/w, 509pp. Pub. for 1st time.

122 ..."History of Tennessee." Nashville, Tenn., 1886 and 1887 edt., 4to, cl, front, plates, ports, fldg. map, viii, (13)-970. or, 1317pp. "Confederate Military History." p.513-617.

123 ..."House Journal 1861-1862 of the First Session of the Thirty-fourth General Assembly of the State of Tennessee. Which convened at Nashville, on the first Monday in October, AD, 1861 and adjourned in Memphis, March, 20, 1862." (Nashville: Benson Print.) (Tennessee Historical Commission, Nashville, 1957) 8vo, cl, 509pp.

124 **TENNEY, Craig D.**
"To Suppress or not to Suppress: Abraham Lincoln and the Chicago Times." In: CWH, Sept. 1981, v.27, #3, p.248-259. Copperheads, Vallandigham, freedom-of-speech. Edt. Storey's hatred of the Negro and abolitionist Republican party and Lincoln in particular. The congress should go back to original policies of peace and reunion. See: Justin Walsh's "To print the news and raise hell-a Biography of Wilbur F. Storey." Chapel Hill, 1968.

125 **TENNEY, S.F.**
"War Letters of S.F. Tenney, a Soldier of the third Georgia Regiment." In: Ga. H.Q., Summer, 1973, v.LVII, #2, p.277-295. $8.

126 **TEPER, Anthony F.**
"Music of the American Civil War." (London) Jour. Confed. Hist. Soc., Winter, 1968, v.6, #4, p.138-161, pl.

127 **TERRELL, "Spot" F.**
"A Confederate private at Fort Donelson, 1862." In: Am. Hist. Rev., Apr. 1926, v.XXXI, p.477-484. Attach on and surrender of Donelson in 1862 by a member of the 49th Tenn. Vols. defending.

128 **TERRELL, Alexander Watkins**
"From Texas to Mexico and the Court of Maximilian in 1865." Dallas: Book Club of Texas, 1933, 8vo, cl, illus., xviii, 94pp. Limited 200 copies $100.

129 **TERRELL, Kate Scurry, Mrs.**
"Terry's Texas Rangers." In: Dudley G. Wooten's "Comprehensive History of Texas." v.II, p.682-694.

130 **TERRELL, Pinkney Lawson**
"Unagrames, Southern Girl in Wartime" Poem." Statesville, N.C., 1902, N.C. Bunyan, 8vo, wraps, 48pp.

131 ..."The Southern Girl, and other Poems." (Greensboro, N.C., Advocate Print, c.1920) 12mo, wraps, cover title, 85pp.

132 **"TERRIFIC COMBAT**
Between the 'Monitor' 2 guns and 'Merrimac' 10 guns, in Hampton Roads, March 9, 1862." N.Y., Currier & Ives, 1862. Small folio, hand-colored litho. #31 of the "Best Fifty". Large folio (20x25") hand color $200.

133 **TERRILL, Charles Frederick**
"Letters of..." In: Helen Terrill's Hist. Stewart Co., Ga., p.275-289.

134 **TERRILL, Helen Eliza and Sara Robertson Dixon**
"History of Stewart County, Georgia (1828-1958). Sponsored by: Roanoke Chap. DAR." Columbus, Ga., Columbus Office Supply, 1958, 8vo, cl, facsms., map, ports, tables, views, xviii, (2), 805pp.

135 **TERRY'S Texas Rangers:**
Isaac Dunbar Affleck; Benj. Franklin Batchelor; James Knox Polk Blackburn; Ephraim Shelby Dodd; John M. Claiborne; Wm. Andrew Fletcher; Leonidas Blanton Giles; Henry William Graber; Charlie C. Jeffries; Harry Larter; "Letters by Terry Rangers."

136 **TERRY, James G.**
"Record of the Alabama State Artillery from its organization in May, 1936 to the surrender in April 1865 and from its reorganization January 1872 to January 1875. Compiled by James G. Terry." In: Ala. Hist. Quart., Summer, 1958, v.20, #2, p.137-447 (relating to CSA). See: Clyde Wilson.

137 **TERRY, William**
"Memorial stone erected in the Wilderness to the Texas Brigade." In: SHSP, 1891, v.19, p.122-124.

138 ..."The Stonewall Brigade" at Chancellorsville." In: SHSP, 1886, v.14, p.364-370. See: Jno. C. Butler, Xavier B. Debray, John C. Walker.

139 **"TEXAN'S account**
of the Battle of Val Verde. A," In: PPHRev., 1964, v.XXXVII, p.33-35. See: Col. M.L. Crimmins.

140 **"TEXAS Almanac-Extra, The."**
Austin, Texas, April 9, 1863. Broadside-4to, 1p. $125. Communications from Rio Grande on Mexican-Federal activities against CSA-Texas and "Harriet Lane" blockade of Galveston.

141 ...Austin, Texas, March 31, 1863. Broadsheet (flimsy) includes articles on Texas Rangers, news of fighting at Vicksburg by "Pony Express"

142 **TEXAS Brigade-**
"Memorial Stone to..." In: SHSP, 1891, v.19, p.122-124.

143 **"TEXAS Civil War**
Centennial Program." 1861-1965 for 1861-1865. n.p., n.d., 12mo, wraps, 24pp., illus.

144 **"TEXAS Confederate."**
Published every Friday. Numbers: 12, 13, 15, and 16. Each one leaf, printed both sides, 9x6". Austin, Texas: Aug. 26, Sept. 2, 16, and 23, 1864. News of war, editorial comment. Pub. by J.D. Buchanan. Not in Crandall/Harwell.

145 **TEXAS Convention, 1861**
"The ordinances and resolutions of the Convention held in Austin, Jan. 28, 1861-Feb. 24, 1861, Austin 1861." (Austin: Gammel Book Co., 1898) 8vo, wraps, 22pp. (double paging, from Gammel's Laws of Texas, 1822-1897, v.4, p.1517-1538.

146 **TEXAS General Order, No. ----**
Headquarters, Expeditionary Forces, Brownsville (Texas) May 12, 1865... ("Every soldier will find himself in readiness to march on the enemy forces at a moment's notice...etc." Broadside, 7x9". Winkler-1350. John S. (Rip) Ford, Commd. One of the last CSA imprints before battle of Palmetto, the last battle of the war. Accompanied is a mssc. map of fortifications, batteries, number Union troops of a report to Ford. Both-$2500.

147 **"TEXAS Johnny Reb."**
Information circular #4, a supplement to the Confederate Alcove. Texas Memorial Museum, Austin, Texas (1962) 4to, wraps (pict.), (4), (1)-12, (2)pp., mimeographed, color flags.

148 **TEXAS Legislature**
"Resolutions of the Legislature of the State of Texas, on the subject of Slavery." Washington, DC, Senate Doc. #106, 8vo 2pp. sheet. "we are prepared to make common-cause with sister-states of South" over issue, in favor slavery.

149 **TEXAS RANGERS-CSA**
See: Ben McCulloch (Victor Rose's Life of), J.P. Blessington, See: list under Terry's Texas Rangers.

150 **TEXAS in the Civil War:**
Frank W. Johnson's "Histo. of Texas and Texans." Chicago: Amer. Hist. Soc., 1916, p.531-550. Clarence Wharton's, "Texas under many flags." Chicago: Amer. Hist. Soc., 1930, v.1, p.77-119. Lewis Worsham's

"History of Texas." Ft. Worth, Texas, 1924, vol. IV, p.301-366, append.IX, p.391-400.

151 **TEXAS in the Confederacy:**
See: Alwyn Barr's "Texas Civil War Historiography." Most complete list. Llerena Friend's "Books on Texas in the Civil War."

152 **TEXAS-SECESSION ,**
"A declaration of the causes which impel the State of Texas to secede from the Federal Union." (Austin, Texas, 1861) $225. 8vo, caption title, 7pp., $500-j, $800-auction '68, $800, see: Crandall #2153, broadside, TxU. Satin and paper.

153 ...(Winkler, II, pg.26, #169) adds: "adopted in Convention, on the second day of February, 1861. O.M. Roberts, president R.T. Brownrigg, secretary."

154 ...Dallas, Texas, Basye Bros., 711 Main St., adds: "and ratified by the people Feb. 23, 1861." 8vo, wraps, 8pp. (Caldwell collection) See: Winkler, II, #159-174, various editions, imprints relating to secession. E.W. Winkler's "Secession Convention."
..."A declaration of causes which impel the State of Texas to secede from the Federal Union-(caption title) adopted in convention, Feb. 2, 1861, O.M. Roberts, President." n.p., n.d. (Austin, Texas?) 8vo sewn, 7pp.
...Reprint: Dallas, Texas, Basye Bros., n.d., 16mo, duofold sheet, 8pp. Border around t.p., not on the original. (title) "A declaration of the causes which impel the State of Texas to secede from the Federal Union; adopted by delegates of the Texas Convention, Feb. 2, 1861. Ratified Feb. 23, 1861." A footnote attributed authorship to John H. Brown. This copy from John Henry Brown's personal collection." See: "Journal of the Secession Convention of Tex." Anthony Banning Norton.

155 ..."Supreme Court of Texas: Austin term, A.D., 1861. Edward A. Pearson, Adm'r. vs. Giles H. Burditt. Brief for Appealle. Chandler, Turner and Scott, for Appellee." (Austin, 1861) (disputed claims: Matagorda Co.) 8vo, orig. yellow printed wraps, 33pp. Not in Crandall. $200.

156 **TEXAS**
"Joint Resolution of the State of Texas. House of Representatives, No. 30." Austin, Texas, May 4, 1861. Broadside 9 1/2x6". Not in Crand./Harw.

157 ..."Circular-Headquarters District of Texas, New Mexico and Arizona." Houston, Texas: June 7, 1864. 8vo, ipp. By J. Hunter Berrien, Surgeon and Medical Director. Rules for disability for duty in field.

158 ..."Order #3, Houston, Texas. Sept. 13, 1864." 1p. broadside, names J.H. Berrien as Medical Director.

158a ...Secession. Broadside. Committee of thirteen 1861 Resolution offered by Phineas Scruggs - 'resolved that the voluntary association of our fellow-citizens of non-slaveholding states is fraught with imminent danger.' Broadside: 19 1/2 cm, unrecorded. $250. G. Hendershott.

159 ..."Texas: Laws of Eighth Legislature of the State of Texas. Extra Session." Austin, Texas, John Marshall and Co., 1861, 8vo sewed, 69, (1)p. not in Crand/Harw. Chap. IX-Joint resolutions, references to CSA, turns US property over to CSA.

160 ..."Special Laws of the Tenth Legislature (Second Extra Session) of the State of Texas." Austin, Texas: State Gazette, 1865. 8vo sewed, 20pp. Unknown to Crandall/Harwell.
...Do: "Special Laws of the Ninth Legislature of the State of Texas." Pub. by Authority. Austin, Texas: Office of Texas Almanac, 1863, 8vo sewed, 66pp. Unknown to Crandall/Harwell.
... Texas & its late Military Occupation &

161 **TEXT BOOKS-**
See: Marinda Branson Moore, Otto H. Olsen, O.L. Davis, New Texas Readers/Spellers.

162 **THARIN, Robert Seymour Symmes**
"Arbitrary arrests in the South; or, scenes from the experience of an Alabama Unionist." N.Y., J. Bradburn, 1863. 12mo,cl, 245pp. Experiences of Wm. L. Yancey's former law partner.

163 **THATCHER, J.W.**
"Letter from a citizen of the Southern Confederacy." In: Ann, Iowa, 3rd. ser., July, 1920, v.XII, p.366-368. Written from Va., May 12, 1861, to brother in Iowa and reflects intense feelings in a divided family.

164 **THAXTER, Sidney W., Major**
"Stonewall Jackson." Read Mar. 6, 1907- MOOLUS: Main Commandery, War Papers, Portland, Me., Lefavor-Tower Pr., 1908, v.III, p.279-295.

165 **THAYER, William S.**
"Politicians in Crisis: The Washington Letters of William S. Thayer, December 1860-March, 1861. Edited by Martin Crawford." In: CWH, Sept. 1981, v.27, #3, p.231-247. Intimate White House insight into politicians maneuvers South to make first move to war.

166 **THEATRE ,**
See: Terry Theodore (below)

167 **THEODORE, Terry**
"The Confederate Theatre. Theatre Personalities and Practices during the Confederacy." In: Lincoln Herald, Winter, 1974, v.76, p.187-195.

168 **THIAN, Raphael P.**
"A collection of Confederate paper money and bonds of Mr. R.P. Thian, together with coins, medals, badges, miniatures, etc., to be sold Missers Bangs and Co., auctioneers on Tues. Dec. 15th, 1885. Catalogues: David Proskey. Patterson, N.J., (1885) 8vo, 24pp., 2nd catalogue, 528 items.

169 ..."The currency of the Confederate States, arranged by issue, denominations and series." Wash: 1884. 8vo, wraps, 20, (36pp.

170 ..."Documentary history of the flag and seal of the Confederate States of America 1861-1865." Wash: 1880.

171 ..."Letter to Gen. E.D. Townsend, Jan. 7, 1887 (with other matters relating to his "Treasury of the Confederate States.") Wash: 1883, 8vo, 10pp., Wash. 1883, 8vo, 10pp.

172 ..."Report of the Secretary of the Treasury of the CSA, 1861-1865. Compiled under director E.D. Townsend by Raphael P. Thian." Wash: 1878-1880. Duke Univ. 4to, vi, 454pp. Append: "Correspondence of the Treasury Dept., pt.v, +pt. iv, 1878-1880, (4 vols.)

173 **THIAN, Raphael Prosper**
"Confederate Note Album, for a complete collection (with descriptive letter-press) of the various designs for face and back- selected by the Confederate Treasury. Authorities for the currency of the Confederate States of America, 1861-1865." (Washington, The Author, 1876) 13 1/2x24cm., 45, 88pp. LC.

174 ..."Register of issues of Confederate States Treasury Notes, together with tabular exhibits of the debt, funded and unfunded of the Confederate States of America, by..., chief clerk Adjutant-General's Office, 1861-1865." Washington, D.C., Gov. Print Office, 1880, 8vo, wraps, 190pp.

175 ..."Register of the Confederate Debt." Boston: Quarterman Publications, 1972. 8vo, cl, pp.xix, 190pp. Front(port) Foreword by Douglas B. Ball. Only five copies known of original. $35-y.

176 **THIBODAUX Sentinel**
"La Sentinelle de Thibodaus" La., Saturday, Feb. 7, 1863, v.11, #xli. Small folio, on red, green and blue flowered wall paper. An article on "Promulgating the Emancipation Proclamation. "Differs from the English edt. Not in Brigham or Crandall.

177 ..."The Confederate Banner: Official Journal of the Parish of Lafourche and the City of Thibodaux (La.) Saturday October 25, 1862. Small folio, on brown and white flowered wallpaper. Not in Brigham or Crandall. Printed the day Yankees entered Donaldsonville. "Startling News! 20,000 Yankees and Eight Gunboats near Donaldsonville!!!". At end of item, presses stopped and was taken over by soldiers who printed the last column and a third. In margins a soldier writes his wife from Camp Stevens, Feb. 20, 1863: "I found this newspaper in a house printed the day our forces landed...in fact, we only had a force of 5000. Paper wasn't plentiful."

178 **"THIN Gray Line, The"**
Pub. by John B. Gordon Camp, Sons of Confed. Vets. Oblong 10 1/2x7 1/2", 94pp., wraps. Souvenir of Confed. Soldier's Home, Ga.

179 **"THIRD Georgia Regiment, Company E, Steward County, Georgia."** Rawson Rangers." In: Helen E. Terrill/Sara R. Dixson's "Hist. of Stewart Co., Ga., Columbus, Ga., 1958. p.255-257.

180 **"THIS They Remembered-**
The history of the four companies and those in other companies, who went from Oglethorpe County to serve in the War Between the States: The Gilmer Blues The Oglethorpe Rifles the Tom Cobb Infantry The Echols Artillery(verse)." Washington, Georgia: Washington Pub. (date in Forward, Jan. 17, 1965-Gussie Reese, "White Oaks", Lexington, Ga.) 8vo, cl, d/w, half-title, (1), (4), 200pp., illus., ports, facsms, map. Compiled and published by Oglethorpe Co., Chapter #1292, United Daughters of the Confederacy, of Lexington, Ga., as their Centennial Project.

181 **THOBURN, Joseph B.**
"The Cherokee Question." In: Ch. Okl. June 1924, v.II, p.141-242. Letters between Union and CSA leaders in Okl. and Ark.

182 **THOM, DeCourey W.**
"Something more of the great Confederate General, "Stonewall" Jackson and one of his humble followers in the South of yesteryear." Md.Hist.Mag., June, 1930, v.XXV, p.129-157.

183 **THOMAS, Anna Hasell**
"The Diary of...July 1864-May 1865. Edt. Charles E. Thomas." In: SCHM, 1973, v.74, #3, p.128-143.

183a **THOMAS, Charles W.**
"Jefferson Davis anniversary celebration to the Confederate veterans association of Waverly, Alabama." Montgomery, Ala., Private Print, 1909.

184 **THOMAS, Clarence**
"General Turner Ashby, the Centaur of the South. A Military Sketch." Winchester, Va., Eddy Press, 1907, 12mo, cl, ports, xii, 211pp. $200.

185 **THOMAS, Cornelius Maria Dickinson**
"Tales of the Cape Fear Blockade. Being a turn of the century account of Blockade-running as told by the Hon. James Sprunt, formerly purser of the Confederate steamer "Lillian"." Wilmington, N.C., 1960, 12mo, cloth, map, 134pp. Ltd. Edt.

186 **THOMAS, David Y.**
"Arkansas in War and Reconstruction 1861-1874." Little Rock, Ark., Ark. Div., United Daughters of the Confederacy, 1926. $45. 12mo, cl, (10), 446pp., front, illus., port. $60.

187 ..."The Confederate State Government in Arkansas." In: SW Pol. & Sci. Ass'n., 6th

Annual Convention, Dallas, Texas, Mar. 30-Apr. 1, 1925, p.145-161.

188 ..."Missouri in the Confederacy." (Columbia, Mo., Mo. Hist. Review, Apr., 1924, v.XVIII, #3, p.382-391.

189 ..."Calling the secession convention in Arkansas." In: SW Pol. Sci. Quart., Dec. 1924, v.V, p.246-254.

190 **THOMAS, Edison**
"The Great Chieftain's Last Ride: the Story of the Jefferson Davis Funeral Train." Louisville, Ky., L & N RRy. Co. (1955) 8vo, wraps, illus., 8pp. Reprint from article in the Feb. 1955 issue, L & N's Co. Magazine.

191 **THOMAS, Edison H.**
"John Hunt Morgan and His Raiders." Lexington: Univ. Press of Kentucky, 1975, 8vo, cl, dj, xiii, 120pp.

192 **THOMAS, Edward J.**
"Memoirs of a Southerner, 1840-1923." Savannah, Ga., Priv. Print, 1923. 16mo, boards, (7)-64pp. Pictures of plantation life in McIntosh County seaboard, serv. as a CSA soldier. And wartime Savannah.

193 **THOMAS, Edward Lloyd, Brig.-Gen.**
"Report: Battle of Gettysburg." In: SHSP, 1880, v.8, p.323.

194 **THOMAS, Emory M.**
"The Confederate State of Richmond: A Biography of the Capital." Austin: Univ. of Texas Press, 1971, 8vo, cl, d/w, viii, 227pp. illus., map.

195 ..."The Confederate Nation, 1861-1865." N.Y., Harper & Row, 1979, 8vo, cl, dj, xvi, 384pp. Bibliog. 50pp., map, facsms., illus., port. "New American Nation ser." paper.

196 ..."The Confederacy as a Revolutionary Experience." New Jersey-Prentice-Hall, Englewood Cliffs, N.J. (1971) 12mo, color wraps, x, 150pp., cloth.

197 ..."To Feed the Citizens. Welfare in Wartime Richmond, 1861-1865." (Richmond) Va. Cavl., Summer, 1972, v.XXII, #1, p.22-29, ports, illus.(color)

198 ..."The lost Confederates of Roanoke." In: CWTI, May 1976, v.15, #2, p.10-17, illus., map, ports.

199 ..."Old Buck"-Admiral Franklin Buchanan." In: CWTI, Oct. 1978, v.16, #6, p.4-10, 43-46, illus., map, ports.

200 ..."Wartime Richmond." June 1977, #3, 50pp., Entire issue on Richmond. Illus., map, ports.

201 ..."The Richmond Bread Riots of 1863." (Richmond) Va. Cavl., Summer 1968, v.XVIII, #1, p.40-47, illus., ports (1-color)

202 ..."Rebel Nationalism: E.H. Cushing and the Confederate Experience." In: SwHQ, Jan. 1970, v.LXXIII, #3, p.343-355.

..."Bold dragoon: the life of J.E.B. Stuart." N.Y., Harper & Row, 1986. 8vo, cl, dj, xi, 354pp. $23.

203 **THOMAS, Frank Morehead**
"Why sleep they here? To the Memory of the Southern men who died in Northern prisons and in hope that every American shall love this new nation, as they loved the Old South. Address delivered at Camp Chase, Ohio, June 1, 1913." cover title, n.p., c.1913. 12mo, wraps, illus., 16pp.

204 **THOMAS, George**
"Maryland Confederate Monument at Gettysburg." In: SHSP, 1886, v.14, p.439-446.

205 **THOMAS, George Henry**
See: Simon Cameron, Dabney H. Maury.

206 **THOMAS, Henry Walter**
"History of the Doles-Cook Brigade Army of Northern Virginia, C.S.A. Containing Muster Rolls of each company of the Fourth, Twelfth, Twenty-first and Forty-fourth Georgia Regiments. With a short sketch of the services of each member and a complete history of each Regiment, by one of its own members and other matters of interest. By Henry W. Thomas Twelfth

Georgia Regiment, Atlanta, Ga., Franklin Print, 1903. Tk.8vo, cl, 2-pls., (61)pp. (unnumbered) ports incl. front, some with multiple ports, x, 632pp. errata, index. $325-r, $200-b-115.

...Dayton, Oh., Morningside, 1980.

...1988, $45..

207 **THOMAS, Herbert A., Jr.**
"The 19th Virginia Regiment, 1861-1865." In: Magazine of Albemarle County Hist." v.25, 1966-1967, p.(4)-35, port.

208 **THOMAS, John Peyre**
"Career and Character of General Micah Jenkins, CSA." Columbia, S.C., The State Co., 1903, 8vo, wraps, front(port), 28pp., limited to 100 copies. $75, $100.

...1908 edition (100 copies)

209 ..."Historical Sketch of the South Carolina Military Academy, with an appendix by John P. Thomas, Sup't. of Carolina Military Academy." Charleston, S.C., Walker, Evans and Cogswell, pubs., 1879. 12mo, cl, 100pp.

...1893 edition, ports, tk. 8vo, cl, 579pp. Enlarged and most desirable edt.

210 ..."James L. Petigru. Address before the joint meeting of Georgia and South Carolina Bar Ass'n., May 30, 1919. By...Pres. South Carolina Bar Ass'n." Columbia, S.C., The State Co., 1919, 8vo, wraps, cover title, 22pp.

...Also in S.C. Bar Ass'n. Trans. of 26th Annual meeting, May 30-31, 1919." Columbia, S.C., The State Co., 1920, p.63-82, title: "James L. Petigru, lawyer and citizen (1789-1863)." See: Wm. J. Grayson and James P. Carson.

211 ..."Oration. The public commemorative of the re-establishment of the South Carolina Military Academy, 22nd, February, 1883. Under the auspices of the Washington Light Infantry and published by order of the Corps." Charleston, S.C., Walker, Evans and Cogswell, 1883. 8vo, wraps, 22pp.

212 **THOMAS, Joseph Peyre**
"Memoirs of Joseph P. Thomas. Dedicated to Arthur D. Thomas." Richmond, Va., 1910, 12mo, wraps, 21pp. cover title.

213 **THOMAS, Lovick P.**
"Their last battle, fight at Bentonville, N.C., between Sherman and Johnston." In: SHSP, 1901, 1975, v.21, #2, p.148-159.

214 **THOMAS, R.S.**
"Yankee Gunboat "Smith Briggs", how it was captured by the Rebels." From: Richmond-Times Dispatch, Mar. 18, 1906 and July 15. In: SHSP, 1906, v.34, p.162-169.

214a **THOMAS, Wilbur D.**
"General James "Pete" Longstreet, Lee's "Old War Horse," scapegoat for Gettysburg." Parsons, W.Va., McClain Print, 1979. 8vo, cl, 377p, xviii, front (port), bibliog. index.

215 **THOMAS, William M., Judge**
"The slaughter at Petersburg, June 18, 1864, some interesting personal reminiscences of the fatal day and those which immediately preceded and succeeded it, by Wm. M. Thomas then an officer of Rion's battalion in Hagood Brigade." In: SHSP, 1897, v.XXV, p.222-230.

216 **THOMASON, John William, Lt. Col.**
"Jeb Stuart, by John W. Thomason, Jr., Captain, US Marine Corps, with illustrations and maps by the author." N.Y., Charles Scribner's Sons, 1930. 8vo, cl, dj, drawings, xiv, (1), 512pp., maps, index. $45-b. Also in Scribner's Mag., 1930, v.LXXXVII/LXXXVIII. Other Edts: 1934; 1936; 1941; 1944; 1946; 1948-New Edition; 1953; 1958; n.d. (1974?)

217 ..."Lone Star Preacher; being a chronicle of the acts of Praxiteles Swan, M.E. Church South, sometimes captain, 5th Texas Regiment, Confederate States Pro-

visional Army." Illus by author, N.Y., Chs. Scribner's, 1941, sm.8vo, cl, front, illus., xii, 2, 3-296pp.

217a **THOMASSON De Thommasson, Capt.**
"Les Procedes D'Exploratin de L'Armee de Nord-Virginie dum la Guerre de Secession Americaine." Paris: Berger-Levrault, 1901. 8vo, wraps, 96pp.

218 **THOMPKINS, Christopher W., Col.**
"The occupation of Richmond, April 1865-the memorandum of events of Col. Christopher Q. Thompkins. Edt: Wm. M.E. Rachal." In: VMHB, April, 1865, v.73, #2, p.189-221. Pl(port). See: Warren F. Spencer.

219 **THOMPSON, Arthur W., Edt.**
"Confederate Finance: a documentary study of a proposal of David L. Yulee." In: FHQ, Oct. 1951, v.30: 193-202pp., notes. Letters from Nancy Yulee to Clement C. Clay; David L. Yulee to Jas. M. Baker, Dec.-Jan. 1863-1864.

220 ..."The Railroad Background of the Florida Senatorial Election of 1851." In: FHQ, Jan. 1953, v.XXXI, #3, p.181-195.

220a **THOMPSON, Bailey**
"John C. C. Sanders (1820-64); Lee's Boy Brigadier." In: Ala. Rev., Apr. 1979, V.32, #2, p.83-107.

221 **THOMPSON, C.L.**
"The Battle of Scary." In: CV, June 1918, v.26, p.275-276. By private in Kanawha Rifles.

222 **THOMPSON, Dorothy Brown**
"A Young Girl in the Missouri Border War." (Columbia, Mo., Mo. Hist. Review, Oct., 1963, v.LVIII-#1, p.55-69, illus., port. Sympathy with CSA, members of family in CSArmy..

223 **THOMPSON, E. Bruce**
"Richard Abbey and the Methodist Publishing House." (Jackson, Miss., Jour. Miss. Hist., July, 1944, v.VI, #3, p.145-160. Trials of publishing before, during and after the CSA.

224 **THOMPSON, Edwin Porter**
"History of the First Kentucky Brigade by Ed. Porter Thompson." Cincinnati: Caxton Publishing House, 1868, Tk. 8vo, cl, 3-ports, incl. front; 4-plates of 7-ports. each, ix, (13)-931pp. $225-bmk-105, $55, $65, Reb: $160.

225 ..."History of the Orphan Brigade." Louisville, Ky., Lewis N. Thompson, 1898, Tk.8vo, decr. cl, front(color flag), music, illus. (13), 110pp., ports (63), index. $175. Note: Essentially the same basic material as "1st Ky. Brig. "revised and extended material". $250-bmk.

...Dayton, Ohio: Morningside Bookshop, 2nd Edition (1973) with an introduction by William C. Davis. Tk. 8vo, cl, vi, xii, (5)-1104pp. op.

226 **THOMPSON, Henry C.**
"Sam Hildebrand Rides Again." Bonne Terre,Mo., 1950. Steinbeck Pub. Co., 8vo, cl, front(port) (6), 113pp. illus. Sam had friends in South, given Com. as Major in CSArmy, raided Federal camps, private enemies alike. Guerrilla fights in S. Missouri.

...Revised and reprinted: Bonne Terre Print. Co., 1967, 8vo, wraps. See: Hildebrand. $20-b

227 **THOMPSON, Henry T.**
"Henry Timrod, Laureate of the Confederacy by Henry T. Thompson." Columbia, S.C., The State Co., 1928, 8vo, cl, front, 147pp. $30.

227a **THOMPSON, Holland**
"Prisons: Prisoners of War; Northern & Southern prisons; Exchange of prisoners; Life of the captured; Soldiers who escaped; Treatment of prisoners; Provost-Marshals - the army police." In: Photo. Hist. of CW, v.7, p.11-212, ills, ports.

228 THOMPSON, J.F.
"Sam Davis, Confederate Hero. Hanged at Nashville, Tenn., when he refused to reveal Confederate War secrets." Kennesaw, Ga., Continental Book Co., 1959. 8vo stiff wraps, 32pp.

229 THOMPSON, J.M.
"Reminiscences of Autauga Rifles. Read before the Historical Association, Dec. 19, 1879, at Autaugaville, Alabama." n.p., n.d. 12mo, wraps, cover title, 12pp.

230 ..."Autauga Rifles, 1861 to 1865." (Montgomery, Ala, Alabama Pr., 1891) 27 1/2x16cm., 13pp. "A unit roster with the individual soldier's record of participation in battles." Dornbusch, III, p.5.

231 THOMPSON, Jacob
"A Leaf from History. Report of J. Thompson secret agent of the late Confederate government stationed in Canada, for the purpose of organizing insurrection in the Northern States and burning their principal cities." Published by Union Republican Congressional Comm...." (Washington: Office of Great Republic, 1868?) 8vo, caption title, 4, 4pp. Report of the Secretary of State, Dec. 3, 1864, "another leaf from history. How rebel emissaries and Northern Democrats plotted in Canada." Report of James P. Holcombe to the Secretary of State, Nov. 16, 1864." 4pp., at end.
...(Washington? 1868)-(another edition with additions to title(above)-"...Plans for a revolt and release of rebel prisoners--Treason of the Democratic leaders and other interesting and important facts...Published by the Union Republican Congressional Commission." 8vo, caption title, 4, 4pp.
...(Toronto, C.W., Dec. 3, 1864)-"Another leaf from history! How rebel emissaries and Northern Democrats plotted in Canada." Report of James P. Holcombe to J.P. Benjamin, Secretary State, C.S.A., Richmond, Nov. 16, 1864." printed double columns, one side paper.
...See: reprint of first title in John F.H. Claiborne's "Mississippi as a province and state, etc." Jackson, Miss., 1880, p.447-466.

232 ...State Department, C.S.A. Official Correspondence. Letters from J.P. Benjamin, J.P. Holcombe, Jacob Thompson and W.J. Almon. In: SHSP, 1879, v.7, p.132-139.

233 THOMPSON, James Monroe, Lt.
"Reminiscences of the Autauga Rifles (Co.G, Sixth Alabama Volunteer Regiment, CSA.) By Lt. James Monroe Thompson. Introduction and Edited by William Stanley Hoole." University, Ala., Confederate Pub. Co., 1984, Confederate Regimental Series, #6. 8vo, stiff wraps, 35pp.

234 THOMPSON, James Thomas
"A Georgia Boy with "Stonewall" Jackson, the letters of James Thomas Thompson and the Walton Infantry." Edited by Aurelia Austin. Athens: Univ. of Georgia Pr., 1967, 8vo, wraps, 99pp.

235 ...(Richmond) Va. Mag. Hist. Biog., 1962, v.LXX, p.314-331.

236 THOMPSON, Jerry Don
"Colonel John Robert Baylor: Texas Indian Fighter and Confederate Soldier." (Hillsboro, Texas) Hill Jr. College, Monograph, #5, 1971. 8vo, wraps, ports, illus., facsms., maps, viii, 114pp. index, bibliog.

237 ..."Santos Benevides and the battle of Laredo (Texas); a stand along the border." In: CWTI, Aug. 1980, v.19, p.26-33.

238 ..."Mexican-Americans in the Civil War. The Battle of Valverde." In: Texana, 1972, v.X, #1, p.1-19, notes.

239 ..."Mutiny and Desertion on the Rio Grande. The Strange Saga of Captain Adrian J. Vidal." In: MHT & Sw., v.XII, #3, 1974, p.159-169.

240 ..."Henry Hopkins Sibley. Military inventor the Texas Frontier." In: TMH, 1972, v.X, #4, p.227-248, plate, port.
...Natchitoches, La., Northwestern State University Press, 1987. 8vo, cl, dj, 399pp, ills, maps. $25.

241 ..."Vaquero in Blue and Gray." Austin: Presidial Press, 1976, 8vo, cl, dj, endpapers, illus., map, bibliog., index, illus., 148pp.

242 **THOMPSON, Jo (Artillery)**
"Muster Roll of Company, Jo Thompson Artillery, of Atlanta, at Beaulieu, below Savannah, from the first day of November, 1862. to the thirty first day of Dec., 1862." In: Ga. H.Q., Sept., 1917, v.1, #3, p.268-269.

243 **THOMPSON, John H., Capt.**
"Shaft to historic Old Portsmouth Artillery. Address of...(from Portsmouth, Va. "Star")." In: SHSP, 1906, v.34, p.144-161.

244 **THOMPSON, John R.**
A Southern response to Mrs. Stowe. Two letters of John H. Thompson. Edt.: William R. Manierre." In: VMHB, Jan. 1961, v.69, #1, p.83-92.

245 **THOMPSON, John Reuben**
"Lee to the Rear (Poem)." In: SHSP, 1882, v.10, p.518-520.

246 **THOMPSON, Joseph Dimmit**
"The Evacuation of Corinth. From the Diary and A Letter of Joseph Thompson." Edt: John G. Biel. (Jackson, Miss., Jour. Miss.Hist., Jan., 1962, v.XXIV, #1, #3, p.40-56. New light on an old debate, seen by a common soldier.

247 ..."The Battle of Shiloh: from the letters and Diary of Joseph Dimmitt Thompson." In: Tenn. HQ, Sept., 1958, v.XVII, p.250-274, soldier in the 38th Tenn. Reg., Apr. 5-10, 1862.

248 **THOMPSON, Lawrence Sidney**
"The War Between the States in the Kentucky novel." In: KyHSR, Jan. 1952, v.50, p.26-34. Annotated checklist.

249 **THOMPSON, Magnus S., Col.**
"From the ranks to brigade commander." In: CV, Aug. 1921, v.XIX, p.298-303. Story of Col. Elijah V. White, CSA in war.

250 ..."Plan to release our men at Point Lookout." In: CV, Feb. 1912, v.XX, p.69-70. Plan to release prisoners in 1864.

251 ..."The strategy of Stonewall Jackson." In: CV, Mar./Apr. 1922, v.XXX, p. 93-96, 133-134.

252 ..."Col. Thompson's CSA Museum." see: George C. Keidel.

253 **THOMPSON, Mattie Thomas**
"History of Barbour County Alabama." Eufaula, Ala., (1939). "Reconstruction Days." (p.180-184, 194-206), "Military", "Veterans rec'd. Cross of Honor", "Grierson's March across the Chattahoochee", p.214-245. Rosters.

254 **THOMPSON, R.L.**
"Webster County History-Folklore from earliest times to present." Webster Springs: Star Print, 1942, p.200. Civil War period, p.60-69; Virginia unites: Co. G, 62nd Inf., Co.F, 31st. Cav., 15th Cav., Co. G, 25th Inf., 40th Cav. Shetler-775.

255 **THOMPSON, Ray M.**
"The Confederate shrine of Beauvoir: the last home of Jefferson Davis." Biloxi, Miss., C.C. Hamill, 1957, 8vo, decr. wraps, facsm., ports, views (1-dbl), 32pp.

256 **THOMPSON, Samuel Bernard**
"Confederate Purchasing Operations Abroad." Chapel Hill, Univ. of N.C. Pr., 1935, 8vo, cl, dj, ix, 137pp. $45-r.

257 ...Nashville, Tenn., Vanderbilt Univ. Bull., Abstracts of theses, 1934, v.XXIV, #9, p.20-21.
...N.Y., H.P. Kraus, 1969, rep. See: Caleb Huse.

258 **THOMPSON, Taylor**
"The Northwest Confederacy." In: CV,

FEb., 1916, v.XXIV, p.87-88. Conspiracy to form a confederacy, by the Copperheads, in Ohio, Indiana, Illinois and Missouri called "Northwest Confederacy."

259 **THOMPSON, W.H.**
"Who lost Gettysburg?" In: CV, June 1915, v.XXIII, p.257-258.

260 **THOMPSON, Wesley S.**
"Tories of the Hills." Vernon (Alabama) U.S.A., Pareil Press, 1960. Cl, 8vo, d/w, 279pp. Reprint: Civil War Centennial Edition. Vernon, U.S.A., The Pareil Press, n.d. Unionist of North Alabama during war. Novel, but more factual than fiction.
...Boston: Christopher Pub. House (1953) 12mo, cl, 362pp. fiction. 1st edition.

261 "The free state of Winston (Ala.). A history of Winston County, Alabama." Winfield, Ala., Pareil Press, 1968. 8vo, cl, 220pp. 2/3 book on the crisis, Unionist in north Alabama.

262 **THOMPSON, William Candace**
"From Shiloh to Port Gibson-an eyewitness account." In: CWTI, Oct., 1964, v.III, #6, p.20-25,illus., map, ports.

263 **THOMPSON, William Y.**
"Robert Toombs, Confederate General." In: CWH, December 1961, v.VI, #4, p.406-420, port, pl.

264 ..."Robert Toombs, Man without a country." In: Ga.H.Q., June 1962, v.XLVI, #2, p.162-168.

265 ..."The Toombs Legend." In: Ga.H.Q., December 1957, v.XLI, #4, p.337-348.

266 **THOMSON, David Whittet**
"Three Confederate Submarines: Operations at New Orleans, Mobile and Charleston, 1862-1864." In: U.S. Naval Inst. Proc., LXVII (1941), p.39-47.

267 **THOMSON, James W., Maj.**
"A Monument to Major James W. Thomson, Confederate States Artillery." In: SHSP, 1893, v.21, p.365-368. (from: Winchester, Va. Times.) See: Wm. N. McDonald.

268 **THORNBERRY, Ruby S.**
"The Alabama." In: CV, July 1923, v.XXXI, p.250-252.

269 **THORNELL, James Henley, Rev.**
"The Collected Writings of James Henley Thornwell. Edt: J.B. Adger." Richmond, Va., Presbyterian Committee of Publications, 1871, 2 vols., 8vo, cl, vi, 659, 622pp.

270 ..."Hear The South! The State of the Country: an article republished from the Southern Presbyterian Review." N.Y., D. appleton & Co., 1861, 12mo, cl, 30pp.
..."Our Danger and Our Duty." Columbia, S.C., Southern Guardian Steam Press, 1862. 12mo, cl, 30pp.

271 ..."Soldiers' Tract Association of the M.E. Church South, 1863." Our Danger and Our Duty." by Rev. J.H. Thornwell, n.p., 16mo, wraps, 16pp.

272 ..."Evangelical Tract Society. Petersburg, Va., #215." "Our Danger and Our Duty." By Rev. J.H. Thornwell. Raleigh, N.C., Register Steam Pr., n.d., 16mo, wraps, 15pp.

273 ..."No. 130. Our Danger and Our Duty." (Pub. by the South Carolina Tract Society (Charleston, S.C.) Evans and Cogswell (1863?) 12mo, wraps, 16pp.

274 ..."Report on the Subject of Slavery, presented to the Synod of South Carolina, at their session in Winnsborough, Nov. 6, 1851." Columbia, S.C., A.S. Johnston, 1852. 8vo, wraps, 16pp.

275 ..."The State of the Country." (New Orleans, La., "True Witness and Sentinel Office, 1861) Crand-2863. 8vo, wraps, 15pp., $100-bmk-96.
..."The State of the Country. An article republished from the "Southern Presbyterian Review", extracted pamphlet, 32pp. Columbia, S.C., 1861, Southern

276 **THORNTON, Ella May**
"Wemyss Fielden, Confederate Soldier." In: GaHQ, Dec. 1959, v.43, p.409-411. On the stay of an English Army officer in the South as aide de camp to the Comd. officer. Dept: S.C., Ga., and Fla. 1862-1865, account in his letters to his future wife, et al.

Guardian. Also: N.Y., D. Appleton, 1861, p.30. A 3rd Edt., 1861, p.32. $60, $125.

277 **THORNTON, Harry Innes, Jr.**
"Recollections of the War by a Confederate Officer from California." In: South. Calif. Quart., 1963, v.XLV, p.195-218. Aide to General Crittenden.

278 **THORNTON, Melvin**
"The escape of Melvin Thornton from Camp Butler, Illinois. Edt: Wm. Warre Rogers." In: AHQ, 1961, v.XXIII, n., p.220-230.

279 **THORNTON, William Mynn**
"John Warwick Daniel." In: SHSP, 1916, v.XLI, p.88-112.

280 **THORPE, John Houston**
"Roster of Nash County Confederate Soldiers, by John H. Thorpe: and copy of Edgecombe County Roster." Raleigh, N.C., Edwards and Broughton, 1925, 12mo, cl, 135pp. $125.

281 **THRALL, James C., Capt.**
"Letter: Battle of Shiloh." In: SHSP, 1878, v.7, p.45-46.

282 **THRUSTON, Gates Phillips, General**
"Chickamauga." In: SB, ns, 1886/1887, v.II, p.406-415.
..."Chickamauga, reprint of an article originally published in the Southern Bivouac, December 1886 and republished in the Century War Book, "Battles and Leaders of the Civil War." v.III, Nashville, Tenn., n.d., large 8vo, wraps, 13pp.

283 ..."The Crisis at Chickamauga." In: B & L, v.III, p.663-665.

284 ..."The Numbers and Rosters of the two armies in the Civil War." (Nashville, Tenn., n.d.) (Phila: Clarence B. Moore.) (June 1909) errata. 8vo, stiff wraps, 13pp. (Reprint of 1st edt., with additions?)

285 ..."Personal recollections of the battle in the rear at Stone's River, Tennessee, by Brevt. Brig-Gen. Gates P. Thruston." Nashville, Tenn., Brandon Print, (1906?) 8vo, wraps, map, 21pp. Also in MOLLUS-Ohio, v.VI, p.219-237.

286 **THRUSTON, Henry C.**
"The tallest Confederate." In: CWTI, March 1975, #7, p.42.

287 **THRUSTON, Stephen C., Col.**
"Report: Conduct of Gen. Geo H. Steuart's Brigade from May 5-12, 1864, inclusive." In: SHSP, 1886, v.14, p.146-154.

288 **THURMAN, A.G.**
"Alleged Traffic with Rebels in Texas." Wash: GPO, 1871, SR-377. 8vo, sewn, caption title, 18pp. Testimony and documents of attempt by Harris Hoyt, supposed Union man, run blockade to Matamoros to move goods out of Texas; or, whether it was a plot to run guns into Texas. Involves John Hay, Sect., Lincoln, Ben Butler, Gov. Sprague of R.E., Gideon Wells, J. Dix.

289 **THURMAN, A.L., Jr.**
"Ratification Speaking in Missouri, 1860." (Columbia, Mo., Mo.Hist.Review, July, 1862, v.LVI, #4, p.365-379.

289a **THURSTON, Arthur**
"Tallahassee Skipper." Yarmouth, Nova Scotia: Lescarbot Press. 8vo, wraps, 434pp. $14. 1981. John Taylor Wood's biography, Lt. on the Merrimac (CSS Virginia, later on the 'Tallahassee.'

290 **THURSTON, Edward N.**
"Memoir of Richard H. Anderson, CSA." In: SHSP, April, 1914, v.XXXIX, p.146-152. See: Cornelius Irvin Walker's Life of...

291 **TIBAULT, C.H., Dr.**
"Losses in the War Between the States." Tibault was Surgeon-General, U.C.V. In: SHSP, 1915, n.s., II, p.316-319.

292 **TICE, Douglas O.**
"Bread or blood."- the Richmond Bread riot. In: CWTI, Feb., 1974, v.12, #10, p.12-19, illus., port.

292a **TICKNOR, Frank O.**
"The Poems of Frank O. Ticknor, M.D., Edt. K.M.R." Phila: J.B. Lippincott & Co., 1879. Intro. by Paul H. Hayne. 8vo, cl, 150p. $40. First rate CSA & Southern poetry. (Rowe).

293 **TILBERG, Frederick**
"Antietam National Battlefield Site, Maryland, by Frederick Tilberg." Wash: Nat'l. Park Ser. Hist. Handbook series, #31, 1960. (revised 1961). 8vo, pict. color stiff wraps, illus., maps, ports, facsm., (4), 60pp. Lee's invasion of Md.

294 ..."Gettysburg National Military Park, Pennsylvania by Frederick Tilberg." Wash: Nat'l. Park Ser. Hist. Handbook, Series #9, 1954. (revised 1962) 8vo, pict. color stiff wraps, facsm., illus., maps (1-dbl. pg.) ports, (4), 50, (14)pp.-Gallery of F.D. Briscoe Battle Paintings.

295 **TILFORD, John E., Jr.**
"The Delicate Track, The L & N's role in the Civil War." In: FCHQ, July, 1962, v.36, #3, p.209-221. Paper read before the Filson Club, June 5, 1961.

296 **TILGHMAN, Lloyd, Brig. Gen.**
"Excerpts from Brig. Gen. Lloyd Tilghmans Official Report of Battle of Fort Henry, Feb. 6, 1862." (London) Jour. Confed. Hist. Soc., Winter, 1969, v.7, #4, p.10-11.

297 ..."Bombardment of and Capture Fort Henry." In: Confed. War Jour., 1893, v.I, p.146-149, 152-153, illus.

298 **TILGHMAN, Tench Francis**
"The Confederate baggage and treasure train ends its flight in Florida; diary of Tench Francis Tilghman." Edt: A.J. Hanna. (Jacksonville, Fla.? 1939) Reprint: Fla. Hist. Quart., Jan. 1939. 8vo, sewn (24pp.) wraps, map, xvii, p.159-180.

298a **TILLETT, Wilbur Fisk**
"Southern Womanhood as affected by the War." In: Cent., Nov. 1892, v.21, p.9-16.

299 **TILLEY, John Shipley**
"The Coming of the Glory." N.Y., Stratford House, 1949, 8vo, cl, dj, x, (4), 290pp., notes (p.269-286), slavery, secession and reconstruction.

300 ..."Facts the Historians Leave Out. (A Youth's Confederate Primer)." Montgomery, Ala., Paragon Pr., (1951). 8vo, 58pp. Editions: 2nd, Jan. '52; 3rd, Feb. '52; 4th, Sept. '52; 5th, Oct. '53; 7th, '55(74pp.) Enlarged '58, (76pp.) '61 (12th print) 76pp. Causes of Civil War, malignancy of Lincoln.

301 ..."Lincoln Takes Command." Chapel Hill: University of North Carolina Press, 1941. 8vo, xxxvii, 334pp. Lincoln wholly responsible for war and the crisis at Sumter.

302 ..."Emancipation Proclamation." In: Ala. HQ, Spring, 1945.

303 **TILLMAN, G.N.**
"Matthew Fontaine Maury: a great Tennesseean (1806-1873)." In: Meth. Quar. Rev., July 1915, v.LXIV, p.533-540.

304 **TIMBERLAKE, W.L.**
"The last days in front of Richmond." In: CV, July 1914, v.XXII, p.303.

305 ..."The retreat from Richmond in 1865." In: CV, Oct. 1914, v.XXII, p.454-456.

306 ..."In the siege of Richmond and after." In: CV, Nov. 1921, v.XXIX, p.412-414.

307 **"TIMES" on the American War: The,**
a Historical Study, by L.S." London: Wm. Ridgway, 1865, 8vo, wraps, 107pp. The Times was sympathetic to the South. (Sir Leslie Stephen)

308 **TIMMONS, Joe T.**
"The Referendum in Texas on the Ordnance of Secession, Feb. 23, 1861: The Vote." In: ETHJ, Fall, 1973, v.XI, #2, p.12-28, notes, tables.

309 **TIMROD, Henry**
"The Poems of Henry Timrod with a sketch of the Poet's Life by Paul H. Hayne." N.Y., E.S. Hale and Sons, 1873. 12mo, cl, 205pp.
...New revised edition, same pub. and date, 8vo, cl, viii, 232pp. See: Paul Hayne and Jay B. Hubbell. Timrod was poet laureate of the CSA. Also: Henry T. Thompson.

310 ..."Notes and documents, Edt: William Fidler." In: Ala. Rev., Apr. 1949, v.2, p.139-149, notes. Letters to Rachel Loyons, Dec. 10, 1861-Sept. 30, 1863. On the author's health, the war, etc.

311 "Unpublished letters in Southern Literary Messenger II" p.527-535 (AR, Oct. 1940) p.605-611, Nov. 1940, II, p.645-651. Dec. 19, 1940.

312 **TINDALL, William**
"The True Story of the Virginia and the Monitor, the account of an eye-witness, with intro: Milledge L. Bonham, Jr. Reprinted from Virginia Historical Magazine, vol.XXXI." Richmond, Va., Old Dominion Press, 1923, 8vo, stiff wraps, map(front), ports, illus., diagrams, 90pp., bibliog.

313 ...Va. Hist. Mag., Jan./Apr. 1923, p.1-38, p.89-143.

314 ..."Booth's escape from Washington after the assassination of Lincoln, his subsequent wanderings and final capture." In: Columbia Hist. Soc. Rec., 1915, v.XVIII, p.1-15.

315 **TINGLEY, Donald F.**
"The Copperheads in Illinois." Pub.: Illinois State Historical Library for the Civil War Centennial Commission of Illinois. #5, n.p., n.d. (1963?) 4to, (4)pp-folder, facsm., pl., 2-ports. Head: "Illinois Civil War Sketches."

316 **TINSLEY, Fanny Gaines**
"Mrs. Tinsley's War Recollections, 1862-1865." In: VaMH, Oct. 1927, v.XXXV, p.393-404.

317 **TINSLEY, Henry C.**
"Observations of a Retired Veteran, by Henry C. Tinsley ("P. Boyzy")." Staunton, Va., Albert Shultz, 1904, 8vo, wraps, (or bds.) front (port), 96, (1)pp. $100. No war content.

318 **"TISHOMINGO CREEK, or Brice's Cross Roads."**
See: Wm. Witherspoon, Robert S. Henry's "As they saw Forrest." reprinted in...

319 **TITTMANN, Edward D.**
"Confederate Courts in New Mexico." (Albuquerque) NMHR, Oct. 1928, v.III, #4, p.347-356, facsms.

320 ..."The Exploitation of Treason." (Albuquerque) NMHR, April, 1929, v.IV, #2, p.128-145. Aftermath of the CSA invasion, N.M.

321 **TITUS, William Albert**
"A Wisconsin burial place of Confederate prisoners of war." In: Wis. Mag. Hist., Spring, 1953, v.36, p.192-194. port, view. Soldiers of 1st. Ala. Reg., Vols. Inf., buried at Forest Hill Cemetery, Madison, 1862.

322 **TOBACCO Premium Booklets/Cards**
See: W. Duke & Co. In additional series to the booklets (above) cards 4 7/8x6 13/16 were published: "Biographical sketches of Union and Confederate military and naval leaders", with chromolith ports on front with battle scenes, c.1888/1890.

322a **TOCHMAN, Gaspard**
"The Case of General Tochman." Richmond, Va., 1863. 8vo, caption title, 14pp. (old)$10. Not in Crand. Harwell. Harwell's

#1105 Tochman's Memorial to Congress. 47pp.

323 **TODD, Frederick Porter**
"Confederate battle honors of the 36th Virginia." In: MC and H, 1951, v.III, p.91-92, illus.

324 ..."Notes on the organization and uniforms of South Carolina military forces, 1860-1861." In: Military Collector, Sept. 1951, v.3, p.53-62, views.

325 ..."Hampton Legion, South Carolina volunteers 1861." In: Mil. Coll. and Hist., 1951, v.III, p.68-71, col. plate, illus.

326 ..."First Virginia cavalry regiment, 1861-1862." In: Mil. Coll. and Hist., Aug. 1949, v.I, #3, p.2-3, col. plate, illus.

327 **TODD, George T.**
"Gaines' Mill - Pickett and Hood." In: CV, 1898, v.6, p.565-570, plate.

328 ..."Sketch of History, the First Texas Regiment, Hood's Brigade, A.N.Va., by Geo. T. Todd, Captain Company A, First Texas 1861-1865. Souvenir Edition, dedicated to Hood's soldiers." (Jefferson, Tex.): Jefferson Jimplecute, 1909. $2000-g, $650, 12mo, wraps, cover title, (27)pp. Ran serially, Apr. 2, Apr. 16, Apr. 30, May 14, June 11, 1909. Set in two columns with identical broken type in both the paper and text of the booklet.
...Waco, Texas, Texian Press, 1961, "First Texas Regiment, by George T. Todd. Notes and Introduction by Harold B. Simpson." 8vo, two-tone cl, facsm. orig. covers, xiii, (1), 45pp. 300 copies, 25 copies: 1/2 Mor. $100.

329 **TODD, Hubert Henry**
"The Building of the Confederate States Navy in Europe." (Nashville, Tenn.) 1941. Private Edt., 8vo, 30pp. Wraps, cover title. Summary of a thesis, Vanderbilt Univ. 1940, distributed by Joint Libraries.

330 **"TODD, Richard Cecil**
"Confederate Finance." Athens, University of Georgia Pr. (1954) 8vo, cl, dj, ports, x, 258pp., notes, bibliog., index, p.201-258, tables. $30.

331 ..."The Produce Loans: a means of financing the Confederacy." In: NCHR, Jan. 1950, v.XXVII, p.46-74. $8.

332 ..."C(hristopher) G(ustavus) Meminger and the Confederate Treasury Department (1861-1864)." In: Ga. Rev., Winter 1958, v.12, p.396-410. ports.

333 **TODD, W.C.**
"The Centralia fight. The killing of Jesse James, by Maj. J.N. Edwards." n.p., n.d. 12mo, wraps, (17)pp. cover title. Dorn-II, 3289. "Not to permit a book pub. in 1882, titles-"The history of Boone Co." to stand unchallenged and undenied with its partial and biased statements and hatreds of the Confederate cause."

334 **TODHUNTER, R.**
"Ector's Texas Brigade at the Battle of Allatoona." In: C.V., August, 1918, v.XXVI, p.340-341. Ector's Texas Brigade, Army of Tenn.

335 **TOLAR, J.R.**
"Brief history of Company B, Tenth Regiment South Carolina volunteers, Confederate States Army, by J.R. Tolar, "child of the regiment"." n.p., n.d. 8vo, cover title, 32pp., roster of Co. B, p.6-8.

336 **TOLBERT, Frank X.**
"Dick Dowling at Sabine Pass." N.Y., McGraw-Hill Book Co. (1962) 12mo, cl, dj, map, 159pp. $60.
...2nd Print, atg. $35.

337 **TOLBERT, Noble J.**
"Daniel Worth: Tar Heel Abolitionist." In: NCHR, July, 1962, v.XXXIX, p.284-304. $8.

338 **TOMB, James H.**
"The last obstructions in Charleston Harbor, 1863." In: CV, Mar. 1924, v.XXXII, p.98-99.

339 **TOMPKINS, Daniel Augustus**
"Company K, Fourteenth South Carolina Volunteers." Prepared for D.A. Tompkins and A.S. Tompkins. Charlotte, N.C., Observer Print, 1897, 16mo, wraps, illus., ports, 36, (1)p. Roster and list of survivors. See: Geo. Taylor Winston-"A Builder of the New South. Being the story of the life work of Daniel Augustus Tompkins." N.Y., Doubleday Page Co., 1926, p.403.

340 **TOMPKINS, Ellen Wilkins**
"The Colonel's Lady: Some letters of Ellen Wilkins Tompkins, July-Dec., 1861." In: Va. MHB, Oct. 1961, v.69, p.(387)-419, illus. Wife of Col. Chris. Q. Tompkins, CSA, daily life on plantation during Federal occupation.

341 **TONEY, Marcus Breckenridge**
"The Privations of a Private, the campaign under Gen. R.E. Lee, the campaign under Gen. Stonewall Jackson, Bragg's Invasion of Kentucky, the Chickamauga Campaign, the Wilderness Campaign, prison life in the North, the privations of a citizen; the Ku Klux Klan; a united citizenship." Nashville, Tenn., Printed for the author, 1905. 12mo, cl, illus., ports, incl. front, 133pp. $100, $125-jk.

342 ...Nashville: M.E. Church South, 1907, Second Edt., revised and enlarged. 12mo, cl, 158pp. $75-bmk.

343 ..."Our Dead at Elmira, Old Days at the Northern Prison." In: SHSP, 1901, v.XXIX, p.193-197.

344 **TOOLE, H. Gresham, Edt.**
"Letters of a Confederate Soldier to his wife in 1864." In: W.Va. Hist., Oct., 1957, v.19, p.69-70. From camp near Winchester, Va.

345 **TOOMBS, Robert Augustus**
"The Correspondence of Robert Toombs, Alexander H. Stephens and Howell Cobb. Edt: Ulrich B. Phillips." Washington, 1913, 8vo, buck, 759pp. Annual Report of Amer. Hist. Assn., 1911, v.2. The 9th report of the Historical Manuscripts Commission. Reprint: N.Y., Da Capo Press: Plenum Pub., 1970. $75-y. See: Henry Whitney Cleveland, Jas U. Vincent.

346 ...Portrait, mezzotint, "R. Toombs" signature in facsimilie, by P.M. Whelpley. Dagpe by Brady (1850), v.XI, 219.

347 ...Portrait, engraving by J.C. Buttre from a Daguerreotype, n.d. Size: 6 1/2x4 3/4". Identical with one in Avery's "Hist. of Ga." 1881, p.140, "engraved expressly for this work"; as well as in White's "Hist. Col. Ga." 3rd Edt., 1855, p.685. DeRenne III, 1270.

348 ..."Speech delivered in Milledgeville, on Tuesday evening, Nov. 13, 1860, before the legislature of Georgia." (Milledgeville, Ga., 1860) 12mo, caption title, 8pp.

349 **TOOMEY, Daniel Carroll**
"The Civil War in Maryland." Baltimore, 1983. 8vo, cl, dj, illus., notes, index, 183pp.

350 **TOPPAN, Geo. L.**
"Stamps and varities, notes upon the US and CSA stamps and their varieties." NY, Scott Stamp and coin, 1906, 8vo, wraps, 27pp., illus.

351 **TORPEDOES ,**
See: Oswald Garrison Villard, Aug. T. Smythe, W.A. Alexander, David (Torpedo Boat), Hunter Davidson, Hunley (Torpedo Boat), P.G.T. Beauregard, John A. Hamilton, Stephen Elliott, Richard L. Maury, Gabriel J. Rains, Milton F. Perry, W.T. Glassell, Dabney H. Maury, Elinor B. MacFarland, W.T. Glassell, C.L. Stanton, C. Welles May, David C. Ebaugh, Jno. W. Rawler, R.O. Crowley.

352 **TORRENCE, Leonidas**
"The Road to Gettysburg. The Diary and Letters of Leonidas Torrence of the Gaston Guards." (Raleigh) NCHRev., October 1959, v.XXXVI, #4, p.476-517.

353 TORRENCE, William Clayton
"Confederate Leaders-Dedicated in loving Memory to Varina Anne Jefferson Davis, Daughter of the Confederacy and to the Atlanta Chapter U.D.C." Atlanta, Ga., Mutual Print, 1898, 16mo, wraps, ports, 64pp.

354 ..."To the People of Western Virginia. The Army of the Confederate States has come among you to expel the enemy...by Command.-Maj. Gen. Loring, Sept. 14, 1862." (Charleston, Va., 1862) Broadside. Forgery-the 6th line ends "Intend to" and the forgery carries "to" in next line. $500.

355 TOTOPOTOMOY, Battle of
See: T.C. Morton.

356 TOTTEN, Joseph Gilbert, Brig. Gen.
"Informe Dirigido Al Hon. Jefferson Davis, Ministro de la Guerra, sobre los efectos de los disparos hechos con piezasde grueso calibre en las Canoneras De Las Casamatas, y sobre-los producidos disparando contra las mismas canoneras diversas clases de proyectiles: Deducidos de la Esperiencias hechas en West Pointmdurant los anos 1852-1855." Traducidos del ingles: D. Rafael Cerero. Madrid: 1861, six fldg. lithos.

357 TOUNG, J.P.
"Gen. Nathan Bedford Forrest." In: CV, June, 1897, v.5, p.277-281.

358 TOWER, Roderick
"Defense of Fort Sumter." Charleston, S.C., Fort Sumter Hotel. 1st Edt. (1938) (Walker, Evans and Cogswell) 12mo, cl, 39pp., illus., fldg-map.

359 TOWN, Franklin E., Capt.
"US Army who took part in the "Battle of New Market", writes of valor of the VMI Cadets." In: SHSP, 1916, v.41, p.179-183.

360 TOWNER, Laura Matilda
"Letters and Diary of...written from the Sea Islands of South Carolina (1862-1884)." Edited by Rupert Sergeant Holland. Cambridge, Mass., Riverside Press, 1912, 8vo, cl, xviii, 310pp. Yankee teacher in the South.

361 TOWNS, W. Stuart
"Honoring the Confederacy in Northwest Florida: The Confederate Monument Ritual." In: FHQ, October 1978, v.LVII, #2, p.205-212. plate.

362 TOWNSEND, George Alfred
"Rustics in Rebellion: A Yankee Reporter on the Road to Richmond, 1861-1865." Chapel Hill: Univ. of North Carolina, 1950. 8vo, cl, dj, xx, 292pp. reprint.

363 ..."Campaigns of a Non-Combatant and his Romaunt abroad during the war." N.Y., Blelock and Co., 1866. 12mo, cl, 368pp. Tho a Yankee war corresp., reported evenly, admired So. way of life.

364 TOWNSEND, Harry C.
"Townsend's Diary, last months of the war, Jan.-May, 1865, a diary from Petersburg to Appomattox, thence to North Carolina to join Johnston's Army." By...Corp. 1st Richmond Howitzers. Richmond: Wm. Ellis Jones, 1907. 8vo, wraps, 31pp., reprint: Southern Historical Soc. Papers, v.XXXIV (1906), p.99-127, Dornbusch-1127.

365 TOWNSEND, Jonathan M.
"Francis Peyre Porcher, Md., 1824-1895)." In: Ann. Med. Hist., 3rd Ser., 1939, v.I, p.177-188. See: Fr. P. Porcher.

366 TOWNSEND, Leah
"The Confederate Gunboat "Pedee"." In: SCHMag., Apr., 1959, v.60, p.66-73, notes. Built CSNavy yard, Pee Dee, S.C., 1864, burned Mar. 15, 1865 to avoid capture. Present condition of its remains.

367 TOWNSEND, Mary Ashley
"The Birthday of Lee. (poem)" In: SHSP, 1900, v.28, p.238-239.

368 ..."Poem to Stonewall Jackson." In: SHSP, 1882, v.10, p.76-78.

369 **TOWNSEND, R. Walter**
"The Passing of the Confederate." Suggested by the account given by the decrepit appearance of the Confederate Veterans, during their march through the streets of Lumberton, N.C., at the unveiling of a monument to the memory of the Confederate Dead from Robeson County, May 10, 1907." N.Y., Neale Pub., 1911. 16mo, cl, 20pp. Verse.

370 **TOWNSEND, Samuel P.**
"The Salvage Operation from the "Modern Greece." (London) Jour. Confed. Hist. Soc., June 1963, v.I, #4, p.111-116.

371 **TOWNSEND, Thomas S.**
"The Townsend Library." In: SHSP, 1890, v.18, p.382-385.

372 **TOWNSEND, William H.**
"Lincoln and the Bluegrass. Slavery and Civil War in Kentucky." University of Kentucky Press, 1955. 8vo, cl, d/w, xiv, 392pp., ports, illus., facsms. "Bluegrass Edt.", atg. for Kentuckians.

373 **TRACY, Albert**
"Freemont's pursuit of Jackson in the Shenandoah Valley, the journal of Colonel . . ., March-July, 1862. Edt: Francis F. Wayland." In: VMHB, 1962, v.LXX, p.165-193, 332-354, illus., map, port.

374 **TRACY, Carlos, Col.**
"An incident of late Col. Tracy." In: SHSP, 1884, v.12, p.547.

375 ..."Operations before Charleston in May and July, 1862." In: SHSP, 1880, v.8, p.541-547.

376 **TRAFFIC with the Rebels**
"Letter of the Secretary of War...in relation to traffic with the Rebels during the war, alleged to have been entered into on the part of Hoyt, Sprague and others." Wash., 1871, Senate Doc. 10, 41st Congress, 3rd Session, pt. 3. 8vo, wraps, 97pp. Concerns, purchase ships, supplies for CSA, running blockade, etc.

377 **TRANS-MISSISSIPPI Department**
Headquarters General Order #45...for purpose of carrying into effect the Conscript Act, passed at last session Confederate Congress." Little Rock, Dec. 8, 1862. 8vo, 3pp. Not in Crandall-Harwell, Allen or Duke suppl.
Bureau of Subsistence, Circular. Marshall, Texas, June 17, 1864. 8vo, sewn, 6pp. Undescribed CSA Imprint.

378 **"TRANS-MISSISSIPPI Dept., CSA."**
Hillsboro, Tex., Jr. College. 1979 Symposiam at Hill Jr. Col. $15.
See: E. K. Smith, Richard Taylor.

TRANSATLANTIC Sketches; or sixty days in America."
London: S. Low, Sons & Co., 1865. Sm4to, wraps, 2pp, 1, (5)-34 numb. 1, 30pls. 27 1/2 x 38 cm. LC Va. Hist. Soc. Jas. I. Robertson, Jr., attributes it to: Edward Kennard, the author of plates, who plagiarizes a newspaper writer's notes given him, named Edward Moseley.
See: Robertson's "English Views..."

379 **TRAPIER, James H., Brig.-Gen.**
"Report: Fight of Apr. 7, 1863, in Charleston Harbor." In: SHSP, 1878, v.VI, p.125-127.

379a **TRAPNELL, Frederica H.**
"Colonel Lawson Botts, CSA." In: Mag. Jefferson Co. Hist. Soc., Dec. 1983, v.49, p.27-34.

380 **TRASK, Benjamin H.**
"9th Virginia Infantry." Lynchburg, Va., H.E. Howard, 1984. (J.P. Bell print) 1st, Lim. Atg. Edt., 820. 8vo, cl, dj, (3), 108p., ill., maps, ports. $17.50.
..."16th Virginia Infantry." Lynchburg, Va., H. E. Howard, 1986. 8vo, cl, dj, (6), 128pp., illus., maps, ports., 1000 copies, numbered, signed.

381 **TRAVELLER (Lee's Horse)**
See: Thomas L. Broun, R. E. Lee, "Gen.

Lee's Horse "Lucy Long," W. Donald Rhinesmith.

382 **TRAYWICK, J. B., Rev.**
"Prison Life at Point Lookout." In: SHSP, 1890, v.18, p.431-435.

383 **"TREASURED Reminiscences,**
Collected by John K. McIver Chapter. South Carolina Chapter, United Daughters of the Confederacy." Columbia, S.C., State Co., 1911. 8vo, wraps, 86pp, cover title, Dorn-II, 519.
...1982. Facsm. Edt., 8vo, stiff wraps, 86pp.

384 **TREASURY of the Confederate States**
See: Micajah H. Clark, John W. Harris, Wm. H. Parker, John F. Wheeless.

385 **"TREATMENT of Prisoners of War**
during the War Between the States." In: SHSP, March and April, 1876, v.1, and 4, p.113-327. Issued in wraps, 8vo.
See: John William Jones.

386 **"TREDEGAR WORKS, The, Richmond, Va."**
Baltimore: E. Sachse, 1865, colored lithograph, after F. Dielman.

387 **TREDWELL, Adam**
"North Carolina Navy." In: Walter Clark's "Hist. of Several Regs. and Batts. from N.C.," Vol.V, p.(298)-313.

388 **TREDWELL, Daniel M.**
"A catalogue of books and pamphlets, belonging to...relating to the great Civil War...with about 500 portraits of military men and civilians who were participants in the strife." Brooklyn, N.Y., E.F. Deselding (Pref. 1874). 8vo, cl, iv, 220pp. (1268 books listed).

389 **TREGLER, Joseph G., Jr.**
"George Eustis, Jr.: Non-Mythis Southerner." La. Hist., 1975, v.XVI, p.383-390.

390 **TRENT AFFAIR**
Alex James Beresford-Hope; "Case of Trent Examined." Col. Evan John Simpson; Geo. H. Warren.

391 **TRENT, William Peterfield**
"Robert E. Lee." Bost: Small, Maynard and Col., 1899. 16mo, cl, front(port), xviii, 135pp. "Beason Biographies."
...In: Photo. Hist. C.W., v.10, p.51-74, ports, incl. composite, ills.

392 ..."William Gilmore Simms." Bost., N.Y., Houghton Mifflin, 1892. 12mo, cl, front(port), viii, 351pp.

393 ..."Southern Statesmen of the Old Regime: Washington, Jefferson, Randolph, Calhoun, Stephens, Toombs and Jefferson Davis." New York: Thos. Y. Crowell (1897). 12mo, cl, ports, 293pp.

394 **TRESCOT, William Henry**
"The Confederacy and the Declaration of Paris." (New York, 1918). Reprint: Amer. Hist. Rev., v.23, #4, July 1918. 8vo, cover title, p.826-835.

395 ..."Memorial of the Life of J. Johnston Pettigrew, Brig. General, Confederate States Army." Charleston, S.C., John Russell (Walker, Evans and Cogswell), 1870. $150-ob, $100-bmk-84. 16mo, wraps (or clo.), 65pp.
See: B. D. Fry's "Pettigrew at Gettsyburg."

396 ..."Three Letters of WHT to Howell Cobb, 1861. Edt: M. Foster Farley." In: SCHM, 1967, v.68, #1, p.22-30.

397 ..."General Stephen Elliott. Address del. in the House Representatives of S.C.." Columbia, S.C., 1926. 8vo, wraps, port, 17pp.
...Do: London: Saunders, Otley Co., 1867, 4to, wraps, 23pp.

398 ..."Memorial of the Life of J. Johnston Pettigrew, Brig.-Gen. Confederate States Army." Charleston, S.C., J. Russell, 1870. 8vo, wraps, 65pp. Sabin-96788. $100, $150.

399 ..."Narrative and Letter of William Henry Trescot, concerning the negotiations between South Carolina and Pres. Buchannan in Dec., 1860, contributed by Gaillard Hunt." (New York, 1908). 8vo,

cover title, p.528-556. Reprinted from Amer. Hist. Rev., v.13, #3, April 1908.

400 **TREVILIANS Battle of**
See: Wade Hampton.

401 **TREW, E. F.**
"Lee' invasion of Maryland; the Sharpsburg Campaign." In: Royal Unit. Ser. Inst. Jour., May 1914, v.LVIII, p.595-604.

401a **TREXLER, H. A.**
"Historical Records Survey, a Calendar of the Ryder collection of Confederate Archives at Tufts College." In: JSH, 1941, v.7, #3, p.427-8.

402 **TREXLER, Harrison A.**
"Causes of Confederate Defeat." In: SWRev., August 1932, v.XVIII, #1, p.87-95.

403 ..."Coaling the Confederate commerce-raiders." In: GaHQ, 1933, v.XVII, p.13-25.

404 ..."The Confederate Navy Department and the Fall of New Orleans." In: SW Review, 1933, v.XIX, p.88-102. $8.

405 ..."The Confederate Ironclad "Virginia" ("Merrimac")." Chicago, Ill., University of Chicago Press (March, 1938). 8vo, cl, dj, sketch, front(map), map liners, vii, 95pp., index, reference-notes, p.73-89.

406 ..."The Davis Administrtion and the Richmond Press, 1861-1865." (Baton Rouge, La.) JSH, May, 1950, v.XVI, #2, p.177-195.

407 ..."The "Harriet Lane" and the Blockade of Galveston." In: SwHQ, Oct. 1931, v.XXXV, #2, p.109-123.

408 ..."Jefferson Davis and the Confederate patronage." In: So. Atl. Quar., Jan. 1929, v.XXVIII, p.45-58. Re. Civil appointments.

409 ..."The opposition of Planters to the employment of slaves as laborers by the Confederacy." In: MVHR, Sept. 1940, v.XXVII, p.211-224. $8.

410 **TREZEVANT, Daniel Henry, Dr.**
"The Burning of Columbia, S.C. A Review of Northern Assertions and Southern Facts." Columbia, S.C., South Carolinian Pr., 1866. $125, $90. 12mo, wraps, 31pp. text: dbl. column.
...(Marietta, Ga., Walton Folk, 1957) 12mo, wraps.

411 **"TRIAL of Abraham Lincoln**
by the Great Statesmen of the Republic. A Council of the past on the tyranny of the present. The Spirit of the Constitution on the Bench-Abraham Lincoln, Prisoner at the Bar, His Own Counsel-1863." Caption title, 8vo, wraps, 8pp. Anti-Lincoln, discredits his administration.
...Do: An 1867 edt., same as the 1863 variant.

412 **"TRIAL of the Officers and Crew**
of the Privateer "Savannah," on the Charge of Piracy, in the U.S. Court for the Southern District of New York. Hon. Judges Nelson and Shopman, presiding. Reported by A. F. Warburton, stenographer and corrected by the Counsel." N.Y., Baker and Godwin Print., 1862. 8vo, cl, xxii, 385pp.

413 **"TRIALS for Treason**
(of Harrison Dodd, Wm. A. Bowles and others), at Indianapolis, disclosing the plans for establishing a North Western Confederacy...Edt: Benn Pittman, recorder to the Military Commission, The." Cincinnati: Moore, Wilstach and Baldwin, 1865. 8vo, cl, 339, (1)p. front group portraits and plate. Sabin-96953.

414 **TRIBBLE, M. P.**
"Report of..., Commissioner of Confederate Rolls to the General Assembly, 1903." Columbia, S.C., State Co., 1904. 8vo, wraps, 5pp.

415 **TRICE, Claude P.**
"Cap't. John H. Dye." In: Indp. Co. (Ark.) Chron. Jan. 1963, v.IV, #2, p.13-28.

416 **TRICE, James Chesley**
"No descendants to honor them. Edt: Mrs.

J. A. Thompson." In: ArkHQ, Spring 1951, v.10, p.85-88. Port. Two letters, Mar. 27, May 15, 1863. From a Pvt. in 19th Ark. Reg., CSArmy, in Mississippi.

417 **TRICKETT, Dean**
"The Civil War in Indian Territory." Oklahoma City: Chron. Okla., Sept. 1939, v.XVII, p.315-327; Dec. 1939, p.401-412; June 1940, v.XVIII, p.142-153; Sept. 1940, p.266-280, v.XVII; Dec. 1941, v.XIX, p.381-396.

418 **TRIMBLE, Isaac Ridgeway**
"The Battle of Gettysburg." In: SHSP, 1898, v.XXVI, p.116-128. From original mssc. by Maj. Graham Daves of N.C.

419 ..."The Civil War Diary of... (edited by Wm. Starr Myers)." In: MdHM, 1922, v.XVII, p.1-20. Chancellorsville and Gettysburg Campaigns.

420 ..."Marylanders in the Confederate Army." In: SHSP, 1909, v.37, p.235.

421 ..."North Carolina at Gettysburg." In: OLOD, Mar. 1876, v.IV, p.53-60; also in: So. Hist. Month., 1876, v.IV, p.56-63.

422 ..."Report of his Operations from Aug. 14-29th, 1862. Charlottesville, Va., Jan 20, 1863." In: SHSP, 1880, v.VIII, p.306-309.

423 ..."North Carolinians at Gettysburg." In: OLOD, March 1876, v.IV, #1, p.53-60. Also in: Southern Hist. Monthly, Jan. 1876, v.1, #1, p.56-63.

424 ..."The campaign and Battle of Gettysburg." In: CV, May 1917, v.XXV, p.209-216.

425 ..."Trinity Church, Portsmouth, Va. - Memorial window." In: SHSP, 1891, v.19, p.207-212.

426 **TROLLOP, Anthony**
"Trollop's North America." In: Black. Edn. Ma., Sept. 1862, c.XCII, p.372-390. Castigates Trollop's view of secession: "He never read the Constitution," we like his plot, he's a good novelist but a bad politician."

427 **TROOP Movements**
at the Battle of Cold Harbor, 1864." Richmond, Va., Civil War Centennial Committee, 1964. Oblong folio, official Pub. #21, (16) unnumbered pages, printed one side, (1)p. introduction.

428 **TROOPS tendered**
to the Confederate War Department, 1861." Washington: War Department Print., 1876. 8vo, sewn, 103pp.

429 **TROP, June F.**
"An update: the Douglas Letters." In: Smith Co. (Tex.) HS, Summer, 1983, v.22, #1, p.13-27, prots. See: Lucia R. Douglas.

430 **TROUBETZKOY, Dorothy Ulrich**
"The horses of Robert E. Lee (from 1846-1870)." In: Va and the Va. County, Jan. 1952, v.6, #1, p.39-49, 18-19, port, view.

431 **TROUBETZKOY, Ulrich**
"The Best Picture of General Stuart." (Richmond) Va. Cavl., Winter 1962-1963, v.XII, #3, p.40-47, illus. (1-color). Controversy involves Frederick Moynihan's work of Stuart.

432 ..."The Confederate Memorial Chapel." (Richmond) Va. Cavl., Winter 1960-1961, v.X, #3, p.23-28, illus., dbl. pg. color.

433 ..."The Lee Monument." (Richmond) Va. Cavl., Spring 1962, v.XI, #4, p.4-10, illus., ports (1-color).

434 ..."W. L. Sheppard: Artist of Action." (Richmond) Va. Cavl., Winter 1961-1962, v.XI, #3, p.20-26, illus. (2-color). Lt. Sheppard of the Richmond Howitzers sketched war from Bethel to Appomattox.
...Same: In: CWTI, Dec. 1962, v.1, #8, p.10-17, line drawings.

435 ..."F. William Sievers, Sculptor." (Richmond) Va. Cavl., Autumn 1962, v.XII, #2, p.4-12, illus (1-color) ports. Famed for his monuments to Confederate war heroes.

436 **TROUP (pseud.)**
"To the People of the South; Senator Hammond and the Tribune, by Troup.

(with extracts from a speech of James H. Hamilton, U.S. Senate, Mar. 4, 1858." Charleston, S.C., 1860, Tract #3, 8vo, sewn, 24pp. caption title. One of the earliest for secession.

437 ..."To the people of the South, Senator Hammond and the Tribune, Tract #3." See: James Henry Hammond.

438 **TROUSDALE, J. A.**
"The Reign of Terror in Tennessee." In: SB, ns, v.1, #10, p.665-670. (1885/1886) $10.

439 **TROW, Harrison, Capt.**
"Charles W. Quantrell." See. John P. Burch.

440 **TROWBRIDGE, John Townsend**
"The South: a tour of its battlefields and ruined cities, a journey through the desolated states and talks with the people; being a description of the present state of the country - its agriculture, railroads, business and finances, giving an account of Confederate misrule, including visits to patriot graves and rebel prisons, and embracing special notes on the labor system, education and moral elevation of the freedman, also on plans of reconstruction and inducements to emigration. From personal observations and experience during months of Southern travel." Hartford, Conn., L. Stebbins, 1867, 8vo, cl, front, illus., maps, xiii, (1), (15)-590.

441 ..."The Desolate South, 1865-1866. Picture of the Battlefields and of the devastated Confederacy. Edt: Gordon Carroll." N.Y., Duell, Sloan and Pearce; Boston: Little, brown and Co., (1956). 8vo, cl, dj, xvi, (16)pp, illus., 320pp.
..."A picture of the desolated states & the work of restoration, 1865-8." Hartford, L. Stebbins, 1868. 8vo, cl, 690p. color t.p., ills. maps. $100.

442 **TROWER, Eva Augusta**
"Mistress Lucy, a true story of the war days, 1861-1865." In: Tyler HGM, July 1949, v.31, p.33-37. On Lucy Ann Diggs (Mrs. Marshall Brownley) at "La Grange," Mathews Co., Co.

443 **"TRUE Conversion.**
A Dialogue Between Hopeful and Christian. From Pilgrim's Progress." Richmond, (c.1863). 12mo, 8pp-folder. Eberstadt- #113 (182).

444 **TRUNDLE, Joseph H.**
"Gettysburg described in two letters from a Maryland Confederate." In: MdHM, June 1959, v.54, p.210-212. To his sister, from Loudoun Co., Va. and Hagerstown, 7 July, 1863, 16 June.

445 **TRUSS, John W.**
"Civil War Letters from Parsons' Texas Cavalry Brigade." In: SwHW, Oct., 1965, v.LXVIII, #2, p.210-223.

446 **TRUSSEL, J.B.B., Jr.**
"Pelham-gallant gunner." In: Field Art. Jour., Mar./Arp., 1949, v.39, p.59-61, map. On John Pelham in CSArmy, 1861-1863.

447 ..."The saga of "Whistling Dick"." In: Artiaircraft Jour., Mar../Apr. 1952, v.95, #2, p.22-23. On an 8 "Blakely rifle" used in CSA defense of Vicksburg, 1863.

448 ..."The Staunton Artillery at Henry Hill." In: Antiaircraft Jour., Nov./Dec., 1954, v.97, p.22-25, map. John D. Imboden's battery at the first battle of Bull Run, 1861.

449 **TRYON, Warren S.**
"The Publications of Ticknor and Fields in the South, 1840-1865." (Baton Rouge, La.) JSH, August, 1948, v.XIV, #3, p.305-330.

450 **"TRYST with the Brace and the True, A."**
Camp Sumter, United Confederate Veterans annual celebration, Charleston, S.C., Apr. 13, 1903. (cover title)---(half-title)- "Heroes Who Wore the Gray. A memorial celebration by Camp Sumter, U.C.V., tributes to dead comrades - reviving treasured recollections - the striking address of Col. Jas. Simons - "Confederate

Soldier," Commander T. George Simons - "Siege of Battery Wagner," and Reb. J. A. B. Scherer - "Teachers in Gray" and Capt. Chs. Inglesby - "Reminiscences on Ft. Sumter"." (Charleston, S.C., Lucas-Richardson, L & P Co.) 8vo, wraps, 17pp.

451 **TUCKER, Beverley**
See: Nathaniel Beverley Tucker.

452 **TUCKER, Beverly D.**
"National Beverly Tucker: prophet of the Confederacy, 1784-1851." Tokyo: Nan'undo, 1979. 8vo, cl, xi, 507pp. $25. Based, in part, on the research of the late Percy Winfield Turrentine, PhD. Tokyo.

453 **TUCKER, Dallas, Rev.**
"The Fall of Richmond." (fron Richmond Dispatch, Feb. 2, 1902) In: SHSP, 1901, v.29, p.152-163.

454 **TUCKER, George Wellford**
"Lee and the Gettysburg Campaign." (Richmond, 1932) 12mo, cl, port(front), xix, 61pp, $25. Pix Va. Monument at Gettysburg on cover. Lynchburg, Va. 1933. Same reprint, added illus. $30.

455 ..."Death of General A. P. Hill, by Sgt. G.W. Tucker." In: SHSP, 1883, v.XI, p.564-569.

456 **TUCKER, Glenn**
"Battle of Chickamauga." Gettysburg, Pa., Civil War Times Illustr., May 1969, v.8, #2, 4to, illus., some color, map, 50pp, bibliog., p.50.

457 ..."The Cavalry invasion of the North." In: CWTI, July, 1963, v.II, #4, p.26-31, illus., map, ports.

458 ..."Chickamauga: Bloody Battle in the West." Indianapolis, Ind., Bobbs-Merrill (1961) 12mo, cl, dj, maps, 448pp. notes, bibliog. and index (p.399-448) $35.
...(Dayton, Ohio) Morningside Pr., 1972. Reprint above, 1976.
...Dayton, Oh., Morningside Press, 1984. 8vo, cl, 448pp., 14 maps. (paper, $9) $17.50.

459 ..."High Tide at Gettysburg. The Campaign in Pennsylvania." Indianapolis, Ind., Bobbs-Merrill (1958) 8vo, cl, dj, maps, viii, (2), 462pp., notes, bibliog., index (p.397-462) $40. "Charter Books," paper, Mar. 1964.
...(Dayton, Ohio) Morningside Bookshop, 1973. Photolith reprint, above. $15.

460 ..."Historical Sketches from Washington Post, 1934." Washington, D.C.: Washington Post, 1934. 4to. "South missed chance to win war: with Northern volunteers put to route in Battle of Bull Run."; "Iron-clad Merrimac periled Union."; "Jackson gave North its worst scare."; "Lee's ragged army invades Maryland."; "Jubal Early's attack on Washington was the three day thriller of the Civil War." Issues: Aug. 12, 19, 26, Sept. 2.

461 ..."Front Rank." Written for the North Carolina Confederate Centennial Commission." Raleigh, North Carolina (1962). $20. 4to, cl, dj, illus., 83pp., ports, facsm.

462 ..."Lee and Longstreet at Gettysburg." Indianapolis: Bobbs-Merrill (1968). 8vo, cl, dj, maps, xi, (2), 286pp., notes, index, p.253-286. $30.

463 ..."Longstreet: culprit or Scapegoat?" In: CWTI, Apr. 1962, v.1, #1, p.4-7, map, ports, cont'd: p.39-44, and a profile.

464 ..."Now he belongs to the entire nation." In: CWTI, April, 1965. v.IV, #1, p.4-11, 35-38, illus., ports. Robert E. Lee universally revered of Amer. soldiers in all parts of the country.

465 ..."Jeb Stuart learned on Fleetwood Hill. Federals could fight on horseback too." In: CWT, Dec. 1960, v.II, #8(OS), p.5-6, 18-19. illus., map.

466 ..."Some Aspects of North Carolina's Participation in the Gettysburg Campaign." (Raleigh) NCHRev., April 1958, v.XXXV, #2, p.191-212. $8.

467 ..."Untutored genius of the war." In: CWTI, June 1964, v.III, #3, p.6-9, 35-39, 49, illus., ports. Nathan Bedford Forrest.

468 ..."Zeb Vance." In: CWTI, April 1968, v.VII, #1, p.10-19, illus., ports.

469 ..."Zeb Vance: Champion of personal freedom." Indianapolis: Bobbs-Merrill (1966) (1965), tk.8vo, cl, dj, maps, port(front), viii, 564pp. $25-bmk.

470 ..."What became of Pickett's report on his assault at Gettysburg?" In: CWTI, Oct., 1967, v.VI, #6, p.36-39, ports.

471 **TUCKER, Henry St. George**
"Memorial address on the life and character of Gen. William Henry Fitzhugh Lee, of Virginia...in the House of Representatives...Feb. 6, 1892." (Richmond, 1893) 8vo, sewn, 8pp. See under principal's name.

472 ..."The treaty-making power under the constitution of the Confederate States of America." In: Va. Law Rev., May 1914, v.1, p.596-603.

472a **TUCKER, John S.**
"The Diary of John S. Tucker: Confederate soldier from Alabama. Edt. Gary Wilson." In: AHQ, 1981, v.43, #1, p.5-33.

473 **TUCKER, Nathaniel Beverley**
"Address of Beverley Tucker, Esq., to the prople of the United States, with appendix relating to President Johnson's proclamation of 2nd May, 1865." Montreal, Longmoore and Co., Print., 1865. 12mo, wraps, 44pp.

474 ...Atlanta, Ga., Library Emory University, 1948. Sources and reprints. Ser. 5, Edt: James Harvey Young. 8vo, wraps, facsm., 32pp. Response to Johnston's broadside accusing he and other leaders inciting assassination of Lincoln.

475 ..."The Partisan Leader; a Tale of the Future. By Edward William Sidney." In two volumes, Printed for the Publishers, by James Caxton, 1856. (i.e., Wash: Printed by D. Green, 1836) Post dated 20 years to make publication contemporary with supposed future events. An extraordinary pre-vision of the Civil War, written 25 years before the fact. From Southern point of view, depicts war for Secession with Virginia background. 12mo, cl, v, 201; (2), 201pp. $100.

476 ..."A Key to the Disunion Conspiracy. The Partisan Leader by Beverly Tucker, of Virginia. Secretly printed in Washington (in the year 1836) by Duff Green, for circulation in the Southern States. But afterwards suppressed." N.Y., Reprinted by Rudd and Carleton, 1861. 12mo, cl, (2), x-xv, 195; iv, (4), 199-392. Also in wraps. Same: 2 vol. in One, 392pp. $150-g.

477 ..."The Partisan Leader; a Novel and an Apocalypse of the Origin and Struggles of the Southern Confederacy. By Judge Beverly Tucker of Virginia." Richmond: West and Johnston, 1862. 8vo, wraps, viii, 220pp. Crandall-3112. Republished and Edt: Rev. Thos. A. Ware. (soiled-$250), $500-bmk.

..."The Partisan Leader." Chapel Hill: University of North Carolina Press, 1971. 8vo, cl, dj, 392pp.

..."Prescience, a Speech delivered by Hon. Beverly Tucker, or Virginia, in the Southern Convention, held at Nashville, Tenn., April 13, 1850." Richmond, Va., West and Johnston, 1862. 12mo, 38pp., wraps.

478 ..."The Partisan leader, edited with an introduction by Carl Bridenbaugh." N.Y., A.A. Knopf, 1933. 12mo, cl, xxxiv, 77, (1)p. Cover: Americana deserta, 1836 edition used for reprint.

479 **TUCKER, Philip C., 3d**
"The United States Gunboat Harriet Lane." In: SwHQ, April, 1918, v.XXI, #4, p.360-380.

479a **TUCKER, Phillip Thomas**
"The exiled Confederates who never returned home: a history of the First Missouri Brigade 1862-65." In: CV, ns, Jan.-Feb. 1988, v.36, #1. p.6-13, map, ills, ports.

480 **TUCKER, Robert Cinnamond**
"The Life and Public Service of E. John Ellis." New Orleans: LHQ, July, 1946, v.29, #3, p.679-770 (CSA and Reconst: 687-737).

481 **TUCKER, Samuel**
"Price raid through Linn Co., Kan., Oct. 24/25, 1864." (n.p., 1958) 4to, 17 leaves, col. map. On a CSA raid led by Gen. Sterling Price and with several narratives by eyewitnesses.

482 **TUNNARD, William H.**
"Running the Mississippi Blockade." In: CV, Jan. 1916, v.XXIV, p.27-28.

483 ..."A Southern record, the history of the Third Regiment Louisiana Infantry, by W. H. Tunnard, containing a complete record of the campaigns in Arkansas and Missouri; the battles of Oak Hills, Elk Horn, Iuka, Corinth; the second siege of Vicksburg, anecdotes, camps, scenery and description of the country through which the regiment marched." Baton Rouge, Printed for the author, 1866. 12mo, cl, xx, (21)-393, (1), front (port), port. Unit roster - (351)-384, ports. of Ben McCulloch and Willie T. Tunnard. $750-bmk.
...Dayton, Oh., Morningside Press, 1970. Edt: Edwin C. Bearss, Ltd. Edt. 1000. 581pp. An added 2200 roster. Note: see Osborn H. Oldroyd's "Soldier's Story of Siege of Vicksburg" among others in append: Tunnard's Reminisc. 3rd La. Inf.
...Dayton, Oh., Morningside Press, 1988. Reprint of 1970 edition. $45.

483a **TUNNELL, Ted**
"Crucible of Reconstruction: War Radicalism, & Race in Louisiana." Baton Rouge: Louisiana State Univ., 1984. 8vo, cl, dj, xi, 257p, maps, notes, appends., bibliog., index. $25.
..."The Negro, the Republican Party & the election of 1876 in Louisiana." In: L.H., spring 1966, v.7, p.101-16.

484 **TUNSTALL, Nannie Whitmell**
"No. 40. A Romance of Fortress Monroe and the Hygea." 2nd Edt. Richmond, Va., J.W. Randolph and english 1884. 16mo, wrasp, 111pp. (1890 edition).

485 **TURLEY, Thomas Battle**
"A Narrative of his Capture and Imprisonment during the War Between the States." (Memphis, Tenn.) Southeastern College, 1961, Burrow Library Monograph #5, 8vo, wraps, illus., ports, vii, 4pp.

486 **TURNER, Arlin**
"George W(ashington) Cable." Durham, N.C., Duke Univ. Pr., 1956, 8vo, cl, ports, xi, 391pp. Service in CSArmy and work in New Orleans.

487 **TURNER, Charles W.**
"The Richmond, Fredericksburg and Potomac, 1861-1865." In: CWH, September, 1961, v.VII, #3, p.255-263.

488 ..."The Virginia Central Railroad at War, 1861-1865." (Baton Rouge, La.) JSH, Nov., 1946, v.XII, #4, p510-533.

489 ..."Virginia Southwestern Railroad System at War, 1861-1865." In: NCHR, Oct., 1947, v.24, p.467-484.

490 **TURNER, Edward Raymond**
"The New Market Campaign, May, 1864." Richmond: Whittet and Shepperson, 1912. Tall 8vo, cl, illus., ports., incl. front, 2-dbl. pg. maps, xiv, 203pp. $60. $85.

491 ..."The Battle of New Market." In: CV, Feb., 1912, v.XX, p.71-75.

492 **TURNER, George Edgar**
"Victory Rode the Rails: The Strategic Place of the Railroads in the Civil War." Indianapolis: Bobbs-Merrill Co., (1953) 8vo, cl, dj, maps, illus., xiv, 419pp. North and South, history and strategy. $40-ob.

493 **TURNER, J. Kelly and Jno. L. Bridges, Jr.**
"History of Edgecombe County, North Carolina." Raleigh, Edwards and Broughton Pr., 1920, 8vo, cl, illus., ports, maps, plats, facsms., 486pp. "Politics after the Revolution" (p.104-155); "Slavery," p.156-185; "War Between States," p.186-236; "Reconstruction," p.237-280.

494 **TURNER, Jesse**
"Correspondence. Hon. Jesse Turner's Position." (Van Buren, Ark., ?1861) Broadside, 31 cm. 3 column, ornamental borders. Dated Van Buren, Ark., Feb. 4, 1861. Relating to secession. Hargrett and Allen.

495 **TURNER, Jim**
"Jim Turner Co. G, 6th Texas Infantry CSA, from 1861 to 1865." In: Texana, 1974, v.XII, #2, p.149-178.

496 **TURNER, John R.**
"The Battle of the Wilderness! The part taken by Mahone's Brigade. An address delivered by Comrade John R. Turner before A. P. Hill Camp of Confederate Veterans of Petersburg, Va., on the evening of March 3rd 1892." n.p., n.d. (1892) 8vo, stitched, 19pp, double columns.
...Also in: SHSP, 1892, v.XX, p.68-95, and Geo. Barnard's WTCV, p.88-106.

497 **TURNER, Josephine M.**
"The Courageous Carolina, Founder of the U.D.C." Montgomery, Ala., Paragon Press (1965). 8vo, wraps, illus., ports. front, privately printed, 63pp.

498 **TURNER, Justin G.**
"Peace conference at Hampton Roads foundered on this basic question, "Our common country" or, "the two countries"?" In: CWT, Jan. 1962, v.III, #9(OS) p.12-16, illus., ports.

499 **TURNER, Maxine**
"Naval Operations on the Apalachicola and Chattahoochee Rivers, 1861-1865." In: AHQ, Fall/Winter, 1974, v.36, p.189-274.

500 **TURNER, Thomas Reed**
"Beware the people weeping: public opinion and the assassination of Abraham Lincoln." Baton Rouge: Louisiana State Univ., 1982, 8vo, cl, dj, xvi, 252pp. $30.

501 **TURNER, Wallace B.**
"Teh Secession Movement in Kentucky." In: RKHS, July 1968, v.66, #3, p.259-278.

502 **TURNER, William A.**
"Even more Confederate faces." Orange, Va., 1983. 8vo, cl, dj, illus.(ports), 224pp. $30. See also: Wm. Albaugh, Largely carte-de-visite photos, from tintypes to embrotypes. Plus an alphabetically listed known photographers. DeLuxe, 100 copies. $41.45.

503 **TURNER, William Dandridge**
"Some War-time Recollections, the Story of a Confederate officer who was at first one of those in charge of and later captive in Libby Prison." In: "American Magazine," Sept. 1910, v.LXX, p.619-631.

504 **TURNEY, Peter**
"The South Justified. Address before Frank Cheatham Bivouac #1, Association of Confederate Soldiers, Tenn., Div., Sat., Aug. 18, 1888." Nashville: Albert B. Tavel, 1888. 8vo, wraps, 25pp. Note: issued also as an append: to Mrs. Ann E. Snyder's "The Civil War from a Southern Stand point."

505 ..."Supplement to - "The South Justified." An address in answer to criticism, delivered before Turney Bivouac #13, Association, Confederate Soldiers, Tenn. Div., Sat., Aug. 17, 1888." 8vo, wraps, 24pp. Nashville: Foster & Webb (1888). In: SHSP, 1888, v.16, p.319-339.

506 ..."Opinion: "Decision of the Supreme Court of Tennessee that the Confederacy was de Jure as well as de facto." In: SHSP, 1878, v.V, p.288-291.

507 **TWAIN, Mark**
"The Letters of Quintus Curtius

Snodgrass." Edt: Ernest E. Leisy. Dallas, Texas: Southern Methodist University Press, 1946. 8vo, cl, port(front) 76pp. Letters in New Orleans (La.) Daily Crescent, 1861. Experiences of a recruit in CSArmy. See. John Gerber.

..."Cave life during the siege of Vicksburg." n.p., n.d. (c.1985). narrow 8vo, 6pp folder. From his 'Life on the Mississippi.'

508 **TWENTIETH Infantry-Tennessee**
See: James L. Cooper, Wm. Martin Clark, Thomas B. Smith, Wm. J. McMurray.

508a **TWENTY-FOURTH Alabama Commemorative Association**
"Memorial tribute. Capt. B. S. Chamberlain, orderly Serg't D. A. Vigo, Corporal William Keifer, Private G. McEvoy." Mobile, Ala., Shields & Co., April 24, 1882. (This regiment was organized in Mobile, August 1861.) Bell pg. 90.

509 **TWIGGS, Hansford**
"Robert E. Lee. An Address by Judge H.D.D. Twiggs." In: Watson's Mag., News stand edition, Mar. 1916. v.XXII, #5, p.244-249. Thomas, Ga., Jeffersonian Pub. Co., 4to.

510 **TWIGGS, Hansford Dade Duncan, Lt.-Col.**
"Address of (on Defense of Battery Wagner) before Confederate Survivors Association in Augusta, Ga." In: "CSA- 14th Annual Reunion on Memorial Day, Apr. 26, 1892," p.7-26. Also in: SHSP, 1892, v.XX, p.166-184.

511 ..."Defense of Battery Wagner, July 18, 1863." In: Addresses delivered before the Confederate Veterans Association of Savannah, Ga., 1898, p.73-89.

512 **TWITCHELL, Ralph Emerson**
"The Confederate Invasion of New Mexico." Albuquerque, New Mexico-Old Santa Fe, 1916, v.III, p.5-43.

513 **TWO Months in Fort Lafayette."**
By a Prisoner. N.Y., Printed for Author, 1862. 12mo, wraps, 53pp. Acct. prison life, July 20-Oct. 28, 1861. List of Prisoners, mostly Southerners, prison conditions by Gov. Morehead of Ky. Author (?) - William Gilchrist.

514 **TWO Months in the Confederate States.**
By an English Merchant. See: W.C. Corsan.

515 **TYLER, Charles Waller**
"The Scout. A Tale of the Civil War." Nashville, Tenn., Cumberland Pr., 1911. 8vo, cl, port(front) CSA-flag, 344. (3)pp.
...Nashville: 1912, p.345. Fact in fiction form. Sam Davis.

516 **TYLER, David Gardiner**
"Address of Welcome to the Confederate Veterans delivered at the auditoruim, June 1, 1915. Twenty-fifth Reunion U.C.V." Richmond, Va., 1915. 8vo, wraps, 70pp.

517 ..."Address...on the occasion of the Anniversary of the birth of Robert E. Lee, delivered at the College of William and Mary, Jan. 19, 1911. (In Bul. College of W&M, v.4, #3, Jan. 1911) 8vo, wraps, 20pp.

519 ..."Diary for 1865 commencing March." In: Tyler QHGM, Jan. 1949, v.30, p.251-255. Diary kept in 1st Va. Art., Rockbridge Bat., Mar. 20-Aug. 10, 1865.

520 **TYLER, H. A.**
"A Review of the Tyler-Latham controversy." n.p., (19070? 8vo, wraps 31pp. + 4pp. insert. C.S. Veteran asserts the Tennessee state UDC president and husband were really Unionist during war. (Carolina)

521 **TYLER, John**
"Historic cannon, brought over by Rockambeau, remolded for service in the War Between the States." In: S.R. Va.- Quart.Mag., April, 1922, v.I, p.3-8. Hist. two brass six-lb. field guns, now on campus

of V.M.I.
See: William Archer Cocke.

522 **TYLER, John, Maj.**
"The Last Hope of the Confederacy - John Tyler to the Governor and Authorities of Texas." Introduction by Chas. W. Ramsdell. In: QTSHA, Oct. 1910, v.XIV, #2, p.129-145.

523 **TYLER, Lyon Gardiner**
"The Bixby Myth." In: Tyler's Quart. Hist. and Geneal. Mag., 1934, v.XV, p.274-276. Raises question if Mrs. Bixby really had five sons.

524 "Barton and the lineage of Lincoln, claim that Lincoln was related to Lee refuted." 2nd Edition. n.p., 1930?, 12mo, wraps, 12pp.

525 ..."Catholicism or slavery-which?" In: TylerQHM, 1934, v.XV, p.220-228.

526 ..."A Confederate Catechism. The War for Southern Self Government." n.p., n.d. (c.1929) 16mo, 8pp.
...Do: 2nd edt., Oct. 21, 1929, wraps, 12pp. (Holdcroft, Charles City County, Va.)
...Do: 3rd., Nov. 21, 1929, wraps, 12pp.
...Do: 4th Rev. Edt., May 25, 1930, wraps, 15pp.
...Do: 5th Enlarged, Nov. 20, 1930, wraps, 43pp.
...Do: 6th Enlarged, Feb. 28, 1931, 60pp.
...Do: 7th Enlarged, July 1935, wraps, 64pp.
...7th Edt., Jan. 1952, 22pp.
...7th Edt., Enlarged, 28 (1)p. Defends South and its right of secession and causes of the war.
...Greenville, S.C., A. Press, 1984. 8vo, wraps, 45pp. $8.

527 ..."A Confederate Catechism." In: Tyler QHGM, Oct. 1951/Jan. 1952, v.33, p.89-106, 157-178. Forty-eight questions and answers on causes, character and ethics of the Civil War. Append: letter from Tyler, Nov. 28, 1934.

528 ..."Confederate leaders and other citizens request house delegates to repeal resolution of respect to Abe Lincoln, the barbarian." (n.p., 1928) 8vo, wraps, 16pp. In: Magazine of History with notes and queries. Tarrytown, N.Y., 1931. Extra number. #169 (v.43, #1) Rare Lincolniana No. 41, p.27-39. Running title: Confederate request, 1928.

529 ..."Confederate forces in the war for Southern independence." In: Tyler's QHG Mag., Jan. 1927, v.VIII, p.155-172.

530 ..."The fiery epoch." In: TylerQHGM, 1934, v.XVI, p.1-15. Critical review of Chs. W. Thompson's "Fiery epoch." Indp., 1931, with copy of a letter by David Rankin Barbee to support criticism.

531 ..."How Lincoln got rich." In: TylerQHGM, 1935, v.XVII, p.3-9.

532 ..."Judicial Murder of Maj. Henry Wirz." In: CV, May 1919, v.XXVII, p.178-180.

533 ..."Major Henry Wirz." In: WMQ, Jan., 1919, v.XXVII, p.145-151.

534 ..."General Lee's Birthday. Address by...at Hollins College on Jan. 18, 1929, repeated before State College for women at East Radford, Jan. 19, 1929, on Gen. Robt. E. Lee." n.p., n.d., 8vo, wraps, 22pp. $10.

535 ..."Lincoln and Fort Sumter." In: Tyl. Quart. Hist. Mag., Jan. 1921, v.II, p.208-214. Re: Connor's "Jno. Arch. Campbell," 1920 and negotiations between Campbell and Seward and Fort Sumter.

536 ..."Lincoln Diplomacy." In: Tyler QHGM, Apr. 1924, v.V, p.217-223.

537 ..."A Northern gentleman and a northern politician." In: TQH & GM, July 1925, v.VII, p.1-8. Re: Seward's attack on loyalty of Franklin Pierce in 1861.

538 ..."The old South and its modern defamers." In: TylerQHGM, 1935, v.XVI, p.139-150.

539 ..."Propaganda in History." Richmond, Va., Richmond Press, 1920. 8vo, cover

title, wraps, 19pp.

...2nd Edt., revised, 20pp., 1921. Monaghan-2488-attacks Rev. Chs. Potter for characterizing Lincoln as a "future social Christ," around a "Amer. Church."

540 ..."Edmund Ruffin. An Address delivered at Virginia Polytechnic Institute, Blacksburg, Virginia, Apr. 25, 1913." (Roanoke, Va., Stone Print, 1913). 8vo, wraps, 15pp.

541 ..."Sectional ambition the cause of the war in 1861." In: TylerQHGM, 1935, v.XVI, p.227-230. A letter from Tyler, Nov. 28, 1934, stating his views on cause of war.

542 ..."Stephen A. Douglas and the war." In: TQHGM, July 1931, wraps, 15pp.

543 ..."The South and self-determination." In: Wm. & Mary Quart., April, 1919, v.XXVII, p.217-225.

544 ..."The New South and the Old South; Myths and Mythmakers." In: TQHGM, Jan. 1926, v.VII, p.145-154.

545 ..."The Old South." In: TQHGM, 1936, v.XVII, p.131-143. Address: Memorial Day, Petersburg, Va., June 9, 1934. Overthrow of South a national disaster.

546 ..."Tyler vs Lincoln." Richmond, Va., Tyler's Quarterly Historical and Genealogical Magazine." v.X, #2, October, 1928, p.75-99. $10.

547 ..."John Tyler and Abraham Lincoln, Who Was the Dwarf? A Reply to a Challenge." Richmond, Va., Press, 1929. 8vo, cl, ports, 41pp. $20.

548 ..."Tyler's Quarterly Historical and Genealogical Magazine, v.1-33; Jyly, 1919-April, 1952." Richmond, Va., Lyon Gardiner Tyler, Edt. 8vo, wraps, illus., ports. Many articles by Tyler on the CSA.

549 ..."Virginia's call for statesmanship, the Peace Convention of 1861." (Richmond) Va. Cavl., Autumn, 1960. v.X, #2, p.12-18, illus., ports (1-color).

550 ..."Virginia Principals, an address to the Waynesboro (Va.) Historical Society, Oct. 11, 1927. Revised and republished Mar. 1, 1928 and July 1951." Richmond, Va., Richmond Press, n.d. 8vo, wraps, 33pp. (1928, p.23).

..."Virginia Principals." In: Tyler's Qrt. Hist. and Geneal. Mag., Jan. 1928, v.IX, p.167-183. An Address of...Principals that led to war. $20.

551 ..."Virginia, founder of the world's navies." In: Tyl. Qurt., Hist. and Genea. Mag., Oct., 1921, v.III, p.84-106. Victory of "Merrimack" changes character of naval warfare, hence Va. claims a 1st.

552 ..."Was Grant magnanimous?" In: TylerQHGM, 1933, v.XV, p.100-106. Re: Grant's actions at Appomattox, NO!

553 **TYLER, Richard**
"Appomattox: the surrender of the Army of Northern Virginia, 1865." In: Picket Post, Nov. 1955-May 1956, v.50, p24-28; v.51, p.34-38; v.52, p.30-35, map, notes.

554 **TYLER, Ronnie Curtis**
"Santiago Vidaurri and the Confederacy." Austin, Texas State Hist. Ass'n., (1973) 8vo, cl, dj, illus., ports., incl. front, map, 196pp., bibliog-index, p.157-196. $12.50.

555 ..."Cotton on the Border, 1861-1865." In: SwHQ, April, 1970, v.LXXIII, #4, p.456-477. Re: John Warren Hunter and traffic of Cotton thru Mexico to Europe.

556 ..."An auspicious agreement (1861) between a Confederate secret agent (Jose A. Quintero) and a Governor (Santiago Vidaurri) of New Mexico." in: Am. West, Jan. 1972, p.38-43, 63.

557 **TYRELL, Henry**
"Shenandoah, love and war in the valley of Virginia 1861-1865, based on the famous play by Bronson Howard, by Henry Terrell." N.Y., G.P. Putnam's Sons, 1912. 12mo, cl, vii, 389pp., col. front, plates.

558 **TYSON, Carl Newton**
"Texas: Men for War; Cotton for

Economy." In: Jour. of West, 1975, v.XIV, p.130-148.

558a **TYSON, Carl P.**
"Highway of War." In: Red River Valley Hist. Rev., Summer, 1978, v.3, p.28-51 Red River Campaign of '64.

559 **TYSON, L. D., Col. (now Brig.-Gen., U.S.A.)**
"Generals Lee and Jackson...address to UDC, Knoxville Chap., Jan. 19, 1917, to celebrate joint anniversaries of Lee and Jackson." In: CV, Dec. 1917, v.25, #12, p.541-547, illus. of "Last meeting of Lee and Jackson."

560 **TYSON, Raymond W.**
"William Barksdale and the Brooks-Summer Assault." (Jackson, Miss.) Jour. Miss. Hist., May, 1964, v.XXXVI, #2, p.135-140.

U

1 **UHLER, John Earle**
"James Ryder Randall in Louisiana." In: LHQ, April 1938, v.21, #2, 1p.532-546. Author: "Maryland, My Maryland."

2 **UHLER, Margaret**
"Maj.-Gen. James Patton Anderson: an autobiography." In: FHQ, Jan. 1987, v.65, #3, p.335-356, port. See also: Jas. P. Anderson.

3 **ULMER, J.B.**
"A glimpse of Albert Sidney Johnston through the smoke of Shiloh." In: ATSHA, April 1907, v.X, #4, p.285-296.

4 **UNDER Both Flags.**
A Panorama of the Great Civil War. As represented in story, anecdote adventure and the romance of reality written by celebrities of both sides; the men and women who created the greatest epoch of our nations history. An unprejudiced representation of the issues that divide our country, as told in the personal recollections of those who participated in the campaigns, marches, sufferings, anecdotes and instances of dauntless heroism which glorified and ennobled this gigantic struggle for the supremacy of the Union. Gorgeously illustrated with about 250 superb illustrations from photographs and drawings accurately picturing the scenes described. Phila: People's Publishing Co., copyright, C.R. Graham, 1896. 4to, cl, pict., illus., incl. front, ports, map, (17), 592pp. Double columns.

5 **UNDERWRITER (Gunboat), USNavy, capture of:**
See: Daniel B. Conrad, Benjamin P. Loyall.

6 **UNDERWOOD, Betsy Swint**
"War seen through a teen-ager's eyes." In: Tenn. HQ, 1961, v.XX, p.177-187.

7 **UNDERWOOD, George C.**
"History of the Twenty-sixth Regiment of North Carolina Troops in the great war, 1861-1865." Goldsboro, N.C., Nash Bros., (1901) $350-ob. 8vo, cl, front, ports, 2, 122, 6pp. Final 6pp., R.M. Tuttle's "Unparalleled loss Co. F, 26th Reg., N.C. troops at Gettysburg, July 1, 1862.
...Wendell, N.C., Broadfoot's Bookmart, 1978. 500 copies. $20.

8 **UNDERWOOD, John C., Maj.-Gen., U.C.V.**
"Report of Proceedings incidental to the erection and dedication of the Monument to the Confederate dead at Chicago. A reception of renowned Southern generals, at Chicago, a banquet at Cincinnati...military greetings at Ft. Thomas, Ky., May 29-June 1, 1895." $75. Chicago: William Johnston Print, 1896, 4to, cl, num. ports, illus., xii, 285pp. 300 copies. Also: in wraps(pict) and 1/2 Mor., atg.

9 **UNDERWOOD, John Levi**
"The Women of the Confederacy, in which is presented the heroism of the women of the Confederacy with accounts of their trials during the War and the period of reconstruction, with their ultimate triumph over adversity. Their motives and their achievements as told by writers and orators now preserved in permanent form. By Rev. J.L. Underwood." N.Y., Wash., Neale Print, 1906. 8vo, cl, front(port), xvii, (19)-313pp. $150, $125.

10 **UNIFORM and Dress of the Army**
Of the Confederate States. Richmond, Va., Chas. H. Wynne, Print, 1861. Lithos: E. Crehen (printed in Petersburg, by Valdry) 4to (14x11") 15pls., orig. boards, paper label. ('58) $500. Note: A NY auction, Feb. 28, 1952 with some plates color

11 ...Of the Confederate States as prescribed by Gen. Order, June 1861-Article XLVII Army Register." Richmond: United Confederate Vets., Virginia Div., R.E. Lee Camp #1 (1911). Also: reprint of Gen. Ord. #9, June 6, 1861; Gen. Ord. #4, Jan. 24, 1864. 8vo, wraps, 10pp. Bound heavy boards, Marcus Wright Book Pl., $100-r.

12 **UNIFORM and Dress of the Army and Navy**
Of the Confederate States of America. Intro: Richard Harwell.N.Y., St. Martin's Press, 1960. Sq. 8vo, xii, 5, iv, 23 plates (colored). This brings together the three CSA editions. (1) "The uniform and dress of the Army of the Confederate States." Richmond: Chas. H. Wynne, 1861. (2) "Uniform and dress of the navy of the Confederate States." Richmond, 1862? and its accompanying, but separately issued set of plates. The Army uniform regulations and plates, as well as the plates illustrating the Navy uniform regulations, were reproduced by litho at the Meriden Gravue Co.: the Navy Uniform regulations, were reset in type on 2 pages of text. These are the University of Virginia and Boston Athenaeum. Note: Two editions of Uniform and Dress of the Army were issued during the war (1861) the first edition had uncolored plates, printed by P.L. Valory of Petersburg, the 2nd January 24, 1862, plates in color. (Nashville: J.F. Wagner) (Columbia, S.C., Blanton Duncan and the same Valory who did the uncolored plates.) The 2nd edition has tipped-in a copy of the Confederate War Dept. General Orders, #4, Jan. 24, 1862, announces changes in regulations re caps and a strip illustrating color for the caps and an error in color of the cavalry sash and the difficulty of obtaining proper colors. The 2nd editions at the Confederate Museum, Duke, Emory, Mellon and Riley Collection and the University of Virginia. NOTE: This research was done by John Mellville Jennings, Va. Mag. Hist. Biog. Vol. 69. Goodspeed's copy (Crandall-1449) #601 $3000.

13 ...Of the Confederate States of America. A facsimilie reproduction from the original regulations of the Confederacy and other authoritative sources. New Hope, Pa., Ray Riling and Robert Halter at The Rive House, 1952. 4to, cl, and boards, (36)pp. some printed on one side., 23 plates, (61)pp. Petersburg, Va. A facsimilie reprint of the Richmond, Va., C.H. Wynne, 1861. With E. Crehen plates. Limited to 400 copies.
...Phila., R. Riling, 1960. Revised edition. Intro: Richard Harwell. 4to, cl, plates (some colored), (12), 5, (4)pp. $75-bmk. See: Fred P. Todd's S.C. Uniforms.
...N.Y., St. Martin's Press, 1960. Intro: Richard Harwell. Sm.4to, boards, (12)pp., reprint: 5, (4)pp. plates, part colored. 2m copies. $75. DeLuxe edition, 50 copies, in full leather, signed by Harwell and Riling, 23 plates, 9-in color.

14 **"UNIFORMS of the Confederacy."**
(London) Jour. Conf. Hist. Soc., Vols. 1-X.
(1)-"Washington Bat. Artly." (I, #4, pp.155-56, pl.)
(2)-"Va. Mil. Inst." (II, #1, p.50-52, pl.)
(3)-"Confed. States Navy", II, #2, p.94-96, pl.)
(4)-"Ensign: Guilford Grays, N.C. Militia." (II, #3, p.135-136, pl.)
(5)-"Charleston Light Dragoons", (ii, #4, p.172-173, pl.)
(6)-"Officers of Confed. States Marine Corps-1862." (III, #1, p.39-40, pl.)
(7)-"Charleston Zouave Cadets-Vol. Militia 1861." (III-#2, p.72-73, pl.)

(8)-"Surgeons-Confed. States Army." (III, #3, p.116-117, pl.)

(9)-"Volunteers - Chatham Artillery Ga., 1860." (III, #4,p.)

(10)-"Georgia Hussars, 1861." (IV, #1, p.39-40, pl.)

(11)-"Savannah Vol. Guards, 1861." (IV, #2, p.84, pl.)

(12)-"First Georgia Regiment, 1861." (IV, #4, p.172, pl.)

(13)- "Fifth Co., Washington Artly. of New Orleans." (IV, #4, p.172, pl.)

(14)-"8th Texas Cavalry (Terry's Texas Raiders.) (V, #1, p.34-35, pl.)

(15)-"Sumter Light Guard-1861." (V, #2, p.77-78, pl.)

(16)-"Danville Blues-Virginia, 1861." (V, #3, p.162-163, pl.)

(17)-"Amherst Rifle Grays, Va., 1861." (V, #4, p.171, pl.)

(18)-"Confederate Infantryman - 1863." (VI, #1, p.39-40, pl.)

(19)-"Confederate Cavalrymen-1863." (VI, #2, p.90-91, pl.)

(21)-"Co. B, 1st Special Artl. Louisiana Inf., 1861." (VI, #4, p.183-185, pl.)

(22)-"Tom Green Rifles, Co. B., 4th Texas Inf., 1861." (VII, #1, p.38-40, pl.)

(23)-"Petersburg Riflemen and Petersburg Grays, Co. B., Virginia, 1861." (VII, #2, p.78-79, pl.)

(24)-"Rutledges Tenn. Batty. Co. A, 1st Tenn. Light Artly, May 1861." (VII, #3, p.118-120, pl.)

(25)-"The City Guard-Petersburg, Va., 1860." (VII, #4, p.159-160, pl.)

(26)-"Maryland Guard, Co. B, 21st. Va. Inf., 1861." (VIII, #1, pl., pg. 20-21)

(27)-"Warrenton Rifles, Co. K, 17th. Va. Inf., 1861." (VIII, #2, p.20-21, pl.)

(28)-"Alexandria Riflemen, Co. A., 17th Va. Inf., 1861." (VIII, #3, p.73-74, pl.)

(29)-"Gen. Simon Bolivar Buckner, 1861." (VIII, #4, p.78-79, pl.)

(30)-"Richmond Grays, Co.A., 1st Reg. Va. Vols., 1861." (IX, #1-2, pl. 56, pl.)

(31)-"Caswell Boys Co.-6th N.C. Inf. Reg., 1861." (p.55, pl.)

(32)-"Mount Vernon Guard, 6th Bat. Va. Vols., 1861." (IX, #3, p.95, pl.)

(33)-"Old Dominion Rifles, 6th Bat., Va. Vals., 1861" (IX, #4, p.33-34, pl.)

(34)-"Col. 4th Reg., European Brigade-1860." (X, #1, p.44, pl.)

(35)-"Maryland Zouaves-1861." (X, #2, p.95-96, pl.)

(36)-"Oglethorpe Light Inf.-Georgia, 1861." (X, #3, p.142-143, pl.)

(37)-"Cadets of the Citadel-Charleston, 1861." (X, #4, p.193, pl.)

UNION, The
Being a Condemnation of Mr. Helper's Scheme, with a plan for the Settlement of the "Irrepressible Conflict". By one who has considered both sides of the question..." N.Y., F.A. Brady (1857?) 8vo, wraps, 32pp., Sabin-97763.

"UNION Theological Seminary,
Hampden Sidney, Virginia, in the Confederate Army." In: SHSP, April 1914, v.XXXIX, p.102-103.

UNIONIST, A
"Abolition & Secession; or, Cause & Effect, together with the Remedy for our sectional troubles. By a Unionist." New York: Van Evrie, Horton & Co., 1862, 12mo, sewn, 24pp.

"UNIT Roster Companies A and E."
In: Alex Duncan's "Roll of officers and members of Georgia Hussars."

"UNITED Confederate Veterans".
See under heads:
Confederate Gray Book; Confederate Vet. Camps, NY, et al; Confederate Women of Ark., S.C.; Flags of the CSA; Grand Camps Confed. Vets; Historical Sketch Explanation of...; Joint History Committee, CV; Minutes of UCV; Offi-

cial Proceedings of...; Organization of 650 camps, etc...; Register of Confed. Soldiers camps; Report of Stars and Bars Comm.; Report on reburials CSA soldiers; United Confederate Veterans, Ga., Fla., Miss., etc.; Robert L. Rodgers Report...; C.H. Tebault.

19a "UNITED CONFEDERATE VETERANS & the Historiography of the Civil War." In: LaH., v.12, p.213-42. (1971); v.16, p.5-37 (1975).

20 UNITED CONFEDERATE VETERANS Constitution and By-Laws for their government. In: CV, Oct. 1894, v.II, #10, p.296-303. emblem.
...NOTE: This list represents UCV taken from the 1913 3rd Edition of "Bibliography or State Participation in the Civil War 1861-1866."

21 ...Minutes U.C.V., v.1-; 1889-. New Orleans, La., (1907-) 21v in 6. 8vo. E485.3.A11. A reissue in bound volumes of the minutes of the various convention. Proceedings of the convention for organization, and adoption of the constitution of the United Confederate veterans, held in the city of New Orleans, La., June 10th, 1889. New Orleans, 1891. 8p. 8vo.
...1st (1890 at Chattanooga.) New Orleans, 1891. 7pp. 8vo;
...2d (1891 at Jackson, Miss.) New Orleans, 1891. 14pp. 8vo;
...3rd (1892 at New Orleans.) New Orleans, 1892. 176pp. 8vo;
...4th (1894 at Birmingham, Ala.) (n.p., 1894?) 23pp. 8vo; Report of the United Confederate veteran historical committee which was unanimously adopted at the Fourth annual reunion, held at Birmingham, Ala., April 25 and 26, 1894...New Orleans, (1894?). 12pp. 8vo. (bound with above.);
...5th (1895 at Houston, Tex.) (n.p., 1895?) 72pp. 8vo.
...6th (1896 at Richmond, Va.) (New Orleans, 1897) 166pp. 8vo;
...7th (1897 at Nashville, Tenn.) (New Orleans, 1898) 113pp. 8vo;
...8th (1898 at Atlanta, Ga.) (New Orleans, 1899) 121pp. 8vo;
...9th (1899 at Charleston, S.C.) (New Orleans, 1900) 228pp. 8vo;
...10th (1900 at Louisville, Ky.) (New Orleans, 1902) 157pp. 8vo;
...11th (1901 at Memphis, Tenn.) (New Orleans, 1901?) 146pp. 8vo;
...12th (1902 at Dallas, Tex.) (New Orleans, 1902?) 88pp. 8vo. Official report of C.H. Tebault, M.D., surgeon general United Confederate veterans. From the minutes of the Twelfth annual meeting of the United Confederate Veterans, held in the city of Dallas, Texas, April 22d, 23d, 24th, and 25th, 1902...New Orleans, (1902). cover-title, 31pp. 8vo. (bound with above);
...13th (1903 at New Orleans) (New Orleans, 1903?) 90pp. 8vo. General Wm. E. Mickle, adjutant-general and chief of staff...April 1st, to December 31st, 1903. (New Orleans 1903?) cover-title, 30pp. 8vo;

22 ...14th (1904 at Nashville, Tenn.) (n.p., 1904?) 63, 34pp. 8vo. The motives and aims of the soldiers of the South in the civil war. Oration delivered...By Randolph H. McKim...(n.p., 1904?) 34pp. 8vo. (Bound with the above as an appendix.) Report of Maj.-General Wm. E. Mickle, adjutant general and chief of staff...April 1st, to December 31st, 1903...(New Orleans? 1904?) cover-title, 30pp. 8vo. (Bound with above) Report of Maj. Gen. Wm. E. Mickle, adjutant general and chief of staff for the year ending December 31st, 1903. Showing increase in the federation, number of camps, comparative statement of expenses, etc...(n.p., 1904?) (4)pp. 8vo. (Bound with above) Official historical

report of C.H. Tebault, M.D., surgeon general... (n.p., 1904?) 20pp. 8vo. (Bound with above);

23 ...15th (1905 at Louisville, Ky.) (n.p., 1905?) 49, (4)pp. 8vo. Report of Major Gen. Wm. E. Mickle, adjutant general and chief of staff, for the year ending December 31, 1904. Showing increase in the federation, number of camps, comparative statements of expenses, etc. (n.p., 1905?) (4)pp. 8vo. (Bound with above). The civil war; its results and lessons. An address delivered at Louisville, Kentucky...June 15th, 1905. By N.E. Harris. Macon, Ga., 1906, 34pp. ports. 8vo. (Bound with above.) Report of Major-Gen'l Wm. E. Mickle, adj't-gen'l and chief of staff...January 1st, 1904 to January 1st, 1905. New Orleans, 1909. 33pp. 8vo. (Bound with above.); 16th (1906 at New Orleans) (New Orleans, 1906?) 86, 32, 9, (4), 13pp., illus. 8vo. Report of Major-gen'l Wm. E. Mickle, adj't-gen'l and chief of staff...January 1st, 1905, to December 31st, 1905. (n.p., 1906?) 32pp. 8vo. (Bound with above.) Report of Maj. Gen. Wm. E. Mickle, adjutant general and chief of staff on delinquent camps...(n.p., 1906?) 9pp. 8vo. (Bound with above.) Report of Maj. Gen. Wm. E. Mickle, adjutant general and chief of staff, for the year ending December 31, 1905. Giving comparative statement of expenses, delinquent camps, etc...(n.p., 1906?) cover title. (4)pp. 8vo. (Bound with above.) Report of committee of co-operation for the women's memorial. (n.p., 1906?) 13pp. 8vo;

24 ...17th (1907 at Richmond, Va.) (n.p., 1907?) 156, 23, (4), 36, 76pp. illus., plates, (partly col.), map, diagrs. 8vo. Speech of Gen. Stephen D. Lee...(and) Speech of Robert E. Lee, Jr...(and) Speech of Col. J.W. Daniel...(n.p., 1907?) 23pp. 8vo. Report of Maj.Gen. Wm. E. Mickle, adjutant-general and chief of staff, for the year ending December 31, 1906. A brief summary of matter connected with his office during that period...(n.p., 1907?) cover-title, (4)pp. 8vo. Report of Major-Gen'l Wm. E. Mickle, Adjt.-Gen. and chief of staff...Receipts and expenditures ...January 1st, 1906, to December 31st, 1906...(n.p., 1907?) 36pp. 8vo. First report of the secretary of the monumental committee of the United Confederate veterans' association. (n.p., 1907?) 76pp. map, diagrs. 8vo. Report of the United Confederate veterans' monumental committee which was unanimously adopted at the seventeenth annual reunion. New Orleans (1907?). 34pp. 8vo. The flags of the Confederate States of America. By authority... (New Orleans? 1907). (4)pp. col. plate. 8vo;

25 ...18th (1908 at Birmingham, Ala.) (New Orleans, 1908?). 144, (4), 35pp., illus., 8vo. Annual address of General Stephen D. Lee...p.139-144. Report of Maj. Gen. Wm. E. Mickle, adjutant general and chief of staff, for the year ending December 31, 1907. A brief summary of matters connected with his office during that period...(n.p., 1908?) cover-title, (4)pp. 8vo. Report of Major-General Wm. E. Mickle, adjutant-general and chief of staff ...statement of receipts and expenditures from January first, nineteen hundred and seven, to December thirty-first, nineteen hundred and seven...(New Orleans?, 1908?) 35pp. 8vo.

...19th (1909 at Memphis, Tenn.) (New Orleans, 1909?). 104, 32, (4), 66pp. illus. 8vo. Report of Major-Gen'l Wm. E. Mickle, adj't-gen'l and chief of staff...statement of receipts and expenditures for the year 1908. (n.p., 1909?) 32pp. 8vo. Report of Maj-Gen. Wm. E. Mickle, adjutant-general and chief of staff, to Gen. Cle-

26 ment A. Evans...June 5th, 1909. A brief summary of matters connected with his office during twelve months...(n.p., 1909?) cover-title, (4)pp. 8vo. Surgeon general Tebault's report...(submitting two letters from Hon. Jeremiah S. Black of Pennsylvania)...(n.p., 1909?) 65pp. 8vo;

...20th (1910 at Mobile, Ala.) (New Orleans, 1910?) 151, 18, (4), 34, 37, 40pp. illus. 8vo. List of delegates. (n.p., 1910?) 18pp. 8vo. Report of Maj.-Gen. Wm. E. Mickle, adjutant-general and chief of staff, to Gen. Clement A. Evans...April 23, 1910. A brief summary of matters connected with his office during twelve months. (n.p., 1901?) (4)pp. 8vo. Annual report of Major-Gen'l Wm. E. Mickle, adj't-gen'l and chief of staff...for year 1909...statement of receipts and expenditures for the year 1909. (New Orleans? 1910?). 34pp. 8vo. Report of the monumental committee of the United Confederate veterans which was unanimously adopted at the twentieth annual reunion...(New Orleans, 1910?) 37pp. illus. 8vo. Surgeon general Tebault's report...(submitting The treatment of President of the Southern Confederacy, Jefferson Davis, as a Federal prisoner, and how he was finally released.) (New Orleans, 1910?) 40pp. 8vo;

...21st (1911 at Little Rock, Ark.) (New Orleans, 1911?). 136, 21, 16, 15, 29, (4)pp. 80pp. illus., plate, ports. 8vo. List of delegates. (n.p., 1911?) 21pp. 8vo. Annual oration delivered...by Dr. R. C. Cave of St. Louis. (n.p., 1911?) 16pp. 8vo. Report of the United Confederate veterans' historical committee which was unanimously adopted at the twenty-first annual reunion...New Orleans, 1911. 15pp. 8vo. Major-General Wm. E. Mickle, adjutant general and chief of staff, in account with United Confederate veterans...statement of receipts and expenditures for the year 1910. (New Orleans, 1911?) 29pp. 8vo. Report of Maj.-Gen. Wm. E. Mickle, adjutant-general and chief of staff, to Gen. Geo. W. Gordon...May 13, 1911. Brief summary of matters connected with his office during twelve months. (n.p., 1911?) (4)pp. 8vo. Fourth annual report of the monumental committee of the United Confederate veterans. 1911. (n.p., 1911?) 80pp. illus., ports. 8vo.

...Historical sketch explanatory of memorial or certificate of membership in the U.C.V.'s...(Charleston, S.C., 1897) 32pp. 8 . E485.3.A173 (In L.C.).

...Orders, U.C.V. General and special. v.1- New Orleans, (1889- v. 8vo. E483.1.A18. v.1-...Issued by General J.B. Gordon, during his term of office, June 10, 1889, to January 9, 1904. v.2-...Issued by General Stephen D. Lee, Lieut. Gen. W.L. Cabell, General Clement A. Evans, General Geo. W. Gordon, Lieut. Gen. C. Irvine Walker. Jan. 10, 1904, to May 7, 1912.

27 ..."Organization of 650 UCV Camps, containing List of Commanders and their Adjutants, Summary of Camps, prepared expressly for use of delegates to the 5th Reunion and Meeting...Houston, Texas, May, 1895." (Cover title) New Orleans: Hopkins Printing Office, n.d., 8vo, wraps, (14)pp.

...Organization of 850 United Confederate veteran camps. Containing names of department, division and brigade commanders and their adjutants general, and address...Prepared expressly for use of delegates to the Sixth reunion and meeting of the association, held at Richmond, Va., June 30th, and July 1st and 2d, 1896...(Richmond, 1896) cover-title, 3, (14)pp. 8vo. E485.3.A175. (In L.C.)

...Organization of 1026 camps in the United Confederate veteran association...prepared expressly for the use of delegates to the Seventh reunion and meeting of the association, held at Nashville, Tenn., on June 22d, 23d and 24th, 1897.

...(n.p., 1897) cover-title, (2)-16, (1)p., 1 l. 4 degrees E485.3.A1751 (In L.C.)

..."List of One thousand two-hundred and sixty Camps, May, 1900." In: CV, 1900, v.8, p.218-226. Alphabetically by states. 1901, v.9, p.357-367.

...Reports of Wm. E. Mickle, adjutant general and chief of staff, from the date of his appointment by General Jno. B. Gordon, January 19th, 1903, to December 31st, 1907...New Orleans, (1903-1907). (209pp. 8vo.

..."Minutes of the Annual meeting and reunion of the UCV." (New Orleans, La., wraps, 8vo, illus., ports. 1917-"Reunion of UCV. Proceedings of the 27th Annual Meeting, the 18th annual convention of the Confederate Southern Memorial Association and the 22nd annual reunion of the Sons of Confederate Veterans, held at Washington, DC, June 4, 5, 6 and 7th, 1917." Washington, DC, 1918.

28 **UNITED CONFEDERATE VETERANS - Alabama.**
"41st Annual Meeting, Souvenir Program." Montgomery, Ala., 1931. Large 8vo, wraps, illus., 40pp.

..."United Confederate Veterans-Alabama Division, Official Programme-25th Annual Reunion, 1925." 8vo, pict. wraps, illus., 12pp., n.p., n.d. Pict. cover, CSA flags in color.

UNITED CONFEDERATE VETERANS - Raphael Semmes Camp No. 11. Mobile.
Confederate gray book, 1912, (n.p., 1912) cover title, 52pp., plates, ports. 8vo. Plates printed on both sides. Advertisements interspersed.

29 **UNITED CONFEDERATE VETERANS - Arkansas Division.**
Confederate women of Arkansas in the civil war, 1861-1865; memorial reminiscences...Little Rock, Ark., 1907. (90)pp. illus., (incl. ports.) of degrees. E487.W852 (In L.C.)

...Confederate women of Arkansas in the civil war, 1861-1865; memorial reminiscences, pub. by the United Confederate veterans of Arkansas...Little Rock, Ark., 1907. 221pp. incl. pl., pl., ports. 8vo. E552.U58 (In L.C.)

...Confederate women of Arkansas in the civil war, 1861-1865. Memorial reminiscences. Pub. by the United Confederate veterans of Arkansas. Nov. 1907. Little Rock, (1907) 2pp. 1, 1 l., 10, (17)-221pp. plates (incl. illus., ports.) 8vo. E553.U51 (In L.C.)

30 **UNITED CONFEDERATE VETERANS - District of Columbia Division.**
Confederate Veterans' Association Camp, No. 171. Joseph E. Johnston. Address delivered...by Leigh Robinson, May 12, 1891...Washington, D.C., 1891. 61pp. 8vo. (In L.C.)

31 **UNITED CONFEDERATE VETERANS - Washington, D.C., Division.**
Charles Broadway Rouss Camp No. 1191. Report on the reburial of the Confederate dead in Arlington cemetery and attention called to the care required for the graves of Confederate soldiers who died in federal prisons and military hospitals now buried in northern states.

...Washington, 1901. 47pp. fold. plates, fold. plans. 8vo. E641.U57 (In L.C.)

"**UNITED CONFEDERATE VETERANS - Florida Division,**
37th Annual Reunion, Marianna, Sept. 26-29, 1927. T.J. Appleyard, Maj.-Gen. commanding, Frank Ironmonger, Adj.-Gen." (Tallahassee, Fla., T.J. appleyard, 1927) sm. 4to, wraps, color flags, ports, illus., 26, (2)pp. Includes a short sketch of Battle of Marianna.

32 **UNITED CONFEDERATE VETERANS - Georgia Div. Atlanta Camp.**
"Battles of Atlanta. Short sketches of the battles around, siege, evacuation and destruction of Atlanta, Ga., in 1864, with map, historic places, directory to battle lines, prominent characters who participated, etc. Prepared under the direction of the committee of the Atlanta Camp, UCV, for information of visitors and sold for benefit of the Camp." Atlanta, Ga., (Bergstrom Print) Sept. 1895. 8vo, wraps, 2, (7)-31pp. $25.

..."Official Programme and Guide Book, Reunion, Georgia Division, UCV, Savannah, Georgia, Nov. 22, 23, 24, 1899." Savannah, Ga., Morning News Pr., (1899) 8vo, wraps, map, 64pp.

..."Lafayette McLaws Camp-" Confederate Gray Book. 1909. Lafayette McLaws Camp, #596. UCV." Savannah, Ga., M.S. and D.A. Byck, (1909) 8vo, wraps, cover title, illus., 22 leaves.

33 ..."Souvenir Book of the United Veterans Reunion 1919. Atlanta's official welcome to the heroic remnant of the South's immortal defenders." Lucian Lamar Knight, Editor, State Hist. n.p., n.d., (Atlanta, Ga., 1919) 4to, wraps, color flags, ports, ads within programs, text, 116pp.

UNITED CONFEDERATE VETERANS - Georgia Division,
Survivors Association, Camp, #435. "Addresses delivered before the Confederate Survivors Association, in Augusta, Georgia, at its annual meetings on Memorial Day; 1879-1897, Nos. 1-19." Augusta, Ga., Jowitt and Shaver Print, 1879-1897. 8vo, wraps, 19 nos. bound in one vol. no general t.p. In 1893 the Confederate Survivors Association of Augusta, Ga., became a camp of the Ga. Div. of the U.C.V., no more published. Individual numbers can also be found under Charles C. Jones.

..."Addresses delivered before the Confederate Veterans Association. (Camp #756) of Savannah, Georgia, to which is added the president's annual report..." 18-. Savannah, Ga., The Association, 18-, 8vo, bound in with the above volume.

UNITED CONFEDERATE VETERANS - Camp 435, Augusta, Ga.
Annual report as submitted in Richmond Co. Court House, to Camp 435, U.C.V., on Memorial Day...by...historian of the association...E485.3.G5.

...1st-7th.

...8th (Apr. 26, 1901. Charles E. Jones, historian.) (n.p., 1901?) 16pp. 8vo.

...9th (Apr. 26, 1902. Charles E. Jones, historian.) (n.p., 1902?). (8)pp. 8vo.

...10th-11th.

...12th (Apr. 26, 1905. Charles E. Jones, historian.) (n.p., 1905?) 8pp. 8vo. (In L.C.)

...13th.

...14th (Apr. 26, 1907. Charles E. Jones, historian.) (n.p., 1907?) 6pp. 8vo.

...15th-

UNITED CONFEDERATE VETERANS - Maryland
"Isaac R. Trimble Camp, Baltimore, Md. Maj. W.M. Cary was on staff of Lee and Johnston." (from Baltimore Democratic Telegram, Jan. 14, 1911.) In: SHSP, 1910, v.38, p.292-295.

UNITED CONFEDERATE VETERANS - Missouri
"Official Proceedings of the Fifth Annual Reunion of Missouri Division, U.C.V... Springfield, Mo., August 8, 9, 10, 1901." St. Louis, Mo., 1901. Tall 8vo, pict. wraps, illus., ports, 103pp.

..."10th Annual Reunion and Convention held at Joplin, Sept. 26, 27th, 1906, with an appendix containing Constitutions of the U.C.V., U.S.C.V., U.D.C., date of historical interest relating to the Civil War, etc."

Jefferson City, 1906. pict. wraps, 8vo, 125pp. $15-bmk.

..."Official proceedings of the First Annual Meeting of the Missouri Division of United Confederate Veterans." (St. Joseph, Missouri, 1897) 8vo, wraps, pls. ports, illus., various reports bound in one vol., imprint varies. The 1st report has a title: "Adjutant general's report of the 1st annual reunion and convention..."

UNITED CONFEDERATE VETERANS - Missouri Division.
Official proceedings of the 1st- , 1897-.
...1st (1897 at Moberly.) St. Louis, (1897?) 53, (1)pp. plates, (incl. illus., ports.) 8vo. (In L.C.)
...2d (1898 at ----)
...3rd (1899 at ----)
...4th (1900 at ----)
...5th (1901 at ----)
...6th (1902 at St. Joseph.) (St. Joseph? 1902?) 131pp. illus., ports. 8vo. (In L.C.)

UNITED CONFEDERATE VETERAN CAMP - New York
"Memorial on the death of Comrade Hugh Smith Thompson." (n.p., 1905?) 12mo, wraps, cover title, 8pp.

UNITED CONFEDERATE VETERANS - North Carolina
Charlotte: "Official Program, 39th Annual Reunion UCV, Charlotte, N.C. Published in honor of the thinning ranks of Gray, June 4-7, 1929." Charlotte, N.C., Washburn Print, 1929. 4to, pict. wraps, illus. (ports of N.C. generals and short articles on war.) (64)pp.

..."Proceedings of the Twenty-fourth Annual Convention of the Oklahoma Div., U.D.C., held in McAlester." Wynnewood, 1932. 8vo, pict. wraps, 125pp. Hosted by Choctaw and Stonewall Jax chaps.

UNITED CONFEDERATE VETERANS - South Carolina
"Annual Meeting at Columbia, S.C., May 12, 13, 14, 1903. Official Souvenir Program. Illustrations and Sketches of people and places of historic interest. Prepared by E.J. Watson, Sect. Chamber of Commerce." Oblong 4to, pict. wraps, (30)pp. Columbia, S.C., 1903.

..."A Tryst with the Brave and True." Camp Sumter, United Confederate Veterans Annual Celebration, April 13, 1903." Charleston, S.C., Lucas-Richardson Pr. '03. 8vo, wraps, 17pp.

..."Souvenir of the United Confederate Veterans' Reunion of 1899. A Guide to points of interest. Charleston, S.C., May 10, 11, 12, 13, 1899." n.p. pub. or date. 12mo, wraps, map, 80pp., about half ads.

..."Official United Confederate Veterans 48th Annual Reunion: UCV: 43rd. Annual Convention Sons of Confederate Veterans: 39th Annual Convention Confederated Southern Memorial Association. August 30, 31, Sept. 1, 2, 1938. Columbia, S.C. "Cradle of the Confederacy." Columbia: The State Co., 1938. 8vo, pict. wraps, 52pp. (McKissick-1844)

..."First Annual Convention United Confederate Veterans. J.B. Gordon, General Commanding. Chattanooga, Tenn., July 3rd, 4th, 5th, 1890." (Chattanooga, Tenn.,1890?) 8vo, colored wraps, 36pp. See: Nath. E. Harris-"Civil War"; Wiley C. Howard; Chas. E. Jones-"Ga. in War", and the 9th, 12th, and 14th Annual Reports $40.

UNITED CONFEDERATE VETERANS - Tennessee
"Twenty-third Annual Reunion United Confederate Veterans, Camp Alexander P. Stewart, "Fifty years after", Chattanooga, Tenn., May 27-29, 1913." (Chattanooga: The Imperial Press, 1913) Oblong wraps 12x9 3/8" colored CSA flag and port. of Gen. Bennett H. Young. (40)pp.

UNITED CONFEDERATE VETERANS - Tennessee Division.
Confederate Historical Association, Camp, No. 28. Memphis. Confederate Gray Book, 1909. Memphis, Tenn., 1909. cover title, (8)pp. pl. 27 port. on 14 1. 8vo. E485.3.T2 (In L.C.)

UNITED CONFEDERATE VETERANS - Texas
"Minutes of the 46th Reunion-First Texas Division, Confederate Veterans, including Ross, Ector, Granbury Brigades." Terrell, Texas, 1920 8vo, wraps, 12pp.

UNITED CONFEDERATE VETERANS - Virginia Division
The Confederate Veterans of Virginia. Roster of the organization. Camps, Grand camps and United Confederate Veterans. (In: So. Hist. Soc. Papers. v.20, p.398-401. 8vo.) E485.4.A14.
..."Official Souvenir, 25th Reunion, United Confederate Veterans, Richmond, Va., June 1st, 2nd and 3rd, 1915." Richmond, 1915. 4to, pict. wraps, illus., ports, 64pp.
..."Address of welcome...see: D.G. Tyler. Col. W.B. Green Speech.
..."Minutes of the 25th Annual Meeting, Richmond, Va., June 1-3, 1915." New Orleans, La., 1915. 8vo, wraps, 148, 24pp.
...Official Souvenir Program, 42nd Reunion, Confederate Veterans, Richmond, Va., June 1932." Richmond, 1932. 4to, pict. wraps, 76pp.

UNITED Grand Camp of Confederate Veterans.
Dept. of Virginia. Proceedings of the...annual meeting(s) of the Grand Camp of Confederate Veterans, Department of Virginia, together with the orders of the Grand commander...v. 8vo. E485.3.V8.
...1st (1886 at ----)
...6th (1893 at ----)
...7th (1894 at Alexandria.) Richmond, 1894, 26pp. 8vo. (In L.C.)
...8th (1895 at Charlottesville.) Richmond, 1895. 32pp. 8vo. (In L.C.)
...9th (1896 at Winchester.) Richmond, 1896. 39pp. 8vo. (In L.C.)
...10th (1897 at Richmond.) Richmond, 1897. 40pp. 8vo. (In L.C.)
...11th (1898 at Culpeper.) Richmond, 1898. 44pp. 8vo. (In L.C.)
...12th (1899 at Pulaski.) Richmond, 1899. 48pp. 8vo. (In L.C.)
...13th (1900 at Staunton.) Richmond, 1900. 62pp. 8vo. (In L.C.)
...14th (1901 at Petersburg.) Richmond, 1901. 72pp. 8vo. (In L.C.)
...15th (1902 at ----)
...16th (1903 at Newport News.) Pulaski, 1904, 61pp. 8vo. (In L.C.)
...17th (1904 at Lynchburg.)
...18th (1905 at Petersburg.) Richmond, 1906. 87pp. 8vo. (In L.C.)
...19th (1906 at Roanoke.) Richmond, 1907. 54pp. 8vo. (In L.C.)
...20th (1907 at Norfolk.) Richmond, 1907. 62pp. 8vo.
...21st (1908 at Charlottesville.) Richmond, 1908, 47pp. 8vo. (In L.C.)
...22nd (1909 at Danville.) Richmond 1909. 51pp. 8vo. (In L.C.)
...23d (1910 at ----)
...24th (1911 at ----)
...25th (1912 at ----)
...26th (1913 at ----)
...27th (1914 at ----)
...28th (1915 at ----)
...29th (1916 at ----)

UNITED CONFEDERATE VETERANS - Virginia Division.
R.E. Lee Camp, No. 1. (Origin, growth and present condition of R.E. Lee Camp.) Address delivered by...N.V. Randolph, before R.E. Lee Camp, No. 1, C.V. December 3, 1886...Richmond, Va., 1887. 15pp. 8vo. (In W.D.L. pamp. v.208)

35 **UNITED CONFEDERATE VETERANS, Annual Meeting,**
Held in Mobile, Alabama, April 26-28, 1910, 20th Annual Meeting. (New Orleans, La.? 1910?) 8vo, wraps, illus., ports, 151, 18, (4), 34, 37, 40pp. (1) List of delegates, (2) Report: Maj.-Gen. Wm. E. Mickle and Annual report (financial), (3) Report of Monument Comm. (4) Surgeon-General Christopher H. Tebault's report of treatment of the President of the Southern Confederacy, Jefferson Davis, as a Federal prisoner and how he was finally released.

..."Report of the United Confederate Veterans Historical Committee, which was unanimously adopted at the 4th Annual Reunion, held at Birmingham, Ala., April 25-26th, 1894." New Orleans: Schumert and Warfield (1894) 8vo, wraps, 12pp. With minutes of annual meeting and reunion. 1st-7th, 1890-1897. New Orleans, 1894-1897.

..."Organization of camps in the UCV, prepared expressly for the use of delegates to the 20th Reunion and meeting of the Association held at Mobile, Ala., April 26-27-28, 1910." New Orleans, La., J.G. Hauser, 1910. 8vo, cover title, wraps, 26pp.

UNITED CONFEDERATE VETERANS - in SHSP.
"Confederate Veterans of Virginia." In: SHSP, 1892, v.20, p.216-220.

..."Report of the History Committee." In: SHSP, 1900, v.28, p.169-198; 1901, v.29, p.99-131.

..."Second Meeting, 1896." In: SHSP, 1890, v.18, p.289-293. See: W.C. Dodson, John Brown Gordon, Joseph Jones.

..."Proceedings of the convention for organization and adoption of the constitution of the UCV held in the City of New Orleans, La., June 10, 1889, New Orleans: Hopkins' Print, 1891. 12mo, wraps, 2pp. (3)-8pp. With minutes of annual meeting and reunion. 1st-7th, 1890-1897, New Orleans, 1891-1897.

..."Reports of the Adjutant General and Chief of Staff, United Confederate Veterans, 1903." New Orleans, La., 1903-. Reports for 1903-1907, bound in 1 vol., with t.p. Reports of: Wm. E. Mickle, Adj-Gen. and chief of staff, from the date of his appointment by Gen. Jno. B. Gordon, Jan. 19, 1903 to Dec. 31st, 1907.

..."Report of Robert L. Rodgers (Georgia) Hist. Atlanta Camp #159. See: under his name.

UNITED CONFEDERATE VETERANS Reunion - Arkansas.
"Little Rock did herself proud: a History of the 1911 United Confederate Veterans Reunion, by Michael David Polston. 21st National meeting." In: Pulaski Co. Hist. Rev., Summer 1981, p.11, illus. Michael David Polston: "Little Rock did herself proud: a History of the 1911 UCV reunion-21st Annual Meet. See: UCV-Arkansas.

..."Report of the United Confederate Veterans' Historical committee, which was unanimously adopted at the 21st annual reunion held at Little Rock, Ark., on May 16-17-18, 1911." New Orleans, La., A.W. Hyatt Print, 1911. 8vo, wraps, cover title, 15pp. List: Gen. and Field Office, CSN, Ark. See: V.Y. Cook

...U.D.C.-Arkansas: Hiram L. Grinsted Chap., #575, Camden, Arkansas. "Garden of Memory" See: Mrs. M.A. Elliott, historian.

36 **UNITED CONFEDERATE VETERANS-Reunion:**
Proceedings of the 27th Annual Reunion of Confederate Veterans, the 18th Annual Convention of the Confederate Southern Memorial Association and the 22nd Annual Reunion of the Sons of Confederate

Veterans, Washington, D.C., June 4, 5, 6, and 7, 1917. "Presented by Mr. Bankhead." 65th Cong. 1st. Sess. Senate Doc. #117. Washington, D.C., GPO, 1918. 8vo, cl, 101pp.

..."Official Souvenir and Handbook. United Confederate Veterans reunion, issued by the Executive Committee." New Orleans, La., May 19 and 22nd, 1903. 8vo, wraps, 134pp., illus., ports, state rosters.

..."Souvenir Program Thirteenth Annual Reunion United Confederate Veterans, May 19, 20, 21, and 22, 1903. New Orleans." Sq. 8vo, stiff color wraps, port of J. Davis, illus., ports, 36pp. Sue H. Walker's-"Hist. Sketch Confederate Southern Memorial Association." (p.20-25); W.C. Chevis-"The Confederate Soldier." p.27-36.

UNITED CONFEDERATE VETERANS. Confederate Survivors' Association,
Camp 435. Augusta, Ga. Address delivered by (Salem Dutcher)...at Augusta, Ga., on Memorial Day, April 26th, 1898, by invitation of the Ladies' Memorial Association...(n.p., 1898) 8pp. 8vo. Caption title.

UNITED CONFEDERATE VETERANS. Ex-Confederate Association of Chicago
Camp, No. 8. Register of Confederate soldiers who died in Camp Douglas, 1862-1865 and lie buried in Oakwoods Cemetery, Chicago, Ill. 1892. Cincinnati, (1892) 58pp. 12 degrees. E615.U58 (In L.C.)

UNITED CONFEDERATE VETERANS. Monument Committee.
Report of the Monument Committee...annual reunion, convention, United Sons of Confederate Veterans... Nashville, Tenn., v. 8vo. E485.31.A.32 (In L.C.)

UNITED CONFEDERATE VETERANS: Report...
"Report of the United Confederate Veterans Historical Committee, which was unanimously adopted at the 5th Annual Reunion held at Houston, Texas, May 22, 23, and 24, 1895, J.B. Gordon, Gen. Comm. Geo. Moorman, Adj.-Gen. and Chief Staff." New Orleans, La., A.W. Hyatt, 1895. 8vo, wraps, color CSA flag, front, back wrap, 12pp. Contains Moorman's Historical Comm. Report, which is also in the Minutes and with other speeches.

..."Minutes of the 5th Annual Meeting and Reunion of the United Confederate Veterans held at Houston, Texas, Wed., Thur., and Fri., 22-24th, 1895. John B. Gordon, Gen. Comm., and Geo. Moorman, Adj.-Gen." n.p. (Houston, Texas, 1895?) 8vo, wraps, 72pp. Contains Gen. Moorman's Historical Comm. Report, same as in Report of the Reunion Report, 12pp.

UNITED DAUGHTERS OF THE CONFEDERACY:
See also under title or following:
..."Confederate Reveille."
..."Confederate Catechism, Secession."
..."Constitution: Mississippi Division."
..."Dixie Dates."
...Mrs. M.A. Elliott.
..."History of Origin of Memorial Day."
..."Illinois Division UDC."
..."Joint History Commission."
..."Minutes of UDC-Florida."
..."Minutes of UDC-Georgia."
..."Mrs. J.W. Parker. Prize essays."
..."Reconstruction period of Ga."
..."Reminiscences of Women of Missouri."
..."Mrs. Orren Randolph Smith."
..."South Carolina Women of the Confederacy."
..."Virginia Leads."

UNITED DAUGHTERS OF THE CONFEDERACY
Minutes of the...annual convention of the Daughters of the Confederacy...Nashville,

(1894?), v. 8vo, E485.33.A12.

...1st (1894 at Nashville) Called meeting at Nashville, Tenn., March 30, 1895.

...2nd (1895 at Atlanta) (n.p. 1896?) cover title, 14pp. 8vo (In L.C.)

...3rd (1896 at Nashville) Nashville, 1897, 63pp. 8vo.

...4th (1897 at Baltimore) Nashville, 1898, 138pp. 8vo.

...5th (1898 at Hot Springs, Ark.)

...6th (1899 at Richmond)

...7th (1900 at Montgomery) Nashville, 1901, 188pp. 8vo. (In L.C.)

...8th (1901 at Wilmington, N.C.)

...9th (1902 at New Orleans) Nashville, 1903, 251pp. 8vo. (In L.C.)

...10th (1903 at Charleston) Nashville, 1904, 307pp. 8vo. (In L.C.)

...11th (1904 at St. Louis) Nashville, 1905, 354pp. 8vo. (In L.C.)

...12th (1905 at San Francisco, Cal.) Nashville, 1906, 308, 77pp. 8vo. (In L.C.)

...13th (1906 at Gulfport, Miss.) Opelika, Ala., 1907, 343, 81pp. 8vo. (In L.C.)

...14th (1907 at Norfolk) Opelika, Ala., 1908, 344, 102pp. 8vo. (In L.C.)

...15th (1908 at Atlanta) Opelika, Ala., 1909, 390, 106pp. 8vo (In L.C.)

...16th (1909 at Houston, Tex.) Opelika, Ala., 1909, 413, 124pp. 8vo. (In L.C.)

...17th (1910 at Little Rock)

...18th (1911 at Richmond) Paducah, Ky., (1911?) 442, 133pp. 8vo. (In L.C.)

...19th (1912 at ----)

...20th (1913 at ----)

...21st (1914 at ----)

UNITED DAUGHTERS OF THE CONFEDERACY. Arkansas Division,

Hiram L. Grinsted Chapter, No. 575, Camden. The garden of memory; stories of the Civil War as told by Veterans and Daughters of the Confederacy; compiled by Mrs. M. A. Elliott, historian...Camden, Arkansas...Camden, Ark., (1911) 3pp. 1, 96pp., 2 1. illus., ports. front. 8vo. E655.U585 (In L.C.)

UNITED DAUGHTERS OF THE CONFEDERACY. Arkansas Division.

"Historical Arkansas. Compliments of the Memorial Chapter, U.D.C., Little Rock, Ark." (Little Rock, Ark., Democrat Print, 1919?) 8vo, wraps, illus., ports, 36pp.

UNITED DAUGHTERS OF THE CONFEDERACY. Florida

...Pensacola Chapter. "Escambia County, Florida. (Notes on Bluff Springs, June 24, 1939. During the Civil War.)" (Pensacola, Fla., 1939?) sm. 4to, wraps, cover title, (i), 3, 3pp. map. Meeting June 24, 1939, Bluff Springs, the remarks of Maggie Crary Coley (Mrs. D. R. Coley). "Some facts about Battle of Bluff Springs, Fla., 1862, by May Crary Weller, both daughters of J.W. Crary, an early settler. UWF.

..."Minutes of the fifty-sixth annual convention held in Pensacola, Florida, Oct. 10-11, 1951." (Kissimmee, Fla., Cattleman Pr., 1951?) 8vo, wraps, 133pp.

UNITED DAUGHTERS OF THE CONFEDERACY. Florida Division.

"Proceedings of the tenth annual convention, held in Pensacola, Florida. May 3-5, 1905." (Pensacola, 1905?) 8vo, wraps, 80pp.

UNITED DAUGHTERS OF THE CONFEDERACY. Georgia

Savannah Chapter, No. 2. "Directory of the Savannah Chapter No. 2. Founded May 19, 1894. (Savannah, 1894?) 8vo, wraps, 30pp.

UNITED DAUGHTERS OF THE CONFEDERACY. History Committee.

"The History of the United Daughters of the Confed. 1894-1955." 2 vols., Ruth Jennings Lawton, Edt. vol. I; Mrs. Albert Lee Thompson, (Bertie S. Thompson) Edt. Vol. 2 consists of sections by various contributors. Raleigh, N.C., Edwards and

Broughton, (1956) 2 Vols. in I, 8vo, cl, (18), 226pp.; (10), 391pp., medals, ports, table, views. First published in 1938, see also under Mary Barnett Poppenheim.

UNITED DAUGHTERS OF THE CONFEDERACY. Illinois. Chicago
Chapter, No. 858, Chicago. Address by W.E. Poulson, Camp 8, U.C.V., to the Chicago Chapter, Daughters of the Confederacy. Chicago, Illinois. February ninth, nineteen hundred and six. (Chicago, 1906) cover-title, (24)pp. 16mo. E650.P87 (In L.C.)

UNITED DAUGHTERS OF THE CONFEDERACY. Louisiana Division.
Camp Moore Chap., #562, Tangiphoa. "Camp Moore Memoirs and recipes. 2nd edition. (1st edt., 1965, p.95.) (Tangipahoa, La., 1968-1969. 8vo, cl, illus., ports, 142pp.

..."History of the Louisiana Division, United Daughters of the Confederacy." (Baton Rouge, La., 1967?) 8vo, wraps, 72pp.

...New Orleans Chap. #72. "Constitution." New Orleans, La., 1899, 12mo, wraps, 5pp.

...New Orleans, La. "The Natal Day of General Lee." In: SHSP, 1900, v.28, p.228-243.

UNITED DAUGHTERS OF THE CONFEDERACY. Mississippi
Ben La Bree Chapter, No. 118, Jackson, Miss. Constitution, objects, rosters of officers, members, etc. Louisville, Ky., 1897. cover-title, 24pp. illus. (incl. ports) 16mo. E485.33.M67 (In L.C.)

UNITED DAUGHTERS OF THE CONFEDERACY. Missouri
St. Louis, Chapter 624. Dixie dates. St. Louis, (1912) cover-title, 1p. 1., (70)pp. col. pl. 8vo. E468.3.U58 (In L.C.)

UNITED DAUGHTERS OF THE CONFEDERACY. North Carolina Division
"Twentieth Annual Convention, Gastonia Chap. #955. Gastonia, N.C., Oct. 10-13, 1916. n.p., n.d., (1916) 8vo, pict. wraps (Gaston Co. CSA Monument on cover), program. (8)pp.

..."United Daughters of the Confederacy. North Carolina Division: Prize Essays presented by the N.C. Div., U.D.C., Mrs. J.W. Parker, historian, 1935-1936." (Raleigh, N.C., Edwards and Broughton) 8vo, cl, port, 178pp. Many essays on CSA personages and places, events and variety.

..."Children of the Confederacy", Prize Essays 1929-1930." n.p., n.d., (1930) 4to, stiff wraps, (31)pp., mimeogr. $40.

...See: "Carolina and Southern Cross."

..."Minutes of the Eleventh Annual Convention 1907." Newton, N.C., Enterprises Print, 1908, 12mo, wraps, 193pp.

...Cape Fear Chapter, No. 3. George Davis. By H.G. Connor...Delivered at the unveiling of a statue of George Davis at Wilmington, N.C., April 20, 1911, by the Cape Fear Chapter, No. 3, United Daughters of the Confederacy (Wilmington?, N.C., 1911?) 53, (1)p. incl. front. (port.) pl. 8vo. F258.D26 (In L.C.)

...Pamlico Chapter, pub. The Confederate reveille, memorial edition. Published by the Pamlico Chapter of the Daughters of the Confederacy, Washington, N.C., May 10, 1898. Raleigh, 1898. 162pp. incl. ports. front. 8vo. E573.U58. (In L.C.)

UNITED DAUGHTERS OF THE CONFEDERACY. South Carolina Division.
South Carolina women in the Confederacy. Records collected by Mrs. A.T. Smythe, Miss M.B. Poppenheim, and Mrs. Thomas Taylor...Columbia, S.C., 1903-1907, 2 v. fronts, ports. 8vo. E577.U58.

...Dixie Chapter, No. 395, Anderson. Dixie. (Anderson), 1905-, v. 8vo. E483.5.S7f. (In L.C.) Published annually.

UNITED SONS OF CONFEDERATE VETERANS.
"By-Laws of H. Burgwyn Camp, #166. Raleigh, N.C., 1900. 8vo, wraps, 13pp. $17.50.
..."Charter members of..., including records of ancestors through whom they derive eligibility." Raleigh, N.C., 1900. 8vo, wraps, 14pp. $25.
...Constitution of the U.S.C.V. Revised and adopted at the seventh annual reunion, Dallas, Texas, April 22-25, 1902. (St. Louis, 1902) 28pp. 12 degrees. E485.31.A122 (In L.C.)
...Minutes of the...U.S.C.V., v. 8vo. E485.31.A15.
...1st (1896 at ----)
...7th (1902 at ----)
...8th (1903 at New Orleans) (n.p., 1903?) 112pp. ports. 8vo (In L.C.)
...9th (1904 at ----)
...10th (1905 at Louisville) (Fort Worth, Tex., 1905?) 96pp. 8vo. (In L.C.)
...11th (1906 at ----)-date. St. Louis.

UNITED SONS OF CONFEDERATE VETERANS.
"Constitution of the United Sons of Confederate Veterans. Revised and adopted at the Seventh Annual Convention, Dallas, Tx. April 22-25, 1902. Minutes of meeting." (St. Louis, Mo., 1902) 8vo, wraps, 144pp. (constitution, 28pp.) See: S.C.V.

UNITED SONS OF CONFEDERATE VETERANS. Missouri.
Camp Sterling Price. "Annual Meeting, March 1906." St. Louis, Missouri, 1906, 11th Annual, 8vo, wraps, 30pp. Contains 3 papers on Gen. Forrest.

UNITED SONS OF CONFEDERATE VETERANS. Relief Committee.
Report of the Relief Committee Annual Reunion, Convention, United Sons of Confederate Veterans...Nashville, Tenn., v. 8vo. E485.31.A135

"**UNITED STATES Military Academy, Bulletin #2.**" West Point, U.S.M.A. Press, Jan. 1902, 8vo, wraps, 93pp. Much on the War: Those in CSArmy (299) and the Union (280) General Officers (CSA-151.) "Important Battles of the Civil War." names and commanders serving both sides. Conflict shows it was in hands of West Pointers."
...West Point, N.Y. "Register of the Officers and Cadets of the U.S. Military Academy, June 1829." (West Point, N.Y., 1829) 8vo, wraps, 22pp. Lee second in his class, along with Joseph E. Johnston, Seth Eastman, Gustavus Brown, et al.
...United States Military Academy, West Point.
See: William Gordon McCabe's CS Graduates, Dabney H. Maury's West Point and Secession.

UNIVERSITY OF NORTH CAROLINA in the War.
See: Stephen B. Weeks.

"**UNIVERSITY OF SOUTH CAROLINA War Records.**"
(Columbia, S.C., The University, 1907. Bul. #VIII, part II, Jan. 1907, years: 1861-1865. sm.8vo, wraps, 48pp.
...(Cont'd.) Bul. #XII, Univ. of S.C., (1908) sm.8vo, wraps, 67pp. Bmk. lists 54pp. $20.

UNIVERSITY OF VIRGINIA
"Circular sent to Federal and Confederate Governments, asking for public documents... for future historians." In: SHSP, 1888, v.16, p.56-58.
..."Honor Roll of the University of Virginia. Students who died in defense of the South's Cause. Preserved in marble." In: SHSP, 1905, v.33, p.42-56. From: Richmond Times-Dispatch, Dec. 3, 1905. See: Robert Stiles.

UNVEILING CEREMONIES
Of the Holmes County Monument at Lex-

ington, Miss., December 2, 1908. Jackson, Miss., Tucker Print House, 1908, 8vo, wraps, 56pp.

"UNVEILING OF SHAFT to Historic Portsmouth Artillery."
See: John H. Thompson, address...

43a **UNVEILING of Confederate Monument,** May 2, 1903-Mount Royal Ave., Baltimore City, May 2, 1903-Order of Ceremonies. Address by McHenry Howard. (Baltimore: Guggenheimer, Weil Co., 1903) 12mo, wraps, cover title-"Gloria Victis 1861-1865." illus. of monument with audience. 39pp.

UNVEILING of Soldier's Monument
In Petersburg, 1890. (Virginia). In: SHSP, 1889, v.17, p.388-403.

"UNVEILING of the Monument
erected by the U.S. government to the Confederate dead in the Pittville national cemetery." Phila., October 12th, 1911. Under the auspices of the Philadelphia chapter of the U.D.C.. 8vo, wraps, (4)p.

UNVEILING of the Monument
To South Carolina's Women of the Confederacy, Columbia, S.C., April 11, 1912. Columbia, S.C., The State Co., 1912, 8vo, wraps, 4pp. (Program.)

"UNVEILING of Monument
to Confederate dead, Warren County, N.C., address & poem delivered at..." Raleigh, N.C., 1906. 8vo, wraps, 20pp. $30-bmk.

UNVEILING of the Soldiers and Sailors
Monument, at Richmond, May 30, 1894. R.C. Cave's noble vindication of the Southern cause. In: SHSP, 1894, XXII, p.336-380.

UPSHUR, John Nottingham
See: Times-Dispatch's "New Market Day at V.M.I."

44 **UPTON, Emory, Gen.**
"Battle of Wilson's Creek." Reprinted from articles by..., in the Springfield News and Leader." (Springfield, Mo., Central Print (195-) 8vo, wraps, cover title, (1), 15pp., print on one side (dble-column). Printed and distributed by Wilson's Creek Battlefield Foundation, Inc. 330 E. Walton St., Springfield, Mo. The Foundation, 1950, acquired 37 acres of the Battlefield as a nucleus of a Memorial Park.
...Copy in photostat, distr. by Park.

45 **URQUHART, David, Col.**
"Bragg's advance & retreat." In: B&L, p.600-9, ills., ports. Bragg's CSArmy, 611-12.

46 **URQUHART, Kenneth Trist, Edt.**
"Vicksburg: Southern city under siege." New Orleans: Historic New Orleans Collection, 1980. 8vo, 107pp. ills. paper $7. $18.

47 **USINA, M.P., Capt.**
"Blockade Running in Confederate Times." In: and read before Confed. Vets. Assn., Savannah, Ga., July 4, 1893. Pres. Annual Report, p.21-39.

48 **UTZ, W.H.**
"Biographical Sketches of the Bartlett Marshall Duncan and Henry Utz families." St. Joseph, Missouri, 1936 (priv. print) 8vo, cl, ports, incl. front, (3), 137pp. Nearly all of book relates to letters of the family during the war, Missouri and the Confederates.

V

1 **VALASQUEZ, Madam**
"Story of the Civil War." N.Y., H.W. Hagemann Pub., 1894. 8vo, decr. cl, front, ports, facsms., maps, illus., (see: Dowie, Menie M.)

2 **VALDEZ, Santiago**
"Letter, dated at Craig, N.M., Jan. 1862." In: NMHR, 1948, v.23, p.242-244, notes. (July) CSA invasion of New Mex., Dec. 1961-Jan. 1962.

3 **VALENTINE, Edward V.**
"Reminiscences of General Lee." In: Outlook, Dec. 22, 1906, v.LXXXIV, p.964-968. Valentine was sculptor of the South. (Richmond)

4 **VALENTINE, L.L.**
"Sue Mundy of Kentucky." In: RKHS, July, 1964, v.62, #3, p.175-205. Part I, Part II, Oct., 1964, #4, p.278-306. Best acct. Celebrated as a woman in CSA uniform. This account of a trial of Jerome Clarke alias Sue Mundy. See: SB, V.XI, 1883/1884, p.126.

5 **VALLANDIGHAM, Clement Laird**
"Clement L. Vallandigham by W.H. Van Fossan, Lisbon, Ohio." In: Ohio Arch. and Hist. Pub., 1914, v.XXIII, p.256-267, port, plate.

6 ..."The Record of...on Abolition, the Union and the Civil War." Cincinnati, Oh., J. Walter and Co., 1863. 8vo, cl, front(port), 248pp. $45.

7 ..."Speeches, Arguments, Addresses and Letters." New York: (1864). 8vo, cl, 580pp., photos. Congr. from Ohio 1858-1863, leader Copperheads during Civil War, court martialed and banished.

8 ..."Rebellion in the North!! Extraordinary disclosures! Vallandigham's plan to overthrow the government! The peace party plot! Full details of the organization. Its declaration, oaths, signs, signals, passwords, grips, etc." (Richmond?) 1864, caption title. 8vo, 16pp. Crandall 2827.

8a ..."The Great Civil War in America. Speech of...of Ohio in the House of Representatives, Jan. 14, 1863." Washington, 1863. 8vo, sewn, 16p. Diatribe against Lincoln.
...Marysville, (Calif.) Daily California express office, 1863. 8vo, wraps, 14pp.

9 **VALLANDIGHAM, Edward N.**
"Clement L. Vallandigham, "Copperhead." In: Putnam's, Aug. 1907, II, p.590-599.

10 ..."A Life of Clement L. Vallandigham." Baltimore: Turnbull Bros., 1872. 8vo, rebound full calf, 573pp., port. Vicious opponent of Lincoln, member of Knights of Golden Circle, banished to CSA by Lincoln; thence back to north by Jeff Davis. See: "New Hampshire Peace Democracy."

11 **VALLANDIGHAM, James L., Rev.**
"Life of Clement L. Vallandigham," by his brother." Baltimore: Turnbull Bros., 1872. 8vo, cl, port(front) illus., 573pp.

12 ..."The Trial of..., by a military commission and the proceedings under his application for a writ of habeas corpus in the circuit court of the U.S. for the southern district: Ohio." Cincinnati, 1863, Rickey and Carroll Print., 8vo, wraps, 272pp. $75-y. Afterwards, banished to the Confederacy.

13 **VALLEY CAMPAIGN**
See: Moses Gibson, T.T. Munford, J.H. Worsham.

14 **"VALLEY Campaign of 1862. The,**
Correspondence of Generals Lee, Jackson and others with General Ewell." In: SHSP, 1874, v.1, p.91-101.

15 **"VALLEY NEWS ECHO."**
Hagerstown, Maryland. The Potomac Edison Co., 1959-1965. sm. folio, 4pp. ea.

issue, illus., ports, facsms, maps, issued v.1, #1-Oct. 1959, #2-Dec., v.2, #1-Apr. 1961 and monthly with final, v.6-#4, Apr. 1965. $35. total-51 issues. Newspaper in style, from papers of the time with ads, and from OR Records, CS and Union armies.

16 "VALOR"
The biennial publication of Hood's Texas Brigade Association." Hillsboro, Texas: Confederate Center of Hill Junior College, #1, 1971 and #2, 1973. 4to, stiff pict. wraps, 300 copies, signed by Col. Harold B. Simpson. illus., ports, facsm., 48, (1), 55pp., (1).

17 VALUABLE War Relic,
Muster roll of a Virginia artillery company. It belonged to Major Boggs Twelfth battalion, composed of North Carolina and Richmonders... In: SHSP, 1889, v.XVII, p.403-407. Co. D.

17a VANAUKEN, Shelton
"The glittering illusion: English sympathy for the Southern Confederacy." Columbia, S.C., Southern Press, 1987. 8vo, wraps, 182pp. $13.

18 VAN BUREN, A. De Puy
"Jottings of a Year's Sojourn in the South; or, First Impressions of the Country and Its People; with a glimpse at Schoolteaching in that Southern Land, and Reminiscences of distinguished Men." Battle Creek, Mich., Review and Herald Print, 1859. 12mo, cl, 320pp. Favorable impression of a Mich. school-teachers' experiences in Mississippi.

19 VAN DEUSEN, John George
"Economic bases of disunion in South Carolina." N.Y., Columbia University Pr., 1928. Studies in History, Economics and public law. Edt. by the faculty of political science of Columbia University, #305. 8vo, cl, front(fldg. map) 360pp.
...N.Y., AMS Press (1970) Reprint." Studies in history, economics and public law, #305.

20 VAN DORN, Earl, Maj.-Gen.
"Regulations for the guidance of troops." (Pocahontas? 1862) Feb. 19, 1862. Broadside, 36cm. Text in 3-columns (Hargrett)

21 ..."A Soldier's Honor with Reminiscences of Major-General Earl Van Dorn; by his comrads." N.Y., Lond: The Abbey Press (1902). 12mo, illus., ports, incl. front, 369pp. $15. $250-ob, Full lt. $200. 12mo, illus., ports, incl. front, 369pp. $15. Van Dorn was killed in Tenn. by a physician in '63 for breaking up "the peace of his home." See: A.F. Brown, Edward Dillon, G.W. Dudley, Robt. G. Hartje, Dabney H. Maury.

22 ..."Van Dorn's Report of the Elkhorn Campaign." In: SHSP, 1878, v.VI, p.37-42.

23 VAN DYKE, Anna Mary Deaderick
"A Southern woman, in 1897, remembers the Civil War." In: East THSP, 1949, v.21, p.111-115. notes. Reminisc. of a CSA woman in Tenn., mostly in Athens.

24 VAN EVRIE, J.H., Md.
"Abolition and Secession: or, Cause and Effect, together with a Remedy for our sectional troubles." by a Unionist. New York: Van Evrie, Horton and Co., 1862, 8vo, orig. wraps, 24pp. "No. 1 Anti-Abolition Tracts." 2nd Edt: "Negroes and Negro Slavery."

25 VAN HOOSE, G.W., Maj., USMC
"The Confederate States Marine Corps." In: Marine Corps. Gazette, Sept., 1928, v.13, #3, p.166-177.

26 VAN HORNE, John Douglass
"Jefferson Davis and Repudiation in Mississippi." n.p., privately printed (Glyndon, Md., Dec., 1915) 8vo, stiff wraps, 14pp. In: SHSP, 1916, v.41, p.49-56.

27 VAN HORNE, Thomas Budd
See: Dabney H. Maury's review "Army of the Cumberland."

28 VAN RIPER, Paul P. and Harry N. Scheiber
"The Confederate Civil Service." (Lexington, Ky.) JSH, Nov., 1959, v.XXV, #4, p.448-470. $8.

29 VAN ZANDT, K.M. and Andrew B. Booth
"List of organized camps of the United Confederate Veterans, corrected to Aug. 31, 1921." n.p., (New Orleans?) 1921. 8vo, pict. wraps, 19pp. Contains 1020 camps, first pub. in 1917.

30 ..."The Seventh Texas at Fort Donelson." In: CV, 1910, v.18, p.501.

31 VAN ZANDT, Khleber Miller
"Force without fanfare; autobiography of Khleber Miller Van Zandt. Edt: Sandra L. Myres, Foreword: Bayard H. Friedman." Fort Worth, Texas: Texas Christian University 1868? Chapters on: Pre-war and KGC, the war years (p.77-109); Reconstruction in Ft. Worth and Tarrant County.

32 VANCE, Maurice M.
"Northerners in late Nineteenth Century Florida: Carpetbaggers or Settlers?" In: FHQ, July 1959, v.XXXVIII, #1, p.1-14.

33 VANCE, Wilson J.
"Stone's River, the turning point of the Civil War." N.Y., Neale Print, 1914. 12mo, cl, 72pp. Also called Murfreesboro.

34 VANCE, Zebulon Baird
"Address at the White Sulphur Springs, W.Va., Aug. 18, 1875 before the Southern Historical Society...North Carolina in the Civil War." In: "Our Living and Our Dead", iii, 612-628.

35 ..."Address before the Southern Historical Society." In: SHSP, 1875, v.14, p.506-521. Also: OLOD, 1875, v.III, p.612-628. On N.C. in the Civil War, del. White Sulphur Springs, W.Va., Aug. 18, 1875.

36 ..."Correspondence between Gov. Vance and President Davis, 1863." In: SHSP, 1875, v.14, p.411-415.

37 ..."Vance, Zebulon Baird-PAPERS." Edt: Frontis W. Johnston, vol. 1(1843-1862). Raleigh: State Dept. Archives and History, 1963. tk 8vo, cl, d/w, ports, illus., 475pp. See: Editor.

38 ..."The Last Days of the War in North Carolina, an address by..., delivered Feb. 23, 1885, at the third annual reunion of the Maryland Line..." Baltimore: Sun Book Off., 1885, 8vo, wraps, 32pp.

39 ..."Memorial addresses on the life and character of..., late Senator from North Carolina delivered in the Senate and House of Representatives, 53rd Cong., 3rd. Cong." mssc. Doc. 151. Wash: Gov. Print Off., 1895. 8vo, wraps, front(port) 192pp. cloth.

40 ..."My Beloved Zebulon: The Correspondence of Zebulon Baird Vance and Harriett Newell Espy." Edt: Elizabeth Roberts Cannon; Intro: Frances Gary Patton. Chapel Hill: Univ. of North Carolina, 1971, 8vo, cl, dj, xxv, 278pp.

41 ..."The Political and Social South during the War, an address in Boston, before the John A. Andrew Post., #15, G.A.R., Dec. 8, 1886." Washington: R.O. Polkinhorn, 1886, 8vo, wraps, 20pp.

42 ..."Restoration is Nature' Law; Lets imitate her...speech of...in Senate of U.S., Monday, May 19, 1879." Washington: R.O. Polkinhard Pr., 1879, 8vo, sewn, 16pp. Carpetbaggers have left South, back to the slums of the North, have quit outrages against South. Representatives invited back to House but still resented!

43 ..."Special Message of the Governor, Document No. 13, delivered Nov. 27, 1863." (Raleigh, 1863) 8vo, sewn, 4pp. Undescribed CSA Imprint. A memorial deploring speculation, extortion and withholding supplies.

44 ..."Statue of...Proceedings in Statuary Hall of the U.S. Capitol and in the Senate and

House of Representatives upon the unveiling, presentation and acceptance of the statue presented by the State of North Carolina, 64th Congress." Washington: Government Printing Hse., 1917, 8vo, cl, port(front) 98pp.

...See: Edward Warren, Rich. Edwin Yates, Glenn Tucker, Vance Papers, Clement Dowd, W.J. Saunders, Richard H. Battle.

45 **VANDIVER, Frank Everson**
"Basic History of the Confederacy." Princeton, N.J., Van Nostrand (1962) 12mo, cl, boards, 192pp.

...Melbourne, Fla., Krieger Press, 1980, 12mo, stiff wraps, 186pp. bibliography. "An Anvil Original." paper edition.

46 ..."The Civil War; its theory and practice." In: Tex. Quart., Summer, 1959, 2(2): 102-108pp. War as a highly profitable industry, especially in publishing, recent years.

47 ..."A collection of Louisiana Confederate Letters." (The Lee Family) In: LHQ, Oct. 1943, v.26, p.937-974.

48 ..."The Confederacy and the American Tradition." (Houston, Texas) In: JSH, Aug. 1962, v.XXVIII, #3, p.277-286. $8.

49 ..."Confederate Blockade Running Through Bermuda, 1861-1865. Letters and Cargo Manifests. Edited by Frank E. Vandiver." $75-ob. Austin, Texas: University of Texas (1947) 8vo, cl, dj, front(plate), xliv, 155pp.

...N.Y., Kraus Reprint Co., 1970.

50 ..."Confederate plans for procuring subsistence stores." In: Tyler QHGMag. Apr. 1946, v.XXVII, p.5.

51 ..."Jefferson Davis and the Confederate state." Oxford, Clarendon Press, 1964. 8vo, wraps, 22pp. An inaugural lecture delivered before the University of Oxford on 26 February, 1964.

52 ..."Jefferson Davis and the unified command." In: L.H.Q., 1955, XXXVIII, p.26-38.

53 ..."Jubal's Raid. General Early's Famous attack on Washington in 1864." N.Y., Lond.: McGraw-Hill Co., (1960) 12mo, cl, dj, illus., maps, ports, xiii, 198pp.

...West Port, Conn., Negro Univ. Press, 1975. $11.

54 ..."Abraham Lincoln and Jefferson Davis 1861-1865." In: "Lincoln for the Ages..." Edt.: Ralph G. Newman. p.282-288. (Garden City, N.Y., Doubleday, 1960)

55 ..."The First Public War, 1861-1865; an address before the conference of the Public Relations Society of America, Shamrock-Hilton Hotel, Nov. 13, 1961." N.Y., (Foundation for Public Relations Research and Education), 1962. 8vo, wraps, 16pp.

56 ..."Josiah Gorgas", Tulane University abstract of a dissertion, 1951, p.44-48.

57 ..."Josiah Gorgas and the Brierfield Iron Works, 1865-1869." In: Ala. Rev., Jan. 1950, v.3, p.5-21, notes.

...Edited: Josiah Gorgas Civil War diary.

58 ..."General Hood as logistician." In: Mil. Affairs, Spring, 1952, v.16, p.1-11. Hood's Tennessee Campaign.

59 ..."How the Yankees are losing the war." In: Southwest Rev., Winter, 1955, v.40, p.62-66. Developing a Southern folklore and traditions about the Civil War.

60 ..."The Idea of the South; pursuit of a central theme. Editor, Frank E. Vandiver. Contributors: Richard B. Harwell, et al." Chicago: Pub. for William Marsh Rice University by the University of Chicago Press, (1964) Rice University Semi-Centennial Publications. Papers presented at a symposium of the History Department of Rice University. 8vo, wraps, xi, 82pp.

61 ..."Essays on the American Civil War." Austin: University of Texas Press, 1968, 8vo, cl, index, bibliog., 107pp. Martin Hardwick Hall and Homer L. Kerr.

62 ..."The Food Supplies of the Confederate Armies, 1865." In: Tyler's Quart. Hist. and Geneal. Mag., 1944/1945, V.XXVI, p.77-89.

63 ..."Charles A. Kingsland: Texas Immortal." In: SwHQ, XLVIII, p.273-274.

64 ..."Letters from the Confederate Medical Service in Texas, 1863-1865." In: SwHQ, v.LV, p.378-401, 459-474.

65 ..."Makeshifts of Confederate Ordnance." In: JSH, 1951, v.XVII, p.180-193. $8.

66 ..."The Making of a President: Jefferson Davis, 1861. A lecture delivered at Richmond, Va., on the 100th Anniversary of the inauguration of Jefferson Davis as president of the permanent Government of the Confederate States of America." Richmond, Va., Civil War Commission (1962) Virginia Civil War Centennial 1961-1965. 8vo, wraps, 14pp.

67 ..."Mighty Stonewall." N.Y., Lond: McGraw-Hill, (1957) Tk. 8vo, cl, dj, illus., maps (1-dbl. pg.) ports, xi, 547, (1)pp., bibliog., index, notes, p.495-547. Civil War Book Club Edition, $40, 7-printings, in print. Also: Limited 1st Edt., with "Hall of Fame plate (Jackson admitted to N.Y. University Hall of Fame, May 19, 1957, numbered and signed by author, solely distributed by the Stonewall Jackson Memorial, Lexington, Va.

68 ..."Ploughshares into Swords, Josiah Gorgas and Confederate Ordnance." Austin: University of Texas Pr., 1952. 8vo, cl, dj, front(port), xiv, 349pp., bibliog. index, notes, p.315-349. $75.
...stiff pict. wraps, from the unbound sheets of the first edition.

69 ..."Proceedings of the Second Confederate Congress, etc., etc." Edited v.50, SHSP, 1959, see under title.

70 ..."Rebel Brass. The Confederate Command System, with introduction by T. Harry Williams." Baton Rouge: Louisiana Univ. Pre. (1956) 12mo, cl, dj, illus., map liners, ports, svii, (3)-142, (1)pp. index, bibliog. $40.
...Civil War Book Club, limited edition, Atg. by author, in dj.
...Reprint: Westport, Conn., Greenwood.

71 ..."The Shelby Iron Company in the Civil War, 1862-1865. A study of a Confederate industry." In: Ala. Rev., Jan./July, 1948, v.1, p.12-26, 111-127, 203-217, notes.

72 ..."A sketch of efforts abroad to equip the Confederate Armory at Macon(Ga.)." In: Ga. H.Q., Mar., 1944, v.XXVIII, #1, p.34-40, illus.

73 ..."The South Carolina Ordnance board 1860-1861." In: S.C. Hist. Assoc. Proceed. (1945), p.14-22.

74 ..."Texas and the Confederate Army's meat problem." In: SWHQ, 1943/1944, v.XLVII, p.225-233.

75 ..."Some problems involved in writing Confederate history." In: JSH, Aug., 1970, v.XXXVI, 11pp. $8-bmk.

76 ..."Their Tattered Flags." N.Y. and Evanston: Harper's Magazine Press Books, (1970) Tall 8vo, cl, dj, front(flags) map as liners, 4-maps (1-fldg.), (6), (10), 362pp. op, $30.

77 ..."Extracts from the diary of Richard H. Gayle, Confederate States Navy." In: TylerQHGM, Oct. 1948, v.30, p.86-114.

78 ..."Lee during the war." 1984 Confederate History symposium, Hill Junior College, Hillsboro, Texas, Apr. 14, 1984. 4to, hardback, 117pp. 75 of 90 copies.

79a **VANDIVER, Frank E.**
"The capture of a Confederate blockade runner, extracts from the journal of a

Confederate Naval officer." In: NCHR, Jan. 1944, v.21, #2, p.136-8.

"Jefferson Davis - leader without legend." In: JSH, Feb. 1977, v.43, #1, p.3-18.

..."Jefferson Davis & Confederate strategy." In: The American Tragedy (Hampden-Sydney, Va.) 1959, p.19-32.

79 **VANDIVER, Joseph L.**
"Capture of Generals Crook and Kelley of the Federal Army-coolest deed on record." In: SHSP, 1891, v.19, p.186-188.

80 **VANDIVER, S. Ernest, Gov., State of Ga.**
"Address by...Dedicating Memorial to Georgia Confederate Dead Antietam National Battlefield Site, Sept. 4, 1961. (Atlanta, Ga., 1961)" 4to, stiff decr. wraps, plastic spiral, photo of governor front. (12pp. printed one side.)

81 **VANDIVER, W.D.**
"Two forgotten heroes-John Hanson McNeill and his son Jesse." In: MHR, April 1927, v.XXI, p.404-419. Capt. and organizer of "McNeill's Rangers", his son served in same organization.

82 **VANFELSON, Charles A.**
"The little Red Book or department directory. For the use of the public in the Confederate States of America. Pub. by C.A. Vanfelson." Richmond: Tyler, Wise and Allegre, 1861, 12mo, wraps, 24pp.

83 **VANN, Samuel King**
"Most Lovely Lizzie." Love Letters of a Young Confederate Soldier." (Birmingham, Ala., 1958: Edt. William Young Elliott) sm. 12mo, plastic wraps, ribbon-tied, ports, 72pp. Mimeographed on colored (several) paper. $30.

84 **VAUGHAN, A.J.**
"Personal record of the 13th Reg., Tenn. Inf. by its old commander." Suffolk, Va., Robt. Hardy Pub., 1986, 8vo, wraps, 40pp., port.

85 **VAUGHAN, Alfred J.**
"Personal Record of the Thirteenth Regiment Tennessee Infantry, by its old commander." (Memphis, Tenn., S.C. Toof and Co., 1897) 12mo, wraps, (cloth), 2-ports, 95pp. $30. 1/2 lt. $125.

...Memphis, Tenn., Burke's Bookstore and Frank Myers, 1975 (500 copies) 8vo, pict. wraps, illust. roster.

86 **VAUGHAN, Jack C., Maj.**
"Brig.-Gen. Alfred Jefferson Vaughan's Brigade, Army of Tennessee, C.S.A." Vol. XI-Vaughan's American Histories. (Grand Prairie, Texas, Box 91) n.d., 4to, buck, 158pp. mimeo (one side) ports, illus., maps, indexed. Pt. I., v.XII-pt. 2, p.(159)-349; v.XIII-pt.3, p.(350)-564; v.XIV-pt.4, p.(565)-775. See also, A.J. Vaughan's "13th Reg." 6 vols. (1171 leaves) facsms., map's, ports, tables, views, notes. His American histories 11-16. On the 13th Tenn. Reg., later also the 154th Tenn. Reg., under his command as Colonel and later as Brig.-Gen., June 1861-Dec., 1863. See: "Tennessee Infantry (CSA) -154th Reg.

87 **VAUGHAN, Myra McAlmont, Mrs.**
"David O. Dodd." n.p., n.d., 32mo, wraps, 15pp. An 18 year old CSA spy, executed Jan. 18, 1864. See: David O. Dodd.

88 **VAUGHAN, Turner**
"Diary of Turner Vaughan, Co. "C", 4th Ala. Reg., CSA." In: AlaHQ, winter 1956, v.18, p.573-601. (while in Va., Md., Ga., and Tenn. 4 Mar. 1863-Feb. 12, 1864.

89 **VAUTIER, John D.**
"The loss at Gettysburg." In: SB, ns, v.1, #10, p.639. 1885/1886. Read in conjunction with Col. Wm. H. Swallow's acct. Battle of Gettysburg.

90 **VEDDER, Charles S., Rev.**
"Diary of the Rev. Charles S. Vedder, May-July 1861. Edt: Willard E. Wight." Savannah, Ga., Georgia Historical Soc. Reprint: GHQ, Mar. 1955, v.39, #1, 25pp.

91 **VEDDER, Charles Stuart, Rev.**
"The Diary of the Reverend Charles S. Vedder (Presbyterian visitor in Monticello, Ga.) May-July, 1861. Edited by Willard E. Wight." In: GaHQ, Mar. 1955, v.XXXIX, p.68-90, notes. $8.

92 ..."A Sermon preached in the Huguenot Church, Charleston, S.C., upon the Sabbath succeeding the death of General Robert E. Lee, by Rev. C.S. Vedder, pastor of that church." Charleston: Walker, Evans & Cogswell, 1870, 8vo, wraps, 12pp.

93 ..."The Diary of...", May-July, 1861. Edt: Willard E. Wight." Rep.: from GaHQ, March, 1955, wraps, 25pp. $10.

94 **VELAZQUEZ, Loreta Janeta**
"The Woman in Battle, a narrative of the exploits, adventures and travel of... Otherwise known as Lt. Harry T. Buford, CSA. Edt: C.J. Worthington." Hartford, Conn., T. Belknap, 1876 (some copies have no date) Richmond, Va., 1876. $40.
...N.Y., Arno Press, 1972. "American Women: images and realities."

95 ..."The Story of the Civil War; or, the exploits, adventures and travels of... Edt: C.J. Worthington, U.S.N." N.Y., Worthington and Co., 1890. 8vo, decr. cl, illus., maps, ports, 606pp.

96 **VENABLE, Andrew Reid**
See: Wm. G. McCabe.

97 **VENABLE, Austin L.**
"The conflict between Douglas and Yancey forces in the Charleston Convention. Offprint, JSH, May 1942, v.8, #2, p.226-241, 8vo, wraps, 16pp. $20.

98 ..."The Role of William L. Yancey in the Secession Movement." Summary of thesis. Nashville, Tenn., Joint University Libraries, 1945, Privately Printed. Vanderbilt University. 8vo, wraps, 33pp.

99 ..."William L. Yancey's Transition from Unionism to States Rights." (Baton Rouge, La.) JSH, Aug., 1944, v.X, #3, p.331-342.
"Public career of William Lowndes Yancey." In: AR, July 1963, v.16, #3, p.200-212.

100 ..."William L. Yancey and the League of United Southerners." In: Pro.SCHA, 1946, p.3-12.

101 **VENABLE, Charles Scott**
"The campaigns from the Wilderness to Petersburg. Address of...(formerly of Gen. R.E. Lee's staff) of the University of Va., before the Virginia division of the Army of Northern Virginia, at their annual meeting, held in the Virginia state capitol, at Richmond, Thursday evening, Oct. 30, 1878." Richmond, Geo. W. Gary, printer, 1879, 8vo, wraps, 20pp. Emory.
...In: SHSP, 1886, v.XIV, p.522-542.

102 ..."Further details of the death of Gen. A.P. Hill." In: SHSP, 1884, v.XII, p.183-187.

103 ..."General Lee in the Wilderness Campaign." In: B & L, v.IV, p.240-246.

104 ..."Major Scheibert's book-"La Guerre Civile Aux Etats-Unis." In: SHSO, 1897, v.IV, p.88-91.

105 **VENABLE, Charles Scott, Colonel**
"Major Scheibert's Book (La Guerre Civile) a review by..." In: SHSP, 1877, v.IV, p.88-91.

106 **VENABLE, Matthew Walton**
"Eighty years after or grandpa's story." Charleston, W.Va., Hood-Misermann-Brodhag, 1929. 8vo, cl, illus., 108pp. $60. Record of service with Co.H, 1st. Regiment CSA Engineers.

107 ..."On the way to Appomattox-War Memories." In: CV, Aug., 1924, v.XXXII, p.303-304. Story of 6 days march from Richmond to Appomattox, in 1865.

108 **"VENDETTA",**
"Four Letters addressed to his Excellency Jefferson Davis in vindication of Captain Randolph, C.S.N., by Vendetta, with an

appendix containing "Cayenne." n.p., n.d., 8vo, sewn, 16pp. Berates Davis for "cruel injustice" to an officer of long and faithful service. Reverse front cover-"With the respects of the author V.M.R." (Henkel sale #1090, May 1913)

109 **VEROT, Augustine, Bishop**
"Esclavage and abolitionisme. Sermon preche dans l'eglise de St. Augustin, Floride, le 4 Janvier 1861, jour d' humiliation, de jeune et de prieres publiques, par Mgr. Verot." Nouvelle Orleans, Imp. du propagateur catholique 1862. 8vo, wraps, cover title, 24pp.

110 ..."Letters of the Bishop of Savannah, 1861-1865. Edited by Willard E. Wight." In: Ga.H.Q., March 1958, v.XL, #1, p.93-106. See: Willard Wight.

111 **VERTEGANS, G.S.**
"Captured a General." In: CV, September, 1918, v. 26, p.389-390. Captures Gen. Eliakim P. Scammon, at Winfield by 16th Va. Cav., by Vertegans.

112 **VETERAN Gunners fire old Battery.**
Inspiring scene at Virginia Military Institute, Lexington, Va., May 10, 1913. In: SHSP, April 1914, v.XXXIX, p.144-145.

113 **VETERANS GUIDE to Charleston, S.C.**
Containing full information to enable veterans, sons and visitors to reach all points, historic points of interest, portraits (22) and sketches of distinguished UCV officers, with map of city. For the U.C.V. Re-Union May 10-13, 1899. Charleston: Walker, Evans and Cogswell Co., 12mo, decr. color wraps, fldg. map, 88pp. ads thru text.

114 **VETERANS Reunion,**
The meeting of the Rockbridge dragoons at Lexington, list of survivors...from Staunton Daily News. In: sHSP, 1894, v.XXII, p.73-75. See: J. Scott Moore.

115 **"VETERANS of the Civil War** Buried in Taylor County, Texas Cemeteries." In: West Tex. Geneal. Soc. Bul. (Abilene, Tx.) In: Jan. 1963, v.5, #1, p.3-9.

116 **VICKERS, George Edward**
"Gettysburg, a Poem by George E. Vickers." (Philadelphia, 1890) 8vo, wraps, (36)pp.

117 ..."Last Charge at Gettysburg, by George Edward Vickers." Philadelphia: Herald Co., 1899, 12mo, wraps, 32pp.
...1902 edition, reprint.

118 **VICKSBURG ,**
"Struggle for Vicksburg. The battle and siege that decided the Civil War. Edt: Dr. Stephen E. Ambrose. Special Edition commemorating-CWTI, July 1967, v.VI, #4, p. 66, illus., portfolio of maps, ports.

118a **VICKSBURG Battlefield Monuments:**
a pictorial record. Text by Steve Walker, David Riggs, Photographs by Harold Young." Jackson: University of Miss. Press, 1984. 4to, wraps, 88pp. $11.

119 **VICKSBURG Memorial Exercises**
"Address: by T.C. Catchings, M.C." In: CV, 1900, v.8, p.313-319, port, illus.

120 **VICKSBURG NAT'L. PARK**
See: Wm. C. Everhart, Edwin C. Bearss, Henry S. Parson's Wall-paper edt. "Daily Citizen.

121 **VICKSBURG, Mississippi**
See: Wm. T. Rigby's CS deat at...; Vicksburg, Siege of; See: J.E. Battaile, J.T. Hogane, Stephen D. Lee, R.W. Memminger, Memphis Appeal-Adalanche, E.R. Montgomery, John C. Pemberton, John B. Pirtle.

122 **VICKSBURG, Mississippi, Siege**
"The Siege of Vicksburg. Its Approaches by Yazoo Pass and other Routes." Mobile, Ala., Goetzel and Co., May 1, 1863. Broadside, mounted, Henkel cat. 1118.

123 **"VIEUX SECONDE" (pseud.)**
"The Second Tennessee regiment at Chickamauga. By Vieux Seconde." In: An-

nals Army of Tenn. and Early Western History, Nashville, 1878, v.1, p.52-62.

124 **"VIEW of the Constitution;**
Report of the Historical Committee of the United Confederate Veterans...May 1914. John R. Deering, Chm." In: Confed. Vet., Aug. 1914, v.XXII, p.353-356. Wm. Rawle's "View of Constitution" used as a text at West Point, when Lee and Davis (students) taught secession was one of constitutional rights of a state.

125 **VILES, Jonas, Edt.**
"Documents illustrative of the troubles on the border, 1858, 1859, and 1865." In: MHR, v.1, (Apr., July, 1907) p.198-215, 293-306; v.II, (Oct. 1907) p.61-77.

126 ..."Sections and sectionalism in a border state." In: MVHR, 1934, p. 3-22, v.XXI. Development of attitude toward slavery in Missouri, 1810-1860, toward extent sectional feelings in 1861 as considered "southern".

127 **VILLARD, Oswald Garrison**
"The submarines and the torpedo in blockade of the Confederacy." In: Harper's, June 1916, v.CXXXIII, p.131-137.

128 **VILLERE, Charles J.**
"Review of certain remarks made by the President when requested to restore Beauregard to the command of Department #2." Charleston, Evans and Cogswell, 1863. 8vo, wraps, 28pp. Crandall 2873.

129 **VILLIERS, Brougham and W.H. Chesson**
"Anglo-American Relations, 1861-1865." London: T. Fisher Unwin (1919) 8vo, cl, vii, 214, (44pp. ads)pp.
...N.Y., Scribner's, 1920. Author's pseud: Frederick John Shaw. $25-bmk. Pro-South ascendancy in Eng., friction of Trent affair, the "Alabama", Lincoln's Emancipation Proc., their effect on the British opinion.

130 **VINCENT, James U.**
"Pen pictures of Gen. Robert Toombs; a glimpse of mental characteristics of Hon. A.H. Stephens and Benj. H. Hill. A circular letter to bodies of 33 degree Free Masons, by Gen. Albert Pike. Also a memorial of Georgia Supreme Court; sketches of Sommerville Co. Bosque, Hood and Johnson Counties." Louisville, Ky., Courier-Journal, 1886, sq. sm. 4to, wraps, 32pp. port.

131 **VINCENT, Louella Styles, Mrs.**
"Sing the South-an address before the McLennon County(Texas) Confederate Association reunion at McGregor on Aug. 10, 1905." cover title. n.p., (c.1905) Emory. 12mo, wraps, 24pp. cover title same 1/2 title.

132 **VINSON, Uriah T., Daniel J. and Ben. W.**
"The Vinson Confederate Letters. Edited by Hugh Buckner Johnston." In: NCHR, Jan. 1948, v.XXV, p.100-110. Notes.

133 **VINTON, Iris**
"The Story of Robert E. Lee." N.Y., Grossett and Dunlap (1952) 8vo, cl, d/w, illus., front, vii, 182pp. Junior Hi-"Signature Books."

134 **VIOLETTE, E.M.**
"The Battle of Kirksville (Mo.) Aug. 6, 1862." (Columbia, Mo., Jan., 1911, v.V, #2, Missouri Historical Review, p.94-112. One of last efforts to keep Missouri as CSA. Massacre Palmyra, Dr. Mudd and Porter, etc. Reprint, in wraps, of above.

135 **VIRGINIA (Ironclad) CSNavy**
See: John M. Brooke, Wm. R. Cline, Joseph G. Fiveash, Catesby R. Jones, H.B. Littlepage, Dabney H. Maury, Monitor (Ironclad) USN, Virginius Newton, Wm. H. Parker, Edward A. Somerset, J.H.D. Wingfield.

135a **VIRGINIA at Gettysburg, 1917.**
See: 'Ceremonies attending dedication...'

136 **"VIRGINIA Battlefield Park.** Fredericksburg's efforts in this direction." (from Richmond Dispatch). In: SHSP, 1908, v.36, p.215-218. Efforts toward US Gov., establish a national park near Fredericksburg and Richmond.

137 **VIRGINIA Civil War Commission.** "The Civil War Centennial; an opportunity for all Virginians..." Richmond, 1960. 12mo, wraps, form, 44pp. cover title. Manual of observance by cities, counties.

138 **VIRGINIA Confederate (pseud.)** "In Vinculis." See: Anthony M. Keiley.

139 **VIRGINIA Confederate Military Records:** "Department of Confederate military records, "General orders and Circulars", Roster of military officers of state and national guards of Virginia, "Report of Virginia Military Institute" (Roster) In: Report of the Adjutant General for the Commonwealth of Virginia of the year ending Oct. 20, 1916." Richmond: D. Bottom, Spt. Print, 1917.

140 **VIRGINIA Forces in the Confederacy-SHSP:** See: W.B. Ashbrooke; Abingdon "Virginian"; R.N. Allen; J.H. Allen; J.S. Apperson; Baltimore Herald; G.W. Beale;; J.C. Birdsong; Black Eagle, Co. H; W.N. Blow; E.E. Bouldin; R.C. Bowles; J.W. Breedlove; J.B. Caddall; Churchville Cavalry; Catlett Conway; Jno. W. Daniel; A.S. Drewry; L.R. Edwards; T.H. Ellis; Farmville Journal; C.D. Fishburne; C.R. Fleet; Joshua Fletcher; C.A. Fonerden; R.D. Funkhouser; E.W. Gaines; J.C. Goolsby; J.P. Gore, L.L. Goss; G.K. Griggs; Hanover Grays; M.W. Hazlewood; Arthur Herbert; R.W. Hunter; R. Irby; Jackson Clarion-Ledger; Mary Johnston; W.F. Johnston; King William Artillery; J.B. Lacy; J.F. Lay; E.H. Lively; C.T. Loehr; Newton McAlpine; J.V.S. McCreery; F.T. Massie; H.F. Miley; H.J. Miller; G.E. Mitchell; J.S. Moore; Muster Roll Co. D; News-Leader Cent. Grime's Batt.; W.A. Parrott; Camm Patterson; Winfield Peters; Petersburg Express; A.H. Plecker; Charles Poindexter; Portsmouth Star; C.H. Powell; C.B. Price; Purcell Battery; E.P. Reeves; "Reunion survivor, Co. D., 18th Va.; Richmond Dispatch's Brunswick Blues and Guards; Cumberland Grays; Co. G., 26th Va. Reg.; Old Dominion Dragoons; Richmond Ambulance Corps.; Roll Co. B.; 9th Va. Roster Lee Rangers; Unveiling Howitzer Monument; Black Horse Troops; T.J. Riddle; B.A. Roberts; Roll Co.I, 13th Va. and 15th Va.; A.H. Roller,; Roster-Amelia Troops; J.H. Shepherd; T.M. Smiley; E.L. Spence; Staunton Daily News; Stuart Horse Artillery; Times-Dispatch: Roster McNeil's Rangers and Co. G, 18th Va. Cav.; H.G. White; J.S. Whitworth; C.M. Wallace; Wm. & Mary Quart; Williamsburg Jr. Guards; C. Wilson; H.E. Wood; W.B. Wooldridge; C.P. Young; L. Zimmer.

142 **"VIRGINIA Generals in the Confederate States Army."** In: SHSP, 1908, v.36, p.105-120.

143 **VIRGINIA Joins the Confederacy;** Chronology of events, November, 1860 through June 1861. (Richmond, Va., 1961) Virginia Civil War Centennial Commission. 12mo, wraps, cover title, 18pp. See: Henry T. Shanks, James Clyde McGregor and Beverley B. Munford.

144 **"VIRGINIA Leads."** n.p., Virginia division, United Daughters of the Confederacy, 1916. 12mo, wraps, 31pp. Prize UDC, historical division. Written by Mrs. W.C.N. Merchant, Mrs. Cabell Smith.

145 **VIRGINIA Legislature** "Message from the President of the U.S., submitting to Congress a series of resolu-

tions adopted by the Legislature of Virginia on the 19th instant, having in view a peaceful settlement of the exciting questions which now threatens the Union." Wash., Jan. 1861, 36th Congress, 2nd Sess., Senate Ex. Doc., #3, 5pp.

146 **VIRGINIA MILITARY INSTITUTE**
"Alphabetical list of graduates of VMI, from 1839 to 1910, with post-office address." Lynchburg, Va., 1910. 8vo, wraps, 46pp. $35-bmk.

..."Register of former cadets. Centennial edition." VMI, Lexington, Va., 1939. Roanoke, Va., Roanoke Print, 1939, 4to, cl, 408pp.

147 ..."The Lieutenant Willis Jefferson Dance, Junior, memorial lectures delivered at the Virginia Military Institute, Lexington, Virginia, 1952-1863." Lexington, V.M.I. Foundation (1965) Imp. 8vo, cl, illus., ports, xiii, 192pp. "What is leadership?" lectures on various CSA leaders, i.e., Freeman's Lee, Chambers Jackson, Wellman, New Market, Maury, A.P. Hill, et al.

148 ..."The Virginia Military Institute." In: SHSP, 1891, v.19, p.273-275. (visitors and staff, 1848-1861., associates of Stonewall.) See: H.W. Fry, Wm. Couper, J.C. and J.S. Wise.

149 ..."New Market Day at V.M.I. Celebrating the thirty-ninth anniversary of the Battle of New Market and unveiling of Ezekiel's statue: Virginia mourning her dead." (Roanoke, Va., Stone Print, 1903) 8vo, wraps, illus., ports, 84pp. Speeches: Jno. N. Upshur, Holmes Conrad and John S. Wise.

150 ..."Seventy-fifth anniversary of the battle of New Market, May 15, 1939. Centennial year, 1839-1939. (Lexington, Va., 1939) 8vo, wraps, illus., 28pp.

151 **VIRGINIA Pension Roster**
"Confederate Pension Law of Virginia compiled by the Auditor of Public accounts 1916." Richmond, Va., D. Bottom, 1916. 8vo, wraps, 12pp. Approved March 21, 1916.

152 ..."Roster of Confederate Pensioners of Virginia. Showing payments from Oct. 1, 1915, to Oct. 1, 1916, to all pensioners enrolled under the several acts of assembly, viz, acts of Mar. 7, 1888, and special acts, "pensions to soldiers and widows". Act of Mar. 7, 1900, as amended, "pensions to soldiers and widows". Act. of Mar. 11, 1902, as amended, "funeral expenses of pensioners", "pensions of Confederate matrons". Compiled by auditor of public accounts." Richmond, Va., D. Bottom, 1916. 26 1/2x11 1/2cm. 152pp. Same for 1917, (148)pp; 1919, (125)pp; 1920, (124)pp; 1921, (125)pp; 1922, (122)pp; 1923, (116)pp; 1925, (113)pp.

153 **"VIRGINIA Record, July 1961."**
"Confederate Centennial Edition, second revised, by Clifford Dowdey (Editor) adding seven great battles." Cover title. (Richmond, Va., Publisher's Wing, Inc., vol. LXXXIII, #1. 4to, pict. color wraps, facsms., illus., maps, ports, largely ads, with text, 170pp.

154 **VIRGINIA State Library-Richmond**
"A list of the official publications of the Confederate States government in the Virginia State Library and the Library of the Confederate Memorial Literary Society." Bul. v.IV, #1, Richmond, 1911, 8vo, wraps, 72pp.

155 **"VIRGINIA'S Contribution to the Confederate Character of Virginia, etc..."**
See: Margarete L. Von der Au

156 **VIRGINIA'S Decision.**
The second Convention of 1861. Richmond: Virginia Civil War Centennial Commission. (1964) 8vo, wraps, illus., ports, 23pp.

157 **"VIRGINIA, History of**
By R.L. Morton. Chi. and NY, Amer. Hist. Soc., 1924. 6 vols., illus., pls, ports, maps. v.III-"Virginia since 1861" by Morton.

158 **VIRGINIA, History, Confederate War**
See: Wm. Baird, George L. Christian, John W. Jones, John Letcher, "Louisiana's Vote of thanks to Virginia." Matthew F. Maury, Wm. and Mary Quart."

159 **VIRGINIA - General Assembly**
"A Bill (#28) to reduce into slavery Emancipated slaves who have forfeited their freedom. (Together with) A Bill (#118) to prohibit the emancipation of slaves by Will Richmond, 1862-1863. Broadside and broadsheet. $350. Wartime attempts to tighten control over slaves and the free black population. Harwell-914 (Bill #118).

160 **"VIRGINIA-MERRIMAC, The"**
Behind the scenes in the Confederate Navy Dept., from the NY Sun. In: United Ser., May 1895, v.XIII, ns, p.493-497.

161 **VIRGINIA. Adjutant General**
"Report: April 17, 1861." In: SHSP, 1886, v.14, p.179-181.

162 **VIRGINIA: Army - C.S.A. - Joseph Jackson.**
Circular, recorder Virginia Forces, giving form to be adopted in each regiment for the gathering of facts regarding the career of each soldier to be used in compilation of statistics and for future history, Nov. 1, 1864. Richmond. (44x41cm) Not in Crandall/Harwell. See: Swem II, #15392. Facsm. reprint in Va. Mag. Hist. and Biog., v.68, #1, Jan. 1960, pg. 48-49.

163 **VIRGINIA: Convention, Richmond, 1861**
"Proceedings of the Virginia State Convention of 1861, Feb. 13-May 1." George H. Reese Edt.-Richmond: Virginia State Library (Historical Publications Division) 1965, 4 ovls. Proceedings and debates of the first session as they were published in the Richmond Enquirer, official reporter of the convention. Supplemented by abstracts from the Daily Dispatch. Append. at end of v.1, with a list of delegates.

164 **VIRGINIA: Topographical Maps.**
Surveyed and drawn by Maj. John E. Weyss, et al. (Military Maps) all 35 1/2x24". Linen mounted. color. "Bermuda Hundred, Va."; "Chancellorsville, Va." "Cold Harbor, Va."; "High Bridge and Farmville"; "Jetersville and Sailor's Creek"; "North Anna" (16 1/2x19); "Richmond, Va. Area."; "Spotsylvania Court House"; "Totopotomoy, Va."; "The Wilderness"; N.Y., 1867-1869.

165 **"VIRGINIAN, A."**
"The Life of Stonewall Jackson by a Virginian." N.Y., Chs. B. Richardson, 1866. See: John Esten Cooke.

166 **"VISIT to the Cities and Camps of the Confederate States, 1863-1864. A,"**
See: FitzGerald Ross.

167 **VOEGELI, V. Jacque**
"Free but Not Equal: The Midwest and the Negro During the Civil War." Chicago: Univ. of Chicago Pr., 1967, 8vo, cl, dj, viii, 215pp. Midwesterner opposed emancipation, afraid of negro migration to North and even lure them back South, against any equality of the negro.

168 **"VOICE from Kentucky, A"**
See: William Coleman.

169 **"VOICE from the South, A"**
Edt: Wm. H. Wroten. In: GaHQ, Oct. 1956, v.40, p.407-410. Reprint: Rocky Mt. News, Denver, Colorado, 2 Jan. 1861. Letter to editor from a Colorado miner, dated Dahlonega, Ga. 3 Dec. 1860, on the proposed secession of Georgia.

"VOICE from the South, A
Comprising Letters from Georgia to Massachusetts, and to the Southern States. With an Append, containing an article from from the Charleston Mercury on the

Wilmot Proviso, together with the 4th Article of the Constitution, the Law of Congress, the Nullification Law of Pennsylvania, the Resolution of Ten of the Free States, Resolutions of Virginia, Georgia and Alabama, Mr. Calhoun's Resolutions in the U.S. Senate." Baltimore: Western Continent Press, 1847, 8vo, wraps, 72pp. (De Renne-11, 514pp. and attributes to Augustus Baldwin Longstreet. $200.

170 **VOLCK, Adalbert Johann**
...A Southern artist on the Civil War." In: Amer. Hertige, Oct. 1958, v.9, #6, p.117-120. Reproductions of 10 Confederate etchings by the Baltimore dentist.

171 **VOLCK, Adelbert J.**
"Confederate War Etchings." (Baltimore?, 1862.) 12x9", complete set 30 etchings and not to be confused with later reprint on thin paper, mounted on cardboard, with printed titles. Printed for private distribution and plates shipped to England, left with De la Rue and Co. of London. LC states 29 plates, Halstead in The Cosmopolitan (Aug. 1890) said only 23, that he was an agent of CSA, ran blockade to get sketches, finally arrested and sent to Ft. McHenry. (Henkel-#1090, May 1913).
...(Baltimore?, 1863?) 8x10 1/2", India paper, mounted on cardboard. 29 plates and "Index" leaf.
..."Confederate War Etchings." (Phila., 1880-1890?) Reissue of the '63 suppressed edt., 100 sets of 29 plates (complete for this issue) Index. $230. Printed on India paper, mounted on heavy white paper, 15x11 1/2". Index leaf in dark red ink. The engraved plate-Worship in the North (9 11x16x7") Portfolio boards cloth back and ties. Phila: (Porter and Coates, 1880-1894) bought plates and printed the edition from them. Some plates have been renumbered. The t.p., 1st Edt. "Sketches from the Civil War in North America, 1861, 1862, 1863 by V. Blada, London, 1863. Four or five sets have been located of this edition. $230, $375.

172 ..."Sketches from the Civil War in North America, 1861, 1862, 1863", by V. Blada, London, 1863. 4to, series of 45 sketches, chiefly in the CSA Army, really pub. in Baltimore and only 12 copies struck off for friends and plates destroyed, for fear of exposing artist, a German dentist in Baltimore. Sabin-#5709.
...Tarrytown, 1917. Extra #60, Magazine of History. 8vo, wraps, 24pp., 30-plates. (See also-Jas. F. McLaughlin, Alison Bishop.)

173 ..."Lincoln and Butler as Don Quixote and Sancho Panza-(untitled)." Etching 9 1/2x12 (incl. margins) Gdsp-(March 1962 in "The Month". Separate etchings from "Great American Tragedians, etc."

174 ..."Lincoln in Cap and Bells, with puppets-untitled." In the final etching this has the series title: "Great American Tragedians." with pencil notation: "Lincoln's "Nobody Hurt, 1861." no doubt in ref. Lincoln made before taking office: "nobody was going to get hurt." The puppets: Union Gov. Thos. H. Hicks of Md., Ben Butler, Gideon Welles, Gen. McClellan, Gen. Fremont and Gen. Scott.

175 ..."Butler as Antony Van Corlear, the man who blew his own trumpet." (title in pencil) Inscribed to Phoebe Elliot.

176 ..."Butler as Blondin Surveying his Conquest at Hatteras." (titled in pencil). Butler captured the fort in Aug., 1861.

177 ..."Jim Lane as Mephistopheles." (titled in pencil) Probably Jno. Lane of Kan.

178 ..."General John C. Fremont." (untitled) Fremont standing on a barrel "Proclamation" (label) Re his independent and premature emancipation proclamation. Goodspeed notes Volck, a Bavarian-born dentist with strong Southern sympathies,

with a gift at satirical etchings... signed them "V. Blada", as a cover since he lived in Baltimore, where a large element were in sympathy with the CSA. The best known were "Conf. War Etchings" (above) greatest rarity being those separates listed last. See: "The Month at Goodspeeds, Mar. 1962, v.33(6).

179 ..."Ye Exploits of ye distinguished Attorney and Gen. B.F.B. (Bombastes Furioso Buncombe) A Series of Pen and Ink Sketches to be continued and most respectfully Dedicated to the "American Napoleon", by his admirer and humble servant, the Author." (Baltimore, 1861?) Series- 6 satirical cartoons, 10 3/4x7", loose, blue printed wraps with single sheet "Explanation of ye Prints". Satire of B.F. Butler, much rarer than above set. Sabin-9619 calls for only 2 plates, no ment. of expl. sheet.

180 **"VOLUNTEER Waltz, The**
Composed by Chas. Young, New Orleans: Blackmar. Reissue of Crandall-3931 with 1863, as copyright first page music, the publisher: Louis Grunewald, 5pp. rear cover ads.

181 **"VOLUNTEERS Wanted!"**
Broadside: 18 1/2"x12", n.p. Oct. 8, 1861. Signed: Jerry Hollis. "Fellow soldiers of South Ark.: the Civil War is now fully upon us, etc. In my opinion, the time has come when our beloved South calls upon everyone. I will be at Hampton on the 15th Inst. Vols. of Ouachita Co. will be received at Camden." (Ark. Hist. Comm.)

182 **VON ABELE, Rudolph Radama**
"Alexander H. Stephens, a Biography." N.Y., Alfred A. Knopf, 1946. 8vo, cl, front, pl., ports, xiii, 337, x, pp. $20.
...Westport, Conn., 1974 ($18.25-y) Greenwood Press, reprint.
...N.Y., Negro Universities Press, (1972) Reprint.

183 **"VON ACHTEN der Letzte (Of Eight the Last)**
Amerikanische Kriegsbilder aus der Sudarmee des Gen. R.E. Lee." Phila: Schafer and Koradi; Wiesbaden: J. Niedner, 1871. 12mo, cl, viii, 1, (1), 276pp. Washington Artillery.

184 **VON DER AU, Margaret L.**
"Virginia's contribution to the Confederacy. Character of Va. previous to the war- institution of slavery." In: CV, Feb. 1915, v.23, #2, p.65-71.

185 **VON KOLNITZ, Alfred Harry**
"The Confederate submarine." In: USN Inst. Proc., 1937, v.LXIII, p.1453-1457. Clarifies some discrepancies re the sub operating off Charleston in winter of 1863-1864.

186 ..."A panorama of three centuries of history viewed from Charleston's famous battery with a description of the guns and monument Charleston: The Historical Commission of the City of Charleston, (1937)." 8vo, pict. wraps, illus.

186a **VOORHEES, Daniel Wolsey, Hon., of Indiana**
"The plunder of eleven states by the Republican Party. Speech of...delivered in the House of Representatives March. 8vo, sewed, 15pp. (not LC) Appeals to North to quit subjugation of the South & send the plunderers home.

187 **VOORHIES, Albert**
"On Conf. Currency & defacto government New Orleans, 1868. 8vo, wraps, cov. title, 15pp. Was justice of the Supreme Court.

188 **VORIS, Alvin C.**
"Charleston in the Rebellion. A paper read before the Ohio Loyal Legion, Mar. 7, 1889." Cincinnati, 1888. 8vo, wraps, 49pp. Splendid pix of Charleston, S.C. in war-days.

W

1 **WAAL, Carla**
"The First original Confederate drams." In: VMHB, Oct. 1962, v.70, #4, p.459-467.

2 **WADDELL, Alfred Moore, Hon.**
"The Confederate Soldier, an address delivered at the written request of 5000 ex-Union Soldiers, at Steinway Hall, N.Y. City. Friday evening, May 3, 1878, for the benefit of the 47th N.Y. Veteran Volunteers (Miles O'Reilly's Regiment)." Washington, D.C., Joseph L. Pearson, 1878, 8vo, wraps, 23pp. Dornbusch-III, 1099. See: Seaton Gales' sketch of G. B. Anderson.

3 ..."General George Burgwyn Anderson, an address by A.M. Waddell." In: SHSP, 1886, v.XIV, p.387-397.

4 ..."The Last Year of the War in North Carolina, including Plymouth, Fort Fisher and Bentonsville. An address before the Association Army of Northern Virginia, delivered in the Hall of the House of Delegates, Richmond, Va., Oct. 28, 1887." Richmond, Va., Wm. Ellis Jones Pr., 1888, 8vo, wraps, 31pp. $85.

5 ..."Life and Character of W.L. Saunders." In: SHSP, 1892, v.XX, p.212-225. Reprinted from: Wilmington, N.C., Jackson and Bell, 1892. 8vo, wraps, 15pp.

6 ..."Some Memories of My Life, 1907." Raleigh, N.C., Edwards and Broughton, 1908, 8vo, cl, front(port), 249pp. index, $45, $100. Wilmington, N.C., during war and a chap. Reconstruction.

7 **WADDELL, I.W., Col., 20th Reg. Ga. Vols.**
"Official Report of Gettysburg." In: SHSP, 1885, v.13, p.199-201.

7a **WADDELL, James A.**
"Uncle Tom's Cabin," reviewed; or American society vindicated from the espersions of Mrs. Harriet Beecher Stowe, by James A. Waddell, Raleigh, N.C., Weekly Post, 1852. 12mo, wraps, iv, (5)-68, (2)pp.

8 **WADDELL, James D., Edt.**
"Biographical sketch of Linton Stephens, (late associate justice of the Supreme Court of Georgia) containing a selection of his letters, speeches, state papers, etc...Edited by James D. Waddell." Atlanta, Ga., Dodson and Scott, 1877. 8vo, cl, 3pp., 434pp. (front) port. $100. Largely extracts from letters to his half-brother, Alexander. See: Linton Stephens.

9 **WADDELL, Joseph Addison**
"Annals of Augusta County, Virginia, with reminiscences illustrative of the vicissitudes of its pioneer settlers; biographical sketches of citizens locally prominent and of those who have founded families in the Southern and Western states; a diary of the War, 1861-1865, and a chapter on Reconstruction." Richmond, Va., Wm. Ellis Jones, 1886. $100-b. 8vo, cl, front, maps, vii, 374pp.

10 ...Richmond, Va., J.W. Randolph, 1888. 8vo, cl, front, maps, vii, 460pp.
...Do., supplement, ii, (381)-492pp. $75.

11 ..."Annals of Augusta County, Virginia, from 1726 to 1871." 2nd Rev. and enlarg. Staunton, Va., C.R. Caldwell, 1902. Large 8vo, cl, front, fldg. map, x, 545pp. Added material on Staunton, Va., and 4 chapters on the War.
...Bridgewater, Va., C.J. Carrier, 1958. Reprint of 2nd Edt., 1902, p.x, 545.
...Same, reprint, 1972.

12 **WADDELL, Lieutenant Commanding**
"C.S.S. Shenandoah. The Memoirs of Lieutenant Commanding James I. Waddell. Edt: James D. Horan." N.Y., Crown Pub., (1960) 12mo, cl, dj, illus., incl. front, ports., facsms, map liners, (3), 200pp. $20.

...\"The Shenandoah. A sketch of the eventful life of the Confederate Cruiser Captain James Iredell Waddell, address by Capt. S.A. Ashe.\" In: SHSP, 1904, v.XXXII, p.320-328.

13 **WADDILL, J.M.**
"A brave man's sensation in battle." In: B & G, 1894, v.III, p.39-41.

14 **WADE, John C.**
"Some neglected aspects of the American Civil War; recollections of John C. Wade. (recorded by) Robert Douthat Meade." In: Wm. & Mary Quart., 2nd Ser., 1936, v.XVI, p.408-413. (recollections of Wade of Yorktown, Va., given in an interview with Robert Meade.

15 **WADLEY, William M.**
"A Postbellum visit with Robert E. Lee: A Letter. Edt: Marshall Scott Legan." In: Ga.H.Q., Winter, 1973, v.LVII, #4, p.585-587.

16 **WADSWORTH, George**
"Camp McDonald. The school of instruction of the 4th Brigade of Georgia Volunteers, organized June 11, 1861." Atlanta, Ga., Franklin Print, (1861) 12mo, wraps, 29, (3)pp. map. Crandall-2556. Roster of 1st/2nd. Regs., rifle batt., artillery batt., and cadets of Ga. Mil. Inst.

17 **WAGANDT, Charles L.**
"The Army versus Maryland Slavery 1862-1864." In: CWH, June 1964, v.X, #2, p.141-148.

18 **WAGERS, Margaret Newman**
"The Education of a Gentleman Jefferson Davis at Transylvania 1821-1824." Lexington, Ky., Buckley and Reading, 1943. 12mo, cl-bds., front(port) 38, (15)pp. 200 numbered copies.

19 **WAGGAMAN, Eugene, Col., 10th La. Reg.**
"Col. Eugene Waggaman, who led the tenth Louisiana Regiment in the famous charge at Malvern Hill." (New Orleans Picayune, Feb. 10, 1889). In: SHSP, 1897, v.25, p.180-186.

20 **WAGNER Battery-Defense of**
See: H.D.D. Twiggs.

21 **WAGNER, Albert**
"The story of the "Jane Campbell", 1857-1863." In: Nautical Research Jour., Jan. 1951, v.3, p.1-2. Her activity as a CSN blockade-runner.

22 **WAGNER, William F.**
"Letters of William F. Wagner, Confederate Soldier. Edt: Joe M. Hatley and Linda Huffman. Wendell, N.C., Broadfoot, 1983. 8vo, wraps, vi, 103pp., bibliog., index. A Catawba Co., N.C., soldier, served in Co. "E", 57th N.C. Inf., 1862-1864.

23 **"WAIF from Dixie. A,"**
(London) Jour. Confed. Hist. Soc., Summer, 1968, v.6, #2, p.44-48. From: "All the Year Round", #288, v.XII, Oct. 29, 1864. Anon., but edt. was Charles Dickens.

24 **WAITT, Robert W., Jr.**
"Confederate Military Hospitals in Richmond." Richmond: Civil War Cent. Comm., 1964, 8vo, pict-wraps, illus., maps, 40pp. #22. $30.

25 ..."Libby Prison. Richmond, Virginia." Richmond: Civil War Cent. Comm., (Jan. 1962) 8vo, wraps, illus., (6)pp. #12.

..."Libby Prison, Richmond, Va." See: under title.

26 ..."A Tribute from the Richmond Civil War Centennial Committee to those business firms, societies, organizations, churches who have served the public for a century or more." (Richmond, Va., Off. Pub. Richmond Civil War Centennial Committee (1961?) Oct., 8vo, decr. wraps, cover title, (8)pp. #4.

27 **WAITZ, Julia Ellen Le Grand**
"The Journal of Julia Le Grand, 1862-1863." Edt: Kate Mason Rowland and Mrs. Morris L. Croxall. Richmond, Va.,

Everett Waddey Co., 1911. sm. 8vo, cl, front, ports, 318pp. $75-dj.

28 **"WAKE FOREST Student (North Carolina)**
Lee Centennial Memorial Number, Jan. 1907, The." 8vo, pict. wraps, 122pp. Personal memoirs by various Confederates.
Memorial Issue, March 1916, The." 8vo, wraps, 175pp. $15-bmk. Charles Elisha Taylor's war letters (21pp.) covering service with Lee and Jackson.

29 **WAKELYN, Jon L.**
"Biographical Dictionary of the Confederacy." Frank Vandiver, Edt. Westport, Conn: Greenwood Pr., 1977, 8vo, cl, xii, 601pp.

30 ..."The changing loyalties of James Henry Hammond: A Reconsideration." In: SCHM, 1974, v.75, #1, p.1-13.

31 ..."The Politics of a Literary Man: Wm. Gilmore Simms." Contributions in American Studies, #5. Westport, Conn., Greenwood Pr., 1973, 8vo, cl, xiv, 306pp.

32 **WALD, Gustavus H.**
"Judah P. Benjamin (1811-1884)." Harvard Grad. Mag., XXXVI (June) p.538-542. Article written in 1887.

33 **WALDEN, James A.**
"Journal of James A. Walden, Confederate Soldier." Fayetteville, Ark: Washington County Historical Society, 1954. Booklet series #8, op. 4to, soft backs, 84pp.

34 **WALDHAUER, David, Capt.**
"The Affair at Frederick City. A correction of Gen. Johnson's Account." In: SHSP, 1885, v.13, p.417-419. Of: Ga. Hussars, Jeff. Davis Legion, Hampton's Brig., ANV.

35 **WALDO, James Curtis**
"The Roll of Honor. Roster of Citizen Soldiery who served Louisiana." Revised and complete, n.p., n.d. (New Orleans, La., J. Curtis Waldo, 1877) 12mo, wraps, 70pp.

36 **WALDRIP, William I.**
"New Mexico During the Civil War." (Albuquerque, N.M., New Mexico Historical Review) July, 1953, v.XXVIII, #3, p.163-182; #4, p.243-290.

37 **WALDROP, John and William Y. Mordecai**
"Diary of...of 2nd Co., combined." In: "Contributions to a History of the Richmond Howitzers." v.3, p.35-57.

37a **WALKER, Alexander**
"A Prisoner's Own Story." n.p., n.d. ('40s ?) 8vo, wraps, 12pp. $10. Lengthy letter from a prisoner on Ship Island, Miss., to Jeff Davis on rigors of imprisonment by Federals.

38 **WALKER, Arthur L.**
"Three Alabama Baptist Chaplains." In: Ala. Rev., 1963, v.XVI, p.174-184.

39 **WALKER, Carroll H.**
"Colonel Walter H. Taylor (1838-1916). CSA." In: Mil. Collector and Hist., Summer 1960, v.12, p.39-41, ports, notes. 2 photos (1855?) and 1861, as a cadet at VMI, as 1st Lieut. Southern Guard, Norfolk, Co. F., 54th Reg., Va. Militia.

40 ..."The Woodis Rifles-1858-1861." In: Mil. Collec. and Hist., Spring 1959, v.11, p.5-6, port. On a Norfolk of 3rd Bat., 54th Reg., Va. Militia, fought during war as Co. C., 6th Va. Reg., CSA.

41 **WALKER, Charles Duy**
"Biographical sketches of the graduates and eleves of the Virginia Military Institute who fell during the War Between the States by Charles D. Walker, last assistant professor V.M.I." Phila: J.B. Lippincott, 1875. $150, $125. 8vo, cl, or calf, 585pp. errata slip. De Luxe edition. Title head: Virginia Military Institute, Memorial. This copy as: a 9pp. pamphlet insert, muster roll, etc., VMI cadets who took part in the Battle of New Market, May 15, 1864. (Edward R. Turner's "New Market

Cadets", ? Append. J, "Roster of Cadet Battalion" p.163-171?)

42 **WALKER, Charles S., Jr.**
"Causes of the Confederate Invasion of New Mexico." (Albuquerque, N. Mex., Historical Society of New Mexico) April, 1933, v.VIII, #2, p.76-97. To annex the southwest and N. Mex.

43 ..."Confederate Government in Dona Ana County." New Mexico Historical Society, July 1931, v.VI, p.253-302.

44 ..."Confederate Government in Dona Ana County, as shown in the records of the Probate Court, 1861-1862." (Albuquerque) NMHR, July, 1931, v.VI, #3, p.253-302.

45 **WALKER, Charles Whiting**
"Battle of Prairie Grove." In: Pub. Ark. Hist. Assn., v.II, 1908, p.354-361.

46 **WALKER, Cornelius Irvine**
"The Life of Lt.-Gen. Richard Heron Anderson of the Confederate States Army." Charleston, S.C., Art. Pub. Co., (1917) 8vo, cl, front(port) illus., 269pp. $100 Bmk-124. $15, $20, $22.50, $25, $30, $32.50, $150-b.

47 ..."Rolls of the Tenth South Carolina Regiment." Alexandria, Va., Stonewall House, 1985. 8vo, cl, 134pp., (84)pp. re: Sol Emanuel + 40pp. introduction by Jim D. Moody. $25.
..."Rolls and Historical Sketch of the 10th Reg., South Carolina volunteers, in the Army of the Confederate States, by...Late Lt.-Col. of the Regiment." Charleston: Walker, Evans and Cogswell, 1881. $300. 12mo, 138pp., unit roster, p.(9)-65.
..."Rolls & Historical sketch of the 10th Reg. S.C. Vol. + S. Emanuel's Georgetown Rifle Guards." Lexington, Va., Stonewall House, 1985. $24.

48 ..."Speech: reunion of the Division U.C.V., at Chester, S.C., July 26, 1899." In: CV, 1900, v.8, p.26-34. "Devoted South Carolina Confederates."

49 ..."What the World Owes the South for Secession." Charleston, S.C. (c.1917) 12mo, sewn, 20pp.

50 ..."The Women of the Southern Confederacy during the War 1861-1865. Original historic incidents of their heroism, suffering and devotion; published in "Our Women in the War", supplements of leading newspapers in Va., N.C., S.C., Ga., Fla. and Ala., clipped from original publications and arranged under direction of Gen. C. Irvine Walker, under whose general supervision aiding the work form the memorials to the women of the Confederacy, the various supplements were published." Charleston, S.C., (1906?) 4to, cl, illus., ports, (297)pp.
...(Same as above but in) "Tenn., Miss., together with Arkansas Memorial, etc." (same wording) Charleston, S.C. (1908) 4to, mounted newspaper clippings, including "Confederate Women of Ark. in the Civil War 1861-1865." Nov. 1901, p.(50)-188.

50a ..."Historic Charleston: Colonial, Revolutionary & Confederate." Charleston, Southern Print., (1927). 8vo, wraps, (20PP. $20.

50b **WALKER, Gary**
"The war in Southwest Virginia, 1861-1865." Roanoke, Va., Gurtner Graphics, 1985. 8vo, cl, dj, 201pp, ills, ports, maps, index, bibliog. $24. CSA military dep't. of SW Virginia.

51 **WALKER, Georgiana Gholson**
"The Private Journal of Georgiana Gholson Walker, 1862-1865. With Selections from the Post War Years, 1865-1876." Edt: Dwight F. Henderson. Tuscaloosa, Ala: Confed. Pub. Co., 1963. Confederate Centennial Studies, #25. 12mo, stiff wraps, 148pp., port. Lim. Edt., 450 copies.

52 **WALKER, Henry L.**
"C.S.S. "Virginia." In: USNIP, Oct. 1952, v.LXX-VIII, p.1143. Misuse of name "Merrimac".

53 **WALKER, James Alexander**
"The Bloody Angle", Confederate disaster at Spotsylvania Court House, May 12, 1864. Gen. Lee to the rear." In: SHSP, 1893, v.XXI, p.228-238.

54 ..."Gettysburg", a report of Brig.-Gen. J.A. Walker, Aug. 17, 1863." In: SHSP, 1880, v.VIII, p.169-170.

55 ..."Gordon's Assault on Fort Stedman, Mar. 25, 1865-brilliant achievement." In: SHSP, 1903, v.XXXI, p.19-31.

56 ..."Operations around Winchester in 1863, report of Gen. J.A. Walker." In: SHSP, 1881, v.IX, p.325-330.

57 ..."Oration at unveiling of a statue of Lt.-Gen. A.P. Hill, in Richmond, Va., 1892." In: SHSP, 1892, v.XX, p.369-386. Reprint: Wytheville, Va., n.d., 8vo, wraps, 24pp.

58 **WALKER, James H.**
"The charge of Pickett's division." In: B & G, 1893, v.1, p.221-223, port.

59 **WALKER, Jeanie Mort**
"Life of Capt. Joseph Fry, the Cuban martyr. Being a faithful record of his remarkable career from childhood to the time of his heroic death at the hands of Spanish executioners; recounting his experience as an officer in the U.S. and Confederate navies, and reveling much of the inner history and secret marine service of the late civil war in America." Hartford, The J.B. Burr Pub., 1875. 12mo, cl, front, pls., ports, 589pp. Same: 1877. Commanded the C.S.S. Morgan.

60 **WALKER, John George, Brig.-Gen.**
"Harper's Ferry and Sharpsburg." In: Cent. June, 1886, ns-X, p.298-308, ports, illus.

61 ..."Jackson's Capture of Harper's Ferry." In: B & L, II, p.604-611.

62 ..."Report of Brig.-Gen. Walker on the Battle of Sharpsburg." In: OLOD, 1874-1875, v.I, p.225-228.

63 ..."Sharpsburg." In: B & L, v.II, p.675-682.

64 **WALKER, M.V., Mrs.**
"The Causes Which Led to Civil War." Fort Worth, Texas, 1919. 12mo, stiff wraps (color flags) port (front) 23pp., (1)p-notes.

65 **WALKER, Noah Dixon**
"Lieut. Noah Dixon Walker to his father Noah Walker." In: MdHM, 1935, v.XXX, p.363-367. Letter Feb. 10, 1863 from Port Royal by Lt. W. Walker, of the Va. Inf., telling exp. of war.

66 **WALKER, Peter Franklin**
"Building a Tennessee Army: Autumn 1861." In: THQ, June 1957, v.XVI, p.99-116. Also: Separate, wraps, 18pp. $8.

67 ..."Citadel: Vicksburg and its People, 1860-1865." Ann Arbor, Mich., University Microfilms 1958 (e.g., 1959). 4to, positive microfilm of typescript, x, 378 leaves, bibliog., Vanderbilt Univ., Abstracted: Dissert, abstracts, 19:3293. June. (Write. Amer. Hist., 1959)

68 ..."Command Failure: The Fall of Forts Henry and Donelson (1862)." In: THQ, Dec. 1957, v.XVI, p.335-360, notes.

69 ..."Holding the Tennessee Line: Winter 1861-1862." In: THQ, Sept. 1957, v.XVI, p.228-249, notes.

70 ..."Vicksburg: a People at War, 1860-1865." Chapel Hill: Univ. North Carolina Press, (1960) 8vo, cl, dj, map, views (1-dble.), xvi, 235pp., notes, bibliog. Thesis, Vanderbilt, 1958.

71 **WALKER, Reuben Lindsay, Col.**
"Report: Battle of Gettysburg." In: SHSP, 1880, v.8, p.427-429. Chief of artillery, 3rd. Corp. ANV.

72 **WALKER, Robert**
"Peripatetic Coffin." In: So. Atlantic Quart., 1940, v.XXXIX, p.438-447. Ac-

tivities of CS submarine "H.L. Hunley", 1864.

73 **WALKER, Robert James**
"American Slavery and Finances." London: W. Ridgway, 1864. 12mo, wraps, 9 pamphlets bound in one vol., 3rd Edt., with appendix. Contrasts CSA and US finances.

74 ..."Jefferson Davis. Repudiation, recognition and slavery. Letters of Hon. Robert J. Walker." London: W. Ridgway, 1863. 2 vols. in one. 12mo, 70pp. (3rd edt.) 12pp. Letter #II.
..."Jefferson Davis. Repudiation of Arkansas Bonds." Letter #3. London: W. Ridgway, 1864. 12mo, sewn, 14pp.

75 **WALKER, Robert M.**
"Marines in Gray: The Forgotten Service of the Confederacy." In: CWT, Aug. 1960, v.2, #5, p.16-17.

76 **WALKER, Robert Sparks**
"Kidnapping the General." In: Ga. Rev., Spring, 1949, v.3, p.70-79. Jas. J. Andrews attempt to steal a CSA Ry. train, but intercepted by the CSAs, Apr. 11, 1862.

77 **WALKER, Sue H.**
"A Confederation of Southern Memorial Associations." In: SHSP, 1900, v.28, p.377-384.

78 **WALKER, T.R.**
"Rock Island Prison Barracks." In: CWH, June, 1962, v.VIII, #2, p.152-163.

79 **WALKER, Thaddeus James**
"Reminiscences of Point Lookout." In: B & G, 1894, v.III, p.59-60.

80 ..."Scouting in the Shenandoah Valley." In: B & G, 1893, v.II, p.449-450.

81 ..."A romantic incident in the war in the death of Col. Ulric Dahlgren." In: B & G, 1894, v.III, p.330-332, port.

82 **WALKER, W.H.S.**
"Honor to W.H.T. Walker. (Georgia)" In: CV, 1902, v.10, p.402-407, port, illus.

83 **WALKER, William**
"The Case of the South against the North, by B.F. Grady-a Review by..." In: SHSP, 1900, v.28, p.56-66.

84 **WALKER, William Stephen**
See: Joseph Eggleston Johnston.

85 **WALKER, Willis H.**
"In service for the old South." In: Aerend 1931, v.II, p.109-122. Letters dated May 18-July 27, 1862. Dornb-II, 3148.

86 **"WALL PAPER NEWS of the sixties."**
Wash. D.C., National Park Service Popular Study Series, History #3, GPO, 1941, Vicksburg, Miss. 8vo, wraps, 13pp. On the famous Vicksburg newspapers, printed on wall paper.

87 **WALL PAPER NEWSPAPERS in the Confederacy.**
See Clarence S. Brigham's "Bibliographica Essays: a Tribute to Wilberforce Eames." Briefly paper was so scarce newspapers were printed on wall paper. Mostly in Louisiana and Mississippi, since no paper mills operated there. Even so, most of extant examples are reproductions, e.g., Vicksburg Daily Citizen." For a genuine example, see Thibodaux (La.) Sentinel.

88 **WALL, Bernardt**
"Gen. Robert E. Lee. A Short Pictorial Biography." 37 original miniature etched plates (both text and illus.) small 4to, bds., d/j, Sierra Madre, Calif., 1949, 100 copies, signed, "personal".

89 **WALL, Henry Clay**
"Historical Sketch of the Pee Dee Guards (Co. D, 23rd. N.C. Regiment), from 1861 to 1865." Raleigh, N.C., Edward, Broughton Co., 1876. 12mo, wraps, 100pp. $275-ob. Gaithersburg, Md., Butternut Press, 1985.
..."The 23rd North Carolina Infantry organized in 1861, as the 13th Regiment of

volunteers, historical sketch." In: SHSP, 1897, v.XXV, p.151-176.

90 **WALL, Joseph Frazier**
"Henry Watterson: Reconstruction Rebel." N.Y., Oxford University Press, 1956, 8vo, cl, dj, illus., bibliog., xvi, 350pp.

91 **WALLACE, C.M.**
"The Light Dragoons, recollections of a celebrated military command." In: SHSP, 1901, v.29, p.366-368. The Roll, 368-371.

92 **WALLACE, David Duncan**
"History of South Carolina." 4 vols. N.Y., American Historical Society, 1934. "The War of Secession, 1861-1865." p.151-222, port, illus. (7). "Reconstruction, 1865-1876." p.222-322. "Waiting for the South, 1852-1860." p.133-150. ("Futile efforts at secession, 1847-1852)

93 **WALLACE, David R., Mrs.**
"An 1864 letter to Mrs. Rufus C. Burleson. Contributed by Merle Mears Duncan." In: SwHQ, Jan. 1961, v.LXIV, #3, p.369-372.

94 **WALLACE, Elizabeth Curtis**
"Glencoe Diary. The War-Time Journal of Elizabeth Curtis Wallace. Edt: by Eleanor P. Cross and Chas. B. Cross, Jr." Chesapeake, Va., Norfolk County Historical Society, 1968. sm.4to, decr. wraps, ports, illus., facsms., maps, 157pp., index. Wendell, N.C., Broadfoot, 1983, cl. (500 copies) $20.

95 **WALLACE, Ernest**
"Texas in Turmoil: The Saga of Texas 1849-1875." Austin, Texas: Steck-Vaugh Co., 1965. 12mo, cl, vii, 293pp.

96 **WALLACE, George Selden**
"Cabell County Annals and Families." Richmond, Va., Garrett and Massie, 1935, illus., 589pp. Narrative military activities in county, p.77-90, 316-321. Huntington Vets., Muster Roll Border Rangers (Co. E, 8th Va. Cav.) Shetler-818.

97 **WALLACE, John H., Jr.**
"The Blue and the Gray; extracts from the address at Daphne, Alabama, July 3, 1909." Montgomery, Ala., Brown Print, 1909. 8vo, wraps, p.

98 **WALLACE, Katie Darling**
"Child of Glencoe-Civil War Journal of Katie Darling Wallace." Chesapeake, Va., Norfolk Historical Society, 1983. 8vo, stiff wraps, (ill. on cover) 110, (5)pp. index, facsm., map, ports.

99 **WALLACE, Lee A., Jr.**
"The Alexandria Militia." (Richmond) Va. Cavl., Winter 1967, v.XVI, #3, p.12-21, illus., ports, 2pp. colored military uniforms. Volunteer military companies were an important part in community affairs.

100 ..."Lt. Francis Hawkes Cameron, Confederate States Marine Corps." In: Mil. Coll. and Hist., Sept. 1954, v.6, #3, port., p.79, notes. Carte de Visit port descp.

101 ..."Coppen's Louisiana Zouaves." In: CWH, September 1962, v.VIII, #3, p.269-282.

102 ..."Drum Major's baldric, First Virginia Regiment, CSA." In: Mil. Col. and Hist., 1953, v.V, illus., p.52-53.
..."The First Regiment of Virginia Volunteers." (Richmond) Va. Cavl., Autumn 1963, v.XIII, #2, p.23-31, ports, facsm., illus. (2-color pls.)

103 ..."The Great Cavalry Encampment of 1860." (Richmond) Va. Cavl., Winter 1970, v.XIX, #3, p.14-21, illus., ports.

104 ..."A Guide to Virginia Military Organizations 1861-1865." Richmond, Virginia Civil War Commissions, 1964. 4to, wraps, frontis, 348pp., index, 44pp. cloth-$125, $75-op.
..."A guide to Virginia Military Organizations, Lynchburg, Va., 1986." Revised edition with new introduction and index. 8vo, cl, dj., $25.

105 …"The C.S. Marine Corps Officers Uniforms." In: Mil. Coll. and Hist., Summer 1971, v.XXIII, #2, p.51-53.

106 …"Musters at Poplar Lawn." (Richmond) Va. Cavl., Winter 1968, v.XVII, #3, p.4-10, illus., ports. Before Civil War, Petersburg militiamen used city park as training ground.

107 …"Sussex light dragoons, Virginia state cavalry, 1861." In: Mil. Coll/Hist., 1955, v.VII, p.22, col. pl, illus.

108 …and Detmar H. Finke. "Virginia Military forces, 1858-1861. The Volunteers of 2nd Brig., 4th Div." In: MC and H, v.X, 1958, p.61-70, 95-101, illus.

108a …"1st Virginia Infantry." Lynchburg, Va., H.E. Howard, 1985. (J.P. Bell Print) Lim-.Atg.Edt. 8vo, cl, dj, (3), 128pp, ills, tables, maps, ports. $17.50.

108b …"3rd Virginia Infantry." Lynchburg, Va., H.E. Howard, 1986. 8vo, cl, dj, (5), 117p, maps, ports. 1,000 copies, signed.

108c …"5th Virginia Infantry." Lynchburg, Va., H.E. Howard, 1988. 8vo, cl, dj, (5), 180pp, ports (incl. groups) maps. 1,000 (#385) copies, atg.

109 **WALLACE, S.L.**
"Address on Lee." Baltimore, 1875, 8vo, wraps, 12pp.

110 **WALLACE, Sarah Agnes, Edt.**
"Confederate exiles in Canada: last letters of James Brown Clay, 1864, Montreal." In: KyHSR, Jan. 1952, v.50, p.41-56. Letters from, to, and about a son of Henry Clay, 1863-1864.

111 …"Confederate Exiles in London, 1865-1870." (Charleston: So. Caro., Hist. Genea. Mag., (Apr.-Oct.) 1951, v.LII, p.74-87; 143-153; p.198-206. From Gen. Louis Trezevant Wigfall to daughter Louis, later Mrs. D. Giraud Wright; his mother Frances M. Cross and his wife Charlotte, son Halsey. See also: Mrs. D. Giraud Wright.

112 **WALLACE, William H.**
"The kid soldiers of the sixties…" Newberry, S.C., 1915. 8vo, wraps, cover title, 15, iv, p. ports. "reprinted from the Newberry "Observer" addenda, ivp. Dorn-II, 3149.

113 …"Operations of second South Carolina Regiment in Campaign of 1864 and 1865." In: SHSP, 1879, v.7, p.128-131.

114 **WALLENSTEIN, Peter**
"Rich man's war, rich man's fight: Civil War and the transformation of public finance in Ga." In: Journal of Southern History, 1984, v.L, p.15-42.

115 **WALLER, George Platt**
"Address delivered at Oakwood Cemetery, Montgomery, Ala., on Confederate Memorial Day, Apr. 26, 1952." In: AlaHQ, v.14, p.99-107. Defends right of secession in '61.

115a **WALLER, James Breckinridge**
"The true doctrine of state rights, with an examination of the record of the Democratic & Republican parties in connection with slavery." Chicago: Jameson & Morse Pr., 1880. 8vo, wraps, 83pp.

116 **WALLER, John L.**
"The Civil War in the El Paso Area." In: WTHAYB, v.XXII, p.3-14.

117 **WALLER, John O.**
"Charles Kingsley and the American Civil War (Confederate Sympathizer in England)." In: Studies in Philology, 1963, v.LX, p.554-568.

118 **WALLER, Sarah Bell, Mrs.**
"Announcement of her death." In: SHSP, 1884, v.12, p.143.

119 **WALLER, W.G.**
"The last of the Confederates." In: Mag. Amer. Hist., June 1886, p.596-611. With W.H. Swallow's "Retreat of the Confed." Gov., from Richmond to the Gulf."

120 **WALLIS, Severn Teackle**
"Reply to the Letter of Hon. John Sherman." (Baltimore, Jan. 3, 1863) 8vo, wraps,

19pp. (Henkel-1090, May 1913) Issued by officers of 1st Maryland Inf., prefatory notes "true position assumed by States Rights party in Md., when Legislative proceedings rudely terminated by the arbitrary and tyrannical arrest, imprisonment of members of legislature."

121 ..."Correspondence between S. Teackle Wallis and Hon. John Sherman, of the U.S. Senate, concerning the arrest of members of the Maryland Legislature and the Mayor and Police Commissioners of Baltimore, 1861." Published by officers of the 1st. Maryland Inf., Baltimore, 1863. 8vo, wraps, cover title, 1, 31pp.

122 ..."Address delivered at Academy of Music, Baltimore, April 10, 1875, on behalf of the Lee Memorial Association." (Baltimore: J. Murphy and Co., 1875) 8vo, wraps, cover title, 12pp. Swem-6220.

123 ..."An Eloquent and Timely Address." Extract from a speech for erection of a statue to Lee. In: OLOD, June 1875, v.2, #4, p.412-419.

124 **WALLS That Talk;** a transcript of the names, initials and sentiments written and graven on the walls, doors and windows of the Libby Prison at Richmond, by the prisoners of 1861-1865." Richmond: Pub. by R.E. Lee Camp #1, Confed. Vets., 1884. (Richmond: Pub. by R.E. Lee Camp #1, Confed. Vets., 1884. (Richmond: Republished by J.W. Randolph and English, 1889) 12mo, wraps, 19pp.

125 **WALMSLEY, James Elliott** "The Last Meeting of the Confederate Cabinet. A paper read at the 12th Annual meeting of the Mississippi Valley Historical Association, May 9, 1919-Rock Hill, South Carolina, Winthrop College, 1919." Winthrop Normal and Industrial College of South Carolina, Bul., v.12, #4, pt. 2, June 1919, wraps, 8vo, 14pp.

...In: Mississippi Valley Historical Review, VI (Dec.) p.336-349.

126 ..."The change of secession sentiment in Virginia in 1861." In: Am. Hist. Rev., Oct., 1925, v.XXXI, p.82-101. Letters written by Judge Edward C. Burks and Bishop Jas. H. Otey, showing change from opposition to secession to accept in 1861.

127 **WALSH, Maurice (pseud: Mon Myrtle?)** "Under the Stars and Bars, or, wearing of the Gray. A thrilling story of Tennessee." N.Y., Novelist Pub., 1883. Pocket Edt. #3, "War Library." 4to, wraps, 96pp.

128 **WALSH, Paul P.** "The seal of the South." In: So. Atl. Quart., 1939, v.XXXVIII, p.392-402. Brief hist. CSA seal, lost 1865, found c.1912.

129 **WALSHE, B.T., Capt.** "Distinguished Dead of the Louisiana Division Army of Northern Virginia." In: SHSP, 1898, v.26, p.377-380.

130 **WALTER, R.S.** "A Ride for Life at Gettysburg." N.Y., A.T. De LaMare Print, 1896, 12mo, wraps (illus. of Lee), 101pp. Poetry.

131 **WALTER, William J.** "A Louisiana volunteer, letters of Wm. J. Walter, 1861-1862." Edt: Edwin A. Davis. Southwest Review: v.19-Oct. 1933, p.78-87; v.20-(1925), p.292-302.

132 **WALTERS, Helen B.** "Confederates in southern California." In: Hist. Soc. South. Calif. Quart., Mar. 1953, v.35, p.41-54, notes, bibliog.

133 **WALTERS, John Bennett** "General William T. Sherman and Total War." (Baton Rouge, La.) JSH, Nov. 1948, v.XIV, #4, p.447-480. $8.

134 **WALTHALL, Edward Cary** "Address: The Confederate Dead of Mississippi." In: SHSP, 1890, v.18, p.282-312-318.

..."Address of E.C. Walthall, delivered at dedication of monument to Confederate dead." Jackson, Miss., June 3, 1891. 8vo, wraps, 19pp.

135 ..."Memorial addresses on the life and character of..., (late senator from Miss.) delivered in the Senate and House of Representatives, 55th Congress, second and third sessions." Washington, D.C., GPO, 1899, 8vo, cl, port., 154pp.

136 ..."Organization of E.C. Walthall, Mississippi Brigade." Memphis, Tenn., 1901, 8vo, wraps, 12pp., cover title-"Gen. E.C. Walthall's Mississippi Brigade." Brig. Gen. CSA, Senator from Miss.

137 ..."Report: Operations about Lookout Mountain." In: SHSP, 1880, v.8, p.275-280.

138 ..."General Walthall." In: Illinois Cent. Mag., Feb. 1916, v.iv, #8, p.9-13, port. See also: E.T. Sykes-"Walthall's Brig.", Ed. A. Smith.

139 **WALTHALL, Ernest Taylor**
"Hidden things brought to light. By author Family history, evacuation day, 60 years in a city, a youth's travels, the business bridge, how capitol square has looked." Richmond, Va., Walthall Print, 1908, 12mo, cl, port, pls., 48pp.
...Reprint, 1933, edt. of 375 copies in slipcase.

140 **WALTHALL, William T.**
"Jefferson Davis. A Sketch of the Life and character of the president of the Confederate States. Presented to the public school children of Louisiana and Mississippi on the Davis Centennial, June 3, 1908, by the..." New Orleans: Times-Democrat, 1908, 8vo, wraps, p.53.

141 ..."The True Story of the Capture of Jefferson Davis." In: SHSP, 1878, v.V, p.97-126.

142 **WALTON, Buck, Major**
"An Epitome of My Life. Civil War Reminiscences." Austin, Texas. The Waterloo Press (1965) 8vo, cl, d/w, port, 99pp., 1000 copies. $35-n.

143 **WALTON, Emily Donelson**
"Autobiography." n.p., n.d., 1922? 12mo, wraps, illus., ports, 63pp.
...Do: 1932? 12mo, front(port), illus., 63pp.
...Do: 1934? private print. 12mo, illus., ports, private print, 63pp.

144 **WALTON, James B.**
"Letters (concerning Walton's rank). Causes of Lee's Defeat at Gettysburg." In: SHSP, 1877/1888, v.5, p.47-53.

145 ..."The Washington Artillery (sketches of the history)." In: SHSP, 1877, v.11, p.210-217.

146 **WALTON, Thomas George**
"Sketches of Pioneers of Burke Co. History." (np, 1961?) (Morganton, N.C.) 8vo, wraps, illus., ports, 89pp., p.5-67, written in 1894 for Morganton Herald, first reprinted in 1924 by same. p.68-89, copies from mssc. of Col. Walton and contains Jno. Murphy Walton diary, May 17-Dec. 28, 1864.

147 **WALWORTH, Jeanette Ritchie Hardemann, Mrs.**
"Southern Silhouette." New York: Henry Holt Co., 1887. 12mo, cl, 376pp. Sketches of life on La. and Miss. plantations during the war.

148 **WANDRUS, Harry and Tom Stich**
"Brief notes on the arms brought into the Confederacy by blockade runners, 1861-1865." In: Hobbies, July/Oct., 1950, v.55 (#'s 5-8) views.

149 **"WAR BULLETIN. The"**
Fayetteville, Arkansas, C.S.A., Jan. 9, 1862. #3-Edt: John Henry Brown. 9 1/2x13, yellow paper, 4pp. (Largely on Gen. McCulloch, Price, et al. Fight with Indians. #4, Jan. 22, 1862, green paper, 4pp., vindication of McCollouch, list of CSA generals, list of West Point men. #5, Feb. 4, 1862, gray paper, 4pp. #6, Feb. 15, 1862, green paper. Few copies printed and distributed in each regiment, to be read

150 **"WAR DAYS in Fayetteville N.C.** Reminiscences of 1861-1865." (Fayetteville, N.C., Judge Print. Co.) 1910. Compiled by J.E.B. Stuart Chap. U.D.C., 8vo, pict. wraps, 60pp.

151 **WAR DEPARTMENT: Adj. and Insp.-Gen.** "General Orders from the Adjutant and Inspector-General's Office, Confederate States Army, from Jan. 1, 1862, to June 30, 1864." Columbia: Evans and Cogswell, 1864. Copy has general t.p., for whole series and independent titles for each portion. 12mo, Mor., 576pp., indexed. Differs with Crandall-1345 (196pp.). Henkels-#1090, May, 1913 auction.

152 **WAR DEPARTMENT: Quartermaster General Circular.** (Regulations for Pay Dept., that acceptance of appointment, renders service) (Richmond, Va., Feb. 19, 1862.) 8vo, (1)p. (Parke-Bernet-#2698, May, 1968)

152a **WAR FINANCE:** A Plan proposing to meet the Governmental expenditure during the war, upon a cotton basis, while the crop remains unsold & left upon the plantations of the South." 8vo, wraps, 15pp. Yates Snowden's note: "This pamphlet is signed "J" & the owner of the copy writes 'By Edward C. Jones, Architect.'"

153 **"WAR Letters."** In: TylerQHGM, 1933, v.XIV, p.145-150. Three Virginia letters, 1861, 1862, and 1864.

154 **"WAR Lyrics and Songs of the South."** London: Spottiswoode and Co., 1866. 16mo, cl, ix, 261pp. Many Ky. writers, compiled there? The proceeds supposed to have gone to crippled CSA soldiers. See: "War Lyrics and Songs of the South." By "Kentucky." (listed on half-title)

154a **WAR Papers of the Confederacy."** Charlottesville, Va., 1961. Pict. wraps, ill., 28pp. $15-bmk-106.

155 **"WAR Poetry of the South."** In: LWL, May 1867, v.III, #1, p.71-74. Poets, e.g., Hayne, Simms, DeLeon, Cooke, etc.

156 **"WAR Poets of the South and Confed. Camp-fire Songs."** See: Charles W. Hubner.

157 **"WAR Recollections** of the Confederate Veterans of Pittsylvania County, Virginia, 1861-1865. Compiled by The Rayley Martin Chapter, Virginia Division U.D.C. Mrs. Kathryne Hobson Powell, President, Mrs. Maude Carter Clement, Historian." (Danville, Va., J.T. Townes Print, 1960?) 8vo, stiff wraps, ports, pl, facsm., 84pp.

158 **"WAR Reminiscences of Columbus,** Mississippi and elsewhere 1861-1865. Compiled by Columbus Chapter U.D.C. Stephen D. Lee Chapter #34." West Point, Miss., Sullivan's Print, 1961. 8vo, stiff wraps, illus., 33pp. $20.

159 **"WAR Scenes, Views and Pointers** of the W. & A.R.R. (Western and Atlantic) and Nashville, Chattanooga and St. Louis RRy." Sm.40, wraps, cover title, battle scenes, illus., map-back cover, dble-pg. RR map. 24pp.

159a **WAR Ships for the Southern Confederacy;** Report of Public Meeting in Free-Trade Hall, Manchester." (England). Manchester, 1863. 8vo, wraps, 36pp.

160 **"WAR Songs of the Blue and the Gray,** as sung by the brave soldiers of the Union and Confederate Armies in camp, on the march and in garrison; with preface by Prof. Henry L. Williams." N.Y., Hurst and

(continued from previous: and passed around. These copies are only known and from John H. Brown's personal collection.)

Co., (1905) 12mo, cl, front, 3-215pp. added t.p., colored borders.

161 **"WAR Songs of the South.**
Edited by "Bohemian", correspondent Richmond Dispatch." Richmond: West and Johnston, 1862. 12mo, wraps, 210pp. Poems clipped from newspapers, many well known writers.

162 **"WAR Times Story of Dahlgren's Raid.**
Gallant defense of Richmond by Departmental Battalion." In: SHSP, 1909, v.XXXVII, p.198-202.

163 **"WAR and Its Heroes, Illustrated, The"**
Richmond, Va., Ayres and Wade, 1864, 8vo, wraps, cover title, ports, (1), 17-88. Cover: "1st Series."

164 **"WAR and Its Heroes, The"**
Freeman: "practically a reprint of a series of articles in "The Southern Illustrated News."

165 **"WAR in Missouri, The"**
In: Confederate Annals, Aug., 1883, v.1, #2, p.55-61. The Wilson Creek Fight.

166 **"WAR of 1861-1865, The**
Virginia and The War." Richmond Times-Dispatch and News Leader, (1961). small folio, 40pp., maps, illus., ports.

167 **"WAR of North and South**
from a "Copperhead" stand-point, The. Its causes, (not pretext) and its meaning." N.Y., Sold for author by N.Y. News (1867?) (Tracts for the Times, #1) 8vo, wraps, 16pp.

168 **"WAR of the Rebellion, The**
Compilation of the Official Records of Union and Confederate Armies..." See: "Official Records"

169 **"WAR Officers of the First Regiment Virginia Volunteer Infantry."**
In: SHSP, 1901, v.29, p.364-366.

170 **"WAR Was the Place.**
Centennial Collection of Confederate Soldier's letters, Old Oakbowery, Chambers Co., Ala." See: "Chattahoochee Valley Hist. Society."

171 **"WAR'S HARVEST in the "Debatable Land."**
In: CV, Jan. 1920, v.28, p.13-16. CSA sketch of Shepherdstown during Harper's Ferry siege, Sept. 13-17, 1862.

172 **"WAR-CHESS, or the Game of Battle."**
Richardson and Co., N.Y., (c.1867) A chess game, for two players, complete with figures representing soldiers, Inf., Cav. and artillery, full length figures in silver and bronze, on level plane, cut by a river, with a bridge, a city to defend, etc. Lithographed board, instructions. A deluxe edition, on fine Morocco, with elegant figures. Advertised in W.G. Simms' "War Poetry of the South", 1867 edition (last page).

173 **WARBURTON, Adolphus Frederick, Reporter**
"Trial of the Officers and Crew of the Privateer Savannah, on the charge of Piracy, in the U.S. Circuit Court for the Southern District of N.Y., Hon. Judges Nelson and Shipman, presiding. Reported by A.F. Warburton, stenographer and corrected by the counsel." N.Y., Baker and Godwin, 1862. 8vo, cl, xxii, 385pp. The first CSA privateer to break the blockade (June 2, 1861) made one prize in the day at sea. Mistrial, after 8 days by a hung jury. All the Savannah's officers and crew hailed from N.Y. City.

174 **WARD, Dallas T.**
"The Last Flag of Truce." (Franklinton, N.C.? 1915) 8vo, cover title, illus. (1 in color) incl. ports, 16pp. Carried last flag of truce, sent by Gov. Z.B. Vance to Sherman, the day before he reached Raleigh.

175 **WARD, Durbin, Colonel**
"The Presidential Campaign of 1864 as viewed by a Federal Army Colonel." Edt:

David Lindsey. In: Ga. H.Q., June 1955, v.XXXIX, #2, p.187-192.

176 **WARD, Evelyn D.**
"The Children of Bladensfield, with an essay by Peter Matthiessen." N.Y., A Sand Dune Press Book, the Viking Press, (1978). sq. 8vo, cl, dj, facsms., incl. front endsheets, illus., incl. front, ports, 141pp. Genealogical chart on back endsheet. Reminiscences of life during the war.

177 **WARD, John Elliott**
"Centennial address of John E. Ward, delivered in Savannah May 4th, 1886, at the request of the Chatham Artillery." (n.p., 1886) 8vo, wraps, cover title, 27pp. Atg-$125.

178 **WARD, John K.**
"Skirmish at Sacramento (Ky.): battles of future Generals." In: RKHS, April 1977, v.75, #2, p.79-91.

179 **WARD, John Shirley**
"Did the Federals fight against superior numbers? An historical paper, prepared by John Shirley Ward of Los Angeles, Cal., Nashville, Tenn., Foster and Webb, 1892, 12mo, wraps, title cover, 17pp. Dornb-II, 3151.

180 ..."The Federal and Confederate Armies." In: SHSP, 1892, v.20, p.238-259.

181 ..."Responsibility for the death of prisoners." In: CV, Jan. 1896, v.IV, #1, p.10-14.

181a **WARD, John W.**
"To the Public! "A coward & a Poltroon." Sardis, Mississippi, May 10, 1861. Broadside: 15 x 23 cm (G. Hendershott). 1,500. Unrecorded. Capt. Ward of the Sardis Blues, 12th Miss. Regt., Corinth, May 16, opposed McClellan at Seven Pines. Challenges R. Abernathy to duel.

182 **WARD, Margaret Ketcham**
"Testimony of Margaret Ketcham Ward on Civil War Times in Georgia. Edt: Aaron M. Bloom." In: Ga.H.Q., Sept.-Dec. 1955, #3 and 4, v.XXXIX, p.268-293; 375-401. $12.

..."Testimony of Mrs. George R. Ward before United States Senate Committee on relations between labor & capital at Relay House in Birmingham on Nov. 15, 1883." Birmingham, Ala., 1965. Private Print. Harwell-186 (Tall Cotton).

183 **WARD, W.C., Capt.**
"Incidents and personal experiences on the Battlefield at Gettysburg." In: CV, 1900, v.8, p.345-349. Address May 5, 1900, in Birmingham, Ala., by a Pvt. Co. G., Fourth Alabama Regiment, Law's Brigade.

184 **WARD, Walter**
"Medical Corps of the Confederate Army." In: N.C. Med. Jour., 1965, v.XXVI, p.458-460.

185 **WARDER, T.B. and Jas. M. Catlett**
"The Battle of Young's Branch; or, Manassas Plain, fought July 21, 1861, with maps of the battlefield made by actual survey and various positions of the regiments and artillery companies placed thereon, with an account of the movements in each, procured from the Commanding officer, or, an officer of the regiment, also an account of the battle. Also the battle ground of the 18th July, 1861, with General Beauregard's report of said battle." Richmond: Enquirer Press, 1862. 16mo, wraps, 2-fldg. maps (20x19"), 156, (1)p. Errata. $200, $550.

186 **WARDLE, Arthur C.**
"Some Blockade-Runners of the Civil War." In: American Neptune (April) 1943, Salem, Mass., v.III, #2, p.131-140.

187 ..."Some British-built blockade-runners of the American Civil War." In: Steamboat Bill of Facts, Dec. 1954, v.11, p.77-80, views. Paper read in Liverpool, 1942.

188 **WARE COUNTY, Georgia**
"History of Ware County, Georgia. Spon-

sored by Waycross Woman's Club." Macon, Ga., J.W. Burke Co., 1934. 8vo, cl, illus., maps, xvii, 547pp. Soldiers from Revolution, CSA to War II, p.197-296; biographies, 1824-1890, p.329-531.

189 **WARE, Charles E.**
"The flags of the Confederate armies returned to the men who bore them by the U.S. Gov." (St. Louis, designed, engraved and printed by Buxton and Skinner) 1905. 8vo, wraps, col. illus., (56)pp. Dorn-II, 157. $100-0b. Souvenir presented to the CS Veterans at their reunion, at Louisville, Ky., June 14, 1905, comps: "Cotton Belt Route."

190 **WARE, James W.**
"Indian Territory (during the Civil War)." In: Jour. of West., April, 1978.

191 **WARE, John N.**
"Sharpsburg." In: CV, April 1921, v.XXIX, p.133-135.

192 **WARE, Lowry P.**
"Att.-Gen. Isaac W. Hayne and the South Carolina Executive Council of 1862." In: Pro.SCHA, 1952, p.5-12.

193 **WARE, Sedley Lunch**
"President Davis, Constitutionalist, a Review." (Sewanee, Tenn.?) reprint of April Number Sewanee Review, 1925, v.XXXIII, 8vo, wraps, cover title, 11pp. p.224-232.

194 **WARE, W.H.**
"The Battle of Kelley's Ford, fought March 17, 1863, written by W.H. Ware, Co. "D", 3rd Virginia Cavalry." Newport News, Va., Warwick Print (1922). Tall 8vo, stiff covers, 11pp. $100-ob. Medical insp., ANV, early life before and during the War.

195 **WARFIELD, Edgar**
"A Confederate soldier's memoirs, by..., member and co-organizer of the "Old Dominion" rifles of Alexandria, later Co. H., Seventeenth Virginia Infantry." Richmond: Masonic Home Press, 1936, Edt: Mr. Otton Wilson. $250-ob, $200. Private edt. of 100 copies. 8vo, port(front), cl, 238pp.

196 **WARING, Malvina Sara, (Mrs. Clark)**
"One Old Reb." Columbia, S.C., State Co., 1929. 12mo, cl, 281pp. $40. See: Elizabeth Waring McMaster, "Girls of the Sixties."

197 **WARING, Martha Gallaudet and Mary Alston**
"Some Observations of the Years 1860 and 1861, as revealed in a packet of old letters." In: GaHQ, Sept. 1931, v.XV, p.272-292.

198 **WARING, Mary**
"Miss. Waring's Journal." Edt: Thad Holt. See: under Holt. Also: "Mobile in 1861-1865."

199 **WARINNER, Napoleon E., Compl.**
"A register of Military Events in Virginia 1861-1865." Richmond: Virginia Civil War Centennial Commission, 1959. 8vo, wraps, 79pp. Alphabetical listing of military events in Va., cross-ref. to "Official Records."

200 **WARLEY, R.L.**
"Letter from General Seymour." In: SHSP, 1882, v.10, p.238-239.

201 **WARMOTH, Henry Clay**
"War, Politics and Reconstruction. Stormy Days in Louisiana." New York: Macmillan Co., 1930. $40. 8vo, cl, port(front) xii, 285pp.
...Westport, Conn., Negro Univ. Pr., 1974.

201a **WARNEFORD, R. N., Lieut.**
"Running the Blockade. Never before published." London, 1863. 16mo, boards, 315pp. Cdsp. $200.

202 **WARNER, Charles Dudley**
"Lee's Birthday." In: SHSP, 1889, v.17, p.350.

203 **WARNER, Charles H., Capt.**
"Capt. Gibbs' Co., CSA, Civil War letters."

In: Indp. Co. (Ark.) Chron., 1961, v.II, p.46-56.

204 **WARNER, Ezra J. and W. Buck Yearns**
"Biographical Register of the Confederate Congress." Baton Rouge: La. State Univ. Press, 1975. 8vo, cl, dj, append-bibliog., xxii, 319pp. Facsm., illus., ports.

205 ..."Generals in Gray. Lives of Confederate Commanders." Baton Rouge: Louisiana State University Press, (1959) 8vo, cl, dj, ports, xxvii, 420pp. $35-b. Editions: 2nd print., 1960; 3rd print, 1965, 4th print., 1970. 1978 edt., 1981 edt.

205 ..."Generals in Gray, 1861-1865." (Houston, Texas, Civil War Round Table.) Address: May 6, 1955. 10pp. (8 1/2x11 heavy paper cover, fldg., 8vo.)

206 ..."Who was General Tyler?" In: CWTI, Oct. 1970, v.IX, #6, p.14-19, illus., ports. A shadowy Confederate who has been a mystery during and since the war.

207 **WARREN BLUES**
See: Robert Funkhouser.

208 **WARREN COUNTY, Va.,**
Civil War Centennial Commission. "Warren County Civil War Centennial Observance, Battle of Front Royal, Va., May 19-20, 1962." (Front Royal, Va., 1962?) 8vo, wraps, illus., (23)pp. See: "Unveiling of Monument CSA dead..."

209 **WARREN, Ebenezer W.**
"Nellie Norton: or, Southern slavery and the Bible. A Scriptural refutation of the principal arguments upon which the Abolitionists rely. A vindication of Southern slavery from the old and new testaments." Macon, Ga., Burke, Boykin Co., 1864. 8vo, wraps, 208pp. Crandall-3113. Goodspeed-$650.

210 **WARREN, Edward**
"A Doctor's Experiences in three Continents, by Edward Warren, formerly Medical Inspector of the Army of Northern Virginia, in a series of letters addressed to John Morris." Baltimore: Cushing and Bailey, 1885. 8vo, cl, ports, xiv, (15)-16pp. (1)p. $65-bmk.

211 ..."An epitome of practical surgery, for field and hospital. By Edward Warren, MD, Surgeon General of the State of North Carolina, formerly professor in the University of Maryland, Frist (sic) edt. Richmond, Va., West and Johnston, 1863. 12mo, cl, 401pp. ($700 and $1000-bmk) Carolina Bks-#10, a long description of this important work. (Cr; 3044) $1500. Richmond, Va., West and Johnston, 1863, 12mo, cl, 409pp. (Crandall-3044) $1000-bmk-114.

212 **WARREN, Gordon H.**
"Fountain of discontent: the "Trent" Affair and freedom of the seas." Boston: Northeastern University Pr., 1981. 8vo, cl, dj, xiv, 301pp., illus.

213 **WARREN, Kittrell J.**
"History of the Eleventh Georgia Vols. embracing the muster rolls, together with a special succinct account of the marches, engagements, casualties, etc., Kittrell J. Warren." Richmond, Va., Smith, Bailey and Co., 1863. 8vo, wraps, 58pp.

214 ..."Life and public services of an army straggler, by..., edited with an introduction by Floyd C. Watkins." Athens, University of Georgia Press, 1961. (University of Georgia Libraries Missc., Pub., #3.) 12mo, cl, dj, (or wraps) facsm., xiv, 98pp.

215 ...Macon, Ga., Phoenix Print., 1865. 8vo, sewn, 90pp. (only known copy?) Orig. pub. anon., "By Chatham."

216 ..."Ups and Downs of Wife Hunting, or Merry Jokes for camp perusal, by a private, Co. B., 11th Ga. Vols." Augusta, Ga., The Constitutionalist, 1861. 12mo, wraps, 43pp. 2nd edt. Crand-3125.

217 ..."A tall tale of the Civil War. Edt: Floyd C. Watkins." Atlanta, Ga." Emory Univ. Quart., Mar. 1957, v.13, p.48-54. 8vo, stiff

wraps, "Recollections of scenes, incidents, and characters around camp-fire in the "happy days gone by", humorous sketch from "The Sunny South", Atlanta Magazine, 1885.

218 **WARREN, Robert Penn**
"Jefferson Davis gets his citizenship back." In: New Yorker, Feb. 25, 1980, v.LVI, #1, p.45-46.
...Lexington: University Press of Ky., 1980. 8vo, wraps, 114pp.

219 ..."To keep his memory green. From "Jefferson Davis gets his citizenship back." In: CWHI, Summer, 1987, v.26, #4, p.22-24, 26, 56-59, 63-67, 69, 74. illus.(incl. color(22) cover.)
..."The legacy of the civil war: mediations on the Centennial." N.Y., Random House, 1961. 12mo, cl, 109pp. $10.

220 **WARREN, Robert and Sam Houston Dixon**
"The Texan Refugee. A Thrilling Story of the Lone Star State during the late Civil War." (fiction, based on fact.) Philadelphia, n.d. (1879) 8vo, cl, 568pp. (1880) $40, $60.
...Phila: John E. Potter and Co. (1879). 12mo, decr. cl, viii, (5)-568pp. Attributed to Saml. Houston Dixon. Based on fact. $60-bmk, $75-bmk-105. Philadelphia: Keystone Pub. Co.
...Reprint: 1890-same stereotype plates with subtitle, "A thrilling story of field and camp-life during the late Civil War.

221 **WARREN, Rose Harlow**
"A Southern home in War-Times." N.Y., Broadway Print, 1914. 12mo, 93pp.

222 **WARRENTON "VIRGINIA",**
"Hanging of Mosby's Men in 1864." In: SHSP, 1896, v.24, p.108-109.

223 **WARRENTON TRUE INDEX**
"A Horror of the War." In: SHSP, 1897, v.25, p.239-244.

224 **WARTHEN, Harry J., M.D.**
"The General and his Surgeon." (London) Jour. Confed. Hist. Soc., Sept. 1965, v.III, #3, p.86-101, ports-2.

225 ..."Some were might hard to kill." In: CWTI, Jan. 1964, v.II, #9, p.18-21. Examples of survival and human endurance, Maj. R. Snoden Andrews, 1st Md. Artly.

226 ..."Medical Manuals of the War Between the States." n.p., n.d., 4to, wraps, 2pp. Reprint: Bul. Richmond Academy Medicine.

227 ..."Medicine and Shockoe Hill." (Richmond, Va.) 1938. 4to, wraps, stapled, 8pp. Reprint: Annals of Medical History, New series, v.10, Jan. 1938. Role played by this region in the War.

228 **WARWICK, A.D., 1st Lieut., 2nd Va. Reg.**
"Demonstration on Harper's Ferry, famous Valley Campaign of 1862." (from Richmond Times-Dispatch, Dec. 9, 1906) In: SHSP, 1906, v.34, p.200-205, same article, v.35, p.341-347.

229 **WARWICK, Bradfute**
"The Rock; a story of the War, by a Rebel." N.Y., Broadway Pub., (1913) 12mo, cl, front, ports, pls., 149pp. Civil War fiction. Sgt. in 18th Ga. Regt.

230 **WASH, W.A.**
"Camp, field and prison life, containing sketches of service in the South and the experience, incidents and observations connected with almost two years' imprisonment at Johnson's Island, Ohio, where 3000 Confederate officers were confined, by W.A. Wash, Capt., with an introduction by Gen. L.M. Lewis and a medical history of Johnson's Island by Col. I.G.W. Steedman." St. Louis: Southwestern Pub., 1870, 12mo, cl, (17)-382pp. $300-ob.

231 **WASHBURN, Wiley A.**
"Reminiscences of Confederate Service by Wiley A. Washburn. Edt: James L.

232 …"Cleburne's Division at Franklin." In: Confed. Vet., Jan. 1905, v.XIII, p.27-28.

233 **WASHBURNE, E.B.**
"Trade with rebellious states, from the Committee on Commerce, made the following report...(including testimony)" Washington: GPO, 1865, serial 1235, 38th Congr., 2nd Sess., H.R., 24. 8vo, sewn, 222pp.

234 **"WASHINGTON Artillery.**
Constitution and By-Laws Adopted Feb. 19, 1861. Roll of the Battalion." New Orleans, La.

235 …"Constitution and By-Laws of New Orleans Military." (New Orleans?, 189?) 5 lf. mounted in portfolio.

236 …"Constitution and By-Laws of the Battalion of Washington Artillery, organized Feb. 22, 1840. Revised Feb. 11, 1861." New Orleans, La., Bulletin Off. 1861, 8vo, wraps, 64pp.

237 …"Washington Artillery, Camp #15, U.C.V., Memorial Hall, Sept. 19, 1899." New Orleans, La., 1899. 8vo, wraps, cover tile, (4)pp.

238 …"Washington Artillery Souvenir." (New Orleans, La., 1894?) 8vo, wraps, cover title, illus., ports, color plates, 40, (19), 41-84, (1)p. Muster Roll Wash. Artly., A.N.Va., 12pp., "Muster Roll of Fifth Co., Wash. Artly., Army of Tenn." 7pp., inserted between p.40-41. By Lt. Col. John B. Richardson.

239 …"Washington Artillery Heroes." In: SHSP, 1900, v.XXVIII, p.301-303. Muster Rolls—

240 …"Washington Artillery of New Orleans." In: LWL, 1868, v.VI, p.150-155. See also: Henry H. Baker, A. Gordon Bakewell, Napier Bartlett, Andrew B. Booth, J.A. Chalaron, B.F. Eschelman, Jno. H. Haney, Harry Larter, Barnes F. Lathrop, Allison Owen, Edward Owen, Wm. Miller Owen, Alfred Roman, Jno. P. Severin and P.D. Stephenson, Jas. B. Walton, Powell A. Casey, "Sketches of Hist. of..."

241 …"Historical military data on Louisiana Militia. Muster Roll Washington Artillery, 1861-1865." U.S., W.P.A., Louisiana. New Orleans, Jackson Barracks, 1939, 4to, 2 vols. (typescript?)

…"The Washington Artillery of New Orleans." In: LWL, Dec. 1868, v.VI, #2, p.150-155, with list of battles engaged.

242 **WASHINGTON COUNTY, Virginia**
"The Historical Society of Washington County, Virginia. Publications series II, No. 7, Winter-Spring, 1968-1969." "History of the 48th Virginia Infantry." Companies and Officers of the 48th Va. Volunteers. (Abington, Va., 1969) 8vo, stiff wraps, 42pp.

243 **WASHINGTON Light Infantry, of South Carolina.**
"An Account of the revival of the company with Proceedings in commemoration of it's 66th Anniversary, including the oration of Hon. Wm. D. Porter, 22nd Feb., 1873." (Charleston: Walker, Evans and Cogswell, 1873) 8vo, wraps, 86pp., seal of the company.

244 …"An address of Donald McKay Frost on the invitation of the WLI at the celebration of its one hundredth Anniversary, Feb. 22, 1907." Charleston, S.C., Walker, Evans, Cogswell, 1907. sq. 8vo, wraps, (3)-4, 26pp., 100 copies printed.

245 …"The Easter Fair of the Washington Light Infantry, March 30th to April 5, 1875." Charleston, S.C., News and Courier Pr., 1875. 8vo, wraps, 2-fld. pls (one double), 54pp.

…"Easter Festival of the Washington Light Infantry, April 2, 1888. Souvenir Program, with poem "Broken Battalion", by Paul H. Hayne." (Charleston, S.C., 1888) 12mo, 6-

light card-sheets, tied at top, ribbon.
..."An Historical Sketch of the Washington Light Infantry. Armory of 240 King St., Charleston, S.C., pub. in the interest of the corps., for use of officers and members, prepared by Louis F. Ostendorff." (Charleston?) November 1943. 8vo, wraps, 11pp.

246 ..."Proceedings of the Washington Light Infantry on the death of William D. Porter." Charleston: News & Courier Press, n.d., 1883, 100 copies printed for Wm. A. Courtenay, 4to, 3lf, (5)-6-39, (1)p. (Turnbull-IV(162)

247 ..."Public ceremonies in connection with the War Memorials of the Washington Light Infantry, with orations by Gen. Wade Hampton, C.H. Simonton and Dr. A. Toomer Porter, with the rolls, monumental inscriptions, etc." Charleston, S.C., Edward Perry and Co., 1894. 8vo, wraps, 75pp. Unit rosters Hampton's Legion, Co's: A & B, 25th Regiment, WLI.

248 ..."Reception of Gen. T.M. Logan, Ex-Capt., WLI Volunteers, Co. A, Hampton Legion Infy., at Hibernian Hall, Charleston, S.C., July 26, 1875, by his comrads of the WLI." Charleston: News and Courier Press, 1875. 8vo, wraps, 16pp. Sabin-88109.

249 ..."Report of M.P. Tribble, commissioner of Confederate Rolls, to the General Assembly, 1903." Columbia, S.C., State Co., 1904. 8vo, wraps, 5pp.

250 ..."Rolls of the WLI in Confederate Service to which is appended the mortuary of the three companies. All corrected by special committee of each of the three companies by WLI Vets." Charleston, S.C., 1888. 8vo, wraps, 17pp., (on cover: Co. A, 25th S.C., Hampton Legion, Co. B, 25th S.C.)

251 ..."A Testimonial of public services of the WLI to Maj. R.C. Gilchrist, Nov. 3, 1891." Charleston, S.C., Walker, Evans and Cogswell, 1892. 8vo, wraps, cover title, 6, (1)p.

252 **WASHINGTON, Amanda Alcenia Strickland (Mrs. J.M. Washington)**
"How beauty was saved and other memories of the sixties, by Mrs. James Madison Washington." NY-Washington: Neale Pub. Co., 1907. 12mo, cl, 75pp. Louisiana during the War.

253 **WASHINGTON, B.C.**
"Bold escape from captivity of B.C. Washington." In: SB, 1883-1884, v.II, p.356-360.

254 **WASHINGTON, D.C.**
See: Jubal A. Early.

255 **WASHINGTON, Ella**
"An army of devils-the diary of Ella Washington. Edt. by James O. Hall." In: CWTI, Feb. 1978, v.16, #10, p.18-25, illus., map, ports.

256 **WASHINGTON, L. Quinton, Col.**
"An address: Hon. R.M.T. Hunter." In: SHSP, 1897, v.XXV, p.193-205.

257 ..."Confederate States State Department." In: SHSP, 1901, v.29, p.341-349.

257a **"WASHINGTON, Missouri.**
The Civil War Years." by Ralph Gregory, Dir., Mark Twain birth place Memorial Shrine at Florida, Mo. 8vo, wraps, ills., 38pp.

258 **WASSON, S.E.**
"Robert Edward Lee, an address at Huntsville, Ala., June 3, 1909." Huntsville, Ala., 1909. 8vo, wraps, 15pp.

259 **WATERLOO, Stanley, Edt.**
"Story of a strange career, being the autobiography of a convict, an authentic document. Edt: Stanley Waterloo." N.Y., D. Appleton, 1902. Civil War, sea and blockade-runners.

260 **WATERMAN, George S.**
"Afloat-Afield-Afloat." In: CV, 1902, v.10, p.496-499, port.

261 ..."Notable events of the Civil War." In: CV, v.6, 1898, p.20-23, 59-63, 170-173, 390-394, illus., ports.

262 ..."Afield, Afloat." Naval reminiscences. v.7, p.449-452, 490-492; v.8, p.21-24, 53-55; v.9, p.24-29; v.10, p.496-499, ports, plates.

263 **WATERS, Willard O.**
"Confederate Imprints in the Henry E. Huntington Library unrecorded in previously published bibliographies of such material." Chicago: University of Chicago Pr. (1930) atg.-$35. Tall 8vo, wraps, facsm., (18)-109pp. Off-print, Papers of the Bibliographical Society of America, v.23, pt. 1, 1929. 550 copies printed, indexed.

264 **WATFORD, W.H.**
"Confederate Western Ambitions." (Austin, Texas: Southwestern Historical Quarterly, Oct. 1940, v.XLIV, #2, p.161-187.

265 **WATIE, Stand, Gen.**
"The Name of General Stand Watie of the Cherokee Nation." Oklahoma City: Chron. Okla., Autumn, 1956, v.XXIV, #3, p.252-253. Spelling and pronunciation of Watie. See: Sherman J. Kline, Mable W. Anderson, Frank Cunningham.

266 ..."Some Letters of Gen. Stand Watie. Edt: Edward E. Dale." In: Chron. Okla., 1921, v.1, p.30-59. +131-149. See: Grant Foreman.

267 **WATKINS, Gipp, Mrs.**
"Kentucky in the War Between the States." In: CV, Dec. 1927, v.XXXV, p.462-465.

268 **WATKINS, Lizzie Stringfellow**
"The Life of Horace Stringfellow with some instances of the life and work of his descendants." Montgomery, Ala., Paragon Press, 1931. 8vo, cl, illus., 151pp., facsm., ports, front. Wartime recollections of family (Raccoon Ford) Horace(?) grandfather of Frank (CSA scout).

269 **WATKINS, Samuel R.**
"1861 vs 1882. "Co. Aytch", Maury Grays, First Tennessee Regiment; or, A side show of the big show." Nashville, Tenn., Cumberland Presbyterian Pub. House, 1882. (cloth or wrappers) $300. 8vo, cl, 236pp., 1-illus., 2000 copies printed. $400.
...Chattanooga, Tenn., Times Print, 1900, 8vo, cl, viii, (9) 223pp., 2nd Edt., 2000 copies.
...Jackson, Tenn., McCowat-Mercer Pr., 1952, cl, d/w, 8vo, illus., ports, facsms., 240pp.
...N.Y., Collier Books (1962). "Collier Books Civil War Classics." 12mo, cl, 255pp., index, reprinted (1970).
...1976.
..."Company Aytch..." Dayton, Oh., Morningside Press, 1985. Reissued, facsm. #67.
...Dayton, Oh., Morningside, 1982. Reprint of 1882 edt., 300 copies. $35.
...Wilmington, N.C., Broadfoot Pub., 1987. 8vo, cl, dj, 231pp, ills. $25. Edt. Bell I. Wiley.

270 ..."The "Fighting" Forty-eighth Tennessee Regiment." In: SB, II, 1883/1884, p.246-251.

271 **WATKINS, Samuel R. and J.S. Jackman**
"Battle of Missionary Ridge." In: SB, 1883-1884, v.II, p.49-58.

272 ..."Reminiscences of Hood's Tennessee Campaign, by Samuel R. Watkins." In: SB, 1883-1884, v.II, p.399-402.

273 **"WATSON'S MAGAZINE"**
v.1-5, Jan. 1907-Dec. 1910; v.12, #4-6, v.13-Jan. 1911. Atlanta, Ga., T.E. Watson, monthly, illus., ports, 8vo, wraps. Title varies: Jan. 1907-Feb. 12, Watson's Jeffersonian Magazine; March 1912, Watson's Magazine. Published in Thomson, Ga., Dec. 1910. Supersedes Watson's Mag.

(earlier Tom Watson's Mag.) N.Y., 1905/1906. Absorbed the Taylor-Trotwood Mag. in Jan. 1911 and continued its volume numbering. (LC) Articles on the CSA.

274 **WATSON, Annah Walker Robinson**
"On the Field of Honor." Memphis, Tenn., Paul and Douglass, (1902) 12mo, cl, ports, 228pp. Stories on the CSA, based on fact, juvenile.
...Detroit, Oh., Sprague Pub., (1902) 12mo, cl, illus., ports, 226pp.

275 ..."Golden Deeds on the Field of Honor." N.Y., Macmillan, 1914. 12mo, cl, 251pp.

276 **WATSON, David Kemper**
"The Trial of Jefferson Davis, an interesting constitutional question." Reprint: Yale Law Journal, June, 1915. (New Haven?, 1915) v.XXIV, p.669-676. 8vo, wraps, 8pp.

276a **WATSON, Elbert L.**
"Lt. Col. David W. Baine: A Confederate hero from the North." In: AHQ, 1968, v.30, #2, p.27-38.

277a **WATSON, Elizabeth, Lady**
"Fight and Survive!" (Conway, Arkansas. River Road Pr. (1974) 8vo, cl, dj, ports, maps, facsm., xiii, 203pp. Append: Rosters, index, 153-2-3. $30.

278 **WATSON, James M.**
"Confederate from East Texas (Rusk Co.): the Civil War Letters of..." Edt: J.W. McClure, Quanah, Texas, Nortex Press, 1976. 8vo, stiff wraps, illus., maps, 66pp. In Col. Locke's Reg., under McCulloch in the Trans-Miss.

279 ..."Confederate from East Texas, the Civil War letters of James M. Watson. Edt: Judy Watson McClure. Austin, Texas, Eakin Pub., 1978. 8vo, wraps, 66pp.

280 **WATSON, James Munroe**
"Confederate East Texas: the Civil War Letters of James Monroe Watson. Edt: Judy Watson McClure." Quanah (Texas) Nortex Press, 1976. 8vo, cl, dj, bibliog., illus., index, maps, orig. letters, notes, 66pp.

281 **WATSON, Robert**
"The Yankees were landing below us", Seaman Watson's daily record of the collapse of the CSNavy." In: CWTI, Apr. 1976, v.15, #1, p.12-21, facsms., illus.

282 **WATSON, Thomas Edward**
"Bethany; a story of the Old South." N.Y., Appleton Pub., 1904, (also 1908) 12mo, cl, front, pls., ports, xv, 383pp. A tale of War Between the States."
...Wash., D.C., 1929.

283 **WATSON, Thomas Shelby, "Bob"**
"The Silent Riders." Louisville, Ky., Beechmont Press, 1972. 8vo, wraps, illus., 82pp. Violence in Ky., coinciding with the close of the War in 1864/1865, e.g., Wm. C. Quantrill, James Bros., the Youngers, etc. This violence was what Lee wanted to resist from those who wanted to carry on the war in the West.

284 **WATSON, Walter C.**
"Sailor's Creek." In: SHSP, Oct. 1917, ns, IV, p.136-151. Battle on Little Sailor's Creek, Va., Apr. 6, 1865. Also in: CV, Oct. 1917, v.XXV, p.448-452.

285 **WATSON, William (of Skelmorlie Scotland)**
"Life in the Confederate Army being the observations and experiences of an alien in the South during the American Civil War." London: Chapman and Hall, Ltd., 1887. 12mo, decr. cl, xvi, (17)-456pp. $250.
...N.Y., Chas. Scribner, 1888. Also: 1908; London Edts: 1892, 1898.
..."Life in the Confederate Army." N.Y., Time-Life Books, 1983. Civil War Series. 8vo, Kivar Bnd., gilt edges, marbled endsheets.

286 ..."Adventures of a Blockade Runner; or, Trade in Time of War." London: T. Fisher Unwin, 1892. "Adventure Series, #13."

$125-white. 12mo, decr., cl, xii, (1), 324pp., illus. 1893 "Popular Edt.", 1898.

287 **WATTERSON, Harvey M.**
"A Southerner views the South, 1865- Letters of Harvey M. Watterson." In: VMHB, Oct. 1960, v.68, #4, p.478-489.

288 **WATTERSON, Henry**
"Lee's Birthday." In: SHSP, 1889, v.17, p.351.

289 ..."Marse Henry", an Autobiography." N.Y., Geo. H. Doran Co., (1919). 8vo, cl, front, pls., ports. xv, (15)-315, 15-214pp. (also 2 vol. in 1)

290 ..."The compromises of life and other lectures and addresses, including some observations on certain tendencies, including modern society." N.Y., Fox, Duffield Co., 1903. 12mo, cl, front(port) x, 477pp. Some sketches re CSA, reuniting two sections. See: Joseph Frazier Wall.

290a **WATTS, Dabney W.**
"Civil War battles in Winchester & Frederick County, Virginia, 1861-1865." See title. $15.

291 **WATTS, Florence G.**
"Death of a Legend." Indiana Magazine of History, Vol.XLV-#3, Sept. 1949, 8vo, wraps, p.233-248. Local tale that Jeff Davis' first wife was daughter of Zach. Taylor (Sarah Knox) is refuted here.

292 **WATTS, Gordon P., Jr., and Jas. A Pleasants, Jr.**
"The Monitor: a bibliography." Raleigh, N.C., Under Water Archaeological Research Branch, N.C., Div. of Archives and History, 1978. 8vo, wraps, 36pp. (425 entries)

293 **WATTS, Hamp B.**
"Babe of the Company-an unfolded leaf from forest of never-to-be-forgotten years." Fayette, Missouri, 1913. 12mo, wraps, cover title, photos, 33pp. $150. Bloody Bill Anderson's man, present at the Centralia Fight. Deals mostly with battle at Fayette, Sept. 20, 1864. See: Donald R. Hale, Jno. McCorkel, Wm. E. Connelly, Kit Dalton, Jno. P. Burch.

294 **WATTS, John**
"The facts of the cotton famine." London: Simpkin, Marshall and Co., 1866. 8vo, cl, front(fldg. diagr.), xii, 472pp.
...N.Y., August M. Kelley, 1968 (Reprint of Economic Classics), London: Cass Print, Library of Industrial Classics, #22. 8vo, cl, illus., 472pp.

295 **WATTS, Legh Richmond**
"Address of Hon. Legh R. Watts of Portsmouth, Va., before the Sidney Lanier Chap. of Daughters of the Confederacy at Macon, Ga., Jan. 19, 1908, Lee's birthday..." Macon, Ga., Anderson Print, 1908, 12mo, cover title, wraps, 16pp.

296 **WATTS, Richard Cannon**
"Memoirs of Richard Cannon Watts, Chief Justice of the Supreme Court of South Carolina. Edited by Rosser H. Taylor and Raven I. McDonald." Columbia, S.C., R.L. Bryan Co., 1938. 8vo, cl, front(port), xiv, 179pp. Much on the C.S.A.

297 **WATTS, Thomas H., Hon.**
"Address on the life and character of Ex-President Jefferson Davis, delivered at the Montgomery (Ala.) Theatre, Dec. 19, 1889. 8vo, wraps, 19pp., n.p.

298 **WAYLAND, Francis F., Edt.**
"Fremont's Pursuit of Jackson in the Shenandoah Valley." In: VMHB, April/July, 1962, v.70, p.165-193, 332-354. illus., maps.

299 **WAYLAND, John Walter**
"The Battle of New Market. Memorial Address, 62nd Anniversary of the Battle of New Market, Va., May 15, 1926." New Market, Va., Henkel Print, 1926. Tall 8vo, wraps, maps, 24pp.

300 ..."A History of Rockingham County, Virginia." Dayton, Va., Ruebush-Elkins, 1912,

8vo, cl, front, illus., ports, maps (part fold.) 4pp, v-vii, (2), 10-466, (7)pp., 1-chap. on war, outstanding. $75.

301 ..."A History of Shenandoah County, Virginia." Strasburg, Va., Shenandoah Pub., 1927, 8vo, cl, illus., ports, maps, plan, 874pp. Reprint: 1976.

302 ..."Stonewall Jackson's Way; Route, Method, Achievement." Staunton, Va., McClure Co., 1940. $150-b. 4to, emb. fabricoid and gold seal of Jackson, xv, 244pp. illus., maps, ports. $75-b
...2nd Edt., 1956. $100.
...3rd Edt., 1969.
...Dayton, Oh., Morningside Books, 1976. 8vo, cl, 244pp, ills., maps, index. $45.
...1984 reprint, Dayton, Oh., Morningside.

303 ..."Robert E. Lee and his Family." Staunton, Va., McClure Print, 1951. 8vo, cl, illus., maps, ports, (8), 104pp.

304 ..."The Pathfinder of the Seas; the Life of Matthew Fontaine Maury (1806-1873)." Richmond, Va., Garrett and Massie, 1930, 8vo, illus., xiii, 191pp.

305 ..."Twenty-five chapters on the Shenandoah Valley; to which is appended a concise history of the Civil War in the Valley." Strasburg, Va., Shenandoah Pub. House, 1957, cl, 8vo, 434pp., illus. $35. Rep: 1976.

306 ..."Virginia Valley Records..." Strasburg, Va., Shenandoah Pub., 1930. See: P.C. Kayor's "Killing of Lt. Meigs, 1864." p.187-196; J.Q. Winfield's "Letters of a cavalry Captain 1861-1862." p.231-299-301pp. $55. Largely genealogical work, but for above. Muster Roll "Brock's Gap Rifles."

307 **WAYNESBORO AFFAIR.**
See: Geo. N. Bliss.

308 **"WEARING OF THE GREY!**
Song arranged for piano by Armand." New Orleans: A.E. Blackmar, 1865, 5, (1)pp.

309 **WEATHER, Willie T.**
"Judith W. McGuire-a lady of Virginia." In: VMHB, Jan. 1974, v.82, #1, p.100-113.

310 **WEATHERFORD, W.D.**
James Dunwoody Brownson DeBow. "Southern Sketches, #3, first series. Gen. Edt: Dr. J.D. Eggleston." Charlottesville, Va., Historical Pub., 1935, large 8vo, stiff wraps, 49pp.

311 **WEATHERLY, A. Earl**
"The first hundred years of historic Guilford, 1771-1871." Greensboro, N.C., 1972. Tall 8vo, cl, 207pp., facsm., illus. CSA and Reconstruction, p.78-201. Philatelic interest.

312 ..."The "new" look in Confederates." In: Amer. Philatelic Cong., Cong. Book, 1959, v.25, p.17-28, facsms. On the present market for Confederates postal collection and new resources for finding and identifying them.

313 **WEAVER, Barry Roland**
"Jesse James in Arkansas: The War Days." In: AHQ, 1964, v.XXIII, p.359-364. Period 1864-1865. Jesse, Frank and Cole Younger, part of an irregular detachment under Lt. Wm. H. Gregg, CSA, later on in Col. Jo Shelby's command.

314 **WEAVER, Blanche Henry Clark**
"Confederate Emigration to Brazil." In: JSH, Feb. 1961, 12pp. $8.
..."Confederate Immigrants and Evangelical Churches in Brazil." (Lexington, Ky.) JSH, November 1952, v.XVIII, #4, p.446-468. $8. See: Herbert Weaver.

314a **WEAVER, Dorothy L., Edt.**
"Survivors of the Union & Confederate Army & Navy 1910, Augusta County." In: Augusta Hist. Bul. 21, #1, Spring 1985, p.50-57.

315 **WEAVER, Fred B.**
"Medical Care in a Confederate Prison." In: N.C. Medical Jour., 1964, v.XXV, p.206-209, (Salisbury, N.C.)

316 **WEAVER, Richard M.**
"Lee the Philosopher." In: Georgia Review, Fall, 1948, v.II, p.297-303.

317 **WEBB, Alexander Stewart**
See: Wm. Allan's Review, "McClellan'd Camp, '62."

318 **WEBB, Elizabeth Yates**
"Cotton Manufacturing and State Regulation in North Carolina, 1861-1865." In: NCHR, Apr. 1932, v.9, p.117-137.

319 **WEBB, Laura S., Mrs.**
"A Requiem for Lee." (N.O., n.d.) (1870?) 16mo, illus., 29pp.
...New Orleans, La., Pelican Pr., 1870, 16mo, wraps, 32pp. $50. Edition for 1880.

320 **WEBB, Walter, Prescott**
"Divided We Stand. The crisis of a frontierless democracy." N.Y., Farrar and Rinehart Pr. (1937) 12mo, cl, vii, 3-239pp. $50-atg.
...Austin, Texas: The Acorn Pr. (1944) Tall 8vo, cl, vi, 151pp., illus., charts. This revised edt., has the famous milk bottle case, told for the first time, how patents stifle local industry. Prescott thesis: that the Civil War is continuing in a sectional struggle. Reprint: $16-y.

321 **WEBB, Willard, Edt.**
"Crucial Moments of the Civil War, with introduction by Bruce Catton." N.Y., Fountainhead Pub. (1961) 12mo, cl, dj, illus., map, ports, 356pp. Bonanza Reprint, n.d.

322 **WEBB, William Larkin**
"Battles and Biographies of Missourians; or, the Civil War Period of our State." Kansas City, Mo., Hudson-Kimberly, 1900. 20cm, illus., ports, incl. front and 19 ports. at end (unnumbered) 369pp.
...Title head, second Edt., 18cm, 404pp. Reprint with additional biographies.

323 **WEBER, Henry**
"The Sword of Robert Lee. Composed by Henry Weber. Words by A.J. Ryan Moina." Nashville, Tenn., J.A. McClure, 1866. (Mitchell-$416)-"This was pub. in 1867 by F. Katzenback of Memphis. Music by Rev. Father Rotchford of Memphis and words by Father A.J. Ryan, Levy Shapiro.

324 **WEBER, L.J.**
"Morgan's Raid." In: Ohio Arch. and Hist. Pub., 1909, v.XVIII, p.79-104, port. map. By a McConnelsville, Oh., attorney.

325 **WEBSTER, Donald B., Jr.**
"The Last Days of Harper's Ferry Armory." In: CWH, March 1959, v.V, #1, p.30-44, port, map, illus.

326 **WEBSTER, Nathan Burnham**
"Robert E. Lee." Phila., J.B. Lippincott, 1890. 12mo, wraps, 7pp.

327 **WEDDELL, Alexander W.**
"Expunged from the Record", Dr. Davis Minton Wright, 1809-1863." Mexico City, 1925. Privately printed. 8vo, wraps, 8pp. Reprint from Richmond News, May 10, 1901.

328 **WEDDLE, Robert S.**
"Plow-Horse Cavalry. The Caney Creek Boys of the Thirty-fourth Texas." Austin, Texas: Madrona Press, (1974) 8vo, cl, dj, map-endsheets, illus., xvi, 210pp. sources, index, p.185-210.

329 **WEDELL, Elizabeth Wright**
"St. Paul's Church, Richmond, Va. It's Historic Years and Memorials." Richmond, Va., Richard Byrd Pr., 1931. 8vo, cl, 2 vols., p.285, (289)-638. Many documents re: J. Davis and St. Paul and public life. (McElroy bibliog.)

330 **WEE NEE Volunteers, S.C.**
See: John G. Pressley.

331 **"WEEKLY Junior Register, The.**
Franklin Attakapas Parish of St. Mary, Louisiana. May 22, 1862." v.1, #24, folio, 2pp. unrecorded newspaper; v.2, Jan. 29, 1863, print on wall-paper. (Titled: "Weekly Register") v.2, #5.

332 **WEEKLY, Robert S.**
"The House in ruins." N.Y., Random House Pub., 1958. 8vo, cl, 248pp. Three

CSA soldiers in Mississippi refuse to accept defeat after Appomattox.

333 **WEEKS, Stephen Beauregard**
"Biographical Sketches of the Confederate Dead of the University of North Carolina. A series of short biographies in the North Carolina University Magazine, 1887-1888." (Chapel Hill, N.C.) vii, 35-40; 83-86; 109-113; 171-176, 232-236, 262-265; 1888-1889, viii, 27-29, 75-79, 176-179, 227-231, 271-274; 1889-1890, ix, 25-28, 80-82, 140-143, 198-201, 240-245; 1890-1891, x, 102-109, 160-166.

334 ..."Confederate Text-Books (1861-1865): A Preliminary Bibliography." In: U.S. Bur. Education. Chapter from Report of Comm. of Education. Chapter from Report of Comm. of Education for 1898-1899. Stamped "Advance Sheet: Chapter 22." p.1139-1155. Washington, D.C., G.P.O., 1900.

335 ..."The First Confederate Martyr." In: SHSP, 1892, v.XX, p.63-68.

336 ..."The University of North Carolina in the Civil War." An address delivered at the Centennial Celebration of the Opening of the Institution June 5, 1895." Richmond: Wm. Ellis Jones, 1896, reprinted from the Southern Historical Society Papers, Vol.xxiv, 8vo, 38pp., p.1-38. $85.

337 ..."Henry Lawson Wyatt, the first Confederate soldier killed in battle." n.p., n.d., Reprint: 300 copies, illus., port., 4pp. First appeared: "National Magazine", Nov. 1892, xvii, p.56-59, port. Also in Southern Historical Papers, xx, p.63-68.

338 **WEEMS, Albert G., Mrs.**
"Work of United Daughters of the Confederacy." In: MHSPub., 1901, v.iv, p.73-78.

339 **WEES, Knight Burns, Comp.**
"Known resting places of our Randolph County soldiers of all wars." Elkins: c.1945. 8vo, stiff wraps, 49pp. Alphabetical listing of CSA and Union soldiers, with birth and death dates and cemetery buried. Shetler-828.

340 **WEGELIN, Oscar**
"A Bibliography of the Separate Writings of John Esten Cooke, of Virginia, 1830-1886." Hattiesburg, Miss: Bookfarm, 1941. 2nd edt. Heartman's Historical Series, #44, p.13.
...Metuchen, N.J., C.F. Heartman, 1925 (55 copies) $75.

341 **WEICHMANN, Louis J.**
"A True History of the Assassination of Abraham Lincoln and of the Conspiracy of 1865." Edt: Floyd E. Risvold. N.Y., Alfred A. Knopf, 1975. 8vo, cl, dj, xxxii, 492, svipp. Accuser of Mrs. Surratt (falsely), wrote the account but never published it, until now. See: Joseph George, Jr.

342 **WEIL, Benjamin (heirs: Alice Weil, et al, Alexandria, La.)**
"The case of U.S. vs Alice Weil, et al, heard in U.S. Court of Claims, in equity, 17916." (Washington, c.1897) 8vo, cl, 106, 377, 5, 61, 32pp. 1/2 Mor. Declared fraudulant but heirs resurrected it in hopes of collecting. Weil was a CSAgent for state of Louisiana and trading cotton with Mexico, bringing back weapons of war thru Brownsville and Eagle Pass. The Mexicans had seized 2000 bales cotton, resulting in the claim. Atg., notes by Asst. Atty. JK(138). $350. Gen. Wm. A. Maury.

343 **WEINBERG, Adelaide**
"John Elliot Cairnes and the American Civil War: A Study in Anglo-American Relations." London: Kingswood Press, 1973. 8vo, cl, dj, 224pp.

344 **WEINERT, Richard P.**
"The Confederate Regular Army." Military Affairs: (1962), p.97-107.

345 ..."The Confederate Regular Cavalry." In: Texana, 1972, v.X, #3, p.244-259, notes.

346 ..."The Confederate Regulars in Louisiana." In: La. Studies, 1967, v.VI, p.53-71.

347 ..."Confederate border troubles with Mexico." In: CWTI, Oct. 1964, v.III, #6, 36-43, illus., ports. Southern officials on Rio Grande troubles with rival Mexican governments, deserters Union sympathizers, little help from Richmond.

348 ..."The Confederate Swamp Fox. John Jackson Dickison with a force of barely 200 men." In: CWTI, Dec. 1966, v.5, #8, p.4-11, 48-50, illus., map, port.

349 ..."The Illinois Confederates, lived in the North but fought for the South." In: CWTI, Oct. 1962, v.1, #6, p.44-45, pl. port. Had migrated to Ill. from Va. and Ky., from Williamson and Jackson Counties.

350 ...Olustee-one sided Southern victory." In: CWTI, June 1962, v.1, #3, p.21-23, map, ports.

351 ..."Yankee Turncoats made poor Confederates." In: CWT, July 1961, v.III, #4, p.7-8, plate.

352 **WEIR, A.M.**
"Old Times in Georgia by "Sarge" Old Man Plunkett." Atlanta, Ga., Constitution Pub., 1903. 8vo, wraps, 126pp., 1p. adv. $50.

353 ..."Old Times in Georgia. Good Time and Bad Times. By "Sarge (A.M. Weir)." Atlanta, Ga., Constitution Pub., 1889, 8vo, wraps, 199pp. Cover: Old Times in Georgia (A.M. Wier). Good Civil War material as fiction.

354 **WEITZEL, Godfrey**
"Richmond Occupied Entry of the United States forces into Richmond, Va., April 3, 1865. Calling together of the Virginia Legislature and revocation of the same." Edited with intro: Louis H. Manarin. (Richmond, Va., Civil War Centennial Committee, 1965) 8vo, stiff wraps, ports, illus., dbl-pg. map, fldg. plate Richmond, 9x30"

355 **WELCH, Spencer Glasgow**
"A Confederate Surgeon's Letters to his Wife. By Spencer Glasgow Welch, Surgeon, Thirteenth South Carolina Volunteers McGowan's Brigade." 16mo, cl, 121pp. N.Y., Wash., Neale, 1911. $350-g, $500-ob.
...Marietta, Ga., Continental Book Co., 1954, 16mo, cl, illus., ports, 127pp. Six family photographs have been added.

356 **WELLER, Jack**
"Bedford Forrest: tactical teamwork was his secret weapon." In: Ordnance, Sept.-Oct., 1853, v.38, p.248-251. Views, on his ordnance, 1861-1864.

357 ..."Nathan Bedford Forrest: an analysis of untutored military genius, 1861-1865." In: Tenn. HQ, Sept. 1959, v.XVIII, p.213-251.

358 ..."The logistics of Nathan Bedford Forrest." In: Mil. Affairs, Winter, 1953, v.17, p.161-169, note.

359 ..."Bedford Forrest: Master at arms." In: Armor., 1955 (May/June) v.64(3), p.40-46. Port, views.
..."The Logistics of Nathan Bedford Forrest." In: Anti-aircraft Jour., 1954 (May/-June) v.97, p.12-16.

360 ..."Confederate 12 PDR. Breech-loading Whitworth Rifle-British cannon in the Confederacy." (London) Jour. Confed. Hist. Soc., Autumn, 1970, v.8, #3, p.48-61, pl.

361 ..."Confederate-made infantry weapons." In: Gun and Cartridge Rec., Dec. 1953, v.2, #9, p.9-11.

362 ..."The Confederate Use of British Cannon." In: CWH, June 1957, v.III, #2, p.135-152, (8)pp. plates.

363 ..."Imported Confederate Shoulder Weapons." In: CWH, June 1959, v.V, #2, p.157-181, (7)pp. plates.

364 ..."Shooting Confederate infantry arms." In: Am. Rifleman, Apr./June, 1954, v.102,

364a ..."The field artillery of the Civil War." In: Mil. Coll. & Hist., June 1953, v.5, #2, p.29-34; Sept. 1953, #3, p.65-70; Dec. 1953, #4, p.95-7. #4, p.42-44; #5, p.22-24; #6, p.41-42. Tables, views. Test on accuracy of arms.

365 **WELLER, John H., Capt.**
"History of the 4th Ky. Inf., address at Louisville (Southern Historical Society)." In: SHSP, 1881, v.9, p.108-115.
..."The Fourth Kentucky." In: SB, 1882-1883, v.1, p.346-354.

366 **WELLES, Gideon**
"The capture and release of Mason and Slidell. Selected essays by Gideon Welles: Civil War and Reconstruction, Edt: Albert Mordell" N.Y., Twayne Pub., 1959, p.256-279. Fron: "Galaxy", May 1873. On unauthorized action of Capt. Chs. Wilkes on USNavy ship seizing CSA emissaries Mason and Slidell en route to England, resulting in Welles' embarrassment.

367 **WELLMAN, Manly Wade**
"Appomattox Road; final adventures of the Iron Scouts." N.Y., Washburn Print, (1960) 12mo, cl, 181pp. fiction.

368 ..."The Ghost Battallion; a story of the Iron Scouts." N.Y., Washburn Print(1958) 12mo, cl, 178pp. Fiction.

369 ..."Giant in Gray. A Biography of Wade Hampton of South Carolina." N.Y., Lond: Chs. Scribner's Son, 1949. $75. 8vo, cl, dj, ports, xv, 387pp. notes, index, bibliog. (335-387) $15, $25, $30, $32.50, $35.
...Dayton, Oh., Morningside, 1980. $15.
...Dayton, Oh., Morningside Press, 1988. 8vo, cl, dj, 387pp, ills, index. ports. $25.

370 ..."Gray Riders: Jeb Stuart and his Men." N.Y., Alladin Books, 1954. American Heritage Series. Fiction. 12mo, cl, illus., 192pp.

371 ..."Harpers Ferry, prize of War (1743-1870)." Charlotte, N.C., McNally Print, 1960. 8vo, cl, dj, illus., vi, (2), 183pp. bibliog. and notes (161-177).

372 ..."Many Are the Hearts; a play in one act." (Raleigh: North Carolina Confederate Centennial Commission, 1961) 12mo, wraps, illus., 37pp.

373 ..."Rebel Boast: First at Bethel-Last at Appomattox." N.Y., Henry Holt, (1956). 8vo, cl, dj, facsms., map, ports, 317pp. $25. Reprint: Westport, Conn., Greenwood Pr., 1874. Enfield Blues of Halifax and Edgecomb Counties, N.C., later 43rd Inf. Reg.

374 ..."Rebel Mail Runner." N.Y., Holiday House (1954). 12mo, cl, illus., 221pp., fiction. Juvenile story based on true account Absalom Grimes, CSA.

375 ..."The Rebel Songster: Songs the Confederates Sang. Music scores by Frances Wellman." Charlotte, N.C., Heritage House (1959) Tall 8vo, cl, dj, ix, 53pp.

376 ..."Ride Rebels! Adventures of the Iron Scouts." N.Y., I. Washburn Print (1959) 12mo, cl, illus., 180pp.

377 ..."They Took Their Stand. The Founders of the Confederacy." N.Y., G.P. Putnam's Sons, (1959) 8vo, cl, dj, 258pp., notes, bibliog., index, p.216-258.

378 **WELLS, Carol**
"William Ross Postell, Adventurer." In: Ga. H.Q., Fall, 1973, v.LVII, #3, p.390-405.

379 **WELLS, Charles F.**
"The Battle of Griswoldville (Ga.), Georgia's Gettysburg." Macon, Ga. (c.1960) 8vo, stiff wraps, 24pp., battle map of area, town hist.

380 **WELLS, Edward Laight**
"The Crisis of the Confederacy." In: SHSP, v.XXXIII, 1905, p.79-82. See: D.B. Rea.

381 ..."Hampton and His Cavalry in '64." Richmond, Va.: B.F. Johnson Pub., 1899. 8vo, cl, (some 3/4 lt) port (front) illus., 429pp., xiv, (4)pp ads. $125-r, $100.

...Richmond, Va., Owens Civil War Books, 1988. $35. New intro: Will Greene, map, index. Lim.Edt.

382 ..."Hampton at Fayetteville." In: SHSP, v.XIII, 1885, p.144-148.

383 ..."A morning call on General Kilpatrick." In: SHSP, v.XII, 1884, p.123-130.

384 ..."A sketch of the Charleston Light Dragoons (5th Cavalry, Troop K) from the earliest formation of the Corps, prepared at the request of the Survivors Association of the company." Charleston: Lucas, Richardson Co., 1888. 8vo, cl, 97pp., illus., errata slip. $100.

385 ..."The Term 'Rebellion' (Notes and Queries." In: SHSP, v.XII, 1884, p.429.

386 ..."Who Burnt Columbia? Testimony of a Confederate Cavalryman." In: SHSP, v.X, 1882, p.109-119.

387 ..."Joseph Wheeler. His rank by commission in the CSArmy-Major General." In: SHSP, v.XXXII, 1904, p.41-42.

388 **WELLS, James M.**
"The Phi Gamma in War. Denunciation of General Shaw." In: SHSP, 1900, v.28, p.309-314.

389 **WELLS, James T.**
"Prison experience, by James T. Wells, Sergeant Company A, Second South Carolina Infantry." In: SHSP, 1879, v.VII, p.324-429, 393-398, 487-491.
..."Prison Experience." Sgt. Co. A., 2nd S.C. Inf." In: SHSP, 1879, v.7, p.324-329, 393-398, 487-491.

390 **WELLS, John D.**
"The scars of war in the Shenandoah." In: Aug., 1908, Metropolitan Mag., N.Y., v.XXVIII, p.488-502.

391 **WELLS, Julian L.**
"The Cause of the War, traced back to the formation of the Constitution." In: SHSP, 1904, v.32, p.13-32.

392 **WELLS, Rosa Lee**
"General Lee: a Great Friend of Youth." N.Y., Vantage Press, (1950). 8vo, cl, dj, illus., ports, 356pp.

393 **WELLS, Tom Henderson**
"The Confederate Navy: A Study in Organization." University, Ala., Univ. of Ala. Press, 1971, 8vo, cl, d/w, ix, 182pp. $15.

394 **WELLS, W. Calvin**
"Oration delivered by..., commander, 1st Brigade Mississippi, U.C.V. Jackson, Miss., on May 6, 1914. Member of Co. B, 22nd Miss. Reg., C.S.A., pub. by order of the reunion, 24th Annual Reunion, U.C.V." (Jackson, Miss., Jones Print, 1914) 8vo, wraps, 19pp. (Ark. Univ.)

395 **WELSH, John P. and James L.**
"A House Divided: the Civil War Letters of a Virginia Family. Edt.: W.G. Bean." Virginia Mag. Hist., v.LIX, p.397-422. Oct. 1951. John was capt. in 27th Va. Reg., James in 78th, Ill. Inf. Reg. Brothers in Lexington.

396 **WELSH, John R.**
"William Gilmore Simms. Critic of the South." (Lexington, Ky.) JSH, May, 1960. v.XXVI, #2, p.201-214.

397 **WELSH, Mary J., Miss**
"The Confederate Orphan's Home of Mississippi." In: Pub. Miss. Hist. Soc., 1904, Oxford, Miss., v.VIII, p.(121)-136.

398 ..."Makeshifts of the War Between the States." In: (Oxford), 1903, Pub. Miss. Hist. Soc., v.VII, p.101-113.

399 **WELTNER, Charles Longstreet**
"Reflections of the War." In: Ga. Rev., 1961, Summer, v.XV, #2, p.144-158. At end: Robert E. Lee; an ode, by Chs. Eator.

399a **WENDER, Herbert**
"The Southern Commercial Convention at Savannah, 1856." In: GaHQ, June 1931, v.XV, #2, p.173-91. Many condemned it as 'secessionist,' but was largely held to protect interests of the South against North, tarrif, etc.

400 **WERLICH, Robert, Edt.**
"Fully Illustrated Catalogue of United States and Canadian and Confederate Currency." With Values. Washington, D.C., Quaker Currency Co., (1963) 8vo, soft covers, illus., 114pp. (CSA-79-98pp.) New Ed.

401 ..."U.S. and Canadian and Confederate Paper Money-large, small and fractional." Editions: 1965, 1966-67, with values.

402 **WERSTEIN, Irving**
"Abraham Lincoln versus Jefferson Davis." N.Y., Crowell Co., 1959. 8vo, cl, dj, ports, views, x, (2), 272pp.

403 **WERT, Jeffry**
"Battle of Fisher's Hill; Confederates 'First fair chance'." In: CWTI, Arp. 1979, #5, p.4-9, 40-45, illus., ports, map.

404 ..."Old John", Maj. Harman Jackson's Wagonmaster." In: CWTI, May 1981, v.20, #2, p.8-13, port, illus. (1-color)

405 ..."Rosser's Rebel Cavalry takes New Creek, W.Virginia." In: CWTI, Feb. 1982, v.20, #10, p.8-17, pl. ports, map.

405a ..."From Winchester to Cedar Creek: the Shenandoah campaign of 1864." Carlisle, 1987. 8vo, cl, dj, 320pp, ills, ports, maps. $22.50.

406 **WERT, Jeffry D.**
"The Confederate Belle." In: CWTI, August, 1976, v.17, #5, p.20-27, illus., sketch, ports.

407 ..."Lee's first year of the War." In: CWTI, April, 1975, v.13, #8, p.4-9, 42-44, illus., ports.

408 ..."Old artillery": William Nelson Pendleton." In: CWTI, June 1974, v.13, #3, p.10-18, illus., ports.

409 ..."Old Jubilee's last battle. Early's last battle against Custer." In: CWTI, Aug. 1977, #5, v.16, p.20-27, illus., map, ports.

410 ..."One great regret: Cold Harbor, a Federal Army went down in a sheet of flame." In: CWTI, Feb. 1979, v.17, #10, p.22-35, illus., map, ports.

411 ..."Robert E. Rodes-so high in rank and brilliant in service and so glorious in death." In: CWTI, Dec. 1977, v.16, #8, p.4-9, 41-45, illus., ports.

412 ..."The Tycoon": Lee and His Staff." In: CWTI, July 1972, v.11, #4, p.10-19, illus., ports, group port.

413 ..."The Valley Campaign in 1862." Part I. In: Va. Cavalcade, Sprint, 1985, v.34, #4, p.150-161, illus., ports, illus. by Wm. L. Sheppard, 1p. color. Part II-Summer, 1985, v.35, #1, p.38-47, illus. (incl. colored view), ports, map.

414 ..."Stephen D. Ramseur-A Profile." In: CWTI, May 1973, v.XII, #2, p.4-7, 42-47, illus., ports.

415 **WESCOAT, Arthur Brailsford**
"Journal of Arthur Brailsford Wescoat, 1863-1864." (Charleston: So. Caro. Hist. and Genea. Mag., April, 1954, v.LV, #2, p.71-102. 15/16 year old boy's diary at Pinopolis Plantation, near Charleston, slipped off, joined Walpole Scouts/J.E. Johnston.

416 **WESCOAT, Joseph Julius**
"Diary of Capt. Joseph Julius Wescoat, 1863-1865. Edt: Anne King Gregorie." In: SCHMag., Jan./Apr. 1958, v.59, 11-23, 86-95. Service in 11th Reg., S.C. Vols. See: Abram Wilson Clement.

417 **WESCOTT, Emma C.**
"Memories of the Old South." (San Antonio, Texas) 1912. Passing Show Printing Co., 12mo, wraps, CSA flag(cover) gray paper, 50pp. All CSA.

418 **WESLEY, Charles Harris**
"The Collapse of the Confederacy." Wash: Associated Publishers, 1937, 12mo, cl, xiii, 225pp. "Complete revision and expansion of an essay, first pub. as a brief account in one of Howard Univ. studies in Hist."

419 ..."The employment of negroes as soldiers in the Confederate Army." In: Jour. Negro Hist., July 1919, v.IV, p.239-253.

420 **WESSELS, William L.**
"Born to be a Soldier. The Military Career of William Wing Loring of St. Augustine, Fla." Ft. Worth: Texas Christian University Press (1971) 8vo, stiff wraps, port, 122pp. CSA, p.51-75. Monograph-#8.

421 **WEST AND JOHNSON**
"Map of the state of Virginia containing the counties, principal towns, railroads, rivers, canals, and all other internal improvements." Richmond, Va., West and Johnston, 1862, 57 1/2x87 1/2cm. $600. Cover title: Map of Virginia.
...Do: "New map of Virginia 1864." $350.
..."Descriptive catalogue of Publications issued by West & Johnston, Richmond. C.H. Wynne, printer. (1864). 8vo, wraps, cover title, 24pp. Crandall-3289.

422 **WEST POINT Military Academy**
See: U.S. Military, West Point, Wm. G. McCabe, Dabney H. Maury, Vincent Joseph Esposito, Ellsworth Eliot.

423 **"WEST VIRGINIA**
and its sturggle for statehood, 1861-1863." Baltimore: Wolk Pub. Co., 1954. 8vo, cl, map, ports, seal, (8), 44pp. notes. bibliog., p.39-42.
See: Wm. Baird, Thomas J. Riddle.

424 ..."West Virginia Battle Ground." In: CV, Sept. 1926, v.34, p.340-341. Military activities Jefferson Co., as marked by Cvets in 1911.

425 ..."West Virginia Doctors in the Civil War." In: W.Va. Medical Journal, June 1963, v.59, p.161-165. Alphabetical listing of 135 regimental surgeons in CSA and Union regiments.

426 ...West Virginia: Dept of Archives and History. "Biennial Report for the period ending June 30, 1932-Jan. 1, 1933." (Charleston, W.Va.) 8vo, wraps, 29pp. Append: p.19-29, contains a list of Confederate companies and their captains and their Va. Regs., about 40 counties included.

427 ..."A Certified Copy of the Constitution of the State of West Virginia, proposed by the Convention assembled at Wheeling, 26 November 1861, and ratified by a vote of the people." Washington, 1862. 8vo, sewn, 28pp.

429 ...Eberstadt-#166(1964) adopted by the "Virginia Restored Govrnm." comprising western counties of Virginia which had voted against secession, thereby themselves seceding from seceded State. But in article XI-"no slave shall be brought, no person of color permitted to come, in state as a permanent resident." It was ratified overwhelmingly by popular vote 3 April 1862.

430 ..."West Virginia Mountains, Raid through..." In: CV, March 1894, v.2, p.83-84. Rosser's Raid from Augusta Co., Val. to Beverly, Jan. 1865.

431 ..."To the people of West Virginia." The Army of Western Virginia has come among you to expel the enemy, to rescue the people from the despotism of the counterfeit State Government imposed on you..." Charleston, Va., Sept. 14, 1862. Oblong 8vo, 1pp. (Chs. Everitt, cat. 40, ns.) Two announcements on one page, both by Maj. Gen. William Wing Loring, CSA.

432 ...West Virginia Records of Confederate and Union Soldiers. Compiled by Clifford R. Myers, State Historian and Archivist, c.1932-1933. 4to, 6 vols.(v.6 is Union, 250 leaves) CSA, vols. 1-5, alphabetically listing counties and under Va. Infantry regiments and separate companies; rosters of men in 31st Va. Inf., diaries of events; rosters of Va. Cav. and Artillery units; record and roll of Co.G, 10th Va. Cav., by Sgt. Henry M. Lowther. Shetler-666

433 ...West Virginia Statehood: From Richard O. Curry's title. pg. 411: Shenandoah Valley less strong for secession than SW Va., Berkely Co., rejected secession but sent twice as many soldiers to the CSA as Union. Charles Town a hotbed for secession. Hampshire as Berkely, but sent ten to one companies to CSA. Wheeling Convention: of 75 counties 45 loyal to the CSA. Lay outside Union lines. See: Willis F. Evans- "Hist. Berkely Co., W.Va.", p.112-119; 150-159 muster rolls and Civil War. Wm. Baird. See: Millard K. Bushong's Jefferson Co.: Hu Maxwell's "Barbour Co." for CSA and muster rolls; and "Hampshire Co., detailed CSA and muster rolls.

434 ..."West Virginia in the Civil War. A series of sketches sponsored by Educational Foundation, Inc. for distribution to West Virginia Newspapers." (Charleston, W.Va., 1958) Published in book form, Charleston, 1963." 107 typed (leaves of 5pp. each) releases, written by Boyd Stutler and Phil Conley. Following titles relate to CSA only, by number. Stutler #220:

435 (5) Death of Col. John Augustine Washington, CSA, at Elkwater. On the shooting of Gen. Lee's aid-de-camp by a detachment of 17th Indiana Inf., Sept. 13, 1861.

436 (6) "The first land battle of the Civil War. On the affair at Philippi, June 3, 1861."

437 (11) "First action in the Kanawha Valley. On the organization of Confederate companies and establishment of camps under Col. Christopher Q. Tomkins and Gen. Henry A. Wise, occupation of Charleston and beginning of CSA withdrawal from the upper valley after action at Scary Creek, July 17, 1861."

438 (12) "Confederate rally to control western Va. On the CSA strategy of July-Aug. 1861 under Gen. W.W. Loring."

439 (13) "Preparing for battle on the Kanawha. Confederate movements around Charleston and the lower valley, June-July 1861."

440 (17) "Wise retreats from the Kanawha Valley. July-Sept., 1861."

441 (21) "Lee fails in mountain campaign. On Gen. Lee in W. Va., Aug.-Oct., 1861."

442 (53) "Morgan's men raid across W. Virginia, July 1862."

443 (54) "McNeill Rangers capture two generals."

444 (55) "The 30 day raid of Jones and Imboden."

445 (57) "Belle Boyd, the Confederate Spy."

446 (65) "John Yates Beall and the Johnson's Island Raid."

447 (72) "The boy colonel of the 25th Infantry CSA (John Higginbotham of Buckhannon, who recruited a co. at the age of 18 and became a Col. of the 25th Va. Inf. at 20.)

448 (81) "Mississippi to honor gallant Infantry at Vicksburg, July 3, 1961."

449 (85) "Virginia troops bring war to Harper's Ferry, April 18, 1861."

450 (93) "Charleston man (Capt. Joseph N. Broun) made last Confederate payroll."

451 (96) "Tuckwiller's Hill skirmish fought by star light. On the night defeat of Col. John C. Paxton's 2nd W. Va. Cavalry by Col. George M. Edgar's 26th Bat. Va. Inf., at Lewisburg, May 2, 1863."

452 (97) "Georgia troops first to aid in '61 campaign. On the 1st and 12th Georgia Reg. in W. Va., 1861-1862.

453 (101) "Stonewall Jackson resigns when Richmond meddles with his army."

454 (102) "The Confederate Postal Service in West Virginia." (103) "Fayetteville Rifles first from Fayette. Organized by Robert Augustus Baily, May 1861, the unit became Co.K, 22nd Va. Inf., under Col. George S. Patton."

455 (104) "Story of a Confederate soldier is told in diary. On James Edmond Hall of the Barbour Greys, later Co.H, 31st Va. Inf. (See: Ruth Woods Dayton)

456 **WEST, A.M., General**
"Circular (caption title) Letter from general West...Meridian, Miss., Aug. 12th, 1863. To my fellow citizens of...Mississippi. As I am a candidate for Governor..." Broadsheet, 16 1/4x6". (Meridian, Miss.?) Goodspeed-$400. Unrecorded. Voting for governor.

457 **WEST, Beckwith**
"Experience of a Confederate States Prisoner, being an ephemeris regularly kept by an officer of the Confederate States Army." Richmond: West and Johnston Pub., 1862. 12mo, wraps, 64pp. $100-$300.

458 **WEST, Decca Lamar**
"Catechism on the History of the Confederate States of America arranged for children of Confederacy Chapters." General United Daughters of the Confederacy." (Austin, Texas: Texas Confederate Museum, 1934)

459 ..."Robert E. Lee in Texas. The sojourn in this state of the leader of the Southern Armies and some of his impressions." Ft. Worth: Texas Monthly, April 1930, v.V, #3, p.323-339.

460 **WEST, Douglass, Col.**
"Recollections of the death of Gen. Lytle." In: SHSP, 1895, v.23, p.82-94.

461 **WEST, George Benjamin**
"When the Yankees Came: Civil War and Reconstruction on the Virginia Peninsula." Richmond, Va., Dietz Press, 1977. 8vo, cl, dj, vii, 199pp. Served in Quarter Master Dept.

462 **WEST, George Mortimer**
"St. Andrews, Florida; historical notes upon St. Andrews and St. Andrews Bay, with map and a portrait of Governor Clark and an appendix containing the official record of the vessels employed on the blockading fleet, of St. Andrews Bay." St. Andrews, Fla., Panama City Pub., 1922. 8vo, cl, (5), 2 lf, 111, (3)pp. port., maps. Reissued, 2nd Ed.t, 1938; 3rd Ed., 1960. Civil War activities, p.56-93; blockade, p.103-111. UWF.

463 ..."The skirmish at "Old Town", St. Andrew's Fla., March 20, 1863." St. Andrews, Panama City Pub., 1918. 8vo, wraps, cover title, 7pp.

464 **WEST, J. Eberle**
"Morgan's Raid." In: Ind. MH, Mar., 1924, v.XXXII, p.92-96. Letter from St. Clairsville, Ohio, July 28, 1863.

465 **WEST, James Durham**
"The Thirteenth Tennessee Regiment-C.S.A." In: TennHM, (Oct., 1921) (Issued Aug. 1923), v.VII, #3, p.180-193. Includes sketch of Rev. Jas. D. West, DD, by Elizabeth Howard West.

466 **WEST, John Camden**
"A Texan in Search of a Fight, being the diaries and letters of a private soldier in Hood's Texas Brigade, by John C. West, Co. E, Fourth Texas." Waco, Texas: J.S. Hill Print, 1901. 12mo, soft cl, 189pp. (at end: "Appendix" to a Texan in Search of a Fight", passed to the higher life, Mrs. Mary Eliza. West, of Waco, her good works and the end." port, 8pp. Insert: (4)pp. folder adv. commendations, with a port. of West. $300-b. $350-g.

...Waco, Texas: Texian Press, 1969. With an intro: Col. Harold B. Simpson. 12mo, cl, dj, (11), 189pp. port (front.)

467 **WEST, Larry L.**
"Douglas H. Cooper, Confederate General." In: Lincoln Herald, 1969, v.LXXI, p.69-76.

468 **WEST, Mabel**
"Jacksonport, Arkansas, in the Civil War." In: AHQ, 1950, v.IX, p.248-251.

469 **WEST, Richard S., Jr.**
"Gunboats in the Swamp: the Yazoo Pass Expedition." In: Civ. War. Hist., June 1963, v.IX, p.157-166.

470 **WEST, W. Reed**
"Contemporary French Opinion on the American Civil War." Baltimore: Johns Hopkins Press, 1924. 8vo, wraps, viii, (9)-159. Johns Hopkins Univ. Stud. Ser. XLII, #1.

471 **"WESTERN Pioneer, The."**
v.1, #1. Fort Lancaster, Texas, Feb. 1, 1862. Folio, 4pp. (C. Dorman David) $500. Mssc. newspaper, entirely in hand script, three columns.

472 **WESTON, James A.**
"Services held in the Chapel of Rest, Yadkin Valley, N.C., at the funeral of the late Captain Walter Waightstill Lenoir, with the sermon by the Rev. James A. Weston and a sketch of the life of the deceased." 12mo, wraps, 27pp. N.Y., E and J.B. Young and Co., 1890. $100.

473 ..."Memorial Sermon and sketch of Gen. Collett Leventhorpe." n.p., n.d., (1890?) 8vo, wraps, 15pp. Subject was a Brig.-Gen., C.S.A.

474 ..."Sketch of Walter W. Lenoir." In: N.C. Univ. Mag., 1890-1891, v.X, p.245-248.

475 **WESTON, James Augustus, Maj.**
"History of the 33rd North Carolina Regiment." Charlotte, N.C., 1900. 8vo, wraps, 35pp. See: Clark, II, p.537-580 and Thos. A. Cowan.

476 **WESTPHALL, David**
"The Battle of Glorieta Pass: Its Importance in the Civil War." (Albuquerque) NMHR, April 1969, v.XLIV, #2, p.137-154.

477 **WESTWOOD, Howard C.**
"Adventure in reporting Civil War News." In: JMH, November 1980, v.XLII, #4, p.316-335.

478 ..."Captive Black Union Soldiers in Charleston-what to do?" In: CWH, Mar. 1982, v.28, #1, p.28-44.

479 ..."The Peace Convention of 1861-where met "The Better Angels of our nature." (London) Jour. Confed. Hist. Soc., Autumn, 1972, v.10, #3, p.99-113.

480 ..."The Real Lost Cause: the Peace Convention of 1861." In: Military Affairs, 1964, v.XXVII, p.119-130.

481 ..."The Second Battle of the Civil War, April 1865-Feb., 1866." (London) Jour. Confed. Hist. Soc., Spring, Summer, 1971, v.9, #1 and 2, p.3-16.

482 ..."The Vicksburg Campaign." The rainment of the Gods of War." In: JMH, August, 1982, v.XVIV, #3, p.193-216, notes. (May 13-14, 1863) See: Ed. C. Bearss, John C. Pemberton.

483 **WETMORE, Elizabeth Bisland, Mrs.**
"A candle of understanding, a novel by..." N.Y., London, Harper and Bros., 1903. 12mo, cl, 305pp., (1) Plantation life in La. during war, ending in New Orleans.

484 **WEYL, Nathaniel and William Marina**
"American Statesmen on Slavery and the Negro." N.Y., Arlington House, 1971. 8vo, cl, d/w, 448pp. Of all times, virtually all believed blacks an alien element, could not be assimilated in society.

485 **WHALING, Thornton**
"Gen. Robert E. Lee." In: CV, November, 1920, v.XXVIII, p.416-418, (also: Centre College Mag., Jan. 1929, v.2, #1, p.12-18.

486 **WHAN, Vorin E., Jr.**
"Fiasco at Fredericksburg." (State College: Penn. State Univ. Press, Himes Printing Co., 1961. 8vo, cl, d/w, 159pp., maps, ends. ...Gaithersburg, Md., Butternut Press, 1986. $25.

487 **WHARTON, Clarence**
"Spruce McCoy Baird (1814-1872)." In: NMHR, Oct. 1952, v.27, p.300-314. On his service as judge in Santa Fe, rancher near

Albuquerque, 1848-1863. Litigation after his death on title to ranch, confiscated by Union as a result of his CSA service.

488 **WHARTON, Henry Marvin, D.D.**
"War Songs and Poems of the Southern Confederacy 1861-1865. A collection of the most popular and impressive songs and poems of war times, dear to every Southern heart. Collected and retold with personal reminiscences of the war." Profusely illustrated. n.p. (Philadelphia, March 1904)(International Pub. Co.) $95/ Large 8vo, 3/4Mor., marbled bds. and endsheet. pls, facsms., music, 412, (4)pp. some copies with decr. cloth. $75-bmk.

489 **WHARTON, T.**
"General Robert E. Lee, the man." Columbia Tenn., 1908. 8vo, wraps, 16pp.

490 **"WHAT Beat the South-**
Strategy or Numbers? A Reply to Gen. W.T. Sherman's Figures." Abingdon, Va. (c.1892) cover title, wraps, 8vo, 24pp.

491 **"WHAT I Saw of the Battle of Chickahominy."**
In: So. Mag., 1872, v.X, p.1-15.

492 **"WHAT Might Have Been.**
An incident in the financial history of the Confederate States, from the Raleigh "News & Observer", Feb. 1896." In: SHSP, 1896, v.XXIV, p.230-231.

493 **"WHAT are the Conditions**
of a Candid and Lasting Reconciliation between the Two Sections of the Country?" New York, 1861 8vo, orig. wraps, 69pp. Rather more favorable to south, in its equalization of slave and non-slave holding states, unrestricted movement of slaves interstate.

494 **"WHAT constituted the Supreme Court**
of the Confederate States of America from 1861 to 1865?" In: Lawyer and Banker, July 1920, v.XIII, p.195-202.

495 **"WHAT is the truth of Dahlgren's Raid?"**
In: Tyler's QHGM, 1946-1947, v.XXVIII, p.65-90.

496 **WHEAT, Chatham Roberdeau**
See: Leo Wheat, Alison Moore

497 **WHEAT, Chatham Roberdeau, Maj.**
See: "Sketch of...", Chas. L. Dufor, Alison Moore, Randy Steffen, Leo Wheat.

498 **WHEAT, Leo**
"Memoir of Gen. C. R. Wheat, Commander of the "Louisiana Tiger Battalion", by his brother." In: SHSP, 1889, v.17, p.47-60.

499 **WHEATON, C.C.**
"The Secession of Louisiana, January 26, 1861." In: East and West Baton Rouge Hist. Soc. Proc., 1918, v.II, p.55-60.

500 **WHEATON, John F.**
"Reminiscences of the Chatham Artillery. During the War 1861-1865, by Capt. John F. Wheaton. Read at Armory Hall, march 21st, 1887. Published by request of the company." (Savannah, Ga.) Press of Morning News, 1887. 8vo, wraps, port(front), 34pp. See: Charles C. Jones.

501 **WHEELER, Joseph, Gen.**
"Address to his command, December 31st, 1864." n.p., n.d., 12mo, (2)pp.

502 ..."Alabama." In vol. VII, Evan's Confederate Mil. Hist. 8vo, illus., ports, 452pp. maps, (biog., p. (383)-452.) Also: Extended Edt., biographies, 865pp.

503 ..."Alabama." v.VIII, 8vo, cl, 865pp. Wilmington, N.C., Broadfoot, 1987.

..."Alabama's Heroes-Pelham and Wheeler. (various addresses) In: SHSP, 1898, v.XXVI, p.291-305.

504 ..."The Battle of Shiloh, a graphic description of that sanguinary engagement." In: SHSP, 1896, v.XXIV, p.119-131.

505 ..."Bragg's invasion of Kentucky." In: B & L, v.III, p.1-25.

506 ..."Causes of the War, speech of...and Slavery and States Rights." In: SHSP, 1904, v.XXXII, p.24-41.

507 ..."An effort to Rescue Jefferson Davis." In: Cent. Mag., May, 1898, v.LVI, p.85-91.

508 ..."General Order #6, Soldiers of the Cavalry Corps. Hdq. Wheeler's Cavalry Corps, June 18, 1864. Virginia, 1864." Broadside, 4 1/2x12" (Argosy-86, #191)

509 ..."Head Quarters, Wheeler's Cavalry Corps., Cleveland, Tenn., Army of Mississippi, Nov. 16, 1863. General Order 16. By order of Gen. Wheeler." Broadside: 35x14cm.

510 ..."Military History of the State of Ala." In: Brant and Fuller's "Memorial Record of Alabama." p.95-153, v.1

511 ..."Light Infantry Tactics, etc." Nashville Imprint (Hill Books) Unrecorded?

512 ..."Proceedings in Statuary Hall of the United States Capitol upon the unveiling and presentation of the statue of Gen. Joseph Wheeler by the State of Alabama. Sixty-ninth Congress. Mar. 12, 1925." Washington: GPO, 1925. 8vo, cl, front, iv, 44pp. 69th Congress, 1st session, House Doc. 480. See: Jno. W. DuBose, Wm. C. Dodson, John P. Dyer, Edward Kennedy, Mrs. C.W. McMahon, Felix H. Robertson, Edward L. Wells.

513 ..."A Revised system of cavalry tactics for the use of the cavalry and mounted infantry, CSA. By Major General Joseph Wheeler, Chief of Cavalry, Army of Tenn." Mobile, Ala., S.H. Goetzel and Co., 1863. 16mo, cl, plates, ii, 220, 104, 47, 97-108, xiv, pp. $375-ob.

514 ..."Synopsis of the Military career of..., commander of the Cavalry Corps., Army of the West." N.Y., 1865, "Taken from official reports by a staff officer." 16mo, front(port) 35pp.
..."Synopsis..." Goodspeed-599 - "False date of imprint on both cover & title not revealed until last few pages, where purpose of biography surfaces: part of a Democratic campaign to replace Alabama carpetbagger in Senate with popular Southern Gen."

515 ..."Joe Wheeler's Cavalry at Murfreesboro." In: AlaHQ, Winter, 1956, v.18, p.601-604. From the Register and Advertiser, Mobile, Ala. 27 Jan. 1863.

516 ..."Wheeler's Raid into Tennessee." In: CV, Oct. 1917, v.XXV, p.460-463. See: John W. DuBose, Wightman Fletcher Melton.

517 ..."Joseph Wheeler." In: Nation, Feb. 1, 1906, v.LXXXV, p.90-91.

518 **WHEELER, Mattie**
"Journal of Mattie Wheeler. A Blue Grass Belle reports on the Civil War. Edt: Frances L.S. Dugan." In: FCHQ, April 1955, v.29, #2, p.118-144. Largely in Winchester, Ky., A brother's war in which Mattie remains loyal to the South.

519 **WHEELER, Richard**
..."We knew Stonewall Jackson." N.Y.: Thomas Crowell, (1977) 8vo, paperback, 129pp. This paperback preceded the bound 1st edition. Advanced proof.
..."We Knew Stonewall Jackson." N.Y., Thos. Y. Crowell Co., (1977) thin 8vo, cl, dj, front, ports, maps, illus., (9), 138pp.

520 ..."The Siege of Vicksburg." N.Y., Thomas Y. Crowell Co. (1978) 8vo, cl, dj, illus., incl. front, maps, ports, x, (2), 257pp.

521 **WHEELER, Woodbury**
"The history of the Battalion of North Carolina Artillery (Volunteers) Confederate States Army, known as "the Tenth". In: Univ. NCMag., March 1895, wraps, 12pp. The 10th, 2nd Battalion, Heavy.

522 **WHEELWRIGHT, Jere Hungerford**
"The Gray Captain." N.Y., Scribner's Sons, 1954. 12mo, cl, dj, 278pp. Story of Capt. Stowell, A.N.V., of a Maryland Company in '64.

523 **WHELAND, Charles E.**
"Bascom Clarke. The Story of a Southern Refugee." Madison, Wisc., American Thresherman (1913) 12mo, cl, front, illus., ports, (7), 216pp. Arkansas during wartime.

524 **WHELESS, John F., Gen.**
"The Confederate Treasure-Statement of Paymaster (JFW)." In: SHSP, 1882, v.10, p.137-141.

525 **"WHERE men only go to die.**
Story of a boy-company, by an ex-boy."
See: Royal W. Figg.

526 **WHERRY, William M.**
"The Battle of Prairie Grove, Arkansas, Dec. 1862." In: Jour. Mil. Ser. Inst., Sept./Oct., 1903, v.XXXIII, p.177-189.

527 ..."The Campaign in Missouri and the Battle of Wilson's Creek, 1861." Missouri Historical Collections, v.1, #1, p.3-18. (St. Louis, 1880)

528 **WHETSTONE, Adam Henry, Captain**
"History of the Fifty-third Alabama Volunteer Infantry (Mounted). Introduction and Edt. by William Stanley and Martha DuBose Hoole with a partial roster of the regiment." University, Ala., Confederate Pub. Co., 1985. Confederate Regimental Series, #9. 8vo, stiff wraps, 87pp. First published in the "Montgomery Advertiser", Oct. 10, 17, 38, Dec. 12, 1897 (again) April 29, May 5, 12, 19, 1901. This being the first edition in book form.
..."Scenes and incidents in the history of the Fifty-third Alabama Regiment." In: Montgomery (Ala.) Advertiser, Oct. 10, 17, 1897. This regiment of cavalry was organized in Montgomery Nov., 1862 (Owens, p.1231)

529 **WHILDEN, Mary S.**
"Recollections of the War 1861-1865." Columbia, S.C., The State Co., 1911. 8vo, wraps, 20pp. Lived thru Sherman's burning spree.

530 **WHIPPLE, Wayne**
"The Heart of Lee an intimate life-story of Robert E. Lee." Phila: John C. Winston Co. (1923). 16mo, cl, front(sketch), 224pp. $25.
...Phil.: Jacobs Print. (1918)

531 **WHITAKER, Walter Claiborne**
"Bishop Richard Hooker Wilmer." Montgomery, Ala. AHS, reprint #9. 8vo, wraps, cover title, p.211-234.

532 ..."Richard Hooker Wilmer, second bishop of Alabama; a Biography." Phila: G.W. Jacobs Co., (1907) 12mo, cl, front(port), 316, (7)pp. See also under R.H. Wilmer.

533 **WHITAKER, William G.**
"A part of war and prison life of Private W.G. Whitaker, Company H, Fourth Georgia Regiment." n.p., n.d. 16mo, wraps, cover title, (11)pp. (another copy reported with 2pp.)

534 **WHITCOMB, Paul S. (Gladstone, Ore.)**
"Lincoln and Democracy." In: Tylers Quart. Hist. and Geneal. Mag., July 1927. v.IX, #1, p.5-33. Lincoln's plots with Northern liberals.

535 **WHITE, Charles**
"John Brown's Raid at Harper's Ferry, Oct. 16-18, 1859: an eyewitness account by Charles White. Edited by Rayburn S. Moore." In: Va. MHB, Oct. 1959, v.67, p.387/395, maps, view, notes.

536 **WHITE, E.V.**
"The first iron clad naval engagement in the world. History of facts of the Great Naval Battle between the Merrimac, Virginia, CSN and the Ericsson Monitor, USN, Hampton Roads, Mar. 8/9, 1862." Suffolk, Va., Robt. Hardy, 1986. 8vo, wraps, (32)pp. port.

537 **WHITE, Edna**
"Mess at Camp Chase." In: ETHJ, Oct., 1968, v.VI, #2, p.124-128, notes. Robert J. Brailsford of Jasper, Texas. Priv. in Co.D,

Whitfield's Cav. Bat., Tex. Vols. Later: Co.E, 1st Tex. Legion, 27th Cav.

538 **WHITE, Elijah Veirs**
"History of the Battle of Ball's Bluff, fought on Oct. 21, 1861." fldg. map. Leesburg, Va., (c.1902) The Washington Print. $100. 8vo, wraps, front(port), 24pp. "Dedicated to Loudoun Chap. UDC, Leesburg, Va., Benefit Monument to be erected in Leesburg to the Confederate Soldiers of Loudon." White was a member of the CSA Engineers Corp.

539 **WHITE, Ellsberry Valentine**
"The first iron clad naval engagement in the word; history of facts of the great naval battle between the Merrimac-Virginia, C.S.N. and the Erricsson Monitor U.S.N., Hampton Roads, Mar. 8 and 9, 1862." (Portsmouth?, Va., c.1906) Report of battle by Commd. of "Gassendi" French man-of-war, p.15-21. sm. 4to, 9-full page pls., ports, (24)pp.
...N.Y., J.S. Ogilvie Print (1906) sm. 4to, tied with silk cord, 33pp. (unnumbered). The LC and Swem-6410 copies (Portsmouth, Va.)

540 **WHITE, Frank, Jr., Ed.**
"The Evacuation of Fort Moultrie, 1860." (Charleston: So. Caro. Hist. and Genea. Mag., Jan. 1952, v.LIII, #1, p.1-5.

541 **WHITE, H.G.**
"Company G, Twenty-Fourth Virginia Infantry List of membersand a Brief History." In: SHSP, 1907, v.35, p.352-256. 1908, v.36, p.356-359.

542 **WHITE, Helen Chappell**
"Surry of Eagle's Nest", by John Esten Cooke." In: Ga. Rev., Spring 1955, v.9, p.104-107. facsm. Memoirs of a first reading of this Civil War novel, c.1900.

543 **WHITE, Henry Alexander**
"Gettysburg Battle. Some literary facts connected therewith. Discussed in light of some late revelations." In: SHSP, 1899, v.XXVII, p.52-60.

544 ..."Lee's wrestle with Grant in the Wilderness, 1864." In: PMHSM, 1897, v.1, p.25-75.

545 ..."Robert E. Lee and the Southern Confederacy, 1807-1870." N.Y., G.P. Putnam's Sons, 1897. fldg. facsm., illus., maps, some fldg., ports, xii, 467pp. 12mo, cl, Half/title: Heroes of History. Copy extra illustrated, 1/2 Mor. Editions: 1900($10); 1902 and 1909; 1910 ($100), N.Y., Haskell House, 1968. (1971).
...N.Y., Greenwood Press (1969) "Famous Epock-makers." series.

546 ..."Was Robert E. Lee Loyal? Southern View by Henry Alexander White. Northern views of Austin Rice and Robert D. Coxe." In: Outlook, Aug. 8, 1903, v.LXXIV, p.887-890.

547 ..."Stonewall Jackson." Phila: George W. Jacobs (c.1908, Pub. January, 1909) $50. 12mo, cl, front (port) dbl-pg. map. 378pp. Half-title and heading-"American Crisis Biographies."

548 **WHITE, Henry M.**
"Confederate Humanity." In: SHSP, 1888, v.16, p.232.

549 **WHITE, Isaiah H., Dr.**
"Andersonville Prison, Dr. White, late surgeon CSArmy, testimony as to treatment of prisoners there." In: SHSP, 1889, v.17, p.383-386.

550 **WHITE, James Jones**
"Lee's Birthday." In: SHSP, 1889, v.17, p.353.

551 **WHITE, James Lowery**
"History of the Confederate General Hospital, located at Farmville, Va., 1862-1865." (Farmville, Va., Martin Press, 1916) 12mo, wraps, cover title, port, pl, 15pp. Pub.: Farmville Chap. UDC, paper read to D.C. Pickett-Thornton Camp, chap. 16,

June 10, 1897.
...1st. Edt., June 10, 1897, wrap, 16cm.

552 WHITE, John E.
"My Old Confederate Address: delivered before Atlanta Camp, #159, U.C.V. and Atlanta Chapters: United Daughters of Confederacy, Oct. 21, 1906." Atlanta, Ga., 1908. 8vo, wraps, xvpp., illus.

553 WHITE, Joseph F.
"Social conditions in the South during the War Between the States." In: CV, Apr./May, 1922, v.XXX, p.142-145, 181-184.

554 WHITE, Laura A.
"Robert Barnwell Rhett: Father of Secession." New York: The Century Co. (1931) American Historical Association. 8vo, cl, front (port) map, illus., ix, 264pp.
...Gloucester, Mass: Peter Smith, 1965.

555 WHITE, Levi S.
"Ordnance Department, CSA. General Josiah Gorgas, Chief." In: SHSP, 1901, v.29, p.319-320.

556 WHITE, Mary Virginia Saunders
"Robert E. Lee." Written for the Folio Club of Cleveland, 1935. 8vo, stiff wraps, 24pp.

557 WHITE, Max E.
"The Thomas G. Jordan Family During the War Between the States." In: Ga. Hist. Quart., 1975, v.LIX, p.134-140.

558 WHITE, Melvin Johnson
"The Secession Movement in the United States, 1847-1852." New Orleans, La: Tulane Univ., 1916, 8vo, wraps, 122pp. Thesis (PhD) Univ. Wisconsin, 1910.

559 ..."The Secession Movement in the United States, 1847-1852." (New Orleans, Tulane Univ. Press, 1916, 8vo, wraps, 122pp.

560 WHITE, Owen P.
"Buckets of Blood." In: Am. Mercury, Mar. 1929, v.XVI, p.296-303. Wm. Quantrill and border wars in Mo. and Kan.

561 WHITE, P.J.
"The Fifth Virginia Cavalry." In: CV, Feb., 1909, v.XVII, p.72-75.

562 WHITE, Richard Grant
"Who and what conquered the South?" In: SHSP, 1883, v.11, p.475-476.
"Book of the Prophet Stephen, Son of Douglas. Wherein marvelous things are foretold of the Reign of Abraham." N.Y., Feeks and Bancker (c.1862) 12mo, wraps, 48pp. See: Monnaghan 254-261, Sabin 6362, 70160, 103445 for variants. "Satire in Biblical form of political scene 1861-1862, concludes "battle of the Copperheads".

563 ..."The New Gospel of Peace according to St. Banjamin." N.Y., Sinclair Tousey (1963) 12mo, wraps, 42pp. Gdsp. $25. Satirical propoganda. Ebrst. $75. Other Edts: 1863-1864-1866. Monaghan.

564 ..."Revelations: A Companion to the "New Gospel of Peace". According to Abraham." N.Y., M. Doolady, 1863. 12mo, wraps, 36pp. Jk-$100. "Troubles with the Devil (alias Niggero)."

565 WHITE, Robert
"West Virginia." Vol.II, Evan's Confed. Mil. Hist. 8vo, cl, plates, maps, port, 138pp. Also: Extended Edt., biographies, p.296.
..."West Virginia." v.II, 8vo, cl, 296pp. Wilmington, N.C., Broadfoot, 1987.

566 WHITE, Robert H.
"Messages of the Governors of Tennessee, 1857-1869." v.5. Nashville: Tennessee Hist. Comm. (1959) Tk. 8vo, cl, facsms., illus., ports, index, (9), 728pp.

567 WHITE, William Spottswood
"A Diary of the War, or What I Saw of it." v.2, in "Richmond Howitzers, Contributions to a History of..." p.89-286. Richmond, Va., Carlton McCarthy Co., 1883, (Corrected by Col. W.E. Cutshaw, v.3, p.61-62.

568 ..."Rev. William S. White, D.D., and His Times. 1800-1873. An autobiography. Edited by his son, Rev. H.M. White, D.D., pastor of the Loudoun Street Presbyterian Church, Winchester, Va." Richmond, Va., Presbyterian Committee of Publications, 1891. 12mo, cl, front(port), 284pp. Much on the Civil War.

569 ..."Sketches of the Life of Captain Hugh A. White of the Stonewall Brigade, by his father." Columbia, S.C., South Carolinian Press, 1864. 12mo, cl, 124pp.

570 ..."Stray leaves from a soldier's Journal." In: SHSP, 1883, v.11, p.552-559.

571 **WHITE, William W.**
"The Confederate Veteran." Tuscaloosa, Ala: Confederate Pub. Co., 1962. Confederate Centennial Studies, #22. Lim. Edt. 450 copies.

572 ..."Mississippi Confederate Veterans in Public Office, 1875-1900." (Jackson, Miss., Jour. Miss. Hist., July, 1958, v.XX, #3, p.147-155.
..."Mississippi Confederate Veterans seek political appointments, 1876-1900." In: Miss. Quar., Winter, 1960, v.13, p.1-5, notes.

573 ..."Report of (Commanding Anderson's Brigade) Battle of Gettysburg." In: SHSP, 1877, v.IV, p.165-167.

573a **WHITEHEAD, Albert Charlton**
"Two Great Southerners, Jefferson Davis & Robert E. Lee." N.Y., etc., American Book Co., 1912. 16mo, decr. cl., ills, ports., 190pp, juvenile. $5. $20.

574 **WHITEHEAD, J.G.E.**
"The study of military history. A reply to "The legend of the Shenandoah Valley"." In: Army Quart. (Loundon), 1932, v.XXV, p.72-80. Author disagrees with conclusions of E.W. Sheppard's "Legends of Shenandoah Valley" in Army Quart., XXIII, p.48.

574a **WHITEHOUSE, J. E.**
"Seventeen days of sunset: the diary of J. Whitehouse, Sergeant Company F, 12th. Virginia, Infantry, CSA." In: Military Engr., 1939, v.31, #177, p.182-6.

575 **WHITFIELD COUNTY, Georgia**
"Official history of Whitfield County, Ga., by the Whitfield County History Commission, July 1930." Dalton, Ga., A.J. Showalter Co., 1930. 8vo, cl, viii, 238pp., illus. "War Between the States" by Mrs. W.C. Martin, "Reconstruction Era.", by Mrs. R.M. Herron.

576 **WHITING, John Downes**
"The Trail of Fire. A story of the famous "Alabama", with illustrations by author." Indianapolis: Bobbs-Merrill (1930) 12mo, cl, 7pp., 17-283pp., front, illus., pls.

577 **WHITLEY, Edythe Johns Rucker**
"Sam Davis Confederate War Hero, 1842-1863." (quote) Copyright 1947, n.p. tall 8vo, cl, illus., ports, 2-maps, 147pp. Sponsorship: The Sam Davis Memorial Ass'n., Sam Davis Home, Smyrna, Tenn. Under special act Tenn. Leg., 1947. Contains genealogical material of Davis and other families.
...Nashville, Tenn., (Blue and Gray Press) 1971. 8vo, cl, illus., maps, ports, ix, 251pp. "Coleman's Scouts" has been added to the above title.

577a **WHITMAN, George Washington**
"Civil War Letters (Feb.-July 1862) of George Washington Whitman. Edt. by Jerome M. Loving." In: NCHR, winter, 1973, p.33-72.
..."The Civil War letters of George Washington Whitman from North Carolina. Edt. Jerome M. Loving." In: NCHR, 1973, v.50, p.73-92.
..."Civil War letters of George Washington Whitman. Edt. Jerome M. Loving." Durham, N.C., Duke University Press, 197?. 8vo, cl, dj, 173p., ills. $10. atg-$13.50.

578 **WHITNEY, Louisa Goddard, Mrs.**
"Goldie's Inheritance: A Story of the Siege of Atlanta." Burlington, Vt., 1903: Free Press Ass'n. 12mo, cl, 263pp.

579 **WHITRIDGE, Arnold**
"The Alabama, 1862-1864. A crisis in Anglo-American relations." In: Hist. Today, Mar. 1955, v.V, p.174-185. Cartoons, ports, views.

580 ..."Anglo-American trouble-makers James Gordon Bennett and John Thadeus Delane." In: Hist. Today, Feb. 1956, v.VI, p.88-95. Cartoons, ports, Journalistic practices.

581 ..."Jefferson Davis and the Collapse of the Confederacy." In: History Today, Feb. 1961. 8vo, wraps, 11pp. article.

582 ..."No Compromise! The Story of the Fanatics Who Paved the Way to the Civil War." New York: Farrar, Straus and Cudahy (1960) 1st. 8vo, cl, d/w, 212pp.

583 ..."Eli Whitney nemesis of the South." In: Amer. Hert., Apr. 1955, v.VI, #3, p.4-11. port, illus. some color. Cotton and guns, industrial North against an agricultural South.

584 ..."The Trent Affair, 1861." In: Hist. Today, June 1954, v.IV, p.394-402. Cartoons, ports.

585 **WHITSELL, Hunter B.**
"Military operations in the Jackson Purchase area of Kentucky, 1862-1865." In: KyHSR, 1965, v.63, p.140-167, 240-267, 323-348, map.

586 ..."Military and Naval activity between Cairo and Columbus." In: KyHSR, April, 1963, v.61, p.107-121.

587 **WHITSITT, William Heth**
"Genealogy of Jefferson Davis: address delivered Oct. 9, 1908, before Lee Camp #1, Confederate Veterans." Richmond, Va., Everett Waddy Co., 1908. 8vo, wraps, 16pp. (McElroy Bibliog.) $10.

588 ..."Genealogy of Jefferson Davis, Pres. of Southern Confederacy and of Samuel Davis, Pres. of Princeton College." N.Y. and Wash., Neale Pub., 1910. 12mo, cl, 65, (1)p. $75-b.
...In: SHSP, Apr., 1914, v.XXXIX, p.73-85.

589 ..."A year with Forrest, address of...before R.E. Lee Camp, Confederate Vets." Richmond, Aug. 1917, v.25, #8, p.357-362. sketch.

590 **WHITSON, Lorenzo Dow, Mrs.**
"Gilbert St. Maurice by Mrs. L.D. Whitson. Published for the Author." Nashville, Tenn: Tavel, Eastman and Howell, 1874. 16mo, cl, front(port), viii, 331pp.

591 ...Louisville, Ky: Bradley and Gilbert, 1875. 16mo, cl, front(port) viii, 337pp. Another edition for 1876, p.337. Life and experiences of a CSA soldier, one of South Carolina's best families.

591a **WHITT, Jane Chapman**
"Elephants and Quaker Guns; a history of Civil War and circus days." N.Y., Vantage Press (1966) 1st. 12mo, cl, dj, facsms., illus., maps and map endsheets, 103pp. Bailey's Crossroads at Fall's Church battlegrounds between Union and Stuart and Mosby.

592 **WHITTINGTON, G.P.**
"Thomas Overton Moore, Governor of Louisiana, 1860-1864." New Orleans: 1930, v.XIII, p.5-31.
..."Papers of Thomas Overton Moore, Governor of Louisiana, 1860-1864." New Orleans: XIII, p.11-22.

593 **WHITTINGTON, Henry B.**
"Four Years of Occupation-Alexandria, Va., 1861-1865. Edt: Ames W. Williams." In: Alexandria Assoc., Yr. Bk., 1957, p.19-23, views. Excerpts from author's diary.

594 **WHITTLE, William C., Capt.**
"The Cruise of the "Shenandoah". The stirring story of her circumnavigation of the globe and many conquests on the high

seas. From the pen of her executive officer, Captain William C. Whittle." Rich: SHSP, 1907, XXXV, p.235-258.

...(Norfolk, Va., 1910?) rep; separate, 8vo, wraps, 32pp. $.50. "Cruise of CSA Steamer "Shenandoah" and "Nashville".

595 **WHITTLE, William Conway, Capt.**
"Cruise of the CS Steamer 'Nashville'." In: SHSP, 1901, v.29, p.207-212; Same, in v.38, 1910, p.334-340.

596 ..."Opening of the lower Mississippi, April, 1862. A reply to Admiral Porter." In: SHSP, 1885, v.13, p.560-572.

597 ..."The Merrimac and the Monitor." In: SHSP, 1915, v.40, p.301-304.

598 **WHITTON, F.E., Lieut. Col.**
"Vicksburg, 4th July 1863." In his "Decisive battles of modern times." Lond: Constable, 1923, p.1-51.

599 **WHITWORTH BATTERY**
See: Cadmus M. Wilcox

600 **WHITWORTH, John S.**
"Elliott Grays of Manchester, Va." In: SHSP, 1902, v.30, p.161-164.

601 **"WHO BURNT COLUMBIA?"**
Part 1st. Official Depositions of Wm. Tecumseh Sherman "General of the Army of the United States" and Gen. O.O. Howard, USA, for the defense; and extracts from some of the depositions for the claimants, filed in certain claims vs United States, pending before "the claims vs United States, pending before "the mixed commission on British and American Claims", in Washington, D.C." Part 2, will contain the Rebuttal Testimony yet to be taken." 1873. Charleston, S.C., Walker, Evans and Cogswell, 16mo, wraps, 121pp. No 2nd part issued. $150-g.

602 **"WHY Pennsylvania Should Become**
one of the Confederate States of America."
See: George McHenry

603 **"WHY Sherman Snubbed Augusta."**
In: CV, Aug., 1914, v.XXII, p.369. Includes letter from Sherman, in re question Oct. 21, 1888.

604 **"WHY the Confederate States of America**
had no Supreme Court. A symposium by Bradley T. Johnson, John V. Wright, J.A. Orr and L.Q. Washington." In: Pub. So. Hist. Ass'n., March 1900, v.IV, #2, p.81-101.

604a **"WHY the Confederacy Failed;**
opinions of Generals: Stephen D. Lee, Jo Wheeler, E. P. Alexander, E. M. Low, Don Carlos Buill, O. O. Howard & Jcob D. Cox." In: Century Mag., Feb. 1897, p.626-33.

605 **"WHY the South Hopes for Lincoln's Re-election.**
Reprint: Richmond Enquirer of Sept. 5, 1864." Broadside: 5 1/2 x 9 1/4" South could get better terms under Lincoln than McClellan.

606 **"WHY We Failed to Win.**
Inquiry into the causes of Confederate defeat." New Orleans "Picayune", Feb. 1, 1903. In: SHSP, 1902, v.XXX, p.368-371.

606a **WIATT, Alex L.**
"26th Virginia Infantry." Lynchburg, Va., H. E. Howard, 1984. J.P. Bell Pr., Lim., Atg.Edt. (916). 8vo, cl, dj, (3), 82p., facsm, maps, ports. $17.50.

607 **WICKERSHAM, John T.**
"The Gray and the Blue." (Berkeley, Ca., 1915) 4to, wraps, cover title, 186pp. mimeogr. Privately printed and distributed. Dornb-II, 3169.

608 **WICKHAM, Julia P. Porcher**
"Matthew Fontaine Maury, pathfinder of the Seas." In: Huguenot Society of South Carolina, Transactions, XXXVI, p.35-59. 8vo, wraps, 1931.

609 ..."Francis Peyre Porcher, M.D., LLd., Physician, botanist, author." In: CV, Dec.

1925, v.XXXIII, p.456-459. 8vo, wraps, 1931.

610 ..."Wade Hampton, the cavalry leader and his times." In: CV, Dec. 1928, v.XXXVI, p.448-450.

611 **WICKHAM, Williams Carter, Col.**
"Battle of Reams's Station." In: SHSP, 1881, v.9, p.107-108.

612 ..."Report of an engagement near Aldie." In: SHSP, 1881, v.9, p.79-80.

613 **WIDENER, Ralph W., Jr.**
"Confederate monuments enduring symbols of the South and the War Between the States." Dedicated to the Confederate soldiers and sailors "some of whom sacrificed all and all of whom sacrificed much." (Produced by Andromeda Associates, Washington, D.C., 1982) 4to, cl, xi, 307, (1)p., illus., plaques, statuary, monuments, cemeteries. Alphabetically arranged as to states. See: Bettie Alder Calhoun Emerson.

614 **WIER, Addison M.**
"Old times in Georgia. Good times and bad. By "Sarge" A.M. Wier." Atlanta, Ga., Constitution, 1903. 8vo, wraps, 126pp.

615 **WIESE, E.R. (author of)**
See: Surg. Gen. Samuel P. Moore.

616 **WIGFALL, Louis Tresvant**
"Speech...on the pending political issues; delivered at Tyler, Smith County, Texas, Sept. 3, 1860. Published by request of the Breckenridge and Lane Club of Smith County." (Tyler, Texas, 1860) 8vo, wraps, 28pp. caption title.

617 ..."Speech of Hon. L.T. Wigfall, of Texas, on relation of states. Delivered in the Senate of the U.S., May 22 and 23, 1860." Wash: Lemuel Towers, 1860. 8vo, wraps, sewn.

618 **WIGGINS, G.**
"Dance and Brothers, Texas Gunmakers of the Confederacy." Orange, Va., Moss Publications, 1986, 4to, cl, 151pp. illus., map, ports. $30.

619 **WIGHT, Levi Lamoni**
"The Reminiscences and Civil War Letters of...Life in a Morman Splinter Colony on the Texas Frontier." Davis Bitton, Edt. Salt Lake City: Univ. of Utah Press (1970) 8vo, fabricoid, front(port) map, facsm., ports, (7), lf, (11), 191pp., table.

620 **WIGHT, Willard Eugene**
"Bishop Elder and the Civil War." In: Cath. Hist. Rev., Oct., 1958, v.XLIV, p.290-306. Conduct of Bishop William Henry Elder of Natchez, 1861-1864.

621 ..."Bishop Verot and the Civil War." In: Catholic Hist. Rev., July 1961. Reprint, 8vo, wraps, 11pp. See also under Verot.

622 ..."The Bishop of Natchez (William Henry Elder) and the Confederate Chaplaincy, 1861-1865." In: Mid-America, v.39: p. 67-72, noteseee: Bishop Lynch Letters.

623 ..."The Churches and the Confederate Cause." In: CWH, December 1960, v.VI, #4, p.361-173.
..."Churches in the Confederacy." Ann Arbor, Mich., University Microfilms, 1979, 4to, paper, 242 leaves. Thesis: Emory Univ., 1919.

624 ..."The Governor of Georgia urges Secession of Arkansas." In: AHQ, v.16, p.192-202.

625 ..."Letters from the Diocese of Little Rock, (Arkansas) 1861-1865. Edt: Willard Wight." In: Ark. HQ, Winter, 1958, v.18, p.366-374. Letters to Archbishop New Orleans from Andrew Byrne, Laurence Smyth and Patrick R. Reilly.

626 ..."Some War Letters of the Bishop of Mobile, 1861-1865." In: Mid-America, Jan., 1961, v.43, p.61-68. See: Benj. J. Blied

627 ..."A Regimental Library in the Confederate Army." In: Jour. Lib. Hist., 1969, v.IV, p.347-352. (27th Virginia.)

628 ..."An unofficial account of the Battle of Wilson Creek, August 10, 1861." In: AHQ, 1956, v.XV, p.360-364, an acct. by Geo. Flournoy to Ed. Clark, Tex. Gov.

629 **WIKE, John**
"Individual decorations of the Confederacy." In: Mil. Collector and Hist., Dec. 1955, v.6, p.93-94. Medal, view, notes.

630 **WILCOX, Cadmus Marcellus**
"The Battle of Gettysburg." In: SHSP, 1878, v.6, p.97-124; v.7, 1879, p.280-287.

631 ..."Battle of Jones' Farm, Sept. 20, 1864." In: SHST, 1875, v.II, p.67-71.

632 ..."Battle of Reams Station." In: SHST, 1875, v.II, p.63-67, 99.

633 ..."Defense of Batteries Gregg and Whitworth and Evacuation of Petersburg." In: SHSP, 1877, v.4, p.18-33; 1882, v.9, p.168-178.

634 ..."Lee and Grant in the Wilderness." In: AW, p.485-501.

635 ..."Letter in reference to Seven Pines." In: sHSP, 1976, v.1, p.364-465.

636 ..."Review of "Four Years with General Lee." In: SHSP, 1878, v.6, p.71-77.

637 ..."Letter from General C.M.W." In: SHSP, 1877, V.4, P.111-117.

638 **WILCOX, Ella Wheeler**
"Sam Davis-a Southern Hero." In: SHSP, 1897, v.25, p.231-234.

639 **WILCOX, G. Griffing, Mrs.**
"War Times in Natchez." (From: New Orleans Picayune, Jan. 18, 1903.) In: SHSP, 1902, v.30, p.135-138.

640 **WILDER, John Augustus, Colonel**
"Key West in the Summer of 1864. Edt. by Millicent Todd Bingham." In: FHQ, January 1965, v.XLIII, #3, p.262-265.

641 **WILDERNESS, Battle of**
See: Goode Bryan, Asher W. Garber, Joseph B. Kershaw, Jas. Longstreet, Wm. Mahone, John R. Turner, "Texas Brigade".

642 **WILEY, Bell Irvin**
"Confederate Women." Contributions in American History, #28. Westport, Conn., London: Greenwood Press, 1975. 8vo, cl, dj, notes, bibliog., index, ports, xiv, 204pp.

643 ..."Camp Newspapers of the Confederate States of America." In: NCHR, 1943, v.XX, p.327-335.

644 ..."The collapse of the Confederacy." In: Emory Alumnus, May 1964, v.XL, p.4-8.

645 ..."The Common Soldier of the Civil War." N.Y., Charles Scribner's Sons, 1975. 8vo, cl, dj, illus., index, 144pp.

646 ...Gettysburg, Pa., Historical Times, Jly. 1973. Special issue of Civil War Times Illustrated, 4to, pict. wraps, illus., 64pp.

647 ..."The Confederate Congress." In: CWTI, Apr. 1968, v.VII, #1, p.22-24, facsms., port.

648 ..."Confederate exiles in Brazil." In: CWTI, Jan. 1977, v.17, #9, p.22-32, illus., port.

649 ..."Diaries from Dixie-Mary Chesnut." In: CWTI, April 1977, v.16, #1, p.22-32, illus., ports.

650 ..."Jefferson Davis." In: CWTI, April 1967, v.VI, #1, p.4-11, 44-49, illus., port+group.

651 ..."Jefferson Davis: an Appreciation." In: CWT, April 1967, v.VI, p.4-11, 44-49.

652 ..."Embattled Confederates. An Illustrated History of Southerners at War." Illus.- Hirst D. Milhollen, compl. N.Y., Harper and Row, 1964. 4to, cl, d/w, illus., ports, 290pp. map, facsms. $20-bmk.
...Bonanza, rep.

653 ..."Holy Joes" of the Sixties: a study of Civil War Chaplains." In: Huntington Lib. Quart., May 1953, v.16, p.287-304; Notes; Reprinted in: Mil. Chaplain, Oct. 1953, 24(2), p.17-22. In: "New Index: Confed. Research Club" (London) I(1956), p.84-93.

654 ..."Robert E. Lee: an Appreciation." In: Emory Univ. Quart., Winter, 1962, v.XVIII, p.240-250.

655 ..."Lincoln and Lee; an innaugural lecture delivered before the University of Oxford

on 19 January 1966." Oxford: Clarendon Press, 1966. 8vo, wraps, 18pp.

656 ..."Life in the South." In: CWTI, Jan. 1970, v.VIII, #9, p.4-9, 44-47, illus. Noncombatants trials on the homefront and morale.

657 ..."The Life of Johnny Reb. The Common Soldier of the Confederacy." Indianapolis-N.Y., Bobbs-Merrill Co. Pres.-$45. (1943) January, 1st Printing; 2nd Print, (1943) March (Cornwall Press, Cornwall, N.Y., verso t/p, dropped after 1st.); 3rd. print. (1943) July; 4th Print(1952) Feb. Imp. 8vo, front, plates, ports, facsms, d/w, 444pp. $30-dj, $85-2vol., 1st. Edt.

...(the 2nd Edt. (March, 1943) was also issued, boxed, with "Life of Billy Yank.")

...(Indianapolis) Charter Books (1962)--"this book a complete text of hardbound", 12mo, wraps, 441, (7)pp. (Amer. Hist. Lib.)

...Garden City: Doubleday & Co., 1971 Reprint, as above, with Billy Yank.

...Grosset, Dunbary, n.p., tk 8vo, 454pp. (vo), N.Y., Doubleday and Co. (1971), 2 vols.

..."Johnny Reb and Billy Yank." In: Emory Univ. Quart. Mar. 1952, v.8, p.1-6. A comparison.

658 ...Baton Rouge; Louisiana State University Press, 1979. 8vo, cl, boxed, 2 vols. Limited and autographed Anniversary Edition, with new rpeface by Bell Wiley. Limited Edt: 500 copies.

..."The Life of Johnny Reb, the Common Soldier of the Confederacy." 8vo, 48-pp. paper, 1979.

659 ..."The movement to humanize the institution of slavery during the Confederacy, 1861-1865." In: Emory Univ. Quart., Dec. 1949, v.5, p.207-220. In: "New Index-Jour. Confed. Research Club (London) I (1956), p.45-47, 55-58, 59-61.

660 ..."The Plain People of the Confederacy." Baton Rouge, La., Louisiana State Univ., 1943. The Walter Lynwood Fleming lectures in Southern History, LSU, 1943. 8vo, cl, d/w, ix, p.2, 1, 104pp. pl. ports. Pres. $40. Do: 1944 (2nd Edt.) $25, $35. N.Y., Grosset and Dunlap (n.d.) Do: Encounter Paperbacks, Quadrangle Books, Chicago (1963) (soft back), cloth, 104pp., Gloucester, Mass. 1971.

..."John Reb and Billy Yank at Shiloh." In: WTHSP, 1972, v.26, p.5-12.

661 ..."Rank and File: Civil War Essays in Honor of Bell Irvin Wiley. Edited by James I. Robertson, Jr., and Richard M. McMurry." San Rafael, Cal., Presidio Pr., 1976, 8vo, cl, dj, 164pp.

662 ..."The Road to Appomattox." Memphis, Tenn., Memphis State College Press (1956). 12mo, cl, dj, facsms., illus., map, ports, x, (1), 121pp. $35.

663 ..."Soldier newspapers of the Civil War." In: SWTI, June 1977, v.16, p.20-29, illus., facsms., port.

664 ..."The soldier's life, North and South, letters home tell adventures of two foes." In: Life Mag. Feb. 3, 1961, p.64-77.

665 ..."Southern reaction to Federal invasion, 1861-1865." In: Jour. South. Hist., Nov. 1950, v.XVI, p.491-510. $8.

666 ...."Southern Negroes 1861-1865." New Haven: Yale University Press, 1938. Cloth, viii, 366pp. (Yale Historical Publications, Mssc., XXXI) $10.

...Reprint: New York: Rinehart & Co., (1953) Intro: Bell Irvin Wiley. 12mo, cl, x, (2), 366pp. illus. Limp. Mor. $75.

...New Haven-Yale Univ. Pr. (1965).

667 ..."Southern Reaction to Federal Invasion." (Baton Rouge, La.) JSH, Nov., 1950, v.XVI, #4, p.491-510.

...Reprint, wraps, 20pp.

668 ..."A story of 3 Southern Officers." In: CWTI, Apr. 1964, v.III, #1, p.6-9, 28-35,

illus., port. Character as revealed in their letters: Jno. Bratton, Winnsboro, S.C., Lt.-Col. D.R.E. Winn, 4th Ga. and Robt. M. Gill, Co. H, 41st, Mississippi Reg.

669 ..."They Who Fought Here." New York: Macmillan Co., 1959, 4to, cl, d/w, illus., ports, vii, 273pp. Largely pictorial, Union and C.S.A.

670 ..."A time of greatness." In: Jour. South. Hist., Feb. 1956, v.XXII, notes, p.3-35. Character of soldiers who wrote home thousands of letters and in many diaries read by Wiley.

671 ..."Vicissitudes of early reconstruction farming in the lower Mississippi Valley." In: JSH, 1937, v.III, p.440-452. Period from 1862-1865, restricted to Federal controlled portions of La., Miss., Ark., Tenn.

672 ..."Why Georgia should commemorate the Civil War." Atlanta, Ga., Dept. State Parks (c.1960) 8vo, wraps(red), 24pp.
...Same (except white cover). Distr. by Nationwide Insurance, Columbus, Ohio.

673 **WILEY, Samuel T.**
"History of Monongalia County, W. Virginia." Kingwood: Preston Pub., 1883. 8vo, cl, 776pp. Shetler-866. Virginia Units: Cavalry: 20th, Cos. A & B; 26th Battalion, p.499-535.

674 **WILGUS, Alva Curtis**
"Some typical London Times views of the Southern Confederacy." In: Tyler's Quart. Hist. and Genea. Hist. Mag., July 1925, v.VII, #1, p.169-175. See also: Edward Tyas Cook's Delane.

675 **WILKES, Abner James**
"A Short History of My Life in the Late War Between the North and South." (Jackson, Miss., 1957) Charlotte Capers, Director of Archives. 4to, mimeo (one side), loose-lf, port, 21pp. Author: 46th Reg. Miss. Inf., CSA.

676 **WILKINS, Benjamin Harrison, Captain**
"War Boy", a true story of the Civil War and Reconstruction Days." Tullahoma, Tenn.: Wilson Bros. Print, 1938, 8vo, stiff wraps, port(front) atg., 84pp., print one side, on pg. 30 a note to "paste Confederate bill here". Some copies have bills. $50.

677 **WILKINS, E.L.**
"Reminiscences of James L. Coker's Confederate service, Memorial Exercises." In: Coker College Quart. Bull. Hartsville, S.C., 1920. 8vo, wraps, 63pp. See: James Lide Coker.

678 **WILKINSON, A.N.**
"John Moncure Daniel (1825-1865)." In: Richmond Coll. Hist. Pap., 1915, v.1, #1, p.73-95. See also Jno. M. Daniel.

679 **WILKINSON, J.W., Mrs.**
"Historical Department, Texas Division, United Daughters of the Confederacy.-..Lee Memorial Yearbook 1922-1923." (Houston, Texas, The Author, 1923?) 8vo, wraps, 35pp.

680 ..."United Confederate Veterans Historical Souvenir Book...Abilene, Texas. 1925." 8vo, wraps, front, 40pp. Roster of Dick Dowling Camp 197 (Houston) with constitution and by-laws.

681 **WILKINSON, John**
"The Narrative of a Blockade-runner." N.Y., Sheldon and Co., 1877. 12mo, 252pp. $275-r, $175.

682 **WILKINSON, Raymond Moore**
"The Confederate paper shortage." In: S.P.A. Jour., Apr., 1955, v.17, p.391-395, facsms. On Materials used for stamps and stp. envps.

683 ..."A permit to see the Postmaster General of the Confederacy." In: Am. Philatelist, Mar. 19, 1953, v.66, p.417-422. Facms., ports. On Atg-letters: Pres. Andrew Johnson, 1865, and Pres. Jefferson Davis, 1867.

684 **WILKS, Washington**
"English Criticism on President Lincoln's Anti-Slavery Proclamation and Message."

London: J. Kenny, 1863. 16mo, wraps, caption title, 8pp.

684a **WILLCOX, William Henry.**
"The Wartime Diary of William Henry Willcox. Edt: Karen T. Perdue." In: Jefferson CHQ, 1972, v.4, #1, p.18-28.

685 **WILLETT, Elbert Decatur, Maj.**
"History of Company B. (originally Pickens Planters), 40th Alabama Regiment, Confederate States Army 1862 to 1865." (Anniston, Norwood Print, Ala., 1902) $375-g. 8vo, wraps, 89pp.
...(Northport, Ala.) Colonial Press, (1963). 12mo, cl, (2), 89pp. Preface signed J.J.W. (Joseph Jackson Willett) "taken without revision or correction from the diary of Captain E.D. Willett of Company B. (preface)" Diary of J.H. Curry, pg. 85-89. See aso in Ala. Hist. Quart., Fall 1955, v.17, #3, p.159-222. "From the diary of J.H. Curry of Pickens Co."

686 **WILLETT, John T.**
"Development of Pea Ridge National Military Park." In: AHQ, 1962, v.XXI, p.166-169.

687 **WILLETT, Robert L., Jr.**
"The first battle of Franklin." In: CWTI, Feb. 1969, v.VII, #10, p.16-23. illus., maps, ports. Best known was the battle Nov. 30, 1864, but another engagement occurred 20 months earlier.

688 ..."We rushed with a yell." In: CWTI, Feb. 1970, v.VIII, #10, p.16-21, illus., map, port. Wheeler's raids on Federal railroads.

689 **WILLEY, William J.**
"The Second Federal Invasion of Indian Territory." Oklahoma City: Chron. Okla., Winter, 1966-1867, V.xliv, #4, P.420-430. See: Gary N. Heath.

690 **WILLIAM & MARY QUARTERLY**
"Virginia's contribution to Confederate States Army." In: Oct., 1904, W & M, p.141-142. In: SHSP, 1904, v.32, p.43-45.

691 **WILLIAMS, A.J.**
"Confederate History of Polk County, Tennessee, 1860-1866." Nashville, Tenn., McQuiddy Print, 1923, 12mo, wraps, 31pp. (Tenn. State Lib.)

692 **WILLIAMS, Ames W.**
"Action Near Vienna Station." (Richmond) Va. Cavl., Summer 1962, v.XII, #1, p.41-47, illus. (1-color) Gregg's South Carolinians ambush of a trainload of Ohioans, little known.

693 ..."The Occupation of Alexandria." (Richmond) Va. Cavl., Winter, 1961, v.XI, #3, p.33-39, facsms., port, illus., one in color.

694 **WILLIAMS, Ben Ames**
"House Divided." Bost: Houghton, Mifflin Co., 1947. Tk. 8vo, cl, xvi, 1514pp. Map and genealogical table as liners.
...Same, but in 2 vols., pres. copy.
...(reader's guide) 27pp., maps. Contains the author's preface to the novel and his bibliog., p.(13)-27, (1963 edt.) (1976 edition)

695 **WILLIAMS, Benjamin**
Note: under Robert McElroy's Davis.

696 **WILLIAMS, Benjamin B.**
"Alabama Civil War poet." In: AR, Oct. 1962, v.15, #4, p.243-252.

697 **WILLIAMS, Benjamin J.**
"Died for their State and Jefferson Davis." In: SHSP, 1886, v.14, p.119-126.

698 **WILLIAMS, Burton J.**
"Missouri State Depredations in Arkansas: a Case of Restitution." In: AHQ, 1964, v.XXIII, p.343-352, plate.

699 **WILLIAMS, C.R.**
"Southern sympathizers: Wood County Confederate soldiers and a sketch of the Nighthawk Rangers of Wood, Jackson, Wirt and Roane Counties in West Virginia." Parkersburg, W.Va., Inland River Books, n.d. (1960's ?) #4/50 copies. Dup. Typescript taken from an anon. memoir,

supposedly written 1930, wraps, $20 ("Book House, #14, Chapel Hill)

700 **WILLIAMS, Charlean Moss**
"Washington Hempstead County Arkansas, Gateway to Texas 1835, Confederate Capital 1863. The Old Town Speaks." Houston, Texas: Anson Jones Press, 1951, 8vo, cl, map endsheets, ports, illus. (CSA-100pp.) (24), 1-338pp.

701 **WILLIAMS, Dewey E.**
"A Civil War camp in North Carolina: Burke County's Camp Vance." Morganton, N.C., Private Print, 1977, 8vo, wraps, 80pp.

702 ..."Fort Macon, N.C., during the Civil War." Newport, N.C., The Author, 1979. 4to, wraps, litho of typed copy, tables, illus., drawings, facsms.

703 **WILLIAMS, Edward F., III**
"Fustest with the Mostest. The Military Career of Confederate Gen. Nathan Bedford Forrest. Born July 13, 1821, Chapel Hill, Tenn., Died Oct. 29, 1877, Memphis, Tenn." Memphis: Historical Hiking Trails, 1969, Memphis Sesquicentennial Edition. 4to, stiff decr. wraps, ports, illus., maps, 32pp. 1973-2nd printing.

704 ..."The Johnsonville Raid and Nathan Bedford Forrest State Park." In: THQ, 1969, v.28, p.225-251. See: SHSP, Nov. 1882, v.10, p.471-488.

705 **WILLIAMS, Edward F., III, and H.K. Humphreys, Edts.**
"Gunboats and Cavalry. The story of Forrest's 1864 Johnsonville Campaign, as told to J.P. Pryor and Thomas Jordan." Memphis, Tenn., Nathan Bedford Forrest Trail Comm., 1965, 8vo, wraps, 24pp.

706 **WILLIAMS, Emily J.**
"A home for the old boys", the Robt. E. Lee Camp Confederate Soldiers' Home." In: VaCavl., Summer, 1979, v.XXIX, #1, p.40-47, facsms., illus., incl. one in color.

707 **WILLIAMS, Fannie R.**
"Why North Carolina claims designer of first flag of the Confederacy, Stars and Bars." Newton, N.C., c.1935. 4to, wraps, 6pp. mimeograph. Issued by N.C. Div., UDC. That Orren Randolph Smith designed the CSA flag. See: Albert L. Cox, Maj. Edgar E. Hume, and Nicola Marschall.

708 **WILLIAMS, Flora McDonald, Mrs.**
"Who's the Patriot? A Story of the Southern Confederacy." (quote) $10. Louisville, Ky.: Courier-Journal, 1886. 12mo, decr. cl., gilt, illus., port, 288pp. Covers social side of war in South.

709 ..."Blue Cockade (Story of the Confederacy.)." Washington, 1905, Neale Pub., 12mo, cl, 381pp.

710 **WILLIAMS, Frances Leigh**
"Mathew Fontaine Maury Scientist of the Sea." New Brunswick, N.J., Rutgers University Press, 1963. 8vo, cl, dj, illus., xx, 720pp.

711 **WILLIAMS, George Walton**
"History of banking in South Carolina, sketch of the life of Geo. W. Williams...Reminiscences of the Confederate War and its effects upon the South." Charleston, S.C., Walker, Evans and Cogswell, 1900. 8vo, cl, 120pp.

712 **WILLIAMS, H. David**
"On the fringes of hell": Billy Yank and Johnny Reb at the siege of Kennesaw Mountain." In: GHQ, Winter, 1986, v.70, #4, p.703-716, ports, illus.

713 **WILLIAMS, H.W., Jr., Lt. Col.**
"A Confederate Marine Corps Button?" In: Mil. Coll. and Hist., Fall 1956, v.8, #3, p.81, illus. A Confed. button "M".

714 **WILLIAMS, Harold**
"Yankee Whaling Fleets Raided by Confederate Cruisers. The Story of the Bark Kireh Swift, Capt. Thomas W. Williams."

In: Amer. Neptune, Oct. 1967, Vol. XXVII, #4, p.263-278.

715 **WILLIAMS, Hattie Eunice**
"A brief history of Company C, 20th Alabama Regiment of the War Between the States." Birmingham (193?) 12mo, wraps, 16pp., illus., port. (Dorn-II, 58) Portions supplied by father: Wm. Alfred.

716 **WILLIAMS, Hermann Warner, Jr.**
"The Civil War: The Artists' Record." Boston: Beacon Press (1961) 4to, cl, and boards, illus. (6 color) 166 from all over the world. 251, (17)pp. d/w. Wash: Corcoran Art Gallery.

717 **WILLIAMS, Ida Belle**
"John Henry Gee, Physician and Soldier." In: Ga. H.Q., Sept. 1961, v.XLV, #3, p.238-244.

718 **WILLIAMS, James**
"The South Vindicated; being a series of letters written for the American press during the canvass for the presidency in 1860, with a letter to Lord Brougham on the John Brown Raid, and a survey of the result of the presidential contest and its consequences, with introduction by John Baker Hopkins." London: Longman, Grenn, 1862. $150-g, 8vo, cl, 1x, 444pp. $125. Supports constitutional justification & secession.

719 ...Nashville, Tenn., Methodist Pub. House, 1861. (1st Edt.)-"Letters on slavery from the Old World; written during the canvass for the presidency of the U.S. in 1860. To which are added a letter to Lord Brougham on the John Brown Raid and a brief reference to the result of the presidential contest and its consequences." 12mo, cl, x, 9-231pp.

720 ..."The rise and fall of the "Model Republic"." London: R. Bentley, 1863. 8vo, cl, xiv, 424pp. See: John Baker Hopkins.

721 **WILLIAMS, James M.**
"From that terrible field, Civil War letters of Jas. M. Williams, Twenty-first Alabama Infantry vols., Edt: John Kent Folmar." University, Ala., University Press, 1981. 8vo, cl, dj, illus., 187pp., xvi, maps.

722 **WILLIAMS, Jay D.**
"Adjutant General's Office, Militia Enrollment List for Carroll County, Ga., 1864." In: Carroll Co. Geneal. Quart., 1985, v.6, #1, p.11-20.

723 **WILLIAMS, John Calvin**
"The fire of hatred"-Rebel Memories of the Red River Campaign." In: CWTI, Jan. 1979, v.17, #9, p.20-31, illus., map, ports. Williams was from Grayson Co., Tex., 34th Tex. Cavl. in the Trans-Miss. campaign.

724 **WILLIAMS, John Jefferson**
See: "Last man killed in war."

725 **WILLIAMS, John Sharp**
"Address to Company "A", Confederate Veterans, at the Lyceum Theatre, Memphis, Tenn." May 31, 1904. Memphis, Tenn., Paul and Douglas Co. (1904) 8vo, wraps, 32pp. Concerns nature of the CSA Vet.

726 ..."Gen. Marcus J. Wright-A Tribute." In: CV, Feb. 1923, v.XXXI, p.49-50.
..."Our advance from Appomattox; address of...at the celebration of the hundredth anniversary of the birthday of General Robert E. Lee, before the Virginia Society of Atlanta, Janaury 1907." (n.p., 1907?) 12mo, wraps, 32pp.

727 **WILLIAMS, John Silas**
"The siege; a novel of love and war." N.Y., Cosmopolitan Press, 1912. 12mo, cl, 410pp. Miss. withdraws from Union, Vicksburg and years at war.

728 **WILLIAMS, John Skelton**
"Advance from Appomattox." In: SHSP, 1906, v.34, p.336-352. How the cotton growers could tie up the commerce of the world.

729 **WILLIAMS, John Stuart**
"Report of Brig. Gen. John S. Williams of operations in East Tennessee, from 27th September to 15th October, 1863. Published by Order of Congress." Richmond, Va., R.M. Smith Print, 1864. 8vo, sewn, 9pp. Crandall-1415.

729a **WILLIAMS, K. J.**
"Ghost ships of the Mersey: a brief history of Confederate Cruisers with Mersey connections." Birkenhead, Merseyside, 1987. 8vo, pict. wraps, 38pp, ills., ports. $5.

730 **WILLIAMS, Lucille Stilwell**
"John Cabell Breckinridge (1821-1875)." In: KyHSR, 1934, v.XXXII, p.301-319. Thesis: KyU, MA Degree.

731 **WILLIAMS, Martha Noyes, (Mrs. H.D. Williams)**
"A year in China; and a narrative of capture and imprisonment...on board the Rebel Pirate "Florida". By Mrs. H. Dwight Williams with an Intro: Wm. Cullen Bryant." N.Y., Hurd and Houghton, 1864. 12mo, cl, xvi, 362pp. $250. About 50pp. her week on the "Florida", her conversations with Maffitt at length.

732 **WILLIAMS, Mary Temple Harrison, Mrs.**
"Grandpapa and one of his stories." Richmond, Va., Enquirer Job. Off., 1863, 16mo, wraps, 14pp.

733 **WILLIAMS, Nannie H.**
"The Tennessee Confederate orphanage." In: CV, June 1923, v.XXXI, p.218-220.

734 **WILLIAMS, Noble Calhoun**
"Echoes from the Battlefields; or, Southern life during the War." Atlanta, Ga., Franklin Print, 1902. 12mo, cl, ix, 94pp. Before and after Sherman's occupation, Atlanta. $40.

735 **WILLIAMS, R. H.**
"Scouting on the Texas Frontier, 1861-1865." In: Frontier Times, July/Aug. 1950, v.27, p.279-287, 303-306. Reminis. CSA officers.

736 **WILLIAMS, R. H. and John W. Sansom**
"The Massacre on the Nueces River the Story of a Civil War tragedy, as related by R.H. Williams and John W. Sansom both of whom participated in the Battle, Williams on the Confederate side and Sansom with the Unionist." Grand Prairie, Texas: Frontier Times (1954) 8vo, stiff wraps, 36pp. Foreword: J. Marvin Hunter, Sr. Taken from "The Border Ruffians".

737 **WILLIAMS, Rebecca Yancey**
"Inauguration of a display of returned Battle Flags of the Confederacy." (Richmond) Va. Mag. Hist. Biog., July 1947, v.55, #3, p.282-285.

738 **WILLIAMS, Richard Hobson**
"General Banks Red River Campaign." New Orleans: LHQ, Jan. 1949, v.32, #1, p.103-144.

739 **WILLIAMS, Robert Gray**
"Address delivered at Washington and Lee University, Jan. 19, 1931." with John Warwick Daniel's speech in 1883. See under John Warwick Daniel.

740 **WILLIAMS, Robert H.**
"With the Border Ruffians; memories of the Far West. 1852-1868, by R.H. Williams, sometimes lieutenant in the Kansas Rangers and afterwards captain in the Texas Rangers; Edt: E.W. Williams." N.Y., E.P. Dutton, 1907. 8vo, cl, 4-pls., 2-ports, incl. front, xiv, xv-xviii, 478pp. See his acc't. "Battle of Nueces River", See his "Massacre on the Nueces". See: John W. Sansom's account.

741 ..."The massacre on the Nueces River, the story of a Civil War tragedy, as related by R.H. Williams and John W. Sansom, both of whom participated in the battle, Williams on the Confederate side and Sansom with the Unionist." Grand Prairie, Texas: Frontier Times, (1954) 8vo, decr. wraps, 36pp. See also under Sansom, Jas. P. Newcomb.

742 **WILLIAMS, Robert W., Jr. and Ralph A. Wooster, Edts.**
"Camp Life in Civil War Louisiana: the Letters of Private Isaac Dunbar Affleck." In: Louisiana Hist., 1964, v.V, p.187-201. Terry's Texas Rangers and Wharton's Cavalry.

743 ..."With the Confederate Cavalry of East Texas: The Civil War Letters of Pvt. Isaac Dunbar Affeck." In: East Texas Hist. Jour., 1963, v.I, p.17-28. Terry's Scouts.

744 **WILLIAMS, Sarah Frances Hicks**
"Plantation experiences of a New York woman. Edt: James C. Bonner." In: NCHR, July/Oct., 1956, v.33, p.384-412, 529-546. Notes. Letters to the author's parents, 1853-1867, Greene Co., N.C. and Ware Co., Ga.

744a **WILLIAMS, Steve A.**
"Charge both ways: the battle of Parker's Crossroads." In: CW(new) Sept. 1985, v.33, #5, p.10-20, plate, ports (Forrest in color), map. Ronald T. Clemmons - 'Reflections on Gen. Forrest.' p.29-20, ports.

745 **WILLIAMS, T. Harry**
"Beauregard at Shiloh." In: C.W.H., Mar. 1955, v.1, #1, p.17-34. From his biography of Beauregard, Vet, to be published by LSU.

746 ..."P.G.T. Beauregard Napoleon in Gray." Baton Rouge: Louisiana State University Press (1954) 8vo, cl, d/w, illus., ports (incl. front) maps, xiii, 345pp. $45.
...Civil War Book Club Edition, limited edition, atg. by author, in dj. $40-bmk-109.
...Southern Biography Series. $27.50
...(1955) second printing.
...(1960) third printing, differs in being thinner book, thicker (stiff) paper.
...Paper-1965 Edt. 4.
..."General Beauregard, Napoleon in Gray." (Houston, Texas, Civil War Round Table. Address Mar. 15, 1955.) 8 1/2x11 heavy paper covers, folded to 8vo, 14pp.

747 ..."The Civil War in Louisiana. A Chronology by T. Harry Williams and A. Otis Hebert, Jr." (Baton Rouge) Louisiana Civil War Centennial Commission, 1961, 8vo, decr. wraps, illus., port, 29pp.

748 ..."Freeman, Historian of the Civil War: An Appraisal." (Lexington, Ky.) JSH, Feb. 1955, v.XXI, #1, p.91-100.

749 ..."Louisiana Commemorates the Civil War." (Baton Rouge: Louisiana Civil War Centennial Commission, 1961) 8vo, decr. wraps, illus., 15pp.

750 ..."The Louisiana Unification Movement of 1873." (Baton Rouge, La.) JSH, Aug. 1945, v.XI, #3, p.249-269.

751 ..."The Military Leadership of the North and the South (1861-1865)." In: "Colorado", (US Air Force Academy) 1960, v.6, port, 23pp. "Harmon Memorial lectures in military history, 2." (Also printed: David Donald's "Why the North won the Civil War.") See: under his name.

752 ..."Selected essays of T. Harry Williams." Baton Rouge: University Press, 1983. 8vo, cl, dj, 276pp. Bibliography of THW's books, articles. Six deal with war and a seventh, works of Douglas S. Freeman.

753 ..."The South's first hero." In: John Art. Garraty, edt., "The unforgettable Americans", Great Neck, NY, Channel Pr.(1960) On P.G.T. Beauregard, US Mil. Acad., US Army in Mexican War, CSA general.

754 **WILLIAMS, Trevor J. Vaughan**
"The C.S.S. Shenandoah in Melbourne, Australia."(London) Jour. Confed. Hist. Soc., Dec. 1963, v.II, #1, p.18-26, port, pls-2.

755 **WILLIAMS, W.A., Civil Engineer**
"Sketch of Charleston Harbor (colored)." 12 3/4x12 3/4", inserts: Plans of Forts Sumter and Moultrie, Castle Pinckney; all

756 shore batteries, armament, torpedoes. Boston: L. Prang and Co., (c.1863).
...."View of Fort Sumter." colored oblong folio lithograph, 7x22" showing city of Charleston, Forts Sumter, Johnson and Moultrie. Boston (c.1861).

757 **WILLIAMSBURG District, S.C.**
See: John G. Pressley.

758 **WILLIAMSBURG Junior Guard**
"Roll of the Company, from Richmond Dispatch, Feb. 9, 1890." In: SHSP, 1890, v.18, p.275-277. See: E.H. Lively.

759 **WILLIAMSBURG Road, Battle of**
See: James Longstreet.

760 **WILLIAMSBURG, Battle of**
"Magruder-Ewell Camp, CV, List of wounded at Williamsburg, Va., May 6, 1862." In: SHSP, 1896, v.24, p.172-175. See: John Bratton, Salem Dutcher, Duncan McRae, Richard L. Maury.

761 **WILLIAMSBURG, South Carolina**
William Willis Boddie's "History of Williamsburg County, S.C., etc." Columbia, S.C., 1923. Index, maps, ports, ix, 609pp.
...Spartanburg, S.C., Reprint Co., 1980. Muster rolls CSA units, officers, deaths of soldiers, excerpts from diaries. Topics as: Nullification, slavery and secession, Reconstr.

762 **WILLIAMSBURG, Va.**
"Sketch of the Battlefield and Confederate Works in front of...5 May, 1862." by Lt. M.D. McAlester. colored: 13x14" Washington: War Dept., Chief Engineers 1876. Confed.-Union forces, positions.

763 **"WILLIAMSON County, Franklin, Tennessee.**
Civil War Centennial, Nov. 28-30, 1964...Battle of Franklin, 1864-1964." 4to, decr-color stiff wraps, illus., maps, 1-fldg. 16pp.

764 **WILLIAMSON, E.M.**
"Confederate Reminiscences 1861-1865." (Danville, Va., McDaniel Print, 1935) Private print, 300 copies, 8vo, wraps, cover title, ports, 39pp. $200-ob.

765 **WILLIAMSON, Hugh P.**
"The Battle of Moore's Mill." Columbia, Mo., Mo. Hist. Review, July 1972, v.LXVI, #4, p.539-548. illus., ports.

766 **WILLIAMSON, J. Pinckney**
"History of the Crater and ten months siege of Petersburg, Virginia." Suffolk, Va., Robt. Hardy Pub., 1986, 8vo, wraps, 32pp.

767 **WILLIAMSON, James J.**
"Mosby's Rangers..." N.Y., Time-Life Pub., 1982. 12mo, fabricoid, "Collector's Library of the Civil War." gilt edges $25.

768 **WILLIAMSON, James Joseph**
"Mosby's Rangers: a record of the operations of the forty-third battalion Virginia Cavalry, from its organization to the surrender, from the diary of a private, supplemented and verified with official reports of Federal officers and also of Mosby; with personal reminiscences, sketches of skirmishes, battles and bivouacs, dashing raids and daring adventures, scenes and incidents in the history of Mosby's Command...Muster Rolls, occupations and present whereabouts of surviving members by James J. Williamson of Co.A." N.Y., Ralph B. Kenyon, Pub., 1896. $200, $165. Tall 8vo, cl-with gilt design, facsms., illus., maps, ports, xii, (13)-511pp.
..."Mosby's Rangers, a record of the operations of the forth-third battalion of Virginia Cavalry from its organization to the surrender. By James J. Williamson. Second edition, revised and enlarged." $150, $100. 12mo, cl, illus., maps, ports, vii, 554pp., plates of 1st Edt, used thru p.473.

769 ..."Prison Life in the Old Capitol and reminiscences of the Civil War, by James J. Williamson." West Orange, N.J., 1911. 12mo, cl, facsms., illus., map, ports, x, 11-162pp. See: Maj. Henry Wirz, p.132-153.

770 **WILLIAMSON, John Coffee**
"The Civil War Diary of John Coffee Williamson. Edt: J.C. Williamson." In: Tenn. HQ, Mar. 1956, v.XV, p.61-74. Commissary Sgt., Co. E, 5th Tenn. Cavl., CSArmy in Tenn., Aug. 11-Oct. 31, 1864.

771 **WILLIAMSON, Mary Lynn Harrison, Mrs.**
"The Life of Gen. Thos. J. Jackson "Stonewall" for the Young, (fourth reader grade) in easy words, illustrated." Richmond, Va., B.F. Johnson Pub., (1899) 12mo, decr. boards (pix of Jackson on cover.) illus., map ports, errata slip, 248pp. front. composite ports., cover sketch of Jackson in black and white.
...(1899) variant edition has a color portrait of Jackson on cover. Front. composite portrait with names under each port. 254pp.
...(1918) title: "Life of Thomas J. Jackson." "Biographical reader"...third and fourth grade with 222pp.

772 ..."The Life of Gen. Robert E. Lee, for children in easy words." Richmond, Va., The Baughman Stationery (1895) 8vo, cl, (illustrated) front, col. pls., 129, (1)pp.
...Richmond, Va., B.F. Johnson Pub. (1895) 12mo, dk. yellow decr. cl., front, illus., maps, ports. This edition has preface dated Sept. 28, 1898. 183pp.
..."Life of Gen. Robert E. Lee." Richmond, Va., Atl., Dal., (1895) 12mo, green decr. cl, 183pp., verso t/p is a list of books: "Life of Lee (3rd gr.); life of Jackson (4th gr.) and Life of Stuart (5th) the latter not pub. until (1914).
...Same, (1918) "Biographical Readers", but with 172pp.

773 ..."Life of J.E.B. Stuart. Edited, arranged by E.O. Wiggins, for school use (5th grade)." Richmond, Va., etc., B.F. Johnson (1914) 12mo, cl, front (port), illus., maps, ports, 215pp. (also bound in boards). $45.

774 **WILLIAMSPORT Hospital**
See: J.M. Gaines.

775 **WILLING, Wildurr**
"Robert Edward Lee." In: Professional Memoirs, Corps of Engineers, U.S. Army and Engineer Department-at-Large. Washington, Engineer School, Washington Barracks." 1917, v.IX, #46, p.361-476.

776 **WILLINGHAM, Robert M.**
"Confederate printing in Augusta." In: Richmond County History, 1985, v.17, #2, p.5-14.

776a **WILLINGHAM, Robert M., Jr.**
"No Jubilee, the story of Confed. Wilkes Co." Washington, Ga., 1976. 8vo, wraps, cl, 343pp. Bmk-$15-28. See: Hanna. Solves mystery of Gold disappearance Jeff Davis flight.

777 **WILLIS, Edward, Col.**
"Letter of Colonel Edward Willis, of the Staff of Lieut-Gen. T.J. Jackson." June 14, 1862. In: SHSP, 1916, v.41, p.161-165.

778 **WILLIS, Edward, Gen.**
"Memorials of...C.S. Army, commandant of the 12th Georgia Infantry, who fell at the head of his regiment in the battle of Mechanicsville, May 31, 1964." Richmond, Va., Southern Hist. Society Papers, 1890, (1889, v.17, p.160-186) 8vo, wraps, 31pp.

779 ..."Valuable American Historical Library of the late Major Edward Willis of Charleston, S.C." (Quartermaster: Beauregard) Phila: 1914. 8vo, wraps, 134pp. Sales Cat., of 892 items, largely Civil War and South Caroliniana.

780 **WILLIS, Francis T.**
"The Twelfth Georgia Infantry." In: SHSP, 1889, v.XVII, p.160-187. See: Edward Willis.

781 **WILLIS, Katherine Jackson and William W. Rogers.**
"Encounter at the Aucilla, 1862." In: FHQ, Oct., 1982, v.LXI, #2, p.148-154. Re: Geo. Washington Scott. See: Marion B. Lucas.

782 **WILLS, David**
"War-the Departed Patriots and Heroes of Macon." In: Scott's Monthly Magazine, March 1968, v.V, p.123-126.

783 **WILLS, George Whitaker, Lt.**
"Its good to be religious"; a loyal slave of God, masters and the Civil War. Edt.: Randall M. Miller." In: NCHR, Jan. 1977, v.54, #1, p.66-71, port.

784 **WILLS, Mary Alice**
"The Confederate Blockade of Washington, D.C., 1861-1862." Parsons, W.Va., McClain Press, 1975. 8vo, cl, dj, illus., maps, bibliog., index, xi, 194pp.

785 **WILLSON, Beckles**
"John Slidell and the Confederates in Paris (1862-1865)." N.Y., Minton, Balch and Co., 1932. 8vo, cl, illus., ports, front, xiii, 196pp. $30.
...N.Y., AMS Print (1969) cl.
...N.Y., (1977) (1970)

786 **WILMER, Joseph Pere Bell, Bishop of La.**
"General Robert E. Lee, an address delivered before students of University of South, Oct. 15, 1870." Nashville: Paul and Tavel, 1872. 8vo, wraps, 12pp., same title on cover.

787 ..."Address on General Lee." In: SHSP, 1886, v.14, p.245-250.

788 ..."A Defense of Louisiana." New Orleans: J.A. Gresham, (1868?) 8vo, wraps, 13pp. Defends Reconstruction in Louisiana.

789 **WILMER, Richard Hooker**
"The Recent Past from a Southern Standpoint. Reminiscences of a Grandfather (quote) by Richard H. Wilmer, Bishop of Alabama." N.Y., Thomas Whittaker, 1887. 8vo, cl, ports, incl. front, 281pp. $30. Editions: 1887, second edt., 294pp. Unreconstructed Rebel after War, when Pres. Johnson had to set an order aside after his and clergy's suspension. See: Walter C. Whitaker.

790 **WILNER, Jonathan M.**
"Female planters and planter's wives in Civil War and Reconstruction: Alabama 1850-1870." In: AR, Arpil 1977, v.30, #2, p.135-149.

791 **WILSHIN, Francis F.**
"Manassas (Bull Run) National Battlefield Park Virginia." Wash: Nat'l. Park Ser. Hist. Handbook, ser.#15, 1953. (reprint, 1961) 8vo, pict. color stiff wraps, illus., maps, 2-dbl. pg., ports, (4), 47, (1)p.

792 **WILSON CREEK, Battle of**
See: W.E. Woodruff, W.H. Tunnard. "Wilson's Creek, from the Richmond Dispatch." In: SHSP, 1910, v.38, p.363-372. See: Robt. A. Austin, Edwin C. Bearss, Geo. M. Flournoy, Return I. Holcombe, John K. Hulston, Wm. Naylor McDonald, J.H. McNamara, H. Clay Neville, Lucile Morris Upton, Albert Castel, Jno. N. Edwards, Jno. McElroy, Jas. Monaghan.

793 **WILSON Co., Tenn., UCV**
See: "Minutes of UCV, Camp #941."

794 **WILSON, Augusta Jane Evans, Mrs.**
"Macaria; or, Alters of Sacrifice." Richmond, Va., West and Johnston, 1864. 8vo, cl, 183pp. dbl. columns.
...N.Y., John Bradburn, 1864. 8vo, cl, 469pp. $35. Novel of the Confederacy. See: Wm. P. Flower.

795 **WILSON, Calvin**
"Roll of the Rockbridge Battery of Artillery, Arpil 10, 1865." In: SHSP, 1888, v.16, p.277-280.

796 **WILSON, Charles Ray**
"The Cincinnati Daily Inquirer and the Civil War Politics: a study in "Copperhead" opinion." Chicago, Ill., 1937, University of Chicago, PH.D. thesis, photolitho, "Private edition, distr. by the Univ. of Chi. Libraries."

796a **WILSON, Charles Reagan**
"Baptized in blood; the religion of the Lost Cause, 1865-1920." Athens: Universi-

ty of Georgia Press, 1980. 8vo, cl, dj, viii, 256pp. $20.

797 **WILSON, Charles Robert**
"Bear Wallow Belles; a love story of the Civil War." Louisville, Ky., B.H. Carothers, 1903, 12mo, cl, 240pp. fiction. Story of Nellie Terrill spying on U.S. Grant.

798 **WILSON, Clyde E.**
"Cotton cards, how secured for the people of Alabama during the period of the War Between the States, 1861-1865." In: Ala.H.Q., 1952, v.14, p.151-156. "carding" was a hand-instrument in preparing cotton.

799 ..."James J. Pettigrew." In: CWTI, Feb. 1973, v.11, #10, p.12-23, illus., ports.
..."Artificial limbs." In: AHQ, 1956, v.18, #4, p.443-62.
..."State Militia, June 1865-Dec. 1865." In: AHQ, 1953, v.14, #3 & 4, p.301-30.
See: James G. Terry.

800 **WILSON, Dell B.**
"The Grandfather and the Globe." Banner Elk, N.C., 1969. 8vo, cl, dj, 264pp. "a chronicle of how the Civil War affected lives of certain families in Grandfather Mt. region of Watauga Co., N.C. and adjacent Globe Valley." Fiction but "events and social history of the war are faithfully recorded."

801 **WILSON, Edmund**
"Patriotic Gore. Studies in the Literature of the American Civil War." N.Y., Oxford University Press, 1962. tk. 12mo, xxxii, 816pp., index. Actual participants in conflict, Union and Confederates (Kate Stone, Sarah Morgan, Mary Chestnut; Rich. Taylor, Jno. Mosby, Lee, Stephens. Geo. Fitzhugh.

802 **WILSON, Francis**
"John Wilkes Booth. Fact and Fiction of Lincoln's Assassination." Boston: Houghton Mifflin, 1929. 8vo, cl, xiv, (i), 321, (1)pp. illus. Also, Edt. 300 copies. $49.50, $30-bmk.

803 **WILSON, Frank I.**
"The Battle of Great Bethel, fought June 10, 1861." Raleigh, N.C., "Standard" office, 1864. 16mo, wraps, 28, (4)pp. Crandall-2665, Goodspeed-$850.

803a **WILSON, Franklin**
"The Life Story of Franklin Wilson, as told by himslef in his journals." Balt., Wharton & Barron, Pub., 1897. 12mo, cl, 132pp, front, pls, ports.

804 **WILSON, Glen O.**
"Old Red River Station." In: SwHQ, Jan. 1958, v.LXI, #3, p.350-358, map. Established during Civil War and afterwards a post on the Chisholm Trail.

805 **WILSON, James Harrison**
"How Jefferson Davis was overtaken." In: Ann. War, p.554-589.

805a **WILSON, James Harrison & William P. Stedman**
"Pursuit & capture of Jefferson Davis." In: Cent., April 1890, v.17, p.587-96. Facsm. of reward poster.

806 **WILSON, Joseph David**
"A Young Confederate stationed in Texas. The Letters of Joseph David Wilson, 1864-1865. By Elvis E. Fleming." In: Texana, 1970, v.VIII, #4, p.352-361.

807 **WILSON, Legrand James**
"The Confederate Soldier, by..., Surgeon Confederate States Army." Fayetteville, Ark., M'Roy Print Co., 1902. 12mo, wraps, cover title, 2pp., 1, (3)-187pp. Was 1st Lt. (surgeon) Co. F, 1st Miss. Inf. after April 1862-Co. F, 42nd Miss. Reg.
...Memphis, Tenn., Memphis State Univ. Press, 1975. 1st Edt-1973.

808 **WILSON, Quintus C.**
"Confederate Press Association: a Pioneer News Agency, 1862-1864." Journalism Quarterly, June 1949, v.XXVI, p.160-166. $7.

809 **WILSON, Robert**
"Medicine in the Days of the Confederacy." In: So. Carol. Med. Assn. Jour., 1970, v.LXVI, p.169-172.

810 **WILSON, Robert Burns**
"Theodore O'Hara." In: Cent., 1890, ns, v.XVIII, p.106-110, plate, port. With O'Hara's noted poem, "The Bivouac of the Dead".

811 **WILSON, Robert T.**
"Some hard fighting; letters of Private Robert T. Wilson, 5th Texas Infantry, Hood Brigade, 1862-1864." In: Mil. Hist. Tex. and Sowst., 1971, #4, p.289-302. (Elvis Fleming, Edt.)

812 **WILSON, Rufus Rockwell**
"Stonewall Jackson's old schoolmaster tells of boyhood days at Weston." In: SHSP, 1894, v.22, p.157-164.

813 **WILSON, T. Paul**
"Delegates of the Five Civilized Tribes to the Confederate Congress." In: Okla. Chronicles, Fall, 1875, v.LIII, #3, p.353-366, ports, plate.

814 **WILSON, Thomas B.**
"Reminiscences of Thomas B. Wilson." n.p., 1939. 8vo, wraps, 47pp. Dorn-II 983. $250-g. Sig: George H. Armistead, Jr.

815 **WILSON, W.**
"Anniversary of Lee's birthday." Chapel Hill, N.C., 1909, 8vo, wraps, 36pp.

816 **WILSON, W. Emerson**
"Fort Delaware-Northern Andersonville." In: CWT, Nov. 1960, v.II, #7 (OS), p.14-15. 2300 CSA prisoners died, or 12 1/2% in contrast to 8% at Andersonville.

817 **WILSON, W.T.**
"Hardships of Bragg's retreat." In: CV, Feb., 1921, v.XXIX, p.51-52. Retreat from mid-Tenn., June 1863.

818 **WILSON, William Edward**
"Thunderbolt of the Confederacy, or King of Horse Theives?" In: Ind. MH, June 1958, v.54, p.119-130, notes. Jno. Hunt Morgan's raid in Southern Indiana and Ohio, 1863.

819 **WILSON, William Lyne**
"A Borderland Confederate." Edt: Festus P. Summers, illus., index, 138pp. (1962) Pittsburg, Pa., Univ. of Pittsburg Press. $30.
...Rep. 1973.

820 ..."Lee's Birthday." In: SHSP, 1889, v.17, p.352-353.

821 **WILSON, Woodrow**
"Robert E. Lee, an Interpretation." Chapel Hill: University of North Carolina Press, 1924. 8vo, wraps, vi, 42pp. $30-bmk. Address Jan. 19, 1909, first printed in North Carolina (Univ.) Record, for May 1909, and here printed.

822 **WILTSHIRE, James G.**
"How Lieut. Walter Bowie of Mosby's Command met his end." In: SHSP, 1900, v.28, p.135-143.

823 **WIMSATT, Josephine Cleary**
"Recollections." Tientsin (China) 1926. 8vo, wraps, 26pp., front. $75-g. Little girl's memoirs of Civil War life in Wash., D.C., rural Virginia.

824 **WINCHESTER, Battle of**
"An incident of the Battle of Winchester, or Opequon." In: SHSP, 1909, v.37, p.232-234. See: Jubal A. Early, James Mercer Garnett, Edward Johnson.

825 **WINCHESTER, Virginia**
See: H.W. Robinson, G.H. Steuart, James A. Walker, "Unveiling Confederate Monument at Winchester." In: SHSP, 1879, v.7, p.349-352.

826 **"WINCHESTER-Frederick County**
Civil War Centennial Commission. Civil War Battles in Winchester and Frederick County, Virginia 1861-1865." (Winchester, Va., Boyce, Virginia: Carr Publishing Co. (1960). 8vo, stiff wraps, cover title, maps (one double pg.) (24)pp. Foreword: James E. Frew.

827 ..."Diaries, Letters and Recollections of the War Between the States." Winchester: 1955, Historical Society Papers, v.3, p.133.

828 **WINDER, William H.**
"Secrets of the American Bastile..." Phila: J. Campbell, 1863. 12mo, cl, viii, 47pp. Pref: sig. W.H. Winder. $60-g. 2nd Edt., 64pp.; 3rd. Edt., 72pp., both 8vo, Nevins- "Brother of the CSA Prison Chief, causes of imprisonment by Federals. Attacks admin. and defends South.

829 **WINDHAM, William T.**
"The Problem of Supply in the Trans-Mississippi Confederacy." (Houston, Tex.) JSH, May, 1961, v.XXVII, #2, p.149-168. $8.

830 **WINDLE, Mary J.**
"Life in Washington and Life Here and There." Philadelphia, 1859. 8vo, cl, xii, 384pp. Howes: A Pennsylvanian with southern sympathies, written when air was charged with imminent disunion.

831 **WINDLER, Penny Nicholas**
"Placid; a collection of authentic Tales centering around Placid Plantation, persons and Granville County, N.C., during period of 1861-1865." Warwick, Va., U.D.C., Hampton Chapter. High-Iron Pub. (1961) 8vo, 73pp. wraps.

832 **WINFIELD, J.Q.**
"Letters of a Cavalry Captain, 1861-1862." Compiled with an addenda by his daughter, Paulina Swife Winfield." separate title-pg., p.231-299. In: John W. Wayland's "Virginia Valley Records", Strasburg, Va., Shenandoah Pub. 1930.

833 **WINGFIELD, Henry Wyatt, Capt.**
"Diary of Capt. H.W. Wingfield." In: W.W. Scott, Edt.-"Two Confederate Items." p.9-47. $25.

834 **WINGFIELD, J.H.D.**
"Thanksgiving Service on the "Virginia", March 10, 1862." In: SHSP, 1891, v.19, p.248-251. signed "Spectator".

835 **WINGFIELD, Marshall**
"Address: Robert E. Lee, at annual birthday banquet, St. Louis, Mo., 1944. Sponsored by Camp Sterling Price #145, Sons of Confederate Veterans." n.p. (St. Louis, Mo., 1944?) 8vo, wraps, 8pp., sewn. ...Also in: AHQ, 1944, v.6, #1, p.23-31.

836 ..."A history of Caroline County, Virginia." Richmond, Va., Trevvet Christian Co., 1924. 8vo, cl, xv, (1), 528pp. front(port), bibliog. (237-243) notes (227-237) 259pp. Early life in Tenn., U.S. Army, a Lt.-Gen. in the CSA, etc. Pres: $85-b, $75. See: Wm. W. Hassler.

837 ..."Old Straight, a sketch of the Life and Campaigns of Lieutenant General Alexander P. Stewart, C.S.A." In: THQ, 1944, v.III, p.99-130.

838 ..."General A.P. Stewart, his life and letters." Memphis, West Tennessee Historical Society, 8vo, cl, 259pp., illus. $50. 1954. Alexander Peter Stewart.

839 **WINKLER, Augusta V. Smith, Mrs.**
"The Confederate Capital and Hood's Texas Brigade." By Mrs. A.V. Winkler. Austin, Texas: Eugene Von Boeckmann, 1894. Tall 8vo, decr. cl, pls., ports, xvi, 312pp. $250, $400-g.

840 ..."Hood's Texas Brigade." In: Dudley G. Wooten's "Texas and Texans in the Civil War." v.II, p.651-681.

841 ..."The Life and Character of Gen. J.B. Hood. Written by request and published by authority of Hood's Texas Brigade Association and read before the Association by the authoress, June 27, 1885." By Mrs. C.M. Winkler. Austin, Texas. (1885) Draughon and Lambert Print., 8vo, wraps, 39pp. In this pamphlet she takes the name of her husband, Clinton M., who was a Capt. in Hood's Brigade. Her larger work was under her maiden initials, Mrs. A.V. Winkler.

842 **WINKLER, Edwin Theodore**
"Our fallen heroes, a memorial sermon on the death of Gen. Robert Edward Lee, delivered in the Citadel Square Baptist Church, on Sunday, Oct. 16, 1870." Charleston, S.C., 1870. 12mo, wraps, caption title, 4pp.

843 **WINKLER, Ernest William, Edt.**
"Platforms of Political Parties in Texas." Austin, Texas: University, (1916) 8vo, wraps, 700pp. TU Bul. #53, Sept. 20, 1916. $100, $64.

844 **WINKS, Robin W.**
"Canada and the United States. The Civil War Years, 1861-1865." Baltimore: Johns Hopkins Press, 1960, 8vo, cl, dj, xviii, (4), 430pp. Bibliog. p.382-397. Based on a thesis. Altho Canada started out friendly to North, politics and events changed this to sentiment towards the South.

845 ..."The St. Albans Raid-A Bibliography." In: Vermont History, Vol. XXVI, #1, Jan. 1958, p.46-51. Vermont Historical Society, Montpelier. Some 93 items.
..."The St. Alban's Raid-1861-a bibliography." In: Vt. Hist., April, 1959, v.27, p.168-169. "A supplement to the 1958 list."

846 ..."The Second Chesapeake Affair." In: Amer. Neptune,, Jan. 1959, Vol. XIX, #1, p.51-72. Attempt to embroil England, via Canada.

847 **WINN, Robert G.**
"Civil War in the Ozarks-personal glimpses." Fayetteville, Ark., Washington County Historical Society, 1985. 8vo, 40pp., illus.

848 **WINNINGHAM, David, Mrs.**
"Sam Houston and Slavery." In: Texana, Summer, 1965, v.III, #2, p.93-104.

849 **WINSLOW, Hattie Lou, Mrs.**
"Camp Morton, 1861-1865. Indianapolis Prison Camp, by Hattie Lou Winslow and Joseph R.H. Moore." Indianapolis, Indiana, Historical Society, 8vo, cl, dj, 2 lf, 229-383pp., illus., 1940, plans, plates, port. See: Jno. A Wyeth's "Cold cheer at Camp Morton." controversy.

850 **WINSOR, Bill**
"Texas in the Confederacy: Military Installations, Economy and People." Hillsboro, Texas: Hill Junior Col., 1978, 8vo, cl, maps, illus., bibliog., index, xix, 154pp. $20.

851 **WINSTON, John R., Col.**
"Daring escape from Johnson's Island." In: CV, Oct., 1924, v.32, p.384-389.

852 **WINSTON, Robert Watson**
"High Stakes and hair-trigger; the Life of Jefferson Davis." N.Y., H. Holt & Co., (1930) 8vo, cl, dj, illus., ports, incl. front, map, viii, 306pp. $40-r.

853 ..."Robert E. Lee, a Biography." N.Y., William Morrow and Co., 1934. 8vo, cl, illus., facsms., ports, incl. front, maps, xi, (1), 428pp.

854 ..."Was the American conflict a war between the states?" In: Social Forces, 1935, v.XIII, p.379-382, (or Civil War? or Rebellion?)

854a **WINTER, George J.**
"Battle of Sutherlands Station (Apr. 1865)." In: Trans. Huguenot Soc. S.C., 1980, p.71.

855 **WINTERS, John D.**
"The Civil War in Louisiana." (Baton Rouge), Louisiana State University Press (1963) (Vail-Ballou Pr., Binghamton, N.Y.) Large 8vo, cl, dj, illus., plan, ports, maps, xiv, (1), 534pp. notes-index, p.433-534. op. $25. 460pp. index.
...Reprint, 1979, 8vo, cl, dj, 552pp. $30.

856 **WIRZ, Henry, Capt.**
"To the Daughters of the Confederacy in Georgia. Columbus, Ga., Feb. 25, 1909. To erect a statue of Capt. Wirz." Folder, 4pp.

857 ..."Pathetic career of Capt. H. Wirz." In: CV, October, 1906, v.XIV, p.448-453.

858 ..."Tennesseans honor Maj. Wirz Memory." In: CV, 1907, v.15, p.239.
...See: Sam'l A. Ashe, J.R. Gibbons, Herman A. Braun, W.J.W. Kerr, Jas. H. M'Neilly, Jas. Madison Page, Mildred Lewis Rutherford, R. Randolph Stevenson, Lyon G. Tyler, Jas. Joseph Williamson, Rev. J. Wm. Jones.

859 ..."The Proceedings of the Trial of Henry Wirz; Testimony, Decisions, Witnesses, Findings and Sentence of the Court." Wash: GPO, 1866. Ex. Doc. 23, 40th Congr., 2nd Session. 8vo, sheep.
..."Trial of Henry Wirz. Letters from the Secretary of War ad interim, in answer to a resolution of the House of April 16, 1866, transmitting a summary of the Trial of Henry Wirz." Wash., GPO, 1868. 8vo, sheep, xxxviii, 850pp. Often a source for the many prisoners of war atrocity stories. See: J.R. Gibbons, James Madison Page, Mildred Lewis Rutherford, R. Randolph Stevenson, Herman A. Braun.
..."The trial and death of Henry Wirz, with other matters pertaining thereto." Raleigh, N.C., E.M. Uzzell and Co., 1908. 8vo, wraps, 62pp.
..."Location of the Wirz Monument." In: CV, 1907, v.15, p.17; Decision: Andersonville. +CV, 1906, v.14, p.445-453, 489-490, 558-559.

860 **WISDOM, John H.**
"Wisdom's Famous Raid. Heroic journey recalled by his death in Alabama." In: SHSP, 1909, v.37, p.372.

861 **WISE'S Brigade**
See: Henry Alex. Wise.

862 **WISE, Barton Haxall**
"The Life and Times of Henry A. Wise of Virginia, 1806-1876." New York: Macmillan Co., 1899. 8vo, cl, xiii, 434pp. front(port). $85, $50. Louisville: Lost Cause Pr., micro-cd. $6.26.

863 **WISE, George**
"Campaigns and Battles of the Army of Northern Virginia." N.Y., Neale Publishing Co., 1916. 8vo, cl, ports (2), incl. front, 432pp., index. $275-g.

864 ..."History of the Seventeenth Virginia Infantry, C.S.A." Baltimore: Kelly, Piet and Co., 1870. $150, $125. 12mo, decr., cl, 312pp.
...Arlington, Va., R.W. Beatty, 1969. Reprint.

865 **WISE, Henry Alexander**
"The cadets at New Market, Va." In: CV, Aug., 1912, v.XX, p.361-362. The Cadets of VMI.

866 ..."Career of Wise's Brigade, 1861-1865." In: SHSP, 1897, v.25, p.1-22.

867 ..."The Private Confederate Soldier." In: SHSP, 1882, v.10, p.417-421.

868 ..."A Tribute to James M. Mason." In: SHSP, 1897, v.25, p.186-192. Lithographed silhouette, tinted background by Kellogg, after Wm. H. Brown, (Hartford) 1844-c. 13 3/8x10 (plate).

869 ..."Richmond Light Infantry Blues: Speech of..., War Roll, Roll of Honorary Members and Present Roll of the Company." Richmond, Va., 1874, Clemmitt and Jones. 8vo, wraps, color frontis., 36pp.
..."Letter from Gen. Wise, Hdq. 6th Military District, Dept. S.C., Ga., Fla., Jan. 3, 1864." Richmond, Va., 1864. 8vo, sewn, 2p. (#11, in vol. pamphlets. On spine: CSA Congress. Communications. Title head: Senate, Jan. 9, 1864 - referred to the committee on military affairs.

870 **WISE, J.D., Mrs.**
"The Great Seal of the Confederacy. Historical Essay by..." Jackson, Tenn., By order of Musidora McCarry Chap. #5, U.D.C. (c.1922) 8vo, wraps, front, (6)pp. cover title.

871 **WISE, Jennings Cropper**
"The Boy Gunners of Lee." Before R.E.

Lee Camp #1, Confederate Veterans, Richmond, Dec. 1, 1916. In: SHSP, Oct. 1917, v.XLII, p.152-173. Also: F.A.J., May-Je., 1923, xiii, p.183-184, 346-355.

872 ..."The artillery mechanics of Gettysburg." In: Field Arty. Jour., Nov. 1923, v.XIII, p.493-497.

873 ..."Robert E. Lee; Unionist; Address delivered by Col... before Rion-Bowman Post #632, VFW of the U.S. Dept. of Va. Lee's Birthday, at Harrisonburg, Va., Jan. 19, 1927." (Harrisonburg, Va., P & L Press, 1927) 8vo, wraps, 1 pl, 21pp.

874 ..."The Long Arm of Lee or the History of the Artillery of the Army of Northern Virginia. With a brief account of the Confederate Bureau of Ordnance." 2 vols. Lynchburg, Va., 3/4lt, J.P. Bell Co., 1915. 8vo, cl, 150, pl, ports, fronts. 496, (8), (505)-996. (1)errata sheet, index. $80-atg.
...N.Y., Barnes and Noble, 1959, original sheets gathered and bound new. $50-y, $65.
...N.Y., Oxford University Pr., 1959. 8vo, cl, dj, xlviii, 957. Reprint of the 2 vol. 1915 edition by J.P. Bell Co., Lynchburg, Va., without the portraits.
...New introduction by Gary Gallagher. Richmond, Va., Owens Civil War Books, 1988. 8vo, 2 vols., 995pp, ills, index. $65.

875 ..."The Military History of the Virginia Military Institute from 1839 to 1865, with appendix, maps, and illustrations." Lynchburg, Va., J.P. Bell Co., 1915. $100-mint. 8vo, cl, front, pls, ports, maps (1-fldg.) 576pp.

876 ..."Personal Memoir of the Life and Services of Gen. Scott Shipp." (Lexington, Va.?) 1915. Privately printed. 8vo, wraps, 56pp., ports (inc. front) addenda, errata. Also, relations with VMI. $75-b.

877 ..."Sunrise of the Virginia Military Institute as a school of arms; spawn of the Cincinnati." (Lexington, Va., 1958) 8vo, cl, illus., 364pp. (wraps) See: Rob't W. Jeffrey.

878 ..."V.M.I. Papers by Jennings C. Wise, Colonel Engineers, Virginia Volunteers, Comandant of Cadets. Published privately by the author for his friends." (Lynchburg, Va., Dulaney-Boatwright Co., n.d.) 8vo, wraps, 53pp. Swem-6621. See also, Col. W. Couper.

879 **WISE, John Sergeant**
"The Battle of New Market, Va., May 15, 1864; an address repeated by John S. Wise, Esq., a cadet in the corps of 1864, before the professors, officers and cadets of the Virginia Military Institute Hall of the Dialectic Society, May 13, 1882." (See below, under diff. title) n.p., n.d. 16mo, wraps, 72pp. $50-b.
..."Battle of New Market, May 15, 1864. By J.S. Wise, Commander Corp. of Cadets at V.M.I. Being four chapters from forthcoming Military History of Institute with account of movement of the corps of cadets to Richmond and its return to Lexington after battle, including the organization and casualties of the battalion in the campaign." Published by the author for benefit of athletics. (Lynchburg, Va., Dulaney-Boatwright Co.) 8vo, wraps, (paste-on ill.) 74pp. See: Virginia Military Institute, Robert W. Jeffrey.

880 ..."The End of an Era. Edited and annotated by Curtis Carroll Davis." N.Y., Thomas Yoseloff (1965) $30-b. 8vo, cl, dj, ports, incl. front 1xiii, (4), 498pp. index, notes, bibliog.
...Boston and N.Y., Houghton Mifflin Co., 1899. $45. First Edition (1900 and 1902) 12mo, cl, iv, 474pp.
...Editions: 1901 ($16.); 1902 (17th impression. $25.)

881 ..."Memorial address, delivered at the unveiling of a monument to the memory of the Southern Soldiers and V.M.I. Cadets

who fell in the Battle of New Market, May 15, 1864. Also rolls of officers and cadets engaged, with official lists of casualties, orders and official report of the battle, from v.xxxvii, pt. 1, series 1, of the Records of Union and Confederate armies, War Records Office, Washington, D.C. By order of the Board of Visitors." (Roanoke, Va., Stone Print, 1898?) 12mo, wraps, cover-title, 2, (5)-62, (1)p.

882 ..."The West Point of the Confederacy. Boys battle of New Market, Va., May 15, 1864." In: Cent., Nov. 1888, v.15, p.461-71, ills., port.

..."The West Point of the Confederacy." In: CV, May, 1915, v.XXIII, p.212-218. Acct. of Va. Mil. Inst., during the war.

883 WISE, L.W.
"Treachery of W.H. Seward brought fire on Sumter. Correspondence with Judge Campbell shows design to deceive Southern leaders." In: SHSP, 1909, v.37, p.360-363.

883a WITHAM, George F.
"Shiloh: Shells & artillery units." Memphis: 1980 Riverside Press. 8vo, cl, 163pp, numbered & signed. $3. Lim.Edt., 1,000 copies.

883b WITHERS, John
"One Year of the War; Civil War diary of John Withers, asst-Adj-Gen., of the Confederate Army. Edt: H.E. Sterkx & L. Y. Trapp." In: AHQ, 1929, #3 &4, p.133+.

884 WITHERS, Robert Enoch
"Autobiography of an Octogenarian, by Robert Enoch Withers, MM.D., Colonel 18th Regiment Virginia Infantry, CSA; Editor, Lynchburg Daily News; Lieutenant-Governor of Virginia; Senator of the United States; member of the board of Regents of the Smithsonian Institute; Consul of the United States at Hong Kong; past Grand Master of the Knights Templar of the U.S., etc." Roanoke, Va., Stone Printing Co., 1907, 8vo, cl, front(port), 550pp. $125-b.

885 WITHERSPOON, J.G.
"Confederate cavalry leaders." In: CV, Nov. 1919, v.XXVII, p.414-417.

886 WITHERSPOON, Thomas Dwight, Rev.
"Prison life at Fort McHenry." In: SHSP, 1880, v.8, p.77-82, 111-119, 163-168. Chaplain of 42nd Miss. Reg.

887 WITHERSPOON, William
"Reminiscences of a Scout, Spy and Soldier of Forrest's Cavalry." Jackson, Tenn: McCowat-Mercer, 1910. 8vo, wraps, 79pp.

...Reprinted in Robert S. Henry's "As they saw Forrest." p.69-110.

888 ..."Tishomingo Creek or Bryce's Cross Roads." Jackson, Tenn. (McCowat-Mercer) 1906. Published by the Author. 8vo, wraps, 21pp. Cover title-"Tishomingo Creek or Bryce's Cross Roads as I saw it and the 7th Tenn. (Confederate Cavalry in the Battle of Tishomingo Creek between General N.B. Forrest (Confederate) and General Sturgis (Federal) on June 10, 1864." errata tip-in.

...Reprinted in Robert S. Henry's "As they saw Forrest", pg. 111-136.

889 WITMER, Edward A.
"The Battle of Bonnie Wilson." Mission, Kan., D. Atkins, Ill. (1941) 12mo, wraps, illus., (incl. ports) 7, 56pp. 1st Edt. June 1941.

890 ..."Battle of Wilson's Creek, 1861." A regiment of Texans in the battle. Note: in MHR, v.36, p.384-385. 2nd Edt.?

891 WITT, John George
"Life in the Law." London: T. Werner Laurie. (?1906) 8vo, cl, ports, plates, 224pp. Reminis. British lawyer, one chap. 141-183pp. on anecdotes of CSA celebrities, while in England during and after the War.

891a **WITTENMYER, Annie**
"Under the guns: a woman's reminiscences of the Civil War." In: Phillips CHQ, Sept., 1979, v.17, p.1-10.

892 **"WOES of War, The.**
A Letter of Sorrow by a Southern Lady." London: J. Ridgway, 1862. Edt: Pauline V.D. Vyver. 16mo, orig. blue wraps bound in, 25pp.
...Also, a 2nd Edition.

893 **WOLF, Edwin, 2nd**
"American Song Sheets, Slip Ballads and Poetical Broadsides, 1850-1870: A Catalogue of the Collection of the Library Company of Philadelphia." Phila: Library Co., of Phila., 1963, p.xxiii, 205.

894 **WOLF, Simon**
"The American Jew as patriot, soldier and citizen, by Simon Wolf. Edited: Louis Edward Levy." Phila: Levytype Co., 1895. 8vo, cl, front, illus., errata, xiii, (2), 576pp. List of Jewish soldiers in Union and CSA during War, alphabetically and by states, p.117-409.

895 **WOLFE, George D.**
"The Confederate raider "Shenandoah", 1863." In: Nautical Research Jour., Feb. 1952, v.4, p.19-20.

896 **WOLFE, Ruth Dantzler**
"Private F.W.D., 1861-1865, experiences of Private F.W. Dantzler during the War Between the States." n.p., n.d., (c.1910) 18mo, wraps, 79pp. $350-0b. Served in 25th S.C. Vols., St. Matthews' Rifles, Eutaw Regiment, Hagood's Brig.

897 **WOLFE, Samuel M., Virginia**
"Helper's Impending Crisis Dissected." New York, 1860. 12mo, cl, (4), 223pp.
...Do: Philadelphia, J.T. Lloyd, 1860. 12mo, cl, (12), 223, (38)pp. An answer to Helper's carelessness with statistics. Defends Slavery.

898 **WOLFORD, Frank, Col.**
"The Case of Colonel Wolford. Another instance of Executive Usurpation. Lincoln's action in the matter. Arbitrary arrest and proffer of an abolition parole. Col. Wolford indignant refusal to bargain for his liberty and his rights! Protest of a loyal Kentuckian. The abolition war policy of Lincoln shown up in its true light." caption title. n.p., (1864) Letter of Wolford: July 30, 1864. 8vo, 4pp-folder, double column, campaign Doc.

899 **WOLSELEY, Lt.-Col. (Field Marshall Lord)**
"The American Civil War; contemporary letters from Lt. Col. G.J. Wolseley. Edt. by Brig.-Gen. H. Biddulph." (London): Society for Army Hist. Research Jour., XVIII (1939), p.38-40; XIX (1940) p.112-117. Titles vary. Written during 1862 when Wolseley was sent to Canada on the Trent Affair (Confederates removed from a British steamer).
...(Edinburgh): Blackwood's Mag., 1863, January. "A Month's Visit to the Confederate Headquarters."
...See also: Charles Francis Adams-"Wolseley and the Confederate Army." extracts from Wolseley's letters above.
..."The American Civil War...An English view." Appeared serially in North American Rev., v.148-149, 1889-1890: Pt. 1 (p.538-562), Pt.II, p.30-43, ; Pt.III (p.164-181); Pt.IV (p.278-292); Pt.V (p.446-459; Pt.VI (p.594-606); Pt.VII (p.711-727).
..."The American Civil War, an English View. Edited, with an intro: James A. Rawley." Charlottesville, Va., University Press of Virginia (1964) 8vo, cl, xxxvii, 230pp. Note: Appeared originally in Macmillan's Magazine for March, 1887.

900 ..."The Battle of Gettysburg and the Campaign in Pennsylvania-Extracts from the diary of an English Officer present with the Confederate Army." In: Blackwoods

Edinburgh Magazine, Sept. 1863, v.XCIV, p.365-394.

901 ..."A month's visit to the Confederate headquarters by an English officer (FM Visc. Wolseley)." In: Blackwood Mag., Jan. 1863, v.XCIII, p.1-29. "the eyes of every Southerner are turned to England."

902 ..."N.B. Forrest, CSArmy." In: SHSP, 1892, v.20, p.325-335.

903 ..."Tribute to Lee." In: SHSP, 1884, v.12, p.232-233.

904 ...."The Story of a Soldier's Life." Westminister: A. Constable and Co., 1903. 8vo, cl, front(ports) illus., fldg. maps, plan, 398, 383pp. 2nd vol. experiences on a visit to CSArmy in 1862.

904a **WOLSELEY, Viscount Garnet**
"An English View of the War; complete in seven parts." Extract from North amer. Review, 1889.
See: Gen. James B. Fry.

905 **WOMACK, J.J., Capt.**
"The Civil War Diary of..., Co. E, Sixteenth Regiment, Tennessee Volunteers (Confederate)." McMinnville, Tenn., Womack Printing Co., 1961. 8vo, wraps, port, 115pp. IBM set. $22.50-y.

906 **WOMEN of the Confederate States**
See: Wm. R. Aylett, Thos. C. DeLeon, Mrs. John Randolph Eggleston, Wm. E. Gonzales, Dabney H. Maury, Joel Chandler Harris.

907 ..."The Women of the Southern Confederacy during the War, 1861-1865, etc..." See: Gen. C. Irvine Walker.

908 **WOOD, Benjamin**
"Fort Lafayette; or, Love and Secession. A Novel." N.Y., Carleton, 1862. 12mo, cl, 300pp. In 50's Wood championed slavery and its extension and Southern way of life. Against Lincoln, "Black Republicans" caused trouble and shouldn't coerce the CSA. However, this novel favors the "Peace Democrats" and moderation. See: Jerome Mushkat's "Ben Woods" Fort Lafayette in CWH, June 1975, v.21, #2, p.160-171.

909 **WOOD, H.E.**
"Black Eagle Company. A typical command of Confederate Soldiers." In: SHSP, 1909, v.37, p.52-59. Roster and history.

910 **WOOD, James H.**
"The War, "Stonewall Jackson", his campaigns and battles, the regiment as I saw them." Cumberland, Md., The Eddy Press, 1910. 12mo, cl, pl. ports, (8), 181pp. Personal narrative of the Capt. of Co. "D", 37th Va., Inf. Reg. during war. $250-ob, $200-b.

911 ..."The War, Stonewall Jackson..." Gaithersburg, Md., Butternut Press, 1984. $20.

912 **WOOD, John Sumner**
"The Virginia Bishop. A Yankee Hero of the Confederacy." Richmond, Va., Garrett and Massie, 1961. 8vo, cl, dj, facsm., illus., ports, incl. front, xiii, 187pp. $20-bmk-84.

913 **WOOD, John Taylor, Col., C.S.A.**
"Escape of the Confederate Secretary of War." In: Cent. Mag., Nov. 1893, #1, v.XLVII, p.110-123.

914 ..."Confederate Commerce-Destroyers the "Tallahassee's" dash into New York waters." In: Cent. Mag., 1898, v.LVI, p.408-417.

915 ..."The first fight of Ironclads, March 9, 1892." In: Cent. Mag., March, 1885, v.XXIX, p.738-754. Lieut. on Merrimac. Reprinted in B & L. See: Royce Gordon Shingleton.

916 **WOOD, Leonora Whitaker**
"Belle Boyd, famous spy of the Confederate States Army." Keyser, W.Va. Mountain Echo, 1940.

917 ...Bloomington captured by McNeill's Confederate Rangers." In: Glades Star, Sept. 1949, v.1, p.369-371. Capture of B & O Ry. bridge across Potomac near

Piedmont by Capt. Jno. H. McNeill and his Rangers, May 1864.

918 **WOOD, Robert Crooke, Edt.**
"Confederate Handbook; a compilation of important data and other interesting an valuable matter relating to the War Between the States 1861-1865." $75, $50. New Orleans, La., Graham Press, 1900. 8vo, wraps, illus. (2-color pls) port, 126pp. type-set two columns.
...Louisville: Micro-cd. Lost Cause Press, $3.98.
..."The Confederate Handbook." N.O., Graham, 1900. Reprint: Falls Church, Va., Sterling Press, 1982. 8vo, cl, (10, p.126, (3)p., (12)p. ads, color, falgs.

919 **WOOD, Robert J., Lieut.-Gen.**
"Lee's Lessons in Leadership." In: Official Army Info. Digest, U.S. Army Mag., August 1961, p.10-21, illus., ports. Address before the Royal Military Academy, Sandhurst, Eng.

920 **WOOD, Walter Birkbeck**
"A History of the Civil War in the United States, 1861-1865, by W. Birkbeck Wood and Maj. J.E. Edmonds. With an introduction by Spencer Wilkinson; with thirteen maps and eleven plans." London: Methuen and Co., (Sept., 1905) 8vo, cl, xxii, 549, (1)p., 13-fldg. maps in pocket, 11-plans (1-fldg.) Two Britishers write one of the best accts.
...London: 2nd Edt., 1908 (Feb.)
...London: 3rd Edt., Nov. 1910.
...London: (1937)-"The Civil War in the United States, with special reference to the Campaigns of 1864 and 1865..." "First pub. in this form, 1937. The bulk of last 10 chapters of 1905 edt. reproduced minimum alterations." 8vo, cl, illus., maps, xix, 328pp.
...N.Y., J. Brussel, (1959)-"Military History of the Civil War, 1861-1865." 8vo, cl, illus., plates (part color), maps, 328, (3)pp. (Globe Lithographing Co.) 35cm, illus., (23 full pg., 13-dble pg., including liners) maps (22) (200)pp. dbl. columns. (8)-double pg. Kurtz and Allison, battle scenes, in full color.
...N.Y., Putnam's (1960) Capricorn Books, CAP 29, 1st Edt. 1905; here reproduced from 1937 Edt. Authors in this edt. listed as Sir James Edward Edmonds, title as '37.

921 ..."The Bull Run Campaign, 1864." In: "National Defence", Oct. 1911, v.V, p.461-482.

921a **WOOD, Wayne**
"The Marble Valley Boys." Hoover, Ala., Interface print, 1986. 4to, wraps, 77, (6)p.

922 **WOOD, William D.**
"A Partial Roster of the Officers and Men Raised in Leon County, Texas. For the service of the Confederate States in the War Between the States, with short biographical sketches of some of the officers and a brief history of Maj. Gould's Battalion. And other matters. Compiled by W.D. Wood, 1899." (San Marcos, Texas, 1899, dates introduction) 8vo, decr. wraps, 49pp.
...Waco, Texas, W.M. Morrison, 1963. 8vo, fabricoid-49pp. print on one side. Lim. Edt., 200 copies. $30. Co. C., Hood's Brig.; Co. D and E-Gould's Bat. Roster: Capt. J.N. Black's Co. A, dismounted Cav., Burnett's Reg. 13th Tex.; Co. E, Baylors Reg.; Roll Co. D, 26th Tex. Reg. Cav. Col. DeBray's Reg.; Muster Roll Co. E, 1st Bat. Inf. Waul's Tex. Legion; Capt. Jno. T. Wilson Co. B, Inf., Hubbard's Reg.

923 ..."Reminiscences of Reconstruction in Texas and Reminiscences of Texas and Texans 50 Years Ago." (San Marcos, Texas?, 1902?) n.d. 8vo, wraps, 58pp. $100. Includes a history of Leon County (Texas).

924 ..."The Ku Klux Klan." In: QTSHA, April, 1906, v.IX, #4, p.262-268.

925 ..."Recollections of the growth and development in the North of the anti-slavery sentiment that led to secession." In: Gulf SHM, July 1903, v.II, p.18-25.

926 ..."Recollections of Judge Wm. D. Wood, of San Marcos, Texas. II Secession." In: Gulf SHM, Sept., 1903, v.II, p.99-109.

927 **WOOD, William Nathaniel**
"Reminiscences of Big I, by Lieut. W.N. Wood." Charlottesville, Va., Michie Pr., 1909. 12mo, cl, 107pp. $700-ob, $600-g, $550.
..."Reminiscences of Big I, by Lieut. William Nathaniel Wood, Monticello Guard, Company A, 19th Virginia Reg. Edited by Bell Irvin Wiley." Jackson, Tenn: McCowat-Mercer, 1956, 8vo, cl, dj, added illus. and ports, not in original edt., xxviii, 138pp., index, $15. Also-a "Rebel Shavetail Edition", with Wiley's signature. $60. Civil War Book Club Edt., $40.

927a **WOODFIN (Buncombe Co., N.C.)**
"Remarks of Mr. Woodfin of . . . on Secession." Raleigh, N.C., 1851. 8vo, sewn, 26pp.

928 **WOODFORD, Milton M.**
"A Connecticut Yankee Fights at Olustee. Letters from the Front and (part 2) "After Olustee", Edited by Vaughn D. Bornet." In: FHQ, Jan and April, 1949, v.XXVII, #3 and 4, p.237-259, p.385-403. See also, Ruth Cole and G.F. Baltzell.

929 **WOODLEY, Robbie Lynn**
"Thomas C. Reynolds and the administration problems of the Confederate government of Missouri, 1863-1865, government-in-exile, Marshall, Texas." In: "Touchstone" (East Tex. Baptist College) 1982.

930 **WOODMAN, Harold D., Edt.**
"The Legacy of the American Civil War." N.Y., 1973. Twenty essays on nationalism, social economic, equality and democracy by Robt. Penn Warren, Frank Vandiver, Allen Nevins and David Potter.

931 **WOODRUFF, William Edward**
"With the Light Guns in '61-'65. Reminiscences of Eleven Arkansas, Missouri and Texas Light Batteries, in the Civil War. (quote), by W.E. Woodruff, Late Major Art. C.S.A." Little Rock, Ark., Central Printing Co., 1903. 12mo, decr. cl, front (port), map, 115pp. $225, $150-(mint), $450, $300.
..."With the Light Guns in '61-'65." Little Rock, Ark., Eagle Press, 1986, 8vo, cl, dj, decr. cloth, 120pp. $25. 50 numbered copies bound in cowhide. $100.
...Louisv.: Lost Cause, micro-cd, $5.62.

932 **WOODS, Gary Doyle**
"The Hicks-Adams-Bass-Floyd-Patillo and Collateral Lines Together with Family Letters 1840-1868." Cover title: "Waldeck Letters Texas-Georgia." Salado, Texas: Anson Jones Press (1963) Privately printed, 100 copies to family, additional 50 copies made by pub. $100.

933 **WOODS, J.H.**
"Stonewall Jackson in West Virginia." In: CV, Nov. 1916, v.XXIV, p.490-493.

934 **WOODS, James M.**
"Devotees and Dissenters: Arkansas in the Confederate Congress, 1861-1865." In: AHQ, Autumn, 1979, v.XXXVIII, #3, p.227-247.
..."Rebellion & realignment Arkansas's road to secession." Fayetteville: University of Arkansas, 1986. 8vo, cl, 277p, append, index. $20.

935 **WOODS, John L.G.**
"Last scenes of war-how I got home: recollections of...Pvt. Co. B, 53rd Reg., Georgia, Sim's Brig., Kershaw's Div., Longstreet's Corp., ANV." In: CV, Apr., 1919, v.27, #4, p.140-144.

936 ..."Semmes' Brigade at Chancellorsville." In: CV, Jan. 1911, v.XIX, p.12-13 (Semme's Ga. Brig.)

937 **WOODS, Mark George, Mrs.**
"Jefferson Davis at St. Johns Episcopal Church, Montgomery, Alabama (1861-1865, 1889, 1925) In: UDCMag., Aug. 1948, v.11, #8, p.18-19.

938 **WOODS, Michael Leonard, Col.**
"Personal Reminiscences of Col. Albert James Pickett." (from Transactions, 1899-1903, Vol. IV) Alabama Historical Society, reprint #27." Montgomery, Alabama, 1904. 8vo, p.597-611, n.p., n.d., reprint. (1967)

939 **WOODS, Robert H.**
"Cruise of the Clarence, Tacony-Archr. Reid's Daring Exploits. How he carried terror to the Northern Ports, etc." In: SHSP, 1895, v.XXI, p.274-282.

939a **WOODS, Rufus**
"The weirdest story in American history the escape of John Wilkes Booth..." Wenatchee, Wash., The Author, 1944. 8vo, wraps, 32pp, ills. $25.

940 **WOODS, Samuel V.**
"An address delivered by request to the United Daughters of the Confederacy and their friends at Parkersburg, W.Va., June 3rd, 1928." 8vo, wraps, 14pp. (n.p., 1928?) Shetler-880.

941 **WOODS, Thomas H.**
"A sketch of the Mississippi Secession Convention of 1861. Its membership and work." In: Pub. Miss. Hist. Soc., v.VI, p.91-104.

942 **WOODS, Walter D.**
"Notes on the Confederate stockade of Florence, S.C., 1864-1865." 8vo, wraps (cover title, 17pp., illus., 194-?) United Daughters of the Confederacy.

943 **WOODSON, A.A., Mrs.**
"South Carolina's representatives in the Confederate Congress." In: CV, Jan. 1927, v.XXXV, p.16-19.

944 **WOODSON, Hortense**
"Come Out, Brave Men of Edgefield." (Headlines from the "Edgefield Advertiser", Nov. 1860-1865, by Faye Christie and Companies from Edgefield in Confederate Service. Compiled by Hortense Woodson." Edgefield, S.C., 1960. 8vo, wraps, 94pp. Company rosters, biographical sketches.

944a **WOODWARD, David**
"Launching the Confederate Navy." 'History Today.,' Mar. 1962, v.12, p.206-12, ills, ports.

945 **WOODWARD, George W. and J.S. Black**
"Secession and coercion." In: TylerQHGM, 1933, v.XV, p.90-98. Corresp. (1860) between Woodward and Black of Penn., justifying secession of the South.

946 **WOODWARD, Grace Steele**
"The White Man's Civil War." In: "The Cherokee", Norman, Okla. U.Pr., (1963) p.253-289, facsms., illus., ports.

947 **WOODWARD, Isaiah Alfonso**
"The stolen original Virginia ordinance of secession-1861." In: W.Va. Hist., Jan. 1956, v.17, p.150-151, facsm. On the seisure or theft of the document at Richmond, Va., 1865, and transferred to Dept. of State, in 1948, transferred to Natl. Archiv.

948 **WOODWARD, Joseph H.**
"Alabama iron manufacturing, 1860-1865." In: Ala. Rev., July 1954, v.7, p.199-207, notes.

949 **WOODWARD, Mary Davis**
"Dr. W.E. Arnold-a Personality Sketch." In: AHQ, 1949, v.VIII, p.331-335. Arnold was an Ass't. Surgeon in the First Arkansas Infantry.

950 **WOODWARD, Thomas E., Major**
"Address delivered before the Survivors Association of the Sixth Regiment SCV, at

Chester, S.C., Aug. 9, 1882; Fort Sumter to Dranesville." Columbia, S.C., Presbyterian Pub., 1883, 8vo, wraps, 32pp. Trumbull IV, 166.

951 **WOODWARD, W.E.**
"Years of Madness." New York: G.P. Putnam's Sons (1951) 8vo, cl, d/w, viii, 311pp., 2 maps. A reappraisal of the Civil War, rather from a southern point of view. ...Cleveland, Ohio: Frontier Press, 8vo, stiff bds., (3), 311pp. 1967.

952 **WOODWORTH, Celia**
"The Confederate Raider 'Shenandoah' at Melbourne." In: US Naval Inst. Proc., IC, 1973, p.66-75.

953 **WOODY, Robert H.**
"Republican Newspapers of S. Carolina." Charlottesville, Va., Historical Pub. Co., 1936. Southern Sketches #10, 1st series. 8vo, soft wraps, 60pp.

954 ..."Some aspects of the economic condition of South Carolina after the Civil War." (Raleigh) NCHRev., July 1930, v.VII, #3, p.346-364.

955 **WOOLDRIDGE, William Beverly, Col.**
"Itinerary of the Fourth Virginia Cavalry." In: SHSP, 1889, v.17, p.376-378.
..."Fourth Virginia Cavalry." In: SHSP, 1910, v.38, p.325-326.

956 **WOOLEY, Robert W.**
"General Albert Sidney Johnston." In: SB(ns), v.II, #5, Oct. 1886, p.320-325.

956a **WOOLSEY, Ronald C.**
"The debate over slavery on the eve of the Charleston Convention." In: MoHR, Oct. 1987, v.82, #1, p.1-23, ills, port.
..."The West becomes a problem: the Missouri controversy & slavery expansion as the Southern dilemma." In: MHR, July 1983, v.77, p.409-32.
..."A Southern dilemma; slavery expansion & the California Statehood issue in 1850-a reconsideration." In: So. Cal. Quart., Summer, 1983, v.65, p.123-44.

957 **WOOLSON, Allen M.**
"Confederates on Lake Erie." In: US Naval Inst. Proc., 1973, v.IC, iv, 69-70.

958 **WOOLWINE, Rufus James**
"The Civil War Diary of R.J.W., Edt.: Louis H. Manarin." In: VMHB, 1963, v.71, p.416-448, port.

959 **WOOSTER, Ralph A.**
"The Alabama Secession Convention, 7-11, Jan. 1861." In: Ala. Rev., Jan. 1959, v.12, p.69-75, notes. On birthplaces, ages, occupations and property of delegates as recorded in 1860 census. Tab. summary of data.

960 ..."An Analysis of the Membership of Secession Conventions in the Lower South." (Lexington, Ky.) JSH, Aug. 1958, v.XXIV, #3, p.360-368, tables.

961 ..."An Analysis of the Membership of the Texas Secession Convention." In: SwHQ, January 1959, v.LXII, #3, p.322-335, charts.

962 ..."An Analysis of the Texas Know Nothings." In: SwHQ, January, 1967. v.LXX, #3, p.414-423, fldg. chart.

963 ..."The Arkansas Secession Convention." In: AHQ, 1954, v.XIII, p.172-195, maps, tables, fldg. tables.

964 "Confederate success at Perryville." In: RKHS, Oct. 1961, v.59, #4, p.318-323.

965 ..."The Florida Secession Convention." In: FHQ, April, 1958, v.XXXVI, #4, p.373-385, tables.

966 ..."The Georgia Secession Convention." In: Ga.H.Q., March, 1956, v.XL, #1, p.21-55, extensive tables.

967 ..."The Louisiana Secesseion Convention, 1861." In: LaHQ, March, 1951, v.34, p.103-133, tables, notes.

968 ..."Life in Civil War East Texas." In: "East Texas History", Edt. by Archie McDonal, p.111-126. Also in: ETHJ, October, 1965, v.III, #2, p.93-102, notes.

969 ..."The Membership of the Mississippi Secession of 1861." (Jackson, Miss., Jour. Miss. Hist., Oct., 1954, v.XVI, #4, p.242-257, tables.

970 ..."Membership of the South Carolina Secession Convention." (Charleston: So. Caro. Hist. and Genea. Mag., Oct., 1954, v.LV, #4, p.185-197, charts.

971 ..."Notes on the Georgia Legislature of 1860." In: Ga.H.Q., March 1961, v.XLV, #1, p.22-36, tables. $10.

972 ..."The Secession Conventions of the South." (Princeton, N.J., University Press, 1962). Maps, bibliog., index, 294pp.
..."Westport, Conn, Greenwood Press, Reprint, 1976.

973 ..."The Secession of the Lower South: an Examination of Changing Interpretations." In: CWH, June 1961, v.VII, #2, p.117-127.
..."The Secession Conventions of the Lower South: A Study of their membership." Austin: Texas University, 1954. 4to, cl, maps, tables, 452pp. $65. Dissertation for Phd. $65.

974 ..."Rarin' for a fight: Texans in the Confederate Army." In: SWHQ, Apr. 1981, #4, v.LXXXIV, p.387-426, ports and group port.

975 ..."With the Confederate Cavalry in the West: The Civil War experiences of Isaac Dunbar Affleck." In: SWHQ, July 1979, v.LXXXIII, #1, p.1-28, vignettes.

976 **WOOTEN, C.S.**
"Jefferson Davis and Robert Toombs." In: CV, April 1912, v.XX, p.170-172.

977 **WOOTEN, Dudley G.**
"Oran Milo Roberts." In: SwHQ, July 1898, v.II, #1, p.1-20. "The President's Annual Message, Life and Services of..."

978 **WOOTEN, Dudley G., Edt.**
"Texas and Texans in the Civil War." In: his "Comprehensive History of Texas", Dallas (Texas): William G. Scarff, 1898, 2 vols., 4to, cl, (or 3/4 Mor.) Part V, v.II, p.517-754, pl., ports. See also under: Mrs. A.V. Winkler-"Hood's Texas Brigade", Mrs. Kate Scurry Terrell's "Terry's Texas Rangers", J.H. McLeary's "Green's Brigade", and O.P. Bowser's "Notes on Granbury's Brigade." $300, $350, (v.II, $155).

979 **WOOTEN, Fred T., Jr.**
"Religious activities in Civil War Memphis." In: THQ, June 1944, v.III, 19pp., p.131-149, 248-272.

980 **WOOTEN, John Morgan**
"A history of Bradley County, Tennessee." (Cleveland, Tenn.?) Bradley Co., Post 81, American Legion. In cooperation with the Tennessee Historical Comm., 1949. 8vo, cl, maps (1 fld.) port, view, 323pp. Extended to 1948, Legion Post 81, by James F. Corn, Chm. Deals particularly with military history, 1861-1945 (p.207-302).

981 **WORDEN, John Lorimer**
"The Monitor and the Merrimac; both sides of the story, told by Lieut. J.L. Worden, USN, Lieut. Greene, USN, of the Monitor and H. Ashton Ramsay, CSN, Chief Engineer of the Merrimac..." N.Y., Lond: Harper and Bros., 1912, 12mo, cl, illus., incl. front, xi, 1, 72, (1)p.

982 **WORK, Philip A., Lieut.-Col., 1st Tex. Reg.**
"Official Report of Gettysburg." In: SHSP, 1885, v.13, p.186-190.

983 **WORLEY, Ted R.**
"The Arkansas Peace Society of 1861: A study in mountain Unionism." (Lexington, Ky.) JSH, Nov. 1958, v.XXIV, #4, p.445-456. Largely CSA in the mountain area Ark.

984 ..."The Civil War Comes to Van Buren." In: AHQ, 1966, v.XXV, p.145-150.

985 ..."Documents relating to Arkansas Peace Society of 1861." In: AHQ, v.17, p.82-111.

986 ..."At Home in Confederate Arkansas. Letters to and from Pulaski Countians 1861-1865." Little Rock, Arkansas: Pulaski

County Hist. Society, Bulletin Series, #2, Dec. 1955. 4to, soft back, (3), 63pp. Reprint: 1985. $14-bmk.

987 ..."Letters from Columbia Co. Confederate." In: Ark. HQ, Summer 1956, v.15, p.172-175. From Newell and Sister Effie McEachern, Pocahontas, Ark., H.B. Harris to Miss. Smith, Camp Harkie, Ark., 11 Sept., 1861.

988 ..."Letters to David Walker relating to Reconstruction in Arkansas, 1866-1874." In: AHQ, v.16, p.319-326.

989 **WORSHAM, John H.**
"Jackson's Valley Campaign, Front Royal and Winchester." In: SHSP, 1910, v.XXXVIII, p.327-333.

990 ..."One of Jackson's Foot Cavalry. His experience and what he saw during the War, 1861-1865. Including a history of "F Company", Richmond, Va., 21st Regiment, Va., Infantry, Second Brigade, Jackson's Div., Second Corps, A.N.V., by John H. Worsham, an Old F., Richmond Va." N.Y., Wash., Neale Pub., 1912, 12mo, cl, illus., incl. front, ports, 353pp. $300, $175-bmk-105, $200-b.
..."One of Jackson's foot cavalrymen." N.Y., Time-Life Books, 1986. $22.50. "Collector's Library of the Civil War." 12mo, fabricoid, gold edges.
...Louisv., Lost Cause Pr., micro-cd, $5.62.
...Jackson, Tenn., McCowat-Mercer Pr., 1964, 12mo, cl, dj, xxix, 215pp., indexed. Edited by Jas. I. Robertson, map liners.

991 ..."The Second Battle of Manassas." In: SHSP, 1904, v.XXXII, p.77-88.

992 **WORSHAM, John H., Co. "F"**
"The Battle of Cedar Run, by an Old "F" Company man." In: SHSP, 1899, v.27, p.144-151.

993 **WORSHAM, William Johnson**
"The Old Nineteenth Tennessee Regiment, C.S.A., June 1861-April 1865. By Dr. W.J. Worsham... Supplementary Chapter by Col. C.W. Heiskell." Knoxville, Tenn., Paragon Print, 1902. 8vo, cl, ports, map, plan, (4), 1, (7)-235pp. $250.
...Blountsville, Tenn., Burmar Books, 1973, 12mo, cl, lim. 300 copies. (op)

994 **WORSLEY, Philip Stanhope**
See: John Wm. Jones.

995 **"WORTH Remembering."**
Edt. Lane Van Hook. United Daughters of the Confederacy, N.Y. Div., (Chicago: Windfall Press, 1963) 12mo, wraps, illus., 56pp. All stories are true events experienced by the families during war and reconstruction.

996 **WORTH, John T.**
"Muster Roll of Company B, First Mo. Cavalry, Trans-Mississippi Dept. CSA." Columbia, Mo., Mo. Hist. Review, v.III, #2, p.161-163.

997 **WORTH, Jonathan**
"The Correspondence of Jonathan Worth." Edt: J.D. De Roulhac Hamilton, 2 vols. Raleigh, N.C., Edwards and Broughton, 1909, Pub: North Carolina Historical Comm., 8vo, cl, v.I-xiii, 656pp. port. 1841-1866. v.II-(657)-1313pp., errata slip. 1866-1869. Worth was in state senate, state treasurer, 1863-1865, Gov., reconstruction period. $60.

998 **WORTHINGTON, D.**
"The Broken Sword or a Pictorial Page in Reconstruction." Wilson, N.C., P.D. Gold and Sons, 1901. 8vo, decr. cl, front, sketches, vii, (9), 326pp. errata, at end.

999 **WORTHINGTON, Glenn H.**
"The battle of Monocacy, being an account of the important engagement at Monocacy River near Frederick, Md., July 9, 1864, together with excerpts from official reports." Frederick, Md., News-Post, 1927. 8vo, wraps, 26pp.

1000 ..."The Battle of Monocacy." In: CV, Jan. 1928, v.XXXVI, p.20-23.

1001 **WORTHINGTON, Thomas Paine**
"Civil War letters of Confederate Cavalryman and Dallasite, Thomas Pain Worthington. Edt: Hazael W. Beckett and Edward W. Sameull, Jr." In: "The Quarterly", Mar. 1980. Wartime letters of Worthington's service in Co.A, 1st Battl. Mississippi Cavalry.

1002 ..."Shiloh: The only correct military history of U.S. Grant and of the Missing Army Records, for which he alone is responsible, to conceal his organized defeat of the Union Army at Shiloh, April 6, 1862." Washington City, 1872, (title page differs-"Shiloh: or the Tennessee Campaign of 1862 witten especially for the Army of Tennessee in 1862 and for the friends and relatives of those patriot soldiers, who sank into their graves on Shiloh's field, unknelled, unnoticed and unknown by a comrade on that battlefield and a West Point graduate of 1827." Washington City: M'Gill and Witherow, 1872, 8vo, wraps, map, 164pp. facsm.
...Wash., 1872, reprint, 179pp. "Shiloh the only correct history of U.S. Grant."

1003 ...Wash., 1880, "A correct history of Shiloh." Howes-11339-"accuses Halleck, Sherman and Grant plot conceived by Wade, Chandler and Cameron, to protract war into 1864-1865 to insure '64 election of Republican Party.

1004 **WRIGHT, Ambrose Ransom, Brig.-Gen.**
"Report: Battle of Gettysburg." In: SHSP, 1880, v.8, p.314-320.

1005 **WRIGHT, Arthur A.**
"The Civil War in the Southwest." Denver: Big Mountain Press (1964) 8vo, cl, d/w, illus., ports, map, 214pp. 2679-Southork St., Denver, 80210.

1006 **WRIGHT, Crafts J.**
"Official journal of the Conference Convention held at Washington City, Feb. 1861." Washington, 1863. 8vo, wraps, 93pp. Virginia's attempt to preserve Union, slavery.

1007 **WRIGHT, D. Giraud, Mrs. (Louise Wigfall)**
"Address of...president of Maryland Div., U.D.C., to the State Convention, Dec. 7, 1903." Baltimore, (1903) cover title, sm 4to, wraps, 10pp. Emory.

1008 ..."A Southern Girl in '61; the War-time Memories of a Confederate Senator's Daughter. Illustrated from contemporary portraits." N.Y., Doubleday, Page, 1905. 8vo, decr. cl, illus., ports, xii, 258pp. $40-dj.

1009 ..."Maryland and the South...nine generals in her army, etc." In: SHSP, 1903, v.XXXI, p.209-214. See: Sarah Agnes Wallace.

1010 **WRIGHT, D.E.**
"English Opinion on Secession: A Note." In: Jour. Amer. Studies, 1971, v.V, p.151-154.

1011 **WRIGHT, David Minton**
"Expunged from the record." David Minton Wright, M.D., 1809-1863. A reprint from the "Richmond News", Richmond, Va., Fri. May 10, 1901." Mexico City, Privately Printed, 1925. Reprinted in: TylerQHGM, Apr. 1948, v.29, p.281-284. On execution of Dr. Wright at Norfolk, Va., Oct. 23, 1863. See: Dr. L.B. Anderson.

1011a **WRIGHT, David R.**
"Up in smoke Soldier's art: carved pipes of the Civil War." In: CV (new) May/June 1986, v.34, #3, p.(30)-(5) ills (1-color facsm).

1011b **WRIGHT, Edmund (pseud.)**
"Narrative of Edmund Wright: his adventure with an escape from Knights of the Golden Circle." Cincinnati: J.R. Hawley, 1864. 12mo, cl, 150, ills. Wright-II, 2802.

1012 **WRIGHT, Edward Needles**
"Conscientious objectors in the Civil War, a thesis in American history, University of

Pa." Phila., University of Pa. Press, 1931. 8vo, stiff wraps, vii, 274pp. $40.

1013 **WRIGHT, Gordon**
"Economic conditions in the Confederacy as seen by the French Consuls." In: JSH, May 1941, p.20, p.195-214. $8.

1014 **WRIGHT, Howard C., Lieut.**
"Confederate Reminiscences." (Albuquerque) NMHR, July 1920, v.V, #3, p.315-324. Wright refutes the generally accepted versions of the Battle of Glorieta Pass. (Bancroft, xvii, p.680-700; Twitchell's "Leading Facts", p.ii, 357-390.

1015 ..."Port Hudson. Its History from an interior point of view. As sketched from the diary of an officer. St. Francisville (1937) Democrat, Lieut. Howard C. Wright 1863." Baton Rouge, reprinted 1961. (1st Ed.t, 1937) Foreword: Charles East. 8vo, stiff wraps, map, 62, (1)pp. Pub. April 15, 1961, by the Comm. for the preservation of the Port Hudson Battlefield, in an edition of 400 copies. Note: First published serially in New Orleans-"Daily True Delta." Anon., and later reproduced in a single issue of "The Weekly True Delta", Sept. 5, 1863. In 1937, Mr. Elrie Robinson, Editor of the St. Francisville, La., Democrat, published the above pamphlet, from which the 1961 imprint was made.

1016 **WRIGHT, Howard Paul**
"Military operations of Brig.-Gen. Marcus J. Wright Confederate States Army, 1861-1865." Atlanta, Ga., 1943. 4to mimeogr. 106 leaves, front(port) References, 9th leaf.

1017 **WRIGHT, James W.A.**
"Bragg's campaign around Chattanooga." In: SB, ns, v.II, p.461-468, 543-549. (1886/1887)

1018 ..."War prisons and poetry." In: SB, ns, v.1, p.716-722, (1885/1886; v.II, p.344-348) (1886/1887.) $10.

1019 ..."Mr. Davis at Montgomery." In: SB, ns, v.II, p.129-120. (1886/1887)

1020 **WRIGHT, John Montgomery**
"A glimpse of Perryville." In: SB, 1885-1886, v.1, ns, plate(map), 130-134. Condensed, in B & L, v.III, p.60-61.

1021 ..."The Trial of Vallandigham." In: SB, ns, II, 1886-1887, p.639-641.

1022 **WRIGHT, Louis Wigfall**
"Memories of the Beginning and the End of the Southern Confederacy." (Dallas, Texas), The Highlands Historical Press, facsimile, n.d. (1965) 8vo, pict. color wraps, ports, illus., (14pp.) Originally appeared in McClure's Magazine, January, 1904.

1023 **WRIGHT, Marcus Joseph, Brig.-Gen.**
"Additional notes on Perryville, Choctaw Nation." In: Ch. Okl., June 1930, v.VIII, p.146-148. Fighting around Perryville.

1024 ..."Attempted sale of the Federal Fleet (on the Mississippi) and desertion of Lt. D.W. Glenney USNavy in 1863." In: SHSP, 1904, v.32, p.58-67. Planned to deliver fleet to CSA and Glenny escapes to Mexico.

1025 ..."Arkansas in the War, 1861-1865." by...Brig.-Gen., Provisional Army, CSA. Batesville, Ark., Independence Co. Hist. Society (1963) (Guard-Record Co., print.) $25-r. 8vo, cl, ($3) wraps ($2) ports, facsm., 98pp. (6).

1026 ..."Catalogue of Pictures, Confederate and Union, belonging to Marcus J. Wright." n.p., n.d., wraps, lists 967 pictures.

1027 ..."The Battle of Belmont." In: SHSP, 1888, v.XVI, p.69-82.

1028 ..."Colonel Elias C. Boudient." In: Sou. Biv. 1883/1884, port, p.433-440. Vol.II.

1029 ..."Battles and commanders of the Civil War; a graphic and pictorical history prepared directly from the Government Records in the Department of War and statistics accompanied by the complete superb collection of the Leslie's famous war pictures drawn upon the spot by the Governments great artists of the time. Narrative and descriptive by John Clark Ridpath, et al. Carefully edited by Gen. Marcus Joseph Wright." Wash: War Records Office (c.1902) 4to, cl, 24-584pp. illus., front, map (part color) 44cm. Wash: (c.1907), 582pp. illus. Phila: (1908) various pagings. Wash: (1908), 34-582pp., facsms., front, illus., maps.

1030 ..."Diary of Brig.-Gen. Marcus J. Wright, CSA, Apr. 23, 1861-Feb. 26, 1863." (n.p., n.d., c.1935) 8vo, wraps, front(port) 8pp. LC

...also, in William and Mary College Qrt., 2nd Ser. (1935), p.89-95 (Dornbusch)

1031 ..."General officers of Confederate Army." In: CV, June-Sept., 1913, v.XXI, p.289-290, 446-448.

..."General Officers of the Confederate Army, officers of the executive departments of the Confederate States, members of the Confederate Congress by states." compl. by N.Y., Neale Pub., 1911. $150-r, $125-r. 12mo, cl, 188pp.

...Mattituck, N.Y., 1983 reprint.

1032 ..."A List of Artillery Officers CSA." (binder's title) 8vo, cl, 186, 37, and 49pp. mssc., copy interleaved. Washington, D.C.? TU Lib., 25 copies printed.

1033 ..."List of staff officers of the Confederate States of America. With a new introduction by John M. Carroll, 1861-1865." Mattituck, N.Y., and Bryan, Texas, J.M. Carroll and Co., (1987). 12mo, cl, (20)pp., facsm., 186pp.

1034 ..."A Glimpse of Perryville." In: SB, v.1, #3, 1885/1886, map, p.129-134.

1035 ..."Local Designations of Confederate Organizations and "Memorandum of Armies, Corps, and Geographical Commands in the Confederate States. 1861-1865." Washington, D.C. (War Dept. Printing Office) n.d., (c.1876) 12mo, cl, 376pp. Only 25 copies, interleaves printed, only three copies survived in War Dep't., another found in 1957 by Wm. Frayne Amann. Reprint: N.Y., Thos. Yoseloff (1961) as "Personnel of the Civil War", 2 vols., as above and "The Fallon Reports (1885)" "The Union Armies", 373pp. See: Wm. F. Amann.

1036 ..."Local Designations of Confederate Troops" and "Memorandum of Armies, Corps., Geographical Commands in the Confederate Army During 1861-1865." n.p., n.d., (Washington, 189?) 8vo, cl, 169pp.

1037 ..."Military operations of Brig.-Gen. Marcus J. Wright..." See: Howard Paul Wright.

1038 ..."Old Boggy Depot." In: Ch. Okl. March 1927, v.V, p.4-17.

1039 ..."Colonel Thomas P. Ochiltree." In: Sou. Biv., v.II, 1883/1884, port, p.481-485. See: Wm. Ruffin Cox's Life and Services of Gen. Marcus J. Wright.

1040 ..."Battle of Shiloh." In: SHSP, 1904, v.32, p.122-133.

1041 ..."Official and Illustrated War Record, embracing nealy one thousand pictorial sketches by the most distinguished American artists of battles by land and sea, camp and field scenes, insignia of rank in the Civil War. Comprehensive and impartial histories of military and Naval operations, compiled from the official data furnished by Union and Confederate departments, commands, Corps., divisions and brigades. Portraits and biographies of Northern and Southern leaders. Elaborate maps, army and navy rosters, battle-lists and descriptions, alphabetically and chronologically arranged. Numerous tabular statements of cemeteries, prisoners, casualties, expenditures and martial matters not hitherto accessible. Authentic articles by eminent officials on the uses of a navy, closing days of conflict, origin and meaning of corps. badges, object and status of the Grand Army of the Republic and Confederate Veterans Associations. Carefully written and edited by Gen. Marcus J. Wright, Col. Benjamin La Bree and James P. Boyd." Washington, 1898. Folio, illus., part colored, maps, ports, fldg. pls. 560pp. $50.

...Folio, some illus. in color, 585pp., ports, fldg. pls.

1042 ..."Official Portfolio of War and Nation; a graphic and pictorial history prepared directly from government records in the department of war and statistics... complete, superb collection of Leslie's famous war pictures-narrative and descriptive by John Clark Ridpath, Rossiter Johnson, Gen. Fitzhugh Lee, Gen. John T. Morgan, Geo. L. Kolmer, and Gen. J.B. Carr." (Philadelphia, 1904-1905) Folio, cl, ix, xxvii, (2), 24-584pp. (i.e., 612pp.) front, illus. $75-ob.

1043 ..."Roster of Confederate General Officers and their Commands." Washington, D.C., 1880. sm.8vo, cl, 453pp. 25 copies printed.

1044 ..."A Roster of the General Officers of the Confederate States of America" giving dates of their commissions." In: The Collector, Mar.-May, 1913, v.XXVI, #5-7, p.51-53, 62-64, 75-77. Edt. W.R. Benjamin states Wright made list Cf. also from "Official Records", also in "Photographic History of Civil war, v.X, 1912.

1045 ..."Sketch of Gen. F.K. Zollicoffer, of Tennessee, by..." Washington, D.C., 1879. 8vo, wraps, 8pp, 50 copies, priv. print.

...also in "Ware's Valley Monthly", of St. Louis, Mo.: also South. Bivouac, v.2, 1883-1884, p.485-499, ports. (Dornbusch)

1046 ..."Tennessee in the War, 1861-1865." Lists of Military Organizations and Officers from Tenn., in both the Confederate and Union Armies, etc., etc." Williamsbridge, N.Y. City, Ambrose Lee Pub. Co., (1908) sm.8vo, cl, 228, (3)pp-ads. $75.

1047 ..."Texas in the War, 1861-1865." Edt: Harold B. Simpson. Hillsboro, Texas: Hill Junior College, 1965, p.xx, 246, illus., notes, index.

...1984, 3rd Print.

1048 ..."Trial of John Brown. Its impartiality and decorum vindicated." (signed MJW) In: SHSP, 1888, v.16, p.357-

..."The trial and execution of John Brown." In: Papers Amer. Hist. Assoc., Oct., 1890, v.IV, pt. 4, p.113-126. To correct a statement by Dr. Herman Von Holst, that Brown's trial was not a fair one.

..."Trial of John Brown. A review of the trial of "Ossawatomie" Brown, in reply to the criticism of Dr. Herman Von Holst, in his work entitled "The Constitutuion and Democracy of the U.S." Richmond, Va., W.E. Jones, 1889, 8vo, cover title, 8pp. Reprinted from SHSP, v.16, p.367-365.

1049 ..."Reminiscences of the early settlement and early settlers of McNairy County, Tenn., Washington, D.C., Commercial Pub., 1882, 8vo, wraps, ports, 96pp. CSA General, of 6th Tenn. See: John Sharp Williams' "Tribute."

1050 ..."West Point before the War." In: SB, ns, v.1, #1, p.13-21.

..."Records of the War between the states." In: Photo. Hist. CW, v.I, p.102-8, ills. ports.

1051 **WRIGHT, Michael F.**
"Vicksburg and the Trans-Mississippi Supply Line (1861-1863)." In: JMH, Aug., 1981, v.XLIII, #3, p.210-225.

1052 **WRIGHT, Muriel H. and LeRoy H. Fischer**
"Civil War Sites in Oklahoma." Oklahoma City: Okla. Hist. Society, 1967, 8vo, wraps, 59pp., illus. Chron. Okla, v.XLIV, #2, p.158-215.

1053 ..."Colonel Cooper's Civil War Report on the Battle of Round Mountain." Oklahoma City: Chron. Okla., Winter, 1961-1962, v.XXXIX, #4, p.352-397, maps, ports, illus.

1054 ..."General Douglas H. Cooper, C.S.A." Oklahoma City: Oklahoma Historical Society - "Chronicles of Oklahoma." v.XXXII-#2, Summer, 1954. 8vo, p.142-184, ports.

1055 ..."Notes on Colonel Elias C. Boudinot." Oklahoma City: Chron. Okla., Winter, 1963-1964, v.XLI, #4, p.382-407, port. Nephew of Gen. Stand Watie, under whom he served. See: Marcus J. Wright/Boudinet.

1056 **WRIGHT, Robert**
"Sinking of the 'Jamestown'. How it was done at Drewry's Bluff." In: SHSP, 1901, v.29, p.371-372.

1057 **WRIGHT, Stuart T.**
"Historical Sketch of Person County, (N.C.)." Danville: The Womack Press, 1974. 8vo, cl, maps, 232pp. 41pp. on war and roster of Person County soldiers.

1058 **WRIGHT, V.C. and Land Payne**
"The Battle of Chalk Bluff which occurred during the Civil War, May 1 and 2, 1863. Battle location: 4 miles NW of St. Francis, Ark., 4 miles SW of Campbell, Mo., other early historical events about NE Ark., and SE Missouri." Piggott, Arkansas, 1953. 8vo, wraps, illus.(ports) (4)pp., 7pp., (1)lf, (1)pp. (9)-17, (1)lf.

1059 **WRIGHT, William C.**
"The Secession Movement in the Middle Atlantic States." Rutherford, Madison, Teaneck: Fairleigh Dickinson University Press, 1973. 8vo, cl, 274pp. $20. Before firing on Sumter, such states as Maryland, Delaware, even Pa. and NY supported the South, strong financial ties with slave states. N.Y., Burt Franklin, 1972, "Research and source works series, American classics in historical and social science."

..."The Confederate Magazine at Fort Wade, Grand Gulf Mississippi Excavations, 1980-1981." Jackson, Miss. State Archives & Hist., 1982. 4to, wraps, 60pp, 4-tables. $5.

..."The Confederate Upper Battery Site, Grant Gulf, Mississippi Excavations. 1982." Jackson, Miss., Archives & History, 1982. 4to, wraps, 72pp., ills. $5.

1060 **WRIGHT, William Troy**
"Devil John Wright of the Cumberlands." Pound, Virginia (1932). 8vo, cl, front, pls., ports, illus., 313pp. Wright in CSA, captured in Morgan's Raid.

1061 **"WRITER'S Program, West Virginia: W.P.A."**
"Of Stars and Bars." Sponsored by State Dept. Education, United Daughters of the Confed. Capt. E.D. Camden, Chap. #1864, Sutton, W.Va., Charleston, W.Va., Writer's Project, 1940. Folklore Series, #11. (Rep: from typed copy) 4to, mimeo, wraps, (5), 18 leaves, illus. A Memorial to Braxton Co. Confederates and Notes on actions at Sutton and Bulltown.

1062 **WUBBEN, Hubery H.**
"Civil War Iowa and the Copperhead Movement." Ames: Iowa University Press, 1980. 8vo, cl, illus., xi, 280pp. bibliog. 263-268.

1063 ..."Copperhead Charles Mason a question of Loyalty." In: CWH, Mar. 1978, v.24, #1, p.46-65.

1064 **WYATT, Henry Lawson**
See: News-Leader, Stephen B. Weeks, Sketch of Wyatt in James C. Birdson's N.C. Troops.

1065 **WYATT, Henry W.**
"Monument to Wyatt, first to die in war." (from Richmond News-Leader, Dec. 30, 1908) In: SHSP, 1908, v.36, p.354-355. See: Stephen B. Weeks.

1066 **WYATT, J.A.G.**
"The Battle of Jonesville." In: CV, Mar. 1922, v.XXX, p.102-103. Jonesville, Va.

1067 **WYATT, Lee T., III**
"William S. Barry, advocate of Secession 1821-1868." In: JMH, November 1977, v.XXXIX, #4, p.339-355.

1068 **WYATT, Lillian Reeves**
"The Reeves, Mercer, Newkirk Families, a compilation." Jacksonville?, Fal., 1956. 8vo, cl, coats-of-arms, facsms., maps, ports, views, notes, (10), 374pp. Concerns Lt. Oliver E. Mercer (1842-1863, CSA) p.241-273; NC diary of Sara Elizabeth Mercer in 1863, p.234-241.

1069 **WYATT-BROWN, Bertram**
"The Antimission Movement in the Jacksonian South: A Study in Regional Folk Culture." (Houston, Tex.) JSH, Nov. 1970, v.XXXVI, #4, p.501-529. Suspicion of Northern missionaries and final break in church before war.

1070 ..."Yankee Saints and Southern Sinners." Baton Rouge: Louisiana State Univ., 1985, 8vo, cl, 656pp. $30.

1071 **WYETH, John Allan, Dr.**
"Addresses at the unveiling of the Statue of Dr. John Allan Wyeth, May 1, 1914, Testimonial." n.p., 1914. 8vo, wraps, illus., 23pp.

1072 ..."Characteristics of General Forrest." In: CV, Oct. 1915, v.XXIII, p.449-452.

1073 ..."Cold Cheer at Camp Morton." In: Cent. Mag., 1891, v.XLI, p.844-852, illus.; p.771-775.

1074 ..."Confederate Raids in the West." In: Photographic Hist. of Civil War., v.4, N.Y., 1911, p.141-156, contains "Morgan's Christmas Raid." Reprint: Glendale, Calif., 1970.

1075 ..."History of La Grange Military Academy and the Cadet Corps, 1857-1862." N.Y. (Brewer Press) Private Print, 1907. 12mo, cl, ports, (8), (9)-202pp. $100-ob.

1076 ..."Life of Nathan Bedford Forrest, with illustrations by T. de Thulstrup, Rogers, Klepper, Redwood, Hitchcock and Carleton." N.Y., Lond: Harper and Bros., 1899. Tk.8vo, cl, facsms. (3) 1-dble., illus., maps (2) 1-dble, ports, incl. front, xix, (1). 655, (1)p. $150-jk-mint copy. Other Edts: 2nd Edt., 1901; 3rd, 1908.

..."Life of Nathan Bedford Forrest." Dayton, Oh., Morningside Press, 1985, 8vo, cl, 656pp. $30.

..."That Devil Forrest. Life of General Nathan Bedford Forrest by John Allan Wyeth. Foreword: Henry Steele Commager, Maps by Jean Tremblay, (other illus. from orig. edt.)." N.Y., Harper and Bros. (1959) Tk.8vo, cl, dj, illus., ports, incl. front, maps, 1-fldg., xxvi, 614pp. $37.50. Orig. text not altered but for modernized spelling, shorten paragraphs, and some flowery speeches, book completely reset, with 21 new maps and an index.

...(Dayton, Ohio) Morningside Print., 1975. 8vo, same binding, 655pp. $30-y.

1077 ..."Maj.-Gen. Forrest at Brice's Crossroads." In: Harper's New Monthly Mag., 1898/1899, XCVIII, 530-545, illus., plan, ports.

1078 ..."Lieut.-Col. Forrest at Fort Donnelson." In: Harper's New Monthly Mag., 1898/1899, XCVIII, p.339-354, illus., port.

1079 ..."General Robert E. Lee. Commemorative address before the N.Y. Southern Society on the anniversary of the great commanders birth, Jan. 19, 1906." N.Y., Unz and Co., 1906. 8vo, wraps, 22pp. Also: in CV, 1907, v.15, p.65-69.

1080 ..."Prisoners North and South." In: SHSP, 1891, v.19, p.47-51.

1081 ..."Rejoiner (re Camp Morton) by Dr. Wyeth." In: Cent. Mag., 1891, v.XLI,

1082 p.771-775. See: Thomas E. Spotswood, Anthony M. Keiley, Hattie Lou Winslow.

1082 ..."Pursuit and capture of Streight's Raiders." In: Harper's Mag., Aug., 1899, v.99, p.435-448. See: Rucker Agee, D.H. Maury, Nathan Bedford Forrest.

1083 ..."A Ride Through Federal Lines at Night." p.204-214.

1084 ..."Storming of Fort Pillow." In: Harpers Mag., Sept. 1899, v.99, p.595-607.

1085 ..."Trials with Gen. John H. Morgan." In: Confed. Vet., Mar./Apr., 1911, p.118-122, 160-164. A chap. from Wyeth's Memoirs-Morgan's Cavalry in 1862-1863.

1086 ..."With Sabre and Scapel. The Autobiography of a soldier and surgeon." N.Y., Lond: Harper and Bros., 1914. $75-atg. 8vo, cl, illus., ports, incl. front, maps, xix, (3), 534, (1)pp.
..."The destruction of Rosecrans' great Wagon-Train." In: Photo. Hist. CW, v.4, p.158-64. Ills, ports.
..."Cold Cheer at Camp Morton." In: Cent. April 1891, v.19, p.844-52. Ills.
See: W. R. Holloway & rejoinder.

1087 **WYLD, James**
"Map of Southern States of North America, with Forts, Harbours, etc." Map 25x38", colored, canvas mounted, fldg. sm.4to. London, n.d. (James Wyld, c.1863) $55.

1088 ..."The United States and relative position of Northern States and Southern Confederated States." Map: 23x17", folded in cloth case. London(c.1861). Few contemporary maps showed CSA as a separate nation.

1089 **WYLLY, Benjamin F.**
"Repulse of Federal Raid on Knoxville, July, 1863." In: SHSP, 1881, v.IX, p.479-481. Served in 9th Batt., artillery.

1090 ..."Repulse of Federal Raid on Knoxville, July, 1863." In: SHSP, 1881, v.9, p.479-481.

1091 **WYNN, William O.**
"Biographical Sketch of the Life of an old Confederate Soldier. Also, three years as a cowboy on the Frontier of Texas." Greenville, Texas, Greenville Print, 1916, 12mo, wraps, illus., port, 159pp.

1092 ..."A Brief Sketch of the life and ups and downs of an ex-Confederate soldier. Also three years a cowboy on the frontier of Texas before the Civil War and a sketch of my pioneer days in the early settling of Texas." (Sulphur Springs, Texas, 1928) 12mo, wraps, front(port), (16)pp. cover title.

1092a **WYNNE, Lewis N. & Guy Porcher Harrison**
"Plain Folk coping in the Confederacy: The Garrett-Asbell Letters." In: GHQ, Spring 1988, v.72, #1, p.102. Ills, facsms, port.

1093 **WYNNE, Thomas Hicks**
"Catalogue of the library collected by the late Thos H. Wynne, of Richmond, Va. Rich in works relating to the history of Virginia and the local history of Richmond and in Confederate States printed and in books relating to the late war. The whole to be sold at auction in Richmond by J. Thompson Brown." (Richmond, Va., Richmond Dispatch, 1875) 8vo, wraps, 158pp. (2628 items)

XYZ

1 **YANCEY Guards**
See: Camm Patterson

2 **YANCEY, Rosa Faulkner**
"Lynchburg and its Neighbors." Richmond, Fergusson, 1935. Orig. cl, pls., 471pp. Chaps: Battle of Lynchburg, biogs. of C.S.A. Gens., Munford, Early, Rodes, etc.

3 **YANCEY, William Lowndes**
"Speech, delivered in the Democratic State Convention, of the State of Alabama on the 11th-14th, January, 1860." Montgomery, Ala., Advitizer Print, 1860. 8vo, wraps, 31pp.

4 ..."Speech delivered in the National Democratic Convention, Charleston, April 28, 1860. With the protest of the Alabama delegation. From the report of the "Charleston Mercury." (Charleston, S.C., Walker, Evans Co.) 8vo, sewn, caption title, 20pp. $40. Alabama withdraws since platform failed to guarantee protection slavery.

5 ..."Substance of the speech made in the Democratic meeting at Marion, Perry County (Ala.), May 19, 1860." n.p., n.d. 8vo, sewn, caption title, 24pp.

6 ..."Speeches of..., Senator from the State of Alabama, made in the Senate of the Confederate States during the session commencing on the 18th day of August, 1862." Montgomery: Advertiser Print, 1862. 12mo, wraps, 54pp.

7 ..."Manuscripts." In: Ala. H.Q., 1940, v.II, p.256-261, 334-341. Letters to and from (above) on life in Alabama, before and during the War and difficulties facing the CSA.

8 ..."Memoranda of the Late Affair of Honor between the Hon. T.L. Clingman of North Carolina and the Hon. William L. Yancey of Alabama." sm4to, sewn, caption title, 8pp.

9 ..."William L. Yancey's European diary, Mar./June, 1861. Edt: W. Stanley Hoole." In: AR, April, 1972, v.25, #2, p.134-142.

10 ..."Yancey and Hill. An account of their difficulty in the Confederate Senate." In: SHSP, 1891, v.XIX, p.374-476. See: Anthony W. Dillard, John W. DuBose, Joseph Hodgson, J.R. Satterfield, George Petrie.

11 **YANKEE Gunboat "Smith Briggs".**
"How it was captured by Rebels. Some interesting war history." In: SHSP, 1906, v.XXXIV, p.162-169. Letters: Wm. W. Rodgers, R.S. Thomas and B.A. Sowell.

12 **YARBROUGH, John Coffee**
"A Tale of Exiles." Boston: Roxburgh Pub., (1921). 12mo, cl, front(map), 13011. Exiles, e.g., Confederates.

13 **YATES, Bowling C.**
"The role of artillery in the Atlanta Campaign." In: Regional Rev., 1940, v.IV, #6, p.25-30.

14 ..."History of Georgia Military Institute." Kennesaw, Ga., Continental Book Co., 1969. 8 1/2x11", stiff wraps, illus., maps, 35pp. Muster roll of two companies from around Atlanta and Savannah, students and faculty. See: Robert L. Rodgers' Confed. Vets. Ass'n.

15 ..."Kennesaw Mountain and the Atlanta Campaign." In: Regional Rev., 1939, v.III, #4-5, 9-12.

16 **YATES, Richard E.**
"The Confederacy and Zeb Vance." Tuscaloosa, Ala: Confed. Pub. Co., 1958. Confederate Centennial Studies, #8. 12mo, stiff wraps, 132pp., port. Lim. Edt. 450 copies.

17 ..."Governor Vance and the Peace Movement." (Raleigh) NCHRev., Jan and Apr., 1940, v.XVII, #1 and 2, p.1-25, 89-113.

18 ..."Zebulon B. Vance as War Governor of North Carolina, 1862-1865." Nashville, Tenn., 1937. Title-head: Vanderbilt University, abstract Thesis (PH.D.) Vanderbilt Univ., 1936. Also in: JSH, 1937, v.III, p.43-75.

19 ..."Governor Vance and the End of the War in North Carolina." In: NCHR, Oct. 1941., v.18, p.315-338.

20 **YAZOO COUNTY, Mississippi**
See: Robert Bowman.

21 **YEAGER, A.H., Edt.**
"Jacob Klodsloe, one of the nobodies. How he came home from the War--how he grew up and into it." Cleaburne, Texas: T.L. Sanders, 1899, 8vo, wraps (cover-title) 129pp., (Jenkins)-$1750. Served in Army of Tenn., "Atlanta Campaign", captured at Kennesaw Mt., imprisoned at Camp Douglas. Unrecorded, fragile paper.

22 **YEAGER, James A., Gen.**
"My Experiences as a Confederate Soldier." (Tulsa, Okla., 1924) 12mo, wraps, port, (14)pp.

23 ..."Memorial-General James A. Yeager of Tulsa, Oklahoma, Dec. 31, 1928, (Okla. Hist. Soc.)

23a **YEARNS, W. Buck, Edt.**
"The Confederate Governors." Athens, Ga., University of Georgia Press, 1985. 8vo, cl, dj, 295p. $27.50.

24 **YEARNS, W. Buck and John G. Barrett, Edt.**
"North Carolina Civil War Documentary." Chapel Hill: North Carolina Press, 1980. 8vo, cl, dj, xvii, 365pp. From secession to surrender at Bennett Farm.... "The Confederate Congress." Athens: University of Georgia Pr.(1960) 8vo, cl, dj, viii, 293pp., notes, bibliog., index, p. (245-293), op, $25.

25 ..."North Carolina in the Confederate Congress." In: NCHR, July 1952, v.XXXVI, p.359-378. See: "North Carolina Civil War Documentary.", Edt. by...

26 ..."The Peace Movement in the Confederate Congress." In: Ga.H.Q., March 1957, v.XLI, #1, p.1-18.

27 **YEARY, Mamie, Miss**
"Reminiscences of the Boys in Gray, 1861-1865." Dallas, Texas, For the Author by Smith and Lamar, M.E. Church South (1912). Sm.4to, 3/4lt., cl, illus., ports, incl. front. 1p-color flags, (6), 904pp. Brief biogs., reminiscences of veterans living in era of 1912. $150, $500-bmk.
...Dayton, Oh., Morningside Press, 1987. Tk4to, decr. cl., 904pp., index. $75.

28 **YEATER, Sarah J.**
"Civil War Experiences of..." Sedalie, Mo., Sedalia Print, 1910, 8vo, wraps, 57pp., priv. print. Southern sympathies, forced to flee south in Ark. and Texas.

29 ..."My Experiences During the War Between the States. (written October 1910, for my granddaughter, Jeanette Brokmeyer)." In: AHW, 1945, v.IV, p.1-55; "My trip to Texas, Fall of 1864", "Winter in Texas and return to Missouri." Written for granddaughters: Christine and Frances Yeater 1909/1910."

30 **"YELL Rifleman's Narrative (Ark.), A."**
In: Confed. Annals, Aug. 1883, v.1, #2, p.66-69. By H.T.W.

31 **YELLOW Tavern, Battle of**
See: Wm. B. Poindexter.

32 **YENCHER, John G.**
"Longstreet, General Lee's War-horse." In: Quartermaster Rev., 1937, v.XVI, #6, p.19-22, 65-66.

33 **YERBY, Frank Garvin**
"Captain Rebel." N.Y., Dial Press (1956) 12mo, cl, dj, 343pp.
...London: Heinemann (1957) 12mo,

313pp., cl, dj. Novel of exploits of a Confederate Blockade Runner.

34 **YERGER, William**
"Address delivered at Jackson (Miss.) Representatives Hall, Thurs., Nov. 29, 1860." Jackson: Power and Cadwallader, 1860., 8vo, wraps, 16pp., On secession.

34a **YONGE, John Eyers Davis**
"The Conservative party in Alabama, 1848-60." Montgomery Ala., 1904. 8vo, cover title, 501-26. Alabama Historical Society, reprint #25. From Transactions, 1899-1903, v.iv.

35 **YONKERS, Tescia Ann**
"Behold his bronze likeness, Rudulph Evan's statue of Robert E. Lee." In: Virginia Cavalcade, Autumn 1984, v.34, #2, p.90-95, ports, plates.

36 **YOPP, William Isaac**
"A Dual Role. A romance of the Civil War." (Dallas, Tex., John F. Worley (1902) 16mo, decr. cl, illus., front(port) 169pp. CSA novel, based on several real events and characters. Tennessee.

37 **YORK RANGERS,**
32nd. Reg., Hunter's Brigade, Virginia Vols. CSA. Roll of Co. "I"
See: Mrs. Conway H. Sheild.

38 **YORK, Richard Watson, Maj.**
"The Old Third Brigade. Death of General Bee." In: OLOD, Feb. 1875, v.1, #6, p.561-566.

39 ..."Gen. Hood's release from arrest-an incident of the Battle of Boonesboro." In: OLOD, June 1875, v.2, #2, p.420-423.

40 **YORK, Zebulon, Brig.-Gen.**
"Report of Brig.-Gen. Z. York, Breckenridge Corps., C.S.A., June and July, 1864." In: Hist. Mag., 1871.

41 **YORKE, J.S., Rev.**
"Texas War Horse. Early Days in Texas, or Experience of a Pioneer Minister." Corsicana, Texas, n.d. (c.1919) Private Print. 8vo, wraps, illus., 86pp. Much on the War.

42 **YOUNCE, W.H.**
"The Adventures of a Conscript. Late 58th NC." Cincinnati: Editor Publishing Co., 1901. 12mo, wraps, 105pp. $135-y. Serial: National Tribune, in Nov. 23 and 30, Dec. 7, 1889; Jan. 4 and 11, 1890.

43 **YOUNG, Abram Hayne**
"Civil War Letters of... Edt: Mary Wyche Burgess." In: SCHM, 1977, v.78, #1, p.56-70.

44 **YOUNG, Bennett Henderson**
"Address: Unveiling of Arlington Monument, June 4, 1914." n.p., 8vo, wraps, port, 11pp.

45 ...In: CV, July 1914, v.22, #7, p.297-299, port.

46 ..."Address, Veterans' Day: Gettysburg." In: CV, Sept. 1913, v.21, #9, p.426-432, illus.

47 ..."John Cabell Breckinridge." In: CV, 1905, v.13, p.257-261, ports. Presentation of Breckinridge's portrait to Robert E. Lee Camp of UCV, March 24 at Richmond, Va.

48 ..."Buried at Red Sulphur Springs, W.Va." In: CV, Dec. 10-5, v.13, p.564-565. Pleas for grave markers CSA dead in Presbyterian Churchyard.

49 ..."Confederate Wizards of the Saddle. Being Reminiscences and Observations of one who rode with Morgan." Boston: Chapple Pub., 1914. $300-b, $350. Large 8vo, decr., cl, illus., maps, ports, incl. front, xxii, 633pp., index.
...Kennesaw, Ga., Continental Book, 1958, Tk. 8vo, cl, 633pp.
...Dayton, Oh., Morningside, 1979, $30.

50 ..."Jefferson Davis Memorial." In: CV, Feb. 1917, v.XXV, p.67-70. 51 = ..."Dedication of the Jefferson Davis Memorial Home." In: CV, July 1909, v.XVII,

52 ..."Memorial Day at Camp Chase, Ohio. Address at Columbus, Ohio, June 10, 1916, decorating graves of Confederate soldiers." In: CV, Aug. 1916, v.24, #8, p.348-352.

p.320-328. Address by..., historical sketch of home.

53 ..."The South in History." In: CV, June 1910, v.XVIII, p.267-272. Largely Civil War period. Report of Young at UCV at Mobile, Ala. Nashville (1910) 16mo, wraps, 23pp. reprint.

54 ..."Texas Cavalry expedition in 1861-1862; perilous and exhaustive expedition into New Mexico." In: CV, Mar. 1913, v.XXI, p.116-119.

55 ..."The Western Army, an address to the United Confederate Veterans at the Memphis reunion. May 28/30, 1901." In: CV, 1901, v.9, p.312-319, port.

56 ..."Zollicoffer's Oak. Recollections of the Battle of Mill Springs and death of this gallant soldier." In: SHSP, v.XXXI, p.165-172.

57 **YOUNG, Cassye Averett**
"The Last Capitol of the Confederacy, Danville, Va., as the president of the Confederacy saw it on his stay here from April 3 to 10, 1865." Danville, Va., Anne Eliz. Johns. Chap., UDC. (1959) An address given Apr. 6, 1954. 12mo, illus.

58 **YOUNG, Charles P.**
"History of Crenshaw Battery, Pegram's Battalion, Third Corps., Army of Northern Virginia, with Roster of the Company...written by Private Charles P. Young and revised by Captain Thomas Ellett." In: SHSP, 1903, v.XXXI, p.275-296.
...Richmond, Va., W.E. Jones Print, 1904, 8vo, wraps, 26pp. $300-r.

59 ..."The Heroism of Pvt. Chew Coleman, of Crenshaw's Battery, Spotsylvania C-H. May 1864." In: SHSP, v.21, p.374-375.

60 **YOUNG, James C.**
"Marse Robert, Knight of the Confederacy." N.Y., Rae D. Henkly Co., (1929) 8vo, cl, ports (incl. front) illus., map, (7), 362pp. Arlington home as endsheets.
...(1929) 2nd Print, December. $25.
...N.Y., Grosset and Dunlap (1931) sm.8vo, cl, (7), 356pp. (3)pp. map, legend.
...DeLuxe Edt. (1929) 3/4 Mor., limited Edt. 150 copies, signed by author, g/t. $50, $35-y.

61 **YOUNG, James R.**
"Confederate Pensions in Georgia, 1886-1929." In: GaHQ, Spring, 1982, v.LXVI, #1, p.47-52, notes and tables.

62 **YOUNG, Jo**
"The Battle of Sabine Pass." In: SwHQ, April 1949, v.LII, #4, p.398-409, map.

63 **YOUNG, John D.**
"A campaign with sharpshooters." In: AW, 1879, p.267-285.

64 **YOUNG, John Preston**
"The Seventh Tennessee Cavalry (Confederate), a History, by J.P. Young, of Company A, printed for the Author." Nashville, Tenn: M.E. Church South, 1890. 8vo, cl, ports, 227pp. $275. Roll of personnel.
...Dayton, Oh., Morningside Press, 1976.

65 ..."Federal Atrocities in the Civil War." In: SHSP, 1907, v.XXXV, p.304-311.

66 ..."Hood's Failure at Spring Hill." In: Confed. Vet., Jan. 1908, v.XVI, p.25-41.
... Do: 1914, v.22, p.126-127, map.

67 **YOUNG, Lot D.**
"Reminiscences of a Soldier of The Orphan Brigade." (Louisville, Courier-Journal, 1897) 8vo, wraps, 99pp.
...Do: Paris, Ky., n.d. (c.1918) $30-auc-173, $35-bmk-86., $10, $15, also micro-cards, in Louisville, Ky: Lost Cause Press, $2.45

68 **YOUNG, M. Clifford**
"Dr. Le Mat's "Grapeshot" revolver." In: Am. Arms Collector, July 1957, v.1, p.91-93, views. A pistol patented by Dr. Alexan-

dre Francois Le Mat of New Orleans, 1856, later made in France for the CSA.

69 **YOUNG, Pierce Manning Butler**
See: E. Edgeworth Eve.

70 **YOUNG, Rogers W.**
"The Construction of Fort Pulaski." In: Ga.HQ, 1936, v.XX, p.41-51. Projected, 1819. Completed 1861, under siege April 10-12, 1862, and captured. East of Savannah.

71 ..."Robert E. Lee and Fort Pulaski." Washington, D.C., U.S. Nat'l. Park Service Popular Study Series, #11, 1947. 12mo, wraps, 28pp., port, facsms., illus.

72 ..."Two Years at Fort Bartow, 1862-1864." In: Ga.H.Q., Sept. 1939, v.XXIII, #3, p.253-264. Causton's Bluff Battery, defenses at Savannah.

73 ..."Vicksburg's Confederate Fort Hill, 1862-1863." (Jackson, Miss., Jour. Miss. Hist., Jan. 1944, v.VI, #1, p.3-29.

74 **YOUNG, Stark**
"Southern Treasury of Life and Literature selected by Stark Young." N.Y., Charles Scribner's Sons, (1937). 12mo, cl, xviii, 748pp., index.

75 ..."So Red the Rose." N.Y., C. Scribner's Sons, 1934. 12mo, cl, dj, 431pp.

76 **YOUNG, T.J.**
"About Jones' Raid into West Virginia." In: CV, May, 1907, v.15, p.211. 6th/7th. Va. Cav. at Greeland Gap, Witcher's Bat., Val. Cav., captures buswhackers.

77 ..."Battle of Balls Bluff." In: CV, 1901-1902, v.10, p.68-69.

78 ..."Capture of Garrison at New Creek." In: CV, Mar. 1904, v.12, p.117-118. Remins. 7th Va. Cav., Nov. 27-1864.

79 ..."More about the capture of Beverly." In: CV, Dec. 1913, v.21, p.585. Ashby Cav., Jan. 11, 1865.

80 **YOUNG., Louis Gourdin**
"The Battle of Gettysburg, an address by Capt. Louis G. Young." (Savannah, Ga., 190?) 8vo, wraps, 8pp. caption title, dbl. column. Also in "Addresses delivered before the Confederate Veterans Association of Savannah, Ga., 1898-1902, p.38-48.

81 ..."Death of Brig.-Gen. J. Johnston Pettigrew, of North Carolina." In: OLOD, v.1, #1, Sept. 1874. p.29-32.

82 ..."Pettigrew's Brigade at Gettysburg." In: OLOD, Feb. 1875, v.1, #6, p.552-558.

82a **YOUNG, William & Joseph Forsythe**
"The Southern Confederates" ? Co. "C", 9th Tenn. Reg. Inft., or Clopton Camp Ground in Tipton County, Tenn., 1861. Note: CV, July 1911, v.19, #7. "A booklet has been published by S. E. Sweet, compiled by ordnance Sgts.... No ref. LC, Dornb., AHA.

83 **YOUNGBLOOD, William**
"Personal observations at Gettysburg." In: CV, June 1911, v.XIX, p.2867-

84 ..."Unwritten history of the Gettysburg Campaign Longstreet's Courier and part played by Hood." In: SHSP, 1910, v.38, p.312-318.

85 **YOUNGE, Julien C.**
"Pensacola in the War for Southern Independence." In: FHQ, January-April, 1959, v.XXXVII, #3/4, p.357-371, facsms., rosters.

86 **"YOUNGEST Confederate General."**
See: Opelika, Ala. Post.

87 **YULEE, C. Wickliffe**
"Senator Yulee of Florida. A biographical sketch by C. Wickliffe Yulee." (cover title) Half-title: "Senator David L. Yulee." n.p., n.d. (Jacksonville, Fla?) 8vo, stiff wraps, front(port), pl (sketches) (1), (4)-42pp. At foot of cover: "Reprinted from the Florida Historical Magazine."

88 ..."Senator Yulee: a biographical sketch." In: Fla.HSW. Apr./July, 1909, v.II, p.26-43, 1-22pp. David Levy Yulee, 1810-1886.

89 **YULEE, David L.**
"Two Letters of David L. Yulee. His opin-

ion on Secession in 1860. A letter to Charles E. Dyke, Edt. "Floridian and Journal", Washington, D.C., May 26, 1860." In: FHQ, Oct. 1950, v.XXIX, #2, p.125-131. See: Leon Huhner.

90 ZAGONYI, Charles
See: Wm. Preston Johnston.

91 ZAMONSKI, Stanley W.
"Colorado Gold and the Confederacy." In: Westerners Brand Book (Denver) 1956, v.12, p.85-117. Activities of Charles Harrison, gambler and a Missouri CSA Cavalry, to raid gold supplies but was murdered by Indians.

92 ZAVALA, Lorenzo de
"Memorial to the Legislature of the State of Texas, of Wm. H. Jones, Administrator of the Estate of Lorenzo de Zavala, deceased, Empresario of Zavala's Colony." (Austin, Texas) 1861. 8vo, 8pp., 3/4 Mor. $175. Not in Crand-Harwell, Winkler, others. His colonization contract from pre-Republic days, petition of recognition.

93 ZELL, Robert R.
"The raid into Pa.- the first armored train." In: CV, July 1920, v.XXVIII, p.260-261.

93a ZENGER LIBRARY of Civil War Classics
Washington, D.C., (Box 42026), 20015.
Munson, Jno. W., Remin. Mosby's Guerrillas.
Baylor, Geo., Bull Run to Bull Run.
Goodlie, Al T., Confederate Echoes.
Batton, S. B., Lone Star Defenders.
McKim (Randolph H.) Soldier's Recoll.

94 ZETTLER, Berrien McPherson
"War Stories and School-day incidents for the Children, by B.M. Zettler, Company B., 8th Ga. Regt." N.Y., Wash., Neale Pub., 1912. 12mo, cl, 168pp. $250, $350-b. Was in Anderson's Brig., Longstreet's Corp., A.N.V.

95 ZIFF, Larzer
"Songs of the Civil War: Civil War Humor." In: CWH, September 1956, v.II, #3, p.7-28.

96 ZIMMER, Louis, Capt.
"Secret Service Episode-affecting success of the First Battle of Manassas." In: SHSP, 1900, v.28, p.14-18.

97 ..."War Officers of 1st Regt., Va. Vol. Infantry." In: SHSP, 1901, v.29, p.364-366.

98 ZINCKE, F. Barham
"The Last Winter in the U.S.; being table talk collected during a tour through the late Southern Confederation, the far West, the Rocky Mountains, etc." London: J. Murray and Co., 1868. 12mo, cl, xvi, 314pp.

99 ZINGG, Paul J.
"John Archibald Campbell and the Hamptons Roads Conference Quixotic Diplomacy, 1865." In: AHQ, Sprint 1974, v.36, p.21-34.

100 ZINN, Jack
"Battle of Rich Mountain." Parsona, W.Va., McClain Print, 1974. 1972, $25-b. op. 8vo, wraps, illus., ports, maps, 51pp.

101 ...R.E. Lee Cheat Mountain Campaign." Parsons, W.Va., McClain Print, 1974. 8vo, cl, illus., xiv, 230pp. $25-b.
..."Military Operations in Jefferson County, Virginia & West Virginia." n.p., 1960. 8vo, wraps, 45pp.

101a ZOLLICOFFER, Felix K., Gen.
"Remorse & repentance: the Death of Gen. Felix K. Zollicoffer." In: THQ, Summer, v.37, #2, p.170-74.

102 ZOLLICOFFER'S Oak
See: Bennett H. Young. Sketch: Felix Zollicoffer. See: Raymond E. Myers.

103 ZOLLINGER, William P., et al
"Gen. George H. Steuart's Brigade at the Battle of Gettysburg." In: SHSP, 1876, v.2, p.105-107.

103a **ZORN, William A.**
"Hold at all hazards, the story of the 29th Alabama Infantry Regiment." Jesup, Ga., The Book Shelf, 1987. 8vo, cl, dj, 300pp. $27.50. Biog. of 1,600 men, letters, orders, casualty lists. Walthall's Div., Army of Miss. Sherman campaign in Georgia.

104 **ZORNOW, William Frank**
"Mississippi State aid for indigent soldiers 1861-1865." In: Mid-America, Han. 1956, v.38, p.38-56, notes.

105 ..."The Missouri Radicals and the Election of 1864." In: Mo.HR, July 1951, v.45, p.354-370.

106 ..."State aid for indigent soldiers and their families in Arkansas, 1861-1865." In: AHQ, 1955, v.XIV, p.97-102.

107 ..."State aid for indigent soldiers and their families in Florida, 1861-1865." In: FHQ, January, 1956, v.XXXIV, #3, p.259-265. Also in: Mid-America, v.XXXVII, p.171-175.

108 ..."State aid for indigent families and soldiers in Louisiana, 1861-1865." In: LHW, July 1956, v.39, p.375-380. notes.

109 ..."State aid for indigent families of South Carolina soldiers, 1861-1865." In: SCHMag., Apr. 1956, v.57, p.82-87. notes.

110 ..."State aid for indigent soldiers and their families in Tennessee, 1861-1865." In: Tenn. HQ, 1954, v.XIII, p.297-300, notes.

111 ..."Texas State aid for indigent soldiers, 1861-1863." In: Mid-Amer., July 1955, v.37, p.171-175. notes.

112 ..."Aid for the indigent families of soldiers in Virginia, 1861-1865." In: VaMHB, Oct. 1958, v.66, p.454-458. notes.

113 **ZUBER, Richard L.**
"Jonathan Worth: a biography of a Southern Unionist." Chapel Hill: Univ. N.C., (1965) 8vo, cl, dj, port, 351pp. Supported CSA reluctantly.

INDEX

> **— IMPORTANT —**
> Author and title listings are alphabetical in this work, thus they are not incorporated into the index.

A

Abbeville County, SC; **C**, 885
   Colonels, **G**, 544
Abbey, Richard; **T**, 223
Abbott, Martin; **S**, 304
Abney's Battalion; **F**, 272
Abolition; **A**, 13, 390, 393, 395, **B**, 28, 787, **C**, 1141, **D**, 410, **H**, 362, **L**, 486, **O**, 197, **S**, 952, **T**, 337, **U**, 17, **V**, 6, 24,
   Conspiracy, **A**, 392
Acadia (ship); **P**, 384
Accoutrements; **G**, 125, 434
Acrostics; **B**, 759
Adair, William Penn, Col.; **M**, 1054
Adams County, MS; **G**, 601, **K**, 181,
   Roster, **R**, 688
Adams Express Co.; **S**, 864
Adams' Brigade; **H**, 705
Adams' Regiment; **A**, 432, **C**, 13
Adams, Charles Francis; **B**, 1183, **M**, 578, **W**, 899
Adams, Daniel Weisiger, Brig.Gen.; **G**, 278
Adams, Henry; **M**, 147
Adams, James Norman; **B**, 285
Adams, John, Brig.Gen.; **M**, 1328
Adams, William Wirt, Brig.Gen.; **A**, 432
Adkins, Sam; **B**, 1307
Admiralty; **R**, 610
Adobe Walls, TX, Battle of; **M**, 422
Advance (ship); **M**, 56
Advance Guards; **M**, 72, 271
Aeronautics; **H**, 579-581
Affleck, Isaac Dunbar; **A**, 79, **T**, 135, **W**, 742, 975
Africa;
   Slave Trade, **B**, 117, 557, **C**, 26, 190
Age, np.; **A**, 20

Agents;
   Confederate, **R**, 119,
   Foreign, **A**, 301,
   Treasury, **R**, 69
Agonistes, Lee; **K**, 255a
Agriculture; **C**, 1302, **G**, 116,
   Mississippi, **J**, 81,
   North Carolina, **C**, 315,
   South, History, **R**, 56
Aiken, SC, Battle of; **B**, 1031
Airplanes; **E**, 261
Alabama; **A**, 113, **C**, 690, **D**, 855, **F**, 318, **L**, 456, 632,
   Blockades, **H**, 32,
   Cadet Corps, **J**, 138,
   Chaplains, Baptist, **W**, 38,
   Churches, **F**, 242,
   Coal & Iron in, **A**, 436,
   Confederate Records, **J**, 137,
   Congress, **S**, 734,
   Conscription, **A**, 95, **F**, 265,
   Conservative Party, **XYZ**, 34a,
   Conventions, **A**, 87, 109, **S**, 735, **XYZ**, 3,
   Cotton, **G**, 639,
   Disloyalty, **L**, 633,
   Federal Raid, **J**, 354,
   Flag, **A**, 100, **M**, 206,
   Heroes, **P**, 218,
   Hill Country, **B**, 26,
   History, **B**, 1241, **M**, 435, 1047, **W**, 502,
   Home Life, **F**, 246,
   Hospitals, **D**, 709, **G**, 643,
   Invasion, **H**, 1074,
   Iron Works, **S**, 1213, **W**, 948,
   Manual, **A**, 92,
   Memorial Records, **B**, 1165,
   Memorials, Vicksburg, **C**, 226,

Alabama

Military Government, **F**, 248-249,
Military Organizations, **B**, 1236, 1242,
Ordinances, **A**, 89,
Politics, **D**, 752,
Postal Arrangements, **A**, 109,
Propaganda, **L**, 626b,
Publications, **C**, 705,
Reconstruction, **B**, 1293,
Secession, **B**, 1167, **D**, 521, **J**, 548, **M**, 362a, 824, **O**, 122,
Secession Commissioners, **L**, 634,
Secession Convention, **D**, 99, **I**, 43, **M**, 1308, **W**, 959,
Soldiers, **A**, 27, 91, 113-114, 249, **C**, 1198, 1216, **D**, 650, **H**, 912,
Southern Rights Association, **B**, 1015,
State Currency, **H**, 1186,
State Memorial, **J**, 547,
States Rights, **A**, 64,
Tories, **H**, 1063,
Unionism, **T**, 260,
Vicksburg Monument, **A**, 116,
Volunteers, **H**, 912,
Wartime Home-front, **M**, 646,
Whiggery in, **A**, 187,
Women, **S**, 1119

Alabama (ironclad); **A**, 94, 101, 302, 442, **B**, 107, 543, 896, 1018, 1087, 1153-1154, 1425, **C**, 175, 369, 395, 712, 1248, 1387, **D**, 317, 501, 504, **E**, 74, **F**, 66, 432, 573, 579-583, **G**, 497, **H**, 222, 609-610, 781, 853, 1073b, 1073c, **J**, 95, **K**, 48, 49, 49b, **L**, 190, 734, 771, **M**, 364a, **N**, 19, 25, 36, 140, **O**, 190, **P**, 611, 785, **R**, 515, 549, 611, **S**, 241, 527, 1393, **W**, 576, 579,
Claims, **B**, 1268, **C**, 514, 1270,
Log, **L**, 740,
Plans to Trade, **D**, 112,
Singapore, **H**, 8

Alabama College; **R**, 335

Alabama Confederate Reader; **M**, 643

Alabama Conscripts; **A**, 108

Alabama Room, Confederate Museum, VA; **C**, 948, **L**, 546

Alabama Troops;
Cadet Corps, **J**, 138,
Cavalry,
1st Regt., **H**, 1063,
2nd Regt., **C**, 717,
3rd Regt., **M**, 902, **S**, 709,
12th Regt., **H**, 702,
Desertion, **M**, 241,
Infantry,
1st Regt., **M**, 649, **P**, 128b, 684, **S**, 604,
1st Regt. Vols., **T**, 321,
2nd Regt., **H**, 1032,
3rd Regt., **C**, 120, **F**, 398,
4th Regt., **H**, 1232, **J**, 505a, **P**, 386, **V**, 88, **W**, 183,
5th Bat., **F**, 600,
5th Regt., **A**, 148, **F**, 565, **H**, 1073,
6th Regt., **R**, 187,
6th Regt. Vols., **T**, 233,
8th Regt. Vols., **H**, 721,
10th Regt., **R**, 273,
12th Regt., **P**, 69-71,
13th Regt., **B**, 705,
13th Regt. Vols., **K**, 62a,
14th Regt., **H**, 1341-1342,
15th Regt., **B**, 1161, **L**, 114, **O**, 39,
19th Regt., **R**, 672, **S**, 83,
20th Regt., **R**, 312, **W**, 715,
21st Regt., **W**, 721,
23rd Regt., **R**, 243,
26th Regt., **S**, 739,
27th Regt., **B**, 125, **C**, 128,
29th Regt., **XYZ**, 103a,
30th Regt. Vol., **M**, 1351b,
35th Regt., **G**, 356,
40th Regt., **H**, 272, **W**, 685,
44th Regt., **G**, 363a,
46th Regt. Vols., **B**, 1235,
47th Regt., **B**, 1612-1613, **C**, 88,
47th Regt. Vols., **B**, 938,
48th Regt., **T**, 55,
55th Regt., **M**, 879,
60th Regt., **S**, 303,
Mounted Infantry,
53rd Regt., **W**, 528,

Roster, **P**, 542,
State Artillery, **T**, 136,
State Troops, **C**, 522
Alabama-Bierce Connections; **H**, 914
Alamance County, NC; **C**, 944,
Troops, **A**, 117-118
Alamance River, Battle of; **M**, 682
Albaugh, William; **T**, 502
Albemarle (ram); **D**, 634, **E**, 156, **J**, 540,
First Battle, **E**, 157
Albemarle County, VA; **L**, 536, **M**, 51
Albert, Alphaeus K.; **B**, 1633
Albright, James G.; **A**, 117
Album, Portrait; **C**, 985
Alcorn, James Lusk, Brig.Gen.; **P**, 263, **R**, 480, 603
Alderman, Edwin A.; **G**, 380
Aldie, VA, Battle of; **R**, 729
Alexander Letters; **A**, 153, **B**, 833
Alexander's Artillery; **T**, 60
Alexander, Edward Porter, Brig.Gen.; **A**, 473, **K**, 211-212, **W**, 604a
Alexander, J.M.; **H**, 861
Alexander, John Brevard, Dr.; **A**, 184
Alexander, William Lee, Capt.; **H**, 77
Alexandra (ship); **M**, 798
Alexandria Militia; **W**, 99
Alexandria Riflemen;
Uniforms, **U**, 14
Alexandria, LA; **M**, 893a
Alexandria, VA; **L**, 367, **M**, 108, **W**, 593, 693,
Federal Occupation, **H**, 718,
History of, **A**, 32,
Monument, **D**, 76
Algebra; **H**, 837
Algeria;
Cotton, **R**, 163
Alice Ball (ship); **B**, 994
Alison, Joseph Dill, Dr.; **A**, 116
Allan's Lone Star Ballads; **A**, 193
Allan, William, Col.; **A**, 196, 218, **K**, 37, **S**, 130
Allatoona, GA, Battle of; **B**, 1366, 1393, **T**, 334
Allegheny Roughs; **F**, 324, **M**, 366b

Allen, H.D.; **B**, 1043
Allen, Henry Watkins, Gov., LA; **C**, 276-277, **E**, 298, **S**, 494a
Allen, J.W., Col.; **C**, 1557
Allen, John; **G**, 150
Allen, Lawrence M., Col.; **G**, 110
Allen, Theodore F., Col.; **S**, 1012
Allen, Thomas C.; **S**, 1113
Allied Indian Nations; **L**, 757
Almanacs; **C**, 1021
Alspaugh, J.C.; **E**, 143
Alstadt Grays, Roster; **A**, 481
Altamaha River; **C**, 1113
Alton Prison, IL;
Roster, **L**, 554
Alverson, James Gibson, Sr.; **G**, 217
Amann, William F.; **G**, 168
Amber, John; **A**, 124
Ambler, Theresa; **J**, 565
Ambrose, Stephen E.; **V**, 118
Amelia Minute Men; **M**, 575
Amendment, Fifteenth; **E**, 78
America (yacht); **N**, 44
American Bastiles; **H**, 1178
American Institute of the History of Pharmacy; **F**, 469
American Knights; **R**, 184
American Medical Association, First Secretary of; **A**, 460
Amherst Rifle Grays;
Uniforms, **U**, 14
Ammunition; **R**, 491,
Cartridge Box Plates, **G**, 126
Amnesty; **B**, 764, **D**, 183, 336, 758, **H**, 128, **J**, 537
Ancestry; **G**, 669
Anderson's Brigade (J.R.); **A**, 331
Anderson's Division; **A**, 481, **P**, 830
Anderson, Archer, Col.; **A**, 291, 450, **L**, 418a
Anderson, Charles, Col.; **C**, 1435
Anderson, D.W., Maj.; **B**, 806
Anderson, Edward C., Maj.; **N**, 43
Anderson, George Burgwyn, Brig.Gen.; **G**, 23, **W**, 3
Anderson, George K.; **C**, 898

Anderson, James Patton, Maj.Gen.;
  A, 311, 314, 341, C, 646, G, 221, H, 958, L, 378, R, 146, U, 2
Anderson, Joseph Reid; D, 559, F, 501
Anderson, Richard Heron, Lt.Gen.;
  A, 343, 449, B, 1174, E, 158, T, 290, W, 46
Anderson, Robert, Maj.Gen.; G, 442
Anderson, S.T.; H, 308
Anderson, SC;
  Pillage, K, 136
Anderson, William; H, 44, S, 1166, W, 293
Anderson, William T., Col.; G, 360
Andersonville Prison, GA; A, 571, B, 100, 823, 1178, 1211, 1543, C, 323, D, 184, 297, E, 230, F, 609, G, 518, J, 431, 486, M, 152, 681, P, 5-6, 68, 261, 293, R, 386, 855, 877-878, S, 383, 1149, W, 549,
  Monument, D, 104
Andersonville Raiders; F, 608
Andrew, John Albion, Gov., MA; C, 1476
Andrews Raid; H, 1198
Andrews' Battalion; A, 370
Andrews' Mounted Artillery; A, 371
Andrews' Raid; S, 593
Andrews, C.H.; L, 530
Andrews, James J.; W, 76
Andrews, John B., Capt.; P, 333
Andrews, Matthew Page; D, 656, E, 93
Andrews, Richard Snowden, Lt.Col.; S, 725
Anecdotes; B, 120, 526, 1294, C, 69, 298, D, 827, F, 41, 320, H, 148, J, 66e, L, 1, M, 618, 1058, N, 84, R, 233, S, 233
Anglo-American Influence; A, 528
Anglo-American Relations; V, 129
Anna F. Schmidt (ship); N, 108
Anniston, AL, Foundry; R, 543
Anti-abolition; C, 456
Anti-Lincoln Sentiment; G, 107, M, 109

Anti-slavery Sentiment; A, 549, C, 101
Antietam National Battlefield, MD; D, 479, T, 293
Antietam, MD, Battle of; A, 316, B, 821, C, 477, D, 65, E, 194, G, 68, 396, H, 748, 774, 1307, M, 1296, S, 203a,
  Secret Service, L, 694
Antimission Movement; W, 1069
Antiques; B, 1151
Apalachicola, FL;
  Blockade, C, 1610,
  Naval Operations, T, 499
Appleton Pub. Co., Lawsuit; B, 1494
Appleyard, T.J.; U, 31
Appomattox County, VA;
  History, S, 992
Appomattox Courthouse National Historical Park; C, 325, H, 260
Appomattox Courthouse, VA; A, 470, C, 772, P, 517,
  Surrender, B, 1020, 1090, 1608, C, 39, 381, M, 212, P, 182, R, 606
Appomattox Road, VA; W, 367
Appomattox, VA; A, 41, 46, 178a, 486, B, 44, 984, 1568, D, 144-145, G, 205, J, 121, K, 187, M, 77, 441, 1030, S, 1168, W, 728,
  Appletree, J, 454,
  Campaign, C, 900, D, 366,
  Lee at, A, 38a,
  North Carolina Soldiers, N, 177,
  Pursuit to, H, 1240,
  Roster, B, 1273,
  Sequel, F, 252,
  Surrender, G, 654, J, 553, P, 634, S, 1280, T, 553
Appomattox, VA, Battle of; B, 691, 952
Aquila (Aquia), VA; A, 238
Arago (schooner); B, 994
Archaeological Excavations; S, 1440
Archbell, L.V.; C, 191
Archer's Brigade; F, 600, H, 1340, L, 197
Archer, William S., Lt.; A, 416, B, 806
Arentschildt, Von, Lt.Col.; B, 1518

Argyle Island, GA; **C**, 683
Arithmetic; **C**, 760
Arizona; **G**, 524, **N**, 35, **P**, 626, **R**, 634,
   Capture of, **G**, 329,
   Spy Company, **M**, 788
Arizona Guards; **H**, 88
Arizona Territory; **D**, 734, **M**, 446, **P**, 539,
   Confiscation Cases, **G**, 317
Arkadelphia, AR; **F**, 85,
   Arsenal, **N**, 62a
Arkansas; **C**, 32, 648, **D**, 172, 517, 775, **E**, 245, **F**, 86, **G**, 237, 541, **J**, 125, 355, **P**, 390, **R**, 197, 315, **S**, 187, 684, 762, **W**, 1025,
   Ancestors, **A**, 421,
   Artillery, **B**, 152,
   Battles in, **A**, 426, **G**, 63,
   Bushwhackers, **H**, 1249,
   Campaigns, **A**, 296,
   Cherokee Indians, **D**, 28,
   Confederate Congress, **W**, 934,
   Confederate Records, **M**, 74,
   Conscription, **G**, 312,
   Convention, **J**, 584, **T**, 189,
   Convention, Secession, **C**, 1623,
   Defends the Mississippi, **H**, 357,
   Economics, **L**, 482,
   Federal Reorganization, **C**, 1342,
   Flags, **A**, 429, **E**, 168,
   General Assembly, **A**, 29-30, **C**, 1140,
   Generals, **C**, 1168a, **M**, 1183, 1190,
   German Settlers, **E**, 250,
   Guerrillas, **H**, 1249,
   History, **H**, 355, **M**, 994,
   Immortal Six Hundred, **L**, 594-595,
   Jayhawkers, **H**, 1249,
   Laws, **M**, 863,
   Martial Law, **H**, 1244,
   Military Board, **H**, 1245,
   Militia, **R**, 336,
   Missouri State Depredations, **W**, 698,
   Officers, **C**, 1168a,
   Peace Society, **A**, 427, **W**, 983,
   Plantations, **C**, 183,
   Political & Military Affairs, **A**, 424,
   Propaganda, **S**, 712,
   Reconstruction, **A**, 531, **T**, 186,
   Scouts, **C**, 795,
   Secession, **B**, 1386, **H**, 731, **M**, 313, **P**, 396, **S**, 188, **W**, 624,
   Secession Convention, **S**, 998, **W**, 963,
   Slavery, **C**, 314, 451,
   Sympathizers, **XYZ**, 28,
   Troops, **K**, 74a,
   UCV, **B**, 700,
   Volunteers, **C**, 521,
   Women, **E**, 217, **F**, 270, **S**, 1413, **U**, 29, **W**, 50
Arkansas (ram); **A**, 430, **B**, 1147, 1370, 1570, **C**, 297, **G**, 365, **J**, 218, **M**, 417, **P**, 113b, **R**, 711
Arkansas Campaign; **C**, 52
Arkansas Gazette, AR, np.; **M**, 1250
Arkansas Post, AR, Battle of; **B**, 378, **C**, 170, **G**, 56
Arkansas Rats; **H**, 791
Arkansas Troops;
   Artillery,
     1st Battery, **D**, 12,
     5th Regt., **A**, 568,
   Burial Lists, **P**, 544-562,
   Cavalry,
     2nd Regt., **D**, 873,
     3rd Regt., **C**, 684,
     45th Regt., **M**, 1125c,
   Infantry,
     1st Regt., **B**, 667, **H**, 168,
     2nd Regt., **H**, 1233,
     3rd Regt., **A**, 228, **C**, 805, **F**, 451,
     4th Regt., **G**, 36, **L**, 142,
     6th Regt., **S**, 989,
     6th Regt., Vols., **A**, 275,
     11th Regt., **P**, 448,
     12th Regt., **J**, 125,
     14th Regt., **C**, 89,
     15th Regt., **C**, 1202,
     16th Regt., Co. I, **A**, 574,
     19th Regt., **T**, 416,
   Mounted Rifles,
     2nd Regt., **L**, 406,
   Roster, **P**, 543
Arkansas Volunteers, Roster; **A**, 425

Arkansas-Texas Desperado; **J**, 165
Arlington Cemetery, VA; **C**, 896, 1197, **R**, 305, **U**, 31
Arlington House, Arlington, VA; **D**, 822
Armes, Ethel; **A**, 437
Armistead's Cavalry; **B**, 495
Armistead, Drury L.; **A**, 439
Armistead, Lewis Addison, Brig.Gen.; **A**, 440, **B**, 149, **P**, 458, 460a,
  Gettysburg, PA, **M**, 255
Armistead, William Ray; **C**, 901
Armor; **E**, 8
Armories; **H**, 1065,
  Macon, GA, **V**, 72
Arms; **K**, 265, **L**, 65, **M**, 150,
  Brought by Blockade-runners, **W**, 148
Armstrong Raid; **A**, 180
Armstrong, James F., Col.; **A**, 95
Army & Navy Prayer Book; **P**, 805
Army & Navy Society; **J**, 527,
  Maryland, **J**, 170,
  Roster, **S**, 782
Army Library; **C**, 556
Army Memorial Hall; **C**, 1024
Army of Mississippi; **L**, 180
Army of New Mexico; **H**, 79
Army of Northern Virginia; **A**, 31, 195, 210, 225, 343, 360, 470, **C**, 270, 381, 1546, **D**, 1, 487, **J**, 72, 443, **K**, 15c, **L**, 615, **M**, 1035, **S**, 1277, **W**, 863,
  Artillery, **P**, 242,
  Campaigns, **F**, 240,
  Cavalry, **H**, 263, **L**, 246, **R**, 726,
  Chaplains, Roster, **L**, 550,
  Food, **N**, 139,
  Last Days, **J**, 534,
  Lee's Report, **M**, 827,
  Louisiana Div., Casualties, **W**, 129,
  Morale, **F**, 523,
  Organization, **M**, 449, **O**, 128-132, 142,
  Paroles, **A**, 408, **B**, 1273, **P**, 109-110, **R**, 551,
  Roster, **K**, 258,
  Morgan's Cavalry, **R**, 745,
  Second Corps, **L**, 8,
  Soldier Life, **M**, 393,
  Surrender, **C**, 325,
  Virginia Division, **A**, 386
Army of Tennessee; **A**, 411, **B**, 763, 839, 1258, 1387, **C**, 235, 375, 564, 1084, **D**, 629, 999, **G**, 446, 448, **H**, 1094, **J**, 133, 308, 335, **M**, 184, **R**, 115, 450, 679, **T**, 119, **W**, 66,
  Annals, **D**, 833,
  Battles of, **C**, 925,
  Hospital Life, **C**, 1553,
  Last Campaign, **S**, 1113,
  Medical Officers, **J**, 491,
  Medical Officers, Roster, **J**, 497,
  Organization, **A**, 451, **O**, 140, 144-148,
  Religion, **H**, 106, **M**, 535
Army of the Cumberland;
  History, **M**, 349
Army of the Frontier; **B**, 373
Army of the James; **G**, 186
Army of the Peninsula; **D**, 792
Army of the Potomac; **C**, 47, **F**, 489
Army of the Southwest; **H**, 747
Army of the Valley;
  Organization, **O**, 139, 141
Army of Virginia;
  Rules, **R**, 812
Army of Western Louisiana;
  Artillery, **B**, 1228
Army Promotion Examinations; **S**, 369
Army, Confederate; **A**, 452, **R**, 240a,
  Conf., Organization, **O**, 150,
  Disbanding, **T**, 41,
  Medical Affairs, **M**, 722a,
  Muster Rolls, **M**, 1351a
Army, Statistics; **L**, 237
Army, Strengths; **A**, 295, **S**, 916
Arnold, Samuel; **M**, 165
Arnold, William E., Lt.Col.; **W**, 949
Arp, Bill; **A**, 561, **C**, 510, **S**, 596-597,
  Peace Papers (humor), **A**, 467
Arrowsmith-Planter, John; **B**, 1615
Arsenal & Naval Foundry, Confederate; **A**, 436

Arsenal Academy, Columbia, SC; **O**, 68a
Arsenals; **B**, 878, 1415,
  Arkadelphia, AR, **N**, 62a,
  Fayetteville, NC, **T**, 57,
  Federal, **P**, 821,
  Selma, AL, **L**, 173a, **S**, 207,
  Southern, **D**, 116
Art; **A**, 284, **C**, 322, 553, 966, 1207, **F**, 438, **G**, 120, 553, **H**, 93, 1279, **J**, 31, 45, **R**, 138, 141-142, **S**, 486, **T**, 294, 434-435, **V**, 3, 170-171, **W**, 716,
  Cyclorama, Atlanta, GA, **C**, 321, **J**, 91, **K**, 268,
  Etchings, Confederate, **B**, 762,
  Lithographs, **C**, 918,
  Pictorial Histories, **B**, 1503,
  Porcelain Portrait, **B**, 556,
  Tyler, TX, **C**, 68
Artifacts;
  Excavated, **P**, 346a
Artificial Limbs; **W**, 799
Artillery; **A**, 155, 158-159, 197, **B**, 629, 1538, **C**, 1465, **D**, 578, **G**, 47, 587, **H**, 516, **N**, 47, 181, **O**, 205, **P**, 9, 242, **R**, 15, 491, 542, **T**, 521,
  Arkansas, **B**, 152,
  Arsenals, Southern, **D**, 116,
  Atlanta Campaign, **XYZ**, 13,
  Battles, **A**, 471,
  Cannon, **D**, 72, 844,
  Drills, **C**, 561,
  Drivers' Saddles, **C**, 851,
  Field, Projectiles, **K**, 111,
  Gettysburg, PA, **W**, 872,
  Handbook, **R**, 541,
  Officers, **A**, 472, **L**, 549, **M**, 767,
  Organizations, **A**, 473,
  Texas, **B**, 153,
  Whistling Dick (gun), **T**, 447,
  Williamsburg, VA, **S**, 1139
Artillery Brigade; **B**, 776, 790
Asboth, Alexander Sandor, Maj.Gen.; **B**, 425
Ashburn Murder Case; **D**, 88
Ashburton Treaty; **B**, 79
Ashby, John William; **F**, 604
Ashby, Thomas Almond; **A**, 484

Ashby, Turner, Brig.Gen.; **A**, 486, 581, **B**, 1618, **C**, 1572, **E**, 109, **K**, 132, **M**, 277, 478, **R**, 360, **T**, 184,
  Death, **G**, 336
Ashcraft, Allan C.; **S**, 1051
Ashe, Samuel A'Court; **A**, 320, **W**, 858
Asheville, NC;
  Vanderbilt Hotel, **S**, 898
Ashton, John; **D**, 588
Association Confederate Soldiers; **A**, 512-513
Atchafalaya River, Battle of; **G**, 595
Athens, AL; **P**, 1
Athens, GA; **B**, 1285, **C**, 793, **S**, 1056,
  Cannon, **D**, 844,
  Monument, **C**, 1293
Athens, MO, Battle of; **G**, 90
Atkinson, Alexander Smith; **C**, 785
Atkinson, J.H.; **A**, 529, **F**, 267
Atkinson, Thomas; **C**, 439, **L**, 407
Atlanta (ironclad); **M**, 22, 749
Atlanta Journal-Constitution, GA, np.; **S**, 304
Atlanta Register, GA, np.; **C**, 520
Atlanta, GA; **B**, 975, **G**, 219, **J**, 2, **M**, 383, 390a, 675, 986,
  Atlas, **S**, 91a,
  Campaign, **B**, 1205, 1395, **C**, 1223, **D**, 386, **E**, 51, **H**, 555, 557, 746, **K**, 86, **M**, 653, **O**, 166, **S**, 91a, 221, **XYZ**, 13,
  Campaign, Medical History, **B**, 1214,
  Capture of, **P**, 264,
  Civilian Life, **H**, 472,
  Confederate Publications, **H**, 468,
  Confederate Treasury, **H**, 379,
  Conference, **P**, 769,
  Cyclorama, **J**, 91, **K**, 268,
  Defenses, **H**, 1052,
  Depopulation, **K**, 26,
  Destruction of, **B**, 309,
  Escape from, **H**, 1334,
  Field Fortifications, **A**, 540,
  Hill Monument, **B**, 722,
  History, **M**, 261,
  Hood, John Bell, Gen., **D**, 6,

Atlanta, GA

    Journalism, **M**, 102,
    Law & Disorder, **L**, 7,
    Map, **A**, 540,
    Military Operations, **R**, 778,
    Murder, **K**, 270,
    Newspapers, **K**, 117a,
    Occupation of, **A**, 539,
    Sherman's Failure, **C**, 630,
    Sherman's March, **J**, 344,
    Siege, **C**, 240, **D**, 536, **W**, 578,
    Significance, **A**, 539
Atlanta, GA, Battle of; **A**, 415, **C**, 25, 321, **F**, 75, **J**, 281, **K**, 135, **S**, 306, **U**, 32,
    Map, **K**, 271
Atlantic Impact (1861); **S**, 495
Atlases; **B**, 663, **O**, 65
Attala County, MS; **H**, 1218
Auchampaugh, Philip G.; **B**, 1502
Aucilla, FL; **W**, 781
Auctions; **F**, 453-454
Augusta Chronicle, GA, np.; **B**, 521
Augusta County, VA; **B**, 1245a,
    History, **W**, 9
Augusta Powder Works, GA; **M**, 747
Augusta, GA; **C**, 595, 1259, **F**, 229,
    Confederate Survivors' Association, **C**, 1045,
    Monument, **C**, 364,
    Sherman's March, **R**, 557
Augusta, KY, Battle of; **A**, 550
Austin, C.W.; **H**, 1168
Austin, J.P.; **A**, 560
Austin, James C.; **A**, 466
Austin, Stephen F.; **A**, 482, **B**, 957
Austin, TX; **G**, 7,
    St. David's Church, **G**, 621
Autauga Rifles; **T**, 229, 233
Autographs, Confederate; **R**, 233a
Avary, Isabella D. Lockett; **C**, 448
Avegno Zouaves; **M**, 553a
Averasboro, NC, Battle of; **D**, 117, **F**, 444, **H**, 339, **M**, 424, **T**, 16
Avery, Isaac Erwin, Col.; **B**, 287
Avery, Myrta L.; **C**, 540
Avirett, James Battle; **A**, 484
Avis, John; **A**, 584, **B**, 1379
Ayer, Lewis M., Gen.; **A**, 589,

B

Bachman's Battery; **B**, 1314, **S**, 492
Bacon, Augustus O.; **B**, 5
Bacon, G.W.; **D**, 215
Badges; **J**, 102
Bagby, Arthur Pendleton, Maj.Gen.; **H**, 80
Bagby, Edward; **P**, 532
Bagby, Ellen M.; **B**, 10
Bagby, George W., Dr.; **S**, 1077
Bailey's Crossroads, VA, Battle of; **M**, 490
Bailey, Robert Augustus, Lt.Col.; **S**, 1365
Bailey, Theodorus; **F**, 65
Bailey, Virginia Griffin; **D**, 990
Baine, David W., Lt.Col.; **W**, 276a
Baird, Spruce McCoy; **W**, 487
Baker's Creek, MS; **J**, 310
Baker's Creek, MS, Battle of; **L**, 374, 688
Baker, Cullen; **B**, 716, 1218, **J**, 165, **O**, 163
Baker, William W.; **B**, 344
Balance of Power; **D**, 774
Baldwin, Briscoe G.; **F**, 105
Baldwin, George J.; **A**, 154, **B**, 833
Ball's Bluff, VA, Battle of; **G**, 212, **H**, 992a, 1331, **M**, 1082, 1199, **P**, 136, **W**, 538
Ball, T.H.; **C**, 615
Ballads; **A**, 380
Balloons; **B**, 1486, **C**, 456, 1262
Baltimore County, MD;
  Gilmor's Raid, **G**, 280
Baltimore, MD; **B**, 1369, **H**, 372, **R**, 120,
  Press, **M**, 342,
  Southern Leanings, **F**, 551a
Baltzell, George F.; **C**, 778
Bande, Haenger; **C**, 55

Bandera, TX; **S**, 64
Bands; **H**, 71, **O**, 111a
Banks, John; **B**, 82
Banks, Nathaniel Prentiss, Maj.Gen.; **B**, 270, **W**, 738
Banks, Robert W.; **B**, 84
Banner Elk, NC; **W**, 800
Bannon, Father; **S**, 1212
Barbee, David Rankin; **D**, 795, **T**, 530
Barbee, Herbert; **C**, 966
Barbiere, Joseph, Maj.; **P**, 825a
Barbour County, AL; **T**, 253
Barbour County, WV;
  History, **M**, 355
Barbour Greys; **S**, 1366, **W**, 455
Bard, William E.; **S**, 508
Barfield, Pinckney; **B**, 579
Barksdale's Brigade; **D**, 648, **M**, 680
Barksdale, William, Brig.Gen.; **M**, 590, **T**, 560
Barlow, Francis Channing, Maj.Gen.; **G**, 504
Barn-Burners; **B**, 1584
Barnard, John Gross, Maj.Gen.; **E**, 19
Barnes, Richard; **P**, 112
Barnes, William; **H**, 411
Barnwell College, Annals; **A**, 591
Barnwell, John; **E**, 161
Barnwell, Robert Woodward; **B**, 139
Barr, Alwyn; **H**, 144, **R**, 203, **T**, 151
Barrancas, FL;
  Spies, **M**, 157
Barre, MA; **M**, 968
Barren Creek, Ind.T., Battle of; **R**, 36
Barrett, J.P., Dr.; **F**, 438
Barrett, John G.; **S**, 976
Barron, S.B.; **XYZ**, 93a
Barrow, James, Lt.Col.; **C**, 1300
Barry, Arthur R., Dr.; **K**, 273

Barry, William S.; **W**, 1067
Bartholomew, Ed; **B**, 49
Bartlett, John R.; **B**, 672
Barton's Brigade; **B**, 839
Barton, James M., Lt.Col.; **N**, 82
Bartow County, FL;
   Saltpetre Works, **D**, 712
Bartow County, GA;
   History, **C**, 1590
Baruch, Bernard; **B**, 203
Bastrop Military Institute; **A**, 73
Bastrop, TX;
   History, **J**, 508
Bate, William Brimage, Maj.Gen.; **C**, 181, **M**, 232
Bates, Dwight E. Lt.; **P**, 842
Batesville, AR;
   Occupation, **M**, 547a
Baton Rouge, LA; **B**, 995,
   Court Records, **C**, 1022,
   Federal Arsenal, **B**, 878
Baton Rouge, LA, Battle of; **B**, 384, 1570, **C**, 1569
Batson, Alfred B.C.; **D**, 550-552
Battery Gregg, SC;
   Defenses, **H**, 382
Battery Wagner, SC; **H**, 28, 327, **T**, 450,
   Defenses, **J**, 388, **T**, 510,
   Evacuation, **J**, 384
Battle Abbey; **B**, 699, **C**, 206, 967, **M**, 227, **R**, 142, 434, **S**, 852
Battle Above the Clouds; **M**, 932
Battle Creek, MI; **V**, 18
Battle Flags; **R**, 324a
Battle Sketches; **B**, 679a
Battle, John D., Jr.; **B**, 285
Battle, William James; **B**, 289
Battlefield Analysis Study; **M**, 740
Battlefields; **T**, 440
Battles; **C**, 184, **O**, 69, **R**, 45, **S**, 876, **U**, 42,
   Chronological & Alphabetical Records, **C**, 1208,
   First, **A**, 258, **C**, 1075, **W**, 436,
   Last, **C**, 1144, **P**, 685,
   Second, **W**, 481,
   Virginia, **C**, 1172

Battles & Leaders (scrapbook); **R**, 846
Bauist, Henry, Capt.; **F**, 272
Baum, Marcus; **B**, 200
Baumgarten, Herman; **G**, 560
Baumgarten, Julius B.; **B**, 317, **C**, 1019
Baxter, Charles N.; **B**, 672
Bayard, George Dashiell, Brig.Gen.; **B**, 600
Baylor University; **N**, 63
Baylor, George, Col.; **XYZ**, 93a
Baylor, John Robert, Col.; **H**, 299, 798a, **N**, 217, **T**, 236,
   as Gov., AZ, **B**, 327
Baylor-Kelley Fight; **H**, 78
Bayne, Thomas L., Lt.Col.; **B**, 329
Bayou Borbeau, LA, Battle of; **B**, 151
Bayou Country; **R**, 118
Bayou des Allemands, LA, Battle of; **M**, 1163
Bazaars; **C**, 996
Beach, Elizabeth Jane; **B**, 332
Beale's Cavalry; **B**, 1281
Beale, Richard Lee T., Brig.Gen.; **B**, 1608, **S**, 547
Beall, John Yates; **C**, 1410, **H**, 41, **L**, 758, **M**, 180, 365b, 689, **R**, 445, **S**, 1358, **W**, 446
Bean's Station, TN, Battle of; **H**, 417, **S**, 917
Bean, W.G.; **B**, 110
Bear Wallow Belles; **W**, 797
Bearss, Edwin C.; **A**, 305, **B**, 1576, **T**, 483
Bearss, Margie Riddle; **A**, 305
Beau Sabreur; **B**, 711
Beaumont, William, Dr.; **C**, 130
Beauregard Volunteers; **C**, 1473
Beauregard, Pierre Gustave T., Gen.; **A**, 206, **B**, 222, 435, 437, 445, 459, 463, 472, 483, 1351, **C**, 478, **D**, 213, **E**, 285, 288, **G**, 128, **H**, 26, **L**, 180, **M**, 711a, 735, 1193, **R**, 704, **T**, 87,
   Manassas, VA, **W**, 185,
   Music, **S**, 822,
   Napoleon in Gray, **W**, 746,
   Operations, **R**, 690,

Religion, **S**, 399,
Shiloh, TN, **L**, 182, **W**, 745,
Songbook, **S**, 134,
West Tennessee, **J**, 579
Beauty & Booty, New Orleans, LA; **S**, 893
Beauvoir, Davis Estate, MS; **D**, 187, **H**, 903, **J**, 484, 559
Beauvoir, MS;
Shrine, **T**, 255
Bedford Light Artillery; **G**, 528
Bee, Barnard Elliott, Brig.Gen.;
Death, **XYZ**, 38
Bee, Hamilton Prioleau, Brig.Gen.; **M**, 741
Beechenbrook; **P**, 720
Beef Packing, Confederate, Jefferson, TX; **A**, 491
Beef Raid; **B**, 1016, **L**, 782
Beers, James H.; **S**, 1197
Beersheba Diary; **F**, 543
Bejach, Louis D.; **F**, 425
Bejach, Wilena Robart; **H**, 172
Belgium; **B**, 573
Bell, Alfreda Eva; **B**, 519
Bell, John; **P**, 102a
Bell, John W., Pvt.; **B**, 527
Bell, Thomas P., Lt.; **S**, 759a
Belle Isle, VA; **S**, 177
Bellona Arsenal; **S**, 225
Belmont, KY, Battle of; **P**, 477, 481
Belmont, MO, Battle of; **W**, 1027
Belt-buckles; **D**, 732, **G**, 126
Benevides, Santos; **T**, 237
Benjamin, Judah Philip; **B**, 562, 566, 568, 570, 573, 1630, **C**, 38, 494, 635, 1593, **D**, 202, 512, **G**, 560, 681-682, **H**, 16, 247, **J**, 75, **K**, 7, 250, **M**, 174, 238, 716-718, **N**, 56, **O**, 176, **P**, 318, 408, **R**, 369, **S**, 120, 1014, **W**, 32,
Memorial, **G**, 34, 114
Bennett Farm, NC; **XYZ**, 24
Bennett, James Gordon; **W**, 580
Bennett, Jonathan McCalley; **M**, 1167, **R**, 348
Benning, Henry L., Brig.Gen.; **A**, 307, **C**, 704
Benson, Berry, Maj.; **B**, 597, 599

Benson, Susan Williams; **B**, 597
Benton, B.F., Capt.; **H**, 228
Bentonville, NC, Battle of; **B**, 148, 380, **H**, 185, 202, 264, **J**, 314a, **L**, 775, 778, **M**, 424, **P**, 383, **T**, 213
Beresford-Hope, Alex James; **T**, 390
Beringer, Richard E.; **D**, 243
Berkeley Border Guards; **B**, 626, **G**, 51
Berkeley Brothers, VA; **B**, 627
Berkeley County, VA; **B**, 626
Berkeley, SC;
Plantation, **J**, 128
Bermuda;
Blockade-running, **V**, 49
Berrien, J. Hunter; **T**, 157
Berryhill, William Harvey, Lt.; **B**, 648
Bertie County, NC;
Veterans' Association, **C**, 202
Bethel Baptist Church, Caroline County, VA; **D**, 17a
Bethel Church, VA, Battle of; **B**, 35, **H**, 1087
Bethel, VA, Battle of; **C**, 762, **F**, 138, **G**, 387, **H**, 829, 846, **W**, 803
Beverly Ford, VA, Battle of; **N**, 109a
Beverly, WV; **N**, 54,
Capture of, **D**, 315, **XYZ**, 79
Bexar County, TX; **A**, 294
Bibles; **H**, 662
Bibliography; **C**, 319, **D**, 753, **K**, 138, **L**, 423, **M**, 771, 945, 1172, **N**, 81, **R**, 499,
Louisiana, **L**, 707,
Marine Corps, **O**, 19
Bickley, George; **C**, 1423, **K**, 6
Bidgood, George L.; **A**, 448
Bidgood, Joseph B.; **B**, 675
Bigelow, John; **B**, 681
Biliography; **M**, 5
Billingsley, William Clyde; **K**, 30
Bills of Fare; **R**, 829
Billy Bowlegs; **P**, 643
Bingham, Barry; **M**, 516
Bingham, Millicent Todd; **W**, 640
Bingham, Robert, Col.; **B**, 692
Birch, E.P.; **B**, 703
Bird, W.H.; **B**, 705

Birkenhead Ironclads; **C**, 1266
Birmingham, AL;
  Pre-Civil War, **M**, 744
Bishops; **B**, 798
Bivins, J.K.; **B**, 49
Bivouac of the Dead; **C**, 728, **R**, 72
Bixby Myth; **T**, 523
Black Eagle Company; **W**, 909
Black Hawk Rifles; **R**, 244
Black Horse Cavalry; **S**, 160
Black Horse Troop; **B**, 750a, **K**, 45
Black Republican Party; **D**, 334
Black Republicanism; **N**, 212
Black Suffrage; **H**, 1188
Black's Cavalry; **M**, 105
Black, J.C.C.; **B**, 722
Black, John Logan, Col.; **M**, 706
Black, John S.; **A**, 543
Blackburn's Ford, VA, Battle of; **E**, 36,
  Engagement, **M**, 962a
Blackford Family, Lynchburg, VA; **B**, 744
Blackford Letters; **B**, 750
Blackford, Charles Minor; **B**, 741, 743, 747
Blackford, Mary Berkeley Minor; **B**, 746
Blackford, Susan Leigh; **B**, 747
Blackman, B.F.; **F**, 401
Blackshear, James Appleton, Capt.; **B**, 758
Blackshear, James Everard; **B**, 758
Blackwater River; **C**, 405
Blackwood's History of the US (book); **D**, 589
Blada, V.; **B**, 762
Blaine, James G.; **A**, 257
Blair's Landing, LA, Battle of; **B**, 158
Blair, Francis Preston, Jr., Maj.Gen.; **B**, 767
Blake, William James; **B**, 789
Blanc, Antoine; **C**, 309
Blankets, A Pair of (book); **S**, 1178
Blanton, L.H., Rev.; **B**, 784
Blease, Cole L.; **P**, 712, **S**, 281
Bledsoe, Albert Taylor; **B**, 580, **H**, 739, **P**, 692, **S**, 523, 1042

Blessington, J.P.; **T**, 149
Bliemel, Emmeran; **P**, 426
Blockade-in Theory; **S**, 521
Blockade-runners; **A**, 104, **B**, 801, 818, 1074, **C**, 169, 545, 614, 712, **D**, 874, 948, **H**, 137, 504, 625, 692, 921-923, 1007, 1107, **J**, 130, **L**, 329, **M**, 50c, **O**, 200, **P**, 384, 737-743, **R**, 298, **S**, 955, 1281, **T**, 75, **U**, 45, **V**, 79a, **W**, 186-187, 259, 285, 681, **XYZ**, 33,
  Arms Shipments, **W**, 148,
  Bermuda, **V**, 49,
  Charter, **P**, 171,
  Inland, **B**, 906,
  Mail, **H**, 1220,
  Texas, **B**, 518
Blockades; **A**, 592, **B**, 216, 637, 1036, **C**, 219, 297, 1610, **G**, 589, **H**, 32, 239, 645, 656, 662, 923, 1087, 1107, **J**, 105, 541, **K**, 63, 208, **L**, 54, 508, **M**, 1128, **O**, 14, **R**, 530, **S**, 755, 1341, **V**, 127, **W**, 201a,
  Cape Fear River, **S**, 960,
  Charleston, SC, **N**, 141,
  Wilmington, NC, **J**, 140
Bloody Angle, Spotsylvania, VA, Battle of; **A**, 299, 316, 445, **B**, 1397, **C**, 48, 244, **S**, 1292, **W**, 53
Bloody Junto; **C**, 1503
Bloomer (ship); **J**, 354
Blount, Thomas William, Capt.; **B**, 808
Blue & the Gray, The; **A**, 560
Blue Springs, TN, Battle of; **E**, 303
Bluff Springs, FL, Battle of; **U**, 38
Boatbuilders, French; **B**, 647
Boaten, Edward W.; **A**, 349a
Bocock, Thomas S.; **S**, 448
Boggs' Battalion; **V**, 17
Boggs, William Robertson, Brig.Gen.; **B**, 1010
Boggstown Resolutions; **N**, 167
Bogle, Joseph, Pvt.; **B**, 839
Bolivar, TN, Battle of; **A**, 180
Bolling Island Plantation, VA; **D**, 446
Bomar, Thomas, Capt.; **B**, 856
Bond, John W.; **B**, 274
Bond, Natalie Jenkins; **C**, 1337

Bonds; **A**, 72, **D**, 492, 687, **H**, 218, 496, 611
Bone, John Wesley; **B**, 867
Bonham, Milledge Luke, Brig.Gen.; **D**, 795, **T**, 312,
　as Gov., SC, **P**, 268
Bonner, Floelle Tongblood; **A**, 95
Bonnet Rock School, SC; **S**, 947
Books; **A**, 144, **B**, 759a, 1271, **C**, 879, **H**, 702, **S**, 771,
　Prices, **J**, 222b,
　School, **A**, 199
Boone County, MO; **A**, 524,
　Slavery, **M**, 543
Boone's Battery;
　Roster, **B**, 620
Boone, Thomas D.; **P**, 112
Boonsborough Gap, MD, Battle of; **G**, 515
Boonville, MO, Battle of; **B**, 130
Booth Family, MD; **K**, 160, **M**, 85
Booth, Andrew B.; **C**, 295, **L**, 716, **M**, 176
Booth, Edwin; **B**, 1057
Booth, John Wilkes; **B**, 233, 1473, **C**, 114, 616, 680, **F**, 394, **G**, 96, 99, 537, **J**, 531, **M**, 182, **P**, 215, 761, **S**, 366, 1002, 1123, **T**, 314, **W**, 802,
　Conspiracy, **G**, 499,
　Escape, **C**, 1503, **W**, 939a,
　Gettysburg, PA, Battle of, **D**, 702
Bootheel Swamp Struggle; **D**, 564
Boots, E.N.; **B**, 913
Boozer, Marie; **C**, 431, 754
Borcke, Heros von, Col.; **B**, 514, **H**, 1282, **S**, 1008
Border & Bastile; **L**, 159
Border Rangers, VA;
　Roster, **W**, 96
Border Ruffians; **R**, 156, **W**, 740
Border States; **E**, 3,
　Convention, **C**, 1136,
　Southern Rights, **J**, 236
Border Wars; **C**, 1079, **J**, 438, **S**, 987
Borglum, Gutzon; **B**, 925
Borglum, Solon H.; **G**, 413
Bosque County, TX; **S**, 222

Boswell, James Keith, Capt.; **B**, 348, **M**, 952, **S**, 547
Botetourt Artillery; **J**, 322-323, **M**, 183, **P**, 434
Botetourt Company; **A**, 243
Botsford, Theophilus F., Pvt.; **B**, 1612
Botts, Lawson, Col.; **T**, 379a
Boudinot, Elias C., Col.; **A**, 337, **W**, 1028, 1055
Bounds, Benjamin H.; **B**, 956
Bounds, Charles L.; **B**, 956
Bounds, Joseph M., Col.; **P**, 295
Bounty; **O**, 50
Bowdoin, Maggie; **B**, 960
Bowen, J.J.; **B**, 964
Bowie, E. Barkley; **S**, 1132
Bowie, Walter, Lt.; **W**, 822
Bowles, William A.; **P**, 419
Bowling Green, KY; **H**, 65
Boy Company; **F**, 120, **J**, 5
Boy Gunners; **W**, 871
Boyce-Hammond Correspondence; **B**, 990
Boyd, Belle; **B**, 779, **C**, 774, **D**, 158, 161, **H**, 54, 315, **K**, 12, **N**, 162, **R**, 388, **S**, 100, 456-457, 942, 1357, **W**, 445, 916
Boyd, Mark; **C**, 408
Boyd, William K.; **B**, 836
Boykin, Alexander Hamilton, Capt.; **B**, 1025
Boykin, Edward M., Maj.; **B**, 1020, 1038, **F**, 19
Boykin, Samuel; **C**, 699
Boyle, Francis Atherton, Adj.; **B**, 1027
Boyle, J.R., Lt.; **B**, 1030
Boyle, John L.; **C**, 553
Boyle, Virginia Frazier; **C**, 1015
Boylston, Samuel L.; **B**, 1031
Boynton, Henry Van Ness, Brig.Gen.; **C**, 357
Bradbeer's Varieties; **D**, 781
Bradford, Augustus W., Gov., MD; **M**, 289
Bragg's Campaign; **D**, 903, **E**, 305, **H**, 220, **M**, 367f, **W**, 1017
Bragg's Headquarters; **E**, 132

Bragg, Braxton, Gen.; **B**, 388, 594, 708, 1126-1127, 1129-1130, 1132, 1134-1139, **H**, 557, 559, **M**, 708, 710, **S**, 230, 1251, **U**, 45,
   Chickamauga, GA, **M**, 268,
   Kentucky, **R**, 269,
   Retreat, **W**, 817,
   Shiloh, TN, **M**, 709
Bragg, Junius Newport; **G**, 118
Braine, John C.; **H**, 608, 979a
Branch History Papers; **A**, 300
Branch, Lawrence O'Bryan, Brig.Gen.; **H**, 1255
Brandenburg, KY; **F**, 354
Brandy Station, VA; **A**, 142, **B**, 919
Brandy Station, VA, Battle of; **B**, 924, **C**, 1229, **D**, 824, **L**, 639, **M**, 980,
   Cavalry, **K**, 82
Branham, Alfred Iverson; **K**, 49
Brannon, Peter A.; **P**, 416
Brantley, William Felix; **B**, 763
Bratton's Brigade; **B**, 1175
Bratton, John, Brig.Gen.; **W**, 668, 760
Brazil;
   Confederate Exiles, **D**, 957, **H**, 864-865, **W**, 314, 648,
   Confederate Warships, **G**, 240,
   Raids, **H**, 250
Bread Riots; **K**, 150, **T**, 201
Breast Plates; **E**, 8
Breathed's Battalion; **B**, 1125
Breckenridge, James M.; **M**, 945
Breckenridge, William Clark; **B**, 1185
Breckinridge & Lane Campaign Democrats; **B**, 191
Breckinridge & Lane Campaign Documents; **B**, 1187, 1196, 1200
Breckinridge & Lane Ticket; **A**, 64, **G**, 556
Breckinridge, John Cabell, Maj.Gen.; **B**, 387, 737, 1188-1193, **D**, 364, 756, **E**, 64, **H**, 234, 424, 643, **J**, 319, **S**, 1208, **W**, 730, **XYZ**, 47,
   Esacape of, **F**, 21,
   Secession, **O**, 6
Breckinridge, William C.P., Col.; **C**, 964
Breeden, James O.; **A**, 139

Brenham, TX, Military Post; **B**, 1588
Brent, Joseph Lancaster, Brig.Gen.; **A**, 473, **B**, 1228
Brice's Crossroads, MS, Battle of; **B**, 375, 1358, **D**, 631, 695, 920, **G**, 147, **H**, 248-249, **L**, 372, 409, 765, **M**, 1186, 1207, **W**, 888,
   Forrest's Cavalry, **W**, 1077
Bridenbaugh, Carl; **T**, 478
Bridges; **K**, 28, **M**, 307
Bridges, Richard C.; **H**, 15
Brierfield Estate, Jackson, MS; **E**, 267, **M**, 1194
Brierfield Iron Works, AL; **V**, 57
Bright, John; **S**, 1302
Brilliant (ship); **A**, 111, **P**, 785
Briscoe, F.D.; **T**, 294
Bristoe Station, VA, Battle of; **B**, 74, **N**, 3
Bristoe, VA;
   Campaign, **L**, 320
British Admiralty Papers; **B**, 323
British Channel;
   Naval Engagement, **E**, 74
British Consuls; **E**, 187
Britton Lane, TN, Battle of; **A**, 180
Broad River Bridge;
   Burning of, **D**, 697
Broadfoot's Pub. Co.; **M**, 441,
   Guide to Civil War Books, **B**, 672
Broadus, John Albert; **R**, 553
Brock's Gap Rifles; **W**, 306
Brockenbrough, L.; **C**, 909
Brocks Crossroads, VA; **R**, 157
Broglie, Albert de; **B**, 1290
Broken Mug; **C**, 1188
Bronaugh, W.C.; **B**, 1294
Brooke, John Mercer, Comdr.; **B**, 1298
Brooks County, GA;
   History, **B**, 1303
Brooks, Edward; **B**, 1307
Brooks, Harold C., Collection; **A**, 478
Brooks, Preston S.; **B**, 1311
Brooks, U.R.; **B**, 1317, 1628, **H**, 449
Brooks, William M.; **A**, 109
Brooks-Baxter Contest; **A**, 531
Brooks-Sumner Assault; **T**, 560

Bropst, John F.; **T,** 49a
Brother against Brother; **D,** 365
Brother, Charles; **S,** 589
Brothers' War; **C,** 634
Brough, Charles Hillman; **C,** 1146
Broun, Ann Eliza; **B,** 1327
Broun, Bessie Lee; **B,** 1328
Broun, Joseph N., Capt.; **S,** 1360, **W,** 450
Broun, Philip Hopkins; **B,** 1327
Broun, Thomas Lee; **B,** 1327
Broun, William LeRoy, Dr.; **B,** 1328
Broward's Neck, FL; **C,** 41
Brown's Gap, VA; **M,** 1039
Brown's Raid; **K,** 136
Brown, Bedford; **B,** 1346, **J,** 425
Brown, Campbell, Col.; **B,** 1353
Brown, Caroline M.; **A,** 139
Brown, George William; **C,** 940
Brown, Gustavus; **U,** 42
Brown, John; **B,** 12, 1371, **H,** 1080, 1189,
　Hanging of, **S,** 1368,
　Insurrection, **D,** 411,
　Raid, **B,** 787, 934, **D,** 786, **S,** 1124, 1303, **W,** 535, 718,
　Trial, **B,** 1379, **W,** 1048
Brown, John Calvin, Maj.Gen.; **B,** 1373
Brown, John Henry; **H,** 1044, **N,** 199, **T,** 154, **W,** 149
Brown, John Thompson, Col.; **B,** 1377
Brown, John, Capt.; **A,** 584
Brown, Joseph Emerson, Gov., GA; **A,** 575, **C,** 121, 811a, 1272, **E,** 236, **F,** 116, **H,** 76, 567, 866, **M,** 657, **N,** 145, **P,** 95, 101, **S,** 918, **T,** 18,
　Richmond, VA, **E,** 287
Brown, Joseph Emerson, Mrs.; **T,** 24
Brown, Joseph Newton, Col.; **B,** 1414
Brown, Norman D.; **F,** 436
Brown, Tom; **C,** 376
Brown, W.L.; **B,** 1628
Browne, S.H.; **B,** 1335
Browne, William Montague, Brig.Gen.; **C,** 1291
Brownley, Marshall, Mrs.; **T,** 442
Brownlow, James P., Col.; **C,** 151
Brownsville, TX; **B,** 664, **C,** 229
Bruce, E.M., Collection of Autographs; **A,** 564
Bruce, Myra; **S,** 866
Brunonians, Confederate; **G,** 161
Brunson, R.J.; **H,** 906
Brunswick Guards; **M,** 956a
Bruton, Joseph H., Capt.; **H,** 45
Bryan's Battery; **B,** 1482, **H,** 1292
Bryan, Goode, Brig.Gen.; **B,** 1474
Bryan, Joseph; **B,** 1477, **M,** 369
Bryan, TX;
　Reunion, **H,** 1058
Bryant, J.M., Capt.; **A,** 355
Bryant, James Fenton; **J,** 13
Buchanan, Franklin, Adm.; **T,** 199
Buchanan, James, Pres.; **A,** 544-545, **F,** 13, **H,** 17, **K,** 209, **N,** 79,
　Cabinet, **A,** 545,
　Dred Scott Case, **A,** 546
Buchel, August; **S,** 1104
Buck Horn, AR, Battle of; **M,** 547
Buck Tails; **B,** 1113
Buck, Irving A.; **M,** 441
Buck, L. Neville; **B,** 1511
Buckhannon, WV; **P,** 447
Buchholtz, L.V.; **B,** 1520
Buckingham County, VA; **M,** 107
Buckingham Yancey Guards; **P,** 145
Buckner, Simon Bolivar, Lt.Gen.; **A,** 453, **F,** 72, 302, **H,** 435, **P,** 276, **S,** 1185,
　Uniforms, **U,** 14
Budwin, Florena; **C,** 745
Buel, Oliver Prince; **B,** 1144
Buell, Don Carlos, Maj.Gen.; **W,** 604a
Buffalo Guards; **B,** 1531
Buford, Harry T., Lt.; **V,** 94
Buford, Jefferson, Maj.; **B,** 1534
Buglers; **L,** 31
Bull Run, VA, Battle of; **A,** 162, 268, **B,** 244, 326, 443, **C,** 861, **D,** 361, 780, **E,** 36, 194, **F,** 429, **G,** 212, **H,** 253, 1336, **I,** 7, **J,** 282, 314b, 332, **N,** 20a, **R,** 834,
　Campaign, **S,** 1435, **W,** 921,

Imboden's Battery, **T**, 448
Bullets; **K**, 118
Bulloch, James Dunwoody; **C**, 1031, 1266, **R**, 550
Burditt, Giles H.; **T**, 155
Bureau of Foreign Supplies; **B**, 331
Burgess, Mary Wyche; **XYZ**, 43
Burgwyn, Henry King, Jr., Col.; **D**, 142, 152
Burials, Confederate; **A**, 400-401
Burkart, Rosamond H.; **D**, 95
Burke County, NC; **W**, 701
Burke Sharpshooters; **B**, 1580
Burleson, Rufus C., Mrs.; **W**, 93
Burlesque; **C**, 1442
Burley, Bennett G.; **A**, 298
Burnett, Edmund Cody; **C**, 736, 937, **M**, 537
Burnett, Henry Cornelius, Col.; **C**, 1378
Burns, Amanda McD.; **B**, 783
Burnside, Ambrose Everett, Maj.Gen.; **K**, 151
Burr, C. Chauncey; **R**, 659
Burton, J.H., Col.; **E**, 104
Bushwhackers; **A**, 141, **B**, 1326, **C**, 1454, **E**, 258, **H**, 300, 1249, **XYZ**, 76
Business; **S**, 1270,
  Confederate Attitudes, **C**, 733,
  Slavery, **F**, 323
Butler's Brigade; **C**, 36
Butler, Benjamin Franklin, Maj.Gen.; **B**, 1314, 1317, **D**, 269, 627, **G**, 489, **K**, 184, **M**, 608
Butler, Emma; **P**, 30a
Butler, Matthew Calbraith, Maj.Gen.; **B**, 1332
Butler-Reagan Ticket; **R**, 169
Butter Preservation; **J**, 19
Butternut & Copperheads; **M**, 337
Button, Charles W.; **E**, 30
Buttons; **A**, 140, **J**, 113, **K**, 106, 109, **S**, 1136, **W**, 713
Byrd Flying Field, Richmond, VA; **N**, 34
Byrd Rifles; **L**, 10a
Byrne, Andrew, Bishop; **L**, 462

C

C. of C.; **U**, 40,
  Raleigh, NC, Manly's Btty. Chap., **B**, 757
Cabarrus County, NC;
  Burial Lists, **P**, 588
Cabell County, VA;
  History, **W**, 96
Cabell's Brigade; **C**, 14
Cabell, H.C.; **A**, 473
Cabell, William Lewis, Brig.Gen.; **A**, 432, **H**, 465, 798a
Cabin Creek, Ind.T.; **C**, 1517, **E**, 220, **H**, 205
Cabin John Bridge, Washington, DC; **D**, 256, **R**, 322, 595
Cabot, S., Dr.; **C**, 1476
Cadenhead, I.B.; **C**, 20
Cadet Corps; **M**, 1299
Cadets; **L**, 153, **M**, 439, 1299, **N**, 5, **O**, 71, **R**, 633
Cage, Josephine (Posey); **C**, 24
Cahaba (Cahawba) Prison, AL; **B**, 1160
Cairns, Kate; **B**, 929
Cairo, IL, Destruction of; **B**, 370
Calcasiey Pass, LA, Battle of; **B**, 157
Caldwell County, NC; **C**, 598, **H**, 351
Caldwell, James F.; **B**, 1348
Calhoun, Frances Boyd; **D**, 837
Calhoun, John Calvin; **B**, 77, 1077, **C**, 90, 145
Calhoun, William L., Capt.; **B**, 839
California; **K**, 146,
  Confederates, **M**, 1052, **W**, 132,
  Southern Sympathizers, **G**, 331, **H**, 342
Call, Richard Keith; **C**, 42
Call, Wilkinson; **R**, 533
Calloway County, MO; **B**, 532
Camden District, SC; **M**, 452

Camden, AR; **J**, 164,
  Fortifications, **S**, 319,
  Steele's Retreat, **F**, 174
Camden, Edwin Duncan, Capt.; **C**, 1161
Cameron, Alexander; **D**, 939
Cameron, Francis Hawkes, Lt.; **C**, 1030, **W**, 100
Cameron, Rebecca; **S**, 439
Camilla Riot; **F**, 190
Camp Bartow, WV; **P**, 816
Camp Beauregard, KY; **S**, 336
Camp Benning, GA; **B**, 146, 547, **C**, 168
Camp Butler Prison, IL; **T**, 278,
  Roster, **L**, 551
Camp Charity, KY; **M**, 1142
Camp Chase Cemetery, OH; **K**, 230,
  Memorial Day, **XYZ**, 50
Camp Chase Prison, OH; **B**, 108, **D**, 884, **K**, 174, 230, **W**, 537
Camp Colorado, TX; **H**, 543
Camp Cooper, TX; **M**, 364
Camp Cutts, VA; **C**, 757
Camp Dennison Prison, OH;
  Roster, **L**, 552
Camp Douglas Prison, IL; **B**, 346, 642, **C**, 3, 1232, **K**, 20, **U**, 37,
  Burials, **C**, 1012,
  Conspiracy, **F**, 94,
  Roster, **L**, 555
Camp Duty; **B**, 1518
Camp Finegan, FL; **J**, 561a
Camp Fires; **L**, 1, **M**, 392
Camp Ford Prison, TX; **G**, 251, **L**, 158, **M**, 605, 963
Camp Groce Prison, TX; **M**, 964
Camp Jackson Prison, MO; **B**, 538, **C**, 1335
Camp Jenkins, WV; **P**, 290

Camp Lawton, GA;
  Stockade, **R**, 649
Camp Lee, GA; **B**, 856
Camp Life; **A**, 76, **C**, 693, **L**, 493, **W**, 216, 230
Camp McDonald, GA;
  School, **W**, 16
Camp Moore, LA; **C**, 263
Camp Morton Prison, IN; **W**, 849, 1073,
  Roster, **L**, 556
Camp Morton, IN; **H**, 1005a, **M**, 779, **S**, 944, **W**, 1086
Camp Newspapers; **W**, 643
Camp Oglethorpe, GA; **M**, 584
Camp Pratt Prison, LA; **B**, 618
Camp Shenandoah, VA; **M**, 10
Camp Vance, NC; **W**, 701
Campaigns; **B**, 591, **F**, 110, 484, **H**, 1273, **S**, 1088
Campaigns, Presidential; **F**, 187
Campbell County, GA; **C**, 1261
Campbell Family, Ireland; **C**, 107
Campbell, J.A.P.; **C**, 51
Campbell, John Angus; **B**, 998
Campbell, John Archibald; **C**, 92, 1094, **D**, 937, **L**, 187, **M**, 159, 1303, **T**, 535, **XYZ**, 99
Campbell, Robert J.; **C**, 308
Camps, UCV; **U**, 27
Canada; **H**, 386, 620, 981, **K**, 51, **S**, 1002, **W**, 844,
  Civil War, Opinion, **M**, 486,
  Confederate Agents, **B**, 959,
  Confederate Exiles, **W**, 110,
  Confederate Operations, **K**, 163,
  Conspiracy, **G**, 537,
  Currency, **W**, 400,
  Secession, Opinions, **L**, 69,
  View of St. Albans Raid, **K**, 19
Canavella, Charles A.; **C**, 120
Candler, Allen D.; **B**, 1383, **C**, 709
Cane Hill, AR, Battle of; **B**, 376, **H**, 462, **O**, 25
Cane-Brake, Battle of; **R**, 808
Cannon; **D**, 72, 844, **F**, 127, **G**, 348, **M**, 443, 891, **S**, 1133, **T**, 521,
  British, **W**, 362

Cannon, Fenelon, Capt.; **G**, 628
Cannon, H.P.; **C**, 126
Cannon, Newton; **M**, 441
Cannoneers; **D**, 74, **J**, 555, **M**, 1057
Canooche-Ogeechee; **H**, 283
Cantata Choir; **M**, 1336
Canteens; **S**, 1458
Cantwell, J.L.; **H**, 218
Cape Fear River; **S**, 956-957, 961,
  Blockades, **T**, 185
Cape Girardeau, MO; **P**, 314
Capers, Charlotte; **B**, 725
Capers, Ellison, Brig.Gen.; **C**, 142, 156, 357, **D**, 860
Capon Valley, VA; **P**, 820
Carbines; **L**, 774, **M**, 1311
Carey, Henry C.; **S**, 638
Carleton, James H., Gen.; **K**, 146
Carlisle, J.M.; **C**, 179
Carlisle, Nora Boone, Mrs.; **B**, 895
Carlisle, PA;
  Invasion of, **G**, 371
Carlota, Mexico; **R**, 497
Carnes, John Elliott; **W**, 343
Carnes, W.W., Capt.; **B**, 1600
Carnifex Ferry, WV, Battle of; **C**, 1168, **H**, 1292, **L**, 750a
Carolina Light Infantry; **A**, 444
Carolina Military Academy; **T**, 209
Carolinas Campaign; **G**, 300
Caroline County, VA; **W**, 836,
  Bethel Baptist Church, **D**, 17a
Carondelet (ship); **B**, 1147
Carpenter's Battery; **F**, 324, 325
Carpenter, James A.; **L**, 788
Carpetbaggers; **B**, 969, **V**, 42
Carr, B.B.; **H**, 275
Carribean Empire, Southern Dream; **M**, 361
Carrington, Henry Alexander, Col.; **C**, 6
Carrington, Henry B.; **K**, 216
Carroll County, GA; **B**, 884,
  Militia Enrollments, **W**, 722
Carroll County, MD; **P**, 196
Carroll County, MS; **H**, 161
Carson, Joseph; **C**, 228
Carson, Kathleen; **A**, 116

Carter House Association; **C**, 1497
Carter, Ellen Timmons; **C**, 242a
Carter, Sidney, Lt.; **L**, 62
Carter, Thomas H., Col.; **B**, 806
Carter, Tod, Capt.; **C**, 238
Cartersville, GA; **C**, 1590
Carthage, MO, Battle of; **S**, 132
Cartography, Military; **C**, 117
Cartoons; **B**, 74
Cary, R. Milton, Col.; **A**, 133
Casey, Silas, Brig.Gen.; **C**, 264
Cash, W.J.; **B**, 868
Cash, William M.; **N**, 215
Cass County, GA; **C**, 1590
Castel, Albert; **A**, 539
Castle Pinckney; **W**, 755
Castle Thunder Prison, Richmond, VA; **E**, 279
Castleman, John B.; **B**, 1363, **C**, 296
Casualties; **A**, 114
Caswell Boys;
   Uniforms, **U**, 14
Catalogues; **D**, 591, 595-596, **E**, 140
Catawba Soldiers, NC; **H**, 37
Cates, Philip; **D**, 503
Cathey, Henry; **A**, 568
Catholic Mission, LA; **M**, 387
Catholics; **H**, 735
Catlett's Station Raid; **C**, 1193
Catoosa County, GA; **C**, 614
Catron, John; **H**, 17
Catterson's Militia; **D**, 515
Cattle; **G**, 124, **T**, 71
Catton, Bruce; **M**, 711b, **S**, 321
Caucuses; **H**, 126, 760
Causton's Bluff Battery; **XYZ**, 72
Cavalry; **D**, 525, 945, **H**, 733, **K**, 226, **L**, 46, 170-171, **M**, 858, 1020, 1218, 1289, **O**, 25-26, **S**, 14, 1312, **T**, 457, **XYZ**, 49,
   Adams (W.), **A**, 54,
   Army of Tennessee, **D**, 999,
   Atlanta Campaign, **S**, 221,
   East, **C**, 1116,
   Gettysburg, PA, **M**, 593,
   Indians, **I**, 36,
   Leaders, **R**, 630, **W**, 885,
   Raids, **G**, 673,
   Revolvers, **L**, 680,
   Scouts, **H**, 186,
   Tactics, **N**, 162a, **W**, 511,
   vs. Infantry, **G**, 337, **M**, 498
Cavalry Corps, ANV; **L**, 146
Cavalrymen; **C**, 234, 236, 1287, **G**, 144,
   Georgia, **H**, 319,
   Uniforms, **U**, 14
Cave, R.C., Rev.; **C**, 342, **S**, 1287
Cave-dwellers; **D**, 689
Cavenaugh, John; **F**, 395
Cease-fire; **J**, 324
Cedar Creek, VA, Battle of; **B**, 1091, 1515, **E**, 12, **G**, 184, **H**, 529, 547, **M**, 1, 549, 679, 1117a
Cedar Keys, FL;
   Reconstruction, **F**, 165
Cedar Mountain, VA, Battle of; **A**, 361, **B**, 1103-1104, **E**, 194, **S**, 197
Cedar Run, VA, Battle of; **A**, 208, **D**, 843, **L**, 89, **W**, 992
Cemeteries; **C**, 895-899, **L**, 457, 551-560,
   Arlington, VA, **C**, 1197, **R**, 305, **U**, 31,
   Beauvoir Soldiers' Home, MS, **D**, 387,
   Camp Chase, OH, **K**, 230, **XYZ**, 50,
   Cave Hill, Louisville, KY, **B**, 1206,
   Columbia, SC, **M**, 777,
   Confederate, First, **K**, 139,
   Confederate, Spotsylvania, PA, **R**, 236b,
   Covington, GA, **H**, 628,
   Cross Roads, Paulding County, GA, **G**, 642,
   Elmwood, Memphis, TN, **B**, 229,
   Elmwood, Norfolk, VA, **C**, 895, **G**, 87,
   Elmwood, Shepherdstown, WV, **H**, 700, **M**, 778, **O**, 191,
   Fayetteville, AR, **M**, 792,
   Finn's Point, Salem, NJ, **P**, 567,
   Forest Hill, Madison, WI, **T**, 321,
   Frederick, MD, **N**, 74,
   Greenwood, New Orleans, LA, **D**, 483, **L**, 11,

Cemeteries

Hagerstown, MD, **D**, 547,
Hollywood, Richmond, VA, **M**, 969, **R**, 239,
Loudon, VA, **K**, 40a,
Mareitta National, **O**, 154,
Mississippi, **J**, 513,
Mt. Olivet, Frederick, MD, **C**, 954,
Oak Hill, Newman, GA, **C**, 921, **O**, 24,
Oakdale, Wilmington, NC, **C**, 825,
Oakwood, Chicago, IL, **M**, 186, **P**, 541, **U**, 37,
Port Gibson, MS, **F**, 336,
Resaca, GA, **R**, 310,
Rose Hill, Macon, GA, **C**, 881,
Shenandoah, Mount Jackson, VA, **M**, 1254a,
Stonewall, Spalding County, GA, **J**, 55,
Stonewall, Winchester, VA, **C**, 899, **K**, 267, 267a, **M**, 499,
Taylor County, TX, **V**, 115,
Union County, NC, **L**, 97,
Vicksburg, MS, **R**, 459,
Westview Cemetery, Fulton County, GA, **C**, 1010,
Woodlawn, Elmira, NY, **H**, 1016
Census; **K**, 77-78,
Tennessee, **S**, 533
Centenary College, AL; **S**, 313
Centennials; **B**, 263, 272-273, 276, 416, 419, 422, 1639, **C**, 423, 529, 536, 792, 872, 944, **D**, 784, **E**, 47, **F**, 354, 365, 537, **G**, 650, **K**, 93, **L**, 12, **M**, 336, 651, 874, 933-934, 1012, 1044, **N**, 86, 178, **O**, 93, **P**, 73, 724, 750-751, 797a, **R**, 352, 394, **S**, 241, 870, 1029, **T**, 461, **V**, 146,
Commission, **C**, 536a,
Studies of, **C**, 893
Central Tennessee;
Cavalry Raid, **C**, 1599
Centralia, MO;
Guerrillas, **D**, 890
Century Quartet; **M**, 1338
Chadwick, Thomas W.; **B**, 1569
Chaleron, J.A., Capt.; **S**, 545
Chalk Bluff, AR, Battle of; **W**, 1058

Chalmers, James Ronald, Brig.Gen.; **C**, 378
Chamber Lye; **K**, 240
Chamberlain, Daniel Henry, Gov., SC; **A**, 254
Chamberlayne, J.L.; **A**, 449
Chamberlayne, John Hampden, Capt.; **T**, 79
Chamberpot Poem; **H**, 340
Chambers County, AL; **W**, 170
Chambersburg, PA; **R**, 140,
Burning of, **M**, 400, 404, 1068a, **S**, 567,
Raid, **P**, 732, **S**, 1310
Chambersburg, PA, Battle of; **O**, 78
Champion's Hill, MS, Battle of; **C**, 752, **L**, 374
Chancellorsville, VA; **H**, 1119, **M**, 824a, **R**, 215,
Campaign, **B**, 336, **M**, 579, **T**, 419,
Salem Church, **C**, 581,
Stuart, James Ewell B., Maj.Gen., **S**, 1320, 1325
Chancellorsville, VA, Battle of; **B**, 713, 795, 1097, **C**, 62, 391, 827, 1366, 1499, 1538, **D**, 446, 692, **F**, 239, **G**, 76, 640-641, **H**, 890, 1340, **L**, 87, 219, 319, **M**, 251, **P**, 270, **R**, 330, 370, 631, **S**, 46, 968,
Lee's Strategy, **T**, 7
Chandler, Daniel; **C**, 92, 102
Chandler, Ralph; **C**, 395
Chantilly, VA, Battle of; **M**, 1077
Chapel Hill, NC; **B**, 297,
Reconstruction, **C**, 380
Chaplains; **G**, 483-484, **M**, 722a, **N**, 201-202, **R**, 869, **S**, 124, 321, 1383, **W**, 653,
Mississippi, **L**, 729,
Roster, **L**, 550
Chapman Pirates; **C**, 396
Chapman's Battery; **J**, 252
Chapman, Beirne, Capt.; **J**, 252
Chapman, Conrad Wise; **B**, 221, **C**, 883, **S**, 484
Chapmen's Fort, SC, Battle of; **R**, 491

Charles City County, VA;
  History, **C**, 1231
Charleston Courier, SC, np.; **D**, 137,
  F, 235, 423, **M**, 101
Charleston Harbor, SC; **O**, 104, **T**,
  379, **W**, 755,
  Defenses, **J**, 215, **K**, 246,
  Torpedoes, **B**, 465, **G**, 297
Charleston Light Dragoons; **E**, 190,
  W, 384,
  Uniforms, **U**, 14
Charleston Mercury, SC, np.; **C**, 539,
  1131, **M**, 978, **S**, 826, 840
Charleston Zouave Cadets;
  Uniforms, **U**, 14
Charleston, SC; **C**, 172, **D**, 421, **G**,
  648, **H**, 776, **I**, 6, **J**, 92, 129, 524, **M**,
  455, **P**, 625, **R**, 647, 817, **S**, 27, 49,
  603, 770, **T**, 375, **V**, 188, **W**, 50a,
  Ashley Hall Plantation, **B**, 1541,
  Battery, **V**, 186,
  Blockades, **M**, 305, **N**, 141, **S**, 755,
  Bombardment, **S**, 1344,
  British Consul, **B**, 1552,
  Campaign, **H**, 1237, 1240,
  Citadel, **O**, 68a,
  Convention, **V**, 97,
  Culture, Early, **B**, 970,
  Defenses, **B**, 461, **J**, 522, **T**, 15,
  Engineers, **R**, 489,
  Fall of, **F**, 306,
  Fire of (1861), **H**, 1017, **M**, 236,
  Forts, **C**, 137, **O**, 159,
  Memorial Day, **G**, 289, **L**, 18,
  Monument, **P**, 770,
  Navy, Confederate, **L**, 579a,
  Retreat, **L**, 161,
  Riots, **C**, 782,
  Secret Discussions (1860), **E**, 125,
  Siege, **B**, 1610, **C**, 178, **J**, 525, **M**,
    840,
  St. Michael's Church, **E**, 160,
  Theater, **H**, 1064,
  Women, **C**, 818, **K**, 124
Charleston, SC, Battle of; **B**, 433
Charlotte Cavalry; **B**, 950-951
Charlotte Grays; **B**, 1210
Charlotte, NC;
  Navy Yard, **D**, 715
Charlton County, MO; **B**, 553
Charming Nellie; **P**, 536
Chase, Salmon P.; **F**, 610
Chatham Artillery; **C**, 351, 421-422,
  561, **J**, 392, 394, **W**, 177, 500,
  Uniforms, **U**, 14
Chattahoochee (ship); **C**, 297
Chattahoochee River; **C**, 122
Chattahoochee Valley; **M**, 333
Chattanooga, TN; **G**, 443, 445, **H**,
  707, 1045a, **M**, 506,
  Atlas, **B**, 663,
  Bragg's Campaign, **W**, 1017,
  Rebel, **L**, 574a
Chattanooga, TN, Battle of; **A**, 335,
  447, **H**, 558, **S**, 1387
Chaudron's Spelling Book; **C**, 425
Cheairs, Nathaniel F., Maj.; **M**, 367g
Cheat Mountain, WV;
  Campaign, **H**, 33, **J**, 349, **S**, 1284,
  XYZ, 101
Cheat Mountain, WV, Battle of; **C**,
  210, **L**, 336, **R**, 144
Cheatham, Benjamin Franklin,
  Maj.Gen.; **L**, 689a, **P**, 639, **Q**, 13,
  Belmont, MO, **J**, 242a
Cheavens, Henry Martyn; **M**, 941
Cheek Indians;
  Treaties, **P**, 395
Cheese Box (ship); **M**, 808
Chemicals; **S**, 3,
  South Acquired, **M**, 90
Cherbourg, France; **N**, 36
Cherokee County, AL; **M**, 198
Cherokee Indian Troops;
  Roster, **P**, 564
Cherokee Indians; **C**, 438, 1485-1486,
  D, 25, 238, **O**, 211, **P**, 392, **T**, 181,
  Arkansas, **D**, 28,
  Burial Lists, **P**, 568,
  Cavalry, **D**, 26,
  Georgia, **C**, 1279,
  Slavery, **D**, 177,
  Treaties, **P**, 394
Cherokee Nation; **A**, 337, **D**, 471, **E**,
  220, **F**, 482, **M**, 1070, **N**, 48, **W**, 265

Cherokee Rangers;
  Roster, C, 1605
Cherokee Script Issuance; M, 1125
Chesapeake & Ohio Canal; S, 45
Chesapeake, VA;
  Second Affair, W, 846
Cheshire, Joseph Blount; L, 612
Cheshire, R.M.; G, 561
Chesney's Campaign; C, 879
Chesney, Charles C., Col.; C, 73
Chesnut, James, Jr., Brig.Gen.; C, 448
Chesnut, Mary Boykin; J, 232a, M, 1269, W, 649
Chestatee Artillery; B, 856
Chester, SC;
  Monuments, B, 1179
Cheves, Langdon, Jr., Capt.; B, 1486, C, 456
Chevis, W.C.; U, 36
Chew's Battery; B, 1125, C, 899, M, 707a
Chew, Roger Preston, Lt.Col.; C, 459
Chewing Gum; C, 985
Chicago Times, IL, np.; T, 124
Chicago, IL;
  Copperhead Convention, C, 1233,
  Democratic National Convention, C, 1242,
  Monument, U, 8,
  Oakwood Cemetery, M, 186, P, 541, U, 37
Chickahominy River; D, 617, H, 822, Map, S, 368
Chickamauga & Chattanooga National Park; B, 225, 1033, S, 1387
Chickamauga Memorial Association; B, 1032
Chickamauga National Military Park; B, 305
Chickamauga, GA; C, 1552a,
  Atlas, B, 663,
  Battlefields, A, 447, S, 1387,
  Crisis, T, 283,
  Monuments, C, 357,
  South Carolina Commission, S, 831
Chickamauga, GA, Battle of; A, 253, 335, B, 589, 1188, 1523, 1600, C, 189, 633, 640, 741, 925, 1370, 1589, D, 636, G, 322, 362, 384, 445, 459, H, 309, 560, 821, 849, 869, 1287, 1315, J, 198, K, 125, L, 644, M, 205, 519, 612, N, 88a, P, 47-48, 488-491, 727, R, 254, 453, 577, S, 499, 653, T, 282, 456, 458, V, 123,
  Bragg's Conduct, M, 268,
  Official Report, N, 13,
  Orphan Brigade, J, 603,
  Roster, P, 491
Chickasaw Bayou Campaign; H, 525
Chickasaw Bayou, MS, Battle of; L, 384
Chickasaw Indians; C, 466, L, 163, P, 392, 398
Chickasaw Nation; M, 1070
Chicora (ship); H, 137
Chicora Wood, SC; P, 760
Chihuahua, Mexico; H, 81
Children; C, 115
Children, Catechism for; S, 1223
Childs, Arney Robinson; R, 129
Chilton, F.B.; C, 473
Chilton, Thomas H.; L, 34
Chimborazo Hospital, Richmond, VA; C, 1539, G, 256, 259, H, 6, 1283, J, 139
Chisolm, Alexander Robert; C, 477, G, 68
Chisolm, Robert, Capt.; C, 484
Choate, Rufus; B, 1424
Choctaw Indians; L, 163, P, 392, 398
Choctaw Nation; H, 1231, M, 1070,
  Slavery, D, 449
Choctaw Warrents; M, 1124
Chowan County, NC; D, 603
Christian Character of Great Leaders; A, 458
Christian County, MO; B, 385
Christian, C.B., Lt.Col.; C, 490
Christian, George L.; C, 501
Christian, Julia Jackson; J, 25b, 29
Christie, Daniel Harvey, Col.; C, 511
Christy, Howard Chandler; C, 17
Church & Religion; A, 61, B, 930, 956, 1491-1492, C, 439, 1478, D, 667, 942, F, 318, 437, 442, G, 3, 39,

314, **H**, 438, 528a, 1042, 1089, **L**, 407, **M**, 692, 1305, **P**, 253, **R**, 695-697, 697a, 858, **W**, 620-623, 783, 796,
Alabama, **F**, 242,
Alabama Chaplains, **W**, 38,
American Church & Civil War, **B**, 613,
Antimission Movement, **W**, 1069,
Arkansas Diocese, **S**, 290,
Army Chaplain, Office of, **D**, 77,
Army of Northern Virginia, **S**, 356,
Army of Tennessee, **H**, 106,
Baptist Split, **G**, 53,
Baptists, **F**, 104, **G**, 53, **M**, 153,
Bethel Baptist Church, VA, **D**, 17a,
Bible Publication, **D**, 82,
Bibles through Blockades, **H**, 662,
Bishops, **B**, 798,
Broad St. Methodist, Richmond, VA, **D**, 699,
Camp Life, **J**, 444,
Catholic Newspaper, **G**, 159,
Catholicism, **B**, 572, 682, **M**, 387, **P**, 410, **S**, 1212, **T**, 525,
Catholics of Diocese of Savannah, GA, **G**, 142,
Chaplains, **B**, 661, 784, **D**, 1, **J**, 321, **N**, 201-202, **P**, 422, **S**, 124, 321, 1383, **W**, 653,
Charleston, SC, **P**, 625,
Christian Association, **D**, 78,
Christian Pantheon, **N**, 209,
Christian Soldiers, **F**, 51,
Circuit Riders, **P**, 424,
Confederate Episcopal Church, **P**, 249-250, 254,
Davis, Nicholas A., **D**, 322,
Devotions, **Q**, 15,
Diocese of Alabama, **P**, 806,
Diocese of Southwest Virginia, **F**, 178,
Diocese of Texas, **G**, 266,
Episcopal Church, **B**, 362, **C**, 513, 652, **D**, 969, **H**, 919, **J**, 592, 599,
Evangelical Tract Society, **T**, 272,
Execution Sermon, **P**, 60,
Florida, **C**, 1611,
Foreign Missions, **P**, 703,
Georgia, **C**, 1279, **F**, 349,
Girardeau, John L., **B**, 733,
Gregg, Maxcy, Gen., **P**, 32,
Huguenots, **V**, 92,
Ireland, **H**, 735,
Jackson, Thomas Jonathan, Lt.-Gen., **J**, 40, **L**, 723, **S**, 255,
Jesuits, **S**, 124,
Jews, **F**, 471, **J**, 134, **K**, 249-251, **L**, 420, **M**, 1245, **W**, 894,
Lee, Robert Edward, Gen., **L**, 332, **M**, 595,
Lincoln Administration, **R**, 329,
Literature, **L**, 611, **P**, 251,
Little Rock Diocese, AR, **W**, 625,
Little Rock, AR, **L**, 462,
Lutheran Church, **M**, 1336,
M.E. Church South, **T**, 271,
Manassas, VA, Battle of, **P**, 480,
Maryland, **R**, 468,
Memphis, TN, **W**, 979,
Mennonites, **H**, 461, 1109,
Methodism, **S**, 631,
Methodist Episcopal Church, **D**, 84, **E**, 154, **M**, 1114, **N**, 205, 208, **S**, 1427, 1437,
Methodist Publishers, **T**, 223, **W**, 719,
Minister/Soldier, **M**, 104,
Mississippi Diocese, **B**, 1567,
Missouri Persecution, **L**, 410,
Mormon Splinter Colony, **W**, 619,
Newspapers, **N**, 204,
Parish Script, **M**, 1327,
Pioneer Minister, **XYZ**, 41,
Polk, Leonidas, Maj.Gen., **C**, 1431, **P**, 475,
Pope Pius IX, **D**, 266, **R**, 635,
Prayers, **P**, 697,
Presbyterian Church, **M**, 998,
Press, **S**, 1304,
Prince Edward County, VA, History, **B**, 1602,
Propaganda, **S**, 464,
Prophecy, **S**, 205,
Protestant Clergy, **D**, 80,

Church & Religion

Protestant Episcopal Church, M, 1306, P, 252, 803, S, 708, 1426,
Protestantism & Patriotism, D, 79,
Quakers, C, 1564, S, 901,
Quebec Missionaries, M, 1278,
Revivals, B, 588, N, 203, P, 757,
Richmond, VA, Old Christ Church, B, 907,
Ryan, Abraham J., Father, B, 849,
Secession, M, 998, P, 44,
Sermons, S, 561,
Shakers, G, 603, M, 1097, N, 37, 41,
Slavery, B, 69, D, 449,
Soldiers, O, 237, S, 399,
South Carolina Presbyterian Church, P, 703,
Southern Baptists, D, 85,
Southern Presbyterians, D, 86,
Southern Protestantism & Secession, D, 87,
Southern Puritanism, D, 77,
St. Michael's Church, Charleston, SC, E, 160,
St. Paul's Church, Richmond, VA, J, 143, W, 329,
State Relations, D, 77, 81,
Stranger's Church, New Orleans, LA, C, 571,
Sudley, VA, N, 4,
Test Oath, L, 410,
Texas, T, 217,
Texas Diocese, F, 98, G, 621,
Trinity Church, Portsmouth, VA, T, 425,
Trinity Church, VA, P, 661,
Vatican, F, 42,
Vicariate Apostolic of Florida, G, 142,
Virginia Baptists, D, 87
Church of Nashville, Second Presbyterian; A, 578
Churchill, Thomas James, Maj.Gen.; C, 411
Chustenahlah, Ind.T., Battle of; S, 420, T, 54
Chustotalasha, Ind.T., Battle of; F, 162
Cigarette Industry; P, 644a

Cincinnati Daily Inquirer, OH, np.; W, 796
Circle of Honor; S, 1188
Citadel, Charleston, SC; B, 864, H, 1302a, O, 68a,
  Cadets, L, 153,
  Uniforms, U, 14
City Point, VA;
  Explosion, O, 10a
Civil War; B, 760, C, 769, 1393-1398, 1504, D, 24, 118, 359, 700, 708, E, 116, 131, 276, F, 35, 536, 592, G, 100, 462, H, 676, 723, 789, J, 278, 575, K, 77, M, 851, 979, R, 245, V, 1,
  American Church, B, 613,
  American Disruption, B, 608,
  Atrocities, S, 1210, XYZ, 65,
  Battles, B, 130, F, 135, G, 374, H, 1314, M, 768, 961, P, 685, S, 1260, 1432, U, 42, W, 436, 481,
  Battles, Errors, E, 31,
  Beginning of, H, 638, S, 1124,
  Bibliography, H, 480, 492, 631, 702, U, 20,
  Books, B, 759a, K, 138, T, 388,
  Causes, H, 363, L, 262, R, 160-161, 782, W, 64,
  Collecting, H, 473,
  Compromise Efforts, G, 309,
  Confederate Forces, J, 121,
  Crimes, D, 467,
  Crucial Moments, W, 321,
  Decisive Battles, S, 1306,
  End of, A, 378,
  Family Life, H, 1192,
  First Shots, C, 1595, M, 367f,
  Foreign Views, B, 40, G, 619,
  Genealogy, G, 141,
  Historic Papers, P, 669,
  Historiography, T, 22,
  History, B, 822, D, 849, H, 1113,
  Home Life, B, 685, J, 572,
  Humor, H, 104,
  Interpretations, R, 47,
  Judicial Relations, CSA & US, A, 262,

Last Days, **B**, 19, **C**, 1549, **H**, 1293, **L**, 730, **S**, 127, 137,
Last Shots, **P**, 91,
Last Victory, **S**, 1176,
Lectures, **H**, 672-673,
Legal Contracts, **D**, 1001,
Liberal Interpretation, **B**, 1183,
Losses, **L**, 573, **T**, 291,
Memoirs, **B**, 916,
Military Events, **K**, 79,
Military Legacy, **L**, 779,
Modernization of Society, **L**, 770,
Names, **C**, 1305, **M**, 724,
Opiate Addiction, Result of War, **C**, 1332,
Origins, **B**, 1289,
Panorama, **U**, 4,
Personnel, **A**, 276,
Photographic History, **R**, 343,
Politics, **F**, 610, **H**, 209,
Popular Views, **B**, 610,
Prints, **A**, 284,
Records Recovered, **C**, 484b,
Regional Allegiances, **T**, 106,
Social & Political Bearings, **B**, 612,
Spain, **P**, 688,
State Participation, **B**, 679,
Strategy, **D**, 463,
Survival, **S**, 1146,
Theories, **D**, 977, **V**, 46,
Union, **V**, 6
Civil War Centennial Series; **A**, 176
Civil War Chronicle, CO, np.; **K**, 27
Civil War Times Illustrated; **C**, 551
Clack, Louise, Mrs.; **C**, 559
Claiborne County, MS; **F**, 334
Claiborne Guards; **C**, 562, **M**, 1115
Claiborne Parish, LA;
 History, **H**, 366
Claiborne, AL;
 Tennessee Soldiers, **C**, 1380
Claiborne, John F.H., Col.; **L**, 99, **R**, 474, **T**, 231
Claiburne Guards; **D**, 490
Clapp, Parson; **C**, 571
Clarence (ship); **W**, 939
Clark County, KY; **O**, 209
Clark, Carrol H.; **C**, 573

Clark, Edward Donaldson;
 Letters from Lamar, **L**, 38
Clark, Edward, Col.; **N**, 217
Clark, Henry Scott; **C**, 13253
Clark, Mary B., Mrs.; **G**, 560
Clark, Pat, Mrs.; **H**, 9
Clark, Sam L.; **C**, 594
Clark, Walter; **B**, 1304, **P**, 210, 362, **S**, 955
Clarke Cavalry; **S**, 363
Clarke County, AL; **C**, 615
Clarke County, VA; **C**, 1196, **M**, 722,
 History, **G**, 325
Clarke's Confederate Almanac; **C**, 619
Clarke, Bascom; **W**, 523
Clarke, Daniel; **C**, 575
Clarke, Jerome (Sue Mundy); **H**, 1037, **V**, 4
Clarke, M.M.; **A**, 139
Clarkson's Cavalry; **A**, 432
Clarkson's Regiment; **C**, 13
Clarksville, TN;
 Soldiers, **J**, 234
Clay Family, AL; **N**, 214
Clay, Brutus J.;
 Papers, **C**, 634
Clay, Clement C.; **N**, 214
Clay, James Brown; **W**, 110
Clay, T.T., Capt.; **C**, 640
Clayton's Division; **C**, 647
Clayton's Militia; **B**, 1635
Clayton, Alexander M.; **C**, 645
Clayton, Henry DeLamar, Maj.Gen.; **A**, 340, **J**, 570
Clayton, Philip A.; **D**, 203
Clayton, W.F.; **C**, 650
Cleburne's Arkansas Brigade; **L**, 505a
Cleburne's Division; **W**, 232
Cleburne, Patrick R., Maj.Gen.; **A**, 283, **B**, 1282, 1406, 1508-1509, **C**, 653-656, **D**, 349, **E**, 275, **F**, 436, **G**, 391, 394, **H**, 294, 512, 798b, 887, **L**, 525, **M**, 441, 1112, **N**, 21, **P**, 826, **R**, 785, 819a, **S**, 1424a
Clemens, Sherrard; **C**, 665

Clement, Abram W.; **C**, 666
Clement, Frank; **D**, 377
Clemson, Florida; **L**, 64, 251
Clemson, Thomas Green; **H**, 1014
Cleveland, Charles Boarman; **C**, 675
Cleveland, Charlotte; **G**, 10
Cleveland, Grover, Pres.; **D**, 140
Cleveland, Henry W.; **H**, 590
Clingman's Brigade; **C**, 686-687
Clingman, Thomas Lanier, Brig.Gen.; **C**, 56, **XYZ**, 8
Clinton, NC; **J**, 87
Clower, George W.; **D**, 168, **M**, 957
Cloyd's Farm, VA, Battle of; **R**, 608
Cloyd's Mountain, VA, Battle of; **B**, 1329
Coal; **A**, 436, **B**, 777
Coastal Defenses; **G**, 694, Treatise, **S**, 118
Cobb County, GA; History, **T**, 104
Cobb's Infantry; **R**, 232, **T**, 180
Cobb's Legion; **D**, 588, **H**, 1190
Cobb, Howell, Maj.Gen.; **B**, 1313, **L**, 36, **M**, 1017, 1019, **R**, 32, **S**, 518-520, 1090, **T**, 396
Cobb, Jessie E.; **A**, 105
Cobb, Thomas Reade Rootes, Brig.Gen.; **B**, 1413, **M**, 398, **P**, 646
Cobb, Viola, Mrs.; **B**, 49
Cobbs, Nicholas H.; **A**, 95, **E**, 163
Cobden, Richard; **B**, 751
Cockade City, VA; Defenses, **G**, 305
Cocke, John K.; **B**, 1544
Cocke, Philip St. George, Brig.Gen.; **A**, 420
Cockrell, Monroe F.; **D**, 879, **P**, 452
Cockrell, Sarah Horton, Mrs.; **G**, 690
Coercion; **B**, 103, **R**, 874, 884, **S**, 214
Cofer Revolvers; **M**, 1291
Cofer, Thomas W.; **M**, 1291
Coffee, John Truesdale, Col.; **H**, 1277
Coffin, Charles E., Capt.; **C**, 1552
Coffman, W.E.; Trial, **M**, 830
Cohen, Marx E.; **H**, 264

Coins; **B**, 1216, 1430, **C**, 1, 158, 1622, **F**, 351, 560, 584, **H**, 452, 1045, **N**, 216, **R**, 75
Coit, Joseph H.; **C**, 750
Coke County, TX; **P**, 185
Coke, Richard; **F**, 96
Coker Family, NC; **S**, 497
Coker, F.M.; **C**, 757
Coker, James L.; **W**, 677
Cold Harbor Campaign; **B**, 145
Cold Harbor, VA, Battle of; **B**, 252, 675, 1103-1104, **C**, 47, **D**, 850, **E**, 117, **G**, 335, 377, **M**, 450, **P**, 57, **S**, 792, **T**, 427, **W**, 410
Cole's Classical & Military School; **C**, 776
Cole, Jim; **B**, 1294
Cole, Ruth; **B**, 75
Coleman's Scouts; **W**, 577
Coleman, Chew, Pvt.; **XYZ**, 59
Coleman, Kenneth; **A**, 523, **B**, 873
Coleman, Lewis Minor, Lt.Col.; **B**, 1604
Coley, Maggie Crary; **U**, 38
Collins, Carvel; **F**, 47
Colorado; **L**, 739,
  Burial Lists, **P**, 570,
  Confederate Sentiment, **J**, 127,
  Conquest, **B**, 1001,
  Gold Fields, **B**, 649, **C**, 1093, **XYZ**, 91,
  Trade, **H**, 203
Colorado Troops;
  Infantry,
    1st Regt. Vols., **H**, 1003
Colquitt County, GA;
  Graves, **C**, 363
Colquitt, Alfred Holt, Brig.Gen.; **G**, 515
Colquitt, Hugh L.; **H**, 571
Colston, Fred M.; **A**, 449, **C**, 829
Colston, J.A. Campbell; **C**, 829
Colston, Raleigh Edward, Brig.Gen.; **C**, 823, 825, 827
Colt Guns; **S**, 1132
Columbia Prison, SC; **F**, 485
Columbia, SC; **D**, 130, 605, **S**, 8, 463,
  Arsenal Academy, **O**, 68a,

Burning of, **B**, 1489, **C**, 36, 214-215, 1431, **E**, 191, **G**, 48, 201, 355, **H**, 197, 857, **L**, 20, 143, 488, 762, **M**, 391, **N**, 135, **S**, 821, 1439, **T**, 410, **W**, 386,
Cemetery, **M**, 777,
Confederate Dead, **C**, 1009,
Confederate Relic Room, **G**, 288,
Destruction of, **C**, 1106, **S**, 487-488,
Evacuation, **R**, 300,
Hospitals, **B**, 1488,
Memorabilia, **S**, 233,
Plantation Life, **M**, 850,
Property Destruction, **B**, 788,
Relics, **C**, 302,
Steam Press, **M**, 636
Columbus Daily Republic Extra, MS, np.; **D**, 21
Columbus, GA; **M**, 249, **S**, 980, Walker Hospital, **C**, 227
Columbus, MS; **N**, 53
Comanche Indians; **M**, 1353-1354
Commanders; **D**, 989
Commerce-raiders; **T**, 403
Commissary-General's Department; **M**, 764
Committee of Manchester, England; **B**, 751
Committee of Thirty-three; **J**, 587
Commonwealth, Magazine of Virginia; **C**, 542
Compromise of 1850; **B**, 1424, **D**, 411, **H**, 139-140, 143
Conecuh Guards; **R**, 470
Confederacy; **D**, 945, **J**, 597, **R**, 383, **W**, 1022,
Aftermath, **H**, 667,
Arkansas Resistance, **A**, 427,
Biographical Dictionary, **W**, 29,
Capitol, **A**, 306,
Character, **J**, 96,
Collapse, **W**, 418,
Commerce, **D**, 13,
Counterfeit Currency, **S**, 144,
Crisis, **W**, 380,
Disloyalty, **C**, 1511, **S**, 292, **T**, 47,
Dissent, **K**, 263,

Failure, **J**, 475, **K**, 196, **M**, 687, **T**, 34,
Fall of, **H**, 1083,
Finance History, **W**, 492,
First Book, **L**, 469,
Foreign Recognition, **L**, 796,
Foreign Relations, **A**, 324,
Freedom Press, **M**, 334,
History, **R**, 54, 121, **V**, 45,
History, Agricultural, **R**, 56,
Inflation, **L**, 442,
Jews, **L**, 420,
Last Capitol, **XYZ**, 57,
Last Days, **H**, 956, **J**, 607, **L**, 124, **P**, 670,
Last Hopes, **R**, 51, 230,
Map, **M**, 170, 471,
Mexican Projects, **R**, 494,
Papers, **P**, 827,
Paris Declaration, **T**, 394,
Prohibition, **R**, 619,
Propaganda, **S**, 467,
Rank & File, **H**, 727,
Rare Books, **H**, 702,
Recognition of, **M**, 308, **R**, 185, **S**, 926,
Resources, **K**, 22, **L**, 166, **M**, 1105, **R**, 320, **S**, 6, 21,
Sea Strategy, **M**, 798,
Transvaal, South Africa, **A**, 37,
Wages, **L**, 441
Confederacy, the (play); **G**, 584
Confederate Agents; **H**, 1090, Canada, **B**, 959
Confederate Ancestry; **P**, 444
Confederate Archives; **H**, 1207, **R**, 905, **T**, 401a
Confederate Army; **L**, 164a, **S**, 385,
Artillery, **K**, 15b,
Command System, **V**, 70,
Food Supplies, **V**, 62,
General Officers, **W**, 1031-1033,
Local Organizations, **W**, 1035,
Northern Enlistments, **J**, 158,
Ranks, **N**, 30,
Regulation, **M**, 729,
Roster, **P**, 78,
Statistics, **D**, 540, **M**, 594, 601,

Confederate Army

Strength of, **H**, 446,
Uniforms, **U**, 12-14
Confederate Artillery; **M**, 580a
Confederate Banners; **C**, 1119
Confederate Catechism; **T**, 526, **U**, 37
Confederate Cemetery, Spotsylvania, PA; **R**, 236b
Confederate Civil Service; **V**, 28
Confederate Collectibles; **M**, 115
Confederate Congress; **D**, 694, **M**, 775, **P**, 771-779, 788, 818, **T**, 377,
Last Session, **R**, 52,
North Carolina, **XYZ**, 25
Confederate Covers; **M**, 119
Confederate Dead; **A**, 435, **G**, 368, **R**, 72, **T**, 203,
Columbia, SC, **C**, 1009,
Johnson's Island, OH, **H**, 661,
Kentucky, **S**, 195,
Reburials, **C**, 957, **U**, 31
Confederate Debt; **R**, 560
Confederate Defeat;
Causes, **T**, 402,
Theory, **C**, 1083
Confederate Department Directory; **V**, 82
Confederate Diplomacy; **J**, 226
Confederate Exiles; **H**, 864-865, **K**, 228, **W**, 110, 648, **XYZ**, 12,
London, England, **W**, 111
Confederate Faces; **A**, 131-132
Confederate Fire-eaters; **O**, 171
Confederate General Hospital, Culpeper, VA; **H**, 941a
Confederate Generals, Last of; **A**, 446
Confederate Government; **B**, 360, **C**, 354, **E**, 237, **G**, 565, **H**, 981, **J**, 461, **K**, 21, **O**, 53,
Administration, **C**, 96, 103, **G**, 449,
Administrative Failure, **S**, 108,
Archives, **B**, 508,
British Consuls, **E**, 187,
Bureau of Foreign Supplies, **B**, 331,
Cabinet, **B**, 875, **M**, 886, **P**, 206, **W**, 125,
Cabinet, Last Meeting, **W**, 125,
Cabinet, Retreat of, **C**, 586,
Canadian Agents, **T**, 231,
Capital, **B**, 826, **O**, 172,
Civil Service, **C**, 150,
Collapse of, **G**, 285,
Commissioners, Treatment, **D**, 457,
Congress, **B**, 622-623, **D**, 337, **G**, 351,
Constitutional Reform, **S**, 163,
Cotton, **R**, 529,
Council Chamber, **K**, 62,
Counterfeiting, **B**, 576,
De Facto Government, **J**, 173,
Debt, **T**, 175,
Defensive Policies, **D**, 532,
Diplomacy, **B**, 686, 816, **D**, 856, **S**, 131,
Diplomatic History, **C**, 43,
Economics, **B**, 681,
England, **G**, 513,
Federal Trade, **F**, 612,
Finances, **T**, 219, 330,
Financial Agents, **D**, 154,
Financial History, **R**, 29,
Fiscal Programs, **L**, 440,
Flees Richmond, VA, **C**, 583,
Foreign Loan, **S**, 142,
Foreign Policy, **M**, 867,
Georgia, **B**, 212,
History, **C**, 397, **S**, 1395,
House of Representatives, **D**, 239,
Imports, **D**, 567,
Indian Tribes, **B**, 820,
Industry, **C**, 161, 164,
Judicial System, **R**, 615-616,
Last Days, **D**, 900, **G**, 409,
Laws, **L**, 452, **M**, 574, 860,
Leadership, **D**, 584, **G**, 576,
Manufacturing Controls, **R**, 48,
Medals, **B**, 515,
Military Departments, **C**, 1264,
Military Records, **H**, 61,
North Carolina, **M**, 1028,
Official Publications, **R**, 293,
Officials, Roster, **J**, 398-401,
Provisional Government, **F**, 1,
Publications, **S**, 1429, **V**, 154,
Purchasing Operations, Foreign, **T**, 256,

Regulations, **U**, 13,
Resources, **B**, 1423, **C**, 86,
Retreat to the Gulf, **S**, 1418,
Seal, **C**, 585, **F**, 109, **G**, 559-560, 564,
Senate, **D**, 239,
State Department, **B**, 563,
State Legislatures, **R**, 481,
Statutes, **S**, 1025-1026,
Supreme Court, **G**, 156,
Supreme Court, Lack of, **J**, 197,
Treasurer, Last, **C**, 588,
Treasury Department, **D**, 153, **R**, 901,
Welfare, **E**, 234,
Whigs, **R**, 621
Confederate Governors; **XYZ**, 23a
Confederate Gray Book, UCV; **U**, 19, 28
Confederate Grays; **F**, 316
Confederate Historical Association; Tennessee Division, **C**, 923
Confederate Historical Society; **J**, 588
Confederate Horsemen; **K**, 226
Confederate Hundred; **H**, 480
Confederate Image; **N**, 45a
Confederate Imprints; **C**, 1385, **G**, 657, **H**, 483-484, 631, **K**, 85, **M**, 311, 727, **P**, 113a, **W**, 263
Confederate Indian Department; **A**, 488
Confederate Indian Territory; **A**, 489
Confederate Indian Troops; **A**, 496
Confederate Leaders; **C**, 935
Confederate Marine Corps; **D**, 713-714, 719, 732-733, 925-926, **M**, 552, 839, **R**, 67, **S**, 1385, **V**, 25, **W**, 75, 100, 105,
Uniforms, **D**, 733, **U**, 14, **W**, 713
Confederate Medical Corps; **H**, 62
Confederate Medical Department; **C**, 1578, **H**, 63
Confederate Medical Officers; **C**, 1574
Confederate Memorial Association; History, **H**, 273
Confederate Memorial Chapel; **T**, 432
Confederate Memorial Halls; **C**, 961, **D**, 190, **J**, 168
Confederate Memorial Institute; **B**, 699, **C**, 206, 507, **M**, 226
Confederate Memorial Literary Society; **S**, 1428
Confederate Messenger, pub.; **C**, 929
Confederate Migrations; **H**, 335
Confederate Military History, pub.; **E**, 251-252
Confederate Military Records; **V**, 139
Confederate Monument Association; **P**, 51
Confederate Museum, Richmond, VA; **C**, 945, **H**, 213
Confederate Nitre & Mining Bureau; **D**, 731
Confederate Note Album; **T**, 173
Confederate Ordnance Department; **A**, 198, **H**, 835
Confederate Ordnance Records; **C**, 162
Confederate Papers; **F**, 508
Confederate Patriotic Covers; **M**, 11
Confederate Pension Law; **S**, 1100a
Confederate Philatelist; **S**, 922
Confederate Point, NC; **L**, 56
Confederate Post Office Department; **B**, 1159, **D**, 592, **G**, 104, **M**, 382, **O**, 52, **P**, 793
Confederate Postal Proclamations; **M**, 12
Confederate Postal Service; **H**, 646, **M**, 838, **R**, 332, **W**, 454,
History, **M**, 5, **C** 1495
Confederate Postmasters; **M**, 13
Confederate Press; **A**, 362, **W**, 808
Confederate Printing; **W**, 776
Confederate Railway Policy; **L**, 116
Confederate Records; **A**, 383-384, **B**, 721, **C**, 709, **D**, 658, 993, **F**, 32, **H**, 61, **L**, 601, **M**, 844, **R**, 901, **T**, 401a,
Alabama, **J**, 137,
Georgia, **B**, 771, **C**, 121,
Louisiana, **B**, 899, **L**, 709,
South Carolina, **C**, 994, **S**, 829,

War Department Collection, **B**, 656
Confederate Refugees; **M**, 316-317, **S**, 301
Confederate Relics; **M**, 922
Confederate Research Club; **N**, 85
Confederate Research Sources; **N**, 36a
Confederate Reveille; **U**, 37
Confederate Saltpetre Works; **D**, 712
Confederate Scrapbook; **D**, 75
Confederate Seal; **J**, 546, **P**, 365, 411, 429, **S**, 199
Confederate Signal Bureau; **B**, 1284
Confederate Soldier's Homes;
Maryland, **M**, 274
Confederate Stamps; **H**, 1217
Confederate State Department; **B**, 563, **C**, 643, **H**, 981
Confederate States Army;
Organizations, **C**, 1515
Confederate States Naval Academy; **F**, 314, **H**, 732
Confederate States Treasury; **P**, 88
Confederate States, Directory; **E**, 315
Confederate Strategy; **C**, 1090
Confederate Survivors' Association; **C**, 1552a, **J**, 374
Confederate Theatre; **T**, 167
Confederate Torpedo Service; **C**, 1490-1491
Confederate Trade Center; **P**, 94
Confederate Treasure; **D**, 612, 810, **F**, 315
Confederate Treasury; **D**, 495, **F**, 238, **H**, 379, **W**, 524
Confederate Treaties; **F**, 478
Confederate Troops;
First Victory, **B**, 260,
Pay, **S**, 108
Confederate Underground; **P**, 285
Confederate Veteran, pub.; **C**, 1430, **G**, 318, **W**, 571
Confederate Veterans; **A**, 12, 173, **C**, 1061, **D**, 747, **G**, 370,
Census, **A**, 421,
Postwar Politics, **G**, 21
Confederate War Department; **T**, 98, 428,

Medical Division, **F**, 443
Confiscation; **G**, 317, **H**, 747, **M**, 334, **R**, 83, **S**, 295
Confiscation Act; **B**, 1433, **N**, 71
Congress (ship); **C**, 1603
Congress, Confederate; **B**, 622-623, **C**, 659, 889, 1034, 1516, **G**, 351, **J**, 516, 589, **M**, 775, **R**, 617, 662, **S**, 461, **T**, 377, **V**, 69, **W**, 647,
Anatomy of, **A**, 189,
Biographical Register, **W**, 204,
Kentucky, **K**, 94,
Last Session, **C**, 888, **L**, 162,
Missouri, **K**, 199,
Secret Acts, **L**, 162
Congress, Provisional; **C**, 1037, **K**, 46
Congress, US; **A**, 59, 62, **B**, 1017, **C**, 250, 367, 935, **V**, 169,
Copperheads, **C**, 1241
Conn-Brantley Letters; **C**, 1076
Connelly, Thomas L.; **C**, 283
Conner's Brigade; **G**, 321
Conner, Anderson; **B**, 1643
Connor, H.G.; **U**, 40
Conrad Boys; **B**, 860
Conrad, Daniel B.; **U**, 5
Conrad, Robert Young; **R**, 461
Conrad, Thomas Nelson; **H**, 438
Conscientious Objectors; **H**, 461, **W**, 1012
Conscript Act; **A**, 434, **B**, 1381, **S**, 314
Conscription; **A**, 433, **B**, 1312, **D**, 208, 783, **F**, 171, **G**, 312, **H**, 427, **J**, 196, **M**, 970, 1043, **R**, 662, **S**, 353, 474,
Alabama, **F**, 265
Conservatism; **S**, 1160
Conspiracy; **B**, 1542, **C**, 1238, **R**, 707, **T**, 476
Constitution, Confederate; **B**, 702, 979, 1457, **C**, 696, 1036, **D**, 448, **F**, 70, 189, **H**, 152, 316, 477, 1274, **J**, 174, 196, **L**, 238, 447, **M**, 340, 376, 1098, **N**, 153, **P**, 807, **Q**, 26, **R**, 618, **S**, 91, 563, 948, 1025-1026,
Manuscript, **C**, 1254,
Washington Artillery, **W**, 236
Constitution, Florida; **F**, 277

Constitution, US; **B**, 567, 773, 979, 1571, **D**, 983, **G**, 227, **N**, 198, **O**, 121, **Q**, 26, **R**, 797, **S**, 13, 833, 1075, **T**, 411, 472, **V**, 124,
   Civil Liberties, **K**, 207,
   Coercion, **E**, 175,
   Fifteenth Amendment, **B**, 1180,
   Secession, **J**, 160
Constitutional Rights; **E**, 271, **G**, 80
Contraband; **E**, 266, **J**, 225
Contracts;
   Effects of War on, **J**, 173
Conventions; **C**, 463, 1242, **H**, 659, **P**, 786, **R**, 286, 552, **S**, 43, 867,
   Alabama, **S**, 735, **W**, 959,
   Arkansas, Secession, **C**, 1623,
   Bogus Texas Delegation, **C**, 258,
   Constitutional, **H**, 285,
   Copperhead, **C**, 1233,
   Debates, **A**, 90,
   Democratic State, **E**, 176, **XYZ**, 3,
   Georgia, **G**, 180-181, **S**, 1097, 1099,
   North Carolina, **M**, 434,
   Peace, **T**, 549, **W**, 479,
   Savannah, GA,
     Convention, **G**, 181,
   Secession, **D**, 99, 129, **H**, 878, 913, **S**, 738, 998, 1097, 1099, **T**, 154,
   South Carolina, **S**, 833,
   Texas, **C**, 1130, **T**, 145,
   UCV, **U**, 21,
   Virginia, **B**, 843, **S**, 293, **V**, 156, 163
Cook & Bro., Armory; **B**, 1286
Cook, Anna Maria Green; **B**, 886
Cook, Harvey T.; **C**, 1150
Cook, James M.; **C**, 1153
Cookbooks; **C**, 993, **H**, 1107a,
   Civil War, **P**, 684a
Cooke, James J.; **O**, 90
Cooke, John Esten; **A**, 443, **B**, 428, **S**, 1004, **W**, 542,
   Bibliography, **W**, 340
Cooke, John Rogers, Brig.Gen.; **B**, 1276
Cooking; **N**, 139, **R**, 219
Cool Spring, VA, Battle of; **M**, 722
Cooling, B. Franklin; **G**, 695
Cooper Guards; **D**, 679
Cooper's History (book); **H**, 443
Cooper, Douglas Hancock, Brig.Gen.; **B**, 390, **W**, 467, 1053-1054
Cooper, Samuel, Gen.; **D**, 280, **J**, 487
Cooper, Walter G.; **F**, 597, **G**, 175
Coopwood, Bethel, Capt.; **M**, 788
Coosawhatchie, SC; **H**, 1208
Coppen's Zouaves; **W**, 101
Copper; **D**, 717
Copperheads; **A**, 20, 22, **B**, 74, 511, 789, 1363, 1598, **C**, 198, 284, 463, 782-783, 1439, **D**, 310, **G**, 158, 489, 543, **H**, 735, **K**, 207, 210, 217-219, **L**, 424, 432, **M**, 296, 337, 888, **P**, 232, **R**, 883, **S**, 289, 546, 706, **T**, 124, 258, 315, **V**, 7, 9, **W**, 167, 562, 796, 1062-1063
Copyrights, Confederate; **R**, 605
Corbett, Julian; **T**, 75
Corbin, Henry; **D**, 571
Corbin, William Francis, Capt.; **D**, 445, **S**, 427
Cordley, R., Rev.; **B**, 949
Corinth, MS; **P**, 729,
   Evacuation of, **T**, 246
Corinth, MS, Battle of; **B**, 595, **C**, 282, 527, 721, 723, 731, **D**, 878-879, **G**, 396, **H**, 970, **P**, 730a, **S**, 1399
Cornish, Jenkins; **B**, 1486
Corona Female College; **G**, 539
Corpus Christi, TX; **D**, 499, **L**, 193
Corse, M.D., Col.; **C**, 1276
Corsicana Invincibles; **S**, 937
Cory, Chappell, Mrs.; **M**, 206
Cosmic Death of a Nation; **L**, 640c
Cotton; **A**, 592, **B**, 793, 1177, 1453, **C**, 1282, 1430, **D**, 89, 682, **E**, 320, **G**, 637-639, **H**, 658, 693, **J**, 485, **K**, 63, 181, **L**, 464, **O**, 113, 234, **P**, 220a, 682, **R**, 163, 529, **S**, 126, **T**, 555, 558, **W**, 342, 583,
   Campaign, **A**, 42,
   Cards, **W**, 798,
   Cotton Rings, **J**, 229,
   Crisis, **A**, 34-35, **M**, 572a,
   Egyptian, **E**, 4,
   Famine, **A**, 50, 459, **W**, 294,

Florida, **D**, 675,
French Substitutes, **P**, 537,
Letters, **C**, 1284,
Loans, **S**, 924,
Manufacturing, **W**, 318,
Scandals, **L**, 66,
Supply, **M**, 570,
Texas, **M**, 741,
Trade, **M**, 569
Cotton Bonds; **G**, 202,
  Committee Report, **C**, 841
Cotton Mill Campaign; **G**, 639
Cotton Production & Slavery in Texas; **A**, 482
Cotton States; **C**, 837
Cotton Whigs; **O**, 9
Coulter Bibliography; **C**, 1296
Coulter, Ellis Merton; **B**, 672, **S**, 279
Counterfeiting; **B**, 576, **H**, 798a
Counterinsurgency; **S**, 728
Couriers; **B**, 600, **D**, 160, **H**, 895, **XYZ**, 84
Court Records; **C**, 1022
Court-martials; **C**, 858, **G**, 470, **H**, 80, **M**, 635, **P**, 137
Courts; **H**, 156, **T**, 319,
  Georgia, **G**, 630,
  Pensions, **S**, 1230
Courts of Admiralty; **R**, 614
Couture, Richard T.; **D**, 446
Covington, GA;
  Cemetery, **H**, 628
Covington, KY; **B**, 778, **K**, 183
Covington, VA;
  McAllister Family, **M**, 366c
Cow Cavalry; **T**, 70
Coward, Osman Latrobe; **C**, 1337
Cowell, John Welsford; **C**, 1339
Coweta County, GA; **C**, 548, 921
Cowper, Pulaski; **G**, 652
Cox, Jacob Dolson, Maj.Gen.; **W**, 604a
Cox, William Ruffin, Brig.Gen.; **S**, 954, **W**, 1039
Crabtree, Beth G.; **E**, 85
Craighead County, AR; **D**, 778
Crandall, Marjorie L.; **B**, 672
Crater Legion, the; **B**, 255

Crater, VA, Battle of; **B**, 146, 631, 634, 636, 1452, **C**, 749, 1389, **F**, 60-61, 223, **H**, 910a, **M**, 633, **R**, 434, **S**, 1167, 1171, 1174,
  Artillery, **R**, 607,
  History, **W**, 766
Craven, John J.; **B**, 1078-1081, **D**, 251
Crawford County, OH; **S**, 721
Crawford, J.H.; **B**, 344
Crawford, W.L., Capt.; **B**, 1544
Creek Indian Troops;
  Roster, **P**, 565
Creek Nation; **D**, 870, **M**, 1070
Creigh, David S.; **D**, 736
Crenshaw's Battery; **C**, 784, **G**, 374, **XYZ**, 58
Crimes; **D**, 467
Crimmins, M.L., Col.; **B**, 1182, **G**, 566
Crisp, Charles Frederick; **M**, 259
Crist, Linda Lasswell; **D**, 243
Critcher, John; **D**, 16
Crittenden Compromise; **C**, 1507
Crook, George, Maj.Gen.; **B**, 33, 978,
  Capture, **M**, 683, **R**, 592,
  Captured, **V**, 79,
  Kidnapping of, **S**, 1057
Cross Keys, VA, Battle of; **G**, 336
Cross Roads Cemetery, Paulding County, GA; **G**, 642
Croushore, James H.; **D**, 419
Crown, Francis J., Jr.; **C**, 987
Crownover, Sims; **B**, 264
Croxall, Morris L., Mrs.; **W**, 27
Croxton, John T., Brig.Gen.; **C**, 690
Crozet, Claudius; **C**, 1315
Crozier, A.R.; **P**, 782
Cruisers; **S**, 645, 1155, **W**, 729a
Crummer, Clyde Lottridge; **H**, 687
Crusader (ship); **R**, 710
Crutchfield's Brigade; **B**, 208
Crutchfield, Stapleton, Col.; **B**, 776
Cuba; **E**, 111, **H**, 656,
  Florida, Relations with, **C**, 1277
Culberson, Charles A.; **G**, 566
Cullen, Joseph P.; **B**, 314
Culpeper County, VA;
  Battles, **G**, 659,
  History, **C**, 33

Culpeper Minute Men, VA; **B**, 527
Culpeper, VA;
  Confederate General Hospital, **H**, 941a
Cumberland (ship); **C**, 1603, **M**, 816, **O**, 18
Cumberland Plateau, TN; **R**, 334
Cumberland, MD;
  Confederate Raid, **S**, 905
Cumming, Arthur, Col.; **D**, 66
Cumming, Bryan, Mrs.; **C**, 1550
Cumming, Joseph B., Col.; **J**, 389, 393
Cumming, Katherine Hubbell; **C**, 1556
Cumming, Mary Gairdner; **C**, 1550
Cunningham, Edward; **B**, 245
Cunningham, Frank; **A**, 484, 580
Cunningham, Sumner Archibald; **M**, 779
Cunyas, Lucy Josephine; **B**, 198
Currency & Notes; **A**, 145, **B**, 317, 780, 1043, **C**, 412-413, 416, 461, 841, 892, 960, 972, 1607, 1622, **D**, 495, 546, 781, 845, **F**, 560, 584, **G**, 572, **H**, 218, 496, 611, **J**, 348, **K**, 110, 113, **L**, 400, **N**, 216, **P**, 55, **R**, 22-28, 262, 267, 710, **S**, 552, **T**, 168-169, 173-175, **V**, 187, **W**, 400,
  Alabama, **H**, 1186,
  Confederate, **A**, 235,
  Counterfeit, **K**, 107-108,
  Criswell's Currency Series, **C**, 1446,
  Georgia, **K**, 115-116,
  Mystery, **K**, 117,
  North Carolina, **B**, 1044, **N**, 180,
  Official Guide, **C**, 1450,
  Redemption, **B**, 689,
  Verse Found on Bill, **C**, 878
Curry, Jabez Lamar Monroe, Lt.Col.; **A**, 148, **R**, 350
Curtis-Lee Mansion, VA; **N**, 57
Cushing, Edward Hopkins; **C**, 1608, **T**, 202
Cushman, George F., Rev.; **A**, 96
Cushman, Joseph D., Jr.; **E**, 219
Custer's Raid; **M**, 1069

Custer, George Armstrong, Maj.Gen.; **C**, 337, **G**, 454, **M**, 1222, **S**, 429
Custis, G.W.P., Mrs.; **F**, 204
Cutrer, Thomas W.; **G**, 452
Cutts' Battery; **C**, 46
Cycloramas; **J**, 91,
  Gettysburg, PA, **G**, 192,

D

Dabney, Robert Lewis; **J**, 242
Dade County, GA;
    Secession from Georgia, **C**, 1303
Daffan, Lawrence Aylett; **D**, 15
Dahlgren's Raid; **B**, 341, **C**, 15, 1483, **J**, 82, **M**, 367d, **R**, 424, **W**, 162
Dahlgren, Ulric, Col.; **A**, 534, **C**, 337, **F**, 355, **H**, 184, **S**, 1333,
    Fredericksburg, VA, **C**, 1452
Dahlonega Mint; **K**, 192c
Daingerfield, Foxhall A., Capt.; **D**, 23, **R**, 682
Dale County, AL; **F**, 237
Dallas County, AL; **S**, 150
Dallas Light Artillery; **G**, 690
Dalton, GA; **J**, 2,
    Snowball Battle, **G**, 390,
    Winter Quarters, **M**, 697
Dalton, J. Frank; **C**, 1092
Dalton-Atlanta Campaign; **J**, 285, **S**, 1144
Damn Yankee Rifles; **A**, 554
Dance & Brothers Gunmakers; **W**, 618
Dance, Willis Jefferson, Lt.; **V**, 147
Dandridge, S.W.; **S**, 1164
Daniel, Dock, Lt.; **D**, 69, **M**, 237
Daniel, Edward M.; **D**, 58
Daniel, John Warwick, Lt.Col.; **A**, 450, 486, **C**, 371, **D**, 56, 216, **E**, 29, **G**, 401, **J**, 192, **T**, 279
Daniel, Junius, Brig.Gen.; **B**, 583
Daniel, L.E.; **M**, 462
Daniel, Lizzie Cary; **C**, 1001
Daniel, Raleigh T.; **D**, 76
Daniel, Robert; **G**, 10
Daniel, W. Harrison; **D**, 1
Daniels, John M.; **B**, 11, **C**, 1181, **W**, 678
Daniels, Selby A.; **C**, 387

Dannelly, Elizabeth; **D**, 549
Dantzler, F.W.; **W**, 896
Danville Blues;
    Uniforms, **U**, 14
Danville, VA;
    Last Capital, **B**, 826, 1437, **XYZ**, 57
Darby, Jemima; **C**, 348
Darden, Annie B.; **P**, 112
Darien, GA; **K**, 178,
    Burning of, **C**, 1307
Darlington County, SC; **B**, 1462
Daugett, Annie F.; **A**, 116
Daughter of the Confederacy; **D**, 381
Daves, Graham, Maj.; **A**, 569, **T**, 418
David (submarine); **C**, 1033, **E**, 58, **M**, 21
Davidson, Greenlee, Capt.; **D**, 123
Davidson, J.O.; **A**, 101
Davidson, Nora Fontaine M.; **D**, 133
Davidson, Theresa Sherrer; **D**, 121
Daviess, Joseph H., Col.; **D**, 141
Davis Historical Foundation (Jefferson); **A**, 321
Davis Legion; **R**, 678
Davis' Bridge, MS, Battle of; **D**, 878
Davis, Curtis Carroll; **B**, 991
Davis, Ezekiel; **C**, 693
Davis, Frances; **C**, 693
Davis, Fredonia; **C**, 693
Davis, George; **G**, 576, **S**, 958,
    Monument, **C**, 1099
Davis, J.C.B.; **R**, 512a
Davis, Jefferson, Mrs.; **B**, 1058, **C**, 1602, **K**, 9, **M**, 522
Davis, Jefferson, Pres.; **A**, 2, 58, 97, 451, 575, **B**, 76, 708, 732, 740, 767, 792, 796, 863, 1266, 1378, 1381, 1440, 1636, **C**, 28, 49, 125, 232, 446, 659, 1619, **D**, 41, 68, 125, 208, 324, 424, 438, 663, 683, 744, **E**, 54, 67,

141, 232, **F**, 11, 83, **G**, 32-33, 229, 379, 567, 569, 582, 605, **H**, 114, 204, 393, 566, 762, 811, 1134, **J**, 71, 98, 192, 221, 227, 291, 336, 393, 468, 474, 559, 579, **K**, 239, **L**, 102, 110, 134a, 310, 625, 712, 755, **M**, 118, 174, 252, 367f, 521, 523, 688, 711c, 907-909, 1068, 1170, 1196, **O**, 111, 175, 233, **P**, 266, 277, 668, 841, **R**, 1a, 90a, 712, 721, 848, **S**, 85, 103, 307, 313, 700, 1066, 1296-1297, 1343, **V**, 26, 51, 54, 66, 79a, **W**, 573a, 650-651, 697, 852, 976,
Administration, T, 406,
Amnesty, B, 764, J, 537,
Analysis of Speeches, A, 465,
Andersonville, GA, F, 251,
Anniversary, S, 1242,
Atlanta Campaign, H, 557,
Bail, B, 1436, S, 641,
Beauvoir, MS, B, 1599, D, 187, E, 263,
Bibliography, T, 43,
Biography, S, 360,
Birthday, N, 88a,
Brierfield Estate, E, 267,
Brother's Will, M, 1194,
Cabinet, H, 698, K, 62, P, 140,
Capture, B, 104, C, 863, D, 610, F, 455, L, 754, P, 81, R, 164, W, 141, 805a,
Character, H, 210, K, 162, S, 658,
Choice as President, R, 382,
Citizenship, M, 244, W, 218,
Collapse of Confederacy, W, 581,
Comparison to Lincoln, R, 849-854,
Comparisons, E, 270,
Confederate Patronage, T, 408,
Constitutional Rights, E, 271,
Constitutionalist, R, 764, W, 193,
Correspondence, C, 1218, M, 156, V, 108, W, 683,
Death, D, 232,
Diseases, E, 262,
Early Life, F, 244,
Escape Attempt, S, 1017,
European Convoy, H, 713,
First Marriage, F, 245, W, 291,
Fort Monroe, VA, A, 67,
Freed, A, 508, H, 454,
Funeral Train, T, 190,
Genealogy, W, 581,
Generalship, C, 1226,
Hampton Roads Peace Conference, G, 352,
Health, R, 475a,
Hill-Blaine Debate, C, 1289,
House, C, 968,
Imprisonment, S, 315-316, U, 35,
Inaugural Speech, C, 1321-1322,
Inauguration, C, 867,
Last Official Meeting, R, 579,
Lawsuit, B, 1493,
Library, Personal, C, 1443,
Life, M, 901, P, 527, W, 297,
Lincoln's Assassination, C, 651, D, 180,
Literary Career, T, 33,
Memorial, D, 619, J, 466, XYZ, 50,
Military Career, M, 3, T, 33,
Misrepresented, H, 1135,
Mississippi Bonds, H, 246,
Montgomery, AL, W, 1019,
Monument, C, 1071,
Overtaken, W, 805,
Papers, H, 469, J, 606, R, 760-761, S, 1296,
Patriotism, M, 1316, 1319,
Political Vindication, E, 324,
Pope, R, 635,
Portrait, R, 768,
Post-war, M, 1273,
Postage Stamps, M, 113-114,
Pre-war Statesmanship, J, 122,
Prison Life, B, 1078-1084, C, 1356, 1403, S, 409, 1179, T, 94,
Propaganda, C, 1542,
Prosecution (1867), A, 548,
Public Services, O, 88,
Release Petition, P, 312,
Religion, F, 250, W, 937,
Rescue Attempt, H, 183, W, 507,
Richmond, VA, K, 161,
Rise & Fall. . . Conf. Govt., B, 1493,
Sectionalism, S, 1109,

Davis, Jefferson, Pres.

Slavery, **E**, 235, **W**, 74,
Song, **H**, 486,
Speeches, **D**, 57, **R**, 384,
State Relations, **B**, 558,
Theories, **S**, 1108,
Trial, **E**, 269, **H**, 18, **M**, 1303, **N**, 129, **R**, 168, **S**, 12, 127, 729, **W**, 276,
UCV Address, **R**, 833,
Unseen Message, **J**, 315,
Vindication, **S**, 11,
vs. Lincoln, **W**, 402
West Point, **F**, 247,
West Point, Teaches Secession, **V**, 124,
Withdrawal Speech, **A**, 100,

Davis, John J.; **D**, 310
Davis, Joseph Claiborne; **D**, 153
Davis, Joseph E.; **M**, 1184
Davis, Moses; **C**, 693
Davis, Oscar L.; **D**, 194
Davis, Robert McElroy; **W**, 695
Davis, Sam; **B**, 1399, **C**, 1584, 1587, **F**, 457, 483, **H**, 132, 906, **K**, 144, **M**, 441, 779, **P**, 612, **R**, 701, 756, **T**, 228, **W**, 577, 638
Davis, Sarah Knox Taylor; **S**, 477, **W**, 291
Davis, Varina Anne Jefferson; **T**, 353
Davis, Varina Howell, Mrs.; **B**, 1601
Davis, William G.M., Brig.Gen.; **D**, 320
Davis, William J.; **J**, 154
Davis, William T.; **D**, 153
Davis, Winnie; **F**, 89
Davis-Hood-Johnston Controversy; **H**, 563
Davis-Stephens Feud; **H**, 510
Dawson, Francis Warrington; **D**, 389
Dawson, George W., Capt.; **D**, 393
Day, James M.; **G**, 529
Day, Samuel Phillips; **D**, 401
Day, Walter E.; **C**, 74
Dayton, Ruth Woods; **H**, 73
De Facto Government; **J**, 173
De Gress Battery; **R**, 641
De Leon, Edwin; **B**, 687, **C**, 1542

De Renne, George Wymberly Jones, Mrs.; **D**, 55
Deasy, Edmond J.; **A**, 492
Deasy, Ella J.; **A**, 492
DeBow, James Dunwoody Brownston; **S**, 550, **W**, 310
DeBray's Cavalry; **D**, 408, 473, **E**, 73
DeBray, Xavier Blanchard, Brig.Gen.; **E**, 73
Debts; **S**, 142, **T**, 175
Decatur County, GA; **D**, 477
Declaration of Independence; **K**, 101
Declaration of Independence, South Carolina; **S**, 833
Deer Creek Expedition; **R**, 502
Defense Strategy; **S**, 974
DeKalb County, TN;
  History, **H**, 58
DeLagnel, Julius Adolph, Brig.Gen.; Rich Mountain, WV, **S**, 689
Delane, John Thadeus; **W**, 580
Delaney, Norman; **A**, 397
Delta Rifles; **B**, 995, **C**, 1379
Democracy; **B**, 847
Democratic Conventions; **C**, 1242, **E**, 176, **G**, 568, **H**, 659, **S**, 777
Democratic Party; **M**, 1295
Democratic Senate; **H**, 140
Democrats; **B**, 52, **C**, 781
Demoralization; **S**, 108
Dempster, Ann; **E**, 106
Denn, George H.; **E**, 44
Dennis, Frank Allen; **H**, 1026
Dent, John Horry; **M**, 332a
Dentists; **F**, 313, **H**, 944
Deparment of Justice; **C**, 1038
Department of Mississippi & East Louisiana; **J**, 310
Department of Tennessee;
  Medical Department, **C**, 592
Derelicts; **S**, 957
Derry, Joseph T.; **C**, 274
Desertion; **B**, 111, 926, **C**, 265, **D**, 548, **L**, 670, **M**, 241, **R**, 251, 259
Destruction; **B**, 1309
Devereaux, J.P.; **C**, 484

Devoy, Robert; S, 820
Dew, Charles B.; A, 333
Dew, Thomas Roderick; B, 893, H, 434
Dial, pub.; F, 253
Diamond Hoax; H, 342
Diana Notes; R, 22
Dickenson County, VA; S, 1410
Dickinson, Elizabeth B.; S, 934
Dickinson, Festus; S, 934
Dickison, John Jackson, Col.; D, 587, W, 348
Dickson County, TN;
 Slavery, C, 1257
Dickson, William, Rev.; F, 171
Didier, Eugene; S, 890
Diggs, Lucy Ann; T, 442
Dinkins, James; C, 540
Diseases;
 Gangrene, J, 488,
 Malaria, J, 495
Dispatches; P, 834,
 Stuart, James Ewell B., Maj.Gen., S, 1329
District of Columbia; D, 723
Disunion; A, 549
Ditch Bayou, AR, Battle of; S, 318
Dix, Mary Seaton; D, 243
Dixie (song); B, 106, M, 363a, S, 657
Dixie Bill; B, 506
Dixie Buckles; B, 1255
Dixie Grays; S, 989
Dixie Readers; M, 1089-1091
Dixie, Origin of; P, 350
Dixon, Archibald; B, 96
Dixon, Kitt; B, 1490
Doctors; C, 1579, H, 464a,
 Woman, H, 550
Documentaries; XYZ, 24
Dodd, David O.; F, 160, H, 730, 1012, P, 59, V, 87
Dodd, Harrison H.; P, 419
Dodd, Henry Martyn; B, 880
Dodd, William E.; O, 228
Dodge, David; B, 756
Doles-Cook Brigade; T, 206
Doll Collection; G, 416
Dona Ana County, NM;
 Confederate Dead, W, 43-44
Donaldsonville Artillery; L, 72
Doniphan Expedition; B, 1185
Doniphan, Alexander W., Brig.Gen.; C, 1543
Doolady, M.; D, 225, 768
Dooley, John Edward; D, 979
Dornbusch, Charles E.; B, 672
Dorris, Jonathan Truman; C, 434
Doubleday's Campaign; A, 213
Douglas Battery; G, 311
Douglas Letters; T, 429
Douglas' Church, TN, Battle of; S, 1002
Douglas, Lucia R.; T, 429
Douglas, Stephen A.; C, 148, F, 440, J, 135, M, 327, 897, T, 542
Dove Creek, TX, Battle of; H, 1312, P, 610
Dover, TN, Battle of; C, 1199
Dow, Neal, Brig.Gen.; B, 1645
Dowling, Richard W., Lt.; M, 1271, N, 217, P, 696, S, 9, 334, 1384,
 Sabine Pass, Tx, T, 336
Downingville Militia; D, 827
Drake, James H., Mrs.; C, 948
Dranesville, VA, Battle of; H, 171
Draper, Lyman; H, 754
Dreaux's Cavalry; S, 539
Dred Scott Case; A, 546, C, 320, 1094, F, 396, H, 17
Dreux, Charles Didier, Col.; D, 513, M, 841
Dreux-Rightor Battalion; D, 814
Drew, John Thompson; M, 525
Drewry's Bluff, VA; C, 692, K, 17a, M, 1178
Drewry's Bluff, VA, Battle of; B, 432, 441, 483, H, 24, 26, 972, L, 582,
 Errors Corrected, S, 1396
Driftwood, Jimmy; M, 1334
Drill & Bayonet Exercise; C, 255
Drills, Artillery; A, 371
Droop Mountain, WV, Battle of; C, 1159
Drugs; C, 1533, J, 74,
 Supplies, F, 465-469
Drunks; N, 49

Dry Creek, WV, Battle of; **R**, 306
DuBose, William Porcher; **G**, 688
Duck River; **B**, 1232
Duels; **C**, 1290, **H**, 118, 1246, **M**, 37
Duffy, John; **C**, 571
Dufor, Charles L.; **W**, 497
Dug Gap, GA, Battle of; **P**, 198
Dugan, Irwin, Mrs.; **M**, 785
Duke of Sonora; **S**, 1250
Duke, Basil Wilson, Brig.Gen.; **A**, 550, **H**, 416, 703
Dunbar (ship); **R**, 350b
Duncan, Alexander M., Lt.; **U**, 18
Duncan, Bartlett Marshall; **U**, 46
Dundee, Scotland; **C**, 207
Dunlop, James N.; **A**, 450, **D**, 954
Dunning, William Archibald; **H**, 349, **S**, 1342
Duplin's Rifles; **S**, 542
Durham, NC;
  Close of War, **S**, 10
Durkin, Joseph T.; **D**, 745
Dutch Gap, VA;
  Negro Soldiers, **S**, 796
Dutcher, Salem; **C**, 1552, **W**, 760
Duval County, FL; **C**, 41, **H**, 537
Dye, Henry L.; **E**, 193
Dye, John H., Capt.; **T**, 415
Dyer, Amelia W.; **D**, 1000

E

Eagleton, George E., Rev.; **P**, 194a
Eakin, John R.; **S**, 711
Eames, Wilberforce; **B**, 1257
Early's Brigade; **E**, 36
Early's Raid; **D**, 943, **G**, 332, **V**, 53
Early's Valley Campaign; **B**, 1585, **L**, 619
Early, Jubal Anderson, Lt.Gen.; **A**, 165, **B**, 7, 1098-1099, 1616, 1620, **C**, 501, 1143, **D**, 62, **E**, 9, 11, **G**, 71, 341, **K**, 253a, **M**, 679, **S**, 1406, **W**, 409
Easter Fair; **W**, 245
Eastern Theatre; **A**, 315
Eastern Virginia Campaign; **B**, 1458
Eastman, Seth; **U**, 42
Eastport, MS;
   History, **K**, 206a
Eaton, Clement; **S**, 529
Ebenezer Church, GA, Battle of; **C**, 1118
Echols' Artillery; **R**, 232, **T**, 180
Economics; **B**, 681, 756, 876, 975, 1557, **C**, 837, 1263, **D**, 394, 690, 945, **G**, 121, 284, 572, **H**, 549, **K**, 137, **R**, 530, **S**, 142, 144, 235, **W**, 1013,
   Cycle, **C**, 1083,
   Florida, **C**, 624, **H**, 537,
   Georgia, **B**, 213,
   Mississippi, **E**, 45,
   North Carolina, **B**, 1009,
   Secession, **R**, 17, **S**, 1243,
   Slavery, **H**, 859, **L**, 696,
   South, **J**, 130,
   South Carolina, **S**, 851, **V**, 19,
   Trade, **D**, 35
Ector's Brigade; **T**, 334
Ector's Cavalry; **B**, 34
Edgar, George, Col.; **S**, 1361
Edgefield County, SC; **C**, 409

Edgefield, SC; **C**, 512,
   Roster, **W**, 944
Edisto Rifles; **H**, 31, **I**, 58, **S**, 34
Editorials; **F**, 520
Edmonds, George (pseudonym); **M**, 793
Edmonds, J.E., Maj.; **W**, 920
Edrington, Angelina Selden; **E**, 89
Edrington, Mary; **E**, 89
Education; **M**, 919,
   Free School for Orphans, **G**, 347,
   North Carolina, **K**, 232,
   School History, **M**, 504,
   South, **F**, 310,
   Teachers, **L**, 532
Edwards, J.N., Maj.; **T**, 333
Edwards, Mike; **S**, 304
Egyptian Cotton; **E**, 4
El Paso, TX; **W**, 116,
   Cannon Captured, **F**, 127
Elbert County, GA; **J**, 561
Elberton, GA; **A**, 86
Elder, John; **C**, 1207, **S**, 485
Elder, William Henry, Bishop; **W**, 620
Elections; **B**, 1340, **C**, 1425, 1427, **L**, 518, **M**, 590, 1006, **O**, 241, **R**, 169,
   (1868), **C**, 781,
   Breckinridge-Lane, **A**, 64,
   Georgia, Gubernatorial, **B**, 214,
   Virginia, **B**, 1292
Elephants; **W**, 591
Elizabethtown, KY; **B**, 369
Elkhorn Tavern, AR; **M**, 1037,
   Campaign, **M**, 349,
   History, **B**, 862
Elkhorn Tavern, AR, Battle of; **J**, 415, **K**, 119a,
   Van Dorn, Earl, Maj.Gen., **V**, 22
Ella & Annie (ship); **P**, 736

Eller, E.M., Adm.; **J**, 541
Ellett, Thomas, Capt.; **XYZ**, 58
Elliott Grays; **W**, 600
Elliott's Brigade; **M**, 634
Elliott, M.A., Mrs.; **U**, 37
Elliott, Stephen, Bishop; **P**, 249
Elliott, Stephen, Jr., Brig.Gen.; **B**, 204, **G**, 688, **H**, 146-147, **T**, 397
Elliott, William; **J**, 507
Ellis, E. John; **T**, 480
Ellis, Frampton Erroll; **E**, 170
Ellis, John Tracy; **G**, 39
Ellison, Rhoda; **A**, 105
Elm Creek, TX;
  Raid, **N**, 50
Elmira Prison, NY; **H**, 1016, 1352, **R**, 567, **S**, 972,
  Roster, **L**, 560
Elmore, Edward C.; **C**, 154
Elmore, Stanton, Col.; **B**, 1419
Elmwood Cemetery, Memphis, TN; **B**, 229
Elmwood Cemetery, Norfolk, VA; **C**, 895, **G**, 87
Elmwood Cemetery, Shepherdstown, WV; **H**, 700, **M**, 778, **O**, 191
Emancipation; **B**, 621, **F**, 212, **N**, 161
Emancipation Proclamation; **M**, 1241, **S**, 238, **T**, 302, **V**, 129
Emmett, Daniel Decatur; **G**, 22, 477, **K**, 8, **M**, 363a
Encyclopedia Brittanica;
  Critcisims, **O**, 80-81
Enfield Guns; **S**, 1449
Engineer Bureau; **C**, 871, **R**, 320
Engineer Corps; **H**, 961
Engineer Troops;
  1st Regt., **R**, 248, **V**, 106,
  Paroles, **T**, 10
Engineers; **B**, 855, **C**, 871, 1419, **E**, 180, **H**, 715, 961, **J**, 219, **K**, 58, **M**, 35, 763, **N**, 119-120, **R**, 489, 613, **S**, 784, **T**, 5, 12, **V**, 106, **W**, 981,
  Morris Island, **C**, 1271
England; **A**, 47, 93, 104, **B**, 611, **C**, 679, **G**, 516-517, 626, **R**, 770,
  Alabama (ironclad), Claims, **C**, 1270,
  Blockade-in Theory, **S**, 521,
  Blockades, **H**, 1087,
  British House Commons, **B**, 1270,
  Cabinet, **G**, 513, **M**, 800,
  Christian Character, **A**, 458,
  Civil War, Policy, **A**, 36,
  Claims, **M**, 975,
  Committee of Manchester, **B**, 751,
  Confederate Agents, **C**, 1273,
  Confederate Consuls, **B**, 877, 976,
  Confederate Finance, **L**, 450,
  Confederate Purchases, **L**, 450,
  Conservatives, **J**, 558,
  Criticism, Lincoln, **W**, 684,
  Intervention, **A**, 50, **T**, 108,
  Labor, **H**, 442,
  Mediation, **B**, 1176,
  Neutral Powers, **S**, 1266,
  Neutrality, **B**, 636a, 639, **G**, 284, **K**, 137,
  Newspapers, Southern, **D**, 575,
  Secession, Opinions of, **C**, 1470,
  Slavery, **O**, 113,
  Soldiers, **B**, 1270,
  South's Debt, **C**, 1275,
  South, View of, **F**, 263,
  Sympathizers, **B**, 1296, **H**, 734, **J**, 602, **W**, 117,
  Working Class' Attitudes, **L**, 593
English Parliamentary Papers; **D**, 670
English Soldiers; **B**, 244, 267
Enlistments;
  Foreign; **A**, 110,
  Negro, **S**, 941
Enloe, Abraham; **C**, 316
Eno, Clara Barton;
  Collection, **A**, 422
Envelopes; **M**, 109-110
Episcopal Church; **H**, 919
Erlanger Loan; **G**, 152
Erosophic & Philomathic Societies; **C**, 99
Erwin, John Seymour; **E**, 228
Escambia County, FL; **U**, 38
Escapes; **B**, 1186, 1546
Esposito, Vincent J.; **S**, 1050
Espy, Harriett Newell; **V**, 40
Estes, Claud; **L**, 541

Estvan, Bela; **C**, 879, **D**, 494
Etchings, Confederate; **B**, 762
Etheridge Conspiracy; **B**, 551
Euphradian Society; **A**, 590
Europe; **J**, 569, **S**, 885,
 Confederate Navy, **S**, 938, **T**, 329,
 Confederate Property, **M**, 463,
 Kenner's Mission, **K**, 83,
 Manley's Mission, **M**, 155,
 Propaganda, Europe, **C**, 1541,
 Recognition of South, **J**, 614,
 Secret Service, **B**, 1548,
 Southern Historical Society Papers,
  S, 117
European Brigade; **U**, 14
Eustis, George, Jr.; **T**, 389
Evans, Augusta Jane; **F**, 100
Evans, Clement Anselm, Brig.Gen.;
 A, 566, **C**, 362, **D**, 540, 668, **U**, 25
Evans, Lemuel Dale; **S**, 131
Evans, Media; **P**, 112
Evans, Samuel, Capt.;
 Texas Scouts, **A**, 414
Eve, F. Edgeworth, Capt.;
 Georgia,
  Military Operations, **J**, 389
Everett, Edward; **A**, 547
Evermore, Tulip; **P**, 30a
Eves, Cora Semmes, Mrs.; **L**, 21
Ewell's Corps; **B**, 208
Ewell's Division; **B**, 1352
Ewell, Eleanor M.B.; **E**, 283
Ewell, Richard Stoddert, Lt.Gen.; **B**,
 350, 1351-1353, **C**, 247, **E**, 284, 287-
 290, **H**, 163-164-164a, 403,
 Correspondence, **V**, 14,
 Loses Leg, **B**, 1355
Ewing, Henry, Maj.; **C**, 1493
Exchelman, B.F., Col.; **S**, 545
Executions; **A**, 334, **B**, 176, 665, 671,
 D, 566, **M**, 157, 1232, **P**, 261, **R**, 881,
 W, 222,
 Hangings, **D**, 786,
 Sermon of, **P**, 60
Exemption Acts; **S**, 314
Exiles; **R**, 680
Explosives; **E**, 261, **H**, 573
Express (ship); **B**, 994

F

Factories;
  Exposé of Conditions, **C**, 221
Fahsel, C.D.; **B**, 1178
Fair Oaks, VA; **T**, 101
Fair Oaks, VA, Battle of; **B**, 1220
Fairchild, Lucius; **D**, 140
Fairfax Courthouse, VA;
  Night Attack, **J**, 106,
  Skirmish at, **S**, 744
Fairfax Courthouse, VA, Battle of; **M**, 489
Fairfax, Randolph; **S**, 560
Fairfax, VA;
  Monument, **F**, 7
Fairfield, PA;
  Cavalry, **P**, 835
Falling Waters, MD; **H**, 768
Falls Church, VA, Battle of; **W**, 591
Fannin County, TX; **D**, 961
Farming; **J**, 582d
Farmington, MS, Battle of; **R**, 811
Farmville, VA;
  Hospital, **W**, 551
Farnsworth, Elon John, Brig.Gen.;
  Death, **P**, 838
Farragut, David G., Adm.; **K**, 89
Faulkner, William; **H**, 1198, **O**, 3
Fauntleroy, James H.; **F**, 49
Fauquier County, VA; **G**, 441, **R**, 33
Fay, Lucy E.; **F**, 52
Fayette Artillery; **B**, 831, **G**, 14
Fayette County, WV; **D**, 738
Fayette Independent Light Infantry; **M**, 703
Fayetteville Independent Light Infantry; **M**, 30
Fayetteville Rifles; **S**, 1365
Fayetteville Road, NC; **N**, 194
Fayetteville, AR; **F**, 58, **W**, 149,
  Cemetery, **M**, 792
Fayetteville, NC; **A**, 326, **D**, 116, **W**, 150,
  Arsenal, **A**, 319, 323, **T**, 57
Fayetteville, NC, Battle of; **D**, 858
Featherston, N.R.; **C**, 772
Federal Fleet, Attempt to Sell; **W**, 1024
Federal Government; **B**, 1465
Federal Military Reoccupation of SW Texas; **A**, 520
Federal Trade; **F**, 612
Federal War Party; **M**, 1154
Federalism, Southern; **A**, 295
Feminism; **M**, 322
Fenner's Battalion; **F**, 81
Ferguson, Champ; **H**, 48, **R**, 452, **S**, 261
Ferguson, John L.; **H**, 168
Ficklin, Benjamin Franklin, Maj.; **M**, 853
Field Artillery; **H**, 615, **K**, 111, **N**, 220, **W**, 364a,
  Officers, **C**, 75
Field Manual; **C**, 916
Field Medical Service; **C**, 1580
Field Officers; **E**, 244, **M**, 762,
  Roster, **L**, 548
Fielden, Wemyss; **T**, 276
Fields & Forests, Southern; **P**, 619-620
Fields, Clara, Mrs.; **A**, 103
Figg, Royal W., Lt.; **E**, 310, **W**, 525
Finances; **A**, 356,
  Slavery, **W**, 73
Financial Agents; **D**, 154
Fingal (ship); **M**, 745
Finke, Detmar H.; **W**, 108
Finley, Jesse Johnson, Brig.Gen.; **F**, 71

Finn's Point National Cemetery, Salem, NJ; **P**, 567
Firearms; **F**, 586,
    Abroad, **S**, 1449,
    Development, **H**, 1171,
    Encyclopedia, **A**, 120-121
First at Bethel; **W**, 373
First Shots; **E**, 311, **F**, 587, **G**, 204, **H**, 116, **M**, 367f, **R**, 794-795
First White House Association; **F**, 140
Fishboat (ship); **S**, 993
Fishers Hill, VA; **C**, 1078, **M**, 1117a
Fishers Hill, VA, Battle of; **B**, 1092, **E**, 12, 42, **L**, 94, **W**, 403
Fitch, Charles, Dr.; **C**, 519
Fitzhugh, William H., Gen.; **A**, 450
Fitzpatrick, Amanda Olive E.W., Mrs.; **F**, 206
Fitzpatrick, Benjamin, Gov., AL; **K**, 54a
Five Forks, VA, Battle of; **C**, 174, **H**, 1355, **S**, 1280
Flags; **B**, 1615, **C**, 906-907, **F**, 218, **H**, 208a, **M**, 222, 304, 306, 1024, 1086, **N**, 109, **O**, 188, 192-195, 210, **P**, 201, 355, 429, 698, **R**, 128, 247, 355, 646, **S**, 37a, 689a, **T**, 170, **V**, 76, **W**, 189, 707, 737,
    Alabama, **A**, 100,
    Arkansas, **E**, 168,
    Arkansas Gallery, **A**, 429,
    Battle, **C**, 12, 193, 481, 908, 1484, **F**, 214, **M**, 369, 394, 805a, **R**, 324a,
    Battle, Army of Tennessee, **M**, 44, 47,
    Black, **D**, 30,
    Bonnie Blue, **M**, 396,
    Cadets, **N**, 5,
    Claiborne Guards, **C**, 562,
    Colors, **E**, 209,
    Confederate, **B**, 133, **C**, 125a, 449, 453, 1299, **F**, 213, **G**, 564, **J**, 171, **R**, 324a,
    Confederate, Designed, **H**, 1279,
    Confederate, First, **C**, 1278, **M**, 206, **S**, 683,
    Confederate, Last, **C**, 908, **L**, 122,
    Confederate, Origin, **C**, 9-10,
    Confederate, Seven Star, **C**, 914,
    Confederate, Washington, **C**, 912,
    Georgia, **B**, 319, **G**, 183,
    History, **C**, 454,
    Illustrations, **C**, 883,
    Independence, **H**, 1201,
    Nighthawk Rangers, **N**, 72,
    Recaptured, **H**, 29,
    Returned, **A**, 234, **C**, 764, **F**, 214, **L**, 48, **M**, 349,
    Secession, **C**, 449, **S**, 731,
    Song Book, **M**, 1116,
    South Carolina, Secession, **B**, 1075,
    Stars & Bars, **B**, 1162, **S**, 704-705, 814,
    Stars & Bars Committee, **S**, 816,
    Stars & Stripes, **H**, 440,
    Texas Lones Star, **B**, 1623,
    Truce, **F**, 589, **J**, 553, **W**, 174,
    Virginia, List, **C**, 911
Fleet Engagement, First; **B**, 1597
Fleetwood, VA, Battle of; **M**, 412
Fleming, C. Seton, Capt.; **F**, 231
Fleming, Elvis E.; **W**, 806
Fleming, Walter Lynwood; **A**, 349a, **B**, 698, **G**, 574, **S**, 1342, **W**, 660
Fletcher, Inglis; **C**, 831
Floating Mines; **S**, 297
Florence Prison, SC; **K**, 172
Florence, SC;
    Stockade, **W**, 942
Florida; **B**, 673, **D**, 585, 587, 674, **F**, 278, **J**, 141-142, 356, **R**, 309a, **T**, 361,
    Burial Lists, **P**, 573,
    Campaign, **B**, 1003, **D**, 608-609,
    Cattle, **T**, 71,
    Confederate Dead, **C**, 360, **D**, 134,
    Confederate Shrine, **G**, 114,
    Conventions, **F**, 277, **J**, 591,
    Cotton, **D**, 675,
    Cotton Mill Campaign, **G**, 639,
    Cuba, Relations with, **C**, 1277,
    Desertion, **R**, 259,
    Designations, **P**, 574,
    Economics, **C**, 624,
    Episcopal Church, **C**, 1611,

Florida

Heroes, **S**, 792,
History, Military, **D**, 586,
House of Representatives, **J**, 593,
Laws, **S**, 789,
Lawyers, **D**, 320,
Legislature, **F**, 285,
Medicine, **S**, 1259,
Railroads, **C**, 623, **T**, 220,
Reconstruction, **D**, 379, **R**, 443,
Roster, **S**, 789,
Salt-making, **L**, 673, **P**, 797,
Secession, **D**, 332, 676, **F**, 284, **M**, 541, **R**, 260, 789, **S**, 211, **W**, 965,
Soldiers, **H**, 1114, **I**, 23, **R**, 558,
Textile Manufacturing, **S**, 426,
Third Conquest, History, **H**, 267,
War Preparations, **B**, 674
Florida (ship); **A**, 94, **B**, 1019, 1167a, **C**, 1387, **H**, 242, 790, **M**, 50, 364a, 1129, **O**, 223-224, **P**, 647, **R**, 710, **S**, 528, **W**, 731
Florida Brigade; **F**, 232
Florida Troops;
  Cavalry,
    5th Regt., **R**, 533,
  Infantry,
    2nd Regt., **F**, 233,
    3rd Regt., **C**, 360,
    4th Regt., **I**, 61,
    7th Regt., Vol., **A**, 71,
  Virginia, **F**, 231
Floyd County, GA; **B**, 240
Floyd, John Buchanan, Brig.Gen.; **B**, 1525, **G**, 673
Floyd, John, Gov., VA; **A**, 280
Fogle, Andrew J.; **L**, 465a
Foley, J.H.; **J**, 31
Folk Culture; **W**, 1069
Folly Islands, SC; **G**, 254
Folmar, John Kent; **W**, 721
Folmsbee, Stanley J.; **T**, 117
Fontaine, Felix Gregory de; **D**, 412-416, **F**, 1, **H**, 1207
Fontaine, Francis; **F**, 328
Food; **J**, 19, **N**, 139, **V**, 62,
  Feeding Troops, Difficulty, **K**, 16,
  Texas, **V**, 74
Foot, Andrew Hull, Adm.; **B**, 1021

Foote, Henry Stuart; **G**, 343
Foote, Shelby; **C**, 1351
Foraging;
  Atlanta, GA, **A**, 539
Ford, John S. (Rip), Maj.; **H**, 1268, **J**, 605, **K**, 266, **O**, 29, **T**, 146
Ford, Lewis de Sassure; **C**, 1042
Ford, Marion Johnstone; **F**, 344
Ford, Tennessee Ernie; **M**, 1339
Foreign Bondholders; **R**, 94
Foreign Inlistment Act; **C**, 712
Foreign Policy; **S**, 966
Foreign Relations; **S**, 1129
Foreign Supplies; **F**, 361
Foreign War, Confederacy's; **H**, 226
Foreigners; **C**, 712, **L**, 671
Foreman, Carolyn T.; **A**, 116
Forest Hill Cemetery, Madison, WI; **T**, 321
Fornell, Earl; **B**, 1476
Forney, John H., Maj.Gen.; **D**, 113
Forrest's Cavalry; **C**, 898, 1156, **D**, 630, **H**, 113, **J**, 239, **M**, 1201, 1205
Forrest's Raid; **H**, 1020, **M**, 1188
Forrest, Nathan Bedford, Lt.Gen.; **A**, 81, **B**, 355, 645, 1246, 1322, 1467, 1594, **C**, 16, 19, 36, 377, 731a, 1239, 1497, **D**, 461, 629, 633, 641, 645-646, **E**, 68, **F**, 193, **G**, 11-12, 149, 260, 278, 384, 580, **H**, 112, 248-249, 708, **J**, 279, 577, 582b, **K**, 182, **L**, 797, **M**, 137, 219, 330, 379, 441, 500, 954, 1184, **P**, 92, 420a, 476, **S**, 370, 670, **T**, 357, **W**, 356, 589, 703, 902, 1072, 1076,
  Brice's Crossroads, MS, **B**, 407, **L**, 765,
  Campaigns, **C**, 722,
  Character, **S**, 662,
  Ebenezer Church, GA, **C**, 1118,
  Johnsonville Raid, **B**, 1349,
  Memphis, TN, **M**, 1053, **R**, 148,
  Okolona, MS, **P**, 53a,
  Operations, **E**, 107,
  State Park, **W**, 704,
  West Tennessee Raid, **P**, 668a
Forrest-Gould Affair; **S**, 629

Forrest-Streight Campaign (1863); **A**, 80
Forrester, Rebel C.; **C**, 340
Fort Beauregard, LA; **M**, 949a
Fort Beauregard, SC;
  Gunboats, **L**, 588
Fort Bragg, NC; **N**, 220
Fort Caswell, NC; **H**, 741
Fort Darling, VA; **K**, 17a
Fort Davis, Ind.T.; **F**, 366
Fort De Russy, LA; **B**, 1641
Fort Delaware Prison, DE; **B**, 205, 1238, **H**, 218, **R**, 256, **S**, 1422, **W**, 816,
  Roster, **L**, 557
Fort Donelson, TN; **C**, 1204a, 1560, **G**, 695, **R**, 664, **T**, 127, **V**, 30,
  Campaign, **C**, 1198, 1202,
  Construction, **B**, 368,
  Evacuation, **R**, 299, 308,
  Fall of, **W**, 68,
  Forrest's Cavalry, **W**, 1078,
  Gunboats, **B**, 498,
  Surrender, **C**, 273,
  Virginians, **C**, 1203
Fort Donelson, TN, Battle of; **B**, 421, **F**, 300-301, **G**, 384, 673, **H**, 145, 401, **M**, 667
Fort Esperanza, TX; **F**, 197
Fort Fillmore, NM; **A**, 441, **B**, 1182, **C**, 1434, **M**, 589
Fort Fisher, NC; **H**, 639, 1199,
  Defenses, **L**, 51-55
Fort Fisher, NC, Battle of; **G**, 388, 498, **P**, 734, **S**, 1344
Fort Gibson, Ind.T.; **F**, 151
Fort Gilmer, VA; **C**, 1479, **J**, 265
Fort Gregg, SC; **R**, 363,
  Artillery, **O**, 214,
  Capture of, **S**, 1301
Fort Gregg, VA; **B**, 187,
  Defenses, **L**, 79
Fort Gregg, VA, Battle of; **J**, 351, **N**, 88a
Fort Hamby, NC; **F**, 298, **G**, 122
Fort Harrison, VA; **S**, 795
Fort Hell, VA; **P**, 310,
  Battlefield, **S**, 1246

Fort Henry, TN; **C**, 1204a, **R**, 664,
  Campaign, **C**, 1198, 1202,
  Construction, **B**, 368,
  Evacuation, **R**, 299, 308,
  Fall of, **W**, 68,
  Tilghman, Lloyd, Brig.Gen., **T**, 296
Fort Henry, TN, Battle of; **B**, 399
Fort Hindman, AR; **F**, 435
Fort Jackson, LA;
  Bombardment, **D**, 941
Fort Lafayette Prison, NY; **P**, 765, **W**, 908
Fort Lafayette, NY; **B**, 1238, **M**, 1329
Fort Lancaster, TX; **W**, 471
Fort Macon, NC; **M**, 1164
Fort Macon, NC, Battle of; **B**, 1149
Fort Mahone, VA; **O**, 168
Fort McAllister, GA; **J**, 610,
  Capture, **J**, 390
Fort McCulloch, AR; **A**, 420, **M**, 886a, **B**, 1518, **P**, 392, 397, 402, **R**, 241
Fort McHenry Prison, MD; **W**, 886
Fort Monroe, VA; **A**, 67, **P**, 151
Fort Morgan, AL; **A**, 556, **C**, 393, **P**, 12, **R**, 353
Fort Moultrie, SC; **F**, 433, **R**, 471,
  Evacuation, **W**, 540,
  First Shots, **E**, 311
Fort Myer, VA; **R**, 684
Fort Pickens, FL; **K**, 104,
  Couriers, **J**, 432
Fort Pillow, TN; **B**, 1597, **D**, 611, **M**, 86a, 139a, **W**, 1084,
  Capture, **C**, 379, **D**, 632, **F**, 186,
  Massacre, **J**, 571, **M**, 138
Fort Pillow, TN, Battle of; **A**, 297, **C**, 292, 519
Fort Pulaski, GA; **J**, 611, **O**, 103, **XYZ**, 71,
  Artillery, **C**, 318,
  Capture, **J**, 403,
  Construction of, **XYZ**, 70,
  Monument, **L**, 138
Fort Sanders, TN; **S**, 274
Fort Smith, AR; **B**, 38, 400-401, 405-406
Fort Smith, AR, Battle of; **B**, 394-395

Fort Stedman, VA;
  Gordon's Assault, W, 55
Fort Stedman, VA, Battle of; B, 1120-1121
Fort Sumter, SC; A, 5, 265, B, 144, C, 96, 139, 280, D, 137, 295, F, 339, 535, H, 588, 775, J, 219, 429, L, 483, R, 54, 147, 395, S, 913, T, 450, W, 755,
  Confederate Diplomacy, J, 226,
  Defenses, J, 215, T, 358,
  Fall of, A, 459, F, 13,
  First Casualties, S, 1419,
  First Shots, L, 192, 398, N, 101, R, 794-795,
  History, C, 1201, H, 388,
  National Monument, B, 129,
  Surrender, S, 1124,
  Washington, DC, Effects on, J, 8,
  Wigfall Mission, R, 482
Fort Sumter, SC, Battle of; C, 436, E, 83, 160, P, 79
Fort Towson, Ind.T.; M, 1175
Fort Wagner, SC; A, 407, 503, C, 152, H, 589
Fort Warren Prison, MA; B, 852, 1238, C, 1432
Fort Washita, Ind.T.; F, 144, M, 1176-1177
Fort Worth, TX; F, 25,
  Reconstruction, V, 31
Fortifications; B, 1520-1521,
  Mobile, B, 1230
Fortress Monroe, VA; B, 940, C, 666, D, 353
Fortune, Porter L.; B, 1596
Foster, Charles Henry; D, 498
Foster, John Gray, Maj.Gen.; K, 194
Foster, Wilbur Fisk, Maj.; C, 1418
Foundries; A, 436, B, 1287, R, 543, S, 1068
Foundry & Machine Works; B, 1287
Fourteen Hundred & Ninety-one Days (book); H, 632-633
France; C, 455,
  Civil War Opinion, W, 470,
  Confederacy, C, 1339-1340,
  Confederate Navy, B, 680,
  Confederate Ships Built, B, 1549,
  Intervention, H, 240, T, 108,
  Mexican War, Intervention, C, 743,
  Secession, G, 514,
  Views, S, 940
Franklin County, NC; F, 502
Franklin County, TN;
  Secession, H, 72
Franklin County, VT;
  Bank Robbery, J, 109
Franklin Guards; S, 581
Franklin, TN; W, 687,
  Battle-ground Academy, B, 226,
  Carter House, M, 536,
  Centennial, B, 263
Franklin, TN, Battle of; B, 85, 989, C, 925, 1232, 1373, 1497, 1586-1587, D, 620, 962, F, 114, 121, G, 290-291, H, 705, 1354, L, 191, M, 231, 507, 511d, 1157, O, 101, R, 568, S, 329-330, 1141,
  Carter House, R, 620,
  Johnson's Division, L, 382
Frantz, Mabel; M, 441
Fraser, Walter, Jr.; H, 9
Frayser (Frazier), C.W., Col.; J, 148
Frayser's Farm, VA, Battle of; L, 404
Frederick City, MD; F, 491, W, 34
Frederick County, MD;
  Confederate Memorial Association, C, 954
Frederick County, VA; W, 826,
  Historical Society, D, 568
Frederick, J.W.; S, 640
Frederick, MD;
  Cemetery, N, 74
Frederick, MD, Mt. Olivet Cemetery; C, 897, 954
Fredericksburg Artillery; F, 227, K, 256b
Fredericksburg, VA; D, 648, G, 373, R, 209, S, 1416, W, 486,
  Battlefields, G, 27,
  Battles of, A, 316,
  Campaign, C, 443,
  Dahlgren's Ride, D, 16,
  History, Q, 11,
  Maps, B, 1181,

Supply Line, **S**, 1332
Fredericksburg, VA, Battle of; **A**, 160, 201, 228, **B**, 51, 244, **C**, 1538, **F**, 239, **G**, 76, **H**, 670, 677, **L**, 9, 44, 91, 104, 575, 645-647, **M**, 610-611, 1067, **R**, 272, 307a, **S**, 92, 179,
  Kershaw's Brigade, **K**, 130,
  Map, **M**, 168,
  Tactics, **H**, 680
Free Trade; **C**, 456
Freedmen;
  Murdered, **C**, 644
Freedmen's Bureau; **H**, 201,
  Louisiana, **E**, 210
Freedom of Conscience; **N**, 133
Freeman, Douglas Southall; **B**, 10, 672, 1012, **D**, 8, **H**, 711, **M**, 100a
Freemasons; **B**, 956, **D**, 36, **P**, 404
Fremantle, Arthur James Lyon, Col.; **H**, 468
Fremont, John Charles, Maj.Gen.; **V**, 178,
  Pursuit of Jackson, **T**, 373, **W**, 298
French, Samuel Gibbs, Maj.Gen.; **K**, 87
Fritchie, Barbara; **J**, 243, **M**, 372
Frobel, Anne S.; **F**, 553
Front Royal, VA; **S**, 932,
  Monuments, **H**, 53
Front Royal, VA, Battle of; **D**, 742, **W**, 208
Frontier Hypothesis; **C**, 307
Frost, Donald McKay; **W**, 244
Fry, Anna M.; **R**, 632
Fry, Birkett Davenport, Brig.Gen.; **B**, 1278
Fry, Joseph, Capt.; **W**, 59
Fullam, G.J.; **A**, 102
Fuller, Richard, Dr.; **B**, 105
Fulton County, GA;
  History, **C**, 1224,
  Westview Cemetery, **C**, 1010
Funkhouser, Robert Daniel, Gen.; **A**, 486, **H**, 56
Fuzzlebug, Fritz; **D**, 951

G

Gailor, Frank M.; **Q**, 3
Gaines' Mill, VA; **H**, 823, 1337, **L**, 149
Gaines' Mill, VA, Battle of; **A**, 330, 332, **B**, 252, **C**, 1534, **H**, 832, **L**, 197, Pickett & Hood, **T**, 327
Gainesville, TX;
  Hangings, **B**, 176, **D**, 566, **R**, 881
Galbreath, Charles B.; **B**, 106
Gales, Seaton, Maj.; **A**, 308
Gallagher, Gary W.; **H**, 164a
Galvanized Yankees; **B**, 1364
Galveston & Dallas News, TX, np.; **B**, 549
Galveston Harbor, TX;
  Naval Raid, **G**, 328
Galveston, TX;
  Artillery Defenses, **D**, 111,
  Blockades, **T**, 140, 407,
  Confederate Loss & Recapture, **C**, 1548,
  Secession, **F**, 372
Galveston, TX, Battle of; **C**, 1591, **E**, 325, **F**, 474, **J**, 538
Gamblers; **XYZ**, 91
Gammage, W.L.; **M**, 441
Gantt, E.W.; **S**, 1087
GAR;
  Race Segregation, **D**, 139
Garber, A.W., Mrs.; **I**, 17
Gardner's Battery; **A**, 373
Garibaldi, Giuseppe; **B**, 1113, **L**, 727
Garnett's Brigade; **P**, 174
Garnett, John J., Col.; **B**, 1274
Garnett, Muscoe Russell Hunter; **G**, 67
Garnett, Richard Brooke, Brig.Gen.; **P**, 299
Garnett, Robert Selden, Brig.Gen.; **M**, 355, **P**, 382, 735

Garnett, Theodore S.; **M**, 369
Garrett County, MD; **R**, 122
Garrett, William Robertson; **H**, 109
Garrison, William Lloyd; **A**, 392
Gary, George W.; **C**, 384
Gaston Guards; **T**, 352
Gaston, John Thomas; **G**, 112
Gastonia, NC; **U**, 409
Gates, E.M.; **B**, 571
Gaughan, T.A., Mrs.; **B**, 1141
Gaul, Gilbert; **R**, 138
Gay, Gatewood, Mrs.; **M**, 456
Gay, Mary; **C**, 540, **F**, 124
Gayle, Richard H., Capt.; **G**, 432, **V**, 77
Gee's Infantry; **C**, 1202
Gee, John Henry, Maj.Gen.; **W**, 717
Gemmill, Chalmers L.; **C**, 622
Genealogy; **A**, 154, **B**, 61, 758, 833, 1148, 1327, **G**, 141, 669, **M**, 431, **N**, 40, **P**, 444, 540
General (locomotive); **R**, 410
General Orders; **U**, 11, **V**, 139,
  No.2, TX, **H**, 621,
  No.3 (Lee's Appointment), **C**, 1221,
  No.9, **F**, 525,
  No.12, **S**, 558,
  No.45 (Conscript Act), **C**, 1516,
  Inspector-General's Office, **W**, 151
Generals; **B**, 759, 894, 1354, **C**, 11, 1372, 1519, **D**, 657, 857, **F**, 17, **H**, 431, 782, 1332, **J**, 70, 407, **M**, 1183, 1190, **R**, 231, **S**, 373, 432, 767-768, 1263, **W**, 205,
  Arkansas, **C**, 1168a,
  British Born, **B**, 1270,
  Histories, **C**, 859,
  Kentucky, **H**, 419,
  Killed, **B**, 18,

Medical Profiles, S, 1060,
Names Confused, C, 81,
North Carolina, K, 185,
Ohio, C, 1559, 1563,
Portraits, H, 93,
Roster, J, 406c,
Souvenirs, C, 1017,
Union, S, 373, 1060,
West Virginia, S, 1353,
Youngest, H, 404, O, 115
Geneva Award; C, 890
Gentry, Meredith Poindexter; S, 1079
Geographical Commands; M, 766
Geographical Conditions, Mississippi; H, 902
Geographical Reader; M, 1092-1093
Geography; R, 350a, S, 1162
Geology; B, 1028
George, James Z., Col.; D, 181
George, Joseph, Jr.; B, 1598
Georgetown Rifle Guards; E, 199
Georgetown, SC; F, 341
Georgia; B, 884, 1483, D, 533, F, 80, J, 385, 409, M, 1359, N, 189, R, 317, S, 1103, W, 182, 352,
  Ashburn Murder Case, D, 88,
  Better Terms Argument, M, 398,
  Burial Lists, P, 575,
  CSA Officers, A, 575,
  Campaign, K, 135,
  Cavalrymen, First, H, 319,
  Churches, F, 349,
  Civil War Sites, M, 851a,
  Coastal Defenses, J, 378,
  Confederate Dead, V, 80,
  Confederate Government, B, 212,
  Confederate Records, C, 121,
  Confederate Veterans, K, 236,
  Conventions, B, 1455, M, 87,
  Cotton, J, 485,
  Courts, G, 630,
  Currency & Notes, K, 115-116,
  Department of Commerce, G, 165,
  Economics, B, 213,
  Famous Georgians, K, 237,
  Financial Operations, R, 287,
  Flags, B, 319,
  G.I. Bill, R, 537,
  Genealogical Survey, C, 962,
  Gubernatorial Elections, B, 214,
  Heroes, F, 319,
  History, A, 575, M, 760,
  House of Representatives, B, 732,
  Impressment, K, 179,
  Johnston's Campaign, J, 286, N, 88a,
  Journalism, Civil War, B, 1166,
  Land & People, M, 956,
  Leaders, H, 753,
  Legislature, R, 304,
  Literature, S, 149,
  Magazines, Early, F, 222,
  Military Cadets, C, 143,
  Military Districts, B, 771,
  Military Operations, J, 404b,
  Militia, B, 1387, H, 746,
  Mountain Campaigns, B, 1396,
  Navy (1861), A, 397,
  Nullification, C, 1304,
  Oratory, S, 1161,
  Peace, T, 19,
  Peace Resolution, H, 76,
  Pensions, XYZ, 61,
  Platform (1850), J, 111,
  Politics, F, 79,
  Railroads, B, 730, M, 567, 1259,
  Reconstruction, B, 1547, 1550, C, 121,
  Religion, C, 1279,
  Role in Civil War, C, 535,
  Roster, B, 1264, L, 27, R, 732a,
  Schoolteachers, L, 532,
  Secession, A, 56, B, 1485, G, 493, 585, H, 913, K, 168, P, 146,
  Secession Convention, J, 231, S, 1097, 1099, W, 966,
  Sherman's March, D, 452, 832, L, 168, S, 143a,
  Slavery, C, 124, E, 233, M, 984,
  Soldiers, C, 411, D, 588, H, 688, I, 26,
  State Line, B, 1142a,
  States Rights, F, 274,
  Suppliers, D, 335,
  Uniforms, D, 724,
  West Point Graduates, N, 75,

Georgia

Women, M, 406
Georgia (ship); A, 94, M, 1324, R, 276, S, 1138a
Georgia Brigade; B, 1106-1108
Georgia Hussars; D, 933, R, 678, Uniforms, U, 14
Georgia Military Institute; H, 998, XYZ, 14,
  Cadet Battalion, R, 633, 639
Georgia Troops; S, 1362,
  Artillery,
    1st Regt., W, 16,
    9th Bat., H, 411,
  Cavalry,
    2nd Regt., M, 1348,
    4th Regt., G, 164,
    5th Regt., G, 167,
    6th Regt., M, 904,
  Infantry,
    1st Regt., M, 1350, R, 145, S, 1215,
    1st Regt. Vols., C, 133, O, 108,
    1st Regt., Reg., A, 375,
    3rd Regt., L, 530, S, 760, T, 125,
    4th Regt., W, 533,
    6th Regt., C, 1473,
    8th Regt., XYZ, 94,
    12th Regt., T, 206, W, 778, 780,
    11th Regt., W, 213,
    12th Regt., P, 82, S, 1362,
    13th Regt., A, 55,
    15th Regt., D, 851,
    18th Regt., B, 208,
    19th Regt., B, 342,
    20th Regt., G, 179,
    26th Regt., C, 785, M, 1312,
    31st Regt., M, 1347,
    30th Regt., A, 55,
    38th Regt., C, 779, H, 1227, M, 974,
    42nd Regt. Vols., C, 37,
    44th Regt., H, 1217,
    53rd Regt., W, 935,
    53rd Regt. Vols., C, 548,
    55th Regt., C, 411,
    59th Regt. Vol., H, 1236,
    61st Regt., N, 117,
    63rd Regt. Vols., G, 389,
  Militia, S, 649-650,
  Reserve Militia, C, 1272,
  Roster, R, 655, 740, 742, T, 206,
  Rosters, B, 839
German Settlement; A, 141
Germans; B, 815, 1528, C, 590,
  Arkansas, Settlers, E, 250
Germany;
  Military Literature, N, 146
Gettysburg of the West; B, 1362, 1418
Gettysburg, PA; A, 502, C, 573a, 732, I, 59b, J, 362, K, 56, S, 122,
  Barksdale's Brigade, M, 680,
  Battle of,
    Longstreet's Charge, M, 835,
  Campaign, B, 338, 1377, C, 7, 246, F, 102-103, G, 406, H, 192, 599, L, 640a, M, 579a-580, 592, 596, 1234, 1239, N, 68, O, 77, S, 71, 1279, 1321, T, 8-9, 419, 466,
  Charge, H, 612,
  Confederate Dead, Re-interment, C, 957,
  Death Roster, K, 256,
  History, J, 119, P, 31, S, 277,
  Lee, Robert Edward, Gen., I, 10, T, 454,
  Maps, Battlefields, B, 1555,
  March to, S, 1177,
  Memorial, C, 358-359,
  Monuments, C, 1102, M, 243, N, 178, T, 204,
  National Park, N, 178, T, 294,
  Official Report, J, 188, 204, M, 467,
  Pickett's Charge, M, 365a,
  Retreat, I, 4,
  Stuart's Cavalry, M, 1228
Gettysburg, PA, Battle of; A, 178, 184, 212, 273, 344, 372, B, 242, 540, 548, 592, 865, 1348, 1414, 1578, C, 212, 326, 328, 515-516, 550, 1366, 1458, D, 52, 63, 70, 796, 804, E, 16, 35, 208, 215, 268, F, 102, 533, G, 77, 250, 399, 570, 658, H, 764, 882, 1055, J, 424, 441, K, 119a, 128, 253a, L, 90, 150a, 585, 617, 728a, M, 79, 213, 254, 270, 464, 592, 607, 613,

788a, **N**, 185, 225, **O**, 97, **P**, 268, 358, 367, 833, 851, **R**, 63, 372, 395, 524-525, 562, 576, 632, **S**, 189, 440, 685, 1130, 1416-1417, **T**, 12, 193, 418, 424, 459, **V**, 89, **W**, 54, 71, 183, 543, 630, 1004, **XYZ**, 80,
Advance Guard, **M**, 271,
Anecdotes, **N**, 84,
Anniversary, **M**, 620,
Army Strengths, Statistics, **T**, 82,
Artillery, **A**, 155, 158, **G**, 79, **L**, 137, **M**, 576, **P**, 829,
Artillery Mechanics, **W**, 872,
Burials, **P**, 567,
Campaign Strategy, **A**, 217,
Cemetery Ridge, **F**, 131,
Confederate Dead, **K**, 256a,
Defeat, **T**, 259,
Failure, **S**, 1278,
Financial Effects, **M**, 25,
First Shots, **F**, 587,
First Soldier to Charge, **J**, 274,
Georgia Troops, **S**, 1056,
Heth's Division, **M**, 1042,
Hood's Charge, **P**, 766,
Kershaw's Brigade, **K**, 126,
Last Charge, **V**, 117,
Lee's Defeat, **L**, 78, 649, **P**, 63, **S**, 110, **W**, 144,
Lee's Defeat, Causes, **T**, 78,
Lee's Hdqrtrs., **M**, 1258,
Lee, Robert Edward, Gen., **P**, 278, **T**, 462,
Longstreet, James, Lt.Gen., **P**, 188, **T**, 462,
Longstreet, James. Lt.Gen., **J**, 350,
Losses, **M**, 1216, **R**, 235,
Mississippi Troops, **L**, 728,
North Carolina Troops, **K**, 191, **T**, 421,
Official Report, **F**, 397, **G**, 131, **J**, 448, **M**, 48, 160, **P**, 242, 283, 453, 662, **S**, 323, 367, **T**, 60, **W**, 7, 573, 982,
Pettigrew's Brigade, **XYZ**, 82,
Pickett's Charge, **H**, 1001, **J**, 274, **O**, 78, **P**, 766,
Pickett's Report, **T**, 470,
Prelude, **N**, 224,
Reinterment of Carolina Dead, **G**, 289,
Statistics, **E**, 34,
Stone Wall, **J**, 274,
Strengths, **P**, 65,
Tennesseans, **K**, 159
Getz, David; **G**, 454
Gholson, Thomas S.; **G**, 200
Ghost Battalion; **W**, 368
Ghost Ship of the Confederacy; **B**, 1018
Ghosts; **J**, 543
Gibbons, Robert; **A**, 539
Gibbs, W.C., Capt.; **W**, 203
Gibbs, W.H.; **F**, 142
Gibralter; **B**, 1629
Gibson, Deanna; **G**, 215
Gift, Ellen Shackleford, Papers; **C**, 297
Gift, George, Lt.; **C**, 297
Gilchrist, R.C., Maj.; **W**, 251
Gilcrease Institute of American History & Art; **C**, 338
Gildersleeve, B.L.; **B**, 641
Giles, L.B.; **C**, 568, **D**, 677
Gill, Robert M.; **W**, 668
Gilleland's Cannon; **M**, 891
Gillette, Charles, Rev.; **F**, 98, **G**, 621
Gilman, Samuel, Mrs.; **G**, 271
Gilmer Blues; **R**, 232, **T**, 180
Gilmer Blues (song); **D**, 659
Gilmer, John A.; **C**, 1466
Gilmer, John H.; **G**, 275
Gilmor, Harry; **B**, 42
Girardeau, John L.; **B**, 733
Glade Spring Rifles; **H**, 34
Gladiator Cotton Claims; **K**, 181
Glazner, Capitola H.; **A**, 421
Glencoe Diary; **W**, 94
Glorieta Pass, NM, Battle of; **D**, 545, **M**, 444, **S**, 65, **W**, 476
Gloucester County, VA; **A**, 357, **M**, 1002
Glover, Robert W.; **C**, 1488, **G**, 113
Godwin, Archibald Campbell, Brig.Gen.; **H**, 530

Gold; **D**, 153, **F**, 307-308, **H**, 379, **P**, 88, **XYZ**, 91
Gold Fields; **B**, 649, **C**, 1093
Goldsboro, NC; **K**, 194
Goldsborough, Effie; **D**, 160
Goldsborough, William W., Maj.; **A**, 485, 514, **L**, 475, **P**, 305, **R**, 503
Goldsmith, W.L., Col.; **F**, 603
Gone with the Wind (book); **M**, 361, 966, **P**, 858
Gone With the Wind (movie); **B**, 1252
Gonzales, Ambrosio Jose, Col.; **J**, 506
Goochland County, VA; **L**, 189, Roster, **L**, 569, **R**, 735
Goochland Light Artillery; **R**, 446
Goochland Light Dragoons; **P**, 677
Good's Brigade;
    Roster, **R**, 735
Good, John J., Capt.; **F**, 194
Goode, John; **G**, 350
Goodloe, Al T.; **XYZ**, 93a
Goolrick, Chester; **B**, 968
Gordon County, GA; **P**, 425
Gordon's Last Assault; **A**, 486
Gordon, George Washington, Brig.Gen.; **M**, 955, **U**, 26
Gordon, James Byron, Brig.Gen.; **B**, 1295, **C**, 1344
Gordon, John Brown, Maj.Gen.; **A**, 470, **F**, 477, **G**, 386, **J**, 532, **M**, 843, **T**, 22,
    as Gov., GA, **J**, 383
Gorgas, Amelia Gayle; **J**, 327
Gorgas, Josiah, Brig.Gen.; **B**, 329, **E**, 104, **F**, 11, **J**, 327, **V**, 56-57,
    Ordnance, **G**, 301
Gorman, William R.; **M**, 143
Gosport Navy Yard, VA; **L**, 631
Gourdin, Robert Mewman; **R**, 483
Government de Facto; **C**, 1027
Government, US; **G**, 565,
    Epitaph, **E**, 218-219
Governor Moore (ship); **K**, 89
Governor's Guards (South Carolina); **B**, 230
Governors, Confederate; **XYZ**, 23a

Gracey, F.P., Capt.; **G**, 457
Gracie's Battalion; **G**, 460
Grady, Donald; **D**, 122
Grady, John C.; **F**, 77
Graham, H.C.; **C**, 952
Graham, Jim; **B**, 1101
Graham, M. Louise Benton; **C**, 954, 1015, **H**, 273
Graham, William A.; **C**, 610, **P**, 210
Grain, Unlawful Distillation; **B**, 1380
Grame, John; **P**, 707
Gramp, W.E.H.; **H**, 1267
Granberry, J.C., Rev.; **J**, 444
Granbury's Brigade; **B**, 983, **F**, 436, **R**, 297
Grancsay, Stephen V.; **G**, 125
Grand Army of the Republic; **B**, 1558
Grand Gulf, MS; **B**, 409
Grand Prairie, TX; **G**, 614
Grand Review; **B**, 1119
Grandfather Mountain, NC; **W**, 800
Grandfathers; **G**, 482
Granger Movement; **K**, 219
Grant County, AR; **B**, 375
Grant's Army;
    Strength of, **E**, 34
Grant, Ulysses Simpson, Gen.; **B**, 1459, **F**, 486, 594, **H**, 852, **M**, 349, 711b, 857, **N**, 137, **O**, 10, **S**, 393, 629a, 919, 1299, **T**, 552, **W**, 544, 1002,
    Comparison to Lee, **P**, 280,
    Dispatch No. Two, **F**, 536,
    Drinking, **R**, 134,
    Generalship, **C**, 853, **G**, 510,
    Leadership, **B**, 1586,
    Lee's Sword, **G**, 507,
    Tabletalk, **J**, 453,
    Virginia, **G**, 511,
    Wilderness, Conduct at, **A**, 174
Grantham, Dewey W., Jr.; **H**, 797
Granville County, NC; **W**, 831
Graves; **B**, 643, **C**, 51, 363, 1007a, **M**, 186-197, **R**, 279
Graves County, KY; **B**, 191
Graves, Henry Lea; **H**, 481
Gray Brigade; **D**, 950
Gray, Edwin Fairfax; **G**, 542

Gray, Samuel Howard; **C**, 900, **H**, 478
Grayson, William John; **P**, 708, **R**, 266
Great Northwestern Conspiracy; **A**, 586
Great Plains; **G**, 213
Great Treason Plot; **A**, 587
Great Valley Campaign; **A**, 271
Green River County, KY; **C**, 1455
Green's Brigade; **M**, 619
Green, Beulah G.; **C**, 998
Green, Fletcher M.; **D**, 379
Green, John Uriah; **M**, 173
Green, Johnny; **K**, 206
Green, Mary; **K**, 139
Green, Nola; **S**, 48
Green, Thomas, Brig.Gen.; **F**, 44, 596
Greenawalt, Bruce S.; **D**, 127
Greenbrier Martyr; **D**, 736
Greenbrier River Battleground; **M**, 699
Greene County, MO; **B**, 385
Greenhow, Rose O'Neal; **B**, 1566, **G**, 501, **N**, 162, **R**, 722, **S**, 458
Greensboro, NC; **A**, 454,
  Reunions, **B**, 1089
Greenville, MS; **D**, 956, **F**, 130
Greenwood Cemetery, New Orleans, LA; **L**, 11
Gregg's Brigade; **G**, 362, **M**, 451
Gregg's Regiment; **C**, 818
Gregg, Alexander, Rev.; **F**, 98, **G**, 266, 625
Gregg, Maxcy, Brig.Gen.; **K**, 257, **P**, 32
Gregg, William; **M**, 262, 953
Gregory, Ralph; **W**, 256a
Grenfell, George St. Leger, Col.; **N**, 163, **S**, 1009
Grier Revolvers; **S**, 1448
Grier, Robert Cooper; **H**, 17
Griffin, John W., Rev.; **B**, 784
Griffith, Lucille; **C**, 1285
Griffith-Barksdale-Humphrey Brigade; **D**, 623
Grime's Battery; **H**, 268
Grime's Division; **G**, 74
Grimes County Rangers; **H**, 91
Grimes, Absalom, Capt.; **B**, 1085, **H**, 1223, **M**, 9, **W**, 374
Grimes, Bryan, Maj.Gen.; **G**, 598, **L**, 607
Grimes, Maxyne Madden; **B**, 725
Grinnan, Andrew G., Dr.; **C**, 1334
Gristmill, Destruction; **H**, 1255a
Griswold Revolvers; **S**, 1448
Griswold, E., Maj.; **M**, 829
Griswoldville, GA; **S**, 1448,
  Campaign, **M**, 583
Griswoldville, GA, Battle of; **W**, 379
Gronauer, Joseph A.; **H**, 1021
Grove, Battle of; **C**, 1566
Grubbs Hussars, GA; **J**, 97
Guerin, H.C., Maj.; **M**, 830
Guerrant, Edward O.; **M**, 366d
Guerrillas; **A**, 405, **B**, 783, 962, 1222, 1224a, 1263, 1435, 1556, **C**, 1331, 1501, 1568, 1600, **D**, 30, 890, 938, **E**, 5, 97, **G**, 122, 360, **H**, 43-44, 1037, 1249, **J**, 544, **M**, 368c, 1005, 1240, 1292-1294, **P**, 752, **Q**, 2, **R**, 42, **S**, 89, 981, 1166, **T**, 226
Guesclin, Bertrand du; **J**, 92
Guess, George W., Lt.Col.; **G**, 690
Guest Station, VA; **H**, 962
Guild, La Fayette; **C**, 410, **P**, 331
Guilford Grays, NC; **S**, 269, 569,
  Uniforms, **U**, 14
Guinea Pete; **S**, 862
Gulf Coast;
  Confederate Corps of Engineers, **E**, 180,
  Military Government, **B**, 1645,
  Slave Rentals, **D**, 574
Gun Makers, Confederate; **H**, 1254
Gunboats; **B**, 498, **F**, 26, **G**, 35, 438, **H**, 910, **J**, 20, **L**, 587, **O**, 76, **R**, 810, **S**, 599, **W**, 469, 705
Gunfights; **B**, 1218
Gunpowder; **J**, 6
Guns; **A**, 454, **R**, 907
Gunter, John; **F**, 364
Gurly, Frank B., Capt.; **C**, 1583
Guy's Battery; **A**, 248
Gwin, William N.; **S**, 1250
Gwinnett County, GA; **M**, 972

H

H.L. Hunley (submarine); **B**, 358, **D**, 946, **S**, 447, 920, 1378, **W**, 72
Habeas Corpus; **R**, 520, **S**, 299, 530
Hagerstown, MD;
   Cemetery, **D**, 547
Hagerstown, MD, Battle of; **P**, 832
Hagood's Brigade; **H**, 27
Hagood, Johnson, Brig.Gen.; **B**, 471, **C**, 484
Hahn, Michael; **S**, 495
Halderman, W.N.; **K**, 101
Haley, M.J.; **A**, 355
Halifax Volunteers; **H**, 622, 622a
Halisey, Dennis J., Col.; **E**, 49
Hall, Bolling, Col.; **J**, 412
Hall, Charles B.; **E**, 198
Hall, Geoffrey, Maj.; **H**, 68
Hall, James Edmond; **S**, 1366
Hall, Martin Hardwick; **A**, 441, **T**, 58
Hall, Thomas W., Jr.; **S**, 854
Halley, Robert Ambrose; **G**, 100
Halpine, Charles Graham; **B**, 91, 1078, **H**, 204
Halstead, Murat; **H**, 760
Halstead, Murray; **B**, 762
Hamilton's Crossing; **M**, 1067
Hamilton, A.J., Gov.; **A**, 500
Hamilton, Holman; **S**, 529
Hamilton, I.M.; **K**, 255
Hamilton, J.G. de Roulhac; **G**, 479, **R**, 798, **S**, 439
Hamilton, James H.; **T**, 436
Hamilton, Paul; **H**, 595
Hamlet, NC; **T**, 51
Hamlin, Percy Gatling, Capt.; **E**, 292
Hammer & Rapier; **C**, 1175
Hammock, Henry Masel; **F**, 206
Hammond, James Henry; **B**, 141, **F**, 51, **K**, 46, **M**, 823, **W**, 30
Hammond, Joseph H.; **M**, 505a

Hampden-Sidney College; **U**, 16
Hampshire County, WV; **S**, 783,
   History, **M**, 355
Hampton Academy, VA; **S**, 781
Hampton Legion; **C**, 473, 1371, **T**, 325, **W**, 248,
   Survivors, **M**, 927
Hampton Roads, VA; **XYZ**, 99,
   Ironclads, **B**, 1272,
   Peace Conference, **C**, 204, 1094, **G**, 349, 352, **H**, 175, **R**, 174, **T**, 498
Hampton Roads, VA, Battle of; **B**, 1466, 1497, **C**, 59, **D**, 33, **G**, 123, **H**, 954, 1269, **K**, 223, **M**, 811, 872, **S**, 410, **T**, 132
Hampton's Cattle Raid; **M**, 505
Hampton's Cavalry; **B**, 1314-1315, **R**, 150
Hampton, Wade, Lt.Gen.; **B**, 652, 1317, 1626, **C**, 173, 222, 478, **D**, 869, **F**, 134, **H**, 257, 949, **R**, 30, **S**, 1032, **W**, 369, 381-382, 610,
   Duel, **M**, 37,
   Family, **C**, 332,
   Strategy, **F**, 355
Handbill, Confederate; **R**, 498
Handbook of Artillery; **R**, 541
Handkerchiefs, Battle of the; **D**, 616, **H**, 1219, **S**, 276
Hangings; **R**, 881
Hanks, Nancy; **C**, 316, 798
Hanleiter, C.R., Capt.; **R**, 639
Hanna, A.J.; **D**, 380
Hanover County, VA; **P**, 15
Hanover Junction, VA; **J**, 319
Hanson, Burton; **B**, 571
Harby, Lee C.; **A**, 25
Hardaway, Robert A., Col.; **A**, 449
Hardee's Corps;
   Last Battles, **F**, 347

Hardee's Tactics; **L**, 257
Hardee, William Joseph, Lt.Gen.; **B**, 1484, **H**, 297-298, 1258, 1258a, **L**, 564, **M**, 897, **P**, 376a,
 Atlanta, GA, **R**, 778
Hardeman, Glen O., Dr.; **H**, 300
Hardeman, Peter, Col.; **H**, 299
Hardesty's Historical & Geographical Encyclopedia; **S**, 749
Harding, Joseph French, Maj.; **C**, 1009
Hargrave, Catherine Perry; **P**, 429
Hargrett, Lester; **B**, 672
Harleston, Francis Huger, Capt.; **C**, 141, **R**, 338
Harmon, John A., Maj.; **G**, 46
Harmony Hall, Columbia, SC; **D**, 100
Harnett County, NC; **A**, 569
Haroldson, John; **K**, 240
Harper's Ferry, WV; **B**, 1495, **C**, 1558, **G**, 72, **H**, 1080, 1189, **I**, 8, **L**, 315, **R**, 294, 412, 724a, **W**, 60, 228, 371, 449, 535,
 Armory, **W**, 325,
 Insurrection, **H**, 343-347,
 Invasion, **C**, 1171,
 Jackson's Capture, **W**, 61,
 Jackson's Intentions, **J**, 186,
 Raid, **S**, 687,
 Richmond Howitzers, **M**, 458,
 Siege, **N**, 131,
 Treason, **T**, 96
Harriet Lane (ship); **B**, 266, **M**, 269, **T**, 140, 407, 479
Harris Letter, the; **F**, 172
Harris' Brigade; **L**, 347
Harris, Bushrod W.; **E**, 95
Harris, George N.; **E**, 95
Harris, Isham Green, Gov., TN; **J**, 246, **M**, 737, **T**, 120
Harris, Joel Chandler; **C**, 621, 1333
Harris, John H., Capt.; **H**, 1217
Harris, N.E.; **U**, 23
Harris, Nathaniel Harrison, Brig.Gen.; **H**, 384
Harrisburg, MS, Battle of; **L**, 371, 373
Harrisburg, PA; **C**, 1445,
 Lee's Invasion, **S**, 967
Harrison County, TX; **S**, 513
Harrison, Burton Norvell, Col.; **H**, 397, 402
Harrison, Charles; **XYZ**, 91
Harrison, Dabney Carr; **H**, 968
Harrison, James Edward, Brig.Gen.; **B**, 43
Harrison, Jesse Burton; **H**, 402
Harrison, Lowell H.; **D**, 378
Hart's Battery; **B**, 1314, **H**, 196, 264, 448, **R**, 464
Hart, Henry; **A**, 25
Hart, James Franklin, Maj.; **A**, 25, **H**, 196
Hart, Martin; **D**, 938, **S**, 88-89
Hartford (ship); **R**, 549
Hartsville, TN; **S**, 162
Hartsville, TN, Battle of; **A**, 84, **B**, 346, 367, **D**, 904
Hartville, MO, Battle of; **R**, 585
Harvey Birch (ship); **C**, 1003
Harvey's Scouts; **C**, 564
Harwell, Richard Barksdale; **B**, 672, 1564, **C**, 890, 900, 1178, 1182, 1554, **M**, 883, **R**, 720, **V**, 60
Harwell, Thomas F.; **H**, 495
Haseltine, John W.; **D**, 546
Haskell Family, SC; **D**, 439
Haskell, Alexander Cheves; **D**, 32
Hastings, Lansford W.; **H**, 1296
Hatcher's Run, VA, Battle of; **G**, 407, **H**, 523
Hatchie Bridge, TN, Battle of; **C**, 723, **M**, 469
Hatteras (ship); **D**, 506
Hatton, Robert Hopkins, Brig.Gen.; **C**, 1562, **D**, 836
Havins, T.R.; **G**, 529
Haw's Shop, VA, Battle of; **H**, 544
Hawes, Lilla Mills; **M**, 894
Hawes, Richard, Gov., KY; **H**, 415
Hawkins, William Stewart, Col.; **B**, 430
Hawley, Joseph R.; **J**, 519
Hay, John; **M**, 577
Hayne, Isaac W.; **W**, 192
Hayne, Paul Hamilton; **P**, 723, **T**, 309

Hayne, Robert Y.; **J**, 131
Hayne, Susanna Shulrick; **M**, 698
Haynes, Landon Carter; **B**, 542
Hayneville, AL; **R**, 830
Hays County, TX; **C**, 194
Hays, Louise Frederick; **M**, 38
Hays, Peregrine; **S**, 1369
Haywood, Edmund Burke; **C**, 1577, **E**, 86
Haywood, Philip Drayton; **A**, 103, **D**, 504, **K**, 49a
Haywood, T. Holt, Mrs.; **B**, 20
Hazardous Service; **B**, 670
Health;
  South, **M**, 967
Heard County, GA; **C**, 548
Heartsill, W.W.; **B**, 1411, **J**, 116, **M**, 441
Heavy Artillery; **K**, 112
Hebert, Paul Octave, Brig.Gen.; **G**, 135, **M**, 729
Heiman, Adolphus; **F**, 463
Heiss, Estell T. Buchanan; **D**, 257
Helena, AR;
  Confiscation, **H**, 747
Helena, AR, Battle of; **A**, 426, **B**, 381, **C**, 279, 1440
Helm, Benjamin Hardin, Brig.Gen.; **M**, 670, 672
Helper, Hinton Rowan; **B**, 28, 97, 99, 505, 817, **G**, 246, 274, **L**, 407a, **P**, 216, **U**, 15, **W**, 897
Hemming, Charles C.; **C**, 360
Hemphill, John; **G**, 622
Henagan, Waring, Mrs.; **J**, 128
Henderson County, TX; **E**, 1
Henderson, Dwight F.; **W**, 51
Henderson, George Francis Robert, Col.; **B**, 1458, **L**, 777
Henderson, KY; **F**, 30
Henderson, Lillian; **C**, 121
Hendersonville, NC; **H**, 1260
Heneberger, E.R. Grymes; **H**, 445a
Henrico County, VA; **B**, 31, **C**, 384
Henry County, GA;
  Volunteers, **H**, 1217
Henry County, TN; **P**, 636,
  History, **R**, 274

Henry Rifle, CSA; **A**, 555
Henry's Raid; **M**, 257
Henry, Robert S.; **D**, 624, **J**, 542, **M**, 441, **P**, 827
Hephzibah Baptist Association; **B**, 89
Herbert, Hilary Abner; **D**, 174, **H**, 167, **S**, 618
Herbert, Philemon Thomas, Col.; **P**, 572
Herd Fighting; **M**, 402
Hergesheimer's Use of Historical Sources, pub.; **F**, 5
Herndon, Dallas T.; **A**, 424-425, **D**, 671
Heroes; **A**, 553, **B**, 1126, 1444, **C**, 203, 784, 1287, 1349, **D**, 543, 704, 831, 921, **E**, 72, 200, **F**, 43, 124, 319, **H**, 1289, **J**, 512, **L**, 56, 785, **M**, 229, 450, 452, 598, 779, **O**, 5, 105, 194-195, **P**, 77, 302, 612, **R**, 338, 682, **S**, 23, 792, 1183, 1269, **T**, 435, **W**, 163, 577, 638, **XYZ**, 59
Hesseltine, William B.; **R**, 69
Hestir, Bluford B., Dr.; **R**, 123
Heth's Division; **D**, 311, **M**, 1042
Heth, Henry, Maj.Gen.; **H**, 509, 766, Gettysburg, PA, **M**, 788a
Hickman County, TN;
  History, **S**, 930
Hickman, John P.; **C**, 907
Hickory Point, KA, Battle of; **R**, 156
Hickory, NC;
  Catawba Soldiers, **H**, 37
Higginbotham, John, Col.; **S**, 1359
Higginson, Thomas Wentworth, Col.; **H**, 28
Hildebrand, Sam; **B**, 1224a, **E**, 258, **T**, 226
Hill's Corps; **A**, 481, **B**, 707, **C**, 46
Hill's Light Division; **S**, 119
Hill, Ambrose Powell, Lt.Gen.; **B**, 255, 1400, **C**, 63, **H**, 505, **J**, 476, **M**, 341, 343a, **R**, 272, 560a, **S**, 500, **T**, 455, **V**, 102, **W**, 57
Hill, Benjamin Harvey, Col.; **B**, 35, **C**, 1290, **H**, 817, **P**, 186, **R**, 227, **V**, 130

Hill, Daniel Harvey, Lt.Gen.; **A**, 290, 449-450, 572, **B**, 1250-1251, **G**, 281, **H**, 863, **L**, 63, 354, **S**, 361
Hill, I. William; **S**, 1118
Hill, William Green; **D**, 837
Hill-Blaine Debate; **C**, 1289
Hill-Jackson Feud; **H**, 508
Hill-McClellan-Marcy Triangle; **H**, 507
Hilliard vs. Yancey; **G**, 330
Hilliard, Henry W., Col.; **J**, 206a
Hillman's Farm, VA, Battle of; **B**, 208
Hillsboro, NC; **C**, 944
Hilton Head Island, SC; **C**, 220
Hindman, Thomas Carmichael, Maj.Gen.; **G**, 135, **H**, 870, 886, **N**, 21, **P**, 402, **R**, 536
Hines, Thomas Henry, Capt.; **C**, 739, **M**, 1136
Hinton, Isaac T.; **H**, 209
Hist, F.B. Heitman; **G**, 63
Historians; **C**, 851
Historical Sites;
  Mississippi, **M**, 933
Historicus (pseudonym); **H**, 280, **J**, 614
History; **F**, 203, **G**, 615
Hitchcock, Alfred, Dr.; **C**, 1476
Hobson, Edwin La Fayette; **B**, 283
Hobson, Richard P.; **P**, 420a
Hodge, Nadine; **C**, 632
Hodges, James Gregory, Col.; **C**, 1459
Hodges, Robert, Jr.; **D**, 110
Hodgkins, William Henry; **B**, 672
Hodgson, Daisy M.L.; **C**, 955, 1015
Hoge, Moses Drury; **B**, 1275
Hoke, Robert Frederick, Maj.Gen.; **N**, 82
Holcombe Guards;
  Roster, **P**, 114
Holcombe, James P.; **T**, 231
Holden, Horace M.; **K**, 234
Holden, Jim; **D**, 436
Holden, William W., Gov., NC; **R**, 117
Hollingsworth, Alan M.; **C**, 1352

Holly Springs, MS; **B**, 1321, **G**, 148,
  Capture, **D**, 593,
  Raid, **H**, 457
Hollywood Cemetery, Richmond, VA; **M**, 969, **R**, 239
Holmann, W.J., Jr.; **G**, 666
Holmes, Theophilus Hunter, Lt.-Gen.; **C**, 281, **F**, 362, **P**, 400
Home Guards; **E**, 182,
  Roster, **M**, 1120
Home, Marshall; **M**, 386
Honey Hill, SC, Battle of; **A**, 11, **C**, 1326, **J**, 380
Honey Springs, Ind.T.; **C**, 432, **E**, 221, **F**, 503,
  National Battlefield, **F**, 158
Hood's Army; **S**, 294
Hood's Brigade; **B**, 205, **C**, 473, 923, **F**, 271, **G**, 113, 263, **H**, 129, 135, 668, 684, 798b, 798a, 1354, **P**, 271, 412, 535, **R**, 575, 578, **S**, 499, 502-512, 516, 1140, **W**, 978
Hood's Brigade Association; **V**, 16
Hood's Campaign; **C**, 550, 1412, **D**, 7, 681, **H**, 556, 565, 1054, **S**, 47
Hood's Tennessee Invasion; **E**, 223
Hood, John Bell, Gen.; **C**, 374, 427, 1373, **D**, 6, 996, **H**, 1315, **M**, 660, **N**, 217, **P**, 149, **S**, 500, 509,
  Death, **E**, 213,
  Logistician, **V**, 58,
  Spring Hill, TN, Failure, **M**, 233,
  Tennessee Invasion, **B**, 357
Hoole, Addie Shirley; **C**, 971a
Hoole, Martha DuBois; **B**, 839, **W**, 528
Hoole, William Stanley; **A**, 301-302, **B**, 839, 1462, 1613, **F**, 398, **G**, 278, 287, 363a, **H**, 912, **J**, 110, **M**, 153, 1071, **T**, 55, **W**, 528
Hooper, Johnson Jones; **H**, 1070, 1075
Hoover, Sallie Wellford Scott; **C**, 1008
Hope, James Barron; **P**, 449
Hopkins, Abner C., Rev.; **B**, 1379
Hopkins, C.A. Porter; **A**, 412
Hopkins, Juliet Opie, Mrs.; **G**, 643

Hopkinsville, KY;
  Confederate Dead, **C**, 898,
  Monument, **M**, 776
Hopson, Winthrop Harlty, Dr.; **H**, 1089
Horan, James D.; **W**, 12
Horn, Stanley F.; **K**, 61a
Horne, Kathleen P.; **B**, 841
Horry County, SC; **B**, 1462
Horse Artillery; **H**, 517
Horse Shoe Bend, KY, Battle of; **C**, 800
Horseman Blue & Gray; **J**, 211
Horses; **D**, 826, **R**, 53, 222, 783,
  Diseases of, **P**, 7,
  Little Sorrel (Jackson), **D**, 746,
  Lucy Long (Lee), **B**, 1330, **C**, 108, **L**, 303,
  Supply, **S**, 1163,
  Thefts, **W**, 818,
  Traveller (Lee), **B**, 1330, 1412, **F**, 183, **H**, 897, **L**, 293, 297, **R**, 342
Horseshoe Bend, KY, Battle of; **G**, 198
Horseshoe, Bloody Angle, Battle of; **O**, 92
Hospitals; **A**, 304, **B**, 724, **H**, 972, **S**, 717,
  Alabama, **D**, 709,
  Army of Tennessee, **C**, 1553,
  Charlottesville, VA, **B**, 1215,
  Chimborazo, Richmond, VA, **C**, 475, 1539, **G**, 256, 259, **H**, 6, 1283, **J**, 139,
  Church Used for, **N**, 4,
  Columbia, SC, **B**, 1488,
  Columbus, GA, Walker Hospital, **C**, 227,
  Confederate, **C**, 1575, **D**, 344,
  Farmville, VA, **W**, 551,
  General, **R**, 536a,
  Marine, New Orleans, LA, **R**, 703,
  Memphis, TN, **L**, 107a,
  Midway, **C**, 622,
  Oxford University, **J**, 213,
  Oxford, MS, **C**, 267, **H**, 115,
  Petersburg, VA, **D**, 384,
  Prototype, **H**, 1124a,
  Raleigh, NC, **C**, 1577, **E**, 86,
  Regulations, **H**, 1117,
  Richmond, VA, **C**, 789, **S**, 7, **W**, 24,
  William & Mary College, VA, **C**, 1476
Hotchkiss Map Collection; **H**, 1120, **L**, 177, **S**, 1115
Hotchkiss, Jedediah, Maj.; **A**, 218, **C**, 270, **M**, 471, 714
Hotel Burners; **K**, 81
Hotze, Henry; **F**, 398, **O**, 28, **R**, 7
Housatonic (ship); **C**, 970
House of Representatives, US; **C**, 1028
Houston, Harry A., Capt.; **G**, 360
Houston, Sam, Gen.; **B**, 1014, **C**, 1518, **F**, 371, **H**, 1139, 1144, **M**, 1271, **R**, 163,
  Secession, **M**, 75,
  Slavery, **W**, 848
Houston, TX; **A**, 493, **J**, 76
Howard College, AL; **I**, 56
Howard County, AR; **B**, 1635
Howard, Ewing Fox, Dr.; **E**, 262
Howard, J.D.; **P**, 852
Howard, James McHenry; **S**, 726, **U**, 43
Howard, Oliver Otis, Maj.Gen.; **O**, 10, **W**, 604a
Howe, John, Capt.; **H**, 1192
Howell Guards; **D**, 854
Howell, Robert Boyte Crawford; **S**, 904
Howell, Varina; **R**, 769
Howlett's House, Richmond, VA; **M**, 1170a
Howorth, Lucy Somerville; **N**, 215
Hubbell, Raynor; **H**, 378
Hubbert, Mike M.; **H**, 1218
Hudson, James Madison; **H**, 330
Hudson, John Rolfe, Dr.; **H**, 1101
Huger, Benjamin, Maj.Gen.; **R**, 342a
Hughes, George; **B**, 785
Hughes, Henry, Col.; **M**, 1114
Huguenin, Thomas A.; **C**, 139
Huguenot Church, Charleston, SC; **V**, 92
Hull, A.L.; **C**, 708

Human, Alfred; **B**, 106
Humanity; **W**, 548
Hume, Edgar E.; **B**, 1041
Humor; **G**, 588,
  Bill Arp, **A**, 467-468
Humphrey's Brigade; **R**, 311a
Humphrey, M.W.; **D**, 738
Humphreys, Andrew Atkinson, Gen.; **A**, 223
Humphreys, Benjamin G., Brig.Gen.; **E**, 268, **P**, 427
Humphreys, West H.; **H**, 75
Hundley, Daniel R., Col.; **B**, 868
Hunt, Alexander; **F**, 449
Hunt, Henry Jackson, Maj.Gen.; **K**, 104
Hunter's Brigade; **J**, 80, **XYZ**, 37
Hunter's Raid; **H**, 1311, **M**, 403, **O**, 211, **S**, 626
Hunter, Alexander; **G**, 68
Hunter, David, Maj.Gen.; **A**, 464, **P**, 237,
  Shenandoah Valley, **A**, 329
Hunter, John Warren; **T**, 555
Hunter, Robert Mercer Taliaferro; **A**, 300, 310, **D**, 285, **H**, 916, 1320, **J**, 382, **S**, 480, **W**, 256
Huntingdon College; **E**, 186
Hunton, Eppa, Brig.Gen.; **F**, 50
Huntsville, AL; **B**, 662, **C**, 366
Huntsville, AL, Battle of; **B**, 379
Hurlbut, William Henry; **C**, 455
Huse, Caleb, Maj.; **G**, 592
Huske, John, Mrs.; **A**, 326
Huxford, Folks; **B**, 1303
Hyman, William; **L**, 132
Hypodermic Syringes; **H**, 211

I

Illinois;
  Burial Lists, **P**, 571, 590,
  Confederates, **W**, 349,
  Copperheads, **T**, 315,
  Secession Spirit, **S**, 210,
  Secret Societies, **K**, 213,
  Slavery, **F**, 255
Illinois Troops;
  Artillery,
    1st Regt., **R**, 641
Imboden Raid; **M**, 674a
Imboden, John Daniel, Brig.Gen.; **A**, 1, 329, **B**, 628, **C**, 1465, **I**, 6, **S**, 1373
Immortal Six-hundred; **C**, 1151, **D**, 951, **F**, 490, **L**, 594-595, **M**, 1314, 1317, **N**, 11, **S**, 537,
  Society, **M**, 926
Immortelles; **R**, 255
Impressment; **J**, 196, **K**, 179, **N**, 58
In Tall Cotton, pub.; **H**, 492
Inaugural Speech, Davis'; **C**, 1321-1322, **D**, 222
India;
  Cotton, **R**, 163
Indian Nations; **M**, 831, 1070
Indian Policy, CSA; **E**, 241
Indian Territory; **B**, 392, 1360, **C**, 52, 132, 466, 1598, **E**, 220, **F**, 149-154, **H**, 935, 1048, 1112, **P**, 392-393, **R**, 37-42, **S**, 417, **T**, 417, **W**, 190,
  Federal Invasion, **H**, 637, **W**, 689,
  Refugees, **F**, 156,
  Surrenders, Confederate, **B**, 1367,
  Treaties, **M**, 674
Indian Territory Department; **C**, 338, **R**, 241
Indian Tribes; **B**, 820, **C**, 794, **W**, 813
Indian Troops; **P**, 397
Indiana;
  Confederate Dead, **C**, 70,
  Conspirators, **M**, 889,
  Knights of the Golden Circle, **K**, 216,
  Morgan's Raid, **B**, 1013,
  Sons of Liberty, **S**, 805
Indiana Troops;
  Infantry,
    46th Regt. Vols., **M**, 1143
Indiana-Ohio Raid; **B**, 554, **D**, 913, 918, **M**, 1137
Indianola (ironclad); **B**, 1225
Indians; **A**, 9, **B**, 1496, **C**, 1571, **D**, 444, **F**, 157, **G**, 524, 530, **H**, 1231, **L**, 757, **R**, 34, **S**, 169, 170, **T**, 236
  Agents, **M**, 34,
  Cavalry, **I**, 35,
  Cherokee, **A**, 337, **B**, 1157, **D**, 25,
  Creek Nation, **D**, 870,
  Fights, **S**, 663,
  Fort Smith, AR, **B**, 390,
  Officers, **C**, 961,
  Organized for CSA Service, **A**, 262,
  Pea Ridge, AR, **C**, 681,
  Reconstruction, **A**, 8,
  Secession, **C**, 796,
  Slave-holding, **A**, 6, **F**, 264,
  Slavery, **D**, 177,
  South Texas, **J**, 605,
  Texas, **N**, 136,
  Treaties, **F**, 478
Indigent Soldiers; **XYZ**, 104-114
Industry; **B**, 1628, **V**, 71,
  Railroad Influence, **J**, 130
Infantry; **H**, 733,
  Arms, **W**, 364,
  First Fight of War, **S**, 1156,
  Tactics, **C**, 264, **L**, 257, **R**, 389, **W**, 511,
  Weapons, **W**, 361,
  vs. Cavalry, **M**, 498

Inflation; **D**, 394, **L**, 442, **S**, 180
Ingraham, Duncan Nathaniel, Como.; **B**, 1073
Inspector of Railroads, Confederate, TX; **A**, 492
Insurrection of Negroes; **A**, 506
Intelligence; **C**, 119, **O**, 54, **S**, 1125
International Law; **H**, 281, 656
International Trade; **G**, 121
Inventions; **S**, 3
Iobst, Richard W.; **N**, 82
Iowa;
    Copperhead Movement, **L**, 432,
    Copperheads, **R**, 883
Irby, Loulie W.; **S**, 94
Irby, Richard, Capt.; **A**, 450, **G**, 483
Iredell County, NC; **S**, 1048
Ireland;
    Confederate Agents, **R**, 903,
    Secession, **H**, 736
Ireys, Henry Tillinghast; **M**, 379a
Iron; **A**, 436, **S**, 1213
Ironclads; **A**, 559, **B**, 1272, **D**, 743, **F**, 26, **G**, 591, **H**, 1168, **J**, 514, **M**, 4, 746, 887, **O**, 76, **S**, 1207, **W**, 597, 915,
    First Battle, **C**, 76, **K**, 223, **W**, 536,
    Origin, **P**, 52
Ironmonger, Frank; **U**, 31
Ironworks; **A**, 333, **D**, 559
Irvine, Josephus Somerville; **R**, 9
Irwin, James P.; **L**, 63
Irwin, R.B.; **H**, 357
Island No.10, TN; **B**, 47, 602
Iuka, MS;
    History, **M**, 491
Iuka, MS, Battle of; **C**, 731, **D**, 879
Ives, Washington; **C**, 2a
Ivy Mountain, Battle of; **S**, 96
Izard, George, Gen.; **M**, 147

J

J.R. Williams (ship); **R**, 34
Jackson County, AR; **L**, 765b
Jackson County, FL; **S**, 991
Jackson Light Infantry; **H**, 268
Jackson Purchase; **C**, 29, 1376
Jackson Railroad Rifles; **C**, 863
Jackson's Cavalry; **C**, 564
Jackson's Corps; **P**, 294
Jackson's Foot Cavalry; **M**, 441, **R**, 217, 624, **W**, 990
Jackson's Raid; **T**, 17
Jackson's Valley Campaign; **A**, 203, 216, 218, 224, 227, **B**, 1618, **C**, 747, **F**, 240, **J**, 120, **K**, 37, 61, **M**, 70, 1290, **P**, 70, **T**, 67, **W**, 990
Jackson's Way (song); **P**, 46a
Jackson, Andrew, Pres.; **K**, 76
Jackson, Anna Morrison (Stonewall, Mrs.); **A**, 458
Jackson, Claiborne Fox, Gov., MO; **G**, 663, **L**, 795, **M**, 948
Jackson, H. Melville, Rev.; **P**, 212
Jackson, H.W.R.; **G**, 347
Jackson, Harmon, Maj.; **W**, 404
Jackson, Henry R., Brig.Gen.; **C**, 1309
Jackson, James W.; **L**, 506a
Jackson, James, Col.; **M**, 492
Jackson, Mary Anna; **C**, 53, 419, **P**, 719
Jackson, MS;
  Siege, **D**, 885,
  Stovall's Brigade, **S**, 1255
Jackson, MS, Battle of; **B**, 374
Jackson, Thomas Jonathan, Lt.Gen.; **A**, 52, 57-58, 182, 195, 462, 558, 582, **B**, 147, 196, 361, 850, 1005, 1021, 1040, 1458, **C**, 21, 388a, 419, 459, 673, 691, 725, 1165, 1180, 1315, 1319, **D**, 92, 150, 225, 314, 486, 744, 787, 819, **E**, 137, 284, 295, **F**, 113, 145, 167, **G**, 46, 58, 293, 339, **H**, 111, 657, 680, 691, 787, 847, 890, 918, 1022, 1170, **J**, 18, 24-29, 186, 465, **M**, 174, 349, 368c, 556, 865, 1000, 1057, 1067, 1228, **N**, 103, **P**, 46, 382, 510, 722, **R**, 116, 214, 222b, 560a, **S**, 114, 121, 320, 500, 617, 624, 674-679, 1363, **T**, 164, 182, 373, **V**, 67, **W**, 302, 547,
  Anecdotes, **R**, 472,
  Campaigns, **B**, 932, **D**, 1-2, **W**, 910,
  Chancellorsville, VA, **B**, 146, **S**, 674,
  Character, **C**, 402, **D**, 53, **P**, 138, **S**, 659,
  Correspondence, **V**, 14,
  Courier, **H**, 895,
  Death, **B**, 713, 1478, **L**, 83, 760, **R**, 71, 258, 646,
  Engineers, **H**, 715,
  Family Life, **C**, 1164,
  Fredericksburg, VA, **E**, 38, **S**, 912,
  Frightened, **J**, 22,
  Generalship, **S**, 232,
  Grave, **J**, 31-32, **L**, 288,
  Harper's Ferry, WV, **I**, 8,
  Last Battle, **P**, 840, **S**, 675,
  Last Days, **C**, 53, **O**, 2,
  Last Hour, **K**, 274,
  Last Orders, **H**, 2,
  Lee, Meetings, **F**, 236, **L**, 200, **T**, 559,
  Lexington, VA, **D**, 128, **M**, 2,
  Liberty Hall Vols., **B**, 352,
  Life, **P**, 712, **V**, 165, **W**, 771,
  Maryland, **D**, 785-786, 789-790,
  Memorials, **C**, 751, **F**, 2,
  Military Career, **C**, 1180,
  Military Road, **L**, 726,

Monument, **D**, 487, **H**, 963, 966, **J**, 31-32, 48, 483, **K**, 68, **M**, 609,
Naval Viewpoint, **M**, 365,
Nickname, **M**, 1297, **R**, 589,
Non-drinker, **B**, 933,
Public Services, **O**, 88,
Raincoat, **R**, 461,
Religion, **J**, 40, **M**, 1315, **S**, 399,
Resigns, **W**, 453,
Richmond, Va, **A**, 349,
Scabbard Speech, **O**, 43,
Schoolmaster of, **W**, 812,
Scouts, **A**, 271,
Shenandoah Valley, **D**, 821, **I**, 9, **S**, 969, **T**, 30-31,
Soldier, **T**, 42,
Spiritually, **S**, 255,
Statue, **A**, 348,
Stonewall Brigade, **C**, 1182,
Strategy, **N**, 23, **T**, 251,
Virginia Campaigns, **A**, 317,
Walton Infantry, **T**, 234,
West Virginia, **C**, 1160, **W**, 933,
Winter Campaign, **H**, 35,
Winter Qrts. (1862), **K**, 193,
Wounded, **L**, 418, **M**, 1117a
Jackson, Thomas Jonathan, Mrs.; **D**, 354, **K**, 10, **S**, 680
Jacksonport, AR; **W**, 468
Jacksonville, FL; **M**, 256, **P**, 795,
    Occupation of, **D**, 972,
    Railroad Battery, **H**, 582
Jacob Bell (ship); **C**, 1040
James & Younger Gang; **C**, 1568
James Brothers; **W**, 283
James City, VA, Cavalry; **A**, 239
James Gray (ship); **B**, 1075
James River; **S**, 368
James, Jason W.; **D**, 606
James, Jesse; **B**, 1643, **C**, 1092, **H**, 44, **W**, 313,
    Death, **T**, 333
Jamestown (ship); **W**, 1056
Jane Campbell (ship); **W**, 21
Jaquess, John A., Col.; **S**, 1437
Jasper County, MO; **S**, 133
Jasper, TN; **C**, 887
Jastremski, Leon, Capt.; **P**, 415

Jayhawkers; **C**, 284, 286, **H**, 1249,
    Missouri, **H**, 726
Jeff Grays, GA; **J**, 97
Jefferson County Guards; **J**, 97
Jefferson County, CO; **E**, 214
Jefferson County, TX; **B**, 801
Jefferson County, VA; **C**, 460, **H**, 699, **M**, 861
Jefferson County, WV;
    History, **B**, 1617
Jefferson Davis (ship); **C**, 467, 1132
Jefferson Davis Bridge; **R**, 322, 595
Jefferson Guards; **B**, 1544
Jefferson Volunteers, GA; **J**, 97
Jenkin's Ferry, AR, Battle of; **A**, 426, **B**, 375, 422, **M**, 485, **R**, 366,
    Steele's Retreat, **F**, 174
Jenkins' Brigade; **S**, 140
Jenkins, Albert Gallatin, Brig.Gen.; **C**, 1158, **D**, 581, **J**, 207
Jenkins, Charles Jones, Jr.; **S**, 279
Jenkins, Dan; **B**, 1633
Jenkins, John Carrell; **J**, 114
Jenkins, John H.; **H**, 492
Jenkins, L.H.; **C**, 493
Jenkins, Micah, Brig.Gen.; **S**, 1423a, **T**, 208
Jericho Ford, VA, Battle of; **L**, 92
Jerli, Frank J.; **G**, 589
Jerome, Father; **B**, 572, 682, **R**, 636
Jessie Scouts; **J**, 4
Jesuits; **S**, 124
Jewish Historical Historical Society; **K**, 249-251
Jewry; **F**, 461
Jews; **H**, 358, 1270, **J**, 134, **L**, 420, 576, **M**, 1245, **W**, 894
Jey, Hobart, Jr., Com.; **G**, 92
Jockusch, Julius W., Capt.; **F**, 475
Joe Thompson Artillery; **H**, 230
Johnny Reb; **K**, 70
Johnny Reb Band; **H**, 71
Johnson County, NC; **B**, 90
Johnson's Island Prison, OH; **A**, 476, 542, **B**, 108, 205, 529, 754, 1277, 1512, **C**, 195, **H**, 463, 661, 783, **J**, 145-153, 369, **K**, 240, **M**, 673a, 1071, 1307, **N**, 165, **P**, 388, 448, **S**, 920,

Johnson's Island Prison, OH
  Burials, **A**, 400,
  Escape, **W**, 851,
  Medical History, **W**, 230,
  Plot, **S**, 355, 357,
  Prisoners, **M**, 923a,
  Raid, **S**, 1358
Johnson's Island, OH, Memorial; **B**, 1281
Johnson, Andrew, Pres.; **C**, 367, 518, **H**, 150, **M**, 898, **R**, 1, **W**, 683,
  Impeachment, **J**, 260a
Johnson, Bradley Tyler, Brig.Gen.; **A**, 449-450, 514, **C**, 967,
  Symposium, **W**, 604
Johnson, Bushrod Rust, Maj.Gen.; **C**, 1560, 1564, **K**, 33
Johnson, Edward, Maj.Gen.; **C**, 940, **H**, 1330, **P**, 148
Johnson, Frank W.; **T**, 150
Johnson, George W., Gov., KY; **H**, 415, **K**, 101
Johnson, Herschel Vespasian, Gov., GA; **F**, 274, **H**, 814, **P**, 651, **R**, 884
Johnson, James; **S**, 280
Johnson, Jane C.; **J**, 183
Johnsonville, TN;
  Forrest's Raid, **B**, 1349,
  Raid, **W**, 704
Johnsonville, TN, Battle of; **C**, 1341, **M**, 1204
Johnston & Brent Diaries; **G**, 447
Johnston Conspiracy; **G**, 245
Johnston's Army; **M**, 1274,
  Surrender, **B**, 1535
Johnston, Albert Sidney, Gen.; **B**, 328, 708, **C**, 417, **D**, 137, 906, **E**, 202, **G**, 17, 226, 489, **H**, 86, 1060, 1353, **J**, 338, 341b, **K**, 146, **L**, 29, **M**, 548, 1051, **R**, 224, 664, **S**, 138, 308-310, 715a, **U**, 3, **W**, 956
Johnston, Eliza; **J**, 258
Johnston, George Burgwyn, Capt.; **L**, 85
Johnston, Hugh Buckner; **B**, 867, **V**, 132
Johnston, Joseph Eggleston, Gen.; **B**, 148, 606, 708, 1054, 1381, **C**, 1088, 1129, 1269, **D**, 198, 298, 859, **E**, 18, 77, **F**, 539, **G**, 261, 367, 393, 433, 444, **H**, 466, 1263, **J**, 69, 191, 563, **L**, 115, 776, 778, **M**, 690-691, **N**, 88a, **P**, 383, **R**, 418, 599, **S**, 61, 223, 500, 651, 784, **U**, 30,
  Bentonville, NC, **T**, 213,
  Memorial, **P**, 624,
  Papers, **S**, 1430,
  Sherman's March, **K**, 53,
  Surrender, **P**, 330, **R**, 300,
  Wounded, **A**, 439
Johnston, Josiah Stoddard; **B**, 1191
Johnston, William Curtis; **J**, 321
Johnston, William Preston, Col.; **A**, 451, **C**, 1211, **D**, 210, 267, **J**, 336, **S**, 312
Jolly, Manson Sherrill; **E**, 5
Jomimi, Baron; **B**, 1537
Jonas, S.A., Maj.; **C**, 972
Jones County, MS; **B**, 866,
  Knight Family, **K**, 233
Jones Raid, WV; **M**, 980
Jones, Ben C.; **O**, 127
Jones, Charles Colcock, Col.; **B**, 886, 1642, **C**, 272, 362, 364, 421, 1041, 1044, 1325, 1552, **G**, 411
Jones, Charles Edgeworth; **J**, 395
Jones, David Rumph, Maj.Gen.; **J**, 413
Jones, Edmund, Capt.; **M**, 982
Jones, Frank S.; **D**, 477
Jones, Henry Francis; **R**, 660
Jones, J. William; **A**, 417, 449, **C**, 1181, **D**, 245, **P**, 63
Jones, James P.; **M**, 1011
Jones, Joseph; **A**, 451, **B**, 1211-1213, 1279, **C**, 1217
Jones, Maggie Mackay; **E**, 85
Jones, Mary G.; **C**, 1343
Jones, MS, Free State; **K**, 233
Jones, Robert Huhn; **B**, 1269
Jones, Thomas Goode, Gov., AL; **A**, 449-450, **J**, 550, 552
Jones, Virgil Carrington; **M**, 1226
Jones, Walter B.; **A**, 116, **D**, 861
Jones, William H.; **XYZ**, 92
Jones-Imboden Raid; **C**, 1194, **S**, 1391

Jonesboro, GA;
  Raid, **H**, 779
Jonesboro, GA, Battle of; **A**, 340, **C**, 142, 646, **D**, 316, **G**, 221, **L**, 378
Jonesville, VA, Battle of; **W**, 1066
Jordan, Thomas G.; **W**, 557
Jordan, Thomas Marshall, Brig.Gen.; **B**, 472, **C**, 264, **F**, 381, **W**, 705
Jordan, Weymouth T.; **D**, 962
Jose, Julian Marti; **G**, 681
Joseph, Josephine; **M**, 1256
Journal of a Secesh Lady; **E**, 85
Journalism; **B**, 1166, **C**, 165, **E**, 259, **G**, 307, **M**, 342, **W**, 477, 808,
  Alabama, **C**, 705,
  Atlanta, GA, **M**, 102,
  Editorial Revolution, **F**, 499,
  Freedom Press, **M**, 334,
  Humor, **F**, 221,
  Kentucky, **C**, 1377, **H**, 1188,
  Missouri, **S**, 1442,
  Press Association, **P**, 704-707,
  Religious, **S**, 1304,
  Sensational Press, **D**, 17
Joyner, Edmund Noah; **D**, 942
Judah (schooner); **S**, 1386
Juhl Letters; **F**, 235
Juniper Meeting House, NC; **B**, 90
Junkin, George G., Lt.; **B**, 349

K

Kaiser; **E**, 270
Kanawha County, WV; **L**, 750
Kanawha Valley, WV; **C**, 1162, **W**, 439-440,
   First Action, **S**, 1348, **W**, 437
Kanawha, WV, Battle of; **S**, 1350
Kansas; **B**, 1185, **C**, 1255, **D**, 172, **N**, 79, **R**, 133,
   Admission as a State, **I**, 59,
   Border Wars, **W**, 560,
   Jayhawkers, **C**, 284, 286,
   Monuments, **B**, 927,
   Sumner Outrage, **F**, 164,
   Territorial, **C**, 1384
Kansas Bill; **B**, 559, **D**, 411
Kansas Rangers; **W**, 740
Kansas Territory; **A**, 26
Kansas-Missouri War;
   Propaganda, **L**, 486
Kansas-Nebraska Bill; **P**, 102
Kaufmann, Patricia A.; **C**, 981
Kautz, August Valentine, Maj.Gen.; **H**, 719
Kearsarge (ironclad); **A**, 112, 442, **B**, 107, 1076, 1425, **E**, 74, **H**, 934, **L**, 190, **N**, 36, **P**, 245, **R**, 515, 611
Keelan, James; **G**, 117
Keiley, Anthony M.; **A**, 386
Kell, John McIntosh, Capt.; **A**, 397, **B**, 1153-1154, **D**, 503, **H**, 610
Kelley's Ford, NC, Battle of; **S**, 1446, **W**, 194
Kelley, Benjamin F. Maj.Gen.; **B**, 33, 978,
   Captured, **C**, 1471, **M**, 683, **R**, 592, **S**, 1057, **V**, 79,
Kelly, James J., Pvt.; **B**, 245
Kelly, John Herbert, Brig.Gen.; **H**, 1073d, **K**, 61b, **P**, 635
Kemble, Fanny; **C**, 305

Kemper County, MS; **H**, 1026, **L**, 786
Kemper's Brigade; **C**, 1276, **J**, 266
Kemper, James Lawson, Maj.Gen.; **C**, 61, 797, **S**, 514
Kendall, George E.; **S**, 798
Kennedy, H., Capt.; **C**, 669
Kennedy, Robert Cobb; **B**, 615, **C**, 1582
Kenner, Duncan F.; **H**, 713
Kennerly, Sarah Law; **B**, 672
Kennesaw Line, GA; **B**, 257
Kennesaw Mountain National Park, GA;
   Confederate Dead, **D**, 480
Kennesaw Mountain, GA;
   Georgia Military Institute, **XYZ**, 14
Kennesaw Mountain, GA, Battle of; **C**, 792, **D**, 481, **F**, 540, **G**, 174, **J**, 342, 613, **M**, 140, 656, 666, **S**, 1244, **XYZ**, 15,
   Bodies Recovered, **B**, 1389,
   Sharpshooters, **B**, 1394,
   Siege, **W**, 712
Kennon, Beverly; **B**, 56
Kent County, MD; **K**, 197a
Kentucky; **A**, 388, **B**, 778, **C**, 1292, **D**, 378, **F**, 445, **G**, 604, **H**, 361, 413-423, **J**, 318, **K**, 93a, 101, 231a, **M**, 120, 669, 911, **O**, 202, **S**, 227, **T**, 248, **W**, 267,
   Abandoned, **B**, 389,
   Battles, **C**, 682,
   Black Suffrage, **H**, 1188,
   Bragg's Invasion, **F**, 172,
   Campaign, **M**, 761, **Q**, 21, **R**, 902,
   Cavaliers, **M**, 441, 1246-1247,
   Civil War Annals, **C**, 814,
   Confederate Dead, **S**, 195,
   Conflicts, **A**, 237,
   Conventions, **K**, 95,

General Assembly, **M**, 61,
Generals, **H**, 419,
History, **M**, 859,
Invasion, **G**, 247, **K**, 97, **M**, 367f, **T**, 38, **W**, 505,
Jackson Purchase, **W**, 585,
Morgan's Raids, **B**, 367, 379, 415, 1323,
Neutrality, **C**, 29, **Q**, 24, **S**, 439,
Operations, **W**, 586,
Pensions, **K**, 103,
Press, Rebel, **C**, 1377,
Provisional Government, **J**, 207a, **K**, 101,
Secession, **B**, 1204, **C**, 1230, **H**, 420, **K**, 4, **Q**, 23, **S**, 196, **T**, 501,
Sectionalism, **R**, 573,
Slavery, **H**, 432, **T**, 372,
Soldiers, **B**, 501,
Verse, **S**, 803,
Volunteers, **K**, 102
Kentucky Brigade; **G**, 157, **H**, 940
Kentucky Rifles; **J**, 516
Kentucky Troops;
  Cavalry,
    4th Regt., **D**, 445,
    9th Regt., **A**, 560,
    11th Regt., **M**, 1345, **Q**, 18,
  Infantry,
    1st Brig., **T**, 224,
    1st Regt., **K**, 99,
    4th Regt., **W**, 365,
    6th Regt., **G**, 481,
    8th Regt., **K**, 96,
    13th Regt., **J**, 321,
  Mounted Rifles,
    1st Bat., **E**, 277,
  Roster, **R**, 743
Keokuk (ship); **H**, 314
Kerksis, Stanley; **B**, 1633
Kerksis, Sydney C.; **K**, 117a
Kernstown, VA, Battle of; **H**, 332
Kerr, Homer L.; **E**, 106, 241
Kerr, William Schomberg Robert; **L**, 695
Kershaw's Brigade; **D**, 576, **K**, 126, 130
Kershaw's Division; **K**, 127
Kershaw, Joseph Brevard, Maj.Gen.; **M**, 515
Kesler Cross Lanes, WV; **C**, 1168
Key West, FL; **B**, 1037, **W**, 640
Key, D.M., Sen.; **A**, 21
Key, Thomas J.; **C**, 308
Keyes, Wade; **D**, 528
Keysville Guards; **R**, 535
Kickapoo Indians; **P**, 610
Kidd, Robert Vaughan; **P**, 386
Killian, Elizabeth, SC; **S**, 947
Kilpatrick, Hugh Judson, Maj.Gen.; **C**, 337, **F**, 355, **H**, 184, 779
Kilpatrick-Dahlgren Raid; **J**, 455
Kincaid's Battery; **C**, 18
Kinchen, Oscar; **B**, 1363
King & Queen County, VA; **B**, 9
King Cotton; **O**, 234
King William Artillery; **K**, 167
King's Mountain, SC; **D**, 67
King, George, Capt.; **C**, 1544
King, Spencer Bidwell, Jr.; **A**, 359, **H**, 5
King, T. Butler; **S**, 1041
King, Thomas E., Capt.; **S**, 1190
Kingsland, Charles A.; **V**, 63
Kinlock, VA; **S**, 54
Kinnaird, M.P.; **F**, 143
Kinney County, TX; **S**, 63
Kiolbassa, Peter; **B**, 1621
Kireh Swift (bark); **W**, 714
Kirkland's Brigade; **E**, 152
Kirkland, Richard; **E**, 183a, **K**, 123, 129, **L**, 104
Kirksville, MO, Battle of; **V**, 134
Kirkwood, W.; **C**, 1556
Kittrell, John B., Mrs.; **A**, 16
Klein, Maury, Dr.; **A**, 176
Klodsoe, Jacob; **XYZ**, 21
Knight Family, MS; **K**, 233
Knight, Lucian Lamar; **U**, 33
Knights of the Golden Circle; **B**, 1247, **C**, 1239, 1423, **F**, 94, **G**, 546, **H**, 784, **K**, 1-6, 216, 221-222a, **L**, 443, **M**, 890, 1180, **P**, 538, **R**, 467, **S**, 52, 219, 862, 1188
Knights Templar, GA; **S**, 800
Know-Nothings; **B**, 345, 354

Knoxville, TN;
  Campaign, **H**, 1237, 1240,
  Cavalry, **M**, 905,
  Federal Raid, **W**, 1089,
  Longstreet's Charge, **R**, 125,
  Siege, **B**, 911, **C**, 1369, **N**, 14
Knoxville, TN, Battle of; **F**, 126
Kollock Family, GA; **K**, 247
Kollock, George J., Mrs.; **K**, 247
Kollock, W.W.; **K**, 247
Kolpatrick, James T.; **B**, 1543
Korn, Bertram W., Dr.; **J**, 134
Krick, Robert K.; **B**, 672
Kriegsfade, Auf dem; **B**, 921
Ku Klux Klan; **B**, 1046-1047, 1422, **F**, 305, **H**, 906, **J**, 84, **M**, 291, 712a, 794a, 955, 977a, 1189, **P**, 512, **R**, 700,
  Origin, **A**, 255
Kurtz & Allison Prints; **B**, 311-312, **C**, 553, **G**, 553, **J**, 45, **W**, 920
Kurtz, Wilbur G.; **A**, 540

L

La Auerre et la Paix; **A**, 229
La Grange Military Academy; **W**, 1075
La Guerre Civile; **V**, 105
Laboratory, Confederate; **H**, 387
Ladies Fuel Society; **N**, 191
Ladies Memorial Association; **B**, 227, **J**, 536, **K**, 124
Lady of Georgia (pseudonym); **D**, 549
LaFayette Guild; **C**, 182
Lafourche District, LA; **L**, 134
Lagree, Simon; **C**, 1258
Laing, Joseph; **F**, 1
Laird Brothers; **C**, 1266, **G**, 1
Lake Bistineau Salt Works; **C**, 1155
Lake Erie; **W**, 957,
   Conspiracy, **R**, 271,
   Raid, **B**, 344,
   Rebels, **F**, 556
Lake Providence; **D**, 175
Lale, Max, Lt.Col.; **G**, 92
Lamar Rifles; **B**, 1560
Lamar, Gazaway Bugg; **H**, 564, **M**, 334
Lamar, Lucius Quintus C., Col.; **A**, 266, **B**, 557, **C**, 306-307, **D**, 577, **H**, 114, **M**, 363, 1309, **N**, 142, **R**, 236, **S**, 287
Lamb, William, Col.; **F**, 405
Lamond, Ben; **H**, 59
Lampasas, TX, Salt Works; **S**, 1101
Lampkin's Battery; **M**, 325
Lancashire Cotton Famine; **H**, 693, 985
Lancashire, England; **A**, 35, **B**, 1296,
   Propaganda, **H**, 986
Lancaster, Dallas M.; **F**, 553
Lancaster, Mary H.; **F**, 553
Land Battle, First; **C**, 188

Land Distribution; **G**, 601
Land of Fadeless Start; **A**, 456
Land We Love (magazine); **A**, 521
Lane's Brigade; **B**, 706, **L**, 82
Lane's Corps; **L**, 84
Lane's Rangers; **H**, 632
Lane, James Henry, Brig.Gen.; **C**, 1358
Lang, David Berkeley, Lt.Col.; **F**, 232, **L**, 101, **N**, 55
Langdon, L.L.; **K**, 104
Lanier, Robert S.; **M**, 873
Lanier, Sidney; **A**, 437, **B**, 1297, **C**, 617, **E**, 202, **M**, 548
Laredo, TX, Battle of; **T**, 237
Las Vegas, NV;
   Capital of New Mexico, **D**, 735
Lasswell, Mary; **G**, 263
Last Shots; **J**, 328, **P**, 91
Latane, William, Capt.; **C**, 116, **M**, 566, **S**, 36,
   Burial, **C**, 1313, **N**, 221
Lathrop, Barnes F.; **L**, 133
Latin America;
   Confederate Exiles, **H**, 864-865
Latrobe, J.H.B.; **F**, 433
Lauderdale County, AL; **D**, 45
Laurel Brigade; **M**, 479,
   History, **M**, 493
Laurel Hill, WV;
   Retreat, **H**, 34, **S**, 1215
Laurel Wood Plantation, MS; **L**, 99
Law, Evander McIvor, Brig.Gen.; **A**, 386, **S**, 1423a, **W**, 604a
Law, Sallie Chapman Gordon; **T**, 26
Law, William; **E**, 227
Lawley, Frank; **J**, 110
Lawrence, F. Lee; **C**, 68, 1488
Lawrence, MO, Massacre; **B**, 948-949

Laws; **C**, 888, **M**, 574, 860, **P**, 818, **R**, 52,
   Atlanta, GA, **L**, 7,
   Florida, **S**, 789,
   Mississippi, **M**, 939
Lawsuits; **B**, 1493
Lay, Henry C., Bishop;
   Papers, **S**, 290
Lay, John Fitzhugh; **P**, 212
Le Gear, Clara Egli; **H**, 1120, **S**, 1115
Le Grand, Julia; **W**, 27
Le Mat Guns; **H**, 20, **L**, 590, **S**, 1449
Le Mat, Alexandre Francois; **XYZ**, 68
Le Mexique et Les Etates
   Confederes; **F**, 458
Leadership; **W**, 751
Leber, Johnny; **L**, 154
Lecutre-lesson, Confederate War; **A**, 475
Ledyard, Erwin; **D**, 436
Lee County, MS;
   Reconstruction, **B**, 1048
Lee Family; **C**, 1287a, **H**, 697,
   Stratford Hall, **A**, 179
Lee Memorial Foundation; **B**, 781
Lee Monument Association; **A**, 291
Lee Rifles; **H**, 268
Lee's Army; **B**, 749, 1051, **C**, 328, **E**, 18, **S**, 77,
   Christmas Dinner, **R**, 4,
   Last Days, **M**, 214, **S**, 327,
   Morale, **J**, 459,
   Strength, **E**, 34, **M**, 216
Lee's Campaigns; **A**, 204, 278, **E**, 14, **G**, 684
Lee's Colonels; **K**, 258, 258a
Lee's Invasion; **G**, 250
Lee's Lieutenants; **L**, 227, **P**, 513
Lee's Tigers; **J**, 529a
Lee, Basil Duke; **T**, 20
Lee, Edmund Jennings, Dr.; **B**, 1274
Lee, Edward Childe; **C**, 468
Lee, Edwin Gray, Brig.Gen.; **L**, 471a, 471b
Lee, Fitzhugh, Maj.Gen.; **A**, 449, **B**, 1351, **C**, 1219, **D**, 525, **G**, 186, **H**, 1329, **L**, 1, 219, 429,
   Monument, **C**, 98,
   as Gov., VA, **D**, 76
Lee, George Washington C., Maj.Gen.; **H**, 1183, **L**, 254, **M**, 369, 377
Lee, John A.I., Lt.; **J**, 274
Lee, Mary Custis; **M**, 489
Lee, Mildred; **M**, 489
Lee, Robert E. (play); **D**, 845
Lee, Robert Edward, Gen.; **A**, 23, 37-38a, 40, 44, 48, 151, 181, 246, 272, 282, 291, 309, 358, 387, 437, 450, **B**, 1, 7, 54, 147, 177, 202, 224, 530, 690, 697, 712, 739, 796, 845, 850, 857, 964, 1012, 1055, 1062-1071, 1122, 1181, 1274, 1319, 1446, 1448, 1451, 1459, 1545, **C**, 2, 58, 82, 180, 233, 248, 283, 386, 445, 468, 835, 1089, 1095, 1177, 1184, 1319, 1324, 1350, 1367, 1386, 1392, **D**, 51, 91, 122, 146, 148, 259, 346, 486, 490-491, 523-524, 685, 806, 973, **E**, 6, 24, 52, 63, 169, 201, **F**, 82, 145, 202, 295, 321, 460, 486, 511-519, 523, 594, **G**, 84, 194, 270, 315-316, 371, 469, 520, 584, 665, **H**, 120, 157, 159, 182, 195, 245, 487, 657, 714, 798b, 798a, 852, 929, 1000, 1098, 1186a, 1339, **J**, 279a, 331a, 341a, 406a, 435, 452, 456, 472-473, 478, 601, **K**, 186, **L**, 261a, 612a, 624, 785, **M**, 24, 131, 174, 204, 297, 346, 368c, 477, 487, 491a, 517, 545, 573, 641, 711b, 827, 899, 915, 961-962, 975a, 999, 1096, 1119, 1214a, 1231, 1243, **N**, 89, **O**, 8, 10, **P**, 103a, 241a, 244, 839, **R**, 116, 143, 234, 473, 527, 566, 588, 698, 711a, **S**, 40, 173, 192, 595, 629a, 919, 1122, 1138, 1196, 1299, **T**, 73, 81, 391, 464, 509, **V**, 78, 133, 183, **W**, 258, 303, 326, 485, 489, 556, 573a, 726, 775, 786, 821, 835, **XYZ**, 35, 60,
   Ancestry, **F**, 332,
   Anecdotes, **B**, 120,
   Appointed Com.-in-Chief, **C**, 1221,
   Appomattox, **A**, 41, 46, 175, **S**, 1046,
   Appreciated, **S**, 727, 758, **W**, 654,

Arlington House, **N**, 57,
Biography, **W**, 88, 853,
Birthday, **G**, 208, **H**, 14, 965, **M**, 421a, 850a, 919a, **N**, 113, **O**, 12, **P**, 37, **S**, 128, **T**, 517, **W**, 202, 550, 815, 819, 1079,
Boy-gunners of, **N**, 181,
Centennial, **A**, 39, **C**, 872, **D**, 784,
Chancellorsville, **B**, 146, **T**, 7,
Character, **A**, 42, **C**, 54, **M**, 1322-1323, **R**, 730, **S**, 660, **T**, 79,
Chickahominy, **H**, 822,
Christmas, **M**, 875,
Clemency, **D**, 548,
Coffin, **C**, 484a,
College, **C**, 1422,
Confederate Government, **B**, 1056,
Correspondence, **M**, 360a, **P**, 49, **V**, 14,
Creed of, **L**, 350,
Daughters, **C**, 1287a,
Death, **F**, 204, **L**, 340, **M**, 1110, **V**, 92, **W**, 842,
Dedications, **J**, 273,
Defeat, Causes of, **A**, 161, 196,
Dispatches, **F**, 510, **L**, 342,
Educator, **C**, 4,
Engineers, **B**, 855,
Eulogy, **L**, 165,
Farewells, **F**, 118, **L**, 343, **M**, 215,
Field Letters, **M**, 6,
First Year of War, **W**, 407,
Florida, **B**, 673,
Fort Pulaski, GA, **XYZ**, 71,
Fredericksburg, **L**, 9,
Freeman's Posthumous Footnote, **G**, 238,
Friend of Youth, **W**, 392,
Funeral, **L**, 346,
General Order No.9, **F**, 525, **L**, 343, 348,
Generals of, **S**, 767-768,
Generalship, **C**, 853, **R**, 668,
Georgia, **B**, 1142,
Gettysburg, **A**, 205, 211, **C**, 515-516, **D**, 804, **E**, 16, **G**, 193, **H**, 764, **I**, 10, **K**, 253a, **L**, 242, 446, 648, **P**, 63, 278, **S**, 681, **T**, 454,
Gettysburg, Hdqrts., **M**, 1257-1258,
Gettysburg, Report, **L**, 345,
Grand Review, **B**, 1119,
Harper's Ferry, **B**, 1495,
Headquarters, **C**, 500,
Health, **R**, 475a,
Historiography, **C**, 1086,
History of ANV, **M**, 983,
Home, Wartime, **R**, 492,
Horses, **D**, 826, **E**, 60, **T**, 430,
Jackson, Meetings, **F**, 236, **L**, 200, **T**, 559,
Ladies, **F**, 517,
Last Campaign, **D**, 808, **G**, 435, **H**, 499, **K**, 171a,
Last Days, **C**, 565,
Last Order, **D**, 10,
Leadership, **B**, 1586, **J**, 112, **W**, 919,
Lexington, VA, **P**, 714,
Life, **E**, 225, **F**, 73, **H**, 153, **M**, 790, 848, **P**, 632, **S**, 358, **W**, 530, 772,
Lost Orders, **D**, 936, **L**, 354,
Loyalty, **H**, 122, **W**, 546,
Medical History, **K**, 253,
Memoirs, **L**, 624,
Memorials, **B**, 781, **C**, 751, **D**, 881, 968, **G**, 15, **K**, 67, **M**, 597,
Military Career, **A**, 31, **P**, 690, **T**, 79,
Military Education, **S**, 1434,
Monuments, **B**, 1558, **D**, 54, **E**, 13, 41, **H**, 931, **L**, 330, **M**, 210, 420, **T**, 433,
Napoleon, **S**, 577,
Naval Influences, **H**, 584,
Ordnance Efficiency, **C**, 821,
Papers, **D**, 814, **L**, 269,
Patriotism, **H**, 123,
Peace Conference, **G**, 349,
Pennsylvania Campaign Report, **L**, 345,
Photographer, **F**, 180,
Post-war, **E**, 65, **F**, 177, **R**, 473,
Prussian Observer, **L**, 780,
Religion, **F**, 178, **J**, 345, **M**, 565, 595, 598,
Requiem, **W**, 319,
Rescues Federal Officer, **G**, 19,

Retirement Requested, **F**, 603,
Retreat, **J**, 99, **M**, 502,
Rich Mountain, WV, **XYZ**, 101,
Richmond Campaign, **C**, 444,
Santa Claus, **C**, 558-559,
School History, **R**, 302,
Seven Days Battles, **D**, 811,
Soldier, **P**, 19-24, **R**, 644,
Songbook, **S**, 135,
Special Order No.191, **L**, 694,
Staff, **T**, 6, **W**, 412,
Strategy, **B**, 145,
Sunday Observances, **S**, 1398,
Surrender, **C**, 381, 1142, **H**, 1035, **L**, 229, **M**, 217, 739, 1157a, **O**, 4,
Sword, **G**, 507, **L**, 298, **M**, 218, **W**, 323,
Tactics, **H**, 21,
Texas, **R**, 496, **S**, 335, 498, **W**, 459,
Tomb, **L**, 268,
Tribute, **C**, 179, **W**, 903,
US Military Academy, **U**, 42,
Unionist, **W**, 873,
Vindication, **S**, 11, 1434,
Virginia, **G**, 511, **T**, 80,
Virginia Retreat, **S**, 264a, 1029a,
Washington & Lee College, **H**, 1099, **N**, 65,
Washington Cathedral, **B**, 207,
West Point Academy, **P**, 726, **R**, 343, **V**, 124,
Wilderness, **A**, 174, **B**, 350, **L**, 574, **V**, 103, **W**, 544,
William & Mary College, **J**, 608,
Writings about, **F**, 179
Lee, Robert Edward, Mrs.; **K**, 11, **M**, 20
Lee, Sidney Smith; **C**, 1573
Lee, Stephen Dill, Lt.Gen.; **A**, 340, **C**, 1367, **D**, 493, 525, **E**, 194, **H**, 526-527, **L**, 370, 392, **M**, 781a, **W**, 604a, UCV, **U**, 24-25
Lee, William H. Fitzhugh, Maj.Gen.; **T**, 471
Leech & Rigdon; **A**, 138
Leeper, Matthew; **H**, 410
Leesburg, VA;
 Confederate Museum, **K**, 34
Leesburg, VA, Battle of; **H**, 948
Legan, Marshall Scott; **W**, 15
Legionares; **C**, 1253
Legislature;
 Voting, **A**, 287
Leiter Library; **L**, 423
Leland, Isabella Middleton; **M**, 846
Lemke, W.J.; **A**, 542, **B**, 275, 1374
Lemley, Harry J.; **R**, 193
Lennox, Mary; **C**, 1154
Lenoir Family Letters; **A**, 524
Lenoir, Walter Waightstill, Capt.; **W**, 472
Leon County, FL;
 Secession, **N**, 211
Leon County, TX;
 Roster, **W**, 922
Leonard, William T.; **R**, 705
Lessee Problems; **B**, 683
Letcher, John, Gov., VA; **B**, 349, 869, **L**, 454, **P**, 728,
 Criticism of Cabinet, **B**, 875,
 Home, **S**, 442
Letford, William; **A**, 98
Letter Express; **B**, 1307
Leventhorpe, Collett, Gen.; **W**, 473
Lewis County, WV; **C**, 1160, 1166
Lewis, Jackson; **K**, 173
Lewis, John A., Dr.; **T**, 40
Lewisburg, WV;
 Law Library, **S**, 1375
Lewisburg, WV, Battle of; **R**, 306
Lexington, KY;
 Morgan's Men, Reunion, **B**, 1545
Lexington, MO; **C**, 790, **M**, 587,
 Centennial, **C**, 529,
 Confederate Advance, **M**, 991,
 Price's Army, **M**, 497,
 Slave Dealers, **C**, 791
Lexington, MO, Battle of; **C**, 293, **L**, 461a, **M**, 401, **S**, 776
Lexington, VA; **B**, 850, **D**, 128, **P**, 714
Lexington, VA, Battle of; **L**, 499
Leyden's Battery; **H**, 411
Libby Prison, Richmond, VA; **B**, 1606, 1644, **S**, 145, **T**, 503, **W**, 25, 124
Liberalism; **D**, 9

Liberty County, GA; **J**, 509, **P**, 608,
  Raids, **M**, 996
Liberty Hall Volunteers; **B**, 110, 352,
  S, 1282
Liberty Independent Troop; **L**, 60
Libraries; **W**, 779, 893, 1093,
  Burned by Sherman, **H**, 757,
  Regimental, **W**, 627
Lieber, Francis; **L**, 601
Light Dragoons; **D**, 179, **W**, 91
Lightburn, Joseph Andrew Jackson, Brig.Gen.; **C**, 1167
Lightfoot, Marise P.; **G**, 94
Lillian (ship); **T**, 185
Lincoln County, NC; **H**, 979,
  Roster, **N**, 150-151
Lincoln, Abraham, Pres.; **A**, 567, **B**, 100, 757, 767, 792, 909, 971, 1144, 1526, **C**, 492, **D**, 611, 685, **E**, 135, **G**, 158, **H**, 390a, 488, 760, **J**, 227, 233, **L**, 133, **M**, 181, 239, 711b, 883, 914, 916-917, **O**, 238, **R**, 55, 79-81, **S**, 414, 619, 919, 974, **T**, 301, 371, **V**, 54,
  Ancestry, **T**, 524,
  Anecdotes, **D**, 827,
  Assassination, **A**, 4, **B**, 1473, **C**, 651, **D**, 180, **F**, 447, 464, **G**, 230, **K**, 225, **L**, 105, **M**, 397, 621, 1263, 1267, **R**, 873, **S**, 1123, **T**, 314, 500, **W**, 341,
  Baldwin Interview, **K**, 25,
  Barbarian, **C**, 1148,
  Cabinet, **C**, 1466,
  Chicago Times, np., **T**, 124,
  Comparisons, **E**, 270, **R**, 849-854, **W**, 402,
  Conduct of War, **P**, 802,
  Conferences, **C**, 1094,
  Conspiracy, **C**, 1594, **R**, 707,
  Constitution, **T**, 411,
  Correspondence, **S**, 1098,
  Cotton Trade, **O**, 9,
  Criticised, **C**, 768, **W**, 684,
  Democracy, **W**, 534,
  Election, **H**, 151,
  Fort Sumter, SC, **R**, 54, 888, **T**, 535,
  Humor, **A**, 3,
  Illegitimacy, **C**, 798, **E**, 280,
  Invasion, **F**, 330,
  Kentucky, **D**, 763, **T**, 372,
  Myths, **B**, 531,
  Negroes, **G**, 556,
  Newspapers, **S**, 1052,
  Pardons Given, **B**, 1542,
  Personal Wealth, **T**, 531,
  Post-assassination, **J**, 531,
  Proclamation, **C**, 95,
  Richmond, VA, **M**, 1356,
  Sherman Peace Fiasco, **N**, 18,
  South's Attitudes toward, **C**, 1400, **R**, 889,
  Treatment of Confederates, **D**, 762, 765,
  Trial, **H**, 311, **S**, 337,
  Tyler, John, Pres., **T**, 546
Lincolnton, NC; **N**, 149
Linn County, KA; **T**, 481
Literary Conspiracy; **M**, 166
Literature; **B**, 1029, 1124, 1305, 1308, 1315, 1356-1357, 1429, **C**, 34, 810, 1352, **E**, 162, **F**, 253, **H**, 471, 475, **J**, 502, **L**, 63, 571, 610, **M**, 368c, **N**, 170, **O**, 84, 87, 206, **P**, 17, 251, 443, **R**, 393, 784, **S**, 490, 855, 890, **W**, 801, **XYZ**, 73,
  Anti-Lincoln, **H**, 474,
  Children's Stories, **B**, 1021,
  Fiction, **B**, 853,
  Georgia, **S**, 149,
  German Military, **N**, 146,
  Military, **B**, 679,
  South, **B**, 320, 935, **H**, 1215a, **J**, 86
Littell, John S., Col.; **C**, 42
Littig, George; **C**, 469
Little Fork Rangers; **H**, 10
Little River Baptist Association; **B**, 90
Little Rock, AR; **R**, 367,
  Conventions, **O**, 123-124,
  Diocese, **W**, 625,
  McAlmont, **M**, 367a,
  Retreat, **E**, 308
Little Sorrel (Jackson's horse); **D**, 746
Little, John, Rev.; **S**, 717

Little, Lewis Henry, Brig.Gen.; **D**, 880,
  Burial, **P**, 354
Little, Magnus Thompson, Col.; **K**, 34
Littlefield, George Washington, Capt.; **G**, 461
Livermore, William R., Col.; **A**, 174
Liverpool Cotton Association; **H**, 658
Liverpool, England; **S**, 924,
  Cotton Trade, **D**, 89
Livingood, James W.; **G**, 445
Llewellyn, David Herbert; **H**, 222
Lloyd Letter; **G**, 523
Loehr, Charles T.; **A**, 450, **P**, 462
Logan County, AR; **L**, 586c
Logan, Thomas Muldrup, Brig.Gen.; **M**, 1161, **W**, 248
Lohse, William R.; **K**, 14
Lomax Rifles; **D**, 442
London News, England, np.; **H**, 214
London Times, England, np.; **A**, 528, **J**, 614, **R**, 266, **S**, 1067, **T**, 307, **W**, 674
London, England;
  Confederate Exiles, **W**, 111,
  Confederate Secret Service, **J**, 89,
  Southern Independence Association, **S**, 877
London, L.F.; **C**, 440
London, Lucy; **A**, 326
Lone Jack, MO, Battle of; **A**, 289
Long Creek Rifles; **G**, 296
Long, Armistead Lindsay, Brig.Gen.; **A**, 450, **L**, 622
Long, Barbara; **N**, 111
Long, George; **J**, 273
Long, John D.; **B**, 1183
Longstreet's Brigade; **A**, 166
Longstreet's Corps; **A**, 168
Longstreet's Division; **A**, 171
Longstreet, Augustus Baldwin; **V**, 169
Longstreet, James, Lt.Gen.; **A**, 156-158, 172, 274, 470, **B**, 350, 1060, 1219, **C**, 8, **E**, 24, 60, 69, **G**, 420, 570, **H**, 636, **J**, 350, **L**, 245, 629, **M**, 349, 488, 1221, **P**, 370, 418a, 843, **R**, 441a, **S**, 55, 57-58, 653, 1423a, **T**, 81, 462-463, **XYZ**, 32,
  Courier, **XYZ**, 84,
  Gettysburg, PA, **J**, 457, **K**, 253a, **M**, 551, **P**, 188, **T**, 214a,
  Pennyslvania Campaign, **L**, 650
Lookout Mountain, TN; **D**, 801, **J**, 23,
  Operations, **L**, 666, **P**, 325, **S**, 1143, **W**, 137
Lookout Mountain, TN, Battle of; **B**, 1373, **M**, 494
Lookout Valley, TN; **B**, 1170, **L**, 146
Loring, William Wing, Maj.Gen.; **S**, 1349, **W**, 420, 431
Los Fieles Catolicos de la Parroquia; **C**, 229
Losses, Confederate; **J**, 487, 493, **L**, 573
Lost Cause Recollections; **A**, 577
Lost Colony of the Confederacy; **H**, 455
Lost Dispatch; **H**, 841
Lost Orders; **M**, 1298
Loudon Cemetery, VA; **K**, 40a
Loudon Guards; **D**, 509,
  Roster, **L**, 696
Loudoun Rangers; **G**, 354
Loughery, Robert W., Col.; **L**, 32, 699
Louisiana; **B**, 1140, **D**, 164-165, 615, **H**, 880-881, **J**, 357a, **L**, 220, **Q**, 7, **U**, 1, **W**, 855,
  Battles, **S**, 68,
  Camp Life, **A**, 75, **W**, 742,
  Campaign, **D**, 939,
  Clergy, **R**, 697a,
  Colonels Killed, **B**, 537,
  Confederate Records, **B**, 899,
  Confederate Regulars, **W**, 346,
  Conventions, **O**, 55-59, **P**, 790,
  Defenses, **W**, 788,
  Disaffection, **L**, 132,
  Discontent, **T**, 51b,
  Elections, Secession, **D**, 561,
  Federal Troops, **O**, 75,
  Freedmen's Bureau, **E**, 210,
  History, **M**, 647,

Legislature, **H**, 324,
Letters, **V**, 47,
Medical Education, **D**, 892,
Military Records, **C**, 295,
Monuments, **S**, 895,
Navy Officers, **N**, 76,
Negro Voters, **C**, 372,
People, **A**, 107,
Pioneer Life, **H**, 366,
Railroads, **E**, 242-243,
Reconstruction, **D**, 395, **H**, 795,
Secession, **B**, 954-955, **C**, 268, **H**, 324, **R**, 670a, **W**, 499, 967,
Segregation, **F**, 163,
Slavery, **M**, 1111,
Soldiers, **H**, 920,
Stories, **E**, 47,
Sugar, **P**, 756, **R**, 669-670,
Voters, **C**, 372,
White Castle, **M**, 1326
Louisiana (ship); **S**, 1199
Louisiana Native Guards; **B**, 644
Louisiana Special Artillery; Uniforms, **U**, 14
Louisiana State University Press; **A**, 147
Louisiana Tigers; **H**, 1022, **J**, 529c, **M**, 356a, 1048, **W**, 498
Louisiana Troops;
  Cavalry,
    1st Regt., **C**, 235, **G**, 628,
    4th Regt., **C**, 228,
  Infantry,
    1st Bat., **D**, 840,
    1st Regt. Vols., **M**, 1351,
    1st Spec. Bat., **S**, 1054,
    2nd Regt., **B**, 846,
    3rd Regt., **T**, 483,
    4th Bat., **L**, 185,
    4th Regt., **C**, 1379, **K**, 72, **L**, 59,
    9th Regt., **R**, 228,
    13th Regt., **M**, 553a,
    18th Regt., **R**, 690,
    19th Regt., **C**, 311,
    22nd Regt., **B**, 614, 619,
    26th Regt., **H**, 108,
    Crescent Regiment, **L**, 180,
  Rosters, **B**, 537

Louisville & Nashville R.R.; **K**, 120, 214, **T**, 295
Louisville Courier Journal, KY, np.; **C**, 554
Louisville, Cincinnati & Charleston R.R.; **J**, 131
Louisville, KY; **E**, 124, **G**, 631, **M**, 516,
  Cave Hill Cemetery, **B**, 1206,
  Destruction, **R**, 719
Love Letters; **V**, 83
Love Stories; **W**, 797
Lovett, Robert, Jr.; **F**, 351, **H**, 1045
Lovingston, VA; **N**, 61
Lowther, Henry M., Sgt.; **W**, 432
Loyal Publications Society; **C**, 1244
Loyall, Benjamin P.; **U**, 5
Loyalty, Divided; **D**, 872
Lubbock, Francis Richard, Gov., TX; **D**, 221, **N**, 217
Lucy Long (Lee's horse); **B**, 1330, **C**, 108, **L**, 303
Lugo Case; **B**, 1227
Lumpkin County, GA; **K**, 192b
Lumsden's Battery; **L**, 562
Lunenburg County, VA; **B**, 528
Lunt, Dolly Sumner; **B**, 1561
Luther, Frank; **M**, 1338
Lux, Rudolph L.; **B**, 556
Lynchburg Home Guards; **B**, 741, **R**, 189
Lynchburg, VA; **C**, 1383, **M**, 1163a, **R**, 632,
  Campaign,
Lynchburg, VA, Battle of; **B**, 742, **XYZ**, 1
Lynde, Isaac, Maj.; **A**, 441
Lyon, Nathaniel; **O**, 32
Lyons, James; **F**, 439
Lytle, R.E., Mrs.; **C**, 972

M

M.E. Church South; **T**, 271
Mackall Journal; **M**, 662
Mackey, T.J.; **M**, 711
Macon City, MO; **N**, 212
Macon County, GA;
  History, **M**, 38
Macon Light Artillery; **H**, 945
Macon, GA; **C**, 706, **L**, 736, **W**, 782,
  Armory, **V**, 72,
  Confederate Laboratory, **H**, 387,
  Justices of Inferior Court, **G**, 178,
  Occupied, **K**, 177,
  Rose Hill Cemetery, **C**, 881
Macon, Nathaniel; **E**, 102
MacPherson (pseudonym); **H**, 880
Madison County, KY; **C**, 434
Madison County, VA;
  Richardson Guard, **C**, 1139
Madison, WI;
  Forest Hill Cemetery, **T**, 321
Maffitt, Emma M.; **R**, 710
Maffitt, John Newland, Capt.; **B**, 1019, 1167a, **C**, 418, **D**, 93, **R**, 710, **S**, 959
Magee, James; **B**, 1076
Magnus, Charles; **C**, 918
Magoffin, Beriah, Gov., KY; **D**, 882-883, **H**, 420
Magruder's Peninsula Campaign; **L**, 234
Magruder, John B., Maj.Gen.; **D**, 792, **N**, 217, **S**, 263,
  General Order No.16, **M**, 65,
  Peninsula, **L**, 743
Magruder, John Bowie, Col.; **S**, 1172
Mahon, John K.; **D**, 496
Mahone's Brigade; **A**, 481, **B**, 255, 1408, **C**, 62, 1389, **H**, 1079, **L**, 140
Mahone's Division; **F**, 60,
  Surrender, **M**, 918

Mahone, William, Maj.Gen.; **B**, 12, 631, 775, **D**, 447, **E**, 15, **H**, 518
Maidstone Literary & Mechanics Institute; **B**, 608
Mail; **B**, 1334, **H**, 1220-1223, **J**, 530, **S**, 346, 380,
  Carriers, **B**, 1085, **G**, 651, **M**, 973, **O**, 210, **W**, 374,
  Censorship, **B**, 1302
Maine; **B**, 994
Mallory, Stephen Russell; **C**, 694, **D**, 155, 978, **M**, 752
Malone, Bartlet Yancey; **M**, 441
Malone, Wallace; **A**, 116
Malvern Hill, VA, Battle of; **B**, 632, **C**, 1457, 1535, **D**, 625, **H**, 47, 824, **L**, 47, **M**, 1084, **W**, 19
Manarin, Louis H.; **C**, 1050, **D**, 814, **W**, 354
Manassas Campaign; **B**, 453
Manassas Gap Railroad; **N**, 6
Manassas, VA, Battle of; **A**, 184, **B**, 448, 477, 1184, **C**, 576, 861, 1163, 1498, 1514, **E**, 129, **F**, 136, **H**, 253, 702a, **N**, 20a, **R**, 395, **S**, 651, 1187, **W**, 185, 791,
  Field Medical Services, **C**, 1580,
  Map, **S**, 203b,
  Official Report, **J**, 309,
  Sermon Preached about, **P**, 480,
  Topography, **E**, 56
Manassas, VA, First Battle of; **B**, 488, 1351, **C**, 720, 886, 1111, 1365, **D**, 65-66, **E**, 288, **G**, 72, **J**, 537a, **M**, 1287, 1320, **P**, 298, **S**, 743, **XYZ**, 96
Manassas, VA, Second Battle of; **A**, 197, 209, **B**, 630, **C**, 471, 1276, 1613, **G**, 69, **L**, 387, 660, **M**, 365c, **P**, 519,
Maney's Brigade; **M**, 141,
  West Point, GA, Battle of, **M**, 533

Maney, George Earl, Brig.Gen.; **E**, 151
Mann, Ambrose Dudley; **B**, 573, **M**, 1068
Manoeuvres de L'Artillerie Legere; **B**, 1538
Manoeuvres de L'Infanterie; **C**, 131
Mansfield, LA; **H**, 772,
  Battle Park Museum, **P**, 440
Mansfield, LA, Battle of; **B**, 892, **P**, 438, **R**, 202
Manual of Rifle Tactics; **R**, 389
Maple Leaf (steamer); **B**, 1432, **G**, 579
Maps; **B**, 1181, **C**, 117, **E**, 240, 254, **H**, 1120, 1347, **O**, 19a, **V**, 164,
  Atlanta, GA, Battle of, **K**, 271,
  Bethel Church, VA, **H**, 1087,
  Chickahominy River, **S**, 368,
  Civil War, **S**, 1114,
  Confederate, **M**, 471, **N**, 122,
  Gettysburg Battlefields, **B**, 1555,
  Hotchkiss Collection, **L**, 177-178a,
  Jackson's Mapmaker, **O**, 172b,
  Lee's Virginia Retreat, **S**, 1029a,
  Lee's, Field, **L**, 624,
  Lost, **C**, 78,
  Manassas, VA, **S**, 203b,
  Middle States, **B**, 1532,
  New Market, VA, **S**, 435,
  North Carolina, **P**, 316,
  Richmond, VA, **R**, 393, **S**, 204,
  South, **W**, 1087,
  South Carolina, **P**, 316,
  Southern States, **S**, 671,
  Valley, **M**, 474a,
  Virginia, **W**, 421,
  War, **S**, 985
March, Bryan; **M**, 175a
Marchmont, John; **M**, 358
Marcus, Jacob Rader; **H**, 728, 745, **L**, 437, **P**, 344, **S**, 1270
Marcy, Ellen; **H**, 507
Marianna, FL, Battle of; **B**, 1004, **C**, 408, **S**, 991
Marietta, GA;
  Centennial, **C**, 792

Marietta, GA, Memorial Association; **C**, 802
Marine Corps, US; **O**, 19
Marine Torpedoes; **M**, 351
Mariners; **D**, 400
Mariners' Museum, VA; **B**, 650
Marines, Confederate; **D**, 713-714, 719, 732-733, **G**, 525, **H**, 481, **L**, 476, **M**, 178, 552, 839, **R**, 67, **S**, 1385
Marion County, MO; **S**, 820
Marion County, NC; **M**, 384
Marion County, SC; **B**, 1462,
  History, **S**, 237
Marion County, TX; **B**, 1544
Marion Hornets, FL; **A**, 71
Maritime Captures, Rights; **H**, 280
Maritime Commerce; **E**, 179
Markham, David; **M**, 358
Markham, Thomas R.; **A**, 451
Markie (Martha Custis Williams); **L**, 358
Marks' Mills, AR, Battle of; **A**, 426, 529, **R**, 365
Marks, Ellen; **G**, 307
Marmaduke, John Sappington, Maj.Gen.; **B**, 398, 813, **C**, 1565, **L**, 258, **M**, 200, **P**, 441, **R**, 585,
  Missouri Raid, **O**, 31
Marmaduke-Walker Duel; **H**, 1246
Marooned Brigade; **B**, 1468
Marschall, Nicola; **B**, 1162, **C**, 1278, **H**, 1279
Marshall Guards; **S**, 513
Marshall Powder Mill; **L**, 765a
Marshall, A.E.; **S**, 1094
Marshall, Charles, Col.; **A**, 450, **E**, 18, **M**, 346
Marshall, George C.; **C**, 1316
Marshall, John, Col.; **G**, 8, **O**, 95,
  Papers, **S**, 1430
Marshall, Thomas F.; **R**, 776
Marshall, TX; **G**, 133, **L**, 30,
  Conf. Capitol, **A**, 306,
  Ordnance Depot, **F**, 218
Marshall, VA;
  History, **G**, 441
Martel, Glenn G.; **D**, 69
Martial Law; **H**, 1244

Martin's Brigade; **E**, 153
Martin, Florance Ashemore Cowles Hamlett; **N**, 219
Martin, James Green, Brig.Gen.; **C**, 601, **D**, 466
Martin, Tom;
  Execution, **D**, 639
Martyr, First Confederate; **W**, 335
Marye, Edward S., Capt.; **F**, 227
Maryland; **A**, 412, **E**, 281, **H**, 464a, **J**, 166, 179, 179a, **M**, 122a, **N**, 110, **T**, 349, **W**, 1009,
  Army & Navy, **C**, 1126, **J**, 170,
  Burials, **P**, 297, 451,
  Campaign, **A**, 200, **B**, 333, **C**, 442, **H**, 774, **J**, 177-178, **L**, 89, **M**, 1296, **R**, 149, **S**, 1313,
  Confederate Dead, **J**, 527,
  Emancipation, **M**, 362,
  History, **S**, 106,
  House of Delegates, **R**, 318,
  House of Representatives, **M**, 360,
  Invasion, **A**, 202, 219, **D**, 943, **L**, 653, **T**, 293, 401,
  Jackson, Thomas Jonathan, Lt.-Gen., **D**, 785,
  Monuments, **J**, 182, **T**, 204,
  Negroes, **B**, 1042,
  Political Crisis, **B**, 1504-1505,
  Political Parties, **B**, 53,
  Proposed Government, **C**, 354,
  Roster, **S**, 782,
  Secession Conflict, **B**, 1369,
  Slavery, **W**, 17,
  Soldier's Home, **P**, 301,
  Soldiers, **E**, 22, **H**, 182, 1180, **J**, 181, **T**, 420,
  Southern Rights, **J**, 236,
  Suppression, **C**, 574,
  Union Parties, **S**, 887,
  Women, **D**, 132
Maryland Guards;
  Uniforms, **U**, 14
Maryland Line; **C**, 842, **E**, 22, **G**, 333, **H**, 577, **J**, 183, **L**, 475, **M**, 774, **S**, 24, **V**, 38
Maryland Line Association; **J**, 169

Maryland Line Soldiers' Home; **B**, 903
Maryland My Maryland (song); **R**, 85-86
Maryland Troops; **H**, 1009,
  Artillery,
    1st Regt., **A**, 370,
    3rd Regt., **R**, 503-507,
  Cavalry,
    1st Regt., **B**, 861, **H**, 575, **M**, 335, **R**, 354, **S**, 1232,
    2nd Regt., **J**, 194,
  Infantry,
    1st Regt., **J**, 185, **M**, 881a, **W**, 120-121,
    2nd Regt., **M**, 603,
  Roster, **P**, 563
Maryland Zouaves;
  Uniforms, **U**, 14
Mason, Charles; **W**, 1063
Mason, Emily V.; **D**, 29
Mason, James M.; **G**, 560, **M**, 312, **W**, 366, 868
Masonry; **F**, 498
Massacres; **F**, 552
Mastin, Thomas J., Capt.; **H**, 88
Matamoros, Mexico; **D**, 507,
  Trade, **D**, 13
Mathews, J.W., Capt.; **F**, 331
Mathias Point, VA, Battle of; **R**, 810
Matthews, W.B.; **D**, 248
Matthiessen, Peter; **W**, 176
Maurice, Gilbert St.; **W**, 590
Maury County, TN; **M**, 346a,
  Soldiers, **G**, 93
Maury Grays; **W**, 269
Maury, Dabney Herndon, Maj.Gen.; **A**, 81, **F**, 27, **W**, 422
Maury, Matthew Fontaine, Como.; **B**, 770, 1410, **C**, 269, 751, 1249-1250, 1338, **D**, 600, **F**, 191, **H**, 323, 552, **L**, 478, **M**, 348, 351, 405, **P**, 343a, **S**, 588, 627, **T**, 303, **V**, 158, **W**, 304, 608, 710,
  as Scientist, **J**, 77
Maxey, Samuel Bell, Brig.Gen.; **H**, 935, 1112, **L**, 508a
Maximilian, Court of; **T**, 128

Maxwell, James R.; **S**, 202
May, Henry; **C**, 940
Mazeppa (ship); **G**, 457
Mazyck, William; **G**, 289
McAllister, Abraham Addams; **M**, 366c
McAllister, Julia Ellen Stratton; **M**, 366c
McAllister, Thompson, Capt.; **M**, 366c
McAlpin, Robert (Simon Lagree); **C**, 1258
McBrien, D.D.; **G**, 64
McCabe, James D., Jr.; **M**, 57
McCabe, William G., Capt.; **A**, 450, **G**, 380, **H**, 439, **W**, 422
McCain, William D.; **G**, 534
McCalla, Margaret; **P**, 127
McCanne, Virginia Yates, Mrs.; **H**, 1038
McCarthy, Carlton; **S**, 1126
McCausland, John, Brig.Gen.; **B**, 1370a, **D**, 737, **E**, 239
McCaw, J.B.; **J**, 139
McClellan's Campaign; **A**, 214
McClellan, George Brinton, Maj.Gen.; **A**, 450, **B**, 711, 1320, **H**, 824, **K**, 41, **M**, 1233, **P**, 276
McClellan, William; **S**, 890
McClurg, Alex. C.; **A**, 569
McCorkle, John; **B**, 194
McCormick, John Gilchrist; **B**, 290
McCrady, Edward; **A**, 449-450
McCreary, Robert N.; **M**, 456
McCulloch, Ben, Brig.Gen.; **B**, 406, 1374, 1376, **H**, 982, **L**, 428, **R**, 713, **S**, 613, **T**, 149
McCulloch, Henry Eustace, Brig.Gen.; **B**, 22
McDaniel, Hester; **M**, 467
McDonald, Archie P.; **A**, 498, **E**, 46, **H**, 1121
McDonald, E.A.H., Maj.; **D**, 312
McDonald, John R., Maj.; **P**, 645
McDonald, William N., Capt.; **C**, 899
McDonough Institute; **A**, 224
McDougle, Ivan E.; **C**, 434
McDowell, Catherine W.; **N**, 124

McDowell, Robert Emmett; **M**, 1358
McDowell, VA, Battle of; **G**, 340
McEldowney, Robert, Capt.; **L**, 58
McElroy, Robert; **C**, 49, **D**, 188
McFerrin, John B.; **F**, 192
McGavock, Randal W., Col.; **G**, 450
McGinty Cannon; **F**, 127
McGowan's Brigade; **B**, 1348, **C**, 31, **W**, 355,
    Spotsylvania, **A**, 445
McGowan, Samuel, Brig.Gen.; **A**, 25, **R**, 464
McGraw, Jefferson; **S**, 427
McGregg's Brigade; **B**, 1462
McGuffey Family, GA; **B**, 236
McGuire, Hunter Holmes; **A**, 582, **H**, 514, **M**, 568, **P**, 261a
McGuire, Judith W.; **W**, 309
McGuire, Patrick; **M**, 736
McHenry, George; **A**, 34, **C**, 26
McIntosh County, GA; **T**, 192
McIntosh's Artillery; **B**, 1460
McIntosh, James T.; **D**, 243
McKee, James Cooper; **A**, 441
McKee, John Miller; **G**, 558
McKim, Randolph H.; **U**, 22, **XYZ**, 93a
McKinney, Elizabeth Ustick, Mrs.; **B**, 1085
McKnight, George, Maj.; **K**, 65a
McLane, Bobby J.; **A**, 421
McLaughlin, William; **G**, 377
McLean, Ross H.; **M**, 723
McLean, Wilmer; **C**, 720
McLemore, Richard Aubrey; **B**, 371, **M**, 938
McLennan County, TX; **D**, 985, **S**, 222
McLeod, Hugh, Col.; **G**, 622
McMahon, T.W.; **M**, 622
McMaster, Elizabeth Waring; **W**, 196
McMillan, John Poynter; **R**, 265a
McMinnville, TN; **H**, 59
McMurray, Richard M.; **M**, 31, 1007
McNair Brigade; **G**, 36
McNairy County, TN; **W**, 1049
McNeil, John, Maj.Gen.; **F**, 53
McNeill's Charge; **D**, 886

McNeill's Rangers; **B**, 33, 1263, **D**, 510, 887-889, **M**, 696, **R**, 416, 592, **S**, 1355, **V**, 81, **W**, 443, 917,
  Kidnapping of Crook & Kelley, **S**, 1057
McNeill, Hanson; **V**, 81
McNeill, James M., Capt.;
  Prison Life, **P**, 196a
McPheeters, William M.; **N**, 147
McPherson, James Birdseye, Brig.Gen.; **C**, 1540
McRae, Colin J.; **D**, 154
McRae, Duncan, Col.; **W**, 760
McRae, J.C.; **L**, 291
McRae, William, Brig.Gen.; **S**, 1037
McSwain, Eleanor D.; **B**, 723
McSweeney, Miles B., Lt.Gov.; **C**, 357
Meade, George Gordon, Maj.Gen.; **P**, 279
Meade, Robert Douthat; **W**, 14
Meares, Kate DeRossett; **D**, 967
Mebane, John; **B**, 672
Mechanicsville, VA, Battle of; **W**, 778
Mecklenburg County, NC; **A**, 183, 185
Medal of Honor, Confederate; **H**, 1284
Medary, Samuel; **C**, 1439
Medical & Surgical Journal; **C**, 1026
Medical Botany; **P**, 619
Medical Corps; **J**, 492, 494, **W**, 184
Medical Department, Confederate; **C**, 592, 1578, **J**, 494, **M**, 1105, **O**, 127a, **S**, 1252
Medical Education;
  Louisiana, **D**, 892
Medical Generals, Profiles; **S**, 1060
Medical History; **B**, 1213-1214, **J**, 490
Medical Journal, pub.; **R**, 423a
Medical Lessons; **G**, 9
Medical Manuals; **W**, 226
Medical Officers; **C**, 1574, **F**, 470, **G**, 256, **M**, 734, **P**, 790a, 808, **T**, 90,
  Roster, **J**, 497
Medical Resources, Southern; **P**, 619
Medical Science;
  South, **F**, 296

Medical Services; **B**, 1088, 1156, **C**, 1576, **E**, 51, **H**, 7, 211, 1197, **P**, 855, **R**, 536a, **S**, 443, **V**, 64,
  Field, **C**, 1580,
  Sanitation, **B**, 1347,
  South, **D**, 891
Medical Society of Virginia; **M**, 558
Medical Statistics; **B**, 1215
Medicine; **A**, 49, **B**, 786, 1088, 1156, **C**, 487, 1026, 1533, **H**, 62, 211, **J**, 74, 488-489, 495-496, **M**, 230, **R**, 475, **W**, 227, 809,
  Florida, **S**, 1259,
  Pharmacy, **F**, 465-469,
  Progress in South, **M**, 559,
  Richmond Academy, VA, **C**, 941,
  Substitutes, **S**, 3
Medico-Chirurgical Lessons; **S**, 69
Medon Station, TN, Battle of; **A**, 180
Meece, T.F.; **H**, 861
Meigs County, TN; **A**, 252
Meigs, John R., Lt.;
  Death, **K**, 18
Melbourne, Australia; **G**, 242, **W**, 754
Memminger, Christopher Gustavus; **C**, 149, 1424, **T**, 332
Memorial Associations; **L**, 11-19
Memorial Day; **C**, 958,
  Origin, **R**, 414
Memorials; **B**, 721, 1281, **C**, 751,
  Arlington National Cemetery, **C**, 1197,
  Norfolk, VA, **C**, 895,
  North Carolina, **C**, 359,
  Virginia, **C**, 358,
  Women, **G**, 345
Memphis & Little Rock R.R.; **H**, 1248
Memphis, TN; **D**, 459, **P**, 96, **T**, 26,
  Capture, **D**, 638,
  Forrest's Raid, **H**, 1020,
  Hospitals, **L**, 107a,
  Occupation of, **R**, 522,
  Postal Provisions, **P**, 694
Memphis, TN, Battle of; **N**, 106
Mennonites; **H**, 1109
Mercantile Education, Southern; **A**, 525

Mercer's Brigade; **C**, 757
Mercer, Oliver E., Lt.; **W**, 1068
Merchant, W.C.N., Mrs.; **V**, 144
Mercier, Henri; **C**, 213
Meredith, Wyndham R.; **B**, 1180
Meridian, MS; **S**, 288,
   Sherman's Advance, **J**, 67, **R**, 385, **S**, 1000-1001
Merrimac (ironclad); **B**, 237, 1300, **C**, 346, 828, 860, 1603, **D**, 33, 653, **E**, 113, **F**, 211, 219, **H**, 1265, 1269, **J**, 372-373, 528, **K**, 223, **L**, 4, **M**, 36, 349, 711, 1179, **N**, 115, **O**, 18, **P**, 89, 151, 420a, 691, 725, **R**, 44, **S**, 220, 526, 531, 568, 580, 606, 723, 766, 794, 1376, **T**, 132, 289a, 405, 551, **W**, 539, 597, 981,
   Construction, **P**, 640
Mesilla Valley, NM;
   Military Operations, **C**, 932
Mesilla, NM, Battle of; **H**, 84
Methodist Publishing House; **T**, 223
Mettham, Henry Clay; **M**, 881a
Mexican War; **B**, 944
Mexico; **C**, 455, **G**, 593, **N**, 183a, **R**, 494,
   Border Problems, **W**, 347,
   Exiles, **B**, 986, **K**, 228, **R**, 680,
   French Intervention, **C**, 743,
   Migrations, **H**, 335,
   Relations, **K**, 80,
   Unionists, **C**, 670
Meynier, Arthur, Jr.; **C**, 934
Micco, Holata; **P**, 643
Michigan (ship); **S**, 355
Michigan Troops;
   Cavalry,
      6th Regt., **P**, 5
Mickle, William E.; **F**, 217, **U**, 22-27
Middle New River Settlement, WV; **J**, 269
Middleburg, VA; **B**, 1327
Midway Hospital; **C**, 622
Midwest;
   Negroes, **V**, 167
Miers, Earl Schenk; **D**, 257
Migration Patterns, Southern; **O**, 225
Mile's Legion;
   Roster, **B**, 620
Miley, Michael; **S**, 37
Milford Station, VA, Battle of; **L**, 583
Military & Naval Laws; **L**, 452
Military Biography; **C**, 441
Military Collectors; **C**, 851
Military Commissions; **M**, 888
Military Courts; **C**, 858
Military Cycle; **C**, 1083
Military Dispatches; **C**, 713
Military Failure; **L**, 800
Military History; **B**, 1165, **W**, 574
Military Institutions; **M**, 202
Military Literature; **B**, 679
Military Memoirs; **A**, 176
Military Organization, Confederate; **D**, 935
Military Schools; **B**, 124
Military Tactics; **M**, 712
Military Telegraph; **P**, 436
Mill Springs, KY, Battle of; **XYZ**, 56
Milledgeville, GA; **B**, 885-886, 888, 1169, **G**, 181,
   Sherman, **B**, 891,
   Sherman's March, **T**, 29
Miller, Ferdinand von; **B**, 678
Miller, G.M.; **R**, 706
Miller, Lowell I.; **B**, 824
Miller, Marion Mills; **G**, 554
Milligan, Lambdin P.; **G**, 546, **K**, 207, **L**, 444
Milliken's Bend, LA, Battle of; **G**, 529
Mills, Luther Rice; **H**, 336
Mills, Roger O.; **B**, 165
Milton, John, Gov., FL; **J**, 526, **P**, 74
Mims, Wilbur F., Capt.; **M**, 902
Mims, William Jemison; **M**, 1065
Mine Creek, KS, Battle of; **L**, 103
Mines; **D**, 578, 718, **P**, 282, 700, **S**, 297, 663
Minnegerode, Charles, Dr.; **C**, 1356
Minor, John B.; **B**, 744
Minor, Kate Pleasants, Mrs.; **S**, 871
Mints; **B**, 1216
Minvielle, Chester Harrington; **R**, 118

Missionary Ridge, TN, Battle of; **B**, 1234, **D**, 801, **F**, 273, **H**, 958, **M**, 141, 495, **S**, 1112, **W**, 271
Mississippi; **B**, 396, 414, **C**, 330, **D**, 333, **H**, 1059, **J**, 365, **P**, 103, **R**, 19, **S**, 466,
   Agriculture, **J**, 81,
   Ante-Bellum Travelers, **B**, 985,
   Army of, **J**, 259a,
   Battles, **L**, 381,
   Blockades, **J**, 105,
   Burial Lists, **P**, 576, **R**, 734,
   Campaigns, **J**, 291, **L**, 381,
   Catholic Church, **P**, 410,
   Cavalry, **H**, 457, **L**, 383,
   Cemeteries, **J**, 513,
   Confederate Dead, **W**, 134,
   Confederate Records, **R**, 758,
   Constitution, **S**, 1221,
   Convention, **J**, 598,
   Department of Archives, **B**, 725-726, **C**, 135a, **G**, 657,
   Economy, **E**, 45,
   Elections, **M**, 590,
   Geographical Conditions, **H**, 902,
   Grant's Campaign, **M**, 349,
   History, **B**, 371, **R**, 765,
   Home Front, **B**, 659,
   Leaders, **H**, 755,
   Military Annals, **R**, 456,
   Monuments, **J**, 513,
   Morale Breakdown, **H**, 1235,
   Nullification, **B**, 1256,
   Plantations, **D**, 932, **P**, 336,
   Politics, **B**, 658, 1342, **D**, 876,
   Post-Vicksburg, **L**, 397,
   Radical Rule, **L**, 786,
   Reconstruction, **G**, 62, **M**, 678,
   Secession, **G**, 61, **R**, 19, **W**, 941, 969,
   Sherman's Campaign, **R**, 725,
   Slavery, **S**, 1220,
   Soldiers, **I**, 27, **J**, 94, **R**, 6, 153,
   Statistical Register, **R**, 766,
   Statistics, **J**, 494,
   UCV, **W**, 572
Mississippi Bonds; **H**, 246
Mississippi Department Army;
   Organization, **O**, 151-154
Mississippi Partisan Rangers; **B**, 1343
Mississippi Rifle (gun); **L**, 681
Mississippi Rifles; **R**, 455
Mississippi River; **C**, 716,
   Blockades, **T**, 482,
   Naval Strategy, **B**, 840
Mississippi Troops;
   Artillery,
     1st Btty., **E**, 112,
   Cavalry,
     1st Btty., **W**, 1001,
     1st Regt., **D**, 553, 594,
     4th Regt., **M**, 427,
     28th Regt., **C**, 228,
   Infantry,
     1st Regt., **M**, 1277,
     3rd Regt., **G**, 609,
     6th Regt., **H**, 1200,
     10th Regt., **R**, 455-456, **S**, 1455,
     11th Regt., **B**, 1403, 1560, **L**, 34, **M**, 526-527, 529,
     12th Regt., **D**, 490, **W**, 181a,
     13th Regt., **H**, 1218,
     14th Regt., **D**, 378,
     15th Regt., **B**, 763,
     16th Regt., **B**, 1294, **H**, 900, 909,
     19th Regt., **C**, 306, **H**, 384,
     21st Regt., **C**, 24,
     22nd Regt., **M**, 202-203, **W**, 394,
     37th Regt., **B**, 85,
     43rd Regt., **B**, 648,
   Roster, **R**, 766
Mississippi Valley; **B**, 87, **S**, 828,
   Commerce, **C**, 1294, 1297,
   Confederate Strategy, **J**, 79
Missouri; **B**, 813, **C**, 430, 927, 1255, 1416, **H**, 312, **K**, 200-201, **M**, 234, 461, 520, 1072, 1260, 1341, **P**, 29, 113c, **R**, 270, **S**, 421-422, 761, 763, **T**, 188, **U**, 46,
   Admitted to Confederacy, **K**, 202-203,
   Battles, **W**, 322,
   Borders, **H**, 300, **W**, 560,
   Burial Lists, **P**, 577-586,
   Bushwhackers, **B**, 1326, **E**, 258,
   Business Neutralism, **B**, 1336,
   Campaigns, **A**, 305, **P**, 748, **W**, 527,

Capital, Marshall, TX, **G**, 133,
Conf. Government, **K**, 199, **W**, 929,
Conf. State Capitol, **A**, 306,
Controversy, **F**, 67,
Conventions, **M**, 88, **S**, 777,
Ex-Confederates, **R**, 284,
Guerrillas, **B**, 962, **C**, 1331, **T**, 226,
History, **M**, 837, 994,
Invasions, **M**, 990,
Jayhawkers, **H**, 726,
Kansas Struggle, **B**, 1185,
Martyrdom, **L**, 410,
Politics, **B**, 1249,
Radicals, **XYZ**, 105,
Raid, **O**, 31,
Ratification, **T**, 289,
Ruffians, **B**, 948,
Scouts, **C**, 795,
Secession, **K**, 204, **L**, 795, **R**, 642, 906,
Slavery, **B**, 73, **V**, 126,
Soldiers, **B**, 502, 989,
Southern Press, **S**, 1442,
State Depridations, Arkansas, **W**, 698,
Sympathizers, **S**, 728, 1142, **T**, 222,
Trials, **E**, 306,
West Point Cadets, **N**, 77,
Women, **U**, 37
Missouri Army Argus, np.; **M**, 940
Missouri Brigades; **B**, 668, 1085, **E**, 223
Missouri Compromise; **B**, 27
Missouri Paw Paw Militia; **C**, 118
Missouri Troops;
Artillery,
1st Regt., **R**, 802,
Cavalry, **C**, 1493,
1st Regt., **F**, 49, **M**, 1346, **W**, 996,
2nd Regt., **B**, 1150,
3rd Regt., **B**, 497,
Infantry,
1st Brig., **A**, 305,
3rd Regt., **C**, 675, **H**, 1214,
6th Regt., **P**, 169
Missouri Valley Historical Society; **J**, 117
Missouri-Kansas Border; **S**, 987

Mitchel, John; **B**, 940, **R**, 340
Mitchell, George E.; **B**, 1464
Mitchell, Margaret; **G**, 672
Mobile Bay, AL; **B**, 976, 1167a, **C**, 418, **G**, 199, 573, **R**, 515
Mobile Bay, AL, Battle of; **B**, 1499, **J**, 276, **R**, 353
Mobile Register, AL, np.; **C**, 971a
Mobile Rifles; **D**, 442, **S**, 540
Mobile Tribune, AL, np.; **R**, 254
Mobile, AL; **C**, 1347, **D**, 497, **F**, 100, **G**, 363, **H**, 158, **M**, 976,
Blockades, **F**, 373,
Confederate Navy, **S**, 1201,
Generals, **S**, 1263,
Monuments, **P**, 784,
Ordnance, **F**, 322,
Siege, **M**, 976b, **N**, 112a, **P**, 83,
Society of Immortal Six-hundred, **M**, 926
Mobile, AL, Battle of; **C**, 64, **D**, 986
Moccasin Rangers; **S**, 1369
Model Republic; **W**, 720
Modern Greece (ironclad); **B**, 1260
Moffett, Dorothy I.; **C**, 901
Mohun; **C**, 1183, 1190
Moise, E. Warren; **A**, 453
Moneyhon, Carl H.; **G**, 541
Monitor (ironclad); **A**, 69, **B**, 651, 1466, 1498, 1501, **C**, 860, 1603, **D**, 33, 653, **F**, 211, 219, **H**, 1010, 1265, 1269, **L**, 4, 764, **M**, 36, 349, 711, 807-818, **N**, 26, **O**, 50, **P**, 89, 151, 691, 725, **R**, 44, 62, **S**, 220, 526, 568, 580, 606, 723, 794, 1376, **T**, 132, 312, **W**, 292, 981
Monocacy, MD, Battle of; **B**, 1093, **G**, 403, **W**, 999
Monographs, Confederate; **H**, 798a
Monongalia County, WV;
History, **M**, 355, **W**, 673
Monroe County, WV;
History, **M**, 1210
Monroe Doctrine; **D**, 426
Monroe's Crossroads, NC; **N**, 220
Monroe, Haskell M., Jr.; **D**, 243
Monroe, John T.; **D**, 453
Montana Territory; **D**, 385

Montauk (ironclad); **N**, 31
Montaye, Ruth; **P**, 414
Monteiro, Aristide; **D**, 95
Montgomery County, VA; **C**, 1513
Montgomery Grays; **D**, 442
Montgomery, AL; **B**, 973, **J**, 353, **S**, 159,
  Baptists, **M**, 153,
  Capital, **M**, 644,
  Confederate Constitution, **J**, 174,
  Convention, **G**, 188,
  Military Adademy, **A**, 98,
  Monument, **F**, 12, **J**, 533, **S**, 53, 176,
  Postoffice, **B**, 1158
Montgomery, Joseph E., Como.; **J**, 73
Monuments; **B**, 678, **E**, 200, **S**, 1247,
  Alexandria, VA, **D**, 76,
  Andersonville, GA, **D**, 104,
  Arlington, VA, **S**, 621,
  Athens, GA, **C**, 1293,
  Atlanta, GA, **B**, 722,
  Augusta, GA, **C**, 364,
  Battlefield, **S**, 1024,
  Charleston, SC, **P**, 770,
  Chester, SC, **B**, 1179,
  Chicago, IL, **U**, 8,
  Confederate, **D**, 345, **W**, 613,
  Courthouse, Union & CSA, **S**, 1024,
  Davis, Jefferson, Pres., **D**, 218,
  Fairfax, VA, **F**, 7,
  Fort Pulaski, GA, **L**, 138,
  Fort Sumter, SC, **B**, 129,
  Fortress Monroe, VA, **B**, 940,
  Front Royal, VA, **H**, 53,
  Gettysburg, PA, **G**, 191, **M**, 243,
  Greenwood Cemetery, New Orleans, LA, **L**, 11,
  Hill, Ambrose Powell, Lt.Gen., **H**, 805,
  Hopkinsville, KY, **M**, 776,
  Jackson, Thomas Jonathan, Lt.-Gen., **H**, 963, 966, **J**, 31-32, 48,
  Kansas, **B**, 927,
  Knoxville, TN, **B**, 227,
  Lee, Fitzhugh, **C**, 98,
  Lee, Robert Edward, Gen., **E**, 13, **H**, 931, **M**, 210,
  Lexington, VA, **E**, 41,
  Louisiana, **S**, 895,
  Maryland, **J**, 182,
  Mississippi, **J**, 513,
  Mobile, AL, **P**, 784,
  Montgomery, AL, **F**, 12, **J**, 533, **S**, 53, 176,
  Munfordville, KY, **S**, 1453,
  New Orleans, LA, **D**, 483, 487,
  North Carolina, **S**, 715,
  Orangeburg, SC, **B**, 1627,
  Palmyra, MO, **P**, 51,
  Paris, TN, **P**, 636,
  Petersburg, VA, **B**, 782, **M**, 369,
  Point Lookout, MD, **M**, 1035a,
  Ramseur, Stephen D., Maj.Gen., **D**, 871,
  Richmond, VA, **C**, 884, 1005, **D**, 482, **G**, 487, **H**, 877, **L**, 330, **S**, 788, 894, **T**, 433,
  Shelbyville, TN, **S**, 326,
  Shiloh, TN, **G**, 228,
  Soldiers & Sailors, **C**, 341,
  Spotsylvania, VA, **M**, 780a,
  Tennessee, **T**, 111,
  Thomaston, GA, **M**, 339,
  Thomson, James W., Maj., **T**, 267,
  Vicksburg, MS, **B**, 238, 419, **M**, 781a,
  Virginia Military Institute, **V**, 149,
  Washington & Lee University, **D**, 54,
  Wilderness, VA, **T**, 137,
  Wilmington, NC, **C**, 825, 1099,
  Winchester, VA, **M**, 1154,
  Wirz, Henry, Capt., **D**, 104,
  Women, **C**, 1381, **M**, 1036
Moon, Anna Mary; **D**, 458
Moore's Mill, MO, Battle of; **W**, 765
Moore, Albert; **B**, 1313
Moore, Glover; **S**, 881
Moore, Hannah; **M**, 489
Moore, James Daniel; **M**, 235
Moore, James Orris; **B**, 956
Moore, John Hammond; **F**, 235
Moore, John W.; **G**, 110, 476, **P**, 112

Moore, Joseph R.H.; **W**, 849
Moore, Marinda Branson; **T**, 161
Moore, Robert; **M**, 441
Moore, Samuel Preston; **A**, 515, **L**, 495, **W**, 615
Moore, Thomas Overton, Gov., LA; **C**, 263, **M**, 1055, **O**, 48, **W**, 592
Moorefield, WV; **F**, 53
Moorman, George; **U**, 37
Morale; **B**, 584, **S**, 464,
   Confederate Press, **A**, 362
Mordecai, Alfred, Maj.; **A**, 14
Morgan & Duke; **A**, 247
Morgan County, GA;
   Volunteers, **H**, 1217
Morgan's Battalion; **G**, 197
Morgan's Cavalry; **B**, 184, 1361, **C**, 296, **D**, 901, 907, **J**, 210, **K**, 253a, **S**, 600
Morgan's Legion, Song of; **D**, 44
Morgan's Men; **A**, 250, **F**, 356, **J**, 210, **Q**, 19, **S**, 1354,
   History, **Q**, 22
Morgan's Raids; **B**, 1013, **C**, 865, 1081, 1353, 1581, **D**, 764, 959, **E**, 282, 307, **F**, 601, **G**, 49-50, **H**, 997, **K**, 50, **M**, 534, **R**, 581, **S**, 482-483, 1198, **W**, 324, 464
Morgan's Rough Riders; **D**, 913, 919, **F**, 21, **H**, 262
Morgan, Asa S., Col.; **J**, 177
Morgan, Jack; **B**, 1164, **J**, 3
Morgan, James Morris; **B**, 882-883
Morgan, John Hunt, Brig.Gen.; **B**, 367, 369, 379, 415, 554, 769, 1323, 1624, **C**, 1072, 1074, 1415, **D**, 44, 703, 899, 909-910, 974, **E**, 216, **F**, 354, **H**, 305a, 369, 433, 893, **J**, 18, **M**, 338, 366, 1248, **N**, 157, **P**, 66, 115, **R**, 32a, 192, 206, 252, **S**, 193, 260, 473, 601, 1438, **T**, 191, **W**, 1085,
   Christmas Raid, **C**, 1581,
   Death, **F**, 570-571,
   Escape, **B**, 1546, **H**, 938,
   Surrender, **R**, 788
Morgan, John Tyler, Brig.Gen.; **A**, 88, **B**, 645
Morgan, Nathaniel Alexander; **L**, 600

Morgan, Thomas J., Col.; **P**, 681
Morgantown, WV;
   Raid, **S**, 300
Morman Splinter Colony; **W**, 619
Morrill, Lily Logan; **L**, 592
Morris Island Prison, SC; **D**, 951, **M**, 704,
   Roster, **L**, 540
Morris Island, SC; **B**, 463, 497, **D**, 580, **F**, 276, 574, **H**, 327, **M**, 367e,
   Confederate Officers, **B**, 128,
   Defenses, **G**, 254,
   Engineers, **C**, 1271,
   Fortifications, **R**, 489
Morrison, Hugh Alexander; **B**, 672, **L**, 423
Morrison, Samuel Elliott; **J**, 569
Morse, Porter; **S**, 890
Morton's Ford, VA, Battle of; **B**, 1111
Morton, J.W., Jr.; **A**, 354
Morton, R.L.; **V**, 157
Mosby's Men; **C**, 1408, **F**, 21, **L**, 768, **R**, 826,
   Hanging of, **W**, 222
Mosby's Night Hawk; **C**, 575
Mosby's Rangers; **A**, 186, **B**, 1477, **R**, 362, **W**, 767
Mosby's Trail; **R**, 212a
Mosby, John Singleton, Col.; **B**, 545, **D**, 90, **G**, 419, 674, **H**, 1309, **J**, 545, **K**, 253a, **L**, 26, **M**, 1292-1294, **R**, 10, 212a, 358, **S**, 165, 455, **T**, 9,
   Destroys Train, **H**, 541
Moscow, TN, Battle of; **B**, 513
Moseley, Alexander; **E**, 247
Moses, Felix; **L**, 576
Mosgrove, George Dallas; **M**, 441
Moss Neck, VA;
   Jackson's Winter Quarters, **K**, 193
Motley, James C., Capt.; **B**, 738
Mount Jackson, VA;
   Shenandoah Cemetery, **M**, 1254a
Mount Vernon Guards;
   Uniforms, **U**, 14
Mount Vernon, VA; **M**, 1271
Mountain Campaign; **M**, 430,
   Failure, **J**, 349

Mounted Raids; **L**, 638
Mouton, Jean J. Alfred A., Brig.Gen.; **A**, 409
Mouton, John Baptist, Rev.; **P**, 730
Mowry, Sylvester; **C**, 672
Mt. Olivet Cemetery, Frederick, MD; **C**, 896, 954
Mt. Pleasant, SC;
Occupation of, **E**, 323
Mudd, Samuel, Dr.; **C**, 241, **H**, 788, **K**, 225, **M**, 1262, **R**, 523, **V**, 134
Muhlenfeld, Elizabeth; **C**, 447
Mulberry Island, VA; **D**, 166
Mullaly, John; **G**, 159
Mulligan, James A., Col.; **B**, 269, **L**, 499
Mullins, Michael; **C**, 1515
Mundy, Jim; **F**, 446
Mundy, Sue; **A**, 260, **H**, 1037, **M**, 63, **V**, 4
Munford, Thomas Taylor, Brig.Gen.; **L**, 49a-50
Munfordville, KY, Battle of; **B**, 132, **S**, 1455
Munitions; **D**, 726, **M**, 524,
Development, **H**, 1171
Munnerlyn's Battalion; **T**, 70
Munson, John W.; **XYZ**, 93a
Murdaugh, William Henry, Capt.; **R**, 225
Murfreesboro, TN; **C**, 637,
Forrest's Attack, **K**, 182
Murfreesboro, TN, Battle of; **G**, 224, **J**, 308, 511, **N**, 118, **P**, 375, **R**, 451
Murrah, Pendleton, Gov., TX; **N**, 217
Murray, J. Ogden, Maj.; **C**, 570
Murray, J. Thomas, Rev.; **B**, 60
Murrell, Cornelia Randolph; **A**, 83
Murrow, Father; **M**, 34
Muscogee (ship); **S**, 236
Museum, Confederate, Leesburg, VA; **K**, 34
Music; **A**, 415, **B**, 783, 859, 1164, 1245, 1490, **C**, 336, 488, 621, 802, 1014, 1236, **D**, 440, 590, 659, **E**, 93, 115, **F**, 3, **G**, 22, 45, 108-109, 477, 505, 584, **H**, 60, 71, 475-476, 482, 486, 488, 491, 592, 602, 641, 1058a, 1225, **J**, 3, 66b, **K**, 8, 245, **L**, 422, 635a, **M**, 363a, 512, 781, 786, 951, 1059, 1062, **O**, 86, 111a, 173, **P**, 47a, **R**, 85-86, 377, 449, 663, 787, **S**, 134-135, 241, 339-340, 387, 508, 593, 657, 798a, 801, 822, 891-892a, 996, 1023, 1237, 1254, **T**, 126, **W**, 154, 160-161, 375, 488, 893, **XYZ**, 95,
Dixie, **B**, 106, **E**, 203-207, 257,
Maryland, My Maryland, **A**, 195, **B**, 72,
NC, 4th Regt. Band, **S**, 1048,
Piano-Forte Primer, **B**, 1603,
Song Books, **C**, 1013,
Southern, **A**, 194, **B**, 62,
Texas, **A**, 192, **S**, 921
Musketoons; **M**, 1311
Muster Rolls; **A**, 275
Muzzle-loader; **P**, 315a
My Father, General Lee (book); **L**, 366
Myers, Abraham Charles, Col.; **B**, 1582
Myers, E.G., Mrs.; **C**, 894
Myres, Sandra L.; **V**, 31
Myths; **T**, 544

N

Nadenbousch, John Quincy Adams, Col.; **B**, 626
Names, Confused; **C**, 81
Nance, David C.; **G**, 30
Napoleon, III; **M**, 1342-1343, **S**, 203, 577
Napoleons (guns); **H**, 614
Nashville (ship); **G**, 83, **P**, 214, **W**, 595
Nashville, Chattanooga & St. Louis R.R.; **S**, 1245, **W**, 159
Nashville, TN; **D**, 605, **G**, 225, **H**, 1045a, 1100, **J**, 94, **M**, 314,
   Battlefields, **S**, 857,
   Campaign, **C**, 550,
   Confederate Underground, **H**, 1101,
   Democratic Association, **B**, 1341,
   Evacuation, **B**, 988,
   Federal Occupation, **B**, 1469,
   Jewry, **F**, 461,
   Medical Officers, **G**, 256,
   Reconstruction, **M**, 292,
   Retreat, **B**, 1233,
   Southern Convention, **C**, 457
Nashville, TN, Battle of; **B**, 357, **C**, 1373, **H**, 1096, **L**, 377, **M**, 1208, **P**, 856
Natchez, MS; **D**, 932, **M**, 265
National Democratic Convention; **C**, 463, **P**, 786
National Gallery Orchestra; **M**, 1336
National Military Parks; **B**, 1035, **S**, 87
National Park Commission; **C**, 840
Nationalism;
   South Carolina, **S**, 139
Natural Bridge, Tallahassee, FL, Battle of; **B**, 1002
Naval Academy, CSA; **F**, 314
Naval Cadets, Confederate; **F**, 238
Naval Life; **K**, 48
Naval Warfare; **C**, 1133, **D**, 970, **H**, 1081, **M**, 349,
   Salt-making, **L**, 673
Naval Weapons, Civil War; **A**, 490
Navy Department, Confederate; **R**, 280
Navy Yards; **D**, 715
Navy, Confederate; **B**, 994, **C**, 59, 368, 650, 1031, **D**, 431, 721, 727-728, 922, 992, **E**, 122, **H**, 225-227, 1033a, 1067, **M**, 49-50b, 367f, 960a, 1171, **O**, 51, 125, **P**, 53, 55a, 87, 89a, 89b, **R**, 155, 238, 408, 550, **S**, 105, 238, 1121, 1193, 1207, **T**, 329, 404, **V**, 160, **W**, 393, 944a,
   Administration, **G**, 594,
   Alabama Claims, **B**, 1268,
   Architecture, **C**, 1133,
   Boatbuilders, French, **B**, 647,
   Charleston, SC, **L**, 579a,
   Development, **J**, 540,
   England, **M**, 801,
   Europe, **S**, 938,
   First Submarine, **F**, 427,
   Georgia, **A**, 397,
   Guns, **T**, 132,
   History, **N**, 29,
   Mississippi River, **B**, 840,
   North Carolina, **T**, 387,
   Policy, **S**, 1205,
   Roster, **J**, 406b,
   Strategy, **S**, 1201,
   Submarines, **B**, 765,
   Uniforms, **U**, 14
Navy, Union;
   History, **N**, 29
Navy, US;
   Cannon, **B**, 237,

Diplomacy, **B**, 638
Necrology; **C**, 971
Neely, Phillip Phillips; **B**, 536
Negroes; **B**, 693, **C**, 518, 1477, **D**, 644, **F**, 606, **G**, 210, 556, **H**, 1188, **J**, 406, **K**, 249, **M**, 414, 663, **N**, 60, **P**, 76, **S**, 862, **V**, 24, **W**, 484, 666,
    Act to Prevent Employment, **C**, 1028,
    Black Republican Party, **D**, 334,
    Confederate, **B**, 1237,
    Enlistments, **S**, 941,
    Garrisons, **H**, 201,
    History, **N**, 58,
    Ironworkers, **B**, 1072,
    Labor, **C**, 183, **S**, 946,
    Life, **N**, 59,
    Louisiana, Voters, **C**, 372,
    Maryland, **B**, 1042,
    Midwest, **V**, 167,
    Music, **E**, 93,
    North Carolina, **B**, 1022-1023,
    Reconstruction, **R**, 438,
    Richmond, VA, **E**, 70,
    Segregation, **D**, 139,
    Soldiers, **B**, 616, 644, 1509, **C**, 655, **G**, 200, **H**, 569, **P**, 699, **S**, 796, **W**, 419
Neibling, C.C.; **E**, 216
Neill, Job; **D**, 815
Neimeyer, William Frederick, Lt.-Col.; **S**, 1170
Nelson County, VA; **N**, 61
Nelson, Allison; **P**, 536a
Nelson, William, Maj.Gen.;
    Assassination, **T**, 35
Nesbit, James Cooper; **M**, 441
Nesson County, VA; **L**, 186
Nettles, T.D., Capt.; **B**, 1431
Neuse (ship); **B**, 1259, **S**, 1202
Neutrality; **B**, 1336, **C**, 29, **H**, 280, 656, **S**, 438
Nevins, Allan; **B**, 672, 729, **N**, 111
New Bern, NC; **B**, 913, **H**, 974, **P**, 362,
    Battle of, **A**, 24, **C**, 1605, **I**, 44,
    Ladies Memorial Association, **L**, 16,

    Raid, **R**, 882,
    Siege, **S**, 454
New Creek Station, WV; **G**, 97
New Creek, WV, Battle of; **W**, 405
New Hanover County, NC;
    Roster, **S**, 20
New Madrid, MO; **M**, 1275
New Market Bridge, VA; **M**, 663
New Market Day, VMI; **V**, 149
New Market, VA; **R**, 682, **S**, 976, **T**, 490
New Market, VA, Battle of; **B**, 1438, **C**, 718, 817, 1314, 1317-1318, **D**, 330, 362, 370, **E**, 64, **I**, 2, **O**, 71, **R**, 407, **S**, 38, 435, 634, **T**, 359, **V**, 149, **W**, 41, 299, 865, 879, 881
New Mexico; **G**, 524, **O**, 94, **P**, 626, **R**, 499, **S**, 988, **W**, 36,
    Army, **H**, 79,
    Campaign, **G**, 478, **H**, 77, 583, **P**, 328, **S**, 1006,
    Cavalry Expeditions, **XYZ**, 54,
    Confederate Arms, **D**, 950,
    Conquest, **B**, 1001,
    Courts, Confederate, **T**, 319,
    Federal Invasion, **P**, 324,
    Hispanos, **M**, 869,
    Invasion, **K**, 47, 105, **S**, 804, **T**, 512, **V**, 2, **W**, 42,
    Operations, **C**, 1098,
    Sectionalism, **G**, 37,
    Supplies, **M**, 870
New Orleans Picayune, LA, np.; **E**, 322
New Orleans, LA; **C**, 211, **D**, 453, **E**, 178, **S**, 893,
    Businesses, **D**, 828,
    Butler's Investment in, **N**, 88a,
    Defenses, **O**, 116,
    Economics, **B**, 883,
    Fall of, **D**, 896, **L**, 733, **P**, 787, **T**, 404,
    German Colony, **C**, 590,
    Greenwood Cemetery, **L**, 11,
    Marine Hspital, **R**, 703,
    Mint, **B**, 1216, **C**, 91,
    Monument, **D**, 483,
    Occupation, **C**, 144-145, 1265,

Schools, **D**, 829,
Social Life, **R**, 487,
Strangers' Church, **C**, 571,
Uncle Tom, **R**, 705,
Women, **D**, 616
New Orleans, LA, Battle of; **M**, 608
New Smyrna, FL; **S**, 1428
New York;
Business & Slavery, **F**, 323,
Chamber of Commerce, **P**, 785,
Confederate Operations, **H**, 620,
Prize Courts, **R**, 602,
UCV Camp, **O**, 208
New York Times, NY, np.; **C**, 539, **G**, 523, **M**, 978
Newman, John P., Bishop; **O**, 10
Newman, Ralph G.; **V**, 54
Newnan, GA;
Oak Hill Cemetery, **C**, 921,
Oakhill Cemetery, **O**, 24
Newport News Point, VA; **R**, 752
Newport, NC; **P**, 452
Newsom-Trader, Ella K., Mrs.; **R**, 357
Newspapers; **C**, 554, 657, 998, 1131, **D**, 18-21, **G**, 571, 657, **H**, 109,
Arkansas Gazette, AR, **M**, 1250,
Atlanta Journal-Constitution, GA, **S**, 304,
Augusta Chronicle, GA, **B**, 521,
Beehive, **L**, 593,
Camp, **W**, 643,
Charleston Courier, SC, **F**, 235, 423, **M**, 101,
Charleston Mercury, SC, **S**, 826, 840,
Charleston, SC, **D**, 137, **M**, 978,
Chicago Times, IL, **T**, 124,
Cincinnati Daily Inquirer, OH, **W**, 796,
Civil War Chronicle, CO, **K**, 27,
Copperheads, **A**, 20, **G**, 159,
Daily Citizen, MS, **V**, 120,
Frank Leslie's Illustrated, **L**, 445,
Galveston & Dallas News, TX, **B**, 549,
London News, England, **H**, 214,
London Times, England, **J**, 614, **L**, 606, **R**, 266, **S**, 1067, **T**, 307, **W**, 674,
Memphis Daily Appeal, TN, **S**, 532,
Mexico, **H**, 233,
Missouri Army Argus, **M**, 940,
Mobile Register, AL, **C**, 971a,
Mobile Tribune, AL, **R**, 254,
Negroes, **A**, 20,
New Orleans Picayune, LA, **E**, 322,
New York Times, **C**, 539, **G**, 523, **M**, 978,
Northern, **K**, 27,
Philadelphia Weekly Times, PA, **M**, 418,
Refugee, **B**, 57,
Religious, **N**, 204,
Republican, SC, **W**, 953,
Richmond Examiner, VA, **D**, 50, **J**, 43,
Richmond Times Dispatch, VA, **R**, 407-421,
Richmond, VA, **R**, 395-396, 424,
Soldier, **W**, 663,
Southern, **K**, 27,
Southern Enterprise, Greenville, SC, **G**, 608, **S**, 863,
Texas, **S**, 1052,
Texas State Gazette, TX, **G**, 8,
Valley News Echo, MD, **V**, 15,
Vicksburg Daily Citizen, MS, **B**, 575,
Virginia, **M**, 923,
Wallpaper, **B**, 1257, **W**, 86-87,
Washington Star, DC, **S**, 1118,
Weekly Atlanta Intelligencer, **M**, 103
Newton County, MS; **B**, 1338
Newton's Regiment; **A**, 296
Newton, John Brockenbrough; **S**, 977
Newton, Mary Barksdale; **B**, 792
Newton, Virginius; **B**, 792
Newtonia, MO, Battle of; **B**, 372
Nichols, James L.; **C**, 903, **M**, 1182
Nicholson, A.O.P.; **J**, 145
Nicholson, John Page; **B**, 672
Nighthawk Rangers; **N**, 72, **W**, 699
Niter Works; **S**, 691

Nobel, Samuel; R, 543
Nolan, L.E., Capt.; N, 162a
Nordendorf, Charles Csaky de; H, 60
Norfolk City Guards; H, 268
Norfolk County, VA; P, 641
Norfolk Light Infantry Blues; H, 268
Norfolk, VA;
  Elmwood Cemetery, C, 895, G, 87,
  History, B, 1611,
  Occupied, C, 388,
  Volunteers, H, 268
Norris, William, Col.; G, 5-6, N, 168
North; C, 1376,
  Appeals to, C, 799,
  Confederate Operations, K, 163,
  Cotton Rings, J, 229,
  Emancipation, A, 390,
  Loyalty Tests, H, 1360,
  Profit, J, 229,
  Resources, S, 6,
  Segregation, D, 139,
  Weakness, A, 285
North Carolina; A, 336, B, 171, 175, C, 502, 506, 1252, F, 208-209, G, 471, 576, H, 842-843, J, 190, S, 98a, 569, 1165,
  Agriculture, C, 315,
  Battalions, C, 599,
  Biographical Sketches, P, 210,
  Blockade-running, R, 298,
  Burial Lists, P, 587-589,
  Centennial, T, 461,
  Cherokee Indians, C, 1486,
  Civil War Documentary, XYZ, 24,
  Commemoration, D, 770,
  Confederate Government, M, 1028,
  Congress, Confederate, N, 169,
  Conscription, D, 783,
  Conventions, M, 434,
  Cotton, W, 318,
  Courts, H, 156,
  Currency & Notes, B, 780, 1044,
  Dersertion, B, 111,
  Disloyalty to Confederacy, D, 143,
  Economics, B, 1009,
  Education, K, 232,
  Emancipation Proclamation, M, 1241,
  Expedition, K, 194,
  Flag Designed, W, 707,
  Forts, E, 174,
  Genealogical Index, N, 40,
  General Assembly, L, 539,
  Generals, C, 603, K, 185,
  Gettysburg, PA, C, 601, 605, T, 421,
  Gettysburg, PA, Memorial, C, 1102,
  History, H, 154, O, 196,
  Last Days of War, R, 832, S, 933, V, 38, W, 4,
  Medical Officers, M, 734,
  Memorial, C, 359,
  Monuments, S, 715,
  Navy, C, 602, T, 387,
  Negroes, B, 1022-1023, N, 59,
  Peace, R, 531, XYZ, 16-19,
  Planters, C, 353,
  Politics, J, 352, K, 264,
  Poverty, E, 238,
  Quakers, S, 901,
  Railroads, P, 733,
  Reconstruction, H, 390a,
  Records, C, 753, 1374,
  Regiments, C, 599,
  Relief, F, 170, N, 175a,
  Reunions, B, 1089,
  Revenue Act, N, 176,
  Roll of Honor, R, 676,
  Roster, F, 137, L, 519,
  Secession, B, 294, 1007,
  Sherman's March, R, 586,
  Slavery, B, 219,
  Soldiers, B, 587, H, 831, I, 28, L, 436,
  State Archives, C, 1374,
  State Regulations, W, 318,
  Supreme Court, J, 420,
  Unionists, D, 498,
  Women, A, 318, C, 1101, H, 825
North Carolina Room, Confederate Museum; C, 951

North Carolina Troops; **C**, 608,
  Alamance County, **A**, 117,
  Armory Guards,
    6th Bat., **T**, 57,
  Arms, **O**, 98,
  Artillery,
    10th Bat., **W**, 521,
  Cavalry,
    1st Regt., **B**, 55, **H**, 198,
    2nd Regt., **H**, 198,
    3rd Regt., **H**, 278, 742, **S**, 701,
    63rd Regt., **C**, 831,
  Infantry,
    1st Regt., **B**, 19, **F**, 137, **L**, 80, 93,
    1st Regt. Vols., **F**, 138, **M**, 367,
    2nd Regt., **S**, 542,
    3rd Regt., **D**, 451,
    4th Regt., **G**, 653, **S**, 107,
    5th Regt., **B**, 1295,
    6th Regt., **I**, 46,
    7th Regt., **H**, 373,
    11th Regt., **M**, 267,
    13th Regt., **B**, 584,
    14th Regt., **F**, 393, **S**, 107, 730,
    20th Regt., **C**, 199, **H**, 275,
    22nd Regt., **D**, 115,
    23rd Regt., **W**, 89,
    24th Regt., **M**, 1057a,
    25th Regt., **G**, 683, **R**, 886,
    26th Regt., **B**, 1578, **D**, 142, **L**, 422, **U**, 7,
    27th Regt., **F**, 451,
    28th Regt., **L**, 77,
    33rd Regt., **W**, 475,
    38th Regt., **F**, 297, **H**, 978,
    39th Regt., **D**, 131,
    43rd Regt., **K**, 69,
    44th Regt., **S**, 1035,
    48th Regt., **B**, 426,
    49th Regt., **D**, 403, **R**, 747, **S**, 1062,
    50th Regt., **C**, 197,
    51st Regt., **M**, 1088,
    54th Regt., **P**, 60,
    56th Regt., **E**, 159, **H**, 356,
    57th Regt., **J**, 419, **W**, 22,
    58th Regt., **C**, 598, **H**, 351-352, **P**, 47,
    59th Regt., **B**, 548,
    64th Regt. State, **G**, 110,
    72nd Regt., **H**, 898,
  Roster, **J**, 582c,
  Roster, **J**, 582e, **M**, 124-128, 1081, **N**, 180a, **S**, 342,
  State Guards, **N**, 172,
  State Troops, **B**, 706,
  Statistics, **F**, 208, **K**, 190,
  Strength of, **H**, 850,
  Union Men (1861), **A**, 118
North West Confederacy; **E**, 40
Northern Incendiarism; **A**, 506
Northern Neck, VA, Soldiers' Reunion; **B**, 335
Northern Wheat & Southern Cotton; **G**, 284
Northrop, Allen C., Maj.; **B**, 824
Northrop, Lucius B.; **F**, 78, **H**, 568
Northwest; **G**, 135, 232
Northwest Conspiracy; **B**, 1363, **C**, 739, **H**, 894, **O**, 114, **S**, 1011, **T**, 258
Northwestern Confederacy; **C**, 716, **F**, 94
Norton, Mary Alice; **N**, 196
Norton, Sarah Mills; **M**, 894
Norwegian-American Soldiers; **C**, 629
Nottoway Grays; **I**, 48
Noxubee Cavalry; **D**, 553
Noyes, Edward, Col.; **E**, 112
Nueces Massacre; **N**, 104
Nueces River; **S**, 63,
  Massacre, **W**, 736
Nueces, TX, Battle of; **S**, 431
Nullification; **B**, 509, 941, 1256, **E**, 272, **F**, 500, **P**, 678, **S**, 56,
  Georgia, **C**, 1304,
  South Carolina, **B**, 77, **H**, 1133
Nullification Law; **V**, 169
Nurses; **C**, 1554, **M**, 229, **R**, 357, **S**, 1257,

O

O'Connell, John C.; **S**, 589
O'Connor, Charles; **A**, 548, **M**, 40
O'Ferral, Charles Triplett, Gov., VA; **F**, 134
O'Hara, Theodore, Col.; **B**, 1041, **C**, 728, **H**, 1001a, 1281, **J**, 320, **R**, 73, **W**, 810
O'Reilly, Miles; **W**, 2
O'Sullivan, John L.; **H**, 383
Oak Hill Cemetery, Newnan, GA; **C**, 921
Oak Hill, GA; **C**, 693
Oak Hills, MO, Battle of; **B**, 999, **H**, 982, 1278, **M**, 673
Oakwood Cemetery, Chicago, IL; **M**, 186, **P**, 541, **U**, 37
Oates, Stephen B.; **F**, 352, **L**, 133
Oaths; **H**, 1360, **P**, 39-40
Obion Avalanche; **C**, 340
Ocean Pond, FL, Battle of; **B**, 75, 469, **C**, 819, **F**, 133, **H**, 405, **J**, 384, 518, **S**, 592
Ochiltree, Thomas P., Col.; **W**, 1039
Officers; **C**, 920, 1515, 1621, **K**, 71, **M**, 769,
  Arkansas, **C**, 1168a,
  Captured, **A**, 314,
  Roster, **J**, 398-401, 406d, **R**, 741, **S**, 871,
  Wilkinson County, MS, Roster, **M**, 885
Officers Corps of Artillery, CSA; **A**, 472
Official Records, Navies, pub.;
  Index, **K**, 242
Official Records, pub.; **I**, 57, **L**, 467, **M**, 73, **W**, 168,
  Making of, **E**, 130
Oglethorpe County, GA; **T**, 180

Oglethorpe Light Infantry; **H**, 302, 689, **R**, 629,
  Uniforms, **U**, 14
Oglethorpe Rifles; **R**, 232, **T**, 180
Ohio; **K**, 5, **R**, 716,
  Confederate Dead, **K**, 229,
  Generals, Confederate, **C**, 1559, 1563
Ohio State Penitentiary; **C**, 1206, **M**, 1136
Okefenokee Swamp, GA; **P**, 235
Oklahoma; **F**, 159,
  Cherokee Nation, **A**, 337,
  Civil War Sites, **W**, 1052,
  First Battle, **R**, 831,
  Historical Sites, **F**, 149,
  UCV, **H**, 40
Okolona, MS, Battle of;
  Forrest at, **P**, 53a
Old Cane Springs, KY; **C**, 434, 636
Old Dominion Guards; **H**, 268
Old Dominion Rifles; **W**, 195,
  Uniforms, **U**, 14
Oldaker, Glenn C.; **F**, 537
Oldham, Kie; **H**, 731
Oldham, Williamson Simpson; **N**, 217
Oldum, F.H., Capt.; **D**, 818
Olin, Viola Parish, Mrs.; **F**, 341
Oliver, Thaddeus; **D**, 114
Olmstead, Charles H., Col.; **H**, 988
Olsen, Stanley J.; **C**, 851
Olustee Campaign; **N**, 215a
Olustee, FL, Battle of; **B**, 75, 469, 1003, 1217, **C**, 553, 778, 819, 832, **D**, 972, **F**, 92, 607, **H**, 329, 406, **J**, 518, **M**, 257, 665, **R**, 349, **W**, 350
Omenhausser, John T.; **M**, 122
Omohundro, J.B.; **L**, 589
Onslow County, NC; **A**, 582
Opera; **G**, 505

Opiate Addiction; **C**, 1332
Opothleyahola, Ind.T.; **B**, 21, **F**, 481
Orange County, VA; **L**, 536,
  History, **O**, 120
Orangeburg, SC;
  Monuments, **B**, 1627
Oratory; **B**, 1049
Ord, Edward Otho Cresap,
  Maj.Gen.; **C**, 1429
Order of American Knights; **F**, 94, **H**, 1033, **K**, 4, 214, 222a, **R**, 295, **S**, 1188
Ordinances; **A**, 88
Ordnance; **A**, 135, 198, **B**, 1331, 1333, 1442, **C**, 162, **F**, 106, 218, 322, **G**, 301, 425, **H**, 546, 835, **J**, 327, **L**, 65, **M**, 729, **P**, 315, **R**, 15, **V**, 65, 68, 73,
  Field Manual, **C**, 916,
  Manual, **G**, 428,
  Naval, **M**, 750
Ordnance Bureau; **A**, 28, **M**, 90, **N**, 10
Ordnance Department; **F**, 74, **W**, 555
Ordway, Sally F.; **B**, 1328
Orphan Brigade; **C**, 986, **J**, 603, **K**, 99, 206, **P**, 170, **T**, 225, **XYZ**, 67,
  Reunion, **O**, 155-156
Orphanages; **W**, 733
Orr Brothers; **A**, 328
Orr's Rifles; **M**, 342b
Orr, Gustavus John; **O**, 157
Orr, J.A.; **W**, 604
Orr, James L.; **L**, 405
Orr, Thomas; **B**, 49
Osborn, George C.; **A**, 313
Ossabaw Sound, GA; **H**, 304
Osterhout, John P.; **S**, 909
Osyka, MS;
  Daily Dispatch, np., **D**, 19
Otey Battery; **A**, 450
Ouachita County, AR; **J**, 164,
  Volunteers, **V**, 181
Ould, Robert, Col.; **H**, 653
Outlaws; **C**, 55, 1501
Outposts; **A**, 420, **C**, 1185, **M**, 72
Outwest, Oliver; **A**, 70
Owen, Richard, Col.; **C**, 1584
Owen, Thomas McAdory; **J**, 137
Owen, W.M., Col.; **S**, 545
Owens, Harry P.; **O**, 90
Owsley, Frank L.; **C**, 1430, **S**, 294a
Ox Hill, VA, Battle of; **S**, 714
Oxford Hospital, MS; **H**, 115
Oxford University;
  War Hospital, **J**, 213
Oxford, MS; **O**, 3,
  Burning of, **D**, 611,
  Hospital, **C**, 267
Ozark Mountains; **D**, 779, **W**, 847

P

P.A.C.S.; **O**, 76
Packard, Thomas J., Rev.; **P**, 4
Packet Markings, Confederate; **A**, 399
Paddle-Steamer Notes; **R**, 25
Paducah, KY; **C**, 1239, **L**, 626c
Page's Battery; **P**, 10, **S**, 541
Page, Thomas Nelson; **B**, 10, **D**, 837, **P**, 14
Page-Barbour Letters; **N**, 80
Pageants; **B**, 1583
Paisley, Clifton; **S**, 154
Paisley, William; **P**, 30a
Palmer, Benjamin; **J**, 240
Palmer, John Williamson; **S**, 1236
Palmer, W.H., Col.; **H**, 890
Palmetto Armory; **A**, 125
Palmetto Flag; **B**, 1075
Palmetto Ranch, TX, Battle of; **K**, 266, **L**, 120-121
Palmetto Riflemen; **H**, 1206, **M**, 470, **R**, 212a
Palmyra, MO;
   Massacre, **B**, 48a, **P**, 51, **S**, 820, **V**, 134
Pamlico District, NC;
   District Court, **R**, 610
Paper Shortages; **F**, 299, **W**, 682
Pardons; **D**, 758-759, **J**, 163
Paris, France; **N**, 36, **W**, 785,
   Declaration, **T**, 394
Paris, Louis, Comte de; **E**, 34, **J**, 450
Paris, Texas; **B**, 1622
Paris, TN;
   Monument, **P**, 636
Park County, CO; **E**, 214
Parker's Battery; **G**, 661, **J**, 5, **K**, 259, **W**, 525
Parker's Crossroads, TN, Battle of; **M**, 139, **W**, 744a

Parker, Nicholas; **M**, 1087
Parker, William Watts, Capt.; **J**, 5, **P**, 85
Parkersburg, WV; **P**, 290
Parkhill, Richard Call, Capt.; **D**, 854
Parliamentary Battle; **M**, 263
Paroles; **P**, 109-110,
   Engineer Troops, **T**, 10
Parson's Brigade; **H**, 959, 1297
Parson's Cavalry; **G**, 197, **H**, 798b, **P**, 117, **T**, 445
Parsons, Jim; **S**, 1215
Parsons, Lewis E.; **S**, 1016
Parsons, Mosby Monroe, Brig.Gen.; **M**, 880a
Parsons, W.H., Gen.; **P**, 117
Partin, Robert Love; **H**, 1031
Partisan Leaders; **T**, 475, 477
Partisan Rangers; **D**, 475, **J**, 154, **N**, 51, **R**, 343, **S**, 165
Partisans; **C**, 285, **G**, 500, **J**, 210, **M**, 676, 1217, **T**, 56a
Paschal, George W.; **F**, 367
Pasha, Hobart, Adm.; **H**, 924
Patrick Henry (ship); **R**, 626
Patrick, Rembert W.; **C**, 1038
Patrick, Robert; **T**, 52
Patriotism & State Sovereignty; **A**, 590
Patterson, Edmund Dewitt; **B**, 170
Patterson, John; **D**, 344
Patton, Frances Gary; **V**, 40
Patton, George S., Col.; **P**, 530, **S**, 1365, 1375, **W**, 454
Patton, James W.; **E**, 85
Patton, Joseph Welch; **G**, 607
Paul, Alfred; **S**, 940
Paxton, Frank "Bull"; **H**, 798b
Paxton, James G., Maj.; **P**, 7
Paxton, John C., Col.; **W**, 450

Payne, J.U.; **C**, 737
Payne, Lewis; **P**, 761
Payne, William Henry F., Brig.Gen.; **R**, 597, **S**, 722
Payroll, Confederate; **L**, 123
Pea Patch Island, DE; **K**, 29
Pea Ridge, AR; **F**, 348,
   Campaign, **F**, 350,
   National Military Park, **W**, 686
Pea Ridge, AR, Battle of; **A**, 426, **B**, 273, 299, 324, 380, 382-383, 603, 1362, 1416, 1418, **C**, 287, 311, 313, 681, 731, **E**, 91, **G**, 578, **H**, 166, 259, **M**, 773, 1037, **O**, 119, **P**, 67, 701, **S**, 1158, 1425
Peabody, Charles; **B**, 549
Peace; **C**, 631, **D**, 613, **H**, 358, **O**, 23, 241,
   Commission, **D**, 244, **H**, 1325,
   Conferences, **G**, 349, 352, **H**, 915, **J**, 189,
   Conventions, **K**, 31-32, **P**, 853, **W**, 479,
   Democrats, **M**, 1329,
   Georgia, **H**, 76, **T**, 19,
   Movement, **XYZ**, 17, 26,
   Negotiations, **A**, 543, **D**, 426,
   North Carolina, **R**, 531
Peace Party; **D**, 566, **V**, 8
Peach Tree Creek, GA, Battle of; **A**, 68
Peacock, Jane; **A**, 539, **D**, 131
Pearce, Thilbert H.; **C**, 387
Pearl River; **E**, 127, **N**, 16
Pearson, Edward A.; **T**, 155
Pearson, John Albert, Jr.; **S**, 1385
Peck, John Calvin; **F**, 286
Peddicord, Kelion Franklin; **L**, 591
Pee Dee Guards, NC; **W**, 89
Pee Dee Light Artillery; **B**, 1460, 1462
Peele, W.J.; **C**, 1359
Pegram Battalion Association; **B**, 1152, **D**, 469, 953, **J**, 14, **M**, 369, **S**, 1285
Pegram's Artillery; **P**, 304, **R**, 733
Pegram's Battalion Association; **F**, 291

Pegram, Robert B., Capt.; **H**, 651
Peifer, James A.; **H**, 337
Pelham's Battalion; **S**, 423
Pelham, John, Lt.Col.; **C**, 1349, **H**, 254, 516-517, **J**, 555, **M**, 245, 338a, 413, 784, 856, 1066a, **P**, 48a, 218-219, **R**, 87, **T**, 446
Pelican Boys; **C**, 236
Pemberton, John Clifford, Lt.Gen.; **J**, 310, **M**, 758a
Pender County, NC;
   Roster, **S**, 20
Pender, William Dorsey, Maj.Gen.; **D**, 599, **H**, 520, **M**, 514, 1027
Pendleton Clemson Area, SC; **B**, 961
Pendleton County, WV;
   History, **M**, 1211
Pendleton's Reserve Artillery; **C**, 46
Pendleton, Alexander S., Col.; **B**, 353, **F**, 105
Pendleton, William Nelson, Brig.Gen.; **A**, 449, 470, 473, **J**, 339, **L**, 309, 399, **W**, 408
Peninsula Campaign; **C**, 1371, **H**, 585, **L**, 584, **N**, 144
Peninsula, VA; **L**, 743
Pennington, Edgar Legare; **C**, 440, 513, **L**, 611
Pennington, William; **B**, 37
Pennsylvania; **P**, 849,
   Campaign, **E**, 215, **F**, 533, **L**, 321, 659, **T**, 77,
   Cavalry Expeditions, **S**, 1314,
   Confederate State, **M**, 572,
   Invasion, **A**, 211, **L**, 652, **N**, 223, **P**, 809,
   Lee's Army, **N**, 185,
   Plundering, **C**, 732,
   Prigg Case, **F**, 129,
   Sympathizers, **E**, 266
Pensacola, FL; **C**, 1481, **M**, 528, **P**, 107, 256, **R**, 442, **S**, 548, **XYZ**, 85,
   Campaign, **S**, 1257,
   Gun Emplacement, **S**, 1440,
   Monuments, **C**, 963
Pensacola, FL, Battle of; **B**, 393
Pension Law, Confederate; **S**, 1100a
Pension Rolls; **C**, 1261

Pensions; **C**, 1052, **G**, 299, **I**, 21, **K**, 103, **P**, 377, **S**, 1230,
  Davis, Jefferson, Pres., **D**, 201,
  Georgia, **XYZ**, 61,
  Missouri, **M**, 943,
  Roster, **V**, 152,
  Texas, **K**, 192,
  Virginia, **V**, 151
Perkins, Steve; **B**, 734
Perrine, C.D.; **K**, 1
Perry, Benjamin F.; **K**, 141
Perry, Edward Aylesworth, Brig.Gen.; **F**, 68-69, 232, **P**, 759
Perry, James S., Capt.; **H**, 875
Perry, Leslie J.; **B**, 1525
Perryville, Ind.T.; **W**, 1020, 1023
Perryville, KY, Battle of; **C**, 429, **F**, 132, **H**, 14a, 1101, **Q**, 21, **R**, 124, **T**, 36-38
Person County, NC; **W**, 1057
Person, Marshall Samuel; **D**, 500
Personne (F.G. Fontaine); **D**, 412-416
Peterhoff Episode; **B**, 637
Peterkin, George William; **C**, 187, **S**, 1284
Peterkin, Joshua; **A**, 349a
Peters, Walter G., Lt.; **B**, 574
Petersburg City Guard;
  Uniforms, **U**, 14
Petersburg Grays; **B**, 707
Petersburg Riflemen;
  Uniforms, **U**, 14
Petersburg, VA; **B**, 710, **C**, 567, **M**, 847,
  Battlefields, **B**, 1290, **G**, 693, **P**, 306,
  Campaign, **R**, 115,
  Crater, The, **M**, 82a,
  Defenses, **A**, 410, **B**, 458,
  Evacuation, **C**, 808, **W**, 633,
  Hospital, **D**, 384,
  Monument, **M**, 369,
  Retreat, **P**, 3,
  Siege, **C**, 1537, **D**, 402, **H**, 1205, **S**, 797, 1169
Petersburg, VA, Battle of; **A**, 169, **B**, 434, 457, **C**, 261, **D**, 138, **H**, 26-27, 31, 975, **L**, 781, **M**, 369, **S**, 182, **T**, 215,
  Fortifications, **B**, 1407
Peterson, Cyrus Asbury; **H**, 255
Peterson, Harold L.; **H**, 615
Peterson, Owen Maurice; **B**, 571
Peticolas, A.B.; **A**, 143
Petigru, James Louis; **C**, 224, **G**, 548, **M**, 886, **T**, 210
Petrel (ship); **M**, 1127
Pettigrew's Charge; **F**, 567
Pettigrew, James J., Brig.Gen.; **B**, 865, **C**, 612, 952, **G**, 473, **R**, 651a, **S**, 1061, **T**, 395, **W**, 799,
  Death, **XYZ**, 81
Peyton, John Lewis; **B**, 819
Peyton, William Madison; **P**, 176
Pharmaceutical Conditions; **F**, 465-469, **H**, 1197
Pharmacy; **F**, 465-469, **S**, 201
Phi Gamma; **W**, 388
Philadelphia Weekly Times, PA, np.; **M**, 418
Philatelic Congress; **C**, 3
Philatelic Society; **S**, 780
Philatelists; **C**, 880, 981, 1019, **S**, 883
Philbrick, Edward S.; **P**, 195
Philippi, WV, Battle of; **C**, 186, **F**, 135, **P**, 672, **S**, 1156,
  Retreat, **M**, 674a
Phillips County, AR; **E**, 87, **M**, 991a
Phillips Expedition; **R**, 35
Phillips' Legion; **C**, 740
Phillips, Benjamin; **P**, 345
Phillips, John G., Capt.; **H**, 90
Phillips, Margaret; **C**, 711
Phillips, Moses; **C**, 711
Phillips, Ulrich Bonnell; **C**, 700, **D**, 607, **L**, 68, **R**, 703a, **S**, 29, 684a, **T**, 345
Photography; **C**, 882, **E**, 90, 246, **F**, 180, **M**, 873, **R**, 343, **S**, 37, 785
Picacho Pass, AZ, Battle of; **S**, 608
Picacho, Arizona Territory; **H**, 85
Pickaway Regiment; **E**, 216
Pickens Planters; **H**, 272
Pickens, Francis Wilkenson, Gov., SC; **C**, 1135, **E**, 88, **H**, 593

Pickens, Lucy Holcombe; **B**, 1539, 1640
Pickersgill, R.H.; **B**, 971
Picket Duty; **B**, 1112
Picket Fights; **C**, 1078
Pickett's Charge; **A**, 157, **B**, 1262, 1308, **C**, 601, 613, 1456, **F**, 131, **P**, 766, **S**, 1159
Pickett's Division; **G**, 155, **W**, 58
Pickett's Mill, GA, Battle of; **M**, 585
Pickett, Albert James, Col.; **W**, 938
Pickett, George Edward, Maj.Gen.; **A**, 157-158, **B**, 865, **D**, 796, **G**, 25, **J**, 260, **N**, 82, **P**, 150
Pickett, John T.; **B**, 573, **G**, 560, **S**, 199
Pickett, LaSalle Corbell; **G**, 25
Pickwick Dam; **B**, 595
Pictorial Battles; **L**, 2
Piedmont, WV, Battle of; **I**, 3-4
Pierce, Franklin, Pres.; **N**, 83, **O**, 21
Pierce, George Foster, Bishop; **S**, 633
Pike County, AL; **M**, 1302,
    Confederate Records, **F**, 32
Pike County, LA; **Q**, 25
Pike, Albert G.; **A**, 193
Pike, Albert, Brig.Gen.; **A**, 261, **B**, 1416-1417, **C**, 438, **D**, 659, 944, **H**, 617, **M**, 831, **V**, 130
Pikes, Confederate; **T**, 97
Pilfering & Plundering; **B**, 788
Pillow, Gideon Johnson, Brig.Gen.; **B**, 534, **G**, 559, **S**, 1234
Pilot Knob, MO, Battle of; **B**, 1434, **C**, 770, **P**, 313
Pine Bluff, AR; **C**, 1405, **M**, 201
Pine Bluff, AR, Battle of; **P**, 261b
Pine Mountain Americans; **H**, 578
Pinkerton Papers; **L**, 516
Pinkerton, Allen; **L**, 105
Pinkney, William; **G**, 66
Pinopolis, SC; **J**, 128
Pioneer (first submarine); **A**, 469
Pipes, Carved; **W**, 1011a
Piracy; **M**, 1304, **S**, 729, **T**, 412, **W**, 173
Pirates; **C**, 396, **G**, 241, **S**, 252
Pitman, Ben; **G**, 230
Pitt County, NC; **K**, 171b
Pittman Family, AR; **P**, 421
Pittsboro, Chatham Record, NC, np.; **C**, 657
Pittsylvania County, VA; **W**, 157
Plantations & Plantation Life; **A**, 152, **B**, 833, 1449, 1541, **C**, 353, 407, 1113, 1306, **D**, 452, 665, **F**, 591, **G**, 386, **H**, 375, 792, **J**, 503, **O**, 127, **P**, 608, **R**, 130, **S**, 226, 987, **T**, 192, 340,
    Architecture, **B**, 889,
    Arkansas, **C**, 183,
    Berkeley, SC, **J**, 128,
    Bolling Island Plantation, VA, **D**, 446,
    Brierfield Plantation, **E**, 267,
    Female Planters, **W**, 790,
    Georgia, **F**, 320,
    Green Mount, KY, **F**, 225-226, 593,
    Harmony Hall, **D**, 100,
    Laurel Wood, MS, **L**, 99,
    Lessee Problems, **B**, 683,
    Louisiana, **R**, 669-670, **W**, 147,
    Medicine, **M**, 230,
    Mississippi, **D**, 932, **P**, 336, **W**, 147,
    Negroes, Free, **B**, 1445,
    Northern, **P**, 680,
    Overseers, **B**, 218,
    Placid Plantation, NC, **W**, 831,
    Pre-Civil War Life, **A**, 582,
    Savannah River Rice Plantation, **C**, 683,
    South Carolina, **C**, 1364, **H**, 179, **M**, 89, 850,
    Teachers, **B**, 1450,
    Tennessee Valley, **K**, 84,
    Texas, **B**, 957, **C**, 1592
Playing Cards, Confederate Personalities; **M**, 58
Plays; **D**, 22, 845, **E**, 222, **G**, 584, **R**, 652
Pleasant Hill, LA, Battle of; **B**, 504, 1228
Pleasant Hill, MO; **C**, 593
Pleasants, Henry, Lt.Col.; **B**, 1452
Pleasants, James; **L**, 189
Plow-Horse Cavalry; **W**, 328
Plummer, Leonard B.; **H**, 208

Plymouth, NC; **B**, 913
Poague, William Thomas, Col.; **P**, 441a
Pocahontas County, WV; **P**, 753
Poems (see Verse);
Poet-Priest; **B**, 849, **H**, 626
Poetical Appeal, Liberate Baltimore, MD; **D**, 223
Poets; **C**, 621
Poindexter, James E.; **A**, 440
Point Lookout Prison, MD; **A**, 542, **B**, 205, 510, **C**, 836, **J**, 371, 417, **L**, 586, **S**, 270, 972, **T**, 382, **W**, 79,
  Monument, **M**, 1035a,
  Roster, **L**, 558
Poison Springs, AR, Battle of; **A**, 426, **F**, 174, **R**, 364
Polemics; **T**, 56a
Polignac, Camille Armand de, Maj.Gen.; **B**, 159, **H**, 533-536, 772
Polish America; **B**, 1621
Political Societies; **F**, 94, **M**, 1180
Politics; **H**, 209, **M**, 84, **P**, 668, **R**, 7, **T**, 165
Polk County, TN;
  History, **W**, 691
Polk County, TX; **H**, 861
Polk, Leonidas, Lt.Gen.; **C**, 486, 1431, **E**, 164, **F**, 539, **G**, 688, **M**, 572b, 659, **P**, 97, 486-489, **S**, 666,
  Ante-bellum Career, **D**, 897,
  Chickamauga, GA, **L**, 183,
  Death, **J**, 289
Pollard, Charleen Plumly; **A**, 233
Pollard, Edward Alfred; **A**, 17, **C**, 879, **E**, 61, 215, **M**, 45, 45a
Pollard, Henry Rives; **P**, 515
Polston, Michael David; **U**, 35
Ponchatoula, LA;
  Military Operations Around, **P**, 268a
Pond, George E.; **A**, 215
Ponsonby, F.; **A**, 420, **B**, 1518
Pontotoc County, MS;
  Soldiers, **H**, 1205
Pope Pius IX; **B**, 572, **D**, 266
Pope's Campaign; **A**, 207

Pope, John, Maj.Gen.; **A**, 222, **B**, 630, **E**, 194, **S**, 500
Poplar Lawn, Richmond, VA; **W**, 106
Poppenheim, M.B., Mrs.; **U**, 41
Porcher, Francis Peyre; **T**, 365, **W**, 609
Porcher, Fredrick Adolphus; **S**, 1239
Port Allen, LA; **B**, 995
Port Clinton, OH; **A**, 298
Port Gibson, MS; **J**, 310,
  Cemeteries, **F**, 336,
  Methodist Episcopal Church, **M**, 1114
Port Hudson, LA; **B**, 879, **D**, 241, **E**, 81, **H**, 772a, **J**, 11,
  Battlefields, **P**, 378,
  Campaign, **C**, 1570,
  Cavalry, **P**, 131,
  History, **P**, 715, **W**, 1015,
  Hospital, **H**, 773,
  Siege, **S**, 692
Port Hudson, LA, Battle of; **M**, 694
Port Republic, VA, Battle of; **J**, 66c
Port Royal Ferry, SC; **P**, 622
Port Royal, SC; **P**, 195,
  Fall of, **F**, 14
Porter, A. Toomer; **W**, 247
Porter, William D., Gov., SC; **E**, 125, **W**, 243
Portsmouth Artillery; **G**, 650, **P**, 660, **T**, 243
Portsmouth Rifle Company; **H**, 268
Portsmouth, VA; **B**, 1632,
  Trinity Church, **T**, 425
Post Office Department, Confederate; **D**, 592, **M**, 382, **O**, 52, **R**, 158
Postal Collections; **W**, 312
Postal History; **S**, 377, 381
Postal Legislation; **A**, 479-480
Postal Rates, Earliest Known Dates; **A**, 480
Postal Records, Confederate; **H**, 642
Postal Routes; **S**, 345, 348
Postal Stamps, General Issue; **A**, 479
Postal System, Confederate; **B**, 1334, **H**, 646, **M**, 838, **R**, 332,
  History, **C**, 1495, **M**, 5,
  Indian Territory, **S**, 415,

West Virginia, **S**, 1364, 1371
Postell, William Ross; **W**, 378
Postmarks, Treasury Notes; **R**, 28
Postmaster Provisionals; **P**, 694, **S**, 375
Postmasters, Confederate; **C**, 1496, **M**, 13, **W**, 683,
   Texas, **R**, 68
Potomac Edison Co.; **V**, 15
Potomac River; **M**, 1094, **N**, 8, 222
Potter County, TX;
   UCV, **H**, 66
Potter, Andrew Jackson; **G**, 524
Potter, David; **D**, 419, **J**, 126
Poulson, W.E.; **U**, 39
Pound, John Thomas; **M**, 1166
Pourtales, Countess; **C**, 431, **S**, 233
Poverty; **E**, 236,
   North Carolina, **E**, 238
Powder Works; **C**, 432, 703, **R**, 14
Powell, Charles Stevens; **C**, 851
Powhatan Troop; **L**, 171
Prairie De Ann, AR, Battle of; **A**, 530
Prairie Grove, AR, Battle of; **A**, 10, 426, **B**, 324, **H**, 888, 1242, **J**, 517, **L**, 596, **M**, 977, **O**, 33, **P**, 701, **W**, 45, 526
Prairie Guards; **L**, 725
Pratt's Battery; **G**, 197
Pratt, Edwin J.; **J**, 569
Prattville Dragoons;
   History, **M**, 902
Praus, Alexander A.; **C**, 1012
Prayer Books; **B**, 1491
Prescott, AR; **A**, 530
Presidential Campaigns;
   (1864), **W**, 175
Presidential Canvass (1860); **R**, 18
Preston County, WV; **M**, 1212
Preston, John Smith, Brig.Gen.; **A**, 307, **S**, 1404
Preston, William, Brig.Gen.; **D**, 749
Price's Campaign; **G**, 675, **P**, 189
Price's Raid; **C**, 14, **D**, 106, **P**, 749
Price, Sterling, Maj.Gen.; **B**, 269, 279, 524, 1359, 1374, **C**, 291, **F**, 561, **G**, 664, **H**, 982, **M**, 673, **P**, 266, **R**, 154, **S**, 286, 764, 971, **T**, 481

Price, William Coleman; **E**, 280
Prichard, John L., Rev.; **H**, 1253
Prince Edward County, VA;
   History, **B**, 1602
Prince George County, VA; **C**, 567
Prince George's County, MD; **C**, 575a
Prince William Cavalry, VA; **B**, 121
Prince William County, VA; **E**, 283,
   Confederate Park, **M**, 132
Printing; **A**, 284, **W**, 776,
   Plates Captured, **B**, 581
Prisoners; **A**, 345, **E**, 224, **F**, 368, **H**, 1178, **I**, 38a, **P**, 643a, **W**, 37a, 1080,
   Autograph Albums, **J**, 145-148,
   Captures, **C**, 237,
   Deaths, **P**, 695, **T**, 203,
   Escapes, **B**, 814, **D**, 38, 914, **F**, 21,
   Exchanges, **G**, 508, **H**, 812, **L**, 513, **M**, 960, **O**, 187, **R**, 282,
   Executions, **M**, 1232,
   Experiences, **A**, 461, **C**, 1458, 1460-1461, **H**, 155, **K**, 36, 39, 174, **L**, 485, **P**, 631, **S**, 357, 396, 587, 635, 710, **W**, 389,
   Immortal Six-hundred, **F**, 490,
   Journals, **F**, 522, **H**, 218,
   Life, **K**, 20,
   Medical Care, **W**, 315,
   Paroled, **C**, 777,
   Punished, **D**, 951,
   Thompson Conspiracy, **J**, 151,
   Treatment, **A**, 369, **B**, 486, 564, **C**, 505, **D**, 289, **G**, 597, **I**, 12, **J**, 446, 498, **K**, 23, 40, **L**, 322, 494, 497, **N**, 62, **T**, 93,
   Wisconsin Burial Sites, **T**, 321
Prisonniers et des Victemes de la Guere; **A**, 229
Prisons; **A**, 398, **B**, 188, **D**, 184, **E**, 26, **G**, 162, **H**, 749, **K**, 36-40, **M**, 84, **T**, 227a, **W**, 1018,
   Alton, IL, **L**, 554,
   Andersonville, GA, **A**, 293, 354, 571, **B**, 100, 823, 1178, 1211, 1543, **C**, 323, **D**, 184, 297, **E**, 230, **F**, 609, **G**, 518, **J**, 431, 486, **M**, 152, 681,

Prisons

P, 5-6, 68, 261, 293, R, 386, 855, 877-878, S, 383, 1149, W, 549,
Monument, D, 104,
Anecdotes, B, 1294,
Cahaba (Cahawba), AL, B, 1160,
Camp Chase, OH, A, 313, B, 108, D, 884, K, 174, 230, W, 537,
Camp Dennison, OH,
Roster, L, 552,
Camp Douglas, IL, B, 346, 642, C, 3, K, 20, U, 37,
Camp Douglas, IL, Roster, L, 555,
Camp Ford, TX, M, 963,
Camp Groce, TX, M, 964,
Camp Jackson, MO, B, 538,
Camp Morton, IN, W, 849,
Camp Morton, IN, Roster, L, 556,
Camp Pratt, LA, B, 618,
Castle Thunder, Richmond, VA, E, 279,
Columbia, SC, F, 485,
Columbus, OH, C, 1205,
Davis, Jefferson, Pres., D, 251,
Elmira, NY, H, 1016, 1352, R, 567, S, 972,
Elmira, NY, Roster, L, 560,
Escapes, B, 66, 598, 852, 1277, T, 278,
Experiences, D, 108,
Florence, SC, K, 172,
Fort Delaware, DE, B, 205, 1238, K, 29, R, 256, S, 1422,
Fort Delaware, DE, Roster, L, 557,
Fort Lafayette, NY, P, 765, W, 908,
Fort McHenry, MD, W, 886,
Fort Warren, MA, B, 852, 1238, C, 1432,
Johnson's Island, OH, A, 244, 400, 542, B, 108, 205, 529, 754, 1277, 1512, C, 195, H, 463, 661, 783, J, 145-153, 369, K, 240, M, 673a, 923a, 1071, 1307, N, 165, P, 388, 448, S, 355, 357, 920, W, 230,
Libby, Richmond, VA, B, 1606, 1644, S, 145, T, 503, W, 25, 124,
Life, B, 1238, E, 72a, P, 196a, 852a,
Ministry, M, 720,
Morris Island, SC, L, 540, M, 704,
Northern, C, 989,
Ohio Penitentiary, H, 893, M, 1136,
Point Lookout, MD, A, 542, B, 205, 510, C, 836, J, 371, 417, L, 586, S, 270, 972, T, 382, W, 79,
Point Lookout, MD, Roster, L, 558,
Propaganda, H, 756,
Richmond, VA, J, 101, M, 902a,
Rock Island, IL, B, 646, L, 559, M, 903, 1249, P, 285, R, 643, W, 78,
Salisbury, NC, B, 704, 1402, J, 418, M, 143,
St. Louis, MO, Roster, L, 553
Pritchard, Benjamin; F, 455
Privateers; A, 104, B, 543, C, 467, 1131, D, 270, 992, E, 74, H, 554, 607, 1302, M, 111, R, 612, W, 173,
California, G, 243,
Vancouver Island, G, 244
Prize Cases; B, 638, R, 602
Prizes; C, 175, M, 269
Prodos, John B., Maj.; R, 275
Prohibition; R, 619
Projectiles; D, 578
Propaganda; C, 864, 1541, D, 182, G, 604, H, 756, 986, S, 467, T, 539,
Arkansas, S, 713,
Church, S, 464,
Davis, Jefferson, Pres., C, 1542,
Kansas-Missouri War, L, 486,
Secession, H, 489,
Southern, S, 884
Prophecy; S, 205
Provisional Army, Confederate; D, 615
Pryor, J.P.; F, 381, W, 705
Pryor, Roger A., Mrs.; B, 1274
Pryor, Roger Atkinson, Brig.Gen.; D, 205, H, 1036
Psychology;
Elections (1860), C, 1425
Publication Rights, Confederate; B, 1484
Publishing; R, 477, S, 772
Puckett, Sam; C, 36
Pulaski Guards; D, 65
Pulaski, TN; H, 906

Pumphrey, William F.; **B**, 672
Purcell Battery; **D**, 843
Purchase Ships; **T**, 376
Puryear, Elmer J.; **G**, 549
Putnam County, TN; **D**, 443

Q

Quaker Guns; **W**, 591
Quakers; **S**, 901,
  Generals, Confederate, **C**, 1564
Quantrell, Charles W.; **B**, 1556, **T**, 439
Quantrill's Raid; **C**, 620
Quantrill, William Clarke; **A**, 405, **B**, 774, 948-949, 962, 1222, 1224, **C**, 285, 289-290, 620, 1079, 1501, 1568, **D**, 30, **F**, 155, **H**, 43, 299, **M**, 432, **R**, 38, **S**, 317, 1166, **W**, 283, 560
Quartermasters; **C**, 404, 676, **G**, 10, **M**, 729, 765, **N**, 121
Quebec, Canada;
  Missionaries, **M**, 1278
Queen City (gunboat); **S**, 599
Quesenbury, William; **B**, 605
Quinine; **J**, 495
Quinlan, John; **L**, 538
Quintard, Charles Todd; **C**, 428, **G**, 688
Quintero, Jose A.; **T**, 556
Quirk's Scouts; **L**, 591
Quitman Guards; **H**, 900
Quitman Rifles; **H**, 277, 909, **N**, 88a
Quitman, John Anthony, Brig.Gen.; **M**, 361

R

Racial Relations; **B**, 28, **E**, 78, **P**, 142
Racoon Roughs; **G**, 395
Rader, Jacob Marcus; **B**, 200
Radicals; **B**, 551
Ragan, Cooper K.; **O**, 1
Ragsdale's Company; **H**, 87
Raiders; **H**, 225, 227, **J**, 543
Railroad Battery; **H**, 582
Railroads; **B**, 178, **H**, 710, **J**, 119, 130, 262-264, **L**, 627, **P**, 128, 211, **R**, 410, **S**, 570a, 1245, 1257, **T**, 487, 492, **W**, 159,
   Armored Trains, **XYZ**, 93,
   Attempts to Steal, **W**, 76,
   Confederate, **B**, 727,
   Construction, **S**, 424,
   Destroyed, **D**, 772, **H**, 541,
   Disloyalty, **J**, 261,
   Florida, **C**, 623,
   Florida Senatorial Election, **T**, 220,
   Georgia, **B**, 730, **M**, 567, 1259,
   Louisiana, **E**, 242-243,
   Military Value, **K**, 120,
   Mississippi, **B**, 397,
   North Carolina, **P**, 733,
   South Carolina, **D**, 529,
   Supply Trains, **C**, 887,
   Texas, **B**, 837,
   Wheeler's Raids, **W**, 688
Rainwater, Percy L.; **A**, 146, **F**, 575
Raleigh, NC;
   Hospital, **C**, 1577,
   Hospitals, **E**, 86
Rams; **G**, 35, **J**, 557, **M**, 417
Ramsay, H. Ashton; **W**, 981
Ramsdell, Charles W.; **B**, 17, **L**, 162, **S**, 1117
Ramseur, Stephen Dodson, Maj.Gen.; **C**, 611, 1359, **D**, 871, **G**, 25, **S**, 1036, 1062, **W**, 414,

Ramsey, James B., Rev.; **R**, 71
Ranck, George Washington; **B**, 1041
Randall, James Ryder; **A**, 195, **U**, 1
Randolph County, NC; **A**, 552
Randolph County, VA;
   Roster, **R**, 91
Randolph County, WV; **C**, 975, 1008, **M**, 353
Randolph, Charles; **H**, 895
Randolph, George Wythe, Brig.Gen.; **J**, 363-364
Randolph, J.W.; **B**, 672, **P**, 8
Randolph, Sarah; **C**, 53
Randolph, Victor, Capt., CSN;
   Abolition, **V**, 109
Ranks; **N**, 30
Ransom's Brigade; **K**, 156, **M**, 1057a
Ransom, Matthew Whitaker, Brig.Gen.; **B**, 1577, **H**, 356
Ranson, WV; **M**, 862
Rapidan River; **J**, 203
Rappahannock (ship); **F**, 378, **G**, 623
Rappannock Bridge, VA; **L**, 220
Ratcliffe, Laura; **R**, 843
Rattlesnake (flag); **R**, 128
Ravenel, Charlotte St. J.; **J**, 128
Rawle, William; **V**, 124
Ray County, MO;
   History, **M**, 947
Raymond Fencibles; **M**, 1025
Raymond, MS, Battle of; **R**, 825
Rea, D.B.; **B**, 1315
Read, Charles W. (Savez), Lt.; **B**, 210, 852, **H**, 858, **M**, 797
Read, F.W.; **B**, 949
Reagan, John H.; **A**, 579, **H**, 647, **M**, 1168, **N**, 217, **P**, 793, **R**, 165, 172
Reams' Station, VA, Battle of; **B**, 1316, **S**, 1034, **W**, 611

Rebel Archives Division, War Dept.;
  L, 549
Rebel Raiders; G, 670
Rebel Reefer; B, 882
Rebel Yell; D, 65, M, 366a, S, 669
Reburials; U, 31
Recipes; J, 19, M, 759,
  Jefferson Davis Cookbook, D, 306
Recollections of Lee (book); L, 365
Reconstruction; A, 149, 241-242, 257, 509, B, 8, 662, 801, 812, 1168, 1309, 1547, 1550, 1571, C, 93, 223, 234, E, 219, F, 243, G, 129, H, 390a, 1361, K, 55, L, 793, O, 162, P, 186, 509, 680, R, 76-77, S, 1409, T, 63, 299, 483a, U, 37, W, 90, 201, 998,
  Alabama, B, 1293,
  Arkansas, T, 186,
  Ashburn Murder Case, D, 88,
  Failure, C, 231,
  Florida, D, 379, R, 443,
  Georgia, C, 121,
  Laws, J, 238,
  Louisiana, D, 395, H, 795,
  Mississippi, B, 980, G, 62, M, 678,
  Nashville, TN, M, 292,
  North Carolina, C, 380,
  Politics, C, 208,
  Tennessee, C, 485, F, 93, P, 155,
  Texas, B, 966, R, 437-438,
  Virginia, C, 496, W, 461,
  Women, W, 790
Reconstruction Acts; S, 91,
  Mississippi, S, 1221
Records, Recovered; C, 484b
Red Artillery; B, 1331
Red Badge; J, 102
Red River Campaign; B, 155, 892, F, 198, L, 66, M, 162, 242, 730, P, 117, 439, S, 15, 60, W, 723
Red River Station; W, 804
Red Shirts; C, 780
Red Sulphur Springs, WV; XYZ, 48
Redwood, Allen C.; R, 141
Reed, Thomas B.; G, 409
Reed, William B.; S, 289
Reese, George H.; V, 163
Reeves, Joseph A.; M, 542

Refugees; B, 65, C, 559, H, 68, 409, 996, M, 316-317, 563, S, 301
Regimental Publications; D, 754
Regiments & Battalions, Confederate;
  Roster, L, 541
Regional Allegiances; T, 106
Reichard, Augustus, Col.; M, 1331
Reiley, James, Col.; H, 81
Reilly, Patrick R.; L, 462
Relics; C, 135, 301-302, 388b, 948, G, 288, M, 922, O, 4, S, 1458
Renne, Wymberley Jones de; F, 510
Republicans;
  Radicals, F, 190
Resaca, GA; M, 655, P, 659,
  Confederate Cemetery, R, 310
Resaca, GA, Battle of; H, 1074a
Research; C, 999, N, 36a
Resolution of Respect; C, 1148
Retaliation; M, 1232
Reunions; C, 884, 1047a, 1508, D, 8, H, 1058, J, 83, M, 349, 1083, O, 155-156, 212, P, 213, 352, 780, R, 326, S, 81, 807, 817
Revenue Cutters; S, 231
Revivalism; F, 51, N, 203
Revolution, Second Great; A, 382
Revolvers; L, 680, S, 419
Reynolds' Brigade; P, 638, R, 331, S, 1451
Reynolds' Raids; E, 214
Reynolds, James Elisha, Capt.; N, 15
Reynolds, Lily; C, 1343
Reynolds, Thomas Caute, Gov., MO;
  C, 873, M, 880b
Rhea County, TN; A, 252
Rhett, Robert Barnwell; B, 139, 1552, W, 554
Rice, John L.; N, 4
Rich Mountain, WV; XYZ, 100,
  Campaign, P, 735
Rich Mountain, WV, Battle of; A, 231, 463
Richard, Sydney K.; B, 1633
Richards, Adolphus Edward; A, 580
Richardson Guards; C, 1139, R, 368
Richardson, David Crockett; G, 661

Richardson, Rufus Bryan; **A**, 349a
Richardson, Rupert N.; **F**, 44
Richardson, Thomas; **B**, 1399
Richmond & Danville R.R.; **H**, 719, **J**, 262
Richmond Academy of Medicine; **C**, 941
Richmond Examiner, VA, np.; **D**, 50, **J**, 43
Richmond Fayette Artillery; **C**, 383
Richmond Grays; **O**, 89, **R**, 247,
  Uniforms, **U**, 14
Richmond Howitzers; **B**, 964, **D**, 37, 48, **E**, 321, **H**, 1228, 1331, **M**, 43, 371, 457-458, 1199, **P**, 433, 456, **R**, 398-399, 598, 673, **S**, 544, **T**, 364, **W**, 37, 567
Richmond Light Infantry Blues; **C**, 1616, **W**, 869
Richmond Sharps Carbine; **A**, 125
Richmond Times Dispatch, VA, np.; **R**, 407-421
Richmond, KY;
  Battle of, **Q**, 20
Richmond, VA; **A**, 184, 349, **B**, 690, 697, 776, 1439, **C**, 525, 786, **D**, 14, **H**, 395, **J**, 542, **K**, 152-155, 157-158, **M**, 654, **P**, 854, **R**, 391, **T**, 34, 200, 304,
  Arsenal, **B**, 1415,
  Attempt to Capture, **H**, 184,
  Battlefields, **B**, 1290, 1573, **C**, 452, **P**, 454-455,
  Boy Company, **J**, 5,
  Bread Riots, **K**, 150, **T**, 201,
  Broad St. Methodist Church, **D**, 699,
  Burning of, **R**, 3,
  Capture, **R**, 486,
  Centenary Church, **D**, 700,
  Chimborazo Hospital, **C**, 1539, **G**, 256, 259, **H**, 6, 1283, **J**, 139,
  City Council (1861-1865), **M**, 130,
  Close of War, **H**, 1181,
  Confederate Government Flees, **C**, 583,
  Confederate Memorial Institute, **C**, 507,
  Confederate Memorial Hall, **J**, 168,
  Confederate Memorial Institute, **M**, 226,
  Confederate Museum, **B**, 661, **C**, 949-951, **H**, 213, **L**, 546,
  Council Chamber, **K**, 62,
  Defenses, **C**, 444, **W**, 162,
  Evacuation, **A**, 570, **B**, 1020, **C**, 97, 104, **D**, 988, **F**, 19, **H**, 1185, **L**, 253, 510,
  Fall of, **A**, 267, **D**, 902, **F**, 15, **P**, 139, **R**, 724a, **S**, 1382, **T**, 453,
  Fall of, France's Views, **S**, 940,
  First Federal Soldier, **S**, 1137,
  Flight from, **M**, 92,
  French Tobacco, **S**, 939,
  Guide, **B**, 1574, **E**, 256,
  Historic Sites, **L**, 261a,
  Historical Catalogue, **S**, 172,
  History, **S**, 978,
  Hollywood Cemetery, **M**, 969, **R**, 239,
  Home Guard, **E**, 182,
  Hospitals, **S**, 7, **W**, 24,
  Howitzer Monument, **S**, 894,
  Howlett's House, **M**, 1170a,
  Libby Prison, **S**, 145,
  Maps, **M**, 167, 169, 171, **R**, 393, **S**, 204,
  Meem's Bottom, **D**, 965,
  Monuments, **C**, 1005, **D**, 482, **G**, 487, **H**, 805, **M**, 562, **S**, 788,
  National Battlefield Park, **C**, 1536,
  Negroes, **E**, 70,
  Occupation of, **T**, 218,
  Old Christ Church, **B**, 907,
  Press, **E**, 259,
  Prisons, **J**, 101, **M**, 902a,
  Retreats, **S**, 1418, **T**, 304,
  Reunion, **D**, 8,
  Richard E. Byrd Flying Field, **N**, 34,
  Siege, **T**, 304,
  Soldiers & Sailors Monument, **M**, 922,
  St. Paul's Church, **J**, 143, **W**, 329,
  Theater, **D**, 750,
  Tredegar Ironworks, **S**, 4,

Richmond, VA

Underground, **S**, 1333,
Valentine Musem, **H**, 213,
Volunteer Companies, **M**, 123,
Welfare, **T**, 197,
Women, **C**, 15, **J**, 501
Richmond, VA, Battle of; **L**, 147, **M**, 429, **R**, 902
Riddell, William R.; **B**, 344
Riddle, T.J.; **G**, 673
Rights, Neutral; **A**, 104
Ring Tournament; **C**, 347
Ringgold, GA; **C**, 614
Ringgold, GA, Battle of; **C**, 654
Rio Grande River; **A**, 143, **M**, 788, **R**, 500, **S**, 194,
Mutiny, **T**, 239
Rio Grande Territory; **L**, 73
Rio Grande Valley, Union Occupation of Lower; **A**, 499
Rion's Battalion; **T**, 215
Ripley, MS; **C**, 771
Ripley, Roswell Sabine, Brig.Gen.; Ordnance, **G**, 301
Rise and Fall... (book); **D**, 257, **R**, 74
Ritchie, Thomas; **A**, 282
River Campaign, LA; **E**, 81
River Rats; **H**, 791
River Wars; **J**, 541
Rivers, William James; **A**, 384
Rives, William C.; **G**, 272, 275, **R**, 511, **S**, 902
Roanoke Grays; **R**, 681
Roanoke, VA;
Lost Confederates, **T**, 198
Roasters; **D**, 720
Robert E. Lee (ship); **O**, 200
Robert the Bruce, King, Scotland; **F**, 332
Roberts, Oran Milo, Col.; **B**, 151, **T**, 153, **W**, 977
Roberts, William Paul, Brig.Gen.; **K**, 136a
Robertson, Felix Huston, Brig.Gen.; **R**, 553
Robertson, James I., Jr.; **B**, 672, 1562, **M**, 1296, **N**, 81, **T**, 79
Robertson, Jerome B., Gen.; **H**, 798b
Robertson, Mary D.; **B**, 1201

Robins, Sally Nelson, Mrs.; **B**, 1274
Robins, William Todd, Col.; **J**, 510
Robinson, Leigh; **A**, 450, **U**, 30
Robinson, Mary Fisher; **A**, 146
Robinson, Raymond V.; **B**, 672
Rock City Guards; **C**, 1419
Rock Island Prison, IL; **B**, 646, **M**, 903, **P**, 285, **R**, 643, **W**, 78,
History, **M**, 1249,
Roster, **L**, 559
Rockbridge Artillery; **F**, 166, **G**, 377, **M**, 1057,
First, **D**, 847,
Roster, **W**, 795,
Second, **D**, 847
Rockbridge Battalion; **T**, 519
Rockbridge Battery, Second; **J**, 333
Rockbridge County, VA; **D**, 129
Rockbridge Dragoons; **M**, 1068a, **S**, 1030, **V**, 114
Rocket Batteries; **D**, 729, **K**, 59
Rockingham County, VA; **C**, 528, **W**, 300
Rodes' Brigade; **C**, 249
Rodes, Robert Emmett, Maj.Gen.; **F**, 565, **W**, 411
Rodgers, Robert L.; **XYZ**, 14
Roffe, Michael; **S**, 232
Rogers, William Warren; **B**, 1598, **M**, 1001
Rogers-Vannerson, J.; **G**, 146
Rogersville, TN, Battle of; **E**, 304
Rollins, Henry B.; **P**, 435
Romans, Alfred, Col.; **A**, 206, **B**, 467, **G**, 128
Rome, GA; **B**, 240
Romney, WV; **A**, 279
Roosevelt, Franklin D., Pres.; **A**, 438
Ropes, John C.; **A**, 222, 225, **S**, 1331
Rosborough, J.T., Capt.; **M**, 423
Rose Hill Cemetery, Macon, GA; **C**, 881
Rose, Victor; **S**, 908, **T**, 149
Rosecrans, William Starke, Maj.Gen.; **W**, 1086
Rosenthal, Albert; **B**, 565
Ross' Brigade; **C**, 1414, **J**, 239, **P**, 780, **R**, 297, 714

Ross' Texas Cavalry; **G**, 662, **H**, 798b, **K**, 119
Ross, Edward B., Rev.; **F**, 402
Ross, John; **C**, 438, **L**, 428, **M**, 331, 459, 1254
Ross, Lawrence Sullivan, Brig.Gen.; **B**, 577-578
Rosser's Cavalry; **W**, 405
Rosser, Thomas Lafayette, Maj.Gen.; **B**, 1274, 1619, **D**, 525, **H**, 258, **S**, 1064
Rosters; **C**, 517, **F**, 282, **I**, 23, 26-30, **J**, 497,
   ANV, Chaplains, **L**, 550,
   Alabama, **P**, 542,
   Alton Prison, IL, **L**, 554,
   Arkansas, **A**, 425, **C**, 1405, **P**, 543,
   Army of Northern Virginia, Officers, **K**, 258,
   Artillery Officers, **L**, 549, **M**, 767,
   Camp Dennison, OH, **L**, 552,
   Camp Douglas Prison, IL, **L**, 555,
   Camp Morton Prison, IN, **L**, 556,
   Cherokee Indians, **C**, 1605, **P**, 564,
   Chickamauga, GA, Battle of, **P**, 491,
   Confederate Army, **P**, 77,
   Creek Indians, **P**, 565,
   Elmira, NY, **L**, 560,
   Engineer Troops, **T**, 10,
   Field Officers, Confederate, **L**, 548,
   Florida, **P**, 574, **S**, 789,
   Fort Delaware Prison, DE, **L**, 557,
   General Officers, **W**, 1031-1036, 1043,
   Georgia, **B**, 839, 1264, **C**, 548, 779, **D**, 135, 933, **H**, 688, **J**, 561, **L**, 27, **M**, 1120, **R**, 655, **T**, 206,
   Gettysburg, PA, **K**, 256,
   Kentucky, **E**, 277, **M**, 1345,
   Local Troop Designations, **L**, 577,
   Louisiana, **B**, 537, **D**, 615, **H**, 763, **K**, 72,
   Maryland, **G**, 91, **P**, 563, **S**, 782,
   Mississippi, **M**, 885, **R**, 688,
   Morris Island Prison, SC, **L**, 540,
   Navy, **J**, 406b,
   North Carolina, **C**, 944, **F**, 137, **G**, 110, 476, 634, 683, **K**, 69, **L**, 93, 519, **M**, 124-128, 1081, **N**, 150-151, **S**, 20, 342,
   Officers, **C**, 1621, **E**, 244, **J**, 398-401, **S**, 871,
   Pensions, **V**, 152,
   Point Lookout Prison, MD, **L**, 558,
   Prisoners, **F**, 490,
   Regiments & Battalions, Confederate, **L**, 541,
   Rock Island Prison, IL, **L**, 559,
   South Carolina, **D**, 576, **F**, 341, **L**, 17, **S**, 910, **W**, 47, 944,
   St. Louis Prison, MO, **L**, 553,
   Texas, **C**, 1024, **H**, 129, **K**, 119, **L**, 545, **P**, 603, **W**, 922,
   US Military Academy, **U**, 42,
   Virginia, **B**, 841, 1273, **C**, 523, 1139, **E**, 100, **F**, 269, 605, **G**, 326, 440-441, **H**, 243, 613, **J**, 119, 368, **K**, 167, 260-262, 267, **L**, 569, 696, **P**, 145, 220, 607, **R**, 401, 681, **V**, 17, 152, **W**, 96,
   Virginia Conf. General Hosp., **H**, 941a,
   Wise Guards, **M**, 650
Roswell, GA, Expulsion of Women; **B**, 1638
Rothert, Otto A.; **D**, 375
Rothrick, Thomas; **E**, 7
Rouden, Lena; **A**, 70, **O**, 201
Rough Riders; **M**, 1138
Round Mountain, AL; **W**, 1053-1054
Round Mountain, Ind.T., Battle of; **D**, 470
Round Top, VA, Battle of; **L**, 150
Rountree, J.A., Mrs.; **C**, 948
Rouss, Charles B.; **A**, 583
Rousseau's Raid; **F**, 544
Rowland, Dunbar; **D**, 223, **F**, 216
Rowland, Kate Mason; **M**, 916, **W**, 27
Rowlands, John; **F**, 40
Royal Military Academy, England; **W**, 919
Rucker, Joseph Lamar; **C**, 700
Ruffin, Edmund; **A**, 347, 396a, **C**, 1399, **S**, 101, 687, 1059, **T**, 540

Ruffner Pamphlet; **B**, 351
Ruggles, Daniel, Brig.Gen.; **S**, 1336
Rusk County, TX; **W**, 278
Russell County, AL; **B**, 1161
Russell, Mattie; **B**, 853
Russell, William Howard; **A**, 45, 528, **C**, 1411, **G**, 52
Ruth, Samuel; **S**, 1332
Rutherford County, NC; **G**, 634, **M**, 1181
Rutherford, Mildred; **C**, 572, **M**, 1253
Rutledge's Battery;
  Uniforms, **U**, 14
Rutledge, Archibald Hamilton; **J**, 124, **S**, 27
Ryan, Abram J., Father; **B**, 849, **H**, 626, 647, **L**, 538a, **M**, 852, 1165
Ryan, Harriet Fitts; **C**, 717
Ryder CSA Archives; **B**, 672

S

S.S. Dee (blockade-runner); **B**, 1335
Sabine Crossroads, TX, Battle of; **H**, 1024
Sabine Pass, TX; **B**, 160, 802, **D**, 818, **T**, 336,
   Military Operations, **K**, 44
Sabine Pass, TX, Battle of; **B**, 1223, **C**, 1253, **G**, 613, **M**, 64, 1270, **S**, 915, **XYZ**, 62
Sacramento, KY, Battle of; **W**, 178
Saddles; **C**, 851
Saint Helena (Parish) Rifles; **R**, 362a
Sala, George Augustus; **B**, 991
Salem Church, VA; **C**, 581
Salem Creek, VA, Battle of; **M**, 550
Salem, NC; **R**, 469
Salem, VA;
   History, **G**, 441
Saline County, AR; **G**, 283
Salisbury Prison, NC; **B**, 704, 1402, **J**, 418, **M**, 143
Salley, Alexander S.; **A**, 265
Salt; **L**, 672-673, **O**, 184, **R**, 5
Saltpetre; **R**, 15
Saltville, VA; **B**, 1587, **R**, 5
Saltworks; **C**, 1155, **P**, 797, **S**, 1101
Saluria, TX; **F**, 197
Salvador;
   Pirates, **G**, 241
Salvage Operations; **T**, 370
Sampson County, NC; **J**, 87
San Antonio, TX; **A**, 294,
   Defenses, **A**, 494,
   Secession, **C**, 1435
San Francisco, CA; **M**, 23
San Jacinto (ship); **C**, 395
Sanders, David Warren, Maj.; **N**, 156
Sanders, John Caldwell Calhoun, Gen.; **H**, 1073d, **T**, 220a
Sanders, Mary Elizabeth; **A**, 264

Sanderson Expose; **K**, 214
Sands, J.G.; **B**, 949
Sanford, Justice; **L**, 117a
Sanitation; **B**, 1347
Sansom, John W.; **W**, 736
Sansone, Emma; **J**, 512, **O**, 210
Santa Rosa Island, FL, Battle of; **L**, 109, **M**, 896
Sappony Church, VA, Battle of; **H**, 188
Sartain, William; **D**, 246
Satire; **B**, 703, **D**, 827
Sattel, Swi Jahre im; **B**, 918
Saunders, W.L.; **W**, 5
Savage, Joseph; **B**, 949
Savannah (ship); **C**, 467, **T**, 412, **W**, 173
Savannah River;
   Rice Plantation, **C**, 683
Savannah Volunteers;
   Uniforms, **U**, 14
Savannah, GA; **C**, 351, **F**, 34, 375, **G**, 635,
   Bishop of, **V**, 110,
   Campaign, **M**, 664,
   Capture, **J**, 404,
   Catholics, **G**, 142,
   Defenses, **XYZ**, 72,
   Flag of Independence, **H**, 1201,
   Hardee's Defense, **H**, 1257,
   Law & Order, **H**, 538,
   Northern Relief, **D**, 998,
   Secession, **L**, 156,
   Sherman's Occupation, **C**, 744, **L**, 156, **S**, 395,
   Siege, **D**, 409, **J**, 386, 404a,
   Volunteer Guards, **H**, 266
Sayler's Creek, VA; **B**, 208, 790
Sayler's Creek, VA, Battle of; **C**, 39, **D**, 988, **H**, 450, 1183, **J**, 80, **W**, 284

Scabbard Speech, Jackson's; **O**, 43
Scalawags; **B**, 16
Scales, Alfred Moore, Brig.Gen.; **A**, 450, **C**, 1104
Scammon, Eliakim Parker, Brig.Gen.; **J**, 521, **V**, 111
Scary Creek, WV, Battle of; **L**, 750
Scary, WV, Battle of; **F**, 85, **T**, 221
Schaller, Frank; **M**, 202-203
Scharf, J. Thomas; **D**, 200
Schatz, Mark Norton; **G**, 307
Schaw, Arthur M.; **A**, 116
Scheibert, Justus, Maj.; **B**, 919, **L**, 780, **P**, 457
Schneider & Glassich; **A**, 125
Schools; **B**, 735,
   History, **J**, 479, **M**, 504
Schoonmaker, J.M.; **R**, 306
Scientific Tradition; **S**, 29
Scientists; **D**, 731
Scorpion (ship); **R**, 779, **S**, 146
Scotland Neck Mounted Riflemen; **H**, 278, **S**, 701
Scott, Edward Herndon; **P**, 754
Scott, George Washington, Col.; **L**, 763
Scott, Winfield, Gen.; **J**, 452
Scottish Rites; **P**, 404
Scouts; **A**, 271, **B**, 597, 670, 1486, **C**, 795, 1004, 1121, 1614, **D**, 958, **E**, 255, **H**, 186, 1108, **J**, 4, **K**, 75, **L**, 589, **M**, 385, **N**, 182, **P**, 197, **Q**, 17, **R**, 756, **S**, 1289-1290, **W**, 735, 887,
   Shenandoah Valley, **W**, 80
Scrapbooks; **C**, 1001
Scratch, Harry (Pseud.); **B**, 1611
Sculptors; **J**, 31, **V**, 3
SCV; **G**, 534,
   Convention, **P**, 801, **U**, 34,
   Gray Book, **A**, 369,
   Hinton, WV, **R**, 327,
   History Commission, **C**, 809,
   New Orleans, LA, **O**, 212,
   Organization, **R**, 861,
   SC Reunion, **B**, 834
Sea Devil of the Confederacy; **B**, 1019
Sea Dogs; **H**, 862
Sea Duels; **R**, 43
Sea King (ship); **M**, 1127
Seal, Confederate; **B**, 317, **C**, 585, 1004, **G**, 559-560, 564, **J**, 546, **S**, 416, 459, 732, **T**, 27, 170, **W**, 128, 870
Seamanship; **P**, 89b
Seaport Strategy, Confederate; **F**, 374
Searcy, James T., Dr.; **L**, 562
Secession; **A**, 38, 62, 88, 280, 307, 390, 403, 456, 498, 506, 588, **B**, 59, 103, 135, 165, 215, 528, 536, 550, 555, 566, 621, 692, 773, 792, 794, 835, 873, 1368, 1391, 1421, **C**, 35, 41-42, 77, 268, 420, 503, 704, 716, 946, 1094, 1138, 1338, **D**, 5, 35, 295, 310, 407, 556, 561, 652, 667, 741, 877, 924, 967, **E**, 125, 185, 299-300, **F**, 371, 430, 546, **G**, 60-61, 80, 568, **H**, 11, 359, 551, 916, 993-994, **J**, 202, 334, 436, **L**, 677, 744, **M**, 19, 75, 539, 615, 707, 726, 735, 771, 1195, **P**, 186, 347-348, 467, 652, 678, **R**, 16, 162, 167, 172, 210, 236, 333, 509, 865, 885, **S**, 39, 56, 185, 365, 480, 523, 534, 573, 823-824, 902, 952, 1028, 1072, 1220, **T**, 61, 217a, 299, **U**, 17, **V**, 24, 97-100, **W**, 92, 115, 558, 925, 945, 1059, 1067, **XYZ**, 34,
   Alabama, **B**, 1167, **I**, 43, **L**, 634, **M**, 362a, 824,
   Arkansas, **B**, 1386, **H**, 731, **M**, 313, **P**, 396, **S**, 188, **W**, 624,
   Canada's Opinions, **L**, 69,
   Conspiracy, **B**, 1204,
   Constitutional Right, **A**, 43, **F**, 48, **J**, 160, **S**, 924,
   Conventions, **B**, 291, **C**, 209, 1623, **D**, 99, 129, **H**, 489, 878, **I**, 43, **M**, 1308, **S**, 738, **T**, 189, **W**, 972,
   Doctrines, **S**, 1086,
   Documents, **H**, 107,
   Economics, **R**, 17, **S**, 1243,
   Editorials, **D**, 930,
   England, **C**, 1470, **W**, 1010,
   Feminine Viewpoint, **P**, 796,
   First Movement, **F**, 139,
   Flag, **C**, 449, **S**, 731,

Florida, **D**, 332, 676, **F**, 284, **M**, 541, **N**, 211, **R**, 260, **S**, 991, **W**, 965,

France, **G**, 514,

Frontier, **R**, 50,

Georgia, **A**, 56, **B**, 1485, **G**, 177, 493, 585, **H**, 913, **J**, 231, 485, **K**, 168, **L**, 156, **P**, 146, **W**, 966,

History, **K**, 4,

Houston, Sam, **C**, 1518,

Indians, **C**, 796,

Ireland, **H**, 736,

Kentucky, **H**, 420, **Q**, 23, **S**, 196, **T**, 501,

Land Seizures, **R**, 656,

Louisiana, **B**, 954-955, **H**, 324, **R**, 670a, **W**, 499, 967,

Methodist Episcopal Church, **E**, 154,

Mississippi, **R**, 19, **W**, 941,

Mississippi Valley Commerce, **C**, 1297,

Missouri, **K**, 199-204, **L**, 795, **R**, 642, 906,

North Carolina, **B**, 294, 1007, **F**, 139,

Northern Editorials, **P**, 265,

Ordinances, **D**, 20, **H**, 1132,

Philosophy, **S**, 948,

Railroads, **K**, 120,

Religion, **P**, 44,

Social Basis, **B**, 136,

South, **C**, 762, **J**, 208, **M**, 505a,

South Carolina, **B**, 140, 945-946, 1310, **C**, 333, 399, 1267, **D**, 425, 427, **H**, 131, **M**, 357, 360b, 1244, **S**, 833, 839, 843, 845, **T**, 74, **W**, 970,

Southern Presbyterians, **M**, 998,

Southern Protestantism, **D**, 87,

Southern Support, **B**, 220,

Southwest, **H**, 947,

Speeches, **S**, 1005,

State Officers, **C**, 91,

States Rights, **S**, 1021,

Tennessee, **F**, 93, **H**, 72, **P**, 129, **Q**, 6,

Texas, **B**, 1527-1530, **G**, 8, **H**, 1145, **J**, 595, **N**, 105, **R**, 882, **S**, 42, 946a, **T**, 152-154, 158a, 308,

Virginia, **E**, 105, 171, **G**, 418, **J**, 462, **K**, 98, **S**, 291, 293, **W**, 126,

West Point Academy, **M**, 349, **V**, 124

Secessionville, SC, Battle of; **H**, 25, **L**, 185

Secret Agents; **B**, 615, **C**, 1266, **G**, 501, **S**, 1334, **T**, 231, 556

Secret Service; **B**, 220, 1284, 1548, **G**, 5, **H**, 619, **J**, 89, **K**, 1, **L**, 694, **S**, 1125, **T**, 51, **XYZ**, 96

Secret Societies; **K**, 213

Secretary of War, Escape; **B**, 1186

Sectionalism; **A**, 402, **B**, 653, 694, 943, **C**, 101, 111, **D**, 764, 892, **F**, 448, **G**, 37, 463, **H**, 365, **K**, 32, **L**, 405, **R**, 573, 717, **S**, 139, 480, 1109, **U**, 17, **V**, 126

Sedberry, T.D., Capt.; **B**, 1544

Segregation; **H**, 983,

Louisiana, **F**, 163

Selma, AL; **C**, 1168a, **H**, 318, **L**, 67, **S**, 150,

Arsenal, **L**, 173a, **S**, 207,

Confederate Navy, **S**, 1193,

Destruction, **R**, 515,

Naval Foundry, **S**, 1068,

Naval Ordnance Works, **M**, 750

Seminole Indians; **P**, 392, **S**, 789

Seminole Nation; **M**, 1070

Semmes' Brigade;

Chancellorsville, VA, **W**, 936

Semmes, Raphael, Adm.; **B**, 939, 1018, 1071, 1629, **C**, 641, **D**, 34, 167, 502, **E**, 149, **F**, 434, 580, **G**, 439, **H**, 1073c, **M**, 50a, 438, 791, **N**, 112, **R**, 549

Semmes, Thomas Jenkins; **A**, 60, **N**, 88a, **S**, 1090

Semple, Henry Churchill, Maj.; **B**, 640

Senac, Felix; **R**, 119

Sensing, Thurman; **H**, 49

Sequestration Act; **D**, 528, **H**, 542, **J**, 196

Sequestration Cases; **S**, 847
Sermons;
  Executions, **P**, 60
Serrono, Don Francisco, Gov., Cuba; **H**, 656
Servants; **B**, 596
Seven Days Campaign; **C**, 1108, **G**, 78
Seven Days, VA, Battle of; **A**, 168, 170, **B**, 252, **C**, 1330, 1368, **E**, 18, **G**, 75, 685, **J**, 284, **L**, 662, **N**, 137a, **P**, 520, 825,
  Roster, **R**, 739
Seven Pines, VA, Battle of; **B**, 150, 1173, 1220, 1470, **C**, 249, 470, **G**, 57, **L**, 657, **S**, 647, 652, 654, **W**, 635,
  Losses, **J**, 283,
  Official Report, **J**, 297
Sevier County, AR; **B**, 1635
Sewanee College, TN; **G**, 688
Sewanee, TN; **P**, 248, **R**, 334,
  Reconstruction, **C**, 485
Sewanee, TN, Battle of; **P**, 248
Seward, William Henry; **A**, 285, **G**, 129, **W**, 883
Sewell Mountain Campaign; **L**, 750b
Seymour, Truman, Maj.Gen.; **W**, 200
Shadbourne, George D.; **H**, 186
Shaffer, Emil; **S**, 281
Shaker Colony; **M**, 1097, **N**, 41
Shakers; **G**, 603, **N**, 37
Shanks, Henry Thomas; **M**, 145
Shannon's Scouts; **S**, 167
Sharkey, William L., Gov., MS; **M**, 702
Sharp, William, Capt.; **G**, 506
Sharpe, William D.; **C**, 1026
Sharpsburg Campaign;
  Campaign, **T**, 401
Sharpsburg, MD, Battle of; **A**, 583, **B**, 590, 1105, **C**, 597, 1620, **D**, 64, **F**, 554, **G**, 68, **H**, 1306, **J**, 277, **M**, 349, 1066a, 1170a, **S**, 1186, **T**, 76, **W**, 191,
  Strategy, **A**, 220-221
Sharpshooters; **B**, 597, 743, **D**, 955, **L**, 140, **S**, 294, **XYZ**, 63
Shaver, Robert G.; **M**, 1189
Shaw, Arthur Marvin; **D**, 267

Shaw, Frederick John; **V**, 129
Shaw, Robert G., Col.; **C**, 1307, **H**, 28
Sheehan, Donald; **B**, 729
Shelby County, TX; **N**, 148
Shelby Iron Company, AL; **V**, 71
Shelby Springs, AL, Hospital; **A**, 97
Shelby's Expedition; **E**, 96
Shelby's Men; **S**, 1142
Shelby's Raid; **O**, 36
Shelby, Joseph Orville, Brig.Gen.; **B**, 134, 927, **D**, 163, **E**, 98-99, **H**, 256, 1074b, **M**, 313a, **O**, 13, 15
Shelbyville, TN;
  Monument, **S**, 326
Shenandoah (ship); **A**, 94, **C**, 1387, **D**, 313, **G**, 239, 242, 649, 670-671, **H**, 430, 1092, 1097, 1299, **L**, 533, **M**, 1126, 1158, **P**, 193, **R**, 476, **W**, 12, 594, 754, 895, 952,
  Surrender of, **A**, 378
Shenandoah Cemetery, Mount Jackson, VA; **M**, 1254a
Shenandoah County, VA; **W**, 301
Shenandoah River; **C**, 1176
Shenandoah Valley; **A**, 215, 315, 487, **B**, 1099, 1244, **C**, 336, **G**, 28, 71, 186, **H**, 332, **P**, 609, **S**, 371, **W**, 305,
  History, **P**, 341-342,
  Legends, **W**, 574,
  Refugee Life, **M**, 475
Shenandoah Valley Campaign; **D**, 488, **W**, 405a,
  Tactics, **K**, 24
Shepherd, Henry; **M**, 899
Shepherdstown, WV; **B**, 821, **W**, 171,
  Elmwood Cemetery, **H**, 700, **M**, 778, **O**, 191,
  History, **D**, 43
Shepherdstown, WV, Battle of; **K**, 60a
Sheppard, E.W.; **W**, 574
Sheppard, W.L.; **T**, 434
Shepperson, William G.; **B**, 842
Sheridan's Raid; **B**, 1584
Sherman's Bummers; **H**, 46, **M**, 1361, **P**, 163
Sherman's Campaign; **F**, 87

Sherman's March; **B**, 173, **C**, 1150, 1298, **D**, 452, **G**, 219, 540, **H**, 160, **J**, 300, 344, 379, 404, 505, **K**, 53, **L**, 168, 775, **M**, 606, **O**, 198, **Q**, 1, 10, **R**, 586, **S**, 143a, 394, 650, 773

Sherman's Meridian Expedition; **L**, 391

Sherman, John; **W**, 121

Sherman, William Tecumseh, Gen.; **A**, 322, **B**, 148, 417, 891, 1489, 1638, **C**, 480, 1129, **D**, 130, 633, **G**, 300, 453, **J**, 67, 344, **L**, 195, 488, **M**, 975, **P**, 329-330, 376, 383, **S**, 221, 1225, **T**, 88, **W**, 133,
    Augusta, GA, **R**, 557,
    Bentonville, NC, **T**, 213,
    Burns Libraries, **H**, 757,
    Columbia, SC, **L**, 762,
    Failure, **C**, 630,
    Gulfport, MS, **K**, 66,
    Leadership, **B**, 1586,
    Meridian, MS, **R**, 385,
    Milledgeville, GA, **T**, 29,
    Peace Fiasco, **N**, 18,
    Savannah, GA, **M**, 664,
    South, **C**, 1308,
    Strategy, **W**, 490

Shiloh National Military Park, TN; **C**, 80, **D**, 601

Shiloh, TN; **F**, 340, **H**, 712,
    Artillery, **W**, 883a,
    Battlefield, **B**, 169,
    Beauregard's Victory, **M**, 711a,
    Campaign, **B**, 431, 466,
    History, **E**, 133,
    Monument, **G**, 228

Shiloh, TN, Battle of; **A**, 269, **B**, 3, 81, 302, 328, 449, 595, **C**, 373, 527, 618, 925, **D**, 459, 462, 464, 531, 635, 905, **E**, 134, 183, **G**, 17, 151, **H**, 296, 601, 717, 1179, 1343, **J**, 423, 574, **K**, 65, **L**, 181, **M**, 508, 511, 511a, 511b, 668, 1074, 1174, **N**, 155, **P**, 484, 683a, 730a, **R**, 223, 263, 582, 807, **S**, 51, 441, 1445-1447, **T**, 247, 281, **W**, 504, 1002, 1040,
    Artillery, **L**, 131,
    Hornet's Nest, **D**, 771,

Slavery, **H**, 1358

Shingleton, Royce Gordon; **C**, 1345

Ship Island, MS; **B**, 1595, **F**, 168, **S**, 787

Shipbuilding, Confederate; **S**, 1203

Shipp, Scott, Gen.; **W**, 876

Ships; **H**, 851, **W**, 159a,
    Acadia, **P**, 383,
    Advance, **M**, 56,
    Alabama (ironclad), **A**, 302, **B**, 107, 543, 896, 1018, 1087, 1153-1154, 1425, **C**, 175, 395, 712, 1248, 1270, 1387, **D**, 317, 501, 504, **E**, 74, **F**, 66, 432, 573, 579-583, **G**, 497, **H**, 8, 222, 609-610, 781, 853, 1073b, 1073c, **J**, 95, **K**, 48-49-49b, **L**, 190, 734, 740, 771, **M**, 364a, **N**, 19, 25, 36, **O**, 190, **P**, 611, 785, **R**, 549, 611, **S**, 241, 527, 1393, **W**, 576, 579,
    Claims, **C**, 514,
    Plans to Trade, **D**, 112,
    Albemarle (ram), **D**, 634, **E**, 156-157, **J**, 540,
    Alexandra, **M**, 798,
    Alice Ball, **B**, 994,
    America (yacht), **N**, 44,
    Anna F. Schmidt, **N**, 108,
    Arago (schooner), **B**, 994,
    Arkansas (ram), **B**, 1147, 1370, 1570, **C**, 297, **G**, 365, **J**, 218, **M**, 417, **P**, 113b, **R**, 711,
    Atlanta (ironclad), **M**, 22, 749,
    Birkenheads, **C**, 1266,
    Bloomer, **J**, 354,
    Brilliant, **P**, 785,
    Carondelet, **B**, 1147,
    Chattahoochee, **C**, 297,
    Cheese Box, **M**, 808,
    Chicora, **H**, 137,
    Clarence, **W**, 939,
    Confederate, Built in France, **B**, 1549,
    Congress, **C**, 1603,
    Construction, **P**, 108, **S**, 1206,
    Cruisers, **B**, 1548, **C**, 369, **S**, 645, 1155, **W**, 729a,
    Crusader, **R**, 710,

Cumberland (ironclad), C, 1603, M, 816, O, 18,
David (submarine), C, 1033, E, 58,
Dunbar, R, 350b,
Ella & Annie, P, 736, 738,
Express, B, 994,
Fingal, M, 745,
Fishboat, S, 993,
Florida, B, 1019, 1167a, C, 1387, H, 242, 790, M, 50, 364a, 1129, O, 223-224, P, 647, R, 710, S, 528, W, 731,
Georgia, M, 1324, R, 276, S, 1138a,
Governor Moore, K, 89,
Gunboats, G, 35, 438, J, 20, R, 810,
H.L. Hunley (submarine), B, 358, D, 946, S, 1378, W, 72,
Harriet Lane (gunboat), B, 266, M, 269, T, 140, 407, 479,
Hartford, R, 549,
Harvey Birch, C, 1003,
Hatteras, D, 506,
Housatonic, C, 970,
Indianola (ironclad), B, 1225,
Ironclads, B, 323, C, 76, D, 372, 743, H, 1168, K, 223, M, 4, P, 52, S, 1207, W, 536,
J.R. Williams, R, 34,
Jacob Bell, C, 1040,
James Gray, B, 1075,
Jamestown, W, 1056,
Jane Campbell, W, 21,
Jefferson Davis, C, 467, 1132,
Judah (schooner), S, 1386,
Kearsarge (ironclad), B, 107, 1076, 1425, E, 74, H, 934, L, 190, N, 36, P, 245, R, 611,
Keokuk, H, 314,
Kireh Swift, W, 714,
Lillian, T, 185,
Lost at Sea, S, 957,
Louisiana, S, 1199,
Maple Leaf (steamer), B, 1432, G, 579,
Mazeppa, G, 457,
Merrimac (ironclad), B, 237, 1300-1301, C, 346, 828, 860, 1603, D, 33, 653, E, 113, F, 211, 219, H, 1265, 1269, J, 372-373, 528, K, 223, L, 4, M, 36, 349, 711, 1179, N, 115, O, 18, P, 89, 151, 420a, 640, 691, 725, R, 44, S, 220, 526, 531, 568, 580, 606, 723, 766, 794, 1376, T, 132, 289a, 405, 551, W, 539, 597, 981,
Michigan, S, 355,
Modern Greece (ironclad), B, 1260,
Monitor (ironclad), B, 651, 1466, 1498, 1501, C, 860, 1603, D, 33, 653, F, 211, 219, H, 1010, 1265, 1269, L, 4, 764, M, 36, 349, 711, N, 26, O, 50, P, 89, 151, 691, 725, R, 44, 62, S, 220, 526, 568, 580, 606, 723, 794, 1376, T, 132, 312, W, 292, 981,
Montauk (ironclad), N, 31,
Muscogee, S, 236,
Nashville, G, 83, P, 214, W, 595,
Neuse (ironclad), B, 1259, S, 1202,
Patrick Henry, R, 626,
Queen City (gunboat), S, 599,
Raiders, C, 1387,
Rams, G, 35, J, 557,
Rappahannock, F, 378, G, 623,
Robert E. Lee, O, 200,
S.S. Dee (blockade-runner), B, 1335,
San Jacinto, C, 395,
Savannah, C, 467, W, 173,
Scorpion, R, 779, S, 146,
Sea King, M, 1127,
Shenandoah, C, 1387, D, 313, G, 239, 242, 649, 670-671, H, 430, 1092, 1097, 1299, L, 533, M, 1126, 1158, P, 193, R, 476, W, 12, 594, 754, 895, 952,
Smith Briggs (gunboat), T, 214, XYZ, 11,
St. Nicholas, H, 1002, S, 25,
St. Patrick (torpedo boat), M, 349,
Star of the West, C, 626, R, 302, S, 665,
Stonewall, B, 848, K, 88, O, 164, P, 16, S, 1298,

Submarines, **B**, 358, **C**, 970, **F**, 427, **K**, 60, **P**, 282, **S**, 525, 920, 993, **T**, 266, **V**, 127, 185,
Sumter, **B**, 1629, **C**, 641, 1387, **K**, 48, **M**, 745, 1128, 1357, **S**, 1393,
Tallahassee, **C**, 1387, **S**, 406,
Tennessee (ram), **B**, 976, **C**, 1109, **J**, 276a,
Torpedo Boats, **C**, 1033, **M**, 21,
Tuscaloosa, **L**, 740,
Underwriter (gunboat), **C**, 1110, **L**, 751,
Virginia, **H**, 1073b,
Virginia (ironclad), **B**, 650, 1272, 1281, 1300, 1466, 1498, 1501, **C**, 685, **D**, 33, **F**, 210, **H**, 1010, **J**, 372-373, 528, **K**, 223, **L**, 474, 568, **N**, 115, 168, **P**, 340, **R**, 62, **S**, 1248, **T**, 312, 405, **W**, 52, 539,
Wachusett, **P**, 647,
Water Witch, **H**, 304,
Webb, **J**, 105
Shockley's Escort Company; **G**, 277, **H**, 1073a
Shotwell, Randolph; **H**, 155
Shreveport, LA; **C**, 1274, **J**, 529b, **M**, 1113,
History, **S**, 778
Shriver Grays; **L**, 58
Shryock, Richard H.; **A**, 460
Shurter, Edwin Dubois; **M**, 1119, **S**, 1157
Sibley's Brigade; **G**, 494, **H**, 82, 368, 451, **P**, 602
Sibley's Campaign; **H**, 81, **P**, 328
Sibley, Henry Hopkins, Brig.Gen.; **B**, 1001, **H**, 1003, **Q**, 9, **S**, 733, **T**, 240,
New Mexico Campaign, **T**, 95
Sidney, Edward William; **T**, 475
Sievers, F. William; **T**, 435
Sifakis, Stewart; **C**, 1215
Signal Corps; **C**, 1567, **H**, 303, **T**, 4
Signal Service; **B**, 1284, **G**, 5-6, **T**, 51
Silver; **P**, 88
Simmons, Edward N.; **A**, 134
Simms, Arthur Benjamin; **A**, 539, **P**, 184a

Simms, William Gilmore; **C**, 1169, **O**, 99, **P**, 657, **S**, 489, **T**, 392, **W**, 31, 396
Simpson, Evan John, Col.; **T**, 390
Simpson, Harold B., Col.; **D**, 259, **P**, 271, **R**, 578, **S**, 206, **T**, 328, **V**, 16
Sims, W.H., Lt.Com.; **M**, 737
Singapore; **H**, 8
Sinkler, Charles; **C**, 1364
Sins; **R**, 858
Sitterson, Joseph Carlyle; **C**, 315
Skinker, Samuel; **S**, 547
Skinner, Tristrim Lowther, Maj.; **D**, 838
Skipper, Elvie Eggleston; **E**, 114
Skipper, Ottis C.; **E**, 2
Skirmish Drill; **C**, 338
Slack, William Yarnell, Brig.Gen.; **B**, 1249
Slander; **J**, 480
Slatter, W.J.; **L**, 121
Slaughter's Mountain, VA, Battle of; **A**, 208
Slaughter, B.G.; **M**, 1200
Slave Labor; **B**, 1443
Slave Taxation; **B**, 1634
Slave Trade; **B**, 1375, **C**, 26, 190,
Africa, **B**, 117, 557, **M**, 755,
Foreign, **S**, 949
Slavery; **A**, 51, 62, 152, 505, **B**, 204, 217, 354, 528, 552, 791-793, 971, 1042, 1077, 1196, 1502, 1581, **C**, 42, 101, 451, 715, 791, 1137, 1225, 1227, 1401, 1592, **D**, 407, 427, 574, 928, **F**, 80, 606, **G**, 80, 554, **H**, 151, 758, 996, **J**, 406, **K**, 76, 249, **L**, 39, **M**, 344, 569, 917, 1111, 1250, **O**, 113, **P**, 521, **R**, 172, **S**, 453b, 529a, 822a, 952, **T**, 274, 299, 525, **W**, 209, 484, 659, 848,
Agitation, **C**, 198,
Agriculture, **F**, 312,
Arkansas, **C**, 314,
Arming of Slaves, **S**, 1110,
Business, **F**, 323,
Catholic Newspapers, **A**, 232,
Charleston Convention, **W**, 956a,
Cherokee Nation, **D**, 177,
Choctaw Nation, **D**, 449,
Defense of, **B**, 582,

Demographic History, **R**, 346,
Dickson County, TN, **C**, 1257,
Dual Revolution, **J**, 237,
Economics, **H**, 859, **L**, 696,
Emancipation, **V**, 159,
Experiments, Vicksburg, MS, **B**, 684,
Finances, **W**, 73,
Georgia, **C**, 124, **D**, 832, **E**, 233, **M**, 984,
Ideology, **G**, 602,
Illinois, **F**, 255,
Impressment Legislation, **N**, 58,
Jews, **K**, 249,
Kentucky, **H**, 432, **T**, 372,
Mississippi, **S**, 1220,
Missouri, **B**, 73, 1185, **M**, 543, **V**, 126,
North Carolina, **A**, 509, **B**, 219,
Northern Wage, **C**, 221,
Opposition of Planters, **T**, 409,
Pennsylvania, **F**, 129,
Protected, **B**, 559,
Railroads, **J**, 130,
Securities, **K**, 98,
Soldiers, Armed, **R**, 242, 257,
South Carolina, **S**, 851, 1305,
Southern View, **B**, 517,
Texas, **A**, 482, **B**, 1536, **L**, 73,
Treatise, **B**, 1375,
Virginia, **M**, 1281,
West Virginia, **M**, 1064
Slavocracy; **B**, 944
Slidell, John; **S**, 203, **W**, 366, 785
Slogans; **W**, 373
Smith Briggs (gunboat); **T**, 214, **XYZ**, 11
Smith County, TX; **C**, 208, 1488,
 Historical Society, **D**, 794
Smith's Brigade; **M**, 825
Smith, A.J., Capt.; **L**, 100
Smith, Aristotle; **D**, 454
Smith, Ashbel, Col.; **M**, 685, **S**, 468
Smith, C. Alphonso; **B**, 1050
Smith, Cabell, Mrs.; **V**, 144
Smith, Charles Henry, Maj.Gen.; **A**, 466, 561
Smith, Charles Jewell; **L**, 120

Smith, D. Howard; **S**, 718
Smith, Edmund Kirby, Gen.; **A**, 474, **D**, 798, **G**, 136, **H**, 169, **K**, 197, **N**, 164, **P**, 99
Smith, Frances Gordon; **G**, 412
Smith, Francis W., Lt.Col.; **S**, 584
Smith, Glenn Curtiss; **D**, 572
Smith, Gustavus Woodson, Maj.Gen.; **S**, 656
Smith, Hank, Memoirs of; **A**, 441
Smith, Henry H., Capt.; **F**, 477
Smith, J. Randolph; **S**, 196
Smith, Leon; **D**, 400
Smith, Orren R.; **W**, 707
Smith, Orren R., Mrs.; **U**, 37
Smith, Thomas W., Col.; **C**, 365
Smith, W. Sooy; **F**, 391
Smith, William (Extra Billy), Maj.Gen.; **B**, 1291, **H**, 56, 519, 652, as Gov., VA, **B**, 527, **F**, 4, **K**, 43
Smith, William Henry; **P**, 538
Smith, William Russell; **E**, 44
Smithfield, VA, Battle of; **B**, 234
Smyth Blues; **A**, 404
Smythe, A.T., Mrs.; **U**, 41
Smythe, Laurence; **L**, 462
Snead, Thomas Lowndes, Col.; **M**, 880
Sneed, S.G.; **P**, 782
Snelling, David Rudolph; **B**, 887
Snodgrass Letters; **B**, 1265
Snodgrass, Quintus Curtius; **B**, 231, **C**, 662, **T**, 507
Snow, E.N.C.; **M**, 1299
Snowball Battles; **G**, 390
Snowden, Edgar, Sr.; **Q**, 8
Snowden, Mary Amarinthia; **H**, 1025, **L**, 19
Snowden, Yates; **B**, 672, **C**, 264
Social Sciences; **M**, 1310
Socialism; **H**, 868
Society, Modern; **L**, 770
Soil Exhaustion; **B**, 17
Soldiers; **C**, 865, **D**, 705, **H**, 836, **M**, 46, 713, **S**, 1307, **W**, 645,
 Anecdotes, **R**, 233,
 Arkansas, **P**, 172,
 Army Life, **L**, 81,

Biographies, **E**, 251,
Black, Union, **W**, 478,
Camp Life, **B**, 1115, **H**, 67, **M**, 393, **S**, 1126,
Christians, **F**, 51,
Concessions, **C**, 1607,
Courage, **H**, 553,
Deceased, **C**, 854,
Difficulty Feeding, **K**, 16,
English, **B**, 244, 267,
First Killed, **M**, 1316,
Florida, **I**, 23,
Food, **C**, 777,
Foreigners, **L**, 671,
Georgia, **C**, 411, **I**, 26,
History, **P**, 61,
Housekeeping, **P**, 90,
Irish, **G**, 54, 636,
Letters, **A**, 264,
Maryland, **J**, 181,
Minors, **B**, 685, 772, **M**, 450, **S**, 1359,
Mississippi, **I**, 27,
Money, **P**, 122,
Morale, **B**, 584, **M**, 677, **S**, 931,
Needy, **A**, 27,
Negroes, **P**, 699, **S**, 796, **W**, 419,
Newspapers, **W**, 663,
North Carolina, **I**, 28, **L**, 539,
Northern Men in Confederate Army, **J**, 158,
Norwegian-American, **C**, 629,
One against Forty, **K**, 28,
Pensions, **C**, 1052,
Rank & File, **H**, 727,
Recreation, **S**, 70,
Regulations, **V**, 20,
Returning Home, **B**, 1110,
Slaves, **H**, 569,
Tennessee, **I**, 29,
Texas, **I**, 30, **N**, 2,
Vermont, **D**, 991,
Wounded, **G**, 18
Soldiers & Sailors Monument, Richmond, VA; **M**, 922
Soldiers' Aid Societies; **P**, 156
Soldiers' Homes;
  Maryland, **B**, 903, **P**, 301, **S**, 408

Soldiers' Relief; **C**, 734
Soldiers' Tract Association; **T**, 271
Sonander (pseudonym); **K**, 70
Sonora, Mexico; **H**, 81
Sons of Liberty; **A**, 586, **C**, 1238, **F**, 94, **G**, 258, **H**, 1033, **K**, 4, 222a, **R**, 184, 295-296, **S**, 1188
Sorrel, Gilbert Moxley, Brig.Gen.; **A**, 290, **M**, 441
South; **B**, 427, 688, 691a, 1123, **C**, 266, 833, 1091, 1310, 1376, 1384, 1416, 1474, **D**, 430, 435, **F**, 51, 257, 330, 473, 530, 563, **G**, 100, 127, 295, 320, 464-465, 474, **H**, 844, 1302, **J**, 383, **K**, 15, **L**, 411, **M**, 28, 350, 1161, 1300, **N**, 17, 90, 152, **O**, 167, 222, 225, **P**, 13, 326, 666-667, 813, **R**, 255, 594, 601, 866, **S**, 82, 143, 226, 229, 535, 1045, 1047, 1231, **T**, 441, 504, **V**, 131, **W**, 282, 287, 789,
Acquisition of Chemicals, **C**, 433,
Africanization, **H**, 983,
Agrarian Tradition, **H**, 212,
Agriculture, **C**, 1302, **F**, 312,
Aliens, **W**, 285,
Alliance with West, **M**, 1155,
Ante-bellum Life, **C**, 1154,
Antimission Movement, **W**, 1069,
Armies, **P**, 616,
Arms, **K**, 265,
Arsenals, **D**, 116,
Attitudes toward Lincoln, **C**, 1400,
Battle Abbey, **M**, 581,
Battlefields, **C**, 23a, 879, **T**, 440,
Belgian Consul, **D**, 422,
Bishops, **B**, 798,
Britsh Intervention, **H**, 1115,
Cadets, **M**, 439,
Carpetbagger Crimes, **B**, 969,
Carribean Empire, Dream of, **M**, 361,
Characteristics, **J**, 96, **M**, 684, **P**, 431,
Chemicals, **M**, 90,
Common Market, **C**, 213,
Confederate Memorial Association, **C**, 955,
Conservatism, **H**, 464,

South

Constitution, US, **D**, 983,
Creed, **G**, 255,
Crises, **F**, 67,
Currency & Notes, **B**, 1043,
Debts, **C**, 1263, 1275, **R**, 560,
Defeat, **B**, 625,
Defenses, **D**, 4, **G**, 405,
Draper, Lyman, **H**, 754,
Economics, **C**, 837, **H**, 549, **J**, 130, **O**, 231, **S**, 235,
Education, **F**, 310,
England, **B**, 751, **F**, 263,
European Recognition, **J**, 614,
Folklore, **B**, 935, **V**, 59,
Formation of the Confederacy, **B**, 820,
Genealogical Records, **P**, 540,
Health, **M**, 967,
Heroes, **E**, 72, **S**, 1183,
History, **B**, 1006, 1420, **C**, 1288, **F**, 524, **H**, 443, **K**, 189, **M**, 361, **P**, 495-509, 614, 857, **R**, 868-869, **S**, 238, 1219, **XYZ**, 53,
Home Life, **C**, 400, **D**, 598, **M**, 320, **O**, 226, **R**, 838, **S**, 1044, **W**, 656, 734,
Humor, **H**, 104,
Identity, **S**, 294a,
Independence, **C**, 398, **N**, 69,
Industry, **C**, 161, 164,
Leadership, **H**, 431,
Liberalism, **D**, 9,
Lincoln, Abraham, Pres., **R**, 55,
Literature, **H**, 1215a, **J**, 86, **N**, 132, **R**, 868, **XYZ**, 73,
Magazines, **M**, 57,
Mail Censorship, **B**, 1302,
Maps, **S**, 671, **W**, 1087,
Martial Image, **M**, 361,
Medical Practice, **D**, 891, **F**, 296, **M**, 559, 967, **S**, 443,
Memorials, **K**, 235,
Mexico, **H**, 240,
Migration, **O**, 225,
Music, **B**, 62, 1490, **F**, 3, **H**, 476, **S**, 1023, 1254,
Nationalism, **M**, 389, **O**, 177,
Newspapers, **C**, 998,
Non-slaveholders, **D**, 407,
Northern Meddling, **B**, 621,
Northern Teachers, **S**, 1443,
Oratory, **B**, 1049, **G**, 526, **S**, 449,
Pension & Relief Programs, **G**, 299,
Personalities, **R**, 20, 74,
Plantations, **J**, 503, **L**, 738,
Poets, **H**, 596, **M**, 900,
Politics, **B**, 1342, **C**, 1225, 1227, **D**, 971, **G**, 273, **R**, 170, **V**, 41,
Post-war, **K**, 74,
Post-war, Social Conditions, **A**, 566,
Propaganda, **P**, 799,
Publishing, **R**, 477,
Raid (1865), **C**, 1301,
Reaction to Federal Invasion, **W**, 665,
Rebellion Organizations, **R**, 295-296,
Recollections, **S**, 1383,
Refugees, **M**, 563,
Reports, **A**, 363-364,
Repression, **A**, 541,
Resolution, **C**, 250,
Resources, **M**, 266, **P**, 619, **S**, 6,
Revivals, **B**, 588,
Rights, **J**, 236, **M**, 541, **O**, 160, **P**, 42-44,
Romanticism, **O**, 177,
Salt, **R**, 5,
Secession, **B**, 220, **C**, 766, 1138, **H**, 551, **J**, 208, **P**, 347, **R**, 162, **S**, 212,
Secession Conventions, **W**, 972,
Secret Societies, **K**, 1,
Sectionalism, **O**, 232,
Sherman's March, **H**, 160,
Slavery, **H**, 569,
  South not Responsible, **J**, 123,
Social Relations, **B**, 868, **E**, 78, **H**, 1295, **P**, 142, **W**, 553,
Soldiers, **C**, 271,
Spirit, **S**, 1181,
States Rights, **S**, 1058,
Statesmen, **D**, 688,
Status, **B**, 695,
Struggle for Democracy, **D**, 686,
Sympathizers, **C**, 812, **E**, 266, **G**, 331, **H**, 342, 734, **W**, 699, **XYZ**, 28,

Tales, **P**, 443,
Territorial Expansion, **G**, 102,
Textbooks, **H**, 837, **L**, 603,
Theater, **D**, 750,
Tradition, **S**, 1219,
Traitors, **K**, 2,
Treason, **B**, 834,
Turner Theories, **C**, 1402,
US Government, **F**, 614,
Verse, **E**, 150, **P**, 199,
    Literature, **D**, 133,
Views of War, **B**, 516,
Vindication, **B**, 1266, **G**, 106, **N**, 210, **O**, 80-81, **R**, 654, 867, **S**, 753,
Women, **A**, 368, **B**, 1148, **C**, 1069, **D**, 748, **H**, 377, **K**, 248, **R**, 818, **T**, 298a,
Writers, **M**, 922
South America; **P**, 470-471
South Atlantic Blockading Squadron; **B**, 1036
South Carolina; **A**, 45, **C**, 136, 140, 348, **H**, 117, **M**, 1361, **N**, 186,
    Assembly, **P**, 34,
    Boy Brigade, **R**, 131,
    Buchanan Negotiations, **T**, 399,
    Citadel, Charleston, SC, **B**, 864,
    Coastal Defenses, **C**, 1326, **O**, 165,
    Commissioners, **M**, 754,
    Confederate Records, **A**, 384, **C**, 994, **R**, 291, **S**, 829,
    Constitution, **M**, 1356a,
    Conventions, **J**, 589, 594, 600,
    Defenses, **J**, 581, **L**, 623,
    Economics, **V**, 19,
    Executive Council (1861-1862), **J**, 596,
    General Assembly, **A**, 28,
    Gettysburg Dead, Reinterment, **G**, 289,
    Governor's Guards, **B**, 230,
    Haskell Familty, **D**, 439,
    Infantry,
        12th Regt. Vols., **B**, 1030,
    Ladies Fuel Society, **N**, 191,
    Laws, **M**, 864,
    Legislature, **O**, 158,
    Manufacturing & Agric., Ante-Bellum, **B**, 942,
    Military Academy, **O**, 68a,
    Military Operations, **D**, 325,
    Monument Association, **P**, 718,
    Monuments, **C**, 357,
    Naval Operations, **D**, 325,
    Newspapers, **W**, 953,
    Nullification, **B**, 77, 941, **F**, 500, **H**, 1133,
    Ordnance Board, **V**, 73,
    Plantations, **C**, 1364, **D**, 665, **H**, 179,
    Politics, **H**, 593,
    Post-war Economics, **N**, 138,
    Railroads, **D**, 529,
    Raising Troops, **R**, 508,
    Representatives, Congress, **W**, 943,
    Sea Islands, **T**, 360,
    Secession, **B**, 140, 835, 945-946, 1310, **C**, 333, 399, 1267, **D**, 425, 427, **H**, 131, **M**, 357, 360b, 1244, **T**, 74,
    Secession Convention, **W**, 970,
    Sectionalism, **B**, 943, **S**, 139,
    Sherman's March, **C**, 1150, **D**, 452,
    Soldiers, **B**, 1414,
    Soldiers' Aid Societies, **P**, 156,
    Statutes, **S**, 1027,
    Survivors' Association, **P**, 789,
    Troops, Raising, **A**, 384,
    Unionism, **K**, 141-142,
    Washington Correspondence, **C**, 1267,
    Women, **S**, 830, **U**, 37, 41
South Carolina College;
    Cadets, **J**, 427, **S**, 769
South Carolina Military Academy; **C**, 139, **H**, 328, **T**, 209, 211
South Carolina Monument Association; **A**, 265
South Carolina Troops; **S**, 31-33,
    Cavalry,
        1st Regt., **H**, 308,
        3rd Regt., **C**, 1327, **J**, 405,
    Infantry,
        1st Regt., **B**, 1462, **C**, 818, **M**, 447,
        1st Regt. Vols., **I**, 58, **M**, 451,

2nd Regt., **W**, 113, 389,
3rd Regt., **N**, 12,
4th Regt., **B**, 1184, **R**, 248,
6th Regt., **B**, 1172-1173, **C**, 756, **M**, 453, **W**, 950,
7th Regt., **M**, 468, **S**, 1380,
9th Regt., **C**, 756,
10th Regt., **T**, 335, **W**, 47,
10th Regt. Vols., **E**, 199,
11th Regt. Vols., **C**, 666, **W**, 416,
12th Regt., **M**, 454,
14th Regt., **T**, 339,
16th Regt., **T**, 55,
17th Regt., **M**, 454,
17th Regt. Vols., **E**, 101,
21st Regt., **D**, 852,
24th Regt., **C**, 142,
26th Regt., **H**, 1234,
Uniforms, **T**, 324
South Mountain, MD, Battle of; **G**, 515, **H**, 748, 820, 840, **S**, 203a
Southern Art Pub. Co.; **G**, 120
Southern Cross (Play); **D**, 22
Southern Enterprise, Greenville, SC, np.; **G**, 608
Southern Historical & Benevolent Association; **C**, 874
Southern Historical Society; **B**, 1280
Southern Historical Society Papers; **M**, 920, **S**, 117
Southern Iron Industry; **C**, 163
Southern Literary Messenger, pub.; **D**, 75
Southern Philatelists; **C**, 880, 981
Southern Press; **C**, 234
Southern Rights; **A**, 544, 589, **C**, 456, **K**, 6, **M**, 758, **O**, 160,
Maryland, **M**, 288
Southern Rights Association; **B**, 1015, 1534, **C**, 100, **M**, 541, **P**, 792
Southern Telegraph Company; **A**, 364, **M**, 1168
Southern Vanguard; **T**, 45
Southern Yeoman; **B**, 29
Southwest; **H**, 1268, **W**, 1005,
Indian Policy, **G**, 530,
Secession, **H**, 947
Southwestern Expansion; **B**, 1177

Souvenirs; **C**, 943, 986, 1017
Sovereign Convention;
Maryland, **M**, 281
Sovereignty; **K**, 149
Spain; **E**, 111,
Civil War, Opinion, **P**, 688
Spalding County, GA;
Stonewall Cemetery, **J**, 55
Spangler's Woods, VA; **S**, 434
Spangler, Edward; **M**, 1263
Spanish Fort, AL; **L**, 505,
Defenses, **M**, 349
Spanish Fort, AL, Battle of; **G**, 222, **S**, 1111
Spanish-American War; **S**, 789
Sparks, James S., Maj.; **A**, 433
Speight's Battalion; **F**, 96
Spencer, Cornelius Phillips; **C**, 380, **P**, 210, **R**, 832
Spies; **A**, 70, **B**, 45, 599, 670-671, 785, 863, 992, 1566, **C**, 669, 774, 1120, 1502, **D**, 158, 161, 519, 563, **F**, 483, **G**, 374, 501, 605-606, **H**, 54, 315, 358, 438, 1012, 1037, 1289, **K**, 12, 166, **M**, 71, 157, 788, **N**, 162, **P**, 521-526, 526a, **R**, 388, 722, **S**, 100, 456-458, 702, 942, 1004, 1040, 1335, 1357, **W**, 445, 797, 916
Spillman, Robert Scott, Mrs.; **R**, 344
Spotswood, William A.W., Dr.; **C**, 487
Spotsylvania Courthouse, VA; **C**, 245, **J**, 203, **R**, 65,
Captured Guns, **G**, 586, **L**, 616
Spotsylvania Courthouse, VA, Battle of; **B**, 806, 1116, 1414, **C**, 1618, **G**, 218, **M**, 553, **P**, 11, **R**, 540, **S**, 741,
Salient, **G**, 504
Spotsylvania, VA;
Campaign, **D**, 37,
Confederate Cemetery, **R**, 236b,
Monument, **M**, 780a
Spratt, L.W.; **S**, 562
Spring Hill College, AL; **S**, 125
Spring Hill, TN; **C**, 1412, **S**, 1003,
Defenses, **H**, 1271,
Hood's Failure, **XYZ**, 66,
Nashville Campaign, **H**, 1103

Spring Hill, TN, Battle of; **H**, 556, **S**, 331,
  Cavalry, **H**, 561
Springfield, MO, Battle of; **R**, 585
Spruill, Frank S.; **C**, 1361
Sprunt, James; **M**, 99, **T**, 185
St. Albans Raid, VT; **A**, 511, **B**, 79, 1145, **C**, 635, **J**, 109, **K**, 19, 164,
  Invasion, **H**, 386,
  Raid, **A**, 374, **L**, 527, **R**, 781, **W**, 845
St. Andrews, FL;
  History, **W**, 462
St. Augustine, FL; **E**, 48
St. Charles, AR, Battle of; **G**, 304
St. Clair, Fitzhugh; **C**, 403
St. George's Hall, Liverpool, England; **S**, 858
St. Johns Bluff, FL; **D**, 350
St. Johns River, FL; **B**, 411, **D**, 350
St. Lawrence (ship); **M**, 1127
St. Louis Prison, MO;
  Roster, **L**, 553
St. Louis, MO; **A**, 346,
  Germans, **B**, 815,
  History, **M**, 947
St. Louis, MO, Benevolent Association; **C**, 874
St. Marks, FL, Battle of; **B**, 1002
St. Martinsville, LA; **C**, 1323
St. Matthews Rifles; **C**, 227, **W**, 897
St. Michael's Parish, Charleston, SC; **A**, 401, **E**, 160, **J**, 74a
St. Nicholas (ship); **H**, 1002, **S**, 25
St. Patrick (torpedo boat); **M**, 349
St. Paul's Church, Richmond, VA; **J**, 143, **W**, 329
St. Philip, LA;
  Bombardment, **D**, 941
St. Simon's Island, GA; **H**, 629,
  Raid, **H**, 616
Stamm, Eim Reis von altem; **B**, 920
Stampless Cover Catalogue; **C**, 1035
Stamps; **B**, 317, **D**, 592, 595-596, 845, **F**, 453-454, **H**, 378, 1217, **L**, 416-417, **M**, 5, 113-114, **N**, 32, **P**, 664, **S**, 147, 349-351, **T**, 350
Stanley, Henry Morton; **F**, 40, **S**, 444
Stanley, William; **C**, 971a
Stanly, Edward; **B**, 1405
Stanton, Edwin McMasters; **A**, 543, **C**, 538, **F**, 447
Star of the West (ship); **C**, 626, **R**, 302, **S**, 665
Starr, James Harper; **C**, 1406
Stars & Bars (flag); **R**, 128
Stars & Bars Committee; **S**, 816
Startk, W.V.; **D**, 779
State Courts; **H**, 152
State Relations; **D**, 236, 334
State Sovereignty; **H**, 364, **S**, 1021
States Rights; **B**, 568, 800, **D**, 279, 764, **G**, 554, **L**, 425, 800, **M**, 41, **O**, 235, 239-240, **P**, 101, **R**, 799, 841, **S**, 72, 573, 1058,
  Georgia, **F**, 274,
  Opposition, **A**, 64,
  Virginia, **S**, 481
States, Seceeding, Officers; **C**, 91
Stationery; **F**, 299
Statistics; **L**, 3,
  Confederate Army, **C**, 274, 870, **D**, 540, **H**, 446, **M**, 594, 601,
  Losses, Confederate, **C**, 1217
Staunton Artillery; **T**, 448
Staunton River Bridge, VA, Battle of; **F**, 27-28, **H**, 623,
  Wilson's Defeat, **L**, 484
Steamer Convoy; **O**, 185
Stedman, Charles M.; **S**, 1038
Steele's Bayou Expedition; **S**, 698
Steele's Campaign; **S**, 1050
Steele, Frederick, Maj.Gen.; **A**, 230, 533, **M**, 200, **P**, 463
Steele, William, Gen.; **B**, 389, 422
Stephens, Alexander Hamilton; **A**, 567, 576, **B**, 491, 519, 1059, 1455-1456, **C**, 677-678, 1290, **D**, 197, **F**, 342, **H**, 76, 1174, **J**, 15, 17, 329, **K**, 234, **M**, 19, **N**, 200, **O**, 79, **P**, 236, **R**, 1a, 373, **S**, 1160, **V**, 130, 182
Stephens, Bertha; **B**, 519
Stephens, E.W.; **R**, 98
Stephens, John; **M**, 586a
Stephens, Linton; **S**, 1078, **W**, 8
Stephenson, P.D.; **A**, 451
Stephenson, Wendell H.; **R**, 46

Sterling, Ada; C, 642
Sterling, Campbell & Albright Pub.; C, 217
Stern, Philip Van Doren; A, 408
Sterry, Jack; J, 4
Steuart's Brigade; T, 287
Steuart, George Hume, Brig.Gen.; H, 1008, 1176, XYZ, 103
Steuart, Richard D.; A, 136, F, 586
Stevens, Daisy McLaurin, Mrs.; A, 435
Stevens, Thadeus; H, 362
Stevens, William C., Maj.; A, 539
Stevenson, Carter Littlepage, Maj.Gen.; D, 798,
Slander, J, 480
Stevenson, Mary; B, 961
Stevenson, R.E.; E, 10
Steward County, GA;
History, T, 179
Steward, John, Pvt.; B, 832
Stewart County, GA; C, 846
Stewart, Alexander Peter, Lt.Gen.; W, 837
Stewart, James L.; S, 1164
Stewart, Jesse M.; S, 1164
Stewart, R.M.; M, 949
Stickles, Arndt M.; B, 1525
Still, William M., Jr.; F, 377
Stockades; R, 649
Stokes, William, Col.; S, 1217
Stone Fleet; N, 27
Stone Mountain, GA; B, 925, D, 973,
History, R, 860,
Memorial, C, 158, M, 971,
Verse, K, 238
Stone River, TN; S, 208, T, 285,
Last Day, M, 511c
Stone River, TN, Battle of; B, 391, C, 925, L, 689a, M, 509, R, 124
Stone, Kate; H, 1027
Stonehouse, Thomas; H, 1029
Stonewall (ship); B, 848, K, 88, O, 164, P, 16, S, 1298
Stonewall Brigade; B, 197, 806, 928, C, 270, 484b, 489, 1111-1112, F, 325, G, 456, R, 565, 569, S, 184, 232, 557, 1235, T, 138

Stonewall Brigade Band; B, 1245, H, 382a
Stonewall Cemetery, Spalding GA; J, 55
Stonewall Cemetery, Winchester, VA; A, 583, C, 899, K, 267, 267a, M, 499
Stonewall's Foot Cavalry; L, 614
Stoney, John Safford; S, 1238
Stoney, Louisa Cheves; S, 751
Stony Creek, VA, Battle of; B, 1318
Storrs, Charles P., Maj.; H, 911
Stoughton, Edwin Henry; R, 359
Stout, S.H.; C, 592
Stovall, F.M.; C, 1552
Stowe, Harriet Beecher; F, 606, W, 7a
Strahl, Otho French, Brig.Gen.; C, 1561
Stratford Hall, VA; A, 438
Stratford-on-the-Potomac; A, 437
Straubing, Harold; D, 573
Strawberry Plains, TN; G, 117
Street, Sol; B, 1344
Streight's Raiders; W, 1082
Streight, Abel D., Col.; B, 1594, C, 1152, D, 626, F, 383-384, M, 349
Strickler, Givens Brown; B, 110
Stringfellow, Benjamin F.; B, 73
Stringfellow, Charles S.; A, 449, C, 343
Stringfellow, Frank; P, 197
Stringfellow, Horace; W, 268
Stringfellow, M.S.; B, 806
Stringtown County, KY; L, 576a
Struthers, D.H.; S, 1368
Stuart's Cavalry; M, 1234-1239, P, 846, T, 8
Stuart's Dumfries Raid; L, 640
Stuart's Horse Artillery; B, 1125, N, 47, S, 423,
Roster, P, 218
Stuart's Raid; F, 489, O, 78, P, 732, R, 150
Stuart's Ride Around McClellan; B, 1320, 1324, C, 116, M, 1233, R, 590
Stuart, Alexander Hugh Holmes; R, 552

Stuart, Dennis; **B**, 1633
Stuart, James Ewell B., Maj.Gen.; **B**, 492, 652, 711, 738, 922, 1052, 1575, **C**, 1174, 1609, **D**, 147, 423, 989, **E**, 255, **F**, 488, **G**, 86, 88, 680, **H**, 12, 1209, **K**, 35, 253a, **L**, 219, **M**, 174, 408-409, 411, 600, 912, 1095, 1230, **N**, 6, 47, 222, **R**, 584, 704, **S**, 76, 79, 661, **T**, 202, 216, 431, 465, **W**, 370, 773,
   Indian Fights, **R**, 821-822,
   Last Battle, **D**, 767,
   Maryland, **P**, 196-197,
   Wounded, **D**, 766
Submarines; **B**, 765, **C**, 970, **H**, 1066, **K**, 60, **P**, 282, **S**, 525, 920, 993, 1378, **T**, 266, **V**, 127, 185, **W**, 72,
   Attacks, **S**, 755,
   First, **F**, 427
Subsistence Department, Confederate; **F**, 78
Subsistence Stores; **V**, 50
Sudley, VA;
   Little Church, **N**, 4
Sudstrom, Helen S.; **K**, 58
Suffolk, VA;
   Siege, **R**, 583
Sugar; **A**, 592, **P**, 756, **R**, 669-670
Suggs, Simon; **H**, 1070, 1075
Summers County, WV; **M**, 877
Summers, Festus P.; **W**, 819
Sumner County, TN; **D**, 976, **F**, 84
Sumner, James C.; **M**, 582
Sumter (ship); **B**, 1629, **C**, 641, 1387, **K**, 48, **M**, 745, 1128, 1357, **S**, 241, 1393
Sumter Light Guards;
   Uniforms, **U**, 14
Supplies; **G**, 319, **H**, 1345, **L**, 65,
   South's Attempt to Buy Northern, **J**, 228
Supply Trains; **C**, 887
Supreme Court;
   Confederacy Lacked, **J**, 197,
   North Carolina, **J**, 420,
   Tennessee, **T**, 506,
   Texas, **R**, 516, **T**, 155,
   US, Military Commissions, **M**, 888

Suratt, Johnny; **C**, 85
Surgeons; **A**, 327, 373, **B**, 201, 724, 1141, 1169, 1211, **C**, 113, 324, 410, 1042, 1379, 1579, **D**, 47, 95, 680, **E**, 43, 193, **G**, 9, 36, 118, **H**, 222, 514, 781, **J**, 139, 489, **L**, 495, **M**, 329, 537, 560, 637, 1003, 1105-1109, **N**, 24, **O**, 213, **P**, 331, 617, 808, **R**, 69, 783, 870, **S**, 283, 1000-1001, 1149, 1238, **T**, 85, 91, 94, 157, 291, **W**, 224, 355, 807, 1086,
   Mississippi, **L**, 729,
   Uniforms, **U**, 14
Surgical Care; **M**, 164, **O**, 182a, **S**, 1000, **T**, 86, **W**, 211,
   Manual, **C**, 483, **M**, 164
Surratt, Mary E., Mrs.; **B**, 316, **C**, 84, **D**, 455, **G**, 160, **M**, 1066, **R**, 652,
   Execution, **D**, 786
Surrenders; **A**, 337, 378,
   Last Confederate, **T**, 64
Surry County, VA; **B**, 841,
   Battle Roll, **J**, 368
Surry Light Artillery; **J**, 367
Surry of Eagle's Nest (book); **C**, 1187, **W**, 542
Susquehanna River;
   Confederate Invasion, **C**, 1444
Sussex Light Dragoons; **B**, 810, **C**, 850, **W**, 107
Sutlers; **C**, 1607, **L**, 683
Swallow, William H., Col.; **V**, 89
Swan, Praxiteles; **T**, 217
Swearingen, Richard Montgomery; **G**, 103
Swem, Earl G.; **M**, 920
Swenson's Salines, Lampasas, TX; **S**, 1101
Swift Creek, VA, Battle of; **C**, 5
Swift, Eben, Maj.; **A**, 174
Swords; **A**, 123, **B**, 1479
Sykes, E.T.; **W**, 138
Sympathizers; **C**, 498,
   Iowa, **A**, 419
Syrett, Harold C.; **B**, 729

T

Tabb, Father; **T**, 1
Taber Collection; **T**, 2
Tactics; **B**, 1522, **C**, 504, **H**, 290-293, 680, **M**, 740,
    Rifle, **R**, 389
Tag, Sam; **K**, 84
Tahlequah, Cherokee Nation; **C**, 438
Talcott, Thomas M.R.; **C**, 902
Tales; **C**, 119
Taliaferro, William Booth, Maj.Gen.; **A**, 569, **D**, 117
Tallahassee (ship); **C**, 1387, **S**, 406
Tallahassee, FL; **P**, 30,
    Gamble Mansion, **G**, 34, 114,
    Occupied, **A**, 413,
    Secession, **N**, 211
Tallahatchie Rifles; **B**, 912
Tallassee, AL;
    Armory, **H**, 1065
Talley, Lavinia Porter, Mrs.; **O**, 173
Tampa Bay, FL;
    History, **S**, 120,
    Naval Engagements, **F**, 10
Taney, Roger Brooke; **J**, 233
Tape Worm R.R.; **J**, 119
Tariff Reform; **S**, 1392
Tarpley's Shop, TN, Battle of; **M**, 1187
Tate, Luke E.; **P**, 356
Tattnall Guards; **H**, 288
Tattnall, Josiah, Como.; **F**, 29, **J**, 402
Tax-in-kind; **N**, 123
Taylor County, FL;
    History, **C**, 265
Taylor County, TX;
    Cemeteries, **V**, 115
Taylor's Ridge, GA, Battle of; **L**, 748, **P**, 485
Taylor, B.F., Dr.; **C**, 1
Taylor, Charles Elisha; **W**, 28
Taylor, Clarissa Walton; **B**, 961
Taylor, John; **S**, 481,
    Secession, **D**, 684
Taylor, Raleigh C.; **M**, 136
Taylor, Richard, Lt.Gen.; **B**, 270, 617, 997, **D**, 176, **H**, 772, **L**, 23, **M**, 349, **S**, 566
Taylor, Sarah Knox (Davis); **S**, 477
Taylor, Thomas, Mrs.; **U**, 41
Taylor, Walter H., Col.; **T**, 69, **W**, 39
Taylor, William Rogers, Adm.; **B**, 436
Taylor, Zachary, Pres.; **S**, 1057
Tazewell County, VA; **P**, 240
Teachers; **T**, 450, **V**, 18
Tebault, C.H.; **U**, 21-22
Teen-agers; **U**, 6
Telegrams; **B**, 1189, **F**, 108, **L**, 380,
    Last Confederate, **D**, 275
Temple Beth-El, History; **C**, 424
Temple, Neville; **F**, 23
Tennessee; **A**, 82, 510, **B**, 755, **C**, 87, 109, 1373, **D**, 647, **G**, 557, **H**, 371, 1104, 1226, **J**, 279, 365, **P**, 637, **T**, 103, **W**, 69, 1046,
    Campaigns, **D**, 460, **F**, 126, **L**, 386, **S**, 1145, **W**, 272,
    Carter's Raid, **B**, 1350,
    Conditions (1865), **A**, 188,
    Confederate Congress, **D**, 694,
    Confederate Generation, **B**, 24,
    Congressional Delegation, **C**, 111,
    Conventions, **B**, 1471, **H**, 285,
    Generals, **H**, 782,
    Guerrillas, **B**, 783,
    Invasion, **E**, 223, **H**, 1053, **S**, 1226,
    Leaders, **H**, 57,
    Marines, **S**, 1386,
    Memorials, **D**, 651, **E**, 151,
    Military Annals, **L**, 531,
    Monuments, **T**, 111,

Nullification Crisis, Response to, **B**, 509,
Reconstruction, **C**, 485, **P**, 155,
Reign of Terror, **T**, 438,
Retreat, **M**, 693,
Revolution, **H**, 704,
Secession, **G**, 153, **P**, 129, **Q**, 6,
Slavery, **B**, 1196,
Soldiers, **B**, 3, **G**, 17, **I**, 29, **J**, 93,
Soldiers, Minors, **B**, 772,
Statistics, **J**, 494,
Supreme Court, **T**, 506,
Wheeler's Raid, **W**, 516,
Whigs, **P**, 102,
Women, **V**, 23
Tennessee (ram); **B**, 976, **C**, 1109, **J**, 276a
Tennessee Brigade; **M**, 368
Tennessee Military Institute; **S**, 980
Tennessee River; **C**, 647
Tennessee Troops;
  Cavalry,
    1st Regt., **C**, 560,
    2nd Regt., **H**, 207,
    5th Regt., **W**, 770,
    7th Regt., **A**, 65, **XYZ**, 64,
    10th Regt., **R**, 609,
    11th Regt., **F**, 173,
  Infantry,
    1st Regt., **C**, 472, **P**, 534, **W**, 269,
    2nd Regt., **S**, 217, **V**, 123,
    6th Regt., **J**, 278,
    7th Regt., **H**, 1212,
    8th Regt., **C**, 210,
    9th Regt., **C**, 340, **F**, 395, **XYZ**, 82a,
    10th Regt., **G**, 636,
    11th Regt., **E**, 143,
    13th Regt., **C**, 1475, **V**, 84, **W**, 465,
    16th Regt. Vols., **C**, 573, **H**, 618, **W**, 905,
    17th Regt., **S**, 267,
    18th Regt., **H**, 178,
    19th Regt., **S**, 1383, **W**, 993,
    20th Regt., **C**, 1213, **M**, 652, **S**, 719,
    21st Regt., **C**, 225,
    30th Regt., **H**, 937,
    41st Regt., **S**, 1164,
    48th Regt., **L**, 468, **W**, 270,
    49th Regt. Vols., **T**, 127,
    154th Regt., **P**, 783, **T**, 116
Tennessee Volunteers; **C**, 1380
Tenniel, John; **L**, 523
Terrell's Cavalry; **S**, 935-936
Terrell, A.W.; **D**, 472
Terrill, James Barbour, Brig.Gen.; **S**, 1063
Terrill, Nellie; **W**, 797
Terrill, William R., Brig.Gen.; **S**, 1063
Territorial Expansion; **G**, 102
Terry's Texas Rangers; **A**, 75, **B**, 223, 734, **C**, 568, 850, **D**, 677, **F**, 200, **G**, 262, 452, **H**, 265, **J**, 103, **L**, 113, **T**, 129, 141, 149
Terry, Tom; **K**, 270
Texas; **A**, 78-79, 497-498, 500, **B**, 716, **C**, 1406, **D**, 794, **E**, 81, **F**, 24, 38, 548-549, **G**, 29, 135, **H**, 682, 1128, 1196, 1204, 1313, 1318, 1350, **J**, 357, **K**, 146, **L**, 756, **N**, 1-2, 183a, **R**, 58-59, 546, **S**, 238, **W**, 95, 466, 850, 978, 1047,
  Annexation, **B**, 945,
  Ballads, **A**, 192,
  Biographical Sketches, **P**, 185,
  Blockade-running, **B**, 518,
  Bogus Delegation, Rep. Nat. Convention, **C**, 258,
  Books, **T**, 151,
  Burial Lists, **P**, 591-601, 604-605,
  Campaign, **D**, 322,
  Cavalry, **O**, 34, **P**, 117, **XYZ**, 54,
  Coastal Defenses, **B**, 163, **F**, 197, **S**, 333,
  Coat of Arms, **B**, 1623,
  Colonels, **F**, 199,
  Confederate Home, **C**, 929,
  Conscription, **G**, 312,
  Constitution, **C**, 1130, **S**, 91,
  Convention Ordinances, **C**, 1130,
  Conventions, **J**, 595, **R**, 547, **T**, 145,
  Cotton Trade, **M**, 741,
  Currency & Notes, **B**, 677,

Defenses, **H**, 991,
Diocese, **G**, 266,
Engineers, **K**, 58,
Executions, **B**, 176,
Field Artillery, **B**, 153,
Finances, **M**, 871,
Flag, **B**, 1623,
Food, **V**, 74,
French Designs, **C**, 1468,
Generals, **F**, 199,
Government, **M**, 462,
Governor's Message, **C**, 578,
Gun Collectors, **A**, 125,
Guns, **T**, 288,
History, **B**, 983,
Independence, **H**, 784,
Indians, **F**, 481, **N**, 136,
Industry, **D**, 898,
Invasion, **R**, 35,
Knights of the Golden Circle, **D**, 962,
Know-nothings, **W**, 959,
Land Grants, **M**, 884,
Legislature, **D**, 400, **N**, 198, **R**, 813, 816, **S**, 256-259,
Life, **B**, 1621,
Locomotives, **B**, 837,
Military Board, **G**, 583,
Military Forces, **F**, 196,
Military Occupation, **P**, 343,
Monuments, **T**, 137,
Mormans, **W**, 619,
Music, **S**, 921,
Naval Engagements, **H**, 584,
Newspapers, **S**, 1052,
Northwest Frontier, **T**, 46,
Operations, **C**, 1099,
Pensions, **K**, 192,
Plantations, **B**, 957, **C**, 1592,
Politics, **B**, 965, **W**, 843,
Ports, **D**, 507,
Postmasters, **R**, 68,
Proclamation, **C**, 577,
Rebels, **T**, 288,
Reconstruction, **B**, 966, **R**, 437-438,
Reconstruction Courts, **N**, 207,
Referendum, **T**, 308,
Refugees, **W**, 220,
Regiments & Battalions, Roster, **L**, 545,
Resists Northern Action, **B**, 1475,
Scouts, **W**, 735,
Secession, **B**, 1527-1530, **D**, 478, **G**, 8, **H**, 1145, **N**, 105, **O**, 37, **R**, 882, **S**, 42, 946a, 1065, **T**, 158a,
Secession Convention, **S**, 43,
Sequestration Act, **H**, 542,
Sheepraising, **F**, 171,
Slavery, **L**, 73,
Soldiers, **B**, 503, 1411, **G**, 420, **I**, 30, **J**, 239,
State Military Board, **R**, 60,
Supreme Court, **N**, 206, **R**, 516,
Surgeons,
    Parson's Texas Cavalry Brigade, **A**, 328,
Sympathizers, **XYZ**, 28,
Texas, **B**, 1536,
Textbooks, **N**, 91-98,
Unionist Sentiment, **E**, 301,
Vicksburg, MS, Monument, **B**, 419,
Yankee Textbooks, **D**, 326
Texas Legion; **F**, 311
Texas Rangers; **S**, 311, **W**, 740
Texas Redskins; **M**, 248
Texas Scouts; **A**, 414
Texas State Gazette, TX, np.; **G**, 8
Texas Troops;
  Artillery,
    Rocket Battery, **K**, 59,
  Cavalry, **A**, 77,
    1st Regt., **S**, 1104,
    2nd Regt., **E**, 126, **K**, 266, **S**, 501,
    3rd Regt., **B**, 1544, **C**, 311, **G**, 624, **J**, 239, **K**, 119, **L**, 31,
    4th Regt., **G**, 235, **H**, 77, **N**, 160,
    5th Regt., **C**, 816,
    6th Regt., **B**, 578, **G**, 92, **K**, 30a, 119,
    8th Regt., **B**, 734, **D**, 678, **F**, 200, **G**, 461, **L**, 113,
    9th Regt., **G**, 662, **K**, 119,
    10th Regt., **H**, 412,
    11th Regt., **P**, 295,
    12th Regt., **A**, 328, **G**, 30,
    13th Bat., **H**, 798a,

13th Regt., **S**, 962,
16th Regt., **D**, 473, **R**, 137,
17th Regt., **D**, 500, **P**, 387,
19th Regt., **G**, 467,
26th Regt., **D**, 408, 475,
27th Regt., **K**, 119,
29th Regt., **F**, 77,
32nd Regt., **G**, 524, **S**, 720,
34th Regt., **S**, 936, **W**, 328,
Cavalry,
32nd Regt., **D**, 875,
Infantry,
1st Regt., **G**, 113, **H**, 129, 135, **R**, 8, 313, **T**, 328,
2nd Regt., **C**, 389-390,
4th Regt., **B**, 78, **G**, 263, **H**, 129, **R**, 313,
5th Regt., **B**, 1480, **R**, 313, **T**, 217, **W**, 811,
6th Regt., **T**, 495,
7th Regt., **V**, 30,
11th Regt., **R**, 297,
15th Regt., **C**, 813,
16th Regt., **C**, 177,
18th Regt., **B**, 1544,
Mounted Rifles,
1st Regt., **M**, 462,
2nd Regt., **D**, 563, **J**, 605,
Mounted Volunteers,
5th Regt., **H**, 87, 91,
Roster, **C**, 1024, **P**, 603
Texas vs. White Case; **P**, 389, 406
Texas-Mexican Border; **C**, 743, **S**, 131
Textbooks; **D**, 326, **F**, 141, **M**, 1089-1093, **N**, 91-98, **R**, 864, **S**, 35, 775, **W**, 334,
History, **B**, 735
Textiles; **S**, 426
Theater; **D**, 750, **F**, 114, **H**, 470, 490, 1064, **T**, 167
Theorie de L'art Militaire; **E**, 314
Theron, Benjamin; **C**, 1468
Thian, Raphael P.; **G**, 564
Thom, Joseph Pembroke; **B**, 180
Thom, William Alex; **B**, 180
Thomas County, FL; **R**, 661
Thomas' Legion; **C**, 1485-1486
Thomas, Charles E.; **T**, 184

Thomas, Clarence; **A**, 485, 580
Thomas, Dean S.; **F**, 107
Thomas, Ella Gertrude Clanton; **M**, 322
Thomas, George Henry, Maj.Gen.; **C**, 57, **M**, 349
Thomas, Herbert A., Jr.; **A**, 139
Thomas, John Peyre; **A**, 383, **R**, 508
Thomas, Z.V., Mrs.; **J**, 97
Thomaston, GA;
Monument, **M**, 339
Thompkins, Sally Louise; **C**, 786
Thompson Conspiracy, Johnson's Island Prison, OH; **J**, 151
Thompson, Bertie S.; **U**, 39
Thompson, G. Harvey, Maj.; **S**, 1215
Thompson, Jacob; **A**, 543, **B**, 96, **R**, 21
Thompson, James Thomas; **A**, 558
Thompson, James Turner Sanford, Lt.; **I**, 1
Thompson, John, Pvt.; **C**, 436
Thompson, Mattie; **B**, 109
Thompson, Meriwether Jefferson, Lt.Col.; **B**, 829, **M**, 588, 988, **S**, 994
Thompson, T.W., Col.; **M**, 228
Thomson, James W., Maj.; **C**, 899
Thornton, Mary Lindsay; **B**, 1027
Thornwell, James Henley; **F**, 31, **P**, 35-36, **T**, 269
Thoroughfare Gap, VA; **C**, 1613
Thrasher, John Sidney, Col.; **K**, 170
Throckmorton, James, Gov., TX; **M**, 237a
Thruston, Gates Phillips, Col.; **H**, 821, 1127, **T**, 285
Thurman, Allen G.; **J**, 16
Thurmond, Philip; **D**, 739
Ticknor & Fields; **J**, 273,
Publications, **T**, 449
Ticknor, Francis Orray; **M**, 1165
Tilberg, Frederick; **A**, 396b
Tilghman, Tench Francis, Col.; **H**, 236
Tilley, Nannie M.; **C**, 645
Timrod, Henry; **T**, 227
Tishomingo Creek, MS, Battle of; **M**, 1207, **W**, 888

Tobacco, French; **S**, 939
Todd Family, KY; **M**, 670
Todd, A.H., Lt.; **B**, 266
Todd, George; **A**, 125
Tokens; **C**, 1607
Tolar, J.R.; **T**, 335
Tom Green Rifles; **G**, 264, **J**, 132,
  Uniforms, **U**, 14
Tomkins, Christopher Q., Col.; **W**, 437
Tompkins, Sally, Capt.; **S**, 7
Toole, H. Gresham; **D**, 465
Toombs, Robert A., Brig.Gen.; **B**, 1053, 1243, **C**, 773, **J**, 381, **R**, 31, **S**, 1090, 1256, **T**, 263-265, **V**, 130, **W**, 976
Topography;
  Bethel Church, VA, **B**, 654,
  Manassas, VA, **E**, 56
Torian, Sarah Hodgson; **H**, 950
Tories; **T**, 260
Torpedo Boats; **M**, 21, 349, **S**, 993
Torpedoes; **B**, 465, 1370, **C**, 1490-1491, **D**, 124, 126, **G**, 297, **H**, 147, **M**, 351, **R**, 13, 135, **S**, 755, **V**, 127
Totopotomoy Creek, VA; **M**, 1214a
Townsend Library; **T**, 371
Townsend, E.D., Gen.; **T**, 171
Townsend, John; **E**, 125
Trade;
  Contraband, **J**, 225
Traitors; **K**, 2
Trans-Mississippi Department; **B**, 418, **G**, 135, **K**, 119a, 195, **L**, 505, **N**, 158, **T**, 65,
  Cavalry, **O**, 27, 35,
  Confederate Association, **C**, 873,
  Mail, **S**, 347,
  Military Operations, **H**, 36,
  Supply Problems, **W**, 829
Trans-Susquehannan Man; **A**, 583
Transvaal, South Africa; **A**, 37
Traveller (Lee's horse); **B**, 1330, 1412, **F**, 183, **H**, 897, **L**, 293, 297, **R**, 342
Travis County, TX; **P**, 782
Traywick, Carrie Buzhardt; **B**, 1637

Treason; **C**, 463, **H**, 18, **M**, 292, 503, **P**, 419, **S**, 52, 532, **T**, 96,
  Trials, **F**, 94
Treasure Hunt; **C**, 1209
Treasure Train; **D**, 924, **T**, 298
Treasury, Confederate; **C**, 588-589, **P**, 88, **S**, 620, **T**, 171
Treaties; **G**, 231, **M**, 674, **P**, 394-395, **S**, 1025-1026
Treatises;
  Coastal Defenses, **S**, 118
Tredegar Ironworks; **A**, 333, **D**, 559, **F**, 501, **S**, 4
Trench Warfare; **H**, 21
Trenholm, George Alfred; **G**, 107, **N**, 73
Trent (ship); **T**, 390
Trent Affair; **B**, 543, **D**, 427, **F**, 90, **V**, 129, **W**, 212, 584
Trenton, TN, Battle of; **M**, 137
Trevilian Station, VA, Battle of; **B**, 1625, **H**, 193, **R**, 904
Trevor, Edward; **F**, 23
Trials; **A**, 586, **B**, 890, **C**, 85, 858, **F**, 129, 367, **G**, 230, 330, **H**, 18, 311, **J**, 420, **K**, 207, **L**, 524, **M**, 830, 1304, **N**, 129, **O**, 184, **P**, 389, 406, 419, **R**, 890, **S**, 13, 127, 337, 353, 1402, **W**, 276, 859
Tribble, M.P.; **W**, 249
Trimble, Isaac Ridgeway, Maj.Gen.; **E**, 22
Trimble, Sarah Ridley; **B**, 755
Trinity Church, Portsmouth, VA; **T**, 425
Trinity College, NC; **G**, 38
Troop Designations;
  Roster, **L**, 577
Trow, Harrison, Capt.; **B**, 1556
Troy, AL; **M**, 1301
True Blues; **D**, 442
Tryon County, NC; **G**, 634
Tucker, Beverly; **B**, 1454, **J**, 223
Tucker, Henry, Pvt.; **C**, 789
Tucker, J.S.; **B**, 1376
Tuckwiller's Hill, WV, Battle of; **S**, 1361, **W**, 451
Tunica Indians; **M**, 1278

Tunnard, W.H.; **W**, 792
Tupelo, MS, Battle of; **S**, 1209
Turkeytown, AL; **A**, 97
Turncoats; **W**, 351
Turner Theories; **C**, 1402
Turner, Charles W.; **D**, 123, **E**, 84
Turner, Joseph Addison; **H**, 1243
Turner, Joseph W.; **H**, 1208
Turner, M.J.; **C**, 972
Turney's Regiment; **C**, 472
Turrentine, Winfield; **T**, 452
Tuscaloosa (ship); **L**, 740
Tuscaloosa, AL; **C**, 689
Twain, Mark; **B**, 1265, **C**, 660-661, 663, 1352, **G**, 185, **M**, 343, 795
Twelve Days Campaign, VA; **D**, 846
Twiggs, David Emanuel, Maj.Gen.; Surrender, **D**, 107
Twiggs, Hansford Dade Duncan, Col.; **C**, 153
Twitchell, Ralph Emerson; **A**, 441
Tygart's Valley Line; **C**, 188
Tyler County, TX; **R**, 8
Tyler, E.A.; **G**, 561
Tyler, Erastus Barnard, Maj.Gen.; **G**, 332
Tyler, John, Pres.; **A**, 544, **P**, 205, **T**, 546
Tyler, Lyon Gardiner; **D**, 196, **H**, 926
Tyler, R.C.; **K**, 6
Tyler, Robert; **A**, 544
Tyler, TX; **A**, 126
Tyler-Latham Controversy; **T**, 520
Tynes, Mary; **D**, 49

U

UCV;
    Alexandria, VA, **R**, 738,
    Anniston, AL, Pelham Camp, **B**, 974,
    Austin, TX, Hood Camp, **C**, 1055,
    Brownsville, TX, Bradford Camp, **M**, 530,
    Camp List, **B**, 897,
    Charleston, SC, Jackson Camp, **C**, 1056,
    Charlottesville, VA, Strange Camp, **M**, 772,
    Confederate Veteran Magazine, **C**, 1048,
    Constitution, **S**, 806,
    Culpeper Courthouse, VA, Grand Camp, **C**, 498,
    Dallas Camp, **B**, 548,
    Danville, VA, Cabell-Graves Camp, **C**, 1057,
    Grand Camp, VA, **G**, 486, **M**, 557, **O**, 74,
    Hinton, WV, **R**, 327,
    Jackson County, AR, **B**, 700,
    Lee Camp, Soldier's Home, **A**, 292,
    Little Rock, AR, **C**, 1069,
    Lynchburg, VA, Garland-Rodes Camp, **B**, 742,
    Memphis, TN, **C**, 1063,
    Mobile, AL, Semmes Camp, **C**, 923,
    Nashville, TN, Cheatham Bivouac, **B**, 701,
    New York, NY, Camp, **O**, 208,
    Ninety-Six, SC, Marshall Camp, **M**, 399,
    Oklahoma, **H**, 40,
    Organization of, **R**, 861,
    Petersburg, VA, Hill Camp, **B**, 633, 635,
    Pittsylvania County, VA, **C**, 667,
    Potter County, TX, **H**, 66,
    Reunions, **J**, 83,
    Richmond, VA, Lee Camp, **C**, 299, **J**, 442,
    Savannah, GA, McLaws Camp, **C**, 923, 1064,
    Soldiers' Homes, **A**, 292,
    Wilmington, NC, Cape Fear Camp, **S**, 20,
    Wilson County, TN, Camp No.941, **M**, 927,
    Yearbook, **M**, 367
UDC; **A**, 151,
    Alabama Division, **M**, 513,
    Alexander Chap., **A**, 437,
    Anderson, SC, Lee Chap., **B**, 1397,
    Anniston, AL, Forney Chap., **B**, 974,
    Baton Rouge, LA, Waddill Chap., **B**, 939,
    Florida Division, **M**, 924,
    Founded, **T**, 497,
    Georgia Division, **M**, 925,
    History, **P**, 615, **R**, 11, 861, **S**, 754, **T**, 28,
    North Carolina, **A**, 336,
    Recipes, **M**, 759,
    Shreveport, LA, **B**, 753,
    Texas Division, **B**, 168, **C**, 304,
    Virginia Division, **S**, 622,
    Warren County Rifles Chap., **B**, 992,
    Washington, NC, Pamlico Chap., **C**, 1000,
    Wilmington, NC, Cape Fear Chap., **B**, 1583, **C**, 135, 301, 922, **M**, 725
Uhler, Margaret Anderson; **A**, 311
Uncle John's Cabin; **R**, 277
Uncle Tom; **F**, 606, **R**, 705

Uncle Tom's Cabin; **C**, 1258, 1451, **E**, 50, **H**, 996, 1019, **P**, 8
Underwriter (gunboat); **C**, 1110, **L**, 751
Uniforms; **A**, 119, **D**, 550-552, 724, **E**, 195, **H**, 603, 1279, **L**, 682, **N**, 172, **P**, 84, **R**, 478,
   Plates & Buckles, **K**, 114
Union City, TN; **D**, 553
Union County, NC; **L**, 97
Union Parties; **J**, 236
Union Records; **D**, 993
Unionism; **P**, 155
Uniontown, AL;
   Postmaster Provisional, **S**, 352
Unity; **B**, 1487
University of Alabama;
   Cadets, **H**, 911,
   Library, **M**, 311
University of Georgia; **R**, 537,
   Confederate Imprints, **H**, 484,
   Libraries, **A**, 523
University of North Carolina; **A**, 325, **C**, 1105, **W**, 336,
   Confederate Dead, **W**, 333
University of South Carolina; **S**, 769
University of Virginia; **C**, 497, 1520,
   Casualties, **U**, 43,
   History of, **B**, 1447
Upperville, VA, Battle of; **S**, 80
Upshur Brothers; **H**, 1106
Urquhart, Kenneth Trist; **F**, 437
US Army;
   Artillery,
     4th Regt., **R**, 541,
   Ranks, **N**, 30,
   Surgical Cases, **O**, 182a
US Government;
   South Carolina, **O**, 159,
   State of the Union, **G**, 80
US Marine Corps; **O**, 19
US Military Academy; **M**, 369,
   Officers & Cadets, **U**, 42
US, History; **C**, 1615, **M**, 33
Utley, Buford; **T**, 116
Utz, Henry; **D**, 934, **U**, 46,

V

Vaccinations; **J**, 496
Valasquez, Loretta; **D**, 816, **H**, 957
Valentine Museum, Richmond, VA; **H**, 213
Valentine, Edward Virginius; **S**, 486
Vallandigham, Clement Laird; **K**, 220-222, **N**, 83, **R**, 184, **T**, 124, **W**, 1021
Valley Campaign; **A**, 487, **B**, 1117, 1458, **C**, 1143, **G**, 220, 632, **H**, 531, **K**, 90, **W**, 413
Valley Mountain; **C**, 187
Valverde Battery; **B**, 1431
Valverde, NM, Battle of; **C**, 815, 932, 1436, **F**, 43, **M**, 445, 638, **P**, 269, **T**, 139, 238
Van Dorn, Earl, Maj.Gen.; **B**, 380, 1337, **C**, 278, **D**, 604-605, 879, **F**, 350, **H**, 457-459, **M**, 349,
  Court-martial, **C**, 721
Van Fossan, W.H.; **V**, 5
Vance, Zebulon Baird, Gov., NC; **B**, 291, 296, **C**, 71, **D**, 271, 800, **J**, 272, **P**, 210, **S**, 73, 418, **T**, 468, **W**, 174, **XYZ**, 16-19
Vanderbilt Hotel, Asheville, NC; **S**, 898
Vandiver, Frank E.; **G**, 130, **L**, 133, **S**, 797, **W**, 29
Vaquero; **T**, 241
Vatican; **F**, 42
Vaughan, Jack C., Maj.; **T**, 116
Veberidge, A.J.; **B**, 92
Vedder, Charles S.; **V**, 90
Venable, Andrew Reid, Jr., Maj.; **M**, 369
Venezuela;
  Confederate Exiles, **H**, 232
Verner, Joseph; **C**, 438
Verot, Augustin; **G**, 39, 142

Verse; **A**, 15, 256, **B**, 703, 731, 1283, 1371, 1428, **C**, 346, 621, 878, 972, 1014, 1178, 1247, **D**, 44, 133, 845, **E**, 10, 150, 317, **F**, 23, 320, 348, **H**, 261, 340, 596, 626, 650, 724, 1224, **J**, 31, 348, 370, 556, 564, 566, **K**, 92, 238, **L**, 1, 173, **M**, 290, 302, 326, 380, 440, 466, 738, 883, 900, 1023, 1061, **N**, 144, **O**, 101, **P**, 199, 257, 273, 346, 359, 449-450, 629, **R**, 96, 183, 309, 663, 787, 892-900, **S**, 134-135, 171, 276, 285, 338, 490, 508, 593, 737, 803, 997, 1211, **T**, 44, 245, 292a, 309, 367-368, **W**, 172, 488, 696, 893, 1018
Veterinarians; **A**, 373
Vickers, George Edward; **V**, 117
Vicksburg Daily Citizen, MS, np.; **B**, 575, **D**, 18
Vicksburg National Millitary Park, MS; **D**, 485
Vicksburg River; **B**, 413
Vicksburg, MS; **D**, 175, **E**, 178, **H**, 165, 208, 654, **J**, 1, 310, **K**, 55, **M**, 106a, 1014a, 1252, 1278, **S**, 1, 493,
  Campaign, **C**, 239, **G**, 502, **J**, 271, 366, 582, **K**, 176, **L**, 374, **M**, 686, 1102, **P**, 160-161, 168, **S**, 187, **W**, 482,
  Cave Life, **L**, 697,
  Cemetery, **R**, 459,
  Confederate Hill, **L**, 396,
  Defenses, **H**, 270, **L**, 579, **P**, 417,
  Fort Hill, **XYZ**, 73,
  History, **R**, 126,
  Hotel Bill of Fare, **R**, 829,
  Hotel de Vicksburg, **B**, 853,
  July 4th (1863), **W**, 598,
  Monument, **B**, 238, **M**, 781a,
  People, **W**, 67, 70,

Rank & File, **J**, 430,
Siege, **C**, 723, **D**, 382, **E**, 146, **F**, 437, 452, **H**, 961, **J**, 320a, **K**, 252, **L**, 375, 385, 686, **O**, 96, **R**, 188, 227a, 514, **S**, 1415, 1419, **T**, 483a, **U**, 46, **W**, 520,
Surrender, **M**, 758a, **P**, 225,
Texas Legion, **F**, 311,
Trans-Mississippi Supply Line, **W**, 1051,
Wallpaper Newspapers, **W**, 86-87
Vicksburg, MS, Battle of; **A**, 17, **B**, 363a, 416, 419, 684, 1231, 1615, **C**, 550, 731, **H**, 103, 1272, **K**, 145, **P**, 224,
Leadership, **H**, 562,
Organization, **O**, 149
Vidaurri, Santiago; **T**, 554, 556
Vienna Station, VA; **W**, 692
Villard, Oswald Garrison; **T**, 351
Villere, Charles J.; **B**, 479
Virginia; **A**, 277, 286, **C**, 502, 506, 1350, 1532, **D**, 565, 580a, **F**, 499, **G**, 51, **H**, 1118, 1333, **M**, 347, 350, 554, 695, 1285, **O**, 11, **P**, 241, **S**, 963, **V**, 184, **W**, 166, 690,
Arms, Manufacture of, **C**, 1467,
Battlefields, **A**, 191, **H**, 1119,
Battles, **C**, 1172,
Bibliography, **H**, 107,
Campaigns, **A**, 223, 317, **C**, 442-443, **D**, 846, **F**, 486, **H**, 774, **L**, 28, **M**, 68, **P**, 284,
Civil War Sites, **R**, 560a,
Civilians, **B**, 960,
Congressional Elections, **B**, 1292,
Conventions, **B**, 843, **G**, 20, **P**, 791,
Defenses, **D**, 4,
Diocese of Virginia, **B**, 1492,
First Gun, **S**, 386,
Founder of Navies, **T**, 551,
General Assembly, **M**, 757,
Governors, **M**, 1069a,
Historical Markers, **S**, 234,
History, **B**, 819, **M**, 53, 1214, **N**, 39, **R**, 572,
House of Representatives, **J**, 590,
Iron Furnaces, **C**, 167,
Iron Industry, **B**, 1443,
Lee's Invasion, **H**, 69,
Legislatures, **O**, 11,
Loyalism, **H**, 354,
Map, **M**, 172, **W**, 421,
Medical Society, **M**, 558,
Medicine, **B**, 786, **C**, 487,
Memorial, **C**, 358,
Military Operations, **F**, 128, **XYZ**, 101,
Military Organizations, Guide, **W**, 104,
Mineral Contribution, **B**, 1028,
Negroes, **B**, 596, 1072, 1237,
Newspapers, **M**, 923,
Ordinance of Secession, Stolen, **W**, 947,
Peace, **N**, 20, **T**, 549,
Peninsula, **C**, 526a,
Political History, **E**, 71,
Politics, **A**, 282, **G**, 21, **M**, 1167,
Prostestant Episcopal Church, **P**, 805,
Reconstruction, **C**, 496, **W**, 461,
Recruits, **C**, 729,
Roster, **P**, 607,
Saltworks, **R**, 5,
Secession, **A**, 307, **E**, 105, 171, **G**, 418, **H**, 107, **J**, 462, **K**, 98, **S**, 291, **W**, 126,
Secession Convention, **S**, 293,
Sectionalism, **A**, 281, **B**, 351,
Slavery, **M**, 1281,
Soldiers, **B**, 539,
State Papers, **F**, 292,
States Rights, **S**, 481,
Stoneman's Raid, **L**, 401,
Tobacco, **L**, 684,
UCV, **U**, 34,
Yankee Press, **C**, 165
Virginia (ironclad); **B**, 650, 1272, 1281, 1300, 1466, 1498, 1501, **C**, 685, **D**, 33, **F**, 210, **H**, 1010, 1073b, **J**, 372-373, 528, **K**, 223, **L**, 474, 568, **N**, 115, 168, **P**, 340, **R**, 62, **S**, 1248, **T**, 312, 405, **W**, 52, 539
Virginia Central R.R.; **T**, 488

Virginia Military Institute; C, 718, D, 330, F, 565, 568, G, 382, J, 100, L, 784, N, 5, O, 44, 71, R, 394, 632, S, 623, 688, V, 112, W, 41, 877,
  Cadets, B, 1427, C, 1317-1318, S, 435,
  Centennial, C, 1317,
  History, W, 875,
  Monument, N, 88,
  New Market Day, R, 413,
  Uniforms, U, 14,
  War Spirit, S, 1389
Virginia Troops; R, 324,
  Artillery,
    10th Btty., A, 534,
    13th Btty., I, 19,
    13th Regt., O, 180, S, 81,
    19th Btty., A, 534,
    38th Bat., C, 383,
  Cavalry,
    1st Regt., H, 12, R, 325, 685, T, 326,
    2nd Regt., L, 249, R, 686, S, 218,
    3rd Regt., R, 687,
    4th Regt., H, 10, I, 59a, S, 1192, W, 955,
    5th Regt., N, 213, W, 561,
    6th Regt., G, 660, R, 678, S, 1318,
    7th Regt., F, 269,
    8th Regt., D, 581,
    9th Regt., B, 337, 339, C, 116, 462, K, 260a, L, 483a, P, 675, R, 674,
    12th Regt., F, 572,
    13th Regt., B, 63, 809, E, 100, H, 441, R, 675, 677,
    14th Regt., M, 981,
    17th Regt., D, 393a,
    18th Regt., D, 511, R, 415,
    35th Regt., D, 655,
    36th Regt., S, 155,
    37th Regt., S, 155,
  Infantry,
    1st Regt., C, 384, L, 534, 584-586a, R, 128, S, 923, 1362, W, 102, 108a, 169,
    1st Regt. Vols., XYZ, 97,
    2nd Regt., B, 626, F, 573,
    3rd Regt., W, 108b,
    4th Bat., B, 707,
    4th Regt., A, 404, R, 571, S, 1282,
    5th Regt., C, 484b, S, 576, W, 108c,
    7th Regt., J, 268, 270, R, 307, 461, S, 923,
    8th Regt., B, 627, 630, D, 564, M, 136, N, 42,
    9th Regt., T, 380,
    10th Regt., B, 968, M, 855a,
    11th Regt., B, 535, G, 484,
    12th Regt., A, 418, B, 256, 707, 1408, H, 695, W, 574a,
    13th Regt., B, 527, 1514, R, 315a, S, 1293,
    14th Regt., C, 1459, E, 260, R, 319,
    15th Regt., D, 64, H, 401, 613, L, 10, M, 1083, 1170a,
    16th Regt., T, 380,
    17th Regt., D, 508, H, 719, R, 307, S, 923, W, 195, 864,
    18th Regt., M, 1088a, R, 560a,
    19th Regt., B, 784, J, 569a, M, 782, T, 207,
    21st Regt., C, 1547, J, 115, S, 1284,
    22nd Regt., H, 1346, S, 670a, 1365,
    23rd Regt., R, 110a,
    24th Regt., W, 541,
    25th Bat., C, 523,
    26th Bat., M, 1214a,
    26th Regt., S, 1361, W, 606a,
    30th Regt., K, 261-262, R, 801,
    31st Regt., C, 1194, S, 1366,
    32nd Regt., P, 58, XYZ, 38,
    32nd Regt. Vols., S, 324,
    33rd Regt., C, 270, 1557, D, 66, R, 257a,
    36th Regt., S, 155, T, 321,
    37th Regt., N, 195, P, 731, R, 110a,
    38th Regt., G, 646,
    40th Regt., D, 931, K, 262a,
    41st Regt., H, 696,
    42nd Regt., C, 401, 404,

44th Regt., **B**, 977, **R**, 801a,
45th Regt., **H**, 875,
48th Regt., **C**, 257, **W**, 242,
49th Regt., **H**, 56, 885, **M**, 874a,
52nd Regt., **D**, 847, **R**, 623,
52nd Regt. Vols., **H**, 333-334,
54th Regt., **J**, 564,
56th Regt., **B**, 1210,
57th Regt., **F**, 326, **S**, 1377,
61st Regt., **M**, 367b, **S**, 1170,
62nd Regt., **D**, 511,
Light Artillery,
  1st Regt., **S**, 560,
Militia,
  54th Regt., **W**, 39,
Officers, **B**, 676,
Rosters, **B**, 841,
State Troops, **B**, 1531
Volck, Adalbert John; **B**, 316, 709, 760, **F**, 313
Voting; **A**, 287

W

Wachusett (ship); **P**, 647
Waddell, A.M.; **A**, 450
Waddell, James D.; **S**, 1102
Waddell, James Iredell; **I**, 41
Waddell, Moses; **L**, 794
Wade, John C.; **M**, 715
Wages, Confederate; **L**, 441
Waggaman, Eugene, Col.; **N**, 88a, **W**, 19
Wagner, Johann Andreas, Gen.; **R**, 127
Wagon Trains;
   Capture, **M**, 868
Wagonmasters; **W**, 404
Wagstaff, Henry McGilbert; **G**, 475, **S**, 1271
Waitz, Julia Ellen LeGrand; **L**, 179
Walden, Alifaire Gaston; **G**, 112
Waldo, FL;
   Davis Captured, **C**, 863
Walker Hospital, Columbus, GA; **C**, 227
Walker's Division; **B**, 797, **H**, 685
Walker, Charles D.; **F**, 565
Walker, Charles S.; **A**, 441
Walker, Cornelius Irvine, Lt.Col.; **C**, 193, **T**, 290, **U**, 26, **W**, 50, 907
Walker, James Alexander, Brig.Gen.; **B**, 806, 1516
Walker, John Burns; **A**, 352
Walker, Leroy Pope; **H**, 390
Walker, Robert J.; **D**, 687
Walker, William Henry T., Maj.Gen.; **C**, 1551, **D**, 342, **K**, 269, **W**, 82
Wallace, George S.; **R**, 344
Wallace, Lee A., Jr.; **C**, 851, **K**, 117a, **N**, 47
Wallace, Lewis, Maj.Gen.; **G**, 332
Wallace, Sarah Agnes; **C**, 904, **H**, 4
Waller, John T.; **J**, 566

Wallpaper Edition, Daily Citizen, np.; **V**, 120
Wallpaper, Newsprint; **A**, 585
Walnut Springs, TX;
   Ex-Confederate Camp, **B**, 48
Walpole Scouts; **W**, 415
Walthall's Brigade; **B**, 763, **S**, 615, 1456, **W**, 138
Walthall, Edward Cary, Maj.Gen.; **B**, 228
Walton Guards; **R**, 206
Walton Infantry; **A**, 558, **T**, 234
Walton, J.B., Col.; **S**, 545
Walton, William M.; **D**, 472
Wapping Heights, VA, Battle of; **H**, 51
War; **B**, 1537,
   Art, **B**, 450,
   Conferences, **D**, 288,
   Conspiracy, **J**, 343,
   Correspondents, **O**, 45, **S**, 532,
   Crimes, **B**, 890,
   Debts, **G**, 173,
   Exiles, **B**, 986,
   Flowers, **A**, 551,
   Journals, **B**, 1376,
   Medals, **B**, 515,
   Music, **C**, 1013,
   Newspapers, **A**, 585, **M**, 1276,
   Orders, Last Official Conf., **P**, 130,
   Principles, **B**, 450,
   Records, **R**, 281, **W**, 1041,
   Relics, **S**, 1458,
   Science, **H**, 674
War College; **M**, 1130
War Department; **B**, 656, 679, **F**, 125, **J**, 437,
   Letters, **C**, 1264
Warburton, A.F.; **T**, 412
Ward, John Elliott; **G**, 2, **W**, 177

Waring, Martha Gallaudet; **H**, 286
Waring, Mary, Miss; **H**, 1034
Waring, Sarah; **M**, 640
Warley, A.F., Capt.; **E**, 157
Warley, Frederick F., Maj.; **S**, 275
Warren Blues; **F**, 605, **H**, 56
Warren County, MS; **B**, 854, **M**, 1278
Warren County, VA; **F**, 529, **H**, 51
Warren Rifles; **H**, 54
Warren, Edward; **B**, 318
Warren, George H.; **T**, 390
Warren, Robert; **D**, 662
Warrenton Rifles;
  Uniforms, **U**, 14
Wash, William D.; **C**, 1311
Washington & Lee University; **C**, 1422, **N**, 65,
  Lee Museum, **L**, 213
Washington Artillery; **A**, 25, **B**, 119, **C**, 262, 375, 850-851, **D**, 401, **E**, 231, **G**, 561, **H**, 105, **L**, 112, **M**, 553, **O**, 207, 217, **P**, 357, **R**, 464, **S**, 268, 545, 943, 1111-1113, **W**, 145,
  History, **O**, 204,
  Uniforms, **U**, 14
Washington College, VA; **C**, 4
Washington County, AR; **B**, 373, **G**, 31
Washington Hempstead County, AR; **W**, 700
Washington Light Infantry; **C**, 1328, **P**, 649, 656, 817, **S**, 494, **T**, 211,
  Easter Fair, **W**, 245
Washington Peace Conference; **C**, 1543
Washington Post, DC, np.; **T**, 460
Washington Star, DC, np.; **S**, 1118
Washington University; **S**, 491
Washington, DC; **W**, 823,
  Blockades, **W**, 784,
  Confederates, **D**, 723,
  Early's Campaign, **S**, 1441,
  Fort Sumter Panic, **J**, 8,
  Peace Conference, **H**, 915,
  Plot to Bomb, **E**, 261,
  Politics, **F**, 13
Washington, George, Pres.; **A**, 181, **E**, 63, **F**, 295,
  Statues, **A**, 23
Washington, James Madison, Mrs.; **W**, 252
Washington, John Augustine, Col.; **H**, 1078, **S**, 1372, **W**, 435
Washington, L. Quinton; **S**, 1014, **W**, 604
Washington, William D.; **C**, 1313
Water Witch (steamer); **H**, 304
Waterman, Robert E.; **E**, 7
Watford, W.H.; **A**, 441
Watie, Stand, Brig.Gen.; **A**, 337, **B**, 1157, **C**, 1571, **D**, 27, **F**, 367, 424, 482, **K**, 42, 224, **N**, 48, **W**, 265
Watkins, Floyd C.; **W**, 214
Watkins, James M.; **M**, 476
Watkins, Sam R.; **M**, 441
Watters, Willard O.; **B**, 672
Watterson, Henry; **W**, 90
Waul's Legion; **H**, 501, **S**, 476
Wautauga County, NC; **W**, 800
Wayfarer Trio; **M**, 1333
Wayland, John W.; **K**, 18, **W**, 832
Wayne, Henry Constantine, Brig.Gen.; **S**, 656
Wayne, James Moore; **L**, 157
Weapons; **A**, 120-121, **C**, 1620, **F**, 586, **H**, 20, **K**, 265, **O**, 98, **S**, 1449,
  Ammunition, **J**, 6, **K**, 118,
  Artillery, **A**, 197, **C**, 761,
    Cannon, Breech-loading, **A**, 251,
  Blakely Rifle, **T**, 447,
  Brooke Guns, **S**, 1068,
  Cannon, **B**, 1287, **M**, 891,
  Carbines, **L**, 774, **M**, 1311,
  Cofer Revolver, **M**, 1291,
  Colt & Whitney, **A**, 129,
  Colt Guns, **A**, 138, **F**, 547, **S**, 1132,
  Confederate-made, **W**, 361,
  Dance & Brothers, **W**, 618,
  Development, **H**, 1171,
  Edged, **A**, 127,
  Equipment, **C**, 742,
  Field Artillery, **K**, 111, **W**, 364a,
  Firearms, **S**, 1134-1135,
  Gun Makers, Conf., **H**, 1254,
  Guns, **A**, 594, **R**, 907,
  Handguns, **A**, 128,

Weapons

Imported, Shoulder, **W**, 363,
Le Mat Revolver, **L**, 590, **XYZ**, 68,
Leech & Rigdon, **A**, 138,
Longarms, **H**, 874,
Mississippi Rifle, **L**, 681,
Muskatoons, **M**, 1311,
Muzzle-loaders, **P**, 315a,
Napoleons, **H**, 614,
Pistols, **A**, 128, **H**, 874,
Revolvers, **B**, 593, **L**, 680, **S**, 419, 1448,
Richmond Sharps Carbine, **A**, 125,
Rifled Musket, **F**, 585,
Rifles, **A**, 554-555,
Rigdon-Ansley, **A**, 138,
Shoulder Arms, **D**, 817,
Small Arms, **C**, 761, **E**, 103, **R**, 177,
Spiller & Burr Revolver, **A**, 124,
Swords, **A**, 123, 136, **B**, 1479

Webb (ship); **J**, 105
Webb, Alexander Stewart, Maj.Gen.; **A**, 214
Webb, William A.; **C**, 1029
Webster County, WV;
   History, **T**, 254
Webster, Daniel; **F**, 430
Wee Nee Volunteers, SC; **P**, 710
Weekly Atlanta Intelligencer, GA, np.; **M**, 103
Weeks, Stephen B.; **U**, 42, **W**, 1064
Wegelin, Oscar; **C**, 1173
Weichmann, Louis J.; **G**, 160
Weisiger, David Addison, Brig.Gen.; **B**, 631
Welder's Brigade; **S**, 1399
Welfare; **T**, 197,
   Confederate, **E**, 234
Weller, Mary Crary; **C**, 1388
Welsh, James L.; **B**, 347
Welsh, John P.; **B**, 347
Welton, Louis A.; **J**, 228
Wentworth Military Academy, MO; **C**, 529
Wescoat, Joseph Julius; **C**, 666
Wessen, Ernest; **K**, 6
West;
   Battles, **F**, 148,
   Confederate Offensive, **J**, 94,
   Divided Command, **G**, 233,
   Early Days of War, **B**, 1554,
   Raids, **S**, 1339, **W**, 1074
West Indies, Emancipation; **B**, 621
West Point Atlas; **E**, 240
West Point Guards; **C**, 424
West Point Military Academy; **A**, 173, 303, **B**, 708, **E**, 144, 188, **M**, 510, 586, **N**, 77, **S**, 517,
   Secession, **M**, 349
West Point of the Confederacy; **W**, 882
West Point, GA; **R**, 375
West Point, MS;
   Smith's Raid, **L**, 391
West Virginia; **C**, 1163, **J**, 267, **L**, 689, **M**, 1063, **S**, 1346, 1369,
   Border Skirmishes, **G**, 91,
   Campaigns, **H**, 502-503, **L**, 621, **P**, 848,
   Floyd's Operations, **R**, 447,
   Generals, **S**, 1353,
   Herd Fighting, **M**, 402,
   History, **W**, 565,
   Imprints, **N**, 166,
   Literature, **S**, 400,
   Military Operations, **XYZ**, 101,
   Morgan's Men, **S**, 1354,
   Postal Service, **S**, 1364, 1371,
   Raids, **B**, 830, **S**, 1373, **XYZ**, 76,
   Scouts, **M**, 385,
   Slavery, **M**, 1064,
   Statehood Movement, **R**, 462
West, Absalom Madden, Brig.Gen.; **S**, 1229
West, James D., Rev.; **W**, 465
Western & Atlantic R.R.; **W**, 159
Western Armies; **XYZ**, 55,
   Battles, **D**, 833
Western Border; **M**, 987
Western Maryland R.R.; **J**, 119
Western States & Territories; **C**, 830, **F**, 146
Western War, Views; **B**, 714
Westminster, MD; **P**, 196
Weston, James A., Rev.; **L**, 470
Westport, MO, Battle of; **B**, 1359, **C**, 1453, **J**, 117-118

Westview Cemetery, Fulton County, GA; **C**, 1010
Wetmore, Louis; **E**, 79
Wetmore, Russell, Mrs.; **C**, 997
Weyss, John E., Maj.; **V**, 164
Whaling Fleets; **W**, 714
Wharton's Cavalry; **A**, 74, **W**, 742
Wharton, Clarence; **T**, 150
Wharton, John A., Maj.Gen.; **G**, 667
Wheat; **S**, 126
Wheat's Tigers; **S**, 1054
Wheat, Chatham Roberdeau, Maj.; **D**, 895, **S**, 538
Wheat, Robert C., Maj.; **M**, 356a
Wheaton's Battery; **S**, 75
Wheeler's Cavalry; **H**, 59, **W**, 508
Wheeler's Raid; **D**, 868
Wheeler's Scouts; **K**, 75
Wheeler, George B., Rev.; **C**, 26
Wheeler, Jacob; **B**, 967
Wheeler, Joseph, Maj.Gen.; **B**, 1165, 1325, 1607, **C**, 1599, **D**, 437, 696, 833, 866, 994, **L**, 164a, **M**, 501, 751, **P**, 218, **R**, 556, **W**, 387, 604a
Whelan, John; **M**, 720
Whigs; **B**, 1177, **G**, 576, **P**, 263, **R**, 621
Whillikens, G.; **S**, 862
Whippy Swamp, SC; **A**, 589
White House of the Confederacy; **D**, 358, **F**, 140, **N**, 15a
White River Expedition; **B**, 424
White Sulphur Springs, WV; **V**, 34, History, **M**, 18
White Sulphur Springs, WV, Battle of; **M**, 18, **S**, 1375
White's Battalion; **M**, 1353-1354
White, Elijah Viers, Lt.Col.; **J**, 72a, **T**, 249
White, Frank F., Jr.; **F**, 433
White, Hugh A., Capt.; **W**, 569
White, Isaiah H.; **A**, 349a
White, Raymond D.; **F**, 188
White, William S., Rev.; **W**, 568
Whitehall, NC; **K**, 194
Whiteman, Maxwell; **F**, 471
Whitfield, George, Maj.; **L**, 116
Whiting, William Henry C., Maj.Gen.; **D**, 519, **R**, 88
Whitman, Walt; **C**, 1352, **S**, 1128
Whittier, John Greenleaf; **E**, 59
Who's Who, Confederates; **D**, 773
Wichita Agency, Ind.T.; **H**, 410
Wichita Indians; **H**, 971
Wierenga, Theron; **O**, 52
Wigfall Mission; **R**, 482
Wigfall, Louis Trezevant, Brig.Gen.; **B**, 763, **K**, 169, **N**, 217
Wight, Willard E.; **B**, 1386, **C**, 513, **F**, 289, **M**, 546, **O**, 47, **S**, 1065, **V**, 90, 110
Wight, William E.; **H**, 231, **L**, 790
Wilby, Jonathan, Maj.; **J**, 330
Wilcox's Brigade; **C**, 580, **F**, 59
Wilcox, Ella Wheeler; **D**, 338
Wildcat Cavalry; **D**, 393a
Wilderness, VA;
Campaign, **A**, 174, **B**, 145, **F**, 241, **L**, 337, 574, **M**, 834, **S**, 1053, 1436,
Lee & Grant, **W**, 634
Wilderness, VA, Battle of; **A**, 272, **B**, 242, 350, 1094, 1114, 1474, **C**, 1531, 1538, **G**, 47, **H**, 635, 681, 1240, **L**, 658, **M**, 80, 553, **O**, 91, **R**, 115, 540, 601, **S**, 102, 911, **T**, 496, **W**, 544
Wiley, Bell I.; **B**, 924, **H**, 19, **M**, 100, 441, 666, **N**, 143, **P**, 452, **S**, 529, **W**, 661
Wilkins, James H.; **H**, 342
Wilkinson County, GA; **B**, 1543, Roster, **D**, 135
Willett, Joseph Jackson; **W**, 685
William & Mary College, VA;
Hospital, **C**, 1476,
Library, **S**, 1430
Williams, Ben Ames; **C**, 448
Williams, Frank B., Jr.; **S**, 1380
Williams, Harry; **V**, 70
Williams, Henry L.; **W**, 160
Williams, J.R.; **M**, 1173
Williams, Julie Carpenter, Mrs.; **C**, 197
Williams, Lawrence Orton, Col.; **B**, 574
Williams, Marjorie Logan, Mrs.; **L**, 5
Williams, Martha Custis; **L**, 358
Williams, R.H.; **W**, 736

Williams, T. Harry; **A**, 176, **S**, 529
Williams, Thomas W., Capt.; **W**, 714
Williamsburg County, SC; **B**, 828
Williamsburg District, SC;
  Wee Nee Volunteers, **P**, 710
Williamsburg Junior Guards; **L**, 570
Williamsburg, VA, Battle of; **B**, 1172, **D**, 982, **G**, 460, **H**, 522, **M**, 351, 700, Artillery, **S**, 1139
Williamson County, TN, Centennial; **B**, 263
Williamsport, MD, Battle of; **P**, 832
Willis, Irvin Cross; **J**, 13
Wills Valley, TN, Battle of; **P**, 275
Wilmer, Richard Hooker, Bishop; **W**, 531
Wilmington Light Infantry, NC; **C**, 134
Wilmington, NC;
  Blockade-runners, **O**, 200, **S**, 1148,
  Blockades, **J**, 140, **T**, 185,
  Medical Officers, **P**, 808
Wilmot Proviso; **F**, 67, **V**, 169
Wilson County, NC; **B**, 131
Wilson's Creek, MO, Battle of; **A**, 562, **B**, 375, 385-386, 999, **C**, 311, 731, **F**, 289, **H**, 982, 1249a, 1278, **M**, 496, 719, 942, 1261, **N**, 78, **P**, 190, 356a, 701, **S**, 136, **U**, 44, **W**, 165, 527, 628, 792, 889-890
Wilson's Raiders; **J**, 434a, 434, **M**, 1188, **S**, 1017
Wilson, Augusta Jane Evans; **F**, 100
Wilson, James Harrison, Maj.Gen.; **K**, 177
Wilson, William H., Capt.; **M**, 265
Wilson, William L.; **S**, 1392
Wilson-Kautz Raid; **C**, 1566
Winchester County, VA; **C**, 530
Winchester, TN; **L**, 121
Winchester, VA; **C**, 155, **D**, 465, **W**, 56,
  Captured, **J**, 205,
  History, **M**, 1213,
  Monument, **M**, 1154,
  Occupied, **Q**, 2a,
  Stonewall Cemetery, **C**, 899, **K**, 267, 267a, **M**, 499

Winchester, VA, Battle of; **B**, 1096, 1101, **E**, 12, 42, **G**, 70, **L**, 496, **M**, 1075
Winder, John Henry, Brig.Gen.; **E**, 26
Windham, Irbia Warren; **J**, 157
Winfield, J.Q.; **W**, 306
Winfield, Judy; **C**, 639
Winfield, Nath; **C**, 639
Winfield, Paulina Swife; **W**, 832
Winfrey, Dorman H.; **C**, 1591
Wingfield, H.W., Capt.; **W**, 833
Wingfield, M.D., Mrs.; **B**, 960
Winkler, E.W.; **C**, 1024, **T**, 154
Winston County, MS; **L**, 498a
Winston, AL;
  History, **T**, 261
Winston, John Anthony, Col.; **M**, 604
Winston, Robert W.; **B**, 1012, **N**, 90
Winton, NC;
  Burning of, **P**, 111
Wirz, Henry, Maj.; **C**, 476, **G**, 207, **K**, 121, **M**, 681, **P**, 5, **R**, 855, 877-878, **T**, 532, **W**, 857,
  Execution, **P**, 261,
  Monument, **D**, 104,
  Trial, **R**, 890, **S**, 1149, **W**, 859
Wisconsin;
  Burial Sites, **T**, 321,
  Copperheads, **B**, 511
Wisdom's Raid; **W**, 860
Wise Guards;
  Roster, **M**, 650
Wise's Brigade; **R**, 318a
Wise, Henry Alexander, Brig.Gen.; **S**, 495a, **W**, 437, 862,
  as Gov., VA, **A**, 544
Wise, Joe R.; **P**, 272
Wise, Obadiah Jennings; **A**, 66
Wishnietsky, Benjamin; **C**, 1035
Wither, William Temple; **H**, 408
Witherspoon, Jim; **C**, 1260
Wolseley, Garnet Joseph, Lord; **A**, 33, **D**, 233, 304, **F**, 569
Women; **B**, 1148, 1510-1511, 1513, 1561, 1564, 1593, 1614, 1638, **C**, 15, 30, 41, 540, 569, 642, 744-745, 754, 774, 802, 804, 818, 1069, 1101, 1113,

1480, 1482, 1554, **D**, 14, 75, 94, 97, 143, 391, 396, 432, 439, 565, 616, 748, 932, **E**, 50, 123, **F**, 80, 124, 130, 226, 270, 341, 517, **G**, 416, 501, 575, 643, **H**, 1, 54, 68, 315, 377, 507, 550, 690, 740, 957, 1025, 1027, 1034, 1037-1038, 1040, 1175, 1309, **I**, 60, **J**, 20, 128, 232a, 243, 258, 500-501, 505, 512, 536, 585, **K**, 9-12, 124, 166, 248, **L**, 11-20, 492, 511, 532, 602-603, **M**, 35, 54, 349, 372, 401, 406, 441, 564, 616, 640, 910, 1038, 1253, 1269, 1313, **N**, 53, 191, **O**, 199, **P**, 25, 113, 221, 414, 796, **Q**, 5, **R**, 488, 539, 818, **S**, 90, 450, 469-470, 702, 830, 982, 1120a, 1147, **T**, 14, 130, 298a, **U**, 9, 29, 37, **V**, 4, 23, **W**, 50, 642, 790, 797, 892, 907,
   Alabama, **S**, 1119,
   Arkansas, **E**, 217, **S**, 1413, **W**, 50,
   Battle, **V**, 94,
   Maryland, **D**, 132,
   Memorial, Confederate, **G**, 345,
   Monument, **C**, 1381, **H**, 825, **M**, 1036,
   North Carolina, **A**, 318,
   Soldiers, **D**, 816,
   Southern, **A**, 368, 593,
   Virginia, **A**, 455,
   War Flowers, **A**, 551,
   War Work, **R**, 879
Wood, Ben; **M**, 1329
Wood, John Taylor, Lt.; **S**, 407, **T**, 289a
Wood, Thomas; **P**, 808
Wood, William N.; **M**, 441
Woodford, Milton M.; **C**, 778
Woodlawn Cemetery, Elmira, NY; **H**, 1016
Woodruff, Mathew, Sgt.; **B**, 874
Woodruff, W.E.; **W**, 792
Woods, Samuel; **D**, 406
Woods, Tommy; **M**, 353
Woodson, Henry Morton; **E**, 172
Woody, Robert H.; **H**, 475
Wooten, Dudley G.; **B**, 983, **T**, 129
Worden, John L.; **J**, 432
Worley, John F.; **XYZ**, 36

Worley, Ted R.; **A**, 422, 427, **D**, 515, **G**, 36, **P**, 822
Worsham, John H.; **M**, 441
Worsham, Lewis; **T**, 150
Worth, Daniel; **T**, 337
Worth, Jonathan; **XYZ**, 113
Worthington, C.J.; **D**, 816, **V**, 95
Wounds; **H**, 7, **M**, 558
Wright, D. Giraud, Mrs.; **W**, 111
Wright, David Minton, Dr.; **A**, 334, **W**, 327
Wright, Edmund; **R**, 467
Wright, Howard C.; **H**, 357
Wright, John; **W**, 604, 1060
Wright, Marcus Joseph, Brig.Gen.; **A**, 276, 386, 417, **C**, 552, 1362, **G**, 168, **L**, 624, **W**, 726, 1016
Wright, Phineas C.; **K**, 214
Wright, Stuart; **B**, 917, 924, **F**, 502
Wright, Thomas R.B.; **G**, 73
Wright-Hawkins-Edwards Family; **B**, 61
Wrightsville, PA, Battle of; **B**, 1095
Wroten, William H.; **V**, 169
Wunder, L.G.; **L**, 2
Wyatt, Henry Lawson; **B**, 706, **C**, 203, **W**, 337
Wyeth, John Allen; **A**, 81, 245, **M**, 1185
Wylly, W.H.; **S**, 148
Wynne, Thomas H.; **B**, 672
Wythe County, VA;
   Lead Mines, **D**, 718
Wytheville, VA, Battle of; **D**, 49

XYZ

Yadkin Valley, NC; **W**, 472
Yale University; **E**, 145
Yancey, William Lowndes; **A**, 87, **D**, 307, 602, 862, **G**, 59, **H**, 586, 1071, **M**, 645, **O**, 171, **P**, 317, 320, **T**, 162, **V**, 97-100
Yandell, David W.; **R**, 544
Yankee Courtesan; **C**, 431
Yankees Are Coming, The (play); **E**, 222
Yazoo County, MS; **B**, 981, Reconstruction, **B**, 980
Yazoo Pass, MS;
  Gunboats, **W**, 469
Yazoo River; **A**, 414
Yeadon, Richard; **E**, 148
Yearns, W. Buck; **N**, 174
Yellow Tavern, AR, Battle of; **C**, 713, **M**, 882
York Rangers; **S**, 324
Yorktown, VA, Battle of; **H**, 1317, **S**, 183
Youghiogheny River; **R**, 122
Young County, TX; **L**, 196, **N**, 50
Young's Branch, VA, Battle of; **W**, 185
Young, Bennett H., Lt.; **B**, 79, **G**, 537, **H**, 386, **K**, 166a
Young, Charles P.; **C**, 784, **V**, 180
Young, David Wendel; **B**, 36a
Young, E.; **D**, 659
Young, Pierce Manning B., Maj.Gen.; **E**, 265, **H**, 999
Young, William Gourdin; **R**, 482
Younger Brothers; **B**, 1221
Younger, Bob; **B**, 1294
Younger, Henry W.; **A**, 405-406
Yulee, David L.; **H**, 1270, **T**, 219

Zacharie, Issachar; **H**, 358
Zagonyi's Charge; **J**, 340
Zamacona, Manuel de; **P**, 366
Zarvona Zouaves;
  Roster, **P**, 563
Zavala's Colony; **XYZ**, 92
Zogbaum, R.F.; **E**, 120
Zollicoffer, Felix Kirk, Brig.Gen.; **M**, 591, 671, **W**, 1045
Zollicoffer, John Jacob; **P**, 93
Zollie Tree; **M**, 1358
Zorn, Roman J.; **A**, 296

NORTH CAROLINA ROOM
NEW HANOVER COUNTY PUBLIC LIBRARY

NEW HANOVER COUNTY
PUBLIC LIBRARY
201 CHESTNUT STREET
WILMINGTON, N. C. 28401

REFERENCE USE ONLY
NEW HANOVER COUNTY PUBLIC LIBRARY

NCr